The
Random House
Dictionary

The Random House Dictionary

JESS STEIN
Editor in Chief

P. Y. SU
Executive Editor

Ballantine Books
New York

Library of Congress Catalog Card Number: 79-88527
ISBN: 0-345-29096-8
o.u/ue
Manufactured in the United States of America

Preface

This new dictionary is intended to meet the needs of those who want up-to-date, comprehensive, reliable information about the English language—and who, at the same time, prefer a dictionary that is compact in format and available at a price they can readily afford.

There are more than 70,000 entries in this book, many thousands more than in any comparable dictionary. This number is necessary to cover the vocabulary—general words, scientific and technical terms, foreign words and phrases, abbreviations, idiomatic expressions, etc.—of present-day users of English. In selecting the vocabulary to be included, we had the special benefit of our large citation file (based on the continuous examination of books, magazines, and newspapers, the analysis of special vocabulary lists, the noting of words used in radio and television broadcasts, etc.).

In the writing of the definitions, we have had two central aims: first, to make them fully reliable in content; second, to write them in clear, precise, modern English. Usage labels and notes have been entered, when necessary, as further guidance for the user. Similarly, when useful, example phrases and sentences have been added to individual definitions. Synonym lists have been given especially when they might help the user achieve greater variety or effectiveness in the choice of words; these lists have been carefully keyed to appropriate individual definitions.

Throughout this book we have tried to free our definitions of sexism, racism, and other prejudices. We believe that we have done so more thoroughly than ever before in lexicographic history.

For pronunciation, we have used a simple and accurate key, shown inside the front cover. The pronunciations given here are the ones usually encountered and may, therefore, be used with confidence in their acceptability.

To increase the usefulness of this book, we have included a basic manual of style, dealing with such matters as punctuation, capitalization, italics, footnotes, manuscript preparation, etc. The recommendations of this manual reflect the practices of most modern writers and conform generally to the preferences of the Modern Language Association.

This dictionary is the latest addition to the series of *Random House Dictionaries*—a widely and generously praised series prepared by our permanent lexicographic staff with the assistance of hundreds of recognized scholars and experts.

STAFF

Editor in Chief	Jess Stein
Executive Editor	P. Y. Su
Managing Editor	Leonore C. Hauck
Editorial Associates	Elizabeth G. Christensen
	Roy Finamore
	Dorothy Gerner Stein
	Lynn St. C. Strong
Editorial Assistants	John Sturman
	Regina B. Wilson
Production Director	Peter Mollman
Production Managers	Patricia W. Ehresmann
	Barry Larit
Typographic Designer	Charlotte Staub

CONTENTS

A Guide to the Dictionary

MAIN ENTRY WORD OR WORDS

TYPEFACE AND SEQUENCE

The main entry word appears in large, boldface type, flush left to the margin of the column. All main entries—words, phrases, names, abbreviations, prefixes, suffixes, etc.—appear in a single alphabetical list in strict sequence of spelling.

GUIDE WORDS

The words at the top left or top right of each page indicate, generally, the first and last entries on that page.

SYLLABIFICATION

Single-word entries of more than one syllable are shown with the syllables separated by a boldface centered dot. These syllabification dots, placed according to the usual American principles of word division, indicate the possible breaks in a word at the end of a line in printing, typing, or writing when a hyphen must be inserted to indicate carryover to the next line. In all hyphenated boldface entries, the hyphen replaces the centered dot as a syllable divider.

The syllable divisions in the boldface entry word—not those in the pronunciation—should be used for guidance in splitting a word at the end of a line.

Examples: **ap·o·plex·y; big-name; fol·low**

STRESS

Entries consisting of two or more words are not fully syllabified (this being done under the separate alphabetical entries for the individual words themselves) but are shown with a pattern of stress in the boldface that reveals the prosodic relationship of each word to the others in the entry. This pattern is not meant to show the relationship of one syllable to another within an individual word. A primary stress mark (′) follows the syllable or syllables that normally have greater stress than those marked with a secondary stress (′). The absence of a stress mark indicates that the syllable or word receives less stress than those marked (′) or (′).

Example: **cane′ sug′ar**

HOMOGRAPHS

Separate main entries are made for all words in the general language that are spelled identically but are of different derivation. When these words are spelled with lower-case rather than capital letters and when they have no distinguishing diacritical markings, each one is followed by a small superscript number.

Example: **will[1], will[2]**

PRONUNCIATION

Pronunciations are shown in this dictionary in parentheses immediately following the entry word. The first pronunciation, if several are shown, is generally the one in most frequent use, although there may be very little difference in frequency between any two consecutive pronunciations.

Example: **dec·a·dence** (dek′ə dəns, di kād′ᵊns)

Pronunciations for plural forms, run-ons, etc., often show only that part which is affected by change.

Example: **syn·the·sis** (sin′thi sis). *n., pl.* **-ses** (-sēz′). the combining of separate parts or elements to form a whole. **—syn′the·size′** (-sīz′). *v.t., v.i.* **—syn′the·siz′er,** *n.*

PRONUNCIATION KEY

The complete Pronunciation Key used in this dictionary appears on pages xv and xvi of this book. The system of pronunciation symbols represents major sound divisions in English. Just as, on a color wheel, the shadings we conventionally name *red* and *orange* have between and around them infinite gradations of color, so certain sounds in English have between and around them infinite gradations of sound coloration. We may well regard certain sounds, then, not as precise points but as general segments of a continuum. The Pronunciation Key is so constructed that the user, by pronouncing the key words given for each symbol, will automatically produce the variety or varieties of each sound appropriate to his or her own dialect.

SYLLABIFICATION

Pronunciations are divided into syllables both as a visual aid and as an aid in producing the appropriate phonetic variant of a given sound.

STRESS

Relative differences in stress between syllables in a word are indicated in the pronunciations. In words of two or more syllables a primary stress mark (′) follows the syllable having greatest stress. A secondary stress mark (′) follows a syllable having slightly less stress, particularly in a word of three or more syllables in which marked, stressed syllables alternate with unmarked, weaker ones. Monosyllables are unmarked and are considered to have primary stress unless otherwise indicated.

PARTS OF SPEECH

A part-of-speech label for each main entry that consists of a single word is
given as an italicized abbreviation preceding the definition or definitions for
that part of speech.

Example: de·gree (di grē′), *n.*

If the entry word is used in more than one grammatical form, the appropriate italicized part-of-speech label precedes each set of definitions given for
that part of speech. Part-of-speech labels subsequent to the first are preceded by a boldface dash.

Example:

e·nough (i nuf′). *adj.* **1.** sufficient for the purpose or
to satisfy desire. —*n.* **2.** an adequate quantity or
number. —*adv.* **3.** sufficiently. **4.** fully or quite. **5.**
tolerably or passably.

If the entry word shows irregularly spelled inflected forms, a summary of all
the parts of speech for the entry is given with the inflected forms following
the pronunciation.

Example:

feed (fēd), *v.*, fed, feed·ing, *n.* —*v.t.* **1.** to give food to.
2. to serve as food for. **3.** to satisfy or gratify. **4.** to
provide with the necessary materials for devel-
opment or operation. —*v.i.* **5.** (esp. of animals) to
eat. —*n.* **6.** food, esp. for farm animals. **7.** *Informal.*
a meal, esp. a lavish one. **8.** the act or process of
supplying a furnace, machine, etc. **9.** the material,
or the amount of it, supplied. **10.** a feeding mechanism. —feed′a·ble, *adj.* —feed′er, *n.*

If an entry word with more than one grammatical form is given a usage,
subject, or other label that applies to all its parts of speech, a boldface dash
precedes the first part-of-speech label as well as the others.

Example:

gyve (jīv), *n.*, *v.*, gyved, gyv·ing. *Archaic.* —*n.* **1.** Usually. gyves. a shackle, esp. for the leg. —*v.t.* **2.** to
shackle.

INFLECTED FORMS

Inflected forms are plurals of nouns, past tenses and participles of verbs,
and comparatives and superlatives of adjectives and adverbs. Such forms
traditionally regarded as "regular" are not generally shown for:

1. nouns whose plural is formed by the addition of *-s* (as in *dog, dogs*) or
   -es (as in *class, classes*).
2. verbs whose past tense is formed by the addition of *-ed* with no alteration of the spelling, whose past participle is formed by the addition of
   -ed with no alteration of the spelling, and whose present participle is
   formed by the addition of *-ing* with no alteration of the spelling (as in
   talk, talked, talking).

3. comparatives and superlatives formed simply by the suffixes *-er* and *-est* (as in *small, smaller, smallest*).
4. the third-person singular, indicative, present tense of verbs, with the exception of auxiliary verbs (as in *heals*).

Inflected forms are shown for those entry words that form inflections in some way other than by the simple addition of appropriate inflectional endings, such as those for:

1. nouns, adjectives, and verbs ending in a consonant plus a *y*, where the *y* changes to an *i* before an inflectional ending is added, as in *steady*.
2. adjectives and verbs ending in *e*, where the *e* is dropped before the inflectional ending is added, as in *fine*.
3. adjectives and verbs doubling the consonant before adding inflectional endings, as in *big, admit*.
4. nouns and verbs changing an internal spelling to form inflections, as in *half, mouse, steal*.
5. adjectives changing their roots to form the comparative and superlative, as in *good*.
6. nouns having plurals that are not native English formations, as in *alumnus*.
7. nouns having the plural and singular spelled identically, as in *Chinese.*
8. nominative pronouns, which show their declensions, as in *I*.

To avoid possible confusion as to their spellings, certain plural forms are also shown, including those for:

1. nouns ending in *-o, -ful, -ey,* or *-us,* as in *potato, cupful, monkey, prospectus.*
2. nouns ending in elements resembling words that form their plurals in a different way, as in *mongoose.*
3. nouns about which there might be confusion as to the pronunciation of the plural, as in *house, path.*
4. entries of two or more words about which there might be confusion as to which element is pluralized, as in *attorney general.*

Where variant inflected forms occur, all forms are shown, with labels when appropriate.

Example: be·get (bi get'), *v.t.,* be·got (-got') or (*Archaic*)
be·gat (-gat'); be·got·ten (-got'ᵊn) or be·got;
be·get·ting. *Literary.* **1.** to be the father of. **2.** to
cause or produce.

Where two inflected forms are given for a verb, the first is the past tense and the past participle and the second is the present participle.

Example: flee (flē), *v.,* fled (fled), flee·ing. —*v.i.* **1.** to run away,
as from danger, pursuers, etc. **2.** to move swiftly.
—*v.t.* **3.** to run away from (a place, person, etc.).

Where three inflected forms are given for a verb, the first is the past tense, the second is the past participle, and the third is the present participle.

DEFINITIONS

Definitions within an entry are individually numbered in a single sequence, regardless of the groupings according to part of speech. In general, the most common part of speech is listed first, and the most frequent meaning appears as the first definition for each part of speech.

Idioms appear in boldface type under the main entry word whose use in the idiom is least clear or denotative, unless that word is a preposition or an adverbial particle. Idioms are listed in alphabetical order after the definitions for the part of speech under which they appear.

> Example: **heel¹** (hēl), *n.* **1.** the back part of the foot, below and behind the ankle. **2.** the part of a stocking, shoe, etc., covering this part. **3.** a solid, raised base attached to the back part of the sole of a shoe. **4.** something resembling a heel in position, shape, etc. **5. down at the heels,** shabby or poor. **6. kick up one's heels,** to frolic. **7. on** or **upon the heels of,** closely following. —*v.t.* **8.** to furnish with heels, as shoes. —*v.i.* **9.** (of a dog) to follow at one's heels on command. —**heel'less,** *adj.*

If two or more definitions belong to the same labeled subject field, they are marked with boldface letters under the same definition number. If an idiomatic phrase has two or more meanings, each meaning is marked with a boldface letter but the idiom itself is listed only once.

Example: See **effect** (def. 6)

For meanings using the entry word in a form slightly different from that shown at the main entry, as with a capital letter or a lower-case letter, the changed form is indicated at the beginning of the definition.

Example: See **republican** (def. 2)

USAGE AND OTHER LABELS

Entries that are limited, in whole or in part, to a particular region, time, subject, or variety of usage, are marked with appropriate labels, as *Brit., Latin; Archaic, Obs.; Physics, Chem.; Slang, Informal.*

1. If the label applies to the entire entry, it appears before the first part-of-speech label if there is more than one part of speech and after it if there is only one part of speech.
2. If the label applies to a certain part of speech only, it follows the part-of-speech label and precedes the subsequent definition numbers.
3. If the label applies to a certain definition only, it follows the definition number and precedes the text of the definition.

4. If a definition has two or more lettered parts and the label applies to both, it precedes the first letter. If the label applies to only one of the lettered parts, it follows that letter.

CROSS REFERENCES

Main entries are defined under the form most commonly encountered in contemporary English. Other forms—for example, less common spellings or shortened forms—are generally listed in their own alphabetical places.

VARIANTS

1. Common variant spellings are shown in boldface type at the form of the entry that is defined, preceded by "Also." Variant names for an entry are preceded by "Also called."

   Examples: See **kerosene; sleeping pill**

2. If a variant applies to a certain definition only, it follows the definition number and precedes the text of the definition.

   Example: See **casino** (def. 2)

3. When a less common form of an entry, as a spelling or other type of variant, appears as a main entry, it is followed by a cross reference to the entry where the definition appears.

   Example: See **inclose**

INFLECTED FORMS

When an inflected form is given its own main entry, it is cross-referred to the defined entry of which it is a part.

   Example: See **lent**

HIDDEN ENTRIES

A hidden entry may be implicitly or explicitly defined within the text of a broader definition in the same field. It is shown in boldface, enclosed in parentheses.

   Example: **a·part·ment** (ə pärt′mənt), *n.* **1.** a room or combination of rooms for use as a dwelling. **2.** a building (**apart′ment house′**) containing such rooms.

ETYMOLOGIES

Etymologies in this dictionary appear in square brackets after the definitions. An etymology key appears on page xiv of this book.

SYMBOLS

The following are the most important symbols in the etymologies:

< This symbol, meaning "from," is used to show descent from one language or group of languages to another, or to show that a word is derived from another word.

= This symbol of equivalence precedes the analysis of a word. It is used to show that a word is made up of the words or elements that follow it.

+ This symbol is used between elements, the members of a compound or a blend, etc., to indicate that these are the immediate constituents of the word being analyzed.

PARENTHESES

Parentheses are used to set off those parts of the source words that do not require analysis or that do not have any bearing on the entry word. They are also used to show various kinds of omission, as in blends and acronyms, variant spellings, etc.

LANGUAGE LABELS

A language label is shown alone, without an accompanying italicized form, when there is no significant difference in form or meaning between the word in the given language and the preceding word.

TYPEFACE

Roman type is used for translations, definitions, and other explanatory matter. Italic type is used for all words or parts of words from which the entry words are formed by derivation or composition.

RUN-ON ENTRIES

Derivatives of the main entry word are often formed by adding a suffix to the root of the main entry. When their meanings are readily understandable from the combined senses of the root word and the suffix, these derivatives are run on at the end of the entry. The run-on entry appears in boldface type at the end of the entry. It is preceded by a lightface dash and followed by an italicized, part-of-speech label.

Example: See **tart** (—**tart′ly,** *adv.* —**tart′ness,** *n.*)

If the pronunciation of a run-on entry is readily derivable from that of the main entry, a preceding variant of the main entry, or a preceding run-on entry, the run-on entry is syllabified with centered dots and stressed in the boldface spelling.

SYNONYMS

At the end of many entries synonym lists appear, preceded by —Syn. They appear in alphabetical order and are usually keyed to the specific definitions to which they relate.

USAGE NOTES

At the end of a number of entries there are usage notes, set flush left to the margin and preceded by —Usage. These describe many of the problems that arise in matters of grammar and usage, and they are intended to reflect the opinions of most educated users of English.

Etymology Key

<	from; derived or descended from	Finn	Finnish	Pers	Persian
		G	German	Pg	Portuguese
		Gael	Gaelic	Pr	Provençal
=	equivalent to	Gk	Greek	Rum	Rumanian
		Gmc	Germanic	Russ	Russian
+	plus; and	Haw	Hawaiian	SAfrD	South African Dutch
AF	Anglo-French	Heb	Hebrew		
		Hung	Hungarian		
Afr	African	Icel	Icelandic	Scand	Scandinavian
AmerInd	American Indian	Ir	Irish		
		It	Italian	Scot	Scottish
Ar	Arabic	Jap	Japanese	Skt	Sanskrit
Aram	Aramaic	L	Latin	Sp	Spanish
CanF	Canadian French	ME	Middle English	Sw	Swedish
				Turk	Turkish
Celt	Celtic	MexSp	Mexican Spanish	WInd	West Indian
Chin	Chinese				
D	Dutch	Norw	Norwegian		
Dan	Danish	OE	Old English	WAfr	West African
F	French				

Pronunciation Key: Foreign Sounds

A as in French **a·mi** (A mē′) [a vowel intermediate in quality between the **a** of *cat* and the **ä** of *calm*, but closer to the former]

KH as in German **ach** (äKH) or **ich** (iKH); Scottish **loch** (lôKH) [a consonant made by bringing the tongue into the position for **k** as in *key, coo*, while pronouncing a strong, rasping **h**]

N as in French **bon** (bôN) [used to indicate that the preceding vowel is nasalized. Four such vowels are found in French: **un bon vin blanc** (œN bôN vaN bläN)]

Œ as in French **feu** (fœ); German **schön** (shœn) [a vowel made with the lips rounded in the position for **o** as in *over*, while trying to say **a** as in *able*]

R as in French **rouge** (Roozh), German **rot** (Rōt), Italian **ma·re** (mä′Re), Spanish **pe·ro** (pe′Rô) [a symbol for any non-English **r**, including a trill or flap in Italian and Spanish and a sound in French and German similar to **KH** but pronounced with voice]

Y as in French **tu** (tY); German **ü·ber** (Y′bər) [a vowel made with the lips rounded in position for **oo** as in *ooze*, while trying to say **ē** as in *east*]

as in French **Bas·togne** (bA·stôn′y²) [a faint prolongation of the preceding voiced consonant or glide]

Pronunciation Key

The symbol ('), as in **moth-er** (mu**th**'ər), **civ'il defense'**, is used to mark primary stress; the syllable preceding it is pronounced with greater prominence than the other syllables in the word or phrase. The symbol ('), as in **grand-moth-er** (grand'mu**th**'ər), **cream' cheese'**, is used to mark secondary stress; a syllable marked for secondary stress is pronounced with less prominence than one marked (') but with more prominence than those bearing no stress mark at all.

a	act, bat, marry	l	low, mellow, all	y	yes, lawyer
ā	aid, cape, way				
â(r)	air, dare, Mary	m	my, simmer, him	z	zeal, lazy, those
ä	alms, art, calm			zh	vision, mirage
		n	now, sinner, on		
b	back, cabin, cab	ng	sing, Washington	ə	occurs only in unaccented syllables and indicates the sound of
ch	chief, butcher, beach				a *in* alone
		o	ox, box, wasp		e *in* system
		ō	over, boat, no		i *in* easily
d	do, rudder, bed	ô	ought, ball, raw		o *in* gallop
		oi	oil, joint, joy		u *in* circus
e	ebb, set, merry	o͝o	book, poor		
ē	equal, seat, bee, mighty	o͞o	ooze, fool, too	ᵊ	occurs in unaccented syllables before l preceded by t, d, or n, or before n preceded by t or d to show syllabic quality, as in **cra-dle** (krād'ᵊl) **red-den** (red'ᵊn) **met-al** (met'ᵊl) **men-tal** (men't'ᵊl) and in accented syllables between ī and r to show diphthongal quality, as in **fire** (fīᵊr) **hire** (hīᵊr)
ēr	ear, mere	ou	out, loud, prow		
f	fit, differ, puff	p	pot, supper, stop		
		r	read, hurry, near		
g	give, trigger, beg	s	see, passing, miss		
h	hit, behave, hear	sh	shoe, fashion, push		
hw	white, nowhere				
		t	ten, butter, bit		
i	if, big, mirror, furniture	th	thin, ether, path		
ī	ice, bite, pirate, deny	th	that, either, smooth		
		u	up, love		
j	just, badger, fudge	û(r)	urge, burn, cur		
		v	voice, river, live		
k	kept, token, make	w	west, away		

xvi

A

A, a (ā), *n., pl.* **A's** or **As, a's** or **as.**
the first letter of the English alphabet, a vowel.

a¹ (ə; *when stressed* ā), *indefinite article.* **1.** any one of some class or group: *a woman.* **2.** any certain one: *one thing at a time.* **3.** one (used before a noun expressing quantity): *a score of times.* **4.** any single: *not a one.*

a² (ə; *when stressed* ā), *prep.* per: *ten cents a ride.*

A, 1. ampere; amperes. **2.** answer.

A, 1. the first in order or in a series. **2.** a grade or mark that indicates the highest quality. **3.** *Music.* the sixth tone in the scale of C major.

a, *Metric System.* are; ares.

a-¹, a prefix meaning: **a.** on: *afoot.* **b.** in: *abed.* **c.** to: *ashore.* **d.** at: *aside.*

a-², a prefix meaning: **a.** of: *akin.* **b.** from: *anew.*

a-³, a prefix meaning: **a.** not: *atypical.* **b.** without: *amoral.*

A., 1. acre; acres. **2.** America. **3.** American. **4.** answer.

a., 1. about. **2.** acre; acres. **3.** adjective. **4.** alto. **5.** anonymous. **6.** answer. **7.** *Metric System.* are; ares.

AA, Alcoholics Anonymous.

A.A., 1. Alcoholics Anonymous. **2.** antiaircraft. **3.** Associate in Arts.

AAA, 1. American Automobile Association. **2.** antiaircraft artillery.

AAM, air-to-air missile.

A and M, Agricultural and Mechanical.

A & R, artists and repertory (used to refer to the profession of selecting recording artists).

aard·vark (ärd'värk'), *n.* a large burrowing mammal of Africa, feeding on ants and termites. [< obs. SAfrD = *aarde* earth + *vark* pig]

ab., 1. about. **2.** *Baseball.* (times) at bat.

A.B., 1. See **able seaman. 2.** Bachelor of Arts. [< L *Artium Baccalaureus*]

A.B.A., American Bar Association.

a·back (ə bak'), *adv.* taken aback, surprised and disconcerted.

ab·a·cus (ab'ə kəs, ə bak'əs), *n., pl.* **ab·a·cus·es, ab·a·ci** (ab'ə sī'). a device for making calculations, consisting of a frame set with movable beads on rods.

a·baft (ə baft', ə bäft'), *Naut.* —*prep.* **1.** to the rear of. —*adv.* **2.** aft.

ab·a·lo·ne (ab'ə lō'nē), *n.* a large mollusk with a rather flat, oval shell, whose flesh is edible.

a·ban·don¹ (ə ban'dən), *v.t.* **1.** to give up or discontinue (a plan or project). **2.** to leave or desert. —**a·ban'don·er,** *n.* —**a·ban'don·ment,** *n.* —**Syn. 1.** relinquish, renounce. **2.** forsake.

a·ban·don² (ə ban'dən), *n.* freedom from constraint or conventionality.

a·ban·doned (ə ban'dənd), *adj.* having no shame or self-control. —**a·ban'doned·ly,** *adv.*

a·base (ə bās'), *v.t.,* **a·based, a·bas·ing.** to humble or degrade (used usually reflexively). —**a·base'ment,** *n.* —**a·bas'er,** *n.*

a·bash (ə bash'), *v.t.* to make ashamed or embarrassed. —**a·bash·ed·ly** (ə bash'id lē), *adv.* —**a·bash'ment,** *n.*

a·bate (ə bāt'), *v.t., v.i.,* **a·bat·ed, a·bat·ing. 1.** to decrease in amount, degree, worth, etc. **2.** *Law.* to put an end (to). —**a·bat'a·ble,** *adj.* —**a·bate'ment,** *n.* —**a·bat'er,** *n.* — **Syn. 1.** ebb, subside, wane.

ab·a·tis (ab'ə tē', -tis, ə bat'ē, ə bat'-is), *n., pl.* **ab·a·tis** (ab'ə tēz', ə bat'-ēz), **ab·a·tis·es** (ab'ə tis'iz, ə bat'ə-siz). an obstacle of felled trees with sharpened branches directed toward an enemy.

ab·at·toir (ab'ə twär'), *n.* a slaughterhouse.

ab·ba·cy (ab'ə sē), *n., pl.* **-cies.** the position or term of office of an abbot.

ab·bé (a bā', ab'ā), *n., pl.* **ab·bés** (a bāz', ab'āz). a title of respect for a French priest.

ab·bess (ab'is), *n.* the female superior of a convent of nuns.

ab·bey (ab'ē), *n., pl.* **-beys. 1.** a monastery or convent. **2.** the church of an abbey.

ab·bot (ab'ət), *n.* the head or superior of a monastery. [< L < Gk < Aram *abbâ* father] —**ab'bot·ship',** *n.*

abbr., 1. abbreviated. 2. abbreviation. Also, **abbrev.**

ab·bre·vi·ate (ə brē'vē āt'), v.t., -at·ed, -at·ing. 1. to shorten (a word or phrase) by omitting letters. 2. to make briefer. —**ab·bre'vi·a'tor,** n.

ab·bre·vi·a·tion (ə brē'vē ā'shən), n. 1. a shortened or contracted form of a word or phrase, used to represent the whole. 2. the act or result of abbreviating.

ABC (ā'bē'sē'), n., pl. **ABC's, ABCs.** 1. the rudiments of a subject. 2. Usually, **ABC's.** the alphabet.

ab·di·cate (ab'də kāt'), v.t., v.i. -cat·ed, -cat·ing. to renounce or relinquish (a throne or power) formally. —**ab'di·ca'tion,** n.

ab·do·men (ab'də mən, ab dō'-), n. 1. the part of the body between the thorax and the pelvis. 2. the posterior section of the body of an arthropod. —**ab·dom'i·nal** (-dom'ə-nəl), adj. —**ab·dom'i·nal·ly,** adv.

ab·duct (ab dukt'), v.t. to carry off (a person) by force, esp. to kidnap. —**ab·duc'tion,** n. —**ab·duc'tor,** n.

a·beam (ə bēm'), adv., adj. at right angles to a ship's keel.

a·be·ce·dar·i·an (ā'bē sē dâr'ē ən), n. a beginner in any field of learning.

a·bed (ə bed'), adv., adj. in bed.

ab·er·ra·tion (ab'ə rā'shən), n. 1. deviation from what is common, normal, or right. 2. mental disorder. 3. failure to form perfect reproduction through a lens or on a mirror. —**ab·er·ra'tion·al,** adj. —**ab·er'rant,** adj.

a·bet (ə bet'), v.t., a·bet·ted, a·bet·ting. to encourage or assist, esp. in wrongdoing. —**a·bet'ment,** n. —**a·bet'tor, a·bet'ter,** n.

a·bey·ance (ə bā'əns), n. temporary inactivity or cessation.

ab·hor (ab hôr'), v.t., -horred, -hor·ring. to detest utterly. —**ab·hor'rence,** n. —**ab·hor'rer,** n.

ab·hor·rent (ab hôr'ənt, -hor'-), adj. causing repugnance or loathing. —**ab·hor'rent·ly,** adv.

a·bide (ə bīd'), v., a·bode or a·bid·ed, a·bid·ing. —v.i. Literary. 1. to remain or stay. 2. to reside. —v.t. 3. Literary. to wait for. 4. to endure or tolerate. 5. abide by, a. to act in accord with. b. to submit to or agree to. —**a·bid'ance,** n.

a·bid·ing (ə bī'diɴg), adj. enduring or steadfast. —**a·bid'ing·ly,** adv.

Ab·i·djan (ab'i jän'), n. the capital of the Ivory Coast.

a·bil·i·ty (ə bil'i tē), n., pl. -ties. 1. power or capacity to act. 2. talent or skill.

ab·ject (ab'jekt, ab jekt'), adj. 1. humiliating and wretched. 2. contemptible or despicable. —**ab·jec'tion,** n. —**ab·ject·ly** (ab jekt'lē, ab'jekt lē), adv. —**ab·ject'ness,** n.

ab·jure (ab jŏŏr'), v.t., -jured, -jur·ing. 1. to retract solemnly. 2. to renounce under oath. —**ab·ju·ra·tion** (ab'jŏŏ rā'shən), n. —**ab·jur'a·to·ry,** adj. —**ab·jur'er,** n.

abl., ablative.

ab·late (a blāt'), v.t., v.i. -lat·ed, -lat·ing. to cause or undergo ablation.

ab·la·tion (ab lā'shən), n. 1. removal by surgery, melting, erosion, etc. 2. Rocketry. burning away of a nose cone by heat in reentry.

ab·la·tive (ab'lə tiv), Gram. —adj. 1. noting a case that indicates the place or manner of an action, as in Latin. —n. 2. the ablative case. —**ab·la·ti·val** (ab'lə tī'vəl), adj.

a·blaze (ə blāz'), adj. 1. on fire. 2. gleaming or brilliant.

a·ble (ā'bəl), adj., a·bler, a·blest. 1. having necessary power, skill, or resources. 2. having or showing intelligence, skill, etc. 3. legally competent. —**a'bly,** adv. —Syn. 1. capable, competent. 2. clever, ingenious.

-able, a suffix meaning: a. able to be: readable. b. worthy of: laudable. c. tending to: changeable.

a·ble-bod·ied (ā'bəl bod'ēd), adj. physically fit.

a'ble sea'man, a skilled or experienced seaman. Also called **a'ble-bodied sea'man.**

a·bloom (ə blōōm'), adj. in bloom.

ab·lu·tion (ab lōō'shən, ə blōō'-), n. a cleansing of the body, esp. as a religious ritual.

ABM, See antiballistic missile.

ab·ne·gate (ab'nə gāt'), v.t., -gat·ed, -gat·ing. to deny oneself (rights, comfort, etc.). —**ab'ne·ga'tion,** n.

ab·nor·mal (ab nôr'məl), adj. not average, typical, or normal. —**ab·nor·mal·i·ty** (ab'nôr mal'i tē), n. —**ab·nor'mal·ly,** adv.

a·board (ə bôrd', ə bōrd'), adv., prep. 1. on, in, or into (a ship, train, etc.). 2. alongside (of a ship or shore).

a·bode¹ (ə bōd'), n. Literary. 1. a house or residence. 2. a stay.

a·bode² (ə bōd'), v. a pt. and pp. of abide.

a·bol·ish (ə bol'ish), v.t. to put an end to. —Syn. abrogate, annul, nullify.

ab·o·li·tion (ab'ə lish'ən), n. 1. the act of abolishing or state of being abolished. 2. (often cap.) the legal termination of slavery in the U.S. —**ab'o·li'tion·ar'y,** adj.

ab·o·li·tion·ism (ab'ə lish'ə niz'əm), n. the policy of abolition of slavery, esp. in the U.S. —**ab'o·li'tion·ist,** n.

A-bomb (ā′bom′), *n.* See **atomic bomb**.

a·bom·i·na·ble (ə bom′ə nə bəl), *adj.* 1. repugnantly hateful. 2. very bad or poor. —**a·bom′i·na·bly,** *adv.*

Abom′inable Snow′man, a large humanlike creature reported to inhabit the Himalayas.

a·bom·i·nate (ə bom′ə nāt′), *v.t.,* -nat·ed, -nat·ing. 1. to loathe intensely. 2. to dislike strongly. —**a·bom′i·na′tion,** *n.* —**a·bom′i·na′tor,** *n.*

ab·o·rig·i·nal (ab′ə rij′ə nol), *adj.* 1. of or pertaining to aborigines. 2. native or indigenous. —*n.* 3. an aborigine.

ab·o·rig·i·ne (ab′ə rij′ə nē), *n.* one of the original inhabitants of a region. [< L *ab origine* from the very first]

a·born·ing (ə bôr′niñg), *adv.* in birth or while coming into being.

a·bort (ə bôrt′), *v.i., v.t.* 1. to undergo or cause abortion. 2. to terminate (a scheduled spaceflight) prematurely. —**a·bor′tive,** *adj.* —**a·bor′tive·ly,** *adv.*

a·bor·tion (ə bôr′shən), *n.* 1. the expulsion of a human fetus before it is viable. 2. an idea or project that has failed to develop fully. —**a·bor·tion·al,** *adj.*

a·bor·tion·ist (ə bôr′shə nist), *n.* a person who induces abortions.

a·bound (ə bound′), *v.i.* 1. to exist in great quantities or numbers. 2. to be well supplied.

a·bout (ə bout′), *prep.* 1. in regard to. 2. connected with. 3. near or close to. 4. on every side of. 5. on the verge of. —*adv.* 6. nearly or approximately. 7. nearby. 8. on every side. 9. in the opposite direction. —*adj.* 10. moving around.

a·bout-face (*n.* ə bout′fās′; *v.* ə bout′-fās′), *n., v.,* -faced, -fac·ing. —*n.* 1. a complete reversal in position, attitude, etc. —*v.i.* 2. to switch to an opposite direction or opinion.

a·bove (ə buv′), *adv.* 1. in or to a higher place. 2. overhead, upstairs, or in the sky. 3. higher in rank or power. 4. before or earlier, esp. in a book, etc. —*prep.* 5. over. 6. more in quantity or number than. 7. superior in rank or standing to. 8. of too fine a character for. 9. above all, principally. 11. —*adj.* 10. mentioned above. —*n.* 11. that which is above.

a·bove·board (ə buv′bôrd′, -bōrd′), *adv., adj.* without tricks or disguise.

abp., archbishop.

abr., 1. abridged. 2. abridgment.

ab·ra·ca·dab·ra (ab′rə kə dab′rə), *n.* 1. a mystical word used as a magical means of warding off misfortune. 2. gibberish or nonsense.

a·brade (ə brād′), *v.t., v.i.,* a·brad·ed, a·brad·ing. 1. to wear or scrape off. 2. to irritate. —**a·brad′er,** *n.* —**a·bra·sion** (ə brā′zhən), *n.*

A·bra·ham (ā′brə ham′, -həm), *n.* the first patriarch of the Hebrew nation.

a·bra·sive (ə brā′siv, -ziv), *n.* 1. any material used for grinding, polishing, etc., as sandpaper. —*adj.* 2. causing abrasion. 3. irritating in manner, tone, etc. —**a·bra′sive·ly,** *adv.* —**a·bra′sive·ness,** *n.*

a·breast (ə brest′), *adv., adj.* 1. side by side. 2. equal to in progress or awareness.

a·bridge (ə brij′), *v.t.,* a·bridged, a·bridg·ing. 1. to shorten by omission while retaining the substance. 2. to diminish or curtail. [< MF *abreg(i)er* < LL *abbreviāre* to shorten] —**a·bridg′er,** *n.* —**a·bridg′ment, a·bridge′ment,** *n.*

a·broad (ə brôd′), *adv.* 1. in or to foreign countries. 2. in general circulation. 3. far and wide. 4. *Obs.* out of doors.

ab·ro·gate (ab′rə gāt′), *v.t.,* -gat·ed, -gat·ing. to abolish by formal means. —**ab′ro·ga′tion,** *n.* —**ab′ro·ga′tor,** *n.* —**Syn.** annul, repeal.

ab·rupt (ə brupt′), *adj.* 1. sudden and unexpected. 2. curt or brusque. 3. terminating suddenly. 4. lacking in continuity. 5. steep or precipitous. —**ab·rupt′ly,** *adv.* —**ab·rupt′ness,** *n.*

abs., 1. absolute. 2. absolutely.

ab·scess (ab′ses), *n.* a localized collection of pus in the tissues of the body. —**ab′scessed,** *adj.*

ab·scise (ab sīz′), *v.i.,* -scised, -scising. to separate by abscission.

ab·scis·sa (ab sis′ə), *n., pl.* -scis·sas, -scis·sae (-sis′ē). (in plane Cartesian coordinates) the horizontal or *x*-coordinate of a point: its distance from the *y*-axis measured parallel to the *x*-axis.

ab·scis·sion (ab sizh′ən, -sish′-), *n.* 1. removal, as by surgery. 2. the normal separation of flowers, fruit, and leaves from plants.

ab·scond (ab skond′), *v.i.* to depart suddenly, esp. to avoid detection. —**ab·scond′er,** *n.*

ab·sence (ab′səns), *n.* 1. state of not being present. 2. a period of being away. 3. lack or want.

ab·sent (*adj.* ab′sənt; *v.* ab sent′), *adj.* 1. not present at a given time. 2. lacking or nonexistent. 3. not attentive. —*v.t.* 4. to take or keep (oneself) away. —**ab′sent·ly,** *adv.*

ab·sen·tee (ab′sən tē′), *n.* a person who is absent. —**ab′sen·tee′ism,** *n.*

ab·sentee bal·lot, the ballot for an absentee vote.

ab·sentee vote', a vote by a person who, because of illness or the like, has been permitted to vote by mail. —**ab'sentee vot'er.**

ab·sent-mind·ed (ab'sənt mīn'did), *adj.* preoccupied so as to be unaware or forgetful of other matters. —**ab'sent-mind'ed·ly,** *adv.* —**ab'sent-mind'ed·ness,** *n.*

ab·sinthe (ab'sinth), *n.* a green, bitter, licorice-flavored liqueur. Also, **ab'sinth.**

ab·so·lute (ab'sə lōōt'), *adj.* 1. being fully as indicated. 2. free from any restriction, limitation, or exception. 3. not comparative or relative. 4. utter or outright. 5. without constitutional restraint. 6. certain. 7. pure. 8. relatively independent in its syntactic relation to other elements. 9. pertaining to a system of units based on some primary units of length, mass, and time. —**ab'so·lute'ly,** *adv.* —**ab'so·lute'ness,** *n.* —Syn. 2. total, unconditional, unqualified. 5. arbitrary, dictatorial, totalitarian.

ab'solute pitch', 1. the exact pitch of a tone in terms of vibrations per second. 2. the ability to sing or recognize the pitch of a tone by ear.

ab'solute val'ue, *Math.* the magnitude of a quantity, irrespective of sign.

ab'solute ze'ro, the lowest possible temperature that the nature of matter admits, being a hypothetical point 273° below the zero of the Celsius scale.

ab·so·lu·tion (ab'sə lōō'shən), *n.* 1. act of absolving. 2. a remission of sin made by a priest in the sacrament of penance.

ab·so·lut·ism (ab'sə lōō tiz'əm), *n.* the principle or the exercise of complete and unrestricted power in government. —**ab'so·lut'ist,** *n., adj.* —**ab'so·lu·tis'tic,** *adj.*

ab·solve (ab zolv', -solv'), *v.t.,* -**solved, -solv·ing.** 1. to free from the consequences or penalties resulting from actions. 2. **a.** to grant remission of sins to. **b.** to remit (a sin) by absolution. —**ab·solv'a·ble,** *adj.*

ab·sorb (ab sôrb', -zôrb'), *v.t.* 1. to suck in (a liquid). 2. to incorporate or assimilate. 3. to engross wholly. 4. to occupy (time). 5. to take in without echo, recoil, or reflection. 6. to assume (an expense). —**ab·sorb'a·ble,** *adj.* —**ab·sorb'er,** *n.* —**ab·sorb'ing,** *adj.* —**ab·sorb'ing·ly,** *adv.*

ab·sorb·ent (ab sôr'bənt, -zôr'-), *adj.* 1. capable of or tending to absorb. —*n.* 2. a thing or material that absorbs. —**ab·sorb'en·cy,** *n.*

ab·sorp·tion (ab sôrp'shən, -zôrp'-), *n.* 1. the process of absorbing or being absorbed. 2. deep engrossment. —**ab·sorp'tive,** *adj.*

ab·stain (ab stān'), *v.i.* to refrain voluntarily. —**ab·stain'er,** *n.* —**ab·sten·tion** (ab sten'shən), *n.*

ab·ste·mi·ous (ab stē'mē əs), *adj.* sparing or moderate, esp. in eating and drinking.

ab·sti·nence (ab'stə nəns), *n.* forbearance from any indulgence of appetite, esp. from alcoholic liquors or from certain kinds of food. —**ab'sti·nent,** *adj.*

abstr., abstract.

ab·stract (*adj.* ab'strakt, ab strakt'; *n.* ab'strakt; *v.* ab strakt'), *adj.* 1. conceived apart from any concrete realities or specific object. 2. expressing a quality or characteristic apart from any specific object or instance. 3. theoretical: *abstract science.* 4. pertaining to the nonrepresentational art styles of the 20th century. —*n.* 5. a summary of a statement, etc. 6. an abstract idea or term. —*v.t.* 7. to take away or remove. 8. to divert the attention of. 9. to summarize. 10. *Informal.* to steal. —**ab·stract'er,** *n.* —**ab'stract·ly,** *adv.* —**ab'stract·ness,** *n.*

ab·stract·ed (ab strak'tid), *adj.* deeply engrossed. —**ab·stract'ed·ly,** *adv.*

ab'stract expres'sionism, art that produces images in or through abstract forms. —**ab'stract expres'sionist.**

ab·strac·tion (ab strak'shən), *n.* 1. the process of abstracting or being abstracted. 2. an abstract idea or thing. 3. engrossment. 4. an abstract work of art.

ab·struse (ab strōōs'), *adj.* hard to understand or grasp. —**ab·struse'ly,** *adv.* —**ab·struse'ness,** *n.*

ab·surd (ab sûrd', -zûrd'), *adj.* contrary to all reason or common sense. —**ab·surd'i·ty, ab·surd'ness,** *n.* —**ab·surd'ly,** *adv.* —Syn. illogical, preposterous, ridiculous.

abt., about.

a·bun·dant (ə bun'dənt), *adj.* 1. present in great quantity. 2. richly supplied. —**a·bun'dance,** *n.* —**a·bun'dant·ly,** *adv.*

a·buse (*v.* ə byōōz'; *n.* ə byōōs'), *v.,* **a·bused, a·bus·ing.** —*v.t.* 1. to use wrongly or improperly. 2. to mistreat or maltreat. 3. to insult. —*n.* 4. wrong or improper use. 5. coarsely insulting language. 6. maltreatment. 7. a corrupt or improper practice. —**a·bu'sive,** *adj.* —**a·bu'sive·ly,** *adv.* —**a·bu'sive·ness,** *n.*

a·but (ə but'), *v.,* **a·but·ted, a·but-**

ting. —*v.i.* **1.** to touch or join at the border. —*v.t.* **2.** to border on. —**a·but′ter,** *n.*

a·but·ment (ə but′mənt), *n.* **1.** a part supporting and receiving the thrust of an arch, vault, etc. **2.** junction (def. 2).

a·but·tal (ə but′əl), *n.* the boundary line of a piece of land in relation to adjacent land.

a·bysm (ə biz′əm), *n.* an abyss.

a·bys·mal (ə biz′məl), *adj.* immeasurably deep or great. —**a·bys′mal·ly,** *adv.*

a·byss (ə bis′), *n.* **1.** a deep, vast chasm. **2.** anything profound or infinite. **3. a.** the primal chaos before the Creation. **b.** hell.

a·byss·al (ə bis′əl), *adj.* **1.** of or like an abyss. **2.** of the lowest depths of the ocean.

Ab·ys·sin·i·a (ab′i sin′ē ə), *n.* former name of **Ethiopia.** —**Ab′ys·sin′i·an,** *adj., n.*

AC, See **alternating current.** Also, **A.C., a.c.**

Ac, actinium.

A/C, 1. account. **2.** account current.

A.C., before Christ. [< L *ante Christum*]

a.c., (in prescriptions) before meals. [< L *ante cibum*]

a·ca·cia (ə kā′shə), *n.* **1.** a tree or shrub bearing clusters of tiny white or yellow to orange flowers. **2.** the locust tree.

acad., 1. academic. **2.** academy.

ac·a·deme (ak′ə dēm′), *n.* **1.** Also, **ac·a·de·mi·a** (ak′ə dē′mē ə). the environment of a university. **2.** *Archaic.* a school.

ac·a·dem·ic (ak′ə dem′ik), *adj.* **1.** of a school or college. **2.** pertaining to areas of study that are not vocational or technical. **3.** not practical or directly useful. **4.** purely theoretical. Also, **ac′a·dem′i·cal.** —**ac′a·dem′i·cal·ly,** *adv.*

a·cad·e·mi·cian (ə kad′ə mish′ən, ak′ə də-), *n.* a member of an association of scholars or artists.

ac·a·dem·i·cism (ak′ə dem′i siz′əm), *n.* traditionalism or conventionalism in art, literature, etc. Also, **a·cad′e·mism′.**

a·cad·e·my (ə kad′ə mē), *n., pl.* **-mies. 1.** a high school, esp. a private one. **2.** a school or college for special training: *a military academy.* **3.** an association of scholars or artists. [< L < Gk *akadēmeia* name of estate where Athenian philosophers met]

a·can·thus (ə kan′thəs), *n., pl.* **-thus·es, -thi** (-thī). **1.** any of several herbs of the Mediterranean region, having toothed leaves. **2.**

an architectural ornament resembling the leaves of this plant.

a cap·pel·la (ä′ kə pel′ə), *Music.* without instrumental accompaniment.

acc., 1. acceleration. **2.** account. **3.** accountant. **4.** accusative.

ac·cede (ak sēd′), *v.i.,* **-ced·ed, -ced·ing. 1.** to yield one's consent. **2.** to attain an office or title. —**ac·ced′ence,** *n.* —**ac·ced′er,** *n.*

ac·cel·er·an·do (ak sel′ə rän′dō), *adv., adj. Music.* gradually increasing in tempo.

ac·cel·er·ate (ak sel′ə rāt′), *v.,* **-at·ed, -at·ing.** —*v.t.* **1.** to cause faster movement in. **2.** to hasten the occurrence of. —*v.i.* **3.** to move or go faster. —**ac·cel′er·a·ble,** *adj.* —**ac·cel′er·a′tion,** *n.* —**ac·cel′er·a′tive,** *adj.*

ac·cel·er·a·tor (ak sel′ə rā′tər), *n.* **1.** one that accelerates. **2.** the gas pedal of an automobile. **3.** a device, as a cyclotron, that produces high-energy particles.

ac·cel·er·om·e·ter (ak sel′ə rom′i tər), *n.* an instrument for measuring acceleration.

ac·cent (*n.* ak′sent; *v.* ak′sent, ak sent′), *n.* **1.** prominence of a syllable of a word in terms of differential loudness or pitch. **2.** degree of prominence of a syllable within a word. **3.** a mark indicating stress. **4.** a characteristic mode of pronunciation: *foreign accent.* **5.** *Music.* a stress or emphasis given to certain notes. —*v.t.* **6.** to pronounce with prominence. **7.** to mark with a written accent. **8.** to give emphasis or prominence to. —**ac·cen′tu·al,** *adj.*

ac·cen·tu·ate (ak sen′chōō āt′), *v.t.,* **-at·ed, -at·ing. 1.** to stress or emphasize. **2.** to mark or pronounce with an accent. —**ac·cen′tu·a′tion,** *n.*

ac·cept (ak sept′), *v.t.* **1.** to receive (something offered). **2.** to agree or accede to. **3.** to answer affirmatively to. **4.** to undertake the duties, etc., of. **5.** to admit to membership. **6.** to believe. **7.** *Com.* to agree to pay.

—**Usage.** ACCEPT and EXCEPT are sometimes confused as verbs because of their similarity in sound. ACCEPT means "to take or receive," *I accept this trophy.* while EXCEPT means "to exclude," *They excepted him from the membership list.*

ac·cept·a·ble (ak sep′tə bəl), *adj.* **1.** capable or worthy of being accepted. **2.** barely adequate or satisfactory. —**ac·cept′a·bil′i·ty, ac·cept′a·ble·ness,** *n.* —**ac·cept′a·bly,** *adv.*

ac·cept·ance (ak sep′təns), *n.* **1.** the act of accepting or state of being accepted or acceptable. **2.** *Com.* a promise to pay a draft.

ac·cep·ta·tion (ak'sep tā'shən), *n.* the usual or accepted meaning of a word.

ac·cept·ed (ak sep'tid), *adj.* generally approved.

ac·cess (ak'ses), *n.* **1.** permission to approach, enter, or use. **2.** a way or means of approach. **3.** *Obs.* an outburst. —*v.t.* **4.** to have or gain access to.

ac·ces·si·ble (ak ses'ə bəl), *adj.* **1.** easy to approach or enter. **2.** easily attainable. —**ac·ces'si·bil'i·ty, ac·ces'si·ble·ness,** *n.* —**ac·ces'si·bly,** *adv.*

ac·ces·sion (ak sesh'ən), *n.* **1.** the act of attaining a throne, power, etc. **2.** an increase by addition. **3.** something added. **4.** formal consent.

ac·ces·so·ry (ak ses'ə rē), *n., pl.* **-ries,** *adj.* —*n.* **1.** a supplementary part, object, etc., to one's basic apparel. **2.** *Law.* a person who, though absent, assists or conceals another who has committed a felony. —*adj.* **3.** supplementary. **4.** *Law.* giving aid as an accessory. Also, **ac·ces'sa·ry** (for defs. 2, 4). —**ac·ces'so·ri·ly,** *adv.* —**ac·ces'so·ri·ness,** *n.*

ac·ci·dence (ak'si dəns), *n.* *Gram.* the study of inflection and word order.

ac·ci·dent (ak'si dənt), *n.* **1.** an unintentional and undesirable happening. **2.** chance or fortune. **3.** an occasional characteristic.

ac·ci·den·tal (ak'si den't°l), *adj.* **1.** happening by chance or accident. —*n.* **2.** *Music.* a sign before a note indicating a chromatic alteration of its pitch. —**ac'ci·den'tal·ly,** *adv.*

ac·claim (ə klām'), *v.t.* **1.** to salute with shouts or sounds of approval. —*n.* **2.** loud applause. —**ac·claim'er,** *n.*

ac·cla·ma·tion (ak'lə mā'shən), *n.* **1.** a loud demonstration of welcome or approval. **2.** an affirmative vote made by shouts, hand clapping, etc.

ac·cli·mate (ə klī'mit, ak'lə māt'), *v.t., v.i.,* **-mat·ed, -mat·ing.** to accustom or become accustomed to a new climate or environment. Also, **ac·cli'ma·tize'** (-tīz'). —**ac·cli·ma·tion** (ak'lə mā'shən), **ac·cli'ma·ti·za'tion,** *n.*

ac·cliv·i·ty (ə kliv'i tē), *n., pl.* **ties.** an upward slope. —**ac·cliv'i·tous,** *adj.*

ac·co·lade (ak'ə lād', ak'ə lād'), *n.* any award, honor, or laudatory notice.

ac·com·mo·date (ə kom'ə dāt'), *v.,* **-dat·ed, -dat·ing.** —*v.t.* **1.** to do a favor for. **2.** to provide suitably. **3.** to provide with lodging. **4.** to

afford space for. **5.** to adapt or adjust. —**ac·com'mo·da'tive,** *adj.*

ac·com·mo·dat·ing (ə kom'ə dā'ting), *adj.* eager to help or please. —**ac·com'mo·dat'ing·ly,** *adv.*

ac·com·mo·da·tion (ə kom'ə dā'shən), *n.* **1.** the act of accommodating or the state of being accommodated. **2.** reconciliation. **3.** anything that supplies a need, want, etc. **4.** Usually, **accommodations. a.** lodging. **b.** facilities for a passenger on a train, plane, etc. **5.** *Com.* a loan.

ac·com·pa·ni·ment (ə kum'pə ni mənt, ə kump'ni-), *n.* **1.** something added for ornament, symmetry, etc. **2.** *Music.* a part serving as background and support.

ac·com·pa·ny (ə kum'pə nē), *v.t.,* **-nied, -ny·ing. 1.** to go with. **2.** to be with. **3.** *Music.* to play or sing an accompaniment to. —**ac·com'pa·nist,** *n.* —**Syn. 1.** attend, convoy, escort.

ac·com·plice (ə kom'plis), *n.* a person who helps another in a crime.

ac·com·plish (ə kom'plish), *v.t.* to bring to a successful conclusion. —**ac·com'plish·er,** *n.*

ac·com·plished (ə kom'plisht), *adj.* **1.** successfully done. **2.** expert or skilled. **3.** polished or refined.

ac·com·plish·ment (ə kom'plish mənt), *n.* **1.** the act of accomplishing. **2.** anything accomplished or achieved. **3.** a social grace or skill.

ac·cord (ə kôrd'), *n.* **1.** exact agreement or harmony. **2. of one's own accord,** voluntarily. —*v.t.* **3.** to make to agree or correspond. **4.** to grant or bestow. —*v.i.* **5.** to agree. —**ac·cord'a·ble,** *adj.* —**ac·cord'er,** *n.*

ac·cord·ance (ə kôr'dəns), *n.* **1.** exact conformity. **2.** the act of granting. —**ac·cord'ant,** *adj.*

ac·cord·ing·ly (ə kôr'ding lē), *adv.* **1.** in accordance. **2.** therefore or so.

according to', **1.** in accord with. **2.** as stated by.

ac·cor·di·on (ə kôr'dē ən), *n.* **1.** a portable musical instrument having a keyboard and a bellows for forcing air through small reeds. —*adj.* **2.** having folds like the bellows of an accordion: *accordion pleat.* —**ac·cor'di·on·ist,** *n.*

ac·cost (ə kôst', ə kost'), *v.t.* to approach, esp. to speak to. —**ac·cost'a·ble,** *adj.*

ac·count (ə kount'), *n.* **1.** a description of events or facts. **2.** an explanatory statement. **3.** reason or basis. **4.** importance or worth. **5.** a business relation allowing a depositor or client certain privileges. **6.** the money or credit available to such a depositor or client. **7.** a statement of transactions. **8. on account,** *Accounting.* as an installment or partial payment. **9. on account of,** because of. **10. on no account,** absolutely not. **11. on (someone's) account,** for the sake of (someone). **12. take into account,** to take into consideration. **13. turn to account,** to derive profit or use from. —*v.i.* **14.** to give an explanation. **15.** to answer concerning one's conduct, duties, etc. **16.** to be a cause (for). —*v.t.* **17.** to consider as. —**Syn. 1.** chronicle, narrative, report.

ac·count·a·ble (ə kount′tə bəl), *adj.* **1.** responsible or answerable. **2.** explainable. —**ac·count′a·bil′i·ty,** *n.* —**ac·count′a·bly,** *adv.*

ac·count·ant (ə koun′t°nt), *n.* a person whose profession is accounting. —**ac·count′an·cy, ac·count′ant·ship′,** *n.*

account′ exec′utive, a company official responsible for managing a client's account.

ac·count·ing (ə koun′tiñg), *n.* the system of organizing, maintaining, and auditing the financial records of a company or an individual.

ac·cou·ter (ə kōō′tər), *v.t.* to equip or outfit (esp. a warrior). Also, *esp. Brit.,* **ac·cou′tre.** —**ac·cou′ter·ment, ac·cou′tre·ment,** *n.*

ac·cred·it (ə kred′it), *v.t.* **1.** to attribute to or credit. **2.** to provide with credentials: *to accredit an envoy.* **3.** to certify as meeting all requirements. **4.** to believe. —**ac·cred′i·ta′tion,** *n.*

ac·cre·tion (ə krē′shən), *n.* **1.** an increase by growth or addition. **2.** the result of this process. **3.** an extraneous addition.

ac·crue (ə krōō′), *v.i.,* **-crued, -cru·ing. 1.** to happen or result as a natural growth, addition, etc. **2.** to be added as a periodic gain. —**ac·cru′al,** *n.* —**ac·crue′ment,** *n.*

acct., **1.** account. **2.** accountant.

ac·cul·tur·a·tion (ə kul′chə rā′shən), *n.* adoption of the traits or patterns of another group.

ac·cu·mu·late (ə kyōō′myə lāt′), *v.t., v.i.,* **-lat·ed, -lat·ing.** to collect or gather, esp. by degrees and over a period of time. —**ac·cu′mu·la′tion,** *n.* —**ac·cu′mu·la′tive,** *adj.* —**ac·cu′mu·la′tor,** *n.*

ac·cu·rate (ak′yər it), *adj.* conforming carefully to truth or fact. —**ac′cu·ra·cy** (-ə sē), *n.* —**ac′cu·rate·ly,** *adv.* —**ac′cu·rate·ness,** *n.* —**Syn.** correct, exact, precise.

ac·curs·ed (ə kûr′sid, ə kûrst′), *adj.* **1.** subject to a curse. **2.** damnable. Also, **ac·curst** (ə kûrst′). —**ac·curs′ed·ly** (ə kûr′sid lē), *adv.* —**ac·curs′ed·ness,** *n.*

accus., accusative.

ac·cu·sa·tive (ə kyōō′zə tiv), *Gram.* —*adj.* **1.** noting a case that indi-

cates the object of a verb or preposition, as in Latin. —*n.* **2.** the accusative case. —**ac·cu′sa·tive·ly,** *adv.*

ac·cuse (ə kyōōz′), *v.t.,* **-cused, -cus·ing. 1.** to charge with a fault, offense, or crime. **2.** to blame. —**ac′cu·sa′tion, ac·cus·al** (ə kyōō′zəl), *n.* —**ac·cus′er,** *n.* —**ac·cus·a·to·ry** (ə kyōō′zə tôr′ē), *adj.* —**Syn. 1.** arraign, impeach, indict.

ac·cused (ə kyōōzd′), *n.* the defendant in a trial.

ac·cus·tom (ə kus′təm), *v.t.* to familiarize by use or habit.

ac·cus·tomed (ə kus′təmd), *adj.* **1.** customary or habitual. **2.** in the habit of.

ace (ās), *n., adj., v.,* **aced, ac·ing.** —*n.* **1.** a playing card bearing a single spot. **2.** (in tennis, etc.) a successful serve that the opponent fails to return. **3.** an expert. **4.** a fighter pilot credited with downing a number of enemy aircraft. **5.** *Golf.* a hole in one stroke. **6. ace in the hole,** an advantage kept in reserve. —*adj.* **7.** excellent or outstanding. —*v.t.* **8.** to score against (an opponent) by an ace.

a·cerb (ə sûrb′), *adj.* **1.** sour in taste. **2.** harsh or severe. Also, **a·cer·bic** (ə sûr′bik). —**a·cer′bi·ty,** *n.*

ac·er·bate (as′ər bāt′), *v.t.,* **-bat·ed, -bat·ing. 1.** to make sour or bitter. **2.** to exasperate.

ac·et·an·i·lide (as′i tan′°līd′, -°lid), *n.* a drug used to treat fever, headache, etc.

ac·e·tate (as′i tāt′), *n.* **1.** a salt or ester of acetic acid. **2.** a fabric composed of an acetic ester of cellulose.

a·ce·tic (ə sē′tik, ə set′ik), *adj.* of, from, or producing vinegar or acetic acid.

ace′tic ac′id, a water-miscible liquid, the essential constituent of vinegar.

a·cet·i·fy (ə set′ə fī′), *v.t., v.i.,* **-fied, -fy·ing.** to turn into vinegar or acetic acid.

ac·e·tone (as′i tōn′), *n.* a volatile, flammable liquid used as a solvent. —**ac·e·ton·ic** (as′i ton′ik), *adj.*

a·ce·tyl·cho·line (ə sēt′°l kō′lēn), *n.* a chemical compound that causes muscle action by transmitting nerve impulses across synapses.

a·cet·y·lene (ə set′°lēn′, -°lin), *n.* a colorless gas, used esp. in metal cutting and welding.

a·ce·tyl·sal·i·cyl′ic ac′id (ə sēt′°l sal′i·sil′ik, ə set′-, as′i t°l-), aspirin.

ache (āk), *v.,* **ached, ach·ing,** *n.* —*v.i.* **1.** to have a continuous, dull pain. **2.** to yearn or long. —*n.* **3.** a continuous, dull pain. —**ach′y,** *adj.* —**ach′i·ness,** *n.*

a·chene (ā kēn′), *n.* a small, dry, one-seeded fruit.

a·chieve (ə chēv′), *v.t.*, **a·chieved**, **a·chiev·ing.** 1. to bring to a successful end. 2. to get by effort. —**a·chiev′a·ble**, *adj.* —**a·chiev′er**, *n.* —**a·chieve′ment**, *n.*

A·chil·les (ə kil′ēz), *n. Class. Myth.* a Greek warrior killed in the Trojan War.

Achil′les heel′, a small but weak or vulnerable spot.

Achil′les ten′don, the tendon joining the calf muscles to the heel bone.

ach·ro·mat·ic (ak′rə mat′ik), *adj.* 1. free from color. 2. able to emit, transmit, or receive light without separating it into colors. —**ach′ro·mat′i·cal·ly**, *adv.*

ac·id (as′id), *n.* 1. a compound usually having a sour taste and capable of neutralizing alkalis and reddening blue litmus paper. 2. a substance with a sour taste. 3. *Slang.* See LSD. —*adj.* 4. belonging or pertaining to acids. 5. sharp or biting to the taste. 6. sharp, biting, or ill-natured. —**a·cid′ic**, *adj.* —**a·cid′i·ty**, *n.*

ac·id·head (as′id hed′), *n. Slang.* a habitual user of LSD.

a·cid·i·fy (ə sid′ə fī′), *v.t.*, *v.i.*, **-fied**, **-fy·ing.** 1. to convert into acid. 2. to make or become sour. —**a·cid′i·fi′a·ble**, *adj.* —**a·cid′i·fi·ca′tion**, *n.* —**a·cid′i·fi′er**, *n.*

ac·i·do·sis (as′i dō′sis), *n.* a blood condition in which the bicarbonate concentration is below normal.

ac′id test′, a severe, conclusive test of worth.

a·cid·u·late (ə sij′ə lāt′, ə sid′yə-), *v.t.*, **-lat·ed**, **-lat·ing.** to make acid. —**a·cid′u·la′tion**, *n.*

a·cid·u·lous (ə sij′ə ləs, ə sid′yə-), *adj.* 1. slightly sour. 2. sharp or caustic.

-acious, a suffix meaning "tending to" or "abounding in": *audacious.*

-acity, a suffix meaning "tendency toward" or "abundance in": *audacity.*

ack., 1. acknowledge. 2. acknowledgment.

ack-ack (ak′ak′), *n.* 1. antiaircraft fire. 2. antiaircraft arms.

ac·knowl·edge (ak nol′ij), *v.t.*, **-edged**, **-edg·ing.** 1. to admit the existence, truth, or fact of. 2. to recognize the authority, validity, or claims of. 3. to express appreciation for. 4. to make known the receipt of. 5. *Law.* to confirm as binding. —**ac·knowl′edg·er**, *n.* —**ac·knowl′edg·ment, ac·knowl′edge·ment**, *n.*

A.C.L.U., American Civil Liberties Union.

ac·me (ak′mē), *n.* highest point or stage.

ac·ne (ak′nē), *n.* a disease of the sebaceous glands characterized esp. by pimples on the face.

ac·o·lyte (ak′ə līt′), *n.* an altar attendant in public worship.

ac·o·nite (ak′ə nīt′), *n.* any plant of the buttercup family, including species with poisonous and medicinal properties.

a·corn (ā′kôrn, ā′kərn), *n.* the typically ovoid fruit or nut of an oak.

a′corn squash′, an acorn-shaped variety of winter squash, dark-green to orange-yellow in color.

a·cous·tic (ə kōō′stik), *adj.* 1. pertaining to the sense or organs of hearing, to sound, or to the science of sound. 2. designed for controlling sound: *acoustic tile.* 3. operated by sound waves. Also, **a·cous′ti·cal**. —**a·cous′ti·cal·ly**, *adv.*

a·cous·tics (ə kōō′stiks), *n.* 1. the branch of physics that deals with sound and sound waves. 2. the qualities of a room, stadium, etc., that determine the quality of sounds in it.

ac·quaint (ə kwānt′), *v.t.* 1. to make familiar or conversant. 2. to make aware. —**ac·quaint′ed**, *adj.*

ac·quaint·ance (ə kwān′təns), *n.* 1. a person whom one knows. 2. personal knowledge. —**ac·quaint′ance·ship′**, *n.*

ac·qui·esce (ak′wē es′), *v.i.*, **-esced**, **-esc·ing.** to consent or comply tacitly. —**ac′qui·es′cence**, *n.* —**ac′qui·es′cent**, *adj.* —**ac′qui·es′cent·ly**, *adv.*

ac·quire (ə kwī°r′), *v.t.*, **-quired**, **-quir·ing.** 1. to get possession of. 2. to gain through one's efforts. —**ac·quir′a·ble**, *adj.* —**ac·quire′ment**, *n.*

ac·qui·si·tion (ak′wi zish′ən), *n.* 1. the act or an instance of getting possession. 2. something acquired.

ac·quis·i·tive (ə kwiz′i tiv), *adj.* tending or seeking to acquire, often greedily. —**ac·quis′i·tive·ly**, *adv.* —**ac·quis′i·tive·ness**, *n.*

ac·quit (ə kwit′), *v.t.*, **-quit·ted**, **-quit·ting.** 1. to relieve from a charge of fault or crime. 2. to release from an obligation. 3. to carry or conduct (oneself). —**ac·quit′tal**, *n.*

a·cre (ā′kər), *n.* 1. a unit of land measure equal to 43,560 square feet or 0.4047 hectare. 2. **acres**, lands.

a·cre·age (ā′kər ij), *n.* area in acres.

ac·rid (ak′rid), *adj.* 1. sharp or biting to the taste or smell. 2. sharply stinging or caustic: *acrid remarks.* —**a·crid·i·ty** (ə krid′i tē), **ac′rid·ness**, *n.* —**ac′rid·ly**, *adv.*

ac·ri·mo·ny (ak′rə mō′nē), *n.* sharpness, harshness, or bitterness of nature, speech, etc. —**ac′ri·mo′ni·ous**, *adj.* —**ac′ri·mo′ni·ous·ness**, *n.*

ac·ro·bat (ak′rə bat′), *n.* a skilled

performer of gymnastic feats. —ac'ro·bat'ic, *adj.*

ac·ro·bat·ics (ak'rə bat'iks), *n.* **1.** the feats of an acrobat. **2.** any remarkably agile feat.

ac·ro·nym (ak'rə nim), *n.* a word formed from the initial letters of words in a phrase, as *scuba* from *self-contained underwater breathing apparatus.*

ac·ro·pho·bi·a (ak'rə fō'bē ə), *n.* pathological dread of high places.

a·crop·o·lis (ə krop'ə lis), *n.* **1.** a fortified hill in an ancient Greek city. **2. the** Acropolis, the citadel of Athens.

a·cross (ə krôs', ə kros'), *prep.* **1.** from one side to the other of. **2.** on or to the other side of. **3.** into contact with. **4.** so as to be transverse to the length of something. —*adv.* **5.** from one side to another. **6.** on the other side. **7.** transversely. **8.** so as to be understood or learned.

a·cross-the-board (ə krôs'<i>th</i>ə bôrd', -bôrd', ə kros'-), *adj.* **1.** applying to all: *an across-the-board pay increase.* **2.** placing a combination bet in a race for win, place, and show.

a·cros·tic (ə krô'stik, ə kros'tik), *n.* a series of written lines or verses in which the first, last, or other particular letters form a word, phrase, etc. —a·cros'ti·cal·ly, *adv.*

a·cryl·ic (ə kril'ik), *n.* **1.** See **acrylic resin. 2.** a paint, esp. for artists, in which an acrylic resin serves as a vehicle.

acryl'ic res'in, any of a group of thermoplastic resins used chiefly where transparency is desired.

act (akt), *n.* **1.** anything done or performed. **2.** the process of doing: *caught in the act.* **3.** a law, decree, or edict: *an act of Congress.* **4.** one of the main divisions of a play or opera. **5.** a short performance, usually part of a variety show, etc. **6.** a piece of insincere conduct. —*v.i.* **7.** to do something or be operative. **8.** to reach a decision. **9.** to function in a particular way. **10.** to produce an effect. **11.** to behave in a particular fashion. **12.** to pretend or feign. **13.** to perform on a stage as an actor or actress. —*v.t.* **14.** to represent (a character): *She acts Cleopatra.* **15. act up,** to exhibit unexpected behavior.

act., active.

ACT, Australian Capital Territory.

actg., acting.

ACTH, a hormone, produced by the pituitary gland, that stimulates the cortical substance of the adrenal glands.

ac·tin (ak'tən), *n.* a muscle protein that is important in muscular contraction.

act·ing (ak'ting), *adj.* **1.** serving temporarily, esp. as a substitute: *the acting mayor.* —*n.* **2.** the art or profession of an actor or actress.

ac'tinide se'ries (ak'tə nīd'), the series of radioactive elements that starts with actinium and ends with lawrencium.

ac·tin·ism (ak'tə niz'əm), *n.* the property of radiation by which chemical effects are produced. —ac·tin·ic (ak tin'ik), *adj.* —ac·tin'i·cal·ly, *adv.*

ac·tin·i·um (ak tin'ē əm), *n. Chem.* a radioactive element. *Symbol:* Ac; *at. wt.:* 227: *at. no.:* 89.

ac·tion (ak'shən), *n.* **1.** the process or state of acting. **2.** act or deed. **3. actions,** conduct. **4.** energetic activity. **5.** effect or influence. **6.** a way of moving: *the action of a machine.* **7.** a mechanism by which something is operated. **8.** a military combat. **9.** a proceeding in a court of justice: *to bring action.*

ac·tion·a·ble (ak'shə nə bəl), *adj.* furnishing grounds for a lawsuit.

ac·ti·vate (ak'tə vāt'), *v.t.*, **-vat·ed, -vat·ing. 1.** to make active. **2.** to render reactive or radioactive. **3.** to aerate (sewage) in order to accelerate decomposition. **4.** *Chem.* to make (carbon, etc.) more active. **5.** to place (a military unit) on an active status. —ac'ti·va'tion, *n.* —ac'ti·va'tor, *n.*

ac'tivated car'bon, a carbon having very fine pores, used chiefly for absorbing gases. Also called **ac'tivated char'coal.**

ac·tive (ak'tiv), *adj.* **1.** constantly in action. **2.** in actual existence. **3.** involving or causing action. **4.** nimble. **5.** currently in action. **6.** not inert. **7.** *Gram.* noting the voice of a verb in which the subject performs the action. **8.** *Accounting.* profitable or busy. **9.** *Mil.* on fulltime duty. —*n.* **10.** *Gram.* the active voice. —ac'tive·ly, *adv.* —**Syn. 1.** busy, energetic, vigorous.

ac·tiv·ism (ak'tə viz'əm), *n.* a doctrine or practice of vigorous action to achieve political or social goals. —ac'tiv·ist, *n.*, *adj.*

ac·tiv·i·ty (ak tiv'i tē), *n., pl.* **-ties. 1.** the state or quality of being active. **2.** a specific deed or action. **3.** work or occupation. **4.** liveliness or alertness.

act' of God', *Law.* a direct and irresistible action of natural forces, as a flood.

ac·to·my·o·sin (ak'tə mī'ə sin), *n.* a complex protein that is the major constituent of skeletal muscle.

ac·tor (ak'tər), *n.* a person who

acts in plays, motion pictures, etc.
—ac′tress, n.fem.

ac·tu·al (ak′chōō əl), adj. existing in
fact: an actual event. —ac′tu·al′i·
ty, n. —ac′tu·al·ly, adv.

ac·tu·al·ize (ak′chōō ə līz′), v.t.,
-ized, -iz·ing. 1. to make actual.
2. to realize in action. —ac′tu·al·
i·za′tion, n.

ac·tu·ar·y (ak′chōō er′ē), n., pl.
-ar·ies. a person who computes
insurance risks, premiums, etc.
—ac·tu·ar·i·al (ak′chōō âr′ē əl),
adj.

ac·tu·ate (ak′chōō āt′), v.t., -at·ed,
-at·ing. 1. to incite to action. 2. to
put into action. —ac′tu·a′tion, n.
—ac′tu·a′tor, n.

a·cu·i·ty (ə kyōō′i tē), n. sharpness
of perception.

a·cu·men (ə kyōō′mən, ak′yə-), n.
superior mental acuteness.

ac·u·punc·ture (ak′yōō pungk′chər),
n. a practice, chiefly in Chinese
medicine, of attempting to cure
illness or relieve pain by puncturing specified areas of the skin with
needles. —ac·u·punc·tur·ist (ak′-
yōō pungk′chər ist), n.

a·cute (ə kyōōt′), adj. 1. sharp at
the end. 2. intense. 3. severe or
crucial. 4. Med. brief and severe.
5. sharp in insight. 6. highly sensitive. 7. (of an angle) less than 90°.
8. of or indicated by the mark ′,
used to indicate quality of a vowel
or stress. —n. 9. the acute accent.
—a·cute′ly, adv. —a·cute′ness, n.

ad (ad), n. advertisement.

A.D., 1. Mil. active duty. 2. in the
year of our Lord (used with dates):
from 20 B.C. to A.D. 50. [< L anno
Domini]

A.D.A., Americans for Democratic
Action.

ad·age (ad′ij), n. a time-honored
proverb.

a·da·gio (ə dä′jō, -zhe ō′), adv., adj.,
n., pl. -gios. —adv. 1. Music.
slowly. —adj. 2. Music. slow. —n.
3. Music. an adagio movement. 4. a
dance emphasizing technical feats.
[< It, for ad agio at ease]

Ad·am (ad′əm), n. Bible. the first
man.

ad·a·mant (ad′ə mənt, -mant′), n.
1. a legendary stone of extreme
hardness. —adj. 2. Also, ad′a·
man′tine (-tin, -tēn, -tīn). utterly unyielding. —ad′a·mant·ly, adv.

Ad·ams (ad′əmz), n. 1. John, 1735-
1826, 2nd president of the U.S.
1797-1801. 2. John Quincy (kwin′-
zē, -sē), 1767-1848, 6th president
of the U.S. 1825-29 (son of John
Adams).

Ad′am's ap′ple, a projection of the
thyroid cartilage at the front of
the neck.

a·dapt (ə dapt′), v.t., v.i. to adjust or
become adjusted to new conditions,
etc. —a·dapt′a·ble, adj. —a·dapt′a·
bil′i·ty, a·dapt′a·ble·ness, n. —ad-
ap·ta·tion (ad′əp tā′shən), n. —
a·dap·tive (ə dap′tiv), adj.

a·dapt·er (ə dap′tər), n. 1. one that
adapts. 2. a device for connecting
parts having different sizes. 3. an
accessory to convert a tool, etc.,
to a new use. Also, a·dap′tor.

add (ad), v.t. 1. to unite or join
so as to produce a greater number,
size, etc. 2. to find the sum of.
3. to say or write further. —v.i.
4. to perform the arithmetic operation of addition. 5. to be an addition. 6. add up, to seem reasonable.
7. add up to, to indicate or imply.
—add′a·ble, add′i·ble, adj. —Syn. 1.
annex, append, subjoin.

add., 1. addenda. 2. addition.

ad·dend (ad′end), n. a number to be
added to another.

ad·den·dum (ə den′dəm), n., pl. -da
(-də). 1. an addition. 2. an appendix to a book.

add·er¹ (ad′ər), n. 1. one that adds.
2. a business machine for adding.

ad·der² (ad′ər), n. 1. the common
European viper. 2. any of various
other venomous or harmless snakes
resembling the viper.

ad·dict (n. ad′ikt; v. ə dikt′), n. 1.
a person who is addicted: a drug
addict. —v.t. 2. to give (oneself)
up to something habitually. 3. to
cause (a person) to depend physiologically on a drug. —ad·dic′tion,
n. —ad·dic′tive, adj.

ad·di·tion (ə dish′ən), n. 1. the act
or process of adding. 2. something
added. 3. in addition to, as well as.
—ad·di′tion·al, adj. —ad·di′tion·al·
ly, adv.

ad·di·tive (ad′i tiv), adj. 1. produced
by addition. —n. 2. something
added to alter or improve the quality.

ad·dle (ad′ºl), v.t., v.i., -dled, -dling.
1. to make or become confused.
2. to make or become rotten, as
eggs.

addn., additional. Also, addnl.

ad·dress (n. ə dres′, ad′res; v.
ə dres′), n. 1. a formal speech
or statement. 2. the designation of
a place where a person or organization may be found or with receive mail. 3. such a designation
placed on mail. 4. Obs. ready skill.
—v.t. 5. to direct a speech to. 6.
to call (a person) by a specific
name. 7. to put the directions for
delivery on. 8. to direct the energy
or attention of.

ad·dress·ee (ad′re sē′, ə dre sē′), n.
a person, etc., to whom a letter,
etc., is addressed.

ad·duce (ə dōōs′, ə dyōōs′), .*v.t.*, **-duced**, **-duc·ing**. to bring forward in argument or as evidence.

-ade, a suffix meaning: a. action: *masquerade*. b. drink made of: *lemonade*.

A·den (äd′ᵊn, ād′ᵊn), n. 1. the capital of the People's Democratic Republic of Yemen. 2. Gulf of, an arm of the Arabian Sea, S of Arabia.

ad·e·nine (ad′ᵊnin, -ᵊnēn′, -ᵊnīn′), n. alkaloid obtained from tea or by synthesis: used chiefly in medicine.

ad·e·noid (ad′ᵊnoid′), n. Usually, **adenoids**. an enlarged mass of lymphoid tissue in the upper pharynx. —ad·e·noi′dal, adj.

ad·en·o·sine tri·phos·phate (ə den′ᵊsēn′ trī fos′fāt). See ATP.

ad·ept (adj. ə dept′; n. ad′ept, ə dept′), adj. 1. very skilled. —n. 2. an expert. —a·dept′ly, adv. —a·dept′ness, n.

ad·e·quate (ad′ᵊ kwit), adj. 1. equal to a requirement. 2. barely sufficient or suitable. —ad′e·quate·ly, adv. —ad′e·qua·cy (-kwə sē), n.

ad·here (ad hēr′), v.i., **-hered**, **-her·ing**. 1. to stick fast. 2. to be a follower or upholder. 3. to hold firmly. —ad·her′ence, n. —ad·her′ent, n., adj. —ad·her′er, n.

ad·he·sion (ad hē′zhən), n. 1. the act or state of adhering. 2. the molecular attraction between unlike bodies contacted. 3. the abnormal union of adjacent tissues.

ad·he·sive (ad hē′siv), adj. 1. sticking fast. 2. sticky or gummed. —n. 3. an adhesive material or substance.

adhe′sive tape′, tape coated on one side with an adhesive substance, used esp. for holding a bandage in place.

ad hoc (ad hok′), for this (special purpose) only.

ad ho·mi·nem (äd hō′mi nem′), appealing to a prejudice rather than to reason.

ad·i·a·bat·ic (ad′ē ə bat′ik, ā′dī ə-), adj. occurring without gain or loss of heat. —ad′i·a·bat′i·cal·ly, adv.

a·dieu (ə dōō′, ə dyōō′), interj., n., pl. **a·dieus**, **a·dieux** (ə dōōz′, ə dyōōz′). goodby. [< MF < a- (L ad- to) + dieu (< L deus god)]

ad in·fi·ni·tum (ad in′fə nī′təm), endlessly.

ad int. See ad interim.

ad in·te·rim (ad in′tə rim), in the meantime.

ad·i·os (ad′ē ōs′, ā′dē-), interj. goodby.

ad·i·pose (ad′ə pōs′), adj. containing or like animal fat. —ad′i·pose′ness, ad·i·pos·i·ty (ad′ə pos′i tē), ad′i·po′sis, n.

Ad′iron′dack Moun′tains (ad′ə ron′-dak), a mountain range in NE New York. Also called **Ad′iron′dacks**.

adj., 1. adjacent. 2. adjective. 3. adjutant.

ad·ja·cent (ə jā′sənt), adj. next to or near by. —ad·ja′cent·ly, adv. —ad·ja′cen·cy, n.

ad·jec·tive (aj′ik tiv), n. a word functioning as a modifier of a noun. —ad·jec·ti·val (aj′ik tī′vəl), adj. —ad′jec·ti′val·ly, adv.

ad·join (ə join′), v.t. 1. to be next to. —v.i. 2. to be connected. —ad·join′ing, adj.

ad·journ (ə jûrn′), v.t. 1. to suspend the meeting of (a legislature, etc.) to a future time or indefinitely. —v.i. 2. to suspend a proceeding for a time. 3. Informal. to go to another place. —ad·journ′ment, n.

ad·judge (ə juj′), v.t., **-judged**, **-judg·ing**. 1. to decide judicially. 2. to award judicially. 3. Archaic. to deem.

ad·ju·di·cate (ə jōō′də kāt′), v., **-cat·ed**, **-cat·ing**. —v.t. 1. to settle judicially. —v.i. 2. to sit in judgment. —ad·ju′di·ca′tion, n. —ad·ju·di·ca·tive (ə jōō′də kā′tiv, -kə tiv), adj. —ad·ju′di·ca′tor, n. —ad·ju′di·ca·to′ry (-kə tōr′ē), adj.

ad·junct (aj′ungkt), n. something added to another thing but not essentially a part of it. —ad·junc′tive, adj.

ad·jure (ə jōōr′), v.t., **-jured**, **-jur·ing**. 1. to charge or command solemnly. 2. to entreat. —ad·ju·ra·tion (aj′-ōō rā′shən), n.

ad·just (ə just′), v.t. 1. to make necessary or desirable changes. 2. to put in working order. 3. to settle properly. 4. Insurance. to determine the amount to be paid in settlement of (a claim). —v.i. 5. to adapt oneself. —ad·just′a·ble, adj. —ad·just′er, ad·jus′tor, n. —ad·just′ment, n. —Syn. 1. accommodate, adapt, fit.

ad·ju·tant (aj′ə tənt), n. 1. a staff officer who assists the commanding officer in issuing orders. 2. an assistant. 3. a large stork.

ad lib (ad lib′, ad′), an ad-libbed remark.

ad-lib (ad lib′, ad′-), v., **-libbed**, **-lib·bing**, adj. —v.t. 1. to improvise (a speech, etc.). —v.i. 2. to speak, etc., without preparation. —adj. 3. impromptu. —ad·lib′ber, n.

ad lib·i·tum (ad lib′i təm), Music. that can be omitted.

ad loc., at the place. [< L ad locum]

Adm., Admiral.

adm., 1. administration. 2. administrative. Also, **admin**.

ad·man (ad′man′, -mən), n. a person who writes, designs, or sells advertisements.

ad·min·is·ter (ad min′i stər), *v.t.*, *v.i.*
1. to manage (affairs, etc.). **2.** to bring into use or operation. **3.** to give remedially. **4.** to tender (an oath). **5.** to dispose of (an estate). —**ad·min·is·tra·ble** (ad min′i stra-bəl), *adj.* —**ad·min·is·trant** (ad min′-i strənt), *adj.*, *n.*

ad·min·is·trate (ad min′i strāt′), *v.t.*, *v.i.*, **-trat·ed, -trat·ing.** to administer.

ad·min·is·tra·tion (ad min′i strā′-shən), *n.* **1.** the act of administering. **2.** the management of an office, agency, or organization. **3.** the duties of an administrator. **4.** an official body serving as an administrator. **5.** the period during which an administrator serves. **6.** the disposition of an estate. —**ad·min′is·tra′tion·al**, *adj.* —**ad·min′is·tra′tive**, *adj.* —**ad·min′is·tra′tive·ly**, *adv.*

ad·min·is·tra·tor (ad min′i strā′tər), *n.* **1.** a person who administers. **2.** a person appointed to dispose of an estate.

ad·mi·ra·ble (ad′mər ə bəl), *adj.* worthy of admiration. —**ad′mi·ra·bly**, *adv.*

ad·mi·ral (ad′mər əl), *n.* **1.** the commander in chief of a fleet. **2.** a naval officer of the second highest rank. —**ad′mi·ral·ship′**, *n.*

ad·mi·ral·ty (ad′mər əl tē), *n., pl.* **-ties.** *Brit.* **1.** (*cap.*) a former department having charge of naval affairs. **2.** a former court dealing with maritime questions, etc.

ad·mire (ad mī″r′), *v.*, **-mired, -mir·ing.** —*v.t.* **1.** to regard with wonder and pleasure. —*v.i.* **2.** to express admiration. —**ad·mi·ra·tion** (ad′-mə rā′shən), *n.* —**ad·mir′er**, *n.* —**ad·mir′ing·ly**, *adv.*

ad·mis·si·ble (ad mis′ə bəl), *adj.* **1.** that may be allowed or conceded. *Law.* capable of being allowed as proof: *admissible evidence.* —**ad·mis′si·bil′i·ty**, *n.* —**ad·mis′si·bly**, *adv.*

ad·mis·sion (ad mish′ən), *n.* **1.** the act of admitting. **2.** the right or means of entering. **3.** the price paid for entrance. **4.** the act of being accepted in a position or office. **5.** confession of a charge, error, or crime.

ad·mit (ad mit′), *v.*, **-mit·ted, -mit·ting.** —*v.t.* **1.** to allow to enter. **2.** to permit to exercise a certain function. **3.** to acknowledge or confess. **4.** to concede as true or valid. —*v.i.* **5.** to permit entrance. —**ad·mit′tance**, *n.* —**ad·mit′ted·ly**, *adv.*

ad·mix (ad miks′), *v.t.*, *v.i.* to mix or become mixed. —**ad·mix′ture**, *n.*

ad·mon·ish (ad mon′ish), *v.t.* **1.** to warn or caution gently. **2.** to reprove mildly. —**ad′mo·ni′tion**, *n.* —**ad-**

mon′ish·ment, *n.* —**ad·mon′i·to′ry** (-mon′i tō′rē), *adj.*

ad nau·se·am (ad nô′zē əm), to a sickening degree.

a·do (ə dōō′), *n.* bustling and confused activity.

a·do·be (ə dō′bē), *n.* **1.** sun-dried brick. **2.** a clay used to make bricks. **3.** a building constructed of such bricks. [< Sp < Ar *aṭ-ṭōb* brick]

ad·o·les·cence (ad′ə les′əns), *n.* the transitional period between puberty and adulthood, mainly covering the teen years. —**ad′o·les′cent**, *adj.*, *n.*

A·do·nis (ə don′is, ə dō′nis), *n.* **1.** *Class. Myth.* a youth whom Aphrodite loved. **2.** a handsome youth.

a·dopt (ə dopt′), *v.t.* **1.** to take as one's own. **2.** to become the legal parent or parents of (another person's child). **3.** to accept (a plan, etc.). —**a·dopt′er**, *n.* —**a·dop′tion**, *n.* —**a·dop′tive**, *adj.* —**a·dop′tive·ly**, *adv.*

a·dor·a·ble (ə dôr′ə bəl, ə dôr′-), *adj.* **1.** delightful and charming. **2.** *Archaic.* worthy of being adored. —**a·dor′a·bil′i·ty**, **a·dor′a·ble·ness**, *n.* —**a·dor′a·bly**, *adv.*

a·dore (ə dôr′, ə dōr′), *v.t.*, **a·dored, a·dor·ing. 1.** to regard with utmost love and respect. **2.** to worship. **3.** to like very much. —**ad·o·ra·tion** (ad′ə rā′shən), *n.* —**a·dor′er**, *n.* —**Syn. 1.** honor, idolize, revere.

a·dorn (ə dôrn′), *v.t.* to add beauty to, as by ornaments. —**a·dorn′er**, *n.* **a·dorn′ment**, *n.*

ad·re·nal (ə drēn′əl), *adj.* **1.** situated near or on the kidneys. **2.** of or produced by the adrenal glands.

adre′nal gland′, one of a pair of ductless glands located above the kidneys.

a·dren·a·line (ə dren′ə lin, -əlēn′), *n.* epinephrine.

a·dre′no·cor·ti·co·trop′ic hor′mone (ə drē″nō kôr″tə kō trop′ik). See **ACTH.**

A′dri·at′ic Sea′ (ā′drē at′ik, ad′rē-), an arm of the Mediterranean between Italy and Yugoslavia.

a·drift (ə drift′), *adj.*, *adv.* **1.** without anchor. **2.** without direction.

a·droit (ə droit′), *adj.* **1.** cleverly skillful or resourceful. **2.** manually dexterous. —**a·droit′ly**, *adv.* —**a·droit′ness**, *n.*

ad·sorb (ad sôrb′, -zôrb′), *v.t.* to gather (a gas, etc.) on a surface in a condensed layer. —**ad·sorb′ent**, *adj.*, *n.* —**ad·sorp′tion** (ad sôrp′-shən, -zôrp′-), *n.* —**ad·sorp′tive**, *adj.*

ad·sorb·ate (ad sôr′bāt, -bit, -zôr′-), *n.* the substance adsorbed.

ad·u·late (aj′ə lāt′), *v.t.*, **-lat·ed, -lat·ing.** to flatter or admire excessively. —**ad·u·la·tion**, *n.* —**ad·u·la·tor**, *n.* —**ad·u·la·to·ry** (aj′ə lə-tōr′ē, -tôr′ē), *adj.*

a·dult (ə dult′, ad′ult), *adj.* **1.** having attained maturity. **2.** of or befitting adults. **3.** intended for adults only: *adult movies.* —*n.* **4.** a person who has attained maturity or legal age. —**a·dult′hood**, *n.* —**a·dult′-ness**, *n.*

a·dul·ter·ant (ə dul′tər ənt), *n.* **1.** a substance that adulterates. —*adj.* **2.** that adulterates.

a·dul·ter·ate (ə dul′tə rāt′), *v.t.,* **-at-ed, -at·ing.** to debase by adding inferior materials or elements. —**a·dul·ter·a′tion**, *n.* —**a·dul·ter·a′-tor**, *n.*

a·dul·ter·y (ə dul′tə rē), *n.,* *pl.* **-ter-ies.** voluntary sexual intercourse of a married person with someone other than his or her lawful spouse. —**a·dul′ter·er**, *n.* —**a·dul·ter·ess** (-tər is, -tris), *n.fem.* —**a·dul′ter·ous**, *adj.* —**a·dul′ter·ous·ly**, *adv.*

ad·um·brate (ad um′brāt, ad′əm brāt′), *v.t.,* **-brat·ed, -brat·ing. 1.** to outline sketchily. **2.** to foreshadow. **3.** to darken partially. —**ad·um·bra′tion**, *n.*

adv., 1. adverb. **2.** advertisement.

ad val., See **ad valorem.**

ad va·lo·rem (ad və lōr′əm, -lôr′-), in proportion to the value: *an ad valorem duty.*

ad·vance (ad vans′, -väns′), *v.,* **-vanced, -vanc·ing,** *n., adj.* —*v.t.* **1.** to bring or send forward. **2.** to present for consideration. **3.** to further the development of. **4.** to promote. **5.** to accelerate. **6.** to supply (money or goods) on credit. **7.** *Rare.* to raise (a price). —*v.i.* **8.** to come or go forward. **9.** to show improvement. **10.** to increase in price, etc. —*n.* **11.** a forward movement. **12.** a noticeable improvement. **13.** a promotion. **14.** an increase in a figure. **15.** an attempt at forming an acquaintance, etc. **16.** a sum of money or quantity of goods furnished on credit. **17. in advance, a.** in front. **b.** beforehand. **18.** before all others. **19.** made or issued beforehand. —**ad·vance′ment**, *n.* —**ad·vanc′er**, *n.*

ad·vanced (ad vanst′, -vänst′), *adj.* **1.** placed forward. **2.** greater than another in development, etc. **3.** relatively old.

ad·van·tage (ad van′tij, -vän′-), *n., v.,* **-taged, -tag·ing.** —*n.* **1.** anything favorable to a desired end. **2.** a superior position. **3.** *Tennis.* the first point scored after deuce. **4. take advantage of, a.** to make use of (an opportunity). **b.** to exploit the weakness of. —*v.t.* **5.** to benefit or gain. —**ad′van·ta′geous**, *adj.* —**ad′van-**

ta′geous·ly, *adv.* —**Syn. 1.** benefit, gain, profit.

ad·vent (ad′vent), *n.* **1.** arrival or coming into being. **2.** (*usually cap.*) the coming of Christ. **3.** (*cap.*) the penitential period beginning four Sundays before Christmas.

ad·ven·ti·tious (ad′vən tish′əs), *adj.* **1.** not intrinsic or essential. **2.** appearing in an abnormal place, as a bud. —**ad′ven·ti′tious·ly**, *adv.* —**ad′ven·ti′tious·ness**, *n.*

ad·ven·ture (ad ven′chər), *n., v.,* **-tured, -tur·ing.** —*n.* **1.** an undertaking involving risk or excitement. **2.** an exciting or remarkable experience. **3.** a venture involving financial risk. —*v.t., v.i.* **4.** to venture. —**ad·ven′ture·some**, *adj.* —**ad·ven′tur·ous**, *adj.* —**ad·ven′tur·ous·ly**, *adv.* —**ad·ven′tur·ous·ness**, *n.*

ad·ven·tur·er (ad ven′chər ər), *n.* **1.** a person who adventures. **2.** See **soldier of fortune. 3.** a speculator. —**ad·ven′tur·ess**, *n.fem.*

ad·verb (ad′vûrb), *n.* a word that modifies a verb, adjective, or another adverb, and typically expresses time, place, manner, etc. —**ad·ver′bi·al**, *adj.* —**ad·ver′bi·al·ly**, *adv.*

ad·ver·sar·y (ad′vər ser′ē), *n., pl.* **-sar·ies.** a determined opponent. —**Syn.** antagonist, enemy, foe.

ad·ver·sa·tive (ad vûr′sə tiv), *adj.* expressing opposition or antithesis. —**ad·ver′sa·tive·ly**, *adv.*

ad·verse (ad vûrs′, ad′vûrs), *adj.* **1.** antagonistic in purpose or effect. **2.** opposing one's interest. —**ad·verse′ly**, *adv.*

ad·ver·si·ty (ad vûr′si tē), *n., pl.* **-ties** for 2. **1.** adverse fortune. **2.** an unfortunate event.

ad·vert (ad vûrt′), *v.i. Literary.* to refer or allude.

ad·vert·ent (ad vûr′tənt), *adj. Rare.* attentive or heedful. —**ad·vert′ence**, *n.*

ad·ver·tise (ad′vər tīz′, ad′vər tīz′), *v.,* **-tised, -tis·ing.** —*v.t.* **1.** to describe (a product, etc.) in some medium in order to induce the public to buy it. **2.** to call public attention to. —*v.i.* **3.** to use an advertisement. Also, **ad′ver·tize′.** —**ad′ver·tis′er**, *n.* —**ad′ver·tis′ing**, *n.*

ad·ver·tise·ment (ad′vər tīz′mənt, ad-vûr′tis mənt, -tiz-), *n.* a public announcement intended or designed to advertise something. Also, **ad′ver·tize′ment.**

ad·vice (ad vīs′), *n.* **1.** an opinion offered as a guide to action, etc. **2.** a communication containing information. —**Syn. 1.** admonition, counsel, recommendation.

ad·vis·a·ble (ad vī′zə bəl), *adj.* proper to be advised or recommended. —**ad·vis′a·bil′i·ty**, *n.*

ad·vise (ad vīz′), *v.t.*, **-vised, -vis·ing.**
1. to give advice to. **2.** to recommend (an action, etc.). **3.** to give notice to. —**ad·vis′er, ad·vi′sor,** *n.*

ad·vised (ad vīzd′), *adj.* thought out (used in combination): *well-advised.* —**ad·vis·ed·ness** (ad vī′zid nis), *n.*

ad·vis·ed·ly (ad vī′zid lē), *adv.* deliberately or by design.

ad·vise·ment (ad vīz′mənt), *n.* careful consideration.

ad·vi·so·ry (ad vī′zə rē), *adj., n., pl.* **-so·ries.** —*adj.* **1.** giving advice. **2.** having the power to advise. —*n.* **3.** an announcement, esp. about the weather.

ad·vo·cate (*v.* ad′və kāt′; *n.* ad′və kit, -kāt′), *v.,* **-cat·ed, -cat·ing,** *n.* —*v.t.* **1.** to plead in favor of or urge publicly. —*n.* **2.** a person who espouses a cause by argument. **3.** a person who pleads for or in behalf of another. [< L *advocāt(us)* legal counselor] —**ad·vo·ca·cy** (ad′-və kə sē), *n.*

advt., advertisement.

adz (adz), *n., pl.* **adz·es.** a heavy, curved tool for dressing timbers, etc. Also, **adze.**

AEC, Atomic Energy Commission.

A.E.F., American Expeditionary Forces.

Ae·ge·an Sea′ (i jē′ən), an arm of the Mediterranean Sea between Greece and Turkey.

ae·gis (ē′jis), *n.* **1.** supporting protection. **2.** sponsorship or patronage.

Ae·ne·as (i nē′əs), *n. Class. Myth.* a Trojan hero, ancestor of the Romans.

ae·o′li·an harp′ (ē ō′lē ən), a box equipped with strings of equal length, sounded by the wind.

ae·on (ē′ən, ē′on), *n.* **1.** an indefinitely long period of time. **2.** eon (def. 1).

aer·ate (âr′āt, ā′ə rāt′), *v.t.,* **-at·ed, -at·ing.** **1.** to expose to or supply with air. **2.** to charge or treat with air or a gas. **3.** to supply (the blood) with oxygen. —**aer·a′tion,** *n.* —**aer′a·tor,** *n.*

aer·i·al (*adj.* âr′ē əl, ā ēr′ē əl; *n.* âr′ē əl), *adj.* **1.** of, in, or produced by the air. **2.** inhabiting the air. **3.** lofty. **4.** unsubstantial or visionary. **5.** pertaining to aircraft. —*n.* **6.** antenna (def. 1). —**aer′i·al·ly,** *adv.*

aer·i·al·ist (âr′ē ə list, ā ēr′ē-), *n.* a trapeze artist or a tightrope walker.

aer·ie (âr′ē, ēr′ē), *n.* the nest of a bird, esp. an eagle, high on a cliff.

aero-, a combining form meaning: **a.** air or the atmosphere: *aerobic.* **b.** aircraft: *aeronautics.*

aero., **1.** aeronautical. **2.** aeronautics.

aer·o·bat·ics (âr′ə bat′iks), *n.pl.* stunts performed by an airplane or glider.

aer·o·bic (â rō′bik), *adj.* (of an organism or tissue) requiring oxygen for life. —**aer·obe** (âr′ōb), *n.* —**aer·o′bi·cal·ly,** *adv.*

aer·o·drome (âr′ə drōm′), *n. Chiefly Brit.* airdrome.

aer·o·dy·nam·ics (âr′ō dī nam′iks), *n.* the science dealing with the motion of air and other gases and with the effects of such motion on objects in such media. —**aer′o·dy·nam′ic, aer′o·dy·nam′i·cal,** *adj.* —**aer′o·dy·nam′i·cal·ly,** *adv.*

aer·ol·o·gy (â rol′ə jē), *n.* a branch of meteorology dealing with the atmosphere. —**aer′o·log′i·cal** (âr′ə loj′i kəl), *adj.* —**aer·ol′o·gist,** *n.*

aeron., aeronautics.

aer·o·naut (âr′ə nôt′, -not′), *n.* the pilot of a balloon or other lighter-than-air craft.

aer·o·nau·tics (âr′ə nô′tiks, -not′iks), *n.* the science or art of flight. —**aer′o·nau′tic, aer′o·nau′tic,** *adj.* —**aer′o·nau′ti·cal·ly,** *adv.*

aer·o·plane (âr′ə plān′), *n. Chiefly Brit.* airplane.

aer·o·sol (âr′ə sōl′, -sôl′, -sol′), *n.* **1.** a system of colloidal particles dispersed in a gas. **2.** a liquid substance, as a disinfectant, etc., sealed in a pressurized container for dispensing a spray, foam, etc.

aer·o·space (âr′ə spās′), *n.* **1.** the atmosphere and the space beyond as a whole. —*adj.* **2.** of missiles, etc., that operate in aerospace.

aer·y (âr′ē, ā′ə rē), *adj.* ethereal.

Aes·chy·lus (es′kə ləs), *n.* 525–456 B.C., Greek poet and dramatist.

Ae·sop (ē′səp, ē′sop), *n.* c620–c560 B.C., Greek writer of fables. —**Ae·so·pi·an** (ē sō′pē ən), *adj.*

aes·thete (es′thēt), *n.* a person who has or affects high sensitivity toward the beautiful in art, poetry, etc.

aes·thet·ic (es thet′ik), *adj.* **1.** of or pertaining to aesthetics. **2.** having a sense or love of beauty. —**aes·thet′i·cal·ly,** *adv.*

aes·thet·ics (es thet′iks), *n.* the philosophical study of the qualities perceived in works of art.

aes·ti·vate (es′tə vāt′), *v.i.,* **-vat·ed, -vat·ing.** to pass the summer in a torpid state.

aet., at the age of. Also, **aetat.** [< L *aetātis*]

AF, **1.** Air Force. **2.** audio frequency.

a.f., audio frequency.

a·far (ə fär′), *adv.* **1.** from, at, or to a distance. —*n.* **2.** a long way off.

AFB, Air Force Base.

AFC, automatic frequency control.

af·fa·ble (af′ə bəl), *adj.* **1.** pleasantly easy to talk to. **2.** showing friendliness. —**af′fa·bil′i·ty**, *n.* —**af′fa·bly**, *adv.*

af·fair (ə fâr′), *n.* **1.** anything requiring action. **2.** affairs, business. **3.** an event, esp. a social one. **4.** an illicit amorous relationship.

af·fect¹ (ə fekt′), *v.t.* **1.** to produce an effect in. **2.** to impress.

af·fect² (ə fekt′), *v.t.* **1.** to feign for effect. **2.** to assume pretentiously. **3.** to use or favor as a personal preference. —**af·fect′er**, *n.*

af·fec·ta·tion (af′ek tā′shən), *n.* a false appearance or assumption of a state, quality, or manner.

af·fect·ed¹ (ə fek′tid), *adj.* influenced or afflicted.

af·fect·ed² (ə fek′tid), *adj.* falsely assumed to impress others: *affected piety.* —**af·fect′ed·ly**, *adv.* —**af·fect′ed·ness**, *n.*

af·fect·ing (ə fek′tiñg), *adj.* moving the feelings or emotions. —**af·fect′ing·ly**, *adv.*

af·fec·tion (ə fek′shən), *n.* **1.** fond devotion. **2.** *Pathol.* a disorder or disease. —**af·fec′tion·ate**, *adj.* —**af·fec′tion·ate·ly**, *adv.*

af·fer·ent (af′fər ənt), *adj.* leading toward a central organ or part, as a nerve.

af·fi·ance (ə fī′əns), *v.t.*, -**anced**, -**anc·ing**. *Literary.* to betroth.

af·fi·da·vit (af′i dā′vit), *n.* a written declaration made upon oath. [< ML: he has taken an oath]

af·fil·i·ate (*v.* ə fil′ē āt′; *n.* ə fil′ē it, -āt′), *v.*, -**at·ed**, -**at·ing**, *n.* —*v.t.* **1.** to bring into close association or connection. —*v.i.* **2.** to be united. —*n.* **3.** a person or concern that is affiliated. —**af·fil′i·a′tion**, *n.*

af·fin·i·ty (ə fin′i tē), *n.*, *pl.* -**ties**. **1.** a natural liking. **2.** relationship or kinship.

af·firm (ə fûrm′), *v.t.* **1.** to declare or assert positively. **2.** to confirm or ratify. —*v.i.* **3.** to declare solemnly but without oath. —**af·firm′a·ble**, *adj.* —**af·firm′a·bly**, *adv.* —**af·fir·ma′tion** (af′ər mā′shən), *n.*

af·firm·a·tive (ə fûr′mə tiv), *adj.* **1.** asserting something as true. **2.** indicating assent. —*n.* **3.** a reply indicating assent. **4.** the side, as in a debate, that affirms a proposition.

affirm′a′tive ac′tion, encouragement for increased representation of women and minority-group members, esp. in employment.

af·fix (*v.* ə fiks′; *n.* af′iks), *v.t.* **1.** to fasten or attach. **2.** to put or append. —*n.* **3.** something affixed. **4.** a prefix or suffix.

af·fla·tus (ə flā′təs), *n.* *Literary.* divine inspiration.

af·flict (ə flikt′), *v.t.* to distress with mental or bodily pain. —**af·flic′tion**, *n.* —**af·flic′tive**, *adj.* —Syn. harass, plague, torment, vex.

af·flu·ent (af′lōō ənt), *adj.* **1.** wealthy and prosperous. **2.** abundant or plenty. —**af′flu·ence**, *n.* —**af′flu·ent·ly**, *adv.*

af·ford (ə fōrd′, ə fôrd′), *v.t.* **1.** to do without serious consequences. **2.** to meet the expense of. **3.** to supply. —**af·ford′a·ble**, *adj.*

af·for·est (ə fôr′ist, ə for′-), *v.t.* to convert into forest. —**af·for′est·a′tion**, *n.*

af·fray (ə frā′), *n.* a public noisy quarrel.

af·front (ə frunt′), *n.* **1.** a personally offensive act or remark. —*v.t.* **2.** to offend by a show of disrespect. **3.** *Literary.* to confront, as death or risk.

afft., affidavit.

Af·ghan (af′gən, -gan), *n.* **1.** a native of Afghanistan. **2.** (*l.c.*) a woolen blanket, knitted, crocheted, or woven. **3.** Also called **Af′ghan hound′.** a hound having a long head and a long, silky coat.

Af·ghan·i·stan (af gan′i stan′), *n.* a country in S Asia, NW of India.

a·fi·cio·na·do (ə fish′yə nä′dō), *n.*, *pl.* -**dos**. an ardent devotee.

a·field (ə fēld′), *adv.* **1.** away from home. **2.** astray. **3.** in the field.

a·fire (ə fīr′), *adj.* **1.** on fire. **2.** aflame (def. 2).

a·flame (ə flām′), *adj.* **1.** ablaze. **2.** eager and excited.

AFL-CIO, American Federation of Labor and Congress of Industrial Organizations.

a·float (ə flōt′), *adv.*, *adj.* **1.** floating freely. **2.** on board a ship, etc. **3.** awash. **4.** drifting without guidance.

a·flut·ter (ə flut′ər), *adj.* in a flutter.

a·foot (ə fōōt), *adv.*, *adj.* **1.** in active progress. **2.** *Archaic.* on foot.

a·fore·men·tioned (ə fōr′men′shənd, ə fôr′-), *adj.* mentioned previously.

a·fore·said (ə fōr′sed′, ə fôr′-), *adj.* said previously.

a·fore·thought (ə fōr′thôt′, ə fôr′-), *adj.* considered or planned beforehand: *with malice aforethought.*

a for·ti·o·ri (ä fōr′shē ōr′ī), for a still stronger reason.

a·foul (ə foul′), *adv.*, *adj.* **1.** in a collision or entanglement. **2. run or fall afoul of,** to come into conflict with.

Afr., **1.** Africa. **2.** African.

a·fraid (ə frād′), *adj.* **1.** feeling fear. **2.** deeply reluctant.

A-frame (ā′frām′), *n.* a building whose main frames are in the form of an inverted V, as Λ.

a·fresh (ə fresh′), *adv.* anew or again.

Af·ri·ca (af'ri kə), *n.* a continent S of Europe and between the Atlantic and Indian oceans. —**Af'·ri·can**, *adj.*, *n.*

Af'rican vi'olet, a popular house plant, having violet, pink, or white flowers.

Af·ri·kaans (af'rə käns', -känz'), *n.* an official language of South Africa, developed from 17th-century Dutch.

Af·ro (af'rō), *adj.* 1. of Afro-Americans or black traditions, etc. —*n.* 2. a hairstyle of black persons in which the hair is allowed to acquire a bushy appearance.

Af·ro-A·mer·i·can (af'rō ə mer'i kən), *adj.* 1. pertaining to Americans of African descent. —*n.* 2. an American of African descent.

aft (aft, äft), *Naut.*, *Aeron.* —*adv.* 1. at, close to, or toward the stern or tail. —*adj.* 2. situated toward or at the stern or tail.

aft., afternoon.

A.F.T., American Federation of Teachers.

af·ter (af'tər, äf'-), *prep.* 1. behind in position. 2. later in time than. 3. as a conclusion to. 4. below in rank or excellence. 5. in imitation of. 6. in search or pursuit of. 7. about. 8. with the name of. 9. in accordance with. —*adv.* 10. behind. 11. afterward. —*adj.* 12. subsequent. 13. aft (def. 2). —*conj.* 14. subsequent to the time that.

af·ter·birth (af'tər bûrth', äf'-), *n.* the placenta and fetal membranes expelled from the uterus after childbirth.

af·ter·burn·er (af'tər bûr'nər, äf'-), *n.* a device for burning exhaust fumes from an internal-combustion engine.

af·ter·care (af'tər kâr', äf'-), *n.* the care of a convalescent patient.

af·ter·deck (af'tər dek', äf'-), *n.* the deck of a vessel behind the midship section.

af·ter·ef·fect (af'tər i fekt', äf'-), *n.* 1. an effect that follows its stimulus. 2. *Med.* a result after the first effect of a drug, etc., has gone.

af·ter·glow (af'tər glō', äf'-), *n.* 1. the glow frequently seen in the sky after sunset. 2. a pleasant remembrance.

af·ter·im·age (af'tər im'ij, äf'-), *n.* a visual image that persists after the stimulus is no longer operative.

af·ter·life (af'tər līf', äf'-), *n.* the life after death.

af·ter·math (af'tər math', äf'-), *n.* 1. a result, esp. a disastrous one. 2. a new growth of grass.

af·ter·most (af'tər mōst'), *adj.* 1. farthest aft. 2. last or hindmost.

af·ter·noon (af'tər nōōn', äf'-), *n.* the time from noon until evening.

af·ter·shave (af'tər shāv'), *n.* a scented lotion applied to the face after shaving.

af·ter·taste (af'tər tāst', äf'-), *n.* a taste lingering in the mouth.

af·ter·thought (af'tər thôt', äf'-), *n.* 1. a later thought. 2. a belated idea.

af·ter·ward (af'tər wərd, äf'-), *adv.* in later time or subsequently. Also, **af'ter·wards**.

Ag, silver. [< L *argentum*]

A.G., 1. Adjutant General. 2. Attorney General.

a·gain (ə gen'), *adv.* 1. once more. 2. additionally. 3. doubly: *as much again as I have.* 4. furthermore. 5. again and again, repeatedly.

a·gainst (ə genst'), *prep.* 1. in a contrary direction to. 2. close beside or in front of. 3. in contact or collision with. 4. in opposition or hostility to. 5. as a protection from. 6. in competition with. 7. in payment for. 8. **over against**, a. near or beside. b. in contrast with.

a·gape[1] (ə gāp', ə gap'), *adv.*, *adj.* with the mouth wide open, esp. in wonder.

a·ga·pe[2] (ä gä'pā, ä'gə pā'), *n.* brotherly love.

a·gar (ä'gär, ag'ər), *n.* 1. Also, **a'gar-a'gar**. a gelatinlike product of certain seaweeds, used as a thickening agent for foods. 2. a culture medium having an agar base.

ag·ate (ag'it), *n.* 1. a variegated chalcedony with colored bands or other markings. 2. a playing marble made of this or of glass in imitation of it. 3. *Print.* a 5½-point type.

a·ga·ve (ə gä'vē, ə gä'-), *n.* a plant native to American deserts, having stiff, fleshy leaves.

agcy., agency.

age (āj), *n.*, *v.*, **aged**, **ag·ing** or **age·ing.** —*n.* 1. the length of time a being or thing has existed. 2. any period of human life. 3. the latter period of a natural term of existence. 4. advanced years or old age. 5. a distinctive historical or geological period. 6. an indefinitely long time. 7. **of age**, being any of several ages at which certain legal rights are acquired. —*v.i.*, *v.t.* 8. to grow or make old. 9. to mature.

-age, a suffix meaning: a. an action or process: *truckage.* b. result: *shrinkage.* c. charge: *brokerage.* d. status: *bondage.* e. residence: *parsonage.*

a·ged (ā'jid *for* 1, 3; ājd *for* 1, 2), *adj.* 1. having grown old. 2. of the age of. —*n.* 3. **the aged**, old persons.

age·ism (āj′iz əm), *n.* discrimination against persons of a certain age, esp. the old. —**age′ist,** *adj., n.*

age·less (āj′lis), *adj.* **1.** never growing old. **2.** lasting forever.

a·gen·cy (ā′jən sē), *n., pl.* **-cies. 1.** a company having a franchise to represent another. **2.** the office, duty, or business of an agent. **3.** a government bureau. **4.** means or instrumentality.

a·gen·da (ə jen′də), *n.* a list of things to be acted on at a meeting, etc.

a·gent (ā′jənt), *n.* **1.** a person or firm authorized to act. **2.** a spy. **3.** a substance that causes a reaction. **4.** a means or instrument.

a·gent pro·vo·ca·teur (A ZHäN′ PRÔ VÔ KA tœR′), *pl.* **a·gents pro·vo·ca·teurs** (A ZHäN′ PRÔ VÔ KA tœR′). *French.* a secret agent hired to incite persons to an illegal act.

age′ of consent′, the legal age at which a person is considered competent to give consent to marriage.

age-old (āj′ōld′), *adj.* from time immemorial.

ag·er·a·tum (aj′ə rā′təm), *n.* any of several composite plants having small, dense, blue or white flower heads.

ag·glom·er·ate (*v.* ə glom′ə rāt′; *adj., n.* ə glom′ər it, -ə rāt′), *v.,* **-at·ed, -at·ing,** *adj., n.* —*v.t.,* *v.i.* **1.** to gather into a cluster or mass. —*adj.* **2.** gathered together into a cluster or mass. —*n.* **3.** a mass of things clustered together. **4.** rock composed of rounded or angular volcanic fragments. —**ag·glom′er·a′tion,** *n.*

ag·glu·ti·nate (*v.* ə glŌŌt′°nāt′; *adj.* ə glŌŌt′°nit, -°nāt′), *v.,* **-nat·ed, -nat·ing,** *adj.* —*v.t.,* *v.i.* **1.** to unite, as with glue. **2.** to clump, as bacteria. —*adj.* **3.** united, as by glue. —**ag·glu′ti·na′tion,** *n.* —**ag·glu′ti·na′tive,** *adj.*

ag·glu·ti·nin (ə glŌŌt′°nin), *n.* an antibody that causes agglutination.

ag·gran·dize (ə gran′dīz, ag′rən diz′), *v.t.,* **-dized, -diz·ing.** to make great or greater in power, wealth, rank, or honor. —**ag·gran·dize·ment** (ə-gran′diz mənt), *n.* —**ag·gran′diz·er,** *n.*

ag·gra·vate (ag′rə vāt′), *v.t.,* **-vat·ed, -vat·ing. 1.** to make worse or more severe. **2.** to annoy or irritate. —**ag′gra·va′tion,** *n.*

ag·gre·gate (*adj., n.* ag′rə git, -gāt′; *v.* ag′rə gāt′), *adj., n., v.,* **-gat·ed, -gat·ing.** —*adj.* **1.** formed by the collection of particulars into a mass. —*n.* **2.** a sum, mass, or assemblage. **3.** a mixture of different mineral substances separable by mechanical means, as granite. —*v.t., v.i.* **4.** to collect into one sum,

mass, or body. **5.** to amount to. —**ag′gre·ga′tion,** *n.*

ag·gres·sion (ə gresh′ən), *n.* **1.** an unprovoked offensive, attack, or invasion. **2.** offensive action in general. **3.** hostile behavior, esp. associated with frustration. —**ag·gres′sor,** *n.*

ag·gres·sive (ə gres′iv), *adj.* **1.** characterized by or tending toward aggression. **2.** vigorously energetic. **3.** boldly assertive. —**ag·gres′sive·ly,** *adv.* —**ag·gres′sive·ness,** *n.*

ag·grieve (ə grēv′), *v.t.,* **-grieved, -griev·ing. 1.** to wrong grievously. **2.** to afflict with pain, anxiety, etc.

a·ghast (ə gast′, ə gäst′), *adj.* struck with shock, amazement, or horror.

ag·ile (aj′əl), *adj.* quick and well-coordinated: *an agile leap.* —**ag′ile·ly,** *adv.* —**a·gil·i·ty** (ə jil′i tē), *n.* —**ag′ile·ness,** *n.* —**Syn,** deft, limber, nimble, spry.

ag·i·tate (aj′i tāt′), *v.,* **-tat·ed, -tat·ing.** —*v.t.* **1.** to move or shake briskly. **2.** to disturb or excite the feelings of. **3.** to call attention to by speech or writing. —*v.i.* **4.** to arouse public interest. —**ag′i·tat′ed·ly,** *adv.* —**ag′i·ta′tion,** *n.* —**ag′i·ta′tor,** *n.*

a·gleam (ə glēm′), *adj.* gleaming.

a·gley (ə glē′, ə glī′), *adv. Chiefly Scot.* awry or wrong.

a·glit·ter (ə glit′ər), *adj.* glittering.

a·glow (ə glō′), *adj.* glowing.

ag·nos·tic (ag nos′tik), *n.* **1.** a person who holds that the ultimate cause (God) and the essential nature of things are unknown and unknowable. —*adj.* **2.** of an agnostic. —**ag·nos′ti·cism′,** *n.*

a·go (ə gō′), *adj.* **1.** gone or past. —*adv.* **2.** in the past.

a·gog (ə gog′), *adj.* **1.** highly excited by eagerness, curiosity, etc. —*adv.* **2.** excitedly.

a go-go (ä gō′gō′), go-go.

ag·o·nize (ag′ə nīz′), *v.i., v.t.,* **-nized, -niz·ing.** to suffer or cause to suffer extreme pain. —**ag′o·niz′ing·ly,** *adv.*

ag·o·ny (ag′ə nē), *n., pl.* **-nies. 1.** extreme and prolonged suffering. **2.** the struggle preceding natural death.

ag·o·ra·pho·bi·a (ag′ər ə fō′bē ə), *n.* an abnormal fear of being in an open space. —**ag′o·ra·pho′bic** (-fō′bik, -fob′ik), *adj.*

agr., **1.** agricultural. **2.** agriculture.

a·grar·i·an (ə grâr′ē ən), *adj.* **1.** of land or land tenure. **2.** of agricultural groups and their welfare. —**a·grar′i·an·ism,** *n.*

a·gree (ə grē′), *v.,* **a·greed, a·gree·ing.** —*v.i.* **1.** to harmonize in opinion or feeling. **2.** to give consent. **3.** to reach an agreement. **4.** to be suitable to each other. **5.** to be consistent or conform. **6.** (of food) to admit of digestion without difficulty. **7.** to correspond in grammatical number, case, etc. —*v.t.* **8.** to concede or grant. —**Syn. 2.** accede, acquiesce, assent, concur.

a·gree·a·ble (ə grē′ə bəl), *adj.* **1.** to one's liking. **2.** willing or ready to agree. **3.** suitable. —**a·gree′a·ble·ness,** *n.* —**a·gree′a·bly,** *adv.*

a·gree·ment (ə grē′mənt), *n.* **1.** the act or state of agreeing. **2.** an arrangement accepted by all parties. **3.** a document delineating such an arrangement. **4.** unanimity of opinion.

agric., 1. agricultural. **2.** agriculture.

ag·ri·busi·ness (ag′rə biz′nis), *n.* a complex of farming with its related industry and business.

ag·ri·cul·ture (ag′rə kul′chər), *n.* the production of crops, livestock, or poultry. —**ag′ri·cul′tur·al,** *adj.* —**ag′ri·cul′tur·al·ly,** *adv.* —**ag′ri·cul′-tur·ist, ag′ri·cul′tur·al·ist,** *n.*

a·gron·o·my (ə gron′ə mē), *n.* the science of soil management and the production of field crops. —**a·gro·nom·ic** (ag′rə nom′ik), *adj.* —**a·gron′o·mist,** *n.*

a·ground (ə ground′), *adv., adj.* **1.** on or onto the ground. **2.** (of a ship) on the ground beneath the water.

agt., agent.

a·gue (ā′gyōō), *n.* a malarial fever with returning cold and sweating fits.

ah (ä), *interj.* (an exclamation to express pain, surprise, appreciation, etc.)

a·ha (ä hä′), *interj.* (an exclamation to express triumph, surprise, etc.)

a·head (ə hed′), *adv.* **1.** in front of or in advance. **2.** onward. **3.** into or for the future. **4.** in a more advantageous situation: *to get ahead in business.* **5. ahead of, a.** in front of. **b.** above or surpassing.

a·hem (ə hem′), *interj.* (an utterance to attract attention, etc.)

a·hoy (ə hoi′), *interj. Naut.* (a call to hail another ship, etc.)

aid (ād), *v.t., v.i.* **1.** to help, esp. in order to provide support or relief. —*n.* **2.** help or assistance. **3.** a helper or auxiliary. —**aid′er,** *n.*

AID, Agency for International Development.

aide (ād), *n.* **1.** an official assistant. **2.** aide-de-camp.

aide-de-camp (ād′də kamp′), *n., pl.* **aides-de-camp.** a military officer acting as a confidential assistant to a superior. Also, **aid′-de-camp′.**

ai·grette (ā′gret, ā gret′), *n.* a tuft or plume of feathers, worn as a head ornament.

ail (āl), *v.t.* **1.** to cause pain or trouble to. —*v.i.* **2.** to be unwell or ill.

ai·lan·thus (ā lan′thəs), *n., pl.* **-thus·es.** an Asiatic tree with pinnate leaves and small green flowers.

ai·ler·on (ā′lə ron′), *n. Aeron.* a movable surface, usually near the trailing edge of a wing, that effects maneuvers.

ail·ment (āl′mənt), *n.* a physical disorder.

aim (ām), *v.i., v.t.* **1.** to position (a weapon) so as to hit. **2.** to direct (one's efforts or objective). **3.** to try. —*n.* **4.** act of aiming. **5.** the direction of a weapon, etc. **6.** purpose. **7. take aim,** to sight a weapon at a target.

aim·less (ām′lis), *adj.* having no direction or purpose. —**aim′less·ly,** *adv.* —**aim′less·ness,** *n.*

ain't (ānt), *Nonstandard.* **1.** am not. **2.** are not, is not, have not, or has not.

—**Usage.** AIN'T is so widely regarded as a nonstandard form that it should be shunned generally. AIN'T occurs occasionally in self-consciously folksy, humorous contexts (*She ain't what she used to be!*), but it is unacceptable in formal writing and speech.

Ai·nu (ī′nōō), *n., pl.* **-nus, -nu. 1.** a member of an aboriginal Caucasoid race of the northernmost islands of Japan. **2.** the language of the Ainus.

air (âr), *n.* **1.** a mixture of oxygen, nitrogen, and other gases that surrounds the earth and forms its atmosphere. **2.** a light breeze. **3.** the apparent character of a person. **4. airs,** affected manners. **5.** *Music.* **a.** a melody. **b.** an aria. **6.** aviation or travel by airplane. **7. in the air,** in circulation. **8. off the air,** not broadcasting. **9. on the air,** being broadcast. **10. up in the air, a.** undecided or unsettled. **b.** angry or perturbed. —*v.t.* **11.** to expose to the air, as for freshening. **12.** to bring to public attention.

air′ bag′, a bag that inflates automatically upon impact in order to protect automobile passengers from injury in a collision.

air′ base′, an operations center for an air force.

air·borne (âr′bôrn′, -bōrn′), *adj.* **1.** carried or transported by air. **2.** in flight.

air′ brake′, 1. a brake operated by compressed air. **2.** a device for reducing an aircraft's speed.

air·brush (âr′brush′), *n.* an atomizer for spraying paint.

air′ cav′alry, airmobile troops.

air·con·di·tion (âr′kən dish′ən), *v.t.* to furnish with an air-conditioning system. —**air′ condi′tioner.**

air′ condi′tioning, a system that controls the temperature and humidity of the air in an office, etc.

air-cool (âr′kōōl′), *v.t.* to cool with circulated air.

air·craft (âr′kraft′, -kräft′), *n., pl.* -**craft.** any vehicle supported for flight in the air by buoyancy, as an airplane, glider, or helicopter.

air′craft car′rier, a warship with a deck for the taking off and landing of aircraft.

air′ cur′tain, compressed air directed across a doorway.

air·drome (âr′drōm′), *n.* an airfield with any buildings and installations.

air·drop (âr′drop′), *v.,* -**dropped,** -**drop·ping,** *n.* —*v.t.* **1.** to drop (personnel or supplies) by parachute from an aircraft in flight. —*n.* **2.** the act or process of airdropping.

Aire·dale (âr′dāl′), *n.* a large terrier having a wiry, black-and-tan coat.

air·field (âr′fēld′), *n.* a level area on which airplanes take off and land.

air·flow (âr′flō′), *n.* air currents caused by a moving aircraft, automobile. etc.

air·foil (âr′foil′), *n.* any surface, as a wing, designed to aid in controlling an aircraft.

air′ force′, the aviation division of a nation's armed forces.

air·frame (âr′frām′), *n.* the framework and external covering of an aircraft or rocket.

air·freight (âr′frāt′), *n.* **1.** freight shipped by aircraft. **2.** the charge for such shipment.

air′ gun′, a gun operated by compressed air.

air′ lane′, a route regularly used by airplanes.

air·less (âr′lis), *adj.* **1.** lacking air. **2.** without fresh air.

air·lift (âr′lift′), *n.* **1.** a system for transporting personnel or supplies by aircraft. —*v.t.* **2.** to transport by airlift.

air·line (âr′līn′), *n.* **1.** a system or company for furnishing transportation by aircraft. **2.** *Archaic.* a direct line.

air·lin·er (âr′lī′nər), *n.* a passenger aircraft operated by an airline.

air′ lock′, 1. an airtight chamber permitting passage between spaces of different pressure. **2.** an air bubble in a pipe that impedes its function.

air·mail (âr′māl′), *n.* **1.** the system of transmitting mail by airplane.

2. mail so transmitted. —*v.t.* **3.** to transmit by airmail.

air·man (âr′mən), *n., pl.* -**men. 1.** an aviator. **2.** *U.S. Air Force.* an enlisted person of one of the three lowest ranks. —**air′man·ship′,** *n.*

air′ mass′, a body of air covering a wide area through any horizontal section.

air′ mile′, mile (def. 2).

air·mo·bile (âr′mō′bēl′, -bil), *adj.* equipped and trained for movement by helicopter to engage in ground combat.

air′ pi′racy, the act of skyjacking. —**air′ pi′rate.**

air·plane (âr′plān′), *n.* a heavier-than-air aircraft kept aloft by the upward thrust exerted by the passing air on its fixed wings and driven by propellers, jet propulsion, etc.

air′ pock′et, a vertical air current that can cause an aircraft to experience a sudden change in altitude.

air′ police′, the organized police of an air force.

air·port (âr′pōrt′, -pôrt′), *n.* a tract of land with facilities for aircraft, esp. one for commercial aircraft and having a passenger terminal.

air′ post′, *Brit.* See **airmail.**

air′ pres′sure, the pressure exerted by the atmosphere or by compressed air.

air′ raid′, a raid by aircraft, esp. for bombing a particular area.

air′ ri′fle, an air gun with rifled bore.

air·ship (âr′ship′), *n.* a self-propelled, lighter-than-air aircraft.

air·sick (âr′sik′), *adj.* ill with motion sickness resulting from air travel. —**air′sick′ness,** *n.*

air·space (âr′spās′), *n.* the region of the atmosphere above a nation over which it has jurisdiction.

air·speed (âr′spēd′), *n.* the forward speed of an aircraft relative to the air.

air′ strike′, an attack by aircraft.

air·strip (âr′strip′), *n.* runway (def. 2).

air′ tax′i, a small aircraft for passengers, cargo, and mail, operated along routes not serviced by regular airlines.

air·tight (âr′tīt′), *adj.* **1.** constructed to prevent the entrance or escape of air. **2.** having no weak points: *an airtight contract.*

air-to-air (âr′tōō âr′, -tə-), *adj.* operating between flying aircraft or directed from one flying aircraft to another.

air·waves (âr′wāvz′), *n.pl.* the media of radio and television broadcasting.

air·way (âr'wā'), *n.* **1.** See **air lane.** **2.** airways, a. airwaves. **b.** *Chiefly Brit.* airline (def. 1).

air·wor·thy (âr'wûr'ᵺē), *adj.* meeting accepted standards for safe flight. —**air'wor'thi·ness,** *n.*

air·y (âr'ē), *adj.*, **air·i·er, air·i·est. 1.** open to a free current of air. **2.** of air. **3.** light or thin. **4.** sprightly or lively. **5.** graceful. **6.** unreal or imaginary. **7.** high or lofty. **8.** affected or haughty. —**air'i·ly,** *adv.* —**air'i·ness,** *n.*

aisle (īl), *n.* a passageway between sections of seats, as in a theater.

a·jar (ə jär'), *adj., adv.* partly open.

AK, Alaska.

a.k.a., also known as.

a·kim·bo (ə kim'bō), *adj., adv.* with hand on hip and elbow bent outward: *to stand with arms akimbo.*

a·kin (ə kin'), *adj.* **1.** related by blood. **2.** allied by nature.

Ak·ron (ak'rən), *n.* a city in NE Ohio.

ak·va·vit (äk'və vēt'), *n.* a dry, ginlike, Scandinavian alcoholic liquor flavored with caraway seeds.

AL, Alabama.

Al, aluminum.

-al, a suffix meaning: **a.** of or pertaining: *national.* **b.** characterized by: *typical.* **c.** act or process: *refusal.*

à la (ä' lä, ä' lə), **1.** according to. **2.** in the manner of. Also, **a la.**

Ala., Alabama.

A.L.A., American Library Association.

Al·a·bam·a (al'ə bam'ə), *n.* a state in SE U.S. *Cap.:* Montgomery. —**Al·a·bam·i·an** (al'ə bam'ē ən), **Al'·a·bam'an,** *adj., n.*

al·a·bas·ter (al'ə bas'tər, -bä'stər), *n.* **1.** a finely granular gypsum, white and translucent, used for figurines, etc. **2.** calcite, often banded, used as alabaster.

à la carte (ä' lə kärt', al' ə), with a stated price for each dish offered.

a·lac·ri·ty (ə lak'ri tē), *n.* **1.** cheerful readiness. **2.** liveliness or briskness.

à la king (ä' lə king'), creamed with pimiento or green pepper.

Al·a·mo (al'ə mō'), *n.* a Franciscan mission in San Antonio, Texas: taken by Mexicans (1836) during the Texan war for independence.

à la mode (ä' lə mōd'), **1.** in the prevailing fashion. **2.** served with ice cream Also, **a' la mode'.**

a·lar (ā'lər), *adj.* **1.** having wings. **2.** wing-shaped.

a·larm (ə lärm'), *n.* **1.** a sudden fear excited by danger. **2.** any signal for an emergency, etc. **3.** any device for such a signal. **4.** *Archaic.* a call to arms. —*v.t.* **5.** to make

fearful. **6.** to warn of an emergency. —**a·larm'ing·ly,** *adv.*

a·larm·ist (ə lär'mist), *n.* **1.** a person who raises alarms by exaggerating dangers, etc. —*adj.* **2.** of an alarmist. —**a·larm'ism,** *n.*

a·las (ə las', ə läs'), *interj.* (used to express sorrow, grief, etc.)

A·las·ka (ə las'kə), *n.* a state of the U.S. in NW North America. *Cap.:* Juneau. —**A·las'kan,** *adj., n.*

alb (alb), *n.* a long-sleeved linen vestment, worn chiefly by priests.

al·ba·core (al'bə kōr', -kôr'), *n., pl.* **-core, -cores.** an edible tuna found in warm or temperate seas.

Al·ba·ni·a (al bā'nē ə, -bān'yə), *n.* a country in S Europe. —**Al·ba'ni·an,** *adj., n.*

Al·ba·ny (ôl'bə nē), *n.* the capital of New York, on the Hudson.

al·ba·tross (al'bə trôs', -tros'), *n.* a large, webfooted sea bird.

al·be·it (ôl bē'it), *conj.* although or even if.

Al·ber·ta (al bûr'tə), *n.* a province in W Canada. *Cap.:* Edmonton. —**Al·ber'tan,** *adj., n.*

al·bi·no (al bī'nō), *n., pl.* **-nos.** a person, animal, or plant deficient in pigmentation, esp. a person with milky skin, light hair, and pink eyes. —**al'bi·nism'** (-bə-), *n.*

al·bum (al'bəm), *n.* **1.** a book of blank leaves for photographs, stamps, etc. **2.** a long-playing phonograph record or tape, or set of such records or tapes.

al·bu·men (al byoo'mən), *n.* **1.** the white of an egg. **2.** albumin.

al·bu·min (al byoo'mən), *n.* any of a class of water-soluble proteins in animal and vegetable juices and tissues. —**al·bu'mi·nous,** *adj.*

Al·bu·quer·que (al'bə kûr'kē), *n.* a city in central New Mexico.

alc., alcohol.

al·cal·de (al kal'dē), *n., pl.* **-des.** (in Spain and Southwestern U.S.) a mayor having judicial powers.

al·ca·zar (al'kə zär', al kaz'ər), *n.* a Spanish castle or fortress.

al·che·my (al'kə mē), *n.* medieval chemistry, aiming chiefly at methods for transmuting baser metals into gold. —**al·chem·ic** (al kem'ik), **al·chem'i·cal,** *adj.* —**al·che·mist** (al'kə mist), *n.*

al·co·hol (al'kə hôl', -hol'), *n.* **1.** a colorless, volatile, flammable liquid produced by fermentation of certain carbohydrates or obtained synthetically: used chiefly as a solvent, in beverages, medicines, lotions, and as a rocket fuel. **2.** any intoxicating liquor containing alcohol. [< NL < ML < Ar *al kuḥul* powdered antimony]

al·co·hol·ic (al′kə hô′lik, -hol′ik), *adj.* 1. of or caused by alcohol. 2. suffering from alcoholism. 3. a person suffering from alcoholism. —**al′co·hol′i·cal·ly**, *adv.*

al·co·hol·ism (al′kə hôl hiz′əm, -ho-), *n.* a diseased condition due to excessive use of alcoholic beverages.

al·cove (al′kōv), *n.* 1. a recess opening out of a room. 2. any recessed space, as in a garden.

ald., alderman.

al·de·hyde (al′də hīd′), *n.* any of a class of organic compounds derived from alcohols by oxidation.

al·der (ôl′dər), *n.* a shrub or tree of the birch family, growing in moist places in colder regions.

al·der·man (ôl′dər mən), *n.*, *pl.* **-men.** a member of a municipal legislative body.

ale (āl), *n.* a malt beverage, darker, heavier, and more bitter than beer.

a·le·a·to·ry (ā′lē ə tōr′ē, -tôr′ē), *adj.* 1. depending on a contingent event. 2. by luck or chance. Also, **a′le·a·tor′ic.**

a·lee (ə lē′), *adv.*, *adj. Naut.* upon or toward the lee side.

ale·house (āl′hous′), *n.* a tavern where ale is sold.

a·lem·bic (ə lem′bik), *n.* a utensil with a beaked cap, formerly used in distilling.

a·lert (ə lûrt′), *adj.* 1. vigilantly attentive or aware. 2. agile or nimble. —*n.* 3. an attitude of vigilance or caution. 4. a warning of danger. 5. the period during which a warning is in effect. 6. **on the alert,** vigilant. —*v.t.* 7. to warn, as to prepare for action. 8. to warn of an attack, storm, etc. [< It *all'erta* = *all(a)* to the + *erta* lookout] —**a·lert′ly,** *adv.* —**a·lert′ness,** *n.* — Syn. keen. observant. watchful.

A·leu′tian Is′lands (ə lōō′shən), an archipelago extending SW from Alaska. —**A·leu′tian,** *adj.*, *n.*

ale·wife (āl′wīf′), *n.*, *pl.* **-wives.** a North American fish resembling a small shad.

Al′ex·an′der the Great′ (al′ig zan′dər, zān′-), 356–323 B.C., king of Macedonia 336–323: conquered Greece and Persia.

Al·ex·an·dri·a (al′ig zan′drē ə, -zän′-), *n.* a seaport in N Egypt.

Al·ex·an·dri·an (al′ig zan′drē ən, -zän′-), *adj.* of Alexander the Great or his rule.

Al·ex·an·drine (al′ig zan′drin, -drēn, -zän′-), *n.* (*often l.c.*) a verse or line of poetry of twelve syllables.

a·lex·i·a (ə lek′sē ə), *n.* a cerebral disorder marked by inability to understand written matter.

al·fal·fa (al fal′fə), *n.* a European leguminous plant, grown for forage in the U.S.

Al′fred the Great′ (al′fred, -frid), A.D. 849–899, king of England 871–899.

al·fres·co (al fres′kō), *adv.*, *adj.* out-of-doors: *to dine alfresco.* Also, **al fres′co.**

alg., algebra.

al·ga (al′gə), *n.*, *pl.* **-gae** (-jē). any of numerous chlorophyll-containing plants ranging from one-celled to many-celled forms, occurring in fresh or salt water. —**al′gal,** *adj.*

al·ge·bra (al′jə brə), *n.* the branch of mathematics utilizing letters and other symbols to represent specific numbers, values, vectors, etc. [< ML < Ar *al* the + *jebr* reunion of parts] —**al′ge·bra′ic** (-brā′ik), *adj.* —**al′ge·bra′i·cal·ly,** *adv.*

Al·ge·ri·a (al jēr′ē ə), *n.* a country in NW Africa. —**Al·ge′ri·an,** *adj.*, *n.*

-algia, a suffix meaning "pain": *neuralgia.*

Al·giers (al jērz′), *n.* the capital of Algeria.

Al·gon·qui·an (al gong′kē ən, -kwē-ən), *n.*, *pl.* **-ans,** **-an.** 1. a family of languages spoken by North American Indians in an area from Labrador to North Carolina and westward to the Rocky Mountains. 2. a member of an Algonquian tribe. Also, **Al·gon′ki·an.**

Al·gon·quin (al gong′kin, -kwin), *n.*, *pl.* **-quins,** **-quin.** 1. a member of a group of Algonquian-speaking tribes. 2. Algonquian. Also, **Al·gon′kin.**

al·go·rithm (al′gə riț̣h′əm), *n.* a set of rules for solving a problem in a finite number of steps, as for finding the greatest common divisor.

a·li·as (ā′lē əs), *n.*, *pl.* **-as·es,** *adv.* —*n.* 1. an assumed name, esp. by a criminal. —*adv.* 2. otherwise: *Simpson alias Smith.*

al·i·bi (al′ə bī), *n.*, *pl.* **-bis,** *v.* —*n.* 1. the defense by an accused person that he or she was elsewhere when the offense was committed. 2. an excuse. —*v.i.* 3. to give an excuse or defense.

al·ien (āl′yən, ā′lē ən), *n.* 1. a person born in and owing allegiance to a country other than the one in which he or she lives. —*adj.* 2. of an alien or aliens. 3. foreign or strange. 4. adverse or hostile.

al·ien·a·ble (āl′yə nə bəl, ā′lē ə-), *adj.* capable of being sold or transferred. —**al′ien·a·bil′i·ty,** *n.*

al·ien·ate (āl′yə nāt′, ā′lē ə-), *v.t.*, **-at·ed, -at·ing.** 1. to make indifferent, unfriendly, or hostile. 2. to transfer (property or title) to another. —**al′ien·a′tion,** *n.*

al·ien·ist (āl′yə nist, ā′lē ə-), *n.* a psychiatrist, esp. one who specializes in related legal matters.

a·light¹ (ə līt′), *v.i.*, **a·light·ed** or **a·lit, a·light·ing.** 1. to dismount from a horse, descend from a vehicle, etc. 2. to settle after descending.

a·light² (ə līt′), *adj.* lighted or burning.

a·lign (ə līn′), *v.t.* 1. to arrange in a straight line. 2. to bring into a line. 3. to ally (oneself) with a group, cause, etc. —*v.i.* 4. to form a line. —**a·lign′ment**, *n.*

a·like (ə līk′), *adv.* 1. in the same manner, form, or degree. —*adj.* 2. having similarity. —**a·like′ness**, *n.*

al·i·ment (al′ə mənt), *n.* food, esp. as nutriment.

al·i·men·ta·ry (al′ə men′tə rē, -trē), *adj.* of food, esp. as nutriment.

alimen′tary canal′, a tubular passage for the digestion and absorption of food, beginning at the mouth and terminating at the anus.

al·i·mo·ny (al′ə mō′nē), *n.* an allowance paid to a divorced person by the former spouse upon legal separation or divorce.

a·line (ə līn′), *v.t., v.i.,* **a·lined, a·lin·ing.** align. —**a·line′ment**, *n.*

A·line (ā′līn′), *adj.* having two A-shaped panels for the front and back: *an A-line coat.*

al·i·quant (al′ə kwənt), *adj.* contained in a number but not dividing it evenly.

a·lit (ə līt′), *v.* a pt. and pp. of alight¹.

a·live (ə līv′), *adj.* 1. having life or animation. 2. in existence or operation. 3. lively or active. 4. alive to, sensitive to. 5. alive with, swarming with. —**a·live′ness**, *n.* —**Syn.** 1. living. 2. active.

a·liz·a·rin (ə liz′ər in), *n.* a reddish-orange or brownish-yellow solid, used chiefly in the synthesis of other dyes.

alk., 1. alkali. 2. alkaline.

al·ka·li (al′kə lī′), *n., pl.* **-lis, -lies.** 1. any of numerous, strong, caustic, water-soluble substances, such as lye, that neutralize acids to form salts and turn red litmus paper blue. 2. any of various other bases, as calcium hydroxide. —**al′ka·line′** (-līn′, -lin), *adj.* —**al·ka·lin′i·ty** (-lin′i-), *n.*

al·ka·lin·ize (al′kə li nīz′), *v.t., v.i.,* **-ized, -iz·ing.** to make into or become an alkali. Also, **al′ka·lize′** (-līz′). —**al′ka·lin·i·za′tion**, *n.*

al·ka·loid (al′kə loid′), *n.* an organic, nitrogen-containing compound having a bitter taste, as nicotine, morphine, or quinine.

al′kyd res′in (al′kid), a sticky resin used chiefly in adhesives and paints. Also called **al′kyd.**

all (ôl), *adj.* 1. the whole of: *all year.* 2. the whole number of: *all men.* 3. the greatest possible: *with all speed.* 4. every: *all manner of men.* 5. any: *beyond all doubt.* —*pron.* 6. the whole amount. 7. the whole number. 8. everything. 9. everything or whole. 10. one's whole interest, energy, or property: *to give one's all.* 11. **after all,** notwithstanding. 12. **all in all,** in general. 13. **at all,** a. in the slightest degree. b. in any way. 14. **in all,** all together: *a hundred guests in all.* 15. **once and for all,** finally. —*adv.* 16. entirely: *all alone.* 17. exclusively. 18. each or apiece: *The score was one all.* 19. **all but,** almost. 20. **all in,** tired or exhausted. 21. **all the better,** more advantageous.

Al·lah (al′ə, ä′lə), *n. Islam.* the Supreme Being.

all-A·mer·i·can (ôl′ə mer′i kən), *adj.* 1. composed exclusively of American members. 2. representing the best in any field of U.S. sport. 3. typically American. —*n.* 4. an all-American player.

all-a·round (ôl′ə round′), *adj.* 1. versatile in ability or usefulness. 2. comprehensive in extent.

al·lay (ə lā′), *v.t.,* **-layed, -lay·ing.** 1. to put (fear, etc.) to rest. 2. to lessen or relieve. —**al·lay′er**, *n.*

all′ clear′, the signal that an air raid is over.

al·le·ga·tion (al′ə gā′shən), *n.* 1. the act of alleging. 2. an assertion made without proof.

al·lege (ə lej′), *v.t.,* **-leged, -leg·ing.** 1. to assert without proof. 2. to give as a reason or excuse. —**al·leged** (ə lejd′), *adj.* —**al·leg′ed·ly**, *adv.* —**al·leg′er**, *n.*

Al·le·ghe′ny Moun′tains (al′ə gā′nē), a mountain range extending from Pennsylvania to Virginia.

al·le·giance (ə lē′jəns), *n.* 1. the loyalty of a citizen to his or her government. 2. devotion to a group or cause. —**al·le′giant**, *adj.*

al·le·go·ry (al′ə gōr′ē, -gôr′ē), *n., pl.* **-ries.** 1. a figurative treatment of one subject under the guise of another. 2. a symbolic narrative. —**al′le·gor′i·cal, al′le·gor′ic,** *adj.* —**al′le·gor′i·cal·ly**, *adv.* —**al′le·go·rist**, *n.*

al·le·gret·to (al′ə gret′ō), *adj., adv. Music.* light and moderately fast.

al·le·gro (ə lā′grō, ə leg′rō), *adj., adv., n., pl.* **-gros.** *Music.* —*adj., adv.* 1. brisk in tempo. —*n.* 2. an allegro movement.

al·lele (ə lēl′), *n.* any of several forms of a gene, usually arising through mutation. —**al·lel·ic** (ə lē′lik), *adj.*

al·le·lu·ia (al′ə lōō′yə), *interj.*, *n.* hallelujah.

Al·len·town (al′ən toun′), *n.* a city in E Pennsylvania.

al·ler·gen (al′ər jen′), *n.* any substance inducing an allergy. —**al′ler·gen′ic** (-jen′ik), *adj.* —**al·ler·gen·ic·i·ty** (al′ər jə nis′i tē), *n.*

al·ler·gist (al′ər jist), *n.* a physician specializing in the treatment of allergies.

al·ler·gy (al′ər jē), *n.*, *pl.* -gies. 1. hypersensitivity, as hay fever or asthma, to pollen, foods, etc., characterized by difficult respiration, skin rashes, etc. 2. an antipathy. —**al·ler·gic** (ə lûr′jik), *adj.*

al·le·vi·ate (ə lē′vē āt′), *v.t.*, -at·ed, -at·ing. to lessen or make easier to endure. —**al·le′vi·a′tion**, *n.* —**al·le′vi·a′tor**, *n.*

al·ley (al′ē), *n.*, *pl.* -leys. 1. a narrow street behind or between buildings. 2. a bowling alley. 3. **up one's alley**, *Slang.* in keeping with one's natural abilities or interests.

al′ley cat′, a homeless cat.

al·ley·way (al′ē wā′), *n.* a narrow passageway.

all-fired (ôl′fīºrd′), *adv. Informal.* extremely or excessively.

All·hal·lows (ôl′hal′ōz), *n.* See **All Saints' Day**.

al·li·ance (ə lī′əns), *n.* 1. the act of allying or the state of being allied. 2. a formal agreement between two or more nations, families, or organizations.

al·lied (ə līd′, al′īd), *adj.* 1. joined by treaty. 2. kindred: *allied species.*

al·li·ga·tor (al′ə gā′tər), *n.* 1. a large reptile of the southern U.S. having a longer and broader snout than the crocodile. 2. a scaly leather made from alligator hide. [< Sp *el lagarto* the lizard < L *lacertus* lizard]

al′ligator pear′, avocado (def. 1).

al·lit·er·ate (ə lit′ə rāt′), *v.i.*, *v.t.*, -at·ed, -at·ing. to show or cause to show alliteration. —**al·lit′er·a′tive**, *adj.*

al·lit·er·a·tion (ə lit′ə rā′shən), *n.* the commencement of two or more stressed words with the same initial sounds.

al·lo·cate (al′ə kāt′), *v.t.*, -cat·ed, -cat·ing. to set apart for a particular purpose. —**al′lo·ca′tion**, *n.*

al·lot (ə lot′), *v.t.*, -lot·ted, -lot·ting. 1. to divide or distribute in shares. 2. to appropriate for a special purpose. —**al·lot′ment**, *n.* —**Syn.** allocate, apportion, assign.

al·lot·ro·py (ə lo′trə pē), *n.* a property of certain chemical elements of existing in two or more distinct forms. —**al′lo·trope** (al′ə trop′), *n.* —**al′lo·trop′ic** (-trop′ik), *adj.*

all-out (ôl′out′), *adj.* using all one's strength or energy: *an all-out assault.*

all-ov·er (ôl′ō′vər), *adj.* over the entire surface.

al·low (ə lou′), *v.t.* 1. to let do or happen, often as a privilege. 2. to grant (a sum of money). 3. to permit by neglect or oversight. 4. to concede: *to allow a claim.* 5. to take into consideration. —*v.i.* 6. to let something happen. 7. **allow for**, to make provision for. —**al·low′a·ble**, *adj.* —**Syn.** 1. permit.

al·low·ance (ə lou′əns), *n.* 1. the act of allowing. 2. something allowed. 3. a sum of money allowed or granted for a particular purpose, as for expenses. 4. a reduction in price, as for damage. 5. **make allowance** or **allowances (for)**, to forgive.

al·loy (*n.* al′oi, ə loi′; *v.* ə loi′), *n.* 1. a substance composed of two or more metals intimately mixed, as by fusion. 2. admixture, as of good with evil. —*v.t.* 3. to mix so as to form an alloy.

all′ right′, 1. safe or unharmed. 2. yes or very well. 3. satisfactory. 4. satisfactorily. 5. without fail. —**Usage.** See **alright**.

all-round (ôl′round′), *adj.* all-around.

All′ Saints′′ Day′, a church festival celebrated November 1 in honor of all the saints.

All′ Souls′′ Day′, a day of solemn prayer for all dead persons, usually on November 2.

all·spice (ôl′spīs′), *n.* 1. an aromatic tree of tropical America. 2. the brown berry of this tree. 3. a mildly sharp spice made from this berry.

all-star (ôl′stär′), *adj.* 1. consisting of star performers. —*n.* 2. a player on an all-star team.

all-time (ôl′tīm′), *adj.* of or for all times on record.

al·lude (ə lōōd′), *v.i.*, -lud·ed, -lud·ing. to mention indirectly or casually. —**al·lu′sion**, *n.* —**al·lu′sive**, *adj.* —**al·lu′sive·ly**, *adv.* —**al·lu′sive·ness**, *n.*

al·lure (ə lōōr′), *v.*, -lured, -lur·ing, *n.* —*v.t.*, *v.i.* 1. to attract by the offer of something desirable. —*n.* 2. fascination or appeal. —**al·lure′ment**, *n.* —**al·lur′ing**, *adj.* —**al·lur′ing·ly**, *adv.*

al·lu·vi·um (ə lōō′vē əm), *n.*, *pl.* -vi·ums, -vi·a (-vē ə). a deposit of sand, mud, etc., formed by flowing water. —**al·lu′vi·al**, *adj.*

al·ly (*v.* ə lī′; *n.* al′ī, ə lī′), *v.*, **-lied,** **-ly·ing,** *n.*, *pl.* **-lies.** —*v.t.,* *v.i.* 1. to unite formally, as by treaty, marriage, or the like. 2. to associate by some mutual relationship. —*n.* 3. a person or country united with another in alliance. —**al·li′a·ble,** *adj.*

al·ma ma·ter (äl′mə mä′tər, al′-; al′mə mä′tər), 1. a school, college, or university at which a person has studied. 2. its anthem.

al·ma·nac (ôl′mə nak′), *n.* a publication containing statistical information, astronomical or meteorological data, and other helpful facts.

al·man·dine (al′mən dēn′, -dīn′), *n.* a deep-red garnet, used as an abrasive. Also, **al·man·dite** (al′mən dīt′).

al·might·y (ôl mī′tē), *adj.* 1. having unlimited or great power. 2. *Informal.* extreme. —*n.* 3. the Almighty, God. —**al·might′i·ly,** *adv.* —**al·might′i·ness,** *n.*

al·mond (ä′mənd, am′ənd, al′mənd), *n.* 1. the nutlike kernel of the fruit of a tree of warm temperate regions. 2. the tree itself.

al·mon·er (al′mə nər, ä′mə-), *n.* a person who distributes alms.

al·most (ôl′mōst, ôl mōst′), *adv.* very nearly.

alms (ämz), *n.* money or other donations given to the poor or needy.

alms·house (ämz′hous′), *n.* *Chiefly Brit.* a poorhouse.

al·oe (al′ō), *n.,* *pl.* **-oes.** 1. any chiefly African plant of the lily family, certain species of which yield a drug and a fiber. 2. Often, **aloes.** a laxative drug made from the juice of several species of aloe.

a·loft (ə lôft′, ə loft′), *adv.* 1. high up. 2. in the air. 3. *Naut.* on the masts.

a·lo·ha (ə lō′ə, ä lō′hä), *interj.,* *n.* 1. hello or welcome. 2. farewell. [< Hawaiian]

a·lone (ə lōn′), *adj.,* *adv.* 1. apart from any other. 2. with nothing else besides. 3. only. 4. **let alone,** **a.** to refrain from interfering with. **b.** not to mention.

a·long (ə lông′, ə long′), *prep.* 1. through, on, or over the length of. 2. during. 3. in accordance with. —*adv.* 4. in a line with the length or direction. 5. onward: *to move along.* 6. some way on: *along toward evening.* 7. in company or in agreement. 8. as a companion: *He took his sister along.* 9. at an advanced state. 10. **all along,** all the time. 11. **be along,** to come.

a·long·shore (ə lông′shōr′), *adv., adj.* by or along the shore or coast.

a·long·side (ə lông′sīd′, ə long′-), *adv.* 1. at or to the side of something. —

prep. 2. Also, **alongside of.** by the side of.

a·loof (ə lōōf′), *adv.* 1. apart in feeling, interest, etc. 2. reserved or indifferent. —**a·loof′ness,** *n.*

al·o·pe·ci·a (al′ə pē′shē ə), *n.* baldness.

a·loud (ə loud′), *adv.* 1. with the natural voice. 2. vocally. 3. loudly: *to cry aloud.*

alp (alp), *n.* a high mountain.

al·pac·a (al pak′ə), *n.* 1. a domesticated, South American animal having long, soft hair or wool. 2. its wool. 3. a fabric made from it.

al·pen·horn (al′pən hôrn′), *n.* a long, powerful horn used by Swiss herdsmen.

al·pen·stock (al′pən stok′), *n.* a strong staff with an iron point, used by mountain climbers.

al·pha (al′fə), *n.* the first letter of the Greek alphabet (A, α).

al·pha·bet (al′fə bet′), *n.* 1. the letters of a language in their customary order. 2. the rudiments. [< LL < Gk *alphábetos* < *alpha* + *bēta* first two letters of Greek alphabet] —**al′pha·bet′i·cal, al′pha·bet′ic,** *adj.* —**al′pha·bet′i·cal·ly,** *adv.*

al·pha·bet·ize (al′fə bi tīz′), *v.t.,* **-ized, -iz·ing.** to put in alphabetical order. —**al·pha·bet·i·za·tion** (al′fə bet′i zā′shən), *n.* —**al′pha·bet·iz′er,** *n.*

al·pha·nu·mer·ic (al′fə nōō mer′ik, -nyōō-), *adj.* *Computer Technol.* including both letters and numbers.

al′pha par′ticle, a positively charged particle consisting of two protons and two neutrons, emitted in radioactive decay or nuclear fission.

al′pha ray′, a stream of alpha particles.

al′pha rhythm′, an electric current from the cerebral cortex running 8 to 13 cycles per second: considered a relaxed state in normal, healthy adults.

al·pine (al′pīn, -pin), *adj.* 1. of lofty mountains. 2. (*cap.*) of or on the Alps. 3. growing on mountains: *alpine plants.*

Alps (alps), *n.* a mountain range in S Europe.

al·read·y (ôl red′ē), *adv.* 1. previous to a given time. 2. so soon: *Is it noon already?*

—**Usage.** ALREADY is sometimes confused with ALL READY. ALREADY means "previously": *The plane had already left the airport.* ALL READY means "completely prepared or ready": *The troops were all ready to attack.*

al·right (ôl rīt′), *adv.* Nonstandard. all right.

—**Usage.** The form ALRIGHT is occasionally seen as a variant of ALL RIGHT, probably by analogy with ALREADY and ALTOGETHER, but it is usually considered unacceptable in standard English.

al·so (ôl′sō), *adv.* in addition or too.

al·so-ran (ol′sō ran′), *n. Informal.* a contestant who is defeated in an election, race, etc.

alt., **1.** alteration. **2.** alternate. **3.** altitude. **4.** alto.

Alta., Alberta.

al·tar (ôl′tər), *n.* **1.** an elevated structure at which religious rites are performed, sacrifices are offered, etc. **2. lead to the altar,** *Informal.* to wed.

al′tar boy′, acolyte.

al·tar·piece (ôl′tər pēs′), *n.* a painted or carved screen behind or above the altar.

al·ter (ôl′tər), *v.t.* **1.** to make different, as in size or appearance. **2.** to castrate or spay. —*v.i.* **3.** to change. —**al′ter·a′tion,** *n.* —**al′ter·a′tive,** *adj.*

al·ter·ca·tion (ôl′tər kā′shən, al′-), *n.* a heated or angry dispute.

al·ter e·go (ôl′tər ē′gō, eg′ō, al′-), **1.** a second self. **2.** an inseparable friend.

al·ter·nate (*v.* ôl′tər nāt′, al′-; *adj., n.* ôl′tər nit, al′-), *v.,* -**nat·ed,** -**nat·ing,** *adj., n.* —*v.i., v.t.* **1.** to interchange or cause to interchange repeatedly. **2.** to change back and forth between conditions, actions, etc. —*adj.* **3.** interchanged repeatedly one for another. **4.** every second one of a series. **5.** being a substitute. —*n.* **6.** a substitute. —**al′ter·nate·ly,** *adv.* —**al′ter·nate·ness,** *n.* —**al′ter·nat′ing·ly,** *adv.* —**al′ter·na′tion,** *n.*

al′ternating cur′rent, an electric current that reverses its direction at regular intervals.

al·ter·na·tive (ôl tûr′nə tiv, al-), *n.* **1.** a choice limited to one of two or more possibilities. **2.** one of these choices. —*adj.* **3.** affording a choice between two things. —**al·ter′na·tive·ly,** *adv.*

al·ter·na·tor (ôl′tər nā′tər, al′-), *n.* a generator of alternating current.

al·though (ôl ᵗħō′), *conj.* in spite of the fact that. Also, **al·tho′.**

al·tim·e·ter (al tim′i tər, al′tə mē′tər), *n.* a device used to measure altitude.

al·ti·tude (al′ti tōōd′, -tyōōd′), *n.* **1.** the height above sea level of a given point. **2.** extent or distance upward. **3.** the angular distance of a heavenly body above the horizon. **4.** the perpendicular distance from the vertex of a figure to the side opposite the vertex.

al·to (al′tō), *n., pl.* -**tos.** **1.** the lowest female voice. **2.** a singer with such a voice.

al·to·geth·er (ôl′tə geᵗħ′ər, ôl′tə-geᵗħ′ər), *adv.* **1.** wholly or entirely. **2.** with everything included. **3.** with everything considered.

al·tru·ism (al′trōō iz′əm), *n.* unselfish concern for the welfare of others. —**al′tru·ist,** *n.* —**al′tru·is′tic,** *adj.* —**al′tru·is′ti·cal·ly,** *adv.*

al·um (al′əm), *n.* **1.** a solid double sulfate, containing aluminum, used as an astringent and styptic, and in dyeing and tanning. **2.** a white, crystalline, water-soluble solid, used chiefly in purifying water.

alum., aluminum.

a·lu·mi·na (ə lōō′mə nə), *n.* the natural or synthetic oxide of aluminum, occurring in nature as corundum.

al·u·min·i·um (al′yə min′ē əm), *n. Chiefly Brit.* aluminum.

a·lu·mi·nize (ə lōō′mə nīz′), *v.t.,* -**nized, -niz·ing.** to treat with aluminum.

a·lu·mi·num (ə lōō′mə nəm), *n. Chem.* a silver-white metallic element, light in weight and not readily corroded or tarnished, used in alloys and for utensils, airplane parts, etc. *Symbol:* Al; *at. wt.:* 26.98; *at. no.:* 13.

a·lum·na (ə lum′nə), *n., pl.* -**nae** (-nē). a female graduate or former student of a specific school, college, or university.

a·lum·nus (ə lum′nəs), *n., pl.* -**ni** (-nī). a male graduate or former student of a specific school, college, or university.

al·ways (ôl′wāz, -wēz), *adv.* **1.** every time. **2.** forever. **3.** in any event or if necessary. **4.** continually.

am (am; *unstressed* əm, m), *v.* 1st pers. sing. pres. indic. of **be.**

AM, 1. See **a.m. 2.** amplitude modulation: **a.** a method of impressing a signal on a radio carrier wave by varying its amplitude. **b.** a system of radio broadcasting by this means.

Am., americium.

Am., 1. America. **2.** American.

A.M., 1. See **a.m. 2.** Master of Arts. [< L *Artium Magister*]

a.m., the period from 12 midnight to 12 noon. [< L *ante meridiem*]

A.M.A., American Medical Association.

a·mah (ä′mə, am′ə), *n.* (in the Orient) **1.** a nurse, esp. a wet nurse. **2.** a maidservant.

a·main (ə mān′), *adv. Archaic.* with or at full speed.

a·mal·gam (ə mal′gəm), *n.* **1.** an alloy of mercury with another metal or metals. **2.** a combination or mixture.

a·mal·ga·mate (ə mal′gə māt′), v.t., v.i., -mat·ed, -mat·ing. to combine or mix. —a·mal′ga·ma′tion, n. — a·mal′ga·ma′tor, n.

a·man·u·en·sis (ə man′yoō en′sis), n., pl. -ses (-sēz). *Now Facetious.* a secretary.

am·a·ranth (am′ə ranth′), n. 1. a legendary undying flower. 2. any of various erect plants, some of which are cultivated for their showy flowers. —am′a·ran′thine (-ran′thin, -thīn), adj.

Am·a·ril·lo (əm′ə ril′ō), n. a city in NW Texas.

am·a·ryl·lis (am′ə ril′is), n. a bulbous plant having large, lilylike, usually rose-colored flowers.

a·mass (ə mas′), v.t. to collect or accumulate, esp. to a great size. — a·mass′ment, n.

am·a·teur (am′ə choōr′, -tyoōr′, am′ə tûr′), n. 1. a person who engages in an activity for pleasure rather than for financial benefit. 2. a person who is inexperienced or unskilled. —am′a·teur′ish, adj. — am′a·teur′ish·ly, adv. —am′a·teur·ism, n.

am·a·tive (am′ə tiv), adj. disposed or inclined to love. —am′a·tive·ly, adv. —am′a·tive·ness, n.

am·a·to·ry (am′ə tôr′ē, -tōr′ē), adj. of lovers, lovemaking, or expressions of love. —am′a·to′ri·al·ly, adv.

a·maze (ə māz′), v.t., a·mazed, a·maz·ing. to overwhelm with surprise or wonder. —a·maz·ed·ly (ə mā′zid lē), adv. —a·maze′ment, n. —a·maz′ing, adj. —a·maz′ing·ly, adv.

Am·a·zon (am′ə zon′, -zən), n. 1. a river in N South America. 2. *Class. Myth.* one of a race of female warriors. 3. (*often l.c.*) a tall, powerful, aggressive woman. — Am·a·zo·ni·an (am′ə zō′nē ən), adj.

amb., ambassador.

am·bas·sa·dor (am bas′ə dər), n. a diplomatic official of the highest rank, sent by one country to another as its representative. — bas·sa·do·ri·al (am bas′ə dōr′ē əl, -dôr′-), adj. —am·bas′sa·dor·ship′, n.

am·ber (am′bər), n. 1. a pale yellow, sometimes reddish or brownish, fossil resin, used in jewelry, etc. 2. a yellowish brown.

am·ber·gris (am′bər grēs′, -gris), n. an ash-colored secretion of the sperm-whale intestine, used in perfumery.

ambi-, a combining form meaning "both": *ambiguous.*

am·bi·dex·trous (am′bi dek′strəs), adj. able to use both hands equally well. —am′bi·dex·ter′i·ty (-dek ster′i tē), n. —am′bi·dex′trous·ly, adv.

am·bi·ence (am′bē əns), n. an environment, esp. its surrounding atmosphere. Also, am′bi·ance.

am·bi·ent (am′bē ənt), adj. surrounding an atmosphere.

am·big·u·ous (am big′yoō əs), adj. 1. having several possible meanings. 2. obscure or indistinct. —am′bi·gu′i·ty (-gyoō′-), am·big′u·ous·ness, n. —am·big′u·ous·ly, adv.

am·bi·tion (am bish′ən), n. 1. an earnest desire for some achievement, power, fame, wealth, etc. 2. an object of such desire.

am·bi·tious (am bish′əs), adj. 1. having ambition. 2. showing or caused by ambition. 3. requiring exceptional effort. —am·bi′tious·ly, adv.

am·biv·a·lence (am biv′ə ləns), n. uncertainty or fluctuation caused by inability to make a choice. —am·biv′a·lent, adj. —am·biv′a·lent·ly, adv.

am·bi·vert (am′bə vûrt′), n. a person whose personality type is intermediate between extrovert and introvert.

am·ble (am′bəl), v., -bled, -bling, n. —v.i. 1. to walk at a slow, leisurely pace. 2. (of a horse) to move at such a pace. —n. 3. an ambling gait. 4. an easy walk. —am′bler, n.

am·bro·sia (am brō′zhə), n. *Class. Myth.* the food and drink of the gods. —am·bro′sial, adj.

am·bu·lance (am′byə ləns), n. a vehicle equipped for transporting sick or injured people.

am·bu·lant (am′byə lənt), adj. walking or moving about.

am·bu·late (am′byə lāt′), v.i., -lat·ed, -lat·ing. to walk or move about. —am′bu·lant (-lənt), adj. —am′bu·la′tion, n. —am′bu·la′tor, n.

am·bu·la·to·ry (am′byə lə tôr′ē, -tōr′ē), adj., n., pl. -ries. —adj. 1. of or capable of walking. 2. adapted for walking 3. moving about. —n. 4. the covered walk of a cloister.

am·bus·cade (am′bə skād′), n., v.t., v.i., -cad·ed, -cad·ing. ambush.

am·bush (am′boōsh), n. 1. the act of lying concealed so as to attack by surprise. 2. the concealed position itself. —v.t., v.i. 3. to attack from ambush.

amdt., amendment.

a·me·ba (ə mē′bə), n., pl. -bas, -bae (-bē). amoeba. —a·me′bic, adj. —a·me′boid, adj.

a·mel·io·rate (ə mēl′yə rāt′), v.t., v.i., -rat·ed, -rat·ing. to make or become better or more tolerable, as in condition. —a·mel′io·ra′tion, n.

a·men (ā′men′, ä′men′), interj. so be it (used after a prayer, creed, etc.). [< LL < Gk < Heb *āmēn* may it be so]

a·me·na·ble (ə mē′nə bəl, ə men′ə-), *adj.* **1.** willing to listen or agree. **2.** willing to yield or submit. —**a·me′na·bil′i·ty,** *n.* —**a·me′na·bly,** *adv.*

a·mend (ə mend′), *v.t.* **1.** to modify (a motion, bill, etc.) formally. **2.** to improve. **3.** to rectify. —*v.i.* **4.** to become better by reforming oneself. —**a·mend′a·ble,** *adj.*

a·mend·ment (ə mend′mənt), *n.* **1.** the act of amending or state of being amended. **2.** an alteration of or addition to a bill, constitution, etc. **3.** a change.

a·mends (ə mendz′), *n.* reparation for a loss, damage, or injury.

a·men·i·ty (ə men′i tē, ə mē′ni-), *n., pl.* **-ties. 1.** amenities, courtesies or civilities. **2.** pleasantness or agreeableness.

Amer., *adj.* **1.** America. **2.** American.

a·merce (ə mûrs′), *v.t.,* **a·merced, a·merc·ing. 1.** to penalize by a fine. **2.** *Archaic.* to punish. —**a·merce′ment,** *n.*

A·mer·i·ca (ə mer′i kə), *n.* **1.** See **United States. 2.** See **North America. 3.** See **South America. 4.** Also called **the Americas.** North and South America, considered together.

A·mer·i·can (ə mer′i kən), *adj.* **1.** of the United States or its inhabitants. **2.** of North or South America. —*n.* **3.** a citizen of the United States. **4.** a native or inhabitant of North or South America.

A·mer·i·ca·na (ə mer′i kan′ə, -kä′nə, -kā′nə), *n.* books, maps, etc., relating to America, esp. to its history.

Amer′ican In′dian, Indian (def. 1).

A·mer·i·can·ism (ə mer′i kə niz′əm), *n.* **1.** devotion to the United States and its institutions. **2.** a custom, trait, or thing peculiar to the U.S. **3.** a word especially characteristic of English spoken in the U.S.

A·mer·i·can·ize (ə mer′i kə nīz′), *v.t., v.i.,* **-ized, -iz·ing.** to make or become American in character, methods, etc. —**A·mer′i·can·i·za′tion,** *n.*

Amer′ican Le′gion, a society of veterans of the U.S. armed forces, organized in 1919.

Amer′ican plan′, a hotel rate covering lodging, service, and meals.

Amer′ican Revolu′tion, the war between Great Britain and her American colonies, 1775–83, by which the colonies won their independence.

a·mer·i·ci·um (am′ə rish′ē əm), *n. Chem.* a radioactive element produced by helium bombardment of uranium and plutonium. *Symbol:* Am; *at. no.:* 95.

Am·er·ind (am′ə rind), *n.* an aboriginal Indian or Eskimo of North or South America. —**Am′er·in′di·an,** *adj., n.*

am·e·thyst (am′i thist), *n.* **1.** a purple quartz, used as a gem. **2.** a purplish tint.

a·mi·a·ble (ā′mē ə bəl), *adj.* friendly and agreeable. —**a′mi·a·bil′i·ty, a′mi·a·ble·ness,** *n.* —**a′mi·a·bly,** *adv.*

am·i·ca·ble (am′ə kə bəl), *adj.* showing friendliness and peaceableness. —**am′i·ca·bil′i·ty, am′i·ca·ble·ness,** *n.* —**am′i·ca·bly,** *adv.*

a·mid (ə mid′), *prep.* **1.** among. **2.** during. Also, **a·midst** (ə midst′).

am·ide (am′id, -id), *n.* an organic compound formed from ammonia.

a·mid·ships (ə mid′ships), *adv.* in or toward the middle part of a vessel or aircraft. Also, **a·mid′ship.**

a·mi·go (ə mē′go, ä mē′-), *n., pl.* **-gos (-gōz).** a friend.

a·mi′no ac′id (ə mē′nō, am′ə nō′), any of a class of organic compounds, some of which are the chief structures of proteins.

A·mish (ä′mish, am′ish, ā′mish), *adj.* **1.** of any of the strict Mennonite groups. —*n.* **2.** the Amish people.

a·miss (ə mis′), *adv.* **1.** out of the proper course or order. **2.** take amiss, to be offended at. —*adj.* **3.** improper or faulty.

am·i·ty (am′i tē), *n.* friendly or peaceful relations.

am·me·ter (am′mē′tər), *n.* an instrument for measuring current in amperes.

am·mo (am′ō), *n. Informal.* ammunition.

am·mo·nia (ə mōn′yə, ə mō′nē ə), *n. Chem.* **1.** a pungent, suffocating, gaseous compound, used chiefly in the manufacture of chemicals and reagents. **2.** Also called **ammo′nia wa′ter, ammonium hydroxide.** this gas dissolved in water.

am·mo·ni·um (ə mō′nē əm), *n.* the univalent ion or group which plays the part of a metal in the salt formed when ammonia reacts with an acid.

ammo′nium chlo′ride, a crystalline powder used chiefly in dry cells and as an expectorant.

ammo′nium hydrox′ide, ammonia (def. 2).

am·mu·ni·tion (am′yə nish′ən), *n.* **1.** projectiles, as powder, shot, shrapnel, bullets, etc. **2.** material used in offense or defense.

am·ne·sia (am nē′zhə), *n.* complete or partial loss of memory. —**am·ne′si·ac′** (-nē′zhē ak′, -zē-), **am·nes′ic** (-nē′sik, -zik), *n., adj.* —**am·nes·tic** (am nes′tik), *adj.*

am·nes·ty (am′ni stē), *n.*, *pl.* **-ties,** *v.*, **-tied, -ty·ing.** —*n.* **1.** a general pardon for offenses against a government. —*v.t.* **2.** to grant amnesty to.

am·ni·o·cen·te·sis (am′nē ō sen tē′sis), *n.* the surgical perforation of the uterus to drain fluid for diagnostic purposes.

a·moe·ba (ə mē′bə), *n.*, *pl.* **-bae** (-bē), **-bas.** a microscopic, one-celled animal consisting of a naked mass of protoplasm constantly changing in shape as it moves and engulfs food. —**a·moe′bic,** *adj.*

a·moe·boid (ə mē′boid), *adj.* resembling or related to amoebae.

a·mok (ə muk′, ə mok′), *adv.* **run amok.** See **amuck.**

a·mong (ə mung′), *prep.* **1.** in the midst of. **2.** with a portion for each of. **3.** in the group of. **4.** familiar to or characteristic of. **5.** in, with, or through the general mass of. **6.** each with the other. Also, **a·mongst** (ə mungst′).
—**Usage.** Precise users of English use AMONG when more than two persons or things are involved (*The winnings were divided among the six men*) and use BETWEEN chiefly when only two persons or things are involved (*to decide between tea and coffee*). This distinction is not very widely maintained in the case of BETWEEN, which is often used when more than two persons or things are involved in individual or reciprocal relationships: *a contract between five companies.*

a·mon·til·la·do (ə mon′tᵊlä′dō), *n.* a pale, dry Spanish sherry.

a·mor·al (ā môr′əl, ā mor′-), *adj.* **1.** neither moral nor immoral. **2.** lacking moral standards. —**a·mo·ral·i·ty** (ā′mə ral′i tē, am′ə-), *n.* —**a·mor′al·ly,** *adv.*

am·or·ous (am′ər əs), *adj.* **1.** inclined to love, esp. sexual love. **2.** enamored. **3.** expressing or pertaining to love. —**am′o·rous·ly,** *adv.* —**am′o·rous·ness,** *n.*

a·mor·phous (ə môr′fəs), *adj.* **1.** lacking definite form. **2.** indeterminate. **3.** not crystalline. —**a·mor′phous·ly,** *adv.* —**a·mor′phous·ness,** *n.*

am·or·tize (am′ər tīz′), *v.t.,* **-tized, -tiz·ing.** to liquidate (a mortgage, debt, etc.), esp. by periodic payments. —**am′or·tiz′a·ble,** *adj.* —**am′or·ti·za′tion,** *n.*

a·mount (ə mount′), *n.* **1.** the total of two or more quantities. **2.** principal and its interest. **3.** quantity or measure. —*v.i.* **4.** to combine to yield a sum or total. **5.** to have a value, effect, or extent.

a·mour (ə mŏŏr′), *n.* **1.** a love affair. **2.** an illicit love affair.

a·mour-pro·pre (A mŏŏR PRô′PRᵊ), *n. French.* self-esteem.

amp., **1.** amperage. **2.** ampere; amperes.

am·per·age (am′pər ij, am pēr′-), *n.* the strength of an electric current measured in amperes.

am·pere (am′pēr), *n.* a unit of electric current equal to the steady current produced by one volt acting through a resistance of one ohm.

am·per·sand (am′pər sand′, am′pər-sand′), *n.* a symbol (& or &) for *and.* [contr. of *and per se and,* lit., (the symbol) & by itself (stands for) and]

am·phet·a·mine (am fet′ə mēn′, -min), *n.* a drug that stimulates the central nervous system: used chiefly to lift the mood or control the appetite.

am·phib·i·an (am fib′ē ən), *n.* **1.** any amphibious animal or plant. **2.** an aircraft designed for taking off from and landing on both land and water. **3.** a military vehicle equipped to move on land or water. —*adj.* **4.** amphibious (def. 2).

am·phib·i·ous (am fib′ē əs), *adj.* **1.** living both on land and in water. **2.** capable of operating on both land and water. **3.** by or trained for both land and naval forces.

am·phi·bole (am′fə bōl′), *n.* any of a group of hydrous silicate minerals containing chiefly calcium, magnesium, sodium, etc.

am·phi·the·a·ter (am′fə thē′ə tər, -thē°′tər), *n.* a building with tiers of seats around an open area. Also, **am′phi·the′a·tre.**

am·pho·ra (am′fər ə), *n.*, *pl.* **-pho·rae** (-fə rē′), **-pho·ras.** *Gk. and Rom. Antiq.* a large, oval, two-handled vase, used for storage, as a trophy, etc.

am·pi·cil·lin (am′pi sil′in), *n.* a semisynthetic penicillin effective against certain bacteria.

am·ple (am′pəl), *adj.,* **-pler, -plest.** of adequate or more than adequate extent, size, or amount. —**am′ple·ness,** *n.* —**am′ply,** *adv.*

am·pli·fy (am′plə fī′), *v.,* **-fied, -fy·ing.** —*v.t.* **1.** to make larger or greater. **2.** to expand or clarify by expanding. **3.** to increase the amplitude of. —*v.i.* **4.** to discourse at length. —**am′pli·fi′a·ble,** *adj.* —**am′pli·fi·ca′tion,** *n.* —**am′pli·fi′er,** *n.*

am·pli·tude (am′pli tŏŏd′, -tyŏŏd′), *n.* **1.** greatness of extent. **2.** large measure or quantity. **3.** the absolute value of the maximum displacement during an oscillation. **4.** the maximum deviation of an alternating current from its average value.

am′plitude modula′tion. See **AM** (def. 2).

am·pule (am′pyōol), *n.* a sealed glass or plastic bulb containing solutions for hypodermic injection. Also, **am′poule.**

am·pu·tate (am′pyōo tāt′), *v.t.,* **-tat·ed, -tat·ing.** to cut off (a limb), as by surgery. —**am′pu·ta′tion,** *n.*

am·pu·tee (am′pyōo tē′), *n.* a person who has lost a limb or limbs by amputation.

Am·ster·dam (am′stər dam′), *n.* the nominal capital of the Netherlands.

amt., amount.

Am·trak (am′trak′), *n.* a national rail-passenger system in the U.S.

amu, See atomic mass unit.

a·muck (ə muk′), *adv.* **run amuck, a.** to rush about in a murderous frenzy. **b.** to lose self-control, as in panic. [< Malay *amoq*]

am·u·let (am′yə lit), *n.* a charm worn to ward off evil.

a·muse (ə myōoz′), *v.t.,* **a·mused, a·mus·ing.** to entertain or divert in a light manner, often by pleasing the sense of humor. —**a·muse′ment,** *n.* —**Syn.** charm, delight, please.

amuse′ment park′, a park equipped with such recreational devices as a Ferris wheel, roller coaster, etc.

AMVETS (am′vets′), *n.* American Veterans of World War II and Korea.

am·yl·ase (am′ə lās′), *n.* any of several enzymes that help convert starch into sugar.

an (ən; *when stressed* an), *indefinite article.* the form of a before an initial vowel sound: *an event; an honor.*

-an, a suffix meaning: **a.** of or belonging to: *republican.* **b.** residing in: *Hawaiian.* **c.** adhering to: *Confucian.*

a·nach·ro·nism (ə nak′rə niz′əm), *n.* **1.** a person or thing that is chronologically out of place. **2.** an error in chronology in which a person or thing is assigned an incorrect date or period. —**a·nach′ro·nis′tic, a·nach′ro·nis′ti·cal,** *adj.* —**a·nach′ro·nis′ti·cal·ly,** *adv.*

an·a·con·da (an′ə kon′də), *n.* a South American boa that often grows to more than 20 feet.

an·a·dem (an′ə dem′), *n. Literary.* a garland or wreath.

a·nae·mi·a (ə nē′mē ə), *n.* anemia. —**a·nae′mic,** *adj.*

an·aer·obe (an âr′ōb, an′ə rōb′), *n.* an organism, esp. a bacterium, that does not require air or free oxygen to live. —**an′aer·o′bic,** *adj.*

an·aes·the·sia (an′is thē′zhə), *n.* anesthesia. —**an·aes·thet·ic** (an′is thet′ik), *adj., n.*

an·a·gram (an′ə gram′), *n.* a word or term formed by transposing the letters of another word or term.

An·a·heim (an′ə hīm′), *n.* a city in SW California.

a·nal (ān′³l), *adj.* **1.** of, involving, or near the anus. **2.** of or pertaining to libidinal development in which attention is centered on the anal region.

anal., **1.** analogous. **2.** analogy. **3.** analysis. **4.** analytic.

an·al·ge·si·a (an′³l jē′zē ə, -sē ə), *n.* absence of sense of pain. —**an′al·ge′sic,** *n., adj.*

an′alog comput′er, a computer that solves a given mathematical problem by using physical analogues, as electric voltages, of the numerical variables in the problem.

a·nal·o·gous (ə nal′ə gəs), *adj.* alike or similar in certain ways. —**a·nal′o·gous·ly,** *adv.*

an·a·logue (an′³l ôg′, -³l og′), *n.* **1.** having analogy to something else. **2.** *Biol.* an organ or part analogous to another. Also, **an′a·log′.**

a·nal·o·gy (ə nal′ə jē), *n., pl.* **-gies. 1.** a partial similarity on which a comparison may be based. **2.** a form of reasoning in which one thing is inferred to be similar to another thing in a certain respect on the basis of the known similarity in other respects. —**an·a·log·i·cal** (an′³l oj′i kəl), *adj.* —**an·a·log′i·cal·ly,** *adv.*

a·nal·y·sand (ə nal′i sand′, -zand′), *n.* a person undergoing psychoanalysis.

a·nal·y·sis (ə nal′i sis), *n., pl.* **-ses** (-sēz′). **1.** the separating of any entity into its constituent elements. **2.** this process as a method of studying the nature of something or of determining its essential features. **3.** psychoanalysis. —**an′a·lyt′ic, an′a·lyt′i·cal,** *adj.* —**an′a·lyt′i·cal·ly,** *adv.*

an·a·lyst (an′³list), *n.* **1.** a person who analyzes. **2.** a psychoanalyst.

an·a·lyze (an′³līz′), *v.t.,* **-lyzed, -lyz·ing. 1.** to examine critically. **2.** to subject to analysis. **3.** to psychoanalyze. —**an′a·lyz′a·ble,** *adj.* —**an′a·lyz′er,** *n.*

an·a·pest (an′ə pest′), *n. Pros.* a foot of three syllables, two unstressed followed by one stressed. —**an′a·pes′tic,** *adj.*

an·ar·chism (an′ər kiz′əm), *n.* **1.** a doctrine advocating the abolition of government as the indispensable condition for full liberty. **2.** the methods of anarchists. —**an′ar·chist,** *n.* —**an′ar·chis′tic,** *adj.*

an·ar·chy (an′ər kē), *n.* **1.** a state of society without government or law. **2.** confusion or disorder —**an·ar′chic** (an är′kik), **an·ar′chi·cal,** *adj.* —**an·ar′chi·cal·ly,** *adv.*

a·nas·to·mo·sis (ə nas′tə mō′sis), n., pl. -ses (-sēz). connection between parts of any branching system, as of blood vessels.

anat., 1. anatomical. 2. anatomist. 3. anatomy.

a·nath·e·ma (ə nath′ə mə), n., pl. -mas. 1. a person or thing detested. 2. a person or thing accused or condemned. 3. a formal ecclesiastical curse involving excommunication.

a·nath·e·ma·tize (ə nath′ə mə tīz′), v.t., v.i., -tized, -tiz·ing. to pronounce an anathema (against).

a·nat·o·mize (ə nat′ə mīz′), v.t., -mized, -miz·ing. 1. to dissect in order to study the structure. 2. to examine in detail.

a·nat·o·my (ə nat′ə mē), n., pl. -mies. 1. the science dealing with the structure of animals and plants. 2. the structure of an animal or plant. 3. an analysis or minute examination. —an·a·tom·i·cal (an′ə tom′i kəl), an′a·tom′ic, adj. —a·nat′o·mist, n.

anc., ancient.

-ance, a suffix meaning: a. action: appearance. b. state or quality: brilliance. c. a thing or object: contrivance.

an·ces·tor (an′ses tər), n. 1. a person from whom one is descended and who is usually more remote than a grandparent. 2. a forerunner or prototype. —an·ces·tral (an ses′trəl), adj. —an′ces·tress, n.fem. —Syn. 1. forebear, forefather, progenitor.

an·ces·try (an′ses trē), n., pl. -tries. 1. ancestral descent or lineage. 2. a series of ancestors.

an·chor (ang′kər), n. 1. any of various devices for dropping by a chain, cable, or rope to the bottom of a body of water to restrict the motion of a vessel or other floating object. 2. at anchor, held in place by an anchor. —v.t. 3. to hold fast by, or as by, an anchor. —v.i. 4. to lie at anchor.

an·chor·age (ang′kər ij), n. a place for anchoring.

an·cho·rite (ang′kə rīt′), n. a hermit, esp. of the early Christian church. —an′cho·ress, n.fem. —an·cho·rit·ic (ang′kə rit′ik), adj.

an′chor man′, 1. a person upon whose performance an organization, team, etc., depends. 2. a newscaster who coordinates a broadcast from different locations. —an′chor wom′an, n.fem.

an·cho·vy (an′chō vē, an chō′vē), n., pl. -vies. any small, marine, herring-like fish used as food.

an·cien ré·gime (än svan′ Rā zhēm′), French. the political and social system of France before the revolution of 1789.

an·cient (ān′shənt), adj. 1. of or in time long past, esp. before the end of the Western Roman Empire A.D. 476: ancient history. 2. old or aged. —n. 3. a person who lived in ancient times, esp. a Greek or Roman. 4. a very old person. —an′cient·ness, n.

an·cient·ly (ān′shənt lē), adv. in ancient times.

an·cil·lar·y (an′sə ler′ē), adj. closely auxiliary.

-ancy, a suffix meaning "state" or "quality": brilliancy.

and (and; unstressed ənd, ən), conj. 1. with or in addition to. 2. as well as. 3. plus or added to. 4. then. 5. then again. 6. Informal. to: Try and do it. 7. and so on or forth, and other things or the rest. —Usage. Since ETC. is an abbreviation for ET CETERA, which means "and others," the form AND ETC. is redundant.

an·dan·te (an dan′tē, än dän′tā), Music. —adj., adv. 1. moderately slow and even. —n. 2. an andante movement.

an·dan·ti·no (an′dan tē′nō, än′dän-), Music. —adj., adv. 1. slightly faster than andante. —n. 2. an andantino movement.

An·des (an′dēz), n. a mountain range in W. South America. —An·de′an, adj.

and·i·ron (and′ī ərn), n. one of a pair of metal supports for logs in a fireplace.

and/or, (used to imply that any or all of the things named may be affected): fire and/or wind damage.

An·dor·ra (an dôr′ə, -dor′ə), n. a country in the E Pyrenees.

an·dro·gen (an′drə jən), n. any substance that promotes masculine characteristics. —an·dro·gen·ic (an′-drə jen′ik), adj.

an·drog·y·nous (an droj′ə nəs), adj. being both male and female. —an·drog′y·ny, n.

an·droid (an′droid), n. an automaton in the form of a human being.

an·ec·dote (an′ik dōt′), n. a short narrative concerning an interesting event. —an·ec·do′tal, adj. —an·ec·dot·ic (an′ik dot′ik), adj. —an′ec·do′tist, n.

an·e·cho·ic (an′e kō′ik), adj. with a very low degree of reverberation.

a·ne·mi·a (ə nē′mē ə), n. a deficiency of the hemoglobin, accompanied by a reduced number of red blood cells, causing pallor, weakness, etc. —a·ne′mic, adj.

an·e·mom·e·ter (an′ə mom′i tər), n. any instrument for measuring the speed of the wind.

a·nem·o·ne (ə nem′ə nē′), n. 1. any of various perennial herbs having delicate whitish flowers. **2.** See sea anemone.

a·nent (ə nent′), *prep. Archaic.* in regard to.

an·er·oid barom′eter (an′ə roid′), a metallic box having an elastic top that is compressed by the external air to serve as a barometer.

an·es·the·sia (an′is thē′zhə), *n.* general or local insensibility to pain and other sensation, induced by certain drugs.

an·es·the·si·ol·o·gy (an′is thē′zē ol′ə jē), *n.* the science of administering anesthetics. **—an′es·the′si·ol′o·gist,** *n.*

an·es·thet·ic (an′is thet′ik), *n.* **1.** a drug that produces anesthesia. **—adj. 2.** of or causing anesthesia.

an·es·the·tist (ə nes′thi tist), *n.* a person who administers anesthetics.

an·es·the·tize (ə nes′thi tīz′), *v.t.,* **-tized, -tiz·ing.** to induce or cause anesthesia in. **—an·es′the·ti·za′tion,** *n.*

an·eu·rysm (an′yə riz′əm), *n.* an arterial dilatation usually caused by arteriosclerosis. Also, **an′eu·rism.**

a·new (ə nōō′, ə nyōō′), *adv.* **1.** once more. **2.** in a new form or manner.

an·gel (ān′jəl), *n.* **1.** a celestial attendant of God. **2.** a conventional representation of such a being, in human form, with wings. **3.** a messenger, esp. of God. **4.** a person who performs acts of great kindness. **5.** a financial backer for some undertaking, esp. a play. [< L *angel(us)* < Gk *ángelos* messenger] **—an·gel·ic** (an jel′ik), **an·gel′i·cal,** *adj.* **—an·gel′i·cal·ly,** *adv.*

an′gel dust′, *Slang.* See PCP.

an·gel·fish (ān′jəl fish′), *n., pl.* **-fish, -fish·es.** a brightly colored, spiny-headed tropical fish.

an′gel food′ cake′, a light, white cake made with stiffly beaten egg whites. Also called **an′gel cake′.**

an·gel·i·ca (an jel′ə kə), *n.* a plant cultivated for its scent, medicinal root, and edible stalks.

an·ger (aṅg′gər), *n.* **1.** a strong feeling of displeasure and belligerence. **—v.t., v.i. 2.** to make or become angry. **—Syn. 1.** fury, indignation.

an·gi·na (an jī′nə), *n.* **1.** any inflammatory affection of the throat or fauces, as quinsy, croup, etc. **2.** See angina pectoris. **—an·gi′nal, an·gi′nous,** *adj.*

angi′na pec′to·ris (pek′tə ris), a syndrome characterized by constricting paroxysmal pain below the sternum.

an·gi·o·sperm (an′jē ə spûrm′), *n.* a plant having its seeds enclosed in an ovary.

Angl., **1.** Anglican. **2.** Anglicized.

an·gle¹ (aṅg′gəl), *n., v.,* **-gled, -gling.** **—n. 1.** *Geom.* **a.** the space within two lines diverging from a common point. **b.** the figure so formed. **c.** the amount of rotation needed to bring one line into coincidence with another. **2.** a projecting corner. **3.** a viewpoint or standpoint. **4.** an aspect or phase of an event, problem, or situation. **—v.t., v.i. 5.** to move, bend, or hit at an angle. **6.** to write from a particular or biased viewpoint.

an·gle² (aṅg′gəl), *v.i.,* **-gled, -gling,** *n.* **—v.i. 1.** to fish with hook and line. **2.** to attempt to get something by artful means. **—n. 3.** *Slang.* a scheme or intrigue. **—an′gler,** *n.* **—an′gling,** *n.*

an′gle i′ron, a piece of iron or steel having a cross section in the form of an L.

An·gles (aṅg′gəlz), *n.pl.* a West Germanic people that migrated to Britain in the 5th century A.D. **—An′gli·an,** *adj., n.*

an·gle·worm (aṅg′gəl wûrm′), *n.* an earthworm, as used for bait in fishing.

An·gli·can (aṅg′glə kən), *adj.* **1.** of or related to the Church of England. **2.** *Obs.* English (def. 1). **—n. 3.** a member of the Church of England. **—An′gli·can·ism′,** *n.*

An·gli·cism (aṅg′gli siz′əm), *n.* a word, idiom, or characteristic feature of English occurring in another language.

An·gli·cize (aṅg′gli sīz′), *v.t., v.i.,* **-cized, -ciz·ing.** **1.** to make or become English in customs, etc. **2.** to conform to the usage of the English language. **—An′gli·ci·za′tion,** *n.*

An·glo (aṅg′glō), *n., pl.* **-glos.** an English-speaking American of northern-European ancestry.

Anglo-, a combining form meaning "English": *Anglophile.*

An·glo·phile (aṅg′glə fīl′, -fil), *n.* a person who greatly admires England or anything English. Also, **An·glo·phil** (aṅg′glə fil). **—An·glo·phil·i·a** (aṅg′glə fil′ē ə, -fēl′yə), *n.*

An·glo·phobe (aṅg′glə fōb′), *n.* a person who hates or fears England or anything English. **—An·glo·pho·bi·a,** *n.*

An·glo-Sax·on (aṅg′glō sak′sən), *n.* **1.** a person whose native language is English. **2.** an Englishman of the period before the Norman Conquest. **3.** a person of English descent. **4.** See Old English. **—adj. 5.** of the Anglo-Saxons.

An·go·la (aṅg gō′lə), *n.* a country in SW Africa. **—An·go′lan,** *adj., n.*

An·go·ra (ang gōr′ə, -gôr′ə, an-), *n.*
1. a cat, goat, or rabbit having
long, silky hair. 2. the hair of such
a cat, goat, or rabbit. 3. yarn, fabric,
or a garment made from this hair.

an·gry (ang′grē), *adj.*, **-gri·er**, **-gri·est**.
1. feeling anger or resentment. 2.
creating a mood associated with
anger or danger: *an angry sea.* 3.
inflamed, as a sore. —**an′gri·ly**, *adv.*
—**Syn.** enraged, infuriated, irate.

angst (ängkst), *n.* a feeling of dread
or anxiety.

ang·strom (ang′strəm), *n.* a unit of
length, equal to one ten-millionth
of a millimeter, primarily used to
express electromagnetic wavelengths.
Also, **ang′strom u′nit.**

an·guish (ang′gwish), *n.* 1. acute
pain, suffering, or distress. —*v.i.,
v.t.* 2. to suffer or cause to suffer
anguish. · —**an′guished**, *adj.*

an·gu·lar (ang′gyə lər), *adj.* 1. having an angle or angles. 2. of, at,
forming, or measured by an angle.
3. bony or gaunt. 4. moving awkwardly. —**an′gu·lar·ly**, *adv.* —**an·
gu·lar·i·ty** (ang′gyə lar′i tē), **an′gu·
lar·ness,** *n.*

An·gus (ang′gəs), *n.* one of a breed
of hornless beef cattle raised originally in Scotland.

an·hy·dride (an hī′drīd, -drid), *n.* a
compound from which water has
been abstracted.

an·hy·drous (an hī′drəs), *adj.* with
all water removed.

an·ile (an′īl, ā′nīl), *adj.* of a weak
old woman. —**a·nil·i·ty** (ə nil′i tē),
n.

an·i·line (an′ᵊlin, -ᵊlīn′), *n.* a colorless liquid used chiefly in the synthesis of dyes and drugs.

an·i·mad·vert (an′ə mad vûrt′), *v.i.* to
comment critically. —**an′i·mad·ver′-
sion,** *n.*

an·i·mal (an′ə məl), *n.* 1. any living
being typically differing from a
plant in having the ability to move
voluntarily, the presence of a nervous system, etc. 2. any such being
other than humans. 3. an inhuman
or brutish person. —*adj.* 4. of or
derived from animals. 5. pertaining to the physical nature of humans,
rather than their spiritual or intellectual nature. —**an′i·mal′i·ty**
(-mal′i tē), *n.*

an·i·mal·cule (an′ə mal′kyōōl), *n.* a
minute or microscopic animal.

an·i·mal·ism (an′ə mə liz′əm), *n.* preoccupation with physical appetites
rather than spiritual or intellectual
forces.

an′imal starch′, glycogen.

an·i·mate (*v.* an′ə māt′; *adj.* an′ə-
mit), *v.,* **-mat·ed,** **-mat·ing,** *adj.* —*v.t.*
1. to make alive. 2. to give zest or

spirit to. 3. to encourage. —*adj.* 4.
alive. 5. lively. —**an′i·mat′ed,** *adj.*
—**an′i·ma′tor, an′i·mat′er,** *n.*

an′imated cartoon′, a motion picture consisting of a sequence of
cartoons.

an·i·ma·tion (an′ə mā′shən), *n.* 1.
animate quality. 2. the act of animating. 3. the process of producing
animated cartoons.

an·i·mism (an′ə miz′əm), *n.* the belief that natural objects and phenomena possess souls or consciousness. —**an′i·mist,** *n.* —**an′i·mis′tic,**
adj.

an·i·mos·i·ty (an′ə mos′i tē), *n., pl.*
-ties. a feeling of ill will.

an·i·mus (an′ə məs), *n.* hostile feeling or attitude.

an·i·on (an′ī′ən), *n.* a negatively
charged ion, as one attracted to the
anode in electrolysis. —**an·i·on·ic**
(an′ī on′ik), *adj.* —**an′i·on′i·cal·ly,**
adv.

an·ise (an′is), *n.* 1. a herbaceous
plant of Mediterranean regions
yielding aniseed. 2. aniseed.

an·i·seed (an′i sēd′, an′is sēd′), *n.*
the aromatic seed of the anise, used
in medicine, in cookery, etc.

an·i·sette (an′i set′, -zet′), *n.* a cordial or liqueur flavored with aniseed.

An·ka·ra (ang′kər ə), *n.* the capital
of Turkey.

ankh (angk), *n. Egyptian Art.* a
cross with a loop at the top, used
as a symbol of life.

an·kle (ang′kəl), *n.* 1. the joint
between the foot and the leg. 2.
the slender part of the leg above
the foot.

an·kle·bone (ang′kəl bōn′), *n.* the
uppermost of the tarsal bones.

an·klet (ang′klit), *n.* 1. a sock that
reaches just above the ankle. 2. an
ornamental circlet worn around
the ankle.

ann., 1. annals. 2. annual. 3. annuity.

an·nals (an′ᵊlz), *n.pl.* 1. a record
of events, esp. a yearly record, in
chronological order. 2. historical
records. —**an′nal·ist,** *n.*

An·nap·o·lis (ə nap′ə lis), *n.* the
capital of Maryland.

an·neal (ə nēl′), *v.t.* 1. to free (glass,
metals, etc.) from internal stress
by heating and gradually cooling.
2. to temper, as the mind. —**an-
neal′er,** *n.*

an·ne·lid (an′ᵊlid), *n.* any segmented
worm, such as the earthworm.

an·nex (*v.* ə neks′; *n.* an′eks), *v.t.*
1. to attach, append, or add. 2. to
incorporate (another state or country) into one state or country. —*n.*

3. something annexed. **4.** a subsidiary building. —**an′nex·a′tion,** n.

an·ni·hi·late (ə nī′ə lāt′), v.t., -**lat·ed,** -**lat·ing.** to reduce to utter ruin or nonexistence. —**an·ni′hi·la′tion,** n. —**an·ni′hi·la′tor,** n.

an·ni·ver·sa·ry (an′ə vûr′sə rē), n., pl. -**ries. 1.** the yearly recurrence of the date of a past event. **2.** the commemoration of such a date.

an·no Dom·i·ni (an′ō dom′ə nī′, -nē′, ä′nō). See **A.D.** (def. 2).

an·no·tate (an′ō tāt′), v.t., v.i., -**tat·ed,** -**tat·ing.** to supply (a text) with notes. —**an·no·ta′tion,** n. —**an′no·ta′tive,** adj. —**an′no·ta′tor,** n.

an·nounce (ə nouns′), v., -**nounced,** -**nounc·ing.** —v.t. **1.** to declare or make known publicly. **2.** to state the approach or presence of. **3.** to serve as an announcer for. —v.i. **4.** to serve as an announcer. —**an·nounce′ment,** n.

an·nounc·er (ə noun′sər), n. a person who announces, esp. one who introduces programs, etc., over radio or television.

an·noy (ə noi′), v.t. to disturb in a way that displeases, troubles, or irritates. —**an·noy′ing,** adj. —**an·noy′ing·ly,** adv. —**Syn.** bother, irk, pester, vex.

an·noy·ance (ə noi′əns), n. **1.** a person or thing that annoys or bothers. **2.** the act of annoying. **3.** the feeling of being annoyed.

an·nu·al (an′yōō əl), adj. **1.** of or relating to a year. **2.** occurring once a year. **3.** performed during a year. **4.** living only one season. —n. **5.** an annual plant. **6.** a book, etc., published annually. —**an′nu·al·ly,** adv.

an′nual ring′, an annual formation of two concentric layers of wood in plants.

an·nu·i·tant (ə nōō′i tənt, ə nyōō′-), n. a person who receives an annuity.

an·nu·i·ty (ə nōō′i tē, ə nyōō′-), n., pl. -**ties. 1.** a specified income payable for a fixed period. **2.** the right to receive such an income.

an·nul (ə nul′), v.t., -**nulled,** -**nul·ling. 1.** to make formally void or null. **2.** to reduce to nothing. —**an·nul′la·ble,** adj. —**an·nul′ment,** n.

an·nu·lar (an′yə lər), adj. having the form of a ring. —**an·nu·lar·i·ty** (an′yə lar′i tē), n.

an′nular eclipse′, an eclipse of the sun in which a portion of its surface is visible as a ring surrounding the dark moon.

an·nu·lus (an′yə ləs), n., pl. -**li** (-lī′), -**lus·es.** a ring or ringlike part, band, or space.

an·nun·ci·ate (ə nun′sē āt′, -shē-), v.t., -**at·ed,** -**at·ing.** Archaic. to announce.

An·nun·ci·a·tion (ə nun′sē ā′shən, -shē-), n. **1.** the announcement by the angel Gabriel to the Virgin Mary of the incarnation of Christ. **2.** the festival on March 25 in memory of this. **3.** (l.c.) Archaic. the act of announcing.

an·nun·ci·a·tor (ə nun′sē ā′tər, -shē-), n. an electrical signaling apparatus that displays a visual indication. —**an·nun′ci·a·to′ry,** adj.

an·ode (an′ōd), n. **1.** the electrode by which current enters an electrolytic cell. **2.** the negative terminal of a battery. **3.** the positive electrode of an electron tube. —**an·o′dal, an·od·ic** (an od′ik), adj. —**an·o′dal·ly, an·od′i·cal·ly,** adv.

an·o·dize (an′ə dīz′), v.t., -**dized,** -**diz·ing.** to coat a metal with a protective film by electrolytic means. —**an′od·i·za′tion,** n.

an·o·dyne (an′ə dīn′), n. a medicine that relieves pain.

a·noint (ə noint′), v.t. **1.** to put oil on. **2.** to consecrate by applying oil. —**a·noint′er,** n. —**a·noint′ment,** n.

a·nom·a·ly (ə nom′ə lē), n., pl. -**lies. 1.** a deviation from the common rule, type, or form. **2.** someone or something abnormal, incongruous, or inconsistent. —**a·nom′a·lis′tic** (-lis′tik), adj. —**a·nom′a·lous,** adj.

an·o·mie (an′ə mē′), n. absence of social norms, as in the case of uprooted people. Also, **an′o·my′.**

a·non (ə non′), adv. Archaic. **1.** soon. **2.** at another time.

anon., 1. anonymous. **2.** anonymously.

a·non·y·mous (ə non′ə məs), adj. **1.** without any name acknowledged as that of author. **2.** whose name is withheld. **3.** without individuality. —**an·o·nym·i·ty** (an′ə nim′i tē), **a·non′y·mous·ness,** n. —**a·non′y·mous·ly,** adv.

a·noph·e·les (ə nof′ə lēz′), n., pl. -**les.** a mosquito which is a vector of the parasite causing malaria in human beings.

an·o·rex·i·a (an′ə rek′sē ə), n. abnormal lack of appetite.

an·oth·er (ə nuth′ər), adj. **1.** one more of the same. **2.** different or distinct. —pron. **3.** an additional one. **4.** a different one. **5.** a person other than oneself or the one specified.

ans., answer.

an·swer (an′sər, än′-), n. **1.** something spoken or written in return to a question, request, etc. **2.** something done in return. **3.** a solution to a problem. —v.i. **4.** to speak or write in answer. **5.** to be responsible or accountable. **6.** to be satisfactory or serve. **7.** to correspond or conform.

—*v.t.* 8. to speak or write in answer to. 9. to act in answer to. 10. to be satisfactory or adequate for. 11. to correspond to or conform to. 12. to **answer back**, to reply rudely. —**an′swer·a·ble,** *adj.* —**an′swer·er,** *n.* — **Syn.** 1. rejoinder, reply, response, retort.

an′swering serv′ice, a commercial service that takes and gives telephone messages for a person away from home or office.

ant (ant), *n.* any of numerous small insects, usually wingless, that exhibit some degree of social organization. —**ant′like′,** *adj.*

ant-. See anti-.

-ant, a suffix meaning: a. promoting or performing: *pleasant.* b. something that does: *pollutant.*.

ant., 1. antenna. 2. antonym.

Ant., Antarctica.

ant·ac·id (ant as′id), *adj.* 1. neutralizing acidity, as of the stomach. —*n.* 2. an antacid agent.

an·tag·o·nism (an tag′ə niz′əm), *n.* 1. active hostility or opposition. 2. an opposing force or tendency. —**an·tag′o·nis′tic,** *adj.* —**an·tag′o·nis′ti·cal·ly,** *adv.*

an·tag·o·nist (an tag′ə nist), *n.* 1. an active opponent. 2. *Literature.* the adversary of the hero or of the protagonist.

an·tag·o·nize (an tag′ə nīz′), *v.t.,* **-nized, -niz·ing.** to provoke or incur the hostility of.

ant·arc·tic (ant ärk′tik, -är′-), *adj.* 1. of, at, or near the South Pole. —*n.* 2. **the Antarctic,** the Antarctic Ocean and Antarctica.

Ant·arc·ti·ca (ant ärk′ti kə, -är′-), *n.* the continent surrounding the South Pole.

Antarc′tic Cir′cle, an imaginary line drawn parallel to the equator, at 23°28′ N of the South Pole.

Antarc′tic O′cean, the waters surrounding Antarctica.

ant′ bear′, a large tropical American anteater.

an·te (an′tē), *n., v.,* **-ted** or **-teed, -te·ing.** —*n.* 1. *Poker.* a stake put into the pot by each player before the deal. 2. *Slang.* the price of something. —*v.t., v.i.* 3. *Poker.* to put (one's initial stake) into the pot. 4. *Informal.* to produce or pay.

ante-, a prefix meaning "before": *antedate.*

ant·eat·er (ant′ē′tər), *n.* any of several mammals feeding chiefly on ants and termites.

an·te·bel·lum (an′tē bel′əm), *adj.* 1. before the war. 2. before the American Civil War.

an·te·ced·ent (an′ti sēd′ənt), *adj.* 1. existing, happening, or going before.

—*n.* 2. a preceding circumstance, event, object, etc. 3. **antecedents,** ancestors. 4. a word, phrase, or clause referred to by a pronoun. —**an′te·ced′ence,** *n.* —**an′te·ced′ent·ly,** *adv.*

an·te·cham·ber (an′tē chām′bər), *n.* a room that serves as a waiting room and entrance to a larger room, as in a palace.

an·te·choir (an′tē kwī°r′), *n.* an enclosed space in front of the choir of a church.

an·te·date (an′ti dāt′), *v.t.,* **-dat·ed, -dat·ing.** 1. to precede in time. 2. to date (a check, etc.) with a date earlier than the actual one.

an·te·di·lu·vi·an (an′tē di lōō′vē ən), *adj.* 1. belonging to the period before the Biblical Flood. 2. antiquated or old-fashioned.

an·te·lope (an′t°lōp′), *n., pl.* **-lopes, -lope.** any of several ruminants having permanent, unbranched horns.

an·te me·rid·i·em (an′tē mə rid′ē əm). See **a.m.**

an·ten·na (an ten′ə), *n., pl.* **-ten·nas** for 1, **-ten·nae** (-ten′ē) for 2. 1. *Radio and Television.* a conductor by which electromagnetic waves are transmitted or received. 2. one of the movable, sensory appendages occurring in pairs on the heads of insects and most other arthropods. —**an·ten′nal,** *adj.*

an·te·pe·nult (an′tē pē′nult), *n.* the last syllable but two in a word, as *te* in *antepenult.* —**an·te·pe·nul·ti·mate** (an′tē pi nul′tə mit), *adj., n.*

an·te·ri·or (an tēr′ē ər), *adj.* 1. situated in or toward the front. 2. *Rare.* earlier. 3. **anterior to,** before. —**an·te′ri·or·ly,** *adv.*

an·te·room (an′tē rōōm′, -rŏŏm′), *n.* an antechamber.

an·them (an′thəm), *n.* 1. a hymn, as of praise or patriotism. 2. a piece of sacred vocal music.

an·ther (an′thər), *n.* the pollenbearing part of a stamen.

ant·hill (ant′hil′), *n.* a mound of dirt, mud, leaves, etc., formed by ants in constructing their nest.

an·thol·o·gy (an thol′ə jē), *n., pl.* **-gies.** a collection of selected writings. —**an·thol′o·gist,** *n.* —**an·thol′o·gize′,** *v.i., v.t.*

an·thra·cite (an′thrə sīt′), *n.* a hard coal that burns almost without flame. —**an·thra·cit·ic** (an′thrə sit′ik), *adj.*

an·thrax (an′thraks), *n.* a malignant, infectious disease of cattle, sheep, and other mammals, including human beings.

anthrop., 1. anthropological. 2. anthropology.

anthropo-, a combining form meaning "human": *anthropology.*

an·thro·po·cen·tric (an'thrə pō sen'-trik), *adj.* viewing everything in terms of human experience and values.

an·thro·poid (an'thrə poid'), *adj.* 1. resembling human beings. —*n.* 2. See **anthropoid ape.**

an'thropoid ape', a tailless ape, as the gorilla, chimpanzee, orangutan, or gibbon.

an·thro·pol·o·gy (an'thrə pol'ə jē), *n.* the science that deals with the origins, customs, etc., of humankind. —**an·thro·po·log·i·cal** (an'thrə pə loj'i kəl), **an'thro·po·log'ic,** *adj.* —**an'thro·po·log'i·cal·ly,** *adv.* —**an'·thro·pol'o·gist,** *n.*

an·thro·po·mor·phic (an'thrə pə môr'fik, -pō-), *adj.* ascribing human form or attributes to a being or thing not human, esp. to a deity. —**an'thro·po·mor'phi·cal·ly,** *adv.* —**an'thro·po·mor'phism,** *n.*

an·ti (an'tī, an'tē), *n., pl.* -tis. *Informal.* a person opposed to a particular practice, policy, action, etc.

anti-, a prefix meaning: **a.** opposed: *antislavery.* **b.** rival or spurious: *antipope.* **c.** opposite of: *antihero.* **d.** not: *antispiritual.* **e.** placed opposite: *antipole.* **f.** moving in a reverse direction: *anticyclone.* **g.** preventive or curative: *antipyretic.*

an'ti·bal·lis'tic mis'sile (an'tē bə lis'tik, an'tī-), a ballistic missile designed to intercept and destroy another ballistic missile.

an·ti·bi·ot·ic (an'tī bī ot'ik, -bē-, an'-tē-, -tī-), *n.* 1. any of a large group of substances, as penicillin or streptomycin, produced by various microorganisms and fungi, having the capacity to inhibit the growth of or to destroy microorganisms: used in the treatment of infectious diseases. —*adj.* 2. of antibiotics.

an·ti·bod·y (an'tī bod'ē, an'tē-), *n., pl.* -bod·ies. a protein, produced in the body, to overcome the toxicity of a specific antigen.

an·tic (an'tik), *n., adj., v.,* -ticked, -tick·ing. —*n.* 1. a playful prank. 2. a grotesque gesture or posture. —*adj.* 3. playful or frisky. 4. *Archaic.* grotesque. —*v.i.* 5. *Obs.* to perform antics. —**an'tic·ly,** *adv.*

An·ti·christ (an'tī krīst'), *n.* 1. (*sometimes l.c.*) any opponent of Christ. 2. a false Christ.

an·tic·i·pate (an tis'ə pāt'), *v.t.,* -pat·ed, -pat·ing. 1. to look forward to. 2. to foresee and act in advance of. 3. to be ahead of in doing or accomplishing. —**an·tic'i·pa'tion,** *n.* —**an·tic'i·pa'tor,** *n.* —**an·tic·i·pa·to·ry** (an tis'ə pə tôr'ē), *adj.*

an·ti·cli·max (an'tī klī'maks), *n.* 1. an event or conclusion that is far less important or powerful than expected. 2. an abrupt descent in quality or power. —**an·ti·cli·mac·tic** (an'tī klī mak'tik), *adj.* —**an'ti·cli·mac'ti·cal·ly,** *adv.*

an·ti·cline (an'tī klīn'), *n.* a fold of rock strata. —**an·ti·cli'nal** (-klīn'əl), *adj.*

an·ti·co·ag·u·lant (an'tē kō ag'yə lənt, an'tī-), *n.* a substance or drug that prevents the coagulation of blood.

an·ti·cy·clone (an'tī sī'klōn), *n.* a circulation of winds around a central region of high atmospheric pressure. —**an·ti·cy·clon·ic** (an'tē sī klon'ik, an'tī-), *adj.*

an·ti·de·pres·sant (an'tē di pres'ənt, an'tī-), *n.* a drug used in the treatment of mental depression for raising the spirits.

an·ti·dote (an'tī dōt'), *n.* 1. a medicine for counteracting the effects of poison, disease, etc. 2. something that prevents or counteracts.

an·ti·freeze (an'tī frēz', an'tē-), *n.* a liquid used in an internal-combustion engine to lower the freezing point of the cooling medium.

an·ti·gen (an'tī jən, -jen'), *n.* a substance that stimulates production of antibodies. —**an·ti·gen·ic** (an'tī jen'ik), *adj.* —**an'ti·gen'i·cal·ly,** *adv.* —**an'ti·ge·nic'i·ty** (-jə nis'i tē), *n.*

an·ti·grav·i·ty (an'tē grav'i tē, an'tī-), *n.* a hypothetical force by which a body of positive mass would repel a body of negative mass.

an·ti·her·o (an'tē hēr'ō, an'tī-), *n., pl.* -he·roes. a protagonist who lacks the attributes that would make him a heroic figure.

an·ti·his·ta·mine (an'ti his'tə mēn', -min), *n.* any of certain medicines that inhibit the effect of histamine in the body, used chiefly in treatment of allergic disorders and colds. —**an·ti·his·ta·min·ic** (an'tē his'tə min'ik, an'tī-), *adj.*

an·ti·hy·per·ten·sive (an'tī hī'pər ten'-siv), *n.* a substance or agent that counteracts high blood pressure.

---

an'ti·a·bor'tion, *n.*
an'ti·air'craft', *adj., n.*
an'ti·A·mer'i·can, *adj., n.*
an'ti·bac·te'ri·al, *adj.*
an'ti·Bol'she·vist, *n., adj.*
an'ti·bus'ing, *adj., n.*
an'ti·can'cer, *adj.*

an'ti·cap'i·tal·ist, *n., adj.*
an'ti·Cath'o·lic, *adj., n.*
an'ti·cler'i·cal, *adj.*
an'ti·co·ag'u·lat'ing, *adj.*
an'ti·com·mu'nism, *n.*
an'ti·com·mu'nist, *adj.*
an'ti·cor·ro'sive, *adj., n.*

an'ti·dem'o·crat'ic, *adj.*
an'ti·e·lec'tron, *n.*
an'ti·fas'cism, *n.*
an'ti·fas'cist, *n., adj.*
an'ti·fer·til'i·ty, *adj.*
an'ti·fun'gal, *adj.*
an'ti·hu'man·ism, *n.*

an·ti·knock (an′tē nok′, an′tī-), *n.* a substance added to fuel for an internal-combustion engine to minimize knock.

An·til·les (an til′ēz), *n.* a chain of islands in the West Indies, including Cuba, Jamaica, etc. (**Great′er An·til′les**), and a group of smaller islands to the SE (**Less′er Antil′les**).

an·ti·log·a·rithm (an′ti lô′gə rith′əm, -log′ə-), *n.* the number of which a given number is the logarithm.

an·ti·ma·cas·sar (an′ti mə kas′ər), *n.* an upholstery covering esp. for the headrest, used chiefly in the 19th century.

an·ti·mag·net·ic (an′tē mag net′ik, an′tī-), *adj.* **1.** resistant to magnetization. **2.** (of a watch, etc.) having the critical parts composed of materials resistant to magnetization.

an·ti·mat·ter (an′tē mat′ər, an′tī-), *n.* matter composed of particles analogous to but having charges opposite to those of common particles of matter, as positrons, antiprotons, etc.

an·ti·mis·sile (an′tē mis′əl, an′tī-), *adj.* designed or used in defense against guided missiles.

ant·i·mo·ny (an′tə mō′nē), *n. Chem.* a brittle, lustrous, white metallic element used chiefly in alloys and in compounds in medicine. *Symbol:* Sb; *at. wt.:* 121.75; *at. no.:* 51.

an·ti·ne·o·plas·tic (an′tē nē′ə pla′stik), *adj.* checking the growth of neoplasms or malignant cells.

an·ti·neu·tri·no (an′tē nōō trē′nō, -nyōō- an′tī-), *n., pl.* **-nos.** the antiparticle to the neutrino.

an·ti·neu·tron (an′tē nōō′tron, -nyōō′-, an′tī-), *n.* the antiparticle to the neutron.

an·ti·no·mi·an (an′ti nō′mē ən), *n.* a person who maintains that Christians are freed from the moral law. —**an′ti·no′mi·an·ism,** *n.*

an·tin·o·my (an tin′ə mē), *n., pl.* **-mies.** a contradiction between two statements, both apparently obtained by correct reasoning.

an·ti·nov·el (an′tē nov′əl), *n.* a literary work in which the author rejects the traditional elements of the novel.

an·ti·nu·cle·on (an′tē nōō′klē on′, -nyōō′-, an′tī-), *n.* an antiproton or an antineutron.

an·ti·ox·i·dant (an′tē ok′si dənt, an′tī-), *n.* any substance inhibiting oxidation.

an·ti·par·ti·cle (an′tē pär′ti kəl, an′tī-), *n.* either of two particles that annihilate each other upon collision, as an electron and a positron.

an·ti·pas·to (an′ti pä′stō, -pas′tō), *n., pl.* **-pas·tos, -pas·ti** (-pä′stē, -pas′tē). an assortment of appetizers, as of olives, anchovies, etc.

an·tip·a·thy (an tip′ə thē), *n., pl.* **-thies. 1.** a basic or habitual repugnance or aversion. **2.** an object of repugnance. —**an·ti·pa·thet·ic** (an′ti pə thet′ik, an tip′ə-), *adj.*

an·ti·per·son·nel (an′tē pûr′sə nel′, an′tī-), *adj.* used against enemy personnel rather than against materiel, etc.

an·ti·per·spi·rant (an′ti pûr′spər ənt), *n.* any preparation for retarding perspiration.

an·ti·phon (an′tə fon′), *n.* a verse or song to be chanted or sung in response. —**an·tiph·o·nal** (an tif′ə nªl), *adj.* —**an·tiph′o·nal·ly,** *adv.*

an·tiph·o·ny (an tif′ə nē), *n., pl.* **-nies.** alternate or responsive singing by a choir in two divisions. —**an·ti·phon·ic** (an′tə fon′ik), *adj.* —**an′ti·phon′i·cal·ly,** *adv.*

an·tip·o·des (an tip′ə dēz′), *n.pl.* places diametrically opposite to each other on the globe. —**an·tip·o·dal** (an tip′ə dªl), *adj.* —**an·tip·o·de·an** (an tip′ə dē′ən), *adj., n.*

an·ti·pope (an′ti pōp′), *n.* a person who claims to be pope in opposition to the one canonically chosen.

an·ti·pov·er·ty (an′tē pov′ər tē, an′tī-), *adj.* aimed at relieving or eliminating poverty.

an·ti·pro·ton (an′tē prō′ton, an′tī-), *n.* the antiparticle to the proton.

an·ti·py·ret·ic (an′tē pī ret′ik, an′tī-), *adj.* **1.** checking or preventing fever. —*n.* **2.** an antipyretic agent. —**an·ti·py·re·sis** (an′tē pī rē′sis, an′tī-), *n.*

antiq., **1.** antiquarian. **2.** antiquity.

an·ti·quar·i·an (an′tə kwâr′ē ən), *adj.* **1.** of antiquaries or the study of antiquities. —*n.* **2.** an antiquary. —**an′ti·quar′i·an·ism,** *n.*

an·ti·quar·y (an′tə kwer′ē), *n., pl.* **-quar·ies. 1.** an expert on antiquities. **2.** a collector of antiquities.

---

an′ti·im·pe′ri·al·ism, *n.*

an′ti·im·pe′ri·al·ist, *adj., n.*

an′ti·in·tel·lec′tu·al, *adj., n.*

an′ti·i′so·la′tion·ist, *n., adj.*

an′ti·la′bor, *adj.*

an′ti·lib′er·al, *adj., n.*

an′ti·ma·lar′i·al, *adj.*

an′ti·mi·cro′bi·al, *adj.*

an′ti·mil′i·ta·rism, *n.*

an′ti·mil′i·ta·ris′tic, *adj.*

an′ti·mon′ar·chist, *n., adj.*

an′ti·mo·nop′o·lis′tic, *adj.*

an′ti·nar·cot′ic, *adj., n.*

an′ti·na′tion·al·ist, *n., adj.*

an′ti·noise′, *adj.*

an′ti·pac′i·fist, *n., adj.*

an′ti·pole′, *n.*

an′ti·pol·lu′tion, *adj., n.*

an′ti·pro·hi·bi′tion, *adj.*

an′ti·Prot′es·tant, *n., adj.*

an·ti·quate (an′tə kwāt′), *v.t.*, **-quat-ed, -quat·ing.** to make obsolete. **—an′ti·quat′ed,** *adj.* **—an′ti·qua′-tion,** *n.*

an·tique (an tēk′), *adj.*, *n.*, *v.*, **-tiqued, ti·quing.** *—adj.* **1.** belonging to the past. **2.** dating from an early period: *antique furniture.* **3.** in the tradition or style of an earlier period. **4.** ancient. *—n.* **5.** any work of art, piece of furniture, etc., produced in a former period. *—v.t.* **6.** to make appear antique. **—an·tique′ly,** *adv.* **—an·tique′ness,** *n.*

an·tiq·ui·ty (an tik′wi tē), *n.*, *pl.* **-ties. 1.** the quality of being ancient. **2.** ancient times. **3.** something of ancient times, as monuments, relics, customs, etc.

an·ti-Sem·ite (an′tē sem′īt, an′tī-), *n.* a person who is hostile to Jews. **—an′ti-Se·mit′ic** (-sə mit′ik, an′tī-), *adj.* **—an′ti-Sem′i·tism** (-sem′i tiz′-əm, an′tī-), *n.*

an·ti·sep·sis (an′ti sep′sis), *n.* destruction of the microorganisms that produce sepsis or septic disease.

an·ti·sep·tic (an′ti sep′tik), *adj.* **1.** of or affecting antisepsis. **2.** free from germs and other microorganisms. **3.** exceptionally clean. *—n.* **4.** an antiseptic substance. **—an′ti·sep′-ti·cal·ly,** *adv.*

an·ti·se·rum (an′ti sēr′əm), *n.* a serum containing antibodies.

an·ti·so·cial (an′tē sō′shəl, an′tī-), *adj.* **1.** not sociable. **2.** antagonistic or hostile toward others. **3.** opposed to the social system. **—an′ti·so′cial·ly,** *adv.*

an·tith·e·sis (an tith′i sis), *n.*, *pl.* **-ses** (-sēz′). **1.** a direct contrast or opposition: *the antithesis of right and wrong.* **2.** the direct opposite. **—an′ti·thet′i·cal** (an′tə thet′i kəl), **an′ti·thet′ic,** *adj.* **—an′ti·thet′i·cal·ly,** *adv.*

an·ti·tox·in (an′ti tok′sin, an′tē-), *n.* **1.** a substance, formed in the body, that counteracts a specific toxin. **2.** the antibody formed in immunization with a given toxin.

an·ti·trust (an′tē trust′, an′tī-), *adj.* opposing or intended to regulate or restrain monopolies or trusts.

an·ti·ven·in (an′tē ven′in, an′tī-), *n.* an antitoxin serum against venom, esp. of snakes.

ant·ler (ant′lər), *n.* the solid horn, usually branched, of an animal of the deer family. **—ant′lered,** *adj.*

ant·li·on (ant′lī′ən), *n.* an insect whose larva digs a pit in sand where it lies in wait for ants or other insects.

an·to·nym (an′tə nim), *n.* a word opposite in meaning to another. **—an·ton·y·mous** (an ton′ə məs), *adj.*

an·trum (an′trəm), *n.*, *pl.* **-tra** (-trə). a cavity in a bone, esp. that in the maxilla. **—an′tral,** *adj.*

Ant·werp (an′twərp), *n.* a seaport in N Belgium.

a·nus (ā′nəs), *n.*, *pl.* **a·nus·es.** the opening at the lower end of the alimentary canal.

an·vil (an′vil), *n.* **1.** a heavy iron block on which metals are hammered into desired shapes. **2.** the incus.

anx·i·e·ty (ang zī′i tē), *n.*, *pl.* **-ties. 1.** uneasiness caused by danger or misfortune. **2.** a state of apprehension and psychic tension found in most forms of mental disorder.

anx·ious (angk′shəs, ang′-), *adj.* **1.** full of or causing anxiety. **2.** eager or desirous: *anxious to please.* **—anx′ious·ly,** *adv.* **—anx′ious·ness,** *n.* **—Usage.** Precise writers and speakers generally avoid the use of ANXIOUS for EAGER in formal contexts.

an·y (en′ē), *adj.* **1.** one, a, an, or some. **2.** whatever it may be. **3.** in whatever quantity or number. **4.** every or all. *—pron.* **5.** anybody. **6.** a quantity or number. *—adv.* **7.** at all.

an·y·bod·y (en′ē bod′ē, -bud′ē), *pron.*, *n.*, *pl.* **-bod·ies.** *—pron.* **1.** any person. *—n.* **2.** a person of some importance.

an·y·how (en′ē hou′), *adv.* **1.** in any way whatever. **2.** under any circumstances.

an·y·more (en′ē mōr′, -môr′), *adv. Informal.* now (used usually in the negative).

an·y·one (en′ē wun′, -wən), *pron.* any person.

an·y·place (en′ē plās′), *adv. Informal.* anywhere.

an·y·thing (en′ē thing′), *pron.* **1.** any thing whatever. *—n.* **2.** a thing of any kind. *—adv.* **3.** to any extent. **4. anything but,** in no degree or respect.

an·y·time (en′ē tīm′), *adv.* at any hour, date, etc.

an·y·way (en′ē wā′), *adv.* **1.** in any manner. **2.** anyhow. **3.** carelessly.

---

an′ti·rad′i·cal, *n.*, *adj.*
an′ti·ra′tion·al, *adj.*; *-ly, adv.*
an′ti·re·li′gious, *adj.*; *-ly, adv.*
an′ti·rev′o·lu′tion·ar′y, *n.*, *pl.* **-ar·ies.**
an′ti-Rus′sian, *adj.*, *n.*
an′ti-slav′er·y, *n.*
an′ti·spas·mod′ic, *adj.*, *n.*
an′ti·sub′ma·rine′, *adj.*
an′ti·tank′, *adj.*
an′ti·un′ion, *adj.*
an′ti·war′, *adj.*
an′ti·viv′i·sec′tion·ist, *n.*
an′ti-Zi′on·ist, *n.*, *adj.*

an·y·where (en'ē hwâr', -wâr'), *adv.*
1. in, at, or to any place. **2.** to
any extent. **3. get anywhere,** *Informal.* to achieve success.

an·y·wise (en'ē wiz'), *adv.* in any
respect.

A/O, account of. Also, **a/o**

A-O.K. (ā'ō kā'), *adj. Informal.* perfectly all right. Also, **A-OK, A-O-kay'.**

A one (ā' wun'), *Informal.* first-class or excellent. Also, **A1.**

a·or·ta (ā ôr'tə), *n.,* *pl.* **-tas, -tae**
(-tē). the main trunk of the arterial
system, conveying blood from the
heart. **—a·or'tic,** *adj.*

aou·dad (ou'dad'), *n.* a wild sheep
of northern Africa.

AP, 1. antipersonnel. **2.** Associated
Press. Also, **A.P.**

Ap., 1. Apostle. **2.** Apothecaries'.
3. April.

A/P, 1. account paid. **2.** accounts
payable.

a.p., additional premium.

A.P.A., American Psychiatric Association.

a·pace (ə pās'), *adv. Literary.* quickly
or swiftly.

a·pache (ə päsh', ə pash'), *n.,* *pl.*
a·pach·es (ə pä'shiz, ə pash'iz). a
Parisian gangster.

A·pach·e (ə pach'ē), *n.,* *pl.* **A·pach·es,
A·pach·e. 1.** a member of an
Athapaskan people of the south-western U.S. **2.** any of the several
Athapaskan languages of Arizona
and the Rio Grande basin.

ap·a·nage (ap'ə nij), *n.* appanage.

a·part (ə pärt'), *adv.* **1.** into pieces
or parts. **2.** separately in place,
time, motion, etc. **3.** to or at one
side. **4.** aside. **5.** apart from, besides. **—adj. 6.** having unique
qualities: *a class apart.*

a·part·heid (ə pärt'hīt, -hāt), *n.* racial
segregation in the Republic of South
Africa.

a·part·ment (ə pärt'mənt), *n.* **1.** a
room or a combination of rooms
for use as a dwelling. **2.** a building
(**apart'ment house'**) containing such
rooms.

ap·a·thy (ap'ə thē), *n.* **1.** absence of
emotion. **2.** lack of interest or concern. **—ap·a·thet·ic** (ap'ə thet'ik),
adj. **—ap'a·thet'i·cal·ly,** *adv.*

ap·a·tite (ap'ə tīt'), *n.* a common
mineral used in the manufacture
of phosphate fertilizers.

APB, all points bulletin (used as a
police call).

APC, a compound consisting of aspirin, phenacetin, and caffeine,
used to relieve headaches, etc.

ape (āp), *n., v.,* **aped, ap·ing. —n.
1.** a tailless monkey or a monkey
with a very short tail. **2.** any

monkey. **3.** See **anthropoid ape. 4.**
a mimic. **5.** a big, clumsy man.
—v.t. 6. to mimic. **—ape'like',** *adj.*

a·peak (ə pēk'), *Naut.* **—adj. 1.**
more or less vertical. **—adv. 2.** more
or less vertically.

ape-man (āp'man'), *n., pl.* **-men.** a
primate representing a transitional
point between true humans and the
higher anthropoid apes.

Ap·en·nines (ap'ə nīnz'), *n.* a mountain range in Italy.

a·per·çu (A peR SY'), *n., pl.* **-çus** (-SY').
French. **1.** a hasty glimpse. **2.** an
insight.

a·pé·ri·tif (ä per'i tēf', ə per'-), *n.*
a small drink of alcoholic liquor
taken before a meal.

ap·er·ture (ap'ər chər), *n.* an opening, as a hole, slit, etc. **—ap·er·tur·al** (ap'ər choor'əl), *adj.*

a·pex (ā'peks), *n., pl.* **a·pex·es, a·pi·ces** (ap'i sēz', ā'pi-). **1.** the tip or
highest point. **2.** climax or acme.

aph·a·nite (af'ə nīt'), *n.* a fine-grained igneous rock.

a·pha·sia (ə fā'zhə), *n.* loss of the
faculty of using or understanding
language. **—a·pha·si·ac** (ə fā'zē ak'),
n. **—a·pha·sic** (ə fā'zik, -sik), *adj.,
n.*

a·phe·li·on (ə fē'lē ən, ə fēl'yən), *n.,
pl.* **a·phe·li·a** (ə fē'lē ə, ə fēl'yə).
the point in the orbit of a planet
or a comet farthest from the sun.
—a·phe'li·an, *adj.*

a·phid (ā'fid, af'id), *n.* any of numerous soft-bodied insects that
suck the sap from various plants.

a·phis (ā'fis, af'is), *n., pl.* **aph·i·des**
(af'i dēz'). an aphid.

aph·o·rism (af'ə riz'əm), *n.* a terse
saying embodying a general truth.
—aph·o·ris·tic (af'ə ris'tik), *adj.*
—aph'o·ris'ti·cal·ly, *adv.*

a·pho·tic (ā fō'tik), *adj.* lightless, as
in the deep-sea zone.

aph·ro·dis·i·ac (af'rə diz'ē ak'), *adj.*
1. arousing sexual desire. **—n. 2.**
an aphrodisiac agent, drug, or food.

Aph·ro·di·te (af'rə dī'tē), *n.* Greek
goddess of love and beauty.

a·pi·ar·y (ā'pē er'ē), *n., pl.* **-ar·ies.**
a place in which bees are kept.
—a'pi·a·rist, *n.*

ap·i·cal (ap'i kəl, ā'pi-), *adj.* of, at,
or forming the apex. **—ap'i·cal·ly,**
adv.

a·piece (ə pēs'), *adv.* for each.

a·plen·ty (ə plen'tē), *adj., adv.* in
generous amounts.

a·plomb (ə plom', ə plum'), *n.* self-possession, poise, or assurance.

apmt., appointment.

APO, Army Post Office.

Apoc., 1. Apocalypse. **2.** Apocrypha.
3. Apocryphal.

a·poc·a·lypse (ə pok′ə lips), *n.* **1.** (*cap.*) revelation (def. 4). **2.** a prophetic revelation, esp. concerning a cataclysm in which good wins over evil. —**a·poc′a·lyp′tic** (ə pok′ə lip′tik), **a·poc′a·lyp′ti·cal**, *adj.* —**a·poc′a·lyp′ti·cal·ly,** *adv.*

a·poc·ry·pha (ə pok′rə fə), *n.* **1.** (*cap.*) a group of 14 books, not considered canonical, included in the Septuagint and the Vulgate as part of the Old Testament. **2.** various religious writings regarded by some as inspired, but rejected by most authorities. **3.** works of doubtful authenticity.

a·poc·ry·phal (ə pok′rə fəl), *adj.* **1.** *Eccles.* **a.** (*cap.*) of the Apocrypha. **b.** of doubtful sanction. **2.** false or spurious. —**a·poc′ry·phal′ly,** *adv.* —**a·poc′ry·phal·ness,** *n.*

ap·o·cyn·thi·on (ap′ə sin′thē ən), *n.* apolune.

ap·o·gee (ap′ə jē), *n.* **1.** the point in the orbit of a heavenly body, esp. of the moon or of a manmade satellite at which it is farthest from the earth. **2.** the highest point or part. —**ap′o·ge′an,** **ap′o·ge′ic,** *adj.*

a·po·lit·i·cal (ā′pə lit′i kəl), *adj.* **1.** not political. **2.** politically indifferent. —**a·po·lit′i·cal·ly,** *adv.*

A·pol·lo (ə pol′ō), *n.* **1.** the ancient Greek and Roman god of healing, music, prophecy, and manly beauty. **2.** a very handsome young man.

a·pol·o·get·ic (ə pol′ə jet′ik), *adj.* **1.** making an apology. **2.** eager to apologize. —**a·pol′o·get′i·cal·ly,** *adv.*

ap·o·lo·gi·a (ap′ə lō′jē ə), *n.* a justification of one's motives or acts.

a·pol·o·gist (ə pol′ə jist), *n.* a person who makes an apology or defense.

a·pol·o·gize (ə pol′ə jīz′), *v.i.,* **-gized, -giz·ing.** to offer an apology. —**a·pol′o·giz′er,** *n.*

a·pol·o·gy (ə pol′ə jē), *n., pl.* **-gies. 1.** an expression of regret for having insulted or wronged another. **2.** a defense, as for a cause or doctrine.

ap·o·lune (ap′ə lōōn′), *n.* the point of a lunar orbit that is farthest from the moon.

ap·o·plex·y (ap′ə plek′sē), *n.* a sudden loss of bodily function due to rupture or occlusion of a blood vessel in the brain. —**ap′o·plec′tic,** *adj.*

a·port (ə pōrt′, ə pôrt′), *adv. Naut.* upon or toward the port side.

a·pos·ta·sy (ə pos′tə sē), *n., pl.* **-sies.** a departure from one's religion, cause, etc.

a·pos·tate (ə pos′tāt, -tit), *n.* a person who forsakes his or her religion, cause, etc. —**a·pos′ta·tize′** (-tə tīz′), *v.i.*

a pos·te·ri·o·ri (ā′ po stēr′ē ôr′ī, -ōr′ī, -ôr′ē, -ōr′ē), based upon actual observation or upon experimental data.

a·pos·tle (ə pos′əl), *n.* **1.** one of the 12 disciples sent forth by Christ to preach the gospel. **2.** a pioneer of any reform movement. —**a·pos′tle·ship′,** *n.*

ap·os·tol·ic (ap′ə stol′ik), *adj.* **1.** of an apostle. **2.** derived from the apostles in regular succession. **3.** papal. Also, **ap′os·tol′i·cal.**

a·pos·tro·phe[1] (ə pos′trə fē), *n.* the sign (′), used to indicate the omission of one or more letters in a word, to indicate the possessive case, or to indicate plurals of abbreviations and symbols.

a·pos·tro·phe[2] (ə pos′trə fē), *n.* a digression in the form of an address to someone not present. —**ap·os·troph·ic** (ap′ə strof′ik), *adj.*

a·pos·tro·phize (ə pos′trə fīz′), *v.t., v.i.,* **-phized, -phiz·ing.** to utter or write an apostrophe (to).

apoth′e·car·ies′ meas′ure, a system of units used in compounding liquid drugs.

apoth′e·car·ies′ weight′, a system of weights used in compounding drugs.

a·poth·e·car·y (ə poth′ə ker′ē), *n., pl.* **-car·ies.** *Obsolesc.* **1.** a pharmacist or druggist. **2.** a pharmacy or drugstore.

ap·o·thegm (ap′ə them′), *n.* a pithy, instructive saying.

ap·o·them (ap′ə them′), *n. Geom.* a perpendicular from the center of a regular polygon to one of its sides.

a·poth·e·o·sis (ə poth′ē ō′sis, ap′ə-thē′ə sis), *n., pl.* **-ses** (-sēz, -sēz′). **1.** the exaltation of a person to the rank of a god. **2.** a deified or glorified ideal.

app., 1. apparatus. **2.** appendix. **3.** apprentice.

Ap·pa·la·chi·a (ap′ə lā′chē ə, -chə, -lach′ē ə, -lach′ə), *n.* a region in the E United States, in the area of the S Appalachian Mountains, marked by poor economic conditions. —**Ap′pa·la′chi·an,** *adj.*

Ap′pa·la′chian Moun′tains, a mountain range in E North America, extending from S Quebec province to N Alabama. Also called **Ap′pa·la′-chi·ans.**

ap·pall (ə pôl′), *v.t.* to fill or overcome with horror or dismay. —**ap·pall′ing,** *adj.*

Ap·pa·loo·sa (ap′ə lōō′sə), *n.* a breed of riding horse, developed in the American West, having a mottled hide and vertically striped hoofs.

ap·pa·nage (ap′ə nij), *n.* **1.** land or revenue granted to a member of a royal family. **2.** a natural accompaniment.

ap·pa·rat (ap'ə rat', -rät'), *n.* a Soviet political machine.

ap·pa·rat·us (ap'ə rat'əs, -rā'təs), *n.*, *pl.* **-tus, -tus·es. 1.** a group of instruments, tools, etc., for a specific use. **2.** any complex instrument or machine. **3.** any system of activities, as for a political goal.

ap·par·el (ə par'əl), *n.*, *v.*, **-eled, -el·ing** or **-elled, -el·ling.** —*n.* **1.** clothing, esp. for outer wear. —*v.t.* **2.** *Archaic.* to dress or clothe.

ap·par·ent (ə par'ənt, ə pâr'-), *adj.* **1.** easily visible. **2.** easily perceived or understood. **3.** ostensible rather than actual. —**ap·par'ent·ly,** *adv.* —**Syn. 2.** evident, obvious. **3.** illusory, seeming.

ap·pa·ri·tion (ap'ə rish'ən), *n.* **1.** a ghostly appearance. **2.** anything that appears, esp. something startling.

ap·peal (ə pēl'), *n.* **1.** an earnest request or entreaty. **2.** a request to some authority for corroboration. **3.** *Law.* an application for review by a higher court. **4.** the power to attract the mind or emotions. —*v.i.* **5.** to ask earnestly, as for aid. **6.** *Law.* to make an appeal in a legal case. **7.** to attract, be of interest, etc. —*v.t.* **8.** *Law.* to make an appeal of (a legal case). —**ap·peal'ing,** *adj.* —**ap·peal'ing·ly,** *adv.* —**Syn. 5.** entreat, request, supplicate.

ap·pear (ə pēr'), *v.i.* **1.** to come into sight. **2.** to seem. **3.** to be made clear by evidence. **4.** to come before the public. **5.** to be present. **6.** *Law.* to come formally before a court.

ap·pear·ance (ə pēr'əns), *n.* **1.** the act or fact of appearing. **2.** the condition in which a person or object appears. **3.** semblance. **4.** *Law.* the coming into court of either party to a suit. **5.** appearances, outward indications or circumstances. **6. keep up appearances,** to maintain a public impression of prosperity despite financial reverses. **7. put in an appearance,** to attend for a very short time, as a party.

ap·pease (ə pēz'), *v.t.*, **-peased, -peasing.** to pacify, allay, or satisfy, esp. in a conciliatory effort. —**ap·pease'ment,** *n.* —**ap·peas'er,** *n.*

ap·pel·lant (ə pel'ənt), *n.* a person who legally appeals, esp. to a higher court.

ap·pel·late (ə pel'it), *adj.* having the authority to review and decide appeals, as a court.

ap·pel·la·tion (ap'ə lā'shən), *n.* an identifying name or title.

ap·pel·lee (ap'ə lē'), *n.* the defendant in an appellate proceeding.

ap·pend (ə pend'), *v.t.* to add as a supplement or appendix.

ap·pend·age (ə pen'dij), *n.* a subordinate part attached to something.

ap·pen·dec·to·my (ap'ən dek'tə mē), *n.*, *pl.* **-mies.** excision of the vermiform appendix.

ap·pen·di·ci·tis (ə pen'di sī'tis), *n.* inflammation of the vermiform appendix.

ap·pen·dix (ə pen'diks), *n.*, *pl.* **-dix·es, -di·ces** (-di sēz'). **1.** supplementary material at the end of a book. **2.** See **vermiform appendix.**

ap·per·tain (ap'ər tān'), *v.i.* to belong as a part, attribute, etc.

ap·pe·stat (ap'i stat'), *n.* a region in the human brain that functions to adjust appetite.

ap·pe·ten·cy (ap'i tən'sē), *n.*, *pl.* **-cies. 1.** intense desire. **2.** a natural tendency. Also, **ap'pe·tence.**

ap·pe·tite (ap'i tīt'), *n.* **1.** a desire for food or drink. **2.** any bodily need or craving.

ap·pe·tiz·er (ap'i tī'zər), *n.* a food or drink that stimulates the appetite.

ap·pe·tiz·ing (ap'i tī'zing), *adj.* appealing to or stimulating the appetite. —**ap'pe·tiz'ing·ly,** *adv.*

appl., applied.

ap·plaud (ə plôd'), *v.i.*, *v.t.* to show approval (of), esp. by clapping the hands. —**ap·plaud'er,** *n.*

ap·plause (ə plôz'), *n.* approval, esp. as expressed by clapping the hands.

ap·ple (ap'əl), *n.* **1.** a round, red or yellow, edible fruit. **2.** a tree that bears this fruit.

ap'ple but'ter, a thick jam made by stewing apples.

ap·ple·jack (ap'əl jak'), *n.* a brandy distilled from fermented cider.

ap·ple·pol·ish (ap'əl pol'ish), *v.i.*, *v.t. Informal.* to curry favor (with), as by gifts. —**ap'ple pol'ish·er.**

ap·ple·sauce (ap'əl sôs'), *n.* **1.** apples stewed to a soft pulp and sweetened. **2.** *Slang.* nonsense or bunk.

ap·pli·ance (ə plī'əns), *n.* an apparatus or machine, esp. one for household use.

ap·pli·ca·ble (ap'lə kə bəl, ə plik'ə-), *adj.* applying or capable of being applied or used. —**ap'pli·ca·bil'i·ty,** *n.* —**ap'pli·ca·bly,** *adv.*

ap·pli·cant (ap'lə kənt), *n.* a person who applies, as for a position.

ap·pli·ca·tion (ap'lə kā'shən), *n.* **1.** the act of applying. **2.** purpose or relevance. **3.** the act or an instance of spreading on, rubbing in, etc. **4.** a salve or healing agent. **5.** the act of requesting. **6.** a written or printed form on which a request is made. **7.** close attention.

ap·pli·ca·tor (ap'lə kā'tər), *n.* a simple device for applying a substance, such as medicine.

ap·plied (ə plīd'), *adj.* having a practical purpose.

ap·pli·qué (ap'lə kā'), *n., v.,* -quéd, qué·ing. —*n.* **1.** ornamentation consisting of sewing a cut piece of material onto another piece, used in dressmaking. —*v.t.* **2.** to apply as appliqué to.

ap·ply (ə plī'), *v.,* -plied, -ply·ing. —*v.t.* **1.** to make practical or active use of. **2.** to assign to a specific purpose. **3.** to spread on. **4.** to bring into physical contact with. **5.** to devote diligently. —*v.i.* **6.** to be pertinent or relevant. **7.** to make a request. —**ap·pli'er,** *n.*

ap·point (ə point'), *v.t.* **1.** to name for an office or position. **2.** to set or fix, as by agreement. **3.** to equip or furnish (used in past participle): *a cozily appointed den.*

ap·point·ee (ə poin tē', ap'oin tē'), *n.* a person who is appointed, as to an office.

ap·poin·tive (ə poin'tiv), *adj.* of or filled by appointment.

ap·point·ment (ə point'mənt), *n.* **1.** the act of appointing. **2.** an office or position to which a person is appointed. **3.** an agreement to meet at a certain place and time. **4.** appointments, equipment or furnishings.

Ap·po·mat·tox (ap'ə mat'əks), *n.* a town in central Virginia where Lee surrendered to Grant, ending the Civil War.

ap·por·tion (ə pōr'shən, ə pôr'-), *v.t.* to distribute proportionately. —**ap·por'tion·ment,** *n.*

ap·pose (ə pōz'), *v.t.,* -posed, -pos·ing. to place side by side or next to. —**ap·pos'a·ble,** *adj.*

ap·po·site (ap'ə zit, ə poz'it), *adj.* suitable and pertinent. —**ap'po·site·ly,** *adj.* —**ap'po·site·ness,** *n.*

ap·po·si·tion (ap'ə zish'ən), *n.* **1.** the act of placing next or side by side. **2.** a syntactic relation between two expressions having the same function and relation to other elements in the sentence, the second expression identifying or supplementing the first, as in *Washington, our first President.* —**ap·pos'i·tive,** *n., adj.*

ap·praise (ə prāz'), *v.t.,* -praised, -prais·ing. **1.** to estimate the nature or quality of. **2.** to estimate the monetary value of. —**ap·prais'al,** *n.* —**ap·prais'er,** *n.* —**ap·prais'ing·ly,** *adv.*

ap·pre·ci·a·ble (ə prē'shē ə bəl, -shə-bəl), *adj.* enough to be readily perceived or measured. —**ap·pre'ci·a·bly,** *adv.*

ap·pre·ci·ate (ə prē'shē āt'), *v.,* -ated, -at·ing. —*v.t.* **1.** to be grateful for. **2.** to value highly. **3.** to be fully aware of. **4.** to raise in value. —*v.i.* **5.** to increase in value. —**ap·pre'ci·a'tor,** *n.* —**ap·pre'cia·to'ry** (-shə tōr'ē), *adj.* —Syn. **2.** cherish, prize, esteem, treasure.

ap·pre·ci·a·tion (ə prē'shē ā'shən), *n.* **1.** appropriate gratefulness. **2.** clear recognition, esp. of aesthetic quality.

ap·pre·cia·tive (ə prē'shə tiv, -shē ā'-), *adj.* feeling or manifesting appreciation. —**ap·pre'cia·tive·ly,** *adv.*

ap·pre·hend (ap'ri hend'), *v.t.* **1.** to arrest by legal authority. **2.** to perceive or understand. **3.** to expect with anxiety.

ap·pre·hen·sion (ap'ri hen'shən), *n.* **1.** uneasiness and fear. **2.** intuitive understanding. **3.** arrest or capture.

ap·pre·hen·sive (ap'ri hen'siv), *adj.* uneasy and fearful. —**ap'pre·hen'sive·ly,** *adv.* —**ap'pre·hen'sive·ness,** *n.*

ap·pren·tice (ə pren'tis), *n., v.,* -ticed, -tic·ing. —*n.* **1.** a person who works for another in order to learn a trade. **2.** a learner or novice. —*v.t.* **3.** to bind to or place as an apprentice. —**ap·pren'tice·ship',** *n.*

ap·prise (ə prīz'), *v.t.,* -prised, -pris·ing. to notify.

ap·proach (ə prōch'), *v.t.* **1.** to come near to. **2.** to come near to in quality, character, etc. **3.** to solicit the interest or favor of. **4.** to begin work on. —*v.i.* **5.** to come near. —*n.* **6.** the act of coming nearer. **7.** close approximation. **8.** any means of access. **9.** the method taken in setting about a task, problem, etc. **10.** Often, **approaches.** an overture or advance. —**ap·proach'a·ble,** *adj.* —**ap·proach'a·bil'i·ty,** *n.*

ap·pro·ba·tion (ap'rə bā'shən), *n.* approval, esp. by authority.

ap·pro·pri·ate (*adj.* ə prō'prē it; *v.* ə prō'prē āt'), *adj., v.,* -at·ed, -at·ing. —*adj.* **1.** suitable for a purpose or use. —*v.t.* **2.** to authorize for some specific use. **3.** to take possession of. —**ap·pro'pri·ate·ly,** *adv.* —**ap·pro'pri·ate·ness,** *n.* —**ap·pro'pri·a'tor,** *n.* —Syn. **1.** apt, fit, proper.

ap·pro·pri·a·tion (ə prō'prē ā'shən), *n.* **1.** the act of appropriating. **2.** money authorized to be paid for a special purpose.

ap·prov·al (ə prōō'vəl), *n.* **1.** the act of approving. **2.** formal permission or sanction. **3. on approval,** without obligation to buy unless satisfactory to the customer.

ap·prove (ə prōov′), v., **-proved**, **-prov·ing.** —v.t. **1.** to speak or think favorably of. **2.** to confirm or ratify. —v.i. **3.** to give sanction or confirmation. —**ap·prov′ing·ly**, adv. —**Syn. 2.** authorize, endorse, sanction.

approx., 1. approximate. **2.** approximately.

ap·prox·i·mate (adj. ə prok′sə mit; v. ə prok′sə māt′), adj., v., **-mat·ed**, **-mat·ing.** —adj. **1.** being nearly as specified. **2.** nearly exact. **3.** close together. —v.t. **4.** to come near to in quantity, quality, or condition. —**ap·prox′i·mate·ly**, adv. —**ap·prox·i·ma·tion** (ə prok′sə mā′shən), n.

appt., 1. appoint. **2.** appointment.

ap·pur·te·nance (ə pûr′t'nəns), n. **1.** something subordinate to another thing. **2.** Law. a right belonging to a principal property. **3.** appurtenances, apparatus or instruments. —**ap·pur′te·nant**, adj.

Apr., April.

après-ski (a′pre skē′, ä′-), n. **1.** the period of relaxation that follows skiing. —adj. **2.** of or suitable for such a time: après-ski clothes.

ap·ri·cot (ap′rə kot′, ā′prə-), n. **1.** a downy, yellow, peachlike fruit. **2.** the tree. **3.** a yellowish pink.

A·pril (ā′prəl), n. the fourth month of the year, containing 30 days.

A′pril Fools′ Day′, April 1, when jokes are played on unsuspecting people.

a pri·o·ri (ä′ prē ôr′ē, -ōr′ē), **1.** from a general law to a particular instance. **2.** existing in the mind prior to and independent of experience.

a·pron (ā′prən), n. **1.** an article of apparel covering the front of the body for protecting the wearer's clothing. **2.** a metal cover for a machine. **3.** a paved area where airplanes are parked or loaded. **4.** the part of a stage floor in front of the curtain line. —**a′pron·like′**, adj.

ap·ro·pos (ap′rə pō′), adv. **1.** to the purpose. **2.** apropos of, as regards. —adj. **3.** opportune or pertinent.

apse (aps), n. a vaulted recess in a building, esp. at the end of the choir of a church.

apt (apt), adj. **1.** inclined by nature. **2.** likely or tending. **3.** quick to learn. **4.** suited to the purpose. —**apt′ly**, adv. —**apt′ness**, n.

apt., apartment.

ap·ti·tude (ap′ti tōōd′, -tyōōd′), n. **1.** a natural talent or ability. **2.** readiness in learning.

aq·ua (ak′wə, ä′kwə), n. **1.** Pharm. **a.** water. **b.** a solution, esp. in water. **2.** a light greenish blue.

aq·ua·cade (ak′wə kād′), n. an aquatic exhibition consisting o[swimming, diving, etc., usually ac[companied by music.

aq·ua·cul·ture (ak′wə kul′chər, ä[kwə-), n. the cultivation of se[animals and plants.

Aq·ua-Lung (ak′wə lung′, ä′kwə-), n[Trademark. a swimmer's underwate[breathing apparatus.

aq·ua·ma·rine (ak′wə mə rēn′, ä[kwə-), n. **1.** a light-blue or gree[ish-blue variety of beryl, used as [gem. **2.** a light blue-green or gree[ish blue.

aq·ua·naut (ak′wə nôt′, -not′, ä[kwə-), n. an underseas explore[esp. one who lives in a submerge[dwelling for an extended period o[time.

aq·ua·plane (ak′wə plān′, ä′kwə[n., v., **-planed**, **-plan·ing.** —n. **1.** [board that skims over water whe[towed at high speed by a moto[boat. —v.i. **2.** to ride an aquaplane[

aq′ua re′gi·a (rē′jē ə), a liquid com[posed of nitric acid and hydr[chloric acid, used to dissolve gol[and platinum.

a·quar·i·um (ə kwâr′ē əm), n., p[a·quar·i·ums, a·quar·i·a (ə kwâr′ē ə[**1.** a tank, etc., in which livin[aquatic animals or plants are kep[**2.** a building in which aquatic an[mals or plants are exhibited, etc.

A·quar·i·us (ə kwâr′ē əs), n. th[eleventh sign of the zodiac. [< L[water bearer] —**A·quar′i·an**, adj., n[

a·quat·ic (ə kwat′ik, ə kwot′-), adj[**1.** living or growing in water. **2.[** practiced on or in water. —n. **3[** aquatics, aquatic sports.

aq·ua·vit (ä′kwə vēt′, ak′wə-), n[akvavit.

aq′ua vi′tae (vī′tē), **1.** spirituous liq[uor, as brandy. **2.** Alchemy. alcohol[

aq·ue·duct (ak′wi dukt′), n. **1.** [conduit or channel for conductin[water from a distance. **2.** a struc[ture that carries a conduit acros[a valley river. **3.** a canal in a bod[organ.

a·que·ous (ā′kwē əs, ak′wē-), adj. of [like, or containing water.

a′queous hu′mor, the watery flui[that fills the space between th[cornea and the lens in the eye.

aq·ui·cul·ture (ak′wə kul′chər), n. **1.[** hydroponics. **2.** aquaculture.

aq·ui·fer (ak′wə fər), n. any geo[logical formation supplying wate[for wells.

aq·ui·line (ak′wə līn′, -lin), adj. **1.[** of or like the eagle. **2.** (of th[nose) shaped like an eagle's beak[

A·qui·nas (ə kwī′nəs), n. Sain[Thomas, 1225?-74, Italian theolo[gian and philosopher.

AR, Arkansas.

Ar, 1. Arabic (def. 2). **2.** argon.

-ar, a suffix meaning "of" or "pertaining to": *regular; singular*.

A/R, account receivable.

ar., 1. arrival. 2. arrive; arrives.

Ar·ab (ar′əb), *n.* 1. a member of a Semitic people mainly inhabiting Arabia and parts of northern Africa. —*adj.* 2. of the Arabs.

ar·a·besque (ar′ə besk′), *n.* any ornament in which plant forms, vases, and figures are represented in an interlaced pattern.

A·ra·bi·a (ə rā′bē ə), *n.* a peninsula in SW Asia. —**A·ra′bi·an,** *adj.*, *n.*

Ara′bian horse′, one of a breed of horses, raised originally in Arabia, noted for their speed.

Ar·a·bic (ar′ə bik), *adj.* 1. of or from Arabia, the Arabs, or Arabic. —*n.* 2. any of the Semitic languages spoken in North Africa, Egypt, Arabia, etc.

Ar′abic nu′merals, the numbers 0, 1, 2, 3, 4, 5, 6, 7, 8, 9.

ar·a·ble (ar′ə bəl), *adj.* suitable for farming.

a·rach·nid (ə rak′nid), *n.* any of a class of arthropods comprising the spiders, scorpions, mites, ticks, etc.

Ar·a·ma·ic (ar′ə mā′ik), *n.* a northwest Semitic language.

A·rap·a·ho (ə rap′ə hō′), *n.*, *pl.* -hos, -ho. a member of a tribe of North American Indians of Algonquian speech stock, now in Oklahoma and Wyoming.

ar·ba·lest (är′bə list, -lest′), *n.* a powerful medieval crossbow. Also, **ar·ba·list** (är′bə list).

ar·bi·ter (är′bi tər), *n.* a person who has the power to judge or decide.

ar·bi·trage (är′bi träzh′), *n.* the simultaneous purchase and sale of the same securities or commodities in different markets to profit from unequal prices. —**ar′bi·trag′er,** *n.*

ar·bit·ra·ment (är bi′trə mənt), *n.* 1. the act of arbitrating. 2. the decision of an arbiter.

ar·bi·trar·y (är′bi trer′ē), *adj.* 1. subject to individual judgment. 2. despotic or autocratic. 3. capricious or unreasonable. —**ar·bi·trar·i·ly** (är′bi trer′ə lē, är′bə trâr′-), *adv.* —**ar′bi·trar′i·ness,** *n.*

ar·bi·trate (är′bi trāt′), *v.*, -trat·ed, -trat·ing. —*v.t.* 1. to decide as arbitrator. 2. to submit to or settle by arbitration. —*v.i.* 3. to act as arbitrator or arbiter. —**ar′bi·tra′tion,** *n.*

ar·bi·tra·tor (är′bi trā′tər), *n.* a person chosen to decide a dispute.

ar·bor¹ (är′bər), *n.* 1. a leafy, shady recess. 2. a latticework bower intertwined with vines.

ar·bor² (är′bər), *n.* a bar that holds, turns, or supports rotating cutting tools.

ar·bo·re·al (är bôr′ē əl, -bōr′-), *adj.* 1. of or like trees. 2. living in trees.

ar·bo·re·tum (är′bə rē′təm), *n.*, *pl.* -tums, -ta (-tə). a plot of land on which trees or shrubs are grown for study or display.

ar·bor vi·tae (är′bər vī′tē), a treelike appearance in a vertical section of the cerebellum, due to the arrangement of the white and gray nerve tissues.

ar·bor·vi·tae (är′bər vī′tē), *n.* any of several ornamental trees of North America and eastern Asia.

ar·bu·tus (är byoo′təs), *n.*, *pl.* -tus·es. 1. an evergreen shrub or tree with scarlet berries. 2. a creeping herb having fragrant white or pink flowers.

arc (ärk), *n.*, *v.*, arced (ärkt) or arcked, arc·ing (är′king) or arck·ing. —*n.* 1. any unbroken part of the circumference of a circle. 2. a luminous bridge formed in a gap between two electrodes. —*v.i.* 3. to form an arc.

ARC, American Red Cross.

ar·cade (är kād′), *n.* 1. a series of arches supported on columns. 2. a covered passageway, usually with shops on each side.

ar·cane (är kān′), *adj.* mysteriously secret or obscure.

arch¹ (ärch), *n.* 1. a curved masonry construction for spanning an opening. 2. any archway. 3. anything resembling an arch. —*v.t.*, *v.i.* 4. to cover with an arch. 5. to form or make into an arch.

arch² (ärch), *adj.* 1. chief or principal. 2. cunning or roguish: *an arch smile.* —**arch′ly,** *adv.* —**arch′ness,** *n.*

arch-, a prefix meaning "chief": *archfiend.*

-arch, a suffix meaning "ruler": *monarch.*

arch., 1. archaic. 2. architect. 3. architectural. 4. architecture.

archaeol., archaeology.

ar·chae·ol·o·gy (är′kē ol′ə jē), *n.* the study of historic or prehistoric peoples and their cultures by analysis of their artifacts, monuments, etc. —**ar′chae·o·log′i·cal, ar′chae·o·log′ic,** *adj.* —**ar′chae·o·log′i·cal·ly,** *adv.* —**ar′chae·ol′o·gist,** *n.*

Ar·chae·o·zo·ic (är′kē ə zō′ik), *adj.*, *n.* Archeozoic.

ar·cha·ic (är kā′ik), *adj.* 1. marked by the characteristics of an earlier period or time. 2. current in an earlier time but rare in present usage. —**ar·cha′i·cal·ly,** *adv.*

ar·cha·ism (är′kē iz′əm, -kā-), *n.* something archaic, as a word or phrase. —**ar′cha·ist,** *n.* —**ar′cha·is′tic,** *adj.*

arch·an·gel (ärk′ān′jəl), *n.* a chief or principal angel.

arch·bish·op (ärch′bish′əp), *n.* a bishop of the highest rank. — **arch′bish′op·ric** (-əp rik), *n.*

arch·dea·con (ärch′dē′kən), *n.* a member of the clergy ranking next below a bishop.

arch·di·o·cese (ärch′dī′ə sēs′, -sis), *n.* the diocese of an archbishop. — **arch·di·oc·e·san** (ärch′dī os′i sən), *adj.*

arch·duke (ärch′dook′, -dyook′), *n.* a prince of imperial Austria. — **arch′duch′ess**, *n.fem.*

arch·en·e·my (ärch′en′ə mē), *n., pl.* **-mies.** 1. a chief enemy. 2. Satan.

ar·che·ol·o·gy (är′kē ol′ə jē), *n.* archaeology.

Ar·che·o·zo·ic (är′kē ə zō′ik), *Geol.* —*adj.* 1. of a period of the Precambrian era, occurring several million years ago, during which the earliest known life came into being. —*n.* 2. the Archeozoic period.

arch·er (är′chər), *n.* 1. a person who shoots with a bow and arrow. 2. **the Archer**, Sagittarius.

ar·cher·y (är′chə rē), *n.* the art or skill of an archer.

ar·che·type (är′ki tīp′), *n.* the original pattern or model after which a thing is made. — **ar·che·typ·al** (är′ki tī′pəl), **ar·che·typ·i·cal** (är′ki tip′i kəl), **ar·che·typ′ic**, *adj.*

arch·fiend (ärch′fēnd′), *n.* 1. a chief fiend. 2. Satan.

ar·chi·e·pis·co·pal (är′kē i pis′kə pəl), *adj.* of an archbishop or his office.

ar·chi·man·drite (är′kə man′drīt), *n. Eastern Ch.* 1. the head of a monastery. 2. a celibate priest.

Ar·chi·me·des (är′kə mē′dēz), *n.* 287?-212 B.C., Greek mathematician. —**Ar·chi·me·de·an** (är′kə mē′dē ən, -mi dē′ən), *adj.*

ar·chi·pel·a·go (är′kə pel′ə gō′), *n., pl.* **-gos, -goes.** 1. any large body of water with many islands. 2. an island group.

archit., architecture.

ar·chi·tect (är′ki tekt′), *n.* 1. a person engaged in the profession of architecture. 2. the planner of anything.

ar·chi·tec·ton·ics (är′ki tek ton′iks), *n.* 1. the science of constructing buildings. 2. structural technique, as in a work of art. —**ar′chi·tec·ton′ic**, *adj.*

ar·chi·tec·ture (är′ki tek′chər), *n.* 1. the profession of designing buildings, communities, etc. 2. the style of building. 3. the design and structure of anything. —**ar′chi·tec′tur·al**, *adj.* —**ar′chi·tec′tur·al·ly**, *adv.*

ar·chi·trave (är′ki trāv′), *n.* the beam in a classical building that rests directly upon the columns.

ar·chive (är′kīv), *n.* 1. Usually, **archives**. documents or records of a

nation, historical figure, etc. 2. **archives**, a place where such records or documents are kept. — **ar·chi·vist** (är′kə vist), *n.*

ar·chon (är′kon), *n.* a chief magistrate in ancient Athens. —**ar′chon·ship′**, *n.*

arch·way (ärch′wā′), *n.* 1. an entrance or passage under an arch. 2. a covering or enclosing arch.

-archy, a suffix meaning "rule" or "government": *monarchy.*

arced (ärkt), *v.* a pt. and pp. of arc.

arck·ing (ar′king), *v.* a ppr. of arc.

arc′ light′, a lamp in which the light source of high intensity is an electric arc between electrodes. Also called **arc′ lamp′.**

arc·tic (ärk′tik, är′tik), *adj.* 1. (*often cap.*) at, or near the North Pole. 2. frigid or bleak. 3. (*often cap.*) the region lying north of the Arctic Circle. 4. **arctics**, warm, waterproof overshoes. [< L *arctic-(us)* < Gk *arktikós* northern, lit., of the Bear (constellation)]

Arc′tic Cir′cle, an imaginary line drawn parallel to the equator, at 23°28′ S of the North Pole.

Arc′tic O′cean, an ocean N of North America, Asia, and the Arctic Circle.

ar·cu·ate (är′kyōō it, -āt′), *adj.* curved like a bow.

-ard, a suffix meaning "a person who does something excessively or habitually": *drunkard; sluggard.*

ar·dent (är′dənt), *adj.* 1. having intense feeling, esp. of desire or devotion. 2. vehement or fierce. 3. *Literary.* burning or fiery. —**ar′dent·ly**, *adv.*

ar·dor (är′dər), *n.* 1. intense feeling, esp. of desire or devotion. 2. *Literary.* burning heat. Also, *esp. Brit.,* **ar′dour.** —**Syn.** 1. fervor, passion, zeal.

ar·du·ous (är′jōō əs), *adj.* 1. involving or demanding great hardship or exertion. 2. energetic or strenuous. —**ar′du·ous·ly**, *adv.* —**ar′du·ous·ness**, *n.*

are¹ (är; *unstressed* ər), *v.* pres. indic. pl. and 2nd pers. sing. of **be.**

are² (âr, är), *n. Metric System.* a surface measure equal to 100 square meters.

ar·e·a (âr′ē ə), *n.* 1. any particular extent of space or surface, as a geographical region. 2. any section reserved for a specific function. 3. extent or scope. 4. field of study. 5. the quantitative measure of a plane or curved surface. — **ar′e·al**, *adj.*

ar′ea code′, a three-digit code that identifies one of the telephone areas, as in the U.S. and Canada.

ar·e·a·way (âr′ē ə wā′), *n.* a sunken area leading to a cellar or basement entrance.

a·re·na (ə rē′nə), *n.* 1. the space in the center of an amphitheater for combats, etc., as in ancient Rome. 2. a field of conflict or activity: *the political arena.*

are′na the′ater, a theater with seats around a central stage.

aren't (ärnt, är′ənt), contraction of: a. *are not.* b. *am not.*
—**Usage.** AREN'T, in the sense of "am not" in such questions as *I'm doing well, aren't I?,* is questioned by precise grammarians and regarded as affected by many users of English.

Ar·es (âr′ēz), *n.* the ancient Greek god of war.

ar·gent (är′jənt), *n.* 1. *Literary.* something silvery or white. —*adj.* 2. Also, **ar·gen·tine** (är′jən tin, -tīn′). like silver.

Ar·gen·ti·na (är′jən tē′nə), *n.* a country in S South America. — **Ar′gen·tine′, Ar′gen·tin′e·an,** *n., adj.*

ar·gen·tite (är′jən tīt′), *n.* a dark lead-gray ore of silver.

ar·gil·la·ceous (är′jə lā′shəs), *adj.* of or resembling clay.

ar·gon (är′gon), *n. Chem.* a chemically inactive, gaseous element: used for filling lamps and electron tubes. Symbol: Ar; at. wt.: 39.948; at. no.: 18.

ar·go·sy (är′gə sē), *n., pl.* **-sies.** 1. a large merchant ship. 2. a fleet of such ships.

ar·got (är′gō, -gət), *n.* the vocabulary peculiar to a particular group of people, esp. that of an underworld group.

ar·gue (är′gyōō), *v.,* **-gued, -gu·ing.** —*v.i.* 1. to present reasons for or against a thing. 2. to contend in argument. —*v.t.* 3 to dispute or debate. 4. to maintain in reasoning. 5. to persuade by reasoning. —*ar′-gu·a·ble, adj.*

ar·gu·ment (är′gyə mənt), *n.* 1. verbal opposition or contention. 2. debate or dispute. 3. a process of reasoning. 4. a statement for or against a point.

ar·gu·men·ta·tion (är′gyə men tā′-shən), *n.* the process of developing an argument.

ar·gu·men·ta·tive (är′gyə men′tə tiv), *adj.* fond of or given to argument.

ar·gyle (är′gīl), *n.* a diamond-shaped pattern of two or more colors, used in knitting socks, etc.

a·ri·a (är′ē ə, âr′ē ə), *n.* an elaborate melody for a single voice, with accompaniment, in an opera, etc.

-arian, a suffix meaning: a. profession: *librarian.* b. advocate: *vegetarian.*

ar·id (ar′id), *adj.* 1. extremely dry, esp. of land. 2. unimaginative or dull. —**a·rid·i·ty** (ə rid′i tē), *n.*

Ar·ies (âr′ēz, -ē ēz′), *n.* the first sign of the zodiac. [< L: ram]

a·right (ə rīt′), *adv.* rightly or correctly.

a·rise (ə rīz′), *v.i.,* **a·rose, a·ris·en** (ə riz′ən), **a·ris·ing.** 1. to come into being or action. 2. to result or issue. 3. to ascend. 4. to get up, as from sitting. 5. to get up, as from sleep.

ar·is·toc·ra·cy (ar′i stok′rə sē), *n., pl.* **-cies.** 1. the hereditary nobility. 2. a state ruled by such a class. 3. any class or group considered to be superior. —**a·ris·to·crat** (ə ris′tə-krat′, ar′i stə-), *n.* —**a·ris′to·crat′ic,** *adj.* —**a·ris′to·crat′i·cal·ly,** *adv.*

Ar·is·toph·a·nes (ar′i stof′ə nēz′), *n.* 448?-385? B.C., Athenian comic dramatist.

Ar·is·tot·le (ar′i stot′əl), *n.* 384–322 B.C., Greek philosopher. —**Ar·is·to·te·lian** (ar′i stə tēl′yən), *adj., n.*

arith., 1. arithmetic. 2. arithmetical.

a·rith·me·tic (*n.* ə rith′mə tik; *adj.* ar′ith met′ik), *n.* 1. the method or process of computation with figures. —*adj.* 2. Also, **ar′ith·met′i·cal.** of arithmetic. —**ar′ith·met′i·cal·ly,** *adv.* —**a·rith′me·ti′cian** (-mi-tish′ən), *n.*

ar′ithmet′ic mean′, the mean obtained by adding several quantities together and dividing the sum by the number of quantities.

Ariz., Arizona.

Ar·i·zo·na (ar′i zō′nə), *n.* a state in SW United States. *Cap.:* Phoenix.

ark (ärk), *n.* 1. (*sometimes cap.*) the boat built by Noah for safety during the Biblical Flood. 2. Also called **ark′ of the cov′enant,** a chest symbolizing the presence of the Deity, carried by the Israelites after the Exodus.

Ark., Arkansas.

Ar·kan·sas (är′kən sô′), *n.* a state in S central United States. *Cap.:* Little Rock. —**Ar·kan·san** (är kan′-zən), *n., adj.*

arm¹ (ärm), *n.* 1. the upper limb of the human body. 2. some part of an organism like an arm. 3. a projecting support for the forearm on a chair or sofa. 4. power or authority. 5. **with open arms,** cordially. —**arm′less,** *adj.*

arm² (ärm), *n.* 1. Usually, **arms.** weapons, esp. firearms. 2. a combat branch of the military service. 3. **arms.** See **coat of arms.** 4. **under arms,** ready for battle. 5. **up in arms,** a. ready to take hostile action. b. indignant. —*v.i.* 6. to prepare for war. —*v.t.* 7. to equip with weapons. —**armed** (ärmd), *adj.*

ar·ma·da (är mä′də, -mā′-), *n.* **1.** a fleet of warships. **2.** a fleet of vehicles, aircraft, etc.

ar·ma·dil·lo (är′mə dil′ō), *n., pl.* **-los.** a burrowing mammal having a protective covering of bony plates.

Ar·ma·ged·don (är′mə ged′ən), *n.* **1.** *Bible.* the place where the final battle will be fought between the forces of good and evil. **2.** a great and decisive battle.

ar·ma·ment (är′mə mənt), *n.* **1.** the weapons with which a military unit is equipped. **2.** Usually, **armaments.** military strength collectively. **3.** the process of arming for war.

ar·ma·ture (är′mə chər), *n.* **1.** a protective covering, as of an animal or plant. **2. a.** the part of an electric machine in which the electromotive force is induced. **b.** the pivoted part of an electric device, as a buzzer or relay. **c.** the iron or steel applied across the poles of an electromagnet.

arm·chair (ärm′châr′), *n.* a chair with sides to support a person's arms.

armed′ forc′es, military, naval, and air forces.

Ar·me·ni·a (är mē′nē ə, -mēn′yə), *n.* an ancient country in W Asia: now a constituent republic of the Soviet Union. —**Ar·me′ni·an,** *adj., n.*

arm·ful (ärm′fŏŏl′), *n., pl.* **-fuls.** the amount that can be held by the arm or both arms.

arm·hole (ärm′hōl′), *n.* an opening for the arm in a garment.

ar·mi·stice (är′mi stis), *n.* a temporary suspension of hostilities by agreement of the warring parties.

Ar′mistice Day′, former name of Veterans Day.

arm·let (ärm′lit), *n.* a band or ring worn on the upper arm.

ar·mor (är′mər), *n.* **1.** any covering used as a defense against weapons. **2.** mechanized units of military forces. —*v.t.* **3.** to cover with armor. Also, *esp. Brit.,* **ar′mour.** —**ar′mored,** *adj.*

ar·mor·er (är′mər ər), *n.* **1.** (formerly) a maker of arms or armor. **2.** a person who services firearms.

ar·mo·ri·al (är môr′ē əl, -mōr′-), *adj.* of heraldry or heraldic bearings.

ar·mor·y (är′mə rē), *n., pl.* **-mor·ies.** **1.** a storage place for weapons. **2.** a military drill center. **3.** arsenal (def. 2).

arm·pit (ärm′pit′), *n.* the hollow under the arm at the shoulder.

arm·rest (ärm′rest′), *n.* arm¹ (def. 3).

ar·my (är′mē), *n., pl.* **-mies.** **1.** the military forces of a nation, esp. those trained to fight on land. **2.** a very large number or group of something.

ar′my ant′, any of the chiefly tropical ants that travel in vast swarms.

ar·my·worm (är′mē wûrm′), *n.* any of various moth larvae that often travel in large numbers.

ar·ni·ca (är′nə kə), *n.* **1.** a perennial plant having golden-yellow flowers. **2.** a tincture of these flowers, used as an external application for sprains and bruises.

Ar·nold (är′nəld), *n.* **Ben·e·dict** (ben′i dikt), 1741–1801, American general in the Revolutionary War who became a traitor.

a·ro·ma (ə rō′mə), *n.* a pleasant or agreeable odor arising from spices, plants, etc. —**ar·o·mat·ic** (ar′ə mat′ik), *adj., n.* —**ar′o·mat′i·cal·ly,** *adv.*

a·rose (ə rōz′), *v.* pt. of **arise.**

a·round (ə round′), *adv.* **1.** in a circle or ring. **2.** on all sides. **3.** in all directions. **4.** in circumference. **5.** in or to another or opposite direction. **6.** nearby. **7.** *Informal.* about or approximately. —*prep.* **8.** on all sides of. **9.** on the edge or border of. **10.** in all or various directions from.

a·rouse (ə rouz′), *v.t.,* **a·roused, a·rous·ing. 1.** to stir to action. **2.** to awaken from sleep. **3.** to provoke or excite. —**a·rous′al,** *n.*

ar·peg·gio (är pej′ē ō′, -pej′ō), *n., pl.* **-gi·os.** the sounding of the notes of a chord in rapid succession instead of simultaneously.

arr., 1. arranged. **2.** arrival. **3.** arrive. **4.** arrived.

ar·raign (ə rān′), *v.t.* **1.** to call or bring before a court to answer to an indictment. **2.** to accuse or charge. —**ar·raign′ment,** *n.*

ar·range (ə rānj′), *v.,* **-ranged, -ranging.** —*v.t.* **1.** to place in proper order. **2.** to come to an agreement regarding. **3.** to prepare or plan. **4.** *Music.* to adapt (a composition) for a particular performance. —*v.i.* **5.** to make preparations. **6.** to come to an agreement. —**ar·range′ment,** *n.* —**ar·rang′er,** *n.*

ar·rant (ar′ənt), *adj.* downright or thorough: *an arrant fool.*

ar·ras (ar′əs), *n.* **1.** a rich tapestry. **2.** a wall hanging, as a tapestry.

ar·ray (ə rā′), *v.t.* **1.** to place in proper order, as troops for battle. **2.** to clothe or attire. —*n.* **3.** an orderly arrangement. **4.** an impressive grouping or organization. **5.** attire.

ar·rear (ə rēr′), *n.* **1.** Usually, **arrears.** the state of being late, esp. in the fulfillment of a payment or obligation. **2. in arrears,** behind in payment.

ar·rest (ə rest′), *v.t.* **1.** to seize (a person) by legal authority. **2.** to

attract and hold (the attention).
3. to stop or slow down. —*n.* **4.** the act of arresting or state of being arrested. —**ar·rest′er,** *n.*

ar·rest·ing (ə res′tĭng), *adj.* attracting or capable of attracting attention.

ar·rhyth·mi·a (ə rĭth̸′mē ə, ə rĭth̸′-), *n.* any disturbance in the rhythm of the heartbeat.

ar·rière-pen·sée (A RYER PÄN sā′), *n. French.* a mental reservation.

ar·ri·val (ə rī′vəl), *n.* **1.** the act of arriving. **2.** a person or thing that arrives.

ar·rive (ə rīv′), *v.i.,* **-rived, -riv·ing. 1.** to reach one's destination. **2.** to come to be present. **3.** to attain a position of success. **4. arrive at,** to reach in a course or process. —**ar·riv′er,** *n.*

ar·ri·ve·der·ci (är′RĔ ve deR′chē), *interj. Italian.* goodby until we meet again.

ar·ro·gant (ar′ə gənt), *adj.* **2.** making unwarrantable claims to superior importance. **2.** haughty or overbearing. —**ar′ro·gance,** *n.* —**ar′ro·gant·ly,** *adv.*

ar·ro·gate (ar′ə gāt′), *v.t.,* **-gat·ed, -gat·ing.** to claim or appropriate to oneself without right. —**ar′ro·ga′tion,** *n.*

ar·row (ar′ō), *n.* **1.** a straight, slender, generally pointed missile equipped with feathers at the end of the shaft, shot from a bow. **2.** a figure having a wedge-shaped end, etc., to indicate direction.

ar·row·head (ar′ō hed′), *n.* the pointed tip of an arrow.

ar·row·root (ar′ō rōōt′, -rŏŏt′), *n.* **1.** a tropical American plant whose rhizomes yield a nutritious starch. **2.** the starch itself.

ar·roy·o (ə roi′ō), *n., pl.* **-os** (-ōz). a small steep-sided gulch, usually dry except after heavy rains.

ar·se·nal (är′sə nᵊl), *n.* **1.** armory (def. 1). **2.** a factory for manufacturing military equipment. **3.** a supply of weapons.

ar·se·nate (är′sə nāt′, -nĭt), *n.* a salt or ester of arsenic acid.

ar·se·nic (*n.* är′sə nĭk. ärs′nĭk; *adj.* är sen′ĭk), *n.* **1.** *Chem.* a grayish-white element, forming poisonous compounds. *Symbol:* As; *at. wt.:* 74.92; *at. no.:* 33. **2.** See **arsenic trioxide.** —*adj.* **3.** Also, **ar·sen′i·cal** (-sen′i kəl). of or containing arsenic. —**ar·se′ni·ous** (-sē′nē əs), *adj.*

arsen′ic ac′id, *Chem.* a water-soluble powder used chiefly in the manufacture of insecticides, glass, etc.

ar′senic tri·ox′ide (trī ok′sīd, -sid), *Chem.* a poisonous powder used

in the manufacture of pigments and glass, as an insecticide, etc.

ar·son (är′sən), *n.* the malicious burning of a house or property. —**ar′son·ist,** *n.* —**ar′son·ous,** *adj.*

art¹ (ärt), *n.* **1.** the quality, production, expression, or realm of what is beautiful. **2.** objects belonging to this realm, as paintings, etc. **3.** a field, genre, or category of this realm. **4.** illustrative or decorative material. **5.** the principles governing any craft, skill, or branch of learning. **6.** a branch of study, esp. one of the fine arts or the humanities. **7. arts.** See **liberal arts. 8.** skilled workmanship or execution. **9.** an artful device.

art² (ärt), *v. Archaic.* 2nd pers. sing. pres. indic. of **be.**

-art. See **-ard.**

art., *n.* **1.** article. **2.** artificial. **3.** artillery. **4.** artist.

Art Deco (är′ dā′kō), a style of art in the 1920's and the 1930's, characterized chiefly by vivid colors and geometric motifs.

Ar·te·mis (är′tə mis), *n.* an ancient Greek goddess characterized as a virgin huntress and associated with the moon.

ar·te·ri·ole (är′tēr′ə ōl′), *n. Anat.* a small artery. —**ar·te′ri·o′lar** (-tē′rē ō′lər), *adj.*

ar·te·ri·o·scle·ro·sis (är tēr′ē ō sklə-rō′sis), *n.* an arterial disease characterized by hardening and thickening of the vessel walls, with lessened blood flow. —**ar·te·ri·o·scle·rot·ic** (är tēr′ē ō sklə rot′ik), *adj.*

ar·ter·y (är′tə rē), *n., pl.* **-ter·ies. 1.** a blood vessel that conveys blood from the heart to any part of the body. **2.** a main highway or channel. —**ar·te·ri·al** (är tēr′ē əl), *adj.*

ar·te′sian well′ (är te′zhən), a deep well in which water rises under pressure from a permeable stratum.

art·ful (ärt′fəl), *adj.* **1.** crafty and tricky. **2.** skillful or ingenious. —**art′ful·ly,** *adv.* —**art′ful·ness,** *n.*

ar·thri·tis (är thrī′tis), *n.* inflammation of a joint, as in rheumatism. —**ar·thrit·ic** (är thrit′ik), *adj.,* *n.*

ar·thro·pod (är′thrə pod′), *n.* any of a major group of segmented invertebrates having jointed legs and including the insects, crustaceans, etc.

Ar·thur (är′thər), *n.* **1. Ches·ter A(l·an)** (ches′tər al′ən), 1830–86, 21st president of the U.S. 1881–85. **2.** a legendary king in ancient Britain. —**Ar·thu′ri·an** (-thŏŏr′ē ən), *adj.*

ar·ti·choke (är′ti chōk′), *n.* a herbaceous, thistlelike plant, having an edible flower head.

ar·ti·cle (är′ti kəl), n. 1. a factual piece of writing on a specific topic. 2. an item or particular: *an article of clothing.* 3. an indefinite object. 4. *Gram.* a member of a small class of words which are linked to nouns and identify the noun as a noun. In English the definite article is *the* and the indefinite article is *a* or *an.* 5. a distinct section of a contract, treaty, etc.

ar·tic·u·lar (är tik′yə lər), adj. of the joints.

ar·tic·u·late (adj. är tik′yə lit; v. är·tik′yə lāt′), adj., v., -lat·ed, -lat·ing. —adj. 1. uttered clearly. 2. capable of speech. 3. using language easily. 4. *Zool.* having joints or composed of segments. —v.t. 5. to pronounce distinctly. 6. to give clarity or distinction to. 7. to unite by joints. —v.i. 8. to pronounce clearly. 9. to form a joint. —ar·tic′u·late·ly, adv. —ar·tic′u·late·ness, n. —ar·tic′u·la′tion, n.

ar·ti·fact (är′tə fakt′), n. any object made or modified by humans, esp. one reflecting workmanship in ancient cultures.

ar·ti·fice (är′tə fis), n. 1. a clever stratagem. 2. cunning or craftiness. 3. ingenuity or skill.

ar·tif·i·cer (är tif′i sər), n. 1. a skilled workman. 2. any ingenious man.

ar·ti·fi·cial (är′tə fish′əl), adj. 1. produced by humans. 2. made in imitation. 3. affected or feigned. —ar·ti·fi·ci·al·i·ty (är′tə fish′ē al′i tē), n. —ar′ti·fi′cial·ly, adv. —ar′ti·fi′cial·ness, n.

artifi′cial respira′tion, the stimulation of natural respiratory functions in persons whose breathing has failed by forcing air into and out of the lungs.

ar·til·ler·y (är til′ə rē), n. 1. mounted projectile-firing guns or missile launchers. 2. the branch of an army concerned with such weapons. —ar·til′ler·y·man, ar·til·ler·ist (är til′ər ist), n.

ar·ti·san (är′ti zən), n. a skilled craftsman. —ar′ti·san·ship′, n.

art·ist (är′tist), n. 1. a person who practices one of the fine arts, esp. a painter or sculptor. 2. artiste. 3. a person who does anything exceptionally well.

ar·tiste (är tēst′), n. a professional artist, esp. a singer, dancer, or other public performer.

ar·tis·tic (är tis′tik), adj. 1. showing skill in execution. 2. exhibiting taste or sensitivity. 3. of the appreciation of art. 4. of an artist. —ar·tis′ti·cal·ly, adv.

art·ist·ry (är′ti strē), n. artistic work, ability, or quality.

art·less (ärt′lis), adj. 1. free from guile or artificiality. 2. natural or simple. 3. lacking art, knowledge, or skill. —art′less·ly, adv. —art′less·ness, n.

Art Nou·veau (är′ nōō vō′, ärt′), a style of art current in the late 19th and early 20th centuries, characterized chiefly by curved-line motifs.

art·y (är′tē), adj., art·i·er, art·i·est. ostentatiously artistic. —art′i·ly, adv. —art′i·ness, n.

arty., artillery.

ar·um (âr′əm), n. a plant having an inflorescence consisting of a spadix enclosed in a large spathe.

A.R.V., American Revised Version.

-ary, a suffix meaning "pertaining to" or "connected with": *honorary; voluntary.*

Ar·y·an (âr′ē ən, âr′yən, ar′-), n. 1. a member or descendant of the prehistoric people who spoke Indo-European. 2. (in Nazi doctrine) a non-Jewish Caucasian. 3. *Archaic.* Indo-European.

as (az; *unstressed* əz), adv. 1. to such a degree or extent. 2. for example. 3. thought to be. —conj. 4. to such a degree or extent that. 5. in the degree, manner, etc., of or that. 6. while or when. 7. since or because. 8. though. 9. that: *I don't know as I do.* 10. as for or to, with reference to it. 11. as if or though, as it would be if. 12. as is, just the way it exists or appears. 13. as it were, in a way. 14. as of, right on, at, or from: *effective as of May 1.* —pron. 15. that, who, or which. 16. a fact that: *The book is good, as I know.* —prep. 17. in the role, function, or status of: *to act as chairperson.*

—Usage. See like.

AS, 1. Anglo-Saxon. 2. antisubmarine.

As, arsenic.

as·a·fet·i·da (as′ə fet′i də), n. a resin having a bitter, acrid taste and an obnoxious odor. Also, a′sa·foet′i·da.

as·bes·tos (as bes′təs, az-), n. a fibrous amphibole, used for making fireproof articles. Also, as·bes′tus.

A.S.C., American Society of Cinematographers.

as·cend (ə send′), v.i., v.t. 1. to mount or move upward gradually. 2. to succeed to (a throne).

as·cend·an·cy (ə sen′dən sē), n. the state of being dominant. Also, as·cend′en·cy.

as·cend·ant (ə sen′dənt), n. 1. a position of dominance. 2. in the ascendant, increasing in power or renown. —adj. 3. ascending or rising. 4. superior or dominant. Also, as·cend′ent.

as·cen·sion (ə sen′shən), *n.* **1.** the act of ascending. **2. the Ascension,** the bodily ascending of Christ from earth to heaven.

Ascen′sion Day′ the 40th day after Easter, commemorating the Ascension of Christ.

as·cent (ə sent′), *n.* **1.** the act or movement of ascending. **2.** a means of ascending, as a stair or slope.

as·cer·tain (as′ər tān′), *v.t.* to find out with assurance. —**as′cer·tain′a·ble,** *adj.*

as·cet·ic (ə set′ik), *n.* **1.** a person who practices extreme self-denial, esp. for religious reasons. —*adj.* **2.** rigorously abstinent or austere. —**as·cet′i·cism,** *n.*

a·scor′bic ac′id (ə skôr′bik, ā skôr′-), a water-soluble vitamin occurring in citrus fruits, green vegetables, etc., essential for normal metabolism. Also called **vitamin C.**

as·cot (as′kət), *n.* a broad scarf or necktie worn looped under the chin.

as·cribe (ə skrīb′), *v.t.,* **-cribed, -crib·ing. 1.** to credit or assign, as to a source. **2.** to attribute as belonging. —**a·scrib′a·ble,** *adj.* —**as·crip·tion** (ə skrip′shən), *n.*

a·sep·tic (ə sep′tik, ā sep′-), *adj.* free from the living germs of disease.

a·sex·u·al (ā sek′shōō əl), *adj.* **1.** having no sex or no sexual organs. **2.** independent of sexual processes: *asexual reproduction.* —**a·sex′u·al·ly,** *adv.*

ash[1] (ash), *n.* **1.** the powdery residue of matter that remains after burning. **2.** finely pulverized lava from a volcano. **3.** a light, silvery-gray color. **4. ashes,** mortal remains.

ash[2] (ash), *n.* a tree whose tough, straight-grained, and elastic wood is valued as timber.

a·shamed (ə shāmd′), *adj.* **1.** feeling shame. **2.** unwilling because of the fear of shame. —**a·sham·ed·ly** (ə shā′mid lē), *adv.*

ash·en (ash′ən), *adj.* **1.** ash-colored. **2.** extremely pale. **3.** consisting of ashes.

ash·lar (ash′lər), *n.* **1.** a squared building stone. **2.** masonry made of such stone.

a·shore (ə shôr′, ə shōr′), *adv.* **1.** to the shore. **2.** on the shore.

ash·ram (ash′rəm), *n. Hinduism.* a place in which people meet for religious instruction.

ash·tray (ash′trā′), *n.* a receptacle for tobacco ashes.

Ash′ Wednes′day, the first day of Lent.

ash·y (ash′ē), *adj.,* **ash·i·er, ash·i·est.** ashen.

A·sia (ā′zhə, ā′shə), *n.* a continent bounded by Europe and the Arctic, Pacific, and Indian Oceans. —**A′sian;** *Often Offensive,* **A·si·at′ic** (ā′zhē at′ik), *adj., n.*

A′sia Mi′nor, a peninsula in W Asia between the Black and Mediterranean Seas.

a·side (ə sīd′), *adv.* **1.** on or to one side. **2.** in reserve: *to lay money aside.* **3.** notwithstanding: *all kidding aside.* **4. aside from, a.** besides. **b.** except for. —*n.* **5.** a comment by an actor intended for the audience and supposedly not heard by others on stage.

as·i·nine (as′ə nīn′), *adj.* **1.** witlessly stupid or silly. **2.** of or like an ass. —**as′i·nine′ly,** *adv.* —**as·i·nin·i·ty** (as′ə nin′i tē), *n.*

ask (ask, äsk), *v.t.* **1.** to inquire of. **2.** to request information about. **3.** to request. **4.** to solicit from. **5.** to demand, expect, or desire. **6.** to invite. —*v.i.* **7.** to inquire. **8.** to request or petition. —**ask′er,** *n.*

a·skance (ə skans′), *adv.* **1.** with suspicion or mistrust. **2.** with a side glance.

a·skew (ə skyōō′), *adv.* **1.** to one side. —*adj.* **2.** crooked or awry.

ask′ing price′, the price originally demanded by the seller.

a·slant (ə slant′, ə slänt′), *adv.* **1.** at a slant. —*adj.* **2.** slanting or oblique. —*prep.* **3.** slantingly across.

a·sleep (ə slēp′), *adv.* **1.** into a state of sleep. —*adj.* **2.** sleeping. **3.** dormant or inactive. **4.** (of the foot, hand, etc.) numb. **5.** dead.

a·so·cial (ā sō′shəl), *adj.* **1.** withdrawn from society. **2.** inconsiderate or selfish.

asp (asp), *n.* any of several venomous snakes of Africa and Europe. —**asp′ish,** *adj.*

as·par·a·gus (ə spar′ə gəs), *n.* **1.** a perennial plant of the lily family with tender edible shoots. **2.** such shoots.

A.S.P.C.A., American Society for Prevention of Cruelty to Animals.

as·pect (as′pekt), *n.* **1.** appearance to the eye or mind. **2.** view or interpretation. **3.** a distinct feature or phase. **4.** an apparent attitude or character.

as·pen (as′pən), *n.* any of several poplars having leaves that tremble in the slightest breeze.

as·per·i·ty (ə sper′i tē), *n.* **1.** roughness of temper or manner. **2.** harshness or roughness.

as·perse (ə spûrs′), *v.t.,* **-persed, -pers·ing.** to attack with aspersions.

as·per·sion (ə spûr′zhən, -shən), *n.* a malicious or damaging statement.

as·phalt (as′fôlt), *n.* **1.** Also, **as·phal·tum** (as fôl′təm). any of various dark-colored, bituminous substances, composed mainly of hydrocarbon mixtures, esp. used for paving. —*v.t.* **2.** to cover or pave with asphalt. —**as·phal′tic,** *adj.*

as′phalt jun′gle, an area of a big city infested with crime and violence.

as·pho·del (as′fə del′), *n.* any of various plants related to the lily family, having white, pink, or yellow flowers.

as·phyx·i·a (as fik′sē ə), *n.* lack of oxygen and excess of carbon dioxide in the blood, produced by interference with respiration, often causing unconsciousness or death.

as·phyx·i·ate (as fik′sē āt′), *v.*, **-at·ed, -at·ing.** —*v.t.* **1.** to produce asphyxia in. —*v.i.* **2.** to become asphyxiated. —**as·phyx′i·a′tion,** *n.*

as·pic (as′pik), *n.* a gelatin used as a coating for meats, seafoods, eggs, etc.

as·pi·dis·tra (as′pi dis′trə), *n.* a smooth, stemless, Asian herb having large evergreen leaves, used as a house plant.

as·pir·ant (as′pər ənt, ə spīr′ənt), *n.* a person who aspires, esp. toward a position, etc.

as·pi·rate (*v.* as′pə rāt′; *n., adj.,* as′pər it), *v.*, **-rat·ed, -rat·ing,** *n., adj.* —*v.t.* **1. a.** to articulate (a sound) so as to produce an audible rush of air, as with the *t* of *time.* **b.** to articulate with an *h*-sound, as in *which* (hwich). **2.** to remove (body fluids) by suction. —*n.* **3.** an aspirated sound. —*adj.* **4.** (of a speech sound) aspirated. —**as′pi·ra′tor,** *n.*

as·pi·ra·tion (as′pə rā′shən), *n.* **1.** strong desire, longing, or ambition. **2.** a goal desired. **3.** act of aspiring.

as·pire (ə spīr′r′), *v.i.,* **-pired, -pir·ing.** to be eagerly desirous: *to aspire to be a doctor.* —**as·pir′ing·ly,** *adv.*

as·pi·rin (as′pə rin, -prin), *n., pl.* **-rin, -rins.** a white, crystalline derivative of salicylic acid used to relieve pain and fever.

ass (as), *n.* **1.** a long-eared, surefooted domesticated mammal, related to the horse, used chiefly as a beast of burden. **2.** a stupid or foolish person. —**ass′like′,** *adj.*

as·sail (ə sāl′), *v.t.* **1.** to attack violently. **2.** to attack with criticism, etc. —**as·sail′a·ble,** *adj.* —**as·sail′ant,** *n.*

as·sas·sin (ə sas′in), *n.* a killer, esp. a fanatic who kills a prominent person. [< ML *assassīnī* (pl.) < Ar *hashshīn* eaters of hashish]

as·sas·si·nate (ə sas′ə nāt′), *v.t.,* **-nat·ed, nat·ing. 1.** to murder treacherously. **2.** to destroy viciously. —**as·sas′si·na′tion,** *n.*

as·sault (ə sôlt′), *n.* **1.** a violent attack. **2.** *Law.* an attempt or threat to do violence to another. **3.** rape[1] (def. 1). —*v.t., v.i.* **4.** to make an assault (upon).

assault′ and bat′tery, *Law.* an assault with actual violence upon another.

as·say (*v.* ə sā′; *n.* ə sā′, as′ā), *v.t.* **1.** to analyze (an ore, etc.) to determine the quantity of gold or other metal in it. **2.** to assess or evaluate. **3.** *Literary.* to attempt. —*v.i.* **4.** to contain, by analysis, a certain proportion of precious metal. —*n.* **5.** determination of the amount of metal, esp. gold, in an ore, etc. —**as·say′er,** *n.*

as·sem·blage (ə sem′blij), *n.* **1.** an assembly or collection. **2.** the act of assembling or state of being assembled. **3.** a sculptural composition made from unrelated objects.

as·sem·ble (ə sem′bəl), *v.*, **-bled, -bling.** —*v.t.* **1.** to gather into one place, body, or whole. **2.** to put or fit together. —*v.i.* **3.** to come together. —**as·sem′bler,** *n.*

as·sem·bly (ə sem′blē), *n., pl.* **-blies. 1.** a body of persons gathered together for a purpose. **2.** (*cap*). a legislative body, esp. a lower house of a legislature. **3.** the act of assembling or state of being assembled. **4.** the putting together of complex machinery. **5.** a signal for troops to assemble.

assem′bly line′, an arrangement of machines, tools, and workers in which a product is assembled by having each perform a specific operation as the unit passes by.

as·sem·bly·man (ə sem′blē mən), *n., pl.* **-men.** a member of a legislative assembly. —**as·sem′bly·wom′an,** *n.fem.*

as·sent (ə sent′), *v.i.* **1.** to express agreement or approval. **2.** to yield or concede. —*n.* **3.** agreement or concurrence. —**Syn. 1.** acquiesce, agree, consent.

as·sert (ə sûrt′), *v.t.* **1.** to state positively but often without support or reason. **2.** to maintain (claims, rights, etc.). **3.** to put (oneself) forward insistently. —**as·sert′er, as·ser′tor,** *n.* —**as·ser′tive,** *adj.* —**Syn. 1.** affirm, avow, declare, profess.

as·ser·tion (ə sûr′shən), *n.* **1.** something asserted. **2.** the act of asserting. —**as·ser′tive·ly,** *adv.* —**as·ser′tive·ness,** *n.*

as·sess (ə ses′), *v.t.* **1.** to estimate officially the value of (property, etc.) for taxation. **2.** to determine the amount of (damages, a fine, etc.). **3.** to evaluate: *to assess one's efforts.* —**as·sess′a·ble,** *adj.* —**as·sess′ment,** *n.* —**as·sess′or,** *n.*

as·set (as′et), *n.* **1.** a useful thing or quality: *Organizational ability is an asset.* **2.** a single item of ownership having exchange value. **3.** **assets, a.** total resources of a person or business, as cash, fixtures, real estate, etc. **b.** *Law.* property available for payment of debts.

as·sev·er·ate (ə sev′ə rāt′), *v.t.,* **-at·ed, -at·ing.** to declare earnestly. —**as·sev′er·a′tion,** *n.*

as·sid·u·ous (ə sij′ō̄ əs), *adj.* **1.** unremittingly attentive. **2.** persevering or industrious. —**as·si·du·i·ty** (as′i-dō̄′i tē, -dyō̄′-), *n.* —**as·sid′u·ous·ly,** *adv.* —**as·sid′u·ous·ness,** *n.*

as·sign (ə sīn′), *v.t.* **1.** to designate or reserve for a specific purpose. **2.** to appoint, as to a duty. **3.** to name or specify. **4.** to ascribe or attribute. **5.** *Law.* to transfer (property), esp. in trust. —**as·sign′a·ble,** *adj.* —**as·sign·ee** (ə sī nē′, as′ə nē′), *n.* —**as·sign′er, as·sign′or,** *n.*

as·sig·na·tion (as′ig nā′shən), *n.* an appointment for a meeting, esp. a rendezvous or tryst.

assigned′ risk′, a risk allocated to an insurance company from a pool of companies who would not otherwise accept it.

as·sign·ment (ə sīn′mənt), *n.* **1.** something assigned, as a particular task. **2.** the act of assigning. **3.** *Law.* the transfer of a right, interest, or title.

as·sim·i·late (ə sim′ə lāt′), *v.,* **-lat·ed, -lat·ing.** —*v.t.* **1.** to take in and incorporate as one's own. **2.** to convert (food) into a substance suitable for absorption into the system. **3.** to take in and make a part of a country or community. —*v.i.* **4.** to be or become assimilated. —**as·sim′i·la·ble,** *adj.* —**as·sim′i·la′tion,** *n.*

as·sist (ə sist′), *v.t., v.i.* **1.** to help, esp. in a subordinate capacity. —*n.* **2.** *Sports.* **a.** *Baseball.* a play that helps to put out a batter or base runner. **b.** a play that helps a teammate in gaining a goal. **3.** *Informal.* an act of assisting. —**as·sist′er, as·sis′tor,** *n.*

as·sis·tance (ə sis′təns), *n.* help, esp. in a subordinate capacity.

as·sis·tant (ə sis′tənt), *n.* **1.** a person who assists or helps. —*adj.* **2.** assisting or helpful. —**Syn. 1.** aid, aide, helper.

as·siz·es (ə sīz′iz), *n.pl.* (formerly). **1.** trial sessions, civil or criminal, held periodically in English counties. **2.** the place or time of these.

assn., association.

assoc., 1. associate. **2.** association.

as·so·ci·ate (*v.* ə sō′shē āt′, -sē-; *n., adj.,* ə sō′shē it, -āt′, -sē-), *v., -at·ed, -at·ing, n., adj.* —*v.t.* **1.** to bring into relation, as thought, memory, etc. **2.** to join as a partner or ally. **3.** to unite or combine. —*v.i.* **4.** to unite or join. —*n.* **5.** a partner or colleague. **6.** a companion or comrade. **7.** a degree conferred by a junior college or community college: *associate of arts.* —*adj.* **8.** connected, joined, or related, esp. as a companion or colleague. **9.** having subordinate status.

as·so·ci·a·tion (ə sō′sē ā′shən, -shē-), *n.* **1.** an organization of people with a common purpose. **2.** act of associating or state of being associated. **3.** friendship or companionship.

associa′tion foot′ball, *Brit.* soccer.

as·so·ci·a·tive (ə sō′shē ā′tiv, -sē-, -shə tiv), *adj.* **1.** pertaining to or resulting from association. **2.** *Math.* giving an equivalent expression when elements are grouped without change of order, as $(a + b) + c = a + (b + c)$.

as·so·nance (as′ə nəns), *n.* **1.** the resemblance of sounds. **2.** *Pros.* rhyme in which the same vowel sounds are used with different consonants. —**as′so·nant,** *adj., n.*

as·sort (ə sôrt′), *v.t.* to distribute or arrange according to kind or class.

as·sort·ed (ə sôr′tid), *adj.* consisting of various kinds: *assorted candies.*

as·sort·ment (ə sôrt′mənt), *n.* **1.** the act of assorting. **2.** a mixed collection.

ASSR, Autonomous Soviet Socialist Republic.

asst., assistant.

as·suage (ə swāj′), *v.t.,* **-suaged, -suag·ing. 1.** to make milder or less severe. **2.** to appease or satisfy.

as·sume (ə sō̄m′), *v.t.,* **-sumed, -sum·ing. 1.** to take for granted. **2.** to take upon oneself. **3.** to take over the duties or responsibilities of. **4.** to take on (a particular character, quality, etc.). **5.** to pretend to have or be. —**as·sum′a·ble,** *adj.* —**as·sum′a·bly,** *adv.* —**as·sum·ed·ly** (ə sō̄′mid lē), *adv.* —**Syn. 5.** affect, feign, simulate.

as·sum·ing (ə sō̄′ming), *adj.* arrogant or presumptuous.

as·sump·tion (ə sump′shən), *n.* **1.** the act of taking for granted or supposing. **2.** a supposition. **3.** act of taking to or upon oneself. **4.** act of taking possession of something. **5.** arrogance or presumption. **6.** *Eccles.* **a.** (*often cap.*) the bodily taking up into heaven of the Virgin Mary. **b.** (*cap.*) a feast commemorating this, celebrated on August 15. —**as·sump′tive,** *adj.*

as·sur·ance (ə shŏŏr'əns), *n.* **1.** a positive declaration intended to give confidence. **2.** pledge or guaranty. **3.** certainty or sureness. **4.** self-confidence. **5.** *Brit.* insurance.

as·sure (ə shŏŏr'), *v.t.,* **-sured, -suring. 1.** to inform or tell positively. **2.** to reassure. **3.** to promise or guarantee. **4.** to make sure or safe. **5.** *Brit.* to insure.

as·sured (ə shŏŏrd'), *adj.* **1.** guaranteed or certain. **2.** bold or confident. **—n. 3.** the beneficiary under an insurance policy. **—as·sur·ed·ly** (ə shŏŏr'id lē), *adv.*

As·syr·i·a (ə shŏŏr'ē ə), *n.* an ancient empire in SW Asia. **—As·syr'i·an,** *adj., n.*

as·ta·tine (as'tə tēn', -tin), *n. Chem.* a rare element of the halogen family. Symbol: At; *at. no.:* 85.

as·ter (as'tər), *n.* any of various plants having white, pink, or blue rays around a yellow disk. [< L < Gk *aster* star]

as·ter·isk (as'tə risk), *n.* the figure of a star (*), used as a reference mark or to indicate omission, etc.

as·ter·ism (as'tə riz'əm), *n.* **1.** a starlike luminous figure in some crystallized minerals. **2. a.** a group of stars. **b.** a constellation.

a·stern (ə stûrn'), *adv.* **1.** at or toward the stern. **2.** in a backward direction.

as·ter·oid (as'tə roid'), *n.* **1.** any of the thousands of small bodies that revolve about the sun in orbits mostly between those of Mars and Jupiter. **2.** a starfish. **—as'ter·oi'dal,** *adj.*

asth·ma (az'mə), *n.* a paroxysmal, often allergic disorder of respiration, characterized by wheezing, constriction in the chest, etc. **—asth·mat·ic** (az mat'ik), *adj., n.*

a·stig·ma·tism (ə stig'mə tiz'əm), *n.* **1.** an aberration of a lens that causes lines in some directions to be focused less sharply than lines in other directions. **2.** a defect in vision due to such an aberration in the eye. **—as·tig·mat·ic** (as'tig mat'ik), *adj.*

a·stir (ə stûr'), *adj., adv.* **1.** in motion. **2.** *Archaic.* out of bed.

As·ti spu·man·te (ä'stē spōō män'te), a sweet, sparkling Italian white wine with a muscat flavor.

as·ton·ish (ə ston'ish), *v.t.* to strike with sudden and overpowering wonder. **—as·ton'ish·ing,** *adj.* **—as·ton'ish·ing·ly,** *adv.* **—as·ton'ish·ment,** *n.*

as·tound (ə stound'), *v.t.* to shock with helpless bewilderment. **—as·tound'ing,** *adj.* **—as·tound'ing·ly,** *adv.*

a·strad·dle (ə strad'ᵊl), *prep., adv., adj.* astride.

as·tra·khan (as'trə kən, -kan'), *n.* a fur of young lambs, with lustrous, closely curled wool, from SE Soviet Union.

as·tral (as'trəl), *adj.* of, pertaining to, or proceeding from the stars.

a·stray (ə strā'), *adv., adj.* **1.** off the correct path. **2.** in or into error.

a·stride (ə strīd'), *prep.* **1.** with a leg on each side of. **2.** on both sides of. **—adv., adj. 3.** with legs apart or with one leg on each side.

as·trin·gent (ə strin'jənt), *adj. Med.* able to constrict living tissues. **2.** stern or austere. **—n. 3.** an astringent substance or agent. **—as·trin'gen·cy,** *n.*

astro-, a combining form meaning "a star" or "outer space": *astrophysics; astronaut.*

as·tro·bi·ol·o·gy (as'trə bī ol'ə jē), *n.* exobiology.

as·tro·dy·nam·ics (as'trə dī nam'iks), *n.* a branch of dynamics that treats of the motions of celestial objects, including space satellites.

astrol., 1. astrologer. **2.** astrological. **3.** astrology.

as·tro·labe (as'trə lāb'), *n.* an ancient instrument for determining the position of the sun or stars.

as·trol·o·gy (ə strol'ə jē), *n.* the study that assumes, and professes to interpret, the influence of the heavenly bodies on human affairs. **—as·trol'o·ger, as·trol'o·gist,** *n.* **—as·tro·log·i·cal** (as'trə loj'i kəl), **as'tro·log'ic,** *adj.* **—as'tro·log'i·cal·ly,** *adv.*

astron., 1. astronomer. **2.** astronomical. **3.** astronomy.

as·tro·naut (as'trə nôt'), *n.* a person engaged in or trained for spaceflight.

as·tro·nau·tics (as'trə nô'tiks), *n.* the science of travel beyond the earth's atmosphere, including interplanetary and interstellar flights. **—as'tro·nau'tic, as'tro·nau'ti·cal,** *adj.* **—as'tro·nau'ti·cal·ly,** *adv.*

as·tro·nom·i·cal (as'trə nom'i kəl), *adj.* **1.** of or connected with astronomy. **2.** inconceivably or enormously large. Also, **as'tro·nom'ic.** **—as'tro·nom'i·cal·ly,** *adv.*

as'tronom'ical u'nit, a unit of length, equal to the mean distance of the earth from the sun: approximately 93 million miles.

as·tron·o·my (ə stron'ə mē), *n.* the science that deals with the material universe beyond the earth's atmosphere. **—as·tron'o·mer,** *n.*

as·tro·phys·ics (as'trō fiz'iks), *n.* the branch of astronomy that deals with the physical properties of celestial bodies. **—as'tro·phys'i·cal,** *adj.* **—as·tro·phys·i·cist** (as'trō fiz'ə sist), *n.*

as·tute (ə stoot′, ə styoot′), *adj.* of keen penetration or discernment. —**as·tute′ly**, *adv.* —**as·tute′ness**, *n.*

a·sun·der (ə sun′dər), *adv., adj.* **1.** in or into pieces. **2.** widely separated.

A.S.V., American Standard Version.

a·sy·lum (ə sī′ləm), *n.* **1.** an institution for care of the blind, insane, orphans, etc. **2.** (formerly) an inviolable refuge. **3.** protection afforded to exiled political offenders.

a·sym·met·ric (ā′sə me′trik, as′ə-), *adj.* lacking symmetry. Also, **a′sym·met′ri·cal.** —**a′sym·met′ri·cal·ly**, *adv.* —**a·sym′me·try**, *n.*

as·ymp·tote (as′im tōt′), *n.* *Math.* a straight line approached by a given curve as one of the variables in the equation of the curve approaches infinity. —**as′ymp·tot·ic** (as′im tot′ik), **as′ymp·tot′i·cal**, *adj.* —**as′ymp·tot′i·cal·ly**, *adv.*

at (at; *unstressed* ət, it), *prep.* **1.** in, on, or near. **2.** (used to indicate a location or position): *at noon.* **3.** (used to indicate location): *at home.* **4.** (used to indicate amount, degree, or rate): *at great speed.* **5.** toward: *Look at that!* **6.** (used to indicate involvement): *at play.* **7.** (used to indicate a condition): *at peace.* **8.** (used to indicate a cause): *She was annoyed at his stupidity.* **9.** (used to indicate a manner): *He spoke at length.* **10.** (used to indicate relative value): *at cost.*

At, astatine.

at., atomic.

at·a·vism (at′ə viz′əm), *n.* the reappearance in a plant or animal of characteristics of some remote ancestor that have been absent in intervening generations. —**at′a·vist,** *n.* —**at·a·vis·tic** (at′ə vis′tik), *adj.*

ate (āt; *Brit.* et), *v.* pt. of **eat.**

-ate[1], a suffix meaning: **a.** in a specified state or condition: *separate.* **b.** office or rule: *caliphate.* **c.** to be or cause to be: *agitate.* **d.** having or showing: *compassionate.*

-ate[2], a suffix meaning "a salt of an acid": *sulfate.*

at·el·ier (at′ºl yā′), *n.* a workshop or studio, esp. of an artist.

Ath·a·pas·kan (ath′ə pas′kən), *n.* **1.** a family of languages spoken by American Indians, including esp. Navaho, Apache, etc. **2.** a member of any of various Athapaskan-speaking peoples. Also, **Ath′a·pas′-can.**

a·the·ism (ā′thē iz′əm), *n.* the belief that there is no God or gods. —**a′the·ist,** *n.* —**a′the·is′tic, a′the·is′ti·cal,** *adj.* —**a′the·is′ti·cal·ly,** *adv.*

A·the·na (ə thē′nə), *n.* the ancient Greek goddess of wisdom, arts, and warfare.

ath·e·nae·um (ath′ə nē′əm), *n.* **1.** an institution for the promotion of learning. **2.** *Archaic.* a library. Also, **ath′e·ne′um.**

Ath·ens (ath′inz), *n.* the capital of Greece, in the SE part. —**A·the·ni·an** (ə thē′nē ən), *adj., n.*

ath·er·o·scle·ro·sis (ath′ə rō skle rō′sis), *n.* a form of arteriosclerosis in which fatty substances deposit in the inner walls of the arteries. —**ath·er·o·scle·rot·ic** (ath′ə rō skle rot′ik), *adj.*

a·thirst (ə thûrst′), *adj.* **1.** eagerly longing. **2.** *Archaic.* thirsty.

ath·lete (ath′lēt), *n.* a trained competitor in a sport, exercise, or game requiring physical skill.

ath·lete's foot′, a fungal infection of the skin of the foot, causing itching, pain, etc.

ath·let·ic (ath let′ik), *adj.* **1.** of or pertaining to athletes or athletics. **2.** physically active and strong. —**ath·let′i·cal·ly,** *adv.*

ath·let·ics (ath let′iks), *n.* athletic sports, exercises, or games.

a·thwart (ə thwôrt′), *adv.* **1.** from side to side. —*prep.* **2.** across. **3.** in opposition to.

a·tilt (ə tilt′), *adj., adv.* at a tilt.

-ation, a suffix meaning "act," "process," or "result": *separation; flirtation.*

-ative, a suffix meaning "tending" or "serving": *regulative.*

Atl., Atlantic.

At·lan·ta (at lan′tə), *n.* the capital of Georgia.

At·lan·tic Cit′y (at lan′tik), a city in SE New Jersey: seashore resort.

Atlan′tic O·cean, an ocean bounded by the Americas in the west and by Europe and Africa in the east. Also called the **Atlan′tic.**

at·las (at′ləs), *n., pl.* **at·las·es. 1.** a bound collection of maps. **2.** the first cervical vertebra, which supports the head. **3.** (*cap.*) *Class. Myth.* a giant condemned to support the sky on his shoulders.

atm., *n.* **1.** atmosphere. **2.** atmospheric.

at·mos·phere (at′məs fēr′), *n.* **1.** the gaseous envelope surrounding the earth or any other celestial body. **2.** a conventional unit of pressure, the normal pressure of the air at sea level, about 14.7 pounds per square inch. **3.** a pervading influence or spirit: *an atmosphere of peace.* **4.** the dominant mood or effect. —**at·mos·pher·ic** (at′məs fer′ik), **at′mos·pher′i·cal,** *adj.*

at·mos·pher·ics (at′məs fer′iks), *n.* noise caused in a radio receiver by natural electromagnetic disturbances in the atmosphere.

at. no., See atomic number.

at·oll (at'ôl, -ol, -ōl), *n.* a ring-shaped coral reef enclosing a lagoon.

at·om (at'əm), *n.* 1. *Physics.* the smallest component of an element having all the properties of the element, consisting of an aggregate of protons, neutrons, and electrons. 2. anything extremely small. 3. See atomic energy.

a·tom·ic (ə tom'ik), *adj.* 1. of or pertaining to an atom or atoms. 2. operated by atomic energy. 3. using atomic bombs: *an atomic explosion.* 4. extremely minute. —**a·tom'i·cal·ly,** *adv.*

atom'ic bomb', a bomb whose explosive force comes from a chain reaction based on nuclear fission. Also, **at'om bomb'.**

atom'ic clock', an extremely accurate electric clock regulated by the resonance frequency of atoms.

atom'ic en'ergy, energy released by rearrangements of atomic nuclei, as in nuclear fission.

atom'ic mass' u'nit, a unit of mass, equal to ½₂ the mass of a carbon-12 atom.

atom'ic num'ber, the number of positive charges or protons in the nucleus of an atom of a given element.

atom'ic pile', reactor (def. 3). Also called **atom'ic reac'tor.**

atom'ic weight', the average weight of an atom of an element based on ½₂ the weight of a carbon-12 atom.

at·om·ism (at'ə miz'əm), *n. Philos.* the theory that minute indivisible elements are the ultimate constituents of all matter. —**at'om·ist,** *n.*

at·om·ize (at'ə mīz'), *v.t.,* **-ized, -iz·ing.** 1. to reduce to atoms. 2. to reduce to fine particles or spray. —**at'om·i·za'tion,** *n.*

at·om·iz·er (at'ə mī'zər), *n.* an apparatus for reducing liquids to a fine spray.

at'om smash'er, accelerator (def. 3).

a·ton·al (ā tōn'°l), *adj. Music.* without tonality. —**a·to·nal·i·ty** (ā'tō-nal'i tē), *n.* —**a·ton'al·ly,** *adv.*

a·tone (ə tōn'), *v.i.,* **a·toned, a·ton·ing.** to make amends or reparation. —**a·ton'a·ble, a·tone'a·ble,** *adj.* —**a·ton'er,** *n.* —**a·ton'ing·ly,** *adv.*

a·tone·ment (ə tōn'mənt), *n.* 1. satisfaction or reparation for a wrong or harmful act. 2. (*sometimes cap.*) the reconciliation of God and humankind through the life and death of Christ.

a·top (ə top'), *adj., adv.* 1. on or at the top. —*prep.* 2. on the top of.

-atory, a suffix meaning "of," "serving," or "characteristic of": *explanatory.*

ATP, an ester serving as a source of energy for physiological reactions, esp. muscle contraction.

a·tri·um (ā'trē əm), *n., pl.* **a·tri·a** (ā'trē ə). 1. the central room of an ancient Roman house. 2. either of the two upper chambers on each side of the heart. —**a'tri·al,** *adj.*

a·tro·cious (ə trō'shəs), *adj.* 1. extremely wicked, cruel, or brutal. 2. shockingly bad: *an atrocious painting.* —**a·tro'cious·ly,** *adv.* —**a·tro'cious·ness,** *n.*

a·troc·i·ty (ə tros'i tē), *n., pl.* **-ties.** 1. an atrocious act, thing, or circumstance. 2. something shockingly bad.

at·ro·phy (a'trə fē), *n., v.,* **-phied, -phy·ing.** —*n.* 1. a wasting away of the body or of an organ or part. —*v.t., v.i.* 2. to affect with or undergo atrophy.

at·ro·pine (a'trə pēn', -pin), *n.* a poisonous alkaloid obtained from belladonna, used chiefly to dilate the pupil of the eye.

att., 1. attached. 2. attention. 3. attorney.

at·tach (ə tach'), *v.t.* 1. to fasten or join, as by gluing or tying. 2. to include as a quality or condition of something. 3. to assign or attribute. 4. to bind by ties of affection or regard. 5. to take (persons or property) by legal authority. 6. to adhere or belong. —**at·tach'a·ble,** *adj.*

at·ta·ché (at'ə shā', a ta-), *n.* a diplomatic or military officer attached to an embassy or legation.

attaché' case', a briefcase with square corners and rigid sides.

at·tach·ment (ə tach'mənt), *n.* 1. the act of attaching or state of being attached. 2. devotion or regard. 3. a fastening or tie. 4. an additional or supplementary device. 5. something attached, as a document added to a letter. 6. seizure of property or person by legal authority.

at·tack (ə tak'), *v.t.* 1. to set upon violently or hostilely. 2. to blame or abuse violently or bitterly. 3. to criticize unfavorably. 4. to set about (a task) vigorously. 5. (of disease, etc.) to begin to affect. —*v.i.* 6. to rape or attempt to rape. —*n.* 7. to make an attack. —*n.* 8. onslaught or assault. 9. a seizure by disease. 10. rape or an attempted rape. —**at·tack'er,** *n.*

at·tain (ə tān'), *v.t.* 1. to reach (an end, goal, etc.), esp. by effort. 2. to come to or arrive at. —*v.i.* 3. attain to, to arrive at, esp. by effort. —**at·tain'a·ble,** *adj.* —**at·tain'a·bil'i·ty,** *n.* —**at·tain'ment,** *n.*

at·tain·der (ə tān′dər), *n.* (formerly) the loss of property and civil rights following a sentence of death.

at·taint (ə tānt′), *v.t.* to condemn by attainder.

at·tar (at′ər), *n.* a perfume obtained from flowers or petals.

at·tempt (ə tempt′), *v.t.* 1. to try to accomplish. —*n.* 2. an effort to accomplish something. 3. an attack or assault. —**at·tempt′er,** *n.* —Syn. 1. endeavor, essay, strive, undertake.

at·tend (ə tend′), *v.t.* 1. to be present at. 2. to accompany. 3. to take care of. 4. to give heed to. —*v.i.* 5. to take care or charge. 6. to apply oneself 7. to be present. —**at·tend′er,** *n.*

at·tend·ance (ə ten′dəns), *n.* 1. the act of attending. 2. the persons present.

at·tend·ant (ə ten′dənt), *n.* 1. a person who attends another. 2. that which follows from or accompanies something. 3. a person who is present. —*adj.* 4. being present or accompanying. 5. associated or related. —**at·tend′ant·ly,** *adv.*

at·ten·tion (ə ten′shən), *n.* 1. the act or faculty of directing the mind to an object. 2. observant or watchful consideration. 3. civility or courtesy. 4. *Mil.* a command to stand or sit in an erect position. —**at·ten′tive,** *adj.* —**at·ten′tive·ly,** *adv.* —**at·ten′tive·ness,** *n.*

at·ten·u·ate (*v.* ə ten′yōō āt′; *adj.* ə ten′yōō it, -āt′), *v.,* **-at·ed, -at·ing,** *adj.* —*v.t.* 1. to make slender or thin, as a thread. 2. to lessen in force, strength, or severity. —*v.i.* 3. to become attenuated. —*adj.* 4. attenuated or thin. —**at·ten′u·a′tion,** *n.*

at·test (ə test′), *v.t.* 1. to bear witness to. 2. to give proof or evidence of. —*v.i.* 3. to testify or bear witness. —**at′tes·ta′tion,** *n.*

Att. Gen., Attorney General.

at·tic (at′ik), *n.* the part of a house directly under a roof.

At·ti·la (at′ələ, ə til′ə), *n.* A.D. 406?-453, king of the Huns.

at·tire (ə tīr′), *v.,* **-tired, -tir·ing,** *n.* —*v.t.* 1. to dress, esp. in rich clothing. —*n.* 2. clothes or apparel.

at·ti·tude (at′i tōōd′, -tyōōd′), *n.* 1. manner, feeling, etc., toward a person or thing. 2. posture of the body expressive of an action, emotion, etc. 3. the inclination of an aircraft relative to the wind, ground, etc. —**at′ti·tu′di·nal,** *adj.*

at·ti·tu·di·nize (at′i tōōd′ən īz′, -tyōōd′-), *v.i.,* **-nized, -niz·ing** to assume an affected attitude.

attn., attention.

at·tor·ney (ə tûr′nē), *n.,* *pl.* **-neys.** a lawyer, esp. an attorney-at-law.

[< AF *attorne,* lit., one (who is) turned to]

at·tor·ney-at-law (ə tûr′nē ət lô′), *n.,* *pl.* **at·tor·neys-at-law.** a legal agent authorized to appear before a court as a representative of a party to a controversy.

attor′ney gen′eral, *pl.* **attorneys gen·eral, attorney generals.** the chief law officer of a country or state and head of its legal department.

at·tract (ə trakt′), *v.t.* 1. to cause to approach, adhere, or unite. 2. to draw by making an appeal to the emotion or interest. 3. to possess attraction. —**at·tract′a·ble,** *adj.* —**at·trac′tive,** *adj.* —**at·trac′tive·ly,** *adv.* —**at·trac′tive·ness,** *n.* —Syn. 2. allure, charm, entice.

at·tract·ant (ə trak′tənt), *n.* an attracting substance or agent.

at·trac·tion (ə trak′shən), *n.* 1. the act, power, or property of attracting. 2. attractive quality. 3. a person or thing that attracts. 4. *Physics.* the tendency of two bodies or particles to draw together.

attrib., 1. attributive. 2. attributively.

at·trib·ute (*v.* ə trib′yōōt; *n.* a′trə byōōt′), *v.,* **-ut·ed, -ut·ing,** *n.* —*v.t.* 1. to regard as caused by, created by, or belonging to. —*n.* 2. an inherent quality or characteristic. 3. an adjective. —**at·trib′ut·a·ble,** *adj.* —**at′tri·bu′tion,** *n.*

at·trib·u·tive (ə trib′yə tiv), *adj.* 1. of or having the character of an attribute. 2. expressing an adjective or adjective equivalent preceding the noun it modifies. —*n.* 3. an attributive word or phrase. —**at·trib′u·tive·ly,** *adv.*

at·tri·tion (ə trish′ən), *n.* 1. a wearing down by friction. 2. a gradual curtailment of personnel, esp. through resignation, retirement, etc. —**at·tri′tion·al,** *adj.*

at·tune (ə tōōn′, ə tyōōn′), *v.t.,* **-tuned, -tun·ing.** to bring into accord or harmony.

atty., attorney.

Atty. Gen., Attorney General.

ATV (ā′tē′vē′), *n.* a small automobile capable of going over any nonroad surface including water. [*a*(*ll*)-*t*(*errain*) *v*(*ehicle*)]

a·twit·ter (ə twit′ər), *adj.* nervously excited.

at. wt., See atomic weight.

a·typ·i·cal (ā tip′i kəl), *adj.* not typical or normal. —**a·typ′i·cal·ly,** *adv.*

Au, gold. [< L *aurum*]

au·burn (ô′bərn), *n.* 1. a reddish-brown color. —*adj.* 2. having auburn color.

au cou·rant (ō kōō Rän′), *French.* up-to-date.

auc·tion (ôk′shən), *n.* **1.** a public sale at which goods are sold to the highest bidder. —*v.t.* **2.** to sell by auction.

auc′tion bridge′, a variety of bridge in which tricks won in excess of the contract are scored toward game.

auc·tion·eer (ôk′shə nēr′), *n.* a person who conducts an auction.

auc·to·ri·al (ôk tōr′ē əl, -tôr′-), *adj. Rare.* of or pertaining to an author.

aud., **1.** audit. **2.** auditor.

au·da·cious (ô dā′shəs), *adj.* **1.** extremely bold or daring. **2.** insolent or brazen. —**au·da′cious·ly,** *adv.* —**au·da′cious·ness,** *n.* —**au·dac·i·ty** (ô das′i tē), *n.* —**Syn. 1.** adventurous, foolhardy, rash.

au·di·ble (ô′də bəl), *adj.* loud enough to be heard. —**au′di·bil′i·ty,** *n.* —**au′di·bly,** *adv.*

au·di·ence (ô′dē əns), *n.* **1.** the listeners or viewers collectively, as at a theater. **2.** the persons reached by a book, radio broadcast, etc. **3.** a formal interview, esp. with a dignitary.

au·di·o (ô′dē ō′), *adj.* **1.** of or using sound or audio frequencies. **2.** of or used in the transmission, reception, or reproduction of sound or audio frequencies. —*n.* **3.** the audio elements of television. **4.** audio equipment.

au′dio fre′quency, a frequency between 15 and 20,000 cycles per second, within the range of normally audible sound.

au·di·ol·o·gy (ô′dē ol′ə jē), *n.* the science of hearing that includes the treatment of persons with impaired hearing. —**au′di·o·log′i·cal** (ô′dē ə loj′i kəl), *adj.* —**au′di·ol′o·gist,** *n.*

au·di·om·e·ter (ô′dē om′i tər), *n.* an instrument for gauging and recording the power of hearing. —**au′di·o·met′ric** (-ə me′trik), *adj.*

au·di·o·phile (ô′dē ə fīl′), *n.* a person who is especially interested in high-fidelity sound reproduction.

au·di·o·tape (ô′dē ō tāp′), *n.* a magnetic tape for recording or reproducing sound.

au·di·o·vis·u·al (ô′dē ō vizh′ōō əl), *adj.* **1.** using media of sound and sight (other than printed materials), such as films, recordings, etc., for education. —*n.* **2.** Usually, **audiovisuals.** audiovisual materials or equipment.

au·dit (ô′dit), *n.* **1.** a formal examination and verification of financial records. —*v.t.* **2.** to make an audit of. **3.** to attend (classes, etc.) as an auditor. —*v.i.* **4.** to make an audit.

au·di·tion (ô dish′ən), *n.* **1.** a trial hearing given to an actor, actress, musician, etc. —*v.t., v.i.* **2.** to try in an audition.

au·di·tor (ô′di tər), *n.* **1.** a person who audits financial records. **2.** a university student registered for a course without receiving credit.

au·di·to·ri·um (ô′di tōr′ē əm, -tôr′-), *n., pl.* **-to·ri·ums, -to·ri·a** (-tōr′ē ə, -tôr′-). **1.** the space set apart for the audience in a public building. **2.** a building for public gatherings.

au·di·to·ry (ô′di tōr′ē, -tôr′ē), *adj.* of hearing or the organs of hearing.

auf Wie·der·seh·en (ouf vē′dər zā′ən), *German.* until we meet again.

Aug., August.

au·ger (ô′gər), *n.* a boring tool, similar to a gimlet.

aught (ôt), *n.* a zero or cipher (0).

aug·ment (ôg ment′), *v.t., v.i.* to increase in size or effect. —**aug·ment′er,** *n.* —**aug′men·ta′tion,** *n.*

au gra·tin (ō grät′ən, ō grat′ən), with a topping of browned crumbs and grated cheese.

au·gur (ô′gər), *n.* **1.** a diviner, esp. from omens. —*v.t.* **2.** to predict, as from omens. **3.** to betoken. —*v.i.* **4.** to be a sign or omen.

au·gu·ry (ô′gyə rē), *n., pl.* **-ries. 1.** divination from omens. **2.** an omen or token.

au·gust (ô gust′), *adj.* inspiring awe and reverence. —**au·gust′ly,** *adv.* —**au·gust′ness,** *n.*

Au·gust (ô′gəst), *n.* the eighth month of the year, containing 31 days.

Au·gus·ta (ô gus′tə), *n.* the capital of Maine.

Au·gus·tan (ô gus′tən), *adj.* of or characteristic of the rule or times of Augustus Caesar, the first Roman emperor.

Au·gus·tine (ô′gə stēn′), *n.* **Saint,** A.D. 354–430, Latin church father. —**Au·gus·tin·i·an** (ô′gə stin′ē ən), *adj.*

Au·gus·tus (ô gus′təs), *n.* 63 B.C.–A.D. 14, first Roman emperor.

au jus (ō zhōōs′, ō jōō′), (of meat) served in its natural juices.

auk (ôk), *n.* a diving bird of northern seas, having webbed feet and small wings.

auld lang syne (ôld′ lang zīn′, -sīn′), *Scot.* old times.

aunt (ant, änt), *n.* **1.** the sister of one's father or mother. **2.** the wife of one's uncle.

au pair (ō pɛr′), *French.* exchanging services for board and room, usually by a young foreign visitor.

au·ra (ôr′ə), *n.* **1.** a subtly pervasive quality surrounding a person or thing. **2.** an invisible radiation.

au·ral (ôr′əl), *adj.* of the ear or the sense of hearing. —**au′ral·ly,** *adv.*

au·re·ate (ôr′ē it, -āt′), *adj.* **1.** golden-colored. **2.** brilliant or splendid. —**au′re·ate·ly,** *adv.* —**au′re·ate·ness,** *n.*

au·re·ole (ôr′ē ōl′), *n.* halo (defs. 1, 3). Also, **au·re·o·la** (ô rē′ə lə).

Au·re·o·my·cin (ôr′ē ō mī′sin), *n. Trademark.* an antibiotic.

au re·voir (ō Rə VWAR′), *French.* goodbye.

au·ri·cle (ôr′i kəl), *n.* **1. a.** the outer portion of the ear. **b.** an ear-shaped appendage projecting from each atrium of the heart. **2.** *Bot., Zool.* a part like an ear. —**au′ri·cled,** *adj.*

au·ric·u·lar (ô rik′yə lər), *adj.* **1.** aural. **2.** perceived by the ear. **3.** shaped like an ear. **4.** pertaining to an auricle of the heart. —**au·ric′u·lar·ly,** *adv.*

au·rif·er·ous (ô rif′ər əs), *adj.* yielding or containing gold.

Au·ro·ra (ô rôr′ə, ô rōr′ə), *n.* **1.** the ancient Roman goddess of the dawn. **2.** (*l.c.*) a radiant luminous emission sporadically seen in night skies of both hemispheres.

auro′ra aus·tra′lis (ô strā′lis), the aurora of the Southern Hemisphere.

auro′ra bo·re·al′is (bôr′ē al′is, bōr′-), the aurora of the Northern Hemisphere.

au·ro·ral (ô rôr′əl, ô rōr′-), *adj.* of or resembling an aurora.

AUS, Army of the United States.

aus·cul·ta·tion (ô′skəl tā′shən), *n.* the act of listening, usually through a stethoscope, to sounds within the body, as a method of diagnosis. —**aus′cul·tate,** *v.t., v.i.*

aus·pice (ô′spis), *n.* **1.** Usually, **auspices.** approving support. **2.** divination, esp. from flight of birds, as by ancient Romans. **3.** any omen or sign.

aus·pi·cious (ô spish′əs), *adj.* promising a good outcome. —**aus·pi′cious·ly,** *adv.* —**aus·pi′cious·ness,** *n.*

Aus·sie (ô′sē), *n. Slang.* an Australian.

Aust., **1.** Austria. **2.** Austrian.

Aus·ten (ô′stən), *n.* **Jane,** 1775–1817, English novelist.

aus·tere (ô stēr′), *adj.* **1.** severely stern or strict, as in manner. **2.** frugal or thrifty. **3.** without ornament. —**aus·tere′ly,** *adv.* —**aus·tere′ness,** *n.* —**aus·ter·i·ty** (ô ster′i tē), *n.*

Aus·tin (ô′stən), *n.* the capital of Texas.

aus·tral (ô′strəl), *adj. Geodesy.* southern.

Aus·tral·ia (ô strāl′yə), *n.* **1.** a continent SE of Asia, between the Indian and the Pacific Oceans. **2.** a

country consisting of this continent and an island state. —**Aus·tral′ian,** *adj., n.*

Austral′ian bal′lot, a ballot to be marked in secret containing the names of all the candidates for public office.

Aus·tri·a (ô′strē ə), *n.* a country in central Europe. —**Aus′tri·an,** *adj., n.*

Aus·tro·ne·sia (ô′strō nē′zhə), *n.* the islands of the central and S Pacific.

Aus·tro·ne·sian (ô′strō nē′zhən, -shən), *adj.* of Austronesia or the Austronesian family of languages.

auth., **1.** authentic. **2.** author. **3.** authority. **4.** authorized.

au·then·tic (ô then′tik), *adj.* **1.** factually accurate or reliable, as a report. **2.** being what it is represented or claimed to be: *authentic Japanese cuisine.* —**au·then′ti·cal·ly,** *adv.* —**au·then·tic·i·ty** (ô′thin tis′i tē, -then-), *n.* —Syn. **2.** genuine, real.

au·then·ti·cate (ô then′tə kāt′), *v.t.,* **-cat·ed, -cat·ing.** to establish as authentic. —**au·then′ti·ca′tion,** *n.* —**au·then′ti·ca′tor,** *n.*

au·thor (ô′thər), *n.* **1.** a person who writes a literary work. **2.** any creator or originator. —*v.t.* **3.** to be the author of. —**au′thor·ess,** *n.fem.*

au·thor·i·tar·i·an (ə thôr′i ter′ē ən, ə thor′-), *adj.* **1.** favoring complete subjection to authority. **2.** of a political system in which individual freedom is subordinate to the authority of the state. —*n.* **3.** a person who favors or acts according to authoritarian principles. —**au·thor′i·tar′i·an·ism,** *n.*

au·thor·i·ta·tive (ə thôr′i tā′tiv, ə thor′-), *adj.* **1.** having the sanction of authority. **2.** accepted by most authorities in a field. —**au·thor′i·ta′tive·ly,** *adv.*

au·thor·i·ty (ə thôr′i tē, ə thor′-), *n., pl.* **-ties.** **1.** the power to judge, act, or command. **2.** a person or body of persons in whom such power is vested. **3.** a person having the legal power to make and enforce the law. **4.** an accepted source of information, etc. **5.** an expert on a subject. **6.** persuasive force.

au·thor·ize (ô′thə rīz′), *v.t.,* **-ized, -iz·ing.** **1.** to give authority or power to. **2.** to sanction formally. **3.** *Archaic.* to warrant or justify. Also, esp. *Brit.,* **au′thor·ise′.** —**au′thor·i·za′tion,** *n.*

Au′thorized Ver′sion, an English version of the Bible prepared under King James I and published in 1611.

au·thor·ship (ô′thər ship′), *n.* **1.** the occupation of an author. **2.** origin of a piece of writing.

au·tism (ô′tiz əm), *n. Psychol.* self-absorption, esp. extreme withdrawal into fantasy. —**au·tis·tic** (ô tis′tik), *adj.*

au·to (ô′tō), *n.*, *pl.* **-tos.** automobile.

auto-, a prefix meaning "self" or "same": *autograph.*

auto., 1. automatic. 2. automobile. 3. automotive.

au·to·bahn (ô′tə bän′), *n.* (in Germany) a superhighway.

au·to·bi·og·ra·phy (ô′tə bī og′rə fē, -bē-), *n.*, *pl.* **-phies.** an account of a person's life written by himself or herself. —**au′to·bi·og′ra·pher,** *n.* —**au·to·bi·o·graph·i·cal** (ô′tə bī′ə graf′i kəl), **au′to·bi′o·graph′ic,** *adj.*

au·toch·tho·nous (ô tok′thə nəs), *adj.* indigenous, as a plant.

au·to·clave (ô′tə klāv′), *n.* an apparatus using steam under pressure, esp. for sterilizing medical equipment.

au·toc·ra·cy (ô tok′rə sē), *n.*, *pl.* **-cies.** 1. unlimited authority over others, invested in a single person. 2. a nation or community ruled by an autocrat.

au·to·crat (ô′tə krat′), *n.* 1. a ruler who holds unlimited powers. 2. a domineering person. —**au′to·crat′ic** (ô′tə krat′ik), *adj.* —**au′to·crat′i·cal·ly,** *adv.*

au·to·di·dact (ô′tō dī′dakt, -dī dakt′), *n.* a self-taught person.

au·to·gi·ro (ô′tə jī′rō), *n.*, *pl.* **-ros.** an aircraft having a propeller for forward motion and a horizontal rotor for lift. Also, **au′to·gy′ro.**

au·to·graph (ô′tə graf′, -gräf′), *n.* 1. a person's signature, esp. for keeping as a memento. 2. a handwritten letter or document, esp. as a collector's item. 3. an ancient or medieval manuscript produced by the author himself. —*v.t.* 4. to sign, esp. as a memento: *to autograph a book.*

au·to·hyp·no·sis (ô′tō hip nō′sis), *n.* self-induced hypnosis or hypnotic state.

au·to·in·tox·i·ca·tion (ô′tō in tok′sə kā′shən), *n.* poisoning with toxic substances formed within the body.

au·to·mat (ô′tə mat′), *n.* a restaurant using coin-operated equipment to dispense food.

au·to·mate (ô′tə māt′), *v.t., v.i.,* **-mat·ed, -mat·ing.** to operate by or undergo automation.

au·to·mat·ic (ô′tə mat′ik), *adj.* 1. self-moving or self-acting. 2. occurring independently of volition or intention. 3. (of a firearm) capable of continuous operation. 4. unconsciously mechanical. —*n.* 5. an automatic rifle, pistol, etc. —**au′to·mat′i·cal·ly,** *adv.*

au·to·mat·ic pi·lot, a control system that automatically maintains an aircraft on a preset heading and altitude.

au·to·ma·tion (ô′tə mā′shən), *n.* the technique or system of operating a mechanical process by highly automatic means, as by electronic devices, reducing human intervention to a minimum.

au·tom·a·tism (ô tom′ə tiz′əm), *n.* action or condition of being automatic, esp. mechanically. —**au·tom′a·ti·za′tion** (-za′shən), *n.* —**au·tom′a·tize′,** *v.t.*

au·tom·a·ton (ô tom′ə ton′, -t°n), *n., pl.* **-tons, -ta** (-tə). 1. a robot. 2. a person who acts in a monotonous, routine manner.

au·to·mo·bile (ô′tə mə bēl′, ô′tə mə-bēl′, ô′tə mō′bēl, -bil), *n.* 1. a passenger vehicle for operation on ordinary roads, typically having four wheels and an internal-combustion gasoline engine. —*adj.* 2. automotive. —**au·to·mo·bil·ist** (ô′tə-mə bē′list, -mō′bi list), *n.*

au·to·mo·tive (ô′tə mō′tiv, ô′tə mō′-tiv), *adj.* 1. of or pertaining to automobiles and motorcycles. 2. propelled by a self-contained motor.

au·ton·o·mic nerv·ous sys·tem (ô′tə-nom′ik), the system of nerves that innervates the heart, viscera, and glands and controls their involuntary functions, consisting of a sympathetic and a parasympathetic division.

au·ton·o·mous (ô ton′ə məs), *adj.* 1. self-governing. 2. of a self-governing state, organization, etc. —**au·ton′o·mous·ly,** *adv.* —**au·ton′o·my,** *n.*

au·to·pi·lot (ô′tō pī′lət), *n.* See **automatic pilot.**

au·top·sy (ô′top sē, ô′təp-), *n., pl.* **-sies.** examination of a body after death, as for determination of the cause of death.

au·to·stra·da (ô′tō strä′də), *n.* an Italian superhighway.

au·to·sug·ges·tion (ô′tō səg jes′chən), *n. Psychol.* suggestion arising from oneself, esp. in the hope of changing behavior.

au·tumn (ô′təm), *n.* the season between summer and winter. —**autum·nal** (ô tum′n°l), *adj.*

autum′nal e′quinox. See under **equinox.**

aux., auxiliary. Also, **auxil.**

aux·il·ia·ry (ôg zil′yə rē, -zil′ə-), *adj., n., pl.* **-ries.** —*adj.* 1. giving additional help. 2. supplemental or subsidiary. —*n.* 3. an auxiliary person, thing, or group. 4. See **auxiliary verb.**

auxil′iary verb′, a word used with a main verb to express distinctions of tense, voice, mood, etc.

aux·in (ôk′sin), *n.* a class of substances that regulate or modify the growth of plants.

av., 1. avenue. **2.** average. **3.** avoirdupois.

A/V, 1. ad valorem. **2.** Also, **A-V** audiovisual.

A.V., 1. audiovisual. **2.** See **Authorized Version.**

a·vail (ə vāl′), *v.t., v.i.* **1.** to be of use or value (to). **2. avail oneself of,** to use to one's advantage. —*n.* **3.** advantage or use: *of little avail.*

a·vail·a·ble (ə vā′lə bəl), *adj.* **1.** ready for use. **2.** readily obtainable. —**a·vail·a·bil·i·ty** (ə vā′lə bil′i tē), *n.*

av·a·lanche (av′ə lanch′, -länch′), *n.* **1.** a large mass of detached snow, ice, etc., sliding suddenly down a mountain slope. **2.** an overwhelming suddenness and destructiveness.

a·vant-garde (ə vänt′gärd′), *n.* **1.** the advance group in any movement, esp. in the arts. —*adj.* **2.** of the experimental treatment of artistic material. **3.** belonging to the avant-garde.

av·a·rice (av′ər is), *n.* insatiable greed for riches. —**av·a·ri·cious** (av′ə rish′əs), *adj.* —**av·a·ri′cious·ly,** *adv.*

a·vast (ə vast′, ə väst′), *interj. Naut.* stop!

av·a·tar (av′ə tär′), *n. Hindu Myth.* the incarnation of a god.

a·vaunt (ə vônt′), *interj. Archaic.* go away!

avdp., avoirdupois.

a·ve (ä′vā, ä′vē), *interj.* **1.** hail! **2.** farewell!

ave., avenue.

A·ve Ma·ri·a (ä′vā mə rē′ə), a prayer and salutation to the Virgin Mary. Also, **A·ve Mar·y** (ä′vē mâr′ē, ä′vā).

a·venge (ə venj′), *v.t., v.i.* **a·venged, a·veng·ing.** —*v.t.* **1.** to take vengeance for. **2.** to take vengeance on behalf of. —*v.i.* **3.** to take vengeance. —**a·veng′er,** *n.* —**a·veng′ing·ly,** *adv.*

av·e·nue (av′ə nyōō′, -nōō′), *n.* **1.** a wide street or main thoroughfare. **2.** means of access or attainment.

a·ver (ə vûr′), *v.t.,* **a·verred, a·ver·ring.** to declare positively. —**a·ver′ment,** *n.*

av·er·age (av′ər ij, av′rij), *n., adj., v.,* **-aged, -ag·ing.** —*n.* **1.** a typical amount, rate, etc. **2.** *Math.* a quantity intermediate to a set of quantities. **3.** See **arithmetic mean. 4. on the** or **an average,** usually or typically. —*adj.* **5.** of an average. **6.** typical or ordinary. —*v.t.* **7.** to find an average value for. **8.** to amount to, as a mean quantity.

—*v.i.* **9.** to have an average. **10. average out,** to reach an average finally.

a·verse (ə vûrs′), *adj.* strongly opposed or unwilling.

a·ver·sion (ə vûr′zhən, -shən), *n.* **1.** a strong desire to avoid because of dislike. **2.** a cause or object of dislike.

a·vert (ə vûrt′), *v.t.* **1.** to turn away or aside. **2.** to ward off or prevent.

avg., average.

a·vi·an (ā′vē ən), *adj.* of birds.

a·vi·ar·y (ā′vē er′ē), *n., pl.* **-ar·ies.** a large enclosure in which birds are kept. —**a′vi·a·rist,** *n.*

a·vi·a·tion (ā′vē ā′shən, av′ē-), *n.* **1.** the science of flying by aircraft. **2.** the design, development, and production of aircraft. [< F = L *avi(s)* bird + *-ation*]

a·vi·a·tor (ā′vē ā′tər, av′ē-), *n.* an aircraft pilot. —**a′vi·a·trix** (-triks), *n.fem.*

av·id (av′id), *adj.* **1.** greedily desirous. **2.** enthusiastic or dedicated. —**a·vid·i·ty** (ə vid′i tē), *n.* —**av′id·ly,** *adv.*

a·vi·on·ics (ā′vē on′iks, av′ē-), *n.* the science and technology of electrical and electronic devices in aviation. —**a′vi·on′ic,** *adj.*

a·vi·ta·min·o·sis (ā vī′tə mə nō′sis), *n.* any disease caused by a lack of one or more vitamins. —**a·vi·ta·min·ot·ic** (ā vī′tə mə not′ik), *adj.*

av·o·ca·do (av′ə kä′dō, ä′və-), *n., pl.* **-dos. 1.** a tropical American fruit, green in color, pear-shaped, and eaten raw. **2.** the tree.

av·o·ca·tion (av′ə kā′shən), *n.* a minor occupation or hobby pursued in addition to one's regular work. —**av′o·ca′tion·al,** *adj.*

av·o·cet (av′ə set′), *n.* a long-legged, web-footed shore bird having a long, slender bill.

a·void (ə void′), *v.t.* to keep or stay away from, as danger. —**a·void′a·ble,** *adj.* —**a·void′a·bly,** *adv.* —**a·void′ance,** *n.* —**a·void′er,** *n.* —**Syn.** elude, escape, evade, shun.

av·oir·du·pois (av′ər də poiz′), *n.* **1.** See **avoirdupois weight. 2.** *Informal.* bodily heaviness.

avoirdupois′ weight′, the system of weights in Britain and the U.S. based on 16 ounces per pound.

a·vouch (ə vouch′), *v.t.* **1.** to make frank affirmation of. **2.** to guarantee.

a·vow (ə vou′), *v.t.* to declare frankly or openly. —**a·vow′al,** *n.* —**a·vowed′,** *adj.* —**a·vow′ed·ly,** *adv.*

a·vun·cu·lar (ə vung′kyə lər), *adj.* of or characteristic of an uncle.

aw (ô), *interj.* (an exclamation of protest, disgust, etc.)

A/W, actual weight.

a·wait (ə wāt′), *v.t.* 1. to wait for. 2. to be in store for. —*v.i.* 3. to wait.

a·wake (ə wāk′), *v.,* **a·woke** or **a·waked, a·wak·ing,** *adj.* —*v.t., v.i.* 1. to rouse from sleep. 2. to become active. 3. to come to an awareness. —*adj.* 4. not sleeping. 5. alert or watchful.

a·wak·en (ə wā′kən), *v.t., v.i.* awake. —**a·wak′en·ing,** *adj., n.*

a·ward (ə wôrd′), *v.t.* 1. to give as merited or due: *to award prizes.* 2. to assign by judicial decree. —*n.* 3. something awarded as a prize. 4. the decision of an arbitrator.

a·ware (ə wâr′), *adj.* having knowledge, esp. in a keenly responsive way. —**a·ware′ness,** *n.* —**Syn.** cognizant, conscious, knowing.

a·wash (ə wosh′, ə wôsh′), *adj., adv.* 1. scarcely above the surface of the water. 2. covered with water. 3. washing about.

a·way (ə wā′), *adv.* 1. from this or that place: *to go away.* 2. far or apart: *away back.* 3. aside or to another place: *to turn your eyes away.* 4. out of one's possession or use: *to give money away.* 5. out of existence or notice: *to fade away.* 6. continuously: *He kept on hammering away.* 7. without hesitation: *Fire away!* 8. **away with,** a. take away. b. go away! leave! 9. **do away with,** a. to abolish or stop. b. to kill. —*adj.* 10. absent: *away from home.* 11. distant: *six miles away.*

awe (ô), *n., v.,* awed, aw·ing. —*n.* 1. an overwhelming feeling of reverence, fear, etc. —*v.t.* 2. to inspire with awe.

a·wea·ry (ə wēr′ē), *adj.* wearied or tired.

a·weigh (ə wā′), *adj.* Naut. (of an anchor) just free of the bottom.

awe·some (ô′səm), *adj.* inspiring awe. —**awe′some·ly,** *adv.* —**awe′some·ness,** *n.*

awe-struck (ô′struk′), *adj.* filled with awe. Also, **awe-strick·en** (ô′strik′-ən).

aw·ful (ô′fəl), *adj.* 1. extremely bad or unpleasant. 2. inspiring fear or dread. 3. inspiring awe. —*adv.* 4. *Informal.* very or extremely. —**aw′-ful·ness,** *n.*

—**Usage.** In informal use, there is no objection to AWFUL in the sense of "very bad, ugly, etc.," but it has been so overworked that it is ineffective.

aw·ful·ly (ô′fə lē, ôf′lē), *adv.* 1. very or extremely. 2. in an awful manner.

a·while (ə hwīl′, ə wīl′), *adv.* for a short time or period.

a·whirl (ə hwûrl′, ə wûrl′), *adj.* rotating rapidly.

awk·ward (ôk′wərd), *adj.* 1. not graceful in bearing. 2. not skillful in movement or behavior. 3. unwieldy or unmanageable. 4. embarrassing or inconvenient. —**awk′ward·ly,** *adv.* —**awk′ward·ness,** *n.* —**Syn.** 2. clumsy, gauche, inept.

awl (ôl), *n.* a pointed instrument for piercing small holes.

awn (ôn), *n.* any of the bristles on a spike of a grass plant. —**awned,** *adj.*

awn·ing (ô′ning), *n.* a rooflike shelter of canvas or other material before a door, etc., to provide protection from the sun.

a·woke (ə wōk′), *v.* a pt. and pp. of awake.

AWOL (*pronounced as initials or* ā′wôl), *Mil.* absent without leave. Also, **awol**

a·wry (ə rī′), *adv., adj.* 1. with a turn or twist to one side: *to look awry.* 2. amiss or wrong.

ax (aks), *n., pl.* **ax·es** (ak′siz), *v.,* axed, ax·ing. —*n.* 1. an implement with a bladed head on a handle, used for chopping, etc. 2. **get the ax,** *Informal.* to be dismissed summarily. 3. **have an ax to grind,** *Informal.* to have a personal motive. —*v.t.* 4. to shape or chop with an ax. Also, **axe.**

ax., axiom.

ax·i·al (ak′sē əl), *adj.* 1. of, characterized by, or forming an axis. 2. situated in or on the axis. —**ax′i·al·ly,** *adv.*

ax·i·om (ak′sē əm), *n.* 1. a self-evident truth. 2. a universally accepted principle or rule. 3. a proposition assumed without proof for the sake of studying its consequences. —**ax·i·o·mat·ic** (ak′sē ə-mat′ik), *adj.* —**ax′i·o·mat′i·cal·ly,** *adv.*

ax·is (ak′sis), *n., pl.* **ax·es** (ak′sēz). 1. the line about which a rotating body turns or may be supposed to turn. 2. a central line bisecting a body or form and in relation to which symmetry is determined. 3. a central or principal structure, about which something is arranged. 4. *Geom.* any line used as a fixed reference in conjunction with one or more other references. 5. an alliance between two or more major countries.

ax·le (ak′səl), *n.* a spindle or shaft on which a wheel rotates.

ax·le·tree (ak′səl trē′), *n.* a fixed bar with a rounded spindle at each end upon which a cartwheel rotates.

Ax′min·ster car′pet (aks′min′stər), a carpet having an even yarn pile that is usually cut.

ax·on (ak′son), *n. Anat.* the appendage of the neuron that transmits impulses away from the cell. Also, **ax·one** (ak′sōn).

ay[1] (ī), *adv., n.* aye[1].

ay[2] (ā), *adv. Archaic.* ever or always.

a·yah (ä′yə), *n.* (in India) a native maid or nurse.

a·ya·tol·lah (ä′yə tō′lə), *n.* **1.** a Muslim scholar with advanced knowledge of Islamic law. **2.** (*cap.*) his title. [< Pers < Ar *āyat* sign or token (of) + ALLAH]

aye[1] (ī), *adv.* **1.** yes. —*n.* **2.** an affirmative vote or voter.

aye[2] (ā), *adv. Archaic.* ay[2].

AZ, Arizona.

az., azimuth.

a·zal·ea (ə zāl′yə), *n.* any of numerous ornamental shrubs with variously colored flowers.

az·i·muth (az′ə məth), *n.* **1.** the arc of the horizon measured clockwise from the south point, in astronomy, or from the north point, in navigation. **2.** the angle of horizontal deviation. —**az·i·muth·al** (az′ə-muth′əl), *adj.*

A·zores (ə zōrz′, ə zôrz′, ā′zōrz, ā′zôrz), *n.* a group of Portuguese islands in the N Atlantic, W of Portugal.

Az·tec (az′tek), *n.* **1.** a member of an Indian people whose empire in Mexico was conquered by Spaniards in 1519. **2.** their language. —**Az′tec·an,** *adj.*

az·ure (azh′ər, ā′zhər), *adj.* **1.** of a sky-blue color. —*n.* **2.** the blue of a clear sky.

B

B, b (bē), *n., pl.* **B's** or **Bs, b's** or **bs.** the second letter of the English alphabet, a consonant.

B, *Chess.* bishop.

B, 1. the second in order or in a series. **2.** a grade that indicates good academic work, etc., but not of the highest quality. **3.** the seventh tone in the scale of C major. **4.** a mediocre or poor motion picture. **5.** *Chem.* boron.

B., 1. bachelor. **2.** bacillus. **3.** *Baseball.* base. **4.** bass. **5.** basso. **6.** Bible. **7.** book. **8.** born. **9.** British.

b., 1. bachelor. **2.** *Baseball.* base. **3.** bass. **4.** basso. **5.** blend of; blended. **6.** book. **7.** born. **8.** breadth. **9.** brother.

Ba, barium.

B.A., 1. Bachelor of Arts. **2.** British Academy. **3.** British Association (for the Advancement of Science).

baa (ba, bä), *n., v.,* **baaed, baa·ing.** bleat.

Ba·al (bā′əl), *n., pl.* **Ba·al·im** (bā′ə-lim). **1.** the fertility god of an ancient Semitic people. **2.** (*sometimes l.c.*) a false god.

ba·ba (bä′bə), *n.* a leavened cake, usually made with raisins and soaked in rum.

Bab′bitt (bab′it), *n.* a self-satisfied person who conforms readily to middle-class attitudes. [after character in *Babbitt*, by Sinclair Lewis (1885–1951), U.S. novelist]

Bab′bitt met′al, an alloy of tin with antimony and copper, used as an antifriction lining for bearings. Also, **bab′bitt met′al.**

bab·ble (bab′əl), *v.,* **-bled, -bling.** —*v.i.* **1.** to utter sounds or words indistinctly. **2.** to talk irrationally or excessively. **3.** to make a continuous, murmuring sound. —*v.t.* **4.** to utter in a foolish or meaningless manner. **5.** to reveal thoughtlessly. —*n.* **6.** the act or sound of babbling. —**bab′bler,** *n.*

babe (bāb), *n.* **1.** a baby or small child. **2.** *Slang.* baby (def. 4). **babe in the woods,** an innocent, helpless person.

ba·bel (bā′bəl, bab′əl), *n.* **1.** a confused mixture of sounds or voices. **2.** a scene of noise and confusion. [< Heb *Bābel* Babylon? *Gen.* 11:4–9]

ba·boon (ba bōōn′), *n.* a large monkey of Africa and Arabia, having a doglike muzzle and a short tail. —**ba·boon′ish,** *adj.*

ba·bush·ka (bə bōōsh′kə, -bōōsh′-), *n.* a woman's scarf, used as a hood tied under the chin.

ba·by (bā′bē), *n., pl.* **-bies,** *adj., v.,* **-bied, -by·ing.** —*n.* **1.** a very young child, esp. an infant. **2.** the youngest member of a family or group. **3.** an immature or childish person. **4.** *Slang.* a girl or woman, esp. an attractive one. **5.** *Slang.* a project or object eliciting a person's special attention or pride. —*adj.* **6.** of, suitable for, or like a baby. —*v.t.* **7.** to pamper. —**ba′by·hood,** *n.* —**ba′by·ish,** *adj.*

ba′by beef′, the beef of a calf 12 to 20 months old.

ba·by car·riage, a small, four-wheeled vehicle with a canopy for pushing an infant about. Also called **ba·by bug·gy.**

ba·by grand', the smallest form of grand piano.

Bab·y·lon (bab'ə lən, -lon'), *n.* the capital of Babylonia: noted for luxury and wickedness.

Bab·y·lo·ni·a (bab'ə lō'nē ə), *n.* an ancient empire in SW Asia. — **Bab'y·lo'ni·an,** *adj., n.*

ba·by's-breath (bā'bēz breth'), *n.* a tall herb having numerous small, fragrant, white or pink flowers.

ba·by-sit (bā'bē sit'), *v.i.,* -sat, -sit-ting. to take charge of a child or children while the parents are temporarily away. — **ba'by sit'ter.**

bac·ca·lau·re·ate (bak'ə lôr'ē it), *n.* 1. See **bachelor's degree.** 2. a sermon delivered at a commencement.

bac·ca·rat (bä'kə rä', bak'ə-), *n.* a French gambling game played with cards. Also, **bac'ca·ra'.**

bac·cha·nal (bä'kə näl', bak'ə nal'), *n.* 1. a follower of Bacchus. 2. an occasion of drunken revelry.

bac·cha·na·li·a (bak'ə nā'lē ə, -näl'-yə), *n., pl.* -li·a, -li·as. a drunken feast. — **bac'cha·na'li·an,** *adj., n.*

Bac·chus (bak'əs), *n.* the Greek and Roman god of wine. — **Bac'chic,** *adj.*

Bach (bäкн), *n.* **Jo·hann Se·bas·ti·an** (yō'hän si bas'сhən), 1685-1750, German composer and organist.

bach·e·lor (bach'ə lər, bach'lər), *n.* 1. an unmarried man. 2. a person who has been graduated to a bachelor's degree. [< OF < VL *baccalār(is)* farm hand] — **bach'e·lor·hood',** **bach'e·lor·ship',** *n.*

bach·e·lor's-but·ton (bach'ə lərz but'-ən, bach'lərz-), *n.* a plant with round flower heads, esp. the corn-flower.

bach'elor's degree', a degree award-ed by a college or university to a person who has completed his or her undergraduate studies.

ba·cil·lus (bə sil'əs), *n., pl.* -cil·li (-sil'ī). 1. any of several rod-shaped, aerobic bacteria that produce spores. 2. any bacterium. — **bac·il·lar·y** (bas'ə ler'ē), *adj.*

back¹ (bak), *n.* 1. the rear part of the human body. 2. the part of the body of animals corresponding to the human back. 3. the area or part that forms the rear. 4. the spine or backbone. 5. *Sports.* a player whose regular position is behind the line, forward line, etc. 6. **in back of** or **back of,** behind. 7. **turn one's back on, a.** to leave behind, as in anger. **b.** to forsake or neglect. — *v.t.* 8. to support or help,

as with money: *to back a Broad-way play.* 9. to substantiate with evidence or reasoning. 10. to bet on. 11. to cause to move backward. — *v.i.* 12. to go or move backward. 13. **back down,** to abandon an argument or claim. 14. **back off,** to back away from something. 15. **back out** or **out of,** to fail to keep an engagement or promise. 16. **back up, a.** to bring or come to a stand-still. **b.** to move backward. **c.** to support. — *adj.* 17. situated at or in the rear. 18. pertaining to the past: *back files.* 19. in arrears or overdue: *back pay.* 20. moving backward. — **back'-less,** *adj.*

back² (bak), *adv.* 1. at, to, or toward the rear. 2. in or into the past. 3. at or toward the original starting place or condition. 4. in direct return. 5. in a state of restraint or retention. 6. **back and forth,** backward and forward. 7. **go back on, a.** to betray. **b.** to fail to keep.

back·ache (bak'āk'), *n.* a pain esp. in the lumbar region of the back.

back·bench·er (bak'ben'chər), *n.* any of the members of a British legislature except the party leaders.

back·bite (bak'bīt'), *v.t., v.i.,* -bit, -bit·ten or -bit, -bit·ing. to slander (an absent person). — **back'bit'er,** *n.*

back·board (bak'bôrd', -bōrd'), *n.* 1. a board placed at or forming the back of anything. 2. *Basketball.* a board to which the basket is at-tached.

back·bone (bak'bōn'), *n.* 1. See **spi-nal column.** 2. strength of charac-ter. 3. a major support.

back·break·ing (bak'brā'king), *adj.* demanding great effort, endurance, etc.

back' burn'er, *Informal.* a state of low priority: *The matter is now on the back burner.*

back·date (bak dāt'), *v.t.,* -dat·ed, -dat·ing. antedate (def. 2).

back·drop (bak'drop'), *n.* 1. the rear curtain of a stage setting. 2. the setting of an event.

back·er (bak'ər), *n.* 1. a supporter or sponsor. 2. a bettor on a con-testant.

back·field (bak'fēld'), *n. Football.* 1. the players stationed behind the linemen. 2. the area stationed by these players.

back·fire (bak'fīr'), *v.,* -fired, -fir-ing, *n.* — *v.i.* 1. to have a prema-ture explosion in the intake mani-fold of an internal-combustion engine. 2. to result in consequences that were to be avoided. — *n.* 3. premature explosion in the intake manifold of an internal-combustion engine.

back′ forma′tion, the creation of a word by dropping the apparent affix in another word, as *typewrite* from *typewriter.*

back·gam·mon (bak′gam′ən), *n.* a game for two persons played on a board, with pieces moved in accordance with throws of the dice.

back·ground (bak′ground′), *n.* 1. the parts situated in the rear, as in a scene. 2. the circumstances whose understanding gives meaning to a fact, event, etc. 3. a person's origin, education, experience, etc. 4. a subordinate or unobtrusive accompaniment.

back·hand (bak′hand′), *n.* 1. (in tennis, squash, etc.) a stroke made from the side of the body opposite to that of the hand holding the racket, paddle, etc. 2. handwriting that slopes toward the left. —*adj.* 3. backhanded. —*adv.* 4. in a backhanded way. —*v.t.* 5. to hit or catch with a backhand.

back·hand·ed (bak′han′did), *adj.* 1. using or performed with a backhand. 2. written in backhand. 3. oblique or ambiguous in meaning. —*adv.* 4. backhand (def. 4).

back·ing (bak′ing), *n.* 1. aid or support of any kind. 2. supporters collectively. 3. something that forms a back.

back·lash (bak′lash′), *n.* 1. any sudden, forceful recoil or reaction. 2. a violent reaction, as to a social change.

back·log (bak′lôg′, -log′), *n., v.,* **-logged, -log·ging.** —*n.* 1. a reserve or accumulation, as of stock, work, or business. 2. a large log at the back of a hearth to keep up a fire. —*v.t., v.i.* 3. to accumulate as a backlog.

back′ or′der, a purchase order not yet filled.

back·pack (bak′pak′), *n.* 1. a pack of supplies carried on one's back, often supported on a metal frame. —*v.i.* 2. to go on an outing, using a backpack. —*v.t.* 3. to carry in a backpack. —**back′pack′er,** *n.*

back·ped·al (bak′ped′ᵊl), *v.i.,* **-aled, -al·ing** or **-alled, -al·ling.** 1. to retard the motion of a bicycle by pressing backward on the pedal. 2. to retreat or reverse.

back·rest (bak′rest′), *n.* a support used by a person for resting his or her back.

back′ road′, a little used country road.

back′-seat driv′er (bak′sēt′), an automobile passenger who offers the driver unsolicited advice.

back·side (bak′sīd′), *n.* the buttocks.

back·slap·ping (bak′slap′ing), *n.* a loud and effusive display of friendliness, etc. —**back′slap′per,** *n.*

back·slide (bak′slīd′), *v.i.,* **-slid** (-slid′), **-slid** or **-slid·den** (-slid′ᵊn), **-slid·ing.** to relapse into error or sin. —**back′slid′er,** *n.*

back·space (bak′spās′), *v.i.,* **-spaced, -spac·ing.** to shift a typewriter carriage one space backward.

back·spin (bak′spin′), *n.* the spin imparted to a ball causing it to roll backward, as in billiards.

back·stage (bak′stāj′), *adv.* 1. behind the proscenium in a theater, esp. in the wings or dressing rooms. —*adj.* 2. located or occurring backstage. 3. of or pertaining to the personal lives of theater people. 4. of or pertaining to activities unknown to the public. —*n.* 5. a backstage area.

back·stairs (bak′stârz′), *adj.* secretively furtive: *backstairs gossip.* Also, **back′stair′.**

back·stop (bak′stop′), *n.* 1. a wall or screen to prevent a ball from going beyond the normal playing area. 2. a safeguard or reinforcement.

back·stretch (bak′strech′), *n.* the straight part of a racetrack opposite the homestretch.

back·stroke (bak′strōk′), *n.* 1. a backhanded stroke. 2. a swimming stroke executed while on one's back.

back·swept (bak′swept′), *adj.* slanting backward or away from the front.

back′ talk′, an impudent response.

back-to-back (bak′tə bak′), *adj., adv.* one after the other.

back·track (bak′trak′), *v.i.* 1. to return over the same course or route. 2. to withdraw from one's position.

back·up (bak′up′), *n.* 1. a person or thing that supports or reinforces another. 2. an accumulation due to a stoppage. 3. a reserve for an emergency.

back·ward (bak′wərd), *adv.* Also, **back′wards.** 1. toward the rear. 2. with the back foremost. 3. in the reverse of the usual way. 4. toward the past. 5. retrogressively. —*adj.* 6. directed toward the back or past. 7. reversed or returning. 8. slow to advance or learn. 9. bashful or hesitant. —**back′ward·ly,** *adv.* —**back′ward·ness,** *n.*

back·wash (bak′wosh′, -wôsh′), *n.* water thrown backward by the motion of oars, propellers, etc.

back·wa·ter (bak′wô′tər, -wot′ər), *n.* 1. water held or forced back by a dam, flood, etc. 2. an isolated or stagnant area or place.

back·woods (bak′wŏŏdz′), *n.pl.* **1.**
wooded or partially unsettled districts. **2.** any remote or isolated
area. —**back′woods′man,** *n.*

ba·con (bā′kən), *n.* **1.** salted and
dried or smoked meat from the
back and sides of a hog. **2. bring
home the bacon, a.** to earn a living.
b. to be successful.

Ba·con (bā′kən), *n.* **Francis,** 1561–
1626, English essayist and philosopher.

bac·te·ri·a (bak tēr′ē ə), *n.pl., sing.*
-te·ri·um (-tēr′ē əm). microscopic,
spherical, rod-shaped, or spiral
organisms involved in fermentation
and putrefaction, the production of
disease, etc. —**bac·te′ri·al,** *adj.*
—**bac·te′ri·al·ly,** *adv.*

bac·te·ri·cide (bak tēr′i sīd′), *n.* an
agent capable of killing bacteria.
—**bac·te·ri·cid′al,** *adj.*

bac·te·ri·ol·o·gy (bak tēr′ē ol′ə jē), *n.*
the science that deals with bacteria.
—**bac·te·ri·o·log′i·cal** (bak tēr′ē ə-
loj′i kəl), —**bac·te′ri·o·log′ic,** *adj.*
—**bac·te·ri·o·log′i·cal·ly,** *adv.* —**bac·
te′ri·ol′o·gist,** *n.*

bac·te·ri·o·phage (bak tēr′ē ə fāj′), *n.*
one of a group of viruses that infect
specific bacteria.

bad (bad), *adj.,* **worse, worst,** *n., adv.*
—*adj.* **1.** not good in any manner
or degree. **2.** lacking moral qualities. **3.** of poor quality. **4.** incorrect or faulty. **5.** suffering from
ill health. **6.** spoiled or rotten.
7. harmful or detrimental. **8.** irritable or surly. **9.** severe or intense.
10. regretful or upset. **11.** unfortunate or unfavorable: *bad news.*
12. vulgar or obscene. **13.** not
collectible or payable: *a bad check.*
—*n.* **14.** something bad. **15. in bad,**
in distress or disfavor. —*adv.* **16.**
Informal. badly. —**bad′ness,** *n.* —
Syn. **2.** evil, immoral, iniquitous,
sinful, wicked.

—Usage. BAD and BADLY are found
with almost equal acceptance in
spoken English when following *feel,*
although *bad* is usually preferred in
formal writing.

bad′ blood′, mutual, long-standing
enmity.

bade (bad), *v.* a pt. of **bid.**

bad′ egg′, *Slang.* an unreliable or
dishonest person. Also called **bad′
ap′ple.**

badge (baj), *n.* **1.** an emblem worn
as a sign of membership, authority,
etc. **2.** any distinctive mark.

badg·er (baj′ər), *n.* **1.** a burrowing
mammal with a round back and
short legs. **2.** its fur. —*v.t.* **3.** to
harass persistently.

bad·i·nage (bad′ə nāzh′), *n., v.,*
-naged, -nag·ing. —*n.* **1.** playful
banter. —*v.t.* **2.** to banter or tease.

bad·lands (bad′landz′), *n.* a barren
area in which soft rock strata are
eroded into varied, fantastic forms.

bad·ly (bad′lē), *adv.* **1.** in a bad
way or manner. **2.** *Informal.* greatly
or very much.

bad·man (bad′man′), *n., pl.* **-men.**
a bandit or outlaw, esp. in the
old West.

bad·min·ton (bad′min tᵊn), *n.* a
game played on a rectangular court
with light rackets used to volley a
shuttlecock over a high net.

bad-mouth (bad′mouth′), *v.t., v.i.*
Slang. to criticize harshly.

bad-tem·pered (bad′tem′pərd), *adj.*
cross or surly.

Bae·de·ker (bā′də kər), *n.* **1.** any
of a series of guidebooks for
travelers issued in Germany. **2.** any
travel guidebook.

baf·fle (baf′əl), *v.,* **-fled, -fling,** *n.*
—*v.t.* **1.** to confuse, esp. in a mysti-
fying or puzzling way. **2.** to frustrate or thwart. —*n.* **3.** a device
for checking or impeding the flow
of gases, sounds, etc. —**baf′fle-
ment,** *n.* —**baf′fler,** *n.* —**baf′fling,**
adj. —Syn. **1.** bewilder, perplex.

bag (bag), *n., v.,* **bagged, bag·ging.**
—*n.* **1.** a container or receptacle
capable of being closed at the
mouth. **2.** a suitcase. **3.** a purse.
4. an amount of game taken in
hunting. **5.** a pouchlike part. **6.**
Baseball. a base. **7.** *Slang.* an unattractive woman. **8.** *Slang.* a person's special interest. **9. in the bag,**
Slang. certain or assured. —*v.i.*
10. to swell or bulge. **11.** to bulge
or hang loosely. —*v.t.* **12.** to put
into a bag. **13.** to kill or catch.
14. to cause to bulge. **15.** *Slang.*
to get or take.

ba·gasse (bə gas′), *n.* crushed sugar-
cane refuse from sugar making.

bag·a·telle (bag′ə tel′), *n.* a trifle.

ba·gel (bā′gəl), *n.* a leavened,
doughnut-shaped, hard roll.

bag·gage (bag′ij), *n.* **1.** the trunks,
suitcases, etc., containing the personal effects of a traveler. **2.** *Facetious.* a pert girl. **3.** *Obs.* an immoral or dishonorable woman.

bag·gy (bag′ē), *adj.,* **-gi·er, -gi·est.**
hanging loosely. —**bag′gi·ly,** *adv.*
—**bag′gi·ness,** *n.*

Bagh·dad (bag′dad), *n.* the capital
of Iraq. Also, **Bag′dad.**

bag·man (bag′mən), *n., pl.* **-men.**
Slang. a racketeer assigned by his
or her superiors to collect or distribute payoff money.

bagn·io (ban′yō, bän′-), *n., pl.* **-ios.**
Archaic. a brothel.

bag·pipe (bag′pīp′), *n.* a reed instrument consisting of a melody
pipe and accompanying drone pipes

protruding from a bag. Also, **bag′- pipes′.** —**bag′pip′er,** n.

ba·guette (ba get′), n. a gem having a rectangular cut.

bah (bä, ba), interj. (an exclamation of contempt or annoyance.)

Ba·ha·mas (bə hä′məz, -hä′-), n. a country on a group of islands in the British West Indies, SE of Florida. Also called **Baha′ma Is′lands.** —**Ba·ha·mi·an** (bə hä′- mē ən, -hä′-), n., adj.

baht (bät), n., pl. **bahts, baht.** the monetary unit of Thailand.

bail¹ (bāl), n. 1. property given as surety that a person released from custody will return at an appointed time. 2. release granted on such surety. 3. the person providing bail. 4. the privilege of being released on bail. —v.t. 5. to release (a person) under bail. —**bail′a·ble,** adj. —**bail′ment,** n. —**bail′or,** n.

bail² (bāl), n. the semicircular handle of a kettle or pail.

bail³ (bāl), v.t., v.i. 1. to dip (water) out of a boat, as with a bucket. 2. **bail out,** a. to parachute from an airplane. b. to relieve (a person, company, etc.) in an emergency. —n. 3. a container for bailing. —**bail′er,** n.

bail·iff (bā′lif), n. a minor court officer authorized to execute processes, protect the courtroom, etc. 2. (in Britain) a. a town administrative official. b. an overseer of a landed estate.

bail·i·wick (bā′lə wik), n. 1. the district of a bailiff. 2. a person's area of skill, knowledge, or operation.

bail·out (bāl′out′), n. the act of bailing out, as of an aircraft or of a financial disaster.

bails·man (bālz′mən), n., pl. **-men.** a person who provides bail or surety.

bairn (bârn; Scot. bārn), n. Scot. a child.

bait (bāt), n. 1. food, etc., used as a lure in angling, trapping, etc. 2. anything that lures. —v.t. 3. to prepare (a hook or trap) with bait. 4. to lure as with bait. 5. to set dogs upon (an animal) for sport. 6. to torment or persecute, esp. with malicious remarks. —**bait′er,** n.

baize (bāz), n. a soft, usually green, woolen fabric.

bake (bāk), v., **baked, bak·ing,** n. —v.t. 1. to cook by dry heat, as in an oven. 2. to harden by heat, as pottery. —v.i. 3. to bake bread, a casserole, etc. 4. to become baked. —n. 5. a social occasion at which the chief food is baked. —**bak′er,** n.

baked′ Alas′ka, a dessert of ice cream on a cake base, covered with meringue and browned in an oven.

bak′er's doz′en, a dozen plus one.

bak·er·y (bā′kə rē), n., pl. **-er·ies.** 1. Also called **bake·shop** (bāk′- shop′). a place where baked goods are made or sold. 2. baked foods.

bak′ing pow′der, a powder used in baking, composed of sodium bicarbonate mixed with an acid substance capable of causing the dough to rise.

bak′ing so′da. See **sodium bicarbonate.**

ba·kla·va (bä′klə vä′), n. a Middle Eastern pastry made of many layers of paper-thin dough with a filling, usually of honey and ground nuts.

bak·sheesh (bak′shēsh), n. (in India, Turkey, etc.) a tip or gratuity.

bal., balance.

bal·a·lai·ka (bal′ə lī′kə), n. a Russian musical instrument having a triangular body and a neck like that of a guitar.

bal·ance (bal′əns), n., v., **-anced, -anc·ing.** —n. 1. an instrument for determining weight, esp. by the equilibrium of weights suspended from opposite ends of a horizontal bar. 2. a state of equilibrium. 3. something that brings about such a state. 4. a state of stability, as of the body or the emotions. 5. a state of harmony, as among the elements of an artistic composition. 6. the remainder or rest. 7. a. equality between the debit total and the credit total of an account. b. the difference between these totals. 8. See **balance wheel.** 9. **in the balance,** at a critical stage. —v.t. 10. to weigh in a balance. 11. to estimate the relative weight or importance of. 12. to counteract or offset. 13. to be equal or proportionate to. 14. to determine the difference between, or to equalize, the debit and credit entries in (an account). —v.i. 15. to have an equivalence in weight, value, etc. 16. to adjust a bookkeeping account. —**Syn.** 5. symmetry, proportion.

bal′ance beam′, a narrow wooden rail set horizontally on posts, used by women for feats of balancing, posture, etc.

bal′ance of pay′ments, the difference between a nation's total payments to and its total receipts from foreign countries.

bal′ance of pow′er, a distribution of forces among nations such that no one is strong enough to dominate the others.

bal'ance of trade', the difference between the values of exports and imports of countries.

bal'ance sheet', a statement of the financial position of a business on a specified date.

bal'ance wheel', a wheel that regulates the rate of running of a watch or clock.

bal·bo·a (bal bō′ə), *n.* the monetary unit of Panama.

bal·brig·gan (bal brig′ən), *n.* a plain-knit cotton fabric, used esp. in underwear.

bal·co·ny (bal′kə nē), *n., pl.* **-nies.** 1. a railed platform projecting from the wall of a building. 2. a gallery in a theater.

bald (bôld), *adj.* 1. lacking hair on the scalp. 2. destitute of natural growth or covering. 3. forthright or undisguised: *a bald lie.* 4. *Zool.* having white on the head. —**bald′ly,** *adv.* —**bald′ness,** *n.*

bal·da·chin (bal′də kin, bôl′-), *n.* an ornamental canopy, as above an altar or throne. Also, **bal·da·chi·no** (bal′də kē′nō).

bald′ ea′gle, a large eagle of the U.S. and Canada, having a white head and tail.

bal·der·dash (bôl′dər dash′), *n.* nonsense or twaddle.

bald-faced (bôld′fāst′), *adj.* barefaced (def. 2).

bal·dric (bôl′drik), *n.* a belt, worn diagonally from shoulder to hip, supporting a sword, horn, etc.

bale (bāl), *n., v.,* **baled, bal·ing.** —*n.* 1. a large bundle of something, often secured by wires, hoops, etc. —*v.t.* 2. to pack in bales. —**bal′er,** *n.*

ba·leen (bə lēn′), *n.* whalebone.

bale·ful (bāl′fəl), *adj.* full of menacing or malign influence. —**bale′ful·ly,** *adv.* —**bale′ful·ness,** *n.*

Ba·li (bä′lē), *n.* an island in Indonesia, E of Java. —**Ba′li·nese′** (-lə nēz′), *adj., n.*

balk (bôk), *v.i.* 1. to stop and refuse to proceed or to do. 2. to hesitate or refuse, esp. abruptly. 3. *Baseball.* to commit a balk. —*v.t.* 4. to hinder or thwart. —*n.* 5. a check or hindrance. 6. *Baseball.* an illegal motion by a pitcher while one or more runners are on base, as a feigned pitch, etc. —**balk′er,** *n.*

Bal·kan (bôl′kən), *adj.* 1. of the Balkans or their inhabitants. 2. of the Balkan Peninsula. —*n.* 3. the **Balkans.** Also called **Bal′kan States′.** the countries in the Balkan Peninsula: Yugoslavia,, Rumania, Bulgaria, Albania, Greece, and European Turkey.

Bal′kan Penin′sula, a peninsula in S Europe, E of Italy.

balk·y (bô′kē), *adj.,* **balk·i·er, balk·i·est.** given to balking, as an animal.

ball¹ (bôl), *n.* 1. a round mass or body. 2. a round or roundish body, for use in games. 3. a game played with a ball, esp. baseball. 4. the throw of a ball. 5. *Baseball.* a pitched ball, not swung at by the batter, that is not a strike. 6. a projectile for a cannon, etc. 7. any part of the human body that is rounded. 8. **on the ball,** *Slang.* a. alert or watchful. b. efficient or competent. —*v.t., v.i.* 9. to make into a ball. 10. **ball up,** *Slang.* to confuse or muddle.

ball² (bôl), *n.* 1. a large party featuring social dancing. 2. *Informal.* a very good time.

bal·lad (bal′əd), *n.* 1. a simple narrative poem of popular origin, composed in short stanzas, esp. one adapted for singing. 2. any light, simple song. —**bal′lad·eer′,** *n.* —**bal′lad·ry,** *n.*

ball′-and-sock′et joint′ (bôl′ən sok′it), a joint in which a ball-like termination on one part is held within a socket on another.

bal·last (bal′əst), *n.* 1. any heavy material carried in a ship or vehicle to provide stability. 2. gravel, broken stone, etc., placed between and under the ties of a railroad. —*v.t.* 3. to furnish with ballast.

ball′ bear′ing, 1. a bearing consisting of a number of hard balls running in grooves. 2. any of the balls so used.

bal·le·ri·na (bal′ə rē′nə), *n.* a female ballet dancer.

bal·let (ba lā′, bal′ā), *n., pl.* **ballets** (ba lāz′, bal′āz). 1. a dance form demanding grace and precision and employing conventional steps and gestures. 2. a theatrical entertainment of such dancing and its accompanying music. 3. a company of ballet dancers.

bal·let·o·mane (ba let′ə mān′, bə-), *n.* a ballet enthusiast.

ballis′tic mis′sile, *Rocketry.* any missile that, after being guided during takeoff, travels unpowered like a falling bomb.

bal·lis·tics (bə lis′tiks), *n.* 1. the science of the motion of projectiles. 2. the art or science of designing projectiles for maximum flight performance. —**bal·lis′tic,** *adj.* —**bal·lis·ti·cian** (bal′i stish′ən), *n.*

ball′ of fire′ *Slang.* an extremely energetic, efficient person.

bal·loon (bə lōōn′), *n.* 1. a bag filled with a gas lighter than air, designed to rise and float in the atmosphere and often having a gondola for passengers or scientific instruments. **2.** an inflatable rubber bag used as a children's plaything. —*v.i.* **3.** to ride in a balloon. **4.** to swell or puff out. —*v.t.* **5.** to inflate or distend. —**bal·loon′like′**, *adj.*

balloon′ tire′, a tire filled with air at low pressure for cushioning shock.

bal·lot (bal′ət), *n.*, *v.*, **-lot·ed**, **-lot·ing.** —*n.* **1.** a sheet of paper used for voting. **2.** the whole number of votes recorded. **3.** the method or right of voting by ballots. —*v.i.* **4.** to vote by ballot. —**bal′lot·er**, *n.*

ball′ park′, a stadium for playing ball games.

ball′-peen ham′mer (bôl′pēn′), a hammer having a round peen (**ball′peen′**) for beating metal.

ball·play·er (bôl′plā′ər), *n.* a person who plays ball professionally, esp. baseball.

ball′point pen′ (bôl′point′), a pen in which the point is a tiny metal ball that deposits ink obtained by rotating at the base of a supply tube. Also called **ball′ pen′**, **ball′point′**.

ball·room (bôl′rōōm′, -rŏŏm′), *n.* a large room, as in a hotel, with a floor for dancing.

bal·lute (ba lōōt′), *n.* a combination balloon and parachute designed to break the fall of an astronaut or a rocket equipped with instruments. [*ball(oon)* + *(parach)ute*]

bal·ly·hoo (*n.* bal′ē hōō′; *v.* bal′ē hōō′), *n.*, *pl.* **-hoos**, *v.*, **-hooed**, **-hoo·ing.** —*n.* **1.** a clamorous attempt to win customers or advance any cause. —*v.t.*, *v.i.* **2.** to advertise or push by ballyhoo.

balm (bäm), *n.* **1.** an oily, fragrant substance of medicinal value. **2.** a plant yielding such a substance. **3.** anything that heals or soothes pain. [< OF *basme* < L *balsam(um)* balsam]

balm·y (bä′mē), *adj.*, **balm·i·er**, **balm·i·est.** **1.** mild and refreshing. **2.** *Brit. Slang.* silly or foolish. —**balm′i·ly**, *adv.* —**balm′i·ness**, *n.*

ba·lo·ney (ba lō′nē), *n.* **1.** *Slang.* foolishness or nonsense. **2.** bologna.

bal·sa (bôl′sa, bäl′-), *n.* **1.** a tree of tropical America yielding an exceedingly light wood. **2.** its wood.

bal·sam (bôl′səm), *n.* **1.** a fragrant exudation from certain trees. **2.** a plant or tree yielding a balsam. **3.** any aromatic ointment for ceremonial or medicinal use.

bal′sam fir′, a North American evergreen tree, often used as a Christmas tree.

Bal·tic (bôl′tik), *adj.* of the Baltic Sea or the countries on its coast.

Bal′tic Sea′, a sea in N Europe, NE of Germany.

Bal·ti·more (bôl′tə môr′, -môr′), *n.* a seaport in N Maryland. —**Bal′ti·mo′re·an**, *n.*

Bal′timore o′riole, an orange and black oriole of North America.

bal·us·ter (bal′ə stər), *n.* any of a number of closely spaced supports for a railing. —**bal′us·tered**, *adj.*

bal·us·trade (bal′ə strād′, bal′ə strād′), *n.* a railing with supporting balusters.

bam·boo (bam bōō′), *n.*, *pl.* **-boos.** a tall, treelike tropical grass with hollow, woody stems, used for making furniture, poles, etc.

bam′boo cur′tain, the barrier of censorship and secrecy maintained by mainland Communist China.

bam·boo·zle (bam bōō′zəl), *v.t.*, **-zled**, **-zling.** to deceive by trickery, flattery, etc. —**bam·boo′zler**, *n.*

ban¹ (ban), *v.*, **banned**, **ban·ning**, *n.* —*v.t.* **1.** to prohibit, esp. by official authority. —*n.* **2.** an act or instance of banning. **3.** *Eccles.* a formal condemnation. —**Syn. 1.** bar, forbid, outlaw.

ban² (bän), *n.*, *pl.* **ba·ni** (bä′nē). a money of account of Rumania.

ba·nal (ba nal′, bān′°l), *adj.* insipid and pointless. —**ba·nal·i·ty** (ba nal′i tē, bā-), —**ba·nal′ly**, *adv.*

ba·nan·a (ba nan′ə), *n.* **1.** a tropical plant, certain species of which are cultivated for their nutritious fruit. **2.** the fruit with yellow or red rind. [< Sp < Pg < WAfr native name]

ba·nan·as (ba nan′əs), *adj.* *Slang.* crazy or insane (usually in the phrase *go bananas*).

band¹ (band), *n.* **1.** a company of persons, animals, or things. **2.** a musical group, usually employing brass, percussion, and often woodwind instruments. —*v.t.*, *v.i.* **3.** to unite in a company or group.

band² (band), *n.* **1.** a thin, flat strip of material for binding, confining, or tying. **2.** a belt or strap. **3.** one of a set of grooves in a long-playing phonograph record that have recorded sound. **4.** a range of frequencies for a specific type of radio service. —*v.t.* **5.** to mark or furnish with a band. —**band′er**, *n.*

band·age (ban′dij), *n.*, *v.*, **-aged**, **-ag·ing.** —*n.* **1.** a strip of material used to dress a wound, sprain, etc. —*v.t.* **2.** to bind or cover with a bandage.

Band-Aid (ban′dād′), *n.* *Trademark.* a small adhesive bandage for minor cuts, etc.

ban·dan·na (ban dan′ə), *n.* a large, colored handkerchief. Also, **ban·dan′a.**

band·box (band'boks'), n. a light, cylindrical box for articles of apparel.

ban·deau (ban dō', ban'dō), n., pl. -deaux (-dōz', -dōz). 1. a narrow band worn around the head. 2. a narrow brassiere.

ban·de·role (ban'də rōl'), n. a small flag or streamer fastened to a lance, masthead, etc. Also, **ban'de·rol'**.

ban·di·coot (ban'də kōot'), n. a small marsupial of Australia and New Guinea.

ban·dit (ban'dit), n., pl. **ban·dits**, **ban·dit·ti** (ban dit'ē). a robber, esp. a member of a marauding band. —**ban'dit·ry**, n.

band·mas·ter (band'mas'tər), n. the conductor of a military band, etc.

ban·do·leer (ban'd°lēr'), n. a belt worn over the shoulder and having pockets for cartridges. Also, **ban'do·lier'**.

band' saw', a saw consisting of an endless toothed steel band passing over two wheels.

bands·man (bandz'mən), n., pl. -men. a musician who plays in a band.

band·stand (band'stand'), n. a platform for a band or orchestra.

band·wag·on (band'wag'ən), n. 1. a wagon, usually ornately decorated, for a musical band, as in a circus parade. 2. **be or jump on or aboard the bandwagon**, Informal. to support a candidate, cause, etc., that seems assured of success.

ban·dy (ban'dē), v., -died, -dy·ing, adj. —v.t. 1. to throw or strike to and fro. 2. to trade or exchange. 3. to circulate freely. —adj. 4. (of legs) curved outward.

ban·dy-leg·ged (ban'dē leg'ïd, -legd'), adj. having crooked legs.

bane (bān), n. 1. a person or thing that harms or spoils. 2. a deadly poison. —**bane'ful**, adj.

bang¹ (bang), n. 1. a loud, sudden, explosive noise, as the discharge of a gun. 2. a resounding blow. 3. Slang. intense pleasure, thrill, or excitement. —v.t. 4. to strike or beat hard and resoundingly. —v.i. 5. to strike violently or noisily. 6. to make a loud, sudden, explosive noise. 7. **bang up**, to damage or impair. —adv. 8. suddenly and loudly. 9. precisely.

bang² (bang), n. 1. hair combed or brushed forward over the forehead. —v.t. 2. to cut (the hair) straight across the forehead.

Bang·kok (bang'kok), n. the capital of Thailand.

Ban·gla·desh (bang'glə desh', bäng'-), n. a country E of India on the Bay of Bengal.

ban·gle (bang'gəl), n. a bracelet or anklet in the form of a ring.

bang-up (bang'up'), adj. Informal. excellent or very good.

ban·ish (ban'ish), v.t. 1. to condemn to exile. 2. to send, drive, or put away. —**ban'ish·ment**, n. —Syn. 1. deport, expatriate. 2. eject, expel, oust.

ban·is·ter (ban'i stər), n. 1. a baluster, esp. a slender one. 2. the balustrade of a staircase.

ban·jo (ban'jō), n., pl. -jos, -joes. a musical instrument having a circular body and either four or five strings. —**ban'jo·ist**, n.

bank¹ (bangk), n. 1. a long heap, as of earth. 2. an upward slope. 3. the slope immediately bordering a river, etc. 4. a broad elevation of the sea floor. 5. the inclination of the bed of a banked road or railroad. 6. Aeron. the lateral inclination of an aircraft. —v.t., v.i. 7. to border with or like a bank. 8. to form into a heap. 9. to slope the bed of (a road or railroad) at curves. 10. to incline (an airplane) laterally. 11. to cover (a fire) with ashes or fuel to make it burn slowly.

bank² (bangk), n. 1. an institution for receiving, lending, and safeguarding money. 2. (in games) the fund of the manager or dealer. 3. a storage place: a blood bank. —v.i. 4. to have an account with a bank. 5. to exercise the functions of a bank or banker. —v.t. 6. to deposit in a bank. 7. **bank on or upon**, to depend on. —**bank'a·ble**, adj. —**bank'er**, n.

bank³ (bangk), n. 1. an arrangement of objects in tiers. 2. a row or tier of oars. —v.t. 3. to arrange in a bank.

bank·book (bangk'book'), n. passbook.

bank' card', a credit card issued by a bank.

bank·ing (bangk'ing), n. the business carried on by a bank or a banker.

bank·note (bangk'nōt'), n. a promissory note issued by an authorized bank and circulating as money.

bank·roll (bangk'rōl'), n. 1. money in one's possession. —v.t. 2. to finance.

bank·rupt (bangk'rupt, -rəpt), n. 1. a person who is adjudged insolvent by a court and whose property is administered for and divided among the creditors. 2. a person lacking in a particular thing or quality. —adj. 3. being declared a bankrupt. 4. lacking or destitute. —v.t. 5. to make bankrupt. —**bank'rupt·cy**, n.

ban·ner (ban′ər), *n.* **1.** the flag of a country, army, troop, etc. **2.** a headline extending across the front page of a newspaper. —*adj.* **3.** leading or foremost: *a banner year for wheat.*

ban·nis·ter (ban′i stər), *n.* banister.

ban·nock (ban′ək), *n.* a flat cake made of oatmeal, usually baked on a griddle.

banns (banz), *n.pl.* the notice of an intended marriage, given in the parish church.

ban·quet (bang′kwit), *n., v., -quet·ed, -quet·ing.* —*n.* **1.** a lavish meal. **2.** a ceremonious public dinner. —*v.t.* **3.** to entertain at a banquet. —**ban′quet·er,** *n.*

ban·quette (bang ket′), *n.* **1.** an upholstered bench, as along a wall. **2.** a platform along the inside of a parapet for gunners.

ban·shee (ban′shē, ban shē′), *n.* (in Irish folklore) a female spirit whose wailing is a sign that a loved one will soon die. [< Ir *bean sīdhe* woman of the fairies]

ban·tam (ban′təm), *n.* **1.** a chicken of very small size. **2.** a small, quarrelsome person. —*adj.* **3.** diminutive or tiny.

ban·tam·weight (ban′təm wāt′), *n.* a boxer weighing up to 118 pounds.

ban·ter (ban′tər), *n.* **1.** light, playful joking. —*v.t.* **2.** to address with banter. —*v.i.* **3.** to use banter. —**ban′ter·ing·ly,** *adv.*

bant·ling (bant′ling), *n.* *Archaic.* a young child.

Ban·tu (ban′tōō), *n., pl.* **-tus, -tu.** a member of a group of Negroid peoples in central and southern Africa. **2.** a group of languages of these peoples.

Ban·tu·stan (ban′tōō stan′), *n.* any of several segregated territories for the Bantu peoples in South Africa.

ban·yan (ban′yən), *n.* an East Indian fig tree whose branches send roots to the ground that become new trunks.

ban·zai (bän zī′, bän′-), *interj.* **1.** (used as a Japanese patriotic shout.) **2.** (used as a shout among Japanese combat troops, when attacking.) —*adj.* **3.** reckless or suicidal. [< Jap = *ban* 10,000 + *zai* year]

ba·o·bab (bā′ō bab′, bä′-), *n.* a large tree which is native to tropical Africa and bears a gourdlike fruit.

Bap., Baptist. Also, **Bapt.**

bap·tism (bap′tiz əm), *n.* **1.** a ceremonial immersion in water, or application of water, as an initiatory rite or sacrament of the Christian church. **2.** any ceremony of initiation. —**bap·tis·mal** (bap tiz′məl), *adj.* —**bap·tis′mal·ly,** *adv.*

baptis′mal name. See **Christian name.**

Bap·tist (bap′tist), *n.* a member of a Christian denomination that baptizes believers by immersion.

bap·tis·ter·y (bap′ti stə rē, -ti strē), *n., pl.* **-ter·ies.** a part of a church used for baptism. Also, **bap′tist·ry.**

bap·tize (bap tīz′, bap′tīz), *v., -tized, -tiz·ing.* —*v.t.* **1.** to administer baptism to. **2.** to initiate by purifying. **3.** to give a name to at baptism. —*v.i.* **4.** to administer baptism. —**bap·tiz′er,** *n.*

bar (bär), *n., v.,* barred, bar·ring, *prep.* —*n.* **1.** a relatively long piece of metal or wood, used as a guard or obstruction. **2.** an oblong piece of any solid material: *a bar of soap.* **3.** an obstacle or hindrance. **4. a.** a counter at which liquors or light meals are served. **b.** barroom. **5.** the legal profession. **6.** the practicing members of the legal profession. **7.** a band or strip. **8.** a railing in a courtroom separating the public from the part occupied by the judges, jury, attorneys, etc. **9.** the line marking the division between two measures of music. —*v.t.* **10.** to equip with a bar. **11.** to shut in or out by or as by bars. **12.** to block (a way, etc.), as with a barrier. **13.** to exclude. **14.** to mark with bars. —*prep.* **15.** but or except: *bar none.*

bar., **1.** barometer. **2.** barometric. **3.** barrel.

barb (bärb), *n.* **1.** a point projecting backward from a main point, as of a fishhook, etc. **2.** an unpleasant or carping remark. **3.** *Bot., Zool.* a beardlike growth. —*v.t.* **4.** to furnish with a barb. —**barbed** (bärbd), *adj.*

Bar·ba·dos (bär bā′dōz, -dōs, bär′bə dōz′, -dōs′), *n.* a country on an island in the E West Indies.

bar·bar·i·an (bär bâr′ē ən), *n.* **1.** a person in a savage, primitive state. **2.** a person without culture or education. —*adj.* **3.** savage or primitive. **4.** not refined or cultured. —**bar′i·an·ism,** *n.*

bar·bar·ic (bär bar′ik), *adj.* **1.** of or characteristic of barbarians. **2.** crude and unrestrained.

bar·ba·rism (bär′bə riz′əm), *n.* **1.** a barbarous or uncivilized condition. **2.** a barbarous act. **3.** the use of words or forms felt to be contrary to the established standards.

bar·bar·i·ty (bär bar′i tē), *n., pl.* **-ties.** **1.** savage cruelty. **2.** an act of cruelty or inhumanity. **3.** crudity or coarseness.

bar·ba·rize (bär′bə rīz′), *v.t., v.i., -rized, -riz·ing.* to make or become barbarous. —**bar′ba·ri·za′tion,** *n.*

bar·ba·rous (bär′bər əs), *adj.* **1.** savagely cruel or harsh. **2.** crude or uncivilized. **3.** not conforming to accepted usage, as language. —**bar′ba·rous·ly,** *adv.*

bar·be·cue (bär′bə kyōō′), *n., v.,* **-cued, -cu·ing.** —*n.* **1.** a social entertainment, at which meats are roasted over an open fire. **2.** meat or fish roasted over an open fire. —*v.t.* **3.** to broil or roast whole or in large pieces before an open fire. **4.** to cook in a highly seasoned sauce. [< Sp *barbacoa* < W Ind *barbacoa* a frame of sticks]

barbed′ wire′, steel wire twisted with barbs at short intervals, used in fences.

bar·bel (bär′bəl), *n.* a whiskerlike growth around the mouths of certain fishes.

bar·bell (bär′bel′), *n.* a bar with adjustable weights fastened to the ends, used in weight lifting.

bar·ber (bär′bər), *n.* **1.** a person whose occupation it is to cut hair, shave beards, etc. —*v.t., v.i.* **2.** to render the services of a barber (to).

bar·ber·ry (bär′ber′ē, -bə rē), *n., pl.* **-ries.** a shrub having red, elongated, acid fruit.

bar·ber·shop (bär′bər shop′), *n.* the place of business of a barber.

bar·bi·can (bär′bə kən), *n.* an outwork of a fortified place, as a castle.

bar·bi·tal (bär′bi tal′, -tôl′), *n.* a barbiturate compound, used as a hypnotic.

bar·bi·tu·rate (bär bich′ə rāt′, -ər it), *n.* any of a group of derivatives of a crystalline powder (**bar′bi·tu′ric ac′id**), used as sedatives and hypnotics.

bar′ car′, a railroad car equipped with a bar that serves liquors or refreshments.

bar·ca·role (bär′kə rōl′), *n.* **1.** a boating song of the Venetian gondoliers. **2.** a piece of music composed in the style of such songs.

Bar·ce·lon·a (bär′sə lō′nə), *n.* a seaport in NE Spain.

bar′ chart′, See bar graph.

bard (bärd), *n.* **1.** an ancient Celtic poet. **2.** any poet. —**bard′ic,** *adj.*

bare (bâr), *adj., v.,* **bar·er, bar·est,** **bared, bar·ing.** —*adj.* **1.** with no outside covering, such as clothes. **2.** without the usual furnishings, etc. **3.** unconcealed or undisguised. **4.** unadorned or plain. **5.** scarcely sufficient: *bare necessities.* —*v.t.* **6.** to make or lay bare. —**bare′ness,** *n.* —**Syn. 1.** naked, nude, unclothed.

bare·back (bâr′bak′), *adv., adj.* without a saddle on the back of a horse. Also, **bare′backed′.**

bare·faced (bâr′fāst′), *adj.* **1.** with

the face uncovered. **2.** without concealment or disguise.

bare·foot (bâr′fŏŏt′), *adj., adv.* with the feet bare. Also, **bare′foot′ed.**

bare·hand·ed (bâr′han′did), *adj., adv.* **1.** with hands uncovered. **2.** without tools, weapons, or other aids.

bare·head·ed (bâr′hed′id), *adj., adv.* with the head uncovered.

bare·leg·ged (bâr′leg′id, -legd′), *adj., adv.* with bare legs.

bare·ly (bâr′lē), *adv.* **1.** only or just. **2.** without disguise or concealment. **3.** nakedly or scantily.

bar·fly (bär′flī′), *n., pl.* **-flies.** *Slang.* a person who frequents barrooms.

bar·gain (bär′gin), *n.* **1.** an agreement settling what each party shall give and take or perform and receive in a transaction. **2.** something acquired by bargaining. **3.** something well worth what is given in exchange, esp. in being cheaper than usual. **4. in or into the bargain,** moreover. —*v.i.* **5.** to negotiate over terms. **6.** to make a bargain. **7. bargain for or on,** to count or rely on. —**bar′gain·er,** *n.*

barge (bärj), *n., v.,* **barged, barg·ing.** —*n.* **1.** a flat-bottomed vessel pushed or towed in transporting freight or passengers. **2.** a ceremonial vessel used in pageants. **3.** a motorboat assigned to a flagship. —*v.t.* **4.** to transport by barge. —*v.i.* **5.** *Informal.* to move clumsily. **6. barge in or into,** *Informal.* to intrude rudely or clumsily.

bar′ graph′, a graph using parallel bars of varying lengths to illustrate comparative costs, etc.

bar·ite (bâr′īt, bar′-), *n.* a common mineral that is the principal ore of barium.

bar·i·tone (bar′i tōn′), *n.* **1.** a male voice or voice part between tenor and bass. **2.** a singer with such a voice.

bar·i·um (bâr′ē əm, bar′-), *Chem.* an active metallic element, occurring in combination chiefly as barite. *Symbol:* Ba; *at. wt.:* 137.34; *at. no.:* 56. —**bar′ic,** *adj.*

bark[1] (bärk), *n.* **1.** the abrupt, explosive cry of a dog or other animal. —*v.i.* **2.** to utter such a cry or a series of such cries. **3.** to speak or cry out sharply or gruffly. —*v.t.* **4.** to utter with a bark or barks. **5. bark up the wrong tree,** to misdirect one's efforts.

bark[2] (bärk), *n.* **1.** the external covering of the woody stems, branches, and roots of plants. —*v.t.* **2.** to strip the bark from. **3.** to rub off the skin of.

bark[3] (bärk), *n.* a sailing vessel having three or more masts, square-rigged on all but the after mast.

bar·keep·er (bär′kē′pər), *n.* **1.** a person who owns or manages a barroom. **2.** bartender. Also, **bar′-keep′.**

bark·en·tine (bär′kən tēn′), *n.* a sailing vessel having three or more masts.

bark·er (bär′kər), *n.* a person who stands before a theater, a sideshow of a carnival, etc., soliciting passers-by to enter.

bar·ley (bär′lē), *n.* **1.** a cereal plant whose awned flowers grow in tightly bunched spikes. **2.** its grain, used as food and in making beer, ale, etc.

bar·maid (bär′mād′), *n.* a female bartender.

bar·man (bär′mən), *n., pl.* **-men.** bartender.

bar mitz·vah (bär mits′və). (*often caps.*) **1.** a ceremony for admitting a Jewish boy as an adult member of the Jewish community, usually at the age of 13. **2.** the boy participating in this ceremony.

barn (bärn), *n.* **1.** a large building, as on a farm, for storing hay, grain, etc., and often for housing livestock. **2.** a garage for streetcars or buses.

bar·na·cle (bär′nə kəl), *n.* a marine crustacean having a calcareous shell, found attached to ship bottoms and rocks. —**bar′na·cled,** *adj.*

barn·storm (bärn′stôrm′), *v.i., v.t.* to tour (rural areas) giving political speeches, theatrical performances, etc. —**barn′storm′er,** *n.*

barn·yard (bärn′yärd′), *n.* a yard, usually fenced, next to or around a barn.

bar·o·graph (bar′ə graf′, -gräf′), *n.* an automatic recording barometer. —**bar·o·graph·ic** (bar′ə graf′ik), *adj.*

ba·rom·e·ter (bə rom′i tər), *n.* **1.** any instrument that measures atmospheric pressure. **2.** anything that indicates changes. —**bar·o·met·ric** (bar′ə me′trik), **bar·o·met′ri·cal,** *adj.* —**bar′o·met′ri·cal·ly,** *adv.* —**ba·rom′e·try,** *n.*

bar·on (bar′ən), *n.* **1.** a member of the lowest grade of nobility. **2.** an important financier or industrialist. —**bar′on·age,** *n.* —**bar·on·ess,** *n. fem.* —**ba·ro·ni·al** (bə rō′nē əl), *adj.* —**bar·o·ny** (bar′ə nē), *n.*

bar·on·et (bar′ə nit, -net′), *n.* a member of a British hereditary order of honor, ranking below the barons and above the knights. —**bar′on·et·cy,** *n.*

ba·roque (bə rōk′), *adj.* **1.** of a style of art and architecture prevailing in Europe during the 17th and first half of the 18th centuries, characterized by elaborate and grotesque forms and ornamentation. **2.** of the musical period following the Renaissance, extending roughly from 1600 to 1750.

ba·rouche (bə rōōsh′), *n.* a four-wheeled carriage with a seat outside for the driver.

barque (bärk), *n.* bark³.

bar·quen·tine (bär′kən tēn′), *n.* barkentine.

barr., barrister.

bar·rack (bar′ək), *n.* Usually, **barracks.** a building or group of buildings for lodging soldiers.

bar·ra·cu·da (bar′ə kōō′də), *n., pl.* **-da, -das.** an elongated, predaceous, tropical marine fish.

bar·rage (bə räzh′), *n., v., -raged, -rag·ing.* —*n.* **1.** a barrier of artillery fire. **2.** an overwhelming quantity. **3.** an artificial obstruction in a watercourse. —*v.t.* **4.** to subject to a barrage.

bar·ra·try (bar′ə trē), *n.* **1.** fraud by a master or crew at the expense of the owners of a ship or its cargo. **2.** the offense of frequently stirring up suits and quarrels. **3.** the purchase or sale of ecclesiastical preferments. —**bar′ra·trous,** *adj.*

barred (bärd), *adj.* **1.** provided with bars or stripes. **2.** closed off with a bar or bolt. **3.** forbidden or prohibited.

bar·rel (bar′əl), *n., v., -reled, -rel·ing** or **-relled, -rel·ling.** —*n.* **1.** a cylindrical container, usually of wood, with slightly bulging sides and flat, parallel ends. **2.** a standard quantity that such a container can hold, 31½ gallons. **3.** any large quantity: *a barrel of fun.* **4.** the tube of a gun. —*v.t.* **5.** to put or pack in a barrel. —*v.i.* **6.** *Slang.* to travel or drive very fast.

bar′rel or′gan, a musical instrument designed to play tunes by means of pins inserted into a revolving barrel.

bar′rel roll′, a maneuver in which an airplane executes a complete roll by revolving once around the longitudinal axis of the airplane.

bar·ren (bar′ən), *adj.* **1.** not producing offspring. **2.** unproductive or unfruitful. **3.** dull or boring. **4.** lacking or devoid. —*n.* **5.** Usually, **barrens.** level land, usually infertile. —**bar′ren·ness,** *n.*

bar·rette (bə ret′), *n.* a clasp for holding a woman's hair.

bar·ri·cade (bar′ə kād′, bar′ə kād′), *n., v., -cad·ed, -cad·ing* —*n.* **1.** a hastily constructed defensive barrier. **2.** any barrier. —*v.t.* **3.** to obstruct or fortify with a barricade. —**bar′·ri·cad′er,** *n.*

bar·ri·er (bar′ē ər), *n.* **1.** anything built to bar passage, as a fence. **2.** anything that restrains or obstructs. **3.** a limit or boundary: *the barriers of caste.*

bar′rier reef′, a reef of coral running parallel to the shore and separated from it by deep water.

bar·ring (bär′ing), *prep.* except for.

bar·rio (bar′ē ō′), *n. U.S.* a section inhabited mainly by Spanish-speaking people.

bar·ris·ter (bar′i stər), *n.* in England) a lawyer who has the privilege of pleading in the higher courts. **—bar·ris·te·ri·al** (bar′i stēr′ē əl), *adj.*

bar·room (bär′rōōm′, -rōōm′), *n.* a place where alcoholic beverages are served.

bar·row¹ (bar′ō), *n.* **1.** a handbarrow. **2.** a wheelbarrow. **3.** *Brit.* a pushcart used by street vendors.

bar·row² (bar′ō), *n.* a burial mound of prehistoric inhabitants.

bar·row³ (bar′ō), *n.* a castrated male swine.

bar·stool (bär′stōōl′), *n.* a high stool used for seating a customer at a bar.

Bart., Baronet.

bar·tend·er (bär′ten′dər), *n.* a person who mixes and serves drinks at a bar.

bar·ter (bär′tər), *v.i.* **1.** to trade by exchange of commodities. **—v.t. 2.** to exchange in trade. **—n. 3.** the act or practice of bartering. **—bar′ter·er,** *n.*

Bart·lett (bärt′lit), *n.* a large, yellow, juicy variety of pear.

bar·y·on (bar′ē on′), *n.* any particle that can be transformed into a nucleon.

ba·sal (bā′səl, -zəl), *adj.* **1.** of or at the base of something. **2.** fundamental or basic. **—ba′sal·ly,** *adv.*

ba′sal metab′olism, the energy turnover of the body in a state of total rest.

ba·salt (bə sôlt′, bā′sôlt), *n.* the dark, dense igneous rock of a lava flow. **—ba·sal′tic,** *adj.*

base¹ (bās), *n., adj., v.,* **based, bas·ing. —n. 1.** the bottom support or part. **2.** a fundamental concept or idea. **3.** the principal element or ingredient. **4.** a starting point. **5.** *Baseball.* any of the four corners of the diamond, esp. first, second, or third base. **6. a.** an area from which military operations proceed. **b.** a supply installation for a large military force. **7.** *Geom.* the line or surface forming the part of a figure that is most nearly horizontal. **8.** *Math.* the number that serves as a starting point for a logarithmic or other numerical system. **9.** *Chem.* a compound that reacts with an acid to form a salt. **10.** the part of a complex word to which affixes may be added. **11. off base, a.** not touching a base. **b.** badly mistaken. **—adj. 12.** serving as or forming a base. **—v.t. 13.** to form a base for. **14.** to establish, as a conclusion.

base² (bās), *adj.,* **bas·er, bas·est. 1.** morally low or mean-spirited. **2.** of little or no value. **3.** debased or poor. **4.** not precious: *a base metal.* **—base′ly,** *adv.* **—base′ness,** *n.*

base·ball (bās′bôl′), *n.* **1.** a game of ball played by two nine-person teams on a diamond formed by lines connecting four bases. **2.** the ball used in this game.

base·board (bās′bōrd′, -bôrd′), *n.* a board forming the foot of an interior wall.

base·born (bās′bôrn′), *adj.* **1.** of humble birth. **2.** born out of wedlock. **3.** mean or contemptible.

base′ exchange′, a post exchange at an air-force base.

base′ hit′, *Baseball.* a fair ball enabling the batter to reach base safely without an error in the field or with no runner forced out.

base·less (bās′lis), *adj.* having no base in reason or fact. **—base′less·ly,** *adv.* **—base′less·ness,** *n.*

base′ line′, 1. a line serving as a base, as for comparison. **2.** *Baseball.* the area between bases within which a player must keep when running from one base to another. **3.** *Tennis.* the line at each end of a court.

base·ment (bās′mənt), *n.* **1.** a story of a building, partly or wholly underground. **2.** the lowermost portion of a structure.

Ba·sen·ji (bə sen′jē), *n.* an African breed of dogs having a chestnut coat, characterized by the inability to bark.

base′ on balls′, *pl.* **bases on balls.** *Baseball.* the advancing to first base of a batter to whom four balls have been pitched.

ba·ses (bā′sēz), *n.* pl. of **basis.**

bash (bash), *n.* **1.** *Informal.* to strike with a crushing blow. **—n. 2.** *Informal.* a crushing blow. **3.** *Slang.* a wildly good time.

bash·ful (bash′fəl), *adj.* **1.** easily embarrassed. **2.** socially timid or awkward. **—bash′ful·ly,** *adv.* **—bash′ful·ness,** *n.*

ba·sic (bā′sik), *adj.* **1.** of, pertaining to, or forming a base or basis: *a basic ingredient.* **2.** *Chem.* **a.** pertaining to, of the nature of, or containing a base. **b.** alkaline. **—n. 3.** something that is fundamental. **—ba′si·cal·ly,** *adv.* **—ba·sic·i·ty** (bā sis′i tē), *n.* **—Syn. 1.** essential, fundamental, underlying, vital.

Ba'sic Eng'lish, a simplified form of English restricted to an 850-word vocabulary and a few simple rules of grammar, intended esp. as an international auxiliary language.

bas·il (baz′əl, bā′zəl), *n.* an aromatic herb, the leaves of which are used in cooking.

bas·i·lar (bas′ə lər), *adj.* pertaining to or situated at the base, esp. the base of the skull. Also, **bas·i·lar·y** (bas′ə ler′ē).

ba·sil·i·ca (bə sil′i kə), *n.* **1.** (in ancient Rome) a large oblong building used for a court and meeting place. **2.** an early medieval church having a nave, aisles, and vaulted apses. **3.** a church accorded certain ceremonial privileges. [< L < Gk *basilikē* hall]

bas·i·lisk (bas′ə lisk, baz′-), *n.* a mythical lizardlike creature, said to kill by its breath or look.

ba·sin (bā′sən), *n.* **1.** a shallow, usually round pan, used chiefly to hold liquid. **2.** the quantity held by such a container. **3.** a sheltered area along a shore. **4.** a. a depression in the earth's surface. **b.** the tract of country drained by a river.

ba·sis (bā′sis), *n., pl.* **-ses. 1.** the basic supporting factor. **2.** the underlying principle. **3.** *Archaic.* the base or foundation.

bask (bask, bäsk), *v.i.* **1.** to lie in pleasant warmth. **2.** to enjoy something: *She basked in royal favor.*

bas·ket (bas′kit, bä′skit), *n.* **1.** a container made of straw, strips of wood, etc., woven together. **2.** the quantity held by such a basket. **3.** *Basketball.* an open net suspended from a metal rim attached to a backboard and through which the ball must pass. **—bas′ket·ful,** *n.*

bas·ket·ball (bas′kit bôl′, bä′skit-), *n.* **1.** a game played by two five-person teams on a court having a raised basket at each end through which a ball must be tossed. **2.** the ball used in this game.

bas′ket case′, *Slang.* **1.** a person who has all four limbs amputated. **2.** a completely incapacitated person.

bas′ket weave′, a textile weave resembling that of a basket.

bas·ket·work (bas′kit wûrk′, bä′skit-), *n.* work made or woven in the manner of a basket.

bas mitz·vah (bäs mits′və). *(often caps.)* See **bath mitzvah.**

Basque (bask), *n.* **1.** a member of a people inhabiting the western Pyrenees. **2.** their language. *—adj.* **3.** of the Basques or their language.

bas-re·lief (bä′ri lēf′), *n.* relief sculpture in which the figures project slightly from the background.

bass[1] (bās), *Music. —n.* **1.** the lowest male voice or voice part. **2.** a singer or instrument with such a voice or part. **3.** See **double bass. 4.** a low pitch or range. *—adj.* **5.** of or in the range of a bass.

bass[2] (bas), *n., pl.* **bass, bass·es.** an edible, spiny-finned, freshwater or marine fish.

bass′ drum′ (bās), a large drum having a cylindrical body and two membrane heads.

bas·set (bas′it), *n.* a hound having short legs, a long body, and long ears. Also called **bas′set hound′.**

bas·si·net (bas′ə net′), *n.* a basket with a hood over one end, for use as a baby's cradle.

bass·ist (bā′sist), *n.* a player of the double bass.

bas·so (bas′ō, bä′sō), *n.* a person who sings bass.

bas·soon (ba sōōn′, bə-), *n.* a large woodwind instrument of low range, with a doubled tube. **—bas·soon′-ist,** *n.*

bass′ re′flex (bās), a loudspeaker equipped with a baffle having openings designed to improve the reproduction of low-frequency sounds.

bass′ vi′ol (bās). See **double bass.**

bass·wood (bas′wood′), *n.* **1.** an American linden tree. **2.** its wood.

bast (bast), *n.* a strong woody fiber used in cordage.

bas·tard (bas′tərd), *n.* **1.** an illegitimate child. **2.** *Slang.* a vicious or despicable person. *—adj.* **3.** illegitimate in birth. **4.** not genuine or real. **—bas′tard·ly,** *adj.* **—bas′tard·y,** *n.*

bas·tard·ize (bas′tər dīz′), *v.t.,* **-ized, -iz·ing. 1.** to declare or prove (someone) to be a bastard. **2.** to lower in condition or worth. **—bas′-tard·i·za′tion,** *n.*

baste[1] (bāst), *v.t.,* **bast·ed, bast·ing.** to sew with long, loose, temporary stitches.

baste[2] (bāst), *v.t.,* **bast·ed, bast·ing.** to moisten (meat or other food) while cooking.

baste[3] (bāst), *v.t.,* **bast·ed, bast·ing. 1.** to beat severely with a stick. **2.** to denounce vigorously.

bas·ti·na·do (bas′tə nā′dō), *n., pl.* **-does. 1.** a beating with a stick, cudgel, etc. **2.** an Oriental mode of punishment, consisting of blows with a stick on the soles of the feet Also, **bas′ti·nade** (-nād′).

bas·tion (bas′chən, -tē ən), *n.* **1.** a projecting portion of a fortification. **2.** a fortified place. **—bas′tioned,** *adj.*

bat[1] (bat), *n., v.,* **bat·ted, bat·ting. —n. 1. a.** the wooden club used in baseball or cricket to strike the ball. **b.** a turn to use such a club. **2.** a heavy stick or club. **3.** *In-*

formal. a blow, as with a bat. **4.**
Slang. a spree or binge. —*v.t.* **5.** to
strike with, or as with, a bat.
—*v.i.* **6.** to take one's turn as a
batter.

bat² (bat), *n.* any nocturnal flying
mammal having modified forelimbs
that serve as wings. —**bat′like′**, *adj.*

bat³ (bat), *v.t.*, **bat·ted, bat·ting.** *Informal.* **1.** to blink or wink. **2.** **not
bat an eye,** to show no emotion or
surprise.

batch (bach), *n.* **1.** a quantity of
the same kind made or handled
at one time or considered as one
group. **2.** the quantity of bread
made at one baking.

bate (bāt), *v.t.*, **bat·ed, bat·ing.** **1.**
Archaic. **a.** to moderate or restrain.
b. to abate. **2. with bated breath,**
with breath drawn in or held because of anticipation.

ba·teau (ba tō′), *n.*, *pl.* **-teaux** (-tōz′).
a double-ended, flat-bottomed row-
boat.

bath (bath, bäth), *n.*, *pl.* **baths**
(bathz, bäthz, baths, bäths). **1.**
a washing, esp. of the body, in
water, steam, etc. **2.** a quantity
of water used for this purpose. **3.** a
bathtub. **4.** a bathroom or any
room equipped for bathing: *a room
and bath.* **5.** an establishment for
bathing, as a steam bath. **6.** Usually, **baths.** spa. **7.** a preparation,
as an acid solution, in which something is immersed.

bathe (bāth), *v.*, **bathed, bath·ing.**
—*v.t.* **1.** to immerse in water or
liquid, as for cleaning. **2.** to wet
or wash. **3.** to apply water or
liquid to. **4.** to cover or surround:
sunlight bathing the room. —*v.i.* **5.**
to take a bath. **6.** to swim for
pleasure. —**bath′er**, *n.*

bath·house (bath′hous′, bäth′-), *n.*
1. a structure containing dressing
rooms for bathers. **2.** a building
having bathing facilities.

bath mitz·vah (bät mits′və). (*often
caps.*) **1.** a ceremony for a girl,
chiefly among Reform and Conservative Jews, paralleling the bar
mitzvah. **2.** the girl participating in
this ceremony.

bath·o·lith (bath′ə lith), *n.* a large
body of bounded igneous rock.
—**bath′o·lith′ic,** *adj.*

ba·thos (bā′thos), *n.* **1.** a ludicrous
descent from the lofty to the commonplace. **2.** triteness or triviality.
3. insincere pathos. —**ba·thet·ic**
(bə thet′ik), *adj.*

bath·robe (bath′rōb′, bäth′-), *n.* a
long, loose, coatlike garment, for
wearing before and after a bath.

bath·room (bath′rōōm′, -rŏŏm′,
bäth′-), *n.* a room containing a

bathtub or shower and, typically, a
washbowl and toilet.

bath·tub (bath′tub′, bäth′-), *n.* a
tub to bathe in.

bath·y·scaphe (bath′i skāf′, -skaf′),
n. a small submarine for deep-sea
exploration. Also, **bath·y·scaph**
(bath′i skaf′).

bath·y·sphere (bath′i sfēr′), *n.* a
spherical diving apparatus from
which to study deep-sea life.

ba·tik (bə tēk′, bat′ik), *n.* **1.** a technique of dyeing fabrics by using
wax to cover parts of a design
not to be dyed. **2.** the fabric so
decorated.

ba·tiste (bə tēst′, ba-), *n.* a fine,
sheer fabric made of any of various
fibers.

bat·man (bat′mən), *n.*, *pl.* **-men.**
a soldier assigned to a British officer
as a servant. —**bat′wom′an,** *n.fem.*

ba·ton (ba ton′, bə-, bat′°n), *n.* **1.**
Music. the wand used by a conductor. **2.** a staff carried and
twirled by a drum major or drum
majorette. **3.** a short staff serving
as a symbol of office.

Bat·on Rouge (bat′°n rōōzh′), the
capital of Louisiana.

ba·tra·chi·an (bə trā′kē ən), *n.* a tailless amphibian, as the toad or frog.

bats (bats), *adj.* *Slang.* batty.

bats·man (bats′mən), *n.*, *pl.* **-men.**
a batter, esp. in cricket.

batt., **1.** battalion. **2.** battery.

bat·tal·ion (bə tal′yən), *n.* **1.** a
ground-force unit composed of a
headquarters and two or more
companies. **2.** an army in battle
array. [< F *bataillon* < It *bat-
taglione* large unit of soldiers]

bat·ten¹ (bat′°n), *n.* **1.** a small
strip of wood used for various
building purposes. —*v.t.* **2.** to furnish or bolster with battens.

bat·ten² (bat′°n), *v.i.* *Archaic.* **1.** to
grow fat, as cattle. **2.** to thrive or
prosper.

bat·ter¹ (bat′ər), *v.t.* **1.** to beat or
pound repeatedly. **2.** to damage by
rough usage. —*v.i.* **3.** to pound
steadily.

bat·ter² (bat′ər), *n.* a mixture of
flour, milk, etc., beaten together
for use in cookery.

bat·ter³ (bat′ər), *n.* a player who
bats or whose turn it is to bat,
as in baseball.

bat′tering ram′, an ancient military
device for battering down walls,
gates, etc.

bat·ter·y (bat′ə rē), *n.*, *pl.* **-ter·ies.**
1. a combination of galvanic cells
for generating an electric current.
2. any group of similar or related
items, parts, etc. **3.** two or more
pieces of artillery used for combined
action. **4.** a group of guns on a

warship. **5.** *Baseball.* the pitcher and catcher in a game. **6.** an unlawful attack upon another person.

bat·ting (bat'ĭng), *n.* **1.** act of using a bat in a game of ball. **2.** cotton or wool in sheets.

bat·tle (bat'ʾl), *n., v.,* **-tled, -tling.** —*n.* **1.** a hostile military encounter or engagement. **2.** a fight or contest. —*v.i., v.t.* **3.** to fight (against). —**bat'tler**, *n.* —Syn. 1, 2. combat, conflict, skirmish.

bat·tle-ax (bat'ʾl aks'), *n., pl.* **-ax·es. 1.** an ax formerly used as a weapon of war. **2.** *Slang.* a domineering, sharp-tempered woman. Also, **bat'tle-axe'.**

bat·tle cry', **1.** a shout of enthusiasm of troops in battle. **2.** a slogan used in any contest.

bat·tle·dore (bat'ʾl dōr', -dôr'), *n.* a light racket used to strike a shuttlecock in a game resembling badminton.

battle fatigue', an emotional disorder resulting from combat duty.

bat·tle·field (bat'ʾl fēld'), *n.* the field or ground on which a battle is fought.

battle jack'et, a waist-length woolen jacket with snugly fitting cuffs and waist, formerly worn as part of the U.S. military uniform.

bat'tle line', the line along which warring troops meet.

bat·tle·ment (bat'ʾl mənt), *n.* Often, **battlements.** a parapet on top of a wall, for defense or decoration. —**bat·tle·ment·ed** (bat'ʾl men'tĭd), *adj.*

bat'tle roy'al, *pl.* **battles royal. 1.** a fight among more than two combatants. **2.** a violent or noisy fight or dispute.

bat·tle·ship (bat'ʾl ship'), *n.* a warship that is the most heavily armored and equipped with the most powerful armament.

bat'tle sta'tion, *Mil.* the place or position that one is assigned to for battle.

bat'tle wag'on, *Informal.* a battleship.

bat·ty (bat'ē), *adj.,* **-ti·er, -ti·est.** *Slang.* insane or crazy.

bau·ble (bô'bəl), *n.* a cheap, showy trinket.

baux·ite (bôk'sīt, bō'zīt), *n.* a claylike mixture of minerals that is the principal ore of aluminum.

bawd (bôd), *n. Archaic.* **1.** a madam of a brothel. **2.** a prostitute.

bawd·y (bô'dē), *adj.,* **bawd·i·er, bawd·i·est.** humorously obscene. —**bawd'i·ly,** *adv.* —**bawd'i·ness,** *n.* —**baw'dry,** *n.*

bawl (bôl), *v.t.* **1.** to shout out. —*v.i.* **2.** to cry loudly. **3. bawl out,** to scold vigorously. —*n.* **4.** a loud shout. **5.** a loud crying. —**bawl'er,** *n.*

bay¹ (bā), *n.* a body of water forming an indentation of the shoreline.

bay² (bā), *n.* **1. a.** any of a number of major vertical divisions of a large interior, wall, etc. **b.** See **bay window** (def. 1). **2.** a compartment set off by walls or bulkheads.

bay³ (bā), *n.* **1.** a deep, prolonged howl, as of a hound. **2.** the situation of a cornered animal or fugitive forced to resist pursuers: *a stag at bay.* —*v.i., v.t.* **3.** to howl (at).

bay⁴ (bā), *n.* **1.** the European laurel. **2. bays,** *Obs.* fame or renown.

bay⁵ (bā), *n.* **1.** a reddish brown. **2.** an animal of this color. —*adj.* **3.** reddish-brown.

bay·ber·ry (bā'ber'ē, -bə rē), *n., pl.* **-ries. 1.** an American shrub bearing small green berries. **2.** its berry.

bay' leaf', the fragrant leaf of the bay tree, used in cookery.

bay·o·net (bā'ə nit, -net', bā'ə net'), *n., v.,* **-net·ed** *or* **-net·ted, -net·ing** *or* **-net·ting.** —*n.* **1.** a daggerlike weapon for attaching to the muzzle end of a gun and used for stabbing. —*v.t., v.i.* **2.** to stab with a bayonet. [< F *baïonnette,* after *Bayonne,* France, where first made]

bay·ou (bī'ōō, bī'ō), *n., pl.* **-ous.** any stagnant or sluggish creek, marshy lake, etc.

bay' rum', a fragrant liquid used chiefly as a cosmetic lotion, prepared by distilling the leaves of the bayberry with rum.

bay' win'dow, 1. an alcove of a room, projecting from an outside wall and having its own windows. **2.** *Informal.* a protruding belly.

ba·zaar (bə zär'), *n.* **1.** a shopping quarter, esp. in the Middle East. **2.** a sale of miscellaneous articles to benefit some charity, etc.

ba·zoo·ka (bə zōō'kə), *n.* a portable rocket launcher that fires an armor-piercing rocket.

BB (bē'bē'), *n.* a size of shot, .18 inch in diameter, for firing from an air rifle (**BB gun**).

bb., 1. ball bearing. **2.** *Baseball.* base on balls.

B.B.A., Bachelor of Business Administration.

BBB, Better Business Bureau.

BBC, British Broadcasting Corporation.

bbl. barrel.

bc, blind [carbon] copy (notation on the carbon copy, esp. of a letter, sent to a third person without the addressee's knowledge). Also, **bcc**

B.C., 1. Bachelor of Commerce. **2.** before Christ (in reckoning dates). **3.** British Columbia.

B.C.S., Bachelor of Commercial Science.

bd., 1. board. 2. bond. 3. bound.

B/D, 1. bank draft. 2. bills discounted. 3. *Accounting.* brought down.

B.D., 1. Bachelor of Divinity. 2. bank draft. 3. bills discounted.

bdl., bundle. Also, **bdle.**

bdrm., bedroom.

be (bē; *unstressed* bē, bi), *v. and auxiliary v., pres. sing. 1st pers.* **am,** *2nd* **are** *or (Archaic)* **art,** *3rd* **is,** *pres. pl.* **are;** *past sing. 1st pers.* **was,** *2nd* **were** *or (Archaic)* **wast** *or* **wert,** *3rd* **was,** *past pl.* **were;** *pres. subj.* **be;** *past subj. sing. 1st pers.* **were,** *2nd* **were** *or (Archaic)* **wert,** *3rd* **were;** *past subj. pl.* **were;** *past part.* **been;** *pres. part.* **be·ing.** —*v.i.* 1. to exist or live. 2. to occur. 3. to occupy a position. 4. to continue as before. 5. *Literary.* to befall. 6. (used as a copula to connect the subject with its predicate adjective, or predicate nominative, in order to describe, identify, or amplify the subject): *Martha is tall.* 7. (used as a copula to introduce or form interrogative or imperative sentences): *Is that right? Be quiet!* —*auxiliary verb.* 8. (used with the present participle of another verb to form the progressive tense): *I am waiting.* 9. (used with the present participle or infinitive of the principal verb to indicate future action): *He is to see me today.* 10. (used with the past participle of another verb to form the passive voice): *The date was fixed.*

Be, beryllium.

be-, a prefix meaning: **a.** about or around: *besiege.* **b.** all over: *bedaub.* **c.** to provide with: *becloud.* **d.** at or regarding: *begrudge.* **e.** to make: *befriend.*

B/E, bill of exchange.

B.E., Board of Education.

beach (bēch), *n.* 1. an expanse of sand or pebbles along a shore. —*v.t., v.i.* 2. *Naut.* to haul or run onto a beach.

beach′ bug′gy, an automobile equipped with oversize tires for sand beaches.

beach·comb·er (bēch′kō′mər), *n.* 1. a person who lives by gathering salable jetsam or refuse from beaches. 2. a vagrant living along the seashore. 3. a long wave rolling onto the beach.

beach′ flea′, any of various small jumping crustaceans, found on beaches.

beach·head (bēch′hed′), *n.* the area that is the first objective of a military force landing on an enemy shore.

bea·con (bē′kən), *n.* 1. a guiding or warning signal, such as a light or fire. 2. a tower or hill used for such purposes. 3. a radio transmitter that sends out signals for navigational aid to aircraft. —**bea′con·less,** *adj.*

bead (bēd), *n.* 1. a small, usually round object of glass or wood, pierced for stringing. 2. **beads, a.** a necklace of such objects. **b.** a rosary. 3. any small, globular body: *beads of sweat.* 4. the front sight of a gun. 5. a reinforced area of a rubber tire. 6. **count, say,** or **tell one's beads,** to say one's prayers with rosary beads. 7. **draw a bead on,** to take careful aim at. —*v.t.* 8. to ornament with beads. —*v.i.* 9. to form in beads. —**bead·ing,** *n.* —**bead′y,** *adj.*

bea·dle (bē′dᵊl), *n.* (formerly) a parish officer who keeps order during services, etc.

bea·gle (bē′gəl), *n.* a small hound having long ears and short legs.

beak (bēk), *n.* 1. the bill of a bird. 2. any similar part in other animals, such as the turtle, etc. —**beaked** (bēkt, bē′kid), *adj.* —**beak′like′,** *adj.*

beak·er (bē′kər), *n.* 1. a large drinking cup or glass with a wide mouth. 2. a flat-bottomed cup with a pouring lip, esp. as used by chemists.

beam (bēm), *n.* 1. a long piece of metal or wood, for use as a rigid part of a structure. 2. a horizontal bearing member, as a joist or lintel. 3. the extreme width of a ship. 4. a ray of light. 5. a group of nearly parallel rays. 6. a radio or radar signal, used to guide pilots. 7. the crossbar of a weighing balance. 8. a radiant smile. 9. **on the beam,** *Slang.* proceeding correctly or exactly. —*v.t.* 10. to emit in beams or rays. 11. to direct (a radio signal). —*v.i.* 12. to emit beams, as of light. 13. to smile radiantly or happily.

bean (bēn), *n.* 1. the edible nutritious seed of various species of leguminous plants. 2. a plant producing such seeds. 3. any beanlike seed or plant, as the coffee bean. 4. *Slang.* a person's head. 5. **spill the beans,** *Informal.* to disclose a secret. —*v.t.* 6. *Informal.* to hit on the head. —**bean′like′,** *adj.*

bean·bag (bēn′bag′), *n.* a small cloth bag filled with beans, used as a toy.

bean′ ball′, a baseball thrown by a pitcher purposely at a batter's head.

bean′ curd′, a creamy, white cake made from soybean, used in Oriental cooking.

bean·er·y (bē′nə rē), *n., pl.* **-er·ies.** *Slang.* a cheap, usually inferior, restaurant.

bean·ie (bē′nē), *n.* a skullcap worn esp. by children and college freshmen.

bean·o (bē′nō), *n.* a form of bingo.

bear[1] (bâr), *v.*, **bore, borne** or **born, bear·ing.** —*v.t.* **1.** to give birth to. **2.** to produce by natural growth. **3.** to support (a load). **4.** to be capable of: *His claim bears close examination.* **5.** to press or push against. **6.** to manage or conduct (oneself, etc.). **7.** to suffer or endure. **8.** to carry or bring: *to bear gifts.* **9.** to give: *to bear testimony.* **10.** to show: *to bear a resemblance.* —*v.i.* **11.** to move or go: *to bear west.* **12.** to be situated. **13.** to bring forth young or fruit. **14. bear down**, **a.** to strive harder. **b.** to approach rapidly. **15. bear on** or **upon**, to affect or relate to. **16. bear out**, to substantiate or confirm. **17. bear up**, to endure. **18. bear with**, to be patient. —**bear′a·ble**, *adj.* —**bear′er**, *n.* —Syn. **7.** abide, stand, tolerate.

bear[2] (bâr), *n.* **1.** a large, four-legged mammal having a massive body and coarse heavy fur. **2.** a gruff, clumsy, or rude person. **3.** a person who believes that the stock or commodities market will decline. —*adj.* **4.** marked by a continuing trend of declining prices, as of stocks: *a bear market.* —**bear′ish**, *adj.* —**bear′-like′**, *adj.*

beard (bērd), *n.* **1.** the growth of hair on the face of an adult man. **2.** a tuft resembling a human beard. —*v.t.* **3.** to pull the beard of. **4.** to oppose boldly. **5.** to supply with a beard. —**beard′ed**, *adj.* —**beard′-less**, *adj.*

bear′ hug′, a forcefully tight embrace.

bear·ing (bâr′ĭng), *n.* **1.** the manner in which one conducts oneself. **2.** the act, capability, or period of bringing forth: *a tree past bearing.* **3.** a crop. **4.** reference or relation. **5.** the support and guide for a shaft, pivot, etc. **6.** Often, **bearings. a.** direction or position. **b.** comprehension of one's position. **7.** a horizontal direction expressed in degrees.

bear·skin (bâr′skin′), *n.* **1.** the skin or pelt of a bear. **2.** an article made from this.

beast (bēst), *n.* **1.** any animal other than humans. **2.** a cruel, coarse person.

beast·ly (bēst′lē), *adj.*, **-li·er, -li·est,** *adv.* —*adj.* **1.** of or like a beast. **2.** *Informal.* nasty or disagreeable. —*adv.* **3.** *Brit. Informal.* very. —**beast′li·ness**, *n.*

beast′ of bur′den, an animal used for carrying heavy loads, as a donkey.

beat (bēt), *v.*, **beat, beat·en** (bēt′°n) or **beat, beat·ing**, *n., adj.* —*v.t.* **1.** to give a series of blows to. **2.** to flutter against. **3.** to stir vigorously. **4.** to make (a path) by repeated treading. **5.** to thrash soundly. **6.** *Music.* to mark (time) with the hand or a metronome. **7.** to scour (the forest or brush) to rouse game. **8.** to defeat. **9.** to be superior to. **10.** *Slang.* to baffle. **11.** to swindle. **12.** *Slang.* to escape or avoid (blame or punishment). —*v.i.* **13.** to pound. **14.** to throb. **15. beat it**, to go away. —*n.* **16.** a stroke or blow. **17.** a throb or pulsation. **18.** a person's regular path or round: *a policeman's beat.* **19.** the marking of the metrical divisions of music. **20.** the accent stress in a rhythmical unit of poetry. **21.** *Informal.* beatnik. —*adj. Informal.* **22.** worn-out. **23.** of or pertaining to beatniks. —**beat′er**, *n.* —**beat′ing**, *n.* —Syn. **1, 5.** buffet, pound, punch, strike.

be·a·tif·ic (bē′ə tĭf′ĭk), *adj.* **1.** bestowing bliss. **2.** blissful or saintly. —**be′a·tif′i·cal·ly**, *adv.*

be·at·i·fy (bē ăt′ə fī′), *v.t.*, **-fied, -fy·ing. 1.** to make blissfully happy. **2.** *Rom. Cath. Ch.* to declare (a deceased person) to be among the blessed in heaven. —**be·at′i·fi·ca′tion**, *n.*

be·at·i·tude (bē ăt′ə tōōd′, -tyōōd′), *n.* **1.** supreme blessedness or happiness. **2.** (*often cap.*) any of the declarations of blessedness pronounced by Jesus in the Sermon on the Mount.

beat·nik (bēt′nĭk), *n.* a young person of the late 1950's, often unconventional in behavior, dress, etc., who espoused mystical detachment and the relaxation of authority and social inhibitions.

beat-up (bēt′up′), *adj. Informal.* dilapidated or worn-out.

beau (bō), *n., pl.* **beaus, beaux** (bōz). *Obsolescent.* **1.** a suitor or lover. **2.** a dandy or fop. —**beau′ish**, *adj.*

Beau′fort scale′ (bō′fort), a scale of wind forces described by name and range of velocity, and classified from force 0 to force 12.

beau geste (bō zhest′), *pl.* **beaux gestes** (bō zhest′). *French.* a fine gesture, often only for effect.

beau′ idé′al, a model of excellence.

Beau·jo·lais (bō′zhə lā′), *n.* a fruity, red Burgundy wine.

beau monde (bō′ mond′), the fashionable world.

Beau·mont (bō′mont), *n.* a city in SE Texas.

beaut (byōōt), *n. Informal.* something or someone beautiful, remarkable, or perfect.

beau·te·ous (byōō′tē əs, -tyəs), *adj. Literary.* beautiful. —**beau′te·ous·ly,** *adv.*

beau·ti·cian (byōō tish′ən), *n.* a cosmetologist.

beau·ti·ful (byōō′tə fəl), *adj.* having beauty. —**beau′ti·ful·ly,** *adv.* —**Syn.** comely, fair, gorgeous, lovely, pretty.

beau′tiful peo′ple, wealthy, sophisticated people who set trends and fashions.

beau·ti·fy (byōō′tə fī′), *v.t., v.i.,* **-fied, -fy·ing.** to make or become beautiful. —**beau·ti·fi·ca·tion** (byōō′tə fə kā′shən), *n.* —**beau′ti·fi′er,** *n.*

beau·ty (byōō′tē), *n., pl.* **-ties** for 2, 3. **1.** quality giving intense aesthetic pleasure. **2.** something having this quality. **3.** a good-looking girl.

beau′ty par′lor, an establishment for hairdressing, manicuring, or other beauty treatment of women. Also called **beau′ty shop′.**

beaux (bōz), *n.* a pl. of **beau.**

beaux arts (bō zär′), the fine arts.

bea·ver (bē′vər), *n.* **1.** a large, furry, amphibious rodent having sharp incisors, webbed hind feet, and a flattened tail. **2.** its fur. **3.** a tall hat for men. **4.** *CB Radio Slang.* a woman.

be·calm (bi käm′), *v.t.* to deprive (a sailing vessel) of the wind necessary to move it.

be·came (bi käm′), *v.* pt. of **become.**

be·cause (bi kôz′, -koz′, -kuz′), *conj.* **1.** for the reason that. **2. because of,** by reason of.
—**Usage. 1.** See **reason.**

beck (bek), *n.* **1.** a beckoning gesture. **2. at someone's beck and call,** ready to do someone's bidding.

beck·on (bek′ən), *v.t., v.i.* **1.** to signal or call by a gesture of the head or hand. **2.** to attract. —**beck′on·er,** *n.* —**beck′on·ing·ly,** *adv.*

be·cloud (bi kloud′), *v.t.* **1.** to darken with clouds. **2.** to make confused.

be·come (bi kum′), *v.,* **be·came, be·come, be·com·ing.** —*v.i.* **1.** to come, change, or grow to be. —*v.t.* **2.** to befit or suit. **3. become of,** to happen to.

be·com·ing (bi kum′ing), *adj.* **1.** suitable or fitting. **2.** attractive or pleasing. —**be·com′ing·ly,** *adv.*

bed (bed), *n., v.,* **bed·ded, bed·ding.** —*n.* **1.** a piece of furniture on which a person sleeps. **2.** a plot of ground where plants are grown. **3.** the bottom of a lake, river, etc. **4.** a foundation or base. **5.** a layer or stratum of rock. —*v.t.* **6.** to provide with a bed. **7.** to put to bed. **8.** to plant in a bed. **9.** to place in layers. **10.** to embed. —*v.i.* **11.** to go to bed. **12.** to form in layers.

be·daub (bi dôb′), *v.t.* to besmear or soil.

be·daz·zle (bi daz′əl), *v.t.,* **-zled, -zling.** to dazzle so as to confuse. —**be·daz′zle·ment,** *n.*

bed′ board′, a thin board placed between the mattress and bedspring to give firm support.

bed·bug (bed′bug′), *n.* a flat, wingless, bloodsucking insect that infests houses and esp. beds.

bed′ check′, an inspection, usually at night, to detect the unauthorized absence of persons.

bed·clothes (bed′klōz′, -klōt͟hz), *n.pl.* coverings for a bed, as sheets, blankets, etc.

bed·da·ble (bed′ə bəl), *adj. Slang.* readily willing to have sexual relations.

bed·ding (bed′ing), *n.* **1.** mattresses, blankets, pillows, etc. **2.** litter, straw, etc., as a bed for animals. **3.** a building foundation.

be·deck (bi dek′), *v.t.* to adorn, esp. gaudily.

be·dev·il (bi dev′əl), *v.t.,* **-iled, -il·ing** or **-illed, -il·ling.** to torment maliciously. —**be·dev′il·ment,** *n.*

be·dew (bi dōō′, -dyōō′), *v.t.* to wet or cover with or as with dew.

bed·fast (bed′fast′, -fäst′), *adj. Archaic.* bedridden.

bed·fel·low (bed′fel′ō), *n.* **1.** a person who shares one's bed. **2.** any close associate.

be·dim (bi dim′), *v.t.,* **-dimmed, -dim·ming.** to make dim.

be·di·zen (bi dī′zən, -diz′ən), *v.t.* to dress in a gaudy or vulgar manner.

bed·lam (bed′ləm), *n.* a scene of wild uproar and confusion. [after *Hospital of St. Mary of Bethlehem,* former insane asylum in London]

Bed′lington ter′rier (bed′ling tən), an English terrier having a thick, fleecy, blue or liver coat.

bed′ of ros′es, *Informal.* a situation of luxurious ease.

Bed·ou·in (bed′ōō in, bed′win), *n., pl.* **-ins, -in.** an Arab of the desert, in Asia or Africa.

bed·pan (bed′pan′), *n.* a shallow toilet pan for use by persons confined to bed.

bed·post (bed′pōst′), *n.* one of the upright supports of a bedstead.

be·drag·gle (bi drag′əl), *v.t.,* **-gled, -gling.** to make limp and soiled, as with rain or dirt.

bed·rid·den (bed′rid′ən), *adj.* confined to bed.

bed·rock (bed′rok′), *n.* **1.** unbroken solid rock, overlaid by soil. **2.** any firm base.

bed·roll (bed′rōl′), *n.* bedding rolled for portability, used esp. out-of-doors.

bed·room (bed'room', -room'), *n.* a room furnished and used for sleeping.

bed·side (bed'sīd'), *n.* **1.** the side of a bed, esp. as the place of one attending the sick. —*adj.* **2.** at or for a bedside.

bed'side man'ner, the behavior of a doctor to his or her patients.

bed·sore (bed'sōr', -sôr'), *n.* a sore caused by prolonged pressure of the body against bedding, as in a long illness.

bed·spread (bed'spred'), *n.* an outer covering, usually decorative, for a bed.

bed·spring (bed'spring'), *n.* a set of springs for the support of a mattress.

bed·stead (bed'sted', -stid), *n.* the framework supporting a bed.

bed·time (bed'tīm'), *n.* the time at which one goes to bed.

bee (bē), *n.* **1.** any of a large group of four-winged insects, usually with a sting, some species of which live in hives and produce honey. **2.** a gathering in order to perform together or to compete: *a sewing bee; a spelling bee.* —**bee'like'**, *adj.*

beech (bēch), *n.* **1.** a tree having a smooth gray bark and bearing a small, edible, triangular nut (**beech'-nut'**). **2.** its wood. —**beech'en**, *adj.*

beef (bēf), *n., pl.* **beeves** (bēvz) for **2, beefs** for **4,** *v.* —*n.* **1.** the flesh of a cow, steer, or bull for use as meat. **2.** an adult cow, steer, or bull raised for its meat. **3.** *Informal.* muscular strength. **4.** *Slang.* a complaint. —*v.i.* **5.** *Slang.* to complain. **6. beef up,** *Informal.* to strengthen.

beef·burg·er (bēf'bûr'gər), *n.* a hamburger.

beef·eat·er (bēf'ē'tər), *n.* **1.** a yeoman of the English royal guard. **2.** *Slang.* an Englishman. **3.** a person who eats beef.

beef·steak (bēf'stāk'), *n.* a steak of beef for broiling, frying, etc.

beef·y (bē'fē), *adj.*, **beef·i·er, beef·i·est.** brawny or thickset.

bee·hive (bē'hīv'), *n.* **1.** a hive for bees. **2.** a crowded, busy place.

bee·keep·er (bē'kē'pər), *n.* a person who raises bees. —**bee'keep'ing**, *n.*

bee·line (bē'līn'), *n.* a direct course.

Be·el·ze·bub (bē el'zə bub'), *n. New Testament.* Satan.

been (bin), *v.* pp. of **be.**

beep (bēp), *n.* **1.** a short, high-pitched tone used as a signal or warning. —*v.i., v.t.* **2.** to make or cause to make such a sound.

beep·er (bē'pər), *n.* a device that transmits a periodic signal to indicate that a telephone conversation is being recorded.

beer (bēr), *n.* **1.** an alcoholic beverage brewed by fermentation from malt and hops. **2.** any of various carbonated beverages: *ginger beer.*

bees·wax (bēz'waks'), *n.* wax[1] (def. 1).

beet (bēt), *n.* **1.** a biennial plant having a fleshy red or white root. **2.** the edible root of this plant.

Bee·tho·ven (bā'tō vən), *n.* **Lud·wig van** (lud'wig van, lōōd'-), 1770–1827, German composer.

bee·tle[1] (bēt'əl), *n.* an insect having hard, horny front wings that cover the membranous flight wings.

bee·tle[2] (bēt'əl), *n.* a heavy hammering or ramming tool.

bee·tle[3] (bēt'əl), *adj., v.,* **-tled, -tling.** —*adj.* **1.** projecting or overhanging. —*v.i.* **2.** to project or overhang.

bee·tle-browed (bēt'əl broud'), *adj.* **1.** having projecting eyebrows. **2.** scowling or frowning.

beeves (bēvz), *n.* a pl. of **beef.**

bef., before.

B.E.F., British Expeditionary Force.

be·fall (bi fôl'), *v.i., v.t.,* **-fell, -fallen, -fall·ing.** to happen (to), esp. something unfortunate.

be·fit (bi fit'), *v.t.,* **-fit·ted, -fit·ting.** to be suitable or appropriate for. —**be·fit'ting**, *adj.*

be·fog (bi fog', -fôg'), *v.t.,* **-fogged, -fog·ging. 1.** to envelop in fog. **2.** to render unclear.

be·fore (bi fōr', -fôr'), *adv.* **1.** in front or ahead. **2.** previously. **3.** earlier or sooner. —*prep.* **4.** in front of or ahead of. **5.** earlier than. **6.** awaiting. **7.** in precedence of. **8.** in the presence or sight of. **9.** under the consideration of. —*conj.* **10.** previously to the time when. **11.** rather than.

be·fore·hand (bi fōr'hand', -fôr'-), *adv., adj.* ahead of time.

be·foul (bi foul'), *v.t.* to make foul or dirty.

be·friend (bi frend'), *v.t.* to act as a friend to.

be·fud·dle (bi fud'əl), *v.t.,* **-dled, -dling.** to confuse thoroughly. —**be·fud'dler**, *n.* —**be·fud'dle·ment**, *n.*

beg (beg), *v.t., v.i.,* **begged, beg·ging. 1.** to ask for (alms or charity). **2.** to ask humbly or earnestly. **3.** to avoid or evade: *to beg the question.* —**Syn. 2.** beseech, entreat, implore, importune, plead.

be·gan (bi gan'), *v.* pt. of **begin.**

be·get (bi get'), *v.t.,* **be·got** (-got') or (*Archaic*) **be·gat** (-gat'); **be·got·ten** (-got'ºn) or **be·got; be·get·ting.** *Literary.* **1.** to be the father of **2.** to cause or produce. —**be·get'ter**, *adv.*

beg·gar (beg'ər), *n.* **1.** a person who lives by begging. —*v.t.* **2.** to impoverish. **3.** to go beyond, as description. —**beg'gar·y**, *n.*

beg·gar·ly (beg′ər lē), *adj.* 1. like a beggar. 2. meanly inadequate. —**beg′gar·li·ness**, *n.*

be·gin (bi gin′), *v.i., v.t.,* **be·gan, be·gun, be·gin·ning.** 1. to do the first part of (something). 2. to come or bring into existence. —**be·gin′ner**, *n.* —**Syn.** 1. commence, initiate, start. 2. inaugurate, institute, originate.

be·gin·ning (bi gin′ĭng), *n.* 1. the act or fact of entering upon an action. 2. the time or place at which anything begins. 3. origin or source.

be·gone (bi gôn′, -gon′), *v.i. Archaic.* go away!: *Begone with you!*

be·gon·ia (bi gōn′yə, -gō′nē ə), *n.* a tropical plant cultivated for its varicolored leaves and waxy flowers.

be·grime (bi grīm′), *v.t.,* **-grimed, -grim·ing.** to make grimy.

be·grudge (bi gruj′), *v.t.,* **-grudged, -grudg·ing.** 1. to envy the pleasure or good fortune of (someone). 2. to be reluctant to give or allow. —**be·grudg′ing·ly**, *adv.*

be·guile (bi gīl′), *v.t.,* **-guiled, -guil·ing.** 1. to influence by guile. 2. to cheat or deceive. 3. to charm or divert. 4. to pass (time) pleasantly. —**be·guile′ment**, *n.* —**be·guil′er**, *n.*

be·guine (bi gēn′), *n.* a West Indian dance in bolero rhythm.

be·gum (bē′gəm), *n.* a high-ranking Muslim lady.

be·gun (bi gun′), *v.* pp. of **begin.**

be·half (bi haf′, -häf′), *n.* **in** or **on behalf of,** as a representative for.

be·have (bi hāv′), *v.i., v.t.,* **-haved, -hav·ing.** 1. to conduct (oneself) in a particular way. 2. to act properly.

be·hav·ior (bi hāv′yər), *n.* 1. manner of behaving or acting. 2. the action or reaction under given circumstances. Also, *esp. Brit.,* **be·hav′iour.** —**be·hav′ior·al**, *adj.*

behav′ioral sci′ence, any of various sciences, as psychology or sociology, concerned with human behavior.

be·hav·ior·ism (bi hāv′yə riz′əm), *n.* the doctrine that regards objective facts of behavior as the only proper subject for psychological study.

be·head (bi hed′), *v.t.* to cut off the head of.

be·held (bi held′), *v.* pt. and pp. of **behold.**

be·he·moth (bi hē′məth, bē′ə-), *n.* a huge animal, perhaps the hippopotamus, mentioned in Job 40:15–24.

be·hest (bi hest′), *n.* 1. an authoritative command. 2. an earnest request.

be·hind (bi hīnd′), *prep.* 1. at or toward the back of. 2. later than or after. 3. in the state of making less progress than. 4. beyond. 5. supporting or promoting. 6. hidden or unrevealed by. —*adv.* 7. at or toward the rear. 8. in a place or

stage already passed. 9. in arrears. 10. slow, as a clock. —*n.* 11. *Slang.* the buttocks.

be·hind·hand (bi hīnd′hand′), *adv., adj.* 1. back in time or progress. 2. in arrears.

be·hold (bi hōld′), *v.,* **be·held, be·hold·ing,** *interj.* —*v.t.* 1. to look at or see. —*interj.* 2. look! see! —**be·hold′er**, *n.*

be·hold·en (bi hōl′dən), *adj. Archaic.* obligated or indebted.

be·hoof (bi hoof′), *n. Archaic.* use or advantage.

be·hoove (bi hoov′), *v.t.,* **-hooved, -hoov·ing.** to be proper or necessary for.

beige (bāzh), *n.* 1. a light grayish brown. —*adj.* 2. of the color beige.

be·ing (bē′ĭng), *n.* 1. the fact of existing. 2. substance or nature. 3. something or someone that exists.

Bei·rut (bā root′), *n.* the capital of Lebanon.

be·jew·el (bi joo′əl), *v.t.,* **-eled, -el·ing** or **-elled, -el·ling.** to adorn with jewels.

be·la·bor (bi lā′bər), *v.t.* 1. to discuss or worry about for an unreasonable amount of time. 2. *Literary.* to beat vigorously.

be·lat·ed (bi lā′tid), *adj.* late or delayed. —**be·lat′ed·ly**, *adv.*

be·lay (bi lā′), *v.t., v.i.,* **-layed, -lay·ing.** *Naut.* 1. to fasten (a rope) by winding around a pin or cleat. 2. to stop (used chiefly in the imperative).

bel can·to (bel′ kan′tō), a smooth, cantabile style of singing. [< It, lit., fine singing]

belch (belch), *v.i., v.t.* 1. to eject (gas) noisily from the stomach through the mouth. 2. to give forth violently, as a volcano. —*n.* 3. an instance of belching.

bel·dam (bel′dəm), *n. Archaic.* an old woman, esp. an ugly one. Also, **bel′dame.**

be·lea·guer (bi lē′gər), *v.t.* 1. to surround with an army. 2. to surround with troubles.

Bel·fast (bel′fast), *n.* the capital of Northern Ireland.

bel·fry (bel′frē), *n., pl.* **-fries.** 1. a bell tower. 2. the part of a structure in which a bell is hung.

Belg., 1. Belgian. 2. Belgium.

Bel·gium (bel′jəm), *n.* a country in W Europe. —**Bel′gian** (-jən), *n., adj.*

Bel·grade (bel grād′, bel′grād), *n.* the capital of Yugoslavia.

be·lie (bi lī′), *v.t., v.i.,* **-lied, -ly·ing.** 1. to show to be false or untrue. 2. to misrepresent. 3. to fail to fulfill or justify. —**be·li′er**, *n.*

be·lief (bi lēf′), *n.* **1.** something believed. **2.** confidence, faith, or trust. **3.** a religious tenet or tenets. —**Syn.** 1. conviction, opinion, view.

be·lieve (bi lēv′), *v.*, **-lieved, -lieving.** —*v.i.* **1.** to accept the truth or reliability of something without proof. —*v.t.* **2.** to accept the truth of (a story, etc.). **3.** to have confidence in (a person). **4.** to suppose. —**be·liev′a·ble,** *adj.* —**be·liev′er,** *n.*

be·like (bi līk′), *adv. Archaic.* very likely.

be·lit·tle (bi lit′°l), *v.t.*, **-tled, -tling.** to consider (something) as less impressive or important. —**be·lit′tle·ment,** *n.* —**be·lit′tler,** *n.*

bell (bel), *n.* **1.** a hollow, metal, cup-shaped instrument that rings when struck. **2.** the stroke or sound of such an instrument. **3.** anything in the form of a bell. **4.** *Naut.* any of the half-hour units of nautical time rung on the bell of a ship. —*v.t.* **5.** to put a bell on. —*v.i.* **6.** to have the shape of a bell.

bel·la·don·na (bel′ə don′ə), *n.* **1.** a poisonous herb having purplish-red flowers and black berries. **2.** a drug made from this plant, used to check spasms and as a cardiac stimulant.

bell-bot·tom (bel′bot′əm), *adj.* **1.** (of trousers) wide and flaring at the bottoms of the legs. —*n.* **2.** **bell-bottoms,** bell-bottom trousers.

bell·boy (bel′boi′), *n.* a man employed to carry luggage, run errands, etc., at a hotel or club.

belle (bel), *n.* a woman or girl admired for her beauty and charm.

belles-let·tres (bel le′tr°), *n.pl.* literature regarded as a fine art. —**bel·let·rist** (bel le′trist), *n.* —**bel·let·ris·tic** (bel′li tris′tik), *adj.*

bell·hop (bel′hop′), *n.* bellboy.

bel·li·cose (bel′ə kōs′), *adj.* inclined or eager to fight or quarrel. —**bel·li·cos·i·ty** (bel′ə kos′i tē), **bel′li·cose′ness,** *n.*

bel·lig·er·ent (bə lij′ər ənt), *adj.* **1.** given to waging war. **2.** aggressively hostile. **3.** waging war. —*n.* **4.** a state or nation at war. —**bel·lig′er·ence, bel·lig′er·en·cy,** *n.* —**bel·lig′er·ent·ly,** *adv.*

bell′ jar′, a bell-shaped glass container for protecting delicate instruments, etc. Also called **bell′ glass′.**

bell·man (bel′mən), *n.*, *pl.* **-men.** a bellhop.

bel·low (bel′ō), *v.i.* **1.** to emit a hollow, loud, animal cry, as a bull. **2.** to roar or bawl. —*v.t.* **3.** to utter in a loud, deep voice. —*n.* **4.** act or sound of bellowing.

bel·lows (bel′ōz, -əs), *n.* **1.** an enclosed boxlike mechanism that can contract and expand to produce air through a tube. **2.** anything resembling a bellows.

bells (belz), *n. Informal.* bell-bottom trousers.

bell·weth·er (bel′weth′ər), *n.* **1.** a male sheep that leads the flock, usually bearing a bell. **2.** a person or thing that takes the lead.

bel·ly (bel′ē), *n.*, *pl.* **-lies,** *v.*, **-lied, -ly·ing.** —*n.* **1.** abdomen (def. 1). **2.** the under part of an animal's body. **3.** the stomach. **4.** the under side of a ship or aircraft. —*v.t.*, *v.i.* **5.** to swell out.

bel·ly·ache (bel′ē āk′), *n.*, *v.*, **-ached, -ach·ing.** —*n.* **1.** a pain in the abdomen. —*v.i.* **2.** *Slang.* to complain.

bel·ly·but·ton (bel′ē but′°n), *n. Informal.* the navel. Also, **bel′ly but′ton.**

bel′ly dance′, a woman's solo dance emphasizing exaggerated movements of the abdominal muscles. —**bel′ly danc′er.** —**bel′ly danc′ing.**

bel′ly flop′, a dive in which the abdomen bears the brunt of the impact with the water.

bel·ly·ful (bel′ē fool′), *n.*, *pl.* **-fuls.** *Slang.* all that one can tolerate.

bel′ly laugh′, *Informal.* a loud, hearty laugh.

be·long (bi lông′, -long′), *v.i.* **1.** to be a member, adherent, etc. **2.** to have the proper qualifications to be a member of a group. **3.** to be proper or due. **4.** **belong to,** to be the property of.

be·long·ings (bi lông′ingz, -long′-), *n.pl.* personal possessions.

be·lov·ed (bi luv′id, -luvd′), *adj.* **1.** greatly loved. —*n.* **2.** a person who is greatly loved.

be·low (bi lō′), *adv.* **1.** in or toward a lower place. **2.** on earth. **3.** in hell. **4.** at a later point in a text. **5.** in a lower rank or grade. —*prep.* **6.** lower than. **7.** too low to be worthy of.

belt (belt), *n.* **1.** a band of flexible material, as leather, for encircling the waist. **2.** any encircling band or strip. **3.** an elongated area having distinctive characteristics: *a belt of cotton plantations.* **4.** an endless band used to transmit motion or to convey objects. **5.** *Slang.* a hard blow. **6.** *Slang.* a drink of liquor. **7.** a thrill or excitement. —*v.t.* **8.** to furnish or mark with a belt. **9.** *Slang.* to give a hard blow to. **10.** *Informal.* to sing (a song) loudly. **11.** *Slang.* to drink (liquor). —**belt′ed,** *adj.*

belt′ tight′ening, a curtailment in spending.

belt·way (belt′wā′), *n.* a highway around the edges of an urban area.

be·lu·ga (bə lōō′gə), *n.* a white sturgeon valued as a source of caviar.

bel·ve·dere (bel′vi dēr′, bel′vi dēr′), *n.* a building designed and situated to look out upon a pleasing view.

be·ma (bē′mə), *n.*, *pl.* **-ma·ta** (-mə tə), **-mas.** **1.** *Eastern Ch.* the sanctuary. **2.** bimah.

be·mire (bi mī′r′), *v.t.*, **-mired, -mir·ing.** **1.** to soil with mire. **2.** to sink in mire.

be·moan (bi mōn′), *v.t.* to express regret over.

be·muse (bi myōōz′), *v.t.*, **-mused, -mus·ing.** to cause to be preoccupied, often to the point of confusion.

bench (bench), *n.* **1.** a long seat for several persons. **2.** a seat occupied by officials, esp. judges. **3.** the office and dignity of a judge. **4.** **a.** a court of law. **b.** judges collectively. **5.** workbench. **6. on the bench, a.** serving as a judge. **b.** *Sports.* not participating in the game. —*v.t.* **7.** to furnish with benches. **8.** to seat on a bench or on the bench. **9.** *Sports.* to remove from a game. **10.** to exhibit in an animal show.

bench′ mark′, a marked point of known or assumed elevation.

bench′ war′rant, a warrant issued by a judge for apprehension of an offender.

bend (bend), *v.*, **bent, bend·ing,** *n.* —*v.t.* **1.** to force (an object) from a straight form into a curved or crooked form. **2.** to cause to submit or yield. **3.** to turn in a particular direction. **4.** to direct (one's energies). **5.** to fasten (a sail). —*v.i.* **6.** to become curved or crooked. **7.** to stoop. **8.** to yield or submit. **9.** to turn in a particular direction: *The road bent toward the south.* **10.** to direct one's energies. —*n.* **11.** the act of bending or state of being bent. **12.** a bent thing or part: *a bend in the road.* **13.** *Naut.* any of various loops for joining the ends of ropes. **14. bends.** See caisson disease. —**bend′a·ble,** *adj.*

bend·er (ben′dər), *n. Slang.* a drinking spree.

be·neath (bi nēth′, -nēth′), *adv.* **1.** in or to a lower position. **2.** underneath. —*prep.* **3.** below or under. **4.** unworthy of: *beneath contempt.*

ben·e·dict (ben′i dikt), *n.* a newly married man, esp. one who has long been a bachelor.

ben·e·dic·tion (ben′i dik′shən), *n.* the invocation of a blessing, esp. at the close of a religious service.

ben·e·fac·tion (ben′ə fak′shən, ben′ə- fak′-), *n.* **1.** act of doing good. **2.** a charitable donation.

ben·e·fac·tor (ben′ə fak′tər, ben′ə- fak′-), *n.* **1.** a kindly helper. **2.** a person who makes a bequest or endowment, as to an institution. —**ben·e·fac·tress** (ben′ə fak′tris, ben′ə fak′-), *n.fem.*

ben·e·fice (ben′ə fis), *n.* a position granted to an ecclesiastic that guarantees a fixed amount of income.

be·nef·i·cence (bə nef′i səns), *n.* **1.** active goodness or kindness. **2.** benefaction.

be·nef·i·cent (bə nef′i sənt), *adj.* **1.** doing good or causing good to be done. **2.** kindly in action. —**be·nef′i·cent·ly,** *adv.*

ben·e·fi·cial (ben′ə fish′əl), *adj.* producing benefits. —**ben′e·fi′cial·ly,** *adv.* —**ben′e·fi′cial·ness,** *n.* —Syn. advantageous, helpful.

ben·e·fi·ci·ar·y (ben′ə fish′ē er′ē, -fish′ə rē), *n.*, *pl.* **-ar·ies.** **1.** a person who receives benefits. **2.** a recipient of funds, etc., under a will, trust, or insurance policy.

ben·e·fit (ben′ə fit), *n.* **1.** anything that is helpful, advantageous, or for the good of a person or thing. **2.** a public entertainment to raise money for a charitable cause. **3.** a payment given by an insurance company, public agency, etc. —*v.t.* **4.** to be of service to. —*v.i.* **5.** to derive advantage.

be·nev·o·lent (bə nev′ə lənt), *adj.* **1.** desiring to do good to others. **2.** intended for benefits rather than profit. —**be·nev′o·lence,** *n.* —**be·nev′o·lent·ly,** *adv.*

Ben·gal (ben gôl′), *n.* **Bay of,** a part of the Indian Ocean, E of India.

be·night·ed (bi nī′tid), *adj.* **1.** intellectually ignorant. **2.** overtaken by darkness of night. —**be·night′ed·ly,** *adv.* —**be·night′ed·ness,** *n.*

be·nign (bi nīn′), *adj.* **1.** having a kindly disposition. **2.** showing or caused by kindness. **3.** favorable or propitious. **4.** not malignant. —**be·nig′ni·ty** (-nig′ni tē), *n.* —**be·nign′ly,** *adv.*

be·nig·nant (bi nig′nənt), *adj.* **1.** kind, esp. to inferiors. **2.** beneficial or favorable.

Be·nin (be nēn′), a country in W Africa.

ben·i·son (ben′i zən, -sən), *n. Archaic.* benediction.

ben·ny (ben′ē), *n.*, *pl.* **-nies.** *Slang.* an amphetamine tablet.

bent (bent), *v.* **1.** pt. and pp. of **bend.** —*adj.* **2.** curved or crooked. **3.** determined or resolved. **4.** inclination or leaning. **5.** capacity of endurance.

ben·thos (ben′thos), *n.* organisms living on or at the bottom of a body of water. —**ben′thic, ben′thal,** *adj.*

ben·ton·ite (ben′t°nīt′), *n.* a clay capable of absorbing much water and swelling considerably. —**ben′ton·it′ic** (-nit′ik), *adj.*

bent·wood (bent′wŏŏd′), *adj.* made of wood steamed and bent.

be·numb (bi num′), *v.t.* **1.** to make numb. **2.** to make inactive. —**be·numbed·ness** (bi numd′nis, -num′id-), *n.*

Ben·ze·drine (ben′zi drēn′), *n. Trademark.* amphetamine.

ben·zene (ben′zēn, ben zēn′), *n.* a flammable liquid obtained chiefly from coal tar: used in chemicals, dyes, and as a solvent.

ben′zene ring′, *Chem.* the graphic representation of the structure of benzene as a hexagon with a carbon atom at each of its points.

ben·zine (ben′zēn, ben zēn′), *n.* a liquid mixture of various hydrocarbons, used in cleaning, dyeing, etc. Also, **ben·zin** (ben′zin).

ben·zo·ate (ben′zō āt′, -it), *n.* a salt or ester of benzoic acid.

ben·zo·caine (ben′zō kān′), *n.* a white powder used as a local anesthetic.

ben·zo·ic (ben zō′ik), *adj.* of or from benzoin or benzoic acid.

benzo′ic ac′id, a powder used chiefly as a preservative and germicide.

ben·zo·in (ben′zō in, -zoin, benzō′in), *n.* a reddish-brown, aromatic resin used in perfume and cosmetics.

ben·zol (ben′zōl, -zôl, -zol), *n.* benzene.

be·queath (bi kwēth′, -kwēth′), *v.t.* **1.** to dispose of (property) by will. **2.** to hand down.

be·quest (bi kwest′), *n.* **1.** a disposition by will of property. **2.** legacy.

be·rate (bi rāt′), *v.t.,* **-rat·ed, -rat·ing.** to scold severely.

Ber·ber (bûr′bər), *n.* **1.** a member of a group of North African tribes. **2.** their language.

ber·ceuse (*Fr.* beR sœz′), *n., pl.* **-ceuses** (*Fr.* -sœz′). **1.** a lullaby. **2.** a musical composition having a lulling quality.

be·reave (bi rēv′), *v.t.,* **-reaved** or **-reft, -reav·ing. 1.** to deprive ruthlessly or by force. **2.** to deprive by death. —**be·reave′ment,** *n.*

be·reft (bi reft′), *v.* **1.** a pt. and pp. of **bereave.** —*adj.* **2.** deprived: *bereft of their senses.*

be·ret (bə rā′, ber′ā), *n.* a soft, visorless cap.

berg (bûrg), *n.* iceberg.

ber·i·ber·i (ber′ē ber′ē), *n.* a disease caused by a deficiency of vitamin B_1, characterized by paralysis of the extremities and emaciation.

Ber′ing Sea′ (bēr′ing, ber′-, bâr′-),

a part of the N Pacific, between Alaska and Siberia.

Berke·ley (bûrk′lē), *n.* a city in W California.

ber·ke·li·um (bər kē′lē əm), *n. Chem.* a synthetic, radioactive, metallic element. *Symbol:* Bk; *at. no.:* 97.

Ber·lin (bər lin′), *n.* a city in E East Germany. —**Ber·lin′er,** *n.*

Ber·mu·da (bər myōō′də), *n.* a group of islands in the Atlantic. —**Bermu·di·an** (bər myōō′dē ən), *adj., n.*

Bermu′da shorts′, short pants extending almost to the knee. Also called **Bermu′das.**

Bermu′da Tri′angle, the triangular area bounded by lines drawn between Bermuda, Puerto Rico, and west of Florida, in which ships and aircraft are alleged to have disappeared mysteriously.

Bern (bûrn), *n.* the capital of Switzerland. Also, **Berne.**

ber·ry (ber′ē), *n., pl.* **-ries,** *v.,* **-ried, -ry·ing.** —*n.* **1.** any small, usually stoneless, juicy fruit, as a strawberry. **2.** a dry seed or kernel, as of wheat. —*v.i.* **3.** to bear berries. **4.** to gather or pick berries. —**ber′ry·like′,** *adj.*

ber·serk (bər sûrk′, -zûrk′), *adj., adv.* in or into a frenzied, violent rage. [< Icel *berserkr* frenzied warrior = *berr* bear + *serkr* skin]

berth (bûrth), *n.* **1.** a shelflike sleeping space on a ship, railroad car, etc. **2.** the space allotted to a vessel at anchor or at a pier. **3.** *Informal.* a job, esp. on a ship. **4. give a wide berth to,** to remain away from. —*v.t.* **5.** to allot a berth to. —*v.i.* **6.** to come into a berth.

ber·yl (ber′əl), *n.* a usually green mineral that is the principal ore of beryllium. —**ber·yl·ine** (ber′ə-lin, -līn′), *adj.*

be·ryl·li·um (bi ril′ē əm), *n. Chem.* a steel-gray, hard, light, metallic element. *Symbol:* Be; *at. wt.:* 9.0122; *at. no.:* 4.

be·seech (bi sēch′), *v.t., v.i.,* **-sought** or **-seeched, -seech·ing.** to beg or ask eagerly (for). —**be·seech′er,** *n.* —**be·seech′ing·ly,** *adv.*

be·seem (bi sēm′), *v.t., v.i. Archaic.* to be suitable (to).

be·set (bi set′), *v.t.,* **-set, -set·ting. 1.** to harass constantly. **2.** to attack on all sides. **3.** to surround or hem in.

be·set·ting (bi set′ing), *adj.* constantly assailing or obsessing.

be·side (bi sīd′), *prep.* **1.** by or at the side of. **2.** compared with. **3.** apart from. **4.** *Archaic.* besides. **5. beside oneself,** almost out of one's senses from a strong emotion. —*adv.* **6.** along the side of something.

—**Usage.** BESIDE, BESIDES may both

be used as prepositions, although with different meanings. BESIDE is almost exclusively used as a preposition meaning by the side of: *beside the house, the stream.* BESIDES is used as a preposition meaning in addition to or over and above: *Besides these honors he received a sum of money.*

be·sides (bi sīdz′), *adv.* **1.** moreover or furthermore. **2.** in addition. **3.** otherwise or else. —*prep.* **4.** in addition to. **5.** except. —Usage. See beside.

be·siege (bi sēj′), *v.t.*, **-sieged, -sieg-ing. 1.** to lay siege to. **2.** to crowd around. **3.** to beset with requests or demands. —**be·siege′ment,** *n.* —**be·sieg′er,** *n.*

be·smear (bi smēr′), *v.t.* to smear all over.

be·smirch (bi smûrch′), *v.t.* **1.** to soil, as with soot. **2.** to detract from the honor of. —**be·smirch′er,** *n.*

be·som (bē′zəm), *n.* a broom, esp. one of brush or twigs.

be·sot (bi sot′), *v.t.,* **-sot·ted, -sot-ting.** to stupefy, as with drink. — **be·sot′ted,** *adj.*

be·sought (bi sôt′), *v.* a pt. and pp. of beseech.

be·span·gle (bi spang′gəl), *v.t.,* **-gled, -gling.** to cover or adorn with spangles.

be·spat·ter (bi spat′ər), *v.t.* **1.** to soil with water, dirt, etc. **2.** to slander.

be·speak (bi spēk′), *v.t.,* **-spoke, -spo-ken** or **-spoke, -speak·ing. 1.** to show evidence of. **2.** *Brit.* to order or reserve (now used only attributively in the pp. form bespoke). **3.** *Archaic.* to speak to.

be·spec·ta·cled (bi spek′tə kəld), *adj.* wearing eyeglasses.

be·spread (bi spred′), *v.t.,* **-spread, -spread·ing.** to spread over (a surface).

be·sprin·kle (bi spring′kəl), *v.t.,* **-kled, -kling.** to sprinkle all over, as with water, flour, etc.

Bes·se·mer convert′er (bes′ə mər), a pear-shaped metal container in which steel is produced by the Bessemer process.

Bes′semer proc′ess, a process of producing steel (**Bes′semer steel′**), in which impurities are removed by forcing a blast of air through molten iron.

best (best), *adj., superl. of good* **with better** *as compar.* **1.** of the highest quality or excellence. **2.** most advantageous, suitable, or desirable. **3.** largest or most. —*adv., superl. of well* **with better** *as compar.* **4.** most excellently. **5.** most fully. **6. had best,** ought to. —*n.* **7.** something that is best. **8.** kind-

est regards. **9. at best,** under the most favorable circumstances. **10. get** or **have the best of, a.** to gain the advantage over. **b.** to defeat. **11. make the best of,** to manage as well as one can under adverse circumstances. —*v.t.* **12.** to defeat or beat.

bes·tial (bes′chəl, best′yəl), *adj.* **1.** of or having the form of a beast. **2.** brutal or inhuman. **3.** carnal. —**bes′ti·al′i·ty** (-chē al′i tē), *n.* —**bes′tial·ly,** *adv.*

bes·tial·ize (bes′chə līz′, best′yə-), *v.t.,* **-ized, -iz·ing.** to make bestial.

bes·ti·ar·y (bes′chē er′ē, -tē-), *n., pl.* **-ar·ies.** a medieval collection of moralized descriptions of actual or mythical animals.

be·stir (bi stûr′), *v.t.,* **-stirred, -stir-ring.** to rouse to action.

best′ man′, the chief attendant of the bridegroom at a wedding.

be·stow (bi stō′), *v.t.* **1.** to present or give as a gift. **2.** *Archaic.* to devote or apply. —**be·stow′al,** *n.*

be·strew (bi strōō′), *v.t.,* **-strewed, -strewed** or **-strewn, -strew·ing.** to scatter about.

be·stride (bi strīd′), *v.t.,* **-strode, -strid-den, -strid·ing. 1.** to get or be astride of. **2.** to step over.

best′ sell′er, a book, etc., that is among those having the largest sales during a given period. Also, **best′-sell′er.**

bet (bet), *v.,* **bet** or **bet·ted, bet·ting,** *n.* —*v.t.* **1.** to pledge (something) as a forfeit if one's forecast of a future event is wrong, usually in return for a similar pledge by another if the forecast is right. —*v.i.* **2.** to make a wager. —*n.* **3.** a pledge made in betting. **4.** that which is pledged. **5.** a person, thing, event, etc., bet on. —**bet′ter,** *n.*

bet., between.

be·ta (bā′tə, bē′-), *n.* the second letter of the Greek alphabet (B, β).

be·take (bi tāk′), *v.t.,* **-took, -tak·en, -tak·ing.** *Chiefly Literary.* to cause (oneself) to go.

be′ta par′ticle, an electron or a positron emitted from a nucleus in radioactive decay or fission.

be′ta ray′, a stream of beta particles.

be·ta·tron (bā′tə tron′, bē′-), *n.* an accelerator for beams of electrons.

be·tel (bēt′ᵊl), *n.* an East Indian pepper plant.

be′tel nut′, the seed of a tall palm (**be′tel palm′**), chewed with dried betel leaves and lime as a stimulant.

bête noire (bet nwAR′), *pl.* **bêtes noires** (bet nwAR′). *French.* something or someone that a person dislikes or dreads.

beth·el (beth′əl), *n.* a church for sailors. [< Heb *bēth ′el* house of God]

be·think (bi thingk′), *v.t.*, **-thought**, **-think·ing.** *Archaic.* to cause (oneself) to recall or remember.

Beth·le·hem (beth′lē əm, -li hem′), *n.* a town in NW Jordan, near Jerusalem: birthplace of Jesus.

be·tide (bi tīd′), *v.t.*, *v.i.*, **-tid·ed**, **-tid·ing.** *Archaic.* to happen (to): *Woe betide the villain!*

be·times (bi tīmz′), *adv.* *Literary.* early or at a good hour.

be·to·ken (bi tō′kən), *v.t.* to serve as a token or sign of.

be·took (bi tŏŏk′), *v.* pt. of betake.

be·tray (bi trā′), *v.t.* **1.** to deliver to an enemy by treachery or disloyalty. **2.** to be unfaithful to: *to betray a trust.* **3.** to reveal or disclose. **4.** to seduce and desert (a woman). —**be·tray′al**, *n.* —**be·tray′er**, *n.*

be·troth (bi trōth′, -trôth′), *v.t.* to promise to give in marriage. —**be·troth′al, be·troth′ment**, *n.*

be·throthed (bi trōthd′, -trôtht′), *adj.* **1.** engaged to be married. —*n.* **2.** the person to whom one is engaged.

bet·ter (bet′ər), *adj., compar.* of good *with* best *as superl.* **1.** of superior quality. **2.** of superior value or use. **3.** larger or greater. **4.** improved in health. —*adv., compar.* of well *with* best *as superl.* **5.** in a more excellent manner. **6.** more completely. **7.** more. **8. better off**, in better circumstances. **9. had better**, ought to. **10. think better of**, to reconsider and decide more wisely. —*v.t.* **11.** to make better or improve. **12.** to surpass or exceed. —*n.* **13.** that which has greater excellence. **14.** Usually, **betters**. those superior to one in wisdom, position, etc. **15. for the better**, in a way that is an improvement. **16. get or have the better of**, to get an advantage over.

bet·ter·ment (bet′ər mənt), *n.* an improvement.

bet·tor (bet′ər), *n.* a person who bets.

be·tween (bi twēn′), *prep.* **1.** in or connecting the space separating. **2.** intermediate in time, quantity, or degree. **3.** by the common action, involvement, or participation of. **4.** distinguishing one from the other. **5. between ourselves**, in strict confidence. Also, **between you and me.** —*adv.* **6.** in the intervening space or time.

—Usage. BETWEEN YOU AND I, occasionally heard in the usage of educated persons, is not the commonly accepted form. Since the pronouns are objects of the preposition BE-

TWEEN, the usual form is *between you and me.*

be·twixt (bi twikst′), *prep., adv.* **betwixt and between**, in a middle position.

bev·el (bev′əl), *n., v.*, **-eled**, **-el·ing** or **-elled**, **-el·ling**, *adj.* —*n.* **1.** the slant or slope of a line or surface when not at right angles with another. **2.** an adjustable instrument for drawing angles, etc. —*v.t.*, *v.i.* **3.** to cut or slant at a bevel. —*adj.* **4.** Also, **beveled, bevelled.** oblique or slanted. —**bev′el·er, bev′el·ler,** *n.*

bev′el gear′, a gear meshing with a similar gear that is set at right angles to it.

bev·er·age (bev′ər ij, bev′rij), *n.* any liquid for drinking, esp. other than water. [< MF *beverage* = *bevr* (< L *bibere* to drink) + *-age*]

bev·y (bev′ē), *n., pl.* **bev·ies.** **1.** a flock of birds, esp. quail. **2.** a group of girls or women.

be·wail (bi wāl′), *v.t., v.i.* to express deep sorrow (for). —**be·wail′er**, *n.*

be·ware (bi wâr′), *v.i., v.t.*, **-wared**, **-war·ing.** to be wary, cautious, or careful (of): *Beware of the dog.*

be·wigged (bi wigd′), *adj.* wearing a wig.

be·wil·der (bi wil′dər), *v.t.* to confuse or puzzle completely. —**be·wil′der·ment**, *n.*

be·witch (bi wich′), *v.t.* **1.** to affect by witchcraft. **2.** to charm or fascinate. —**be·witch′ment**, *n.*

bey (bā), *n., pl.* **beys.** **1.** a former Turkish provincial governor. **2.** the former native ruler of Tunis or Tunisia.

be·yond (bē ond′, bi yond′), *prep.* **1.** on or to the farther side of. **2.** farther on than. **3.** outside the limits or reach of. —*adv.* **4.** farther on or away. —*n.* **5. the great beyond**, the life after the present one.

bez·el (bez′əl), *n.* **1.** the beveled edge of a cutting tool. **2.** that part of a ring, bracelet, etc., to which gems are attached. **3.** the grooved rim holding a gem or watch crystal in its setting.

b.f., *Print.* boldface. Also, **bf.**

B/F, *Accounting.* brought forward.

B.F.A., Bachelor of Fine Arts.

bg., bag.

B.G., Brigadier General.

B-girl (bē′gûrl′), *n.* a woman employed by a bar, etc., to act as a companion to male customers and induce them to buy expensive drinks.

bhang (bang), *n.* **1.** the Indian hemp plant. **2.** a preparation of its leaves and tops used in India as an intoxicant and narcotic.

bhd., bulkhead.

Bhu·tan (bōō tän′), *n.* a country in the Himalayas. —**Bhu′tan·ese′**, *n., adj.*

Bi, bismuth.

bi-, a prefix meaning: **a.** two: *bicycle*. **b.** twice: *biannual*. **c.** having two: *biped*. **d.** every two: *biweekly*.

bi·a·ly (bē ä′lē), *n., pl.* **-lys.** a flat, onion-flavored roll made of white flour.

bi·an·nu·al (bī an′yōō əl), *adj.* occurring twice a year. —**bi·an′nu·al·ly**, *adv.*

bi·as (bī′əs), *n., adj., adv., v.,* **bi·ased, bi·as·ing** or **bi·assed, bi·as·sing.** —*n.* **1.** a predisposed point of view. **2.** a diagonal line of direction, esp. across a fabric. **3.** a steady voltage applied to an electrode, as of a transistor. —*adj.* **4.** cut or set diagonally. —*adv.* **5.** slantingly. — *v.t.* **6.** to cause to have a bias. —Syn. **2.** partiality, preconception, prejudice.

bi·ath·lon (bī ath′lon), *n.* a sports contest combining skiing with rifle shooting.

bib (bib), *n., v.,* **bibbed, bib·bing.** —*n.* **1.** a cloth for tying under the chin of a child to protect its clothing from spilled food. **2.** the upper part of an apron. —*v.t., v.i.* **3.** *Archaic.* to tipple or drink. —**bib′ber**, *n.*

Bib., **1.** Bible. **2.** Biblical.

bi·be·lot (bib′lō), *n., pl.* **-lots.** a small object of curiosity, beauty, or rarity.

bibl., **1.** biblical. **2.** bibliographical.

Bibl., Biblical.

Bi·ble (bī′bəl), *n.* **1.** the sacred writings of the Christian religion, comprising the Old and New Testaments. **2.** the sacred writings of the Jewish religion, comprising the Old Testament only. **3.** (*l.c.*) any book accepted as authoritative or reliable. [< OF < LL < Gk *biblíon* book < *býblos* book, papyrus < *Byblos* Phoenician city noted for export of papyrus] —**Bib·li·cal** (bib′li-kəl), *adj.*

biblio-, a combining form meaning "book" or "of books": *bibliophile*.

bibliog., **1.** bibliographer. **2.** bibliography.

bib·li·og·ra·phy (bib′lē og′rə fē), *n., pl.* **-phies.** **1.** a list of writings on a particular subject or by a particular author. **2.** the science that deals with the history of books, their publication, editions, etc. —**bib·li·og′ra·pher,** *n.* —**bib·li·o·graph·ic** (bib′lē ə graf′ik), **bib′li·o·graph′i·cal,** *adj.* —**bib′li·o·graph′i·cal·ly,** *adv.*

bib·li·o·phile (bib′lē ə fīl′, -fil), *n.* a person who loves or collects books.

bib·u·lous (bib′yə ləs), *adj.* addicted to alcoholic drinking.

bi·cam·er·al (bī kam′ər əl), *adj.* having two branches, as a legislative body.

bi·car·bo·nate (bī kär′bə nit, -nāt′), *n.* an acid carbonate, as sodium bicarbonate.

bicar′bonate of so′da. See **sodium bicarbonate.**

bi·cen·te·nar·y (bī sen′t°ner′ē, bī-sen ten′ə rē), *adj., n., pl.* **-nar·ies.** bicentennial.

bi·cen·ten·ni·al (bī′sen ten′ē əl), *adj.* **1.** of or in honor of a 200th anniversary. **2.** consisting of or lasting 200 years. **3.** occurring every 200 years. —*n.* **4.** a 200th anniversary. —**bi′cen·ten′ni·al·ly,** *adv.*

bi·ceps (bī′seps), *n., pl.* **-ceps, -ceps·es** (-sep siz). a muscle on the front of the arm, the action of which bends the elbow.

bi·chlo·ride (bī klôr′īd, -id, -klōr′-), *n.* **1.** a compound in which two atoms of chlorine are combined with another element or group. **2.** See **mercuric chloride.**

bick·er (bik′ər), *v.i.* **1.** to engage in an angry, petty dispute. —*n.* **2.** an angry, petty dispute. —**bick′er·er,** *n.*

bi·con·cave (bī kon′kāv, bī′kon kāv′), *adj.* concave on both sides, as a lens. —**bi·con·cav·i·ty** (bī′kon kav′i tē), *n.*

bi·con·vex (bī kon′veks, bī′kon veks′), *adj.* convex on both sides, as a lens. —**bi·con·vex·i·ty** (bī′k°n vek′si tē), *n.*

bi·cor·po·ral (bī kôr′p°r əl), *adj.* having two bodies or main divisions. Also, **bi·cor·po·re·al** (bī′kôr pōr′ē-əl, -pôr′-).

bi·cul·tur·al·ism (bī kul′chər ə liz′əm), *n.* the presence of two different cultures in the same country. —**bi·cul′tur·al,** *adj.*

bi·cus·pid (bī kus′pid), *adj.* **1.** having two cusps or points, as certain teeth. —*n.* **2.** a bicuspid tooth.

bi·cy·cle (bī′si kəl, -sik′əl), *n., v.,* **-cled, -cling.** —*n.* **1.** a vehicle with two wheels in tandem, propelled by pedals and having handlebars for steering. —*v.i.* **2.** to ride a bicycle. —**bi′cy·clist, bi′cy·cler,** *n.*

bid (bid), *v.,* **bade** or **bid; bid·den** (bid′°n) or **bid; bid·ding;** *n.* —*v.t.* **1.** to tell or ask (someone) to do something, esp. commandingly. **2.** to say as a greeting or wish. **3.** to make an offer of (a price at an auction) to secure a contract. **4.** *Cards.* to enter a bid of a given quantity or suit. **5.** *Archaic.* to invite. —*v.i.* **6.** to make a bid. **7.** the act or an instance of bidding. **8.** *Cards.* **a.** an offer to make a specified number of points or tricks. **b.** the amount of such an offer. **c.** the turn of a person to bid. **9.**

Informal. an invitation. 10. an attempt to attain some goal or purpose. **—bid′der,** *n.* **—Syn.** 1. command, order, direct.

b.i.d., (in prescriptions) twice a day. [< L *bis in die*]

bid·da·ble (bid′ə bəl), *adj.* 1. *Cards.* adequate to bid upon. 2. *Archaic.* obedient or docile.

bid·dy¹ (bid′ē), *n., pl.* **-dies.** *Dial.* a chicken.

bid·dy² (bid′ē), *n., pl.* **-dies.** *Slang.* a fussy old woman.

bide (bīd), *v.t.* **bid·ed** or **bode, bid·ed, bid·ing.** 1. *Archaic.* to abide. 2. **bide one's time,** to wait for a favorable opportunity.

bi·det (bē dā′, bi det′), *n.* a low, basinlike bath, used esp. in France, for bathing one's private parts.

bi·en·ni·al (bī en′ē əl), *adj.* 1. happening every two years. 2. enduring for two years. 3. completing the normal term of life in two years, flowering and fruiting the second year, as beets. *—n.* 4. any event occurring once in two years. 5. a biennial plant. **—bi·en′ni·al·ly,** *adv.*

bi·en·ni·um (bī en′ē əm), *n., pl.* **-en·ni·ums, -en·ni·a** (-en′ē ə). a period of two years.

bier (bēr), *n.* a frame on which a corpse or coffin is laid before burial.

bi·fo·cal (bī fō′kəl, bī′fō–), *adj.* 1. (of an eyeglass lens) having two portions, one for near and one for far vision. *—n.* 2. **bifocals,** eyeglasses with bifocal lenses.

bi·fur·cate (bī′fər kāt′, bī fûr′kāt), *v.t., v.i.,* **-cat·ed, -cat·ing.** to divide or fork into two branches. **—bi′fur·ca′tion,** *n.*

big (big), *adj.,* **big·ger, big·gest,** *adv.* *—adj.* 1. large, as in size, amount, etc. 2. important. 3. boastful. 4. generous or kindly: *a big heart.* 5. loud: *a big voice.* 6. near the full term of pregnancy: *a big with child.* 7. outstanding: *a big liar.* *—adv.* 8. *Informal.* boastfully. 9. *Slang.* successfully. **—big′gish,** *adj.* **—big′ness,** *n.*

big·a·my (big′ə mē), *n., pl.* **-mies.** the crime of marrying while one has a legal wife or husband still living. **—big′a·mist,** *n.* **—big′a·mous,** *adj.*

Big′ Ap′ple, the, *Slang.* any large city, esp. New York City.

big′-bang′ the′ory (big′bang′), the theory that the universe was created from the explosion of a mass of hydrogen atoms and is still expanding.

big′ broth′er, 1. an elder brother. 2. a man who assists a boy in need of help. 3. the head of a totalitarian state.

Big′ Dip′per, dipper (def. 3a).

big′ game′, 1. large wild animals hunted for sport, as deer, tigers, etc. 2. a major objective that involves risk.

big·gie (big′ē), *n. Slang.* 1. See big shot. 2. something large, important, or very successful.

big-heart·ed (big′här′tid), *adj.* generous or kind.

big·horn (big′hôrn′), *n., pl.* **-horns, -horn.** a wild sheep of the Rocky Mountains, with large, curving horns.

bight (bīt), *n.* 1. the middle, loop, or bent part of a rope. 2. a curve in the shore of a sea or river. 3. a bay or gulf.

big-league (big′lēg′), *adj.* major: *the big-league oil companies.*

big·mouth (big′mouth′), *n. Slang.* a loud, talkative person, esp. one who lacks discretion.

big-name (big′nām′), *adj.* famous or widely acclaimed.

big·ot (big′ət), *n.* a person who is intolerant of any creed, belief, or race that is not his or her own. **—big′ot·ed,** *adj.* **—big′ot·ry,** *n.*

big′ shot′, *Slang.* an important or influential person.

big-tick·et (big′tik′it), *adj.* expensive, as an appliance.

big′ time′, *Slang.* 1. the top rank in any occupation. 2. a very good time. **—big′-time′,** *adj.* **—big′-tim′er,** *n.*

big′ top′, 1. the main tent of a circus. 2. a circus.

big·wig (big′wig′), *n. Informal.* an important person, esp. an official.

bike (bīk), *n. Informal.* 1. a bicycle. 2. a motorcycle. 3. a motorbike.

bike·way (bīk′wā′), *n.* a road or path built or reserved for bicycle traffic.

bi·ki·ni (bi kē′nē), *n.* a very brief two-piece bathing suit for women.

bi·lat·er·al (bī lat′ər əl), *adj.* 1. of or having two sides. 2. pertaining to or affecting two or both sides, parties, etc. **—bi·lat′er·al·ly,** *adv.*

bile (bīl), *n.* 1. a bitter, alkaline, yellow or greenish liquid, secreted by the liver, that aids in digestion, esp. of fats. 2. ill temper.

bilge (bilj), *n.* 1. *Naut.* the bottom part inside the hull. 2. seepage accumulated in a bilge. 3. *Slang.* foolish or worthless talk.

bi·lin·gual (bī ling′gwəl), *adj.* 1. able to speak two languages. 2. spoken or written in two languages.

bil·ious (bil′yəs), *adj.* 1. of the bile. 2. suffering from or attended by trouble with the liver. 3. peevish or irritable. **—bil′ious·ness,** *n.*

bilk (bilk), *v.t.* to defraud or cheat. **—bilk′er,** *n.*

bill¹ (bil), *n.* **1.** a statement of money owed for goods or services supplied. **2.** See **bill of exchange.** **3.** a piece of paper money. **4.** a draft of a statute presented to a legislature. **5.** a public notice or advertisement: *Post no bills.* **6.** a written paper containing a statement of particulars. **7.** *Law.* a written statement, usually of a complaint, presented to a court. **8.** a theater program. **9. fill the bill,** *Informal.* to fulfill all requirements. —*v.t.* **10.** to enter (charges) in a bill. **11.** to send a bill to. **12.** to advertise by bill. **13.** to schedule on a program.

bill² (bil), *n.* **1.** the parts of a bird's jaws that are covered with a horny sheath. **2.** any mouthpart resembling these. —*v.i.* **3.** to join beaks, as doves. **4. bill and coo,** to whisper endearments, as lovers. — **billed** (bild), *adj.*

bill·board (bil′bōrd′, -bôrd′), *n.* a board, usually outdoors, on which large advertisements are posted.

bil·let (bil′it), *n., v.,* **-let·ed, -let·ing.** —*n.* **1.** lodging for soldiers in nonmilitary buildings. **2.** an official order directing a person to provide such lodging. **3.** *Informal.* a job or appointment. —*v.t.* **4.** to assign lodging by billet.

bil·let-doux (bil′ē dōō′, bil′ā-), *n., pl.* **bil·lets-doux** (bil′ē dōōz′, bil′ā-). a love letter.

bill·fold (bil′fōld′), *n.* a wallet.

bill·head (bil′hed′), *n.* a printed form on which a statement of money due is rendered.

bil·liards (bil′yərdz), *n.* a game played with hard balls that are driven with a cue on a cloth-covered table enclosed by a cushioned rim. —**bil′liard,** *adj.*

bill·ing (bil′ing), *n.* the relative position in which a performer or act is listed on a playbill.

bil·lings·gate (bil′ingz gāt′), *n.* coarsely or vulgarly abusive language. [after *Billingsgate,* a London fish market]

bil·lion (bil′yən), *n., pl.* **-lions, -lion.** **1.** *U.S.* a thousand millions. **2.** *Brit.* a million millions. —**bil′lionth,** *adj., n.*

bil·lion·aire (bil′yə nâr′), *n.* a person who has assets worth a billion or more dollars, pounds, etc.

bill′ of exchange′, a written order to pay a specified sum to a specified person.

bill′ of fare′, *Chiefly Brit.* a menu.

bill′ of lad′ing, a receipt given by a carrier for goods accepted for transportation.

Bill′ of Rights′, a statement of the fundamental rights of the people, incorporated in the U.S. Constitution as Amendments 1–10.

bill′ of sale′, a document transferring title in personal property from seller to buyer.

bil·low (bil′ō), *n.* **1.** a great wave or surge of the sea. **2.** any surging mass: *billows of smoke.* —*v.i.* **3.** to surge or roll in billows. —**bil′low·y,** *adj.*

bil·ly (bil′ē), *n., pl.* **-lies.** a police officer's club. Also, **bil′ly club′.**

bil′ly goat′, a male goat.

bi·mah (bē′mə, bim′ə), *n.* a platform in a synagogue holding the reading table.

bi·me·tal·lic (bī′mə tal′ik), *adj.* made or consisting of two metals.

bi·met·al·lism (bī met′ʲliz′əm), *n.* the policy of using two metals, ordinarily gold and silver, at a fixed relative value, as a monetary standard. —**bi·met′al·list,** *n.*

bi·month·ly (bī munth′lē), *adj., n., pl.* **-lies,** *adv.* —*adj.* **1.** occurring every two months. **2.** semimonthly. —*n.* **3.** a bimonthly publication. —*adv.* **4.** every two months. **5.** semimonthly.

—Usage. Since it is not always clear which meaning of BIMONTHLY is intended—"twice a month" or "every two months"—the use of SEMIMONTHLY for "twice a month" is preferable because it is unambiguous. Since there is no single, unambiguous term for "every two months," this phrase itself is the least confusing to use.

bin (bin), *n.* a box or enclosed place for storing grain, coal, etc.

bi·na·ry (bī′nə rē, -ne-), *adj., n., pl.* **-ries.** —*adj.* **1.** consisting of, indicating, or involving two. **2.** of a system of numerical notation to the base 2, in which each place of a number, expressed as 0 or 1, corresponds to a power of 2. **3.** of the digits or numbers used in binary notation. —*n.* **4.** a whole composed of two.

bi′nary star′, a system of two stars that revolve around their common center of gravity.

bin·au·ral (bī nôr′əl, bin ôr′əl), *adj.* **1.** of, with, or for both ears. **2.** of or pertaining to the earlier technique of stereophonic reproduction in which each ear hears only one recording channel.

bind (bīnd), *v.,* **bound, bind·ing,** *n.* —*v.t.* **1.** to fasten or encircle with a band. **2.** to bandage: *to bind up one's wounds.* **3.** to cause to cohere. **4.** to unite by any legal or moral tie. **5.** to hold to a particular state, place, etc. **6.** to put under legal obligation. **7.** to make compulsory or obligatory. **8.**

(of clothing) to chafe or restrict. **9.** to constipate. **10.** to fasten within a cover, as a book. **11.** to cover the edge of, as for protection or ornament. —*v.i.* **12.** to be compact or solid. **13.** to be obligatory. —*n.* **14.** something that binds. **15.** *Slang.* a predicament. —**bind′a·ble,** *adj.* —**bind′er,** *n.*

bind·er·y (bīn′də rē, -drē), *n.*, *pl.* **-er·ies.** a place where books are bound.

bind·ing (bīn′diñg), *n.* **1.** anything that binds. —*adj.* **2.** having power to bind or oblige.

binge (binj), *n.* *Informal.* a period of excessive indulgence, as in eating, drinking, etc.

bin·go (biñg′gō), *n.* a game similar to lotto, played usually by a large number of persons in competition for prizes.

bin·na·cle (bin′ə kəl), *n.* a stand or case for a ship's compass.

bin·oc·u·lar (bə nok′yə lər, bī-), *adj.* **1.** involving two eyes. —*n.* **2.** Usually, **binoculars.** an optical device, as field glasses, for use with both eyes. [< L *bin-* double + *ocul(us)* eye + *-ar*] —**bin·oc′u·lar·ly,** *adv.*

bi·no·mi·al (bī nō′mē əl), *n.* **1.** an expression that is a sum or difference of two terms, as $3x + 2y$ and $x^2 - 4x$. **2.** *Zool., Bot.* a taxonomic name consisting of a generic and specific term. —*adj.* **3.** of two terms or names.

bi·o (bī′ō), *n.*, *pl.* **bi·os.** *Informal.* biography.

bio-, a prefix meaning "life" or "living matter": *biography; biology.*

bi·o·as·tro·nau·tics (bī′ō as′trə nô′-tiks), *n.* the science dealing with the effects of space travel upon life.

bi·o·chem·is·try (bī′ō kem′i strē), *n.* the science dealing with the chemistry of living matter. —**bi·o·chem·i·cal** (bī′ō kem′i kəl), *adj.*, *n.* —**bi′o·chem′ic,** *adj.* —**bi′o·chem′i·cal·ly,** *adv.* —**bi′o·chem′ist,** *n.*

bi·o·cide (bī′ō sīd′), *n.* a chemical substance that destroys life, esp. plant life. —**bi′o·cid′al** (-ə sīd′ºl), *adj.*

bi·o·clean (bī′ō klēn′), *adj.* free or almost free from harmful living germs.

bi·o·de·grad·a·ble (bī′ō di grā′də bəl), *adj.* capable of decaying and being absorbed by the environment, as paper and kitchen scraps. —**bi′o·de·grad′a·bil′i·ty,** *n.* —**bi′o·de·gra·da′tion,** *n.*

bi·o·feed·back (bī′ō fēd′bak′), *n.* a method of learning to control one's bodily and mental functions with the aid of a visual or auditory display of one's own brain waves, blood pressure, etc.

biog., **1.** biographer. **2.** biographical. **3.** biography.

bi·o·ge·og·ra·phy (bī′ō jē og′rə fē), *n.* the study of the geographical distribution of living things. —**bi′o·ge·og′ra·pher,** *n.* —**bi·o·ge·o·graph·ic** (bī′ō jē′ə graf′ik), **bi′o·ge′o·graph′i·cal,** *adj.*

bi·og·ra·phy (bī og′rə fē, bē-), *n.*, *pl.* **-phies. 1.** a written account of another person's life. **2.** such writings collectively. —**bi·og′ra·pher,** *n.* —**bi·o·graph·i·cal** (bī′ə graf′i kəl), **bi′o·graph′ic,** *adj.*

biol., **1.** biological. **2.** biologist. **3.** biology.

biolog′ical clock′, the innate system in people, animals, etc., that causes regular cycles of function or behavior, esp. on a daily basis.

biolog′ical war′fare, warfare using bacteria, viruses, etc., to destroy people, animals, and crops.

bi·ol·o·gy (bī ol′ə jē), *n.* **1.** the science of living matter in all its forms and phenomena. **2.** the phenomena of an organism or a group of organisms. —**bi·o·log·i·cal** (bī′ə loj′i kəl), **bi·o·log′ic,** *adj.* —**bi′o·log′i·cal·ly,** *adv.* —**bi·ol′o·gist,** *n.*

bi·o·med·i·cine (bī′ō med′i sin), *n.* clinical medicine dealing with the relationship of body chemistry and function. —**bi′o·med′i·cal,** *adj.*

bi·on·ics (bī on′iks), *n.* the design of computers and other electronic equipment that perform after the manner of human beings and animals. —**bi·on′ic,** *adj.*

bi·o·phys·ics (bī′ō fiz′iks), *n.* the branch of biology dealing with the study of biological structures and processes by means of the methods of physics. —**bi′o·phys′i·cal,** *adj.* —**bi·o·phys·i·cist** (bī′ō fiz′i sist), *n.*

bi·op·sy (bī′op sē), *n.*, *pl.* **-sies.** the excision for diagnostic study of a piece of tissue from a living body. —**bi·op·tic** (bī op′tik), *adj.*

bi·o·sat·el·lite (bī′ō sat′ºlīt′), *n.* a space satellite designed to carry people, animals, or plants.

bi·o·sci·ence (bī′ō sī′əns), *n.* any science that deals with the biological aspects of living organisms, esp. while in outer space.

bi·o·sphere (bī′ə sfēr′), *n.* the part of the earth's crust, waters, and atmosphere where living organisms can subsist.

bi·o·te·lem·e·try (bī′ō tə lem′i trē), *n.* the remote sensing and measuring of biological functions of living things, as in spacecraft. —**bi′o·te·le·met′ric,** *adj.*

bi·ot·ic (bī ot′ik), *adj.* *Biol.* pertaining to life. Also, **bi·ot′i·cal.**

biot′ic poten′tial, the capacity of a population of animals or plants to increase in number under optimum environmental conditions.

bi·o·tin (bī′ə tin), *n.* a growth vitamin of the vitamin-B complex.

bi·o·tite (bī′ə tīt′), *n.* a common mineral of the mica group, an important constituent of igneous rocks.

bi·pa·ren·tal (bī pə ren′t°l), *adj.* of or characteristic of two parents.

bi·par·ti·san (bī pär′ti zən), *adj.* representing or including members from two parties. —**bi·par′ti·san·ship′,** *n.*

bi·par·tite (bī pär′tīt), *adj.* **1.** divided into or consisting of two parts. **2.** shared by two parties: *a bipartite pact.* —**bi·par·ti·tion** (bī′pär tish′ən), *n.*

bi·ped (bī′ped), *n.* a two-footed animal.

bi·plane (bī′plān′), *n.* an airplane with two sets of wings, one above the other.

bi·po·lar (bī pō′lər), *adj.* **1.** having two poles, as the earth. **2.** pertaining to or found at both poles. —**bi·po·lar·i·ty** (bī′pō lar′i tē), *n.*

bi·ra·cial (bī rā′shəl), *adj.* representing or including members from two races. —**bi·ra′cial·ism,** *n.*

birch (bûrch), *n.* **1.** a tree with a smooth, laminated outer bark and close-grained wood. **2.** its wood. **3.** a birch rod, or a bundle of birch twigs, used as a whip. —*v.t.* **4.** to beat with a birch rod. —**birch′en,** *adj.*

Birch·er (bûr′chər), *n.* a member or follower of the John Birch Society, an ultraconservative U.S. organization. Also, **Birch·ite** (bûr′chīt). —**Birch′ism,** *n.*

bird (bûrd), *n.* **1.** a warm-blooded vertebrate having a body covered with feathers and forelimbs modified into wings. **2.** *Slang.* a person. **3. birds of a feather,** people with interests or opinions in common. **4. for the birds,** *Slang.* contemptible or ridiculous.

bird·bath (bûrd′bath′, -bäth′), *n.* a tublike garden ornament for birds to drink from or bathe in.

bird·brain (bûrd′brān′), *n. Slang.* a dolt or scatterbrain.

bird·house (bûrd′hous′), *n., pl.* **-hous·es** (-hou′ziz). a houselike box for birds to live in.

bird·ie (bûr′dē), *n. Golf.* a score of one stroke under par on a hole.

bird·lime (bûrd′līm′), *n.* a sticky material smeared on twigs to catch birds that light on it.

bird′ of par′adise, any of several birds of the New Guinea region with ornate, colorful plumage.

bird·seed (bûrd′sēd′), *n.* a mixture of small seeds, used as food for birds.

bird's-eye (bûrdz′ī′), *adj.* **1.** seen from above: *a bird's-eye view of the city.* **2.** having markings resembling birds' eyes.

bi·ret·ta (bə ret′ə), *n. Rom. Cath. Ch.* a square cap with three projecting pieces, worn by the clergy.

Bir·ming·ham (bûr′ming əm *for 1;* bur′ming ham′ *for 2*), *n.* **1.** a city in central England. **2.** a city in central Alabama.

birth (bûrth), *n.* **1.** fact or act of being born or of bearing offspring. **2.** lineage or descent. **3.** supposedly natural heritage. **4.** any coming into being or existence. **5. give birth to,** a. to bear, as an offspring. b. to originate.

birth′ control′, regulation of the number of one's children through the restriction of ovulation or conception.

birth·day (bûrth′dā′), *n.* the day or anniversary of a person's birth.

birth·mark (bûrth′märk′), *n.* a mark or blemish on a person's skin at birth.

birth·place (bûrth′plās′), *n.* place of birth or origin.

birth·rate (bûrth′rāt′), *n.* the number of births in a place in a given time, usually as a quantity per 1000 of population.

birth·right (bûrth′rīt′), *n.* any right or privilege to which a person is entitled by birth.

birth·stone (bûrth′stōn′), *n.* a gem considered appropriate for wear by persons born within a particular month and believed to be lucky.

bis·cuit (bis′kit), *n.* **1.** a kind of bread in small cakes, raised with baking powder or soda. **2.** *Brit.* a. a cookie. b. a cracker. [< MF *biscuit,* var. of *bescuit* seamen's bread, lit., twice cooked]

bi·sect (bī sekt′, bī′sekt), *v.t.* **1.** to cut or divide into two equal parts. **2.** to intersect or cross. —**bi·sec′tion,** *n.* —**bi·sec′tion·al,** *adj.* —**bi·sec′tion·al·ly,** *adv.* —**bi·sec′tor,** *n.*

bi·sex·u·al (bī sek′shōō əl), *adj.* **1.** of both sexes. **2.** combining male and female organs in one individual. **3.** sexually responsive to both sexes. —*n.* **4.** a person who is bisexual. —**bi·sex′u·al·ism, bi′·sex·u·al′i·ty,** *n.* —**bi·sex′u·al·ly,** *adv.*

bish·op (bish′əp), *n.* **1.** a prelate who oversees a number of local churches or a diocese. **2.** *Chess.* a piece that may be moved any unobstructed distance diagonally. [< LL *episcopus* < Gk *epískopos* overseer]

bish·op·ric (bish′əp rik), *n.* the see, diocese, or office of a bishop.

Bis·marck (biz′märk), *n.* **1.** Ot·to von (ot′ō von), 1815–98, German statesman. **2.** the capital of North Dakota.

bis·muth (biz′məth), *n. Chem.* a metallic element used in the manufacture of fusible alloys and in medicine. *Symbol:* Bi; *at. wt.:* 208.980; *at. no.:* 83. —**bis′muth·al**, *adj.* —**bis·mu′thic** (-myōō′thik, -muth′ik), *adj.*

bi·son (bī′sən, -zən), *n., pl.* **-son.** a North American, oxlike ruminant having a large head and high, humped shoulders.

bisque (bisk), *n.* **1.** a heavy cream soup of puréed shellfish, game, or vegetables. **2.** ice cream made with powdered macaroons or nuts.

bis·tro (bis′trō), *n.* a small, unpretentious bar or restaurant.

bit¹ (bit), *n.* **1.** the mouthpiece of a bridle. **2.** a removable drilling tool for use in a brace, drill press, etc.

bit² (bit), *n.* **1.** a small piece or quantity of anything. **2.** a short time: *Wait a bit.* **3.** *Slang.* a. 12½ cents: *two bits.* b. an act, performance, or routine. **4.** a very small role, as in a play. **5.** any small coin. **6.** a bit, rather or somewhat: *a bit drunk.* **7.** bit by bit, by degrees or gradually. **8.** do one's bit, to contribute one's share to an effort.

bit³ (bit), *n.* a single, basic unit of information, used in connection with computers. [*b*(*inary*) + (*dig*)*it*]

bitch (bich), *n.* **1.** a female dog. **2.** *Slang.* a. a malicious, selfish woman. b. a lewd woman. **3.** *Slang.* a. a complaint. b. anything difficult or unpleasant. —*v.i.* **4.** *Slang.* to complain. —**bitch′y**, *adj.*

bite (bīt), *v., bit* (bit), *bit·ten* (bit′ən) or *bit, bit·ing, n.* —*v.t.* **1.** to cut, wound, or tear with the teeth. **2.** to grip with the teeth. **3.** to sting, as an insect. **4.** to cause to smart or sting. **5.** to sever with the teeth. **6.** to corrode, as an acid does. —*v.i.* **7.** to attack with the jaws, bill, etc. **8.** (of fish) to take bait. **9.** to accept an offer, esp. one intended to deceive. **10.** to grip or hold. **11.** bite the bullet, to face up to an unavoidable, unpleasant situation. **12.** bite the dust, to be killed, esp. in battle. —*n.* **13.** act of biting. **14.** a wound made by a bite or sting. **15.** a cutting, stinging, or nipping effect. **16.** *Slang.* an exacted portion. **17.** a morsel of food: *not a bite to eat.* **18.** a small meal. —**bit′er**, *n.*

bit·ing (bī′tiŋ), *adj.* **1.** nipping or keen. **2.** cutting or sarcastic. —**bit′ing·ly**, *adv.*

bit·ter (bit′ər), *adj.* **1.** having a harsh, acrid taste. **2.** hard to accept: *a bitter lesson.* **3.** piercing or stinging. **4.** characterized by intense hostility **5.** resentful or cynical. —**bit′ter·ly**, *adv.* —**bit′ter·ness**, *n.*

bit·tern (bit′ərn), *n.* a tawny brown heron that inhabits reedy marshes.

bit·ters (bit′ərz), *n.* a liquid, often an alcoholic liquor, in which bitter herbs or roots have steeped, used in mixed drinks or as a tonic.

bit·ter·sweet (*n.* bit′ər swēt′; *adj.* bit′ər swēt′), *n.* **1.** a climbing or trailing plant having scarlet berries. **2.** a climbing plant bearing orange capsules opening to expose red-coated seeds. **3.** pleasure mingled with pain or regret. —*adj.* **4.** both bitter and sweet to the taste. **5.** both pleasant and painful.

bi·tu·men (bī tōō′mən, -tyōō′-, bi-), *n.* any of various natural substances, as asphalt, etc., consisting mainly of hydrocarbons. —**bi·tu′mi·nous** (-mə nəs), *adj.*

bitu′minous coal′, a coal that burns with a yellow, smoky flame.

bi·va·lent (bī vā′lənt, biv′ə-), *adj. Chem.* having a valence of two.

bi·valve (bī′valv′), *n.* a mollusk having two shells hinged together, as the clam.

biv·ou·ac (biv′ōō ak′, biv′wak), *n., v., -acked, -ack·ing.* —*n.* **1.** a temporary military encampment made with tents or shelters. —*v.i.* **2.** to rest or assemble in a bivouac.

bi·week·ly (bī wēk′lē), *adj., n., pl. -lies, adv.* —*adj.* **1.** occurring every two weeks. **2.** semiweekly. —*n.* **3.** a periodical issued every other week. —*adv.* **4.** every two weeks. **5.** twice a week.
—Usage. Since it is not always clear which meaning of BIWEEKLY is intended—"twice a week" or "every two weeks"—the use of SEMIWEEKLY for "twice a week" is preferable because it is unambiguous. Since there is no single, unambiguous term for "every two weeks," this phrase itself is the least confusing to use.

bi·year·ly (bī yēr′lē), *adj.* **1.** biennial (defs. 1, 2). —*adv.* **2.** biennially. **3.** twice yearly.

bi·zarre (bi zär′), *adj.* markedly unusual, strange, or odd. —**bi·zarre′ly**, *adv.*

Bk, berkelium.

bk., **1.** black. **2.** book.

bkg., banking.

bkgd., background.

bkpg., bookkeeping.

bks., barracks.

bkt., **1.** basket. **2.** bracket.

B/L, See **bill of lading.**

bl., **1.** bale. **2.** barrel. **3.** black. **4.** blue.

blab (blab), *v., blabbed, blab·bing, n.* —*v.t.* **1.** to reveal indiscreetly and thoughtlessly —*v.i.* **2.** to talk indiscreetly and thoughtlessly. —*n.* **3.** idle, indiscreet chattering. —**blab′ber**, *n.*

black (blak), *adj.* **1.** lacking hue and brightness.. **2.** (*sometimes cap.*) of or belonging to an ethnic group of African descent characterized by dark skin pigmentation. **3.** soiled or stained. **4.** dark: *a black night.* **5.** gloomy or dismal. **6.** sullen or hostile. **7.** evil or wicked. **8.** indicating disgrace, etc. **9.** (of coffee) without milk or cream. —*n.* **10.** the color opposite to white, absorbing all light incident upon it. **11.** (*sometimes cap.*) a member of a dark-skinned people of African descent. **12.** black clothing: *He wore black at the funeral.* **13.** in the black, operating at a profit. —*v.t., v.i.* **14.** to make or become black or dark. **15.** black out, to lose consciousness. —**black'ish,** *adj.* —**black'ly,** *adv.* —**black'ness,** *n.*

black·a·moor (blak'ə mŏŏr'), *n.* Archaic. a black (def. 11).

black-and-blue (blak'ən blōō'), *adj.* discolored, as by bruising.

black' art', necromancy (def. 1).

black·ball (blak'bôl'), *v.t.* **1.** to vote against (a candidate, etc.). **2.** to ostracize (a person or group). —*n.* **3.** a negative vote, esp. on a candidate.

black' bass' (bas), a freshwater, American game fish.

black belt, **1.** **a.** a rank of proficient skill in judo or karate: so called from the color of the belt of the costume worn by a rank holder. **b.** a player who holds such a rank. **2.** (*sometimes caps.*) the predominantly black section of a city.

black·ber·ry (blak'ber'ē, -bə rē), *n., pl.* -ries. **1.** the fruit, black or very dark purple when ripe, of certain brambles. **2.** its plant.

black·bird (blak'bûrd'), *n.* any of several American birds having black plumage.

black·board (blak'bôrd', -bōrd'), *n.* a smooth, hard surface for writing on with chalk.

black' bod'y, Physics. a hypothetical body that absorbs all of the radiation incident on its surface.

black' box', any electronic device that has its function, but not its components, specified.

Black' Death', a bubonic plague in Europe in the 14th century.

black·en (blak'ən), *v.t.* **1.** to make black or dark. **2.** to sully or defame. —*v.i.* **3.** to grow or become black. —**black'en·er,** *n.*

black' eye', a discoloration of the skin around the eye, resulting from a blow, etc.

black'-eyed Su'san (sōō'zən), a plant having flowers with a dark center against a lighter, usually yellow, background.

Black·foot (blak'fŏŏt'), *n., pl.* -feet, -foot. a member of a North American tribe of Indians of Algonquian stock.

black' gold', Informal. petroleum.

black·guard (blag'ärd, -ərd), *n.* a low, contemptible scoundrel.

black·head (blak'hed'), *n.* a small, black-tipped, fatty mass in a skin follicle, esp. of the face.

black' hole', a region in outer space, hypothetically caused by the collapse of a star, in which the density is so great that even light cannot escape the gravitational force.

black·ing (blak'ing), *n.* a preparation for producing a black finish.

black·jack (blak'jak'), *n.* **1.** a short, leather-covered club with a flexible handle. **2.** Cards. twenty-one. —*v.t.* **3.** to beat with a blackjack.

black' light', invisible infrared or ultraviolet light.

black·list (blak'list'), *n.* **1.** a list of persons or organizations under suspicion, disfavor, etc. —*v.t.* **2.** to put on a blacklist.

black' lung', a respiratory ailment caused by frequent inhalation of fine coal-dust particles.

black' mag'ic, sorcery.

black·mail (blak'māl'), *n.* **1.** any payment extorted by intimidation, as by threats of revelation. —*v.t.* **2.** to obtain blackmail from. [*black* + ME *mal*(*e*) rent < Scand] —**black'mail'er,** *n.*

black' mark', a detrimental fact, as in one's record.

black' mar'ket, a market of illicit buying and selling in violation of controls. —**black' mar·ke·teer'.**

Black' Mass', a blasphemous ceremony mocking the Christian Mass, esp. one by an alleged worshiper of the devil.

Black' Mus'lim, a member of an organization of blacks advocating Islam and complete separation of races.

black' na'tionalism, a social and political movement advocating separatism and self-government for black people. —**black' na'tionalist.**

black·out (blak'out'), *n.* **1.** the extinguishing or concealment of lights, as from a power failure or to reduce visibility in an air raid. **2.** temporary unconsciousness. **3.** suspension or suppression, as of news.

Black' Pan'ther, a member of a militant black organization.

black' pow'er, the political and economic power of black Americans as a group, esp. such power used for achieving racial equality.

Black' Sea', a sea between SE Europe and Asia.

black′ sheep′, a person considered embarrassingly disreputable by his or her family or group.

black·smith (blak′smith′), *n.* **1.** a person who makes horseshoes and shoes horses. **2.** a person who forges objects of iron.

black·thorn (blak′thôrn′), *n.* a thorny shrub having white flowers and small plumlike fruits.

black′ tie′, a black bow tie, worn with a tuxedo.

black·top (blak′top′), *n., v.,* **-topped, -top·ping.** —*n.* **1.** a bituminous substance, usually asphalt, for paving roads, etc. —*v.t.* **2.** to pave with blacktop.

black′ wid′ow, a small, jet-black, venomous spider, widely distributed in the U.S.

blad·der (blad′ər), *n.* **1.** a membranous sac or organ serving as a receptacle for a fluid or gas, esp. urine. **2.** something resembling such a sac.

blade (blād), *n.* **1.** the flat cutting part of a sword, knife, etc. **2.** a sword. **3.** the leaf of a plant, esp. of grass. **4.** the broad part of a leaf. **5.** the sharp part of a skate in contact with the ice. **6.** a thin, flat part of something, as of an oar. **7.** *Informal.* a dashing young man. **8.** a swordsman.

blain (blān), *n.* an inflammatory swelling or sore.

blame (blām), *v.,* **blamed, blam·ing.** *n.* —*v.t.* **1.** to place the responsibility for (a fault, error, etc.) on (a person). **2.** to censure or condemn. **3. to blame,** at fault. —*n.* **4.** censure or reproof. **5.** responsibility for anything deserving of censure. —**blam′a·ble,** *adj.* —**blam′a·ble·ness,** *n.* —**blam′a·bly,** *adv.* —**blam′er,** *n.* —**blame′less,** *adj.* —**blame′less·ly,** *adv.* —**blame′less·ness,** *n.* —**Syn. 1, 2.** accuse, criticize, denounce, reproach.

blame·wor·thy (blām′wûr′thē), *adj.* deserving blame. Also, **blame′ful.** —**blame′wor′thi·ness,** *n.*

blanch (blanch, blänch), *v.t.* **1.** to bleach or whiten. **2.** to scald briefly to facilitate removal of skins. **3.** to make pale. —*v.i.* **4.** to become white or pale.

blanc·mange (blə mänj′, -mänzh′), *n.* a flavored, sweet pudding made with milk and cornstarch.

bland (bland), *adj.* **1.** pleasantly agreeable. **2.** soothing and nonirritating: *a bland diet.* **3.** unemotional or indifferent. —**bland′ly,** *adv.* —**bland′ness,** *n.*

blan·dish (blan′dish), *v.t., v.i.* to coax by cajolery. —**blan′dish·er,** *n.* —**blan′dish·ment,** *n.*

blank (blangk), *adj.* **1.** not written or printed on. **2.** not filled in: *a blank check.* **3.** unrelieved by ornament, etc.: *a blank wall.* **4.** void of interest, results, etc. **5.** showing no interest or emotion. **6.** complete or utter: *a blank denial.* —*n.* **7.** a place or space where something is lacking. **8.** a printed form containing such spaces. **9.** a gun cartridge containing powder only, without a bullet. **10. draw a blank,** to fail in an attempt. —*v.t.* **11.** to cross out or delete. **12.** to keep (an opponent) from scoring in a game. —**blank′ly,** *adv.* —**blank′ness,** *n.*

blank′ check′, **1.** a bank check bearing a signature but no stated amount. **2.** unrestricted authority.

blan·ket (blang′kit), *n.* **1.** a large piece of soft fabric used as a covering for warmth, esp. on a bed. **2.** any extended covering: *a blanket of snow.* —*v.t.* **3.** to cover with a blanket. **4.** to obscure or obstruct. —*adj.* **5.** covering all things, conditions, etc.

blank′ verse′, unrhymed iambic pentameter in verse.

blare (blâr), *v.,* **blared, blar·ing,** *n.* —*v.i., v.t.* **1.** to sound or utter raucously. —*n.* **2.** a loud raucous noise.

blar·ney (blär′nē), *n.* flattering or wheedling talk.

Blar′ney stone′, a stone in Blarney Castle near Cork, Ireland, said to impart skill in flattery to those who kiss it.

bla·sé (blä zā′, blä′zā), *adj.* indifferent to or bored, as from an excess of worldly pleasures.

blas·pheme (blas fēm′, blas′fēm), *v.,* **-phemed, -phem·ing.** —*v.t.* **1.** to speak irreverently of (God or sacred things). **2.** to curse or slander. —*v.i.* **3.** to speak blasphemy. —**blas·phem′er,** *n.*

blas·phe·my (blas′fə mē), *n., pl.* **-mies.** impious or irreverent utterance or action concerning God or sacred things. —**blas′phe·mous,** *adj.* —**blas′phem·ous·ly,** *adv.*

blast (blast, bläst), *n.* **1.** a sudden and violent gust of wind. **2.** the blowing of a trumpet, whistle, etc. **3.** a loud, sudden sound or noise. **4.** air forced into a furnace by a blower to increase the rate of combustion. **5.** a vigorous criticism. **6.** *Slang.* a party, esp. a wild one. **7.** an explosion. **8.** a blight, as of a plant. **9. at full blast,** or with full volume or speed. —*v.t.* **10.** to blow or blow up. **11.** to shrivel or wither. **12.** to curse or damn. **13.** to criticize vigorously. —*v.i.* **14.** to produce a loud, blaring sound. **15. blast off,** (of a rocket) to leave a launch pad under self-propulsion.

blast′ fur′nace, a large vertical furnace for smelting iron from ore.

blast-off (blast′ôf′, -of′, bläst′-), *n.* the launching of a rocket or guided missile.

bla·tant (blāt′ᵊnt), *adj.* **1.** brazenly obvious: *a blatant error.* **2.** noisy or clamorous. —**bla′tan·cy,** *n.* —**bla′tant·ly,** *adv.*

blath·er (blaŧẖ′ᵊr), *n.* **1.** foolish talk. —*v.i., v.t.* **2.** to speak foolishly.

blath·er·skite (blaŧẖ′ᵊr skīt′), *n.* a person given to voluble, empty talk.

blaze¹ (blāz), *n., v.,* **blazed, blaz·ing.** —*n.* **1.** a bright fire. **2.** a bright, hot glow. **3.** a sparkling brightness. **4.** a sudden, intense outburst of passion, fury, etc. —*v.i.* **5.** to blaze brightly. **6.** to shine like flame. **7.** to burn with intense feeling.

blaze² (blāz), *n., v.,* **blazed, blaz·ing.** —*n.* **1.** a mark made on a tree to indicate a path in a forest. **2.** a white area on the face of a horse, cow, etc. —*v.t.* **3.** to mark with blazes.

blaze³ (blāz), *v.t.,* **blazed, blaz·ing.** to spread (news) widely.

blaz·er (blā′zər), *n.* a solid-color sports jacket, often with metal buttons.

bla·zon (blā′zən), *v.t.* **1.** to display conspicuously. **2.** *Archaic.* to proclaim. —*n.* **3.** a coat of arms. **4.** conspicuous display.

bldg., building.

bldr., builder.

bleach (blēch), *v.t., v.i.* **1.** to make or become whiter or lighter in color. —*n.* **2.** a bleaching agent.

bleach·er (blē′chər), *n.* Usually, **bleachers.** a roofless section of seats in tiers, esp. at an athletic stadium.

bleak (blēk), *adj.* **1.** bare, desolate, and windswept. **2.** cold and raw. **3.** offering little hope. —**bleak′ish,** *adj.* —**bleak′ly,** *adv.* —**bleak′ness,** *n.*

blear (blēr), *v.t.* **1.** to make (the eyes) dim, as with tears. —*adj.* **2.** (of the eyes) dim.

blear·y (blēr′ē), *adj.,* **blear·i·er, blear·i·est. 1.** (of the eyes) blurred or dimmed. **2.** indistinct or unclear.

bleat (blēt), *n.* **1.** the cry of a sheep, goat, or calf. —*v.i.* **2.** to utter a bleat.

bleed (blēd), *v.,* **bled** (bled), **bleed·ing.** —*v.i.* **1.** to lose blood from the vascular system. **2.** to exude sap, resin, etc. **3.** (of dye or paint) to run or become diffused. **4.** to feel pity, sorrow, or anguish. —*v.t.* **5.** to cause to lose blood, esp. surgically. **6.** to drain sap, water, etc., from (something). **7.** *Slang.* to extort money from.

bleed·er (blē′dər), *n.* a hemophiliac.

bleed′ing heart′, 1. a common garden plant having racemes of red, heart-shaped flowers. **2.** *Disparaging.* a person who makes a display of concern for others.

bleep (blēp), *n., v.,* beep.

blem·ish (blem′ish), *v.t.* **1.** to destroy or diminish the perfection of. —*n.* **2.** a defect or flaw.

blench¹ (blench), *v.i. Archaic.* to flinch. —**blench′er,** *n.* —**blench′ing·ly,** *adv.*

blench² (blench), *v.t., v.i.* to blanch.

blend (blend), *v.,* **blend·ed** or **blent, blend·ing,** *n.* —*v.t., v.i.* **1.** to mix smoothly and inseparably together. **2.** to fit or relate harmoniously. —*n.* **3.** act or manner of blending. **4.** a mixture produced by blending. **5.** a word made by putting together parts of other words, as *smog* from *smoke and fog.* —**blend′er,** *n.*

blend′ed whis′key, a blend of two or more whiskeys or of whiskey and neutral spirits.

bleph·a·ri·tis (blef′ə rī′tis), *n.* inflammation of the eyelids.

bless (bles), *v.t.,* **blessed** or **blest** (blest), **bless·ing. 1.** to pronounce holy. **2.** to request divine favor for. **3.** to bestow good of any kind upon. **4.** to extol as holy. **5.** to make the sign of the cross over or upon.

bless·ed (bles′id *for 1;* blest *for 1, 2*), *adj.* **1.** sacred or holy. **2.** favored or fortunate. **3.** beatified. Also, **blest.** —**bless′ed·ly,** *adv.* —**bless′ed·ness,** *n.*

Bless′ed Sac′rament, the consecrated Host.

Bless′ed Vir′gin, the Virgin Mary.

bless·ing (bles′ing), *n.* **1.** the act or words of a person who blesses. **2.** a special favor, mercy, or benefit. **3.** a gift bestowed by God. **4.** the invocation of God's favor upon a person. **5.** grace said before a meal. **6.** approval.

blew (blōō), *v.* pt. of **blow²**.

blight (blīt), *n.* **1.** the wilting and death of plant tissues. **2.** any cause of ruin or frustration. —*v.t.* **3.** to cause to wither or decay. **4.** to destroy or ruin. —**blight′ing·ly,** *adv.*

blimp (blimp), *n.* a small, nonrigid airship. [? from *Type B, limp* a nonrigid dirigible]

blind (blīnd), *adj.* **1.** unable to see. **2.** not characterized by reason or control: *blind chance.* **3.** characterized by a lack of awareness: *a blind stupor.* **4.** hidden from immediate view: *a blind corner.* **5.** having no outlets: *a blind alley.* **6.** using instruments alone: *blind flying.* **7.** of, pertaining to, or for blind persons. —*v.t.* **8.** to make blind. **9.** to dazzle. **10.** to deprive of reason or judgment. —*n.* **11.** something that obstructs vision or keeps out light. **12.** a lightly built structure, esp. one in which hunters conceal themselves. **13.** subterfuge. **14.** a decoy. —**blind′ly,** *adv.* —**blind′ness,** *n.*

blind′ cop′y. See **bc**

blind′ date′, a prearranged date between a man and a woman who have never met before.

blind·er (blīn′dər), *n.* a blinker for a horse.

blind·fold (blīnd′fōld′), *v.t.* **1.** to cover the eyes of, as with a cloth. **2.** to impair the awareness or clear thinking of. —*n.* **3.** a cloth covering the eyes to prevent seeing. —*adj.* **4.** with the eyes covered. **5.** rash or reckless.

blind·man's buff (blīnd′manz′ buf′), a game in which a blindfolded player tries to catch and identify one of the others.

blind′ spot′, 1. a small area on the retina where the optic nerve leaves the eye and which is insensitive to light. **2.** a subject, area, etc., about which one is uninformed.

blink (blingk), *v.i.* **1.** to open and close the eye quickly. **2.** to evade or shirk. **3.** to twinkle. —*v.t.* **4.** to cause (the eye) to blink. **5.** to evade or shirk. —*n.* **6.** act of blinking. **7.** a gleam or glimmer. **8. on the blink,** *Slang.* not in working order.

blink·er (bling′kər), *n.* **1.** a device for flashing light signals. **2.** either of two flaps on a bridle, to prevent a horse from seeing sideways.

blintze (blints), *n.* a thin pancake folded around a filling, as of cheese or fruit. Also, **blintz** (blints).

blip (blip), *n., v.,* **blipped, blip·ping.** —*n.* **1.** a spot of light on a radar screen indicating the position of an object. —*v.t.* **2.** to erase (an unwanted word, etc.) from a videotape.

bliss (blis), *n.* **1.** supreme happiness. **2.** the joy of heaven. —**bliss′ful,** *adj.* —**bliss′ful·ly,** *adv.* —**bliss′ful·ness,** *n.*

blis·ter (blis′tər), *n.* **1.** a thin vesicle on the skin, containing watery matter, caused by a burn or other injury. **2.** any similar swelling. —*v.t.* **3.** to raise a blister on. **4.** to criticize or rebuke severely. —*v.i.* **5.** to become blistered.

blithe (blīth, blīth), *adj.* joyously merry. Also, **blithe′some** (-səm). —**blithe′ly,** *adv.* —**blithe′ness,** *n.*

blitz (blits), *n.* **1.** an overwhelming all-out attack. **2.** an intensive aerial bombing. **3.** any swift attack. —*v.t.* **4.** to attack with a blitz. [*blitz-(krieg)* < G, lit., lightning war]

blitz·krieg (blits′krēg′), *n., v.t.* blitz.

bliz·zard (bliz′ərd), *n.* a heavy and windy snowstorm.

blk., **1.** black. **2.** block. **3.** bulk.

bloat (blōt), *v.t., v.i.* **1.** to expand or swell with or as with air or water. **2.** to inflate or become inflated, as with pride.

bloat·er (blō′tər), *n.* a herring or mackerel cured by being salted and briefly smoked and dried.

blob (blob), *n., v.,* **blobbed, blob·bing.** —*n.* **1.** a small lump or splotch. —*v.t.* **2.** to mark with blobs.

bloc (blok), *n.* **1.** a group working for some particular interest. **2.** a group of peoples or nations having a common objective.

block (blok), *n.* **1.** a solid mass of wood, stone, etc., usually with one or more flat faces. **2.** a platform from which an auctioneer sells. **3.** a part enclosing one or more pulleys about which ropes pass to form a hoisting tackle. **4.** an obstacle or hindrance. **5.** an obstruction, as of a nerve. **6.** a quantity taken as a unit. **7.** a small section of a city, enclosed by neighboring streets or the length of one side of such a section. **8.** *Philately.* a group of four or more unseparated stamps, not in a strip. **9.** a sudden stoppage of thought, usually caused by emotional tension. **10.** *Slang.* a person's head. —*v.t.* **11.** to furnish or support with a block. **12.** to mount or shape on a block. **13.** to obstruct or hinder. **14. block in** or **out,** to outline roughly. —**block·age** (blok′ij), *n.* —**block′er,** *n.*

block·ade (blo kād′), *n., v.,* **-ad·ed, -ad·ing.** —*n.* **1.** the isolating of a place, esp. a port, by ships or troops to prevent entrance or exit. **2.** any obstruction of passage. —*v.t.* **3.** to subject to a blockade. —**block·ad′er,** *n.*

block′ and tack′le, the ropes or chains and blocks used in a hoisting tackle.

block·bust·er (blok′bus′tər), *n.* **1.** an aerial bomb for large-scale demolition. **2.** something overwhelmingly impressive.

block·bust·ing (blok′bus′ting), *n.* the practice of exploiting racial prejudice to induce home owners to sell their property at a low price, as upon the entrance into the neighborhood of a single black family.

block·head (blok′hed′), *n.* a stupid person.

block·house (blok′hous′), *n.* **1.** a fortified structure with loopholes through which defenders may direct gunfire. **2.** a structure for protecting personnel during rocket-launching operations.

bloke (blōk), *n. Brit. Slang.* guy[1].

blond (blond), *adj.* 1. (of hair, fur, etc.) light-colored. 2. (of a person) having light-colored hair and skin. 3. (of wood) light in tone. —*n.* 4. a blond person. Also, *referring to a woman,* **blonde.** —**blond′ness,** *n.*

blood (blud), *n.* 1. the fluid that circulates in the vascular system of humans and other vertebrates. 2. life. 3. a fresh source of energy, vitality, or vigor, as personnel. 4. slaughter or murder. 5. the juice of a plant. 6. temperament. 7. a high-spirited youth. 8. physical and cultural extraction. 9. descent from a common ancestor. 10. **in cold blood,** deliberately or ruthlessly. —**blood′less,** *adj.*

blood′ bank′, a place where blood or plasma is collected, stored, and distributed.

blood′ bath′, a massacre.

blood′ count′, the number of red and white corpuscles in a specific volume of blood.

blood·cur·dling (blud′kûrd′ling), *adj.* terrifyingly horrible. —**blood′cur′dling·ly,** *adv.*

blood·ed (blud′id), *adj.* having a good pedigree: *blooded cattle.*

blood′ group′, one of several classes into which human blood can be separated according to the presence or absence in the red corpuscles of specific substances. Also called **blood′ type′.**

blood·hound (blud′hound′), *n.* a large-sized hound having long ears and an acute sense of smell.

blood·let·ting (blud′let′ing), *n.* 1. phlebotomy. 2. bloodshed.

blood·line (blud′līn′), *n.* (usually of animals) the line of desent.

blood·mo·bile (blud′mə bēl′), *n.* a truck with medical equipment for receiving blood donations for blood transfusions.

blood′ poi′soning, a condition of the blood caused by presence of harmful toxic matter or microorganisms.

blood′ pres′sure, the pressure of the blood against the inner walls of the blood vessels.

blood′ rel′ative, a person related to one by birth. Also, **blood′ re·la′tion.**

blood·root (blud′root′, -root′), *n.* a North American plant having a red root and root sap.

blood·shed (blud′shed′), *n.* destruction of life, as in war, murder, etc.

blood·shot (blud′shot′), *adj.* (of the eyes) exhibiting dilated blood vessels.

blood·stained (blud′stānd′), *adj.* 1. stained with blood. 2. guilty of bloodshed.

blood·stone (blud′stōn′), *n.* a greenish variety of chalcedony with small bloodlike spots.

blood·stream (blud′strēm′), *n.* the blood flowing through a circulatory system.

blood·suck·er (blud′suk′ər), *n.* an animal that sucks blood, esp. a leech. —**blood′suck′ing,** *adj.*

blood′ sug′ar, glucose in the blood.

blood′ test′, a test of a sample of blood to determine blood group, presence of infection, etc.

blood·thirst·y (blud′thûr′stē), *adj.* eager to shed blood or cause bloodshed. —**blood′thirst′i·ly,** *adv.* —**blood′thirst′i·ness,** *n.*

blood′ ves′sel, any of the vessels, as arteries, veins, or capillaries, through which the blood circulates.

blood·y (blud′ē), *adj.,* **blood·i·er, blood·i·est,** *v.,* **blood·ied, blood·y·ing,** *adv.* —*adj.* 1. stained with blood or bleeding. 2. characterized by bloodshed. 3. bloodthirsty or cruel. 4. *Brit. Slang.* damned or extraordinary. —*v.t.* 5. to stain with blood. —*adv.* 6. *Brit. Slang.* damned or damnably. —**blood′i·ly,** *adv.* —**blood′i·ness,** *n.*

Blood′y Mar′y, a mixed drink made principally with vodka and tomato juice.

bloom (bloom), *n.* 1. the flower of a plant. 2. flowers collectively. 3. the state of having the buds open. 4. the period of greatest beauty, artistry, etc. 5. a glow on the cheek indicative of youth and health. 6. a whitish powdery coating, as on certain fruits and leaves. —*v.i.* 7. to produce blossoms. 8. to flourish. 9. to be in a state of beauty and vigor. —**bloom′er,** *n.* —**bloom′y,** *adj.*

bloom·ers (bloo′mərz), *n.pl.* a woman's athletic costume or undergarment of loose trousers gathered at the knee. [after Amelia *Bloomer* (1818–94), U.S. advocate of the costume]

bloom·ing (bloo′ming), *adj.* 1. in bloom. 2. flourishing or prospering. 3. *Informal.* damned (def. 2b).

bloop·er (bloo′pər), *n.* 1. *Slang.* a blunder, as one spoken over radio or TV. 2. *Baseball.* a fly ball that carries just beyond the infield.

blos·som (blos′əm), *n.* 1. the flower of a plant. 2. the state of flowering. —*v.i.* 3. to produce blossoms. 4. to flourish or develop. —**blos′som·y,** *adj.*

blot[1] (blot), *n., v.,* **blot·ted, blot·ting.** —*n.* 1. a spot or stain, esp. of ink on paper. 2. a blemish on one's reputation. —*v.t.* 3. to spot or stain. 4. to darken or hide entirely. 5. to dry, as with absorbent paper. —*v.i.* 6. to make a blot. 7.

to become blotted. **8. blot out**, to destroy or annihilate.

blot² (blot), *n. Backgammon.* an exposed piece liable to be taken or forfeited.

blotch (bloch), *n.* **1.** a large, irregular spot or blot. **2.** a skin blemish. —*v.t.* **3.** to mark with blotches. —**blotch′y**, *adj.*

blot·ter (blot′ər), *n.* **1.** a piece of blotting paper. **2.** a book in which events, as sales, arrests, etc., are recorded as they occur: *a police blotter.*

blot′ting pa′per, a soft, absorbent paper, used esp. to dry ink.

blouse (blous, blouz), *n., v.,* **bloused, blous·ing.** —*n.* **1.** a garment for women and children, covering the body from the neck to the waistline. **2.** a jacket worn as part of the U.S. Army uniform. —*v.i.* **3.** to puff out in a drooping fullness.

blou·son (bloo′son′), *n.* a woman's amply cut blouse or dress that is drawn tight at the waistline.

blow¹ (blō), *n.* **1.** a sudden, hard stroke with a hand, fist, or weapon. **2.** a sudden shock, calamity, etc. **3.** a sudden attack or action. **4. come to blows**, to begin to fight.

blow² (blō), *v.,* **blew, blown** (blōn), **blow·ing,** *n.* —*v.i.* **1.** (of the wind) to move forcefully. **2.** to move along, carried by or as by the wind. **3.** to produce a current of air, as with the mouth. **4.** to sound shrilly. **5.** (of horses) to pant. **6.** (of a whale) to spout. **7.** (of a fuse) to stop functioning by overloading. **8.** *Informal.* to boast. —*v.t.* **9.** to drive by means of a current of air. **10.** *Slang.* to leave. **11.** to clear by forcing air through. **12.** to shape (glass) with a current of air. **13.** to cause to sound. **14.** to explode. **15.** to burn out or destroy by overloading. **16.** *Slang.* **a.** to squander. **b.** to depart from. **c.** to botch or bungle. **17. blow off,** *Informal.* to reduce tension, as by loud talking. **18. blow over,** to subside. **19. blow up,** *Informal.* to lose one's temper. —*n.* **20.** a blast of air or wind. **21.** a windstorm. **22.** the act of blowing. —**blow′er,** *n.*

blow³ (blō), *v.i., v.t.,* **blew, blown, blow·ing.** to blossom or cause to blossom (chiefly used in combination in past participle): *a full-blown rose.*

blow-by-blow (blō′bī′blō′), *adj.* (of an account) precisely detailed.

blow·fly (blō′flī′), *n., pl.* **-flies.** a fly that deposits its eggs on decaying flesh, etc.

blow·gun (blō′gun′), *n.* a pipe through which missiles are blown by the breath.

blow·out (blō′out′), *n.* **1.** a sudden bursting, as of an automobile tire. **2.** the melting of a fuse under excessive load. **3.** *Slang.* a big, lavish party.

blow·pipe (blō′pīp′), *n.* **1.** a tube through which air is forced into a flame to increase its heating action. **2.** a long metal pipe used to gather and blow molten glass.

blows·y (blou′zē), *adj.,* **blows·i·er, blows·i·est.** blowzy.

blow·torch (blō′tôrch′), *n.* a small apparatus that gives an extremely hot flame.

blow·up (blō′up′), *n.* **1.** an explosion. **2.** a violent outburst of temper. **3.** *Photog.* an enlargement.

blow·y (blō′ē), *adj.,* **blow·i·er, blow·i·est.** windy. —**blow′i·ness,** *n.*

blowz·y (blou′zē), *adj.,* **blowz·i·er, blowz·i·est.** disheveled or unkempt.

B.L.S., Bachelor of Library Science.

BLT, bacon, lettuce, and tomato (sandwich).

blub·ber (blub′ər), *n.* **1.** the fat of marine mammals, as whales. **2.** a noisy weeping. —*v.i.* **3.** to weep noisily. —**blub′ber·er,** *n.* —**blub′ber·y,** *adj.*

blu·cher (bloo′kər, -chər), *n.* a shoe with the vamp continued up beneath the top.

bludg·eon (bluj′ən), *n.* **1.** a short club with one end heavier than the other. —*v.t.* **2.** to strike with a bludgeon. **3.** to coerce or bully.

blue (bloo), *n., adj.,* **blu·er, blu·est,** *v.,* **blued, blu·ing** or **blue·ing.** —*n.* **1.** the pure color of a clear sky. **2.** bluing. **3.** something having a blue color. **4. out of the blue,** suddenly and unexpectedly. **5. the blue, a.** the sky. **b.** the sea. —*adj.* **6.** of the color blue. **7.** discolored or livid. **8.** depressed or melancholy. **9.** indecent: *blue movies.* —*v.t., v.i.* **10.** to make or become blue. —**blu′ish,** *adj.*

blue′ bab′y, an infant born with bluish skin resulting from a congenital heart or lung defect.

blue·bell (bloo′bel′), *n.* a plant with blue, bell-shaped flowers.

blue·ber·ry (bloo′ber′ē, -bə rē), *n., pl.* **-ries. 1.** the edible, usually bluish berry of various shrubs. **2.** any of these shrubs.

blue·bird (bloo′bûrd′), *n.* a small North American songbird having predominantly blue plumage.

blue·black (bloo′blak′), *adj.* black with bluish highlights.

blue′ blood′, 1. an aristocrat or a member of the nobility. **2.** aristocratic lineage. —**blue′-blood′ed,** *adj.*

blue·bon·net (bloo′bon′it), *n.* **1.** the cornflower. **2.** a blue-flowered lupine.

blue·book (blōō′bŏŏk′), *n.* **1.** a directory of socially prominent persons. **2.** a blank booklet used in taking college examinations, usually with a blue paper cover.

blue·bot·tle (blōō′bŏt′ᵊl), *n.* a fly with an iridescent blue body.

blue′ box′, *Slang.* an illegal electronic device used in conjunction with a telephone to avoid charges for long-distance calls.

blue′ cheese′, a rich, blue-veined cheese made from cow's milk.

blue′ chip′, a high-quality common-stock issue of a leading company that pays regular dividends.

blue-col·lar (blōō′kŏl′ər), *adj.* of or pertaining to factory workers or manual labor.

blue·fish (blōō′fĭsh′), *n., pl.* **-fish, -fish·es.** a bluish or greenish food fish, found along the Atlantic coast.

blue·gill (blōō′gĭl′), *n.* a freshwater sunfish, used for food.

blue·grass (blōō′grăs′, -gräs′), *n.* **1.** See **Kentucky bluegrass.** **2.** a type of country music of the southern U.S., played on unamplified stringed instruments.

blue·jack·et (blōō′jăk′ĭt), *n.* a sailor, esp. an enlisted person in the navy.

blue′ jay′, a common, crested jay having a bright blue back and a gray breast.

blue′ jeans′, blue denim trousers having reinforced pockets and seams.

blue′ laws′, puritanical laws that forbid drinking or working on Sunday, dancing, etc.

blue′ moon′, *Informal.* a very long time: *once in a blue moon.*

blue·nose (blōō′nōz′), *n.* a puritanical person.

blue-pen·cil (blōō′pĕn′səl), *v.t.,* **-ciled, -cil·ing** or **-cilled, -cil·ling.** to edit with or as with a blue pencil.

blue′ plate′, a main course, as of meat and vegetables, offered at a special price on a menu.

blue·point (blōō′point′), *n.* a small oyster, esp. one from Blue Point, Long Island.

blue·print (blōō′prĭnt′), *n.* **1.** a photographic print, esp. of architectural drawings, using a white line on a blue background. **2.** a detailed outline or plan. *—v.t.* **3.** to make a blueprint of.

blue′ rib′bon, the highest award or distinction, as the first prize in a contest.

blues (blōōz), *n.* **1.** despondency or melancholy. **2.** *Jazz.* a song of black American origin that is marked by frequent minor intervals.

blue′-sky′ law′, a law regulating the sale of securities, esp. one

designed to prevent the promotion of fraudulent stocks.

blue·stock·ing (blōō′stŏk′ĭng), *n.* a woman with considerable intellectual ability or interest.

blu·et (blōō′ĭt), *n.* a plant having blue flowers, as the cornflower.

bluff¹ (blŭf), *adj.* **1.** good-naturedly abrupt or frank. **2.** presenting a nearly perpendicular front. *—n.* **3.** a broad, steep bank or cliff.

bluff² (blŭf), *v.t., v.i.* **1.** to mislead (someone) by feigning confidence. *—n.* **2.** the act of bluffing. **3.** a person who bluffs. **—bluff′er,** *n.*

blu·ing (blōō′ĭng), *n.* a substance used to whiten clothes or give them a bluish tinge. Also, **blue′ing.**

blun·der (blŭn′dər), *n.* **1.** a gross or stupid mistake. *—v.i.* **2.** to move or act blindly or stupidly. **3.** to make a gross or stupid mistake. *—v.t.* **4.** to bungle or botch. **—blun′der·er,** *n.*

blun·der·buss (blŭn′dər bŭs′), *n.* **1.** a short musket of wide bore with expanded muzzle. **2.** a stupid, blundering person.

blunt (blŭnt), *adj.* **1.** having a thick or dull edge or point. **2.** abrupt in manner. **3.** insensitive or obtuse. *—v.t., v.i.* **4.** to make or become blunt. **—blunt′ly,** *adv.* **—blunt′ness,** *n.*

blur (blŭr), *v.,* **blurred, blur·ring,** *n.* *—v.t., v.i.* **1.** to make or become indistinct. **2.** to blot or smear. **3.** to make or become dull or insensible. *—n.* **4.** a smudge or smear that obscures. **5.** a blurred condition or thing. **—blur′ry,** *adj.*

blurb (blŭrb), *n.* a brief advertisement, as on a book jacket.

blurt (blŭrt), *v.t.* to utter inadvertently or indiscreetly.

blush (blŭsh), *v.i.* **1.** to redden, esp. in the face, from modesty or embarrassment. **2.** to feel embarrassment. *—n.* **3.** a reddening, as of the face in modesty or embarrassment. **4.** rosy tinge. **5. at first blush,** at first glance. **—blush′ful,** *adj.*

blus·ter (blŭs′tər), *v.i.* **1.** to blow gustily, as wind. **2.** to be loud, noisy, or swaggering. *—n.* **3.** boisterous noise and violence. **4.** inflated talk. **—blus′ter·er,** *n.* **—blus′ter·y,** *adj.*

blvd., boulevard.

BM, 1. basal metabolism. **2.** *Informal.* bowel movement.

BMR, basal metabolic rate.

bn., battalion.

B'nai B'rith (bə nā′ brĭth′), a Jewish organization seeking to promote the social, educational, and cultural betterment of Jews and of the general public.

B.O., **1.** body odor. **2.** box office.

b.o., **1.** branch office. **2.** buyer's option.

bo·a (bō′ə), *n., pl.* **bo·as. 1.** a nonvenomous, chiefly tropical snake, such as the boa constrictor. **2.** a stole of feathers or fur.

bo′a con·stric′tor (kən strik′tər), a boa of tropical America, noted for its ability to crush its prey in its coils.

boar (bōr, bôr), *n.* **1.** the uncastrated male of swine. **2.** a wild swine.

board (bōrd, bôrd), *n.* **1.** a long piece of timber sawed thin. **2.** a sheet of wood, cardboard, paper, etc.: *a cutting board.* **3. boards,** the stage. **4.** a table, esp. to serve food on. **5.** daily meals, esp. as provided for pay: *room and board.* **6.** an official group of persons who direct or supervise some activity: *a board of directors.* **7.** the side of a ship. **8. on board,** on or in a ship, train, or other vehicle. —*v.t.* **9.** to cover or close with or as with boards: *to board up a house.* **10.** to furnish with meals, or with meals and lodging, esp. for pay. **11.** to go on board of or enter (a ship, train, etc.). —*v.i.* **12.** to take one's meals. or be supplied with food and lodging, at a fixed price. —**board′er,** *n.*

board·ing·house (bōr′ding hous′, bôr′-), *n.* a house at which meals, or meals and lodging, may be obtained for payment.

board·walk (bōrd′wôk′, bôrd′-), *n.* a promenade made of wooden boards, esp. at a commercial beach.

boast (bōst), *v.i.* **1.** to speak with exaggeration and pride. —*v.t.* **2.** to speak of with excessive pride or vanity. **3.** to be proud in the possession of. —*n.* **4.** the act or an instance of boasting. **5.** a thing boasted of. —**boast′er,** *n.* —**boast′ing·ly,** *adv.* —**Syn. 1.** brag, crow.

boast·ful (bōst′fəl), *adj.* given to or characterized by boasting. —**boast′ful·ly,** *adv.* —**boast′ful·ness,** *n.*

boat (bōt), *n.* **1.** a vessel for transport by water. **2.** a small ship, generally for specialized use: *a fishing boat.* **3.** a serving dish resembling a boat: *a gravy boat.* **4. in the same boat,** in the same circumstances. **5. rock the boat,** *Informal.* to disrupt the existing state of a situation. —*v.i.* **6.** to go in a boat. —**boat′ing,** *n.*

boat·el (bō tel′), *n.* a waterside hotel with dock space for persons who travel by private boat.

boat·er (bō′tər), *n.* **1.** a person who boats. **2.** a stiff straw hat with a flat-topped crown.

boat·man (bōt′mən), *n.* a person who operates, sells, or works on boats.

boat′ peo′ple, *Informal.* Indochinese refugees fleeing esp. from Vietnam in large numbers in the late 1970's, many by small, overcrowded, unseaworthy boats.

boat·swain (bō′sən), *n.* a warrant officer or petty officer in charge of rigging, anchors, etc.

bob¹ (bob), *n., v.,* **bobbed, bob·bing.** —*n.* **1.** a short, jerky motion. —*v.t., v.i.* **2.** to move quickly down and up. **3. bob up,** to appear, esp. unexpectedly. —**bob′ber,** *n.*

bob² (bob), *n., v.,* **bobbed, bob·bing.** —*n.* **1.** a short haircut for women and children. **2.** a small, dangling object, as the weight on a plumb line. **3.** a float for a fishing line. —*v.t.* **4.** to cut short.

bob³ (bob), *n., pl.* **bob.** *Brit. Slang.* (formerly) a shilling.

bob·bin (bob′in), *n.* a reel or spool upon which thread is wound.

bob·ble (bob′əl), *n., v.,* **-bled, -bling.** —*n.* **1** a momentary fumbling of a ball. —*v.t.* **2.** to fumble (a ball) momentarily.

bob·by (bob′ē), *n., pl.* **-bies.** *Brit. Informal.* a policeman. [after Sir Robert ("*Bobby*") Peel, 1788–1850, organizer of London police system]

bob′by pin′, a flat, springlike metal hairpin.

bob·by·socks (bob′ē soks′), *n.pl. Informal.* anklets, esp. as worn by teenage girls. Also, **bob′by·sox′.**

bob·by·sox·er (bob′ē sok′sər), *n. Informal.* an adolescent girl.

bob·cat (bob′kat′), *n., pl.* **-cats, -cat.** an American wildcat having a brownish coat with black spots.

bob·o·link (bob′ə lingk′), *n.* a common American passerine songbird.

bob·sled (bob′sled′), *n., v.,* **-sled·ded, -sled·ding.** —*n.* **1.** a sled having two pairs of runners, a brake, and a steering mechanism. **2.** a sled formed of two short sleds in tandem. —*v.i.* **3.** to ride on a bobsled. —**bob′sled′der,** *n.*

bob·tail (bob′tāl′), *n.* **1.** a short or docked tail. **2.** an animal with such a tail.

bob·white (bob′hwīt′, -wīt′), *n.* a common North American quail.

Boc·cac·ci·o (bō kä′chē ō′), *n.* **Giovan·ni** (jē′ə vä′nē), 1313–75, Italian writer.

boc·cie (boch′ē), *n.* an Italian variety of lawn bowling. Also, **boc′ci, boc′ce.**

bock′ beer′ (bok), a heavy, dark beer.

bode¹ (bōd), *v.t.,* **bod·ed, bod·ing.** to be an omen of.

bode² (bōd), *v.* a pt. of **bide.**

bod·ice (bod′is), *n.* the part of a woman's dress covering the body above the waist.

bod·i·less (bŏd′ē lis), *adj.* lacking a body or a material form.

bod·i·ly (bŏd′°lē), *adj.* 1. of the body. —*adv.* 2. in person. 3. as a physical entity.

bod·kin (bŏd′kin), *n.* 1. a small, pointed instrument for making holes in cloth. 2. a needlelike instrument for drawing tape or cord through a loop or hem. 3. *Obs.* a small dagger.

bod·y (bŏd′ē), *n., pl.* **bod·ies.** 1. the physical structure and substance of an animal or plant. 2. a corpse. 3. the main mass of a thing. 4. *Zool., Anat.* the trunk. 5. *Informal.* a person. 6. a collective group of people: *a student body.* 7. a separate physical mass: *a heavenly body.* 8. richness or substance: *This wine has good body.* —*Syn.* 2. cadaver, carcass.

bod·y Eng·lish, a twisting of the body by a player as if to help a ball to travel in the desired direction.

bod·y·guard (bŏd′ē gärd′), *n.* a person or persons employed to guard an individual from bodily harm.

bod′y lan′guage, kinesics.

bod′y pol′itic, a people as forming a political unit under an organized state.

bod′y rub′, massage, esp. as given in a massage parlor.

bod′y shirt′, a closefitting shirt having a shape and seams that follow the contours of the body. Also, **bod·y·suit** (bŏd′ē sōōt′).

bod′y stock′ing, a woman's closefitting, one-piece sheer garment covering the feet, legs, trunk, and arms.

Boer (bōr, bôr), *n.* a South African of Dutch extraction.

bog (bog, bôg), *n., v.,* **bogged, bog·ging.** —*n.* 1. wet, spongy ground. —*v.t., v.i.* 2. to sink in or as in a bog. —**bog′gy,** *adj.*

bo·gey (bō′gē), *n., pl.* **-geys.** 1. bogy. 2. *Golf.* a score of one stroke over par on a hole. Also, **bo′gie.**

bo·gey·man (bō′gē man′, bŏŏ′-, bŏŏg′ē-), *n.* a hobgoblin supposed to carry off naughty children.

bog·gle (bog′əl), *v.,* **-gled, -gling.** —*v.i.* 1. to start with fright. 2. to hesitate in doubt. —*v.t.* 3. to astound or overwhelm.

Bo·go·ta (bō′gə tä′), *n.* the capital of Colombia.

bo·gus (bō′gəs), *adj.* counterfeit or spurious.

bo·gy (bō′gē), *n., pl.* **-gies.** an evil spirit. Also, **bo′gie.**

Bo·he·mi·an (bō hē′mē ən, -hēm′yən), *n. (often l.c.)* 1. a person, typically one with artistic or intellectual

aspirations, who lives an unconventional life. —*adj.* 2. of or characteristic of a bohemian.

boil[1] (boil), *v.i.* 1. to change from a liquid to a gaseous state, as a result of heat, producing bubbles of gas. 2. to reach the boiling point. 3. to move about like boiling water. 4. to be intensely angry. 5. to undergo cooking in boiling water. —*v.t.* 6. to cause to boil. 7. to cook in boiling water. 8. **boil down,** a. to reduce by boiling off some liquid. b. to shorten or condense. —*n.* 9. the act or state of boiling.

boil[2] (boil), *n.* a painful inflammatory sore containing pus.

boil·er (boi′lər), *n.* 1. a container, together with a heat source, in which steam is generated. 2. a tank in which water is heated and stored, as for supplying hot water.

boil·er·mak·er (boi′lər mā′kər), *n.* 1. a person who makes and repairs boilers. 2. whiskey with beer as a chaser.

boil′ing point′, the temperature at which a liquid boils, equal to 212°F or 100°C for water at sea level.

Boi·se (boi′zē, -sē), *n.* the capital of Idaho.

bois·ter·ous (boi′stər əs, -strəs), *adj.* 1. noisily jolly or rowdy. 2. rough and stormy. —**bois′ter·ous·ly,** *adv.* —**bois′ter·ous·ness,** *n.*

Bol., Bolivia.

bo·la (bō′lə), *n., pl.* **-las (-ləz).** a South American weapon consisting of balls secured to the ends of a strong cord, hurled to entangle the legs of animals.

bold (bōld), *adj.* 1. courageous and daring. 2. forward or immodest. 3. flashy or showy: *a bold pattern.* 4. steep or abrupt. 5. **make bold,** to venture or dare. —**bold′ly,** *adv.* —**bold′ness,** *n.*

bold·face (bōld′fās′), *n.* a typeface that has thick, heavy lines, used for emphasis, headings, etc.

bold·faced (bōld′fāst′), *adj.* 1. impudent or brazen. 2. set in boldface.

bole (bōl), *n.* the stem or trunk of a tree.

bo·le·ro (bə lâr′ō, bō-), *n., pl.* **-ros.** 1. a lively Spanish dance in triple meter. 2. the music for this dance. 3. a waist-length jacket, worn open in front.

bol·i·var (bol′ə vər), *n.* the monetary unit of Venezuela.

Bol·i·var (bol′ə vər), *n.* **Si·món** (sē′mən), 1783-1830, South American statesman and revolutionary leader.

Bo·liv·i·a (bō liv′ē ə, bə-), *n.* a country in W South America. —**Bo·liv′i·an,** *adj., n.*

boll (bōl), *n.* a rounded seed pod of a plant, esp. that of flax or cotton.

boll′ wee′vil, a small beetle that attacks the bolls of cotton.

bo·lo (bō′lō), *n., pl.* **-los.** a large, heavy military knife or machete, used in the Philippines.

bo·lo·gna (bə lō′nē, -nə, -lōn′yə), *n.* a large smoked sausage made of finely ground beef and pork. [after *Bologna*, Italy, where first made]

bo′lo tie′, a stringlike necktie with an ornamental clasp.

Bol·she·vik (bōl′shə vik, bol′-), *n., pl.* **-viks, -vik·i** (-vik′ē, -vē′kē). **1.** a member of the radical Russian Marxists who seized control of the government in 1917. **2.** a member of any communist party. **—Bol′she·vism**, *n.* **—Bol′she·vist**, *n., adj.*

bol·ster (bōl′stər), *n.* **1.** a long cushion for a bed, sofa, etc. **—v.t.** **2.** to prop up or support with or as if with a bolster. **—bol′ster·er**, *n.*

bolt¹ (bōlt), *n.* **1.** a movable bar for fastening a door or gate. **2.** the part of a lock that is moved out and drawn back into the case, as by the key. **3.** a strong fastening rod, usually threaded to receive a nut. **4.** a sudden dash or escape. **5.** a length of woven goods, esp. as it comes on a roll. **6.** an arrow, esp. a short, heavy one for a crossbow. **7.** thunderbolt. **—v.t.** **8.** to fasten with a bolt. **9.** to break with: *to bolt a political party.* **10.** to utter hastily. **11.** to swallow (food or drink) hurriedly. **—v.i.** **12.** to make a sudden dash or escape. **13.** to break away, as from one's political party. **—adv.** **14.** **bolt upright**, stiffly upright.

bolt² (bōlt), *v.t.* to sift.

bo·lus (bō′ləs), *n., pl.* **-lus·es.** **1.** a round mass of medicine, larger than an ordinary pill. **2.** a soft, roundish mass of chewed food.

bomb (bom), *n.* **1.** a missile exploded by means of a fuze, by impact, or otherwise. **2.** a container filled with an aerosol that is released as a spray under pressure. **3.** *Slang.* a complete failure. **—v.t.** **4.** to drop bombs on. **5.** *Slang.* to be a complete failure.

bom·bard (bom bärd′), *v.t.* **1.** to attack or batter with artillery fire. **2.** to assail vigorously. **3.** to direct high-energy particles or radiations against. **—bom·bard′ment**, *n.*

bom·bar·dier (bom′bər dēr′), *n.* the member of a bomber crew who operates the bombing equipment.

bom·bast (bom′bast), *n.* pretentious, pompous language. **—bom·bas′tic**, *adj.* **—bom·bas′ti·cal·ly**, *adv.*

Bom·bay (bom bā′), *n.* a seaport in W India.

bom·ba·zine (bom′bə zēn′), *n.* a twill fabric constructed of a silk or rayon warp and worsted filling, often dyed black.

bomb·er (bom′ər), *n.* an airplane equipped to carry and drop bombs.

bomb·proof (bom′prōōf′), *adj.* able to withstand the impact of bombs.

bomb·shell (bom′shel′), *n.* **1.** a bomb. **2.** any sudden, startling surprise.

bomb·sight (bom′sīt′), *n.* an instrument on an aircraft for aiming bombs.

bo·na fide (bō′nə fīd′, bon′ə; bō′nə fī′dē), **1.** in good faith without fraud. **2.** genuine or real.

bo·nan·za (bə nan′zə, bō-), *n.* **1.** a rich mass of ore. **2.** a source of great wealth or luck.

bon ap·pé·tit (bô nА pā tē′), *French.* (I wish you) a hearty appetite.

bon·bon (bon′bon′), *n.* a small, fondant-coated candy, typically having a jam filling.

bond (bond), *n.* **1.** something that binds, fastens, or confines. **2.** something that binds a person or persons to a certain line of behavior. **3.** something, as a binding agreement, that unites individuals or peoples. **4.** any written obligation under seal. **5.** a written promise of a surety or the amount assured. **6.** the state of dutiable goods stored without payment of duties or taxes until withdrawn. **7.** a certificate of debt due to be paid by a government or corporation to an individual holder and usually bearing a fixed rate of interest. **8.** a substance that causes particles to bind or adhere. **9.** the attraction between atoms in a molecule. **10.** See **bond paper**. **11.** **bonds**, *Literary.* shackles or fetters. **—v.t.** **12.** to put (goods, an employee, etc.) on or under bond. **13.** to connect or bind.

bond·age (bon′dij), *n.* slavery or involuntary servitude.

bond·hold·er (bond′hōl′dər), *n.* a holder of a bond issued by a government or corporation.

bond·man (bond′mən), *n., pl.* **-men.** a male slave. **—bond′wom′an**, *n. fem.*

bond′ pa′per, a durable paper of high quality, used esp. for stationery.

bonds·man (bondz′mən), *n., pl.* **-men.** **1.** a person who by bond becomes surety for another. **2.** bondman.

bone (bōn), *n., v.,* **boned, bon·ing.** **—n.** **1.** one of the structures composing the skeleton of a vertebrate. **2.** such a structure from an edible animal. **3.** any of various similarly hard or structural animal substances, as ivory, whalebone, etc. 4. have a bone to pick with, to have cause to disagree or argue with. 5. make no bones about, to deal with in a direct manner. —v.t. 6. to remove the bones from. —v.i. 7. Slang. to study intensely. —bone'less, adj.

bone·black (bōn'blak'), n. a black, carbonaceous substance obtained by calcining bones, used as a pigment.

bone' chi'na, a fine, naturally white china.

bone-dry (bōn'drī'), adj. Informal. very dry.

bone·fish (bōn'fish'), n., pl. -fish·es, -fish. a marine game fish, found in tropical waters.

bone·head (bōn'hed'), n. a stupid, obstinate person.

bone' meal', bones ground to a coarse powder, used as fertilizer or feed.

bon·er (bō'nər), n. Slang. a foolish and obvious blunder.

bon·fire (bon'fīr'), n. a large fire in the open air.

bong (bông, bong), n. 1. a dull, resonant sound, as of a large bell. —v.i. 2. to produce this sound.

bon·go (bông'gō, bông-), n., pl. -gos, -goes. one of a pair of small tuned drums played by beating with the fingers. Also called bon'go drum'.

bon·ho·mie (bon'ə mē'), n. a genial manner.

bo·ni·to (bə nē'tō), n., pl. -to, -tos. any of several striped tunas found in warm ocean waters.

bon·jour (bôɴ zhŌor'), interj. French. good day.

bon mot (bon'mō'), pl. bons mots (bon' mōz'). a clever or witty saying.

Bonn (bon), n. the capital of West Germany, on the Rhine River.

bon·net (bon'it), n. 1. a head covering tied under the chin, worn chiefly by children. 2. a bonnetlike headdress: an Indian war bonnet. 3. any of various covers or protective devices. 4. Brit. an automobile hood.

bon·ny (bon'ē), adj. Chiefly Scot. 1. handsome or pretty. 2. pleasing or agreeable. Also, bon'nie. —bon'ni·ness, n.

bon·ny·clab·ber (bon'ē klab'ər), n. Dial. sour, thick milk.

bon·sai (bōn'sī, bon'-), n., pl. -sai. a potted tree or shrub that has been dwarfed by pruning, etc.

bon·soir (bôɴ swar'), interj. French. good evening.

bo·nus (bō'nəs), n., pl. -nus·es. something given or paid over and above what is due.

bon vi·vant (bôn vē väɴ'), pl. bons vi·vants (bôɴ vē väɴ'), French. a person who lives luxuriously and enjoys good food and drink.

bon vo·yage (bon' voi äzh'), (Have a) pleasant trip.

bon·y (bō'nē), adj., bon·i·er, bon·i·est. 1. of or like bone. 2. full of bones. 3. thin or gaunt. —bon'i·ness, n.

bon·zer (bon'zər), adj. Australian. 1. very big. 2. remarkable or wonderful.

boo (bōō), interj., v., booed, boo·ing. —interj. 1. (an exclamation of contempt, disapproval, etc., or to frighten or startle.) —v.i., v.t. 2. to cry "boo" (at).

boo-boo (bōō'bōō'), n., pl. -boos. Slang. a silly mistake.

boo·by (bōō'bē), n., pl. -bies. a stupid person. Also, boob (bōōb).

boo'by hatch', Slang. an insane asylum.

boo'by prize', a prize given to the worst player in a contest.

boo'by trap', a hidden explosive set off by an unsuspecting person, as by moving an apparently harmless object.

boo·dle (bōōd'əl), n. Slang. 1. a bribe or other illicit payment. 2. loot or booty.

book (bŏŏk), n. 1. a printed work of some length on consecutive sheets of paper bound together in a volume. 2. a volume used in recording business transactions. 3. a division of a literary work. 4. the Book, the Bible. 5. libretto. 6. by the book, according to the correct form. —v.t. 7. to enter in a book or list. 8. to engage (rooms, transportation, or entertainers) beforehand. 9. to enter a charge against (an arrested suspect) on a police register.

book·bind·er (bŏŏk'bīn'dər), n. a person whose business or work is the binding of books. —book'bind'ing, n.

book·case (bŏŏk'kās'), n. a set of shelves for books.

book' club', a business organization that sells books at reduced prices to its members by mail.

book·end (bŏŏk'end'), n. a support for holding a row of books upright, usually used in pairs.

book·ie (bŏŏk'ē), n. Informal. bookmaker.

book·ing (bŏŏk'ing), n. a scheduled engagement or performance, as for a concert.

book·ish (bŏŏk'ish), adj. 1. devoted to reading. 2. more acquainted with books than with real life.

book·keep·ing (bŏŏk'kē'pĭng), n. the work or skill of keeping account books or systematic records of business transactions. —**book'keep'-er**, n.

book' learn'ing, knowledge from books rather than from experience.

book·let (bŏŏk'lĭt), n. a little book.

book·mak·er (bŏŏk'mā'kər), n. a person who makes a business of accepting and paying off bets. —**book'mak'ing**, n., adj.

book·mark (bŏŏk'märk'), n. a ribbon, strip of paper, etc., placed between pages of a book to mark a place.

book' match', a match in or from a matchbook.

book·mo·bile (bŏŏk'mə bēl'), n. a truck constructed to serve as a traveling library.

book·plate (bŏŏk'plāt'), n. a label bearing the owner's name for pasting inside a book.

book·sel·ler (bŏŏk'sel'ər), n. the owner or manager of a bookstore.

book·shelf (bŏŏk'shelf'), n., pl. **-shelves.** a shelf for books, esp. one in a bookcase.

book·store (bŏŏk'stōr', -stôr), n. a store where books are sold. Also called **book·shop** (bŏŏk'shŏp').

book·worm (bŏŏk'wûrm'), n. 1. a person devoted to reading or studying. 2. an insect that feeds on books.

boom[1] (bŏŏm), v.i., v.t. 1. to make or cause to make a deep, prolonged, resonant sound. 2. to flourish or cause to flourish vigorously. —n. 3. a deep, prolonged, resonant sound. 4. a rapid increase, as in development, sales, or popularity. 5. a period of rapid economic growth.

boom[2] (bŏŏm), n. 1. a horizontal spar for extending the feet of sails, etc. 2. a chain, cable, etc., serving to confine floating timber. 3. a beam projecting from the mast of a derrick for supporting or guiding the weights to be lifted. 4. a beam on a mobile crane for holding a microphone or camera. —v.i. 5. to sail at full speed.

boom·er·ang (bŏŏ'mə rang'), n. 1. a curved wooden club which can be thrown so as to return to the thrower. 2. a scheme, etc., that recoils upon the user. —v.i. 3. to act as a boomerang. [< native Australian language]

boom' town', a town that has grown rapidly as a result of sudden prosperity.

boon[1] (bŏŏn), n. 1. a benefit greatly enjoyed. 2. Archaic. a favor sought.

boon[2] (bŏŏn), adj. jovial or convivial: a boon companion.

boon·docks (bŏŏn'dŏks'), n.pl. Slang. 1. the backwoods or marsh. 2. a remote rural area.

boon·dog·gle (bŏŏn'dôg'əl), n., v., **-gled, -gling.** Informal —n. 1. work of little value done merely to keep or look busy. —v.i. 2. to do such work. —**boon'dog'gler**, n.

boor (bŏŏr), n. 1. a rude, unmannerly person. 2. a rustic or yokel. —**boor'ish**, adj. —**boor'ish·ly**, adv.

boost (bŏŏst), v.t. 1. to lift or raise by pushing from below. 2. to advance or aid by speaking well of. 3. to increase or raise. —n. 4. an upward shove or raise. 5. an increase or rise: a boost in food prices. 6. an act or remark that helps one's progress, morale, etc.

boost·er (bŏŏ'stər), n. 1. a person or thing that boosts. 2. a rocket used as the principal source of thrust in takeoff. 3. Also, **boost'er shot'.** a dose of an immunizing substance given to maintain the effect of a previous one.

boot[1] (bŏŏt), n. 1. a covering of leather, rubber, etc., for the foot and all or part of the leg. 2. any sheathlike protective covering. 3. U.S. Navy, Marines. a recruit. 4. Brit. an automobile trunk. 5. a kick. 6. Slang. a dismissal or discharge. —v.t. 7. to kick. 8. to put boots on. 9. Slang. to dismiss or discharge.

boot[2] (bŏŏt), n. 1. Archaic. something given into the bargain. 2. **to boot,** besides. —v.i., v.t. 2. Archaic. to profit.

boot·black (bŏŏt'blak'), n. a person whose occupation is shining shoes, boots, etc.

boot' camp', U.S. Navy, Marines. a camp for training recruits.

boot·ee (bŏŏ'tē), n. 1. a baby's socklike shoe, usually knitted or crocheted. 2. any boot having a short leg.

boot·er·y (bŏŏ'tə rē), n., pl. **-er·ies.** a store selling boots, shoes, etc.

booth (bŏŏth, bŏŏth), n., pl. **booths** (bŏŏthz, bŏŏths). 1. a stall for display purposes, as at a fair. 2. a small compartment: a telephone booth; voting booth. 3. a partly enclosed compartment, as in a restaurant.

boot·leg (bŏŏt'leg'), v., **-legged, -legging,** adj., n. —v.t., v.i. 1. to make, transport, or sell (something, esp. liquor) illegally. —adj. 2. made, transported, or sold illegally. —n. 3. bootlegged liquor. —**boot'leg'ger,** n.

boot·less (bŏŏt'lĭs), adj. offering no advantage. —**boot'less·ly,** adv.

boot·lick (bŏŏt'lĭk'), Informal. —v.t. 1. to seek the favor of (someone) in a servile way. —v.i. 2. to be a toady.

boot′ tree′, shoetree.

boo·ty (bōō′tē), *n., pl.* **-ties. 1.** plunder seized in war. **2.** any prize.

booze (bōōz), *n., v.,* **boozed, booz·ing.** *Informal.* —*n.* **1.** liquor. —*v.t., v.i.* **2.** to drink (liquor) excessively. —**booz′er,** *n.* —**booz′y,** *adj.*

bop (bop), *v.,* **bopped, bop·ping,** *n. Slang.* —*v.t.* **1.** to strike, as with the fist, etc. —*n.* **2.** a blow.

BOQ, bachelor officers' quarters.

bor., borough.

bo·rate (bôr′āt, -it, bôr′-), *n.* a salt or ester of boric acid.

bo·rax[1] (bôr′aks, -əks, bôr′-), *n.* a white substance occurring naturally or obtained from borates: used as a flux, cleansing agent, etc.

bo·rax[2] (bôr′aks, -əks, bôr′-), *n. Slang.* cheap, showy merchandise.

bor·del·lo (bôr del′ō), *n., pl.* **-los.** a brothel.

bor·der (bôr′dər), *n.* **1.** the edge of a surface or area that forms its outer boundary. **2.** the line that separates one country, state, etc., from another. **3.** an ornamental strip or design around an edge. —*v.t.* **4.** to make a border about. **5.** to form a border to. **6.** to adjoin. **7. border on** or **upon,** to verge on. —**Syn. 1.** brim, brink, margin.

bor·der·land (bôr′dər land′), *n.* **1.** land forming a border or frontier. **2.** an uncertain condition.

bor·der·line (bôr′dər līn′), *adj.* **1.** on or near a border. **2.** indefinite or uncertain.

bore[1] (bôr, bōr), *v.,* **bored, bor·ing,** *n.* —*v.t.* **1.** to pierce (a solid substance), as with a drill. **2.** to make (a hole) with such an instrument. **3.** to make (a tunnel, well, etc.) by drilling. —*v.i.* **4.** to make a hole, as with a drill. —*n.* **5.** a hole made or enlarged by boring. **6.** the inside diameter of a hole, gun barrel, etc. —**bor′er,** *n.*

bore[2] (bôr, bōr), *v.,* **bored, bor·ing,** *n.* —*v.t.* **1.** to weary by dullness, tedious repetition, etc. —*n.* **2.** a dull, tiresome person, thing, etc. —**Syn. 1.** fatigue, tire, annoy.

bore[3] (bôr, bōr), *n.* an abrupt rise of tidal water.

bore[4] (bôr, bōr), *v.* pt. of **bear**[1].

bo·re·al (bôr′ē əl, bōr′-), *adj.* **1.** of the north wind. **2.** *Geodesy.* northern.

bore·dom (bôr′dəm, bōr′-), *n.* the state of being mentally bored.

bo′ric ac′id (bôr′ik, bōr′-), a white, crystalline acid used as a mild antiseptic.

bor·ing (bôr′iṅg, bōr′-), *adj.* dull or tedious.

born (bôrn), *v.* **1.** a pp. of **bear**[1]. —*adj.* **2.** brought forth by birth. **3.**

possessing from birth the quality stated: *a born musician.*

born-a·gain (bôrn′ə gen′), *adj. Informal.* **1.** recommitted to religious faith: *a born-again Christian.* **2.** enthusiastically committed: *a born-again jogger.*

borne (bôrn, bōrn), *v.* a pp. of **bear**[1].

Bor·ne·o (bôr′nē ō′), *n.* an island in the Malay Archipelago.

bo·ron (bôr′on, bōr′-), *n. Chem.* a nonmetallic element occurring naturally only in combination, as in borax, boric acid, etc. *Symbol:* B; *at. wt.:* 10.81; *at. no.:* 5.

bor·ough (bûr′ō, bur′ō), *n.* **1.** an incorporated municipality smaller than a city. **2.** one of the five administrative divisions of New York City. **3.** *Brit.* a town, area, or constituency represented by a member of Parliament.

bor·row (bor′ō, bōr′ō), *v.t., v.i.* **1.** to obtain (something) with the promise to return it. **2.** to appropriate (an idea, etc.) from another source. —**bor′row·er,** *n.*

borscht (bôrsht), *n.* a soup containing beets, often served with sour cream. Also, **borsch** (bôrsh), **borsht.**

bor·stal (bôr′stəl), *n.* (in England) a school for delinquent boys.

bort (bôrt), *n.* a quantity of low-quality diamonds in crushed form.

bor·zoi (bôr′zoi), *n., pl.* **-zois.** a tall, slender dog having long, silky hair, raised originally in Russia.

bosh (bosh), *n. Informal.* nonsense.

bosk·y (bos′kē), *adj.,* **bosk·i·er, bosk·i·est.** covered with bushes or trees.

bo′s'n (bō′sən), *n.* boatswain.

bos·om (bōōz′əm, bōō′zəm), *n.* **1.** the breast or chest of a human being. **2.** the part of a garment that covers the breast. **3.** the breast conceived of as the center of feelings. **4.** any warm, comfortable place: *the bosom of the family.* —*adj.* **5.** intimate or confidential.

bos·om·y (bōōz′ə mē, bōō′zə-), *adj.* (of a woman) having a large or prominent bosom.

boss[1] (bôs, bos), *n.* **1.** a person who employs or superintends others. **2.** a politician who controls the party organization. —*v.t.* **3.** to direct or control. **4.** *Informal.* to order, esp. in a domineering manner. —*adj.* **5.** *Slang.* first-rate [< D *baas* master]

boss[2] (bôs, bos), *n.* **1.** an ornamental protuberance of metal, ivory, etc. —*v.t.* **2.** to ornament with bosses.

bos·sa no·va (bos′ə nō′və), jazz-influenced music of Brazilian origin.

boss·ism (bô′siz əm, bos′iz-), *n.* control by bosses, esp. political bosses.

boss·y (bô′sē, bos′ē), *adj.* **boss·i·er,
boss·i·est.** *Informal.* domineering or
overbearing. —**boss′i·ly,** *adv.* —
boss′i·ness, *n.*

Bos·ton (bô′stən, bos′tən), *n.* the
capital of Massachusetts. —**Bos·to′ni·an** (-tō′nē ən), *adj., n.*

Bos′ton ter′rier, a small, pug-faced,
short-haired dog having a brindled
or black coat with white markings.

bo·sun (bō′sən), *n.* boatswain.

bot., 1. botanical. 2. botanist. 3.
botany. 4. bottle.

bot·a·ny (bot′ə·nē, bot′nē), *n., pl.*
-nies. the branch of biology that
deals with plant life. —**bo·tan·i·cal**
(bə tan′i kəl), **bo·tan′ic,** *adj.* —**bot′-
a·nist,** *n.*

botch (boch), *v.t.* 1. to spoil by poor
work or clumsiness. 2. to patch
clumsily. —*n.* 3. a clumsy or poor
piece of work. —**botch′er,** *n.*

botch·y (boch′ē), *adj.,* **botch·i·er,
botch·i·est.** clumsily or poorly done.
—**botch′i·ly,** *adv.*

both (bōth), *adj., pron.* 1. one and
the other: *Both girls were beautiful.*
—*conj.* 2. alike or equally: *He is
both ready and willing.*

both·er (both′ər), *v.t., v.i.* 1. to annoy (someone), esp. mildly. 2. to
trouble or inconvenience (oneself).
—*n.* 3. something or someone troublesome or annoying. —**both′er-
some,** *adj.*

Bot·swa·na (bot swä′nä), *n.* a country in S Africa.

Bot·ti·cel·li (bot′l chel′ē), *n.* **San-
dro,** 1444?–1510, Italian painter.

bot·tle (bot′əl), *n., v.,* **-tled, -tling.**
—*n.* 1. a container for liquids,
characteristically having a neck and
mouth and made of glass. 2. its
contents. 3. bottled cow's milk
and milk formulas given to infants:
raised on the bottle. 4. **hit the bottle,** *Slang.* to drink excessively. —
v.t. 5. to put into or seal in a bottle. 6. **bottle up,** to repress or restrain. —**bot′tler,** *n.*

bot·tle·neck (bot′əl nek′), *n.* 1. a narrow entrance or passageway. 2. a
place or a stage at which progress
is impeded.

bot·tom (bot′əm), *n.* 1. the lowest
part of anything. 2. the under or
lower side. 3. the ground under
any body of water. 4. the seat of a
chair. 5. the buttocks or rump. 6.
the cause or origin. 7. lowest limit,
as of status. 8. **at bottom,** fundamentally. —*adj.* 9. lowest: *bottom
prices.* 10. fundamental. —*v.i.* 11.
bottom out, to reach the lowest
state or level. —**bot′tom·less,** *adj.*

bot′tom land′, low land next to a
river.

bot′tom line′, *Informal.* 1. the final
figure, showing profit or loss, in a
financial statement. 2. the ultimate
result or consideration.

bot·u·lism (boch′ə liz′əm), *n.* a disease of the nervous system caused
by a toxin developed in spoiled
foods.

bou·clé (bōō klā′), *n.* 1. yarn with
loops producing a rough, nubby appearance on fabrics. 2. a fabric
made of this yarn. Also, **bou·cle′.**

bou·doir (bōō′dwär, -dwôr), *n.* 1. a
lady's private sitting room, as esp.
in the Victorian era. 2. *Facetious.*
a lady's bedroom. [< F: lit., a sulking place]

bouf·fant (bōō fänt′), *adj.* puffed
out: *a bouffant hairdo.*

bou·gain·vil·lae·a (bōō′gən vil′ē ə,
-vil′yə), *n.* a climbing shrub having
small flowers, cultivated for ornament.

bough (bou), *n.* a branch of a tree,
esp. one of the larger branches.

bought (bôt), *v.* pt. and pp. of **buy.**

bouil·la·baisse (bōōl′yə bās′, bōōl′-
yə bäs′), *n.* a stew containing several kinds of fish.

bouil·lon (bōōl′yon, -yən), *n.* a clear
broth flavored with beef, chicken,
etc.

boul·der (bōl′dər), *n.* a large
rounded or worn rock.

boule (bōōl), *n.* a cylindrical lump
of material for synthetic gems.

boul·e·vard (bōōl′ə värd′, bōō′lə-), *n.*
a broad avenue, often lined with
trees.

bounce (bouns), *v.,* **bounced, bouncing,** *n.* —*v.i.* 1. to strike a surface
and rebound. 2. to spring suddenly
or leap. 3. *Informal.* (of a check)
to be refused, due to insufficient
funds on deposit for payment. —
v.t. 4. to cause to bounce. 5. *Slang.*
to eject, expel, or dismiss summarily or forcibly. —*n.* 6. a bound
or rebound. 7. a sudden spring or
leap. 8. resilience. 9. vitality or
energy. 10. *Slang.* dismissal. —
boun′cy, *adj.*

bounc·er (boun′sər), *n.* *Slang.* a
person employed at a bar, etc., to
eject disorderly persons.

bounc·ing (boun′sing), *adj.* stout,
strong, or vigorous. —**bounc′ing·ly,**
adv.

bound¹ (bound), *v.* 1. pt. and pp. of
bind. —*adj.* 2. tied or confined: *a
bound prisoner.* 3. made fast as if
by a band. 4. secured within a
cover, as a book. 5. under obligation. 6. sure or certain. 7. determined or resolved.

bound² (bound), *v.i.* 1. to move by
leaps. 2. to rebound or bounce.
—*n.* 3. a jump. 4. a bounce.

bound³ (bound), *n.* **1.** Usually, **bounds.** limits or boundaries: *within the bounds of reason.* **2. bounds,** territories on or near a boundary. **3. out of bounds,** a. beyond prescribed limits. b. prohibited. —*v.t.* **4.** to limit by bounds. **5.** to form the boundary of. **6.** to name the boundaries of. —**bound′less,** *adj.* —**bound′less·ly,** *adv.*

bound⁴ (bound), *adj.* going or intending to go: *The train is bound for Denver.*

bound·a·ry (boun′də rē, -drē), *n., pl.* **-ries.** something that indicates bounds or limits.

bound·en (boun′dən), *adj.* made obligatory: *my bounden duty.*

bound·er (boun′dər), *n. Chiefly Brit. Slang.* an obtrusive, ill-bred person.

boun·te·ous (boun′tē əs), *adj.* **1.** giving generously. **2.** plentiful or abundant. Also, **boun′ti·ful** (-tə fəl). —**boun′te·ous·ly,** *adv.* —**boun′te·ous·ness,** *n.*

boun·ty (boun′tē), *n., pl.* **-ties. 1.** generosity in giving. **2.** a generous gift. **3.** a reward, esp. one offered by a government. —**boun′ty·less,** *adj.*

bou·quet (bō kā′, boō-), *n.* **1.** a bunch of flowers. **2.** the characteristic aroma of wines, etc.

bour·bon (bŏor′bən), *n.* a whiskey distilled from a mash having 51 percent or more corn.

bour·geois (boŏr zhwä′, boōr′zhwä), *n., pl.* **-geois,** *adj.* —*n.* **1.** a member of the middle class. **2.** a person whose values and beliefs are petty and materialistic. —*adj.* **3.** belonging to the middle class. **4.** lacking refinement or culture.

bour·geoi·sie (boŏr′zhwä zē′), *n.* **1.** the bourgeois class. **2.** (in Marxist theory) the class opposed to the proletariat.

bourn (bôrn, bōrn, boōrn), *n. Archaic.* **1.** a limit. **2.** a destination. Also, **bourne.**

Bourse (boŏrs), *n.* the stock exchange of Paris, France.

bout (bout), *n.* **1.** a contest, as of boxing. **2.** a spell or period: *a bout of illness.*

bou·tique (boō tēk′), *n.* a small shop that sells fashionable clothes and accessories.

bou·ton·niere (boōt′ᵊnēr′, -°nyâr′), *n.* a flower or small bouquet worn on a lapel.

bo·vine (bō′vīn, -vin, -vēn), *adj.* **1.** of or resembling an ox or cow. **2.** stolid or dull. —*n.* **3.** a bovine animal.

bow¹ (bou), *v.i.* **1.** to bend the body or head, as in submission, salutation, etc. **2.** to yield or sub-

mit. —*v.t.* **3.** to bend (the body or head). **4.** to burden or crush. —*n.* **5.** an inclination of the body or head, as in submission, salutation, etc. **6. take a bow,** to stand up to receive applause, etc. —**bowed′ness,** *n.*

bow² (bō), *n.* **1.** a flexible strip of wood, bent by a string stretched between its ends, esp. for propelling arrows. **2.** a bend or curve. **3.** a readily loosened knot having two projecting loops. **4.** a long rod strung with horsehairs used for playing an instrument of the violin family. —*adj.* **5.** curved: *bow legs.* —*v.t., v.i.* **6.** to bend or curve. **7.** to play (a stringed instrument) with a bow. —**bow′like,** *adj.*

bow³ (bou), *n.* the forward end of a vessel or airship.

bowd·ler·ize (bōd′lə rīz′, boud′-), *v.t.,* **-ized, -iz·ing.** to expurgate in a prudish manner. [after Thomas *Bowdler* (1754–1825), English editor who expurgated Shakespeare] —**bowd′ler·ism,** *n.* —**bowd′ler·i·za′tion,** *n.*

bow·el (bou′əl, boul), *n.* **1.** a. Usually, **bowels.** the intestine. b. a part of the intestine. **2. bowels,** the interior parts: *the bowels of the earth.* **3. move one's or the bowels,** to defecate.

bow·er (bou′ər), *n.* a shaded, leafy shelter. —**bow′er·like′,** *adj.*

bow′ie knife′ (bō′ē, boō′ē), a heavy knife having a long, single-edged, pointed blade. [after James *Bowie* (1799–1836), U.S. pioneer]

bow·knot (bō′not′), *n.* a readily loosened knot for joining the ends of two cords.

bowl¹ (bōl), *n.* **1.** a deep, round dish for liquids or food. **2.** its contents. **3.** a rounded, cuplike, hollow part. **4.** a large drinking cup. **5.** an amphitheaterlike stadium. —**bowl′ful,** *n.*

bowl² (bōl), *n.* **1.** a ball used in bowling. **2. bowls,** a bowling game played on a bowling green. **3.** a cast of the ball in bowling. —*v.i., v.t.* **4.** to roll (a ball) or perform in bowling. **5.** to move along smoothly and rapidly. **6. bowl over,** *Informal.* to surprise greatly. —**bowl′er,** *n.*

bowl·der (bōl′dər), *n.* boulder.

bow·leg (bō′leg′), *n.* an outward curvature of one or both legs. —**bow′leg·ged** (bō′leg′id, bō′legd′), *adj.*

bowl·er (bō′lər), *n. Chiefly Brit.* a derby hat.

bow·line (bō′lin, -līn), *n.* a knot used to make a nonslipping loop on the end of a rope.

bowl·ing (bō′ling), *n.* any of several games in which players roll balls along a grassy lane (**bowl′ing green′**) or a wooden lane (**bowl′ing al′ley**) at a mark or a group of pins.

bow·man (bō′mən), *n., pl.* **-men.** an archer.

bow·sprit (bou′sprit, bō′-), *n.* a spar projecting from the upper end of the bow of a sailing vessel.

bow·string (bō′string), *n.* the string of an archer's bow.

bow′ tie′ (bō), a small necktie tied in a bow.

box[1] (boks), *n.* **1.** a container, often rectangular and having a lid. **2.** the quantity contained in a box. **3.** a compartment for a small number of people, as in a theater. **4.** a small enclosure or area, as in a courtroom. **5.** a small shelter: *a sentry's box.* **6.** an awkward predicament. **7.** any of various spaces on a baseball diamond marking the playing positions of the pitcher, catcher, batter, or coaches. —*v.t.* **8.** to put into a box. **9.** to furnish with a box. **10.** to block. —**box′-like′**, *adj.*

box[2] (boks), *n.* **1.** a blow, as with the fist. —*v.t.* **2.** to strike with the fist. **3.** to fight against (someone) in a boxing match. —*v.i.* **4.** to fight in a boxing match. —*v.i.*

box[3] (boks), *n.* an evergreen shrub used for ornamental borders, hedges, etc.

box·car (boks′kär′), *n.* a completely enclosed freight car.

box·er (box′sər), *n.* **1.** a person who boxes, esp. a prizefighter. **2.** a medium-sized, stocky, short-haired, tan, pug-faced dog.

box·ing (bok′sing), *n.* the act, technique, or profession of fighting with the fists.

box′ of′fice, **1.** the office of a theater, at which tickets are sold. **2.** entertainment popular enough to attract paying audiences.

box·wood (boks′wŏŏd′), *n.* the hard, fine-grained, compact wood of the box shrub.

boy (boi), *n.* **1.** a male child. **2.** any man, esp. when referred to familiarly. **3.** a male servant or waiter. —*interj.* **4.** (an exclamation of wonder, contempt, etc.) —**boy′hood**, *n.* —**boy′ish**, *adj.* —**boy′ish·ly**, *adv.* —**boy′ish·ness**, *n.*

boy·cott (boi′kot), *v.t.* **1.** to abstain from dealing with or buying, as a means of coercion. —*n.* **2.** the act of boycotting. [after C. C. *Boycott* (1832-97), British land agent, first victim]

boy·friend (boi′frend′), *n.* **1.** a male

friend. **2.** a frequent or favorite male companion.

boy′ scout′, a member of an organization of boys (**Boy′ Scouts′**), that stresses the development of character and self-reliance.

boy·sen·ber·ry (boi′zən ber′ē), *n., pl.* **-ries.** a blackberrylike fruit with a flavor similar to that of raspberries.

bp., bishop.

B.P., 1. bills payable. **2.** blood pressure.

b.p., 1. bills payable. **2.** boiling point.

bpl., birthplace.

B.P.O.E., Benevolent and Protective Order of Elks.

Br, bromine.

Br., 1. Britain. **2.** British.

br., 1. branch. **2.** brass. **3.** brother. **4.** brown.

b.r., bills receivable. Also, **B.R.**

bra (brä), *n.* brassiere. —**bra′less**, *adj.*

brace (brās), *n., v.,* **braced, brac·ing.** —*n.* **1.** something that holds parts in place, as a clamp. **2.** anything that imparts steadiness, as to a framework. **3.** a device for holding and turning a bit. **4.** Often, **braces.** an appliance for straightening irregularly arranged teeth. **5.** an appliance for supporting a weak joint or joints. **6. braces,** *Chiefly Brit.* suspenders. **7.** one of two marks { or } used to enclose words or lines to be considered together. —*v.t.* **8.** to furnish, fasten, or strengthen with a brace. **9.** to steady (oneself), as against a shock. **10.** to stimulate or invigorate. **11. brace up,** *Informal.* to summon up one's courage or determination.

brace′ and bit′, a boring tool consisting of an auger rotated by a brace.

brace·let (brās′lit), *n.* an ornamental band or circlet for the wrist or arm.

bra·ce·ro (brə sâr′ō), *n., pl.* **-ce·ros** (-sâr′ōz). a Mexican admitted into the U.S. to perform seasonal farm labor.

brack·en (brak′ən), *n.* **1.** a large or coarse fern. **2.** a cluster or thicket of such ferns.

brack·et (brak′it), *n.* **1.** a support projecting from a wall to hold the weight of a shelf, etc. **2.** a shelf so supported. **3.** one of two marks [or] used to enclose interpolations. **4.** a class or grouping: *the low-income bracket.* —*v.t.* **5.** to furnish with brackets. **6.** to place within brackets. **7.** to associate or class together.

brack·ish (brack′ish), *adj.* **1.** salty or briny. **2.** distasteful or unpleasant. —**brack′ish·ness**, *n.*

bract (brakt), *n.* a specialized leaf or leaflike part at the base of a flower or inflorescence.

brad (brad), *n.* a slender wire nail having a small, deep head.

brae (brā, brē), *n. Scot.* a hillside.

brag (brag), *v.,* **bragged, brag·ging,** *n.* —*v.i., v.t.* 1. to speak boastfully. —*n.* 2. boastful or arrogant talk. —**brag′ger,** *n.*

brag·ga·do·ci·o (brag′ə dō′shē ō′), *n., pl.* **-os.** 1. empty boasting. 2. a braggart.

brag·gart (brag′ərt), *n.* a person given to bragging.

Brah·ma (brä′mə), *n. Hinduism.* "the Creator," the first and chief member of the trinity, along with Vishnu and Shiva.

Brah·man (brä′mən), *n., pl.* **-mans.** 1. a member of the highest, or priestly, caste among the Hindus. 2. a breed of Indian cattle, esp. a grayish, heat-resistant American breed.

Brah·man·ism (brä′mə niz′əm), *n.* the religious and social system of the Brahmans and orthodox Hindus. Also, **Brah′min·ism.** —**Brah′man·ist, Brah′min·ist,** *n.*

Brah·min (brä′min), *n., pl.* **-min, -mins.** 1. Brahman (def. 1). 2. a person of great culture and intellect.

Brahms (brämz), *n.* **Jo·han·nes** (yō hä′nəs), 1833-97, German composer.

braid (brād), *v.t.* 1. to weave together three or more strands of: *to braid hair.* 2. to trim with braid, as a garment. —*n.* 3. a braided length or plait, esp. of hair. 4. a plaited or woven band of silk, cotton, etc., used as trimming. —**braid′er,** *n.*

Braille (brāl), *n.* a system of lettering devised for use by the blind, in which raised dots are read by touch. [after L. *Braille* (1809-52), French deviser of system]

brain (brān), *n.* 1. the part of the central nervous system enclosed in the cranium of vertebrates, serving to control and coordinate the mental and physical actions. 2. Sometimes, **brains.** intelligence. —*v.t.* 3. to hit (someone) on the head. —**brained** (brānd), *adj.* —**brain′less,** *adj.*

brain·child (brān′chīld′), *n. Informal.* a product of one's work or thought.

brain′ drain′, the loss of trained professional personnel to a foreign country.

brain·storm (brān′stôrm′), *n. Informal.* a sudden impulse, idea, etc.

brain·storm·ing (brān′stôr′mĭng), *n.* a conference technique of solving problems, developing ideas, etc., by unrestrained discussion.

brain·teas·er (brān′tē′zər), *n.* a very difficult puzzle or problem requiring ingenuity and patience for its solution.

brain′ trust′, a group of experts who serve a government, corporation, etc., as consultants. —**brain′ trust′er.**

brain·wash (brān′wŏsh′, -wôsh′), *v.t.* to subject to brainwashing. —**brain′wash′er,** *n.*

brain·wash·ing (brān′wŏsh′ĭng, -wô′shĭng), *n.* 1. a method for changing attitudes or beliefs, esp. through torture, drugs, or psychological-stress techniques. 2. any method of controlled indoctrination.

brain′ wave′, 1. Usually, **brain waves.** electrical impulses given off by brain tissue. 2. *Informal.* a sudden idea or thought.

brain·y (brā′nē), *adj.,* **brain·i·er, brain·i·est.** *Informal.* intelligent or intellectual. —**brain′i·ly,** *adv.* —**brain′i·ness,** *n.*

braise (brāz), *v.t.,* **braised, brais·ing.** to cook by sautéeing in fat and then simmering slowly in very little liquid.

brake[1] (brāk), *n., v.,* **braked, brak·ing.** —*n.* 1. a device for slowing or stopping a vehicle or mechanism. —*v.t., v.i.* 2. to slow or stop by a brake. 3. to use a brake (on). —**brake′less,** *adj.*

brake[2] (brāk), *n.* a place overgrown with bushes or shrubs.

brake[3] (brāk), *n.* a large or coarse fern.

brake·age (brā′kij), *n.* the action of a brake.

brake′ flu′id, the liquid used in a brake cylinder, as of an automobile.

brake·man (brāk′mən), *n., pl.* **-men.** a trainman who assists the conductor in the operation of a train.

brake′ shoe′, a rigid plate, usually of steel in the shape of an arc of a cylinder, tightened to produce a braking action.

bram·ble (bram′bəl), *n.* a prickly shrub, as the blackberry. —**bram′bly,** *adj.*

bran (bran), *n.* the partly ground husk of wheat or other grain, separated from flour meal by sifting.

branch (branch, bränch), *n.* 1. a division or subdivision of the stem or axis of a tree or plant. 2. a limb, offshoot, or ramification of any main stem. 3. any section or subdivision: *branches of learning.* 4. a local operating division of an organization. 5. a division of a family. 6. a tributary stream. —*v.i.* 7. to spread in branches. 8. to diverge, as a branch from a tree trunk. 9. **branch out,** to expand or extend, as business activities. —**branched,** *adj.* —**branch'like,** *adj.*

branch' wa'ter, water in or from a branch, creek, stream, etc.

brand (brand), *n.* **1.** kind, grade, or make, as indicated by a stamp, trademark, etc. **2.** a mark made by burning or otherwise, to indicate kind, ownership, etc. **3.** stigma. **4.** an iron for branding. **5.** a burning or partly burned piece of wood. —*v.t.* **6.** to mark with a brand. **7.** to stigmatize. —**brand'er,** *n.*

bran·dish (bran'dish), *v.t.* to shake or wave threateningly, as a weapon. —**bran'dish·er,** *n.*

brand-new (brand'nŏō', -nyŏō', bran'-), *adj.* entirely new.

bran·dy (bran'dē), *n., pl.* **-dies,** *v.,* **-died, -dy·ing.** —*n.* **1.** a spirit distilled from wine or from the fermented juice of grapes, apples, etc. —*v.t.* **2.** to mix, flavor, or preserve with brandy. [*brandy (wine)* < D *brandewijn* burnt (now distilled) wine]

brash (brash), *adj.* **1.** recklessly hasty. **2.** impudent or tactless. —**brash'ly,** *adv.* —**brash'ness,** *n.* —Syn. **1.** rash, impetuous.

Bra·síl·ia (brä zēl'yə), *n.* the capital of Brazil.

brass (bras, bräs), *n.* **1.** a metal alloy consisting mainly of copper and zinc. **2.** articles made of such an alloy. **3.** **a.** an instrument of the trumpet or horn family. **b.** such instruments collectively. **4.** *Slang.* high-ranking military officers. **5.** *Informal.* impudence or effrontery. —**brass'y,** *adj.*

bras·se·rie (bras'ə rē'), *n.* an unpretentious restaurant that serves beer.

brass' hat', *Slang.* a high-ranking military officer.

brass·ie (bras'ē, brä'sē), *n.* a golf club with a wooden head and a brass-plated face, for hitting long, low drives.

bras·siere (brə zēr'), *n.* a woman's undergarment for supporting and shaping the breasts. Also, **bras·sière'.**

brass' tacks', *Informal.* the essentials of a subject under discussion.

brat (brat), *n.* a spoiled or impolite child. —**brat'ty,** *adj.* —**brat'ti·ness,** *n.*

brat·wurst (brat'wərst), *n.* sausage made of pork, spices, and herbs.

Braun·schwei·ger (broun'shwī'gər), *n.* a spiced liver sausage, usually smoked.

bra·va·do (brə vä'dō), *n., pl.* **-does, -dos.** a pretentious, swaggering display of courage.

brave (brāv), *adj.,* **brav·er, brav·est,** *n., v.,* **braved, brav·ing.** —*adj.* **1.** possessing or exhibiting courage.

2. making a fine appearance. —*n.* **3.** a warrior, esp. among American Indian tribes. —*v.t.* **4.** to meet or face courageously. **5.** to defy or challenge. —**brave'ly,** *adv.* —**brave'ness,** *n.* —Syn. **1.** bold, courageous, daring, dauntless.

brav·er·y (brā'və rē, brāv'rē), *n., pl.* **-er·ies.** brave spirit or conduct.

bra·vo (brä'vō, brä vō'), *interj., n., pl.* **-vos.** —*interj.* **1.** well done! good! —*n.* **2.** a shout of "bravo!"

bra·vu·ra (brə vyŏōr'ə), *n.* **1.** *Music.* a passage or piece requiring great skill. **2.** a brilliant performance.

brawl (brôl), *n.* **1.** a noisy quarrel or fight. —*v.i.* **2.** to quarrel angrily and noisily. —**brawl'er,** *n.*

brawn (brôn), *n.* **1.** well-developed muscles. **2.** muscular strength. —**brawn·y,** *adj.* —**brawn'il·y,** *adv.* —**brawn'i·ness,** *n.*

bray (brā), *n.* **1.** a harsh, breathy cry, as of a donkey. —*v.i.* **2.** to make such a cry.

braze (brāz), *v.t.,* **brazed, braz·ing.** to unite (metal objects), by soldering with materials that have a high melting point. —**braz'er,** *n.*

bra·zen (brā'zən), *adj.* **1.** made of brass. **2.** like brass, as in sound, color, or strength. **3.** shameless or impudent. —*v.t.* **4.** to make bold. —**bra'zen·ly,** *adv.* —**bra'zen·ness,** *n.*

bra·zier¹ (brā'zhər), *n.* a person who makes articles of brass.

bra·zier² (brā'zhər), *n.* a metal receptacle for holding live coals, as for heating a room or cooking.

Bra·zil (brə zil'), *n.* a country in South America. —**Bra·zil·ian** (brə·zil'yən), *adj., n.*

Brazil' nut', the triangular edible seed of a South American tree.

breach (brēch), *n.* **1.** a gap made in a wall, line of defense, etc. **2.** an infraction or violation, as of a law. **3.** a severance of friendly relations. —*v.t.* **4.** to make a breach in.

breach' of prom'ise, a violation of one's promise, esp. to marry a specific person.

bread (bred), *n.* **1.** a food made of baked dough or batter. **2.** livelihood or sustenance. **3.** *Slang.* money. **4.** break bread, to eat a meal. —*v.t.* **5.** to cover with bread crumbs. —**bread'less,** *adj.*

bread' and but'ter, *Informal.* a source of livelihood.

bread·bas·ket (bred'bas'kit, -bä'skit), *n.* an area that provides large amounts of grain.

bread·board (bred'bôrd', -bōrd'), *n.* an experimental assembly of electronic components for a proposed circuit.

bread·fruit (bred′frōōt′), *n.* **1.** a large, round, starchy fruit borne by a tropical tree, used, baked or roasted, for food. **2.** the tree bearing this fruit.

bread·stuff (bred′stuf′), *n.* grain, flour, or meal.

breadth (bredth, bretth), *n.* **1.** the measure of the side-to-side dimension of something **2.** freedom from narrowness, as of viewpoint. **3.** extent or scope.

bread·win·ner (bred′win′ər), *n.* a person who earns a livelihood for his or her dependents.

break (brāk), *v.,* **broke, bro·ken, break·ing.** —*v.t.* **1. a.** to separate into pieces or parts forcefully or suddenly. **b.** to crack or fracture, as a leg. **2.** to injure so as to render useless. **3.** to burst or pierce, as a blister. **4.** to interrupt (a continuous action). **5.** to terminate. **6.** to end the otherwise perfect condition of. **7.** to reveal at a certain time, as news. **8.** to train to obedience, as an animal. **9.** to train away from a habit. **10.** to overcome emotionally or master. **11.** to find the meaning of: *to break a code.* **12.** to bankrupt. **13.** to reduce in rank. **14.** to surpass: *to break the record.* **15.** to violate: *to break the law.* **16.** to make a way through. —*v.i.* **17.** to become cracked or divided. **18.** to become useless or inoperative. **19.** to burst. **20.** to appear, as the dawn. **21.** to become public, as news. **22.** to subside. **23.** to be overwhelmed, as by grief. **24.** to change suddenly or unpleasantly. **25.** to take place. **26. break down, a.** to cease to function. **b.** to have a physical or mental collapse. **c.** to decompose. **d.** to analyze. **e.** to classify. **27. break in, a.** to enter enclosed property by force. **b.** to train or initiate. **c.** to begin to use. **d.** to interrupt. **28. break off, a.** to stop suddenly. **b.** to sever a relationship. **29. break out, a.** to begin abruptly. **b.** (of certain diseases) to appear in eruptions. **c.** to escape, as from confinement. **30. break up, a.** to separate or scatter. **b.** to discontinue. **c.** to laugh or make laugh. **31. break with,** to separate from. —*n.* **32.** the act of breaking or an instance of being broken. **33.** a crack or opening made by breaking. **34.** an interruption. **35.** a brief respite or rest. **36.** a sudden dash, as in making an escape. **37.** *Informal.* a stroke of luck. **38.** *Informal.* a social blunder. —**break′a·ble,** *adj.* —**Syn. 1.** burst, shatter, smash, split.

break·age (brā′kij), *n.* **1.** the act of breaking or state of being broken. **2.** the value of things broken. **3.** an allowance for articles broken.

break·down (brāk′doun′), *n.* **1.** a breaking down. **2.** a physical or mental collapse. **3.** decomposition. **4.** analysis. **5.** classification.

break·er (brā′kər), *n.* **1.** a person or thing that breaks. **2.** a wave that breaks into foam. **3.** *CB Radio Slang.* a person who indicates a wish to transmit a message.

break·e·ven (brāk′ē′vən), *adj.* having income exactly equal to expenditure or costs.

break·fast (brek′fəst), *n.* **1.** the first meal of the day. —*v.i.* **2.** to eat breakfast.

break·front (brāk′frunt′), *adj.* **1.** having a central section extending forward from those at either side. —*n.* **2.** a breakfront cabinet.

break·in (brāk′in′), *n.* an illegal entry into a home, car, office, etc.

break·neck (brāk′nek′), *adj.* (of speed) dangerously excessive.

break·out (brāk′out′), *n.* **1.** an escape, as from a prison. **2.** an appearance, as of a disease.

break·through (brāk′thrōō′), *n.* **1.** a movement through and beyond an enemy's defensive system. **2.** a significant advance, as in technology.

break·up (brāk′up′), *n.* **1.** disintegration or disruption. **2.** a separation, as between friends.

break·wa·ter (brāk′wô′tər, -wot′er), *n.* a barrier that breaks the force of waves, as before a harbor.

bream (brēm), *n., pl.* **bream, breams.** a freshwater fish with a compressed, deep body.

breast (brest), *n.* **1.** the front part of the body from the neck to abdomen. **2.** either of two projecting, milk-secreting organs on the chest of a woman or certain female mammals. **3.** the part of a garment that covers the chest. **4.** the bosom conceived of as the center of feelings. **5. make a clean breast of,** to confess. —*v.t.* **6.** to meet or oppose.

breast·bone (brest′bōn′), *n.* the sternum.

breast·feed (brest′fēd′), *v.t.,* **-fed, -feed·ing.** to nurse (a baby) at the breast.

breast·plate (brest′plāt′), *n.* a piece of plate armor for the front of the torso.

breast·stroke (brest′strōk′), *n.* a swimming stroke in which both hands move simultaneously forward, outward, and rearward from the front of the chest while the legs kick outward.

breast·work (brest'wûrk'), *n.* a hastily constructed fortification, usually breast high.

breath (breth), *n.* **1.** the air inhaled and exhaled in respiration. **2.** respiration. **3.** life or vitality. **4.** the ability to breathe easily. **5.** a single inhalation. **6.** the slightest suggestion: *not a breath of scandal.* **7.** a light current of air. **8.** a voiceless sound. **9. below** or **under one's breath,** in a low whisper. **10. catch one's breath, a.** to rest or pause. **b.** to gasp, as in fear. **11. out of breath,** gasping for breath. **12. take one's breath away,** to stun or thrill. —**breath'less,** *adj.* —**breath'less·ly,** *adv.*

breathe (breth), *v.t., v.t.,* **breathed** (brethd), **breath·ing. 1.** to inhale and exhale (air) in respiration. **2.** to pause, as to rest. **3.** to live or exist. **4.** to whisper. **5. breathe freely** or **again,** to have relief from anxiety. —**breath'a·ble,** *adj.*

breath·er (brē'thər), *n.* **1.** a pause, as for breath. **2.** a vigorous exercise.

breath·tak·ing (breth'tā'king), *adj.* causing extreme awe or excitement. —**breath'tak'ing·ly,** *adv.*

breath·y (breth'ē), *adj.* marked by excessive emission of breath.

brec·ci·a (brech'ē ə, bresh'-), *n.* rock composed of angular fragments of older rocks melded together.

breech (brēch), *n.* **1.** the buttocks. **2.** the rear part of the bore of a gun.

breech·cloth (brēch'klôth'), *n.* loincloth.

breech' deliv'ery, the birth of an infant with the feet or breech appearing first.

breech·es (brich'iz), *n.pl.* **1.** knee-length trousers. **2.** *Informal.* trousers.

breed (brēd), *v.,* **bred** (bred), **breed·ing,** *n.* —*v.t.* **1.** to produce (offspring). **2.** to cause to be born. **3.** to raise (cattle, etc.). **4.** to rear or bring up. **5.** to produce (a fissionable element) by absorbing neutrons. —*v.i.* **6.** to produce offspring. **7.** to be produced. —*n.* **8.** a homogenous group of animals within a species, developed by humans. **9.** a sort or kind. —**breed'er,** *n.*

breed·ing (brē'ding), *n.* **1.** the production of offspring. **2.** the improvement of livestock or plants by selection. **3.** training or nurture. **4.** manners, esp. good manners.

breeze (brēz), *n., v.,* **breezed, breez·ing.** —*n.* **1.** a light wind. **2.** *Informal.* an easy task. —*v.i.* **3.** *Informal.* to progress quickly and easily. —**breez'y,** *adj.* —**breez'i·ly,** *adv.* —**breez'i·ness,** *n.*

breeze·way (brēz'wā'), *n.* a roofed passageway with open sides, for connecting two buildings.

Brem·en (brem'ən), *n.* a port in N West Germany.

br'er (brûr, brâr), *n. Dial.* brother.

breth·ren (breth'rin), *n.pl.* **1.** fellow members. **2.** (*cap.*) members of a Protestant group originating in Germany in the 18th century and practicing the simple Christian life. **3.** *Archaic.* brothers.

Bret·on (bret'ən), *n.* **1.** a native or inhabitant of Brittany, in NW France. **2.** the Celtic language of Brittany.

breve (brēv, brev), *n.* a mark (˘) over a vowel to show that it is short, as ŭ in (kŭt) *cut.*

bre·vet (brə vet'), *n., v.,* **-vet·ted, -vet·ting** or **-vet·ed, -vet·ing.** (formerly) —*n.* **1.** a commission promoting an army officer to a higher rank without increase in pay. —*v.t.* **2.** to promote by brevet.

bre·vi·ar·y (brē'vē er'ē, brev'ē-), *n., pl.* **-ar·ies.** *Rom. Cath. Ch.* a book containing all daily hymns, prayers, lessons, etc.

brev·i·ty (brev'i tē), *n.* **1.** shortness of duration. **2.** conciseness or terseness.

brew (broo), *v.t.* **1.** to make (beer, ale, etc.) by steeping, boiling, and fermenting malt and hops. **2.** to make (a beverage, as tea), by steeping, soaking, etc. **3.** to contrive or bring about. —*v.i.* **4.** to make beer, ale, etc. **5.** to form, esp. in an ominous manner: *Trouble was brewing.* —*n.* **6.** a quantity brewed at one time. —**brew'er,** *n.*

brew·er·y (broo'ə rē, broor'ē), *n., pl.* **-er·ies.** a place for brewing beer or other malt beverages.

Brezh·nev (brezh'nef), *n.* **Le·o·nid Il·yich** (le o nēt' il yēch'), born 1906, Russian political leader.

bri·ar (brī'ər), *n.* **1.** brier[1]. **2.** brier[2].

bribe (brīb), *n., v.,* **bribed, brib·ing.** —*n.* **1.** anything promised or given as illicit payment. —*v.t.* **2.** to give or promise a bribe to. —**brib'er,** *n.* —**brib'er·y,** *n.*

bric-a-brac (brik'ə brak'), *n.* small articles of antiquarian, decorative, or other interest.

brick (brik), *n.* **1.** a rectangular block of clay hardened by heat and used for building, paving, etc. —*v.t.* **2.** to pave or build with brick.

brick·bat (brik'bat'), *n.* **1.** a piece of brick, used as a missile. **2.** *Informal.* a caustic criticism or remark.

brick·lay·ing (brik'lā'ing), *n.* the process or occupation of laying bricks in construction. —**brick'lay'er,** *n.*

brid·al (brīd′ᵊl), *adj.* **1.** of a bride or a wedding. —*n.* **2.** a wedding. —**brid′al·ly,** *adv.*

bride (brīd), *n.* a newly married woman or a woman about to be married.

bride·groom (brīd′grōōm′, -grŏŏm′), *n.* a newly married man or a man about to be married.

brides·maid (brīdz′mād′), *n.* a young woman who attends the bride at the wedding ceremony.

bridge¹ (brij), *n., v.,* **bridged, bridging.** —*n.* **1.** a structure providing passage over a river, etc. **2.** a connection between two adjacent elements, conditions, etc. **3.** a raised platform, esp. that from which a ship is navigated. **4.** the ridge of the nose. **5.** an artificial replacement for a missing tooth or teeth. **6.** a thin, fixed wedge raising the strings of a musical instrument above the sounding board. **7.** a transitional passage connecting major sections of a musical composition. **8. burn one's bridges (behind one),** to eliminate all possibilities of retreat. —*v.t.* **9.** to make a bridge over. —**bridge′a·ble,** *adj.*

bridge² (brij), *n.* a card game in which one partnership of two players attempts to fulfill a certain declaration against an opposing partnership.

bridge·head (brij′hed′), *n.* a position gained on the enemy side of a river or other obstacle, to cover the crossing of friendly troops.

Bridge·port (brij′pōrt′, -pôrt′), *n.* a seaport in SW Connecticut.

bridge·work (brij′wûrk′), *n.* a dental bridge or bridges.

bri·dle (brīd′ᵊl), *n., v.,* **-dled, -dling.** —*n.* **1.** part of the harness of a horse, consisting usually of a headstall, bit, and reins. **2.** anything that restrains. —*v.t.* **3.** to put a bridle on. **4.** to restrain or curb. —*v.i.* **5.** to show disdain or resentment. —**bri′dler,** *n.*

bri′dle path′, a wide path for riding horses.

Brie (brē), *n.* a white, soft cheese, ripened with bacterial action, originating in France.

brief (brēf), *adj.* **1.** of short duration. **2.** concise or succinct. —*n.* **3.** a synopsis or summary. **4.** a memorandum of points of fact or of law for use in conducting a case. **5. briefs,** closefitting, legless underpants. —*v.t.* **6.** to make a summary of. **7.** to instruct by a brief. —**brief′ing,** *n.* —**brief′ly,** *adv.* —**brief′ness,** *n.*

brief·case (brēf′kās′), *n.* a flat, rectangular case for carrying papers, books, etc.

bri·er¹ (brī′ᵊr), *n.* a prickly plant or shrub. —**bri′er·y,** *adj.*

bri·er² (brī′ᵊr), *n.* a white heath, the woody root of which is used for tobacco pipes.

brig (brig), *n.* **1.** a two-masted vessel square-rigged on both masts. **2.** a place of detention, esp. in the U.S. Navy.

brig., **1.** brigade. **2.** brigadier.

bri·gade (bri gād′), *n.* **1.** a military unit having its own headquarters, consisting of two or more regiments or battalions. **2.** a group organized for a particular purpose.

brig′a·dier′ gen′eral (brig′ᵊ dēr′), *pl.* **brigadier generals.** *U.S. Army.* an officer of the rank between colonel and major general.

brig·and (brig′ᵊnd), *n.* a bandit, esp. one of a roving gang. —**brig′and·age,** *n.*

brig·an·tine (brig′ᵊn tēn′, -tĭn′), *n.* a two-masted vessel, square-rigged and having a fore-and-aft mainsail. **Brig. Gen.,** Brigadier General.

bright (brīt), *adj.* **1.** radiating much light. **2.** vivid or brilliant. **3.** illustrious or glorious. **4.** quickwitted or intelligent. **5.** animated or lively. **6.** favorable or auspicious. —**bright′ly,** *adv.* —**bright′ness,** *n.* —**Syn. 1, 2.** brilliant, luminous, lustrous, radiant.

bright·en (brīt′ᵊn), *v.i., v.t.* to become or make bright or brighter. —**bright′en·er,** *n.*

bril·liant (bril′yᵊnt), *adj.* **1.** shining brightly. **2.** distinguished or illustrious. **3.** having great intelligence or talent. —*n.* **4.** a gem cut with many facets. —**bril′liance, bril′lian·cy,** *n.* —**bril′liant·ly,** *adv.*

bril·lian·tine (bril′yᵊn tēn′), *n.* a preparation for making the hair lustrous.

brim (brim), *n., v.,* **brimmed, brimming.** —*n.* **1.** the upper edge of anything hollow. **2.** a projecting edge, as of a hat. —*v.i., v.t.* **3.** to be full or fill to the brim. —**brim′less,** *adj.*

brim·ful (brim′fŏŏl′), *adj.* full to the brim. Also, **brim′full′.**

brim·stone (brim′stōn′), *n.* sulfur.

brin·dle (brin′d′ᵊl), *n.* **1.** a brindled coloring. —*adj.* **2.** brindled.

brin·dled (brin′d′ᵊld), *adj.* gray or tawny with darker streaks or spots.

brine (brīn), *n.* **1.** water saturated with salt. **2.** the sea or ocean. —**brin′y,** *adj.* —**brin′i·ness,** *n.*

bring (bring), *v.t.,* **brought, bring·ing. 1.** to cause to come to or with oneself. **2.** to cause to happen to one. **3.** to persuade, convince, or compel. **4.** to sell for. **5. bring about,** to accomplish or cause. **6. bring forth, a.** to produce. **b.** to present for consideration. **7. bring off,** to accomplish or achieve. **8. bring out, a.** to reveal. **b.** to publish, as a book, etc. **9. bring to,** to revive. **10. bring up, a.** to rear, as a child. **b.** to mention for consideration. **c.** to vomit. **d.** to stop or cause to stop. —**bring′er,** n. —Syn. 1. bear, carry, convey, lead.

brink (bringk), n. **1.** the edge of a steep place or of land bordering water. **2.** any extreme position.

brink·man·ship (bringk′mən ship′), n. the policy of maneuvering a risky situation to the limits of safety. Also, **brinks′man·ship′.**

bri·o (brē′ō), n. Italian. vigor or vivacity.

bri·oche (brē′ōsh, -osh), n. a light, sweet roll made with eggs and butter.

bri·quette (bri ket′), n. a small brick of compressed coal dust or charcoal used for fuel, esp. in barbecuing. Also, **bri·quet′.**

Bris·bane (briz′bān, -bən), n. a seaport in E Australia.

brisk (brisk), adj. **1.** quick and active. **2.** sharp and stimulating. —**brisk′ly,** adv. —**brisk′ness,** n.

bris·ket (bris′kit), n. the breast of an animal.

bris·ling (bris′ling), n. the sprat.

bris·tle (bris′əl), n., v., **-tled, -tling.** —n. **1.** a short, stiff hair of an animal. —v.i. **2.** to stand or rise stiffly. **3.** to become rigid with anger or irritation. **4.** to be thickly filled. —**bris′tly,** adj.

Bris·tol (bris′təl), n. a seaport in SW England.

Brit., 1. Britain. **2.** British.

Brit·ain (brit′ən), n. See **Great Britain.**

Bri·tan′ni·a met′al (bri tan′ē ə, -tan′- yə), a white alloy of tin, antimony, and copper.

Bri·tan·nic (bri tan′ik), adj. British.

britch·es (brich′iz), n.pl. Informal. breeches.

Brit·i·cism (brit′i siz′əm), n. a word or phrase characteristic of British English.

Brit·ish (brit′ish), adj. **1.** of Great Britain, the British Commonwealth, or its inhabitants. —n. **2.** the people of Great Britain or the British Commonwealth. **3.** See **British English.**

Brit′ish Colum′bia, a province in W Canada. Cap.: Victoria.

Brit′ish Com′monwealth of Na′tions, former name of **Commonwealth of Nations.**

Brit′ish Eng′lish, English as used in England.

Brit·ish·er (brit′i shər), n. a native or inhabitant of Great Britain, esp. of England.

Brit′ish Isles′, a group of islands in W Europe, including Great Britain, Ireland, etc.

Brit′ish ther′mal u′nit, the amount of heat required to raise the temperature of one pound of water one degree F.

Brit·on (brit′ən), n. **1.** a native or inhabitant of Great Britain, esp. of England. **2.** one of the Celtic people occupying ancient Britain.

brit·tle (brit′əl), adj. **1.** easily broken. **2.** inflexible, as a person. —n. **3.** a brittle, crunchy candy. —**brit′- tle·ness,** n.

bro., brother.

broach (brōch), n. **1.** a tapered tool for shaping and enlarging holes. **2.** a gimlet for tapping casks. —v.t. **3.** to mention for the first time. **4.** to tap or pierce. —**broach′er,** n.

broad (brôd), adj. **1.** of great breadth. **2.** measured from side to side. **3.** of great area. **4.** open or full. **5.** of extensive range or scope. **6.** liberal or tolerant. **7.** main or general. **8.** plain or clear. —n. **9.** Slang. a woman. —**broad′ly,** adv. —**broad′ness,** n. —Syn. **3.** spacious, vast, wide.

broad a., the a-sound (ä) when used in place of the more common a-sound (a) in such words as half or laugh.

broad·band (brôd′band′), adj. of or responsive to a continuous, wide range of radio frequencies.

broad·cast (brôd′kast′, -käst′), v., **-cast** or **-cast·ed, -cast·ing,** n., adj., adv. —v.t., v.i. **1.** to transmit (programs) over radio or television. **2.** to scatter over an area, as seed. **3.** to spread widely, as news. —n. **4.** that which is broadcast. **5.** a single radio or television program. — adj. **6.** of or by radio or television transmission. **7.** widely spread. — adv. **8.** cast abroad over an area. —**broad′cast′er,** n.

broad·cloth (brôd′klôth′, -kloth′), n. **1.** a woolen fabric having a compact texture. **2.** a closely woven fabric of cotton, rayon, or silk, having a soft finish.

broad·en (brôd′ən), v.i., v.t. to become or make broad.

broad′ jump. See **long jump.**

broad·loom (brôd′lōōm′), n. any carpet woven on a wide loom, esp. one wider than 54 inches.

broad·mind·ed (brôd′mīn′did), adj. free from prejudice or bigotry. — **broad′-mind′ed·ly,** adv. —**broad′- mind′ed·ness,** n.

broad·side (brôd′sīd′), n. **1.** the side of a ship above the water line. **2.** simultaneous discharge of all the guns on one side of a warship. **3.** any strong or comprehensive attack. **4.** a sheet of paper printed on one or both sides, as for advertising.

broad-spec·trum (brôd′spek′trəm), *adj.* noting an antibiotic effective against a wide range of organisms.

broad·sword (brôd′sōrd′, -sôrd′), *n.* a sword having a straight, broad, flat blade.

broad·tail (brôd′tāl′), *n.* the wavy fur of a young or stillborn karakul lamb.

Broad·way (brôd′wā′), *n.* a street in New York City noted for its theaters.

bro·cade (brō kād′), *n., v., -cad·ed, -cad·ing.* —*n.* 1. fabric woven with a raised design. —*v.t.* 2. to weave with a raised design.

broc·co·li (brok′ə lē), *n.* a plant resembling the cauliflower, the green flower head and stalk of which are a common vegetable.

bro·chette (brō shet′), *n.* a skewer for use in cookery.

bro·chure (brō shoŏr′), *n.* a free pamphlet, esp. for promotional purposes.

bro·gan (brō′gən), *n.* a coarse, ankle-high work shoe.

brogue[1] (brōg), *n.* a dialectal pronunciation, esp. an Irish accent. —**bro′guish,** *adj.*

brogue[2] (brōg), *n.* a durable oxford shoe.

broi·der (broi′dər), *v.t. Archaic.* to embroider.

broil (broil), *v.t., v.i.* 1. to cook by direct heat, as on a gridiron. —*n.* 2. something broiled.

broil·er (broi′lər), *n.* 1. a grate, pan, etc. for broiling. 2. a young chicken suitable for broiling.

broke (brōk), *v.* 1. pt. of **break.** —*adj.* 2. *Informal.* a. without money. b. bankrupt.

bro·ken (brō′kən), *v.* 1. pp. of **break.** —*adj.* 2. fragmented or fractured. 3. not working or functioning 4. infringed or violated: *a broken promise.* 5. interrupted or disconnected. 6. reduced to submission. 7. imperfectly spoken. 8. ruined or bankrupt. 9. disunited or divided: *a broken family.* —**bro′ken·ly,** *adv.* —**bro′ken·ness,** *n.*

bro·ken-heart·ed (brō′kən här′tid), *adj.* burdened with great sorrow or disappointment.

bro·ker (brō′kər), *n.* a person engaged, for a commission or fee, in bargaining or negotiating between two or more parties for agreements, purchases, or sales.

bro·ker·age (brō′kər ij), *n.* 1. the business of a broker. 2. the commission of a broker.

bro·mide (brō′mīd, -mid), *n.* 1. a compound containing bromine. 2. See **potassium bromide.** 3. *Informal.* a. a platitude. b. a boring person. —**bro·mid·ic** (brō mid′ik), *adj.*

bro·mine (brō′mēn, -min), *n. Chem.* a nonmetallic element that is a dark-reddish, fuming liquid, used in antiknock compounds, pharmaceuticals, etc. *Symbol:* Br; *at. wt.:* 79.909; *at. no.:* 35.

bron·chi·al (brong′kē əl), *adj.* pertaining to the bronchi. —**bron′chi·al·ly,** *adv.*

bron·chi·tis (brong kī′tis), *n.* inflammation of the membrane lining of the bronchial tubes. —**bron·chit·ic** (brong kit′ik), *adj.*

bron·chus (brong′kəs), *n., pl.* **-chi** (-kī). either of the two main branches of the trachea.

bron·co (brong′kō), *n., pl.* **-cos.** a wild or untamed pony or horse of the western U.S. Also, **bron′cho.**

bron·co·bust·er (brong′kō bus′tər), *n.* a person who breaks broncos to the saddle.

bron·to·saur (bron′tə sôr′), *n.* an amphibious, herbivorous dinosaur of North America. Also, **bron·to·saurus** (bron′tə sôr′əs). [< Gk *brontē* thunder + *saur(os)* lizard]

Bronx (brongks), *n.* the, a borough of New York City.

Bronx′ cheer′, *Slang.* raspberry (def. 3).

bronze (bronz), *n., v.,* **bronzed, bronz·ing.** —*n.* 1. an alloy essentially of copper and tin. 2. a metallic brownish color. 3. a work of art, as a statue, made of bronze. —*v.t.* 4. to give the appearance of bronze to. —**bronz′y,** *adj.*

Bronze′ Age′, a period of human history between the Stone Age and the Iron Age, during which bronze weapons and implements were used.

brooch (brōch, brōōch), *n.* an ornamental clasp or pin.

brood (brōōd), *n.* 1. a number of young produced or hatched at one time. —*v.i.* 2. to sit upon eggs to be hatched. 3. to dwell on a subject with morbid persistence. —*adj.* 4. kept for breeding purposes: *brood hens.*

brood·er (brōō′dər), *n.* 1. a heated structure for raising young chickens. 2. a person who broods.

brood·y (brōō′dē), *adj.,* **brood·i·er, brood·i·est.** moody or gloomy.

brook[1] (brōōk), *n.* a small, natural stream of fresh water.

brook[2] (brōōk), *v.t.* to bear or tolerate (used usually in the negative).

brook·let (brōōk′lit), *n.* a small brook.

Brook·lyn (brōōk′lin), *n.* a borough of New York City.

brook′ trout′, a trout of eastern North America.

broom (brōōm, brōōm), *n.* 1. a long-handled implement for sweeping, with a brush of straw or similar material. **2.** a shrubby plant having long, slender branches with yellow flowers. —**broom′y,** adj.

broom·stick (broom′stik′, broom′-), n. the long sticklike handle of a broom.

bros., brothers.

broth (brôth, broth), n. **1.** thin soup that has been boiled with meat, fish, or vegetables. **2.** a liquid suitable for cultivating bacteria. —**broth′y,** adj.

broth·el (broth′əl, broth′-, brô′thəl, -thəl), n. a house of prostitution.

broth·er (bruth′ər), n., pl. **brothers,** (Archaic) **brethren. 1.** a male offspring having both parents in common with another offspring. **2.** Also called **half brother.** a male offspring having only one parent in common with another offspring. **3.** a male numbered among the same kinship group, nationality, profession, etc., as another. **4.** a male who devotes himself to a religious order without taking holy orders. —**broth′er·ly,** adj. —**broth′er·li·ness,** n.

broth·er·hood (bruth′ər hood′), n. **1.** the state of being a brother or brothers. **2.** fraternality or fellowship. **3.** all those engaged in a particular trade, profession, etc.

broth·er-in-law (bruth′ər in lô′), n., pl. **broth·ers-in-law. 1.** the brother of one's husband or wife. **2.** the husband of one's sister. **3.** the husband of one's wife's or husband's sister.

brough·am (broo′əm, broom, brô′əm), n. **1.** a four-wheeled closed carriage having the driver's perch outside. **2.** a limousine having an open driver's compartment.

brought (brôt), v. pt. and pp. of **bring.**

brou·ha·ha (broo hä′hä, broo′hä hä′), n. an uproar or bustle.

brow (brou), n. **1.** the ridge over the eye. **2.** the eyebrow. **3.** the forehead. **4.** the edge of a steep place: *the brow of a hill.*

brow·beat (brou′bēt′), v.t., -**beat,** -**beat·en,** -**beat·ing.** to intimidate by overbearing looks or words.

brown (broun), n. **1.** a dark shade with a yellowish or reddish hue. —adj. **2.** of the color brown. **3.** sunburned or tanned. —v.t., v.i. **4.** to make or become brown. —**brown′ish,** adj.

brown-bag (broun′bag′), v.t., -**bagged,** -**bag·ing.** to bring (one's lunch) to work, usually in a small brown paper bag. —**brown′-bag′ger,** n. —**brown′-bag′ging,** adj., n.

brown·ie (brou′nē), n. **1.** a little fairy, esp. one who helps secretly in household work. **2.** a small, chewy, chocolate cake. **3.** (cap.)

a member of the youngest group (ages 7–8) of the Girl Scouts.

Brown·ing (brou′ning), n. **Robert,** 1812–89, English poet.

brown·out (broun′out′), n. the elimination of some or reduction of all electric lights of a city, esp. as a conservation measure.

brown′ rice′, unpolished rice.

brown·stone (broun′stōn′), n. **1.** a reddish-brown sandstone. **2.** a building, esp. a row house, fronted with this stone.

brown′ stud′y, deep, serious thought.

brown′ sug′ar, unrefined or partially refined sugar.

browse (brouz), v., **browsed, brows·ing,** n. —v.t., v.i. **1.** to eat or nibble at (leaves, etc.). **2.** to look through or over (something) in a casual, unhurried manner. —n. **3.** tender shoots, twigs, and leaves as food for cattle. —**brows′er,** n.

bru·in (broo′in), n. a bear, esp. a brown bear.

bruise (brooz), v., **bruised, bruis·ing,** n. —v.t. **1.** to injure without breaking the skin. **2.** to hurt superficially: *to bruise a person's feelings.* **3.** to crush (drugs or food) by beating or pounding. —v.i. **4.** to bruise the body tissue, etc. **5.** to become bruised. —n. **6.** a bruised area of the body tissue.

bruis·er (broo′zər), n. Informal. a strong, tough person.

bruit (broot), v.t. to spread a rumor of.

brunch (brunch), n. a late-morning meal that serves both as breakfast and lunch.

bru·nette (broo net′), adj. **1.** (of a female) having dark hair, eyes, or skin. —n. **2.** a brunette woman. Also, *referring to a man,* **bru·net′.**

Bruns′wick stew′ (brunz′wik), a stew consisting of rabbit or squirrel meat, onions, and other vegetables.

brunt (brunt), n. the main shock, force, or impact, as of an attack or blow.

brush¹ (brush), n. **1.** an implement consisting of bristles, hair, etc., set in a handle, used for painting, cleaning, grooming, etc. **2.** a light, stroking touch. **3.** the bushy tail of an animal, esp. a fox. **4.** a slight encounter: *a brush with the law.* **5.** a conductor serving to maintain electric contact between the stationary and moving parts of a machine, generator, etc. —v.t. **6.** to paint, clean, or groom with a brush. **7.** to touch lightly in passing. **8.** to remove by brushing. —v.i. **9.** to brush one's teeth. **10. brush aside,** to ignore. **11. brush off,** Slang. to rebuff. **12. brush up,** to review.

brush² (brush), *n.* **1.** a dense growth of bushes, shrubs, etc. **2.** lopped or broken branches. Also, **brush·wood** (brush′wŏŏd′).

brush-off (brush′ôf′, -of′), *n. Slang.* an abrupt dismissal or rebuff.

brusque (brusk), *adj.* abrupt in manner or speech. Also, **brusk.** —**brusque′ly,** *adv.* —**brusque′ness,** *n.*

Brus·sels (brus′əlz), *n.* the capital of Belgium.

Brussels sprout (brus′əl sprout′), a plant having small, cabbagelike, edible heads or sprouts along the stalk.

brut (brōōt), *adj.* (of wine) very dry.

bru·tal (brōōt′⁹l), *adj.* **1.** savagely cruel. **2.** crude or coarse. —**brutal′i·ty,** *n.* —**bru′tal·ly,** *adv.*

bru·tal·ize (brōōt′⁹līz′), *v.t., v.i.,* **-ized, -iz·ing. 1.** to make or become brutal. **2.** to treat with brutality. —**bru′tal·i·za′tion,** *n.*

brute (brōōt), *n.* **1.** a nonhuman creature. **2.** a brutal, crude person. —*adj.* **3.** like an animal. **4.** unreasoning or irrational. **5.** savage or cruel. —**brut′ish,** *adj.* —**brut′ish·ly,** *adv.*

B.S., 1. Bachelor of Science. **2.** See **bill of sale.**

b.s., 1. See **balance sheet. 2** See **bill of sale.**

B.S.A., Boy Scouts of America.

B.Sc., Bachelor of Science.

bsh., bushel; bushels.

bskt., basket.

Bt., Baronet.

btry., battery.

Btu, See **British thermal unit.** Also, **BTU**

bu., 1. bureau. **2.** bushel; bushels.

bub·ble (bub′əl), *n., v.,* **-bled, -bling.** —*n.* **1.** a nearly spherical body of gas contained in a liquid. **2.** a small globule of gas in a thin liquid envelope. **3.** anything that lacks firmness or substance. **4.** an inflated speculation. **5.** a transparent canopy. —*v.i.* **6.** to form or produce bubbles. **7.** to flow with a gurgling noise. —**bub′bly,** *adj.*

bub′ble gum′, a chewing gum that can be blown into large bubbles.

bub·bler (bub′lər), *n.* a drinking fountain that spouts water directly into the mouth.

bub·ble·top (bub′əl top′), *n.* a transparent dome of bulletproof plastic protecting the passengers of a limousine.

bu·bo (byōō′bō), *n., pl.* **-boes.** an inflammatory swelling of a lymphatic gland, esp. in the groin or armpit. —**bu·bon·ic** (byōō bon′ik, bōō-), *adj.*

bubon′ic plague′, a form of plague characterized by buboes, chills, and fevers.

buc·ca·neer (buk′ə nēr′), *n.* a pirate, esp. one of those active in the 17th century. [< F *boucanier,* lit., barbecuer]

Bu·chan·an (byōō kan′ən, bə-), *n.* **James,** 1791-1868, 15th president of the U.S. 1857-61.

Bu·cha·rest (bōō′kə rest′, byōō′-), *n.* the capital of Rumania.

buck¹ (buk), *n.* **1.** the male of the deer, antelope, etc. **2.** an impetuous or spirited man or youth. **3.** *Slang* a dollar **4. pass the buck,** *Informal* to shift responsibility to another person.

buck² (buk), *v.i.* **1.** to leap with arched back to dislodge a rider or pack. **2.** *Informal.* to resist or object strongly **3.** *Informal.* (of a vehicle) to move by jerks and bounces. —*v.t.* **4.** to throw (a rider) by bucking **5.** *Informal.* to resist or object strongly to. **6.** *Football.* to charge into (the opponent's line). **7. buck for,** *Slang* to strive in any way for (a promotion, etc.). **8. buck up,** *Informal* to make or become more cheerful. —*n.* **9.** the act of bucking —*adj.* **10.** *Slang.* of the lowest military rank: *buck private* —**buck′er,** *n.*

buck³ (buk) *n.* **1.** a sawhorse. **2.** a sawhorselike frame for gymnastic vaulting

buck·board (buk′bōrd′, -bôrd′), *n.* a light four-wheeled carriage in which a long elastic board is used in place of body and springs.

buck·et (buk′it) *n.* **1.** a cylindrical container for carrying or holding water, etc **2.** a scoop, as on a power shovel **3.** Also called **buck′et·ful′.** the amount that a bucket can hold **4. kick the bucket,** *Slang.* to die.

buck′et seat′, an individual seat with a rounded back, as in some cars, airplanes, etc.

buck·eye (buk′ī′), *n.* **1.** any of various trees or shrubs allied to the horse chestnut. **2.** its inedible seed.

buck′ fe′ver, nervous excitement of an inexperienced hunter upon the approach of game.

buck·ish (buk′ish), *adj.* impetuous or dashing —**buck′ish·ly,** *adv.*

buck·le (buk′əl), *n., v.,* **-led, -ling.** —*n.* **1.** a device for fastening two loose ends, as of a belt or strap. **2.** a bend, bulge, or kink. —*v.t., v.i.* **3.** to fasten with a buckle. **4.** to bend or warp **5. buckle down,** to apply oneself. —**buck′le·less,** *adj*

buck·ler (buk′lər), *n.* a round shield.

buck·ram (buk'rəm), *n.* a stiff cotton fabric for interlinings, book-bindings, etc.

buck·saw (buk'sô'), *n.* a two-handed saw consisting of a blade set across an upright frame.

buck·shot (buk'shot'), *n.* a large size of lead shot used for hunting game.

buck·skin (buk'skin'), *n.* **1.** the skin of a deer. **2.** a strong, soft leather, usually from sheepskins.

buck' slip', a piece of paper attached to and showing the routing and handling of an interoffice memo, file, etc. Also called **buck' sheet'**.

buck·tooth (buk'tōōth'), *n., pl.* **-teeth** (-tēth'). a projecting tooth, esp. an upper front tooth. **—buck'-toothed'**, *adj.*

buck·wheat (buk'hwēt', -wēt'), *n.* **1.** a herbaceous plant cultivated for its triangular seeds, which are used as feed or made into flour. **2.** the seeds of this plant.

bu·col·ic (byōō kol'ik), *adj.* **1.** pertaining to shepherds. **2.** of or suggesting an idyllic rural life. **—n.** **3.** a pastoral poem. **—bu·col'i·cal·ly**, *adv.*

bud (bud), *n., v.,* **bud·ded, bud·ding.** **—n.** **1.** a small protuberance on a plant, which develops into a flower, leaf, or branch. **2.** *Anat.* any small rounded part, as a taste bud. **3.** an undeveloped person or thing. **—v.i.** **4.** to produce buds, as a plant. **5.** to begin to develop. **—bud'der**, *n.* **—bud'like**, *adj.*

Bu·da·pest (bōō'də pest', bōō'də-pest'), *n.* the capital of Hungary.

Bud·dha (bōōd'ə, bōō'də), *n.* 566?-c480 B.C., Indian religious leader: founder of Buddhism.

Bud·dhism (bōōd'iz əm, bōō'diz-), *n.* a religion, originated by Buddha, holding that suffering is caused by desire and that the way to end this suffering is through an enlightenment. **—Bud'dhist**, *n., adj.*

bud·dy (bud'ē), *n., pl.* **-dies.** *Informal.* a comrade or chum.

budge (buj), *v.t., v.i.,* **budged, budging.** **1.** to move slightly. **2.** to change or cause to change one's opinion or position.

budg·er·i·gar (buj'ə rē gär'), *n.* an Australian parakeet bred as a pet.

budg·et (buj'it), *n., v.,* **-et·ed, -et·ing.** **—n.** **1.** an estimate, often itemized, of expected income and expense. **2.** a plan of operations based on such an estimate. **3.** the total sum of money for a specific purpose. **4.** *Obs.* a limited stock or collection. **—v.t.** **5.** to plan or schedule (time, etc.). **6.** to deal with in a budget. **—budg·et·ar·y** (buj'i ter'ē), *adj.* **—budg'et·er**, *n.*

budg·ie (buj'ē), *n. Informal.* budgerigar.

bue·nas no·ches (bwe'näs nô'chɛs), *Spanish.* good night.

Bue·nos Ai·res (bwā'nəs ī°r'iz), the capital of Argentina.

bue·nos dí·as (bwe'nôs dē'äs), *Spanish.* good morning or good day.

buff (buf), *n.* **1.** a thick, light-yellow leather with a napped surface. **2.** a military coat made of buff leather. **3.** medium or dark tan. **4.** *Informal.* the bare skin: *in the buff.* **5.** *Informal.* a devotee of some activity or subject. **—adj.** **6.** made of buff leather. **7.** having the color of buff. **—v.t.** **8.** to clean or polish with a buffer.

buf·fa·lo (buf'ə lō'), *n., pl.* **-loes, -los, -lo,** *v.,* **-loed, -lo·ing.** **—n.** **1.** any of several large wild oxen. **—v.t.** *Informal.* **2.** to baffle or mystify. **3.** to impress or intimidate. [< It < LL *būfalus* var. of L *būbalus* < Gk *boúbalos*]

Buf·fa·lo (buf'ə lō'), *n.* a port in W New York, on Lake Erie.

buff·er¹ (buf'ər), *n.* **1.** anything used for absorbing shock, as during collision. **2.** any substance that, added to a solution, is capable of neutralizing both acids and bases.

buff·er² (buf'ər), *n.* a device for polishing or buffing.

buff'er state', a small neutral state lying between potentially hostile larger powers.

buf·fet¹ (buf'it), *n., v.,* **-fet·ed, -fet·ing.** **—n.** **1.** a blow, as with the fist. **—v.t.** **2.** to strike, as with the fist. **3.** to strike against or push repeatedly: *The wind buffeted the house.* **—v.i.** **4.** to struggle with blows. **5.** to force one's way. **—buf'fet·er**, *n.*

buf·fet² (bə fā', bōō-), *n., pl.* **buffets** (bə fāz', bōō-). **1.** a cabinet for holding china, linen, etc. **2.** a counter for serving meals or refreshments. **3.** a meal laid out on a table or sideboard so that guests may serve themselves.

buf·foon (bə fōōn'), *n.* a person who amuses others by tricks, odd postures, etc. **—buf·foon·er·y** (bə-fōō'nə rē), *n.* **—buf·foon'ish**, *adj.*

bug (bug), *n., v.,* **bugged, bug·ging.** **—n.** **1.** any of a group of insects that have sucking mouthparts. **2.** any insect. **3.** *Informal.* any microorganism, esp. a virus. **4.** *Informal.* a defect, as in a mechanical device. **5.** *Slang.* a fan or hobbyist. **6.** *Slang.* a hidden microphone. **—v.t.** *Slang.* **7.** to install a hidden microphone in. **8.** to bother or annoy.

bug·bear (bug'bâr'), *n.* a source of fears, often groundless. Also, **bug·a·boo** (bug'ə bōō). **—bug'bear'-ish**, *adj.*

bug-eyed (bug'īd'), *adj. Slang.* with bulging eyes, as from surprise

bug-gy (bug'ē), *n., pl.* **-gies.** 1. a light, four-wheeled carriage with a single seat 2. See **baby carriage.**

bu-gle (byōō'gəl), *n., v.,* **-gled, -gling.** —*n.* 1. a brass wind instrument resembling a cornet and sometimes having valves. —*v.i., v.t.* 2. to signal by or with a bugle. —**bu'gler,** *n*

bugs (bugz), *adj. Slang.* crazy or insane.

build (bild), *v.,* **built** (bilt) or (*Archaic*) **build-ed; build-ing;** *n* —*v.t.* 1. to make or erect by joining parts or materials. 2. to establish or strengthen. 3. to form or create —*v.i* 4. to engage in building. 5. to develop toward a maximum 6. **build up,** a. to increase or strengthen b. to prepare in stages. —*n* 7. the mode or form of structure, physique, etc. —**build'er,** *n* —**Syn.** 1. construct, fabricate raise

build-ing (bil'ding), *n.* 1. a relatively permanent construction having a roof and walls, used for living, manufacturing, etc. 2. the act or business of constructing houses etc.

build-up (bild'up'), *n.* 1. strengthening and development. 2. *Informal.* a publicity campaign.

built-in (bilt'in'), *adj.* 1. built as part of a larger construction: *a built-in bookcase.* 2. inherent or intrinsic

built-up (bilt'up'), *adj.* 1. made or enlarged by adding something. 2. filled in with houses.

bulb (bulb), *n.* 1. a. an underground bud having fleshy leaves, rooting from the underside as in the onion, tulip, etc b. a plant growing from such a bud. 2. any round enlarged part. 3. an incandescent electric lamp. —**bulb'ar,** *adj* —**bulb'ous** *adj.*

bul-bul (bōōl'bōōl), *n.* a songbird often mentioned in Persian poetry.

Bulg. 1. Bulgaria 2. Bulgarian.

Bul-gar-i-a (bul gâr'ē ə bōōl-), *n.* a country in SE Europe. —**Bul-gar'i-an,** *n adj.*

bulge (bulj), *n., v.,* **bulged, bulg-ing.** —*n.* 1. a rounded projection or protruding part. —*v.i. v.t.* 2. to swell outward. —**bulg'y** *adj.*

bul-gur (bōōl'gŭr bōōl'gər), *n.* a highly nutritious form of wheat that has been parboiled, cracked, and dried.

bulk (bulk), *n.* 1. magnitude in three dimensions: *a ship of great bulk.* 2. the main mass or body. 3. food that forms a fibrous residue in digestion. 4. **in bulk,** unpackaged. —*v.i.* 5. to be or appear to be of

great weight, size, or importance. —*adj.* 6. being or traded in bulk: *bulk grain* —**bulk'y,** *adj.*

bulk-head (bulk'hed'), *n.* 1. a wall-like construction inside a ship for forming watertight compartments. 2. a retaining structure for shore protection 3. a boxlike structure covering a stairwell.

bull¹ (bōōl), *n.* 1. the male of a bovine animal and certain other animals *an elephant bull.* 2. a person who believes that the stock or commodities market will advance 3. **the Bull.** Taurus —*adj.* 4. male, esp of animals *a bull whale.* 5. marked by a continuing trend of rising prices as of stocks: *a bull market* —**bull'ish,** *adj.*

bull² (bōōl), *n.* a formal papal document

bull³ (bōōl), *n. Slang.* exaggerations, lies, or nonsense.

bull., bulletin

bull-dog (bōōl'dôg', -dog'), *n., v.,* **-dogged, -dog-ging.** —*n.* 1. a medium-sized short-haired, muscular dog with a prominent undershot jaw. —*v.t* 2. to throw (a steer) to the ground by seizing the horns and twisting the head.

bull-doze (bōōl'dōz'), *v.t.,* **-dozed, -doz-ing** 1. to clear or level by a bulldozer 2. *Informal.* to coerce or intimidate

bull-doz-er (bōōl'dō'zər), *n.* a tractor having a vertical blade at the front for moving earth, rocks, etc.

bul-let (bōōl'it), *n.* a small metal projectile for firing from small arms

bul-le-tin (bōōl'i tⁿn, -tin), *n.* 1. a brief public statement as of late news. 2. a periodical publication, as of a learned society

bul-let-proof (bōōl'it prōōf'), *adj.* 1. capable of resisting the impact of a bullet. —*v.t.* 2. to make bullet-proof.

bull-fight (bōōl'fit'), *n.* a traditional Spanish spectacle in which a bull is fought and killed by a matador —**bull'fight'er,** *n.* —**bull'fight'ing** *n*

bull-finch (bōōl'finch'), *n.* a European songbird with a rosy breast.

bull-frog (bōōl'frog' -frôg'), *n.* a large frog having a deep voice.

bull-head (bōōl'hed' *n.* a North American freshwater catfish.

bull-head-ed (bōōl'hed'id), *adj.* obstinate or stubborn. —**bull'head'ed-ness.** *n*

bull-horn (bōōl'hôrn'), *n.* a high-powered electrical loudspeaker or an electrical megaphone.

bul-lion (bōōl'yən), *n.* gold or silver in bars or ingots.

bull·ock (bŏŏl′ək), *n.* **1.** a castrated bull, as a steer. **2.** *Obs.* a young bull.

bull·pen (bŏŏl′pen′), *n.* **1.** *Informal.* a temporary detention room for prisoners. **2.** *Baseball.* a place where relief pitchers warm up during a game.

bull·ring (bŏŏl′rĭng′), *n.* a bullfight arena.

bull′ ses′sion, *Slang.* an informal, spontaneous group discussion.

bull′s-eye (bŏŏlz′ī′), *n.*, *pl.* **-eyes.** **1.** the circular spot at the center of a target. **2.** a shot that hits this.

bul·ly (bŏŏl′ē), *n.*, *pl.* **-lies,** *v.*, **-lied, -ly·ing,** *adj., interj.* **—n. 1.** a person who habitually intimidates smaller or weaker people. **—**v.t.*, *v.i.* **2.** to behave as a bully (toward). **—adj. 3.** *Informal.* excellent or very good. **—interj. 4.** *Informal.* well done!

bul′ly beef′, canned or pickled beef.

bul·rush (bŏŏl′rŭsh′), *n.* a tall grasslike plant growing in marshes.

bul·wark (bŏŏl′wərk, bŭl′-), *n.* **1.** a wall or rampart built for defense. **2.** any protection against external danger.

bum (bŭm), *n., v.,* **bummed, bum·ming,** *adj.,* **bum·mer, bum·mest. —n.** *Informal.* **1.** a shiftless person, esp. a tramp or hobo. **2.** *Slang.* an enthusiast of a recreational pastime: *a ski bum.* **3. on the bum, a.** living as a hobo. **b.** out of order. **—v.t. 4.** *Informal.* to borrow without expectation of returning. **—v.i. 5.** to live as a hobo. **—adj.** *Slang.* **6.** wretched or bad. **7.** false or misleading: *a bum steer.*

bum·ble·bee (bŭm′bəl bē′), *n.* any of various large, hairy social bees.

bum·bling (bŭm′blĭng), *adj.* incompetent or ineffectual.

bum·mer (bŭm′ər), *n. Slang.* **1.** a failure or mistake. **2.** an unpleasant experience of any kind, esp. with a hallucinogenic drug.

bump (bŭmp), *v.t., v.i.* **1.** to come violently in contact (with). **2.** to bounce along in jolts. **3. bump into,** *Informal.* to meet by chance. **4. bump off,** *Slang.* to kill. **—n. 5.** a collision or blow. **6.** a swelling from a blow. **7.** a small area higher than the surrounding surface. **—bump′y,** *adj.*

bump·er (bŭm′pər), *n.* **1.** a horizontal metal guard for protecting the front or rear of an automobile, etc. **2.** a cup or glass filled to the brim. **3.** something unusually large. **—adj. 4.** unusually abundant: *bumper crops.*

bump′er stick′er, a gummed paper strip bearing a printed slogan, advertisement, etc., for sticking on the bumper of a motor vehicle.

bump·kin (bŭmp′kĭn), *n.* an awkward, clumsy yokel. **—bump′kin·ish,** *adj.*

bump·tious (bŭmp′shəs), *adj.* offensively self-assertive. **—bump′tious·ly,** *adv.*

bun (bŭn), *n.* **1.** a bread roll, either plain or slightly sweetened. **2.** hair gathered into a round coil.

bunch (bŭnch), *n.* **1.** a connected group or cluster: *a bunch of grapes.* **2.** *Informal.* a group of people or things. **—v.t., v.i. 3.** to gather into a bunch. **—bunch′y,** *adj.*

bun·co (bŭng′kō), *n., pl.* **-cos.** *Informal.* a swindle or misrepresentation.

bun·combe (bŭng′kəm), *n.* bunkum.

bun·dle (bŭn′d ə l), *n., v.,* **-dled, -dling. —n. 1.** a quantity of material gathered or bound together. **2.** a package. **3.** *Slang.* a large amount of money. **—v.t. 4.** to tie or wrap in a bundle. **5.** to send away hurriedly: *They bundled her off to the country.* **—v.i. 6.** (esp. of sweethearts in early New England) to sleep or lie in the same bed while fully clothed. **7. bundle up,** to dress warmly. **—bun′dler,** *n.*

bung (bŭng), *n.* a stopper for the opening of a cask.

bun·ga·low (bŭng′gə lō′), *n.* **1.** a small house, esp. today at the seashore. **2.** (in India) a one-story house with a low-pitched roof.

bung·hole (bŭng′hōl′), *n.* a hole for filling or tapping a cask.

bun·gle (bŭng′gəl), *v.,* **-gled, -gling,** *n.* **—v.t., v.i. 1.** to do awkwardly or badly. **—n. 2.** something bungled. **—bun′gler,** *n.* **—Syn. 1.** botch, spoil.

bun·ion (bŭn′yən), *n.* a swelling on the foot caused by the inflammation of a bursa, esp. of the great toe.

bunk[1] (bŭngk), *n.* **1.** a built-in platform bed, as on a ship. **—v.i. 2.** to occupy a bunk. **—v.t. 3.** to furnish with a bunk.

bunk[2] (bŭngk), *n. Slang.* bunkum.

bunk·er (bŭng′kər), *n.* **1.** a large bin or box. **2.** *Golf.* any obstacle, as a mound of dirt, constituting a hazard. **3.** a fortification set mostly below the surface of the ground.

bunk·house (bŭngk′hous′), *n.* a rough building housing ranch hands, etc.

bun·ko (bŭng′kō), *n., pl.* **-kos.** bunco.

bun·kum (bŭng′kəm), *n.* insincere, empty talk. [after *Buncombe* (N.C. county)]

bun·ny (bŭn′ē), *n., pl.* **-nies.** *Informal.* a rabbit, esp. a young one.

Bun′sen burn′er (bŭn′sən), a gas burner commonly used in chemical laboratories. [after R. W. *Bunsen* (1811–99), Ger. chemist]

bunt (bunt), *v.t.*, *v.i.* **1.** (of a goat) to push with the horns or head **2.** *Baseball.* to bat (a pitched ball) very gently so that it does not roll far into the infield. —*n.* **3.** butt³. **4.** *Baseball.* **a.** the act of bunting. **b.** a bunted ball.

bun·ting (bun′ting), *n.* **1.** a coarse open fabric for flags, etc. **2.** flags collectively.

bun·ting² (bun′ting), *n.* a small, seed-eating, short billed finch.

bun·ting³ (bun′ting), *n.* a hooded sleeping garment for infants.

bu·oy (boo′ē boi), *n.* **1.** a marked float, anchored to mark a channel, anchorage etc. **2.** a ringlike life preserver. —*v.t.* **3.** to keep from sinking. **4.** to mark with a buoy. **5.** to sustain or encourage. *Her courage was buoyed up by the doctor's calmness.*

buoy·an·cy (boi′ən sē, boo′yən sē), *n.* **1.** the tendency to float in a fluid. **2.** the upward pressure exerted by the fluid in which an object is immersed. **3.** cheerfulness. —**buoy·ant**, *adj* —**buoy′ant·ly**, *adv*

bur (bûr), *n.* **1.** the rough, prickly case around the seeds of certain plants. **2.** any bur-bearing plant. **3.** burr (defs. 1, 2).

Bur., Burma.

bur., bureau.

bur·den¹ (bûr′d⁰n), *n.* **1.** something heavy that is carried **2.** something that is borne with difficulty. **3.** *Brit.* the carrying capacity of a ship. —*v.t.* **4.** to load heavily **5.** to oppress or trouble —**bur′den·some** *adj.*

bur·den² (bûr′d⁰n), *n* **1.** the principal idea. **2.** the refrain or chorus of a song.

bur·dock (bûr′dok), *n.* a coarse, broad-leaved weed bearing prickly heads of burs.

bu·reau (byoor′ō), *n.*, *pl.* **bu·reaus, bu·reaux** (byoor′ōz) **1.** a chest of drawers, often with a mirror at the top. **2.** a division of a government department. **3.** a business office or agency *a travel bureau*

bu·reauc·ra·cy (byoo rok′rə sē) *n.*, *pl.* **-cies. 1.** government characterized by a rigid hierarchy of bureaus, administrators, and petty officials **2.** a body of officials and administrators. **3.** administration characterized by excessive red tape and routine. —**bu·reau·crat** (byoor′ə krat′) *n.* —**bu′reau·crat′ic**, *adj.* —**bu′reau·crat′i·cal·ly**, *adv*

bu·reauc·ra·tize (byoo rok′rə tīz′), *v.t.*, *v.i.*, **-tized**, **-tiz·ing.** to make or become bureaucratic. —**bu·reauc′ra·ti·za′tion** *n*

bu·rette (byoo ret′), *n.* a graduated glass tube for measuring out small quantities of liquid. Also, **bu·ret′.**

burg (bûrg), *n. Informal.* a small, quiet city or town.

bur·gee (bûr′jē), *n.* a triangular or swallow-tail-shaped identification flag, used esp by yachts.

bur·geon (bûr′jən) *v.i.* **1.** to begin to put forth buds shoots, etc. **2.** to grow or develop suddenly.

burg·er (bûr′gər), *n. Informal.* a hamburger

bur·gess (bûr′jis), *n.* **1.** (formerly) a representative of a borough in the British Parliament. **2.** *Rare.* an inhabitant of an English borough.

burgh (bûrg) *n* (in Scotland) an incorporated town.

burgh·er (bûr′gər), *n.* a townsman, esp. a middle class citizen.

bur·glar (bûr′glər), *n.* a person who commits burglary.

bur·glar·ize (bûr′glə rīz′), *v.t.*, *v.i.*, **-ized**, **-iz·ing.** to commit burglary (in).

bur·glar·proof (bûr′glər proof′), *adj.* safeguarded against burglary.

bur·gla·ry (bûr′glə rē), *n.*, *pl.* **-ries.** the felony of breaking into and entering a building with intent to steal. —**bur·glar·i·ous** (bər glâr′ē əs), *adj.*

bur·gle (bûr′gəl), *v.t.*, *v.i.*, **-gled**, **-gling.** *Informal.* to burglarize.

bur·go·mas·ter (bûr′gə mas′tər, -mä′stər), *n* the chief magistrate of a municipal town of Holland, Flanders, Germany or Austria.

Bur·gun·dy (bûr′gən dē), *n.*, *pl.* **-dies. 1.** (*often l.c.*) any of various red or white table wines. **2.** (*l.c.*) a reddish-purple color.

bur·i·al (ber′ē əl), *n.* the act or ceremony of burying.

burl (bûrl), *n* a dome-shaped growth on the trunk of a tree, sliced to make veneer —**burled**, *adj.*

bur·lap (bûr′lap), *n.* a plain-woven, coarse fabric of jute or hemp for making bags

bur·lesque (bər lesk′), *n.*, *v.*, **-lesqued**, **-les·quing.** —*n* **1.** a ludicrous parody or grotesque caricature. **2.** a stage show featuring slapstick humor and striptease acts. —*v.t.*, *v.i.* **3.** to mock by burlesque.

bur·ley (bûr′lē) *n* *pl.* **-leys.** an American tobacco grown esp. in Kentucky and Ohio

bur·ly (bûr′lē), *adj.* **-li·er**, **-li·est. 1.** big and sturdy in bodily size. **2.** bluff or brusque —**bur′li·ness**, *n.*

Bur·ma (bûr′mə), *n.* a country in SE Asia. —**Bur·mese′** (-mēz′, -mēs′), *n.*, *adj.*

burn (bûrn), *v.*, **burned** or **burnt**, **burn·ing** *n* —*v.i* **1.** to be on fire. **2.** to feel heat or pain from or as from a fire. **3.** to glow brightly. **4.** to give off heat or be hot. **5.** to feel strong emotion. —*v.t.* **6.**

to cause to be consumed by fire. 7. to use as fuel or as a source of light. 8. to destroy by fire. 9. to redden (a person's skin). 10. to injure with or as with fire. 11. to produce (a hole, etc.) by fire. 12. to cause pain or a stinging sensation. 13. **burn down,** to burn to the ground. 14. **burn up,** *Slang* a. to incite to anger. b. to become angry. —*n.* 15. a burned place or area. 16. an injury caused by burning. 17. the process of burning. 18. a firing of an engine in spaceflight —**burn'a·ble,** *adj.*

burn·er (bûr'nər), *n.* 1. the part of a gas or electric fixture from which flame or heat issues. 2. a device for burning fuel: *a gas burner.*

bur·nish (bûr'nish), *v.t., v.i.* 1. to polish or become polished by friction. —*n.* 2. gloss or luster —**bur'nish·er,** *n.* —**bur'nish·ing,** *n., adj.*

bur·noose (bər nōōs', bûr'nōōs), *n.* a hooded cloak worn by Arabs. Also, **bur·nous'.**

burn·out (bûrn'out'), *n.* termination of the powered portion of a rocket's fight upon exhaustion of the propellant.

Burns (bûrnz), *n.* **Robert,** 1759–96, Scottish poet.

burnt (bûrnt), *v.* a pt. and pp. of **burn.**

burp (bûrp), *n.* 1. a belch. —*v.i.* 2. to belch. —*v.t.* 3. to help (esp. a baby) to belch.

burp' gun', a fully automatic pistol.

burr[1] (bûr), *n.* 1. a small, hand-held, power-driven milling cutter used for deepening, widening, etc. 2. a ragged metal edge raised on a surface in drilling, shearing, etc. 3. bur (defs. 1, 2). —*v.t.* 4. to form a rough edge on.

burr[2] (bûr), *n.* 1. a guttural pronunciation of the r-sound, as in certain Northern English dialects. 2. a whirring sound.

bur·ro (bûr'ō, bōōr'ō, bur'ō), *n., pl.* -**ros.** a small donkey used as a pack animal.

bur·row (bûr'ō, bur'ō), *n.* 1. a hole in the ground made by an animal, as for refuge. 2. any shelter or refuge. —*v.i.* 3. to make a burrow. 4. to lodge or hide in a burrow. 5. to proceed by or as if by digging. —*v.t.* 6. to put burrows into (a hill, etc.). 7. to make by or as by burrowing —**bur'row·er,** *n.*

bur·sa (bûr'sə), *n., pl.* -**sae** (-sē), -**sas.** a pouch or sac to facilitate motion, as between a tendon and a bone.

bur·sar (bûr'sər, -sär), *n.* a treasurer, esp. of a college or university.

bur·si·tis (bər sī'tis), *n.* inflammation of a bursa.

burst (bûrst), *v.,* **burst, burst·ing,** *n.* —*v.i.* 1. to break or fly apart with sudden violence. 2. to issue forth suddenly and forcibly. 3. to give sudden expression to or as to emotion. 4. to be extremely full: *The house was bursting with people.* 5. to become visible, audible, etc. —*v.t.* 6. to cause to burst. —*n.* 7. the act or an instance of bursting. 8. a sudden display of intense activity. 9. a sudden expression of emotion. 10. a group of shots fired.

Bu·run·di (bə run'dē, bōō rōōn'dē), *n.* a country in central Africa. —**Bu·run'di·an** *adj., n.*

bur·y (ber'ē) *v.t.,* **bur·ied, bur·y·ing.** 1. to put in the ground and cover with earth 2. to put (a corpse) in the ground or a grave 3. to cover in order to conceal from sight. 4. to immerse: *He buried himself in his work.*

bus (bus), *n., pl.* **bus·es, bus·ses,** *v.,* **bused** or **bussed, bus·ing** or **bus·sing.** —*n* 1. a large motor vehicle for passengers. —*v.t.* 2. to transport by bus. —*v.i.* 3. to travel by bus. 4. to work as a busboy. [(*omni*)*bus*]

bus., business.

bus·boy (bus'boi'), *n.* a waiter's helper who clears dishes, resets tables etc.

bus·by (buz'bē), *n. pl.* -**bies.** a tall bearskin hat worn by certain British guardsmen

bush (bōōsh) *n* 1. a low plant having many branches arising from or near the ground 2. something like a bush 3. a large uncleared area 4. **beat around** or **about the bush,** to avoid coming to the point —*v.i.* 5. to spread like a bush —**bush'y,** *adj.*

bushed (bōōsht) *adj Informal.* exhausted or tired out

bush·el (bōōsh'əl) *n* 1. a dry measure in the U S equal to 4 pecks or 2150.42 cubic inches 2. a liquid and dry measure in Great Britain, equal to 2219.36 cubic inches.

bush·ing (bōōsh'ing) *n* a lining for a hole to insulate and/or protect from abrasion conductors that pass through it

bush' league', *Slang.* a secondary baseball league. —**bush'-league',** *adj.* —**bush' lea'guer.**

bush·man (bōōsh'mən), *n., pl.* -**men.** 1. a dweller in the Australian bush. 2. (*cap.*) a member of a nomadic, racially distinct people of southern Africa.

bush·mas·ter (bōōsh'mas'tər, -mä'stər), *n.* a pit viper of tropical America that grows to a length of 12 feet.

bush·whack (boosh′hwak′, -wak′), v.i. 1. to make one's way through woods by cutting at undergrowth, branches, etc. —v.t. 2. to ambush. —bush′whack′er, n.

busi·ness (biz′nis), n. 1. a profit-seeking enterprise or concern. 2. an occupation, profession, or trade. 3. trade or patronage. 4. a person's principal concern. 5. affair or situation. 6. a task or duty. 7. **mean business**, to be serious in intent.

busi′ness col′lege, a school offering instruction in typing, bookkeeping, etc.

busi·ness·like (biz′nis līk′), adj. efficient, practical, or serious.

busi·ness·man (biz′nis man′), n., pl. **-men.** a man who engages in business or commerce. —busi′ness-wom′an, n.fem.

bus·ing (bus′ing), n. the transporting of pupils by bus to more distant schools, esp. as a compulsory integration measure. Also, **bus′-sing.**

bus·kin (bus′kin), n. 1. a high, thick-soled shoe worn in ancient tragedy. 2. Obs. tragic drama.

buss (bus), v.t., v.i., n. Informal. kiss.

bust[1] (bust), n. 1. a sculpture of the head and shoulders of a human subject. 2. the chest or breast, esp. a woman's bosom.

bust[2] (bust), Informal. —v.i. 1. to burst. 2. to go bankrupt. —v.t. 3. to burst. 4. to ruin financially. 5. to demote. 6. to tame or break. 7. to arrest. 8. to hit. —n. 9. a failure. 10. a hit or punch. 11. a spree or binge 12. a business depression. 13. an arrest.

bus·tle[1] (bus′əl), v.i., -tled, -tling, n. —v.i. 1. to move or act with a great show of energy. —n. 2. busy and energetic activity. —bus′tler, n.

bus·tle[2] (bus′əl), n. a pad or framework formerly worn by women to expand the back of a skirt.

bus·y (biz′ē), adj., bus·i·er, bus·i·est, v., bus·ied, bus·y·ing. —adj. 1. actively engaged in work. 2. not at leisure. 3. full of activity. 4. (of a telephone line) in temporary use. 5. officious or meddlesome. 6. ornate or fussy: a busy design. —v.t. 7. to keep occupied. —bus′i·ly, adv. —bus′y·ness, n. —Syn. 1. diligent, industrious. 2, 3. absorbed, engrossed.

bus·y·bod·y (biz′ē bod′ē), n., pl. **-bodies.** a person who meddles in the affairs of others.

bus·y·work (biz′ē wûrk′), n. active but valueless work.

but (but; unstressed bət), conj. 1. on the contrary or yet: My brother went, but I did not. 2. except or save: Overcome with grief, they could do nothing but weep. 3. unless, if not, or except that: Nothing would do but that I should come in. 4. without the circumstance that: It never rains but it pours. 5. otherwise than: There is no hope but by prayer. 6. that: I don't doubt but he will do it. 7. who or which not: No leader ever existed but he was an optimist. —prep. 8. with the exception of: No one replied but me. —adv. 9. only or just: There is but one God. 10. but for, except for. —n. 11. Often, **buts.** a restriction or objection.

—**Usage.** Many users of English regard BUT WHAT as informal (I have no doubt but what he'll protest), preferring BUT THAT (I have no doubt but that he'll protest) or THAT alone (I have no doubt that he'll protest).

bu·tane (byoo′tān, byoo tān′), n. a colorless, flammable gas used chiefly in the manufacture of rubber and fuel.

butch (booch), n. 1. a short haircut, like a crew cut. 2 Slang. a lesbian who assumes the dominant role.

butch·er (booch′ər), n. 1. a dealer in meat. 2. a person who slaughters or dresses animals or fish for food. 3. a person guilty of brutal murder. —v.t. 4. to slaughter or dress (animals or fish) for food. 5. to kill indiscriminately or brutally. 6. to bungle or botch: to butcher a job. —butch′er·y, n.

but·ler (but′lər), n. the chief male servant of a household.

butt[1] (but), n. 1. the end or extremity of anything, esp. the larger end: a rifle butt. 2. an unused end or remnant: a cigar butt. 3. Slang. a cigarette.

butt[2] (but), n. 1. an object of sarcasm, contempt, etc. 2. a target. —v.t., v.i. 3. to set end to end.

butt[3] (but), v.t., v.i. 1. to strike or push with the head or horns. 2. **butt in** or **into**, Slang. to intrude or meddle. —n. 3. a push or blow with the head or horns.

butt[4] (but), n. a large cask or barrel, esp. for wine, beer, or ale.

butte (byoot), n. an isolated hill having a flat top and rising abruptly.

but·ter (but′ər), n. 1. the fatty portion of milk, separating as a soft yellowish solid when milk is churned. 2. any substance like butter: peanut butter. —v.t. 3. to put butter on or in. 4. **butter up**, Informal. to flatter to gain a favor. —but′ter·y, adj.

but·ter-and-eggs (but′ər ən egz′), n. a perennial plant whose flowers are of two shades of yellow.

but·ter bean′, 1. See **lima bean. 2.** See **wax bean.**

but·ter·cup (but′ər kup′), *n.* a plant having red, white, or esp. yellow flowers.

but·ter·fat (but′ər fat′), *n.* the fatty constituent of milk, from which butter is made.

but·ter·fin·gers (but′ər fiñg′gerz), *n.*, *pl.* **-gers.** a person who is likely to drop things, as a clumsy person. —**but′ter·fin′gered,** *adj.*

but·ter·fish (but′ər fish′), *n.*, *pl.* **-fish·es, -fish.** a small, flattened, edible fish found off the Atlantic coast of the U.S.

but·ter·fly (but′ər flī′), *n.* any of numerous diurnal insects having a slender body and broad, often brightly marked wings.

but·ter·milk (but′ər milk′), *n.* the sour liquid remaining after the butter has been separated from milk or cream.

but·ter·nut (but′ər nut′), *n.* **1.** the edible oily nut of an American tree of the walnut family. **2.** the tree itself.

but·ter·scotch (but′ər skoch′), *n.* a flavoring or a hard, brittle taffy made with butter, brown sugar, etc.

butt′ joint′, a joint formed by two pieces of wood or metal united end to end without overlapping.

but·tock (but′ək), *n.* either of the two fleshy protuberances forming the lower and back part of the body trunk.

but·ton (but′ən), *n.* **1.** a small disk or knob for attaching to an article, as of clothing, serving as a fastener. **2.** anything resembling a button. **3.** a badge or emblem bearing a printed catchword for wear on the lapel: *campaign buttons.* **4.** on the button, *Informal.* exactly as desired or specified. —*v.t., v.i.* **5.** to fasten with a button or buttons.

but·ton-down (but′ən doun′), *adj.* **1.** having buttonholes on a collar so it can be fastened to the shirt. **2.** conventional or prosaic.

but·ton·hole (but′ən hōl′), *n., v.,* **-holed, -hol·ing.** —*n.* **1.** the hole or loop through which a button is passed. —*v.t.* **2.** to detain in conversation.

but·tress (bu′tris), *n.* **1.** a projecting support built into or against a wall. **2.** any prop or support. —*v.t.* **3.** to support or prop up.

bux·om (buk′səm), *adj.* **1.** shapely and full-bosomed. **2.** healthy, plump, and lively. —**bux′om·ness,** *n.*

buy (bī), *v.,* **bought, buy·ing,** *n.* —*v.t.* **1.** to acquire by paying an equivalent, esp. in money. **2.** to acquire by exchange or concession. **3.** to bribe. **4.** *Slang.* to accept or be-

lieve: *I don't buy that explanation.* —*v.i.* **5.** to be or become a purchaser. **6.** buy off, to bribe. **7.** buy out, to acquire all of the share or interest of. **8.** buy up, to purchase as much as one can of. —*n.* **9.** something bought. **10.** *Informal.* a bargain. —**Syn. 1.** procure, purchase.

buy·er (bī′ər), *n.* **1.** a person who buys or purchases. **2.** a purchasing agent, as for a retail store.

buy′ers′ mar′ket, a market in which goods and services are plentiful and prices relatively low.

buzz (buz), *n.* **1.** a low, vibrating, humming sound, as of bees. —*v.i.* **2.** to make such a sound. **3.** to whisper or murmur. **4.** to move busily or noisily. —*v.t.* **5.** to fly an airplane very low over. [imit.]

buz·zard (buz′ərd), *n.* **1.** a broad-winged, soaring hawk. **2.** See **turkey buzzard.**

buzz·er (buz′ər), *n.* a signaling apparatus similar to an electric bell, but producing a buzzing sound.

buzz′ saw′, a power-operated circular saw.

buzz·word (buz′ wûrd′), *n.* a word or phrase, sometimes sounding technical, that is a popular cliché of a particular group or field.

B.V., Blessed Virgin.

BW, black and white (as opposed to color).

bwa·na (bwä′nə), *n.* (in Africa) master or boss.

B.W.I., British West Indies.

BX, See **base exchange.**

bx., box.

by (bī), *prep., adv., n., pl.* **byes.** —*prep.* **1.** near to or next to: *an estate by a lake.* **2.** over, through, along, or using as a route: *She arrived by air.* **3.** on, as a means of conveyance: *They arrived by ship.* **4.** to and beyond: *The girl went by the church.* **5.** within the extent or time of: *by night.* **6.** at or before: *I finish work by five o'clock.* **7.** to the extent or amount of: *taller by three inches.* **8.** according to: *by his own account.* **9.** through the agency or authority of: *The document was distributed by a local group.* **10.** from the hand or mind of: *a poem by Keats.* **11.** on behalf of: *He did well by his children.* **12.** after: *little by little.* **13.** taken with (a certain number of) times or (of a shape longer than wide) the other dimension: *Multiply 18 by 57. The room was 10 feet by 12 feet.* **14.** using as a divisor. **15.** as a unit of measure: *Apples are sold by the bushel.* **16.** into, at, or to: *Drop by my office this afternoon.* —*adv.* **17.** near

or at hand: *The school is close by.*
18. past: *The car drove by.* **19.**
aside or away: *Put your work by.*
20. over: *in times gone by.* **21.**
by and by, before long or soon.
22. by and large, in general. —*n.* **23.**
bye. **24. by the by.** See **bye** (def. 2).
by-and-by (bī′ən bī′), *n.* the future.
bye (bī), *n.* **1.** the position of a
player not paired with a competitor in an early round and thus
automatically advanced to play in
the next round, as in a tournament.
2. by the bye, incidentally.
bye-bye (bī′bī′), *interj. Informal.*
goodby.
by-e·lec·tion (bī′i lek′shən), *n. Brit.*
a special election not held at the
time of a general election, to fill
a vacancy in Parliament. Also,
bye′-e·lec′tion.
Bye·lo·rus·sia (byel′ō rush′ə, bel′ō-),
n. a constituent republic of the
Soviet Union, in the W part.
Official name, **Byelorus′sian So′viet
So′cialist Repub′lic.** —**Bye′lo·rus′-
sian,** *adj., n.*
by·gone (bī′gôn′, -gon′), *adj.* **1.**
past or gone by. —*n.* **2. let bygones
be bygones,** to forget past disagree-
ments.
by·law (bī′lô′), *n.* a standing rule
governing a corporation's or
society's affairs. Also, **bye′law′.**
by·line (bī′līn′), *n.* a line accompanying a newspaper or magazine
article, giving the author's name.
—**by′lin′er,** *n.*

by·pass (bī′pas′, -päs′), *n.* **1.** a road
enabling motorists to avoid a city
or to drive around an obstruction.
—*v.t.* **2.** to avoid by following a bypass. **3.** to neglect to consult.
by·path (bī′path′, -päth′), *n.* a secondary or indirect path or road.
by·play (bī′plā′), *n.* an action carried on to the side while the main
action proceeds, esp. on the stage.
by·prod·uct (bī′prod′əkt), *n.* a secondary or incidental product, as in
a process of manufacture.
by·road (bī′rōd′), *n.* a secondary road.
By·ron (bī′rən), *n.* **George Gordon,
Lord,** 1788-1824, English poet. —**By·
ron′ic,** *adj.*
by·stand·er (bī′stan′dər), *n.* a person present but not involved.
by·street (bī′strēt′), *n.* a side street.
byte (bīt), *n.* a unit of information
for processing in certain kinds of
electronic computers, equal to one
character or eight bits [*bi*(*nary*) +
(*digi*)*t*, perh. infl. by *bite* to contrast
with *bit*]
by·way (bī′wā′), *n.* **1.** a secluded,
private road. **2.** a subsidiary or
obscure field of research, etc.
by·word (bī′wûrd′), *n.* **1.** a word
associated with some person or
idea. **2.** an object of general scorn.
3. *Obs.* a proverb.
Byz·an·tine (biz′ən tēn′, -tīn′, bi zan′-
tin), *adj.* **1.** of the Byzantine Empire
or its art, esp. its architecture style.
2. puzzlingly intricate.
Byz·an′tine Em′pire, an empire, A.D.
476-1453, in SE Europe and SW Asia.

C

C, c (sē), *n., pl.* **C's** or **Cs, c's** or
cs. the third letter of the English
alphabet, a consonant.
C, 1. Celsius. **2.** centigrade.
C, 1. the third in order or in a
series. **2.** a grade indicating fair or
average work. **3.** *Music.* the first
tone in the scale of C major.
4. (*sometimes l.c.*) the Roman
numeral for 100. **5.** capacitance.
6. carbon.
c, circa.
C., 1. Cape. **2** Catholic. **3.** Celsius.
4. Centigrade.
c., 1. cape. **2.** carat. **3.** *Baseball.*
catcher. **4.** cent; cents. **5.** *Football.* center. **6.** centigrade. **7.** centimeter. **8.** century. **9.** chapter.
10. church. **11.** circa. **12.** city.

13. college. **14.** copy. **15.** Also, ©.
copyright. **16.** corps. **17.** court.
18. cubic. **19.** cup. **20.** cycle.
CA, California.
Ca, calcium.
ca., circa.
C.A., 1. chartered accountant. **2.**
chief accountant. **3.** chronological
age.
cab (kab), *n.* **1.** a taxicab. **2.** the
enclosed part of a truck, crane,
etc., where the operator sits. **3.** a
horse-drawn vehicle, esp. one for
public hire.
CAB, Civil Aeronautics Board.
Also, **C.A.B.**
ca·bal (kə bal′), *n., v.,* **-balled, -bal-
ling.** —*n.* **1.** a small group of
plotters. —*v.i.* **2.** to form a cabal.

cab·a·la (kab′ə lə, kə bä′-), *n.* **1.** a system of esoteric theosophy developed by medieval rabbis. **2.** any occult doctrine or science.

ca·bal·le·ro (kab′əl yâr′ō, kab′ə-lâr′ō), *n., pl.* **ca′bal·le′ros.** **1.** a Spanish gentleman. **2.** *Southwestern U.S.* **a.** a horseman. **b.** a lady's escort.

ca·ban·a (kə ban′ə, -ban′yə), *n.* a small structure for use as a bathhouse at a beach.

cab·a·ret (kab′ə rā′), *n.* a large restaurant providing liquor and musical entertainment.

cab·bage (kab′ij), *n.* a vegetable having leaves formed into a compact, edible head. [< OF < L *caput* head]

cab·by (kab′ē), *n., pl.* **-bies.** *Informal.* a person who drives a cab. Also, **cab′bie.**

cab·in (kab′in), *n.* **1.** a small house or cottage, usually of simple design and construction. **2.** a stateroom in a ship. **3.** the enclosed space for the pilot, passengers, or cargo in an air or space vehicle.

cab′in boy′, a boy employed to wait on the officers and passengers on a ship.

cab′in class′, the class of accommodations on a passenger ship less costly and luxurious than first class but more so than tourist class.

cab′in cruis′er, a power-driven pleasure boat having a cabin equipped for living aboard.

cab·i·net (kab′ə nit), *n.* **1.** (*often cap.*) a council advising a sovereign, president, etc. **2.** a piece of furniture with shelves, drawers, etc., for holding or displaying objects. **3.** a box containing a radio or television set.

cab·i·net·mak·er (kab′ə nit mā′kər), *n.* a person who makes fine furniture, esp. cabinets, chests, etc. —**cab′i·net·mak′ing,** *n.*

cab·i·net·work (kab′ə nit wûrk′), *n.* fine woodwork, as cabinets or chests.

ca·ble (kā′bəl), *n., v.,* **-bled, -bling.** —*n.* **1.** a heavy, strong rope. **2.** an insulated electrical conductor, often in strands. **3.** cablegram. —*v.t., v.i.* **4.** to send a cablegram (to).

ca′ble car′, a vehicle moved on rails by an underground cable or suspended and pulled along an elevated cable.

ca·ble·gram (kā′bəl gram′), *n.* a telegram sent by underwater cable.

ca′ble TV′, a system offering television programs on channels other than those available over the air, by coaxial cable to paying subscribers.

cab·o·chon (kab′ə shon′), *n.* a precious stone of convex or oval form.

ca·boo·dle (kə bōōd′əl), *n. Informal.* the lot, pack, or crowd: *the whole caboodle.*

ca·boose (kə bōōs′), *n.* a car for the crew of a freight train, esp. when attached to the rear.

cab·ri·o·let (kab′rē ə lā′), *n.* **1.** a light, two-wheeled, one-horse carriage with a folding top. **2.** a former type of convertible coupe.

ca·ca·o (kə kā′ō, -kä′ō), *n., pl.* **-ca·os.** **1.** a small, evergreen tree of tropical America, cultivated for its seeds: the source of cocoa, chocolate, etc. **2.** Also called **caca′o bean′.** the fruit and seeds of this tree.

cac·cia·to·re (kä′chə tôr′ē, -tôr′ē), *adj.* prepared with tomatoes, mushrooms, herbs, etc.

cache (kash), *n., v.,* **cached, caching.** —*n.* **1.** a hiding place for provisions, treasures, etc. **2.** anything hidden or stored. —*v.t.* **3.** to put in a cache.

cache·pot (kash′pot′, -pō′), *n.* an ornamental container for holding a flowerpot.

ca·chet (ka shā′, kash′ā), *n.* **1.** an official seal, as in 18th-century France. **2.** a distinguishing mark. **3.** a sign or expression of approval. **4.** high standing. **5.** an inscription stamped or printed on mail. **6.** *Med.* a seal-shaped capsule.

cack·le (kak′əl), *v.,* **-led, -ling,** *n.* —*v.i.* **1.** to utter the shrill, broken sound of a hen. **2.** to laugh or chatter with such a sound. —*n.* **3.** the act or sound of cackling. —**cack′ler,** *n.*

ca·coph·o·ny (kə kof′ə nē), *n., pl.* **-nies.** harsh discordant sound. — **ca·coph′o·nous,** *adj.* —**ca·coph′o·nous·ly** *adv*

cac·tus (kak′təs), *n., pl.* **-tus·es, -ti** (-tī). a fleshy-stemmed desert plant, usually leafless and spiny, often producing showy flowers. —**cac′toid.** *adj*

cad (kad) *n.* a man who behaves crudely toward women. —**cad′dish,** *adj.* —**cad′dish·ly,** *adv.* —**cad′dish·ness,** *n.*

ca·dav·er (kə dav′ər), *n.* a dead body as for dissection. —**ca·dav′er·ic.** *adj*

ca·dav·er·ous (kə dav′ər əs), *adj.* **1.** of or like a corpse. **2.** pale or wan.

cad·die (kad′ē) *n., v.,* **-died -dy·ing.** *Golf* —*n* **1.** a person hired to carry a player's clubs, find the ball, etc. —*v i* **2.** to work as a caddie. Also **cad′dy.**

cad·dy (kad′ē) *n., pl.* **-dies.** *Chiefly Brit.* a small box, can, or chest: *a tea caddy.*

-cade, a suffix meaning "procession": *motorcade.*

ca·dence (kād′°ns), *n.* **1.** rhythmic flow of sounds in language. **2.** the general modulation of the voice. **3.** *Music.* a sequence of chords indicating the end of a composition. —ca′denced, *adj.*

ca·den·za (kə den′zə), *n.* an elaborate flourish or showy passage, as near the end of an aria.

ca·det (kə det′), *n.* **1.** a student in training at a service academy. **2.** *Brit.* a younger or youngest son of a noble family. —ca·det′ship′, *n.*

Ca·dette (kə det′), *n.* a member of the Girl Scouts from 12 through 14 years old.

cadge (kaj), *v.t., v.i.,* **cadged, cadg·ing.** to get (something) by begging or by sponging on another. —cadg′er, *n.*

cad·mi·um (kad′mē əm), *n. Chem.* a white, ductile metallic element, used in plating and in making alloys. Symbol: Cd; *at. wt.:* 112.41; *at. no.:* 48. —cad′mic, *adj.*

ca·dre (kā′drə; *Mil.* usually kad′rē), *n.* **1.** the key group of people needed to establish and train a new military unit. **2.** a cell of trained and devoted workers in communist countries. **3.** a member of a cadre.

ca·du·ce·us (kə dōō′sē əs, -dyōō′-), *n., pl.* **-ce·i** (-sē ī′). a staff with wings and two entwined snakes, used as an emblem of the medical profession.

cae·cum (sē′kəm), *n., pl.* **-ca** (-kə). cecum.

Cae·sar (sē′zər), *n.* **1.** a title of the Roman emperors after the reign of Julius Caesar. **2.** a tyrant or dictator. **3.** **Ga·ius** (gā′əs) **Jul·ius** (jōōl′yəs), c100–44 B.C., Roman general and statesman.

Cae·sar·e·an (si zâr′ē ən), *adj.* **1.** of Caesar. —*n.* **2.** (*sometimes l.c.*) Also called **Caesar′ean sec′tion.** the delivery of a baby by incision through the walls of the abdomen and uterus: so called because Julius Caesar was supposedly born this way. Also, **Cae·sar′i·an.**

Cae·sar·ism (sē′zə riz′əm), *n.* military despotism. —Cae′sar·ist, *n., adj.*

cae·si·um (sē′zē əm), *n.* cesium.

cae·su·ra (si zhōōr′ə, -zōōr′ə), *n., pl.* **cae·su·ras, cae·su·rae** (si zhōōr′ē, -zōōr′ē). a pause near the middle of a verse. —cae·su′ral, cae·su′ric, *adj.*

CAF, cost and freight.

ca·fé (ka fā′, kə-), *n.* **1.** a restaurant, usually unpretentious. **2.** a barroom, cabaret, or night club. Also, **ca·fe′.** [< F: lit., coffee]

ca·fé au lait (kaf′ā ō lā′, ka fā′), hot

coffee poured in equal portions with scalded milk.

caf·e·te·ri·a (kaf′i tēr′ē ə), *n.* a restaurant in which the patrons carry their food to their tables from service counters.

caf·feine (ka fēn′, kaf′ēn, kaf′ē in), *n.* a bitter alkaloid, usually obtained from coffee or tea: used chiefly as a stimulant and diuretic. Also, **caf′fein.**

caf·tan (kaf′tən, käf tän′), *n.* a long coatlike garment with wide sleeves, worn in the Middle East.

cage (kāj), *n., v.,* **caged, cag·ing.** —*n.* **1.** an enclosure having wires, bars, etc., for confining birds or animals. **2.** any enclosure like a cage in structure, as for a cashier, etc. —*v.t.* **3.** to put or confine in or as in a cage.

cage·ling (kāj′ling), *n.* a caged bird.

cag·er (kā′jər), *n. Informal.* a basketball player.

cage·y (kā′jē), *adj.* **cag·i·er, cag·i·est.** *Informal.* **1.** cautious not to be trapped or tricked. **2.** shrewd or cunning. Also, **cag′y.** —cag′i·ly, *adv.* —cag′i·ness, *n.*

ca·hoot (kə hōōt′), *n. Slang.* **in cahoot** or **cahoots, a.** in league. **b.** in conspiracy.

cai·man (kā′mən), *n., pl.* **-mans.** any of several tropical American crocodiles related to the alligators.

Cain (kān), *n.* **1.** the first son of Adam and Eve, who murdered his brother Abel. **2. raise Cain,** *Slang.* to cause a disturbance.

cairn (kârn), *n.* a heap of stones set up as a landmark, tombstone, etc.

Cai·ro (kī′rō), *n.* the capital of Egypt.

cais·son (kā′sən, -son), *n.* **1.** a structure used in underwater work, containing air under sufficient pressure to exclude the water. **2.** a two-wheeled ammunition wagon.

cais′son disease′, a condition marked by paralysis, pain, etc., developed in coming from an atmosphere of high pressure, as in a caisson, to air of ordinary pressure.

cai·tiff (kā′tif), *n. Archaic.* a base, despicable person.

ca·jole (kə jōl′), *v.t., v.i.,* **-joled, -jol·ing.** to persuade by flattery or promises. —ca·jole′ment, *n.* —ca·jol′er, *n.* —ca·jol′er·y, *n.* —Syn. coax, wheedle.

Ca·jun (kā′jən), *n. Dial.* a native of Louisiana originally descended from French immigrants from Acadia (now the Nova Scotia areas).

cake (kāk), *n., v.,* **caked, cak·ing.** —*n.* **1.** a sweet, baked, breadlike food, often covered with frosting. **2.** a flat, thin mass of fried or baked batter. **3.** a shaped mass: *a cake of soap.* **4. take the cake,** *Informal.* to surpass all others. —*v.t., v.i.* **5.** to form into a crust or compact mass. —**cak′y,** *adj.*

cake·walk (kāk′wôk′), *n.* a promenade of black American origin, in which the couples performing the most intricate steps receive cakes as prizes.

Cal., California.

cal., **1.** calendar. **2.** caliber. **3.** calorie.

cal·a·bash (kal′ə bash′), *n.* **1.** any of various gourd fruits. **2.** the shell of the calabash, used as a container.

cal·a·boose (kal′ə bōōs′, kal′ə bōōs′), *n. Informal.* a jail.

ca·la·di·um (kə lā′dē əm), *n.* an ornamental plant of tropical America, cultivated for its variegated, colorful leaves.

cal·a·mine (kal′ə mīn′, -min), *n.* a powder consisting of oxides of zinc and iron, used in skin lotions, etc.

ca·lam·i·ty (kə lam′i tē), *n., pl.* **-ties. 1.** grievous affliction or adversity. **2.** a great misfortune. —**ca·lam′i·tous,** *adj.* —**ca·lam′i·tous·ly,** *adv.* —**ca·lam′i·tous·ness,** *n.*

calc., calculate.

cal·car·e·ous (kal kâr′ē əs), *adj.* of, containing, or like calcium carbonate. —**cal·car′e·ous·ness,** *n.*

cal·cic (kal′sik), *adj.* of or containing lime or calcium.

cal·cif·er·ous (kal sif′ər əs), *adj.* containing calcium carbonate.

cal·ci·fy (kal′sə fī′), *v.t., v.i.,* **-fied, -fy·ing.** to make or become calcareous or bony. —**cal′ci·fi·ca′tion,** *n.*

cal·ci·mine (kal′sə mīn′, -min), *n., v.,* **-mined, -min·ing.** —*n.* **1.** a white or tinted wash for walls, ceilings, etc. —*v.t.* **2.** to wash or cover with calcimine.

cal·cine (kal′sīn, -sin), *v.t., v.i.,* **-cined, -cin·ing. 1.** to convert or be converted into an ashlike powder by heat. **2.** to oxidize by heating. —**cal′ci·na′tion,** *n.*

cal·cite (kal′sīt), *n.* one of the commonest minerals, calcium carbonate, a major constituent of limestone, marble, and chalk. —**cal·cit·ic** (kal sit′ik), *adj.*

cal·ci·um (kal′sē əm), *n. Chem.* a silver-white metal, occurring combined in limestone, chalk, gypsum, etc. *Symbol:* Ca; *at. wt.:* 40.08; *at. no.:* 20.

cal′cium car′bonate, a powder occurring in various forms, as calcite, chalk, and limestone: used chiefly in dentifrices, polishes, etc.

cal′cium hydrox′ide, a powder obtained by the action of water on lime, used in mortars, etc.

cal·cu·late (kal′kyə lāt′), *v.,* **-lat·ed, -lat·ing.** —*v.t.* **1.** to figure by using mathematics. **2.** to determine or estimate by reasoning or practical experience. **3.** to make fit for a purpose: *a remark calculated to inspire confidence.* —*v.i.* **4.** to make a computation. **5.** to count or rely. —**cal′cu·la·ble,** *adj.* —**cal′cu·la·bly,** *adv.* —**Syn. 1.** compute, estimate, reckon.

cal·cu·lat·ed (kal′kyə lā′tid), *adj.* carefully thought out or planned. —**cal′cu·lat′ed·ly,** *adv.*

cal·cu·lat·ing (kal′kyə lā′ting), *adj.* shrewd or selfishly scheming. —**cal′cu·lat′ing·ly,** *adv.*

cal·cu·la·tion (kal′kyə lā′shən), *n.* **1.** the act or process of calculating. **2.** the result or product of calculating. **3.** forethought or careful planning. —**cal′cu·la′tive,** *adj.*

cal·cu·la·tor (kal′kyə lā′tər), *n.* **1.** a person who calculates. **2.** Also called **cal′culating machine′.** a machine that performs mathematical operations.

cal·cu·lous (kal′kyə ləs), *adj.* characterized by the presence of stone.

cal·cu·lus (kal′kyə ləs), *n., pl.* **-li** (-lī′), **-lus·es. 1.** a method of calculation or reasoning by a special system of algebraic notations. **2.** a stone found in the gallbladder, kidneys, etc. [< L: pebble, small stone (used in calculating)]

Cal·cut·ta (kal kut′ə), *n.* a seaport in E India.

cal·de·ra (kal der′ə), *n.* a large, basinlike depression resulting from the explosion of the center of a volcano.

cal·dron (kôl′drən), *n.* cauldron.

cal·e·fa·cient (kal′ə fā′shənt), *adj.* providing heat or warmth.

cal·en·dar (kal′ən dər), *n.* **1.** a system of reckoning the beginning, length, and divisions of the year. **2.** a tabular arrangement of the days, weeks, and months in a year. **3.** a list or schedule of appointments, cases to be tried in a court, etc. —*v.t.* **4.** to enter in a calendar.

cal·en·der (kal′ən dər), *n.* **1.** a machine in which cloth or paper is smoothed or glazed by pressing between revolving cylinders. —*v.t.* **2.** to press in a calender.

cal·ends (kal′əndz), *n.* the first day of the month in the ancient Roman calendar.

ca·len·du·la (kə len′jə lə), *n.* a common marigold grown for its annual flowers.

calf[1] (kaf, käf), *n., pl.* **calves** (kavz, kävz). **1.** the young of the domestic cow or of other bovine animals. **2.** the young of certain other mammals, as the elephant or whale. **3.** calfskin leather.

calf² (kaf, käf), n., pl. calves (kavz, kävz). the fleshy part of the back of the human leg below the knee.

calf·skin (kaf′skin′, käf′-), n. 1. the skin or hide of a calf. 2. leather made from this skin.

Cal·ga·ry (kal′gə rē), n. a city in S Alberta, Canada.

cal·i·ber (kal′ə bər), n. 1. the diameter of something of circular section, esp. the inside of a tube. 2. the diameter of the bore of a gun or of a bullet, usually measured in hundredths of an inch and expressed as a decimal fraction: a .22-caliber pistol. 3. competence, merit, or importance. Also, esp. Brit., cal′ibre.

cal·i·brate (kal′ə brāt′), v.t., -brat·ed, -brat·ing. 1. to determine the caliber of. 2. to divide with gradations of degree, quantity, etc., as on a thermometer. —cal′i·bra′tion, n. —cal′i·bra′tor, n.

cal·i·co (kal′ə kō), n., pl. -coes, -cos, adj. —n. 1. a plain-woven cotton cloth printed with a figured pattern. —adj. spotted like calico: a calico cat.

Calif., California.

Cal·i·for·nia (kal′ə fôr′nyə, -fôr′nē ə), n. a state in the W United States, on the Pacific coast. Cap.: Sacramento. —Cal′i·for′nian, adj., n.

Cal′ifor′nia pop′py, an herb having showy, orange-yellow flowers.

cal·i·for·ni·um (kal′ə fôr′nē əm), n. Chem. a synthetic, radioactive, metallic element. Symbol: Cf; at no.: 98.

cal·i·per (kal′ə pər), n. 1. Usually, calipers. an instrument for measuring thicknesses and diameters, usually a pair of pivoted legs adjustable at any distance. —v.t., v.i. 2. to measure with calipers. Also, cal′li·per.

cal·iph (kal′if, kā′lif, kä lēf′), n. a leader of Islam, claiming succession from Muhammad. Also, cal′if. —cal′iph·ate′, n.

cal·is·then·ics (kal′is then′iks), n. gymnasic exercises for health. —cal′is·then′ic, adj.

calk (kôk), v.t. caulk.

call (kôl), v.t. 1. to cry out in a loud voice. 2. to rouse from sleep. 3. to telephone to. 4. to summon. 5. to proclaim or order. 6. to end (a contest) because of inclement weather. 7. to demand payment of (a loan). 8. to give a name to: The boys call him Tex. 9. to designate as something specified: He called me a liar. 10. to consider. 11. Cards. to demand of (a player) that his or her hand be shown. —v.i. 12. to shout. 13. to make a short visit. 14. to telephone a person. 15. to utter a characteristic cry. 16. call down, to reprimand. 17. call for, a. to fetch. b. to require. 18. call in, a. to request payment of. b. to ask for help. c. to inform by telephone. 19. call off, to cancel. 20. call up, a. to evoke. b. to communicate with by telephone. c. to summon for service. —n. 21. a cry or shout. 22. the cry of a bird or other animal. 23. a short visit. 24. a summons, invitation, or bidding. 25. a demand or claim. 26. the act or an instance of telephoning. 27. a demand for payment. 28. on call, available for duty. —call′er, n. —Syn. 4. convene, convoke.

cal·la (kal′ə), n. a plant, native to Africa, having a large white leaf enclosing a yellow spike. Also called cal′la lil′y.

call·back (kôl′bak′), n. recall (def. 9).

call·board (kôl′bôrd′, -bōrd′), n. a board on which notices are posted announcing rehearsals, etc., in a theater.

call′ girl′, a prostitute with whom an appointment can be arranged by telephone.

cal·lig·ra·phy (kə lig′rə fē), n. 1. the art of beautiful handwriting. 2. penmanship. —cal·lig′ra·pher, n. —cal·li·graph·ic (kal′ə graf′ik), adj.

call-in (kôl′in′), n. a telephone conversation, intended for broadcasting, between a host or hostess and a listener or viewer.

call·ing (kô′ling), n. 1. the act of a person or thing that calls. 2. vocation, profession, or occupation. 3. a strong impulse or inclination.

cal·li·o·pe (kə lī′ə pē, kal′ē ōp′), n. a musical instrument consisting of a set of harsh-sounding steam whistles.

call′ let′ters, the identifying letters and numbers of a broadcasting station.

call′ num′ber, a number assigned to a library book to indicate its specific location on the shelves.

cal·los·i·ty (kə los′i tē), n., pl. -ties. 1. a callous condition. 2. callus (def. 1).

cal·lous (kal′əs), adj. 1. thick and hardened, as skin. 2. insensitive or unsympathetic. 3. having a callus. —v.t., v.i. 4. to make or become callous. —cal′lous·ly, adv. —cal′lous·ness, n.

cal·low (kal′ō), adj. immature and inexperienced. —cal′low·ness, n.

call-up (kôl′up′), n. an order to report for active military service.

cal·lus (kal′əs), n., pl. -lus·es, v., -lused, -lus·ing. —n. 1. a hardened or thickened part of the skin. —v.i., v.t. 2. to form or cause to form a callus.

calm (käm), *adj.* **1.** without rough motion. **2.** not windy. **3.** tranquil or serene. —*n.* **4.** freedom from motion or disturbance. **5.** absence of wind. **6.** tranquility or serenity. —*v.t., v.i.* **7.** to make or become calm. —**calm′ly**, *adv.* —**calm′ness**, *n.* —**Syn. 3.** peaceful, placid, quiet, still.

cal·o·mel (kal′ə mel′, -məl), *n.* a white, tasteless powder used chiefly as a purgative and fungicide.

cal·lor·ic (kə lôr′ik, -lor′-), *adj.* **1.** of calories. **2.** of heat.

cal·o·rie (kal′ə rē), *n.* **1.** the amount of heat necessary to raise the temperature of one gram of water by 1°C (**small′ cal′orie**), or of one kilogram of water by 1°C (**large′ cal′orie**). **2.** a unit equal to the large calorie, used to express the heat output of an organism and the fuel or energy value of food. Also, **cal′o·ry.**

cal·o·rif·ic (kal′ə rif′ik), *adj.* pertaining to conversion into heat.

cal·o·rim·e·ter (kal′ə rim′i tər), *n.* an apparatus for measuring quantities of heat. —**cal·o·ri·met·ric** (kal′ər ə me′trik, kə lôr′-, -lor′-), *adj.* —**cal′o·ri·met′ri·cal·ly**, *adv.* —**cal′o·rim′e·try**, *n.*

cal·u·met (kal′yə met′, kal′yə met′), *n.* a long, ornamented tobacco pipe used by North American Indians on ceremonial occasions, esp. in token of peace.

ca·lum·ni·ate (kə lum′nē āt′), *v.t., -at·ed, -at·ing.* to make false and malicious statements about. —**ca·lum′ni·a′tion**, *n.* —**ca·lum′ni·a′tor**, *n.*

cal·um·ny (kal′əm nē), *n., pl.* **-nies.** a false and malicious statement to injure someone. —**ca·lum′ni·ous**, *adj.* —**ca·lum′ni·ous·ly**, *adv.*

Cal·va·ry (kal′və rē), *n.* the site outside ancient Jerusalem where Jesus was crucified.

calve (kav, käv), *v.i., v.t., calved, calv·ing.* to give birth to (a calf).

calves (kavz, kävz), *n. pl.* of **calf.**

Cal·vin (kal′vin), *n.* **John,** 1509–64, French Protestant theologian and reformer.

Cal·vin·ism (kal′və niz′əm), *n.* the doctrines and teachings of John Calvin or his followers, emphasizing predestination. —**Cal′vin·ist**, *n., adj.* —**Cal′vin·is′tic**, *adj.*

cal·vi·ti·es (kal vish′ē ēz′), *n.* baldness.

ca·lyp·so (kə lip′sō), *n., pl.* **-sos.** a topical ballad of West Indian origin.

ca·lyx (kā′liks, kal′iks), *n., pl.* **ca·lyx·es, ca·ly·ces** (kal′i sēz′, kā′li-). the outermost group of floral parts, usually green.

cam (kam), *n. Mach.* an irregularly shaped disk or cylinder that imparts a rocking motion to any contiguous part.

ca·ma·ra·de·rie (kä′mə rä′də rē), *n.* comradeship or good fellowship.

cam·ber (kam′bər), *v.t., v.i.* **1.** to arch slightly. —*n.* **2.** a slight arching, upward curve, or convexity.

cam·bi·um (kam′bē əm), *n., pl.* **-bi·ums, -bi·a** (bē ə). a layer of tissue between the inner bark and the wood, that produces all secondary growth in plants and is responsible for the annual rings of wood. —**cam′bi·al**, *adj.*

Cam·bo·di·a (kam bō′dē ə), *n.* a country in SE Asia. —**Cam·bo′di·an**, *adj., n.*

Cam·bri·an (kam′brē ən), *adj.* **1.** noting or pertaining to a period of the Paleozoic era, occurring 500–600 million years ago and characterized by the presence of algae and marine invertebrates. —*n.* **2.** the Cambrian period.

cam·bric (kām′brik), *n.* a thin cotton or linen fabric of fine close weave.

Cam·bridge (kām′brij), *n.* **1.** a city in E England. **2.** a city in E Massachusetts.

Cam·den (kam′dən), *n.* a port in SW New Jersey.

came (kām), *v.* pt. of **come.**

cam·el (kam′əl), *n.* a large, humped, cud-chewing mammal, used in Asian and Arabian deserts for carrying heavy loads. [< L *camēl(us)* < Gk *kāmēlos* < Sem, as Heb *gāmāl*]

cam·el·back (kam′al bak′), *n.* a compound of synthetic or reclaimed rubber for retreading tires.

ca·mel·lia (kə mēl′yə, -mē′lē ə), *n.* **1.** a woody plant having glossy evergreen leaves and waxy, roselike flowers. **2.** its flower. [after G. J. *Camellus* (1661–1706), Jesuit missionary, who brought it to Europe from Asia]

ca·mel·o·pard (kə mel′ə pärd′), *n. Obs.* a giraffe.

cam′el's hair′, 1. the hair of a camel or of a substitute. **2.** cloth made of this hair, sometimes mixed with wool.

Cam·em·bert (kam′əm bâr′), *n.* a mellow, soft cheese, with a creamy center. [after *Camembert,* village in France]

cam·e·o (kam′ē ō), *n., pl.* **cam·e·os**, *adj.* **1.** a gem or medallion engraved with a low-relief design against a background of contrasting color. **2.** a prominent bit role.

cam·er·a (kam′ər ə, kam′rə), *n.*, *pl.* **-er·as. 1.** a boxlike device having an aperture that, when opened, admits light enabling an object to be focused by means of a lens on a photosensitive film or plate, thereby producing a photographic image. **2.** *Television.* the device in which the picture to be transmitted is formed before it is changed into electric impulses. **3. in camera,** *Law.* privately.

cam·er·a·man (kam′ər ə man′, -mən, kam′rə-), *n.*, *pl.* **-men** (-men′, -mən). a person who operates a camera, esp. a motion-picture camera.

Cam·e·roon (kam′ə rōōn′), *n.* a country in W Africa. Also, **Cam·e·roun′.** —**Cam′e·roon′i·an,** **Cam′e·roun′i·an,** *adj., n.*

cam·i·sole (kam′i sōl′), *n.* a short garment worn underneath a sheer bodice.

cam·o·mile (kam′ə mīl′), *n.* a plant having strongly scented foliage and daisylike flowers that are used in medicine.

cam·ou·flage (kam′ə fläzh′), *n., v.,* **-flaged, -flag·ing.** —*n.* **1.** *Mil.* the disguising of things to deceive an enemy, as by painted patterns of foliage. **2.** disguise or deception. —*v.t., v.i.* **3.** to deceive by means of camouflage. —**cam′ou·flag′er,** *n.*

camp¹ (kamp), *n.* **1.** a place where a body of persons is lodged in tents or other temporary shelter. **2.** such tents or shelters collectively. **3.** the persons so sheltered. **4.** a group of persons favoring the same ideals, doctrines, etc. **5.** a recreation area in the country, equipped with extensive facilities for sports. **6. break camp,** to pack up and leave a campsite. —*v.i.* **7.** to establish or pitch a camp. **8.** to live temporarily in or as in a camp: *The boys will camp out for a week.* [< L *camp(us)* field]

camp² (kamp), *n.* **1.** pretentious gesture or style, esp. when amusing or when consciously contrived. —*adj.* **2.** campy.

cam·paign (kam pān′), *n.* **1.** a series of military operations for a specific objective. **2.** any systematic course of aggressive activities for some special purpose, esp. a commercial or political one. —*v.i.* **3.** to conduct a campaign. —**campaign′er,** *n.*

cam·pa·ni·le (kam′pə nē′lē), *n., pl.* **-ni·les, -ni·li** (-nē′lē). a bell tower, esp. one detached from the body of a church.

cam·pa·nol·o·gy (kam′pə nol′ə jē), *n.* the art of making bells, bell ringing, etc. —**cam′pa·nol′o·gist,** *n.*

camp′ chair′, a lightweight folding chair.

camp·craft (kamp′kraft′, -kräft′), *n.* the methods or techniques of outdoor camping.

camp·er (kam′pər), *n.* **1.** a person who camps out for recreation. **2.** a pickup truck with a roomlike addition over the truck bed, outfitted as temporary living quarters for use in camping.

camp·fire (kamp′fī°r′), *n.* **1.** an outdoor fire, as at a camp. **2.** a gathering around such a fire.

camp′fire girl′, a member of an organization (**Camp′ Fire Girls′,** Inc.) for girls aged 6–18.

camp′ fol′lower, a prostitute who follows an army or settles near an army camp.

camp·ground (kamp′ground′), *n.* a place for a camp or for a camp meeting.

cam·phor (kam′fər), *n.* an aromatic whitish compound used esp. as a moth repellent. —**cam·phor·ic** (kam·fôr′ik, -for′-), *adj.*

cam·pho·rate (kam′fə rāt′), *v.t.,* **-rat·ed, -rat·ing.** to impregnate with camphor. —**cam′phor·at′ed,** *adj.*

camp′ meet′ing, a religious gathering, usually for some days, in a tent.

camp·o·ree (kam′pə rē′), *n.* a small camp gathering of Boy Scouts, usually from a given district.

camp·site (kamp′sīt′), *n.* a place used or suitable for camping.

camp·stool (kamp′stōōl′), *n.* a lightweight folding seat.

cam·pus (kam′pəs), *n., pl.* **-pus·es.** the grounds, often including the buildings, of a college or other school.

camp·y (kam′pē), *adj.,* **camp·i·er, camp·i·est.** *Slang.* amusingly outlandish, affected, or theatrical. —**camp′i·ly,** *adj.* —**camp′i·ness,** *n.*

cam·shaft (kam′shaft′, -shäft′), *n.* a shaft bearing integral cams.

can¹ (kan; *unstressed* kən), *auxiliary v., past* **could. 1.** to be able to. **2.** to know how to. **3.** to have the power or means to. **4.** to have the right or qualifications to. **5.** may: *Can I speak to you a moment?*

can² (kan), *n., v.,* **canned, can·ning.** —*n.* **1. a.** a small container of thin metal in which foodstuffs are sealed for preservation. **b.** its contents. **2.** a receptacle for garbage, ashes, etc. **3.** *Slang.* jail. —*v.t.* **4.** to preserve by sealing in a can, jar, etc. **5.** *Slang.* to dismiss or fire. **6.** *Slang.* to stop. **7.** *Slang.* to record, as on tape. —**can′ner,** *n.*

Can., 1. Canada. **2.** Canadian.

can., 1. canceled. **2.** cancellation. **3.** canon. **4.** canto.

Ca·naan (kā′nən), *n.* the ancient region between the Jordan and the Mediterranean: the Promised Land. —**Ca′naan·ite′,** *n.*

Canad., Canadian.

Can·a·da (kan′ə də), *n.* a country in N North America. *Cap.:* Ottawa. —**Ca·na·di·an** (kə nā′dē ən), *adj., n.*

Can′ada goose′, a common wild goose of North America.

Cana′dian ba′con, bacon taken from a boned strip of pork loin.

Ca·na·di·an·ism (kə nā′dē ə niz′əm), *n.* a custom, trait, English usage, or thing peculiar to Canada or its citizens.

ca·naille (kə nāl′), *n.* riffraff or rabble.

ca·nal (kə nal′), *n.* **1.** an artificial waterway for navigation, irrigation, etc. **2.** a tubular passage or cavity, esp. in an animal or plant.

ca·nal·ize (kə nal′īz, kan′ə līz′), *v.t.,* **-ized, -iz·ing. 1.** to make a canal or canals through. **2.** to convert into a canal. —**ca·nal′i·za′tion,** *n.*

Canal′ Zone′, a zone in central Panama, on both sides of the Panama Canal.

can·a·pé (kan′ə pē, -pā′), *n.* a thin piece of bread, toast, etc., topped with appetizing food.

ca·nard (kə närd′), *n.* a false story or report, usually derogatory.

ca·nar·y (kə nâr′ē), *n., pl.* **-nar·ies. 1.** a yellow finch, native to the Canary Islands and often kept as a pet. **2.** a light, clear yellow. **3.** a sweet white wine resembling sherry.

Canar′y Is′lands, a group of Spanish islands near the NW coast of Africa.

ca·nas·ta (kə nas′tə), *n.* a variety of rummy played with two decks of cards plus four jokers.

Can·ber·ra (kan′ber ə, -bər ə), *n.* the capital of Australia.

canc., **1.** canceled. **2.** cancellation.

can·can (kan′kan′), *n.* an exhibition dance marked by high kicking.

can·cel (kan′səl), *v.,* **-celed, -cel·ing** or **-celled, -cel·ling,** *n.* —*v.t.* **1.** to call back or call off, as an appointment. **2.** to annul or make void. **3.** to mark or perforate (a postage stamp, admission ticket, etc.) to render it invalid for reuse. **4.** to neutralize or counterbalance. **5.** to eliminate or offset. **6.** to eliminate by striking out a factor common to both the denominator and numerator of a fraction, etc. —*n.* **7.** the act of canceling. **8.** *Print.* **a.** an omission. **b.** the replacement for an omitted part. —**can′cel·a·ble,** *adj.* —**can′cel·er,** *n.* —**can′cel·la′tion,** *n.*

can·cer (kan′sər), *n.* **1.** a malignant growth or tumor that tends to spread. **2.** any evil that spreads destructively. **3.** (*cap.*) the fourth sign of the zodiac. —**can′cer·ous,** *adj.* —**can′cer·ous·ly,** *adv.*

can·de·la·brum (kan′dᵊlä′brəm, -dᵊlä′-), *n., pl.* **-bra** (-brə), **-brums.** an ornamental branched holder for more than one candle. Also, **can′-de·la′bra.**

can·des·cent (kan des′ənt), *adj.* glowing, esp. with heat. —**can·des′cence,** *n.*

can·did (kan′did), *adj.* **1.** honest and direct. **2.** free from bias. **3.** informal or unposed: *a candid photo.* —**can′did·ly,** *adv.* —**can′did·ness,** *n.* —**Syn. 1.** frank, open, outspoken, truthful.

can·di·date (kan′di dāt′, -dit), *n.* a person who seeks or is nominated for an office, honor, etc. [< L *candidāt(us)* clothed in white (toga)] —**can′di·da·cy** (-də sē); *Brit.,* **can·di·da·ture** (kan′di də chər), *n.*

can·died (kan′dēd), *adj.* **1.** prepared by cooking in sugar or syrup. **2.** flattering or ingratiating.

can·dle (kan′dᵊl), *n., v.,* **-dled, -dling.** —*n.* **1.** a long, usually slender piece of tallow or wax with an embedded wick, burned to give light. —*v.t.* **2.** to examine (eggs) for freshness by holding them up to a bright light. —**can′dler,** *n.*

can·dle·light (kan′dᵊl līt′), *n.* **1.** the light of a candle. **2.** a dim artificial light. **3.** twilight or dusk.

Can·dle·mas (kan′dᵊl məs, -mas′), *n.* a religious festival, February 2, in honor of the presentation of the infant Jesus in the temple.

can·dle·pin (kan′dᵊl pin′), *n.* a bowling pin that is almost cylindrical, used in a game resembling tenpins.

can·dle·pow·er (kan′dᵊl pou′ər), *n.* luminous intensity of light: often used as a unit for its measurement.

can·dle·stick (kan′dᵊl stik′), *n.* a holder having a socket or a spike for a candle.

can·dle·wick (kan′dᵊl wik′), *n.* **1.** the wick of a candle. **2.** a fabric, esp. a bedspread, embroidered with tufts of soft, short yarn.

can·dor (kan′dər), *n.* **1.** honesty and directness. **2.** freedom from bias. Also, *esp. Brit.,* **can′dour.**

C. and W., *Music.* country and western.

can·dy (kan′dē), *n., pl.* **-dies,** *v.,* **-died, -dy·ing.** —*n.* **1.** a confection made with sugar, syrup, etc., combined with other ingredients. —*v.t.* **2.** to cook in sugar or syrup, as yams. **3.** to cook in heavy syrup until transparent, as fruit. **4.** to reduce to a crystalline form. **5.** to make pleasant or agreeable. [ME *sugre candy* candied sugar < MF *sucre candi* < Ar *qandī* of sugar]

can'dy strip'er, *Slang.* a young girl who works as a volunteer in a hospital.

cane (kān), *n., v.,* caned, can·ing. —*n.* **1.** a short stick, used as a support in walking. **2.** a long, jointed woody stem, as that of bamboo, etc. **3.** a plant having such a stem. **4.** split rattan, used for chair seats, etc. **5.** any rod used for flogging. —*v.t.* **6.** to flog with a cane. **7.** to make with cane: *to cane chairs.* —**can'er,** *n.*

cane·brake (kān'brāk'), *n.* a thicket of canes.

cane' sug'ar, sugar obtained from sugar cane.

ca·nine (kā'nīn, kə nīn'), *adj.* **1.** of or like a dog. **2.** of the four pointed teeth next to the incisors. —*n.* **3.** any animal of the dog family, including the wolves and foxes. **4.** a dog. **5.** a canine tooth.

can·is·ter (kan'i stər), *n.* **1.** a small box for holding tea, coffee, etc. **2.** a can of shot or fragments that explodes when fired from a cannon. **3.** the part of a gas mask containing the neutralizing filter.

can·ker (kang'kər), *n.* a gangrenous or ulcerous sore, esp. in the mouth. —**can'ker·ous,** *adj.*

can·ker·worm (kang'kər wûrm'), *n.* the larva of any of several moths, which destroys fruit and shade trees.

can·na (kan'ə), *n.* a tropical plant having large leaves and showy flowers.

can·na·bis (kan'ə bis), *n.* **1.** the hemp plant. **2.** the dried flowering parts of Indian hemp.

canned (kand), *adj.* **1.** preserved in a can or jar: *canned peaches.* **2.** *Slang.* recorded or taped: *canned music.*

can'nel coal' (kan'²l), an oily, compact coal, burning readily and brightly.

can·ner·y (kan'ə rē), *n., pl.* -ner·ies. a factory where foodstuffs are canned.

can·ni·bal (kan'ə bəl), *n.* **1.** a person who eats human flesh. **2.** any animal that eats its own kind. —*adj.* **3.** of cannibals. —**can'ni·bal·ism,** *n.* —**can'ni·bal·is'tic,** *adj.*

can·ni·bal·ize (kan'ə bə līz'), *v.t., v.i.,* -ized, -iz·ing. to take from one thing, as a part from a machine, for use on another. —**can'ni·bal·i·za'tion,** *n.*

can·non (kan'ən), *n., pl.* -nons, -non. **1.** a mounted gun for firing heavy projectiles. **2.** a large automatic gun on an aircraft. **3.** *Brit.* a carom in billiards.

can·non·ade (kan'ə nād'), *n., v.,* -ad·ed, -ad·ing. —*n.* **1.** a continued discharge of cannon. —*v.t., v.i.* **2.** to attack with or discharge cannon.

can·non·ball (kan'ən bôl'), *n.* **1.** a round missile designed to be fired from a cannon. **2.** *Informal.* to move with great rapidity.

can·non·eer (kan'ə nēr'), *n.* an artilleryman.

can·not (kan'ot, ka not', kə-), *v.* **1.** a negative form of can. **2.** cannot but, must.

can·nu·la (kan'yə lə), *n., pl.* -las, -lae (-lē'), a tube for insertion into the body, used to draw off fluid.

can·ny (kan'ē), *adj.,* -ni·er, -ni·est. **1.** careful and prudent. **2.** astute or shrewd. —**can'ni·ly,** *adv.* —**can'ni·ness,** *n.*

ca·noe (kə nōō'), *n., v.,* -noed, -noe·ing. —*n.* **1.** a slender, open boat propelled by paddles. —*v.i.* **2.** to paddle a canoe. **3.** to go in a canoe. —**ca·noe'ist,** *n.*

can·on¹ (kan'ən), *n.* **1.** a rule or law enacted by a church council. **2.** the body of church law. **3.** an accepted rule. **4.** a standard or criterion. **5.** the books of the Bible recognized as holy by any Christian church.

can·on² (kan'ən), *n.* a clergyman or clergywoman who is a member of a cathedral —**can'on·ry,** *n.*

ca·ñon (kan'yən), *n.* canyon.

ca·non·i·cal (kə non'i kəl), *adj.* **1.** pertaining to, established by, or conforming to a canon. **2.** authorized or accepted —*n* **3.** canonicals, garments prescribed by canon for officiating clergy —**ca·non'i·cal·ly** *adv* —**can·on·ic·i·ty** (kan'ə nis'i tē) *n.*

can·on·ize (kan'ə nīz'), *v.t.,* -ized, -iz·ing. **1.** to declare to be a saint. **2.** to glorify or exalt. —**can'on·i·za'tion** *n*

can'on law', the body of codified law governing a church.

can'on reg'ular. *pl.,* canons regular. *Rom Cath Ch* one of the members of certain religious orders.

can·o·py (kan'ə pē), *n., pl.* -pies, *v.,* -pied -py·ing —*n* **1.** a covering, usually of fabric suspended above a bed, throne etc. **2.** a covering from a doorway to the curb. —*v.t.* **3.** to cover with a canopy.

canst (kanst), *v. Archaic or Literary.* 2nd pers sing. pres of can.

cant¹ (kant), *n.* **1.** insincere statements esp pious platitudes **2.** the special language spoken by a particular class, profession, etc. **3.** monotonous songlike speech. —*v.i.* **4.** to use or speak in cant. —**cant'ing·ly,** *adv.*

cant² (kant), *n.* **1.** a salient angle. **2.** a slanting or tilted position. **3.** an oblique line or surface. —*v.t.*, *v.i.* **4.** to tilt or tip.

can't (kant, känt), contraction of *cannot.*

Cant., Cantonese.

can·ta·bi·le (kän tä′bi lā, -bē-, kən-), *adj., adv. Music.* songlike and flowing in style.

can·ta·loupe (kan′tə lōp′), *n.* **1.** a variety of melon having a hard, scaly, or warty rind. Also, **can′-ta·loup′.**

can·tan·ker·ous (kan tang′kər əs), *adj.* quarrelsome, grouchy, and irritable. —**can·tan′ker·ous·ly,** *adv.* —**can·tan′ker·ous·ness,** *n.*

can·ta·ta (kən tä′tə), *n.* a choral composition resembling a short oratorio.

can·teen (kan tēn′), *n.* **1.** a small container for carrying water. **2.** a place where free entertainment is provided for enlisted persons. **3.** a store, esp. one at a military base, selling refreshments, drugstore items, etc. [< F *cantine* < It *cantin(a)* cellar]

can·ter (kan′tər), *n.* **1.** an easy gallop. —*v.t.*, *v.i.* **2.** to ride at a canter.

Can′ter·bur·y bell′ (kan′tər ber′ē), a plant cultivated for its showy violet-blue, pink, or white flowers.

can·thar·i·des (kan thar′i dēz′), *n. pl., sing.* **can·tha·ris** (kan′thar′is). See **Spanish fly.**

can·thus (kan′thəs), *n., pl.* **-thi** (-thī). the corner on each side of the eye, formed by the junction of the upper and lower lids. —**can′thal,** *adj.*

can·ti·cle (kan′ti kəl), *n.* a liturgical hymn from the Bible, similar to a Psalm but not directly drawn from the Book of Psalms.

can·ti·lev·er (kan′tə lev′ər, -tə lē′vər), *n.* **1.** any rigid horizontal structural member projecting well beyond its vertical support, used as a structural element of a bridge, etc. —*v.t.* **2.** to construct by means of cantilevers. —**can′ti·le′vered,** *adj.*

can·tle (kan′təl), *n.* the hind part of a saddle.

can·to (kan′tō), *n., pl.* **-tos.** one of the main or larger divisions of a long poem.

can·ton (kan′tən, -ton, kan ton′ *for 1, 2;* kan ton′, -tōn′ *for 3*), *n.* **1.** a small territorial district, esp. one of the states of Switzerland. —*v.t.* **2.** to divide into cantons. **3.** to allot quarters to (soldiers, etc.). —**can′ton·al,** *adj.*

can·ton (kan′tən, -ton, kan ton′ *for 1,* kan′tən *for 2*), *n.* **1.** Western name of **Kwangchow. 2.** a city in NE Ohio.

Can·ton·ese (kan′tə nēz′, -tə nēs′), *n., pl.* **-ese. 1.** a Chinese language spoken in Canton, southern China, and Hong Kong. **2.** a native or inhabitant of Canton, China.

can·ton·ment (kan ton′mənt, -tōn′-), *n.* **1.** a camp where persons are trained for military service. **2.** military quarters.

can·tor (kan′tər, -tôr), *n.* the religious official of a synagogue who sings the prayers designed as solos.

can·vas (kan′vəs), *n.* **1.** a closely woven, heavy cloth used for tents, sails, etc. **2.** a piece of such material on which an oil painting is made. **3.** sailcloth. **4.** sails collectively. **5.** the floor of a boxing ring.

can·vas·back (kan′vəs bak′), *n., pl.* **-backs, -back.** a North American wild duck, the male of which has a whitish back.

can·vass (kan′vəs), *v.t.*, *v.i.* **1.** to solicit votes, sales, opinions, etc., from (a district, etc.). **2.** to discuss or debate. —*n.* **3.** a soliciting of votes, sales, etc. —**can′vass·er,** *n.*

can·yon (kan′yən), *n.* a deep valley with steep sides. [< Sp *cañón* a long tube, hollow]

caou·tchouc (kou′chŏŏk, kou chŏŏk′), *n.* rubber¹ (def. 1).

cap (kap), *n., v.,* **capped, cap·ping.** —*n.* **1.** a covering for the head, usually closefitting and having a visor. **2.** anything resembling a covering for the head in shape or use: *a cap on a bottle.* **3.** a noise-making device for toy pistols. —*v.t.* **4.** to provide with a cap. **5.** to complete. **6.** to surpass with something better.

CAP, Civil Air Patrol.

cap., **1.** capacity. **2.** capital. **3.** capitalize. **4.** capitalized.

ca·pa·ble (kā′pə bəl), *adj.* **1.** having the ability for satisfactory performance. **2.** **capable of, a.** qualified or fitted for. **b.** able to. —**ca′pa·bil′i·ty,** *n.* —**ca′pa·ble·ness,** *n.* —**ca′pa·bly,** *adv.*

ca·pa·cious (kə pā′shəs), *adj.* able to hold or contain much. —**ca·pa′cious·ly,** *adv.* —**ca·pa′cious·ness,** *n.*

ca·pac·i·tance (kə pas′i təns), *n.* **1.** the ratio of the charge on either of a pair of conductors of a capacitor to the potential difference between the conductors. **2.** the property of being able to collect a charge of electricity. —**ca·pac′-i·tive,** *adj.* —**ca·pac′i·tive·ly,** *adv.*

ca·pac·i·tate (kə pas′i tāt′), *v.t.*, **-tat·ed, -tat·ing.** to make capable. —**ca·pac′i·ta′tion,** *n.*

ca·pac·i·tor (kə pas′i tər), *n.* a device for accumulating and holding a charge of electricity, consisting of two conductors separated by a dielectric.

ca·pac·i·ty (kə pas′i tē), *n., pl.* **-ties,** *adj.* —*n.* **1.** the ability to receive or contain. **2.** cubic contents or volume. **3.** mental ability. **4.** ability to do something. **5.** position or relation. **6.** *Elect.* **a.** capacitance. **b.** maximum possible output. —*adj.* **7.** holding or packed to fullest capacity: *a capacity audience.*

cap′ and gown′, a mortarboard and gown worn as academic costume.

cap-a-pie (kap′ə pē′), *adv.* from head to foot. Also, **cap′-à-pie′.**

ca·par·i·son (kə par′i sən), *n.* **1.** a decorative covering for a horse. —*v.t.* **2.** to cover with a caparison.

cape¹ (kāp), *n.* a sleeveless garment fastened at the neck and falling loosely from the shoulders. —**caped,** *adj.*

cape² (kāp), *n.* **1.** a piece of land jutting into a large body of water. **2.** capeskin.

Cape′ Cod′, a rectangular one- or one-and-a-half-story house covered by a gable roof.

ca·per¹ (kā′pər), *v.i.* **1.** to leap or skip about in a sprightly manner. —*n.* **2.** a playful leap. **3.** a frivolous, carefree episode. **4.** *Slang.* a criminal act, as a robbery.

ca·per² (kā′pər), *n.* a shrub of Mediterranean regions whose flower bud is pickled and used for seasoning.

cape·skin (kāp′skin′), *n.* a light, pliable leather made from lambskin or sheepskin and used esp. for gloves.

Cape′ Town′, a seaport in and the legislative capital of the Republic of South Africa. Also, **Cape′town′.**

cap·ful (kap′fŏŏl′), *n.* the amount that a cap will hold.

cap·il·lar·i·ty (kap′ə lar′i tē), *n.* a manifestation of surface tension by which the portion of the surface of a liquid coming in contact with a solid is elevated or depressed. Also called **cap′illary ac′tion.**

cap·il·lar·y (kap′ə ler′ē), *n., pl.* **-lar·ies,** *adj.* —*n.* **1.** one of the minute blood vessels between the terminations of the arteries and the beginnings of the veins. —*adj.* **2.** of or occurring in a tube of fine bore. **3.** resembling hair in growth or shape. **4.** of or pertaining to capillaries or capillarity.

cap·i·tal¹ (kap′i təl), *n.* **1.** the city or town that is the official seat of government in a county, state, etc. **2.** a capital letter. **3.** the wealth, whether in money or property, accumulated by or employed in business. **4.** the net worth of a business.

5. an advantage or asset. **6.** capitalists as a group or class. —*adj.* **7.** pertaining to financial capital. **8.** highly important. **9.** chief, esp. as being the seat of government. **10.** excellent or first-rate. **11.** (of an alphabetical letter) of a form different from and higher than its corresponding lower-case letter. **12.** punishable by death: *a capital crime.* [< L *capitāl(is)* of the head]

cap·i·tal² (kap′i təl), *n. Archit.* the uppermost portion of a column.

cap′ital gain′, profit from the sale of capital assets, such as stocks.

cap′ital goods′, machines and tools used in the production of other goods.

cap·i·tal·ism (kap′i təliz′əm), *n.* an economic system in which investment in and ownership of production and distribution is made and maintained chiefly by private individuals or corporations.

cap·i·tal·ist (kap′i təlist), *n.* **1.** a person who has capital invested in business. **2.** an advocate of capitalism. **3.** a very wealthy person. —**cap′i·tal·is′tic,** *adj.* —**cap′i·tal·is′ti·cal·ly,** *adv.*

cap·i·tal·i·za·tion (kap′i təli zā′shən), *n.* **1.** the act or process of capitalizing. **2.** the total investment in a business.

cap·i·tal·ize (kap′i təlīz′), *v.t.,* **-ized, -iz·ing. 1.** to write or print in capital letters or with an initial capital. **2.** to convert into or utilize as financial capital. **3.** to supply with financial capital. **4.** to take advantage of.

cap′ital loss′, loss from the sale of capital assets, such as stocks.

cap·i·tal·ly (kap′i təlē), *adv.* **1.** excellently. **2.** in a manner involving capital punishment.

cap′ital pun′ishment, punishment by death for a crime.

cap′ital ship′, a large warship, such as a battleship or aircraft carrier.

cap′ital stock′, the total stock authorized or issued by a corporation.

cap·i·ta·tion (kap′i tā′shən), *n.* a tax levied against each person.

Cap·i·tol (kap′i təl), *n.* (*often l.c.*) a building occupied by a legislature.

Cap′itol Hill′, *Figurative.* U.S. Congress.

ca·pit·u·late (kə pich′ə lāt′), *v.i.,* **-lat·ed, -lat·ing. 1.** to surrender unconditionally or on stipulated terms. **2.** to give up resistance. —**ca·pit′u·la′tion,** *n.*

ca·pon (kā′pon, -pən), *n.* a rooster castrated to improve its flesh for use as food.

cap′ pis′tol, a toy gun using caps.

ca·pric·ci·o (kə prē′chē ō′), *n., pl.*

-ci·os. *Music.* a composition in a free, irregular style.

ca·price (kə prēs′), *n.* **1.** a sudden, unpredictable change. **2.** a tendency to change one's mind without motive. **3.** capriccio. —**ca·pri·cious** (kə prish′əs, -prē′shəs), *adj.* —**ca·pri′cious·ly,** *adv.* —**ca·pri′cious·ness,** *n.*

Cap·ri·corn (kap′rə kôrn′), *n.* the 10th sign of the zodiac. [< L: goat]

cap·ri·ole (kap′rē ōl′), *n.* **1.** a movement in which the horse jumps up with its forelegs drawn in and kicks out with its hind legs. **2.** a jump or leap.

caps., **1.** *Print.* capitals. **2.** capsule.

cap·si·cum (kap′sə kəm), *n.* any of various tropical plants, such as the red pepper, used for pickling or flavoring.

cap·size (kap′sīz, kap sīz′), *v.,* **-sized, -siz·ing.** —*v.i., v.t.* (of a boat) to overturn or upset.

cap·stan (kap′stən), *n.* **1.** a windlass, chiefly on ships, rotated in a horizontal plane, for winding in ropes, cables, etc. **2.** a spindle that rotates against a recording tape in motion.

cap·stone (kap′stōn′), *n.* a finishing stone of a structure.

cap·su·late (kap′sə lāt′), *adj.* enclosed in a capsule.

cap·sule (kap′səl), *n., v.,* **-suled, -sul·ing,** *adj.* —*n.* **1.** a gelatinous case enclosing a dose of medicine. **2.** a dry fruit composed of two or more carpels. **3.** a membranous sac or integument. **4.** a small pressurized cabin of a spacecraft. —*v.t.* **5.** to encapsulate. **6.** to summarize. —*adj.* **7.** compact or brief. —**cap′su·lar,** *adj.*

Capt., Captain.

cap·tain (kap′tən, -tin), *n.* **1.** a person in command of others. **2.** an army officer above a first lieutenant and below a major. **3.** a naval officer above a commander and below a rear admiral or a commodore. **4.** the pilot of an airplane. **5.** headwaiter. **6.** the master of a merchant vessel. **7.** the field leader of a sports team. —*v.t.* **8.** to lead as a captain. —**cap′tain·cy, cap′tain·ship,** *n.*

cap·tion (kap′shən), *n.* **1.** a legend for a picture or illustration. **2.** a subtitle on a motion picture. **3.** *Archaic.* a title, as of a chapter. —*v.t.* **4.** to supply a caption for.

cap·tious (kap′shəs), *adj.* **1.** exaggerating trivial defects. **2.** designed to ensnare or perplex. —**cap′tious·ly,** *adv.* —**cap′tious·ness,** *n.*

cap·ti·vate (kap′tə vāt′), *v.t.,* **-vat·ed, -vat·ing.** to enthrall or charm, as by beauty. —**cap′ti·va′tion,** *n.* —**cap′ti·va′tor,** *n.*

cap·tive (kap′tiv), *n.* **1.** a prisoner. **2.** a person who is captivated. —*adj.* **3.** held prisoner, esp. in war. **4.** kept in confinement or restraint. **5.** captivated. —**cap·tiv′i·ty,** *n.*

cap·tor (kap′tər), *n.* a person who captures.

cap·ture (kap′chər), *v.,* **-tured, -tur·ing,** *n.* —*v.t.* **1.** to take by force or stratagem. **2.** to preserve permanently. —*n.* **3.** the act or process of capturing. **4.** the thing or person captured.

Cap·u·chin (kap′yŏŏ chin, -shin), *n. Rom. Cath. Ch.* a friar belonging to a branch of the order of St. Francis engaged in missionary and social work.

car (kär), *n.* **1.** an automobile. **2.** a vehicle running on rails, as a streetcar. **3.** the part of an elevator, balloon, etc., that carries the passengers, freight, etc. [< AF < L *carra* < Celt]

car., carat.

ca·ra·ba·o (kär′ə bä′ō), *n.* (in the Philippines) the water buffalo.

car·a·bi·neer (kär′ə bə nēr′), *n.* carbineer. Also, **car′a·bi·nier′.**

Ca·ra·cas (kə rä′kəs), *n.* the capital of Venezuela.

car·a·cole (kar′ə kōl′), *n.* a half turn executed by a mounted horse.

car·a·cul (kar′ə kəl), *n.* karakul.

ca·rafe (kə raf′, -räf′), *n.* a bottle for holding water or other beverages.

car·a·mel (kar′ə məl, -mel′, kär′məl), *n.* **1.** burnt sugar, used for coloring and flavoring food. **2.** a chewy candy, made from sugar, butter, milk, etc.

car·a·mel·ize (kar′ə mə līz′), *v.t., v.i.,* **-ized, -iz·ing.** to convert or be converted into caramel.

car·a·pace (kar′ə pās′), *n.* a hard shell covering the back of an animal.

car·at (kar′ət), *n.* **1.** a unit of weight in gemstones, 200 milligrams. **2.** karat.

car·a·van (kar′ə van′), *n.* **1.** a group of travelers banded together for safety in journeying through deserts, etc. **2.** any group, as of vehicles, traveling in a file. **3.** a vehicular van. [< It *carovan(a)* < Pers *kārwān*]

car·a·van·sa·ry (kar′ə van′sə rē), *n., pl.* **-ries.** (in the Near East) an inn for caravans. Also, **car′a·van′se·rai** (-rī′).

car·a·vel (kar′ə vel′), *n.* a small Spanish or Portuguese sailing vessel of the 15th-16th centuries.

car·a·way (kar′ə wā′), *n.* an aromatic herb, the seedlike fruit of which is used in cooking and medicine.

car′ bed′, a portable basketlike crib for use esp. in an automobile.

car·bide (kär′bīd, -bid), *n.* a compound of carbon with another element or group.

car·bine (kär′bīn, -bēn), *n.* **1.** a light, gas-operated, semiautomatic rifle. **2.** (formerly) a short rifle used in the cavalry.

car·bi·neer (kär′bə nēr′), *n.* (formerly) a cavalry soldier armed with a carbine.

carbo-, a combining form meaning "carbon": *carbohydrate*.

car·bo·hy·drate (kär′bō hī′drāt, -bə-), *n.* any of a class of organic compounds composed of carbon, hydrogen, and oxygen, including starches and sugars.

car·bo·lat·ed (kär′bə lā′tid), *adj.* containing carbolic acid.

car·bol′ic ac′id (kär bol′ik), phenol.

car·bon (kär′bən), *n.* **1.** *Chem.* an element that forms organic compounds in combination with hydrogen, oxygen, etc., and that occurs in a pure state as the diamond and as graphite, and in an impure state as charcoal. *Symbol:* C; *at. wt.:* 12.011; *at. no.:* 6. **2.** a sheet of carbon paper. **3.** Also called **car′bon cop′y.** a duplicate made by using carbon paper. —**car′bon·less,** *adj.*

carbon 12, a stable isotope of carbon that comprises 99 percent of naturally occurring carbon.

carbon 14, radiocarbon.

car·bo·na·ceous (kär′bə nā′shəs), *adj.* of, like, or containing carbon.

car·bon·ate (*n.* kär′bə nāt′, -nit; *v.* kär′bə nāt′), *n., v.,* -at·ed, -at·ing. —*n.* **1.** a salt or ester of carbonic acid. —*v.t.* **2.** to charge or impregnate with carbon dioxide. —**car′bon·a′tion,** *n.* —**car′bon·a′tor,** *n.*

car′bon black′, any of various finely divided forms of amorphous carbon used in pigments, etc.

car·bon-date (kär′bən dāt′), *v.t.,* -dat·ed, -dat·ing. to estimate the age of (objects) by means of the radioactivity of the carbon content. —**car′bon dat′ing.**

car′bon diox′ide, an incombustible gas present in the atmosphere and formed during respiration: used in carbonated beverages, fire extinguishers, etc.

car·bon′ic ac′id (kär bon′ik), the acid formed when carbon dioxide dissolves in water.

Car·bon·if·er·ous (kär′bə nif′ər əs), *adj.* **1.** of or noting a period of the Paleozoic era, from 270 million to 350 million years ago. **2.** (*l.c.*) producing carbon or coal. —*n.* **3.** the Carboniferous period.

car′bon monox′ide, an odorless, poisonous, flammable gas produced when carbon burns with insufficient air.

car′bon pa′per, a paper coated with a pigmented material, used between two sheets of plain paper to reproduce on the lower sheet that which is written on the upper.

car′bon tet′ra·chlo′ride, (te′trə klōr′īd, -id, -klôr′-), a nonflammable, vaporous, toxic liquid, used as a fire extinguisher, cleaning fluid, etc.

Car·bo·run·dum (kär′bə run′dəm), *n. Trademark.* an abrasive of carbon, silicon, and other materials.

car·boy (kär′boi), *n.* a large bottle protected by basketwork, used esp. for corrosive liquids.

car·bun·cle (kär′bung kəl), *n.* a painful inflammation of the skin tissue, resulting in a boil, somewhat like a boil. —**car·bun·cu·lar** (kär·bung′kyə lər), *adj.*

car·bu·re·tor (kär′bə rā′tər, -byə-), *n.* a device for mixing vaporized fuel with air to produce an explosive mixture, as for an internal-combustion engine.

car·bu·rize (kär′bə rīz′, -byə-), *v.t.,* -rized, -riz·ing. to cause to unite with carbon. —**car′bu·ri·za′tion,** *n.*

car·cass (kär′kəs), *n.* **1.** the dead body of an animal. **2.** a framework or basic structure.

car·cin·o·gen (kär sin′ə jən), *n.* a substance that tends to produce a cancer. —**car·cin·o·gen′ic** (kär′sə nō jen′ik), *adj.* —**car·ci·no·ge·nic·i·ty** (kär′sə nō jə nis′i tē), *n.*

car·ci·no·ma (kär′sə nō′mə), *n., pl.* -mas, -ma·ta (-mə tə). a malignant tumor made up chiefly of epithelial cells. —**car′ci·no′ma·tous,** *adj.*

car′ coat′, a hip-length overcoat for informal wear.

card[1] (kärd), *n.* **1.** a piece of stiff paper or thin pasteboard, for various uses. **2.** one of a set of small cardboards used in playing various games. **3. cards, a.** a game played with such a set. **b.** the playing of such a game. **4.** a piece of paper or thin cardboard, printed with a message of holiday greeting, congratulations, etc. **5.** postcard. **6.** a program of the events at races, boxing matches, etc. **7.** *Informal.* a person who is amusing. **8. put one's cards on the table,** to conceal nothing. —*v.t.* **9.** to provide with a card. **10.** to fasten on a card. **11.** to write or list on cards.

card[2] (kärd), *n.* **1.** a machine for combing fibers of cotton, flax, wool, etc. **2.** a similar implement for raising the nap on cloth. —*v.t.* **3.** to dress (wool or the like) with a card. —**card′er,** *n.*

Card., Cardinal.

car·da·mom (kär′də məm), *n.* **1.** the aromatic seed capsule of a plant native to tropical Asia, used as a spice or condiment and in medicine. **2.** its plant

card·board (kärd′bōrd′, -bôrd′), *n.* a thin, stiff pasteboard, used for signs, boxes, etc

card-car·ry·ing (kärd′kar′ē iṅg), *adj.* admittedly belonging to a group or party.

card′ cat′alog, a file of cards in alphabetical sequence listing the items in a library collection.

car·di·ac (kär′dē ak′), *adj.* **1.** pertaining to the heart. **2.** pertaining to heart disease.

car·di·gan (kär′də gən), *n.* a knitted jacket or sweater collarless and open in front [after Earl of *Cardigan* (1797-1868), British hero in Crimean War]

car·di·nal (kär′dən°l), *n.* **1.** Rom. Cath. Ch a high official appointed by the pope and standing next in rank. **2.** a crested grosbeak of North America, the male of which is bright red. **3.** a deep rich red. —*adj.* **4.** of prime importance **5.** of the color cardinal. —**car′di·nal·ly**, *adv.*

car·di·nal·ate (kär′dən°lāt′), *n.* Rom. Cath Ch. **1.** the body of cardinals **2.** the office or dignity of a cardinal

car′dinal flow′er, a North American plant with showy red flowers.

car·di·nal·i·ty (kär′də nal′i tē), *n., pl.* **-ties.** the condition of being able to be represented by a cardinal number

car′dinal num′ber, a number that expresses amount, as *1, 2, 3,* etc.

car′dinal points′, the four chief directions of the compass (north, south, east and west).

cardio-, a combining form meaning "heart" *cardiogram*.

car·di·o·gram (kär′dē ə gram′), *n.* electrocardiogram

car·di·o·graph (kär′dē ə graf′, -gräf′), *n.* electrocardiograph —**car·di·o·graph·ic** (kär′dē ə graf′ik) *adj.* —

car·di·og·ra·phy (kär′dē og′rə fē), *n.*

car·di·ol·o·gy (kär′dē ol′ə jə) *n* the study of the heart and its functions in health and disease —**car·di·o·log·ic** (kär′dē ə loj′ik), **car·di·o·log′i·cal**, *adj* —**car′di·ol′o·gist**, *n.*

car·di·o·pul·mo·nar·y (kär′dē ō pul′mə ner′ē -pool′-), *adj.* of or for the heart and lungs

car·di·o·vas·cu·lar (kär′dē ō vas′kyə lər), *adj* of or affecting the heart and blood vessels.

card·sharp (kärd′shärp′), *n.* a person who cheats at card games. Also, **card′sharp′er**.

care (kâr), *n. v., cared, car·ing.* —*n.* **1.** an uneasy state of mind as arising from burdens or anxiety. **2.** a cause or object of this **3.** close or serious attention **4.** protection, charge or supervision **5.** care of, at the following address **6.** take care, to be careful or alert **7.** take care of, a. to watch over b. to attend to —*v.i* **8.** to be concerned or solicitous **8.** to look out Will *you care for the children while I am away* **10.** to have an inclination, liking fondness or affection. —*v.t.* **11.** to feel concern about: He *doesn't care what others say.* **12.** to desire or want Do *you care to have a drink* —**car′er,** *n* —**Syn. 1.** concern solicitude worry

CARE (kâr Cooperative for American Relief Everywhere.

ca·reen (kə rēn′) *v.t., v.i.* to lean or cause to lean over to one side. —**ca·reen′er** *n*

ca·reer (kə rēr′) *n.* **1.** progress of a person through life as in some profession **2.** an occupation followed as one's lifework. —*v.i.* **3.** to go at full speed .

care·free (kâr′frē′ *adj* **1.** without worry **2.** requiring little care, esp. in laundering *carefree fabrics.*

care·ful (kâr′təl) *adj* **1.** cautious in one's actions **2.** done with accuracy or caution —**care′ful·ly**, *adv.* —**care′ful·ness** *n* —Syn. **1.** circumspect prudent wary.

care·less (kâr′lis) *adj* **1.** not paying enough attention to what one does. **2.** not exact or thorough **3.** done or said heedlessly **4.** having no care or concern —**care′less·ly**, *adv.* —**care′less·ness** *n* —Syn. heedless inadvertent neglectful.

ca·ress (kə res′) *n.* **1.** a gentle stroking of a kiss or embrace —*v.t.* **2.** to touch or stroke gently with affection —**ca·ress′er,** *n.*

car·et (kar′it) *n* a mark (∧) made in written or printed matter to show where something is to be inserted. [< L (there) is lacking]

care·tak·er (kâr′tā′kər) *n.* **1.** a person in charge of the maintenance of a building estate etc **2.** a person or group that temporarily performs the duties of an office.

care·worn (kâr′wôrn′, -wôrn′), *adj.* showing signs of care or worry.

car·fare (kär′fâr′), *n.* the amount charged for a ride on a bus, streetcar, etc

car·go (kär′gō), *n., pl.* **-goes, -gos.** the load carried by a ship, airplane etc comprising freight, express. and mail.

car·hop (kär′hop′), *n.* a waiter or waitress at a drive-in restaurant.

Car·ib·be·an (kar′ə bē′ən, kə rib′ē-), *n.* **1.** Also called **Car′ibbe′an Sea′.** the sea between the West Indies and Central and South America. —*adj.* **2.** of the Caribbean Sea and its islands.

car·i·bou (kar′ə bōō′), *n., pl.* **-bous, -bou.** a large, North American deer related to the reindeer of the Old World. [< CanF < Algonquian *khalibu*]

car·i·ca·ture (kar′ə kə chər, -chŏŏr′), *n., v.,* **-tured, -tur·ing.** —*n.* **1.** a picture, description, etc., ludicrously exaggerating the peculiarities of persons or things. **2.** any imitation so inferior as to be ludicrous. —*v.t.* **3.** to make a caricature of. —**car′i·ca·tur′ist,** *n.*

car·ies (kâr′ēz, -ē ēz), *n., pl.* **-ies.** decay, as of bone or teeth.

car·il·lon (kar′ə lon′, -lən), *n.* a set of stationary bells in a tower, sounded mainly by keyboard.

car·il·lon·neur (kar′ə lə nûr′), *n.* a person who plays a carillon.

ca·ri·na (kə rī′nə, -rē′-), *n., pl.* **-nas, -nae** (-nē). *Bot., Zool.* a keellike part or ridge.

car·i·ous (kâr′ē əs), *adj.* having caries.

car·load (kär′lōd′), *n.* the amount carried by a car, esp. a freight car.

car·min·a·tive (kär min′ə tiv, kär′mə nā′tiv), *adj.* **1.** expelling gas from the body. —*n.* **2.** a carminative drug.

car·mine (kär′min, -mīn), *n.* a crimson or purplish red.

car·nage (kär′nij), *n.* the slaughter of many people, as in battle.

car·nal (kär′n°l), *adj.* **1.** of the body or flesh. **2.** sensual or sexual: *carnal pleasures.* —**car·nal′i·ty,** *n.* —**car′nal·ly,** *adv.* —**Syn. 1.** earthly, temporal, worldly.

car·na·tion (kär nā′shən), *n.* **1.** a cultivated plant having fragrant flowers of various colors. **2.** its flower.

car·nau·ba (kär nou′bə), *n.* a wax derived from the young leaves of a Brazilian tree, used esp. as a polish.

car·nel·ian (kär nēl′yən), *n.* a red or reddish variety of chalcedony, used in jewelry.

car·ni·val (kär′nə vəl), *n.* **1.** a traveling amusement show, having sideshows, merry-go-rounds, etc. **2.** any merrymaking, revelry, or festival. **3.** the season of merrymaking preceding Lent. [< It *carnevale(e)*, OIt *carnelevare* taking meat away]

car·ni·vore (kär′nə vōr′, -vôr′), *n.* any chiefly flesh-eating mammal of an order comprising dogs, cats, bears, seals, etc.

car·niv·o·rous (kär niv′ər əs), *adj.* **1.** flesh-eating. **2.** of the carnivores. —**car·niv′o·rous·ly,** *adv.* —**car·niv′o·rous·ness,** *n.*

car·ny (kär′nē), *n., pl.* **-nies.** *Informal.* **1.** a person employed by a carnival. **2.** carnival (def. 1).

car·ol (kar′əl), *n., v.,* **-oled, -ol·ing** or **-olled, -ol·ling.** —*n.* **1.** a song, esp. of joy. **2.** a Christmas song or hymn. —*v.i., v.t.* **3.** to sing joyously. —**car′ol·er, car′ol·ler,** *n.*

car·om (kar′əm), *n.* **1.** *Billards, Pool.* a shot in which the cue ball hits two balls in succession. **2.** any strike and rebound. —*v.i.* **3.** to make a carom. **4.** to strike and rebound.

car·o·tene (kar′ə tēn′), *n.* any of three isomeric red hydrocarbons found in many plants, esp. carrots, and transformed to vitamin A in the liver.

ca·rot·id (kə rot′id), *n.* either of the two large arteries, one on each side of the head, that carry blood to the head. —**ca·rot′id·al,** *adj.*

ca·rous·al (kə rou′zəl), *n.* a noisy or drunken feast.

ca·rouse (kə rouz′), *n., v.,* **-roused, -rous·ing.** —*n.* **1.** carousal. —*v.i.* **2.** to engage in a drunken revel. —**ca·rous′er,** *n.*

car·ou·sel (kar′ə sel′, -zel′; kar′ə sel′, -zel′), *n.* carrousel.

carp[1] (kärp), *v.i.* to find fault unreasonably. —**carp′er,** *n.*

carp[2] (kärp), *n., pl.* **carp** or **carps.** a large, freshwater food fish.

car·pal (kär′pəl), *adj.* **1.** pertaining to the carpus. —*n.* **2.** a carpal bone.

car·pe di·em (kär′pe dē′em), *Latin.* enjoy the present. [lit., seize the day]

car·pel (kär′pəl), *n.* a simple pistil regarded as a modified leaf.

car·pen·ter (kär′pən tər), *n.* a person who builds or repairs wooden structures. —**car′pen·try,** *n.*

car·pet (kär′pit), *n.* **1.** a heavy fabric for covering floors. **2.** any covering like a carpet. **3. on the carpet,** before an authority for a reprimand. —*v.t.* **4.** to cover with a carpet.

car·pet·bag (kär′pit bag′), *n., v.,* **-bagged, -bag·ging.** —*n.* **1.** a bag for traveling, esp. one made of carpeting. —*v.i.* **2.** to act as a carpetbagger.

car·pet·bag·ger (kär′pit bag′ər), *n.* a Northerner who went to the South seeking private gain after the Civil War. —**car′pet·bag′ger·y,** *n.*

car·pet·ing (kär′pi ting), *n.* **1.** material for carpets. **2.** carpets in general.

car′ pool′, an arrangement among automobile owners by which each in turn drives the others to and from work.

car·port (kär′pōrt′, -pôrt′), *n.* a simple roof projecting from the side of a building for sheltering an automobile.

car·pus (kär′pəs), *n., pl.* **-pi** (-pī). 1. the wrist. 2. the wrist bones collectively.

car·ra·geen·in (kar′ə gēn′in), *n.* a substance extracted from seaweed, chiefly used as an emulsifying ingredient in foods, cosmetics, etc.

car·rel (kar′əl), *n.* a small recess in a library stack, for individual study.

car·riage (kar′ij), *n.* 1. a wheeled vehicle for passengers, esp. one drawn by horses. 2. a movable part, as of a machine: *the carriage of a typewriter.* 3. the manner of carrying the head and body. 4. *Chiefly Brit.* transportation or conveyance.

car′riage trade′, wealthy patrons of a store.

car·ri·er (kar′ē ər), *n.* 1. a person or thing that carries. 2. See **aircraft carrier.** 3. See **common carrier.** 4. an individual harboring specific pathogenic organisms who may transmit the disease to others. 5. Also called **car′rier wave′.** the radio wave whose amplitude, frequency, or phase is to be varied or modulated to transmit a signal.

car′rier pig′eon, a homing pigeon trained to carry messages.

car·ri·on (kar′ē ən), *n.* dead and putrefying flesh.

car·rot (kar′ət), *n.* 1. a plant widely cultivated for its edible orange root. 2. its root. —**car′rot·y,** *adj.*

car·rou·sel (kar′ə sel′, -zel′; kar′ə-sel′, -zel′), *n.* merry-go-round (def. 1).

car·ry (kar′ē), *v.,* **-ried, -ry·ing,** *n., pl.* **-ries.** —*v.t.* 1. to move while supporting or holding. 2. to wear or hold. 3. to serve as a medium for the transmission of. 4. to put forward or transfer. 5. to bear the weight, burden, etc., of. 6. to bear or sustain. 7. to hold (the body, head, etc.) in a certain manner. 8. to secure the adoption of (a motion or bill). 9. to get a majority of votes in (a district). 10. to bring or communicate, as news. 11. to lead or influence. 12. to convey or conduct. 13. to have as an attribute, consequence, etc. 14. to keep on hand or in stock. 15. to keep on one's account books. —*v.i.* 16. to act as a bearer. 17. to be transmitted or sustained. 18. **carry away,** to influence greatly or unreasonably. 19. **carry on, a.** to manage or conduct. **b.** to behave in an agitated or indiscreet manner. **c.** to continue without stopping. 20. **carry out, a.** to put into operation. **b.** to complete. 21. **carry over, a.** to postpone. **b.** to be left. 22. **carry through,** to complete. —*n.* 23. range, as of a gun. 24. portage.

car·ry·all¹ (kar′ē ôl′), *n.* 1. a light, four-wheeled, covered carriage for four persons. 2. a passenger automobile having two facing benches running the length of the body.

car·ry·all² (kar′ē ôl′), *n.* a large basket, bag, etc.

car′rying charge′, 1. a charge made for paying for goods by installments. 2. cost incurred while an asset is unproductive.

car·ry·on (kar′ē on′, -ôn′), *adj.* 1. suitable for being kept with an airplane passenger during flight. —*n.* 2. a piece of carry-on luggage.

car·ry·out (kar′ē out′), *adj.* take-out.

car·ry·o·ver (kar′ē ō′vər), *n.* something carried over, as to a later time.

car·sick (kär′sik′), *adj.* ill with a feeling of nausea resulting from the motion of the car in which one is traveling. —**car′sick′ness,** *n.*

Car′son Cit′y (kär′sən), the capital of Nevada.

cart (kärt), *n.* 1. a two-wheeled vehicle drawn by a horse, ox, etc. 2. any small vehicle. —*v.t., v.i.* 3. to carry in a cart. —**cart′a·ble,** *adj.* —**cart′er,** *n.*

cart·age (kär′tij), *n.* the act or cost of carting.

carte blanche (kärt′ blanch′, blänch′), *pl.* **cartes blanches** (kärts′ blanch′, blänch′). full discretionary power.

car·tel (kär tel′, kär′tl), *n.* an international combine formed to regulate prices and output in some field of business.

Car·ter (kär′tər), *n.* **Jim·my** (jim′ē) (*James Earl, Jr.*), born 1924, 39th president of the U.S., since 1977.

Car·te·sian (kär tē′zhən), *adj.* of Descartes or his mathematical methods or philosophy. —**Carte′-sian·ism,** *n.*

Carte′sian coor′dinates, *Math.* a system of coordinates for locating a point on a plane by its distance from each of two perpendicular intersecting lines, or in space by its distance from each of three mutually perpendicular planes intersecting at a point.

car·ti·lage (kär′təlij, kärt′lij), *n.* a firm, elastic, flexible type of connective tissue. —**car·ti·lag·i·nous** (kär′təlaj′ə nəs), *adj.*

car·tog·ra·phy (kär tog′rə fē), *n.* the production of maps. —**car·tog′ra·pher,** *n.* —**car·to·graph·ic** (kär′tə-graf′ik), *adj.*

car·ton (kär′tən), *n.* a large cardboard box.

car·toon (kär tōōn′), *n.* **1.** a drawing caricaturing some action or subject. **2.** See **comic strip. 3.** See **animated cartoon. 4.** a preliminary full-scale drawing, as for a fresco. —*v.t., v.i.* **5.** to draw a cartoon (of). —**car·toon′ist,** *n.*

car·top (kär′top′), *adj.* that can be carried on the top of an automobile.

car·tridge (kär′trij), *n.* **1.** a cylindrical case for holding a complete charge of powder for a firearm. **2.** a small container for ready insertion into some mechanism: *a typewriter-ribbon cartridge.* **3.** a lightproof container for a roll of film. **4.** a flat, compact container enclosing an endless loop of audio tape: playable by slipping into a slot in a player. **5.** pickup (def. 4).

cart·wheel (kärt′hwēl′, -wēl′), *n.* **1.** the wheel of a cart. **2.** a handspring done to the side. **3.** *Slang.* any large coin.

carve (kärv), *v.*, **carved, carv·ing.** —*v.t.* **1.** to cut so as to form something. **2.** to form by cutting: *to carve a statue out of stone.* **3.** to decorate with designs cut on the surface. **4.** to cut into slices, as meat. —*v.i.* **5.** to form designs by cutting. **6.** to cut meat. —**carv′er,** *n.* —**carv′ing,** *n.*

car·wash (kär′wosh, -wôsh), *n.* a place having special equipment for washing automobiles.

car·y·at·id (kar′ē at′id), *n., pl.* **-ids, -i·des** (-i dēz′). *Archit.* a sculptured female figure used as a column.

ca·sa·ba (kə sä′bə), *n.* a winter muskmelon, having a yellow rind and sweet, juicy flesh. [after *Kassaba,* Turkey, which exported it]

Ca·sa·blan·ca (kä′sä bläng′kä, kas′ə-bläng′kə), *n.* a seaport in NW Morocco.

Cas·a·no·va (kaz′ə nō′və, kas′-), *n.* **1.** Gio·van·ni (jō vän′nē), 1725–98, Italian amorous adventurer and writer. **2.** a man known for his amorous adventures.

cas·cade (kas kād′), *n., v.,* **-cad·ed, -cad·ing.** —*n.* **1.** a waterfall over a steep, rocky surface. **2.** a series of shallow waterfalls, either natural or artificial. —*v.i., v.t.* **3.** to fall or cause to fall in or like a cascade.

cas·car·a (kas kâr′ə), *n.* **1.** a thorny shrub of the Pacific coast of the U.S. **2.** a laxative made from its dried bark.

case¹ (kās), *n.* **1.** a specific instance or example. **2.** the actual state of things. **3.** situation, condition, or plight. **4.** a person or thing whose plight or situation calls for attention. **5.** a state of things requiring discussion, decision, or investigation. **6.** a statement of facts, etc., to support an argument. **7.** an instance of disease, injury, etc. **8.** a patient. **9.** a suit or action at law. **10.** a category in the inflection of nouns or pronouns, noting their syntactic relation to other words. **11. in any case,** anyhow. **12. in case,** if. **13. in case of,** in the event of. **14. in no case,** never.

case² (kās), *n., v.,* **cased, cas·ing.** —*n.* **1.** a container for something, as for carrying, safekeeping, etc.: *a jewel case.* **2.** an outer covering. **3.** a pair or couple. **4.** a surrounding framework, as of a door. **5.** *Print.* a tray divided into compartments for holding types. —*v.t.* **6.** to put or enclose in a case. **7.** *Slang.* to examine (a bank, etc.) in planning a crime.

case·hard·en (kās′här′dᵊn), *v.t.* to harden the outside of (an alloy) by carburizing and heat treatment.

case′ his′tory, a record of information about an individual, family, etc.

ca·sein (kā′sēn, -sē in, kā sēn′), *n.* a protein precipitated from milk, forming the basis of cheese and certain plastics, paints, etc.

case·load (kās′lōd′), *n.* the number of cases handled by a court, a social worker, etc.

case·ment (kās′mənt), *n.* **1.** a window sash opening on hinges. **2.** a window with such a sash or sashes. **3.** a covering.

case·work (kās′wûrk′), *n.* a close study and treatment by a social worker of an individual or family. —**case′work′er,** *n.*

cash (kash), *n.* **1.** money in the form of coins or banknotes. **2.** money or an equivalent, as a check, paid at the time of making a purchase. —*v.t.* **3.** to give or obtain cash for (a check, etc.). **4. cash in, a.** to turn into ready money. **b.** to withdraw from a business agreement.

cash′ dis′count, a term of sale by which the purchaser deducts a percentage if payment is made within a stipulated period.

cash·ew (kash′ōō, kə shōō′), *n.* **1.** a tropical American tree that bears kidney-shaped, edible nuts. **2.** its nut.

cash·ier¹ (ka shēr′), *n.* **1.** an employee, as in a store, etc., who collects payments for purchases, etc. **2.** an executive who has charge of monetary transactions, as in a bank.

cash·ier² (ka shēr′), *v.t.* to dismiss (a military officer), esp. with disgrace.

cashier's' check', a check drawn by a bank on its own funds and signed by its cashier.

cash·mere (kazh′mēr, kash′-), *n.* **1.** fine, downy wool from goats of N India. **2.** a fabric made from this wool.

cash' reg'ister, a business machine that records and totals receipts and has a money drawer.

cas·ing (kā′sing), *n.* **1.** a framework, as around a door. **2.** the outer covering of an automobile tire. **3.** the skin of a sausage or salami.

ca·si·no (kə sē′nō), *n.*, *pl.* **-nos. 1.** a place, usually licensed, with facilities for gambling. **2.** Also, **cas·si·no.** a card game for two, three, or four players.

cask (kask, käsk), *n.* **1.** a container resembling a barrel but larger and stronger. **2.** its contents.

cas·ket (kas′kit, kä′skit), *n.* **1.** a coffin, esp. an expensive one. **2.** *Brit.* a small box, as for jewels.

Cas'pi·an Sea' (kas′pē ən), a salt lake between SE Europe and Asia.

casque (kask), *n.* an open, conical helmet with a nose guard.

Cas·san·dra (kə san′drə), *n.* **1.** *Class. Myth.* a prophetess cursed by Apollo so that her prophecies, though true, were fated never to be believed. **2.** a person who prophesies disaster.

cas·sa·va (kə sä′və), *n.* **1.** a tropical plant cultivated for its starchy edible root. **2.** a starch from the root, the source of tapioca.

cas·se·role (kas′ə rōl′), *n.* **1.** a baking dish of glass, pottery, etc., usually with a cover. **2.** food cooked in such a dish.

cas·sette (ka set′, kə-), *n.* **1.** a compact case enclosing audio tape that runs between two reels: recordable or playable by pushing into a holder in a recorder or player. **2.** cartridge (def. 3).

cas·sia (kash′ə, kas′ē ə), *n.* **1.** a variety of cinnamon derived from a tropical Asian tree. **2.** an ornamental tropical tree having long pods whose pulp is a mild laxative.

cas·sit·er·ite (kə sit′ə rīt′), *n.* a common mineral that is the principal ore of tin.

cas·sock (kas′ək), *n.* a long garment worn by members of the clergy.

cas·so·war·y (kas′ə wer′ē), *n.*, *pl.* **-war·ies.** a large, flightless bird resembling the ostrich.

cast (kast, käst), *v.*, **cast**, **cast·ing**, *n.* —*v.t.* **1.** to throw, as esp. a light object. **2.** to direct (the eye, glance, etc.). **3.** to send forth: *to cast a soft light.* **4.** to shed or drop (hair, fruit, etc.). **5.** to deposit (a ballot or vote). **6.** to select (performers) for (a play or role). **7.** to form (an object) by pouring into a mold. **8.** to compute, as a column of figures. —*v.i.* **9.** to throw or hurl. **10. cast about,** to look. **11. cast aside** or **away,** to reject or discard. **12. cast off, a.** to abandon or disown. **b.** to let go, as a vessel from a mooring. **c.** to estimate the space the text will occupy when set in type. **13. cast up,** to add up or total. —*n.* **14.** act of casting or throwing. **15.** something thrown off or out. **16.** a throw of dice. **17.** the performers in a play or motion picture. **18.** something formed from a material poured into a mold. **19.** a rigid surgical dressing, usually made of plaster of Paris. **20.** sort, kind, or style. **21.** a permanent twist or turn: *to have a cast in one's eye.* **22.** a hue or shade.

cas·ta·net (kas′tə net′), *n.* either of a pair of concave pieces of wood held in the hand and clicked together, usually to accompany dancing.

cast·a·way (kast′ə wā′, käst′-), *n.* **1.** a shipwrecked person. **2.** an outcast. —*adj.* **3.** cast adrift. **4.** thrown away.

caste (kast, käst), *n.* **1. a.** a hereditary social group limited to persons of the same rank, occupation, etc. **b.** any rigid system of social distinctions. **2.** any of the four hereditary divisions into which Hindu society is traditionally divided. **3.** social position: *to lose caste.*

cas·tel·lan (kas′t°lən, ka stel′ən), *n.* the governor of a feudal castle.

cas·tel·lat·ed (kas′t°lā′tid), *adj.* built like a castle, esp. with battlements.

cast·er (kas′tər, kä′stər), *n.* **1.** a person or thing that casts. **2.** a small wheel on a swivel, set under a piece of furniture, etc., to facilitate moving it. **3.** a cruet or shaker for condiments. Also, **cas·tor** (for defs. 2, 3).

cas·ti·gate (kas′tə gāt′), *v.t.*, **-gat·ed**, **-gat·ing.** to punish or criticize severely. —**cas′ti·ga′tion**, *n.* —**cas′ti·ga′tor**, *n.*

cast·ing (kas′ting, kä′sting), *n.* **1.** something thrown off. **2.** any article cast in a mold. **3.** the selection of actors or actresses, as in a play.

cast'ing vote', a deciding vote of a presiding officer made when the other votes are equally divided.

cast' i′ron, an alloy of iron, carbon, and other elements, cast as a hard, brittle iron.

cas·tle (kas′əl, kä′səl), *n., v.,* **-tled, -tling.** —*n.* **1.** a fortified residence, as of a noble in feudal times. **2.** a strongly fortified stronghold. **3.** *Chess.* the rook. —*v.i. Chess.* **4.** to move the king two squares laterally and bring the appropriate rook to the first square the king has passed over. [< L *castell(um)* stronghold]

cas′tle in the air′, a fanciful, impracticable plan.

cast·off (kast′ôf′, -of′, käst′-), *adj.* **1.** thrown away or discarded. —*n.* **2.** a person or thing that has been cast off.

cas·tor oil′ (kas′tər, kä′stər), a colorless to pale-yellow oil obtained from the bean of a tropical plant: used as a lubricant, cathartic, etc.

cas·trate (kas′trāt), *v.t.,* **-trat·ed, -trat·ing.** to remove the testes of. —**cas·tra′tion,** *n.* —**cas′tra·tor,** *n.*

cas·u·al (kazh′ᴏᴏ əl), *adj.* **1.** happening by chance. **2.** offhand or cursory. **3.** seeming to be indifferent. **4.** (of clothes) informal. **5.** occasional. —**cas′u·al·ly,** *adv.* —**cas′u·al·ness,** *n.*

cas·u·al·ty (kazh′ᴏᴏ əl tē), *n., pl.* **-ties. 1.** a military person lost through death, wounds, capture, or because his or her whereabouts are unknown. **2.** a person injured or killed in an accident. **3.** a severe accident.

cas·u·ist (kazh′ᴏᴏ ist), *n.* an oversubtle or disingenuous reasoner. —**cas′u·is′tic, cas′u·is′ti·cal,** *adj.* —**cas′u·ist·ry,** *n.*

ca·sus bel·li (kā′səs bel′ī). *Latin.* an event that causes war.

cat (kat), *n.* **1.** a domesticated carnivore, popular as a pet, bred in a number of varieties. **2.** any related carnivore, as the lion, tiger, jaguar, etc. **3.** *Informal.* a spiteful or malicious woman. **4.** *Slang.* **a.** any person. **b.** a devotee of jazz. **5.** a cat-o′-nine-tails. **6. let the cat out of the bag,** to divulge a secret.

CAT, clear air turbulence.

cat., catalog; catalogue.

ca·tab·o·lism (kə tab′ə liz′əm), *n.* the metabolic breaking down of more complex substances into simpler ones. —**cat·a·bol·ic** (kat′ə-bol′ik), *adj.* —**cat′a·bol′i·cal·ly,** *adv.*

cat·a·clysm (kat′ə kliz′əm), *n.* any violent upheaval. —**cat′a·clys′mic, cat′a·clys′mal,** *adj.*

cat·a·comb (kat′ə kōm′), *n.* an underground cemetery, esp. one consisting of tunnels with recesses for tombs.

cat·a·falque (kat′ə falk′, -fôk′, -fôlk′), *n.* a raised structure on which the body of a deceased person lies in state.

cat·a·lep·sy (kat′ə lep′sē), *n.* a physical condition characterized by suspension of sensation, muscular rigidity, etc. —**cat′a·lep′tic,** *adj./n.*

cat·a·log (kat′əlôg′, -°log′), *n.* **1.** a systematic list of the contents of a library. **2.** a list with brief notes on the names, articles, etc., listed. **3.** a book, leaflet, or file containing such a list or record. —*v.t., v.i.* **4.** to make a catalog (of). —**cat′a·log′er,** *n.*

cat·a·logue (kat′°lôg′, -°log′), *n., v.,* **-logued, -logu·ing.** catalog. —**cat′a·logu′er,** *n.*

ca·tal·pa (kə tal′pə), *n.* a tree of the U.S., having large leaves and bell-shaped white flowers.

ca·tal·y·sis (kə tal′i sis), *n., pl.* **-ses** (-sēz′). the causing or accelerating of a chemical change by the addition of a substance that is not permanently affected by the reaction. —**cat·a·lyt·ic** (kat′°lit′ik), *adj., n.* —**cat′a·lyt′i·cal·ly,** *adv.*

cat·a·lyst (kat′°list), *n.* a substance that causes catalysis.

cat′alyt′ic convert′er, an antipollution device containing a catalyst that reduces the volume of undesirable substances, such as carbon monoxide, from automotive exhaust.

cat·a·lyze (kat′°līz′), *v.t.,* **-lyzed, -lyz·ing.** to act upon by catalysis. —**cat′a·lyz′er,** *n.*

cat·a·ma·ran (kat′ə mə ran′), *n.* **1.** a sailing raft formed of logs tied side by side. **2.** a vessel formed of two hulls.

cat·a·mount (kat′ə mount′), *n.* **1.** the cougar. **2.** the lynx.

cat·a·pult (kat′ə pult′, -pᴏᴏlt′), *n.* **1.** an ancient military engine for hurling stones, etc. **2.** a device for launching an airplane from the deck of a ship. —*v.t.* **3.** to hurl from a catapult. —*v.i.* **4.** to spring up.

cat·a·ract (kat′ə rakt′), *n.* **1.** a large waterfall. **2.** a downpour or deluge. **3. a.** an abnormality of the eye, characterized by opacity of the lens. **b.** the opaque area.

ca·tarrh (kə tär′), *n.* inflammation of a mucous membrane, esp. of the respiratory tract. —**ca·tarrh′al, ca·tarrh′ous,** *adj.*

ca·tas·tro·phe (kə tas′trə fē), *n.* **1.** a sudden and widespread disaster. **2.** a fiasco. —**cat·a·stroph·ic** (kat′ə-strof′ik), *adj.* —**cat′a·stroph′i·cal·ly,** *adv.*

cat·a·to·ni·a (kat′ə tō′nē ə), *n.* a pathological syndrome, esp. of schizophrenia, characterized by muscular rigidity and mental stupor. —**cat·a·ton·ic** (kat′ə ton′ik), *adj., n.*

Ca·taw·ba (kə tô′bə), *n.* **1.** a red
grape of the eastern U.S. **2.** a dry
white wine made from this grape.
cat·bird (kat′bûrd′), *n.* a slate-
colored North American songbird,
having a call resembling the mew-
ing of a cat.
cat·boat (kat′bōt), *n.* a boat having
one mast set well forward and one
large sail.
cat·call (kat′kôl′), *n.* **1.** a cry like
that of a cat, made by the human
voice and used for expressing disapproval. —*v.i., v.t.* **2.** to sound
catcalls (at).
catch (kach), *v.,* **caught, catch·ing,**
n. —*v.t.* **1.** to capture, as in a trap
or after pursuit. **2.** to deceive.
3. to get aboard (a train, boat, etc.).
4. to see or attend: *to catch a show.*
5. to come upon suddenly. **6.** to
intercept and hold: *to catch a ball.*
7. to receive, incur, or contract:
to catch cold. **8.** to grasp or clasp.
9. to grip, hook, or entangle. **10.**
to attract. **11.** to comprehend.
—*v.i.* **12.** to become gripped or
entangled. **13.** to take hold. **14.**
catch at, to grasp at eagerly. **15.**
catch on, *Informal.* **a.** to become
popular. **b.** to understand. **16.**
catch up, **a.** to lift suddenly. **b.** to
come up to. —*n.* **17.** act of catching. **18.** anything that catches, as
a latch on a door. **19.** a slight break
in the voice. **20.** something caught,
as a quantity of fish. **21.** a person
or thing worth getting. **22.** any
tricky or concealed drawback. **23.**
a fragment: *catches of a song.* **24.**
a game in which a ball is thrown
from one person to another: *to
play catch.*
Catch-22, *n. Informal.* a frustrating
situation in which one is trapped by
conflicting regulations. [from the
novel *Catch-22* by J. Heller, b. 1923,
U.S. author]
catch·all (kach′ôl′), *n.* a receptacle
for odds and ends.
catch-as-catch-can (kach′əz kach′-
kan′), *adj.* taking advantage of
any opportunity that comes to hand.
catch·er (kach′ər), *n.* **1.** a person
or thing that catches. **2.** *Baseball.*
the player behind home plate.
catch·ing (kach′ing), *adj.* **1.** contagious or infectious. **2.** attractive
or fascinating.
catch·ment (kach′mənt), *n.* **1.** act of
catching water. **2.** something for
catching water, as a basin. **3.** the
water so caught.
catch·pen·ny (kach′pen′ē), *adj.* made
to sell readily at a low price.
catch·up (kach′əp, kech′-), *n.* ketchup.
catch·word (kach′wûrd′), *n.* **1.** a
word or phrase repeated so often
that it becomes a slogan. **2.** a

word at the top of a page in a
reference book to indicate the first
or last article on that page.
catch·y (kach′ē), *adj.,* **catch·i·er,
catch·i·est.** **1.** pleasing and easily
remembered. **2.** tricky or deceptive.
cat·e·chism (kat′ə kiz′əm), *n.* a
summary of the principles of a
religion, in the form of questions
and answers. —**cat′e·chist,** *n.* —
cat′e·chize, *v.t.*
cat·e·chu·men (kat′ə kyōō′mən), *n.*
a convert undergoing instruction in
Christianity.
cat·e·gor·i·cal (kat′ə gôr′i kəl, -gôr′-),
adj. **1.** unqualified and unconditional: *a categorical denial.* **2.** of,
pertaining to, or in a category.
Also, **cat′e·gor′ic.** — **cat′e·gor′i-
cal·ly,** *adv.* —**cat′e·gor′i·cal·ness,** *n.*
cat·e·go·rize (kat′ə gə rīz′), *v.t.,*
-rized, -riz·ing. to arrange in categories or classes. —**cat′e·go·ri·za′-
tion,** *n.*
cat·e·go·ry (kat′ə gôr′ē, -gôr′ē), *n.,
pl.* **-ries.** a class or division in a
system.
cat·e·nar·y (kat′ə ner′ē), *n., pl.* **-nar-
ies.** *Math.* the curve assumed approximately by a heavy uniform
cord or chain hanging freely from
two points not in the same vertical
line.
ca·ter (kā′tər), *v.i.* **1.** to provide
food, service, etc. **2.** to supply
something desired or demanded: *to
cater to popular demand.* —**ca′-
ter·er,** *n.*
cat·er-cor·nered (kat′ə kôr′nərd,
kat′ē-, kat′ər-), *adj.* **1.** diagonal.
—*adv.* **2.** diagonally. Also, **cat′er-
cor′ner.**
cat·er·pil·lar (kat′ə pil′ər, kat′ər-),
n. the wormlike larva of a butterfly or a moth.
cat·er·waul (kat′ər wôl′), *v.i.* **1.** to
cry as cats in the time of rut. —*n.*
2. such a cry.
cat·fish (kat′fish′), *n., pl.* **-fish,
-fish·es.** a fish having a scaleless
skin and feelers around the mouth.
cat·gut (kat′gut′), *n.* a strong cord
made by twisting the dried intestines
of animals, as sheep.
Cath., Catholic.
ca·thar·sis (kə thär′sis), *n.* **1.** purga-
tion of the bowels. **2.** the purging
of an audience's emotions through
a work of art.
ca·thar·tic (kə thär′tik), *adj.* **1.**
of or producing catharsis. —*n.* **2.**
a purgative.
ca·the·dral (kə thē′drəl), *n.* the
principal church of a diocese, containing the bishop's throne.
cath·e·ter (kath′i tər), *n.* a hollow
tube employed to drain fluids from
body cavities or to distend body
passages. —**cath′e·ter·ize′** (-īz′), *v.t.*

cath·ode (kath′ōd), n. 1. the negative electrode by which current leaves an electrolytic cell, etc. 2. the positive terminal of a battery. 3. the negative electrode in an electron tube. —ca·thod·ic (ka thod′ik, -thō′dik, kə-), adj.

cath′ode ray′, a flow of electrons emanating from a cathode in a vacuum tube.

cath·o·lic (kath′ə lik, kath′lik), adj. universal in extent or broad-minded: catholic interests. —ca·thol·i·cal·ly, adv.

Cath·o·lic (kath′ə lik, kath′lik), adj. 1. of the Roman Catholic Church. —n. 2. a member of the Roman Catholic Church. —Ca·thol·i·cism (kə thol′i siz′əm), n.

cath·o·lic·i·ty (kath′ə lis′i tē), n. 1. universality or broad-mindedness. 2. (cap.) the Roman Catholic Church or its doctrines.

cat·i·on (kat′ī′on, -on), n. a positively charged ion attracted to the cathode in electrolysis..

cat·kin (kat′kin), n. a spike-shaped, drooping flower cluster, as of the willow.

cat·like (kat′līk′), adj. 1. resembling a cat. 2. stealthy or noiseless.

cat·nap (kat′nap′), n., v., -napped, -nap·ping. —n. 1. a short, light nap. —v.i. 2. to doze or sleep lightly.

cat·nip (kat′nip′), n. a plant of the mint family, having strongly scented leaves of which cats are fond. Also called **cat·mint** (kat′mint′).

cat-o′-nine-tails (kat′ə nīn′tālz′), n., pl. -tails. a whip, usually having nine knotted cords fastened to a handle, used for flogging.

cat's′ cra′dle, a game in which two players alternately stretch a looped string over their fingers to produce different designs.

cat's-eye (kats′ī′), n., pl. -eyes. a gem having a changeable luster.

Cats′kill Moun′tains (kat′skil), a mountain range in E New York. Also called **Cats′kills.**

cat's-paw (kats′pô′), n. a person used by another as a dupe. Also, **cats′-paw′.**

cat·sup (kat′səp, kech′əp, kach′-), n. ketchup.

cat·tail (kat′tāl′), n. a tall, reed-like, marsh plant having flowers in long, dense, cylindrical spikes.

cat·tle (kat′əl), n. bovine animals, as cows and steers —**cat′tle·man,** n.

cat·ty (kat′ē), adj., -ti·er, -ti·est. 1. catlike or feline. 2. slyly malicious. —**cat′ti·ly,** adv. —**cat′ti·ness,** n.

cat·ty-cor·nered (kat′ē kôr′nərd), adj., adv. cater-cornered. Also, **cat′ty-cor′ner.**

CATV, a system of distributing satisfactory television signals to poor-reception areas, as by cable through an elevated antenna. [c(ommunity) a(ntenna) TV]

cat·walk (kat′wôk′), n. any narrow walkway, esp. one high above a surrounding area.

Cau·ca·sian (kô kā′zhən, -shən, -kazh′ən, -kash′-), n. 1. a person having Caucasoid characteristics. 2. a native of the Caucasus. —adj. 3. Caucasoid (def. 2). 4. of the Caucasus, its people, or their language.

Cau·ca·soid (kô′kə soid′), n. 1. a member of one of the major racial groups of mankind, predominantly thin-lipped and having minimum skin pigmentation. —adj. 2. of or belonging to this group.

Cau·ca·sus (kô′kə səs), n. a region and mountain range in the SW Soviet Union.

cau·cus (kô′kəs), n., pl. -cus·es, v. —n. 1. a meeting of the local members of a political party to nominate candidates, determine policy, etc. —v.i. 2. to hold or meet in a caucus.

cau·dal (kôd′°l), adj. of, at, or near the tail or the posterior end of the body. —**cau′dal·ly,** adv.

cau·dil·lo (kô dēl′yō, -dē′ō), n., pl. -dil·los. (in Spanish-speaking countries) the military leader.

caught (kôt), v. pt. and pp. of **catch.**

caul·dron (kôl′drən), n. a large kettle or boiler.

cau·li·flow·er (kô′lə flou′ər, -lē-, kol′ə-, kol′ē-), n. 1. a cultivated plant whose inflorescence forms a compact, fleshy head, used as a vegetable. 2. the head itself.

cau′liflower ear′, an ear deformed by repeated injury and scar tissue.

caulk (kôk), v.i. 1. to fill (a seam, joint, etc.) to make watertight, etc., as in a boat. 2. to make (a tank, window, etc.) watertight or airtight by filling the seams with some material. —**caulk′er,** n.

caus·al (kô′zəl), adj. 1. of, constituting, or implying a cause. 2. Gram. expressing a cause, as a conjunction. —**cau·sal·i·ty** (kô zal′i tē), n. —**caus′al·ly,** adv.

cau·sa·tion (kô zā′shən), n. 1. the action of causing. 2. the relation of cause to effect.

cause (kôz), n., v., caused, caus·ing. —n. 1. a person or thing that produces a result. 2. reason or motive. 3. good or sufficient reason. 4. a. a ground of legal action. b. a case for judicial decision. 5. the ideal or goal to which a person or group is dedicated: the cause of equal rights. —*v.t.* **6.** to be the cause or reason of. —**caus′a·tive,** *adj.* —**cause′less,** *adj.* —**caus′er,** *n.*

cause cé·lè·bre (kôz′ sə leb′rə, -leb′), any controversy that attracts great public attention.

cau·se·rie (kō′zə rē′), *n.* **1.** an informal talk. **2.** a short, informal essay.

cause·way (kôz′wā′), *n.* a raised road or path, as across low or wet ground.

caus·tic (kô′stik), *adj.* **1.** severely biting or sarcastic. **2.** capable of burning or corroding living tissue. —*n.* **3.** a caustic substance. —**caus′ti·cal·ly,** *adv.* —**caus·tic′i·ty** (-tis′i tē), *n.*

cau·ter·ize (kô′tə rīz′), *v.t.,* **-ized, -iz·ing.** to burn with a hot iron or a caustic, esp. fo. curative purposes. —**cau′ter·i·za′tion,** *n.*

cau·tion (kô′shən), *n.* **1.** alertness and prudence. **2.** a warning. **3.** *Informal.* someone or something that astonishes. —*v.t.* **4.** to give warning to. —**cau′tion·ar′y,** *adj.*

cau·tious (kô′shəs), *adj.* manifesting or characterized by caution. —**cau′tious·ly,** *adv.* —**cau′tious·ness,** *n.* —Syn. careful, circumspect, prudent, wary.

cav., cavalry.

cav·al·cade (kav′əl kād′, kav′əl kād′), *n.* **1.** a procession, esp. of persons riding on horses or in horse-drawn vehicles. **2.** a pageant or pageant-like sequence.

cav·a·lier (kav′ə lēr′, kav′ə lēr′), *n.* **1.** (formerly) a horseman, esp. one who is armed. **2.** a person having the manner of a courtier. —*adj.* **3.** haughty or disdainful. **4.** offhand or unceremonious. [< MF horseman < OPr < LL *caballāri(us)* groom] —**cav′a·lier′ly,** *adv.,* *adj.* —**cav′a·lier′ness,** *n.*

cav·al·ry (kav′əl rē), *n., pl.* **-ries. 1.** troops that serve on horseback. **2.** the motorized, armored units of a military force. —**cav′al·ry·man,** *n.*

cave (kāv), *n., v.,* **caved, cav·ing.** —*n.* **1.** a hollow in the earth, esp. one opening into a hill, etc. —*v.t., v.i.* **2. cave in, a.** to collapse or cause to collapse. **b.** *Informal.* to yield or surrender.

ca·ve·at (ka′vē at′, kā-, kä-), *n.* a warning, as in business dealings.

ca′veat emp′tor (emp′tôr), the principle that the seller cannot be held responsible for the quality of his or her product unless guaranteed in a warranty.

cave-in (kāv′in′), *n.* **1.** a collapse, as of a mine. **2.** a place or site of such a collapse.

cave′ man′, 1. a cave dweller, esp. of the Stone Age. **2.** a rough, brutal man.

cav·ern (kav′ərn), *n.* a cave, esp. one that is large and mostly underground. —**cav′ern·ous,** *adj.* —**cav′ern·ous·ly,** *adv.*

cav·i·ar (kav′ē är′, kav′ē är′), *n.* the roe of sturgeon, usually served as an appetizer. Also, **cav′i·are′.**

cav·il (kav′əl), *v.,* **-iled, -il·ing** or **-illed, -il·ling,** *n.* —*v.i.* **1.** to raise irritating and trivial objections. —*n.* **2.** a trivial and annoying objection. —**cav′il·er, cav′il·are′.**

cav·i·ta·tion (kav′i tā′shən), *n.* **1.** the rapid formation and collapse of vapor pockets in a flowing liquid in regions of very low pressure. **2.** such a pocket formed.

cav·i·ty (kav′i tē), *n., pl.* **-ties. 1.** any hollow place. **2.** a hollow place in a tooth structure, caused by decay. —**cav′i·tied,** *adj.*

ca·vort (kə vôrt′), *v.i.* to caper about.

ca·vy (kā′vē), *n., pl.* **-vies.** any of several short-tailed or tailless South American rodents, as the guinea pig.

caw (kô), *n.* **1.** the harsh cry of a crow or raven. —*v.i.* **2.** to utter this cry.

cay (kā, kē), *n.* a small low island.

cay·enne (kī en′, kā-), *n.* a hot condiment composed of the ground pods and seeds of the pepper plant.

cay·man (kā′mən), *n., pl.* **-mans.** caiman.

Ca·yu·ga (kā yōō′gə, kī-), *n., pl.* **-gas, -ga.** a member of a tribe of North American Indians, formerly in New York State.

cay·use (kī yōōs′, kī′ōōs), *n. Western U.S.* an Indian pony.

CB, 1. See **citizens band. 2.** *Mil.* construction battalion.

Cb, columbium.

CBC, Canadian Broadcasting Corporation.

C.B.D., cash before delivery.

C.B.W., chemical and biological warfare.

cc, 1. carbon copy. **2.** cubic centimeter. Also, **c.c.**

cc., chapters.

CCC, 1. Civilian Conservation Corps. **2.** Commodity Credit Corporation.

CCTV, closed-circuit television.

ccw, counterclockwise.

Cd, cadmium.

cd., cord; cords. Also, **cd**

CD, 1. See **certificate of deposit. 2.** Civil Defense. Also, **C.D.**

c.d., cash discount.

Cdr., Commander. Also, **CDR**

Ce, cerium.

C.E., 1. Chemical Engineer. **2.** Civil Engineer. **3.** Corps of Engineers.

cease (sēs), *v.i.*, *v.t.*, **ceased, ceas·ing,** *n.* **1.** to stop, esp. formally or often permanently. —*n.* **2.** cessation.

cease-fire (sēs′fī°r′), *n.* a temporary cessation of hostilities.

cease·less (sēs′lis), *adj.* without stop or pause. —**cease′less·ly,** *adv.* —**cease′less·ness,** *n.*

ce·cro′pi·a moth′ (si krō′pē ə), a large North American silkworm moth.

ce·cum (sē′kəm), *n.*, *pl.* **-ca** (-kə). the pouch forming the first part of the large intestine. —**ce′cal,** *adj.*

ce·dar (sē′dər), *n.* **1.** any of several cone-bearing, evergreen trees with aromatic durable wood. **2.** its wood.

ce′dar chest′, a chest made of cedar for storing woolen clothing, etc., esp. to prevent insect damage.

cede (sēd), *v.t.*, **ced·ed, ced·ing.** to yield or turn over to another, as by treaty. —**ced′er,** *n.*

ce·dil·la (si dil′ə), *n.* a mark ( ) placed under a consonant letter, as under *c* in French, to indicate that it is pronounced (s).

ceil·ing (sē′ling), *n.* **1.** the overhead interior lining of a room. **2.** the top limit, as one set by law on prices. **3.** the maximum altitude to which a particular aircraft can rise under specified conditions. **4.** *Meteorol.* the height of the lowest layer of clouds or other obscuring phenomena in the atmosphere. **5. hit the ceiling,** *Slang.* to become enraged.

cel·an·dine (sel′ən dīn′), *n.* a plant of the poppy family having small yellow flowers in clusters.

cel·e·brant (sel′ə brənt), *n.* **1.** the officiating priest in the celebration of the Eucharist. **2.** a participant in any celebration.

cel·e·brate (sel′ə brāt′), *v.*, **-brat·ed, -brat·ing.** —*v.t.* **1.** to observe (a day) or commemorate (an event) with ceremonies or festivities. **2.** to praise or honor widely. **3.** to perform with appropriate rites, as a Mass. —*v.i.* **4.** to observe a day or commemorate an event with ceremonies or festivities. **5.** to perform a religious ceremony. **6.** *Informal.* to have a merry time, esp. by drinking. —**cel′e·bra′tion,** *n.* —**cel′e·bra′tor,** *n.*

cel·e·brat·ed (sel′ə brā′tid), *adj.* well-known and widely recognized.

ce·leb·ri·ty (sə leb′ri tē), *n.*, *pl.* **-ties 1.** a celebrated person. **2.** the state of being celebrated.

ce·ler·i·ty (sə ler′i tē), *n.* swiftness or speed.

cel·er·y (sel′ə rē), *n.* a plant of the parsley family widely grown for its edible stalks.

ce·les·ta (sə les′tə), *n.* a keyboard instrument consisting of graduated steel plates struck with hammers.

ce·les·tial (sə les′chəl), *adj.* **1.** pertaining to the sky. **2.** heavenly or divine: *celestial bliss.* —**ce·les′tial·ly,** *adv.*

celes′tial equa′tor, the great circle of the celestial sphere, lying in the same plane as the earth's equator.

celes′tial guid′ance, a guidance system in a missile or spacecraft that automatically takes periodic fixes on celestial bodies.

celes′tial naviga′tion, navigation by observing the position of heavenly bodies.

celes′tial sphere′, the imaginary, infinite, spherical shell formed by the sky.

ce·li·ac (sē′lē ak′), *adj.* of or located in the cavity of the abdomen.

cel·i·ba·cy (sel′ə bə sē), *n.* **1.** state of being unmarried. **2.** abstention by vow from marriage. **3.** sexual abstinence.

cel·i·bate (sel′ə bit, -bāt′), *n.* **1.** a person who remains unmarried, esp. for religious reasons. —*adj.* **2.** not married.

cell (sel), *n.* **1.** a small room, as in a convent or prison. **2.** any of various small compartments forming part of a whole. **3.** a small unit within a larger organization. **4.** a usually microscopic plant or animal structure containing nuclear material enclosed by a membrane and, in plants, a cellulosic wall: the structural unit of plant and animal life. **5.** a device that generates electricity, usually consisting of two different conducting substances placed in an electrolyte. **6.** a device for producing electrolysis, consisting essentially of the electrolyte, its container, and the electrodes. —**celled** (seld), *adj.*

cel·lar (sel′ər), *n.* **1.** a room or rooms wholly or partly underground and usually beneath a building. **2.** See **wine cellar. 3.** the lowest position among a sports group.

cel·lar·age (sel′ər ij), *n.* **1.** cellar space. **2.** storage charge for a cellar.

cel·lar·et (sel′ə ret′), *n.* a cabinet or stand for wine bottles. Also, **cel′lar·ette′.**

cell′ block′, a unit of a prison consisting of a number of cells.

cel·lo (chel′ō), *n.*, *pl.* **-los.** the third largest member of the violin family. Also, **'cel′lo.** —**cel′list, 'cel′list,** *n.*

cel·lo·phane (sel′ə fān′), *n.* a transparent, paperlike product of viscose used for wrapping.

cel·lu·lar (sel′yə lər), *adj.* pertaining to or characterized by cells.

Cel·lu·loid (sel′yə loid′), n. *Trademark.* a substance consisting essentially of soluble guncotton and camphor, used for toys, film, etc.

cel·lu·lose (sel′yə lōs′), n. an inert carbohydrate, the chief constituent of the walls of plant cells, used to make paper, rayon, etc. —**cel·lu·lo·sic** (sel′yə lō′sik), adj., n.

cel′lulose ac′etate, any of a group of acetic esters of cellulose, used to make yarns, textiles, etc.

cel′lulose ni′trate, any of a group of nitric esters of cellulose, used for lacquers and explosives.

Cel·si·us (sel′sē əs, -shē-), adj. pertaining to a temperature scale in which 0° represents the freezing point of water and 100° the boiling point. [after A. *Celsius,* 1701–44, Swed. astronomer]

Celt (selt, kelt), n. a member of a Celtic-speaking people.

Celt·ic (sel′tik, kel′-), n. 1. a branch of the Indo-European family of languages including esp. Irish and Welsh. —adj. 2. of the Celts or their languages.

cem·ba·lo (chem′bə lō′), n., pl. -li (-lē′), -los. harpsichord.

ce·ment (si ment′), n. 1. any of various calcined mixtures of clay and limestone, usually mixed with water and sand, gravel, etc., to form concrete, that are used as building material. 2. any sticky substance, as an adhesive. 3. anything that binds or unites. 4. a hardening, adhesive substance, used in the repair of teeth. —v.t. 5. to unite by cement. 6. to cover with cement. —v.i. 7. to cohere or unite. —ce′men·ta′tion, n. —ce·ment′er, n.

ce·men·tum (si men′təm), n. the bonelike tissue that forms the outer surface of the root of the tooth.

cem·e·ter·y (sem′i ter′ē), n., pl. -ter·ies. an area for graves or tombs.

cen., 1. central. 2. century.

ce·no·bite (sē′nə bīt′, sen′ə-), n. a member of a religious order living in a convent or community. —**ce·no·bit·ic** (sē′nə bit′ik, sen′ə-), **ce·no·bit′i·cal,** adj.

cen·o·taph (sen′ə taf′, -täf′), n. a monument erected in memory of a deceased person whose body is buried elsewhere. —**cen′o·taph′ic,** adj.

Ce·no·zo·ic (sē′nə zō′ik, sen′ə-), adj. 1. noting or pertaining to the present era, beginning 70,000,000 years ago and characterized by the appearance of mammals. —n. 2. the Cenozoic era.

cen·ser (sen′sər), n. a container in which incense is burned.

cen·sor (sen′sər), n. 1. an official who examines books, plays, films, etc., to suppress anything objectionable. 2. (in the ancient Roman republic) one of two officials who kept the census. —v.t. 3. to examine and act upon as a censor. —**cen·so·ri·al** (sen sōr′ē əl, -sôr′-), adj.

cen·so·ri·ous (sen sōr′ē əs, -sôr′-), adj. severely or harshly critical. —**cen·so′ri·ous·ly,** adv. —**cen·so′ri·ous·ness,** n.

cen·sor·ship (sen′sər ship′) n. 1. act of censoring. 2. the office or power of a censor.

cen·sure (sen′shər), n., v., -sured, -sur·ing. —n. 1. strong disapproval. —v.t., v.i. 2. to criticize in a harsh manner. —**cen′sur·a·ble,** adj. —**cen′sur·er,** n.

cen·sus (sen′səs), n., pl. -sus·es. a periodic official enumeration of the population, with details as to age, sex, occupation, etc.

cent (sent), n. 1. a 100th part of a basic monetary unit, as a dollar. 2. a coin representing this value. [< L *cent(ēsimus)* hundredth]

cent., 1. centigrade. 2. central. 3. century.

cen·taur (sen′tôr), n. *Class. Myth.* one of a race of creatures having the head, trunk, and arms of a human, and the body and legs of a horse.

cen·ta·vo (sen tä′vō), n., pl. -vos. the 100th part of the monetary units of various Spanish American nations.

cen·te·nar·i·an (sen′tᵊnâr′ē ən), n. a person who has reached the age of 100.

cen·te·nar·y (sen′tᵊner′ē, sen ten′ə rē, -tē′nə rē), adj., n., pl. -nar·ies. —adj. 1. of a centennial. 2. of a century. —n. 3. a centennial. 4. a century.

cen·ten·ni·al (sen ten′ē əl), adj. 1. of a 100th anniversary. 2. lasting 100 years. 3. 100 years old. —n. 4. a 100th anniversary or its celebration.

cen·ter (sen′tər), n. 1. the middle point, as the point within a circle equally distant from all points of the circumference. 2. a pivot, axis, etc. 3. the source of an influence, action, force, etc. 4. a principal point, place, or object: *a shipping center.* 5. the core or middle of anything. 6. (sometimes cap.) the part of a legislative assembly holding political views intermediate between those of the Right and Left. 7. a player who primarily plays in the center. —v.t. 8. to place in a center. 9. to focus. —v.i. 10. to be at or come to a center.

cen·ter·board (sen′tər bôrd′, -bôrd′), *n. Naut.* a pivoted keel able to be swung upward and aft when not in use.

cen·tered (sen′tərd), *adj.* having a central axis.

cen·ter·fold (sen′tər fōld′), *n.* a double-page spread at the center of a magazine, etc.

cen′ter of grav′ity, the point through which the resultant of gravitational forces on a body passes.

cen·ter·piece (sen′tər pēs′), *n.* an ornamental object used in the center of a dining table.

cen′ter punch′, a punch for making shallow indentations in metalwork, as to center drill bits.

cen·tes·i·mal (sen tes′ə məl), *adj.* pertaining to division into hundredths.

centi-, a combining form meaning: **a.** hundredth: *centimeter.* **b.** hundred: *centipede.*

cen·ti·grade (sen′tə grād′), *adj.* Celsius.

cen·ti·gram (sen′tə gram′), *n.* one hundredth of a gram. Also, *Brit.,* **cen′ti·gramme′.**

cen·ti·li·ter (sen′t°lē′tər), *n.* one hundredth of a liter or 0.338 ounce. Also, *Brit.,* **cen′ti·li·tre.**

cen·time (sän′tēm), *n.* the 100th part of the francs of France, Belgium, Switzerland, etc.

cen·ti·me·ter (sen′tə mē′tər), *n.* one hundredth of a meter or 0.3937 inch. Also, *Brit.,* **cen′ti·me′tre.**

cen·ti·me·ter-gram-sec·ond (sen′tə-mē′tər gram′sek′ənd), *adj.* of or pertaining to the system of units in which the centimeter, gram, and second are the principal units of length, mass, and time.

cen·ti·pede (sen′tə pēd′), *n.* a small animal having a long, flat body composed of many segments, each with a pair of legs.

cen·tral (sen′trəl), *adj.* **1.** of or forming the center. **2.** in, at, or near the center. **3.** constituting that from which other related things proceed or upon which they depend: *a central agency.* **4.** principal or dominant —*n.* **5.** (formerly) a main telephone exchange. —**cen′tral·ly,** *adv.*

Cen′tral Af′rican Repub′lic, a country in central Africa.

Cen′tral Amer′ica, continental North America, S of Mexico. —**Cen′tral Amer′ican.**

cen′tral cit′y, a city at the core or center of a metropolitan area.

cen·tral·ism (sen′trə liz′əm), *n.* a centralizing system or authority. —**cen′tral·ist,** *n., adj.* —**cen·tral·is·tic** (sen′trə lis′tik), *adj.*

cen·tral·i·ty (sen tral′i tē), *n., pl.* -**ties.** a central position or state.

cen·tral·ize (sen′trə līz′), *v.,* -**ized,** -**iz·ing.** —*v.t.* **1.** to draw to a central point. **2.** to bring under one control. —*v.i.* **3.** to become centralized. —**cen′tral·i·za′tion,** *n.* —**cen′tral·iz′er,** *n.*

cen′tral nerv′ous sys′tem, the part of the nervous system comprising the brain and spinal cord.

cen·tre (sen′tər), *n., v.,* -**tred,** -**tring.** *Chiefly Brit.* center.

cen·trif·u·gal (sen trif′yə gəl, -ə gəl), *adj.* **1.** moving outward away from a center or axis. **2.** pertaining to or operated by centrifugal force. —**cen·trif′u·gal·ly,** *adv.*

centrif′ugal force′, the force repelling a body away from the axis around which it rotates or away from the center of curvature of a curved path.

cen·tri·fuge (sen′trə fyōōj′), *n.* an apparatus that uses centrifugal force to separate substances of different densities. —**cen·trif·u·ga·tion** (sen trif′yə gā′shən, -trif′ə-), *n.*

cen·trip·e·tal (sen trip′i t°l), *adj.* **1.** moving inward toward a center or axis. **2.** pertaining to or operated by centripetal force. —**cen·trip′e·tal·ly,** *adv.*

centrip′etal force′, a force attracting a body toward the axis around which it rotates or toward the center of curvature of a curved path.

cen·trist (sen′trist), *n.* (*sometimes cap.*) a member of a political party of the center.

cen·tu·ri·on (sen tŏŏr′ē ən, -tyŏŏr′-), *n.* (in the ancient Roman army) the commander of a century.

cen·tu·ry (sen′chə rē), *n., pl.* -**ries. 1.** a period of 100 years. **2.** (in the ancient Roman army) a company, consisting of approximately 100 men.

cen′tury plant′, a Mexican agave, erroneously believed to flower only once every century.

CEO, chief executive officer.

ce·phal·ic (sə fal′ik), *adj.* **1.** of the head. **2.** situated or directed toward the head.

cephal′ic in′dex, the ratio of the greatest breadth of a head to its greatest length from front to back, multiplied by 100.

ce·ram·ic (sə ram′ik), *adj.* **1.** of products made from clay and similar materials, as pottery, brick, etc. —*n.* **2.** ceramic material.

ce·ram·ics (sə ram′iks), *n.* **1.** the art or technology of making objects of clay and similar materials treated by firing. **2.** articles of earthenware, porcelain, etc. —**cer·a·mist** (ser′ə-mist, sə ram′ist), **ce·ram′i·cist,** *n.*

ce·re·al (sēr′ē əl), *n.* **1.** a plant yielding an edible grain, as wheat, rye, or corn. **2.** the grain itself. **3.** some preparation of it, esp. a breakfast food. —*adj.* **4.** of grain or the plants producing it.

cer·e·bel·lum (ser′ə bel′əm), *n.*, *pl.* **-bel·lums, -bel·la** (-bel′ə). a large portion of the brain, serving to coordinate voluntary movements and balance in human beings. —**cer′e·bel′lar**, *adj.*

cer·e·bral (ser′ə brəl, sə rē′-), *adj.* **1.** of or pertaining to the cerebrum or the brain. **2.** characterized by the use of the intellect. —**cer′e·bral·ly**, *adv.*

cer′ebral cor′tex, the outermost layer of the cerebrum, functioning as the center of intellectual activity.

cer′ebral pal′sy, a form of paralysis caused by brain injury during or before birth, characterized by difficulty in control of the voluntary muscles.

cer·e·brate (ser′ə brāt′), *v.i.*, *v.t.*, **-brat·ed, -brat·ing.** *Chiefly Physiol.* to think (about). —**cer′e·bra′tion,** *n.*

cer·e·brum (ser′ə brəm, sə rē′-), *n.*, *pl.* **-brums, -bra** (-brə). the anterior and largest part of the brain, serving to control voluntary movements and coordinate mental actions.

cere·cloth (sēr′klôth′, -kloth′), *n.*, *pl.* **-cloths** (-klôthz′, -kloṯhz′, -klôths′, -kloths′). cloth coated with wax so as to be waterproof, formerly used for wrapping the dead.

cere·ment (sēr′mənt), *n.* a cerecloth used for wrapping the dead.

cer·e·mo·ni·al (ser′ə mō′nē əl), *adj.* **1.** of or characterized by ceremony. —*n.* **2.** a system of rites or formalities. —**cer′e·mo′ni·al·ist,** *n.* —**cer′e·mo′ni·al·ly,** *adv.*

cer·e·mo·ni·ous (ser′ə mō′nē əs), *adj.* **1.** elaborately polite. **2.** of or marked by ceremony. —**cer′e·mo′ni·ous·ly,** *adv.* —**cer′e·mo′ni·ous·ness,** *n.*

cer·e·mo·ny (ser′ə mō′nē), *n.*, *pl.* **-nies. 1.** the formalities observed on some solemn occasion. **2.** a formal rite. **3.** any meaningless formal act. **4.** strict formality. **5. stand on ceremony,** to behave in a formal manner.

ce·re·us (sēr′ē əs), *n.*, *pl.* **-us·es.** any of various columnar cactuses of tropical America and the western U.S.

ce·rise (sə rēs′, -rēz′), *adj.*, *n.* moderate to deep red.

ce·ri·um (sēr′ē əm), *n. Chem.* a gray, ductile metallic element found only in combination. *Symbol:* Ce; *at. wt.:* 140.12; *at. no.:* 58.

cer·met (sûr′met), *n.* a durable, heat-resistant alloy formed by compacting a metal and a ceramic substance.

cert., 1. certificate. **2.** certification. **3.** certified. **4.** certify.

cer·tain (sûr′t°n), *adj.* **1.** free from doubt or reservation. **2.** quite sure. **3.** inevitable. **4.** established as true. **5.** fixed or agreed upon. **6.** definite but not specified: *a certain woman.* **7.** trustworthy. **8. for certain,** without a doubt. —**cer′tain·ly,** *adv.* —**Syn. 1, 2.** assured, confident, positive.

cer·tain·ty (sûr′t°n tē), *n.*, *pl.* **-ties** for **2. 1.** the state of being certain. **2.** something certain.

certif., certificate.

cer·tif·i·cate (*n.* sər tif′ə kit; *v.* sər·tif′ə kāt′), *n.*, *v.*, **-cat·ed, -cat·ing.** —*n.* **1.** a document serving as evidence or testimony, as of status, qualifications, etc. **2.** a document attesting to the completion of an educational course. —*v.t.* **3.** to attest or authorize by a certificate. **4.** to issue a certificate to.

certif′icate of depos′it, a receipt issued by a bank for a specified sizable amount of funds for a fixed period of time earning a higher interest rate than normally available.

cer·ti·fi·ca·tion (sûr′tə fə kā′shən, sər·tif′ə-), *n.* **1.** act of certifying or state of being certified. **2.** a certified statement.

cer′tified check′, a check bearing a guarantee of payment by the bank on which it is drawn.

cer′tified mail′, uninsured first-class mail requiring proof of delivery.

cer′tified milk′, milk processed in dairies conforming to official standards of sanitation.

cer′tified pub′lic account′ant, a person holding an official certificate as an accountant, having fulfilled all the legal requirements.

cer·ti·fy (sûr′tə fī′), *v.*, **-fied, -fy·ing.** —*v.t.* **1.** to attest as true or accurate. **2.** to guarantee or endorse. **3.** to guarantee in writing on (a check) that the funds to meet the payment are on deposit. **4.** *Brit.* to declare (a person) legally insane. —**cer′ti·fi′a·ble,** *adj.* —**cer′ti·fi′a·bly,** *adv.* —**cer′ti·fi′er,** *n.*

cer·ti·tude (sûr′ti tōōd′, -tyōōd′), *n.* freedom from doubt.

ce·ru·le·an (sə rōō′lē ən), *adj.*, *n. Chiefly Literary.* azure.

ce·ru·men (si rōō′mən), *n.* a yellowish, waxlike secretion from the ear. —**ce·ru′mi·nous,** *adj.*

Cer·van·tes (sər van′tēz), *n.* **Mi·guel de** (mi gel′ dā), 1547–1616, Spanish novelist.

cer·vix (sûr′viks), *n.*, *pl.* **cer·vix·es, cer·vi·ces** (sər vī′sēz, sûr′vi sēz′). *Anat.* **1.** the neck, esp. the back. **2.** any necklike part, esp. the constricted lower end of the uterus. —**cer′vi·cal** (-vi kəl), *adj.*

Ce·sar·e·an (si zâr′ē ən), *adj., n.* Caesarean. Also, **Ce·sar′i·an.**

ce·si·um (sē′zē əm), *n. Chem.* a rare, highly reactive, soft, metallic element, used chiefly in photoelectric cells. *Symbol:* Cs; *at. wt.:* 132.905; *at. no.:* 55.

cess (ses), *n. Irish Eng. Informal.* luck: *Bad cess to them!*

ces·sa·tion (se sā′shən), *n.* a temporary or complete ceasing.

ces·sion (sesh′ən), *n.* 1. the act of ceding, as by treaty. 2. that which is ceded, as territory.

cess·pool (ses′pōōl′), *n.* an underground tank or pit for the sewage from sinks, toilets, etc.

ce·ta·cean (si tā′shən), *adj.* 1. belonging to aquatic, chiefly marine mammals, including the whales, dolphins, etc. —*n.* 2. a cetacean mammal.

Cey·lon (si lon′), *n.* former name of Sri Lanka. —**Cey′lo·nese′,** *adj., n.*

Cf, californium.

c/f, *Bookkeeping.* carried forward.

cf., 1. *Baseball.* center fielder. 2. compare. [< L *confer*]

C.F., cost and freight. Also, **c.f.**

C.F.I., cost, freight, and insurance. Also, **c.f.i.**

cg., centigram; centigrams.

C.G., 1. Coast Guard. 2. Commanding General 3. Consul General.

c.g., center of gravity.

cgm., centigram; centigrams

cgs, centimeter-gram-second. Also, **c.g.s., CGS**

ch, *Survey.* chain; chains.

Ch., 1. *TV.* Channel. 2. Chapter. 3. China. 4. Chinese. 5. Church.

ch., 1. chaplain. 2. chapter. 3. check. 4. chief. 5. child; children. 6. church.

c.h., 1. clearinghouse. 2. courthouse. 3. customhouse.

Chab·lis (shab′lē, shä blē′), *n.* a dry, white Burgundy table wine.

cha-cha (chä′chä′), *n., pl.* -**chas.** a Latin-American dance similar to the mambo.

Chad (chad), *n.* a country in W central Africa. —**Chad′i·an,** *adj., n.*

chafe (chāf), *v.,* **chafed, chaf·ing.** —*v.t.* 1. to warm by rubbing. 2. to make sore by rubbing. 3. to irritate or annoy. —*v.i.* 4. to rub. 5. to be irritated or annoyed.

chaf·er (chā′fər), *n.* any large dark beetle.

chaff¹ (chaf, chäf), *n.* 1. the husks of grains and grasses separated during threshing. 2. worthless matter.

chaff² (chaf, chäf), *v.t., v.i.* 1. to mock or tease in a good-natured manner. —*n.* 2. good-natured ridicule or teasing. —**chaff′er,** *n.*

chaf·fer (chaf′ər), *Rare.* —*n.* 1. bargaining or haggling. —*v.i.* 2. to bargain or haggle. —**chaff′er·er,** *n.*

chaf·finch (chaf′inch), *n.* a common finch of the Old World, often kept as a pet.

chaf′ing dish′ (chā′fing), a metal dish with a lamp or heating appliance beneath it, for cooking or keeping food hot at the table.

cha·grin (shə grin′), *n., v.,* -**grined** or -**grinned,** -**grin·ing** or -**grin·ning.** —*n.* 1. a feeling of vexation, marked by disappointment or humiliation. —*v.t.* 2. to cause to feel chagrin.

chain (chān), *n.* 1. a series of metal rings passing through one another. 2. something that binds or restrains. 3. **chains,** a. shackles or fetters. b. bondage or servitude. 4. a series of things connected in succession: *a chain of events.* 5. a number of similar establishments under one ownership. 6. *Survey.* a distance-measuring device consisting of a chain of 100 links having a total length of 66 feet. —*v.t.* 7. to fasten with a chain. 8. to confine or secure.

chain′ gang′, a group of convicts chained together, esp. when working outside.

chain′ let′ter, a letter sent to a number of persons, each of whom sends copies to other persons who do likewise.

chain mail, *Armor.* mail².

chain-re·act (chān′rē akt′), *v.i.,* to undergo a chain reaction.

chain′ reac′tion, 1. a self-sustaining reaction in which the fission of nuclei produces particles that cause the fission of other nuclei. 2. *Chem.* a reaction that results in a product necessary for the continuance of the reaction. 3. any series of events each of which is the result of the one preceding.

chain′ saw′, a power saw, usually portable, having teeth set on an endless chain.

chain′ smok′er, a person who smokes cigarettes or cigars continually. —**chain′-smoke′,** *v.i., v.t.*

chain′ stitch′, a looped stitch resembling links in a chain.

chain′ store′, one of a group of retail stores under the same ownership.

chair (châr), *n.* 1. a seat, esp. for one person, usually having a rest for the back. 2. a seat of office or authority. 3. a position of authority, as of a′ judge, professor, etc. 4. the chairperson of a meeting. 5. See **electric chair.** —*v.t.* 6. to preside over.

chair′ lift′, a series of chairs suspended from an endless cable driven by motors, as for conveying skiers up a slope.

chair·man (châr′mən), *n.* **1.** a man who presides over a meeting, etc. **2.** a man who heads a board, committee, etc. —**chair′man·ship′,** *n.* —**chair′wom′an,** *n.fem.*

chair·per·son (châr′pûr′sən), *n.* a person who presides over a meeting, committee, etc. —**Usage.** This term is now often used in preference to *chairman* or *chairwoman.*

chaise (shāz), *n.* a light, open carriage, usually with a hood.

chaise longue (shāz′ lông′, chāz′), *pl.* **chaise longues.** a couch in the form of a long reclining chair. Also, **chaise lounge** (shāz′ lounj′, chāz′).

chal·ced·o·ny (kal sed′°nē, kal′sa-dō′nē), *n., pl.* **-nies.** a translucent variety of quartz, often milky or grayish. —**chal′ce·don′ic,** *adj.*

chal·co·py·rite (kal′kə pī′rīt, -pēr′īt), *n.* a very common mineral constituting the most important ore of copper.

cha·let (sha lā′, shal′ā), *n.* **1.** a herdsman's hut in the Swiss mountains. **2.** a cottage, villa, ski lodge, etc., built in this style, with wide eaves, balconies, etc.

chal·ice (chal′is), *n.* **1.** a cup for the wine of the Eucharist. **2.** *Literary.* a drinking cup.

chalk (chôk), *n.* **1.** a soft, white, powdery limestone. **2.** a prepared piece of chalk or chalklike substance for marking on a blackboard. —*v.t.* **3.** to mark with chalk. **4.** to treat with chalk. **5. chalk up, a.** to score or earn. **b.** to charge or ascribe to. —*adj.* **6.** of, made of, or drawn with chalk. —**chalk′y,** *adj.* —**chalk′i·ness,** *n.*

chalk·board (chôk′bôrd′, -bōrd′), *n.* a blackboard, esp. a smooth, light-colored one.

chal·lah (кнä′lə, hä′-), *n.* a loaf of bread, often braided before baking, prepared esp. for the Jewish Sabbath.

chal·lenge (chal′inj), *n., v.,* **-lenged, -leng·ing.** —*n.* **1.** a call to engage in a contest of skill, strength, etc. **2.** a call to fight, as a battle, a duel, etc. **3.** a demand to explain or justify. **4.** the demand of a sentry for identification **5.** a formal objection to the qualifications of a juror. **6.** a difficulty in an undertaking that is stimulating. —*v.t.* **7.** to subject to a challenge. —*v.i.* **8.** to make or issue a challenge. —**chal′lenge·a·ble,** *adj.* —**chal′leng·er,** *n.*

chal·lis (shal′ē), *n.* a soft, usually printed, fabric of plain weave in wool, cotton, or rayon. Also, **chal′lie.**

cham·ber (chām′bər), *n.* **1.** a legislative, judicial, or deliberative body. **2.** the meeting hall of such a body. **3.** a council or board, as for business purposes. **4. chambers,** an office in which a judge hears matters not requiring action in open court. **5.** a room in a palace or official residence. **6.** *Literary.* a private room, as a bedroom. **7.** an enclosed compartment. **8.** a receptacle for cartridges in a firearm. —**cham′bered,** *adj.*

cham·ber·lain (chām′bər lin), *n.* **1.** an official manager of a sovereign's living quarters. **2.** *Brit.* a treasurer of public revenues, esp. of a municipality. **3.** a high official of a royal court.

cham·ber·maid (chām′bər mād′), *n.* a maid who cleans bedrooms, esp. in a hotel.

cham′ber mu′sic, music for a small number of solo instruments.

cham′ber of com′merce, an association of business people to protect and promote the commercial interests in a community.

cham′ber pot′, a portable container formerly used as a bedroom toilet.

cham·bray (sham′brā), *n.* a fine cloth of cotton, silk, or linen, commonly of plain weave with a colored warp.

cha·me·le·on (kə mē′lē ən, -mēl′yən), *n.* any of numerous lizards characterized by the ability to change the color of their skin. [< L < Gk *chamailéōn,* lit. dwarf lion]

cham·fer (cham′fər), *n.* **1.** an oblique face formed at a corner of a board, etc. —*v.t.* **2.** to cut or make a chamfer on.

cham·ois (sham′ē), *n., pl.* **cham·ois** (sham′ēz). **1.** a small, agile, goatlike antelope of high mountains of Europe and southwestern Russia. **2.** Also, **cham′my,** a soft, pliable leather from any of various skins dressed with oil.

cham·o·mile (kam′ə mīl′, -mēl′), *n.* camomile.

champ¹ (champ), *v.t., v.i.* **1.** to chew vigorously or noisily. **2. champ at the bit,** to show impatience.

champ² (champ), *n. Informal.* a champion.

cham·pagne (sham pān′), *n.* a sparkling, dry, white table wine, esp. one from the region of Champagne, France.

cham·paign (sham pān′), *n. Literary.* level, open country.

cham·pi·on (cham′pē ən), *n.* **1.** a person who has defeated all opponents in competition and thus holds first place. **2.** anything that takes first place in competition. **3.** a person who fights for a person or cause. —*v.t.* **4.** to defend or support. —*adj.* **5.** first among all competitors. —**cham′pi·on·ship′**, *n.*

Chanc., **1.** Chancellor. **2.** Chancery.

chance (chans, chäns), *n., v.,* **chanced, chanc·ing,** *adj.* —*n.* **1.** the unpredictable element in an occurrence. **2.** luck: *a game of chance.* **3.** a possibility or probability. **4.** an opportunity. **5.** a risk or hazard: *Take a chance.* **6.** a share or ticket in a lottery. **7. by chance,** without plan or intent. **8. on the off chance,** against the very slight possibility. —*v.i.* **9.** to happen or occur by accident. —*v.t.* **10.** to take the risks of. **11. chance on** or **upon,** to come upon by accident. —*adj.* **12.** occurring by accident: *a chance encounter.* —**Syn. 2.** accident, fate, fortune.

chan·cel (chan′səl, chän′-), *n.* the space about the altar of a church, usually enclosed, for the clergy and choir.

chan·cel·ler·y (chan′sə lə rē, -slə rē, chän′-), *n., pl.* **-ler·ies. 1.** the position or department of a chancellor. **2.** a building occupied by a chancellor's department. **3.** the office attached to an embassy.

chan·cel·lor (chan′sə lər, chän′slər, chän′-), *n.* **1.** the chief minister of state, as in West Germany. **2.** a secretary, as to a king. **3.** the chief administrative officer in certain American universities. **4.** the judge of a U.S. court of equity in some states. —**chan′cel·lor·ship′**, *n.*

chance-med·ley (chans′med′lē, chäns′-), *n. Law.* a sudden quarrel, with violence.

chan·cer·y (chan′sə rē, chän′-), *n., pl.* **-cer·ies. 1.** a court having jurisdiction in equity. **2.** an office of public records, esp. in England **3.** chancellery (def. 1).

chan·cre (shang′kər), *n.* the initial lesion of syphilis, commonly a distinct sore with a hard base.

chan·croid (shang′kroid), *n.* an infectious venereal ulcer with a soft base.

chanc·y (chan′sē, chän′-), *adj.,* **chanc·i·er, chanc·i·est.** *Informal.* uncertain or risky.

chan·de·lier (shan′də lēr′), *n.* a light fixture suspended from a ceiling.

chan·dler (chand′lər, chänd′-), *n.* **1.** a dealer in supplies, esp. for ships. **2.** *Archaic.* a person who makes or sells candles. —**chan′dler·y,** *n.*

change (chānj), *v.,* **changed, changing,** *n.* —*v.t.* **1.** to make different. **2.** to exchange for something else. **3.** to give or get money in smaller denominations in exchange for. **4.** to give or get different money in exchange for. **5.** to remove and replace the covering or coverings of. —*v.i.* **6.** to become different. **7.** to make a change or an exchange. **8.** to change trains, airplanes, etc. **9.** to change one's clothes. **19. change off,** to alternate. —*n.* **11.** the act or fact of changing or being changed. **12.** a variation or deviation. **13.** a fresh set of clothing. **14.** money given in exchange for an equivalent of higher denomination. **15.** a balance of money that is returned when the sum tendered in payment is larger than the sum due. **16.** small coins. **17. ring the changes,** to repeat with variations. —**change′a·ble,** *adj.* —**change′ful,** *adj.* —**change′less,** *adj.* —**chang′er,** *n.* —**Syn. 1.** alter, modify, transform, vary.

change·ling (chānj′ling), *n.* a child surreptitiously or unintentionally substituted for another.

change′ of life′, menopause.

change·o·ver (chānj′ō′vər), *n.* a complete change from one thing or system to another.

change′ ring′ing, the art of ringing bells of different tones according to various sequences.

chan·nel (chan′əl), *n., v.,* **-neled, -nel·ing** or **-nelled, -nel·ling.** —*n.* **1.** the bed of a stream or waterway. **2.** the deeper part of a waterway. **3.** a wide strait, as between a continent and an island. **4.** a navigable route between two bodies of water. **5.** a means of access. **6. channels,** the prescribed course of communication. **7.** a frequency band wide enough for one-way communication from a radio or television station. **8.** a tubular passage, as for fluids. **9.** a groove or furrow. —*v.t.* **10.** to convey through a channel. **11.** to direct: *to channel one's interests.*

Chan′nel Is′lands, a British island group in the English Channel.

chan·nel·ize (chan′əl īz′), *v.t.,* **-ized, -iz·ing.** to channel. —**chan′nel·i·za′tion,** *n.*

chan·son (shan′sən), *n.* a song, esp. one with French lyrics.

chant (chant, chänt), *n.* **1.** a simple melody, esp. one in which several syllables are intoned, used in the church service. **2.** a monotonous intonation of the voice in speaking. —*v.t., v.i.* **3.** to sing or utter in a chant. **4.** to celebrate in song. —**chant′er,** *n.*

chan·teuse (shän tooz′), *n.* a female singer, esp. a woman who sings in nightclubs.

chant·ey (shan′tē, chan′-), *n., pl.* **-eys.** a sailors' song, esp. one sung in rhythm to work. Also, **chant′y.**

chan·ti·cleer (chan′tə klēr′), *n.* a rooster, used as a proper name in medieval fables.

chan·try (chan′trē, chän′-), *n., pl.* **-tries. 1.** an endowment for the singing or saying of Mass. **2.** a chapel so endowed.

Cha·nu·kah (KHä′nə kə, -noo kä′, hä′-), *n.* Hanukkah.

cha·os (kä′os), *n.* **1.** utter confusion or disorder. **2.** the formless matter supposed to have preceded the existence of the ordered universe. —**cha·ot·ic** (kā ot′ik), *adj.* —**cha·ot′i·cal·ly,** *adv.*

chap[1] (chap), *v.,* **chapped, chap·ping,** *n.* —*v.t.* **1.** to crack or roughen (the skin). —*v.i.* **2.** to become chapped. —*n.* **3.** a fissure or crack.

chap[2] (chap), *n. Informal.* a man or boy.

chap[3] (chop, chap), *n.* chop[2].

chap., **1.** chaplain. **2.** chapter.

chap·ar·ral (chap′ə ral′), *n.* a dense thicket.

chap·book (chap′book′), *n.* a pamphlet of popular tales, etc., formerly sold by peddlers.

cha·peau (sha pō′), *n., pl.* **-peaux** (-pōz′), **-peaus.** *Facetious.* a hat.

chap·el (chap′əl), *n.* **1.** a private or subordinate place of worship. **2.** a room or building for worship in a school, hospital, etc.

chap·er·on (shap′ə rōn′), *n.* **1.** a person, usually married or older, who, for propriety, accompanies a young unmarried woman in public. —*v.t., v.i.* **2.** to act as chaperon (for). Also, **chap′er·one′.** —**chap′er·on′age,** *n.*

chap·fall·en (chop′fô′lən, chap′-), *adj.* dispirited or dejected.

chap·lain (chap′lin), *n.* a member of the clergy attached to a chapel, a military unit, etc. —**chap′lain·cy,** *n.*

chap·let (chap′lit), *n.* **1.** a wreath for the head. **2.** a third of a complete rosary. **3.** *Archaic.* a string of beads. —**chap′let·ed,** *adj.*

chap·man (chap′mən), *n. Obs.* a hawker or peddler.

chaps (chaps, shaps), *n.pl.* strong, trouserlike leggings of leather, often widely flared, worn esp. by cowboys.

chap·ter (chap′tər), *n.* **1.** a main division of a book, treatise, etc. **2.** a branch of a society, fraternity, etc. **3.** an assembly of the monks or the canons of a church.

char[1] (chär), *v.,* **charred, char·ring.** —*v.t.* **1.** to burn or reduce to char-coal. **2.** to burn slightly. —*v.i.* **3.** to become charred.

char[2] (chär), *n., pl.* **char, chars.** any of a widely found genus of trout.

char[3] (chär), *n., v.,* **charred, char·ring.** *Brit.* —*n.* **1.** a charwoman. —*v.i.* **2.** to work as a charwoman.

char·à·banc (shar′ə bang′, -bangk′), *n. Obsolesc.* a sightseeing bus.

char·ac·ter (kar′ik tər), *n.* **1.** the aggregate of features and traits that form the individual nature of some person or thing. **2.** trait or characteristic. **3.** moral quality or integrity. **4.** good repute. **5.** status or capacity. **6.** a person, esp. with reference to behavior or personality. **7.** *Informal.* an odd or eccentric person. **8.** a person represented in a drama, story, etc. **9.** a letter or symbol used in writing or printing. **10.** any symbol that represents information and is usable by a computer.

char·ac·ter·is·tic (kar′ik tə ris′tik), *adj.* **1.** showing the usual character. —*n.* **2.** a distinguishing feature or quality. —**char′ac·ter·is′ti·cal·ly,** *adv.*

char·ac·ter·ize (kar′ik tə rīz′), *v.t.* **-ized, -iz·ing. 1.** to be a characteristic of. **2.** to describe the individual quality of. **3.** to attribute character to. —**char′ac·ter·i·za′tion,** *n.*

char·ac·ter·y (kar′ik tə rē, -trē), *n.* characters or symbols collectively.

cha·rade (shə rād′), *n.* **1.** **charades.** a game in which a player acts out in pantomime a word or phrase that other players must guess. **2.** a false pretense or show.

char·broil (chär′broil′), *v.t., v.i.* to broil (food) over a charcoal fire.

char·coal (chär′kōl′), *n.* **1.** a black, carbon-containing substance obtained by heating wood in the absence of air. **2.** a drawing pencil of charcoal. **3.** a drawing made with charcoal.

chard (chärd), *n.* a variety of beet having large leafstalks, used as a vegetable (**Swiss chard**).

charge (chärj), *v.,* **charged, charg·ing,** *n.* —*v.t.* **1.** to ask as a price. **2.** to hold liable for payment. **3.** to list or record as a debt. **4.** to attack or rush violently. **5.** to accuse or blame. **6.** to lay a task or duty upon. **7.** to fill or load with something, as bullets. **8.** to supply with a quantity of electrical energy: *to charge a storage battery.* **9.** to ascribe the responsibility for. —*v.i.* **10.** to attack or rush violently. **11.** to require payment. —*n.* **12.** the quantity that an apparatus is fitted to hold at one time. **13.** a duty or responsibility. **14.** care, custody, or superintendence. **15.** anything or anybody committed to one's care or management. **16.** an accusation or indictment. **17.** an instructional address by a judge to a jury. **18.** expense or cost. **19.** a fee or price charged. **20.** an assault or attack, as of soldiers. **21.** the quantity of electricity or electric energy in or upon an object or substance. **22.** *Slang.* a thrill or kick. **23.** in charge, in command or having supervisory power. —**charge′a·ble,** *adj.*

charge′ account′, an account that permits a customer to buy merchandise to be billed at a later date.

charge′ card′. See **credit card.** Also called **charge′ plate′.**

char·gé d'af·faires (shär zhä′ də fâr′, shär′zhā), *pl.* **char·gés d'af·faires** (shär′zhāz′ də fâr′, shär′zhāz). a diplomatic official in temporary charge of an embassy or legation.

charg·er (chär′jər), *n.* **1.** a person or thing that charges. **2.** a horse ridden in battle.

char·i·ot (char′ē ət), *n.* (in ancient Egypt, Greece, Rome, etc.) a light two-wheeled vehicle, used in warfare, races, and parades. —**char′i·ot·eer′** (-ə tēr′), *n.*

cha·ris·ma (kə riz′mə), *n.* the special quality that gives an individual influence, charm, or inspiration over large numbers of people. —**char′is·mat′ic,** *adj.*

char·i·ta·ble (char′i tə bəl), *adj.* **1.** generous to the poor. **2.** kindly or lenient. **3.** concerned with charity. —**char′i·ta·ble·ness,** *n.* —**char′i·ta·bly,** *adv.*

char·i·ty (char′i tē), *n., pl.* **-ties. 1.** generosity toward the poor. **2.** alms or aid. **3.** a charitable fund or institution. **4.** benevolent feeling. **5.** leniency or forbearance. **6.** Christian love.

char·la·tan (shär′lə tªn), *n.* a person who pretends to knowledge or skill. —**char′la·tan·ism, char′la·tan·ry,** *n.*

Char·le·magne (shär′lə mān′), *n.* A.D. 742–814, emperor of the Holy Roman Empire 800–814.

Charles·ton (chärlz′tən, chärl′stən), *n.* **1.** a vigorous, rhythmic ballroom dance popular in the 1920's. **2.** the capital of West Virginia.

char′ley horse′ (chär′lē), a painful contraction of an arm or leg muscle.

Char·lotte (shär′lət), *n.* a city in S North Carolina.

char′lotte russe′ (shär′lət rōōs′), a dessert made by lining a mold with sponge cake and filling it with custard.

Char·lotte·town (shär′lət toun), *n.* the capital of Prince Edward Island.

charm (chärm), *n.* **1.** a power of pleasing or attracting, as through personality or beauty. **2.** a trinket worn on a bracelet, etc. **3.** any ac-

tion or verse credited with magical power. —*v.t., v.i.* **4.** to delight or please by beauty, etc. **5.** to act (upon) with a charm. —**charm′er,** *n.* —**charm′ing,** *adj.* —**charm′ing·ly,** *adv.*

char·nel (chär′nªl), *n.* a house or room in which dead bodies or bones are deposited. Also called **char′nel house′.**

Char·on (kâr′ən, kar′-), *n. Class. Myth.* the ferryman on the Styx.

chart (chärt), *n.* **1.** a sheet exhibiting information in tabular form. **2.** any graphic representation. **3.** a map, esp. for nautical use. —*v.t.* **4.** to make a chart of. **5.** to plan in detail.

char·ter (chär′tər), *n.* **1.** a governmental document outlining the conditions under which a corporation, colony, or city is organized. **2.** a document defining the formal organization of a corporate body. **3.** authorization from a parent organization to establish a new branch, etc. **4.** a temporary lease of a vessel or aircraft. —*v.t.* **5.** to establish by charter. **6.** to hire by charter. —**char′ter·er,** *n.*

char′ter mem′ber, an original member of a club, organization, etc.

char·treuse (shär trōōz′), *n.* **1.** green or yellow aromatic liqueur. **2.** a clear, yellowish green.

char·wom·an (chär′wōōm′ən), *n. Brit.* a woman hired to do general cleaning.

char·y (châr′ē), *adj.,* **char·i·er, char·i·est. 1.** discerningly or mistrustfully careful. **2.** not lavish. —**char′i·ly,** *adv.* —**char′i·ness,** *n.*

chase¹ (chās), *v.,* **chased, chas·ing,** *n.* —*v.t.* **1.** to pursue in order to seize, overtake, etc. **2.** to hunt. **3.** to devote attention to with the hope of attracting, etc. **4.** to drive by pursuing. —*v.i.* **5.** *Informal.* to run or hasten. **6.** to follow in pursuit. —*n.* **7.** the act of chasing or pursuing. **8.** something chased. **9.** the chase, the sport of hunting. **10. give chase,** to pursue.

chase² (chās), *n.* a groove cut in a wall, as for a pipe.

chase³ (chās), *v.t.,* **chased, chas·ing.** to ornament (metal) by engraving or embossing.

chas·er (chā′sər), *n.* **1.** a person or thing that chases. **2.** *Informal.* a mild beverage taken after a drink of liquor.

chasm (kaz′əm), *n.* **1.** a deep cleft in the earth's surface, as a gorge. **2.** a gap or break. —**chas′mal,** *adj.*

chas·sis (shas′ē, -is, chas′ē), *n., pl.* **chas·sis** (shas′ēz, chas′-). **1.** the frame, wheels, and machinery of a motor vehicle, on which the body is supported. 2. a frame for mounting the circuit components of a radio or television set. 3. the main landing gear of an aircraft.

chaste (chāst), *adj.*, **chast·er, chast·est.** 1. not having engaged in unlawful sexual intercourse. 2. free from obscenity: *chaste conversation.* 3. pure or simple in style. —**chaste′ly,** *adv.* —**chaste′ness,** *n.* —Syn. 1. decent, pure, virginal, virtuous.

chas·ten (chā′sən), *v.t.* 1. to inflict suffering upon for moral improvement. 2. to restrain or subdue. 3. to make chaste in style. —**chas′ten·er,** *n.*

chas·tise (chas tīz′, chas′tīz), *v.t.,* **-tised, -tis·ing.** 1. to punish, esp. by whipping. 2. to criticize sharply. —**chas·tise·ment** (chas′tiz mənt, chas tīz′-), *n.* —**chas·tis′er,** *n.*

chas·ti·ty (chas′ti tē), *n.* the state or quality of being chaste.

chas·u·ble (chaz′yə bəl, -ə bəl, chas′-), *n.* a sleeveless outer vestment worn by the celebrant at Mass.

chat (chat), *v.,* **chat·ted, chat·ting,** *n.* —*v.i.* 1. to converse informally. —*n.* 2. informal conversation.

châ·teau (sha tō′), *n., pl.* **-teaus, -teaux** (-tōz′). 1. a castle in a French-speaking country. 2. a stately European country estate, esp. in France. Also, **cha·teau′.**

chat·e·laine (shat′°lān′), *n.* 1. the mistress of a castle. 2. a hooklike clasp for suspending keys, trinkets, etc.

Chat·ta·noo·ga (chat′ə nōō′gə), *n.* a city in SE Tennessee.

chat·tel (chat′°l), *n.* 1. *Law.* a movable article of personal property. 2. *Archaic.* a slave.

chat·ter (chat′ər), *v.i.* 1. to talk rapidly, constantly, and pointlessly. 2. to utter quick, inarticulate, speechlike sounds. 3. to make a rapid clicking noise by striking together. —*n.* 4. idle or foolish talk. 5. the act or sound of chattering. —**chat′ter·er,** *n.*

chat·ter·box (chat′ər boks′), *n.* an excessively talkative person.

chat·ty (chat′ē), *adj.,* **-ti·er, -ti·est.** given to or full of chatting. —**chat′ti·ly,** *adv.* —**chat′ti·ness,** *n.*

Chau·cer (chô′ sər), *n.* **Geoffrey,** 1340?–1400, English poet.

chauf·feur (shō′fər, shō fûr′), *n.* 1. a person employed to drive a private automobile. —*v.t., v.i.* 2. to drive or work as a chauffeur (for).

chau·vin·ism (shō′və niz′əm), *n.* 1. zealous and belligerent patriotism. 2. prejudiced devotion to any attitude or cause: *male chauvinism.* —**chau′vin·ist,** *n.* —**chau′vin·is′tic,** *adj.* —**chau′vin·is′ti·cal·ly,** *adv.*

cheap (chēp), *adj.* 1. of a low price.

2. costing little labor or trouble. 3. charging low prices. 4. of little worth or value. 5. vulgar or contemptible. 6. stingy or miserly. —*adv.* 7. at a low price. —**cheap′ly,** *adv.* —**cheap′ness,** *n.*

cheap·en (chē′pən), *v.t., v.i.* to make or become cheap or cheaper.

cheap′ shot′, *Slang.* a mean, unfair remark or act.

cheap·skate (chēp′skāt′), *n. Slang.* a stingy person.

cheat (chēt), *n.* 1. a person who defrauds. 2. a fraud or swindle. —*v.t.* 3. to defraud or swindle. 4. to deprive of something expected. —*v.i.* 5. to practice fraud or deceit. 6. to violate regulations unfairly, as on an examination or at cards. 7. *Slang.* to be sexually unfaithful. —**cheat′er,** *n.* —**cheat′ing·ly,** *adv.* —Syn. 3. deceive, dupe, hoodwink, victimize.

check (chek), *v.t.* 1. to stop the motion of suddenly. 2. to restrain or curb. 3. to verify as to correctness. 4. to make an inquiry into, search through, etc. 5. to mark (something) to indicate correctness, preference, etc. 6. to leave in temporary custody. 7. to ship (baggage) on a passenger ticket for pickup at destination. 8. to mark in a pattern of squares. 9. *Chess.* to place (an opponent's king) under direct attack. —*v.i.* 10. to correspond accurately. 11. to make an inquiry, etc., as for verification. 12. **check in,** to register, as at a hotel. 13. **check out, a.** to pay a hotel bill and leave. **b.** to figure out the total purchase for collection of payment. **c.** to fulfill requirements. —*n.* 14. a person or thing that stops or restrains. 15. a sudden stoppage. 16. a test or inspection that ascertains performance. 17. an inquiry or examination. 18. a mark (√) to indicate approval or verification. 19. a written order directing a bank to pay money. 20. a bill at a restaurant. 21. a ticket or token showing identification or ownership. 22. a pattern formed of squares. 23. *Chess.* the exposure of the king to direct attack. 24. **in check,** under restraint. —*interj.* 25. *Slang.* all right! agreed! —**check′a·ble,** *adj.* —**check′less,** *adj.*

check·book (chek′bŏŏk′), *n.* a book containing blank checks on a bank.

check·er¹ (chek′ər), *n.* 1. a small, usually red or black disk used in playing checkers. 2. **checkers,** a game played by two persons, each with 12 playing pieces, on a checkerboard. —*v.t.* 3. to mark like a checkerboard. 4. to diversify in color. 5. to diversify in character.

check·er² (chek'ər), n. **1.** a person or thing that checks. **2.** a person who checks coats, etc.

check·er·board (chek'ər bôrd', -bôrd'), n. a board marked off into sixty-four squares of two alternating colors, on which checkers is played.

check'ing account', a bank deposit against which checks can be drawn.

check' list', items listed together for convenience of comparison or other checking purposes.

check·mate (chek'māt'), n., v., -mat·ed, -mat·ing. —n. **1.** Chess. **a.** the act of maneuvering the opponent's king into a check from which it cannot escape. **b.** this position. **2.** defeat or overthrow. —v.t. **3.** Chess. to put in checkmate. **4.** to defeat or overthrow.

check·off (chek'ôf', -of'), n. the withholding of union dues by employers.

check·out (chek'out'), n. **1.** the act or place of checking out, as purchases in a supermarket. **2.** the time before which one must check out of a hotel.

check·point (chek'point'), n. a place, as at a border, where vehicles or travelers are stopped for inspection.

check·room (chek'rōōm', -rōōm'), n. a room where hats, coats, etc., may be checked.

check·up (chek'up'), n. **1.** an examination or verification as to accuracy, etc. **2.** a comprehensive medical examination.

Ched·dar (ched'ər), n. a hard, smooth-textured cheese. [after Cheddar, England, where first made]

cheek (chēk), n. **1.** either side of the face below the eye and above the jaw. **2.** something resembling the side of the human face in form or position. **3.** Informal. impudence or effrontery.

cheek·bone (chēk'bōn'), n. the bone just below the eye.

cheek·y (chē'kē), adj., cheek·i·er, cheek·i·est. Informal. impudent or insolent. —cheek'i·ly, adv. —cheek'i·ness, n.

cheep (chēp), v.i., v.t., n. chirp. —cheep'er, n.

cheer (chēr), n. **1.** a shout of encouragement, approval, etc. **2.** a traditional shout used by spectators to encourage an athletic team, contestant, etc. **3.** encouragement or comfort. **4.** a state of feeling or spirits. **5.** gladness or gaiety. —interj. **6.** cheers, (used as a toast to one's drinking companions.) —v.t. **7.** to salute with shouts of approval, triumph, etc. **8.** to restore cheerfulness or hope to. —v.i. **9.** to utter cheers. **10.** to become more cheerful.

cheer·ful (chēr'fəl), adj. **1.** full of cheer. **2.** pleasant or bright. **3.** hearty or ungrudging. —cheer'ful·ly, adv. —cheer'ful·ness, n.

cheer·i·o (chēr'ē ō', chēr'ē ō'), interj. Brit. **1.** goodby! **2.** (used as a toast to one's drinking companions.)

cheer·lead·er (chēr'lē'dər), n. a person who leads spectators in cheering, esp. at a game.

cheer·less (chēr'lis), adj. joyless or gloomy. —cheer'less·ly, adv. —cheer'less·ness, n.

cheer·y (chēr'ē), adj., cheer·i·er, cheer·i·est. joyous or gay. —cheer'i·ly, adv. —cheer'i·ness, n.

cheese (chēz), n. the curd of milk separated from the whey and prepared in many ways as a food. [< L *cāse(us)*]

cheese·burg·er (chēz'bûr'gər), n. a hamburger cooked with a slice of cheese on top of it.

cheese·cake (chēz'kāk'), n. **1.** a rich, custardlike cake prepared with cottage cheese or cream cheese. **2.** Slang. photographs featuring the legs and body of an attractive woman.

cheese·cloth (chēz'klôth', -kloth'), n. a coarse, lightweight cotton fabric of open texture.

cheese·par·ing (chēz'pâr'ing), adj. Brit. meanly economical.

chees·y (chē'zē), adj., chees·i·er, chees·i·est. **1.** of or like cheese. **2.** Slang. of poor quality. —chees'i·ness, n.

chee·tah (chē'tə), n. a cat of southwestern Asia and Africa, resembling a leopard.

chef (shef), n. a cook, esp. a male head cook.

chef-d'oeu·vre (she dœ'/vʀ°), n., pl. **chefs-d'oeu·vre** (she dœ'/vʀ°). a masterpiece, esp. in art.

Che·khov (chek'ôf, -of), n. **An·ton Pa·vlo·vich** (än tôn' pä vlô'vich), 1860–1904, Russian writer.

che·la (kē'lə), n., pl. -lae (-lē). the pincerlike organ or claw terminating certain limbs of crustaceans.

chem., **1.** chemical. **2.** chemist. **3.** chemistry.

chem·i·cal (kem'i kəl), adj. **1.** of, used in, produced by, or concerned with chemistry, or its actions or properties. —n. **2.** a substance used in a chemical process. —chem'i·cal·ly, adv.

chem'ical engineer'ing, the science or profession of applying chemistry to industrial processes. —chem'ical engineer'.

chem'ical war'fare, warfare using poisonous, corrosive, or debilitating gases, oil flames, etc.

che·mise (shə mēz′), *n.* **1.** a woman's loose-fitting, shirtlike undergarment. **2.** a dress with an unfitted waistline.

chem·ist (kem′ist), *n.* **1.** a person skilled in chemistry. **2.** *Brit.* a druggist.

chem·is·try (kem′i strē), *n.*, *pl.* **-tries. 1.** the science that deals with or investigates the composition, properties, and transformations of substances and various elementary forms of matter. **2.** a group of chemical properties, reactions, etc.

chem·o·ster·i·lant (kem′ō ster′ə lənt, kēm′ə-), *n.* any of various chemical compounds that cause sterility in insects or birds without hampering their normal life.

chem·o·ther·a·py (kem′ə ther′ə pē, kē′mə-), *n.* the treatment of disease by means of chemicals. —**chem′o·ther′a·peu′tic** (-pyōō′tik), **chem′o·ther′a·peu′ti·cal**, *adj.* —**chem′o·ther′a·pist**, *n.*

chem·ur·gy (kem′ûr jē), *n.* chemistry concerned with the industrial use of organic substances, esp. from farm produce. —**chem·ur′gic**, *adj.*

che·nille (shə nēl′), *n.* **1.** a velvety cord of silk or worsted. **2.** fabric made of this.

cheque (chek), *n.* *Brit.* check (def. 19).

cher·ish (cher′ish), *v.t.* **1.** to hold dear. **2.** to nurture. **3.** to cling fondly to. —**cher′ish·er**, *n.*

Cher·o·kee (cher′ə kē′, cher′ə kē′), *n.*, *pl.* **-kees**, **-kee.** a member of a tribe of North American Indians whose present center is in Oklahoma.

che·root (shə rōōt′), *n.* a cigar having open, untapered ends.

cher·ry (cher′ē), *n.*, *pl.* **-ries. 1.** a berrylike red fruit that contains one round pit. **2.** the tree it grows on. **3.** its wood. **4.** a bright red.

cher·ry·stone (cher′ē stōn′), *n.* a small, round clam.

chert (chûrt), *n.* a compact rock consisting of fine-grained quartz. —**chert′y**, *adj.*

cher·ub (cher′əb), *n.*, *pl.* **cher·ubs** for 2; **cher·u·bim** (cher′ə bim, -yōō bim) for 1. **1.** a member of the second order of angels, often represented as a winged child. **2.** an innocent person, esp. a child. —**che·ru·bic** (chə rōō′bik), **che·ru′bi·cal**, *adj.* —**che·ru′bi·cal·ly**, *adv.*

cher·vil (chûr′vil), *n.* a plant of the parsley family, having aromatic leaves used to flavor soups, salads, etc.

Ches′a·peake Bay′ (ches′ə pēk′), an inlet of the Atlantic, in Maryland and Virginia.

chess (ches), *n.* a game played by two persons, each with sixteen chessmen, on a chessboard.

chess·board (ches′bôrd′, -bōrd′), *n.* the board, identical with a checkerboard, used in chess.

chess·man (ches′man′, -mən), *n.* one of the pieces used in the game of chess.

chest (chest), *n.* **1.** the trunk of the body from the neck to the abdomen. **2.** a box, usually a large, strong one, for storage, etc. **3.** See **chest of drawers.**

ches·ter·field (ches′tər fēld′), *n.* a topcoat or overcoat with a narrow velvet collar. [after Earl of *Chesterfield*, 19th century]

chest·nut (ches′nut′, -nət), *n.* **1.** the edible nut of trees of the beech family. **2.** any of these trees. **3.** the wood of these trees. **4.** a dark reddish brown. **5.** *Informal.* an old or stale joke, anecdote, etc.

chest′ of drawers′, a piece of furniture with a set of drawers for keeping clothes.

che·val′ glass′ (shə val′), a full-length mirror mounted in a frame so that it can be tilted.

chev·a·lier (shev′ə lēr′, shə val′yā, -väl′-), *n.* a member of certain orders of honor or merit.

chev·i·ot (shev′ē ət), *n.* a woolen fabric in a coarse twill weave, for coats, suits, etc.

chev·ron (shev′rən), *n.* a badge consisting of stripes meeting at an angle, worn on the sleeve of a uniform as an indication of rank or service.

chew (chōō), *v.t.*, *v.i.* **1.** to crush or bite with the teeth. **2. chew out,** *Slang.* to scold harshly. **3. chew the fat** or **rag,** *Slang.* to have a chat. —*n.* **4.** the act or an instance of chewing. **5.** something chewed or suitable for chewing. —**chew′a·ble**, *adj.* —**chew′er**, *n.*

chew′ing gum′ (chōō′ing), a preparation for chewing, usually made of flavored chicle.

chew·y (chōō′ē), *adj.*, **chew·i·er**, **chew·i·est.** (of food) not easily chewed.

Chey·enne (shī en′, -an′), *n.*, *pl.* **-ennes**, **-enne** for 1. **1.** a member of an American Indian people of the western plains, living in Montana and Oklahoma. **2.** the capital of Wyoming.

chg., **1.** change. **2.** charge.

chi (kī), *n.* the 22nd letter of the Greek alphabet (X, χ).

Chi·an·ti (kē än′tē, -an′-), *n.* a dry, red, Italian table wine.

chi·a·ro·scu·ro (kē ä′rə skyōōr′ō), *n.*, *pl.* **-ros.** the distribution of light and shade in a picture.

chic (shēk, shik), *adj.* 1. attractive and fashionable in style. —*n.* 2. style and elegance. 3. stylishness or fashionableness. —**chic′ly,** *adv.*

Chi·ca·go (shi kä′go, -kô′-), *n.* a city in NE Illinois. —**Chi·ca′go·an,** *n.*

chi·can·er·y (shi kā′nə rē), *n., pl.* **-er·ies.** petty trickery and deception. Also, **chi·cane** (shi kān′).

Chi·ca·no (chi kä′nō, -kä′nō), *n., pl.* **-nos.** 1. a U.S. citizen or resident of Mexican descent. —*adj.* 2. of Chicanos.

chi·chi (shē′shē′), *adj.* showily elegant, sophisticated, or stylish.

chick (chik), *n.* 1. a young chicken or other bird. 2. *Slang.* a girl or young woman.

chick·a·dee (chik′ə dē′), *n.* a small gray North American bird having the throat and top of the head black.

Chick·a·saw (chik′ə sô′), *n., pl.* **-saws, -saw.** a member of a tribe of North American Indians now in Oklahoma.

chick·en (chik′ən, -in), *n.* 1. the common domestic fowl. 2. the young of this bird. 3. the flesh of the chicken, used as food. —*adj.* 4. *Slang.* cowardly. —*v.i.* 5. **chicken out,** *Slang.* to refrain because of cowardice.

chick′en feed′, *Slang.* an insignificant sum of money.

chick·en-heart·ed (chik′ən här′tid, chik′in-), *adj.* timid or cowardly. Also, **chick·en-liv·ered** (chik′ən-liv′ərd).

chick′en pox′, a mild, contagious, eruptive children's disease.

chick′en wire′, a light, wire netting used esp. in building fences or barriers.

chick·pea (chik′pē′), *n.* 1. a leguminous plant bearing edible pealike seeds, used for food. 2. its seed.

chick·weed (chik′wēd′), *n.* a common weed whose small leaves and seeds are relished by birds.

chic·le (chik′əl), *n.* a gumlike substance from the latex of certain tropical American trees, used chiefly in the manufacture of chewing gum.

chic·o·ry (chik′ə rē), *n., pl.* **-ries.** 1. a perennial plant having bright-blue flowers, cultivated as a salad plant. 2. its root, used ground as a substitute or additive for coffee.

chide (chīd), *v.t., v.i.,* **chid·ed** or **chid** (chid), **chid·ed** or **chid** or **chid·den** (chid′ən), **chid·ing.** to scold mildly. —**chid′er,** *n.* —**chid′ing·ly,** *adv.*

chief (chēf), *n.* 1. the leader of an organized group of people. 2. the head of a tribe: *Indian chief.* 3.

Slang. a boss or manager. —*adj.* 4. highest in rank. 5. most important. —**chief′ly,** *adv., adj.* —**Syn.** 5. foremost, leading, prime, principal.

Chief′ Exec′utive, the President of the United States.

chief′ jus′tice, 1. the presiding judge of a court having several members. 2. (*caps.*) the presiding judge of the U.S. Supreme Court.

chief′ mas′ter ser′geant, *U.S. Air Force.* a noncommissioned officer of the top grade.

chief′ of staff′, the senior officer in command of a general staff, esp. that of the military forces.

chief′ of state′, the titular head of a nation.

chief′ pet′ty of′ficer, *U.S. Navy and Coast Guard.* a noncommissioned rank below senior chief petty officer.

chief·tain (chēf′tən, -tin), *n.* the chief of a clan or a tribe. —**chief′tain·cy, chief′tain·ship′,** *n.*

chief′ war′rant of′ficer, a warrant officer ranking immediately below a second lieutenant or ensign.

chif·fon (shi fon′, shif′on), *n.* 1. a sheer fabric of silk in plain weave. —*adj.* 2. of chiffon. 3. having a light, frothy texture, as with beaten egg whites.

chif·fo·nier (shif′ə nēr′), *n.* a high chest of drawers, often with a mirror. Also, **chif′fon·nier′.**

chif·fo·robe (shif′ə rōb′), *n.* a piece of furniture having both drawers and space for hanging clothes.

chig·ger (chig′ər), *n.* 1. the six-legged larva of a mite parasitic on humans and other vertebrates, causing severe skin itching. 2. chigoe.

chi·gnon (shēn′yon, shēn yun′), *n.* a large, smooth knot of hair, worn at the back of the head.

chig·oe (chig′ō), *n.* a tropical flea that burrows into the skin.

Chi·hua·hua (chi wä′wä, -wə), *n.* a very small dog with large erect ears.

chil·blain (chil′blān′), *n.* an inflammation of the hands and feet caused by exposure to cold.

child (chīld), *n., pl.* **chil·dren.** 1. a boy or girl. 2. a son or daughter. 3. a baby or infant. 4. a childish person. 5. any person or thing regarded as the result of particular influences, etc.: *a child of poverty.* 6. **with child,** pregnant. —**child′ish,** *adj.* —**child′ish·ly,** *adv.* —**child′ish·ness,** *n.* —**child′less,** *adj.* —**child′less·ness,** *n.* —**child′like,** *adj.*

child·bear·ing (chīld′bâr′ing), *n.* 1. the act of producing children. —*adj.* 2. of or pertaining to childbearing.

child·birth (chīld′bûrth′), *n.* the act or an instance of bringing forth a child.

child·hood (chīld′hŏŏd), *n.* the state or period of being a child.

child·proof (chīld′prōōf′), *adj.* so designed that children cannot tamper with, esp. to harm themselves: *a childproof cap on an aspirin bottle.*

chil·dren (chil′drən, -drin), *n.* pl. of **child.**

Chil′dren of God′, a highly disciplined, fundamentalist Christian sect whose converts, mostly young, live in a commune.

chil′dren of Is′rael, the ancient Hebrews or modern Jews.

child′s′ play′, something very easily done.

Chil·e (chil′ē), *n.* a country in SW South America. —**Chil′e·an,** *adj., n.*

chil·i (chil′ē), *n., pl.* **chil·ies.** 1. the hot pungent pod of a variety of red pepper. 2. See **chili con carne.** Also, **chil′e, chil′li.**

chil·i con car·ne (chil′ē kon kär′nē), a Mexican dish of meat, beans, onion, chopped pepper, etc.

chil′i sauce′, a sauce of tomatoes simmered with chili peppers and spices.

chill (chil), *n.* 1. coldness, esp. when moderate but penetrating. 2. a sensation of cold, usually with shivering. 3. a depressing influence or sensation. —*adj.* 4. chilly. —*v.i., v.t.* 5. to make or become cold. 6. to cause a sensation of fear (in). —**chill′ing·ly,** *adv.* —**chill′ness,** *n.*

chill·er (chil′ər), *n. Informal.* a frightening story of murder.

chill′ fac′tor. See **wind chill.**

chill·y (chil′ē), *adj.,* -**i·er,** -**i·est,** *adv.* —*adj.* 1. mildly cold. 2. feeling cold. 3. without warmth of feeling. —*adv.* 4. Also, **chil′li·ly.** in a chill manner. —**chil′li·ness,** *n.*

chime (chīm), *n., v.,* **chimed, chiming.** —*n.* 1. Often, **chimes.** a set of bells producing musical tones when struck. 2. the musical tones thus produced. 3. harmonious sound in general. —*v.i.* 4. to sound in chimes. 5. to harmonize or agree. —*v.t.* 6. to indicate or announce (the hour) by chiming. 7. **chime in, a.** to break into, as a conversation. **b.** to harmonize, as in singing. —**chim′er,** *n.*

chi·me·ra (ki mēr′ə, kī), *n., pl.* -**ras.** 1. (*often cap.*) a mythological fire-breathing monster, represented with a lion's head, a goat's body, and a serpent's tail. 2. a vain or idle fancy. Also, **chi·mae′ra.**

chi·mer·i·cal (ki mer′i kəl, -mēr′-, kī), *adj.* unreal, imaginary, or wildly fanciful. Also, **chi·mer′ic.**

chim·ney (chim′nē), *n., pl.* -**neys.** 1. a structure, usually vertical, containing a passage by which the smoke, etc., of a fire or furnace are carried off. 2. a tube, usually of glass, surrounding the flame of a lamp.

chimp (chimp), *n. Informal.* chimpanzee.

chim·pan·zee (chim′pan zē′, chimpan′zē), *n.* a humanlike ape of equatorial Africa.

chin (chin), *n., v.,* **chinned, chin·ning.** —*n.* 1. the lower extremity of the face, below the mouth. —*v.t.* 2. to bring one's chin up to (a horizontal bar, from which one is hanging by the hands), by bending the elbows. —*v.i.* 3. *Informal.* to talk or chatter.

Chin., 1. China. 2. Chinese.

chi·na (chī′nə), *n.* 1. a translucent ceramic material. 2. any porcelain ware. 3. plates, cups, saucers, etc., collectively. Also called **chi′na·ware′.**

Chi·na (chī′nə), *n.* 1. **People's Republic of,** a country in E Asia. 2. **Republic of,** a country consisting of Taiwan and adjacent small islands.

Chi·na·town (chī′nə toun′), *n.* the Chinese quarter of a city.

chinch′ bug′ (chinch), a small black-and-white bug that feeds on corn, wheat, etc.

chin·chil·la (chin chil′ə), *n.* 1. a small, South American rodent having a soft, silvery gray fur. 2. the fur of this animal. 3. a thick, napped, woolen fabric for coats.

chine (chīn), *n.* 1. the backbone or spine. 2. a cut of meat from the backbone. 3. a ridge or crest.

Chi·nese (chī nēz′, -nēs′), *n., pl.* -**nese,** *adj.* —*n.* 1. the language of China. 2. a native of China. —*adj.* 3. of China, its people, or their language.

Chi′nese check′ers, a board game in which marbles resting in holes are moved to the opposite side.

Chi′nese lan′tern, a collapsible lantern of thin, colored paper.

Chi′nese-res′taurant syn′drome, physical distress believed to be caused by the monosodium glutamate often used in Chinese food.

Chi′nese Wall′, an insuperable barrier, as to understanding.

chink¹ (chingk), *n.* 1. a crack, as in a wall. —*v.t.* 2. to fill up chinks in.

chink² (chingk), *n., v., v.i.* 1. to make or cause to make a short, sharp, ringing sound. —*n.* 2. a chinking sound.

chi·no (chē′nō), *n., pl.* -**nos** for 2. 1. a tough, twilled cotton cloth used for uniforms, etc. 2. Usually, **chinos.** a pair of trousers made of this material.

Chi·nook (shi nook', -nook', chi-), n., pl. -nooks, -nook. a member of a North American Indian people originally inhabiting Oregon.

chintz (chints), n. a printed cotton fabric, used esp. for draperies.

chintz·y (chint'sē), adj., chintz·i·er, chintz·i·est. 1. decorated with chintz. 2. Informal. cheap or gaudy.

chin·up (chin'up'), n. the act or an instance of chinning a horizontal bar, rod, etc.

chip (chip), n., v., chipped, chip·ping. —n. 1. a small piece, as of wood, separated by chopping or breaking. 2 a very thin slice of food: potato chips. 3. a flaw made by the breaking off of a small piece. 4. a small disk used as a counter, as in roulette. 5. a tiny square piece of thin semiconducting material on which an integrated circuit is formed. 6. chip on one's shoulder, a disposition to quarrel. 7. in the chips, Slang. wealthy or rich. 8. when the chips are down, in a crucial situation. —v.t. 9. to break off chips from. —v.i. 10. to break off in chips. 11. chip in, Informal. a. to contribute money, as to a fund. b. to interrupt or interject. —chip'per, n.

chip·munk (chip'mungk), n. a small, striped squirrel of North America.

chipped' beef', very thin slices of dried, smoked beef.

chip·per (chip'or), adj. Informal. lively or cheerful.

Chip·pe·wa (chip'ə wä', -wä', -wə), n., pl. -was, wa. Ojibwa.

chip·py (chip'ē), n., pl. -pies. Informal. a prostitute.

chip' shot', Golf. a shot hit fairly high into the air in approaching the green.

chiro- a combining form meaning "hand": chiromancy.

chi·rog·ra·phy (kī rog'rə fē), n. the style of handwriting. —chi·rog'ra·pher, n. —chi·ro·graph·ic (kī'rə-graf'ik), chi'ro·graph'i·cal, adj.

chi·ro·man·cy (kī'rə man'sē), n. divination by analyzing the appearance of the hand.

chi·rop·o·dy (kī rop'ə dē, ki-, shə-), n. podiatry. —chi·rop'o·dist, n.

chi·ro·prac·tic (kī'rə prak'tik), n. a therapeutic system based upon adjusting the segments of the spinal column. —chi'ro·prac'tor, n.

chirp (chûrp), v.i. 1. to make a short, sharp sound, as small birds. —v.t. 2. to utter in a chirping manner. —n. 3. a chirping sound.

chir·rup (chêr'əp, chûr'-), v.i., v.t., -ruped, -rup·ing, n. chirp.

chis·el (chiz'əl), n., v., -eled, -el·ing or -elled, -el·ing. —n. 1. a wedgelike, sharp-edged tool used for cutting or shaping wood, stone, etc.

—v.t., v.i. 2. to cut or work with a chisel. 3. Slang. a. to swindle (someone). b. to get by trickery. —chis'el·er, n.

chit¹ (chit), n. a voucher of money owed for food, drink, etc.

chit² (chit), n. a child or young person, esp. a pert girl.

chit·chat (chit'chat'), n. 1. light conversation. 2. idle talk.

chi·tin (kī'tin), n. a horny, organic component of the outer covering of arthropods. —chi'tin·ous, adj.

chit·ter·lings (chit'linz), n. the small intestine of swine, usually fried or in a sauce. Also, chit'lings, chit'·lins.

chiv·al·rous (shiv'əl rəs), adj. 1. courageous, generous, and courteous. 2. courteous or gallant to women. 3. of chivalry. Also, chiv·al·ric (shiv'əl rik, shi val'rik). —chiv'al·rous·ly, adv. —chiv'al·rous·ness, n.

chiv·al·ry (shiv'əl rē), n. 1. the qualities expected of a knight, as courage, generosity, and courtesy. 2. medieval knighthood. 3. courtesy or gallantry toward women.

chive (chīv), n. a small bulbous plant related to the onion, having long, slender leaves used as a seasoning in cookery.

chlo·ral (klôr'əl, klōr'-), n. 1. an oily liquid that combines with water to form chloral hydrate. 2. Also called chlo'ral hy'drate. a white crystalline solid used as a hypnotic.

chlor·dane (klôr'dān, klōr'-), n. a toxic liquid used as an insecticide. Also, chlor'dan (-dan).

chlo·ride (klôr'īd, -id, klōr'-), n. a salt of hydrochloric acid consisting of two elements, one of which is chlorine.

chlo·rin·ate (klôr'ə nāt', klōr'-), v.t., -at·ed, -at·ing. 1. to combine or treat with chlorine. 2. to disinfect (water) with chlorine. —chlo'rin·a'tion, n. —chlo'rin·a'tor, n.

chlo·rine (klôr'ēn, -in, klōr'-), n. Chem. a greenish-yellow, incombustible, poisonous, gaseous element that is highly irritating to the respiratory organs, used for water purification, in making bleaching powder, etc. Symbol: Cl; at. wt: 35.453; at. no.: 17.

chlo·rite (klôr'īt, klōr'-), n. a group of minerals occurring in green platelike crystals or scales.

chlo·ro·form (klôr'ə fôrm', klōr'-), n. 1. a colorless, volatile, nonflammable liquid, used as an anesthetic and as a solvent. —v.t. 2. to administer chloroform to.

chlo·ro·phyll (klôr'ə fil, klōr'-), *n.* the green coloring matter of leaves and plants, essential in photosynthesis. Also, **chlo'ro·phyl.**

chm., chairman.

chock (chok), *n.* **1.** a wedge for holding an object steady, preventing motion, etc. —*v.t.* **2.** to furnish with chocks. —*adv.* **3.** as tight as possible.

chock-a-block (chok'ə blok'), *adv.* in a jammed or crowded condition.

chock-full (chok'fōōl'), *adj.* full to the utmost or limit.

choc·o·late (chô'kə lit, chok'ə-, chŏk'-lit, chok'-), *n.* **1.** a preparation of the seeds of cacao, often sweetened and flavored. **2.** a beverage or candy made from this. **3.** a dark brown.

Choc·taw (chok'tô), *n., pl.* **-taws, -taw** a member of a tribe of North American Indians living in Oklahoma.

choice (chois), *n., adj.,* **choic·er, choic·est.** —*n.* **1.** the act of choosing or selecting. **2.** the right or opportunity to choose. **3.** a person or thing that is or may be chosen. **4.** an alternative. **5.** a variety from which one may choose. **6.** the best part of anything. —*adj.* **7.** excellent or superior. **8.** carefully selected.

choir (kwīr), *n.* **1.** a group of singers, as for a church. **2.** the part of a church occupied by such a group. **3.** any group of musicians or musical instruments: *string choir.* [< OF *cuer* < *chor(us)* chorus]

choir' loft', a raised gallery for a choir.

choir·mas·ter (kwīr'mas'tər, -mä'stər), *n.* the leader or director of a choir.

choke (chōk), *v.,* **choked, chok·ing, n.** —*v.t.* **1.** to hinder the breathing of, as by obstructing the windpipe. **2.** to obstruct, as a pipe. **3.** to arrest the growth or activity of. **4.** to suppress, as an emotion: *She choked back her tears.* **6.** to enrich the fuel mixture of (an internal-combustion engine) by diminishing the air supply to the carburetor. —*v.i.* **6.** to suffer from suffocating. **7.** to become obstructed. **8.** **choke up,** to become speechless, as from emotion. —*n.* **9.** the act or sound of choking. **10.** any mechanism that, by blocking a passage, regulates the flow of air, gas, etc.

chok·er (chō'kər), *n.* a necklace that fits snugly around the neck.

chol·er (kol'ər), *n. Literary.* irascibility or anger.

chol·er·a (kol'ər ə), *n.* an acute, infectious, often epidemic fatal disease, characterized by profuse diarrhea, vomiting, etc.

chol·er·ic (kol'ər ik, kə ler'ik), *adj. Literary.* irascible or angry.

cho·les·ter·ol (kə les'tə rōl', -rôl', -rol'), *n.* a colorless crystalline substance occurring in tissues of the animal organism.

cho·line (kō'lēn, kol'ēn, -in), *n.* one of the B-complex vitamins, found in lecithin.

chomp (chomp), *v.t., v.i. Dial.* to munch.

chon·drite (kon'drīt), *n.* a stony meteorite containing chondrules.

chon·drule (kon'drōōl), *n.* a small round mass of olivine found in stony meteorites.

choose (chōōz), *v.,* **choose, cho·sen, choos·ing.** —*v.t., v.i.* **1.** to select in preference. **2.** to decide or desire. **3.** **cannot choose but,** cannot do otherwise than. —**choos'er,** *n.* —**Syn. 1.** elect, opt, pick, prefer.

choos·y (chōō'zē), *adj.,* **choos·i·er, choos·i·est.** *Informal.* fastidious, esp. in making a choice. Also, **choos'ey.** —**choos'i·ness,** *n.*

chop[1] (chop), *v.,* **chopped, chop·ping, n.** —*v.t., v.i.* **1.** to cut with quick, heavy blows. **2.** to cut into small pieces. **3.** (in tennis, etc.) to hit (a ball) with a short downward stroke. —*n.* **4.** the act or instance of chopping. **5.** a cutting blow. **6.** a slice or portion of lamb, pork, etc. **7.** a short, irregular, broken motion of waves.

chop[2] (chop), *n.* **1.** Usually, **chops.** the jaw. **2. chops,** the mouth.

chop[3] (chop), *n.* **1.** (in India, China, etc.) an official or private seal. **2.** *Anglo-Indian.* quality or grade.

chop' chop', (in pidgin English) quickly!

chop·house (chop'hous'), *n., pl.* **-hous·es** (-hou'ziz), a restaurant specializing in chops and steaks.

Cho·pin (shō'pan), *n.* **Fré·dé·ric** (frēd'ə rik), 1810–49, Polish composer and pianist.

chop·per (chop'ər), *n.* **1.** a person or thing that chops. **2.** *Informal.* a helicopter. **3. choppers,** *Slang.* the teeth.

chop·py (chop'ē), *adj.,* **-pi·er, -pi·est. 1.** (of the sea, etc.) forming short, broken waves. **2.** uneven in style or quality. —**chop'pi·ly,** *adv.* —**chop'pi·ness,** *n.*

chop·stick (chop'stik'), *n.* one of a pair of thin sticks used as eating utensils by certain Oriental peoples.

chop' su'ey (sōō'ē), a Chinese-style dish of meat, onions, bean sprouts, etc., served with rice.

cho·ral (kôr'əl, kōr'-), *adj.* **1.** of, for, or sung by a chorus or a choir. —*n.* **2.** chorale. —**cho'ral·ly,** *adv.*

cho·rale (kə ral′, -räl′, kō-, kô-; kôr′-əl, kôr′-), *n.* **1.** a hymn, either played or sung, esp. one sung in unison or in parts. **2.** a choral group.

chord[1] (kôrd), *n.* **1.** the line segment between two points on a given curve. **2.** a feeling or emotion. **3.** *Anat.* cord (def. 5).

chord[2] (kôrd), *n. Music.* a combination of three or more different tones sounded simultaneously. —**chord′al**, *adj.*

chore (chōr, chôr), *n.* **1.** a small job, esp. around a house or farm. **2.** a hard or unpleasant task.

cho·re·a (kə rē′ə, kō-, kô-), *n.* a nervous disorder characterized by jerky, involuntary movements.

cho·re·o·graph (kôr′ē ə graf′, -gräf′, kôr′-), *v.t., v.i.* to provide the choreography for (a ballet, etc.).

cho·re·og·ra·phy (kôr′ē og′rə fē, kôr′-), *n.* the art of composing ballets and other dances for the stage. —**cho′re·og′ra·pher,** *n.* —**cho·re·o·graph·ic** (kôr′ē ə graf′ik, kôr′-), *adj.* —**cho′re·o·graph′i·cal·ly,** *adv.*

cho·rine (kôr′in, kôr′ēn), *n.* a chorus girl.

chor·is·ter (kôr′i stər, kor′-), *n.* a singer in a choir.

cho·roid (kôr′oid, kōr′-), *n.* a delicate, highly vascular layer of the eye. Also called **cho′roid coat′.**

chor·tle (chôr′t°l), *v.,* -**tled,** -**tling,** *n.* —*v.t., v.i.* **1.** to chuckle or utter with glee. —*n.* **2.** a gleeful chuckle. [b. *chuckle* and *snort*, coined by English writer Lewis Carroll (1832-98)] —**chor′tler,** *n.*

cho·rus (kôr′əs, kōr′-), *n., pl.* -**rus·es,** *v.,* -**rused,** -**rus·ing.** —*n.* **1. a.** a musical composition to be sung by a large group. **b.** a group performing such a composition. **c.** (in an opera, etc.) a company of singers, dancers, or both. **d.** a part of a song, as the refrain. **2.** simultaneous utterance by many. **3.** the sounds so uttered. —*v.t., v.i.* **4.** to sing or speak in chorus.

chose (chōz), *v.* pt. of **choose.**

cho·sen (chō′zən), *v.* **1.** pp. of **choose.** —*adj.* **2.** selected or preferred.

chow[1] (chou), *n. Slang.* food.

chow[2] (chou), *n.* See **chow chow.**

chow chow (chou′ chou′), one of a Chinese breed of medium-sized dogs having a thick black, blue, red, or cream coat and a black tongue.

chow-chow (chou′chou′), *n.* a relish or mixed pickles in mustard.

chow·der (chou′dər), *n.* a thick soup made of clams or fish and various vegetables.

chow mein (chou′ mān′), a dish of mushrooms and other vegetables, topped with shrimp, shredded chicken, etc., and served with fried noodles.

Chr., 1. Christ. **2.** Christian.

chrism (kriz′əm), *n.* a consecrated oil used in various rites, as in baptism.

Christ (krīst), *n.* Jesus of Nazareth, held by Christians as the Messiah. [< L *Christ(us)* < Gk *christós* anointed] —**Christ′like′,** *adj.* —**Christ′ly,** *adj.*

chris·ten (kris′ən), *v.t.* **1.** to name in a religious ceremony, esp. of an infant. **2.** to administer baptism to. **3.** to name (a ship, etc.) at its launching. —**chris′ten·er,** *n.* —**chris′ten·ing,** *n.*

Chris·ten·dom (kris′ən dəm), *n.* **1.** Christians collectively. **2.** the Christian world.

Chris·tian (kris′chən), *adj.* **1.** of or derived from Jesus Christ or His teachings. **2.** of or adhering to the religion based on the teachings of Jesus Christ. **3.** of or pertaining to Christians. —*n.* **4.** an adherent of Christianity.

Chris′tian E′ra, the period, in Christian countries, since the assumed year of Jesus' birth.

Chris·tia·ni·a (kris′chə an′ē ə, -tē-), *n. Skiing.* a turn in which the body is swung around with the skis kept parallel.

Chris·ti·an·i·ty (kris′chē an′i tē), *n., pl.* -**ties. 1.** the Christian religion, including the Catholic, Protestant, and Eastern Orthodox churches. **2.** the state of being a Christian. **3.** Christendom.

Chris·tian·ize (kris′chə nīz′), *v.t.,* -**ized,** -**iz·ing.** to make Christian. —**Chris′tian·i·za′tion,** *n.*

Chris′tian name′, 1. the name given at baptism. **2.** a person's given name.

Chris′tian Sci′ence, a religion teaching the treatment of disease by spiritual means. —**Chris′tian Sci′entist.**

Chris·tie (kris′tē), *n.* Christiania. Also, **Chris′ty.**

Christ·mas (kris′məs), *n.* the annual celebration, on December 25, of the birth of Jesus.

Christ′mas club′, a savings account for periodic deposits, designed to provide for Christmas shopping.

Christ·mas·tide (kris′məs tīd′), *n.* the season of Christmas.

Christ′mas tree′, an evergreen tree decorated at Christmas with ornaments and lights.

chro·mat·ic (krō mat′ik, krə-), *adj.* **1.** pertaining to color or colors. **2.** *Music.* progressing by half tones. —**chro·mat′i·cal·ly,** *adv.* —**chro·mat′i·cism,** *n.*

chro·ma·tic·i·ty (krō'mə tis'i tē), *n.* the quality of a color as determined by its dominant wavelength and its purity.

chro·ma·tog·ra·phy (krō'mə tog'rə fē), *n.* the chemical separation of mixtures into their constituents by preferential adsorption by a solid, as a column of silica. —**chro·ma·to·graph·ic** (krō'mə tə graf'ik, krō·mat'ō-, krə-), *adj.* —**chro'ma·to·graph'i·cal·ly,** *adv.*

chrome (krōm), *n., v.,* **chromed, chrom·ing.** —*n.* **1.** chromium, esp. as a source of various pigments, as chrome green. **2.** chromium-plated trim, as on an automobile. —*vt.* **3.** to plate with chromium.

chrome' green', any of several green pigments made from chromium compounds.

chrome' yel'low, any of several yellow pigments made from chromium compounds.

chro·mic (krō'mik), *adj.* of or containing chromium.

chro·mi·um (krō'mē əm), *n. Chem.* a lustrous, metallic element used in alloy steels for hardness. *Symbol:* Cr; *at. wt.:* 51.996; *at. no.:* 24.

chro·mo (krō'mō), *n., pl.* **-mos.** a picture produced by lithography in colors.

chro·mo·some (krō'mə sōm'), *n.* any of several threadlike bodies that are found in a cell nucleus and carry the genes in a linear order. —**chro'mo·so'mal,** *adj.*

chro·mo·sphere (krō'mə sfēr'), *n.* a gaseous envelope surrounding a star. —**chro·mo·spher·ic** (krō'mə·sfer'ik), *adj.*

Chron., Chronicles.

chron., **1.** chronicle. **2.** chronological. **3.** chronology.

chron·ic (kron'ik), *adj.* **1.** continuing over a long time or recurring frequently, as a disease. **2.** habitual or of long standing: *a chronic liar.* —**chron'i·cal·ly,** *adv.* —**chro·nic·i·ty** (kro nis'i tē), *n.*

chron·i·cle (kron'i kəl), *n., v.,* **-cled, -cling.** —*n.* **1.** a chronological record of events. —*v.t.* **2.** to record in a chronicle. —**chron'i·cler,** *n.*

chrono-, a combining form meaning "time": *chronometer.* Also, **chron-.**

chron·o·graph (kron'ə graf', -gräf', krō'nə-), *n.* a timepiece capable of measuring extremely brief intervals of time accurately. —**chron·o·graph·ic** (kron'ə graf'ik), *adj.* —**chro·nog·ra·phy,** *n.*

chronol., **1.** chronological. **2.** chronology.

chro·nol·o·gy (krə nol'ə jē), *n., pl.* **-gies.** **1.** an order of events from earliest to latest. **2.** the science of arranging time in periods and as-

certaining the dates of past events. **3.** a chronological work of reference. —**chron'o·log'i·cal,** *adj.* —**chron'o·log'i·cal·ly,** *adv.* —**chro·nol'o·gist,** *n.*

chro·nom·e·ter (krə nom'i tər), *n.* a highly accurate timepiece.

chrys·a·lis (kris'ə lis), *n., pl.* **chrys·a·lis·es, chrys·al·i·des** (kri sal'i dēz'), the hard-shelled pupa of a moth or butterfly.

chry·san·the·mum (kri san'thə məm), *n.* any of many cultivated varieties of plants notable for the diversity of color and size of their autumnal flowers.

chrys·o·lite (kris'ə līt'), *n.* olivine.

chub (chub), *n., pl.* **chub, chubs.** a common, freshwater fish, esp. the whitefish, found in the Great Lakes.

chub·by (chub'ē), *adj.,* **-bi·er, -bi·est.** round and plump. —**chub'bi·ness,** *n.*

chuck[1] (chuk), *v.t.* **1.** to pat lightly, as under the chin. **2.** to toss. **3.** *Informal.* to throw out. **4.** *Informal.* **a.** to resign from. **b.** to give up. —*n.* **5.** a light pat, as under the chin.

chuck[2] (chuk), *n.* **1.** the cut of beef between the neck and the shoulder blade. **2.** a device for centering and clamping work in a lathe or other machine tool.

chuck·full (chuk'fool'), *adj.* chockfull.

chuck·hole (chuk'hōl'), *n.* a hole or depression in a road or street.

chuck·le (chuk'əl), *v.,* **chuck·led, chuck·ling.** —*v.i.* **1.** to laugh softly or to oneself. —*n.* **2.** a soft, amused laugh. —**chuck'ler,** *n.*

chuck' wag'on, a wagon carrying cooking facilities and food, as at a ranch.

chug (chug), *n., v.,* **chugged, chug·ging.** —*n.* **1.** a short, dull, explosive sound. —*v.i.* **2.** to make this sound. **3.** to move with this sound.

chuk·ka boot' (chuk'ə), an ankle-high shoe with two pairs of eyelets. Also called **chuk'ka.**

chuk·ker (chuk'ər), *n. Polo.* one of the periods of play.

chum[1] (chum), *n., v.,* **chummed, chum·ming.** —*n.* **1.** an intimate friend. —*v.i.* **2.** to associate closely.

chum[2] (chum), *n.* cut or ground bait dumped into the water to attract fish.

chum·my (chum'ē), *adj.,* **-mi·er, -mi·est.** intimately friendly. —**chum'mi·ly,** *adv.* —**chum'mi·ness,** *n.*

chump (chump), *n. Informal.* a blockhead or dolt.

Chung·king (chŏŏng'king'), *n.* a city in SW China.

chunk (chungk), *n.* **1.** a thick mass or lump of anything. **2.** a substantial amount.

chunk·y (chung′kē), *adj.*, **chunk·i·er,
chunk·i·est. 1.** thick and stout. **2.** in
a chunk or chunks. —**chunk′i·ly,**
adv. —**chunk′i·ness,** *n.*

church (chûrch), *n.* **1.** a building for
public Christian worship. **2.** an
occasion of such worship. **3.** (*sometimes cap.*) the whole number of
Christian believers. **4.** (*sometimes
cap.*) any Christian denomination.
5. an organized religious congregation. [< Gk *kȳri(a)kón* (*dôma*) the
Lord's (house)]

church·go·er (chûrch′gō′ər), *n.* a person who goes to church, esp. habitually. —**church′go′ing,** *n., adj.*

Church·ill (chûr′chil, -chəl), *n.* **Sir
Winston,** 1874–1965, British statesman and author.

church·less (chûrch′lis), *adj.* not belonging to or attending any church.

church·man (chûrch′mən), *n.* **1.** a
clergyman. **2.** a church member.

Church′ of Christ′, Sci′entist, the
official name of the Christian Science Church.

Church′ of Eng′land, the established
church in England.

**Church′ of Je′sus Christ′ of Lat′ter-
day Saints′,** the official name of
the Mormon Church.

church·ward·en (chûrch′wôr′d'n), *n.
Anglican and Episcopal Ch.* a lay
officer who looks after the secular
affairs of the church.

church·wom·an (chûrch′wŏŏm′ən), *n.*
a female member of a church.

church·yard (chûrch′yärd′), *n.* the
ground adjoining a church, often
used as a graveyard.

churl (chûrl), *n.* **1.** a rude, boorish,
or surly person. **2.** *Archaic.* a peasant or rustic. —**churl′ish,** *adj.* —
churl′ish·ly, *adv.* —**churl′ish·ness,** *n.*

churn (chûrn), *n.* **1.** a container in
which cream or milk is agitated to
make butter. —*v.t., v.i.* **2.** to stir
or agitate to make into butter. **3.**
to make (butter) by the agitation of
cream. **4.** to agitate with violent motion. **5. churn out,** to produce in a
mechanical manner —**churn′er,** *n.*

chute¹ (shōōt), *n.* an inclined trough
or shaft for conveying water, coal,
etc.

chute² (shōōt), *n. Informal.* a parachute.

chut·ney (chut′nē), *n.* a sweet and
sour relish of fruits, herbs, etc.,
with spices and other seasoning.
Also, **chut′nee.**

chutz·pa (ᴋʜŏŏt′spə), *n. Slang.* unmitigated effrontery or impudence.
Also, **chutz′pah.** [< Yiddish < Heb]

CIA, Central Intelligence Agency (of
the U.S. Government).

Cía., Company. [< Sp. *Compañía*]

cia·o (chou), *interj. Italian Informal.* **1.** hi. **2.** so long.

ci·ca·da (si kā′də, -kä′-), *n., pl.* **-das,
-dae** (-dē) a large insect, the male
of which produces a shrill sound.

cic·a·trix (sik′ə triks, si kā′triks), *n.,
pl.* **cic·a·tri·ces** (sik′ə trī′sēz). new
tissue that forms over a wound and
later contracts into a scar.

Cic·e·ro (sis′ə rō), *n.* **Marcus Tul-
li·us** (tul′ē əs), 106–43 B.C., Roman
statesman and orator.

cic·e·ro·ne (sis′ə rō′nē, chich′ə), *n.*
a tour guide in Italy.

C.I.D., Criminal Investigation Department (of Scotland Yard).

-cide, a suffix meaning: **a.** killer: *insecticide.* **b.** killing: *homicide.*

ci·der (sī′dər), *n.* the juice pressed
from apples, used for drinking or
for making applejack, vinegar, etc.

Cie., Company. [< F *Compagnie*]

C.I.F., cost, insurance, and freight
(included in the price quoted).

ci·gar (si gär′), *n.* a roll of tobacco
leaves for smoking.

cig·a·rette (sig′ə ret′, sig′ə ret′), *n.* a
short roll of finely cut tobacco
wrapped in paper for smoking.
Also, **cig′a·ret′.**

cig·a·ril·lo (sig′ə ril′ō), *n., pl.* **-los.** a
small, thin cigar.

cil·i·a (sil′ē ə), *n.pl., sing.* **cil·i·um**
(sil′ē əm). **1.** the eyelashes. **2.** *Biol.*
minute, hairlike processes.

cil·i·ar·y (sil′ē er′ē), *adj.* **1.** noting
or pertaining to various anatomical
structures in or about the eye. **2.**
pertaining to cilia.

cil·i·ate (sil′ē it, -āt′), *n.* a protozoan having cilia on part or all of
the body.

C. in C., Commander in Chief.

cinch (sinch), *n.* **1.** a strong girth
for securing a pack or saddle. **2.**
Slang. something sure or easy. —
v.t. **3.** to gird or bind firmly. **4.**
Slang. to make sure of.

cin·cho·na (sin kō′nə), *n.* **1.** a South
American tree whose bark yields
quinine and other alkaloids. **2.** its
medicinal bark.

Cin·cin·nat·i (sin′sə nat′ē), *n.* a city
in SW Ohio.

cinc·ture (singk′chər), *n., v.,* **-tured,
-tur·ing.** *Literary.* —*n.* **1.** a belt or
girdle. —*v.t.* **2.** to encircle with a
cincture.

cin·der (sin′dər), *n.* **1.** a partially
burned piece of coal, wood, etc.
2. cinders, **a.** any residue of combustion, as ashes. **b.** *Geol.* coarse
scoriae thrown out of volcanoes.
—**cin′der·y, cin′der·ous,** *adj.*

cin′der block′, a concrete building
block made with cinders and cement.

cin·e·ma (sin′ə mə), *n.* **1.** *Chiefly
Brit.* See **motion picture. 2.** the
cinema, motion pictures collectively.
3. *Chiefly Brit.* a motion-picture

theater. —**cin·e·mat·ic** (sin′ə mat′ik), *adj.* —**cin′e·mat′i·cal·ly**, *adv.*

cin·e·ma·theque (sin′ə mə tek′), *n.* a motion-picture house showing experimental films.

cin·e·ma·tog·ra·phy (sin′ə mə tog′rə fē), *n.* the art or technique of motion-picture photography. —**cin·e·ma·tog·ra·pher** (sin′ə mə tog′rə fər), *n.* —**cin·e·mat·o·graph·ic** (sin′ə mat′ə graf′ik), *adj.*

cin·é·ma vé·ri·té (sē nä mä′ vā Rē tā′), a technique of film making in which life and people are recorded as they actually are.

cin·e·rar·i·um (sin′ə râr′ē əm), *n., pl.* **-rar·i·a** (-râr′ē ə). a place for depositing the ashes of the cremated dead. —**cin·e·rar·y** (sin′ə rer′ē), *adj.*

cin·na·bar (sin′ə bär′), *n.* a red mineral that is the principal ore of mercury.

cin·na·mon (sin′ə mən), *n.* **1.** the aromatic inner bark of an East Indian tree, used as a spice. **2.** a yellowish or reddish brown.

cinque·foil (singk′foil′), *n.* any of several plants of the rose family, having five-lobed leaves.

C.I.O., Congress of Industrial Organizations. Also, **CIO**

CIP, Cataloging in Publication.

ci·pher (sī′fər), *n.* **1.** a secret method of writing by coded symbols. **2.** the key to such a method. **3.** *Arith. Brit.* zero. **4.** *Rare.* an Arabic numeral. —*v.i.* **5.** to write in cipher. **6.** *Rare.* to use numerals arithmetically. —*v.t.* **7.** to convert into cipher. **8.** *Rare.* to calculate numerically.

cir., **1.** circa. **2.** circular.

circ., **1.** circa. **2.** circular. **3.** circuit. **4.** circulation. **5.** circumference.

cir·ca (sûr′kə), *prep., adv.* about: used esp. in approximate dates.

cir·ca·di·an (sûr kā′dē ən), *adj.* of rhythmic biological cycles recurring at approximately 24-hour intervals.

cir·cle (sûr′kəl), *n., v.,* **-cled, -cling.** —*n.* **1.** a closed plane curve of which all points are at an equal distance from the center. **2.** any circular object, formation, or arrangement. **3.** a realm or sphere. **4.** a cycle or round. **5.** a number of persons bound by a common tie. —*v.t.* **6.** to enclose in or as in a circle. **7.** to move or revolve around. —*v.i.* **8.** to move in a circle. —**cir′cler,** *n.*

cir·clet (sûr′klit), *n.* **1.** a small circle. **2.** a ring-shaped ornament, esp. for the head.

cir·cuit (sûr′kit), *n.* **1.** a circular journey or course. **2.** a periodic tour of duty in an appointed territory,

as by judges, ministers, etc. **3.** the line bounding any area. **4.** a chain of theaters, nightclubs, etc. **5.** the complete path of an electric current, including the source of the current, etc. —*v.t.* **6.** to make the circuit of. —*v.i.* **7.** to go in a circuit. —**cir′cuit·al,** *adj.*

cir′cuit break′er, a device for interrupting an electric circuit when the current becomes excessive.

cir′cuit court′, a court holding sessions at various intervals in different sections of a district.

cir·cu·i·tous (sər kyōo′i təs), *adj.* roundabout or not direct. —**cir·cu′i·tous·ly,** *adv.* —**cir·cu′i·ty,** *n.*

cir·cuit·ry (sûr′ki trē), *n.* **1.** electric or electronic circuits collectively. **2.** the components of such circuits collectively.

cir·cu·lar (sûr′kyə lər), *adj.* **1.** having the form or shape of a circle. **2.** moving in or forming a circle. **3.** circuitous. **4.** intended for general circulation. —*n.* **5.** a letter or advertisement for general circulation. —**cir·cu·lar·i·ty** (sûr′kyə lar′i tē), *n.*

cir·cu·lar·ize (sûr′kyə lə rīz′), *v.t.,* **-ized, -iz·ing.** **1.** to send circulars to. **2.** to publicize, esp. with circulars. —**cir·cu·lar·i·za′tion,** *n.* —**cir′cu·lar·iz′er,** *n.*

cir′cular saw′, a power saw having a disk-shaped blade.

cir·cu·late (sûr′kyə lāt′), *v.,* **-lat·ed, -lat·ing.** —*v.i.* **1.** to move in a circle or circuit. **2.** to pass from place to place, from person to person, etc. —*v.t.* **3.** to disseminate or distribute. —**cir′cu·la·tor,** *n.* —**cir·cu·la·to·ry** (sûr′kyə lə tôr′ē, -tōr′ē), *adj.*

cir·cu·la·tion (sûr′kyə lā′shən), *n.* **1.** the act or an instance of circulating. **2.** the continuous movement of blood through the heart and blood vessels. **3.** the distribution of copies of a periodical among readers. **4.** the number of copies distributed or sold.

cir′cu·la·to·ry sys′tem, the system of organs and tissues involved in circulating blood and lymph through the body.

circum., circumference.

circum-, a prefix meaning "around" or "about": *circumpolar.*

cir·cum·am·bu·late (sûr′kəm am′byə lāt′), *v.t., v.i.,* **-lat·ed, -lat·ing.** to walk or go about or around, esp. affectedly. —**cir′cum·am′bu·la′tion,** *n.*

cir·cum·cise (sûr′kəm sīz′), *v.t.,* **-cised, -cis·ing.** to remove the prepuce of (a male), esp. as a religious rite. —**cir′cum·ci′sion,** *n.*

cir·cum·fer·ence (sər kum′fər əns, -frəns), *n.* **1.** the outer boundary, esp. of a circular area. **2.** the length of such a boundary.

cir·cum·flex (sûr′kəm fleks′), *n.* a mark (ˆ, ˆ, or ˜) placed over a vowel to indicate nasalization, length, etc.

cir·cum·lo·cu·tion (sûr′kəm lō kyōō′shən), *n.* a roundabout way of speaking. —**cir′cum·loc′u·to·ry** (sûr′kəm lok′yə tōr′ē, -tôr′ē), *adj.*

cir·cum·lu·nar (sûr′kəm lōō′nər), *adj.* rotating about or surrounding the moon.

cir·cum·nav·i·gate (sûr′kəm nav′ə gāt′), *v.t.*, -**gat·ed**, -**gat·ing.** to sail or fly around. —**cir′cum·nav′i·ga′tion,** *n.*

cir·cum·po·lar (sûr′kəm pō′lər), *adj.* around or near one of the poles of the earth.

cir·cum·scribe (sûr′kəm skrīb′, sûr′kəm skrīb′), *v.t.*, -**scribed**, -**scrib·ing.** **1.** to draw or trace a line around. **2.** to limit or confine the scope of. —**cir′cum·scrip′tion,** *n.*

cir·cum·so·lar (sûr′kəm sō′lər), *adj.* around the sun.

cir·cum·spect (sûr′kəm spekt′), *adj.* discreet and prudent. —**cir′cum·spec′tion,** *n.*

cir·cum·stance (sûr′kəm stans′), *n.* **1.** a condition or attribute that accompanies or determines a fact or event. **2.** Usually, **circumstances.** the existing conditions or state of affairs. **3. circumstances,** the condition with respect to material welfare. **4.** an incident or occurrence. **5.** *Literary.* ceremonious display: *pomp and circumstance.* **6. under no circumstances,** never. **7. under the circumstances,** because of the conditions. —**cir′cum·stanced′,** *adj.*

cir·cum·stan·tial (sûr′kəm stan′shəl), *adj.* **1.** of or derived from circumstances. **2.** unessential or incidental. **3.** giving details. —**cir′cum·stan′tial·ly,** *adv.*

cir′cumstan′tial ev′idence, proof of facts offered as evidence from which other facts are to be inferred.

cir·cum·stan·ti·ate (sûr′kəm stan′shē āt′), *v.t.*, -**at·ed**, -**at·ing.** to set forth or support with circumstances or particulars. —**cir′cum·stan′ti·a′tion,** *n.*

cir·cum·vent (sûr′kəm vent′, sûr′kəm vent′), *v.t.* to outwit, avoid, or get the better of, esp. by stratagem or craft. —**cir′cum·ven′tion,** *n.*

cir·cus (sûr′kəs), *n., pl.* -**cus·es.** **1.** a large public entertainment featuring performing animals, clowns, feats of skill and daring, etc. **2.** a circular arena, surrounded by tiers of seats and often covered by a tent, used for such shows. **3.** *Informal.* fun, excitement, or uproar.

cirque (sûrk), *n.* a circular space, esp. a natural amphitheater, as in mountains.

cir·rho·sis (si rō′sis), *n.* a disease of the liver characterized by increase of connective tissue. —**cir·rhot·ic** (si rot′ik), *adj.*

cir·ro·cu·mu·lus (sir′ō kyōō′myə ləs), *n., pl.* -**lus.** a cloud of a class characterized by thin, white, granular patches at high altitude.

cir·ro·stra·tus (sir′ō strā′təs, -strat′əs), *n., pl.* -**tus.** a cloud of a class characterized by a composition of ice crystals and appearing as a whitish fibrous veil at high altitude.

cir·rus (sir′əs), *n., pl.* **cir·rus.** a cloud of a class characterized by thin white bands and ice crystals at high altitude.

cis·lu·nar (sis lōō′nər), *adj.* lying between the earth and the orbit of the moon.

cis·tern (sis′tərn), *n.* a reservoir or tank for storing water or other liquid.

cit., **1.** citation. **2.** cited. **3.** citizen.

cit·a·del (sit′ə dᵊl, -ə del′), *n.* **1.** a fortress for defending a city. **2.** any strongly fortified place.

cite (sīt), *v.t.*, **cit·ed**, **cit·ing.** **1.** to quote (a book, author, etc.), esp. as an authority. **2.** to mention in support or proof. **3.** to summon to appear in court. **4.** to commend, as for outstanding service, etc. —**ci·ta′tion,** *n.*

cit·i·fy (sit′i fī′), *v.t.*, -**fied**, -**fy·ing.** to cause to conform to city habits, fashions, etc. —**cit′i·fi·ca′tion,** *n.* —**cit′i·fied′,** *adj.*

cit·i·zen (sit′i zən, -sən), *n.* **1.** a native or naturalized member of a nation who owes allegiance to its government and is entitled to its protection. **2.** an inhabitant of a city or town. —**cit′i·zen·ly,** *adj.* —**cit′i·zen·ship′,** *n.*

cit·i·zen·ry (sit′i zən rē, -sən-), *n., pl.* -**ries.** citizens collectively.

cit′izens band′, federally designated frequencies for two-way radio communication between licensed individuals with mobile or base stations.

cit·rate (si′trāt, sī′-), *n.* a salt or ester of citric acid.

cit·ric (si′trik), *adj.* of or derived from citric acid.

cit′ric ac′id, a powder having a sour taste, occurring in limes, lemons, etc., used as a flavoring.

cit·ron (si′trən), *n.* **1.** a pale yellow fruit, larger than the lemon, borne by an Asiatic tree. **2.** the tree itself. **3.** the rind of the fruit, candied and preserved.

cit·ron·el·la (si'trə nel'ə), *n.* **1.** a fragrant grass of southern Asia, cultivated as the source of citronella oil. **2.** See **citronella oil.**

citronel'la oil', a pungent oil, distilled from citronella, used in the manufacture of liniment, perfume, and soap, and as an insect repellent.

cit·rus (si'trəs), *n., pl.* **-rus·es.** **1.** any tree or shrub of the genus which includes the lemon, lime, orange, grapefruit. etc. —*adj.* **2.** Also, **cit'rous.** of such trees or shrubs.

cit·y (sit'ē), *n., pl.* **cit·ies.** **1.** a large or important town. **2.** an incorporated municipality, usually governed by a mayor. **3.** the inhabitants of a city collectively. [< OF *cite(t)* < L *civitāt-* (s. of *civitās*)]

cit'y hall', (*often caps.*) the administration building of a city government.

cit'y man'ager, an administrator appointed by a city council to manage a city.

cit·y-state (sit'ē stāt'), *n.* a sovereign state consisting of an autonomous city with its dependencies.

civ., **1.** civil. **2.** civilian.

civ·et (siv'it), *n.* **1.** Also called **civ'et cat'.** a catlike mammal that secretes a yellowish, unctuous substance with a strong musklike odor. **2.** this substance, used in perfumery.

civ·ic (siv'ik), *adj.* of or pertaining to a city, citizenship, or citizens.

civ·ics (siv'iks), *n.* the science of civic affairs.

civ·il (siv'əl), *adj.* **1.** of citizens: *civil society.* **2.** of the ordinary life of citizens, as distinguished from military and ecclesiastical life. **3.** civilized or cultured. **4.** formally polite. **5.** pertaining to the private rights of individuals and to legal proceedings connected with these. —**civ'il·ly,** *adv.* —**civ'il·ness,** *n.* —**Syn.** 4. affable, courteous, polite.

civ'il defense', emergency civilian plans for the protection of population and property in times of war, floods, etc.

civ'il disobe'dience, the refusal to obey the government in order to influence legislation or policy, characterized by nonviolent techniques as boycotting, picketing, etc.

civ'il engineer', a person trained to design and build public works, as roads, bridges, etc. —**civ'il engineer'ing.**

ci·vil·ian (si vil'yən), *n.* **1.** a person engaged in civil pursuits, as distinguished from a member of an armed service. —*adj.* **2.** of or pertaining to civilians.

ci·vil·i·ty (si vil'i tē), *n., pl.* **-ties** for 2. **1.** formal politeness. **2.** a polite attention or expression.

civ·i·li·za·tion (siv'ə li zā'shən), *n.* **1.** an advanced state of human society, in which a high level of culture and science has been reached. **2.** those people or nations that have reached such a state. **3.** the type of culture of a specific place, time, or group: *Greek civilization.*

civ·i·lize (siv'ə līz'), *v.t.,* **-lized, -liz·ing. 1.** to bring out of a primitive or uneducated state. **2.** to enlighten or refine. —**civ'i·liz'a·ble,** *adj.* —**civ'i·lized,** *adj.* —**civ'i·liz'er,** *n.*

civ'il law', the body of laws regulating ordinary private matters.

civ'il lib'erty, the liberty to exercise rights guaranteed by the laws of a country.

civ'il rights', the rights to full legal, economic, and social equality.

civ'il serv'ant, *Chiefly Brit.* a civil-service employee.

civ'il serv'ice, those branches of public service concerned with all governmental functions outside the armed services.

civ'il war', **1.** a war between factions within the same country. **2.** (*caps.*) *U.S.* the war between the North and the South, 1861–65.

civ·vies (siv'ēz), *n.pl. Informal.* civilian clothes. Also, **civ'ies.**

CJ, Chief Justice.

ck., **1.** cask. **2.** check. **3.** cook.

Cl, chlorine.

cl, centiliter; centiliters.

cl., **1.** centiliter; centiliters. **2.** class. **3.** classification. **4.** clause. **5.** clearance. **6.** clerk.

c.l., **1.** carload. **2.** civil law. **3.** common law.

clab·ber (klab'ər), *n.* bonnyclabber.

clack (klak), *v.i., v.t.* **1.** to make or cause to make a quick, sharp sound, as by striking or cracking. **2.** to babble or prattle. —*n.* **3.** a clacking sound. **4.** chatter or prattle. —**clack'er,** *n.*

clad¹ (klad), *v.* **1.** a pt. and pp. of **clothe.** —*adj.* **2.** clothed or dressed.

clad² (klad), *v.t.,* **clad, clad·ding.** to bond a metal to (another metal), esp. to provide wtih a protective coat.

claim (klām), *v.t.* **1.** to demand as a right. **2.** to assert as a fact. **3.** to require as due or fitting. —*n.* **4.** a demand for something as due. **5.** an assertion of something as a fact. **6.** a right to claim or demand. **7.** something claimed. —**claim'a·ble,** *adj.* —**claim'er,** *n.* —**Syn.** 2. allege, avow, maintain.

claim·ant (klā′mənt), *n.* a person who makes a claim.

clair·voy·ant (klâr voi′ənt), *adj.* **1.** having the alleged supernatural power of seeing objects beyond the range of vision. —*n.* **2.** a clairvoyant person. —**clair·voy′ance,** *n.* —**clair·voy′ant·ly,** *adv.*

clam (klam), *n., v.,* **clammed, clam·ming.** —*n.* **1.** any of various bivalve mollusks, esp. certain edible species. —*v.i.* **2.** to gather or dig clams. **3. clam up,** *Slang.* to restrain oneself from talking.

clam·bake (klam′bāk′), *n.* **1.** a seashore picnic at which clams and other foods are baked. **2.** *Informal.* any social gathering.

clam·ber (klam′bər, -ər), *v.t., v.i.* to climb with difficulty.

clam·my (klam′ē), *adj.,* **-mi·er, -mi·est.** cold and damp. —**clam′mi·ness,** *n.*

clam·or (klam′ər), *n.* **1.** a persistent uproar, as from a crowd of people. **2.** a vehement expression of desire or dissatisfaction. **3.** popular outcry. —*v.i.* **4.** to make a clamor. —**clam′or·ous,** *adj.*

clamp¹ (klamp), *n.* **1.** a device for holding, joining, or compressing parts together. —*v.t.* **2.** to fasten with a clamp. **3. clamp down,** *Informal.* to impose controls.

clam·shell (klam′shel′), *n.* **1.** the shell of a clam. **2.** a dredging bucket opening at the bottom.

clan (klan), *n.* **1.** a group of families, as among the Scottish Highlanders, whose heads claim descent from a common ancestor. **2.** a group of people of common descent or interest. —**clan′nish,** *adj.* —**clan′nish·ly,** *adv.* —**clan′nish·ness,** *n.* —**clans′man,** *n.* —**clans′wom·an,** *n.fem.*

clan·des·tine (klan des′tin), *adj.* done in secrecy, esp. for subversion or deception. —**clan·des′tine·ly,** *adv.*

clang (klang), *v.i., v.t.* **1.** to make or cause to make a loud, resonant sound, as that produced by a large bell. —*n.* **2.** a clanging sound.

clang·or (klang′or, klang′gor), *n.* a loud, resonant sound. —**clang′or·ous,** *adj.*

clank (klangk), *n.* **1.** a sharp, hard, nonresonant sound. —*v.i., v.t.* **2.** to make or cause to make such a sound.

clap (klap), *v.,* **clapped, clap·ping,** *n.* —*v.t.* **1.** to strike (an object) against something forcefully, producing a sharp sound. **2.** to strike the palms of (one's hands) against one another repeatedly, esp. to express approval. **3.** to put or place quickly or forcefully. —*v.i.* **4.** to make an abrupt, sharp sound. **5.** to clap the hands, as in applause. —*n.* **6.** the act or sound of clapping. **7.** a resounding blow or slap. **8.** a loud and abrupt or explosive noise, as of thunder.

clap² (klap), *n. Slang.* gonorrhea.

clap·board (klab′ərd, klap′bôrd′, -bōrd′), *n.* **1.** a thin board, thicker along one edge than along the other, used in covering the outer walls of buildings. —*v.t.* **2.** to cover with clapboards.

clap·per (klap′ər), *n.* **1.** a person or thing that claps. **2.** the tongue of a bell.

clap·trap (klap′trap′), *n.* pretentious but insincere language.

claque (klak), *n.* a group of persons hired to applaud an act or performer, as in a nightclub.

clar·et (klar′it), *n.* a dry, red table wine.

clar·i·fy (klar′ə fī′), *v.t., v.i.,* **-fied, -fy·ing.** to make or become clear or pure. —**clar′i·fi·ca′tion,** *n.* —**clar′i·fi′er,** *n.*

clar·i·net (klar′ə net′), *n.* a woodwind instrument in the form of a cylindrical tube with a single reed attached to its mouthpiece. —**clar′i·net′ist, clar′i·net′tist,** *n.*

clar·i·on (klar′ē ən), *adj.* clear and shrill.

clar·i·ty (klar′i tē), *n.* **1.** clearness or lucidity as to understanding. **2.** the quality of being clear to the eye.

clash (klash), *v.i.* **1.** to make a loud, harsh noise. **2.** to collide, esp. noisily. **3.** to conflict or disagree. —*v.t.* **4.** to strike with a resounding or violent collision. —*n.* **5.** a loud, harsh noise. **6.** a conflict, as of views.

clasp (klasp, kläsp), *n.* **1.** a device for fastening things or parts together. **2.** a firm grasp or grip. **3.** a tight embrace. —*v.t.* **4.** to fasten with a clasp. **5.** to grasp or grip with the hand. **6.** to hold in a tight embrace. —**clasp′er,** *n.*

class (klas, kläs), *n.* **1.** a number of persons or things forming a group by reason of common traits or attributes. **2.** any division of persons or things according to rank or grade. **3.** a number of students pursuing the same studies or graduated in the same year. **4.** a social stratum having the same position. **5.** *Slang.* elegance of dress and behavior. **6.** any of several grades of passenger accommodations. —*v.t.* **7.** to place in a class or kind. —**class′less,** *adj.* —**Syn. 1.** kind, sort.

class., **1.** classic. **2.** classical.

class′ ac′tion, a legal proceeding against a single party filed on behalf of all people having a common complaint.

class′ con′sciousness, awareness of one's social or economic rank in society. —**class-con·scious** (klas′-kon′shəs, kläs′-), *adj.*

clas·sic (klas′ik), *adj.* **1.** of the highest rank. **2.** serving as a standard. **3.** of or pertaining to ancient Greek and Roman literature and art. **4.** of or adhering to an established set of standards or methods. **5.** of enduring interest, quality, or style. **6.** traditional or typical. —*n.* **7.** an author or a literary production of the first rank. **8. the classics,** the literature of ancient Greece and Rome. **9.** a traditional or typical event.

clas·si·cal (klas′i kəl), *adj.* **1.** classic (defs. 1–5). **2.** versed in the ancient classics. **3.** of or constituting the formally and artistically more sophisticated and enduring types of music. **4.** accepted as standard and authoritative: *classical physics.* —**clas′si·cal·ly,** *adv.*

clas·si·cism (klas′i siz′əm), *n.* **1.** the principles of classic literature and art. **2.** adherence to such principles. **3.** the classical style in literature and art. —**clas′si·cist,** *n.*

clas′sified ad′, a brief advertisement, typically one column wide, as in a newspaper. Also called **clas′sified advertise′ment.**

clas·si·fy (klas′ə fī′), *v.t.,* **-fied, -fy·ing. 1.** to arrange or organize in classes or categories. **2.** to assign a level of secrecy to (government documents). —**clas′si·fi′a·ble,** *adj.* —**clas′si·fi·ca′tion,** *n.* —**clas′si·fied,** *adj.*

class·mate (klas′māt′, kläs′-), *n.* a member of the same class at a school or college.

class·room (klas′rōōm′, -rŏŏm′, kläs′-), *n.* a room in a school or college in which classes meet.

class′ strug′gle, (in Marxist thought) the struggle for political and economic power carried on between capitalists and workers.

class·y (klas′ē), *adj.,* **class·i·er, class·i·est.** *Slang.* elegant or stylish.

clas·tic (klas′tik), *adj.* composed of particles of older rocks.

clat·ter (klat′ər), *v.i., v.t.* **1.** to make or cause to make a loud, rattling sound. —*n.* **2.** a clattering sound. **3.** a noisy disturbance.

clause (klôz), *n.* **1.** a syntactic construction containing a subject and predicate and forming part of a compound or complex sentence. **2.** part of an article, document, etc., as a distinct provision of a law. —**claus′al,** *adj.*

claus·tro·pho·bi·a (klô′strə fō′bē ə), *n.* an abnormal fear of enclosed or confined places. —**claus′tro·pho′bic,** *adj.*

clav·i·chord (klav′ə kôrd′), *n.* an early keyboard instrument whose strings are struck by metal blades.

clav·i·cle (klav′ə kəl), *n.* either of two slender bones, each joining the sternum and a scapula. —**cla·vic·u·lar** (klə vik′yə lər), *adj.*

cla·vier (klə vēr′, klav′ē ər, klä′vē-), *n.* **1.** the keyboard of a musical instrument. **2.** an early keyboard instrument, esp. the clavichord.

claw (klô), *n.* **1.** a sharp, usually curved, nail on the foot of an animal. **2.** a similar curved process at the end of the leg of an insect. **3.** any part or thing resembling a claw, as the cleft end of a hammer. —*v.t., v.i.* **4.** to tear, scratch, or dig with claws. —**clawed** (klôd), *adj.*

clay (klā), *n.* **1.** a natural earthy material that is plastic when wet, used for making bricks, pottery, etc. **2.** earth or mud. **3.** the mortal human body. —**clay′ey, clay′ish,** *adj.*

clay·more (klā′mōr′, -môr′), *n.* a two-handed double-edged sword used by Scottish Highlanders in the 16th century.

clay′ pig′eon, *Trapshooting.* a disk of baked clay hurled into the air as a target.

cld., **1.** called. **2.** cleared.

clean (klēn), *adj.* **1.** free from dirt or filth. **2.** free from defect or blemish. **3.** pure or not adulterated. **4.** upright or honorable: *a clean life.* **5.** habitually free of dirt. **6.** fair, esp. in sports. **7.** shapely or trim. **8.** complete or thorough. —*adv.* **9.** in a clean manner. **10.** wholly or completely. **11. come clean,** *Slang.* to tell the truth. —*v.t., v.i.* **12.** to make or become clean. **13. clean out,** to empty or use up. **14. clean up, a.** to wash or tidy up. **b.** to finish. **c.** to make a large profit. —**clean′er,** *n.* —**clean′ness,** *n.*

clean-cut (klēn′kut′), *adj.* **1.** having a distinct, regular shape. **2.** clearly outlined. **3.** neat and wholesome.

clean′ en′ergy, energy, such as electricity, which does not pollute the atmosphere when used.

clean·ly (klen′lē), *adj.,* **-li·er, -li·est. 1.** personally neat. **2.** habitually clean. —**clean·li·ness** (klen′lē nis), *n.*

clean′ room′, a room or area where all contaminants in the air are excluded, as for assembly of delicate instruments.

cleanse (klenz), *v.t., v.t.,* **cleansed, cleans·ing,** to clean, esp. thoroughly. —**cleans′er,** *n.*

clean·up (klēn'up'), *n.* **1.** the act or process of cleaning up. **2.** an elimination of vice or crime. **3.** a large profit. **4.** *Baseball Slang.* the fourth position in the batting order.

clear (klēr), *adj.* **1.** free from darkness or cloudiness. **2.** bright or shining. **3.** transparent or limpid. **4.** easily seen. **5.** easily heard. **6.** easily understood. **7.** evident or plain. **8.** free from confusion or doubt. **9.** free from blame or guilt. **10.** free from obstructions or obstacles. **11.** free from contact or entanglement. **12.** without limitation or qualification. **13.** free from debt. **14.** net: *a clear profit.* —*adv.* **15.** in a clear manner. **16.** entirely or completely. —*v.t.* **17.** to make clear or transparent. **18.** to free from impurities. **19.** to make understandable. **20.** to remove or get rid of. **21.** to relieve (the throat) of phlegm. **22.** to free from suspicion or accusation. **23.** to pass by or over without contact. **24.** to gain as clear profit. **25.** to receive authorization before taking action on. —*v.i.* **26.** to become clear. **27.** **clear away** or **off, a.** to leave. **b.** to remove in order to make room. **28. clear out, a.** to remove the contents of. **b.** to remove. **c.** to go away, esp. abruptly. **29. clear up,** to explain or solve. —*n.* **30.** a clear or unobstructed space. **31. in the clear,** absolved of guilt. —**clear'·a·ble,** *adj.* —**clear'er,** *n.* —**clear'ly,** *adv.* —**clear'ness,** *n.*

clear·ance (klēr'əns), *n.* **1.** the act of clearing. **2.** the clear space or distance between two things. **3.** the disposal of merchandise at reduced prices.

clear-cut (klēr'kut'), *adj.* **1.** formed with clearly defined outlines. **2.** evident or definite.

clear·head·ed (klēr'hed'id), *adj.* having an alert, wide-awake mind.

clear·ing (klēr'ing), *n.* **1.** a tract of land, as in a forest, that contains no trees or bushes. **2.** the reciprocal exchange between banks of checks and drafts, and the settlement of the differences.

clear·ing·house (klēr'ing hous'), *n.* an institution where banks exchange checks and drafts drawn on one another for settlement of outstanding balances.

cleat (klēt), *n.* a piece of wood or metal fastened to or projecting from an object to serve as a support or to give a foothold.

cleav·age (klē'vij), *n.* **1.** the act of splitting or state of being cleft. **2.** a split or division.

cleave¹ (klēv), *v.t.*, *v.i.*, **cleaved** or **cleft** or **clove; cleaved** or **cleft** or **clo·ven; cleav·ing.** to split or divide by or as by a cutting blow.

cleave² (klēv), *v.i.*, **cleaved, cleav·ing.** *Archaic.* to adhere closely.

cleav·er (klē'vər), *n.* a heavy knife or long-bladed hatchet, esp. one used by butchers.

clef (klef), *n.* *Music.* a symbol placed on a staff to indicate the pitches of the notes corresponding to its lines and spaces.

cleft¹ (kleft), *n.* a space made by cleavage.

cleft² (kleft), *v.* **1.** a pt. and pp. of **cleave¹.** —*adj.* **2.** split or divided.

clem·a·tis (klem'ə tis), *n.* a flowering vine or erect shrub having white or purple flowers.

Clem·ens (klem'ənz), *n.* **Samuel Lang·horne** (lang'hôrn, -ərn). See **Twain, Mark.**

clem·ent (klem'ənt), *adj.* **1.** merciful or lenient in disposition. **2.** (of the weather) mild or pleasant. —**clem'en·cy** (-ən sē), *n.* —**clem'ent·ly,** *adv.*

clench (klench), *v.t.* **1.** to close (the hands, teeth, etc.) tightly. **2.** to grasp or grip firmly. **3.** clinch (defs. 1, 2). —*n.* **4.** a firm grasp.

Cle·o·pa·tra (klē'ə pa'trə, -pä'-, -pā'-), *n.* 69–30 B.C., queen of Egypt.

clere·sto·ry (klēr'stôr'ē, -stōr'ē), *n., pl.* **-ries.** a portion of an interior rising above adjacent rooftops and having windows.

cler·gy (klûr'jē), *n., pl.* **-gies.** the group of ordained persons in a religion.

cler·gy·man (klûr'jē mən), *n.* a member of the clergy. —**cler'gy·wom'an,** *n.fem.*

cler·ic (kler'ik), *n.* **1.** clergyman. —*adj.* **2.** clerical (def. 2).

cler·i·cal (kler'i kəl), *adj.* **1.** of or pertaining to office clerks. **2.** of or characteristic of the clergy or a member of the clergy.

cler·i·cal·ism (kler'i kə liz'əm), *n.* clerical power or influence in government, politics, etc. —**cler'i·cal·ist,** *n.*

clerk (klûrk), *n.* **1.** a person employed to do general office work. **2.** salesclerk. **3.** an official who keeps the records of a court, legislature, etc. **4.** *Archaic.* cleric. —*v.i.* **5.** to serve as a clerk. —**clerk'ship,** *n.*

Cleve·land (klēv'lənd), *n.* **1. (Stephen) Gro·ver** (grō'vər), 1837–1908, 22nd and 24th president of the U.S. 1885–89, 1893–97. **2.** a port in NE Ohio.

clev·er (klev'ər), *adj.* **1.** mentally bright. **2.** superficially skillful or witty. **3.** ingenious or smart. —**clev'er·ly,** *adv.* —**clev'er·ness,** *n.* —**Syn. 3.** adroit, cunning, resourceful.

clev·is (klev'is), *n.* a U-shaped yoke at the end of a chain or rod, between the ends of which a lever, hook, etc., can be bolted.

clew (klōō), *n.* **1.** a ball of thread, yarn, etc. **2.** either lower corner of a square sail. **3.** *Obsolesc.* clue (def. 1).

cli·ché (klē shā', kli-), *n.* a trite, stereotyped expression. —**cli·chéd,** *adj.*

click (klik), *n.* **1.** a slight, sharp sound: *the click of a latch.* —*v.i.* **2.** to make a click or series of clicks. **3.** *Informal.* **a.** to succeed. **b.** to function well together. —*v.t.* **4.** to cause to click. —**click'er,** *n.*

cli·ent (klī'ənt), *n.* **1.** a person who engages the services of a lawyer or other professional. **2.** a patron or customer. —*adj.* **3.** dependent upon a major nation: *a client state.*

cli·en·tele (klī'ən tel'), *n.* the clients (as of a lawyer) or the customers (as of a shop) collectively.

cliff (klif), *n.* the high steep face of a rocky mass overlooking a lower area.

cliff·hang·er (klif'hang'ər), *n.* **1.** a melodramatic adventure serial in which each installment ends in suspense. **2.** a contest whose outcome is suspensefully uncertain.

cli·mac·ter·ic (klī mak'tər ik, klī'mak ter'ik), *n.* **1.** the period of decreasing reproductive capacity, culminating in women in menopause. **2.** any critical period.

cli·mate (klī'mit), *n.* **1.** the prevailing weather conditions of a region averaged over a series of years. **2.** a region characterized by its prevailing weather. **3.** a prevailing attitude, atmosphere, or condition. —**cli·mat·ic** (klī mat'ik), **cli·mat'i·cal, cli·mat·al,** *adj.* —**cli·mat'i·cal·ly,** *adv.*

cli·ma·tol·o·gy (klī'mə tol'ə jē), *n.* the science that deals with climatic conditions. —**cli·ma·to·log·ic** (klī'mə t'loj'ik), **cli·ma·to·log'i·cal,** *adj.* —**cli·ma·to·log'i·cal·ly,** *adv.* —**cli'ma·tol'o·gist,** *n.*

cli·max (klī'maks), *n.* **1.** the highest or most intense point in the development of something. **2.** a decisive point in the plot of a dramatic or literary work. **3.** an orgasm. —*v.t., v.i.* **4.** to bring to or reach a climax. —**cli·mac'tic** (-mak'tik), *adj.*

climb (klīm), *v.i.* **1.** to move upward or toward the top of something. **2.** to slope upward. **3.** to ascend by twining. **4.** to move by using the hands and feet. **5.** to ascend in prominence or fortune. —*v.t.* **6.** to ascend, esp. by the use of the hands and feet. **7.** **climb down,** to move downward. —*n.* **8.** the act or an instance of climbing. **9.** a place to be climbed. —**climb'a·ble,** *adj.* —**climb'er,** *n.*

clime (klīm), *n. Literary.* **1.** a region of the earth. **2.** climate.

clinch (klinch), *v.t.* **1.** to fasten (a nail, etc.) in position by beating down the protruding point. **2.** to settle (a matter) decisively. —*v.i.* **3.** *Boxing.* to engage in a clinch. **4.** *Slang.* to embrace passionately. —*n.* **5.** the act of clinching. **6.** *Boxing.* a holding about the opponent's arms or body to prevent punching. **7.** *Slang.* a passionate embrace.

clinch·er (klin'chər), *n.* **1.** a person or thing that clinches. **2.** a point, argument, or fact that is conclusive.

cling (kling), *v.i.,* **clung, cling·ing.** **1.** to adhere closely. **2.** to hold tight. **3.** to remain attached, as to an idea. —**cling'er,** *n.*

cling·stone (kling'stōn'), *n.* a peach having a stone to which the pulp adheres closely.

clin·ic (klin'ik), *n.* **1.** a place for treatment of outpatients, as in a hospital. **2.** a class of medical students assembled for instruction in diagnosis and treatment of patients. **3.** any group convening for instruction, advice, etc.: *a speech clinic.* [< L *clīnic(us)* < Gk *klīnikós* of a sickbed]

clin·i·cal (klin'ĭ kəl), *adj.* **1.** pertaining to a clinic. **2.** concerned with observation and treatment of patients rather than medical theory. **3.** dispassionately critical. —**clin'i·cal·ly,** *adv.*

cli·ni·cian (kli nish'ən), *n.* a physician who is skilled in clinical methods.

clink[1] (klingk), *v.t., v.i.* **1.** to make, or cause to make, a light, sharp, ringing sound. —*n.* **2.** a clinking sound.

clink[2] (klingk), *n. Slang.* a jail.

clink·er[1] (kling'kər), *n.* **1.** a partially vitrified mass as of ash. **2.** a hard Dutch paving brick.

clink·er[2] (kling'kər), *n. Slang.* any mistake or error.

clip[1] (klip), *v.,* **clipped, clip·ping,** *n.* —*v.t.* **1.** to cut, cut off, or trim with shears or scissors. **2.** to cut short. **3.** *Informal.* to hit with a quick, sharp blow. **4.** *Slang.* to swindle or cheat. —*v.i.* **5.** to clip or cut something. **6.** to move swiftly. —*n.* **7.** the act of clipping. **8.** anything clipped off. **9.** *Informal.* a quick, sharp blow. **10.** *Informal.* a rate of speed or pace: *at a rapid clip.*

clip² (klip), *n., v.,* **clipped, clip·ping.**
—*n.* **1.** a device that grips and holds tightly. **2.** See **paper clip. 3.** a metal frame for holding rifle cartridges. —*v.t., v.i.* **4.** to fasten with a clip. **5.** *Football.* to block (an opponent) illegally, usually from behind.

clip·board (klip′bôrd′, -bôrd′), *n.* a board with a heavy spring clip at one end for holding papers.

clip′ joint′, *Slang.* a nightclub, bar, etc., that makes a practice of overcharging customers.

clipped′ word′, a shortened form of a word, as *deli* for *delicatessen.* Also called **clipped′ form′.**

clip·per (klip′ər), *n.* **1.** a person or thing that clips or cuts. **2.** Often, **clippers.** a cutting tool, esp. shears. **3.** a sailing vessel built and rigged for speed.

clip·ping (klip′ing), *n.* **1.** the act of a person or thing that clips. **2.** a piece clipped off or out, as from a newspaper.

clip·sheet (klip′shēt′), *n.* a sheet of paper containing news items, etc., printed on one side for convenience in cutting and printing.

clique (klēk, klik), *n.* a small, exclusive group of people. —**cli′quey, cli′quy,** *adj.* —**cli′quish,** *adj.* — **cli′quish·ly,** *adv.* —**cli′quish·ness,** *n.*

clit·o·ris (klit′ər is, klī′tər is), *n.* the erectile organ of the vulva. —**clit′o·ral, cli·tor′ic** (-tôr′ik), *adj.*

clk., **1.** clerk. **2.** clock.

clo., clothing.

cloak (klōk), *n.* **1.** a loose outer garment. **2.** disguise or pretense. —*v.t.* **3.** to cover with a cloak. **4.** to conceal or disguise.

cloak-and-dag·ger (klōk′ən dag′ər), *adj.* of or characteristic of espionage.

cloak·room (klōk′rōōm′, -rōōm′), *n.* a room in which coats, hats, etc., may be left temporarily, as in a club.

clob·ber (klob′ər), *v.t. Slang.* **1.** to batter severely. **2.** to defeat decisively.

cloche (klōsh, klôsh), *n.* a bell-shaped, closefitting hat for women.

clock¹ (klok), *n.* **1.** a timepiece not designed to be worn or carried about. —*v.t.* **2.** to record the time of (a race or runner), as with a stopwatch. —**clock′er,** *n.*

clock² (klok), *n.* a short ornament on the side of a stocking.

clock·wise (klok′wīz′), *adv.* in the direction of the rotation of the hands of a clock. —*adj.* **2.** directed clockwise.

clock·work (klok′wûrk′), *n.* **1.** the mechanism of a clock. **2.** like clockwork, with precision.

clod (klod), *n.* **1.** a lump, esp. of earth or clay. **2.** a stupid person. —**clod′dy,** *adj.* —**clod′dish,** *adj.*

clod·hop·per (klod′hop′ər), *n.* **1.** a clumsy or rude person. **2.** **clodhoppers,** heavy shoes.

clog (klog, klôg), *v.,* **clogged, clogging,** *n.* —*v.t.* **1.** to hinder or obstruct with thick matter. **2.** to encumber or hamper. —*v.i.* **3.** to become clogged. —*n.* **4.** anything that impedes motion or action. **5.** a shoe with a thick sole of wood. —**clog′gy,** *adj.*

cloi·son·né (kloi′zə nā′), *n.* enamelwork in which colored areas are separated by thin, metal bands.

clois·ter (kloi′stər), *n.* **1.** a place of religious seclusion, as a monastery or convent. **2.** a covered walk, having an open arcade and opening onto a courtyard. —*v.t.* **3.** to confine, as in a cloister.

clone (klōn), *n., v.,* **cloned, clon·ing.** —*n.* **1.** a group of organisms derived from a single individual by various types of asexual reproduction. —*v.i., v.t.* **2.** to grow or cause to grow as or into a clone.

clop (klop), *n., v.,* **clopped, clopping.** —*n.* **1.** a sound made by or as if by a horse's hoof. —*v.i.* **2.** to make or walk with such a sound.

close (v. klōz; *adj.* klōs; *adv.* klōs; *n.* klōz), *v.,* **closed, clos·ing,** *adj.,* **clos·er, clos·est,** *adv., n.* —*v.t.* **1.** to block or bar an opening or passage through. **2.** to obstruct. **3.** to join or unite: *Close up those ranks!* **4.** to bring to an end. —*v.i.* **5.** to become closed. **6.** to unite. **7.** to grapple. **8.** to come to terms. **9.** to come to an end. **10.** **close down** or **up,** to stop entirely. **11.** **close in,** to advance and surround. **12.** **close out,** a. to reduce the price of for quick sale. b. to dispose of finally and completely. —*adj.* **13.** compact or dense. **14.** being in or having proximity in space or time. **15.** similar in degree, action, feeling, etc. **16.** near in kind or relationship. **17.** left flush with the surface or very short. **18.** strict or searching. **19.** not deviating from a model. **20.** nearly equal: *a close contest.* **21.** shut or shut tight. **22.** shut in or enclosed. **23.** confined or narrow: *close quarters.* **24.** lacking fresh air: *a hot, close room.* **25.** narrowly confined. **26.** secretive or reticent. **27.** parsimonious or stingy. **28.** scarce as money. —*adv.* **29.** in a close manner. **30.** near or close by. —*n.* **31.** the act of closing. **32.** the end or conclusion. —**clos·a·ble, close·a·ble** (klō′zə bəl), *adj.* — **close·ly** (klōs′lē), *adv.* —**close·ness** (klōs′nis), *n.* —**clos·er** (klō′zər), *n.* —**Syn. 4.** complete, conclude, finish, terminate.

close′ call′ (klōs), *Informal.* a narrow escape from danger or failure. Also called **close′ shave′.**

closed′ cir′cuit, a system of televising by means of cable to viewing sets. Also called **closed′-cir′cuit tel′evision.**

closed′ shop′, a shop in which union membership is a condition of employment.

close·fist·ed (klōs′fis′tid), *adj.* stingy or miserly.

close·fit·ting (klōs′fit′ing), *adj.* fitting snugly to the body.

close·knit (klōs′nit′), *adj.* tightly connected or organized.

close-mouthed (klōs′mouᵗʰd′, -moutʰt′), *adj.* reticent or uncommunicative.

close·out (klōz′out′), *n.* a sale on all goods in liquidating a business.

clos·et (kloz′it), *n.* 1. a small room or compartment for storing utensils, clothing, etc. 2. *Obs.* a small private room. —*v.t.* 3. to shut up in a private room for a conference, interview, etc.

close-up (klōs′up′), *n.* 1. a picture taken at close range. 2. an intimate view of something.

clo·sure (klō′zhər), *n.* 1. the act or state of being closed. 2. a conclusion or end. 3. something that closes. 4. a cloture.

clot (klot), *n., v.,* **clot·ted, clot·ting.** —*n.* 1. a thickened mass or lump. —*v.i., v.t.* 3. to form into clots.

cloth (klôtʰ, klotʰ), *n., pl.* **cloths** (klôtʰz, klotʰz, klôtʰs, klotʰs). 1. a fabric formed by weaving, etc., for garments, upholstery, etc. 2. a piece of such a fabric for a particular purpose: *an altar cloth.* 3. the particular attire of any profession, esp. that of the clergy. 4. **the cloth,** the clergy.

clothe (klōtʰ), *v.t.,* **clothed** or **clad, cloth·ing.** 1. to provide clothing for. 2. to cover with or as with clothing.

clothes (klōz, klōtʰz), *n.pl.* 1. garments for the body. 2. *Obs.* bedclothes. —*Syn.* 1. apparel, attire, garb.

clothes·horse (klōz′hôrs′, klōtʰz′-), *n.* 1. *Informal.* a person whose chief interest and pleasure is dressing fashionably. 2. a frame on which to hang wet laundry for drying.

clothes·pin (klōz′pin′, klōtʰz′-), *n.* a device for fastening clothes to a line, esp. for drying.

clothes·press (klōz′pres′, klōtʰz′-), *n.* *Obs.* an upright cabinet for clothes.

cloth·ier (klōtʰ′yər, -ē ər), *n.* 1. a retailer of clothing, esp. for men. 2. *Obs.* a person who makes cloth.

cloth·ing (klō′tʰing), *n.* 1. garments collectively. 2. a covering.

clo·ture (klō′chər), *n. Parl. Proc.* a method of closing debate and causing an immediate vote to be taken.

cloud (kloud), *n.* 1. a visible collection of particles of water or ice suspended in the air. 2. any similar mass, esp. of smoke or dust. 3. anything that obscures something or causes gloom, etc. 4. a great number of insects, birds, etc., flying together. 5. **in the clouds.** a. lost in reverie. b. impractical or fanciful. 6. **under a cloud,** in disgrace or under suspicion. —*v.t.* 7. to cover with clouds. 8. to overshadow or darken. 9. to make gloomy. 10. to place under suspicion or disgrace. —*v.i.* 11. to become clouded. —**cloud′less,** *adj.* —**cloud′y,** *adj.* —**cloud′i·ness,** *n.*

cloud·burst (kloud′bûrst′), *n.* a sudden and very heavy rainfall.

cloud·let (kloud′lit), *n.* a small cloud.

cloud′ nine′, *Informal.* a state of perfect happiness or bliss: *The newlyweds seemed to be on cloud nine.*

clout (klout), *n.* 1. a blow, esp. with the hand. 2. *Informal.* the influential effect of an idea, personality, etc. —*v.t.* 3. to strike, esp. with the hand.

clove¹ (klōv), *n.* the dried flower bud of a tropical tree, used whole or ground as a spice.

clove² (klōv), *n.* a small section of a bulb, as of garlic.

clove³ (klōv), *v.* a pt. of **cleave¹.**

clo·ven (klō′vən), *v.* 1. a pp. of **cleave¹.** —*adj.* 2. split or divided.

clo·ver (klō′vər), *n.* any of various herbs having three leaflets and dense flower heads, many species of which are cultivated as forage plants.

clo·ver·leaf (klō′vər lēf′), *n., pl.* **-leaves.** a road arrangement for permitting easy traffic movement between two intersecting high-speed highways.

clown (kloun), *n.* 1. a comic performer, esp. in a circus, who entertains by pantomime, tumbling, etc. 2. a coarse, ill-bred person. —*v.i.* 3. to act like a clown. [akin to Icel *klunni* boor] —**clown′ish,** *adj.* —**clown′ish·ly,** *adv.* —**clown′ish·ness,** *n.*

cloy (kloi), *v.t., v.i.* to weary by excess, as of sweetness.

clr., clear.

CLU, 1. Chartered Life Underwriter. 2. Civil Liberties Union.

club (klub), *n., v.,* **clubbed, clubbing.** —*n.* 1. a heavy stick, suitable for use as a weapon. 2. a stick or bat used in various games, as golf. 3. a group of persons organized for

a social, literary, or other purpose.
4. its meeting place. 5. a black
trefoil-shaped figure on a playing
card. 6. a card bearing such figures.
—*v.t.*, *v.i.* 7. to beat with or as
with a club. 8. to unite or join
together.

club′ chair′, a heavily upholstered
chair having solid sides and a low
back.

club·foot (klub′foŏt′), *n.*, *pl.* -feet
for 1. 1. a deformed or distorted
foot. 2. the condition of having
such a foot. —**club′foot′ed,** *adj.*

club·house (klub′hous′), *n.* 1. a
building or room occupied by a
club. 2. a room for dressing by an
athletic club.

club′ sand′wich, a sandwich having
two layers of sliced meat, lettuce,
etc., between three slices of bread.

club′ so′da. See soda water (def. 1).

club′ steak′, a beefsteak cut from
the rib end of the short loin.

cluck (kluk), *v.i.* 1. to utter the
cry of a hen brooding. —*n.* 2. a
clucking sound. 3. *Slang.* a dull-
witted person.

clue (kloō), *n.*, *v.*, **clued,** **clu·ing.**
—*n.* 1. any guide in the solution
of a problem, mystery, etc. 2. clew
(defs. 1, 2). —*v.t.* 3. to direct by
a clue.

clump (klump), *n.* 1. a cluster,
esp. of trees or other plants. 2. a
lump or mass. 3. a heavy, thumping
sound. —*v.i.* 4. to walk heavily
and clumsily. —*v.t.* 5. to gather
into a clump. —**clump′y,** *adj.*

clum·sy (klum′zē), *adj.* **-si·er, -si·est.**
1. without agility or grace in mo-
tion or action. 2. awkwardly done
or made. —**clum′si·ly,** *adv.* —**clum′-
si·ness,** *n.* —**Syn.** 1. awkward, stiff,
ungainly.

clung (klung), *v.* pt. and pp. of
cling.

clus·ter (klus′tər), *n.* 1. a number
of things of the same kind, growing or held together. —*v.t.*, *v.i.* 2.
to gather or grow in a cluster.

clutch¹ (kluch), *v.t.* 1. to seize with
or as with the hands or claws.
—*v.i.* 2. to try to seize or grasp.
—*n.* 3. the hand, etc., when grasping. 4. power of disposal or control. 5. a tight grip or hold. 6. a
mechanism for engaging or disengaging a shaft with or from
another shaft or rotating part. 7.
Informal. a critical situation.

clutch² (kluch), *n.* 1. a hatch of
eggs. 2. a brood of chickens.

clut·ter (klut′ər), *v.t.* 1. to litter
with things in a disorderly manner.
—*n.* 2. a disorderly heap. 3. disorderly mess.

clys·ter (klis′tər), *n. Rare.* an enema.

C.M., Congregation of the Mission.

Cm, curium.

cm, centimeter; centimeters. Also,
cm.

cmdg., commanding.

Cmdr., Commander.

cml., commercial.

CMSgt, Chief Master Sergeant.

C/N, 1. circular note. 2. credit note.

CNO, Chief of Naval Operations.

CNS, central nervous system.

CO, 1. Colorado. 2. Commanding
Officer. 3. conscientious objector.

Co, cobalt.

co-, a prefix meaning: **a.** together:
cooperate. **b.** joint: *coauthor.* **c.**
equally: *coextensive.*

C/O, cash order.

c/o, 1. care of. 2. carried over.
3. cash order.

Co., 1. Company. 2. County. Also,
co.

C.O., 1. cash order. 2. Commanding
Officer. 3. conscientious objector.

c.o., 1. care of. 2. carried over.

coach (kōch), *n.* 1. a large, horse-
drawn, four-wheeled carriage. 2. a
public motor bus. 3. the least
expensive class of passenger accommodation on a railroad, airline, etc. 4. a person who instructs
or trains an athlete or performer,
etc. 5. a private tutor. —*v.t.* 6. to
instruct or train. —*v.i.* 7. to act
as a coach. —**coach′er,** *n.*

coach·man (kōch′mən), *n.* a person
employed to drive a coach or carriage.

co·ad·ju·tor (kō aj′ə tər, kō′ə jōō′tər),
n. 1. *Literary.* an assistant. 2. a
bishop who assists another bishop
and has the right of succession.

co·ag·u·lant (kō ag′yə lənt), *n.* a
substance that aids coagulation.

co·ag·u·late (kō ag′yə lāt′), *v.t.*, *v.i.*,
-lat·ed, -lat·ing. to change from a
fluid into a thickened mass. —**co·
ag′u·la′tion,** *n.* —**co·ag′u·la′tive,**
adj. —**co·ag′u·la′tor,** *n.*

coal (kōl), *n.* 1. a black combustible
mineral, used as a fuel. 2. an
ember. 3. rake, haul, or drag over
the coals, to reprimand severely.

co·a·lesce (kō′ə les′), *v.i.*, *v.t.*, -lesced,
-lesc·ing. to unite so as to form
one mass, community, etc. —**co′a·
les′cence,** *n.* —**co′a·les′cent,** *adj.*

coal′ field′, an area containing coal
deposits.

coal′ gas′, a gas used for heating,
produced by distilling bituminous
coal.

co·a·li·tion (kō′ə lish′ən), *n.* 1. an alliance, esp. a temporary one be-
tween factions, etc. 2. union or
fusion.

coal′ oil′, *Chiefly Dial.* kerosene.

coal′ tar′, a thick, black liquid
formed during the distillation of
coal, used in dyes, drugs, etc.

coarse (kōrs, kôrs), *adj.*, **coars·er, coars·est.** 1. of inferior or faulty quality. 2. composed of large parts or particles. 3. lacking fineness of texture: *coarse fabric.* 4. lacking refinement. —**coarse′ly,** *adv.* —**coarse′ness,** *n.*

coars·en (kōr′sən, kôr′-), *v.t., v.i.* to make or become coarse.

coast (kōst), *n.* 1. the land next to the sea. 2. a slide down a hill, as on a sled. —*v.i.* 3. to slide on a sled down a hill. 4. to sail along a coast. 5. to continue to move on momentum. —**coast′al,** *adj.*

coast·er (kō′stər), *n.* 1. a person or thing that coasts. 2. a small dish or mat, esp. for placing under a glass to protect a table from moisture. 3. a ship engaged in coastal trade.

coast′er brake′, a brake on a bicycle, operated by back pressure on the pedals.

coast′ guard′, a military service that enforces maritime laws, saves lives and property at sea, etc. —**coast-guards·man** (kōst′gärdz′mən), *n.*

coast·line (kōst′līn′), *n.* the contour of a coast.

coat (kōt), *n.* 1. an outer garment covering at least the upper part of the body. 2. a natural covering, as hair, fur, bark, etc. 3. Also called **coat′ing.** a layer of anything that covers a surface. —*v.t.* 4. to cover or provide with a coat.

co·a·ti (kō ä′tē), *n., pl.* **-tis.** a tropical American carnivore related to the raccoon.

coat′ of arms′, 1. a garment embroidered with heraldic devices, worn by medieval knights over their armor. 2. heraldic insignia.

coat′ of mail′, a long defensive garment made of interlinked metal rings.

coat-tail (kōt′tāl′), *n.* 1. the back of the skirt on a man's coat or jacket. 2. **on someone's coattails,** aided by association with another person.

co·au·thor (kō ô′thər, kō′ô′-), *n.* one of two or more joint authors.

coax (kōks), *v.t., v.i.* to attempt to influence (a person) by gentle persuasion, etc. —**coax′er,** *n.* —**coax′ing·ly,** *adv.* —**Syn.** cajole, persuade, wheedle.

co·ax·i·al (kō ak′sē əl), *adj.* having a common axis or axes. —**co·ax′i·al·ly,** *adv.*

coax′ial ca′ble, an insulated conducting tube through which a central conductor runs, used for transmitting high-frequency television signals.

cob (kob), *n.* 1. a corncob. 2. a male swan. 3. a short-legged, thickset horse.

co·balt (kō′bôlt), *n. Chem.* a silver-white metallic element, occurring in compounds that provide blue coloring substances. *Symbol:* Co; *at. wt.:* 58.933; *at. no.:* 27.

cob·ble (kob′əl), *v.t.,* **-bled, -bling.** 1. to mend (shoes, boots, etc.). 2. to put together roughly or clumsily.

cob·bler (kob′lər), *n.* 1. a person who mends shoes. 2. a deep-dish fruit pie with a rich biscuit crust.

cob·ble·stone (kob′əl stōn′), *n.* a naturally rounded stone formerly used for paving.

COBOL (kō′bôl, -bôl′), *n.* a programming language for writing computer programs to process uniformly related data items. [*co(m*mon) *b(usiness) o(riented) l(anguage)*]

co·bra (kō′brə), *n.* a venomous African or Asian snake that flattens the neck into a hoodlike form when disturbed.

cob·web (kob′web′), *n.* 1. a web spun by a spider to entrap its prey. 2. anything finespun, flimsy, or insubstantial.

co·caine (kō kān′, kō′kān), *n.* a narcotic alkaloid obtained from the leaves of a South American shrub, used as a surface anesthetic.

co·cain·ism (kō kā′niz əm, kō′kə-niz′əm), *n.* an abnormal condition caused by excessive or habitual use of cocaine.

coc·cus (kok′əs), *n., pl.* **-ci** (-sī). a spherical bacterium.

coc·cyx (kok′siks), *n., pl.* **coc·cy·ges** (kok sī′jēz, kok′si jēz′). a small triangular bone forming the lower extremity of the spinal column. —**coc·cyg·e·al** (kok sij′ē əl), *adj.*

coch·i·neal (koch′ə nēl′, koch′ə nēl′), *n.* a red dye prepared from the dried bodies of a tropical insect.

coch·le·a (kok′lē ə), *n., pl.* **coch·le·ae** (kok′lē ē′, -lē ī′), **coch·le·as.** a spiral-shaped cavity forming a division of the internal ear. —**coch′le·ar,** *adj.*

cock[1] (kok), *n.* 1. a rooster or other male bird. 2. a leader or chief. 3. a hand-operated valve or faucet. 4. a. the hammer of a firearm. b. its position when in preparation for firing. —*v.t.* 5. to pull back and set the cock of (a firearm).

cock[2] (kok), *v.t.* 1. to turn up or to one side, often in a jaunty way. 2. the act of turning the head to one side in a jaunty way.

cock[3] (kok), *n.* a conical pile of hay, dung, etc.

cock·ade (ko kād′), *n.* a rosette, knot of ribbon, etc., worn on the hat as an indication of rank.

cock·a·ma·mie (kok′ə mā′mē), *adj.*
Slang. ridiculous or nonsensical.

cock′-and-bull′ sto′ry (kok′ ən bŏŏl′),
an absurd, improbable story presented as the truth.

cock·a·too (kok′ə tōō′, kok′ə tōō′), *n.*,
pl. **-toos.** a crested parrot of the
Australian region.

cock·a·trice (kok′ə tris), *n.* a legendary monster with a deadly
glance.

cock·crow (kok′krō′), *n.* *Literary.*
daybreak.

cocked′ hat′, a man's wide-brimmed
hat, turned up on two or three
sides.

cock·er·el (kok′ər əl, kok′rəl), *n.* a
young domestic cock.

cock′er span′iel (kok′ər), a small
spaniel having a flat or slightly
waved, soft, dense coat.

cock·eye (kok′ī′), *n.* a squinting
eye.

cock·eyed (kok′īd′), *adj.* **1.** crosseyed. **2.** having a squinting eye.
3. *Slang.* **a.** twisted to one side.
b. foolish or absurd. **c.** completely
wrong.

cock·fight (kok′fīt′), *n.* a fight between gamecocks, usually fitted
with spurs.

cock·horse (kok′hôrs′), *n.* a child's
rocking horse.

cock·le¹ (kok′əl), *n.* **1.** a bivalve
mollusk having heart-shaped valves.
2. cockles of one's heart, the depths
of one's emotions or feelings.

cock·le² (kok′əl), *n.* any of various
common weeds found in areas
where grain is grown.

cock·le·shell (kok′əl shel′), *n.* **1.** a
shell of the cockle. **2.** a light or
frail boat.

cock·ney (kok′nē), *n.*, *pl.* **-neys.**
(*sometimes cap.*) **1.** a native of the
East End district of London, England. **2.** the pronunciation or dialect
of cockneys.

cock·pit (kok′pit′), *n.* **1.** a separate
area in some airplanes for the
pilot and copilot. **2.** a pit or enclosed place for cockfights.

cock·roach (kok′rōch′), *n.* an insect
characterized by a flattened body
and nocturnal habits, a common
household pest.

cocks·comb (koks′kōm′), *n.* **1.** the
comb of a rooster. **2.** the cap,
resembling it, formerly worn by
professional fools. **3.** a garden
plant with flowers resembling a
rooster's comb. **4.** coxcomb.

cock·sure (kok′shŏŏr′), *adj.* overly
sure or self-confident.

cock·tail (kok′tāl′), *n.* **1.** a chilled,
mixed drink of liquor and juice or
other flavorings. **2.** an appetizer,
as of seafood, juice, etc. —*adj.* **3.**

styled for semiformal wear: *a
cocktail dress.*

cock·y (kok′ē), *adj.*, **cock·i·er, cock·
i·est.** arrogantly conceited. —**cock′·
i·ly,** *adv.* —**cock′i·ness,** *n.*

co·co (kō′kō), *n.*, *pl.* **-cos.** **1.** See
coconut palm. 2. coconut.

co·coa (kō′kō), *n.* **1.** the roasted,
husked, and ground seeds of the
cacao. **2.** a beverage made from
cocoa powder.

co′coa but′ter, a fatty substance obtained from cacao seeds.

co·co·nut (kō′kə nut′, -nət), *n.* the
large, hard-shelled seed of the
coconut palm, lined with a white
edible meat and containing a milky
liquid (**co′conut milk′**). Also, **co′·
coa·nut′.**

co′conut palm′, a tall, tropical palm
bearing a large, edible fruit.

co·coon (kə kōōn′), *n.* the silky
envelope spun by the larvae of
many insects, as silkworms, that
serves as a covering while they
are in the pupal stage.

cod (kod), *n.*, *pl.* **cod, cods.** a food
fish found in the colder waters of
the North Atlantic.

C.O.D., **1.** cash on delivery. **2.** collect on delivery. Also, **COD, c.o.d.**

co·da (kō′də), *n.* *Music.* a more or
less independent passage concluding
a composition.

cod·dle (kod′ᵊl), *v.t.*, **-dled, -dling.**
1. to treat too protectively or indulgently. **2.** to cook in water just below the boiling point. —**cod′dler,** *n.*
—**Syn. 1.** baby, pamper, spoil.

code (kōd), *n.*, *v.*, **cod·ed, cod·ing.**
—*n.* **1.** a system of signals for
communication by telegraph, etc.
2. a system of symbols used for
brevity or secrecy of communication. **3.** a systematic collection of
the existing laws of a country.
4. any system of principles. —*v.t.*
5. to put into code.

co·deine (kō′dēn), *n.* an alkaloid
obtained from opium: used as an
analgesic and to inhibit coughing.

co·dex (kō′deks), *n.*, *pl.* **co·di·ces**
(kō′di sēz′, kod′i-). an ancient manuscript, usually of a classic or the
Scriptures.

cod·fish (kod′fish′), *n.*, *pl.* **-fish,
-fish·es.** cod.

codg·er (koj′ər), *n.* an odd or eccentric man, esp. one who is old.

cod·i·cil (kod′i səl), *n.* a supplement to a will, containing an addition, modification, etc.

cod·i·fy (kod′ə fī′, kō′də-), *v.t.*,
-fied, -fy·ing. 1. to reduce (laws,
etc.) to a code. **2.** to arrange in
a systematic collection. —**cod′i·
fi·ca′tion,** *n.* —**cod′i·fi′er,** *n.*

cod·ling (kod′ling), *n.* **1.** the young
of the cod. **2.** hake.

co·ed (kō'ed', -ed'), *Informal.* —*n.* **1.** a female college student. —*adj.* **2.** coeducational.

co·ed·u·ca·tion (kō'ej ŏŏ kā'shən, -ed yŏŏ-), *n.* the education of both sexes in the same classes. —**co'ed·u·ca'tion·al,** *adj.* —**co'ed·u·ca'tion·al·ly,** *adv.*

co·ef·fi·cient (kō'ə fish'ənt), *n.* **1.** a number or quantity multiplying another quantity, as *3* in *3x.* **2.** a number that is constant for a given substance or process under certain conditions, serving as a measure of one of its properties.

coe·len·ter·ate (si len'tə rāt', -tər it), *n.* an invertebrate animal having a single internal cavity for digestion and excretion, such as the hydra, jellyfish, or sea anemone.

co·e·qual (kō ē'kwəl), *adj.* **1.** equal with another. —*n.* **2.** a coequal person or thing. —**co·e·qual·i·ty** (kō'i kwol'i tē), *n.* —**co·e'qual·ly,** *adv.*

co·erce (kō ûrs'), *v.t.,* **-erced, -erc·ing. 1.** to compel by force, intimidation, etc. **2.** to dominate or control. —**co·erc'er,** *n.* —**co·er'cion,** *n.* —**co·er'sive,** *adj.*

co·e·val (kō ē'vəl), *adj.* **1.** of the same era, epoch, or duration. —*n.* **2.** a coeval person. —**co·e'val·ly,** *adv.*

co·ex·ist (kō'ig zist'), *v.i.* **1.** to exist together or at the same time. **2.** to exist together peacefully. —**co'ex·ist'ence,** *n.* —**co'ex·ist'ent,** *adj.*

co·ex·ten·sive (kō'ik sten'siv), *adj.* extending equally in space, time, or scope.

C. of C., Chamber of Commerce.

co·fea·ture (kō fē'chər), *n.* a feature, as a motion picture, presented as a subordinate attraction to the main one.

cof·fee (kô'fē, kof'ē), *n.* **1.** a beverage consisting of an infusion of the roasted ground or crushed seeds (**cof'fee beans'**) of the two-seeded fruit (**cof'fee ber'ry**) of a tropical tree. **2.** the seeds. **3.** the coffee tree. **4.** a dark brown.

cof·fee break', a short intermission from work for coffee or other refreshments.

cof·fee·cake (kô'fē kāk', kof'ē-), *n.* a cake or bread, usually containing nuts and raisins.

cof·fee·house (kô'fē hous', kof'ē-), *n.* a café serving different kinds of coffee, often with pastries or snacks.

cof'fee klatsch' (klach, kläch), a social gathering for informal conversation at which coffee is served.

cof·fee·pot (kô'fē pot', kof'ē-), *n.* a utensil for brewing and serving coffee.

cof'fee shop', a small restaurant where refreshments and light meals are served.

cof'fee ta'ble, a low table, usually placed in front of a sofa, for holding ashtrays, glasses, etc.

cof·fer (kô'fər, kof'ər), *n.* **1.** a box or chest, esp. for valuables. **2.** coffers, a treasury or funds.

cof·fer·dam (kô'fər dam', kof'ər-), *n.* a watertight enclosure placed under water and pumped dry to allow construction or repairs.

cof·fin (kô'fin, kof'in), *n.* the box in which a corpse is placed for burial.

C. of S., Chief of Staff.

cog (kog, kôg), *n.* **1.** a gear tooth. **2.** a minor person in a large organization, etc. —**cogged** (kogd, kôgd), *adj.*

cog., cognate.

co·gent (kō'jənt), *adj.* convincing by forcible, clear presentation. —**co'gen·cy,** *n.* —**co'gent·ly,** *adv.*

cog·i·tate (koj'i tāt'), *v.i., v.t.,* **-tat·ed, -tat·ing.** to think hard (about). —**cog'i·ta'tion,** *n.* —**cog'i·ta'tive,** *adj.* —**cog'i·ta'tor,** *n.* —**Syn.** meditate, ponder.

co·gnac (kōn'yak, kon'-), *n.* (*often cap.*) a brandy distilled in the French town of Cognac and its surrounding area.

cog·nate (kog'nāt), *adj.* **1.** related by birth. **2.** descended from the same earlier form: *cognate words.* **3.** similar in nature. —*n.* **4.** a cognate person or thing.

cog·ni·tion (kog nish'ən), *n.* **1.** the act or process of knowing or perceiving. **2.** something known or perceived. —**cog·ni'tion·al,** *adj.* —**cog·ni·tive** (kog'ni tiv), *adj.*

cog·ni·za·ble (kog'ni zə bəl, kon'i-, kog nī'-), *adj.* **1.** capable of being perceived or known. **2.** being within the jurisdiction of a court.

cog·ni·zance (kog'ni zəns, kon'i-), *n.* **1.** knowledge, esp. through perception or reason. **2.** notice or acknowledgment. —**cog'ni·zant,** *adj.*

cog·no·men (kog nō'mən), *n., pl.* **-no·mens, -nom·i·na** (-nom'ə nə). **1.** a surname, esp. the third and family name of an ancient Roman. **2.** any name, esp. a nickname.

co·gno·scen·ti (kon'yə shen'tē, kog'nə-), *n.pl., sing.* **-te** (-tē). those who have superior knowledge of a particular field.

cog' rail'way, a railway having locomotives with a cogged center driving wheel engaging with a cogged rail for climbing steep grades.

cog·wheel (kog'hwēl', -wēl'), *n.* a wheel having cogs or teeth placed around its edge.

co·hab·it (kō hab′it), *v.i.* to live together as husband and wife without being legally married. —**co·hab′i·ta′tion,** *n.*

co·heir (kō âr′), *n.* a joint heir.

co·here (kō hēr′), *v.i.,* **-hered, -hering. 1.** to stick together. **2.** to be naturally or logically connected.

co·her·ent (kō hēr′ənt), *adj.* **1.** sticking together. **2.** consistent or logical. —**co·her′ence, co·her′en·cy,** *n.* —**co·her′ent·ly,** *adv.*

co·he·sion (kō hē′zhən), *n.* **1.** the act or state of cohering or uniting. **2.** the molecular force between particles within a body that acts to unite them. —**co·he′sive,** *adj.* —**co·he′sive·ly,** *adv.* —**co·he′sive·ness,** *n.*

co·ho (kō′hō), *n., pl.* **-hos, -ho.** a small salmon native to the Pacific Ocean, introduced into the Great Lakes.

co·hort (kō′hôrt), *n.* **1.** *Informal.* one's companion or associate. **2.** a group, esp. of warriors.

coif (koif *for 1;* kwäf *for 2*), *n.* **1.** a hood-shaped cap. **2.** *Informal.* coiffure.

coif·feur (kwä fər′), *n. French.* hairdresser. —**coif′feuse** (kwä fōos′, -fōoz′), *n. fem.*

coif·fure (kwä fyŏor′), *n.* a style of arranging the hair.

coil (koil), *v.t., v.i.* **1.** to wind into rings one above or around the other. —*n.* **2.** a series of spirals or rings into which a rope or the like is wound. **3.** a single such ring. **4.** *Elect.* a conductor, as a copper wire, wound up in a spiral or other form.

coin (koin), *n.* **1.** a piece of metal stamped and issued by the government for use as money. **2.** a number of such pieces. —*v.t.* **3.** to make (money) by stamping metal. **4.** to invent or make up: *to coin words.* —**coin′er,** *n.*

coin·age (koi′nij), *n.* **1.** the act or process of coining. **2.** coins collectively.

co·in·cide (kō′in sīd′), *v.i.,* **-cid·ed, -cid·ing. 1.** to occupy the same place in space or the same period in time. **2.** to correspond exactly, as in nature, etc.

co·in·ci·dence (kō in′si dəns), *n.* **1.** the fact of coinciding. **2.** an instance of this. **3.** an event happening at the same time or place, apparently by mere chance. —**co·in′ci·dent, co·in′ci·den′tal,** *adj.* —**co·in′ci·den′tal·ly,** *adv.*

co·i·tus (kō′i təs), *n.* See **sexual intercourse.** Also, **co·i·tion** (kō ish′ən). —**co′i·tal,** *adj.*

coke¹ (kōk), *n.* the solid product

resulting from the destructive distillation of coal, used as a fuel.

coke² (kōk), *n. Slang.* cocaine.

Coke (kōk), *n. Trademark.* a soft drink formally called Coca-Cola.

COL, cost of living.

Col., 1. Colonel. **2.** Colorado.

col., 1. collect. **2.** college. **3.** collegiate. **4.** colony. **5.** color. **6.** colored. **7.** column.

co·la¹ (kō′lə), *n.* a carbonated soft drink made with a syrup from the seeds of kola nuts.

co·la² (kō′lə), *n.* a pl. of **colon.**

col·an·der (kul′ən dər, kol′-), *n.* a container with a perforated bottom, for draining foods.

cold (kōld), *adj.* **1.** having relatively low temperature. **2.** feeling an uncomfortable lack of warmth or heat. **3.** *Informal.* unconscious because of a severe blow, shock, etc. **4.** lacking in passion, enthusiasm, etc.: *cold reason.* **5.** not affectionate or cordial. **6.** lacking sensual desire. **7.** depressing or dispiriting. **8.** (of a hunting scent) faint or weak. —*n.* **9.** the relative absence of heat. **10.** a respiratory virus infection characterized by sneezing, sore throat, coughing, etc. **11.** cold weather. —*adv.* **12.** with complete certainty. **13** without preparation or prior notice: *to play the lead role cold.* **14.** **catch** or **take cold,** to suffer from a cold. **15. left out in the cold,** neglected or ignored. —**cold′ly,** *adv.* —**cold′ness,** *n.* —**Syn. 4.** indifferent, unconcerned. **5.** reserved, unfeeling.

cold-blood·ed (kōld′blud′id), *adj.* **1.** designating animals, as fishes and reptiles, whose blood temperature varies with the surroundng medium. **2.** without emotion or feeling. **3.** sensitive to cold. —**cold′-blood′ed·ness,** *n.*

cold′ cream′, a cosmetic for soothing and cleansing the skin.

cold′ cuts′, various meats and sometimes cheeses, sliced and served cold.

cold′ duck′, a beverage made of a mixture of sparkling burgundy and champagne.

cold′ feet′, *Informal.* uncertainty or fear.

cold′ front′, the zone separating two air masses, of which the cooler, denser mass is advancing and replacing the warmer.

cold′ shoul′der, deliberate indifference.

cold′ sore′, an infection around the mouth caused by a virus, often accompanying a cold or fever.

cold′ sweat′, a chill accompanied by perspiration, caused by fear or nervousness.

cold′ tur′key, *Slang.* 1. the sudden and complete withholding of narcotics from an addict, as to effect a cure. 2. impromptu.

cold′ war′, intense rivalry between nations just short of military conflict.

cold-weld (kōld′weld′), *v.t.*, *v.i.* to weld (metals) by forcing heavy pressure without heat, used in sealing transistors.

cole·slaw (kōl′slô′), *n.* a salad of finely sliced or chopped raw cabbage. [< D *koolsla* = *kool* cabbage + *sla* salad]

co·le·us (kō′lē əs), *n., pl.* **-us·es.** a plant cultivated for its colored foliage and blue flowers.

col·ic (kol′ik), *n.* a severe cramping pain in the abdomen or bowels. —**col·ick·y** (kol′ə kē), *adj.*

col·i·se·um (kol′i sē′em), *n.* a large, usually oval building for conventions, exhibitions, or sports.

co·li·tis (kə lī′tis, kō-), *n.* inflammation of the colon. —**co·lit·ic** (kō-lit′ik), *adj.*

coll., 1. collect. 2. college. 3. collegiate. 4. colloquial.

col·lab·o·rate (kə lab′ə rāt′), *v.i.*, **-rat·ed, -rat·ing.** 1. to work with another or others, esp. in literary pursuits. 2. to cooperate with an enemy nation. —**col·lab′o·ra′tion,** *n.* —**col·lab′o·ra′tive,** *adj.* —**col·lab′o·ra′tor,** *n.*

col·lage (kə läzh′, kō-), *n.* a work of art made by pasting various materials on a single surface.

col·lapse (kə laps′), *v.*, **-lapsed, -laps-ing,** *n.* —*v.i.* 1. to fall or cave in. 2. to fold together compactly. 3. to break down or fail. 4. to fall unconscious from a stroke or exhaustion. —*v.t.* 5. to cause to collapse. —*n.* 6. a falling in or together. 7. a breakdown or failure. —**col·laps′i·ble,** *adj.*

col·lar (kol′ər), *n.* 1. anything worn around the neck. 2. the part of a shirt, coat, etc., around the neck. 3. a band or chain fastened around the neck of an animal as a means of restraint or identification. —*v.t.* 4. to put a collar on. 5. to seize or detain. —**col′lar·less,** *adj.*

col·lar·bone (kol′ər bōn′), *n.* the clavicle.

col·lard (kol′ərd), *n.* a variety of kale grown in the southern U.S.

collat., collateral.

col·late (ko lāt′, kə-, kol′āt, kō′lāt), *v.t.*, **-lat·ed, -lat·ing.** 1. to collect or arrange (pages) in proper order. 2. to compare (texts) critically. —**col·la′tor,** *n.*

col·lat·er·al (kə lat′ər əl), *adj.* 1. situated or running side by side. 2.

accompanying or auxiliary. 3. additional: *collateral evidence.* 4. secured by collateral: *a collateral loan.* 5. secondary or indirect. 6. descended from the same stock, but in a different line: *a collateral relative.* —*n.* 7. security pledged for the payment of a loan. 8. a collateral kinsman.

col·la·tion (ko lā′shən, kə-, kō-), *n.* 1. the act of collating. 2. *Rom. Cath. Ch.* the light meal allowed on fasting days.

col·league (kol′ēg), *n.* an associate in an office or profession.

col·lect[1] (kə lekt′), *v.t.*, *v.i.* 1. to gather together. 2. to gather or accumulate (stamps, etc.) as a hobby or for study. 3. to receive or compel payment (of): *to collect a bill.* 4. to regain control (of oneself, etc.). —*adj., adv.* 5. requiring payment by the recipient: *a collect telephone call.* —**col·lect′i·ble, col·lect′a·ble,** *adj.* —**col·lec′tion,** *n.* —**col·lec′tor,** *n.*

col·lect[2] (kol′əkt), *n.* a brief prayer used in some churches.

col·lect·ed (kə lek′tid), *adj.* having control of one's faculties or emotions. —**col·lect′ed·ly,** *adv.*

col·lec·tive (kə lek′tiv), *adj.* 1. formed by collecting. 2. of a group of individuals taken together. —*n.* 3. See **collective noun.** 4. a collective body. —**col·lec′tive·ly,** *adv.*

collec′tive bar′gaining, negotiation between a union and an employer for determining wages, hours, rules, etc.

collec′tive noun′, a noun, as *herd, jury,* or *clergy,* that appears singular but denotes a group.

col·lec·tiv·ism (kə lek′tə viz′əm), *n.* the principle of centralized economic control, esp. of all means of production. —**col·lec′tiv·ist,** *n., adj.*

col·lec·ti·vize (kə lek′tə vīz′), *v.t.*, **-vized, -viz·ing.** to organize (a people, etc.) under collectivism.

col·leen (kol′ēn, ko lēn′), *n.* a young Irish girl.

col·lege (kol′ij), *n.* 1. an institution of higher learning granting degrees. 2. a constituent unit of a university. 3. an institution for specialized instruction: *a barber college.* 4. an organized association of persons having certain powers and rights: *the electoral college.* —**col·le·giate** (kə lē′jit), *adj.*

col·le·gi·al (kə lē′jē əl, -jəl), *adj.* characterized by the collective responsibility shared by each of the colleagues, esp. in a church. —**col·le′gi·al′i·ty,** *n.*

col·le·gian (kə lē′jən, -jē ən), *n.* a college student.

col·le·gi·um (kə lē′jē əm), *n., pl.* **-gi·a** (-jē ə), **-gi·ums.** a group of ruling officials each with the same rank and power, esp. one that formerly functioned for a Soviet commissariat.

col·lide (kə līd′), *v.i.,* **-lid·ed, -lid·ing.** 1. to come into violent contact. 2. to clash or conflict. **—col·li·sion** (ke lizh′ən), *n.*

col·lie (kol′ē), *n.* a large dog having a usually long, black, tan, and white coat, raised originally for herding sheep.

col·lier (kol′yər), *n. Brit.* 1. a ship for carrying coal. 2. a coal miner.

col·liery (kol′yə rē), *n., pl.* **-lier·ies.** *Brit.* a coal mine.

col·lin·e·ar (kə lin′ē ər, kō-), *adj.* lying in the same straight line.

col·lins (kol′inz), *n.* a tall drink made with gin, whiskey, rum, or vodka, lemon or lime juice, soda water, and sugar.

col·lo·cate (kol′ə kāt′), *v.t.,* **-cat·ed, -cat·ing.** 1. to place together, esp. side by side. 2. to arrange (esp. words) in proper order. **—col′lo·ca′tion,** *n.*

col·lo·di·on (kə lō′dē ən), *n.* a solution of cellulose nitrate in ether and alcohol: used in the manufacture of photographic film, etc.

col·loid (kol′oid), *n.* 1. See **colloidal system.** 2. the suspended matter in a colloidal system. **—col·loi′dal,** *adj.*

colloi′dal sys′tem, a mixture of a solid, liquid, or gas in a solid, liquid, or gas that does not separate on standing, as a solid solution, gel, emulsion, or fog.

colloq., 1. colloquial. 2. colloquialism.

col·lo·qui·al (kə lō′kwē əl), *adj.* characteristic of ordinary conversation rather than formal speech or writing. **—co·lo′qui·al·ism,** *n.* **—col·lo′qui·al·ly,** *adv.*

col·lo·qui·um (kə lō′kwē əm), *n., pl.* **-qui·ums, -qui·a** (-kwē ə). an informal conference or group discussion.

col·lo·quy (kol′ə kwē), *n., pl.* **-quies.** a conversation or conference, esp. one formally arranged.

col·lude (kə lood′), *v.i.,* **-lud·ed, -lud·ing.** to act together through a secret understanding. **—col·lu′sion,** *n.* **—col·lu′sive,** *adj.*

col·lu·vi·um (kə loo′vē əm), *n.* a deposit of soil and fragmentary matter at the base of a slope. **—col·lu′vi·al,** *adj.*

Colo., Colorado.

co·logne (kə lōn′), *n.* a toilet water consisting of alcohol and perfume oils. **—co·logned′** (-lōnd′), *adj.*

Co·logne (kə lōn′), *n.* a city in W West Germany.

Co·lom·bi·a (kə lum′bē ə), *n.* a country in NW South America. **—Co·lom′bi·an,** *adj., n.*

co·lon[1] (kō′lən), *n.* the sign (:) used to mark a major division in a sentence, to indicate that what follows is an elaboration, etc.

co·lon[2] (kō′lən), *n., pl.* **-lons, -la** (-lə). the part of the large intestine extending from the cecum to the rectum. **—co·lon′ic,** *adj.*

co·lon[3] (kō lōn′), *n., pl.* **-lons, -lo·nes** (-lō′nes). the monetary unit of El Salvador or Costa Rica.

colo·nel (kûr′n³l), *n.* a commissioned officer, as in the army, ranking just below a brigadier general. **—colo′nel·cy, colo′nel·ship,** *n.*

co·lo·ni·al (kə lō′nē əl), *adj.* 1. of or concerning a colony or colonies. 2. *(often cap.)* pertaining to the 13 British colonies that became the United States of America. **—n.** 3. an inhabitant of a colony. **—co·lo′ni·al·ly,** *adv.*

co·lo·ni·al·ism (kə lō′nē ə liz′əm), *n.* the policy of a nation seeking to extend its power over other territories. **—co·lo′ni·al·ist,** *n., adj.*

col·o·nist (kol′ə nist), *n.* 1. an inhabitant of a colony. 2. a member of a colonizing expedition.

col·o·nize (kol′ə nīz′), *v.i., v.t.,* **-nized, -niz·ing.** 1. to establish a colony (in). 2. to settle in a colony. **—col′o·ni·za′tion,** *n.* **—col′o·niz′er,** *n.*

col·on·nade (kol′ə nād′), *n.* a series of columns usually supporting one side of a roof. **—col′on·nad′ed,** *adj.*

col·o·ny (kol′ə nē), *n., pl.* **-nies.** 1. a group of people who form in a new land a settlement subject to a parent state. 2. the country settled. 3. any people or territory separated from but subject to a ruling power. 4. **the Colonies,** those British colonies that formed the original 13 states of the United States. 5. any group having the same nationality or occupations. 6. the district inhabited by such a group: *an artists′ colony.* 7. a group of animals or plants of the same kind living together in close association.

col·o·phon (kol′ə fon′, -fən), *n.* a publisher's distinctive emblem.

co·lor (kul′ər), *n.* 1. the quality of an object or substance with respect to light reflected by it. 2. the natural appearance of the skin. 3. vivid or distinctive quality. 4. pigment or tint. 5. colors, **a.** a badge, ribbon, etc. **b.** a flag, ensign, etc. **c.** attitude or personality: *to reveal one′s true colors.* 6. outward ap-

pearance or aspect. —*v.t.* **7.** to give
or apply color to. **8.** to cause to
appear different from the reality.
9. to give a special character to.
—*v.i.* **10.** to take on or change
color. **11.** to flush or blush. —**col′-
or·less,** *adj.*

Col·o·rad·o (kol′ə rad′ō, -rä′dō), *n.*
a state in the W United States.
Cap.: Denver. —**Col′o·rad′an,**
adj., n.

Colora′do pota′to bee′tle, a black-
and-yellow beetle that attacks the
leaves of the potato.

col·or·ant (kul′ər ənt), *n.* a pigment or dye.

col·or·a·tion (kul′ə rā′shən), *n.* arrangement or use of colors.

col·o·ra·tu·ra (kul′ər ə tŏŏr′ə -tyŏŏr′ə,
kol′-, kōl′-), *n.* **1.** florid decorations in vocal music. **2.** a lyric
soprano who specializes in such
music.

col′or bar′. See **color line.**

col·or-blind (kul′ər blīnd′), *adj.* of
or affected with the inability to
perceive certain colors. —**col′or
blind′ness.**

col·or·cast (kul′ər kast′, -käst′), *n.,
v.,* **cast, -cast·ing.** —*n.* **1.** a television program broadcast in color.
—*v.t., v.i.* **2.** to televise in color.

col·ored (kul′ərd), *adj.* **1.** having
color. **2.** (*often cap.*) belonging to
a race other than the white, esp.
to the black race. **3.** influenced
or biased.

col·or-fast (kul′ər fast′, -fäst′), *adj.*
(of fabrics) maintaining color without fading or running, esp. in washing. —**col′or-fast′ness,** *n.*

col·or·ful (kul′ər fəl), *adj.* **1.**
abounding in color. **2.** richly
picturesque. —**col′or·ful·ly,** *adv.*
—**col′or·ful·ness,** *n.*

col·or·ing (kul′ər iṅg), *n.* **1.** act or
method of applying color. **2.** appearance as to color. **3.** aspect or
tone.

col′or line′, social or political distinction based on differences of skin
pigmentation, as between white and
black people.

co·los·sal (kə los′əl), *adj.* awesomely
large. —**co·los′sal·ly,** *adv.* —**Syn.**
enormous, huge, gigantic.

co·los·sus (kə los′əs), *n., pl.* **-los·si**
(-los′ī), **-los·sus·es. 1.** a statue
of gigantic size. **2.** anything gigantic
or very powerful.

co·los·to·my (kə los′tə mē), *n., pl.*
-mies. incision of an artificial opening into the colon to effect an
artificial anus.

col·our (kul′ər), *n., v.t., v.i.* Brit.
color.

col·por·teur (kol′pōr′tər, -pôr′-), *n.*
a traveling vendor of religious
books.

colt (kōlt), *n.* a young male horse,
zebra, etc. —**colt′ish,** *adj.*

Co·lum·bi·a (kə lum′bē ə), *n.* **1.** a
river in SW Canada and the NW
United States. **2.** the capital of
South Carolina.

col·um·bine (kol′əm bīn′), *n.* a
garden plant of the buttercup
family having showy bluish-purple
flowers.

co·lum·bi·um (kə lum′bē əm), *n.*
(formerly) niobium. —**co·lum′bic,**
adj.

Co·lum·bus (kə lum′bəs), *n.* **1.**
Christopher, 1446?–1506, Italian dis-
coverer of America 1492. **2.** the
capital of Ohio. **3.** a city in W
Georgia.

Colum′bus Day′, October 12, a legal
holiday in various states of the
U.S. in commemoration of the discovery of America by Columbus:
now officially observed on the
second Monday in October.

col·umn (kol′əm), *n.* **1.** a pillar,
typically having a cylindrical or
polygonal shaft with a capital and
usually a base. **2.** any columnlike
thing. **3.** a vertical arrangement
on a page of horizontal lines of
type. **4.** a regular article in a
newspaper or magazine. **5.** a long,
narrow row of troops, ships, etc.
—**col·lum·nar** (kə lum′nər), *adj.*
—**col·umned** (kol′əmd), *adj.*

col·umn·ist (kol′əm nist, -ə mist), *n.*
the writer or editor of a journalistic
column.

com-, a prefix meaning: **a.** with or
together: *combine.* **b.** completely:
commit.

Com. 1. Commander. **2.** Commission. **3.** Commissioner. **4.** Committee. **5.** Commonwealth.

com., 1. comma. **2.** command. **3.**
commander. **4.** commerce. **5.** commercial. **6.** commission. **7.** commissioner. **8.** committee. **9.** common.

co·ma (kō′mə), *n.* prolonged unconsciousness due to disease, injury,
etc.

Co·man·che (kō man′chē, kə-), *n.,
pl.* **-ches, -che.** a member of a
Shoshonean tribe, formerly ranging
from Wyoming to Texas, now in
Oklahoma.

com·a·tose (kom′ə tōs′, kō′mə-), *adj.*
1. affected with coma. **2.** lethargic
or torpid.

comb (kōm), *n.* **1.** a toothed strip
of plastic, etc., for arranging the
hair. **2.** a machine for separating
choice cotton or worsted fibers. **3.**
the fleshy, serrated growth on the
head, esp. of the domestic fowl.
4. a honeycomb. —*v.t.* **5.** to arrange
with a comb. **6.** to search everywhere in: *to comb the files.* **7.** to
separate (wool fibers) with a comb.

comb., 1. combination. 2. combining.

com·bat (v. kəm bat′, kom′bat; n. kom′bat), v., **-bat·ed, -bat·ing** or **-bat·ted, -bat·ting,** n. —v.t., v.i. 1. to fight (against), esp. in direct contact. —n. 2. active fighting between enemy forces. 3. any fight or struggle. —**com·bat·ant** (kəm bat′°nt, kom′bə t°nt), n. —**com·bat′ive,** adj.

com′bat fatigue′. See battle fatigue.

comb·er (kō′mər), n. 1. a person or thing that combs. 2. a long, curling wave.

com·bi·na·tion (kom′bə nā′shən), n. 1. the act of combining or state of being combined. 2. something formed by combining. 3. an alliance of persons or parties. 4. the series of numbers or letters used to open a special lock without a key.

com·bine (v. kəm bīn′; n. kom′bīn), v., **-bined, -bin·ing,** n. —v.t., v.i. 1. to join into a close union or whole. —n. 2. Informal. a business combination, such as a syndicate or trust. 3. a machine for cutting and threshing grain in the field. —**com·bin′er,** n.

comb·ings (kō′mingz), n.pl. hairs removed with a comb or a brush.

combin′ing form′, a linguistic form used only in compound words, never independently, as hemo- in hemoglobin.

com·bo (kom′bō), n., pl. **-bos.** a small jazz or dance band.

com·bus·ti·ble (kəm bus′tə bəl), adj. capable of catching fire and burning, as gas. —**com·bus′ti·bil′i·ty,** n. —**com·bus′ti·bly,** adv.

com·bus·tion (kəm bus′chən, -bush′-), n. 1. the act or process of burning. 2. rapid oxidation accompanied by heat and, usually, light. —**com·bus′tive,** adj.

comdg., commanding.

Comdr., Commander. Also, **comdr.**

Comdt., Commandant. Also, **comdt.**

come (kum), v., **came, come, com·ing,** interj. —v.i. 1. to move toward a person or place. 2. to arrive. 3. to move into view. 4. to extend or reach. 5. to happen or occur. 6. to be available. 7. to issue or be derived. 8. to result. 9. to enter into a specified state. 10. to do or manage. 11. Slang. to have an orgasm. 12. **come about, a.** to happen or occur. **b.** to change direction. 13. **come across** or **upon,** to find or meet, esp. by chance. 14. **come along, a.** to accompany someone. **b.** to succeed. **c.** to appear. 15. **come around** or **round, a.** to change one's opinion. **b.** to revive. **c.** to cease being angry. 16. **come between,** to estrange or separate. 17. **come by,** to obtain or acquire. 18. **come down with,** to become af-

flicted with (an illness). 19. **come into, a.** to acquire. **b.** to inherit. 20. **come off, a.** to happen. **b.** to reach the end. **c.** to be completed. 21. **come out, a.** to be published or released. **b.** to make a debut. **c.** to end. 22. **come out for,** to endorse publicly. 23. **come through, a.** to finish successfully. **b.** to do as expected. 24. **come to, a.** to recover consciousness. **b.** to total. 25. **come up,** to be referred to. 26. **come up with,** to present or propose. —interj. 27. (an exclamation of impatience or mild anger.)

come·back (kum′bak′), n. 1. a return to a former position, prosperity, etc. 2. Slang. a clever retort.

co·me·di·an (kə mē′dē ən), n. 1. a professional entertainer who amuses by telling jokes, etc. 2. an actor in comedy. —**co·me·di·enne′** (-en′, -mā′-), n. fem.

com·e·do (kom′i dō′), n., pl. **com·e·dos, com·e·do·nes** (kom′i dō′nēz). blackhead.

come·down (kum′doun′), n. a descent from dignity, importance, or prosperity.

com·e·dy (kom′i dē), n., pl. **-dies.** 1. a play, movie, etc., of light and humorous character. 2. the comic element of drama, literature, or of life. 3. any comic incident or incidents. —**co·me·dic** (kə mē′dik, -med′ik), adj.

come·ly (kum′lē), adj., **-li·er, -li·est.** pleasing in appearance. —**come′li·ness,** n.

come-on (kum′on′, -ôn′), n. Slang. inducement or lure.

com·er (kum′ər), n. Informal. a person or thing that is very promising.

co·mes·ti·ble (kə mes′tə bəl), n. 1. Usually, **comestibles.** Facetious. food. —adj. 2. Obs. edible.

com·et (kom′it), n. a celestial body moving about the sun, consisting of a central mass surrounded by a misty envelope, that may form a tail that streams away from the sun.

come·up·pance (kum′up′əns), n. Informal. a deserved rebuke or reprimand.

com·fit (kum′fit, kom′-), n. a sweetmeat containing a nut or piece of fruit.

com·fort (kum′fərt), v.t. 1. to soothe or console, as someone grieved. —n. 2. consolation or solace. 3. a person or thing that comforts. 4. a state of ease and satisfaction of bodily wants. —**com′fort·ing·ly,** adv. —**com′fort·less,** adj.

com·fort·a·ble (kumf′tə bəl, kum′fər tə bəl), adj. 1. allowing physical comfort or ease. 2. contented or at ease. 3. adequate or sufficient.

—com'fort·a·ble·ness, *n.* —com'fort·a·bly, *adv.*

com·fort·er (kum'fər tər), *n.* **1.** a person or thing that comforts. **2.** a thick, quilted bed cover.

com'fort sta'tion, a place with toilet and lavatory facilities for public use.

com·fy (kum'fē), *adj.,* **-fi·er, -fi·est.** *Informal.* comfortable.

com·ic (kom'ik), *adj.* **1.** of or pertaining to comedy. **2.** humorous or funny. —*n.* **3.** a comic actor or actress. **4.** *Informal.* **a.** See **comic book. b. comics,** comic strips. —com'i·cal, *adj.* —com'i·cal'i·ty, *n.* —com'i·cal·ly, *adv.*

com'ic book', a booklet of comic strips.

com'ic strip', a sequence of drawings relating a comic incident, an adventure story, etc.

com·ing (kum'ing), *adj.* **1.** approaching, esp. in time. **2.** promising future fame or success. —*n.* **3.** approach or arrival.

com·i·ty (kom'i tē), *n., pl.* **-ties.** mutual courtesy.

coml., commercial.

comm., 1. commission. **2.** committee. **3.** commonwealth.

com·ma (kom'ə), *n.* the sign (,), a mark of punctuation used for indicating a division in a sentence.

com·mand (kə mand', -mänd'), *v.t.* **1.** to direct with authority. **2.** to demand. **3.** to be master of. **4.** to receive (respect, etc.). **5.** to dominate by location. —*v.i.* **6.** to have authority. —*n.* **7.** the act of commanding or ordering. **8.** an order so given. **9.** a body of troops or a station, ship, etc., under a commander. **10.** the possession of controlling authority. **11.** mastery. —**Syn. 1.** bid, charge, enjoin, order.

com·man·dant (kom'ən dant', -dänt'), *n.* the commanding officer of a place, group, etc.

com·man·deer (kom'ən dēr'), *v.t.* to seize (property) for military or other public use.

com·mand·er (kə man'dər, -män'-), *n.* **1.** a person who commands. **2.** a leader or chief officer. **3.** the commissioned officer in command of a military unit. **4.** a naval officer ranking just below a captain.

comman'der in chief', *pl.* **commanders in chief.** the supreme commander of the armed forces of a nation.

com·mand·ment (kə mand'mənt, -mänd'-), *n.* **1.** a divine command. **2.** (*sometimes cap.*) any of the Ten Commandments.

com·man·do (kə man'dō, -män'-), *n., pl.* **-dos, -does.** a member of a specially trained military unit used for surprise destructive raids.

command' ser'geant ma'jor, *U.S. Army.* a noncommissioned officer ranking just above a first sergeant.

comme il faut (kum' ēl fō'), *French.* proper or as it should be.

com·mem·o·rate (kə mem'ə rāt'), *v.t.,* **-rat·ed, -rat·ing. 1.** to serve as a memorial of. **2.** to honor the memory of. —**com·mem'o·ra'tion,** *n.* —**com·mem'o·ra'tive,** *adj.* —**com·mem'o·ra'tor,** *n.*

com·mence (kə mens'), *v.i., v.t.,* **-menced, -menc·ing.** to begin, esp. formally or ceremonially.

com·mence·ment (kə mens'mənt), *n.* **1.** a formal beginning. **2.** the ceremony of graduation, as in a college.

com·mend (kə mend'), *v.t.* **1.** to mention as worthy of confidence, notice, etc. **2.** to entrust. **3.** to cite with special praise. —**com·mend'a·ble,** *adj.* —**com·mend'a·bly,** *adv.* —**com'men·da'tion,** *n.* —**com·mend'a·to'ry,** *adj.*

com·men·su·ra·ble (kə men'sər ə bəl, -shər ə-), *adj.* having a common measure or divisor. —**com·men'su·ra·bly,** *adv.*

com·men·su·rate (kə men'sər it, -shər-), *adj.* **1.** having the same measure. **2.** corresponding in amount or degree. **3.** proportionate or adequate. —**com·men'su·rate·ly,** *adv.*

com·ment (kom'ent), *n.* **1.** a note in explanation or criticism. **2.** a remark or observation. —*v.i.* **3.** to make a comment or comments. —*v.t.* **4.** to make comments on.

com·men·tar·y (kom'ən ter'ē), *n., pl.* **-tar·ies. 1.** a series of comments. **2.** an explanatory essay.

com·men·ta·tor (kom'ən tā'tər), *n.* a person who analyzes news events on radio or television.

com·merce (kom'ərs), *n.* an interchange of goods, esp. among people in one area.

com·mer·cial (kə mûr'shəl), *adj.* **1.** of or characteristic of commerce. **2.** done or acting for profit. —*n.* **3.** *Radio and Television.* a paid advertising or promotional announcement. —com·mer'cial·ly, *adv.*

com·mer·cial·ism (kə mûr'shə liz'əm), *n.* the principles, practices, and spirit of commerce.

com·mer·cial·ize (kə mûr'shə līz'), *v.t.,* **-ized, -iz·ing.** to make commercial in character, esp. for making profit. —**com·mer'cial·i·za'tion,** *n.*

com·mi·na·tion (kom'ə nā'shən), *n.* a denunciation or threat of punishment, esp. of sinners. —**com·min·a·to·ry** (kə min'ə tôr'ē, -tōr'ē, kom'in ə-), *adj.*

com·min·gle (kə ming'gəl), v.t., v.i., -gled, -gling. to mix or mingle together.

com·mis·er·ate (kə miz'ə rāt'), v.t., v.i., -at·ed, -at·ing. 1. to feel or express compassionate pity (with). —**com·mis'er·a'tion,** n. —**com·mis'er·a'tive,** adj.

com·mis·sar (kom'i sär', kom'i sär'), n. (formerly) the head of a commissariat.

com·mis·sar·i·at (kom'i sâr'ē ət), n. (formerly) a major governmental division in the U.S.S.R.

com·mis·sar·y (kom'i ser'ē), n., pl. -sar·ies. 1. a store that sells food and supplies, esp. in a military post. 2. a dining room or cafeteria, as one in a motion-picture studio.

com·mis·sion (kə mish'ən), n. 1. the act of committing or giving in charge. 2. an authoritative order. 3. authority granted. 4. a document granting such authority. 5. a document conferring authority issued to officers of the armed forces. 6. the power thus granted. 7. the rank thus conferred. 8. a group of persons authoritatively charged with particular functions. 9. a sum or percentage paid to an agent for his or her services. 10. **in commission,** in operating order. 11. **out of commission,** not in operating order. —v.t. 12. to give a commission to. 13. to authorize. 14. to order (a warship) to active duty.

commis'sioned of'ficer, a military officer holding a commission.

com·mis·sion·er (kə mish'ə nər), n. 1. a person commissioned to act officially. 2. a member of a commission. 3. a government official in charge of a department. —**com·mis'sion·er·ship',** n.

com·mit (kə mit'), v.t., -mit·ted, -mit·ting. 1. to perform or perpetrate, as a crime. 2. to pledge (oneself), as to a position on an issue. 3. to give in trust or charge. 4. to place in confinement or custody. —**com·mit'ment,** n. —**com·mit'ta·ble,** adj. —**com·mit'tal,** n.

com·mit·tee (kə mit'ē), n. a group of persons chosen to perform some service or function. —**com·mit'tee·man,** n. —**com·mit'tee·wom'an,** n. fem.

com·mode (kə mōd'), n. 1. a low ornamental chest of drawers. 2. (formerly) a closed cabinet or chair containing a chamber pot. 3. any portable toilet, as for an invalid.

com·mo·di·ous (kə mō'dē əs), adj. spacious and roomy. —**com·mo'di·ous·ly,** adv. —**com·mo'di·ous·ness,** n.

com·mod·i·ty (kə mod'i tē), n., pl. -ties. 1. an article of trade or com-

merce. 2. something of use, advantage, or value.

com·mo·dore (kom'ə dōr', -dôr'), n. 1. U.S. Navy. a commissioned officer ranking just below a rear admiral: a wartime rank only. 2. the senior captain of a line of merchant vessels. 3. the president of a yacht club.

com·mon (kom'ən), adj. 1. belonging equally to all. 2. belonging equally to an entire community: common welfare. 3. widespread or general. 4. of frequent or usual occurrence. 5. of inferior quality. 6. coarse or vulgar. 7. noting a noun, as woman or pen, that is not the name of any particular person or thing. —n. 8. Often, **commons.** a tract of land owned jointly by the members of a community. 9. **commons,** a. the body of people not of noble birth. b. a dining hall at some colleges. 10. **Commons.** See **House of Commons.** 11. **in common,** shared equally. —**com'mon·ly,** adv. —**com'mon·ness,** n. —Syn. 3. current, customary, familiar, popular.

com·mon·al·ty (kom'ə nəl tē), n., pl. -ties. the ordinary or common people.

com'mon car'rier, an individual or company, as an airline, engaged in transporting passengers or cargo for payment.

com'mon coun'cil, the local legislative body of a municipal government.

com'mon denom'inator, 1. a number that is a multiple of all the denominators of a set of fractions. 2. a trait or characteristic in common.

com'mon divi'sor, a number that is an exact divisor of two or more given numbers. Also called **com'mon fac'tor.**

com·mon·er (kom'ə nər), n. a member of the common people.

com'mon frac'tion, a fraction represented as a numerator above and a denominator below a horizontal or diagonal line.

com'mon law', the unwritten law, based on custom or court decision, as distinct from statutory law.

com'mon log'arithm, a logarithm having 10 as the base.

com'mon mar'ket, an economic association of nations, chiefly for abolition of trade barriers, esp. one created in Europe in 1958.

com'mon mul'tiple, a number that is a multiple of all the numbers of a given set.

com·mon·place (kom'ən plās'), adj. 1. widespread and ordinary. 2. platitudinous or dull. —n. 3. a trite or uninteresting saying. 4. anything common or ordinary.

com'mon sense', normal native intelligence.

com·mon·weal (kom'ən wēl'), n. 1. the common welfare. 2. Archaic. a commonwealth.

com·mon·wealth (kom'ən welth'), n. 1. a group of sovereign states and their dependencies. 2. a self-governing territory. 3. the people of a nation or state.

Com'monwealth of Na'tions, the worldwide political association of nations and dependencies under the British monarch.

com·mo·tion (kə mō'shən), n. 1. tumultuous agitation. 2. disturbance or upheaval.

com·mu·nal (kə myōōn'ºl, kom'yə-nºl), adj. 1. of a commune or a community. 2. of, by, or belonging to a community. 3. marked by common ownership and sharing of property and responsibilities. —com'mu·nal'i·ty, n. —com·mu'nal·ly, adv.

com·mune¹ (kə myōōn'), v.i., -muned, -mun·ing. to talk together intimately.

com·mune² (kom'yōōn), n. 1. the smallest administrative division in France, Italy, etc. 2. a close-knit community of people who share common interests. 3. a place for group living and sharing of work and income by people seeking radical personal changes.

com·mu·ni·ca·ble (kə myōō'nə kə bəl), adj. 1. capable of being easily transmitted: a communicable disease. 2. Archaic. talkative. —com·mu'ni·ca·bil'i·ty, com·mu'ni·ca·ble·ness, n. —com·mu'ni·ca·bly, adv.

com·mu·ni·cant (kə myōō'nə kənt), n. 1. a church member entitled to receive the Eucharist. 2. a person who communicates.

com·mu·ni·cate (kə myōō'nə kāt'), v., -cat·ed, -cat·ing. —v.t. 1. to make known. 2. to transmit to another, as a disease. —v.i. 3. to give or interchange thoughts or information. 4. to express one's true feelings easily. 5. to receive the Eucharist. 6. Brit. to be joined or connected, as rooms. —com·mu'nu·ca'tive, adj. —com·mu'ni·ca'tive·ness, n. —com·mu'ni·ca'tor, n. —Syn. 1. announce, disclose, reveal, tell.

com·mu·ni·ca·tion (kə myōō'nə kā'-shən), n. 1. the act or process of communicating. 2. interchange of thoughts or information. 3. something imparted or transmitted. 4. a message, letter, etc. 5. **communications**, the means of communicating.

com·mun·ion (kə myōōn'yən), n. 1. a sharing, as of thoughts or emotions.

2. association or fellowship. 3. a religious denomination. 4. (often cap.) Eccles. **a.** the act of receiving the Eucharistic elements. **b.** the elements of the Eucharist. **c.** the celebration of the Eucharist.

com·mu·ni·qué (kə myōō'nə kā', kə-myōō'nə kā'), n. an official bulletin.

com·mun·ism (kom'yə niz'əm), n. 1. a theory or system of social organization based on common ownership of property. 2. (sometimes cap.) a system of social organization in which all economic and social activity is controlled by a totalitarian state. [< L commūn(is) common + -ism] —com'mun·ist, n., adj. —com·mu·nis'tic, adj. —com'mu·nis'ti·cal·ly, adv.

com·mu·ni·ty (kə myōō'ni tē), n., pl. -ties. 1. a social group whose members live in a specific locality, share government, and have a common heritage. 2. such a locality. 3. a social or occupational group. 4. the plant and animal populations occupying a given area. 5. joint possession. 6. similar or common character: community of interests. 7. the public or society.

commu'nity anten'na tel'evision. See CATV.

commu'nity chest', a fund for local welfare activities collected by voluntary contributions.

commu'nity col'lege, a junior college serving the needs of a local area.

commu'nity prop'erty, (in some states) property acquired by a husband, wife, or both together, that is considered by law to be jointly owned and equally shared.

com·mu·ta·tion (kom'yə tā'shən), n. 1. the act of commuting. 2. the act or process of using a commutator. —com·mu'ta·tive, adj.

commuta'tion tick'et, a passenger ticket issued at a reduced rate over a given route and for a fixed number of trips.

com·mu·ta·tor (kom'yə tā'tər), n. Elect. a device for reversing the direction of a current.

com·mute (kə myōōt'), v., -mut·ed, -mut·ing, n. —v.t. 1. to change (a punishment or penalty) to a less severe one. 2. to exchange for something else. —v.i. 3. to travel regularly over some distance between one's home and office. —n. 4. a trip or travel made in commuting. —com·mut'er, n.

comp., 1. comparative. 2. compilation. 3. compiled. 4. compiler. 5. complete. 6. composition. 7. compositor. 8. compound.

com·pact[1] (*adj.*, *v.* kəm pakt'; *n.* kom'pakt), *adj.* **1.** joined or packed together. **2.** arranged within a small space. **3.** small in size. **4.** terse or pithy. —*v.t.* **5.** to join or pack closely together. **6.** to form by putting together. —*n.* **7.** a small case containing a mirror, face power, a puff, etc. **8.** a compact automobile. —**com·pact'ly**, *adv.* —**com·pact'ness**, *n.*

com·pact[2] (kom'pakt), *n.* a formal agreement or contract.

com·pac·tor (kəm pak'tər), *n.* a kitchen appliance for grinding and compressing refuse, esp. to facilitate disposal.

com·pan·ion (kəm pan'yən), *n.* **1.** a frequent associate with another or others. **2.** a person employed to accompany or live with another. **3.** a mate or match for something. —**com·pan'ion·a·ble**, *adj.* —**com·pan'ion·a·bly**, *adv.* —**com·pan'ion·less**, *adj.* —**com·pan'ion·ship'**, *n.*

com·pan·ion·way (kəm pan'yən wā'), *n.* a stair or ladder within the hull of a vessel. Also called **com·pan'ion.**

com·pa·ny (kum'pə nē), *n.*, *pl.* **-nies.** —*n.* **1.** a number of individuals together. **2.** an assemblage for social purposes. **3.** companionship. **4.** a guest or guests. **5.** a number of persons associated for joint action, esp. for business. **6.** the smallest body of troops, consisting of a headquarters and two or three platoons. **7.** a ship's crew, including officers. **8. keep company, a.** to be a friend (of). **b.** to go together, as in courtship. **9. part company,** to cease association (with).

compar., comparative.

com·pa·ra·ble (kom'pər ə bəl), *adj.* **1.** capable of being compared. **2.** worthy of comparison. —**com'pa·ra·bil'i·ty**, *n.* —**com'pa·ra·bly**, *adv.*

com·par·a·tive (kəm par'ə tiv), *adj.* **1.** of, pertaining to, or proceeding by comparison. **2.** relative: *in comparative affluence.* **3.** *Gram.* noting the intermediate degree of the comparison of adjectives and adverbs, as *surer* and *more carefully.* —*n.* **4.** *Gram.* the comparative degree. —**com·par'a·tive·ly**, *adv.*

com·pare (kəm pâr'), *v.*, **-pared, -par·ing,** *n.* —*v.t.* **1.** to examine for similarities and differences. **2.** to liken. **3.** to form the degrees of comparison of (an adjective or adverb). —*v.i.* **4.** to be held equal. **5.** to make comparisons. —*n.* **6.** comparison: *Her beauty is beyond compare.* —**com·par'er**, *n.*

com·par·i·son (kəm par'i sən), *n.* **1.** the act of comparing or state of

being compared. **2.** comparative estimate. **3.** the modification of an adverb or adjective that indicates the degree of quality, quantity, or intensity, as *mild, milder, mildest.*

com·part·ment (kəm pärt'mənt), *n.* **1.** a space partitioned off. **2.** a separate room, section, etc. —**com·part·men·tal** (kəm pärt men't[ə]l, kom'pärt-), *adj.*

com·part·men·tal·ize (kəm pärt men't[ə]līz', kom'pärt-), *v.t.*, **-ized, -iz·ing.** to divide into compartments.

com·pass (kum'pəs), *n.* **1.** an instrument for determining directions, as by means of a freely rotating magnetized needle that indicates magnetic north. **2.** the enclosing limits of an area. **3.** extent or range. **4.** due or proper limits. **5.** Often, **compasses.** an instrument for drawing circles, etc., consisting generally of two movable legs hinged at one end. —*v.t.* **6.** to go or move round. **7.** to surround or encircle. **8.** to attain or achieve. **9.** to contrive or plot.

com·pas·sion (kəm pash'ən), *n.* a feeling of deep sympathy for another's suffering or misfortune. —**com·pas'sion·ate**, *adj.* —**com·pas'sion·ate·ly**, *adv.*

com·pat·i·ble (kəm pat'ə bəl), *adj.* capable of existing together in harmony. —**com·pat'i·bil'i·ty, com·pat'i·ble·ness**, *n.* —**com·pat'i·bly**, *adv.*

com·pa·tri·ot (kəm pā'trē ət), *n.* a fellow countryman or countrywoman.

com·peer (kəm pēr', kom'pēr), *n. Literary.* **1.** a peer or colleague. **2.** close friend or comrade.

com·pel (kəm pel'), *v.*, **-pelled, -pel·ling.** —*v.t.* **1.** to force or drive, esp. to a course of action. —*v.i.* **2.** to have a powerful effect, influence, etc. —**com·pel'la·ble**, *adj.* —**com·pel'ling·ly**, *adv.*

com·pen·di·um (kəm pen'dē əm), *n.*, *pl.* **-di·ums, -di·a** (-dē ə). a handy collection of a field of information.

com·pen·sate (kom'pən sāt'), *v.*, **-sat·ed, -sat·ing.** —*v.t.* **1.** to make a suitable payment to. **2.** to be equivalent to, as in substance. —*v.i.* **3.** to make amends. —**com'pen·sa'tion**, *n.* —**com·pen·sa·to·ry** (kəm·pen'sə tôr'ē, -tōr'ē), *adj.* —**Syn. 1.** pay, recompense, remunerate.

com·pete (kəm pēt'), *v.i.*, **-pet·ed, -pet·ing.** to strive to outdo another, as for supremacy.

com·pe·tence (kom'pi t[ə]ns), *n.* **1.** the quality of being competent. **2.** *Literary.* an income sufficient for the modest comforts of life. **3.** legal capacity or qualification. Also, **com'pe·ten·cy.**

com·pe·tent (kom'pi tənt), *adj.* **1.** having suitable skill, experience, etc., for some purpose. **2.** adequate or sufficient. **3.** having legal competence. **—com'pe·tent·ly,** *adv.*

com·pe·ti·tion (kom'pi tish'ən), *n.* **1.** the act or process of competing. **2.** a contest for some prize, honor, etc. **—com·pet'i·tive,** *adj.* **—com·pet'i·tive·ly,** *adv.* **—com·pet'i·tive·ness,** *n.*

com·pet·i·tor (kəm pet'i tər), *n.* a person, team, or company that competes.

com·pile (kəm pīl'), *v.t.,* **-piled, -pil·ing. 1.** to put together (materials or data) in one book or work. **2.** to make (a book, etc.) of materials from various sources. **—com·pi·la·tion** (kom'pə lā'shən), *n.* **—com·pil'er,** *n.*

com·pla·cen·cy (kəm plā'sən sē), *n.* self-satisfaction or smug satisfaction. Also, **com·pla·cence** (kəm plā'səns). **—com·pla'cent,** *adj.* **—com·pla'cent·ly,** *adv.*

com·plain (kəm plān'), *v.i.* **1.** to express discontent, pain, etc. **2.** *Law.* to make a formal accusation. **—com·plain'er,** *n.*

com·plain·ant (kəm plā'nənt), *n.* a person or group that files a complaint, as in a legal action.

com·plaint (kəm plānt'), *n.* **1.** an expression of discontent, pain, etc. **2.** a cause of discontent, pain, etc. **3.** an ailment or disease. **4.** *Law.* a formal accusation.

com·plai·sant (kəm plā'sənt, -zənt, kom'plə zant'), *adj.* inclined or disposed to please. **—com·plai'sance,** *n.* **—com·plai'sant·ly,** *adv.*

com·pleat (kəm plēt'), *adj. Facetious.* complete (in the archaic sense of "accomplished"): *a compleat hunter.*

com·plect·ed (kəm plek'tid), *adj.* complexioned.

com·ple·ment (*n.* kom'plə mənt; *v.* kom'plə ment'), *n.* **1.** something that completes or makes perfect. **2.** the amount that completes anything. **3.** complete allowance. **4.** the full number of ship officers and crew. **5.** a word or words used to complete a grammatical construction. **6.** the quantity by which an angle or an arc falls short of 90°. **—v.t. 7.** to form a complement to. **—com'ple·men'ta·ry,** *adj.*

com·plete (kəm plēt'), *adj., v.,* **-plet·ed, -plet·ing. —adj. 1.** having all its parts or elements. **2.** finished or concluded. **3.** thorough or perfect. **—v.t. 4.** to make whole or complete. **5.** to bring to completion. **—com·plete'ly,** *adv.* **—com·plete'ness,** *n.* **—com·ple·tion** (kəm plē'shən), *n.* **—Syn. 1.** entire, perfect, whole.

com·plex (*adj.* kəm pleks', kom'-pleks; *n.* kom'pleks), *adj.* **1.** com-posed of interconnected parts. **2.** complicated or involved. **—n. 3.** an intricate assemblage of parts, units, etc. **4.** a system of interrelated, emotion-charged ideas and impulses that gives rise to abnormal behavior. **—com·plex'i·ty,** *n.* **—Syn. 2.** intricate, knotty, perplexing.

com·plex frac·tion, a fraction in which the numerator or the denominator or both contain one or more fractions.

com·plex·ion (kəm plek'shən), *n.* **1.** the natural color and appearance of a person's skin, esp. of the face. **2.** appearance or character. **—com·plex'ion·al,** *adj.*

com·plex·ioned (kəm plek'shənd), *adj.* having a specified complexion: *fair-complexioned.*

com·plex num·ber, a mathematical expression $(a + bi)$ in which a and b are real numbers and i is defined as $\sqrt{-1}$

com·plex sen·tence, a sentence containing one or more dependent clauses in addition to the main clause.

com·pli·ance (kəm plī'əns), *n.* **1.** the act of conforming or acquiescing. **2.** a tendency to yield readily to others. Also, **com·pli'an·cy.** **—com·pli'ant,** *adj.* **—com·pli'ant·ly,** *adv.*

com·pli·cate (kom'plə kāt'), *v.t., v.i.,* **-cat·ed, -cat·ing.** to make or become complex, intricate, or involved. **—com'pli·ca'tion,** *n.*

com·pli·cat·ed (kom'plə kā'tid), *adj.* **1.** composed of elaborately connected parts. **2.** difficult to analyze or understand. **—com'pli·cat'ed·ly,** *adv.* **—com'pli·cat'ed·ness,** *n.*

com·plic·i·ty (kəm plis'i tē), *n., pl.* **-ties.** partnership or involvement in wrongdoing.

com·pli·ment (*n.* kom'plə mənt; *v.* kom'plə ment'), *n.* **1.** an expression of praise or admiration. **2.** a formal act of respect or regard. **3.** compliments, good wishes or regards. **—v.t. 4.** to pay a compliment to.

com·pli·men·ta·ry (kom'plə men'tə rē, -trē), *adj.* **1.** of, conveying, or expressing a compliment. **2.** given free as a gift or courtesy.

com·ply (kəm plī'), *v.i.,* **-plied, -ply·ing.** to act in accordance, as with requests, requirements, etc.

com·po·nent (kəm pō'nənt), *adj.* **1.** being or serving as an element (in something larger). **—n. 2.** a component part.

com·port (kəm pōrt', -pôrt'), *v.t.* **1.** to conduct or behave (oneself). **—v.i. 2.** *Literary.* to be in agreement. **—com·port'ment,** *n.*

com·pose (kəm pōz′), v., **-posed, -pos·ing.** —v.t. **1.** to make by combining things, parts, etc. **2.** to be a part of. **3.** to create (a literary or musical work). **4.** to calm or quiet. **5.** *Print.* to set (type). —v.i. **6.** to create a literary or musical work. —**com·pos′er,** n.

com·posed (kəm pōzd′), adj. calm and self-possessed. —**com·pos·ed·ly** (kəm pō′zid lē), adv.

compos′ing stick′, a hand-held tray for the compositor to place and gather type.

com·pos·ite (kəm poz′it), adj. **1.** made up of separate elements. **2.** belonging to the family of plants, as the daisy, in which the florets are borne in a close head. —n. **3.** something composite. **4.** a composite plant. —**com·pos′ite·ly,** adv.

com·po·si·tion (kom′pə zish′ən), n. **1.** the act of combining parts to form a whole. **2.** the resulting product. **3.** makeup or constitution. **4.** the art of writing. **5.** a short essay written as a school exercise. **6.** the art of composing music. **7.** a piece of music. **8.** the setting up of type for printing.

com·pos·i·tor (kəm poz′i tər), a person who sets up type.

com·post (kom′pōst), n. a mixture of decaying organic substances for fertilizing land.

com·po·sure (kəm pō′zhər), n. calmness and self-possession.

com·pote (kom′pōt), n. **1.** fruit stewed in a syrup, served as a dessert. **2.** a dish having a stem, used for serving fruit, nuts, etc.

com·pound¹ (adj. kom′nound, kompound′; n. kom′pound; v. kəmpound′), adj. **1.** composed of two or more parts or ingredients. —n. **2.** something formed by combining parts, elements, etc. **3.** a substance composed of two or more elements chemically united. **4.** a word composed of two or more parts that are also words or word elements. —v.t. **5.** to combine or mix. **6.** to make by combining parts, elements, etc. **7.** to intensify or make more serious. **8.** to pay (interest) on the accrued interest as well as the principal. **9.** to agree, for payment, not to prosecute (a crime or felony). **10.** *Brit.* to settle (a debt, etc.) by compromise. —**com·pound′a·ble,** adj.

com·pound² (kom′pound), n. an enclosure containing living quarters, etc., esp. in the Far East.

com′pound-com′plex sen′tence (kom′pound kom′pleks), a compound sentence having one or more dependent clauses.

com′pound frac′ture, a fracture in which the broken bone is exposed through a wound in the skin.

com′pound in′terest, interest paid on both the principal and accrued interest.

com′pound sen′tence, a sentence containing two or more coordinate independent clauses, but no dependent clause.

com·pre·hend (kom′pri hend′), v.t. **1.** to understand thoroughly. **2.** *Literary.* to include. —**com·pre·hen′sion,** n.

com·pre·hen·si·ble (kom′pri hen′səbəl), adj. capable of being understood thoroughly. —**com′pre·hen′si·bil′i·ty,** n. —**com′pre·hen′si·bly,** adv.

com·pre·hen·sive (kom′pri hen′siv), adj. **1.** wide in scope or content. **2.** *Literary.* understanding much. —**com′pre·hen′sive·ly,** adv. —**com′pre·hen′sive·ness,** n. —Syn. **1.** broad, extensive, inclusive.

com·press (v. kəm pres′; n. kom′pres), v.t. **1.** to press together and force into less space. —n. **2.** a soft cloth pad to provide pressure or to supply moisture, cold, heat, or medication. —**com·press′i·bil′i·ty,** n. —**com·press′i·ble,** adj. —**com·pres′sion,** n. —**com·pres′sive,** adj.

compressed′ air′ (kəm prest′), air whose density is raised to a pressure higher than that of the atmosphere.

com·pres·sor (kəm pres′ər), n. a machine for increasing the pressure of gases.

com·prise (kəm prīz′), v.t., **-prised, -pris·ing. 1.** to consist of. **2.** *Informal.* a. to include or contain. b. to form or constitute.

com·pro·mise (kom′prə mīz′), n., v., **-mised, -mis·ing.** —n. **1.** a settlement of differences by mutual concessions. **2.** the result of such a settlement. **3.** something intermediate between different things. —v.t. **4.** to settle by a compromise. **5.** to make liable to suspicion, scandal, etc. —v.i. **6.** to make a compromise. —**com′pro·mis′er,** n.

comp·trol·ler (kən trō′lər), n. (in some titles only) controller (def. 1).

com·pul·sion (kəm pul′shən), n. **1.** the act of compelling or state of being compelled. **2.** a strong, irresistible impulse. —**com·pul′sive,** adj. —**com·pul′sive·ly,** adv. —**com·pul′sive·ness,** n.

com·pul·so·ry (kəm pul′sə rē), adj. **1.** compelled, as by law: *compulsory education.* **2.** compelling or constraining. —**com·pul′so·ri·ly,** adv. —Syn. **1.** mandatory, obligatory.

com·punc·tion (kəm puñgk'shən), *n.* uneasiness resulting from feelings of guilt.

com·pute (kəm pyōōt'), *v.t., v.i.,* **-put·ed -put·ing.** to determine by arithmetic means. —**com·put'a·ble,** *adj.* —**com'pu·ta'tion,** *n.*

com·put·er (kəm pyōō'tər), *n.* **1.** an electronic machine capable of accepting and processing data and producing results by carrying out repetitious and highly complex mathematical operations at high speeds. **2.** a person or thing that computes.

com·pu·ter·ize (kəm pyōō'tə rīz'), *v.t.,* **-ized, -iz·ing.** to control, perform, or execute by or in an electronic computer. —**com'pu'ter·i·za'tion,** *n.*

Comr., Commissioner.

com·rade (kom'rad), *n.* **1.** an intimate companion. **2.** a fellow member of a fraternal group, political party, etc. —**com'rade·ly,** *adj.* —**com'rade·ship,** *n.*

Com·sat (kom'sat'), *n.* Communications Satellite Corporation (created by U.S. Congress 1962). Also, **COM·SAT.**

con¹ (kon), *adv.* **1.** against. —*n.* **2.** an opposing argument or vote.

con² (kon), *adj., v.,* **conned, con·ning.** *Slang.* —*adj.* **1.** involving abuse of confidence. —*v.t.* **2.** to swindle or defraud. **3.** to persuade by deception, cajolery, etc.

con³ (kon), *n. Slang.* a convict.

con⁴ (kon), *v.t.,* **conned, con·ning.** *Archaic.* **1.** to lean carefully. **2.** to commit to memory.

Con., Consul.

con., continued.

con bri·o (kon brē'ō, kōn), with vigor (used as a musical direction).

conc., concentrated.

con·cat·e·nate (kon kat'°nāt'), *v.t.,* **-nat·ed, -nat·ing.** to unite in a chain, as of events. —**con·cat'e·na'tion,** *n.*

con·cave (kon kāv', kon'kāv), *adj.* curved like a segment of the interior of a hollow sphere. —**con·cav·i·ty** (kon kav'i tē), *n.*

con·ceal (kən sēl'), *v.t.* **1.** to cover or keep from sight, esp. intentionally. **2.** to keep secret. —**con·ceal'·er,** *n.* —**con·ceal'ment,** *n.*

con·cede (kən sēd'), *v.,* **-ced·ed, -ced·ing.** —*v.t.* **1.** to acknowledge as true, just, or proper. **2.** to grant as a right or privilege. —*v.i.* **3.** to make concession.

con·ceit (kən sēt'), *n.* **1.** an exaggerated estimate of one's own ability, importance, etc. **2.** an elaborate, fanciful metaphor in poetry. —**con·ceit·ed** (kən sē'tid), *adj.* —**Syn. 1.** egotism, self-esteem, vanity.

con·ceive (kən sēv'), *v.,* **-ceived,**

-ceiv·ing. —*v.t.* **1.** to form (a notion, purpose, etc.). **2.** to imagine or think. **3.** to become pregnant with. —*v.i.* **4.** to form an idea. **5.** to become pregnant. —**con·ceiv'a·ble,** *adj.* —**con·ceiv'a·bil'i·ty,** *n.* —**con·ceiv'a·bly,** *adv.* —**con·ceiv'er,** *n.*

con·cel·e·brate (kon sel'ə brāt'), *v.i.,* **-brat·ed, -brat·ing.** to participate in the joint celebration of a Mass by two or more members of the clergy. —**con'cel·e·bra'tion,** *n.*

con·cen·trate (kon'sən trāt'), *v.,* **-trat·ed, -trat·ing,** *n.* —*v.t.* **1.** to bring or draw to a common center or point. **2.** to put or bring into a single place, group, etc. **3.** to make denser, stronger, etc. —*v.i.* **4.** to bring one's efforts, faculties, etc., to bear on one thing. —*n.* **5.** a concentrated product. —**con'cen·tra'tion,** *n.*

concentra'tion camp', a guarded camp for the confinement of and forced labor by political prisoners.

con·cen·tric (kən sen'trik), *adj.* having a common center, as spheres. —**con·cen'tri·cal·ly,** *adv.* —**con'·cen·tric'i·ty** (-tris'i tē), *n.*

con·cept (kon'sept), *n.* a general notion or idea. —**con·cep'tu·al,** *adj.* —**con·cep'tu·al·ly,** *adv.*

con·cep·tion (kən sep'shən), *n.* **1.** the act of conceiving or state of being conceived. **2.** inception of pregnancy. **3.** origination or beginning. **4.** something that is conceived. **5.** a notion or idea. —**con·cep'tion·al,** *adj.*

con·cep·tu·al·ize (kən sep'chōō ə līz'), *v.,* **-ized, -iz·ing.** —*v.t.* **1.** to make a concept of. —*v.i.* **2.** think in concepts. —**con·cep'tu·al·i·za'tion,** *n.*

con·cern (kən sûrn'), *v.t.* **1.** to relate to or be connected with. **2.** to interest, engage, or involve. **3.** to trouble, worry, or disquiet. —*n.* **4.** something that relates to a person. **5.** a matter that engages a person's attention or that affects one's welfare. **6.** solicitude or anxiety. **7.** a commercial company.

con·cerned (kən sûrnd'), *adj.* **1.** directly involved or interested. **2.** troubled or anxious.

con·cern·ing (kən sûr'ning), *prep.* relating to or regarding.

con·cert (*n.* kon'sûrt, -sərt; *v.* kən·sûrt'), *n.* **1.** a public musical performance. **2.** *Literary.* a combined action. **3. in concert,** together or jointly. —*v.t.* **4.** *Literary.* to arrange by agreement. —*v.i.* **5.** *Literary.* to plan or act together.

con·cert·ed (kən sûr'tid), *adj.* **1.** planned or designed together. **2.** done in cooperation. —**con·cert'ed·ly,** *adv.*

con·cer·ti·na (kon'sər tē'nə), *n.* a small musical instrument resembling an accordion but having buttonlike keys.

con·cert·ize (kon'sər tīz'), *v.i.,* **-ized, -iz·ing.** to give concerts or recitals professionally, esp. while on tour.

con·cert·mas·ter (kon'sərt mas'tər, -mä'stər), *n.* the leader of the first violins in a symphony orchestra, usually the assistant to the conductor.

con·cer·to (kən cher'tō), *n., pl.* **-tos.** a composition for one or more instruments with orchestral accompaniment.

con·ces·sion (kən sesh'ən), *n.* **1.** the act of conceding or yielding. **2.** the thing or point yielded. **3.** something conceded by a government, as a franchise. **4.** a space within certain premises for a subsidiary business.

con·ces·sion·aire (kən sesh'ə nâr'), *n.* the holder of a concession, esp. one allowing him or her to operate an enterprise.

con·ces·sive (kən ses'iv), *adj.* tending or serving to concede.

conch (kongk, konch), *n., pl.* **conchs** (kongks), **con·ches** (kon'chiz). **1.** the spiral shell of a gastropod, often used as a horn. **2.** the gastropod itself. [< L *concha* < Gk *kónchē* shell]

con·cierge (kon'sē ârzh'), *n.* (esp. in France) a person who has charge of the entrance of a building.

con·cil·i·ate (kən sil'ē āt'), *v.t.,* **-at·ed, -at·ing. 1.** to overcome the distrust or hostility of. **2.** to win (regard or favor). **—con·cil·i·a'tion,** *n.* **—con·cil·i·a·to·ry** (kən sil'ē ə tôr'ē, -tōr'ē), *adj.*

con·cise (kən sīs'), *adj.* expressing much in few words. **—con·cise'ly,** *adv.* **—con·cise'ness,** *n.* **—Syn.** pithy, succinct, terse.

con·clave (kon'klāv, kong'-), *n.* a private or secret meeting, esp. of Roman Catholic cardinals to elect a pope.

con·clude (kən klood'), *v.,* **-clud·ed, -clud·ing. —v.t. 1.** to end, esp. formally. **2.** to bring to a settlement. **3.** to deduce or infer. **4.** to determine or resolve. **—v.i. 5.** to come to an end. **6.** to decide. **—con·clud'er,** *n.*

con·clu·sion (kən kloo'zhən), *n.* **1.** ending or termination. **2.** a result or outcome. **3.** final settlement. **4.** final decision. **5.** a deduction or inference.

con·clu·sive (kən kloo'siv), *adj.* decisively final. **—con·clu'sive·ly,** *adv.* **—con·clu'sive·ness,** *n.*

con·coct (kon kokt', kən-), *v.t.* **1.** to prepare by combining ingredients.

2. to devise or contrive. **—con·coc'tion,** *n.*

con·com·i·tant (kon kom'i tənt, kən-), *adj.* **1.** existing along or in association with. **—n. 2.** a concomitant quality or thing. **—con·com'i·tant·ly,** *adv.*

con·cord (kon'kôrd, kong'-), *n.* **1.** harmonious agreement in ideas, feelings, etc. **2.** peace or amity.

Con·cord (kong'kərd), *n.* **1.** a city in E Massachusetts: second battle of the Revolution, April 19, 1775. **2.** the capital of New Hampshire.

con·cord·ance (kon kôr'd°ns, kən-), *n.* **1.** an alphabetical index of the words of a book with reference to the passage in which each occurs. **2.** a state of concord.

con·cord·ant (kon kôr'd°nt, kən-), *adj.* being in concord.

con·cor·dat (kon kôr'dat), *n.* Rom. Cath. Ch. an official agreement.

Con'cord grape' (kong'kərd, kon'-kôrd), a large, dark-blue grape grown for table use.

con·course (kon'kōrs, -kôrs, kong'-), *n.* **1.** a large open space for crowds, as in an airline terminal. **2.** *Literary.* confluence (defs. 1, 3).

con·cres·cence (kon kres'əns), *n.* a growing together, as of parts, cells, etc. **—con·cres'cent,** *adj.*

con·crete (kon'krēt, kong'-, kon-krēt'), *adj., n., v.,* **-cret·ed, -cret·ing. —adj. 1.** of an actual or real thing or instance that can be seen. **2.** particular, not general. **3.** made of concrete. **—n. 4.** a concrete idea or term. **5.** a mass formed by coalescence of particles of matter. **6.** a stonelike building material, made by mixing cement and sand or gravel. **—v.t.,** *v.i.* **7.** to treat or cover with concrete. **8.** to make or become solid. **—con·crete'ly,** *adv.* **—con·crete'ness,** *n.*

con·cre·tion (kon krē'shən), *n.* **1.** the act or process of becoming substantial. **2.** a solid mass formed by coalescence or cohesion..

con·cu·bine (kong'kyə bīn', kon'-), *n.* a woman who cohabits with a man to whom she is not married. **—con·cu'bi·nage,** *n.*

con·cu·pis·cence (kon kyoo'pi səns), *n.* strong sexual desire. **—con·cu'pis·cent,** *adj.*

con·cur (kən kûr'), *v.i.,* **-curred, -cur·ring. 1.** to agree in opinion. **2.** to work together. **3.** to occur simultaneously. **—con·cur'rence,** *n.*

con·cur·rent (kən kûr'ənt, -kur'-), *adj.* **1.** occurring at the same time. **2.** acting in conjunction. **3.** *Law.* having equal authority. **4.** intersecting at the same point. **—con·cur'rent·ly,** *adv.*

con·cus·sion (kən kush′ən), *n.* **1.** a violent shock or blow. **2.** jarring of the brain, spinal cord, etc., from a violent blow.

con·demn (kən dem′), *v.t.* **1.** to express strong disapproval of. **2.** to pronounce guilty or sentence to punishment. **3.** to pronounce unfit for use or service. **4.** to take over (land) for a public purpose. —**con·dem·na·tion** (kon′dem nā′shən, -dəm-), *n.* —**con·dem′na·to′ry** (-nə tôr′ē), *adj.* —**con·demn′er**, (-dem′ər), *n.* —**Syn. 1.** censure, criticize, denounce.

con·den·sate (kən den′sāt), *n.* something formed by condensation.

con·dense (kən dens′), *v.*, **-densed, -dens·ing.** —*v.t.* **1.** to make compact. **2.** to shorten or abridge. **3.** to reduce to another and denser form, as a vapor to a liquid. —*v.i.* **4.** to become condensed. —**con·den·sa·tion** (kon′den sā′shən, -dən-), *n.*

condensed′ milk′, whole milk reduced by evaporation to a thick consistency, with sugar added.

con·dens·er (kən den′sər), *n.* **1.** a person or thing that condenses. **2.** any device for liquefying gases. **3.** a lens that concentrates light in a specified direction. **4.** capacitor.

con·de·scend (kon′di send′), *v.i.* **1.** to lower oneself to do something. **2.** to behave as if one is conscious of descending from a superior position. —**con′de·scend′ing,** *adj.* —**con′de·scend′ing·ly,** *adv.* —**con·de·scen·sion** (kon′di sen′shən), *n.*

con·dign (kən dīn′), *adj.* well-deserved: *condign punishment.* —**con·dign′ly,** *adv.*

con·di·ment (kon′də mənt), *n.* something to give additional flavor to food, as a spice.

con·di·tion (kən dish′ən), *n.* **1.** a particular state or situation of a person or thing. **2.** state of health. **3.** social position. **4.** a modifying circumstance. **5.** a prerequisite. **6.** a bodily disorder: *a heart condition.* **7.** on or upon condition that, provided that or if. —*v.t.* **8.** to put in a fit state. **9.** to accustom. **10.** to impose a condition upon. **11.** to make (something) a condition. —**con·di′tion·er,** *n.*

con·di·tion·al (kən dish′ə n°l), *adj.* **1.** imposing, containing, or depending on a condition. **2.** involving a condition, as by the first clause in the sentence *If it rains, he won't go.* —**con·di′tion·al·ly,** *adv.*

con·di·tioned (kən dish′ənd), *adj.* **1.** subject to conditions. **2.** characterized by a consistent pattern of behavior. **3.** acquired or learned: *conditioned behavior patterns.*

con·do (kon′dō), *n., pl.* **-dos.** *Informal.* condominium (def. 1).

con·dole (kən dōl′), *v.i.,* **-doled, -dol·ing.** to express sympathy with a person in sorrow or pain. —**con·do′lence,** *n.* —**con·dol′er,** *n.*

con·dom (kon′dəm, kun′-), *n.* a thin rubber sheath worn over the penis during intercourse to prevent conception or infection.

con·do·min·i·um (kon′də min′ē əm), *n., pl.* **-ums. 1.** an apartment house in which the apartments are individually owned. **2. a.** joint sovereignty over a territory by several states. **b.** the territory itself.

con·done (kən dōn′), *v.t.,* **-doned, -don·ing.** to overlook (an offense) with relative tolerance. —**con·don′a·ble,** *adj.* —**con·do·na·tion** (kon′dō nā′shən), *n.* —**con·don′er,** *n.*

con·dor (kon′dər), *n.* a large, New World vulture: the largest flying bird in the Western Hemisphere.

con·duce (kən dōōs′, -dyōōs′), *v.i.,* **-duced, -duc·ing.** to lead or contribute to a result. —**con·du′cive,** *adj.*

con·duct (*n.* kon′dukt; *v.* kən dukt′), *n.* **1.** personal behavior. **2.** direction or management. —*v.t.* **3.** to behave (oneself). **4.** to manage or carry on: *to conduct a meeting.* **5.** to direct, as an orchestra. **6.** to lead or escort: *to conduct a tour.* **7.** to serve as a medium for (heat, electricity, etc.). —*v.i.* **8.** to act as musical conductor. —**con·duc′tion,** *n.* —**con·duc′tive,** *adj.* —**con′duc·tiv′i·ty** (-tiv′i tē), *n.*

con·duct·ance (kən duk′təns), *n. Elect.* the ability of a conductor to transmit current.

con·duc·tor (kən duk′tər), *n.* **1.** a leader, director, or manager. **2.** the person in charge of a train, bus, etc. **3.** a person who directs an orchestra or chorus. **4.** a substance or device that conducts heat, electricity, etc.

con·duit (kon′dwit, -dōō it, -dyōō it, -dit), *n.* **1.** a pipe or channel for water or other fluid. **2.** a pipe or tube for protecting electric wires.

con·dyle (kon′dīl, -d°l), *n.* a rounded protuberance on a bone.

cone (kōn), *n.* **1.** a solid with a circular base and a plane curve tapering uniformly to a vertex. **2.** something resembling this shape. **3.** the conical multiple fruit of the pine, fir, etc. **4.** one of the cone-shaped cells in the retina of the eye.

Con·es·to·ga wag′on (kon′i stō′gə, kon′-), a broad-wheeled covered wagon, used esp. in North America during the early westward migration.

co·ney (kō′nē, kun′ē), *n., pl.* **-neys.** cony.

conf., conference.

con·fab (kon′fab), *n., v.,* **-fabbed, -fab·bing.** *Informal.* —*n.* **1.** a confabulation. —*v.i.* **2.** to confabulate.

con·fab·u·late (kən fab′yə lāt′), *v.i.,* **-lat·ed, -lat·ing.** to converse informally. —**con·fab′u·la′tion,** *n.*

con·fec·tion (kən fek′shən), *n.* a sweet preparation of fruit or the like, as a preserve or candy.

con·fec·tion·er (kən fek′shə nər), *n.* a person who makes or sells candies, etc.

con·fec·tion·er·y (kən fek′shə ner′ē), *n., pl.* **-er·ies.** **1.** confections collectively. **2.** a confectioner's shop.

Confed., Confederate.

con·fed·er·a·cy (kən fed′ər ə sē, -fed′rə sē), *n., pl.* **-cies.** **1.** a united alliance. **2. the Confederacy.** See Confederate States of America.

con·fed·er·ate (*adj., n.* kən fed′ər it, -fed′rit; *v.* kən fed′ə rāt′), *adj., n., v.,* **-at·ed -at·ing.** —*adj.* **1.** united in an alliance. **2.** (*cap.*) of the Confederate States of America. —*n.* **3.** a person, group, nation, etc., in a confederacy. **4.** an accomplice. **5.** (*cap.*) an adherent of the Confederate States of America. —*v.t., v.i.* **6.** to unite in an alliance.

Confed′erate States′ of Amer′ica, the group of 11 Southern states that seceded from the United States in 1860–61.

con·fed·er·a·tion (kən fed′ə rā′shən), *n.* **1.** the act of confederating or state of being confederated. **2.** an alliance or league. **3. the Confederation,** the union of the 13 original American states 1781–1789. —**con·fed′er·a′tive,** *adj.*

con·fer (kən fûr′), *v.,* **-ferred, -fer·ring.** —*v.t.* **1.** to bestow upon, as an honor. —*v.i.* **2.** to consult together. —**con·fer·ee** (kon′fə rē′), *n.* —**con·fer′ment,** *n.* —**con·fer′rer,** *n.*

con·fer·ence (kon′fər əns, -frəns), *n.* **1.** a meeting for discussion. **2.** an association of athletic teams, schools, or churches.

con·fess (kən fes′), *v.t.* **1.** to admit or reveal (a secret, fault, etc.). **2.** to declare (one's sins) to a priest. **3.** (of a priest) to hear the confession of. —*v.i.* **4.** to make confession. **5.** to make confession of sins. —**con·fess′a·ble,** *adj.*

con·fess·ed·ly (kən fes′id lē), *adv.* as confessed willingly.

con·fes·sion (kən fesh′ən), *n.* **1.** an admission of a fault, etc. **2.** acknowledgment of sin, esp. to a priest to obtain absolution. **3.** something that is confessed. **4.** a church group having a particular creed.

con·fes·sion·al (kən fesh′ə n°l), *n.* **1.** the place set apart for the hearing of confessions by a priest. —*adj.* **2.** of or like a confession.

con·fes·sor (kən fes′ər), *n.* **1.** a person who confesses. **2.** a priest authorized to hear confessions.

con·fet·ti (kən fet′ē), *n.* small bits of colored paper for throwing to enhance the gaiety of a parade, wedding, etc.

con·fi·dant (kon′fi dant′, -dänt′), *n.* a person to whom secrets are confided. —**con′fi·dante,** *n. fem.*

con·fide (kən fīd′), *v.,* **-fid·ed, -fid·ing.** —*v.i.* **1.** to disclose secrets trustfully. —*v.t.* **2.** to tell in assurance of secrecy. **3.** to entrust. —**con·fid′er,** *n.*

con·fi·dence (kon′fi dəns), *n.* **1.** full trust. **2.** self-reliance, assurance, or boldness. **3.** a confidential communication: *to exchange confidences.* **4. in confidence,** with reliance on another's keeping a secret. —**con′fi·dent,** *adj.* —**con′fi·dent·ly,** *adv.*

con′fidence game′, any swindle technique in which the swindler (**con′fidence man′**), gaining the confidence of the victim, robs him or her by cheating.

con·fi·den·tial (kon′fi den′shəl), *adj.* **1.** communicated in confidence. **2.** indicating confidence or intimacy. **3.** entrusted with private affairs. —**con′fi·den′ti·al′i·ty,** *n.* —**con′fi·den′tial·ly,** *adv.* —**Syn. 1.** private, restricted, secret.

con·fig·u·ra·tion (kən fig′yə rā′shən), *n.* the relative disposition of the parts or elements of a thing. —**con·fig′u·ra′tive, con·fig′u·ra′tion·al,** *adj.*

con·fine (kən fīn′ *for 1, 2;* kon′fīn *for 3*), *v.,* **-fined, -fin·ing,** *n.* —*v.t.* **1.** to keep within bounds. **2.** to shut up, as in prison. —*n.* **3.** Usually, **confines.** a boundary or border. —**con·fine′ment,** *n.* —**con·fin′er,** *n.*

con·firm (kəm fûrm′), *v.t.* **1.** to prove to be right or true. **2.** to sanction or ratify: *to confirm an agreement.* **3.** to make firm or fast. **4.** to administer the rite of confirmation to. —**con·firm′a·ble,** *adj.* —**Syn. 1.** corroborate, substantiate, verify.

con·fir·ma·tion (kon′fər mā′shən), *n.* **1.** the act of confirming or state of being confirmed. **2.** corroboration or proof. **3.** a rite administered to a baptized person by which he or she is admitted to full communion with the church. **4.** a solemn ceremony among certain Jews to admit boys and girls formally as adult members of the Jewish community. —**con·firm′a·to·ry** (-fûr′mə tō′rē), *adj.*

con·firmed (kən fûrmd′), *adj.* 1. proved to be right or true. 2. habitual or inveterate: *a confirmed bachelor.*

con·fis·cate (kon′fi skāt′, kən fis′kāt), *v.t.,* **-cat·ed, -cat·ing.** 1. to seize as forfeited for public use. 2. to seize by or as by authority. —**con′fis·ca′tion,** *n.* —**con′fis·ca′tor,** *n.* —**con·fis′ca·to′ry** (-fis′kə tô′rē), *adj.*

con·fla·gra·tion (kon′flə grā′shən), *n.* a large and destructive fire.

con·flict (*v.* kən flikt′; *n.* kon′flikt), *v.i.* 1. to come into direct disagreement, as of ideas or interests. —*n.* 2. a battle or struggle. 3. antagonism or opposition. 4. incompatibility or interference. —**con·flic′tive,** *adj.*

con·flict of in′terest, the situation of a public officeholder whose private financial interests might benefit from his or her official actions.

con·flu·ence (kon′floo əns), *n.* 1. a coming or flowing together, as of streams. 2. their place of junction. 3. a crowd or throng. Also called **con·flux** (kon′fluks). —**con′flu·ent,** *adj.*

con·fo·cal (kon fō′kəl), *adj. Math.* having the same focus or foci.

con·form (kən fôrm′), *v.i.* 1. to act in accordance with a standard or norm. 2. to be or become similar in form or character. 3. to be in harmony or accord. —*v.t.* 4. to make similar in form or character. 5. to bring into harmony. —**con·form′a·ble,** *adj.* —**con·form′er,** *n.*

con·for·ma·tion (kon′fôr mā′shən), *n.* 1. general structure or form. 2. symmetrical arrangement of parts.

con·form·ist (kən fôr′mist), *n.* a person who conforms to a particular practice of a group, society, etc. —**con·form′ism,** *n.*

con·form·i·ty (kən fôr′mi tē), *n., pl.* **-ties.** 1. correspondence in form or character. 2. compliance or acquiescence. Also, **con·form′ance.**

con·found (kon found′, kən-; *for 3 usually* kon′found′), *v.t.* 1. to dismay or amaze utterly. 2. to throw into confusion or disorder. 3. to damn: *Confound it!* —**con·found′ed,** *adj.* —**con·found′er,** *n.*

con·fra·ter·ni·ty (kon′frə tûr′ni tē), *n., pl.* **-ties.** a lay brotherhood devoted to some religious or charitable service.

con·frere (kon′frâr), *n.* a fellow member of a fraternity, profession, etc.

con·front (kən frunt′), *v.t.* 1. to stand or come direct in front of. 2. to face in hostility. —**con′fron·ta′tion,** *n.*

Con·fu·cian·ism (kən fyoo′shə niz′əm), *n.* the system of ethics, education, and statesmanship taught by Confucius.

Con·fu·cius (kən fyoo′shəs), *n.* 551?-479 B.C., Chinese philosopher and teacher. —**Con·fu′cian,** *n., adj.*

con·fuse (kən fyooz′), *v.t.,* **-fused, -fus·ing.** 1. to make unclear or uncertain. 2. to throw into disorder. 3. to associate by mistake. —**con·fus′ed·ly,** *adv.* —**con·fus′ing·ly,** *adv.* —**Syn.** 1. bewilder, confound, perplex.

con·fu·sion (kən fyoo′zhən), *n.* 1. the act of confusing or state of being confused. 2. disorder or chaos. 3. embarrassment or bewilderment.

con·fute (kən fyoot′), *v.t.,* **-fut·ed, -fut·ing.** to prove to be wrong by argument or proof. —**con′fu·ta′tion,** *n.*

Cong. 1. Congregational. 2. Congress. 3. Congressional.

con·ga (kong′gə), *n.* a Cuban dance performed by a group in a single line.

con·geal (kən jēl′), *v.t., v.i.* 1. to change from a fluid state to a solid state, as by freezing. 2. to curdle or coagulate. —**con·geal′a·ble,** *adj.* —**con·geal′ment,** *n.*

con·ge·ner (kon′jə nər), *n.* 1. one of the same kind or class. 2. a plant or animal belonging to the same genus as another. —**con·ge·ner·ic** (kon′jə ner′ik), *adj.*

con·gen·ial (kən jēn′yəl), *adj.* 1. suited in disposition or taste. 2. agreeable in nature or character. —**con·ge·ni·al·i·ty** (kən jē′nē al′i tē), *n.* —**con·gen′ial·ly,** *adv.*

con·gen·i·tal (kən jen′i təl), *adj.* existing at or from one's birth. —**con·gen′i·tal·ly,** *adv.*

con′ger eel′ (kong′gər), a large, marine eel, used for food.

con·ge·ries (kon jēr′ēz), *n.* an aggregation of objects or ideas.

con·gest (kən jest′), *v.t.* 1. to fill to excess. 2. to cause an unnatural accumulation of blood in the vessels of. —**con·ges′tion,** *n.* —**con·ges′tive,** *adj.*

con·glom·er·ate (*n., adj.* kən glom′ər·it; *v.* kən glom′ə rāt′), *n., adj., v.,* **-at·ed, -at·ing.** —*n.* 1. anything composed of heterogeneous elements. 2. a rock consisting of pebbles or the like cemented together. 3. a company consisting of a number of subsidiary companies in unrelated industries. —*adj.* 4. clustered or collected. 5. of the nature of a conglomerate. —*v.t., v.i.* 6. to collect or cluster together. —**con·glom′er·a′tion,** *n.*

Con·go (kong'gō), *n.* **1.** a country in central Africa, W of Zaire. **2.** a former name of **Zaire** (def. 1). **3.** former name of the Zaire River. —**Con'go·lese'** (-gə lēz'), *adj., n.*

con·grat·u·late (kən grach'ə lāt'), *v.t.,* **-lat·ed, -lat·ing.** to express one's joy to (a person), as on a happy occasion. —**con·grat'u·la'tion,** *n.* — **con·grat·u·la·to·ry** (kən grach'ə lə tōr'ē, -tôr'ē), *adj.*

con·gre·gate (kong'grə gāt'), *v.i., v.t.,* **-gat·ed, -gat·ing.** to gather in a body or crowd.

con·gre·ga·tion (kong'grə gā'shən), *n.* **1.** the act of congregating. **2.** an assemblage, as of persons gathered for religious worship. —**con'gre·gant,** *n.*

con·gre·ga·tion·al (kong'grə gā'shə nºl), *adj.* **1.** of or pertaining to a congregation. **2.** (*cap.*) pertaining to a Protestant denomination in which each local religious society is self-governing.

Con·gre·ga·tion·al·ism (kong'grə gā'shə nºliz'əm), *n.* the doctrine of Congregational churches. —**Con'gre·ga'tion·al·ist,** *n., adj.*

con·gress (kong'gris), *n.* **1.** (*cap.*) the legislative body of the U.S., consisting of the Senate and the House of Representatives. **2.** the legislative body of a nation. **3.** a formal meeting for the discussion and solution of some matter. —**con·gres·sion·al** (kən gresh'ə nºl), *adj.* —**con·gres'sion·al·ly,** *adv.*

con·gress·man (kong'gris mən), *n., pl.* **-men.** a male member of the U.S. Congress. —**con'gress·wom'an,** *n. fem.*

con·gru·ent (kong'grōō ənt), *adj.* **1.** *Geom.* coinciding at all points when superimposed: *congruent triangles.* **2.** agreeing or corresponding. —**con'gru·ence, con'gru·en·cy,** *n.* —**con'gru·ent·ly,** *adv.*

con·gru·i·ty (kən grōō'i tē, kon-), *n., pl.* **-ties. 1.** the quality of being geometrically congruent. **2.** agreement or harmony. —**con'gru·ous,** *adj.* —**con'gru·ous·ly,** *adv.*

con·ic (kon'ik), *adj.* of, having the form of, or resembling a cone. Also, **con'i·cal.** —**con'i·cal·ly,** *adv.*

co·ni·fer (kō'nə fər, kon'ə-), *n.* a cone-bearing evergreen tree or shrub, as a pine. —**co·nif'er·ous,** *adj.*

conj., **1.** conjugation. **2.** conjunction.

con·jec·ture (kən jek'chər), *n., v.,* **-tured, -tur·ing.** —*n.* **1.** the formation of an opinion without sufficient evidence for proof. **2.** the opinion so formed. —*v.t., v.i.* **3.** to conclude from evidence insufficient to ensure reliability. —**con·jec'tur·a·ble,** *adj.* —**con·jec'tur·al,** *adj.*

con·join (kən join'), *v.t., v.i.* to join or act together. —**con·join'er,** *n.* —**con·joint',** *adj.* —**con·joint'ly,** *adv.*

con·ju·gal (kon'jə gəl), *adj.* of marriage or the relation of husband and wife. —**con'ju·gal·ly,** *adv.*

con·ju·gate (*v.* kon'jə gāt'; *adj.* kon'jə git, -gāt'), *v.,* **-gat·ed, -gat·ing,** *adj.* —*v.t.* **1.** to give the inflected forms of (a verb), in a fixed order. **2.** *Obs.* to join, esp. in marriage. —*adj.* **3.** joined together, esp. in pairs. **4.** (of words) having a common derivation. **5.** *Math.* so related as to be interchangeable in the enunciation of certain properties. —**con'ju·ga'tor,** *n.*

con·ju·ga·tion (kon'jə gā'shən), *n.* **1.** the inflection of verbs. **2.** the whole set of inflected forms of a verb. **3.** union or conjunction. **4.** the sexual process in protozoans, involving temporary fusion. —**con'ju·ga'tion·al,** *adj.*

con·junct (kən jungkt', kon'jungkt), *adj.* joined together.

con·junc·tion (kən jungk'shən), *n.* **1.** a joining together. **2.** a combination, as of events. **3.** a word functioning as connector between words, phrases, clauses, or sentences, as *and, but, however.*

con·junc·ti·va (kon'jungk tī'və), *n., pl.* **-vas, -vae** (-vē). the mucous membrane that lines the inner surface of the eyelids. —**con'junc·ti'val,** *adj.*

con·junc·tive (kən jungk'tiv), *adj.* **1.** connective. **2.** joint or linked. **3.** *Gram.* of the nature of a conjunction.

con·junc·ti·vi·tis (kən jungk'tə vī'tis), *n.* inflammation of the conjunctiva.

con·junc·ture (kən jungk'chər), *n.* **1.** a combination of circumstances or a particular state of affairs. **2.** a critical state of affairs.

con·jure (kon'jər; kən jŏŏr' *for* 4), *v.,* **-jured, -jur·ing.** —*v.t.* **1.** to summon (a devil or spirit) by invocation or spell. **2.** to produce by magic. **3.** to bring to mind by or as if by magic. **4.** *Literary.* to appeal to solemnly or earnestly. —*v.i.* **6.** to summon a devil or spirit by invocation or spell. **6.** to practice magic. —**con'ju·ra'tion,** *n.* —**con'jur·er, con'jur·or,** *n.*

conk (kongk, kôngk), *Slang.* —*v.t.* **1.** to hit on the head. —*v.i.* **2.** conk out, **a.** to break or fail, as a machine. **b.** to faint.

Conn., Connecticut.

con·nect (kə nekt'), *v.t., v.i.* **1.** to band or link together. **2.** to associate mentally. —**con·nect'ed·ly,** *adv.* —**con·nec'tor, con·nect'er,** *n.*

Con·nect·i·cut (kə net'ə kət), *n.* a state in the NE United States. *Cap.:* Hartford.

con·nec·tion (kə nek'shən), *n.* **1.** the act of connecting or state of being connected. **2.** link or bond. **3.** association or relationship. **4.** association with something observed, discussed, etc. **5.** Often, **connections.** the meeting of trains, planes, etc., for transfer of passengers. **6.** Usually, **connections.** associates, relations, or friends having some influence or power. Also, *Brit.,* **con·nex'ion.**

con·nec·tive (kə nek'tiv), *adj.* **1.** serving to connect. —*n.* **2.** something that connects. **3.** a word used to connect words, phrases, clauses, or sentences, as a conjunction.

con·nip·tion (kə nip'shən), *n. Informal.* a fit of hysteria, anger, etc.

con·nive (kə nīv'), *v.i.,* **-nived, -niv·ing. 1.** to give aid to wrongdoing by pretending not to know or notice. **2.** to cooperate secretly. [< L *con·niv(ēre)* (to) wink at] —**con·ni'vance,** *n.* —**con·niv'er,** *n.*

con·nois·seur (kon'ə sûr', -sŏōr'), *n.* an expert judge in art or in matters of taste.

con·no·ta·tion (kon'ə tā'shən), *n.* the associated or secondary meaning of a word or expression. —**con'no·ta'tive,** *adj.*

con·note (kə nōt'), *v.t.,* **-not·ed, -not·ing. 1.** to suggest (certain meanings, etc.) in addition to the explicit meaning. **2.** to involve as a condition or accompaniment.

con·nu·bi·al (kə nōō'bē əl, -nyōō'-), *adj.* of or characteristic of marriage.

con·quer (kong'kər), *v.t.* **1.** to acquire by force of arms. **2.** to overcome by force. **3.** to obtain by effort. **4.** to surmount. —*v.i.* **5.** to be victorious. —**con'quer·a·ble,** *adj.* —**con'quer·or,** *n.* —Syn. **2.** defeat, overwhelm, vanquish.

con·quest (kon'kwest, kong'-), *n.* **1.** the act of conquering or state of being conquered. **2.** the winning of favor or affection. **3.** anything acquired by conquering.

con·quis·ta·dor (kon kwis'tə dôr'), *n.* one of the 16th-century Spanish conquerors in the Americas.

Con·rail (kon'rāl), *n. U.S.* a quasi-governmental network of railroads set up in 1976. Also, **ConRail.** [*Con(solidated) Rail (Corporation)*]

Cons., 1. Constable. **2.** Consul.

cons., 1. consolidated. **2.** consonant.

con·san·guin·e·ous (kon'sang̱ gwin'ē-əs), *adj.* having the same ancestry, esp. related by blood. —**con'san·guin'i·ty,** *n.*

con·science (kon'shəns), *n.* the sense of what is right or wrong in one's conduct or motives. —**con'science·less,** *adj.*

con·sci·en·tious (kon'shē en'shəs, kon'sē-), *adj.* **1.** controlled by or done according to conscience. **2.** careful and painstaking. —**con'sci·en'tious·ly,** *adv.* —**con'sci·en'tious·ness,** *n.*

conscien'tious objec'tor, a person who refuses to perform military service for his country for moral or religious reasons.

con·scious (kon'shəs), *adj.* **1.** knowing one's own existence, surroundings, etc. **2.** having the mental faculties fully active. **3.** known to oneself: *conscious guilt.* **4.** deliberate or intentional. —**con'scious·ly,** *adv.* —**con'scious·ness,** *n.*

con·script (*v.* kən skript'; *n.* kon'-skript), *v.t.* **1.** to draft for military service. —*n.* **2.** a recruit obtained by conscription. —**con·scrip'tion,** *n.*

con·se·crate (kon'sə krāt'), *v.t.,* **-crat·ed, -crat·ing. 1.** to make or declare sacred. **2.** to devote to some purpose. **3.** to ordain to a sacred office, esp. to that of bishop. —**con'se·cra'tion,** *n.*

con·sec·u·tive (kən sek'yə tiv), *adj.* following one another in uninterrupted order. —**con·sec'u·tive·ly,** *adv.*

con·sen·sus (kən sen'səs), *n., pl.* **-sus·es. 1.** general agreement or harmony. **2.** majority of opinion.

con·sent (kən sent'), *v.i.* **1.** to agree to or comply with what is done or proposed by another. —*n.* **2.** agreement or compliance thus obtained.

con·se·quence (kon'sə kwens', -kwəns), *n.* **1.** the effect or result of an earlier occurrence. **2.** importance or significance.

con·se·quent (kon'sə kwent', -kwənt), *adj.* following as an effect or result. —**con'se·quent'ly,** *adv.*

con·se·quen·tial (kon'sə kwen'shəl), *adj.* **1.** consequent. **2.** of importance. **3.** self-important or conceited. —**con'se·quen'tial·ly,** *adv.*

con·serv·an·cy (kən sûr'vən sē), *n., pl.* **-cies.** conservation (def. 2).

con·ser·va·tion (kon'sər vā'shən), *n.* **1.** the act of conserving. **2.** the wise use of natural resources. —**con'ser·va'tion·al,** *adj.*

con·ser·va·tion·ist (kon'sər vā'shə-nist), *n.* a person who advocates conservation of the natural resources of a country. —**con'ser·va'tion·ism,** *n.*

con·ser·va·tism (kən sûr'və tiz'əm), *n.* the disposition to preserve what is established and to resist change.

con·serv·a·tive (kən sûr′və tiv), *adj.*
1. disposed to preserve existing conditions, institutions, etc., and to resist change. 2. cautious or moderate. 3. traditional in style or manner. 4. of political conservatism. —*n.* 5. a conservative person. —**con·serv′a·tive·ly**, *adv.*

con·ser·va·tor (kon′sər vā′tər, kən-sûr′və-), *n. Law.* a guardian or custodian.

con·ser·va·to·ry (kən sûr′və tōr′ē, -tôr′ē), *n., pl.* **-ries.** 1. a music school. 2. a small greenhouse.

con·serve (*v.* kən sûrv′; *n.* kon′sûrv, kən sûrv′), *v.,* -served, -serv·ing, *n.* —*v.t.* 1. to keep from loss, decay, waste, or injury. 2. to preserve (fruit). —*n.* 3. Often, **conserves**, preserves prepared from mixed fruits. —**con·serv′a·ble**, *adj.*

con·sid·er (kən sid′ər), *v.t.* 1. to think carefully about. 2. to regard, think, believe, or suppose. 3. to bear in mind. 4. to pay attention to. —**con·sid′ered**, *adj.* —**Syn.** 1. contemplate, ponder, weigh.

con·sid·er·a·ble (kən sid′ər ə bəl), *adj.* 1. rather large or great, as in size, distance, etc. 2. worthy of consideration. —*n.* 3. *Informal.* much. —**con·sid′er·a·bly**, *adv.*

con·sid·er·ate (kən sid′ər it), *adj.* having regard for another's feelings, etc. —**con·sid′er·ate·ly**, *adv.*

con·sid·er·a·tion (kən sid′ə rā′shən), *n.* 1. careful thought or deliberation. 2. something kept in mind in making a decision, evaluating facts, etc. 3. a payment or compensation. 4. thoughtful or sympathetic concern. 5. **take into consideration**, to bear in mind.

con·sid·er·ing (kən sid′ər ing), *prep.* 1. in view of. —*conj.* 2. taking into consideration that.

con·sign (kən sīn′), *v.t.* 1. to deliver formally. 2. to entrust. 3. to relegate. 4. to ship, as by common carrier, esp. for sale or custody. —**con·sign·ee′,** *n.* —**con·sign′or,** *n.*

con·sign·ment (kən sīn′mənt), *n.* something that is consigned, esp. property sent to an agent for sale, storage, or shipment.

con·sist (kən sist′), *v.i.* 1. to be made up or composed of. 2. to inhere or exist.
—**Usage.** 1, 2. CONSIST OF and CONSIST IN are often confused. With CONSIST OF, parts or ingredients are spoken of: *Bread consists of flour, yeast, etc.* With CONSIST IN, something resembling a definition is given: *Cooperation consists in helping one another.*

con·sist·en·cy (kən sis′tən sē), *n., pl.* **-cies.** 1. the condition of holding together and retaining form. 2. degree of density or firmness. 3. steadfast adherence to the same principles, course, etc. 4. agreement among parts or things. Also, **con·sist′ence.** —**con·sist′ent,** *adj.* —**con·sist′ent·ly,** *adv.*

con·sis·to·ry (kən sis′tə rē), *n., pl.* **-ries.** a solemn assembly of the whole body of Roman Catholic cardinals, presided over by the pope. —**con·sis·to·ri·al** (kon′si stōr′ē əl, -stôr′-), *adj.*

consol., consolidated.

con·sole¹ (kən sōl′), *v.t.,* -soled, -sol·ing. to attempt to lessen the grief of. —**con·so·la·tion** (kon′sə lā′shən), *n.* —**con·sol′a·to·ry,** *adj.* —**con·sol′er,** *n.* —**con·sol′ing·ly,** *adv.*

con·sole² (kon′sōl), *n.* 1. a desklike structure containing the keyboards, pedals, etc., of an organ. 2. a radio, phonograph, or television cabinet that stands on the floor. 3. the control unit of an electrical or electronic system.

con·sol·i·date (kən sol′i dāt′), *v.t., v.i.,* -dat·ed, -dat·ing. 1. to unite into a single whole. 2. to make or become firm or secure. —**con·sol′i·da′tion,** *n.* —**con·sol′i·da′tor,** *n.*

con·som·mé (kon′sə mā′, kon′sə mā′), *n.* a clear soup made by boiling meat or vegetables.

con·so·nance (kon′sə nəns), *n.* 1. accord, as of elements. 2. the repetition of consonants as a rhyming device. Also, **con′so·nan·cy.**

con·so·nant (kon′sə nənt), *n.* 1. a speech sound produced by obstructing the flow of air from the lungs. 2. a letter that represents such a sound. —*adj.* 3. in accord or agreement. —**con·so·nan·tal** (kon′sə nan′t°l), *adj.* —**con′so·nant·ly,** *adv.*

con·sort (*n.* kon′sôrt; *v.* kən sôrt′), *n.* 1. a husband or wife, esp. of a reigning monarch. 2. one vessel or ship accompanying another. —*v.i.* 3. to keep company. 4. to agree or harmonize.

con·sor·ti·um (kən sôr′shē əm), *n., pl.* **-ti·a** (-shē ə). a combination of financial institutions for a common end requiring large resources of capital.

con·spec·tus (kən spek′təs), *n., pl.* **-tus·es.** 1. a general survey. 2. a digest or summary.

con·spic·u·ous (kən spik′yōō əs), *adj.* 1. easily seen or noticed. 2. attracting special attention. —**con·spic′u·ous·ly,** *adv.* —**con·spic′u·ous·ness,** *n.*

con·spir·a·cy (kən spir′ə sē), *n., pl.* **-cies.** an evil, unlawful plot. —**con·spir′a·to′ri·al** (-spir′ə tor′ē əl, -tôr′-), *adj.*

con·spire (kən spī′r′), *v.i.*, **-spired,
-spir·ing. 1.** to agree together, esp.
secretly, to do something wrong,
evil, or illegal. **2.** to act together
toward the same goal. **—con·spir·**
a·tor (kən spir′ə tər), **con·spir′er,** *n.*

Const., 1. Constable. **2.** Constitution.

const., 1. constable. **2.** constant. **3.**
constitution. **4.** constitutional.

con·sta·ble (kon′stə bəl), *n.* **1.** a
peace officer in a rural district. **2.**
Brit. a policeman or policewoman.

con·stab·u·lar·y (kən stab′yə ler′ē), *n.*,
pl. **-lar·ies. 1.** the body of constables of a locality. **2.** a body of
peace officers organized on a military basis.

con·stan·cy (kon′stən sē), *n.* **1.** firmness of mind or faithfulness. **2.**
uniformity or stability.

con·stant (kon′stənt), *adj.* **1.** not
changing or varying. **2.** regularly
recurrent. **3.** steadfast or resolute.
—n. 4. something that does not
change or vary. **—con′stant·ly,** *adv.*
—Syn. 2. continuous, incessant, unremitting.

Con·stan·ti·no·ple (kon′stan t′nō′-
pəl), *n.* former name of Istanbul.

con·stel·la·tion (kon′stə lā′shən), *n.*
1. any of various configurations of
stars to which names have been
given. **2.** the relative position of
the stars as supposed to influence
events, esp. at a person's birth.

con·ster·na·tion (kon′stər nā′shən), *n.*
a sudden, alarming amazement or
dread.

con·sti·pate (kon′stə pāt′), *v.t.*, **-pat-**
ed, -pat·ing. to cause constipation
in.

con·sti·pa·tion (kon′stə pā′shən), *n.*
a condition of the bowels in which
evacuation is difficult and infrequent.

con·stit·u·en·cy (kən stich′ōō ən sē),
n., pl. **-cies. 1.** the voters of a
district represented by an elective
officer. **2.** the district itself.

con·stit·u·ent (kən stich′ōō ənt), *adj.*
1. necessary to make up a whole
thing. **2.** having power to elect,
as a representative: *a constituent
body.* **3.** having power to frame
or alter a political constitution.
—n. 4. a constituent element. **5.** a
voter in a district represented by
an elected official.

con·sti·tute (kon′sti tōōt′, -tyōōt′),
v.t., **-tut·ed, -tut·ing. 1.** to make
up or form (a whole). **2.** to appoint
to an office or function. **3.** to set up
or establish (laws, etc.). **—con′sti-**
tu′tive, *adj.*

con·sti·tu·tion (kon′sti tōō′shən,
-tyōō′-), *n.* **1.** the way in which
something is constituted or put
together. **2.** the physical charac-

ter of the body. **3. a.** the system of
principles according to which a nation or organization is governed.
b. the document embodying these
principles. **4.** (*cap.*) the Constitution of the U.S., carried into effect
in 1789.

con·sti·tu·tion·al (kon′sti tōō′shə n′l,
-tyōō′-), *adj.* **1.** of the makeup of
a person's body or mind. **2.** of the
constitution of a nation or organization. **—n. 3.** *Informal.* a walk taken
for the benefit of one's health. **—**
con′sti·tu′tion·al′i·ty (-nal′i tē), *n.*
—con′sti·tu′tion·al·ly, *adv.*

const., construction.

con·strain (kən strān′), *v.t.* **1.** to
compel or restrict, esp. morally. **2.**
to confine forcibly. **3.** to repress or
restrain. **—con·strain′a·ble,** *adj.* **—**
con·strained′, *adj.* **—con·strain′ed-**
ly (-strā′nid lē), *adv.* **—con·strain′-**
er, *n.*

con·straint (kən strānt′), *n.* **1.** moral
compulsion. **2.** confinement or restriction. **3.** repression of natural
feelings and impulses.

con·strict (kən strikt′), *v.t.* to make
narrow, as by squeezing. **—con·**
stric′tion, *n.* **—con·stric′tive,** *adj.*
—con·stric′tor, *n.*

con·struct (*v.* kən strukt′; *n.* kon′-
strukt), *v.t.* **1.** to build, esp. systematically. **—n. 2.** something constructed. **—con·struc′tor,** *n.*

con·struc·tion (kən struk′shən), *n.*
1. the act or art of constructing. **2.**
a structure. **3.** the arrangement of
two or more forms in a grammatical unit. **4.** explanation or
interpretation.

con·struc·tion·ist (kən struk′shə nist),
n. a person who interprets, esp.
laws, in a specific manner.

con·struc·tive (kən struk′tiv), *adj.* **1.**
helping to improve. **2.** of or pertaining to construction. **—con·struc′-**
tive·ly, *adv.*

con·strue (kən strōō′), *v.t.,* **-strued,**
-stru·ing. 1. to show or explain the
meaning or intention of. **2.** to
translate, esp. literally. **3.** to analyze the syntax of: *to construe a
sentence.* **—con·stru′a·ble,** *adj.* **—**
con·stru′er, *n.*

con·sub·stan·ti·a·tion (kon′səb stan′-
shē ā′shən), *n.* the doctrine that
the substance of the body and
blood of Christ coexist in and with
the substance of bread and wine
of the Eucharist.

con·sul (kon′səl), *n.* **1.** a foreign-
service officer stationed abroad to
promote trade, protect the rights of
resident fellow citizens, etc. **2.** either
of the two chief magistrates of the
ancient Roman republic. **—con′-**
su·lar, *adj.* **—con′sul·ship′,** *n.*

con·su·late (kon′sə lit), *n.* **1.** the premises officially occupied by a consul. **2.** the position or authority of a consul.

con·sult (kən sult′), *v.t.* **1.** to seek advice from. **2.** to consider, esp. in making plans. —*v.i.* **3.** to confer: *He consulted with his doctor.* —**con′sul·ta′tion,** *n.* —**con·sul′ta·tive** (-sul′tə tiv), *adj.*

con·sult·ant (kən sul′t°nt), *n.* **1.** a person who consults someone or something. **2.** a person who gives expert advice.

con·sume (kən sōōm′), *v.t.,* **-sumed, -sum·ing. 1.** to expend by using up. **2.** to eat or drink up. **3.** to destroy, as by burning. **4.** to spend (money, time, etc.) wastefully. **5.** to absorb or engross. —**con·sum′a·ble,** *adj.*

con·sum·er (kən sōō′mər), *n.* **1.** a person or thing that consumes. **2.** a person who uses a commodity or service.

con·sum·er·ism (kən sōō′mər iz′əm), *n.* a movement for the protection of the consumer against inferior or dangerous products, misleading advertising, etc.

con·sum·mate (*v.* kon′sə māt′; *adj.* kən sum′it, kon′sə mit), *v.,* **-mat·ed, -mat·ing,** *adj.* —*v.t.* **1.** to bring to fulfillment. **2.** to complete (a marriage) by sexual intercourse. —*adj.* **3.** perfect or superb. —**con·sum′mate·ly,** *adv.* —**con′sum·ma′tion,** *n.*

con·sump·tion (kən sump′shən), *n.* **1.** the act of consuming. **2.** an amount consumed. **3.** *Econ.* the using up of goods and services. **4.** a wasting disease, esp. tuberculosis of the lungs.

con·sump·tive (kən sump′tiv), *adj.* **1.** pertaining to or affected by bodily consumption. **2.** destructive or wasteful. —*n.* **3.** a person who suffers from consumption. —**con·sump′tive·ly,** *adv.* —**con·sump′tive·ness,** *n.*

cont., 1. containing. **2.** contents. **3.** continent. **4.** continental. **5.** continue. **6.** continued. **7.** contract. **8.** contraction. **9.** control.

con·tact (kon′takt), *n.* **1.** a touching or meeting, as of two things, people, etc. **2.** association or relationship. **3.** an acquaintance through whom one can get information or favors. **4.** a junction of electric conductors. **5.** See **contact lens.** —*v.t.* **6.** to put into contact. **7.** to communicate with. —*v.i.* **8.** to enter into contact.

con′tact fly′ing, aircraft piloting in which visual reference is made to the horizon, esp. the landmarks.

con′tact lens′, one of a pair of small, inconspicuous lenses of plastic placed over the cornea to aid defective vision.

con·ta·gion (kən tā′jən), *n.* **1.** the communication of disease by contact. **2.** a disease so communicated. **3.** the medium by which a contagious disease is transmitted. **4.** the spread as of an idea, emotion, etc.

con·ta·gious (kən tā′jəs), *adj.* **1.** capable of being transmitted by contact: *contagious diseases.* **2.** spreading a contagious disease. **3.** tending to spread from person to person: *contagious laughter.* —**con·ta′gious·ly,** *adv.* —**con·ta′gious·ness,** *n.*

con·tain (kən tān′), *v.t.* **1.** to hold or include within a volume or area. **2.** to have capacity for. **3.** to prevent or restrict the success of (an enemy or disaster). —**con·tain′ment,** *n.*

con·tain·er (kən tā′nər), *n.* anything that contains something, as a box, crate, etc.

con·tain·er·i·za·tion (kən tā′nər i zā′shən), *n.* a method of shipping a large amount of crated cargo by consolidating it into one standard, sealed, reusable van.

con·tain·er·ize (kən tā′nə rīz′), *v.t.,* **-ized, -iz·ing.** to pack and ship by containerization.

con·tain·er·ship (kən tā′nər ship′), *n.* a ship built to accommodate containerized cargoes.

con·tam·i·nant (kən tam′ə nənt), *n.* something that contaminates.

con·tam·i·nate (kən tam′ə nāt′), *v.t.,* **-nat·ed, -nat·ing.** to make impure or unsuitable by contact or mixture. —**con·tam′i·na′tion,** *n.* —**con·tam′i·na·tive,** *adj.*

contd., continued.

con·temn (kən tem′), *v.t. Literary.* to treat or regard with contempt.

contemp., contemporary.

con·tem·plate (kon′təm plāt′, kən tem′plāt), *v.,* **-plat·ed, -plat·ing.** —*v.t.* **1.** to view thoughtfully. **2.** to plan or expect. —*v.i.* **3.** to consider deliberately. —**con′tem·pla′tion,** *n.* —**con·tem′pla·tive** (kən tem′plə tiv), *adj.* —**con′tem·pla′tor,** *n.*

con·tem·po·ra·ne·ous (kən tem′pə rā′nē əs), *adj.* (esp. of events) contemporary (def. 1).

con·tem·po·rar·y (kən tem′pə rer′ē), *adj., n., pl.* **-rar·ies.** —*adj.* **1.** occurring or existing at the same time. **2.** of the same age or date. **3.** of the present time. —*n.* **4.** a person or thing belonging to the same time with another or others. **5.** a person of the same age as another. —**con·tem′po·rar′i·ly,** *adv.*

con·tempt (kən tempt′), n. 1. the feeling with which one regards anything mean or worthless. 2. dishonor or disgrace. 3. willful disobedience to or disrespect for a court or legislative body.

con·tempt·i·ble (kən temp′tə bəl), adj. deserving or held in contempt. —**con·tempt′i·bly,** adv. —Syn. abominable, despicable, hateful, mean.

con·temp·tu·ous (kən temp′chŏŏ əs), adj. showing or expressing contempt or disdain. —**con·temp′tu·ous·ly,** adv. —**con·temp′tu·ous·ness,** n.

con·tend (kən tend′), v.i. 1. to struggle in opposition. 2. to strive in rivalry. 3. to dispute earnestly. —v.t. 4. to assert earnestly. —**contend′er,** n.

con·tent¹ (kon′tent), n. 1. Usually, **contents. a.** something that is contained. **b.** the subjects, chapters, etc., covered in a book. 2. something expressed in a book, speech, or other medium. 3. significance or meaning. 4. the amount contained.

con·tent² (kən tent′), adj. 1. contented. —v.t. 2. to satisfy modestly. —n. 3. contentment. —**con·tent′ly,** adv.

con·tent·ed (kən ten′tid), adj. modestly satisfied. —**con·tent′ed·ly,** adv. —**con·tent′ed·ness,** n.

con·ten·tion (kən ten′shən), n. 1. heated dispute or controversy. 2. a point affirmed in this. 3. struggle or contest. —**con·ten′tious,** adj. —**con·ten′tious·ly,** adv. —**con·ten′tious·ness,** n.

con·tent·ment (kən tent′mənt), n. modest satisfaction.

con·ter·mi·nous (kən tûr′mə nəs), adj. 1. having a common boundary. 2. having the same boundary. —**con·ter′mi·nous·ly,** adv. —**con·ter′mi·nous·ness,** n.

con·test (n. kon′test; v. kən test′), n. 1. a competition, esp. for a prize. 2. a struggle or fight. —v.t. 3. to fight for, as in battle. 4. to dispute or challenge. —**con·test′a·ble,** adj.

con·test·ant (kən tes′tənt), n. 1. a competitor, as in a race. 2. a challenger, as in legal proceedings.

con·text (kon′tekst), n. 1. the parts of a statement that precede or follow a word or passage, influencing its meaning or effect. 2. the circumstances that surround an event, situation, etc. —**con·tex·tu·al** (kən teks′chŏŏ əl), adj. —**con·tex′tu·al·ly,** adv.

contg., containing.

con·tig·u·ous (kən tig′yŏŏ əs), adj. 1. touching or in contact. 2. near or next. —**con·ti·gu·i·ty** (kon′tə gyŏŏ′i tē), n.

con·ti·nence (kon′tə nəns), n. 1. self-restraint, esp. in sexual passion or activity. 2. the ability to retain feces or urine voluntarily. —**con′ti·nent,** adj.

con·ti·nent (kon′tə nənt), n. 1. one of the main land masses of the globe. 2. **the Continent,** the mainland of Europe, as distinguished from the British Isles.

con·ti·nen·tal (kon′tə nen′t'l), adj. 1. of or of the nature of a continent. 2. (usually cap.) European. 3. (cap.) of the American colonies of the Revolutionary period. —n. 4. (cap.) a soldier of the Continental army in the American Revolution. —**con′ti·nen′tal·ly,** adv.

continen′tal divide′, a divide separating river systems which flow to opposite sides of a continent.

con′tinen′tal shelf′, the part of a continent submerged in relatively shallow sea.

con′tinen′tal slope′, a steep slope separating a continental shelf and a deep ocean basin.

con·tin·gen·cy (kən tin′jən sē), n., pl. -cies. 1. dependence on chance. 2. an uncertain event.

con·tin·gent (kən tin′jənt), adj. 1. dependent on something not yet certain. 2. accidental or fortuitous. —n. 3. a quota of troops furnished. 4. any one of the representative groups composing an assemblage.

con·tin·u·al (kən tin′yŏŏ əl), adj. happening at frequent intervals: continual demands. —**con·tin′u·al·ly,** adv.

con·tin·u·ance (kən tin′yŏŏ əns), n. 1. an act or instance of continuing. 2. duration or prolongation. 3. an uninterrupted succession. 4. a postponement of a legal proceeding.

con·tin·u·a·tion (kən tin′yŏŏ ā′shən), n. 1. the act or state of continuing or being continued. 2. extension or lengthening in time. 3. a sequel, as to a story.

con·tin·ue (kən tin′yŏŏ), v., -ued, -u·ing. —v.i. 1. to go on or keep on. 2. to go on after interruption. 3. to last or endure. 4. to remain or stay in a place. 5. to remain in a particular state. —v.t. 6. to go on with. 7. to prolong or extend. 8. to carry on from the point of interruption. 9. to cause to last or endure. 10. to keep pending, as a legal proceeding. —**con·tin′u·er,** n. **con·tin′u·a·ble,** adj.

con·ti·nu·i·ty (kon′ti nŏŏ′i tē, -nyŏŏ′-), n., pl. -ties for 3. 1. the state of being continuous. 2. a continuous whole. 3. a motion-picture scenario.

con·tin·u·ous (kən tin′yŏŏ əs), adj. going on without stop: a continuous rain. —**con·tin′u·ous·ly,** adv. —**con·tin′u·ous·ness,** n. —Syn. endless, incessant, unremitting.

con·tin·u·um (kən tin′yŏŏ əm), *n.*, *pl.* **-tin·u·a** (-tin′yŏŏ ə). a continuous extent, series, or whole.

con·tort (kən tôrt′), *v.t.* to twist or bend out of shape. —**con·tor′tion**, *n.* —**con·tor′tive**, *adj.*

con·tor·tion·ist (kən tôr′shə nist), *n.* a person who performs gymnastic feats involving contorted postures. —**con·tor′tion·is′tic**, *adj.*

con·tour (kon′tŏŏr), *n.* **1.** the outline of a figure or shape. **2.** the representation of this. —*v.t.* **3.** to form or shape to the contour of. —*adj.* **4.** following the contour lines of the land in order to prevent erosion.

con′tour line′, (on a map) a line joining points of equal elevation on a surface.

contr., **1.** contract. **2.** contraction. **3.** contralto.

contra-, a prefix meaning "against," "opposite," or "opposing": *contradict; contraception.*

con·tra·band (kon′trə band′), *n.* **1.** anything prohibited by law from being imported or exported. **2.** smuggled goods.

con·tra·cep·tion (kon′trə sep′shən), *n.* the prevention of conception or impregnation. —**con′tra·cep′tive**, *adj.*, *n.*

con·tract (*n.* and usually for *v.* 8, 10 kon′trakt; *otherwise v.* kən trakt′), *n.* **1.** an agreement, esp. one enforceable by law. **2.** Also called **con′tract bridge′.** a bridge game in which the side that wins the bid can earn toward game only that number of tricks named in the contract. **3.** *Slang.* a hired murder. —*v.t.* **4.** to draw together: *to contract a muscle.* **5.** to shorten (a word, phrase, etc.) by omitting some of its elements. **6.** to get or acquire, as a disease. **7.** to incur, as a debt. **8.** to establish by contract. —*v.i.* **9.** to shrink. **10.** to enter into a contract. —**con·tract′i·ble**, *adj.* —**con·trac′tion**, *n.* —**con·trac′tive**, *adj.* —**con·trac′tor**, *n.* —**con·trac′tu·al** (-trak′chŏŏ əl), *adj.* —**con·trac′tu·al·ly**, *adv.*

con·trac·tile (kən trak′t°l, -til), *adj.* capable of contraction. —**con·trac·til·i·ty** (kon′trak til′i tē), *n.*

con′tract man′, *Slang.* See **hit man**.

con·tra·dict (kon′trə dikt′), *v.t.* **1.** to assert the contrary of. **2.** to speak contrary to the assertions of. **3.** to imply a denial of. —*v.i.* **4.** to utter a contrary statement. —**con·tra·dic′tion**, *n.* —**con′tra·dic′to·ry**, *adj.*

con·tra·dis·tinc·tion (kon′trə di stingk′shən), *n.* distinction by contrast. —**con′tra·dis·tinc′tive**, *adj.*

con·trail (kon′trāl), *n.* a visible condensation of water droplets or ice crystals in the wake of an aircraft, rocket, etc. [*con*(*densation*) + *trail*]

con·tra·in·di·cate (kon′trə in′də kāt′), *v.t.*, **-cat·ed**, **-cat·ing**. to give indication against the advisability of (a particular remedy or treatment). —**con′tra·in′di·ca′tion**, *n.*

con·tral·to (kən tral′tō), *n.*, *pl.* **-tos**. **1.** the lowest female voice or voice part. **2.** a singer with such a voice.

con·trap·tion (kən trap′shən), *n. Informal.* a mechanical contrivance.

con·tra·pun·tal (kon′trə pun′t°l), *adj. Music.* of or pertaining to counterpoint.

con·tra·ri·e·ty (kon′trə rī′i tē), *n.*, *pl.* **-ties** for 2. **1.** the quality or state of being contrary. **2.** something contrary.

con·tra·ri·wise (kon′trer ē wīz′, kən·trâr′ē wīz′), *adv.* **1.** in the opposite way. **2.** on the contrary.

con·tra·ry (kon′trer ē; *for 4 also* kən trâr′ē), *adj.*, *n.*, *pl.* **-ries**, *adv.* —*adj.* **1.** opposite in nature or character. **2.** mutually opposed. **3.** unfavorable or adverse. **4.** stubbornly opposed or willful. —*n.* **5.** something opposite. **6. on the contrary,** from another point of view. **7. to the contrary,** to the opposite effect. —*adv.* **8.** oppositely or counter.

con′tra·ri·ly, *adv.* —**con′tra·ri·ness**, *n.*

con·trast (*v.* kən trast′; *n.* kon′trast), *v.t.* **1.** to compare to show differences. —*v.i.* **2.** to exhibit unlikeness. —*n.* **3.** a striking exhibition of unlikeness. **4.** a thing or person strikingly unlike in comparison. **5.** *Photog.* the difference between light and dark areas of a print or negative. —**con·trast′a·ble**, *adj.* —**con·trast′ing·ly**, *adv.*

con·tra·vene (kon′trə vēn′), *v.t.*, **-vened**, **-ven·ing**. **1.** to go or act contrary to: *to contravene a law.* **2.** to dispute or contradict, as a statement.

con·tre·temps (kon′trə tän′), *n.* an embarrassing or inopportune occurrence.

contrib., **1.** contribution. **2.** contributor.

con·trib·ute (kən trib′yŏŏt), *v.t.*, *v.i.*, **-ut·ed**, **-ut·ing**. **1.** to give (money, etc.) along with others to a supply, fund, etc., as for charitable purposes. **2.** to furnish (an article) for publication. **3. contribute to,** to have a large share in causing (something). —**con·tri·bu·tion** (kon′trə byŏŏ′shən), *n.* —**con·trib·u·tor** (kən trib′yə tər), *n.* —**con·trib·u·to·ry** (kən trib′yə tôr′ē, -tōr′ē), *adj.*

con·trite (kən trīt′, kon′trīt), *adj.* sincerely remorseful. —**con·trite′ly**, *adv.* —**con·trite′ness**, **con·tri·tion** (-trish′ən), *n.*

con·triv·ance (kən trī′vəns), n. 1. a mechanical device. 2. a plan or scheme.

con·trive (kən trīv′), v.t., **-trived, -triv·ing.** 1. to plan with ingenuity. 2. to plot or frame. 3. to bring about or effect by a scheme. —**con·triv′ed·ly**, adv. —**con·triv′er,** n.

con·trol (kən trōl′), v., **-trolled, -trol·ling,** n. —v.t. 1. to exercise restraint or direction over. 2. to hold back or in check. 3. to verify (an experiment) by a standard of comparison. —n. 4. the act or power of controlling. 5. a person or thing that provides a standard of comparison. 6. a device for regulating a machine. —**con·trol′la·ble,** adj.

con·trol·ler (kən trō′lər), n. 1. a person who checks finances, etc., as of a business firm. 2. a person or thing that controls something or another thing.

con·tro·ver·sy (kon′trə vûr′sē), n., pl. **-sies.** 1. a prolonged public argument or debate. 2. a dispute or quarrel. —**con′tro·ver′sial** (-vûr′shəl), adj. —**con′tro·ver′sial·ly,** adv.

con·tro·vert (kon′trə vûrt′, kon′trə-vûrt′), v.t. to dispute about or deny. —**con′tro·vert′i·ble,** adj.

con·tu·ma·cious (kon′tŏŏ mā′shəs, -tyŏŏ-), adj. stubbornly rebellious or disobedient. —**con′tu·ma′cious·ly,** adv. —**con′tu·ma·cy** (-mə sē), n.

con·tu·me·ly (kon′tŏŏ mə lē, -tyŏŏ-), n., pl. **-lies.** an insulting display of contempt. —**con·tu·me·li·ous** (kon′-tŏŏ mē′lē əs, -tyŏŏ-), adj.

con·tuse (kən tŏŏz′, -tyŏŏz′), v.t., **-tused, -tus·ing.** Med. to bruise (def. 1). —**con·tu′sion,** n.

co·nun·drum (kə nun′drəm), n. 1. a riddle whose answer involves a pun. 2. anything that puzzles.

con·ur·ba·tion (kon′ər bā′shən), n. a large, continuous group of cities or towns.

con·va·lesce (kon′və les′), v.i., **-lesced, -lesc·ing.** to recover health after illness. —**con′va·les′cence,** n. —**con′va·les′cent,** adj., n.

con·vect (kən vekt′), v.t. to transfer by convection. —**con·vec′tive,** adj.

con·vec·tion (kən vek′shən), n. the transfer of heat by the circulation or movement of the heated parts of a liquid or gas. —**con·vec′tion·al,** adj.

con·vene (kən vēn′), v.t., v.i., **-vened, -ven·ing.** to assemble, esp. for a meeting. —**con·ven′er,** n.

con·ven·ience (kən vēn′yəns), n. 1. the quality of being convenient. 2. a convenient situation or time. 3. comfort or ease. 4. anything that saves work, adds to comfort, etc. 5. at one's convenience, whenever or however suitable to one's wishes or needs.

con·ven·ient (kən vēn′yənt), adj. 1. agreeable to the needs or purposes. 2. accessible or at hand. —**con·ven′·ient·ly,** adv.

con·vent (kon′vent), n. 1. a community devoted to religious life, esp. of nuns. 2. the building occupied by such a society. —**con·ven·tu·al** (kən ven′chŏŏ əl), adj.

con·ven·ti·cle (kən ven′ti kəl), n. a secret meeting, esp. for religious worship.

con·ven·tion (kən ven′shən), n. 1. a meeting, as of delegates, for action on matters of common concern. 2. a representative party assembly to nominate candidates and adopt platforms. 3. an agreement, compact, or contract. 4. accepted usage. 5. an established practice or custom.

con·ven·tion·al (kən ven′shə nəl), adj. 1. conforming to accepted standards. 2. established by accepted usage. 3. ordinary or usual. —**con·ven′tion·al·ism,** n. —**con·ven·tion·al·i·ty** (kən ven′shə nal′i tē), n. —**con·ven′tion·al·ly,** adv.

con·ven·tion·al·ize (kən ven′shə-nəlīz′), v.t., **-ized, -iz·ing.** to make conventional.

con·ven·tio·neer (kən ven′shə nēr′), n. a person who attends a convention.

con·verge (kən vûrj′), v.i., **-verged, -verg·ing.** to tend to meet in a point or line. —**con·ver′gence,** con·ver′gen·cy,** n. —**con·ver′gent,** adj.

con·ver·sant (kən vûr′sənt, kon′vər-), adj. familiar by use or study: *conversant with Spanish history.*

con·ver·sa·tion (kon′vər sā′shən), n. informal oral communication between persons. —**con′ver·sa′tion·al,** adj. —**con′ver·sa′tion·al·ly,** adv.

con·ver·sa·tion·al·ist (kon′vər sā′shə-nəlist), n. a person who enjoys or is adept at conversation.

conversa′tion piece′, any object that arouses comment because of some striking quality.

con·verse¹ (v. kən vûrs′; n. kon′vûrs), v., **-versed, vers·ing,** n. —v.i. 1. to talk informally with another or others. —n. 2. conversation.

con·verse² (adj. kən vûrs′, kon′vûrs; n. kon′vûrs), adj. 1. opposite or contrary in direction, action, etc. —n. 2. the opposite of another. —**con·verse′ly,** adv.

con·ver·sion (kən vûr′zhən, -shən), n. 1. the act of converting or state or process of being converted. 2. a change from one religion, belief, etc., to another. 3. the exchange of one currency into another. 4. unauthorized takeover and use of property belonging to another.

con·vert (v. kən vûrt′; n. kon′vûrt), v.t. 1. to change into a different form, etc. 2. to change from one religion, belief, etc., to another. 3. to obtain an equivalent value for in an exchange of currencies. 4. to take over and use another's property unlawfully. —v.i. 5. to become converted. —n. 6. a person who has been converted, as from one religion to another. —con·vert′er, con·ver′tor, n. —Syn. 1. alter, transform, transmute.

con·vert·i·ble (kən vûr′tə bəl), adj. 1. capable of being converted. 2. having a folding top. —n. 3. an automobile having such a top.

con·vex (kon veks′, kən-, kon′veks), adj. having a surface that is curved or rounded outward. —con·vex′i·ty, n.

con·vey (kən vā′), v.t. 1. to carry, bring, or take from one place to another. 2. to impart, as information. 3. Law. to transfer. —con·vey′a·ble, adj. —con·vey′or, con·vey′er, n.

con·vey·ance (kən vā′əns), n. 1. the act of conveying. 2. a means of transporting, esp. a vehicle. 3. a legal document by which transfer of property is effected.

con·vict (v. kən vikt′; n. kon′vikt), v.t. 1. to prove or declare guilty of an offense. —n. 2. a convicted person, esp. one serving a prison sentence.

con·vic·tion (kən vik′shən), n. 1. the act of convicting or state of being convicted. 2. a fixed belief.

con·vince (kən vins′), v.t., -vinced, -vinc·ing. to persuade by argument or proof. —con·vinc′er, n. —con·vinc′ing, adj. —con·vinc′ing·ly, adv.

con·viv·i·al (kən viv′ē əl), adj. 1. fond of feasting, drinking, and companionship. 2. festive or jovial. —con·viv′i·al′i·ty, n. —con·viv′i·al·ly, adv.

con·vo·ca·tion (kon′və kā′shən), n. 1. the act of convoking or state of being convoked. 2. an assembly, esp. of the clergy.

con·voke (kən vōk′), v.t., -voked, -vok·ing. to call together to a meeting.

con·vo·lut·ed (kon′və lōō′tid), adj. 1. intricately coiled. 2. complicated or involved.

con·vo·lu·tion (kon′və lōō′shən), n. 1. a coiled condition. 2. a coiling together. 3. a turn of anything coiled. 4. one of the folds or ridges of the surface of the brain.

con·voy (v. kon′voi, kon voi′; n. kon′voi), v.t. 1. to escort, usually for protection. —n. 2. an armed force, warship, etc., that convoys or is convoyed. 3. any group of military vehicles moving together under the same orders.

con·vulse (kən vuls′), v.t., -vulsed, -vuls·ing. 1. to shake violently. 2. to cause to shake violently with laughter, anger, etc.

con·vul·sion (kən vul′shən), n. 1. contortion of the body caused by violent, involuntary muscular contractions. 2. violent disturbance. —con·vul′sive, adj. —con·vul′sive·ly, adv.

co·ny (kō′nē, kun′ē), n., pl. -nies. 1. the fur of a rabbit. 2. a rabbit or similar small animal.

coo (kōō), v., cooed, coo·ing, n. —v.i. 1. to utter the murmur of pigeons or doves. —n. 2. a cooing sound.

cook (kōōk), v.t. 1. to prepare (food) by heat, as by boiling, baking, etc. —v.i. 2. (of food, etc.) to undergo cooking. 3. cook up, Informal. to concoct or contrive. —n. 4. a person who cooks. —cook′er, n.

cook·book (kōōk′bōōk′), n. a book containing recipes and instructions for cooking.

cook·er·y (kōōk′ə rē), n. the art of cooking.

cook·ie (kōōk′ē), n. a small cake made from stiff, sweet dough. Also, **cook′y.**

cook·out (kōōk′out′), n. a party featuring the cooking and eating of a meal out of doors.

cool (kōōl), adj. 1. moderately free of heat. 2. allowing one to feel so, as clothes. 3. unaffected by emotions, as anger or fear. 4. lacking in enthusiasm or cordiality. 5. calmly audacious. 6. Informal. without exaggeration: a cool million dollars. 7. Slang. great or fine. —n. 8. something that is cool: the cool of the evening. 9. Slang. calmness or composure: Don't lose your cool. —v.i., v.t. 10. to make or become cool. —cool′ly, adv. —cool′ness, n. —Syn. 3. collected, composed, imperturbable, unruffled. 4. apathetic, indifferent, distant.

cool·ant (kōō′lənt), n. a substance used to reduce the temperature of a system below a specified level.

cool·er (kōō′lər), n. 1. a container in which something may be cooled or kept cool. 2. a tall, iced drink. 3. Slang. a jail.

Cool·idge (kōō′lij), n. Calvin, 1872–1933, 30th president of the U.S. 1923–29.

coo·lie (kōō′lē), n. an unskilled, cheaply employed laborer, esp. formerly in India and China.

coon (kōōn), n. raccoon.

coon·hound (kōōn′hound′), n. a hound of any of several breeds developed esp. for hunting raccoons.

coon's' age', *Informal.* a long time.
coon·skin (kōōn'skin'), *n.* **1.** the pelt of a raccoon. **2.** an article of clothing made of coonskin.
co-op (kō'op, kō op'), *n. Informal.* cooperative (defs. 2, 3). Also, **co'op.**
coop (kōōp, kōop), *n.* **1.** an enclosure or pen for fowls. **2.** *Slang.* a prison. —*v.t.* **3.** to place in or as in a coop.
coop., cooperative.
coop·er (kōō'pər, kōōp'ər), *n.* a person who makes or repairs casks, barrels, etc. —**coop'er·age** (-ij), *n.*
co·op·er·ate (kō op'ə rāt'), *v.i.*, **-at·ed, -at·ing.** to work together, esp. willingly, for a common purpose. —**co·op'er·a'tion,** *n.* —**co·op'er·a'tor,** *n.*
co·op·er·a·tive (kō op'ə rā'tiv, -ər ə tiv), *adj.* **1.** working together or willing to cooperate. —*n.* **2.** a jointly owned means of production or distribution of goods or services operated by the consumers. **3.** Also called **co·op'er·a'tive apart'ment.** an apartment house in which the apartments are individually occupied by shareholders of a corporation that owns the entire property. —**co·op'er·a'tive·ly,** *adv.* —**co·op'er·a'tive·ness,** *n.*
co·opt (kō opt'), *v.t.* **1.** to elect or appoint as a fellow member. **2.** to win over or assimilate.
co·or·di·nate (*adj., n.* kō ôr'dᵊnit, -dᵊnāt'; *v.* kō ôr'dᵊnāt'), *adj., n., v.,* **-nat·ed, -nat·ing.** —*adj.* **1.** of the same order or rank. **2.** involving coordination. **3.** *Math.* using coordinates. **4.** of the same rank in a grammatical construction, as *"Jack"* and *"Jill"* in *"Jack and Jill."* —*n.* **5.** a coordinate person or thing. **6.** *Math.* any of the linear quantities that define the position of a point by reference to a fixed figure. **7.** **coordinates,** women's outer garments, harmonizing in color or style, designed to be worn together. —*v.t.* **8.** to place in the same order or rank. **9.** to place in proper order or relation. —*v.i.* **10.** to act in harmonious combination. —**co·or'di·nate·ly,** *adv.* —**co·or'di·na'tor,** *n.*
coor'dinating conjunc'tion, a conjunction that connects coordinate words, as *"and"* in *"Sue and Barbara."*
co·or·di·na·tion (kō ôr'dᵊnā'shən), *n.* **1.** the act of coordinating or state of being coordinated. **2.** harmonious combination or interaction.
coot (kōōt), *n.* **1.** a dark-gray, water-dwelling bird resembling a duck. **2.** *Informal.* a foolish old man.
coot·ie (kōō'tē), *n.* a louse, esp. the body louse.

cop¹ (kop), *v.*, **copped, cop·ping.** *Slang.* —*v.t.* **1.** to steal or filch. —*v.i.* **2. cop out, a.** to give up or back out. **b.** to renege. **c.** to plead guilty.
cop² (kop), *n. Informal.* a policeman or policewoman.
cop., copyright.
co·part·ner (kō pärt'nər, kō'pärt'-), *n.* a fellow associate, as in a business.
cope¹ (kōp), *v.i.*, **coped, cop·ing.** to struggle or contend, esp. with some degree of success.
cope² (kōp), *n.* a long mantle worn by priests, esp. in processions.
Co·pen·ha·gen (kō'pən hā'gən, -hä'-), *n.* the capital of Denmark.
Co·per·ni·cus (kō pûr'nə kəs, kə-), *n.* **Nic·o·la·us** (nik'ə lā'əs), 1473–1543, Polish astronomer.
cop·i·er (kop'ē ər), *n.* **1.** a person or thing that copies. **2.** an electrically operated machine for making instant copies of material.
co·pi·lot (kō'pī'lət), *n.* an assistant aircraft pilot.
cop·ing (kō'ping), *n.* the top covering of an exterior masonry wall.
co·pi·ous (kō'pē əs), *adj.* plentifully abundant. —**co'pi·ous·ly,** *adv.* —**co·pi·ous·ness,** *n.* —**Syn.** ample, extensive, liberal, profuse.
co·pol·y·mer (kō pol'ə mər), *n.* a mixed polymer of two or more different monomers.
cop·out (kop'out'), *n. Slang.* an act of copping out, as by giving up, reneging, or pleading guilty.
cop·per¹ (kop'ər), *n.* **1.** *Chem.* a metallic element having a light reddish-brown color, used as an electrical conductor. *Symbol:* Cu; *at. wt.:* 63.54; *at. no.:* 29. **2.** a coin composed of copper, as the old British penny. [< LL *cuprum*] —**cop'per·y,** *adj.*
cop·per² (kop'ər), *n. Slang.* a policeman or policewoman.
cop·per·as (kop'ər əs), *n.* a bluish-green crystal used in dyeing wool, making inks, etc.
cop·per·head (kop'ər hed'), *n.* a venomous snake of the eastern U.S., having a copper-red body.
cop·ra (kop'rə), *n.* the dried, oil-bearing meat of the coconut.
copse (kops), *n.* a thicket or small wood. Also, *esp Brit.*, **cop·pice** (kop'is).
cop·ter (kop'tər), *n. Informal.* helicopter.
cop·u·la (kop'yə lə), *n., pl.* **-las, -lae** (-lē'). a verb, as *be* or *seem,* that acts as a connecting link between subject and predicate. —**cop'u·lar,** *adj.* —**cop'u·la·tive** (-lā'tiv, -lə tiv), *adj.*

cop·u·late (kop′yə lāt′), *v.i.*, **-lat·ed,** **-lat·ing.** to engage in sexual intercourse. —**cop′u·la′tion,** *n.* —**cop′-u·la·to′ry** (-lə tôr′ē, -tōr′ē), *adj.*

cop·y (kop′ē), *n., pl.* **cop·ies** for 1, 4, *v.,* **cop·ied, cop·y·ing.** —*n.* 1. an imitation, reproduction, or transcript of an original. 2. matter to be reproduced in printed form. 3. any text material, as in an advertisement. 4. a specimen of the same book or engraving. —*v.t.* 5. to make a copy of. 6. to be like or imitate. —**cop′y·ist,** *n.*

cop·y·book (kop′ē bŏŏk′), *n.* a book of models, usually of penmanship, formerly used by learners to imitate.

cop·y·boy (kop′ē boi′), *n.* an office boy employed by a newspaper.

cop·y·cat (kop′ē kat′), *n. Informal.* a person who imitates the actions or work of another.

cop′y desk′, a desk at which newspaper copy is edited and prepared for printing.

cop·y·ed·it (kop′ē ed′it), *v.t.* to edit (a manuscript, etc.) for publication, esp. for punctuation, spelling, etc. —**cop′y·ed′i·tor.**

cop·y·read·er (kop′ē rē′dər), *n.* a person who edits copy and writes headlines for a newspaper.

cop·y·right (kop′ē rīt′), *n.* 1. the exclusive right, granted by law for a certain number of years, to make and dispose of copies of a literary, musical, or artistic work. —*v.t.* 2. to secure a copyright on.

cop·y·writ·er (kop′ē rī′tər), *n.* a writer of copy, esp. for advertisements or publicity releases.

co·quette (kō ket′), *n., v.,* **-quet·ted,** **-quet·ting.** —*n.* 1. a girl or woman who flirts frivolously with men. —*v.i.* 2. Also, **co·quet.** to behave as a coquette or flirt. —**co·quet′ry** (kō′ki trē, kō ke′trē), *n.* —**co·quet′tish,** *adj.* —**co·quet′tish·ly,** *adv.*

Cor., Coroner.

cor., 1. corner. 2. cornet. 3. coroner. 4. corpus. 5. correct. 6. corrected. 7. correction. 8. correspondence. 9. correspondent. 10. corresponding.

cor·a·cle (kôr′ə kəl, kor′-), *n.* a small, round boat made of wickerwork covered with animal skin or canvas.

cor·al (kôr′əl, kor′-), *n.* 1. the hard skeleton secreted by certain tiny sea animals. 2. such skeletons collectively, forming reefs, islands, etc. 3. a light yellowish red or pink.

cor′al snake′, a venomous snake found chiefly in the New World tropics, often brilliantly marked with bands of red, yellow, and black.

cor·bel (kôr′bəl), *n.* any bracket, esp. one of brick or stone, usually of slight extent.

cord (kôrd), *n.* 1. a string or thin rope made of several strands twisted or woven together. 2. *Elect.* a small, flexible, insulated cable. 3. a ribbed fabric. 4. a rib on the surface of cloth. 5. a cordlike structure: *the spinal cord.* 6. a unit of volume used chiefly for fuel wood, equal to 128 cubic feet. —*v.t.* 7. to fasten with a cord or cords. 8. to pile (wood) in cords. —**cord′er,** *n.*

cord·age (kôr′dij), *n.* ropes, lines, etc., esp. with reference to the rigging of a vessel.

cor·dial (kôr′jəl), *adj.* 1. courteous and gracious. —*n.* 2. an aromatic alcoholic liqueur. 3. *Med.* a stimulating remedy. —**cor′dial′i·ty** (-jal′i tē), *n.* —**cor′dial·ly,** *adv.*

cor·dil·le·ra (kôr′dil yâr′ə, kôr dil′ər ə), *n.* a chain of mountains. —**cor′dil·le′ran,** *adj.*

cord·ite (kôr′dīt), *n.* a smokeless explosive powder composed of nitroglycerin, cellulose nitrate, and petrolatum.

cord·less (kôrd′lis), *adj.* operated by a self-contained, rechargeable power supply.

cor·do·ba (kôr′də bə), *n.* the monetary unit of Nicaragua.

cor·don (kôr′d°n), *n.* 1. a line of troops, police, etc., enclosing or guarding an area. 2. a cord or ribbon worn for ornament. —*v.t.* 3. to blockade with a cordon.

cor·do·van (kôr′də vən), *n.* a soft, smooth leather.

cor·du·roy (kôr′də roi′, kôr′də roi′), *n.* 1. a cotton-filling pile fabric with lengthwise ridges. 2. **corduroys,** trousers made of this fabric.

core (kôr, kōr), *n., v.,* **cored, cor·ing.** —*n.* 1. the central part of a fleshy fruit, containing the seeds. 2. the central or most essential part. —*v.t.* 3. to remove the core of (fruit). —**cor′er,** *n.*

CORE (kôr, kōr), *n.* Congress of Racial Equality.

core′ cur·ric′u·lum, *Educ.* a curriculum in which the subjects are correlated to a central theme.

co·re·spond·ent (kō′ri spon′dənt), *n.* a joint defendant, charged along with the respondent, as in cases of adultery.

co·ri·an·der (kôr′ē an′dər, kōr′-), *n.* a plant bearing seeds and seedlike fruit used in cookery and medicine.

Cor·inth (kôr′inth, kor′-), *n.* an ancient city in Greece.

cork (kôrk), *n.* **1.** the outer bark of an oak of Mediterranean countries, used for making stoppers, floats, etc. **2.** Also called **cork′ oak′.** the tree itself. **3.** something made of cork, as a stopper or float. —*v.t.* **4.** to stop with a cork. —**cork′y,** *adj.*

cork·er (kôr′kər), *n. Slang.* someone or something of astonishing or excellent quality.

cork·ing (kôr′kiṅg), *Informal.* —*adj.* **1.** excellent or fine. —*adv.* **2.** very: *a corking good time.*

cork·screw (kôrk′skrōō′), *n.* **1.** an augerlike, spiral instrument for drawing corks from bottles. —*adj.* **2.** spiral or winding. —*v.t., v.i.* **3.** to twist or wind.

corm (kôrm), *n.* a fleshy, bulblike base of a stem, as in the crocus.

cor·mo·rant (kôr′mər ənt), *n.* a voracious seabird having a long neck.

corn¹ (kôrn), *n.* **1.** a tall, annual cereal plant having a jointed, solid stem and bearing the kernels on large ears. **2.** the kernels, used as food. **3.** the ears. **4.** the edible seed of certain other cereal plants, esp. wheat in England and oats in Scotland. **5.** *Slang.* old-fashioned, trite, or sentimental material. —*v.t.* **6.** to preserve and season with brine.

corn² (kôrn), *n.* a small, hard thickening of skin, formed esp. on the toes or feet.

corn·ball (kôrn′bôl′), *adj. Slang.* corny.

corn′ bread′, a bread made of cornmeal.

corn·cob (kôrn′kob′), *n.* the woody core in which the grains of an ear of corn are embedded.

corn·crib (kôrn′krib′), *n.* a ventilated structure for the storage of unhusked corn.

cor·ne·a (kôr′nē ə), *n.* the transparent anterior part of the external coat of the eye covering the iris and the pupil. —**cor′ne·al,** *adj.*

corn′ ear′worm (ēr′wûrm′), *n.* a moth whose larvae are highly destructive to crops of corn.

cor·ne·ous (kôr′nē əs), *adj.* consisting of a horny substance.

cor·ner (kôr′nər), *n.* **1.** the meeting place of two converging lines or surfaces. **2.** the angle converged. **3.** the point where two streets meet. **4.** a narrow, secluded place. **5.** an awkward position, esp. one from which escape is impossible. **6.** a monopolizing of the supply of a stock or commodity to permit control of price. **7.** region or part: *from every corner of the empire.* **8. cut corners,** to reduce costs or care in execution. —*v.t.* **9.** to place

in or drive into a corner. **10.** to gain control of (a stock, commodity, etc.). —*v.i.* **11.** (of an automobile) to turn, esp. at a relatively high speed. —**cor′nered,** *adj.*

cor·ner·stone (kôr′nər stōn′), *n.* **1.** a stone uniting two masonry walls at an intersection. **2.** a stone representing the starting place in the construction of a building. **3.** something essential or basic.

cor·net (kôr net′), *n.* a valved wind instrument of the trumpet family. —**cor·net′ist,** *n.*

corn′ flour′, *Brit.* cornstarch.

corn·flow·er (kôrn′flou′ər), *n.* a composite plant having blue to white flowers.

cor·nice (kôr′nis), *n.* a projecting horizontal feature located at or near the top of an architectural composition.

corn·meal (kôrn′mēl′), *n.* meal made of corn.

corn′ pone′, *Southern U.S.* corn bread, esp. of a plain kind.

corn′ snow′, *Skiing.* snow in the form of small pellets produced by alternate melting and freezing.

corn·stalk (kôrn′stôk′), *n.* the stalk or stem of corn.

corn·starch (kôrn′stärch′), *n.* a starchy flour made from corn and used for thickening gravies and sauces.

corn′ sug′ar, dextrose.

corn′ syr′up, the syrup prepared from corn.

cor·nu·co·pi·a (kôr′nē kō′pē ə), *n.* **1.** *Class. Myth.* a goat's horn containing food, drink, etc., in endless supply. **2.** an abundant supply. [< LL = L *cornu* horn + *cōpiae* of plenty] —**cor′nu·co′pi·an,** *adj.* — **cor·nu·co·pi·ate** (kôr′nə kō′pē it), *adj.*

corn·y (kôr′nē), *adj.,* **corn·i·er, corn·i·est.** *Informal.* old-fashioned, trite, or sentimental.

co·rol·la (kə rol′ə), *n.* the internal envelope of floral leaves of a flower.

cor·ol·lar·y (kôr′ə ler′ē, kor′-), *n., pl.* **-lar·ies. 1.** a proposition that is incidentally proved in proving another proposition. **2.** a consequence or result.

co·ro·na (kə rō′nə), *n., pl.* **-nas, -nae** (-nē). **1.** a white or colored circle or set of concentric circles seen around a luminous body, esp. the sun or moon. **2.** a crownlike part. **3.** *Elec.* a discharge, frequently luminous, at the surface of a conductor.

cor·o·nach (kôr′ə nəKH, kor′-), *n.* (in Scotland and Ireland) a dirge.

cor·o·nal (kôr′ə nəl, kor′-), *n.* a circlet, esp. of precious metals.

cor·o·nar·y (kôr′ə ner′ē, kor′-), *adj.,
n., pl.* **-nar·ies.** —*adj.* **1.** pertaining
to the arteries that supply the heart
tissues and originate in the root
of the aorta. **2.** of the human
heart, with respect to health. —*n.*
3. See **coronary thrombosis.**

cor′onary throm·bo′sis, a coronary
occlusion in which there is blockage
of a coronary arterial branch by a
blood clot within the vessel.

cor·o·na·tion (kôr′ə nā′shən, kor′-),
n. the act or ceremony of crowning
a monarch.

cor·o·ner (kôr′ə nər, kor′-), *n.* a
public official whose chief function
is to investigate any death not
clearly resulting from natural causes.

cor·o·net (kôr′ə nit, -net′, kor′-), *n.*
1. a small crown worn by peers or
peeresses. **2.** a crownlike ornament
for the head.

corp., **1.** corporal. **2.** corporation.

corpn., corporation.

cor·po·ra (kôr′pər ə), *n.* pl. of
corpus.

cor·po·ral[1] (kôr′pər əl, -prəl), *adj.* of
or affecting the human body.

cor·po·ral[2] (kôr′pər əl, -prəl), *n.* a
noncommissioned officer ranking
just below a sergeant, as in the
U.S. Army.

cor′poral pun′ishment, bodily punishment, as flogging.

cor·po·rate (kôr′pər it, -prit), *adj.*
1. forming a corporation. **2.** of or
belonging to a corporation. **3.**
united into one. —**cor′po·rate·ly,**
adv.

cor·po·ra·tion (kôr′pə rā′shən), *n.*
1. an association of individuals,
created by and existing as an
entity with powers and liabilities
independent of those of its members. **2.** such a body created for
political purposes and to act as a
government agency.

cor·po·re·al (kôr pôr′ē əl, -pōr′-), *adj.*
1. of the nature of the physical
body. **2.** material or tangible. —**cor-
po′re·al′i·ty,** *n.* —**cor·po′re·al·ly,**
adv.

corps (kôr, kōr), *n., pl.* **corps** (kōrz,
kôrz). **1.** a military organization consisting of officers and enlisted persons or of officers alone. **2.** an army
unit consisting of two or more divisions and other troops. **3.** a group of
persons associated or acting together.

corpse (kôrps), *n.* a dead body,
usually of a human being.

corps·man (kôr′mən, kōr′-), *n., pl.*
-men. an enlisted person in the
medical corps who accompanies
troops into battle to give first aid,
etc.

cor·pu·lence (kôr′pyə ləns), *n.* fleshy
fatness. Also, **cor′pu·len·cy.** —**cor′-
pu·lent,** *adj.* —**cor′pu·lent·ly,** *adv.*

cor·pus (kôr′pəs), *n., pl.* **-po·ra**
(-pər ə). **1.** a large or complete
collection of writings. **2.** *Anat.* a
body or part having a special function. **3.** *Facetious.* the body of a
human or animal, esp. when dead.

Cor·pus Chris·ti (kôr′pəs kris′tē), a
seaport in S Texas.

cor·pus·cle (kôr′pə səl, -pus əl), *n.* **1.**
a cell, esp. a blood cell. **2.** a minute
body forming a distinct part of an
organism. **3.** any minute particle.
Also, **cor′pus·cule** (kôr pus′kyool). —
cor·pus·cu·lar (kôr pus′kyə lər), *adj.*

cor·pus de·lic·ti (kôr′pəs di lik′tī),
the basic element of a crime, as, in
murder, the death of the murdered
person.

corr., 1. corrected. **2.** correction. **3.**
correspond. **4.** correspondence. **5.**
correspondent. **6.** corresponding.

cor·ral (kə ral′), *n., v.,* **-ralled,
-ral·ing.** —*n.* **1.** an enclosure or
pen for horses, cattle, etc. **2.** an
enclosure of wagons for defense.
—*v.t.* **3.** to confine in a corral. **4.**
Informal. to seize or capture.

cor·rect (kə rekt′), *v.t.* **1.** to set or
make right. **2.** to point out or mark
the errors in. **3.** to rebuke or
punish. **4.** to counteract the operation of (something hurtful). —*adj.*
5. free from error or fault. **6.** in
accordance with an acknowledged
or accepted standard. —**cor·rect′a-
ble,** *adj.* —**cor·rec′tive,** *adj., n.* —
correct′ly, *adv.* —**cor·rect′ness,** *n.*
—**Syn. 5.** accurate, appropriate, exact, faultless.

cor·rec·tion (kə rek′shən), *n.* **1.** the
act of correcting. **2.** something
substituted for what is wrong. **3.**
punishment or chastisement. **4.** a
quantity applied to increase accuracy. —**cor·rec′tion·al,** *adj.*

correl., correlative.

cor·re·late (kôr′ə lāt′, kor′-), *v.t.,
v.i.,* **-lat·ed, -lat·ing.** **1.** to be in or
bring into mutual or reciprocal relation.

cor·re·la·tion (kôr′ə lā′shən, kor′-),
n. **1.** mutual relation of two or
more things, parts, etc. **2.** the act
or state of correlating or being
correlated.

cor·rel·a·tive (kə rel′ə tiv), *adj.* **1.**
so related that each implies the
other. **2.** *Gram.* complementing one
another, as *either* and *or.* —*n.* **3.**
either of two things, as two terms,
that are correlative. **4.** a correlative
expression.

cor·re·spond (kôr′i spond′, kor′-),
v.i. **1.** to be in agreement or conformity. **2.** to be similar or analogous. **3.** to communicate by exchange of letters. —**cor′re·spond′-
ing,** *adj.* —**cor′re·spond′ing·ly,** *adv.*

cor·re·spond·ence (kôr′i spon′dəns, kor′-), *n.* **1.** communication by exchange of letters. **2.** letters between correspondents. **3.** conformity or similarity.

cor·re·spond·ent (kôr′i spon′dənt, kor′-), *n.* **1.** a person who communicates by letters. **2.** a person employed, as by a newspaper, periodical, etc. to contribute news, articles, etc., regularly from a distant place. **3.** a thing that corresponds to something else. —*adj.* **4.** conforming or similar.

cor·ri·dor (kôr′i dər, -dôr′, kor′-), *n.* **1.** a long main passage in a building providing access to separate rooms. **2.** a main railroad route linking cities. **3.** a narrow tract of land forming an outlet through foreign territory.

cor·ri·gen·dum (kôr′i jen′dəm, kor′-), *n., pl.* **-da** (-də). **1.** an error in print. **2.** corrigenda, a list of corrections of errors in a publication.

cor·ri·gi·ble (kôr′i jə bəl, kor′-), *adj.* capable of being corrected or improved.

cor·rob·o·rate (kə rob′ə rāt′), *v.t.,* **-rat·ed, -rat·ing.** to support with additional proof. —**cor·rob′o·ra′tion,** *n.* —**cor·rob′o·ra′tive** (kə rob′ə rā′tiv, -ər ə tiv), **cor·rob·o·ra·to·ry** (kə rob′ər ə tôr′e, -tōr′e), *adj.* —**cor·rob′o·ra′tor,** *n.*

cor·rode (kə rōd′), *v.,* **-rod·ed, -rod·ing.** —*v.t.* **1.** to eat away gradualy, esp. by chemical action. —*v.i.* **2.** to become corroded. —**cor·rod′er,** *n.* —**cor·rod′i·bil′i·ty,** *n.* —**cor·rod′i·ble,** *adj.* —**cor·ro′sion,** *n.* —**cor·ro′sive,** *adj.,* *n.* —**cor·ro′sive·ly,** *adv.*

cor·ru·gate (kôr′ə gāt′, kor′-), *v.t., v.i.,* **-gat·ed, -gat·ing.** to bend into folds or alternate furrows and ridges. —**cor′ru·gat′ed,** *adj.* —**cor′ru·ga′tion,** *n.* —**cor′ru·ga′tor,** *n.*

cor·rupt (kə rupt′), *adj.* **1.** guilty of dishonest practices, as bribery. **2.** debased in character. **3.** decayed or putrid. —*v.t., v.i.* **4.** to make or become corrupt. —**cor·rupt′i·ble,** *adj.* —**cor·rup′tive,** *adj.* —**cor·rupt′ly,** *adv.* —**cor·rup′tion,** *n.*

cor·sage (kôr säzh′), *n.* a small bouquet worn at the waist or on the shoulder by a woman.

cor·sair (kôr′sâr), *n.* a pirate or pirate vessel, esp. formerly of Barbary, a region in N Africa.

cor·set (kôr′sit), *n.* a closefitting and usually boned undergarment, worn by women, to shape and support the body.

cor·tege (kôr tezh′, -tāzh′), *n.* **1.** a procession, esp. a funeral procession. **2.** a group of attendants. Also, **cor·tège.**

cor·tex (kôr′teks), *n., pl.* **-ti·ces** (-ti sēz′). **1.** the outer portion of a stem between the epidermis and the vascular tissue. **2. a.** the rind of an organ, as the outer wall of the kidney. **b.** the layer of gray matter that covers much of the surface of the brain. —**cor′ti·cal,** *adj.* —**cor′ti·cal·ly,** *adv.*

cor·ti·sone (kôr′ti sōn′, -zōn′), *n.* a hormone active in carbohydrate metabolism and used chiefly in the treatment of arthritis and certain allergies.

co·run·dum (kə run′dəm), *n.* a common mineral notable for its hardness: transparent varieties used as gems, other varieties, as abrasives.

cor·us·cate (kôr′ə skāt′, kor′-), *v.i.,* **-cat·ed, -cat·ing.** to emit vivid flashes of light, as metal. —**cor′us·ca′tion,** *n.*

cor·vette (kôr vet′), *n.* **1.** a warship of the old sailing class. **2.** *Brit.* a small, lightly armed, fast vessel used mostly for convoy escort.

co·ry·za (kə rī′zə), *n.* acute inflammation of the mucous membrane of the nasal cavities.

C.O.S., 1. cash on shipment. **2.** Chief of Staff.

co·sig·na·to·ry (kō sig′nə tōr′e, -tôr′e), *n., pl.* **-ries.** a person or party who signs a document jointly with another or others.

co·sign·er (kō′sī′nər, kō′sī′), *n.* **1.** a joint signer of a negotiable instrument, esp. a promissory note. **2.** cosignatory.

cos·met·ic (koz met′ik), *n.* **1.** a powder, lotion, or other preparation for beautifying the skin, hair, nails, etc. —*adj.* **2.** imparting beauty. **3.** correcting physical defects or injuries: *cosmetic surgery.* —**cos·met′i·cal·ly,** *adv.*

cos·me·tol·o·gy (koz′mi tol′ə jē), *n.* the art of applying cosmetics. —**cos′me·tol′o·gist,** *n.*

cos·mic (koz′mik), *adj.* **1.** of the cosmos. **2.** vast or grandiose. Also, **cos′mi·cal.** —**cos′mi·cal·ly,** *adv.*

cos′mic ray′, a radiation of extremely high penetrating power that originates in outer space and consists partly of high-energy atomic nuclei.

cos·mo·chem·is·try (koz′mə kem′i·strē), *n.* the science dealing with the occurrence and distribution of the chemical elements in the universe. —**cos′mo·chem′i·cal,** *adj.*

cos·mog·o·ny (koz mog′ə nē), *n., pl.* **-nies.** a theory of the origin and development of the universe. —**cos′mo·gon′ic** (-mə gon′ik), *adj.* —**cos·mog′o·nist,** *n.*

cos·mol·o·gy (koz mol′ə jē), *n.* the study of the origin and general structure of the universe. **—cos·mo·log·i·cal** (koz′mə loj′i kəl), *adj.* **—cos·mol′o·gist,** *n.*

cos·mo·naut (koz′mə nôt′, -not′), *n.* an astronaut, esp. a Russian one.

cos·mop·o·lis (koz mop′ə lis), *n.* an internationally important city inhabited by many different peoples.

cos·mo·pol·i·tan (koz′mə pol′i t°n), *adj.* 1. not limited to just one part of the world. 2. free from local, provincial, or national ideas, prejudices, or attachments. **—n.** 3. Also, **cos·mop′o·lite** (-mop′ə līt′). a cosmopolitan person. **—cos′mo·pol′i·tan·ism,** *n.*

cos·mos (koz′məs, -mōs), *n., pl.* **-mos, -mos·es** for 2, 4. 1. the universe regarded as an orderly system. 2. a complete, orderly system. 3. order or harmony. 4. a composite plant cultivated for its showy flowers. [< Gk *kósmos* order, world, universe]

co·spon·sor (kō′spon′sər), *n.* 1. a joint sponsor, as of a legislative proposal. **—v.t.** 2. to be a co-sponsor of or for. **—co′spon′sor·ship′,** *n.*

Cos·sack (kos′ak, -ək), *n.* a member of various tribes of warriors living chiefly in SE Russia and forming an elite corps of horsemen in czarist Russia.

cost (kôst, kost), *n., v.,* **cost, cost·ing. —n.** 1. the price paid to acquire or accomplish anything. 2. a sacrifice or penalty. 3. outlay of money, trouble, etc. 4. at all costs, by any means necessary. **—v.t.** 5. to require the payment of. 6. to result in the loss or injury of.

co-star (*n.* kō′stär′; *v.* kō′stär′), *n., v.,* **-starred, -star·ring. —n.** 1. an actor or actress who shares star billing with another. **—v.t., v.i.** 2. to feature or appear as a co-star.

Cos·ta Ri·ca (kos′tə rē′kə, kô′stə, kō′-), a country in Central America, between Panama and Nicaragua. **—Cos′ta Ri′can.**

cos·tive (kos′tiv, kô′stiv), *adj.* suffering from constipation.

cost·ly (kôst′lē, kost′-), *adj.,* **-li·er, -li·est.** 1. costing very much. 2. resulting in great detriment: *a costly mistake.* 3. of great value. **—cost′li·ness,** *n.* **—Syn.** 1. dear, expensive.

cost′ of liv′ing, the average cost of food, clothing, and other necessities paid by a person, family, etc.

cost-plus (kôst′plus′, kost′-), *n.* the cost of production plus an agreed rate of profit.

cos·tume (*n.* kos′tōōm, -tyōōm; *v.* ko stōōm′, -styōōm′), *n., v.,* **-tumed, -tum·ing. —n.** 1. a style of dress, esp. that typical of a nation, social class, or historical period. 2. a set of garments for wear at a single time. **—v.t.** 3. to furnish with a costume. **—cos·tum·er** (ko stōō′mər, -styōō′-), *n.* **—cos·tum·i·er** (ko stōō′mē ər, -styōō′-), *n.*

cos′tume jew′elry, jewelry made of nonprecious metals, often set with imitation stones.

co·sy (kō′zē), *adj.,* **-si·er, -si·est,** *n., pl.* **-sies.** cozy. **—co′si·ly,** *adv.* **—co′si·ness,** *n.*

cot[1] (kot), *n.* a light portable bed, esp. one of canvas stretched on a frame.

cot[2] (kot), *n. Literary.* a cottage

cote (kōt), *n.* a shelter for sheep, pigs, pigeons, etc.

co·te·rie (kō′tə rē), *n.* a group of people who associate closely because of common interests. [< F: association of tenant farmers]

co·ter·mi·nous (kō tûr′mə nəs), *adj.* conterminous.

co·til·lion (kō til′yən, kə-), *n.* 1. a formalized dance in which a head couple leads the other dancers through elaborate figures. 2. a formal ball given esp. for debutantes.

cot·tage (kot′ij), *n.* a small, one-story house, esp. one in the country. **—cot′tag·er,** *n.*

cot′tage cheese′, a loose, white, mild-flavored cheese made from skim-milk curds.

cot·ter[1] (kot′ər), *n.* a pin, wedge, or key fitted into an opening to hold parts together.

cot·ter[2] (kot′ər), *n. Scot.* a farmer occupying a small plot of land. Also, **cot′tar.**

cot′ter pin′, a cotter having a split end that is spread after being pushed through a hole.

cot·ton (kot′°n), *n.* 1. a soft, white, downy substance consisting of the fibers attached to the seeds of certain warm-area plants, used in making fabrics, thread, etc. 2. cloth, thread, a garment, etc., of cotton. **—v.i.** 3. cotton to, *Informal.* a. to begin to like. b. to approve of. **—cot′ton·y,** *adj.*

cot′ton gin′, a machine for separating the fibers of cotton from the seeds.

cot·ton·mouth (kot′°n mouth′), *n., pl.* **-mouths** (-mouths′, -mouthz′). a venomous snake of swamps of the southeastern U.S.

cot·ton·seed (kot′°n sēd′), *n., pl.* **-seeds, -seed.** the seed of the cotton plant, yielding an oil used in cooking, medicine, etc.

cot·ton·tail (kot′°n tāl′), *n.* a North American rabbit having a fluffy white tail.

cot·ton·wood (kot′ən wŏŏd′), *n.* an American poplar having cottonlike tufts on the seeds.

cot·y·le·don (kot′ə lēd′ən), *n.* the primary leaf of the embryo of seed plants. —**cot′y·le′don·al, cot′-y·le′don·ar′y** (-er′ē), **cot′y·le′don·ous,** *adj.*

couch (kouch), *n.* **1.** a long piece of furniture for sitting or reclining on. —*v.t.* **2.** to express in a special manner. —**couch′er,** *n.*

couch·ant (kou′chənt), *adj. Heraldry.* lying on its stomach with its legs pointed forward.

cou·gar (kŏŏ′gər), *n.,* pl. **-gars, -gar.** a large, tawny cat of North and South America.

cough (kôf, kof), *v.i.* **1.** to expel air from the lungs suddenly with a harsh noise. —*v.t.* **2.** to expel by coughing: *to cough up a fish bone.* —*n.* **3.** the act or sound of coughing. **4.** an illness characterized by frequent coughing.

could (kŏŏd; *unstressed* kəd), *v.* **1.** pt. of **can[1]. 2.** (used as an auxiliary verb to express politeness [*Could you come?*] or doubt [*It could not be true*].)

could·n't (kŏŏd′ənt), contraction of *could not.*

cou·lee (kŏŏ′lē), *n.* **1.** *Western U.S.* a deep ravine. **2.** a small valley. **3.** a small intermittent stream.

cou·lomb (kŏŏ′lom, -lōm), *n.* a unit of electric charge, equal to the quantity of charge transferred in one second by a constant current of one ampere. [after C.A. de Coulomb, 1736–1806, Fr. physicist]

coun·cil (koun′səl), *n.* **1.** an assembly of persons convened for deliberation or advice. **2.** a group chosen to act in an advisory or legislative capacity.

coun·cil·man (koun′səl mən), *n.,* pl. **-men.** a member of a council, esp. the legislative body of a city. — **coun′cil·wom′an,** *n. fem.*

coun·ci·lor (koun′sə lər, -slər), *n.* a member of a council. Also, *esp. Brit.,* **coun′cil·lor.**

coun·sel (koun′səl), *n., v.,* **-seled, -sel·ing** *or* **-selled, -sel·ling.** —*n.* **1.** advice given in directing the judgment of another. **2.** interchange of opinions as to future procedure. **3.** a lawyer or lawyers. **4.** deliberate purpose. —*v.t., v.i.* **5.** to give advice (to). **6.** to recommend (a plan, etc.).

coun·se·lor (koun′sə lər), *n.* **1.** a person who counsels. **2.** a lawyer, esp. a trial lawyer. Also, *esp. Brit.,* **coun′sel·lor.**

count[1] (kount), *v.t.* **1.** to check over one by one to determine the total number. **2.** to calculate or compute. **3.** to take into account. **4.** to consider or regard. —*v.i.* **5.** to list or name numerals in order. **6.** to have a specified numerical value. **7.** to have merit or value: *Every bit of help counts.* **8.** count on or upon, to depend or rely on. —*n.* **9.** the act of counting. **10.** the total. **11.** an accounting. **12.** *Law.* a distinct charge in an indictment. —**count′a·ble,** *adj.*

count[2] (kount), *n.* a European nobleman equivalent in rank to an English earl.

count·down (kount′doun′), *n.* the backward counting in fixed time units from the initiation of a project, as a rocket launching, with firing designated as zero.

coun·te·nance (koun′tᵊnəns), *n., v.,* **-nanced, -nanc·ing.** —*n.* **1.** appearance, esp. the expression of the face. **2.** the face or facial features. **3.** approval or support. —*v.t.* **4.** to tolerate or approve.

count·er[1] (koun′tər), *n.* **1.** a long table on which goods can be shown, business transacted, food served, etc. **2.** anything used in keeping account, as a disk of wood, esp. as used in some games.

count·er[2] (koun′tər), *n.* a device for counting revolutions of a wheel, items produced, etc.

coun·ter[3] (koun′tər), *adv.* **1.** in the reverse direction. **2.** in opposition. —*adj.* **3.** opposite or contrary. —*n.* **4.** something opposite or contrary to something else. —*v.t., v.i.* **5.** to act in opposition (to).

counter-, a combining form meaning: **a.** against: *countermand.* **b.** complementary: *counterbalance.* **c.** duplicate: *counterfeit.*

coun·ter·act (koun′tər akt′), *v.t.* to act in opposition to. —**coun′ter·ac′-tion,** *n.* —**coun′ter·ac′tive,** *adj.*

coun·ter·at·tack (*n.* koun′tər ə tak′; *v.* koun′tər ə tak′), *n.* **1.** an attack made as an offset to another attack. —*v.t., v.i.* **2.** to make a counterattack (against).

coun·ter·bal·ance (*n.* koun′tər bal′əns; *v.* koun′tər bal′əns), *n., v.,* **-anced, -anc·ing.** —*n.* **1.** a weight balancing another weight. —*v.t., v.i.* **2.** to act as a counterbalance (to).

coun·ter·claim (*n.* koun′tər klām′; *v.* koun′tər klām′), *n.* **1.** a claim made to offset another claim, esp. in law. —*v.t., v.i.* **2.** to make a counterclaim (against or of).

coun·ter·clock·wise (koun′tər klok′-wīz′), *adj., adv.* in a direction opposite to that of the normal rotation of the hands of a clock.

coun·ter·cul·ture (koun'tər kul'chər), *n.* the culture of those people, esp. among the young, who reject the established values and behavior of society.

coun·ter·es·pi·o·nage (koun'tər es'pē ə näzh', -nij), *n.* the detection and frustration of enemy espionage.

coun·ter·feit (koun'tər fit), *adj.* 1. made in imitation with intent to be passed off as genuine. 2. pretended or unreal. —*n.* 3. an imitation intended to be passed off as genuine. —*v.t., v.i.* 4. to make a counterfeit, as of money. 5. to feign or dissemble. —**coun'ter·feit'er,** *n.* —**Syn.** 1. bogus, fake, sham, spurious.

coun·ter·in·sur·gen·cy (koun'tər in·sûr'jən sē), *n.* a program or an act of combating guerrilla warfare and subversion.

coun·ter·in·tel·li·gence (koun'tər in·tel'i jəns), *n.* the activity of an intelligence service employed in thwarting the efforts of an enemy's intelligence agents.

count·er·man (koun'tər man'), *n.* a person who waits on customers from behind a counter, as in a cafeteria.

coun·ter·mand (koun'tər mand', -mänd'), *v.t.* 1. to revoke or cancel (a command, etc.). 2. to recall or stop by a contrary order.

coun·ter·meas·ure (koun'tər mezh'ər), *n.* an opposing or retaliatory measure.

coun·ter·of·fen·sive (koun'tər ə fen'siv), *n.* an attack against an attacking enemy force.

coun·ter·pane (koun'tər pān'), *n. Obsolesc.* a bedspread.

coun·ter·part (koun'tər pärt'), *n.* 1. a person or thing closely resembling another, esp. in function. 2. *Law.* a duplicate or copy of an indenture.

coun·ter·point (koun'tər point'), *n.* 1. the art of combining melodies. 2. the pattern resulting from the combining of individual melodic lines.

coun·ter·poise (koun'tər poiz'), *n., v.,* **-poised, -pois·ing.** —*n.* 1. a counterbalancing weight. 2. any equal and opposing power or force. 3. balance. —*v.t.* 4. to balance by an opposing weight.

coun·ter·pro·duc·tive (koun'tər prə·duk'tiv), *adj.* resulting in something contrary to what is intended.

coun·ter·rev·o·lu·tion (koun'tər rev'ə·lōo'shən), *n.* a revolution against a government recently established by a revolution. —**coun'ter·rev·o·lu'tion·ar'y,** *n., adj.*

coun·ter·sign (*n., v.* koun'tər sīn'; *v. also* koun'tər sīn'), *n.* 1. a signature added to another signature, esp. for authentication. 2. a secret sign that must be given in order to pass through a guarded area. —*v.t.* 3. to sign (a document that has been signed by someone else), esp. in authentication. —**coun'ter·sig'na·ture** (-sig'nə chər), *n.*

coun·ter·sink (koun'tər singk'), *v.,* **-sank, -sunk, -sink·ing,** *n.* —*v.t.* 1. to enlarge the upper part of (a hole) to receive the head of a screw, bolt, etc. 2. to cause (the head of a screw, bolt, etc.) to sink into such a hole. —*n.* 3. a tool for countersinking a hole.

coun·ter·spy (koun'tər spī'), *n.* a person who spies against spies of an enemy nation.

coun·ter·ten·or (koun'tər ten'ər), *n.* an adult male with a voice higher than that of a tenor.

coun·ter·vail (koun'tər vāl'), *v.t.* to oppose with equal power or effect.

coun·ter·weight (koun'tər wāt'), *n.* a weight that balances another.

coun·tess (koun'tis), *n.* 1. the wife or widow of a count or earl. 2. a woman having the rank of a count or earl in her own right.

count'ing house', *Rare.* a place used by the accounting department of a business.

count·less (kount'lis), *adj.* too many to count.

coun·tri·fied (kun'tri fīd'), *adj.* rustic or rural in appearance, conduct, etc. Also, **coun'try·fied'.**

coun·try (kun'trē), *n., pl.* **-tries,** *adj.* —*n.* 1. territory demarcated by specific conditions: *mountainous country.* 2. the territory of a nation. 3. a state or nation. 4. the people of a district, state, or nation. 5. the land of one's birth or citizenship. 6. rural districts. —*adj.* 7. rural or rustic. 8. of or pertaining to country music.

coun'try and wes'tern. See **country music.**

coun'try club', a suburban club with facilities for outdoor sports, social activities, etc.

coun'try dance', an English dance in which the dancers face each other in two rows.

coun·try·man (kun'trē mən), *n.* 1. a native or inhabitant of one's own country. 2. an inhabitant of a rural area. —**coun'try·wom'an,** *n. fem.*

coun'try mu'sic, music derived from folk and cowboy songs, spirituals, and blues.

coun·try·side (kun'trē sīd'), *n.* 1. a rural section. 2. its inhabitants.

coun·ty (koun'tē), *n., pl.* **-ties.** the largest administrative division of a state or nation.

coup (kōō), *n., pl.* **coups** (kōōz). 1. a highly successful stroke or move. 2. See **coup d'état.**

coup de grâce (kōōd° gräs′), *pl.* **coups de grâce** (kōōd° gräs′). *French.* **1.** a deathblow, esp. one delivered to end suffering. **2.** any decisive stroke.

coup d'é·tat (kōō′ dā tä′), *pl.* **coups d'é·tat** (kōōz′ dā tä′). a sudden overthrow of government by force.

coupe (kōōp), *n.* a closed, two-door automobile. Also, **cou·pé** (kōō pā′).

cou·ple (kup′əl), *n., v.,* **-pled, -pling.** —*n.* **1.** a combination of two of the same kind. **2.** a man and woman considered together, as a married pair, lovers, etc. **3.** a couple of, *Informal.* a few. —*v.t.*, *v.i.* **4.** to join or link together. —**cou′pler,** *n.*

cou·plet (kup′lit), *n.* a pair of successive rhyming lines of verse.

cou·pling (kup′ling), *n.* **1.** the act of coupling. **2.** a device for joining two things or parts together.

cou·pon (kōō′pon, kyōō′-), *n.* **1.** a certificate or ticket entitling the holder to a gift or discount, or for use as an order blank, a contest entry form, etc. **2.** one of a number of small certificates calling for periodic interest payments on a bond.

cour·age (kûr′ij, kur′-), *n.* the ability to face difficulty or danger with firmness and without fear. —**cou·ra·geous** (kə rā′jəs), *adj.* —**cou·ra′geous·ly,** *adv.* —**cou·ra′geous·ness,** *n.*

cou·ri·er (kûr′ē ər, kŏŏr′-), *n.* **1.** a messenger bearing diplomatic messages, important reports, etc. **2.** *Brit.* a tour escort or arranger.

course (kōrs, kôrs), *n., v.,* **coursed, cours·ing.** —*n.* **1.** advance in a particular direction. **2.** a direction or route taken. **3.** a path, route, or channel. **4.** regular or natural order of events. **5.** conduct or behavior. **6.** a particular manner of proceeding. **7.** a systematized series. **8.** a program of instruction, as in a university. **9.** a part of a meal served at one time. **10. in due course,** at some time. **11. of course,** without doubt. —*v.t.* **12.** to run through or over. **13.** to hunt (game) with dogs. —*v.i.* **14.** to run or move swiftly. **15.** to hunt game with dogs.

cours·er (kōr′sər, kôr′-), *n. Literary.* a swift horse.

court (kōrt, kôrt), *n.* **1.** an open area surrounded by buildings, walls, etc. **2.** a short street. **3.** a smooth, level quadrangle on which to play tennis, handball, basketball, etc. **4.** a royal palace. **5.** a sovereign with the councilors and retinue. **6.** a formal assembly held by a sovereign. **7.** homage paid to a king. **8.** *Literary.* wooing or courtship: *to pay court to a lady.* **9.** *Law.* **a.** a place where justice is administered. **b.** a judicial body duly constituted for the hearing and determination of cases. **c.** a session of a judicial body. **10. out of court,** without a legal trial. —*v.t.* **11.** to try to win the favor of. **12.** to woo. **13.** to act in such a manner as to lead to. —*v.i.* **14.** to woo a person. —**court′er,** *n.*

cour·te·ous (kûr′tē əs), *adj.* having or showing good manners. —**cour′te·ous·ly,** *adv.* —**cour′te·ous·ness,** *n.*

cour·te·san (kôr′ti zən, kôr′-, kûr′-), *n.* (formerly) a prostitute associating with men of nobility or wealth. Also **cour′te·zan.**

cour·te·sy (kûr′ti sē), *n., pl.* **-sies. 1.** polite behavior. **2.** a courteous act or expression.

court·house (kōrt′hous′, kôrt′-), *n.* **1.** a building in which courts of law are held. **2.** a building housing government offices of a U.S. county.

cour·ti·er (kōr′tē ər, kôr′-), *n.* an attendant at a royal palace.

court·ly (kōrt′lē, kôrt′-), *adj.,* **-li·er, -li·est.** polite, refined, and elegant. —**court′li·ness,** *n.*

court-mar·tial (kōrt′mär′shəl, -mär′-, kôrt′-), *n., pl.* **courts-mar·tial, court-mar·tials,** *v.,* **-tialed, -tial·ing** or **-tialled, -tial·ling.** —*n.* **1.** a court of military personnel appointed to try offenses by members of the armed forces against military law. **2.** a trial by such a court. —*v.t.* **3.** to try by court-martial.

court·room (kōrt′rōōm′, -rŏŏm′, kôrt′-), *n.* a room in which sessions of a law court are held.

court·ship (kōrt′ship, kôrt′-), *n.* the act or period of courting or wooing a woman.

court·yard (kōrt′yärd′, kôrt′-), *n.* a court open to the sky, esp. one enclosed on all sides.

cous·in (kuz′ən), *n.* the child of an uncle or aunt.

cou·ture (kōō tōōr′), *n.* **1.** the occupation of a couturier. **2.** couturiers collectively.

cou·tu·ri·er (kōō tōōr′ē ā′, -ē ər, -tōōr′yā), *n., pl.* **-tu·riers** (-tōōr′ē āz′, -ē ərz, -tōōr′yāz). a person who designs, makes, and sells fashionable clothes for women. —**cou·tu′ri·ere** (-ər, -ē er′) *n. fem.*

co·va·lence (kō vā′ləns), *n.* the bond (**cova′lent bond′**) formed by the sharing of a pair of electrons by two atoms. —**co·va′lent,** *adj.* —**co·va′lent·ly,** *adv.*

cove (kōv), *n.* a small recess in the shoreline.

cov·en (kuv′ən, kō′vən), *n.* an assembly of witches.

cov·e·nant (kuv′ə nənt), *n.* **1.** an agreement, usually formal, between two or more persons. **2.** the conditional promises made to humanity by God, as revealed in the Scripture. —*v.i.* **3.** to enter into a covenant. —*v.t.* **4.** to promise by covenant.

cov·er (kuv′ər), *v.t.* **1.** to place something over or upon. **2.** to extend over. **3.** to clothe. **4.** to shelter or protect. **5.** to hide from view. **6.** to aim at. **7.** to include, deal with, or provide for. **8.** to offset (a loss). **9.** to insure against risk or loss. **10.** to buy (shares of stock sold short) in order to return ones previously borrowed. **11.** to gather news of. **12.** to travel over. —*v.i. Informal.* **13.** to spread over. **14.** to provide an alibi. **15.** cover up, **a.** to enfold completely. **b.** to keep from being known. —*n.* **16.** something that covers, as the lid of a vessel or the binding of a book. **17.** protection, shelter, or concealment. **18.** anything that veils or shuts from sight. **19.** a set of a knife, fork, napkin, etc., for a person. **20.** an envelope or outer wrapping for mail. **21. take cover,** to seek shelter or safety. **22. under cover,** in secrecy. —**cov′er·er,** *n.*

cov·er·age (kuv′ər ij), *n.* **1.** protection provided by an insurance policy against a risk. **2.** the reporting and publishing or broadcasting of news.

cov·er·all (kuv′ər ôl′), *n.* Often, **coveralls.** a one-piece work garment worn to protect other clothing.

cov′er charge′, a fee charged by a restaurant, nightclub, etc., for service.

cov′er crop′, a crop planted to keep soil from eroding, as during the winter.

cov′ered wag′on, a large wagon with a bonnetlike canvas top, esp. used by early American pioneers.

cov·er·ing (kuv′ər ing), *n.* something laid over a thing, as for concealment.

cov·er·let (kuv′ər lit), *n.* a bed quilt that does not cover the pillow.

cov′er sto′ry, an article in a magazine related to an illustration on its cover.

cov·ert (kō′vərt, kuv′ərt), *adj.* **1.** not openly and easily observable. **2.** *Archaic.* covered or sheltered. —*n.* **3.** a shelter or hiding place. **4.** a thicket giving shelter to wild animals or game. **5.** See **covert cloth.** —**cov′ert·ly,** *adv.* —**cov′ert·ness,** *n.* — Syn. **1.** hidden, secret.

cov′ert cloth′, a cotton, woolen, or worsted cloth of twill weave.

cov·er·up (kuv′ər up′), *n.* any action or other means of preventing investigation or exposure.

cov·et (kuv′it), *v.t., v.i.* to desire (another's property) wrongfully. —**cov′et·ous,** *adj.* —**cov′et·ous·ly,** *adv.* —**cov′et·ous·ness,** *n.*

cov·ey (kuv′ē), *n., pl.* **-eys.** a small flock of partridges or similar birds.

cow¹ (kou), *n.* **1.** the mature female of a bovine animal. **2.** the female of various other large animals, as the elephant, whale, etc.

cow² (kou), *v.t.* to frighten with threats, violence, etc.

cow·ard (kou′ərd), *n.* a person who lacks courage in facing danger, pain, etc. —**cow′ard·li·ness,** *n.* —**cow′ard·ly,** *adj., adv.*

cow·ard·ice (kou′ər dis), *n.* lack of courage to face danger, pain, etc.

cow·bird (kou′bûrd′), *n.* an American blackbird that lays its eggs in other birds' nests.

cow·boy (kou′boi′), *n.* a man, usually on horseback, who herds and tends cattle on a ranch, esp. in the western U.S. Also called **cow·hand** (kou′hand′). —**cow′girl′,** *n. fem.*

cow·catch·er (kou′kach′ər), *n.* a frame at the front of a locomotive, streetcar, etc., designed for clearing the track.

cow·er (kou′ər), *v.i.* to crouch in fear.

cow·hide (kou′hīd′), *n.* **1.** the hide of a cow. **2.** the leather made from it. **3.** a strong whip made of braided leather.

cowl (koul), *n.* **1.** a hooded garment worn by monks. **2.** the hood of this garment. **3.** the forward part of the automobile body supporting the rear of the hood and the windshield and housing the instrument panel.

cow·lick (kou′lik′), *n.* a tuft of hair that grows in a direction different from the rest.

cowl·ing (kou′ling), *n.* a streamlined housing for an aircraft engine.

cow·man (kou′mən), *n., pl.* **-men.** a cattle owner.

co-work·er (kō′wûr′kər, kō′wûr′-), *n.* a fellow worker.

cow·poke (kou′pōk′), *n. Slang.* a cowboy.

cow′ po′ny, a horse used by cowboys in herding cattle.

cow·pox (kou′poks′), *n.* an eruptive disease of cows that forms in small pustules containing a virus used in smallpox vaccine.

cow·punch·er (kou′pun′chər), *n. Informal.* a cowboy.

cow·rie (kou′rē), *n.* **1.** the highly polished, usually brightly colored shell of a marine gastropod of the tropics. **2.** the gastropod itself. Also, **cow′ry.**

cow·slip (kou'slip'), n. **1.** an English primrose having yellow flowers. **2.** See **marsh marigold.**

cox·comb (koks'kōm'), n. a conceited, foolish dandy.

cox·swain (kok'sən, -swān'), n. a person who steers a racing shell.

coy (koi), adj. **1.** falsely modest. **2.** artfully shy or reserved. —**coy'ly,** adv. —**coy'ness,** n.

coy·ote (kī'ōt, kī ō'tē), n., pl. **-tes, -te.** a carnivorous, wolflike mammal of western North America. [< Mex Sp < Amer Ind]

coy·pu (koi'pōō), n. a large, South American, aquatic rodent yielding the fur nutria.

coz·en (kuz'ən), v.t., v.i. Literary. to cheat or swindle. —**coz'en·age** (-nij), n. —**coz'en·er,** n.

co·zy (kō'zē), adj., **-zi·er, -zi·est,** n., pl. **-zies.** —adj. **1.** snugly warm and comfortable. —n. **2.** a padded covering for a teapot, etc., to retain the heat. —**co'zi·ly,** adv. —**co'zi·ness,** n.

cp., compare.

C.P. 1. Command Post. **2.** Common Prayer. **3.** Communist Party.

c.p., 1. candlepower. **2.** chemically pure.

C.P.A., See **certified public accountant.**

cpd., compound.

CPFF, cost plus fixed fee.

CPI, consumer price index.

cpl., corporal.

CPO, See **chief petty officer.**

CPR, cardiopulmonary resuscitation.

cps, cycles per second. Also, **c.p.s.**

CQ, Mil. charge of quarters.

Cr, chromium.

cr., 1. credit. **2.** creditor. **3.** crown.

crab¹ (krab), n. **1.** a crustacean having a short, broad, flattened body. **2. the Crab,** the zodiacal constellation or sign Cancer. —**crab'ber,** n.

crab² (krab), n., v., **crabbed, crabbing.** Informal. —n. **1.** an ill-tempered or grouchy person. —v.i. **2.** to complain. —v.t. **3.** to criticize. —**crab'ber,** n.

crab' ap'ple, a small, sour, wild apple.

crab·bed (krab'id), adj. **1.** grouchy and irritable. **2.** difficult to decipher, as handwriting. —**crab'bed·ness,** n.

crab·by (krab'ē), adj., **-bi·er, -bi·est.** crabbed (def. 1). —**crab'bi·ly,** adv. —**crab'bi·ness,** n.

crab' grass', an annual grass common as a weedy pest in lawns.

crab' louse', a louse that attacks the human pubic region or armpits.

crack (krak), v.i. **1.** to make a sudden, sharp sound, as in breaking or snapping. **2.** to break with a sudden, sharp sound. **3.** to break without complete separation of parts.

4. (of the voice) to break abruptly and discordantly. **5.** Chem. to decompose as a result of being subjected to heat. **6.** Informal. to succumb, as to torture. —v.t. **7.** to cause to make a sudden, sharp sound. **8.** to strike. **9.** to break without complete separation of parts. **10.** Informal. to break into (a safe, etc.). **11.** Informal. to decipher: to crack the code. **12.** to tell: to crack jokes. **13.** to subject to the process of cracking as in the distillation of petroleum. **14. crack down,** Informal. to take severe measures, esp. in enforcing laws. **15. cracked up to be,** Informal. alleged to be. **16. crack up, a.** Slang. to suffer a mental or emotional breakdown. **b.** to crash, as in a vehicle. **c.** to laugh or cause to laugh unrestrainedly. **17. get cracking,** Slang. to start. —n. **18.** a sudden, sharp noise. **19.** a resounding blow. **20.** a break without complete separation of parts. **21.** a slight opening. **22.** a broken tone of the voice. **23.** Informal. opportunity or try. **24.** Informal. a wisecrack. —adj. **25.** Informal. first-rate or excellent.

crack·down (krak'doun'), n. Informal. a severe enforcing of laws or regulations.

cracked (krakt), adj. **1.** broken or fractured. **2.** broken in tone, as the voice. **3.** Informal. mad or insane.

crack·er (krak'ər), n. **1.** a thin, crisp biscuit. **2.** a firecracker. **3.** Disparaging. one of a class of poor whites in parts of the southeastern U.S.

crack·er·jack (krak'ər jak'), Slang. —n. **1.** a person or thing of marked excellence. —adj. **2.** exceptionally fine.

crack·ing (krak'ing), n. (in the distillation of petroleum) the process of breaking down certain hydrocarbons into simpler ones of lower boiling points, as by excess heat, etc.

crack·le (krak'əl), v., **-led, -ling,** n. —v.i. **1.** to make slight, sudden, sharp noises, rapidly repeated. **2.** to form a network of fine cracks on the surface. —n. **3.** a crackling noise. **4.** a network of fine cracks, as in some glazes. —**crack'ly,** adj.

crack·pot (krak'pot'), Informal. —n. **1.** an eccentric person. —adj. **2.** eccentric or impractical.

crack·up (krak'up'), n. **1.** a crash, as of a car. **2.** Informal. a physical or mental breakdown.

-cracy, a combining form meaning "rule" or "government body": democracy.

cra·dle (krād′əl), *n., v.,* **-dled, -dling.**
—*n.* **1.** a little bed for an infant, usually built on rockers. **2.** a place of origin. **3.** a device, framework, etc., for holding or supporting something. —*v.t.* **4.** to place or rock in or as in a cradle. **5.** to nurture during infancy.

cra·dle·song (krād′əl sông′, -song′), *n.* a lullaby.

craft (kraft, kräft), *n., pl.* **crafts, craft** for 6. **1.** special manual skill. **2.** cunning or guile. **3.** a trade requiring manual skill. **4.** the members of such a trade collectively. **5.** ships, aircraft, etc., collectively. **6.** a single ship, airplane, etc.

crafts·man (krafts′mən, kräfts′-), *n.* a person who practices a craft. —**crafts′man·ly,** *adj.* —**crafts′man·ship′,** *n.*

craft·y (kraf′tē, kräf′-), *adj.,* **craft·i·er, craft·i·est.** ingeniously cunning. —**craft′i·ly,** *adv.* —**craft′i·ness,** *n.* —Syn. deceitful, sly, wily.

crag (krag), *n.* a steep, rugged rock. —**crag′gy,** *adj.* —**crag′gi·ness,** *n.*

cram (kram), *v.,* **crammed, cram·ming.** —*v.t.* **1.** to fill (something) tightly by force. **2.** to force or stuff. **3.** to feed too much. —*v.i.* **4.** to eat greedily or to excess. **5.** *Informal.* to study for an examination by hastily memorizing facts at the last minute. —**cram′mer,** *n.*

cramp[1] (kramp), *n.* **1.** Often, **cramps. a.** a sudden, involuntary, persistent contraction of a muscle or group of muscles. **b.** a piercing pain in the abdomen. **2.** See **writer's cramp.** —*v.t.* **3.** to affect with or as with a cramp.

cramp[2] (kramp), *v.t.* to restrain, esp. from free action or expression.

cran·ber·ry (kran′ber′ē, -bə rē), *n., pl.* **-ries. 1.** the red, acid fruit or berry of a trailing plant. **2.** its plant.

crane (krān), *n., v.,* **craned, cran·ing.** —*n.* **1.** a large wading bird having long legs, bill, and neck. **2.** a device for lifting and moving heavy weights. —*v.t., v.i.* **3.** to stretch (the neck).

crane′ fly′, any of numerous insects that resemble a large mosquito with extremely long legs.

cra·ni·um (krā′nē əm), *n., pl.* **-ni·ums, -ni·a** (-nē ə). **1.** the skull of a vertebrate. **2.** the part of the skull that encloses the brain. —**cra′ni·al,** *adj.*

crank (krangk), *n.* **1.** an angular arm for imparting rotary or oscillatory motion to a rotating shaft. **2.** *Informal.* a grouchy person. **3.** an eccentric person. —*v.t.* **4.** to start or operate with a crank. **5. crank out,** to make or produce in a mechanical way.

crank·case (krangk′kās′), *n.* the housing that encloses the crankshaft, the connecting rods, and allied parts.

crank·shaft (krangk′shaft′, -shäft′), *n.* a shaft having one or more cranks, usually formed as integral parts.

crank·y (krang′kē), *adj.,* **crank·i·er, crank·i·est. 1.** ill-tempered and grouchy. **2.** eccentric or queer. —**crank′i·ly,** *adv.* —**crank′i·ness,** *n.*

cran·ny (kran′ē), *n., pl.* **-nies.** a small, narrow opening in a wall, etc.

crap[1] (krap), *n.* **1.** (in craps) a losing throw. **2.** craps.

crap[2] (krap), *n. Slang.* **1.** nonsense or absurdity. **2.** something worthless. —**crap′py,** *adj.*

crape (krāp), *n.* crepe.

crap·pie (krap′ē, kräp′ē), *n.* a small sunfish found in the central U.S.

craps (kraps), *n.* a gambling game in which two dice are thrown.

crap·shoot·er (krap′shoo′tər), *n.* a person who plays the game of craps.

crash[1] (krash), *v.t.* **1.** to break into pieces suddenly, violently, and noisily. **2.** to force or drive with violence and noise. **3.** *Informal.* to gain admittance to though without a ticket, invitation, etc. —*v.i.* **4.** to break or fall to pieces noisily. **5.** to make a loud, clattering noise. **6.** to collapse suddenly, as the stock market. **7.** to crash-land. —*n.* **8.** a breaking to pieces with loud noise. **9.** the shock of collision and breaking. **10.** a collision, as of automobiles. **11.** a sudden collapse, as of the stock market. **12.** a sudden loud noise. —*adj.* **13.** *Informal.* intensive, esp. to meet an emergency. —**crash′er,** *n.*

crash[2] (krash), *n.* a fabric of rough, irregular, or lumpy yarns, for toweling, dresses, etc.

crash-land (krash′land′), *v.t., v.i.* to land in an emergency, in such a way as to damage the aircraft. —**crash′land′ing.**

crash′ pad′, *Slang.* a temporary place for sleep or lodging.

crass (kras), *adj.* without refinement or sensitivity. —**crass′ly,** *adv.* —**crass′ness,** *n.*

-crat, a combining form meaning "member or advocate of a particular form of government": *democrat.*

crate (krāt), *n., v.,* **crat·ed, crat·ing.** —*n.* **1.** a packing case made of wooden slats. **2.** any solid packing case. —*v.t.* **3.** to pack in a crate.

cra·ter (krā′tər), *n.* **1.** the cup-shaped depression marking the orifice of a volcano. **2.** a similar depression formed by the impact of a meteorite. [< L < Gk *krátēr* mixing bowl]

cra·ton (krā′ton), *n.* a relatively rigid and immobile region of the earth's crust.

cra·vat (krə vat′), *n.* a necktie, esp. a broad, frilly one formerly worn.

crave (krāv), *v.t.*, **craved, crav·ing. 1.** to long for eagerly. **2.** to ask earnestly for. **—crav′er,** *n.*

cra·ven (krā′vən), *adj.* **1.** contemptibly timid. **—n. 2.** a coward. **—cra′ven·ly,** *adv.* **—cra′ven·ness,** *n.*

crav·ing (krā′viṅg), *n.* deep longing. **—crav′ing·ly,** *adv.*

craw (krô), *n.* **1.** the crop of a bird or insect. **2.** the stomach of an animal.

craw·fish (krô′fish′), *n., pl.* **-fish, -fish·es.** crayfish.

crawl (krôl), *v.i.* **1.** to move slowly with the body resting on the ground. **2.** to progress slowly or laboriously. **3.** to feel or be overrun with or as with crawling things. **—n. 4.** the act of crawling. **5.** a swimming stroke in a prone position. See crawl. **—crawl′er,** *n.*

crawl′ space′, a shallow space, as under a roof, of much less than human height.

crawl·y (krô′lē), *adj.,* **crawl·i·er, crawl·i·est.** *Informal.* creepy.

cray·fish (krā′fish′), *n., pl.* **-fish, -fish·es.** a freshwater crustacean closely related to but smaller than the lobster.

cray·on (krā′on, -ən), *n.* **1.** a pointed stick of colored clay, chalk, wax, etc., used for drawing. **2.** a drawing in crayons. **—cray′on·ist,** *n.*

craze (krāz), *v.,* **crazed, craz·ing,** *n.* **—v.t., v.i. 1.** to make or become insane. **—n. 2.** a widespread fad.

cra·zy (krā′zē), *adj.,* **-zi·er, -zi·est,** *n., pl.* **-zies.** **—adj. 1.** mentally unbalanced. **2.** senseless or impractical. **3.** *Informal.* intensely enthusiastic. **4.** very enamored. **—n. 5.** *Slang.* an unpredictable, nonconforming person. **—cra′zi·ly,** *adv.* **—cra′zi·ness,** *n.*

cra′zy bone′. See funny bone.

cra′zy quilt′, a patchwork quilt made of irregular patches.

CRC, Civil Rights Commission.

creak (krēk), *v.i.* **1.** to make a harsh squeaking sound. **—n. 2.** a creaking sound. **—creak′y** *adj.* **—creak′i·ly,** *adv.* **—creak′i·ness,** *n.*

cream (krēm), *n.* **1.** the part of whole milk that is rich in butterfat. **2.** a soft solid or thick liquid containing medicaments or other specific ingredients, as for cosmetic purposes. **3.** a soft-centered confection coated with chocolate. **4.** the best part. **5.** a yellowish white. **—v.t. 6.** to add cream to or on. **7.** to work into a creamy consistency. **8.** to prepare in a cream sauce. **—cream′y,** *adj.* **—cream′i·ness,** *n.*

cream′ cheese′, a soft, white, smooth-textured cheese made of sweet milk and cream.

cream·er (krē′mər), *n.* **1.** a small jug for holding cream. **2.** a nondairy product in powder or liquid form,

chiefly made from corn-syrup solids, used as a substitute for cream.

cream·er·y (krē′mə rē), *n., pl.* **-er·ies.** a place where milk and cream are processed and where butter and cheese are produced.

crease (krēs), *n., v.,* **creased, creas·ing.** **—n. 1.** a ridge or groove produced in anything by folding, heat, etc. **2.** a wrinkle or fold. **—v.t. 3.** to make a crease or creases in or on. **—v.i. 4.** to become creased. **—creas′er,** *n.*

cre·ate (krē āt′), *v.t.,* **-at·ed, -at·ing. 1.** to cause to exist. **2.** to produce or cause.

cre·a·tion (krē ā′shən), *n.* **1.** the act of creating. **2. the Creation,** the original bringing into existence of the universe by God. **3.** a thing that has been created. **4.** the world or universe.

cre·a·tive (krē ā′tiv), *adj.* **1.** having the power of creating. **2.** resulting from originality of thought or expression. **3.** productive or generative. **—cre·a·tiv·i·ty** (krē′ə tiv′i tē), *n.*

cre·a·tor (krē ā′tər), *n.* **1.** a person or thing that creates. **2. the Creator,** God.

crea·ture (krē′chər), *n.* **1.** anything created. **2.** an animal, esp. one other than a human. **3.** a human being.

crèche (kresh, krāsh), *n.* a tableau of the birth of Jesus in the stable at Bethlehem.

cre·dence (krēd′°ns), *n.* belief as to the truth of something.

cre·den·tial (kri den′shəl), *n.* **1.** anything that provides the basis for confidence, belief, etc. **2.** Usually, **credentials.** evidence of authority or qualification, usually in written form.

cre·den·za (kri den′zə), *n.* a low sideboard.

cred·i·bil′i·ty gap′, public distrust expressed about the veracity of statements, esp. by the government.

cred·i·ble (kred′ə bəl), *adj.* **1.** capable of being believed. **2.** reliable or trustworthy. **—cred′i·bil′i·ty, cred′i·ble·ness,** *n.* **—cred′i·bly,** *adv.*

cred·it (kred′it), *n.* **1.** commendation or honor given for some action, quality, etc. **2.** trustworthiness or credence. **3.** a source of commendation or honor. **4.** official acceptance of the work of a student in a particular course of study. **5.** time allowed for payment for goods obtained on trust. **6.** confidence in a purchaser's ability and intention to pay. **7.** reputation of solvency and probity. **8.** a sum of money due to a person. **9.** an entry of payment or value received on an account. **10. on credit,** by deferred payment. **—v.t. 11.** to believe or trust. **12.** to give credit for or to. **13 credit to** or **with,** to ascribe to.

cred·it·a·ble (kred′i tə bəl), *adj.* deserving credit or esteem. —**cred′it·a·ble·ness, cred′it·a·bil′i·ty,** *n.* —**cred′it·a·bly,** *adv.*

cred′it card′, a card allowing the bearer to charge certain purchases or services.

cred·i·tor (kred′i tər), *n.* a person to whom money is due.

cred′it un′ion, a cooperative group that makes loans to its members at low-interest rates.

cre·do (krē′dō, krā′-), *n., pl.* **-dos.** a creed or formula of belief.

cred·u·lous (krej′ə ləs), *adj.* unduly willing to believe or trust. —**cre·du·li·ty** (kri dōō′li tē, -dyōō′-), *n.* —**cred′u·lous·ly,** *adv.*

Cree (krē), *n., pl.* **Crees, Cree.** 1. a member of an American Indian people of Manitoba and Saskatchewan. 2. their language.

creed (krēd), *n.* 1. a system of religious belief. 2. any system of belief or of opinion. [< L *crēdō* I believe]

creek (krēk, krik), *n.* 1. a watercourse smaller than a river. 2. **up the creek,** *Slang.* in a predicament.

Creek (krēk), *n., pl.* **Creeks, Creek.** 1. a member of an American Indian people of Alabama and Georgia. 2. their language.

creel (krēl), *n.* a wicker basket for holding fish, lobsters, etc.

creep (krēp), *v.,* **crept, creep·ing,** *n.* —*v.i.* 1. to move with the body on or close to the ground. 2. to move slowly or stealthily. 3. to have a sensation as of something creeping over the skin. 4. to grow along the ground, a wall, etc., as a plant. 5. **make one's flesh creep,** to cause one to experience uneasiness. —*n.* 6. *Slang.* a boring, eccentric person. 7. **the creeps,** *Slang.* a sensation of horror, fear, etc. —**creep′er,** *n.*

creep·ing (krē′piṅg), *adj.* progressing or materializing by extremely gradual steps: *creeping socialism.*

creep·y (krē′pē), *adj.,* **creep·i·er, creep·i·est.** having or causing a sensation of horror or fear. —**creep′i·ly,** *adv.* —**creep′i·ness,** *n.*

cre·mate (krē′māt), *v.t.,* **-mat·ed, -mat·ing.** to reduce (a dead body) to ashes by fire. —**cre·ma·tion** (kri mā′shən), *n.* —**cre′ma·tor,** *n.*

cre·ma·to·ry (krē′mə tōr′ē, -tôr′ē, krem′ə-), *n., pl.* **-ries.** a place or furnace for cremating. Also, **cre′ma·to′ri·um** (-ē əm).

crème (krem, krēm), *n., pl.* **crèmes** (kremz, krēmz). a thick liqueur.

crème de menthe (krem′ də menth′, mint′, krēm′). a white or green liqueur flavored with mint.

cren·el·ate (kren′°lāt′), *v.t.,* **-at·ed, -at·ing.** to furnish with battlements.

Also, *esp. Brit.,* **cren·el·late.** —**cren′e·la′tion,** *n.*

Cre·ole (krē′ōl), *n.* 1. a person born in the West Indies but of European ancestry. 2. a person of French ancestry born in Louisiana. 3. the French patois spoken in parts of Louisiana. 4. (*l.c.*) a person of mixed Spanish and black or French and black ancestry. 5. (*usually l.c.*) (of a sauce) made with tomatoes, peppers, seasonings, etc.

cre·o·sote (krē′ə sōt′), *n.* an oily liquid obtained by the distillation of wood tar and used as a preservative and antiseptic.

crepe (krāp), *n.* 1. a thin fabric of silk, cotton, etc., with a crinkled surface. 2. Also called **crepe′ pa′per.** thin paper densely wrinkled like this fabric. 3. a silk fabric, usually black, used for mourning veils, bands, etc. 4. Also called **crepe′ rub′ber.** a crinkled crude rubber. 5. a thin delicate pancake. Also, **crêpe** (for defs. 1, 3, 5).

crêpe su·zette (krāp′ sōō zet′), *pl.* **crêpe su·zettes** (krāp′ sōō zets′). a thin dessert pancake, flavored with liqueur and served flaming.

crept (krept), *v.* pt. and pp. of **creep.**

cre·pus·cu·lar (kri pus′kyə lər), *adj.* 1. of or resembling twilight. 2. appearing or flying in the twilight.

cres., crescendo.

cre·scen·do (kri shen′dō, -sen′dō), *n., pl.* **-dos,** *adj., adv.* —*n.* 1. a gradual increase in force or loudness. 2. a crescendo passage. —*adj., adv.* 3. gradually increasing in force or loudness.

cres·cent (kres′ənt), *n.* 1. the figure of the moon in its last or first quarter, resembling a segment of a ring tapering to points at the ends. 2. any crescent-shaped object. —**cres·cen·tic** (krə sen′tik), *adj.*

cress (kres), *n.* a plant having pungent-tasting leaves often used for salad.

crest (krest), *n.* 1. a tuft or other natural growth on the top of the head of an animal, as the comb of a cock. 2. a heraldic device, as on stationery. 3. the highest part of a hill or mountain range. 4. the highest or best of the kind. —*v.i.* 5. to form or rise to a crest. —**crest′ed,** *adj.* —**crest′less,** *adj.*

crest·fall·en (krest′fô′lən), *adj.* dejected or depressed. —**crest′fall′en·ly,** *adv.*

cre·ta·ceous (kri tā′shəs), *adj.* 1. of the nature of, resembling, or containing chalk. 2. (*cap.*) noting a period of the Mesozoic era, characterized by the extinction of the giant reptiles and the advent of modern insects. —n. **3.** (cap.) the Cretaceous period.

Crete (krēt), n. a Greek island in the Mediterranean. —**Cre′tan**, adj., n.

cre·tin (krēt′°n, krē′tin), n. a person suffering from cretinism.

cre·tin·ism (krēt′°niz′əm), n. a chronic disease due to thyroid deficiency, characterized by physical deformity, idiocy, etc.

cre·tonne (kri ton′, krē′ton), n. a heavy cotton material in printed designs, used esp. for drapery and slipcovers.

cre·vasse (krə vas′), n. a deep cleft in glacial ice or the earth's surface.

crev·ice (krev′is), n. a crack forming a narrow opening.

crew[1] (krōō), n. **1.** a group of persons working together: a wrecking crew. **2.** the company of persons who man a boat, airplane, etc. **3.** the team that mans a racing shell. **4.** the sport of racing with racing shells. —**crew′man**, n.

crew[2] (krōō), v. a pt. of **crow**[2].

crew′ cut′, a man's closely cropped haircut.

crew·el (krōō′əl), n. a worsted yarn for embroidery. —**crew′el·work′**, n.

crib (krib), n., v., **cribbed, crib·bing.** —n. **1.** a child's bed with enclosed sides. **2.** a manger for fodder. **3.** a bin for storing grain, salt, etc. **4.** Informal. a translation, list of correct answers, or other illicit aid used by students in taking exams, etc. —v.t. **5.** to confine in a crib. **6.** to provide with a crib. **7.** Informal. to plagiarize. —v.i. **8.** Informal. to use a crib in examinations, etc. —**crib′ber**, n.

crib·bage (krib′ij), n. a card game, basically for two players, scored on a small board (**crib′bage board′**) having holes for pegs.

crick (krik), n. a sharp, painful spasm of the muscles, as of the neck or back.

crick·et[1] (krik′it), n. a leaping insect, the male of which makes a sharp chirping sound.

crick·et[2] (krik′it), n. a game played with a bat and ball by two teams using wickets. —**crick′et·er**, n.

cried (krīd), v. pt. and pp. of **cry.**

cri·er (krī′ər), n. See **town crier.**

crime (krīm), n. an action, or an instance of negligence, that is legally prohibited.

Cri·me·a (krī mē′ə, kri-), n. a peninsula in the SW Soviet Union jutting into the Black Sea. —**Cri·me′an**, adj.

crim·i·nal (krim′ə n°l), adj. **1.** of crime or its punishment. **2.** guilty of crime. —n. **3.** a person guilty of a crime. —**crim·i·nal·i·ty** (krim′ə nal′i tē), n. —**crim′i·nal·ly**, adv.

crim·i·nol·o·gy (krim′ə nol′ə jē), n. the study of crime and criminals. —**crim·i·no·log·i·cal** (krim′ə n°loj′i kəl), adj. —**crim′i·nol′o·gist**, n.

crimp (krimp), v.t. **1.** to press into small, regular folds. **2.** to curl (hair). —n. **3.** the act of crimping. **4.** a crimped condition or form. **5. put a crimp in,** Informal. to interfere with. —**crimp′er**, n.

crim·son (krim′zən, -sən), adj. **1.** deep purplish-red. —n. **2.** a crimson color. —v.t., v.i. **3.** to make or become crimson.

cringe (krinj), v.i., **cringed, cring·ing.** to shrink back or crouch, esp. from fear or servility. —**Syn.** cower, wince.

crin·kle (kring′kəl), v., **-kled, -kling,** n. —v.t., v.i. **1.** to turn or wind in many little bends and twists. **2.** to wrinkle or ripple. —n. **3.** a wrinkle or ripple. —**crin′kly**, adj.

crin·o·line (krin′°lin, -°lēn′), n. **1.** See **hoop skirt.** **2.** a stiff, coarse cotton material for interlining.

crip·ple (krip′əl), n., v., **-pled, -pling.** —n. **1.** a lame person or animal. **2.** a person who is disabled in any way. —v.t. **3.** to make a cripple of. **4.** to disable or impair.

cri·sis (krī′sis), n., pl. **-ses** (-sēz). **1.** a crucial stage at which future events are determined. **2.** a decisive change in the course of a serious disease, as for the worse.

crisp (krisp), adj. **1.** hard but easily breakable: crisp toast. **2.** firm and fresh. **3.** brisk or decided. **4.** lively or pithy. **5.** crinkled or curly. —v.t., v.i. **6.** to make or become crisp. —**crisp′ly**, adv. —**crisp′ness**, n. —**crisp′y**, adj. —**crisp′i·ness**, n.

criss·cross (kris′krôs′, -kros′), adj. **1.** having many crossing lines, paths, etc. —n. **2.** a crisscross mark, etc. —adv. **3.** crosswise. **4.** awry or askew. —v.t., v.i. **5.** to mark with or form crossing lines. **6.** to move in a crisscross manner. **7.** to move back and forth.

crit., **1.** critic. **2.** critical. **3.** criticism. **4.** criticized.

cri·te·ri·on (krī tēr′ē ən), n., pl. **-te·ri·a** (-tēr′ē ə), **-te·ri·ons.** a standard of judgment or criticism.

crit·ic (krit′ik), n. **1.** a person who judges literary or artistic works. **2.** a person who tends to make trivial or harsh judgments.

crit·i·cal (krit′i kəl), adj. **1.** inclined to find fault. **2.** occupied with or skilled in criticism. **3.** involving judgment as to merit, etc. **4.** of critics or criticism. **5.** being or of the nature of a crisis. —**crit′i·cal·ly**, adv. —**crit′i·cal·ness**, n.

crit·i·cism (krit′i siz′əm), *n.* **1.** the act or art of judging the quality of a literary or artistic work. **2.** fault-finding or censure. **3.** a critical comment or article.

crit·i·cize (krit′i sīz′), *v.i., v.t.,* -cized, -ciz·ing. **1.** to make judgments as to merits (of). **2.** to find fault (with). Also, *esp. Brit.,* **crit′i·cise′.** —**crit′i·ciz′a·ble,** *adj.* —**crit′i·ciz′er,** *n.* —**Syn. 2.** blame, censure, condemn.

cri·tique (kri tēk′), *n.* a critical evaluation or analysis.

crit·ter (krit′ər), *n. Dial.* a creature.

croak (krōk), *v.i.* **1.** to utter a low, hoarse cry, as a frog. **2.** *Slang.* to die. —*v.t.* **3.** to utter by croaking. —*n.* **4.** a croaking sound. —**croak′er,** *n.* —**croak′i·ly,** *adj.* —**croak′i·ly,** *adv.*

cro·chet (krō shā′), *n., v.,* -cheted (-shād′), -chet·ing (-shā′ing). —*n.* **1.** needlework done with a needle having a small hook at one end. —*v.t., v.i.* **2.** to form by crochet. —**cro·chet′er,** *n.*

crock (krok), *n.* an earthen pot or jar.

crocked (krokt), *adj. Slang.* drunk or intoxicated.

crock·er·y (krok′ə rē), *n.* crocks collectively.

Crock-Pot (krok′pot′), *n. Trademark.* an electric ceramic pot for slow cooking by very low-watt heat.

croc·o·dile (krok′ə dīl′), *n.* a large thick-skinned reptile found in sluggish waters and swamps of the tropics, having a pointed snout. [< *crocodīl(us)* < Gk *krokódeilos* lizard]

cro·cus (krō′kəs), *n., pl.* -cus·es. a small bulbous plant cultivated for its showy, solitary flowers.

crois·sant (*Fr.* krwä säN′), *n., pl.* -sants (-säN′). a rich crescent-shaped roll.

Crom·well (krom′wəl, -wel, krum′-), *n.* **Oliver,** 1599–1658, British general, Puritan statesman, and Lord Protector of England 1653–58.

crone (krōn), *n.* an ugly, withered old woman.

cro·ny (krō′nē), *n., pl.* -nies. an intimate friend or companion.

crook (krŏok), *n.* **1.** a bent or curved implement, part, etc. **2.** *Informal.* a dishonest person, esp. a swindler or thief. —*v.t., v.i.* **3.** to bend or curve.

crook·ed (krŏok′id), *adj.* **1.** not straight in form or shape. **2.** deformed or misshapen. **3.** dishonest or fraudulent. —**crook′ed·ly,** *adv.* —**crook′ed·ness,** *n.*

crook·neck (krŏok′nek′), *n.* a squash having a long curving neck.

croon (krŏon), *v.i., v.t.* **1.** to sing or hum in a low, soothing voice. —*n.* **2.** the act or sound of crooning. —**croon′er,** *n.*

crop (krop), *n., v.,* **cropped, crop·ping.** —*n.* **1.** the cultivated produce of the ground. **2.** the yield of such produce for a particular season. **3.** a group of persons or things. **4.** the handle of a whip. **5.** a short riding whip. **6.** a close-cropped hairstyle. **7.** a pouchlike enlargement of the gullet of many birds, in which food is held and softened. —*v.t.* **8.** to cut off the top of (a plant, grass, etc.). **9.** to cut off the ends or a part of. **10.** to clip the ears, hair, etc., of. **11.** to trim (a print or negative). **12.** to reap or harvest. —*v.i.* **13.** to bear or yield a crop. **14. crop out,** to rise to the surface. **15. crop up,** to appear unexpectedly.

crop-dust·ing (krop′dus′ting), *n.* the spraying of powdered fungicides or insecticides on crops, as from an airplane. —**crop′-dust′er,** *n.*

crop·land (krop′land′), *n.* land suitable for the cultivation of crops.

crop·per (krop′ər), *n.* **1.** a person or thing that crops. **2.** a person who raises a crop. **3. come a cropper,** *Informal.* to fail completely.

cro·quet (krō kā′), *n.* an outdoor game played by knocking wooden balls through a series of wire wickets by means of mallets.

cro·quette (krō ket′), *n.* a small mass of minced meat, fish, etc., fried in deep fat.

cro·sier (krō′zhər), *n.* a ceremonial staff carried by a bishop or an abbot.

cross (krôs, kros), *n.* **1.** a structure consisting of an upright and a transverse piece, upon which persons were formerly put to death. **2. the Cross,** the cross upon which Jesus died. **3.** a figure of the Cross as a Christian emblem, badge, etc. **4.** a crossing of animals or plants. **5.** an animal, plant, etc., produced by crossing. **6.** a punch thrown across and over the lead of an opponent. **7. bear one's cross,** to accept troubles patiently. —*v.t.* **8.** to make the sign of the cross upon or over, as in devotion. **9.** to cancel by marking with a cross or with a line or lines. **10.** to lie or pass across so as to intersect. **11.** to move or extend from one side to the other side of (a street, river, etc.). **12.** to meet and pass. **13.** to thwart or frustrate. **14.** to hybridize. —*v.i.* **15.** to lie or be athwart. **16.** to move or extend from one side or place to another. **17. cross one's mind,** to occur suddenly to one. **18. cross one's path,** to meet unexpectedly. —*adj.* **19.** lying or passing crosswise. **20.** contrary or opposite. **21.** angry and annoyed. **22.** hybrid or crossbred. —**cross′ly,** *adv.* —**cross′ness,** *n.*

cross·bar (krôs′bär′, kros′-), *n.* a transverse bar, line, or stripe.

cross·beam (krôs′bēm′, kros′-), n. a transverse beam in a structure, as a joist.

cross·bones (krôs′bōnz′, kros′-), n.pl. two bones placed crosswise, usually below a skull, symbolizing death.

cross·bow (krôs′bō′, kros′-), n. a medieval weapon consisting of a bow fixed transversely on a grooved wooden stock.

cross·breed (krôs′brēd′, kros′-), v., **-bred** (-bred), **-breed·ing**, n. —v.t., v.i. 1. to hybridize. —n. 2. hybrid (def. 1).

cross·coun·try (adj. krôs′kun′trē, kros′-; n. krôs′kun′trē, -kun′-, kros′-), adj. 1. proceeding over fields, through woods, etc. 2. from one end of the country to the other. —n. 3. a cross-country sport or sports.

cross·cur·rent (krôs′kûr′ənt, -kur′-, kros′-), n. 1. a current, as in a stream, moving across the main current. 2. a conflicting tendency or movement.

cross·cut (krôs′kut′, kros′-), adj., n., v., **-cut**, **-cut·ting**. —adj. 1. used for cutting crosswise. 2. cut across the grain. —n. 3. a transverse cut or course. —v.t. 4. to cut or go across.

cross·ex·am·ine (krôs′ig zam′in, kros′-), v.t., **-ined**, **-in·ing**. to examine by questions intended to check a previous examination. —**cross′-ex·am′i·na′tion,** n.

cross·eye (krôs′ī′, kros′ī′), n. a deviation of vision in which both eyes turn toward the nose. —**cross′-eyed′,** adj.

cross·file (krôs′fīl′, kros′-), v.i., **-filed**, **-fil·ing**. to register as a candidate in the primary elections of more than one party.

cross′ fire′, 1. a brisk exchange, as of words or opinions. 2. lines of gunfire crossing one another.

cross′ hairs′, fine wires or threads crossing in a focal plane of an optical instrument and serving to obtain accurate sighting.

cross·hatch (krôs′hach′, kros′-), v.t. to shade with two or more intersecting series of parallel lines. —**cross′hatch′ing,** n.

cross·ing (krô′sing, kros′ing), n. 1. an intersection, as of lines, streets, tracks, etc. 2. a place at which a road, river, etc., may be crossed.

cross·o·ver (krôs′ō′vər, kros′-), n. 1. a bridge or other structure for crossing a river, highway, etc. 2. a voter who switches to another party from the one he or she usually voted for in the past.

cross·patch (krôs′pach′, kros′-), n. Informal. a bad-tempered person.

cross·piece (krôs′pēs′, kros′-), n. a transverse piece.

cross·pol·li·nate (krôs′pol′ə nāt′, kros′-), v.t., **-nat·ed**, **-nat·ing**. to subject to cross-pollination.

cross·pol·li·na·tion (krôs′pol′ə nā′shən, kros′-), n. the transfer of pollen from the flower of one plant to the flower of a plant having a different genetic constitution.

cross·pur·pose (krôs′pûr′pəs, kros′-), n. 1. an opposing or contrary purpose. 2. **at cross purposes**, in a way that involves or produces mutual misunderstanding.

cross·ques·tion (krôs′kwes′chən, kros′-), v.t. to cross-examine.

cross·re·fer (krôs′ri fûr′, kros′-), v.t., v.i., **-ferred**, **-fer·ring**. to refer by a cross reference.

cross′ ref′erence, a reference from one part of a book or index to another part.

cross·road (krôs′rōd′, kros′-), n. 1. a road that crosses another road. 2. the place where roads intersect.

cross′ sec′tion, 1. a section made by a plane cutting anything transversely, esp. at right angles to the longest axis. 2. a piece so cut off. 3. a pictorial representation of such a section. 4. a typical selection or a sample. —**cross′-sec′tion·al,** adj.

cross′ talk′, interference by other sound on a telephone, radio, etc.

cross·town (krôs′toun′, kros′-), adj. traveling in a direction extending across a city.

cross·walk (krôs′wôk′, kros′-), n. a lane for pedestrians crossing a street.

cross·wise (krôs′wīz′, kros′-), adv. across or transversely. Also, **crossways** (krôs′wāz′, kros′-).

cross′word puz′zle (krôs′wûrd′, kros′-), a puzzle in which words corresponding to numbered clues are fitted into a pattern of horizontal and vertical squares. Also, **cross′word′.**

crotch (kroch), n. 1. a forked piece, support, etc. 2. a place of forking, as between the legs. 3. the part of a pair of trousers, etc., formed by the joining of the two legs. —**crotched** (krotcht), adj.

crotch·et (kroch′it), n. an odd fancy or whimsical notion. —**crotch′et·y,** adj. —**crotch′et·i·ness,** n.

crouch (krouch), v.i. 1. to stoop or bend low. 2. to cringe or cower. —n. 3. a stooping or bending low.

croup (kroop), n. any condition of the larynx or trachea characterized by a hoarse cough and difficult breathing. —**croup′y,** adj.

crou·pi·er (kroo′pē ər, -pē ā′), n. an attendant who collects and pays the money at a gaming table.

crou·ton (kroo′ton, kroo ton′), n. a small piece of fried or toasted bread, used in soups, etc.

crow[1] (krō), *n.* **1.** a large bird having lustrous black plumage. **2. as the crow flies,** by the most direct route. **3. eat crow,** *Informal.* to suffer humiliation.

crow[2] (krō), *v.,* **crowed** or, for 1 **crew; crowed; crow·ing;** *n.* —*v.i.* **1.** to utter the cry of a rooster. **2.** to utter an inarticulate cry of pleasure. **3.** to exult or boast loudly. —*n.* **4.** the cry of the rooster.

Crow (krō), *n.* **1.** a member of a Siouan people of eastern Montana. **2.** their language.

crow·bar (krō′bär′), *n.* a steel bar, usually slightly bent at one or both ends, used as a lever.

crowd (kroud), *n.* **1.** a large number of persons gathered closely together. **2.** any social group, esp. with something in common. —*v.i.* **3.** to gather in large numbers. **4.** to press forward. —*v.t.* **5.** to push or shove. **6.** to fill to excess. —**crowd′ed,** *adj.* —**crowd′er,** *n.* —**Syn. 1.** horde, multitude, throng.

crow·foot (krō′foot′), *n., pl.* **-foots.** a plant in the buttercup family, having leaves like the feet of birds.

crown (kroun), *n.* **1.** a headgear worn by a monarch as a symbol of sovereignty. **2.** an ornamental wreath for the head as a mark of victory. **3.** the distinction of a great achievement. **4. the Crown,** the sovereign as head of the state, or the power of a monarch. **5.** any of various coins bearing the figure of a crown or crowned head. **6.** a former British silver coin. **7.** something having the form of a crown. **8.** the top of anything, as of the head, a hat, a mountain, etc. **9.** the part of a tooth that is covered by enamel. **10.** an artificial substitute, as of porcelain, for the crown of a tooth. **11.** the highest state of anything. —*v.t.* **12.** to put a crown upon. **13.** to invest with regal power. **14.** to surmount as with a crown. **15.** to complete worthily. **16.** to confer distinction upon. **17.** to cap (a tooth) with a dental crown. —**crowned** (kround), *adj.*

crown′ prince′, the heir apparent of a monarch.

crown′ vetch′, an Old World plant having pink flowers, naturalized in the U.S.

crow's-foot (krōz′foot′), *n., pl.* **-feet.** a wrinkle at the outer corner of the eye.

crow's-nest (krōz′nest′), *n.* a platform for a lookout at or near the top of a mast.

cro·zier (krō′zhər), *n.* crosier.

cru·cial (krōō′shəl), *adj.* **1.** involving a final and supreme decision. **2.** severe or trying. —**cru′cial·ly,** *adv.*

cru·ci·ble (krōō′sə bəl), *n.* **1.** a container of metal or refractory material employed for heating substances to high temperatures. **2.** a severe test.

cru·ci·fix (krōō′sə fiks), *n.* a cross with the figure of Jesus upon it.

cru·ci·fix·ion (krōō′sə fik′shən), *n.* **1.** the act of crucifying. **2.** (*cap.*) the death of Jesus by being nailed upon a cross.

cru·ci·form (krōō′sə fôrm′), *adj.* shaped in a cross.

cru·ci·fy (krōō′sə fī′), *v.t.,* **-fied, -fy·ing. 1.** to put to death by nailing or binding a person to a cross. **2.** to torture or persecute.

crude (krōōd), *adj.,* **crud·er, crud·est,** *n.* —*adj.* **1.** in a raw or unprepared state. **2.** lacking finish, polish, etc.: *a crude summary.* **3.** lacking culture, refinement, tact, etc. —*n.* **4.** See **crude oil.** —**crude′ly,** *adv.* —**crude′ness, cru′di·ty,** *n.*

crude′ oil′, petroleum before refining.

cru·el (krōō′əl), *adj.* causing pain or distress to others. —**cru′el·ly,** *adv.* —**cru′el·ty,** *n.*

cru·et (krōō′it), *n.* a glass bottle, esp. one for vinegar, oil, etc., for the table.

cruise (krōōz), *v.,* **cruised, cruis·ing,** *n.* —*v.i.* **1.** to sail about from port to port. **2.** to travel about without a particular purpose. **3.** to fly at the speed that permits maximum operating efficiency. **4.** to travel about slowly, looking for customers, etc. —*v.t.* **5.** to cruise in: *to cruise the Caribbean.* —*n.* **6.** a cruising tour, esp. by ship.

cruise′ mis′sile, a jet-powered, radar-guided, low-flying missile designed to deliver a nuclear or a conventional warhead.

cruis·er (krōō′zər), *n.* **1.** a warship of medium tonnage, designed for high speed and long cruising radius. **2.** a pleasure vessel intended for cruising. **3.** See **squad car.**

crul·ler (krul′ər), *n.* a light, sweet cake fried in deep fat.

crumb (krum), *n.* **1.** a small particle broken off, as of bread, cake, etc. **2.** a small portion of anything. —*v.t.* **3.** to prepare with bread crumbs. **4.** to break into crumbs. —**crumb·y** (krum′ē), *adj.*

crum·ble (krum′bəl), *v.t., v.i.* **-bled, -bling. 1.** to break into small fragments. **2.** to disintegrate gradually. —**crum′bly,** *adj.*

crum·my (krum′ē), *adj.,* **-mi·er, -mi·est.** *Slang.* **1.** shabby or seedy. **2.** cheap or worthless.

crum·pet (krum′pit), *n. Chiefly Brit.* a soft bread resembling a muffin.

crum·ple (krum′pəl), *v.t., v.i.,* **-pled, -pling. 1.** to contract into wrinkles. **2.** to collapse.

crunch (krunch), *v.t., v.i.* **1.** to chew with a crushing noise. **2.** to crush noisily. —*n.* **3.** act or sound of crunching. **4.** *Slang.* a pinch or cutback: *monetary crunch.* —**crunch′y,** *adj.*

crup·per (krup′ər, krōōp′-), *n.* a leather strap fastened to the saddle of a harness and looping under the horse's tail.

cru·sade (krōō sād′), *n., v.,* -**sad·ed,** -**sad·ing.** —*n.* **1.** (*often cap.*) any of the military expeditions undertaken by the Christians of Europe in the 11th, 12th, and 13th centuries to recover the Holy Land. **2.** any vigorous movement for a cause, etc. —*v.i.* **3.** to engage in a crusade. —**cru-sad′er,** *n.*

cruse (krōōz, krōōs), *n. Archaic.* an earthen pot, bottle, etc., for liquids.

crush (krush), *v.t.* **1.** to press with a force that destroys or deforms. **2.** to pound into small fragments. **3.** to force out by squeezing. **4.** hug or embrace strongly. **5.** to subdue or suppress utterly: *to crush a revolt.* —*n.* **6.** the act of crushing. **7.** a great crowd. **8.** *Informal.* an intense infatuation. —**crush′er,** *n.*

crust (krust), *n.* **1.** the hard outer portion of bread, roll, etc. **2.** the baked shell of a pie. **3.** any hard external covering. **4.** *Slang.* unabashed nerve. —*v.t., v.i.* **5.** to cover or become covered with a crust. —**crus′tal,** *adj.* —**crust′y,** *adj.*

crus·ta·cean (kru stā′shən), *n.* any chiefly aquatic arthropod typically having the body covered with a hard shell, including the lobsters, shrimps, crabs, etc.

crutch (kruch), *n.* **1.** a support to assist a lame person in walking, usually with a crosspiece fitting under the armpit. **2.** anything that gives support.

crux (kruks), *n., pl.* **crux·es. 1.** a basic or decisive point. **2.** a perplexing difficulty.

cru·zei·ro (krōō zâr′ō), *n., pl.* -**zei·ros** (-zâr′ōz). the monetary unit of Brazil.

cry (krī), *v.,* **cried, cry·ing,** *n., pl.* **cries.** —*v.i.* **1.** to utter sounds of grief or suffering, usually with tears. **2.** to weep or sob. **3.** to shout or yell. **4.** to make a characteristic call, as an animal does. —*v.t.* **5.** to utter loudly. **6.** to announce publicly as for sale. —*n.* **7.** a shout, scream, or wail. **8.** clamor or outcry. **9.** an entreaty or appeal. **10.** an oral proclamation. **11.** a fit of weeping. **12.** the characteristic call of an animal. **13. a far cry,** quite some distance or difference.

cry·ba·by (krī′bā′bē), *n., pl.* -**bies.** a person who cries readily for very little reason.

cry·ing (krī′ing), *adj.* demanding attention or remedy: *a crying evil.*

cry·o·gen·ics (krī′ō jen′iks), *n.* the branch of physics that deals with very low temperatures, esp. those at or near absolute zero. —**cry′o·gen′ic,** *adj.* —**cry′o·gen′i·cal·ly,** *adv.*

cry·o·lite (krī′ə līt′), *n.* a colorless mineral used as a flux in producing aluminum.

cry·o·sur·ger·y (krī′ō sûr′jə rē), *n.* the use of extreme cold to destroy tissue for therapeutic purposes.

crypt (kript), *n.* **1.** a subterranean chamber or vault, esp. one used as a burial place. **2.** *Anat.* a small glandular cavity. [< L *crypt(a)* < Gk *kryptē* hidden place]

cryp·tic (krip′tik), *adj.* **1.** intended to be puzzling or baffling. **2.** secret or occult. —**cryp′ti·cal·ly,** *adv.* —**Syn. 1.** ambiguous, enigmatic.

cryp·to·gram (krip′tə gram′), *n.* a message in code or cipher.

cryp·tog·ra·phy (krip tog′rə fē), *n.* the art of ciphering and deciphering messages in code. —**cryp·tog′ra·pher,** *n.*

cryst., crystalline.

crys·tal (kris′təl), *n., adj.* —*n.* **1.** a clear, transparent mineral or glass resembling ice. **2.** the transparent form of crystallized quartz. **3.** a solid enclosed by symmetrically arranged plane surfaces, intersecting at definite angles. **4.** anything of or resembling such a substance. **5.** the glass cover over the face of a watch. —*adj.* **6.** composed of crystal. **7.** clear or transparent. —**crys·tal·line** (kris′t°lin, -t°līn′), *adj.*

crys·tal·lize (kris′t°līz′), *v.i., v.t.,* -**lized, -liz·ing. 1.** to form into crystals. **2.** to assume or cause to assume a definite form. —**crys·tal·li·za·tion** (kris′t°li zā′shən), *n.*

crys·tal·log·ra·phy (kris′t°log′rə fē), *n.* the science dealing with crystallization and crystals. —**crys′tal·log′ra·pher,** *n.* —**crys′tal·lo·graph′ic** (-lə graf′ik), *adj.*

Cs, cesium.

cs., case; cases.

C/S, cycles per second.

C.S., 1. Chief of Staff. **2.** Christian Science. **3.** Christian Scientist. **4.** Civil Service.

c.s., 1. capital stock. **2.** civil service.

C.S.A., Confederate States of America.

CST, Central Standard Time. Also, **C.S.T., c.s.t.**

Ct., 1. Connecticut. **2.** Count.

ct., 1. carat. **2.** cent. **3.** county. **4.** court.

CT. Connecticut.

C.T., Central Time.

ctf., certificate.

ctg., cartage. Also, **ctge.**

ctn., carton.

ctr., center.

cts., 1. centimes. 2. cents.

Cu, copper. [< L *cuprum*]

cu., 1. cubic. 2. cumulus.

cub (kub), *n.* 1. the young of certain animals, as the fox, bear, etc. 2. a young, inexperienced person, esp. an unseasoned newspaper reporter.

Cu·ba (kyōō′bə), *n.* a country in the Caribbean, S of Florida. **—Cu′ban,** *adj., n.*

cub·by·hole (kub′ē hōl′), *n.* a small, snug place or room. Also, **cub·by** (kub′ē).

cube (kyōōb), *n., v.,* **cubed, cub·ing.** **—n.** 1. a solid bounded by six equal squares. 2. *Math.* the third power of a quantity, expressed as $a^3 = a \cdot a \cdot a$. **—v.t.** 3. to make into a cube. 4. *Math.* to raise to the third power. **—cub′er,** *n.*

cube′ root′, *Math.* a quantity of which a given quantity is the cube: *The cube root of 64 is 4.*

cu·bic (kyōō′bik), *adj.* 1. of or having three dimensions. 2. Also, **cu′bi·cal.** having the form of a cube. 3. pertaining to a unit of linear measure that is multiplied by itself twice to form a unit of measure for volume: *a cubic foot.*

cu·bi·cle (kōō′bi kəl), *n.* a small space or compartment formed by partitioning.

cu′bic meas′ure, the measurement of volume by means of cubic units.

Cub·ism (kyōō′biz əm), *n.* (*often l.c.*) a style of painting and sculpture developed in the early 20th century, characterized chiefly by reduction of natural forms to their geometrical equivalents. **—cub′ist,** *n., adj.* **—cu·bis′tic,** *adj.*

cu·bit (kyōō′bit), *n.* an ancient linear unit usually from 17 to 21 inches.

cub′ scout′, a member of the junior division (ages 8–10) of the Boy Scouts.

cuck·old (kuk′əld), *n.* 1. the husband of an unfaithful wife. **—v.t.** 2. to make a cuckold of. **—cuck′old·ry** (-rē), *n.*

cuck·oo (kōō′kōō, kōōk′ōō), *n., pl.* **-oos,** *adj.* **—n.** 1. a common, European bird noted for its two-note call. **—adj.** 2. *Slang.* crazy or foolish.

cu·cum·ber (kyōō′kum bər), *n.* the edible, fleshy, usually long, cylindrical fruit of a common plant.

cud (kud), *n.* the portion of food that a ruminant returns from the first stomach to the mouth to chew a second time.

cud·dle (kud′∂l), *v.,* **-dled, -dling.** **—v.t.** 1. to hug tenderly. **—v.i.** 2. to

lie close and snug. **—cud·dle·some** (kud′∂l səm), **cud′dly,** *adj.*

cudg·el (kuj′əl), *n., v.,* **-eled, -el·ing,** or **-elled, -el·ling.** **—n.** 1. a short, thick stick used as a weapon. **—v.t.** 2. to beat with a cudgel.

cue¹ (kyōō), *n., v.,* **cued, cu·ing.** **—n.** 1. *Theat.* anything said or done that is followed by a specific line or action. 2. a hint or intimation. **—v.t.** 3. to give a cue to.

cue² (kyōō), *n.* a long, tapering rod used to strike the ball in billiards, pool, etc.

cue′ ball′, the ball struck by the cue as distinguished from the other balls on the table.

cues·ta (kwes′tə), *n.* a long ridge with a relatively steep face on one side and a gentle slope on the other.

cuff¹ (kuf), *n.* 1. a fold, band, etc., at the bottom of a sleeve. 2. a turned-up fold, as at the bottom of a trouser leg. 3. **off the cuff,** *Slang.* extemporaneously. 4. **on the cuff,** *Slang.* on credit.

cuff² (kuf), *v.t.* 1. to strike with the open hand. **—n.** 2. a blow or slap.

cuff′ link′, one of a pair of linked buttons or buttonlike ornaments for fastening a French cuff.

cui·sine (kwi zēn′), *n.* 1. a style of cooking. 2. the food cooked, esp. at a restaurant.

cul-de-sac (kul′də sak′, -sak′, kōōl′-), *n., pl.* **culs-de-sac** (kulz′də sak′, -sak′, kōōlz′-). 1. a street closed at one end. 2. any situation in which further progress is impossible.

cu·li·nar·y (kyōō′lə ner′ē, kul′ə-), *adj.* of or used in cooking or the kitchen.

cull (kul), *v.t.* 1. to pick the best elements or parts from. 2. to collect or gather. **—n.** 3. anything picked out and put aside as inferior.

cul·len·der (kul′ən dər), *n.* colander.

cul·mi·nate (kul′mə nāt′), *v.i.,* **-nat·ed, -nat·ing.** 1. to terminate at the highest point, summit, etc. 2. to end or conclude. **—cul′mi·na′tion,** *n.*

cu·lottes (kōō lots′, kyōō-; kōō′lots, kyōō′-), *n.pl.* women's casual trousers cut full to resemble a skirt. Also, **cu·lotte′.**

cul·pa·ble (kul′pə bəl), *adj.* deserving blame or censure. **—cul′pa·bil′i·ty,** *n.* **—cul′pa·bly,** *adv.*

cul·prit (kul′prit), *n.* a person accused or guilty of an offense or fault.

cult (kult), *n.* 1. a particular system of religious worship. 2. intense devotion to a person, ideal, or thing. 3. such a group or sect bound together by devotion. **—cul′tic,** *adj.* **—cult′ism,** *n.* **—cult′ist,** *n.*

cul·ti·vate (kul′tə vāt′), *v.t.,* **-vat·ed, -vat·ing.** 1. to prepare and work on (land) in order to raise crops. 2. to promote the growth of (a plant, crop, etc.). **3.** to develop by education or training. **4.** to promote or foster. **5.** to seek the friendship of (a person). —**cul'ti·va·ble** (-və bəl), **cul'ti·vat'a·ble**, *adj.* —**cul'ti·va'tion**, *n.* —**cul'ti·va'tor**, *n.*

cul·ture (kul'chər), *n., v.,* **-tured, -tur·ing.** —*n.* **1.** the quality in a person or society that arises from interest in arts, letters, scholarly pursuits, etc. **2.** a particular form or stage of civilization: *Greek culture.* **3.** the cultivation of microorganisms or tissues for scientific study, etc. **4.** the product resulting from such cultivation. **5.** the cultivation of land. **6.** the raising of plants or animals. —*v.t.* **7.** to subject to culture. —**cul'tur·al**, *adj.* —**cul'tur·al·ly**, *adv.*

cul'ture shock', a state of bewilderment in an individual suddenly exposed to a cultural environment radically different from his or her own.

cul·vert (kul'vərt), *n.* a drain crossing under a road, sidewalk, etc.

cum., cumulative.

cum·ber (kum'bər), *v.t. Literary.* **1.** to hinder or hamper. **2.** to overload or burden.

cum·ber·some (kum'bər səm), *adj.* **1.** heavy and burdensome. **2.** unwieldy or clumsy. Also, **cum·brous** (kum'brəs). —**cum'ber·some·ness,** *n.*

cum·in (kum'ən), *n.* a small plant bearing aromatic, seedlike fruit, used in cookery and medicine.

cum·mer·bund (kum'ər bund'), *n.* a wide sash worn as a waistband beneath a tuxedo.

cu·mu·la·tive (kyōō'myə lā'tiv, -lə tiv), *adj.* increasing by successive additions: *cumulative evidence.* —**cu'mu·la·tive·ly,** *adv.*

cu·mu·lo·nim·bus (kyōō'myə lō nim'bəs), *n., pl.* **-bus.** a cloud of a class indicative of thunderstorm conditions, characterized by large, dense, and very tall towers.

cu·mu·lus (kyōō'myə ləs), *n., pl.* **-lus.** a cloud of a class characterized by dense individual elements in the form of puffs and heaps.

cu·ne·i·form (kyōō nē'ə fôrm', kyōō'nē ə-), *adj.* **1.** composed of slim triangular elements, as writing by the ancient Babylonians and others. **2.** wedge-shaped. —*n.* **3.** cuneiform writing.

cun·ner (kun'ər), *n.* a small food fish found off the North Atlantic coast of the U.S.

cun·ni·lin·gus (kun'ə ling'gəs), *n.* oral stimulation of the female genitals, esp. to orgasm.

cun·ning (kun'ing), *n.* **1.** artful craftiness or slyness. **2.** *Archaic.* skill or ingenuity. —*adj.* **3.** crafty or sly. **4.** *Informal.* charmingly cute. **5.** *Archaic.* skillful or ingenious. —**cun'-**

ning·ly, *adv.*

cup (kup), *n., v.,* **cupped, cup·ping.** —*n.* **1.** a small, open container, of china, metal, etc., used for drinking. **2.** the quantity in a cup. **3.** a unit of capacity, equal to 8 fluid ounces. **4.** the chalice or the wine used in communion. **5.** any cuplike utensil, part, etc. —*v.t.* **6.** to form into a cuplike shape.

cup·bear·er (kup'bâr'ər), *n.* an attendant who fills and passes wine cups, as in a royal palace.

cup·board (kub'ərd), *n.* a closet or cabinet with shelves for dishes, cups, etc.

cup·cake (kup'kāk'), *n.* a small cake baked in a cup-shaped pan.

cup·ful (kup'fōōl'), *n., pl.* **-fuls.** the amount a cup can hold.

Cu·pid (kyōō'pid), *n.* the ancient Roman god of love, usually represented as a winged, naked infant boy with a bow and arrows.

cu·pid·i·ty (kyōō pid'i tē), *n.* eager or inordinate desire, esp. for wealth.

cu·po·la (kyōō'pə lə), *n.* a small structure on a dome or roof.

cu·prite (kyōō'prīt, kōō'-), *n.* a red mineral that is an important ore of copper.

cu·pro·nick·el (kyōō'prə nik'əl, kōō'-), *n.* an alloy of copper with nickel.

cur (kûr), *n.* **1.** a mongrel dog. **2.** a low, despicable person.

cur., **1.** currency. **2.** current.

cu·ra·re (kyōō rär'ē), *n.* a resinlike substance derived from tropical plants, used by South American Indians for poisoning arrows and used in modern medicine as a muscle relaxant.

cu·rate (kyōōr'it), *n.* **1.** *Chiefly Brit.* a member of the clergy who assists a rector or vicar. **2.** *Archaic.* a parish priest. —**cu·ra·cy** (kyōōr'ə sē), *n.*

cur·a·tive (kyōōr'ə tiv), *adj.* **1.** serving to cure. —*n.* **2.** a remedy. —**cur'a·tive·ly,** *adv.*

cu·ra·tor (kyōō rā'tər, kyōōr'ā-), *n.* the person in charge of a museum, art collection, etc. —**cu·ra·to·ri·al** (kyōōr'ə tôr'ē əl, -tōr'-), *adj.*

curb (kûrb), *n.* **1.** an edging, esp. of concrete or stone, for a sidewalk. **2.** a bit used with a chain for control of a horse. **3.** a restraint or control. —*v.t.* **4.** to restrain or control. **5.** to put a curb on (a horse).

curb·ing (kûr'bing), *n.* **1.** Also, **curb'-stone'.** the material forming a curb. **2.** a curb or a section of a curb.

curb' serv'ice, service given to people in parked cars, as at a roadside eating place.

curd (kûrd), *n.* Often, **curds.** a substance obtained from milk by coagulation, used as food or made into cheese.

cur·dle (kûr'dəl), *v.t.*, *v.i.*, **-dled**, **-dling.** 1. to change into curd. 2. **curdle one's blood**, to terrify one.

cure (kyŏŏr), *n.*, *v.*, **cured, cur·ing.** —*n.* 1. a method or course of remedial treatment, as for disease. 2. restoration to health. 3. a remedy. 4. spiritual charge of the people in a certain district. —*v.t.* 5. to restore to health. 6. to relieve of (an illness, a bad habit, etc.). 7. to prepare (meat, etc.) for preservation, esp. by salting or drying. 8. to process (rubber, tobacco, etc.), as by fermentation, aging, etc. —*v.i.* 9. to effect a cure. —**cur'a·ble,** *adj.* —**cure'less,** *adj.* —**cur'er,** *n.* —Syn. 5, 6. heal, remedy, treat.

cu·ré (kyŏŏ rā', kyŏŏr'ā), *n.* a parish priest in France.

cure-all (kyŏŏr'ôl'), *n.* panacea.

cu·ret·tage (kyŏŏ ret'ij, kyŏŏr'i tazh'), *n.* the surgical removal of tissues from body cavities, as the uterus.

cur·few (kûr'fyŏŏ), *n.* an order establishing a specific time during which no unauthorized persons may be outdoors. [< MF *cuevre-feu*, lit., cover (the) fireplace]

cu·ri·a (kyŏŏr'ē ə), *n.*, *pl.* **cu·ri·ae** (kyŏŏr'ē ē'). (*often cap.*) the body of congregations or offices that assist the pope in the administration of the church.

cu·rie (kyŏŏr'ē, kyŏŏ rē'), *n.* the unit of radioactivity, equivalent to 3.70 × 10¹⁰ disintegrations per second. [after Marie *Curie*, 1867–1935, Fr. physicist]

cu·ri·o (kyŏŏr'ē ō'), *n.*, *pl.* **-ri·os.** any article, object of art, etc., valued as a curiosity.

cu·ri·os·i·ty (kyŏŏr'ē os'i tē), *n.*, *pl.* **-ties.** 1. the desire to know about anything. 2. a rare or novel thing.

cu·ri·ous (kyŏŏr'ē əs), *adj.* 1. desirous of knowing. 2. prying or meddlesome. 3. odd or strange. —**cu'ri·ous·ly,** *adv.* —**cu'ri·ous·ness,** *n.* —Syn. 2. inquisitive, nosy. 3. singular, unusual.

cu·ri·um (kyŏŏr'ē əm), *n.* *Chem.* a radioactive element found among the products of plutonium after bombardment by high-energy helium ions. Symbol: Cm; at. no.: 96.

curl (kûrl), *v.t.* 1. to form into coils or ringlets. —*v.i.* 2. to grow in or form ringlets, as the hair. 3. to coil or curve. —*n.* 4. a coil or ringlet of hair. 5. anything of a spiral or curved shape. —**curl'er,** *n.* —**curl'y,** *adj.* —**curl'i·ness,** *n.*

cur·lew (kûr'lŏŏ), *n.* a shorebird having a long, slender, downward curved bill.

curl·i·cue (kûr'lə kyŏŏ'), *n.* an ornamental, fancy curl or twist.

curl·ing (kûr'lĭng), *n.* a game played on ice in which players slide large, round stones toward a center mark.

cur·mudg·eon (kər muj'ən), *n.* an irascible, churlish person.

cur·rant (kûr'ənt, kur'-), *n.* 1. a small seedless raisin. 2. the small, edible, acid, round berry of certain shrubs. 3. its shrub.

cur·ren·cy (kûr'ən sē, kur'-), *n.*, *pl.* **-cies.** 1. any form of money that is actually circulated in a country. 2. general acceptance or use.

cur·rent (kûr'ənt, kur'-), *adj.* 1. belonging to the time actually passing: *the current month.* 2. generally accepted or used. 3. widely circulating or circulated. —*n.* 4. a flow, as of a river. 5. a large portion of air, water, etc., moving in a certain direction. 6. the movement or flow of electric charge. 7. the rate of flow. 8. the general tendency. —**cur'rent·ly,** *adv.*

cur·ric·u·lum (kə rik'yə ləm), *n.*, *pl.* **-la** (-lə), **-lums.** the aggregate of courses of study given in a school, college, etc. —**cur·ric'u·lar,** *adj.*

cur·ry¹ (kûr'ē, kur'ē), *n.*, *pl.* **-ries,** *v.*, **-ried, -ry·ing.** —*n.* 1. a dish, as meat, vegetables, etc., flavored with curry powder. 2. See **curry powder.** —*v.t.* 3. to cook or flavor (food) with curry powder.

cur·ry² (kûr'ē, kur'ē), *v.t.*, **-ried, -ry·ing.** 1. to rub and clean (a horse) with a currycomb. 2. to dress (tanned hides) by scraping. 3. **curry favor,** to seek to advance oneself through flattery or fawning.

cur·ry·comb (kûr'ē kōm', kur'-), *n.* a comb, usually with rows of metal teeth, for currying horses. —*v.t.* 2. to clean with this comb.

cur·ry pow·der, a powdered mixture of turmeric, coriander, and other spices.

curse (kûrs), *n.*, *v.*, **cursed** or **curst** (kûrst), **curs·ing.** —*n.* 1. the wish that misfortune, evil, etc., befall another. 2. a profane oath. 3. an evil that has been invoked upon a person. 4. something accursed. —*v.t.* 5. to wish calamity upon. 6. to swear at. 7. to afflict with great evil. —*v.i.* 8. to swear profanely. —**curs'er,** *n.*

curs·ed (kûr'sid, kûrst), *adj.* 1. under a curse. 2. hateful or abominable.

cur·sive (kûr'siv), *adj.* (of handwriting) in flowing strokes with the letters joined together.

cur·so·ry (kûr'sə rē), *adj.* hasty and superficial. —**cur'so·ri·ly,** *adv.*

curt (kûrt), *adj.* 1. rudely brief in speech or manner. 2. terse or concise. —**curt'ly,** *adv.* —**curt'ness,** *n.*

cur·tail (kər tāl'), *v.t.* to cut short or lessen, as in extent. —**cur·tail'ment,** *n.*

cur·tain (kûr′t∍n, -tin), *n.* **1.** a hanging piece of fabric to shut out the light from a window, adorn a room, etc. **2.** drapery concealing the stage from the audience. —*v.t.* **3.** to provide, conceal, or adorn with a curtain.

curt′ain call′, the return of performers to the stage in response to the applause of the audience.

curt·sy (kûrt′sē), *n., pl.* **-sies,** *v.,* **-sied, -sy·ing.** —*n.* **1.** a bow by women in recognition or respect, consisting of bending the knees. —*v.i.* **2.** to make a curtsy. Also, **curt′sey.**

cur·va·ceous (kûr vā′shəs), *adj.* (of a woman) having a well-shaped figure with pronounced, voluptuous curves. Also, **cur·va′cious.** —**cur·va′ceous·ly,** *adv.*

cur·va·ture (kûr′və chər), *n.* **1.** curved condition, often abnormal. **2.** the degree of curving.

curve (kûrv), *n., v.,* **curved, curv·ing.** —*n.* **1.** a continuously bending line, without angles. **2.** a curving movement. **3.** any curved form. **4.** *Baseball.* a pitched ball that veers from a normal straight path. —*v.t., v.i.* **5.** to bend in a curve. —**curv·ed·ly** (kûr′vid lē), *adv.* —**curv′y,** *adj.*

cur·vet (kûr′vit), *n.* a leap of a horse from a rearing position.

cush·ion (kŏŏsh′ən), *n.* **1.** a soft pad or pillow on which to sit, kneel, or lie. **2.** anything for absorbing shocks. **3.** the padded, raised rim encircling the top of a billiard table. —*v.t.* **4.** to furnish with a cushion. **5.** to lessen or soften the effects of.

cush·y (kŏŏsh′ē), *adj.,* **cush·i·er, cush·i·est.** *Slang.* easy or pleasant.

cusp (kusp), *n.* a pointed end, as on the crown of a tooth.

cus·pid (kus′pid), *n.* (in man) a tooth with a single projection point.

cus·pi·dor (kus′pi dôr′), *n.* a bowl-shaped receptacle formerly used for spit, tobacco ash, etc.

cuss (kus), *Informal.* —*n.* **1.** curse word. **2.** a person or animal: *a strange but likable cuss.* —*v.t., v.i.* **3.** to curse.

cus·tard (kus′tərd), *n.* a dish made of eggs and milk folded together, sweetened, and baked, boiled, or frozen.

cus·to·di·an (ku stō′dē ən), *n.* **1.** a person who has custody. **2.** janitor.

cus·to·dy (kus′tə dē), *n., pl.* **-dies. 1.** guardianship and care. **2.** imprisonment or legal restraint. —**cus·to·di·al** (ku stō′dē əl), *adj.*

cus·tom (kus′təm), *n.* **1.** a habitual practice. **2.** social habits or practices collectively. **3.** customs, duties imposed by law on imported or exported goods. **4.** *Chiefly Brit.* regular business patronage. —*adj.* **5.**
made specially for individual customers. **6.** dealing in things so made, or doing work to order.

cus·tom·ar·y (kus′tə mer′ē), *adj.* **1.** of or established by custom. **2.** usual or habitual. —**cus′tom·ar′i·ly,** *adv.*

cus·tom-built (kus′təm bilt′), *adj.* built to individual order: *a custom-built limousine.*

cus·tom·er (kus′tə mər), *n.* **1.** a patron, buyer, or shopper. **2.** *Informal.* a person one has to deal with: *a tough customer.*

cus·tom·house (kus′təm hous′), *n.* a government office, often at a seaport, for collecting customs.

cus·tom·ize (kus′tə mīz′), *v.t.,* **-ized, -iz·ing.** to modify or alter to suit individual needs.

cus·tom-made (kus′təm mād′), *adj.* made to individual order: *custom-made shoes.*

cut (kut), *v.,* **cut, cut·ting,** *adj., n.* —*v.t.* **1.** to penetrate with a sharp-edged instrument. **2.** to strike sharply. **3.** to wound the feelings of. **4.** to divide with or as with a sharp-edged instrument. **5.** to hew or fell. **6.** to reap or harvest. **7.** to trim or pare. **8.** to intersect or cross. **9.** to abridge or shorten. **10.** to reduce or curtail. **11.** to make by cutting, as a statue, garment, etc. **12.** to grow (a tooth or teeth). **13.** *Informal.* to cease or discontinue. **14.** to refuse to recognize socially. **15.** to absent oneself from. **16.** to mix (a pack of cards). **17.** to hit (a ball) to cause it to spin. —*v.i.* **18.** to penetrate or divide something, as with a sharp-edged instrument. **19.** to admit of being cut. **20.** to traverse or cross. **21.** to make a sharp change in direction. **22. cut back,** to curtail or discontinue. **23. cut down,** to lessen or decrease. **24. cut in, a.** to thrust oneself abruptly between others. **b.** to stop a dancing couple in order to take one for one's partner. **25. cut it out,** *Slang.* to stop doing something. **26. cut off, a.** to stop or shut off. **b.** to sever or separate. **27. cut out, a.** to omit or delete. **b.** *Slang.* to leave suddenly. **c.** to be naturally fit: *not cut out to be a diplomat.* **28. cut up, a.** to cut into pieces. **b.** *Informal.* to play pranks. —*adj.* **29.** that has been cut. —*n.* **31.** the act of cutting. **32.** a piece cut off. **33.** *Informal.* a share, esp. of earnings. **34.** the result of cutting, as an incision, wound, etc. **35.** the fashion in which anything is cut. **36.** a passage or course straight across. **37.** a reduction, as in price. **38.** an act, speech, etc., that wounds the feelings. **39.** an engraved plate or block used for printing. **40.** a printed picture or illustration. **41.** an absence, as from a school class. **42. a cut above,** *Informal.* somewhat better than.

cut-and-dried (kut'ən drīd'), *adj.* **1.** fixed in advance. **2.** lacking freshness.

cu·ta·ne·ous (kyōō tā'nē əs), *adj.* of or affecting the skin. —**cu·ta'ne·ous·ly,** *adv.*

cut·a·way (kut'ə wā'), *n.* a man's formal coat cut so as to taper toward the tails.

cut·back (kut'bak'), *n.* reduction in rate, quantity, etc.

cute (kyōōt), *adj.,* **cut·er, cut·est. 1.** pleasingly pretty or dainty. **2.** *Informal.* clever and shrewd. —**cute'ly,** *adv.* —**cute'ness,** *n.*

cu·ti·cle (kyōō'ti kəl), *n.* the epidermis, esp. the nonliving one that surrounds the edges of the fingernail. —**cu·tic·u·lar** (kyōō tik'yə lər), *adj.*

cut·lass (kut'ləs), *n.* a short, heavy, slightly curved sword.

cut·ler (kut'lər), *n.* a person who makes, sells, or repairs cutlery.

cut·ler·y (kut'lə rē), *n.* cutting instruments collectively, esp. those for use in serving or eating food.

cut·let (kut'lit), *n.* **1.** a slice of meat, esp. of veal or mutton, for broiling or frying. **2.** a flat croquette of minced chicken or lobster.

cut·off (kut'ôf', -of'), *n.* **1.** something that is cut off. **2.** the point, time, or stage for a cutting off. **3.** a road that provides a shortcut. **4.** a device that stops, cuts off, etc.

cut·out (kut'out'), *n.* something that cuts out or is cut out from something else.

cut-rate (kut'rāt'), *adj.* offered or on sale at a reduced charge or price.

cut·ter (kut'ər), *n.* **1.** a person or thing that cuts. **2.** a single-masted sailing vessel. **3.** a ship's boat for carrying passengers, supplies, etc. **4.** a lightly armed vessel, used by a government to enforce regulations. **5.** a small, light sleigh.

cut·throat (kut'thrōt'), *adj.* **1.** ruinously ruthless, as competition. **2.** cruel or murderous. —*n.* **3.** a murderer.

cut·ting (kut'ing), *n.* **1.** a root, stem, or leaf cut from a plant and used for propagation. —*adj.* **2.** penetrating by or as by a cut. **3.** piercing, as a wind. **4.** wounding the feelings severely.

cut·tle·fish (kut'əl fish'), *n., pl.* **-fish, -fish·es.** a marine mollusk having ten arms with suckers and a thick internal shell (**cut'tle·bone'**) used for making polishing powder.

cut·up (kut'up'), *n. Informal.* a show-off or prankster.

cut·worm (kut'wûrm'), *n.* the caterpillar of certain moths that feeds on young plants at night.

cw, clockwise.

CWO, *Mil.* chief warrant officer.

c.w.o., cash with order.

cwt, hundredweight.

-cy, a suffix meaning: **a.** state or condition: *expediency.* **b.** rank or office: *magistracy.*

cy·an (sī'an, sī'ən), *n.* a hue between blue and green.

cy·a·nide (sī'ə nīd', -nid), *n.* a highly toxic compound containing sodium or potassium, used in various chemical processes. Also, **cy·a·nid** (sī'ə-nid).

cy·ber·na·tion (sī'bər nā'shən), *n.* the use of computers to control automatic processes, esp. in manufacturing. —**cy'ber·nat'ed** (-nāt'əd), *adj.*

cy·ber·net·ics (sī'bər net'iks), *n.* the study of human-control functions and of mechanical and electric systems designed to replace them.

cyc., cyclopedia.

cy·cla·mate (sī'klə māt', sik'lə māt'), *n.* a white, artificial sweetening powder consisting of a salt of calcium or sodium.

cyc·la·men (sik'lə mən, -men'), *n.* a low plant having white, pink, or crimson flowers.

cy·cla·zo·cine (sī'klə zō'sēn), *n.* a drug that hinders the effects of morphine or heroin chiefly by preventing its action on the nervous system.

cy·cle (sī'kəl), *n., v.,* **-cled, -cling.** —*n.* **1.** a recurring period of time, esp. one in which certain events repeat themselves in the same order and intervals. **2.** any complete series of occurrences that repeats or is repeated: *a cycle of alternating current.* **3.** any group of poems or narratives about a central theme or figure: *the Arthurian cycle.* **4.** a bicycle, motorcycle, etc. —*v.i.* **5.** to travel by bicycle, motorcycle, etc. **6.** to pass through cycles. —**cy·clic** (sī'klik, sik'lik), *adj.* —**cy·cli·cal** (sī'kli kəl, sik'-), *adj.* —**cy'cli·cal·ly,** *adv.*

cy·clist (sī'klist), *n.* a person who rides or travels by bicycle, motorcycle, etc. Also, **cy'cler.**

cyclo-, a combining form meaning "cycle" or "wheel": *cyclometer.*

cy·cloid (sī'kloid), *adj.* like a circle. —**cy·cloi'dal,** *adj.*

cy·clom·e·ter (sī klom'i tər), *n.* a device for recording the revolutions of a wheel and the distance traversed.

cy·clone (sī'klōn), *n.* **1.** a large-scale storm characterized by low pressure at its center and by circular wind motion. **2.** tornado. [< Gk *kyklôn* revolving] —**cy·clon·ic** (sī klon'ik), *adj.*

cy·clo·pe·di·a (sī′klə pē′dē ə), *n.* an encyclopedia. Also, **cy′clo·pae′di·a.**

cy·clo·tron (sī′klə tron′, sik′lə-), *n.* an accelerator in which particles move in a spiral path under the influence of an alternating voltage and a magnetic field.

cyg·net (sig′nit), *n.* a young swan.

cyl., cylinder.

cyl·in·der (sil′in dər), *n.* **1.** a surface or solid bounded by two parallel planes and generated by a line tracing a closed curve perpendicular to the given planes. **2.** any cylinderlike object or part. **3.** the rotating part of a revolver. **4.** a cylindrical chamber in which a sliding piston moves. —**cy·lin·dri·cal** (si lin′dri kəl), *adj.*

cym·bal (sim′bəl), *n. Music.* a concave plate of brass that produces a sharp, ringing sound when struck. —**cym′bal·ist,** *n.*

cyme (sīm), *n.* an inflorescence in which the primary axis bears a single terminal flower that develops first, the inflorescence being continued by secondary, tertiary, and other axes. —**cy·mose** (sī′mōs, sī mōs′), *adj.*

cyn·ic (sin′ik), *n.* a person who believes that only selfishness motivates human actions. —**cyn′i·cal,** *adj.* —**cyn′i·cal·ly,** *adv.*

cyn·i·cism (sin′i siz′əm), *n.* the disposition, character, or belief of a cynic.

cy·no·sure (sī′nə shŏŏr′, sin′ə-), *n.* something that strongly attracts attention.

CYO, Catholic Youth Organization.

cy·pher (sī′fər), *n., v.i., v.t. Chiefly Brit.* cipher.

cy·press (sī′prəs), *n.* an evergreen tree having dark-green, scalelike, overlapping leaves.

Cy·prus (sī′prəs), *n.* an island country in the Mediterranean, S of Turkey. —**Cyp·ri·ot** (sip′rē ət), **Cyp·ri·ote′,** *n., adj.*

cyst (sist), *n.* a closed, bladderlike sac formed in animal tissues, containing fluid or semifluid matter. —**cyst·ic** (sis′tik), *adj.*

cys′tic fibro′sis, a hereditary, chronic disease of the pancreas, lungs, etc., in which there is inability to digest foods and difficulty in breathing.

cy·tol·o·gy (sī tol′ə jē), *n.* the branch of biology dealing with the study of cells. —**cy·to·log·ic** (sīt′°loj′ik), **cy′to·log′i·cal,** *adj.* —**cy′to·log′i·cal·ly,** *adv.* —**cy·tol′o·gist,** *n.*

cy·to·plasm (sī′tə plaz′əm), *n. Biol.* the protoplasm of a cell exclusive of the nucleus. —**cy′to·plas′mic,** *adj.*

cy·to·sine (sī′tə sēn′), *n.* a white, crystalline pyrimidine, used in the study of cell metabolism.

CZ, Canal Zone. Also **C.Z.**

czar (zär), *n.* **1.** (*often cap.*) the former emperor of Russia. **2.** any person in a position of power, as a high public official. [< Russ *tsar′* < L *Caesar*] —**cza·ri·na** (zä rē′nə), *n. fem.* —**czar′ist,** *adj., n.*

czar·das (chär′däsh), *n.* a Hungarian dance in two movements, one slow and the other fast.

Czech (chek), *n.* **1.** a native or inhabitant of Czechoslovakia. **2.** the Slavic language of the Czechs.

Czech·o·slo·va·ki·a (chek′ə slə vä′kē ə, -vak′ē ə), *n.* a country in central Europe. —**Czech′o·slo′vak, Czech′o·slo·va′ki·an,** *adj., n.*

D

D, d (dē), *n., pl.* **D's** or **Ds, d's** or **ds.** the fourth letter of the English alphabet, a consonant.

D, Dutch.

D, 1. the fourth in order or in a series. **2.** (*sometimes l.c.*) a grade, as of academic work, that indicates poor quality. **3.** the second tone in the scale of C major. **4.** the Roman numeral for 500. **5.** deuterium.

D., 1. December. **2.** Democrat. **3.** Democratic. **4.** Doctor. **5.** dose. **6.** Dutch.

d., 1. date. **2.** daughter. **3.** day. **4.** deceased. **5.** degree. **6.** *Brit.* penny. [< L *dēnārius*] **7.** deputy. **8.** diameter. **9.** died. **10.** dose. **11.** drachma.

D/A, 1. days after acceptance. **2.** deposit account.

D.A., 1. Department of Agriculture. **2.** District Attorney. **3.** doesn't answer; don't answer.

dab (dab), *v.,* **dabbed, dab·bing,** *n.* —*v.t., v.i.* **1.** to touch or strike gently. **2.** to apply (a substance) by light strokes. —*n.* **3.** a quick or light pat. **4.** a small quantity.

dab·ble (dab′əl), *v.*, **-bled**, **-bling.**
—*v.i.* **1.** to play in or as if in water.
2. to work at anything in a superficial manner. —*v.t.* **3.** to wet slightly.
—**dab′bler**, *n.*

dace (dās), *n., pl.* **dace**, **dac·es.** a
small, slim, freshwater fish of the
carp family.

da·cha (dä′chə), *n.* a country house
in Russia.

dachs·hund (däks′hōŏnd′, -ənd, dash′-),
n. a dog having short legs, a long
body and ears, and a usually tan
coat. [< G = *Dachs* badger +
Hund dog]

Da·cron (dä′kron, dak′ron), *n. Trademark.* a synthetic textile fiber that is
wrinkle-resistant and strong.

dac·tyl (dak′t⁹l, -til), *n. Pros.* a foot
of three syllables, one stressed followed by two unstressed. —**dac·tyl′ic**,
adj., n.

dad (dad), *n. Informal.* father (def. 1).

Da·da (dä′dä), *n.* (*sometimes l.c.*)
the style of a group of artists, writers,
etc., of the early 20th century who
exploited accidental and incongruous
effects in their work. —**Da′da·ism**,
n. —**Da′da·ist**, *n.*

dad·dy (dad′ē), *n., pl.* **-dies.** a diminutive of **dad.**

dad·dy-long·legs (dad′ē lông′legz′,
-lông′-), *n.* an arachnid having a
compact body and extremely long,
slender legs.

da·do (dä′dō), *n., pl.* **-does**, **-dos. 1.**
the part of a pedestal between the
base and the cornice. **2.** the lower
broad part of an interior wall finished in wallpaper, a fabric, etc.

dae·mon (dē′mən), *n.* demon. —**dae-
mon·ic** (di mon′ik), *adj.*

daf·fo·dil (daf′ə dil), *n.* a plant having yellow, nodding flowers that
bloom in the spring.

daff·y (daf′ē), *adj.*, **daff·i·er**, **daff·i·est.**
Informal. silly or crazy. —**daff′i-
ness**, *n.*

daft (daft, däft), *adj.* **1.** daffy. **2.**
simple or foolish. —**daft′ness**, *n.*

dag, dekagram; dekagrams.

dag·ger (dag′ər), *n.* **1.** a short, sword-
like weapon with a pointed blade.
2. a mark (†) used esp. for references.

da·guerre·o·type (də ger′ə tīp′), *n.* an
early photographic print made on a
silvered copper plate. [after L. J. M.
Daguerre, 1789–1851, Fr. inventor]

dahl·ia (dal′yə, däl′- *or, esp. Brit.*,
dāl′-), *n.* a composite plant widely
cultivated for its showy, variegated
flowers. [after Anders *Dahl*, d. 1789,
Sw. botanist]

Da·ho·mey (də hō′mē), *n.* former
name of **Benin.** —**Da·ho·man** (də-
hō′mən), **Da·ho′me·an** (-mē ən), *adj.,
n.*

dai·ly (dā′lē), *adj., n., pl.* **-lies**, *adv.*
—*adj.* **1.** done, occurring, or issued
each day or each weekday. **2.** computed by the day. —*n.* **3.** a daily
newspaper. —*adv.* **4.** every day.

dai′ly dou′ble, a betting system in
horse racing in which one bet is
made in a special pool on the outcome of two consecutive races.

dai′ly doz′en, a set of exercises to
be done each day.

dain·ty (dān′tē), *adj.*, **-ti·er**, **-ti·est**, *n.,
pl.* **-ties.** —*adj.* **1.** of delicate beauty.
2. delicious or nice. **3.** excessively
particular or fastidious. —*n.* **4.** a
delicacy. —**dain′ti·ly**, *adv.* —**dain′-
ti·ness**, *n.*

dai·qui·ri (dī′kə rē, dak′ə-), *n., pl.* **-ris.**
a cocktail consisting of rum, lemon
or lime juice, and sugar.

dair·y (dâr′ē), *n., pl.* **dair·ies. 1.** a shop
or company that makes or sells milk,
butter, etc. **2.** a farm concerned with
the production of milk, cheese, etc.

dair·y·ing (dâr′ē ing), *n.* the business
of a dairy.

dair·y·maid (dâr′ē mād′), *n.* a girl or
woman employed in a dairy.

dair·y·man (dâr′ē mən), *n.* **1.** an owner
or manager of a dairy. **2.** an employee in a dairy.

da·is (dā′is, dī′-, dās), *n.* a raised
platform, as for a throne.

dai·sy (dā′zē), *n., pl.* **-sies.** a plant
whose flowers have a yellow disk
and white rays.

Da·ko·ta (də kō′tə), *n.* **1.** a member
of a large group of American Indian
peoples formerly living on the pla-
teau region in the western U.S. **2.**
their language.

dal, dekaliter; dekaliters.

dale (dāl), *n. Literary.* a valley.

Dal·las (dal′əs), *n.* a city in NE
Texas.

dal·ly (dal′ē), *v.i.*, **-lied**, **-ly·ing. 1.**
to play, esp. amorously. **2.** to play
mockingly. **3.** to waste time playfully. —**dal′li·ance** (-ē əns), *n.* —
dal′li·er, *n.*

Dal·ma·tian (dal mā′shən), *n.* a short-
haired dog having a white coat
marked with black spots.

dam¹ (dam), *n., v.*, **dammed**, **damming.** —*n.* **1.** a barrier to obstruct
the flow of water, esp. one built
across a stream. —*v.t.* **2.** to furnish
with a dam. **3.** to obstruct or confine.

dam² (dam), *n.* the female parent
of a four-footed animal.

dam, dekameter; dekameters.

dam·age (dam′ij), *n., v.*, **-aged**, **-ag-
ing.** —*n.* **1.** injury or harm that
impairs value or usefulness. **2. damages**, *Law.* the estimated money
equivalent for detriment or injury
sustained. —*v.t.* **3.** to cause damage

to. —**dam′age·a·ble,** *adj.* —**dam′ag-ing·ly,** *adv.*

Dam·a·scene (dam′ə sēn′), *v.t.* to decorate (steel or iron) with wavy lines or with inlaid patterns of silver or gold.

Da·mas·cus (də mas′kəs), *n.* the capital of Syria.

Damas′cus steel′, an ancient type of hard steel having a wavy appearance, used chiefly for sword blades.

dam·ask (dam′əsk), *n.* **1.** a reversible fabric woven with patterns, used esp. for table linen. **2.** See **Damascus steel. 3.** a pink color.

dame (dām), *n.* **1.** (*cap.*) (in Britain) the title of the wife of a knight. **2.** an elderly woman. **3.** *Slang.* any woman.

damn (dam), *v.t.* **1.** to declare to be bad, unfit, or a failure. **2.** to condemn to eternal punishment in hell. **3.** to curse, using the word "damn." —*interj.* **4.** (an expletive to express anger, disgust, etc.) —*n.* **5.** the utterance of "damn" in swearing. —*adj.* **6.** *Informal.* damned (def. 2a). —*adv.* **7.** *Informal.* damned.

dam·na·ble (dam′nə bəl), *adj.* **1.** worthy of damnation. **2.** detestable or abominable. —**dam′na·bly,** *adv.*

dam·na·tion (dam nā′shən), *n.* **1.** the act or state of damning or of being damned. —*interj.* **2.** (an exclamation of anger, etc.)

damned (damd), *adj., superl.* **damned-est, damnd·est,** *adv.* —*adj.* **1.** condemned as bad, etc. **2.** *Informal.* **a.** detestable or loathsome. **b.** utter: *a damned fool.* —*adv.* **3.** *Informal.* very.

Dam·o·cles (dam′ə klēz′), *n. Class. Myth.* a flatterer who was forced by his king to sit at a banquet under a sword suspended by a single hair to show him the perilous nature of a king's happiness. —**Dam·o·cle·an** (dam′ə klē′ən), *adj.*

damp (damp), *adj.* **1.** moderately wet, often unpleasantly so. —*n.* **2.** a moderate wetness. **3.** a noxious gas, esp. in a mine. —*v.t.* **4.** to make damp. **5.** to deaden or bank, as a fire. **6.** to dampen (def. 2). —**damp′-ness,** *n.*

damp-dry (damp′drī′, -drī′), *v.,* **-dried, dry·ing,** *adj.* —*v.t.* **1.** to dry (laundry) partially so that some moisture remains. —*adj.* **2.** of laundry so dried.

damp·en (dam′pən), *v.t.* **1.** to make damp. **2.** to check or retard the intensity or force of. **3.** to discourage, as one's spirits. —*v.i.* **4.** to become damp. —**damp′en·er,** *n.*

damp·er (dam′pər), *n.* **1.** a person or thing that damps. **2.** a movable plate for regulating the draft in a stove, furnace, etc.

dam·sel (dam′zəl), *n. Archaic.* a maiden.

dam·sel·fly (dam′zəl flī′), *n.* a slender, slow-flying insect related to the dragonflies.

dam·son (dam′zən), *n.* a small dark-blue or purple plum.

Dan., 1. Daniel. **2.** Danish.

dance (dans, däns), *v.,* **danced, danc·ing,** *n.* —*v.i.* **1.** to move rhythmically in a pattern of steps, esp. to music. **2.** to leap, skip, etc., as from emotion. **3.** to bob up and down. —*v.t.* **4.** to perform (a dance). **5.** to cause to dance. —*n.* **6.** a group of rhythmic bodily motions, usually to music. **7.** the art of dancing. **8.** a social gathering for dancing. **9.** a piece of music suited to dancing. —**danc′er,** *n.* —**danc′ing,** *n., adj.* —**danc′ing·ly,** *adv.*

dan·de·li·on (dan′d°lī′ən), *n.* a weed having deeply notched leaves and golden-yellow flowers. [< MF *dent de lion* tooth of (a) lion]

dan·der (dan′dər), *n. Informal.* anger or temper.

dan·di·fy (dan′də fī′), *v.t.,* **-fied, -fy-ing.** to make into a dandy or fop. —**dan′di·fi·ca′tion,** *n.*

dan·dle (dan′d°l), *v.t.,* **-dled, -dling.** to move (a baby) lightly up and down, as on one's knee.

dan·druff (dan′drəf), *n.* a scurf that forms on the scalp and comes off in scales.

dan·dy (dan′dē), *n., pl.* **-dies,** *adj.* **-di·er, -di·est.** —*n.* **1.** a man excessively concerned about appearance. **2.** *Informal.* something of exceptional quality. —*adj.* **3.** *Informal.* fine or first-rate.

Dane (dān), *n.* a native or inhabitant of Denmark.

dan·ger (dān′jər), *n.* **1.** liability to harm, injury, or evil. **2.** an instance or cause of such a menace.

dan·ger·ous (dān′jər əs), *adj.* **1.** full of or exposing to danger. **2.** able or likely to do physical injury: *a dangerous criminal.* —**dan′ger·ous·ly,** *adv.* —**dan′ger·ous·ness,** *n.* —**Syn. 1.** hazardous, perilous, risky, unsafe.

dan·gle (dang′gəl), *v.,* **-gled, -gling.** —*v.i.* **1.** to hang loosely, esp. with a swaying motion. —*v.t.* **2.** to cause to dangle.

dan′gling par′ticiple, a participle or participial phrase that appears to modify an element of the sentence other than the one intended, as *burning* in *Burning with enthusiasm, the car brought us to Rome.*

Dan·iel (dan′yəl), *n. Bible.* a Hebrew prophet who escaped alive from the lions' den.

Dan·ish (dā′nish), *adj.* **1.** of the Danes, their country, or their language. —n. 2. the language of Denmark.

Dan·ish pas′try, a light pastry leavened with yeast and often filled with fruit, etc.

dank (dangk), *adj.* unpleasantly moist or humid. —**dank′ly,** *adv.* —**dank′ness,** *n.*

dan·seuse (dän sōōz′), *n.* a female ballet dancer.

Dan·te (dan′tē, dän′tā), *n.* (*Dante Alighieri*), 1265–1321, Italian poet.

Dan·ube (dan′yōōb), *n.* a river in central and SE Europe.

dap·per (dap′ər), *adj.* 1. neat and trim. 2. small and active.

dap·ple (dap′əl), *n., v.,* **-pled, -pling.** —*n.* 1. a mottled marking. —*v.t., v.i.* 2. to mark or become marked with spots.

D.A.R., Daughters of the American Revolution.

dare (dâr), *v.,* **dared** or (*Archaic*) **durst, dared,** **dar·ing,** *n.* —*v.i.* 1. to have the courage for something. —*v.t.* 2. to have the courage (to do something). 3. to face (something) boldly. 4. to challenge (a person) to do something. 5. **I dare say, I** assume. —*n.* 6. an act of daring. —**dar′er,** *n.* —**Syn.** 6. challenge, defiance.

dare·dev·il (dâr′dev′əl), *n.* 1. a recklessly daring person. —*adj.* 2. recklessly daring.

dar·ing (dâr′ing), *n.* 1. adventurous courage. —*adj.* 2. venturesomely courageous. —**dar′ing·ly,** *adv.*

dark (därk), *adj.* 1. having little or no light. 2. admitting or reflecting little light: *a dark color.* 3. somber in hue. 4. gloomy or dismal. 5. evil or wicked. 6. ignorant or unenlightened. 7. hidden or secret. —*n.* 8. the absence of light. 9. night or nightfall. 10. a dark color. 11. **in the dark, a.** in ignorance. **b.** in secrecy. —**dark′ish,** *adj.* —**dark′ly,** *adv.* —**dark′ness,** *n.* —**Syn.** 1. dim, dusky, murky, obscure.

dark′ adapta′tion, the reflex adjustment of the eye to sudden dim light. —**dark′-a·dapt′ed,** *adj.*

Dark′ Ag′es, the Middle Ages, esp. the early part.

dark·en (där′kən), *v.t., v.i.* 1. to make or become dark or darker. 2. to make or become gloomy or dull. —**dark′en·er,** *n.*

dark′ horse′, a competitor, nominee, etc., about whom little is known or who unexpectedly wins.

dark·ling (därk′ling), *adv. Chiefly Literary.* in the dark.

dark·room (därk′rōōm′, -rōōm′), *n.* a lightless room illuminated by a special-color lamp for processing photographic materials.

dark·some (därk′səm), *adj. Chiefly Literary.* dark or darkish.

dar·ling (där′ling), *n.* 1. a person very dear to another. 2. a person or thing in great favor. —*adj.* 3. dearly loved. 4. favorite or cherished. 5. *Informal.* charming or lovable.

darn[1] (därn), *v.t.* 1. to mend, esp. by interweaving stitches. —*n.* 2. a darned place. —**darn′er,** *n.*

darn[2] (därn), *v.t., interj., n., adj., adv. Informal.* damn. —**darned** (därnd), *adj., adv.*

dar·nel (där′n[ə]l), *n.* an annual grass often growing as a weed in grain fields.

darn′ing nee′dle, 1. a long needle with a long eye used in darning. 2. *Dial.* a dragonfly.

dart (därt), *n.* 1. a small, slender, pointed missile, usually feathered. 2. **darts,** a game in which darts are thrown at a target. 3. a sudden swift movement. 4. a tapered seam of fabric. —*v.i.* 5. to move swiftly. —*v.t.* 6. to thrust or move suddenly.

dart·er (där′tər), *n.* 1. a person or thing that darts or moves swiftly. 2. a small, darting, freshwater fish of the perch family.

Dar·von (där′von), *n. Trademark.* a nonnarcotic compound used to relieve pain.

Dar·win (där′win), *n.* **Charles (Robert),** 1809–82, English naturalist: noted for his theory of evolution. —**Dar·win′i·an,** *adj., n.*

Dar·win·ism (där′wə niz′əm), *n.* the theory that the origin of species is derived by descent, with variation, from parent forms, through the natural selection of those best adapted to survive in the struggle for existence. —**Dar′win·ist, Dar′win·ite′** (-nīt′), *n., adj.*

dash (dash), *v.t.* 1. to strike violently, esp. so as to break to pieces. 2. to throw suddenly. 3. to splash violently. 4. to apply roughly, as by splashing. 5. to ruin or frustrate (hopes, plans, etc.). 6. to depress or dispirit. 7. to accomplish quickly: *to dash a letter off.* —*v.i.* 8. to strike with violence. 9. to rush. 10. **dash off,** to leave or go hurriedly. —*n.* 11. the splashing of liquid against something. 12. a small quantity added: *a dash of salt.* 13. the sign (—) used to note an abrupt break or pause in a sentence, etc. 14. a sudden onset. 15. a short race. 16. spirited action. 17. a signal of longer duration than a dot, used in groups of dots, dashes, and spaces to represent letters, as in Morse code.

dash·board (dash′bôrd′, -bōrd′), *n.* an instrument panel beneath the front window in an automobile, aircraft, etc.

dash·er (dash′ər), *n.* a plunger for mixing liquids in a churn, ice-cream freezer, etc.

da·shi·ki (də shē′kē), *n.* a loose, colorful pullover shirt for men, originally worn mainly in western Africa.

dash·ing (dash′ing), *adj.* 1. vigorously lively. 2. brilliant or showy. —**dash′ing·ly,** *adv.*

dash·pot (dash′pot′), *n.* a device for cushioning, damping, or reversing the motion of a piece of machinery.

das·tard (das′tərd), *n.* a mean, sneaking coward. —**das′tard·ly,** *adj.* —**das′tard·li·ness,** *n.*

dat., dative.

da·ta (dā′tə, dat′ə, dä′tə), *n.pl., sing.* **da·tum.** (*often construed as sing.*) facts or information collected for analysis or computation.

da′ta bank′, a fund of special information gathered and organized for quick use or analysis, usually on a computer.

da·ta·ma·tion (dā′tə mā′shən), *n.* automatic electronic data processing.

da′ta proc′essing, the high-speed handling of information by computer. —**da′ta proc′ess·or.**

date¹ (dāt), *n., v.,* **dat·ed, dat·ing.** —*n.* 1. the day of the month. 2. a particular time at which some event happened or will happen. 2. an inscription on a writing, coin, etc., that shows the time of writing, casting, etc. 3. the period or age to which any event or thing belongs. 4. a social appointment. 5. a person of the opposite sex with whom one has such an appointment. 6. to date, up to the present time. —*v.i.* 7. to have a date. 8. to belong to a particular period. 9. to go out on dates with persons of the opposite sex. —*v.t.* 10. to furnish with a date. 11. to assign a period or point in time to. 12. to show the age of. 13. show to be old-fashioned. 14. to make a date with (a person of the opposite sex). —**dat′er,** *n.* —**date′less,** *adj.*

date² (dāt), *n.* the oblong, fleshy fruit of a tropical palm tree.

dat·ed (dā′tid), *adj.* 1. having or showing a date. 2. out-of-date or old-fashioned. —**dat′ed·ness,** *n.*

date·line (dāt′līn′), *n.* a line giving the place of origin and date of a news dispatch.

dat′ing bar′, a bar patronized by unmarried people, esp. as a meeting place.

da·tive (dā′tiv), *Gram.* —*adj.* 1. noting a case that indicates the indirect object of a verb. —*n.* 2. the dative case.

da·tum (dā′təm, dat′əm, dä′təm), *n., pl.* **da·ta.** an individual piece of data.

dau., daughter.

daub (dôb), *v.t., v.i.* 1. to cover with soft, adhesive matter. 2. to smear or soil. 3. to paint unskillfully. —*n.* 4. anything daubed on. 5. a crude, inartistic painting. —**daub′er,** *n.*

daugh·ter (dô′tər), *n.* 1. a female child. 2. any female descendant. —**daugh′ter·ly,** *adj.*

daugh·ter-in-law (dô′tər in lô′), *n., pl.* **daugh·ters-in-law.** the wife of one's son.

daunt (dônt, dänt), *v.t.* 1. to overcome by frightening. 2. to dishearten.

daunt·less (dônt′lis, dänt′-), *adj.* not to be daunted or discouraged. —**daunt′less·ly,** *adv.* —**daunt′less·ness,** *n.*

dau·phin (dô′fin), *n. Hist.* the eldest son of a king of France.

dav·en·port (dav′ən pôrt′, -pōrt′), *n. Obsolesc.* a large sofa convertible into a bed.

Da·vid (dā′vid), *n.* died c970 B.C., the second king of Israel.

Da·vis (dā′vis), *n.* **Jefferson,** 1808–89, president of the Confederate States of America 1861–65.

dav·it (dav′it, dā′vit), *n.* any of various cranelike devices used for supporting, raising, and lowering boats, anchors, etc.

daw·dle (dôd′²l), *v.i., v.t.,* **-dled, -dling.** to waste (time) by trifling. —**daw′dler,** *n.* —**Syn.** dally, idle, loiter.

dawn (dôn), *n.* 1. the first appearance of daylight in the morning. 2. the beginning of anything. —*v.i.* 3. to begin to grow light in the morning. 4. to begin to open or develop. 5. to begin to be perceived.

day (dā), *n.* 1. the interval of light between two successive nights. 2. the period of 24 hours during which the earth makes one rotation on its axis. 3. the portion of a day allotted to work. 4. Often, **days.** a particular time or period: *in days of old.* 5. period of existence, power, or influence. 6. the contest or battle on hand: *to win the day.* 7. call it a day, to stop temporarily. 8. day in, day out, every day.

day′ bed′, a couch that is convertible into a bed at night.

day·book (dā′book′), *n.* an appointment book.

day·break (dā′brāk′), *n.* dawn.

day′-care cen′ter, an institution for the daytime care of infants and preschool children of working mothers. Also called **day′ nurs′ery.**

day·dream (dā′drēm′), *n.* 1. a visionary fancy indulged in while awake. —*v.i.* 2. to indulge in daydreams. —**day′dream′er,** *n.*

day·flow·er (dā′flou′ər), *n.* a plant having small, blue flowers that last only one day.

day·light (dā′līt′), *n.* 1. the light of day. 2. openness or publicity. 3. daytime. 4. dawn. 5. clear understanding or solution, as of an intricate problem: *to see daylight.* 6. **daylights,** *Informal.* sense or conciousness: *to beat the daylights out of him.*

day′light-sav′ing time′ (dā′līt′sā′vĭng), time one hour later than standard time, usually used in summer.

Day′ of Atone′ment. See **Yom Kippur.**

day′ school′, a private school for pupils living at home.

day′ stud′ent, a student who attends a daytime session, esp. one who lives at home or one who does not attend classes in the evening.

day·time (dā′tīm′), *n.* the time between sunrise and sunset.

day-to-day (dā′tə dā′), *adj.* 1. occurring each day. 2. routine or normal.

Day·ton (dāt′ən), *n.* a city in SW Ohio.

daze (dāz), *v.,* **dazed, daz·ing,** *n.* —*v.t.* 1. to stun or stupefy, as with a blow. 2. to dazzle. —*n.* 3. a dazed condition. —**daz′ed·ly,** *adv.*

daz·zle (daz′əl), *v.,* **-zled, -zling,** *n.* —*v.t., v.i.* 1. to overpower or be overpowered by intense light. 2. to bewilder or excite admiration by brilliance, splendor, etc. —*n.* 3. an act of dazzling. —**daz′zler,** *n.*

dB, decibel; decibels. Also, **db**

D.B., Bachelor of Divinity.

dbl., double.

DC, 1. See **direct current.** 2. District of Columbia. Also, **D.C.**

dc, See **direct current.** Also, **d.c.**

D.C.M., Distinguished Conduct Medal.

D/D, days after date.

DD, dishonorable discharge.

D.D., 1. demand draft. 2. Doctor of Divinity. [< L *Divinitatis Doctor*]

D-day (dē′dā′), *n.* the day set for beginning some action, as a military offensive.

D.D.S., 1. Doctor of Dental Science. 2. Doctor of Dental Surgery.

DDT, a water-insoluble solid, used as an insecticide.

DE, Delaware.

de-, a prefix meaning: **a.** removal: *dehumidify.* **b.** negation: *demerit.* **c.** descent: *degrade.* **d.** reversal: *detract.*

de·ac·ces·sion (dē′ak sesh′ən), *v.t.* to withdraw (a painting, etc.) from a museum collection, as for sale or exchange.

dea·con (dē′kən), *n.* 1. a member of the clergy ranking just below a priest. 2. a lay official having various duties in Protestant churches. —**dea′con·ess,** *n.fem.*

de·ac·ti·vate (dē ak′tə vāt′), *v.t.,* **-vat·ed, -vat·ing.** to cause to be inactive. —**de·ac′ti·va′tion,** *n.*

dead (ded), *adj.* 1. no longer living. 2. not endowed with life. 3. deathlike or deadly. 4. bereft of sensation. 5. insensitive or unresponsive. 6. incapable of being moved emotionally. 7. obsolete or no longer in general use. 8. utterly exhausted. 9. stagnant or not circulating. 10. no longer functioning. 11. extinguished or put out. 12. tasteless or flat. 13. without resilience or bounce. 14. without vitality or spirit. 15. complete or absolute. 16. sudden or abrupt. 17. accurate or unerring: *a dead shot.* 18. exact or precise. 19. out of play: *a dead ball.* —*n.* 20. the period of greatest darkness, coldness, etc. 21. dead persons collectively. —*adv.* 22. absolutely or completely. 23. with abrupt stoppage of motion. 24. directly or exactly: *dead ahead.* —**dead′ness,** *n.* —**Syn.** 1. deceased, lifeless, inanimate.

dead·beat (ded′bēt′), *n.* Informal. a person who avoids paying his or her debts or share of expenses.

dead·en (ded′ən), *v.t.* 1. to make less sensitive, active, energetic, or forcible. 2. to make impervious to sound.

dead′ end′, 1. a street, etc., that is closed at one end. 2. a position that offers no hope of progress. —**dead′-end′,** *adj.*

dead′ heat′, a race ending in a tie.

dead′ let′ter, 1. a law or regulation that has lost its force. 2. a letter that cannot be delivered or returned because of incorrect address, etc.

dead·line (ded′līn′), *n.* the latest time for finishing something, as copy for a publication.

dead·lock (ded′lok′), *n.* 1. a complete standstill, as in a dispute. —*v.t., v.i.* 2. to bring or come to a deadlock.

dead·ly (ded′lē), *adj.,* **-li·er, -li·est,** *adv.* —*adj.* 1. causing or tending to cause death. 2. implacable or mortal: *a deadly enemy.* 3. like death. 4. excessive or inordinate. 5. extremely accurate. 6. excruciatingly boring. —*adv.* 7. in a manner suggesting death. 8. completely. —**dead′li·ness,** *n.* —**Syn.** 1. fatal, lethal, mortal.

dead′ly sins′, the seven sins of pride, covetousness, lust, anger, gluttony, envy, and sloth.

dead·pan (ded′pan′), *adj.* marked by a careful pretense of seriousness or detachment.

dead′ reck′oning, *Navig.* calculation of one's position on the basis of distance run on various headings since the last precisely observed position.

Dead′ Sea′, a salt lake between Israel and Jordan.

dead′ weight′, 1. the heavy, unrelieved weight of anything inert. 2. an oppressive burden.

dead·wood (ded′wŏŏd′), n. 1. dead branches or trees. 2. useless and burdensome persons or things.

deaf (def), adj. 1. partially or wholly unable to hear. 2. refusing to listen. **—deaf′ly,** adv. **—deaf′ness,** n.

deaf·en (def′ən), v.t. 1. to make deaf. 2. to stun with noise.

deaf-mute (def′myŏŏt′, -myŏŏt′), n. a person unable to hear or speak.

deal¹ (dēl), v., **dealt** (delt), **deal·ing,** n. **—v.i.** 1. to be engaged or concerned, as with a subject or matter. 2. to take action with respect to a thing or person. 3. to behave oneself. 4. to do business. 5. to distribute cards in a game. **—v.t.** 6. to apportion or distribute. 7. to deliver or administer. **—n.** 8. Informal. a. a business transaction. b. a bargain or agreement. c. a secret agreement or bargain. d. treatment received. 9. an indefinite quantity, amount, extent, etc.: a great deal of work. 10. an act of dealing or distributing. **—deal′·er,** n.

deal² (dēl), n. fir or pine wood.

deal·er·ship (dē′lər ship′), n. 1. authorization to sell a commodity. 2. a sales agency having such authorization.

deal·ing (dē′ling), n. 1. Often, **dealings.** relations or transactions, esp. in business. 2. conduct in relation to others.

dean (dēn), n. 1. the head of a faculty in a university or college. 2. any college or school official in charge of some aspect of administration. 3. the head of the chapter of a cathedral in the Anglican church. 4. the senior member, in length of service, of any group, profession, etc. **—dean′ship,** n.

dean·er·y (dē′nə rē), n., pl. **-er·ies.** the office, jurisdiction, or residence of an ecclesiastical dean.

dean′s′ list′, a list of students of high scholastic standing compiled by a college.

dear (dēr), adj. 1. tenderly loved. 2. (in the salutation of a letter) highly esteemed: Dear Sir. 3. heartfelt or earnest. 4. expensive or costly. **—n.** 5. a beloved one: my dear. **—interj.** 6. (an exclamation of surprise, distress, etc.) **—dear′ly,** adv. **—dear′ness,** n.

Dear·born (dēr′bərn, -bôrn), n. a city in SE Michigan.

Dear′ John′, Slang. a letter from a woman informing her boyfriend or fiancé that she is jilting him.

dearth (dûrth), n. great scarcity.

death (deth), n. 1. the act of dying or state of being dead. 2. extinction or destruction. 3. bloodshed or murder. 4. a cause of death. **—death′like,** adj.

death·bed (deth′bed′), n. 1. the bed on which a person dies. 2. the last few hours before death.

death·blow (deth′blō′), n. a blow causing death.

death·less (deth′lis), adj. immortal or imperishable. **—death′less·ly,** adv. **—death′less·ness,** n.

death·ly (deth′lē), adj. 1. like or characteristic of death. 2. deadly or fatal. **—adv.** 3. in the manner of death. 4. very or utterly.

death′ rat′tle, a sound produced by a dying person, caused by the passage of air through the mucus in the throat.

death′ row′, a row of prison cells for prisoners awaiting execution.

death′s-head (deths′hed′), n. a human skull, esp. as a symbol of mortality.

death·trap (deth′trap′), n. a structure or situation involving imminent risk of death.

Death′ Val′ley, an arid basin in E California and S Nevada.

death·watch (deth′woch′, -wôch′), n. 1. a vigil beside a dying or dead person. 2. a beetle that makes a ticking sound.

deb (deb), n. Informal. a debutante.

de·ba·cle (dā bä′kəl, -bak′əl, də-), n. a general breakup or collapse.

de·bar (di bär′), v.t., **-barred, -bar·ring.** 1. to exclude from a place or condition. 2. to hinder or prohibit. **—de·bar′ment,** n.

de·bark (di bärk′), v.t., v.i. to disembark. **—de·bar·ka·tion** (dē′bär kā′shən), n.

de·base (di bās′), v.t., **-based, -bas·ing.** to reduce in quality or value. **—de·base′ment,** n.

de·bate (di bāt′), n., v., **-bat·ed, -bat·ing. —n.** 1. a discussion involving a proposed solution to an issue. 2. a formal contest in which the affirmative and negative sides of a proposition are advocated by opposing speakers. **—v.i., v.t** 3. to discuss (an issue) for the best solution. 4. to participate in a formal debate with (a speaker) or on (an issue). **—de·bat′a·ble,** adj. **—de·bat′er,** n.

de·bauch (di bôch′), v.t. to corrupt by sensuality, intemperance, etc. **—deb′au·chee′,** n. **—de·bauch′er·y,** n.

de·ben·ture (di ben′chər), n. a corporate bond unsecured by any mortgage, dependent on the credit of the issuer.

de·bil·i·tate (di bil′i tāt′), *v.t.*, **-tat·ed,** **-tat·ing.** to make weak or feeble. —**de·bil′i·ta′tion,** *n.* —**de·bil′i·ta′-tive,** *adj.*

de·bil·i·ty (di bil′i tē), *n., pl.* **-ties.** a weakened or enfeebled state.

deb·it (deb′it), *n.* **1.** the recording of debt in an account. **2.** a recorded item of debt. —*v.t.* **3.** to charge (a person, account, etc.) with a debt. **4.** to enter as a debt.

deb′it card′, a type of credit card that allows the settlement of bills electronically through direct deduction from bank accounts.

deb·o·nair (deb′ə nâr′), *adj.* **1.** courteous and charming. **2.** gay and carefree. —**deb′o·nair′ly,** *adv.*

de·bouch (di bōōsh′, -bouch′), *v.i.* to march out into open country, as a body of troops.

de·brief (dē brēf′), *v.t.* to interrogate (a pilot, astronaut, etc.) on return from a mission. —**de·brief′ing,** *n.*

de·bris (də brē′, dā′brē), *n.* **1.** the remains of anything broken down or destroyed. **2.** an accumulation of loose fragments of rock. Also, **dé·bris′.**

debt (det), *n.* **1.** something that is owed. **2.** an obligation to pay or render something. **3.** the condition of being under such an obligation. **4.** *Theol.* sin or trespass. —**debt′or,** *n.*

de·bug (dē bug′), *v.t.,* **-bugged, -bugging.** *Informal.* **1.** to detect and remove defects or errors from. **2.** to remove electronic bugs from (a room or building).

de·bunk (di bungk′), *v.t. Informal.* to strip of false opinions or claims. —**de·bunk′er,** *n.*

De·bus·sy (deb′yōō sē′, də byōō′sē), *n.* **Claude,** 1862–1918, French composer.

de·but (dā byōō′, di-, dā′byōō, deb′-yōō), *n.* **1.** a first public appearance, as on a stage. **2.** a formal introduction into society, esp. of a girl. **3.** the beginning of a career, etc. Also, **dé·but′.**

deb·u·tante (deb′yōō tänt′, -tant′), *n.* a girl making a debut into society. Also, **déb′u·tante′.**

Dec., December.

dec., **1.** deceased. **2.** decimeter. **3.** decrease.

deca-, a combining form meaning "ten": *decagon.* Also, **dec-.**

dec·ade (dek′ād), *n.* a period of 10 years.

dec·a·dence (dek′ə dəns, di kād′°ns), *n.* **1.** the process of decay. **2.** decline in morals or art. —**dec′a·dent,** *adj., n.* —**dec′a·dent·ly,** *adv.*

de·caf·fein·ate (dē kaf′ə nāt′, -kaf′ē-ə-), *v.t.,* **-at·ed, -at·ing.** to extract caffeine from.

dec·a·gon (dek′ə gon′), *n.* a polygon having 10 angles and 10 sides.

dec·a·gram (dek′ə gram′), *n.* dekagram.

dec·a·he·dron (dek′ə hē′drən), *n., pl.* **-drons, -dra** (-drə). a solid figure having 10 faces.

de·cal (dē′kal, di kal′, dek′əl), *n.* **1.** the art or process of transferring pictures or designs from specially prepared paper to metal, glass, etc. **2.** the paper bearing such a picture or design.

de·cal·ci·fy (dē kal′sə fī′), *v.t.,* **-fied, -fy·ing.** to deprive of lime or calcareous matter, as a bone.

dec·a·li·ter (dek′ə lē′tər), *n.* dekaliter.

Dec·a·logue (dek′ə lôg′, -log′), *n.* See **Ten Commandments.**

dec·a·me·ter (dek′ə mē′tər), *n.* dekameter.

de·camp (di kamp′), *v.i.* **1.** to pack up and leave a camping ground. **2.** to depart quickly or secretly.

de·cant (di kant′), *v.t.* to pour (wine) gently so as not to disturb the sediment.

de·cant·er (di kan′tər), *n.* an ornamental bottle for wine, brandy, etc.

de·cap·i·tate (di kap′i tāt′), *v.t.,* **-tat·ed, -tat·ing.** to behead. —**de·cap′i·ta′tion,** *n.*

dec·a·syl·la·ble (dek′ə sil′ə bəl), *n.* a word or line of verse of 10 syllables. —**dec·a·syl·lab·ic** (dek′ə si lab′ik), *adj.*

de·cath·lon (di kath′lon), *n.* an athletic contest comprising 10 different track-and-field events.

de·cay (di kā′), *v.i.* **1.** to become decomposed or rot. **2.** to decline in excellence, prosperity, health, etc. **3.** to undergo radioactive disintegration. —*v.t.* **4.** to cause to decay. —*n.* **5.** decline or deterioration. **6.** decomposition or rot. —**Syn. 1.** disintegrate, putrefy, spoil.

de·cease (di sēs′), *n., v.,* **-ceased, -ceasing.** *Chiefly Law.* —*n.* **1.** death. —*v.i.* **2.** to die.

de·ce·dent (di sēd′°nt), *n. Law.* a deceased person.

de·ceit (di sēt′), *n.* **1.** the act or practice of deceiving. **2.** trick or stratagem. **3.** falseness or deceitfulness. —**Syn.** duplicity, fraud, guile.

de·ceit·ful (di sēt′fəl), *adj.* **1.** given to deceiving. **2.** misleading or deceptive. —**de·ceit′ful·ly,** *adv.* —**de·ceit′ful·ness,** *n.*

de·ceive (di sēv′), *v.t., v.i.,* **-ceived, -ceiving.** to mislead (a person) by a false appearance or statement. —**de·ceiv′er,** *n.* —**de·ceiv′ing·ly,** *adv.*

de·cel·er·ate (dē sel′ə rāt′), *v.t., v.i.,* **-at·ed, -at·ing.** to slow down. —**de·cel′er·a′tion,** *n.* —**de·cel′er·a′tor,** *n.*

De·cem·ber (di sem'bər), *n.* the 12th month of the year, containing 31 days.

de·cen·cy (dē'sən sē), *n., pl.* **-cies.** the state or quality of being decent.

de·cen·ni·al (di sen'ē əl), *adj.* **1.** of or for 10 years. **2.** occurring every 10 years. —*n.* **3.** a decennial anniversary. —**de·cen'ni·al·ly,** *adv.*

de·cent (dē'sənt), *adj.* **1.** conforming to the recognized standard of propriety, good taste, etc. **2.** respectable or worthy. **3.** not obscene. **4.** adequate or fair: *a decent wage.* **5.** kind or generous. **6.** *Informal.* adequately dressed. —**de'cent·ly,** *adv.*

de·cen·tral·ize (dē sen'trə līz'), *v.t.,* **-ized, -iz·ing. 1.** to distribute the powers or functions of over a less concentrated area. **2.** to disperse (something) from an area of concentration. —**de·cen'tral·i·za'tion,** *n.*

de·cep·tion (di sep'shən), *n.* **1.** the act of deceiving or state of being deceived. **2.** fraud or trick. —**de·cep'tive,** *adj.* —**de·cep'tive·ly,** *adv.*

dec·i·bel (des'ə bel'), *n.* **1.** a unit used to compare two voltages or currents. **2.** a unit of intensity of sound.

de·cide (di sīd'), *v.,* **-cid·ed, -cid·ing.** —*v.t.* **1.** to solve or end (a question or struggle) by giving victory to one side. **2.** to make up one's mind about. **3.** to bring (a person) to a decision. —*v.i.* **4.** to arrive at a decision. —**de·cid'a·ble,** *adj.* —**de·cid'er,** *n.* —**Syn.** determine, resolve, settle.

de·cid·ed (di sī'did), *adj.* **1.** definite and unquestionable. **2.** resolute or determined. —**de·cid'ed·ly,** *adv.*

de·cid·u·ous (di sij'ōō əs), *adj.* **1.** shedding the leaves annually. **2.** falling off at a particular season or stage of growth, as leaves, horns, or teeth.

dec·i·gram (des'ə gram'), *n.* a metric unit of weight of ¹⁄₁₀ gram, equivalent to 1.543 grains.

dec·i·li·ter (des'ə lē'tər), *n.* a metric unit of capacity of ¹⁄₁₀ liter, equivalent to 6.102 cubic inches, or 3.381 U.S. fluid ounces.

dec·i·mal (des'ə məl), *adj.* **1.** pertaining to tenths or to the number 10. **2.** based on ten: *a decimal system.* —*n.* **3.** See decimal fraction. —**dec'i·mal·ly,** *adv.*

dec'imal frac'tion, a fraction whose denominator is some power of 10, usually indicated by a dot (**dec·imal point'**) written before the numerator: $0.4 = \frac{4}{10}$.

dec·i·mal·ize (des'ə mə līz'), *v.t.,* **-ized, -iz·ing.** to convert to a decimal system. —**dec'i·mal·i·za'tion,** *n.*

dec·i·mate (des'ə māt'), *v.t.,* **-mat·ed, -mat·ing. 1.** to destroy a great number of. **2.** to select by lot and kill every tenth person of. —**dec'i·ma'tion,** *n.*

dec·i·me·ter (des'ə mē'tər), *n.* a metric unit of length equal to ¹⁄₁₀ meter.

de·ci·pher (di sī'fər), *v.t.* **1.** to make out the meaning of. **2.** to decode. —**de·ci'pher·a·ble,** *adj.*

de·ci·sion (di sizh'ən), *n.* **1.** the act of deciding. **2.** a judgment, as one pronounced by a court. **3.** the act of making up one's mind. **4.** firmness in deciding.

de·ci·sive (di sī'siv), *adj.* **1.** marked by or displaying decision. **2.** unquestionable or unmistakable. **3.** having the power or quality of deciding. —**de·ci'sive·ly,** *adv.* —**de·ci'sive·ness,** *n.*

dec·i·stere (des'i stēr'), *n.* a metric unit of volume equal to ¹⁄₁₀ stere.

deck (dek), *n.* **1.** a floorlike surface occupying one level of a hull. **2.** any platform suggesting a deck of a ship. **3.** a pack of playing cards. —*v.t.* **4.** to clothe or array in something decorative. **5.** *Informal.* to knock down.

deck' hand', a sailor who works on deck.

deck'le edge (dek'əl), the irregular, untrimmed edge of paper.

decl., declension.

de·claim (di klām'), *v.i., v.t.* to speak aloud rhetorically. —**de·claim'er,** *n.* —**dec·la·ma·tion** (dek'lə mā'shən), *n.* —**de·clam·a·to·ry** (di klam'ə tōr'ē, -tôr'ē), *adj.*

de·clar·a·tive (di klar'ə tiv), *adj.* serving to declare. Also, **de·clar·a·to·ry** (di klar'ə tōr'ē, -tôr'ē), *adj.*

de·clare (di klâr'), *v.,* **-clared, -clar·ing.** —*v.t.* **1.** to make known clearly, esp. in formal terms. **2.** to announce officially: *to declare a state of emergency.* **3.** to state emphatically. **4.** *Bridge.* to bid (a trump suit or no-trump). —**de·clar'a·ble,** *adj.* —**dec·la·ra·tion** (dek'lə rā'shən), *n.* —**de·clar'er,** *n.* —**Syn.** 1–3. assert, avow, proclaim.

de·clas·si·fy (dē klas'ə fī'), *v.t.,* **-fied, -fy·ing.** to remove the security classification from. —**de·clas'si·fi·ca'tion,** *n.*

de·clen·sion (di klen'shən), *n.* **1.** the inflection of nouns, pronouns, and adjectives. **2.** a slope or descent. **3.** deterioration or decline.

de·cline (di klīn'), *v.,* **-clined, -clin·ing,** *n.* —*v.t.* **1.** to refuse courteously. **2.** to cause to slope or incline downward. **3.** to give the grammatical declension of. —*v.i.* **4.** to refuse courteously. **5.** to deteriorate or weaken. **6.** to fall or drop. **7.** to bend or descend. **8.** to draw toward the close, as the day. **9.** to condescend, as to an unworthy level. —*n.* **10.** a gradual loss, as in strength. **11.** a downward movement, as of prices. **12.** declivity. —**de·clin′a·ble,** *adj.* —**dec·li·na·tion** (dek′lə nā′shən), *n.* —**de·clin′er,** *n.*

de·cliv·i·ty (di kliv′i tē), *n., pl.* **-ties.** a downward slope, as of ground.

de·code (dē kōd′), *v.t., v.i.,* **-cod·ed, -cod·ing.** to convert (a coded message) into plain language. —**de·cod′er,** *n.*

dé·col·le·té (dā′kol tā′, -kol ə-, dek′ə lə-), *adj.* **1.** (of a garment) low-necked. **2.** wearing a low-necked garment.

de·col·o·nize (dē kol′ə nīz′), *v.t.* **-nized, -niz·ing.** to free from the status of a colony. —**de·col′o·ni·za′tion,** *n.*

de·com·mis·sion (dē′kə mish′ən), *v.t.* to retire (a ship, etc.) from active service.

de·com·pen·sate (dē kom′pən sāt′), *v.i.,* **-sat·ed, -sat·ing.** to undergo decompensation.

de·com·pen·sa·tion (dē′kom pən sā′shən), *n.* the inability of a diseased heart to compensate for its defect.

de·com·pose (dē′kəm pōz′), *v.t., v.i.,* **-posed, -pos·ing. 1.** to separate into constituent parts or elements. **2.** to rot or putrefy. —**de·com·po·si·tion** (dē′kom pə zish′ən), *n.*

de·com·press (dē′kəm pres′), *v.t.* to release from air pressure, as within a cabin. —**de′com·pres′sion,** *n.*

de·con·ges·tant (dē′kən jes′tənt), *n.* a drug that relieves congestion, esp. in the nose.

de·con·tam·i·nate (dē′kən tam′ə nāt′), *v.t.,* **-nat·ed, -nat·ing.** to free of contamination or harmful substance. —**de′con·tam′i·na′tion,** *n.*

de·con·trol (dē′kən trōl′), *v.,* **-trolled, -trol·ling,** *n.* —*v.t.* **1.** to remove controls from. —*n.* **2.** the removal of control.

dé·cor (dā kôr′, di-, dā′kôr), *n.* style of decoration, as of a room. Also, **de·cor′.**

dec·o·rate (dek′ə rāt′), *v.t.,* **-rat·ed, -rat·ing. 1.** to furnish with something beautiful. **2.** to plan and execute the furnishings, wall coverings, etc., of (a house or room). **3.** to confer a medal, honor, etc., upon. —**dec·o·ra·tive** (dek′ər ə tiv, dek′rə-, dek′ə rā′-), *adj.* —**dec′o·ra·tive·ly,** *adv.* —**dec′o·ra·tive·ness,** *n.* —**Syn. 1.** adorn, embellish, ornament.

dec·o·ra·tion (dek′ə rā′shən), *n.* **1.** the act of decorating. **2.** adornment or ornament. **3.** a badge, medal, etc., conferred.

dec·o·ra·tor (dek′ə rā′tər), *n.* a person who decorates, esp. an interior decorator.

dec·o·rous (dek′ər əs, di kōr′əs, -kôr′-), *adj.* characterized by propriety in conduct, appearance, etc. —**dec′o·rous·ly,** *adv.*

de·co·rum (di kōr′əm, -kôr′-), *n.* **1.** propriety of behavior, speech, dress, etc. **2.** an observance or requirement of polite society.

de·cou·page (dā′kōō päzh′), *n.* the art of decorating something with cutouts of paper, linoleum, plastic or other flat materials. Also, **dé′cou·page′.**

de·coy (*n.* di koi′, dē′koi; *v.* di koi′), *n.* **1.** a person or thing that entices another person or thing, as into danger. **2.** an artificial or trained bird, used to entice game into a trap or within gunshot. —*v.t.* **3.** to lure by or as if by a decoy. [< D *de kooi* the cage]

de·crease (*v.* di krēs′; *n.* dē′krēs, di krēs′), *v.,* **-creased, -creas·ing,** *n.* —*v.i., v.t.* **1.** to lessen in extent, power, etc. —*n.* **2.** the act or process of decreasing. **3.** the amount by which a thing is lessened.

de·cree (di krē′), *n., v.,* **-creed, -cree·ing.** —*n.* **1.** a formal and authoritative order having the force of law. **2.** a judicial decision. —*v.t., v.i.* **3.** to ordain or decide by decree.

dec·re·ment (dek′rə mənt), *n.* **1.** gradual decrease. **2.** the amount lost by reduction.

de·crep·it (di krep′it), *adj.* **1.** weakened by old age. **2.** worn out by long use. —**de·crep′i·tude′,** *n.*

de·cre·scen·do (dē′kri shen′dō, dā′-), *adj., adv., n.* Music. —*adj., adv.* **1.** gradually reducing force of loudness. —*n.* **2.** a gradual reduction in force or loudness. **3.** a decrescendo passage.

de·crim·i·nal·ize (dē′krim′ə nᵊ līz′), *v.t.,* **-ized, -iz·ing.** to eliminate criminal penalties for possession or use of: *to decriminalize marijuana.* —**de·crim′i·nal·i·za′tion,** *n.*

de·cry (di krī′), *v.t.,* **-cried, -cry·ing.** to speak disparagingly of.

ded·i·cate (ded′ə kāt′), *v.i.,* **-cat·ed, -cat·ing. 1.** to consecrate to a deity or to a sacred purpose. **2.** to devote wholly and earnestly, as to some purpose. **3.** to inscribe (a book, etc.) to a person or cause. —**ded′i·ca′tion,** *n.* —**ded′i·ca′tor,** *n.* —**ded′i·ca·to·ry** (ded′ə kə tōr′ē), *adj.*

de·duce (di dōōs′, -dyōōs′), *v.t.,* **-duced, -duc·ing. 1.** to conclude by logical deduction. **2.** to trace the course of. —**de·duc′i·ble,** *adj.*

de·duct (di dukt′), *v.t.* to take away, as from a sum. —**de·duct′i·ble,** *adj.*

de·duc·tion (di duk′shən), *n.* **1.** the act or process of deducting. **2.** something deducted. **3.** the act or process of deducing. **4.** something deduced. **5. a.** the process of reasoning from the general to the specific. **b.** a conclusion reached by this process. —de·duc′tive, *adj.*

deed (dēd), *n.* **1.** something done. **2.** an exploit or achievement. **3.** a document executed under seal and delivered to effect a conveyance, esp. of real estate. —*v.t.* **4.** to convey by deed.

dee·jay (dē′jā′), *n.* See disc jockey.

deem (dēm), *v.t.* to believe or judge, esp. after deliberation.

de·em·pha·size (dē em′fə sīz′), *v.t.*, -sized, -siz·ing. to place less emphasis upon. —de·em′pha·sis (-sis), *n.*

deep (dēp), *adj.* **1.** extending far down from the top or surface. **2.** extending far in or back from the front. **3.** having a specified depth. **4.** difficult to understand. **5.** grave or serious. **6.** profound or intense: *deep sleep.* **7.** dark and vivid: *a deep red.* **8.** low in pitch: *deep tones.* **9.** mysterious or obscure: *deep, dark secrets.* **10.** involved or immersed. **11.** absorbed or engrossed. —*n.* **12.** the deep part of the sea, a river, etc. **13.** the part of greatest intensity, as of winter. **14.** the deep, *Literary.* the ocean. —*adv.* **15.** to or at a considerable or specified depth. **16.** far on in time —deep′ly, *adv.* — deep′ness, *n.*

deep·en (dē′pən), *v.t., v.i.* to make or become deep or deeper.

deep-freeze (dēp′frēz′), *v.t.,* -freezed or -froze, -freezed or -fro·zen, -freez·ing. to quick-freeze (food).

deep-fry (dēp′frī′), *v.t.,* -fried, -fry·ing. to fry in a quantity of fat sufficient to cover the food being cooked.

deep-root·ed (dēp′rōō′tid, -rōōt′id), *adj.* firmly implanted.

deep-sea (dēp′sē′), *adj.* of, pertaining to, or in the deeper parts of the sea.

deep-seat·ed (dēp′sē′tid), *adj.* firmly established.

deep-set (dēp′set′), *adj.* placed far in.

deep-six (dēp′siks′), *v.t.* Slang. to get rid of, as by throwing overboard.

deep′ space′, space beyond the limits of the solar system.

deer (dēr), *n., pl.* deer. a hoofed mammal, the males of which have solid, deciduous horns or antlers.

deer′ fly′, a horsefly that sucks the blood of deer.

deer·skin (dēr′skin′), *n.* **1.** the skin of a deer. **2.** leather made from this. **3.** a garment made of such leather.

de·es·ca·late (dē es′kə lāt′), *v.t., v.i.,* -lat·ed, -lat·ing. to decrease in intensity, magnitude, etc. —de·es′ca·la′tion, *n.*

def., **1.** defective. **2.** defense. **3.** definite. **4.** definition.

de·face (di fās′), *v.t.,* -faced, -fac·ing. to mar the appearance of. —de·face′ment, *n.*

de fac·to (dē fak′tō), actually existing, esp. when without lawful authority.

de·fal·cate (di fal′kāt, -fôl′-), *v.i.,* -cat·ed, -cat·ing. to misappropriate money entrusted to one. —de·fal·ca·tion (dē′fal kā′shən), *n.*

de·fame (di fām′), *v.t.,* -famed, -fam·ing. to attack the good reputation of, as by slander or libel. —def·a·ma·tion (def′ə mā′shən, dē′fə-), *n.* — de·fam·a·to·ry (di fam′ə tôr′ē, -tōr′ē), *adj.* —de·fam′er, *n.*

de·fault (di fôlt′), *n.* **1.** failure to act. **2.** failure to meet financial obligations. **3.** failure to perform an act legally required. **4.** failure to participate in or complete a scheduled match. —*v.i.* **5.** to fail in fulfilling an engagement, obligation, etc. — *v.t.* **6.** to lose by default. —de·fault′er, *n.*

de·feat (di fēt′), *v.t.* **1.** to overcome in a contest, battle, etc. **2.** to thwart or frustrate. —*n.* **3.** the act of defeating or state of being defeated. —de·feat′er, *n.* —Syn. **1.** conquer, overthrow, vanquish.

de·feat·ism (di fē′tiz əm), *n.* the attitude or conduct of a person who admits or expects defeat. —de·feat′ist, *n., adj.*

def·e·cate (def′ə kāt′), *v.i.,* -cat·ed, -cat·ing. to void excrement from the bowels. —def′e·ca′tion, *n.*

de·fect (*n.* dē′fekt, di fekt′; *v.i.* di-fekt′), *n.* **1.** a moral or physical imperfection. **2.** lack of something essential to completeness. —*v.i.* **3.** to desert a cause, country, etc. — de·fec′tion, *n.* —de·fec′ter, *n.* —Syn. **1.** blemish, fault, flaw.

de·fec·tive (di fek′tiv), *adj.* having a defect or defects. —de·fec′tive·ly, *adv.* —de·fec′tive·ness, *n.*

de·fend (di fend′), *v.t.* **1.** to guard against assault or injury. **2.** to maintain or uphold by argument, etc. **3. a.** to contest (a legal charge, etc.). **b.** to serve as attorney for (a defendant). —de·fend′a·ble, *adj.* —de·fend′er, *n.*

de·fend·ant (di fen′dənt), *n. Law.* a person against whom a claim or charge is brought in court.

de·fense (di fens′), *n.* **1.** resistance against attack. **2.** something that defends. **3.** the defending of a cause by speech, etc. **4.** a speech, argument, etc., in vindication. **5.** the denial of the defendant in answer to the claim or charge against him or her. **6.** a defendant and his or her counsel. **7.** the side that is defending or protecting a goal, etc., against scoring. Also, *Brit.,* de·fence′. —de·fense′less, *adj.* —de·fense′less·ly, *adv.* —de·fen′si·ble, *adj.* —de·fen′sive, *adj., n.* —de·fen′sive·ly, *adv.*

defense′ mech′anism, an unconscious process that opposes unacceptable or painful ideas and impulses.

de·fer¹ (di fûr′), v.t., v.i., **-ferred, -fer·ring.** —v.t. **1.** to put off (action, etc.) to a future time. **2.** to exempt (a person) temporarily from military service. —**de·fer′ment, de·fer·ral** (di fûr′əl), n. —**de·fer′rer,** n.

de·fer² (di fûr′), v.i., **-ferred, -fer·ring.** to yield in judgment or opinion. —**de·fer′rer,** n.

def·er·ence (def′ər əns), n. **1.** yielding to the opinion, will, etc., of another. **2.** respectful regard. —**def′er·en′tial, def′er·ent,** adj. —**def′er·en′tial·ly,** adv.

de·fi·ance (di fī′əns), n. **1.** a bold resistance to authority. **2.** open disregard. —**de·fi′ant,** adj. —**de·fi′ant·ly,** adv.

defi′ciency disease′, an illness due to an insufficiency of one or more essential nutrients.

de·fi·cient (di fish′ənt), adj. **1.** lacking some element or characteristic. **2.** insufficient or inadequate. —**de·fi′cien·cy,** n. —**de·fi′cient·ly,** adv.

def·i·cit (def′i sit), n. the amount by which a sum of money falls short of the required amount.

def′icit spend′ing, the practice of spending funds in excess of income, esp. by a government.

de·file¹ (di fīl′), v.t., **-filed, -fil·ing. 1.** to make dirty or unclean. **2.** to desecrate or profane. **3.** to sully, as a person's reputation. **4.** Obs. to violate the chastity of. —**de·file′ment,** n. —**de·fil′er,** n. —**de·fil′ing·ly,** adv.

de·file² (di fīl′, dē′fīl), n., v., **-filed, -fil·ing.** —n. **1.** any narrow passage, esp. between mountains. —v.i. **2.** to march in a line or by files.

de·fine (di fīn′), v.t., **-fined, -fin·ing. 1.** to state the exact meaning of (a word, etc.). **2.** to describe exactly: *to define judicial functions.* **3.** to fix the boundaries of. **4.** to make clear the outline or form of. —**de·fin′a·ble,** adj. —**de·fin′a·bly,** adv. —**de·fin′er,** n.

def·i·nite (def′ə nit), adj. **1.** clearly defined or determined. **2.** having fixed limits. **3.** certain or sure. —**def′i·nite·ly,** adv. —**def′i·nite·ness,** n.

def′inite ar′ticle, the article *the,* which particularizes the noun it modifies.

def·i·ni·tion (def′ə nish′ən), n. **1.** the act of defining or making definite or clear. **2.** the exact statement of the meaning of a word, phrase, etc. **3.** condition of being definite.

de·fin·i·tive (di fin′i tiv), adj. **1.** most reliable or complete, as of a text: *a definitive biography.* **2.** serving to specify definitely. **3.** having its fixed and final form. —**de·fin′i·tive·ly,** adv. —**de·fin′i·tive·ness,** n.

def·la·grate (def′lə grāt′, dē′flə-), v.t., v.i., **-grat·ed, -grat·ing.** to burn, esp. suddenly and violently. —**def′la·gra′tion,** n.

de·flate (di flāt′), v., **-flat·ed, -flat·ing.** —v.t. **1.** to release the air or gas from. **2.** to reduce (prices, etc.) from an inflated condition. **3.** to reduce (a person's ego, hopes, etc.). —v.i. **4.** to become deflated. —**de·fla′tion,** n. —**de·fla′tion·ar·y** (di flā′shə ner′ē), adj. —**de·fla′tor,** n.

de·flect (di flekt′), v.t., v.i. to bend or turn aside. —**de·flect′a·ble,** adj. —**de·flec′tion,** n. —**de·flec′tive,** adj. —**de·flec′tor,** n.

def·lo·ra·tion (def′lə rā′shən, dē′flə-), n. the act of deflowering.

de·flow·er (di flou′ər), v.t. **1.** to deprive of flowers. **2.** to deprive (a woman) of virginity.

De·foe (di fō′), n. **Daniel,** 1659?–1731, English novelist.

de·fog (dē fog′), v.t., **-fogged, -fog·ging.** to remove the fog or moisture from (a car window, etc.). —**de·fog′ger,** n.

de·fo·li·ant (dē fō′lē ənt), n. a chemical spray for defoliating plants.

de·fo·li·ate (dē fō′lē āt′), v.t., **-at·ed, -at·ing. 1.** to strip of leaves. **2.** to destroy (a forest, etc.), as by chemical sprays to give enemy troops no concealment. —**de·fo′li·a′tion,** n. —**de·fo′li·a′tor,** n.

de·for·est (dē fôr′ist, -for′-), v.t. to divest of forests or trees. —**de·for′est·a′tion,** n.

de·form (di fôrm′), v.t. **1.** to mar the natural shape of. **2.** to make ugly. —**de·form′a·ble,** adj. —**de·for·ma′tion,** n.

de·formed (di fôrmd′), adj. misshapen or disfigured.

de·form·i·ty (di fôr′mi tē), n., pl. **-ties. 1.** the quality or state of being deformed. **2.** a deformed part.

de·fraud (di frôd′), v.t. to deprive of a right or property by fraud. —**de·fraud′er,** n.

de·fray (di frā′), v.t. to bear or pay (the costs, etc.). —**de·fray′a·ble,** adj. —**de·fray′al,** n.

de·frock (dē frok′), v.t. to unfrock.

de·frost (dē frôst′, -frost′), v.t. **1.** to remove the frost or ice from. **2.** to thaw (frozen food). —**de·frost′er,** n.

defs., definitions.

deft (deft), adj. quick and skillful. —**deft′ly,** adv. —**deft′ness,** n. —**Syn.** adept, adroit, dexterous.

de·funct (di fungkt′), adj. no longer existing or functioning. —**de·func′tive,** adj. —**de·funct′ness,** n.

de·fuse (dē fyōōz′), v.t., **-fused, -fus·ing. 1.** to make harmless or powerless. **2.** to remove the fuse from (a bomb, etc.).

de·fy (di fī′), *v.t.*, **-fied, -fy·ing. 1.** to resist boldly or openly. **2.** to withstand or baffle. **3.** to challenge to do something deemed impossible.

deg., degree; degrees.

de·gas (dē gas′), *v.t.*, **-gassed, -gassing.** to free from gas.

de Gaulle (də gōl′), **Charles,** 1890–1970, French general and statesman.

de·gauss (dē gous′), *v.t.* to neutralize the magnetism of.

de·gen·er·ate (*v.* di jen′ə rāt′; *adj., n.* di jen′ər it), *v.*, **-at·ed, -at·ing.** *adj., n.* —*v.i.* **1.** to fall below a normal or desirable quality or condition. —*adj.* **2.** having fallen below a normal or desirable quality or condition. —*n.* **3.** a degenerate person. **4.** a sexual deviate. —**de·gen·er·a·cy** (jen′ər ə sē), *n.* —**de·gen′er·ate·ly,** *adv.* —**de·gen′er·ate·ness,** *n.* —**de·gen′era′tion,** *n.* —**de·gen′er·a′tive,** *adj.*

de·grad·a·ble (dē grā′də bəl), *adj.* capable of being chemically decomposed: *degradable wastes.*

de·grade (di grād′), *v.*, **-grad·ed, -grad·ing.** —*v.t.* **1.** to reduce to a lower rank, degree, etc. **2.** to debase or deprave. **3.** to lower in dignity or estimation. —**deg·ra·da·tion** (deg′rə dā′shən), *n.* —**de·grad′ed·ly,** *adv.* —**de·grad′ed·ness,** *n.* —**de·grad′er,** *n.*

de·gree (di grē′), *n.* **1.** any of a series of steps or stages. **2.** relative standing in society, business, etc. **3.** a stage in a scale of intensity or amount. **4.** extent, measure, scope, or the like. **5.** the 360th part of a complete circle. **6.** a unit of measure, as of temperature. **7.** a line or point on the earth or the celestial sphere, the position of which is defined by its angular distance, as from the equator. **8.** the distinctive classification of a crime according to its gravity: *murder in the first degree.* **9.** an academic title conferred by colleges as an indication of the completion of study or as an honorary recognition of achievement. **10.** one of the parallel formations of adjectives and adverbs used to express differences in quality, quantity, or intensity. **11.** the sum of the exponents of the variables in an algebraic expression. **12.** *Music.* a tone or step of the scale.

de·horn (dē hôrn′), *v.t.* to deprive (cattle) of horns.

de·hu·man·ize (dē hyoo′mə nīz′), *v.t.*, **-ized, -iz·ing.** to deprive of human qualities. —**de·hu′man·i·za′tion,** *n.*

de·hu·mid·i·fy (dē′hyoo mid′ə fī′), *v.t.*, **-fied, -fy·ing.** to remove moisture from. —**de·hu·mid′i·fi·ca′tion,** *n.* —**de·hu·mid′i·fi′er,** *n.*

de·hy·drate (dē hī′drāt), *v.*, **-drat·ed, -drat·ing.** —*v.t.* **1.** to deprive of water. —*v.i.* **2.** to lose water or moisture. —**de′hy·dra′tion,** *n.* —**de·hy′dra·tor,** *n.*

de·hy·dro·gen·ate (dē hī′drə jə nāt′, -hī droj′ə-), *v.t.*, **-at·ed, -at·ing.** to remove hydrogen from (a compound). —**de·hy′dro·gen·a′tion,** *n.*

de·ice (dē īs′), *v.t.*, **-iced, -ic·ing. 1.** to free of ice. **2.** to remove ice formation on (the wing of an airplane). —**de·ic′er,** *n.*

de·i·fy (dē′ə fī′), *v.t.*, **-fied, -fy·ing. 1.** to make a god of. **2.** to adore or worship. —**de′i·fi·ca′tion,** *n.*

deign (dān), *v.i., v.t.* to condescend (to do or grant).

de·i·on·ize (dē ī′ə nīz′), *v.t.*, **-ized, -iz·ing.** to remove ions from. —**de·i′·on·i·za′tion,** *n.*

de·ism (dē′iz əm), *n.* belief in the existence of God on the evidence of reason only. —**de′ist,** *n.* —**de·is′·tic,** *adj.*

de·i·ty (dē′i tē), *n., pl.* **-ties. 1.** a god or goddess. **2.** divinity. **3. the Deity,** God.

de·ject·ed (di jek′tid), *adj.* depressed in spirits. —**de·ject′ed·ly,** *adv.* —**de·ject′ed·ness,** *n.*

de·jec·tion (di jek′shən), *n.* depression or lowness of spirits.

de ju·re (dē joor′ē), by right or according to law.

dek·a·gram (dek′ə gram′), *n.* a metric unit of 10 grams, or 0.353 ounce.

dek·a·li·ter (dek′ə lē′tər) *n.* a metric unit of 10 liters, equivalent to 9.08 quarts U.S. dry measure or 2.64 gallons U.S. liquid measure.

dek·a·me·ter (dek′ə mē′tər), *n.* a metric unit of 10 meters, or 32.8 feet.

Del., Delaware.

del., delegate; delegation.

Del·a·ware (del′ə wâr′), *n., pl.* **-wares, -ware** for 2. **1.** a state in the eastern United States. *Cap.:* Dover. **2.** a member of an Indian people formerly occupying most of New Jersey. **3.** their language. —**Del′a·war′e·an,** *n., adj.*

de·lay (di lā′), *v.t.* **1.** to put off to a later time. **2.** to retard or hinder. —*v.i.* **3.** to put off action. —*n.* **4.** the act of delaying. **5.** an instance of being delayed. **6.** the period or amount of time during which something is delayed. —**de·lay′er,** *n.*

de·le (dē′lē), *v.t.*, **de·led, de·le·ing.** *Print.* to delete.

de·lec·ta·ble (di lek′tə bəl), *adj.* **1.** highly pleasing. **2.** delicious. —**de·lec′ta·bly,** *adv.*

de·lec·ta·tion (dē′lek tā′shən), *n.* enjoyment, as from an entertainment.

del·e·gate (n. del′ə gāt′, -git; v. del′ə-gāt′), n., v., **-gat·ed, -gat·ing.** —n. **1.** a person designated to act for or represent another or others. **2.** a member of the lower house of the legislatures of Maryland, Virginia, and West Virginia. —v.t. **3.** to send or appoint (a person) as a delegate. **4.** to commit (powers, etc.) to another as deputy.

del·e·ga·tion (del′ə gā′shən), n. **1.** the act of delegating or state of being delegated. **2.** a group or body of delegates.

de·lete (di lēt′), v.t., **-let·ed, -let·ing.** to strike out or remove (something written or printed). —**de·le′tion,** n.

del·e·te·ri·ous (del′i tēr′ē əs), adj. **1.** injurious to health. **2.** hurtful or harmful. —**del′e·te′ri·ous·ly,** adv. —**del′e·te′ri·ous·ness,** n.

delft (delft), n. an earthenware having an opaque white glaze with an overglaze decoration, usually blue. Also called **delft′ ware′.**

Del·hi (del′ē), n. a city in N India.

del·i (del′ē), n., pl. **del·is** (del′ēz). Informal. a delicatessen.

de·lib·er·ate (adj. di lib′ər it; v. di lib′ə rāt′), adj., v., **-at·ed, -at·ing.** —adj. **1.** carefully weighed or considered. **2.** careful or slow in deciding. **3.** unhurried or leisurely. —v.t. **4.** to weigh or consider carefully. —v.i. **5.** to confer formally in order to reach a decision. —**de·lib′er·ate·ly,** adv. —**de·lib′er·ate·ness,** n.

de·lib·er·a·tion (di lib′ə rā′shən), n. **1.** careful consideration. **2.** formal discussion before reaching a decision. **3.** slowness or carefulness. —**de·lib·er·a·tive** (di lib′ə rā′tiv, -ər ə tiv), adj. —**de·lib′er·a′tive·ly,** adv.

del·i·ca·cy (del′ə kə sē), n., pl. **-cies. 1.** the quality or state of being delicate. **2.** something delightful or pleasing, esp. a choice food.

del·i·cate (del′ə kit), adj. **1.** fine in texture, quality, construction, etc. **2.** easily damaged. **3.** frail or sickly. **4.** pleasing to the senses in a subtle way. **5.** fine or precise in action or execution. **6.** requiring great care or tact. **7.** keenly sensitive, as of feeling. —**del′i·cate·ly,** adv. —**del′i·cate·ness,** n.

del·i·ca·tes·sen (del′ə kə tes′ən), n. **1.** a store selling foods ready for serving, as cooked meats, salads, etc. **2.** the food products sold in such a store.

de·li·cious (di lish′əs), adj. **1.** highly pleasing to the taste or smell. **2.** delightful or enjoyable. —**de·li′cious·ly,** adv. —**de·li′cious·ness,** n. —Syn. **1.** delectable, luscious, savory.

de·light (di līt′), n. **1.** great pleasure or enjoyment. **2.** something that

gives great pleasure. —v.t. **3.** to give great pleasure or enjoyment to. —v.i. **4.** to have great pleasure.

de·light·ed (di lī′tid), adj. highly pleased. —**de·light′ed·ly,** adv.

de·light·ful (di līt′fəl), adj. highly pleasing. —**de·light′ful·ly,** adv. —**de·light′ful·ness,** n.

de·lim·it (di lim′it), v.t. to fix or mark the limits of. —**de·lim′i·ta′tion,** n.

de·lin·e·ate (di lin′ē āt′), v.t., **-at·ed, -at·ing. 1.** to sketch in outline. **2.** to portray or depict in words. —**de·lin′e·a′tion,** n. —**de·lin′e·a′tive,** adj.

de·lin·quent (di ling′kwənt), adj. **1.** failing in or neglectful of a duty or obligation. **2.** past due, as a debt. —n. **3.** a delinquent person. —**de·lin′quen·cy,** n. —**de·lin′quent·ly,** adv.

del·i·quesce (del′ə kwes′), v.i., **-quesced, -quesc·ing.** Chem. to melt and become liquid by absorbing moisture from the air. —**del′i·ques′cent,** adj.

de·lir·i·ous (di lēr′ē əs), adj. **1.** affected with or characteristic of delirium. **2.** wild with excitement, enthusiasm, etc. —**de·lir′i·ous·ly,** adv. —**de·lir′i·ous·ness,** n.

de·lir·i·um (di lēr′ē əm), n., pl. **-lir·i·ums, -lir·i·a** (-lēr′ē ə). **1.** a temporary disorder of the mental faculties, characterized by excitement, delusions, etc. **2.** a state of violent excitement or emotion.

delir′i·um tre′mens (trē′mənz), a violent restlessness due to excessive use of alcohol, characterized by trembling.

de·liv·er (di liv′ər), v.t. **1.** to carry (letters, goods, etc.) to the intended recipient. **2.** to give into another's possession or keeping. **3.** to utter or pronounce: to deliver a speech. **4.** to strike or throw: to deliver a blow. **5.** to set free. **6.** to assist in bringing forth young. **7.** to assist at the birth of. —v.i. **8.** to give birth. **9.** to provide delivery service. —**de·liv′er·er,** n.

de·liv·er·ance (di liv′ər əns), n. liberation from bondage or rescue from danger.

de·liv·er·y (di liv′ə rē), n., pl. **-er·ies. 1.** the delivering of letters, goods, etc. **2.** transfer or surrender. **3.** vocal and bodily behavior in speaking. **4.** the act or manner of striking or throwing. **5.** childbirth or parturition. **6.** something delivered.

dell (del), n. a small, usually wooded valley.

de·louse (dē lous′, -louz′), v.t., **-loused, -lous·ing.** to remove lice from.

del·phin·i·um (del fin′ē əm), n., pl. **-i·ums, -i·a** (-ē ə). a plant whose tall branching stalks bear colorful spurred flowers.

del·ta (del′tə), *n.* **1.** the fourth letter of the Greek alphabet (Δ, δ). **2.** a flat plain of alluvial deposit between diverging branches of the mouth of a river, often triangular. —**del·ta·ic** (del tā′ik), *adj.*

del′ta ray′, an electron emitted by a substance after bombardment by high-energy particles.

del′ta wing′, the triangular surface that serves as both wing and horizontal stabilizer of some supersonic aircraft.

de·lude (di lōōd′), *v.t.,* **-lud·ed, -lud·ing.** to cause to believe as true what is false or wrong. —**Syn.** deceive, mislead.

del·uge (del′yōōj), *n., v.,* **-uged, -ug·ing.** —*n.* **1.** a great flood. **2.** a drenching rain. **3.** anything that overwhelms like a flood. —*v.t.* **4.** to flood or inundate. **5.** to overwhelm or overrun.

de·lu·sion (di lōō′zhən), *n.* **1.** an act of deluding or state of being deluded. **2.** a false belief, esp. as a persistent psychotic symptom. —**de·lu·sion·al, de·lu·sive,** *adj.*

de luxe (də lōōks′, -luks′), *adj.* **1.** of special elegance or sumptuousness. —*adv.* **2.** in a luxurious or sumptuous manner.

delve (delv), *v.i.,* **delved, delv·ing. 1.** to carry on thorough research for data, information, etc. **2.** *Archaic.* to dig. —**delv′er,** *n.*

del·y., delivery.

Dem., 1. Democrat. **2.** Democratic.

de·mag·net·ize (dē mag′ni tīz′), *v.t.,* **-ized, -iz·ing.** to remove magnetization from. —**de·mag′net·i·za′tion,** *n.*

dem·a·gogue (dem′ə gôg′, -gog′), *n.* a person, esp. a political leader, who gains power and popularity by arousing the emotions and prejudices of people. Also, **dem′a·gog′.** —**dem·a·gog·ic** (dem′ə goj′ik), *adj.* —**dem′a·go′gy** (-gō′jē, -goj′ē), *n.* —**dem′a·gogu′er·y** (-gô′gə rē), *n.*

de·mand (di mand′, -mänd′), *v.t.* **1.** to ask for with authority. **2.** to claim as a right. **3.** to ask for peremptorily or urgently. **4.** to require as proper or necessary. —*v.i.* **5.** to make a demand. —*n.* **6.** the act of demanding. **7.** something that is demanded. **8.** an urgent or pressing requirement. **9.** the desire to purchase coupled with the power to do so. **10.** the state of being in request for purchase or use: *an article in great demand.* **11.** on demand, when requested, esp. for payment. —**de·mand′er,** *n.*

de·mand·ing (di man′ding), *adj.* claiming more than is generally felt by others to be due. —**de·mand′ing·ly,** *adv.*

de·mar·cate (di mär′kāt, dē′mär kāt′), *v.t.,* **-cat·ed, -cat·ing. 1.** to mark off the boundaries of. **2.** to separate distinctly. —**de′mar·ca′tion,** *n.* —**de·mar′ca·tor,** *n.*

dé·marche (dā märsh′), *n.* (formerly in British diplomacy) a decisive step or action.

de·mean[1] (di mēn′), *v.t.* to lower in dignity or standing.

de·mean[2] (di mēn′), *v.t.* to conduct or behave (oneself) in a specified manner.

de·mean·or (di mē′nər), *n.* outward manner of behavior. Also, *esp. Brit.,* **de·mean′our.**

de·ment·ed (di men′tid), *adj.* affected with dementia. —**de·ment′ed·ly,** *adv.*

de·men·tia (di men′shə, -shē ə), *n.* **1.** severe impairment of intellectual capacity. **2.** mental deterioration, esp. when due to physical causes.

de·men′tia prae′cox (prē′koks), *Obs.* schizophrenia.

de·mer·it (dē mer′it), *n.* a mark against a person for misconduct or deficiency.

de·mesne (di mān′, -mēn′), *n.* **1.** the possession of land as one's own. **2.** an estate occupied and worked by the owner. **3.** any territory or domain.

De·me·ter (di mē′tər), *n.* the ancient Greek goddess of agriculture.

demi-, a prefix meaning "half" or "lesser": *demitasse.*

dem·i·god (dem′ē god′), *n.* a mythological being who is partly divine and partly human.

dem·i·john (dem′i jon′), *n.* a large bottle having a short, narrow neck and encased in wickerwork.

de·mil·i·ta·rize (dē mil′i tə rīz′), *v.t.,* **-rized, -riz·ing.** to remove military forces, equipment, etc., from. —**de·mil′i·ta·ri·za′tion,** *n.*

dem·i·mon·daine (dem′ē mon dān′), *n.* a woman of the demimonde.

dem·i·monde (dem′ē mond′), *n.* a class of women who have lost their standing in respectable society, usually because of their sexual promiscuity.

de·min·er·al·ize (dē min′ər ə līz′), *v.t.,* **-ized, -iz·ing.** to deprive of mineral content.

de·mise (di mīz′), *n.* **1.** *Chiefly Literary.* death or decease. **2.** termination of existence or operation. **3.** transfer of sovereignty, as by death.

dem·i·tasse (dem′i tas′, -täs′), *n.* a small cup of or for strong black coffee after dinner.

dem·o (dem′ō), *n. Informal.* a phonograph or tape recording of a new song distributed to demonstrate its merits.

de·mo·bi·lize (dē mō′bə līz′), *v.t.,* **-lized, -liz·ing. 1.** to disband (an army, etc.). **2.** to discharge from military service. —**de·mo′bi·li·za′tion,** *n.*

de·moc·ra·cy (di mok′rə sē), *n.*, *pl.* **-cies. 1.** government in which su-preme power is vested in the people and exercised by them or their elected representatives. **2.** a state having such government. **3.** political or social equality.

dem·o·crat (dem′ə krat′), *n.* **1.** an advocate of democracy. **2.** one who maintains social equality. **3.** (*cap.*) a member of the Democratic Party.

dem·o·crat·ic (dem′ə krat′ik), *adj.* **1.** of or advocating democracy. **2.** per-taining to or characterized by social equality. **3.** (*cap.*) of the Democratic Party. **—dem′o·crat′i·cal·ly,** *adv.*

Dem′ocrat′ic Par′ty, one of the two major political parties in the U.S., founded in 1828.

de·moc·ra·tize (di mok′rə tīz′), *v.t.,* *v.i.,* **-tized, -tiz·ing.** to make or become democratic.

dé·mo·dé (dā mô dā′), *adj. French.* no longer in fashion.

de·mod·u·late (dē moj′ə lāt′, -mod′-yə-), *v.t.,* **-lat·ed, -lat·ing.** to rectify the radio wave in (a receiver). **—de·mod′u·la′tion,** *n.*

de·mog·ra·phy (di mog′rə fē), *n.* the science of vital and social statistics, as of the births, marriages, etc., of populations. **—de·mog′ra·pher,** *n.* **—de·mo·graph·ic** (dē′mə graf′ik, dem′ə-), *adj.* **—de′mo·graph′i·cal·ly,** *adv.*

dem·oi·selle (dem′wä zel′, dem′ə-), *n.* an unmarried girl.

de·mol·ish (di mol′ish), *v.t.* **1.** to tear down (a building). **2.** to destroy or finish. **3.** to ruin utterly. **—dem·o·li·tion** (dem′ə lish′ən), *n.*

de·mon (dē′mən), *n.* **1.** an evil spirit. **2.** a person considered extremely wicked or cruel. **3.** a person with great energy, drive, etc. **—de·mon·ic** (di mon′ik), **de·mon′i·cal,** *adj.*

de·mon·e·tize (dē mon′i tīz′, -mun′-), *v.t.,* **-tized, -tiz·ing.** to divest (a mon-etary standard) of value. **—de·mon′·e·ti·za′tion,** *n.*

de·mo·ni·ac (di mō′nē ak′, dē′mə nī′ak), *adj.* **1.** of or like a demon. **2.** fiendish or frantic. Also, **de·mo·ni·a·cal** (dē′mə nī′ə kəl).

de·mon·ol·o·gy (dē′mə nol′ə jē), *n.* **1.** the study of demons. **2.** beliefs about demons.

de·mon·stra·ble (di mon′strə bəl, dem′ən-), *adj.* **1.** capable of being demonstrated. **2.** obvious or evident. **—de·mon′stra·bly,** *adv.*

dem·on·strate (dem′ən strāt′), *v.,* **-strat·ed, -strat·ing. —v.t. 1.** to de-scribe or explain by examples. **2.** to manifest or show. **3.** to establish by reasoning. **4.** to exhibit the oper-ation or use of (a product). **—v.i. 5.** to make a public exhibition of group

feelings, as by parading. **—dem′on·stra′tion,** *n.* **—dem′on·stra′tor,** *n.*

de·mon·stra·tive (də mon′strə tiv), *adj.* **1.** expressing one's feelings openly. **2.** serving to prove, show, or illus-trate. **3.** *Gram.* indicating the thing referred to. **—***n.* **4.** a demonstrative word. **—de·mon′stra·tive·ly,** *adv.* **—de·mon′stra·tive·ness,** *n.*

de·mor·al·ize (di môr′ə līz′, -mor′-), *v.t.,* **-ized, -iz·ing. 1.** to deprive of spirit, courage, etc. **2.** to corrupt the morals of. **—de·mor′al·i·za′tion,** *n.* **—de·mor′al·iz′er,** *n.*

De·mos·the·nes (di mos′thə nēz′), 384?–322 B.C., Athenian orator.

de·mote (di mōt′), *v.t.,* **-mot·ed, -mot·ing.** to reduce to a lower grade or class. **—de·mo′tion,** *n.*

de·mul·cent (di mul′sənt), *n.* a sub-stance for soothing an irritated mu-cous membrane.

de·mur (di mûr′), *v.i.,* **-murred, -mur·ring.** to make objection. **—de·mur′ra·ble,** *adj.* **—de·mur′ral,** *n.*

de·mure (di myŏŏr′), *adj.,* **-mur·er, -mur·est. 1.** shy and modest. **2.** coyly decorous or sedate. **—de·mure′ly,** *adv.* **—de·mure′ness,** *n.*

de·mur·rage (di mûr′ij, -mur′-), *n.* **1.** the detention of a vessel, railroad car, truck, etc., as in loading or un-loading, beyond the time agreed upon. **2.** a charge for such deten-tion.

de·mur·rer (di mûr′ər, -mur′-), *n. Law.* a pleading that the facts alleged by the opposite party do not sustain the contention based on them.

den (den), *n.* **1.** a secluded place, as the lair of a predatory animal. **2.** a cave used as a place of shelter or concealment. **3.** a squalid abode or place. **4.** a small, secluded room in a house or apartment.

Den., Denmark.

de·na·ture (dē nā′chər), *v.t.,* **-tured, -tur·ing. 1.** to deprive of its natural properties, etc. **2.** to render (alcohol) unfit for drinking. **—de·na′tur·ant,** *n.*

den·drite (den′drīt), *n.* the branching process of a neuron which conducts impulses toward the cell. **—den·drit·ic** (-drit′ik), *adj.*

den·drol·o·gy (den drol′ə jē), *n.* the branch of botany dealing with trees and shrubs. **—den·dro·log·i·cal** (den′drə loj′i kəl), **den′dro·log′ic,** *adj.* **—den·drol·o·gist** (den drol′ə-jist), *n.*

den·gue (deng′gā, -gē), *n.* an infec-tious, eruptive fever of warm climates.

de·ni·al (di nī′əl), *n.* **1.** an assertion that an allegation is false. **2.** refusal to believe a doctrine, theory, etc. **3.** the refusal to satisfy a claim, request, etc. **4.** disavowal or repudiation. **5.** self-denial.

de·nic·o·tin·ize (dē nik′ə ti nīz′), v.t., -ized, -iz·ing. to remove nicotine from (tobacco).

de·nier (də nēr′, den′yər), n. a unit of weight indicating the fineness of fiber filaments and yarns.

den·i·grate (den′ə grāt′), v.t., -grat·ed, -grat·ing. 1. to attack the reputation of. 2. to belittle. —den′i·gra′tion, n. —den′i·gra′tor, n.

den·im (den′əm), n. 1. a heavy twill cotton for work garments. 2. denims, overalls or trousers made of denim. [< F, short for serge de Nimes serge of Nimes (city in France)]

den·i·zen (den′i zən), n. Chiefly Liter-.ary. an inhabitant or resident: denizens of the deep.

Den·mark (den′märk), n. a country in N Europe.

de·nom·i·nate (di nom′ə nāt′), v.t., -nat·ed, -nat·ing. to give a specific name to.

de·nom·i·na·tion (di nom′ə nā′shən), n. 1. a name or designation, esp. one for a class of things. 2. a class of persons or things having a specific name. 3. a particular religious group. 4. one of the grades or degrees in a series of values, as of currency. —de·nom′i·na′tion·al, adj. —de·nom′i·na′tion·al·ly, adv.

de·nom·i·na·tor (di nom′ə nā′tər), n. the term of a fraction, usually written under the line, that indicates the number of equal parts into which the unit is divided.

de·no·ta·tion (dē′nō tā′shən), n. 1. the specific association that a word or expression usually elicits. 2. the act or fact of denoting.

de·no·ta·tive (dē′nō tā′tiv, di nō′tə-tiv), adj. able or tending to denote.

de·note (di nōt′), v.t., -not·ed, -not·ing. 1. to be a specific indication of. 2. to have a specific meaning of. 3. to stand as a symbol for.

de·noue·ment (dā′nōō män′), n. the final resolution of a plot, as of a drama or novel. Also, dé′noue·ment′.

de·nounce (di nouns′), v.t., -nounced, -nounc·ing. 1. to condemn publicly. 2. to make a formal accusation against. 3. to give formal notice of the termination of (a treaty, etc.). —de·nounce′ment, n. —de·nounc′er, n.

de no·vo (dē nō′vō), Latin. anew.

dense (dens), adj., dens·er, dens·est. 1. closely compacted together: a dense forest. 2. intense or extreme. 3. stupid or dull. —dense′ly, adv. —dense′ness, n.

den·si·tom·e·ter (den′si tom′i tər), n. an instrument for measuring the density of photographic negatives.

den·si·ty (den′si tē), n., pl. -ties. 1. the state or quality of being dense. 2. Physics. mass per unit volume.

3. the quantity per unit of area at a point on a surface, as of population. 4. stupidity or dullness.

dent (dent), n. 1. a depression in a surface, as from a blow. 2. a slight progress. —v.t. 3. to make a dent in or on. —v.i. 4. to become indented.

dent., 1. dental. 2. dentist. 3. dentistry.

den·tal (den′t°l), adj. 1. of the teeth. 2. of dentistry or a dentist. —den′tal·ly, adv.

den′tal floss′, a soft, waxed thread for cleaning the spaces between the teeth.

den·tate (den′tāt), adj. Bot., Zool. having toothlike projections.

den·ti·frice (den′tə fris), n. a powder, paste, or other preparation for cleaning the teeth.

den·tin (den′t°n, -tin), n. the hard, calcareous tissue, similar to but denser than bone, that forms the major portion of a tooth. Also, den·tine (den′tēn). —den′tin·al, adj.

den·tist (den′tist), n. a person whose profession is dentistry.

den·tist·ry (den′ti strē), n. the prevention and treatment of diseases of the teeth, gums, and oral cavity.

den·ti·tion (den tish′ən), n. 1. the kind, number, and arrangement of the teeth of humans and animals. 2. the process of teething.

den·ture (den′chər), n. an artificial replacement of one or more teeth.

de·nu·cle·ar·ize (dē nōō′klē ə rīz′), v.t., -ized, -iz·ing. to forbid the deployment or construction of nuclear weapons in (a country or zone). —de·nu′cle·ar·i·za′tion, n.

de·nude (di nōōd′, -nyōōd′), v.t., -nud·ed, -nud·ing. to make naked or bare. —den·u·da·tion (den′yōō dā′shən), n.

de·nun·ci·a·tion (di nun′sē ā′shən, -shē-), n. 1. an act of denouncing. 2. an accusation of crime.

Den·ver (den′vər), n. the capital of Colorado.

de·ny (di nī′), v.t., -nied, -ny·ing. 1. to state that (something) is not true: to deny an accusation. 2. to refuse to agree to. 3. to withhold the possession, use, or enjoyment of. 4. to disown or repudiate. —de·ni′a·ble (-nī′ə bəl), adj. —de·ni′er, n. —Syn. 1. contradict, gainsay, oppose.

de·o·dar (dē′ə där′), n. a large Himalayan cedar yielding a durable wood.

de·o·dor·ant (dē ō′dər ənt), n. 1. a substance for destroying or masking odors. —adj. 2. capable of destroying odors.

de·o·dor·ize (dē ō′də rīz′), v.t., -ized, -iz·ing. to rid of odor, esp. of unpleasant odor. —de·o·dor·iz′er, n.

De·o gra·ti·as (dā′ō grāt′sē äs′), Latin. thanks be to God.

de·ox·i·dize (dē ok′si dīz′), v.t., -dized, -diz·ing. to remove oxygen from. — **de·ox′i·diz′er**, n.

de·ox·y·ri′bo·nu·cle′ic ac′id (dē ok′si-rī′bō nōō klē′ik, -nyōō-, -rī′-). See DNA.

dep., 1. depart. 2. department. 3. departure. 4. deposit. 5. deputy.

de·part (di pärt′), v.i. 1. to go away. 2. to diverge or deviate. 3. to pass away, as from life. —v.t. 4. to go away from.

de·part·ment (di pärt′mənt), n. 1. an operational or functional division, as of a business, government, or university. 2. a particular field of knowledge or activity. —**de·part·men·tal** (di pärt men′t°l, dē′pärt-), adj.

de·part·men·tal·ize (di pärt men′t°līz′, dē′pärt-), v.t., -ized, -iz·ing. to divide into departments. —**de′part·men′tal·i·za′tion**, n.

depart′ment store′, a large retail store organized into departments of merchandise.

de·par·ture (di pär′chər), n. 1. an act or instance of departing. 2. deviation, as from a standard.

de·pend (di pend′), v.i. 1. to place confidence. 2. to rely for support, help, etc. 3. to be contingent.

de·pend·a·ble (di pen′də bəl), adj. worthy of trust. —**de·pend′a·bil′i·ty, de·pend′a·ble·ness,** n. —**de·pend′a·bly,** adv.

de·pend·ence (di pen′dəns), n. 1. the state of depending on someone or something for aid, support, or the like. 2. reliance or trust. 3. the state of being contingent on something. 4. the state of psychologically depending on a drug after a prolonged period of use. Also, Rare, **de·pend′ance.**

de·pend·en·cy (di pen′dən sē), n., pl. -cies. 1. a subject territory that is not part of the ruling country. 2. something dependent. 3. dependence (defs. 1, 3).

de·pend·ent (di pen′dənt), adj. 1. depending on someone or something else for aid, support, etc. 2. determined by something else. 3. subject to another's rule. 4. Gram. subordinate (def. 4). —n. 5. Also, Brit., **de·pend′ant.** a person who depends on someone or something for aid, support, etc. —**de·pend′ent·ly,** adv.

de·per·son·al·ize (dē pûr′sə n°līz′), v.t., -ized, -iz·ing. 1. to make impersonal. 2. to deprive of personality or individuality.

de·pict (di pikt′), v.t. 1. to represent by or as by painting. 2. to represent in words. —**de·pic′tion,** n. —Syn. delineate, describe, portray.

de·pil·a·to·ry (di pil′ə tōr′ē, -tôr′ē), adj., n., pl. -ries. —adj. 1. capable

of removing hair. —n. 2. a depilatory substance.

de·plane (dē plān′), v.i., -planed, -plan·ing. to disembark from an airplane.

de·plete (di plēt′), v.t., -plet·ed, -plet·ing. to use up or exhaust the supply of. —**de·plet′a·ble,** adj. —**de·ple′tion,** n.

de·plor·a·ble (di plôr′ə bəl, -plōr′-), adj. 1. causing grief or regret. 2. worthy of censure or disapproval. —**de·plor′a·ble·ness,** n. —**de·plor′a·bly,** adv.

de·plore (di plôr′, -plōr′), v.t., -plored, -plor·ing. 1. to regret deeply. 2. to disapprove of.

de·ploy (di ploi′), v.t. to spread out (troops) so as to form an extended front or line. —**de·ploy′ment,** n.

de·po·lar·ize (dē pō′lə rīz′), v.t., -ized, -iz·ing. to deprive of polarity or polarization. —**de·po′lar·i·za′tion,** n. —**de·po′lar·iz′er,** n.

de·po·lit·i·cize (dē pə lit′i sīz′), v.t., -cized, -ciz·ing. to deprive of political character or bias.

de·po·nent (di pō′nənt), n. a person who testifies, under oath, esp. in writing.

de·pop·u·late (dē pop′yə lāt′), v.t., -lat·ed, -lat·ing. to remove or reduce the population of, as by destruction or expulsion. —**de·pop′u·la′tion,** n. —**de·pop′u·la′tor,** n.

de·port (di pōrt′, -pôrt′), v.t. 1. to expel (an alien) from a country. 2. to behave in a particular manner. —**de·port′a·ble,** adj. —**de′por·ta′tion,** n.

de·port·ment (di pōrt′mənt, -pôrt′-), n. behavior in relation to arbitrary rules, as at school.

de·pose (di pōz′), v.t., -posed, -pos·ing. 1. to remove from office or position, esp. high office. 2. to testify under oath, esp. in writing. —**de·pos′a·ble,** adj. —**de·pos′er,** n.

de·pos·it (di poz′it), v.t. 1. to place for safekeeping in a bank account. 2. to give as security or in part payment. 3. to put or set down. 4. to throw down or precipitate. —n. 5. money placed in a bank account. 6. anything given as security or in part payment. 7. something accumulated or precipitated, as sediment. —**de·pos′i·tor,** n.

dep·o·si·tion (dep′ə zish′ən, dē′pə-), n. 1. removal from an office or position. 2. the act or process of depositing or precipitating. 3. something deposited or precipitated. 4. written testimony under oath intended to be used in court.

de·pos·i·to·ry (di poz′i tōr′ē, -tôr′ē), n., pl. -ries. a place where anything is deposited for safekeeping.

de·pot (dē′pō; *Mil.* dep′ō), *n.* **1.** a railroad or bus station. **2.** a place at which military supplies are stored for distribution. **3.** a warehouse.

depr., depreciation.

de·prave (di prāv′), *v.t.,* **-praved, -prav·ing.** to make morally bad or evil. —**de·praved′,** *adj.* —**de·prav·i·ty** (di prav′i tē), *n.*

dep·re·cate (dep′rə kāt′), *v.t.,* **-cat·ed, -cat·ing. 1.** to express disapproval of. **2.** to depreciate or belittle. —**dep′re·ca′tion,** *n.* —**dep′re·ca′tive,** *adj.* —**dep′re·ca′tor,** *n.* —**dep·re·ca·to·ry** (dep′rə kə tōr′ē, -tôr′ē), *adj.*

de·pre·ci·ate (di prē′shē āt′), *v.,* **-at·ed, -at·ing.** —*v.t.* **1.** to lessen the value or price of. **2.** to belittle or disparage. —*v.i.* **3.** to decline in value. —**de·pre′ci·a′tion,** *n.* —**de·pre′ci·a′tor,** *n.*

dep·re·da·tion (dep′ri dā′shən), *n.* the act of preying upon or plundering.

de·press (di pres′), *v.t.* **1.** to make sad or gloomy. **2.** to lower in force or activity. **3.** to lower in amount or value. **4.** to press down. —**de·press′or,** *n.*

de·pres·sant (di pres′ənt), *adj.* **1.** lowering the vital activities. —*n.* **2.** a depressant drug.

de·pressed (di prest′), *adj.* **1.** sad or gloomy. **2.** undergoing economic hardship, esp. poverty and unemployment.

de·pres·sion (di presh′ən), *n.* **1.** the act of depressing or state of being depressed. **2.** a sunken place or part. **3.** sadness or gloom. **4.** emotional dejection greater than that warranted by any objective reason. **5.** a period during which business, employment, etc., decline or remain at a low level of activity.

de·pres·sive (di pres′iv), *adj.* **1.** tending to depress. **2.** characterized by depression, esp. mental depression. —*n.* **3.** a mentally depressive person. —**de·pres′sive·ly,** *adv.*

dep·ri·va·tion (dep′rə vā′shən), *n.* **1.** the act of depriving or fact of being deprived. **2.** dispossession or loss. **3.** privation.

de·prive (di prīv′), *v.t.,* **-prived, -priv·ing. 1.** to take away from. **2.** to withhold something from the enjoyment or possession of.

de·pro·gram·mer (dē prō′gram ər), *n.* a person engaged in intensive persuasion to free a convert from a cult or indoctrination. Also, **de·pro′gram·er.** —**de·pro′gram,** *v.t.* —**de·pro′gram·ming,** *adj., n.*

dept., **1.** department. **2.** deputy.

depth (depth), *n.* **1.** a dimension taken through an object, usually downward or horizontally inward. **2.** the quality of being deep. **3.** intensity, as of silence. **4.** the farthest, innermost, or extreme part or state. **5.** Usually, **depths.** a low intellectual or moral condition. **6.** the part of greatest intensity, as of night or winter. **7. in depth,** thoroughly.

depth′ charge′, an explosive device for use against submarines and other underwater targets.

dep·u·ta·tion (dep′yə tā′shən), *n.* **1.** the act of appointing a deputy. **2.** a body of deputies.

de·pute (də pyōōt′), *v.t.,* **-put·ed, -put·ing. 1.** to appoint as one's substitute. **2.** to assign (authority, etc.) to a deputy.

dep·u·tize (dep′yə tīz′), *v.t.,* **-tized, -tiz·ing.** to appoint as deputy.

dep·u·ty (dep′yə tē), *n., pl.* **-ties. 1.** a person authorized to act as a substitute for another or others. **2.** an assistant to a public official. **3.** a person representing a constituency in certain legislative bodies.

der., **1.** derivation. **2.** derivative. **3.** derive.

de·rail (dē rāl′), *v.t., v.i.* to run off or cause to run off the rails of a track. —**de·rail′ment,** *n.*

de·rail·leur (də rā′lər), *n.* a gear mechanism on a bicycle in which the chain can readily be switched among sprockets of different sizes.

de·range (di rānj′), *v.t.,* **-ranged, -rang·ing. 1.** to disturb the condition, action, or function of. **2.** to make insane. —**de·range′ment,** *n.*

Der·by (dûr′bē), *n., pl.* **-bies. 1.** a race for three-year-old horses run annually. **2.** (*l.c.*) a race or contest, usually open to all. **3.** (*l.c.*) a man's stiff felt hat with rounded crown and narrow brim.

de·reg·u·late (dē reg′yə lāt′), *v.t. v.i.,* **-lat·ed, -lat·ing.** to remove regulatory controls (from). —**de·reg′u·la′tion,** *n.*

der·e·lict (der′ə likt), *adj.* **1.** left or abandoned, as by the owner: *a derelict ship.* **2.** delinquent or negligent. —*n.* **3.** personal property abandoned by the owner. **4.** a vessel abandoned in open water. **5.** a person abandoned by society.

der·e·lic·tion (der′ə lik′shən), *n.* **1.** deliberate neglect: *dereliction of duty.* **2.** the act of abandoning something. **3.** the state of being abandoned.

de·ride (di rīd′), *v.t.,* **-rid·ed, -rid·ing.** to attack with scornful laughter. —**de·ri′si·ble** (-riz′ə bəl), *adj.* —**de·ri′sion** (-rizh′ən), *n.* —**de·ri·sive** (di·rī′siv), *adj.* —**de·ri′sive·ly,** *adv.* —**de·ri′so·ry** (-rī′sə rē), *adj.* —**Syn.** mock, scoff.

de ri·gueur (də ri gûr′), *French.* strictly required, as by etiquette, usage, or fashion.

deriv., 1. derivation. 2. derivative. 3. derived.

der·i·va·tion (der′ə vā′shən), *n.* 1. the act or fact of deriving or of being derived. 2. the process of deriving. 3. the source or origin of something. 4. the origin and evolution of a word.

de·riv·a·tive (di riv′ə tiv), *adj.* 1. derived from another. —*n.* 2. something derived. 3. a form that has undergone derivation from another, as *atomic* from *atom.*

de·rive (di rīv′), *v.,* -**rived, -riv·ing.** —*v.t.* 1. to receive or obtain from a source or origin. 2. to trace from a source or origin. 3. to reach by reasoning. —*v.i.* 4. to be derived.

der·ma (dûr′mə), *n. Anat.* the skin. Also, **der·mis** (dûr′mis). —**der′mal,** *adj.*

der·ma·ti·tis (dûr′mə tī′tis), *n.* inflammation of the skin.

der·ma·tol·o·gy (dûr′mə tol′ə jē), *n.* the science dealing with the skin and its diseases. —**der·ma·to·log·i·cal** (dûr′mə t°loj′i kəl), *adj.* —**der′ma·tol′o·gist,** *n.*

der·o·gate (der′ə gāt′), *v.,* -**gat·ed, -gat·ing.** —*v.i.* 1. to detract, as from authority, estimation, etc. —*v.t.* 2. *Rare.* to disparage or belittle. —**der′o·ga′tion,** *n.*

de·rog·a·to·ry (di rog′ə tōr′ē, -tôr′ē), *adj.* tending to lessen the merit or reputation of a person or thing: *a derogatory remark.*

der·rick (der′ik), *n.* 1. a crane having a boom hinged near the base of the mast for moving heavy loads. 2. a towerlike framework that lowers and raises equipment to drill an oil well.

der·ri·ère (der′ē âr′), *n. French.* the buttocks. Also, **der′ri·ere′.**

der·ring-do (der′ing dōō′), *n. Literary.* daring deeds.

der·rin·ger (der′in jər), *n.* an early short-barreled pocket pistol. [after H. *Deringer,* 19th century U.S. gunsmith]

der·ris (der′is), *n.* an East Indian plant whose roots are used as an insecticide.

der·vish (dûr′vish), *n.* a member of any of various Muslim ascetic orders, some of which carry on ecstastic observances, such as dancing and whirling.

de·sal·i·nate (dē sal′ə nāt′), *v.t.,* -**nat·ed, -nat·ing.** desalt. —**de·sal′i·na′tion,** *n.*

de·sa·lin·ize (dē sā′lə nīz′, -lī, -sal′ə-), *v.t.,* -**ized, -iz·ing.** desalt. —**de·sa′lin·i·za′tion,** *n.*

de·salt (dē sôlt′), *v.t.* to remove the salt from (esp. sea water), usually to make it drinkable. —**de·salt′er,** *n.*

des·cant (des kant′, dis-), *v.i.* 1. to comment or discourse at length. 2. to sing a part song.

Des·cartes (dā kärt′), *n.* **Re·né** (rə nā′), 1596–1650, French philosopher and mathematician.

de·scend (di send′), *v.i.* 1. to move to a lower place, level, standard, etc. 2. to slope or lead downward 3. to be inherited or transmitted. 4 to come down from. 5. to attack, esp. with violence. —*v.t.* 6. to move downward upon or along.

de·scend·ant (di sen′dənt), *n.* 1. a person who is descended from a specific ancestor. 2. something deriving from an earlier form. —*adj.* 3. descendent

de·scend·ent (di sen′dənt), *adj.* 1. going or coming down. 2. descending from an ancestor.

de·scent (di sent′), *n.* 1. the act or process of descending. 2. a downward slope. 3. a passage or stairway leading down. 4. lineage or ancestry. 5. any decline in degree or state. 6 a sudden raid.

de·scribe (di skrīb′), *v.t.,* -**scribed, -scrib·ing.** 1. to depict in words. 2. to draw the outline of. —**de·scrib′a·ble,** *adj.* —**de·scrib′er,** *n.*

de·scrip·tion (di skrip′shən), *n.* 1. a statement or picture in words that describes. 2. the act or method of describing. 3. sort or variety. —**de·scrip′tive,** *adj.*

de·scry (di skrī′), *v.t.,* -**scried, -scry·ing.** 1. to catch sight of (something unclear). 2. to discover, esp. by observation.

des·e·crate (des′ə krāt′), *v.t.,* -**crat·ed, -crat·ing.** to treat with sacrilege. —**des′e·cra′tion,** *n.*

de·seg·re·gate (dē seg′rə gāt′), *v.t., v.i.,* -**gat·ed, -gat·ing.** to eliminate racial segregation in (schools, etc.). —**de′seg·re·ga′tion,** *n.*

de·se·lect (dē si lekt′), *v.t.,* to discharge (esp. a trainee).

de·sen·si·tize (dē sen′si tīz′), *v.t.* -**tized, -tiz·ing.** to lessen the sensitiveness of. —**de·sen′si·ti·za′tion,** *n.* —**de·sen′si·tiz′er,** *n.*

des·ert¹ (dez′ərt), *n.* a region so arid that it supports only sparse vegetation or none at all.

de·sert² (di zûrt′), *v.t., v.i.* 1. to leave (a person, place, etc.) without intending to return. 2. to run away from (service, duty, etc.) with the intention of never returning. —**de·sert′er,** *n.* —**de·ser′tion,** *n.*

de·sert³ (di zûrt′), *n.* reward or punishment that is deserved: *to get one's just deserts.*

de·serve (di zûrv′), *v.t., v.i.,* -**served, -serv·ing.** to be rightfully worthy of (reward, punishment, etc.). —**de·served′,** *adj.* —**de·serv′ed·ly** (-zûr′vid lē), *adv.* —**de·serv′ing,** *adj.* —

de·serv'ing·ly, *adv.* —Syn. earn, merit.

des·ic·cant (des'ə kənt), *adj.* a drying substance or agent.

des·ic·cate (des'ə kāt'), *v.t., v.i.,* -cat·ed, -cat·ing. to dry up or become dried up. —des'ic·ca'tion, *n.* —des'ic·ca'tive, *adj.* —des'ic·ca'tor, *n.*

de·sid·er·a·tum (di sid'ə rā'təm), *n., pl.* -ta (-tə). something wanted or needed.

de·sign (di zīn'), *v.t.* 1. to prepare the plans for: *to design a new bridge.* 2. to plan and fashion skillfully. 3. to intend, esp. for a definite purpose. 4. to form in the mind. —*v.i.* 5. to make drawings or plans. 6. to plan an object, work of art, etc. —*n.* 7. an outline, sketch, or plan. 8. the organization of elements in a work of art. 9. an ornamental pattern. 10. a plan or project. 11. a plot or intrigue. 12. intention or end. —de·sign'er, *n.*

des·ig·nate (v. dez'ig nāt'; *adj.* dez'ig nit, -nāt'), *v.,* -nat·ed, -nat·ing. *adj.* —*v.t.* 1. to mark or point out. 2. to indicate. 3. to denote or call by a particular name. 4. to select for a duty, office, etc. —*adj.* 5. selected for an office, position, etc., but not yet installed. —des'ig·na'tion, *n.*

de·sign·ing (di zī'ning), *adj.* 1. selfishly scheming. —*n.* 2. the art of making designs or patterns.

de·sir·a·ble (di zīr'ə bəl), *adj.* 1. worth desiring. 2. arousing desire. 3. advisable or recommendable. —de·sir'a·bil'i·ty, *n.* —de·sir'a·bly, *adj.*

de·sire (di zīr'), *v.,* -sired, -sir·ing, *n.* —*v.t.* 1. to long for intensely. 2. to ask for. —*v.i.* 3. to have or feel a desire. —*n.* 4. an intense longing. 5. an expressed wish. 6. something desired. 7. sexual urge. —de·sir'er, *n.* —Syn. 1. covet, crave, fancy, wish.

de·sir·ous (di zīr'əs), *adj.* having or characterized by desire.

de·sist (di zist', -sist'), *v.i.* to cease, as from some action.

desk (desk), *n.* 1. an article of furniture having a level writing surface. 2. a specialized section of a large organization: *news desk.*

Des Moines (də moin', moinz'), the capital of Iowa.

des·o·late (*adj.* des'ə lit; *v.* des'ə lāt'), *adj., v.,* -lat·ed, -lat·ing. —*adj.* 1. barren or laid waste. 2. uninhabited or deserted. 3. isolated or lonely. 4. feeling abandoned, as by friends. 5. dismal. —*v.t.* 6. to make desolate. —des'o·late·ly, *adv.* —des'o·late·ness, *n.*

des·o·la·tion (des'ə lā'shən), *n.* 1. the act of making desolate or state of being desolated. 2. devastation or ruin. 3. loneliness or wretchedness.

4. sorrow or grief. 5. a desolate place.

des·ox·y·ri'bo·nu·cle·ic ac'id (des ok·si rī'bō nōō klē'ik, -nyōō-). See DNA.

de·spair (di spâr'), *n.* 1. loss of hope. 2. someone or something causing this. —*v.i.* 3. to be without hope. —de·spair'ing, *adj.* —de·spair'ing·ly, *adv.*

des·patch (di spach'), *v.t., n.* dispatch. —des·patch'er, *n.*

des·per·a·do (des'pə rä'dō, -rā'-), *n., pl.* -does, -dos. a bold, reckless criminal.

des·per·ate (des'pər it, -prit), *adj.* 1. reckless or dangerous because of despair. 2. having an urgent need, desire, etc. 3. very serious. 4. extreme or excessive. —des'per·ate·ly, *adv.* —des'per·ate·ness, *n.*

des·per·a·tion (des'pə rā'shən), *n.* 1. the state of being desperate. 2. recklessness caused by hopelessness.

des·pi·ca·ble (des'pi kə bəl, di spik'ə bəl), *adj.* deserving to be despised. —des'pi·ca·bly, *adv.*

de·spise (di spīz'), *v.t.,* -spised, -spis·ing. 1. to regard with contempt or disdain. 2. to regard as disagreeable or useless. —Syn. 1. abhor, detest, loathe, scorn.

de·spite (di spīt'), *prep.* in spite of.

de·spoil (di spoil'), *v.t.* to strip of possessions by force. —de·spoil'er, *n.* —de·spoil'ment, *n.*

de·spo·li·a·tion (di spō'lē ā'shən), *n.* 1. the act of plundering. 2. the fact or circumstance of being despoiled.

de·spond (di spond'), *v.i.* to be depressed by loss of hope or courage. —de·spond'ing·ly, *adv.*

de·spond·en·cy (di spon'dən sē), *n.* depression from loss of courage or hope. Also, de·spond'ence. —de·spond'ent, *adj.* —de·spond'ent·ly, *adv.*

des·pot (des'pət, -pot), *n.* 1. a ruler having absolute power. 2. any tyrant or oppressor. —des·pot·ic (di spot'ik), *adj.* —des·pot'i·cal·ly, *adv.* —des'pot·ism, *n.*

des·sert (di zûrt'), *n.* pastry, ice cream, etc., served as the final course of a meal. [< F *dessert(ir)* (to) clear the table]

des·ti·na·tion (des'tə nā'shən), *n.* 1. the place to which a person or thing travels or is sent. 2. an ultimate end or design.

des·tine (des'tin), *v.t.,* -tined, -tin·ing. 1. to set apart for a particular purpose. 2. to foreordain, as by divine decree. 3. **destined for,** bound for (a certain destination).

des·ti·ny (des'tə nē), *n., pl.* -nies. 1. something that is to happen to a particular person or thing. 2. the predetermined course of events.

des·ti·tute (des'ti tōōt', -tyōōt'), *adj.* 1. without means of subsistence. 2.

deprived or lacking. —**des'ti·tu'·tion,** *n.*

de·stroy (di stroi'), *v.t.* **1.** to injure beyond repair or renewal. **2.** to put an end to. **3.** to kill or slay. —*v.i.* **4.** to engage in destruction. —**Syn. 1.** demolish, devastate, wreck.

de·stroy·er (di stroi'ər), *n.* **1.** a person or thing that destroys. **2.** a fast warship used as an escort in convoys, etc.

destroy'er es'cort, a warship somewhat smaller than a destroyer.

de·struct (di strukt'), *n.* **1.** the intentional destruction of a missile. —*v.t.* **2.** to destroy. —*v.i.* **3.** to be destroyed automatically.

de·struct·i·ble (di struk'tə bəl), *adj.* capable of being destroyed. —**de·struct'i·bil'i·ty,** *n.*

de·struc·tion (di struk'shən), *n.* **1.** the act of destroying. **2.** the fact or condition of being destroyed. **3.** a cause or means of destroying. —**de·struc'tive,** *adj.* —**de·struc'tive·ly,** *adv.* —**de·struc'tive·ness,** *n.*

de·struc·tor (di struk'tər), *n. Brit.* incinerator.

des·ue·tude (des'wi tōōd', -tyōōd'), *n.* disuse or discontinuance.

des·ul·to·ry (des'əl tōr'ē, -tōr'ē), *adj.* **1.** lacking in consistency or visible order. **2.** random or digressing.

det., 1. detach. **2.** detachment. **3.** detail.

de·tach (di tach'), *v.t.* **1.** to unfasten and separate. **2.** to send (a regiment, etc.) on a special mission. —**de·tach'a·ble,** *adj.* —**de·tach'a·bly,** *adv.*

de·tached (di tacht'), *adj.* **1.** not attached or joined. **2.** disinterested or unbiased: *a detached judgment.*

de·tach·ment (di tach'mənt), *n.* **1.** the act of separating or condition of being separated. **2.** lack of interest. **3.** freedom from partiality. **4.** the act of sending out a detached force of troops or naval ships. **5.** the force sent.

de·tail (*n.* di tāl', dē'tāl; *v.* di tāl'), *n.* **1.** an individual or minute part or particular. **2.** such particulars collectively. **3.** attention to a subject in individual or minute parts. **4.** *Mil.* **a.** an appointment or assignment for a special task. **b.** the party or person so selected: *the kitchen detail.* **5.** in detail, item by item. —*v.t.* **6.** to relate with complete particulars. **7.** to specify or list. **8.** *Mil.* to assign for a particular duty.

de·tain (di tān'), *v.t.* **1.** to keep from proceeding. **2.** to keep under restraint or in custody. —**de·tain'ment,** *n.*

de·tect (di tekt'), *v.t.* to discover the presence or fact of. —**de·tect'a·ble, de·tect'i·ble,** *adj.* —**de·tec'tion,** *n.* —**de·tec'tor,** *n.*

de·tec·tive (di tek'tiv), *n.* a person

employed or engaged in investigating, solving, and preventing crimes.

dé·tente (dā tänt'), *n.* a relaxation of international tension. Also, **de·tente'.**

de·ten·tion (di ten'shən), *n.* **1.** the act of holding back or state of being detained. **2.** maintenance of a person in custody or confinement.

deten'tion home', a house of correction for juvenile offenders or delinquents.

de·ter (di tûr'), *v.t.,* -terred, -ter·ring. **1.** to discourage or restrain from acting, as through fear. **2.** to prevent or check. —**de·ter'ment,** *n.*

de·ter·gent (di tûr'jənt), *n.* a water-soluble cleaning agent that has wetting and emulsifying properties.

de·te·ri·o·rate (di tēr'ē ō rāt'), *v.t., v.i.,* -rat·ed, -rat·ing. to make or become worse in quality, value, etc. —**de·te'ri·o·ra'tion,** *n.*

de·ter·mi·nant (di tûr'mə nənt), *n.* a determining agent or factor.

de·ter·mi·nate (di tûr'mə nit), *adj.* **1.** having defined limits. **2.** settled or positive. —**de·ter'mi·na·cy** (-nə sē), *n.* —**de·ter'mi·nate·ness,** *n.*

de·ter·mi·na·tion (di tûr'mə nā'shən), *n.* **1.** the act or condition of determining or being determined. **2.** ascertainment, as after investigation. **3.** the decision arrived at or pronounced. **4.** a fixed purpose or intention.

de·ter·mine (di tûr'min), *v.t.,* -mined, -min·ing. —*v.t.* **1.** to settle by an authoritative or conclusive decision. **2.** to ascertain, as after observation. **3.** to fix the position of. **4.** to cause, affect, or control. **5.** to give direction to. **6.** to decide upon. —*v.i.* **7.** to come to a decision. —**de·ter'mi·na·ble,** *adj.* —**de·ter'mi·na·bly,** *adv.*

de·ter·mined (di tûr'mind), *adj.* **1.** unwaveringly decided. **2.** settled or resolved. —**de·ter'mined·ly,** *adv.* —**de·ter'mined·ness,** *n.*

de·ter·min·ism (di tûr'mə niz'əm), *n.* the doctrine that all events, including human choices and decisions, have sufficient causes. —**de·ter'min·ist,** *n., adj.*

de·ter·rent (di tûr'ənt, -tur'-, -ter'-), *adj.* **1.** serving to deter. —*n.* **2.** something that deters, esp. against nuclear attack. —**de·ter'rence,** *n.*

de·test (di test'), *v.t.* to dislike intensely. —**de·test'a·ble,** *adj.* —**de·tes·ta'tion,** *n.*

de·throne (dē thrōn'), *v.t.,* -throned, -thron·ing. to remove from a throne. —**de·throne'ment,** *n.*

det·o·nate (det'°nāt'), *v.t., v.i.,* -nat·ed, -nat·ing. to explode with suddenness and violence. —**det'o·na·ble,** *adj.* —**det'o·na'tion,** *n.* —**det'o·na'tor,** *n.*

de·tour (dē'tōōr, di tōōr'), *n.* **1.** a roundabout course, esp. one used temporarily instead of the main one. —*v.i.*, *v.t.* **2.** to make or cause to make a detour.

de·tox·i·fy (dē tok′sə fī′), *v.t.*, **-fied, -fy·ing.** to rid of poison or the effect of poison. —**de·tox′i·fi·ca′-tion,** *n.*

de·tract (di trakt′), *v.i.* **1.** to take away a part, as from quality, value, or reputation. —*v.t.* **2.** to divert or distract. —**de·trac′tion,** *n.* —**de·trac′tive,** *adj.* —**de·trac′tor,** *n.*

de·train (dē trān′), *v.i.*, *v.t.* to alight or cause to alight from a railroad train.

det·ri·ment (de′trə mənt), *n.* **1.** anything that causes damage or harm. **2.** such damage. —**det·ri·men·tal** (de′trə men′t°l), *adj.* —**det′ri·men′-tal·ly,** *adv.*

de·tri·tus (di trī′təs), *n.* rock in small particles or other material broken away from a mass. —**de·tri′tal** (-t°l), *adj.*

De·troit (di troit′), *n.* a city in SE Michigan.

deuce (dōōs, dyōōs), *n.* **1.** a card or die having two pips. **2.** *Tennis.* a tie that can be broken by a player scoring two successive points to win the game. **3.** *Informal.* the devil (used as a mild oath).

deu·te·ri·um (dōō tēr′ē əm, dyōō-), *n.* an isotope of hydrogen, having twice the mass of ordinary hydrogen. *Symbol:* D; *at. no.:* 1; *at. wt.:* 2.01.

deu·ter·on (dōō′tə ron′, dyōō′-), *n.* a positively charged particle consisting of a proton and a neutron.

Deut′sche mark′ (doi′chə), the monetary unit of West Germany.

dev., deviation.

de·val·ue (dē val′yōō), *v.t.*, **-val·ued, -val·u·ing.** **1.** to reduce the value of. **2.** to fix a lower legal value on (a currency). Also, **de·val′u·ate′** (-āt′). —**de·val′u·a′tion,** *n.*

dev·as·tate (dev′ə stāt′), *v.t.*, **-tat·ed, -tat·ing.** **1.** to cause widespread ruin and desolation to, as by war. **2.** *Informal.* to overwhelm or overpower. —**dev′as·ta′tion,** *n.* —**dev′as·ta′tor,** *n.*

de·vel·op (di vel′əp), *v.t.* **1.** to bring to a more advanced or effective state. **2.** to cause to grow or expand. **3.** to expand in detail. **4.** to bring into being or activity. **5.** to make visible (the latent image on an exposed film). —*v.i.* **6.** to grow into a more advanced state. **7.** to come gradually into existence or operation. **8.** to become evident or manifest. —**de·vel′op·er,** *n.* —**de·vel′op·ment,** *n.* —**de·vel′op·men′tal,** *adj.*

de·vel·op·ing (di vel′ə piñg), *adj.* not yet fully developed industrially and economically, as a nation.

de·vi·ant (dē′vē ənt), *adj.* **1.** deviating from the norm. —*n.* **2.** a deviant person or thing. —**de′vi·ance, de′-vi·an·cy,** *n.*

de·vi·ate (*v.* dē′vē āt′; *adj.*, *n.* dē′vē it), *v.*, **-at·ed, -at·ing,** *adj.*, *n.* —*v.i.* **1.** to turn aside, as from a course, norm, pattern, or subject. —*adj.* **2.** deviant. —*n.* **3.** a deviant, esp. a sexual pervert. —**de′vi·a′tion,** *n.* —**de′vi·a′tor,** *n.*

de·vice (di vīs′), *n.* **1.** something made, usually for a particular working purpose. **2.** a plan or trick for effecting a purpose. **3.** a design used as an emblem, badge, trademark, etc. **4. leave to one's own devices,** to leave alone to do as one pleases.

dev·il (dev′əl), *n.*, *v.*, **-iled, -il·ing** or **-illed, -il·ling.** —*n.* **1.** *Theol.* **a.** (*sometimes cap.*) the supreme spirit of evil: Satan. **b.** a subordinate evil spirit. **2.** an atrociously wicked person. **3.** a person of great cleverness, energy, or recklessness. **4.** an apprentice in a printing office. **5.** a person, esp. one in unfortunate circumstances. —*v.t.* **6.** *Informal.* to annoy or harass. [< L *diabolus* < Gk *diábolos*]

dev·iled (dev′əld), *adj.* prepared with hot or savory seasoning.

dev·il·ish (dev′ə lish, dev′lish), *adj.* **1.** of, like, or befitting a devil. **2.** *Informal.* very great: *a devilish mess.* —*adv.* **3.** *Informal.* extremely. —**dev′-il·ish·ly,** *adv.* —**dev′il·ish·ness,** *n.*

dev·il·may·care (dev′əl mā kâr′), *adj.* reckless or careless.

dev·il·ment (dev′əl mənt), *n.* mischievous prank.

dev′il's ad′vocate, a person who advocates an opposing cause for the sake of argument.

dev′il's food′ cake′, a rich chocolate cake.

dev·il·try (dev′əl trē), *n.*, *pl.* **-tries. 1.** reckless mischief. **2.** diabolic magic or art. Also, *Brit.*, **dev′il·ry** (-rē).

de·vi·ous (dē′vē əs), *adj.* **1.** departing from the shortest way. **2.** shifty or crooked. —**de′vi·ous·ly,** *adv.* —**de′-vi·ous·ness,** *n.*

de·vise (di vīz′), *v.*, **-vised, -vis·ing,** *n.* —*v.t.* **1.** to create from existing ideas: *to devise a method.* **2.** to transmit (property) by will. —*n.* **3.** the act of disposing of property by will. **4.** a will or clause in a will disposing of property. —**de·vis′er,** *n.* —**Syn. 1.** concoct, contrive, invent.

de·vi·tal·ize (dē vīt′°līz′), *v.t.*, **-ized, -iz·ing.** to deprive of vitality.

de·void (di void′), *adj.* not possessing or using: *devoid of humor.*

de·voir (də vwär′, dev′wär), *n. Archaic.* **1.** an act of civility or respect. **2.** duty or responsibility.

de·volve (di volv'), *v.t., v.i.,* **-volved, -volv·ing.** to pass or be passed on from one to another, as an obligation. —**de·volve'ment,** *n.*

De·vo·ni·an (də vō'nē ən), *adj.* **1.** noting a period of the Paleozoic era, occurring from 350,000,000 to 400,-000,000 years ago, characterized by the dominance of fishes and the advent of amphibians. —*n.* **2.** the Devonian period.

de·vote (di vōt'), *v.t.,* **-vot·ed, -vot·ing. 1.** to give up or appropriate to a particular pursuit, cause, etc.: *devoting himself to science.* **2.** to consecrate or dedicate.

de·vot·ed (di vō'tid), *adj.* **1.** zealous or ardent in attachment. **2.** consecrated or dedicated. —**de·vot'ed·ly,** *adv.*

dev·o·tee (dev'ə tē'), *n.* a person devoted to or enthusiastic over something.

de·vo·tion (di vō'shən), *n.* **1.** profound dedication. **2.** earnest attachment to a cause, person, etc. **3.** an assignment to any purpose, cause, etc. **4.** religious observance or worship. —**de·vo'tion·al,** *adj.*

de·vour (di vour'), *v.t.* **1.** to eat up voraciously. **2.** to consume wantonly. **3.** to take in greedily with the senses or intellect. —**de·vour'er,** *n.*

de·vout (di vout'), *adj.* **1.** deeply devoted to divine worship or service. **2.** expressing devotion or piety: *devout prayer.* **3.** sincere or hearty. —**de·vout'ly,** *adv.* —**de·vout'ness,** *n.* —Syn. **1.** pious, religious.

dew (dōō, dyōō), *n.* **1.** moisture condensed from the atmosphere, esp. at night, and deposited in small drops on a cool surface. **2.** something like or compared to dew, as in purity. —**dew'y,** *adj.* —**dew'i·ly,** *adv.* —**dew'i·ness,** *n.*

DEW (dōō, dyōō), *n. Mil.* distant early warning.

dew·ber·ry (dōō'ber'ē, -bə rē, dyōō'-), *n.* the fruit of any of several trailing blackberries.

dew·claw (dōō'klô', dyōō'-), *n.* a claw in the foot of some dogs, not reaching the ground in walking.

dew·drop (dōō'drop', dyōō'-), *n.* a drop of dew.

dew·lap (dōō'lap', dyōō'-), *n.* a pendulous fold of skin under the throat, esp. of a bovine animal.

dew' point', the temperature to which air must be cooled for dew to form.

dex·ter·i·ty (dek ster'i tē), *n.* skill in using the hands, body, or mind.

dex·ter·ous (dek'strəs, -stər əs), *adj.* **1.** possessing dexterity. **2.** done with dexterity. Also, **dex'trous.** —**dex'ter·ous·ly,** *adv.* —**dex'ter·ous·ness,** *n.*

dex·trin (dek'strin), *n.* a gummy substance formed from starch, used chiefly as a thickening agent and a mucilage, and as a substitute for gum arabic.

dex·trose (dek'strōs), *n.* glucose, commercially obtainable from starch by acid hydrolysis.

D.F.C., Distinguished Flying Cross.

D.F.M., Distinguished Flying Medal.

D.G., 1. by the grace of God. [< L *Dei gratia*] **2.** Director General.

dg, decigram; decigrams.

dhole (dōl), *n.* a fierce, wild dog of India, that hunts in packs which attack large game.

dho·ti (dō'tē), *n., pl.* **-tis.** a loincloth worn by Hindu men in India.

dhow (dou), *n.* an Arab sailing vessel common on the Arabian and Indian coasts, generally having two or three masts.

DI, 1. Department of the Interior. **2.** drill instructor.

di-, a prefix meaning "two," "twice," or "double": *diphthong.*

dia., diameter.

di·a·be·tes (dī'ə bē'tis, -tēz), *n.* a disease that impairs the ability of the body to use sugar and causes sugar to appear abnormally in the urine. Also called **diabetes mel·li·tus** (mə lī'təs). —**di·a·bet·ic** (dī'ə bet'ik), *adj., n.*

di·a·bol·ic (dī'ə bol'ik), *adj.* outrageously wicked or fiendish: *a diabolic plot.* Also, **di'a·bol'i·cal.** —**di'a·bol'i·cal·ly,** *adv.*

di·a·crit·ic (dī'ə krit'ik), *n.* **1.** Also called **diacrit'ical mark'.** a mark added or attached to a letter to give it a particular phonetic value. —*adj.* **2.** diacritical.

di·a·crit·i·cal (dī'ə krit'i kəl), *adj.* serving to distinguish.

di·a·dem (dī'ə dem'), *n.* a crown or cloth headband worn as a symbol of power.

di·aer·e·sis (dī er'i sis), *n.* dieresis.

diag., 1. diagonal. **2.** diagram.

di·ag·nose (dī'əg nōs', -nōz', dī'əg nōs', -nōz'), *v.t., v.i.,* **-nosed, -nos·ing.** to make a diagnosis (of).

di·ag·no·sis (dī'əg nō'sis), *n., pl.* **-ses** (-sēz). **1.** the process of determining by examination and analysis the nature and circumstances of a diseased condition. **3.** the conclusion reached from such a process. —**di·ag·nos·tic** (dī'əg nos'tik), *adj.* —**di·ag·nos·ti·cal·ly,** *adv.* —**di·ag·nos·ti·cian** (-tish'ən), *n.*

di·ag·o·nal (dī ag'ə nəl), *adj.* **1.** connecting two nonadjacent vertices of a polygon, as a straight line. **2.** having an oblique direction. **3.** having oblique lines, markings, etc. —*n.* **4.** a diagonal line or plane. **5.** slash (def. 7). —**di·ag·o·nal·ly,** *adv.*

di·a·gram (dī′ə gram′), *n.*, *v.*, **-gramed,** **-gram·ing** or **-grammed,** **-gram·ming.** **—n.** **1.** a drawn figure illustrating a mathematical demonstration, etc. **2.** a drawing or plan that outlines and explains the parts, operation, etc., of something. **—v.t.** **3.** to make a diagram of. **—di′a·gram·mat·ic** (dī′ə grə mat′ik), **di′a·gram·mat′i·cal,** *adj.* **—di′a·gram·mat′i·cal·ly,** *adv.*

di·al (dī′əl, dīl), *n.*, *v.*, **di·aled, di·al·ing** or **di·alled, di·al·ling.** **—n.** **1.** a graduated face upon which time or degree is indicated by a pointer, as of a clock. **2.** a rotatable disk having a knob used for regulating a mechanism, etc. **3.** a rotatable disk on a telephone, used in making calls. **—v.t., v.i.** **4.** to show on or as on a dial. **5.** to tune in (on a radio). **6.** to work the dial of a telephone to call. **—di′al·er,** *n.*

dial., **1.** dialect. **2.** dialectal. **3.** dialectic. **4.** dialectical.

di·a·lect (dī′ə lekt′), *n.* a variety of a language used by a group of speakers who are set off from others geographically or socially. **—di′a·lec′tal,** *adj.*

di·a·lec·tic (dī′ə lek′tik), *adj.* **1.** of logical argumentation. **—n.** **2.** the art or practice of logical discussion, as of the truth of a theory or opinion.

di·a·lec·ti·cal (dī′ə lek′ti kəl), *adj.* **1.** dialectic. **2.** *Obsolesc.* of a dialect.

di·a·logue (dī′ə lôg′, -log′), *n.* **1.** conversation between two or more persons, characters in a novel, etc. **2.** an exchange of ideas, esp. on a political issue. Also, **di′a·log′.**

Di′alogue Mass′, *Rom. Cath. Ch.* a Mass at which the responses are made aloud by the congregation.

di′al tone′, a steady humming sound which indicates that the telephone line is ready for dialing.

di·al·y·sis (dī al′i sis), *n.*, *pl.* **-ses** (-sēz′). the separation of different components in a chemical solution by diffusion through a semipermeable membrane.

diam., diameter.

di·a·mag·net·ic (dī′ə mag net′ik), *adj.* noting a substance, as bismuth or copper, whose induced magnetism is in a direction opposite to that of iron. **—di′a·mag′net·ism** (-ni tiz′əm), *n.*

di·am·e·ter (dī am′i tər), *n.* **1.** a straight line passing through the center of a circle or sphere and meeting at each end the circumference or surface. **2.** the length of such a line. **3.** the width of a circular or cylindrical object.

di·a·met·ri·cal (dī′ə me′tri kəl), *adj.* **1.** of or along a diameter. **2.** direct or complete: *diametrical opposites.* Also, **di′a·met′ric.** **—di′a·met′ri·cal·ly,** *adv.*

dia·mond (dī′mənd, dī′ə-), *n.* **1.** a form of carbon, naturally crystallized in the isometric system, of extreme hardness. **2.** a piece of this stone, valued as a precious gem or used in a cutting tool. **3.** a geometrical figure having four equal sides, two equal obtuse angles, and two equal acute angles. **4.** a red lozenge-shaped figure on a playing card. **5.** a card of the suit bearing such figures. **6.** *Baseball.* the space enclosed by home plate and the three bases.

dia·mond·back (dī′mənd bak′, dī′ə-), *n.* a large, highly venomous rattlesnake having diamond-shaped markings on the back.

Di·an·a (dī an′ə), *n.* an ancient Roman deity, goddess of the moon and of hunting, and protectress of women.

di·an·thus (dī an′thəs), *n.* a plant of the pink family, as the carnation.

di·a·pa·son (dī′ə pā′zən, -sən), *n.* **1.** a full, rich outpouring of melodious sound. **2.** either of two principal stops of a pipe organ.

dia·per (dī′pər, dī′ə pər), *n.* **1.** a piece of cloth or other absorbent material folded and worn about an infant's loins. **—v.t.** **2.** to put a diaper on (a baby).

di·aph·a·nous (dī af′ə nəs), *adj.* almost transparent or translucent.

dia·pho·ret·ic (dī′ə fə ret′ik), *Med.* **—adj.** **1.** producing perspiration. **—n.** **2.** a diaphoretic medicine.

di·a·phragm (dī′ə fram′), *n.* **1.** a muscular, membranous wall, esp. one separating the chest from the abdomen. **2.** a thin disk that vibrates when receiving or producing sound waves, as in a telephone. **3.** a contraceptive device, usually of rubber, that fits over the uterine cervix. **4.** a plate with a hole, usually variable in size, in a camera to control light. **—di′a·phrag·mat′ic** (-frag mat′ik), *adj.*

di·ar·rhe·a (dī′ə rē′ə), *n.* an intestinal disorder that causes frequent, fluid bowel movements. Also, **di′ar·rhoe′a.**

di·a·ry (dī′ə rē), *n.*, *pl.* **-ries.** **1.** a daily record, esp. of the writer's own experiences, attitudes, etc. **2.** a book for keeping such a record. **—di′a·rist,** *n.*

Di·as·po·ra (dī as′pər ə), *n.* the scattering of the Jews to countries outside of Palestine after the Babylonian captivity.

di·as·to·le (dī as′t°lē′), *n.* the normal rhythmical dilatation of the heart during which the chambers are filling with blood. **—di·as·tol·ic** (dī′ə stol′ik), *adj.*

di·as·tro·phism (dī as′trə fiz′əm), *n.* the action of the forces that cause the earth's crust to be deformed. —**di·a·stroph·ic** (dī′ə strof′ik), *adj.*

di·a·ther·my (dī′ə thûr′mē), *n.* the production of heat in body tissues by electric currents, for therapeutic purposes. —**di′a·ther′mic**, *adj.*

di·a·tom (dī′ə təm, -tom′), *n.* any of numerous microscopic, unicellular, marine or freshwater algae having siliceous cell walls.

di·at·o·mite (dī at′ə mīt′), *n.* a fine siliceous earth, used in filtration, as an abrasive, etc.

di·a·tom·ic (dī′ə tom′ik), *adj.* 1. having two atoms in the molecule. 2. containing two replaceable atoms or groups.

di·a·ton·ic (dī′ə ton′ik), *adj.* using a scale composed of five whole tones and two half tones, as the major, minor, and certain modal scales.

di·a·tribe (dī′ə trīb′), *n.* a bitter, abusive denunciation.

di·az·e·pam (dī az′ə pam′), *n.* a tranquilizer that relieves anxiety, depression, and muscular tension.

dib·ble (dib′əl), *n.* a pointed implement for making holes in the ground for planting seeds, bulbs, etc.

dice (dīs), *n.pl., sing.* **die,** *v.,* **diced, dic·ing.** —*n.* 1. small cubes, marked on each side with one to six spots, usually used in pairs in games or gambling. 2. **no dice,** *Slang.* a. a negative response. b. without success. —*v.t.* 3. to cut into small cubes. —*v.i.* 4. to play at dice. —**dic′er,** *n.*

dic·ey (dī′sē), *adj.,* **dic·i·er, dic·i·est.** *Informal.* risky or uncertain.

di·chot·o·my (dī kot′ə mē), *n., pl.* **-mies.** division into two, esp. mutually exclusive, groups. —**di·chot′o·mous,** *adj.* —**di·chot′o·mous·ly,** *adv.*

dick (dik), *n. Slang.* a detective.

dick·ens (dik′inz), *n.* the devil (used as a mild oath.)

Dick·ens (dik′inz), *n.* **Charles,** 1812–70, English novelist. —**Dick·en·si·an** (di ken′zē ən), *adj., n.*

dick·er (dik′ər), *v.i., v.t.* to trade with petty bargaining.

dick·ey (dik′ē), *n., pl.* **-eys.** 1. a detachable insert worn to simulate the front of a shirt. 2. Also called **dick′ey bird′.** a small bird. 3. *Brit.* an outside seat in a carriage. Also, **dick′y.**

di·cot·y·le·don (dī kot′əl lēd′°n, dī′-kot°lēd′-), *n.* a plant producing seeds with two cotyledons. Also, **di′cot.** —**di′cot·y·le′don·ous,** *adj.*

dict., 1. dictation. 2. dictator. 3. dictionary.

Dic·ta·phone (dik′tə fōn′), *n. Trademark.* a phonographic machine that records and reproduces dictation.

dic·tate (*v.* dik′tāt, dik tāt′; *n.* dik′-tāt), *v.,* **-tat·ed, -tat·ing,** *n.* —*v.t.,*

v.i. 1. to say (something) for another to transcribe or for a machine to record. 2. to command with authority. —*n.* 3. an authoritative order or command. —**dic·ta′tion,** *n.*

dic·ta·tor (dik′tā tər, dik tā′tər), *n.* 1. a person exercising absolute power. 2. a person who dictates, as to a secretary.

dic·ta·to·ri·al (dik′tə tôr′ē əl, -tôr′-), *adj.* 1. of a dictator or dictatorship. 2. imperious or overbearing. —**dic′ta·to′ri·al·ly,** *adv.* —**dic′ta·to′ri·al·ness,** *n.*

dic·ta·tor·ship (dik tā′tər ship′, dik′-tā-), *n.* 1. a country or government in which absolute power is exercised by a dictator. 2. absolute, imperious, or overbearing power or control. 3. the position held by a dictator.

dic·tion (dik′shən), *n.* 1. style of speaking or writing as dependent upon choice of words. 2. enunciation or delivery.

dic·tion·ar·y (dik′shə ner′ē), *n., pl.* **-ar·ies.** a book containing words of a language, usually arranged alphabetically, with their meanings, pronunciations, etymologies, etc.

dic·tum (dik′təm), *n., pl.* **-ta** (-tə), **-tums.** 1. an authoritative pronouncement. 2. a saying or maxim.

did (did), *v.* pt. of **do**[1].

di·dac·tic (dī dak′tik), *adj.* 1. intended for instruction: *didactic poetry.* 2. preaching or moralizing. —**di·dac′-ti·cal·ly,** *adv.* —**di·dac′ti·cism,** *n.*

did·dle (did′°l), *v.,* **-dled, -dling.** *Informal.* —*v.t.* 1. *Brit.* to cheat or swindle. —*v.i.* 2. to waste time.

did·n't (did′°nt), contraction of **did not.**

di·do (dī′dō), *n., pl.* **-dos, -does.** *Informal.* a prank or antic.

die[1] (dī), *v.i.,* **died, dy·ing.** 1. to cease to live. 2. to cease to exist. 3. to cease to function. 4. to pass gradually: *The storm slowly died down.* 5. *Informal.* to desire keenly: *I'm dying for a cup of coffee.* 6. **die off,** to die one after another until the number is greatly reduced. 7. **die out,** to cease existing completely.

die[2] (dī), *n., pl.* **dies** for 1, **dice** for 2. 1. a device for cutting or forming material in a press or a stamping machine. 2. sing. of **dice.**

die·hard (dī′härd′), *n.* a person who vigorously maintains a hopeless position, outdated attitude, etc.

diel·drin (dēl′drin), *n.* a poisonous insecticide.

di·e·lec·tric (dī′i lek′trik), *n.* an electrically nonconducting substance.

di·er·e·sis (dī er′i sis), *n., pl.* **-ses** (-sēz′). a sign (¨) over the second of two adjacent vowels to indicate separate pronunciation, as in *naïve.*

die·sel (dē′zəl), *n.* **1.** See **diesel engine**. **2.** a vehicle powered by a diesel engine. [after R. *Diesel*, 1858–1913, Ger. engineer]

die′sel en′gine, an internal-combustion engine in which a spray of fuel, introduced into air heated by compression, ignites at a virtually constant pressure.

di·et[1] (dī′it), *n., v.,* **-et·ed, -et·ing.** —*n.* **1.** food considered in terms of its effects on health. **2.** a particular selection of food, esp. as prescribed to cure a disease, lose weight, etc. —*v.i., v.t.* **3.** to go or put on a prescribed diet. —**di·e·tar·y** (dī′i ter′ē), *adj.* —**di′et·er,** *n.*

di·et[2] (dī′it), *n.* the legislative body of certain countries, as Japan.

di·e·tet·ic (dī′i tet′ik), *adj.* **1.** pertaining to diet. **2.** suitable for special diets. —*n.* **3.** **dietetics,** the science concerned with the nutritional planning and preparation of foods.

di·e·ti·tian (dī′i tish′ən), *n.* an expert in dietetics. Also, **di′e·ti′cian.**

diff., **1.** difference. **2.** different. Also, **dif.**

dif·fer (dif′ər), *v.i.* **1.** to be unlike in nature or qualities. **2.** to disagree in opinion or belief.

dif·fer·ence (dif′ər əns, dif′rəns), *n.* **1.** the state, relation, or an instance of being different. **2.** the degree in which one person or thing differs from another. **3.** discrimination or distinction. **4.** a disagreement in opinion. **5.** a dispute or quarrel. **6.** the amount by which one quantity is greater or less than another.

dif·fer·ent (dif′ər ənt, dif′rənt), *adj.* **1.** differing in character or quality. **2.** not identical. **3.** various or several. **4.** not ordinary. —**dif′fer·ent·ly,** *adv.* —**Syn. 1.** disparate, dissimilar, diverse, unlike.
—**Usage.** Most grammarians, chiefly on semantic grounds, regard any preposition but FROM after DIFFERENT as a solecism: *He is different from me.* But in the comparative of the sense "not ordinary," DIFFERENT is used in the same way as other adjectives: *He is more different than you are.*

dif·fer·en·ti·a (dif′ə ren′shē ə), *n., pl.* **-ti·ae** (-shē ē′). the attribute by which one species is distinguished from all others of the same genus.

dif·fer·en·tial (dif′ə ren′shəl), *adj.* **1.** of difference or diversity. **2.** exhibiting or depending upon a difference or distinction. —*n.* **3.** the amount of difference, as in cost or degree, between things that are comparable. **4.** Also called **differential gear.** a train of gears designed to permit two or more shafts to revolve at different speeds. **5.** *Math.* a function of two variables that is obtained from a given function.

dif·fer·en·ti·ate (dif′ə ren′shē āt′), *v.,* **-at·ed, -at·ing.** —*v.t.* **1.** to form or mark differently from other such things. **2.** to change or alter. **3.** to perceive the difference in or between. —*v.i.* **4.** to become unlike or dissimilar. **5.** to make a distinction. —**dif′fer·en′ti·a′tion,** *n.*

dif·fi·cult (dif′ə kult′, -kəlt), *adj.* **1.** requiring much labor or skill to be accomplished. **2.** hard to understand or solve. **3.** hard to deal with. **4.** hard to please or satisfy.

dif·fi·cul·ty (dif′ə kul′tē, -kəl tē), *n., pl.* **-ties. 1.** the fact or condition of being difficult. **2.** an embarrassing situation, esp. of financial affairs. **3.** a trouble or struggle. **4.** a disagreement or dispute. **5.** an impediment or obstacle.

dif·fi·dent (dif′i dənt), *adj.* lacking confidence in oneself. —**dif′fi·dence,** *n.* —**dif′fi·dent·ly,** *adv.*

dif·frac·tion (di frak′shən), *n.* the bending or spreading out of waves, esp. sound and light waves, around obstacles in their path. —**dif·frac′tive,** *adj.*

dif·fuse (*v.* di fyo͞oz′; *adj.* di fyo͞os′), *v.,* **-fused, -fus·ing,** *adj.* —*v.t., v.i.* **1.** to pour out and spread widely or thinly. —*adj.* **2.** discursive or wordy. **3.** widely spread or scattered. —**dif·fuse′ly** (di fyo͞os′lē), *adv.* —**dif·fuse′ness,** *n.* —**dif·fu′sion,** *n.* —**dif·fu′sive,** *adj.*

dig (dig), *v.,* **dug, dig·ging,** *n.* —*v.i.* **1.** to break up, turn over, or remove earth, sand, etc. **2.** to make one's way by turning over material: *to dig through the files.* —*v.t.* **3.** to break up, turn over, or loosen (earth, sand, etc.). **4.** to make (a hole, tunnel, etc.) by removing material. **5.** to unearth, obtain, or remove by digging. **6.** to find out by search. **7.** to thrust or poke. **8.** *Slang.* to understand or appreciate. **9. dig in, a.** to build trenches for cover. **b.** to work energetically. **10. dig up,** to discover in the course of digging. —*n.* **11.** a thrust or poke. **12.** a cutting, sarcastic remark. **13.** an archaeological site undergoing excavation. —**dig′ger,** *n.*

dig., digest.

di·gest (*v.* di jest′, dī-; *n.* dī′jest), *v.t.* **1.** to convert (food) in the alimentary canal for assimilation into the system. **2.** to assimilate mentally, as an argument. **3.** to condense, abridge, or summarize. —*v.i.* **4.** to undergo digestion, as food. —*n.* **5.** a collection or compendium, esp. when classified or condensed. —**di·gest′i·bil′i·ty,** *n.* —**di·gest′i·ble,** *adj.* —**di·ges′tion,** *n.* —**di·ges′tive,** *adj.*

dig·it (dij′it), *n*. **1.** any of the Arabic figures of 1 through 9 and 0. **2.** a finger or toe.

dig·it·al (dij′i t°l), *adj*. **1.** of a digit. **2.** resembling a finger. **3.** (of a timepiece) that tells time in digits rather than by the conventional hands: *a digital watch*. —*n*. **4.** a digital watch. —**dig′it·al·ly**, *adv*.

dig′ital comput′er, a computer that processes information expressed in numerical format.

dig·i·tal·is (dij′i tal′is, -tā′lis), *n*. the dried leaves of the foxglove, used as a heart stimulant.

dig·ni·fied (dig′nə fīd′), *adj*. marked by dignity of aspect or manner. —**dig′ni·fied·ly** (dig′nə fīd′lē, -fī′id-), *adv*.

dig·ni·fy (dig′nə fī′), *v.t.*, **-fied, -fy·ing.** to give dignity to.

dig·ni·tar·y (dig′ni ter′ē), *n*., *pl*. **-tar·ies**. a person who holds a high office, as in the government.

dig·ni·ty (dig′ni tē), *n*., *pl*. **-ties. 1.** formal, grave, or noble bearing, conduct, or speech. **2.** nobility or elevation of character. **3.** elevated rank, office, station, etc.

di·graph (dī′graf, -gräf), *n*. a pair of letters representing a single speech sound, as *th* in *path*.

di·gress (di gres′, dī-), *v.i.* to wander away from the main topic. —**di·gres′sion**, *n*. —**di·gres′sive**, *adj*.

dike (dīk), *n*. an embankment for controlling the waters of the sea or a river.

dil., dilute.

Di·lan·tin (di lan′tin), *n*. *Trademark*. a drug used to arrest convulsions in epilepsy.

di·lap·i·dat·ed (di lap′i dā′tid), *adj*. fallen into partial ruin or decay, as from neglect. —**di·lap′i·da′tion**, *n*.

di·late (dī lāt′, di-), *v.*, **-lat·ed, -lat·ing.** —*v.t.* **1.** to make wider or larger. —*v.i.* **2.** to speak or write at length. —**dil·a·ta·tion** (dil′ə tā′shən, dī′lə-), *n*. —**di·la′tion**, *n*. —**di·la′tive**, *adj*.

dil·a·to·ry (dil′ə tôr′ē, -tōr′ē), *adj*. **1.** inclined to delay. **2.** intended to bring about delay.

di·lem·ma (di lem′ə), *n*. a situation requiring a choice between equally undesirable alternatives.

dil·et·tante (dil′i tänt′, dil′i tänt′, dil′i-tan′tē, -tän′tā), *n*., *pl*. **-tantes, -tan·ti** (-tan′tē), (-tän′tē). a person who takes up an art or subject merely for amusement. —**dil′et·tan′tish**, *adj*. —**dil′et·tant′ism**, *n*.

dil·i·gent (dil′i jənt), *adj*. **1.** constant in effort to accomplish something. **2.** done with persevering attention. —**dil′i·gence**, *n*. —**dil′i·gent·ly**, *adv*.

dill (dil), *n*. a plant bearing a seed-like fruit used in medicine, in cookery, for flavoring pickles, etc.

dil·ly (dil′ē), *n*., *pl*. **-lies.** *Informal*. something remarkable of its kind.

dil·ly·dal·ly (dil′ē dal′ē, -dal′-), *v.i.*, **-lied, -ly·ing.** to waste time, esp. by indecision.

dil·u·ent (dil′yoo ənt), *n*. a diluting substance.

di·lute (di loot′, -dī-; *adj*. also dī′loot), *v.*, **-lut·ed, -lut·ing.** *adj*. —*v.t.* **1.** to make (a liquid) thinner or weaker by the addition of water. —*adj*. **2.** diluted or weak. —**di·lu′tion**, *n*.

dim (dim), *adj*., **dim·mer, dim·mest**, *v.*, **dimmed, dim·ming.** —*adj*. **1.** obscure from lack or weakness of light. **2.** indistinct or faint. **3.** dull in luster. **4.** not seeing clearly. **5.** not understanding clearly. **6.** take a dim view of, to regard with pessimism, skepticism, etc. —*v.t.*, *v.i.* **7.** to make or become dim or dimmer. —**dim′ly**, *adv*. —**dim′ness**, *n*.

dim., **1.** dimension. **2.** diminished. **3.** diminuendo. **4.** diminutive.

dime (dīm), *n*. a U.S. or Canadian coin worth 10 cents.

di·men·sion (di men′shən, dī-), *n*. **1.** magnitude measured in a particular direction. **2.** measurement in width, length, and thickness. **3.** scope or extent. —**di·men′sion·al**, *adj*. —**di·men′sion·al′i·ty**, *n*.

dime′ store′, five-and-ten.

di·min·ish (di min′ish), *v.t.*, *v.i.* to make or become smaller, less important, etc. —**dim·i·nu·tion** (dim′ə noo′shən, -nyoo′-), **di·min′ish·ment**, *n*.

di·min·u·en·do (di min′yoo en′dō), *adj*., *adv*. *Music*. gradually reducing in force or loudness.

di·min·u·tive (di min′yə tiv), *adj*. **1.** extremely small. **2.** denoting smallness, familiarity, or triviality, as the suffix *-let*, in *droplet*, from *drop*. —*n*. **3.** a small thing or person. **4.** a diminutive element or word.

dim·i·ty (dim′i tē), *n*., *pl*. **-ties.** a thin, cotton fabric woven with a stripe or check of heavier yarn.

dim·mer (dim′ər), *n*. **1.** a person or thing that dims. **2.** a rheostat or similar device for varying the intensity of illumination.

di·mor·phism (dī môr′fiz əm), *n*. the occurrence of two forms distinct in structure, among animals of the same species. —**di·mor′phous**, **di·mor′phic**, *adj*.

dim·ple (dim′pəl), *n*., *v.*, **-pled, -pling.** —*n*. **1.** a small, natural hollow area, esp. one formed in the cheek in smiling. —*v.t.*, *v.i.* **2.** to produce dimples (in). —**dim′ply**, *adj*.

dim·wit (dim′wit′), *n*. *Slang*. a stupid or slow-thinking person. —**dim′wit′ted**, *adj*. —**dim′wit′ted·ness**, *n*.

din (din), *n., v.,* **dinned, din·ning.**
—*n.* **1.** a loud, confused noise. —*v.t.*
2. to assail with din. **3.** to utter
with persistent repetition.

di·nar (di när'), *n.* the monetary unit
of Yugoslavia, Iraq, Jordan, Kuwait,
etc.

din-din (din'din'), *n. Baby Talk.*
dinner.

dine (dīn), *v.,* **dined, din·ing.** —*v.i.* **1.**
to have dinner. —*v.t.* **2.** to entertain
at dinner.

din·er (dī'nər), *n.* **1.** a person who
dines. **2.** a railroad dining car. **3.**
a restaurant built like such a car.

di·nette (dī net'), *n.* a small space
serving as an informal dining room.

ding (ding), *n.* the sound of a bell.
Also called **ding'-dong'** (-dông').

ding-a-ling (ding'ə ling'), *n. Informal.*
a stupid, befuddled, dimwitted person.

din·ghy (ding'ē, ding'gē), *n., pl.* **-ghies.**
a ship's small boat. [< Hindi *dingi,*
dim. of *dingā* boat]

din·gle (ding'gəl), *n.* a deep, narrow,
shady valley.

din·go (ding'gō), *n., pl.* **-goes.** a wolflike, wild dog of Australia, having
a reddish-brown coat.

ding·us (ding'əs), *n., pl.* **-us·es.** *Informal.* a gadget or whatever whose
name is unknown or forgotten.

din·gy (din'jē), *adj.,* **-gi·er, -gi·est.** **1.**
of a dark, dull, or dirty color or as-
pect. **2.** shabby or dismal. —**din'-
gi·ly,** *adv.* —**din'gi·ness,** *n.*

din'ing room', a room in which meals
are eaten, as in a home or hotel.

dink·y (ding'kē), *adj.,* **dink·i·er, dink·
i·est.** *Informal.* of small size or importance.

din·ner (din'ər), *n.* **1.** the main meal
of the day, eaten in the evening or
at midday. **2.** a banquet in honor of
some person or occasion.

din'ner jack'et, a man's jacket worn
for semiformal occasions.

din·ner·ware (din'ər wâr'), *n.* china,
glasses, and silver used for table
service.

di·no·saur (dī'nə sôr'), *n.* an extinct,
chiefly terrestrial, often huge reptile
of the Mesozoic era. [< NL *dino-
saur(us)* < Gk *deino-* terrible +
Gk *saúros* lizard]

dint (dint), *n.* **1.** force or power (used
chiefly in the phrase *by dint of*). **2.**
dent.

di·o·cese (dī'ə sēs', -sis), *n.* a district
under the jurisdiction of a bishop. —
di·oc·e·san (dī os'i sən), *adj.*

di·ode (dī'ōd), *n.* any electronic device through which current can pass
only in one direction.

Di·og·e·nes (dī oj'ə nēz'), *n.* 412?-
323 B.C., Greek philosopher.

Di·o·ny·sus (dī'ə nī'səs), *n. Class.
Myth.* the god of fertility, wine, and

drama. Also, **Di·o·ny'sos.** —**Di·o·
ny·sian** (dī'ə nish'ən), *adj.*

di·op·ter (dī op'tər), *n.* a unit of
measure of the refractive power of
a lens.

di·o·ra·ma (dī'ə ram'ə, -rä'mə), *n.* a
scene reproduced in three dimensions
against a painted background.

di·ox·ide (dī ok'sīd, -sid), *n.* an oxide
containing two atoms of oxygen in
the molecule.

dip (dip), *v.,* **dipped, dip·ping,** *n.* —*v.t.*
1. to plunge briefly into a liquid. **2.**
to take up by scooping. **3.** to lower
and raise: *to dip a flag in salutation.*
4. to immerse (cattle, etc.) in a solution to destroy germs. —*v.i.* **5.** to
plunge briefly into water or other
liquid. **6.** to put the hand, a dipper,
etc., down into a liquid or a container, esp. to remove something.
7. to sink or drop down. **8.** to slope
downward. **9.** to decline slightly or
temporarily. **10.** to engage slightly
in a subject. —*n.* **11.** the act of
dipping. **12.** that which is taken
up by dipping. **13.** a liquid or soft
substance into which something is
dipped. **14.** a creamy mixture for
scooping with potato chips, crackers,
etc. **15.** a momentary lowering. **16.**
a downward slope or course. **17.** a
brief swim.

diph·the·ri·a (dif thēr'ē ə, dip-), *n.* a
severe infectious disease characterized by fever and the formation of
a false membrane in the air passages,
esp. the throat. —**diph·the·rit·ic**
(dif'thə rit'ik, dip'-), **diph·the'ri·al,**
diph·ther·ic (dif ther'ik, dip'-), *adj.*

diph·thong (dif'thông, -thong, dip'-),
n. a gliding speech sound varying
continuously in phonetic quality but
held to be a single sound, as the
oi-sound of *boil.*

dipl., **1.** diplomat. **2.** diplomatic.

dip·loid (dip'loid), *adj.* having two
similar complements of chromosomes.

di·plo·ma (di plō'mə), *n.* a document
given by an educational institution
conferring a degree or certifying
satisfactory completion of a course of
study.

di·plo·ma·cy (di plō'mə sē), *n.* **1.** the
conduct by government officials of
negotiations and other relations between nations. **2.** tactful dealing
with others.

dip·lo·mat (dip'lə mat'), *n.* **1.** a government official or representative
engaged in international diplomacy.
2. a tactful person.

dip·lo·mate (dip'lə māt'), *n.* a person
who has received a diploma, as a
doctor who has been certified as a
specialist.

dip·lo·mat·ic (dip/lə mat/ik), *adj.* **1.** of or engaged in diplomacy. **2.** tactful or suave. —**dip/lo·mat/i·cal·ly,** *adv.*

diplomat/ic immu/nity, exemption from arrest, customs duties, etc., enjoyed by diplomatic officials under international law.

di·plo·ma·tist (di plō/mə tist), *n.* *Chiefly Brit.* a diplomat.

di·pole (dī/pōl/), *n.* an antenna of a transmitter or receiver consisting of two equal rods extending in opposite directions.

dip·per (dip/ər), *n.* **1.** a person or thing that dips. **2.** a cuplike container with a long, straight handle, used for dipping liquids. **3.** (*cap.*) *Astron.* **a.** Also called **Big Dipper.** the group of seven bright stars in Ursa Major resembling such a container in outline. **b.** Also called **Little Dipper.** a similar group in Ursa Minor. **4.** any of various diving birds.

dip·py (dip/ē), *adj.,* **-pi·er, -pi·est.** *Slang.* foolish or crazy.

dip·so·ma·ni·a (dip/sə mā/nē ə), *n.* an irresistible, typically periodic, craving for intoxicating drink. —**dip/so·ma/ni·ac/, n.**

dip·stick (dip/stik/), *n.* a graduated metal rod for measuring or ascertaining depth.

dip·ter·ous (dip/tər əs), *adj.* belonging to an order of insects comprising the houseflies, mosquitoes, etc., characterized by a single pair of wings. Also, **dip/ter·an.**

dip·tych (dip/tik), *n.* a pair of pictures or carvings on two panels, usually hinged together.

dir., director.

dire (dīⁱr), *adj.,* **dir·er, dir·est. 1.** causing dreadful fear or suffering. **2.** indicating disaster. **3.** urgent or desperate.

di·rect (di rekt/, dī-), *v.t.* **1.** to guide by advice, instruction, etc. **2.** to manage or supervise. **3.** to command or order. **4.** to serve as director for (a play, motion picture, etc.). **5.** to show (a person) the way to a place. **6.** to aim or send toward a place or object. **7.** to cause to move, act, or work toward a given end or result. **8.** to address (a remark, etc.) to a person or persons. **9.** to mark (a letter, etc.) with the destination. —*v.i.* **10.** to give guidance or orders. **11.** to be a director, as of a film. —*adj.* **12.** proceeding in a straight line or by the shortest course. **13.** proceeding in an unbroken line of descent. **14.** frank or candid. **15.** absolute or exact. **16.** consisting exactly of the words originally used: *direct quotation.* **17.** of or by action of voters, which takes effect without

any intervening agency such as representatives. —*adv.* **18.** in a direct manner. —**di·rect/ly,** *adv.* —**di·rect/ness, n.**

direct/ cur/rent, an electric current that flows continuously in one direction.

di·rec·tion (di rek/shən, dī-), *n.* **1.** the act or an instance of directing. **2.** the line along which anything lies, faces, moves, etc., with reference to the point toward which it is directed. **3.** tendency or inclination. **4.** instruction for making, using, etc. **5.** order or command. **6.** management or supervision. —**di·rec/tion·al,** *adj.*

di·rec·tive (di rek/tiv, dī-), *adj.* **1.** serving to direct. —*n.* **2.** an authoritative instruction or order.

direct/ mail/, mail, usually consisting of advertising matter, appeals for donations, etc., sent individually to large numbers of people.

direct/ ob/ject, a word or words representing the person or thing upon which the action of a verb is performed, as *it* in *He saw it.*

di·rec·tor (di rek/tər, dī-), *n.* **1.** a person or thing that directs. **2.** one of a body of persons chosen to govern a corporation: *a board of directors.* **3.** the person responsible for the interpretive aspects of a play, film, etc. **4.** the musical conductor of an orchestra, chorus, etc. —**di·rec/tor·ship/, n.**

di·rec·to·rate (di rek/tər it, dī-), *n.* **1.** the office of a director. **2.** a body of directors.

di·rec·to·ry (di rek/tə rē, -trē, dī-), *n., pl.* **-ries.** an alphabetical list of the names, addresses, etc., of a specific group of people.

direct/ pri/mary, a primary in which a party nominates its candidates by direct vote.

dire·ful (dīⁱr/fəl), *adj. Literary.* dire (defs. 1, 2). —**dire/ful·ly,** *adv.*

dirge (dûrj), *n.* a funeral song or a song in commemoration of the dead.

dir·i·gi·ble (dir/ə jə bəl, di rij/ə-), *n.* an early steerable airship.

dirk (dûrk), *n.* a dagger, esp. of the Highlands.

dirn·dl (dûrn/dᵊl), *n.* a dress with a closefitting bodice and full skirt.

dirt (dûrt), *n.* **1.** any foul or filthy substance, as mud, dust, etc. **2.** earth or soil. **3.** moral filth or corruption. **4.** obscene language. **5.** gossip, esp. of a malicious nature.

dirt-cheap (dûrt/chēp/), *adj.* very inexpensive.

dirt·y (dûr/tē), *adj.,* **dirt·i·er, dirt·i·est,** *v.,* **dirt·ied, dirt·y·ing.** —*adj.* **1.** soiled or soiling with dirt. **2.** vile or contemptible. **3.** obscene or lewd. **4.** not fair or sportsmanlike. **5.** stormy: *dirty weather.* —*v.t., v.i.* **6.** to make

or become dirty. —**dirt′i·ly,** *adv.*
—**dirt′i·ness,** *n.* —**Syn. 1.** filthy,
foul, squalid, unclean.

dis-, a prefix meaning "privation,"
"negation," or "reverse": *dispel; dishonor; disconnect.*

dis·a·ble (dis ā′bəl), *v.t.,* -**bled,** -**bling.
1.** to deprive of physical or mental
ability. **2.** to make legally incapable.
—**dis′a·bil′i·ty,** *n.*

dis·a·buse (dis′ə byōoz′), *v.t.,* -**bused,**
-**bus·ing.** to free from deception or
error.

di·sac·cha·ride (dī sak′ə rīd′), *n.* a
carbohydrate, such as lactose, which
yields two simple sugars on hydrolysis.

dis·ad·van·tage (dis′əd van′tij, -văn′-),
n. **1.** an unfavorable circumstance
or condition. **2.** something that puts
one into an unfavorable position or
condition. **3.** injury to interest, reputation, etc. —**dis·ad′van·ta′geous**
(-ad′vən tā′jəs), *adj.* —**dis·ad′van-
ta′geous·ly,** *adv.* —**Syn. 1.** drawback,
hindrance.

dis·ad·van·taged (dis′əd van′tijd,
-văn′-), *adj.* lacking the normal advantages, comforts, etc., esp. through
poverty.

dis·af·fect (dis′ə fekt′), *v.t.* to make
discontented or disloyal. —**dis′af-
fect′ed·ly,** *adv.* —**dis′af·fec′tion,** *n.*

dis·af·fil·i·ate (dis′ə fil′ē āt′), *v.t., v.i.,*
-**at·ed,** -**at·ing.** to sever affiliation
(with). —**dis′af·fil′i·a′tion,** *n.*

dis·a·gree (dis′ə grē′), *v.i.,* -**greed,**
-**gree·ing. 1.** to fail to agree. **2.** to
differ in opinion. **3.** to quarrel or
dispute. **4.** to cause physical discomfort or ill effect. —**dis′a·gree′ment,**
n.

dis·a·gree·a·ble (dis′ə grē′ə bəl), *adj.*
1. not to one's liking or taste. **2.** unpleasant in manner or nature. —**dis′-
a·gree′a·ble·ness,** *n.* —**dis′a·gree′a-
bly,** *adv.*

dis·al·low (dis′ə lou′), *v.t.* **1.** to refuse
to allow. **2.** to refuse to admit the
truth or validity of. —**dis′al·low′-
ance,** *n.*

dis·ap·pear (dis′ə pēr′), *v.i.* **1.** to cease
to be seen. **2.** to cease to exist. —
dis′ap·pear′ance, *n.*

dis·ap·point (dis′ə point′), *v.t.* **1.** to
fail to fulfill the expectations or
wishes of. **2.** to thwart or frustrate.
—**dis′ap·point′ment,** *n.*

dis·ap·pro·ba·tion (dis′ap rə bā′shən),
n. disapproval, esp. by authority.

dis·ap·prov·al (dis′ə prōo′vəl), *n.* a
condemnatory feeling, look, or utterance.

dis·ap·prove (dis′ə prōov′), *v.t., v.i.,*
-**proved,** -**prov·ing. 1.** to think (something) wrong or reprehensible. **2.** to
withhold approval (from). —**dis′-
ap·prov′ing·ly,** *adv.*

dis·arm (dis ärm′), *v.t.* **1.** to deprive
of a weapon or weapons. **2.** to deprive of means of attack or defense.
3. to divest of hostility, suspicion.
etc. —*v.i.* **4.** to lay down one's
weapons. **5.** to reduce the size of
the armed forces. —**dis·ar′ma·ment,**
n.

dis·arm·ing (dis är′ming), *adj.* removing hostility, suspicion, etc.: *a dis-
arming smile.* —**dis·arm′ing·ly,** *adv.*

dis·ar·range (dis′ə rānj′), *v.t.,* -**ranged,**
-**rang·ing.** to disturb the arrangement
of. —**dis′ar·range′ment,** *n.*

dis·ar·ray (dis′ə rā′), *v.t.* **1.** to throw
into disorder. —*n.* **2.** disorder or
confusion.

dis·as·sem·ble (dis′ə sem′bəl), *v.t.,*
-**bled,** -**bling.** to take apart.

dis·as·so·ci·ate (dis′ə sō′shē āt′, -sē-),
v.t., -**at·ed,** -**at·ing.** to dissociate.

dis·as·ter (di zas′tər, -zäs′tər), *n.* a
calamitous event, esp. one causing
great damage or hardship. —**dis·as′-
trous,** *adj.* —**dis·as′trous·ly,** *adv.* —
Syn. accident, catastrophe, mishap.

dis·a·vow (dis′ə vou′), *v.t.* to disclaim
knowledge of, connection with, or
responsibility for. —**dis′a·vow′al,** *n.*

dis·band (dis band′), *v.t., v.i.* to break
up or disperse. —**dis·band′ment,** *n.*

dis·bar (dis bär′), *v.t.,* -**barred,** -**barring.** to expel from the legal profession. —**dis·bar′ment,** *n.*

dis·be·lieve (dis′bi lēv′), *v.t., v.i.,*
-**lieved,** -**liev·ing.** to refuse or reject
belief (in). —**dis′be·lief′,** *n.* —**dis′-
be·liev′er,** *n.*

dis·bur·den (dis bûr′d'n), *v.t.* to remove a burden from.

dis·burse (dis bûrs′), *v.t.,* -**bursed,**
-**burs·ing.** to pay out (money), esp.
for expenses. —**dis·burse′ment,** *n.*

disc (disk), *n.* **1.** a phonograph record.
2. disk (defs. 1, 2).

disc., 1. discount. **2.** discovered.

dis·card (*v.* di skärd′; *n.* dis′kärd),
v.t., v.i. **1.** to dismiss, esp. from use.
2. *Cards.* to throw out (cards) from
one's hand. —*n.* **3.** the act of dis-
carding. **4.** a person or thing discarded.

dis·cern (di sûrn′, -zûrn′), *v.t., v.i.* **1.**
to perceive by the sight or by the
intellect. **2.** to distinguish mentally.
—**dis·cern′er,** *n.* —**dis·cern′i·ble,**
adj. —**dis·cern′ment,** *n.*

dis·cern·ing (di sûr′ning, -zûr′-), *adj.*
showing good judgment and understanding. —**dis·cern′ing·ly,** *adv.*

dis·charge (*v.* dis chärj′; *n.* dis′chärj,
dis chärj′), *v.,* -**charged,** -**charg·ing,**
n. —*v.t.* **1.** to relieve of a load or
burden. **2.** to remove or send forth.
3. to fire or shoot (a firearm). **4.** to
pour forth or emit. **5.** to relieve oneself of (an obligation). **6.** to relieve
of obligation, etc. **7.** to fulfill (a
duty). **8.** to dismiss from service.

9. to release or allow to go. **10.** to pay (a debt). **11.** to rid (a battery, etc.) of a charge of electricity. —*v.i.* **12.** to get rid of a burden or load. **13.** to go off, as a firearm. —*n.* **14.** the act of discharging a ship, load, etc. **15.** the act of firing a weapon. **16.** ejection or emission. **17.** something emitted. **18.** fulfillment of an obligation. **19.** the payment of a debt. **20.** a release or dismissal, as from prison, employment, etc. **21.** the separation of a person from military service. **22.** the removal of an electric charge, as by the conversion of chemical energy to electrical energy. **23.** the spark produced by an electric current passing through a gas. —**dis·charge′a·ble,** *adj.* —**dis·charg′er,** *n.*

dis·ci·ple (di sī′pəl), *n.* **1.** any professed follower of Christ in His lifetime, esp. one of the 12 apostles. **2.** a pupil or an adherent of another. —**dis·ci′ple·ship,** *n.*

dis·ci·pli·nar·i·an (dis′ə plə när′ē ən), *n.* a person who enforces or advocates discipline.

dis·ci·pli·nar·y (dis′ə plə ner′ē), *adj.* of or for discipline.

dis·ci·pline (dis′ə plin), *n., v.,* **-plined, -plin·ing.** —*n.* **1.** training to act in accordance with rules: *military discipline.* **2.** instruction designed to train to proper conduct or action. **3.** punishment inflicted by way of correction and training. **4.** the training effect of experience, adversity, etc. **5.** behavior in accord with rules of conduct. **6.** a system of regulations. **7.** a branch of instruction or learning. —*v.t.* **8.** to train by instruction and exercise. **9.** to bring to order and obedience by training and control. **10.** to punish in order to train and control. —**dis′ci·plin′er,** *n.*

disc′ jock′ey, a performer who conducts a radio program featuring recorded music and informal talk.

dis·claim (dis klām′), *v.t.* to repudiate or deny interest in or connection with. —**dis·claim′er,** *n.*

dis·close (di sklōz′), *v.t.,* **-closed, -clos·ing.** to make known. —**dis·clo·sure** (di sklō′zhər), *n.*

dis·co (dis′kō), *n., pl.* **-cos.** *Informal.* discotheque.

dis·coid (dis′koid), *adj.* **1.** Also, **dis·coi′dal.** having the form of a discus or disk. —*n.* **2.** something in the form of a disk.

dis·col·or (dis kul′ər), *v.t., v.i.* to change in color or hue. Also, *esp. Brit.,* **dis·col′our.** —**dis·col′o·ra′tion,** *n.*

dis·com·bob·u·late (dis′kəm bob′yə lāt′), *v.t.,* **-lat·ed, -lat·ing.** *Informal.* to upset or confuse.

dis·com·fit (dis kum′fit), *v.t.* **1.** to confuse and deject. **2.** to frustrate the plans of. **3.** *Archaic.* to defeat utterly. —**dis·com′fit·ure,** *n.*

dis·com·fort (dis kum′fərt), *n.* **1.** uneasiness, hardship, or mild pain. **2.** anything that disturbs the comfort. —*v.t.* **3.** to make uncomfortable or uneasy.

dis·com·mode (dis′kə mōd′), *v.t.,* **-mod·ed, -mod·ing.** *Archaic.* to inconvenience.

dis·com·pose (dis′kəm pōz′), *v.t.,* **-posed, -pos·ing.** **1.** to disturb the composure of. **2.** to upset the order of. —**dis′com·pos′ure** (-pō′zhər), *n.*

dis·con·cert (dis′kən sûrt′), *v.t.* to disturb the self-possession of. —**dis′con·cert′ing·ly,** *adv.*

dis·con·nect (dis′kə nekt′), *v.t.* to sever or interrupt the connection of or between. —**dis′con·nec′tion,** *n.*

dis·con·nect·ed (dis′kə nek′tid), *adj.* **1.** disjointed or broken. **2.** not coherent.

dis·con·so·late (dis kon′sə lit), *adj.* **1.** without consolation. **2.** cheerless or gloomy. —**dis·con′so·late·ly,** *adv.* —**dis·con′so·late·ness,** *n.*

dis·con·tent (dis′kən tent′), *adj.* **1.** discontented. —*n.* **2.** Also, **dis′con·tent′ment,** lack of contentment. —*v.t.* **3.** to make discontented. —**Syn.** **2.** displeasure, dissatisfaction.

dis·con·tent·ed (dis′kən ten′tid), *adj.* not contented or easy in mind. —**dis′con·tent′ed·ly,** *adv.* —**dis′con·tent′ed·ness,** *n.*

dis·con·tin·ue (dis′kən tin′yōō), *v.,* **-tin·ued, -tin·u·ing.** —*v.t.* **1.** to cause to cease. **2.** to cease to take, use, etc. —*v.i.* **3.** to stop or cease. —**dis′con·tin′u·ance,** **dis′con·tin′u·a′tion,** *n.* —**dis′con·tin′u·ous,** *adj.* —**dis′con·tin′u·ous·ly,** *adv.*

dis·con·ti·nu·i·ty (dis′kon t°nōō′i tē, -t°nyōō′-), *n., pl.* **-ties.** **1.** absence of or a break in continuity. **2.** a break or gap.

dis·cord (dis′kôrd), *n.* **1.** lack of concord or harmony. **2.** difference of opinion. **3.** an inharmonious combination of musical sounds. **4.** any confused or harsh noise. —**dis·cord′ant,** *adj.* —**dis·cord′ant·ly,** *adv.*

dis·co·theque (dis′kə tek′), *n.* a cabaret in which patrons may dance to popular music, esp. on recordings. Also, **dis′co·thèque′.**

dis·count (*v.* dis′kount, dis kount′; *n.* dis′kount), *v.t.* **1.** to deduct (an amount) from a bill, etc. **2.** to sell at a reduced price. **3.** to lend money with deduction of interest on. **4.** to purchase or sell (a bill or note) before maturity at a reduction based on the interest still to be earned. **5.** to disregard or minimize. —*n.* **6.** a reduction from the usual list price.

7. a payment of interest in advance upon a loan of money. **—dis′count·a·ble,** *adj.* **—dis·count′er,** *n.*

dis·coun·te·nance (dis koun′t°nəns), *v.t.*, **-nanced, -nanc·ing. 1.** to show disapproval of. **2.** to disconcert or embarrass.

dis′count house′, a store that sells merchandise for less than the usual price. Also called **dis′count store′.**

dis·cour·age (di skûr′ij, -skur′-), *v.t.*, **-aged, -ag·ing. 1.** to deprive of courage or confidence. **2.** to dissuade or deter. **3.** to hinder or hamper. **—dis·cour′age·ment,** *n.* **—dis·cour′ag·ing·ly,** *adv.*

dis·course (*n.* dis′kōrs, -kôrs, dis kōrs′, -kôrs′; *v.* dis kōrs′, -kôrs′), *n., v.,* **-coursed, -cours·ing. —n. 1.** communication of thought by words. **2.** a formal discussion of a subject in speech or writing. **—v.i. 3.** to talk or converse. **4.** to treat a subject formally in speech or writing. **—dis·cours′er,** *n.*

dis·cour·te·ous (dis kûr′tē əs), *adj.* not courteous or considerate. **—dis·cour′te·ous·ly,** *adv.*

dis·cour·te·sy (dis kûr′ti sē), *n., pl.* **-sies. 1.** lack or breach of courtesy. **2.** a discourteous act.

dis·cov·er (di skuv′ər), *v.t.* **1.** to gain sight or knowledge of for the first time. **2.** to notice or realize. **—dis·cov′er·a·ble,** *adj.* **—dis·cov′er·er,** *n.* **—dis·cov′er·y,** *n.*

dis·cred·it (dis kred′it), *v.t.* **1.** to injure the reputation of. **2.** to destroy confidence in. **3.** to refuse to believe. **—n. 4.** loss or lack of belief or confidence. **5.** disrepute or disgrace. **—dis·cred′it·a·ble,** *adj.*

dis·creet (di skrēt′), *adj.* tactful and judicious in one's conduct or speech. **—dis·creet′ly,** *adv.* **—Syn.** circumspect, prudent.

dis·crep·an·cy (di skrep′ən sē), *n., pl.* **-cies** for 2. **1.** difference or disagreement, esp. between statements. **2.** an instance of this.

dis·crep·ant (di skrep′ənt), *adj.* marked by discrepancy. **—dis·crep′ant·ly,** *adv.*

dis·crete (di skrēt′), *adj.* **1.** detached from others. **2.** consisting of distinct parts. **—dis·crete′ly,** *adv.*

dis·cre·tion (di skresh′ən), *n.* **1.** the power to decide or act according to one's own judgment. **2.** quality of being discreet. **—dis·cre′tion·ar′y, dis·cre′tion·al,** *adj.*

dis·crim·i·nate (*v.* di skrim′ə nāt′), *v.i.*, **-nat·ed, -nat·ing. 1.** to make a distinction in favor of or against a person or thing on the basis of prejudice. **2.** to distinguish accurately. **—dis·crim′i·nate·ly,** *adv.* **—dis·crim′i·na′tion,** *n.*

dis·crim·i·nat·ing (di skrim′ə nā′ting), *adj.* **1.** able or serving to discriminate. **2.** fastidious, esp. in selection: *discriminating consumers.*

dis·crim·i·na·to·ry (di skrim′ə nə tôr′ē, -tōr′ē), *adj.* characterized by prejudice or bias.

dis·cur·sive (di skûr′siv), *adj.* passing aimlessly from one subject to another. **—dis·cur′sive·ly,** *adv.* **—dis·cur′sive·ness,** *n.*

dis·cus (dis′kəs), *n., pl.* **dis·cus·es.** a circular disk, usually wooden with a metal rim, for throwing for distance in athletic competition.

dis·cuss (di skus′), *v.t.* to consider or examine by argument, comment, etc., esp. to explore solutions. **—dis·cus′sion,** *n.* **—Syn.** debate, deliberate, reason.

dis·cus·sant (di skus′ənt), *n.* a person who participates in a formal discussion or symposium.

dis·dain (dis dān′), *v.t.* **1.** to look upon or treat as beneath oneself. **2.** to think unworthy of notice, performance, etc. **—n. 3.** haughty contempt. **—dis·dain′ful,** *adj.* **—dis·dain′ful·ly,** *adv.*

dis·ease (di zēz′), *n.* **1.** a condition of the body in which there is incorrect function. **2.** any deranged condition, as of the mind, society, etc. **—dis·eased′,** *adj.* **—Syn. 1.** ailment, complaint, disorder, malady.

dis·em·bark (dis′em bärk′), *v.t., v.i.* to put or go on shore from a ship. **—dis·em·bar·ka·tion** (dis em′bär kā′-shən), *n.*

dis·em·bod·y (dis′em bod′ē), *v.t.*, **-bod·ied, -bod·y·ing.** to divest (a soul, etc.) of a body. **—dis·em·bod′i·ment,** *n.*

dis·em·bow·el (dis′em bou′əl), *v.t.*, **-eled, -el·ing** or **-elled, -el·ling.** to eviscerate (def. 1). **—dis·em·bow′el·ment,** *n.*

dis·em·ploy (dis′em ploi′), *v.t.* to put out of work. **—dis·em·ploy′ment,** *n.*

dis·en·chant (dis′en chant′, -chänt′), *v.t.* to free from enchantment. **—dis·en·chant′ment,** *n.*

dis·en·cum·ber (dis′en kum′bər), *v.t.* to free from encumbrance.

dis·en·fran·chise (dis′en fran′chīz), *v.t.*, **-chised, -chis·ing.** to disfranchise. **—dis·en·fran′chise·ment,** *n.*

dis·en·gage (dis′en gāj′), *v.*, **-gaged, -gag·ing. —v.t. 1.** to release from attachment or connection. **—v.i. 2.** to become disengaged. **—dis′en·gage′ment,** *n.*

dis·en·tan·gle (dis′en tang′gəl), *v.t.*, *v.i.*, **-gled, -gling.** to free or become free from entanglement. **—dis′en·tan′gle·ment,** *n.*

dis·es·tab·lish (dis′ə stab′lish), *v.t.* **1.** to deprive of the character of being established. **2.** to withdraw exclusive state support from (a church). — **dis′es·tab′lish·ment,** *n.*

dis·es·teem (dis′ə stēm′), *n.* lack of esteem.

di·seuse (dē zŒz′), *n., pl.* **-seuses** (-zŒz′). a female professional entertainer who talks or recites.

dis·fa·vor (dis fā′vər), *n.* **1.** unfavorable regard or dislike. **2.** the state of being regarded unfavorably.

dis·fig·ure (dis fig′yər), *v.t.,* **-ured, -ur·ing.** to mar the appearance or beauty of. — **dis·fig′ure·ment,** *n.*

dis·fran·chise (dis fran′chīz), *v.t.,* **-chised, -chis·ing. 1.** to deprive (a person) of a right of citizenship. **2.** to deprive of a franchise, privilege, or right. — **dis·fran·chise·ment** (dis-fran′chiz mənt, -chīz-), *n.* — **dis-fran′chis·er,** *n.*

dis·gorge (dis gôrj′), *v.t., v.i.,* **-gorged, -gorg·ing. 1.** to eject (something) from the throat or stomach. **2.** to discharge forcefully.

dis·grace (dis grās′), *n., v.,* **-graced, -grac·ing. —n. 1.** loss of respect, honor, or esteem. **2.** a person, act, or thing that is dishonorable. —*v.t.* **3.** to bring or reflect shame or dishonor upon. — **dis·grace′ful,** *adj.* — **dis·grace′ful·ly,** *adv.* — **dis·grac′er,** *n.* —**Syn. 1.** dishonor, ignominy, infamy, shame.

dis·grun·tle (dis grun′t°l), *v.t.,* **-tled, -tling.** to put into a state of sulky dissatisfaction.

dis·guise (dis gīz′, di skīz′), *v.,* **-guised, -guis·ing,** *n.* —*v.t.* **1.** to change the appearance of so as to conceal identity. **2.** to conceal the real character of. —*n.* **3.** a deceptive covering, manner, etc. **4.** the state of being disguised. — **dis·guise′ment,** *n.*

dis·gust (dis gust′, di skust′), *v.t.* **1.** to cause loathing in. **2.** to offend the good taste, moral sense, etc., of. —*n.* **3.** a strong distaste. — **dis·gust′-ed,** *adj.* — **dis·gust′ed·ly,** *adv.* — **dis·gust′ing,** *adj.* — **dis·gust′ing·ly,** *adv.*

dish (dish), *n.* **1.** a shallow container of pottery, glass, etc., used esp. for holding food. **2.** something served or contained in a dish. **3.** a particular article or preparation of food. **4.** the quantity held by a dish. **5.** anything like a dish in form or use. **6.** a radio or radar antenna having a concave reflector for directional transmission and reception. —*v.t.* **7.** to put into or serve in a dish. **8. dish out,** *Informal.* to distribute. [< L *disc(us)*]

dis·ha·bille (dis′ə bēl′, -bē′), *n.* the state of being carelessly or partly dressed.

dis·har·mo·ny (dis här′mə nē), *n.* lack of harmony or accord. — **dis′har-mo′ni·ous,** *adj.*

dish·cloth (dish′klôth′, -kloth′), *n.* a cloth for washing dishes.

dis·heart·en (dis här′t°n), *v.t.* to depress the courage or spirits of. — **dis·heart′en·ing·ly,** *adv.*

dished (disht), *adj.* concave: *a dished face.*

di·shev·el (di shev′əl), *v.t.,* **-eled, -el-ing** or **-elled, -el·ling.** to let down, as hair, or wear in loose disorder, as clothing. — **di·shev′eled,** *adj.* — **di·shev′el·ment,** *n.*

dis·hon·est (dis on′ist), *adj.* **1.** not honest or trustworthy. **2.** fraudulent or deceitful. — **dis·hon′est·ly,** *adv.* — **dis·hon′es·ty,** *n.* —**Syn. 1.** corrupt, crooked, lying, unscrupulous.

dis·hon·or (dis on′ər), *n.* **1.** lack or loss of honor. **2.** a cause of shame or disgrace. —*v.t.* **3.** to deprive of honor. **4.** to refuse to honor or pay (a draft). — **dis·hon′or·a·ble,** *adj.* — **dis·hon′or·a·bly,** *adv.*

dish·rag (dish′rag′), *n.* dishcloth.

dish·tow·el (dish′tou′əl), *n.* a towel for drying dishes.

dish·wash·er (dish′wosh′ər, -wô′shər), *n.* **1.** a person who washes dishes. **2.** a machine for washing dishes.

dis·il·lu·sion (dis′i lŒ′zhən), *v.t.* **1.** to free from or deprive of illusion. —*n.* **2.** a freeing or a being freed from illusion. — **dis′il·lu′sion·ment,** *n.*

dis·in·cline (dis′in klīn′), *v.t., v.i.,* **-clined, -clin·ing.** to make or be averse or unwilling. — **dis·in′cli·na′-tion,** *n.*

dis·in·fect (dis′in fekt′), *v.t.* to cleanse (clothing, wounds, etc.) to destroy harmful microorganisms. — **dis′in-fect′ant,** *n., adj.* — **dis′in·fec′tion,** *n.*

dis·in·gen·u·ous (dis′in jen′yŒ əs), *adj.* lacking in frankness or candor.

dis·in·her·it (dis′in her′it), *v.t.* to exclude from inheritance. — **dis′in-her′i·tance,** *n.*

dis·in·te·grate (di sin′tə grāt′), *v.t., v.i.,* **-grat·ed, -grat·ing.** to separate into component parts. — **dis′in′te-gra′tion,** *n.* — **dis·in′te·gra′tor,** *n.*

dis·in·ter (dis′in tûr′), *v.t.,* **-terred, -ter-ring.** to take out of the place of interment.

dis·in·ter·est (dis in′tər ist, -trist), *n.* absence of interest.

dis·in·ter·est·ed (dis in′tə res′tid, -tri-stid), *adj.* **1.** unbiased by personal interest or advantage. **2.** *Nonstandard.* uninterested (def. 1). — **dis-in′ter·est′ed·ly,** *adv.* — **dis·in′ter-est′ed·ness,** *n.*

dis·in·tox·i·ca·tion (dis′in tok′sə kā′-shən), *n.* the medical treatment of freeing an addict from his or her narcotic habit.

dis·join (dis join′), v.t., v.i. to disunite or separate.

dis·joint (dis joint′), v.t. 1. to separate the joints of. 2. to put out of order.

dis·joint·ed (dis join′tid), adj. 1. having the joints separated. 2. disconnected or incoherent. —**dis·joint′ed·ly**, adv. —**dis·joint′ed·ness**, n.

disk (disk), n. 1. any thin, flat, circular plate or object. 2. a roundish, flat structure or part, as in a plant. 3. disc (def. 1).

disk′ brake′, an automotive brake set by pressure from large disks against the inside of the wheels.

dis·like (dis līk′), n., v., -liked, -liking. —n. 1. a feeling of not liking or being set against. —v.t. 2. to regard with dislike. —**Syn.** 1. aversion, distaste, repugnance.

dis·lo·cate (dis′lō kāt′), v.t., -cat·ed, -cat·ing. 1. to put out of place. 2. to put out of joint or out of position, as a limb. 3. to upset or disrupt. —**dis′lo·ca′tion**, n.

dis·lodge (dis loj′), v.t., -lodged, -lodging. 1. to remove or force out of a particular place. 2. to drive out of a military position, etc.

dis·loy·al (dis loi′əl), adj. not loyal or faithful. —**dis·loy′al·ly**, adv. —**dis·loy′al·ty**, n.

dis·mal (diz′məl), adj. 1. causing gloom or dejection. 2. very bad or poor. —**dis′mal·ly**, adv. —**dis′mal·ness**, n. —**Syn.** 1. bleak, cheerless, desolate, dreary.

dis·man·tle (dis man′t°l), v.t., -tled, -tling. 1. to strip of furniture, equipment, etc. 2. to take apart. —**dis·man′tle·ment**, n.

dis·may (dis mā′), v.t. 1. to break down the courage of completely. —n. 2. sudden or complete loss of courage.

dis·mem·ber (dis mem′bər), v.t. 1. to deprive of limbs. 2. to cut to pieces. —**dis·mem′ber·ment**, n.

dis·miss (dis mis′), v.t. 1. to direct to disperse. 2. to discharge, as from office or service. 3. to put aside from consideration. 4. Law. to put out of court, as a complaint or appeal. —**dis·miss′al**, n.

dis·mount (dis mount′), v.i. 1. to get off a horse, bicycle, etc. —v.t. 2. to bring down, as from a horse. 3. to remove (a thing) from its mounting, etc. 4. to take (a mechanism) to pieces. —**dis·mount′a·ble**, adj.

dis·o·be·di·ence (dis′ə bē′dē əns), n. neglect or refusal to obey. —**dis′o·be′di·ent**, adj. —**dis′o·be′di·ent·ly**, adv.

dis·o·bey (dis′ə bā′), v.t., v.i. to neglect or refuse to obey. —**dis′o·bey′er**, n.

dis·o·blige (dis′ə blīj′), v.t., -bliged, -blig·ing. 1. to act contrary to the desire of. 2. to offend or inconvenience.

dis·or·der (dis ôr′dər), n. 1. lack of order or tidiness. 2. a public disturbance. 3. a derangement of physical or mental health. —v.t. 4. to destroy the order of. 5. to derange the physical or mental health of.

dis·or·der·ly (dis ôr′dər lē), adj. 1. untidy or confused. 2. unruly or tumultuous. 3. Law. intentionally disturbing the public order and peace.

dis·or·gan·ize (dis ôr′gə nīz′), v.t., -ized, -iz·ing. to destroy the organization of. —**dis·or′gan·i·za′tion**, n. —**dis·or′gan·iz′er**, n.

dis·o·ri·ent (dis ôr′ē ent′, -ôr′-), v.t. 1. to cause to lose one's way. 2. to cause to lose perception of place or identity.

dis·o·ri·en·tate (dis ôr′ē ən tāt′, -ôr′-), v.t., -tat·ed, -tat·ing. to disorient. —**dis·o′ri·en·ta′tion**, n.

dis·own (dis ōn′), v.t. to refuse to acknowledge as belonging to oneself.

dis·par·age (di spar′ij), v.t., -aged, -ag·ing. 1. to speak of or treat slightingly. 2. to bring reproach or discredit upon. —**dis·par′age·ment**, n. —**dis·par′ag·ing·ly**, adv.

dis·pa·rate (dis′pər it, di spar′-), adj. distinct in kind or essentially different. —**dis′pa·rate·ly**, adv. —**dis·par′i·ty** (di spar′i tē), n.

dis·pas·sion (dis pash′ən), n. freedom from passion or bias.

dis·pas·sion·ate (dis pash′ə nit), adj. free from or unaffected by passion or bias. —**dis·pas′sion·ate·ly**, adv.

dis·patch (di spach′), v.t. 1. to send off with speed, as a messenger, etc. 2. to dispose of (a matter) speedily. 3. to put to death quickly. —n. 4. the sending off of a messenger, etc., to a destination. 5. speedy action. 6. a message sent with speed, by special messenger, etc. 7. a news story sent in by a reporter to a newspaper. 8. a summary killing. —**dis·patch′er**, n.

dis·pel (di spel′), v.t., -pelled, -pel·ling. 1. to drive off by scattering. 2. to cause to vanish: dispel my fears.

dis·pen·sa·ble (di spen′sə bəl), adj. 1. not essential. 2. capable of being dispensed or administered.

dis·pen·sa·ry (di spen′sə rē), n., pl. -ries. a place where medicines are dispensed.

dis·pen·sa·tion (dis′pən sā′shən, -pen-), n. 1. the act or an instance of dispensing. 2. something dispensed. 3. a specified order, system, or arrangement. 4. the divine ordering of the affairs of the world. 5. a doing without something. 6. Rom. Cath. Ch. a relaxation of law in a particular case granted by a competent superior.

dispense □ dissatisfaction

dis·pense (di spens′), v., **-pensed,
-pens·ing.** —v.t. **1.** to give or deal
out. **2.** to administer, as the law. **3.**
to prepare and distribute (medicine),
esp. on prescription. **4.** *Rom. Cath.
Ch.* to grant a dispensation to. —v.i.
5. to grant dispensation. **6.** dispense
with, **a.** to forgo. **b.** to rid of. —**dis·
pens′er,** n.

dis·perse (di spûrs′), v., **-persed, -pers·
ing.** —v.t. **1.** to send off in various
directions. **2.** to spread widely. **3.** to
cause to vanish. —v.i. **4.** to become
scattered. —**dis·per′sion, dis·per′·
sal,** n.

dis·pir·it (di spir′it), v.t. to deprive
of spirit, enthusiasm, etc. —**dis·pir′·
it·ed,** adj.

dis·place (dis plās′), v.t., **-placed,
-plac·ing. 1.** to take the place of. **2.**
to compel (a person) to leave home,
country, etc. **3.** to put out of the
usual or proper place. **4.** to remove
from a position, office, etc.

displaced′ per′son, a person driven
or expelled from his or her homeland
by war or tyranny.

dis·place·ment (dis plās′mənt), n. **1.**
the act of putting out of place or
state of being displaced. **2.** the
weight or the volume of fluid displaced by a floating or submerged
body. **3.** the distance of an oscillating body from its central position at
any given moment.

dis·play (di splā′), v.t. **1.** to present
to view, esp. to best advantage. —n.
2. an exhibition, as to impress. **3.**
something displayed. —**Syn. 1.** exhibit, manifest, show.

dis·please (dis plēz′), v.t., v.i., **-pleased,
-pleas·ing.** to incur the dislike or
disapproval (of).

dis·pleas·ure (dis plezh′ər), n. dissatisfaction, disapproval, or annoyance.

dis·port (di spôrt′, -spôrt′), *Literary.*
—v.t. **1.** to divert or amuse (oneself). —v.i. **2.** to play or frolic.

dis·pos·a·ble (di spō′zə bəl), adj. **1.**
designed to be thrown away after
a single use. **2.** retained after payment of taxes: *disposable personal
income.*

dis·pos·al (di spō′zəl), n. **1.** a getting
rid of something, as by throwing
away or by sale. **2.** settlement or
management. **3.** arrangement, as of
troops. **4. at one's disposal,** available for one's use.

dis·pose (di spōz′), v., **-posed, -pos·
ing.** —v.t. **1.** to put in a particular
or the proper arrangement. **2.** to
give an inclination to. **3.** to make
fit or ready. —v.i. **4.** to decide
matters. **5. dispose of, a.** to settle.
b. to give away. **c.** to do away with.
—**dis·pos′er,** n.

dis·po·si·tion (dis′pə zish′ən), n. **1.**
mental outlook or mood: *a pleasant

disposition. **2.** an inclination or tendency. **3.** arrangement or placing. **4.**
the final settlement of a matter. **5.**
transfer or bestowal. **6.** the power
to settle or control. —**dis·pos′i·tive,**
adj. —**Syn. 1.** temperament.

dis·pos·sess (dis′pə zes′), v.t. to put
(a person) out of possession, esp.
of real property.

dis·pro·por·tion (dis′prə pôr′shən,
-pôr′-), n. lack of proportion. —
**dis′pro·por′tion·al, dis′pro·por′tion-
ate,** adj.

dis·prove (dis prōōv′), v.t., **-proved,
-prov·ing.** to prove to be false or
wrong. —**dis·proof′,** n. —**dis·prov′·
a·ble,** adj.

dis·pu·tant (di spyōōt′³nt), n. a person who disputes.

dis·pu·ta·tion (dis′pyōō tā′shən), n. **1.**
the act of disputing. **2.** the argument
of an academic thesis, as between
two parties.

dis·pu·ta·tious (dis′pyōō tā′shəs), adj.
given to disputing.

dis·pute (di spyōōt′), v., **-put·ed, -put·
ing,** n. —v.i. **1.** to engage in argument involving differing opinions.
2. to wrangle or quarrel. —v.t. **3.** to
argue or debate about. **4.** to call in
question. **5.** to struggle over or
against. —n. **6.** an argument or debate. **7.** a wrangle or quarrel. —
dis·put′a·ble, adj. —**dis·put′er,** n.

dis·qual·i·fy (dis kwol′ə fī′), v.t., **-fied,
-fy·ing. 1.** to deprive of qualification or fitness. **2.** to declare ineligible or unqualified. —**dis·qual′·
i·fi·ca′tion,** n.

dis·qui·et (dis kwī′it), n. **1.** Also, **dis·
qui′e·tude′** (-i tōōd′). lack of calm
or peace. —v.t. **2.** to deprive of calm
or peace. —**dis·qui′et·ing·ly,** adv.

dis·qui·si·tion (dis′kwi zish′ən), n. a
formal discourse or treatise.

dis·re·gard (dis′ri gärd′), v.t. **1.** to
pay no attention to. **2.** to treat
without due regard. —n. **3.** lack of
attention. **4.** lack of due regard.
—**dis′re·gard′ful,** adj.

dis·re·pair (dis′ri pâr′), n. the condition of being in need of repair.

dis·rep·u·ta·ble (dis rep′yə tə bəl), adj.
1. having a bad reputation. **2.** shabby
or shoddy.

dis·re·pute (dis′ri pyōōt′), n. bad
repute or low regard.

dis·re·spect (dis′ri spekt′), n. lack of
respect or courtesy. —**dis′re·spect′·
ful,** adj.

dis·robe (dis rōb′), v.t., v.i., **-robed,
-rob·ing.** to undress. —**dis·rob′er,** n.

dis·rupt (dis rupt′), v.t. **1.** to cause
disorder in. **2.** to interrupt or disturb. —**dis·rup′tion,** n. —**dis·rup′-
tive,** adj.

dis·sat·is·fac·tion (dis′sat is fak′shən,
dis sat′-), n. the state or attitude of
not being satisfied.

dis·sat·is·fy (dis sat′is fī′), *v.t.*, **-fied**, **-fy·ing.** to cause to be displeased, esp. by failing to provide something expected or desired. —**dis′sat′is·fac′-tion,** *n.* —**dis′sat′is·fied′,** *adj.*

dis·sect (di sekt′, dī-), *v.t.* **1.** to cut apart (an animal body, etc.) to examine the structure, parts, etc. **2.** to analyze minutely. —**dis·sect′ed,** *adj.* —**dis·sec′tion,** *n.* —**dis·sec′tor,** *n.*

dis·sem·ble (di sem′bəl), *v.t.*, *v.i.*, **-bled, -bling. 1.** to conceal (one's true motives or thoughts) by pretense. **2.** to feign or pretend. —**dis·sem′blance,** *n.* —**dis·sem′bler,** *n.*

dis·sem·i·nate (di sem′ə nāt′), *v.t.*, **-nat·ed, -nat·ing.** to scatter or spread widely. —**dis·sem′i·na′tion,** *n.*

dis·sen·sion (di sen′shən), *n.* strong disagreement.

dis·sent (di sent′), *v.i.* **1.** to differ in opinion. **2.** to reject the doctrines or authority of an established church. —*n.* **3.** difference in opinion. **4.** separation from an established church. —**dis·sent′er,** *n.* —**dis·sen·tient** (di-sen′shənt), *adj.*, *n.*

dis·ser·ta·tion (dis′ər tā′shən), *n.* an extended treatise, esp. one written for a doctor's degree.

dis·serv·ice (dis sûr′vis), *n.* a harmful act or action.

dis·sev·er (di sev′ər), *v.t.*, *v.i.* to disunite or separate completely.

dis·si·dent (dis′i dənt), *adj.* **1.** strongly dissenting, as in attitude. —*n.* **2.** a strong dissenter. —**dis′si·dence,** *n.* —**dis′si·dent·ly,** *adv.*

dis·sim·i·lar (di sim′ə lər, dis sim′-), *adj.* not similar or like. —**dis·sim·i·lar·i·ty** (dis sim′ə lar′itē), *n.*

dis·si·mil·i·tude (dis′si mil′i tōōd′, -tyood′), *n.* lack of similitude.

dis·sim·u·late (di sim′yə lāt′), *v.t.*, *v.i.*, **-lat·ed, -lat·ing.** to dissemble. —**dis·sim′u·la′tion,** *n.* —**dis·sim′u·la′tor,** *n.*

dis·si·pate (dis′ə pāt′), *v.*, **-pat·ed, -pat·ing.** —*v.t.* **1.** to break up and send away. **2.** to cause to vanish. **3.** to waste or squander. —*v.i.* **4.** to become dissipated. **5.** to indulge in intemperate or dissolute pleasure. —**dis′si·pat′ed,** *adj.* —**dis′si·pat′er, dis′si·pa′tor,** *n.* —**dis′si·pa′tion,** *n.*

dis·so·ci·ate (di sō′shē āt′, -sē-), *v.t.*, *v.i.*, **-at·ed, -at·ing.** to separate from association with another. —**dis·so′ci·a′tion,** *n.* —**dis·so′ci·a′tive,** *adj.*

dis·so·lute (dis′ə lōōt′), *adj.* given to immoral or improper conduct. —**dis′so·lute′ly,** *adv.* —**dis′so·lute′ness,** *n.*

dis·so·lu·tion (dis′ə lōō′shən), *n.* **1.** the act or process of dissolving into parts or elements. **2.** the breaking of a bond, tie, etc. **3.** the breaking up of an assembly or organization. **4.** death or decease. **5.** disintegration or termination.

dis·solve (di zolv′), *v.*, **-solved, -solv·ing,** *n.* —*v.t.* **1.** to make a solution of, as by mixing with a liquid. **2.** to melt or liquefy. **3.** to break up (a union, etc.). **4.** to terminate (an assembly or organization). **5.** to separate into parts or elements. —*v.i.* **6.** to become dissolved. **7.** to disappear gradually. **8.** to become emotionally weakened.

dis·so·nance (dis′ə nəns), *n.* **1.** an inharmonious or harsh sound. **2.** lack of harmony or agreement. —**dis′so·nant,** *adj.* —**dis′so·nant·ly,** *adv.*

dis·suade (di swād′), *v.t.*, **-suad·ed, -suad·ing.** to deter by advice or persuasion. —**dis·sua′sion,** *n.* —**dis·sua′sive,** *adj.*

dist., **1.** distance. **2.** distant. **3.** district.

dis·taff (dis′taf, -täf), *n.* **1.** a staff with a cleft end for holding wool, flax, etc., in spinning. **2.** the female sex. **3.** woman's work. —*adj.* **4.** female or maternal.

dis′taff side′, the female side of a family.

dis·tal (dis′t°l), *adj.* situated away from the point of origin or attachment, as of a limb or bone. —**dis′tal·ly,** *adv.*

dis·tance (dis′təns), *n.*, *v.*, **-tanced, -tanc·ing.** —*n.* **1.** the extent of space between two points. **2.** the state or fact of being apart in space or time. **3.** an expanse or area. **4.** remoteness or difference in any respect. **5.** an amount of progress. **6.** a distant region. —*v.t.* **7.** to leave behind at a distance, as at a race.

dis·tant (dis′tənt), *adj.* **1.** far off or apart in space or time. **2.** separate or distinct. **3.** remote or far apart in any respect: *a distant relative.* **4.** reserved or aloof. **5.** arriving from or going to a distance. —**dis′tant·ly,** *adv.* —**dis′tant·ness,** *n.*

dis·taste (dis tāst′), *n.* natural or fixed dislike. —**dis·taste′ful,** *adj.* —**dis·taste′ful·ly,** *adv.*

dis·tem·per (dis tem′pər), *n.* an infectious disease of dogs, cats, etc., caused by a virus and characterized by fever, vomiting, and convulsions.

dis·tend (di stend′), *v.t.*, *v.i.* to stretch out or swell. —**dis·ten′si·ble,** *adj.* —**dis·ten′tion, dis·ten′sion,** *n.*

dis·tich (dis′tik), *n.* *Pros.* a unit of two lines of verse.

dis·till (di stil′), *v.t.*, *v.i.* **1.** to undergo or subject to distillation. **2.** to give forth in drops. Also, *esp. Brit.,* **dis·til′.** —**dis·till′er,** *n.* —**dis·till′er·y,** *n.*

dis·til·late (dis′t°lit, -t°lāt′, di stil′it), *n.* the product obtained from the condensation of vapors in distillation.

dis·til·la·tion (dis'tᵊlā'shən), n. 1. the evaporation and subsequent condensation of a liquid, as when water is boiled in a retort and the steam is condensed in a cool receiver. 2. distillate.

dis·tinct (di stingkt'), adj. 1. not identical or alike. 2. different in kind, nature, or quality. 3. clear to the senses or intellect. 4. unusual or notable. —dis·tinct'ly, adv. — dis·tinct'ness, n.

dis·tinc·tion (di stingk'shən), n. 1. a distinguishing as different. 2. the recognizing of differences. 3. a distinguishing quality or characteristic. 4. a special honor. 5. marked superiority.

dis·tinc·tive (di stingk'tiv), adj. serving to make distinct. —dis·tinc'tive·ly, adv. —dis·tinc'tive·ness, n.

dis·tin·guish (di sting'gwish), v.t. 1. to mark off as different. 2. to recognize as distinct. 3. to perceive or make out clearly. 4. to make prominent or conspicuous. 5. to divide into categories. —v.i. 6. to indicate or show a difference. —dis·tin'guish·a·ble, adj. —dis·tin'guish·a·bly, adv.

dis·tin·guished (di sting'gwisht), adj. 1. marked or characterized by distinction or excellence. 2. dignified or elegant. —Syn. 1. celebrated, eminent, famous.

dis·tort (di stôrt'), v.t. 1. to give a false meaning to. 2. to twist awry or out of shape. 3. to reproduce (a recording sound) inaccurately. —dis·tort'er, n. —dis·tor'tion, n.

distr., 1. distribute. 2. distribution. 3. distributor.

dis·tract (di strakt'), v.t. 1. to divert, as the mind or attention. 2. to trouble greatly in mind. —dis·tract'ed, adj. —dis·tract'ing, adj. —dis·trac'·tion, n. —dis·trac'tive, adj.

dis·trait (di strā'), adj. inattentive because of distracting worries, etc.

dis·traught (di strôt'), adj. 1. utterly bewildered, esp. because of worry, etc. 2. mentally deranged.

dis·tress (di stres'), n. 1. acute physical or mental suffering. 2. anything that causes pain, anxiety, strain, or sorrow. 3. a state of extreme necessity or misfortune. —v.t. 4. to afflict with great pain, anxiety, or strain. —dis·tress'ful, adj. —Syn. 1. agony, misery, tribulation.

dis·trib·ute (di strib'yoot), v.t., -ut·ed, -ut·ing. 1. to divide and give out in shares. 2. to spread over an area. 3. to sell, promote, and ship (merchandise) to customers. 4. to divide or arrange by kinds. —dis'tri·bu'·tion, n. —dis·trib'u·tive, adj. — dis·trib'u·tive·ly, adv. —Syn. 1. allocate, allot, dispense.

dis·trib·u·tor (di strib'yə tər), n. 1. a person or thing that distributes something or another thing. 2. a person or firm, esp. a wholesaler, that distributes merchandise. 3. a device in an engine for distributing the voltage to the spark plugs in a definite sequence.

dis·trict (dis'trikt), n. 1. a division of territory marked off for administrative or other purposes. 2. a region or locality.

dis'trict attor'ney, an officer who acts as attorney for the government within a specified district.

Dis'trict of Colum'bia, a federal area in the E United States, on the Potomac, coextensive with the federal capital, Washington.

dis·trust (dis trust'), v.t. 1. to regard with doubt or suspicion. —n. 2. lack of trust or confidence. —dis·trust'ful, adj. —dis·trust'ful·ly, adv. —dis·trust'ful·ness, n.

dis·turb (di stûrb'), v.t. 1. to interrupt the quiet, rest, or peace of. 2. to interfere with. 3. to throw into disorder. 4. to perplex or trouble. — dis·turb'ance, n. —dis·turb'ing·ly, adv. —dis·turb'er, n.

dis·turbed (di stûrbd'), adj. marked by symptoms of neurosis or psychosis.

dis·u·nite (dis'yōō nīt'), v.t., v.i., -nit·ed, -nit·ing. to sever the union (of). —dis·u·nit'er, n.

dis·u·ni·ty (dis yōō'ni tē), n., pl. -ties. lack of unity or accord.

dis·use (dis yōōs'), n. discontinuance of use or practice.

ditch (dich), n. 1. a long, narrow excavation dug in the ground. —v.t. 2. to dig a ditch in. 3. to run or drive into a ditch. 4. to crash-land (an aircraft) on water and abandon it. 5. Slang. to get rid of. —ditch'·less, adj.

dith·er (dith'ər), n. Informal. a state of flustered excitement.

dit·to (dit'ō), n., pl. -tos. 1. the above or the same (used in lists, etc., to avoid repetition). 2. See ditto mark. [< It < L dictus said]

dit'to mark', Often, ditto marks. two small marks (") used as a sign for ditto.

dit·ty (dit'ē), n., pl. -ties. a short, simple song.

di·u·ret·ic (dī'yōō ret'ik), adj. 1. increasing the volume of urine excreted. —n. 2. a diuretic medicine or agent. —di'u·ret'i·cal·ly, adv.

di·ur·nal (dī ûr'nᵊl), adj. 1. of a day or each day. 2. of or belonging to the daytime. —di·ur'nal·ly, adv.

Div., 1. Divine. 2. Divinity.

div., 1. divided. 2. dividend. 3. division. 4. divisor. 5. divorced.

di·va (dē′vä), *n., pl.* **-vas, -ve** (-ve). a distinguished female singer, as in an opera.

di·va·gate (dī′və gāt′), *v.i.,* **-gat·ed, -gat·ing.** *Literary.* to wander or stray, esp. in speech. —**di·va·ga′-tion,** *n.*

di·va·lent (dī vā′lənt), *adj.* having a valence of two.

di·van (di van′, dī′van), *n.* a sofa or couch without arms or back, usually usable as a bed.

dive (dīv), *v.,* **dived** *or* **dove, dived, div·ing,** *n.* —*v.i.* **1.** to plunge, esp. headfirst, as into water. **2.** to submerge, as a submarine. **3.** to plunge, fall, or descend through the air, etc. **4.** to dart or dash. —*v.t.* **5.** to cause to plunge, submerge, or descend. —*n.* **6.** the act or an instance of diving. **7.** the vertical descent of an airplane at a speed surpassing the possible speed of the same plane in level flight. **8.** a sudden decline, as of stock prices, etc. **9.** a disreputable bar or nightclub. —**div′er,** *n.*

di·verge (di vûrj′, dī-), *v.i.,* **-verged, -verg·ing. 1.** to move in different directions from a common point. **2.** to differ in opinion, form, etc. **3.** to turn aside or deviate, as from a path, practice, or plan. —**di·ver′-gence,** *n.* —**di·ver′gent,** *adj.* —**di·ver′gent·ly,** *adv.*

di·vers (dī′vərz), *adj. Archaic.* several.

di·verse (di vûrs′, dī-, dī′vûrs), *adj.* **1.** of a different kind, character, etc. **2.** varied or multiform. —**di·verse′ly,** *adv.* —**di·verse′ness,** *n.* —**Syn. 1.** dissimilar, separate, unlike.

di·ver·si·fy (di vûr′sə fī′, dī-), *v.,* **-fied, -fy·ing.** —*v.t.* **1.** to make diverse, as in form or character. —*v.i.* **2.** to invest in the securities of different companies in different industries. **3.** to add various lines or products, esp. for different markets. —**di·ver′si·fi·ca′tion,** *n.*

di·ver·sion (di vûr′zhən, -shən, dī-), *n.* **1.** the act of diverting. **2.** distraction from business or care as a pastime. **3.** a feint to draw off attention from the point of main attack. —**di·ver′-sion·ar′y,** *adj.*

di·ver·si·ty (di vûr′si tē, dī-), *n., pl.* **-ties. 1.** the state or fact of being diverse. **2.** a point of difference.

di·vert (di vûrt′, dī-), *v.t.* **1.** to turn aside from a path or course. **2.** to draw off to a different course, purpose, etc. **3.** to entertain or amuse, esp. momentarily or as a pastime. —*v.i.* **4.** to turn aside. —**di·vert′er,** *n.*

di·ver·tic·u·li·tis (dī′vər tik′yə līt′is), *n.* inflammation of a tubular sac (**dī′ver·tic′u·lum**) branching off from a canal or cavity, esp. in the colon.

di·vest (di vest′, dī-), *v.t.* **1.** to strip of clothing, ornament, etc. **2.** to deprive of anything, esp. property or rights.

di·vide (di vīd′), *v.,* **-vid·ed, -vid·ing,** *n.* —*v.t.* **1.** to separate into parts or groups. **2.** to sever or cut off. **3.** to distribute in shares. **4.** to separate in opinion or feeling. **5.** to distinguish the kinds of. **6. a.** to separate into equal parts by the process of mathematical division. **b.** to be a divisor of, without a remainder. —*v.i.* **7.** to become divided. **8.** to share with others. **9.** to diverge or branch. **10.** to perform mathematical division. —*n.* **11.** a ridge separating two drainage basins. —**di·vid′-a·ble,** *adj.*

div·i·dend (div′i dend′), *n.* **1. a.** a share in an amount to be distributed. **b.** a sum of money paid to shareholders of a corporation out of earnings. **2.** *Math.* a number that is to be divided by a divisor. **3.** anything received as a bonus.

di·vid·er (di vī′dər), *n.* **1.** a person or thing that divides. **2. dividers,** a pair of compasses, as used for dividing lines, measuring, etc. **3.** a partition, as a room.

div·i·na·tion (div′ə nā′shən), *n.* **1.** the attempt to foretell events or discover knowledge by occult or supernatural means. **2.** perception by intuition.

di·vine (di vīn′), *adj., n., v.,* **-vined, -vin·ing.** —*adj.* **1.** of, like, being, or proceeding from a god, esp. the Supreme Being. **2.** religious or sacred: *divine worship.* **3.** *Informal.* extremely good. —*n.* **4.** a theologian. **5.** *Informal.* a clergyman or clergywoman. —*v.t.* **6.** to declare by divination. **7.** to discover (water, etc.) by means of a divining rod. **8.** to perceive by intuition or insight. —*v.i.* **9.** to prophesy. **10.** to conjecture. [< L *divīn(us)*] —**di·vine′ly,** *adv.* —**di·vin′er,** *n.*

divin′ing rod′, a forked stick supposed to be useful in locating underground water, metal deposits, etc.

di·vin·i·ty (di vin′i tē), *n., pl.* **-ties. 1.** the quality of being divine. **2.** a divine being. **3. the Divinity,** God. **4.** theology.

di·vis·i·ble (di viz′ə bəl), *adj.* capable of being divided, esp. of being evenly divided, without remainder. —**di·vis′i·bil′i·ty,** *n.*

di·vi·sion (di vizh′ən), *n.* **1.** the act of dividing or state of being divided. **2.** the operation of determining the number of times that one quantity is contained in another. **3.** something that divides, as a boundary or partition. **4.** any section or segment. **5.** disagreement or dissension. **6.** one of the major parts into which a country or an organization is divided for administrative or functional purposes. **7.** a major tactical unit of the army or navy. —**di·vi′sion·al,** *adj.*

di·vi·sive (di vī′siv, -vī′siv), *adj.* creating dissension. —**di·vi′sive·ly,** *adv.* —**di·vi′sive·ness,** *n.*

di·vi·sor (di vī′zər), *n.* a number by which another number, the dividend, is divided.

di·vorce (di vôrs′, -vôrs′), *n.,* *v.,* **-vorced, -vorc·ing.** —*n.* **1.** a judicial declaration dissolving a marriage. **2.** total separation. —*v.t.,* *v.i.* **3.** to separate by divorce. —**di·vorce′ment,** *n.*

di·vor·cee (di vôr sē′, -sā′, -vôr-, -vôr′sē, -vôr′-), *n.* a divorced woman. Also, **di·vor·cée′.**

div·ot (div′ət), *n.* a piece of turf gouged out with a golf club in making a stroke.

di·vulge (di vulj′, dī-), *v.t.,* **-vulged, -vulg·ing.** to disclose or reveal (something secret). —**di·vul′gence,** *n.* —**di·vulg′er,** *n.*

div·vy (div′ē), *v.t.,* *v.i.,* **-vied, -vy·ing.** *Informal.* to divide or share.

Dix·ie (dik′sē), *n.* the southern states of the United States, esp. those that were part of the Confederacy.

Dix·ie·land (dik′sē land′), *n.* a style of jazz played by a small group of instruments and marked by strongly accented rhythm and improvisation.

diz·zy (diz′ē), *adj.,* **-zi·er, -zi·est.** **1.** having a sensation of whirling and a tendency to fall. **2.** bewildered or confused. **3.** causing giddiness or confusion. **4.** *Informal.* foolish or silly. —**diz′zi·ly,** *adv.* —**diz′zi·ness,** *n.*

D.J., 1. See **disc jockey. 2.** District Judge. **3.** Doctor of Law. [< L *Doctor Juris*]

Dja·kar·ta (jə kär′tə), *n.* the capital of Indonesia.

dk., 1. dark. **2.** deck. **3.** dock.

dl, deciliter; deciliters.

D.Lit., Doctor of Literature. [< L *Doctor Literārum*]

D.Litt., Doctor of Letters. [< L *Doctor Litterārum*]

D.L.O., Dead Letter Office.

dlr., dealer.

dlvy., delivery.

DM, Deutsche mark.

dm, decimeter; decimeters.

D.M.D., Doctor of Dental Medicine. [< L *Dentariae Medicinae Doctor*]

DMZ, demilitarized zone.

dn., down.

DNA, any of the class of nucleic acids found chiefly in the nucleus of cells: responsible for transmitting hereditary characteristics and for the building of proteins.

Dnie·per (nē′pər, dnye′per), *n.* a river in the W Soviet Union in Europe

flowing S to the Black Sea. Also, **Dne′pr.**

do¹ (dōō; *unstressed* dŏŏ, də), *v.,* **did, done, do·ing,** *n.,* *pl.* **dos, do's.** —*v.t.* **1.** to perform (an act, duty, role, etc.). **2.** to execute (a piece or amount of work). **3.** to accomplish or finish. **4.** to put forth or exert. **5.** to be the cause of (good, harm, etc.). **6.** to render or pay (justice, etc.). **7.** to deal with (anything) as the case may require. **8.** to travel (a distance). **9.** to suffice for. **10.** to make or prepare. **11.** to serve (a term of time). **12.** to create or form. **13.** to study or work at. **14.** to travel through as a sightseer. —*v.i.* **15.** to act or behave. **16.** to get along. **17.** to be in health, as specified. **18.** to be enough. **19.** to take place. **20.** (used in interrogative and negative constructions): *Do you think so? I don't agree.* **21.** (used to lend emphasis): *Do visit us!* **22.** (used to avoid repetition of a verb): *I think as you do.* **23.** do away with, **a.** to put an end to. **b.** to murder. **24.** do by, to deal with. **25.** do for, to cause the defeat or death of. **26.** do in, *Slang.* **a.** to murder. **b.** to injure gravely or exhaust. **27.** do over, *Informal.* to redecorate. **20.** do up, *Informal.* **a.** to wrap and tie up. **b.** to wash or clean. **29.** do with, to make use of. **30.** do without, to forgo. **31.** make do with, to manage or cope. —*n.* **32.** *Chiefly Brit.* a party or social gathering. **33.** dos and don'ts, customs, rules, or regulations. —**do′a·ble,** *adj.*

do² (dō), *n.,* *pl.* **dos.** the syllable used for the first tone of a diatonic scale.

do., ditto.

D.O., 1. Doctor of Optometry. **2.** Doctor of Osteopathy.

D.O.A., dead on arrival.

D.O.B., date of birth. Also, **d.o.b.**

dob·bin (dob′in), *n.* a quiet, plodding horse.

Do·ber·man pin·scher (dō′bər mən pin′shər), a medium-sized, short-haired dog.

doc (dok), *n. Informal.* doctor.

doc., document.

do·cent (dō′sənt), *n.* a college or university lecturer.

doc·ile (dos′əl; *Brit.* dō′sīl), *adj.* easily managed or taught. —**doc′ile·ly,** *adv.* —**do·cil·i·ty** (do sil′i tē), *n.*

dock¹ (dok), *n.* **1.** *Chiefly Brit.* the waterway between two piers or beside a pier, as for receiving a ship while in port. **2.** Often, **docks.** such a waterway together with the surrounding piers. **3.** (loosely) a landing pier. **4.** a platform for loading trucks, freight cars, etc. —*v.t.* **5.** to bring (a ship) into a dock. —*v.i.* **6.** to come or go into a dock. **7.** (of a space vehicle) to join together with another vehicle in outer space.

dock² (dok), *n.* **1.** the solid or fleshy part of an animal's tail. —*v.t.* **2.** to cut off the end of: *to dock the ears of cattle.* **3.** to deduct from the wages of.

dock³ (dok), *n.* the place in a criminal court for a defendant during trial.

dock⁴ (dok), *n.* a coarse, weedy plant of the buckwheat family.

dock·age (dok'ij), *n.* **1.** a charge for the use of a dock. **2.** docking accommodations.

dock·et (dok'it), *n.* **1.** a list of cases in court for trial. **2.** the list of business to be transacted, as by a legislative assembly. **3.** *Brit.* a label on a package showing its address, contents, etc. —*v.t.* **4.** to enter in a docket.

dock·yard (dok'yärd'), *n.* a waterside area containing dry docks for building or repairing ships.

doc·tor (dok'tər), *n.* **1.** a person licensed to practice medicine, esp. a physician, dentist, or veterinarian. **2.** a person who has been awarded a doctor's degree. —*v.t.* **3.** to give medical treatment to. **4.** to treat (an ailment). **5.** to repair or mend. **6.** to tamper with. **7.** to revise or adapt. —*v.i.* **8.** to practice medicine. [< L = doc(ēre) (to) teach + -tor] —**doc'tor·al,** *adj.*

doc·tor·ate (dok'tər it), *n.* See **doctor's degree.**

doc'tor's degree', the highest academic degree awarded in graduate study.

doc·tri·naire (dok'trə nâr'), *n.* **1.** a person who tries to apply a theory dogmatically without regard for practicalities. —*adj.* **2.** of a doctrinaire. —**doc'tri·nair'ism,** *n.*

doc·trine (dok'trin), *n.* **1.** a particular principle or position taught or advocated, as of a religion, government, etc. **2.** any basic creed. —**doc'tri·nal,** *adj.* —**doc'tri·nal·ly,** *adv.*

doc·u·ment (n. dok'yə mənt; v. dok'yə ment'), *n.* **1.** a written or printed paper furnishing information or evidence. —*v.t.* **2.** to furnish with or support by documents. —**doc'u·men·ta'tion,** *n.*

doc·u·men·ta·ry (dok'yə men'tə rē), *adj.,* *n., pl.* **-ries.** —*adj.* **1.** Also, **doc·u·men·tal** (dok'yə men't°l). of or pertaining to documents. **2.** portraying and interpreting an actual event, life of a real person, etc., in factual, usually dramatic form. —*n.* **3.** a documentary film or television program. —**doc'u·men'ta·ri·ly,** *adv.*

DOD, Department of Defense.

dod·der¹ (dod'ər), *v.i.* to shake or totter, esp. from old age. —**dod'der·ing,** *adj.*

dod·der² (dod'ər), *n.* a leafless parasitic plant having a threadlike stem.

dodge (doj), *v.,* **dodged, dodg·ing,** *n.* —*v.i.* **1.** to move aside or change position suddenly, as to avoid a blow or get behind something. **2.** to use evasive methods. —*v.t.* **3.** to elude or evade by a sudden shift: *to dodge a question.* —*n.* **4.** a quick evasive movement. **5.** *Informal.* an ingenious expedient or trick. —**dodg'er,** *n.*

do·do (dō'dō), *n., pl.* **-dos, -does.** **1.** a clumsy, flightless, extinct bird. **2.** *Slang.* a dull, slow-reacting person.

doe (dō), *n., pl.* **does, doe.** the female of the deer, goat, rabbit, etc.

DOE, Department of Energy.

do·er (dōō'ər), *n.* a person who does something, esp. one who gets things done with vigor and efficiency.

does (duz), *v.* 3rd pers. sing. pres. ind. of **do¹.**

doe·skin (dō'skin'), *n.* **1.** the skin of a doe. **2.** leather made from this. **3.** a closely woven woolen cloth.

does·n't (duz'ənt), contraction of *does not.*

doff (dof, dôf), *v.t.* **1.** to take off, as clothing. **2.** to tip (the hat), as in greeting. **3.** to get rid of. —**doff'er,** *n*

dog (dôg, dog), *n., v.,* **dogged, dog·ging.** —*n.* **1.** a domesticated carnivore bred in a great many varieties. **2.** any animal belonging to the same family, including the wolves and foxes. **3.** the male of such an animal. **4.** *Slang.* a despicable person. **5.** *Informal.* a fellow in general, as specified: *a wily dog.* **6.** a mechanical device for gripping or holding something. **7. go to the dogs,** *Informal.* to go to ruin. —*v.t.* **8.** to follow or track like a dog, esp. with hostile intent. —**dog'gy,** *adj.*

dog·bane (dôg'bān', dog'-), *n.* a perennial herb yielding an acrid milk juice and having an intensely bitter root.

dog·cart (dôg'kärt', dog'-), *n.* a light, two-wheeled, horse-drawn vehicle with two seats set back to back.

dog·catch·er (dôg'kach'ər, dog'-), *n* a person employed by a municipal pound to capture stray dogs or cats.

doge (dōj), *n.* the chief magistrate in the former republics of Venice and Genoa.

dog·ear (dôg'ēr', dog'-), *n.* the corner of a page folded over, as by careless use, or to mark a place. —**dog'eared',** *adj.*

dog·fight (dôg'fīt', dog'-), *n.* a violent engagement of highly maneuverable fighter planes at close range.

dog·fish (dôg'fish', dog'-), *n., pl.* **-fish, -fish·es.** any of several small sharks that are destructive to food fishes.

dog·ged (dô'gid, dog'id), *adj.* stub-

bornly persistent. **—dog′ged·ly,** *adv.*
—dog′ged·ness, *n.*

dog·ger·el (dô′gər əl, dog′ər-), *n.* verse that is comic and usually loose or irregular in measure.

dog′gie bag′, a small bag provided by a restaurant for carrying home leftovers, esp. meat. Also, **dog′gy bag′.**

dog·gone (dôg′gôn′, -gon′, dog′-), *v.,* **-goned, -gon·ing,** *adj., superl.* **-gon-est,** *adv Informal.* **—v.t.** **1.** to damn. **—adj., adv.** **2.** damned.

dog·gy (dô′gē, dog′ē), *n., pl.* **-gies.** a little dog. Also, **dog′gie.**

dog·house (dôg′hous′, dog′-), *n.* **1.** a small shelter for a dog. **2. in the doghouse,** *Slang.* in disgrace.

do·gie (dō′gē), *n. Western U.S.* a motherless calf in a cattle herd. Also, **do′gy.**

dog·leg (dôg′leg′, dog′-), *n.* something bent at a sharp angle.

dog·ma (dôg′mə, dog′-), *n.* **1.** a system of principles or tenets, as of a church. **2.** a specific tenet or doctrine authoritatively put forth: *the dogma of the Assumption.*

dog·mat·ic (dôg mat′ik, dog-), *adj.* **1.** of or of the nature of dogma. **2.** asserting opinions in an arrogant manner **—dog·mat′i·cal·ly,** *adv.* **— Syn. 2.** authoritarian, doctrinaire, opinionated.

dog·ma·tism (dôg′mə tiz′əm, dog′-), *n.* arrogant assertion of opinions as truths. **—dog′ma·tist,** *n.*

do-good·er (dōō′good′ər), *n.* a well-intentioned but naive social reformer.

dog-tired (dôg′tī′rd′, dog′-), *adj. Informal.* utterly exhausted.

dog·tooth (dôg′tōōth′, dog′-), *n.* a canine tooth.

dog′tooth vi′olet, a bulbous, spring-blooming plant of the lily family having purple flowers.

dog·trot (dôg′trot′, dog′-), *n.* a gentle trot.

dog·wood (dôg′wŏŏd′ dog′-), *n.* a tree or shrub having showy pink or white blossoms in spring

doi·ly (doi′lē), *n., pl.* **-lies.** any small, ornamental mat, as of embroidery or lace. [after a London draper of the 17th century]

do·ing (dōō′ing), *n.* **1.** behavior or responsibility **2. doings,** happenings or events.

do-it-your·self (dōō′it yər self′ or, *commonly* ı chər-), *adj* of or designed for construction or use by amateurs without special training. **—do′-it-your·self′er,** *n*

dol., dollar.

dol·drums (dōl′drəmz, dol′-), *n.* **1.** a state of inactivity or stagnation, as in business, art, etc. **2. the doldrums,** a belt of calms and light

variable winds near the equator. **3.** a dull, listless, depressed mood.

dole (dōl), *n., v.,* **doled, dol·ing.** *—n.* **1.** a portion of money, food, etc., esp. as given at regular intervals in charity. **2.** a dealing out or distributing, esp. in charity. **3.** *Brit. Informal.* a weekly payment by a government to the unemployed. *—v.t.* **4.** to distribute in charity. **5.** to give out sparingly or in small quantities.

dole·ful (dōl′fəl), *adj.* mournfully sad. **—dole′ful·ly,** *adv.* **—dole′ful·ness,** *n.*

doll (dol), *n.* **1.** a toy representing a baby or other human being, esp. a child's toy. **2.** *Slang.* a girl or woman, esp. one who is very attractive. *—v.t., v.i.* **3. doll up,** *Slang.* to dress in an elegant or stylish manner. **—doll′ish,** *adj.* **—doll′ish·ly,** *adv.*

dol·lar (dol′ər), *n.* **1.** the monetary unit of the U.S., equal to 100 cents. **2.** the monetary unit of various other nations, as Canada, Australia, etc., equal to 100 cents. **3.** a currency bill or coin equivalent to one dollar.

dol·lars-and-cents (dol′ərs and′ sents′), *adj.* considered strictly in terms of money.

dol·lop (dol′əp), *n.* **1.** a lump or blob, as of paint or mud. **2.** a small serving or portion.

dol·ly (dol′ē), *n., pl.* **dol·lies. 1.** *Baby Talk.* a doll. **2.** a low truck or cart with small wheels for moving heavy loads. **3.** a mobile platform for moving a motion-picture or television camera about a set.

dol·men (dōl′men, -mən, dol′-), *n.* a prehistoric structure consisting of two or more upright stones with a space between and capped by a horizontal stone.

do·lo·mite (dō′lə mīt′, dol′ə-), *n.* a soft mineral composed of carbonates of calcium and magnesium.

do·lor (dō′lər), *n. Literary.* sorrow or grief.

do·lor·ous (dō′lər əs, dol′ər-), *adj.* full of or causing pain or sorrow. **— do′lor·ous·ly,** *adv.* **—do′lor·ous·ness,** *n.*

dol·phin (dol′fin, dôl′-), *n.* **1.** a marine mammal resembling a small whale, with a head elongated into a beaklike snout. **2.** either of two large, slender fishes found in warm and temperate seas.

dolt (dōlt), *n.* a dull, stupid person. **—dolt′ish,** *adj.* **—dolt′ish·ly,** *adv.*

-dom, a suffix meaning: **a.** domain: *kingdom.* **b.** collection of persons: *officialdom.* **c.** rank or dignity: *earldom.* **d.** general condition: *freedom.*

Dom., Dominican.

dom., **1.** domain. **2.** domestic. **3.** dominant. **4.** dominion.

do·main (dō mān′), *n.* **1.** the territory governed by a single ruler or government. **2.** a field of action, knowledge, etc.: *the domain of technology.* **3.** ultimate ownership and control over the use of land.

dome (dōm), *n.* a hemispheric vault of a building or room.

do·mes·tic (də mes′tik), *adj.* **1.** of the home, the household, or the family. **2.** devoted to home life. **3.** tame or domesticated. **4.** of one's own or a particular country. **5.** from or produced within one's own country. — *n.* **6.** a hired household servant. — **do·mes′ti·cal·ly,** *adv.*

do·mes·ti·cate (də mes′tə kāt′), *v.t.,* -cat·ed, -cat·ing. **1.** to tame to domestic use or uses. **2.** to accustom to household life and affairs. —**do·mes′ti·ca′tion,** *n.*

do·mes·tic·i·ty (dō′me stis′i tē), *n., pl.* -ties. **1.** the state of being domestic. **2.** domestic or home life.

dom·i·cile (dom′i sil′, -səl, dō′mi-), *n., v.,* -ciled, -cil·ing. —*n.* **1.** one's legal residence. —*v.t.* **2.** to establish in a domicile. —**dom·i·cil·i·ar·y** (dom′i·sil′ē er′ē, dō′mi-), *adj.*

dom·i·nant (dom′ə nənt), *adj.* **1.** exerting authority or influence. **2.** occupying a commanding position. **3.** most important or prominent. —**dom′i·nance,** *n.* —**dom′i·nant·ly,** *adv.*

dom·i·nate (dom′ə nāt′), *v.t., v.i.,* -nat·ed, -nat·ing. **1.** to rule or control, esp. by strength. **2.** to occupy a commanding or elevated position (over). **3.** to have a controlling or preeminent place (in). —**dom′i·na′-tion,** *n.* —**dom′i·na′tor,** *n.*

dom·i·neer (dom′ə nēr′), *v.i.* **1.** to rule arbitrarily or despotically. **2.** to behave overbearingly. —**dom′i·neer′-ing,** *adj.*

Do·min′i·can Repub′lic (də min′i-kən), a country in the West Indies on the E part of Hispaniola. —**Do·min′i·can,** *adj., n.*

dom·i·nie (dom′ə nē, dō′mə-), *n.* **1.** *Chiefly Scot.* a schoolmaster. **2.** *Dial.* a minister.

do·min·ion (də min′yən), *n.* **1.** supreme or sovereign authority. **2.** realm or domain. **3.** the former title used for some of the self-governing member nations of the British Commonwealth.

dom·i·no¹ (dom′ə nō′), *n., pl.* -noes, -nos. **1.** a large, loose cloak, usually hooded, worn with a small mask in masquerade. **2.** the mask. **3.** a person wearing such dress.

dom·i·no² (dom′ə nō′), *n., pl.* -noes. **1.** a flat, thumb-sized, rectangular tile bearing dots. **2.** dominoes, a game played with such tiles.

dom′ino the′ory, a theory that if one country, esp. in Southeast Asia, is taken over by communism, nearby nations will be taken over one after another.

don¹ (don; *Sp.* dôn), *n.* **1.** (*cap.*) Mr. or Sir: a Spanish title of respect. **2.** a Spanish lord or gentleman. **3.** a head, fellow, or tutor of an English college.

don² (don), *v.t.,* donned, don·ning. to put on or dress in.

Don (don), *n.* a river in the S Soviet Union.

Do·ña (dō′nyä), *n.* Madam: a Spanish title of respect.

do·nate (dō′nāt, dō nāt′), *v.t., v.i.,* -nat·ed, -nat·ing. to make a donation (of). —**do′na·tor,** *n.*

do·na·tion (dō nā′shən), *n.* **1.** the act of presenting something as a gift or contribution. **2.** a gift or contribution.

done (dun), *v.* **1.** pp. of do¹. —*adj.* **2.** completed or through. **3.** cooked sufficiently. **4.** in conformity with fashion, good taste, prosperity. **5.** done for, *Informal.* **a.** tired. **b.** ruined. **c.** dead or close to death. **6.** done in, *Informal.* very tired.

dong (dông), *n.* the monetary unit of Vietnam.

Don Juan (don wän′ *or* don jōō′ən), a legendary Spanish nobleman famous for his seductions and dissolute life.

don·key (dong′kē, dung′-), *n., pl.* -keys. **1.** the domesticated ass. **2.** a stupid, silly, or obstinate person.

don·ny·brook (don′ē brŏŏk′), *n.* (*of-ten cap.*) a wild, noisy fight.

do·nor (dō′nər), *n.* **1.** a person who donates. **2.** a person or animal furnishing biological tissue, esp. blood for transfusion.

Don Quix·o·te (don′ kē hō′tē, don kwik′sət), a person inspired by chivalrous but impractical ideals. [after the hero of Cervantes' romance *Don Quixote de la Mancha* (1605, 1615)]

don't (dōnt), contraction of do not.

do·nut (dō′nət, -nut′), *n.* doughnut.

doo·dad (dōō′dad), *n. Informal.* dingus.

doo·dle (dōōd′ºl), *v.,* -dled, -dling, *n.* —*v.t., v.i.* **1.** to draw or scribble idly. —*n.* **2.** a design, figure, etc., made by doodling. —**doo′dler,** *n.*

doom (dōōm), *n.* **1.** fate or destiny, esp. adverse fate. **2.** ruin or death. **3.** an unfavorable judgment or sentence. —*v.t.* **4.** to destine, esp. to an adverse fate. **5.** to pronounce judgment against.

dooms·day (dōōmz′dā′), *n.* the day of the Last Judgment.

door (dōr, dôr), *n.* **1.** a movable, usually solid barrier for opening and closing an entrance, cabinet, etc. **2.** doorway. **3.** any means of access.

door·jamb (dôr′jam′, dōr′-), *n.* either of the two sidepieces of a door.

door·knob (dôr′nob′, dōr′-), *n.* the handle for opening a door.

door·man (dôr′man′, -mən, dōr′-), *n.* the door attendant of an apartment house, etc., who performs minor services for entering and departing people.

door·mat (dôr′mat′, dōr′-), *n.* a mat placed before a door for wiping dirt from shoes.

door·plate (dôr′plāt′, dōr′-), *n.* a small identification plate on the outside door of a house or room.

door·step (dôr′step′, dōr′-), *n.* a step or one of a series of steps leading to a door from the ground outside.

door·way (dôr′wā′, dōr′-), *n.* the passage into a building, room, etc., commonly opened by a door.

door·yard (dôr′yärd′, dōr′-), *n.* a yard in front of the door of a house.

dop·ant (dō′pənt), *n.* an impurity deliberately added to a semiconducting material to modify its electrical property.

dope (dōp), *n., v.,* **doped, dop·ing.** —*n.* **1.** any thick liquid preparation, as a lubricant, used in preparing a surface. **2.** a varnishlike product used esp. for waterproofing the fabric of airplane wings. **3.** any narcotic drug. **4.** *Slang.* information or news. **5.** *Slang.* a stupid person. —*v.t.* **6.** *Slang.* to affect with dope or drugs. **7.** to treat with dope. **8. dope out,** *Slang.* to figure out. —**dop′er,** *n.*

dop·ey (dō′pē), *adj.,* **dop·i·er, dop·i·est.** *Informal.* **1.** befuddled, as from the use of narcotics or alcohol. **2.** stupid or inane. Also, **dop′y.**

Dor·ic (dôr′ik, dor′-), *adj.* noting a style of ancient Greek architecture characterized by massive, fluted shafts with simple capitals.

dorm (dôrm), *n. Informal.* dormitory.

dor·mant (dôr′mənt), *adj.* **1.** in a state of rest or inactivity. **2.** temporarily inactive: *dormant buds.* —**dor′man·cy,** *n.*

dor·mer (dôr′mər), *n.* a vertical window in a projection built out from a sloping roof. Also called **dor′mer win′dow.**

dor·mi·to·ry (dôr′mi tôr′ē, -tōr′ē), *n., pl.* **-ries.** **1.** a building, as at or near a college, providing living and recreational facilities. **2.** a room serving as communal sleeping quarters.

dor·mouse (dôr′mous′), *n., pl.* **-mice** (-mīs′). a furry-tailed, Old World rodent resembling a small squirrel.

dor·sal (dôr′səl), *adj.* of or situated on the back, as of an organ or part: *dorsal nerves.* —**dor′sal·ly,** *adv.*

do·ry (dôr′ē, dōr′ē), *n., pl.* **-ries.** a boat with a narrow, flat bottom and high sides that curve outward.

dose (dōs), *n., v.,* **dosed, dos·ing.** —*n.* **1.** a quantity of medicine prescribed to be taken at one time. **2.** *Physics.* the quantity of radiation absorbed by a given mass of material, esp. tissue. —*v.t.* **3.** to administer in doses. **4.** to give a dose of medicine to. —**dos′age,** *n.* —**dos′er,** *n.*

do·sim·e·ter (dō sim′i tər), *n.* a device for measuring the quantity of radiation to which one has been exposed. —**do·sim′e·try,** *n.*

dos·si·er (dos′ē ā′, -ē ər, dô′sē ā′, -sē ər), *n.* a group of documents on the same subject, containing detailed information.

dost (dust), *v. Archaic.* 2nd pers. sing. pres. ind. of **do**[1].

Dos·to·ev·sky (dos′tə yef′skē, -toi-, dus′-), *n.* **Feo·dor** (fyô′dor), 1821–81, Russian novelist. Also, **Dos′to·yev′ski.**

dot (dot), *n., v.,* **dot·ted, dot·ting.** —*n.* **1.** a minute or small spot. **2.** a small, roundish mark made with or as with a pen. **3.** a signal of shorter duration than a dash, used in groups with dashes and spaces to represent letters, as in Morse code. **4. on the dot,** *Informal.* precisely on time. —*v.t.* **5.** to mark with or as with a dot or dots. **6.** to stud or cover with dots. —**dot′ter,** *n.* —**dot′ty,** *adj.*

DOT, Department of Transportation.

dot·age (dō′tij), *n.* feebleness of mind, esp. resulting from old age. —**do′tard,** *n.*

dote (dōt), *v.i.,* **dot·ed, dot·ing.** **1.** to bestow excessive love or fondness. **2.** to be weak-minded, esp. from old age. —**dot′er,** *n.* —**dot′ing·ly,** *adv.*

doth (duth), *v. Archaic.* 3rd pers. sing. pres. ind. of **do**[1].

dot·tle (dot′əl), *n.* half-burnt tobacco in the bottom of a pipe after smoking.

dot·ty (dot′ē), *adj.,* **-ti·er, -ti·est.** *Informal.* crazy or eccentric.

Dou′ay Bi′ble (dōō′ā), an English translation of the Bible prepared by Roman Catholic scholars. Also called **Don′ay Ver′sion.**

dou·ble (dub′əl), *adj., n., v.,* **-bled, -bling,** *adv.* —*adj.* **1.** twice as large, heavy, strong, etc. **2.** twofold in form, number, extent, etc. **3.** composed of two like parts. **4.** (of flowers) having many more than the normal number of petals. **5.** made or designed for two. **6.** deceitful or insincere. **7.** in the service of two rival countries: *a double agent.* **8.** folded in two. —*n.* **9.** something that is twice the usual size, amount, strength, etc. **10.** a duplicate or counterpart. **11.** a fold or plait. **12.** a sudden backward turn. **13.** a substitute or understudy. **14.** *Baseball.*

a base hit that enables a batter to reach second base safely. **15. doubles**, a game between two pairs of players, as in tennis. **16.** (in bridge) a doubling of an opponent's bid. **17. on the double**, *Informal.* without delay. —*v.i.* **18.** to make double or twice as great. **19.** to bend or fold. **20.** to clench (the fist). **21.** to duplicate or repeat. **22.** (in bridge) to challenge (the bid of an opponent) by making a call that increases the value of tricks won or lost. —*v.i.* **23.** to become double. **24.** to bend or fold. **25.** to turn back on a course. **26.** to serve in two capacities. **27.** (in bridge) to double the bid of an opponent. **28.** *Baseball.* to make a double. **29. double up**, to share quarters planned for only one person or family. —*adv.* **30.** twofold. **31.** in pairs. —**dou′ble·ness**, *n.* —**dou′bler**, *n.* —**dou′bly**, *adv.*

dou·ble-bar·reled (dub′əl bar′əld), *adj.* **1.** having two barrels mounted, as a shotgun. **2.** serving a double purpose.

dou′ble bass′ (bās), the largest and lowest-pitched instrument of the violin family.

dou′ble boil′er, a cooking utensil consisting of two pots, one of which fits into the other.

dou·ble-breast·ed (dub′əl bres′tid), *adj.* overlapping partway in front, as a coat.

dou·ble-cross (dub′əl krôs′, -kros′), *v.t. Informal.* to betray or deceive. —**dou′ble-cross′er**, *n.*

dou′ble date′, *Informal.* a date which two couples go on together.

dou·ble-deal·ing (dub′əl dē′liŋg), *n.* **1.** deceitful acts or behavior. —*adj.* **2.** treacherous or deceitful. —**dou′ble-deal′er**, *n.*

dou·ble-deck·er (dub′əl dek′ər), *n.* **1.** something with two decks or tiers, as a bus with two decks. **2.** a sandwich with two layers of filling.

dou′ble-dip′per (dub′əl dip′ər), *n. Slang.* a retired military employee who works full-time for a federal agency while drawing a pension. —**dou′ble-dip′ping**, *adj., n.*

dou·ble en·ten·dre (dub′əl än tän′drə, -tänd′), *pl.* **dou·ble en·ten·dres** (dub′-el än tän′drəz, -tändz′). a word or expression with two meanings, one of which is usually risqué.

dou·ble-head·er (dub′əl hed′ər), *n.* two games between the same teams or two different pairs of teams, in immediate succession.

dou·ble-joint·ed (dub′əl join′tid), *adj.* having unusually flexible joints that can bend in unusual ways or to an abnormally great extent.

dou·ble-knit (dub′əl nit′), *n.* a firmly heavy fabric made of a double stitch bonded together.

dou′ble play′, a baseball play in which two players are put out.

dou·ble-space (dub′əl spās′), *v.t., v.i.* to typewrite using a full space between lines.

dou′ble stand′ard, any set of principles containing different provisions for one group of people than for another, as the unwritten code that permits men more sexual freedom than women.

dou·blet (dub′lit), *n.* **1.** a closefitting jacket worn by men in the Renaissance. **2.** a pair of like things. **3.** one of a pair of like things.

dou′ble take′, a rapid or surprised second look at a person or situation whose significance had not been completely grasped at first.

dou·ble-talk (dub′əl tôk′), *n.* **1.** speech using nonsense syllables along with words in a rapid patter. **2.** evasive or ambiguous language.

dou·bloon (du blōōn′), *n.* a former gold coin of Spain and Spanish America.

doubt (dout), *v.t.* **1.** to be uncertain and undecided about. **2.** to distrust or disbelieve. —*v.i.* **3.** to be uncertain and undecided. —*n.* **4.** a feeling of uncertainty and indecision about something or someone. **5.** distrust or suspicion. **6.** a state of affairs such as to cause uncertainty. **7. beyond doubt**, with certainty. Also, **without doubt**. **8. no doubt**, **a.** probably. **b.** certainly. —**doubt′a·ble**, *adj.* —**doubt′er**, *n.* —**doubt′ing·ly**, *adv.*

doubt·ful (dout′fəl), *adj.* **1.** admitting of or causing doubt. **2.** of uncertain outcome or result. **3.** questionable or suspect. **4.** undecided or hesitating. —**doubt′ful·ly**, *adv.* —**doubt′ful·ness**, *n.*

doubt·less (dout′lis), *adv.* Also, **doubt′less·ly.** **1.** unquestionably. **2.** probably. —*adj.* **3.** free from doubt or uncertainty.

douche (dōōsh), *n., v.,* **douched, douch·ing.** —*n.* **1.** a jet of water applied to a body part or cavity for medicinal or hygienic purposes. **2.** the application of such a jet. **3.** an instrument, as a syringe, for administering it. —*v.t., v.i.* **4.** to apply a douche (to).

dough (dō), *n.* **1.** flour or meal combined with water, milk, etc., in a mass for baking into bread, cake, etc. **2.** any soft, pasty mass. **3.** *Slang.* money. —**dough′y**, *adj.*

dough·boy (dō′boi′), *n. Informal.* an American infantryman, esp. one in World War I.

dough·nut (dō′nət, -nut′), *n.* a small, usually ring-shaped cake of sweetened dough fried in deep fat.

dough·ty (dou′tē), *adj.*, **-ti·er**, **-ti·est**. *Often Facetious.* courageous and resolute. **—dough′ti·ly**, *adv.* **—dough′ti·ness**, *n.*

Doug′las fir′ (dug′ləs), a tall evergreen tree of western North America, yielding a strong, durable timber.

dour (door, dour, dou′ər), *adj.* **1.** sullenly gloomy. **2.** severe or stern. **—dour′ly**, *adv.* **—dour′ness**, *n.*

douse (dous), *v.t.*, **doused**, **dous·ing.** **1.** to plunge into water or other liquid. **2.** to splash or throw water on. **3.** *Informal.* to put out or extinguish, as a light or fire.

dove¹ (duv), *n.* **1.** a bird resembling a small pigeon. **2.** a symbol of peace and gentleness. **3.** *Informal*, a person who advocates peace or a conciliatory national attitude. **—dov′ish,** *adj.*

dove² (dōv), *v.* a pt. of **dive.**

dove·cote (duv′kōt′), *n.* a structure, usually above the ground, for housing domestic pigeons. Also, **dove·cot** (duv′kot′).

Do·ver (dō′vər), *n.* the capital of Delaware.

dove·tail (duv′tāl′), *n.* **1.** a tapered projection on a board. **2.** a joint formed of one or more such tenons fitting tightly within corresponding mortises. **—v.t., v.i. 3.** to join together by means of dovetails. **4.** to fit together harmoniously.

dow·a·ger (dou′ə jər), *n.* **1.** a woman who holds some title or property from her deceased husband, esp. the widow of a king, duke, etc. **2.** an elderly society woman.

dow·dy (dou′dē), *adj.*, **-di·er**, **-di·est.** not neat or stylish, as in dress. **—dow′di·ness**, *n.*

dow·el (dou′əl), *n., v.*, **-eled**, **-el·ing** or **-elled**, **-el·ling. —n. 1.** a pin, usually round, fitting into holes in two adjacent pieces to prevent their slipping or to align them. **—v.t. 2.** to reinforce or furnish with dowels.

dow·er (dou′ər), *n.* **1.** the portion of a deceased husband's real property allowed to his widow for her lifetime. **2.** *Archaic.* dowry. **—v.t. 3.** to provide with a dower.

dow·itch·er (dou′ich ər), *n.* a long-billed, snipelike shorebird.

down¹ (doun), *adv.* **1.** toward, into, or in a lower physical position. **2.** on or to the ground or bottom. **3.** to or in a sitting or lying position. **4.** to or in a position geographically lower, as to the south. **5.** to or at a lower value, volume, amount, strength, etc. **6.** from an earlier to later time. **7.** in an attitude of earnest application. **8.** on paper. **9.** in cash at the time of purchase. **10.** completely or thoroughly: *loaded*

down with gifts. **11.** to the source or actual position. **12.** confined to bed with illness. **13.** in or into a lesser state or condition. **14. down with!** do away with! stop! **—prep. 15.** in a descending or more remote direction on, over, or along. **—adj. 16.** going or directed downward. **17.** being at a low position or on the ground or bottom. **18.** downcast or dejected. **19.** behind an opponent in points, games, etc. **20.** losing the amount indicated, esp. at gambling. **21.** finished or done. **22. down and out,** destitute. **23. down on,** *Informal.* hostile to. **—n. 24.** a downward movement or turn. **25.** a turn for the worse. **26.** one of a series of plays during which a football team must advance the ball. **—v.t. 27.** to knock or throw down. **28.** *Informal.* to defeat, as in a game.

down² (doun), *n.* **1.** the soft under plumage of birds. **2.** a growth of soft, fine hair. **—down′y,** *adj.*

down³ (doun), *n.* Usually, **downs.** open, rolling, upland country with grassy slopes.

down·beat (doun′bēt′), *n.* the downward stroke of a conductor's arm or baton indicating the first or accented beat of a measure.

down·cast (doun′kast′, -käst′), *adj.* **1.** dejected in spirit. **2.** directed downward, as the eyes.

down·court (doun′kōrt′, -kôrt′), *adv.*, *adj.* *Basketball.* in, into, or toward a team's offensive half of the court.

down·er (dou′nər), *n.* *Slang.* **1.** a depressant or sedative drug, esp. a barbiturate. **2.** a depressing experience, person, or thing.

down·fall (doun′fôl′), *n.* **1.** a sudden fall to a lower position or standing. **2.** something causing this. **3.** a sudden or heavy fall, as of rain or snow. **—down′fall′en,** *adj.*

down·grade (doun′grād′), *n., v.*, **-grad·ed**, **-grad·ing. —n. 1.** a downward slope, esp. of a road. **2. on the downgrade,** falling from success, wealth, etc. **—v.t. 3.** to reduce in rank, income, importance, etc.

down·heart·ed (doun′här′tid), *adj.* dejected or depressed. **—down′heart′ed·ly,** *adv.*

down·hill (doun′hil′), *adv.* **1.** down the slope of a hill. **2.** into a worse condition. **—adj. 3.** going or tending downward.

down·home (doun′hōm′), *adj.* *Informal.* warm and folksy.

down′ pay′ment, an initial amount paid at the time of purchase in installment buying, etc.

down·pour (doun′pōr′, -pôr′), *n.* a drenching rain.

down·range (*adj.* doun′rānj′; *adv.* doun′rānj′), *adj.*, *adv.* in the designated path away from a launch pad.

down·right (doun′rīt′), *adj.* **1.** thorough or absolute. **2.** frankly direct. —*adv.* **3.** thoroughly.

down·shift (doun′shift′), *v.i.* **1.** to shift the automobile transmission into a lower gear. —*n.* **2.** the act or instance of downshifting.

down·size (doun′sīz′), *v.*, **-sized, -siz·ing,** *adj.* —*v.t.* **1.** to make a smaller version of (a standard car). —*adj.* **2.** Also, **down′sized′.** of a smaller version, esp. of a car.

Down's syn′drome (dounz), Mongolism. [after J. L. H. *Down* (1828–96), English physician]

down·stage (*adv.* doun′stāj′; *adj.* doun′stāj′), *adv.*, *adj.* at or toward the front of the stage.

down·stairs (*adv.*, *n.* doun′stârz′; *adj.* doun′stârz′), *adv.* **1.** down the stairs. **2.** to or on a lower floor. —*adj.* **3.** Also, **down′stair′.** on or pertaining to a lower floor, esp. the ground floor. —*n.* **4.** the lower floor of a building.

down·state (*adj.* doun′stāt′; *adv.* doun′stāt′), *adj.*, *adv.* in, to, or from the southern part of the state.

down·stream (doun′strēm′), *adv.*, *adj.* in the direction of the current of a stream.

down·stroke (doun′strōk′), *n.* a downward stroke, as of a piston.

down·swing (doun′swing′), *n.* **1.** a downward swing, as of a golf club. **2.** downturn.

down-to-earth (doun′tōō ûrth′, -tə-), *adj.* practical and realistic.

down·town (doun′toun′), *adv.*, *adj.* **1.** to, toward, or in the main business section of a city. —*n.* **2.** the business section of a city.

down·trod·den (doun′trod′°n), *adj.* oppressed or subjugated.

down·turn (doun′tûrn′), *n.* a downward trend, esp. in business.

down′ un′der, *Informal.* Australia or New Zealand.

down·ward (doun′wərd), *adv.* **1.** Also, **down′wards.** from a higher to a lower place or condition. **2.** from a past time or ancestor. —*adj.* **3.** moving to a lower place or condition.

down·wind (doun′wind′), *adv.*, *adj.* in the direction that the wind is blowing.

down′y mil′dew, **1.** a fungus that causes many plant diseases and produces a white, downy mass, usually on the undersurface of the leaves. **2.** a plant disease caused by this.

down′y wood′pecker, a small, North American woodpecker having black and white plumage.

dow·ry (dou′rē), *n.*, *pl.* **-ries.** the money, goods, or estate that a bride brings to her husband.

dowse[1] (douz), *v.i.*, **dowsed, dows·ing.** to search for underground water, metal, etc., by the use of a divining rod. —**dows′er,** *n.*

dowse[2] (dous), *v.t.*, **dowsed, dows·ing.** douse.

dox·ol·o·gy (dok sol′ə jē), *n.*, *pl.* **-gies.** a hymn of praise to God.

doy·en (doi en′, doi′ən), *n. Chiefly Brit.* dean (def. 4). —**doy·enne′,** *n.fem.*

doz., dozen; dozens.

doze (dōz), *v.*, **dozed, doz·ing,** *n.* —*v.i.* **1.** to sleep lightly or briefly, often unintentionally. —*n.* **2.** such a sleep. —**doz′er,** *n.* —**doz′y,** *adj.*

doz·en (duz′ən), *n.*, *pl.* **doz·ens, doz·en.** a group of twelve. —**doz′enth,** *adj.*

D.P., See **displaced person.** Also, **DP**

dpt., department.

D.R., See **dead reckoning.**

Dr., **1.** Doctor. **2.** Drive.

dr., **1.** debit. **2.** debtor. **3.** drachma; drachmas. **4.** dram; drams. **5.** drum.

drab (drab), *n.*, *adj.*, **drab·ber, drab·best.** —*n.* **1.** dull brownish gray. —*adj.* **2.** having a drab color. **3.** dull or cheerless. —**drab′ly,** *adv.* —**drab′ness,** *n.*

drach·ma (drak′mə), *n.*, *pl.* **-mas, -mae** (-mē). the monetary unit of Greece.

draft (draft, dräft), *n.* **1.** a preliminary form of any writing. **2.** a drawing, sketch, or design. **3.** a current of air in any enclosed space. **4.** a device for regulating the current of air in a stove, fireplace, etc. **5. a.** a selection of persons for military service. **b.** the persons so selected. **6.** the act of pulling loads. **7.** that which is drawn or hauled. **8.** the force required to pull a load. **9.** the taking of supplies, forces, etc. **10.** a written order for payment of money. **11.** the depth to which a loaded vessel is immersed. **12.** draught (defs. 1–4). **13. on draft,** available from a cask: *beer on draft.* —*v.t.* **14.** to draw the outlines of. **15.** to compose in written form. **16.** to select by draft, esp. for military service. **17.** to draw or pull. —*adj.* **18.** used for drawing loads: *a draft ox.* **19.** drawn from a cask. **20.** being a preliminary version or sketch. —**draft′er,** *n.* —**draft′a·ble,** *adj.*

draft·ee (draf tē′, dräf-), *n.* a person drafted into military service.

drafts·man (drafts′mən, dräfts′-), *n.* a person who draws plans and blueprints. —**drafts′man·ship′,** *n.*

draft·y (draf′tē, dräf′-), *adj.*, **draft·i·er, draft·i·est.** characterized by or admitting drafts of air. —**draft′i·ly,** *adv.* —**draft′i·ness,** *n.*

drag (drag), v., **dragged, drag·ging,** n.
—v.t. **1.** to draw or pull heavily or
slowly along. **2.** to search with a
drag. **3.** to bring in, as an irrelevant
matter. **4.** to protract (something)
or pass (time) tediously. —v.i. **5.** to
be drawn or hauled along. **6.** to trail
on the ground. **7.** to move heavily
or with effort. **8.** to proceed slowly.
9. to lag behind. —n. **10.** any device
for dragging the bottom of a body
of water to recover objects. **11.** a
heavy harrow. **12.** a boring
person or thing. **13.** anything that
retards progress. **14.** the act of
dragging. **15.** Informal. a puff on a
cigarette, etc. **16.** Slang. a city street.
17. Slang. influence that gains special
favor. **18.** Slang. transvestite attire.
19. See drag race. —drag'ger, n.

drag·gy (drag'ē), adj., **-gi·er, -gi·est.**
1. sluggish or lethargic. **2.** Slang.
extremely dull or tiresome.

drag·net (drag'net'), n. **1.** a net drawn
along a river bottom, etc., to catch
fish. **2.** a network for catching
criminals by the police.

drag·o·man (drag'ə mən), n., pl. -mans,
-men. a professional interpreter in
the Near East.

drag·on (drag'ən), n. a fabulous
monster represented generally as a
huge, winged reptile, often spout-
ing fire.

drag·on·fly (drag'ən flī'), n., pl. -flies.
an insect having a long, straight
body and four wings.

dra·goon (drə gōon'), n. **1.** a former
European cavalryman of a heavily
armed troop. —v.t. **2.** to oppress or
coerce.

drag' race', Slang. a short race between automobiles, the winner being
the car that accelerates fastest.

drag' strip', a straight, paved course
for drag races.

drain (drān), v.t. **1.** to draw off (a
liquid) gradually. **2.** to empty by
drawing off liquid. **3.** to draw off
completely. **4.** to exhaust (resources,
spiritual strength, etc.) gradually.
—v.i. **5.** to flow off or become empty
gradually. —n. **6.** that by which
anything is drained, as a pipe. **7.**
outflow or expenditure. **8.** the act
of draining. **9. down the drain,** being lost or wasted. —drain'er, n.

drain·age (drā'nij), n. **1.** the act or
process of draining. **2.** a system of
drains. **3.** an area drained, as by
a river. **4.** that which is drained off.

drain·pipe (drān'pīp'), n. a large pipe
that carries away water, waste, etc.

drake (drāk), n. a male duck.

dram (dram), n. **1.** a unit of apothecaries' weight, equal to ⅛ ounce.
2. 1/16 ounce, avoirdupois weight. **3.**
a small drink of liquor.

dra·ma (drä'mə, dram'ə), n. **1.** a composition presenting a story in dialogue, esp. one acted out on the
stage. **2.** the art dealing with the
writing and production of plays. **3.**
any series of vivid, conflicting
events: the drama of a murder trial.
—dra·mat·ic (drə mat'ik), adj. —
dra·mat'i·cal·ly, adv.

Dram·a·mine (dram'ə mēn'), n. Trademark. an antihistamine used to prevent motion sickness.

dra·mat·ics (drə mat'iks), n. **1.** the
art of producing or acting dramas.
2. overemotional behavior.

dram·a·tist (dram'ə tist, drä'mə-), n.
playwright.

dram·a·tize (dram'ə tīz', drä'mə-), v.t.,
-tized, -tiz·ing. **1.** to make into a
drama. **2.** to express vividly or
strikingly. —dram·a·ti·za'tion, n.

drank (drangk), v. pt. and a pp. of
drink.

drape (drāp), v., **draped, drap·ing,** n.
—v.t. **1.** to cover or hang with
fabric, esp. in graceful folds. **2.** to
adjust (curtains, clothes, etc.) into
graceful folds. **3.** to arrange or let
fall carelessly. —n. **4.** a draped curtain. **5.** manner or style of hanging.
—drap'a·ble, drape'a·ble, adj.

drap·er (drā'pər), n. Brit. a retail
merchant or clerk who sells clothing and dry goods.

dra·per·y (drā'pə rē), n., pl. -per·ies.
1. hangings, clothing, etc., of fabric
in loose folds. **2.** Often, draperies.
long curtains of heavy fabric. **3.**
Brit. See dry goods.

dras·tic (dras'tik), adj. **1.** acting with
violence. **2.** extremely severe. —
dras'ti·cal·ly, adv.

draught (draft, dräft), n. **1.** the drawing of a liquid from its receptacle:
ale on draught. **2.** the act of drinking
or inhaling. **3.** a drink or dose. **4.**
a quantity of fish caught. **5. draughts,**
Brit. the game of checkers. **6.** Chiefly
Brit. draft (defs. 1–11). —v.t. **7.**
Chiefly Brit. draft (defs. 14–17).
—adj. **8.** Chiefly Brit. draft (defs.
18–20).

draw (drô), v., **drew, drawn, draw·ing,**
n. —v.t. **1.** to cause to move in a
particular direction by or as by pulling. **2.** to take or pull out, as from
a receptacle. **3.** to attract or bring:
The concert drew a large audience.
4. to sketch (someone or something)
in lines or words. **5.** to frame or
formulate (a distinction). **6.** to inhale
or suck in. **7.** to deduce or infer:
to draw a conclusion. **8.** to get or
receive, as from a source. **9.** to
produce or bring in: The deposits
draw interest. **10.** to write out (a
check or draft). **11.** to withdraw
(funds) from a place of deposit. **12.**
to disembowel, as a fowl. **13.** to

stretch or extend. **14.** to bend (a bow) by pulling back its string. **15.** to choose or to have assigned to one at random. **16.** to wrinkle or shrink by contraction. **17.** (of a vessel) to need (a specific depth of water) to float in. **18.** to take or be dealt (a card or cards) from the pack. —*v.i.* **19.** to exert a pulling or attracting force. **20.** to move or pass, esp. slowly or continuously: *The day draws near.* **21.** to take out a sword, pistol, etc., for action. **22.** to hold a lottery: *to draw for prizes.* **23.** to sketch or to trace figures. **24.** to shrink or contract. **25.** to make a draft or demand: *to draw on one's imagination.* **26.** to produce or permit a draft, as a pipe or flue. **27.** to leave a contest undecided. **28. draw on,** to come nearer. **29. draw out, a.** to pull out. **b.** to prolong. **c.** to persuade someone to speak freely. **30. draw up, a.** to draft, esp. in legal form: *to draw up a will.* **b.** to arrange. **c.** to stop. —*n.* **31.** the act or result of drawing. **32.** something that attracts customers, an audience, etc. **33.** that which is moved by being drawn. **34.** that which is drawn at random. **35.** a contest that ends in a tie.

draw·back (drô′bak′), *n.* a disadvantageous feature.

draw·bridge (drô′brij′), *n.* a bridge that can be raised or turned to leave a passage for boats, barges, etc.

draw·er (drôr *for 1, 2;* drô′ər *for 3*), *n.* **1.** a sliding, lidless, horizontal compartment, as in a piece of furniture. **2. drawers,** an undergarment, with legs, that covers the lower part of the body. **3.** a person or thing that draws.

draw·ing (drô′ing), *n.* **1.** the act of a person or thing that draws. **2.** a graphic representation by lines of an object or idea, as with a pencil. **3.** a picture, sketch, etc. **4.** the art or technique of making these. **5.** something decided by drawing lots.

draw′ing card′, an entertainer, performance, sale, etc., that attracts many customers.

draw′ing room′, **1.** a formal reception room. **2.** a private room for two or three passengers in a railroad car.

drawl (drôl), *v.t., v.i.* **1.** to speak in a slow manner, usually prolonging the vowels. —*n.* **2.** the act or utterance of a person who drawls.

drawn (drôn), *v.* **1.** pp. of **draw.** —*adj.* **2.** tense or haggard. **3.** eviscerated, as a fowl.

drawn′ but′ter, melted butter, often seasoned with herbs.

draw·string (drô′string′), *n.* a string, cord, etc., that tightens or closes an opening, as of a bag.

dray (drā), *n.* a low, strong cart without fixed sides, for carrying heavy loads. —**dray′age,** *n.*

dread (dred), *v.t.* **1.** to fear greatly. **2.** to be reluctant to experience. —*n.* **3.** great fear, as of something in the future. —*adj.* **4.** greatly feared. **5.** held in awe.

dread·ful (dred′fəl), *adj.* **1.** causing great dread. **2.** extremely bad or unpleasant. —**dread′ful·ly,** *adv.* —**dread′ful·ness,** *n.*

dread·nought (dred′nôt′), *n.* a battleship armed with heavy-caliber guns. Also, **dread′naught′.**

dream (drēm), *n., v.,* **dreamed** or **dreamt** (dremt), **dream·ing.** —*n.* **1.** a succession of images, thoughts, or emotions occurring during sleep. **2.** a daydream or reverie. **3.** a goal or aim. **4.** a wild fancy. **5.** something of unreal beauty. —*v.i.* **6.** to have dreams. **7.** to indulge in daydreams. **8.** to conceive of something remotely. —*v.t.* **9.** to have a dream of. **10.** to pass or spend (time) in dreaming. **11. dream up,** *Informal.* to devise or concoct. —**dream′er,** *n.* —**dream′less,** *adj.* —**dream′like′,** *adj.*

dream·land (drēm′land′), *n.* **1.** a lovely land that exists only in the imagination. **2.** sleep or slumber.

dream′ world′, the world of imagination or illusion.

dream·y (drē′mē), *adj.,* **dream·i·er, dream·i·est.** **1.** full of or characterized by dreams. **2.** vague or dim. **3.** soothing or restful. **4.** *Informal.* wonderful or marvelous. —**dream′i·ly,** *adv.* —**dream′i·ness,** *n.*

drear (drēr), *adj. Literary.* dreary.

drear·y (drēr′ē), *adj.,* **drear·i·er, drear·i·est.** **1.** depressingly dismal. **2.** dull or boring. —**drear′i·ly,** *adv.* —**drear′i·ness,** *n.*

dredge[1] (drej), *n., v.,* **dredged, dredg·ing.** —*n.* **1.** a powerful machine for scooping earth from the bottom of a river. —*v.t.* **2.** to clear out or gather with a dredge. —*v.i.* **3.** to use a dredge. —**dredg′er,** *n.*

dredge[2] (drej), *v.t.,* **dredged, dredg·ing.** to coat (food) with flour.

dregs (dregz), *n.pl.* **1.** the sediment of liquids, esp. of a beverage. **2.** the least valuable part of anything.

drench (drench), *v.t.* to wet thoroughly. —**drench′er,** *n.*

dress (dres), *n.* **1.** the most common outer garment of women, consisting of waist and skirt in one piece. **2.** clothing or apparel. —*adj.* **3.** of or for dresses. **4.** of or for a formal occasion. **5.** requiring formal dress. —*v.t.* **6.** to put clothing upon. **7.** to provide or furnish with clothing. **8.** to trim or adorn. **9.** to prepare (meat, fowl, skins, fabrics, etc.) for cooking or other use. **10.** to comb

out and arrange (hair). **11.** to cultivate (land, etc.). **12.** to apply medication to (a wound). **13.** to bring
(troops) into line: *to dress the ranks.*
—*v.i.* **14.** to clothe oneself. **15.** to
put on formal or fancy clothes. **16.**
to come into line, as troops. **17.**
dress down, *Informal.* to reprimand.
18. dress up, to put on one's best
or fanciest clothing.

dres·sage (drə säzh′), *n.* the art of
training a horse in obedience and in
precision of movement.

dress′ cir′cle, a circular or curving
division of seats in a theater, usually
the first gallery.

dress·er¹ (dres′ər), *n.* **1.** a person who
dresses. **2.** a person employed to
dress others, care for costumes, etc.

dress·er² (dres′ər), *n.* a chest of
drawers, usually with a mirror.

dress·ing (dres′ing), *n.* **1.** the act of a
person or thing that dresses. **2.** a
sauce for a salad, etc. **3.** stuffing
for a fowl. **4.** material to dress a
wound.

dress·ing-down (dres′ing doun′), *n.* a
severe scolding.

dress′ing gown′, a robe worn for
lounging or when dressing.

dress·mak·er (dres′mā′kər), *n.* a person who makes women's dresses,
coats, etc. —**dress′mak′ing,** *n.*

dress′ rehears′al, a final rehearsal of
a play, in costume and with scenery,
etc.

dress·y (dres′ē), *adj.,* **dress·i·er, dress-
i·est. 1.** shown in dress. **2.** stylish or
smart. —**dress′i·ness,** *n.*

drew (drōō), *v.* pt. of **draw.**

drib·ble (drib′əl), *v.,* **-bled, -bling,** *n.*
—*v.i., v.t.* **1.** to fall or let fall in
drops. **2.** to let (saliva) trickle from
the mouth. **3.** to advance (a ball
or puck) by bouncing it or giving
it a series of short kicks or pushes.
—*n.* **4.** a small trickle or drop. **5.**
the dribbling of a ball or puck.
—**drib′bler,** *n.*

drib·let (drib′lit), *n.* a small portion,
part, or sum.

dried (drīd), *v.* pt. and pp. of **dry.**

dri·er¹ (drī′ər), *n.* **1.** a person or
thing that dries. **2.** any substance
added to paints, varnishes, etc., to
make them dry quickly. **dryer**
(def. 1).

dri·er² (drī′ər), *adj.* comparative of
dry.

drift (drift), *n.* **1.** the act or an
instance of being carried along by
currents of water or air. **2.** the deviation of a plane or boat from a set
course due to winds. **3.** a meaning or
intent: *the drift of a statement.* **4.**
something driven, as animals, rain,
etc. **5.** a heap of any matter driven
together. —*v.i.* **6.** to be carried
along by currents of water or air.

7. to wander aimlessly. **8.** to be
driven into heaps, as by the wind.
—*v.i.* **9.** to drive into heaps. —
drift′y, *adj.*

drift·er (drif′tər), *n.* a person who
moves frequently from place to
place, job to job, etc.

drift·wood (drift′wood′), *n.* wood
floating on or cast ashore by the
water.

drill¹ (dril), *n.* **1.** a shaftlike tool with
cutting edges for making holes in
firm materials, esp. by rotation. **2.**
training or an exercise in formal
marching or other precise military
movements. **3.** any strict, methodical
training or exercise. —*v.t., v.i.* **4.** to
pierce or bore with a drill. **5.** to
perform or make perform training
drills. —**drill′er,** *n.*

drill² (dril), *n.* **1.** a small furrow
made in the soil in which to sow
seeds. **2.** a machine for sowing in
rows and for covering the seeds
when sown.

drill³ (dril), *n.* a strong, twilled cotton
fabric.

drill·mas·ter (dril′mas′tər, -mä′stər),
n. a person who trains others by
routine drills.

drill′ press′, a drilling machine used
chiefly on metals.

dri·ly (drī′lē), *adv.* dryly.

drink (dringk), *v.,* **drank; drunk** or,
often, **drank; drink·ing;** *n.* —*v.i.* **1.**
to take liquid into the mouth and
swallow it. **2.** to consume alcoholic
liquors, esp. in excess. **3.** to propose
or participate in a toast. —*v.t.* **4.**
to take into the mouth and swallow
(a liquid). **5.** to absorb (a liquid).
6. to take in eagerly through the
senses: *He drank in the beauty of
the scene.* **7.** to swallow the contents
of (a glass, etc.). —*n.* **8.** any liquid
for drinking. **9.** alcoholic liquor.
10. excessive indulgence in alcoholic
liquor. **11.** a draft of liquid. —**drink′-
a·ble,** *adj.* —**drink′er,** *n.*

drip (drip), *v.,* **dripped** or **dript, dripping,** *n.* —*v.i.* **1.** to let drops fall.
2. to fall in drops, as a liquid. —*v.t.*
3. to let fall in drops. —*n.* **4.** the act
of dripping. **5.** the liquid that drips.
6. the sound made by falling drops.
7. *Slang.* an unattractive, colorless
person. —**drip′per,** *n.* —**drip′py,**
adj.

drip-dry (drip′drī′), *adj.* wash-and-
wear.

drip′ grind′, finely ground coffee
beans.

drip·ping (drip′ing), *n.* Often, **drip-
pings.** fat and juices exuded from
meat in cooking.

drive (drīv), *v.,* **drove, driv·en** (driv′-
ən), **driv·ing,** *n.* —*v.t.* **1.** to send,
expel, or otherwise force to move.
2. to force to work or overwork. **3.**

to guide the movement of: *to drive a car.* **4.** to transport in a vehicle. **5.** to compel or constrain. **6.** to carry vigorously through: *He drove a hard bargain.* **7.** to dig (a well, etc.) horizontally. **8.** to hit (a ball or puck) very hard. —*v.i.* **9.** to be impelled. **10.** to rush violently. **11.** to cause and guide the movement of a vehicle or animal. **12.** to go or travel in a driven vehicle. **13.** to hit a ball or puck very hard. **14.** to strive vigorously toward an objective. **15. drive at,** to suggest or allude to. **16. drive in,** *Baseball.* to cause (a run or runner) to be scored. —*n.* **17.** the act of driving. **18.** a trip in a vehicle. **19.** an impelling along, as of game or floating logs, in a particular direction. **20.** the animals, logs, etc., thus driven. **21.** *Psychol.* a basic or instinctive need. **22.** a vigorous effort toward a goal. **23.** a strong military offensive. **24.** energy and initiative: *a person with great drive.* **25.** a road for vehicles, esp. a scenic highway. **26.** a driving mechanism, as of an automobile. **27.** *Sports.* a propelling, forcible stroke. —**driv′er,** *n.*

drive-in (drīv′in′), *n.* a motion-picture theater, bank, etc., designed to accommodate patrons in their automobiles.

driv·el (driv′əl), *v.,* **-eled, -el·ing** or **-elled, -el·ling,** *n.* —*v.i., v.t.* **1.** to let (saliva) flow from the mouth. **2.** to talk childishly or idiotically. —*n.* **3.** childish, silly talk. —**driv′el·er, driv′el·ler,** *n.*

drive′ shaft′, a shaft for imparting torque from a power source to machinery.

drive·way (drīv′wā′), *n.* a road, esp. a private one, from a street to a house, garage, etc.

driz·zle (driz′əl), *v.,* **-zled, -zling,** —*v.t., v.i.* **1.** to rain gently and steadily in fine drops. —*n.* **2.** a very light rain. —**driz′zly,** *adj.*

drogue (drōg), *n.* a parachutelike device for braking.

droll (drōl), *adj.* amusing in an odd way. —**droll′er·y,** *n.* —**droll′ness,** *n.* —**drol′ly,** *adv.*

drom·e·dar·y (drom′i der′ē, drum′-), *n., pl.* **-dar·ies.** the one-humped camel of Arabia and northern Africa. [< LL *dromedāri(us) camēlus* running camel]

drone¹ (drōn), *n.* **1.** a male bee, stingless and making no honey. **2.** a parasitic loafer. **3.** a remote-control mechanism, as a radio-controlled airplane or boat.

drone² (drōn), *v.,* **droned, dron·ing,** —*v.i.* **1.** to make a dull, continued, monotonous sound. **2.** to speak in

a monotonous tone. —*v.t.* **3.** to say in a dull, monotonous tone. —*n.* **4.** a droning sound.

drool (drōōl), *v.i.* **1.** to water at the mouth, as in anticipation of food. **2.** to show excessive pleasure. **3.** to talk foolishly.

droop (drōōp), *v.i.* **1.** to sag, sink, bend, or hang down, as from weakness. **2.** to become weak. **3.** to lose spirit. —*v.t.* **4.** to let sink or drop. —*n.* **5.** a drooping. —**droop′y,** *adj.* —**droop′i·ness,** *n.*

drop (drop), *n., v.,* **dropped, drop·ping.** —*n.* **1.** a small quantity of liquid that falls in a more or less spherical mass. **2.** a very small quantity of liquid. **3.** a minute quantity of anything. **4.** Usually, **drops.** liquid medicine from a medicine dropper. **5.** something resembling a drop, as an earring, etc. **6.** a piece of candy. **7.** the act or an instance of dropping. **8.** the distance or depth to which anything drops. **9.** that which drops or is used for dropping. **10.** a central depository: *a main drop.* **11.** a decline in amount, value, etc. **12.** persons or supplies dropped by parachute. —*v.i.* **13.** to fall in drops. **14.** to fall vertically. **15.** to sink to the ground, as if inanimate. **16.** to cease or vanish. **17.** *Informal.* to withdraw: *to drop out of a race.* **18.** to fall lower in degree, value, etc. **19.** to pass without effort into some condition. **20.** to move to a position that is farther back, inferior, etc. **21.** to make an unexpected visit: *Let′s drop in at Tom′s.* —*v.t.* **22.** to let fall in drops. **23.** to let or cause to fall. **24.** to cause or allow to sink to a lower position. **25.** to reduce in value, quality, etc. **26.** to utter casually: *to drop a hint.* **27.** to send or mail (a note, etc.). **28.** to set down or unload. **29.** to cease to employ or keep up with. **30. drop behind,** to fall short of the required pace. Also, **drop back. 31. drop off, a.** to fall asleep. **b.** to decline. **32. drop out,** *Slang.* to withdraw from established society, esp. to take drugs or live in a commune.

drop′ kick′, a kick made by dropping a football to the ground and kicking it as it starts to bounce up. —**drop-kick** (drop′kik′), *v.t., v.i.* —**drop′-kick′er,** *n.*

drop·let (drop′lit), *n.* a little drop.

drop-off (drop′ôf′, -of′), *n.* **1.** a very steep descent. **2.** a decline or decrease.

drop·out (drop′out′), *n.* a person who withdraws, esp. a student who withdraws before graduation.

drop·per (drop′ər), *n.* a glass tube with a hollow rubber bulb at one end, for drawing in a liquid and expelling it in drops.

drop·sy (drop′sē), *n.* an excessive accumulation of fluid in a body cavity or in the tissue. —**drop′si·cal** (-si-kəl), *adj.*

dross (drôs, dros), *n.* 1. a waste product taken off molten metal during smelting. 2. waste matter. —**dross′y**, *adj.* —**dross′i·ness**, *n.*

drought (drout), *n.* an extended period of dry weather, esp. one injurious to crops. Also, **drouth** (drouth).

drove[1] (drōv), *v.* pt. of **drive.**

drove[2] (drōv), *n.* 1. a number of oxen, sheep, etc., driven in a group. 2. a large crowd of human beings, esp. in motion.

dro·ver (drō′vər), *n.* a person who drives cattle, sheep, etc., to market.

drown (droun), *v.i.* 1. to be suffocated by immersion in water. —*v.t.* 2. to suffocate by such immersion. 3. to flood or inundate. 4. to overwhelm so as to be inaudible, as by a louder noise.

drowse (drouz), *v.*, **drowsed, drowsing**, *n.* —*v.i.* 1. to be half asleep. —*n.* 2. a sleepy condition.

drow·sy (drou′zē), *adj.*, **-si·er, -si·est.** 1. half asleep. 2. inducing sleepiness. —**drow′si·ly**, *adv.* —**drow′si·ness**, *n.*

drub (drub), *v.t.*, **drubbed, drub·bing.** 1. to beat with a stick. 2. to defeat decisively, as in a game. —**drub′ber**, *n.* —**drub′bing**, *n.*

drudge (druj), *n.*, *v.*, **drudged, drudging.** —*n.* 1. a person who does menial, dull, or hard work. —*v.i.* 2. to perform such work. —**drudg′er·y**, *n.*

drug (drug), *n.*, *v.*, **drugged, drug·ging.** —*n.* 1. a chemical substance taken to cure disease or improve health. 2. a narcotic. 3. **drug on the market**, a commodity that is overabundant. —*v.t.* 4. to mix (food or drink) with a drug, esp. a stupefying or poisonous drug. 5. to stupefy or poison with a drug. [< MF *drogus* < Gmc]

drug·gist (drug′ist), *n.* 1. pharmacist. 2. the owner of a drugstore.

drug·store (drug′stōr′, -stôr′), *n.* the place of business of a pharmacist, usually also selling cosmetics, stationery, etc.

Dru·id (drŌ̄′id), *n.* (*often l.c.*) a priest among the ancient Celts of France, Britain, and Ireland. —**dru′id·ism**, *n.*

drum (drum), *n.*, *v.*, **drummed, drumming.** —*n.* 1. a percussion instrument consisting of a hollow, usually cylindrical body covered at one or both ends with a tightly stretched membrane. 2. the sound produced by such instrument. 3. any cylindrical object, esp. a large, metal receptacle for storing or transporting

liquids. 4. the eardrum. —*v.i.* 5. to beat a drum. 6. to tap one's fingers rhythmically on a hard surface. —*v.t.* 7. to perform by beating a drum. 8. to drive or force by persistent repetition: *to drum an idea into someone.* 9. **drum out**, to dismiss in disgrace. 10. **drum up**, to create (customers, etc.) through vigorous effort.

drum·beat (drum′bēt′), *n.* the sound of a drum.

drum·lin (drum′lin), *n.* a long, narrow or oval hill of glacial drift.

drum′ ma′jor, the marching leader of a band.

drum′ majorette′, a girl who twirls a baton, esp. while marching with a band, as in a parade.

drum·mer (drum′ər), *n.* 1. a person who plays a drum. 2. a traveling salesman.

drum·stick (drum′stik′), *n.* 1. a stick for beating a drum. 2. the meaty leg of a fowl.

drunk (drungk), *adj.* 1. having one's faculties impaired by an excess of alcoholic liquor. 2. dominated by emotion. 3. of or caused by intoxication. —*n.* 4. a drunken person. 5. a drinking party. —*v.* 6. a pp. of **drink.** —**Syn.** 1. inebriated, intoxicated, tipsy.

drunk·ard (drung′kərd), *n.* a person who is habitually or frequently drunk.

drunk·en (drung′kən), *adj.* 1. drunk. 2. given to drunkenness. 3. of or proceeding from intoxication. —**drunk′en·ly**, *adv.* —**drunk′en·ness**, *n.*

drupe (drŌ̄p), *n.* a fruit, as a peach, having a hard and woody inner seed and usually enclosing a single seed.

dry (drī), *adj.*, **dri·er, dri·est,** *v.*, **dried, dry·ing,** *n.*, *pl.* **drys.** —*adj.* 1. free from moisture. 2. having or characterized by little or no rain or ordinary moisture. 3. not under or on water. 4. not now containing water. 5. not yielding milk. 6. drained or evaporated away. 7. desiring drink. 8. served without butter, jam, etc. 9. lacking enough moisture to be succulent. 10. plain or unadorned. 11. dull or uninteresting. 12. expressed in a straight-faced, matter-of-fact way: *dry humor.* 13. indifferent or cold. 14. not productive. 15. (of wines) not sweet. 16. of nonliquid substances or commodities. 17. not allowing the manufacture and sale of alcoholic beverages: *a dry state.* —*v.t.*, *v.i.* 18. to make or become dry. 19. **dry up, a.** to make or become completely dry. **b.** to cease to exist. **c.** *Informal.* to stop talking. —*n.* 20. *Informal.* a prohibitionist. —**dry′a·ble**, *adj.* —**dry′ly**, *adv.* —**dry′ness**, *n.* —**Syn.** 2. arid, dehydrated, parched.

dry·ad (drī'əd, -ad), n. (often cap.) Class, Myth. a nymph of the woods.

dry' cell', an electric cell in which the electrolyte exists in the form of a paste.

dry-clean (drī'klēn'), v.t. to clean (garments, etc.) with a liquid other than water, as benzine. —**dry' clean'er**. —**dry' clean'ing**.

dry' dock', a dock in which a vessel can be lifted above the water for repairs, painting, etc.

dry·er (drī'ər), n. 1. a machine or appliance for removing moisture, as by forced ventilation or heat. 2. drier¹ (defs. 1, 2).

dry' farm'ing, farming in regions of insufficient rainfall, by rendering the soil more receptive of moisture. —**dry' farm'er**.

dry' goods', textile fabrics and related merchandise.

Dry' Ice', Trademark. solidified carbon dioxide, used as a refrigerant.

dry' meas'ure, the system of units of capacity used esp. in measuring dry commodities.

dry' run', 1. practice in firing arms without live ammunition. 2. a rehearsal or trial.

dry·wall (drī'wôl'), n. a prefabricated panel of dried plaster, used in wall construction.

D.S., Music. repeat from the sign. [< It dal segno]

ds, decistere; decisteres.

d.s., Com. 1. days after sight. 2. document signed.

D.S.C., 1. Distinguished Service Cross. 2. Doctor of Surgical Chiropody.

D.S.M., Distinguished Service Medal.

D.S.O., Distinguished Service Order.

d.s.p., died without offspring. [< L decessit sine prole]

DST, 1. daylight-saving time. 2. Doctor of Sacred Theology. Also, **D.S.T.**

d.t., See delirium tremens. Also, **d.t.'s**.

Du., 1. Duke. 2. Dutch.

du·al (dōō'əl, dyōō'-), adj. 1. of two. 2. composed of two people, items, etc., together. 3. having a double character or nature. —**du'al·ism'**, n. —**du'al·ist**, n., adj. —**du'al·is'tic**, adj. —**du·al'i·ty**, n. —**du'al·ly**, adv.

dub¹ (dub), v.t., **dubbed, dub·bing**. 1. to designate as a knight. 2. to give a name or nickname to. 3. to strike, rub, or make smooth, as leather. 4. Slang. to hit (a golf ball) clumsily. —**dub'ber**, n.

dub² (dub), n. Slang. an awkward, unskillful person.

dub³ (dub), v.t., **dubbed, dub·bing**. 1. to furnish (a film or tape) with a new sound track, as one in another language. 2. to add (music, speech, etc.) to a film or tape. —**dub'ber**, n.

dub·bin (dub'in), n. a mixture of tallow and oil used in dressing leather.

du·bi·e·ty (dōō bī'i tē, dyōō-), n., pl. **-ties** for 2. 1. great doubtfulness or doubt. 2. a matter of great doubt.

du·bi·ous (dōō'bē əs, dyōō'-), adj. 1. marked by or occasioning great doubt. 2. of doubtful quality. 3. inclined to doubt. —**du'bi·ous·ly**, adv. —**du'bi·ous·ness**, n. —Syn. 3. doubtful, irresolute, skeptical.

Dub·lin (dub'lin), n. the capital of Ireland.

du·cal (dōō'kəl, dyōō'-), adj. of a duke or dukedom.

duc·at (duk'ət), n. any of various gold coins formerly issued in parts of Europe.

duch·ess (duch'is), n. 1. the wife or widow of a duke. 2. a woman who rules a duchy.

duch·y (duch'ē), n., pl. **duch·ies**. the territory ruled by a duke or duchess.

duck¹ (duk), n., pl. **ducks, duck**. any of numerous webfooted swimming birds with a broad, flat bill and short legs.

duck² (duk), v.t., v.i. 1. to plunge or dip in water momentarily. 2. to lower (the head, body, etc.) suddenly, esp. to evade a blow. 3. to evade (a blow, unpleasant task, etc.).

duck³ (duk), n. 1. a heavy cotton fabric for tents, clothing, etc. 2. ducks, trousers made of this material.

duck·bill (duk'bil'), n. a small, aquatic, egg-laying mammal of Australia, having webbed feet and a bill like that of a duck.

duck·board (duk'bôrd', -bōrd'), n. boards laid as a floor over wet or muddy ground.

duck·ling (duk'ling), n. a young duck.

duck·pin (duk'pin'), n. 1. a short bowling pin used in a game resembling tenpins. 2. **duckpins**, the game.

duck·y (duk'ē), adj., **duck·i·er, duck·i·est**. Informal. fine or excellent.

duct (dukt), n. 1. any tube, canal, or pipe by which a fluid, air, glandular secretion, etc., is conveyed. 2. a single enclosed runway for electric cables. —**duct'less**, adj.

duc·tile (duk'tᵊl, -til), adj. 1. capable of being hammered out thin or drawn out into wire. 2. pliable or tractable. —**duc·til'i·ty**, n.

duct'less gland'. See endocrine gland.

dud (dud), n. Informal. 1. a failure. 2. a shell that fails to explode after being fired. 3. **duds**, clothes or belongings.

dude (dōōd, dyōōd), n. 1. a dandy or fop. 2. an Easterner vacationing on a ranch.

dude' ranch', a ranch operated as a vacation resort.

dudg·eon (duj'ən), *n. Literary.* anger (in the phrase *in high dudgeon*).

due (dōō, dyōō), *adj.* 1. owed or owing: *This bill is due.* 2. owing as a right. 3. proper or fitting. 4. adequate or sufficient. 5. expected or scheduled. 6. **due to,** a. attributable, as to a cause. b. because of. —*n.* 7. something owed or naturally belonging to someone. 8. Usually, **dues.** a regular fee or charge, esp. to a group. 9. **pay one's dues,** *Slang.* to gain experience, esp. by having gone through hardships. —*adv.* 10. directly or exactly: *a due east course.*

du·el (dōō'əl, dyōō'-), *n., v.,* **-eled, -el·ing** or **-elled, -el·ling.** —*n.* 1. a prearranged combat between two persons, fought with deadly weapons, esp. to settle a private quarrel. 2. any contest between two parties. —*v.t., v.i.* 3. to fight in a duel. —**du'el·ist, du'el·er,** *n.*

du·en·na (dōō en'ə, dyōō-), *n.* 1. (in Spain and Portugal) an older woman serving as chaperon of a young lady. 2. a governess.

due' proc'ess of law', the regular administration of the law, according to which no citizen may be denied his or her legal rights.

du·et (dōō et', dyōō-), *n.* a musical composition for two voices or instruments.

duf'fel bag', a large, cylindrical canvas bag for carrying personal effects.

duff·er (duf'ər), *n. Informal.* a plodding, clumsy, incompetent person.

dug¹ (dug), *v.* pt. and pp. of **dig.**

dug² (dug), *n.* the nipple of a female mammal.

dug·out (dug'out'), *n.* 1. a rough shelter dug in the ground, esp. one used by soldiers. 2. a boat made by hollowing out a log. 3. a roofed structure in which baseball players sit when not on the field.

duke (dōōk, dyōōk), *n.* 1. (in Continental Europe) the sovereign of a small state. 2. a British nobleman ranking immediately below a prince. 3. **dukes,** *Slang.* fists or hands. [< OF *duc* < L *dūc-* (s. of *dux* leader] —**duke'dom,** *n.*

dul·cet (dul'sit), *adj.* pleasant to the ear.

dul·ci·mer (dul'sə mər), *n.* a musical instrument with metal strings that are struck with light hammers.

dull (dul), *adj.* 1. mentally slow. 2. lacking keenness of perception. 3. not intense or acute. 4. slow in motion or action. 5. not lively. 6. boring or tedious. 7. not sharp or pointed. 8. lacking richness or intensity of color. 9. not bright or clear. —*v.t., v.i.* 10. to make or become dull. —**dull'ness, dul'ness,** *n.* —**dul'ly,** *adv.* —**Syn.** 1. obtuse, stupid,

unimaginative. 6. dreary, monotonous, uninteresting.

Du·luth (də lōōth'), *n.* a port in E Minnesota, on Lake Superior.

du·ly (dōō'lē, dyōō'-), *adv.* 1. in a proper manner. 2. in due time.

dumb (dum), *adj.* 1. without the power of speech, now esp. of animals. 2. temporarily unable to speak. 3. *Informal.* stupid or silly. —**dumb'ly,** *adv.* —**dumb'ness,** *n.* —**Usage.** 1. In referring to people, it is now preferable to use *mute.*

dumb·bell (dum'bel'), *n.* 1. a gymnastic device consisting of two weighted balls connected by a bar, used for exercising. 2. *Slang.* a stupid person.

dumb·wait·er (dum'wā'tər), *n.* a small elevator for moving food, garbage, etc., between floors.

dum·dum (dum'dum'), *n.* a soft-nosed bullet that expands greatly on impact.

dum-dum (dum'dum'), *n. Slang.* a silly, stupid person.

dum·found (dum found', dum'found'), *v.t.* to make speechless with amazement. Also, **dumb'found'.**

dum·my (dum'ē), *n., pl.* **-mies,** *adj.* —*n.* 1. an imitation or copy of something. 2. a representation of a human figure, as for displaying clothes in store windows. 3. *Informal.* a stupid person. 4. a person put forward to act for others while ostensibly acting for himself or herself. 5. *Bridge.* a. a player whose hand is exposed and played by his or her partner. b. the hand of cards so exposed. 6. an advance copy of a book or magazine, usually with only blank pages, made to show size, shape, etc. —*adj.* 7. counterfeit or fictitious.

dump (dump), *v.t.* 1. to drop or let fall in a mass. 2. to unload or empty out. 3. *Informal.* to rid oneself of suddenly and irresponsibly. 4. to put (goods) on the market in large quantities and at a low price, esp. in a foreign country. —*n.* 5. a place where garbage, refuse, etc., is deposited. 6. a collection of ammunition, stores, etc. 7. *Slang.* a dilapidated or disreputable place. —**dump'er,** *n.*

dumps (dumps), *n. Informal.* a depressed state of mind: *to be in the dumps.*

dump·ling (dump'ling), *n.* 1. a ball of steamed and seasoned dough, often served in soup or with stewed meat. 2. a dessert consisting of dough enclosing an apple or other fruit.

dump·y (dum'pē), *adj.,* **dump·i·er, dump·i·est.** short and stout. —**dump'i·ness,** *n.*

dun¹ (dun), *v.t.,* **dunned, dun·ning.** to

make repeated demands upon, esp. for the payment of a debt.

dun² (dun), *adj.* dull, grayish-brown.

dunce (duns), *n.* a stupid or ignorant person.

dun·der·head (dun′dər hed′), *n.* dunce.

dune (dōōn, dyōōn), *n.* a sand hill or ridge formed by the wind.

dune′ bug′gy. See beach buggy.

dung (dung), *n.* animal excrement.

dun·ga·ree (dung′gə rē′), *n.* **1.** a denim fabric, esp. blue denim. **2.** **dungarees,** work clothes, overalls, etc., of dungaree.

dun·geon (dun′jən), *n.* a strong, usually underground prison or cell.

dung·hill (dung′hil′), *n.* a heap of dung.

dunk (dungk), *v.t.* **1.** to dip (a doughnut, etc.) into coffee, etc., before eating. **2.** to submerge in a liquid. —*v.i.* **3.** to submerge oneself in water. —**dunk′er,** *n.*

du·o (dōō′ō, dyōō′ō), *n., pl.* **du·os. 1.** a couple or pair. **2.** duet.

du·o·dec·i·mal (dōō′ə des′ə məl, dyōō′-), *adj.* **1.** pertaining to twelfths or to the number twelve. —*n.* **2.** one of twelve equal parts.

du·o·de·num (dōō′ə dē′nəm, dyōō′-; dōō od′ən əm, dyōō-), *n., pl.* **du·o·de·na** (-nə), **du·o·de·num.** the first portion of the small intestine. —**du′o·de′nal,** *adj.*

dup., duplicate.

dupe (dōōp, dyōōp), *n., v.,* **duped, dup·ing.** —*n.* **1.** a person easily deceived or fooled. —*v.t.* **2.** to make a dupe of. —**dup′er,** *n.* —**dup′er·y,** *n.*

du·ple (dōō′pəl, dyōō′-), *adj. Music.* having two or sometimes a multiple of two beats in a measure.

du·plex (dōō′pleks, dyōō′-), *adj.* **1.** having two parts. —*n.* **2.** an apartment which has rooms on two floors. **3.** a house for two families.

du·pli·cate (*adj., n.* dōō′plə kit, dyōō′-; *v.* dōō′plə kāt′, dyōō′-), *adj., n., v.,* -**cat·ed, -cat·ing,** *adj.* —*n.* **1.** an exact copy. **2.** anything corresponding in all respects to something else. —*v.t.* **3.** to make an exact copy of (something). **4.** to do or make again. —*adj.* **5.** having or consisting of two identical parts. **6.** exactly like something else. —**du′pli·ca′tion,** *n.*

du·pli·ca·tor (dōō′plə kā′tər, dyōō′-), *n.* a machine for making duplicates, as a mimeograph. Also called **du′plicating machine′.**

du·plic·i·ty (dōō plis′i tē, dyōō-), *n., pl.* **·ties.** deceitfulness in speech or conduct.

du·ra·ble (dōōr′ə bəl, dyōōr′-), *adj.* highly resistant to wear, decay, etc. —**du′ra·bil′i·ty,** *n.* —**dur′a·bly,** *adv.*

du′rable press′. See permanent press.

dur·ance (dōōr′əns, dyōōr′-), *n. Liter-*

ary. imprisonment, esp. long confinement.

du·ra·tion (dōō rā′shən, dyōō-), *n.* **1.** continuance in time. **2.** the length of time during which something continues or exists. —**du·ra′tion·al,** *adj.*

du·ress (dōō res′, dyōō-, dōōr′is, dyōōr′-), *n.* **1.** compulsion by threat. **2.** wrongful imprisonment.

dur·ing (dōōr′ing, dyōōr′-), *prep.* **1.** throughout the duration of. **2.** at some point in the course of.

durst (dûrst), *v. Archaic.* pt. of dare.

du·rum (dōōr′əm), *n.* a wheat whose grain yields flour used in making macaroni, spaghetti, etc.

dusk (dusk), *n.* **1.** the period of partial darkness between day and night. **2.** shade or gloom. —**dusk′y,** *adj.* —**dusk′i·ness,** *n.*

dust (dust), *n.* **1.** earth or other matter in fine, dry particles. **2.** the earth's surface. **3.** what is left of anything after death or destruction. **4.** anything worthless. **5.** **bite the dust,** to be killed, esp. in battle. —*v.t.* **6.** to wipe the dust from. **7.** to sprinkle with a powder or dust. —*v.i.* **8.** to wipe dust from furniture, etc. —**dust′less,** *adj.*

dust′ bowl′, an area subject to dust storms.

dust′ dev′il, a small whirlwind made visible by dust and sand.

dust·er (dus′tər), *n.* **1.** a person or thing that dusts. **2.** a cloth, brush, etc., for removing dust. **3.** an outer garment worn to protect the clothing from dust. **4.** a woman's lightweight housecoat or summer coat.

dust·pan (dust′pan′), *n.* a short-handled, shovellike pan into which dust is swept.

dust′ storm′, a storm of dust-filled wind during a period of drought.

dust·y (dus′tē), *adj.,* **dust·i·er, dust·i·est. 1.** filled or covered with dust. **2.** like or consisting of dust. **3.** grayish: *dusty pink.* —**dust′i·ly,** *adv.* —**dust′i·ness,** *n.*

Dutch (duch), *adj.* **1.** of the Netherlands, its people, or their language. **2.** *Slang.* German. **3.** **go Dutch,** *Informal.* to have each person pay his or her own share. —*n.* **4.** the people of the Netherlands collectively. **5.** the language of the Netherlands. **6.** **in Dutch,** *Slang.* in trouble or disfavor. —**Dutch′man,** *n.*

Dutch′ door′, a door consisting of two units horizontally divided so that they can be opened separately.

Dutch′ elm′ disease′, a fungous disease of elms, characterized by wilting, yellowing, and falling of the leaves.

Dutch′ ov′en, a heavy kettle with a close-fitting lid, for pot roasts, stews, etc.

Dutch′ treat′, *Informal.* a meal or entertainment for which each person pays his or her own share.

Dutch′ un′cle, *Informal.* a person who criticizes with unsparing frankness.

du·te·ous (dŌŌ′tē əs, dyŌŌ′-), *adj. Literary.* dutiful. —**du′te·ous·ly,** *adv.*

du·ti·a·ble (dŌŌ′tē ə bəl, dyŌŌ′-), *adj.* subject to customs duty.

du·ti·ful (dŌŌ′ti fəl, dyŌŌ′-), *adj.* **1.** performing the duties expected or required of one. **2.** proceeding from a sense of duty: *dutiful attention.* —**du′ti·ful·ly,** *adv.* —**du′ti·ful·ness,** *n.*

du·ty (dŌŌ′tē, dyŌŌ′-), *n., pl.* **-ties. 1.** something that one is required to do by moral or legal obligation. **2.** action required by one's position or occupation. **3.** respectful conduct due to a parent, etc. **4.** assigned service or work, esp. military service: *his Vietnam duty.* **5.** a tax imposed by law on the import or export of goods. **6.** the measure of effectiveness of any machine. **7. off duty,** not at one's work. **8. on duty,** at one's work.

D.V., 1. God willing. [< L *Deo volente*] **2.** Douay Version (Bible).

D.V.M., Doctor of Veterinary Medicine.

dwarf (dwôrf), *n., pl.* **dwarfs, dwarves** (dwôrvz), *adj., v.* —*n.* **1.** a person, animal, or plant of abnormally small size. —*adj.* **2.** unusually small. —*v.t.* **3.** to cause to appear smaller in size, character, etc. **4.** to stunt the growth of. —**dwarf′ish,** *adj.* —**dwarf′ism,** *n.*

dwell (dwel), *v.i.,* **dwelt** (dwelt) or **dwelled, dwell·ing. 1.** *Literary.* to live permanently. **2. dwell on** or **upon,** to linger over in thought or language. —**dwell′er,** *n.*

dwell·ing (dwel′ing), *n.* a place of residence.

dwin·dle (dwin′dəl), *v.i., v.t.,* **-dled, -dling.** to make or become smaller and smaller.

dwt, pennyweight. [< L *d(enarius* penny) + *w(eigh)t*]

DX, distance (used esp. to designate difficult shortwave reception).

Dy, dysprosium.

dyb·buk (dib′ək), *n., pl.* **dyb·buks, dyb·buk·im** (di bŏŏk′im) *Jewish Folklore.* a demon that enters the body of a person and controls it.

dye (dī), *n., v.,* **dyed, dye·ing.** —*n.* **1.** a substance used to color textiles, paper, hair, etc. **2.** a color or hue produced by dyeing. —*v.t., v.i.* **3.** to color with a dye. —**dye′er,** *n.*

dyed-in-the-wool (dīd′ən t͟hə wŏŏl′), *adj.* complete or absolute.

dye·stuff (dī′stuf′), *n.* a material yielding or used as a dye.

dy·ing (dī′ing), *adj.* **1.** approaching death. **2.** given or uttered just before death. **3.** drawing to a close. —*v.* **4.** ppr. of **die¹.**

dyke (dīk), *n.* dike.

dy·nam·ic (dī nam′ik), *adj.* **1.** forceful and energetic. **2.** of or pertaining to physical force related to motion. Also, **dy·nam′i·cal.** —**dy·nam′i·cal·ly,** *adv.*

dy·nam·ics (dī nam′iks), *n.* **1.** the branch of mechanics that deals with the motion and equilibrium of systems under the action of forces. **2.** the moving forces in any field.

dy·na·mism (dī′nə miz′əm), *n.* great force or power. —**dy′na·mist,** *n.* —**dy′na·mis′tic,** *adj.*

dy·na·mite (dī′nə mīt′), *n., v.,* **-mit·ed, -mit·ing.** —*n.* **1.** a high explosive of nitroglycerin mixed with an absorbent substance. —*v.t.* **2.** to blow up with dynamite. —**dy′na·mit′er,** *n.*

dy·na·mo (dī′nə mō′), *n., pl.* **-mos. 1.** an electric generator, esp. for direct current. **2.** *Informal.* an energetic, forceful person.

dy·na·mom·e·ter (dī′nə mom′i tər), *n.* a device for measuring mechanical force or power.

dy·nas·ty (dī′nə stē), *n., pl.* **-ties.** a sequence of rulers from the same family or group. —**dy·nas·tic** (dī-nas′tik), *adj.*

dys-, a prefix meaning "ill" or "bad": *dysfunction.*

dys·en·ter·y (dis′ən ter′ē), *n.* an infectious disease of the colon, with painful diarrhea that becomes mucous and hemorrhagic. —**dys′en·ter′ic,** *adj.*

dys·func·tion (dis fungk′shən), *n.* malfunctioning, as of a body organ.

dys·lex·i·a (dis lek′sē ə), *n.* an impairment of the ability to read due to a brain defect. —**dys·lex′ic,** *adj., n.*

dys·pep·sia (dis pep′shə, -sē ə), *n.* impaired digestion. Also, **dys·pep·sy** (dis pep′sē). —**dys·pep′tic,** *adj., n.*

dys·pro·si·um (dis prō′sē əm, -shē-), *n. Chem.* a rare-earth metallic element. *Symbol:* Dy; *at wt.:* 162.50; *at no.:* 66.

dys·tro·phy (dis′trə fē), *n.* any of a number of disorders characterized by weakening or abnormal development of muscle. Also, **dys·tro·phi·a** (di strō′fē ə). —**dys·troph·ic** (dis-trof′ik), *adj.*

dz., dozen; dozens.

E

E, e (ē), *n., pl.* **E's** or **Es, e's** or **es.**
the fifth letter of the English alpha-
bet, a vowel.

E, 1. east. **2.** eastern. **3.** English.
4. excellent.

E, 1. the fifth in order or in a series.
2. (*sometimes l.c.*) a grade, as of
academic work, that indicates work
that is unacceptable. **3.** *Music.* the
third tone in the scale of C major.
4. See **electromotive force. 5.** *Physics.* energy.

e, a constant equal to 2.7182818 . . .,
used as the base of natural loga-
rithms.

E., 1. Earl. **2.** Earth. **3.** east. **4.**
Easter. **5.** eastern. **6.** engineer. **7.**
engineering. **8.** English.

e., 1. eldest. **2.** engineer. **3.** engineering. **4.** *Baseball.* error.

ea., each.

each (ēch), *adj.* **1.** every one of two
or more considered individually.
—*pron.* **2.** each one. —*adv.* **3.** to
or for each.
—**Usage. 2.** Careful writers and
speakers make certain that EACH,
which is a singular pronoun, is always used with a singular verb:
*Each of the houses is painted a
different color.*

each′ oth′er, one toward the other
or others: *The two men distrust each
other.*
—**Usage.** Careful users of English
restrict EACH OTHER to two persons,
things, etc., and prefer ONE ANOTHER
for more than two.

ea·ger (ē′gər), *adj.* **1.** impatiently
longing. **2.** enthusiastic or earnest.
—**ea′ger·ly,** *adv.* —**ea′ger·ness,** *n.*
—**Syn.** anxious, avid, keen.

ea·gle (ē′gəl), *n.* **1.** a large bird of
prey noted for its size, strength, and
powers of flight and vision. **2.** a
former gold coin of the U.S., equal
to 10 dollars. **3.** a golf score of two
below par on any hole.

ea·glet (ē′glit), *n.* a young eagle.

-ean, var. of **-an:** *European.*

E.&O.E., errors and omissions excepted.

ear¹ (ēr), *n.* **1.** the organ of hearing
in man and other vertebrates. **2.** the
external part of this. **3.** the sense
of hearing. **4.** keen perception of
the differences of sound. **5.** any
part that resembles an ear. **6.** **be all
ears,** to listen with all one's attention. **7.** **give ear,** to listen carefully.
Also, **lend an ear. 8. play by ear,**
to play (music) without the aid of

a score. **9. play it by ear,** to improvise. —**eared,** *adj.* —**ear′less,**
adj.

ear² (ēr), *n.* the grain-bearing part of
a cereal plant, as corn, wheat, etc.

ear·ache (ēr′āk′), *n.* a pain in the
ear.

ear·drum (ēr′drum′), *n.* See **tympanic
membrane.**

ear·flap (ēr′flap′), *n.* either of a pair
of flaps attached to a cap, for covering the ears in cold weather. Also
called **ear·lap** (ēr′lap′).

earl (ûrl), *n.* a British nobleman of
a rank below a marquis and above
a viscount. —**earl′dom,** *n.*

ear·lobe (ēr′lōb′), *n.* the soft, pendulous, lower part of the external
ear.

ear·ly (ûr′lē), *adv., adj.,* **-li·er, -li·est.**
1. in the first part of a period of
time, series of events, etc. **2.** before
the usual or appointed time. **3.** belonging far back in time. **4.** occurring in the near future. **5. early on,**
during an early stage. —**ear′li·ness,**
n.

ear·mark (ēr′märk′), *n.* **1.** an identifying or distinguishing mark, originally made on the ear of an animal.
—*v.t.* **2.** to mark with an earmark.
3. to set aside for a specific purpose.

ear·muff (ēr′muf′), *n.* one of a pair
of adjustable coverings for the ears
in cold weather.

earn (ûrn), *v.t.* **1.** to gain in return
for one's service. **2.** to get through
merit. **3.** to gain as due return
or profit. —**earn′er,** *n.*

ear·nest¹ (ûr′nist), *adj.* **1.** serious in
intention, purpose, or effort. **2.** showing depth of feeling. **3.** seriously
important. —*n.* **4.** full seriousness,
as of intention or purpose: *in earnest.*
—**ear′nest·ly,** *adv.* —**ear′nest·ness,** *n.*

ear·nest² (ûr′nist), *n.* something given
or done in advance as a pledge of
the remainder.

earn·ings (ûr′ningz), *n.pl.* money
earned, esp. wages or profits.

ear·phone (ēr′fōn′), *n.* a receiver for
a radio, etc., fitted over or into
the ear.

ear·plug (ēr′plug′), *n.* a plug for the
opening of the outer ear to keep
out water or noise.

ear·ring (ēr′ring′, -ing), *n.* an ornament worn on the earlobe.

ear·shot (ēr′shot′), *n.* the range within which a sound, etc., can be heard.

ear·split·ting (ēr′split′ing), *adj.* irritatingly loud.

283

earth (ûrth), *n.* **1.** (*often cap.*) the planet on which man lives, third in order from the sun. **2.** this planet in contrast to heaven and hell. **3.** the surface of this planet. **4.** soil and dirt. —**earth′ward,** *adj., adv.*

earth·en (ûr′thən), *adj.* composed of earth or baked clay.

earth·en·ware (ûr′thən wâr′), *n.* pottery of baked or hardened clay.

earth·ling (ûrth′ling), *n.* an inhabitant of earth.

earth·ly (ûrth′lē), *adj.,* **-li·er, -li·est. 1.** of the earth or this world, esp. as opposed to heaven. **2.** possible or conceivable: *of no earthly use.* —**earth′li·ness,** *n.* —**Syn. 1.** mundane, worldly.

earth′ moth′er, the earth conceived of as the female principle of fertility and the source of all life.

earth·quake (ûrth′kwāk′), *n.* a vibration or movement of a part of the earth's surface.

earth′ sci′ence, any of various sciences, as geography, geology, etc., that deal with the earth, its composition, or any of its changing aspects.

earth-shak·ing (ûrth′shā′king), *adj.* affecting basic beliefs, attitudes, etc.

earth·work (ûrth′wûrk′), *n.* a construction formed chiefly of earth for protection against enemy fire.

earth·worm (ûrth′wûrm′), *n.* a long, slender worm that burrows in soil.

earth·y (ûr′thē), *adj.,* **earth·i·er, earth·i·est. 1.** of, consisting of, or like earth or soil. **2.** realistic or practical. **3.** coarse or unrefined. —**earth′i·ly,** *adv.* —**earth′i·ness,** *n.*

ear·wax (ēr′waks′), *n.* cerumen.

ear·wig (ēr′wig′), *n.* an elongated nocturnal insect having a pair of large, movable pincers at the rear of the abdomen.

ease (ēz), *n., v.,* **eased, eas·ing.** —*n.* **1.** freedom from labor, pain, or anxiety. **2.** freedom from difficulty. **3.** freedom from stiffness or formality. —*v.t.* **4.** to give rest or relief to. **5.** to free from care. **6.** to lighten or lessen. **7.** to move with great care. **8.** to facilitate. —*v.i.* **9.** to become less painful, difficult, etc. —**eas′er,** *n.*

ea·sel (ē′zəl), *n.* a stand for supporting an artist's canvas, etc.

ease·ment (ēz′mənt), *n.* **1.** *Law.* a right held by one property owner to make use of the land of another. **2.** *Rare.* an easing or relief.

eas·i·ly (ē′zə lē, ēz′lē), *adv.* **1.** with ease. **2.** by far. **3.** most likely.

east (ēst), *n.* **1.** a cardinal point of the compass, 90° to the right of north. **2.** the direction in which this point lies. **3.** (*usually cap.*) a quarter or territory situated in this direc-

tion. **4. the East,** a. the Orient. b. the eastern part of the U.S. —*adj.* **5.** in, from, or toward the east. —*adv.* **6.** toward or from the east.

East′ A′sia, the area of China, Japan, Korea, and the Soviet Union in Asia.

East′ Ber′lin′, the capital of East Germany.

East′ Chi′na Sea′, a part of the N Pacific, bounded by China and Japan.

East·er (ē′stər), *n.* an annual Christian festival in commemoration of the resurrection of Jesus Christ.

east·er·ly (ē′stər lē), *adj., adv.* **1.** toward the east. **2.** from the east.

east·ern (ē′stərn), *adj.* **1.** toward or situated in the east. **2.** coming from the east. **3.** (*often cap.*) of the East. **4.** (*cap.*) of or pertaining to the Christian churches originating in countries formerly comprising the Eastern Roman Empire.

east·ern·er (ē′stər nər), *n.* (*often cap.*) a native or inhabitant of an eastern area, esp. of the eastern U.S.

East′ern Hem′isphere, the eastern part of the earth, including Asia, Africa, Australia, and Europe.

East′ Ger′many, a country in central Europe bounded by the Baltic Sea to the north.

East′ In′dies, the Malay Archipelago. —**East′ In′dian.**

east·ward (ēst′word), *adj.* **1.** moving or situated toward the east. —*adv.* **2.** Also, **eastwards.** toward the east. —**east′ward·ly,** *adj., adv.*

eas·y (ē′zē), *adj.,* **eas·i·er, eas·i·est,** *adv.* —*adj.* **1.** not difficult. **2.** free from pain, worry, etc. **3.** comfortable or pleasant. **4.** easygoing or relaxed. **5.** not harsh or strict. **6.** not forced or hurried. **7.** gradual, as a flight of stairs. —*adv.* **8.** *Informal.* in an easy manner: *to take it easy.* —**eas′i·ness,** *n.*

eas′y chair′, an upholstered armchair for lounging.

eas·y·go·ing (ē′zē gō′ing), *adj.* calm and unworried.

eat (ēt), *v.,* **ate, eat·en** (ēt′ən), **eat·ing,** *n.* —*v.t.* **1.** to take into the mouth and swallow for nourishment. **2.** to wear away or corrode. **3.** to ravage or devastate. **4.** to make (a hole, etc.), as by gnawing or corrosion. —*v.i.* **5.** to consume food. **6. be eating someone,** *Slang.* to cause someone to be greatly troubled. —*n.* **7. eats,** *Slang.* food. —**eat′a·ble,** *adj., n.* —**eat′er,** *n.*

eat·er·y (ēt′ə rē), *n., pl.* **-er·ies.** *Slang.* a restaurant, usually small and cheap.

eaves (ēvz), *n.pl.* the overhanging lower edge of a roof. —**eaved,** *adj.*

eaves·drop (ēvz′drop′), *v.i.*, **-dropped,**
-drop·ping. to listen secretly to a
private conversation. —**eaves′drop′-**
per, *n.*

ebb (eb), *n.* **1.** the flowing back of
the tide as the water returns to the
sea. **2.** a point of decline. —*v.i.* **3.**
to flow back or away. **4.** to decline
or decay.

eb·on·ite (eb′ə nīt′), *n.* vulcanite.

eb·on·y (eb′ə nē), *n.*, *pl.* **-on·ies,** *adj.*
—*n.* **1.** a hard, heavy wood, highly
prized when black, from various
tropical trees of southern India and
Ceylon. —*adj.* **2.** made of ebony.
3. of a deep, lustrous black.

e·bul·lient (i bul′yənt), *adj.* **1.** overflowing with enthusiasm. **2.** boiling
up. —**e·bul′lience,** *n.* —**e·bul′lient-**
ly, *adv.*

eb·ul·li·tion (eb′ə lish′ən), *n.* **1.** an
outburst, as of passion or feeling. **2.**
a boiling up of a liquid.

EC, European Community (encom-
passing the European Common
Market).

ec·cen·tric (ik sen′trik, ek-), *adj.* **1.**
deviating from the customary char-
acter, practice, etc. **2.** not concentric: *eccentric circles.* **3.** (of an axle,
etc.) not situated in the center. **4.**
deviating from a circular form, as
an elliptic orbit. —*n.* **5.** an eccentric
person. **6.** a device for converting
circular motion into reciprocating
rectilinear motion, consisting of a
disk fixed out of center to a shaft.
—**ec·cen′tri·cal·ly,** *adv.* —**ec·cen-**
tric′i·ty (ek′sən tris′i tē, ek′sen-), *n.*

Eccl., Ecclesiastes. Also, **Eccles.**

eccl., **1.** ecclesiastic. **2.** ecclesiastical.
Also, **eccles.**

Ec·cle·si·as·tes (i klē′zē as′tēz), *n.* a
book of the Bible.

ec·cle·si·as·tic (i klē′zē as′tik), *n.* **1.** a
member of the clergy. —*adj.* Rare.
2. ecclesiastical.

ec·cle·si·as·ti·cal (i klē′zē as′ti kəl),
adj. of the church or the clergy.

ECG, electrocardiogram.

ech·e·lon (esh′ə lon′), *n.* **1.** a level of
command, authority, or rank. **2.** a
steplike formation of troops, airplanes, etc.

ech·o (ek′ō), *n.*, *pl.* **ech·oes,** *v.*, **ech-**
oed, ech·o·ing. —*n.* **1.** a repetition
of sound produced by the reflection
of sound waves from an obstructing
surface. **2.** a sound so produced. **3.**
any repetition or close imitation. **4.**
the reflection of a radio wave, as in
radar. —*v.i.* **5.** to resound with an
echo. **6.** to be repeated by an echo.
—*v.t.* **7.** to repeat by or as by an
echo. **8.** to repeat or imitate. —**ech′-**
o·er, *n.* —**e·cho·ic** (e kō′ik), *adj.*
—**ech′o·less,** *adj.*

ech·o·lo·ca·tion (ek′ō lō kā′shən), *n.*
a method of locating objects by

determining the time for an echo
to return and the direction from
which it returns, as by radar and
sonar.

é·clair (ā klâr′, ā′klâr), *n.* a cream
puff of oblong shape, filled with
whipped cream or custard.

é·clat (ā klä′), *n.* **1.** brilliance of
success. **2.** showy display. **3.** ac-
claim or praise.

ec·lec·tic (i klek′tik), *adj.* selecting
or made up of elements from different sources. —**ec·lec′ti·cal·ly,** *adv.*
—**ec·lec′ti·cism,** *n.*

e·clipse (i klips′), *n.*, *v.*, **e·clipsed,**
e·clips·ing. —*n.* **1.** the darkening of
the light of the moon by the intervention of the earth between it and
the sun or of the light of the sun by
the intervention of the moon between it and a point on the earth. **2.**
a loss of status, reputation, etc. —*v.t.*
3. to cause to undergo eclipse. **4.**
to surpass or outshine

e·clip·tic (i klip′tik), *n.* the apparent
annual path of the sun in the
heavens.

ec·logue (ek′lôg, -log), *n.* a pastoral
poem.

E.C.M., European Common Market.

e·co·cide (ek′ō sīd′, ē′kō-), *n.* the
ruin of the human environment, esp.
through the use of pollutants.

ecol., **1.** ecological. **2.** ecology.

e·col·o·gy (i kol′ə jē), *n.* the branch
of biology dealing with the relations
between organisms and their environment. —**ec·o·log·i·cal** (ek′ə loj′i kəl,
ē′kə-), **ec′o·log′ic,** *adj.* —**ec′o·log′i-**
cal·ly, *adv.* —**e·col′o·gist,** *n.*

econ., **1.** economic. **2.** economics. **3.**
economy.

e·co·nom·ic (ē′kə nom′ik, ek′ə-), *adj.*
1. pertaining to the production, distribution, and use of income, wealth,
and commodities. **2.** of the science
of economics. **3.** pertaining to one's
personal finances.

e·co·nom·i·cal (ē′kə nom′i kəl, ek′ə-),
adj. **1.** avoiding waste or extravagance. **2.** economic. —**e′co·nom′-**
i·cal·ly, *adv.* —**Syn. 1.** frugal, thrifty.

e·co·nom·ics (ē′kə nom′iks, ek′ə-), *n.*
1. the science treating of the production, distribution, and consumption
of goods and services. **2.** financial
considerations. —**e·con·o·mist** (i-
kon′ə mist), *n.*

e·con·o·mize (i kon′ə mīz′), *v.i.,*
-mized, -miz·ing. to avoid waste or
extravagance. —**e·con′o·miz′er,** *n.*

e·con·o·my (i kon′ə mē), *n.*, *pl.* **-mies.**
1. thrifty management of money,
materials, etc. **2.** an instance of this.
3. the management of the resources
of a community, country, etc. **4.** an
organized system or method. —*adj.*
5. economical: *economy size.*

ec·o·sys·tem (ek′ō sis′təm, ē′kō-), *n.* a system formed by the interaction of a community of organisms with their environment.

ec·ru (ek′rōō, ā′krōō), *adj., n.* pale tan.

ec·sta·sy (ek′stə sē), *n., pl.* **-sies. 1.** rapturous delight. **2.** an overpowering emotion or exaltation. —**ec·stat·ic** (ek stat′ik), *adj.* —**ec·stat′i·cal·ly,** *adv.*

-ectomy, a combining form meaning "surgical excision": *tonsillectomy.*

ec·to·plasm (ek′tə plaz′əm), *n.* the supposed emanation from the body of a medium.

Ecua., Ecuador.

Ec·ua·dor (ek′wə dôr′), *n.* a country in NW South America.

ec·u·men·i·cal (ek′yōō men′i kəl), *adj.* **1.** pertaining to the whole Christian church. **2.** promoting or fostering religious, esp. Christian, unity throughout the world. —**ec′u·men′i·cal·ism′,** *n.* —**ec·u·me·nic′i·ty** (-mə nis′i tē, -me-), *n.* —**ec·u·me·nism** (ek′yōō mə niz′əm), **ec·u·men·i·cism** (ek′yōō men′i siz′əm), *n.* —**ec′u·men′i·cal·ly,** *adv.*

ec·ze·ma (ek′sə mə, eg′zə-, ig zē′-), *n.* an inflammatory disease of the skin attended with itching and red, scaly patches. —**ec·zem·a·tous** (ig zem′ə-təs), *adj.*

-ed¹, a suffix forming the past tense of most verbs: *She waited.*

-ed², a suffix used to form: **a.** the past participle of most verbs: *He had crossed the river.* **b.** a participial adjective indicating "conditioned" or "quality": *inflated balloons.*

-ed³, a suffix forming adjectives from nouns: *moneyed.*

ed., **1.** edited. **2.** edition. **3.** editor. **4.** education.

E·dam (ē′dəm, ē′dam), *n.* a mild, hard, yellow cheese.

ed·dy (ed′ē), *n., pl.* **-dies,** *v.,* **-died, -dy·ing.** —*n.* **1.** a current at variance with the main current in a stream of liquid or gas. **2.** a small whirlpool. —*v.t., v.i.* **3.** to whirl in eddies.

e·del·weiss (ād′°l vīs′, -wīs′), *n.* a small Alpine herb having white woolly leaves and flowers.

e·de·ma (i dē′mə), *n., pl.* **-ma·ta** (-mə-tə). excessive fluid in body cavities or tissues. —**e·dem·a·tous** (i dem′ə-təs), *adj.*

E·den (ēd′°n), *n.* **1.** the place where Adam and Eve first lived. **2.** paradise (def. 3).

edge (ej), *n., v.,* **edged, edg·ing.** —*n.* **1.** a line at which a surface terminates or ends. **2.** a brink or verge: *the edge of a precipice.* **3.** the thin, sharp side of a cutting blade. **4.** keenness of language, appetite, etc. **5.** *Informal.* advantage: *He gained the edge on his opponent.* **6. on edge, a.** nervous or tense. **b.** impatient or eager. —*v.t.* **7.** to provide with an edge. **8.** to make (one's way) gradually. —*v.i.* **9.** to move gradually. —**edg′er,** *n.*

edge·wise (ej′wīz′), *adv.* **1.** with the edge forward. **2.** sideways. Also, **edge·ways** (ej′wāz′).

edg·ing (ej′ing), *n.* something that forms or is placed along an edge.

edg·y (ej′ē), *adj.,* **edg·i·er, edg·i·est. 1.** nervously irritable. **2.** having a sharp edge. —**edg′i·ness,** *n.*

ed·i·ble (ed′ə bəl), *adj.* **1.** fit to be eaten as food. —*n.* **2.** Usually, **edibles.** food. —**ed′i·bil′i·ty, ed′i·ble·ness,** *n.*

e·dict (ē′dikt), *n.* a decree issued by the sovereign of a nation.

ed·i·fi·ca·tion (ed′ə fə kā′shən), *n.* enlightenment or moral improvement.

ed·i·fice (ed′ə fis), *n.* a large, usually impressive building.

ed·i·fy (ed′ə fī′), *v.t.,* **-fied, -fy·ing.** to instruct or benefit, esp. morally. —**ed′i·fi′er,** *n.*

Ed·in·burgh (ed′°n bûr′ō, -bur′ō), *n.* the capital of Scotland.

Ed·i·son (ed′i sən), *n.* **Thomas Al·va** (al′və), 1847–1931, U.S. inventor.

ed·it (ed′it), *v.t.* **1.** to supervise or direct the preparation of (a newspaper, magazine, etc.). **2.** to prepare and arrange (materials) for publication. —**ed′i·tor,** *n.* —**ed′i·tor·ship′,** *n.*

edit., **1.** edited. **2.** edition. **3.** editor.

e·di·tion (i dish′ən), *n.* **1.** the format in which a literary work is published. **2.** the whole number of impressions or copies of a book, newspaper, etc., printed at one time. **3.** a version of anything.

ed·i·to·ri·al (ed′i tôr′ē əl, -tôr′-), *n.* **1.** an article or statement in a newspaper or other medium presenting the opinion of the publisher, editor, or owner. —*adj.* **2.** of an editor or editing. **3.** of or involved in the preparation of an editorial. —**ed′i·to′ri·al·ly,** *adv.*

ed·i·to·ri·al·ize (ed′i tôr′ē ə līz′, -tôr′-), *v.i.,* **-ized, -iz·ing. 1.** to set forth opinions in an editorial. **2.** to inject opinions into a factual account. —**ed′i·to′ri·al·i·za′tion,** *n.* —**ed′i·to′ri·al·iz′er,** *n.*

Ed·mon·ton (ed′mən tən), *n.* the capital of Alberta, Canada.

EDP, electronic data processing.

EDT, Eastern daylight time. Also, **E.D.T.**

educ., **1.** education. **2.** educational.

ed·u·ca·ble (ej′ōō kə bəl, ed′yōō-), *adj.* capable of being educated. —**ed′u·ca·bil′i·ty,** *n.*

ed·u·cate (ej'ōō kāt', ed'yōō-), v.t., -cat·ed, -cat·ing. 1. to develop the faculties and powers of (a person) by teaching. 2. to send to school. —ed'u·ca'tor, n.

ed·u·ca·tion (ej'ōō kā'shən, ed'yōō-), n. 1. the act or process of educating a person. 2. the result thus produced. 3. the science or art of teaching. —ed'u·ca'tion·al, adj. —ed'u·ca'tion·al·ly, adv.

educa'tional tel'evision, any television program that is educational, whether on a commercial or a non-commercial station.

e·duce (i dōōs', i dyōōs'), v.t., e·duced, e·duc·ing. 1. to draw out (something latent, etc.). 2. to infer or deduce.

-ee, a suffix denoting a person who is the object of some action, or who undergoes or receives something: mortgagee; employee.

E.E., Electrical Engineer.

EEC, European Economic Community.

EEG, electroencephalogram.

eel (ēl), n., pl. eel, eels. a snakelike fish. —eel'y (-ē), adj.

e'er (âr), adv. Chiefly Literary. ever.

-eer, a suffix denoting a person who is concerned with, employed in connection with, or busies himself or herself with something: profiteer.

ee·rie (ēr'ē), adj., -ri·er, -ri·est. uncannily weird. Also, ee'ry. —ee'ri·ly, adv.

eff., efficiency.

ef·face (i fās'), v.t., -faced, -fac·ing. 1. to remove by or as if by rubbing out. 2. to make (oneself) inconspicuous. —ef·face'a·ble, adj. —ef·face'a·bly, adv. —ef·face'ment, n. —ef·fac'er, n.

ef·fect (i fekt'), n. 1. something that is produced by an agent or cause. 2. power to produce or cause results. 3. operation or execution. 4. a mental impression produced. 5. main idea or meaning: He wrote to that effect. 6. in effect, a. virtually. b. essentially. c. in force. 7. take effect, to go into operation. —v.t. 8. to bring about or accomplish. 9. to produce or make. —Syn. 1. consequence, outcome, result.

ef·fec·tive (i fek'tiv), adj. 1. producing an expected effect. 2. operative or functioning. 3. impressive or striking. —ef·fec'tive·ly, adv. —ef·fec'tive·ness, n.

ef·fects (i fekts'), n.pl. personal property.

ef·fec·tu·al (i fek'chōō əl), adj. 1. producing an intended effect or result. 2. valid or binding. —ef·fec'tu·al·ly, adv.

ef·fec·tu·ate (i fek'chōō āt'), v.t., -at·ed, -at·ing. to effect (def. 8).

ef·fem·i·nate (i fem'ə nit), adj. (of a man) soft or delicate to an unmanly degree in traits, tastes, habits, etc. —ef·fem'i·na·cy (-nə sē), n. —ef·fem'i·nate·ly, adv.

ef·fen·di (i fen'dē), n. (in eastern Mediterranean countries) a well-educated or aristocratic man.

ef·fer·ent (ef'ər ənt), adj. Physiol. conducting away from an organ or part.

ef·fer·vesce (ef'ər ves'), v.i., -vesced, -vesc·ing. 1. to give off bubbles of gas, as fermenting liquors. 2. to show liveliness, etc. —ef·fer·ves'cence, n. —ef·fer·ves'cent, adj. —ef·fer·ves'cent·ly, adv.

ef·fete (i fēt'), adj. 1. exhausted of vigor or energy. 2. decadent or weak. —ef·fete'ly, adv. —ef·fete'ness, n.

ef·fi·ca·cious (ef'ə kā'shəs), adj. effective as a means, remedy, etc. —ef'fi·ca'cious·ly, adv. —ef·fi·ca·cy (ef'ə kə sē), n.

ef·fi·cient (i fish'ənt), adj. performing or functioning in the least wasteful manner. —ef·fi'cien·cy, n. —ef·fi'cient·ly, adv.

ef·fi·gy (ef'i jē), n., pl. -gies. 1. an image, as on a monument. 2. a crude representation of someone disliked.

ef·flo·resce (ef'lə res'), v.i., -resced, -resc·ing. to burst into bloom.

ef·flo·res·cence (ef'lə res'əns), n. 1. the state or a period of flowering. 2. an example or result of growth and development. —ef'flo·res'cent, adj.

ef·flu·ence (ef'lōō əns), n. 1. the process or action of flowing out. 2. something that flows out. —ef'flu·ent, adj., n.

ef·flu·vi·um (i flōō'vē əm), n., pl. -vi·a (-vē ə), -vi·ums. a disagreeable or noxious vapor. —ef·flu'vi·al, adj.

ef·fort (ef'ərt), n. 1. exertion of physical or mental power. 2. a strenuous attempt. 3. an achievement or accomplishment. —ef'fort·less, adj. —ef'fort·less·ly, adv.

ef·fron·ter·y (i frun'tə rē), n., pl. -ter·ies. impudent boldness.

ef·ful·gent (i ful'jənt), adj. shining forth brilliantly. —ef·ful'gence, n. —ef·ful'gent·ly, adv.

ef·fu·sion (i fyōō'zhən), n. 1. the act or result of pouring forth. 2. an unrestrained expression of feelings. —ef·fu'sive, adj. —ef·fu'sive·ly, adv. —ef·fu'sive·ness, n.

eft (eft), n. a newt in its immature terrestrial stage.

E.F.T., electronic funds transfer.

Eg., 1. Egypt. 2. Egyptian.

e.g., for example. [< L exempli grātia]

e·gad (i gad', ē'gad'), interj. (a mild oath.)

e·gal·i·tar·i·an (i gal/i târ/ē ən), *adj.*
1. asserting or characterized by belief in the equality of all people, esp. in economic or social life. —*n.* 2. an advocate of such belief. —**e·gal/i·tar/i·an·ism,** *n.*

egg[1] (eg), *n.* 1. the roundish reproductive body produced by the female of certain animals, as birds and some snakes. 2. such a body produced by a domestic bird, esp. the hen, used as food. 3. Also called **egg/ cell/.** the female reproductive cell. 4. *Slang.* person: *a good egg.*

egg[2] (eg), *v.t.* to incite or urge: *They egged me on to punch him.*

egg·beat·er (eg/bē/tər), *n.* a small rotary device for beating eggs, whipping cream, etc.

egg/ foo young/ (fōō yung/), a Chinese-American dish of a pancake-shaped omelet with a mixture of chopped onions, mushrooms, and pork. [< *egg* + Chin *fu jung:* lit., lotus]

egg·head (eg/hed/), *n. Informal.* an intellectual.

egg·nog (eg/nog/), *n.* a drink made of eggs, milk or cream, sugar, and, usually, liquor.

egg·plant (eg/plant/, -plänt/), *n.* a plant cultivated for its edible, dark-purple fruit, used as a vegetable.

egg/ roll/, (in Chinese cuisine) a cylindrical casing of egg dough filled with minced roast pork, bamboo shoots, etc., and browned in deep fat.

egg·shell (eg/shel/), *n.* the shell of a bird's egg.

e·gis (ē/jis), *n.* aegis.

eg·lan·tine (eg/lən tīn/, -tēn/), *n.* sweetbrier.

e·go (ē/gō, eg/ō), *n., pl.* **e·gos.** 1. the "I" or self of any person. 2. *Psychoanal.* the part of the psyche that experiences and reacts to the outside world. 3. egotism or self-importance.

e·go·cen·tric (ē/gō sen/trik, eg/ō-), *adj.* regarding the self as the center of all worldly things.

e/go ide/al, *Psychoanal.* a conscious ideal of personal excellence toward which an individual strives.

e·go·ism (ē/gō iz/əm, eg/ō-), *n.* 1. the habit of valuing everything only in reference to one's personal interest. 2. conceit or self-esteem. —**e/go·ist,** *n.* —**e/go·is/tic, e/go·is/ti·cal,** *adj.* —**e/go·is/ti·cal·ly,** *adv.*

e·go·tism (ē/gə tiz/əm, eg/ə-), *n.* 1. excessive and objectionable reference to oneself, in conversation or writing. 2. self-conceit or boastfulness. —**e/go·tist,** *n.* —**e/go·tis/tic, e/go·tis/ti·cal,** *adj.* —**e/go·tis/ti·cal·ly,** *adv.*

e/go trip/, an act undertaken primarily to satisfy one's vanity or self-image.

e·gre·gious (i grē/jəs, -jē əs), *adj.* glaringly bad, as an error. —**e·gre/gious·ly,** *adv.* —**e·gre/gious·ness,** *n.*

e·gress (ē/gres), *n. Chiefly Literary.* a means of existing.

e·gret (ē/grit, eg/rit), *n.* a white heron that grows long, ornamental plumes.

E·gypt (ē/jipt), *n.* a country in NE Africa.

E·gyp·tian (i jip/shən), *adj.* 1. of Egypt or its people. —*n.* 2. a native or inhabitant of Egypt. 3. the extinct language of the ancient Egyptians.

eh (ā, e), *interj.* (an utterance expressing surprise or doubt or seeking confirmation.)

EHF, See **extremely high frequency.**

ei·der·down (ī/dər doun/), *n.* soft feathers from the breast of the female eider duck, used to stuff quilts.

ei/der duck/ (ī dər), a large sea duck of the Northern Hemisphere. Also, **ei/der.**

ei·do·lon (ī dō/lən), *n., pl.* **-la** (-lə), **-lons.** 1. an unreal image. 2. an ideal figure.

eight (āt), *n.* 1. a cardinal number, seven plus one. 2. a symbol for this number, as 8 or VIII. —*adj.* 3. amounting to eight in number. —**eighth** (ātth), *adj., n., adv.*

eight·ball (āt/bôl/), *n.* 1. (in pool) a black ball bearing the number eight. 2. **behind the eightball,** *Slang.* in a disadvantageous situation.

eight·een (ā/tēn/), *n.* 1. a cardinal number, ten plus eight. 2. a symbol for this number, as 18 or XVIII. —**eight·eenth** (ā/tēnth/), *adj., n.*

eight-track (āt/trak/), *n.* a magnetic-tape cartridge, esp. one carrying eight parallel tracks of prerecorded sound or music. Also, **8-track.**

eight·y (ā/tē), *n., pl.* **eight·ies.** 1. a cardinal number, ten times eight. 2. a symbol for this number, as 80 or LXXX. —**eight·i·eth** (ā/tē ith), *adj., n.*

eight·y-six (ā/tē siks/), *v.t. Slang.* to refuse to serve (an undesirable customer in a restaurant or bar).

Ein·stein (īn/stīn), *n.* **Albert,** 1879–1955, U.S. physicist, born in Germany.

ein·stein·i·um (īn stī/nē əm), *n. Chem.* a synthetic, radioactive, metallic element. *Symbol:* Es; *at. no.:* 99.

Eir·e (âr/ə, ī/rə), *n.* a former name of the country of Ireland.

Ei·sen·how·er (ī/zən hou/ər), *n.* **Dwight David,** 1890–1969, U.S. general and statesman: 34th president of the U.S. 1953–61.

eis·tedd·fod (ī steth′vod), *n.* (in Wales) an annual competition among poets and minstrels. [< Welsh]

ei·ther (ē′thər, ī′thər), *adj.* **1.** one or the other of two: *Sit at either end of the table.* **2.** each of two. —*pron.* **3.** one or the other. —*conj.* **4.** (used before a word or statement that is followed by *or,* to emphasize the possibility of choice): *Either come or write.* —*adv.* **5.** also or too: *He is not fond of parties, and I am not either.*

—**Usage.** The pronoun EITHER is commonly followed by a singular verb: *Either is good enough.*

e·jac·u·late (i jak′yə lāt′), *v.t., v.i., -lat·ed, -lat·ing.* **1.** to say suddenly and briefly. **2.** to eject (semen). —**e·jac·u·la′tion,** *n.* —**e·jac′u·la′tor,** *n.* —**e·jac′u·la·to′ry** (-lə tôr′ē), *adj.*

e·ject (i jekt′), *v.t.* to drive or throw out, as from within. —**e·jec′tion,** *n.* —Syn. expel, evict.

ejec′tion seat′, an airplane seat that can be ejected with the pilot in an emergency.

eke (ēk), *v.t.,* eked, ek·ing. eke out, **1.** to supply what is lacking. **2.** to make (a living) or support (existence) laboriously.

EKG, 1. electrocardiogram. **2.** electrocardiograph.

e·kis·tics (i kis′tiks), *n.* the science that deals with urban planning and development, based on diverse disciplines including sociology and economics. —**e·kis′tic,** *adj.*

el., elevation.

e·lab·o·rate (*adj.* i lab′ər it; *v.* i lab′ə·rāt′), *adj., v., -rat·ed, -rat·ing.* — *adj.* **1.** worked out with great care and detail. **2.** complicated and ornate. —*v.t.* **3.** to work out carefully or minutely. —*v.i.* **4.** to add details in writing, speaking, etc.: *to elaborate upon a theme.* —**e·lab′o·rate·ly,** *adv.* —**e·lab′o·rate·ness,** *n.* —**e·lab′o·ra′tion,** *n.* —**e·lab′o·ra′tor,** *n.*

é·lan (ā län′, ā lan′), *n.* impetuous ardor.

e·land (ē′lənd), *n.* a large, African antelope having long, spirally twisted horns. [< SAFrD]

e·lapse (i laps′), *v.i.,* e·lapsed, e·laps·ing. (of time) to slip by or pass away.

e·las·tic (i las′tik), *adj.* **1.** capable of returning to its original length, shape, etc., after being stretched or deformed. **2.** flexible or accommodating. **3.** spring or resilient. —*n.* **4.** an elastic band or fabric. —**e·las′ti·cal·ly,** *adv.* —**e·las·tic·i·ty** (i la·stis′i tē, ē′la stis′-), *n.* —**e·las′ti·cize′,** *v.t.*

e·las·to·mer (i las′tə mər), *n.* a natural or synthetic elastic substance, as rubber. —**e·las·to·mer·ic** (i las′tə·mer′ik), *adj.*

e·late (i lāt′), *v.t.,* e·lat·ed, e·lat·ing. to make very happy or proud. —**e·la′tion,** *n.*

el·bow (el′bō), *n.* **1.** the bend or joint of the arm between upper arm and forearm. **2.** something bent like an elbow. **3. out at the elbows,** poorly dressed. —*v.t., v.i.* **4.** to push with the elbow. **5.** to make (one's way) by so pushing.

el′bow grease′, *Informal.* strenuous physical exertion.

el·bow·room (el′bō rōōm′, -rŏŏm′), *n.* room or space in which to move freely.

eld·er¹ (el′dər), *adj. a compar. of* old *with* eldest *as superl.* **1.** older. **2.** of higher rank. **3.** earlier. —*n.* **4.** a person who is older or higher in rank than oneself. **5.** one of the older and more influential persons of a community. **6.** a layman or laywoman who is a church officer.

eld·er² (el′dər), *n.* a tree or shrub having red or black berrylike fruit.

el·der·ber·ry (el′dər ber′ē, -bə rē), *n., pl.* -ries. **1.** the fruit of the elder, used in making wine and jelly. **2.** elder².

eld·er·ly (el′dər lē), *adj.* **1.** somewhat old. **2.** of persons in later life.

eld·est (el′dist), *adj. a superl. of* old *with* elder *as compar.*

El Do·ra·do (el′ də rä′dō, -rā′-), any fabulously wealthy place.

e·lect (i lekt′), *v.t.* **1.** to select by vote, as for an office. **2.** to pick out or choose: *to elect a course in school.* —*v.i.* **3.** to choose or select someone or something. —*adj.* **4.** selected for an office, but not yet inducted: *the governor-elect.* **5.** chosen or select. [< L *ēlect(us)* chosen] —**e·lect·ee′,** *n.*

elect., 1. electric. **2.** electrical. **3.** electrician. **4.** electricity. Also, **elec.**

e·lec·tion (i lek′shən), *n.* **1.** the selection of a person or persons for office by vote. **2.** a public vote upon a proposition submitted **3.** the act of electing.

e·lec·tion·eer (i lek′shə nēr′), *v.i.* to work for a candidate, party, etc., in an election.

e·lec·tive (i lek′tiv), *adj.* **1.** appointed by or derived from election. **2.** having the power of electing. **3.** optional, as a study. —*n.* **4.** an elective study or course. —**e·lec′tive·ly,** *adv.*

e·lec·tor (i lek′tər), *n.* **1.** a person who elects, esp. a qualified voter. **2.** a member of the electoral college. —**e·lec·tor·al** (i lek′tər əl), *adj.* **e·lec′tor·al·ly,** *adv.*

elec′toral col′lege, *U.S.* a body of electors chosen by the voters in each state to elect the President and Vice President.

e·lec·tor·ate (i lek′tər it), *n.* the body of persons entitled to vote in an election.

e·lec·tric (i lek′trik), *adj.* **1.** pertaining to, produced by, or involving electricity. **2.** producing or operated by electric currents. **3.** thrilling or exciting. Also, **e·lec′tri·cal.** —**e·lec′tri·cal·ly,** *adv.*

elec′trical storm′, thunderstorm. Also, **elec′tric storm′.**

elec′tric chair′, a chair used to electrocute criminals sentenced to death.

elec′tric eye′. See photoelectric cell.

e·lec·tri·cian (i lek trish′ən, ē′lek-), *n.* a person who installs, operates, or repairs electric equipment.

e·lec·tric·i·ty (i lek tris′i tē, ē′lek-), *n.* **1.** a physical agency caused by the motion of electrons, protons, and other charged particles, manifesting itself as attraction, repulsion, magnetic, luminous and heating effects, etc. **2.** the science dealing with this agency. **3.** electric current.

e·lec·tri·fy (i lek′trə fī′), *v.t.,* **-fied, -fying.** **1.** to charge with or subject to electricity. **2.** to supply with or equip for electric power. **3.** to startle greatly or thrill. —**e·lec′tri·fi·ca′tion,** *n.* —**e·lec′tri·fi′er,** *n.*

electro-, a combining form meaning "electric" or "electricity": *electromagnet.*

e·lec·tro·car·di·o·gram (i lek′trō kär′dē ə gram′), *n.* the graphic record produced by an electrocardiograph.

e·lec·tro·car·di·o·graph (i lek′trō kär′dē ə graf′, -gräf′), *n.* a device that records the minute changes of potential in each heartbeat. —**e·lec′tro·car′di·o·graph′ic,** *adj.* —**e·lec·tro·car·di·og·ra·phy** (i lek′trō kär′dē og′rə fē), *n.*

e·lec·tro·chem·is·try (i lek′trō kem′i-strē), *n.* the branch of chemistry that deals with the relation between chemical changes and electricity. —**e·lec·tro·chem·i·cal** (i lek′trō kem′i-kəl), *adj.* —**e·lec′tro·chem′i·cal·ly,** *adv.*

e·lec·tro·cute (i lek′trə kyōōt′), *v.t.,* **-cut·ed, -cut·ing.** to kill or execute by electricity. —**e·lec′tro·cu′tion,** *n.*

e·lec·trode (i lek′trōd), *n.* a conductor through which a current enters or leaves an electric or electronic device.

e·lec·tro·dy·nam·ics (i lek′trō dī nam′iks), *n.* the branch of physics that deals with the interactions of electric, magnetic, and mechanical phenomena. —**e·lec′tro·dy·nam′ic,** *adj.*

e·lec·tro·en·ceph·a·lo·gram (i lek′trō-en sef′ə lə gram′), *n.* a graphic record produced by an electroencephalograph.

e·lec·tro·en·ceph·a·lo·graph (i lek′trō-en sef′ə lə graf′, -gräf′), *n.* an instrument for measuring and recording the electric activity of the brain. —**e·lec·tro·en·ceph·a·lo·graph·ic** (i-lek′trō en sef′ə lə graf′ik), *adj.* —**e·lec·tro·en·ceph·a·log·ra·phy** (i lek′trō en sef′ə log′rə fē), *n.*

e·lec·trol·o·gist (i lek trol′ə jist), *n.* a person skilled in the use of electrolysis for removing warts, moles, or excess hair.

e·lec·trol·y·sis (i lek trol′i sis, ē′lek-), *n.* **1.** the passage of an electric current through an electrolyte with subsequent migration of ions to the electrodes. **2.** the destruction of tumors, hair roots, etc., by an electric current.

e·lec·tro·lyte (i lek′trə līt′), *n.* any substance that dissociates into ions when dissolved in a suitable medium or melted and thus forms a conductor of electricity.

e·lec·tro·lyt·ic (i lek′trə lit′ik), *adj.* **1.** pertaining to or derived by electrolysis. **2.** pertaining to an electrolyte. —**e·lec′tro·lyt′i·cal·ly,** *adv.*

e·lec·tro·mag·net (i lek′trō mag′nit), *n.* a device consisting of an iron or steel core that is magnetized by electric current in a coil surrounding it. —**e·lec′tro·mag·net′ic** (-mag net′ik), *adj.* —**e·lec′tro·mag·net′i·cal·ly,** *adv.*

elec′tromagnet′ic wave′, a wave produced by the acceleration of an electric charge.

e·lec·tro·mag·ne·tism (i lek′trō mag′ni tiz′əm), *n.* **1.** the phenomena associated with the relations between electric current and magnetism. **2.** the science that deals with these phenomena.

e·lec·tro·mo·tive (i lek′trə mō′tiv), *adj.* pertaining to, producing, or tending to produce a flow of electricity.

elec′tromo′tive force′, a difference in electric potential that causes an electric current to flow.

e·lec·tron (i lek′tron), *n.* an elementary particle that is a fundamental constituent of matter, having a negative charge and existing as the component outside the nucleus of an atom.

e·lec·tron·ic (i lek tron′ik, ē′lek-), *adj.* **1.** of electronics or equipment developed through electronics. **2.** of electrons. —**e·lec·tron′i·cal·ly,** *adv.*

electron′ic mu′sic, electronically produced sounds recorded on tape, and arranged into combinations by the composer.

e·lec·tron·ics (i lek tron′iks, ē′lek-), *n.* the science dealing with the flow of electrons in a vacuum, in conductors, and in semiconductors.

electron′ic surveil′lance, the gathering of information by surreptitious use of electronic devices, esp. by wiretapping, as in crime detection, espionage, etc.

elec′tron mi′croscope, a microscope of extremely high power that uses beams of electrons instead of rays of light.

elec′tron tube′, a sealed glass bulb containing two or more electrodes, used to generate, amplify, and rectify electric oscillations and alternating currents.

e·lec·tro·plate (i lek′trə plāt′), *v.t.,* **-plat·ed, -plat·ing.** to coat with a metal by electrolysis.

e·lec·tro·scope (i lek′trə skōp′), *n.* a device for detecting the presence and determining the sign of electric charges.

e·lec·tro·shock (i lek′trə shok′), *n.* shock therapy administered by means of electrical currents.

e·lec·tro·stat·ics (i lek′trə stat′iks), *n.* the branch of physics dealing with electric phenomena not associated with electricity in motion. **—e·lec′-tro·stat′ic,** *adj.*

e·lec·tro·ther·a·py (i lek′trō ther′ə pē), *n.* treatment of diseases by means of electricity.

e·lec·tro·type (i lek′trə tīp′), *n.* a facsimile of a block of type, an engraving, etc., for use in printing.

el·ee·mos·y·nar·y (el′ə mos′ə ner′ē, -moz′-, el′ē ə-), *adj.* of or supported by gifts, charity, etc.

el·e·gant (el′ə gənt), *adj.* **1.** tastefully fine or luxurious in dress, style, design, etc. **2.** gracefully refined and dignified. **3.** excellent or fine. **—el′-e·gance,** *n.* **—el′e·gant·ly,** *adv.*

el·e·gi·ac (el′ə jī′ək, -ak, i lē′jē ak′), *adj.* **1.** expressing sorrow or lamentation. **2.** used in, suitable for, or like an elegy. Also, **el′e·gi′a·cal.**

el·e·gy (el′i jē), *n., pl.* **-gies.** a mournful, melancholy, or plaintive poem, esp. a lament for the dead. **—el′e·gize′,** *v.t., v.i.*

elem., **1.** element. **2.** elementary. **3.** elements.

el·e·ment (el′ə mənt), *n.* **1.** a component or constituent of a whole. **2.** one of the substances, esp. earth, water, air, and fire, formerly regarded as constituting the material universe. **3.** the natural environment of someone or something. **4. elements, a.** atmospheric forces, as wind, rain, and cold. **b.** the rudimentary principles of an art, science, etc. **5.** *Chem.* any of a class of substances, of which 103 are now recognized, that cannot be separated into simpler substances by chemical means.

el·e·men·tal (el′ə men′t°l), *adj.* **1.** of the four elements of the universe. **2.** of the atmospheric elements. **3.** simple or primal. **—el′e·men′tal·ly,** *adv.*

el·e·men·ta·ry (el′ə men′tə rē, -trē), *adj.* **1.** essentially basic. **2.** uncomplicated or undeveloped. **3.** of a single chemical element. **—el·e·men·ta·ri·ly** (el′ə men ter′ə lē), *adv.* **—el′e·men′ta·ri·ness,** *n.* **—Syn. 1.** fundamental, rudimentary.

el′emen′tary par′ticle, any of several entities that are less complex than an atom and are the constituents of all matter.

elemen′tary school′, a school teaching elementary subjects and extending from six to eight years.

el·e·phant (el′ə fənt), *n.* a large mammal of Africa and India, with a flexible trunk, flapping ears, and ivory tusks.

el·e·phan·ti·a·sis (el′ə fən tī′ə sis, -fan-), *n.* a chronic disease characterized by enormous enlargement of the parts affected, esp. of the legs and scrotum.

el·e·phan·tine (el′ə fan′tin, -tīn, -tēn), *adj.* **1.** of or resembling an elephant. **2.** ponderous or clumsy.

elev., elevation.

el·e·vate (el′ə vāt′), *v.t.,* **-vat·ed, -vat·ing.** **1.** to raise to a higher place. **2.** to raise to a higher rank or office. **3.** to improve intellectually or spiritually. **4.** to put in high spirits.

el·e·va·tion (el′ə vā′shən), *n.* **1.** the height to which something is elevated. **2.** the altitude of a place above sea level or ground level. **3.** an elevated place, thing, or part.

el·e·va·tor (el′ə vā′tər), *n.* **1.** a moving platform or cage for carrying passengers or freight from one level to another, as in a building. **2.** a building in which grain is stored and handled. **3.** a hinged horizontal surface on an airplane used to control inclination.

e·lev·en (i lev′ən), *n.* **1.** a cardinal number, ten plus one. **2.** a symbol for this number, as 11 or XI. **—***adj.* **3.** amounting to 11 in number. **—e·lev′enth,** *adj., n.*

elf (elf), *n., pl.* **elves** (elvz). a small, mischievous fairy with magical powers. **—elf·in** (el′fin), **elf·ish** (el′fish), *adj.* **—elf′ish·ly,** *adv.* **—elf′ish·ness,** *n.*

El Gre·co (el grek′ō), 1541–1614, Spanish painter, born in Crete.

el·hi (el′hī), *adj.* elementary- and high-school.

e·lic·it (i lis′it), *v.t.* to bring out or forth, esp. with skill or effort. **—e·lic′i·ta′tion,** *n.* **—e·lic′i·tor,** *n.* **—Syn.** evoke.

e·lide (i līd′), *v.t.*, **e·lid·ed, e·lid·ing.** to omit (a vowel, consonant, or syllable) in pronunciation. —**e·li·sion** (i lizh′ən), *n.*

el·i·gi·ble (el′i jə bəl), *adj.* **1.** fit to be chosen. **2.** legally qualified for office. —*n.* **3.** an eligible person. —**el·i·gi·bil·i·ty** (el′i jə bil′i tē), *n.* —**el′i·gi·bly,** *adv.*

E·li·jah (i lī′jə), *n.* a Hebrew prophet of the 9th century B.C.

e·lim·i·nate (i lim′ə nāt′), *v.t.*, **-nat·ed, -nat·ing. 1.** to remove or get rid of, esp. as being undesirable. **2.** to omit or ignore. **3.** to void or expel from an organism. [< L *ēlīmināt(us)* sent out of doors] —**e·lim′i·na′tion,** *n.* —**e·lim′i·na·to′ry** (-nə tôr′ē, -tôr′ē), *adj.*

e·lite (i lēt′, ā lēt′), *n.* **1.** the best or most powerful of anything considered collectively, esp. of a group or class of persons. **2.** a typewriter type having 12 characters to the inch. Also, **é·lite′.**

e·lit·ism (i lē′tiz əm, ā lē′-), *n.* practice of or belief in rule by an elite. —**e·lit′ist,** *n., adj.*

e·lix·ir (i lik′sər), *n.* **1.** a sweetened medicinal solution of alcohol. **2.** an alchemic preparation supposedly capable of transmuting base metals into gold or of prolonging life.

E·liz·a·beth I (i liz′ə bəth), 1533–1603, queen of England 1558–1603.

Elizabeth II, born 1926, queen of Great Britain since 1952.

E·liz·a·be·than (i liz′ə bē′thən, -beth′-ən), *adj.* **1.** of or characteristic of Queen Elizabeth I. —*n.* an English person, esp. a poet or dramatist, of the Elizabethan period.

elk (elk), *n., pl.* **elks, elk. 1.** a large deer of Europe and Asia. **2.** a large North American deer with spreading antlers.

ell¹ (el), *n.* an extension usually at right angles to one end of a building.

ell² (el), *n.* a former measure of length in England, equal to 45 inches.

el·lipse (i lips′), *n.* a closed symmetrical curve resembling a flattened circle.

el·lip·sis (i lip′sis), *n., pl.* **-ses** (-sēz). **1.** the omission from a sentence of a word or words that would complete the construction. **2.** marks (...) to indicate an omission of a words or words.

el·lip·soid (i lip′soid), *n. Geom.* a solid figure all plane sections of which are ellipses or circles. —**el·lip·soi·dal** (i lip soid′°l, el′ip-), *adj.*

el·lip·ti·cal (i lip′ti kəl), *adj.* **1.** of or having the form of an ellipse. **2.** of or marked by grammatical ellipsis. Also, **el·lip′tic.** —**el·lip′ti·cal·ly,** *adv.*

elm (elm), *n.* **1.** a tall shade tree

with gradually spreading branches. **2.** its wood.

el·o·cu·tion (el′ə kyōō′shən), *n.* the study and practice of public speaking. —**el′o·cu′tion·ist,** *n.*

e·lon·gate (i lông′gāt, i lông′-), *v.t., v.i.,* **-gat·ed, -gat·ing.** to lengthen spatially. —**e·lon·ga′tion,** *n.*

e·lope (i lōp′), *v.i.,* **e·loped, e·lop·ing.** to run off secretly to be married. —**e·lope′ment,** *n.* —**e·lop′er,** *n.*

el·o·quent (el′ə kwənt), *adj.* having, exercising, or characterized by fluent, forceful speech. —**el′o·quence,** *n.* —**el′o·quent·ly,** *adv.*

El Pas·o (el pas′ō), a city in W Texas.

El Sal·va·dor (el sal′və dôr′), a country in NW Central America.

else (els), *adj.* **1.** other or different: *something else.* **2.** in addition: *Who else was there?* —*adv.* **3.** if not: *I'll come, or else I'll call.* **4.** otherwise: *How else could I have acted?*

else·where (els′hwâr′, -wâr′), *adv.* somewhere else.

e·lu·ci·date (i lōō′si dāt′), *v.t., v.i.,* **-dat·ed, -dat·ing.** to make clear, usually by illustration or explanation. —**e·lu′ci·da′tion,** *n.* —**e·lu′ci·da·tor,** *n.*

e·lude (i lōōd′), *v.t.,* **e·lud·ed, e·lud·ing. 1.** to avoid or escape by speed, cleverness, etc. **2.** to escape the mind of. —**e·lud′er,** *n.*

e·lu·sive (i lōō′siv), *adj.* **1.** eluding perception or mental grasp: *an elusive concept.* **2.** cleverly evasive. —**e·lu′sive·ly,** *adv.* —**e·lu′sive·ness,** *n.*

el·ver (el′vər), *n.* a young eel.

elves (elvz), *n., pl.* of **elf.**

E·lys·i·um (i lizh′ē əm, i liz′-), *n.* **1.** *Class. Myth.* the abode of the blessed after death. **2.** any place or state of perfect happiness. —**E·ly·sian** (i lizh′-ən), *adj.*

em (em), *n., pl.* **ems.** the square of any size of type, used as the unit of measurement for matter printed in that type size.

EM, enlisted man; enlisted men.

'em (əm), *pron. Informal.* them.

em-, var. of **en-** before *b, p,* or *m*: *embalm.*

e·ma·ci·ate (i mā′shē āt′), *v.t.,* **-at·ed, -at·ing.** to make very thin, as by lack of nutrition or by disease. —**e·ma′ci·a′tion,** *n.*

em·a·nate (em′ə nāt′), *v.i.,* **-nat·ed, -nat·ing.** to flow out, as from a source. —**em′a·na′tion,** *n.* —**em′a·na′tive,** *adj.*

e·man·ci·pate (i man′sə pāt′), *v.t.,* **-pat·ed, -pat·ing. 1.** to free from restraint or influence. **2.** to free (a slave) from bondage. —**e·man′ci·pa′tion,** *n.* —**e·man′ci·pa′tor,** *n.*

e·mas·cu·late (i mas′kyə lāt′), v.t., -lat·ed, -lat·ing. 1. to deprive of masculinity or procreative power. 2. to deprive of strength or vigor. — e·mas′cu·la′tion, n. —e·mas′cu·la′tor, n.

em·balm (em bäm′), v.t. to treat (a dead body) so as to preserve it, as with chemicals or drugs. —em·balm′er, n.

em·bank (em bangk′), v.t. to enclose or protect with a bank or mound. —em·bank′ment, n.

em·bar·go (em bär′gō), n., pl. -goes, v., -goed, -go·ing. —n. 1. a government order prohibiting the movement of merchant vessels from or into its ports. 2. any legal restriction on commerce. —v.t. 3. to impose an embargo on. [< Sp embargar to hinder]

em·bark (em bärk′), v.t. 1. to put or receive on board a ship or aircraft. —v.i. 2. to board a ship or aircraft. 3. to engage in an enterprise, business, etc. —em·bar·ka′tion (em′bär-kā′shən), n.

em·bar·rass (em bar′əs), v.t. 1. to make feel uncomfortably self-conscious. 2. to impede or hinder. 3. to beset with financial difficulties. —em·bar′rassed·ly (em bar′əst lē, -ə sid lē), adv. —em·bar′rass·ing·ly, adv. —em·bar′rass·ment, n. —Syn. 1. abash, disconcert, fluster.

em·bas·sy (em′bə sē), n., pl. -sies. 1. an ambassador and his or her staff. 2. the official headquarters of an ambassador. 3. the function or office of an ambassador.

em·bat·tled (em bat′°ld), adj. disposed or prepared for battle.

em·bed (em bed′), v.t., -bed·ded, -bed·ding. to fix into a surrounding mass.

em·bel·lish (em bel′ish), v.t. 1. to beautify by ornamentation. 2. to enhance (a statement) with fictitious additions. —em·bel′lish·er, n. —em·bel′lish·ment, n.

em·ber (em′bər), n. 1. a small live piece of coal or wood, as in a dying fire. 2. embers, the smoldering remains of a fire.

em·bez·zle (em bez′əl), v.t., -zled, -zling. to appropriate fraudulently to one's own use, as money entrusted to one's care. —em·bez′zle·ment, n. —em·bez′zler, n.

em·bit·ter (em bit′ər), v.t. to cause to feel bitter or resentful. —em·bit′ter·ment, n.

em·bla·zon (em blā′zən), v.t. 1. to depict, as on a heraldic shield. 2. to decorate with brilliant colors. 3. to extol or celebrate. —em·bla′zon·ment, n.

em·blem (em′bləm), n. 1. an object or figure symbolizing something else.

2. a sign or badge that identifies or represents something. —em·blem·at·ic (em′blə mat′ik), em·blem·at′i·cal, adj.

em·bod·y (em bod′ē), v.t., -bod·ied, -bod·y·ing. 1. to give a definite form to. 2. to collect into or include in an organized whole. 3. to provide with a body. —em·bod′i·ment, n.

em·bold·en (em bōl′dən), v.t. to make bold or bolder.

em·bo·lism (em′bə liz′əm), n. the occlusion of a blood vessel by some undissolved material, as a blood clot. —em·bol′ic (-bol′ik), adj.

em·bon·point (än bôn pwan′), n. French. excessive plumpness.

em·boss (em bôs′, -bos′), v.t. 1. to raise (surface designs) in relief. 2. to decorate (a surface) with raised ornament. —em·boss′er, n. —em·boss′ment, n.

em·bou·chure (äm′bōō shŏŏr′, äm′-bōō shŏŏr′), n. 1. the mouthpiece of a wind instrument. 2. the adjustment of a player's mouth to such a mouthpiece.

em·bow·er (em bou′ər), v.t., v.i. to shelter in or as in a bower.

em·brace (em brās′), v., -braced, -brac·ing, n. —v.t. 1. to take or clasp in the arms lovingly. 2. to adopt or accept eagerly. 3. to avail oneself of: to embrace an opportunity. 4. to encircle or surround. 5. to include or contain. —v.i. 6. to join in an embrace. —n. 7. an act of embracing. —em·brace′a·ble, adj.

em·bra·sure (em brā′zhər), n. 1. an opening in a wall through which a gun may be fired. 2. an enlargement of a door or window toward the inner face of a wall.

em·bro·cate (em′brō kāt′), v.t., -cat·ed, -cat·ing. to moisten and rub with a liniment or lotion. —em′bro·ca′tion, n.

em·broi·der (em broi′dər), v.t. 1. to decorate with ornamental needlework. 2. to embellish rhetorically. —v.i. 3. to do embroidery. —em·broi′der·er, n.

em·broi·der·y (em broi′də rē, -drē), n., pl. -der·ies. 1. the art of embroidering. 2. embroidered work or ornamentation. 3. elaboration or embellishment.

em·broil (em broil′), v.t. 1. to bring into conflict. 2. to complicate or entangle. —em·broil′ment, n.

em·bry·o (em′brē ō), n., pl. -os. 1. an organism in the earlier stages of its development, as the young of a mammal in the womb. 2. the beginning stage of anything. —em′bry-on′ic (-on′ik), adj.

embryol., embryology.

em·bry·ol·o·gy (em′brē ol′ə jē), *n., pl.* **-gies.** the science dealing with the development of embryos. —**em·bry·o·log·i·cal** (em′brē ə loj′i kəl), **em·bry·o·log′ic,** *adj.* —**em′bry·o·log′i·cal·ly,** *adv.* —**em′bry·ol′o·gist,** *n.*

em·cee (em′sē′), *n., v., -ceed, -cee·ing.* —*n.* **1.** See **master of ceremonies.** —*v.t., v.i.* **2.** to act as master of ceremonies (for).

e·mend (i mend′), *v.t.* to edit (a text) by removing errors, flaws, etc. — **e·men·da·tion** (ē′mən dā′shən, em′-ən-), *n.*

em·er·ald (em′ər əld, em′rəld), *n.* **1.** a rare, green beryl valued as a gem. **2.** a clear, deep green.

e·merge (i mûrj′), *v.i.,* **e·merged, e·merg·ing. 1.** to come forth, as from water. **2.** to come into view or notice. **3.** to develop or evolve. — **e·mer′gence,** *n.* —**e·mer′gent,** *adj.*

e·mer·gen·cy (i mûr′jən sē), *n., pl.* **-cies.** a sudden, urgent, unforeseen occurrence requiring immediate action.

e·mer·i·tus (i mer′i təs), *adj.* retired from active duty but retaining the title or rank: *a professor emeritus.*

Em·er·son (em′ər sən), *n.* **Ralph Waldo,** 1803–82, U.S. essayist and poet.

em·er·y (em′ə rē, em′rē), *n.* a granular mineral substance used for grinding and polishing.

e·met·ic (ə met′ik), *adj.* **1.** inducing vomiting. —*n.* **2.** an emetic medicine or agent. —**e·met′i·cal·ly,** *adv.*

emf, See **electromotive force.** Also, **EMF**

-emia, a suffix referring to the state of the blood: *leukemia.*

em·i·grate (em′ə grāt′), *v.i., -grat·ed, -grat·ing.* to leave one country or region to settle in another. —**em′i·grant** (-grənt), *n., adj.* —**em′i·gra′tion,** *n.*

é·mi·gré (em′ə grā′), *n.* a person forced to emigrate because of political conditions.

em·i·nence (em′ə nəns), *n.* **1.** high rank or repute. **2.** a high place or part. **3.** (*cap.*) *Rom. Cath. Ch.* a title of honor applied to cardinals.

em·i·nent (em′ə nənt), *adj.* **1.** high in rank or repute. **2.** conspicuous or noteworthy: *eminent fairness.* **3.** lofty or high. —**em′i·nent·ly,** *adv.* —**Syn. 1.** celebrated, illustrious, prominent, renowned.

em′inent domain′, the power of the state to take private property for public use upon compensating the owner.

e·mir (ə mēr′), *n.* an Arab chieftain or prince. —**em·ir·ate** (em′ə rit, -āt′), *n.*

em·is·sar·y (em′i ser′ē), *n., pl. -sar·ies.* an agent, esp. of a national government, sent on a mission.

e·mit (i mit′), *v.t.,* **e·mit·ted, e·mit·ting. 1.** to send forth (liquid, light, heat, etc.). **2.** to utter or voice. **3.** *Archaic.* to issue (paper money). — **e·mis′sion,** *n.* —**e·mit′ter,** *n.*

e·mol·lient (i mol′yənt), *adj.* **1.** softening or soothing, esp. to the skin. —*n.* **2.** an emollient medicine or agent.

e·mol·u·ment (i mol′yə mənt), *n.* salary or fee arising from an office or employment held, esp. in the government.

e·mote (i mōt′), *v.i.,* **e·mot·ed, e·mot·ing.** *Informal.* to show emotion, esp. exaggeratedly. —**e·mot′er,** *n.*

e·mo·tion (i mō′shən), *n.* **1.** feeling or reaction stirred up. **2.** an instance of this, as love, hate, sorrow, or fear. —**e·mo′tion·al,** *adj.* —**e·mo′tion·al·ly,** *adv.* —**e·mo′tion·al·ism** (i mō′shə n°liz′əm), *n.*

Emp., 1. Emperor. **2.** Empire. **3.** Empress.

em·pa·thize (em′pə thīz′), *v.i.,* **-thized, -thiz·ing.** to experience empathy.

em·pa·thy (em′pə thē), *n.* identification with or vicarious experiencing of the feelings or thoughts of another person. —**em·path·ic** (em-path′ik), *adj.*

em·pen·nage (äm′pə näzh′), *n.* the tail assembly of an airplane or airship.

em·per·or (em′pər ər), *n.* the supreme ruler of an empire.

em·pha·sis (em′fə sis), *n., pl. -ses* (-sēz′). **1.** special attention or importance given to something. **2.** prominence given to particular words or syllables by means of voice or underscoring.

em·pha·size (em′fə sīz′), *v.t., -sized, -siz·ing.* to give emphasis to. —**Syn.** stress, underline.

em·phat·ic (em fat′ik), *adj.* **1.** uttered or done with emphasis. **2.** using emphasis in speech or action. **3.** clearly or boldly outlined. —**em·phat′i·cal·ly,** *adv.*

em·phy·se·ma (em′fi sē′mə, -zē′-), *n.* abnormal distention of a part of the body, esp. the lungs, with air or other gas.

em·pire (em′pīr′), *n.* **1.** a group of nations or peoples ruled over by one sovereign. **2.** imperial power or supreme control. **3.** a powerful enterprise: *an oil empire.* [< L *imper(ium)*]

em·pir·i·cal (em pir′i kəl), *adj.* derived from or depending upon experience or experiment alone. Also, **em·pir′ic.** —**em·pir′i·cal·ly,** *adv.*

em·pir·i·cism (em pir′i siz′əm), *n.* **1.** empirical method or practice. **2.** the doctrine that all knowledge is derived from sense experience. — **em·pir′i·cist,** *n., adj.*

em·place·ment (em plās′mənt), *n.* the space or platform for a gun or battery and its accessories.

em·ploy (em ploi′), *v.t.* **1.** to hire the services of. **2.** to use (an instrument, means, etc.). **3.** to occupy or devote (time, energies, etc.). —*n.* **4.** employment or service. —**employ′a·ble,** *adj.* —**employ′er,** *n.*

em·ploy·ee (em ploi′ē, em′ploi ē′), *n.* a person working for another person or an organization for pay. Also, **employ′e.**

em·ploy·ment (em ploi′mənt), *n.* **1.** the act of employing someone or something, or the state of being employed. **2.** an occupation, work, or activity. **3.** the total number of people of a nation gainfully employed or working.

em·po·ri·um (em pōr′ē əm, -pôr′-), *n.,* *pl.* **-po·ri·ums, -po·ri·a** (-pōr′ē ə, -pôr′-). a large retail store selling a great variety of articles.

em·pow·er (em pou′ər), *v.t.* **1.** to give power or authority to. **2.** to enable or permit.

em·press (em′pris), *n.* **1.** a female ruler of an empire. **2.** the consort of an emperor.

emp·ty (emp′tē), *adj.,* **-ti·er, -ti·est,** *v.,* **-tied, -ty·ing,** *n.,* *pl.* **-ties.** —*adj.* **1.** containing nothing. **2.** vacant or unoccupied. **3.** without force, effect, or significance. —*v.t.* **4.** to make empty. **5.** to discharge (contents). —*v.i.* **6.** to become empty. **7.** to discharge contents, as a river. —*n.* **8.** something empty, as a box, bottle, etc. —**emp′ti·ly,** *adv.* —**emp′ti·ness,** *n.*

emp·ty-hand·ed (emp′tē han′did), *adj.,* *adv.* **1.** having nothing in the hands. **2.** having gained nothing.

emp′ty nest′er, *Informal.* an elderly couple without children or whose children no longer live with them.

em·py·re·an (em′pə rē′ən, -pī-, empir′ē ən), *n.* **1.** the highest heaven. **2.** the visible heavens.

EMU, electromagnetic unit.

e·mu (ē′myōō), *n.* a large, flightless bird of Australia, resembling the ostrich but smaller.

em·u·late (em′yə lāt′), *v.t.,* **-lat·ed, -lat·ing.** to imitate with effort to equal or surpass. —**em′u·la′tion,** *n.* —**em′u·la′tive,** *adj.* —**em′u·la′tor,** *n.* —**em′u·lous,** *adj.*

e·mul·si·fy (i mul′sə fī′), *v.t.,* *v.i.,* **-fied, -fy·ing.** to make into an emulsion. —**e·mul′si·fi′a·ble,** *adj.* —**e·mul′si·fi·ca′tion,** *n.* —**e·mul′si·fi′er,** *n.*

e·mul·sion (i mul′shən), *n.* **1.** a combination of two liquids that do not ordinarily mix, such as oil and water, in which tiny drops of one liquid

are evenly distributed in the other. **2.** a photosensitive material used for coating photographic film. —**e·mul′sive,** *adj.*

en-, a prefix meaning: **a.** in or into: *engulf.* **b.** to put in or on: *encircle.* **c.** to cause to be: *enslave.*

-en, a suffix used to form: **a.** verbs from adjectives: *sweeten.* **b.** verbs from nouns: *lengthen.* **c.** adjectives from nouns: *ashen.* **d.** past participles: *proven.* **e.** plurals: *oxen.* **f.** diminutives: *kitten.*

en·a·ble (en ā′bəl), *v.t.,* **-bled, -bling. 1.** to make able. **2.** to give power or means to. **3.** to make possible or easy. —**en·a′bler,** *n.*

en·act (en akt′), *v.t.* **1.** to make into law. **2.** to act the part of: *to enact Romeo.* —**en·act′ment,** *n.* —**en·ac′tor,** *n.*

e·nam·el (i nam′əl), *n.,* *v.,* **-eled, el·ing** or **-elled, -el·ing.** —*n.* **1.** a glassy substance, usually opaque, applied to coat the surface of metal, pottery, etc. **2.** any of various enamellike varnishes, paints, etc. **3.** the hard, glossy covering of the crown of a tooth. —*v.t.* **4.** to coat or decorate with enamel. —**e·nam′el·er, e·nam′el·ler,** *n.* —**e·nam′el·work′,** *n.*

e·nam·el·ware (i nam′el wâr′), *n.* metal utensils covered with an enamel surface.

en·am·or (en am′ər), *v.t.* to inflame with love: *to be enamored of a lady.* Also, *Brit.,* **en·am′our.**

en bloc (en blok′), *French.* as a whole.

enc., **1.** enclosed. **2.** enclosure.

en·camp (en kamp′), *v.i., v.t.* to settle or lodge in a camp. —**en·camp′ment,** *n.*

en·cap·su·late (en kap′sə lāt′), *v.t.,* *v.i.,* **-lat·ed, -lat·ing.** to make, form, or place in or as in a capsule. Also, **en·cap′sule** (-səl). —**en·cap′su·la′tion,** *n.*

en·case (en kās′), *v.t.,* **-cased, -cas·ing.** to enclose in or as in a case.

-ence, a suffix meaning: **a.** act or fact: *abhorrence.* **b.** state or quality: *absence.*

en·ceinte (än saNt′), *adj. French.* pregnant.

en·ceph·a·li·tis (en sef′ə lī′tis), *n.* inflammation of the substance of the brain. —**en·ceph·a·lit·ic** (en sef′ə·lit′ik), *adj.*

en·ceph·a·lo·my·e·li·tis (en sef′ə lō·mī′ə lī′tis), *n.* inflammation of the brain and spinal cord.

en·ceph·a·lon (en sef′ə lon′), *n.,* *pl.* **-la** (-lə). *Anat.* the brain.

en·chain (en chān′), *v.t.* to fasten with or as with chains. —**en·chain′ment,** *n.*

en·chant (en chant', -chänt'), v.t. **1.** to cast a magic spell upon. **2.** to delight or charm greatly. —**en·chant'er,** n. —**en·chant'ing·ly,** adv. —**en·chant'ment,** n. —**en·chant'ress,** n.

en·chi·la·da (en'chə lä'də, -lad'ə), n. a rolled tortilla filled with meat and served with cheese and a chili-flavored sauce.

en·ci·pher (en sī'fər), v.t. to convert (a message, etc.) into cipher. —**en·ci'pher·ment,** n.

en·cir·cle (en sûr'kəl), v.t., -cled, -cling. **1.** to form a circle around. **2.** to go around. —**en·cir'cle·ment,** n.

encl., 1. enclosed. **2.** enclosure.

en·clave (en'klāv), n. a territory entirely or mostly surrounded by the territory of another country.

en·close (en klōz'), v.t., -closed, -clos-ing. **1.** to shut or hem in. **2.** to insert in the same envelope or package with the main letter or memo. —**en·clos'a·ble,** adj. —**en·clos·ure** (en klō'zhər), n.

en·code (en kōd'), v.t., -cod·ed, -cod-ing. to convert (a message, etc.) into code. —**en·cod'er,** n.

en·co·mi·um (en kō'mē əm), n., pl. -mi·ums, -mi·a (-mē ə). formal praise.

en·com·pass (en kum'pəs), v.t. **1.** to include comprehensively. **2.** to surround, as for protection.

en·core (äng'kōr, -kôr, än'-), n. **1.** a demand, as by applause, for an additional performance or appearance. **2.** a performance or appearance in response to such a demand.

en·coun·ter (en koun'tər), v.t. **1.** to meet with, esp. unexpectedly. **2.** to meet in battle. —n. **3.** a meeting, esp. casual or unexpected. **4.** a meeting of enemies in battle. —**en·coun'ter·er,** n.

encoun'ter group', a group of persons who meet regularly to increase social- and self-awareness and to change behavior through confrontation, self-disclosure, and strong emotional expression.

en·cour·age (en kûr'ij, -kur'-), v.t., -aged, -ag·ing. **1.** to inspire with courage or confidence. **2.** to stimulate by assistance or approval. —**en·cour'age·ment,** n. —**en·cour'ag·er,** n. —**en·cour'ag·ing·ly,** adv.

en·croach (en krōch'), v.i. to intrude or trespass, esp. stealthily or gradually. —**en·croach'ment,** n.

en·crust (en krust'), v.t., v.i. incrust. —**en·crus·ta'tion,** n.

en·cum·ber (en kum'bər), v.t. **1.** to hinder, esp. with cares. **2.** to burden or weigh down. —**en·cum'brance,** n.

-ency, a suffix meaning "state" or "quality": consistency.

ency., encyclopedia. Also, **encyc., encycl.**

en·cyc·li·cal (en sik'li kəl, -sī'kli-), n. a letter from the pope to all the bishops of the church.

en·cy·clo·pe·di·a (en sī'klə pē'dē ə), n. a book or set of books containing articles on all subjects and facts, usually in alphabetical or topical arrangement. Also, **en·cy·clo·pae'di·a** [< NL < Gk enkýklios paideía circular (i.e., well rounded) education] —**en·cy·clo·pe'dic,** adj. —**en·cy·clo·pe'di·cal·ly,** adv.

en·cyst (en sist'), v.t., v.i. to enclose or become enclosed in a cyst. —**en·cyst'ment,** n.

end (end), n. **1.** the extremity of anything. **2.** a point that indicates the full extent or limit of something. **3.** a part or place at an extremity. **4.** a termination or conclusion. **5.** a purpose or aim. **6.** an issue or result. **7.** death or ruin. **8.** a remnant or fragment: mill end. **9.** a share or part in something. **10.** Football. either of the linemen stationed farthest from the center. **11. make both ends meet,** to live within one's means. **12. no end,** Informal. very much. **13. put an end to,** to terminate or finish. —v.t. **14.** to bring to an end. **15.** to form the end of. —v.i. **16.** to come to an end. **17.** to issue or result. —adj. **18.** final or ultimate: the end result.

en·dan·ger (en dān'jər), v.t. to expose to danger. —**en·dan'ger·ment,** n.

en·dan·gered (en dān'jərd), adj. threatened with extinction: endangered wildlife.

en·dear (en dēr'), v.t. to make dear or beloved. —**en·dear'ing·ly,** adv.

en·dear·ment (en dēr'mənt), n. an action or utterance showing affection.

en·deav·or (en dev'ər), n. **1.** an earnest, continued effort. —v.i. **2.** to make such an effort. Also, Brit. **en·deav'our.**

en·dem·ic (en dem'ik), adj. peculiar to a particular people or locality, as a disease.

end·ing (en'ding), n. **1.** the concluding part. **2.** death or destruction. **3.** an inflected form at the end of a word, as -ed in granted.

en·dive (en'dīv, än'dēv), n. a plant having finely divided, curled leaves used for salads.

end·less (end'lis), adj. **1.** having or seeming to have no end or termination. **2.** made continuous. —**end'less·ly,** adv. —**end'less·ness,** n. —**Syn. 1.** boundless, limitless, interminable.

end' man', a man at either end of the line of performers of a minstrel troupe who carries on a dialogue with the interlocutor.

end·most (end′mōst′), *adj.* most distant.

endo-, a combining form meaning "within": *endogenous.*

en·do·crine (en′də krin, -krīn′, -krēn′), *adj.* **1.** secreting internally. **2.** of an endocrine gland or its secretion.

en′docrine gland′, any of various glands, as the thyroid or pituitary, that secrete hormones directly into the blood or lymph.

en·do·cri·nol·o·gy (en′dō krə nol′ə jē, -krī-), *n.* the science dealing with the endocrine glands and their secretions. —**en′do·cri·nol′o·gist**, *n.*

en·dog·e·nous (en doj′ə nəs), *adj. Biol.* growing or proceeding from within. —**en·dog′e·nous·ly**, *adv.*

end′ or′gan, a specialized structure at the peripheral end of sensory or motor nerve fibers.

en·dorse (en dôrs′), *v.t.*, **-dorsed, -dorsing. 1.** to support actively. **2.** to designate oneself as payee of (a check) by signing, usually on the back. **3.** to sign one's name on (a check). —**en·dors′a·ble**, *adj.* —**en·dorse′ment**, *n.* —**en·dors′er**, *n.*

en·do·scope (en′də skōp′), *n.* a slender, tubular instrument used to examine the interior of a body cavity or hollow organ. —**en·do·scop·ic** (en′də skop′ik), *adj.* —**en·dos′co·py** (en dos′kə pē), *n.*

en·do·ther·mic (en′dō thûr′mik), *adj. Chem.* accompanied by an absorption of heat. Also, **en′do·ther′mal.**

en·dow (en dou′), *v.t.* **1.** to provide with a permanent fund or source of income. **2.** to furnish, as with some gift, faculty, or quality. —**en·dow′er**, *n.* —**en·dow′ment**, *n.*

en·drin (en′drin), *n.* a solid isomer of dieldrin, used as an insecticide.

end′ run′, *Football.* a running play in which the ball carrier attempts to outflank the defensive end.

end′ ta′ble, a small table placed beside a chair or at the end of a sofa.

en·due (en dōō′, -dyōō′), *v.t.*, **-dued, -du·ing.** to provide with some quality or faculty.

en·dur·ance (en dōōr′əns, -dyōōr′-), *n.* **1.** the fact or power of enduring or bearing anything. **2.** lasting quality.

en·dure (en dōōr′, -dyōōr′), *v.*, **-dured, -dur·ing.** —*v.t.* **1.** to sustain without yielding. **2.** to bear with patience. —*v.i.* **3.** to continue in existence. **4.** to suffer patiently. —**en·dur′a·ble**, *adj.* —**en·dur′ing**, *adj.*

en·du·ro (en dōō′rō, -dyōō′rō), *n., pl.* **-du·ros.** a long-distance race, as for motorcycles, for going farthest, usually in 24 hours.

end·ways (end′wāz′), *adv.* **1.** on end. **2.** with the end upward or forward.

3. lengthwise. Also, **end·wise** (end′wīz′).

-ene, a combining form indicating unsaturated hydrocarbons: *benzene.*

ENE, east-northeast.

en·e·ma (en′ə mə), *n.* **1.** the injection of a fluid into the rectum. **2.** the fluid injected.

en·e·my (en′ə mē), *n., pl.* **-mies. 1.** a person who feels hatred for or fosters harmful designs against another. **2.** an opposing military force. **3.** a hostile nation or state. **4.** something harmful. —**Syn. 1.** adversary, foe, opponent.

en·er·get·ic (en′ər jet′ik), *adj.* possessing or exhibiting energy or vigor. —**en′er·get′i·cal·ly**, *adv.*

en·er·get·ics (en′ər jet′iks), *n.* the branch of physics that deals with energy.

en·er·gize (en′ər jīz′), *v.t.*, **-gized, -gizing.** to give energy to. —**en′er·giz′er**, *n.*

en·er·gy (en′ər jē), *n., pl.* **-gies. 1.** the capacity for vigorous activity. **2.** an exertion of such power. **3.** *Physics.* the capacity of matter or radiation to perform physical work. **4.** such capacity converted into heat from any of various forms, as crude oil, electricity, etc.

en·er·vate (en′ər vāt′), *v.t.*, **-vat·ed, -vat·ing.** to deprive of nerve, force, or strength. —**en′er·va′tion**, *n.* —**en′er·va′tor**, *n.*

en·fee·ble (en fē′bəl), *v.t.*, **-bled, -bling.** to make feeble. —**en·fee′ble·ment**, *n.*

en·fi·lade (en′fə lād′, en′fə lād′), *n.* a sweeping fire from along the length of a line of troops.

en·fold (en fōld′), *v.t.* **1.** to envelop or wrap up as if in folds. **2.** to clasp or embrace. —**en·fold′er**, *n.*

en·force (en fôrs′, -fōrs′), *v.t.*, **-forced, -forc·ing. 1.** to compel obedience to: *to enforce laws strictly.* **2.** to obtain or impose by force. —**en·force′a·ble**, *adj.* —**en·force′ment**, *n.*

en·fran·chise (en fran′chīz), *v.t.*, **-chised, -chis·ing. 1.** to admit to citizenship, esp. to the right of voting. **2.** to set free, as from slavery. —**en·fran·chise·ment** (en fran′chiz·mənt, -chīz·), *n.*

Eng., **1.** England. **2.** English.

eng., **1.** engine. **2.** engineer. **3.** engineering. **4.** engraved.

en·gage (en gāj′), *v.*, **-gaged, -gag·ing.** —*v.t.* **1.** to occupy the attention or efforts of (a person or persons). **2.** to secure for employment, use, aid, etc. **3.** to attract and hold fast: *The novel engaged his interest.* **4.** to bind, as by pledge. **5.** to betroth (usually used in the passive). **6.** to bring (troops) into conflict. **7.** to cause (gears) to become interlocked.

—*v.i.* **8.** to occupy oneself. **9.** to assume an obligation. **10.** to enter into conflict. **11.** to interlock. —**en·gag'er,** *n.*

en·gage·ment (en gāj'mənt), *n.* **1.** the act of engaging or state of being engaged. **2.** a promise of marriage. **3.** employment, usually in the performing arts. **4.** an appointment for a meeting. **5.** a conflict or battle.

en·gag·ing (en gā'jiṅg), *adj.* pleasingly attractive. —**en·gag'ing·ly,** *adv.*

en·gen·der (en jen'dər), *v.t.* **1.** to cause or give rise to: *Hatred engenders violence.* **2.** *Rare.* to beget or procreate.

en·gine (en'jən), *n.* **1.** a machine for converting thermal energy into mechanical power to produce motion. **2.** a railroad locomotive. **3.** a fire engine. **4.** any mechanical contrivance. —**en'gine·less,** *adj.*

en·gi·neer (en'jə nēr'), *n.* **1.** a person skilled in any branch of engineering. **2.** a person who operates an engine or a locomotive. —*v.t.* **3.** to plan, construct, or manage as an engineer. **4.** to carry through skillfully.

en·gi·neer·ing (en'jə nēr'iṅg), *n.* **1.** the science of making practical application of pure sciences, as physics, chemistry, etc., as in the construction of engines, buildings, etc. **2.** the work or profession of an engineer.

Eng·land (iṅg'glənd *or, often,* -lənd), *n.* the largest division of the United Kingdom, in S Great Britain.

Eng·lish (iṅg'glish), *adj.* **1.** of or characteristic of England or its inhabitants, etc. **2.** of or used in the English language. —*n.* **3.** the people of England. **4.** the Germanic language of the British Isles, standard in the U.S. and most of the British Commonwealth.

Eng'lish Chan'nel, an arm of the Atlantic between S England and N France.

Eng'lish horn', a large oboe, lower in pitch than the ordinary oboe.

Eng·lish·man (iṅg'glish mən *or, often,* -lish-), *n., pl.* -**men.** a native or a naturalized citizen of England. — **Eng'lish·wom'an,** *n. fem.*

engr., 1. engineer. **2.** engraved. **3.** engraving.

en·graft (en graft', -gräft'), *v.t.* to insert, as a scion of one plant into another, for propagation.

en·gram (en'gram), *n.* a structural change in the nervous system effected by an experience, considered to be the physical basis of memory.

en·grave (en grāv'), *v.t.,* -**graved,** -**grav·ing. 1.** to carve (letters or designs) on a hard surface, as of metal or stone. **2.** to print from such a surface. **3.** to mark or ornament with carved letters or designs. **4.** to impress deeply. —**en·grav'er,** *n.*

en·grav·ing (en grā'viṅg), *n.* **1.** the act of a person or thing that engraves a plate or block. **2.** the design engraved. **3.** an engraved plate or block. **4.** a print from this.

en·gross (en grōs'), *v.t.* to occupy completely, as the mind or attention. —**en·gross'er,** *n.* —**en·gross'ing,** *adj.* —**en·gross'ment,** *n.*

en·gulf (en gulf'), *v.t.* to swallow up in or as in a gulf.

en·hance (en hans', -häns'), *v.t.,* -**hanced,** -**hanc·ing.** to raise to a higher degree, as in value or quality. —**en·hance'ment,** *n.*

e·nig·ma (ə nig'mə), *n., pl.* -**mas,** -**ma·ta** (-mə tə). **1.** a baffling and inexplicable situation or person. **2.** a mysterious riddle. —**en·ig·mat'ic** (en'ig mat'ik, ē'nig-), **en'ig·mat'i·cal,** *adj.* —**en'ig·mat'i·cal·ly,** *adv.*

en·jamb·ment (en jam'mənt, -jamb'-), *n.* the running on of the thought from one line to the next without a syntactical break. Also, **en·jambe'ment.**

en·join (en join'), *v.t.* **1.** to prohibit by an injunction. **2.** to direct or order. —**en·join'er,** *n.*

en·joy (en joi'), *v.t.* **1.** to experience with joy. **2.** to have and use with satisfaction. —**en·joy'a·ble,** *adj.* —**en·joy'er,** *n.* —**en·joy'ment,** *n.*

enl., 1. enlarge. **2.** enlarged. **3.** enlisted.

en·large (en lärj'), *v.t., v.i.,* -**larged,** -**larg·ing. 1.** to make or grow larger in scope or size. **2.** to speak or write at length. —**en·large'ment,** *n.* —**en·larg'er,** *n.*

en·light·en (en līt'ᵊn), *v.t.* **1.** to give intellectual or spiritual light to. **2.** to instruct or teach. —**en·light'en·er,** *n.* —**en·light'en·ment,** *n.*

en·list (en list'), *v.i., v.t.* **1.** to engage for military service. **2.** to enter into some cause, enterprise, etc. —**en·list·ee',** *n.* —**en·list'er,** *n.* —**en·list'·ment,** *n.*

en·list'ed man', a member of the U.S. armed services who is not a commissioned officer or a warrant officer. —**enlist'ed wom'an.**

en·liv·en (en lī'vən), *v.t.* to make lively, active, or gay. —**en·liv'en·ment,** *n.*

en masse (än mas', en), in a group or as a whole.

en·mesh (en mesh'), *v.t.* to catch or entangle in or as in net meshes. —**en·mesh'ment,** *n.*

en·mi·ty (en'mi tē), *n., pl.* -**ties.** a bitter feeling of hatred.

en·no·ble (en nō'bəl), *v.t.,* -**bled,** -**bling.** to elevate in degree, excellence, or respect. —**en·no'ble·ment,** *n.* —**en·no'bler,** *n.*

en·nui (än wē′, än′wē), *n.* discontented boredom.

e·nor·mi·ty (i nôr′mi tē), *n., pl.* **-ties.**
1. outrageous character. 2. something outrageous, as an offense. 3. greatness of size or scope.

e·nor·mous (i nôr′məs), *adj.* greatly exceeding the common size, extent, etc. —**e·nor′mous·ly,** *adv.* —**e·nor′mous·ness,** *n.* —**Syn.** colossal, immense, vast.

e·nough (i nuf′), *adj.* 1. sufficient for the purpose or to satisfy desire. —*n.* 2. an adequate quantity or number. —*adv.* 3. sufficiently. 4. fully or quite. 5. tolerably or passably.

en·plane (en plān′), *v.i.,* **-planed, -planing.** to board an aircraft.

en·quire (en kwīr′), *v.t., v.i.,* **-quired, -quir·ing.** inquire.

en·quir·y (en kwīr′ē, en′kwə rē), *n., pl.* **-quir·ies.** inquiry.

en·rage (en rāj′), *v.t.,* **-raged, -rag·ing.** to put into a rage.

en·rap·ture (en rap′chər), *v.t.,* **-tured, -tur·ing.** to move to rapture.

en·rich (en rich′), *v.t.* 1. to make rich or richer. 2. to make better or finer, as in quality. —**en·rich′er,** *n.* —**en·rich′ment,** *n.*

en·rol (en rōl′), *v.t., v.i.,* **-rolled, -rolling.** enroll.

en·roll (en rōl′), *v.t., v.i.* 1. to write (a name), or insert the name of (a person), in a roll or register. 2. to enlist (oneself). —**en·roll′er,** *n.* —**en·roll′ment,** *n.*

en route (än rōōt′, en), on the way. **Ens.,** Ensign.

en·sconce (en skons′), *v.t.,* **-sconced, -sconc·ing.** to settle securely or snugly: *ensconced in an armchair.*

en·sem·ble (än säm′bəl, -sämb′), *n.* 1. all the parts of a thing taken together that produce a general effect. 2. a person's entire costume. 3. the united performance of an entire group of musicians, actors, etc. 4. the group so performing: *a string ensemble.*

en·sheathe (en shēth′), *v.t.,* **-sheathed, -sheath·ing.** to enclose in or as in a sheath.

en·shrine (en shrīn′), *v.t.,* **-shrined, -shrin·ing.** 1. to place in or as in a shrine. 2. to cherish as sacred. —**en·shrine′ment,** *n.*

en·shroud (en shroud′), *v.t.* to shroud or conceal.

en·sign (en′sīn; *Mil.* en′sən), *n.* 1. the national flag flown by naval vessels. 2. *U.S. Navy & Coast Guard.* the lowest commissioned officer.

en·si·lage (en′sə lij), *n.* silage.

en·sile (en sīl′, en′sīl), *v.t.,* **-siled, -sil·ing.** 1. to preserve (green fodder) in a silo. 2. to make into silage.

en·slave (en slāv′), *v.t.,* **-slaved, -slav·ing.** to make a slave of. —**en·slave′ment,** *n.*

en·snare (en snâr′), *v.t.,* **-snared, -snar·ing.** to trap in or as in a snare. —**en·snare′ment,** *n.*

en·sue (en sōō′), *v.i.,* **-sued, -su·ing.** 1. to follow afterward. 2. to follow as a consequence.

en·sure (en shōōr′), *v.t.,* **-sured, -sur·ing.** 1. to secure or guarantee. 2. to make sure or certain.

-ent, a suffix appearing in nouns and adjectives of Latin origin: *accident; different.*

en·tail (en tāl′), *v.t.* 1. to cause or involve by necessity. 2. to limit the passage of (a landed estate) to a specified line of heirs. —**en·tail′er,** *n.* —**en·tail′ment,** *n.*

en·tan·gle (en tang′gəl), *v.t.,* **-gled, -gling.** 1. to catch in or as in a tangle. 2. to confuse. —**en·tan′gler,** *n.* —**en·tan′gle·ment,** *n.*

en·tente (än tänt′), *n.* 1. an understanding between nations in respect to international policy. 2. the parties to such an understanding.

en·ter (en′tər), *v.t.* 1. to come or go in. 2. to be admitted into. 3. to make a beginning: *We have entered upon a new phase in history.* —*v.t.* 4. to come or go into. 5. to penetrate or pierce. 6. to put in or insert. 7. to become a member of. 8. to cause to be admitted. 9. to record or register. 10. *Law.* a. to make a formal record of (a fact). b. to occupy or to take possession of (lands). 11. **enter into,** a. engage in. b. to form a part or ingredient of. —**en′ter·a·ble,** *adj.* —**en′ter·er,** *n.*

en·ter·i·tis (en′tə rī′tis), *n.* inflammation of the intestines.

en·ter·prise (en′tər prīz′), *n.* 1. a project, esp. an important or difficult one. 2. dynamic boldness or ingenuity. 3. a business venture.

en·ter·pris·ing (en′tər prī′zing), *adj.* full of initiative and energy. —**en′ter·pris·ing·ly,** *adv.*

en·ter·tain (en′tər tān′), *v.t.* 1. to hold the attention of so as to bring about pleasure. 2. to treat as a guest. 3. to hold or keep in the mind. —*v.i.* 4. to have guests, as for a party. —**en′ter·tain′er,** *n.* —**en′ter·tain′ing,** *adj.* —**en′ter·tain′ment,** *n.* —**Syn.** 1. amuse, divert. 3. consider.

en·thral (en thrôl′), *v.t.,* **-thralled, -thral·ling.** enthrall.

en·thrall (en thrôl′), *v.t.* 1. to charm fascinatingly. 2. *Rare.* to enslave. —**en·thrall′ing·ly,** *adv.* —**en·thrall′ment,** *n.*

en·throne (en thrōn′), *v.t.,* **-throned, -thron·ing.** 1. to place on or as on a throne. 2. to exalt or revere. —**en·throne′ment,** *n.*

en·thuse (en thōoz′), *v.*, **-thused,
-thus·ing.** *Informal.* —*v.i.* **1.** to show
enthusiasm. —*v.t.* **2.** to move to
enthusiasm.
—**Usage.** Although it is now widely
encountered, ENTHUSE is disapproved
by some careful users of English,
and in formal writing it is best to
avoid it.
en·thu·si·asm (en thōō′zē az′əm), *n.*
1. lively, absorbing, keen interest. **2.**
an activity in which such interest is
shown. —**en·thu′si·ast** (-ast′), *n.*
—**en·thu′si·as′tic,** *adj.* —**en·thu′sias′ti·cal·ly,** *adv.*
en·tice (en tīs′), *v.t.*, **-ticed, -tic·ing.**
to lead on by exciting desire. —**en·
tice′ment,** *n.*
en·tire (en tī°r′), *adj.* having unbroken unity, with no part omitted.
—**en·tire′ly,** *adv.* —**en·tire′ness,** *n.*
—**Syn.** complete, total, whole.
en·tire·ty (en tī°r′tē), *n., pl.* **-ties. 1.**
the state of being entire. **2.** something entire or whole.
en·ti·tle (en tīt′°l), *v.t.*, **-tled, -tling.
1.** to give a title, right, or claim to.
2. to name or designate.
en·ti·ty (en′ti tē), *n., pl.* **-ties. 1.** something that has a real existence. **2.**
being or existence.
en·tomb (en tōōm′), *v.t.* to bury or
place in a tomb. —**en·tomb′ment,** *n.*
entomol., 1. entomological. **2.** ento-
mology. Also, **entom.**
en·to·mol·o·gy (en′tə mol′ə jē), *n.* the
branch of zoology dealing with insects. —**en·to·mo·log·i·cal** (en′tə-
mə loj′i kəl), *adj.* —**en·to·mo·log′-
i·cal·ly,** *adv.* —**en·to·mol′o·gist,** *n.*
en·tou·rage (än′tōō räzh′), *n.* a body
of attendants or associates, esp. when
traveling together with a dignitary.
en·tr'acte (än trakt′), *n.* **1.** the interval
between two acts of a theatrical
performance. **2.** music, dancing,
etc., during such an interval.
en·trails (en′trālz, -trəls), *n.pl.* the
internal parts of an animal, esp.
the intestines.
en·train (en trān′), *v.i., v.t.* to put or
go aboard a train.
en·trance¹ (en′trəns), *n.* **1.** the act
of entering. **2.** a point or place of
entering, as a doorway. **3.** the right
or permission to enter.
en·trance² (en trans′, -träns′), *v.t.*,
-tranced, -tranc·ing. to fill with
delight or wonder. —**en·trance′-
ment,** *n.* —**en·tranc′ing·ly,** *adv.*
en·trant (en′trənt), *n.* **1.** a person
who enters. **2.** a competitor in a
contest.
en·trap (en trap′), *v.t.*, **-trapped, -trap-
ping.** to catch in or as in a trap.
—**en·trap′ment,** *n.*
en·treat (en trēt′), *v.t., v.i.* to ask
or beg imploringly. —**en·treat′ing·ly,**
adv. —**en·treat′y,** *n.*

en·trée (än′trā), *n.* **1.** the main course
of a meal. **2.** a dish served before
the main course or between the
regular courses. **3.** the right of entry.
Also, **en′tree.**
en·trench (en trench′), *v.t.* **1.** to dig
trenches for defensive purposes
around. **2.** to place in a position of
strength: *safely entrenched behind
undeniable facts.* —**en·trench′ment,** *n.*
en·tre·pre·neur (än′trə prə nûr′,
-nōōr′), *n.* a person who organizes,
manages, and assumes responsibility
for a business or other enterprise.
—**en′tre·pre·neur′i·al,** *adj.*
en·tro·py (en′trə pē), *n.* **1.** a measure
of the amount of energy unavailable
for work during a natural process.
2. hypothesized tendency toward uniform inertness, esp. of the universe.
en·trust (en trust′), *v.t.* **1.** to charge
with a trust or responsibility. **2.** to
commit (something) in trust.
en·try (en′trē), *n., pl.* **-tries. 1.** en-
trance¹. **2.** the act of recording something in a book, register, etc. **3.** the
item so recorded. **4.** a person or
thing entered in a contest. **5.** a word,
phrase, etc., listed alphabetically in
a dictionary or reference book, usually with its definition or explanation.
en·twine (en twīn′), *v.t., v.i.,* **-twined,
-twin·ing.** to twine with, around, or
together.
e·nu·mer·ate (i nōō′mə rāt′, i nyōō′-),
v.t., **-at·ed, -at·ing. 1.** to name one
by one. **2.** to count or compute.
—**e·nu′mer·a′tion,** *n.* —**e·nu′mer·a′-
tor,** *n.*
e·nun·ci·ate (i nun′sē āt′, -shē-), *v.t.,
v.i.*, **-at·ed, -at·ing. 1.** to pronounce
(words), esp. in an articulate manner.
2. to declare definitely. **3.** *Rare.* to
proclaim. —**e·nun′ci·a′tion,** *n.* —
e·nun′ci·a′tor, *n.*
en·u·re·sis (en′yə rē′sis), *n.* involuntary urination.
env., envelope.
en·vel·op (en vel′əp), *v.t.* **1.** to wrap
or cover thoroughly. **2.** to surround
entirely. —**en·vel′op·er,** *n.* —**en·
vel′op·ment,** *n.*
en·ve·lope (en′və lōp, än′-), *n.* **1.** a
flat paper container, as for a letter,
usually having a gummed flap. **2.** a
wrapper or surrounding cover.
en·ven·om (en ven′əm), *v.t.* **1.** to make
poisonous. **2.** to embitter.
en·vi·a·ble (en′vē ə bəl), *adj.* causing
or worthy of envy. —**en′vi·a·bly,**
adv.
en·vi·ous (en′vē əs), *adj.* full of or
expressing envy. —**en′vi·ous·ly,** *adv.*
—**en′vi·ous·ness,** *n.*
en·vi·ron·ment (en vī′rən mənt, -vī′-
ərn-), *n.* the aggregate of surrounding things, conditions, or influences.
—**en·vi′ron·men′tal,** *adj.*

en·vi·ron·men·tal·ist (en vī′rən men′tə-list), *n.* any person who advocates or works to protect the air, water, and other natural resources from pollution. —**en·vi′ron·men′tal·ism,** *n.*

en·vi·rons (en vī′rənz, -vī′ərnz), *n.pl.* surrounding parts, as of a city.

en·vis·age (en viz′ij), *v.t.,* -aged, -ag·ing. to imagine and visualize.

en·vi·sion (en vizh′ən), *v.t.* to picture mentally.

en·voy[1] (en′voi, än′-), *n.* 1. a diplomatic agent, esp. one next in rank after an ambassador. 2. any accredited representative.

en·voy[2] (en′voi), *n.* a final stanza of some forms of poetry. Also, **en′voi.**

en·vy (en′vē), *n., pl.* -vies, *v.,* -vied, -vy·ing. —*n.* 1. a sense of discontent or jealousy about or desire for another's advantages, possessions, etc. 2. an object of envious feeling. —*v.t.* 3. to regard with envy. —**en′vy·ing·ly,** *adv.*

en·zyme (en′zīm), *n.* a complex protein molecule, originating from living cells and capable of producing certain chemical changes in organic substances by catalytic action, as in digestion. —**en·zy·mat·ic** (en′zī mat′ik, -zī-), *adj.*

E·o·cene (ē′ə sēn′), *adj.* 1. noting or pertaining to an epoch of either the Tertiary or Paleogene period. —*n.* 2. the Eocene period.

e·o·li·an (ē ō′lē ən), *adj.* blown, carried, or arranged by the wind: *eolian sand.*

e.o.m., *Chiefly Com.* end of the month.

e·on (ē′ən, ē′on), *n.* 1. a division of geologic time comprising two or more eras. 2. aeon (def. 1).

-eous, a suffix meaning "of the nature of" or "like": *gaseous.*

EPA, Environmental Protection Agency.

ep·au·let (ep′ə let′, -lit, ep′ə let′), *n.* an ornamental shoulder piece worn on uniforms. Also, **ep′au·lette′.** [< F *épaulette* = *épaule* shoulder + *-et(te)*]

é·pée (ā pā′), *n.* Fencing. a rapier with a three-sided blade and a guard over the tip. Also, **e·pee′.** —**é·pée′-ist,** *n.*

e·pergne (i pûrn′, ā pârn′), *n.* an ornamental dish for fruit, flowers, etc.

e·phed·rine (i fed′rin; Chem. ef′i-drēn′, -drin), *n.* a crystalline alkaloid used chiefly for the treatment of respiratory ailments.

e·phem·er·al (i fem′ər əl), *adj.* lasting a very short time, esp. for only one day.

epi-, a prefix meaning "upon," "on," or "over": *epidermis.*

ep·ic (ep′ik), *adj.* 1. noting a long

poetic composition, usually centered upon a hero or heroine, in which great achievements are narrated in elevated style. 2. resembling such poetry. 3. heroic or majestic. —*n.* 4. an epic poem. 5. any composition resembling an epic poem.

ep·i·cene (ep′i sēn′), *adj.* 1. belonging to or having the characteristics of both sexes. 2. effeminate or unmanly. —*n.* 3. an epicene person or thing.

ep·i·cen·ter (ep′i sen′tər), *n.* a point on the surface of the globe which lies directly above the center of an earthquake. —**ep′i·cen′tral,** *adj.*

ep·i·cure (ep′ə kyŏor′), *n.* a person who cultivates a refined taste, esp. in food and wine. [< *Epicurus,* 342?–270 B.C., Greek philosopher]

e·pi·cu·re·an (ep′ə kyŏŏ rē′ən, -kyŏŏr′ē-), *adj.* 1. having luxurious tastes or habits, esp. in eating and drinking. 2. fit for an epicure. —*n.* 3. epicure.

ep·i·dem·ic (ep′i dem′ik), *adj.* 1. affecting at the same time a large number of persons in a locality, as a contagious disease. —*n.* 2. an epidemic disease. 3. a rapid spread of something. —**ep′i·dem′i·cal·ly,** *adv.*

ep·i·der·mis (ep′i dûr′mis), *n.* the outer layer of the skin. —**ep′i·der′mal, ep′i·der′mic,** *adj.*

ep·i·glot·tis (ep′ə glot′is), *n., pl.* -glot·tis·es. a thin, valvelike, cartilaginous structure that covers the glottis during swallowing.

ep·i·gram (ep′ə gram′), *n.* any witty or pointed saying or poem, tersely expressed. —**ep·i·gram·mat·ic** (ep′ə grə mat′ik), *adj.* —**ep′i·gram·mat′i·cal·ly,** *adv.*

e·pig·ra·phy (i pig′rə fē), *n.* the study or science of inscriptions, esp. of ancient inscriptions.

ep·i·lep·sy (ep′ə lep′sē), *n.* a disorder of the nervous system, usually characterized by fits or convulsions that end with loss of consciousness. —**ep·i·lep·tic** (ep′ə lep′tik), *adj., n.* —**ep·i·lep·toid** (ep′i lep′toid), *adj.*

ep·i·logue (ep′ə lôg′, -log′), *n.* 1. a concluding part added to a literary work. 2. a speech delivered by one of the actors or actresses at the end of a play. Also, **ep′i·log′.**

ep·i·neph·rine (ep′ə nef′rin, -rēn), *n.* 1. a hormone produced by the adrenal glands and causing a rise in blood pressure. 2. a commercial form of this substance, used chiefly as a heart stimulant, to constrict the blood vessels, and to relax the bronchi in asthma. Also, **ep′i·neph′rin.**

E·piph·a·ny (i pif′ə nē), *n., pl.* **-nies.** a Christian festival, observed on January 6, commemorating the manifestation of Christ to the gentiles in the persons of the Magi.

Episc., **1.** Episcopal. **2.** Episcopalian.

e·pis·co·pa·cy (i pis′kə pə sē), *n., pl.* **-cies. 1.** government of the church by bishops. **2.** episcopate.

e·pis·co·pal (i pis′kə pəl), *adj.* **1.** of a bishop. **2.** based on or recognizing a governing order of bishops. **3.** (*cap.*) designating the Anglican Church or some branch of it, as the Protestant Episcopal Church. **—e·pis′co·pal·ly,** *adj.*

E·pis·co·pa·lian (i pis′kə pāl′yən, -pā′lē ən), *adj.* **1.** pertaining or adhering to the Protestant Episcopal Church. **—n. 2.** a member of the Protestant Episcopal Church.

e·pis·co·pate (i pis′kə pit, -pāt′), *n.* **1.** the office, dignity, or term of a bishop. **2.** the order or body of bishops.

ep·i·sode (ep′i sōd′, -zōd′), *n.* **1.** an incident in a person's life or experience. **2.** an incident, scene, etc., within a narrative. **—ep·i·sod·ic** (ep′i sod′ik, -zod′-), *adj.* **—ep·i·sod′i·cal·ly,** *adv.*

e·pis·te·mol·o·gy (i pis′tə mol′ə jē), *n.* a branch of philosophy that investigates the origin, methods, and limits of human knowledge.

Epist., Epistle.

E·pis·tle (i pis′əl), *n.* **1.** one of the apostolic letters in the New Testament. **2.** (*l.c.*) *Now Facetious.* a letter, esp. a long, elegant one. **—e·pis·to·lar·y** (i pis′tə ler′ē), *adj.*

ep·i·taph (ep′i taf′, -täf′), *n.* an inscription, esp. on a tomb, in memory of a deceased person.

ep·i·tha·la·mi·on (ep′ə thə lā′mē ən), *n., pl.* **-mi·a** (-mē ə). a wedding song or poem.

ep·i·tha·la·mi·um (ep′ə thə lā′mē əm), *n., pl.* **-mi·ums, -mi·a** (-mē ə). epithalamion.

ep·i·the·li·um (ep′ə thē′lē əm), *n., pl.* **-li·ums, -li·a** (-lē ə). *Biol.* any tissue that covers a surface or lines a cavity. **—ep′i·the′li·al,** *adj.*

ep·i·thet (ep′ə thet′), *n.* **1.** any descriptive word or phrase replacing or added to the name of a person or thing. **2.** a word, phrase, etc., used in abuse, contempt, etc.

e·pit·o·me (i pit′ə mē), *n.* **1.** a person or thing that has the ideal features of a whole class: *She is the epitome of goodness.* **2.** a summary.

e·pit·o·mize (i pit′ə mīz′), *v.t.,* **-mized, -miz·ing.** to be or make an epitome of.

e plu·ri·bus u·num (ē′ plŏŏr′ə bəs yōō′nəm), *Latin.* out of many, one (motto of the U.S.).

ep·och (ep′ək), *n.* **1.** a period of time marked by new developments and other crucial changes: *an epoch of electronics.* **2.** the beginning of a distinctive period in the history of anything. **3.** any of several divisions of a geological period. **—ep′och·al,** *adj.* **—ep′och·al·ly,** *adv.*

ep·ox·y (e pok′sē), *n., pl.* **-ox·ies.** a synthetic substance used in adhesives, coatings, etc. Also called **epox′y res′in.**

ep·si·lon (ep′sə lon′, -lən), *n.* the fifth letter of the Greek alphabet (E, ε).

Ep′som salts′ (ep′səm), a white crystalline magnesium salt used as a cathartic. [from its presence in the mineral water at *Epsom,* England]

eq., **1.** equal. **2.** equation. **3.** equivalent.

eq·ua·ble (ek′wə bəl, ē′kwə-), *adj.* **1.** uniform, as motion or temperature. **2.** tranquil, as the mind. **—eq′ua·bil′i·ty,** *n.* **—eq′ua·bly,** *adv.*

e·qual (ē′kwəl), *adj., n., v.,* **e·qualed, e·qual·ing** or **e·qualled, e·qual·ling.** **—adj. 1.** of the same quantity, degree, merit, etc. **2.** having the same rights, privileges, etc. **3.** evenly balanced. **4.** uniform in operation or effect. **5.** adequate in power, ability, etc.: *He wasn't equal to the task.* **—n. 6.** a person or thing that is equal. **—v.t. 7.** to be or become equal to. **8.** to make or do something equal to. **—e·qual·i·ty** (i kwol′i tē), *n.* **—e′qual·ly,** *adv.* **—Syn. 1.** equivalent, tantamount.

e·qual·ize (ē′kwəl līz′), *v.t.,* **-ized, -iz·ing.** to make equal or uniform. **—e′qual·i·za′tion,** *n.* **—e′qual·iz′er,** *n.*

e′qual sign′, the symbol (=) used in a mathematical equation to indicate that the terms it separates are equal. Also, **e′quals sign′.**

e′qual time′, a doctrine that a television or radio station must give or sell equal air time to all qualified political candidates if it gives or sells any time to one of them.

e·qua·nim·i·ty (ē′kwə nim′i tē, ek′wə-), *n.* composure, esp. under tension.

e·quate (i kwāt′), *v.,* **e·quat·ed, e·quat·ing. —v.t. 1.** to state the equality of or between, as in an equation. **2.** to regard, treat, or represent as equivalent. **—v.i. 3.** to be equal. **—e·quat′a·ble,** *adj.*

e·qua·tion (i kwā′zhən, -shən), *n.* **1.** the act of equating or state of being equated. **2.** an expression or a proposition, often algebraic, asserting the equality of two quantities. **—e·qua′tion·al,** *adj.* **—e·qua′tion·al·ly,** *adv.*

e·qua·tor (i kwā′tər), *n.* the great circle of the earth that is equidistant from the North Pole and South Pole.

—e·qua·to·ri·al (ē′kwə tôr′ē əl, -tôr′-, ek′wə-), adj.

Equato′rial Guin′ea, a country in W equatorial Africa.

eq·uer·ry (ek′wə rē), n., pl. **-ries. 1.** (formerly) an officer who supervised royal horses. **2.** an officer who attends the British royal family.

e·ques·tri·an (i kwes′trē ən), adj. **1.** of horsemen or horsemanship. **2.** mounted on horseback. **3.** representing a person on a horse. —n. **4.** a person who rides horses. —e·ques′tri·an·ism, n. —e·ques′tri·enne′ (-trē en′), n. fem.

equi-, a combining form meaning "equal": equidistant.

e·qui·an·gu·lar (ē′kwē ang′gyə lər), adj. having all the angles equal.

e·qui·dis·tant (ē′kwi dis′tənt), adj. equally distant. —e′qui·dis′tant·ly, adv.

e·qui·lat·er·al (ē′kwə lat′ər əl), adj. having all the sides equal.

e·qui·lib·ri·um (ē′kwə lib′rē əm), n., pl. **-ri·ums, -ri·a** (-rē ə). a state of balance between any powers, forces, influences, etc.

e·quine (ē′kwīn), adj. of or resembling a horse.

e·qui·nox (ē′kwə noks′, ek′wə-), n. the times when the sun crosses the equator, making night and day of approximately equal length all over the earth, occurring about March 21 (**vernal equinox**) and September 22 (**autumnal equinox**). —e·qui·noc·tial (ē′kwə nok′shəl), adj.

e·quip (i kwip′), v.t., **e·quipped, e·quip·ping.** to provide with, esp. for a specific service or function.

equip., equipment.

eq·ui·page (ek′wə pij), n. a carriage, often with its horses and attendants.

e·quip·ment (i kwip′mənt), n. **1.** anything kept, furnished, or provided for a specific purpose. **2.** the act of equipping a person or thing. **3.** the state of being equipped.

e·qui·poise (ē′kwə poiz′, ek′wə-), n. **1.** an equal distribution of weight. **2.** a counterpoise or counterbalance.

eq·ui·ta·ble (ek′wi tə bəl), adj. fair and just. —eq′ui·ta·bly, adv.

eq·ui·ta·tion (ek′wi tā′shən), n. the act or skill of riding on horseback.

eq·ui·ty (ek′wi tē), n., pl. **-ties. 1.** fairness and justice. **2.** a system of jurisprudence serving to supplement and remedy the common law. **3.** the value, less liabilities, of a property or business.

equiv., equivalent.

e·quiv·a·lent (i kwiv′ə lənt), adj. **1.** equal in value, measure, force, significance, etc. —n. **2.** something equivalent. —e·quiv′a·lence, n. —e·quiv′a·lent·ly, adv.

e·quiv·o·cal (i kwiv′ə kəl), adj. **1.** having two possible meanings, usually purposely deceptive. **2.** uncertain or doubtful. **3.** questionable or dubious. —e·quiv′o·cal·ly, adv. —e·quiv′o·cal·ness, n. —Syn. **1.** ambiguous, misleading.

e·quiv·o·cate (i kwiv′ə kāt′), v.i., **-cat·ed, -cat·ing.** to use equivocal or deceptive expressions. —e·quiv′o·ca′tion, n. —e·quiv′o·ca′tor, n.

Er, erbium.

-er¹, a suffix meaning: a. a person who makes or works at something: hatter. b. a person who lives in or comes from a certain place: Icelander. c. a person or thing that has or does: three-master; harvester.

-er², a suffix forming the comparative degree of adjectives: harder.

ERA, Equal Rights Amendment (to the U.S. Constitution, esp. referring to sexual equality).

e·ra (ēr′ə, er′ə), n. **1.** a period of time characterized by notable historical change. **2.** a system of chronological notation reckoned from a given date. **3.** a major division of geological time composed of a number of periods.

e·rad·i·cate (i rad′ə kāt′), v.t., **-cat·ed, -cat·ing. 1.** to destroy utterly. **2.** to erase or remove. —e·rad′i·ca·ble, adj. —e·rad′i·ca′tion, n. —e·rad′i·ca′tor, n.

e·rase (i rās′), v.t., **e·rased, e·ras·ing. 1.** to rub out or remove, as writing, sounds, etc. **2.** to obliterate, as from something tangible or intangible. —e·ras′a·ble, adj. —e·ras′er, n. —e·ras·ure (i rā′shər), n.

E·ras·mus (i raz′məs), n. **Des·i·de·ri·us** (dez′i dēr′ē əs), 1466?–1536, Dutch scholar and theologian.

er·bi·um (ûr′bē əm), n. **Chem.** a metallic element, having pink salts. Symbol: Er; at. wt.: 167.26; at. no.: 68.

ere (âr), prep., conj. **Poetic.** before.

e·rect (i rekt′), adj. **1.** straight up in position or posture. —v.t. **2.** to construct or put up by fitting materials together. **3.** to raise and set in an upright position: to erect a telegraph pole. **4.** to set up or establish. —e·rect′a·ble, adj. — e·rect′ly, adv. —e·rect′ness, n. — e·rec′tor, n.

e·rec·tile (i rek′təl, -til, -tīl), adj. **1.** capable of being erected or set upright. **2.** capable of being distended with blood and becoming rigid, as tissue.

e·rec·tion (i rek′shən), n. **1.** something erected, as a building. **2.** a rigid state of an organ or part containing erectile tissue, esp. of the penis or the clitoris.

ere·long (âr lông′, -long′), *adv. Archaic.* before long.

er·e·mite (er′ə mīt′), *n.* a hermit, esp. one under a religious vow.

erg (ûrg), *n. Physics.* a unit of work or energy.

er·go (ûr′gō, er′gō), *adv. Chiefly Logic.* therefore. [< L]

er·gos·ter·ol (ûr gos′tə rōl′, -rôl′, -rol′), *n.* a compound that occurs in ergot and yeast and that, when irradiated with ultraviolet light, is converted into vitamin D.

er·got (ûr′gət, -got), *n.* **1.** a disease of rye and other cereal grasses, caused by a fungus. **2.** the resulting substance, used medicinally.

E·rie (ēr′ē), *n., pl.,* for 2, **E·ries,** **E·rie.** **1.** Lake, the southernmost lake of the Great Lakes. **2.** a member of a tribe of American Indians formerly living along the southern shore of Lake Erie.

Er·in (er′in, ēr′in, âr′in), *n. Literary.* Ireland.

er·mine (ûr′min), *n., pl.* **-mines, -mine.** **1.** a weasel having a white winter coat. **2.** its fur.

e·rode (i rōd′), *v.,* **e·rod·ed, e·rod·ing.** —*v.t.,* **1.** to eat out or away. **2.** to wear away by erosion. —*v.i.* **3.** to become eroded. —**e·rod′i·ble,** *adj.*

e·rog·e·nous (i roj′ə nəs), *adj.* sexually sensitive, esp. of certain zones of the human body. Also, **e·ro·to·gen·ic** (i rō′tə jen′ik).

E·ros (ēr′os, er′os), *n.* the ancient Greek god of love.

e·ro·sion (i rō′zhən), *n.* **1.** the act or state of eroding. **2.** the state of being eroded. **3.** the process by which the surface of the earth is worn away by the action of water, winds, waves, etc. —**e·ro′sion·al,** *adj.*

e·ro·sive (i rō′siv), *adj.* causing erosion. —**e·ro′sive·ness,** *n.*

e·rot·ic (i rot′ik), *adj.* of or arousing sexual love or desire. [< Gk. erōtik-(ós) of love] —**e·rot′i·cal·ly,** *adv.*

e·rot·i·ca (i rot′i kə), *n.* literature or art dealing with sexual love.

err (ûr, er), *v.i.* **1.** to be in or fall into error. **2.** to sin or do wrong.

er·rand (er′ənd), *n.* **1.** a short or quick trip to do something, usually for someone else. **2.** the object of such a trip.

er·rant (er′ənt), *adj.* **1.** wandering in quest of adventure. **2.** erring or doing wrong. **3.** moving aimlessly. —**er′rant·ly,** *adv.*

er·rat·ic (i rat′ik), *adj.* **1.** unpredictably eccentric. **2.** wandering or not fixed: *erratic winds.* —**er·rat′i·cal·ly,** *adv.*

er·ra·tum (i rā′təm, i rä′-), *n., pl.* **-ta** (-tə) an error in writing or printing.

erron., **1.** erroneous. **2.** erroneously.

er·ro·ne·ous (ə rō′nē əs, e rō′-), *adj.* containing or marked by error. —**er·ro′ne·ous·ly,** *adv.*

er·ror (er′ər), *n.* **1.** a deviation from accuracy or correctness. **2.** belief in something untrue. **3.** the condition of believing what is not true. **4.** a sin or wrongdoing. **5.** *Baseball.* a defensive misplay in fielding. —**er′ror·less,** *adj.*

er·satz (er′zäts, -sats), *adj.* **1.** serving as a substitute, esp. something synthetic. —*n.* **2.** a substitute, esp. of inferior quality.

erst (ûrst), *adv. Archaic.* formerly.

erst·while (ûrst′hwīl′, -wīl′), *adj.* **1.** former or previous. —*adv.* **2.** *Archaic.* formerly.

e·ruct (i rukt′), *v.t., v.i.* **1.** to belch forth. **2.** to emit violently, as matter from a volcano.

er·u·dite (er′yoo dīt′, er′oo-), *adj.* profoundly learned: *an erudite commentary.* —**er′u·dite′ly,** *adv.*

er·u·di·tion (er′yoo dish′ən, er′oo-), *n.* profound learning acquired by study, research, etc.

e·rupt (i rupt′), *v.i.* **1.** to burst forth, as volcanic matter. **2.** (of a volcano, etc.) to eject matter. **3.** to break out of a pent-up state. **4.** to break out in a skin rash. —*v.t.* **5.** to cause to erupt. —**e·rup′tion,** *n.* —**e·rup′tive,** *adj.* —**e·rup′tive·ly,** *adv.*

-ery, a suffix meaning: **a.** business: *grocery.* **b.** state or condition: *slavery.* **c.** art or practice: *archery.* **d.** place or establishment: *bakery.* **e.** goods or products: *pottery.* **f.** things collectively: *finery.* **g.** qualities: *trickery.* **h.** actions: *foolery.*

er·y·sip·e·las (er′i sip′ə ləs, ēr′i-), *n.* an acute, infectious bacterial disease characterized by inflammation of the skin.

er·y·the·ma (er′ə thē′mə), *n.* abnormal redness of the skin due to local congestion, as in inflammation.

e·ryth·ro·cyte (i rith′rə sīt′), *n.* one of the red cells of the blood that contain hemoglobin and that carry oxygen to the cells and tissues.

Es, einsteinium.

-es¹, an ending marking the plural of certain nouns ending as in *s, z, ch, sh: losses; fuzzes; riches; ashes.*

-es², an ending marking the third person sing. indicative present of certain verbs ending as in *s, z, ch, sh: passes; buzzes; pitches; dashes.*

es·ca·late (es′kə lāt′), *v.t., v.i.,* **-lat·ed, -lat·ing.** to increase in intensity, magnitude, etc. —**es′ca·la′tion,** *n.* —**es·ca·la·to·ry** (es′kə lə tôr′ē, -tôr′ē), *adj.*

es·ca·la·tor (es′kə lā′tər), *n.* a continuously moving stairway for carrying passengers up or down.

es·cal·lop (e skol′əp, e skal′-), *v.t.* to bake in sauce, with crumbs on top.

es·ca·pade (es′kə pād′, es′kə pād′), *n.* a reckless adventure or wild prank.

es·cape (e skāp′), *v.*, **-caped, -cap·ing**, *n.*, *adj.* —*v.i.* **1.** to get away, as from imprisonment. **2.** to avoid capture, punishment, etc. **3.** to issue from a confining enclosure, as a fluid. —*v.t.* **4.** to slip away from. **5.** to succeed in avoiding (any threatened evil). **6.** to elude (one's memory, etc.). **7.** to slip from or be uttered inadvertently by, as a remark. —*n.* **8.** a means of escaping. **9.** avoidance of reality. **10.** leakage, as of water. —*adj.* **11.** for or providing an escape: *an escape hatch.* —**es·cap′a·ble,** *adj.* —**Syn. 4.** avoid, elude, evade.

es·ca·pee (e skā′pē′), *n.* a person who has escaped, as from imprisonment.

es·cape·ment (e skāp′mənt), *n.* the portion of a watch or clock that measures beats and controls the speed of wheels in gear.

escape′ veloc′ity, the minimum speed an object must have to free itself from the gravitational pull of a body.

es·cap·ism (e skā′piz əm), *n.* the avoidance of reality by absorption of the mind in entertainment or in an imaginative situation, etc. —**es·cap′ist,** *adj.*, *n.*

es·ca·role (es′kə rōl′), *n.* a broadleaved chicory, used for salads.

es·carp·ment (e skärp′mənt), *n.* a long clifflike ridge of land or rock.

-escence, a suffix of nouns corresponding to adjectives ending in *-escent: convalescence.*

-escent, a suffix of adjectives meaning: **a.** beginning: *adolescent.* **b.** giving off light: *fluorescent.*

es·chew (es chōō′), *v.t.* to keep away from, as something wicked. —**eschew′al,** *n.* —**es·chew′er,** *n.*

es·cort (*n.* es′kôrt; *v.* e skôrt′), *n.* **1.** a person or body of persons accompanying another for protection, guidance, or courtesy. **2.** a man who accompanies a woman in public. —*v.t.* **3.** to accompany as an escort.

es·cri·toire (es′kri twär′), *n.* a writing desk, esp. of an antique type.

es·crow (es′krō, e skrō′), *n.* a contract, money, etc., deposited with a third person, by whom it is to be delivered to the grantee on the fulfillment of some condition.

es·cu·do (e skōō′dō), *n.*, *pl.* **-dos.** the monetary unit of Portugal.

es·cutch·eon (e skuch′ən), *n.* a shield on which a coat of arms is depicted.

ESE, east-southeast.

-ese, a suffix referring to: **a.** nationality: *Chinese.* **b.** language: *Japanese.* **c.** literary style: *journalese.*

Esk., Eskimo.

Es·ki·mo (es′kə mō′), *n.*, *pl.* **-mos, -mo.** **1.** a member of a people inhabiting Greenland, northern Canada, Alaska, and northeastern Siberia. **2.** the language spoken by the Eskimos.

Es′kimo dog′, a strong, medium-sized dog used in arctic regions for drawing sleds.

e·soph·a·gus (i sof′ə gəs, ē sof′-), *n.*, *pl.* **-gi** (-jī′). a tube connecting the mouth with the stomach gullet. —**e·soph·a·ge·al** (i sof′ə jē′əl, ē′sə faj′ē-əl), *adj.*

es·o·ter·ic (es′ə ter′ik), *adj.* **1.** understood by or meant for only a select few. **2.** private or secret.

ESP, extrasensory perception: communication outside of normal sensory activity, as in telepathy.

esp., especially. Also, **espec.**

es·pa·drille (es′pə dril′), *n.* a flat sandal, usually with a canvas upper.

es·pal·ier (e spal′yər), *n.* **1.** a trellis on which fruit trees or shrubs are trained to grow flat. **2.** a plant so trained.

es·pe·cial (e spesh′əl), *adj.* very special or particular. —**es·pe′cial·ly,** *adv.*

Es·pe·ran·to (es′pə rän′tō, -ran′-), *n.* an artificial international language based on the most common words in the important European languages.

es·pi·o·nage (es′pē ə näzh′, -nij, es′pē-ə näzh′), *n.* the practice of spying on others.

es·pla·nade (es′plə nād′, -näd′), *n.* any open, level space, esp. one serving for public walks or drives.

es·pouse (e spouz′), *v.t.*, **-poused, -pous·ing. 1.** to adopt or advocate, as a cause. **2.** *Archaic.* to take or give in marriage. —**es·pou′sal,** *n.* —**es·pous′er,** *n.*

es·pres·so (e spres′ō), *n.* a strong coffee prepared by forcing live steam through ground dark-roast coffee beans.

es·prit (e sprē′), *n.* sprightliness of spirit or wit.

es·prit de corps (e sprē′ də kôr′), a sense of union developed among a group of persons associated together.

es·py (e spī′), *v.t.*, **-pied, -py·ing.** to catch sight of.

Esq., Esquire. Also, **Esqr.**

-esque, a suffix indicating: **a.** style or manner: *Romanesque.* **b.** resemblance: *statuesque.*

es·quire (e skwī°r′, es′kwī°r), *n.* **1.** (*cap.*) *Chiefly Brit.* an unofficial title of respect. **2.** a man of the English gentry ranking next below a knight. **3.** *Archaic.* squire (def. 2).

-ess, a suffix forming feminine nouns: *hostess.*

es·say (n. es′ā for 1; es′ā, e sā′ for 2; v. e sā′), n. 1. a short literary composition on a particular theme or subject. 2. an attempt or endeavor. —v.t. 3. to try or attempt. —es·say′er, n. —es′say·ist, n.

es·sence (es′əns), n. 1. the basic or intrinsic constituent or quality of a thing. 2. a substance obtained from a plant or drug, by distillation or infusion, and containing its characteristic properties in concentrated form. 3. Literary. a perfume.

es·sen·tial (ə sen′shəl), adj. 1. absolutely necessary and important. 2. of or constituting the essence of a thing. —n. 3. an essential thing or element. —es·sen′tial·ly, adv. —Syn. 1. indispensable, requisite.

EST, Eastern Standard Time.

-est¹, a suffix forming the superlative degree of adjectives and adverbs: warmest.

-est², a suffix used to form the archaic second person sing. indicative present and past of verbs: knowest.

est., 1. established. 2. estate. 3. estimate. 4. estimated.

estab., established.

es·tab·lish (e stab′lish), v.t. 1. to bring into being on a firm or stable basis. 2. to install or settle in a position, place, business, etc. 3. to cause to be accepted or recognized. 4. to prove or demonstrate. 5. to enact or appoint for permanence, as a law. 6. to bring about permanently: to establish order.

es·tab·lish·ment (e stab′lish mənt), n. 1. the act of establishing or state of being established. 2. the Establishment, the existing power structure in society. 3. a place of business or residence together with its staff, members, property, etc. 4. a permanent civil, military, or other force or organization.

es·tate (e stāt′), n. 1. a piece of landed property, esp. one of large extent. 2. property or possessions. 3. the property of a deceased person. 4. a major political or social class. 5. Literary. a period or condition of life.

es·teem (e stēm′), v.t. 1. to regard highly or favorably. 2. Literary. to consider or regard. —n. 3. high regard.

es·ter (es′tər), n. a compound produced by the reaction between an acid and an alcohol.

es·thet·ics (es thet′iks), n. aesthetics. —es′thete, n. —es·thet′ic, adj.

'es·ti·ma·ble (es′tə mə bəl), adj. deserving respect or admiration.

es·ti·mate (v. es′tə māt′; n. es′tə mit, -māt′), v., -mat·ed, -mat·ing, n. —v.t. 1. to make an approximate calculation of (value, amount, size, etc.).

2. to judge or evaluate. —v.i. 3. to make an estimate. —n. 4. an approximate calculation, as of value. 5. a statement of such a calculation. 6. a judgment or opinion. —es′ti·ma′tor, n. —Syn. 1. appraise, assess, value.

es·ti·ma·tion (es′tə mā′shən), n. 1. estimate (defs. 4, 6). 2. Archaic. esteem.

Es·to·ni·a (e stō′nē ə), n. a constituent republic of the Soviet Union, on the Baltic, S of the Gulf of Finland. —Es·to′ni·an, adj., n.

es·trange (e strānj′), v.t., -tranged, -trang·ing. to turn away in feeling or affection. —es·trange′ment, n.

es·tro·gen (es′trə jən), n. a female hormone capable of inducing estrus in immature, spayed mammals. —es′tro·gen′ic (-jen′ik), adj.

es·trus (es′trəs), n. the period of maximum sexual receptivity of the female.

es·tu·ar·y (es′chōō er′ē), n., pl. -ar·ies. 1. the mouth of a river in which the river's current meets the sea's tide. 2. an arm of the sea at the lower end of a river.

E.T., Eastern Time.

e·ta (ā′tə, ē′tə), n. the seventh letter of the Greek alphabet (H, η).

ETA, estimated time of arrival:

é·ta·gère (ā tA zher′), n. French. whatnot.

et al. (et al′, äl′, ôl′). and others. [< L et alii]

etc. (often et set′ər ə, -se′trə). See et cetera.

—Usage. See and.

et cet·er·a (et set′ər ə, -se′trə), and others, esp. of the same sort. [< L]

etch (ech′), v.t. 1. to produce (a design, image, etc.) on (copper or glass) by the corrosive action of an acid. 2. to outline clearly or sharply. —v.i. 3. to practice etching. —etch′er, n.

etch·ing (ech′iñg), n. 1. the act or art of etching designs or pictures. 2. a print made from an etched plate. 3. the design so produced.

ETD, estimated time of departure.

e·ter·nal (i tûr′nəl), adj. 1. lasting forever. 2. ceaseless or endless. 3. enduring or immutable. —e·ter′nal·ly, adv. —e·ter′nal·ness, n.

e·ter·ni·ty (i tûr′ni tē), n., pl. -ties. 1. duration without beginning or end. 2. eternal existence. 3. the state into which the soul passes at death. 4. a seemingly endless period of time.

-eth¹, a suffix used to form the archaic third person sing. present indicative of verbs: doeth.

-eth², var. of -th²: thirtieth.

eth·ane (eth′ān), n. a colorless, odorless, flammable gas of the methane series, used chiefly as a fuel.

eth·a·nol (eth'ə nōl', -nôl', -nol'), *n.* alcohol (def. 1).

e·ther (ē'thər), *n.* **1.** a highly volatile, flammable liquid, used as a solvent and as an inhalant anesthetic. **2.** one of a class of compounds in which two organic groups are attached directly to an oxygen atom. **3.** the upper regions of space. **4.** a hypothetical substance once supposed to occupy all space.

e·the·re·al (i thēr'ē əl), *adj.* **1.** light, airy, or tenuous. **2.** extremely delicate or refined. **3.** heavenly or celestial. —**e·the're·al·ly,** *adv.* —**e·the're·al·ness,** *n.*

eth·ic (eth'ik), *n.* a body of moral principles or values.

eth·i·cal (eth'i kəl), *adj.* **1.** of or pertaining to ethics. **2.** in accordance with professional standards for right conduct or practice. **3.** (of drugs) sold only upon medical prescription. —**eth'i·cal·ly,** *adv.*

eth·ics (eth'iks), *n.pl.* **1.** a system of moral principles. **2.** the branch of philosophy dealing with right and wrong of certain actions and with good and bad of such actions.

E·thi·o·pi·a (ē'thē ō'pē ə), *n.* a country in E Africa. —**E'thi·o'pi·an,** *adj., n.*

eth·nic (eth'nik), *adj.* **1.** of or pertaining to a group of people of the same race or nationality sharing common and distinctive cultural characteristics. —*n.* **2.** a member of a minority group that retains a distinctive tradition. —**eth'ni·cal·ly,** *adv.*

eth·nic·i·ty (eth nis'ə tē), *n.* ethnic trait, background, or mentality.

ethnol., **1.** ethnological. **2.** ethnology.

eth·nol·o·gy (eth nol'ə jē), *n.* a branch of anthropology dealing with the origin, distribution, and distinguishing characteristics of the races of humankind. —**eth·no·log·i·cal** (eth'nə loj'i kəl), **eth'no·log'ic,** *adj.* —**eth·nol'o·gist,** *n.*

e·thol·o·gy (e thol'ə jē, ē thol'-), *n.* the scientific study of animal behavior. —**eth·o·log·i·cal** (eth'ə loj'i kəl, *adj.* —**e·thol'o·gist,** *n.*

e·thos (ē'thos, eth'os), *n.* the underlying sentiment that informs the beliefs, customs, or practices of a person or society.

eth·yl (eth'əl), *n.* a type of antiknock fluid, containing tetraethyl lead and other ingredients for an even combustion.

eth'yl al'cohol, alcohol (def. 1).

eth·yl·ene (eth'ə lēn'), *n.* a flammable gas, used to improve the color of citrus fruits and as an inhalant anesthetic.

e·ti·ol·o·gy (ē'tē ol'ə jē), *n., pl.* **-gies.**

1. the study of the causes of diseases. **2.** the cause or origin of a disease. **3.** the study of causes, causation, or causality. —**e'ti·o·log'ic** (-ə loj'ik), **e'ti·o·log'i·cal,** *adj.* —**e'ti·o·log'i·cal·ly,** *adv.*

et·i·quette (et'ə kit, -ket'), *n.* **1.** conventional requirements as to social behavior. **2.** a prescribed or accepted code of usage in matters of ceremony.

E·tru·ri·a (i trŏor'ē ə), *n.* an ancient country located in W Italy.

E·trus·can (i trus'kən), *n.* **1.** an inhabitant of Etruria. **2.** the extinct language of Etruria.

et seq., *pl.* **et seqq., et sqq.** and the following. [< L *et sequens*]

-ette, a suffix meaning: **a.** little or small: *kitchenette.* **b.** female or feminine: *majorette.*

é·tude (ā'tōōd, ā'tyōōd, ā tōōd', ā tyōōd'), *n.* a musical composition intended mainly for the practice of technique.

ETV, See educational television.

etym., **1.** etymological. **2.** etymology.

et·y·mol·o·gy (et'ə mol'ə jē), *n., pl.* **-gies.** **1.** the study of historical linguistic change, esp. as applied to individual words. **2.** an account of the history of a particular word. **3.** the derivation of a word. —**et·y·mo·log·i·cal** (et'ə mə loj'i kəl), *adj.* —**et'y·mol'o·gist,** *n.*

Eu, europium.

eu-, a prefix meaning "good" or "well": *euphoria.*

eu·ca·lyp·tus (yōō'kə lip'təs), *n., pl.* **-ti** (-tī), **-tus·es.** a mainly Australian aromatic evergreen.

Eu·cha·rist (yōō'kə rist), *n.* **1.** the sacrament of Holy Communion. **2.** the consecrated bread and wine of the Holy Communion, esp. the bread. —**Eu'cha·ris'tic, Eu'cha·ris'ti·cal,** *adj.*

eu·chre (yōō'kər), *n., v.,* **-chred, -chring.** —*n.* **1.** a game played with the 32 highest cards in the pack. —*v.t.* **2.** *Informal.* to get the better of.

Eu·clid (yōō'klid), *n.* 330?–275 B.C., Greek geometrician. —**Eu·clid'e·an, Eu·clid'i·an,** *adj.*

eu·gen·ics (yōō jen'iks), *n.* the science of improving the qualities of a breed or species, esp. the human race, by the careful selection of parents. —**eu·gen'ic,** *adj.* —**eu·gen'i·cal·ly,** *adv.* —**eu·gen'i·cist** (-i sist), *n.*

eu·lo·gize (yōō'lə jīz'), *v.t.,* **-gized, -giz·ing.** to praise highly, esp. in a eulogy. —**eu'lo·gist, eu'lo·giz'er,** *n.*

eu·lo·gy (yōō'lə jē), *n., pl.* **-gies.** **1.** a speech or writing in praise of a person or thing, esp. one in honor of a deceased person. **2.** *Brit.* high praise. —**eu·lo·gis·tic** (yōō'lə jis'tik), *adj.*

eu·nuch (yŏŏ′nək), *n.* a castrated man, esp. formerly, one employed by Oriental rulers as a harem attendant.

eu·phe·mism (yŏŏ′fə miz′əm), *n.* **1.** the substitution of a mild, indirect, or vague expression for one thought to be offensive, harsh, or blunt. **2.** the expression so substituted. —**eu′phe·mis′tic**, *adj.* —**eu′phe·mis′ti·cal·ly**, *adv.*

eu·pho·ni·ous (yŏŏ fō′nē əs), *adj.* pleasant in sound.

eu·pho·ny (yŏŏ′fə nē), *n., pl.* **-nies.** agreeableness of sound, esp. in speech.

eu·pho·ri·a (yŏŏ fōr′ē ə, -fôr′-), *n.* a feeling of well-being, esp. an exaggerated one having no basis in reality. —**eu·phor·ic** (yŏŏ fôr′ik, -for′-), *adj.*

Eu·phra·tes (ū frā′tēz), *n.* a river in SW Asia.

Eur., **1.** Europe. **2.** European.

Eur·a·sia (yŏŏ rā′zhə, -shə), *n.* Europe and Asia considered as a whole.

Eur·a·sian (yŏŏ rā′zhən, -shən), *adj.* **1.** of Eurasia. **2.** of mixed European and Asian descent. —*n.* **3.** the offspring of a European and an Asian.

eu·re·ka (yŏŏ rē′kə), *interj.* I have found (it) (an exclamation of triumph at a discovery). [Gk *heúrēka* I have discovered]

Eu·rip·i·des (yŏŏ rip′i dēz′), *n.* c480-406? B.C., Greek dramatist.

Euro-, **1.** a combining form meaning "of or in Europe, esp. Western Europe": *Eurocommunism; Europort.* **2.** a combining form meaning "issued or circulated in Europe and usually in a currency of the country of origin": *Eurobond; Eurosterling.*

Eu·ro·dol·lars (yŏŏr′ə dol′ərz), *n.pl.* dollars deposited abroad, esp. in Europe, and used as a medium of international credit, esp. to finance trade or investment.

Eu·rope (yŏŏr′əp), *n.* a continent in the W part of Eurasia, separated from Asia by the Ural Mountains. —**Eu′ro·pe′an** (-ə pē′ən), *adj., n.*

Europe′an plan′, a hotel rate covering only lodging and service.

eu·ro·pi·um (yŏŏ rō′pē əm), *n. Chem.* a rare-earth metallic element. *Symbol:* Eu; *at. wt.:* 151.96; *at. no.:* 63.

Eu·sta′chian tube′ (yŏŏ stā′shən, -stā′-kē ən), a canal extending from the middle ear to the pharynx. [after B. *Eustachio,* 1524?–1574, Ital. anatomist]

eu·tha·na·sia (yŏŏ′thə nā′zhə, -zhē ə, -zē ə), *n.* the act of putting to death painlessly a person suffering from an incurable disease.

eu·then·ics (yŏŏ then′iks), *n.* a science concerned with bettering the condition of human beings through improvement of their environment.

eu·troph·ic (yŏŏ trof′ik), *adj.* (of a lake, etc.) abundant in nutrients for plant and animal life but shallow and lacking in oxygen in summer. —**eu·troph′i·ca′tion,** *n.* —**eu·tro·phy** (yŏŏ′trə fē), *n.*

Ev, electron volt. Also, **ev**

EVA, extravehicular activity.

e·vac·u·ate (i vak′yŏŏ āt′), *v.,* **-at·ed, -at·ing.** —*v.t.* **1.** to leave empty. **2.** to remove from, esp. for safety. **3.** to discharge or eject, esp. from the bowels. —*v.i.* **4.** to leave or withdraw. —**e·vac′u·a′tion,** *n.* —**e·vac′u·a′tor,** *n.*

e·vac·u·ee (i vak′yŏŏ ē′, i vak′yŏŏ ē′), *n.* a person evacuated from a place of danger.

e·vade (i vād′), *v.t., v.i.,* **e·vad·ed, e·vad·ing. 1.** to escape (from) by trickery or cleverness. **2.** to avoid doing. **3.** to avoid answering directly. —**e·vad′er,** *n.*

e·val·u·ate (i val′yŏŏ āt′), *v.t.,* **-at·ed, -at·ing.** to determine or judge the value or worth of. —**e·val′u·a′tion,** *n.* —**e·val′u·a′tor,** *n.*

ev·a·nes·cent (ev′ə nes′ənt), *adj.* **1.** vanishing or fading away. **2.** scarcely perceptible —**ev′a·nes′cence,** *n.* —**ev′a·nes′cent·ly,** *adv.*

e·van·gel·i·cal (ē′van jel′i kəl, ev′ən-), *adj.* Also, **e′van·gel′ic. 1.** of or in keeping with the gospel and its teachings. **2.** of certain Protestant movements that stress the importance of personal experience of guilt for sin, and of reconciliation to God through Christ. **3.** ardent or zealous. —*n.* **4.** an adherent of evangelical doctrines. —**e′van·gel′i·cal·ism** (-kə liz′əm), *n.* —**e′van·gel′i·cal·ly,** *adv.*

e·van·ge·lism (i van′jə liz′əm), *n.* **1.** the preaching or promulgation of the gospel, esp. by itinerant preachers. **2.** missionary zeal or activity.

e·van·ge·list (i van′jə list), *n.* **1.** a preacher of the gospel. **2.** (*cap.*) any of the writers of the four Gospels. **3.** a Protestant missionary who preaches personal conversion. —**e·van′ge·lis′tic,** *adj.* —**e·van′ge·lis′ti·cal·ly,** *adv.*

e·van·ge·lize (i van′jə līz′), *v.,* **-lized, -liz·ing.** —*v.t.* **1.** to convert to Christianity. —*v.i.* **2.** to preach the gospel.

Ev·ans·ville (ev′ənz vil′), *n.* a city in SW Indiana.

evap., evaporate.

e·vap·o·rate (i vap′ə rāt′), *v.,* **-rat·ed, -rat·ing.** —*v.i.* **1.** to turn to vapor. **2.** to give off moisture. **3.** to vanish or fade. —*v.t.* **4.** to convert into vapor. **5.** to extract moisture from, as by heat, so as to reduce to a denser state. —**e·vap′o·ra′tion,** *n.*

—e·vap′o·ra′tive (-rā′tiv), adj. —
e·vap′o·ra′tor, n.
e·vap·o·rite (i vap′ə rīt′), n. any sedimentary rock formed by precipitation from evaporating seawater. —
e·vap′o·ri′tic, adj.
e·va·sion (i vā′zhən), n. 1. the act or
an instance of evading. 2. a means
of evading. —e·va′sive, adj. —e·va′-
sive·ly, adv. —e·va′sive·ness, n.
eve (ēv), n. 1. the evening or the day
before a holiday. 2. the period preceding any event. 3. Literary. evening.
Eve (ēv), n. Bible. the first woman:
wife of Adam.
e·ven (ē′vən), adj. 1. constantly or
completely flat. 2. on the same level
or line. 3. free from variation.
4. equal in measure or quantity. 5.
divisible by two. 6. exactly expressible without fractional parts. 7.
leaving no balance or debt on either
side. 8. calm or placid. —adv. 9.
still or yet. 10. (used to suggest an
extreme case or an unlikely instance): Even the slightest noise disturbs him. Even if he attends, he may
not participate. 11. just or exactly:
Even as he lay dying, they argued
over his estate. 12. fully or quite.
13. indeed. 14. break even, to have
one's profits equal one's losses. 15.
get even, to retaliate. —v.t., v.i. 16.
to make or become even. —e′ven·ly,
adv. —e′ven·ness, n.
e·ven-hand·ed (ē′vən han′did), adj.
impartial or equitable.
eve·ning (ēv′ning), n. 1. the latter
part of the day and early part of
the night. 2. the period from sunset
to bedtime.
eve′ning gown′, a woman's formal
dress, usually having a floor-length
skirt.
eve′ning prim′rose, a plant having
yellow flowers that open at nightfall.
eve′ning star′, a bright planet, esp.
Venus, seen in the west directly
after sunset.
e′ven mon′ey, equal odds in a wager.
e·ven·song (ē′vən sông′, -song′), n. 1.
Anglican Ch. a prayer said or sung
at evening. 2. vesper (def. 1).
e·vent (i vent′), n. 1. an occurrence,
esp. one of some importance. 2. an
outcome or consequence. 3. any of
the contests in a program. 4. at all
events, in any case. Also, in any
event. 5. in the event (of), in case
(of).
e·vent·ful (i vent′fəl), adj. 1. full of
events or incidents. 2. having important results. —e·vent′ful·ly, adv.
—e·vent′ful·ness, n.
e·ven·tide (ē′vən tīd′), n. Literary.
evening.
e·ven·tu·al (i ven′chōō əl), adj. happening at some indefinite future
time. —e·ven′tu·al·ly, adv.

e·ven·tu·al·i·ty (i ven′chōō al′i tē), n.,
pl. -ties. a possible occurrence or
circumstance.
e·ven·tu·ate (i ven′chōō āt′), v.i., -at-
ed, -at·ing. to result ultimately. —
e·ven′tu·a′tion, n.
ev·er (ev′ər), adv. 1. at any time. 2.
in any possible case. 3. at all times.
4. ever so, exceedingly.
ev·er·bloom·ing (ev′ər blōō′ming), adj.
in bloom through most of the growing months of the year.
Ev·er·est (ev′ər ist), n. Mount, a
mountain in S Asia, in the Himalayas: the highest mountain in the
world.
ev·er·glade (ev′ər glād′), n. a tract
of low, swampy land.
ev·er·green (ev′ər grēn′), adj. 1. having green leaves throughout the entire year. —n. 2. an evergreen plant.
ev·er·last·ing (ev′ər las′ting, -lä′sting),
adj. 1. lasting forever. —n. 2. eter-
nity. —ev′er·last′ing·ly, adv.
ev·er·more (ev′ər mōr′, -môr′), adv.
always or forever.
ev·er·y (ev′rē), adj. 1. each. 2. all
possible. 3. every bit, Informal.
completely. 4. every other, every
alternate. 5. every so often, on occasion. 6. every which way, Informal. in disorganized fashion.
ev·er·y·bod·y (ev′rē bod′ē), pron. every
person.
eve·ry·day (ev′rē dā′), adj. 1. of every
day. 2. of or for ordinary days:
everyday clothes. 3. ordinary or
commonplace.
eve·ry·one (ev′rē wun′, -wən), pron.
every person.
eve·ry·place (ev′rē plās′), adv. everywhere.
eve·ry·thing (ev′rē thing), pron. every
particular of an aggregate or total.
eve·ry·where (ev′rē hwâr′, -wâr′), adv.
in every place or part.
evg., evening.
e·vict (i vikt′), v.t. to expel (a tenant) by legal process. —e·vic′tion,
n. —e·vic′tor, n.
ev·i·dence (ev′i dəns), n., v., -denced,
-denc·ing. —n. 1. that which tends
to prove or disprove something. 2.
an indication or sign. 3. Law. data
presented to a court to decide an
alleged matter of fact. 4. in evidence, plainly visible. —v.t. 5. to
show clearly.
ev·i·dent (ev′i dənt), adj. plain or
clear to the sight or understanding.
—ev′i·dent·ly, adv. —Syn. apparent,
manifest, obvious.
e·vil (ē′vəl), adj. 1. morally wrong
or bad. 2. harmful or injurious. 3.
unfortunate or disastrous. —n. 4.
an evil quality or conduct. 5. harm
or misfortune: to wish one evil. —
e′vil·ly, adv.

e·vil·do·er (ē'vəl dōō'ər, ē'vəl dōō'ər),
n. a person who does evil or wrong.

e'vil eye', the power, superstitiously
attributed to certain persons, of inflicting injury or bad luck by a look.
—e'vil-eyed', adj.

e·vil-mind·ed (ē'vəl mīn'did), adj.
having an evil disposition or malicious intentions.

e·vince (i vins'), v.t., e·vinced, e·vinc·
ing. to show clearly. —e·vin'ci·ble,
adj.

e·vis·cer·ate (i vis'ə rāt'), v.t., -at·ed,
-at·ing. 1. to remove the entrails
from. 2. to deprive of vital parts.
—e·vis'cer·a'tion, n.

e·voke (i vōk'), v.t., e·voked, e·vok·
ing. 1. to call up or bring out, as
memories. 2. to draw forth, esp. in
response. —ev·o·ca·tion (ev'ə kā'-
shən), n. —e·voc·a·tive (i vok'ə tiv),
adj. —e·vok'er, n.

ev·o·lu·tion (ev'ə lōō'shən or, esp.
Brit., ē'və-), n. 1. any process of
formation or growth. 2. something
evolved. 3. Biol. a. the development
of complex animals and plants from
earlier simpler forms. b. a theory
that all living things have acquired
their present forms through successive generations. 4. a pattern formed
by a series of movements. —ev'o·
lu'tion·ar'y, adj. —ev'o·lu'tion·ism,
n. —ev'o·lu'tion·ist, n.

e·volve (i volv'), v.t., v.i., e·volved,
e·volv·ing. 1. to develop gradually.
2. to develop by biological evolution.
—e·volve'ment, n.

ev·zone (ev'zōn), n. an infantryman
belonging to an elite corps in the
Greek army.

EW, enlisted woman; enlisted
women.

ewe (yōō; Dial. yō), n. an adult female sheep.

ew·er (yōō'ər), n. a pitcher with a
wide spout.

ex¹ (eks), prep. 1. without: ex dividend. 2. out of: ex warehouse.

ex² (eks), n. Informal. one's former
spouse.

ex-, a prefix meaning: a. out of or
from: export. b. utterly or thoroughly: exacerbate. c. former: ex-
governor.

Ex., Exodus.

ex., 1. examination. 2. examined. 3.
example. 4. except. 5. exception.
6. exchange. 7. express. 8. extra.

ex·ac·er·bate (ig zas'ər bāt', ik sas'-),
v.t., -bat·ed, -bat·ing. to increase
the bitterness or violence of (disease,
ill feeling, etc.). —ex·ac'er·bat'ing·
ly, adv. —ex·ac'er·ba'tion, n.

ex·act (ig zakt'), adj. 1. perfectly in
accord with fact. 2. not approximate
or variant. —v.t. 3. to call for or
demand. 4. to force the payment or

yielding of. —ex·act'er, n. —ex·
ac'tion, n. —ex·act'ly, adv. —ex·
act'ness, n. —Syn. 1. accurate, correct. 2. precise.

ex·act·ing (ig zak'ting), adj. 1. unduly severe in demands: an exacting
teacher. 2. requiring close attention. —ex·act'ing·ly, adv. —ex·act'-
ing·ness, n.

ex·act·i·tude (ig zak'ti tōōd', -tyōōd'),
n. the quality of being exact.

exact' sci'ence, a science, as chemistry or physics, that deals with quan-
titatively measurable phenomena of
the material universe.

ex·ag·ger·ate (ig zaj'ə rāt'), v.t., v.i.,
-at·ed, -at·ing. to magnify beyond
the limits of truth. —ex·ag'ger·at'-
ed·ly, adv. —ex·ag'ger·a'tion, n. —
ex·ag'ger·a'tive, adj. —ex·ag'ger·a'-
tor, n.

ex·alt (ig zôlt'), v.t. 1. to elevate in
rank, power, character, etc. 2. to
praise or extol. —ex·al·ta'tion, n.

ex·am (ig zam'), n. Informal. an examination.

exam., 1. examination. 2. examiner.

ex·am·ine (ig zam'in), v.t., -ined, -in·
ing. 1. to look over carefully in order
to find or learn about 2. to test the
knowledge or qualifications of (a
pupil, etc.), as by questions. —ex·
am'i·na'tion, n. —ex·am'in·er, n. —
Syn. 1. inspect, scrutinize.

ex·am·ple (ig zam'pəl, -zäm'-), n. 1.
one of a number of things taken to
show the character of the whole.
2. a pattern or model to be imitated
or avoided. 3. an instance illustrating a rule or method. 4. an instance,
esp. of punishment, serving as a
warning.

ex·as·per·ate (ig zas'pə rāt'), v.t., -at·
ed, -at·ing. to irritate to a high
degree. —ex·as'per·a'tion, n.

exc., 1. excellent. 2. except. 3. exception. 4. excursion.

ex·ca·vate (eks'kə vāt'), v.t., -vat·ed,
-vat·ing. 1. to make a hole or
cavity in. 2. to make (a hole, tunnel,
etc.) by removing material. 3. to dig
out (earth, etc.). 4. to lay bare by
digging. —ex'ca·va'tion, n. —ex'-
ca·va'tor, n.

ex·ceed (ik sēd'), v.t., v.i. 1. to go
beyond the limits (of). 2. to be
superior (to).

ex·ceed·ing (ik sē'ding), Literary.
—adj. 1. extraordinary or exceptional.
—adv 2. exceedingly.

ex·ceed·ing·ly (ik sē'ding lē), adv. to
an extreme degree.

ex·cel (ik sel'), v.i., v.t., -celled, -cel·
ling. to be better or finer than
(others).

ex·cel·lence (ek'sə ləns), n. 1. superiority, as in worth. 2. an excellent
quality or feature.

Ex·cel·len·cy (ek′sə lən sē), *n.*, *pl.* **-cies. 1.** a title of honor given to certain high officials, as ambassadors. **2.** (*l.c.*) *Archaic.* excellence.

ex·cel·lent (ek′sə lənt), *adj.* **1.** possessing superior merit. **2.** remarkably good. —**ex′cel·lent·ly**, *adv.*

ex·cel·si·or (ik sel′sē ər, ek-), *n.* wood shavings, used for stuffing, packing, etc. [< L: higher (former trademark)]

ex·cept¹ (ik sept′), *prep.* **1.** Also, **ex·cept′ing.** with the exclusion of. —*conj.* **2.** only or but.

ex·cept² (ik sept′), *v.t.* to exclude or leave out.
—Usage. See accept.

ex·cep·tion (ik sep′shən), *n.* **1.** the act of excepting something. **2.** the fact of being excepted. **3.** something excepted. **4. take exception,** to make an objection.

ex·cep·tion·a·ble (ik sep′shə nə bəl), *adj.* liable to exception or objection.

ex·cep·tion·al (ik sep′shə nəl), *adj.* **1.** beyond the normal measure. **2.** unusually excellent. —**ex·cep′tion·al′i·ty,** *n.* —**ex·cep′tion·al·ly,** *adv.* —Syn. extraordinary, uncommon, unusual.

ex·cerpt (*n.* ek′sûrpt; *v.* ik sûrpt′), *n.* **1.** a passage taken out of a book, film, etc. —*v.t.* **2.** to take (a passage) from a book, film, etc.

ex·cess (*n.* ik ses′; *adj.* ek′ses, ik ses′), *n.* **1.** the fact of exceeding specified limits in amount. **2.** the amount by which one thing exceeds another. **3.** a superabundance. **4.** intemperance in eating, drinking, etc. —*adj.* **5.** more than usual or specified: *excess baggage.*

ex·ces·sive (ik ses′iv), *adj.* exceeding the usual or proper limit or degree. —**ex·ces′sive·ly,** *adv.* —**ex·ces′sive·ness,** *n.* —Syn. exorbitant, immoderate, inordinate, unreasonable.

exch., **1.** exchange. **2.** exchequer.

ex·change (iks chānj′), *v.*, **-changed, -chang·ing.** *n.* —*v.t.*, *v.i.* **1.** to give up (something) for something else. **2.** to give and receive (similar things) reciprocally: *to exchange blows.* —*n.* **3.** the act or an instance of exchanging. **4.** something exchanged. **5.** a place for buying and selling commodities, securities, etc. **6.** a central station: *a telephone exchange.* **7.** the reciprocal transfer of equivalent sums of money, as in the currencies of two different countries. —**ex·change′a·ble,** *adj.*

exchange′ rate′, the ratio at which money of one country can be exchanged for money of another country.

ex·cheq·uer (eks′chek ər, iks chek′ər), *n. Chiefly Brit.* a treasury, as of a state or nation.

ex·cise¹ (ek′sīz, -sīs), *n.* a tax on certain commodities, as tobacco, levied on their manufacture, sale, or consumption within the country.

ex·cise² (ik sīz′), *v.t.*, **-cised, -cis·ing.** to cut out or off, as a tumor. —**ex·cis′a·ble,** *adj.* —**ex·ci·sion** (ek sizh′ən, ik-), *n.*

ex·cit·a·ble (ik sī′tə bəl), *adj.* **1.** capable of being excited. **2.** easily excited. —**ex·cit′a·bil′i·ty,** *n.*

ex·cite (ik sīt′), *v.t.*, **-cit·ed, -cit·ing. 1.** to arouse the emotions or feelings of. **2.** to arouse or stir up (emotions or feelings). **3.** to stimulate: *to excite a nerve.* —**ex′ci·ta′tion,** *n.* —**ex·cit′ed·ly,** *adv.* —**ex·cit′er,** *n.* —**ex·cit′ing,** *adj.* —Syn. 1, 2. kindle, provoke, quicken.

ex·cite·ment (ik sīt′mənt), *n.* **1.** an excited state or condition. **2.** something that excites.

excl., 1. exclamation. **2.** excluding. **3.** exclusive.

ex·claim (ik sklām′), *v.i.*, *v.t.* to cry out or speak suddenly and vehemently, as in surprise. —**ex·claim′er,** *n.* —**ex·cla·ma·tion** (ek′sklə mā′shən), *n.* —**ex·clam·a·to·ry** (ik sklam′ə tōr′ē, -tôr′ē), *adj.*

exclama′tion point′, the sign (!) used in writing after an exclamation. Also called **exclama′tion mark′.**

ex·clave (eks′klāv), *n.* a portion of a country separated from the main part by surrounding alien territory.

ex·clude (ik sklood′), *v.t.*, **-clud·ed, -clud·ing. 1.** to prevent the entrance of. **2.** to shut out from consideration, membership, etc. **3.** to expel or eject. —**ex·clud′er,** *n.* —**ex·clu·sion,** *n.*

ex·clu·sive (ik skloo′siv), *adj.* **1.** excluding all others from a part or share. **2.** single or sole: *an exclusive dealership.* **3.** disposed to resist the admission of outsiders. **4.** snobbish or expensive: *an exclusive residential area.* **5.** exclusive of, excluding. —**ex·clu′sive·ly,** *adv.* —**ex·clu′sive·ness, ex·clu·siv·i·ty** (eks′kloo siv′i·tē), *n.*

ex·cog·i·tate (eks koj′i tāt′), *v.t.*, **-tat·ed, -tat·ing.** *Often Facetious.* to think out or up.

ex·com·mu·ni·cate (eks′kə myoo′nə kāt′), *v.t.*, **-cat·ed, -cat·ing.** to cut off from communion or membership, esp. from a church. —**ex′com·mu′ni·ca′tion,** *n.* —**ex′com·mu′ni·ca′tor,** *n.*

ex·co·ri·ate (ik skōr′ē āt′, -skôr′-), *v.t.*, **-at·ed, -at·ing. 1.** to strip off the skin from. **2.** to denounce or berate severely. —**ex·co′ri·a′tion,** *n.*

ex·cre·ment (ek′skrə mənt), *n.* waste matter discharged from the body, esp. feces. —**ex·cre·men·tal** (ek′skrə·men′t°l), *adj.*

ex·cres·cence (ik skres′əns), n. 1. abnormal growth. 2. an abnormal outgrowth, as a mole. —ex·cres′cent, adj.

ex·cre·ta (ik skrē′tə), n.pl. excreted matter, as sweat, urine, feces, etc. —ex·cre′tal, adj.

ex·crete (ik skrēt′), v.t., -cret·ed, -cret·ing. to separate and eliminate (waste) from the body, blood, or tissues. —ex·cre′tion, n. —ex·cre·to·ry (ek′skri tōr′ē, -tôr′ē, ik skrē′tə·rē), adj.

ex·cru·ci·at·ing (ik skrōō′shē ā′ting), adj. extremely painful. —ex·cru′ci·at·ing·ly, adv.

ex·cul·pate (ek′skul pāt′, ik skul′pāt), v.t., -pat·ed, -pat·ing. to clear from a charge of guilt or fault. —ex′cul·pa′tion, n.

ex·cur·sion (ik skûr′zhən, -shən), n. 1. a short journey, usually for pleasure. 2. a round trip on a train, ship, etc., at a reduced rate. 3. deviation or digression. —ex·cur′sion·ist, n.

ex·cur·sive (ik skûr′siv), adj. digressive, as in writing. —ex·cur′sive·ly, adv. —ex·cur′sive·ness, n.

ex·cur·sus (ek skûr′səs), n., pl. -sus·es, -sus. a detailed discussion of some point in a book, esp. one added as an appendix.

ex·cuse (v. ik skyōōz′; n. ik skyōōs′), v., -cused, -cus·ing, n. —v.t. 1. to overlook indulgently (a trivial fault, error, etc.). 2. to offer an apology for. 3. to justify or absolve. 4. to release from an obligation or duty. 5. to allow to leave. —n. 6. an explanation offered as a reason for being excused. 7. a ground or reason for being excused. —ex·cus′a·ble, adj. —ex·cus′a·ble·ness, n. —Syn. 1. condone, forgive, pardon.

exec., 1. executive. 2. executor.

ex·e·cra·ble (ek′sə krə bəl), adj. 1. utterly detestable. 2. very bad or inferior. —ex′e·cra·bly, adv.

ex·e·crate (ek′sə krāt′), v.t., -crat·ed, -crat·ing. 1. to detest utterly. 2. to denounce harshly. —ex′e·cra′tion, n. —ex′e·cra′tor, n.

ex·e·cute (ek′sə kyōōt′), v.t., -cut·ed, -cut·ing. 1. to carry out: to execute a plan. 2. to perform or do. 3. to put to death according to law. 4. to produce in accordance with a plan. 5. to complete (a contract, will, etc.) by fulfilling the legal requirements. —ex′e·cut′er, n. —ex′e·cu′tion, n.

ex·e·cu·tion·er (ek′sə kyōō′shə nər), n. an official who inflicts capital punishment.

ex·ec·u·tive (ig zek′yə tiv), n. 1. a person who has managerial and policy-making authority in an organization. 2. the executive branch of a government. —adj. 3. of, for, or suited for carrying out plans, duties, etc. 4. pertaining to or charged with the execution of laws, policies, and public affairs.

ex·ec·u·tor (ig zek′yə tər), n. a person named by a decedent in his or her will to carry out its provisions.

ex·ec·u·trix (ig zek′yə triks), n., pl. ex·ec·u·tri·ces (ig zek′yə trī′sēz), ex·ec·u·trix·es. a female executor.

ex·e·ge·sis (ek′si jē′sis), n., pl. -ses (-sēz). critical explanation or interpretation, esp. of Scripture.

ex·e·gete (ek′si jēt′), n. a person skilled in exegesis.

ex·em·plar (ig zem′plər, -plär), n. 1. a model or pattern to be imitated. 2. a typical example or instance.

ex·em·pla·ry (ig zem′plə rē, eg′zem·pler′ē), adj. 1. worthy of imitation. 2. serving as a model or pattern.

ex·em·pli·fy (ig zem′plə fī′), v.t., -fied, -fy·ing. 1. to show by example. 2. to serve as an example of. —ex·em′pli·fi·ca′tion, n.

ex·empt (ig zempt′), v.t. 1. to free from an obligation to which others are subject. —adj. 2. released from, or not subject to, an obligation, liability, etc. —exempt′i·ble, adj. —ex·emp′tion, n.

ex·er·cise (ek′sər sīz′), n., v., -cised, -cis·ing. —n. 1. bodily or mental exertion, esp. for the sake of training. 2. something done or performed as training. 3. a putting into action, use, or operation: the exercise of caution. 4. Often, exercises. a traditional ceremony: graduation exercises. —v.t. 5. to put through exercises. 6. to put (faculties, rights, etc.) into action, use, or operation. 7. to use or display in one's action or procedure. 8. to worry or make uneasy. —v.i. 9. to go through exercises. —ex′er·cis′er, n.

ex·ert (ig zûrt′), v.t. 1. to put into vigorous action. 2. to put (oneself) into great effort. —ex·er′tion, n.

ex·hale (eks hāl′, ig zāl′), v.t., v.i., -haled, -hal·ing. 1. to emit (breath or vapor). 2. to pass off as vapor. —ex·ha·la·tion (eks′hə lā′shən, eg·zə-), n.

ex·haust (ig zôst′), v.t. 1. to use up completely. 2. to fatigue greatly. 3. to treat or study thoroughly. 4. to empty by drawing out the contents. —n. 5. the escape of steam or gases from an engine. 6. the steam or gases ejected. 7. the parts of an engine through which the exhaust is ejected. —ex·haust′i·ble, adj. —ex·haus·tion (ig zôs′chən, -zôsh′-), n. —ex·haust′less, adj.

ex·haus·tive (ig zôs′tiv), adj. thorough and comprehensive.

ex·hib·it (ig zib′it), v.t. **1.** to offer or expose to view. **2.** to manifest or display. **3.** to present something to public view. —n. **4.** an act or instance of exhibiting. **5.** something exhibited. **6.** a document or object submitted to a court as evidence. —**ex·hi·bi·tion** (ek′sə bish′ən), n. —**ex·hib′i·tor, ex·hib′it·er,** n. — Syn. **2.** evince, reveal, show.

ex·hi·bi·tion·ism (ek′sə bish′ə niz′əm), n. a tendency to behave in such a way as to attract attention, esp. by indecent exposure. —**ex′hi·bi′tion·ist,** n.

ex·hil·a·rate (ig zil′ə rāt′), v.t., **-rat·ed, -rat·ing. 1.** to make very lively and cheerful. **2.** to invigorate or stimulate. —**ex·hil′a·ra′tion,** n. —**ex·hil′a·ra′tive,** adj.

ex·hort (ig zôrt′), v.t., v.i. to urge, advise, or caution earnestly. —**ex′hor·ta′tion,** n.

ex·hume (ig zōōm′, -zyōōm′, eks-hyōōm′), v.t., **-humed, -hum·ing.** to dig (something buried, esp. a dead body) out of the earth. —**ex·hu·ma·tion** (eks′hyōō mā′shən), n.

ex·i·gen·cy (ek′si jən sē), n., pl. **-cies. 1.** Often, **exigencies.** the requirements intrinsic to a circumstance, condition, etc. **2.** a case demanding prompt action. —**ex′i·gent,** adj.

ex·ig·u·ous (ig zig′yōō əs, ik sig′-), adj. extremely scanty. —**ex·i·gu·i·ty** (ek′sə gyōō′i tē), n.

ex·ile (eg′zīl, ek′sīl), n., v., **-iled, -il·ing.** —n. **1.** prolonged separation from one's country, usually by force. **2.** a person in such status. —v.t. **3.** to send (a person) into exile.

ex·ist (ig zist′), v.i. **1.** to have actual being. **2.** to continue to be or live. **3.** to be found or occur.

ex·ist·ence (ig zis′təns), n. **1.** the state or fact of existing. **2.** continuance in being or life. **3.** all that exists. —**ex·ist′ent,** adj.

ex·is·ten·tial (eg′zi sten′shəl, ek′si-), adj. **1.** of existence. **2.** of existentialism.

ex·is·ten·tial·ism (eg′zi sten′shə liz′-əm, ek′si-), n. a philosophic doctrine of beliefs that people have absolute freedom of choice and that the universe is absurd, with an emphasis on the phenomena of anxiety and alienation. —**ex′is·ten′tial·ist,** adj., n.

ex·it (eg′zit, ek′sit), n. **1.** a way or passage out. **2.** a going out or away: to make one's exit. **3.** a departure of an actor or actress from the stage. —v.i. **4.** to go out or leave. [< L exīre to go out]

exo-, a prefix meaning "outside," "outer," or "external": exosphere.

ex·o·bi·ol·o·gy (ek′sō bī ol′ə jē), n. the study of life beyond the earth's atmosphere, as on other planets. —**ex′o·bi′o·log′i·cal,** adj. —**ex′o·bi·ol′o·gist,** n.

ex·o·crine (ek′sə krin, -krīn′, -krēn′), adj. of an exocrine gland or its secretion.

ex′ocrine gland′, any of several glands, as the salivary glands, that secretes externally through a duct.

Exod., Exodus.

ex·o·dus (ek′sə dəs), n. **1.** a mass departure or emigration. **2. the Exodus,** the departure of the Israelites from Egypt under Moses.

ex of·fi·ci·o (eks ə fish′ē ō′), by virtue of office or official position.

ex·og·e·nous (ek soj′ə nəs), adj. Biol. growing or proceeding from outside. —**ex·og′e·nous·ly,** adv.

ex·on·er·ate (ig zon′ə rāt′), v.t., **-at·ed, -at·ing.** to free from blame. —**ex·on′er·a′tion,** n. —**ex·on′er·a′tor,** n.

exor., executor.

ex·or·bi·tant (ig zôr′bi t°nt), adj. exceeding the bounds of propriety or reason, esp. in amount. —**ex·or′bi·tance,** n. —**ex·or′bi·tant·ly,** adv.

ex·or·cise (ek′sôr sīz′), v.t., **-cised, -cis·ing. 1.** to seek to expel (an evil spirit) by solemn ceremonies. **2.** to free (a person, place, etc.) of evil spirits or influences. —**ex′or·cis′er,** n. —**ex·or·cism** (ek′sôr siz′əm), n. —**ex′or·cist,** n.

ex·or·di·um (ig zôr′dē əm, ik sôr′-), n., pl. **-di·ums, -di·a** (-dē ə). the introductory part of an oration or discourse.

ex·o·sphere (ek′sō sfēr′), n. the highest, least dense region of the atmosphere. —**ex·o·spher·ic** (ek′sō sfer′ik), adj.

ex·o·ther·mic (ek′sō thûr′mik), adj. Chem. accompanied by a liberation of heat. Also, **ex′o·ther′mal.**

ex·ot·ic (ig zot′ik), adj. **1.** of foreign origin or character. **2.** strikingly unusual or strange. —**ex·ot′i·cal·ly,** adv. —**ex·ot·i·cism** (ig zot′i siz′əm), n.

exp., 1. expenses. **2.** expired. **3.** export. **4.** express.

ex·pand (ik spand′), v.t., v.i. **1.** to increase in extent, size, etc. **2.** to spread or stretch out. —**ex·pand′a·ble, ex·pand′i·ble,** adj. —**ex·pand′er,** n.

ex·panse (ik spans′), n. an uninterrupted space or area.

ex·pan·sion (ik span′shən), n. **1.** the act or state of expanding. **2.** the state of being expanded. **3.** the amount or degree of expanding. **4.** an expanded portion or form of a thing. —**ex·pan′sion·ar′y,** adj.

ex·pan·sion·ism (ik span′shə niz′əm), n. a policy of expansion, as of territory. —**ex·pan′sion·ist,** n., adj.

ex·pan·sive (ik span'siv), *adj.* 1. tending to expand. 2. causing expansion. 3. having a wide range. 4. unrestrained or open. —**ex·pan'sive·ly**, *adv.* —**ex·pan'sive·ness**, *n.*

ex par·te (eks pär'tē), *Latin.* from one side only, as in a controversy.

ex·pa·ti·ate (ik spā'shē āt'), *v.i.*, -at·ed, -at·ing. to enlarge in discourse or writing. —**ex·pa'ti·a'tion**, *n.* —**ex·pa'ti·a'tor**, *n.*

ex·pa·tri·ate (*v.* eks pā'trē āt'; *n.* eks pā'trē it, -āt'), *v.*, -at·ed, -at·ing, *n.* —*v.t.*, *v.i.* 1. to banish (a person) from his or her native country. 2. to withdraw (oneself) from residence in one's native country. —*n.* 3. an expatriated person. —**ex·pa'tri·a'tion**, *n.*

ex·pect (ik spekt'), *v.t.* 1. to regard as likely or sure to happen or arrive. 2. to look for with reason or justification. 3. *Informal.* to suppose or surmise. —*v.i.* 4. **be expecting**, to be pregnant. —**ex·pect'er**, *n.* —**Syn.** 1. anticipate, await, foresee.

ex·pect·an·cy (ik spek't°n sē), *n., pl.* -cies. expectation (defs. 1, 3).

ex·pect·ant (ik spek't°nt), *adj.* expecting, as a baby. —**ex·pect'ant·ly**, *adv.*

ex·pec·ta·tion (ek'spek tā'shən), *n.* 1. the act or state of expecting. 2. an expectant mental attitude. 3. something expected. 4. Often, **expectations**. a prospect of future good or profit.

ex·pec·to·rant (ik spek'tər ənt), *adj.* 1. promoting the secretion of fluid from the respiratory tract. —*n.* 2. an expectorant medicine.

ex·pec·to·rate (ik spek'tə rāt'), *v.i.*, *v.t.*, -rat·ed, -rat·ing. spit[1] (defs. 1, 2). —**ex·pec'to·ra'tion**, *n.* —**ex·pec'to·ra'tor**, *n.*

ex·pe·di·en·cy (ik spē'dē ən sē), *n., pl.* -cies. 1. the quality of being expedient. 2. a regard for what is politic or advantageous rather than for what is right or just. 3. an expedient. Also, **ex·pe'di·ence**.

ex·pe·di·ent (ik spē'dē ənt), *adj.* 1. tending to promote some proposed or desired object. 2. conducive to advantage or interest. —*n.* 3. a means to an end. —**ex·pe'di·en'tial** (-en'shəl), *adj.* —**ex·pe'di·ent·ly**, *adv.*

ex·pe·dite (ek'spi dīt'), *v.t.*, -dit·ed, -dit·ing. 1. to speed up the progress of: *to expedite shipments.* 2. to accomplish promptly.

ex·pe·dit·er (ek'spi dīt'ər), *n.* a person who expedites something, esp. one employed to move shipments on schedule, as for a railroad.

ex·pe·di·tion (ek'spi dish'ən), *n.* 1. a journey for some specific purpose, as of war. 2. the body of persons, ships, etc., engaged in such an activity. 3. promptness in accomplishing something.

ex·pe·di·tion·ar·y (ek'spi dish'ə ner'ē), *adj.* pertaining to or composing an expedition.

ex·pe·di·tious (ek'spi dish'əs), *adj.* acting with or characterized by promptness. —**ex'pe·di'tious·ly**, *adv.* —**ex'pe·di'tious·ness**, *n.*

ex·pel (ik spel'), *v.t.*, -pelled, -pel·ling. 1. to drive or force out or away. 2. to cut off from membership or relations. —**ex·pel'la·ble**, *adj.* —**ex·pel'ler**, *n.*

ex·pend (ik spend'), *v.t.* 1. to use up. 2. to pay out.

ex·pend·a·ble (ik spen'də bəl), *adj.* 1. capable of being expended. 2. consumed in use or not reusable. 3. (of men, equipment, etc.) capable of being sacrificed to accomplish a military objective.

ex·pend·i·ture (ik spen'di chər), *n.* 1. the act of expending something, esp. funds. 2. something expended.

ex·pense (ik spens'), *n.* 1. cost involved in operating an activity. 2. a cause of spending. 3. charges incurred in a business assignment, trip, etc. 4. **at the expense of**, at the sacrifice of.

ex·pen·sive (ik spen'siv), *adj.* entailing great expense. —**ex·pen'sive·ly**, *adv.*

ex·pe·ri·ence (ik spēr'ē əns), *n., v.*, -enced, -enc·ing. —*n.* 1. the process or an instance of personally encountering or undergoing something. 2. knowledge gained from such a process. 3. the encountering or undergoing of things as they occur in the course of time. —*v.t.* 4. to have or feel as an experience.

ex·pe·ri·enced (ik spēr'ē ənst), *adj.* skillful in a particular field through experience.

ex·per·i·ment (*n.* ik sper'ə mənt; *v.* ek sper'ə ment'), *n.* 1. a tentative procedure used to discover facts or test ideas about something. —*v.i.* 2. to conduct experiments. —**ex·per'i·men'tal**, *adj.* —**ex·per'i·men'tal·ly**, *adv.* —**ex·per'i·men·ta'tion**, *n.* —**ex·per'i·ment'er**, *n.*

ex·pert (*n.* ek'spûrt; *adj.* ik spûrt', ek'spûrt), *n.* 1. a person who has special skill or knowledge in some field. —*adj.* 2. possessing special skill or knowledge. —**ex·pert'ly**, *adv.* —**ex·pert'ness**, *n.*

ex·per·tise (ek'spər tēz'), *n.* expert skill or knowledge.

ex·pi·ate (ek'spē āt'), *v.t.*, -at·ed, -at·ing. to make amends for (a sin, etc.). —**ex'pi·a'tion**, *n.* —**ex'pi·a'tor**, *n.* —**ex·pi·a·to·ry** (ek'spē ə tōr'ē, -tôr'ē).

ex·pir·a·to·ry (ik spi°r'ə tōr'ē, -tôr'ē), *adj.* pertaining to the expiration of air from the lungs.

ex·pire (ik spī^ər′), *v.i.,* **-pired, -pir·ing.**
1. to lapse or terminate, as a con-
tract. **2.** to breathe out. **3.** *Literary.*
to die. —**ex′pi·ra′tion,** *n.*

ex·plain (ik splān′), *v.t.* **1.** to make
plain or clear. **2.** to assign a meaning to. **3.** to give reasons for. —*v.i.*
4. to give an explanation. —
plain′a·ble, *adj.* —**ex·plain′er,** *n.* —
ex·pla·na·tion (ek′splə nā′shən), *n.*
—**ex·plan·a·to·ry** (ik splan′ə tōr′ē,
-tôr′ē), *adj.* —**Syn. 1.** elucidate, expound, interpret.

ex·ple·tive (ek′spli tiv), *n.* an inter-
jectory word or expression, frequently profane.

ex·pli·ca·ble (ek′splə kə bəl, ik splik′-
ə bəl), *adj.* capable of being explained.

ex·pli·cate (ek′splə kāt′), *v.t.,* **-cat·ed,
-cat·ing.** to explain and interpret in
detail. —**ex′pli·ca′tion,** *n.* —**ex′pli·
ca′tor,** *n.*

ex·plic·it (ik splis′it), *adj.* fully and
clearly expressed. —**ex·plic′it·ly,**
adv. —**ex·plic′it·ness,** *n.*

ex·plode (ik splōd′), *v.,* **-plod·ed,
-plod·ing.** —*v.i.* **1.** to expand with
force and noise because of rapid
chemical change, as gunpowder. **2.**
to burst violently with a loud noise.
3. to burst forth violently or emotionally. —*v.t.* **4.** to cause (gunpowder, a boiler, etc.) to explode.
5. *Informal.* to discredit or disprove:
to explode a theory. —**ex·plod′er,** *n.*

ex·plod·ed (ik splō′did), *adj.* showing
the parts separately but in their
proper relationship: *an exploded
view of an engine.*

ex·ploit¹ (ek′sploit, ik sploit′), *n.* a
striking or notable deed.

ex·ploit² (ik sploit′), *v.t.* **1.** to utilize,
esp. for profit. **2.** to use selfishly
for one's own ends. —**ex·ploit′a·
ble,** *adj.* —**ex·ploit′a·tive,** *adj.* —
ex′ploi·ta′tion, *n.* —**ex·ploit′er,** *n.*

ex·plore (ik splōr′, -splôr′), *v.,* **-plored,
-plor·ing.** —*v.t.* **1.** to traverse (a
region, etc.) for the purpose of discovery. **2.** to examine or look into
closely. —*v.i.* **3.** to engage in exploring. —**ex′plo·ra′tion,** *n.* —**ex·
plor·a·to·ry** (ik splōr′ə tōr′ē, -splôr′ə-
tôr′ē), *adj.* —**ex·plor′er,** *n.*

ex·plo·sion (ik splō′zhən), *n.* **1.** the
act or an instance of exploding. **2.**
the noise itself. **3.** a violent outburst, as of laughter, anger, etc. **4.**
a sudden, rapid, or great increase:
a population explosion.

ex·plo·sive (ik splō′siv), *adj.* **1.** tending or serving to explode. **2.** of or of
the nature of an explosion. —*n.* **3.**
an explosive agent or substance, as
dynamite. —**ex·plo′sive·ly,** *adv.* —
ex·plo′sive·ness, *n.*

ex·po (eks′pō), *n.* (*often cap.*) *Informal.* exposition (def. 1).

ex·po·nent (ik spō′nənt *or, esp for 3,*
ek′spō nənt), *n.* **1.** a person or thing
that expounds. **2.** a person or thing
that is an advocate or symbol of
something. **3.** *Math.* a symbol placed
above and after another symbol to
denote the power to which the letter
is to be raised, as *n* in the expression
x^n. —**ex·po·nen·tial** (ek′spō nen′-
shəl), *adj.* —**ex′po·nen′tial·ly,** *adv.*

ex·port (*v.* ik spōrt′, -spôrt′, ek′spōrt,
-spôrt; *n.* ek′spōrt, -spôrt), *v.t.,* *v.i.*
1. to ship (commodities) to other
countries for sale, exchange, etc.
—*n.* **2.** the act of exporting. **3.** that
which is exported. —**ex′por·ta′tion,**
n. —**ex·port′er,** *n.*

ex·pose (ik spōz′), *v.t.,* **-posed, -pos-
ing. 1.** to lay open to danger, harm,
etc. **2.** to bare to the air, cold, etc.
3. to present to view. **4.** to disclose
or reveal. **5.** to subject (a photosensitive material) to the action of
light. —**ex·pos′er,** *n.*

ex·po·sé (ek′spō zā′), *n.* a public revelation, as of something discreditable.

ex·po·si·tion (ek′spə zish′ən), *n.* **1.** a
large-scale public exhibition, as of
the products of manufacture. **2.** the
act of expounding or explaining. **3.**
an explanatory treatise.

ex·pos·i·tor (ik spoz′i tər), *n.* a person who expounds or explains.

ex·pos·i·to·ry (ik spoz′i tōr′ē, -tôr′ē),
adj. serving to expound or explain.

ex post fac·to (eks′ pōst′ fak′tō), ret-
rospectively or retroactively.

ex·pos·tu·late (ik spos′chə lāt′), *v.i.,*
-lat·ed, -lat·ing. to reason earnestly
with a person against some action.
—**ex·pos′tu·la′tion,** *n.*

ex·po·sure (ik spō′zhər), *n.* **1.** the act
of exposing. **2.** the act or time of
exposing a photosensitive material.
3. placement with regard to sunlight or wind. **4.** public appearance,
esp. on the mass media.

ex·pound (ik spound′), *v.t.,* *v.i.* **1.** to
set forth or state (a view) in detail.
2. to explain or interpret. —**ex·
pound′er,** *n.*

ex·press (ik spres′), *v.t.* **1.** to put
(thought) into words. **2.** to show
or reveal. **3.** to represent by a symbol. **4.** to send express. **5.** *Obs.* to
press or squeeze out. —*adj.* **6.** clearly
indicated. **7.** special or definite. **8.**
specially direct or fast: *an express
bus.* —*n.* **9.** an express train, bus,
etc. **10. a.** a system for the fast pickup, transportation, and delivery of
parcels, small freight shipments, etc.:
air express. **b.** a shipment by such
a system. —*adv.* **11.** by express.
—**ex·press′i·ble,** *adj.* —**ex·press′ly,** *adv.*

ex·pres·sion (ik spresh'ən), *n.* 1. the act of expressing something, esp. in words. 2. a particular word or phrase. 3. the manner in which a thing is expressed in words. 4. indication of feeling, character, etc., as in the voice. 5. a look or intonation expressing personal reaction, feeling, etc. 6. *Math.* a symbol or a combination of symbols representing a value or relation. —**ex·pres'sion·less,** *adj.*

ex·pres·sion·ism (ik spresh'ə niz'əm), *n.* (*sometimes cap.*) a stylistic movement in art, literature, etc., stressing the subjective element in experience and the symbolic aspects of objects. —**ex·pres'sion·ist,** *n.,* *adj.* —**ex·pres'sion·is'tic,** *adj.*

ex·pres·sive (ik spres'iv), *adj.* 1. serving to express. 2. full of meaning or feeling. —**ex·pres'sive·ly,** *adv.* —**ex·pres'sive·ness,** *n.*

ex·press·way (ik spres'wā'), *n.* a divided highway especially planned for high-speed traffic, usually having few if any intersections.

ex·pro·pri·ate (eks prō'prē āt'), *v.t.,* -at·ed, -at·ing. to take (property) from another, esp. without permission. —**ex·pro'pri·a'tion,** *n.*

expt., experiment.

exptl., experimental.

ex·pul·sion (ik spul'shən), *n.* 1. the act of expelling. 2. the state of being expelled.

ex·punge (ik spunj'), *v.t.,* -punged, -pung·ing. to delete emphatically, as from writing or records.

ex·pur·gate (ek'spər gāt', ik spûr'gāt), *v.t.,* -gat·ed, -gat·ing. to amend by removing offensive or objectionable matter, esp. from a book. —**ex'pur·ga'tion,** *n.* —**ex'pur·ga'tor,** *n.*

expwy., expressway.

ex·qui·site (ek'skwi zit, ik skwiz'it), *adj.* 1. of special beauty, charm, or excellence. 2. intense or keen, as pleasure. 3. keenly sensitive or responsive. 4. of peculiar refinement. —**ex'qui·site·ly,** *adv.*

ext., 1. extension. 2. exterior. 3. external. 4. extinct. 5. extra. 6. extract.

ex·tant (ek'stənt, ik stant'), *adj.* still in existence.

ex·tem·po·ra·ne·ous (ik stem'pə rā'nē-əs), *adj.* done or spoken without special preparation. Also, **ex·tem'po·rar'y** (-rer'ē). —**ex·tem'po·ra'ne·ous·ly,** *adv.*

ex·tem·po·re (ik stem'pə rē), *adv.* 1. on the spur of the moment. —*adj.* 2. extemporaneous. [< L = *ex* out of + *tempore* (abl. sing. of *tempus* time)]

ex·tem·po·rize (ik stem'pə rīz'), *v.i.,* *v.t.,* -rized, -riz·ing. to speak or perform (something) extemporaneously.

ex·tend (ik stend'), *v.t.* 1. to stretch or draw out. 2. to stretch in a given direction or to a particular point. 3. to prolong or lengthen. 4. to expand or widen. 5. to grant or give. 6. to exert (oneself) to an unusual degree. —*v.i.* 7. to be or become extended. —**ex·tend'ed,** *adj.* —**ex·tend'er,** *n.* —**ex·tend'i·bil'i·ty,** *n.* —**ex·tend'i·ble,** **ex·tend'a·ble,** **ex·ten'si·ble,** *adj.*

extend'ed care', minimum health service provided on a continuous basis, as in a nursing home having required special facilities.

extend'ed fam'ily, a special group consisting of a family nucleus and various near relatives.

ex·ten·sion (ik sten'shən), *n.* 1. the act of extending or state of being extended. 2. that by which something is extended, as a construction added to a house. 3. an extra telephone that operates on the principal line.

ex·ten·sive (ik sten'siv), *adj.* 1. of great extent. 2. far-reaching or comprehensive. —**ex·ten'sive·ly,** *adv.* —**ex·ten'sive·ness,** *n.*

ex·tent (ik stent'), *n.* 1. length, area, volume, or scope: *the extent of his lands.* 2. something extended.

ex·ten·u·ate (ik sten'yōō āt'), *v.t.,* -at·ed, -at·ing. to serve to make (a fault, offense, etc.) be or seem less serious. —**ex·ten'u·a'tion,** *n.*

ex·te·ri·or (ik stēr'ē ər), *adj.* 1. being on the outer side. 2. suitable for outdoor use. —*n.* 3. the outer surface or part. —**ex·te'ri·or·ly,** *adv.*

ex·ter·mi·nate (ik stûr'mə nāt'), *v.t.,* -nat·ed, -nat·ing. to destroy totally. —**ex·ter'mi·na'tion,** *n.* —**ex·ter'mi·na'tor,** *n.*

ex·tern (ek'stûrn), *n.* a person connected with an institution but not residing in it, as a doctor.

ex·ter·nal (ik stûr'nəl), *adj.* 1. of the outside or outer part. 2. situated, acting, or coming from outside. 3. superficial or outward. 4. pertaining to foreign countries: *external affairs.* 5. independent of the perceiving mind. —*n.* 6. an external feature, circumstance, etc. —**ex·ter'nal·ly,** *adv.*

ex·tinct (ik stingkt'), *adj.* 1. not existing now: *an extinct species.* 2. having ceased eruption, as a volcano. —**ex·tinc'tion,** *n.*

ex·tin·guish (ik sting'gwish), *v.t.* 1. to put out (a fire, light, etc.). 2. to put an end to: *to extinguish hope.* —**ex·tin'guish·a·ble,** *adj.* —**ex·tin'guish·er,** *n.*

ex·tir·pate (ek'stər pāt', ik stûr'pāt), *v.t.,* -pat·ed, -pat·ing. 1. to destroy totally. 2. to pull up by or as by the roots. —**ex'tir·pa'tion,** *n.*

ex·tol (ik stōl', -stol'), *v.t.,* -tolled, -tol·ling. to praise highly. Also, **extoll'.** —**ex·tol'ler,** *n.*

ex·tort (ik stôrt′), *v.t.* to force (money, information, etc.) from a person by intimidation or abuse of authority. —**ex·tor′tion,** *n.* —**ex·tor′tion·ist, ex·tor′tion·er,** *n.*

ex·tor·tion·ate (ik stôr′shə nit), *adj.* grossly excessive. —**ex·tor′tion·ate·ly,** *adv.*

ex·tra (ek′strə), *adj.* **1.** beyond what is expected. **2.** better than what is usual. —*n.* **3.** an extra thing or person. **4.** an additional charge. **5.** a special edition of a newspaper. **6.** a performer hired for a minor part, esp. in a movie scene. **7.** an additional worker. —*adv.* **8.** beyond the ordinary degree.

extra-, a prefix meaning "outside" or "beyond": *extraterritorial.*

ex·tract (*v.* ik strakt′; *n.* ek′strakt), *v.t.* **1.** to pull or draw out, esp. by force: *to extract a tooth.* **2.** to deduce (a principle, etc.). **3.** to copy out (matter), as from a book. **4.** to obtain (a juice, etc.) from a mixture by pressure or distillation. —*n.* **5.** something extracted. **6.** an excerpt or selection. **7.** an essence in concentrated form. —**ex·trac′tor,** *n.*

ex·trac·tion (ik strak′shən), *n.* **1.** the act or process of extracting something. **2.** descent or lineage.

ex·tra·cur·ric·u·lar (ek′strə kə rik′yə lər), *adj.* outside the regular curriculum.

ex·tra·dite (ek′strə dīt′), *v.t.* -dit·ed, -dit·ing. to surrender (an alleged fugitive or criminal) to another state or authority. —**ex′tra·di′tion** (-dish′ən), *n.*

ex·tra·dos (ek′strə dos′, -dōs′, ek strā′dos, -dōs), *n., pl.* -dos (-dōz′, -dōz), -dos·es. the exterior curve of an arch or vault.

ex·tra·ga·lac·tic (ek′strə gə lak′tik), *adj.* outside the Milky Way system.

ex·tra·le·gal (ek′strə lē′gəl), *adj.* beyond the authority of law.

ex·tra·mar·i·tal (ek′strə mar′i təl), *adj.* pertaining to sexual relations with someone other than one's spouse.

ex·tra·mu·ral (ek′strə myŏor′əl), *adj.* involving representatives of more than one school.

ex·tra·ne·ous (ik strā′nē əs), *adj.* **1.** not pertinent or relevant: *an extraneous remark.* **2.** not belonging or proper to a thing or organism. —**ex·tra′ne·ous·ly,** *adv.* —**ex·tra′ne·ous·ness,** *n.*

ex·traor·di·nar·y (ik strôr′d°ner′ē, ek′strə ôr′d°ner′ē), *adj.* **1.** beyond what is ordinary or established. **2.** exceeding the ordinary extent or degree. **3.** (of an official, etc.) additional to the ordinary staff. —**ex·traor′di·nar′i·ly** (ik strôr′d°nâr′ə lē, ek′strə ôr′-), *adv.*

ex·trap·o·late (ik strap′ə lāt′, ek′strə

pə-), *v.t., v.i.* -lat·ed, -lat·ing. to infer (an unknown) from something that is known. —**ex·trap′o·la′tion,** *n.*

ex·tra·sen·so·ry (ek′strə sen′sə rē), *adj.* outside of normal sense perception.

ex·tra·ter·res·tri·al (ek′strə tə res′trē əl), *adj.* outside, or originating outside, the limits of the earth.

ex·tra·ter·ri·to·ri·al (ek′strə ter′i tôr′ē əl, -tôr′-), *adj.* beyond local territorial jurisdiction.

ex·tra·ter·ri·to·ri·al·i·ty (ek′strə ter′i tôr′ē al′i tē, -tôr′-), *n.* immunity from the jurisdiction of a state granted to foreign diplomatic officials, warships, etc.

ex·tra·u·ter·ine (ek′strə yōō′tər in, -tə rīn′), *adj.* being or developing outside the uterus.

ex·trav·a·gant (ik strav′ə gənt), *adj.* **1.** spending much more than is necessary or prudent. **2.** exceeding the bounds of reason, as passions, etc. —**ex·trav′a·gant·ly,** *adv.* —**ex·trav′a·gance, ex·trav′a·gant·ness,** *n.* —Syn. **1.** imprudent, lavish. **2.** immoderate, inordinate.

ex·trav·a·gan·za (ik strav′ə gan′zə), *n.* an elaborate musical or dramatic composition, as musical comedy.

ex·tra·ve·hic·u·lar (ek′strə vē hik′yə lər), *adj.* performed outside a space vehicle during a spaceflight.

ex·tra·vert (ek′strə vûrt′), *n.* extrovert.

ex·treme (ik strēm′), *adj.* **1.** of a character farthest removed from the ordinary: *extreme measures.* **2.** exceedingly great. **3.** outermost or endmost. **4.** exceeding the bounds of moderation. **5.** radical, as in action or opinion. —*n.* **6.** one of two things as remote or different from each other as possible: *the extremes of joy and grief.* **7.** an extreme act, measure, condition, etc. —**ex·treme′ly,** *adv.* —**ex·treme′ness,** *n.*

extreme′ high′ fre′quency, any radio frequency between 30,000 and 300,000 megahertz.

extreme′ unc′tion, *Rom. Cath. Ch.* a sacrament administered to a person in danger of dying.

ex·trem·ism (ik strē′miz əm), *n.* a tendency to go to extremes, esp. in politics. —**ex·trem′ist,** *n., adj.*

ex·trem·i·ty (ik strem′i tē), *n., pl.* -ties. **1.** the extreme or terminal point or part of something. **2.** a limb or body, esp. a hand or foot. **3.** a condition of extreme need, distress, etc. **4.** any extreme degree. **5.** an extreme measure, act, etc.

ex·tri·cate (ek′strə kāt′), *v.t.* -cat·ed, -cat·ing. to free from entanglement. —**ex′tri·ca·ble** (-kə bəl, ik strik′ə bəl), *adj.* —**ex′tri·ca′tion,** *n.*

ex·trin·sic (ik strin′sik), *adj.* **1.** not essential or inherent. **2.** outward or external. —**ex·trin′si·cal·ly,** *adv*

ex·tro·vert (ek′strō vûrt′, -strə-), *n.* a person who is primarily interested in things outside the self. —**ex′tro·ver′sion,** *n.* —**ex′tro·ver′sive,** *adj.* —**ex′tro·vert′ed,** *adj.*

ex·trude (ik strōōd′), *v.,* **-trud·ed, -trud·ing.** —*v.t.* **1.** to thrust, force, or press out. **2.** to form (metal, plastic, etc.) by forcing through a die. —*v.i.* **3.** to be extruded. —**ex·tru·sion** (ik strōō′zhən), *n.*

ex·tru·sive (ik strōō′siv), *adj.* (of rocks) having been forced to the surface of the earth while in a molten or plastic condition.

ex·u·ber·ant (ig zōō′bər ənt), *adj.* **1.** extremely joyful and vigorous. **2.** lavish and unreserved: *an exuberant welcome.* **3.** profuse in growth. —**ex·u′ber·ance,** *n.* —**ex·u′ber·ant·ly,** *adv.*

ex·u·date (eks′yōō dāt′, ek′sə-, eg′zə-), *n.* a substance exuded.

ex·ude (ig zōōd′, ik sōōd′), *v.i., v.t.,* **-ud·ed, -ud·ing.** **1.** to pass out gradually through the pores. **2.** to give forth or off. —**ex′u·da′tion,** *n.*

ex·ult (ig zult′), *v.i.* to rejoice exceedingly. —**ex·ult′ant,** *adj.* —**ex·ult′ing·ly,** *adv.* —**ex′ul·ta′tion,** *n.*

ex·urb (ek′sûrb, eg′zûrb), *n.* a small, usually fashionable community situated beyond the suburbs of a city. —**ex·ur·ban** (eks ûr′bən), *adj.*

ex·ur·ban·ite (eks ûr′bə nīt′), *n.* a person living in an exurb.

ex·ur·bi·a (eks ûr′bē ə), *n.* a generalized area comprising the exurbs.

-ey¹, var. of **-y**¹: *clayey.*

-ey², See **-y**².

eye (ī), *n., v.,* **eyed, ey·ing** or **eye·ing.** —*n.* **1.** the organ of sight, typically one of two spherical bodies at the front of the skull. **2.** the region surrounding the eye: *a black eye.* **3.** sight or vision. **4.** discriminating visual perception. **5.** look, glance, or gaze. **6.** an attentive look, close observation, or watch. **7.** regard, view, or intention. **8.** estimation or opinion. **9.** something suggesting the eye in appearance, shape, etc. **10.** **have an eye for,** to be discerning about. **11.** **keep an eye on,** to watch over attentively. **12.** **lay, clap,** or **set eyes on,** to catch sight of. **13.** **make eyes at,** to gaze flirtatiously or amorously at. **14.** **see eye to eye,** to be in complete agreement. **15.** **with an eye to,** with an object or advantage in mind. —*v.t.* **16.** to view or observe. —**eyed** (īd), *adj.* —**eye′less,** *adj.* —**ey′er,** *n.*

eye·ball (ī′bôl′), *n.* **1.** the ball or globe of the eye. **2.** **have** or **get an eyeball on,** *CB Radio Slang.* to see. —*v.t.* **3.** *Slang.* to view or observe very closely.

eye′ bank′ a place for the storage of corneas that have been removed from the eyes of people recently dead, used for transplanting to the eyes of persons having corneal defects.

eye·brow (ī′brou′), *n.* **1.** the ridge forming the upper part of the orbit of the eye. **2.** the hairs growing on this.

eye′ catch′er, *Informal.* something that specially attracts the eye. —**eye′-catch′ing,** *adj.*

eye·drop·per (ī′drop′ər), *n.* a dropper for eye drops.

eye′ drops′, medicinal drops to relieve discomfort in the eye.

eye·ful (ī′fŏŏl′), *n.* **1.** an amount of foreign matter in the eye. **2.** the amount that a person can or wants to see. **3.** *Informal.* a very beautiful woman.

eye·glass (ī′glas′, ī′gläs′), *n.* **1.** a lens used to aid defective vision. **2.** **eyeglasses,** a pair of such lenses set in a frame.

eye·lash (ī′lash′), *n.* **1.** one of the short hairs growing on the edge of an eyelid. **2.** the fringe of hairs itself.

eye·let (ī′lit), *n.* **1.** a small hole, finished along the edge, for the passage of a cord or as in embroidery for decoration. **2.** a metal ring for lining a small hole.

eye·lid (ī′lid′), *n.* the movable lid of skin that serves to cover and uncover the eyeball.

eye·lin·er (ī′lī′nər), *n.* a cosmetic used to outline the eye close to the lashes.

eye-o·pen·er (ī′ō′pə nər), *n.* a startling or enlightening experience or disclosure. —**eye′-o′pen·ing,** *adj.*

eye·piece (ī′pēs′), *n.* the lens or combination of lenses in an optical instrument through which the eye views the image.

eye·shade (ī′shād′), *n.* a visor worn on the head or forehead to shield the eyes from overhead light.

eye′ shad′ow, a cosmetic coloring material applied to the eyelids.

eye·sight (ī′sīt′), *n.* **1.** the power or faculty of seeing. **2.** the range of the eye.

eye·sore (ī′sōr′, ī′sôr′), *n.* something unpleasant or ugly to look at.

eye·strain (ī′strān′), *n.* discomfort produced in the eyes by their excessive or improper use.

eye·tooth (ī′tōōth′), *n., pl.* **-teeth** (-tēth′). a canine tooth of the upper jaw.

eye·wash (ī′wosh′, ī′wôsh′), *n.* **1.** a solution applied locally to the eye for administering medication. **2.** *Slang.* nonsense or bunk.

eye·wit·ness (ī′wit′nis, ī′wit′nis), *n.* a person who sees some act or occurrence and can give a firsthand account of it.

ey·rie (âr′ē, ēr′ē), *n.* aerie. Also, **ey′ry.**

F

F, f (ef), *n., pl.* **F's** or **Fs, f's** or **fs.**
the sixth letter of the English al-
phabet, a consonant.
F, 1. Fahrenheit. 2. farad. 3. French.
4. *Math.* function (of).
F, 1. the sixth in order or in a series.
2. a grade indicating academic work
of the lowest quality. 3. the fourth
tone in the scale of C major. 4.
fluorine.
f, 1. farad. 2. *Music.* forte.
f, 1. See focal length. 2. frequency.
F., 1. Fahrenheit. 2. false. 3. family.
4. February. 5. French. 6. Friday.
f., 1. farad. 2. female. 3. feminine.
4. folio. 5. following. 6. foot. 7.
franc; francs.
f/, See f number.
fa (fä), *n.* the fourth tone of a
diatonic scale.
FAA, Federal Aviation Agency.
fa·ba·ceous (fə bā′shəs), *adj.* belonging to the bean family of plants
that bear seeds in pods or legumes.
Fa·bi·an (fā′bē ən), *adj.* 1. of or belonging to an English organization
(**Fa′bian Soci′ety**) founded in 1884,
favoring the gradual and peaceful
spread of socialism. —*n.* 2. a member of this society. —**Fa′bi·an·ism,**
n.
fa·ble (fā′bəl), *n.* 1. a short tale to
teach a moral, often with animals
as characters. 2. a story about
supernatural persons or incidents. 3.
an untruth or falsehood.
fa·bled (fā′bəld), *adj.* 1. celebrated
in fables. 2. unreal or fictitious.
fab·ric (fab′rik), *n.* 1. a cloth made
by weaving or knitting fibers. 2.
framework or structure.
fab·ri·cate (fab′rə kāt′), *v.t.,* -cat·ed,
-cat·ing. 1. to make by art and labor.
2. to make by assembling standard
sections. 3. to devise (a story, lie,
etc.). —**fab′ri·ca′tion,** *n.* —**fab′ri·
ca′tor,** *n.*
fab·u·lous (fab′yə ləs), *adj.* 1. aston-
ishingly incredible. 2. marvelous or
superb. 3. told or known through
fables or legends. —**fab′u·lous·ly,**
adv.
fac., 1. facsimile. 2. factor. 3. factory. 4. faculty.
fa·cade (fə säd′, fa-), *n.* 1. the front
of a building, esp. an imposing one.
2. a false or superficial appearance.
Also, **fa·cade′.**
face (fās), *n., v.,* faced, fac·ing. —*n.*
1. the front part of the head. 2. a
look or expression on this part. 3. a
grimace: *to make a face.* 4. In-

formal. boldness or impudence. 5.
outward appearance. 6. prestige or
dignity: *to lose face.* 7. the characteristics of a land surface. 8. the
side upon which the use of a thing
depends: *the face of a watch.* 9. face
to face, a. turning towa.d each other.
b. in direct opposition. 10. in the
face of, a. notwithstanding. b. when
confronted with. 11. on the face
of it, seemingly. 12. to one's face,
openly in one's presence. —*v.t.*
13. to look towar‹ 14. to have the
front toward or permit a vie٧ of. 15.
to confront directly. 16 to confront
boldly or impudently. 17. to cover
with a different material in front.
18. to finish the edge of (a garment)
with facing. —*v.i.* 19. to turn or
be turned. 20. to be placed with the
front in a certain direction. 21. face
up to, a. to acknowledge or admit.
b. to meet courageously. —**faced**
(fāst), *adj.* —**face′less,** *adj.* —**face′-
less·ness,** *n.*
face-lift (fās′lift′), *n.* 1. plastic surgery on the face for elevating sag-
ging tissues and eliminating wrinkles, etc. 2. *Informal.* a renovation
or improvement, esp. of a building.
Also called **face′ lift′ing.**
face-off (fās′ôf′, -of′), *n.* 1. *Ice
Hockey.* the start of a game or period when the referee puts the puck
between two opposing players. 2.
Informal. a decisive confrontation.
face-sav·ing (fās′sā′viñg), *adj.* serving
to save one's prestige or dignity.
fac·et (fas′it), *n., v.,* -et·ed, -et·ing or
-et·ted, -et·ting. —*n.* 1. one of the
small, polished plane surfaces of a
cut gem. 2. an aspect or phase.
—*v.t.* 3. to cut facets on.
fa·ce·tious (fə sē′shəs), *adj.* frivolously amusing. —**fa·ce′tious·ly,** *adv.*
—**fa·ce′tious·ness,** *n.*
face′ val′ue, 1. the value printed on
the face of a stock, bond, etc. 2. apparent value.
fa·cial (fā′shəl), *adj.* 1. of the face.
2. for the face: *facial tissues.* —*n.* 3.
a massage or other treatment to
beautify the face. —**fa′cial·ly,** *adv.*
fac·ile (fas′il), *adj.* 1. acting, working, or proceeding with ease. 2. easily
performed or used. 3. affable, agreeable, or complaisant. —**fac′ile·ly,**
adv.
fa·cil·i·tate (fə sil′i tāt′), *v.t.,* -tat·ed,
-tat·ing. to make easier or less
difficult, as a process, etc. —**fa·cil′-
i·ta′tion,** *n.*

319

fa·cil·i·ty (fə sil′i tē), *n., pl.* **-ties. 1.** something designed, built, or installed to serve a specific function: *educational facilities.* **2.** the quality of being easily or conveniently done or performed. **3.** something that permits the easier performance of an action, etc. **4.** freedom from difficulty. **5.** ease due to skill, aptitude, or practice.

fac·ing (fā′sing), *n.* **1.** a covering in front, as an outer layer of stone on a brick wall. **2.** a lining applied to the edge of a garment. **3.** material turned outward or inward, as a hem.

fac·sim·i·le (fak sim′ə lē), *n.* **1.** an exact copy, as of a book, painting, etc. **2.** a method of transmitting drawings, printed material, etc., by means of radio or telegraph. —*v.t.* **3.** to make a facsimile of. [< L *fac simile* make similar]

fact (fakt), *n.* **1.** something known to exist or to have happened. **2.** a truth known by actual experience or observation. **3.** actuality or truth. **4.** *Law.* an action or deed, esp. a crime committed: *after the fact.* **5.** in fact, indeed. —**fact′ful,** *adj.*

fac·tion (fak′shən), *n.* **1.** a group or clique within a larger body, party, government, etc. **2.** party strife and intrigue. —**fac′tion·al,** *adj.* —**fac′tion·al·ism,** *n.*

fac·tious (fak′shəs), *adj.* **1.** given to or causing faction. **2.** of or proceeding from faction. —**fac′tious·ly,** *adv.* —**fac′tious·ness,** *n.*

fac·ti·tious (fak tish′əs), *adj.* not spontaneous or natural: *factitious enthusiasm.* —**fac·ti′tious·ly,** *adv.* —**fac·ti′tious·ness,** *n.*

fac·tor (fak′tər), *n.* **1.** one of the elements contributing to a particular result. **2.** one of two or more numbers that when multiplied together produce a given product. **3.** gene. **4.** a selling agent, esp. in the textile trade. —*v.t.* *Math.* to resolve into factors.

fac·to·ri·al (fak tōr′ē əl, -tôr′-), *Math.* —*n.* **1.** the product of a given positive integer multiplied by all lesser positive integers. —*adj.* **2.** of factors or factorials.

fac·to·ry (fak′tə rē), *n., pl.* **-ries.** a building or group of buildings with facilities for the manufacture of goods.

fac·to·tum (fak tō′təm), *n.* *Chiefly Brit. and Facetious.* a person employed to do all kinds of work. [< ML < *fac* do + *tōtum* all]

facts′ of life′, the facts concerning sex, reproduction, and birth.

fac·tu·al (fak′chōō əl), *adj.* **1.** of or concerning facts. **2.** based on facts. —**fac′tu·al·ly,** *adv.*

fac·u·la (fak′yə lə), *n., pl.* **-lae** (-lē′). an unusually bright patch on the sun's surface.

fac·ul·ty (fak′əl tē), *n., pl.* **-ties. 1.** an ability for a particular kind of action. **2.** one of the powers of the mind, as memory, speech, etc. **3.** an inherent capability of the body. **4.** one of the departments of learning in a university. **5.** the teaching and administrative force of an educational institution. **6.** *Brit.* the members of a learned profession.

fad (fad), *n.* a temporary, popular fashion, manner of conduct, etc. —**fad′dish,** *adj.* —**fad′dist,** *n.*

fade (fād), *v.,* **fad·ed, fad·ing.** —*v.i.* **1.** to lose brightness or vividness of color. **2.** to become dim. **3.** to lose freshness, vigor, or health. **4.** to disappear gradually. —*v.t.* **5.** to cause to fade.

fade·less (fād′lis), *adj.* not fading or diminishing.

FAdm, Fleet Admiral.

fae·ces (fē′sēz), *n.pl.* feces. —**fae·cal** (fē′kəl), *adj.*

fae·rie (fā′ə rē, fâr′ē), *n.* *Archaic.* **1.** fairyland. **2.** a fairy. Also, **fa′er·y.**

fag¹ (fag), *v.,* **fagged, fag·ging.** —*v.t., v.i.* **1.** to make or become tired or exhausted. —*n.* **2.** *Slang.* a cigarette. **3.** *Brit. Informal.* a hard, menial task.

fag² (fag), *n.* faggot².

fag′ end′, 1. the last part of something. **2.** the unfinished end of a piece of cloth.

fag·got¹ (fag′ət), *n.* *Brit.* fagot.

fag·got² (fag′ət), *n.* *Slang.* a male homosexual.

fag·ot (fag′ət), *n.* a bundle of sticks, twigs, or branches used as fuel.

fag·ot·ing (fag′ə ting), *n.* an openwork decoration of fabric in which the thread is drawn in crisscross stitches across an open seam. Also, *Brit.,* **fag′got·ing.**

Fahr., Fahrenheit. Also, **Fah.**

Fahr·en·heit (far′ən hīt′), *adj.* noting or pertaining to a temperature scale in which 32° represents the freezing point of water and 212° the boiling point. [after G. D. *Fahrenheit,* 1686–1736, Ger. physicist]

fa·ience (fī äns′, fā-), *n.* glazed earthenware or pottery. Also, **fa·ience′.**

fail (fāl), *v.i.* **1.** to fall short of success in something expected or approved. **2.** to receive less than the passing grade. **3.** to be insufficient or absent. **4.** to dwindle or die away. **5.** to become weaker. **6.** to become insolvent or bankrupt. **7.** to stop functioning. —*v.t.* **8.** to be unsuccessful in the performance of. **9.** to prove of no use or help to. **10.** to abandon or desert. **11.** to receive less than a passing grade in. **12.** to declare (a person) unsuccessful in a test, course of study, etc. —*n.* **13. without fail,** with certainty.

fail·ing (fā′ling), *n.* **1.** a minor shortcoming. **2.** *Rare.* a failure. —*prep.* **3.** in the absence of. —**fail′ing·ly,** *adv.*

faille (fīl, fāl), *n.* a soft ribbed fabric of silk, rayon, etc.

fail-safe (fāl′sāf′), *adj.* of or noting a mechanism built into a system to ensure safety if the system fails to operate properly.

fail·ure (fāl′yər), *n.* **1.** the act or an instance of failing. **2.** nonperformance of something due or expected. **3.** an insufficiency. **4.** deterioration or decay. **5.** a condition of being bankrupt. **6.** a becoming bankrupt. **7.** a person or thing that proves unsuccessful.

fain (fān), *Archaic.* —*adv.* **1.** gladly or willingly. —*adj.* **2.** content or willing.

faint (fānt), *adj.* **1.** lacking brightness or clearness. **2.** feeble or slight. **3.** feeling weak or dizzy. **4.** cowardly or timorous. —*v.i.* **5.** to lose consciousness temporarily. —*n.* **6.** temporary loss of consciousness. —**faint′er,** *n.* —**faint′ly,** *adv.* —**faint′ness,** *n.*

faint·heart·ed (fānt′här′tid), *adj.* lacking courage. —**faint′heart′ed·ly,** *adv.* —**faint′heart′ed·ness,** *n.*

fair[1] (fâr), *adj.* **1.** free from dishonesty or injustice. **2.** proper under the rules. **3.** moderately large. **4.** moderately good. **5.** likely or promising. **6.** bright and sunny. **7.** free from blemish or imperfection. **8.** legitimate or liable to pursuit or attack: *fair game.* **9.** easy to read. **10.** not dark: *fair skin.* **11.** beautiful or attractive. —*adv.* **12.** in a fair manner. **13.** straight or directly. —**fair′ness,** *n.* —**Syn. 1.** equitable, just, impartial, unprejudiced.

fair[2] (fâr), *n.* **1.** a competitive exhibition of farm products, livestock, etc. **2.** *Chiefly Brit.* a periodic gathering of buyers and sellers in an appointed place. **3.** an exhibition and sale of articles to raise money, often for some charitable purpose.

fair·ground (fâr′ground′), *n.* a place where fairs, horse races, etc., are held.

fair-haired (fâr′hârd′), *adj.* **1.** having light-colored hair. **2. fair-haired boy,** a youth or man favored by a superior.

fair·ly (fâr′lē), *adv.* **1.** justly or impartially. **2.** moderately or tolerably. **3.** actually or completely. **4.** properly or legitimately.

fair′ play′, just and honorable treatment, action, or conduct.

fair′ shake′, *Slang.* an equal opportunity or treatment.

fair-spo·ken (fâr′spō′kən), *adj.* courteous or smooth in speech.

fair-trade (fâr′trād′), *adj.* subject to an agreement between a manufacturer and a retailer to sell a branded product at no less than a specific price.

fair·way (fâr′wā′), *n. Golf.* the mowed part of any hole between the tee and the green.

fair·y (fâr′ē), *n., pl.* **fair·ies,** *adj.* —*n.* **1.** an imaginary supernatural being having a diminutive human form and magical powers. **2.** *Slang.* a male homosexual. —*adj.* **3.** of fairies. **4.** like a fairy.

fair·y·land (fâr′ē land′), *n.* **1.** the imaginary realm of the fairies. **2.** an enchantingly beautiful region.

fair′y tale′, 1. a story about fairies, usually for children. **2.** an incredible statement or report.

fait ac·com·pli (fe tA kôn plē′), *pl.* **faits ac·com·plis** (fe zA kôn plē′). *French.* an accomplished fact.

faith (fāth), *n.* **1.** complete confidence or trust. **2.** belief in God or the doctrines of religion. **3.** a system of religious belief. **4.** loyalty or fidelity. **5. bad faith,** deceit or duplicity. **6. good faith,** honesty or sincerity. **7. in faith,** *Archaic.* indeed. —**faith′ful,** *adj.* —**faith′ful·ly,** *adv.* —**faith′ful·ness,** *n.* —**faith′less,** *adj.* —**faith′less·ly,** *adv.* —**faith′less·ness,** *n.*

fake (fāk), *v.,* **faked, fak·ing,** *n., adj.* —*v.t., v.i.* **1.** to make (something) seem genuine, esp. by fraud. **2.** to pretend or simulate. —*n.* **3.** a counterfeit or fraud. **4.** a person who fakes. —*adj.* **5.** sham or fraudulent. —**fak′er,** *n.* —**fak′er·y,** *n.*

fa·kir (fə kēr′, fā′kər), *n.* a Muslim or Hindu religious ascetic or mendicant monk commonly considered a wonder worker.

fal·chion (fôl′chən, -shən), *n.* a broad, short medieval sword having a convex edge.

fal·con (fal′kən, fôl′-, fô′kən), *n.* a hawk having long, pointed wings and a notched bill, esp. one trained to hunt other birds as a sport. —**fal′con·er,** *n.* —**fal′con·ry,** *n.*

fall (fôl), *v.,* **fell, fall·en** (fô′lən), **fall·ing,** *n.* —*v.i.* **1.** to descend under the force of gravity. **2.** to come or drop down suddenly to a lower position. **3.** to move to a lower level, degree, quality, etc. **4.** to subside or abate. **5.** to hang down. **6.** to become directed downward, as the eyes. **7.** to succumb to temptation. **8.** to lose status, dignity, etc. **9.** to succumb to attack. **10.** to be overthrown. **11.** to drop down wounded or dead. **12.** to pass into some physical or emotional condition: *to fall in love.* **13.** to envelop, as stillness, night, etc.

14. to issue forth. **15.** to come by lot or chance. **16.** to come by chance into a particular position. **17.** to occur or become at a certain time: *The rent falls due today.* **18.** to have its proper place. **19.** to come by right. **20.** to be naturally divisible. **21.** to appear disappointed, as the face. **22.** to slope or extend downward. **23.** to be directed, as light, sight, etc. **24.** to collapse or topple. **25. fall back on or upon, a.** Also, **fall back to.** to retreat to. **b.** to rely on. **26. fall flat,** to fail to produce the desired effect. **27. fall for,** *Slang.* **a.** to be deceived by. **b.** to fall in love with. **28. fall foul of, a.** to collide with. **b.** to come into conflict with. **29. fall in, a.** to sink inward. **b.** to take one's place in the ranks, as a soldier. **30. fall off,** to deteriorate or decline. **31. fall on or upon,** to assault or attack. **32. fall out, a.** to quarrel or disagree. **b.** to leave one's place in the ranks, as a soldier. **33. fall all over oneself,** to show unusual eagerness. **34. fall through,** to fail of realization. **35. fall to,** to begin. **b.** to begin to eat. —*n.* **36.** the act or an instance of falling. **37.** something that falls or drops. **38.** autumn. **39.** a decline to a lower level. **40.** the distance through which anything falls. **41.** Usually, **falls.** a cataract or waterfall. **42.** downward slope or declivity. **43.** a falling from an erect position, as to the ground. **44.** a hanging down: *a fall of long hair.* **45.** lapse into sin. **46.** surrender or capture, as of a city. **47.** a hairpiece consisting of long hair, usually hanging at the back of one's hairdo.

fal·la·cious (fə lā′shəs), *adj.* **1.** logically unsound. **2.** deceptive or misleading. —**fal·la′cious·ly,** *adv.*

fal·la·cy (fal′ə sē), *n., pl.* -**cies.** **1.** a logically unsound argument. **2.** a deceptive or misleading idea.

fall′ guy′, *Slang.* **1.** an easy victim. **2.** a scapegoat.

fal·li·ble (fal′ə bəl), *adj.* **1.** liable to err or be mistaken. **2.** liable to be erroneous or false. —**fal′li·bil′i·ty, fal′li·ble·ness,** *n.* —**fal′li·bly,** *adv.*

fall·ing-out (fô′ling out′), *n., pl.* **fall-ings-out, fall·ing-outs.** a quarrel or estrangement.

fall′ing sick′ness, *Archaic.* epilepsy.

fall′ing star′, an incandescent meteor.

fall′ line′, an imaginary line where rivers descend abruptly from an upland to a lowland.

fall-off (fôl′ôf′, -of′), *n.* a decline in quantity, vigor, etc.

Fal·lo′pi·an tube′ (fə lō′pē ən), either of a pair of slender tubes that carries ova from the ovary to the uterus. [after G. *Fallopio* (d. 1562), Ital. anatomist]

fall·out (fôl′out′), *n.* **1.** the settling to the ground of airborne radioactive particles that result from a nuclear explosion. **2.** the particles themselves. **3.** an unexpected outcome, effect, or product.

fal·low (fal′ō), *adj.* **1.** plowed and left unseeded for a season or more. **2.** undeveloped or inactive.

fal′low deer′, a Eurasian deer with broad antlers and a yellowish coat.

false (fôls), *adj., fals·er, fals·est, adv.* —*adj.* **1.** not true or correct. **2.** uttering what is untrue. **3.** not faithful or loyal. **4.** deceptive or misleading. **5.** counterfeit or fake. **6.** based on mistaken or erroneous ideas: *false pride.* **7.** used as a substitute or supplement. **8.** not accurate: *a false balance.* **9.** inaccurate in pitch, as a musical note. —*adv.* **10.** dishonestly or treacherously. —**Syn.** 1. erroneous, mistaken, wrong.

false′ alarm′, **1.** a false report of fire to a fire department. **2.** something that excites unfounded alarm or expectation.

false·hood (fôls′hŏŏd), *n.* **1.** a false statement. **2.** the lack of conformity to truth or fact. **3.** an untrue idea, belief, etc.

fal·set·to (fôl set′ō), *n., pl.* -**tos.** an unnaturally or artificially high-pitched voice or register, esp. in a man.

fals·ie (fôl′sē), *n.* *Informal.* either of a pair of shaped pads for wearing inside a brassiere to give the breasts a larger or more shapely appearance.

fal·si·fy (fôl′sə fī′), *v.t.,* -**fied,** -**fy·ing.** **1.** to make false, esp. so as to deceive. **2.** to alter fraudulently. **3.** to represent falsely. **4.** to show to be false. —**fal·si·fi·ca·tion** (fôl′sə fə kā′shən), *n.* —**fal′si·fi′er,** *n.*

fal·si·ty (fôl′si tē), *n., pl.* -**ties.** **1.** the quality or condition of being false. **2.** something false.

falt·boat (fält′bōt′), *n.* a small boat having a collapsible wooden frame.

fal·ter (fôl′tər), *v.i.* **1.** to hesitate or waver in action or purpose. **2.** to speak hesitatingly or brokenly. **3.** to move or walk unsteadily. —*n.* **4.** an unsteadiness of gait, voice, action, etc. —**fal′ter·ing·ly,** *adv.*

fame (fām), *n.* widespread reputation, esp. of a favorable character. —**famed,** *adj.*

fa·mil·ial (fə mil′yəl), -**mil′ē əl), *adj.* **1.** of or characteristic of a family. **2.** appearing in individuals by heredity.

fa·mil·iar (fə mil′yər), *adj.* **1.** commonly known or seen. **2.** well-acquainted. **3.** informal or unceremonious. **4.** closely intimate. **5.** unduly intimate. —**fa·mil′iar·ly,** *adv.* —**fa·mil′iar·ness,** *n.*

fa·mil·i·ar·i·ty (fə mil′ē ar′i tē), *n., pl.* **-ties. 1.** thorough knowledge of a thing, subject, etc. **2.** friendly relationship. **3.** informality. **4.** undue intimacy.

fa·mil·iar·ize (fə mil′yə riz′), *v.t.,* **-ized, -iz·ing. 1.** to make (oneself or another) well-acquainted with something. **2.** to bring into common knowledge or use. —**fa·mil·iar·i·za′-tion,** *n.*

fam·i·ly (fam′ə lē, fam′lē), *n., pl.* **-lies. 1.** parents and their children. **2.** the spouse and children of one person. **3.** any group of persons closely related by blood or marriage. **4.** all descendants of a common progenitor. **5.** a group of related things or people. [< L *familia*]

fam′ily tree′, a genealogical chart of a family.

fam·ine (fam′in), *n.* **1.** extreme and general scarcity of food. **2.** any extreme scarcity.

fam·ish (fam′ish), *v.t., v.i.* to suffer or cause to suffer extreme hunger.

fam·ished (fam′isht), *adj.* very hungry.

fa·mous (fā′məs), *adj.* **1.** having a widespread reputation. **2.** *Informal.* first-rate or excellent. —**fa′mous·ly,** *adv.* —**Syn. 1.** celebrated, eminent, illustrious, renowned.

fan¹ (fan), *n., v.,* **fanned, fan·ning.** —*n.* **1.** any device, as a hand-waved triangular piece or a mechanism with blades, for producing a current of air for cooling, circulating, or ventilating. —*v.t.* **2.** to move (the air) with a fan. **3.** to cause air to blow upon, as from a fan. **4.** to stir to activity: *to fan emotions.* **5.** *Baseball.* to strike out (a batter). —*v.i.* **6.** to spread like a fan.

fan² (fan), *n.* an enthusiastic devotee or follower. [*fan*(*atic*)]

fa·nat·ic (fə nat′ik), *n.* **1.** a person with extreme enthusiasm or zeal, as in religion, politics, etc. —*adj.* **2.** fanatical. —**fa·nat′i·cism** (fə nat′ə siz′əm), *n.*

fa·nat·i·cal (fə nat′i kəl), *adj.* actuated or characterized by excessive enthusiasm or zeal, as in religion, politics, etc. —**fa·nat′i·cal·ly,** *adv.*

fan·ci·er (fan′sē ər), *n.* a person having a special interest in something, esp. in breeding animals, plants, etc.

fan·ci·ful (fan′si fəl), *adj.* **1.** capricious or whimsical in appearance. **2.** imaginary or unreal. **3.** imaginative or inventive. —**fan′ci·ful·ly,** *adv.* —**fan′ci·ful·ness,** *n.*

fan·cy (fan′sē), *n., pl.* **-cies,** *adj.,* **-ci-er, -ci·est,** *v.,* **-cied, -cy·ing.** —*n.* **1.** imagination, esp. as exercised in a

capricious manner. **2.** a mental image. **3.** an illusion or delusion. **4.** a caprice or whim. **5.** a capricious preference. **6.** *Rare.* critical judgment. —*adj.* **7.** of superfine quality or exceptional appeal. **8.** ornamental or decorative. **9.** whimsical or irregular. **10.** *Informal.* unreasonably costly: *fancy prices.* **11.** bred for excellence, as an animal. —*v.t.* **12.** to picture to oneself. **13.** to take a liking to. **14.** to suppose or presume. —**fan′ci·ly,** *adv.* —**fan′ci·ness,** *n.*

fan′cy dress′, a costume for a masquerade, chosen to please the fancy.

fan·cy-free (fan′sē frē′), *adj.* free from any influence, esp. that of love.

fan·cy·work (fan′sē wûrk′), *n.* ornamental needlework.

fan·dan·go (fan dang′gō), *n., pl.* **-gos.** a lively Spanish or Spanish-American dance.

fan·dom (fan′dəm), *n.* fans collectively, as of a motion-picture star.

fan·fare (fan′fâr), *n.* **1.** a flourish played on trumpets. **2.** an ostentatious display.

fang (fang), *n.* **1.** a long, sharp, hollow or grooved tooth of a venomous snake by which poison is injected. **2.** a canine tooth. —**fanged** (fangd), *adj.*

fan·jet (fan′jet′), *n.* **1.** a turbojet engine with the addition of an exhausting fan to reduce fuel consumption. **2.** an aircraft powered by such an engine.

fan·light (fan′līt′), *n.* a transom window, esp. one having the form of a semicircle.

fan·ny (fan′ē), *n., pl.* **-nies.** *Informal.* buttocks.

fan·tail (fan′tāl′), *n.* **1.** a tail, end, or part shaped like a fan. **2.** a domestic pigeon having a fan-shaped tail. **3.** a fancy goldfish with double anal and caudal fins. —**fan′-tailed′,** *adj.*

fan·ta·sia (fan tā′zhə, -zhē ə, fan′tə zē′ə), *n.* a musical composition in fanciful or irregular form.

fan·ta·size (fan′tə sīz′), *v.,* **-sized, -siz·ing.** —*v.i.* **1.** to conceive fanciful ideas or views. —*v.t.* **2.** to portray in one's fancy. —**fan·ta·sist** (-sist), *n.*

fan·tas·tic (fan tas′tik), *adj.* **1.** imaginative in an unrestrained or grotesque way. **2.** fanciful or capricious. **3.** imaginary or groundless. **4.** *Informal.* extraordinarily good. Also, **fan·tas′ti·cal.** —**fan·tas′ti·cal·ly,** *adv.* —**fan·tas′ti·cal·ness,** *n.*

fan·ta·sy (fan′tə sē, -zē), *n., pl.* **-sies. 1.** imagination, esp. when unrestrained. **2.** the forming of grotesque mental images. **3.** a daydream. **4.** caprice or whim. **5.** fantasia.

fan·zine (fan′zēn′), *n.* **1.** a mimeographed periodical distributed by science-fiction or comic-strip devotees. **2.** a magazine containing information and gossip about celebrities. [*fan* + (*maga*)*zine*]

FAO, Food and Agriculture Organization (of the United Nations).

far (fär), *adv., adj.,* **far·ther** or **fur·ther, far·thest** or **fur·thest.** —*adv.* **1.** at or to a great distance or a long way off. **2.** at or to a remote or advanced time. **3.** to a great degree or very much: *far worse.* **4.** at or to a definite point of progress. **5. as far as,** to the degree or extent that. **6. by far,** very much. **7. far and away,** undoubtedly. **8. far and wide,** over great distances. **9. far be it from me,** I do not wish or dare (to interrupt, criticize, etc.). **10. go far, a.** to attain success. **b.** to help. **11. in so far as,** to the extent that. Also, **so far as. 12. so far, a.** up to now. **b.** up to a certain point or extent. —*adj.* **13.** being at a great distance. **14.** extending far or remote. **15.** more distant of the two.

far·ad (far′əd, -ad), *n.* *Elect.* the unit of capacitance equal to the change in the number of coulombs of charge per volt of change of potential. [after M. *Faraday,* 1791–1867, Eng. physicist]

far·a·way (fär′ə wā′), *adj.* **1.** distant or remote. **2.** abstracted or dreamy: *a faraway look.*

farce (färs), *n.* **1.** a light, humorous play in which the plot depends upon a skillfully exploited situation. **2.** humor of the type displayed in such works. **3.** a ridiculous sham. —**far′ci·cal,** *adj.*

fare (fâr), *n., v.,* **fared, far·ing.** —*n.* **1.** the price charged for transporting a passenger. **2.** a paying passenger. **3.** food served at a meal, as in a restaurant. —*v.i.* **4.** to get on or along. **5.** *Archaic.* **a.** to turn out or happen. **b.** to eat and drink.

Far′ East′, (broadly) the countries of East Asia and Southeast Asia.

fare·well (fâr′wel′), *interj.* **1.** goodby. —*n.* **2.** good wishes at parting. **3.** leave-taking or departure. —*adj.* **4.** parting or final: *a farewell performance.*

far-fetched (fär′fecht′), *adj.* not naturally pertinent.

far-flung (fär′flung′), *adj.* **1.** extending over a great distance. **2.** widely distributed.

fa·ri·na (fə rē′nə), *n.* flour or meal made from cereal grains and cooked as cereal, used in puddings, etc.

far·i·na·ceous (far′ə nā′shəs), *adj.* **1.** consisting or made of flour or meal, as food. **2.** mealy in appearance or nature.

farm (färm), *n.* **1.** a tract of land on which crops and often livestock are raised. —*v.t.* **2.** to cultivate (land). —*v.i.* **3.** to operate a farm. **4. farm out,** to assign (work, etc.) to be done by others. —**farm′a·ble,** *adj.* —**farm′er,** *n.*

farm′ cheese′, a pressed cheese made from whole milk, similar to dry cottage cheese.

farm′ hand′, a hired worker on a farm.

farm·house (färm′hous′), *n.* a house on a farm, esp. the chief dwelling.

farm·ing (fär′ming), *n.* the business of operating a farm.

farm·land (färm′land′), *n.* land under cultivation or capable of being cultivated.

farm·stead (färm′sted′), *n.* a farm with its buildings.

farm·yard (färm′yärd′), *n.* a yard surrounded by or connected with farm buildings.

far·o (fâr′ō), *n.* a gambling game in which players bet on cards.

far-off (fär′ôf′, -of′), *adj.* distant or remote.

far-out (fär′out′), *adj.* *Slang.* **1.** unconventional or offbeat. **2.** radical or extreme.

far·ra·go (fə rä′gō, -rā′-), *n., pl.* **-goes.** a confused mixture or jumble.

far-reach·ing (fär′rē′ching), *adj.* extending far in influence, effect, etc.

far·ri·er (far′ē or), *n.* *Brit.* a blacksmith.

far·row (far′ō), *n.* **1.** a litter of pigs. —*v.t., v.i.* **2.** (of swine) to bring forth (young).

far·sight·ed (fär′sī′tid, -sī′tid), *adj.* **1.** seeing distant objects more clearly than nearby ones. **2.** Also, **far′see′ing.** wise, as in forseeing future developments. —**far′sight′ed·ness,** *n.*

far·ther (fär′T͟Hər), *adv.* **1.** at or to a greater distance. **2.** at or to a greater degree or extent. **3.** *Nonstandard.* further (def. 2). —*adj.* **4.** more distant or remote. **5.** *Nonstandard.* further (def. 5).

far·ther·most (fär′T͟Hər mōst′, -məst), *adj.* farthest.

far·thest (fär′T͟Hist), *adj.* **1.** most distant or remote. —*adv.* **2.** at or to the greatest distance. **3.** at or to the most advanced point. **4.** at or to the greatest degree or extent.

far·thing (fär′T͟Hing), *n.* a former bronze coin of Great Britain of very small value.

far·thin·gale (fär′T͟Hing gāl′), *n.* a framework for expanding a woman's skirt, worn esp. in the 16th century.

F.A.S., *Com.* free alongside ship.

fas·ci·cle (fas′i kəl), *n.* **1.** a small bundle or tight cluster. **2.** a section of a book being published in installments.

fas·ci·nate (fas′ə nāt′), *v.t.*, **-nat·ed,** **-nat·ing.** **1.** to attract and hold spellbound by a unique power, personal charm, etc. **2.** to arouse the interest or curiosity of. **—fas′ci·na′tion,** *n.*

fas·cism (fash′iz əm), *n.* (*sometimes cap.*) **1.** a totalitarian governmental system led by a dictator and emphasizing an aggressive nationalism and often racism. **2.** the philosophy, principles, or methods of fascism. [< It *fascism(o)* < L *fasc(is)* bundle, political group + *-ism*] **—fas′-cist,** *n., adj.* **—fa·scis·tic** (fə shis′-tik), *adj.*

fash·ion (fash′ən), *n.* **1.** a prevailing custom or style of dress, etiquette, etc. **2.** conventional usage in dress, manners, etc. **3.** manner or mode. **4.** the make or form of anything. **5.** after or in a fashion, in some manner or other. **—***v.t.* **6.** to give a particular shape or form to. **7.** to accommodate or adapt. **—fash′ion·er,** *n.* **—Syn. 1.** fad, mode, vogue.

fash·ion·a·ble (fash′ə nə bəl), *adj.* **1.** conforming to the fashion. **2.** of, characteristic of, or patronized by the world of fashion. **—fash′ion·a·ble·ness,** *n.* **—fash′ion·a·bly,** *adv.*

fast¹ (fast, fäst), *adj.* **1.** acting or moving with speed. **2.** done in relatively little time. **3.** indicating a time in advance of the correct time, as a clock. **4.** adapted to rapid movement. **5.** characterized by unrestrained conduct. **6.** resistant: *acidfast.* **7.** held or caught firmly. **8.** firmly tied. **9.** closed and made secure. **10.** loyal: *fast friends.* **11.** permanent: *a fast color.* **12.** deep or sound, as sleep. **13.** *Photog.* **a.** (of a lens) able to transmit a large amount of light in a short time. **b.** (of a film) requiring relatively little exposure to attain a given density. **—***adv.* **14.** tightly or firmly. **15.** soundly: *fast asleep.* **16.** quickly or rapidly. **17.** in a wild or dissipated way. **—Syn. 1.** fleet, quick, rapid. **5.** dissolute, immoral.

fast² (fast, fäst), *v.i.* **1.** to abstain from all food. **2.** to eat only sparingly or of certain kinds of food. **—***n.* **3.** the act or a period of fasting.

fast·back (fast′bak′, fäst′-), *n.* **1.** a form of back for an automobile body consisting of a single, unbroken curve from the top to the bumper. **2.** a car having such a back.

fas·ten (fas′ən, fä′sən), *v.t.* **1.** to attach firmly or securely. **2.** to make secure, as a door with a lock. **3.** to direct (the eyes, thoughts, etc.) intently. **—***v.i.* **4.** to become fastened. **—fas′ten·er,** *n.*

fas·ten·ing (fas′ə ning, fä′sə-), *n.* something that fastens, as a clasp.

fast-food (fast′food′), *adj.* of or specializing in standardized foods, such as fried chicken, hamburgers, etc., that can be quickly served or taken out.

fas·tid·i·ous (fa stid′ē əs), *adj.* **1.** excessively critical or demanding. **2.** requiring or characterized by excessive care or delicacy. **—fas·tid′i·ous·ly,** *adv.* **—fas·tid′i·ous·ness,** *n.*

fast·ness (fast′nis, fäst′-), *n.* **1.** the quality of being fast, as of dyes. **2.** a secure place, esp. a stronghold.

fast-talk (fast′tôk′, fäst′-), *v.t. Informal.* to persuade with facile argument, usually in order to deceive.

fast′ time′, *Informal.* See daylight-saving time.

fat (fat), *adj.*, **fat·ter, fat·test,** *n., v.,* **fat·ted, fat·ting.** **—***adj.* **1.** having excess adipose tissue. **2.** plump or well-fed. **3.** containing fat. **4.** abounding in a particular element. **5.** fertile, as land. **6.** profitable, as an office or position. **7.** thick or broad. **8. a fat chance,** *Slang.* a very slight chance. **—***n.* **9.** any of several greasy substances, composed of carbon, hydrogen, and oxygen, that form the chief part of adipose tissue of animals and also occur in plants. **10.** the richest or best part of anything. **11.** obesity or corpulence. **12.** an overabundance or excess. **—***v.t., v.i.* **13.** to make or become fat. **—fat′ly,** *adv.* **—fat′ness,** *n.*

fa·tal (fāt′ᵊl), *adj.* **1.** causing or capable of causing death: *a fatal dose.* **2.** causing destruction or ruin. **3.** decisively important. **—fa·tal·ly,** *adv.* **—fa′tal·ness,** *n.*

fa·tal·ism (fāt′ᵊliz′əm), *n.* the doctrine that all events are subject to fate. **—fa′tal·ist,** *n.* **—fa′tal·is′tic,** *adj.* **—fa′tal·is′ti·cal·ly,** *adv.*

fa·tal·i·ty (fā tal′i tē, fə-), *n., pl.* **-ties.** **1.** a disaster resulting in death. **2.** a death resulting from a disaster. **3.** a fatal effect. **4.** predetermined liability to disaster, misfortune, etc.

fat·back (fat′bak′), *n.* the fat and fat meat from the upper part of a side of pork, usually cured by salting.

fat′ cat′, *Slang.* **1.** a wealthy person who makes large political campaign contributions. **2.** a person who gains special privileges because of wealth.

fate (fāt), *n.* **1.** the ultimate power by which the order of things is prescribed. **2.** something supposed to be caused by such power. **3.** a prophetic declaration of what must be. **4.** death or ruin. **5. Fates,** *Class. Myth.* the three goddesses of destiny. **—Syn. 1, 2.** destiny, fortune, lot.

fat·ed (fā′tid), *adj.* subject to or guided by fate.

fate·ful (fāt′fəl), *adj.* **1.** involving momentous consequences. **2.** deadly or disastrous. **3.** controlled by destiny. **4.** prophetic or portentous. —**fate′ful·ly,** *adv.* —**fate′ful·ness,** *n.*

fat′ farm′, *Informal.* a resort that specializes in helping people lose weight.

fath., fathom.

fat·head (fat′hed′), *n.* *Informal.* a stupid person.

fa·ther (fä′thər), *n.* **1.** a male parent. **2.** any male ancestor, esp. the founder of a race or family. **3.** any man who exercises paternal care over another or others. **4.** one of the leading men in a city, town, etc. **5.** a person who has originated or established something: *the founding fathers.* **6.** a precursor or early form. **7.** (*cap.*) God. **8.** (*often cap.*) a title for a Christian priest. —*v.t.* **9.** to be the father of. **10.** to originate or create. **11.** to act as a father toward. —**fa′ther·hood′,** *n.* —**fa′ther·less,** *adj.* —**fa′ther·ly,** *adj.* —**fa′ther·li·ness,** *n.*

fa·ther-in-law (fä′thər in lô′), *n.,* *pl.* **fa·thers-in-law.** the father of one's husband or wife.

fa·ther·land (fä′thər land′), *n.* **1.** one's native country. **2.** the land of one's ancestors.

fath·om (fa*th*′əm), *n.,* *pl.* **fath·oms,** **fath·om,** *v.* —*n.* **1.** a nautical unit of length equal to six feet. —*v.t.* **2.** to measure the depth of, esp. by a sounding line. **3.** to understand thoroughly. —**fath′om·a·ble,** *adj.*

fath·om·less (fa*th*′əm lis), *adj.* **1.** incapable of being fathomed. **2.** impossible to understand.

fa·tigue (fə tēg′), *n.,* *v.,* **-tigued, -ti·guing.** —*n.* **1.** weariness from exertion. **2.** *Mech.* the weakening or breakdown of material subjected to stress. **3.** Also called **fatigue′ du′ty.** nonmilitary labor done by soldiers. **4.** **fatigues,** a military uniform for fatigue duty. —*v.t.,* *v.i.* **5.** to weary with exertion. —**fa·tigue′less,** *adj.*

fat·ten (fat′ᵊn), *v.t.,* *v.i.* to make or grow fat.

fat·ty (fat′ē), *adj.,* **-ti·er, -ti·est,** *n.* —*adj.* **1.** consisting of, containing, or resembling fat. —*n.* **2.** a fat person.

fat′ty ac′id, any of a class of organic acids derived from hydrocarbons and present in animal and vegetable fats.

fa·tu·i·ty (fə tōō′i tē, -tyōō′-), *n.,* *pl.* **-ties.** **1.** complacent stupidity. **2.** something foolish.

fat·u·ous (fach′ōō əs), *adj.* complacently foolish or silly. —**fat′u·ous·ly,** *adv.* —**fat′u·ous·ness,** *n.*

fau·bourg (fō′bŏŏr, -bōŏrg), *n.* a suburb or a quarter just outside a French city.

fau·ces (fô′sēz), *n., pl.* **-ces.** the cavity at the back of the mouth, leading into the pharynx.

fau·cet (fô′sit), *n.* any device for controlling the flow of liquid from a pipe.

Faulk·ner (fôk′nər), *n.* **William,** 1897–1962, U.S. novelist.

fault (fôlt), *n.* **1.** a moral imperfection. **2.** a misdeed or transgression. **3.** responsibility for failure or a wrongful act. **4.** a break in the continuity of a body of rock, with dislocation along the plane of fracture. **5.** failure to serve the ball according to the rules, as in tennis. **6. at fault,** open to censure. **7. find fault,** to complain or criticize. **8. to a fault,** extremely. —*v.t.* **9.** to blame or censure. **10.** *Geol.* to cause a fault in. —*v.i.* **11.** *Geol.* to undergo a fault or faults. **12.** to make a fault, as in tennis. —**fault′less,** *adj.* —**fault′less·ly,** *adv.* —**Syn. 1.** defect, flaw, foible.

fault·find·er (fôlt′fīn′dər), *n.* a person who complains or objects, esp. in a petty way. —**fault′find′ing,** *n.,* *adj.*

fault·y (fôl′tē), *adj.,* **fault·i·er, fault·i·est.** having faults or defects. —**fault′i·ly,** *adv.* —**fault′i·ness,** *n.*

faun (fôn), *n.* *Class. Myth.* a half-human deity with the hind legs of a goat.

fau·na (fô′nə), *n., pl.* **-nas, -nae (-nē).** the animals of a given region or period. —**fau′nal,** *adj.*

Faust (foust), *n.* a legendary magician and astrologer who sold his soul to the devil in exchange for knowledge and power. —**Faus′ti·an,** *adj.*

Fauve (fōv), *n.* one of a group of French artists of the early 20th century whose works are characterized by the use of vivid colors, contours in marked contrast, etc. —**Fauv′ism,** *n.* —**Fauv′ist,** *n.,* *adj.*

faux pas (fō pä′), *pl.* **faux pas** (fō päz′). a blunder in manners or conduct.

fa·vor (fā′vər), *n.* **1.** a kind act: *to ask a favor.* **2.** good will. **3.** the state of being approved or held in regard: *to be in favor.* **4.** unfair partiality. **5.** a gift given as a token of good will, love, etc. **6.** a ribbon, badge, etc., worn in evidence of good will or loyalty. **7.** a small gift or party item, as a noisemaker or paper hat. **8.** Usually, **favors.** sexual intimacy. **9.** *Obs.* a letter, esp. a commercial one. **10. in favor of,** a. in support of. b. to the advantage of. —*v.t.* **11.** to regard with favor. **12.** to treat with partiality. **13.** to show favor to. **14.** to facilitate. **15.** to deal with gently. **16.** *Informal.* to resemble. Also, *Brit.,* **fa′vour.** —**fa′vor·er,** *n.*

fa·vor·a·ble (fā′vər ə bəl), *adj.* **1.** inclined to aid or approve. **2.** advantageous: *a favorable position.* **3.** pleasing: *a favorable impression.* **4.** promising well. **—fa′vor·a·ble·ness.** *n.* **—fa′vor·a·bly,** *adv.*

fa·vor·ite (fā′vər it), *n.* **1.** a person or thing regarded with special favor or preference. **2.** a competitor considered likely to win. **—adj. 3.** regarded with particular favor or preference.

fa′vorite son′, a person nominated as a presidential candidate at a national political convention by the delegates from his own state.

fa·vor·it·ism (fā′vər i tiz′əm), *n.* the unfair favoring of one person or group over others.

fawn¹ (fôn), *n.* **1.** a young deer, esp. an unweaned one. **2.** a light yellowish-brown color.

fawn² (fôn), *v.i.* **1.** to seek favor by servile demeanor. **2.** to show fondness, as a dog does. **—fawn′er,** *n.* **—fawn′ing·ly,** *adv.*

fay (fā), *n. Literary.* fairy (def. 1).

faze (fāz), *v.t.,* **fazed, faz·ing.** *Informal.* to cause to be disconcerted.

f.b., **1.** freight bill. **2.** fullback. Also, **fb.**

FBI, Federal Bureau of Investigation.

FCC, Federal Communications Commission.

fcp., foolscap.

fcy., fancy.

F.D., Fire Department.

FDA, Food and Drug Administration.

FDIC, Federal Deposit Insurance Corporation.

Fe, iron. [< L *ferrum*]

fe·al·ty (fē′əl tē), *n., pl.* **-ties. 1.** loyalty to a feudal lord. **2.** *Archaic.* faithfulness or allegiance.

fear (fēr), *n.* **1.** a distressing emotion aroused by an impending pain, danger, etc. **2.** a specific instance of such a feeling. **3.** excessive anxiety. **4.** reverential awe. **5.** something of which one is afraid or that causes fright. **—v.t. 6.** to be frightened of. **7.** to have reverential awe of. **—v.i. 8.** to be frightened. **— fear′less,** *adj.* **—fear′less·ly,** *adv.* **—fear′less·ness,** *n.* **—Syn. 1.** alarm, dread, fright, terror.

fear·ful (fēr′fəl), *adj.* **1.** causing fear. **2.** feeling fear. **3.** showing or caused by fear. **4.** extreme in intensity or badness. **—fear′ful·ly,** *adv.* **—fear′ful·ness,** *n.*

fear·some (fēr′səm), *adj.* **1.** causing fear and awe. **2.** afraid or timid. **— fear′some·ly,** *adv.*

fea·si·ble (fē′zə bəl), *adj.* **1.** capable of being done or accomplished. **2.** suitable. **3.** probable or likely. **—fea-**

si·bil·i·ty (fē′zə bil′i tē), **fea′si·ble·ness,** *n.* **—fea′si·bly,** *adv.*

feast (fēst), *n.* **1.** a periodic celebration commemorating an event, person, etc. **2.** a sumptuous meal for many guests. **—v.i. 3.** to have a feast. **—v.t. 4.** to provide with a feast. **5.** to gratify or delight. **— feast′er,** *n.*

feat (fēt), *n.* a noteworthy or extraordinary act or achievement. **— Syn.** deed, exploit.

feath·er (feth′ər), *n.* **1.** one of the horny structures forming the principal covering of birds. **2.** condition, as of health, spirits, etc.: *in fine feather.* **3.** kind or character. **4.** something like a feather, as a tuft or fringe of hair. **5.** *Archaic.* attire. **6.** *Obs.* plumage. **7.** a feather in one's cap, a praiseworthy accomplishment. **—v.t. 8.** to provide with feathers. **9.** to clothe or cover with or as with feathers. **10.** feather one's nest, to look after one's own interests. **—feath′ered,** *adj.* **—feath′er·y,** *adj.* **—feath′er·i·ness,** *n.*

feath′er bed′, a quilt or sack stuffed with feathers and used as a mattress.

feath·er·bed·ding (feth′ər bed′ing), *n.* the practice of requiring an employer to hire unnecessary employees or limit production according to a union rule or a safety statute.

feath′er dust′er, a brush for dusting, made of a bundle of feathers attached to a handle.

feath·er·edge (feth′ər ej′), *n.* an edge that thins out like that of a feather.

feath·er·weight (feth′ər wāt′), *n.* **1.** a professional boxer weighing more than 118 but not exceeding 126 pounds. **2.** an insignificant person or thing.

fea·ture (fē′chər), *n., v.,* **-tured, turing. —n. 1.** any part of the face, as the nose, chin, etc. **2.** features, the face or countenance. **3.** the form or cast of the face: *delicate of feature.* **4.** a conspicuous part or characteristic. **5.** something offered as a special attraction. **6.** the main motion picture in a program. **7.** a column, cartoon, etc., appearing regularly in a newspaper or magazine. **—v.t. 8.** to be a feature or distinctive mark of. **9.** to give prominence to. **10.** to outline or depict. **—v.i. 11.** to play a major part. **— fea′ture·less,** *adj.*

feaze (fēz, fāz), *v.t.,* **feazed, feaz·ing.** faze.

Feb., February.

feb·ri·fuge (feb′rə fyōōj′), *adj.* **1.** serving to relieve fever, as a medicine. **—n. 2.** a febrifuge medicine.

fe·brile (fē′brəl, feb′rəl), *adj.* pertaining to or marked by fever.

Feb·ru·ar·y (feb′rōō er′ē, feb′yōō-er′ē), *n.*, *pl.* **-ar·ies.** the second month of the year, containing 28 days and in leap years 29 days.

fec., he (she) made it: formerly used on works of art after the name of the artist. [< L *fecit*]

fe·ces (fē′sēz), *n.pl.* waste matter discharged from the intestines. —**fe·cal** (fē′kəl), *adj.*

feck·less (fek′lis), *adj.* **1.** feeble in mind. **2.** irresponsible and careless. —**feck′less·ly,** *adv.*

fe·cund (fē′kund, -kənd, fek′und, -ənd), *adj.* satisfactorily prolific or fruitful. —**fe·cun·di·ty** (fi kun′di tē), *n.*

fe·cun·date (fē′kən dāt′, fek′ən-), *v.t.*, **-dat·ed, -dat·ing. 1.** to make fecund. **2.** to impregnate or fertilize. —**fe′-cun·da′tion,** *n.*

fed¹ (fed), *v.* **1.** pt. and pp. of **feed. 2.** fed up, *Informal.* disgusted, bored, or impatient.

fed² (fed), *n. Informal.* a federal official or law-enforcement officer.

fed., **1.** federal. **2.** federated. **3.** federation.

Fed., Federal.

fe·da·yeen (fe dä yēn′), *n.pl.* Palestinian guerrilla commandos, operating esp. against Israel.

fed·er·al (fed′ər əl), *adj.* **1.** pertaining to or of the nature of a union of states under a central government distinct from the individual governments of the separate states. **2.** of or noting such a central government. **3.** (*often cap.*) of the central government of the U.S. **4.** (*cap.*) **a.** of the Federalists or the Federalist Party. **b.** (in the Civil War) of or supporting the government. —*n.* **5.** an advocate of federalism. **6.** (*cap.*) (during the Civil War) an adherent of the Union government, esp. a Union soldier. [< L *foeder-* (s. of *foedus*) league + *-al*] —**fed′er·al·ly,** *adv.*

Fed′eral Dis′trict, a district in which the central government of a federation is located.

fed·er·al·ism (fed′ər ə liz′əm), *n.* **1.** the federal principle of government. **2.** (*cap.*) **a.** advocacy of the federal system of government. **b.** the principles of the Federalist Party.

fed·er·al·ist (fed′ər ə list), *n.* **1.** an advocate of federalism. **2.** (*cap.*) **a.** member or supporter of the Federalist Party —*adj.* **3.** of federalism or the Federalists.

Fed′eralist Par′ty, a political group that favored the adoption by the states of the Constitution and advocated a strong central government.

fed·er·al·ize (fed′ər ə līz′), *v.t.*, **-ized, -iz·ing. 1.** to bring under a federal government. **2.** to bring together in a federal union. —**fed′er·al·i·za′-tion,** *n.*

fed·er·ate (fed′ə rāt′), *v.t.*, *v.i.*, **-at·ed, -at·ing.** to unite in a federation.

fed·er·a·tion (fed′ə rā′shən), *n.* **1.** the act of federating. **2.** the formation of a political unity, with a central government, by a number of separate states. **3.** a federated body or government.

fedn., federation.

fe·do·ra (fi dôr′ə, -dōr′ə), *n.* a soft felt hat with a curled brim.

fee (fē), *n.* **1.** a charge for professional services. **2.** a sum charged, as for a license, etc. **3.** *Law.* an estate of inheritance in land. **4.** an inheritable estate in land held of a feudal lord. **5.** *Archaic.* a gratuity or tip.

fee·ble (fē′bəl), *adj.*, **-bler, -blest. 1.** physically weak, as from age, etc. **2.** lacking in force or effectiveness: *feeble arguments.* —**fee′ble·ness,** *n.* —**fee′bly,** *adv.*

fee·ble-mind·ed (fē′bəl mīn′did), *adj.* lacking normal mental powers. —**fee′ble-mind′ed·ness,** *n.*

feed (fēd), *v.*, **fed, feed·ing,** *n.* —*v.t.* **1.** to give food to. **2.** to serve as food for. **3.** to satisfy or gratify. **4.** to provide with the necessary materials for development or operation. —*v.i.* **5.** (esp. of animals) to eat. —*n.* **6.** food, esp. for farm animals. **7.** *Informal.* a meal, esp. a lavish one. **8.** the act or process of supplying a furnace, machine, etc. **9.** the material, or the amount of it, supplied. **10.** a feeding mechanism. —**feed′a·ble,** *adj.* —**feed′er,** *n.*

feed·back (fēd′bak′), *n.* **1.** the return of part of the output to the input of a mechanism, process, or system. **2.** informative reaction or response.

feed·lot (fēd′lot′), *n.* land where livestock are fed and fattened prior to slaughter.

feed·stuff (fēd′stuf′), *n.* a substance used for feed.

feel (fēl), *v.*, **felt, feel·ing,** *n.* —*v.t.* **1.** to perceive or examine by touch. **2.** to find (one's way) by touching or cautious moves. **3.** to be or become conscious of. **4.** to be emotionally affected by. **5.** to have a particular sensation or impression of. **6.** to think or consider. —*v.i.* **7.** to have perception by touch. **8.** to grope. **9.** to perceive a state of mind or a condition of body: *to feel happy.* **10.** to have sympathy or compassion. **11.** to have a sensation of being: *to feel warm.* **12.** to seem. **13. feel like,** *Informal.* to have a desire for. **14. feel out,** *Informal.* to attempt to ascertain by indirect means. **15. feel up to,** *Informal.* to be capable of. —*n.* **16.**

a quality of an object that is perceived by touching. **17.** the sense of touch. **18.** native ability or acquired sensitivity.

feel·er (fē'lər), *n.* **1.** a remark, hint, etc., designed to bring out the opinions or purposes of others. **2.** an organ of touch, as an antenna or a tentacle.

feel·ing (fē'lĭng), *n.* **1.** the function or the power of perceiving by touch. **2.** a particular sensation of this kind. **3.** a consciousness or awareness. **4.** an emotion. **5.** capacity for compassion. **6.** a sentiment or opinion. **7.** feelings, sensibilities or susceptibilities. —*adj.* **8.** sensitive or sentient. **9.** readily affected by emotion. —**feel'ing·ly,** *adv.*

feet (fēt), *n.* pl. of **foot.**

feign (fān), *v.t.* **1.** to put on a false appearance of, often elaborately. —*v.i.* **2.** to pretend or simulate. —**feign'er,** *n.*

feint (fānt), *n.* **1.** an attack aimed at one place merely as a distraction from the real place of attack. —*v.i., v.t.* **2.** to make a feint (at or on).

feist·y (fī'stē), *adj.* quick-tempered or quarrelsome.

feld·spar (feld'spär', fel'-), *n.* any of a group of minerals, principally silicates of aluminum with potassium, sodium, and calcium.

fe·lic·i·tate (fi lis'i tāt'), *v.t.,* -tat·ed, -tat·ing. to compliment upon a happy event. —**fe·lic'i·ta'tion,** *n.* —**fe·lic'i·ta'tor,** *n.*

fe·lic·i·tous (fi lis'i təs), *adj.* **1.** well-suited for the occasion. **2.** having a special ability for suitable expression. —**fe·lic'i·tous·ly,** *adv.*

fe·lic·i·ty (fi lis'i tē), *n., pl.* -ties. **1.** the state of being happy: *marital felicity.* **2.** a source of happiness. **3.** a skillful capacity, esp. for expression. **4.** an instance or display of this.

fe·line (fē'līn), *adj.* **1.** of the cat family, which includes domestic cats, lions, tigers, etc. **2.** sly or stealthy. —*n.* **3.** an animal of the cat family.

fell¹ (fel), *v.,* pt. of **fall.**

fell² (fel), *v.t.* **1.** to knock, strike, or cut down. **2.** to finish (a seam) by sewing the edge down flat. —**fell'a·ble,** *adj.*

fell³ (fel), *adj. Literary.* **1.** fierce or cruel. **2.** destructive or deadly. —**fell'ness,** *n.*

fell⁴ (fel), *n.* the skin or hide of an animal.

fel·lah (fel'ə), *n., pl.* **fel·lahs, fel·la·hin, fel·la·heen** (fel'ə hēn'), a peasant or laborer in Egypt, Syria, etc.

fel·la·ti·o (fə lā'shē ō', fe-), *n.* oral stimulation of the penis, esp. to orgasm.

fel·loe (fel'ō), *n.* the circular rim or a part of the rim of a wheel.

fel·low (fel'ō), *n.* **1.** *Informal.* a man or boy. **2.** *Informal.* a beau or suitor. **3.** *Informal.* a person in general. **4.** a companion or associate. **5.** a peer or colleague. **6.** one of a pair. **7.** a graduate student to whom an allowance is granted for special study. **8.** a member of any of certain learned societies. —*adj.* **9.** belonging to the same class or group: *fellow students.*

fel·low·man (fel'ō man'), *n.* a kindred member of the human race.

fel·low·ship (fel'ō ship'), *n.* **1.** friendly relationship or companionship. **2.** community of interest, feeling, etc. **3.** an association of persons having similar interests, etc. **4.** the position or stipend of an academic fellow. **5.** a foundation for the maintenance of academic fellows.

fel'low trav'eler, a nonmember who supports or sympathizes with a political party, esp. the Communist Party.

fel·ly (fel'ē), *n., pl.* -lies. felloe.

fel·on¹ (fel'ən), *n.* a person who has committed a felony.

fel·on² (fel'ən), *n.* an inflammation of the deeper tissues of a finger or toe, usually near the nail.

fel·o·ny (fel'ə nē), *n., pl.* -nies. any of various offenses, as murder or burglary, of graver character than misdemeanors. —**fe·lo·ni·ous** (fə lō'-nē əs), *adj.* —**fe·lo'ni·ous·ly,** *adv.*

felt¹ (felt), *v.* pt. and pp. of **feel.**

felt² (felt), *n.* **1.** a nonwoven fabric of wool, fur, or hair, matted together by heat, moisture, and pressure. **2.** any matted fabric or material.

fem., 1. female. **2.** feminine.

fe·male (fē'māl), *adj.* **1.** belonging to the sex that bears young or produces eggs. **2.** of or pertaining to this sex or to women: *female suffrage.* **3.** *Mach.* made with a recessed part into which a corresponding part fits. —*n.* **4.** a female person, animal, or plant. —**fe'male·ness,** *n.*

fem·i·nine (fem'ə nin), *adj.* **1.** characteristic of a woman or girl. **2.** gentle, soft, and delicate. **3.** noting the gender that has among its members many nouns referring to females. —*n.* **4.** the feminine gender. **5.** a noun or other element in that gender. —**fem'i·nine·ly,** *adv.* —**fem'i·nin'i·ty,** *n.*

fem·i·nism (fem'ə niz'əm), *n.* **1.** the doctrine advocating social and political rights for women equal to those of men. **2.** an organized movement for the attainment of such rights for women. —**fem'i·nist,** *n., adj.*

femme fa·tale (fem′ fə tal′, -täl′), *pl.* **femmes fa·tales** (fem fə talz′, -tälz′). *French.* an irresistibly attractive woman who leads men into danger.

fe·mur (fē′mər), *n.*, *pl.* **fe·murs**, **fem·o·ra** (fem′ər ə). a bone in the leg, extending from the pelvis to the knee —**fem′o·ral**, *adj.*

fen (fen), *n.* *Brit.* boggy land.

fence (fens), *n.*, *v.*, **fenced**, **fenc·ing.** —*n.* 1. a barrier enclosing a field, yard, etc., usually of posts and wire or wood, used to prevent entrance or mark a boundary. 2. a person who receives and disposes of stolen goods. 3. the place of business of such a person. 4. **on the fence**, *Informal.* neutral or undecided. —*v.t.* 5. to enclose with a fence. 6. to separate by a fence. —*v.i.* 7. to practice the sport of fencing. 8. to strive to avoid giving direct answers. —**fenc′er**, *n.*

fenc·ing (fen′sing), *n.* 1. the art or sport in which an épée, foil, or saber is used for defense and attack. 2. fences collectively. 3. material for fences.

fend (fend), *v.t.* 1. to ward off: *to fend off blows.* —*v.i.* 2. to shift or provide: *to fend for oneself.*

fend·er (fen′dər), *n.* 1. a sheet-metal part over the wheel of an automobile, bicycle, etc., to reduce splashing of mud or water. 2. a low metal guard before an open fireplace.

fen·es·tra·tion (fen′i strā′shən), *n.* the design and disposition of windows and other exterior openings of a building.

Fe·ni·an (fē′nē ən, fēn′yon), *n.* a member of a 19th-century Irish revolutionary organization that advocated an independent Irish republic.

fen·nel (fen′ªl), *n.* a plant having yellow flowers whose aromatic seeds are used in cookery and medicine.

FEPC, Fair Employment Practices Committee.

fe·ral (fēr′ɔl, fer′-), *adj.* 1. existing in a natural state, as animals or plants. 2. having reverted to the wild state, as from domestication.

fer·de·lance (fer′d°lans′, -d°läns′), *n.* a large pit viper of tropical America.

fer·ment (*n.* fûr′ment; *v.* fər ment′), *n.* 1. a living organism, as yeast, that causes fermentation. 2. agitation or unrest: *political ferment.* —*v.t.* 3. to cause to undergo fermentation. 4. to inflame or foment. —*v.i.* 5. to undergo fermentation. 6. to seethe with agitation or unrest. —**fer·ment′a·ble**, *adj.*

fer·men·ta·tion (fûr′men tā′shən), *n.* 1. a change brought about by enzymes which convert grape sugar into ethyl alcohol. 2. ferment (def. 2).

fer·mi·um (fûr′mē əm), *n.* *Chem.* a synthetic, radioactive element. *Symbol:* Fm; *at. no.:* 100. [after E. *Fermi,* 1901–54., It. physicist]

fern (fûrn), *n.* a flowerless, seedless plant having fronds of leaflets.

fern·er·y (fûr′nə rē), *n.*, *pl.* **-er·ies.** 1. a place in which ferns are grown. 2. a collection of ferns, as in a garden.

fe·ro·cious (fə rō′shəs), *adj.* 1. savagely fierce, as a wild beast. 2. extreme or intense. —**fe·ro′cious·ly**, *adv.* —**fe·ro′cious·ness**, *n.*

fe·roc·i·ty (fə ros′i tē), *n.* savage fierceness.

-ferous, a suffix meaning "bearing," "yielding," or "conveying": *coniferous.*

fer·ret (fer′it), *n.* 1. a domesticated polecat used in Europe for driving rabbits and rats from their burrows. —*v.t.* 2. to drive out by means of a ferret. 3. to search out or bring to light.

fer·ric (fer′ik), *adj.* *Chem.* of or containing iron.

fer′ric ox′ide, a dark-red solid occurring naturally, as hematite and rust: used chiefly as a pigment.

Fer′ris wheel′ (fer′is), an amusement ride consisting of a large upright wheel rotating on a permanent stand and having seats suspended freely around its rim. [after G. W. G. *Ferris* (d. 1896), Am. engineer]

fer·rite (fer′īt), *n.* a compound formed when ferric oxide is combined with a more basic metallic oxide.

ferro-, a combining form meaning "iron": *ferromagnetic.*

fer·ro·mag·net·ic (fer′ō mag net′ik), *adj.* noting a substance, as iron, that can possess magnetization in the absence of an external magnetic field. —**fer·ro·mag·ne·tism** (fer′ō·mag′ni tiz′əm), *n.*

fer·ro·type (fer′ə tīp′), *n.* tintype.

fer·rous (fer′əs), *adj.* of or containing iron, esp. in the bivalent state.

fer·rule (fer′ɔl, -ōōl), *n.* a ring put around the end of a post, cane, etc., to prevent splitting.

fer·ry (fer′ē), *n.*, *pl.* **-ries**, *v.*, **-ried**, **-ry·ing.** —*n.* 1. a commercial service with boats for transporting persons, etc., across a river, bay, etc. 2. ferryboat. 3. a service for flying airplanes over a particular route. —*v.t.* 4. to carry or convey over water in a boat or plane. —*v.i.* 5. to pass over water in a boat or by ferry. —**fer′ry·man**, *n.*

fer·ry·boat (fer′ē bōt′), *n.* a boat for ferrying passengers, vehicles, etc.

fer·tile (fûr'təl), *adj.* **1.** bearing or producing abundantly: *fertile land.* **2.** capable of bearing offspring. **3.** abundantly productive: *a fertile imagination.* **4.** capable of growth or development, as seeds or eggs. —**fer'tile·ness,** *n.* —**fer·til'i·ty,** *n.* — Syn. fecund, fruitful, prolific.

fer·ti·lize (fûr'təlīz'), *v.t.,* -lized, -liz·ing. **1.** to render (the female gamete) capable of development by uniting it with the male gamete. **2.** to impregnate (an animal or plant). **3.** to make fertile: *to fertilize farmland.* —**fer'ti·liz'a·ble,** *adj.* —**fer'ti·li·za'·tion,** *n.*

fer·ti·liz·er (fûr'təlī'zər), *n.* any substance used to fertilize the soil.

fer·ule (fer'əl, -ool), *n.* a rod or cane for punishing children.

fer·vent (fûr'vənt), *adj.* **1.** showing great warmth or intensity of spirit, feeling, etc. **2.** hot or glowing. —**fer'ven·cy,** *n.* —**fer'vent·ly,** *adv.*

fer·vid (fûr'vid), *adj.* fervent (def. 1). —**fer'vid·ly,** *adv.* —**fer'vid·ness,** *n.*

fer·vor (fûr'vər), *n.* **1.** great warmth and earnestness of feeling. **2.** intense heat. —Syn. **1.** ardor, zeal.

fes·cue (fes'kyoo), *n.* a type of grass often cultivated for pasture or lawns.

fes·tal (fes'təl), *adj.* festive.

fes·ter (fes'tər), *v.i.* **1.** to form pus. **2.** to rankle or cause, as a feeling of resentment. —*v.t.* **3.** to cause to fester or rankle. —*n.* **4.** a small pus-filled sore.

fes·ti·val (fes'tə vəl), *n.* **1.** a time of celebration, marked by feasting, ceremonies, or other observances. **2.** a period or program of festive activities, cultural events, or entertainment: *a music festival.* **3.** gaiety or merrymaking.

fes·tive (fes'tiv), *adj.* **1.** of or suitable for a feast or festival. **2.** joyous or merry. —**fes'tive·ly,** *adv.* —**fes'·tive·ness,** *n.*

fes·tiv·i·ty (fe stiv'ī tē), *n.,* pl. **-ties.** **1.** festival (def. 1). **2.** festivities, festive events or activities. **3.** festive character or quality.

fes·toon (fe stoon'), *n.* **1.** a chain of flowers suspended in a curve between two points. **2.** a decorative representation of this, as in architectural work. —*v.t.* **3.** to adorn with festoons.

Fest·schrift (fest'shrift'), *n.,* pl. **-schrif·ten** (-shrif'tən), **-schrifts.** (*sometimes l.c.*) a volume of articles, essays, etc., contributed by many authors in honor of a colleague.

F.E.T., Federal Excise Tax.

fe·tal (fēt'əl), *adj.* of or having the character of a fetus.

fetch (fech), *v.t.* **1.** to go for and bring back. **2.** to cause to come. **3.** to sell for (a price, etc.). **4.** to take (a breath). **5.** to utter (a sigh, etc.). **6.** to deliver (a blow, etc.). —**fetch'er,** *n.*

fetch·ing (fech'ing), *adj. Informal.* charming or captivating. —**fetch'·ing·ly,** *adv.*

fete (fāt, fet), *n., v.,* fet·ed, fet·ing. —*n.* **1.** a religious feast or festival. **2.** a festive celebration or entertainment. —*v.t.* **3.** to entertain at or honor with a fete. Also, **fête.**

fe·ti·cide (fē'tī sīd'), *n.* the act of destroying a fetus or causing an abortion.

fet·id (fet'id, fē'tid), *adj.* having an offensive odor. —**fet'id·ness,** *n.*

fet·ish (fet'ish, fē'tish), *n.* **1.** an object regarded as having magical power. **2.** any object, idea, etc., eliciting unquestioning reverence or devotion. **3.** any object that causes a habitual erotic response. Also, **fet'ich.** —**fet'·ish·ism,** *n.* —**fet'ish·ist,** *n.* —**fet'ish·is'tic,** *adj.*

fet·lock (fet'lok'), *n.* **1.** the projection of the leg of a horse behind the hoof, bearing a tuft of hair. **2.** the tuft of hair itself.

fet·ter (fet'ər), *n.* **1.** a chain or shackle placed on the feet. **2.** Usually, **fetters.** anything that confines or restrains. —*v.t.* **3.** to put fetters upon. **4.** to confine or restrain.

fet·tle (fet'əl), *n.* state or condition: *in fine fettle.*

fet·tu·ci·ni (fet'ə chē'nē), *n.* pasta in the form of narrow strips.

fe·tus (fē'təs), *n.,* pl. **-tus·es.** the young of an animal while in the womb or egg, esp. in the later stages of development.

feud (fyood), *n.* **1.** a bitter, continuous hostility, esp. between families or clans —*v.i.* **2.** to engage in a feud.

feu·dal (fyood'əl), *adj.* **1.** of or like the feudal system. **2.** of or of the nature of a fief or fee.

feu·dal·ism (fyood'əl iz'əm), *n.* the principles and practices of the feudal system. —**feu'dal·ist,** *n.* —**feu'dal·is'tic,** *adj.*

feu'dal sys'tem, the system of social and economic organization in medieval Europe, based on the holding of lands in fief or fee and on the resulting relations between lord and vassal.

feu·da·to·ry (fyoo'də tōr'ē, -tôr'ē), *n.,* pl. **-ries,** *adj.* —*n.* **1.** a feudal vassal. **2.** a fief or fee. —*adj.* **3.** owing feudal allegiance to a lord. **4.** holding or held by feudal tenure.

fe·ver (fē'vər), *n.* **1.** an abnormal condition of the body, characterized by undue rise in temperature. **2.** any disease in which high temperature is a prominent symptom. **3.** intense nervous excitement. —**fe'·ver·ish,** *adj.* —**fe'ver·ish·ly,** *adv.* — **fe'ver·ish·ness,** *n.*

few (fyo̅o̅), *adj.* 1. not many. 2. **few and far between**, infrequent. —*n.* 3. a small number or amount. 4. **quite a few**, *Informal.* many. 5. **the few, the minority.** —*pron.* 6. a small number of persons or things. —**few'ness,** *n.*

few·er (fyo̅o̅'ər), *adj.* 1. comparative of few. —*pron.* 2. a smaller number. —**Usage.** 1. FEWER, LESS are sometimes confused because both imply a comparison with something larger. FEWER is used with plural nouns or pronouns and applies only to number: *Fewer streetcars are running now than ten years ago.* LESS is used with singular nouns and pronouns and is commonly applied to material in bulk, in reference to amount: *There was less gasoline than we had thought.*

fey (fā), *adj.* 1. *Chiefly Scot.* appearing to be under a spell. 2. supernatural or unreal. 3. in a state of impending death. 4. strange or otherworldly.

fez (fez), *n., pl.* **fez·zes.** a red cap, shaped like a truncated cone, with a black tassel, worn esp. by men in the Near East. [< Turk *fes*]

ff, *Music.* fortissimo.

ff., 1. folios. 2. following (pages, etc.).

FHA, Federal Housing Administration.

fi·an·cé (fē'än sā', fē än'sā), *n.* a man engaged to be married.

fi·an·cée (fē'än sā', fē än'sā), *n.* a girl or woman engaged to be married.

fi·as·co (fē as'kō), *n., pl.* **-cos, -coes.** a disastrous failure.

fi·at (fī'ət, -at), *n.* an arbitrary decree or order. [< L: let it be done]

fi'at mon'ey, paper currency that has value only by law and is not backed by gold or silver.

fib (fib), *n., v.,* **fibbed, fib·bing.** —*n.* 1. a trivial lie. —*v.i.* 2. to tell a fib. —**fib'ber,** *n.*

fi·ber (fī'bər), *n.* 1. a fine, threadlike piece, as of cotton, jute, or asbestos. 2. a slender filament. 3. matter or material composed of filaments: *a plastic fiber.* 4. an essential character, quality, or strength: *strong moral fiber.* Also, *Brit.,* **fi'bre.** —**fi'brous** (-brəs), *adj.*

fi·ber·board (fī'bər bōrd', -bôrd'), *n.* a building material made of wood fibers compressed into rigid sheets.

fi·ber·fill (fī'bər fil'), *n.* synthetic fibers, as polyester, used as filling for pillows, etc.

fi·ber·glass (fī'bər glas', -gläs'), *n.* a material consisting of extremely fine filaments of glass woven into fabrics, used as an insulator, etc.

fi'ber op'tics, 1. the technique of transmitting light, images, etc., through long, thin transparent fibers, as of glass, plastic, etc. 2. the fibers so used. —**fi'ber-op'tic,** *adj.*

fi·bril (fī'brəl, fib'rəl), *n.* a small or fine fiber.

fi·bril·la·tion (fī'brə lā'shən, fib'rə-), *n.* uncontrolled twitching or quivering of muscular filaments, as of the cardiac muscles.

fi·brin (fī'brin), *n.* a white, strongly elastic fibrous protein, formed in the coagulation of blood. —**fi'brin·ous,** *adj.*

fi·brin·o·gen (fī brin'ə jən), *n.* a globulin occurring in blood and yielding fibrin in the coagulation of blood.

fi·broid (fī'broid), *adj.* resembling or composed of fibrous tissue, as a tumor.

fi·bro·sis (fī brō'sis), *n.* the development in an organ of excess fibrous connective tissue.

fib·u·la (fib'yə lə), *n., pl.* **-lae** (-lē'), **-las.** the outer and thinner of the two bones of the leg. —**fib'u·lar,** *adj.*

-fic, a suffix meaning "making" or "causing": *prolific.*

F.I.C.A., Federal Insurance Contributions Act (for social-security tax).

fiche (fēsh), *n.* microfiche.

fich·u (fish'o̅o̅), *n.* a light neck scarf of muslin, lace, etc.

fick·le (fik'əl), *adj.* casually changeable or inconstant. —**fick'le·ness,** *n.*

fic·tion (fik'shən), *n.* 1. the class of literature comprising works of imaginative narration, esp. in prose form. 2. works of this class, as novels or short stories. 3. a made-up story. —**fic'tion·al,** *adj.* —**fic'tion·al·ly,** *adv.*

fic·tion·al·ize (fik'shə nºlīz'), *v.t.,* **-ized, -iz·ing.** to make into fiction: *to fictionalize a biography.*

fic·ti·tious (fik tish'əs), *adj.* 1. imaginatively produced or set forth. 2. created or assumed for deception or disguise: *fictitious names.* —**Syn.** 2. false, feigned, spurious.

fic·tive (fik'tiv), *adj.* 1. capable of creating fiction. 2. *Rare.* fictitious.

fid·dle (fid'ºl), *n., v.,* **-dled, -dling.** —*n.* 1. *Informal.* violin. —*v.i.* 2. *Informal.* to play on the fiddle. 3. to make fussing movements with the hands. 4. to trifle or waste time. —**fid'dler,** *n.*

fid'dler crab', a small, burrowing crab, the male of which has one greatly enlarged claw.

fid·dle·stick (fid'ºl stik'), *n. Informal.* a violin bow.

fid·dle·sticks (fid'ºl stiks'), *interj.* nonsense.

fi·del·i·ty (fi del′i tē, fī-), *n., pl.* **-ties.** 1. strict observance of or faithfulness to promises, duties, etc. 2. accuracy or exactness. 3. the degree of exactness with which sound is recorded or reproduced. —Syn. 1. allegiance, devotion, loyalty.

fidg·et (fij′it), *v.i.* 1. to move about restlessly or nervously —*n.* 2. Often, **fidgets.** the condition of being nervously restless or uneasy. 3. a person who fidgets. —**fidg′et·y,** *adj.* —**fidg′et·i·ness,** *n.*

fi·du·ci·ar·y (fi dōō′shē er′ē, -dyōō′-), *n., pl.* **-ar·ies,** *adj.* —*n.* 1. a person to whom property is entrusted for the benefit of another. —*adj.* 2. of the relation between a fiduciary and his or her principal.

fie (fī), *interj.* (used to express disapproval.)

fief (fēf), *n.* an estate in land held from a feudal lord.

field (fēld), *n.* 1. a piece of open or cleared ground, esp. one suitable for pasture or tillage. 2. an area or piece of ground devoted to sports or contests. 3. all the contestants in a particular event. 4. the area of active military operations. 5. a battleground. 6. a battle. 7. an expanse of anything: *a field of ice.* 8. any region characterized by a particular feature, product, etc.: *a gold field.* 9. the ground of each division, as in a flag. 10. a sphere of activity, interest, etc. 11. the area or region drawn on or serviced by a business or profession. 12. a region of space under the influence of some agent, as electricity or magnetism. 13. **play the field,** to vary one's activities. —*v.t.* 14. to catch or pick up (the ball) in play. 15. to place (a player or a team) in the field to play. 16. to answer skillfully: to *field a difficult question.* —**field′er,** *n.*

field′ day′, 1. a day devoted to outdoor sport or athletic contests. 2. an occasion for unrestricted activity, amusement, etc.

field′ e·vent′, an event in a track meet that involves throwing, as a discus or javelin, or jumping and is not performed on the running track.

field′ glass′es, a compact, easily portable binocular telescope for use out-of-doors.

field′ goal′, 1. *Football.* a score made by kicking the ball over the crossbar between the opponent's goal posts. 2. *Basketball.* a goal made while the ball is in play.

field′ hock′ey, a game, played on a rectangular field, in which two teams of 11 players each compete in driving a small ball into each other's goal, using hockey sticks.

field′ mar′shal, an officer of the highest rank, as in the British army.

field·piece (fēld′pēs′), *n.* a cannon mounted on a carriage for service in the field.

field′stone (fēld′stōn′), *n.* stone found in fields and used for building purposes.

field·test (fēld′test′), *v.t.* to test (a new product or method) by actually using it outside the factory or laboratory.

fiend (fēnd), *n.* 1. a diabolically cruel or wicked person. 2. an evil spirit. 3. *Informal.* an addict to some pernicious habit: *an opium fiend.* 4. *Informal.* a person excessively interested in some game, sport, etc. —**fiend′ish,** *adj.* —**fiend′ish·ly,** *adv.* —**fiend′ish·ness,** *n.*

fierce (fērs), *adj.,* **fierc·er, fierc·est.** 1. menacingly wild, savage, or hostile. 2. violent in force or intensity. 3. furiously eager or intense: *fierce competition.* 4. *Informal.* extremely bad or severe. [< OF < L *ferus*] —**fierce′ly,** *adv.* —**fierce′ness,** *n.* —Syn. 1. barbarous, ferocious.

fier·y (fī°r′ē, fī′ə rē), *adj.,* **fier·i·er, fier·i·est.** 1. consisting of or containing fire. 2. intensely hot. 3. like or suggestive of fire. 4. intensely impetuous or passionate: *a fiery speech.* 5. easily angered or provoked. —**fier′i·ly,** *adv.* —**fier′i·ness,** *n.*

fi·es·ta (fē es′tə), *n.* 1. a religious festival, as in Spain. 2. any festive celebration. [< Sp < L *festa*]

fife (fīf), *n.* a high-pitched flute used esp. in marching bands.

FIFO (fī′fō), *n.* first-in, first-out (a method of inventory evaluation).

fif·teen (fif′tēn′), *n.* 1. a cardinal number, ten plus five. 2. a symbol for this number, as 15 or XV. —*adj.* 3. amounting to 15 in number. —**fif′-teenth′,** *adj., n.*

fifth (fifth), *adj.* 1. being number five in a series. 2. being one of five equal parts. —*n.* 3. a fifth part, esp. of one (⅕). 4. the fifth member of a series. 5. a fifth part of a gallon of liquor or spirits: ⅘ of a quart.

Fifth′ A·mend′ment, an amendment to the U.S. Constitution, providing chiefly that no person be required to testify against himself or herself in a criminal case.

fifth′ col′umn, a group of people who, although residing in a country, act traitorously out of secret sympathy with an enemy. —**fifth′ col′-umnist.**

fifth′ wheel′, 1. a horizontal wheel on a carriage designed to support the forepart of the body. 2. a superfluous or unwanted person or thing.

fif·ty (fif′tē), *n., pl.* **-ties,** *adj.* **—n.**
1. a cardinal number, ten times five.
2. a symbol for this number, as 50 or L. **—adj.** 3. amounting to 50 in number. **—fif′ti·eth,** *adj., n.*

fif·ty-fif·ty (fif′tē fif′tē), *Informal.* **—adv.** 1. equally or evenly. **—adj.** 2. shared equally. 3. half good or likely and half bad or unlikely: *a fifty-fifty chance of winning.*

fig (fig), *n.* 1. a tree or shrub of warm climates bearing an edible pear-shaped fruit. 2. its fruit. 3. the least bit.

fig., 1. figurative. 2. figuratively. 3. figure; figures.

fight (fit), *n., v.,* **fought, fight·ing.** **—n.** 1. an open or hand-to-hand clash, esp. between two persons. 2. any contest or struggle. 3. an angry argument or disagreement. 4. ability or inclination to fight. **—v.i.** 5. to engage in battle, as to attempt to defeat an adversary. 6. to contend in any manner. **—v.t.** 7. to contend with in battle. 8. to contend with or against in any manner: *to fight crime.* 9. to carry on (a battle, duel, etc.). 10. to make (one's way) by fighting or striving. 11. to cause or set (a boxer, cock, etc.) to fight.

fight·er (fi′tər), *n.* 1. a professional boxer. 2. an aircraft designed to intercept and destroy enemy aircraft in the air. 3. a person having the will to struggle or resist.

fig·ment (fig′mənt), *n.* a product of mental invention.

fig·u·ra·tion (fig′yə rā′shən), *n.* 1. the act of shaping into a particular figure. 2. the resulting figure or shape.

fig·ur·a·tive (fig′yər ə tiv), *adj.* 1. of the nature of or involving a figure of speech, esp. a metaphor. 2. abounding in or fond of figures of speech. 3. representing by a figure or emblem. **—fig′ur·a·tive·ly,** *adv.* **—fig′ur·a·tive·ness,** *n.*

fig·ure (fig′yər), *n., v.,* **-ured, -ur·ing.** **—n.** 1. a written symbol other than a letter. 2. a numerical symbol, esp. an Arabic numeral. 3. an amount or value expressed in numbers. 4. figures, arithmetic. 5. the form or shape of something. 6. a character or personage, esp. one of distinction. 7. the appearance or impression made by a person or sometimes a thing. 8. a representation, pictorial or sculptured, esp. of the human form. 9. a figure of speech. 10. a design or pattern, as in cloth. 11. a movement or series of movements in skating. **—v.t.** 12. to compute or calculate. 13. to express in figures. 14. to mark or adorn with a design or pattern. 15. to picture or depict. 16. *Informal.* to conclude or reason. **—v.i.** 17. to compute or work with

numerical figures. 18. to be or appear, esp. conspicuously. 19. (of a situation, act, etc.) to be logical or expected. 20. **figure in,** to add in. 21. **figure on,** *Informal.* **a.** to rely on. **b.** to plan on. 22. **figure out,** *Informal.* **a.** to understand. **b.** to solve. 23. **figure up,** to total.

fig·ure·head (fig′yər hed′), *n.* 1. a head of a group, etc., in title but with no real authority. 2. a carved figure or bust on a ship's prow.

fig′ure of speech′, any expressive use of language, as a metaphor, simile, etc.

fig·ur·ine (fig′yə rēn′), *n.* a small ornamental figure of pottery, metal-work, etc.

Fi·ji (fē′jē), *n.* a country on a group of islands (**Fi′ji Is′lands**) in the S Pacific.

fil·a·ment (fil′ə mənt), *n.* 1. a very fine thread or threadlike structure. 2. a threadlike wire, often of tungsten, heated to incandescence in an electric lamp. **—fil′a·men′tous, fil′a·men′ta·ry,** *adj.*

fi·lar (fi′lər), *adj.* of a thread or threads.

fil·bert (fil′bərt), *n.* 1. the thick-shelled, edible nut of a European hazel. 2. its tree.

filch (filch), *v.t.* to steal (esp. something of small value). **—filch′er,** *n.*

file¹ (fil), *n., v.,* **filed, fil·ing.** **—n.** 1. a folder, cabinet, or other container in which papers, letters, etc., are arranged in convenient order. 2. a collection of papers, etc., so arranged. 3. a line of persons or things arranged one behind another. 4. **on file,** kept in a reference file. **—v.t.** 5. to arrange (papers, etc.) in convenient order for preservation or reference. 6. to submit (an application, petition, etc.). 7. to send in (news copy). **—v.i.** 8. to march in a file or line, as soldiers. 9. to make an application, as for a permit. **—file′a·ble,** *adj.* **—fil′er,** *n.*

file² (fil), *n., v.,* **filed, fil·ing.** **—n.** 1. a metal tool having a series of ridges on its surfaces for smoothing, grinding, or polishing. **—v.t.** 2. to smooth, grind, or polish with or as with a file. **—file′a·ble,** *adj.* **—fil′er,** *n.*

fi·let mi·gnon (fi lā′ min yon′, min′yon), *pl.* **fi·lets mi·gnons** (fi lā′ min-yonz′, min′yonz), a small, tender round of steak cut from the thick end of a beef tenderloin.

fil·i·al (fil′ē əl), *adj.* of or befitting a son or daughter. **—fil′i·al·ly,** *adv.*

fil·i·bus·ter (fil′ə bus′tər), *n.* 1. the use of obstructive tactics, as exceptionally long speeches, to prevent or block action on a legislative bill. 2. an irregular military adventurer in the 19th century. —v.i., v.t. 3. to impede (legislation) by a filibuster. —fil′i·bus′ter·er, n.

fil·i·gree (fil′ə grē), n., v., -greed, -gree·ing. —n. 1. ornamental work of fine wires. —v.t. 2. to adorn with filigree.

fil·ings (fī′lingz), n.pl. particles removed by a file.

Fil·i·pi·no (fil′ə pē′nō), n., pl. -nos, adj. —n. 1. an inhabitant of the Philippines. —adj. 2. of the Philippines or Filipinos.

fill (fil), v.t. 1. to make full. 2. to occupy to the full capacity. 3. to feed fully. 4. to put into a receptacle. 5. to pervade completely. 6. to furnish (a vacancy or office) with an occupant. 7. to perform the duties of (a position, etc.). 8. to execute (a purchase order). 9. to meet satisfactorily, as requirements. 10. to make up (a medical prescription). 11. to stop up or close (a hole, etc.): to fill a tooth. —v.i. 12. to become full. 13. fill in, a. to supply missing or desired information. b. to complete (a document, etc.) by filling spaces. c. to substitute for. d. to supply (someone) with information. 14. fill out, a. to complete (a document, etc.) by supplying missing or desired information. b. to become larger or fuller. 15. fill up, to make or become full. —n. 16. a full supply. 17. a quantity of earth and stones.

filled′ milk′, milk containing a substitute for the butterfat.

fill·er (fil′ər), n. 1. a person or thing that fills. 2. a substance used to fill cracks, etc. 3. a liquid, paste, etc., used to give solidity, bulk, etc., to a substance.

fil·let (fil′it; usually fi lā′, fil′ā for 1, 3), n. 1. a boneless cut or slice of meat or fish, esp. the beef tenderloin. 2. a ribbon or strip of any material used for binding. —v.t. 3. to cut or prepare (meat or fish) as a fillet. 4. to bind with or as with a decorative fillet.

fill-in (fil′in′), n. 1. a person or thing that fills in, as a substitute or insertion. 2. Informal. a brief, informative summary.

fill·ing (fil′ing), n. 1. something that is put in as a filler: the filling of a pie. 2. a substance in plastic form, as cement or gold foil, used to close a cavity in a tooth. 3. yarn interlacing the warp in woven cloth.

fill′ing sta′tion. See service station.

fil·lip (fil′əp), v.t. to strike with the nail of a finger snapped from the end of the thumb. —n. 2. the act or an instance of filliping. 3. anything that tends to rouse or stimulate.

Fill·more (fil′mōr, -môr), n. **Mil·lard** (mil′ərd), 1800–74, 13th president of the U.S. 1850–53.

fil·ly (fil′ē), n., pl. -lies. a young female horse.

film (film), n. 1. a thin layer or coating. 2. a cellulose composition made in thin sheets or strips and coated with a sensitive emulsion for taking photographs. 3. a motion picture. 4. a thin skin or membrane. —v.t., v.i. 5. to make a motion picture (of). 6. to cover or be covered with a film.

film·dom (film′dəm), n. the motion-picture industry or its personnel.

film·go·er (film′gō′ər), n. a person who attends motion-picture performances.

film·og·ra·phy (fil′mog′rə fē), n., pl. -phies. a listing of motion pictures on a particular theme, or of a particular producer, director, or actor or actress.

film·strip (film′strip′), n. a length of film containing a series of still pictures, diagrams, etc., for projection on a screen.

film·y (fil′mē), adj., film·i·er, film·i·est. 1. of, resembling, or covered with a film. 2. gauzy or blurred.

fil·ter (fil′tər), n. 1. any substance through which liquid or gas is passed to remove suspended impurities or to recover solids. 2. any device containing such a substance for filtering. 3. Photog. a lens screen of dyed gelatin or glass for controlling the rendering of color. 4. a device that selectively damps oscillations of certain frequencies. —v.t., v.i. 5. to remove by a filter. 6. to pass (something) through or as through a filter. —fil′ter·a·ble, fil′tra·ble (-trə bəl), adj.

fil′ter tip′, 1. a mouthpiece for a cigarette with a means of filtering the smoke. 2. a cigarette with such a mouthpiece.

filth (filth), n. 1. foul matter. 2. a foul condition: to live in filth. 3. moral impurity or corruption. 4. vulgar or obscene language. —filth′y, adj. —filth′i·ness, n.

fil·trate (fil′trāt), v., -trat·ed, -trat·ing, n. —v.t., v.i. 1. to filter. —n. 2. liquid that has been filtered. —fil·tra′tion, n.

fin (fin), n. 1. a membranous, winglike organ on the body of fishes, used for propulsion, steering, or balancing. 2. any part, as of a mechanism, resembling a fin. 3. Usually, fins. flipper (def. 2). —finned (find), adj.

Fin., 1. Finland. 2. Finnish.

fin., 1. finance. 2. financial. 3. finish.

fi·na·gle (fi nā′gəl), v., **-gled, -gling.** *Informal.* —v.i. 1. to practice deception or fraud. —v.t. 2. to trick or cheat. 3. to get or achieve by guile or trickery. —**fi·na′gler**, n.

fi·nal (fīn′°l), adj. 1. of or coming at the end. 2. conclusive or decisive: *a final decision.* 3. Often, **finals. a.** the last and decisive game, contest, or round in a series. **b.** the last examination in a course of study. —**fi·nal′i·ty** (-nal′i tē), n. —**fi′nal·ly**, adv.

fi·nal·e (fi nal′ē, -nä′lē), n. the concluding part of a musical composition.

fi·nal·ist (fīn′°list), n. a person entitled to take part in the finals, as of an athletic contest.

fi·na·lize (fīn′°līz′), v., **-lized, -liz·ing.** —v.t. 1. to put into final form. —v.i. 2. to complete an agreement. —**fi′na·li·za′tion**, n.

—**Usage.** Although FINALIZE is regarded by many as a recent, bureaucratic coinage, the word has been current in English for at least 50 years.

fi·nance (fi nans′, fī′nans), n., v., **-nanced, -nanc·ing.** —n. 1. the management or transaction of money matters generally. 2. **finances,** the monetary resources, as of a government, organization, etc. —v.t. 3. to supply with capital or obtain money or credit for. —**fi·nan′cial** (-nan′-shəl), adj. —**fi·nan′cial·ly**, adv.

finance′ com′pany, a nonbank institution engaged in making loans to businesses (usually by discounting installment contracts) or to individuals (chiefly to finance their purchase of durable goods).

fin·an·cier (fin′ən sēr′, fī′nən-), n. a person who is skilled in or engaged in financial operations.

finch (finch), n. any of numerous small birds, including the buntings, sparrows, etc., most of which have a short, conical bill.

find (fīnd), v., **found, find·ing,** n. —v.t. 1. to come upon by chance. 2. to learn or obtain by search or effort: *to find a job.* 3. to recover (something lost). 4. to gain or regain the use of. 5. to perceive or learn by experience. 6. to ascertain by study or calculation. 7. to determine after judicial inquiry. —v.i. 8. to determine an issue after judicial inquiry. 9. **find out,** to discover or confirm the truth of. —n. 10. an act of finding. 11. something found.

find·er (fīn′dər), n. 1. a person or thing that finds. 2. a camera device for fixing the view of the subject to be photographed.

fin de siè·cle (faɴ də sye′kl°), *French.* end of the century, esp. of the 19th century.

find·ing (fīn′diɴg), n. 1. the act of a person or thing that finds. 2. something found or ascertained. 3. a decision or verdict after judicial inquiry.

fine¹ (fīn), adj., **fin·er, fin·est,** adv. —adj. 1. of superior or best quality. 2. consisting of minute particles. 3. keen or sharp, as a tool. 4. polished or refined: *fine manners.* 5. delicate or subtle: *a fine distinction.* 6. bright and clear, as the weather. 7. free from impurities, as gold. 8. *Informal.* in good health. —adv. 9. *Informal.* very well. 10. delicately. —**fine′ly**, adv. —**fine′ness**, n.

fine² (fīn), n., v., **fined, fin·ing.** —n. 1. a sum of money exacted as a penalty. —v.t. 2. to punish by a fine.

fine′ art′, art, as painting or sculpture, considered primarily in relation to aesthetic criteria.

fin·er·y (fī′nə rē), n. fine or showy dress, ornaments, etc.

fine·spun (fīn′spun′), adj. highly or excessively refined or subtle.

fi·nesse (fi nes′), n. 1. delicacy or subtlety in performance, skill, etc. 2. skill and adroitness in handling a highly sensitive situation. 3. an artifice or stratagem.

fin·ger (fiɴg′gər), n. 1. any of the terminal members of the hand, esp. one other than the thumb. 2. a part of a glove made to receive a finger. 3. something like a finger in form or use. 4. **keep one's fingers crossed,** to wish for success. 5. **lay or put one's finger on,** to indicate exactly. —v.t. 6. to touch with the fingers. 7. to play on (an instrument) with the fingers. 8. to perform or mark (a passage of music) with a certain fingering. —**fin·gered** (fiɴg′gərd), adj.

fin·ger·board (fiɴg′gər bōrd′, -bôrd′), n. the part of a stringed instrument against which the strings are pressed by the fingers.

fin′ger bowl′, a small bowl to hold water for rinsing the fingers at table.

fin·ger·ing (fiɴg′gər iɴg), n. 1. the act of a person who fingers. 2. the action or method of using the fingers in playing on an instrument. 3. the indication of the way the fingers are to be used in performing a piece of music.

fin·ger·ling (fiɴg′gər liɴg), n. a young or small fish.

fin·ger·nail (fiɴg′gər nāl′), n. the nail at the end of a finger.

fin′ger paint′, a jellylike paint used chiefly by children in painting with their fingers.

fin′ger paint′ing, 1. the technique of applying paint to wet paper with the fingers to produce a painting. 2. a painting produced in this way.

fin·ger·print (fiṅg′gər print′), *n.* 1. an impression of the markings of the inner surface of the fingertip, esp. when made with ink for purposes of identification. —*v.t.* 2. to take the fingerprints of.

fin·ger·tip (fiṅg′gər tip′), *n.* 1. the tip of a finger. 2. **at one′s fingertips,** easily available.

fin′ger wave′, a wave set by impressing the fingers into hair dampened by lotion or water.

fin·i·al (fin′ē əl, fī′nē-), *n.* a small, ornamental, terminal feature at the top of a gable, piece of furniture, etc. —**fin′i·aled,** *adj.*

fin·ick·y (fin′ə kē), *adj.* excessively particular or fastidious. Also, **fin·i·cal** (fin′i kəl), **fin·i·king** (fin′ə kiṅg).

fin·is (fin′is, fī′nis), *n.* (formerly) the end, as of a book.

fin·ish (fin′ish), *v.t.* 1. to bring to an end. 2. to come to the end of. 3. to use completely. 4. to complete and perfect in detail. 5. to put a finish on (wood, metal, etc.). —*v.i.* 6. to come to an end. 7. **finish off,** to destroy or kill. 8. **finish with,** to bring to completion. —*n.* 9. the end or conclusion. 10. the end of a hunt, race, etc. 11. death. 12. educational or social polish. 13. the surface coating or texture of wood, metal, etc. 13. something used or serving to complete or perfect a thing. —**fin′ish·er,** *n.*

fi·nite (fī′nīt), *adj.* 1. having bounds or limits. 2. *Math.* capable of being completely counted. 3. not infinite or infinitesimal. —**fi′nite·ly,** *adv.* —**fi′nite·ness,** *n.*

fink (fiṅk), *n. Slang.* 1. a strikebreaker. 2. an informer. 3. a contemptible person.

Fin·land (fin′lənd), *n.* a country in N Europe.

Finn (fin), *n.* an inhabitant or native of Finland.

Finn., Finnish.

fin·nan had·die (fin′ən had′ē), smoked haddock.

Finn·ish (fin′ish), *n.* 1. the principal language of Finland. —*adj.* 2. of Finland, its inhabitants, or their language.

fin·ny (fin′ē), *adj.,* **-ni·er, -ni·est.** 1. of or abounding in fish. 2. like or having fins.

F.I.O., free in and out (in ship chartering).

fiord (fyôrd, fyōrd), *n.* fjord.

fir (fûr), *n.* 1. a pyramidal cone-bearing tree of the pine family. 2. its wood.

fire (fīʳr), *n., v.,* **fired, fir·ing.** —*n.* 1. the light, heat, and flame of burning substances. 2. a burning mass of material, as in a furnace. 3. the destructive burning of a building, town, forest, etc. 4. burning passion. 5. the discharge of firearms: *to open fire.* 6. **catch fire,** to become ignited. 7. **hang fire, a.** to fail to explode. **b.** to be undecided or delayed. 8. **on fire, a.** ignited or burning. **b.** ardent or zealous. 9. **open fire, a.** to start shooting. **b.** to begin or commence. 10. **under fire,** under attack. —*v.t., v.i.* 11. to discharge or shoot (a gun, bullet, etc.). 12. to ignite or be ignited. 13. to attend to the fire (of). 14. to bake (pottery) in a kiln. 15. to inflame or become inflamed with passion. 16. *Informal.* to dismiss (an employee) from a job. 17. *Informal.* to hurl or throw. —**fire′less,** *adj.*

fire′ alarm′, 1. a signal that a fire has started. 2. a bell, siren, etc., that gives such a signal.

fire·arm (fīʳr′ärm′), *n.* a small-arms weapon, as a pistol, from which a projectile is fired by gunpowder.

fire·ball (fīʳr′bôl′), *n.* 1. a ball of fire, as the sun. 2. a luminous meteor. 3. the highly luminous central portion of a nuclear explosion. 4. *Informal.* an unusually energetic worker.

fire·base (fīʳr′bās′), *n.* an artillery base, esp. one set up quickly to support advancing troops.

fire·boat (fīʳr′bōt′), *n.* a powered vessel fitted for fire fighting.

fire·bomb (fīʳr′bom′), *n.* 1. a crude incendiary device. —*v.t., v.i.* 2. to attack with a firebomb.

fire·box (fīʳr′boks′), *n.* 1. the box or chamber containing the fire of a steam boiler, furnace, etc. 2. a box with a device for notifying the fire station of an outbreak of fire.

fire·brand (fīʳr′brand′), *n.* 1. a piece of burning wood or other material. 2. a person who kindles strife, unrest, etc.

fire·break (fīʳr′brāk′), *n.* a strip of plowed or cleared land made to check the spread of a prairie or forest fire.

fire·brick (fīʳr′brik′), *n.* a brick made of fire clay.

fire·bug (fīʳr′bug′), *n. Informal.* a pyromaniac or arsonist.

fire′ clay′, a refractory clay used for making crucibles, firebricks, etc.

fire·crack·er (fīʳr′krak′ər), *n.* a paper cylinder filled with an explosive and having a fuse, for exploding to make a noise, as during a celebration.

fire·damp (fīʳr′damp′), *n.* a combustible gas consisting chiefly of methane.

fire·dog (fīʳr′dôg′, -dog′), *n.* an andiron.

fire′ en′gine, a truck equipped for fire fighting.

fire′ escape′, a metal stairway down an outside wall for escaping from a burning building.

fire′ extin′guisher, a portable apparatus, usually containing chemicals, for putting out a fire.

fire′ fight′, a skirmish, as one preceding a major assault.

fire′ fight′er, fireman (def. 1). —**fire′ fight′ing.**

fire·fly (fī°r′flī′), n. a soft-bodied nocturnal beetle having light-producing organs at the rear of the abdomen.

fire·house (fī°r′hous′), n. See **fire station.**

fire′ i′rons, the implements used for tending a fireplace, as tongs, poker, etc.

fire·man (fī°r′mən), n. 1. a person employed to extinguish or prevent fires. 2. a person employed to tend fires, as on a locomotive.

fire·place (fī°r′plās′), n. 1. the part of a chimney which opens into a room and in which a fire is built and held. 2. any open structure, usually of masonry, for containing fire, as at a campsite

fire·plug (fī°r′plug′), n. a hydrant.

fire·pow·er (fī°r′pou′ər), n. the ability to deliver gunfire.

fire·proof (fī°r′proof′), adj. 1. capable of preventing destruction by fire. —v.t. 2. to make fireproof.

fire·re·sist·ant (fī°r′ri zis′t°nt), adj. resisting though not entirely preventing destruction by fire.

fire′ screen′, a screen placed in front of an open fireplace as a protection.

fire·side (fī°r′sīd′), n. 1. the space about a fire or hearth. 2. home or family life. —adj. 3. informal in manner.

fire′ sta′tion, a building in which fire-fighting apparatus and often fire fighters are housed.

fire′ storm′, a large fire drawing in strong winds, often accompanied by rain.

fire′ tow′er, a tower, as on a mountain, from which a watch for fires is kept.

fire·trap (fī°r′trap′), n. a building which, because of its age, structure, etc., is especially dangerous in case of fire.

fire′ truck′, an automotive vehicle fitted for fire fighting.

fire·wa·ter (fī°r′wô′tər, -wot′ər), n. Informal. alcoholic drink.

fire·wood (fī°r′wood′), n. wood for fuel.

fire·work (fī°r′wûrk′), n. a combustible or explosive device for producing a striking display of light or a loud noise.

fir′ing line′, 1. the positions at which troops are stationed to fire upon the enemy or targets. 2. the forefront of any action or activity.

fir′ing squad′, a military detachment assigned to execute a condemned person.

firm¹ (fûrm), adj. 1. not soft or yielding when pressed: firm ground. 2. securely fixed in place. 3. not shaking or trembling. 4. fixed or unalterable: a firm belief. 5. steadfast or unwavering. 6. indicating firmness. —v.t., v.i. 7. to make or become firm. —**firm′ly**, adv. —**firm′ness**, n.

firm² (fûrm), n. 1. a partnership or unincorporated association of two or more persons for carrying on a business. 2. any business company.

fir·ma·ment (fûr′mə mənt), n. the expanse of the heavens.

first (fûrst), adj. 1. being before all others with respect to time, order, rank, importance, etc. —adv. 2. before all others or anything else. 3. for the first time 4. rather or sooner: I'd die first 5. in the first place. —n. 6. something that is first in time, order, rank, etc. 7. the beginning. 8. Auto low gear. 9. the first place in a race or other competition.

first′ aid′, emergency aid or treatment given before regular medical services can be obtained.

first-born (fûrst′bôrn′), adj. 1. first in the order of birth. —n. 2. a first-born child.

first′ class′, 1. the best or highest class or grade, as of accommodations on an airplane. 2. a class of mail for matter sealed against inspection —**first′-class′**, adj., adv.

first-hand (fûrst′hand′), adv., adj. from the first or the original source.

first′ la′dy, (often caps.) the wife of the chief executive of a country, state, or city

first′ lieuten′ant, a commissioned officer, as in the U.S. Army, ranking above a second lieutenant and below a captain.

first·ling (fûrst′ling), n. 1. the first of a kind. 2. a first product or result.

first·ly (fûrst′lē), adv. first (def. 5).

first′ mate′, a ship's officer next in command below the captain.

first-night·er (fûrst′nīt′ər), n. a person who habitually attends the theater, etc., on opening night.

first′ per′son, Gram. the form of a pronoun or verb that refers to the speaker.

first-rate (fûrst′rāt′), adj. 1. of the first order or class. —adv. 2. Informal. very well.

first′ ser′geant, 1. a noncommissioned officer, as in the U.S. Air Force, responsible for personnel and administration of a company, squadron, etc. **2.** a noncommissioned rank in the U.S. Army below a command sergeant major and in the U.S. Marine Corps above a gunnery sergeant.

first-string (fûrst′strĭng′), *adj. Informal.* composed of regular members, players, etc., as in football. —**first′-string′er,** *n.*

firth (fûrth), *n. Chiefly Scot.* a long, narrow indentation of the seacoast.

fis·cal (fĭs′kəl), *adj.* **1.** of the public treasury or revenues. **2.** pertaining to financial matters in general. —**fis′cal·ly,** *adv.*

fish (fĭsh), *n., pl.* **fish, fish·es,** *v.* —*n.* **1.** any of various aquatic, cold-blooded vertebrates, having gills, commonly fins, and typically scales. **2.** the flesh of fishes used as food. **3.** **the Fishes,** Pisces. —*v.t.* **4.** to catch or attempt to catch (fish). **5.** to try to catch fish in (a stream, lake, etc.). **6.** to search through as by fishing. —*v.i.* **7.** to catch or attempt to catch fish. **8.** to seek to obtain something indirectly or by artifice.

fish′ and chips′, *Chiefly Brit.* fried fish fillets and French fried potatoes.

fish·bowl (fĭsh′bōl′), *n.* **1.** a glass bowl for goldfish, etc. **2.** any place or area where there is no privacy.

fish′ cake′, a fried ball or cake of shredded fish, esp. salt codfish, and mashed potato.

fish·er (fĭsh′ər), *n.* **1.** a fisherman. **2.** a dark-brown or blackish, somewhat foxlike marten of northern North America. **3.** its fur.

fish·er·man (fĭsh′ər mən), *n.* **1.** a person who fishes as a livelihood or for pleasure. **2.** a ship employed in fishing.

fish·er·y (fĭsh′ə rē), *n., pl.* **-er·ies. 1.** the occupation or industry of catching fish. **2.** a place where such an industry is regularly carried on.

fish′eye lens′ (fĭsh′ī), a camera lens for photographing in a full 180° in all directions.

fish-hook (fĭsh′hŏŏk′), *n.* a hook used in fishing.

fish·ing (fĭsh′ĭng), *n.* the technique, occupation, or diversion of catching fish.

fish′ing rod′, a flexible rod for use with a reel and line in catching fish.

fish′ lad′der, a series of ascending pools constructed to enable fish to swim around or over a dam.

fish′ pro′tein con′centrate′, an odorless and tasteless powder ground from dried fish to yield protein content.

fish′ sto′ry, *Informal.* an exaggerated or incredible story.

fish-wife (fĭsh′wīf′), *n.* **1.** a woman who sells fish. **2.** a coarse, vulgar woman.

fish·y (fĭsh′ē), *adj.,* **fish·i·er, fish·i·est. 1.** like a fish in smell, taste, etc. **2.** *Informal.* of questionable character. **3.** dull and expressionless. —**fish′i·ness,** *n.*

fis·sile (fĭs′əl), *adj.* **1.** capable of being split or divided. **2.** *Physics.* capable of undergoing fission. —**fis·sil·i·ty** (fĭ sĭl′ə tē), *n.*

fis·sion (fĭsh′ən), *n.* **1.** act of cleaving or splitting into parts. **2.** the division of an organism into new organisms as a process of reproduction. **3.** the splitting of the nucleus of an atom into nuclei of lighter atoms, accompanied by the release of energy. —**fis′sion·a·ble,** *adj.*

fis·sure (fĭsh′ər), *n.* a narrow opening produced by cleavage.

fist (fĭst), *n.* **1.** the hand closed tightly, with the fingers doubled into the palm. **2.** index (def. 4).

fist·ful (fĭst′fŏŏl), *n.* handful (defs. 1, 2).

fist·i·cuff (fĭs′tə kŭf′), *n.* **1.** a blow with the fist. **2.** fisticuffs, **a.** combat with the fists. **b.** the sport of boxing.

fis·tu·la (fĭs′chŏŏ lə), *n., pl.* **-las, -lae** (-lē′). a narrow passage formed by disease, as one leading from an abscess. —**fis′tu·lous,** *adj.*

fit¹ (fĭt), *adj.,* **fit·ter, fit·test,** *v.,* **fit·ted** or **fit, fit·ting,** *n.* —*adj.* **1.** adequately suited. **2.** proper or becoming. **3.** qualified or competent. **4.** prepared for ready. **5.** in good condition or health. —*v.t.* **6.** to be adapted to or suitable for. **7.** to be of the right size or shape for. **8.** to adjust or make conform to something. **9.** to make qualified or competent. **10.** to make ready. **11.** to place with care. **12.** to provide or equip. —*v.i.* **13.** to be suitable or proper. **14.** to be of the right size or shape. —*n.* **15.** the manner in which a thing fits. **16.** something that fits. —**fit′ly,** *adv.* —**fit′ness,** *n.* —**fit′ter,** *n.* —**Syn. 1.** appropriate, apt, suitable.

fit² (fĭt), *n.* **1.** a sudden, acute attack, as of a convulsive disease. **2.** a sudden, temporary spasm, as of laughing. **3.** a highly emotional reaction. **4.** **by fits and starts,** at irregular intervals. Also, **by fits. 5.** **throw a fit,** *Informal.* to become extremely excited or angry.

fit·ful (fĭt′fəl), *adj.* **1.** appearing or acting in fits. **2.** recurring irregularly. —**fit′ful·ly,** *adv.* .—**fit′ful·ness,** *n.*

fit·ting (fĭt′ĭng), *adj.* **1.** suitable and proper. —*n.* **2.** the act of trying on clothes that are being made or altered. **3.** anything provided as equipment or parts. **4.** Usually, **fittings.** *Chiefly Brit.* furniture, fixtures, etc. —**fit′ting·ly,** *adv.* —**fit′ting·ness,** *n.*

five (fīv), *n.* **1.** a cardinal number, four plus one. **2.** a symbol for this number, as 5 or V. —*adj.* **3.** amounting to five in number.

five-and-ten (fīv′ən ten′), *n.* a retail store offering a wide assortment of inexpensive items. Also called **five′-and-ten′-cent store′.**

fix (fiks), *v.,* **fixed, fix·ing,** *n.* —*v.t.* **1.** to make firm, stable, or stationary. **2.** to attach or place permanently. **3.** to direct (the eyes, attention, etc.) steadily. **4.** to attract and hold (the eye, attention, etc.). **5.** to make set or rigid. **6.** to put into permanent form. **7.** to place (responsibility, blame, etc.) on a person. **8.** to assign or refer to a definite place, time, etc. **9.** to repair or mend. **10.** to put in order. **11.** to arrange matters with respect to, esp. privately or dishonestly. **12.** to prepare (a meal or food). **13.** *Informal.* to get even with. **14.** to render (a photographic negative) permanent by removing silver salts. —*v.i.* **15.** to become fixed. **16.** *Dial.* to prepare or plan. **17. fix on** or **upon,** to decide on. **18. fix up,** *Informal.* **a.** to arrange for. **b.** to provide with. **c.** to repair. —*n.* **19.** *Informal.* a predicament or difficulty. **20.** a charted position of a vessel or aircraft. **21.** *Slang.* an injection of heroin or other narcotic. **22.** *Slang.* an underhanded or illegal arrangement. —**fix′a·ble,** *adj.* —**fix′er,** *n.*

fix·a·tion (fik sā′shən), *n.* **1.** the act of fixing or state of being fixed. **2.** a partial arrest of emotional and instinctual development at an early point in life. **3.** a preoccupation or obsession.

fix·a·tive (fik′sə tiv), *adj.* **1.** serving to fix or making fixed. —*n.* **2.** a substance sprayed on a drawing to prevent blurring.

fixed (fikst), *adj.* **1.** firmly implanted or stationary. **2.** rendered stable or permanent, as color. **3.** set or intent upon something. **4.** definitely and permanently placed. **5.** not fluctuating or varying. —**fix·ed·ly** (fik′-sid lē), *adv.* —**fix′ed·ness,** *n.*

fixed′ sat′ellite, an earth satellite that remains over a particular point on the earth's surface.

fixed′ star′, any of the stars that appear always to retain the same position in respect to one another.

fix·ings (fik′singz), *n.pl.* appropriate accompaniments or trimmings.

fix·i·ty (fik′si tē), *n.* the state or quality of being fixed or stable.

fix·ture (fiks′chər), *n.* **1.** something securely, and usually permanently, attached: *a light fixture.* **2.** a person or thing long established in the same place or position.

fizz (fiz), *v.i.* **1.** to make a hissing or sputtering sound. —*n.* **2.** a fizzing sound. **3.** an effervescent drink, as soda water.

fiz·zle (fiz′əl), *v.,* **-zled, -zling,** *n.* —*v.i.* **1.** to fizz. **2.** *Informal.* to fail ignominiously after a good start. —*n.* **3.** *Informal.* a fiasco or failure.

fjord (fyôrd, fyōrd), *n.* a long, narrow arm of the sea bordered by steep cliffs.

FL, Florida.

Fl, **1.** Flanders. **2.** Flemish.

fl., **1.** floor. **2.** flourished. [< L *floruit*] **3.** fluid.

Fla., Florida.

flab (flab), *n. Informal.* fat, flabby flesh.

flab·ber·gast (flab′ər gast′), *v.t. Informal.* to overcome with bewilderment.

flab·by (flab′ē), *adj.,* **-bi·er, -bi·est. 1.** hanging loosely or limply, as flesh. **2.** lacking firmness or determination. —**flab′bi·ly,** *adv.* —**flab′bi·ness,** *n.*

flac·cid (flak′sid, flas′id), *adj.* soft and limp: *flaccid biceps.*

flack¹ (flak), *n. Slang.* See **press agent.**

flack² (flak), *n.* flak.

flac·on (flak′ən), *n.* a small bottle or flask with a stopper.

flag¹ (flag), *n., v.,* **flagged, flag·ging.** —*n.* **1.** a piece of cloth, varying in design, used as the symbol of a nation, as a means of signaling, etc. **2.** a stroke attached to the vertical line of certain musical notes. —*v.t.* **3.** to decorate with flags. **4.** to signal with, or as with, a flag.

flag² (flag), *n.* any of various plants with long, sword-shaped leaves.

flag³ (flag), *v.i.,* **flagged, flag·ging. 1.** to hang loosely or limply. **2.** to diminish in vigor, energy, interest, etc.

flag⁴ (flag), *n., v.,* **flagged, flag·ging.** —*n.* **1.** flagstone. —*v.t.* **2.** to pave with flagstones.

flag·el·lant (flaj′ə lənt, flə jel′ənt), *n.* a person who flagellates, esp. one in former times who publicly scourged himself for religious discipline.

flag·el·late (flaj′ə lāt′), *v.t.,* **-lat·ed, -lat·ing.** to whip or scourge. —**flag′el·la′tion,** *n.* —**flag′el·la′tor,** *n.*

fla·gel·lum (flə jel′əm), *n., pl.* **-gel·la** (-jel′ə), **-gel·lums.** a long, lashlike appendage serving as an organ of locomotion in certain reproductive bodies, bacteria, protozoa, etc.

flag·eo·let (flaj′ə let′, -lā′), *n.* a small flute with four finger holes in front and two in the rear.

fla·gi·tious (flə jish′əs), *adj.* shamefully wicked.

flag·man (flag′mən), *n.* a person who signals with a flag or lantern.

flag·on (flag′ən), *n.* a large bottle, esp. with a handle, a spout, and a cover.

flag·pole (flag′pōl′), *n.* a staff or pole on which a flag is displayed. Also called **flag·staff** (flag′staf′, -stäf′).

fla·grant (flā′grənt), *adj.* outrageously evident: *a flagrant error.* —**fla′gran·cy, fla′grance,** *n.* —**fla′grant·ly,** *adv.* —Syn. conspicuous, glaring, gross.

fla·gran·te de·lic·to (flə grän′tē di lik′-tō), while the crime is, or was, being committed.

flag·ship (flag′ship′), *n.* a ship carrying the commander of a fleet or squadron and displaying his or her flag.

flag·stone (flag′stōn′), *n.* a flat slab used esp. for paving.

flail (flāl), *n.* **1.** an instrument for threshing grain by hand. —*v.t.* **2.** to beat with a flail. —*v.i.* **3.** to toss about.

flair (flâr), *n.* **1.** a natural talent or ability. **2.** smartness of style, manner, etc. **3.** keen perception or discernment.

flak (flak), *n.* **1.** antiaircraft fire. **2.** *Informal.* annoying criticism or opposition.

flake (flāk), *n., v.,* **flaked, flak·ing.** —*n.* **1.** a small, flat piece, esp. one detached from a larger piece. **2.** any small piece or mass. —*v.i.* **3.** to peel off in flakes. —*v.t.* **4.** to break flakes from. —**flak′y,** *adj.*

flam·bé (fläm bā′), *adj.* (of food) served in flaming liquor, esp. brandy.

flam·beau (flam′bō), *n., pl.* **-beaux** (-bōz), **-beaus.** a flaming torch.

flam·boy·ant (flam boi′ənt), *adj.* **1.** strikingly bold or brilliant. **2.** conspicuously dashing and colorful. **3.** elaborately styled. —**flam·boy′ance, flam·boy′an·cy,** *n.* —**flam·boy′ant·ly,** *adv.*

flame (flām), *n., v.,* **flamed, flam·ing.** —*n.* **1.** burning gas or vapor, as from ignited wood or coal. **2.** Often, **flames.** the state of blazing combustion. **3.** any flamelike condition. **4.** brilliant light. **5.** intense zeal or passion. **6.** *Informal.* a sweetheart. —*v.i.* **7.** to burn with a flame. **8.** to glow like flame. **9.** to break into anger, etc. —**flam·ing** (flā′ming), *adj.*

fla·men·co (flə meng′kō), *n.* a strongly rhythmic style of dancing, characteristic of the gypsies in southern Spain. [< Sp: gypsylike]

flame·out (flām′out′), *n.* the failure of a jet engine due to faulty combustion.

flame·throw·er (flām′thrō′ər), *n.* a weapon that squirts ignited incendiary fuel.

fla·min·go (flə ming′gō), *n., pl.* **-gos, -goes.** a tropical bird having very long legs and neck, and pinkish to scarlet plumage.

flam·ma·ble (flam′ə bəl), *adj.* easily set on fire. —**flam′ma·bil′i·ty,** *n.*

Flan·ders (flan′dərz), *n.* a region in W Belgium, and the adjacent parts of N France and SW Netherlands.

flange (flanj), *n.* a projecting rim on a shaft, pipe, etc., to give additional strength or supporting area.

flank (flangk), *n.* **1.** the side of an animal or a human between the ribs and hip. **2.** a slice of meat from the flank of an animal. **3.** the side of anything, as of a building. **4.** the extreme right or left side of a military formation, fortification, etc. —*v.t.* **5.** to be at the flank or side of. **6.** to defend or guard at the flank. **7.** to menace or attack the flank of. **8.** to pass around or turn the flank of.

flank·er (flang′kər), *n.* a person or thing that flanks.

flan·nel (flan′əl), *n.* **1.** a warm, soft, napped fabric of wool or cotton. **2. flannels,** a. trousers made of flannel. b. woolen undergarments. —**flan′nel·ly,** *adj.*

flan·nel·et (flan′əl et′), *n.* a cotton fabric napped on one side. Also, **flan′nel·ette′.**

flap (flap), *n., v.,* **flapped, flap·ping.** —*v.i., v.t.* **1.** to swing or cause to swing loosely, esp. with noise. **2.** to move (the wings) up and down. **3.** to strike (a blow) with something broad and flexible. —*n.* **4.** a flapping motion. **5.** the noise produced by something that flaps. **6.** a blow given with something broad and flexible. **7.** something broad and flexible, or flat and thin, that hangs loosely, attached at one side only. **8.** a movable surface used for increasing the lift or drag of an airplane. **9.** *Slang.* a state of nervous excitement.

flap·jack (flap′jak′), *n.* pancake.

flap·pa·ble (flap′ə bəl), *adj. Slang.* easily upset or confused, esp. in a crisis.

flap·per (flap′ər), *n.* **1.** a person or thing that flaps. **2.** a young woman, esp. an unconventional one, during the 1920's.

flare (flâr), *v.,* **flared, flar·ing,** *n.* —*v.i.* **1.** to burn with an unsteady, swaying flame, as a torch in the wind. **2.** to develop or erupt suddenly. **3.** to spread gradually outward, as the bottom of a wide skirt, etc. —*v.t.* **4.** to cause to flare. —*n.* **5.** a flaring or swaying flame. **6.** a bright blaze of light used as a signal, etc. **7.** a device to produce such a blaze. **8.** a sudden burst, as of zeal or temper. **9.** outward curvature.

flare-up (flâr′up′), *n.* **1.** a sudden outburst of anger. **2.** a sudden outbreak of violence, disease, etc.

flash (flash), *n.* 1. a brief, sudden burst of bright light. 2. a sudden, brief display, as of wit. 3. a very brief period of time. 4. flashlight. 5. gaudy showiness. 6. a brief dispatch sent by a wire service. 7. *Photog.* bright artificial light thrown briefly upon a subject during an exposure. —*v.i.* 8. to break forth into sudden flame or light. 9. to gleam or sparkle. 10. to burst suddenly into view or perception. —*v.t.* 11. to emit (fire or light) in sudden flashes. 12. to cause to flash. 13. to transmit or communicate instantaneously, as by telegraph. 14. *Informal.* to make an ostentatious display of. —*adj.* 15. showy or ostentatious. 16. sudden and brief: *a flash storm.* 17. caused by or used as protection against flash. —**flash′er,** *n.*

flash·back (flash′bak′), *n.* a scene representing an earlier event inserted into a current situation depicted in a novel, motion picture, etc.

flash·bulb (flash′bulb′), *n.* *Photog.* a glass bulb, burning with a brilliant flash when ignited electrically, for momentarily illuminating a subject. Also called **flash·lamp** (flash′lamp′).

flash′ card′, a card bearing words, numerals, or pictures, designed for gaining a rapid response from pupils when held up briefly by a teacher.

flash·cube (flash′kyoōb′), *n.* a cube, for attaching to a camera, that contains a flashbulb in each vertical side for taking four flash pictures in rapid succession.

flash′ flood′, a sudden and destructive rush of water, as down a narrow gully.

flash·for·ward (flash′fôr′wərd), *n.* a scene representing a future event inserted into a current situation depicted in a novel, motion picture, etc.

flash′ gun′, a device that simultaneously discharges a flashbulb and operates a camera shutter.

flash·ing (flash′ing), *n.* sheet metal used to cover and protect certain joints and angles, as of a roof.

flash·light (flash′līt′), *n.* 1. a small, portable electric lamp powered by dry batteries. 2. *Photog.* a burst of artificial illuminating light.

flash′ point′, the lowest temperature at which a liquid will give off sufficient vapor to ignite on application of a flame.

flash·tube (flash′toōb′, -tyoōb′), *n.* an electronic flashlamp having a tube that is powered by a high-voltage source and can be ignited any number of times.

flash·y (flash′ē), *adj.,* **flash·i·er, flash·i·est.** 1. briefly sparkling or brilliant. 2. showy or gaudy: *flashy clothes.* —**flash′i·ly,** *adv.* —**flash′i·ness,** *n.*

flask (flask, fläsk), *n.* 1. a bottle having a rounded body and a narrow neck, used to hold wine, oil, etc. 2. a flat metal or glass bottle for carrying in the pocket.

flat¹ (flat), *adj.,* **flat·ter, flat·test,** *n., v.,* **flat·ted, flat·ting,** *adv.* —*adj.* 1. level, even, or without inequalities of surface. 2. lying horizontally at full length, as a person. 3. not deep or thick. 4. spread out, as an unrolled map. 5. deflated or collapsed: *a flat tire.* 6. absolute, downright, or positive. 7. without modification or variation: *a flat price.* 8. lifeless or dull. 9. having lost its flavor, sharpness, or life. 10. pointless, as a remark. 11. without gloss. 12. *Music.* **a.** lowered a half step in pitch: *B flat.* **b.** below an intended pitch, as a note. —*n.* 13. something flat. 14. **flats,** women's shoes with flat heels. 15. a flat surface, side, or part of anything: *the flat of his hand.* 16. flat ground. 17. *Music.* **a.** a tone one chromatic half step below a given tone. **b.** the symbol (♭) indicating this. 18. a deflated automobile tire. —*v.t., v.i.* 19. to make or become flat. —*adv.* 20. horizontally or levelly. 21. completely or utterly: *flat broke.* 22. exactly or precisely. 23. below the true pitch: *to sing flat.* —**flat′ly,** *adv.* —**flat′ness,** *n.* —**flat′tish,** *adj.*

flat² (flat), *n.* *Chiefly Brit.* a residential apartment.

flat·bed (flat′bed′), *n.* a motortruck having an enclosed cab and a platform over the rear wheels, without stakes around its edges.

flat·boat (flat′bōt′), *n.* a flat-bottomed boat for use in shallow water, esp. on rivers.

flat·car (flat′kär′), *n.* a railroad car without sides or top.

flat·fish (flat′fish′), *n.* any fish, including the halibut, sole, flounder, etc., having a greatly compressed body, with both eyes on the upper side.

flat·foot (flat′fŏŏt′), *n., pl.* **feet** for 1; **foots** for 2. 1. a condition in which the arch of the foot is flattened so that the entire sole rests upon the ground. 2. *Slang.* a police officer. —**flat′-foot′ed,** *adj.*

Flat·head (flat′hed′), *n.* a member of a tribe of Indians of NW Montana.

flat·i·ron (flat′ī′ərn), *n.* any of various early types of laundry iron.

flat-out (flat′out′), *Slang.* —*adj.* 1. downright or thorough: *a flat-out recession.* —*adv.* Also, **flat out** 2. brusquely or candidly. 3. at full speed.

flat·ten (flat′ᵊn), *v.t.*, *v.i.* to make or become flat. —**flat′ten·er,** *n.*

flat·ter (flat′ər), *v.t.* 1. to try to please by complimentary speech or attention. 2. to compliment insincerely. 3. to praise excessively. 4. to represent favorably. —*v.i.* 5. to use flattery. —**flat′ter·er,** *n.* —**flat′ter·ing·ly,** *adv.*

flat·ter·y (flat′ə rē), *n.*, *pl.* **-ter·ies.** 1. the act of flattering. 2. a flattering compliment or speech.

flat·top (flat′top′), *n.* 1. *Informal.* an aircraft carrier. 2. *Slang.* a type of crew cut.

flat·u·lent (flach′ə lənt), *adj.* 1. having or generating gas in the alimentary canal. 2. pompous or turgid. —**flat′u·lence,** *n.* —**flat′u·lent·ly,** *adv.*

fla·tus (flā′təs), *n.* gas accumulated in the stomach or intestines.

flat·ware (flat′wâr′), *n.* flat tableware, as plates or saucers.

flaunt (flônt), *v.t.*, *v.i.* 1. to display (oneself) ostentatiously. 2. *Nonstandard.* to flout. —**flaunt′er,** *n.* —**flaunt′ing·ly,** *adv.*
—**Usage.** 2. This sense of FLAUNT stems from its confusion with FLOUT. Although this confusion is quite common, FLAUNT in this meaning is still regarded as nonstandard usage.

flau·tist (flô′tist, flou′-), *n.* *Brit.* flutist.

fla·vor (flā′vər), *n.* 1. distinctive taste. 2. a substance that provides a particular flavor. 3. characteristic quality. —*v.t.* 4. to give flavor to. Also, *Brit.,* **fla′vour.** —**fla′vor·ful,** *adj.* —**fla′vor·less,** *adj.* —**fla′vor·some,** *adj.*

fla·vor·ing (flā′vər ing), *n.* flavor (def. 2).

flaw (flô), *n.* 1. a feature that mars the perfection of something. 2. a crack or fissure. —**flaw′less,** *adj.* —**flaw′less·ly,** *adv.* —**flaw′less·ness,** *n.*

flax (flaks), *n.* 1. a slender, erect plant having narrow leaves and blue flowers, cultivated for its fiber and seeds. 2. its fiber, manufactured into linen yarn.

flax·en (flak′sən), *adj.* 1. of or resembling flax. 2. pale-yellow. Also, **flax′y.**

flay (flā), *v.t.* 1. to strip off the skin of. 2. to criticize with scathing severity. —**flay′er,** *n.*

flea (flē), *n.* a small, wingless, bloodsucking, leaping insect, parasitic upon mammals and birds.

flea·bag (flē′bag′), *n.* *Slang.* a cheap, run-down hotel or rooming house.

flea·bane (flē′bān′), *n.* any of various plants of the daisy family, reputed to drive away fleas.

flea·bite (flē′bīt′), *n.* the bite of a flea.

flea-bit·ten (flē′bit′ᵊn), *adj.* 1. bitten by a flea. 2. infested with fleas.

flea′ mar′ket, an open-air market where old or used articles are sold.

fleck (flek), *n.* 1. a spot or patch of color, light, etc. 2. a speck: *a fleck of dirt.* —*v.t.* 3. to mark with flecks. —**fleck′y,** *adj.*

fledg·ling (flej′ling), *n.* 1. a young bird with new flight feathers. 2. an inexperienced person. Also, *esp. Brit.,* **fledge′ling.**

flee (flē), *v.,* **fled** (fled), **flee·ing.** —*v.i.* 1. to run away, as from danger, pursuers, etc. 2. to move swiftly. —*v.t.* 3. to run away from (a place, person, etc.).

fleece (flēs), *n.,* *v.,* **fleeced, fleec·ing.** —*n.* 1. the coat of wool that covers a sheep or similar animal. 2. a fabric with a soft, silky pile. —*v.t.* 3. to remove the fleece of (a sheep). 4. to swindle or cheat. —**fleec′er,** *n.* —**fleec′y,** *adj.* —**fleec′i·ness,** *n.*

fleer (flēr), *v.i.* to grin or laugh coarsely or mockingly.

fleet¹ (flēt), *n.* 1. the largest organization of warships under the command of a single officer. 2. a large group of ships, airplanes, trucks, etc., operated by a single company.

fleet² (flēt), *Literary.* —*adj.* 1. swift or rapid: *to be fleet of foot.* —*v.i.* 2. to move swiftly. —**fleet′ly,** *adv.* —**fleet′ness,** *n.*

fleet′ ad′miral, the highest ranking naval officer.

fleet·ing (flē′ting), *adj.* passing swiftly. —**fleet′ing·ly,** *adv.* —**fleet′ing·ness,** *n.*

Flem, Flemish. Also, **Flem.**

Flem·ing (flem′ing), *n.* 1. a native of Flanders. 2. a Flemish-speaking Belgian.

Flem·ish (flem′ish), *adj.* 1. of Flanders, its people, or their language. —*n.* 2. the people of Flanders. 3. one of the official languages of Belgium.

flesh (flesh), *n.* 1. the soft substance of an animal or human body, consisting of muscle and fat. 2. muscular and fatty tissue. 3. meat, usually excluding fish or fowl. 4. the body, as distinguished from the soul. 5. *Literary.* mankind. 6. living creatures generally. 7. one's family, relatives, or kindred. 8. the soft, pulpy portion of a fruit, vegetable, etc. 9. **in the flesh, a.** in person. **b.** alive or living.

flesh′ fly′, a two-winged insect that deposits its larvae in flesh of living animals.

flesh·ly (flesh′lē), *adj.,* **-li·er, -li·est.** 1. of the flesh or body. 2. carnal or sensual. 3. worldly, rather than spiritual.

flesh·pot (flesh′pot′), *n.* a place offering luxurious and unrestrained pleasure.

flesh·y (flesh′ē), *adj.*, **flesh·i·er, flesh·i·est.** 1. having much fat or flesh. 2. of or resembling flesh.

fleur-de-lis (flûr′d°lē′, -lēs′, floor′-), *n.*, *pl.* **fleurs-de-lis** (flûr′d°lēz′, floor′-). a heraldic device somewhat resembling three petals of an iris tied by an encircling band.

flew (floo), *v.* a pt. of **fly**[1].

flex (fleks), *v.t.*, *v.i.* 1. to bend, as a part of the body. 2. to tighten (a muscle).

flex·i·ble (flek′sə bəl), *adj.* 1. capable of being easily flexed or bent. 2. adaptable to change: *a flexible schedule.* 3. willing or disposed to yield: *a flexible personality.* —**flex′i·bil′i·ty**, *n.* —**flex′i·bly**, *adv.*

flex·i·time (flek′sə tīm′), *n.* the system of working hours under which employees are individually allowed to choose, within limits, when to go to work and when to go home. Also, **flex′time**′.

flex·ure (flek′shər), *n.* a bend or fold.

flib·ber·ti·gib·bet (flib′ər tē jib′it), *n.* a chattering or flighty person.

flick[1] (flik), *n.* 1. a sudden light blow or stroke. 2. the sound made by this. 3. a daub or splash. —*v.t.* 4. to strike lightly with the finger, etc. —*v.i.* 5. to flutter or twitch.

flick[2] (flik), *n.* *Slang.* a motion picture.

flick·er[1] (flik′ər), *v.i.* 1. to burn unsteadily. 2. to vibrate or quiver. —*v.t.* 3. to cause to flicker. —*n.* 4. an unsteady flame or light. 5. a flickering movement. 6. a brief occurrence: *a flicker of hope.*

flick·er[2] (flik′ər), *n.* a large woodpecker native to wooded areas in North America.

flied (flīd), *v.* a pt. and pp. of **fly**[1].

fli·er (flī′ər), *n.* 1. something that flies. 2. an aviator. 3. a person or thing that moves with great speed. 4. *Informal.* a financial venture outside of one's ordinary business. 5. a small handbill.

flight[1] (flīt), *n.* 1. the act, manner, or power of flying. 2. the distance covered or the course taken by a flying object. 3. a number of beings or things flying together: *a flight of swallows.* 4. a trip by an airplane, etc. 5. a scheduled trip on an airline. 6. a journey into or through outer space, as of a rocket. 7. swift movement or transition: *the flight of time.* 8. a soaring above ordinary bounds: *a flight of fancy.* 9. a series of steps between any landing and the next.

flight[2] (flīt), *n.* an act or instance of fleeing.

flight′ bag′, a small bag, usually of canvas, used by airline passengers to carry personal belongings.

flight·less (flīt′lis), *adj.* incapable of flying.

flight′ line′, the general area in an airfield for parking and servicing of aircraft.

flight′ path′, the locus of the center of gravity of an airplane during flight.

flight′ strip′, a strip of cleared land used as an emergency runway for aircraft.

flight-test (flīt′test′), *v.t.* to test (an airplane) in flight.

flight·y (flī′tē), *adj.*, **flight·i·er, flight·i·est.** 1. given to flights of fancy. 2. mildly crazy. 3. irresponsible or unstable. —**flight′i·ness**, *n.*

flim·flam (flim′flam′), *n.* *Informal.* a trick or deception.

flim·sy (flim′zē), *adj.*, **-si·er, -si·est.** 1. without material strength or solidity. 2. not effective or convincing. —**flim′si·ly**, *adv.* —**flim′si·ness**, *n.*

flinch (flinch), *v.i.* to shrink from what is difficult or painful. —**flinch′er**, *n.* —**flinch′ing·ly**, *adv.*

fling (fling), *v.*, **flung, fling·ing**, *n.* —*v.t.* 1. to throw with force or violence. 2. to move (oneself) violently with impatience or contempt. 3. to put suddenly or violently. —*n.* 4. an act of flinging. 5. a short period of unrestrained indulgence of one's impulses. 6. a lively Scottish dance. 7. take a fling at, to make an attempt at something. —**fling′er**, *n.*

flint (flint), *n.* 1. a hard kind of stone, a form of silica. 2. a piece of this, esp. as used for striking fire. —**flint′y**, *adj.*

Flint (flint), *n.* a city in SE Michigan.

flint′ glass′, durable glass of high dispersion containing lead of oxide, used to make lenses.

flint·lock (flint′lok′), *n.* 1. an outmoded gunlock in which a flint ignites the charge. 2. a firearm with such a lock.

flip[1] (flip), *v.*, **flipped, flip·ping**, *n.* —*v.t.* 1. to toss with a snap of a finger and thumb. 2. to move (something) suddenly. 3. to turn over. —*v.i.* 4. to move with a jerk or jerks. 5. *Slang.* to react excitedly. 6. **flip one's lid**, *Slang.* to lose self-control. —*n.* 7. an instance of flipping.

flip[2] (flip), *n.* a mixed drink made with liquor or wine, sugar, and egg, topped with nutmeg.

flip[3] (flip), *adj.*, **flip·per, flip·pest.** *Informal.* flippant.

flip·pant (flip′ənt), *adj.* frivolously shallow and disrespectful. —**flip′pan·cy**, *n.* —**flip′pant·ly**, *adv.*

flip·per (flĭp'ʻor), *n.* 1. a broad, flat limb, as of a seal, etc., especially adapted for swimming. 2. a paddle-like rubber device worn on the foot as an aid in swimming.

flip' side', *Informal.* the reverse and usually less important side of a phonograph record.

flirt (flûrt), *v.i.* 1. to act amorously without serious intentions. 2. to trifle or toy, as with an idea. 3. to dart about. —*v.t.* 4. *Archaic.* to throw with a toss or jerk. —*n.* 5. a person who flirts. 6. a quick throw or toss. —**flir·ta·tion** (flĭr tā'shon), *n.* —**flir·ta'tious**, *adj.* —**flir·ta'tious·ly**, *adv.* —**flirt'ing·ly**, *adv.*

flit (flĭt), *v.i.*, **flit·ted**, **flit·ting.** to fly, dart, or skim along. —**flit'ter**, *n.*

flitch (flĭch), *n.* the side of a hog salted and cured: *a flitch of bacon.*

fliv·ver (flĭv'ʻor), *n. Facetious.* an old, small, or cheap automobile.

float (flōt), *v.i.* 1. to remain on the surface of a liquid. 2. to move gently on the surface of a liquid. 3. to rest or move in a liquid, the air, etc.: *a balloon floating on high.* 4. to move or drift about. 5. (of a currency) to find its own value without a fixed rate in the foreign-exchange market. —*v.t.* 6. to cause to float. 7. to issue in order to raise money, as a government bond. 8. to let (a currency) float. —*n.* 9. something that floats, as a raft. 10. a hollow ball that through its buoyancy automatically regulates the supply of a liquid in a cistern. 11. a cork for supporting a baited line in the water. 12. a vehicle bearing a display in a parade or procession. —**float'er**, *n.*

flock[1] (flŏk), *n.* 1. a number of animals of one kind keeping, feeding, or herded together, as sheep, goats, or birds. 2. a large number of people, esp. under the guidance of a single person. 4. a group of things. —*v.i.* 5. to gather or go in a flock.

flock[2] (flŏk), *n.* finely powdered wool, cloth, etc., for decorating wallpaper, covering phonograph turntables, etc.

floe (flō), *n.* a sheet of floating ice.

flog (flŏg, flôg), *v.t.*, **flogged**, **flogging.** to beat hard with a whip, stick, etc. —**flog'ger**, *n.*

flood (flŭd), *n.* 1. a great overflowing of water, esp. over land not usually submerged. 2. any great outpouring: *a flood of words.* 3. the flowing in of the tide. 4. the **Flood**, the universal deluge in the days of Noah. —*v.t.* 5. to cover with a flood of water or other liquid. 6. to fill or occupy completely. 7. to overwhelm with an abundance of something. —*v.i.* 8. to flow or pour in, or as in, a flood.

flood-gate (flŭd'gāt'), *n.* a gate designed to regulate the flow of water.

flood-light (flŭd'līt'), *n.*, *v.*, **-light·ed** or **-lit**, **-light·ing.** —*n.* 1. an artificial light that gives illumination over a large area. 2. a lamp or projector that produces such a light. —*v.t.* 3. to illuminate with a floodlight.

flood' plain', a flat land area along a stream that is subject to flooding.

flood' tide', 1. flood (def. 3). 2. a tide at its greatest height. 3. a peak or climax.

floor (flōr, flôr), *n.* 1. the lower part of a room upon which one walks. 2. a story or level in a building. 3. a flat extent of surface. 4. the part of a legislative chamber, etc., where the members sit. 5. the right of one member to speak from such a place. 6. the bottom limit, as one set by law. —*v.t.* 7. to cover or furnish with a floor. 8. to bring down to the floor or ground. 9. to overwhelm or defeat. 10. *Informal.* to confound or nonplus.

floor-board (flōr'bôrd', flôr'bôrd'), *n.* 1. any of the boards composing a floor. 2. the floor of an automotive vehicle.

floor' ex'ercise, a gymnastic act performed on the mat-covered floor without apparatus.

floor-ing (flōr'ĭng, -flôr'-), *n.* 1. a floor. 2. floors collectively. 3. materials for making floors.

floor' lead'er, the majority or minority leader in the Senate or House of Representatives.

floor' man'ager, a person employed in a department store, etc., to direct customers, supervise sales people, etc.

floor-shift (flōr'shĭft', flôr'-), *n.* a gearshift set in the floor of an automobile.

floor' show', an entertainment in a nightclub.

floor-walk·er (flōr'wô'kor, flôr'-), *n. Obsolete.* See **floor manager.**

floo·zy (floo'zē), *n.*, *pl.* **-zies.** *Slang.* a gaudily dressed, immoral woman. Also, **floo'zie.**

flop (flŏp), *v.*, **flopped**, **flop·ping**, *n.* —*v.i.* 1. to fall or drop with a sudden bump or thud. 2. to move or flap around loosely or softly. 3. *Informal.* to fail totally: *The play flopped dismally.* —*v.t.* 4. to cause to flop. —*n.* 5. an act or sound of flopping. 6. *Informal.* a total failure. —**flop'per**, *n.* —**flop'py**, *adj.*

flop-house (flŏp'hous'), *n.* a cheap, run-down hotel.

flop·o·ver (flŏp'ō'vor), *n.* a continuous, vertical movement of the picture on a television screen, caused as by interference in reception.

flo·ra (flôr′ə, flōr′ə), *n., pl.* **flo·ras,**
flo·rae (flôr′ē, flōr′ē). the plants of
a particular region or period.

flo·ral (flôr′əl, flōr′-), *adj.* pertaining
to or consisting of flowers. —**flo′-**
ral·ly, *adv.*

Flor·ence (flôr′əns, flor′-), *n.* a city
in central Italy. —**Flor′en·tine′** (-ən-
tēn′, -tīn′), *adj., n.*

flo·res·cence (flō res′əns, flô-, flə-), *n.*
act, state, or period of flowering.
—**flo·res′cent,** *adj.*

flo·ret (flôr′it, flōr′-), *n.* a small
flower.

flor·id (flôr′id, flor′-), *adj.* 1. ruddy,
esp. of the complexion. 2. excessively ornate.

Flor·i·da (flôr′i də, flor′-), *n.* a state
in SE U.S. *Cap.:* Tallahassee. —
Flo·rid′i·an (-rid′ē ən), **Flor′i·dan,**
adj., n.

flor·in (flôr′in, flor′-), *n.* 1. a former
coin of Great Britain, equal to two
shillings. 2. the Dutch guilder, esp.
its former gold coin.

flo·rist (flôr′ist, flōr′-, flor′-), *n.* a
grower or retailer of flowers.

floss (flôs, flos), *n.* 1. the cottony
fiber of silk. 2. silk filaments with
little or no twist, used in embroidery. 3. any silky, filamentous
matter, as the silk of corn.

floss·y (flô′sē, flos′ē), *adj.,* **floss·i·er,**
floss·i·est. 1. made of or resembling
floss. 2. *Slang.* showily stylish.

flo·ta·tion (flō tā′shən), *n.* 1. the act
or state of floating. 2. the floating
of a bond issue.

flota′tion col′lar, a large, inflated
tubular device attached to a space
vehicle immediately after splash-
down to prevent sinking.

flo·til·la (flō til′ə), *n.* 1. a group of
small naval vessels. 2. a small fleet.

flot·sam (flot′səm), *n.* the wreckage
of a ship and its cargo found floating
on the water.

flounce¹ (flouns), *v.,* **flounced, flounc-**
ing, *n.* —*v.i.* 1. to go with an impatient or angry movement of the
body. 2. to twist or jerk abruptly.
—*n.* 3. the action of flouncing.

flounce² (flouns), *n.* a strip of material, wider than a ruffle, gathered
at one edge, esp. on a woman's
skirt.

floun·der (floun′dər), *v.i.* 1. to
struggle with stumbling or plunging
movements. 2. to struggle clumsily
or helplessly in embarrassment or
confusion. —**floun′der·ing·ly,** *adv.*

floun·der² (floun′dər), *n., pl.* **-der,**
ders. a flatfish used for food.

flour (flour, flou′ər), *n.* 1. the finely
ground meal of grain, esp. wheat. 2.
any fine, soft powder. —*v.t.* 3. to
sprinkle or dredge with flour. —
flour′y, *adj.*

flour·ish (flûr′ish, flur′-), *v.i.* 1. to be

or grow in a vigorous state. 2. to be
at the height of fame, excellence,
influence, etc. 3. to be successful
markedly. —*v.t.* 4. to brandish or
wave (a sword, etc.) about in the
air. —*n.* 5. a brandishing or waving,
as of a sword. 6. a decoration or
embellishment in writing. 7. a dramatic display, act, etc. 8. *Music.*
an elaborate passage largely for
display. —Syn. 1-3. prosper, thrive.

flout (flout), *v.t., v.i.* 1. to show disdainful disregard (for). —*n.* 2. *Ar-*
chaic. a flouting remark or act. —
flout′er, *n.*
—Usage. See flaunt.

flow (flō), *v.i.* 1. to move along in
a stream. 2. to circulate, as the
blood. 3. to stream or well forth. 4.
to issue from a source. 5. to men-
struate. 6. to proceed continuously
and smoothly, as speech, etc. 7. to
fall or hang loosely at full length,
as hair. 8. to abound. 9. to rise
and advance, as the tide. —*v.t.* 10.
to cause or permit to flow. —*n.* 11.
the act of flowing. 12. movement in
a stream. 13. any continuous movement, as of thought, etc. 14. the
rate of flowing. 15. something that
flows. 16. an outpouring or discharge. 17. menstruation. 18. an
overflowing. 19. the rise of the tide.

flow′ chart′, a schematic representation of a sequence of steps involved,
as in a manufacturing process or
computer operation. Also called
flow′ di′agram.

flow·er (flou′ər), *n.* 1. that part of a
seed plant comprising the reproductive organs and their envelopes if
any, esp. when such envelopes are
more or less conspicuous in form and
color, and often sweet-smelling. 2.
a plant cultivated for its beauty. 3.
a state of efflorescence or bloom.
4. the most flourishing state or period. 5. the finest product or example: *the flower of American youth.*
—*v.i.* 6. to produce flowers. 7. to
come out into full development. —
flow′ered (flou′ərd), *adj.* —**flow′er-**
less, *adj.*

flow′er girl′, a young girl at a wedding ceremony who precedes the
bride and carries flowers.

flow′er head′, a dense cluster of
florets.

flow·er·pot (flou′ər pot′), *n.* a container, usually a clay pot, in which
to grow plants.

flow·er·y (flou′ə rē), *adj.* 1. covered
with or having many flowers. 2. full
of highly ornate language, etc. —
flow′er·i·ness, *n.*

flown (flōn), *v.* a pp. of **fly¹.**

fl. oz., See **fluid ounce.**

flu (floo), *n. Informal.* influenza.

flub (flub), v., **flubbed, flub·bing,** n. *Informal.* —v.t., v.i. **1.** to make an embarrassing bungle (of). —n. **2.** something flubbed.

fluc·tu·ate (fluk′chŏŏ āt′), v.i., **-at·ed, -at·ing. 1.** to change continually from one position, condition, etc., to another. **2.** to move in waves or like waves. —**fluc′tu·a′tion,** n. — Syn. 1. vacillate, waver.

flue (flŏŏ), n. a passage or duct for smoke in a chimney.

flu·ent (flŏŏ′ənt), adj. **1.** spoken or written effortlessly: *fluent French.* **2.** able to speak or write smoothly, easily, or readily. **3.** capable of flowing, or fluid, as liquids or gases. —**flu′en·cy,** n. —**flu′ent·ly,** adv. — Syn. 1, 2. facile, glib, voluble.

fluff (fluf), n. **1.** light, downy particles, as of cotton. **2.** a soft, light, downy mass. **3.** a light, frivolous thing. **4.** *Informal.* an error or blunder, esp. one made by an actor. —v.t., v.i. **5.** to shake or puff out (feathers, etc.) into a fluffy mass. **6.** *Informal.* to make a mistake (in).

fluff·y (fluf′ē), adj., **fluff·i·er, fluff·i·est. 1.** of, resembling, or covered with fluff. **2.** light or airy. **3.** having little or no intellectual weight.

flu·id (flŏŏ′id), n. **1.** a substance, as a liquid or gas, which changes its shape at a steady rate when acted upon by a force. —adj. **2.** capable of flowing. **3.** consisting of or pertaining to fluids. **4.** changing readily, as a plan. **5.** convertible into cash, as assets. —**flu·id′i·ty, flu′id·ness,** n. —**flu′id·ly,** adv.

flu′id dram′, the eighth part of a fluid ounce.

flu′id drive′, *Auto.* a coupling mechanism consisting of two rotors with vanes operating in oil, to permit the car's smooth starting.

flu·id·ics (flŏŏ id′iks), n. the technology dealing with the use of a flowing liquid or gas in various devices, as controls, to perform functions, as sensing, amplifying, or computing.

flu′id ounce′, a measure of capacity equal to 1.8047 cubic inches (2.957 centiliters) in the U.S. and to 1.7339 cubic inches in Great Britain.

fluke¹ (flŏŏk), n. **1.** the part of an anchor that catches in the ground. **2.** the barbed head of a harpoon, spear, etc. **3.** either half of the triangular tail of a whale.

fluke² (flŏŏk), n. a stroke of good luck.

fluke³ (flŏŏk), n. **1.** any of several flounders or various other flatfishes. **2.** a trematode that infects human beings.

fluk·y (flŏŏ′kē), adj., **fluk·i·er, fluk·i·est.** *Informal.* obtained by chance rather than skill. —**fluk′i·ness,** n.

flume (flŏŏm), n. **1.** a deep narrow valley containing a stream or torrent. **2.** an artificial channel for conducting water.

flung (flung), v. pt. and pp. of fling.

flunk (flungk), v.i., v.t. *Informal.* to fail, as in a recitation or examination.

flun·ky (flung′kē), n., pl. **-kies. 1.** *Disparaging.* a male servant in livery. **2.** a servile follower. Also, flun′key.

flu·o·resce (flŏŏ′ə res′, flŏŏ res′, flō-, flō-), v.i., **-resced, -resc·ing.** to exhibit fluorescence.

flu·o·res·cence (flŏŏ′ə res′əns, flŏŏ-res′-, flō-, flō-), n. **1.** the emission of radiation, esp. of visible light, by a substance during exposure to external radiation, as light or x-rays. **2.** the radiation so produced. —**flu′o·res′cent,** adj.

fluores′cent lamp′, a tubular electric lamp in which light is produced by the fluorescence of phosphors coating the inside of the tube.

fluor·i·date (flŏŏr′i dāt′, flōr′-, flōr′-), v.t., **-dat·ed, -dat·ing.** to introduce a fluoride into. —**fluor′i·da′tion,** n.

flu·o·ride (flŏŏ′ə rīd′, flŏŏr′īd, flōr′-, flōr′-), n. **1.** a salt of hydrofluoric acid. **2.** a compound containing fluorine.

fluor·i·nate (flŏŏr′ə nāt′, -flōr′-, flōr′-), v.t., **-nat·ed, -nat·ing.** to treat or combine with fluorine. —**fluor′i·na′tion,** n.

flu·o·rine (flŏŏ′ə rēn′, -rin, flŏŏr′ēn, -in, flōr′-, flōr′-), n. *Chem.* the most reactive nonmetallic element, a pale-yellow, corrosive toxic gas that occurs combined, esp. in minerals. *Symbol:* F; *at. wt.:* 18.9984; *at. no.:* 9.

flu·o·rite (flŏŏ′ə rīt′, flŏŏr′īt, flōr′-, flōr′-), n. a common mineral, the principal source of fluorine.

flu·o·ro·car·bon (flŏŏ′ə rō kär′bən, flŏŏr′ō-, flōr′-, flōr′-), n. any of a class of compounds produced by substituting fluorine for hydrogen in a hydrocarbon: used chiefly as a lubricant.

fluor·o·scope (flŏŏr′ə skōp′, flōr′-, flōr′-, flŏŏ′ər ə-), n. a tube or box fitted with a screen coated with a fluorescent substance, used for viewing objects by means of x-ray or other radiation. —**fluor·o·scop·ie** (flŏŏr′ē skop′ik, flōr′-, flōr′-, flŏŏ′ər ə-), adj. —**fluo·ros′co·pist,** n. —**fluor·os·co·py** (flŏŏ ros′kə pē, flō-, flō-, flŏŏ′ə ros′-), n.

flur·ry (flûr′ē, flur′ē), n., pl. **-ries,** v., **-ried, -ry·ing.** —n. **1.** a shower of snow. **2.** *Chiefly Brit.* a sudden gust of wind. **3.** sudden commotion, excitement, or confusion. **4.** a brief, unusual activity of stock trading. —v.t. **5.** to put (a person) into a flurry. —v.i. **6.** to move in a flurry. [*fl(utter)* + *(h)urry*]

flush¹ (flush), *n.* **1.** a rosy glow. **2.** a rushing flow, as of water. **3.** a sudden rise of emotion or excitement: *a flush of anger.* **4.** glowing freshness or vigor. **5.** the hot stage of a fever. —*v.t.* **6.** to cause to blush or glow. **7.** to flood with water, as for cleansing purposes. **8.** to wash out (a sewer, toilet, etc.) by a sudden rush of water. **9.** to excite or inflame. —*v.i.* **10.** to blush or redden. **11.** to flow and spread suddenly. **12.** to become flushed with water.

flush² (flush), *adj.* **1.** even or level, as with a surface. **2.** having or in direct or immediate contact. **3.** well-supplied, as with money. **4.** abundant or plentiful. **5.** having a ruddy color. **6.** full of vigor. **7.** full to overflowing. —*adv.* **8.** on the same level or directly in a straight line. **9.** squarely.

flush³ (flush), *Hunting.* —*v.t.* **1.** to rouse and cause to start up or fly off. —*v.i.* **2.** to fly out or start up suddenly.

flush⁴ (flush), *n.* a hand or set of cards all of one suit.

flus·ter (flus′tər), *v.t., v.i.* **1.** to make or become nervously confused. —*n.* **2.** nervous confusion.

flute (floot), *n.* **1.** a musical wind instrument consisting of a tube with a series of finger holes or keys, in which the wind is directed against a sharp edge. **2.** a channel or groove, as on the shaft of a column. —*fluted*, *adj.* —*fluting*, *n.*

flut·ist (floo′tist), *n.* a flute player.

flut·ter (flut′ər), *v.t.* **1.** to wave, flap, or toss about in the air, as a flag. **2.** (of birds) to flap the wings. **3.** to move in quick, irregular motions. **4.** to beat rapidly and irregularly, as the heart. —*v.t.* **5.** to cause to flutter. —*n.* **6.** a fluttering movement. **7.** a state of nervous excitement or mental agitation. **8.** sensation or stir: *to cause a flutter.* —*flut′ter·er*, *n.* —*flut′ter·y*, *adj.*

flux (fluks), *n.* **1.** a flowing or flow. **2.** continuous change. **3.** an abnormal discharge of liquid matter from the bowels. **4.** a substance used to remove oxides from and prevent further oxidation of fused metal, as in soldering. —*v.t.* **5.** to melt or make fluid. **6.** to fuse by the use of flux.

fly¹ (flī), *v.*, **flew** or, for 8, **flied;** **flown** or, for 8, **flied; fly·ing;** *n., pl.* **flies.** —*v.i.* **1.** to move through the air on wings, as a bird. **2.** to be carried through the air by the wind or any other force. **3.** to float or flutter in the air, as a kite or flag. **4.** to travel through the air or outer space in an aircraft, rocket, or satellite. **5.** to move suddenly and quickly. **6.** to flee or escape. **7.** to pass swiftly. **8.** *Baseball.* to bat a fly ball. —*v.t.* **9.** to make (something) float or move through the air. **10.** to operate (an aircraft, spaceship, or the like). **11.** to hoist aloft, as for display, signaling, etc. **12.** to operate an aircraft over. **13.** to transport or convey (something) by air. **14.** to escape from. **15.** **fly at** or **into,** to attack, either verbally or physically. **16.** **let fly, a.** to hurl or propel (a weapon, etc.). **b.** to give free rein to an emotion. —*n.* **17.** a fold of material along one edge of a garment opening for concealing buttons or other fasteners. **18.** a flap forming the door of a tent. **19.** See **fly ball. 20. flies,** the space above the stage, used chiefly for storing scenery and equipment. **21. on the fly, a.** during flight. **b.** without pausing. —*fly′a·ble, adj.*

fly² (flī), *n., pl.* **flies. 1.** any of numerous two-winged insects, esp. the common housefly. **2.** a fishhook dressed with feathers, etc., to resemble an insect.

fly′ ball′, *Baseball.* a ball that is batted up into the air.

fly-blown (flī′blōn′), *adj.* spoiled or tainted, as by flies' eggs.

fly-by (flī′bī′), *n., pl.* **-bys.** a flight, usually at low altitude, past a given point by an airplane, helicopter, or spacecraft.

fly-by-night (flī′bī nīt′), *adj.* **1.** not reliable or responsible, esp. in business. **2.** dubiously transitory. —*n.* **3.** a person or thing that is fly-by-night.

fly-by-wire (flī′bī wī°r′), *adj.* activated entirely by electrical controls connected by fine but strong wires between the device and the controller: *a fly-by-wire helicopter.*

fly′ cast′ing, the act or technique of casting with an artificial fly as the lure.

fly·catch·er (flī′kach′ər), *n.* a bird that feeds on insects captured in the air.

fly·er (flī′ər), *n.* flier.

fly′ing boat′, a seaplane whose main body consists of a single hull that supports it on water.

fly′ing but′tress, a segmental arch which carries the thrust of the nave wall over the aisle to a solid pier buttress.

fly′ing col′ors, triumphal success.

fly′ing fish′, a fish having stiff, enlarged fins enabling it to glide considerable distances through the air.

fly′ing sau′cer, any of various disk-shaped objects allegedly seen flying at high speeds and altitudes, and generally presumed to be from outer space.

fly′ing squir′rel, a squirrellike animal

having folds of skin connecting the fore and hind legs, that enable it to take long gliding leaps.

fly'ing start', a vigorous and enthusiastic beginning.

fly-leaf (flī'lēf'), *n., pl.* **-leaves.** a blank leaf in the front or the back of a book.

fly-pa-per (flī'pā'pər), *n.* paper designed to kill flies by poisoning them or catching them on its sticky surface.

fly-speck (flī'spek'), *n.* **1.** a tiny stain from the excrement of a fly. **2.** a minute spot.

fly-way (flī'wā'), *n.* specific air route taken by birds during migration.

fly-weight (flī'wāt'), *n.* a boxer weighing up to 112 pounds.

fly-wheel (flī'hwēl', -wēl'), *n.* a heavy disk rotating on a shaft so that its momentum gives almost uniform rotational speed.

FM, 1. frequency modulation: a method of impressing a signal on a radio carrier wave by varying the frequency of the carrier wave. **2.** a system of radio broadcasting by this means.

Fm, fermium.

fm., 1. fathom. **2.** from.

fn, footnote.

f number, a number corresponding to the ratio of the focal length to the diameter of a lens system.

fo., folio.

F.O., 1. Foreign Office. **2.** *Mil.* forward observer.

foal (fōl), *n.* **1.** a young horse, mule, etc., esp. one less than one year of age. —*v.t., v.i.* **2.** to give birth to (a colt or filly).

foam (fōm), *n.* **1.** a collection of minute bubbles formed on the surface of a liquid by agitation, fermentation, etc. **2.** the froth formed on the skin of a horse or other animal. **3.** a lightweight material of stiff, porous plastic, used esp. in packaging. —*v.i.* **4.** to form or gather foam. —**foam'y,** *adj.* —**foam'-ness,** *n.*

foam' rub'ber, a light, spongy rubber used for mattresses, cushions, etc.

fob¹ (fob), *n.* **1.** a short chain or ribbon attached to a watch and worn hanging from a pocket. **2.** a medallion or other ornament worn on such a chain.

fob² (fob), *v.t.,* **fobbed, fob-bing. 1.** *Archaic.* to deceive. **2. fob off, a.** to cheat by substituting something inferior. **b.** to put off by deception or trickery.

f.o.b., free on board (for the quoted price that includes delivery onto a carrier). Also, **F.O.B.**

fo-cal (fō'kəl), *adj.* of or pertaining to focus. —**fo'cal-ly,** *adv.*

fo'cal length', the distance between a focal point of a lens or mirror and the corresponding principal plane.

fo'cal plane', a plane through a focal point and normal to the axis of a lens, mirror, or other optical system.

fo'cal point', 1. the centre or principal point of focus. **2.** the center of activity or attention.

fo'c's'le, (fōk'səl), *n.* forecastle. Also, **fo'c's'le.**

fo-cus (fō'kəs), *n., pl.* **-cus-es,** or **(-sī)** *v.,* **-cused, -cus-ing** or **-cussed, -cus-sing.** —*n.* **1.** a point at which rays of light, heat, or other radiation meet after being refracted or reflected. **2. a.** the focal length. **b.** the position of a viewed object or the adjustment of an optical device necessary to produce a clear image: *out of focus.* **3.** See **focal point.** —*v.t.* **4.** to bring to a focus or into focus. **5.** to concentrate —*v.i.* **6.** to become focused.

fod-der (fod'ər), *n.* coarse food for livestock.

foe (fō), *n.* **1.** a person who feels enmity or malice toward another. **2.** an enemy in war. **3.** an opponent in a game or contest.

foehn (fān), *n.* a warm, dry wind descending a mountain. Also, **föhn.**

foe-man (fō'mən), *n. Archaic.* an enemy.

foe-tus (fē'təs), *n.* fetus. —**foe'tal,** *adj.*

fog (fog, fôg), *n., v.,* **fogged, fog-ging.** —*n.* **1.** a cloudlike mass of minute water droplets near the surface of the earth, reducing visibility. **2.** a state of mental confusion or obscurity. **3.** *Photog.* a hazy effect on a negative or positive. —*v.t., v.i.* **4.** to envelop or obscure or to become enveloped or obscured with or as with fog. —**fog'gy,** *adj.* —**fog'gi-ly,** *adv.* —**fog'gi-ness,** *n.*

fog-horn (fog'hôrn', fôg'-), *n.* a deep, loud horn for sounding warning signals to ships in time of fog.

fo-gy (fō'gē), *n., pl.* **-gies.** an excessively conservative or old-fashioned person. Also, **fo'gey.** —**fo'gy-ish,** *adj.*

foi-ble (foi'bəl), *n.* a slight, often amusing weakness of character

foil¹ (foil), *v.t.* **1.** to prevent the success of (a plan, etc.). **2.** to keep (a person) from succeeding in a plan, etc.

foil² (foil), *n.* **1.** metal in very thin sheets: *aluminum foil.* **2.** a person or thing that makes another seem better by contrast.

foil³ (foil), *n.* a flexible four-sided rapier having a blunt point.

foist (foist), *v.t.* to force upon or impose fraudulently or unjustifiably.

fol., 1. folio. 2. followed. 3. following.

fold[1] (fōld), *v.t.* 1. to bend (cloth, paper, etc.) over upon itself. 2. to bring into a compact form by bending and laying parts together. 3. to bring (the arms, hands, etc.) together in an intertwined or crossed manner. 4. to enclose or wrap. 5. to clasp or embrace. 6. to mix in or add by gently turning one part over another. —*v.i.* 7. to be folded or be capable of folding. 8. to end or close, esp. through lack of patronage. 9. to fail or collapse. —*n.* 10. a part that is folded. 11. a crease made by folding.

fold[2] (fōld), *n.* 1. an enclosure for sheep or other domestic animals. 2. a flock of sheep. 3. a group sharing common beliefs, values, etc. —*v.t.* 4. to confine (sheep) in a fold.

-fold, a suffix meaning "of so many parts" or denoting the multiplication by the number indicated: *manifold; twofold.*

fold·a·way (fōld′ə wā′), *adj.* designed to be folded out of the way when not in use: *a foldaway bed.*

fold·boat (fōld′bōt′), *n.* faltboat.

fold·er (fōl′dər), *n.* 1. a person or thing that folds. 2. a printed sheet, as a circular, folded into pagelike sections. 3. a folded sheet of light cardboard used to cover or hold papers, letters, etc.

fol·de·rol (fol′də rol′), *n.* 1. mere nonsense. 2. a flimsy trifle.

fold·out (fōld′out′), *n.* an outsize page of a book or periodical, folded so as not to extend beyond the edges.

fo·li·age (fō′lē ij), *n.* the leaves of a plant, collectively.

fo·li·ar (fō′lē ər), *adj.* of or having the nature of a leaf or leaves.

fo·li·at·ed (fō′lē ā′tid), *adj.* shaped like a leaf or leaves: *foliated ornaments.*

fo′lic ac′ld (fō′lik, fol′ik), a synthetic form of one of the B-complex vitamins, used in treating anemia.

fo·li·o (fō′lē ō′), *n., pl.* **-li·os.** 1. the number of each page. 2. a sheet of paper folded once to make two leaves (four pages) of a book. 3. a volume having pages of the largest size formerly made from such a sheet.

folk (fōk), *n.* 1. Usually, **folks.** people in general. 2. Often, **folks.** people of a specified class or group: *poor folks.* 3. **folks,** *Informal.* members of one's family. —*adj.* 4. originating among the common people: *folk music.*

folk·lore (fōk′lōr′, -lôr′), *n.* the traditional beliefs, legends, customs, etc., of a people. —**folk′lor′ist,** *n.*

folk′ mass′, a liturgical mass in which folk music is used in place of traditional music.

folk′ mu′sic, music, usually of anonymous origin and usually simple in melody and lyric.

folk′ rock′, a style of music combining characteristics of rock-'n'-roll and folk music.

folk′ sing′er, a singer who specializes in folk songs —**folk′ sing′ing.**

folk·sy (fōk′sē), *adj.,* **-si·er, -si·est.** 1. sociable or neighborly. 2. casual or familiar.

folk·ways (fōk′wāz′), *n.pl.* the traditional patterns of life common to a people.

foll., following.

fol·li·cle (fol′i kəl), *n.* a small cavity, sac, or gland.

fol·low (fol′ō), *v.t.* 1. to come after in sequence, time, etc. 2. to go or come after. 3. to comply with or obey. 4. to imitate or copy. 5. to move forward along (a road, etc.). 6. to result from. 7. to engage in as a pursuit. 8. to watch the movements or course of. 9. to keep up with and understand. —*v.i.* 10. to come next after something or someone else in sequence, time, etc. 11. to result as an effect. 12. **follow out** or **up,** to carry to a conclusion. 13. **follow through,** to carry out fully. —**fol′lower,** *n.*

fol·low·ing (fol′ō ing), *n.* 1. a body of followers, adherents, etc. 2. —*adj.* 2. that follows. 3. that comes next in order or time.

fol·low-up (fol′ō up′), *n.* subsequent attention, action, etc.

fol·ly (fol′ē), *n., pl.* **-lies.** 1. the state or quality of being foolish. 2. a foolish action, idea, etc. 3. a costly and foolish undertaking, as an unwise investment.

fo·ment (fō ment′), *v.t.* 1. to instigate or foster (discord, etc.). 2. to apply warm liquid, ointments, etc., to (the surface of the body). —**fo′men·ta′tion,** *n.* —**fo·ment′er,** *n.*

fond (fond), *adj.* 1. having a liking for: *fond of sweets.* 2. loving or affectionate: *a fond look.* 3. excessively tender. 4. cherished with unreasoning feeling. —**fond′ly,** *adv.* —**fond′ness,** *n.*

fon·dant (fon′dənt), *n.* a thick, creamy sugar paste, the basis of many candies.

fon·dle (fon′dəl), *v.t.,* **-dled, -dling.** to handle or touch lovingly or tenderly.

fon·due (fon dōō′, fon′dōō), *n.* melted cheese and seasonings, together with dry white wine, served with bread. Also, **fon·du′.**

font[1] (font), *n.* **1.** a receptacle for the water used in baptism. **2.** stoup. **3.** *Archaic.* **a.** a fountain. **b.** a source.

font[2] (font), *n.* *Print.* a complete assortment of type of one style and size.

fon·ti·na (fon tē′nə), *n.* a type of Italian cheese, semisoft to firm, made of ewe's milk.

food (fōōd), *n.* **1.** any nourishing substance eaten or otherwise taken into the body to sustain life, promote growth, etc. **2.** solid nourishment, as distinguished from liquids. **3.** any nourishment: *a plant food.* **4.** anything serving for consumption or use: *food for thought.*

food′ chain′, a series of organisms interrelated in their feeding habits, each being fed upon by a larger one that in turn feeds a still larger one.

food′ poi′soning, an acute gastrointestinal condition caused by foods that are toxic or contaminated.

food′ proc′essor, a powerful multipurpose kitchen appliance for the grinding, slicing, shredding, pureeing, etc., of foods.

food′ stamp′, any of the coupons sold under a federal program to eligible needy persons at a price lower than their face value, redeemable at face value only for food.

food·stuff (fōōd′stuf′), *n.* a substance used or capable of being used as nutriment.

food′ web′, a series of interrelated food chains. Also called **food′ cy′cle.**

fool (fōōl), *n.* **1.** a silly or stupid person. **2.** a person who has been made to appear silly or stupid. **3.** jester (def. 2). —*v.t.* **4.** to trick or deceive. —*v.i.* **5.** to act like a fool. **6.** to jest or pretend. **7. fool around, a.** to putter aimlessly. **b.** to philander. **8. fool with,** to play with idly. [< L *foll(is)* bag]

fool·er·y (fōō′lə rē), *n.,* *pl.* **-er·ies. 1.** foolish behavior. **2.** a foolish action or thing.

fool·har·dy (fōōl′här′dē), *adj.,* **-di·er, -di·est.** bold without judgment. —**fool′har′di·ly,** *adv.* —**fool′har′di·ness,** *n.*

fool·ish (fōō′lish), *adj.* **1.** lacking common sense or good judgment. **2.** resulting from or showing a lack of forethought or prudence. **3.** abashedly embarrassed. —**fool′ish·ly,** *adv.* —**fool′ish·ness,** *n.* —Syn. **1, 2.** fatuous, inane, unwise.

fool·proof (fōōl′prōōf′), *adj.* involving no risk or harm, even when tampered with.

fools·cap (fōōlz′kap′), *n.* *Chiefly Brit.* a size of drawing or printing paper, 13½ × 17 inches.

fool's′ gold′, chalcopyrite or iron pyrites, sometimes mistaken for gold.

fool's′ par′adise, enjoyment based on false beliefs or hopes.

foot (fōōt), *n.,* *pl.* **feet,** *v.* —*n.* **1.** the terminal part of the leg, below the ankle joint, on which the body stands and moves. **2.** any part similar in position or function. **3.** a unit of length equal to 12 inches or equivalent to 30.48 centimeters. **4.** *Chiefly Brit.* infantry. **5.** the part of a stocking, sock, etc., covering the foot. **6.** the lowest part, or bottom, as of a hill, ladder, page, etc. **7.** the part of anything opposite the top or head: *the foot of a bed.* **8.** a group of stressed and unstressed syllables constituting a metrical unit of a verse. **9. on foot,** by walking. **10. put one's foot down,** to take a firm stand. **11. under foot,** in the way. —*v.i.* **12.** to walk. **13.** to move the feet rhythmically, as in dance. —*v.t.* **14.** to walk or dance on. **15.** *Informal.* to pay or settle, as a bill.

foot·age (fōōt′ij), *n.* **1.** length or extent in feet. **2.** a motion-picture scene or scenes: *newsreel footage.*

foot·ball (fōōt′bôl′), *n.* **1.** *U.S.* **a.** a game, played with a ball, in which two opposing teams of 11 players each defend goals at opposite ends of a field. **b.** the ball used in this game. **2.** *Brit.* **a.** Rugby. **b.** soccer.

foot·board (fōōt′bôrd′, -bōrd′), *n.* **1.** a board or platform on which to support the feet. **2.** an upright piece across the foot of a bedstead.

foot·bridge (fōōt′brij′), *n.* a bridge intended for pedestrians only.

foot·can·dle (fōōt′kan′dəl), *n.* a unit of illumination, equivalent to the illumination produced by a source of one candle at a distance of one foot.

foot·ed (fōōt′id), *adj.* having a foot or feet (often used in combination): *a four-footed animal.*

foot·fall (fōōt′fôl′), *n.* the sound of a footstep.

foot·hill (fōōt′hil′), *n.* a low hill at the base of a mountain or mountain range.

foot·hold (fōōt′hōld′), *n.* **1.** a place where a person may stand or tread securely. **2.** a firm basis for further progress.

foot·ing (fōōt′ing), *n.* **1.** a secure and established position or basis. **2.** the basis or foundation on which anything is established. **3.** a place or support for the feet. **4.** a moving on foot, as in walking. **5.** a firm placing of the feet. **6.** position or status assigned to a person, group, etc. **7.** *Bookkeeping.* **a.** the act of adding up a column of figures. **b.** the total of such a column.

foot·less (foŏt′lis), *adj.* **1.** lacking feet. **2.** having no support or basis. **3.** *Informal.* awkward or inefficient. —**foot′less·ness**, *n.*

foot·light (foŏt′līt′), *n.* **1.** Usually, **footlights.** the lights at the front of a stage that are nearly on a level with the feet of the performers. **2.** **the footlights.** the acting profession.

foot·lock·er (foŏt′lok′ər), *n.* a small trunk for containing personal effects.

foot·loose (foŏt′lōōs′), *adj.* free to go or travel about.

foot·man (foŏt′mən), *n.* a liveried servant who attends the door or carriage, waits on table, etc.

foot·note (foŏt′nōt′), *n.*, *v.*, **-not·ed,** **-not·ing.** —*n.* **1.** an explanatory comment or reference note at the bottom of a page. —*v.t.* **2.** to add footnotes to.

foot·pad¹ (foŏt′pad′), *n.* *Archaic.* a highwayman or robber who goes on foot.

foot·pad² (foŏt′pad′), *n.* one of the broad, padded legs of a lunar spacecraft.

foot·path (foŏt′path′, -päth′), *n.* a path for pedestrians.

foot·pound (foŏt′pound′), *n.* a unit of energy equal to the work done by a force of one pound through a distance of one foot.

foot·print (foŏt′print′), *n.* a mark left by the foot, as in earth, sand, etc.

foot·rest (foŏt′rest′), *n.* a support for a person's feet.

foot′ sol′dier, an infantryman.

foot·sore (foŏt′sōr′, -sôr′), *adj.* having sore or tender feet, as from much walking.

foot·step (foŏt′step′), *n.* **1.** the setting down of a foot, or the sound so produced. **2.** the distance covered by a step. **3.** a footprint. **4.** a step by which to ascend or descend.

foot·stool (foŏt′stōōl′), *n.* a low stool upon which to rest one's feet while seated.

foot·wear (foŏt′wâr′), *n.* articles to be worn on the feet, as shoes or slippers.

foot·work (foŏt′wûrk′), *n.* the use of the feet, as in boxing.

fop (fop), *n.* a man who is excessively vain and concerned about his manners and appearance. —**fop′per·y,** *n.* —**fop′pish,** *adj.*

for (fôr; *unstressed* fər), *prep.* **1.** with the object or purpose of: *to run for exercise.* **2.** intended to belong to or be used in connection with: *a closet for dishes.* **3.** suiting the purposes or needs of: *medicine for the aged.* **4.** directed to or focused upon: *a longing for something.* **5.** in consideration of or in return for: *three for a dollar.* **6.** appropriate or

adapted to: *clothes for winter.* **7.** with regard or respect to: *pressed for time.* **8.** during the continuance of: *for a long time.* **9.** in favor of: *to be for honest government.* **10.** instead of. **11.** on behalf of: *to act for a client.* **12.** in exchange for: *blow for blow.* **13.** in honor of: *to give a dinner for a person.* **14.** with the purpose of reaching: *to start for London.* **15.** in assignment to: *That's for you to decide.* **16.** such as results in: *her reason for going.* **17.** in proportion or with reference to: *He's tall for his age.* **18.** as being: *to know a thing for a fact.* **19.** because of: *to shout for joy.* **20.** in spite of: *He's a decent guy for all that.* **21.** to the extent or amount of. **22.** (used to introduce an infinitive phrase equivalent to a construction with a relative clause): *It's time for me to go.* —*conj.* **23.** because.

for., **1.** foreign. **2.** forester. **3.** forestry.

F.O.R., *Com.* free on rails.

fo·ra (fôr′ə, fōr′ə), *n.* a pl. of **forum.**

for·age (fôr′ij, for′-), *n.*, *v.*, **-aged,** **-ag·ing.** —*n.* **1.** food for horses or cattle. **2.** the seeking of such food. —*v.i.* **3.** to go in search of provisions. **4.** to search about. **5.** to make a raid. —*v.t.* **6.** to collect forage from. —**for′ag·er,** *n.*

fo·ra·men (fō rā′mən, fō-, fə-), *n.*, *pl.* **-ram·i·na** (-ram′ə nə). an opening or orifice, as in a bone.

for·as·much as (fôr′əz much′-, fôr′-), *Chiefly Law.* in view of the fact that.

for·ay (fôr′ā, for′ā), *n.* **1.** a quick raid, usually for plunder. **2.** a quick, sudden attack. —*v.i.,* *v.t.* **3.** to raid or ravage, esp. in search of plunder.

for·bear¹ (fôr bâr′), *v.,* **-bore,** **-borne,** **-bear·ing.** —*v.t.* **1.** to refrain patiently from. —*v.i.* **2.** to hold back. **3.** to be patient or self-controlled. —**for·bear′ance,** *n.* —**for·bear′er,** *n.*

for·bear² (fôr′bâr′), *n.* *Brit.* forebear.

for·bid (fər bid′, fôr-), *v.t.,* **-bade** (-bad′, -bād′) *or* **bad** (-bad′), **-bid·den** (-bid′n) *or* (*Archaic*) **-bid,** **-bid·ding.** **1.** to command (a person) not to do something, have something, etc. **2.** to prohibit, esp. directly or personally. **3.** to hinder or prevent. **4.** to exclude or bar. —**Syn.** 1, 2. ban, interdict, proscribe.

for·bid·ding (fər bid′ing, fôr-), *adj.* **1.** grimly hostile. **2.** dangerous or threatening. —**for·bid′ding·ly,** *adv.*

force (fōrs, fôrs), *n.,* *v.,* **forced, forc·ing.** —*n.* **1.** strength exerted. **2.** power to influence, affect, or control. **3.** physical coercion or violence. **4.** persuasive power or power to convince. **5.** Often, **forces.** the military or fighting strength, esp. of a nation. **6.** any body of persons combined for joint action: *a police force.* **7.** an influence on a body or system, producing a change in movement or in shape. **8. in force, a.** effective or valid. **b.** at full strength. —*v.t.* **9.** to compel unwillingly. **10.** to bring about or effect by force. **11.** to impose forcibly on or upon a person. **12.** to overcome the resistance of. **13.** to obtain by or as if by force. **14.** to break open (a door, etc.). **15.** to cause (plants, fruits, etc.) to grow faster by artificial means. —**forced** (fôrst, fōrst), *adj.* —**force′less,** *adj.* —Syn. **9.** coerce, constrain, oblige.

forced′ march′, any march that is longer or faster than troops are accustomed to.

force-feed (fôrs′fēd′, fōrs′-), *v.t.,* **-fed, -feed-ing.** to compel to eat or take food into the body.

force-ful (fôrs′fəl, fōrs′-), *adj.* **1.** full of force. **2.** powerful or vigorous. —**force′ful-ly,** *adv.* —**force′ful-ness,** *n.*

for-ceps (fôr′səps, -seps), *n., pl.* **-ceps.** an instrument for seizing and holding objects, esp. in surgical operations.

for-ci-ble (fôr′sə bəl, fōr′-), *adj.* **1.** effected by force. **2.** producing a powerful effect. —**for′ci-ble-ness,** *n.* —**for′ci-bly,** *adv.*

ford (fôrd, fōrd), *n.* **1.** a place where a river is shallow enough to be crossed by wading. —*v.t.* **2.** to cross by a ford.

Ford (fôrd, fōrd), *n.* **1. Gerald R.,** born 1913, 38th president of the U.S. 1974–76. **2. Henry,** 1863–1947, U.S. automobile manufacturer.

fore¹ (fôr, fōr), *adj.* **1.** situated at or toward the front. **2.** first in place, time, order, etc. —*adv.* **3.** *Naut.* at or toward the bow. —*n.* **4.** the forepart of anything.

fore² (fôr, fōr), *interj.* *Golf.* (a cry of warning to persons on a course who are in danger of being struck by the ball.)

fore-, a prefix meaning: **a.** before in time: *foretell.* **b.** front: *forehead.*

fore-and-aft (fôr′ənd aft′, -äft′, fōr′-), *adj.* *Naut.* located along or parallel to a line from the stem to the stern.

fore-arm¹ (fôr′ärm′, fōr′-), *n.* the part of the arm between the elbow and the wrist.

fore-arm² (fôr ärm′, fōr-), *v.t.* to arm beforehand.

fore-bear (fôr′bâr′, fōr′-), *n.* *Literary.* Usually, **forebears.** ancestors.

fore-bode (fôr bōd′, fōr-), *v.t., v.i.,* **-bod-ed, bod-ing. 1.** to indicate beforehand (esp. something harmful). **2.** *Literary.* to have a presentiment of (esp. coming evil). —**fore-bod′ing,** *n., adj.*

fore-cast (fôr′kast′, -käst′, fōr′-), *v.,*

-**cast** or **-cast-ed, -cast-ing,** *n.* —*v.t.* **1.** to state expected future occurrences in (esp. weather conditions). **2.** to serve as a prediction of. —*n.* **3.** a prediction, esp. as to the weather. —**fore′cast′er,** *n.*

fore-cas-tle (fōk′səl, fôr′kas′əl, -kä′səl, fōr′-), *n.* **1.** a superstructure at or immediately aft of the bow of a vessel. **2.** the quarters for sailors, located in the forward part of a vessel.

fore-close (fôr klōz′, fōr-), *v.t.,* **-closed, -clos-ing. 1.** to deprive (a mortgagor) of the right to redeem the property, esp. on failure to make payment when due. **2.** to exclude or bar.

fore-clos-ure (fôr klō′zhər, fōr-), *n.* the act of foreclosing a mortgage.

fore-doom (*v.* fôr dōōm′, fōr-; *n.* fôr′dōōm′, fōr′-), *v.t.* to doom beforehand.

fore-fa-ther (fôr′fä′t͟hər, fōr′-), *n.* *Chiefly Literary.* an ancestor.

fore-fend (fôr fend′, fōr-), *v.t.* *Obs.* to forfend.

fore-finger (fôr′fiñg′gər, fōr′-), *n.* the finger next to the thumb.

fore-foot (fôr′fŏŏt′, fōr′-), *n.* one of the front feet of a quadruped.

fore-front (fôr′frunt′, fōr′-), *n.* **1.** the foremost part or place. **2.** the position of major prominence.

fore-gath-er (fôr ga͟th′ər, fōr-), *v.i.* forgather.

fore-go¹ (fôr gō′, fōr-), *v.t.* **-went, -gone, -go-ing.** forgo.

fore-go² (fôr gō′, fōr-), *v.t., v.i.,* **-went, -gone, -go-ing.** *Rare.* to go before.

fore-go-ing (fôr gō′iñg, fōr-), *adj.* previously stated.

fore-gone (fôr gôn′, -gon′, fōr-; fôr′gôn′, -gon′, fōr′-), *adj.* just past.

fore′gone′ conclu′sion, an inevitable result.

fore-ground (fôr′ground′, fōr′-), *n.* **1.** the ground or parts situated in the front, as in a scene. **2.** forefront (def. 2).

fore-hand (fôr′hand′, fōr′-), *adj.* (in tennis, etc.) **1.** of or noting a stroke made from the same side of the body as that of the hand holding the racket, etc. —*n.* **2.** a forehand stroke.

fore-hand-ed (fôr′han′did, fōr′-), *adj.* **1.** forehand. **2.** *Obs.* thrifty or prudent.

fore-head (fôr′id, for′-; fôr′hed′, for′-), *n.* the part of the face above the eyes.

for-eign (fôr′in, for′-), *adj.* **1.** of or derived from another nation. **2.** of contact or dealings with other countries: *foreign policy.* **3.** carried on with other countries: *foreign trade.* **4.** belonging to or coming from another district, province, etc. **5.** not belonging to the place or body where found: *a speck of foreign matter.* —**fore'eign·ness,** *n.*

for·eign·er (fôr'ə nər, for'-), *n.* a person not native to or naturalized in a given country.

for'eign min'ister, the cabinet minister who conducts and supervises foreign and diplomatic relations with other states.

fore·know (fôr nō', fōr-), *v.t.,* -knew, -known, -know·ing. to know beforehand. —**fore'knowl·edge,** *n.*

fore·la·dy (fôr'lā'dē, fōr'-), *n.* a forewoman.

fore·land (fôr'land', fōr'-), *n.* a cape or promontory.

fore·leg (fôr'leg', fōr'-), *n.* one of the front legs of a quadruped.

fore·limb (fôr'lim', fōr'-), *n.* a front limb of a quadruped.

fore·lock (fôr'lok', fōr'-), *n.* the lock of hair that grows from the forepart of the head.

fore·man (fôr'mən, fōr'-), *n.* 1. a person in charge of a group of workers, etc. 2. the chairman of a jury.

fore·mast (fôr'mast', -mäst', fōr'-; *Naut.* fôr'məst, fōr'-), *n.* the mast nearest the bow of a vessel.

fore·most (fôr'mōst', -most, fōr'-), *adj., adv.* first in place, order, rank, etc.

fore·name (fôr'nām', fōr'-), *n. Rare.* a person's given name.

fore·named (fôr'nāmd', fōr'-), *adj.* named before.

fore·noon (fôr'nōōn', fōr'-; fōr'nōōn', fôr'-), *n.* the period of daylight before noon.

fo·ren·sic (fə ren'sik), *adj.* 1. pertaining to or used in legal proceedings, esp. with respect to questions of crime: *forensic medicine.* 2. of forensics. —*n.* 3. forensics, the art or study of argumentation and formal debate.

fore·or·dain (fôr'ôr dān', fōr'-), *v.t.* 1. to ordain or appoint beforehand. 2. to predestine or predetermine. —**fore'or·dain'ment,** *n.*

fore·part (fôr'pärt', fōr'-), *n.* the fore, front, or early part.

fore·play (fôr'plā', fōr'-), *n.* sexual stimulation intended as a prelude to sexual intercourse.

fore·quar·ter (fôr'kwôr'tər, fōr'-), *n.* the forward end of half of a carcass, as of beef.

fore·run·ner (fôr'run'ər, fōr'-, fôr-run'ər, fōr-), *n.* 1. a predecessor, as in technical progress. 2. a sign of something to follow. 3. a herald or harbinger.

fore·sail (fôr'sāl', fōr'-; *Naut.* fôr'səl, fōr'-), *n.* 1. the lowest sail on a foremast. 2. a triangular sail, set immediately forward of the mainmast of a yawl, ketch, etc.

fore·see (fôr sē', fōr-), *v.t., v.i.,* -saw,

-seen, -see·ing. to see or know beforehand. —**fore'see'a·ble,** *adj.* —**fore·se·er,** *n.* —**Syn.** anticipate, divine, forecast, predict.

fore·shad·ow (fôr shad'ō, fōr-), *v.t.* to show or warn of beforehand.

fore·sheet (fôr'shēt', fōr'-), *n.* 1. foresheets, the foremost space in an open boat. 2. the sheet of a foresail.

fore·shore (fôr'shōr', fōr'shôr'), *n.* the part of the shore between the high-water and low-water marks.

fore·short·en (fôr shôr't'n, fōr-), *v.t.* to reduce or distort (a represented object) in order to convey the illusion of three-dimensional space.

fore·sight (fôr'sīt', fōr'-), *n.* 1. care in planning and preparing for the future. 2. the act or power of foreseeing. 3. the act of looking forward. —**fore'sight'ed,** *adj.* —**fore'sight'ed·ness,** *n.*

fore·skin (fôr'skin', fōr'-), *n.* prepuce.

for·est (fôr'ist, for'-), *n.* a large tract of land covered with trees and underbrush. —**for·est·ed** (fôr'i stid, for'-), *adj.*

fore·stall (fôr stôl', fōr-), *v.t.* 1. to prevent, hinder, or thwart by action in advance. 2. to deal with or realize beforehand.

for·est·a·tion (fôr'i stā'ʃən, for'-), *n.* the planting of forests.

for·est·er (fôr'i stər, for'-), *n.* a person who is expert in forestry.

for'est ran'ger, an officer supervising the care of a forest, esp. a public forest.

for·est·ry (fôr'i strē, for'-), *n.* the science of planting and taking care of forests.

fore·taste (*n.* fôr'tāst', fōr'-; *v.* fôr-tāst', fōr-), *n., v.,* -tast·ed, -tast·ing. —*n.* 1. a slight taste, experience, or knowledge of something to come. —*v.t.* 2. to have a foretaste of.

fore·tell (fôr tel', fōr-), *v.t.,* -told, -tell·ing. to tell of or announce beforehand. —**fore·tell'er,** *n.* —**Syn.** augur, forecast, predict, prophesy.

fore·thought (fôr'thôt', fōr'-), *n.* 1. thoughtful provision beforehand. 2. previous consideration.

fore·to·ken (fôr tō'kən, fōr-), *v.t.* to be or give a sign of beforehand.

fore·top (fôr'top', fōr'-; *also* fôr'təp, fōr'-), *n.* a platform at the head of a fore lower mast.

for·ev·er (fôr ev'ər, fər-), *adv.* 1. without ever ending in time. 2. constantly or incessantly.

for·ev·er·more (fôr ev'ər môr', -mōr', fər-), *adv. Literary.* forever.

fore·warn (fôr wôrn', fōr-), *v.t.* to warn beforehand.

fore·wing (fôr'wing', fōr'-), *n.* either of the anterior wings of an insect having four wings.

fore·wom·an (fōr′wŏŏm′ən, fôr′-), *n.*
1. a woman in charge of a group of workers, etc. 2. the chairwoman of a jury.

fore·word (fōr′wûrd′, -word, fôr′-), *n.*
a short introductory statement in a book, etc., often by someone other than the author or writer.

for·feit (fôr′fit), *n.* 1. something to which the right is lost as a result of committing a crime, violating a contract, etc. 2. a. **forfeits**, an old-fashioned game in which an article is surrendered by a loser and redeemable by performing a specified act. b. an article so surrendered. 3. forfeiture. —*v.t.* 4. to lose as a forfeit.

for·fei·ture (fôr′fi chər), *n.* 1. the act of forfeiting. 2. something forfeited.

for·fend (fôr fend′), *v.t. Obs.* to defend, secure, or protect.

for·gath·er (fôr gaₜₕ′ər), *v.i.* 1. to gather together. 2. to meet, esp. by accident.

for·gave (fər gāv′), *v.* pt. of forgive.

forge[1] (fōrj, fôrj), *n., v.,* **forged, forging.** —*n.* 1. an open furnace in which metal is heated before shaping. 2. smithy. —*v.t.* 3. to form by heating and hammering. 4. to form or make in any way. 5. to imitate (a signature, etc.) fraudulently. —*v.i.* 6. to commit forgery. 7. to work at a forge. —**forg′er,** *n.*

forge[2] (fōrj, fôrj), *v.i.,* **forged, forging.** 1. to progress slowly or with difficulty. 2. to move ahead with increased speed or effectiveness.

for·ger·y (fôr′jə rē, fôr′-), *n., pl.* **-ger·ies.** 1. the crime of forging signatures, documents, etc., for purposes of fraud. 2. something produced by forgery.

for·get (fər get′), *v.,* **-got** (-got′), **-got·ten** (-got′ᵊn) or **-got, -get·ting.** —*v.t.* 1. to cease or fail to remember. 2. to neglect unintentionally. 3. to overlook or disregard. —*v.i.* 4. to cease or omit to think of something. 5. **forget oneself,** to lose one's self-control. —**for·get′ful,** *adj.* —**for·get′ful·ly,** *adv.* —**for·get′ful·ness,** *n.* —**for·get′ta·ble,** *adj.*

for·get-me-not (fər get′mē not′), *n.* a small plant having a light-blue flower.

forg·ing (fōr′jiṅg, fôr′-), *n.* a piece of forged work in metal.

for·give (fər giv′), *v.t., v.i.,* **-gave, -giv·en, -giv·ing.** 1. to cease to blame or feel resentment about (an offense or offender). 2. to cancel or let off (a debt). —**for·giv′a·ble,** *adj.* —**for·give′ness,** *n.* —**for·giv′er,** *n.* —**Syn.** condone, excuse, pardon.

for·giv·ing (fər giv′iṅg), *adj.* disposed to forgive.

for·go (fôr gō′), *v.t.,* **-went, -gone, -go·ing.** to do without, esp. in mild self-denial.

for·int (fôr′int), *n.* the monetary unit of Hungary.

fork (fôrk), *n.* 1. an instrument having two or more prongs for holding, lifting, etc., esp. food. 2. a division into branches. 3. the point or part at which a thing branches. 4. any of such branches. —*v.t.* 5. to pierce, raise, or pitch with a fork. 6. to divide into branches. 7. **fork over** or **out** or **up,** *Informal.* to hand over or pay out. —**fork′like′,** *adj.*

forked (fôrkt, fôr′kid), *adj.* 1. having a fork or forklike branches. 2. zigzag, as lightning.

fork-lift (fôrk′lift′), *n.* a small vehicle with a power-operated pronged platform at the front for lifting and moving heavy loads, etc.

for·lorn (fôr lôrn′), *adj.* 1. lonely and wretched. 2. abandoned or forsaken. 3. hopeless or despairing. —**for·lorn′ly,** *adv.*

forlorn′ hope′, 1. an undertaking almost certain to fail. 2. a perilous enterprise.

form (fôrm), *n.* 1. external appearance of a clearly defined area. 2. the shape of a thing or person. 3. a body, esp. that of a human being. 4. a dummy used for fitting or displaying clothing. 5. something that gives, holds, or determines shape. 6. a particular condition, character, or mode in which something appears. 7. the manner or style of arranging and coordinating parts for a pleasing or effective result. 8. due or proper shape. 9. the structure, pattern, or essential nature of anything. 10. a prescribed or customary order or method of doing something. 11. a set order of words, as in a legal document. 12. a document with blank spaces to be filled in. 13. formality or ceremony. 14. procedure or conduct. 15. particular manner or method of performing something. 16. physical condition or fitness, as for performing. 17. a particular shape of word as it occurs in a specific context. 18. a word with a particular inflectional ending. 19. a grade or class in certain schools. 20. types, leads, etc., secured in a frame to print from. —*v.t.* 21. to construct or frame. 22. to make or produce. 23. to compose or constitute. 24. to arrange or organize. 25. to frame (ideas, etc.) in the mind. 26. to contract or develop (habits, friendships, etc.). 27. to shape or fashion. 28. to mold by discipline or instructions. —*v.i.* 29. to be formed.

-form, a suffix meaning "having the form of": *cruciform.*

for·mal (fôr′məl), *adj.* **1.** being in accordance with the usual requirements, customs, etc. **2.** marked by form or ceremony: *a formal occasion.* **3.** ceremonious or stiff. **4. a.** for wear at ceremonial or elaborate occasions: *formal attire.* **b.** requiring the wear of such type of dress: *a formal dance.* **5.** nominal or perfunctory. **6.** made or done in accordance with procedures that ensure validity. —*n.* **7.** a formal dance. **8.** formal attire for evening wear.

form·al·de·hyde (fôr mal′də hīd′, fər-), *n.* a colorless, toxic gas used chiefly in aqueous solution as a disinfectant and preservative.

for·mal·ism (fôr′mə liz′əm), *n.* strict adherence to prescribed or traditional forms.

for·mal·i·ty (fôr mal′i tē), *n., pl.* **-ties. 1.** condition or quality of being formal. **2.** adherence to established rules, procedures, etc. **3.** a formal act or observance.

for·mal·ize (fôr′mə līz′), *v.t.,* **-ized, -iz·ing. 1.** to make formal, esp. for official acceptance. **2.** to give a definite shape to. —**for′mal·i·za′tion,** *n.*

for·mat (fôr′mat), *n.* **1.** the shape and size of a book. **2.** the general appearance of a publication. **3.** the organization, style, or type of something.

for·ma·tion (fôr mā′shən), *n.* **1.** the act of forming or state of being formed. **2.** structure or arrangement. **3.** a particular disposition of troops, as in columns, etc. **4.** something formed.

form·a·tive (fôr′mə tiv), *adj.* **1.** giving form or shape. **2.** pertaining to formation or development.

for·mer (fôr′mər), *adj.* **1.** belonging to or existing in the past. **2.** being the first mentioned of two. —**Syn. 1.** earlier, previous, prior.

for·mer·ly (fôr′mər lē), *adv.* in time past.

form·fit·ting (fôrm′fit′ing), *adj.* designed to fit snugly: *a formfitting blouse.*

for·mic (fôr′mik), *adj.* **1.** of ants. **2.** of a corrosive acid found in ants, etc.

For·mi·ca (fôr mī′kə), *n. Trademark.* a laminated plastic used as a chemical-proof and heat-proof covering for table surfaces, etc.

for·mi·da·ble (fôr′mi də bəl), *adj.* **1.** causing great fear or dread. **2.** extremely difficult or demanding. —**for′mi·da·bly,** *adv.*

form·less (fôrm′lis), *adj.* lacking a definite form or shape.

form′ let′ter, a printed or typed letter that can be sent to any number of persons.

For·mo·sa (fôr mō′sə), *n.* Taiwan.

for·mu·la (fôr′myə lə), *n., pl.* **-las, -lae** (-lē′). **1.** any fixed or conventional method for doing something. **2.** a set form of words for use on some ceremonial occasion. **3.** a rule or principle frequently expressed in algebraic symbols. **4.** *Chem.* an expression of the constituents of a compound by symbols and figures. **5.** a recipe or prescription. **6.** a mixture of milk and other ingredients for feeding a baby.

for·mu·late (fôr′myə lāt′), *v.t.,* **-lat·ed, -lat·ing. 1.** to express definitely or systematically. **2.** to devise or develop, as a method, etc. **3.** to express in a formula. —**for′mu·la′tion,** *n.* —**for′mu·la′tor,** *n.*

for·ni·ca·tion (fôr′nə kā′shən), *n.* voluntary sexual intercourse between two unmarried persons or two persons not married to each other. —**for′ni·cate,** *v.i.* —**for′ni·ca′tor,** *n.*

for·sake (fôr sāk′), *v.t.,* **-sook** (-sŏŏk′), **-sak·en** (-sā′kən), **-sak·ing. 1.** to quit or leave entirely. **2.** to give up or renounce (a belief, etc.).

for·sooth (fôr sŏŏth′), *adv. Archaic.* indeed.

for·swear (fôr swâr′), *v.,* **-swore** (-swōr′, -swôr′), **-sworn** (-swôrn′, -swōrn′), **-swear·ing.** —*v.t.* **1.** to reject or renounce upon oath or firmly. **2.** to deny vehemently or upon oath. —*v.i.* **3.** to commit perjury.

for·syth·i·a (fôr sith′ē ə, -sī′thē ə, fər-), *n.* a shrub much cultivated for its showy yellow flowers. [after W. Forsyth (1737–1804), Eng. horticulturist]

fort (fôrt, fōrt), *n.* **1.** a strong or fortified place occupied by troops. **2.** any permanent army post.

fort., **1.** fortification. **2.** fortified.

forte[1] (fôrt, fōrt), *n.* something in which one excels.

for·te[2] (fôr′tā), *Music.* —*adj.* **1.** loud. —*adv.* **2.** loudly.

forth (fôrth, fōrth), *adv.* **1.** forward or onward: *from that day forth.* **2.** into view or consideration.

forth·com·ing (fôrth′kum′ing, fōrth′-), *adj.* **1.** coming or about to appear. **2.** ready or available when needed.

forth·right (fôrth′rīt′, fōrth′-), *adj.* direct and straightforward. —**forth′right′ly,** *adv.* —**forth′right′ness,** *n.*

forth·with (fôrth′with′, -with′, fōrth′-), *adv.* without delay.

for·ti·fy (fôr′tə fī′), *v.,* **-fied, -fy·ing.** —*v.t.* **1.** to strengthen against attack. **2.** to impart strength or endurance to. **3.** to increase the quality or effectiveness of. **4.** to strengthen mentally or morally. **5.** to confirm or corroborate. **6.** to add alcohol to (wines). —**for′ti·fi·ca′tion,** *n.* —**for′ti·fi′er,** *n.*

for·tis·si·mo (fôr tis′ə mō′), *Music.* —*adj.* **1.** very loud. —*adv.* **2.** very loudly.

for·ti·tude (fôr′ti tōōd′, -tyōōd′), *n.* patient courage under affliction or privation.

Fort′ Knox′, a military reservation in N Kentucky: U.S. gold depository.

Fort′ Lau′der·dale (lô′dər dāl′), a city in SE Florida: seashore resort.

fort·night (fôrt′nīt′, -nit), *n. Chiefly Brit.* two weeks.

fort·night·ly (fôrt′nīt′lē), *Chiefly Brit.* —*adj.* **1.** occurring or appearing once a fortnight. —*adv.* **2.** once a fortnight.

for·tress (fôr′tris), *n.* a large fortified place.

for·tu·i·tous (fôr tōō′i təs, -tyōō′-), *adj.* **1.** happening or produced by chance: *a fortuitous encounter.* **2.** lucky or fortunate. —**for·tu′i·tous·ly,** *adv.*

for·tu·i·ty (fôr tōō′i tē, -tyōō′-), *n., pl.* **-ties. 1.** the state or fact of being fortuitous. **2.** an accidental occurrence.

for·tu·nate (fôr′chə nit), *adj.* **1.** having good fortune. **2.** bringing or indicating good fortune. —**for′tu·nate·ly,** *adv.*

for·tune (fôr′chən), *n.* **1.** position in life as determined by wealth. **2.** great wealth. **3.** chance or luck. **4.** Often, **fortunes.** something that happens to a person in his or her life or in some particular incident. **5.** lot or destiny. [< OF < L *fortūna*]

for′tune hunt′er, a person who hopes to gain wealth, esp. through marriage.

for·tune-tell·er (fôr′chən tel′ər), *n.* a person who professes to predict the future. —**for′tune-tell′ing,** *n., adj.*

Fort′ Wayne′, a city in NE Indiana.

Fort′ Worth′, a city in N Texas.

for·ty (fôr′tē), *n., pl.* **-ties,** *adj.* —*n.* **1.** a cardinal number, ten times four. **2.** a symbol for this number, as 40 or XL. —*adj.* **3.** amounting to 40 in number. —**for′ti·eth** (-ith), *adj., n.*

for·ty-five (fôr′tē fīv′), *n.* **1.** Also, **.45.** a .45-caliber pistol or revolver. **2.** Also, **45.** a phonograph record devised to be played at 45 revolutions per minute.

for·ty-nin·er (fôr′tē nī′nər), *n.* a person who went to California in 1849 during the gold rush.

for′ty winks′, *Informal.* a short nap.

fo·rum (fôr′əm, fōr′əm), *n., pl.* **fo·rums, fo·ra. 1.** the marketplace or public square of an ancient Roman city. **2.** an assembly for discussion of questions of public interest. **3.** an outlet for discussion of matters of interest to a given group, as a radio show. **4.** a court or tribunal.

for·ward (fôr′wərd), *adv.* Also, **for′-**

wards. 1. onward or ahead: *to move forward.* **2.** toward the front. **3.** into view or consideration: *to bring forward.* —*adj.* **4.** going or moving ahead: *a forward motion.* **5.** well-advanced. **6.** ready or eager. **7.** presumptuous or bold. **8.** situated in the front. **9.** of or pertaining to the future. **10.** radical or extreme, as opinions. —*n.* **11.** a player stationed in advance of others on the team, as in hockey. —*v.t.* **12.** to transmit, esp. to a new address: *to forward a letter.* **13.** to advance or promote. —**for′ward·ness,** *n.*

for·ward·er (fôr′wər dər), *n.* **1.** a person who forwards or sends forward. **2.** a person or firm that handles freight shipments.

for·went (fôr went′), *v.* pt. of **forgo.**

F.O.S., *Com.* free on steamer.

fos·sil (fos′əl), *n.* **1.** any remains, impression, or trace of an animal or plant of a former geological age. **2.** *Informal.* an outdated or old-fashioned person or thing. —*adj.* **3.** of the nature of a fossil: *fossil insects.* **4.** dug out of the earth: *fossil fuel.* —**fos′sil·like′,** *adj.*

fos·sil·ize (fos′ə līz′), *v.t., v.i.,* **-ized, -iz·ing.** to convert into a fossil. —**fos′sil·i·za′tion,** *n.*

fos·ter (fô′stər, fos′tər), *v.t.* **1.** to promote the growth or development of. **2.** to bring up or rear. —*adj.* **3.** giving or receiving parental care though not kin by blood or related legally: *a foster daughter.*

fos′ter home′, a household in which a child is raised by someone other than its own parents.

fos·ter·ling (fô′stər ling, fos′tər-), *n.* a foster child.

F.O.T., *Com.* free on truck.

fought (fôt), *v.* pt. and pp. of **fight.**

foul (foul), *adj.* **1.** grossly offensive to the senses. **2.** charged with or characterized by offensive matter. **3.** filthy or dirty. **4.** unfavorable or stormy, as weather. **5.** grossly offensive in a moral sense. **6.** abominable or wicked, as crime, etc. **7.** scurrilous or profane. **8.** contrary to the rules or established usages, as of a sport. **9.** *Baseball.* pertaining to a foul ball or a foul line. **10.** entangled or jammed: *a foul anchor.* —*adv.* **11.** in a foul manner. —*n.* **12.** something that is foul. **13.** a collision or entanglement. **14.** a violation of the rules of a sport or game. **15.** See **foul ball.** —*v.t.* **16.** to make foul. **17.** to clog or obstruct. **18.** to collide with. **19.** to cause to become entangled, as a rope. **20.** to defile or disgrace. **21.** *Baseball.* to hit (a pitch) foul. —*v.i.* **22.** to become foul. **23. foul up,** *Slang.* to bungle or spoil. —**foul′ly,** *adv.* —**foul′ness,** *n.*

fou·lard (fōō lärd', fə-), *n.* a soft, lightweight silk, rayon, or cotton with printed design.

foul' ball', *Baseball.* a batted ball that rolls or passes outside the foul lines.

foul·ing (fou'ling), *n.* a deposit, esp. on the hull of a ship.

foul' line', **1.** *Baseball.* either of the two lines connecting home plate with first and third base respectively. **2.** *Basketball.* a line on the court 15 feet from the backboard.

foul·mouthed (foul'mouṭhd', -mouṭht'), *adj.* using obscene or scurrilous language.

foul' play', any treacherous or unfair dealing, esp. one that involves murder.

foul-up (foul'up'), *n. Informal.* confusion or disorder caused by inefficiency, stupidity, mechanical failure, etc.

found¹ (found), *v.* pt. and pp. of **find**.

found² (found), *v.t.* **1.** to set up or establish on a firm basis. **2.** to build on a firm base or ground: *a house founded on solid rock.* **3.** to base or ground. —**found'er**, *n.*

found³ (found), *v.t.* **1.** to melt and pour (metal, etc.) into a mold. **2.** to make (an article) by founding metal.

foun·da·tion (foun dā'shən), *n.* **1.** the natural or prepared ground or base on which some structure rests. **2.** basis or groundwork. **3.** the act of founding. **4.** an institution financed by a donation or legacy to aid research, education, arts, etc. **5.** an endowment for such an institution. **6.** a corset or girdle. —**founda'tion·al**, *adj.*

found·er (foun'dər), *v.i.* **1.** (of a ship, etc.) to fill with water and sink. **2.** to fail utterly. **3.** to stumble, break down, or go lame, as a horse.

found·ling (found'ling), *n.* an infant of unknown parentage found abandoned.

found' ob'ject, a natural or manufactured object that is perceived as being aesthetically satisfying.

found·ry (foun'drē), *n., pl.* -ries. an establishment for producing castings in molten metal.

fount (fount), *n. Literary.* **1.** a fountain or spring. **2.** a source or origin.

foun·tain (foun't'n), *n.* **1.** a spring or source of water. **2.** source or origin. **3.** a mechanically created jet of water. **4.** a structure for such a jet. **5.** a reservoir for a liquid to be supplied.

foun·tain·head (foun't'n hed'), *n.* a source from which a stream flows.

foun'tain pen', a pen with a reservoir that provides a continuous supply of ink to the point.

four (fōr, fôr), *n.* **1.** a cardinal number, three plus one. **2.** a symbol for this number, as 4 or IV. —*adj.* **3.** amounting to four in number.

four-flush (fōr'flush', fôr'-), *v.i. Informal.* to bluff. —**four'flush'er**, *n.*

four-fold (fōr'fōld', fôr'-), *adj.* **1.** comprising four parts. **2.** four times as much. —*adv.* **3.** in fourfold measure.

Four'-H' Club' (fōr'āch', fôr'-), an organization sponsored by the U.S. Department of Agriculture, established chiefly to instruct young people of rural communities in modern farming methods. Also, **4-H Club**. —**4-H'er**, *n.*

Four' Hun'dred, the exclusive social set of a city or area. Also, **400**.

four-in-hand (fōr'in hand', fôr'-), *n.* **1.** a necktie tied in a slipknot with the ends left hanging. **2.** a vehicle drawn by four horses and driven by one person. **3.** a team of four horses.

four-o'clock (fōr'ə klok', fôr'-), *n.* a common garden plant having red, white, yellow, or variegated flowers that open in the late afternoon.

four-pen·ny (fōr'pen'ē, -pə nē, fôr'-), *adj. Carpentry.* noting a nail 1½ inches long.

four-post·er (fōr'pō'stər, fôr'-), *n.* a bed with four corner posts, as for supporting a canopy.

four-score (fōr'skôr', fôr'skōr'), *n. Chiefly Literary.* eighty.

four-some (fōr'səm, fôr'-), *n.* **1.** a match between two pairs of golf players. **2.** a company or set of four.

four-square (fōr'skwâr', fôr'-), *adj.* **1.** having a square shape **2.** firm or steady. **3.** forthright or blunt. —*adv.* **4.** frankly or forthrightly.

four·teen (fōr'tēn', fôr'-), *n.* **1.** a cardinal number, ten plus four. **2.** a symbol for this number, as 14 or XIV. —*adj.* **3.** amounting to 14 in number. —**four'teenth'**, *adj., n.*

fourth (fōrth, fôrth), *adj.* **1.** next after the third. **2.** being one of four equal parts. —*n.* **3.** a fourth part. **4.** the fourth member of a series. —*adv* **5.** in the fourth place.

fourth' class', a class of mail consisting of merchandise and sent at the lowest rate. —**fourth'-class'**, *adj., adv.*

fourth' dimen'sion, the dimension of time, in addition to three spatial dimensions.

fourth' estate', (*often caps.*) the journalistic profession or its members.

Fourth' of July'. See **Independence Day**.

four-wheel (fōr'hwēl', -wēl', fôr'-), *adj.* functioning on or by four wheels: *a truck with four-wheel drive.*

fowl (foul), *n.*, *pl.* **fowls, fowl. 1.** the domestic hen or rooster. **2.** any of several other birds, as the duck, turkey, or pheasant. **3.** the meat of a domestic fowl. —*v.i.* **4.** to hunt wildfowl.

fox (foks), *n.*, *pl.* **fox·es, fox,** *v.* —*n.* **1.** a carnivore of the dog family having a pointed muzzle, erect ears, and a long, bushy tail. **2.** the fur of this animal. **3.** a cunning or crafty person. —*v.t.* **4.** *Informal.* to deceive or trick.

foxed (fokst), *adj.* stained a yellowish brown, as an old book.

fox-fire (foks'fīᵊr'), *n.* **1.** organic luminescence, esp. from certain fungi on decaying wood. **2.** any of various fungi causing luminescence in decaying wood.

fox·glove (foks'gluv'), *n.* a plant having drooping, tubular, purple or white flowers, and leaves that are used as digitalis in medicine.

fox·hole (foks'hōl'), *n.* a small pit used for cover in a battle area.

fox·hound (foks'hound'), *n.* a medium-sized hound trained to hunt foxes.

fox' ter'rier, a small terrier having either a long, wiry coat or a short, flat coat.

fox' trot', a social dance, in quadruple meter, performed by couples.

fox-trot (foks'trot'), *v.i.* -**trot·ted, trot·ting.** to dance a fox trot.

fox·y (fok'sē), *adj.*, **fox·i·er, fox·i·est.** cunning or crafty. —**fox'i·ly,** *adv.* —**fox'i·ness,** *n.*

foy·er (foi'ᵊr, foi'ā), *n.* **1.** the lobby of a theater. **2.** an entrance hall in an apartment.

fp., **1.** foolscap. **2.** foot-pound. **3.** freezing point.

FPC, 1. Federal Power Commission. **2.** See **fish protein concentrate.**

fpm, feet per minute. Also, **ft/min**

FPO, 1. field post office. **2.** fleet post office.

fps, feet per second.

Fr, francium.

Fr., 1. Father. **2.** *pl.* **Fr., Frs.** franc. **3.** France. **4.** French. **5.** Friar. **6.** Friday.

fr., 1. fragment. **2.** *pl.* **fr., frs.** franc. **3.** from.

frab·jous (frab'jus), *adj. Informal.* wonderful or superb. [coined by English writer Lewis Carroll (1832–98) in *Through the Looking-Glass*]

fra·cas (frā'kᵊs), *n.* a disorderly noise or fight.

frac·tion (frak'shᵊn), *n.* **1.** the ratio between any two numbers or algebraic quantities. **2.** a portion or section. **3.** a fragment or bit. —**frac'tion·al,** *adj.* —**frac'tion·al·ly,** *adv.*

frac·tious (frak'shᵊs), *adj.* **1.** peevish-

ly quarrelsome. **2.** refractory or unruly. —**frac'tious·ly,** *adv.*

frac·ture (frak'chᵊr), *n.*, *v.*, -**tured, -tur·ing.** —*n.* **1.** the breaking of a bone or the resulting condition. **2.** the characteristic manner of breaking. **3.** a break, breach, or split. —*v.t.*, *v.i.* **4.** to break or crack.

frag (frag), *v.t.*, **fragged, frag·ging.** *Slang.* to injure or assault (esp. one's unpopular superior) with a grenade. [*frag(mentation)*] —**frag'ging,** *n.*

frag·ile (fraj'ᵊl; *Brit.* fraj'īl), *adj.* **1.** easily broken or damaged, as china. **2.** flimsy: *a fragile excuse.* —**fra·gil·i·ty** (fro jil'i tē), **frag'ile·ness,** *n.*

frag·ment (frag'mᵊnt), *n.* **1.** a part broken off or detached. **2.** a portion that is unfinished or incomplete. —*v.i.*, *v.t.* **3.** to break into fragments. —**frag'men·ta'tion,** *n.*

frag·men·tar·y (frag'mᵊn ter'ē), *adj.* consisting of fragments.

fra·grant (frā'grᵊnt), *adj.* having a pleasant odor. —**fra'grance,** *n.* —**fra'grant·ly,** *adv.*

frail (frāl), *adj.* **1.** in delicate health. **2.** easily destroyed. **3.** morally weak. —**frail'ly,** *adv.*

frail·ty (frāl'tē), *n.*, *pl.* -**ties 1.** the quality or state of being frail. **2.** a fault resulting from moral weakness.

frame (frām), *n.*, *v.*, **framed, fram·ing.** —*n.* **1.** an open border or case for enclosing a picture, mirror, etc. **2.** a rigid structure used as a major support for a house, etc. **3.** a human body, with reference to its size or build. **4.** a structure for admitting or enclosing something: *a window frame.* **5.** Usually, **frames.** the framework for a pair of eyeglasses. **6.** a particular state, as of the mind. **7.** form or structure. **8.** *Bowling.* one of the 10 divisions of a game. **9.** one of the successive small pictures on a strip of film. **10.** *Slang.* frame-up. —*v.t.* **11.** to form or make. **12.** to contrive, devise, or compose, as a plan, law, poem, etc. **13.** *Informal.* to contrive fraudulently or falsely, as in a scheme, race, etc. **14.** *Informal.* to incriminate (an innocent person). **15.** to provide with or put into a frame, as a picture. —**fram'er,** *n.*

frame' house', a house constructed with a skeletal frame of timber.

frame-up (frām'up'), *n. Informal.* a fraudulent incrimination of an innocent person.

frame·work (frām'wûrk'), *n.* **1.** a structure composed of parts joined together. **2.** a skeletal structure to support or enclose something.

franc (frangk), *n.* the monetary unit of France, Belgium, Liechtenstein, Luxembourg, Senegal, Switzerland, etc.

France (frans, fräns), *n.* a country in W Europe.

fran·chise (fran′chīz), *n.*, *v.*, **-chised**, **-chis·ing.** —*n.* **1.** a right granted by a large business chain, as a fast-food company, allowing an investor to operate an outlet for its product or service by using its chain name and management knowhow. **2.** the right of suffrage. **3.** a regional dealership, as in automobiles. **4.** a privilege of a public nature conferred on an individual or a company by a governmental grant. —*v.t.* **5.** to grant (an investor, individual, etc.) a franchise.

fran·chis·ee (fran′chī zē′), *n.* an investor or individual to whom a franchise is granted.

fran·chis·er (fran′chī′zər), *n.* a person or company that holds a franchise. Also, **fran′chis′or.**

Fran′cis of As·si′si (fran′sis əv ə sē′zē), Saint, 1182?–1226, Italian friar. —**Fran·cis′can** (-kən), *adj.*, *n.*

fran·ci·um (fran′sē əm), *n. Chem.* a radioactive element of the alkali metal group. *Symbol:* Fr; *at. no.:* 87.

Fran·co (frang′kō), **Fran·cis·co** fran sis′kō), 1892–1975, Spanish military leader and dictator.

Franco-, a combining form meaning "French" or "France": *Franco-American.*

fran·gi·ble (fran′jə bəl), *adj.* capable of being broken. —**fran′gi·bil′i·ty,** *n.*

frank[1] (frangk), *adj.* **1.** unreserved in expressing oneself. —*n.* **2.** a mark affixed by special privilege to a piece of mail for free transmission. **3.** this privilege of free mail accorded to members of Congress. —*v.t.* **4.** to send (mail) free. —**frank′ly,** *adv.* — **frank′ness,** *n.* —Syn. **1.** candid, open, outspoken, straightforward.

frank[2] (frangk), *n. Informal.* frankfurter.

Frank·en·stein (frang′kən stīn′), *n.* **1.** a person who creates a destructive agency that he cannot control or that brings about his own ruin. **2.** Also called **Frank′enstein mon′ster.** the destructive agency itself. [after a novel (1818) by Mary Shelley, Eng. author, 1797–1851]

Frank·fort (frangk′fərt), *n.* the capital of Kentucky, in the N part.

frank·furt·er (frangk′fər tər), *n.* a small, smoked sausage, usually of beef and pork. Also, **frank′fort·er, frank′fort, frank′furt.**

frank·in·cense (frang′kin sens′), *n.* an aromatic resin used as incense, in perfumery, etc.

Frank·lin (frangk′lin), *n.* **Benjamin,** 1706–90, American statesman, diplomat, author, and scientist.

fran·tic (fran′tik), *adj.* wild with ex-

citement, passion, fear, pain, etc. — **fran′ti·cal·ly, fran′tic·ly,** *adv.*

frap·pé (fra pā′), *n.* **1.** a fruit juice mixture frozen to a mush. **2.** a liqueur poured over cracked ice. **3.** Also, **frappe** (frap). See **milk shake.**

fra·ter·nal (frə tûr′n°l), *adj.* **1.** of or befitting a brother or brothers. **2.** of or being a society of men in brotherly union. —**fra·ter′nal·ism,** *n.* —**fra·ter′nal·ly,** *adv.*

fra·ter·ni·ty (frə tûr′ni tē), *n., pl.* **-ties. 1.** a local or national organization of male students, primarily for social purposes. **2.** a group of persons having common purposes, interests, etc.: *the medical fraternity.* **3.** an organization of laymen for religious or charitable purposes. **4.** brotherhood or brotherliness.

frat·er·nize (frat′ər nīz′), *v.i.*, **-nized, -niz·ing. 1.** to associate in a fraternal way. **2.** to associate cordially or intimately with enemy troops, natives of a conquered country, etc. —**frat′er·ni·za′tion,** *n.*

frat·ri·cide (fra′tri sīd′, frā′-), *n.* **1.** a person who kills his or her brother. **2.** the act of killing one's brother. — **frat′ri·cid′al,** *adj.*

Frau (frou), *n., pl.* **Frau·en** (frou′ən), *Eng.* **Fraus** (frouz). *German.* Mrs.

fraud (frôd), *n.* **1.** deceit or trickery used to gain unfair or dishonest advantage. **2.** any deception or trickery. **3.** a cheat or impostor.

fraud·u·lent (frô′jə lənt), *adj.* **1.** given to or using fraud. **2.** characterized by or involving fraud. —**fraud′u·lence,** *n.* —**fraud′u·lent·ly,** *adv.*

fraught (frôt), *adj.* accompanied or filled: *an undertaking fraught with danger.*

Fräu·lein (froi′līn, frŏ′-, frou′-), *n., pl.* **Fräu·lein,** *Eng.* **Fräu·leins.** *German.* Miss (a term of address).

fray[1] (frā), *n.* a noisy quarrel.

fray[2] (frā), *v.t.* **1.** to wear (cloth, etc.) to loose, raveled threads at the edge. **2.** to wear by rubbing. **3.** to strain or upset. —*v.i.* **4.** to become frayed.

fraz·zle (fraz′əl), *v.*, **-zled, -zling,** *n. Informal.* —*v.i.*, *v.t.* **1.** to wear to shreds. **2.** to tire out. —*n.* **3.** the state of being frazzled.

FRB, Federal Reserve Board.

freak (frēk), *n.* **1.** a sudden and apparently causeless turn of events, the mind, etc. **2.** any abnormal or curiously unusual person or animal. **3.** *Slang.* a devoted fan or enthusiast. **4.** *Slang.* a narcotics user. —*v.i.*, *v.t.* **5.** **freak out,** *Slang.* **a.** to react with wild excitement, as when under the influence of a hallucinogenic drug. **b.** to lose one's sanity or composure. —**freak′ish, freak′y,** *adj.* — **freak′ish·ly,** *adv.* —**freak′ish·ness,** *n.*

freak·out (frēk'out'), *n. Slang.* a period or event characterized by wild excitement or loss of sanity.

freck·le (frek'əl), *n., v.,* -led, -ling. —*n.* a small, brownish spot on the skin. —*v.t., v.i.* 2. to cover or become covered with freckles. —**freck'ly,** *adj.*

Fred'er·ick the Great' (fred'rik, -ər-ik), 1712–86, king of Prussia 1740–86.

Fred·er·ic·ton (fred'or ik tən), *n.* the capital of New Brunswick, in SE Canada.

free (frē), *adj.,* fre·er, fre·est, *adv., v.,* freed, free·ing. —*adj.* 1. enjoying personal rights or liberty. 2. possessing civil and political liberties. 3. exempt from external restriction. 4. able to do something at will. 5. not subject to special regulations, duties, etc. 6. not literal, as a translation. 7. not subject to set forms, etc. 8. clear of obstacles, as a road. 9. not occupied or in use. 10. exempt or released from something that controls, restrains, burdens, etc. 11. unattached or not held fast. 12. frank and open. 13. loose or licentious. 14. liberal or lavish. 15. without, or not subject to, a charge or payment. —*adv.* 16. in a free manner. 17. without cost or charge. 18. **make free with,** to use as one's own. —*v.t.* 19. to make free. 20. to exempt or deliver. 21. to relieve or rid. 22. to disengage or clear. —**free'ly,** *adv.* —**free'ness,** *n.* —**Syn.** 19. emancipate, liberate, release.

free·bie (frē'bē), *n. Slang.* something given without charge or cost, as a theater ticket or pass. Also, **free'bee.**

free·board (frē'bôrd', -bôrd'), *n. Naut.* the distance between the uppermost deck considered fully watertight and the official water line.

free·boot·er (frē'bōō'tər), *n.* a person who goes about in search of plunder.

free·born (frē'bôrn'), *adj.* 1. born free, rather than in slavery or vassalage. 2. of or befitting a person who is freeborn.

freed·man (frēd'mən), *n.* a person who has been freed from slavery.

free·dom (frē'dəm), *n.* 1. the state of being free. 2. personal or political independence. 3. exemption or immunity from controls, duties, etc. 4. ease or facility of movement or action. 5. frankness of manner or speech. 6. unrestricted use, access, etc. 7. right of citizenship, membership, etc.

free' en'terprise, a private business system with a minimum of governmental intervention and control.

free' fall', the fall of a body entirely by the pull of gravity alone.

free' flight', a flight, as of a rocket, that is not assisted by any preset or remote control.

free-for-all (frē'fər ôl'), *n.* 1. a fight, argument, etc., open to everyone and usually without rules. —*adj.* 2. open to everyone.

free·hand (frē'hand'), *adj., adv.* by hand without guiding instruments or other aids.

free·hold (frē'hōld'), *n. Law.* an estate in land, inherited or held for life. —**free'hold'er,** *n.*

free' lance', a person who works as a writer, designer, etc., but not on a regular salary basis for any one employer. —**free'lance',** *v.i., adj., adv.*

free·load (frē'lōd'), *v.i. Informal.* to take advantage of others for free food, entertainment, etc. —**free'load'er,** *n.* —**free'load'ing,** *n., adj.*

free' love', the practice of having sexual relations without legal marriage.

free·man (frē'mən), *n.* a person who enjoys personal, civil, or political liberty. 2. a person entitled to the rights of citizenship.

Free·ma·son (frē'mā'sən, frē'mā'-), *n.* a member of a secret fraternity having for its object mutual assistance and the promotion of brotherly love. —**Free'ma'son·ry,** *n.*

free' school', a school organized as an alternative to the traditional public or private school, usually following a highly flexible approach to the curriculum and teaching methods.

free·stand·ing (frē'stan'ding), *adj.* (of sculpture, etc.) unattached to a supporting unit or background.

free·stone (frē'stōn'), *n.* 1. a stone that can be cut well without splitting. 2. a fruit, esp. a peach, having a stone from which the pulp is easily separated.

free·think·er (frē'thing'kər), *n.* a person who forms his or her opinions independently of authority or tradition, esp. in religious matters. —**free'think'ing,** *adj., n.*

free' trade', trade between different countries, free from governmental restrictions or duties.

free' univer'sity, a school run informally by and for college students, organized to offer courses and approaches not usually offered at the established universities.

free' verse', verse without a fixed metrical pattern.

free·way (frē'wā'), *n.* an express highway, usually having traffic routed on and off by means of cloverleaves.

free·wheel·ing (frē'hwē'ling, -wē'-), *adj. Informal.* 1. (of a person) moving about independently or irresponsibly. 2. (of words, actions, etc.) unrestrained or irresponsible.

free′ will′, 1. voluntary decision. 2. the doctrine that human action expresses personal choice and is not determined solely by physical or divine forces.

free·will (frē′wil′), *adj.* voluntarily decided.

free′ world′, the nations not under communist or totalitarian control or influence.

freeze (frēz), *v.,* **froze, fro·zen, freez·ing,** *n.* —*v.i.* 1. to become hardened into ice. 2. to become hard or rigid because of loss of heat. 3. to be of the degree of cold at which water freezes. 4. to suffer the effects of intense cold. 5. to die of frost or cold. 6. to be chilled with fear, shock, etc. 7. to become immobilized through fear, shock, etc. 8. to become stiff or unfriendly. —*v.t.* 9. to harden into ice. 10. to form ice on the surface of (a river, etc.). 11. to harden or stiffen by cold. 12. to subject (something) to freezing temperature, as in a freezer. 13. to cause to suffer the effects of intense cold. 14. to kill by frost or cold. 15. to dampen the enthusiasm of. 16. to make stiff or unfriendly. 17. to fix (rents, prices, etc.) at a specific amount. 18. *Finance Informal.* to render impossible of liquidation or collection. 19. **freeze out,** *Informal.* to exclude or eliminate, as by severe competition. 20. **freeze over,** to coat or become coated with ice. —*n.* 21. the act of freezing or state of being frozen. 22. a spell of freezing weather. —**freez′a·ble,** *adj.*

freeze-dry (frēz′drī′), *v.t.,* **-dried, -dry·ing.** to dry (food, antibiotics, etc.) in a high vacuum after frozen, for preservation in compact form. —**freeze′-dried′,** *adj.*

freez·er (frē′zər), *n.* 1. a person or thing that freezes. 2. a refrigerator or compartment that holds its contents at or below 32°F. 3. a machine for making ice cream, sherbet, etc.

freez′ing point′, the temperature at which a liquid freezes.

freight (frāt), *n.* 1. the ordinary conveyance or means of transport of goods provided by common carriers. 2. the charges for such transportation. 3. the goods so transported. 4. Also called **freight′ train′.** a railroad train for carrying such goods. —*v.t.* 5. to ship as or by freight. 6. *Rare.* to load (a ship) with freight

freight·er (frā′tər), *n.* a vessel used mainly for carrying cargo.

French (french), *adj.* 1. of France, its inhabitants, or their language. —*n.* 2. the people of France. 3. the language of France. —**French′man,** *n.* —**French′wom′an,** *n.fem.*

French′ cuff′, a sleeve cuff folded back and fastened with a cuff link.

French′ door′, a door having glass panes throughout its length.

French′ dress′ing, salad dressing prepared from oil, vinegar, and seasonings.

French′-fried′ pota′toes, thin strips of potatoes, deep-fried. Also called **French′ fries′.**

French-fry (french′frī′), *v.t.,* **-fried, -fry·ing.** to fry in deep fat: *to French-fry onion rings.*

French′ Gui·an′a (gē an′ə, gē ä′nə), an overseas department of France, on the NE coast of South America.

French′ horn′, a brass wind instrument with a long, coiled tube, having a conical bore and a flaring bell.

French′ leave′, a departure without ceremony, permission, or notice.

French′ toast′, bread dipped in a batter of egg and milk and sautéed until brown.

fre·net·ic (frə net′ik), *adj.* marked by or driven to frenzy. —**fre·net′i·cal·ly,** *adv.*

fren·zy (fren′zē), *n., pl.* **-zies.** 1. wild excitement or enthusiasm. 2. violent mental agitation. 3. temporary delirium. —**fren′zied,** *adj.*

Fre·on (frē′on), *n. Trademark.* a fluorinated hydrocarbon used as a refrigerant.

freq., 1. frequency. 2. frequent. 3. frequently.

fre·quen·cy (frē′kwən sē), *n., pl.* **-cies.** 1. the state or fact of being frequent. 2. rate of recurrence. 3. *Physics.* a. the number of periods or regularly occurring events of any given kind in unit time, usually in one second. b. the number of cycles or completed alternations per unit time of a wave or oscillation.

fre′quency modula′tion. See FM.

fre·quent (*adj.* frē′kwənt; *v.* fri kwent′, frē′kwənt), *adj.* 1. happening at short intervals. 2. constant or habitual: *a frequent guest.* —*v.t.* 3. to visit often or habitually. —**frequent′er,** *n.* —**fre′quent·ly,** *adv.* —**fre′quent·ness,** *n.*

fres·co (fres′kō), *n., pl.* **-coes, -cos.** 1. the art of painting on a moist, plaster surface with colors ground in water. 2. a picture so painted. —**fres′co·er, fres′co·ist,** *n.*

fresh (fresh), *adj.* 1. newly made or obtained. 2. newly arrived. 3. new or novel. 4. additional or further: *fresh supplies.* 5. not salt, as water. 6. not deteriorated. 7. not frozen or canned. 8. not fatigued. 9. not faded, worn, obliterated, etc. 10. looking youthful and healthy. 11. pure, cool, or refreshing, as air. 12. (of wind) moderately strong or brisk. 13. inexperienced: *fresh recruits.* 14.

Informal. forward or presumptuous. —*adv.* 15. newly or recently. —**fresh′ly,** *adv* —**fresh′ness,** *n.*

fresh·en (fresh′ən), *v.t., v.i.* 1. to make or become fresh. 2. **freshen up,** to wash and change clothes. —**fresh′en·er,** *n.*

fresh·et (fresh′it), *n.* 1. a sudden rise in the level of a stream due to heavy rains or the rapid melting of snow and ice.

fresh·man (fresh′mən), *n.* 1. a student in the first year of the course, as at a university 2. a novice or beginner.

fresh·wa·ter (fresh′wô′tər, -wot′ər), *adj.* 1. of or living in water that is fresh or not salt. 2. accustomed to sailing on inland water only.

Fres·no (frez′nō), *n.* a city in central California.

fret¹ (fret), *v.,* **fret·ted, fret·ting,** *n.* —*v.i., v.t.* 1. to be or cause to be vexed and uneasy. 2. to wear away, as by gnawing, corrosion, etc. 3. to move or cause to move in agitation, as water. —*n.* 4. a fretted state of mind. 5. gnawing of corrosion 6. a worn or eroded place. —**fret′ter,** *n.*

fret² (fret), *n.* an angular design of bands within a border.

fret³ (fret), *n.* any of the ridges of wood or metal set across the fingerboard of a guitar or similar instrument.

fret·ful (fret′fəl), *adj.* tending to fret emotionally. —**fret′ful·ly,** *adv.* —**fret′ful·ness,** *n.* —**Syn.** irritable, peevish.

fret′ saw′, a long, narrow-bladed saw used to cut ornamental work from thin wood.

fret·work (fret′wûrk′), *n.* 1. ornamental work consisting of interlacing parts. 2. any pattern of dark and light resembling this.

Freud (froid), *n.* **Sig·mund** (sig′mənd), 1856–1939, Austrian neurologist: founder of psychoanalysis. —**Freud′i·an,** *adj., n.*

Fri., Friday.

fri·a·ble (frī′ə bəl), *adj.* easily crumbled or reduced to powder. —**fri′a·bil′i·ty, fri′a·ble·ness,** *n.*

fri·ar (frī′ər), *n.* Rom. Cath. Ch. a member of a religious order, mostly mendicant. [< OF *frere* < L *frāter* brother]

fri·ar·y (frī′ə rē), *n., pl.* **-ar·ies.** a monastery of friars.

fric·as·see (frik′ə sē′), *n., v.,* **-seed, -see·ing.** —*n.* 1. meat, esp. chicken or veal, browned lightly, stewed, and served in a sauce. —*v.t.* 2. to prepare as a fricassee.

fric·tion (frik′shən), *n.* 1. surface resistance to relative motion, as of a body sliding or rolling. 2. the rubbing of the surface of one body against that of another. 3. dissension or conflict between persons, nations, etc. —**fric′tion·al,** *adj.*

fric′tion tape′, a cloth adhesive tape used esp. to insulate electrical conductors.

Fri·day (frī′dā, -dā), *n.* the sixth day of the week, following Thursday.

fried (frīd), *v.* pt. and pp. of **fry¹.**

fried-cake (frīd′kāk′), *n.* a doughnut or other small cake cooked in deep fat.

friend (frend), *n.* 1. a person attached to another by feelings of affection or personal regard. 2. a patron or supporter. 3. a person who is not hostile. 4. (*cap.*) a member of the Society of Friends: Quaker. 5. **make friends with,** to become a friend to. —**friend′less,** *adj.* —**friend′ship,** *n.* —**Syn.** 1. acquaintance, companion, comrade.

friend·ly (frend′lē), *adj.,* **-li·er, -li·est.** 1. characteristic of or befitting a friend. 2. kind or helpful. 3. favorably disposed. 4. amicable or peaceable: *friendly natives.* —**friend′li·ness,** *n.*

frieze (frēz), *n.* any decorative band bearing lettering, sculpture, etc., as around the walls of a room.

frig·ate (frig′it), *n.* 1. a fast naval war vessel of the late 18th and early 19th centuries. 2. a warship larger than a destroyer.

fright (frīt), *n.* 1. sudden and extreme fear. 2. a person or thing of shocking or grotesque appearance.

fright·en (frīt′ᵊn), *v.t.* 1. to throw into a fright. 2. to set in motion by scaring. —*v.i.* 3. to become frightened. —**fright′en·ing·ly,** *adv.* —**Syn.** 1. alarm, intimidate, scare, terrify.

fright·ful (frīt′fəl), *adj.* 1. causing fright. 2. horrible or shocking. 3. *Informal.* unpleasant or disagreeable. 4. *Informal.* very great. —**fright′ful·ly,** *adv.* —**fright′ful·ness,** *n.*

frig·id (frij′id), *adj.* 1. very cold in temperature. 2. without warmth of feeling. 3. (of a woman) incapable of being sexually aroused. —**fri·gid′i·ty,** *n.* —**frig′id·ly,** *adv.*

Frig′id Zone′, either of two regions, one between the Arctic Circle and the North Pole, or one between the Antarctic Circle and the South Pole.

frill (fril), *n.* 1. a trimming, as a strip of lace, gathered at one edge and loose at the other. 2. something superfluous. —**frill′y,** *adj.* —**frill′i·ness,** *n.*

fringe (frinj), *n., v.,* **fringed, fring·ing.** —*n.* 1. a decorative border of short threads or cords. 2. anything resembling this. 3. a marginal part of something without being fully typical of it. —*v.t.* 4. to furnish with a fringe. 5. to serve as a fringe for. —**fringe′less,** *adj.* —**fringe′like′,** *adj.*

fringe′ ar′ea, a region in which television reception is weak or distorted because of distance from the station, obstruction, etc.

fringe′ ben′efit, a benefit, as free insurance, received by an employee in addition to his or her pay.

frip·per·y (frip′ə rē), *n., pl.* **-per·ies.** 1. finery in dress, esp. when gaudy. 2. empty display.

Fris., Frisian.

Fris·bee (friz′bē), *n. Trademark.* a thin plastic disk, about nine inches across, sailed between players in an outdoor game.

Fri·sian (frizh′ən, frē′zhən), *adj.* 1. of the Frisian Islands, their inhabitants, or their language. —*n.* 2. a native or inhabitant of the Frisian Islands. 3. the Germanic language of the Frisian Islands.

Fri′sian Is′lands, a chain of islands in the North Sea, extending along the coasts of the Netherlands, West Germany, and Denmark.

frisk (frisk), *v.i.* 1. to dance, leap, or skip, as in frolic. —*v.t.* 2. to search (a person) for concealed weapons, etc., by feeling his or her clothing. —**frisk′er,** *n.*

frisk·y (fris′kē), *adj.,* **frisk·i·er, frisk·i·est.** lively and frolicsome. —**frisk′i·ly,** *adv.* —**frisk′i·ness,** *n.*

frit·ter¹ (frit′ər), *v.t., v.i.* 1. to waste little by little. 2. to break into small pieces. —**frit′ter·er,** *n.*

frit·ter² (frit′ər), *n.* a small cake of batter, sometimes containing fruit or clams, fried in deep fat or sautéed.

friv·o·lous (friv′ə ləs), *adj.* 1. given to undue levity. 2. of little or no worth or importance. —**fri·vol·i·ty** (fri vol′i tē), *n.* —**friv′o·lous·ly,** *adv.*

friz (friz), *v.,* **frizzed, friz·zing,** *n., pl.* **friz·zes.** —*v.t., v.i.* 1. to form into small, crisp curls or little tufts. —*n.* 2. something frizzed, esp. hair. Also, **frizz.** —**friz′zy,** *adj.* —**friz′zi·ly,** *adv.* —**friz′zi·ness,** *n.*

friz·zle¹ (friz′əl), *v.,* **-zled, -zling,** *n.* —*v.t., v.i.* 1. to friz. —*n.* 2. a short, crisp curl. —**friz′zly,** *adj.*

friz·zle² (friz′əl), *v.,* **-zled, -zling.** —*v.i.* 1. to make a sizzling noise in frying. —*v.t.* 2. to make (food) crisp by frying.

fro (frō), *adv.* **to and fro,** alternating from one place to another.

frock (frok), *n.* 1. a coarse outer garment worn by monks. 2. *Brit.* a dress worn by a woman. 3. a loose outer garment worn by peasants and workers.

frock′ coat′, a man's closefitting coat, usually double-breasted, with skirts extending to the knees, worn esp. in 19th-century England.

frog¹ (frog, frôg), *n.* 1. a tailless amphibian having long hind legs adapted for jumping. 2. a small holder made of heavy material, placed in a bowl or vase to hold flower stems in position. 3. **frog in the** or **one's throat,** *Informal.* a slight hoarseness.

frog² (frog, frôg), *n.* an ornamental fastening for the front of a coat, consisting of a button and a loop through which it passes.

frog·man (frog′man′, -mən, frôg′-), *n.* a swimmer specially equipped for underwater demolition, salvage, etc.

frol·ic (frol′ik), *n., v.,* **-icked, -ick·ing.** —*n.* 1. merry play. 2. a merrymaking or party. —*v.i.* 3. to gambol merrily. 4. to play in a frisky, light-spirited manner. —**frol′ick·er,** *n.* —**frol′ic·some** (-səm), *adj.*

from (frum, from; *unstressed* frəm), *prep.* 1. (used to specify a starting point in spatial movement). 2. (used to specify a starting point in an expression of limits). 3. (used to express removal or separation, as in space, time, order, etc.) 4. (used to express discrimination or distinction): *to differ from one's father.* 5. (used to indicate source or origin): *to come from the Midwest.* 6. (used to indicate agent or instrumentality): *death from starvation.* 7. (used to indicate cause or reason): *From the evidence, he must be guilty.*

frond (frond), *n.* an often large, finely divided leaf, esp. of a fern.

front (frunt), *n.* 1. the foremost part or surface of anything. 2. the part that seems to be directed forward. 3. a place or position directly before anything. 4. the place where combat operations are carried on. 5. land abutting on a road, river, lake, etc. 6. *Informal.* someone or something that serves as a cover or disguise for another activity, esp. one of a disreputable nature. 7. *Informal.* outward impression of position or wealth. 8. bearing or demeanor: *a calm front.* 9. the forehead, or the entire face. 10. an interface separating two dissimilar air masses. 11. **in front of,** before or ahead of. —*adj.* 12. of or at the front. —*v.t., v.i.* 13. to face. 14. to serve as a front (for). —**fron′tal,** *adj.*

front., frontispiece.

front·age (frun′tij), *n.* 1. the front of a building or lot. 2. the lineal extent of this front. 3. the direction it faces. 4. front (def. 5).

front′ burn′er, *Informal.* a state of top priority: *Welfare reform is on the front burner.*

fron·tier (frun tēr′), *n.* 1. the part of a country that borders another country. 2. land that forms the farthest extent of a country's settled regions. 3. Often, **frontiers.** the limit of knowledge or achievement in a particular field. —*adj.* 4. of or characteristic of the frontier. —**fron·tiers'·man,** *n.*

fron·tis·piece (frun'tis pēs', fron'-), *n.* an illustrated leaf preceding the title page of a book.

front' of'fice, the executive or administrative office of a company.

front' run'ner, a person who leads in any competition.

frost (frôst, frost), *n.* 1. a covering of minute ice needles, formed from atmospheric vapor upon the ground and exposed objects. 2. a state of coldness sufficient to freeze water. —*v.t.* 3. to cover with frost. 4. to give a frostlike surface to (glass, etc.). 5. to put frosting on (a cake, etc.). 6. to kill or injure by frost. 7. *Brit.* to quick-freeze. —*v.i.* 8. to become frosted. —**frost'i·ness,** *n.* —**frost'like',** *adj.*

Frost (frôst, frost), *n.* **Robert (Lee),** 1874–1963, U.S. poet.

frost·bite (frôst'bīt', frost'-), *n., v.,* **-bit, -bit·ten, -bit·ing.** —*n.* 1. the inflamed, gangrenous effect of excessive exposure to extreme cold. —*v.t.* 2. to injure by extreme cold. —**frost'bit'ten,** *adj.*

frost' heave', an uplift in soil caused by the freezing of internal moisture.

frost·ing (frô'sting, fros'ting), *n.* 1. a sweet mixture for coating or filling cakes, cookies, etc. 2. a lusterless finish, as of metal or glass.

froth (frôth, froth), *n.* 1. a mass of bubbles, as on agitated liquid. 2. a foam of saliva. 3. something unsubstantial or evanescent. —*v.t.* 4. to cover with froth. —*v.i.* 5. to give out froth. —**froth'y,** *adj.* —**froth'i·ly,** *adv.* —**froth'i·ness,** *n.*

frou-frou (frōō'frōō'), *n.* 1. a rustling, as of silk. 2. elaborate decoration, esp. on women's clothing.

fro·ward (frō'word, frō'ord), *adj.* Archaic. perverse or willfully contrary. —**fro'ward·ness,** *n.*

frown (froun), *v.i.* 1. to contract the brow, as in displeasure or deep thought. 2. to look displeased. 3. to look disapprovingly: *to frown upon a scheme.* —*v.t.* 4. to express by a frown. —*n.* 5. a frowning look.

frowz·y (frou'zē), *adj.,* **frowz·i·er, frowz·i·est.** dirty and untidy. —**frowz'i·ly,** *adv.* —**frowz'i·ness,** *n.*

froze (frōz), *v.* pt. of **freeze.**

fro·zen (frō'zən), *v.* 1. pp. of **freeze.** —*adj.* 2. congealed by cold or covered with ice. 3. very cold. 4. injured or killed by cold. 5. chilly or cold in manner. 6. chilled or refrigerated. 7. not readily turned into cash: *frozen assets.*

FRS, Federal Reserve System.

frt., freight.

fruc·ti·fy (fruk'tə fī', frōōk'-), *v.,* **-fied, -fy·ing.** —*v.i.* 1. to bear fruit. —*v.t.* 2. to make fruitful or productive.

fruc·tose (fruk'tōs, frōōk'-), *n.* an extremely sweet sugar occurring in honey and many fruits, used in foods.

fru·gal (frōō'gəl), *adj.* 1. economical in use or expenditure. 2. meager or scanty. —**fru·gal·i·ty** (frōō gal'i tē), *n.* —**fru'gal·ly,** *adv.*

fruit (frōōt), *n., pl.* **fruits, fruit,** *v.* —*n.* 1. *Bot.* a. the developed ovary of a seed plant, as the nut, tomato, etc. b. the edible part of a plant developed from a flower, as the peach, banana, etc. 2. any useful part of a plant. 3. anything produced or accruing. —*v.i., v.t.* 4. to bear or cause to bear fruit. —**fruit'ed** (-id), *adj.*

fruit·cake (frōōt'kāk'), *n.* a rich cake containing raisins, nuts, etc.

fruit·er·er (frōō'tər ər), *n.* Chiefly Brit. a dealer in fruit.

fruit' fly', any of numerous small two-winged insects whose larvae feed on fruit.

fruit·ful (frōōt'fəl), *adj.* 1. bearing fruit abundantly. 2. producing an abundant growth, as of fruit. 3. productive of good results. —**fruit'-ful·ly,** *adv.* —**fruit'ful·ness,** *n.*

fru·i·tion (frōō ish'ən), *n.* 1. attainment of anything desired. 2. enjoyment, as of something attained. 3. the state of bearing fruit.

fruit·less (frōōt'lis), *adj.* 1. without results or success. 2. bearing no fruit. —**fruit'less·ly,** *adv.* —**fruit'less·ness,** *n.*

fruit·y (frōō'tē), *adj.,* **fruit·i·er, fruit·i·est.** having the taste or flavor of fruit. —**fruit'i·ness,** *n.*

frump (frump), *n.* a dowdy and drab woman. —**frump'ish, frump'y,** *adj.*

frus·trate (frus'trāt), *v.t.,* **-trat·ed, -trat·ing.** 1. to block in an endeavor. 2. to cause disheartening feelings in. 3. to make (efforts, etc.) worthless or of no avail. —**frus'trat·ing·ly,** *adv.* —**frus·tra'tion** (-strā'shən), *n.* —**Syn.** baffle, disappoint, foil, thwart.

frus·tum (frus'təm), *n., pl.* **-tums, -ta** (-tə). *Geom.* the part of a conical solid left after cutting off a top portion with a plane parallel to the base.

frwy., freeway.

fry¹ (frī), *v.,* **fried, fry·ing,** *n., pl.* **fries.** —*v.t.* 1. to cook with fat, oil, etc., usually over direct heat. —*v.i.* 2. to undergo cooking in fat. —*n.* 3. a dish of something fried. 4. an occasion at which the chief food is fried, frequently outdoors. [< OF *fri(re)* < L *frigere*]

fry² (frī), *n., pl.* **fry. 1.** the young of fish. **2.** the young of various other animals, as frogs.

fry·er (frī′ər), *n.* **1.** a person or thing that fries. **2.** something, as a young chicken, for frying.

FSLIC, Federal Savings and Loan Insurance Corporation.

f-stop (ef′stop′), *n.* a camera-lens aperture setting calibrated to an f number.

ft, foot; feet.

ft., **1.** foot; feet. **2.** fort.

FTC, Federal Trade Commission.

ft-lb, foot-pound; foot-pounds.

fuch·sia (fyōō′shə), *n.* **1.** a plant cultivated for its handsome drooping flowers. **2.** a shrub having large crimson flowers. **3.** a bright, purplish-red color.

fud·dle (fud′³l), *v.,* **-dled, -dling.** —*v.t.* **1.** to muddle or stupefy with or as with liquor. —*n.* **2.** a fuddled state.

fud·dy-dud·dy (fud′ē dud′ē, -dud′ē), *n., pl.* **-dud·dies.** *Informal.* a person who is stuffy, old-fashioned, conservative, or fussy about details.

fudge¹ (fuj), *n.* a candy made of sugar, butter, milk, chocolate, and flavoring.

fudge² (fuj), *n.* nonsense or foolishness (often used interjectionally).

fudge³ (fuj), *v.t.,* **fudged, fudg·ing. 1.** to avoid coming to grips with something: *to fudge on an issue.* **2.** to cheat or deceive.

Fueh·rer (fyōōr′ər), *n.* Führer.

fu·el (fyōō′əl), *n., v.,* **-eled, -el·ing** or **-elled, -el·ling.** —*n.* **1.** combustible matter used to maintain fire, as coal, wood, oil, etc. **2.** something that gives nourishment or incentive. —*v.t.,* *v.i.* **3.** to supply with or obtain fuel.

fu′el cell′, a device in which the chemical energy of a fuel is converted into continuous electrical energy.

fu′el injec′tion, the spraying of liquid fuel into the cylinders or combustion chambers of an engine. —**fu′el injec′tor.**

fu·gi·tive (fyōō′ji tiv), *n.* **1.** a person who is fleeing, as from prosecution. —*adj.* **2.** having taken flight or run away: *a fugitive slave.* **3.** fleeting or transitory. —**fu′gi·tive·ly,** *adv.*

fugue (fyōōg), *n.* **1.** *Music.* a polyphonic composition based upon one or more themes that are enunciated by several voices or parts in turn. **2.** *Psychiatry.* a period during which a patient suffers from loss of memory and, upon recovery, remembers nothing of the amnesic period. —**fu′gal,** *adj.*

Füh·rer (fyōōr′ər), *n.* German. **1.** leader. **2.** der Führer (der), the leader, applied to Adolf Hitler.

-ful, a suffix meaning: **a.** full of or characterized by: *shameful; beautiful.* **b.** tending to or able to: *wakeful; harmful.* **c.** as much as will fill: *spoonful.*

ful·crum (fŏŏl′krəm, ful′-), *n., pl.* **crums, -cra** (-krə). **1.** the support on which a lever turns in moving a body. **2.** any means of wielding power or influence.

ful·fill (fŏŏl fil′), *v.t.* **1.** to bring to realization, as a prophecy. **2.** to perform or do, as duty. **3.** to satisfy (requirements, etc.). **4.** to finish or complete, as a period of time. Also, **ful·fil′.** —**ful·fill′er,** *n.* —**fulfill′ment,** *n.*

full¹ (fŏŏl), *adj.* **1.** filled to utmost capacity. **2.** complete or entire. **3.** of the maximum amount, extent, etc.: *full pay.* **4.** (of garments, etc.) wide or having ample folds. **5.** abundant or well-supplied: *a cabinet full of medicine.* **6.** filled or rounded out, as in form: *a full bust.* **7.** engrossed or occupied: *He was full of his own anxieties.* **8.** of the same parents: *full brothers.* **9.** *Music.* ample in volume or richness of sound. **10.** (of wines) having considerable body. —*adv.* **11.** exactly or directly. **12.** very: *You know it full well.* —*n.* **13.** the fullest state, amount, or degree. —**full′ness, ful′ness,** *n.*

full² (fŏŏl), *v.t.,* *v.i.* to cleanse and thicken (cloth) by special processes in manufacture. —**full′er,** *n.*

full·back (fŏŏl′bak′), *n.* *Football.* a running back who lines up behind the quarterback.

full-blood·ed (fŏŏl′blud′id), *adj.* **1.** of unmixed ancestry or breed. **2.** vigorous or virile.

full-blown (fŏŏl′blōn′), *adj.* **1.** in full bloom. **2.** completely developed.

full-bod·ied (fŏŏl′bod′ēd), *adj.* of full flavor or richness.

full′ dress′, a ceremonial or formal style of dress.

full-fledged (fŏŏl′flejd′), *adj.* **1.** fully developed. **2.** of full rank or standing.

full′ moon′, the moon when the whole of its disk is illuminated.

full-scale (fŏŏl′skāl′), *adj.* **1.** having the exact size or proportions of the original. **2.** using all possible means or facilities.

full′ tilt′, at the full potential, speed, or energy.

full-time (fŏŏl′tīm′), *adj., adv.* working or operating the customary number of hours in a given period. —**full′-tim′er,** *n.*

ful·ly (fŏŏl′ē), *adv.* **1.** entirely or wholly. **2.** quite or at least.

ful·mi·nate (ful'mə nāt'), v.i., v.t., -nat·ed, -nat·ing. 1. to explode with a loud noise. 2. to issue denunciations (against). —ful'mi·na'tion, n.

ful·some (fŏŏl'səm, ful'-), adj. 1. offensive to good taste, esp. as being excessive. 2. disgusting or repulsive. —ful'some·ly, adv. —ful'some·ness, n.

fu·ma·role (fyŏŏ'mə rōl'), n. a hole, in or near a volcano, from which vapor rises. —fu·ma·rol·ic (fyŏŏ'mə rol'ik), adj.

fum·ble (fum'bəl), v., -bled, -bling, n. —v.i., v.t. 1. to feel or grope (about) clumsily. 2. to make or handle (a thing) clumsily or inefficiently. 3. Sports. to fail to hold (a ball) after having touched it. —n. 4. the act of fumbling. 5. Sports. a ball that is fumbled. —fum'bler, n.

fume (fyŏŏm), n., v., fumed, fum·ing. —n. 1. any smokelike or vaporous exhalation from matter, esp. of an odorous nature. —v.i. 2. to emit or exhale, as fumes. 3. to treat with fumes. —v.i. 4. to emit fumes. 5. to show fretful irritation or anger.

fu·mi·gant (fyŏŏ'mi gənt), n. any chemical compound used in fumigating.

fu·mi·gate (fyŏŏ'mə gāt'), v.t., -gat·ed, -gat·ing. to expose to fumes, as in disinfecting. —fu'mi·ga'tion, n. —fu'mi·ga'tor, n.

fum·y (fyŏŏ'mē), adj., fum·i·er, fum·i·est. emitting or full of fumes.

fun (fun), n. 1. something that provides mirth or amusement. 2. enjoyment or playfulness. 3. make fun of, to ridicule or deride. —Syn. 1, 2. entertainment, merriment, pleasure.

func·tion (fungk'shən), n. 1. the kind of action or activity proper to any person or thing. 2. the purpose for which something is designed or exists. 3. any ceremonious public or social gathering or occasion. 4. a factor related to or dependent upon other factors. 5. Math. a relation between two sets in which one or more elements of the second set are assigned to each element of the first set. —v.i. 6. to perform a function. 7. to serve or operate. —func'tion·less, adj.

func·tion·al (fungk'shə nᵊl), adj. 1. of a function. 2. having or performing a function. 3. capable of functioning. 4. Psychol. without a known organic cause or structural change. —func'tion·al·ly, adv.

func·tion·ar·y (fungk'shə ner'ē), n., pl. -ar·ies. a person who functions in a specified capacity, esp. a government official.

func'tion word', a word, as a preposition, used to show syntactic relationship.

fund (fund), n. 1. a stock of money or pecuniary resources, as for some purpose. 2. a supply or stock of something, as information. 3. funds, money in hand. 4. an organization created to administer or manage money contributed or invested. —v.t. 5. to convert (a short-term debt) into a long-term obligation, as a bond. 6. to provide funds for.

fun·da·men·tal (fun'də men't ᵊl), adj. 1. serving as, or being an essential part of, a foundation or basis: fundamental principles. 2. of or affecting the foundation or basis: a fundamental revision. 3. being an original or primary source: a fundamental idea. —n. 4. a basic principle, rule, law, etc. 5. Physics. the component of lowest frequency in a composite wave. —fun'da·men'tal·ly, adv.

fun·da·men·tal·ism (fun'də men'tᵊliz'əm), n. (sometimes cap.) a Protestant movement that stresses the infallibility of the Bible in all matters of faith. —fun'da·men'tal·ist, n., adj.

fu·ner·al (fyŏŏ'nər əl), n. 1. the ceremonies for a dead person prior to burial or cremation. 2. a funeral procession.

fu'neral direc'tor, a person who manages a funeral home.

fu'neral home', an establishment where the dead are prepared for burial or cremation and where funeral services are held. Also called **fu'neral par'lor**.

fu·ner·ar·y (fyŏŏ'nə rer'ē), adj. of or pertaining to a funeral or burial.

fu·ne·re·al (fyŏŏ nēr'ē əl), adj. 1. of or suitable for a funeral. 2. mournful and gloomy. —fu·ne're·al·ly, adv.

fun·gi·cide (fun'ji sīd'), n. an agent used for destroying fungi. —fun'gi·cid'al, adj.

fun·gus (fung'gəs), n., pl. fun·gi (fun'jī), fun·gus·es. any of a group of simple plants that have no chlorophyll and comprise the mushrooms, molds, mildews, smuts, etc. —fun'gal (-gəl), fun'goid (-goid), fun'gous, adj.

fu·nic·u·lar (fyŏŏ nik'yə lər), adj. 1. worked by a rope or cord. —n. 2. a short, steep cable railway operating in such a way that the ascending and descending cars are counterbalanced.

funk (fungk), n. Informal. 1. cowering fear. 2. a dejected mood.

funk·y (fung'kē), adj., funk·i·er, funk·i·est. Slang. 1. Jazz. having an earthy, blues-based quality. 2. pleasantly unconventional or offbeat.

fun·nel (fun'ᵊl), *n.*, *v.*, **-neled, -nel·ing** or **-nelled, -nel·ling.** —*n.* **1.** a cone-shaped utensil with a tube at the apex, for conducting liquid through a small opening, as into a bottle. **2.** a smokestack, esp. of a steamship. —*v.t.*, *v.i.* **3.** to pass or cause to pass through or as through a funnel.

fun·ny (fun'ē), *adj.*, **-ni·er, -ni·est,** *n.*, *pl.* **-nies.** —*adj.* **1.** provoking laughter. **2.** *Informal.* odd or strange. **3.** *Informal.* deceitful or underhanded. —*n.* **4.** funnies, comic strips. —**fun'·ni·ly,** *adv.* —**fun'ni·ness,** *n.* —Syn. **1.** amusing, comical, humorous, laughable.

fun'ny bone', a place at the bend of the elbow which when struck causes a tingling sensation in the hand.

fun'ny mon'ey, *Slang.* **1.** counterfeit currency. **2.** money from undisclosed or questionable sources.

fur (fûr), *n.* **1.** the fine, soft, thick, hairy coat of the skin of a mammal. **2.** such a coat, as of sable, used for lining or garments. **3.** a garment made of fur. **4.** any coating resembling fur. —*adj.* **5.** of fur. —**furred** (fûrd), *adj.*

fur., furlong; furlongs.

fur·be·low (fûr'bə lō'), *n.* **1.** a festooned flounce. **2.** any bit of showy trimming.

fur·bish (fûr'bish), *v.t.* to restore to freshness of appearance or condition.

fur·cu·la (fûr'kyə lə), *n.*, *pl.* **-lae** (-lē'). any forked bone, esp. the wishbone of a bird. Also, **fur'cu·lum** (-ləm). —**furc'u·lar,** *adj.*

fu·ri·ous (fyŏŏr'ē əs), *adj.* **1.** full of fury or rage. **2.** intensely violent, as wind. —**fu'ri·ous·ly,** *adv.*

furl (fûrl), *v.t.* **1.** to roll up and bind securely, as a flag against its staff. —*v.i.* **2.** to become furled. —**furl'er,** *n.*

fur·long (fûr'lông, -long), *n.* a unit of distance, equal to 220 yards or ⅛ mile.

fur·lough (fûr'lō), *n.* **1.** vacation granted to an enlisted person. —*v.t.* **2.** to grant a furlough to.

fur·nace (fûr'nəs), *n.* a structure in which heat is generated, as for heating houses.

fur·nish (fûr'nish), *v.t.* **1.** to give what is useful, as for necessity or comfort. **2.** to fit out (a room, etc.) with furniture. —Syn. **1.** provide, supply.

fur·nish·ings (fûr'ni shingz), *n.pl.* **1.** furniture, carpeting, etc., for a house. **2.** articles of dress and accessories for men.

fur·ni·ture (fûr'ni chər), *n.* the movable articles, as tables, chairs, desks, cabinets, etc., required for use or ornament in a house or office.

fu·ror (fyŏŏr'ôr), *n.* **1.** a general outburst of enthusiasm or controversy. **2.** a prevailing mania or craze. **3.** fury or rage. Also, *esp. Brit.*, **fu'rore** (for defs. **1, 2**).

fur·ri·er (fûr'ē ər), *n.* a fur dealer or fur dresser. —**fur'ri·er·y** (-ə rē), *n.*

fur·ring (fûr'ing), *n.* strips of wood or metal attached to a wall or other surface, as to provide an even support.

fur·row (fûr'ō, fur'ō), *n.* **1.** a narrow groove made in the ground, esp. by a plow. **2.** a narrow, groovelike depression, as a wrinkle. —*v.t.* **3.** to make furrows in. —*v.i.* **4.** to become furrowed. —**fur'row·y,** *adj.*

fur·ry (fûr'ē), *adj.*, **fur·ri·er, fur·ri·est.** **1.** consisting of or resembling fur. **2.** covered with fur. —**fur'ri·ness,** *n.*

fur·ther (fûr'ʦhər), *adv.*, *compar. of* **far** *with* **furthest** *as superl.* **1.** to a greater extent. **2.** in addition. **3.** farther (def. **1**). —*adj.*, *compar. of* **far** *with* **furthest** *as superl.* **4.** more extended. **5.** additional. **6.** farther (def. **4**). —*v.t.* **7.** to help forward (an undertaking, cause, etc.). —**fur'ther·ance,** *n.*

fur·ther·more (fûr'ʦhər môr', -môr'), *adv.* moreover or besides.

fur·ther·most (fûr'ʦhər mōst'), *adj.* most distant.

fur·thest (fûr'ʦhist), *adj.*, *adv.*, *superl. of* **far** *with* **further** *as compar.* farthest.

fur·tive (fûr'tiv), *adj.* **1.** taken, done, used, etc., by stealth. **2.** sly or sneaky. —**fur'tive·ly,** *adv.* —**fur'tive·ness,** *n.*

fu·ry (fyŏŏr'ē), *n.*, *pl.* **-ries.** **1.** unrestrained or violent anger. **2.** vehemence or fierceness. [< L *furia*]

furze (fûrz), *n.* a low, many-branched, spiny shrub having yellow flowers, native to Europe.

fuse¹ (fyōōz), *n.*, *v.*, **fused, fus·ing.** —*n.* **1.** a tube filled or saturated with combustible matter, for igniting an explosive. **2.** fuze (def. **1**). —*v.t.* **3.** fuze (def. **3**). —**fuse'less,** *adj.*

fuse² (fyōōz), *v.*, **fused, fus·ing,** *n.* —*v.t.*, *v.i.* **1.** to combine by melting together. **2.** to blend into a whole, as if by melting together. —*n.* **3.** *Elect.* a protective device containing a piece of metal that melts under heat produced by an excess current in a circuit, thereby breaking the circuit. —**fu'si·ble,** *adj.* —**fu'si·ble·ness,** *n.*

fu·see (fyōō zē'), *n.* **1.** a wooden match having a large head and ignited by friction. **2.** a red flare light, used on a railroad as a warning signal to approaching trains. **3.** fuse¹ (def. **1**).

fu·se·lage (fyŏŏ′sə läzh′, -lij, -zə-), *n.* the central structure to which the wing, tail surfaces, and engines are attached on an airplane.

fu′sel oil′ (fyŏŏ′zəl, -səl), a colorless liquid mixture of alcohols used to make varnishes.

fu·sil·lade (fyŏŏ′sə lād′, -läd′, -zə-), *n.* **1.** a simultaneous or continuous discharge of firearms. **2.** a general outpouring of anything: *a fusillade of questions.*

fu·sion (fyŏŏ′zhən), *n.* **1.** the process of fusing or state of being fused. **2.** something that is fused. **3.** a coalition of political parties or factions. **4.** a thermonuclear reaction in which nuclei of light atoms join to form nuclei of heavier atoms under the influence of extreme heat.

fuss (fus), *n.* **1.** an excessive display of anxious attention or activity. **2.** an argument or noisy dispute. **3.** a complaint or protest, esp. about something unimportant. —*v.i.* **4.** to make a fuss. **5.** to complain or fret.

fuss·budg·et (fus′buj′it), *n.* a needlessly faultfinding person. Also called **fuss·pot** (fus′pot′).

fuss·y (fus′ē), *adj.*, **fuss·i·er, fuss·i·est. 1.** excessively anxious or particular about petty details. **2.** elaborately made, as clothes. **3.** full of details, esp. in excess. —**fuss′i·ly,** *adv.* —**fuss′i·ness,** *n.*

fus·tian (fus′chən), *n.* **1.** a stout fabric of cotton and flax. **2.** pompous or bombastic language.

fus·ty (fus′tē), *adj.*, **-ti·er, -ti·est. 1.** having a stale smell. **2.** old-fashioned or out-of-date. —**fus′ti·ly,** *adv.* — **fus′ti·ness,** *n.*

fut., future.

fu·tile (fyŏŏt′[ə]l, fyŏŏ′tīl), *adj.* **1.** incapable of producing any useful result. **2.** trifling or frivolous. —**fu′tile·ly,** *adv.* —**fu·til·i·ty** (fyŏŏ til′i tē), *n.* —**Syn. 1.** ineffectual, useless.

fu·ture (fyŏŏ′chər), *n.* **1.** time that is to be or come hereafter. **2.** something that will exist or happen in

time to come. **3.** a chance of success or failure to come. **4.** *Gram.* **a.** the future tense. **b.** a verb form in the future. —*adj.* **5.** that is to be or come hereafter. **6.** pertaining to time to come. **7.** *Gram.* designating a verb tense that refers to events or states in time to come. —**fu′ture·less,** *adj.*

fu′ture shock′, the inability of people to cope with very rapid social and technological change. [coined by Alvin *Toffler* (b.1928), U.S. author]

fu·tur·ism (fyŏŏ′chə riz′əm), *n. (often cap.)* an Italian movement in the arts begun in 1909 which extolled the vigor and energy of the machine age. —**fu′tur·ist,** *n., adj.*

fu·tur·is·tic (fyŏŏ′chə ris′tik), *adj.* **1.** well-advanced and ahead of the times: *futuristic technology.* **2.** *(often cap.)* of or pertaining to futurism.

fu·tu·ri·ty (fyŏŏ tōŏr′i tē, -tyŏŏr′-, -chŏŏr′-), *n., pl.* **-ties. 1.** future time. **2.** a future state or condition.

fu·tu·rol·o·gy (fyŏŏ′chə rol′ə jē), *n.* the study or practice of forecasting trends or developments in science, technology, political or social structure, etc. —**fu′tu·rol′o·gist,** *n.*

fuze (fyŏŏz), *n., v.*, **fuzed, fuz·ing.** —*n.* **1.** a mechanical or electronic device to detonate an explosive charge. **2.** fuse[1] (def. 1). —*v.t.* **3.** to attach a fuze to (a bomb, etc.).

fu·zee (fyŏŏ zē′), *n.* fusee.

fuzz (fuz), *n., pl.,* **fuzz. 1.** loose, light, fibrous, or fluffy matter. **2.** *Slang.* a police officer or the police.

fuzz·y (fuz′ē), *adj.*, **fuzz·i·er, fuzz·i·est. 1.** resembling or covered with fuzz. **2.** indistinct or blurred. —**fuzz′i·ness,** *n.*

FWD, four-wheel drive.

fwd., forward.

-fy, a suffix meaning: **a.** to make, render, or cause to be: *simplify; beautify.* **b.** to become or be made: *liquefy.*

FY, fiscal year.

FYI, for your information.

G

G, g (jē), *n., pl.* **G's** or **Gs, g's** or **gs.** the seventh letter of the English alphabet, a consonant.

G, *Slang.* a sum of $1,000.

G, 1. the seventh in order or in a series. **2.** *Music.* the fifth tone in the scale of C major. **3.** a designation for motion pictures regarded as acceptable for all age groups.

g, 1. good. **2.** gram; grams. **3.** *Physics.* gravity.

g, acceleration of gravity.

G., 1. German. **2.** Gulf.

g., 1. gauge. **2.** gender.

Ga, gallium.

Ga., Georgia.

GA, 1. General of the Army. **2.** Georgia.

G.A., 1. General Assembly. 2. general average.

gab (gab), v., **gabbed, gab·bing,** n. Informal. —v.i. 1. to talk idly. —n. 2. idle talk. —**gab′ber,** n.

gab·ar·dine (gab′ər dēn′, gab′ər dēn′), n. 1. firm, woven fabric of worsted, cotton, or spun rayon, with a twill weave. 2. gaberdine (def. 1).

gab·ble (gab′əl), v., **-bled, -bling,** n. —v.i., v.t. 1. to speak rapidly and unintelligibly. —n. 2. rapid, unintelligible talk. —**gab′bler,** n.

gab·bro (gab′rō), n., pl. **-bros.** a granular igneous rock. —**gab·bro·ic** (gə brō′ik), adj.

gab·by (gab′ē), adj., **-bi·er, -bi·est.** very talkative. —**gab′bi·ness,** n.

gab·er·dine (gab′ər dēn′, gab′ər dēn′), n. 1. a long, loose coat or frock for men, worn in the Middle Ages, esp. by Jews. 2. gabardine (def. 1).

gab·fest (gab′fest′), n. Informal. a gathering at which there is a great deal of conversation.

ga·ble (gā′bəl), n. the portion of the front or side of a building enclosed by the end of or masking the end of a pitched roof.

Ga·bon (gΛ bôN′), n. a country in W Africa.

Ga·bri·el (gā′brē əl), n. one of the archangels, appearing usually as a divine messenger.

gad (gad), v.i., **gad·ded, gad·ding.** to move restlessly or aimlessly about. —**gad′der,** n.

Gad (gad), interj. Archaic. (a euphemism for God, used as a mild oath.) Also, **gad.**

gad·a·bout (gad′ə bout′), n. a person who moves restlessly or aimlessly about, esp. for curiosity or gossip.

gad·fly (gad′flī′), n. 1. a fly that bites or annoys domestic animals. 2. a person who repeatedly and persistently annoys others.

gadg·et (gaj′it), n. a mechanical contrivance or device. —**gadg′e·teer′,** n. —**gadg′et·ry,** n.

gad·o·lin·i·um (gad′°lin′ē əm), n. Chem. a rare-earth metallic element. Symbol: Gd; at. wt.: 157.25; at. no.: 64.

Gael (gāl), n. a Gaelic-speaking Celt. **Gael,** Gaelic. Also, **Gael.**

Gael·ic (gā′lik), n. 1. any Celtic language spoken in Ireland and the Highlands. —adj. 2. of or pertaining to the Gaels or their languages.

gaff (gaf), n. 1. an iron hook with a handle for landing large fish. 2. a spar used to support the head of a fore-and-aft sail. 3. **stand the gaff,** Slang. to weather hardship or strain.

gaffe (gaf), n. a social blunder.

gaf·fer (gaf′ər), n. an old fellow, esp. an elderly rustic.

gag¹ (gag), v., **gagged, gag·ging,** n. —v.t. 1. to stop up the mouth of (a person) by putting something in it, thus preventing speech, shouts, etc. 2. to restrain from speaking freely. 3. to hold open the jaws of, as in surgical operations. 4. to cause to retch or choke. —v.i. 5. to retch or choke. —n. 6. something put into a person's mouth to prevent speech, shouting, etc. 7. any suppression of free speech. 8. a surgical instrument for holding the jaws open.

gag² (gag), v., **gagged, gag·ging,** n. Informal. —v.t. 1. to tell a joke or jokes. —n. 2. a joke. 3. any contrived piece of wordplay or horseplay.

gage¹ (gāj), n. 1. something, as a glove, thrown down by a medieval knight in token of challenge to combat. 2. Archaic. a. a challenge. b. a pledge or pawn.

gage² (gāj), v.t., **gaged, gag·ing,** n. Chiefly Technical. gauge.

gag·gle (gag′əl), n. a flock of geese.

gai·e·ty (gā′i tē), n., pl. **-ties.** 1. the state of being gay or cheerful. 2. merrymaking or festivity. 3. showiness or finery.

gai·ly (gā′lē), adv. 1. merrily or cheerfully. 2. with showiness.

gain (gān), v.t. 1. to get (something desired), esp. as a result of one's efforts. 2. to win: to gain the prize. 3. to acquire as an increase or addition: to gain weight. 4. to reach by effort. —v.i. 5. to improve: to gain in health. 6. to get nearer, as in pursuit: Our racehorse was gaining on the favorite. —n. 7. something gained. 8. gains, profits or winnings. 9. an increase or advance. —**gain·er** (gā′nər), n. —Syn. 1. earn, obtain. 7. advantage, profit.

gain·ful (gān′fəl), adj. producing gain or profit. —**gain′ful·ly,** adv. —**gain′ful·ness,** n. —Syn. lucrative, profitable.

gain·say (gān′sā′), v.t., **-said, -say·ing.** Literary. 1. to deny. 2. to speak or act against. —**gain′say′er,** n.

gait (gāt), n. 1. a manner of walking, stepping, or running. 2. any of the manners in which a horse moves, as a trot, canter, gallop, etc. —**gait′ed,** adj.

gait·er (gā′tər), n. 1. a covering of cloth or leather for the ankle, instep, and the lower leg. 2. a cloth or leather shoe with elastic insertions at the sides. 3. a high overshoe having a fabric top.

gal (gal), n. Informal. a girl.

gal, gallon; gallons.

ga·la (gā′lə, gal′ə, gä′lə), adj. 1. showily festive. —n. 2. a showy celebration or festive occasion.

ga·lac·tose (gə lak′tōs), *n.* a simple sugar obtained from lactose.

Gal·a·had (gal′ə had′), *n.* **1.** Sir, *Arthurian Romance.* the noblest knight, who found the Holy Grail. **2.** a man of knightly purity.

gal·ax·y (gal′ək sē), *n., pl.* **-ax·ies.** **1. a.** a large system of stars held together by mutual gravitation. **b.** (*usually cap.*) See **Milky Way. 2.** any large and brilliant assemblage of persons or things. [< ML < Gk: milky] **—ga·lac·tic** (gə lak′tik), *adj.*

gale (gāl), *n.* **1.** a strong wind. **2.** a noisy outburst: *a gale of laughter.*

ga·le·na (gə lē′nə), *n.* a common, heavy mineral: the principal ore of lead.

Gal·i·lee (gal′ə lē′), *n.* Sea of, a lake in NE Israel.

Gal·i·le·o (gal′ə lē′ō, -lā′ō), *n.* 1564-1642, Italian physicist and astronomer.

gall¹ (gôl), *n.* **1.** something bitter or severe. **2.** bitterness of spirit. **3.** bile, esp. that of the ox. **4.** impudence or effrontery.

gall² (gôl), *v.t.* **1.** to make sore by rubbing. **2.** to vex or irritate. **—n. 3.** a sore on the skin, esp. of a horse, due to rubbing. **4.** something vexing or irritating.

gall³ (gôl), *n.* any abnormal growth on plants, caused by insects, fungi, bacteria, etc.

gal·lant *adj.* gal′ənt *for 1, 2;* gə lant′, -länt′, gal′ənt *for 3, 4; n.* gə lant′, -länt′, gal′ənt), *adj.* **1.** brave, high-spirited, or chivalrous. **2.** stately or grand. **3.** polite and attentive to women. **4.** amorous or amatory. **— n. Rare. 5.** a brave, high-spirited, or chivalrous man. **6.** a gay and dashing man. **7.** a man particularly attentive to women. **—gal′lant·ly,** *adv.*

gal·lant·ry (gal′ən trē), *n., pl.* **-ries. 1.** heroic bravery. **2.** gallant or courtly attention to women. **3.** a gallant act, action, or speech.

gall·blad·der (gôl′blad′ər), *n.* a small sac resting under the right lobe of the liver, which stores and concentrates the bile.

gal·le·on (gal′ē ən, gal′yən), *n.* a large Spanish sailing vessel of the 15th and 16th centuries.

gal·ler·y (gal′ə rē, gal′rē), *n., pl.* **-leries. 1.** a raised, balconylike platform or passageway running along the exterior wall of a building. **2.** a raised area, often with a sloping floor, in a theater, church, etc., to accommodate spectators, exhibits, etc. **3.** the uppermost of such areas in a theater, usually containing the cheapest seats. **4.** the public taste. **5.** any group of spectators or observers, as at a Congressional session. **6.** a room or building devoted to the exhibition and often the sale of works of art. **7.** a collection of art for exhibition. **8.** a large room or building used for photography, target practice, etc. **9.** a long, covered area, open at one side, used as a walk or corridor. **10.** a small tunnel in a dam, mine, or rock. **11.** *Southern U.S.* a porch or portico. **—gal′ler·ied,** *adj.*

gal·ley (gal′ē), *n., pl.* **-leys. 1.** a seagoing vessel propelled mainly by oars, used in ancient and medieval times. **2.** a kitchen aboard a vessel or airplane. **3.** *Print.* **a.** a long, narrow tray for holding type that has been set. **b.** Also called **gal′ley proof′.** a proof printed from type in such a tray.

Gal·lic (gal′ik), *adj.* **1.** of the Gauls or Gaul. **2.** French: *Gallic humor.*

Gal·li·cism (gal′i siz′əm), *n.* a French idiom, trait, etc. Also, **gal′li·cism.**

gal·li·mau·fry (gal′ə mô′frē), *n., pl.* **-fries.** *Literary.* a confused medley.

gal·li·nule (gal′ə nōol′, -nyōol′), *n.* an aquatic bird having elongated, webless toes.

gal·li·um (gal′ē əm), *n. Chem.* a rare, steel-gray metallic element used in high-temperature thermometers. Symbol: Ga; *at. wt.:* 69.72; *at. no.:* 31.

gal·li·vant (gal′ə vant′), *v.i.* to gad about gaily or frivolously. **—gal′li·vant′er,** *n.*

gal·lon (gal′ən), *n.* a unit of capacity equal to four quarts or 3.785 liters.

gal·lop (gal′əp), *v.i., v.t.* **1.** to run or cause to run full speed. **—n. 2.** a fast gait of the horse or other quadruped in which all four feet are off the ground at once. **—gal′lop·er,** *n.*

gal·lows (gal′ōz, -əz), *n., pl.* **-lows·es, -lows. 1.** a frame, consisting of a cross beam on two uprights, on which condemned persons are executed by hanging. **2.** a similar structure from which something is suspended.

gall·stone (gôl′stōn′), *n.* an abnormal stonelike mass formed in the gallbladder or bile passages.

Gal′lup poll′. a representative sampling of public opinion concerning a certain issue. [after G. H. *Gallup* (b. 1901), U.S. statistician]

gal·lus·es (gal′əs, -iz), *n.pl. Chiefly Dial.* a pair of trouser suspenders.

ga·lore (gə lôr′, -lōr′), *adv.* in plentiful amounts.

ga·losh (gə losh′), *n.* a high overshoe. Also, **ga·loshe′.**

galv., galvanized.

gal·va·nism (gal′və niz′əm), *n. Elect.* electricity, esp. as produced by chemical action. **—gal·van′ic** (-van′ik), *adj.* **—gal·van′i·cal·ly,** *adv.*

gal·va·nize (gal′və nīz′), *v.t.*, **-nized,** **-niz·ing.** **1.** to stimulate by or as by a galvanic current. **2.** to startle into sudden activity. **3.** to coat (metal, esp. iron or steel) with zinc. —**gal′va·ni·za′tion,** *n.* —**gal′va·niz′er,** *n.*

gal·va·nom·e·ter (gal′və nom′i tər), *n.* an instrument for detecting the existence and determining the strength of small electric currents. —**gal′va·no·met′ric** (-nō met′trik), *adj.*

gam (gam), *n. Slang.* a person's leg, esp. an attractive female leg.

Ga·ma (gam′ə), *n.* **Vas·co da** (vas′kō də), c1460–1524, Portuguese navigator.

Gam·bi·a (gam′bē ə), *n.* a country in W Africa. —**Gam′bi·an,** *adj., n.*

gam·bit (gam′bit), *n.* **1.** *Chess.* an opening in which the player seeks by sacrificing a pawn or piece to obtain some advantage. **2.** any maneuver by which one seeks to gain an advantage.

gam·ble (gam′bəl), *v.,* **-bled,** **-bling,** *n.* —*v.i.* **1.** to play at any game of chance for stakes. **2.** to stake or risk money on the outcome of something involving chance. —*v.t.* **3.** to bet or stake (something of value). —*n.* **4.** any matter or thing involving risk. —**gam′bler,** *n.*

gam·bol (gam′bəl), *v.,* **-boled, -bol·ing** or **-bolled, -bol·ling,** *n.* —*v.i.* **1.** to skip about, as in dancing or playing. —*n.* **2.** a skipping or frisking about.

gam′brel roof′ (gam′brəl), a gable roof, each side of which has a shallower slope above a steeper one.

game¹ (gām), *n., adj.,* **gam·er, gam·est,** *v.,* **gamed, gam·ing.** —*n.* **1.** a form of playing for amusement, esp. as a pastime of children. **2.** the equipment needed for such a pastime. **3.** a competitive activity involving skill, chance, or endurance played according to rules. **4.** a single occasion of such an activity. **5.** the number of points required to win. **6.** a particular manner or style of playing in competition. **7.** a trick or strategy. **8.** wild animals, including birds and fishes, such as are hunted or taken for sport or profit. **9.** the flesh of such wild animals, used as food. **10.** any object of attack, abuse, etc. **11.** *Informal.* a business or profession. —*adj.* **12.** pertaining to wild animals hunted for sport or food. **13.** plucky or hardy. **14.** *Informal.* having the required spirit or will. —*v.i.* **15.** to play games of chance for stakes. —**game′ly,** *adv.* —**game′ness,** *n.*

game² (gām), *adj. Informal.* lame: *a game leg.*

game·cock (gām′kok′), *n.* a rooster of a fighting breed, or one bred and trained for fighting.

game′ fish′, an edible fish capable of affording sport to the angler in its capture.

game·keep·er (gām′kē′pər), *n.* a person in charge of the breeding and protection of game animals, as on an estate.

game′ plan′, a carefully thought-out strategy or course of action.

game′ point′, the point that if won by the scorer would enable his or her side to win the game, as in tennis.

games·man·ship (gāmz′mən ship′), *n.* skill in winning games by dubious methods without infringing the rules.

game·some (gām′səm), *adj.* playful or frolicsome. —**game′some·ly,** *adv.*

game·ster (gām′stər), *n.* a person who gambles habitually.

gam·ete (gam′ēt, gə mēt′), *n.* a mature sexual reproductive cell that unites with another cell to form a new organism. —**ga·met·ic** (gə met′ik), *adj.*

game′ the′ory, a mathematical theory that deals with strategies for maximizing gains and minimizing losses, as in business.

gam·in (gam′in), *n.* a neglected child left to run about the streets.

gam·ine (gam′ēn, -in, ga mēn′), *n.* a diminutive girl who is playfully mischievous.

gam·ma (gam′ə), *n.* the third letter of the Greek alphabet. (γ, Γ).

gam′ma glob′ulin, a protein component of blood plasma, containing antibodies effective against certain microorganisms.

gam′ma ray′, a highly energetic, penetrating radiation from certain radioactive elements.

gam·mer (gam′ər), *n. Archaic.* an old woman.

gam·mon¹ (gam′ən), *n.* **1.** a smoked or cured ham. **2.** the lower end of a side of bacon.

gam·mon² (gam′ən), *n. Brit. Informal.* deceitful nonsense.

gam·ut (gam′ət), *n.* **1.** the entire scale or range. **2.** the whole series of musical notes.

gam·y (gā′mē), *adj.,* **gam·i·er, gam·i·est.** **1.** having the flavor of game, esp. game kept uncooked until slightly tinted. **2.** plucky or spirited. **3.** risqué or ribald. —**gam′i·ly,** *adv.* —**gam′i·ness,** *n.*

gan·der (gan′dər), *n.* **1.** the male of the goose. **2.** *Slang.* a look or glance: *Take a gander.*

Gan·dhi (gän′dē, gan′-), *n.* **Mo·han·das K.** (mō′hən däs′), (*Mahatma Gandhi*), 1869–1948, Hindu religious leader and nationalist.

gang (gang), *n.* **1.** a group of persons working or associated together. **2.** a group of persons associated for some criminal purpose. **3.** a set of tools, oars, etc., arranged to work together. **5. gang up on,** *Informal.* to combine against.

Gan·ges (gan'jēz), *n.* a river in N India flowing into the Bay of Bengal.

gang·land (gang'land', -lĕnd), *n.* the criminal underworld.

gan·gling (gang'gling), *adj.* awkwardly tall and spindly. Also, **gan'gly** (-glē).

gan·gli·on (gang'glē ən), *n., pl.* **-gli·a'** (-glē ə), **-gli·ons.** a gray mass of nerve tissue existing outside the brain and spinal cord. —**gan'gli·on'ic** (-glē on'ik), *adj.*

gang·plank (gang'plangk'), *n.* a movable bridgelike structure for use by persons boarding or leaving a vessel at a pier.

gang' plow', a combination of two or more plows in one frame.

gan·grene (gang'grēn, gang grēn'), *n.* the dying or death of a part of body tissue, as from the interruption of circulation. —**gan'gre·nous** (-grənəs), *adj.*

gang·ster (gang'stər), *n.* a member of a gang of criminals. —**gang'ster·ism,** *n.*

gang·way (*n.* gang'wā'; *interj.* gang'wā'), *n.* **1.** a passageway, as a temporary path of planks at a building site. **2.** gangplank. —*interj.* **3.** clear the way!

gan·net (gan'it), *n.* a large web-footed bird having a long, pointed bill.

gant·let (gant'lit, gônt'-), *n.* **1.** gauntlet[1]. **2.** gauntlet[2].

gan·try (gan'trē), *n., pl.* **-tries. 1.** a spanning framework, as a bridgelike portion of certain cranes. **2.** a frame consisting of scaffolds on various levels used to launch missiles.

GAO, General Accounting Office.

gaol (jāl), *n., v.t. Brit.* jail. —**gaol'er,** *n.*

gap (gap), *n.* **1.** a break or opening, as in a fence or wall. **2.** an empty space or interval. **3.** a wide divergence or difference. **4.** a deep ravine, as in a mountain.

gape (gāp, gap), *v.*, **gaped, gap·ing,** *n.* —*v.i.* **1.** to stare with open mouth, as in wonder. **2.** to open the mouth wide involuntarily, as the result of sleepiness. **3.** to become open wide. —*n.* **4.** a wide opening or gap. **5.** the act or an instance of gaping. —**gap'er,** *n.* —**gap'ing·ly,** *adv.*

gar (gär), *n., pl.* **gar, gars.** a North American freshwater fish having a long beak with large teeth.

gar., garage.

G.A.R., Grand Army of the Republic.

ga·rage (gə räzh', -räj'), *n., v.*, **-raged, -rag·ing.** —*n.* **1.** a building for sheltering, cleaning, or repairing motor vehicles. —*v.t.* **2.** to put or keep in a garage.

garage' sale', a sale of a family's used unwanted household goods, etc., usually held in one's garage.

garb (gärb), *n.* **1.** a mode of dress, esp. of a distinctive, uniform kind. **2.** outward semblance. —*v.t.* **3.** to dress or clothe.

gar·bage (gär'bij), *n.* **1.** refuse matter from a kitchen. **2.** anything worthless, inferior, or vile.

gar·ban·zo (gär ban'zō, -bän'-), *n., pl.* **-zos.** chickpea.

gar·ble (gär'bəl), *v.t.*, **-bled, -bling.** to distort or jumble (a report, message, etc.) so as to be misleading or unintelligible. —**gar'bler,** *n.*

gar·çon (GAR SôN'), *n., pl.* **-çons** (-SôN'). *French.* (usually in direct address) a waiter in a restaurant.

gar·den (gär'dən), *n.* **1.** a plot of ground where flowers, vegetables, or herbs are cultivated. **2.** a parklike area with displays of plants or animals for public recreation. **3.** a fertile and delightful spot. —*adj.* **4.** pertaining to or produced in a garden. —*v.i.* **5.** to cultivate a garden. [< OF *jardin* < Gmc] —**gar·den·er** (gärd'nər), *n.*

gar·de·nia (gär dē'nyə, -nē ə), *n.* **1.** an evergreen tree or shrub cultivated for its fragrant, white flowers. **2.** its flower.

gar·den-va·ri·e·ty (gär'dən və rī'ĭ tē), *adj. Informal.* common or ordinary.

Gar·field (gär'fēld), *n.* James Abram, 1831–81, 20th president of the United States, 1881.

gar·fish (gär'fish'), *n., pl.* **-fish, -fishes.** gar.

gar·gan·tu·an (gär gan'chŏŏ ən), *adj.* of enormous size or capacity.

gar·gle (gär'gəl), *v.*, **-gled, -gling,** *n.* —*v.t., v.i.* **1.** to rinse (the throat) with a liquid held in the throat and kept in motion by a stream of air from the lungs. —*n.* **2.** any liquid used for gargling.

gar·goyle (gär'goil), *n.* a waterspout, terminating in a grotesque representation of a human or animal figure, projecting from the gutter of a building. —**gar'goyled,** *adj.*

Gar·i·bal·di (gar'ə bôl'dē), *n.* Giuseppe (jə sep'ē), 1807–82, Italian patriot and general.

gar·ish (gâr'ish, gar'-), *adj.* crudely or tastelessly colorful, showy, or elaborate. —**gar'ish·ly,** *adv.* —**gar'ish·ness,** *n.*

gar·land (gär'lənd), *n.* **1.** a wreath or festoon of flowers, leaves, etc. —*v.t.* **2.** to deck with a garland or garlands.

gar·lic (gär'lik), *n.* **1.** a hardy plant of the family whose strong-scented, pungent bulb is used in cooking. **2.** its bulb. —**gar'lick·y,** *adj.*

gar·ment (gär'mənt), *n.* any article of clothing.

gar·ner (gär'nər), *v.t.* **1.** to gather and store. **2.** to get or acquire. **3.** to accumulate or collect.

gar·net (gär'nit), *n.* **1.** a deep-red transparent mineral used as a gem and as an abrasive. **2.** a deep-red color. —**gar'net·like′,** *adj.*

gar·nish (gär'nish), *v.t.* **1.** to provide with something ornamental. **2.** to provide (a food) with something that adds flavor, decorative color, etc. **3.** to garnishee. —*n.* **4.** something used to garnish food. **5.** adornment or decoration.

gar·nish·ee (gär'ni shē′), *v.t.,* -**nish·eed,** -**nish·ee·ing.** *Law.* **1.** to attach (money or property) by garnishment. **2.** to serve with a garnishment.

gar·nish·ment (gär'nish mənt), *n.* **1.** *Law.* a warning served on a person holding the money or property of a debtor not to give it to the defendant. **2.** garnish (def. 5).

gar·ni·ture (gär'ni chər), *n.* something that garnishes.

gar·ret (gar'it), *n.* an attic, often a small, wretched one.

gar·ri·son (gar'i sən), *n.* **1.** troops stationed in a fortified place. **2.** the fort where such troops are stationed. **3.** any military post, esp. a permanent one. —*v.t.* **4.** to put (troops) on duty in a fort, post, etc.

gar·rote (gə rot′, -rōt′), *n., v.,* -**rot·ed,** -**rot·ing.** —*n.* **1.** a former Spanish method of execution in which an iron collar is tightened around a condemned person's neck until death occurs by strangulation. **2.** strangulation, esp. in the course of a robbery. —*v.t.* **3.** to execute by the garrote. Also, **ga·rotte′.** —**gar·rot′er,** *n.*

gar·ru·lous (gar'ə ləs, gar'yə-), *adj.* **1.** given to excessive chatter or talkativeness. **2.** wordy or diffuse. —**gar·ru·li·ty** (gə rōō'li tē), **gar'ru·lous·ness,** *n.* —**gar'ru·lous·ly,** *adv.*

gar·ter (gär'tər), *n.* **1.** an elastic band for holding up a stocking or sock. —*v.t.* **2.** to fasten with a garter.

gar′ter snake′, a harmless snake common in North America.

Gar·y (gâr'ē, gar'ē), *n.* a port in NW Indiana.

gas (gas), *n., pl.* **gas·es,** *v.,* **gassed, gas·sing.** —*n.* **1.** a substance possessing perfect molecular mobility and the property of indefinite expansion, as opposed to a solid or liquid. **2.** any such fluid used as an anesthetic. **3.** any such combustible fluid used as fuel, esp. natural gas. **4.** *Informal.* **a.** gasoline. **b.** the accelerator of an automobile. **5.** any toxic mistlike substance dispersed in air, used in warfare to poison an enemy. —*v.t.* **6.** to supply with gas. **7.** to poison with gas. **8.** to treat with gas. —**gas'e·ous** (-ē əs), *adj.*

gas′ cham′ber, a room used for the execution of people by means of a poisonous gas.

gash (gash), *n.* **1.** a long, deep wound or cut. —*v.t.* **2.** to make a gash in.

gas·ket (gas'kit), *n.* a rubber, metal, or rope ring, for packing a piston to make it watertight.

gas·light (gas'līt′), *n.* **1.** light produced by the combustion of illuminating gas. **2.** a gas burner for producing such light.

gas′ mask′, an air-purifying device for the face to protect the wearer against noxious gases.

gas·o·hol (gas'ə hôl′, -hol′), *n.* a mixture of 90% gasoline and 10% alcohol, used esp. as an automobile fuel. [*gas(oline) + (alc)ohol*]

gas·o·line (gas'ə lēn′, gas'ə lēn′), *n.* a volatile, flammable liquid mixture of hydrocarbons, obtained from petroleum and used chiefly as fuel for internal-combustion engines. Also, **gas′o·lene′.**

gasp (gasp, gäsp), *n.* **1.** a sudden, short breath. **2.** a short, convulsive utterance. —*v.i.* **3.** to catch the breath with one's mouth open. —*v.t.* **4.** to utter with gasps.

gas′ sta′tion. See **service station.**

gas·sy (gas'ē), *adj.,* -**si·er,** -**si·est.** full of or resembling gas. —**gas'si·ness,** *n.*

gas·tric (gas'trik), *adj.* pertaining to the stomach.

gas′tric juice′, a digestive fluid secreted by gastric glands.

gas·tri·tis (ga strī'tis), *n.* inflammation of the stomach.

gastro-, a combining form meaning "stomach": *gastrointestinal.*

gas·tro·en·ter·i·tis (gas'trō en'tə rī'tis), *n.* inflammation of the stomach and intestines.

gas·tro·en·ter·ol·o·gy (gas'trō en'tə rol'ə jē), *n.* the study of the structure and diseases of digestive organs. —**gas'tro·en'ter·ol'o·gist,** *n.*

gas·tro·in·tes·ti·nal (gas'trō in tes'tə nəl), *adj.* of or affecting the stomach and intestines.

gas·trol·o·gy (ga strol'ə jē), *n.* the study of the structure and diseases of the stomach. —**gas·trol'o·gist,** *n.*

gas·tron·o·my (ga stron'ə mē), *n.* the art or science of good eating. —**gas·tro·nom·ic** (gas'trə nom'ik), **gas'tro·nom'i·cal,** *adj.* —**gas'tro·nom'i·cal·ly,** *adv.*

gas·tro·pod (gas'trə pod′), *n.* any mollusk of the class comprising the snails.

gas·works (gas'wûrks'), *n.* a plant where illuminating gas is made.

gate (gāt), *n.* **1.** a movable structure closing an opening in a fence or wall. **2.** an opening permitting passage through an enclosure. **3.** any movable barrier, as at a road. **4.** a sliding barrier for regulating the passage of water, as in a dam. **5.** the total number of paid admissions at a public event. **6.** **give (someone) the gate,** *Slang.* to reject or dismiss.

gate·crash·er (gāt'krash'ər), *n. Informal.* a person who enters without an invitation or a ticket.

gate·fold (gāt'fōld'), *n.* foldout.

gate·keep·er (gāt'kē'pər), *n.* a person in charge of a gate.

gate·post (gāt'pōst'), *n.* the vertical post on which a gate is suspended by hinges.

gate·way (gāt'wā'), *n.* **1.** a passage or entrance that may be closed by a gate. **2.** any place at which a region may be entered.

gath·er (gath'ər), *v.t.* **1.** to bring together into one group or place. **2.** to pick or harvest. **3.** to pick up piece by piece. **4.** to wrap or draw around or closer, as a garment. **5.** to take from among other things. **6.** to assemble or collect (one's energies or oneself), as for an effort. **7.** to conclude from observation. **8.** to draw (cloth) up on a thread in fine folds or puckers by means of even stitches. **9.** to increase (speed, etc.). —*v.i.* **10.** to come together or assemble. **11.** to grow or increase. **12.** to come to a head, as a sore. —*n.* **13.** Often, **gathers.** a fold or pucker, as in gathered cloth. —**gath'er·er,** *n.* —**gath'er·ing,** *n.* —**Syn.** 1. accumulate, amass, assemble, collect.

GATT, General Agreement on Tariffs and Trade.

gauche (gōsh), *adj.* lacking social grace or tract. —**gauche'ness,** *n.*

gau·che·rie (gō'shə rē'), *n.* a gauche act or movement.

gau·cho (gou'chō), *n., pl.* **-chos** (-chōz). a cowboy of the South American pampas.

gaud (gôd), *n.* a showy ornament.

gaud·y (gô'dē), *adj.,* **gaud·i·er, gaud·i·est.** showy without taste. —**gaud'i·ly,** *adv.* —**gaud'i·ness,** *n.* —**Syn.** flashy, garish, ostentatious.

gauge (gāj), *v.,* **gauged, gaug·ing,** *n.* —*v.t.* **1.** to determine the exact dimensions, capacity, quantity, or force of. **2.** to appraise or judge. —*n.* **3.** a standard of measure or measurement. **4.** any device for measuring or testing something. **5.** a means of estimating or judging. **6.** the size of the internal diameter of a shotgun. **7.** the distance between the two rails in a railroad track. **8.** the thickness or diameter of various thin objects, as wire. —**gaug'er,** *n.*

Gaul (gôl), *n.* **1.** an ancient region of the Roman Empire, in W Europe. **2.** an inhabitant of Gaul.

gaunt (gônt), *adj.* **1.** haggard and drawn, as from great hunger. **2.** bleak or grim, as places or things. —**gaunt'ly,** *adv.* —**gaunt'ness,** *n.*

gaunt·let[1] (gônt'lit, gänt'-), *n.* **1.** a glove, as of mail or plate, worn by an armored knight. **2.** a glove with an extended cuff for the wrist. **3.** **throw down the gauntlet,** to challenge, as to a fight.

gaunt·let[2] (gônt'lit, gänt'-), *n.* **1.** a form of punishment in which the offender is made to run between two rows of people who strike at him or her. **2.** trying ordeals.

gauss (gous), *n., pl.* **gauss.** the centimeter-gram-second unit of magnetic induction.

gauze (gôz), *n.* any thin, transparent fabric made in a loose weave, used esp. for surgical dressings. —**gauz'y,** *adj.* —**gauz'i·ly,** *adv.* —**gauz'i·ness,** *n.*

ga·vage (gə väzh'), *n.* forced feeding, as by a flexible tube.

gave (gāv), *v.* pt. of **give.**

gav·el (gav'əl), *n.* a small mallet used, as by a judge, for signaling for attention or order.

ga·votte (gə vot'), *n.* an old French dance in quadruple meter.

G.A.W., guaranteed annual wage.

gawk (gôk), *v.i.* to stare stupidly.

gawk·y (gô'kē), *adj.,* **gawk·i·er, gawk·i·est.** awkwardly tall and ungainly. Also, **gawk·ish** (gô'kish).

gay (gā), *adj.* **1.** having or showing a joyous mood. **2.** bright or showy: *gay colors.* **3.** given to or abounding in social pleasures. **4.** *Slang.* of, for, or frequented by gays. —*n.* **5.** *Slang.* a homosexual person. —**gay'ness,** *n.* —**Syn.** 1. cheerful, jolly, lively.

gay·e·ty (gā'i tē), *n., pl.* **-ties.** gaiety.

gay·ly (gā'lē), *adv.* gaily.

gay' pow'er, the organized influence exerted by homosexuals as a group, esp. to ensure equal rights in employment, housing, etc.

gaz., **1.** gazette. **2.** gazetteer.

gaze (gāz), *v.,* **gazed, gaz·ing,** *n.* —*v.i.* **1.** to look steadily and intently, as with great interest. —*n.* **2.** a steady or intent look. —**gaz'er,** *n.*

ga·ze·bo (gə zē'bō, -zā'-), *n., pl.* **-bos, -boes.** a structure, as a pavilion, built on a site affording an enjoyable view.

ga·zelle (gə zel'), *n., pl.* **-zelles, -zelle.** a small antelope noted for graceful movements and lustrous eyes.

ga·zette (gə zet′), *n., v.,* -zett·ed, -zett·ing. **1.** a newspaper (used chiefly in the names of newspapers). **2.** (*cap.*) *Brit.* a government journal containing official notices. —*v.t.* **3.** *Brit.* to publish in an official gazette.

gaz·et·teer (gaz′i tēr′), *n.* **1.** a geographical dictionary. **2.** *Archaic.* a journalist.

G.B., Great Britain.

GCA, ground-controlled approach.

G clef, *Music.* treble clef.

G.C.T., Greenwich Civil Time.

Gd, gadolinium.

gd., **1.** good. **2.** guard.

gds., goods.

Ge, germanium.

gear (gēr), *n.* **1.** *Mach.* **a.** a moving part receiving or imparting force by means of teeth engaging with teeth in, a corresponding part. **b.** an assembly of such parts. **c.** the state of such parts engaging with each other: *out of gear.* **d.** a possible combination of such parts: *in low gear.* **e.** any of various mechanisms: *a steering gear.* **2.** implements, tools, or apparatus: *fishing gear.* **3.** *Brit. Informal.* clothes or attire. —*v.t.* **4.** to provide with or connect by gears. **5.** to put in or into gear. **6.** to adjust or regulate so as to match or conform to something.

gear·box (gēr′boks′), *n.* a transmission, as in an automobile.

gear·shift (gēr′shift′), *n.* a lever for engaging and disengaging gears for a power-transmission system, esp. in a motor vehicle.

gear·wheel (gēr′hwēl′, -wēl′), *n.* a wheel having teeth or cogs that engage with those of another wheel.

gee (jē), *interj. Informal.* (used to express surprise, etc.)

geese (gēs), *n.* a pl. of **goose.**

gee·zer (gē′zər), *n. Slang.* an odd or strange person.

ge·fil′te fish′ (gə fil′tə), *Jewish Cookery.* balls of boneless fish, blended with eggs, matzo meal, etc.

Gei′ger count′er (gī′gər), an instrument for detecting ionizing radiations, used chiefly to measure radioactivity.

gei·sha (gā′shə, gē′-), *n., pl.* -sha, -shas. a Japanese girl trained as a professional singer, dancer, and companion for men. [< Jap: art person]

gel (jel), *n.* colloidal solution that has the consistency of a jelly.

gel·a·tin (jel′ə tin, -ə t′n), *n.* a nearly transparent glutinous substance, obtained by boiling animal tissue, used as a food, in photography, etc. Also, **gel′a·tine.** [< F *gélatine* < ML *gelātin(a)* = L *gelāt(us)* frozen + -*in*] —**ge·lat·i·nous** (jə lat′ʷnəs), *adj.*

geld (geld), *v.t.,* geld·ed or gelt (gelt), geld·ing. to castrate (esp. a horse).

geld·ing (gel′diṅg), *n.* a castrated horse.

gel·id (jel′id), *adj.* very cold. —**gel′id·ly,** *adv.*

gem (jem), *n.* **1.** a cut and polished precious stone or pearl fine enough for use in jewelry. **2.** something prized because of its beauty or worth.

gem·i·nate (jem′ə nāt′), *v.t., v.i.,* -nat·ed, -nat·ing. to make or become doubled or paired. —**gem′i·na′tion,** *n.*

Gem·i·ni (jem′ə nī′, -nē, jim′-), *n.* the third sign of the zodiac. [< L: twins]

gem·ol·o·gy (je mol′ə jē), *n.* the science dealing with gemstones. Also, **gemmol′o·gy.** —**gem·o·log·i·cal, gem·mo·log·i·cal** (jem′ə loj′i kəl), *adj.* —**gem·ol′o·gist, gem·mol′o·gist,** *n.*

gem·stone (jem′stōn′), *n.* a precious stone suitable for cutting and polishing for use as a gem.

ge·müt·lich (gə mʏt′likʜ), *adj. German.* congenial or agreeable.

-gen, a suffix meaning "production (of)": *hydrogen.*

Gen., **1.** *Mil.* General. **2.** Genesis.

gen., **1.** gender. **2.** general. **3.** genitive. **4.** genus.

gen·darme (zhän′därm), *n.* an armed police officer, esp. in France.

gen·dar·me·rie (zhän där′mə rē), *n.* gendarmes collectively. Also, **gendarm′er·y.**

gen·der (jen′dər), *n.* a grammatical classification of nouns and pronouns into masculine, feminine, and neuter.

gene (jēn), *n.* the unit of heredity transmitted in the chromosome that controls the development of hereditary character. —**gen·ic** (jen′ik), *adj.*

ge·ne·al·o·gy (jē′nē ol′ə jē, -al′-, jen′ē-), *n., pl.* -gies. **1.** a record or account of one's ancestry. **2.** the study of family ancestries. **3.** descent from an ancestor or progenitor. —**ge·ne·a·log·i·cal** (jē′nē ə loj′i kəl, jen′ē-), *adj.* —**ge′ne·a·log′i·cal·ly,** *adv.* —**ge′ne·al′o·gist,** *n.*

gen·er·a (jen′ər ə), *n.* a pl. of **genus.**

gen·er·al (jen′ər əl), *adj.* **1.** of or pertaining to all persons or things belonging to a group or category. **2.** of or true of such persons or things in the main. **3.** not limited to one class, field, etc.: *the general public.* **4.** dealing with all or the overall aspects of a subject: *a general description.* **5.** not specific or definite. **6.** having superior rank: *a general manager.* —*n.* **7. a.** *U.S. Army and Air Force.* an officer ranking below a general of the army or general of the air force. **b.** an officer holding the highest rank in the U.S. Marine Corps. **8.** a statement involving or applicable to the whole. **9. in general,**

a. as a whole. **b.** as a rule. —**gen′er·al·ly,** *adv.*

Gen′eral Assem′bly, 1. the main deliberative body of the United Nations. **2.** the legislature in some states of the U.S.

gen′eral deliv′ery, a postal service delivering mail to a specific post office where it is held for pickup by an addressee.

gen·er·al·is·si·mo (jen′ər ə lis′ə mō′), *n., pl.* **-mos,** the supreme commander of the armed forces in certain countries.

gen·er·al·i·ty (jen′ə ral′i tē), *n., pl.* **-ties. 1.** an unspecific or undetailed statement. **2.** a general principle or rule. **3.** the greater part or majority. **4.** the state or quality of being general.

gen·er·al·ize (jen′ər ə līz′), *v.,* **-ized, -iz·ing.** —*v.t.* **1.** to give a general rather than a specific character to. **2.** to infer (a general principle, etc.) from particular facts, etc. **3.** to form a general principle from. **4.** to make general. —*v.i.* **5.** to form general principles. **6.** to think or speak in generalities. —**gen′er·al·i·za′tion,** *n.*

gen′eral of the air′ force′, the highest ranking officer in the U.S. Air Force.

gen′eral of the ar′my, the highest ranking officer in the U.S. Army.

gen′eral practi′tioner, a medical practitioner who does not limit his or her practice to a particular branch of medicine.

gen′eral seman′tics, semantics (def. 2).

gen·er·al·ship (jen′ər əl ship′), *n.* **1.** skill as a military commander. **2.** management or tactics. **3.** the rank or office of a general.

gen′eral staff′, *Mil.* a group of officers whose duty is to assist high commanders in planning and carrying out orders.

gen′eral store′, a store, usually in a rural area, that sells a wide variety of merchandise but is not divided into departments.

gen·er·ate (jen′ə rāt′), *v.t.,* **-at·ed, -at·ing. 1.** to bring into being or existence. **2.** to reproduce or procreate. —**gen′er·a·tive,** *adj.*

gen·er·a·tion (jen′ə rā′shən), *n.* **1.** the entire body of individuals born and living at about the same time. **2.** the average period between the birth of parents and the birth of their offspring. **3.** a single step in natural descent, as of human beings. **4.** the act or process of generating. —**gen′er·a′tion·al,** *adj.*

genera′tion gap′, the wide difference between the outlook or tastes of one generation and those of another.

gen·er·a·tor (jen′ə rā′tər), *n.* **1.** a person or thing that generates. **2.** a machine that converts mechanical energy into electrical energy, as a dynamo.

ge·ner·ic (jə ner′ik), *adj.* **1.** of or referring to an entire class, group, or kind. **2.** not protected by trademark registration. **3.** *Biol.* of or pertaining to a genus. —**ge·ner′i·cal·ly,** *adv.*

gen·er·ous (jen′ər əs), *adj.* **1.** liberal in giving or sharing. **2.** free from smallness of mind or character. **3.** abundant or ample. —**gen·er·os·i·ty** (jen′ə ros′i tē), *n.* —**gen′er·ous·ly,** *adv.* —**gen′er·ous·ness,** *n.* —**Syn. 1.** bountiful, lavish, munificent.

gen·e·sis (jen′i sis), *n., pl.* **-ses** (-sēz′). the coming into being of something, esp. through a process of development. —**Syn.** creation, origin.

Gen·e·sis (jen′i sis), *n.* the first book of the Bible.

genet′ic code′, the order in which the four DNA bases are arranged to link to the determination of inherited traits.

ge·net·ics (jə net′iks), *n.* the science of heredity, dealing with resemblances and differences of related organisms. —**ge·net′ic,** *adj.* —**ge·net′i·cal·ly,** *adv.* —**ge·net′i·cist** (-i sist), *n.*

Ge·ne·va (jə nē′və), *n.* a city in SW Switzerland.

Gen·ghis Khan (jeng′gis kän′), 1162–1227, Mongol conqueror.

gen·ial (jēn′yəl, jē′nē əl), *adj.* **1.** sympathetically cheerful and pleasant. **2.** favorable for life or growth: *the genial climate of Hawaii.* —**ge·ni·al·i·ty** (jē′nē al′i tē), *n.* —**gen′ial·ly,** *adv.*

ge·nie (jē′nē), *n.* jinn.

genit., genitive.

gen·i·tal (jen′i təl), *adj.* **1.** of or noting reproduction or the sexual organs. **2.** *Psychoanal.* **a.** of or pertaining to the final stage of psychosexual development during which the pubescent child is drawn toward heterosexuality. **b.** of or pertaining to the centering of sexual interest around the genitalia.

gen·i·ta·li·a (jen′i tā′lē ə, -tāl′yə), *n.pl.* the organs of reproduction, esp. the external organs. —**gen·i·tal·ic** (jen′i tal′ik), *adj.*

gen·i·tals (jen′i təlz), *n.pl.* genitalia.

gen·i·tive (jen′i tiv), *Gram.* —*adj.* **1.** noting a case that expresses possession or origin, as in Latin. —*n.* **2.** the genitive case.

gen·i·to·u·ri·nar·y (jen′i tō yŏŏr′ə ner′ē), *adj.* of the genital and urinary organs.

gen·ius (jēn′yəs), *n., pl.* **gen·ius·es. 1.** an exceptional natural capacity of intellect. **2.** a person having such capacity. **3.** natural ability or capacity. **4.** distinctive character or spirit, as of a nation, period, language, etc.

Genl., General.

Gen·o·a (jen′ō ə), *n.* a seaport in NW Italy.

gen·o·cide (jen′ə sīd′), *n.* the systematic extermination of a national or racial group. —**gen′o·cid′al,** *adj.*

gen·o·type (jen′ə tīp′), *n.* **1.** the genetic constitution of an organism or group of organisms. **2.** a group or class sharing a specific genetic constitution. —**gen·o·typ·ic** (jen′ə tip′ik), *adj.*

-genous, a suffix of adjectives corresponding to nouns ending in **-gen:** *erogenous.*

gen·re (zhän′rə), *n.* **1.** a class or category of artistic endeavor having a particular form or content. **2.** a style of painting in which scenes of everyday life form the subject matter.

gens (jenz), *n., pl.* **gen·tes** (jen′tēz). (in ancient Rome) a group of families constituting a clan and having a common name.

gent (jent), *n. Informal.* gentleman.

gen·teel (jen tēl′), *adj.* **1.** affectedly or pretentiously polite or delicate. **2.** *Often Facetious.* well-bred or refined. **3.** *Archaic.* belonging or suited to polite society.

gen·tian (jen′shən), *n.* a flowering plant usually having blue blossoms.

gen·tile (jen′tīl), *adj.* **1.** of or pertaining to any people not Jewish. —*n.* **2.** a person who is not Jewish, esp. a Christian. Also, **Gen′tile.**

gen·til·i·ty (jen til′i tē), *n.* **1.** affected or pretentious politeness or elegance. **2.** *Often Facetious.* good breeding or refinement. **3.** *Archaic.* **a.** the status of belonging to polite society. **b.** members of polite society collectively.

gen·tle (jen′t°l), *adj.,* **-tler, -tlest,** *v.,* **-tled, -tling.** —*adj.* **1.** amiably kind. **2.** mild or moderate. **3.** gradual: *a gentle slope.* **4.** easily handled or managed. **5.** soft or low: *a gentle sound.* **6.** polite or refined. **7.** of good birth or family. —*v.t.* **8.** to tame or render tractable. **9.** to modify or calm. —**gen′tle·ness,** *n.* —**gen′tly,** *adv.*

gen·tle·folk (jen′t°l fōk′), *n.* persons of good family and breeding. Also, **gen′tle·folks′.**

gen·tle·man (jen′t°l mən), *n.* **1.** a civilized, educated, or well-mannered man. **2.** a polite term for any man. **3.** a man of good breeding and social standing. —**gen′tle·man·ly,** *adj.* —**gen′tle·wom′an,** *n. fem.*

gen·try (jen′trē), *n.* **1.** wellborn and well-bred people. **2.** (in England) the class under the nobility. **3.** *Informal.* people, esp. considered as a specific group or class.

gen·u·flect (jen′yōō flekt′), *v.i.* to bend the knee in worship. —**gen′u·flec′tion,** *n.*

gen·u·ine (jen′yōō in), *adj.* **1.** unquestionably not false, copied, or adulterated: *a genuine diamond.* **2.** free from pretense or hypocrisy: *genuine love.* —**gen′u·ine·ly,** *adv.* —**gen′u·ine·ness,** *n.* —**Syn. 1.** authentic, real.

ge·nus (jē′nəs), *n., pl.* **gen·er·a** (jen′ər ə), **ge·nus·es. 1.** a classification of plants and animals usually consisting of more than one species. **2.** a kind, sort, or class.

geo-, a prefix meaning "the earth": *geochemistry.*

ge·o·cen·tric (jē′ō sen′trik), *adj.* **1.** measured as from the center of the earth. **2.** having or representing the earth as a center. —**ge′o·cen′tri·cal·ly,** *adv.*

ge·o·chem·is·try (jē′ō kem′i strē), *n.* the science dealing with the chemical changes in and the composition of the earth's crust. —**ge′o·chem′i·cal** (jē′ō kem′i kəl), *adj.* —**ge′o·chem′ist,** *n.*

ge·ode (jē′ōd), *n.* a hollow nodular stone often lined with crystals.

ge·o·des·ic (jē′ə des′ik, -dē′sik), *n.* **1.** Also called **ge′odes′ic line′.** the shortest line lying on a curved surface and connecting two given points. —*adj.* **2.** of or pertaining to geodesic lines.

ge′odes′ic dome′, a light, domelike structure developed to combine the structurally desirable properties of the tetrahedron and the sphere.

ge·od·e·sy (jē od′i sē), *n.* the branch of applied mathematics that deals with the curvature, shape, and dimensions of the earth. —**ge·od′e·sist,** *n.*

ge·o·det·ic (jē′ə det′ik), *adj.* **1.** pertaining to geodesy. **2.** geodesic.

geog., 1. geographer. **2.** geographic; geographical. **3.** geography.

ge·og·ra·phy (jē og′rə fē), *n., pl.* **-phies. 1.** the science dealing with the earth's surface and such elements as climate, etc. **2.** the topographical features of a region. —**ge·og′ra·pher,** *n.* —**ge′o·graph′i·cal** (-ə graf′i kəl), **ge′o·graph′ic,** *adj.* —**ge′o·graph′i·cal·ly,** *adv.*

geol., 1. geologic; geological. **2.** geologist. **3.** geology.

ge·ol·o·gy (jē ol′ə jē), *n., pl.* **-gies. 1.** the science that deals with the history of the earth, its rocks and physical changes, etc. **2.** the features and processes occurring in a given region on the earth or on a celestial body. —**ge′o·log′ic** (-ə loj′ik), **ge′o·log′i·cal,** *adj.* —**ge′o·log′i·cal·ly,** *adv.* —**ge·ol′o·gist,** *n.*

geom., 1. geometric; geometrical. **2.** geometry.

ge·o·mag·net·ic (jē'ō mag net'ik), *adj.* of or pertaining to terrestrial magnetism. —**ge·o·mag·net·ism** (jē'ō-mag'ni tiz'əm), *n.*

ge'omet'ric mean', the mean of *n* positive numbers obtained by taking the *n*th root of the product of the numbers: *The geometric mean of 6 and 24 is 12.*

geomet'ric progres'sion, a sequence of terms in which the ratio between any two successive terms is the same, as the progression 1, 3, 9, 27, 81.

ge·om·e·try (jē om'i trē), *n.* the branch of mathematics that deals with the deduction of the properties, measurement, and relationships of points, lines, angles, and figures in space. —**ge'o·met'ric** (-ə mə'trik), **ge'o·met'-ri·cal,** *adj.* —**ge'o·met'ri·cal·ly,** *adv.* —**ge·om'e·tri'cian** (-om'i trish'ən), **ge·om'e·ter,** *n.*

ge·o·mor·phol·o·gy (jē'ə môr fol'ə jē), *n.* the study of the characteristics, origin, and development of land forms.

ge·o·phys·ics (jē'ō fiz'iks), *n.* the physics of the earth, including oceanography, geomagnetism, etc. —**ge'-o·phys'i·cal,** *adj.* —**ge'o·phys'i·cist,** *n.*

ge·o·pol·i·tics (jē'ō pol'i tiks), *n.* the study of the influence of political and economic geography on the national power and foreign policy of a nation.

George III (jôrj), 1738–1820, king of England 1760–1820.

Geor·gia (jôr'jə), *n.* **1.** a state in the SE United States. *Cap.:* Atlanta. **2.** a constituent republic of the Soviet Union bordering on the Black Sea. —**Geor'gian,** *adj., n.*

ge·o·sci·en·tist (jē'ō sī'ən tist), *n.* a specialist in earth science.

ge·o·sta·tion·ar·y (jē'ō stā'shə ner'ē), *adj. Aerospace.* moving at the same speed as the earth does so as to remain fixed above the equator. Also, **ge'o·syn'chro·nous** (-siNG'krə nəs).

ge·o·syn·cline (jē'ō sin'klīn), *n.* a portion of the earth's crust subjected to downward warping. —**ge'o·syn·cli'-nal,** *adj.*

ge·o·ther·mal (jē'ō thûr'məl), *adj.* of or pertaining to the internal heat of the earth. Also, **ge'o·ther'mic.**

Ger., 1. German. **2.** Germany.

ger., gerund.

ge·ra·ni·um (ji rā'nē əm), *n.* **1.** a plant with heart-shaped leaves cultivated for its clusters of red, white, or pink flowers. **2.** a related wild flower grown for forage.

ger·bil (jûr'bəl), *n.* a burrowing rodent of Asia, Africa, and southern Russia. Also, **ger'bille.**

ger·i·at·rics (jer'ē a'triks), *n.* the medical science dealing with the diseases and care of aged persons. —**ger'i·at'ric,** *adj.*

germ (jûrm), *n.* **1.** a microorganism, esp. when disease-producing. **2.** the rudiment of a living organism. **3.** any initial stage for further development. [< F *germe* < L *germen* seed]

Ger·man (jûr'mən), *adj.* **1.** of Germany, its inhabitants, or their language. —*n.* **2.** a native or inhabitant of Germany. **3.** the language of Germany, Austria, etc.

ger·mane (jər mān'), *adj.* closely or significantly related. —**ger·mane'ly,** *adv.* —**ger·mane'ness,** *n.* —**Syn.** pertinent, relevant.

Ger·man·ic (jər man'ik), *adj.* **1.** Teutonic. **2.** German. —*n.* **3.** a branch of the Indo-European family of languages including German, Dutch, English, etc.

ger·ma·ni·um (jər mā'nē əm), *n.* a scarce, metallic element, used chiefly in transistors. *Symbol:* Ge; *at. wt.:* 72.59; *at. no.:* 32.

Ger'man mea'sles, a contagious virus disease characterized by a rash resembling that of scarlet fever.

Ger·ma·ny (jûr'mə nē), *n.* a former country in central Europe, now divided into East Germany and West Germany.

germ' cell', a sexual reproductive cell, esp. a sperm or ovum.

ger·mi·cide (jûr'mi sīd'), *n.* an agent for killing germs or microorganisms. —**ger'mi·cid'al,** *adj.*

ger·mi·nal (jûr'mə nəl), *adj.* **1.** of or pertaining to a germ or germ cell. **2.** being in the earliest stage of development: *germinal ideas.*

ger·mi·nate (jûr'mə nāt'), *v.i., v.t., -nat·ed, -nat·ing.* to begin to grow or develop. —**ger'mi·na'tion,** *n.*

germ' plasm', the protoplasm of the germ cells containing the units of heredity.

ger·on·tol·o·gy (jer'ən tol'ə jē), *n.* the branch of science that deals with aging and the special problems of aged persons. —**ge·ron·to·log·i·cal** (jə rän'tə loj'i kəl), *adj.* —**ger'on·tol'o·gist,** *n.*

ger·ry·man·der (jer'i man'dər, ger'-), *v.t., v.i.* to divide (a state, country, etc.) into election districts so as to gain partisan advantage.

ger·und (jer'ənd), *n.* the English -*ing* form of a verb when functioning as a noun.

Ge·sta·po (gə stä'pō), *n.* the German state secret police during the Nazi regime.

ges·ta·tion (je stā'shən), *n.* the process or period during which developing young are carried in the womb.

ges·tic·u·late (je stik′yə lāt′), v.i., -lat-ed, -lat·ing. to make or use gestures, esp. in speaking. —**ges·tic′u·la′tion,** n.

ges·ture (jes′chər, jesh′-), n., v., -tured, -tur·ing. —n. 1. a movement of the body, head, or hands that is expressive of an idea, emotion, etc. 2. any action or proceeding intended for effect or as a formality. —v.i. 3. to make or use gestures. —**ges′tur·al,** adj.

ge·sund·heit (gə zŏŏnt′hīt), interj. (used to wish good health, or esp. to a person who has just sneezed.)

get (get), v., got; got ·· or gotten; get-ting; n. —v.t. 1. to receive or come to have possession of. 2. to obtain or acquire, as for one's use. 3. to go after (something). 4. to cause or cause to become, do, etc.: to get one's hair cut. 5. to communicate with over a distance: You can get me by telephone. 6. to hear: I didn't get your last name. 7. to learn or understand: I don't get your meaning. 8. to capture or seize. 9. to receive as punishment: to get 20 years in jail. 10. to influence or persuade: We'll get him to go with us. 11. to prepare: to get dinner. 12. (esp. of animals) to beget. 13. to affect emotionally: Her tears got me. 14. to take vengeance on. 15. to suffer from: He's got a bad cold. 16. Slang. to puzzle or irritate. —v.i. 17. to come to or reach a specified place: What time do we get there? 18. to become or to cause oneself to become as specified: to get promoted. 19. to succeed in coming or going: I don't get into town very often. 20. to earn money. 21. Informal. to leave promptly. 22. to start or enter upon the action of: to get moving. 23. get about, a. to move about. b. to become known. c. to be socially active. Also, **get around.** 24. **get across,** to make or become understandable. 25. **get ahead,** to be successful. 26. **get along,** a. to go away or leave. b. See get (def. 39). 27. **get around,** a. to circumvent or outwit. b. to ingratiate oneself with (someone) through flattery or cajolery. 28. **get at,** a. to reach or touch: to stretch in order to get at a top shelf. b. to hint at or imply: What are you getting at? c. to discover or determine: to get at the root of a problem. 29. **get away,** a. to escape. b. to start out. 30. **get away with,** to accomplish without detection or punishment. 31. **get back,** a. to recover or regain. b. to be revenged: She waited for a chance to get back at her accuser. 32. **get by,** to manage to exist or survive. 33. **get down,** to concentrate or at-

tend: to get down to the matter at hand. 34. **get going,** to begin or act. 35. **get in,** a. to go into a place. b. to arrive: They both got in on the same train. 36. **get it,** Informal. a. to be punished. b. to understand something. 37. **get nowhere,** to be unsuccessful. 38. **get off,** a. to escape or to help (someone) escape. b. to begin or start a journey. c. to leave (a train, etc.). 39. **get on,** a. to make progress. b. to have sufficient means to manage or survive. c. to be on good terms. d. to advance in age. 40. **get out,** a. to leave: Get out of here! b. to become publicly known. c. to withdraw or retire. d. to produce or complete. 41. **get over,** to recover from: to get over an illness. 42. **get there,** to reach one's goal. 43. **get through,** a. to complete or finish. b. to make oneself understood. 44. **get to,** a. to contact. b. Informal. to affect. 45. **get together,** a. to accumulate or gather. b. to come to an accord. 46. **get up,** a. to rise from bed. b. to arrange or organize. 47. **has** or **have got,** a. (used in place of "has" or "have"): She's got a new hat. b. (used in place of "has" or "have" to indicate obligation or necessity): He's got to get to a doctor right away. —n. 48. the offspring, esp. of a male animal: the get of a stallion.

get·a·way (get′ə wā′), n. 1. an escape. 2. the start of a race: a fast getaway.

get-to·geth·er (get′tə geth′ər), n. an informal and usually small social gathering.

Get·tys·burg (get′iz bûrg′), n. a borough in S Pennsylvania: the site of a major Civil War battle in 1863.

get-up (get′up′), n. Informal. 1. format or style. 2. costume or outfit.

gew·gaw (gyŏŏ′gô, gŏŏ′-), n. something gaudy and useless.

gey·ser (gī′zər, -sər), n. a hot spring that intermittently sends up jets of water and steam.

Gha·na (gä′nə, gan′ə), n. a country in West Africa. —**Gha·na·ian, Gha·ni·an** (gä′nē ən, gan′ē-), n., adj.

ghast·ly (gast′lē, gäst′-), adj., -li·er, -li·est. 1. shockingly frightful. 2. resembling a ghost, esp. in being very pale. 3. very bad: a ghastly error. —**ghast′li·ness,** n.

ghat (gôt), n. (in India) a passage or stairway descending to a river. Also, **ghaut.**

gher·kin (gûr′kin), n. a small, immature cucumber, used in pickling.

ghet·to (get′ō), n., pl. -tos, -toes. 1. (formerly) a section of a city in most European countries in which all Jews were required to live. 2. any section of a city inhabited predominantly by a minority group. [< It, perh. (*bor*)*ghetto*, dim. of *borgo* settlement outside city wall]

ghet·to·ize (get′ō īz′), *v.t.*, **-ized, -iz·ing.** to segregate in or as if in a ghetto.

ghost (gōst), *n.* **1.** the disembodied spirit of a dead person imagined as wandering among or haunting living persons. **2.** a mere shadow or semblance. **3.** a remote possibility: *He hasn't a ghost of a chance.* **4.** an undesired secondary image, esp. one appearing on a television screen. **5.** **give up the ghost,** to die. —*v.i.* **6.** to ghostwrite. —**ghost′ly,** *adj.*

ghost·write (gōst′rīt′), *v.t., v.i.,* **-wrote, -writ·ten, writ·ing.** to write (a speech, etc.) for and in the name of someone, esp. a famous person. —**ghost′writ′er,** *n.*

ghoul (gool), *n.* an evil demon supposed to rob graves and prey on corpses. —**ghoul′ish,** *adj.* —**ghoul′ish·ly,** *adv.*

GHQ, *Mil.* general headquarters.

GI (jē′ī′), *n., pl.* **GI's** or **GIs,** *adj. Informal.* —*n.* **1.** a member or former member of the U.S. armed forces, esp. an enlisted person. —*adj.* **2.** of or characteristic of a GI or U.S. military regulations and practices. **3.** of a standardized style or type issued by the U.S. armed forces: *GI shoes.* Also, **G.I.**

gi., gill; gills.

G.I., **1.** galvanized iron. **2.** gastrointestinal. **3.** general issue. **4.** government issue. Also, **GI**

gi·ant (jī′ənt), *n.* **1.** an imaginary being of human form but superhuman size and strength. **2.** a person or thing of unusually great size, power, importance, etc. —*adj.* **3.** huge or gigantic. —**gi′ant·ess,** *n. fem.*

gib·ber (jib′ər, gib′-), *v.i.* to speak inarticulately and often foolishly.

gib·ber·ish (jib′ər ish, gib′-), *n.* meaningless or unintelligible talk or writing.

gib·bet (jib′it), *n., v.,* **-bet·ed, -bet·ing.** —*n.* **1.** a gallows with a projecting arm for suspending and displaying the bodies of criminals after hanging. —*v.t.* **2.** to hang on a gibbet. **3.** to hold up to public scorn.

gib·bon (gib′ən), *n.* a small, slender, long-armed ape of the East Indies and southern Asia.

gib·bous (gib′əs, jib′-), *adj.* convex at both edges, as the moon when more than half full. —**gib′bous·ly,** *adv.* —**gib′bous·ness,** *n.*

gibe (jīb), *n., v.,* **gibed, gib·ing.** —*n.* **1.** a taunting and sarcastic remark. —*v.i., v.t.* **2.** to mock or jeer. —**gib′er,** *n.* —**gib′ing·ly,** *adv.*

gib·let (jib′lit), *n.* Usually, **giblets.** the viscera of a fowl, often cooked separately.

Gi·bral·tar (ji brôl′tər), *n.* a British colony comprising a fortress and seaport on a promontory near the S tip of Spain.

Gib·son (gib′sən), *n.* a dry martini cocktail garnished with a tiny onion.

gid·dy (gid′ē), *adj.,* **-di·er, -di·est. 1.** frivolous and lighthearted. **2.** causing dizziness: *a giddy climb.* —**gid′di·ly,** *adv.* —**gid′di·ness,** *n.*

gift (gift), *n.* **1.** something given, esp. formally. **2.** the act or power of giving. **3.** a special natural ability.

gift·ed (gif′tid), *adj.* having a special natural ability.

gig[1] (gig), *n.* **1.** a light ship's boat for rowing or sailing. **2.** a light, two-wheeled, one-horse carriage.

gig[2] (gig), *n.* a spearlike device for fishing.

gig[3] (gig), *n. Slang.* a demerit or reprimand, as in the army.

gig[4] (gig), *n. Slang.* a single engagement for a jazz musician.

gi·gan·tic (jī gan′tik), *adj.* **1.** exceedingly big, as in size. **2.** of or like a giant. —**gi·gan′ti·cal·ly,** *adv.* —**Syn. 1.** colossal, enormous, huge, mammoth.

gig·gle (gig′əl), *v.,* **-gled, -gling,** *n.* —*v.i.* **1.** to laugh in a silly, undignified way, esp. with short, repeated gasps. —*n.* **2.** a silly, spasmodic laugh. —**gig′gler,** *n.* —**gig′gling·ly,** *adv.* —**gig′gly,** *adj.*

gig·o·lo (jig′ə lō′, zhig′-), *n., pl.* **-los.** a male professional escort or dancing partner.

Gi′la mon′ster (hē′lə), a large, venomous lizard of the southwestern U.S.

gild[1] (gild), *v.t.,* **gild·ed** or **gilt, gild·ing. 1.** to coat with gold or a gold-colored substance. **2.** to give a bright, pleasing, or specious aspect to. —**gild·ed** (gil′did), *adj.* —**gild′er,** *n.* —**gild′ing,** *n.*

gild[2] (gild), *n.* guild.

gill[1] (gil), *n.* a respiratory organ, as of a fish, for obtaining oxygen dissolved in the water.

gill[2] (jil), *n.* a liquid measure equal to ¼ pint.

gilt[1] (gilt), *v.* **1.** a pt. and pp. of **gild**[1] —*adj.* **2.** covered with gilt. **3.** gold in color. —*n.* **4.** the gold or other material applied in gilding.

gilt[2] (gilt), *n.* a young female swine.

gilt-edged (gilt′ejd′), *adj.* of the highest or best quality, kind, etc.; *gilt-edged securities.* Also, **gilt′-edge′.**

gim·bals (jim′bəlz, gim′-), *n.* a contrivance consisting of a ring or base on an axis which permits a ship's compass to remain horizontal even when its support is tipped.

gim·crack (jim′krak′), *n.* **1.** a showy, useless trifle. —*adj.* **2.** showy but useless. —**gim′crack′er·y**, *n.*

gim·let (gim′lit), *n.* a small screw-pointed tool for boring holes.

gim·mick (gim′ik), *n.* **1.** *Slang.* an ingenious or novel device, scheme, deception, or hidden disadvantage, as one used to promote sales. **2.** *Informal.* a hidden mechanical device by which a magician works a trick. —**gim′mick·ry**, *n.* —**gim′mick·y**, *adj.*

gimp (gimp), *n.* *Slang.* **1.** a limp. **2.** a cripple. —**gimp′y**, *adj.*

gin¹ (jin), *n.* an alcoholic liquor made by distilling grain mash with juniper berries.

gin² (jin), *n.*, *v.*, **ginned, gin·ning.** —*n.* **1.** See **cotton gin. 2.** a trap or snare for game. —*v.t.* **3.** to clear (cotton) of seeds with a gin. —**gin′ner**, *n.*

gin·ger (jin′jər), *n.* **1.** the pungent, spicy rhizome of a reedlike plant, used in cookery and medicine. **2.** this plant. **3.** *Informal.* liveliness or animation. —**gin′ger·y**, *adj.*

gin′ger ale′, a carbonated soft drink flavored with ginger extract.

gin·ger·bread (jin′jər bred′), *n.* **1.** a cake flavored with ginger and molasses. **2.** elaborate, gaudy, or superfluous ornamentation.

gin·ger·ly (jin′jər lē), *adv.* **1.** very warily. —*adj.* **2.** cautious or wary.

gin·ger·snap (jin′jər snap′), *n.* a thin, brittle cookie flavored with ginger and molasses.

ging·ham (ging′əm), *n.* yarn-dyed, plain-weave cotton fabric, usually striped or checked. [< F *guingan* < Malay *ginggang* striped]

gin·gi·vi·tis (jin′jə vī′tis), *n.* *Pathol.* inflammation of the gums.

gink·go (gingk′gō, jingk′-), *n.*, *pl.* **-goes.** a large, ornamental tree, native to China, having fan-shaped leaves. Also, **ging′ko.**

gin′ mill′ (jin), *Slang.* a bar or saloon, esp. a cheap or disreputable one.

gin′ rum′my, a variety of rummy for two players. Also called **gin.**

gin·seng (jin′seng), *n.* **1.** a perennial plant of China and Korea having an aromatic root used in medicine by the Chinese. **2.** its root.

gip (jip), *v.t.*, *v.i.*, **gipped, gip·ping,** *n.* gyp.

Gip·sy (jip′sē), *n.* *Chiefly Brit.* Gypsy.

gi·raffe (jə raf′), *n.* a tall, long-necked, spotted ruminant mammal of Africa. [< F *girafe* < Ar *zarāfah,* prob. of Afr origin]

gird (gûrd), *v.t.*, **gird·ed** or **girt, gird·ing. 1.** to encircle with a belt or band. **2.** to surround or hem in. **3.** to prepare (oneself) for action.

gird·er (gûr′dər), *n.* a large beam, as of steel or wood, for supporting masonry, joists, etc.

gir·dle (gûr′dᵊl), *n.*, *v.*, **-dled, -dling.** —*n.* **1.** a woman's supporting undergarment for the abdomen and hips. **2.** a belt or cord worn about the waist. **3.** anything that encircles or confines. —*v.t.* **4.** to encircle with a belt.

girl (gûrl), *n.* **1.** a female child. **2.** a young unmarried woman. **3.** a female servant or employee. **4.** a man's or boy's sweetheart. **5.** *Informal.* a woman. —**girl′hood**, *n.* —**girl′ish**, *adj.*

girl′ Fri′day, a female employee with a wide variety of office tasks.

girl·friend (gûrl′frend′), *n.* **1.** a female friend. **2.** a boy's or man's sweetheart.

girl′ scout′, a member of an organization of girls (**Girl′ Scouts′**) for promoting health, character, and outdoor life.

girt¹ (gûrt), *v.* a pt. and pp. of **gird.**

girt- (gûrt), *v.t.* gird (def. 1).

girth (gûrth), *n.* **1.** the measure around anything. **2.** a band that passes underneath an animal to hold a saddle in place.

gis·mo (giz′mō), *n.* *Informal.* gizmo.

gist (jist), *n.* the main or essential part of a matter.

give (giv), *v.*, **gave, giv·en, giv·ing,** *n.* —*v.t.* **1.** to present voluntarily: *to give a present.* **2.** to place in someone's care. **3.** to hand to someone: *Give me a match.* **4.** to pay or deliver in exchange: *What will you give for my car?* **5.** to grant (permission, opportunity, etc.): *Give me a chance.* **6.** to furnish or proffer: *to give evidence.* **7.** to produce or yield. **8.** to put forth or utter: *to give a cry.* **9.** to impart or communicate: *to give advice.* **10.** to deal or administer: *to give medicine.* **11.** to relinquish or sacrifice: *to give one's life for a cause.* **12.** to perform publicly: *to give a concert.* **13.** to provide as an entertainment: *to give a dinner.* **14.** to assign or allot, as a ration, name, etc. **15.** to attribute or ascribe. **16.** to cause or occasion. **17.** to award, as after consideration: *A decision was given for the defendant.* **18.** to inflict as a punishment. **19.** to concede or grant, as a point in an argument. —*v.i.* **20.** to make a gift. **21.** to afford a view or passage: *The window gives on the sea.* **22.** to yield under force, pressure, etc. **23. give away, a.** to give as a present. **b.** to present (the bride) to the bridegroom at a wedding. **c.** to expose or betray. **24. give back,** to return or restore. **25. give in, a.** to acknowledge defeat. **b.** to hand in. **26. give**

it to, *Informal.* to reprimand or punish. **27. give off,** to put forth or emit, as odors. **28. give or take,** to add or subtract. **29. give out, a.** to make public. **b.** to distribute or issue. **c.** to become exhausted. **30. give up, a.** to abandon hope. **b.** to desist from. **c.** to surrender or relinquish. **d.** to devote (oneself) entirely to. —*n.* **31.** *Informal.* resilience or springiness. —**give′a·ble,** *adj.* —**giv′er,** *n.*

give-and-take (giv′ən tāk′), *n.* **1.** mutual concession or cooperation. **2.** good-humored exchange of talk, ideas, etc.

give·a·way (giv′ə wā′), *n.* **1.** a betrayal or disclosure, usually unintentional. **2.** a premium, as given to promote sales. **3.** a radio or television program on which prizes are given to contestants.

giv·en (giv′ən), *v.* **1.** pp. of **give.** —*adj.* **2.** stated or specified: *at a given time.* **3.** addicted or disposed: *given to talking.* **4.** bestowed or conferred. **5.** granted or assumed. **6.** executed as of the date shown.

giv′en name′, the name given to one, as contrasted with an inherited family name.

giz·mo (giz′mō), *n.* *Informal.* any gadget or device.

giz·zard (giz′ərd), *n.* the muscular portion of the stomach of birds, in which food is crushed.

Gk., Greek.

gl., **1.** glass. **2.** gloss.

gla·brous (glā′brəs), *adj.* *Zool., Bot.* having a surface devoid of hair or pubescence.

gla·cé (gla sā′), *adj., v.,* **-céed, -cé·ing.** —*adj.* **1.** candied, as fruits. **2.** finished with a gloss, as silk. —*v.t.* **3.** to make glacé.

gla·cial (glā′shəl), *adj.* **1.** of or pertaining to glaciers. **2.** bitterly cold. —**gla′cial·ly,** *adv.*

gla′cial ep′och, the Pleistocene epoch, during which much of the earth was covered by glaciers.

gla·cier (glā′shər), *n.* an extended mass of ice formed from snow moving very slowly from high mountains. —**gla′ciered,** *adj.*

gla·ci·ol·o·gy (glā′shē ol′ə jē, -sē-), *n.* the branch of geology that deals with the nature, distribution, and action of glaciers. —**gla′ci·ol′o·gist,** *n.*

glad¹ (glad), *adj., v.,* **glad·der, glad·dest. 1.** feeling joy or pleasure. **2.** causing or showing joy or pleasure. **3.** very pleased. —**glad′ly,** *adv.* —**glad′ness,** *n.* —**Syn. 1.** delighted, elated, joyful, pleased.

glad² (glad), *n.* *Informal.* gladiolus.

glad·den (glad′ən), *v.t.* to make glad.

glade (glād), *n.* an open space in a forest. —**glade′like′,** *adj.*

glad′ hand′, *Informal.* a hearty welcome that is often hypocritical. —**glad′-hand′,** *v.t., v.i.*

glad·i·a·tor (glad′ē ā′tər), *n.* **1.** (in ancient Rome) an armed person, often a slave, who was compelled to fight for the entertainment of the spectators. **2.** a person who engages in a fight or controversy. —**glad·i·a·to·ri·al** (glad′ē ə tōr′ē əl, -tôr′-), *adj.*

glad·i·o·lus (glad′ē ō′ləs), *n., pl.* **-lus·es, -li** (-lī). a garden plant having erect leaves and spikes of variously colored flowers. [< L: small sword]

glad·some (glad′səm), *adj.* *Literary.* glad. —**glad′some·ly,** *adv.*

Glad′stone bag′ (glad′stōn′, -stən), a small suitcase hinged to open into two compartments of equal size.

glam·or·ize (glam′ə rīz′), *v.t.,* **-ized, -iz·ing.** to make glamorous. —**glam′or·i·za′tion,** *n.*

glam·our (glam′ər), *n.* alluring charm, fascination, and attractiveness. **2.** magic or enchantment. Also, **glam′or.** —**glam′or·ous, glam′our·ous,** *adj.*

glance (glans, gläns), *v.,* **glanced, glanc·ing,** *n.* —*v.i.* **1.** to look quickly or briefly. **2.** to gleam or flash. **3.** to strike an object obliquely and bounce off at an angle. —*n.* **4.** a quick or brief look. **5.** a gleam or flash of light. **6.** a deflected movement or course.

gland (gland), *n.* **1.** a cell, group of cells, or organ producing a secretion. **2.** any of various organs or structures resembling the shape but not the function of true glands. —**glan·du·lar** (glan′jə lər), *adj.*

glans (glanz), *n., pl.* **glan·des** (glan′dēz). the head of the penis or of the clitoris.

glare (glâr), *n., v.,* **glared, glar·ing.** —*n.* **1.** a very harsh, dazzling light. **2.** a fiercely piercing stare. **3.** dazzling or showy appearance. —*v.i.* **4.** to shine with a very harsh, dazzling light. **5.** to stare with a fiercely piercing look. —*v.t.* **6.** to express with a glare.

glar·ing (glâr′ing), *adj.* **1.** dazzlingly bright. **2.** staring fiercely. **3.** very conspicuous or obvious: *glaring defects.* **4.** excessively showy. —**glar′ing·ly,** *adv.*

Glas·gow (glas′gō, -kō *or* glaz′-), *n.* a seaport in SW Scotland.

glass (glas, gläs), *n.* **1.** a hard, brittle, more or less transparent substance produced by fusion, usually consisting of mutually dissolved silica and silicates that also contain soda and lime, used for windows, bottles, etc. **2.** something made of glass, as a window, tumbler, or mirror. **3.** glasses, eyeglass (def. 2). **4.** glassware. **5.** a glassful. —*adj.* **6.** of or made of glass. —*v.t.* **7.** to fit with panes of glass.

glass·blow·ing (glas′blō′ing), *n.* the art of forming a mass of molten or heat-softened glass into ware by blowing air into it through a tube. —**glass′blow′er,** *n.*

glass·ful (glas′fool, gläs-), *n.* an amount contained by a glass or tumbler.

glass·ware (glas′wâr′, gläs′-), *n.* articles of glass, esp. glasses for a table setting.

glass′ wool′, spun glass similar to wool, used for insulation, filters, etc.

glass·y (glas′ē, glä′sē), *adj.,* **glass·i·er, glass·i·est.** **1.** resembling glass, as in transparency. **2.** having an expressionless, dull stare: *glassy eyes.* —**glass′i·ly,** *adv.* —**glass′i·ness,** *n.*

glau·co·ma (glô kō′mə, glou-), *n.* a disease of the eye characterized by increased pressure within the eyeball and progressive loss of vision. —**glau·co·ma·tous** (glô kō′mə təs, -kom′ə-, glou-), *adj.*

glaze (glāz), *v.,* **glazed, glaz·ing,** *n.* —*v.t.* **1.** to furnish with sheets of glass. **2.** to cover with a smooth, glossy surface or coating. —*v.i.* **3.** to become glazed or glassy. —*n.* **4.** a smooth, glossy surface or coating. **5.** a thin coating of ice on land, trees, etc. —**glaz′er,** *n.*

gla·zier (glā′zhər), *n.* a person who fits windows with glass or panes of glass.

gleam (glēm), *n.* **1.** a flash or beam of light. **2.** a dim or subdued light. **3.** a brief or slight manifestation: *a gleam of hope.* —*v.i.* **4.** to send forth a gleam. To appear suddenly and clearly. —**gleam′y,** *adj.*

glean (glēn), *v.t.,* *v.i.* **1.** to gather (grain) after the reapers or regular gatherers. **2.** to collect (facts) slowly and patiently. —**glean′a·ble,** *adj.* —**glean′er,** *n.*

glebe (glēb), *n.* *Brit.* the cultivable land owned by a parish church or ecclesiastical benefice.

glee (glē), *n.* **1.** demonstrative joy. **2.** an unaccompanied part song for three or more voices.

glee′ club′, a chorus organized for singing choral music.

glen (glen), *n.* a small, narrow, secluded valley.

Glen·dale (glen′dāl′), *n.* a city in SW California.

glen·gar·ry (glen gar′ē), *n., pl.* **-ries.** a Scottish cap with straight sides. [after *Glengarry,* valley in NW Scotland]

glib (glib), *adj.,* **glib·ber, glib·best.** ready and fluent, often thoughtlessly or insincerely so. —**glib′ly,** *adv.* —**glib′ness,** *n.*

glide (glīd), *v.,* **glid·ed, glid·ing,** *n.* —*v.i.* **1.** to move smoothly and effortlessly, as a flying bird. **2.** *Aeron.*

to descend at an easy angle, with little or no engine power. —*v.t.* **3.** to cause to glide. —*n.* **4.** a gliding movement, as in dancing. **5.** *Aeron.* a gliding descent.

glid·er (glī′dər), *n.* **1.** a person or thing that glides. **2.** *Aeron.* a motorless, heavier-than-air craft for gliding or soaring. **3.** a couchlike porch swing suspended from a steel framework.

glim·mer (glim′ər), *n.* **1.** a faint or unsteady light. **2.** a dim perception. —*v.i.* **3.** to shine faintly or unsteadily. **4.** to appear faintly or dimly. —**glim′mer·ing,** *n.*

glimpse (glimps), *n., v.,* **glimpsed, glimps·ing.** —*n.* **1.** a very brief, passing look. —*v.t.* **2.** to catch a glimpse of. —*v.i.* **3.** to look briefly. —**glimps′er,** *n.*

glint (glint), *n.* **1.** a tiny, quick flash of light. —*v.i.* **2.** to shine with a glint.

glis·san·do (gli sän′dō), *adj., n., pl.* **-di** (-dē). *Music.* —*adj.* **1.** performed with a gliding effect, as by sliding fingers rapidly over the keys of a piano. —*n.* **2.** a glissando passage.

glis·ten (glis′ən), *v.i.* **1.** to shine lustrously. —*n.* **2.** a glistening or sparkle.

glitch (glich), *n.* *Slang.* a minor defect or malfunction in a machine or plan.

glit·ter (glit′ər), *v.i.* **1.** to reflect light with a brilliant show. **2.** to make a brilliant show. —*n.* **3.** a sparkling reflected light. **4.** showy splendor. **5.** small glittering ornaments.

gloam·ing (glō′ming), *n.* *Literary.* twilight or dusk.

gloat (glōt), *v.i.* to look at or think about with great or excessive satisfaction.

glob (glob), *n.* **1.** a drop or globule. **2.** a rounded lump of something.

glob·al (glō′bəl), *adj.* worldwide or universal. —**glob′al·ly,** *adv.*

glob·al·ism (glō′bəliz′əm), *n.* an idea or policy of placing the interests of the entire world above those of individual nations. —**glob′al·ist,** *n., adi.*

globe (glōb), *n.* **1.** the planet earth. **2.** a sphere on which is depicted a map of the earth. **3.** anything more or less spherical. as a glass fishbowl.

globe·trot·ter (glōb′trot′ər), *n.* a person who travels frequently to countries all over the world. —**globe′trot′ting.** *n.. adi.*

glob·ule (glob′yōōl). *n.* a small spherical body. —**glob′u·lar** (-yə lər), *adj.*

glob·u·lin (glob′yə lin). *n.* any of a group of proteins occurring in plant and animal tissue. insoluble in pure water but soluble in dilute salt water.

glock·en·spiel (glok′ən spēl′, -shpēl′), *n.* a musical instrument composed of a set of graduated steel bars mounted in a frame, played with hammers. [< G = *Glocke* bell + *Spiel* play]

gloom (gloom), *n.* **1.** low spirits or deep sadness. **2.** a despondent look or expression. **3.** total or partial darkness. **—gloom′y,** *adj.* **—gloom′- i·ly,** *adv.* **—gloom′i·ness,** *n.* **—Syn.** **1.** dejection, despondency, despair.

glop (glop), *n. Informal.* any messy, viscous substance.

glo·ri·fy (glôr′ə fī′, glōr′-), *v.t.,* **-fied, -fy·ing.** **1.** to magnify with praise. **2.** to treat as more splendid or ex- cellent than would normally be con- sidered. **3.** to make glorious. **4.** to promote the glory of (God). **—glo′- ri·fi·ca′tion,** *n.* **—glo′ri·fi′er,** *n.*

glo·ri·ous (glôr′ē əs, glōr′-), *adj.* **1.** delightful and wonderful. **2.** con- ferring glory: *a glorious victory.* **3.** full of glory. **4.** brilliantly beautiful or magnificent. **—glo′ri·ous·ly,** *adv.* **—glo′ri·ous·ness,** *n.*

glo·ry (glôr′ē, glōr′ē), *n., pl.* **-ries,** *v.,* **-ried, -ry·ing.** **—n.** **1.** exalted praise, honor, or distinction. **2.** something that makes one honored or illustri- ous. **3.** adoring praise or worshipful thanksgiving. **4.** resplendent beauty or magnificence. **5.** a state of abso- lute happiness: *to be in one's glory.* **6.** the splendor and bliss of heaven. **7.** a halo or nimbus. **—v.i.** **8.** to exult with triumph.

gloss¹ (glos, glôs), *n.* **1.** a superficial luster or shine. **2.** a false or decep- tive appearance. **—v.t.** **3.** to put a gloss upon. **4.** to give a speciously good appearance to: *to gloss over flaws in the woodwork.* **—gloss′y,** *adj.* **—gloss′i·ly,** *adv.* **—gloss′i- ness,** *n.*

gloss² (glos, glôs), *n.* a marginal or interlinear note or translation, esp. one added to an ancient text. **—v.t.** **2.** to insert glosses on. **3.** to explain away: *to gloss over a serious problem with a pat solution.*

glos·sa·ry (glos′ə rē, glô′sə-), *n., pl.* **-ries.** a list of special or difficult terms with accompanying definitions, usually appearing at the end of a book. **—glos·sar·i·al** (glo sâr′ē əl, glō-). *adj.*

glos·so·la·li·a (glos′ō lā′lē ə, glô′sō-), *n.* See **speaking in tongues.**

glot·tis (glot′is). *n., pl.* **glot·tis·es, glot·ti·des** (glot′i dēz′). the opening at the upper part of the larynx, be- tween the vocal cords. **—glot′tal.** *adj.*

glove (gluv). *n.* **1.** a covering for the hand made with a separate sheath for each finger and for the thumb. **2.** any of various leather-padded coverings for the hand used in base- ball, boxing, etc. **—gloved.** *adj.*

glow (glō). *n.* **1.** a light emitted by or as by a heated substance. **2.** brightness of color, esp. ruddiness. **3.** a sensation of bodily heat. **4.** warmth of emotion or passion. **—v.i.** **5.** to emit bright light and heat with- out flame. **6.** to shine like something intensely heated. **7.** to exhibit a strong, bright color. **8.** to feel very warm or hot. **9.** to become filled with emotion: *to glow with pride.* **—glow′ing,** *adj.*

glow·er (glou′ər), *v.i.* **1.** to stare with sullen discontent or anger. **—n.** **2.** a glowering look.

glow·worm (glō′wûrm′), *n.* a wingless female beetle or larva that emits a greenish light.

gloze (glōz), *v.t.,* **glozed, gloz·ing.** **gloss²** (def. 3).

glu·cose (gloo′kōs), *n.* **1.** a white sugar occurring in many fruits and having a sweetness about one half that of ordinary sugar. **2.** a thick syrup made from cornstarch, used in making candies, etc.

glue (gloo), *n., v.,* **glued, glu·ing.** **—n.** **1.** a protein gelatin obtained by boiling animal substances in water and used as a strong adhesive. **2.** any of various similar preparations. **—v.t.** **3.** to stick with or as with glue. **—glue′y,** *adj.*

glue′ sniff′ing, the inhaling of the fumes of certain kinds of glue for effects of euphoria, hallucination, etc. **—glue′ sniff′er.**

glum (glum), *adj.,* **glum·mer, glum- mest.** sullenly or silently gloomy. **—glum′ly,** *adv.* **—glum′ness.** *n.*

glut (glut), *v.,* **glut·ted, glut·ting,** *n.* **—v.t.** **1.** to feed or fill to excess. **2.** to flood (a market) with more merchandise than can be readily absorbed. **—v.i.** **3.** to eat to excess. **—n.** **4.** an excessive supply or amount.

glu·ten (gloot′ᵊn), *n.* the tough, viscid substance remaining when flour is washed to remove the starch. [< L: glue]

glu·ti·nous (gloot′ᵊnəs), *adj.* viscid or sticky. **—glu′ti·nous·ly.** *adv.*

glut·ton (glut′ᵊn), *n.* **1.** a person who eats excessively. **2.** a person with a great desire or capacity for some- thing. **—glut′ton·ous,** *adj.* **—glut′- ton·ous·ly,** *adv.* **—glut′ton·y,** *n.*

glyc·er·in (glis′ər in), *n.* glycerol. Also, **glyc·er·ine.**

glyc·er·ol (glis′ə rōl′, -rôl′, -rol′), *n.* a colorless, odorless, syrupy liquid made from fats, used in food, cosmetics, medicine, etc.

gly·co·gen (glī′kə jən), *n.* an odorless, white powder constituting the prin- cipal carbohydrate stored in animal cells. **—gly·co·gen·ic** (glī′kə jen′ik), *adj.*

gly·co·side (glī'kə sīd'), *n.* any of the class of compounds that yield a sugar upon hydrolysis. —**gly·co·sid·ic** (glī'kə sid'ik), *adj.*

gm., gram; grams.

G.M., 1. General Manager. **2.** guided missile.

G-man (jē'man'), *n. U.S.* an agent of the Federal Bureau of Investigation.

Gmc, Germanic. Also, **Gmc.**

GMT, Greenwich Mean Time. Also, **G.M.T.**

gnarl (närl), *n.* a knotty protuberance on a tree. —**gnarled,** *adj.*

gnash (nash), *v.t., v.i.* to grind (the teeth) together, esp. in rage or pain.

gnat (nat), *n.* any of various small flies, most of which bite or suck.

gnaw (nô), *v.,* **gnawed, gnawed** or **gnawn** (nôn), **gnaw·ing.** —*v.t.* **1.** to wear away by persistent biting. **2.** to torment by constant annoyance. —*v.i.* **3.** to bite or chew on persistently. **4.** to cause constant annoyance: *Her mistake gnawed at her conscience.* —**gnaw'er,** *n.* —**gnaw'ing·ly,** *adv.*

gneiss (nīs), *n.* a metamorphic rock made up of light or dark bands.

gnome (nōm), *n.* a legendary dwarflike person who lives in the ground and guards its treasures. —**gnom'ish,** *adj.*

GNP, See **gross national product.**

gnu (nōō, nyōō), *n., pl.* **gnus, gnu.** an African antelope having an oxlike head and curved horns.

go (gō), *v.,* **went, gone, go·ing,** *n., pl.* **goes,** *adj.* —*v.i.* **1.** to move along, esp. to or from something. **2.** to leave a place. **3.** to function: *The engine's going now.* **4.** to become as specified: *to go mad.* **5.** to act as specified: *Go warily.* **6.** to act so as to come into a certain condition: *to go to sleep.* **7.** to be known: *to go by a false name.* **8.** to reach or extend. **9.** (of time) to pass or elapse. **10.** to be applied to a particular purpose. **11.** to be sold: *The house went for a song.* **12.** to be considered usually: *This player is short, as pitchers go.* **13.** to conduce or tend. **14.** to result or end. **15.** to belong: *This book goes on the top shelf.* **16.** (of colors, etc.) to harmonize. **17.** to fit into: *This belt won't go around my waist.* **18.** to be consumed or spent. **19.** to develop or progress. **20.** to pass or circulate: *The rumor has gone around.* **21.** to make a certain sound. **22.** to be written or composed: *How does that song go?* **23.** to resort: *to go to court.* **24.** to become worn out. **25.** to die. **26.** to fail or give away. **27.** to begin: *Go when you hear the bell.* **28.** to be requisite: *Sixteen ounces go to the pound.* **29.** to be able to be divided into: *Three goes into fifteen five times.* **30.** to contribute to an end result. **31.** to be about or intending: *He is going to write.* **32.** to be considered acceptable: *Anything goes.* **33.** to be authoritative: *What I say goes!* **34.** to subject oneself: *Don't go to any trouble.* **35.** (used in the infinitive to intensify a verb that follows): *He decided to go borrow it.* —*v.t.* **36.** *Informal.* to tolerate: *I can't go his preaching.* **37.** *Informal.* to afford or bet: *I'll go two dollars on number seven.* **38.** to share in to the extent of: *to go halves.* **39.** to weigh or grow to: *These tomatoes will go half a pound each.* **40.** to assume the obligation of: *His father went ball for him.* **41. go at, a.** to assault or attack. **b.** to begin vigorously. **42. go for, a.** to try for. **b.** to assault. **c.** to favor. **43. go in for,** to occupy oneself with. **44. go off, a.** to explode. **b.** to happen. **45. go on, a.** to continue: *Go on working.* **b.** to happen or take place. **46. go (someone) one better,** to be superior to. **47. go out, a.** to cease or fail to function. **b.** to participate in social activities. **48. go over, a.** to repeat. **b.** to be successful. **c.** to examine. **49. go through, a.** to experience. **b.** to examine carefully. **c.** to use up or spend completely. **50. go through with,** to complete. **51. go together, a.** to be harmonious. **b.** to keep company or date. **52. go under,** to fail. **53. let go, a.** to release or free. **b.** to dismiss from employment. **54. let oneself go,** to free oneself of restraint. **55. to go,** *Informal.* **a.** (of food) for consumption off the premises where sold. **b.** remaining: *two pages to go.* —*n.* **56.** the act of going. **57.** energy or spirit. **58.** an attempt or try. **59. no go,** *Informal.* futile or useless. **60. on the go,** very busy. —*adj.* **61.** functioning properly.

G.O., general order.

goad (gōd), *n.* **1.** a pointed stick for driving cattle. **2.** anything that pricks or urges. —*v.t.* **3.** to drive with or as with a goad.

go-a·head (gō'ə hed'), *n.* permission or a signal to proceed.

goal (gōl), *n.* **1.** the result toward which effort is directed. **2.** the terminal point in a race. **3.** a place toward or into which players of various sports must drive an object to score. **4.** the score thus made.

goal·keep·er (gōl'kē'pər), *n.* (in ice hockey, etc.) a player whose chief duty is to prevent the puck or ball from crossing the goal. Also called **goal·ie** (gō'lē), **goal'tend'er** (-ten'dər).

goal′ post′, a post supporting a crossbar and, with it, forming a goal, as in football.

goat (gōt), *n.* **1.** an agile, hollow-horned ruminant related to the sheep. **2.** *Informal.* a scapegoat. **3.** **the Goat,** Capricorn. **4. get one's goat,** *Informal.* to anger or annoy a person.

goat·ee (gō tē′), *n.* a man's beard trimmed to a tuft on the chin.

goat·herd (gōt′hûrd′), *n.* a person who tends goats.

goat·skin (gōt′skin′), *n.* **1.** the skin or hide of a goat. **2.** leather made from it.

gob[1] (gob), *n.* a mass or lump.

gob[2] (gob), *n.* *Informal.* a seaman in the U.S. Navy.

gob·bet (gob′it), *n.* *Archaic.* a fragment or piece, esp. of raw flesh.

gob·ble[1] (gob′əl), *v.,* **-bled, -bling.** —*v.t.* **1.** to swallow hungrily. **2.** *Informal.* to seize upon eagerly. —*v.i.* **3.** to eat hastily.

gob·ble[2] (gob′əl), *v.,* **-bled, -bling,** *n.* —*v.i.* **1.** to make the throaty cry of a male turkey. —*n.* **2.** the cry itself.

gob·ble·dy·gook (gob′əl dē gŏŏk′), *n.* language characterized by circumlocution and jargon. Also, **gob′ble·de·gook′.**

gob·bler (gob′lər), *n.* a male turkey.

go-be·tween (gō′bi twēn′), *n.* a person who acts as an intermediary between parties.

Go·bi (gō′bē), *n.* a desert in E Asia, mostly in Mongolia.

gob·let (gob′lit), *n.* a drinking glass with a foot and stem.

gob·lin (gob′lin), *n.* a grotesque, mischievous sprite.

go-by (gō′bī′), *n.* *Informal.* an intentional snub.

go-cart (gō′kärt′), *n.* **1.** a small wagon for children. **2.** kart.

God (god), *n.* **1.** the creator and ruler of the universe, regarded as almighty. **2.** (*l.c.*) one of several deities, esp. a male diety, presiding over some portion of worldly affairs. **3.** (*l.c.*) an image of a diety. **4.** (*l.c.*) any deified person or object.

god·child (god′chīld′), *n.* a child for whom a godparent serves as sponsor, as at baptism.

god·daugh·ter (god′dô′tər), *n.* a female godchild.

god·dess (god′is), *n.* **1.** a female god. **2.** a greatly adored woman.

god·fa·ther (god′fä′ᵗħər), *n.* **1.** a male godparent. **2.** (*often cap.*) any powerful leader, as of the Mafia.

God·head (god′hed′), *n.* the essential being, nature, or condition of God.

god·hood (god′hŏŏd), *n.* divine character or condition.

god·less (god′lis), *adj.* **1.** atheistic or irreligious. **2.** wicked or evil. —**god′-**

less·ly, *adv.* —**god′less·ness,** *n.*

god·like (god′līk′), *adj.* like or befitting God or a god.

god·ly (god′lē), *adj.,* **-li·er, -li·est. 1.** devout or pious. **2.** *Archaic.* godlike. —**god′li·ness,** *n.*

god·moth·er (god′muᵗħ′ər), *n.* a female godparent.

god·par·ent (god′pâr′ənt, -par′-), *n.* a person who serves as a sponsor for a child, as at baptism.

god·send (god′send′), *n.* an unexpected thing that is particularly welcome and timely, as if sent by God.

god·son (god′sun′), *n.* a male godchild.

God·speed (god′spēd′), *n.* a wish of good fortune to a departing person.

Goe·the (gûr′tə, *Ger.* gœ′tə), *n.* **Jo·hann Wolf·gang von** (yō′hän vôlf′gäng fən), 1749–1832, German poet.

go·fer (gō′fər), *n.* *Slang.* a person who runs menial errands for another person, other employees, etc.

go-get·ter (gō′get′ər, -get′-), *n.* *Informal.* an enterprising, aggressive person. —**go′-get′ting,** *adj.*

gog·gle (gog′əl), *n., v.,* **-gled, -gling.** —*n.* **1. goggles,** large eyeglasses to prevent injury to the eyes from strong wind, etc. —*v.i.* **2.** to stare with bulging or wide-open eyes.

go-go (gō′gō′), *adj.* *Informal.* **1.** engaged in performing dances, sometimes in topless costumes, at a discotheque, etc. **2. a.** full of energy or vitality. **b.** modern or up-to-date.

go·ings-on (gō′ingz on′), *n.* *Informal.* behavior or events, esp. when open to criticism.

goi·ter (goi′tər), *n.* an enlargement of the thyroid gland, on the front and sides of the neck. Also, **goi′tre.** —**goi′trous** (-trəs), *adj.*

gold (gōld), *n.* **1.** *Chem.* a precious, yellow, highly malleable metallic element, used in jewelry. *Symbol:* Au; *at. wt.:* 196.967; *at no.:* 79. **2.** wealth or riches. **3.** a bright, metallic yellow color.

gold·brick (gōld′brik′), *n.* *Slang.* a person, esp. a soldier, who loafs on his or her job. Also, **gold′brick′er.** —**gold′·brick′,** *v.i.*

gold′ bug′, *Slang.* a person who believes in the holding of gold as a good investment.

gold′ dig′ger, *Informal.* a woman who associates with or marries a man chiefly for material gain.

gold·en (gōl′dən), *adj.* **1.** of the color of gold. **2.** made or consisting of gold. **3.** exceptionally valuable. **4.** full of happiness or prosperity. —**gold′en·ly,** *adv.*

gold′en ag′er (āj′ər), *Informal.* an elderly person who has retired.

gold·en·rod (gōl′dən rod′), *n.* a North American plant with wandlike stems and small, yellow flowers.

gold′en rule′, a rule of ethical conduct, usually phrased "Do unto others as you would have them do unto you."

gold·finch (gōld′finch′), *n.* an American finch, the male of which has yellow body plumage in the summer.

gold·fish (gōld′fish′), *n.* a small, usually yellow or orange fish of the carp family, often kept in aquariums and pools.

gold′ leaf′, gold in the form of very thin foil, as for gilding.

gold·smith (gōld′smith′), *n.* a person who makes or sells articles of gold.

golf (golf, gôlf), *n.* **1.** a game in which each player uses a number of golf clubs to hit a small, white ball into a succession of holes, usually 9 or 18 in number. —*v.i.* **2.** to play golf. —**golf′er,** *n.*

Go·li·ath (gə lī′əth), *n.* the giant warrior of the Philistine army killed by David.

gol·ly (gol′ē), *interj. Informal.* (a mild exclamation of surprise, etc.)

-gon, a combining form meaning "angled" or "angular": *polygon.*

go·nad (gō′nad, gon′ad), *n.* either of the two sex glands: an ovary or testis. —**go·nad′al,** *adj.*

gon·do·la (gon′d°lə), *n.* **1.** a long, narrow, flat-bottomed boat, used on the canals in Venice, Italy. **2.** Also called **gon′dola car′.** an open railroad freight car with low sides for bulk goods. **3.** the car of a dirigible. **4.** the passenger-carrying basket suspended beneath a balloon.

gon·do·lier (gon′d°lēr′), *n.* a person who rows or poles a gondola.

gone (gôn, gon), *v.* **1.** pp. of **go.** —*adj.* **2.** departed. **3.** lost or hopeless. **4.** ruined. **5.** dead. **6.** past. **7.** weak and faint. **8.** used up. **9.** pregnant. **10.** gone on, *Informal.* in love with.

gon·er (gô′nər, gon′ər), *n. Informal.* a person or thing that is dead or lost.

gon·fa·lon (gon′fə lən), *n.* a banner suspended from a crossbar.

gong (gông, gong), *n.* a large bronze disk that produces a vibrant, hollow tone when struck.

gon·o·coc·cus (gon′ə kok′əs), *n., pl.* **-coc·ci** (-kok′sī). a bacterium that causes gonorrhea. —**gon′o·coc′cal,** **gon′o·coc′cic,** *adj.*

gon·or·rhe·a (gon′ə rē′ə), *n.* a venereal, purulent inflammation of the urethra or the vagina. —**gon′or·rhe′al,** *adj.*

goo (gōō), *n. Informal.* **1.** a thick or sticky substance. **2.** maudlin sentimentality. —**goo′ey,** *adj.*

goo·ber (gōō′bər), *n. Chiefly Southern U.S.* a peanut.

good (gŏŏd), *adj.*, **bet·ter, best,** *n., adv.* —*adj.* **1.** morally excellent. **2.** satisfactory in quality, quantity, or degree: *good health.* **3.** proper or fit. **4.** well-behaved. **5.** kind or friendly. **6.** honorable or worthy: *a good name.* **7.** not counterfeit: *good money.* **8.** sound or valid: *good judgment.* **9.** healthful or beneficial. **10.** not spoiled or tainted. **11.** agreeable or genial: *Have a good time.* **12.** attractive: *She has a good figure.* **13.** sufficient or ample. **14.** competent or skillful. **15.** skillfully or expertly done: *a really good job.* **16.** best or most dressy. **17.** full: *a good day's journey away.* **18.** as good as, equivalent to. **19.** good for, a. certain to repay (money owed). b. equivalent in value of. c. that can be used for (the length of time or the distance indicated). **20.** make good, a. to repay. b. to fulfill. c. to be successful. d. to substantiate. —*n.* **21.** profit or benefit. **22.** excellence or merit: *to do good.* **23.** moral righteousness. **24.** goods, a. possessions. b. merchandise. c. *Informal.* evidence of guilt. d. cloth or textile material. **25.** for good, forever. Also, **for good and all. 26.** the good, good persons collectively. **27.** to the good, richer in profit or gain. —*adv.* **28.** *Informal.* well. **29.** good and, *Informal.* completely.

—Usage. **28.** In the speech and writing of educated people, GOOD is rarely encountered as an adverb: *He did well* (not *good*) *on the test. She sees well* (not *good*) *with her new glasses.* Some confusion arises because WELL can be an adjective meaning "healthy": *He is a well man again.*

good·by (gŏŏd′bī′), *interj.* (used as a closing expression of good wishes at parting). Also, **good′bye′.** [contr. of *God be with you* (ye)]

good-for-noth·ing (gŏŏd′fər nuth′ing, -nuth′-), *n.* a worthless person.

Good′ Fri′day, the Friday before Easter, commemorating the Crucifixion of Jesus.

good-heart·ed (gŏŏd′här′tid), *adj.* kind or considerate. —**good′-heart′ed·ly,** *adv.* —**good′-heart′ed·ness,** *n.*

Good′ Hope′, Cape of, a cape in SW South Africa.

good′ hu′mor, a cheerful or amiable mood. —**good′-hu′mored,** *adj.* —**good′-hu′mored·ly,** *adv.*

good·ish (gŏŏd′ish), *adj.* fairly good.

good-look·ing (gŏŏd′lŏŏk′ing), *adj.* of good or attractive appearance.

good·ly (gŏŏd′lē), *adj.,* **-li·er, -li·est. 1.** of substantial size or amount. **2.** *Literary.* of good quality or appearance.

good·man (gŏŏd′mən), *n.*, *Archaic.*
1. the master of a household. 2.
(*cap.*) a title similar to *Mr.*

good-na·tured (gŏŏd′nā′chərd), *adj.*
having a pleasant, kindly disposition. —**good′-na′tured·ly,** *adv.*

good·ness (gŏŏd′nis), *n.* 1. the state
or quality of being good. 2. moral
excellence or virtue. 3. kindly feeling. 4. a euphemism for God: *Thank
goodness!* —*interj.* 5. (an exclamation of surprise, alarm, etc.) —**Syn.**
2. integrity, probity, uprightness.

good′ Samar′itan, a person who gratuitously gives help to someone in
distress.

good·wife (gŏŏd′wīf′), *n.* (*cap.*) *Archaic.* a title similar to *Mrs.*

good·will (gŏŏd′wil′), *n.* 1. friendly
disposition. 2. cheerful consent. 3.
Com. an intangible, salable asset
arising from the reputation of a
business and its relations with its
customers. Also, **good′ will′.**

good·y (gŏŏd′ē), *n.*, *pl.* **good·ies.** *Informal.* something very good, esp. to
eat.

good·y-good·y (gŏŏd′ē gŏŏd′ē), *adj.*
affecting goodness. —*n.* 2. a goody-
goody person.

goof (gŏŏf), *Slang.* —*n.* 1. a stupid
person. 2. a mistake or blunder. —
v.i. 3. to make an error, etc. 4. to
kill time or evade work: *We just
goofed off till train time.* —**goof′y,**
adj. —**goof′i·ness,** *n.*

goof-ball (gŏŏf′bôl′), *n. Slang.* 1. a
pill containing a barbituate drug. 2.
an extremely eccentric person.

goof-off (gŏŏf′ôf′, -of′), *n. Slang.* a
person who habitually shirks responsibility.

gook (gŏŏk, gook), *n. Slang.* any
grimy or viscid substance.

goon (gŏŏn), *n.* 1. *Slang.* a stupid
person. 2. *Informal.* a hired hoodlum or thug.

goose (gŏŏs), *n.*, *pl.* **geese** for 1–4, 6,
goos·es for 5. 1. a web-footed, swimming bird larger than a duck and
having a longer neck. 2. the female
of this bird. 3. its flesh, used as
food. 4. a silly or foolish person.
5. *Obs.* a tailor's smoothing iron.
6. **cook one's goose,** *Informal.* to
ruin one's chances.

goose·ber·ry (gŏŏs′ber′ē, -bə rē,
gŏŏz′-), *n.* 1. the small, edible, acid
berry of a prickly shrub. 2. its shrub.

goose′ flesh′, a rough condition of
the skin, induced by cold or fear.
Also called **goose′ pim′ples.**

G.O.P., Grand Old Party (the Republican Party of the U.S.).

go·pher (gō′fər), *n.* any of several
ground squirrels of the prairie regions of North America.

gore¹ (gōr, gôr), *n.* blood that is shed,
esp. when clotted.

gore² (gōr, gôr), *v.t.,* **gored, gor·ing.**
(of an animal) to pierce with the
horns or tusks.

gore³ (gōr, gôr), *n.* a triangular piece
of material inserted in a garment,
sail, etc.

gorge (gôrj), *n.,* *v.,* **gorged, gorg·ing.**
—*n.* 1. a narrow ravine with steep,
rocky walls. 2. an obstructing mass:
an ice gorge. 3. *Archaic.* the throat.
—*v.t.,* *v.i.* 4. to stuff (oneself) with
food.

gor·geous (gôr′jəs), *adj.* 1. sumptuous
in appearance or coloring. 2. extremely enjoyable. —**gor′geous·ly,**
adv. —**gor′geous·ness,** *n.*

Gor·gon·zo·la (gôr′gan zō′lə), *n.* a
strongly flavored, Italian milk
cheese.

go·ril·la (gə ril′ə), *n.* a humanlike
large ape of western equatorial
Africa having long arms and huge
shoulders.

Gor·ki (gôr′kē), *n.* a city in the central Soviet Union, on the Volga
River.

gor·mand·ize (gôr′mən dīz′), *v.i.,* *v.t.,*
-ized, -iz·ing. to eat like a glutton.
—**gor′mand·iz′er,** *n.*

gorse (gôrs), *n. Chiefly Brit.* furze.

gor·y (gôr′ē, gōr′ē), *adj.,* **gor·i·er, gor·i·est.** 1. covered or stained with
gore. 2. involving much bloodshed.
—**gor′i·ly,** *adv.* —**gor′i·ness,** *n.*

gosh (gosh), *interj.* (an exclamation
or mild oath.)

gos·hawk (gos′hôk′), *n.* a powerful,
short-winged hawk having a long
tail.

gos·ling (goz′ling), *n.* a young goose.

gos·pel (gos′pəl), *n.* 1. the teachings
of Jesus and the apostles. 2. (*usually cap.*) any of the first four books
of the New Testament. 3. something regarded as true and implicitly
believed. —*adj.* 4. pertaining to or
proclaiming the gospel or its teachings: *a gospel singer.*

gos·sa·mer (gos′ə mər), *n.* 1. a fine,
filmy cobweb. 2. any thin, light
fabric. 3. something extremely light
and delicate. —*adj.* 4. thin and light.

gos·sip (gos′əp), *n.,* *v.,* **-siped, -sip·ing.**
—*n.* 1. idle talk or rumor, esp.
about the private affairs of others.
2. a person given to such talk. 3. a
casual conversation. —*v.i.* 4. to relate or spread gossip. —**gos′sip·y,**
adj.

got (got), *v.* pt. and a pp. of **get.**

Goth (goth), *n.* a member of a Teutonic people who, in the 3rd to 5th
centuries, invaded and settled in
parts of the Roman Empire.
Goth, Gothic. Also, **Goth.**

Goth·ic (goth′ik), *adj.* **1.** noting a style of architecture of western Europe from the 12th to 16th centuries, marked by pointed arches, tall columns, etc. **2.** of the Goths or their language. —*n.* **3.** the Gothic architectural style. **4.** the extinct Germanic language of the Goths. **5.** (*l.c.*) a novel involving mystery and horror in a medieval setting.

got·ten (got′ən), *v.* a pp of **get.**

Gou·da (gou′də, gōō′-), *n.* a cream-colored Dutch cheese, usually coated with red wax.

gouge (gouj), *n., v.,* **gouged, goug·ing.** —*n.* **1.** a chisel having a partly cylindrical blade. **2.** a groove or hole made by gouging. —*v.t.* **3.** to scoop out with or as with a gouge. **4.** *Informal.* to swindle or overcharge. —**goug′er,** *n.*

gou·lash (gōō′läsh, -lash), *n.* a stew of beef, veal, vegetables, etc., with paprika seasoning. [< Hung *gulyas,* short for *gulyas hus* herdsman's meat]

gourd (gōrd, gôrd, gōōrd), *n.* **1.** the fruit of any of various plants whose dried shell is used for bottles and sometimes for ornament. **2.** a plant bearing such a fruit. **3.** a dried and excavated gourd shell used as a bottle, etc.

gourde (gōōrd), *n.* the monetary unit of Haiti.

gour·mand (gōōr′mənd), *n.* a person who is fond of good eating, usually indiscriminatingly and often to excess. [< OF *gormant* glutton]

gour·met (gōōr mā′, gôr mā′), *n.* a connoisseur of fine food and drink.

gout (gout), *n.* a disease characterized by painful inflammation of the joints, esp. in the great toe. —**gout′y,** *adj.*

gov., **1.** governor. **2.** government.

gov·ern (guv′ərn), *v.t.* **1.** to rule by right of authority. **2.** to exercise a directing influence over. **3.** to control or hold in check. **4.** to serve as a law for. —*v.i.* **5.** to exercise the function of government. —**gov′ern·a·bil′i·ty, gov′ern·a·ble·ness,** *n.* —**gov′ern·a·ble,** *adj.* —**gov′ern·ance,** *n.*

gov·ern·ess (guv′ər nis), *n.* a woman employed to take charge of a child's upbringing, education, etc.

gov·ern·ment (guv′ərn mənt, -ər mənt), *n.* **1.** the political direction and control exercised over a nation, state, community, etc. **2.** the form or system of rule by which a nation, state, community, etc., is governed. **3.** a governing body of persons. **4.** control or rule. —**gov·ern·men·tal** (guv′ərn men′təl), *adj.*

gov′ernment is′sue, (*often cap.*) issued or supplied by the government or one of its agencies.

gov·er·nor (guv′ər nər), *n.* **1.** the executive head of a state in the U.S. **2.** a ruler appointed to govern a province, etc. **3.** a device for maintaining uniform speed or power of a vehicle. —**gov′er·nor·ship′,** *n.*

govt., government.

gown (goun), *n.* **1.** a woman's dress, esp. a formal one. **2.** a loose, flowing outer garment worn as distinctive of the wearer's office or profession. **3.** any loose robe, as a nightgown.

G.P., general practitioner.

gp., group.

GPO, 1. general post office. **2.** Government Printing Office.

GQ, General Quarters.

Gr., 1. Greece. **2.** Greek.

gr., 1. grade. **2.** grain; grains. **3.** gram; grams. **4.** grammar. **5.** gravity. **6.** gross (def. 9). **7.** group.

grab (grab), *v.,* **grabbed, grab·bing,** *n.* —*v.t.* **1.** to seize suddenly. **2.** to seize forcibly or unscrupulously. **3.** *Slang.* to arouse interest in. —*n.* **4.** the act of grabbing. —**grab′ber,** *n.* —**grab′by,** *adj.*

gra·ben (grä′bən), *n.* a portion of the earth's crust, bounded on at least two sides by faults.

grace (grās), *n., v.,* **graced, grac·ing.** —*n.* **1.** elegance or beauty of form, manner, or motion. **2.** a pleasing or attractive quality. **3.** favor or goodwill. **4.** mercy or clemency. **5.** favor shown in granting a delay. **6. a.** the freely given, unmerited favor and love of God. **b.** the condition of being in God's favor. **7.** a short prayer before or after a meal. **8.** (*usually cap.*) a formal title for a duke, duchess, or archbishop. **9. in someone's good** or **bad graces,** in or out of favor with. —*v.t.* **10.** to adorn or decorate. **11.** to favor or honor. —**grace′ful,** *adj.* —**grace′ful·ly,** *adv.* —**grace′ful·ness,** *n.* —**grace′less,** *adj.* —**grace′less·ly,** *adv.* —**grace′less·ness,** *n.*

gra·cious (grā′shəs), *adj.* **1.** disposed to show grace or favor. **2.** characterized by good taste, comfort, ease, or luxury. **3.** beneficent in a pleasantly condescending way, esp. to inferiors. **4.** merciful or compassionate. —**gra′cious·ly,** *adv.* —**gra′cious·ness,** *n.* —**Syn. 1.** benign, courteous, kindly.

grack·le (grak′əl), *n.* any of several long-tailed American birds having usually iridescent black plumage.

grad (grad), *n. Informal.* a graduate.

gra·da·tion (grā dā′shən), *n.* **1.** any change through a series of stages or by degrees. **2.** a stage or degree in such a series. **3.** an advance by very small degrees. **4.** the act of grading. —**gra·da′tion·al,** *adj.*

grade (grād), *n., v.,* **grad·ed, grad·ing.** —*n.* **1.** a degree in a scale, as of rank, quality, etc. **2.** a class of persons or things of the same relative rank, quality, etc. **3.** a step or stage in a course or process. **4.** any of the divisions corresponding to a year's work in school. **5.** the pupils in such a division. **6. the grades,** elementary school. **7.** a rating in a school examination or assignment. **8. a.** the inclination of a road. **b.** the degree of such slope. **9. make the grade,** to attain a specific goal. —*v.t.* **10.** to arrange in a series of grades. **11.** to determine the grade of. **12.** to assign a grade to. **13.** to reduce the inclination of: *to grade a road.*

-grade, an element occurring in loan words from Latin, where it meant "step": *retrograde.*

grade′ cross′ing, an intersection of a railroad track and another track at the same level.

grad·er (grā′dər), *n.* a machine for grading ground.

grade′ school′. See **elementary school.**

gra·di·ent (grā′dē ənt), *n.* grade (def. 8).

grad·u·al (graj′ōō əl), *adj.* changing or moving by degrees or little by little. —**grad′u·al·ly,** *adv.*

grad·u·al·ism (graj′ōō ə liz′əm), *n.* the principle of achieving some goal by gradual steps rather than by drastic change.

grad·u·ate (*n., adj.* graj′ōō it, -āt′; *v.* graj′ōō āt′), *n., adj., v.,* **-at·ed, -at·ing.** —*n.* **1.** a person who has received an academic degree or diploma. **2.** a graduated container for measuring. —*adj.* **3.** holding an academic degree or diploma. **4.** of or pertaining to academic study beyond the bachelor's degree: *a graduate student.* —*v.i.* **5.** to receive an academic degree or diploma: *to graduate from college.* —*v.t.* **6.** to grant an academic diploma to. **7.** to arrange in grades or graduations. **8.** to divide into or mark with degrees or other divisions. —**grad′u·a′tor,** *n.*

grad·u·a·tion (graj′ōō ā′shən), *n.* **1.** the act of graduating or state of being graduated from a college or school. **2.** the ceremony of conferring academic degrees or diplomas. **3.** marks on an instrument for indicating degrees, quantity, etc.

graf·fi·to (grə fē′tō), *n., pl.* **-ti** (-tē). Usually, **graffiti.** messages or slogans, often of a social or political nature, scrawled on walls of public buildings or conveyances.

graft¹ (graft, gräft), *n.* **1. a.** a bud or shoot of a plant inserted into another plant in which it continues to grow. **b.** the plant resulting from this. **2.** skin surgically transplanted to another part of the body. —*v.t., v.i.* **3.** to insert (a graft). **4.** to transplant (skin) as a graft. —**graft′er,** *n.*

graft² (graft, gräft), *n.* **1.** the acquisition of money or position by dishonest means, esp. through the abuse of power in politics. **2.** the money or position so acquired. —*v.t., v.i.* **3.** to obtain (money or position) by graft. —**graft′er,** *n.*

gra·ham (grā′əm), *adj.* made of whole-wheat flour. [after S. *Graham* (1794–1851), U.S. dietitian]

Grail (grāl), *n.* the cup or chalice allegedly used at the Last Supper.

grain (grān), *n.* **1.** a small, hard seed of any food plant, as wheat, rye, etc. **2.** the gathered seeds of one of the food plants, esp. of cereal plants. **3.** the plants themselves. **4.** any small, hard particle, as of sand. **5.** the smallest unit of weight. **6.** a tiny amount: *a grain of truth.* **7.** the arrangement of fibers in wood. **8.** texture: *sugar of fine grain.* **9.** natural character: *to go against one's grain.* —**grained,** *adj.*

grain′ al′cohol, alcohol (def. 1).

grain·y (grā′nē), *adj.,* **grain·i·er, grain·i·est. 1.** made of or resembling grains. **2.** having a natural or simulated grain, as wood. —**grain′i·ness,** *n.*

gram (gram), *n.* a metric unit of mass equal to 1/1000 of a kilogram or 0.035 ounce. Also, *Brit.,* **gramme.**

-gram¹, a combining form meaning "something written" or "drawing": *diagram; cablegram.*

-gram², a combining form of **gram:** *kilogram.*

gram., 1. grammar. **2.** grammarian. **3.** grammatical.

gram·mar (gram′ər), *n.* **1.** the study of the formal features of a language, as the ways in which words are used in sentences. **2.** a book dealing with these features. **3.** criteria for evaluating speech or writing. **4.** usage of the preferred forms in speaking or writing. —**gram·mar·i·an** (grə mar′-ē ən), *n.* —**gram·mat·i·cal** (grə mat′i kəl), *adj.* —**gram·mat′i·cal·ly,** *adv.*

gram′mar school′, 1. *Brit.* a secondary school corresponding to an American high school. **2.** *Brit.* (formerly) a secondary school in which Latin and Greek were among the principal subjects taught. **3.** *Obsolesc.* an elementary school.

Gram·o·phone (gram′ə fōn′), *n. Trademark.* an early type of phonograph.

gram·pus (gram′pəs), *n., pl.* **-pus·es.** a blunt-nosed mammal of the dolphin family, widely distributed in northern seas.

gra·na·ry (grā′nə rē, gran′ə-), *n., pl.* **-ries.** a storehouse or repository for grain.

grand (grand), *adj., n., pl.* **grands** for 10, **grand** for 11. —*adj.* 1. impressive in size, appearance, or general effects. 2. stately or dignified. 3. highly ambitious. 4. magnificent or splendid. 5. highest in rank or official dignity: *a grand potentate.* 6. main or principal. 7. of great importance or pretension. 8. complete or comprehensive: *a grand total.* 9. very good or splendid. —*n.* 10. See **grand piano.** 11. *Informal.* a thousand dollars. —**grand′ly,** *adv.* —**grand′ness,** *n.*

grand-, a prefix meaning "one generation more remote": *grandfather; grandnephew.*

gran·dam (gran′dəm, -dam), *n.* *Archaic.* 1. a grandmother. 2. an old woman. Also, **gran·dame** (gran′dām, -dəm).

Grand′ Can′yon, an immense gorge in N Arizona.

grand·child (gran′chīld′), *n.* a child of one's son or daughter.

grand·daugh·ter (gran′dô′tər), *n.* a daughter of one's son or daughter.

grand dame (gränd dȧm′), *French.* a usually old lady of dignified bearing.

gran·dee (gran dē′), *n.* a Spanish or Portuguese nobleman.

gran·deur (gran′jər, -jŏŏr), *n.* 1. the state or quality of being grand. 2. something grand. —*Syn.* 1. magnificence, majesty, splendor.

grand·fa·ther (gran′fä′thər, grand′-), *n.* 1. the father of one's father or mother. 2. a forefather.

grand′father's clock′, a pendulum floor clock having a case as tall as a person. Also, **grand′father clock′.**

gran·dil·o·quent (gran dil′ə kwənt), *adj.* speaking or expressed in a lofty or pompous style. —**gran·dil′o·quence,** *n.* —**gran·dil′o·quent·ly,** *adv.*

gran·di·ose (gran′dē ōs′), *adj.* 1. grand in an imposing way. 2. affectedly grand or stately. —**gran′di·ose′ly,** *adv.* —**gran·di·os·i·ty** (gran′dē os′i tē), **gran′di·ose′ness,** *n.*

grand′ ju′ry, a jury designated to inquire into alleged violations of the law in order to ascertain whether the evidence is sufficient to warrant trial.

grand·ma (gran′mä′, grand′-, gram′-, gram′mə), *n.* *Informal.* grandmother.

grand mal (gran′ mal′), the most severe form of epilepsy.

grand′ mas′ter, a highly ranked chess player.

grand·moth·er (gran′muth′ər, grand′-, gram′-), *n.* 1. the mother of one's father or mother. 2. an ancestress.

grand′ op′era, an opera in which the text is sung throughout.

grand·pa (gran′pä′, grand′-, gram′-, gram′pə), *n.* *Informal.* grandfather.

grand·par·ent (gran′pâr′ənt, -par′-, grand′-), *n.* a parent of a parent.

grand′ pian′o, a harp-shaped horizontal piano.

Grand Prix (grän prē′), *pl.* **Grand Prix** (grän prēz′). an international automobile race over a long, arduous course.

Grand′ Rap′ids, a city in SW Michigan.

grand′ slam′, 1. *Bridge.* See under **slam³.** 2. *Baseball.* a home run hit with three players on base. 3. *Informal.* complete success.

grand·son (gran′sun′, grand′-), *n.* a son of one's son or daughter.

grand·stand (gran′stand′, grand′-), *n.* a seating area of a stadium, racecourse, etc.

grange (gränj), *n.* 1. *Brit.* a farm with its nearby buildings. 2. (*cap.*) a lodge or local branch of a farmers' association in the U.S.

gran·ite (gran′it), *n.* a granular igneous rock composed chiefly of feldspar and quartz. —**gra·nit·ic** (grə nit′ik), *adj.*

gran·ny (gran′ē), *n., pl.* **-nies,** *adj.* —*n.* 1. *Informal.* a grandmother. 2. an old woman. 3. a fussy person. 4. *Southern U.S.* a nurse or midwife. —*adj.* 5. old-fashioned: *granny glasses.* Also, **gran′nie.**

gra·no·la (grə nō′lə), *n.* a breakfast food consisting of a dry mixture of cereals, nuts, dried fruit, etc., usually served in milk. [< L *gran(um)* grain + arbitrary suffix]

grant (grant, gränt), *v.t.* 1. to bestow or confer, esp. by a formal act. 2. to give or accord. 3. to agree to accede to. 4. to admit or concede. 5. to transfer (property), esp. by deed. 6. **take for granted,** to accept as true, completed, etc. —*n.* 7. something granted, as a right or funds. 8. the act of granting. 9. a transfer of property. —**grant′er,** or, **gran·tor,** *n.*

Grant (grant), *n.* Ulysses S(imp·son) (simp′sən), 1822–85, Union general in the Civil War: 18th president of the U.S. 1869–77.

gran·tee (gran tē′, grän-), *n.* *Law.* a person to whom a grant is made.

grant-in-aid (grant′in ād′), *n., pl.* **grants-in-aid.** financial assistance given, as by a foundation, to an individual or institution for educational purposes, etc.

grants·man (grants′mən), *n.* an expert in grantsmanship.

grants·man·ship (grants′mən ship′), *n.* the art of securing grants-in-aid.

gran·u·lar (gran′yə lər), *adj.* 1. of or like granules. 2. composed of or bearing granules or grains. —**gran·u·lar·i·ty** (gran′yə lar′i tē), *n.* —**gran′u·lar·ly,** *adv.*

gran·u·late (gran′yə lāt′), v.t., v.i., -lat·ed, -lat·ing. to form into granules or grains. —**gran′u·lat·ed,** adj. —**gran′u·la′tion,** n. —**gran′u·la′tor,** n.

gran·ule (gran′yool), n. 1. a little grain. 2. a small particle.

grape (grāp), n. 1. an edible, pulpy, smooth-skinned berry which grows in clusters on a vine and from which wine is made. 2. grapevine (def. 1). 3. a dark, purplish-red color. 4. grapeshot.

grape·fruit (grāp′froot′), n. a large, roundish, yellow-skinned, edible citrus fruit.

grape′ hy′acinth, a plant of the lily family, having globular, blue flowers resembling tiny grapes.

grape·shot (grāp′shot′), n. a cluster of small cast-iron balls formerly used as a charge for cannon.

grape·vine (grāp′vīn′), n. 1. a vine that bears grapes. 2. a person-to-person method of relaying information. 3. rumor or gossip.

graph (graf, gräf), n. 1. a diagram representing a system of or interrelations among things by a number of dots, lines, bars, etc. —v.t. 2. to represent by means of a graph.

-graph, a combining form meaning: **a.** drawn or written: monograph. **b.** an instrument that writes or records: phonograph.

graph·ic (graf′ik), adj. 1. giving a clear and effective picture. 2. pertaining to the use of graphs or diagrams. 3. of or pertaining to the graphic arts. Also, **graph′i·cal.** —**graph′i·cal·ly,** adv.

graph′ic arts′, the arts of engraving, etching, printing, lithography, etc.

graph·ics (graf′iks), n. 1. the art of drawing, esp. as used in mathematics, engineering, etc. 2. See **graphic arts.**

graph·ite (graf′īt), n. a soft carbon used for pencil leads, as a lubricant, etc. —**gra·phit·ic** (grə fit′ik), adj.

graph·ol·o·gy (gra fol′ə jē), n. the study of handwriting, esp. as regarded as an expression of the writer's character. —**graph·ol′o·gist,** n.

graph′ pa′per, paper having a pattern of straight or curved lines, for plotting graphs and curves.

-graphy, a combining form meaning: **a.** a process or form of writing, recording, or describing: biography; photography. **b.** a descriptive art or science: choreography; geography.

grap·nel (grap′n°l), n. a small anchor with three or more flukes or claws.

grap·ple (grap′əl), n., v., -pled, -pling. —n. 1. a gripping and holding. 2. a hand-to-hand fight, as in wrestling. 3. a hook formerly used for fastening onto an enemy ship in a sea battle. —v.t. 4. to seize or hold with or as with a grapple. 5. to grab tightly. —v.i. 6. to seize another in a firm grip, as in wrestling. 7. to struggle or cope: to grapple with a problem. 8. to use a grapple. —**grap′pler,** n.

grasp (grasp, gräsp), v.t. 1. to seize and hold with or as with the hand. 2. to seize upon. 3. to comprehend or understand. —v.i. 4. to make a motion of grasping something. —n. 5. the act of grasping. 6. a hold or grip. 7. one's power of seizing and holding. 8. possession or mastery. 9. comprehension or understanding. —**grasp′a·ble,** adj.

grasp·ing (gras′ping, gräs′-), adj. unscrupulously greedy for material gain. —**grasp′ing·ly,** adv. —**grasp′ing·ness,** n.

grass (gras, gräs), n. 1. any of several widely distributed plants with jointed stems, sheathing leaves, and seedlike fruit 2. herbage in general. 3. the grass-covered ground, as a pasture or lawn. 4. Slang. marijuana. —**grass′y,** adj.

grass·hop·per (gras′hop′ər, gräs′-), n. any of numerous insects having the hind legs adapted for leaping.

grass·land (gras′land′, gräs′-), n. an area in which the natural vegetation consists largely of perennial grasses.

grass′ roots′, 1. the common people or rural people not ordinarily regarded as politically influential. 2. the basic popular support. —**grass-roots** (gras′roots′, -roots′, gräs′-), adj.

grass′ wid′ow, a woman who is separated, divorced, or lives apart from her husband.

grate¹ (grāt), n. 1. a frame of metal bars for holding burning fuel, as in a fireplace. 2. a framework of parallel or crossed bars, used as a partition or guard.

grate² (grāt), v., grat·ed, grat·ing. —v.t. 1. to have an irritating effect. 2. to make a sound of or as of rough scraping. —v.t. 3. to rub together with a harsh, jarring sound. 4. to reduce to small particles by rubbing against a rough surface. 5. to irritate or annoy. —**grat′er,** n.

grate·ful (grāt′fəl), adj. 1. deeply thankful. 2. expressing gratitude. 3. agreeable or welcome. —**grate′ful·ly,** adv. —**grate′ful·ness,** n.

grat·i·fy (grat′ə fī′), v.t.i., -fied, -fy·ing. 1. to give satisfying pleasure to. 2. to humor or indulge. —**grat′i·fi·ca′tion,** n.

grat·ing (grā′ting), n. grate¹ (def. 2).

grat·ing² (grā′ting), adj. 1. irritatingly unpleasant. 2. harsh or rasping. —**grat′ing·ly,** adv.

grat·is (grat′is, grā′tis), adv., adj. without charge or payment.

grat·i·tude (grat'i tood', -tyood'), *n.* deep thankfulness.

gra·tu·i·tous (grə too'i təs, -tyoo'-), *adj.* 1. provided or done without charge or payment. 2. without apparent reason or justification.

gra·tu·i·ty (grə too'i tē, -tyoo'-), *n., pl.* **-ties.** a gift of money, esp. for service, as a tip.

grau·pel (grou'pəl), *n.* crisp, white ice particles.

gra·va·men (grə vā'mən), *n., pl.* **-vam·i·na** (-vam'ə nə). the part of an accusation that weighs most heavily against the accused.

grave¹ (grāv), *n.* 1. an excavation made in the earth to bury a dead body. 2. any place of interment.

grave² (grāv; *for 4, 6 also* gräv), *adj.,* **grav·er, grav·est** *for 1–3, 5, n.* —*adj.* 1. weighty and important. 2. critical and serious. 3. solemn or sedate. 4. *Gram.* noting or having a particular accent (ˋ) indicating the pitch of a vowel. 5. (of colors) dull or somber. —*n.* 6. the grave accent. —**grave'ly,** *adv.* —**grave'ness,** *n.* —**Syn.** 1. critical, momentous, significant.

grave³ (grāv), *v.t.,* **graved, grav·en** (grā'vən) *or* **graved, grav·ing.** 1. to impress deeply. 2. *Archaic.* to carve or engrave.

grav·el (grav'əl), *n.* small stones and pebbles, or a mixture of these with sand. —**grav'el·ly,** *adj.*

grave·stone (grāv'stōn'), *n.* a stone marking a grave.

grave·yard (grāv'yärd'), *n.* a burial ground.

grave'yard shift', *Slang.* a work shift usually beginning at midnight.

grav·id (grav'id), *adj. Literary.* pregnant.

gra·vim·e·ter (grə vim'i tər), *n.* 1. an instrument for measuring specific gravity. 2. an instrument for measuring the strength of a gravitational field.

grav·i·met·ric (grav'ə me'trik), *adj.* of or pertaining to measurement by weight.

grav·i·tate (grav'i tāt'), *v.t.,* **-tat·ed, -tat·ing.** 1. to move or tend to move under the influence of gravitational force. 2. to be strongly attracted.

grav·i·ta·tion (grav'i tā'shən), *n.* 1. the force of mutual attraction between all bodies. 2. a movement toward something or someone: *the gravitation of people toward the suburbs.* —**grav'i·ta'tion·al,** *adj.* —**grav'i·ta'tion·al·ly,** *adv.* —**grav'i·ta'tive,** *adj.*

grav·i·ty (grav'i tē), *n., pl.* **-ties.** 1. the force of attraction by which terrestrial bodies tend to fall toward the center of the earth. 2. gravitation in general. 3. seriousness or importance.

gra·vure (grə vyoor', grā'vyər), *n.* a process of photomechanical printing, such as rotogravure.

gra·vy (grā'vē), *n., pl.* **-vies.** 1. a sauce of the fat and juices from cooked meat, often thickened and seasoned. 2. *Slang.* something valuable obtained easily or unexpectedly.

gray (grā), *adj.* 1. of a color between white and black. 2. dismal or gloomy. 3. having gray hair. 4. indeterminate in character. —*n.* 5. any achromatic color made by mixing black and white. 6. something of this color. —*v.t., v.i.* 7. to make or become gray. —**gray'ish,** *adj.* —**gray'ness,** *n.*

gray·beard (grā'bērd'), *n. Often Contemptuous.* an old man.

gray·ling (grā'ling), *n.* a freshwater fish related to the trout.

gray' mat'ter, 1. the reddish-gray nerve tissue of the brain and spinal cord. 2. *Informal.* one's brains or intellect.

gray' pow'er, the organized influence exerted by elderly people as a group, esp. for social or political purposes.

graze¹ (grāz), *v.,* **grazed, graz·ing.** —*v.i.* 1. to feed on growing herbage. —*v.t.* 2. to put (cattle, etc.) out to graze. 3. *Literary.* to feed on (growing herbage). 4. *Obs.* to tend (cattle, etc.) at pasture. —**graz'er,** *n.*

graze² (grāz), *v.t., v.i.,* **grazed, graz·ing.** to touch or scrape (something) lightly in passing. —**graz'ing·ly,** *adv.*

Gr. Br., Great Britain. Also, **Gr. Brit.**

grease (*n.* grēs; *v.* grēs, grēz), *n., v.,* **greased, greas·ing.** —*n.* 1. the melted fat of animals. 2. fatty or oily matter in general. —*v.t.* 3. to cover or lubricate with grease.

grease' paint', an oily makeup used by actors, clowns, etc.

greas·y (grē'sē, -zē), *adj.,* **greas·i·er, greas·i·est.** 1. soiled with grease. 2. containing grease or fat. —**greas'i·ness,** *n.*

great (grāt), *adj.* 1. unusually or comparatively large in size or dimensions. 2. large in number. 3. considerable in degree, intensity, etc.: *great pain.* 4. notable or remarkable. 5. distinguished or famous. 6. important or consequential. 7. having unusual merit or skill. 8. of marked duration: *a great while.* 9. *Informal.* very good. 10. noting one generation more remote from the family relative indicated: *a great-grandson.* —*adv.* 11. *Informal.* very well. —**great'ly,** *adv.* —**great'ness,** *n.*

Great' Brit'ain, an island of NW Europe, comprising England, Scotland, and Wales.

great' cir'cle, 1. a circle on a sphere such that the plane containing the circle passes through the center of the sphere. 2. the line of shortest distance between two points on the surface of the earth.

great·coat (grāt′kōt′), *n. Chiefly Brit.* a heavy overcoat.

Great′ Dane′, a large, powerful, short-haired dog.

great·heart·ed (grāt′här′tid), *adj.* 1. generous or magnanimous. 2. high-spirited or courageous.

Great′ Lakes′, a series of five lakes between the U.S. and Canada.

Great′ Pow′er, a nation that plays a major, often decisive role in international affairs.

Great′ Salt′ Lake′, a shallow salt lake in NW Utah.

grebe (grēb), *n.* a diving bird related to the loons, having short wings and a flattened body.

Gre·cian (grē′shən), *adj.* Greek, esp. of ancient Greece. —*n.* 2. a Greek.

Greece (grēs), *n.* a country in S Europe.

greed (grēd), *n.* excessive or rapacious desire, esp. for wealth.

greed·y (grē′dē), *adj.*, **greed·i·er, greed·i·est.** 1. excessively desirous of wealth, profit, etc. 2. having a great desire for food or drink. —**greed′i·ly,** *adv.* —**greed′i·ness,** *n.* —Syn. 1. avaricious, grasping.

Greek (grēk), *adj.* 1. of Greece, the Greeks, or their language. 2. pertaining to the Greek Orthodox Church. —*n.* 3. a native of Greece. 4. the language of the ancient Greeks and any of the languages that have developed from it.

Greek′ Or′thodox Church′, that branch of the Orthodox Church constituting the national church of Greece.

green (grēn), *adj.* 1. of the color of growing foliage, between yellow and blue in the spectrum. 2. covered with foliage. 3. made of green vegetables: *a green salad.* 4. unseasoned or unripe. 5. immature or inexperienced. 6. sickly or pale. —*n.* 7. a color intermediate in the spectrum between yellow and blue. 8. grassy land. 9. *Golf.* the area of closely cropped grass surrounding the hole. 10. **greens,** the leaves and stems of plants, used for decoration or for food. —*v.t., v.i.* 11. to make or become green. —**green′ish,** *adj.* —**green′ness,** *n.*

green·back (grēn′bak′), *n.* a U.S. legal-tender note printed in green on the back.

green′ bean′. See **string bean.**

green′ belt′, an area of parks or unoccupied ground surrounding a community.

green·er·y (grē′nə rē), *n.* foliage or vegetation.

green-eyed (grēn′īd′), *adj.* bitterly jealous.

green·gro·cer (grēn′grō′sər), *n. Brit.* a retailer of fresh vegetables and fruit.

green·horn (grēn′hôrn′), *n. Slang.* 1. a raw, inexperienced person. 2. a person easily imposed upon.

green·house (grēn′hous′), *n.* a building, chiefly of glass, with controlled temperature, used for cultivating plants.

Green·land (grēn′lənd, -land′), *n.* a Danish island located NE of North America.

green′ manure′, a crop of growing plants plowed under to enrich the soil.

green′ pep′per. See **sweet pepper.**

green′ pow′er, the power of money, as a social force.

green·room (grēn′rōōm′, -rŏŏm′), *n.* a lounge in a theater for the use of performers.

Greens·bo·ro (grēnz′bûr′ō, -bur′ō), *n.* a city in N North Carolina.

greens′ fee′, a fee for playing on a golf course.

green·sward (grēn′swôrd′), *n.* green, grassy turf.

green′ thumb′, an aptitude for gardening.

Green′wich Time′ (grin′ij, -ich, gren′-), the time as measured on the prime meridian running through Greenwich, England: used in England and as a basis of calculation elsewhere.

green·wood (grēn′wŏŏd′), *n.* a wood or forest when green, as in summer.

greet (grēt), *v.t.* 1. to address with some form of salutation. 2. to receive: *to greet a proposal with boos.* 3. to manifest (itself) to: *Music greeted our ears.* —**greet′er,** *n.*

greet·ing (grē′tiṅg), *n.* 1. the act or words of a person who greets. 2. **greetings,** an expression of friendly regard.

gre·gar·i·ous (gri gâr′ē əs), *adj.* 1. seeking or fond of the company of others. 2. living in herds, as animals. —**gre·gar′i·ous·ly,** *adv.* —**gre·gar′i·ous·ness,** *n.* —Syn. 1. sociable.

Gre·go′ri·an cal′endar (gri gōr′ē ən, -gôr′-), the calendar now in use. [after Pope *Gregory* XIII, 1502–85]

grem·lin (grem′lin), *n.* a mischievous invisible being.

gre·nade (gri nād′), *n.* a small explosive shell for throwing by hand or firing from a rifle.

gren·a·dier (gren′ə dēr′), *n.* 1. a member of a British infantry regiment. 2. (formerly) a soldier who threw grenades.

gren·a·dine (gren′ə dēn′, gren′ə dēn′), *n.* a syrup made from pomegranate juice.

grew (grōō), *v.* pt. of **grow.**

grey (grā), *adj., n., v.t., v.i. Chiefly Brit.* gray.

grey·hound (grā'hound'), *n.* a tall, slender, short-haired dog, noted for its swiftness.

grid (grid), *n.* **1.** a grating of crossed bars. **2. a.** a metallic framework in a storage battery for conducting the electric current. **b.** a system of electrical distribution serving a large area. **3.** an electrode in a vacuum tube, for controlling the flow of electrons between the other electrodes.

grid·dle (grid'əl), *n.* a frying pan with a slightly raised edge, for cooking pancakes, etc.

grid·dle·cake (grid'əl kāk'), *n.* pancake.

grid·i·ron (grid'ī'ərn), *n.* **1.** a utensil consisting of parallel metal bars on which to broil food. **2.** any framework resembling a gridiron. **3.** a football field.

grief (grēf), *n.* **1.** keen mental suffering over affliction or loss. **2.** a cause of such suffering. —*Syn.* **1.** mourning, sorrow, woe.

griev·ance (grē'vəns), *n.* **1.** a wrong considered as grounds for complaint. **2.** resentment or complaint against an unjust act.

grieve (grēv), *v.t., v.i.,* grieved, grieving. to feel or cause to feel grief. —**griev'er,** *n.*

griev·ous (grē'vəs), *adj.* **1.** causing or expressing grief. **2.** flagrant or atrocious. **3.** burdensome or oppressive. **4.** causing great physical suffering. —**griev'ous·ly,** *adv.*

grif·fin (grif'in), *n.* a fabled monster with the head and wings of an eagle and the body of a lion.

grill¹ (gril), *n.* **1.** a grated utensil for broiling food. **2.** a dish of grilled food. **3.** a restaurant serving grilled food. —*v.t.* **4.** to broil on a grill. **5.** *Informal.* to question severely and persistently.

grill² (gril), *n.* grille.

grille (gril), *n.* a grating or openwork barrier forming a screen. —**grilled,** *adj.*

grim (grim), *adj.,* grim·mer, grimmest. **1.** stern and unyielding. **2.** having a sinister or ghastly character: *a grim joke.* **3.** savage or cruel. —**grim'ly,** *adv.* —**grim'ness,** *n.*

grim·ace (grim'əs, gri mās'), *n., v., -aced, -ac·ing.* —*n.* **1.** a facial expression that indicates disapproval, pain, etc. —*v.i.* **2.** to make grimaces.

grime (grīm), *n.* dirt or foul matter, esp. lying upon or embedded in a surface. —**grim'y,** *adj.*

grin (grin), *v.,* grinned, grin·ning, *n.* —*v.i.* **1.** to smile broadly, esp. in amusement. **2.** to draw back the lips and show the teeth, as in scorn.

—*n.* **3.** the act or expression of grinning. —**grin'ner,** *n.*

grind (grīnd), *v.,* ground, grind·ing, *n.* —*v.t.* **1.** to smooth or sharpen by abrasion or friction. **2.** to reduce to fine particles, as by crushing. **3.** to oppress or harass. **4.** to grate together: *to grind one's teeth.* **5.** to operate or produce by turning a crank. —*v.i.* **6.** to rub harshly. **7.** to become ground. **8.** *Informal.* to work or study laboriously. —*n.* **9.** the act or a sound of grinding. **10.** laborious, uninteresting work. **11.** *Slang.* an excessively diligent student. —**grind'ing·ly,** *adv.*

grind·er (grīn'dər), *n.* **1.** a person or thing that grinds. **2.** a molar tooth. **3.** grinders, *Informal.* the teeth. **4.** *Slang.* See **hero sandwich.**

grind·stone (grīnd'stōn'), *n.* **1.** a rotating solid stone wheel used for sharpening, shaping, etc. **2. keep one's nose to the grindstone,** to work or make someone work incessantly.

gri·ot (grē ō'), *n.* (in western Africa) a tribal poet, musician, and narrator of history.

grip (grip), *n., v.,* gripped, grip·ping. —*n.* **1.** a secure hold or firm, tight grasp. **2.** the power of gripping. **3.** mastery or firm control. **4.** mental or intellectual hold. **5.** a special mode of clasping hands. **6.** a device that seizes and holds. **7.** a handle or hilt. **8.** a small traveling bag. **9. come to grips with,** to deal with directly or firmly. —*v.t.* **10.** to grasp or seize firmly. **11.** to hold the interest of. —*v.i.* **12.** to get a grip. —**grip'per,** *n.* —**grip'ping·ly,** *adv.*

gripe (grīp), *v.,* griped, grip·ing, *n.* —*v.i.* **1.** *Informal.* to complain naggingly. —*v.t.* **2.** *Informal.* to annoy or irritate. **3.** to cause a pain in the bowels of. **4.** *Archaic.* to distress or oppress. **5.** *Obs.* to grasp or clutch. —*n.* **6.** *Informal.* a nagging complaint. **7.** Usually, **gripes.** a pain in the bowels. —**grip'er,** *n.* —**grip'y,** *adj.*

grippe (grip), *n.* *Obsolesc.* influenza. —**grip'py,** *adj.*

gris-gris (grē'grē'), *n., pl.* gris-gris (-grēz'). an African charm or amulet.

gris·ly (griz'lē), *adj.,* -li·er, -li·est. shudderingly horrible. —**Syn.** ghastly, gruesome.

grist (grist), *n.* **1.** grain to be ground. **2.** ground grain.

gris·tle (gris'əl), *n.* cartilage, esp. in meats. —**gris'tly** (-lē), *adj.*

grit (grit), *n., v.,* grit·ted, grit·ting. —*n.* **1.** fine, abrasive particles as those deposited as dust from the air. **2.** indomitable courage. —*v.t.* **3.** to grate or grind: *to grit the teeth.* —*v.i.* **4.** to make a grating sound. —**grit'ty,** *adj.*

grits (grits), *n.* grain hulled and coarsely ground.

griz·zled (griz′əld), *adj.* gray or partly gray.

griz·zly (griz′lē), *adj.*, **-zli·er, -zli·est.** somewhat gray.

griz′zly bear′, a large, ferocious bear of western North America, varying in color from grayish to brownish. Also called **griz′zly.**

gro., gross (def. 9).

groan (grōn), *n.* 1. a low, mournful sound uttered in pain, grief, disapproval, etc. 2. a creaking sound due to overburdening, as with a great weight. —*v.i., v.t.* 3. to utter (with) a groan.

groats (grōts), *n.* hulled grain, as oats, broken into fragments.

gro·cer (grō′sər), *n.* a dealer in general food supplies for the table and in other articles of household use. [< OF *gross(i)er* wholesale merchant]

gro·cer·y (grō′sə rē), *n., pl.* **-cer·ies.** 1. a grocer's store. 2. Usually, **groceries.** the goods sold by a grocer.

grog (grog), *n.* 1. a mixture of alcoholic liquor and water. 2. strong drink.

grog·gy (grog′ē), *adj.*, **-gi·er, -gi·est.** staggering or dazed, as from exhaustion or blows. —**grog′gi·ly,** *adv.* —**grog′gi·ness,** *n.*

groin (groin), *n.* 1. the fold where either thigh joins the abdomen. 2. *Archit.* the curved edge formed by the intersection of two vaults.

grom·met (grom′it), *n.* 1. a metal eyelet, as in leather. 2. a short length of rope, as for securing ship spars.

groom (grōom, grŏom), *n.* 1. a man or boy in charge of horses or a stable. 2. a bridegroom. —*v.t.* 3. to tend carefully as to person and dress. 4. to tend (horses). 5. to prepare (a person) for a position, etc. —**groom′er,** *n.*

grooms·man (grōomz′mən, grŏomz′-), *n. Obsolesc.* See best man.

groove (grōov), *n., v.,* **grooved, grooving.** —*n.* 1. a long, narrow cut in a surface. 2. the track of a phonograph record. 3. a fixed routine. —*v.t.* 4. to cut a groove in. —*v.i.* 5. *Slang.* to understand or appreciate someone fully

groov·y (grōo′vē), *adj.*, **groov·i·er, groov·i·est.** *Slang.* highly stimulating or attractive.

grope (grōp), *v.*, **groped, grop·ing.** —*v.i.* 1. to feel about with the hands. 2. to search blindly or uncertainly. —*v.t.* 3. to seek by groping: *He groped his way up the stairs.* —**grop′ing·ly,** *adv.*

gros·beak (grōs′bēk′), *n.* a finch having a thick, conical bill.

gro·schen (grō′shən), *n., pl.* **-schen.** a money of account of Austria.

gros·grain (grō′grān′), *n.* a heavy, corded ribbon or cloth of silk or rayon.

gross (grōs), *adj.*, *n., pl.* **gross** for 9, **gross·es** for 10, *v.* —*adj.* 1. without deductions: *gross profits.* 2. unqualified or rank. 3. flagrant and extreme. 4. indelicate or vulgar. 5. lacking in refinement, good manners, etc. 6. big or bulky. 7. extremely or excessively fat. 8. dense or heavy: *gross vegetation.* 9. twelve dozen. 10. income without deductions. —*v.t.* 11. to earn a total of before the deduction of taxes, expenses, etc. —**gross′er,** *n.* —**gross′ly,** *adv.* —**gross′ness,** *n.*

gross′ na′tional prod′uct, the total monetary value of all final goods and services produced in a country during one year.

grot (grot), *n. Chiefly Literary.* a grotto.

gro·tesque (grō tesk′), *adj.* 1. odd or unnatural in shape, appearance, or character. 2. fantastic or bizarre. —**gro·tesque′ly,** *adv.* —**gro·tesque′ness,** *n.*

grot·to (grot′ō), *n., pl.* **-toes, -tos.** 1. a cave or cavern. 2. an artificial cavernlike recess or structure.

grouch (grouch), *Informal.* —*v.i.* 1. to be sulky or discontented. —*n.* 2. a sulky or complaining person. 3. a sulky mood. —**grouch·y** (grou′chē), *adj.*

ground[1] (ground), *n.* 1. the solid surface of the earth. 2. earth or soil. 3. Often, **grounds.** a. a tract of land: *picnic grounds.* b. the foundation or basis on which a belief or action rests: *grounds for divorce.* 4. subject for discussion. 5. the background in painting, etc. 6. **grounds,** a. dregs or sediment. b. the gardens, lawn, etc., surrounding and belonging to a building. 7. a conducting connection between an electric circuit or equipment and the earth or some other conducting body. 8. **gain** or **lose ground,** to gain or lose approval or acceptance. 9. **give ground,** to yield or retreat. 10. **hold** or **stand one's ground,** to be steadfast. 11. **run into the ground,** to go beyond a reasonable point. —*adj.* 12. of, on, at, or adjacent to the ground. —*v.t.* 13. to lay on the ground. 14. to place on a firm foundation or basis. 15. to instruct in first principles. 16. *Elect.* to establish a ground for (a circuit, etc.). 17. to cause (a vessel) to run aground. 18. to restrict (an aircraft) to the ground because of bad weather, etc. —*v.i.* 19. to come to or strike the ground. 20. *Naut.* to run aground.

ground² (ground), *v.* pt. and pp. of **grind**.

ground' ball', *Baseball.* a batted ball that rolls or bounces along the ground. Also called **ground·er** (groun'dər).

ground' cov'er, any of several low plants used in place of grass.

ground' floor', 1. the floor of a building on or nearest to ground level. 2. **get in on the ground floor,** to share in the founding of a promising enterprise.

ground' glass', glass that has had its polished surface removed by fine grinding and that is used to diffuse light.

ground' hog', woodchuck.

ground·less (ground'lis), *adj.* without rational basis. —**ground'less·ly,** *adv.* —**ground'less·ness,** *n.*

ground·ling (ground'ling), *n.* 1. a plant or animal that lives on or close to the ground. 2. an uncritical or uncultured person.

ground' rule', a basic or governing principle of conduct in any situation or field of endeavor.

ground·swell (ground'swel'), *n.* 1. a broad, deep swell or rolling of the sea. 2. any surging enthusiasm, esp. among the general public.

ground·work (ground'wûrk'), *n.* the foundation basis of an undertaking.

group (groop), *n.* 1. a number of persons or things ranged or considered together as being related in some way. —*v.t., v.i.* 2. to form into a group.

group·er (groo'pər), *n,* pl. **-er, -ers.** a large-mouthed food fish of tropical seas.

group·ie (groo'pē), *n.* *Slang.* a young girl follower of rock-'n'-roll musicians.

group' ther'apy, psychotherapy in which a group of patients participate in a discussion of their problems in an attempt to solve them.

grouse¹ (grous), *n.,* pl. **grouse, grouses.** a game bird related to the pheasant, having brown, red, and gray plumage.

grouse (grous), *v.i.,* **groused, grousing.** *Informal.* to grumble or complain.

grout (grout), *n.* a thin, coarse mortar used for filling masonry joints, etc.

grove (grōv), *n.* a small wood or orchard.

grov·el (gruv'əl, grov'-), *v.i.,* **-eled, -el·ing** or **-elled, -el·ling.** 1. to humble oneself. 2. to lie or crawl with the face downward, as in abject humility, fear, etc. —**grov'el·er,** *n.*

grow (grō), *v.,* **grew, grown, grow·ing.** —*v.i.* 1. to increase by natural development 2. to arise or issue as a natural development. 3. to increase gradually in size, amount, etc. 4. to become united by or as by growth. 5. to become by degrees: *to grow old.* —*v.t.* 6. to cause or allow to grow. 7. **grow on,** to increase in influence. 8. **grow up, a.** to be fully grown. **b.** to arise or develop. —**grow'er,** *n.*

growl (groul), *v.i.* 1. to utter a deep guttural sound of anger or hostility. 2. to complain angrily. —*v.t.* 3. to express by growling. —*n.* 4. the act or sound of growling. —**growl'er,** *n.*

grown (grōn), *adj.* 1. advanced in growth: *a grown boy.* 2. mature or adult: *a grown man.* —*v.* 3. pp. of **grow.**

grown-up (grōn'up'), *adj.* 1. having reached maturity. 2. of or for adults.

grown-up (grōn'up'), *n.* a mature adult.

growth (grōth), *n.* 1. the act or process, or a manner of growing. 2. size or stage of development: *to reach one's full growth.* 3. completed development. 4. something that has grown or developed. 5. an abnormal increase in a mass of tissue, as a tumor. —*adj.* 6. of a business or equity security that moves ahead year after year: *a growth stock; a growth industry.*

grub (grub), *n., v.,* **grubbed, grub·bing.** —*n.* 1. a thick-bodied, sluggish larva, as of a beetle. 2. *Informal.* a drudge, esp. a dull, unkempt person. 3. *Informal.* food or victuals. —*v.t.* 4. to clear of roots, etc. 5. to uproot: *to grub up tree stumps.* 6. *Slang.* scrounge (def. 1). —*v.i.* 7. to search by or as by digging. 8. to lead a laborious life. —**grub'ber,** *n.*

grub·by (grub'ē), *adj.,* **-bi·er, -bi·est.** dirty or slovenly. —**grub'bi·ness,** *n.*

grub·stake (grub'stāk'), *n.* provisions, outfit, etc., furnished to a prospector on condition that he or she share the profits of any discoveries.

grudge (gruj), *n., v.,* **grudged, grudging.** —*n.* 1. a feeling of ill will or resentment. —*v.t.* 2. to give or permit with reluctance. 3. to resent the good fortune of (another). —*v.i.* 4. *Obs.* to feel dissatisfaction. —**grudg'-ing·ly,** *adv.*

gru·el (groo'əl), *n.* a thin cereal.

gru·el·ing (groo'ə ling, groo'ling), *adj.* arduously severe. Also, **gru'el·ling.** —**gru'el·ing·ly,** *adv.*

grue·some (groo'səm), *adj.* horribly repugnant. —**grue'some·ly,** *adv.* —**grue'some·ness,** *n.*

gruff (gruf), *adj.* 1. low and harsh. 2. rough and brusque. —**gruff'ly,** *adv.* —**gruff'ness,** *n.*

grum·ble (grum'bəl), *v.,* **-bled, -bling,** *n.* —*v.i.* 1. to mutter in discontent. 2. to growl. 3. to rumble. —*v.t.* 4.

to utter by grumbling. —*n.* 5. a grumbling expression. —**grum′bler,** *n.* —Syn. 1. complain, whine.

grump·y (grum′pē), *adj.,* **grump·i·er, grump·i·est.** surly and moody. —**grump′i·ly,** *adv.* —**grump′i·ness,** *n.*

grun·gy (grun′jē), *adj.,* **-gi·er, -gi·est.** *Slang.* ugly, run-down, or dilapidated.

grun·ion (grun′yən), *n.* a small, slender food fish found in southern California.

grunt (grunt), *v.i., v.t.* 1. to utter (with) the deep, guttural sound characteristic of a hog. —*n.* 2. a sound of grunting. —**grunt′ing·ly,** *adv.*

gr. wt., gross weight.

GSA, 1. Girl Scouts of America. 2. General Services Administration.

G-suit (jē′sōōt′), *n.* a garment for a flier or astronaut designed to protect the wearer against effects of excessive acceleration forces.

G.T., gross ton.

gt., 1. great. 2. (in prescriptions) a drop. [< L *gutta*]

Gt. Br., Great Britain. Also, **Gt. Brit.**

gtd., guaranteed.

GU, Guam.

g.u., genitourinary. Also, **GU**

gua·ca·mo·le (gwä′kə mō′lē), *n. Mexican Cookery.* a thick sauce consisting of mashed avocado flavored with hot peppers, etc.

Guam (gwäm), *n.* an island belonging to the U.S. in the N Pacific.

gua·nine (gwä′nēn), *n.* a colorless solid used chiefly in biochemical research.

gua·no (gwä′nō), *n.* a natural manure composed chiefly of the excrement of seabirds, valued as a fertilizer.

guar., guaranteed.

gua·ra·ni (gwär′ə nē′, gwär′ə nē′), *n., pl.* **-nis, -nies.** the monetary unit of Paraguay.

guar·an·tee (gar′ən tē′), *n., v.,* **-teed, -tee·ing.** —*n.* 1. guaranty (def. 1). 2. a written assurance that something is of specified quality, or that it will perform satisfactorily for a given time: *a money-back guarantee.* 3. a guarantor. 4. guaranty (def. 2). —*v.t.* 5. to make or give a guarantee or guaranty for. 6. to promise or affirm.

guar·an·tor (gar′ən tôr′, -tər), *n.* a person who makes or gives a guaranty or guarantee.

guar·an·ty (gar′ən tē′), *n., pl.* **-ties,** *v.,* **-tied, -ty·ing.** —*n.* 1. a formal assurance given as security that another's debt or obligation will be fulfilled. 2. something taken or presented as security. 3. the act of giving security. 4. a guarantor. —*v.t.* 5. to guarantee.

guard (gärd), *v.t.* 1. to keep safe from harm or danger. 2. to keep under close watch. 3. *Sports.* to try to im-

pede the progress of (an opponent). —*v.i.* 4. to take precautions: *to guard against errors.* 5. to keep watch. —*n.* 6. a person or group of persons that guards. 7. a close watch, as over a prisoner. 8. a device or attachment that prevents injury, loss, etc. 9. a posture of defense or readiness, as in boxing, etc. 10. a football or basketball player who guards an opponent. —**guard′er,** *n.* —Syn. 1. defend, protect.

guard·ed (gär′did), *adj.* 1. cautious or prudent. 2. protected or watched. —**guard′ed·ly,** *adv.*

guard·house (gärd′hous′), *n., pl.* **-hous·es** (-hou′ziz). a building housing military guards or for the temporary detention of prisoners.

guard·i·an (gär′dē ən), *n.* 1. a person who guards, protects, or preserves. 2. a person entrusted by law with the care of the person or property, or both, of another, as a minor. —**guard′i·an·ship,** *n.*

guards·man (gärdz′mən), *n., pl.* **-men.** 1. a man who acts as a guard. 2. a member of the U.S. National Guard.

Gua·te·ma·la (gwä′tə mä′lə), *n.* a country in N Central America. —**Gua′te·ma′lan,** *adj., n.*

gua·va (gwä′və), *n.* a tree of the myrtle family, having a berrylike fruit. 2. its fruit.

gu·ber·na·to·ri·al (gōō′bər nə tôr′ē əl, -tôr′-, gyōō′-), *adj.* of a state governor or his or her office.

guer·don (gûr′dⁿn), *n. Literary.* a reward or recompense.

Guern·sey (gûrn′zē), *n., pl.* **-seys.** one of a breed of dairy cattle producing rich, golden-colored milk.

guer·ril·la (gə ril′ə), *n.* a member of a small independent band of soldiers that harasses the enemy by surprise raids, etc. Also, **gue·ril′la.** [< Sp *guerilla* band, dim. of *guerra* war < Gme]

guerill′la the′ater, the unannounced presentation of short plays on themes such as war, justice, etc., to street audiences.

guess (ges), *v.t., v.i.* 1. to risk an estimate or judgment about (something), often haphazardly. 2. to estimate about correctly: *to guess a riddle.* 3. to think or suppose. —*n.* 4. an opinion reached by guessing. 5. the act of guessing. —**guess′er,** *n.* —Syn. 1. conjecture, speculate, surmise.

guest (gest), *n.* 1. a person who receives the hospitality of another person, organization, etc. 2. a person who patronizes a hotel, restaurant, etc. —*adj.* 3. performing as or done by a person who is not a member of the cast or staff involved: *a guest star in a movie; a guest editorial.*

guf·faw (gu fô′, gə-), *n.* **1.** a burst of loud laughter. —*v.i.* **2.** to laugh loudly and boisterously.

guid·ance (gīd′°ns), *n.* **1.** the act or function of guiding. **2.** advice or counseling service.

guide (gīd), *v.,* **guid·ed, guid·ing,** *n.* —*v.t.* **1.** to lead or show the way to. **2.** to direct the movement or course of. **3.** to lead or direct in any course or action. —*v.i.* **4.** to act as a guide. —*n.* **5.** a person who guides, esp. one hired to conduct or lead tours. **6.** something that guides, as a mark, tab, or sign. **7.** guidebook. **8.** a contrivance for regulating progressive motion or action: *a sewing-machine guide.* —**guid′a·ble,** *adj.* —**guid′er,** *n.* —**Syn.** **1.** conduct, escort.

guide·book (gīd′boŏk′), *n.* a book of directions and information for travelers, tourists, etc.

guid′ed mis′sile, a projectile that can be steered during its flight to a target, as by a radar beam.

guide·line (gīd′līn′), *n.* any guide or indication of a future course of action.

guide′ word′, catchword (def. 2).

gui·don (gīd′°n), *n.* *Mil.* a small flag carried as a guide, for marking or identification.

guild (gild), *n.* **1.** an organization of persons with related interests, goals, etc. **2.** a medieval association of merchants or tradesmen.

guil·der (gil′dər), *n.* the monetary unit of the Netherlands.

guile (gīl), *n.* insidious cunning in attaining a goal. —**guile′ful,** *adj.* —**guile′less,** *adj.* —**guile′less·ness,** *n.*

guil·lo·tine (*n.* gil′ə tēn′, gē′ə tēn′; *v.* gil′ə tēn′), *n., v.,* **-tined, -tin·ing.** —*n.* **1.** a device for beheading persons by means of a heavy blade that is dropped between two posts. —*v.t.* **2.** to behead by a guillotine. [after J. I. *Guillotin* (1738–1814), French physician]

guilt (gilt), *n.* **1.** the fact or state of being guilty. **2.** criminal conduct. **3.** a feeling of responsibility for some real or imagined offense, crime, etc. —**guilt′less,** *adj.*

guilt·y (gil′tē), *adj.,* **guilt·i·er, guilt·i·est.** **1.** having committed an offense, crime, etc., esp. against moral or penal law: *He is guilty of murder.* **2.** connected with or involving guilt. **3.** having or showing guilt. —**guilt′i·ly,** *adv.* —**guilt′i·ness,** *n.*

guin·ea (gin′ē), *n.* (formerly) the sum of 21 British shillings, often used in quoting professional fees or expensive items.

Guin·ea (gin′ē), *n.* a country in W Africa. —**Guin′e·an,** *adj., n.*

guin′ea fowl′, an African game bird having dark gray plumage spotted with white, raised for its flesh and eggs. Also called **guin′ea hen′.**

guin′ea pig′, 1. a short-eared, tailless rodent used in scientific experiments. **2.** *Informal.* the subject of any experiment.

guise (gīz), *n.* **1.** general external appearance. **2.** assumed appearance or mere semblance. **3.** *Archaic.* style of dress.

gui·tar (gi tär′), *n.* a musical instrument with typically six strings plucked with the fingers or with a plectrum. [< Sp *guitar(ra)* < Gk *kithára* cithara] —**gui·tar′ist,** *n.*

gulch (gulch), *n.* a deep, narrow ravine, esp. one marking the course of a stream.

gul·den (goŏl′d°n), *n., pl.* **-dens, -den.** guilder.

gulf (gulf), *n.* **1.** a portion of an ocean or sea partly enclosed by land. **2.** a chasm or abyss. **3.** any wide separation, as in education. —**gulf′like′,** *adj.*

gull[1] (gul), *n.* a long-winged, web-toed seabird having usually white plumage with a gray back and wings. —**gull′-like′,** *adj.*

gull[2] (gul), *Archaic.* —*v.t.* **1.** to deceive or trick. —*n.* **2.** a person easily gulled.

gul·let (gul′it), *n.* **1.** the esophagus. **2.** the throat or pharynx.

gul·li·ble (gul′ə bəl), *adj.* easily deceived or cheated. —**gul′li·bil′i·ty,** *n.*

gul·ly (gul′ē), *n., pl.* **-lies.** a small valley or ravine worn away by running water.

gulp (gulp), *v.t.* **1.** to swallow eagerly or in large drafts or morsels: *to gulp down one's food.* **2.** to choke back as if by swallowing. —*v.i.* **3.** to gasp or choke. —*n.* **4.** the act of gulping. **5.** a mouthful. —**gulp′er,** *n.*

gum[1] (gum), *n., v.,* **gummed, gumming.** —*n.* **1.** a sticky substance exuded from plants, hardening on exposure to air and soluble in or forming a viscid mass with water. **2.** any of various similar substances, as resin. **3.** See **chewing gum.** —*v.t.* **4.** to seal or stick together with gum. —*v.i.* **5.** to become clogged with gum. **6.** **gum up,** *Slang.* to spoil or ruin. —**gum′like′,** *adj.* —**gum′my,** *adj.*

gum[2] (gum), *n.* Often, **gums.** the firm, fleshy tissue enveloping the necks of the teeth.

gum′ ar′abic, a gum obtained from several species of acacia: used as mucilage, a food thickener, etc.

gum·bo (gum′bō), *n.* a thick soup containing okra and chicken or seafood.

gum·boil (gum′boil′), *n.* a small abscess on the gum.

gum·drop (gum′drop′), *n.* a small, soft or chewy candy made of gum arabic, gelatin, etc.

gump·tion (gump′shən), *n. Informal.* **1.** initiative or resourcefulness. **2.** courage or spunk.

gum·shoe (gum′shōō′), *n.* **1.** a rubber shoe. **2.** *Slang.* a police officer or detective.

gun (gun), *n., v.,* **gunned, gun·ning.** —*n.* **1.** a weapon consisting of a metal tube, with its mechanical attachments, from which projectiles are shot by the force of an explosive. **2.** any portable firearm, as a rifle, shotgun, etc. **3.** a long-barreled cannon. **4.** any device for shooting something under pressure. **5. jump the gun,** *Slang.* to act hastily. **6. stick to one's guns,** to stand firm. —*v.i.* **7.** to hunt or shoot with a gun. —*v.t.* **8.** to shoot with a gun: *to gun down a killer.* **9.** to feed gasoline to, suddenly and quickly: *to gun an engine.* **10. gun for,** to try earnestly to obtain. —**gun′ner,** *n.*

gun·boat (gun′bōt′), *n.* a small vessel carrying mounted guns.

gun′boat diplo′macy, foreign relations backed by a nation's military supremacy, esp. as formerly conducted in bullying a weaker nation.

gun·cot·ton (gun′kot′ᵊn), *n.* an explosive made from cotton and used in making smokeless powder.

gun·fight (gun′fīt′), *n.* a battle between people in which the principal weapon is a gun. —**gun′fight′er,** *n.*

gun·fire (gun′fīᵊr′), *n.* the firing of a gun or guns.

gung ho (gung′ hō′), *Informal.* wholeheartedly loyal and enthusiastic.

gunk (gungk), *n. Informal.* greasy, sticky, or slimy matter.

gun·lock (gun′lok′), *n.* the mechanism of a firearm by which the charge is exploded.

gun·man (gun′mən), *n.* a man armed with or expert in the use of a gun, esp. one ready to use a gun unlawfully.

gun·nel (gun′ᵊl), *n. Naut.* gunwale.

gun·ner·y (gun′ə rē), *n.* the art and science of constructing and managing guns, esp. large guns.

gun′nery ser′geant, *U.S. Marine Corps.* a noncommissioned officer ranking below a first sergeant.

gun·ny (gun′ē), *n.* a strong, coarse material made commonly from jute.

gun·ny·sack (gun′ē sak′), *n.* a sack made of gunny or burlap.

gun·point (gun′point′), *n.* **1.** the point or aim of a gun. **2. at gunpoint,** under threat of being shot.

gun·pow·der (gun′pou′dər), *n.* an explosive mixture of potassium nitrate, sulfur, and charcoal.

gun·shot (gun′shot′), *n.* **1.** a projectile or other shot fired from a gun. **2.** the range of a gun: *out of gunshot.*

gun-shy (gun′shī′), *adj.* frightened by the shooting of a gun.

gun·sling·er (gun′sling′ər), *n. U.S. Slang.* a gunfighter, esp. in the old West. —**gun′sling′ing,** *n., adj.*

gun·smith (gun′smith′), *n.* a person who makes or repairs firearms.

gun·wale (gun′ᵊl), *n.* (loosely) the upper edge of the side or bulwark of a vessel.

gup·py (gup′ē), *n., pl.* **-pies.** a small, freshwater fish often kept in aquariums.

gur·gle (gûr′gəl), *v.,* **-gled, -gling,** *n.* —*v.i.* **1.** to flow in a broken, irregular, noisy current. **2.** to make a sound as of water doing this. —*n.* **3.** the act or sound of gurgling.

gu·ru (gōō′rōō, gōō rōō′), *n.* **1.** a Hindu spiritual instructor. **2.** any wise or respected leader. (< Hindi *gurū* < Skt *guru* venerable]

gush (gush), *v.i.* **1.** to flow out or issue copiously or forcibly. **2.** to talk effusively. —*v.t.* **3.** to cause to gush. —*n.* **4.** a copious or forcible outflow.

gush·er (gush′ər), *n.* **1.** a flowing oil well, usually of large capacity. **2.** a person who gushes.

gush·y (gush′ē), *adj.,* **gush·i·er, gush·i·est.** given to or marked by effusive talk, behavior, etc. —**gush′i·ly,** *adv.*

gus·set (gus′it), *n.* a small, triangular piece of material inserted into a garment to improve the fit or for reinforcement.

gus·sy (gus′ē), *v.t.,* **-sied, -sy·ing.** *Slang.* to dress up or decorate: *all gussied up for the celebration.*

gust (gust), *n.* **1.** a sudden, strong blast of wind. **2.** an outburst of passion. —*v.i.* **3.** to blow or rush in gusts. —**gust′less,** *adj.* —**gust′y,** *adj.* —**gust′i·ly,** *adv.*

gus·ta·to·ry (gus′tə tôr′ē), *adj.* of taste or tasting.

gus·to (gus′tō), *n.* hearty enjoyment or enthusiasm.

gut (gut), *n., v.,* **gut·ted, gut·ting,** *adj.* —*n.* **1.** the alimentary canal or some portion of it. **2. guts, a.** the bowels or entrails. **b.** *Slang.* courage or stamina. **3.** intestinal tissue or fiber. **4.** a strong cord made from animal intestines. —*v.t.* **5.** to eviscerate or disembowel. **6.** to destroy the interior of, as by fire. —*adj.* **7.** *Informal.* **a.** basic or essential: *gut issues.* **b.** based on emotions: *a gut reaction.* —**gut′less,** *adj.* —**gut′like′,** *adj.*

gut′ course′, *Chiefly Northeastern U.S. Informal.* a college course requiring little effort.

est. *Slang.* **1.** having a great deal of courage. **2.** forceful or lusty.

gut·ta-per·cha (gut′ə pûr′chə), *n.* the milky juice of various Malaysian trees, used as a dental cement and for insulating electric wires.

guts·y (gut′sē), *adj.*, **guts·i·er, guts·i·est.**

gut·ter (gut′ər), *n.* a channel for leading off water, as at the side of a road or along the eaves of a roof.

gut·ter·snipe (gut′ər snīp′), *n.* a person belonging to the lowest social group.

gut·tur·al (gut′ər əl), *adj.* **1.** of the throat. **2.** harsh or throaty. **3.** pronounced in the throat. —**gut′tur·al·ly,** *adv.*

gut·ty (gut′ē), *adj.*, **-ti·er, -ti·est.** *Slang.* gutsy.

guy¹ (gī), *n.*, *v.*, **guyed, guy·ing.** —*n.* **1.** *Informal.* a fellow or man. —*v.t.* **2.** *Chiefly Brit.* to ridicule.

guy² (gī), *n.*, *v.*, **guyed, guy·ing.** —*n.* **1.** a rope, cable, or appliance used to guide or steady an object. —*v.t.* **2.** to guide or steady with a guy.

Guy·a·na (gī an′ə, -än′ə), *n.* a country on the NE coast of South America. —**Guy′a·nese′** (-ə nēz′), *n., adj.*

guz·zle (guz′əl), *v.i., v.t.,* **-zled, -zling.** to drink or eat greedily. —**guz′zler,** *n.*

gym (jim), *n. Informal.* **1.** gymnasium¹. **2.** See physical education.

gym·kha·na (jim kä′nə), *n.* a sporting event, as a gymnastics exhibition, auto race, etc.

gym·na·si·um¹ (jim nā′zē əm), *n., pl.* **-si·ums, -si·a** (-zē ə, -zhə). a building or room for physical-education activities.

gym·na·si·um² (jim nā′zē əm), *n.* (esp. in Germany) a classical school preparatory to the universities.

gym·nas·tics (jim nas′tiks), *n.* physical exercises performed to develop strength and agility. —**gym′nast,** *n.* —**gym·nas′tic,** *adj.* —**gym·nas′ti·cal·ly,** *adv.*

gym·no·sperm (jim′nə spûrm′), *n.* a plant having its seeds exposed and not enclosed in an ovary.

gyn., gynecology.

gy·ne·col·o·gy (gī′nə kol′ə jē, jin′ə-, jī′nə-), *n.* the branch of medical science that deals with the reproductive organs of women. —**gyn′e·co·log′i·cal** (-kə loj′i kəl), **gyn′e·co·log′ic** (-kə loj′ik), *adj.* —**gy′ne·col′o·gist,** *n.*

gyp (jip), *v.*, **gypped, gyp·ping,** *n. Informal.* —*v.t., v.i.* **1.** to swindle or cheat. —*n.* **2.** a swindle. **3.** Also, **gyp′per, gyp′ster** (-stər). a swindler or cheat.

gyp·sum (jip′səm), *n.* a common mineral used to make plaster of Paris, as a fertilizer, etc.

Gyp·sy (jip′sē), *n., pl.* **-sies. 1.** a member of a nomadic, Caucasoid people of generally swarthy complexion, who migrated originally from India. **2.** Romany (def. 2). **3.** (*l.c.*) a person who resembles or lives like a Gypsy.

gyp′sy moth′, a moth introduced into the U.S. from Europe, the larvae of which feed on the foliage of trees.

gy·rate (jī′rāt, jī rāt′), *v.i.,* **-rat·ed, -rat·ing.** to move in a circle or spiral. —**gy·ra′tion,** *n.* —**gy′ra·tor,** *n.*

gyr·fal·con (jûr′fal′kən, -fôl′-, -fô′-), *n.* a large falcon of arctic and subarctic regions.

gy·ro (jī′rō), *n., pl.* **-ros. 1.** gyrocompass. **2.** gyroscope.

gyro-, a combining form meaning "circle" or "spiral": *gyroscope.*

gy·ro·com·pass (jī′rō kum′pəs), *n.* a navigational compass containing a gyroscope rotor, that registers the direction of true north along the surface of the earth.

gy·ro·scope (jī′rə skōp′), *n.* a rotating wheel so mounted that its axis can turn freely in certain or all directions. —**gy·ro·scop′ic** (jī′rə skop′ik), *adj.* —**gy′ro·scop′i·cal·ly,** *adv.*

Gy. Sgt., Gunnery Sergeant.

gyve (jīv), *n., v.,* **gyved, gyv·ing.** *Archaic.* —*n.* **1.** Usually, **gyves.** a shackle, esp. for the leg. —*v.t.* **2.** to shackle.

H

H, h (āch), *n., pl.* **H's** or **Hs, h's** or **hs.** the eighth letter of the English alphabet, a consonant.

H, 1. hard. **2.** *Slang.* heroin.

H, 1. the eighth in order or in a series. **2.** hydrogen.

h., 1. harbor. **2.** hard. **3.** hardness. **4.** height. **5.** high. **6.** *Baseball.* hit; hits. **7.** hour; hours. **8.** hundred. **9.** husband. Also, **H.**

ha (hä), *interj.* (an exclamation of surprise, suspicion, triumph, etc.)

ha, hectare; hectares.

ha·ba·ne·ra (hä′bə när′ə), *n.* **1.** a slow dance of Cuban origin. **2.** the music for this dance.

ha·be·as cor·pus (hä′bē əs kôr′pəs), a writ requiring a person to be brought before a judge or court, used as a protection against illegal imprisonment. [< L: lit. have the body]

hab·er·dash·er (hab′ər dash′ər), *n.* a dealer in men's furnishings, as shirts, ties, etc.

hab·er·dash·er·y (hab′ər dash′ə rē), *n.,* pl. **-er·ies. 1.** a haberdasher's shop. **2.** the goods sold there.

ha·bil·i·ment (hə bil′ə mənt), *n.* **1.** Usually, **habiliments.** *Facetious.* clothes or clothing. **2.** habiliments. *Rare.* accouterments or trappings.

hab·it (hab′it), *n.* **1.** an acquired behavior pattern regularly followed until it has become almost involuntary. **2.** customary practice or use. **3.** a particular custom or usage. **4.** an addiction to narcotics, esp. to heroin. **5.** garb of a particular rank, religious order, etc.: *monk's habit.*

hab·it·a·ble (hab′i tə bəl), *adj.* capable of being inhabited. **—hab′it·a·bil′i·ty, hab′it·a·ble·ness,** *n.* **—hab′it·a·bly,** *adv.*

hab·it·ant (hab′i t°nt), *n.* an inhabitant.

hab·i·tat (hab′i tat′), *n.* **1.** the natural environment of an animal or plant. **2.** the place where a person or thing is usually found. **3.** habitation (def. 1).

hab·i·ta·tion (hab′i tā′shən), *n.* **1.** a place of residence. **2.** the act of inhabiting.

hab·it-form·ing (hab′it fôr′ming), *adj.* tending to become a habit, esp. when based upon physiological dependence.

ha·bit·u·al (hə bich′ōō əl), *adj.* **1.** fixed by or resulting from habit. **2.** being such by habit: *a habitual gossip.* **3.** customary or usual. **—ha·bit′u·al·ly,** *adv.* **—ha·bit′u·al·ness,** *n.* **—Syn. 2.** confirmed, inveterate. **3.** accustomed, regular.

ha·bit·u·ate (hə bich′ōō āt′), *v.t.,* **-at·ed, -at·ing.** to accustom, as to a particular situation. **—ha·bit′u·a′tion,** *n.*

ha·bit·u·é (hə bich′ōō ā′), *n.* a habitual frequenter of a place.

ha·ci·en·da (hä′sē en′də), *n.* (in Spanish America) **1.** a landed estate, esp. one used for farming or ranching. **2.** the main house on such an estate.

hack¹ (hak), *v.t.* **1.** to cut or notch with heavy, irregular blows. **—v.i. 2.** to make rough cuts or notches. **3.** to cough harshly, usually in short and repeated spasms. **4. hack it,** *Slang.* to handle the situation well. **—n. 5.**

a cut or notch. **6.** a tool for hacking. **7.** a short, rasping cough. **—hack′er,** *n.*

hack² (hak), *n.* **1.** a writer who exploits his or her ability primarily for money. **2.** a horse for hire, esp. an old or worn-out one. **3.** a coach or carriage kept for hire. **4.** *Informal.* **a.** a taxi. **b.** a cab driver. **—v.i. 5.** to work as a hack. **—adj. 6.** hired as a hack. **7.** hackneyed or trite.

hack·ie (hak′ē), *n. Informal.* hack² (def. 4b).

hack·le (hak′əl), *n., v.,* **-led, -ling. —n. 1.** one of the long, slender feathers on the neck of certain birds, as the domestic rooster. **2. hackles, a.** the hair on the back of the neck of an animal. **b.** anger, esp. when aroused in a challenging or challenged manner: *to raise the hackles of someone.*

hack·man (hak′mən, -man′), *n.* the driver of a hack.

hack·ney (hak′nē), *n., pl.* **-neys. 1.** a horse for ordinary riding or driving. **2.** a carriage or coach for hire.

hack·neyed (hak′nēd), *adj.* made commonplace or trite.

hack·saw (hak′sô′), *n.* a saw for cutting metal, consisting of a fine-toothed blade fixed in a frame.

had (had), *v.* pt. and pp. of **have.**

had·dock (had′ək), *n., pl.* **-dock, -docks.** a food fish of the cod family, found in the North Atlantic.

Ha·des (hā′dēz), *n.* **1.** *Class. Myth.* the underworld inhabited by departed souls. **2.** (*often l.c.*) hell.

had·n't (had′°nt), contraction of **had not.**

hadst (hadst), *v. Archaic.* a 2nd pers. sing. pt. indic. of **have.**

haem·or·rhage (hem′ər ij), *n., v.,* **-rhaged, -rhag·ing.** hemorrhage.

haf·ni·um (haf′nē əm, häf′-), *n. Chem.* a metallic element found in zirconium ores. *Symbol:* Hf; *at. wt.:* 178.49; *at. no.:* 72.

haft (haft, häft), *n.* a handle, esp. of a knife, sword, dagger, etc.

hag (hag), *n.* **1.** an ugly old woman, esp. a vicious or malicious one. **2.** a witch or sorceress. **—hag′gish,** *adj.*

hag·gard (hag′ərd), *adj.* having a gaunt or exhausted appearance, as from suffering, anxiety, etc. **—hag′gard·ly,** *adv.*

hag·gis (hag′is), *n. Scot.* a dish made of the heart, liver, etc., of a sheep or calf, minced with suet and oatmeal.

hag·gle (hag′əl), *v.,* **-gled, -gling,** *n.* **—v.i. 1.** to bargain in a petty, quibbling manner. **—n. 2.** the act of haggling. **—hag′gler,** *n.*

hag·i·og·ra·pher (hag′ē og′rə fər, hā′jē-), *n.* a writer of lives of the saints. **—hag′i·og′ra·phy,** *n.*

Hague, The (hāg), a city in the W Netherlands: seat of the government.

hah (hä), *interj.* ha.

ha-ha (hä′hä′), *interj., n.* (an exclamation or representation of laughter.)

hai·ku (hī′kōō), *n., pl.* -ku for 2. **1.** a major form of Japanese verse, written in 3 lines and employing highly evocative allusions. **2.** a poem in this form.

hail[1] (hāl), *v.t.* **1.** to greet by calling. **2.** to call out to in order to stop, ask aid, etc. **3.** to approve enthusiastically. —*v.i.* **4.** to call out. **5.** hail from, to have as one's place of birth. —*n.* **6.** a shout or call. **7.** a salutation or greeting. **8.** the act of hailing. —*interj.* **9.** (a greeting or acclamation.)

hail[2] (hāl), *n.* **1.** precipitation in the form of irregular pellets of ice. **2.** a shower of anything. —*v.i., v.t.* **3.** to pour down (like) hail.

Hail′ Mar′y. See Ave Maria.

hail·stone (hāl′stōn′), *n.* a pellet of hail.

hail·storm (hāl′stôrm′), *n.* a storm with hail.

hair (hâr), *n.* **1.** any of the fine, cylindrical filaments growing from the skin of humans and animals. **2.** an aggregate of such filaments, as that covering the human head. **3.** any fine, filamentous outgrowth. **4.** a very small amount, degree, etc. **5.** get in someone's hair, *Slang.* to annoy someone. **6.** split hairs, to make petty distinctions. —haired (hârd), *adj.* —hair′less, *adj.* —hair′like′, *adj.*

hair·ball (hâr′bôl′), *n.* a ball of hair accumulated in the intestines of a cat or other animal that licks its coat.

hair·breadth (hâr′bredth′, -bretth′), *n., adj.* hairsbreadth.

hair·brush (hâr′brush′), *n.* a brush for the hair.

hair·cloth (hâr′klôth′, -kloth′), *n.* a stiff, wiry cloth from the manes and tails of horses, used in upholstery, etc.

hair·cut (hâr′kut′), *n.* **1.** the act or an instance of cutting the hair. **2.** the style in which the hair is cut and worn.

hair·do (hâr′dōō), *n., pl.* -dos. **1.** the style in which a woman's hair is cut, arranged, and worn. **2.** the hair itself.

hair·dress·er (hâr′dres′ər), *n.* a person who arranges or cuts women's hair. —hair′dress′ing, *n.*

hair·line (hâr′līn′), *n.* **1.** a very slender line. **2.** the lower edge of the hair, esp. along the upper forehead.

hair·piece (hâr′pēs′), *n.* a toupee or any type of wig.

hair·pin (hâr′pin′), *n.* **1.** a slender U-shaped piece of wire used to fasten up the hair or hold a headdress. —*adj.* **2.** sharply curved: *a hairpin turn.*

hair-rais·ing (hâr′rā′zing), *adj.* terrifying or horrifying.

hairs·breadth (hârz′bredth′, -bretth′), *n.* **1.** a very small space or distance. —*adj.* **2.** very narrow or close.

hair·split·ter (hâr′split′ər), *n.* a person who makes fine or unnecessary distinctions. —hair′split′ting, *n., adj.*

hair·spray (hâr′sprā′), *n.* a cosmetic liquid in an aerosol container, for holding the hair in place.

hair·spring (hâr′spring′), *n.* a fine, usually spiral spring used for oscillating the balance of a timepiece.

hair·style (hâr′stīl′), *n.* a creative style of arranging the hair, esp. for women. —hair′styl′ist, *n.* —hair′styl′ing, *n.*

hair-trig·ger (hâr′trig′ər), *adj.* easily activated or set off.

hair-weav·ing (hâr′wē′ving), *n.* the attachment of matching hair to a base of nylon thread interwoven with a person's remaining hair, to cover a bald area. —hair′weav′er, *n.*

hair·y (hâr′ē), *adj.,* hair·i·er, hair·i·est. **1.** covered with hair. **2.** of or resembling hair. **3.** *Informal.* difficult or risky. —hair′i·ness, *n.*

Hai·ti (hā′tē), *n.* a country in the West Indies occupying the W part of the island of Hispaniola. —Haitian (hā′shən, -tē ən) *adj., n.*

haj·ji (haj′ē), *n., pl.* haj·jis. a Muslim who has gone on a pilgrimage to Mecca.

hake (hāk), *n., pl.* hake, hakes. a food fish closely related to the cod.

hal·berd (hal′bərd, hôl′-, hol′-), *n.* a weapon with an axlike cutting blade, used esp. in the 15th and 16th centuries. Also, hal·bert (hal′bərt, hôl′-, hol′-).

hal·cy·on (hal′sē ən), *adj.* peaceful and calm.

hale[1] (hāl), *adj.* free from infirmity, esp. in an elderly person (used usually in the phrase *hale and hearty*). —hale′ness, *n.*

hale[2] (hāl), *v.t.,* haled, hal·ing. **1.** to bring as by dragging: *to hale a man into court.* **2.** *Archaic.* to haul or drag.

half (haf, häf), *n., pl.* halves (havz, hävz), *adj., adv.* —*n.* **1.** one of two equal parts, as of an object, unit of measure or time, etc. **2.** a quantity or amount equal to such a part. —*adj.* **3.** being a half. **4.** being half or about half of anything in degree, amount, etc. **5.** partial or incomplete. —*adv.* **6.** in or to the extent of half. **7.** partly or incompletely. **8.** not half, not really.

half-and-half (haf′ən haf′, häf′ən häf′), *n.* milk and light cream combined in equal parts, esp. for table use.

half·back (haf′bak′, häf′-), *n.* *Football.* one of two backs who typically line up on each side of the fullback.

half-baked (haf′bākt′, häf′-), *adj.* **1.** insufficiently baked. **2.** insufficiently planned or prepared.

half-breed (haf′brēd′, häf′-), *n.* the offspring of parents of different races.

half′ broth′er, brother (def. 2).

half-caste (haf′kast′, häf′käst′), *n.* a person of mixed race.

half-cocked (haf′kokt′, häf′-), *adj.* **1.** lacking mature consideration or preparation. **2.** go off half-cocked, to act or happen prematurely.

half-heart·ed (haf′här′tid, häf′-), *adj.* having or showing little enthusiasm. —**half′heart′ed·ly,** *adv.* —**half′-heart′ed·ness,** *n.*

half-life (haf′līf′, häf′-), *n.* the time required for one half the atoms of a radioactive substance to disintegrate.

half-mast (haf′mast′, häf′mäst′), *n.* a position approximately halfway between the top of a mast, staff, etc., and its base: a mark of mourning or a signal of distress.

half·pen·ny (hā′pə nē, hāp′nē), *n.,* *pl.* **half·pence** (hā′pəns), **half·pen·nies.** a British coin worth one half of a penny.

half′ pint′, **1.** a half of a pint: equal to 2 gills. **2.** *Informal.* a very short person.

half′ sis′ter, sister (def. 2).

half′ size′, any size in women's garments designated by a fractional number from 12½ through 24½, designed for a short-waisted, full figure.

half-slip (haf′slip′, häf′-), *n.* a skirtlike undergarment.

half′ sole′, a sole of a shoe that extends from the shank to the end of the toe.

half′ step′, *Music.* a pitch interval halfway between two whole tones.

half-tone (haf′tōn′, häf′-), *n.* **1.** a process in which gradation of tone is obtained by a system of minute dots. **2.** a print from such a process.

half-track (haf′trak′, häf′-), *n.* an armored vehicle with rear driving wheels on special treads.

half-truth (haf′trooth′, häf′-), *n.* a statement that is only partly true, esp. one intended to deceive or evade blame.

half·way (haf′wā′, häf′-), *adv.* **1.** to the midpoint. **2.** almost or nearly. **3.** meet halfway, to compromise with. —*adj.* **4.** midway, as between two places. **5.** partial or inadequate.

half′way house′, a special residence for former mental patients, prisoners, etc., during their adjustment back to normal life.

half-wit (haf′wit′, häf′-), *n.* **1.** a feebleminded person. **2.** a foolish or senseless person. —**half′-wit′ted,** *adj.*

half′-ad·mit′ted, *adj.;* -ly, *adv.*	**half′ dol′lar**	**half′-na′ked,** *adj.*
half′-a·fraid′, *adj.*	**half′-done′,** *adj.*	**half′ note′**
half′-a·live′, *adj.*	**half′-doz′en,** *n.,* *adj.*	**half′-o′pen,** *adj.*
half′-a·shamed′, *adj.*	**half′-dressed′,** *adj.*	**half′-pet′ri·fied′,** *adj.*
half′-a·sleep′, *adj.*	**half′ drowned′,** *adj.*	**half′-play′ful,** *adj.*
half′-a·wake′, *adj.*	**half′-earn′est,** *adj.*	**half′-pleased′,** *adj.*
half′-bur′ied, *adj.*	**half′-eat′en,** *adj.*	**half′-pound′,** *n.*
half′-cen′tu·ry, *n.,* *pl.* -ries.	**half′-Eng′lish,** *adj.*	**half′-proved′,** *adj.*
half′-civ′il·ized′, *adj.*	**half′-fam′ished,** *adj.*	**half′-ques′tion·ing,** *adj.*
half′-clad′, *adj.*	**half′-filled′,** *adj.*	**half′-raw′,** *adj.*
half′-closed′, *adj.*	**half′-fin′ished,** *adj.*	**half′-rea′son·a·ble,** *adj.*
half′-coax′ing, *adj.*	**half′-full′,** *adj.*	**half′-re·luc′tant,** *adj.*
half′-com·plet′ed, *adj.*	**half′-gal′lon,** *n.,* *adj.*	**half′-re·mem′bered,** *adj.*
half′-con·cealed′, *adj.*	**half′-grown′,** *adj.*	**half′-right′,** *adj.,* *n.*
half′-con′scious, *adj.*	**half′-heard′,** *adj.*	**half′-rot′ten,** *adj.*
half′-con·sumed′, *adj.*	**half′-hid′den,** *adj.*	**half′-ru′ined,** *adj.*
half′-con·temp′tu·ous, *adj.*	**half′-hour′,** *n.,* *adj.*	**half′-sav′age,** *adj.*
half′-con·vinced′, *adj.*	**half′-inch′,** *n.*	**half′-seen′,** *adj.*
half′-cooked′, *adj.*	**half′-in·clined′,** *adj.*	**half′-se′ri·ous,** *adj.*
half′-cov′ered, *adj.*	**half′-in·formed′,** *adj.*	**half′-shut′,** *adj.*
half′-crazed′, *adj.*	**half′-in·tel′li·gi·ble,** *adj.*	**half′ starved′,** *adj.*
half′-day′, *n.*	**half′-in·tox′i·cat′ed,** *adj.*	**half′-stat′ed,** *adj.*
half′-dazed′, *adj.*	**half′-look′ing,** *adj.*	**half′-sub·merged′,** *adj.*
half′-dead′, *adj.*	**half′-jus′ti·fied′,** *adj.*	**half′-tast′ed,** *adj.*
half′-de·fi′ant, *adj.*	**half′-mad′,** *adj.*	**half′-term′,** *n.*
half′-di·gest′ed, *adj.*	**half′-meant′,** *adj.*	**half′-un·der·stood′,** *adj.*
	half′-mile′, *n.,* *adj.*	**half′-used′,** *adj.*
	half′-min′ute, *n.*	**half′-wild′,** *adj.*
	half′-moon′, *n.*	**half′-wrong′,** *adj.*

hal·i·but (hal′ə bət, hol′-), *n.*, *pl.* **-but, -buts.** either of two large flatfishes found in the North Atlantic, used for food.

Hal·i·fax (hal′ə faks′), *n.* the capital of Nova Scotia, in SE Canada.

hal·ite (hal′īt, hā′līt), *n.* See **rock salt.**

hal·i·to·sis (hal′i tō′sis), *n.* a condition of having offensive-smelling breath.

hall (hôl), *n.* **1.** a building corridor, as in a home. **2.** the large entrance room of a house or building. **3.** a large room or building for public gatherings. **4.** a large building at a college or university. **5.** *Brit.* a mansion or large residence, esp. one on a large estate. **6.** the castle of a medieval noble.

hal·lah (hä′lə, кнä′-), *n.* challah.

hal·le·lu·jah (hal′ə loo′yə), *interj.* **1.** Praise ye the Lord! —*n.* **2.** an exclamation of "hallelujah!" Also, **hal′le·lu′iah.**

hall·mark (hôl′märk′), *n.* **1.** any mark or indication of genuineness, quality, etc. **2.** any distinguishing feature or characteristic.

hal·lo (hə lō′), *interj.* **1.** (used to call someone or to incite dogs in hunting.) —*n.* **2.** the cry "hallo!" Also, **hal·loo** (hə loo′)

hal·low (hal′ō), *v.t.* **1.** to make holy. **2.** to honor as holy. —**hal′low·er**, *n.*

hal·lowed (hal′ōd; *in liturgical use often* hal′ō id), *adj.* venerated or sacred.

Hal·low·een (hal′ə wēn′, -ō ēn′, hol′-), *n.* the evening of October 31, celebrated by children as a merrymaking festival. [(*All*)*hallow*(*s*) + *e*(*v*)*en*]

hal·lu·ci·nate (hə loo′sə nāt′), *v.i.*, *v.t.*, **-nat·ed, -nat·ing.** to have or cause to have hallucinations.

hal·lu·ci·na·tion (hə loo′sə nā′shən), *n.* **1.** a sensory experience of something that does not exist outside the mind. **2.** the sensation caused by a hallucinatory condition or the object experienced. **3.** a false notion or impression. —**hal·lu·ci·na·tive** (hə loo′sə nā′tiv, -nə tiv), *adj.* —**hal·lu·ci·na·to·ry** (hə loo′sə nə tôr′ē, -tōr′ē), *adj.*

hal·lu·cin·o·gen (hə loo′sə nə jen′, hal′yə sin′ə-), *n.* a substance that produces hallucinations. —**hal·lu·ci·no·gen·ic** (hə loo′sə nō jen′ik), *adj.*

hall·way (hôl′wā′), *n.* **1.** a corridor, esp. in a private house. **2.** hall (def. 2).

ha·lo (hā′lō), *n.*, *pl.* **-los, -loes. 1.** a symbolic circle of radiant light circling the head in pictures of divine or sacred personages. **2.** an atmosphere or quality of glory or sanctity. **3.** a bright circle or arc centered on the sun or moon.

hal·o·gen (hal′ə jən, hā′lə-), *n.* any of the nonmetallic elements fluorine, chlorine, iodine, bromine, and astatine. —**hal′o·gen·oid′**, *adj.* —**ha·log·e·nous** (hə loj′ə nəs), *adj.*

halt[1] (hôlt), *v.i.*, *v.t.* **1.** to stop or cause to stop, either permanently or temporarily. —*n.* **2.** a permanent or temporary stop.

halt[2] (hôlt), *v.i.* **1.** to falter, as in speech or reasoning. **2.** to waver between alternatives. —*adj.* **3.** *Archaic.* lame or limping.

hal·ter (hôl′tər), *n.* **1.** a rope or strap for leading or restraining horses or cattle. **2.** a woman's garment, worn above the waist and tied behind the neck and across the back. **3.** a hangman's noose. —*v.t.* **4.** to put a halter on. **5.** to restrain as by a halter.

halt·ing (hôl′ting), *adj.* **1.** faltering or hesitating, esp. in speech. **2.** faulty or imperfect. **3.** limping or lame. —**halt′ing·ly**, *adv.*

hal·vah (häl vä′, häl′vä), *n.* a sweet, candylike confection of Turkish origin, consisting chiefly of ground sesame seeds and honey. Also, **hal·va′**. [Yiddish < Rumanian < Turk *helva* < Ar *halwa*]

halve (hav, häv), *v.t.*, **halved, halv·ing. 1.** to divide into halves. **2.** to share equally. **3.** to reduce to half.

halv·ers (hav′ərz), *n.pl.* half shares or portions.

halves (havz, hävz), *n.* **1.** pl. of **half. 2.** go halves, to share equally or divide evenly.

hal·yard (hal′yərd), *n.* a line or tackle for hoisting a spar, sail, flag, etc.

ham[1] (ham), *n.* **1.** a cut of meat from a hog's heavy-muscled rear part between hip and hock, usually cured. **2.** that part of a hog's hind leg. **3.** the part of the leg back of the knee. **4.** Often, **hams.** the back of the thigh, or the thigh and the buttock together.

ham[2] (ham), *n.*, *v.*, **hammed, hamming.** —*n.* **1.** *Slang.* an actor who overacts. **2.** *Informal.* an operator of an amateur radio station. —*v.i.* **3.** *Slang.* to overact. —**ham′my**, *adj.*

Ham·burg (ham′bûrg), *n.* a seaport in N West Germany.

ham·burg·er (ham′bûr′gər), *n.* **1.** a patty of ground or chopped beef, fried or broiled. **2.** ground or chopped beef. **3.** a sandwich consisting of a cooked beef patty between two halves of a roll. Also, **ham′burg.**

Ham·il·ton (ham′əl tən), *n.* **Alexander,** 1757–1804, American statesman.

ham·let (ham′lit), *n.* a small village.

ham·mer (ham′ər), *n.* **1.** a tool consisting of a metal head set crosswise on a handle, used for driving nails, etc. **2.** something resembling this in form, action, or use. **3.** the part of a gun that, by its fall or action, causes the discharge. **4.** malleus. —v.t. **5.** to beat or drive with a hammer. **6.** to shape or construct with a hammer. **7.** to accomplish by repeated or strenuous effort: *to hammer out an agreement.* —v.i. **8.** to strike blows with or as with a hammer. **9.** to work at laboriously: *He hammered away at his speech for hours* —ham′mer·er, *n.*

ham·mer·head (ham′ər hed′), *n.* **1.** the part of a hammer designed for striking. **2.** a shark having the head expanded laterally so as to resemble a double-headed hammer. —ham′mer·head′ed, *adj.*

ham·mer·lock (ham′ər lok′), *n.* a wrestling hold in which one arm of an opponent is twisted and forced upward behind his back.

ham·mer·toe (ham′ər tō′), *n.* a deformed toe in which there is a permanent angular bending of the second and third joints.

ham·mock (ham′ək), *n.* a hanging bed made of canvas with cords attached to two supports at each end.

ham·per[1] (ham′pər), *v.t.* to hold back, esp. by putting an embarrassing restraint upon. —ham′per·er, *n.* —Syn. hinder, impede.

ham·per[2] (ham′pər), *n.* a large covered basket or wickerwork receptacle.

ham·ster (ham′stər), *n.* a short-tailed, burrowing rodent having large cheek pouches.

ham·string (ham′string′), *n., v., -strung, -string·ing.* —*n.* **1.** a tendon that bounds the hollow of the knee. —*v.t.* **2.** to disable by cutting the hamstring. **3.** to render powerless or useless.

hand (hand), *n.* **1.** the terminal part of the upper limb below the wrist. **2.** something resembling a hand in shape or function, as a pointer. **3.** a worker or crew member. **4.** a person who performs a specific work or skill. **5.** skill or workmanship. **6.** a person with reference to ability or skill: *a poor hand at running a business.* **7.** Often, **hands. a.** possession or power. **b.** control or care. **8.** a bargaining position. **9.** agency or instrumentality: *death by his own hand.* **10.** assistance or aid. **11.** an active participation: *Give me a hand.* **12.** side or direction. **13.** handwriting or penmanship. **14.** a round of applause for a performer. **15.** a pledge, as of marriage. **16.** a linear measure equal to four inches, used esp. in determining the height of horses. **17.** *Cards.* **a.** the cards dealt to or held by each player at one time. **b.** a single part of a game, in which all the cards

dealt at one time are played. **18. at hand, a.** nearby. **b.** soon. **c.** ready for use. **19. by hand,** by using the hands, as opposed to machines. **20. hand and glove,** very intimately associated. Also, **hand in glove. 21. hand in hand,** close together. **22. hand over fist,** *Informal.* speedily and in abundance. **23. hands down, a.** without difficulty. **b.** without question. **b.** in one's possession. **24. in hand, a.** under control. **b.** in one's possession. **c.** under consideration **25. on hand, a.** at one's disposal. **b.** about to occur. **c.** present. **26. on the other hand,** from another aspect. **27. out of hand,** beyond control. —*v.t.* **28.** to deliver or pass with or as with the hand. **29.** to help or guide with the hand. **30. hand down, a.** to deliver (the decision of a court). **b.** to bequeath to posterity. **31. hand it to,** *Informal.* to give just credit to. —*adj.* **32.** of, for, belonging to, using, or used by the hand. **33.** made by hand. **34.** operated by hand. —hand′less, *adj.*

hand·bag (hand′bag′), *n.* a woman's bag for carrying money, toilet articles, etc.

hand·ball (hand′bôl′), *n.* a game played by striking a small ball against a wall with the hand.

hand·bar·row (hand′bar′ō), *n.* a frame with handles at each end by which it is carried.

hand·bill (hand′bil′), *n.* a small printed announcement for distribution by hand.

hand·book (hand′book′), *n.* a book of instruction, guidance, or information.

hand·car (hand′kär′), *n.* a small railroad car on four wheels propelled by hand.

hand·cart (hand′kärt′), *n.* a small cart drawn or pushed by hand.

hand·clasp (hand′klasp′, -kläsp′), *n.* a gripping of hands by two or more people, esp. to show a spiritual bond of friendship, sympathy, etc.

hand·craft (*n.* hand′kraft′, -kräft′; *v.* hand′kraft′, -kräft′), *n.* **1.** handicraft. —*v.t.* **2.** to make (something) by manual skill.

hand·cuff (hand′kuf′), *n.* **1.** a ring-shaped metal device that can be locked around a prisoner's wrist, usually one of a pair connected by a short chain. —*v.t.* **2.** to put handcuffs on.

hand·ed (han′did), *adj.* **1.** having a hand or hands. **2.** preferring the use of a particular hand: *left-handed.* **3.** requiring a specified number of persons: *four-handed.*

Han·del (han′d°l), *n.* **George Frederick,** 1685–1759, German composer in England after 1712.

hand·ful (hand′fŏŏl′), *n., pl.* -fuls. 1. the quantity or amount that the hand can hold. 2. a small amount or quantity. 3. *Informal.* a difficult person or thing to manage.

hand·gun (hand′gun′), *n.* any firearm that can be held and fired with one hand.

hand·i·cap (han′dē kap′), *n., v.* -capped, -cap·ping. —*n.* 1. a contest in which certain disadvantages or advantages of weight, distance, etc., are placed upon competitors to equalize their chances of winning. 2. the disadvantage or advantage itself. 3. any disadvantage or disability. —*v.t.* 4. to place at a disadvantage. 5. to assign handicaps to (competitors).

hand·i·capped (han′dē kapt′), *adj.* 1. physically disabled. 2. mentally deficient. —*n.* 3. handicapped persons collectively.

hand·i·cap·per (han′dē kap′ər), *n.* a person who predicts the outcome of horse races, as for a newspaper.

hand·i·craft (han′dē kraft′, -kräft′), *n.* 1. manual skill. 2. an art, craft, or trade requiring manual skill. 3. the articles made by handicraft. —**hand′i·crafts′man,** *n.*

hand·i·work (han′dē wûrk′), *n.* 1. work done by hand. 2. the work of a particular person.

hand·ker·chief (hang′kər chif, -chēf′), *n.* a small piece of fabric, usually square, used for personal or decorative purposes.

han·dle (han′dᵊl), *n., v.,* -dled, -dling. —*n.* 1. a part of a thing made specifically to be grasped or held by the hand. 2. *CB Radio Slang.* a nickname adopted by an operator. 3. **fly off the handle,** *Informal.* to become very agitated or angry. —*v.t.* 4. to touch, pick up, carry, or feel with the hands. 5. to manage, deal with, operate, or be responsible for. 6. to deal or trade in: *to handle dry goods.* —*v.i.* 7. to perform in a particular way when handled: *The jet was handling poorly.* —**han′dler,** *n.*

han·dle·bar (han′dᵊl bär′), *n.* Usually, **handlebars.** the curved steering bar of a bicycle, motorcycle, etc.

hand·made (hand′mād′), *adj.* made by hand, rather than by machine.

hand·maid (hand′mād′), *n. Archaic.* a female attendant. Also, **hand′maid′en.**

hand-me-down (hand′mē doun′, han′-), *n.* 1. *Informal.* a piece of clothing passed on to another person after being used for some time. 2. anything cheap or inferior.

hand·out (hand′out′), *n.* 1. *Informal.* something, as food or clothing, given to a needy person. 2. a prepared statement distributed to the press for information or publicity. 3. anything given away for nothing.

hand·pick (hand′pik′), *v.t.* to select personally and with care.

hand·rail (hand′rāl′), *n.* a rail serving as a support at the side of a stairway, platform, etc.

hand·saw (hand′sô′), *n.* any saw with a handle at one end for manual operation with one hand.

hand·set (hand′set′), *n.* a telephone with the receiver and transmitter at the ends of a handle.

hand·shake (hand′shāk′), *n.* a grasping and shaking of right hands by two individuals, as to symbolize greeting, agreement, farewell, etc.

hand·some (han′səm), *adj.* 1. having an attractive, well-proportioned, and imposing appearance. 2. ample or liberal in amount. 3. gracious or generous. 4. dexterous or graceful. —**hand′some·ly,** *adv.* —**hand′some·ness,** *n.*

hand·spring (hand′spring′), *n.* an acrobatic feat in which a person starts from a standing position and turns the body forward or backward in a complete circle, landing first on the hands and then on the feet.

hand·stand (hand′stand′), *n.* an act of supporting the body in a vertical position by balancing on the palms of the hands.

hand-to-hand (hand′tə hand′), *adj.* at close quarters: *hand-to-hand combat.*

hand-to-mouth (hand′tə mouth′), *adj.* providing barely enough to live on.

hand·work (hand′wûrk′), *n.* work done by hand, not by machine.

hand·write (hand′rīt′), *v.t.,* -wrote, -writ·ten, -writ·ing. to write (something) by hand.

hand·writ·ing (hand′rī′ting), *n.* 1. writing done with the hand. 2. the style of writing characteristic of a person. —**hand′writ′ten,** *adj.*

hand·y (han′dē), *adj.,* hand·i·er, hand·i·est. 1. conveniently available. 2. skillful in manual work. 3. easily handled or manipulated. —**hand′i·ly,** *adv.* —**hand′i·ness,** *n.*

hand·y·man (han′dē man′), *n.* a person hired to do various small jobs.

hang (hang), *v.,* hung *or (esp. for 3, 11)* hanged; hang·ing; *n.* —*v.t.* 1. to fasten or attach (a thing) so that it is supported from above or near its own top. 2. to attach so as to allow free movement. 3. to execute by suspending from a gallows, as a capital punishment. 4. to decorate with something suspended: *to hang a room with pictures.* 5. to fasten at a proper angle. 6. to attach (wallpaper, curtains, etc.) to a wall. 7. to bow downward: *She hung her head.* 8. to keep (a jury) from rendering a

verdict. —*v.i.* 9. to be or remain
suspended. 10. to swing freely, as on
a hinge. 11. to die by punitive hanging. 12. to incline downward or lean
over. 13. to float in the air. 14. to
fit or drape in graceful lines: *That
coat hangs well in back.* 15. **hang
around** or **about**, *Informal.* to loiter.
16. **hang back,** to hesitate. 17. **hang
in,** *Slang.* to persevere in the face of
adversity. Also, **hang in there.** 18.
hang on, a. to hold fast. **b.** to be
contingent on. **c.** to keep a telephone
line open. 19. **hang out,** *Slang.* to idle
away one's free time. 20. **hang up, a.**
to suspend from a hook or hanger.
b. to hold back. **c.** to break a telephone connection by replacing the
receiver. —*n.* 21. the way in which
a thing hangs. 22. *Informal.* the precise manner of doing or using something. 23. *Informal.* meaning or concept.

hang·ar (hang'ər), *n.* an enclosed
structure for housing airplanes. [< F]

hang·dog (hang'dôg', -dog'), *adj.* 1.
defeated or abject: *a hangdog look.*
2. shamefaced or guilty.

hang·er (hang'ər), *n.* 1. a frame with
a hook at the top, for hanging a
garment. 2. a contrivance on which
things are hung, as a hook. 3. a person who hangs something.

hang·er-on (hang'ər on', -ôn'), *n., pl.*
hang·ers-on. a self-seeking follower.

hang'glid'ing, the sport of jumping
from a hilltop and soaring through
the air while harnessed beneath a
kitelike glider. —**hang' glid'er.**

hang·ing (hang'ing), *n.* 1. an execution in which a convicted criminal is
hanged from a gallows. 2. Often,
hangings, something hung on the
walls, as a drapery or tapestry.

hang·man (hang'mən), *n.* a person
who hangs criminals condemned to
death.

hang·nail (hang'nāl'), *n.* a small piece
of partly detached skin at the side or
base of the fingernail.

hang·out (hang'out'), *n.* *Informal.* a
place where a person frequently visits.

hang·o·ver (hang'ō'vər), *n.* 1. the disagreeable physical aftereffects of
drunkenness. 2. something remaining
behind.

hang·up (hang'up'), *n.* *Slang.* a psychological block or disturbance.

hank (hangk), *n.* 1. a skein, as of
thread or yarn. 2. a coil or loop: *a
hank of hair.*

han·ker (hang'kər), *v.i.* to have a
restless or incessant longing. —**han'-
ker·ing,** *n.*

han·ky (hang'kē), *n., pl.* **-kies.** *Informal.* a handkerchief. Also, **han'kie.**

han·ky-pan·ky (hang'kē pang'kē), *n.*
Informal. unethical behavior.

Ha·noi (ha noi', hä'noi'), *n.* the cap-

ital of Vietnam: formerly of North
Vietnam before reunification.

han·som (han'səm), *n.* a two-wheeled
covered carriage, the driver being
mounted on an elevated seat behind.
[after J. A. *Hansom* (1803–82), English architect]

Ha·nuk·kah (hä'nə kə, -nŏŏ kä', -kə),
n. an eight-day Jewish festival celebrated in December or late November, commemorating an ancient victory over the Syrians.

hap (hap), *n.* *Archaic.* luck or lot.

hap·haz·ard (hap haz'ərd), *adj.* without order or planning. —**hap·haz'-
ard·ly,** *adv.* —**hap·haz'ard·ness,** *n.*

hap·less (hap'lis), *adj.* unfortunate or
unlucky. —**hap'less·ly,** *adv.* —**hap'-
less·ness,** *n.*

hap·loid (hap'loid), *adj.* pertaining
to a single set of chromosomes.

hap·ly (hap'lē), *adv.* *Archaic.* by
chance.

hap·pen (hap'ən), *v.i.* 1. to take place.
2. to come to pass by chance. 3. to
have the fortune: *I happened to see
him on the street.* 4. to meet or discover by chance: *to happen on a clue
to the mystery.*

hap·pen·ing (hap'ə ning), *n.* 1. an occurrence or event. 2. any special
event or performance in which the
audience is to play a spontaneous
creative part.

hap·pen·stance (hap'ən stans'), *n.*
Informal. chance or accident.

hap·py (hap'ē), *adj.,* **-pi·er, -pi·est.** 1.
feeling or providing contented pleas-
ure or joy. 2. fortunate or lucky. 3.
apt or felicitous. —**hap'pi·ly,** *adv.*
—**hap'pi·ness,** *n.*

hap·py-go-luck·y (hap'ē gō luk'ē), *adj.*
trusting cheerfully to luck.

ha·ra-ki·ri (här'ə kēr'ē, har'ə-, har'ē-),
n. (in Japan) ceremonial suicide by
ripping open the abdomen with a
knife. [< Jap: belly cutting]

ha·rangue (hə rang'), *n., v.,* **-rangued,
-rangu·ing.** —*n.* 1. a long, passionate, and pompous speech. —*v.t.* 2.
to address in a harangue. —*v.i.* 3. to
deliver a harangue. —**ha·rangu'er,** *n.*

har·ass (har'əs, hə ras'), *v.t.* 1. to
trouble by repeated attacks, incur-
sions, etc. 2. to disturb persistently.
—**har'ass·er,** *n.* —**har'ass·ment,** *n.*

Har·bin (här'bin), *n.* a city in NE
China.

har·bin·ger (här'bin jər), *n.* a person
or thing that heralds the approach of
someone or something.

har·bor (här'bər), *n.* 1. a sheltered
portion of a body of water along the
shore deep enough for anchoring
ships. 2. any place of shelter or refuge. —*v.t.* 3. to give shelter to. 4.
to keep or hold in the mind: *to harbor suspicion.* —*v.i.* 5. to take shelter in a harbor. Also, *Brit.,* **har'bour.**

hard (härd), *adj.* **1.** solid and firm to the touch. **2.** firmly formed or tight. **3.** difficult to do, accomplish, deal with, understand, etc. **4.** involving or expending a great deal of effort or persistence. **5.** forceful or violent. **6.** bad or unbearable. **7.** oppressive or harsh. **8.** realistic or undeniable. **9.** unfriendly or resentful. **10.** stern or searching. **11.** disreputable or tough. **12.** supported by sufficient gold reserves: *hard currency.* **13.** containing more than 22.5 percent alcohol by volume. **14.** (of water) containing mineral salts that interfere with the action of soap. **15. hard of hearing,** partly deaf. **16. hard up,** *Informal.* in need of money. —*adv.* **17.** with great effort, force, or intensity. **18.** so as to be solid, tight, or firm. **19.** excessively or immoderately. —**hard′ness,** *n.*

hard-and-fast (härd′ən fast′, -fäst′), *adj.* not to be violated: *hard-and-fast rules.*

hard·back (härd′bak′), *n., adj.* hardcover.

hard·ball (härd′bôl′), *n.* baseball.

hard-bit·ten (härd′bit′ən), *adj.* unyieldingly tough.

hard-boiled (härd′boild′), *adj.* **1.** boiled until hard, as an egg. **2.** *Informal.* tough and unsentimental.

hard·bound (härd′bound′), *adj.* (of a book) bound with a stiff cover.

hard′ cash′, actual money as distinguished from checks or credit.

hard′ ci′der, fully fermented cider.

hard-core (härd′kôr′), *adj.* **1.** unswerving and uncompromising. **2.** pruriently explicit, as pornography. **3.** chronically persistent, as unemployment.

hard·cov·er (härd′kuv′ər), *n.* **1.** a hardbound book. —*adj.* **2.** hardbound.

hard′ drug′, any drug that is physiologically addictive and physically and psychologically harmful, such as heroin.

hard·en (här′dən), *v.t., v.i.* to make or become hard or unfeeling. —**hard′en·er,** *n.*

hard-hat (härd′hat′), *n. Informal.* **1.** a construction worker. **2.** any working-class conservative.

hard·head·ed (härd′hed′id), *adj.* **1.** practical and shrewd. **2.** stubborn or willful. —**hard′head′ed·ly,** *adv.* — **hard′head′ed·ness,** *n.*

hard·heart·ed (härd′här′tid), *adj.* unfeeling or pitiless. —**hard′heart′ed·ly,** *adv.* —**hard′heart′ed·ness,** *n.*

har·di·hood (här′dē hŏŏd′), *n.* **1.** determined boldness. **2.** audacity or impudence.

Har·ding (här′diñg), *n.* **Warren G(amaliel),** 1865–1923. 29th president of the U.S. 1921–23.

hard′ line′, an uncompromising or unyielding stand, esp. in politics. — **hard′-line′,** *adj.* —**hard′-lin′er,** *n.*

hard·ly (härd′lē), *adv.* **1.** barely or scarcely. **2.** not quite. **3.** with little likelihood: *He will hardly come now.* —**Usage.** HARDLY, BARELY, and SCARCELY all have a negative connotation, and the use of any of them with a supplementary negative is considered nonstandard, as in *I can't hardly wait* for *I can hardly wait.*

hard-nosed (härd′nōzd′), *adj. Slang.* unsentimentally practical.

hard′ pal′ate, the anterior bony portion of the palate.

hard·pan (härd′pan′), *n.* any layer of clay underlying soft soil.

hard′ rock′, the original form of rock-'n'-roll, basically dependent on a very loud, strong beat.

hard′ rub′ber. rubber vulcanized with a large amount of sulfur, to render it inflexible.

hard′ sell′, a forceful and insistent method of advertising or selling.

hard-shell (härd′shel′), *adj.* rigid and uncompromising.

hard·ship (härd′ship), *n.* **1.** a condition difficult to endure, as poverty. **2.** an instance or cause of this.

hard·stand (härd′stand′), *n.* a paved area, usually set up near a runway, for parking airplanes or surface vehicles.

hard·tack (härd′tak′), *n.* a hard, saltless biscuit, formerly much used for naval rations.

hard·top (härd′top′), *n.* an automobile having a rigid metal top and no center posts between windows.

hard·ware (härd′wâr′), *n.* **1.** metalware, as tools, locks, etc. **2,** the mechanical equipment necessary for conducting an activity. **3.** any electronic or mechanical equipment used in association with data processing.

hard·wood (härd′wŏŏd′), *n.* the hard, compact wood of various trees, as the oak. cherry, etc.

hard·work·ing (härd′wûr′kiñg), *adj.* industrious or laborious.

har·dy (här′dē), *adj.,* **-di·er, -di·est. 1.** capable of enduring hardship, exposure, etc. **2.** (of plants) able to withstand the cold of winter in the open air. **3.** bold or courageous. —**har′di·ly,** *adv.* —**har′di·ness,** *n.*

hare (hâr), *n., pl.* **hares, hare.** a rodentlike mammal related to but larger than the rabbit. —**hare′like′,** *adj.*

hare·bell (hâr′bel′), *n.* a low herb having blue, bell-shaped flowers.

hare·brained (hâr′brānd′), *adj.* giddy or reckless.

hare·lip (hâr′lip′), *n.* a congenital deformity in which there is a vertical fissure in the upper lip. —**hare′-lipped′,** *adj.*

har·em (hâr′əm, har′-), *n.* **1.** that part of a Muslim household reserved for the residence of women. **2.** the women there. [< Ar *harīm,* lit., forbidden]

hark (härk), *v.i.* **1.** to listen (used chiefly in the imperative). **2. hark back,** to return to a previous subject or point.

hark·en (här′kən), *v.i.* hearken.

har·le·quin (här′lə kwin, -kin), *n.* **1.** (*often cap.*) a character in comic theater, usually masked, dressed in multicolored tights, and carrying a wooden sword. **2.** a clown or buffoon.

har·lot (här′lət), *n. Now Rare.* a prostitute. —**har′lot·ry,** *n.*

harm (härm), *n.* **1.** physical injury or mental damage. **2.** moral impairment. —*v.t.* **3.** to do or cause harm to. —**harm′ful,** *adj.* —**harm′ful·ness,** *n.* —**harm′less,** *adj.* —**harm′less·ly,** *adv.* —**harm′less·ness,** *n.*

har·mon·ic (här mon′ik), *adj.* **1.** of or in musical harmony. —*n.* **2.** a musical harmony. —**har·mon′i·cal·ly,** *adv.*

har·mon·i·ca (här mon′ə kə), *n.* a small wind instrument played by exhaling or inhaling the air through a set of metal reeds.

har·mon·ics (här mon′iks), *n.* the science of musical sounds.

har·mo·ni·ous (här mō′nē əs), *adj.* **1.** agreeing in feeling or action. **2.** blending well: *harmonious colors.* **3.** tuneful or melodious. —**har·mo′ni·ous·ly,** *adv.* —**har·mo′ni·ous·ness,** *n.*

har·mo·ni·um (här mō′nē əm), *n.* an organlike keyboard instrument with small metal reeds.

har·mo·nize (här′mə nīz′), *v.,* -nized, -niz·ing. —*v.t.* **1.** to bring into harmony or agreement. —*v.i.* **2.** to be in agreement. **3.** to sing in harmony. —**har′mo·ni·za′tion,** *n.* —**har′mo·niz′er,** *n.*

har·mo·ny (här′mə nē), *n., pl.* -nies. **1.** agreement or accord, as of thoughts. **2.** a pleasing arrangement of parts. **3.** *Music.* the simultaneous combination of tones, esp. when blended into chords pleasing to the ear. [< L *harmoni(a)* < Gk: melody]

har·ness (här′nis), *n.* **1.** the combination of straps, bands, and other parts forming the working gear of a draft animal. **2. in harness,** engaged in one's usual routine of work. —*v.t.* **3.** to put a harness on. **4.** to gain control over and use. —**har′ness·er,** *n.*

harp (härp), *n.* **1.** a large musical instrument having strings stretched across a triangular frame, played by plucking with the fingers. —*v.i.* **2.** to play on a harp. **3. harp on** or **upon,** to dwell on persistently or tediously. —**harp′er,** *n.* —**harp′ist,** *n.*

har·poon (här pōōn′), *n.* **1.** a barbed, spearlike missile attached to a rope, used mainly in whaling. —*v.t.* **2.** to strike with a harpoon. —**har·poon′-er,** *n.*

harp·si·chord (härp′si kôrd′), *n.* a keyboard instrument in which the strings are plucked by leather or quill points.

Har·py (här′pē), *n., pl.* -pies. **1.** *Class. Myth.* a ravenous monster having a woman's head and a bird's body. **2.** (*l.c.*) **a.** a rapacious, grasping person. **b.** a scolding, nagging woman.

har·ri·dan (har′i dᵊn), *n.* a scolding, vicious old woman.

har·ri·er¹ (har′ē ər), *n.* **1.** a person or thing that harries. **2.** a predatory hawk.

har·ri·er² (har′ē ər), *n.* **1.** a medium-sized hunting hound. **2.** a cross-country runner.

Har·ris·burg (har′is bûrg′), *n.* the capital of Pennsylvania.

Har·ri·son (har′i sən), *n.* **1. Benjamin,** 1833–1901, 23rd president of the U.S. 1889–93. **2. William Henry,** 1773–1841, U.S. general: 9th president of the U.S. 1841.

har·row (har′ō), *n.* **1.** an agricultural implement with spikelike teeth or upright disks, for breaking up plowed land. —*v.t.* **2.** to draw a harrow over (land). **3.** to disturb keenly or painfully. —**har′row·ing,** *adj.*

har·ry (har′ē), *v.t.,* -ried, -ry·ing. **1.** to torment constantly. **2.** to ravage, as in war.

harsh (härsh), *adj.* **1.** ungentle in action or effect: *harsh treatment.* **2.** grim or cruel. **3.** unpleasant to the senses. —**harsh′ly,** *adv.* —**harsh′-ness,** *n.* —**Syn. 2.** austere, severe.

hart (härt), *n.* a male of the deer, commonly the red deer.

Hart·ford (härt′fərd), *n.* the capital of Connecticut.

har·um-scar·um (hâr′əm skâr′əm), *adj.* **1.** wild and irresponsible. —*adv.* **2.** in a harum-scarum manner. —*n.* **3.** a harum-scarum person.

har·vest (här′vist), *n.* **1.** the gathering of crops. **2.** the season when ripened crops are gathered. **3.** a crop or yield of one growing season. **4.** the result of any act, process, or event. —*v.t., v.i.* **5.** to gather or reap. —**har′vester,** *n.*

has (haz), *v.* a 3rd pers. sing. pres. indic. of **have.**

has-been (haz′bin′), *n. Informal.* a person or thing that is no longer successful or popular.

ha·sen·pfef·fer (hä′sən fef′ər), *n.* a stew of marinated rabbit meat.

hash¹ (hash), *n.* **1.** a dish of chopped meat, as of leftover beef, potatoes, and sometimes vegetables sautéed in a frying pan. **2.** a mess or muddle. —*v.t.* **3.** to chop into small pieces. **4. hash over,** *Slang.* to bring up again for discussion or review. [< F *hach*(*er*) (to) cut up]

hash² (hash), *n. Slang.* hashish.

hash·head (hash′hed′), *n. Slang.* a hashish addict.

hash·ish (hash′ēsh, -ish), *n.* a narcotic and intoxicant made from the flowering tops and leaves of Indian hemp.

hash′ mark′, *Mil. Slang.* a service stripe worn on the left sleeve by an enlisted person.

Ha·sid (hä′sid, кнä′-), *n., pl.* **Ha·sid·im** (hä sid′im, кнä-). a member of a mystic Jewish sect founded in Poland in the 18th century. —**Ha·sid·ic** (hə sid′ik), *adj.*

has·n't (haz′ənt), contraction of *has not.*

hasp (hasp, häsp), *n.* a clasp for a door, lid, etc., esp. one passing over a staple and fastened by a pin or padlock.

has·sle (has′əl), *n., v.,* **has·sled, has·sling.** *Informal.* —*n.* **1.** a disorderly dispute. **2.** a bother or irritation. —*v.i.* **3.** to have a disorderly dispute. —*v.t.* **4.** to bother or irritate.

has·sock (has′ək), *n.* a thick firm cushion used as a footstool or for kneeling.

hast (hast), *v. Archaic.* 2nd pers. sing. pres. indic. of **have.**

has·ta la vis·ta (hä′stə lə vē′stə), *Spanish.* goodby.

haste (hāst), *n.* **1.** swiftness of motion. **2.** urgent need of quick action. **3.** rash or undue speed.

has·ten (hā′sən), *v.i.* **1.** to move or act with haste. —*v.t.* **2.** to cause to hasten. —**Syn. 2.** accelerate, expedite.

hast·y (hā′stē), *adj.,* **hast·i·er, hast·i·est. 1.** acting with haste. **2.** unduly quick: *a hasty decision.* —**hast′i·ly,** *adv.* —**hast′i·ness,** *n.* —**Syn. 1.** hurried, speedy. **2.** precipitate, rash.

hat (hat), *n.* **1.** a shaped covering for the head, usually with a crown and brim. **2. pass the hat,** *Informal.* to ask for contributions of money. **3. talk through one's hat,** *Informal.* to speak without knowing the facts. **4. throw** or **toss one's hat into the ring,** to declare one's candidacy for political office. **5. under one's hat,** *Informal.* confidential or secret. —**hat′less,** *adj.*

hatch¹ (hach), *v.t.* **1.** to bring forth (young) from the egg. **2.** to cause young to emerge from (the egg), as by incubating. **3.** to bring forth or contrive. —*v.i.* **4.** to be hatched. —**hatch′a·ble,** *adj.*

hatch² (hach), *n.* **1. a.** a large, covered, usually rectangular opening in a ship's deck through which cargo is lowered into or lifted from a hold. **b.** Also called **hatch′ cov′er.** the covering for this. **2. a.** a small opening in the floor or roof of a building. **b.** the cover over such an opening.

hatch³ (hach), *v.t.* to mark with lines, esp. closely set parallel lines, as for shading in drawing or engraving. —**hatch′ing,** *n.*

hatch·back (hach′bak′), *n.* an automobile whose rear deck lid and window lift open as a unit, with a folding back seat for additional cargo space.

hatch·er·y (hach′ə rē), *n., pl.* **-er·ies.** a place for hatching eggs of hens, fish, etc.

hatch·et (hach′it), *n.* **1.** a small, short-handled ax. **2.** a tomahawk. **3. bury the hatchet,** to make peace. —**hatch′et·like′,** *adj.*

hatch′et job′, *Informal.* a maliciously destructive criticism or act.

hatch′et man′, *Informal.* **1.** a professional murderer. **2.** a person whose job it is to execute unpleasant tasks for a superior, as dismissing.

hatch·way (hach′wā′), *n.* **hatch²** (defs. 1a, 2a).

hate (hāt), *v.,* **hat·ed, hat·ing,** *n.* —*v.t.* **1.** to dislike intensely or passionately. **2.** to be unwilling. —*v.i.* **3.** to feel intense dislike or hostility. —*n.* **4.** intense dislike or hostility. **5.** the hated object. —**hate′ful,** *adj.* —**hate′ful·ly,** *adv.* —**hate′ful·ness,** *n.* —**hat′er,** *n.* —**Syn. 1.** abhor, detest, loathe.

hath (hath), *v. Archaic.* 3rd pers. sing. pres. indic. of **have.**

ha·tred (hā′trid), *n.* intense dislike, aversion, or hostility.

hat·ter (hat′ər), *n.* a maker or seller of hats.

hau·berk (hô′bûrk), *n. Armor.* a long coat of mail.

haugh·ty (hô′tē), *adj.,* **-ti·er, -ti·est.** disdainfully proud. —**haugh′ti·ly,** *adv.* —**haugh′ti·ness,** *n.*

haul (hôl), *v.t., v.i.* **1.** to pull or draw with force. **2.** to cart or transport. **3. haul off,** *Informal.* to prepare to deal a blow. —*n.* **4.** the act or an instance of hauling. **5.** a load hauled. **6.** the distance over which anything is hauled. **7.** *Informal.* something taken or collected. **8. long haul,** a long period of time. —**haul′er,** *n.*

haul·age (hô′lij), *n.* **1.** the act or labor of hauling. **2.** a charge made for hauling.

haunch (hônch, hänch), *n.* **1.** the hip. **2.** the fleshy part of the body about the hip. **3.** a hind quarter of an animal. **4.** the leg and loin of an animal, used for food.

haunt (hônt, hänt), *v.t.* **1.** to visit habitually or appear to frequent as a spirit or ghost. **2.** to recur persistently to the consciousness of: *Memories haunted him.* **3.** to visit frequently. —*n.* **4.** a place frequently visited. —**haunt′er,** *n.* —**haunt′ing,** *adj.* —**haunt′ing·ly,** *adv.*

haute cou·ture (ōt kōō tYR′), *French.* the most fashionable and influential dressmaking and designing.

haute cui·sine (ōt kwē zēn′), *French.* fine cooking.

hau·teur (hō tûr′), *n.* haughty manner or spirit.

Ha·van·a (hə van′ə), *n.* the capital of Cuba.

have (hav; *unstressed* həv, əv), *v.* and *auxiliary v.,* **had, hav·ing,** *n.* —*v.t.* **1.** to hold in possession or for one's use. **2.** to be related to or accept in some relation. **3.** to get, receive, or take. **4.** to be obliged to: *I have to go out.* **5.** to experience, undergo, or engage in. **6.** to hold in mind, etc.: *to have doubts.* **7.** to cause to, as by command, invitation, etc. **8.** to show or exhibit in action or words. **9.** to eat or drink. **10.** to permit or allow. **11.** to assert or maintain: *Rumor has it.* **12.** to know or be skilled in. **13.** to beget or give birth to: *to have a baby.* **14.** to hold at a disadvantage. **15.** *Slang.* **a.** to outwit or cheat. **b.** to bribe. **16.** to engage in sexual intercourse with. —*auxiliary v.* **17.** (used with a past participle to form perfect tenses): *She has gone.* **18. have at,** to attack. **19. have coming,** to merit. **20. have had it,** *Slang.* to be unable or unwilling to endure more. **21. have it out,** to come to an understanding through discussion. **22. have on,** to be clothed in. **23. have to do with, a.** to deal with. **b.** to have dealings or social relations with. —*n.* **24.** Usually, **haves.** a person or nation having social position, wealth, etc.

ha·ven (hā′vən), *n.* **1.** a place of shelter and safety. **2.** *Literary.* a harbor or port.

have-not (hav′not′, -not′), *n.* Usually, **have-nots.** a person or nation without social position, wealth, etc.

have·n't (hav′ənt), contraction of *have not.*

hav·er·sack (hav′ər sak′), *n.* a single-strapped shoulder bag for provisions.

hav·oc (hav′ək), *n.* **1.** ruinous damage and confusion. **2. play havoc with,** to destroy or ruin.

haw[1] (hô), *n.* **1.** the fruit of the hawthorn. **2.** the hawthorn.

haw[2] (hô), *v.i.* to hesitate or falter in or as in speech (used usually in the phrase *to hem and haw*).

Ha·wai·i (hə wī′ē, -wä′-, -wä′yə), *n.* a state of the United States comprising a group of islands in the N Pacific. *Cap.:* Honolulu. —**Ha·wai′ian** (-yən), *adj., n.*

hawk[1] (hôk), *n.* **1.** a bird of prey, smaller than the eagle, with a hooked beak and powerful claws. **2.** *Informal.* a person who advocates a belligerent national attitude. —**hawk′ish,** *adj.*

hawk[2] (hôk), *v.t., v.i.* to peddle, esp. to offer for sale by calling aloud in public. —**hawk′er,** *n.*

hawk[3] (hôk), *v.i.* **1.** to clear the throat noisily. —*v.t.* **2.** to raise by hawking: *to hawk up phlegm.*

hawk-eyed (hôk′īd′), *adj.* having very keen eyes.

haw·ser (hô′zər, -sər), *n.* a heavy rope for mooring or towing a ship.

baw·thorn (hô′thôrn′), *n.* a thorny shrub or tree with white or pink blossoms and bright-colored fruits.

Haw·thorne (hô′thôrn′), *n.* **Nathaniel,** 1804–64, U.S. novelist.

hay (hā), *n.* **1.** grass, alfalfa, etc., cut and dried for use as forage. **2.** *Slang.* a small sum of money. **3. hit the hay,** *Slang.* to go to bed. —*v.i.* **4.** to cut grass, etc., and store for use as forage.

hay·cock (hā′kok′), *n.* a small conical pile of hay awaiting removal to a barn.

Hay·dn (hīd′ən), *n.* **Franz Jo·seph** (frants jō′zəf), 1732–1809, Austrian composer.

Hayes (hāz), *n.* **Rutherford B(ir·chard)** (ruᵗʰ′ər fərd bur′chərd), 1822–93, 19th president of the U.S. 1877–81.

hay′ fe′ver, *Pathol.* inflammation of the mucous membranes of the eyes and respiratory tract caused by an allergic response to the pollen of certain plants.

hay·fork (hā′fôrk′), *n.* **1.** a forklike tool for pitching hay. **2.** a machine for loading or unloading hay.

hay·loft (hā′lôft′, -loft′), *n.* a loft in a stable or barn for the storage of hay.

hay·mak·er (hā′mā′kər), *n.* **1.** *Informal.* a knockout punch. **2.** a person or a machine that cuts hay and spreads it to dry.

hay·mow (hā′mou′), *n.* **1.** a mass of hay stored in a barn. **2.** hayloft.

hay·seed (hā′sēd′), *n.* *Informal.* a yokel or hick.

hay·stack (hā′stak′), *n.* a stack of hay built up in the open air for preservation. Also called, *esp. Brit.,* **hay′rick′** (-rik′).

hay·wire (hā′wīr′), *adj. Informal.*
1. out of control or order. **2.** mentally disturbed or upset.

haz·ard (haz′ərd), *n.* **1.** a foreseeable but unavoidable danger: *occupational hazards.* **2.** something causing this. **3.** *Golf.* an obstacle, such as a bunker. —*v.t.* **4.** to venture or risk. —**haz′ard·ous,** *adj.* —**haz′ard·ous·ly,** *adv.*

haze[1] (hāz), *n., v.,* **hazed, haz·ing. 1.** an aggregation in the atmosphere of very fine, widely dispersed particles, giving the air a blurred appearance. **2.** vagueness or obscurity, as of the mind. —*v.t., v.i.* **3.** to make or become hazy.

haze[2] (hāz), *v.t.,* **hazed,) haz·ing.** to subject (freshmen, etc.) to abusive or humiliating tricks and ridicule. —**haz′er,** *n.*

ha·zel (hā′zəl), *n.* **1.** a shrub or small tree related to the birch, bearing an edible nut (**ha′zel·nut′**). **2.** a light golden brown.

ha·zy (hā′zē), *adj.,* **-zi·er, -zi·est. 1.** full of or obscured by haze. **2.** vague or confused. —**ha′zi·ly,** *adv.* —**ha′zi·ness,** *n.*

Hb, hemoglobin.

H.B.M., His (or Her) Britannic Majesty.

H-bomb (āch′bom′), *n.* See **hydrogen bomb.**

H.C., 1. Holy Communion. **2.** House of Commons.

h.c., for the sake of honor. [< L *honoris causa*]

h.c.l., high cost of living.

hd., 1. hand. **2.** head.

h.d., heavy duty.

hdbk., handbook.

hdkf., handkerchief.

hdqrs., headquarters.

hdw., hardware. Also, **hdwe.**

he (hē; *unstressed* ē), *pron., n., pl.* **hes.** —*pron.* **1.** the male being in question or last mentioned. **2.** anyone: *He who hesitates is lost.* —*n.* **3.** any male person or animal.

HE, high explosive.

He, helium.

H.E., 1. high explosive. **2.** His Eminence. **3.** His (or Her) Excellency.

head (hed), *n.* **1.** the upper part of the body, containing the brain, eyes, ears, nose, and mouth. **2.** intellect or mind. **3.** the position or place of leadership. **4.** a leader or chief. **5.** the top or upper end. **6.** a front end or a forward projecting part. **7.** the part of a weapon, etc., used for striking. **8.** one of a number, herd, or group: *ten head of cattle.* **9.** a crisis or climax: *to bring matters to a head.* **10.** froth or foam at the top of a liquid. **11.** any dense flower cluster or compact part of a plant, as that composed of leaves in the lettuce. **12.** the main side of a coin. **13.** the source of a river or stream. **14.** headline (def. 1). **15. come to a head, a.** to suppurate, as a boil. **b.** to reach a crisis. **16. go to one's head, a.** to make a person dizzy or drunk. **b.** to make one conceited. **17. head over heels,** intensely or completely. **18. heads up!** *Informal.* be careful! **19. keep or lose one's head,** to keep (or lose) one's poise. **20. on one's head,** as one's responsibility. **21. over one's head, a.** to one having a superior position. **b.** beyond one's comprehension. **22. turn one's head,** to cause one to become conceited. —*adj.* **23.** first in rank, grade, or position. **24.** situated at the top or front. **25.** moving or coming from in front: *head sea.* —*v.t.* **26.** to be or go at the head of. **27.** to be the chief of. **28.** to direct the course of. —*v.i.* **29.** to move forward toward a point specified. **30. head off,** to go before in order to hinder. —**head′ed** (-id), *adj.* —**head′less,** *adj.*

head·ache (hed′āk′), *n.* **1.** a pain in the head. **2.** *Informal.* anything or anyone bothersome.

head·band (hed′band′), *n.* a band worn around the head.

head·board (hed′bōrd′, -bôrd′), *n.* a board forming the head of anything, esp. of a bed.

head′ cold′, a common cold characterized esp. by nasal congestion.

head·dress (hed′dres′), *n.* a covering or decoration for the head.

head·first (hed′fûrst′), *adv.* **1.** with the head in front or bent forward. **2.** rashly or precipitately.

head·gear (hed′gēr′), *n.* any covering for the head, as a hat, cap, helmet, etc.

head·hunt·ing (hed′hun′tĭng), *n.* (among certain primitive peoples) the practice of hunting down and decapitating victims and preserving their heads as trophies. —**head′hunt′er,** *n.*

head·ing (hed′ĭng), *n.* **1.** something that serves as a head, top, or front. **2.** a title or caption of a page, chapter, section, etc. **3.** the compass direction toward which a traveler or vehicle is moving.

head·land (hed′lənd), *n.* a promontory extending into a large body of water.

head·light (hed′līt′), *n.* a light equipped with a reflector, on the front of a vehicle.

head·line (hed′līn′), *n., v.,* **-lined, -lin·ing.** —*n.* **1.** a heading in a newspaper for any written material. **2.** the largest such heading on the front page, usually at the top. —*v.t.* **3.** to mention prominently, as in a headline. **4.** to be the featured performer of (a show, nightclub, etc.).

head·lock (hed′lok′), *n.* a hold in which a wrestler locks his or her arm around the opponent's head.

head·long (hed′lông′, -long′), *adv.* **1.** with the head foremost. **2.** hastily. **3.** rashly. —*adj.* **4.** hasty. **5.** rash or impetuous. **6.** with the head foremost.

head·mas·ter (hed′mas′tər, -mä′stər), *n.* a principal of a private school. —**head′mis′tress,** *n. fem.*

head-on (hed′on′, -ôn′), *adj., adv.* with the front or head foremost.

head·phone (hed′fōn′), *n.* Usually, **headphones.** a headset.

head·piece (hed′pēs′), *n.* **1.** any covering for the head. **2.** a decorative piece at the head of a chapter.

head·quar·ters (hed′kwôr′tərz), *n., pl.* **-ters.** a center of operations, as of a military commander or a business, from which orders are issued.

head·rest (hed′rest′), *n.* a support for the head.

head·room (hed′rōōm′, -rŏŏm′), *n.* clear vertical space, esp. overhead.

head·set (hed′set′), *n.* a device consisting of one or two earphones with a headband for holding them over the ears.

heads·man (hedz′mən), *n.* a public executioner who beheads condemned persons.

head·stall (hed′stôl′), *n.* the part of a bridle that encompasses the head of an animal.

head′ start′, an advantage given or acquired in any competition.

head·stone (hed′stōn′), *n.* a stone marker at the head of a grave.

head·strong (hed′strông′, -strong′), *adj.* willfully stubborn.

head′ ta′ble, the table in a principal position, as in a large meeting room, at which the chairperson, speakers, and special guests are seated.

head·wait·er (hed′wā′tər), *n.* the chief waiter in a restaurant.

head·wa·ters (hed′wô′tərz, -wot′ərz), *n.pl.* the upper tributaries of a river.

head·way[1] (hed′wā′), *n.* **1.** movement forward. **2.** any progress, as in work.

head·way[2] (hed′wā′), *n.* headroom.

head·wind (hed′wind′), *n.* a wind opposed to the course of a vessel or aircraft.

head·word (hed′wûrd′), *n. Brit.* a word constituting a heading, as an entry word in a dictionary.

head·work (hed′wûrk′), *n.* mental labor.

head·y (hed′ē), *adj.,* **head·i·er, head·i·est. 1.** intoxicating: *a heady wine.* **2.** rashly impetuous. —**head′i·ly,** *adv.* —**head′i·ness,** *n.*

heal (hēl), *v.t.* **1.** to make whole or well, as of a wound. **2.** to settle or reconcile. —*v.i.* **3.** to effect a cure. **4.** to mend or get well. —**heal′er,** *n.* —**Syn. 1.** cure, remedy.

health (helth), *n.* **1.** the general condition of the body or mind: *poor health.* **2.** freedom from disease or ailment. **3.** a toast to a person's health, happiness, etc. **4.** vigor or vitality. —*adj.* **5.** of, for, or promoting health: *health food; health aids.*

health·ful (helth′fəl), *adj.* **1.** conducive to health. **2.** *Rare.* healthy (def. 1). —**health′ful·ly,** *adv.* —**health′ful·ness,** *n.*

health·y (hel′thē), *adj.,* **health·i·er, health·i·est. 1.** possessing good health. **2.** of or characteristic of good health. **3.** healthful (def. 1). **4.** *Informal.* fairly large. —**health′i·ly,** *adv.* —**health′i·ness,** *n.* —**Syn. 1.** hale, robust, well.

heap (hēp), *n.* **1.** a group of things lying one on another. **2.** *Informal.* a great quantity or number. —*v.t.* **3.** to put or pile in a heap. **4.** to give or assign in great quantity. **5.** to load or fill abundantly. —*v.i.* **6.** to become heaped.

hear (hēr), *v.,* **heard** (hûrd), **hear·ing.** —*v.t.* **1.** to perceive by the ear. **2.** to be informed of. **3.** to listen to or attend. **4.** to consider officially, as a judge: *to hear a case.* —*v.i.* **5.** to be capable of perceiving sound by the ear. **6.** to receive information by the ear or otherwise: *to hear from a friend.* **7.** to listen with favor or assent: *I will not hear of your going.* —**hear′er,** *n.*

hear·ing (hēr′ing), *n.* **1.** the faculty or sense by which sound is perceived. **2.** the act of perceiving sound. **3.** an opportunity to be heard. **4.** an instance or a session in which official testimony and arguments are presented. **5.** earshot.

heark·en (här′kən), *v.i. Literary.* to hear attentively.

hear·say (hēr′sā′), *n.* unverified information acquired from another.

hearse (hûrs), *n.* a vehicle for carrying a dead person to the place of burial.

heart (härt), *n.* **1.** a hollow, muscular organ that by rhythmic contractions and relaxations keeps the blood in circulation throughout the body. **2.** the center of the total personality, esp. with reference to intuition, feeling, or emotion. **3.** love or sympathy. **4.** courage or enthusiasm. **5.** the innermost or central part of anything. **6.** a conventional figure representing a heart. **7.** a playing card of the suit bearing such figures. **8. after one's own heart,** according to one's taste. **9. at heart,** fundamentally or basically. **10. by heart,** by memory. **11. set one's heart on,** to determine on. **12. take to heart, a.** to think seriously about. **b.** to be deeply affected by.

heart·ache (härt′āk′), *n.* emotional distress.

heart′ attack′, a sudden inability of the heart to function, usually due to an embolism or increased blood pressure.

heart·beat (härt′bēt′), *n.* a pulsation of the heart.

heart·break (härt′brāk′), *n.* great sorrow or grief. —**heart′break′ing**, *adj.* —**heart′bro′ken**, *adj.*

heart·burn (härt′bûrn′), *n.* uneasy burning sensation in the chest caused by an acid fluid from the stomach.

heart·en (här′tən), *v.t.* to give courage or confidence to.

heart′ fail′ure, a condition in which the heart ceases to function.

heart·felt (härt′felt′), *adj.* deeply felt.

hearth (härth), *n.* **1.** the floor of a fireplace, usually of stone or brick. **2.** home or family life. **3.** the lower part of a blast furnace, in which the molten metal collects.

hearth·side (härth′sīd′), *n.* fireside (def. 1).

hearth·stone (härth′stōn′), *n.* **1.** a stone forming a hearth. **2.** hearth (def. 2).

heart·less (härt′lis), *adj.* unfeeling or cruel. —**heart′less·ly**, *adv.* —**heart′less·ness**, *n.*

heart·rend·ing (härt′ren′ding), *adj.* causing or expressing intense grief or anguish.

heart·sick (härt′sik′), *adj.* extremely depressed or unhappy. —**heart′sick′ness**, *n.*

heart·strings (härt′stringz′), *n.pl.* the deepest feelings or the strongest affections.

heart·throb (härt′throb′), *n.* **1.** a rapid beat of the heart. **2.** a passionate emotion. **3.** sweetheart.

heart-to-heart (härt′tə härt′), *adj.* frank and sincere: *a heart-to-heart talk.*

heart·warm·ing (härt′wôr′ming), *adj.* tenderly moving.

heart·y (här′tē), *adj.*, **heart·i·er**, **heart·i·est**, *n.*, *pl.* **heart·ies**. —*adj.* **1.** warmhearted and cordial. **2.** heartfelt or sincere. **3.** physically vigorous: *hale and hearty.* **4.** abundant or nourishing: *a hearty meal.* —*n.* **5.** *Archaic.* a brave or good fellow, esp. a shipmate. —**heart′i·ness**, *n.*

heat (hēt), *n.* **1.** the state of a body perceived as having or generating a relatively high degree of warmth. **2.** the condition or quality of being hot. **3.** the degree of hotness. **4.** the sensation of hotness. **5.** added or external energy that causes a rise in temperature, expansion, evaporation, or other physical change. **6.** hot season or weather. **7.** warmth or intensity of feeling: *He spoke with much heat.* **8.** a single course or division of a race or other contest. **9.** sexual excitement in animals, esp. females. **10.** *Slang.* great pressure, esp. in police searches for criminals. .—*v.t.*, *v.i.* **11.** to make or become hot or warm. **12.** to excite or become excited. —**heat′ed**, *adj.* —**heat′ed·ly**, *adv.* —**heat′less**, *adj.*

heat·er (hē′tər), *n.* any of various apparatus for heating, as for heating water.

heath (hēth), *n.* **1.** *Brit.* a tract of open and uncultivated land. **2.** any of various low, evergreen shrubs common on waste land, as the heather. —**heath′y**, *adj.*

hea·then (hē′thən), *n.*, *pl.* **-thens**, **-then**, *adj.* —*n.* **1.** an irreligious or uncivilized person. **2.** an unconverted individual of a people that do not acknowledge the God of the Christians, Jews, or Muslims. —*adj.* **3.** irreligious or unenlightened. **4.** of the heathen. —**hea′then·dom**, *n.* —**hea′then·ish**, *adj.* —**hea′then·ism′**, *n.*

heath·er (heth′ər), *n.* any of various heaths, esp. of England and Scotland, having small, pinkish purple flowers. —**heath′ered**, *adj* —**heath′er·y**, *adj.*

heat′ light′ning, flashes of light unaccompanied by thunder, seen near the horizon on summer evenings.

heat′ shield′, a coating or structure for protecting a spacecraft from excessive heating during reentry.

heat·stroke (hēt′strōk′), *n.* collapse or fever caused by exposure to excessive heat.

heave (hēv), *v.*, **heaved** or (*esp. Naut.*) **hove**; **heav·ing**; *n.* —*v.t.* **1.** to raise or lift with effort. **2.** to lift and throw with force or violence. **3.** to utter laboriously or painfully: *to heave a sigh.* **4.** to haul or pull on (a rope, cable, etc.). —*v.i.* **5.** to rise and fall rhythmically. **6.** to vomit or retch. **7.** to rise and swell as if thrust up, as a hill. **8.** to pull, haul, or push. **9.** *Naut.* to move in a certain direction or into a certain situation: *to heave about.* **10.** **heave to**, *Naut.* to stop the headway of (a vessel). —*n.* **11.** the act or effort of heaving. **12.** a throw, toss, or cast. **13. heaves**, a disease of horses characterized by difficult breathing. —**heav′er**, *n.*

heav·en (hev′ən), *n.* **1.** the dwelling place of God, the angels, and the spirits of the righteous after death. **2.** (*often cap.*) the Supreme Being. **3.** Usually, **heavens**. the sky or firmament. **4.** a place or state of supreme happiness. —**heav′en·ly**, *adj.* —**heav′en·ward**, *adv.*, *adj.*

heav·y (hev′ē), *adj.*, **heav·i·er**, **heav·i·est**, *n.*, *pl.* **heav·ies**, *adv.* —*adj.* **1.**

of great weight. **2.** of great amount, intensity, or size. **3.** of great force, turbulence, etc. **4.** of more than the usual or average density or weight: *a heavy person.* **5.** profound or serious. **6.** *Mil.* **a.** thickly armed or equipped. **b.** of the more powerful sizes: *heavy weapons.* **7.** burdened or burdensome. **8.** indulging to an unusually great degree: *a heavy drinker.* **9.** broad, thick, or coarse. **10.** dull or depressed. **11.** clumsy or slow. **12.** overcast or cloudy. **13.** not easily digested. **14.** pregnant: *heavy with child.* **15.** producing or refining basic materials, as steel or coal, used in manufacturing: *heavy industry.* **16.** *Slang.* excellent. —*n.* **18.** *Theat.* **a.** a villainous part or character. **18.** an actor who plays such parts. —*adv.* **19.** in a heavy manner. —**heav′i·ly,** *adv.* —**heav′i·ness,** *n.*

heav·y-du·ty (hev′ē dōō′tē, dyōō′-), *adj.* made to withstand great physical strain.

heav·y-hand·ed (hev′ē han′did), *adj.* **1.** oppressive or harsh. **2.** clumsy or graceless.

heav·y-heart·ed (hev′ē här′tid), *adj.* sorrowful or dejected.

heav′y·set (hev′ē set′), *adj.* having a stocky build.

heav′y wa′ter, water in which hydrogen atoms have been replaced by deuterium.

heav·y·weight (hev′ē wāt′), *n.* **1.** a person of more than average weight. **2.** a boxer or wrestler weighing more than 175 pounds.

Heb., **1.** Hebrew. **2.** Hebrews. Also, **Hebr.**

He·bra·ic (hi brā′ik), *adj.* of or characteristic of the Hebrews, their language, or their culture. —**He·bra′i·cal·ly,** *adv.*

He·bra·ism (hē′brā iz′əm, -brē-), *n.* the character, spirit, or practices distinctive of the Hebrew people. —**He′bra·ist,** *n.*

He·brew (hē′brōō), *n.* **1.** a member of a group of Semitic peoples inhabiting ancient Palestine and claiming descent from Abraham, Isaac, and Jacob. **2.** the Semitic language of the ancient Hebrews, now the national language of Israel. —*adj.* **3.** Hebraic.

He·brews (hē′brōōz), *n.* a book of the New Testament.

heck (hek), *interj.* (a mild expression of annoyance, disgust, etc.)

heck·le (hek′əl), *v.t.,* **-led,** **-ling.** to harass with impertinent questions or gibes. —**heck′ler,** *n.*

hec·tare (hek′târ), *n.* a metric unit of land measure equal to 10,000 square meters: equivalent to 2.471 acres.

hec·tic (hek′tik), *adj.* **1.** full of excitement, confused and rapid movement, etc. **2.** feverish or flushed, as from an illness. —**hec′ti·cal·ly,** *adv.*

hec·to·gram (hek′tə gram′), *n.* a metric unit of 100 grams, equivalent to 3.527 ounces avoirdupois.

hec·to·li·ter (hek′tə lē′tər), *n.* a metric unit of capacity of 100 liters, equivalent to 2.8378 U.S. bushels, or 26.418 U.S. gallons.

hec·to·me·ter (hek′tə mē′tər), *n.* a metric unit of length equal to 100 meters, or 328.08 feet.

Hec·tor (hek′tər), *n.* **1.** *Class. Myth.* the greatest Trojan hero, killed by Achilles. —*v.t.* **2.** (*l.c.*) to treat with insolence.

he'd (hēd; *unstressed* ēd), contraction of: **a.** *he had.* **b.** *he would.*

hedge (hej), *n., v.,* **hedged, hedg·ing.** —*n.* **1.** a row of bushes or small trees forming a boundary. **2.** any barrier or boundary. **3.** a protection against loss. —*v.t.* **4.** to enclose with or surround by or as by a hedge. **5.** to protect against a possible loss by counterbalancing (bets, etc.). —*v.i.* **6.** to avoid a rigid commitment. —**hedg′er,** *n.*

hedge·hog (hej′hog′, -hôg′), *n.* **1.** an Old World insect-eating mammal having spiny hairs on the back and sides. **2.** the porcupine.

hedge-hop (hej′hop′), *v.i.,* **-hopped, -hop·ping.** to fly an airplane at a very low altitude.

he·don·ism (hēd′³niz′əm), *n.* **1.** the doctrine that pleasure or happiness is the highest good. **2.** devotion to pleasure as a way of life. —**he′don·ist,** *n., adj.* —**he·do·nis′tic,** *adj.*

heed (hēd), *v.t., v.i.* **1.** to give careful attention (to). —*n.* **2.** careful attention. —**heed′ful,** *adj.* —**heed′ful·ly,** *adv.* —**heed′ful·ness,** *n.* —**heed′less,** *adj.* —**heed′less·ly,** *adv.* —**heed′less·ness,** *n.*

heel¹ (hēl), *n.* **1.** the back part of the foot, below and behind the ankle. **2.** the part of a stocking, shoe, etc., covering this part. **3.** a solid, raised base attached to the back part of the sole of a shoe. **4.** something resembling a heel in position, shape, etc. **5. down at the heels,** shabby or poor. **6. kick up one's heels,** to frolic. **7. on** or **upon the heels of,** closely following. —*v.t.* **5.** to furnish with heels, as shoes. —*v.i.* **6.** (of a dog) to follow at one's heels on command. —**heel′less,** *adj.*

heel² (hēl), *v.i., v.t.* **1.** to lean or cause to lean to one side, esp. of a ship. —*n.* **2.** a heeling movement.

heel³ (hēl), *n.* *Informal.* a low, despicable person.

heeled (hēld), *adj.* *Slang.* having money.

heft (heft), *Informal.* —*v.t.* **1.** to try the weight of by lifting. —*n.* **2.** weight or heaviness. —**heft′er,** *n.*

heft·y (hef′tē), *adj.,* **heft·i·er, heft·i·est.** *Informal.* **1.** big and muscularly strong. **2.** weighty or heavy. —**hef′ti·ness,** *n.*

he·gem·o·ny (hi jem′ə nē), *n., pl.* **-nies.** leadership or dominance, esp. of one nation over others.

He·gi·ra (hi jī′rə, hej′ər ə), *n.* **1.** the flight of Muhammad from Mecca, A.D. 622. **2.** (*l.c.*) any flight or journey to a more congenial place.

heif·er (hef′ər), *n.* a cow that has not produced a calf.

height (hīt), *n.* **1.** extent or distance upward. **2.** the distance between the lowest and highest points of a person standing upright. **3.** altitude or elevation. **4.** a high place above a level. **5.** the highest part or utmost degree.

height·en (hīt′ən), *v.t., v.i.* **1.** to make or become higher. **2.** to increase in degree or amount. —**Syn. 2.** enhance, intensify.

hei·nous (hā′nəs), *adj.* hateful or totally reprehensible. —**hei′nous·ly,** *adv.* —**hei′nous·ness,** *n.*

heir (âr), *n.* a person who inherits or is entitled to inherit the property or title of another. —**heir′ship,** *n.*

heir′ appar′ent, *pl.* **heirs apparent.** an heir whose right is indefeasible, provided he survives the ancestor.

heir·ess (âr′is), *n.* a female heir, esp. to considerable wealth.

heir·loom (âr′lōōm′), *n.* **1.** any family possession transmitted from generation to generation. **2.** an item of personal property that goes directly to the heir by inheritance.

heir′ presump′tive, *pl.* **heirs presumptive.** a person whose current right of inheritance may be defeated by the birth of a nearer heir.

heist (hīst), *Slang.* —*v.t.* **1.** to rob or steal, esp. by burglary. —*n.* **2.** a robbery, esp. a burglary.

held (held), *v.* pt. and pp. of **hold**[1].

Hel′en of Troy′ (hel′ən), *Class. Myth.* the beautiful daughter of Zeus and queen of Sparta whose abduction by Paris was the cause of the Trojan War.

Hel·e·na (hel′ə nə), *n.* the capital of Montana.

hel·i·cal (hel′i kəl), *adj.* having the form of a helix.

hel·i·coid (hel′ə koid′, hē′lə-), *adj.* coiled or curving like a spiral. Also, **hel′i·col′dal.**

hel·i·cop·ter (hel′ə kop′tər, hē′lə-), *n.* an aircraft that is lifted and sustained in the air by rotating blades turning on vertical axes. [< F *hélicoptère* < Gk *helix* helix + *pteron* wing]

he·li·o·cen·tric (hē′lē ō sen′trik), *adj.* having or representing the sun as a center. —**he·li·o·cen′tri·cal·ly,** *adv.* —**he·li·o·cen·tric′i·ty** (hē′lē ō sen·tris′i tē), *n.*

he·li·o·graph (hē′lē ə graf′, -gräf′), *n.* a device for signaling by means of a movable mirror that reflects beams of light.

he·li·o·trope (hē′lē ə trōp′), *n.* **1.** an herb or shrub having small, fragrant, purple flowers. **2.** a light tint of purple.

hel·i·pad (hel′ə pad′, hē′lə-), *n.* a takeoff and landing area for helicopters, usually without commercial facilities.

hel·i·port (hel′ə pôrt′, -pōrt′, hē′lə-), *n.* a landing place for helicopters, often the roof of a building.

he·li·um (hē′lē əm), *n. Chem.* an inert, gaseous element used as a substitute for flammable gases in lighter-than-air craft. *Symbol:* He; *at. wt.:* 4.0026; *at. no.:* 2. [< NL < Gk *hélios* sun]

he·lix (hē′liks), *n., pl.* **he·lix·es, hel·i·ces** (hel′i sēz′). something spiral in shape.

hell (hel), *n.* **1.** the place or state of punishment of the wicked after death. **2.** the abode of evil and condemned spirits. **3.** any place or state of torment or misery. **4.** **get** or **catch hell,** *Slang.* to receive a harsh reprimand. **5.** **hell of a,** *Slang.* **a.** very bad. **b.** extremely. **6.** **raise hell,** *Slang.* to create an uproar. —*interj.* **7.** (to express irritation, disgust, etc.)

he′ll (hēl; *unstressed* ēl, hil, il), contraction of: **a.** *he will.* **b.** *he shall.*

hell·bent (hel′bent′), *adj. Informal.* **1.** recklessly determined. **2.** going at terrific speed.

hell·cat (hel′kat′), *n.* **1.** a bad-tempered, unmanageable woman. **2.** a sorceress or witch.

hel·le·bore (hel′ə bōr′, -bôr′), *n.* a coarse herb of the lily family whose powdered root is used to kill lice and caterpillars.

Hel·lene (hel′ēn), *n.* a modern Greek.

Hel·len·ic (he len′ik, -lē′nik), *adj.* of or characteristic of the ancient Greeks or their language, culture, thought, etc. —**Hel·len·ism** (hel′ə niz′əm), *n.* —**Hel′len·ist** (-nist), *n.* —**Hel′len·is′tic,** *adj.*

hell·gram·mite (hel′grə mīt′), *n.* the aquatic larva of a fly, used as bait in fishing.

hell·hole (hel′hōl′), *n.* a place totally lacking in comfort and cleanliness.

hel·lion (hel′yən), *n. Informal.* a disorderly, troublesome or rowdy person.

hell·ish (hel′ish), *adj.* **1.** of or like hell. **2.** wicked or devilish. —**hell′-ish·ly,** *adv.* —**hell′ish·ness,** *n.*

hel·lo (he lō′, hə-, hel′ō), *interj.* (to express a greeting or attract attention.)

helm (helm), *n.* **1.** a wheel or tiller by which a ship is steered. **2.** the place or post of control.

hel·met (hel′mit), *n.* any of various forms of protective head covering worn by soldiers, cyclists, etc.

helms·man (helmz′mən), *n.* a person who steers a ship.

hel·ot (hel′ət, hē′lət), *n.* a serf or slave.

help (help), *v.t.* **1.** to contribute strength, means, or be of service to. **2.** to refrain from: *He can't help doing it.* **3.** to relieve (someone) in need or distress. **4.** to remedy or prevent. **5.** to serve food to at table. —*v.i.* **6.** to give aid or be of service. **7. help out,** to be of aid to. **8. cannot help but,** to be obliged to. **9. help oneself to,** to take or appropriate at will. —*n.* **10.** aid or assistance. **11.** relief or succor. **12.** a person or thing that helps. **13.** a hired helper. **14.** a body of such helpers. —**help′-er,** *n.* —**Syn. 1.** aid, assist, succor. —**Usage.** HELP BUT, in sentences like *She's so beautiful you can't help but admire her,* has been condemned by purists. It is so widely used that it can be accepted as standard English.

help·ful (help′fəl), *adj.* giving or rendering help. —**help′ful·ly,** *adv.* —**help′ful·ness,** *n.*

help·ing (hel′piñg), *n.* a portion of food served to a person at one time.

help·less (help′lis), *adj.* **1.** unable to help oneself or manage by oneself. **2.** without help or aid. **3.** deprived of strength or power. —**help′less·ly,** *adv.* —**help′less·ness,** *n.*

help·mate (help′māt′), *n. Literary.* a helpful companion, esp. a spouse. Also, **help′meet′** (-mēt′).

Hel·sin·ki (hel′siñ kē, hel siñg′-), *n.* the capital of Finland.

hel·ter·skel·ter (hel′tər skel′tər), *adv., adj.* **1.** in headlong and disorderly haste. **2.** in a haphazard manner.

helve (helv), *n.* a handle, esp. of an ax.

Hel·ve·tia (hel vē′shə), *n. Obsolesc.* Switzerland. —**Hel·ve′tian,** *adj., n.*

hem[1] (hem), *v.,* **hemmed, hem·ming,** *n.* —*v.t.* **1.** to fold back and sew down the edge of. **2.** to enclose or confine: *hemmed in by enemies.* —*n.* **3.** the edge or border of a garment, drape, etc., made by hemming. —**hem′mer,** *n.*

hem[2] (hem), *interj., n., v.,* **hemmed, hem·ming.** —*interj.* **1.** (an utterance resembling a slight clearing of the throat, used to attract attention, express doubt, etc.) —*n.* **2.** the utterance or sound of "hem." —*v.i.* **3.** to utter the sound "hem." **4. hem and haw,** to speak noncommittally.

he·man (hē′man′), *n. Informal.* a strong, tough, virile man.

hem·a·tite (hem′ə tīt′, hē′mə-), *n.* a very common mineral consisting chiefly of an oxide of iron: the principal ore of iron.

hem·a·tol·o·gy (hem′ə tol′ə jē, hē′mə-), *n.* the study of the nature and diseases of the blood and blood-forming organs. —**hem·a·to·log·ic** (hem′ə t°loj′ik, hē′mə-), **hem′a·to·log′i·cal,** *adj.* —**hem′a·tol′o·gist,** *n.*

heme (hēm), *n.* a deep-red pigment obtained from hemoglobin.

hemi-, a prefix meaning "half": *hemisphere.*

hem·i·sphere (hem′i sfēr′), *n.* (*often cap.*) half of the terrestrial globe or celestial sphere, esp. any of the halves into which the earth is divided: *Eastern Hemisphere.* —**hem·i·spher·ic** (hem′i sfer′ik), **hem′i·spher′i·cal,** *adj.*

hem·i·stich (hem′i stik′), *n.* half of a poetic verse or line, esp. as divided by a caesura.

hem·line (hem′līn′), *n.* the bottom edge of a coat, skirt, etc.

hem·lock (hem′lok′), *n.* **1.** a poisonous herb having finely divided leaves and small white flowers. **2.** a poisonous drink made from this herb. **3.** an evergreen tree characterized by its pyramidal manner of growth. **4.** the wood of this tree.

hemo-, a combining form meaning "blood": *hemoglobin.*

he·mo·glo·bin (hē′mə glō′bin, hem′ə-; hē′mə glō′bin, hem′ə-), *n.* the protein coloring matter of the red blood corpuscles that serves to convey oxygen to the tissues.

he·mo·phil·i·a (hē′mə fil′ē ə, -fēl′yə, hem′ə-), *n.* an abnormal condition of males inherited through the mother, characterized by a tendency to bleed excessively. —**he′mo·phil′i·ac′** (-ak′), *n., adj.*

hem·or·rhage (hem′ər ij, hem′rij), *n., v.,* **-rhaged, -rhag·ing.** —*n.* **1.** a profuse discharge of blood, as from a ruptured blood vessel. —*v.i.* **2.** to bleed profusely. —**hem·or·rhag·ic** (hem′ə raj′ik), *adj.*

hem·or·rhoid (hem′ə roid′, hem′roid), *n.* Usually, **hemorrhoids.** a painful enlargement of internal or external veins in the rectum. —**hem′or·rhoi′-dal,** *adj.*

he·mo·stat (hē′mə stat′, hem′ə-), *n. Med.* an instrument or agent used to stop hemorrhage.

hemp (hemp), *n.* **1.** a tall Asiatic herb cultivated for its tough fiber. **2.** its fiber, used for making rope, coarse fabric, etc. **3.** a narcotic preparation, as bhang, obtained from the Indian hemp. —**hemp'en,** *adj.*

hem·stitch (hem'stich'), *v.t.* **1.** to hem along a line from which threads have been drawn out, stitching the cross threads into a series of little groups. —*n.* **2.** the stitch used in hemstitching.

hen (hen), *n.* **1.** the female of the domestic fowl. **2.** the female of any bird.

hence (hens), *adv.* **1.** as an inference from this fact. **2.** from this time: *a month hence.* **3.** *Rare.* henceforth. **4.** *Archaic.* from this place. **5.** *Obs.* from this source or origin.

hence·forth (hens'fôrth', -fôrth'; hens'fôrth', -fôrth'), *adv.* from now on. Also, **hence·for·ward** (hens'fôr'-wərd).

hench·man (hench'mən), *n.* **1.** a political supporter, esp. one motivated by the hope of personal gain. **2.** a trusted attendant or follower.

hen·na (hen'ə), *n., v., -naed, -na·ing.* —*n.* **1.** a shrub of warm countries prized for its fragrant white or pink flowers. **2.** a dye made from the leaves of this plant, used esp. as a hair tint. **3.** a red brown. —*v.t.* **4.** to tint or dye with henna.

hen·peck (hen'pek'), *v.t.* to domineer over (one's husband), esp. by persistent nagging.

hen·ry (hen'rē), *n., pl. -ries, -rys. Elect.* the meter-kilogram-second unit of inductance.

Hen·ry VIII (hen'rē), 1491–1547, king of England 1509–47.

hep (hep), *adj. Slang.* hip[3].

hep·a·rin (hep'ə rin), *n.* an acid occurring in various tissues, esp. the liver, that prevents coagulation of the blood.

he·pat·ic (hi pat'ik), *adj.* of, like, or pertaining to the liver.

he·pat·i·ca (hi pat'i kə), *n.* an herb of the buttercup family having delicate purplish, pink, or white flowers.

hep·a·ti·tis (hep'ə tī'tis), *n.* inflammation of the liver.

hep·cat (hep'kat'), *n. Slang.* an enthusiast for jazz, esp. swing.

hep·tam·e·ter (hep tam'i tər), *n.* a verse of seven metrical feet.

her (hûr; *unstressed* hər, ər), *pron.* **1.** the objective case of **she.** **2.** the possessive case of **she.**

He·ra (hēr'ə), *n.* the ancient Greek queen of heaven and the wife of Zeus.

her·ald (her'əld), *n.* **1.** (formerly) a royal or official messenger similar to a modern ambassador. **2.** (formerly) an official crier of public proclamations. **3.** a forerunner or harbinger. **4.** a person or thing that proclaims or announces. —*v.t.* **5.** to announce or proclaim. **6.** to usher in.

he·ral·dic (he ral'dik), *adj.* of or pertaining to heraldry or heralds.

her·ald·ry (her'əl drē), *n., pl. -ries.* **1.** the art of designing and blazoning armorial bearings, of tracing and recording genealogies, etc. **2.** armorial bearings. **3.** heraldic pomp or ceremony. —**her'ald·ist,** *n.*

herb (ûrb, hûrb), *n.* **1.** a flowering plant whose stem above ground does not become woody. **2.** such a plant when valued for its medicinal properties, flavor, or scent. —**her·ba·ceous** (hûr bā'shəs, ûr-), *adj.* —**herb'al,** *adj.*

herb·age (ûr'bij, hûr'-), *n.* **1.** herbs collectively, esp. those suitable for grazing. **2.** the succulent leaves of herbaceous plants.

herb·al·ist (hûr'bə list, ûr'-), *n.* a person who collects or deals in herbs.

her·bar·i·um (hûr bâr'ē əm), *n., pl. -bar·i·ums, -bar·i·a** (-bâr'ē ə).* **1.** a collection of dried plants systematically arranged. **2.** a place in which such a collection is kept.

herb·i·cide (ûr'bi sīd', hûr'-), *n.* a substance or preparation for killing plants, esp. weeds. —**her'bi·cid'al,** *adj.*

her·bi·vore (hûr'bə vōr', -vôr'), *n.* a herbivorous animal.

her·biv·o·rous (hûr biv'ər əs), *adj.* feeding on plants. —**her·biv'o·rous·ly,** *adv.*

her·cu·le·an (hûr'kyə lē'ən, hûr kyōō'-lē ən), *adj.* **1.** requiring exceptional strength or effort. **2.** having enormous strength, courage, or size.

Her·cu·les (hûr'kyə lēz'), *n. Class. Myth.* a celebrated hero possessing exceptional strength.

herd (hûrd), *n.* **1.** a number of animals kept, feeding, or traveling together. **2.** *Informal.* a large group of people. **3. the herd,** *Disparaging.* the common people. —*v.i., v.t.* **4.** to assemble or move as a herd. —**herd'er,** *n.*

herds·man (hûrdz'mən), *n., pl. -men.* a person who tends, drives, or owns a herd. —**herds'wom'an,** *n.fem.*

here (hēr), *adv.* **1.** in this place. **2.** to or toward this place: *Come here.* **3.** at this point. **4.** in the present life or existence. **5. neither here nor there,** immaterial. —*n.* **6.** this place. —*interj.* **7.** (used to command attention, give comfort, etc.)
—**Usage.** It is generally considered nonstandard to place HERE, for emphasis, in an adjectival position between a demonstrative adjective and a noun, as in *This here book is the one you're looking for.*

here·a·bout (hēr′ə bout′), *adv.* in this neighborhood. Also, **here′a·bouts′**.

here·af·ter (hēr af′tər, -äf′-), *adv.* **1.** after this in time or order. **2.** in the world to come. —*n.* **3.** a life after death.

here·by (hēr bī′, hēr′bī′), *adv.* as a result of this.

he·red·i·tar·y (hə red′i ter′ē), *adj.* **1.** passing, or capable of passing, genetically from parents to offspring. **2.** existing by reason of opinions or prejudices held by predecessors. **3.** holding title, rights, etc., by inheritance.

he·red·i·ty (hə red′i tē), *n., pl.* -ties. **1.** the transmission of genetic characters from parents to offspring. **2.** the genetic characters so transmitted.

Her·e·ford (hûr′fərd, her′ə-), *n.* one of an English breed of red beef cattle having a white face and white body markings.

here·in (hēr in′), *adv.* **1.** in or into this. **2.** in view of this.

here·of (hēr uv′, -ov′), *adv.* **1.** of this. **2.** concerning this.

here·on (hēr on′, -ôn′), *adv.* hereupon.

her·e·sy (her′i sē), *n., pl.* -sies. **1.** religious opinion or doctrine at variance with the orthodox or accepted doctrine. **2.** any belief or theory that is strongly at variance with established beliefs, mores, etc.

her·e·tic (her′i tik), *n.* a professed believer who maintains religious opinions contrary to those of his or her church. —**he·ret·i·cal** (hə ret′i kəl), *adj.* —**he·ret′i·cal·ly**, *adv.*

here·to (hēr tōō′), *adv.* to this matter, document, subject, etc. Also, **here·un·to** (hēr un′tōō, hēr′un tōō′).

here·to·fore (hēr′tə fôr′, -fōr′), *adv.* before this time.

here·un·der (hēr un′dər), *adv.* under or below this.

here·up·on (hēr′ə pon′, -pôn′), *adv.* **1.** upon or on this. **2.** immediately following this.

here·with (hēr with′, -with′), *adv.* **1.** along with this. **2.** by means of this.

her·it·a·ble (her′i tə bəl), *adj.* capable of being inherited.

her·it·age (her′i tij), *n.* **1.** something that comes or belongs to a person by reason of birth. **2.** any property, esp. land, that devolves by right of inheritance.

her·maph·ro·dite (hûr maf′rə dīt′), *n.* an animal, as an earthworm, or plant having normally both the male and female organs of generation. —**her·maph·ro·dit·ic** (hər maf′rə dit′ik), *adj.* —**her·maph′ro·dit′i·cal·ly**, *adv.*

Her·mes (hûr′mēz), *n.* the ancient Greek messenger of the gods.

her·met·ic (hûr met′ik), *adj.* **1.** made airtight by fusion or sealing. **2.** not affected by outward influence or power. Also, **her·met′i·cal.** —**her·met′i·cal·ly**, *adv.*

her·mit (hûr′mit), *n.* a person who has withdrawn to a solitary place for a life of religious seclusion.

her·mit·age (hûr′mi tij), *n.* **1.** the dwelling of a hermit. **2.** any secluded place of residence.

her·ni·a (hûr′nē ə), *n., pl.* -ni·as, -ni·ae (-nē ē′). the protrusion of an organ or tissue through an opening in its surrounding walls, esp. in the abdominal region. —**her′ni·al**, *adj.*

her·ni·ate (hûr′nē āt′), *v.i.,* -ated, -ating. to protrude so as to constitute a hernia. —**her′ni·a′tion**, *n.*

he·ro (hēr′ō), *n., pl.* -roes; for 4 also -ros. **1.** a man of distinguished courage or ability, admired for his brave deeds. **2.** a man who is regarded as having heroic qualities. **3.** the principal male character in a story, play, etc. **4.** See **hero sandwich.**

He·rod·o·tus (hi rod′ə təs), *n.* 484?–425? B.C., Greek historian.

he·ro·ic (hi rō′ik), *adj.* Also, **he·ro′i·cal. 1.** of or like a hero. **2.** suitable to the character of a hero in size or concept. **3.** extraordinarily bold, altruistic, or determined. —*n.* **4. heroics,** extravagant language or behavior. —**he·ro′i·cal·ly**, *adv.* —**he·ro′i·cal·ness**, *n.*

her·o·in (her′ō in), *n.* an addictive narcotic derived from morphine.

her·o·ine (her′ō in), *n.* **1.** a female hero. **2.** the principal female character in a story, play, etc.

her·o·ism (her′ō iz′əm), *n.* **1.** the qualities of a hero or heroine. **2.** heroic conduct.

her·on (her′ən), *n.* a long-legged, long-necked bird having a long bill and large wings.

he′ro sand′wich, a large sandwich consisting of a small loaf of white bread filled with meats, cheeses, onions, etc.

her·pes (hûr′pēz), *n.* an inflammation of the skin, characterized by clusters of tiny blisters. —**her·pet·ic** (hər pet′-ik), *adj.*

her′pes zos′ter (zos′tər), shingles.

her·pe·tol·o·gy (hûr′pi tol′ə jē), *n.* the branch of zoology dealing with reptiles and amphibians. —**her·pe·to·log·ic** (hûr′pi t°loj′ik), **her′pe·to·log′i·cal,** *adj.* —**her′pe·tol′o·gist**, *n.*

Herr (heR), *n., pl.* **Her·ren** (heR′ən). *German.* Mr. or sir.

her·ring (her′ing), *n., pl.* -ring, -rings. an important food fish found in the North Atlantic.

her·ring·bone (her′ing bōn′), *n.* **1.** a pattern consisting of adjoining vertical rows of slanting lines, any two contiguous lines forming either a V or an inverted V. **2.** something, as a fabric, having this pattern.

hers (hûrz), *pron.* **1.** a form of the possessive case of **she. 2.** that or those belonging to her: *Hers are the red ones.*

her·self (hər self'), *pron.* **1.** an emphatic appositive of *her* or *she: She .herself wrote the letter.* **2.** a reflexive form of *her: She supports herself.* **3.** her normal self: *After a few weeks of rest, she will be herself again.*

hertz (hûrtz), *n., pl.* **hertz.** a unit of frequency, equal to one cycle per second.

he's (hēz; *unstressed* ēz), contraction of: **a.** *he is.* **b.** *he has.*

hes·i·tant (hez'i tənt), *adj.* inclined to hesitate. —**hes'i·tan·cy,** *n.* —**hes'i·tant·ly,** *adv.*

hes·i·tate (hez'i tāt'), *v.i.,* **-tat·ed, -tat·ing. 1.** to wait to act because of fear, indecision, or disinclination. **2.** to have scruples or doubts. **3.** to pause or stop. **4.** to falter in speech. —**hes'i·tat'er,** *n.* —**hes'i·tat'ing·ly,** *adv.* —**hes'i·ta'tion,** *n.* —**Syn. 1.** vacillate, waver.

hetero-, a combining form meaning "different" or "other": *heterogeneous.*

het·er·o·dox (het'ər ə doks'), *adj.* **1.** not in accordance with established doctrines, esp. in theology. **2.** holding unorthodox doctrines. —**het'er·o·dox'y,** *n.*

het·er·o·ge·ne·ous (het'ər ə jē'nē əs, -jēn'yəs), *adj.* **1.** different in kind. **2.** composed of parts of different kinds. —**het'er·o·ge'ne·ous·ly,** *adv.* —**he'ter·o·ge'ne·ous·ness,** **het·er·o·ge·ne·i·ty** (het'ə rō jə nē'i tē), *n.*

het·er·o·sex·u·al (het'ər ə sek'shōō əl), *adj.* **1.** erotically directed toward the opposite sex. **2.** pertaining to the opposite sex or to both sexes. —*n.* **3.** a heterosexual person. —**het'er·o·sex'u·al'i·ty** (-al'i tē), *n.*

heu·ris·tic (hyōō ris'tik), *adj.* encouraging the student to discover for himself or herself.

hew (hyōō), *v.,* **hewed, hewed** or **hewn** (hyōōn), **hew·ing.** —*v.t.* **1.** to strike forcibly with an ax, sword, etc. **2.** to make or shape with cutting blows. —*v.i.* **3.** to uphold or conform: *to hew to the party line.* —**hew'er,** *n.*

HEW, Department of Health, Education, and Welfare.

hex (heks), *v.t.* **1.** to practice witchcraft on. —*n.* **2.** a spell or charm, usually associated with witchcraft.

hex., **1.** hexagon. **2.** hexagonal.

hexa-, a combining form meaning "six": *hexagon.*

hex·a·gon (hek'sə gon', -gən), *n.* a polygon having six angles and six sides. —**hex·ag·o·nal** (-sag'ə nəl), *adj.*

hex·a·he·dron (hek'sə hē'drən), *n., pl.* **-drons, -dra** (-drə). a solid figure having six faces. —**hex'a·he'dral,** *adj.*

hex·am·e·ter (hek sam'i tər). *n.* a line of verse in six metrical feet.

hex·a·pod (hek'sə pod'), *n.* an arthropod having six feet, esp. an insect.

hey (hā), *interj.* (an exclamation to call attention or to express pleasure, surprise, etc.)

hey·day (hā'dā'), *n.* the period of greatest vigor, strength, success, etc.

HF, See **high frequency.**

Hf, hafnium.

hf., half.

HG, High German.

Hg, *Chem.* mercury. [< L *hydrargyrum*]

hgt., height.

hgwy., highway.

H.H., 1. His (or Her) Highness. **2.** His Holiness.

hhd, hogshead; hogsheads.

hi (hī), *interj.* (an exclamation of greeting.)

HI, Hawaii.

H.I., Hawaiian Islands.

hi·a·tus (hī ā'təs), *n., pl.* **-tus·es, -tus.** a break or interruption in the continuity of a work, series, action, etc.

hi·ba·chi (hē bä'chē), *n.* a small Japanese charcoal stove. [< Jap: fire pot]

hi·ber·nate (hī'bər nāt'), *v.i.,* **-nat·ed, -nat·ing.** to spend the winter in a dormant condition, as certain animals. —**hi'ber·na'tion,** *n.* —**hi'ber·na'tor,** *n.*

hi·bis·cus (hī bis'kəs, hi-), *n.* a plant of the mallow family having large, showy flowers.

hic·cup (hik'up, -əp), *n., v.,* **-cuped** or **-cupped, -cup·ing** or **-cup·ping.** —*n.* **1.** a quick, involuntary inspiration suddenly checked by closure of the glottis, producing a short, relatively sharp sound. **2.** Usually, **hiccups.** the condition of having such spasms. —*v.i.* **3.** to make the sound of a hiccup. **4.** to have the hiccups. Also, **hic·cough** (hik'up, -əp).

hick (hik), *n. Informal.* a boorish, provincial person.

hick·ey (hik'ē), *n., pl.* **-eys.** any gadget or contrivance.

hick·o·ry (hik'ə rē, hik'rē), *n., pl.* **-ries. 1.** a North American tree of the walnut family which bears edible nuts or yields a valuable wood. **2.** its wood.

hi·dal·go (hi dal'gō), *n., pl.* **-gos.** a man of the lower nobility in Spain.

hid'den tax'. See **indirect tax.**

hide¹ (hīd), *v.,* **hid** (hid), **hid·den** (hid'ºn) or **hid, hid·ing.** —*v.t.* **1.** to prevent from being seen or discovered. **2.** to obstruct the view of. **3.** to keep secret. —*v.i.* **4.** to conceal oneself. **5.** to lie concealed. —**hid'er,** *n.*

hide² (hīd), *n.* the skin of an animal, raw or dressed.

hide-and-seek (hīd′ən sēk′), *n.* a children's game in which one player gives the other players a chance to hide and then attempts to find them.

hide·a·way (hīd′ə wā′), *n.* a place to which one can retreat.

hide·bound (hīd′bound′), *adj.* narrow and rigid in opinion.

hid·e·ous (hid′ē əs), *adj.* **1.** horrible or frightful to the senses. **2.** shocking to the moral sense. —**hid′e·ous·ly,** *adv.* —**hid′e·ous·ness,** *n.*

hide·out (hīd′out′), *n.* a safe place for hiding, esp. from the law.

hie (hī), *v.i., v.t.,* **hied, hie·ing** or **hy·ing.** *Literary.* to hasten (oneself).

hi·er·ar·chy (hī′ə rär′kē, hī′rär-), *n., pl.* **-chies.** **1.** any system of persons or things ranked one above another. **2.** government by ecclesiastical rulers. **3.** government by an elite group. —**hi′er·ar′chi·cal, hi′er·ar′chic,** *adj.* —**hi′er·ar′chi·cal·ly,** *adv.*

hi·er·o·glyph·ic (hī′ər ə glif′ik, hī′rə-), *n.* **1.** a symbol in a system of a pictographic script, esp. that of the ancient Egyptians. **2.** a symbol or character difficult to decipher.

hi·er·o·phant (hī′ər ə fant′, hī′rə-, hī er′ə-), *n.* a high priest in ancient Greece.

hi-fi (hī′fī′), *n.* **1.** See **high fidelity. 2.** equipment for sound reproduction with high fidelity.

hig·gle·dy-pig·gle·dy (hig′əl dē pig′əl-dē), *adv.* in a jumbled confusion.

high (hī), *adj.* **1.** reaching far upward. **2.** having a certain extent upward. **3.** exceeding the common degree or measure: *high speed; high color.* **4.** expensive or costly: *high prices.* **5.** exalted in rank, station, etc. **6.** acute in pitch. **7.** sharp or shrill. **8.** extending to or from an elevation: *a high dive.* **9.** grave or serious: *high treason.* **10.** haughty or arrogant. **11.** advanced to the utmost extent: *high tide.* **12.** elated or hilarious. **13.** extravagant or luxurious: *high living.* **14.** *Informal.* intoxicated with alcohol or drugs. **15.** remote: *high latitude.* **16.** (of meat, esp. game) slightly tainted. —*adv.* **17.** at or to a high point, place, or level. **18.** luxuriously or extravagantly. **19. high and low,** in every possible place. —*n.* **20.** a high point, place, or level. **21.** *Auto.* a transmission gear producing the highest speed. **22.** *Meteorol.* a center of relatively high pressure. **23.** a euphoric state, as one induced by drugs. **24. on high,** in heaven. —**high′ly,** *adv.* —**Syn. 1.** elevated, lofty, tall.

high·ball (hī′bôl′), *n.* a drink of whiskey or other liquor mixed with water, soda, or ginger ale.

high′ beam′, an automobile headlight beam providing long-range illumination.

high·born (hī′bôrn′), *adj.* of noble rank by birth.

high·boy (hī′boi′), *n.* a tall chest of drawers on legs.

high·bred (hī′bred′), *adj.* of superior breed.

high·brow (hī′brou′), *Informal.* —*n.* **1.** a person having or affecting superior intellectual interests and tastes. —*adj.* **2.** of or characteristic of a highbrow.

high·er-up (hī′ər up′), *n. Informal.* a person in a position of major authority in a organization.

high·fa·lu·tin (hī′fə lōōt′ən), *adj. Informal.* pompous or pretentious. Also, **hi′fa·lu′tin.**

high′ fidel′ity, sound reproduction over the full range of audible frequencies with very little distortion of the original. —**high′-fi·del′i·ty,** *adj.*

high-flown (hī′flōn′), *adj.* **1.** extravagant in aims, etc. **2.** pretentiously lofty.

high′ fre′quency, a radio frequency between 3 and 30 megahertz.

high′ gear′, high (def. 21).

High′ Ger′man, the West Germanic language as used in central and southern Germany.

high-hand·ed (hī′han′did), *adj.* arbitrarily overbearing. —**high′hand′ed·ly,** *adv.* —**high′hand′ed·ness,** *n.*

high-hat (hī′hat′), *v.,* **-hat·ted, -hat·ting,** *adj. Informal.* —*v.* **1.** to treat condescendingly. —*adj.* **2.** snobbish or disdainful.

high·land (hī′lənd), *n.* **1.** an elevated region. **2. highlands,** a mountainous region or elevated part of a country.

High·land·er (hī′lən dər), *n.* **1.** an inhabitant of the Highlands **2.** (*l.c.*) an inhabitant of any highland region.

High·lands (hī′ləndz), *n.* a mountainous region in N Scotland.

high-lev·el (hī′lev′əl), *adj.* **1.** by or of members having a high status. **2.** having high status.

high·light (hī′līt′), *v.,* **-light·ed, -lighting,** *n.* —*v.t.* **1.** to make prominent. **2.** to create highlights in (a photograph, etc.). —*n.* **3.** an important or conspicuous event, scene, etc. **4.** *Art.* the point of most intense light on a represented form.

high-mind·ed (hī′mīn′did), *adj.* having high, exalted principles or feelings. —**high′-mind′ed·ly,** *adv.* —**high′-mind′ed·ness,** *n.*

high·ness (hī′nis), *n.* **1.** the quality or state of being high. **2.** (*cap.*) a title of honor for a royal family.

high·pres·sure (hī′presh′ər), *adj.*, *v.*, **-sured, -sur·ing.** —*adj.* **1.** involving a pressure above the normal. **2.** making use of aggressively forceful and unrelenting methods, esp. in selling or advertising. —*v.t.* **3.** to persuade or promote by high-pressure methods.

high-rise (hī′rīz′), *adj.* **1.** (of a building) having a comparatively large number of stories and equipped with elevators. **2.** of or pertaining to high-rise buildings. —*n.* **3.** a high-rise apartment or office building.

high′ road′ (hī′rōd′), *n.* **1.** *Chiefly Brit.* a main road. **2.** an easy or certain course.

high′ school′, a school following elementary school and usually consisting of grades 9 through 12. —**high′-school′**, *adj.*

high′ sea′, the sea or ocean beyond the territorial waters of a country.

high′ sign′, *Slang.* a gesture, glance, etc., used as a warning or signal.

high-sound·ing (hī′soun′ding), *adj.* having a pretentious sound: *high-sounding titles.*

high-spir·it·ed (hī′spir′i tid), *adj.* **1.** characterized by energetic enthusiasm or vivacity. **2.** boldly courageous. —**high′-spir′it·ed·ness,** *n.*

high-strung (hī′strung′), *adj.* highly tense or nervous.

high-tail (hī′tāl′), *v.i. Informal.* to go away or leave rapidly.

high-ten·sion (hī′ten′shən), *adj.* operating under relatively high voltage.

high-test (hī′test′), *adj.* (of gasoline) boiling at a relatively low temperature.

high′ tide′, the tide at its highest level of elevation.

high′ time′, the time just before it is too late.

high-toned (hī′tōnd′), *adj.* **1.** marked by dignified, well-bred character. **2.** affectedly stylish.

high·way (hī′wā′), *n.* **1.** a main road, esp. one between towns or cities. **2.** any public passage.

high·way·man (hī′wā′mən), *n.* (formerly) a holdup man, esp. one on horseback, who robbed travelers along a public road.

hi·jack (hī′jak′), *v.t.* **1. a.** to steal (something) from a moving vehicle by stopping it. **b.** to rob (a moving vehicle) in similar manner. **c.** to seize (a moving vehicle) by force or threat of force. **2.** to skyjack. —*n.* **3.** the act or an instance of hijacking. Also, **high′jack′.** —**hi′jack′er,** *n.*

hike (hīk), *v.*, **hiked, hik·ing,** *n.* —*v.i.* **1.** to walk or march a great distance, esp. through rural areas for pleasure. —*v.t.* **2.** to move or raise with a jerk: *to hike up one's socks.* **3.** to increase or raise, often sharply. —*n.* **4.** a

long walk or march. **5.** an increase or rise. —**hik′er,** *n.*

hi·lar·i·ous (hi lâr′ē əs, -lar′-, hī-), *adj.* boisterously gay or merry. —**hi·lar′i·ous·ly,** *adv.* —**hi·lar′i·ty** (-lar′i tē), *n.*

hill (hil), *n.* **1.** a natural elevation of the earth's surface smaller than a mountain. **2.** an artificial heap, pile, or mound. —**hill′y,** *adj.* —**hill′i·ness,** *n.*

hill·bil·ly (hil′bil′ē), *n., pl.* **-lies.** *Informal.* a person from a backwoods area. [*hill* + *Billy* nickname for *William*]

hill·ock (hil′ək), *n.* a little hill.

hill·side (hil′sīd′), *n.* the side or slope of a hill.

hill·top (hil′top′), *n.* the top or summit of a hill.

hilt (hilt), *n.* **1.** the handle of a sword or dagger. **2. to the hilt,** completely or fully.

him (him; *unstressed* im), *pron.* the objective case of *he*.

Him·a·la·yas (him′ə lā′əz, hi mäl′yəz), *n. the,* a mountain range extending across central Asia. —**Him′a·la′yan,** *adj.*

him·self (him self′), *pron.* **1.** an emphatic appositive of *him* or *he*: *He himself spoke to the men.* **2.** a reflexive form of *him*: *He cut himself.* **3.** his normal self.

hind[1] (hīnd), *adj.* situated in the rear or back, esp. of an animal.

hind[2] (hīnd), *n.* the female of the deer, chiefly the red deer.

hind[3] (hīnd), *n. Brit. Dial.* a farm laborer.

Hind., **1.** Hindi. **2.** Hindu. **3.** Hindustan. **2.** Hindustani.

hin·der[1] (hin′dər), *v.t.* **1.** to cause delay or difficulty in. **2.** to prevent from doing or happening. —**hin′der·er,** *n.* —**Syn. 1.** hamper, impede, obstruct.

hind·er[2] (hīn′dər), *adj.* hind[1].

Hin·di (hin′dē), *n.* the official and most widely spoken language in India.

hind·most (hīnd′mōst′), *adj.* nearest the rear.

hind·quar·ter (hīnd′kwôr′tər), *n.* **1.** the posterior end of a halved carcass of beef, lamb, etc. **2. hindquarters,** the rear part of an animal.

hin·drance (hin′drəns), *n.* **1.** the act of hindering or state of being hindered. **2.** a person or thing that hinders.

hind·sight (hīnd′sīt′), *n.* recognition of the nature and requirements of a situation or event after its occurrence.

Hin·du (hin′dōō), *n.* **1.** a person who adheres to Hinduism. **2.** a native of Hindustan or India. —*adj.* **3.** of the people of Hindustan or India. **4.** of Hindus or Hinduism.

Hin·du·ism (hin′dōō iz′əm), *n.* the common and dominant religion of India.

Hin·du·stan (hin′dōō stän′, -stan′), *n.* 1. a region in N central India. 2. the predominantly Hindu areas of India.

Hin·du·sta·ni (hin′dōō stä′nē, -stan′ē), *n.* a language of northern India based on a dialect of Hindi.

hinge (hinj), *n., v.,* **hinged, hing·ing.** —*n.* 1. a jointed device on which a door, gate, or lid turns or swings. 2. a natural anatomical joint, as that of the knee. —*v.i.* 3. to be dependent or contingent: *Everything hinges on his decision.* —*v.t.* 4. to furnish with or attach by hinges. —**hinge′less,** *adj.*

hint (hint), *n.* 1. an indirect or covert suggestion or implication. 2. a hardly noticeable amount. —*v.t., v.i.* 3. to give a hint (of). —**hint′er,** *n.* —Syn. 3. imply, intimate, suggest.

hin·ter·land (hin′tər land′), *n.* 1. the land lying behind a coastal district. 2. the remote area of a country.

hip[1] (hip), *n.* 1. the projecting part of each side of the body formed by the side of the pelvis and the upper part of the thighbone. 2. See **hip joint.** —**hip′py,** *adj.*

hip[2] (hip), *n.* the ripe fruit of a rose, esp. of a wild rose.

hip[3] (hip), *adj.,* **hip·per, hip·pest.** *Slang.* 1. familiar with the latest ideas, styles, etc. 2. informed or knowledgeable.

hip·bone (hip′bōn′), *n.* See **innominate bone.**

hip·hug·gers (hip′hug′ərz), *n.* slacks that are belted or fastened at the hips rather than at the waist.

hip′ joint′, the joint between the thighbone and the pelvis.

hipped[1] (hipt), *adj.* 1. having hips. 2. having hips as specified: *narrowhipped.*

hipped[2] (hipt), *adj. Informal.* greatly interested or preoccupied: *He's hipped on golf.*

hip·pie (hip′ē), *n.* a usually middleclass, young nonconformist who often lives in a commune, wears nonconventional clothing, and often takes psychedelic drugs. Also, **hip′py.** —**hip′pie·dom,** *n.*

hip·po (hip′ō), *n., pl.* **-pos.** *Informal.* hippopotamus. [by shortening]

Hip·poc·ra·tes (hi pok′rə tēz′), *n.* c460–c377? B.C., Greek physician.

hip·po·drome (hip′ə drōm′), *n.* an arena for equestrian and other spectacles.

hip·po·pot·a·mus (hip′ə pot′ə məs), *n., pl.* **-mus·es, -mi** (-mī′), a large mammal having a thick hairless body, found in and near rivers in Africa. [< L < Gk *hippopótamos* river horse]

hip·ster (hip′stər), *n. Slang.* a person who is hip, esp. to the latest ideas, styles, etc

hire (hī°r), *v.,* **hired, hir·ing,** *n.* —*v.t.* 1. to engage the services of for pay. 2. to engage the temporary use of at a set price. 3. **hire out,** to offer one's services for pay. —*n.* 4. the price or compensation paid in hiring. 5. the act of hiring or condition of being hired.

hire·ling (hī°r′ling), *n.* a person who serves for pay, esp. one motivated only by a desire for pay or gain.

Hi·ro·shi·ma (hēr′ō shē′mə, hi rō′shi-mə), *n.* a seaport on SW Honshu, in SW Japan: first military use of atomic bomb August 6, 1945.

hir·sute (hûr′sōōt, hûr sōōt′), *adj.* unusually hairy. —**hir′sute·ness,** *n.*

his (hiz; *unstressed* iz), *pron.* 1. the possessive form of **he.** 2. that or those belonging to him: *I borrowed a tie of his.*

His·pan·ic (hi span′ik), *adj.* 1. Spanish. 2. Latin-American. —*n.* 3. Also, **His·pa′no** (-pa′nō, -pä′nō). an American citizen or resident of Spanish descent.

His·pan·io·la (his′pən yō′lə; *Sp.* ēs′pän yō′lä), *n.* an island in the West Indies.

hiss (his), *v.i.* 1. to make a sharp sound like that of the letter *s* when prolonged. 2. to express disapproval by making this sound. —*v.t.* 3. to express disapproval of by hissing. —*n.* 4. a hissing sound, esp. one made in disapproval. —**hiss′er,** *n.*

hist., 1. historian. 2. historical. 3. history.

his·ta·mine (his′tə mēn′, -min), *n.* an organic compound released from human tissues during allergic reactions. —**his·ta·min·ic** (his′tə min′ik), *adj.*

his·to·gram (his′tə gram′), *n. Statistics.* a graph of a frequency distribution in which rectangles with bases on the horizontal axis are given widths equal to the class intervals and heights equal to the corresponding frequencies.

his·tol·o·gy (hi stol′ə jē), *n.* the branch of biology dealing with the study of tissues. —**his·tol′o·gist,** *n.*

his·tol·y·sis (hi stol′i sis), *n.* the disintegration or dissolution of organic tissues. —**his·to·lyt·ic** (his′tə lit′ik), *adj.*

his·to·ri·an (hi stôr′ē ən, -stôr′-), *n.* 1. an authority on history. 2. a writer of history.

his·tor·ic (hi stôr′ik, -stor′-), *adj.* 1. well-known in history. 2. historical (defs. 1, 2).

his·tor·i·cal (hi stôr'i kəl, -stor'-), *adj.*
1. of or pertaining to history. 2.
based on history or on documented
material from the past. 3. historic
(def. 1). —**his·tor'i·cal·ly,** *adv.*

his·to·ric·i·ty (his'tə ris'i tē), *n.* historical authenticity.

his·to·ri·og·ra·pher (hi stôr'ē og'rə fər, -stôr'-), *n.* an official historian, as of a court.

his·to·ri·og·ra·phy (hi stôr'ē og'rə fē, -stôr'-), *n.* the body of techniques and principles of historical research.

his·to·ry (his'tə rē, his'trē), *n., pl.* -ries.
1. the branch of knowledge dealing with past events. 2. a systematic narrative of past events as relating to a particular people, country, etc. 3. the record of past events. 4. a past that is full of important events.

his·tri·on·ic (his'trē on'ik), *adj.* 1. of actors or acting. 2. affected in behavior or speech. —**his'tri·on'i·cal·ly,** *adv.*

his·tri·on·ics (his'trē on'iks), *n.* 1. dramatic representation. 2. affected behavior or speech done for effect.

hit (hit), *v.*, **hit, hit·ting,** *n.* —*v.t.* 1. to give a blow to. 2. to come against with an impact or collision. 3. to reach with a missile or a weapon, as by throwing or shooting. 4. *Baseball.* to make (a hit). 5. to request or demand of: *He hit me for a loan.* 6. to reach or attain (a specified level or amount): *The new train can hit 100 mph.* 7. to meet with or find: *to hit the right answer.* 8. to suit exactly. —*v.i.* 9. to deal a blow. 10. to come or light: *to hit on a new way.* 11. **hit it off,** *Informal.* to be congenial. —*n.* 12. an impact or collision. 13. a stroke that reaches an object. 14. *Baseball.* See **base hit.** 15. a successful stroke, performance, or production: *The play is a hit.* 16. **hit or miss,** haphazardly. —**hit'ter,** *n.*

hit-and-run (hit'ᵊn run'), *adj.* guilty of leaving the scene of an accident caused by a vehicle driven by oneself: *a hit-and-run driver.*

hitch (hich), *v.t.* 1. to fasten or tie, as with a hook, rope, etc. 2. to raise with jerks: *to hitch up one's trousers.* 3. to hitchhike (a ride). 4. *Slang.* to unite in marriage. —*v.i.* 5. to stick or become fastened. 6. to move roughly or jerkily. 7. to hitchhike. —*n.* 8. a kind of knot or loop. 9. *Slang.* a period of military service. 10. an unexpected delay or obstruction. 11. a jerk or pull. 12. a hobble or limp. —**hitch'er,** *n.*

hitch·hike (hich'hīk'), *v.*, -hiked, -hiking. —*v.i.* 1. to travel by getting free automobile rides. —*v.t.* 2. to get (a ride) by hitchhiking. —**hitch'hik'er,** *n.*

hith·er (hiᵗʰ'ər), *Literary.* —*adv.* 1. toward this place. —*adj.* 2. being on this side.

hith·er·to (hiᵗʰ'ər tōō'), *adv.* until now.

Hit·ler (hit'lər), *n.* **Ad·olf** (ad'olf, ä'dolf), 1889–1945, Nazi dictator of Germany 1933–45.

Hit·ler·ism (hit'lə riz'əm), *n.* Nazism as developed by Hitler.

hit' man', *Slang.* a professional killer for hire.

hit-or-miss (hit'ər mis'), *adj.* careless or haphazard.

hive (hīv), *n., v.,* **hived, hiv·ing.** —*n.* 1. a shelter for honeybees. 2. the bees inhabiting a hive. 3. a place swarming with busy occupants. 4. a swarming or teeming multitude. —*v.t.* 5. to gather into a hive. —*v.i.* 6. to enter a hive, as bees.

hives (hīvz), *n.* urticaria.

H.J., here lies. [< L *hīc jacet*]

H.L., House of Lords.

H.M., His (or Her) Majesty.

HMO, health maintenance organization.

H.M.S., 1. His (or Her) Majesty's Service. 2. His (or Her) Majesty's Ship.

Ho, holmium.

ho., house.

hoa·gy (hō'gē), *n., pl.* **-gies.** *Northeastern U.S.* See **hero sandwich.** Also, **hoa'gie.**

hoard (hōrd, hôrd), *n.* 1. a supply that is hidden or carefully guarded for future use. —*v.t., v.i.* 2. to accumulate a hoard (of). —**hoard'er,** *n.*

hoard·ing (hōr'ding, hôr'-), *n. Brit.* 1. a billboard. 2. a temporary fence enclosing a construction site.

hoar·frost (hōr'frôst', -frost', hôr'-), *n.* frost (def. 1).

hoarse (hōrs, hôrs), *adj.,* **hoars·er, hoars·est.** 1. harsh and low in sound. 2. having a raucous voice. —**hoarse'ly,** *adv.* —**hoarse'ness,** *n.*

hoars·en (hōr'sən, hôr'-), *v.t., v.i.* to make or become hoarse.

hoar·y (hōr'ē, hôr'ē), *adj.,* **hoar·i·er, hoar·i·est.** 1. gray or white, esp. with age. 2. ancient or venerable. —**hoar'i·ness,** *n.*

hoax (hōks), *n.* 1. a mischievous deception, esp. a practical joke. 2. something intended to deceive or defraud. —*v.t.* 3. to deceive by a hoax. —**hoax'er,** *n.*

hob¹ (hob), *n.* a projection at the back or side of a fireplace, used for keeping food warm.

hob² (hob), *n.* 1. a hobgoblin or elf. 2. **play or raise hob with,** *Informal.* to cause mischief or trouble.

hob·ble (hob'əl), *v.,* **-bled, -bling,** *n.* —*v.i.* 1. to walk lamely. —*v.t.* 2. to cause to limp. 3. to fasten together the legs of (a horse, etc.) by a rope to prevent free motion. **4.** to hamper the progress of. —*n.* **5.** an uneven, halting gait. **6.** a rope, strap, etc., used to hobble an animal. —**hob′bler,** *n.*

hob·ble·de·hoy (hob′əl dē hoi′), *n.* an awkward, clumsy youth.

hob′ble skirt′, a woman's skirt that is very narrow at the bottom.

hob·by (hob′ē), *n., pl.* **-bies. 1.** an activity or interest pursued for pleasure or relaxation. **2.** a child's hobbyhorse. —**hob′by·ist,** *n.*

hob·by·horse (hob′ē hôrs′), *n.* **1.** a stick with a horse's head, or a rocking horse, ridden by children. **2.** a pet idea or project.

hob·gob·lin (hob′gob′lin), *n.* **1.** anything causing superstitious fear. **2.** a mischievous goblin.

hob·nail (hob′nāl′), *n.* a large-headed nail for protecting the soles of heavy boots and shoes. —**hob′nailed′** (-nāld′), *adj.*

hob·nob (hob′nob′), *v.i.,* **-nobbed, -nob·bing.** to associate on very friendly terms.

ho·bo (hō′bō), *n., pl.* **-bos, -boes. 1.** a vagabond tramp. **2.** a migratory worker.

Ho Chi Minh (hō′ chē′ min′), 1890?–1969, North Vietnamese political leader.

Ho′ Chi′ Minh′ Cit′y, a port city in S Vietnam. Formerly, Saigon.

hock¹ (hok), *n.* the joint in the hind leg of a horse, cow, etc., corresponding to the ankle in a human.

hock² (hok), *v.t., n. Informal.* pawn¹ (defs. 1, 3, 4).

hock·ey (hok′ē), *n.* **1.** See **ice hockey. 2.** See **field hockey.**

hock·shop (hok′shop′), *n. Informal.* a pawnshop.

ho·cus-po·cus (hō′kəs pō′kəs), *n.* **1.** a meaningless formula used in conjuring or incantation. **2.** a juggler's trick or sleight of hand. **3.** trickery or deception. [sham-Latin formula used by magicians]

hod (hod), *n.* **1.** a portable trough for carrying mortar, bricks, etc., on the shoulder. **2.** a coal scuttle.

hodge·podge (hoj′poj′), *n.* a heterogeneous mixture.

Hodg·kin's disease′ (hodj′kinz), a disease characterized by progressive chronic inflammation and enlargement of the lymph nodes.

hoe (hō), *n., v.,* **hoed, hoe·ing.** —*n.* **1.** a long-handled implement having a thin, flat blade usually set transversely, used to break up the surface of the ground or destroy weeds. —*v.t., v.i.* **2.** to dig or weed. —**ho′er,** *n.*

hoe·cake (hō′kāk′), *n. Southern U.S.* a cake made with cornmeal.

hoe·down (hō′doun′), *n.* **1.** a community party typically featuring square

dancing. **2.** the country music typical of a hoedown.

hog (hôg, hog), *n., v.,* **hogged, hogging.** —*n.* **1.** a domesticated swine raised for market. **2.** *Informal.* a selfish, gluttonous, or filthy person. **3. go the whole hog,** *Informal.* to carry to the utmost extent. Also, **go whole hog. 4. live or eat high off the hog,** *Informal.* to be in prosperous circumstances. —*v.t.* **5.** *Slang.* to take more than one's share of. —**hog′gish,** *adj.* —**hog′gish·ly,** *adv.*

ho·gan (hō′gôn, -gən), *n.* a Navaho Indian dwelling constructed of earth and branches and covered with mud or sod.

hog·back (hôg′bak′, hog′-), *n.* a long, sharply crested ridge formed of steeply inclined strata.

hogs·head (hôgz′hed′, hogz′-), *n.* **1.** a large cask, esp. one containing from 63 to 140 gallons. **2.** a liquid measure equivalent to 63 gallons.

hog·tie (hôg′tī, hog′-), *v.t.,* **-tied, -ty·ing. 1.** to tie (an animal) with all four feet together. **2.** *Informal.* to hamper or thwart.

hog·wash (hôg′wosh′, -wôsh′, hog′-), *n.* **1.** refuse given to hogs. **2.** *Slang.* meaningless or insincere talk, writing, etc.

hog-wild (hôg′wīld′, hog′-), *adj. Informal.* wildly enthusiastic or excited.

hoi pol·loi (hoi′ pə loi′), *Often Contemptuous.* the common people (often preceded by *the*). [< Gk: the many]

hoist (hoist), *v.t.* **1.** to raise or lift, esp. by some mechanical appliance. —*n.* **2.** an apparatus for hoisting, as a block and tackle. **3.** the act of hoisting. **4.** the height of a flag as flown from a vertical staff. —**hoist′er,** *n.*

hoke (hōk), *v.,* **hoked, hok·ing.** *n. Slang.* —*v.t.* **1.** to contrive or fake. —*n.* **2.** hokum. —**ho′key,** *adj.*

ho·kum (hō′kəm), *n. Informal.* **1.** nonsense or bunk. **2.** sentimental matter of a stereotyped kind introduced into a play, novel, etc.

hold¹ (hōld), *v.,* **held, hold·ing,** *n.* —*v.t.* **1.** to keep in the hand. **2.** to reserve or retain. **3.** to sustain or support, as with the hands. **4.** to keep in a specified state or relation: *He held them spellbound.* **5.** to detain or delay. **6.** to engage in or carry on: *to hold a meeting.* **7.** to keep back from action. **8.** to occupy: *to hold political office.* **9.** to contain: *This bottle holds a quart.* **10.** to think or believe. **11.** to regard or consider: *I hold you responsible.* **12.** to keep forcibly, as against an adversary. —*v.i.* **13.** to continue in a specified state or relation: *to hold still.* **14.** to remain fast. **15.** to maintain one's position against opposition. **16.** to remain attached or faithful: *to hold to one's purpose.* **17.** to remain valid: *The rule does not hold.* **18. hold forth, a.** to extend or offer. **b.** to talk at great length. **19. hold out, a.** to present or offer. **b.** to continue to exist. **c.** to refuse to yield. **d.** *Slang.* to withhold something expected. **20. hold over, a.** to postpone. **b.** to remain beyond the arranged period. **21. hold up, a.** to present to notice. **b.** to hinder or delay. **c.** to stop by force in order to rob. **d.** to support or uphold. **e.** to endure. **22. hold with, a.** to be in agreement with or concur with. **b.** to approve of or condone. —*n.* **23.** the act of holding fast by a grasp of the hand: *Take hold. Get hold of the rope.* **24.** something to hold a thing by. **25.** a thing that holds something else. **26.** an order reserving something. **27.** a dominating influence: *to have a hold on a person.* **28.** a pause or delay, as in a continuing series. **29.** a prison or prison cell. **30.** a receptacle for something. **31.** *Archaic.* a stronghold. —**hold′er,** *n.*

hold² (hōld), *n.* **1.** the entire cargo space in the hull of a vessel. **2.** the cargo compartment of an aircraft.

hold·ing (hōl′dǐng), *n.* **1.** a section of land leased. **2.** Often, **holdings.** legally owned property, esp. stocks, bonds, or real estate.

hold′ing pat′tern, a traffic pattern for planes while waiting to be cleared for landing.

hold·o·ver (hōld′ō′vər), *n.* a person or thing remaining from a former period.

hold·up (hōld′ŭp′), *n.* **1.** a forcible stopping and robbing of a person. **2.** a stop or delay.

hole (hōl), *n., v.,* **holed, hol·ing.** —*n.* **1.** an opening through something. **2.** a hollow place in a solid body. **3.** an animal's burrow. **4.** a small, dingy, or shabby place. **5.** an embarrassing position or predicament. **6.** a fault or flaw. **7.** *Golf.* **a.** the cup in a green into which the ball is to be played. **b.** a part of a golf course leading to it. **8.** *Electronics.* a mobile vacancy in the electronic structure of a semiconductor that acts as a positive charge carrier. **9. in the hole,** in debt. —*v.t., v.i.* **10.** to make a hole (in). **11. hole up, a.** to retire for the winter, as a hibernating animal. **b.** *Slang.* to hide, as from the police.

hol·i·day (hǒl′ǐ dā′), *n.* **1.** a day fixed by law or custom on which ordinary business is suspended in commemoration of some event or person. **2.** any day of exemption from work. **3.**

a religious feast day. **4.** *Chiefly Brit.* a vacation. —*adj.* **5.** festive or joyous.

ho·li·er-than-thou (hō′lē ər t͟hən t͟hou′), *adj.* sanctimonious or self-righteous.

ho·li·ness (hō′lē nis), *n.* **1.** the quality or state of being holy. **2.** (*cap.*) a title of the pope (prec. by *His* or *Your*).

ho·lism (hō′liz əm), *n.* **1.** *Philos.* the theory that whole entities of reality have an existence greater than the mere sum of their parts. **2.** the principle that a part is understandable only in its relationship to the whole. —**ho′list,** *n.* —**ho·lis′tic,** *adj.*

Hol·land (hǒl′ənd), *n.* the Netherlands. —**Hol′land·er,** *n.*

hol′lan·daise sauce′ (hǒl′ən dāz′, hǒl′-ən dāz′), a rich sauce made of egg yolks, butter, lemon juice, etc.

hol·ler (hǒl′ər), *v.i., v.t. Informal.* to shout or yell.

hol·low (hǒl′ō), *adj.* **1.** having a space or cavity inside. **2.** having a depression or concavity. **3.** sunken, as the eyes. **4.** dull or muffled: *a hollow voice.* **5.** without worth: *a hollow victory.* **6.** having an empty feeling. —*n.* **7.** a hollow place. **8.** a valley. —*v.t.* **9.** to make or become hollow. —**hol′low·ness,** *n.*

hol·low·ware (hǒl′ō wâr′), *n.* silver dishes having some depth.

hol·ly (hǒl′ē), *n., pl.* **-lies.** a tree or shrub having glossy leaves, whitish flowers, and red berries.

hol·ly·hock (hǒl′ē hok′, -hôk′), *n.* a tall plant of the mallow family having showy flowers of various colors.

Hol·ly·wood (hǒl′ē wood′), *n.* the NW part of Los Angeles, California: motion-picture studios.

hol·mi·um (hōl′mē əm), *n. Chem.* a rare-earth element. *Symbol:* Ho; *at. wt.:* 164.930; *at. no.:* 67.

hol·o·caust (hǒl′ə kôst′, hō′lə-), *n.* devastation, esp. by fire.

Hol·o·cene (hǒl′ə sēn′, hō′lə-), *Geol.* —*adj.* **1.** recent (def. 3). —*n.* **2.** recent (def. 4).

hol·o·crine (hǒl′ə krin, -krīn′, hō′lə-), *adj.* producing a secretion formed by disintegration of glandular cells.

ho·lo·gram (hō′lə gram′, hǒl′ə-), *n.* a true three-dimensional photograph recorded on film by a reflected laser beam of a subject.

hol·o·graph (hǒl′ə graf′, -gräf′, hō′lə-), *n.* a document wholly written by the person in whose name it appears. —**hol′o·graph′ic,** *adj.*

ho·log·ra·phy (hə log′rə fē), *n.* the process or technique of making holograms. —**hol·o·graph′ic,** *adj.*

Hol·stein (hōl′stīn, hōl′stēn), *n.* a breed of black-and-white dairy cattle yielding large quantities of low-fat milk. Also called **Hol'stein-Frie'sian** (-frē'zhən).

hol·ster (hōl'stər), *n.* a leather case for a pistol, attached to a belt.

ho·ly (hō'lē), *adj.*, **-li·er**, **-li·est**. **1.** declared sacred by religious use: *holy ground.* **2.** of religious purity or exaltation: *a holy love.* **3.** entitled to religious reverence: *a holy relic.* —**Syn. 1.** consecrated, hallowed.

Ho'ly Commun'ion, communion (def. 4).

Ho'ly Grail', Grail.

Ho'ly Land', Palestine.

Ho'ly Ro'man Em'pire, an empire in central and W Europe from 962 to 1806.

Ho'ly Spir'it, the third person of the Trinity. Also called **Ho'ly Ghost'**.

ho·ly·stone (hō'lē stōn'), *n.* a soft sandstone used in scrubbing the decks of a vessel.

ho'ly wa'ter, water blessed by a priest.

hom·age (hom'ij, om'-), *n.* reverential respect.

hom·burg (hom'bûrg), *n.* a man's felt hat with a soft crown dented lengthwise and a slightly rolled brim.

home (hōm), *n., adj., adv., v.,* **homed**, **hom·ing.** —*n.* **1.** a place of residence. **2.** the place in which one's domestic affections are centered. **3.** an institution for the homeless, sick, etc.: *a veterans' home.* **4.** the dwelling place or retreat of an animal. **5.** the native place or region of a thing. **6.** any place of refuge. **7.** a person's native place or country. **8.** a principal base of operations or activities. **9.** *Baseball.* See **home plate**. **10. at home, a.** in one's own house. **b.** at ease. **c.** well-informed or proficient. —*adj.* **11.** of or pertaining to one's home, country, or government. **12.** *Sports.* played in a team's home town: *a home game.* **13.** principal or main: *a home office.* —*adv.* **14.** to, toward, or at home. **15.** deeply or to the heart. **16.** to the mark aimed at: *Her arguments hit home.* **17. bring home to,** to make evident to. **18. home free,** *Slang.* safe, secure, or settled. —*v.i.* **19.** to go or return home. —**home'less**, *adj.* —**home'like**, *adj.*

home' base', **1.** *Baseball.* See **home plate**. **2.** home (def. 8).

home·bod·y (hōm'bod'ē), *n.* a person whose pleasures and activities center around the home.

home·bred (hōm'bred'), *adj.* **1.** bred or raised at home. **2.** native or domestic.

home·com·ing (hōm'kum'ing), *n.* **1.** a return to one's home. **2.** an annual event held by a university for visiting alumni.

home' econom'ics, the art and science

of home management, including nutrition, child development, etc.

home-grown (hōm'grōn'), *adj.* **1.** grown or produced at home: *home-grown tomatoes.* **2.** native or indigenous.

home·land (hōm'land'), *n.* a person's native land.

home·ly (hōm'lē), *adj.*, **-li·er**, **-li·est.** **1.** not beautiful or attractive. **2.** not having elegance. **3.** plain or unpretentious. **4.** commonly seen or known. —**home'li·ness**, *n.*

home-made (hōm'mād'), *adj.* **1.** made or prepared at home. **2.** not professionally made or done.

home·mak·er (hōm'mā'kər), *n.* a person who manages a home, esp. a housewife. —**home'mak'ing**, *n.*

ho·me·op·a·thy (hō'mē op'ə thē), *n.* the method of treating disease by drugs, given in minute doses, that would produce in a healthy person symptoms similar to those of the disease. —**ho·me·o·path·ic** (hō'mē ə path'ik), *adj.*

ho·me·o·sta·sis (hō'mē ə stā'sis), *n.* the tendency of a physiological system to maintain internal stability, owing to the coordinated response of its parts to any disruptive situation or stimulus. —**ho·me·o·stat·ic** (hō'mē ə stat'ik), *adj.*

home' plate', *Baseball.* the base at which the batter stands and which a base runner must reach safely in order to score a run.

Ho·mer (hō'mər), *n.* 8th century B.C., Greek epic poet —**Ho·mer·ic** (hō-mer'ik), *adj.*

home·room (hōm'rōom', -rōom'), *n.* a school classroom in which pupils of the same grade meet at certain times, as at the beginning of the day.

home' run', *Baseball.* a hit that enables a batter to score a run by making a nonstop circuit of the bases. Also called **hom·er** (hō'mər).

home' screen', *Informal.* television.

home·sick (hōm'sik'), *adj.* longing for home while away from it, as when traveling a long time. —**home'sick'ness**, *n.*

home·spun (hōm'spun'), *adj.* **1.** spun or made at home: *homespun cloth.* **2.** made of such cloth. **3.** plain or unpolished. —*n.* **4.** a plain-weave cloth made at home or of homespun yarn. **5.** any cloth of similar appearance.

home·stead (hōm'sted, -stid), *n.* a dwelling with its land and buildings. —**home'stead'er**, *n.*

home·stretch (hōm'strech'), *n.* **1.** the straight part of a racetrack from the last turn to the finish line. **2.** the final phase of any endeavor.

home·ward (hōm'wərd), *adv.* **1.** Also, **home'wards.** toward home. —*adj.* **2.** directed toward home.

home·work (hōm'wûrk'), *n.* **1.** schoolwork assigned to be done outside the classroom. **2.** any work done at home, esp. piecework.

home·y (hō'mē), *adj.*, **hom·i·er, hom·i·est.** comfortably informal and inviting. —**home'y·ness,** *n.*

hom·i·cide (hom'i sīd'), *n.* **1.** the killing of one human being by another. **2.** a person who kills another. —**hom'i·ci'dal,** *adj.*

hom·i·let·ics (hom'ə let'iks), *n.* the art of writing and preaching sermons. —**hom'i·let'ic,** *adj.*

hom·i·ly (hom'ə lē), *n., pl.* **-lies. 1.** a sermon, esp. of a plain, nondoctrinal nature. **2.** an admonitory or moralizing discourse.

hom·ing (hō'ming), *adj.* **1.** capable of returning home, usually over a great distance. **2.** guiding or directing homeward or to a destination, esp. by mechanical means.

hom'ing pi'geon, any pigeon used to carry messages and equipped by training and breeding to fly home.

hom·i·ny (hom'ə nē), *n.* whole or ground hulled corn with the bran and germ removed.

hom'iny grits', finely ground hominy.

ho·mo (hō'mō), *adj., n., pl.* **-mos.** *Slang.* homosexual.

Ho·mo (hō'mō), *n.* the primate genus that includes modern human beings and a number of related extinct species.

homo-, a combining form meaning "same" or "like": *homogeneous.*

ho·mo·ge·ne·ous (hō'mə jē'nē əs, -jēn'yəs, hom'ə-), *adj.* **1.** composed of parts all of the same kind. **2.** of the same kind or nature. —**ho'mo·ge·ne'i·ty** (-jə nē'i tē), **ho'mo·ge'ne·ous·ness,** *n.* —**ho'mo·ge'ne·ous·ly,** *adv.*

ho·mog·e·nize (hə moj'ə nīz', hō-), *v.t.,* **-nized, -niz·ing. 1.** to make homogeneous. **2.** to break up the fat globules in (milk or cream) in order to distribute them throughout. —**ho·mog'e·ni·za'tion,** *n.* —**ho·mog'e·niz'er,** *n.*

hom·o·graph (hom'ə graf', -gräf'), *n.* a word of the same written form as another but of different origin and meaning, whether pronounced the same way or not, as *lead* (to conduct) and *lead* (the metal). —**hom·o·graph·ic** (hom'ə graf'ik), *adj.*

ho·mol·o·gous (hə mol'ə gəs, hō-), *adj.* corresponding in relative position, structure, etc.

hom·o·nym (hom'ə nim), *n.* **1.** a word the same as another in sound and spelling but different in meaning, as *chase* (to pursue) and *chase* (to ornament metal). **2.** (loosely) a. a homophone. **b.** a homograph. —**hom'o·nym'ic,** *adj.*

ho·mo·phile (hō'mə fīl'), *n.* **1.** a homosexual person. —*adj.* **2.** advocating the civil rights and welfare of homophiles: *a homophile organization.*

hom·o·phone (hom'ə fōn', hō'mə-), *n.* a word pronounced the same as but differing in meaning from another, whether spelled the same way or not, as *heir* and *air.*

Ho'mo sa'pi·ens (sā'pē ənz), the human race.

ho·mo·sex·u·al (hō'mə sek'shōō əl, -mō-), *adj.* **1.** of or exhibiting sexual desire toward a person of one's own sex. —*n.* **2.** a homosexual person. —**ho'mo·sex'u·al'i·ty,** *n.*

hom·y (hō'mē), *adj.,* **hom·i·er, hom·i·est.** homey.

Hon., 1. Honorable. **2.** Honorary.

hon., 1. honor. **2.** honorable.

hon·cho (hon'chō'), *n., pl.* **-chos.** *Informal.* a chief or boss. [< Jap: *han* squad + *cho* leader]

Hon·du·ras (hon dŏŏr'əs, -dyŏŏr'-), *n.* a country in NE Central America. —**Hon·du'ran,** *adj., n.*

hone (hōn), *n., v.,* **honed, hon·ing.** —*n.* **1.** a whetstone of fine, compact texture. —*v.t.* **2.** to sharpen on or as on a hone. —**hon'er,** *n.*

hon·est (on'ist), *adj.* **1.** honorable in principles, intentions, and actions. **2.** gained fairly: *honest wealth.* **3.** sincere and frank: *an honest face.* **4.** genuine or unadulterated: *honest weights.* **5.** having a good reputation. **6.** truthful or creditable. —**hon'est·ly,** *adv.* —**hon'es·ty, hon'est·ness,** *n.* —**Syn. 1.** fair, just, upright.

hon'est bro'ker, *Informal.* an impartial intermediary or arbitrator.

hon·ey (hun'ē), *n.* **1.** a sweet, viscid fluid produced by bees from the nectar collected from flowers. **2.** something sweet or delicious. **3.** (*often cap.*) darling or sweetheart. —**hon'eyed,** *adj.*

hon'ey·bee (hun'ē bē'), *n.* a bee that collects and stores honey.

hon·ey·comb (hun'ē kōm'), *n.* **1.** a structure of hexagonal wax cells, formed by bees to store honey and their eggs. **2.** anything whose appearance suggests such a structure. —*v.t.* **3.** to cause to be full of holes like a honeycomb.

hon·ey·dew (hun'ē dōō', -dyōō'), *n.* a sugary material secreted by aphids.

hon'eydew mel'on, a sweet-flavored, white-fleshed muskmelon having a smooth, pale-green rind.

hon·ey·moon (hun'ē mōōn'), *n.* **1.** a vacation taken by a newly married couple. **2.** any new relationship characterized by an initial period of harmony. —*v.i.* **3.** to spend one's honeymoon. —**hon'eymoon'er,** *n.*

hon'eymoon bridge', *Cards.* any of several varieties of bridge for two players.

hon·ey·suck·le (hun′ē suk′əl), *n.* an upright or climbing shrub cultivated for fragrant white, yellow, or red tubular flowers.

Hong·kong (hong′kong′), *n.* a British colony in SE China. Also, **Hong′ Kong′**.

honk (hongk, hôngk), *n.* **1.** the cry of a goose. **2.** any similar sound, as of an automobile horn. —*v.i., v.t.* **3.** to make or cause to make a honk. —**honk′er,** *n.*

hon·ky (hong′kē), *n., pl.* **hon·kies.** *Disparaging.* a white person: used esp. by blacks. Also, **hon′key, hon′kie.**

honk·y·tonk (hong′kē tongk′, hông′kē tôngk′), *n. Informal.* a cheap, noisy nightclub or dance hall.

Hon·o·lu·lu (hon′ə lōō′lōō), *n.* the capital of Hawaii.

hon·or (on′ər), *n.* **1.** high public esteem. **2.** honesty or integrity in one's beliefs and actions. **3.** a source of credit or distinction. **4.** high respect, as for worth, merit, or rank. **5.** such respect manifested. **6.** (*cap.*) a title of respect, esp. for judges and mayors (prec. by *Your, His,* or *Her*). **7. honors, a.** an academic recognition given to an outstanding student. **b.** an advanced course of study for superior students. **8.** chastity or purity in a woman. **9. do the honors,** to serve as host. —*v.t.* **10.** to hold in high respect. **11.** to confer honor or distinction upon. **12.** to show a courteous regard for. **13.** to accept or pay (a draft, check, etc.). —*adj.* **14.** of, pertaining to, or noting honor. Also, *esp. Brit.,* **hon′our.** —**hon′or·er,** *n.* —**Syn. 1.** fame, glory, repute. **4.** deference, reverence.

hon·or·a·ble (on′ər ə bəl), *adj.* **1.** characterized by principles of honor or integrity. **2.** of high rank or distinction. **3.** worthy of honor and high respect. **4.** bringing honor or credit. **5.** (*cap.*) **a.** (used as a title of respect for certain ranking government officials.) **b.** *Brit.* (used as a title of courtesy for children of peers ranking below a marquis.)

hon·o·rar·i·um (on′ə râr′ē əm), *n., pl.* **-rar·i·ums, -rar·i·a** (-râr′ē ə). a reward for professional services for which custom or propriety forbids a price to be set.

hon·or·ar·y (on′ə rer′ē), *adj.* **1.** given for honor only: *an honorary degree.* **2.** holding a title or position conferred for honor only: *an honorary president.* **3.** given or serving as a token of honor. —**hon′or·ar′i·ly,** *adv.*

hon·or·if·ic (on′ə rif′ik), *adj.* **1.** doing or conferring honor. —*n.* **2.** a title or term of respect. —**hon′or·if′i·cal·ly,** *adv.*

Hon·shu (hon′shōō), *n.* an island in central Japan: chief island of the country.

hooch (hōōch), *n. Slang.* alcoholic liquor.

hood[1] (hōōd), *n.* **1.** a soft or flexible covering for the head and neck, often attached to a coat or cloak. **2.** something resembling or suggesting such a covering, esp. in shape. **3.** the part of an automobile body covering the engine. —**hood′ed,** *adj.*

hood[2] (hōōd, hŏŏd), *n.* .*Slang.* hoodlum.

-hood, a suffix meaning: **a.** state or condition: *childhood.* **b.** character or nature: *likelihood.* **c.** a body of persons of a particular class: *priesthood.*

hood·lum (hōōd′ləm, hŏŏd′-), *n.* a young street ruffian, esp. one belonging to a gang.

hoo·doo (hōō′dōō), *n.* **1.** bad luck. **2.** a person or thing that brings bad luck. **3.** voodoo.

hood·wink (hŏŏd′wingk′), *v.t.* to deceive, esp. by trickery.

hoo·ey (hōō′ē), *Informal.* —*interj.* **1.** (to express disapproval or disbelief.) —*n.* **2.** nonsense or hokum.

hoof (hŏŏf, hōōf), *n., pl.* **hoofs** or **hooves,** *v.* —*n.* **1.** the horny covering protecting the ends of the toes or encasing the foot in certain animals, as the ox, horse, etc. **2.** the entire foot of a horse, donkey, etc. —*v.t.* **3.** *Slang.* to walk: *Let's hoof it to the supermarket.* —*v.i.* **4.** *Slang.* to dance. —**hoofed** (hŏŏft, hōōft), *adj.*

hook (hŏŏk), *n.* **1.** a curved or angular piece of metal, etc., for catching, pulling, or suspending something. **2.** a fishhook. **3.** something having a curve or angle like a hook. **4.** *Boxing.* a short, circular punch delivered with the elbow bent. **5. by hook or by crook,** by any means. Also, by **hook or crook. 6. hook, line, and sinker.** *Informal.* entirely or completely. **7. off the hook,** *Slang.* out of trouble. —*v.t.* **8.** to seize, fasten, or suspend from, with or as with a hook. **9.** to catch (fish) with a fishhook. **10.** *Slang.* to seize by stealth. —*v.i.* **11.** to become hooked. **12.** to curve or bend like a hook. **13. hook up, a.** to fasten with a hook or hooks. **b.** to assemble or connect, often for temporary or experimental use: *to hook up water to a mobile home.*

hook·ah (hŏŏk′ə), *n.* a tobacco pipe of Near Eastern origin with a long, flexible tube by which the smoke is drawn through a jar of water and thus cooled. Also, **hook′a.**

hook′ and eye′, a clothing fastener consisting of a metal hook attached to a loop.

hooked (hŏŏkt), *adj.* **1.** bent like a hook. **2.** made with a hook or by hooking. **3.** *Slang.* addicted to or obsessed with anything, esp. narcotics. **4.** *Slang.* married.

hook·er (hŏŏk'ər), *n. Slang.* prostitute.

hook·up (hŏŏk'up'), *n.* an assembly and connection of circuits or equipment, often for temporary or experimental use.

hook·worm (hŏŏk'wûrm'), *n.* a bloodsucking worm that is parasitic in the intestine of human beings and animals.

hook·y (hŏŏk'ē), *n. Informal.* truancy (usually used in the phrase *to play hooky*).

hoo·li·gan (hōō'lə gən), *n. Chiefly Brit.* hoodlum.

hoop (hōōp, hŏŏp), *n.* **1.** a circular band of metal or wood, used esp. for holding together the staves of a cask, tub, etc. **2.** a large ring of iron or plastic, used as a plaything. **3.** a ringlike object, figure, etc. **4.** a circular band of stiff material used to expand a woman's skirt. —**hoop'less,** *adj.*

hoop·la (hōōp'lä), *n. Informal.* **1.** bustling excitement or activity. **2.** speech or writing intended to mislead or bewilder.

hoop' skirt', a woman's skirt made to bell out by a framework of flexible hoops.

hoo·ray (hŏŏ rā'), *interj., v.i., n.* hurrah.

hoose·gow (hōōs'gou), *n. Slang.* a jail. Also, **hoos'gow.** [< MexSp *jusga(d)o*]

Hoo·sier (hōō'zhər), *n.* a native or inhabitant of Indiana.

hoot (hōōt), *v.i.* **1.** to cry out or shout, esp. in disapproval or derision. **2.** to utter the cry characteristic of an owl. —*v.t.* **3.** to drive out, off, or away by hooting. —*n.* **4.** the cry of an owl. **5.** a cry or shout, esp. of disapproval or derision. —**hoot'er,** *n.*

hoot·en·an·ny (hōōt'ə nan'ē), *n., pl.* **-nies.** a social gathering featuring folk singing.

Hoo·ver (hōō'vər), *n.* Herbert (Clark), 1874–1964, 31st president of the U.S. 1929–33.

hop¹ (hop), *v., hopped, hop·ping, n.* —*v.i.* **1.** to make a short, bouncing leap. **2.** to spring or leap on one foot. **3.** to make a flight or any short, quick trip. —*v.t.* **4.** to jump over. **5.** *Informal.* to board or get onto a vehicle. —*n.* **6.** a short leap. **7.** a leap on one foot. **8.** *Informal.* a short trip, esp. by air. **9.** *Informal.* a dance or dancing party.

hop² (hop), *n., v., hopped, hop·ping.* —*n.* **1.** a twining plant grown for its conelike flowers. **2. hops,** its

dried female flower cones, used in brewing, medicine, etc. —*v.t.* **3. hop up,** *Slang.* **a.** to stimulate, esp. with drugs. **b.** to add to the power of.

hope (hōp), *n., v., hoped, hop·ing.* —*n.* **1.** the feeling that what is wanted can be had or that events will turn out for the best. **2.** a particular instance of this feeling. **3.** grounds for this feeling in a particular instance. **4.** a person in whom or thing in which expectations are centered. —*v.t.* **5.** to look forward to with desire and reasonable confidence. **6.** to believe or trust. —*v.i.* **7.** to have hope. **8. hope against hope,** to continue to hope, although the situation does not warrant it. —**hope'less,** *adj.* —**hope'less·ly,** *adv.* —**hope'less·ness,** *n.* —**hop'er,** *n.*

hope·ful (hōp'fəl), *adj.* **1.** full of hope. **2.** exciting hope. —*n.* **3.** a promising or aspiring young person. —**hope'ful·ness,** *n.*

hope·ful·ly (hōp'fə lē), *adv.* **1.** in a hopeful manner. **2.** it is hoped.

hop·head (hop'hed'), *n. Slang.* a drug addict.

Ho·pi (hō'pē), *n., pl.* **-pis, -pi. 1.** a member of an Indian people of northern Arizona. **2.** the language of the Hopi Indians.

hop·per (hop'ər), *n.* **1.** a person or thing that hops. **2.** any jumping insect. **3.** a funnel-shaped bin with an opening at the bottom for dispensing its contents.

hop·sack·ing (hop'sak'ing), *n.* a coarse fabric of cotton, wool, etc., similar to burlap, used for apparel.

hop·scotch (hop'skoch'), *n.* a children's game in which a player tosses a small stone into one of several numbered sections of a diagram marked on the ground and then hops on one foot from section to section, picking up the stone on his or her return.

hor., **1.** horizon. **2.** horizontal.

ho·ra (hôr'ə, hōr'ə), *n.* a traditional Israeli round dance. [< Heb < Rum < Turk]

Hor·ace (hôr'is, hor'-), *n.* 65–8 B.C., Roman poet. —**Ho·ra·tian** (hə rā'shən), *adj.*

horde (hôrd, hōrd), *n., v., hord·ed, hord·ing.* —*n.* **1.** a large, moving throng. —*v.i.* **2.** to gather in a horde.

hore·hound (hôr'hound', hōr'-), *n.* **1.** a perennial herb containing a bitter, medicinal juice. **2.** a brittle candy or lozenge flavored with its juice.

ho·ri·zon (hə rī'zən), *n.* **1.** the line that forms the apparent boundary between earth and sky. **2.** the range of perception or knowledge. [< L < Gk *horízōn (kýklos)* bounding (circle)]

hor·i·zon·tal (hôr′i zon′t°l, hor′-), adj.
1. parallel to the horizon. 2. flat
or level. 3. of, near, or on the
horizon. —**hor′i·zon′tal·ly**, adv.

hor·mone (hôr′mōn), n. an internally
secreted compound formed in endocrine organs which affects the functions of specifically receptive organs
or tissues when carried to them by
the body fluids. —**hor·mo′nal**, adj.

horn (hôrn), n. 1. one of the bony
paired growths on the head of certain
hoofed mammals. 2. the bony substance of which such animal growths
are composed. 3. something resembling or suggesting an animal horn.
4. a. a wind instrument, usually
made of metal or plastic. b. See
French horn. 5. an instrument for
sounding a warning signal: an automobile horn. —v.t. 6. **horn in,** Slang.
to intrude or interrupt. —**horned**
(hôrnd), adj. —**horn′less,** adj. —
horn′like′, adj. —**horn′y,** adj.

Horn (hôrn), n. **Cape,** a headland
at the S extremity of South America
on an island belonging to Chile.

horn·book (hôrn′bŏŏk′), n. 1. a leaf
or page containing the alphabet, a
prayer, etc., covered with a sheet of
transparent horn, formerly used in
teaching children to read. 2. a book
of rudiments.

horned′ toad′, a small harmless lizard
with flattened body and hornlike
spines.

hor·net (hôr′nit), n. a large, stinging
social wasp.

horn′ of plen′ty, cornucopia.

horn·pipe (hôrn′pīp′), n. a lively
jiglike dance performed usually by
one person, esp. a sailor.

horol., horology.

ho·rol·o·gy (hō rol′ə jē, hô-), n. the
science of making timepieces or of
measuring time. —**hor′o·log′i·cal,**
adj. —**ho·rol′o·gist,** n.

hor·o·scope (hôr′ə skōp′, hor′-), n.
a diagram of the heavens, showing
the relative positions of planets and
the signs of the zodiac, for use in
foretelling events in a person's life.

hor·ren·dous (hô ren′dəs, ho-), adj.
perfectly horrible. —**hor·ren′dous·ly,**
adv.

hor·ri·ble (hôr′ə bəl, hor′-), adj. 1.
causing or tending to cause horror.
2. extremely unpleasant. —**hor′ri-
ble·ness,** n. —**hor′ri·bly,** adv.

hor·rid (hôr′id, hor′-), adj. 1. such as
to cause horror. 2. extremely disagreeable. —**hor′rid·ly,** adv. —**hor′-
rid·ness,** n.

hor·ri·fy (hôr′ə fī′, hor′-), v.t., **-fied,**
-fy·ing. 1. to cause to feel horror.
2. to shock extremely.

hor·ror (hôr′ər, hor′-), n. 1. an
overwhelming and painful feeling
caused by something frightfully

shocking. 2. anything that causes
such a feeling. 3. a strong aversion.
—Syn. 1. dread, fear, terror.

hors de com·bat (ôr də kôn bA′),
French. no longer able to fight.

hors d'oeu·vre (ôr dûrv′), pl. **hors
d'oeuvre, hors d'oeuvres** (ôr dûrvz′).
an appetizer, often served on crackers or small pieces of toast.

horse (hôrs), n., pl. **hors·es, horse,** v.,
horsed, hors·ing, adj. —n. 1. a large,
solid-hoofed, herbivorous quadruped
domesticated as a draft and riding
animal. 2. a frame with legs on
which something is supported. 3.
Slang. horsepower. 4. **hold one's
horses,** to check one's impulsiveness.
—v.t. 5. to provide with a horse or
horses. 6. to set on horseback. 7.
horse around, Slang. to indulge in
horseplay. —**horse′less,** adj.

horse·back (hôrs′bak′), n. 1. the back
of a horse. —adv. 2. on horseback.

horse′ chest′nut, 1. a tree having
large leaves and upright clusters of
showy white, red, or yellow flowers.
2. its seed.

horse·feath·ers (hôrs′feth′ərz), Slang.
—n. 1. something not worth considering. —interj. 2. (to express
contemptuous rejection.)

horse·flesh (hôrs′flesh′), n. 1. the flesh
of a horse. 2. horses collectively,
esp. for riding, racing, etc.

horse·fly (hôrs′flī′), n. a large bloodsucking fly that is a serious pest to
horses, cattle, etc.

horse·hair (hôrs′hâr′), n. 1. the hair
of a horse, esp. from the mane or
tail. 2. a sturdy fabric woven of
this hair.

horse·hide (hôrs′hīd′), n. 1. the hide
of a horse. 2. leather made from
this. 3. Slang. a baseball.

horse′ laugh′ (hôrs′laf′, -läf′), n. a loud,
coarse laugh, esp. of derision.

horse·man (hôrs′mən), n. 1. a man
who rides on horseback. 2. a man
skilled in riding horses. 3. a man
who owns, breeds, or tends horses.
—**horse′man·ship′,** n. —**horse′wom-
an,** n. fem.

horse′ op′era, Slang. a film or television play dealing with the Wild West.

horse·play (hôrs′plā′), n. rough or
boisterous play or pranks.

horse·play·er (hôrs′plā′ər), n. a habitual bettor on horse races.

horse·pow·er (hôrs′pou′ər), n. a unit
for computing the power of an engine, equivalent to 550 foot-pounds
per second.

horse·rad·ish (hôrs′rad′ish), n. 1. a
perennial plant cultivated for its
fleshy, pungent root. 2. a condiment
made by grinding this root.

horse′ sense′, *Informal.* plain, practical common sense.

horse·shoe (hôrs′shŏŏ′, hôrsh′-), *n.* **1.** a U-shaped metal plate nailed to a horse's hoof to protect it from wear on hard surfaces. **2.** something U-shaped, as a valley. **3. horseshoes,** a game in which horseshoes or other U-shaped pieces of metal or plastic are tossed at a stake. **—horse′sho′-er,** *n.*

horse·tail (hôrs′tāl′), *n.* a perennial plant having hollow, jointed stems.

horse·whip (hôrs′hwip′, -wip′), *n., v.,* **-whipped, -whip·ping. —n. 1.** a whip for controlling horses. **—v.t. 2.** to beat with a horsewhip.

hors·y (hôr′sē), *adj.,* **hors·i·er, hors·i·est. 1.** of, pertaining to, or characteristic of a horse or horses. **2.** dealing with horses or sports involving them. Also, **hors′ey.**

hort., **1.** horticultural. **2.** horticulture.

hor·ta·to·ry (hôr′tə tôr′ē, -tōr′ē), *adj.* urging to some course of good conduct or action. Also, **hor′ta·tive** (-tiv).

hor·ti·cul·ture (hôr′tə kul′chər), *n.* the science and art of cultivating flowers, fruits, vegetables, or ornamental plants. **—hor′ti·cul′tur·al,** *adj.* **—hor′ti·cul′tur·ist,** *n.*

ho·san·na (hō zan′ə), *interj.* (an exclamation in praise of God or Christ.)

hose (hōz), *n., pl.* **hos·es** for 1, **hose** for 2; *v.,* **hosed, hos·ing. —n. 1.** a flexible tube for conveying a liquid, as water, to a desired point. **2.** stockings or socks. **—v.t. 3.** to water, wash, or spray with a hose.

ho·sier·y (hō′zhə rē), *n.* stockings and socks of any kind.

hosp., hospital.

hos·pice (hos′pis), *n.* a shelter for pilgrims or strangers, esp. one kept by a religious order.

hos·pi·ta·ble (hos′pi tə bəl, ho spit′ə-bəl), *adj.* receiving or treating guests or strangers warmly and generously. **2.** favorably receptive: *to be hospitable to new ideas.* **—hos′pi·ta·ble·ness,** *n.* **—hos′pi·ta·bly,** *adv.*

hos·pi·tal (hos′pi t°l), *n.* an institution in which sick or injured persons are given medical or surgical treatment.

hos·pi·tal·i·ty (hos′pi tal′i tē), *n., pl.* **-ties.** hospitable reception, treatment, quality, or disposition.

hos·pi·tal·ize (hos′pi t°liz′), *v.t.,* **-ized, -iz·ing.** to place in, or admit to, a hospital. **—hos′pi·tal·i·za′tion,** *n.*

host[1] (hōst), *n.* **1.** a person who receives or entertains guests. **2.** a master of ceremonies or moderator for a television or radio program. **3.** a living animal or plant from which a parasite obtains nutrition. **—v.t. 4.** to act as host at, to, or for.

host[2] (hōst), *n.* **1.** a great number of persons or things. **2.** *Archaic.* an army.

Host (hōst), *n.* the consecrated wafer of the Eucharist.

hos·tage (hos′tij), *n.* a person given or held as security for the fulfillment of certain conditions or terms.

hos·tel (hos′t°l), *n.* a supervised lodging place for young people. [< OF < LL *hospitāle* guest room]

hos·tel·ry (hos′t°l rē), *n., pl.* **-ries.** *Literary.* an inn.

host·ess (hō′stis), *n.* **1.** a female host. **2.** a woman employed to assist patrons, as at a restaurant. **—v.t. 3.** to act as hostess at, to, or for.

hos·tile (hos′t°l *or, esp. Brit.,* -tīl), *adj.* **1.** opposed in feeling, action, or character. **2.** of or characteristic of an enemy. **—hos′tile·ly,** *adv.* **—Syn. 1.** antagonistic, unfriendly.

hos·til·i·ty (ho stil′i tē), *n., pl.* **-ties. 1.** a hostile state, condition, or attitude. **2.** a hostile act. **3. hostilities,** acts of warfare.

hos·tler (hos′lər, os′lər), *n.* a person who takes care of horses, esp. at an inn.

hot (hot), *adj.,* **hot·ter, hot·test,** *adv.* **—adj. 1.** having a relatively or extremely high temperature. **2.** having or causing a sensation of great bodily heat. **3.** peppery or pungent. **4.** having or showing intense or violent feeling: *hot temper.* **5.** lustful or lascivious. **6.** violent, furious, or intense: *the hottest battle of the war.* **7.** absolutely new: *hot from the press.* **8.** *Slang.* following very closely: *hot pursuit.* **9.** *Slang.* extremely lucky: *a hot crapshooter.* **10.** *Slang.* sensational or scandalous: *a hot news story.* **11.** *Slang.* stolen recently. **12.** actively conducting an electric current: *a hot wire.* **13.** of or noting radioactivity. **14. make it hot for,** *Informal.* to cause trouble for. **—adv. 15.** in a hot manner. **—hot′ly,** *adv.* **—hot′ness,** *n.*

hot′ air′, *Slang.* boastful talk or writing.

hot·bed (hot′bed′), *n.* **1.** a glass-covered bed of earth heated by fermenting manure, for growing plants out of season. **2.** a place or environment favoring the rapid growth of something, esp. something bad.

hot-blood·ed (hot′blud′id), *adj.* **1.** excitable or impetuous. **2.** ardent or passionate.

hot·box (hot′boks′), *n. Railroads.* a metal journal shaft overheated by excessive friction.

hot′ cake′, **1.** a pancake. **2. sell or go like hot cakes,** to be disposed of very quickly.

hot′ dog′, a cooked frankfurter, esp. one served in a split roll.

ho·tel (hō tel′), *n.* a commercial establishment offering lodging and usually meals to the general public. [< F *hôtel* < OF *hostel* hostel]

ho·tel·ier (ō tel yā′), *n.* a manager or owner of a hotel.

hot′ flash′, a sensation of heat passing over the entire body, often experienced by women before and during the menopause.

hot·foot (hot′fŏot′), *n.* a practical joke in which a match, inserted surreptitiously between the sole and upper of the victim's shoe, is lighted and allowed to burn down.

hot·head (hot′hed′), *n.* a hotheaded person.

hot·head·ed (hot′hed′id), *adj.* 1. fiery in temper. 2. easily angered. —**hot′-head′ed·ly,** *adv.* —**hot′head′ed·ness,** *n.*

hot·house (hot′hous′), *n.* a heated greenhouse for tender plants.

hot′ line′, 1. a direct Teletype or telephone line for instant communication between two chiefs of state in case of international crisis. 2. any direct telephone line used for instant contact, counseling, etc.

hot′ plate′, a portable electric appliance for cooking.

hot′ pota′to, *Informal.* a situation or issue that is unpleasant or risky to deal with.

hot′ rod′, *Slang.* a car, esp. an old one, whose engine has been altered or replaced for increased speed. —**hot′ rod′der.**

hot′ seat′, *Slang.* See **electric chair.**

hot·shot (hot′shot′), *n. Slang.* a flamboyantly skillful person.

hot′ wa′ter, *Informal.* a troublesome predicament.

hound (hound), *n.* 1. a dog trained to pursue game either by sight or by scent, esp. one with a long face and large drooping ears. 2. *Informal.* an addict or devotee: *an autograph hound.* —*v.t.* 3. to hunt or track with hounds. 4. to pursue or harass without respite. 5. *Informal.* to urge (a person) to do something. —**hound′er,** *n.*

hound′s′ tooth′, a pattern of broken or jagged checks, often used on fabrics. Also, **hound′s-tooth check′.**

hour (our, ou′ər), *n.* 1. the 24th part of a day, equivalent to 60 minutes. 2. any specific time of day. 3. a customary or usual time: *dinner hour.* 4. **hours,** time spent for work, business, etc.: *store hours.* 5. one unit of academic credit, usually representing attendance at one scheduled period of instruction per week.

hour·glass (our′glas′, -gläs′, ou′ər-), *n.*

an instrument for measuring time by the draining of sand or mercury from a top to a bottom glass bulb.

hou·ri (hŏor′ē, hour′ē), *n., pl.* **-ris.** one of the beautiful virgins of the Muslim paradise.

hour·ly (our′lē, ou′ər-), *adj.* 1. of, occurring, or done each successive hour. 2. frequent or continual. —*adv.* 3. at each hour. 4. frequently or continually.

house (*n.* hous; *v.* houz), *n., pl.* **houses** (hou′ziz), *v.,* **housed, hous·ing.** —*n.* 1. a building in which people live. 2. a household. 3. (*often cap.*) a family, including ancestors and descendants. 4. a building for any purpose: *a house of worship.* 5. a theater. 6. the audience of a theater or concert hall. 7. a place of shelter for an animal, bird, etc. 8. (*cap.*) a legislative or deliberative body. 9. (*often cap.*) a commercial establishment. 10. **keep house,** to maintain a home. 11. **on the house,** as a gift from management. —*v.t.* 12. to provide a house or living quarters. 13. to hold, store, or shelter. —**house′ful,** *n.* —**house′less,** *adj.*

house′ arrest′, confinement of an arrested person to his or her residence.

house·boat (hous′bōt′), *n.* a flat-bottomed, bargelike boat fitted for use as a floating dwelling.

house·boy (hous′boi′), *n.* a man employed for general domestic work, esp. a native male servant employed in a white family's home in Asia.

house·break·ing (hous′brā′king), *n.* the breaking into and entering of a house with felonious intent. —**house′-break′er,** *n.*

house·bro·ken (hous′brō′kən), *adj.* (of a pet) trained to avoid excreting in improper places.

house·coat (hous′kōt′), *n.* a woman's one-piece garment for casual wear.

house·fly (hous′flī′), *n.* a common two-winged fly that lives in houses and feeds on food, garbage, etc.

house·hold (hous′hōld′, -ōld′), *n.* 1. the people of a house collectively. 2. a home and its related affairs. —*adj.* 3. of a household. 4. common or usual.

house·hold·er (hous′hōl′dər, -ōl′-), *n.* 1. a person who holds title to or occupies a house. 2. the head of a family.

house′hold word′, a well-known word or phrase. Also, **house′hold name′.**

house·hus·band (hous′huz′bənd), *n.* a man who is married to a working wife and who stays home to manage their household.

house·keep·er (hous′kē′pər), *n.* a person, usually hired, who runs or manages a home. —**house′keep′ing,** *n.*

house·lights (hous′līts′), *n.pl.* the lamps providing illumination of the seating area of a theater.

house·maid (hous′mād′), *n.* a female servant for housework.

house·man (hous′man′, -mən), *n.* **1.** a houseboy. **2.** *Brit.* a medical intern.

house·moth·er (hous′muth′ər), *n.* a woman in charge of a residence, esp. for young women, who acts as chaperon, and often housekeeper.

House′ of Com′mons, the lower house of the British or Canadian Parliament.

House′ of Lords′, the upper house of the British Parliament.

House′ of Represen′tatives, the lower legislative branch in many national and state bicameral governing bodies, as in the United States, etc.

house·sit (hous′sit′), *v.t.* -sat, -sitting. to take charge of a house while the owner is temporarily away. — **house′ sit′ter.**

house·top (hous′top′), *n.* the roof of a house.

house·wares (hous′wârz′), *n.pl.* articles of household equipment.

house·warm·ing (hous′wôr′ming), *n.* a party to celebrate a person's or family's occupancy of a new house.

house·wife (hous′wīf′ *or, usually,* huz′if *for* 2), *n.* **1.** a married woman who manages her own household, esp. as her principal occupation. **2.** *Brit. Obsolesc.* a small case or box for needles, thread, etc. —**house′wife/ly,** *adj.* —**house′wife/li·ness,** *n.* —**house′wif′er·y,** *n.*

house·work (hous′wûrk′), *n.* the work of cleaning, cooking, etc., to be done in housekeeping. —**house′work′er,** *n.*

hous·ing¹ (hou′zing), *n.* **1.** any shelter or lodging. **2.** houses collectively. **3.** the providing of houses for a community. **4.** anything that covers or protects.

hous·ing² (hou′zing), *n.* **1.** a protective or ornamental covering for a saddle. **2.** housing, the trappings on a horse.

Hous·ton (hyōō′stən), *n.* a city in SE Texas.

hove (hōv), *v.* a pt. and pp. of **heave.**

hov·el (huv′əl, hov′-), *n.* a wretched hut.

hov·er (huv′ər, hov′-), *v.i.* **1.** to hang fluttering or suspended in the air. **2.** to keep lingering about. **3.** to remain in an uncertain state.

Hov·er·craft (huv′ər kraft′, -kräft′), *n.* *Trademark.* a vehicle that can travel rapidly over water or smooth terrain on a cushion of air.

how (hou), *adv.* **1.** in what way or manner? **2.** to what extent, degree, etc.?: *How damaged is the car?* **3.** in what state or condition? **4.** for what reason? **5.** with what meaning?: *How is one to interpret his ac-*

tion? **6.** what?: *If they don't have vanilla, how about chocolate?* **7.** at what price: *How do you sell these tomatoes?* **8.** (used as an intensifier): *How seldom I go there!* **9. how come?** why? —*conj.* **10.** the manner or way in which: *He knew how to solve the problem.* **11.** however: *You can travel how you please.*

how·be·it (hou bē′it), *adv.* **1.** *Archaic.* nevertheless. —*conj.* **2.** *Obs.* although.

how·dah (hou′də), *n.* a seat placed on the back of an elephant.

how-do-you-do (hou′də yə dōō′), *n. Informal.* an awkward or unpleasant situation. Also, **how-de-do** (hou′dē-dōō′).

how·e′er (hou âr′), *adv., conj. Literary.* however.

how·ev·er (hou ev′ər), *adv.* **1.** nevertheless or yet. **2.** to whatever extent or degree. —*conj.* **3.** in whatever manner or state.

how·itz·er (hou′it sər), *n.* a cannon that fires shells at a high angle of elevation.

howl (houl), *v.i.* **1.** to utter a loud, prolonged, mournful cry, as that of a dog or wolf. **2.** to utter a similar cry in distress, rage, etc. **3.** *Informal.* to laugh loudly. —*v.t.* **4.** to utter with howls. **5.** to drive or force by howls. —*n.* **6.** the cry of a dog, wolf, etc. **7.** any similar cry or sound. **8.** something hilariously funny.

howl·er (hou′lər), *n.* **1.** a person or thing that howls. **2.** *Informal.* a humorous or embarrassing blunder.

howl·ing (hou′ling), *adj.* **1.** producing a howling noise. **2.** *Informal.* tremendous: *a howling success.*

how·so·ev·er (hou′sō ev′ər), *adv.* **1.** to whatsoever extent or degree. **2.** in whatsoever manner.

how-to (hou′tōō), *adj.* giving basic instructions to lay people on some methods: *a how-to book.*

hoy·den (hoid′ᵊn), *n.* a boisterous, ill-bred girl.

Hoyle (hoil), *n.* **1.** a handbook on card games originally prepared by English writer Edmond Hoyle (1672–1769). **2. according to Hoyle,** according to the rules or authority.

hp, horsepower. Also, **HP**

H.P., 1. *Elect.* high power. **2.** high pressure. **3.** horsepower. Also, **h.p.**

H.Q., headquarters. Also, **h.q., HQ**

hr., hour; hours. Also, **hr**

H.R., House of Representatives.

H.R.H., His (or Her) Royal Highness.

H.S., High School.

HST, 1. Hawaiian Standard Time. **2.** hypersonic transport.

H.T., *Elect.* high-tension.

ht., height.

Hts., Heights (used in place names).

hua·ra·che (wə rä′chē), *n.* a Mexican sandal having the upper woven of leather strips.

hub (hub), *n.* **1.** the central part of a wheel, propeller, fan, etc. **2.** a center of activity.

hub·bub (hub′ub), *n.* **1.** a loud, confused noise, as of many voices. **2.** a tumult or uproar.

hub·cap (hub′kap′), *n.* a removable metal covering for the hub of an automobile wheel.

hu·bris (hyōō′bris, hōō′-), *n.* excessive pride or self-confidence.

huck·le·ber·ry (huk′əl ber′ē), *n.* **1.** the dark-blue or black edible berry of a shrub closely related to the blueberry. **2.** the shrub itself.

huck·ster (huk′stər), *n.* **1.** a peddler, esp. of fruits and vegetables. **2.** *Informal.* **a.** a persuasive and aggressive salesperson. **b.** a person who prepares advertising, esp. for radio and TV.

HUD (hud), *n.* Department of Housing and Urban Development.

hud·dle (hud′əl), *v.,* **-dled, -dling,** *n.* —*v.t., v.i.* **1.** to crowd together closely. **2.** to draw (oneself) closely together. —*n.* **3.** a closely gathered group or heap. **4.** a conference or consultation, esp. a private one. **5.** *Football.* a gathering of the team behind the line of scrimmage for instructions, signals, etc. —**hud′dler,** *n.*

Hud·son (hud′sən), *n.* a river in E New York.

Hud′son Bay′, a large inland sea in N Canada.

hue (hyōō), *n.* **1.** the property of light by which the color of an object is classified as red, blue, green, or yellow in reference to the spectrum. **2.** a gradation or variety of a color. —**hued** (hyōōd), *adj.*

hue′ and cry′, any public clamor or protest.

huff (huf), *n.* **1.** a mood of sulking anger. —*v.i.* **2.** to puff or blow. —**huff′y,** *adj.* —**huff′i·ness,** *n.*

hug (hug), *v.,* **hugged, hug·ging,** *n.* —*v.t.* **1.** to clasp tightly in the arms, esp. with affection. **2.** to cling firmly or fondly to: *to hug an opinion.* **3.** to keep close to. —*v.i.* **4.** *Archaic.* to cling together. —*n.* **5.** a tight clasp with the arms. —**hug′ger,** *n.*

huge (hyōōj *or, often,* yōōj), *adj.,* **hug·er, hug·est.** extraordinarily large in bulk, extent, etc. —**huge′ly,** *adv.* —**huge′ness,** *n.* —**Syn.** enormous, gigantic, immense.

hug·ger·mug·ger (hug′ər mug′ər), *n. Archaic.* **1.** muddled disorder. **2.** secrecy or concealment.

Hu·go (hyōō′gō), *n.* **Vic·tor** (vik′tər), 1802–85, French poet and novelist.

Hu·gue·not (hyōō′gə not′), *n.* a French Protestant in the 16th and 17th centuries.

huh (hu), *interj.* (an exclamation of surprise, contempt, or interrogation.)

hu′la hoop′ (hōō′lə), a plastic hoop for rotating about the body, used for physical exercise.

hu·la-hu·la (hōō′lə hōō′lə), *n.* a sinuous Hawaiian native dance with intricate arm movements. Also called **hu′la.**

hulk (hulk), *n.* **1.** the body of an old or dismantled ship. **2.** a bulky or unwieldy person.

hulk·ing (hul′king), *adj.* heavy and clumsy.

hull¹ (hul), *n.* **1.** the husk, shell, or outer covering of a seed or fruit, as of a nut. —*v.t.* **2.** to remove the hull of. —**hull′er,** *n.*

hull² (hul), *n.* the watertight frame of a vessel or a flying boat. **2.** the outer covering of a rocket or missile.

hul·la·ba·loo (hul′ə bə lōō′), *n.* a clamorous noise or disturbance.

hum (hum), *v.,* **hummed, hum·ming,** *n.* —*v.i.* **1.** to make a low, continuous, droning sound. **2.** to sing with closed lips, without articulating words. **3.** to be in a state of busy activity. —*v.t.* **4.** to sing by humming. —*n.* **5.** an inarticulate or indistinct murmur. —**hum′mer,** *n.*

hu·man (hyōō′mən), *adj.* **1.** of, pertaining to, or characteristic of mankind. **2.** having or showing the form or attributes of a human being. —*n.* **3.** Also called **hu′man be′ing.** a person as distinguished from other animals. —**hu′man·ness,** *n.*

hu·mane (hyōō mān′), *adj.* **1.** characterized by tenderness, compassion, and sympathy for human beings and animals. **2.** of or pertaining to the humanities. —**hu·mane′ly,** *adv.* —**hu·mane′ness,** *n.*

hu·man·ism (hyōō′mə niz′əm), *n.* **1.** any system of thought in which human interests and values are taken to be of primary importance. **2.** devotion to or study of the humanities. **3.** (*sometimes cap.*) the study of the cultures of ancient Rome and Greece as pursued by scholars of the Renaissance. —**hu′man·ist,** *n., adj.* —**hu′man·is′tic,** *adj.* —**hu′man·is′ti·cal·ly,** *adv.*

hu·man·i·tar·i·an (hyōō man′i târ′ē ən), *adj.* **1.** having concern for the welfare of humanity. —*n.* **2.** a person actively engaged in promoting human welfare. —**hu·man′i·tar′i·an·ism,** *n.*

hu·man·i·ty (hyōō man′i tē), *n., pl.* **-ties. 1.** the human race. **2.** the condition or quality of being human or humane. **3. the humanities,** literature, philosophy, art, etc., as distinguished from the sciences.

hu·man·ize (hyōō′mə nīz′), v.t., v.i., -ized, -iz·ing. to make or become human or humane. —hu′man·i·za′·tion, n. —hu′man·iz′er, n.

hu·man·kind (hyōō′mən kīnd′, -kīnd′), n. human beings collectively

hu·man·ly (hyōō′mən lē), adv. 1. in a human manner. 2. by human means.

hu·man·oid (hyōō′mə noid′), adj. 1. having human characteristics and functions. —n. 2. a humanoid robot.

hu′man rights′, fundamental rights of an individual to speak, act, work, etc., within limits, without harassment or arrest, including esp. the right to dissent from the government.

hum·ble (hum′bəl, um′-), adj., -bler, -blest, v., -bled, -bling. —adj. 1. not proud or arrogant. 2. feeling insignificant, inferior, or subservient. 3. low in rank, position, or status. 4. courteously respectful. —v.t. 5. to destroy the independence, power, or pride of. 6. to lower in rank, position, or status. —hum′ble·ness, n. —hum′bly, adv. —Syn. 1. modest, unpretentious. 2. meek, submissive.

hum·bug (hum′bug′), n., v., -bugged, -bug·ging, interj. —n. 1. something intended to delude or deceive. 2. an impostor or charlatan. 3. something devoid of sense or meaning. —v.t. 4. to delude or deceive. —interj. 5. nonsense! —hum′bug′ger, n.

hum·ding·er (hum′ding′ər), n. Slang. a person or thing of remarkable excellence.

hum·drum (hum′drum′), adj. unexcitingly monotonous.

hu·mer·us (hyōō′mər əs), n., pl. -mer·i (-mə rī′). the long bone in the arm of a human extending from the shoulder to the elbow. —hu′mer·al, adj.

hu·mid (hyōō′mid), adj. permeated with much water vapor, esp. of the air. —hu′mid·ly, adv.

hu·mid·i·fy (hyōō mid′ə fī′), v.t., -fied, -fy·ing. to make humid. —hu·mid′·i·fi·ca′tion, n. —hu·mid′i·fi′er, n.

hu·mid·i·ty (hyōō mid′i tē), n. humid condition, esp. of the atmosphere.

hu·mi·dor (hyōō′mi dôr′), n. a container for cigars or tobacco, fitted with means for keeping the tobacco suitably moist.

hu·mil·i·ate (hyōō mil′ē āt′), v.t., -ated, -at·ing. to lower or injure the self-respect of, esp. in public. —hu·mil′i·at′ing·ly, adv. —hu·mil′i·a′tion, n. —Syn. embarrass, humble.

hu·mil·i·ty (hyōō mil′i tē), n. the quality or condition of being humble.

hum·ming·bird (hum′ing bûrd′), n. a very small, American bird having narrow wings, the rapid beating of which produces a humming sound.

hum·mock (hum′ək), n. a small, low, rounded hill.

hu·mon·gous (hyōō mung′gəs, -mong′-),
adj. Slang. extraordinarily large. [perh. hu(ge) + mon(strous) + g(reat) + (enorm)ous]

hu·mor (hyōō′mər or, often, yōō′-), n. 1. a comic quality causing amusement. 2. the faculty of perceiving or expressing what is amusing or comical. 3. comical writing or talk in general. 4. mental disposition or temperament. 5. a temporary mood or frame of mind. 6. a capricious or freakish inclination. 7. **out of humor**, displeased or irritable. —v.t. 8. to comply with the humor or mood of. Also, Brit., hu′mour. —hu′mor·ist, n. —hu′mor·less, adj. —hu′mor·less·ly, adv. —hu′mor·less·ness, n.

hu·mor·ous (hyōō′mər əs or, often, yōō′-), adj. expressing or full of humor. —hu′mor·ous·ly, adv. —hu′mor·ous·ness, n. —Syn. amusing, comical, funny, witty.

hump (hump), n. 1. a rounded protuberance, esp. a fleshy protuberance on the back, as of a camel. 2. a low, rounded rise of ground. 3. **over the hump**, past the most difficult part or period. —v.t. 4. to raise (the back) in a hump.

hump·back (hump′bak′), n. 1. a back that is humped. 2. hunchback. —hump′backed′, adj.

humph (humf), interj. (an expression resembling a snort, used to indicate disbelief, contempt, etc.)

hu·mus (hyōō′məs), n. the dark organic material in soils, produced by the decomposition of plants.

Hun (hun), n. a member of a nomadic and warlike Asian people who invaded the Roman Empire in the 4th and 5th centuries A.D.

Hun. 1. Hungarian. 2. Hungary.

hunch (hunch), v.t. 1. to thrust out or up in a hump. —v.i. 2. to thrust oneself forward jerkily. —n. 3. Informal. a premonition or suspicion.

hunch·back (hunch′bak′), n. a person whose back is humped. —hunch′backed′, adj.

hun·dred (hun′drid), n., pl., -dreds, -dred, adj. —n. 1. a cardinal number, ten times ten. 2. a symbol for this number, as 100 or C. 3. **hundreds**, the numbers between 100 and 999. —adj. 4. amounting to one hundred in number. —hun′dredth (-dridth), adj., n.

hun·dred·fold (hun′drid fōld′), adj. a hundred times as great or as much.

hun·dred·weight (hun′drid wāt′), n., pl. -weights, -weight. a unit of weight equivalent to 100 pounds in the U.S. and 112 pounds in England.

hung (hung), v. 1. a pt. and pp. of hang. 2. **hung over**, Slang. suffering the effects of a hangover. 3. **hung up on**, a. Slang. to be obsessively interested in. b. to be infatuated with.

Hung., 1. Hungarian. 2. Hungary.

Hun·gar·i·an (hung gâr′ē ən), *adj.* 1. of Hungary, its people, or their language. —*n.* 2. a native or inhabitant of Hungary. 3. the language of Hungary.

Hun·ga·ry (hung′gə rē), *n.* a country in central Europe.

hun·ger (hung′gər), *n.* 1. a compelling need or desire for food. 2. discomfort or weakness caused by need of food. 3. a strong desire or craving. —*v.i.* 4. to feel hunger. 5. to have a strong desire. —**hun′ger·less,** *adj.* —**hun′gry,** *adj.* —**hun′gri·ly,** *adv.*

hun′ger strike′, a deliberate refusal to eat, undertaken in protest against imprisonment, objectionable conditions, etc.

hunk (hungk), *n. Informal.* a large piece or lump.

hun·ker (hung′kər), *Scot.* —*v.i.* 1. to squat on one's heels. —*n.* 2. hunkers, buttocks or haunches.

hunk·y (hung′kē), *n., pl.* **hunk·ies.** honky.

hunk·y-do·ry (hung′kē dōr′ē, -dôr′ē), *adj. Slang.* pretty good or satisfactory.

Hun·nish (hun′ish), *adj.* 1. of or pertaining to the Huns. 2. (*sometimes l.c.*) barbarous or destructive. —**Hun′nish·ness,** *n.*

hunt (hunt), *v.t., v.i.* 1. to chase or search for (game) for food or sport. 2. to chase or drive with force or hostility. 3. to endeavor to find. 4. to scour (an area) in pursuit of game. —*n.* 5. an act of hunting game. 6. a search or pursuit. 7. an association of huntsmen. —**hunt′er,** *n.* —**hunt′ress,** *n. fem.*

hunts·man (hunts′mən), *n.* a person who hunts, esp. one who manages the hounds during the hunt.

hur·dle (hûr′d°l), *n., v.,* **-dled, -dling.** —*n.* 1. a portable barrier over which runners or horses must jump in certain races. 2. a difficult problem to be overcome. —*v.t.* 3. to leap over, as in a race. 4. to master (a difficulty, etc.). —**hur′dler,** *n.*

hur·dy-gur·dy (hûr′dē gûr′dē, -gûr′-), *n., pl.* **-gur·dies.** a barrel organ or similar instrument played by turning a crank.

hurl (hûrl), *v.t.* 1. to throw with great force. 2. to throw or cast down. 3. to utter with vehemence. —*v.i.* 4. *Baseball.* to pitch a ball. —**hurl′er,** *n.*

hurl·y-burl·y (hûr′lē bûr′lē, -bûr′-), *n.* noisy disorder and confusion.

Hu·ron (hyŏŏr′ən, -on), *n.* 1. a member of an Indian tribe living west of Lake Huron. 2. the Iroquoian language of the Huron Indians. 3. **Lake,** a lake between the U.S. and Canada.

hur·rah (hə rä′, -rô′), *interj.* 1. (an exclamation of joy, exultation, encouragement, etc.) —*v.i.* 2. to shout "hurrah." —*n.* 3. an exclamation of "hurrah." Also, **hur·ray** (hə râ′).

hur·ri·cane (hûr′ə kān′, hur′- or, esp. *Brit.,* -kən), *n.* a violent, tropical, cyclonic storm having wind speeds of or in excess of 73 miles per hour. [< Sp *huracán* < WInd *hurakán*]

hur·ry (hûr′ē, hur′ē), *v.,* **-ried, -ry·ing,** *n., pl.* **-ries.** —*v.i.* 1. to move, proceed, or act with haste. —*v.t.* 2. to drive, carry, or cause to move or perform with speed. 3. to hasten or urge forward. 4. to impel or perform with undue haste. —*n.* 5. a state of urgency or eagerness. 6. hurried movement or action. —**hur′ried·ly,** *adv.* —**hur′ried·ness,** *n.*

hurt (hûrt), *v.,* **hurt, hurt·ing,** *n.* —*v.t.* 1. to cause bodily or mental pain to. 2. to damage or injure. 3. to offend or distress. —*v.i.* 4. to feel or suffer bodily or mental pain. 5. to cause damage or injury. —*n.* 6. bodily or mental pain. 7. injury or distress. 8. *Archaic.* harm or damage. —**hurt′ful,** *adj.*

hur·tle (hûr′t°l), *v.,* **-tled, -tling.** —*v.i.* 1. to move with great speed. —*v.t.* 2. to fling or throw forcibly.

hus·band (huz′bənd), *n.* 1. a married man. —*v.t.* 2. to manage, esp. with prudent economy.

hus·band·man (huz′bənd mən), *n. Archaic.* a farmer.

hus·band·ry (huz′bən drē), *n.* 1. farming, as of livestock. 2. thrifty management, as of resources.

hush (hush), *interj.* 1. (a command to be silent or quiet.) —*v.t., v.i.* 2. to make or become silent or quiet. 3. to calm or lull. 4. to suppress mention (of). —*n.* 5. silence or quiet, esp. after noise.

hush-hush (hush′hush′), *adj. Informal.* highly secret or confidential.

hush′ pup′py, *Southern U.S.* a deep-fried, cornmeal cake.

husk (husk), *n.* 1. the dry external covering of certain fruits or seeds, esp. of corn. 2. the outer part of anything, esp. when dry or worthless. —*v.t.* 3. to remove the husk from. —**husk′er,** *n.*

husk′ing bee′, a gathering of farm families to husk corn. Also called **husk′ing.**

husk·y¹ (hus′kē), *adj.,* **husk·i·er, husk·i·est.** 1. big and strong. 2. somewhat hoarse and rough, as a voice. —**husk′i·ly,** *adv.* —**husk′i·ness,** *n.*

husk·y² (hus′kē), *n.* (*sometimes cap.*) See **Eskimo dog.**

hus·sar (hŏŏ zär′), *n.* one of a body of European light cavalry, usually with striking or flamboyant uniforms. [< Hung *huszár*]

hus·sy (hus′ē, huz′ē), *n., pl.* **-sies. 1.** a bold or lewd woman. **2.** a mischievous or ill-behaved girl.

hus·tings (hus′tiĭgz), *n.* **1.** any place from which political campaign speeches are made. **2.** the political campaign trail.

hus·tle (hus′əl), *v.,* **-tled, -tling,** *n.* — *v.i.* **1.** to proceed or work rapidly or energetically. **2.** to push or force one's way. **3.** *Slang.* to earn one's living by illicit or unethical means. —*v.t.* **4.** to jostle or shove roughly. **5.** to force to leave, esp. roughly or hurriedly. —*n.* **6.** energetic activity, as in work. **7.** discourteous shoving or jostling. **8.** a recent kind of social dancing.

hus·tler (hus′lər), *n.* **1.** a person who hustles. **2.** *Slang.* a prostitute.

hut (hut), *n.* a small or humble dwelling, esp. one made of logs, grass, etc.

hutch (huch), *n.* **1.** a pen or enclosed coop for small animals. **2.** a chest, bin, etc., for storage. **3.** a chestlike cabinet having open shelves. **4.** a small cottage.

hutz·pa (ᴋʜŏŏt′spə), *n. Slang.* chutzpa. Also, **hutz′pah.**

huz·zah (hə zä′), *interj., v.i., n. Archaic.* hurrah. Also, **huz·za′.**

H.V., 1. high velocity. **2.** high voltage. Also, **h.v.**

hvy., heavy.

hwy., highway.

hy·a·cinth (hī′ə sinth), *n.* a plant of the lily family, cultivated for its spikes of fragrant, bell-shaped flowers. —**hy·a·cin·thine** (hī′ə sin′thin, thin), *adj.*

hy·ae·na (hī ē′nə), *n.* hyena.

hy·brid (hī′brid), *n.* **1.** the offspring of two animals or plants of different breeds or species. **2.** anything derived from mixed sources. —*adj.* **3.** of or characteristic of a hybrid. —**hy′brid·ism,** *n.*

hy·brid·ize (hī′bri dīz′), *v.t., v.i.,* **-ized, -iz·ing.** to produce or cause to produce hybrids. —**hy′brid·i·za′tion,** *n.* —**hy′brid·iz′er,** *n.*

hy·dra (hī′drə), *n., pl.* **-dras, -drae** (-drē). *Zool.* any freshwater polyp having a thin tubular body.

hy·dran·gea (hī drān′jə, -jē ə, -dran′-), *n.* a shrub cultivated for its large, showy, white, pink, or blue flower clusters.

hy·drant (hī′drənt), *n.* an upright pipe with an outlet for drawing water from a main pipe.

hy·drate (hī′drāt), *n., v.,* **-drat·ed, -drat·ing.** —*n.* **1.** any of a class of compounds containing chemically combined water. —*v.t., v.i.* **2.** to form or become a hydrate. —**hy·dra′tion,** *n.* —**hy′dra·tor,** *n.*

hy·drau·lic (hī drô′lik, -drol′ik), *adj.* **1.** operated by or employing water or other liquids in motion **2.** operated by water or other liquids under pressure. **3.** of or pertaining to hydraulics. **4.** hardening under water, as a cement. —**hy·drau′li·cal·ly,** *adv.*

hy·drau·lics (hī drô′liks, -drol′iks), *n.* the science that deals with the laws governing water or other liquids in motion and their applications in engineering.

hy·dro (hī′drō), *adj.* hydroelectric.

hydro-¹, a combining form meaning "water": *hydroplane.*

hydro-², *Chem.* a combining form of **hydrogen:** *hydrocarbon.*

hy·dro·car·bon (hī′drə kär′bən), *n.* any compound containing only hydrogen and carbon, as methane.

hy·dro·ceph·a·lus (hī′drə sef′ə ləs), *n.* an accumulation of serous fluid within the cranium, esp. in infancy, often causing great enlargement of the head. Also, **hy·dro·ceph·a·ly** (hī′drə sef′ə lē). —**hy′dro·ce·phal′ic** (-sə fal′ik), *adj.*

hy′dro·chlo′ric ac′id (hī′drə klôr′ik, -klōr′-), a corrosive and fuming liquid, used chiefly in chemical and industrial processes.

hy·dro·dy·nam·ics (hī′drō dī nam′iks, -di-), *n.* the science that deals with the forces in or motions of fluids. —**hy′dro·dy·nam′ic,** *adj.*

hy·dro·e·lec·tric (hī′drō i lek′trik), *adj.* pertaining to the generation and distribution of electricity by waterpower. —**hy′dro·e·lec′tric′i·ty,** *n.*

hy′dro·flu·or′ic ac′id (hī′drō flŏŏ ôr′ik, -ōr′-), a colorless, fuming, corrosive liquid, used chiefly for etching glass.

hy·dro·foil (hī′drə foil′), *n.* **1.** a winglike structure designed to lift the hull of a moving vessel out of water when traveling at high speed. **2.** a vessel equipped with hydrofoils.

hy·dro·gen (hī′drə jən), *n. Chem.* a colorless, odorless, flammable gas that combines chemically with oxygen to form water: the lightest of the known elements. *Symbol:* H; *at. wt.:* 1.00797; *at. no.:* 1. —**hy·drog′-e·nous** (-droj′ə nəs), *adj.*

hy·dro·gen·ate (hī′drə jə nāt′, hī droj′-ə-), *v.t.,* **-at·ed, -at·ing.** to combine or treat with hydrogen. —**hy′dro·gen·a′tion,** *n.*

hy′drogen bomb′, a bomb, more powerful than an atomic bomb, that derives its explosive energy from the thermonuclear fusion reaction of hydrogen isotopes.

hy′drogen perox′ide, an unstable liquid used as an antiseptic and a bleaching agent.

hy·drog·ra·phy (hī drog′rə fē), *n.* the science of the measurement and description of the surface waters of the earth. —**hy·drog′ra·pher**, *n.* —**hy·dro·graph·ic** (hī′drə graf′ik), *adj.*

hy·drol·o·gy (hī drol′ə jē), *n.* the science that deals with the circulation, distribution, and properties of the water of the earth. —**hy·dro·log·ic** (hī′drə loj′ik), **hy′dro·log′i·cal**, *adj.* —**hy·drol′o·gist**, *n.*

hy·drol·y·sis (hī drol′i sis), *n., pl.* **-ses** (-sēz′), decomposition in which a compound is split into other compounds by taking up the elements of water. —**hy′dro·lyt′ic** (-drə lit′ik), *adj.*

hy·drom·e·ter (hī drom′i tər), *n.* an instrument for determining the specific gravity of a liquid.

hy·dro·pho·bi·a (hī′drə fō′bē ə), *n.* 1. an abnormal dread of water. 2. rabies. [< LL < Gk: horror of water]

hy·dro·phone (hī′drə fōn′), *n.* a device for locating sources of sound under water.

hy·dro·plane (hī′drə plān′), *n.* 1. a light, high-powered speedboat designed to skim over the water. 2. seaplane.

hy·dro·pon·ics (hī′drə pon′iks), *n.* the cultivation of plants in liquid nutrient solutions. —**hy′dro·pon′ic**, *adj.*

hy·dro·sphere (hī′drə sfēr′), *n.* the water on or surrounding the surface of the globe.

hy·dro·stat·ics (hī′drə stat′iks), *n.* the branch of hydrodynamics that deals with the statics of fluids. —**hy′dro·stat′ic**, **hy′dro·stat′i·cal**, *adj.*

hy·dro·ther·a·py (hī′drə ther′ə pē), *n.* the treatment of disease by the scientific application of water.

hy·dro·ther·mal (hī′drə thûr′məl), *adj.* noting hot water within or on the surface of the earth.

hy·drous (hī′drəs), *adj.* containing water, esp. in some kind of chemical combination.

hy·drox·ide (hī drok′sīd, -sid), *n.* a compound of oxygen and hydrogen grouped together with one atom each.

hy·e·na (hī ē′nə), *n.* a nocturnal, doglike animal of Africa and Asia, feeding chiefly on carrion.

hy·giene (hī′jēn, -jē ēn′), *n.* 1. the science that deals with the preservation of health. 2. a condition or practice conducive to health, as cleanliness. —**hy·gi·en·ic** (hī′jē en′ik, hī jē′nik), *adj.* —**hy·gi·en′i·cal·ly**, *adv.* —**hy·gien′ist** (-jē′nist, -jen′ist), *n.*

hy·grom·e·ter (hī grom′i tər), *n.* any instrument for measuring the water-vapor content of the atmosphere. —**hy·grom′e·try** (-trē), *n.*

hy·gro·scop·ic (hī′grə skop′ik), *adj.* absorbing or attracting moisture from the air.

hy·ing (hī′ing), *v.* a ppr. of **hie**.

hy·men (hī′mən), *n.* a fold of mucous membrane partially closing the external orifice of the vagina in a virgin.

hy·me·ne·al (hī′mə nē′əl), *adj. Literary.* of marriage or a wedding.

hymn (him), *n.* a song in praise of God.

hym·nal (him′n°l), *n.* a book of hymns. Also called **hymn′book′**.

hym·no·dy (him′nə dē), *n.* 1. the singing or the composition of hymns. 2. hymns collectively.

hyp., 1. hypotenuse. 2. hypothesis. 3. hypothetical.

hype (hīp), *v.,* **hyped, hyp·ing,** *n. Slang.* —*v.t.* 1. to stimulate, excite, or agitate. 2. to intensify (publicity) by ingenious or questionable methods. —*n.* 3. an ingenious or questionable method used in publicity to intensify the effect. 4. a drug addict, esp. one who uses a hypodermic needle.

hyper-, a prefix meaning "over," "excessive," or "exaggerated": *hyperbole.*

hy·per·a·cid·i·ty (hī′pər ə sid′i tē), *n.* excessive acidity, as of the gastric juice. —**hy·per·ac·id** (hī′pər as′id), *adj.*

hy·per·ac·tive (hī′pər ak′tiv), *adj.* abnormally or excessively active, esp., as in children, almost unable to sit still for a while. —**hy′per·ac·tiv′i·ty,** *n.*

hy·per·bar·ic (hī′pər bar′ik), *adj.* of, utilizing, or supplied with oxygen at higher pressure than normal.

hy·per·bo·la (hī pûr′bə lə), *n. Geom.* the set of points in a plane whose distances to two fixed points in the plane have a constant difference.

hy·per·bo·le (hī pûr′bə lē), *n.* an intentional exaggeration not intended to be taken literally. —**hy·per·bol·ic** (hī′pər bol′ik), *adj.* —**hy′per·bol′i·cal·ly,** *adv.*

hy·per·bo·re·an (hī′pər bôr′ē ən, -bôr′-, -bə rē′-), *adj.* of or living in a far northern region.

hy·per·crit·i·cal (hī′pər krit′i kəl), *adj.* captiously critical. —**hy′per·crit′i·cal·ly,** *adv.*

hy·per·o·pi·a (hī′pə rō′pē ə), *n.* a vision defect in which distant objects are seen more distinctly than near ones. —**hy′per·op′ic** (-rop′ik), *adj.*

hy·per·sen·si·tive (hī′pər sen′si tiv), *adj.* 1. excessively sensitive. 2. allergic to a substance to which a normal individual does not react. —**hy′per·sen′si·tiv′i·ty, hy′per·sen′si·tive·ness,** *n.*

hy·per·son·ic (hī'pər son'ik), *adj.* pertaining to speed at least five times that of sound in the same medium.

hy·per·ten·sion (hī'pər ten'shən), *n.* 1. elevation of the blood pressure, esp. the diastolic pressure. 2. a condition of extreme emotional tenseness. —**hy'per·ten'sive,** *adj.*

hy·per·thy·roid·ism (hī'pər thī'roi diz'əm), *n.* overactivity of the thyroid gland, resulting in increased metabolism, extreme nervousness, etc. —**hy'per·thy'roid,** *adj.*

hy·per·tro·phy (hī pûr'trə fē), *n., pl.* **-phies,** *v.,* **-phied, -phy·ing.** —*n.* 1. abnormal enlargement of a body part or organ. —*v.t., v.i.* 2. to affect with or undergo hypertrophy. —**hy·per·troph·ic** (hī'pər trof'ik), *adj.*

hy·per·ven·ti·la·tion (hī'pər ven'tºlā'shən), *n. Med.* excessively rapid and deep breathing, resulting esp. in the decrease of carbon dioxide in the blood.

hy·phen (hī'fən), *n.* 1. a short line (-) used to connect the parts of a compound word or the parts of a word divided for any purpose. —*v.t.* 2. to hyphenate. [< LL < Gk: together (adv.)]

hy·phen·ate (hī'fə nāt'), *v.t.,* **-at·ed, -at·ing.** to connect or write with a hyphen. —**hy'phen·a'tion,** *n.*

hyp·no·sis (hip nō'sis), *n., pl.* **-ses** (-sēz). an artificially induced state resembling sleep, characterized by heightened susceptibility to suggestion. —**hyp'no·tiz'a·ble** (-ne tī'zə bəl), *adj.* —**hyp'no·tize'** (-nə tīz'), *v.t., v.i.*

hyp·not·ic (hip not'ik), *adj.* 1. of or pertaining to hypnosis or hypnotism. 2. inducing sleep. —*n.* 3. an agent or drug that produces sleep. —**hyp·not'i·cal·ly,** *adv.*

hyp·no·tism (hip'nə tiz'əm), *n.* the act or theory of inducing hypnosis. —**hyp'no·tist,** *n.*

hy·po¹ (hī'pō), *n.* See **sodium thiosulfate.**

hy·po² (hī'pō), *n. Informal.* a hypodermic syringe or injection.

hypo-, a prefix meaning: a. under or beneath: *hypodermic.* b. lacking or insufficient: *hypothyroidism.*

hy·po·cen·ter (hī'pə sen'tər), *n.* an underground point from which an earthquake originates.

hy·po·chon·dri·a (hī'pə kon'drē ə), *n.* an abnormal condition characterized by a depressed emotional state and imaginary ill health. —**hy'po·chon'dri·ac'** (-ak'), *n., adj.*

hy·poc·ri·sy (hi pok'rə sē), *n., pl.* **-sies.** a pretense of having desirable or

publicly approved attitudes, beliefs, principles, etc., that one does not actually possess.

hyp·o·crite (hip'ə krit), *n.* a person given to hypocrisy. —**hyp'o·crit'i·cal,** *adj.* —**hyp'o·crit'i·cal·ly,** *adv.*

hy·po·der·mic (hī'pə dûr'mik), *adj.* 1. introduced or administered into or under the skin: *a hypodermic medication.* —*n.* 2. a hypodermic remedy. 3. a hypodermic injection. 4. See **hypodermic syringe.**

hypoder'mic syringe', a small syringe having a detachable, hollow needle (**hypoder'mic nee'dle**) for use in injecting material into or under the skin.

hy·po·gly·ce·mi·a (hī'pō glī sē'mē ə), *n.* an abnormally low level of glucose in the blood. —**hy'po·gly·ce'mic,** *adj.*

hy·pot·e·nuse (hī pot'ºnoos', -nyoos'), *n. Geom.* the side of a right triangle opposite the right angle.

hypoth., 1. hypothesis. 2. hypothetical.

hy·poth·e·cate (hī poth'ə kāt', hī-), *v.t., v.i.,* **-cat·ed, -cat·ing.** hypothesize.

hy·poth·e·sis (hī poth'i sis, hī-), *n., pl.* **-ses** (-sēz'). an unproved or unverified assumption that can be either used or accepted as probable in the light of established facts. —**hy·poth'e·sist,** *n.*

hy·poth·e·size (hī poth'i sīz', hī-), *v.t., v.i.,* **-sized, -siz·ing.** to assume as or from a hypothesis. —**hy·poth'e·siz'er,** *n.*

hy·po·thet·i·cal (hī'pə thet'i kəl), *adj.* 1. assumed by hypothesis. 2. presumed to exist. —**hy'po·thet'i·cal·ly,** *adv.*

hy·po·thy·roid·ism (hī'pə thī'roi diz'əm), *n.* deficient activity of the thyroid gland, resulting in goiter, and, in children, cretinism. —**hy'po·thy'roid,** *adj., n.*

hys·sop (his'əp), *n.* an aromatic herb having blue flowers.

hys·ter·ec·to·my (his'tə rek'tə mē), *n., pl.* **-mies.** surgical removal of the uterus. —**hys'ter·ec'to·mize'** (-mīz'), *v.t.*

hys·te·ri·a (hi stēr'ē ə, -ster'-), *n.* 1. an uncontrollable outburst of emotion or fear. 2. a psychiatric disorder characterized by violent emotional outbreaks, disturbances of sensory and motor functions, etc. —**hys·ter'ic,** *n., adj.* —**hys·ter'i·cal,** *adj.* —**hys·ter'i·cal·ly,** *adv.*

hys·ter·ics (hi ster'iks), *n.* a fit of uncontrollable laughter or weeping.

Hz, hertz.

I

I, i (ī), *n., pl.* **I's** or **Is, i's** or **is.** the ninth letter of the English alphabet, a vowel.

I (ī), *pron.* the nominative singular pronoun, used by a speaker in referring to himself or herself.

I, 1. the ninth in order or in a series. **2.** (*sometimes l.c.*) the Roman numeral for 1. **3.** iodine.

I, Interstate (Highway).

I., 1. Island; Islands. **2.** Isle; Isles.

i., 1. interest. **2.** intransitive. **3.** island. **4.** isle; isles.

IA, Iowa. Also, **Ia.**

-ial, var. of **-al:** *imperial.*

i·amb (ī′am, ī′amb), *n.* a metrical foot of two syllables, a stressed followed by an unstressed one. Also, **i·am·bus** (-bəs). **—i·am·bic,** *adj., n.*

-ian, var. of **-an:** *humanitarian.*

-iatrics, a combination of **-iatry** and **-ics:** *pediatrics.*

-iatry, a combining form meaning "medical care": *psychiatry.*

ib., ibidem.

I·be·ri·a (ī bēr′ē ə), *n.* a peninsula in SW Europe, comprising Spain and Portugal. Also called **Ibe′rian Penin′sula. —I·be′ri·an,** *adj., n.*

i·bex (ī′beks), *n., pl.* **i·bex·es, ib·i·ces** (ib′i sēz′, ī′bi-), **i·bex** a wild goat of Asia, North Africa, and Europe, having long, backward-curving horns.

ibid. (ib′id), ibidem.

i·bi·dem (ib′i dem, i bī′dem), *adv. Latin.* in the same book, chapter, page, etc., previously cited.

i·bis (ī′bis), *n., pl.* **i·bis·es** (ī′bi siz), **i·bis.** a large wading bird related to the heron and having a long thin, downward-curved bill.

-ible, var. of **-able:** *horrible; reducible.*

Ib·sen (ib′sən), *n.* **Hen·rik** (hen′rik), 1828–1906, Norwegian dramatist.

-ic¹, a suffix meaning: **a.** of or pertaining to: *metallic.* **b.** like or characteristic of: *idyllic.* **c.** containing or made of: *alcoholic.* **d.** made or produced by: *telegraphic.* **e.** affected with: *lethargic.* **f.** suggestive of: *Homeric.* **g.** showing the higher of two valances: *ferric.*

-ic², a suffix meaning: **a.** a person afflicted with: *arthritic.* **b.** an agent or drug: *cosmetic.* **c.** a follower or adherent: *Socratic.*

-ical, a combination of **-ic¹** and **-al:** *rhetorical; poetical; economical.*

ICBM, intercontinental ballistic missile.

ICC, Interstate Commerce Commission.

ice (īs), *n., v.,* **iced, ic·ing. —n. 1.** the solid form of water, produced by freezing. **2.** a frozen dessert made of sweetened water and fruit juice. **3.** *Slang.* diamonds. **4. break the ice,** to overcome reserve or formality between people. **5. cut no ice,** *Informal.* to fail to make a favorable impression. **6. on thin ice,** in a risky situation. **—v.t. 7.** to change into ice. **8.** to cool with or as with ice. **9.** to cover with icing. **—v.i. 10.** to be covered with ice: *The windshield has iced up.* **—iced** (īst), *adj.*

Ice., 1. Iceland. **2.** Icelandic.

ice′ age′. See **glacial epoch.**

ice′ bag′, a bag for holding ice, applied to cool the head.

ice·berg (īs′bûrg), *n.* **1.** a large floating mass of ice, detached from a glacier. **2.** *Informal.* an emotionally cold person.

ice·bound (īs′bound′), *adj.* hemmed in or obstructed by ice.

ice·box (īs′boks′), *n. Obsolesc.* a refrigerator.

ice·break·er (īs′brā′kər), *n.* a vessel especially built for forcing navigable passages through ice.

ice·cap (īs′kap′), *n.* a thick cover of ice over an area, sloping in all directions from the center.

ice′ cream′, a frozen food made of milk products, sweetened and variously flavored.

ice′ floe′, floe.

ice′ hock′ey, a game played on ice between two teams, each having six players, who compete by hitting the puck into each other's goal.

Icel., 1. Iceland. **2.** Icelandic.

Ice·land (īs′lənd), *n.* an island country in the N Atlantic. **—Ice·land·er** (īs′lan′dər, -lən dər), *n.*

Ice·lan·dic (īs lan′dik), *adj.* **1.** of Iceland, its inhabitants, or their language. **—n. 2.** the language of Iceland.

ice·man (īs′man′), *n.* a man who sells or delivers ice.

ice′ milk′, a kind of ice cream made of skimmed milk.

ice′ pick′, a pick or other tool for chipping ice.

ice-skate (īs′skāt′), *v.i.,* **-skat·ed, -skat·ing.** to skate on ice. **—ice′ skat′er,** *n.*

i·chor (ī′kôr, ī′kər), *n. Class. Myth.* an ethereal fluid supposed to flow in the veins of the gods.

ich·thy·ol·o·gy (ik′thē ol′ə jē), *n.* the branch of zoology dealing with fishes. **—ich′thy·ol′o·gist,** *n.*

i·ci·cle (ī'si kəl), *n.* a hanging, tapering mass of ice formed by the freezing of dripping water.

ic·ing (ī'sĭng), *n.* any sweet, usually creamy covering for cakes, cookies, etc., esp. frosting.

ICJ, International Court of Justice.

ick·y (ik'ē), *adj.,* **ick·i·er, ick·i·est.** *Slang.* **1.** repulsive or disgusting. **2.** sticky or viscid.

i·con (ī'kon), *n.* **1.** *Eastern Ch.* a representation of a sacred personage, usually painted on a wood or ivory surface. **2.** anything devotedly admired.

i·con·o·clast (ī kon'ə klast'), *n.* a person who attacks cherished beliefs, traditional institutions, etc. —**i·con'o·clasm'** (-klaz'əm), *n.* —**i·con'o·clas'tic,** *adj.*

-ics, a suffix meaning "science" or "art": *physics; politics; tactics.*

ic·tus (ik'təs), *n. Pros.* rhythmical or metrical stress.

ICU, *Med.* intensive-care unit.

i·cy (ī'sē), *adj.,* **i·ci·er, i·ci·est. 1.** full of or covered with ice. **2.** of or resembling ice. **3.** cold: *icy wind.* **4.** slippery: *an icy road.* **5.** without warmth of feeling. —**i'ci·ly,** *adv.* —**i'ci·ness,** *n.*

id (id), *n. Psychoanal.* the part of the psyche that is the source of instinctive energy.

ID, 1. Also, **Id., Ida.** Idaho. **2.** identification.

I'd (īd), contraction of: **a.** *I would.* **b.** *I should.* **c.** *I had.*

id., idem.

I.D., identification.

i.d., inside diameter.

I·da·ho (ī'də hō'), *n.* a state in the NW United States. *Cap.:* Boise.

i·de·a (ī dē'ə, ī dē'ə'), *n.* **1.** any conception existing in the mind. **2.** a thought or notion. **3.** an impression or mental image. **4.** an opinion, view, or belief. **5.** a plan of action.

i·de·al (ī dē'əl, ī dēl'), *n.* **1.** a conception of something in its perfection. **2.** a standard of perfection. **3.** a person or thing regarded as conforming to such a standard. **4.** an ultimate aim of endeavor. —*adj.* **5.** conceived as constituting a standard of perfection. **6.** regarded as perfect of its kind. **7.** existing only in the imagination.

i·de·al·ism (ī dē'ə liz'əm), *n.* **1.** the cherishing or pursuit of one's ideals. **2.** perception of people or things as they should be rather than as they are. —**i·de'al·ist,** *n.* —**i·de'al·is'tic,** *adj.* —**i·de'al·is'ti·cal·ly,** *adv.*

i·de·al·ize (ī dē'ə līz'), *v.t.,* **-ized, -izing.** to represent or regard as ideal. —**i·de'al·i·za'tion,** *n.*

i·de·al·ly (ī dē'ə lē), *adv.* **1.** in accordance with an ideal. **2.** in theory or principle.

i·de·a·tion (ī'dē ā'shən), *n.* the process of forming ideas or images. —**i'de·a'tion·al,** *adj.*

i·dem (ī'dem, id'em), *pron., adj. Latin.* the same as previously given or mentioned.

i·den·ti·cal (ī den'ti kəl, i den'-), *adj.* **1.** exactly the same. **2.** similar or alike in every way. —**i·den'ti·cal·ly,** *adv.*

i·den·ti·fi·ca·tion (ī den'tə fə kā'shən, i den'-), *n.* **1.** the act of identifying or state of being identified. **2.** something that identifies one.

i·den·ti·fy (ī den'tə fī', i den'-), *v.t.,* **-fied, -fy·ing. 1.** to verify the identity of. **2.** to make or represent to be identical. **3.** to associate in feeling, interest, action, etc. —**i·den'ti·fi'a·ble,** *adj.*

i·den·ti·ty (ī den'ti tē, i den'-), *n., pl.* **-ties. 1.** the state or fact of remaining the same. **2.** the condition of being oneself or itself, and not another. **3.** the state or fact of being the same one as described.

iden'ti·ty cri'sis, a period of psychological distress, normative in adolescence, when a person is struggling consciously for a clear sense of unified self.

id·e·o·gram (id'ē ə gram', ī'dē-), *n.* a written symbol that represents an idea or object directly rather than a particular word or speech sound. Also, **id'e·o·graph'** (-graf', ī'dē-).

i·de·ol·o·gy (ī'dē ol'ə jē, id'ē-), *n., pl.* **-gies. 1.** the body of doctrines or beliefs that guides a particular individual, class, or culture. **2.** such a body of doctrines or beliefs. with reference to some political and social plan. —**i'de·o·log'i·cal,** *adj.*

ides (īdz), *n.* (in the ancient Roman calendar) the 15th day of March, May, July, or October, or the 13th day of the other months.

id est (id est'), *Latin.* See **i.e.**

id·i·o·cy (id'ē ə sē), *n., pl.* **-cies** for 2. **1.** extreme degree of mental deficiency. **2.** an idiotic act or statement.

id·i·om (id'ē əm), *n.* **1.** an expression whose meaning cannot be derived from its constituent elements, as *kick the bucket* in the sense of "to die." **2.** a language, dialect, or style of speaking peculiar to a people. **3.** a construction or expression peculiar to a language. **4.** a distinct style or character, as in music or art. —**id'i·o·mat'ic** (-ə mat'ik), *adj.* —**id'i·o·mat'i·cal·ly,** *adv.*

id·i·o·path·ic (id'ē ə path'ik), *adj.* of unknown cause, as a disease. —**id'i·op'a·thy** (-op'ə thē), *n.*

id·i·o·syn·cra·sy (id′ē ə siṅg′krə sē, -sin′-), n., pl. -sies. a habit or mannerism that is peculiar to an individual. —**id′i·o·syn·crat′ic** (-ō sin-krat′ik), adj.

id·i·ot (id′ē ət), n. 1. an utterly foolish or senseless person. 2. Obsolesc. a person lacking the capacity to develop beyond the mental age of three or four years. [< L idiōt(a) < Gk idiṓtēs] —**id′i·ot′ic** (-ot′ik), adj. —**id′i·ot′i·cal·ly**, adv.

id′iot light′, Auto. a warning light on the instrument panel that turns on automatically when there are deficiencies or malfunctions in the battery, oil supply, etc.

i·dle (īd′əl), adj., i·dler, i·dlest, v., i·dled, i·dling. —adj. 1. not working or active. 2. not filled with activity: idle hours. 3. lazy or shiftless. 4. of no real worth: idle talk. 5. having no basis or reason: idle fears. —v.i. 6. to pass time doing nothing. 7. to move or saunter aimlessly. 8. to operate without doing useful work. —v.t. 9. to pass (time) doing nothing: to idle away the afternoon. 10. to cause to be idle. —**i′dle·ness**, n. —**i′dler**, n. —**i′dly**, adv.

i·dol (īd′əl), n. 1. an image, as a statue, worshiped as a deity. 2. any person or thing devotedly admired.

i·dol·a·try (ī dol′ə trē), n., pl. -tries. 1. the religious worship of idols. 2. blind adoration or devotion. —**i·dol′a·ter**, n. —**i·dol′a·trous**, adj.

i·dol·ize (īd′ə līz′), v.t., -ized, -iz·ing. 1. to regard with blind adoration or devotion. 2. to worship as an idol.

i·dyll (īd′əl), n. 1. a short poem on pastoral or rural life. 2. material suitable for such a work. 3. a charmingly simple episode. Also, **i′dyl**. —**i·dyl′lic** (ī dil′ik), adj.

IE, Indo-European.

I.E., 1. Indo-European. 2. Industrial Engineer.

i.e., that is. [< L id est]

-ier, var. of -eer: gondolier.

if (if), conj. 1. supposing that: I'll go if he goes. 2. even though: an enthusiastic if small audience. 3. whether: He asked if I knew Spanish. —n. 4. Often, ifs. a condition, requirement, or stipulation.

—Usage. IF meaning WHETHER, as in I haven't decided if I'll go, is sometimes criticized, but the usage has been established in standard English for a long time.

IF, intermediate frequency.

if·fy (if′ē), adj. Informal. full of unresolved points or questions.

ig·loo (ig′lōō), n., pl. -loos. an Eskimo hut usually built of blocks of hard snow and shaped like a dome. Also, **ig′lu**.

ig·ne·ous (ig′nē əs), adj. 1. produced under intense heat, as rocks of volcanic origin. 2. of or characteristic of fire.

ig·nite (ig nīt′), v., -nit·ed, -nit·ing. —v.t. 1. to set on fire. —v.i. 2. to catch fire. —**ig·nit′a·ble, ig·nit′i·ble**, adj.

ig·ni·tion (ig nish′ən), n. 1. the act or fact of igniting. 2. the state of being ignited. 3. the process that ignites the fuel in the cylinder of an internal-combustion engine.

ig·no·ble (ig nō′bəl), adj. 1. of low character, aims, etc. 2. Archaic. of humble birth or origin. —**ig′no·bil′i·ty**, n. —**ig·no′bly**, adv.

ig·no·min·i·ous (ig′nə min′ē əs), adj. 1. marked by disgrace or dishonor. 2. bearing or deserving contempt or shame. —**ig′no·min′i·ous·ly**, adv. —**ig·no·min·y** (ig′nə min′ē), n.

ig·no·ra·mus (ig′nə rā′məs, -ram′əs), n., pl. -mus·es. an extremely ignorant person.

ig·no·rant (ig′nər ənt), adj. 1. lacking in knowledge or training. 2. lacking knowledge about a particular subject or fact. 3. uninformed or unaware. —**ig′no·rance**, n. —**ig′no·rant·ly**, adv. —Syn. 1. illiterate, uneducated.

ig·nore (ig nōr′, ˌnôr′), v.t., -nored, -nor·ing. to refuse deliberately to consider or take notice of. —Syn. disregard, neglect, slight.

i·gua·na (i gwä′nə), n. a large green lizard of tropical America.

IGY, International Geophysical Year.

IHP, indicated horsepower.

IHS, Jesus (used as a monogram or symbol). [< LL < Gk IHΣ, short for IHΣOYΣ Jesus]

i·kon (ī′kon), n. icon.

IL, Illinois.

il·e·i·tis (il′ē ī′tis), n. Pathol. inflammation of the ileum.

il·e·um (il′ē əm), n., pl. -e·a (-ə). the third and lowest division of the small intestine, extending from the jejunum to the cecum. —**il′e·al**, adj.

ILGWU, International Ladies' Garment Workers' Union.

Il·i·ad (il′ē əd), n. a Greek epic poem describing the siege of Troy, ascribed to Homer.

il·i·um (il′ē əm), n., pl. il·i·a (il′ē ə). the broad, upper portion of either innominate bone.

ilk (ilk), n. Now facetious. family, class, or kind.

ill (il), adj., worse, worst, n., adv. —adj. 1. of unsound physical or mental health. 2. wicked or bad: of ill repute. 3. objectionable or faulty: ill manners. 4. hostile or unkindly: ill feeling. 5. unfavorable or adverse: ill fortune. 6. ill at ease, uncomfortable or nervous. —*n.* 7. trouble or affliction. 8. a disease or ailment. 9. evil or bad. —*adv.* 10. wickedly or badly. 11. unsatisfactorily or poorly. 12. scarcely: *an expense we can ill afford.* —**ill'ly,** *adv.*

I'll (īl), contraction of: a. *I will.* b. *I shall.*

Ill., Illinois.

ill., 1. illustrated. 2. illustration. 3. illustrator.

ill-ad·vised (il'əd vīzd'), *adj.* acting or done without due consideration. —**ill-ad·vis·ed·ly** (il'əd vī'zid lē), *adv.*

ill-bred (il'bred'), *adj.* unmannerly or rude.

il·le·gal (i lē'gəl), *adj.* 1. forbidden by law or statute. 2. contrary to official rules, regulations, etc. —**il·le·gal·i·ty** (il'ē gal'i tē), *n.* —**il·le'gal·ly,** *adv.*

il·leg·i·ble (i lej'ə bəl), *adj.* impossible or hard to read or decipher, esp. because of poor handwriting. —**il·leg'i·bil'i·ty,** *n.* —**il·leg'i·bly,** *adv.*

il·le·git·i·mate (il'i jit'ə mit), *adj.* 1. born out of wedlock. 2. not sanctioned by law and custom. 3. not in good usage. 4. not in accordance with logic. —**il'le·git'i·ma·cy** (-mə sē), *n.* —**il'le·git'i·mate·ly,** *adv.*

ill-fat·ed (il'fā'tid), *adj.* 1. destined, as though by fate, to an unhappy end. 2. bringing bad fortune.

ill-fa·vored (il'fā'vərd), *adj.* 1. unpleasant in appearance. 2. offensive or unpleasant.

ill-got·ten (il'got'ᵊn), *adj.* acquired by evil or improper means.

ill' hu'mor, a disagreeable or surly mood. —**ill'-hu'mored,** *adj.*

il·lib·er·al (i lib'ər əl, i lib'rəl), *adj.* narrow-minded or bigoted.

il·lic·it (i lis'it), *adj.* not legally permitted. —**il·lic'it·ly,** *adv.* —**il·lic'it·ness,** *n.*

il·lim·it·a·ble (i lim'i tə bəl), *adj.* limitless or boundless. —**il·lim'it·a·bly,** *adv.*

Il·li·nois (il'ə noi', -noiz'), *n.* a state in the midwestern United States. *Cap.:* Springfield. —**Il·li·nois·an** (il'ə noi'ən, -zən), *n., adj.*

Il·li·nois (il'ə noi', -noiz'), *n., pl.* **-nois** (-noi', -noiz') a member of a North American Indian people, formerly occupying Illinois and adjoining regions westward.

il·lit·er·ate (i lit'ər it), *adj.* 1. unable to read and write. 2. lacking education. 3. showing lack of culture, esp. in language and literature. —*n.* 4. an illiterate person. —**il·lit'er·a·cy** (-ə sē), *n.*

ill-man·nered (il'man'ərd), *adj.* having bad manners.

ill-na·tured (il'nā'chərd), *adj.* having an unkindly or unpleasant disposition. —**ill'-na'tured·ly,** *adv.*

ill·ness (il'nis), *n.* the state or period of being ill.

il·log·i·cal (i loj'i kəl), *adj.* contrary to or disregardful of the rules of logic. —**il·log'i·cal'i·ty,** *n.* —**il·log'i·cal·ly,** *adv.*

ill-starred (il'stärd'), *adj.* unlucky or doomed to misfortune or disaster.

ill-suit·ed (il'sōō'tid), *adj.* not suitable or appropriate.

ill' tem'per, bad or irritable disposition. —**ill'-tem'pered,** *adj.*

ill-timed (il'tīmd'), *adj.* badly timed.

ill-treat (il'trēt'), *v.t.* to treat badly or improperly. —**ill'-treat'ment,** *n.*

il·lu·mi·nate (i lōō'mə nāt'), *v.t.,* **-nat·ed, -nat·ing.** 1. to supply with light. 2. to throw light on (a subject). 3. to decorate with lights, as in celebration. 4. to enlighten, as with knowledge. 5. to decorate (a manuscript or book) with colors and gold or silver, as done in the early Middle Ages. —**il·lu'mi·na·ble,** *adj.* —**il·lu'mi·nat'ing·ly,** *adv.* —**il·lu'mi·na'tion,** *n.* —**il·lu'mi·na'tor,** *n.*

il·lu·mine (i lōō'min), *v.t.,* **-mined, -min·ing.** *Literary.* to illuminate.

illus., 1. illustrated. 2. illustration.

ill-use (*v.* il'yōōz'; *n.* il'yōōs'), *v.,* **-used, -us·ing,** *n.* —*v.t.* 1. to treat unjustly or cruelly. —*n.* 2. Also, **ill'-us'age.** unjust or cruel treatment.

il·lu·sion (i lōō'zhən), *n.* 1. something that deceives by producing a false impression. 2. a misapprehension or misconception. 3. a perception that represents what is perceived in an unreal way.

il·lu·sion·ism (i lōō'zhə niz'əm), *n.* a technique of using pictorial methods in order to deceive the eye. —**il·lu'sion·ist,** *n.*

il·lu·so·ry (i lōō'sə rē, -zə-), *adj.* causing or of the nature of an illusion. Also, **il·lu·sive** (i lōō'siv).

illust., 1. illustrated. 2. illustration.

il·lus·trate (il'ə strāt', i lus'trāt), *v.t.,* **-trat·ed, -trat·ing.** 1. to make clear or intelligible, as by examples. 2. to furnish (a book, etc.) with drawings or pictorial representations intended for elucidation or adornment. —**il'lus·tra'tor,** *n.*

il·lus·tra·tion (il'ə strā'shən), *n.* 1. something that illustrates, as a picture in a magazine. 2. a comparison or an example intended for explanation or corroboration. 3. the act or process of illustrating.

il·lus·tra·tive (i lus'trə tiv, il'ə strā'tiv), *adj.* serving to illustrate. —**il·lus'tra·tive·ly,** *adv.*

il·lus·tri·ous (i lus'trē əs), *adj.* reputable because of achievement or character. —**il·lus'tri·ous·ly,** *adv.* —**il·lus'tri·ous·ness,** *n.* —**Syn.** celebrated, distinguished, eminent.

ill' will', hostile feeling.

ILO, International Labor Organization.

ILS, instrument landing system.

I'm (īm), contraction of *I am.*

im·age (im′ij), *n., v.,* **-aged, -ag·ing.** —*n.* **1.** a physical likeness or representation of a person or thing, esp. a statue. **2.** an optical counterpart of an object, such as is produced by reflection from a mirror. **3.** a mental representation. **4.** form or semblance: *God created man in His own image.* **5.** counterpart or copy: *the image of his mother.* **6.** a type or embodiment: *He was the image of frustration.* **7.** the impression that a public personage, a corporation, or a country creates or tries to create, esp. through the mass media. **8.** a metaphor or a simile. —*v.t.* **9.** to form an image of. **10.** to reflect the likeness of.

im·age·ry (im′ij rē, im′ij ə rē), *n., pl.* **-ries. 1.** mental images collectively. **2.** figurative description or illustration.

im·ag·i·na·ble (i maj′ə nə bəl), *adj.* capable of being imagined or conceived. —**im·ag′i·na·bly,** *adv.*

im·ag·i·nar·y (i maj′ə ner′ē), *adj.* existing only in the imagination. —**Syn.** fanciful, illusory, unreal.

imag′inary num′ber, 1. the imaginary part of a complex number, as *bi* in the expression $a + bi$ where a and b are real numbers and i^2 is defined as —1. **2.** a complex number having its real part equal to zero.

imag′inary u′nit, the positive square root of —1.

im·ag·i·na·tion (i maj′ə nā′shən), *n.* **1.** the act or faculty of imagining. **2.** the power of reproducing images stored in the memory under the suggestion of associated images or of recombining former experiences to create new images. **3.** the faculty of producing ideal creations consistent with reality. **4.** a popular conception or creation. **5.** ability to meet and resolve difficulties. —**im·ag·i·na·tive** (i maj′ə nə tiv, -nā′tiv), *adj.* —**im·ag′i·na·tive·ly,** *adv.*

im·ag·ine (i maj′in), *v.t., v.i.* **-ined, -in·ing. 1.** to form a mental image (of something not actually present to the senses). **2.** to believe or suppose. **3.** *Archaic.* to plan, scheme, or plot.

im·ag·ism (im′ə jiz′əm), *n.* a style of poetry that employs free verse and precise imagery, esp. as developed by English and American poets in the 1910's. —**im′ag·ist,** *n., adj.*

i·ma·go (i mā′gō), *n., pl.* **im·a·goes, i·ma·gi·nes** (i maj′ə nēz′). an adult insect. —**im·ag·i·nal** (i maj′ə nəl), *adj.*

i·mam (i mäm′), *n.* **1.** (*cap.*) a recognized Muslim religious leader. **2.** the prayer leader in a mosque.

im·bal·ance (im bal′əns), *n.* the state or condition of lacking balance.

im·be·cile (im′bi sil, -səl), *n.* **1.** a dull, stupid person. **2.** *Obsolesc.* a person lacking the capacity to develop beyond a mental age of seven or eight years. —*adj.* **3.** mentally feeble. **4.** silly or absurd. —**im·be·cil·ic** (im′bi sil′ik), *adj.* —**im′be·cil′i·ty,** *n.*

im·bed (im bed′), *v.t.* **-bed·ded, -bed·ding.** embed.

im·bibe (im bīb′), *v.,* **-bibed, -bib·ing.** —*v.t.* **1.** *Literary.* to consume (liquids) by drinking. **2.** to take or receive into the mind. —*v.i.* **3.** *Literary.* to absorb liquid or moisture. —**im·bib′er,** *n.* —**im·bi·bi·tion** (im′bi bish′ən), *n.* —**im′bi·bi′tion·al,** *adj.*

im·bri·ca·tion (im′brə kā′shən), *n.* **1.** an overlapping, as of tiles or shingles. **2.** a pattern resembling this. —**im·bri·cate** (im′brə kit, -kāt′), *adj.*

im·bro·glio (im brōl′yo), *n., pl.* **-glios. 1.** a complicated or difficult situation. **2.** a misunderstanding of a complicated or bitter nature. **3.** a confused heap.

im·brue (im brōō′), *v.t.,* **-brued, -bru·ing.** to drench or stain, esp. with blood.

im·bue (im byōō′), *v.t.,* **-bued, -bu·ing. 1.** to impregnate or inspire, as with feelings, opinions, etc. **2.** to saturate with moisture, color, etc.

IMF, International Monetary Fund.

im·i·tate (im′i tāt′), *v.t.,* **-tat·ed, -tat·ing. 1.** to endeavor to follow in action or manner. **2.** to copy or mimic. **3.** to reproduce closely. **4.** to assume the appearance of —**im′i·ta·ble** (-tə-bəl), *adj.* —**im′i·ta′tor,** *n.* —**Syn.** ape, mock, simulate.

im·i·ta·tion (im′i tā′shən), *n.* **1.** a result or product of imitating. **2.** the act of imitating. **3.** a counterfeit or copy. **4.** a literary composition that imitates the manner or subject of another author or work. —*adj.* **5.** designed to imitate a genuine article or thing. —**im′i·ta′tion·al,** *adj.*

im·i·ta·tive (im′i tā′tiv), *adj.* **1.** given to imitation. **2.** of or characterized by imitation. **3.** made in imitation of something. —**im′i·ta′tive·ly,** *adv.* —**im′i·ta′tive·ness,** *n.*

im·mac·u·late (i mak′yə lit), *adj.* **1.** spotlessly clean. **2.** free from moral blemish or impurity. **3.** free from fault or flaw —**im·mac′u·late·ly,** *adv.* —**im·mac′u·late·ness,** *n.*

im·ma·nent (im′ə nənt), *adj.* **1.** existing or operating within. **2.** (of the Deity) indwelling the universe, time, etc. —**im′ma·nence, im′ma·nen·cy,** *n.* —**im′ma·nent·ly,** *adv.*

im·ma·te·ri·al (im′ə tēr′ē əl), *adj.* **1.** of no essential consequence. **2.** incorporeal or spiritual. —**im′ma·te′ri·al′i·ty** (-al′ə tē), *n.* —**im′ma·te′ri·al·ly,** *adv.*

im·ma·ture (im′ə toŏr′, -tyoŏr′, -choŏr′), *adj.* **1.** not mature, ripe, developed, perfected, etc. **2.** childish or silly. —**im′ma·ture′ly,** *adv.* —**im′-ma·tu′ri·ty,** *n.*

im·meas·ur·a·ble (i mezh′ər ə bəl), *adj.* incapable of being measured **2.** limitless or vast. · —**im·meas′ur·a·bly,** *adv.*

im·me·di·a·cy (i mē′dē ə sē), *n.* **1.** the state or quality of being immediate. **2.** relevance to the present time or subject. **3.** a sense of urgency.

im·me·di·ate (i mē′dē it), *adj.* **1.** occurring without delay. **2.** of or pertaining to the present time. **3.** following without a lapse of time. **4.** having no object or space intervening. **5.** without intervening medium or agent. —**im·me′di·ate·ly,** *adv.* —**im·me′di·ate·ness,** *n.*

im·me·mo·ri·al (im′ə môr′ē əl, -môr′-), *adj.* extending back beyond memory, record, or knowledge. —**im′me·mo′ri·al·ly,** *adv.*

im·mense (i mens′), *adj.* **1.** vast and extensive. **2.** *Informal.* very good. —**im·mense′ly,** *adv.* · —**im·men′si·ty,** *n.*

im·merse (i mûrs′), *v.t.,* -mersed, -mers·ing. **1.** to plunge into ɔr place under a liquid. **2.** to absorb deeply. **3.** to baptize by submerging in the water. —**im·mer′sion,** *n.*

immer′sion heat′er, a small, rodlike, electric apparatus for heating water by directly submerging in it.

im·mi·grant (im′ə grənt), *n.* **1.** a person who immigrates. **2.** a plant or animal found living in a new habitat.

im·mi·grate (im′ə grāt′), *v.i.* -grat·ed, -grat·ing. to come into another country for permanent residence. —**im′-mi·gra′tion,** *n.*

im·mi·nent (im′ə nənt), *adj.* **1.** likely to occur at any moment. **2.** threateningly near or at hand. · —**im′mi·nence,** *n.* —**im′mi·nent·ly,** *adv.*

im·mis·ci·ble (i mis′ə bəl), *adj.* incapable of being mixed. —**im·mis′ci·bil′i·ty,** *n.*

im·mit·i·ga·ble (i mit′ə gə bəl), *adj.* not to be mitigated.

im·mo·bile (i mō′bil, -bēl), *adj.* **1.** incapable of moving or being moved. **2.** not mobile or moving. · im′mo·bil′i·ty, *n.* ·—**im·mo′bi·li·ize′** (-līz′), *v.t.* —**im·mo′bi·li·za′tion.** *n.*

im·mod·er·ate (i mod′ər it). *adj.* exceeding just or reasonable limits. —**im·mod′er·a·cy** (-ə sē). *n.* —**im·mod′er·ate·ly,** *adv.* · —**im·mod′er·a·cy** (-ə sē). *n.* —**im·mod′er·a′tion,** *n.*

im·mod·est (i mod′ist), *adj.* **1.** lacking restraint in conduct or speech. **2.** boastful or impudent. —**im·mod′-**

est·ly, *adv.* —**im·mod′es·ty,** *n.* — **Syn. 1.** indecent, shameless.

im·mo·late (im′ə lāt′), *v.t.,* -lat·ed, -lat·ing. to kill as a sacrificial victim, as by fire. —**im′mo·la′tion,** *n.*

im·mor·al (i môr′əl, i mor′-), *adj.* **1.** violating moral principles. **2.** licentious or lascivious. —**im·mor′al·ly,** *adv.* —**Syn. 1.** corrupt, unethical. **2.** depraved, wicked.

im·mo·ral·i·ty (im′ə ral′i tē, im′ô-), *n.,* *pl.* -ties. **1.** immoral character or conduct. **2.** sexual misconduct. **3.** an immoral act.

im·mor·tal (i môr′t°l), *adj.* **1.** not liable or subject to death. **2.** remembered or celebrated through all time. **3.** not liable to perish or decay. —*n.* **4.** an immortal being. **5.** a person, esp. an author, of enduring fame. **6.** (*often cap.*) any of the gods of classical mythology. —**im·mor′tal·ly,** *adv.*

im·mor·tal·i·ty (im′ôr tal′i tē), *n.* **1.** unending life. **2.** enduring fame.

im·mor·tal·ize (i môr′t°līz′), *v.t.,* -ized, -iz·ing. to make immortal, esp. in fame.

im·mo·tile (i mōt′°l), *adj. Biol.* not able to move. —**im′mo·til′i·ty,** *n.*

im·mov·a·ble (i moō′və bəl), *adj.* **1.** incapable of being moved. **2.** emotionless or impassive. **3.** steadfast or unyielding. —**im·mov′a·bil′i·ty,** *n.* —**im·mov′a·bly,** *adv.*

im·mune (i myoōn′), *adj.* **1.** protected from a disease, as by inoculation. **2.** exempt, as from taxation. —**im·mu′ni·ty,** *n.*

im·mu·nize (im′yə nīz′, i myoō′nīz′), *v.t.,* -nized, -niz·ing. to make immune. —**im′mu·ni·za′tion,** *n.*

im·mu·nol·o·gy (im′yə nol′ə jē), *n.* the branch of medicine dealing with immunity from disease. —**im·mu·no·log·ic** (i myoō′n°loj′ik), **im·mu′no·log′i·cal,** *adj.* —**im·mu·nol′o·gist,** *n.*

im·mu·no·sup·pres·sive (im′yə nō sə-pres′iv), *adj.* acting to suppress the body's natural reactions to foreign agents or tissues. —**im′mu·no·sup·pres·sant** (-sə pres′ənt), *n., adj.*

im·mure (i myoōr′), *v.t.,* -mured, -mur·ing. **1.** to enclose within walls. **2.** to shut in or confine.

im·mu·ta·ble (i myoō′tə bəl), *adj.* not mutable or changeable. —**im·mu′-ta·bil′i·ty,** *n.* —**im·mu′ta·bly,** *adv.*

imp (imp), *n.* **1.** a little devil or demon. **2.** a mischievous child.

imp., 1. imperative. **2.** imperfect. **3.** imperial. **4.** import. **5.** important. **6.** imported. **7.** importer.

im·pact (*n.* im′pakt; *v.* im pakt′), *n.* **1.** the striking of one body against another. **2.** the force of such a striking. **3.** influence or effect. —*v.t.* **4.** to drive or press closely. **5.** to strike forcefully.

im·pact·ed (im pak′tid), *adj.* noting a tooth so confined in its socket as to be incapable of normal eruption.

im·pair (im pâr′), *v.t.* to diminish in quality, strength, etc. —**im·pair′·ment,** *n.*

im·pa·la (im pal′ə, -pä′lə), *n., pl.* **-pal·as, -pal·a.** an African antelope, the male of which has long lyre-shaped horns.

im·pale (im pāl′), *v.t.,* **-paled, -pal·ing.** to pierce with a sharpened stake thrust up through the body, as for torture or punishment. —**im·pal′er,** *n.* —**im·pale′ment,** *n.*

im·pal·pa·ble (im pal′pə bəl), *adj.* **1.** incapable of being touched or felt. **2.** incapable of being readily grasped by the mind. —**im·pal′pa·bly,** *adv.*

im·pan·el (im pan′əl), *v.t.,* **-eled, -el·ing or -elled, -el·ling. 1.** to enter on a panel or list for jury duty. **2.** to select (a jury) from the panel.

im·part (im pärt′), *v.t.* **1.** to make known. **2.** to give a share of.

im·par·tial (im pär′shəl), *adj.* not partial or biased. —**im·par·ti·al·i·ty** (im pär′shē al′i tē), *n.* —**im·par′tial·ly,** *adv.*

im·pass·a·ble (im pas′ə bəl, -pä′sə-), *adj.* not allowing passage over, through or along.

im·passe (im′pas, im pas′), *n., pl.* **-pass·es** (-pas iz, -pas′iz). **1.** a position from which there is no escape. **2.** a road or way that has no outlet.

im·pas·si·ble (im pas′ə bəl), *adj.* **1.** incapable of suffering pain. **2.** incapable of emotion. —**im·pas′si·bil′-i·ty,** *n.* —**im·pas′si·bly,** *adv.*

im·pas·sioned (im pash′ənd), *adj.* filled with passion or fervor.

im·pas·sive (im pas′iv), *adj.* showing no sign of emotion or feeling. —**im·pas′sive·ly,** *adv.* —**im·pas·siv·i·ty** (im′pa siv′i tē), *n.*

im·pas·to (im pä′stō, -pas′tō), *n.* **1.** the laying on of paint thickly. **2.** the paint so laid on.

im·pa·tience (im pā′shəns), *n.* **1.** lack of patience. **2.** eager desire for relief or change. **3.** intolerance of anything that thwarts or hinders.

im·pa·ti·ens (im pā′shē enz′), *n.* any annual plant having irregular flowers in which the calyx and corolla are not clearly distinguishable.

im·pa·tient (im pā′shənt), *adj.* **1.** not patient. **2.** indicating lack of patience. **3.** restless in desire or expectation. —**im·pa′tient·ly,** *adv.*

im·peach (im pēch′), *v.t.* **1.** to accuse (a public official) before an appropriate tribunal of misconduct in office. **2.** *Chiefly Law.* to challenge the credibility of: *to impeach a witness.* —**im·peach′a·ble,** *adj.* —**im·peach′er,** *n.* —**im·peach′ment,** *n.*

im·pearl (im pûrl′), *Chiefly Literary.* **1.** to form into pearls. **2.** to adorn with pearls.

im·pec·ca·ble (im pek′ə bəl), *adj.* **1.** without flaw or fault. **2.** not liable to sin. —**im·pec′ca·bil′i·ty,** *n.* —**im·pec′ca·bly,** *adv.*

im·pe·cu·ni·ous (im′pə kyōō′nē əs), *adj.* having very little or no money. —**im′pe·cu′ni·ous·ly,** *adv.* —**im′pe·cu′ni·ous·ness,** *n.*

im·ped·ance (im pēd′əns), *n.* the total opposition to alternating current by an electric circuit.

im·pede (im pēd′), *v.t.,* **-ped·ed, -ped·ing.** to slow in movement or progress by interference. —**im·ped′er,** *n.* —**Syn.** hinder, obstruct, retard.

im·ped·i·ment (im ped′ə mənt), *n.* something that impedes, esp. a speech disorder.

im·ped·i·men·ta (im ped′ə men′tə), *n. pl.* things that impede, as supplies carried by an army.

im·pel (im pel′), *v.t.,* **-pelled, -pel·ling. 1.** to drive or urge forward. **2.** to drive or cause to move onward. —**im·pel′ler,** *n.*

im·pend (im pend′), *v.i.* **1.** to be imminent or near at hand. **2.** to be a threat or menace. [< L *impend(ere)* (to) hang over, threaten]

im·pen·e·tra·ble (im pen′i trə bəl), *adj.* **1.** unable to be penetrated or pierced. **2.** incapable of being comprehended. —**im·pen′e·tra·bil′i·ty,** —**im·pen′e·tra·ble·ness,** *n.* —**im·pen′e·tra·bly,** *adv.*

im·pen·i·tent (im pen′i tənt), *adj.* not feeling sorrow for sin. —**im·pen′i·tence,** *n.*

imper., imperative.

im·per·a·tive (im per′ə tiv), *adj.* **1.** not to be avoided or evaded. **2.** expressing a command. **3.** *Gram.* noting the mood of the verb used in commands, requests, etc. —*n.* **4.** something imperative. **5.** *Gram.* **a.** the imperative mood. **b.** a verb in this mood. —**im·per′a·tive·ly,** *adv.*

im·per·cep·ti·ble (im′pər sep′tə bəl), *adj.* **1.** very slight, gradual, or subtle. **2.** not perceived by or affecting the senses. —**im′per·cep′ti·ble·ness,** *n.* —**im′per·cep′ti·bly,** *adv.*

im·per·cep·tive (im′pər sep′tiv), *adj.* lacking perception. Also, **im′per·cip′i·ent** (-sip′ē ənt). —**im′per·cep′tive·ness,** *n.*

imperf., imperfect.

im·per·fect (im pûr′fikt), *adj.* **1.** of or pertaining to defects. **2.** not perfect. **3.** *Gram.* designating a verb tense noting incompleted action or state, esp. with reference to the past. —*n. Gram.* **4.** the imperfect tense. **5.** a verb form in this tense. —**im·per′fect·ly,** *adv.* —**im·per′fect·ness,** *n.*

im·per·fec·tion (im′pər fek′shən), n.
1. something imperfect in makeup.
2. the quality or condition of being
imperfect.

im·per·fo·rate (im pûr′fər it, -fə rāt′),
adj. 1. not perforated. 2. Philately.
lacking the perforations usually separating individual stamps. —n. 3.
an imperforate stamp.

im·pe·ri·al (im pēr′ē əl), adj. 1. of
an empire, emperor, or empress. 2.
characterizing the rule or authority
of a sovereign state over its dependencies. 3. domineering or imperious.
4. of special size or quality. —im·
pe′ri·al·ly, adv. —im·pe′ri·al·ness, n.

im·pe·ri·al² (im pēr′ē əl), n. a small,
pointed beard beneath the lower lip.

impe′rial gal′lon, a British gallon
equivalent to 1⅕ U.S. gallons.

im·pe·ri·al·ism (im pēr′ē ə liz′əm), n.
1. the policy of extending the rule or
authority of an empire or nation
over foreign countries. 2. imperial
government. 3. an imperial system
of government. —im·pe′ri·al·ist, n.,
adj. —im·pe′ri·al·is′tic, adj.

im·per·il (im per′əl), v.t., -iled, -il·ing
or -illed, -il·ling. to put in peril. —
im·per′il·ment, n.

im·pe·ri·ous (im pēr′ē əs), adj. 1.
commandingly arrogant. 2. urgent or
imperative. —im·pe′ri·ous·ly, adv.
—im·pe′ri·ous·ness, n. —Syn. 1.
domineering, overbearing.

im·per·ish·a·ble (im per′i shə bəl), adj.
not subject to decay. —im·per′ish·
a·bly, adv.

im·per·ma·nent (im pûr′mə nənt), adj.
not permanent or enduring. —im·
per′ma·nence, n. —im·per′ma·nent·
ly, adv.

im·per·me·a·ble (im pûr′mē ə bəl), adj.
1. not permeable. 2. not permitting
the passage of a fluid through the
pores, etc. —im·per′me·a·bly, adv.

im·per·mis·si·ble (im′pər mis′ə bəl),
adj. not permissible or allowable.

impers., impersonal.

im·per·son·al (im pûr′sə nəl), adj. 1.
without personal reference or connection. 2. having no personality or
human traits. 3. Gram. (of a verb)
having only third person singular
forms, usually with the pronoun its
as the subject. —im·per′son·al′i·ty,
n. —im·per′son·al·ly, adv.

im·per·son·ate (im pûr′sə nāt′), v.t.,
-at·ed, -at·ing. to assume the character or role of. —im·per′son·a′-
tion, n. —im·per′son·a′tor, n.

im·per·ti·nent (im pûr′t°nənt), adj. 1.
unseemingly intrusive or rude. 2. not
pertinent. —im·per′ti·nence, n. —
im·per′ti·nent·ly, adv. —Syn. 1. impudent, insolent, presumptuous.

im·per·turb·a·ble (im′pər tûr′bə bəl),
adj. incapable of being perturbed or

agitated. —im′per·turb′a·bil′i·ty, n.
—im′per·turb′a·bly, adv.

im·per·vi·ous (im pûr′vē əs), adj. 1.
not permitting penetration or passage. 2. incapable of being influenced or affected. —im·per′vi·ous·
ly, adv.

im·pe·ti·go (im′pi tī′gō), n. a contagious skin disease marked by a
superficial eruption of pustules.

im·pet·u·ous (im pech′oo əs), adj. 1.
characterized by sudden or rash action, emotion, etc. 2. moving with
great force. —im·pet′u·os′i·ty (-os′-
i tē), n. —im·pet′u·ous·ly, adv.

im·pe·tus (im′pi təs), n., pl. -tus·es. 1.
a moving or motivating force. 2. the
force with which a moving body
tends to maintain its velocity and
overcome resistance.

im·pi·e·ty (im pī′i tē), n., pl. -ties. 1.
lack of piety. 2. lack of respect. 3.
an impious act.

im·pinge (im pinj′), v.i., -pinged,
-ping·ing. 1. to have an effect or
impact. 2. to make steady inroads:
to impinge upon another's rights. 3.
to come into violent contact. —im·
pinge′ment, n.

im·pi·ous (im′pē əs), adj. not pious
or religious —im′pi·ous·ly, adv.

imp·ish (im′pish), adj. 1. of or like an
imp. 2. mischievous. —imp′ish·ly,
adv. —imp′ish·ness, n.

im·plac·a·ble (im plak′ə bəl, -plā′kə-),
adj. not to be appeased or pacified.
—im·plac′a·bil′i·ty, n. —im·plac′a·
bly, adv.

im·plant (im plant′, -plänt′), v.t. 1.
to fix or put firmly. 2. to plant securely. 3. to insert (a tissue) into the
body by grafting.

im·plau·si·ble (im plô′zə bəl), adj. not
having the appearance of truth or
credibility. —im·plau′si·bil′i·ty, im·
plau′si·ble·ness, n. —im·plau′si·bly,
adv.

im·ple·ment (n. im′plə mənt; v. im′·
plə ment′), n. 1. a device for assisting in manual work, as one used
in agriculture. —v.t. 2. to put into
effect according to a procedure. —
im′ple·men·ta′tion, n.

im·pli·cate (im′pli kāt′), v.t., -cat·ed,
-cat·ing. 1. to show to be also involved, usually in an incriminating
manner. 2. Chiefly Logic. to imply.

im·pli·ca·tion (im′plə kā′shən), n. 1.
something implied or suggested. 2.
the act of implying or state of being
implied. 3. the act of implicating or
state of being implicated.

im·plic·it (im plis′it), adj. 1. implied,
rather than expressly stated. 2. potentially contained. 3. unquestioning
or unreserved. —im·plic′it·ly, adv.
—im·plic′it·ness, n.

im·plode (im plōd′), *v.i., v.t.,* **-plod·ed, -plod·ing.** to burst inward. —**im·plo′sion** (-plō′zhən), *n.* —**im·plo′sive,** *adj.*

im·plore (im plôr′, -plōr′), *v.t.,* **-plored, -plor·ing.** 1. to beg urgently or piteously, as for aid or mercy. 2. to beg urgently or piteously for. —**im·plo·ra′tion,** *n.* —**im·plor′ing·ly,** *adv.*

im·ply (im plī′), *v.t.,* **-plied, -ply·ing.** 1. to indicate or suggest without express statement. 2. to require as a necessary condition: *Speech implies a speaker.*

—Usage. See **infer.**

im·po·lite (im′pə līt′), *adj.* not polite or courteous. —**im·po·lite′ly,** *adv.*

im·pol·i·tic (im pol′i tik), *adj.* not politic or expedient. —**im·pol′i·tic·ly,** *adv.*

im·pon·der·a·ble (im pon′dər ə bəl), *adj.* 1. that cannot be precisely measured or evaluated. —*n.* 2. an imponderable thing.

im·port (*v.* im pôrt′, -pōrt′; *n.* im′pôrt, -pōrt), *v.t.* 1. to ship (commodities) from foreign countries for sale, use, etc. 2. *Literary.* to convey as meaning or implication. —*v.i.* 3. *Literary.* to be of consequence. —*n.* 4. something imported. 5. meaning or implication. 6. consequence or importance. —**im·port′a·ble,** *adj.* —**im·port′er,** *n.*

im·por·tance (im pôr′təns), *n.* 1. the quality or state of being important. 2. significance or consequence.

im·por·tant (im pôr′tənt), *adj.* 1. of much significance or consequence. 2. of considerable influence, authority, or distinction: *important guests.* —**im·por′tant·ly,** *adv.*

im·por·ta·tion (im′pôr tā′zhən, -pōr-), *n.* 1. the act of importing. 2. something imported.

im·por·tu·nate (im pôr′chə nit), *adj.* 1. urgent or persistent in solicitation. 2. pertinacious, as demands. —**im·por′tu·nate·ly,** *adv.* —**im·por′tu·nate·ness,** *n.*

im·por·tune (im′pôr tōōn′, -tyōōn′, im pôr′chən), *v.t., v.i.,* **-tuned, -tun·ing.** to entreat urgently or persistently. —**im′por·tu′ni·ty,** *n.*

im·pose (im pōz′), *v.,* **-posed, -pos·ing.** —*v.t.* 1. to lay on or set as something to be borne, endured, paid, etc. 2. to obtrude or thrust (oneself) upon others. —*v.i.* 3. **impose on** or **upon, a.** to take unfair advantage of. **b.** to defraud or deceive. —**im·pos′er,** *n.* —**im·po·si′tion** (-pə ish′ən), *n.*

im·pos·ing (im pō′zing), *adj.* very impressive, as because of great size, stately appearance, etc. —**im·pos′ing·ly,** *adv.*

im·pos·si·ble (im pos′ə bəl), *adj.* 1. unable to be or happen. 2. unable to be done or effected. 3. not to be

done or endured with any degree of reason or propriety. 4. utterly impracticable. 5. hopelessly difficult or objectionable. —**im·pos′si·bil′i·ty,** *n.* —**im·pos′si·bly,** *adv.*

im·post[1] (im′pōst), *n. Archaic.* a customs duty. —**im′post·er,** *n.*

im·post[2] (im′pōst), *n. Archit.* the point of springing of an arch.

im·pos·tor (im pos′tər), *n.* a person who practices deception under an assumed character or name. Also, **im·post′er.**

im·pos·ture (im pos′chər), *n.* the act, way, or practice of an impostor.

im·po·tent (im′pə tənt), *adj.* 1. lacking physical power or strength. 2. without force or effectiveness. 3. (of a male) incapable of having normal coitus. —**im′po·tence, im′po·ten·cy,** *n.* —**im′po·tent·ly,** *adv.*

im·pound (im pound′), *v.t.* 1. to shut up in a pound, as a stray animal. 2. to seize and retain in custody of the law. 3. to confine within an enclosure: *water impounded in a reservoir.* —**im·pound′ment,** *n.*

im·pov·er·ish (im pov′ər ish, -pov′rish), *v.t.* 1. to reduce to poverty. 2. to exhaust the strength or richness of. —**im·pov′er·ish·ment,** *n.*

im·prac·ti·ca·ble (im prak′tə kə bəl), *adj.* incapable of being done or put into practice.

im·prac·ti·cal (im prak′tə kəl), *adj.* 1. not practical or useful. 2. impracticable. —**im·prac′ti·cal′i·ty,** *n.*

im·pre·cate (im′prə kāt′), *v.t.,* **-cat·ed, -cat·ing.** to invoke (evil or curses). —**im′pre·ca′tion,** *n.* —**im′pre·ca′tor,** *n.*

im·pre·cise (im′pri sīs′), *adj.* not precise or exact. —**im′pre·cise′ly,** *adv.* —**im′pre·ci′sion** (-sizh′ən), **im′pre·cise′ness,** *n.*

im·preg·na·ble (im preg′nə bəl), *adj.* 1. strong enough to resist attack, as a fortress. 2. not to be overcome, as an argument. —**im·preg′na·bil′i·ty,** *n.* —**im·preg′na·bly,** *adv.*

im·preg·nate (im preg′nāt, im′preg-), *v.t.,* **-nat·ed, -nat·ing.** 1. to make pregnant. 2. to cause to be infused, as with a substance. 3. to imbue or permeate, as with ideas. —**im·preg′na·ble,** *adj.* —**im′preg·na′tion,** *n.*

im·pre·sa·ri·o (im′pri sär′ē ō′, -sär′-), *n., pl.* **-sa·ri·os.** a person who organizes or manages public entertainments, esp. operas, ballets, or concerts.

im·press[1] (*v.* im pres′; *n.* im′pres), *v.,
n.* —*v.t.* 1. to affect deeply or strongly. 2. to fix deeply in the mind. 3. to produce (a mark, figure, etc.) by pressure. 4. to apply with pressure so as to leave a mark. —*n.* 5. the act of impressing. 6. a mark made by or as by pressure. —**im·press′er,** *n.*

im·press² (im pres′), *v.t.* to take by force for public service, as men or goods, esp. as formerly done by the British navy. —**im·press′ment**, *n.*

im·press·i·ble (im pres′ə bəl), *adj.* impressionable. —**im·press′i·bil′i·ty**, *n.*

im·pres·sion (im presh′ən), *n.* 1. a strong effect produced on the intellect, feelings, or conscience. 2. the effect produced by an agency or influence. 3. a notion, belief, etc., often of a vague nature. 4. a mark, figure, etc., produced by pressure. 5. *Brit.* printing (def. 3). 6. an imitation of recognizable traits of famous persons, as by an entertainer.

im·pres·sion·a·ble (im presh′ə nə bəl, -presh′nə-), *adj.* easily impressed or influenced

im·pres·sion·ism (im presh′ə niz′əm), *n.* (*often cap.*) a movement in art, esp. in painting, which attempts to convey general impressions rather than objective reality.

im·pres·sion·ist (im presh′ə nist), *n.* 1. (*often cap.*) an artist who practices impressionism. 2. an entertainer who does impersonating impressions. —*adj.* 3. of impressionism or impressionists. —**im·pres′sion·is′tic**, *adj.*

im·pres·sive (im pres′iv), *adj.* tending to make a profound impression. —**im·pres′sive·ly**, *adv.* —**im·pres′sive·ness**, *n.*

im·pri·ma·tur (im′pri mä′tər, -mā′-, -prī-), *n.* 1. a license to publish a book, esp. one granted by the Roman Catholic Church. 2. any sanction or approval. [< NL: let it be printed]

im·print (*n.* im′print; *v.* im print′), *n.* 1. something impressed or printed. 2. any impressed effect. 3. the publisher's name, usually with the place and date of publication, printed on the title page. —*v.t.* 4. to produce (a mark) on something by pressure. —**im·print′er**, *n.*

im·pris·on (im priz′ən), *v.t.* to put into a prison. —**im·pris′on·ment**, *n.*

im·prob·a·ble (im prob′ə bəl), *adj.* unlikely to be true or to happen. —**im′prob·a·bil′i·ty**, *n.* —**im·prob′a·bly**, *adv.*

im·promp·tu (im promp′tōo, -tyōo), *adj., adv.* without previous preparation.

im·prop·er (im prop′ər), *adj.* 1. not proper or fit. 2. not strictly applicable or correct. 3. not in accordance with propriety of behavior, manners, etc. —**im·prop′er·ly**, *adv.* —**im·prop′er·ness**, *n.*

improp′er frac′tion, a fraction having the numerator greater than the denominator.

im·pro·pri·e·ty (im′prə prī′i tē), *n., pl.* -ties. 1. the quality or condition of being improper. 2. an improper act, expression, or usage.

im·prove (im prōōv′), *v.,* -proved, -prov·ing. —*v.t.* 1. to bring into a more desirable condition. 2. to make (land) more valuable by enclosure, cultivation, etc. 3. to make good use of. —*v.i.* 4. to become better. 5. **improve on** or **upon**, to make improvements in, as by revision or addition. —**im·prov′a·ble**, *adj.*

im·prove·ment (im prōōv′mənt), *n.* 1. the act of improving or state of being improved 2. a change or addition by which a thing is improved. 3. something done or added to real property which increases its value.

im·prov·i·dent (im prov′i dənt), *adj.* lacking prudent foresight. —**im·prov′i·dence**, *n.* —**im·prov′i·dent·ly**, *adv.*

im·pro·vise (im′prə vīz′), *v.,* -vised, -vis·ing. —*v.t.* 1. to compose and perform without previous preparation. 2. to devise or provide from whatever material is available. —*v.i.* 3. to improvise something. —**im·prov′i·sa′tion** (-prov′i zā′shən), *n.* —**im·prov′i·sa′tion·al** *adj.* —**im′pro·vis′er**, **im′pro·vis′or**, *n.*

im·pru·dent (im prōōd′ənt), *adj.* not prudent or judicious. —**im·pru′dence**, *n.*

im·pu·dent (im′pyə dənt), *adj.* characterized by boldness, impertinence, or effrontery —**im′pu·dence**, *n.* —**im′pu·dent·ly**, *adv.*

im·pugn (im pyōōn′), *v.t.* to attack forcefully by words or arguments, as veracity, motives, etc. —**im·pugn′er**, *n.*

im·pu·is·sant (im pyōō′i sənt, im·pwis′ənt), *adj. Archaic.* feeble or weak —**im·pu′is·sance**, *n.*

im·pulse (im′puls). *n.* 1. the influence of a particular feeling or mental state. 2. sudden inclination prompting to action 3. an impelling force. 4. the effect of such a force. 5. *Mech.* the product of the average force acting upon a body.

im·pul·sion (im pul′shən), *n.* 1. the act of impelling or state of being impelled 2. an impelling force. 3. mental impulse.

im·pul·sive (im pul′siv), *adj.* 1. swayed by emotional impulses. 2. having the power of impelling. —**im·pul′sive·ly**, *adv.* —**im·pul′sive·ness**, *n.*

im·pu·ni·ty (im pyōō′ni tē), *n.* exemption from punishment or detrimental effects.

im·pure (im pyōōr′), *adj.* 1. not pure or clean. 2. mixed with extraneous matter. 3. unchaste or obscene. —**im·pure′ly**, *adv.* —**im·pu′ri·ty**, **im·pure′ness**, *n.*

im·pute (im pyōōt'), *v.t.*, **-put·ed, -put·ing.** to attribute (something discreditable), as to a person. —**im·put'a·ble,** *adj.* —**im·pu·ta'tion,** *n.*

in (in), *prep., adv., adj., n.* —*prep.* **1.** (to indicate inclusion within space or a place): *walking in the park.* **2.** (to indicate inclusion within something immaterial): *in politics.* **3.** to indicate inclusion within or occurrence during a period or limit of time): *in ancient times.* **4.** (to indicate limitation or qualification, as of situation, manner, action, etc.): *to speak in a whisper; to be similar in appearance.* **5.** (to indicate means): *spoken in French.* **6.** (to indicate motion or direction from outside to a point within): *Let's go in the house.* **7.** (to indicate transition from one state to another): *to break in half.* **8.** (to indicate object or purpose): *speaking in honor of the event.* **9. in that,** because. —*adv.* **10.** in or into some place, position, etc. **11.** on the inside. **12.** in one's house or office. **13.** in office or power. **14. have it in for,** *Informal.* to wish harm to. **15. in with,** on friendly terms with. —*adj.* **16.** located or situated within. **17.** stylish or fashionable. **18.** *Informal.* comprehensible only to a special group: *an in joke.* **19.** incoming or inbound. **20.** being in power, control, etc.: *the in party.* —*n.* **21.** Usually, **ins.** persons in office or political power. **22.** pull or influence: *He's got an in with important people.*

In, indium.

IN, Indiana.

in-[1], a prefix meaning "in": *incarcerate; incantation.*

in-[2], a prefix meaning "not" or "lack of": *indelicate; inexperience.*

-in, a combining form of **in** to form compound nouns that refer to various organized social or cultural activities: *be-in.*

in., inch; inches. Also, **in**

in·a·bil·i·ty (in'ə bil'i tē), *n.* lack of ability or capacity.

in ab·sen·tia (in ab sen'shə, -shē ə, -tē ə), *Latin.* in absence.

in·ac·ti·vate (in ak'tə vāt'), *v.t.,* **-vat·ed, -vat·ing.** to make inactive. —**in·ac'ti·va'tion,** *n.*

in·ad·e·quate (in ad'ə kwit), *adj.* not adequate or sufficient. —**in·ad'e-**

qua·cy, **in·ad'e·quate·ness,** *n.* —**in·ad'e·quate·ly,** *adv.*

in·ad·vert·ent (in'əd vûr't°nt), *adj.* **1.** not attentive or mindful. **2.** unintentional or thoughtless. —**in'ad·vert'ence, in·ad·vert'en·cy,** *n.* —**in'ad·vert'ent·ly,** *adv.*

in·al·ien·a·ble (in āl'yə nə bəl, -ā'lē-ə-), *adj.* not alienable or transferable to another. —**in·al'ien·a·bil'ity,** *n.* —**in·al'ien·a·bly,** *adv.*

in·am·o·ra·ta (in am'ə rä'tə, in'am-), *n.* a woman who is loved.

in·ane (i nān'), *adj.* **1.** lacking sense or ideas: *inane questions.* **2.** empty or void. —**in·an·i·ty** (i nan'i tē), *n.* —Syn. **1.** foolish, pointless, silly.

in·an·i·mate (in an'ə mit), *adj.* **1.** not animate or alive. **2.** spiritless or dull. —**in·an'i·mate·ly,** *adv.* —**in·an'i·mate·ness,** *n.*

in·ap·pre·ci·a·ble (in'ə prē'shē ə bəl, -shə bəl), *adj.* too small to be readily perceived or measured. —**in'ap·pre'ci·a·bly,** *adv.*

in·ar·tic·u·late (in'är tik'yə lit), *adj.* **1.** not uttered with intelligible modulations, **2.** unable to use articulate speech. **3.** lacking the ability to express oneself in clear and effective speech. **4.** not fully expressed or expressible. —**in'ar·tic'u·late·ly,** *adv.* —**in'ar·tic'u·late·ness,** *n.*

in as much' as' (in'əz much'), **1.** seeing that. **2.** to such a degree as.

in·at·ten·tion (in'ə ten'shən), *n.* **1.** lack of attention. **2.** an act of neglect. —**in'at·ten'tive,** *adj.*

in·au·gu·ral (in ô'gyər əl, -gər əl), *adj.* **1.** of an inauguration. **2.** marking the beginning of a new venture or series. —*n.* **3.** an address, as of a president, at the beginning of a term of office. **4.** an inaugural ceremony.

in·au·gu·rate (in ô'gyə rāt', -gə-), *v.t.,* **-rat·ed, -rat·ing. 1.** to begin formally. **2.** to induct into office with formal ceremonies. **3.** to introduce into public use by some formal ceremony. —**in·au'gu·ra'tion,** *n.*

in·board (in'bōrd', -bôrd'), *adj., adv.* **1.** located inside a hull or aircraft. **2.** located nearer the center, as of an airplane. —*n.* **3.** an inboard motor. **4.** a boat equipped with an inboard motor.

in·born (in'bôrn'), *adj.* possessed by one as if existing at birth.

in·bound (in'bound'), *adj.* inward bound: *inbound ships.*

---

in·bred (in′bred′), *adj.* **1.** resulting from or involved in inbreeding. **2.** naturally inherent.

in·breed·ing (in′brē′ding), *n.* **1.** the mating of related individuals or self-fertilized plants, esp. in order to produce desired characteristics. **2.** excessive narrowness or limitation, as in choice of personnel. —**in′-breed′** (-brēd′), *v.t., v.i.*

Inc. (*sometimes* ingk), Incorporated.

inc., **1.** incorporated. **2.** increase.

In·ca (ing′kə), *n.* a member of a dominant South American Indian people who established an empire in Peru (c. A.D. 1400) prior to the Spanish conquest.

in·cal·cu·la·ble (in kal′kyə lə bəl), *adj.* **1.** unable to be calculated or determined. **2.** incapable of being forecast or predicted. —**in·cal′cu·la·ble·ness,** *n.* —**in·cal′cu·la·bly,** *adv.*

in·can·des·cent (in′kən des′ənt), *adj.* **1.** glowing or white with heat. **2.** intensely bright. —**in′can·des′cence,** *n.* —**in′can·des′cent·ly,** *adv.*

in′candes′cent lamp′, a lamp that emits light due to the glowing of a heated material, as a filament.

in·can·ta·tion (in′kan tā′shən), *n.* **1.** the chanting or uttering of words purporting to have magical power. **2.** the formula employed.

in·ca·pa·ble (in kā′pə bəl), *adj.* **1.** not capable or able. **2.** utterly incompetent. —**in·ca′pa·bil′i·ty,** *n.* —**in·ca′pa·bly,** *adv.*

in·ca·pac·i·tate (in′kə pas′i tāt′), *v.t.,* **-tat·ed, -tat·ing. 1.** to make incapable or unfit. **2.** to deprive of the legal ability to act. —**in′ca·pac′i·ta′tion,** *n.*

in·ca·pac·i·ty (in′kə pas′i tē), *n.* **1.** lack of capacity or ability. **2.** lack of the legal ability to act.

in·car·cer·ate (in kär′sə rāt′), *v.t.,* **-at·ed, -at·ing.** to imprison, esp. legally. —**in·car′cer·a′tion,** *n.* —**in·car′cer·a′tor,** *n.*

in·car·na·dine (in kär′nə dīn′, -din, -dēn′), *v.t.,* **-dined, -din·ing.** *Literary.* to make crimson.

in·car·nate (*adj.* in kär′nit, -nāt; *v.* in kär′nāt), *adj., v.,* **-nat·ed, -nat·ing.** —*adj.* **1.** having a bodily, esp. a human, form. **2.** personified or typified. —*v.t.* **3.** to give a bodily, esp. a human, form to. **4.** to be the embodiment or type of. **5.** to put into a concrete form. —**in′car·na′tion,** *n.*

in·case (in kās′), *v.t.,* **-cased, -cas·ing.** encase.

in·cen·di·ar·y (in sen′dē er′ē), *adj., n., pl.* **-ar·ies.** —*adj.* **1.** designed to cause combustion or fires. **2.** of or pertaining to arson. **3.** tending to arouse strife, sedition, etc. —*n.* **4.**

an incendiary bomb, bullet, etc. **5.** a person who commits arson.

in·cense[1] (in′sens), *n.* **1.** an aromatic substance producing a sweet odor when burned. **2.** the perfume or smoke of such a substance.

in·cense[2] (in sens′), *v.t.,* **-censed, -cens·ing.** to make exceedingly angry.

in·cen·tive (in sen′tiv), *n.* something that incites to action, as a reward offered to stimulate greater effort.

in·cep·tion (in sep′shən), *n.* an act or period of beginning. —**in·cep′tive,** *adj.*

in·cer·ti·tude (in sûr′ti tood′, -tyood′), *n.* **1.** lack of certitude or confidence. **2.** insecurity or instability.

in·ces·sant (in ses′ənt), *adj.* continuing without interruption. —**in·ces′sant·ly,** *adv.*

in·cest (in′sest), *n.* sexual intercourse between persons so closely related that marriage is legally forbidden. —**in·ces·tu·ous** (in ses′choo əs), *adj.* —**in·ces′tu·ous·ly,** *adv.* —**in·ces′tu·ous·ness,** *n.*

inch (inch), *n.* **1.** a unit of length equal to 1/12 foot, or 2.54 centimeters. **2. by inches,** by small degrees. Also, **inch by inch. 3.** every inch, in every respect. **4. within an inch of,** close to. —*v.t., v.i.* **5.** to move by small degrees.

in·cho·ate (in kō′it), *adj.* **1.** *Literary.* just or only begun. **2.** not organized or orderly. —**in·cho′ate·ly,** *adv.*

inch·worm (inch′wûrm′), *n.* the larva of a moth that moves in a looping motion.

in·ci·dence (in′si dəns), *n.* the rate or range of occurrence.

in·ci·dent (in′si dənt), *n.* **1.** a distinct occurrence. **2.** an occurrence of seemingly minor importance that can lead to serious consequences. —*adj.* **3.** likely or apt to happen. **4.** falling or striking on something, as light rays.

in·ci·den·tal (in′si den′t°l), *adj.* **1.** happening in fortuitous or subordinate conjunction with something else. **2.** incurred casually. —*n.* **3.** something incidental, as a circumstance. **4. incidentals,** minor expenses. —Syn. **1.** accidental, casual.

in·ci·den·tal·ly (in′si den′t°lē), *adv.* **1.** in an incidental manner. **2.** aside from the main subject of discussion.

in·cin·er·ate (in sin′ə rāt′), *v.t.,* **-at·ed, -at·ing.** to burn or reduce to ashes. —**in·cin′er·a′tion,** *n.*

in·cin·er·a·tor (in sin′ə rā′tər), *n.* a furnace or apparatus for incinerating.

in·cip·i·ent (in sip′ē ənt), *adj.* beginning to exist or appear. —**in·cip′i·ence,** *n.*

---

in·cau′tious, *adj.*   **in·cau′tious·ly,** *adv.*

in·cise (in sīz′), *v.t.*, **-cised**, **-cis·ing.**
1. to cut marks, figures, etc., upon.
2. to make (marks, figures, etc.) by cutting.

in·ci·sion (in sizh′ən), *n.* **1.** a cutting into something, esp. flesh, as for surgical purposes. **2.** a wound resulting from this.

in·ci·sive (in sī′siv), *adj.* **1.** mentally sharp and forceful: *an incisive wit.* **2.** penetrating or cutting. **—in·ci′sive·ly,** *adv.* **—in·ci′sive·ness,** *n.* **—Syn. 1.** acute, keen.

in·ci·sor (in sī′zər), *n.* one of the four anterior teeth in each jaw, used for cutting.

in·cite (in sīt′), *v.t.,* **-cit·ed, -cit·ing.** to stimulate or prompt to action. **—in·ci·ta·tion** (in′sī tā′shən, -si-), *n.* **—in·cite′ment,** *n.* **—in·cit′er,** *n.* **—Syn.** arouse, instigate, provoke.

in·ci·vil·i·ty (in′sə vil′i tē), *n., pl.* **-ties.**
1. uncivil behavior or treatment. **2.** an uncivil act. **—in·civ·il** (in siv′əl), *adj.*

incl., 1. inclosure. **2.** including. **3.** inclusive.

in·clem·ent (in klem′ənt), *adj.* **1.** severe or stormy, as the weather. **2.** not kind or merciful. **—in·clem′en·cy,** *n.*

in·cli·na·tion (in′klə nā′shən, *n.* **1.** a liking for something. **2.** something to which a person is inclined. **3.** the act of inclining or state of being inclined. **4.** a tendency toward a certain condition, action, etc. **5.** an inclined surface.

in·cline (*v.* in klīn′; *n.* in′klīn, in-klīn′), *v.,* **-clined, -clin·ing,** *n. —v.i.*
1. to have a mental tendency, preference, etc. **2.** to deviate from the vertical or horizontal. **3.** to tend in character or in course of action. **4.** to lean or bend. **—v.t. 5.** to dispose (a person) in mind, habit, etc. **6.** to bow or bend (the head, body, etc.). **7.** to cause to lean or bend in a particular direction. **—n. 8.** a sloping surface. **—in·clin′a·ble** (-klī′nə bəl), *adj.*

in·close (in klōz′), *v.t.,* **-closed, -clos·ing.** enclose. **—in·clo′sure** (-klō′-zhər), *n.*

in·clude (in klood′), *v.t.,* **-clud·ed, -clud·ing. 1.** to contain, as a whole does parts. **2.** to take in or consider as a part or member of. **—in·clu′sion** (-kloo′zhən), *n.*

in·clu·sive (in kloo′siv), *adj.* **1.** including the stated limit or extremes: *from six to ten inclusive.* **2.** including everything concerned. **3.** inclusive of, including. **—in·clu′sive·ly,** *adv.* **—in·clu′sive·ness,** *n.*

incog., incognito.

in·cog·ni·to (in kog′ni tō′, in′kog nē′-), *adj., adv.* with the real identity concealed, as under an assumed name, esp. to avoid notice. [< It < L *incognitus* unknown]

in·co·her·ent (in′kō hēr′ənt), *adj.* **1.** without logical connection. **2.** characterized by such thought or language. **—in′co·her′ence,** *n.* **—in′co·her′ent·ly,** *adv.*

in·com·bus·ti·ble (in′kəm bus′tə bəl), *adj.* incapable of burning or being burned.

in·come (in′kum), *n.* the monetary payment received for goods or services, or from other sources, as rents, investments, etc.

in′come tax′, a tax levied on individual or corporate income.

in·com·ing (in′kum′ing), *adj.* **1.** coming in: *the incoming tide.* **2.** succeeding, as an officeholder: *the incoming mayor.*

in·com·men·su·rate (in′kə men′shər it, -sər it), *adj.* not commensurate or adequate. **—in′com·men′su·rate·ly,** *adv.*

in·com·mode (in′kə mōd′), *v.t.,* **-mod·ed, -mod·ing.** *Literary.* to inconvenience.

in·com·mu·ni·ca·do (in′kə myoo′nə kä′dō), *adj.* (esp. of a prisoner) deprived of communication with others.

in·com·pa·ra·ble (in kom′pər ə bəl, -prə bəl), *adj.* **1.** not validly comparable. **2.** matchless or unequaled.

in·com·pat·i·ble (in′kəm pat′ə bəl), *adj.* **1.** incapable of existing together in harmony. **2.** opposed in character: *incompatible colors.* **—in′com·pat′i·bil′i·ty,** *n.* **—in′com·pat′i·bly,** *adv.*

in·com·pe·tent (in kom′pi tənt), *adj.* **1.** lacking qualification or ability. **2.** not legally qualified. **—n. 3.** an incompetent person. **—in·com′pe·tence, in·com′pe·ten·cy,** *n.* **—in·com′pe·tent·ly,** *adv.* **—Syn. 1.** inadequate, incapable, unfit.

in·com·plete (in′kəm plēt′), *adj.* **1.** lacking some part or parts. **2.** imperfect or unfinished. **—in′com·plete′ly,** *adv.* **—in′com·plete′ness,** *n.*

in·com·pre·hen·si·ble (in′kom pri hen′-sə bəl, in kom′-), *adj.* not comprehensible or intelligible. **—in′com·pre·hen′sion,** *n.*

in·com·press·i·ble (in′kəm pres′ə bəl), *adj.* that cannot be compressed. **—in′com·press′i·bil′i·ty,** *n.* **—in′com·press′i·bly,** *adv.*

in·con·gru·ous (in kong′groo əs), *adj.* **1.** out of keeping or place. **2.** not harmonious in character. **—in′con·gru′i·ty** (-groo′i tē), *n.* **—in·con′gru·ous·ly,** *adv.*

---

in′com·men′su·ra·ble, *adj.*

in′com·mo′di·ous, *adj.*

in′com·mu′ni·ca·ble, *adj.*

in′con·ceiv′a·ble, *adj.*

in′con·ceiv′a·bly, *adv.*

in′con·clu′sive, *adj.*

in′con·clu′sive·ly, *adv.*

in·con·se·quen·tial (in′kon sə kwen′-shəl, in kon′-), *adj.* 1. of no consequence or significance. 2. illogical or irrelevant. —**in′con·se·quen′tial·ly,** *adv.*

in·con·sid·er·a·ble (in′kən sid′ər ə-bəl), *adj.* not worthy of consideration or notice.

in·con·sid·er·ate (in′kən sid′ər it), *adj.* 1. without due regard for the rights or feelings of others. 2. acting without consideration. —**in′con·sid′er·ate·ly,** *adv.* —**in′con·sid′er·ate·ness,** *n.*

in·con·sol·a·ble (in′kən sō′lə bəl), *adj.* that cannot be consoled. —**in′con·sol′a·bly,** *adv*

in·con·spic·u·ous (in′kən spik′yōō əs), *adj.* not conspicuous or noticeable. —**in′con·spic′u·ous·ly,** *adv.* —**in′con·spic′u·ous·ness,** *n.*

in·con·stant (in kon′stənt), *adj.* not constant or steadfast. —**in·con′stan·cy,** *n.* —**in·con′stant·ly,** *adv.*

in·con·test·a·ble (in′kən tes′tə bəl), *adj.* not contestable or disputable. —**in′con·test′a·bil′i·ty,** *n.* —**in′con·test′a·bly,** *adv*

in·con·ti·nent (in kon′t°nənt), *adj.* 1. lacking in moderation or control, esp. in seeking sexual gratification. 2. unable to restrain natural discharges or evacuations —**in·con′ti·nence,** *n.* —**in·con′ti·nent·ly,** *adv.*

in·con·tro·vert·i·ble (in′kon trə vûr′tə bəl, in kon′-), *adj.* that cannot be disputed or questioned. —**in′con·tro·vert′i·bly,** *adv*

in·con·ven·ience (in′kən vēn′yəns), *n.,* *v.,* **-ienced, -ienc·ing.** —*n.* 1. the quality or state of being inconvenient. 2. an inconvenient circumstance or thing. —*v.t.* 3. to put to inconvenience.

in·con·ven·ient (in′kən vēn′yənt), *adj.* 1. not agreeable to the needs or purposes. 2. not accessible or at hand. —**in′con·ven′ient·ly,** *adv.*

in·cor·po·rate (in kôr′pə rāt′), *v.,* **-rat·ed, -rat·ing.** —*v.t.* 1. to form into a corporation. 2. to introduce into a body as a part. 3. to include as a part. 4. to combine into one uniform substance. —*v.t.* 5. to combine so as to form one body. 6. to form a corporation. —**in·cor′po·rat′ed,** *adj.* —**in·cor′po·ra′tion,** *n.* —**in·cor′po·ra′tor,** *n.*

in·cor·po·re·al (in′kôr pôr′ē əl, -pōr′-), *adj.* not corporeal or material.

in·cor·rect (in′kə rekt′), *adj.* 1. not correct as to fact. 2. improper or unbecoming. —**in′cor·rect′ly,** *adv.* —**in′cor·rect′ness,** *n.*

in·cor·ri·gi·ble (in kôr′i jə bəl, -kor′-), *adj.* bad beyond reform: *an incorri-*

gible liar. —**in·cor′ri·gi·bil′i·ty,** *n.* —**in·cor′ri·gi·bly,** *adv.*

in·cor·rupt·i·ble (in′kə rup′tə bəl), *adj.* 1. incapable of corruption. 2. that cannot be perverted or bribed. 3. that will not dissolve or decay: *an incorruptible metal.* —**in′cor·rupt′i·bil′i·ty,** *n.* —**in′cor·rupt′i·bly,** *adv.*

incr., 1. increase. 2. increased. 3. increasing.

in·crease (*v.* in krēs′; *n.* in′krēs), *v.,* **-creased, -creas·ing,** *n.* —*v.t., v.i.* 1. to make or become greater or more numerous. —*n.* 2. growth or augmentation in numbers 3. the amount by which something is increased. —**in·creas′er,** *n* —**in·creas′ing·ly,** *adv.* —**Syn.** 1. augment enlarge expand.

in·cred·i·ble (in kred′ə bəl), *adj.* so extraordinary as to seem impossible or unbelievable. —**in·cred′i·bil′i·ty,** *n.* —**in·cred′i·ble·ness,** *n.* —**in·cred′i·bly,** *adv.*

in·cred·u·lous (in krej′ə ləs), *adj.* 1. not willing to believe or trust 2. expressing disbelief. —**in·cre·du·li·ty** (in′kri dōō′li tē, -dyōō′-), *n* —**in·cred′u·lous·ly,** *adv.* —**Syn.** 1. skeptical, unbelieving

in·cre·ment (in′krə mənt, iñg′-), *n.* 1. an increase in value, as of land. 2. something added or gained. —**in·cre·men·tal** (in′krə men′t°l, iñg′-), *adj.*

in·crim·i·nate (in krim′ə nāt′), *v.t.,* **-nat·ed, -nat·ing.** 1. to charge with a crime. 2. to involve in an accusation. —**in·crim′i·na′tion,** *n.* —**in·crim′i·na·to·ry** (in krim′ə nə tôr′ē, -tōr′ē), *adj.*

in·crust (in krust′), *v.t.* 1. to cover with a crust or hard coating. —*v.i.* 2. to form a crust. —**in′crus·ta′tion,** *n.*

in·cu·bate (in′kyə bāt′, iñg′-), *v.t., v.i.* **-bat·ed, -bat·ing.** 1. to sit upon (eggs) for the purpose of hatching 2. to keep (premature babies) in favorable conditions for growth. 3. to develop or produce (ideas) as if by hatching. —**in′cu·ba′tion,** *n.* —**in′cu·ba′tive,** *adj.*

in·cu·ba·tor (in′kyə bā′tər, iñg′-), *n.* 1. an apparatus for hatching eggs. 2. an apparatus in which premature babies are kept in favorable conditions for growth.

in·cu·bus (in′kyə bəs, iñg′-), *n., pl.* **-bi** (-bī′), **-bus·es.** 1. a demon supposed to descend upon sleeping persons. 2. something that oppresses one like a nightmare.

in·cul·cate (in kul′kāt, in′kul kāt′), *v.t.,* **-cat·ed, -cat·ing.** to teach persistently and earnestly. —**in′cul·ca′tion,** *n.*

in·cul·pa·ble (in kul′pə bəl), *adj.* free from blame or guilt.

---

in′con·sist′en·cy, *n.*　　　　**in′con·sist′ent,** *adj.*　　　　**in′con·sist′ent·ly,** *adv.*

in·cul·pate (in kul′pāt, in′kul pāt′), *v.t.*, **-pat·ed, -pat·ing.** to incriminate.

in·cum·ben·cy (in kum′bən sē), *n., pl.* **-cies.** 1. the position or term of an incumbent. 2. a duty or obligation.

in·cum·bent (in kum′bənt), *adj.* 1. holding an indicated office: *the incumbent senator.* 2. obligatory: *a duty incumbent upon me.* 3. *Archaic.* resting or lying on something. *—n.* 4. the holder of an office. **—in·cum′bent·ly,** *adv*

in·cum·ber (in kum′bər), *v.t.* encumber. **—in·cum′brance,** *n.*

in·cu·nab·u·la (in′kyōō nab′yə lə), *n. pl., sing.* **-lum** (-ləm). books produced before 1500.

in·cur (in kûr′), *v.t.,* **-curred, -cur·ring.** 1. to run or fall into: *to incur a loss.* 2. to bring upon oneself: *to incur someone's displeasure.*

in·cur·a·ble (in kyōōr′ə bəl), *adj.* that cannot be cured or remedied **—in·cur′a·bil′i·ty,** *n* **—in·cur′a·bly,** *adv.*

in·cu·ri·ous (in kyōōr′ē əs), *adj.* not curious or inquisitive.

in·cur·sion (in kûr′zhən, -shən), *n.* a hostile, usually sudden invasion of a place.

in·cus (ing′kəs), *n., pl.* **in·cu·des** (in-kyōō′dēz). the middle one of the three small bones in the middle ear.

Ind., 1. India 2. Indian. 3. Indiana.

ind., 1. independent 2. index. 3. indicative 4. industrial 5. industry.

in·debt·ed (in det′id), *adj.* 1. owing money. 2. owing gratitude. **—in·debt′ed·ness,** *n.*

in·de·cent (in dē′sənt), *adj.* 1. offensive to propriety or good taste. 2. unbecoming or unseemly. **—in·de′cen·cy,** *n* **—in·de′cent·ly,** *adv.* — Syn. 1. improper, vulgar.

in·de·ci·pher·a·ble (in′di sī′fər ə bəl), *adj.* that cannot be deciphered or decoded

in·de·ci·sion (in′di sizh′ən), *n.* inability to decide.

in·de·ci·sive (in′di sī′siv), *adj.* 1. not decisive or conclusive. 2. characterized by indecision **—in′de·ci′sive·ly,** *adv.* **—in′de·ci′sive·ness,** *n.*

in·dec·o·rous (in dek′ər əs, in′di kôr′əs, -kōr′-), *adj.* violating propriety or good taste. **—in·dec′o·rous·ly,** *adv.* **—in·dec′o·rous·ness,** *n.*

in·deed (in dēd′), *adv.* 1. truly. *—interj.* 2. (an expression of surprise, incredulity, irony, etc.)

in·de·fat·i·ga·ble (in′di fat′ə gə bəl), *adj.* incapable of being tired out. **—in′de·fat′i·ga·bly,** *adv.*

in·de·fea·si·ble (in′di fē′zə bəl), *adj.* not to be annulled or made void. **—in′de·fea′si·bly,** *adv.*

in·de·fen·si·ble (in′di fen′sə bəl), *adj.* 1. not justifiable or excusable 2. incapable of being defended as against attack. **—in′de·fen′si·bly,** *adv.*

in·de·fin·a·ble (in′di fī′nə bəl), *adj.* not readily identified, described, or analyzed

in·def·i·nite (in def′ə nit), *adj.* 1. without fixed limit. 2. not clearly defined or determined. 3. not certain or clear. 4. *Gram.* not particularizing the noun modified· *A is an indefinite article* **—in·def′i·nite·ly,** *adv.* **—in·def′i·nite·ness,** *n.*

in·del·i·ble (in del′ə bəl), *adj.* 1. incapable of being deleted or obliterated. 2. making indelible marks. **—in·del′i·bly,** *adv*

in·del·i·cate (in del′ə kit), *adj.* 1. not delicate or subtle. 2. offensive to propriety or decency. **—in·del′i·ca·cy,** *n* **—in·del′i·cate·ly,** *adv.*

in·dem·ni·fy (in dem′nə fī′), *v.t.,* **-fied, -fy·ing.** 1. to compensate for damage or loss sustained. 2. to give security against future damage or loss. **—in·dem′ni·fi·ca′tion,** *n.*

in·dem·ni·ty (in dem′ni tē), *n., pl.* **-ties.** 1. protection or security against future damage or loss. 2. compensation for damage or loss sustained.

in·dent¹ (in dent′), *v.t., v.i.* 1. to form deep recesses (in): *The sea indents the coast.* 2. to set in or back from the margin, as the first line of a paragraph. **—in·dent′er, in·den′tor,** *n.*

in·dent² (in dent′), *v.t.* to make a dent in.

in·den·ta·tion (in′den tā′shən), *n.* 1. a cut, notch, or deep recess. 2. a series of incisions or notches. 3. a notching or being notched. 4. indention or notch.

in·den·tion (in den′shən), *n.* 1. the act of indenting or state of being indented. 2. the blank space left by indenting. 3. *Archaic.* an indentation or notch.

in·den·ture (in den′chər), *n., v.,* **-tured, -tur·ing.** *—n.* 1. a written agreement or contract, esp. one by which an apprentice is bound to service. *—v.t.* 2. to bind by indenture.

in·de·pend·ence (in′di pen′dəns), *n.* 1. the state or quality of being independent. 2. freedom from the control of others.

Independ′ence Day′, *U.S.* July 4, a holiday commemorating the adoption of the Declaration of Independence in 1776.

---

in′de·cid′u·ous, *adj.*   **in′de·mon′stra·ble,** *adj.*   **in′de·ter′mi·na·ble,** *adj.*

in·de·pend·ent (in′di pen′dənt), *adj.*
1. not influenced or controlled by
others. **2.** not subject to another's
authority or jurisdiction. **3.** not
depending upon something else for
existence, operation, etc. **4.** not
relying on another or others for aid
or support. **5.** free from party commitments in politics. **6.** *Gram.* main
(def. 3). **—***n.* **7.** an independent
person, esp. a voter who is not registered as a member of any political
party. **—in′de·pend′ent·ly,** *adv.*

in-depth (in′depth′), *adj.* extensive,
thorough, or profound.

in·de·scrib·a·ble (in′di skrī′bə bəl),
adj. **1.** incapable of being described
in words. **2.** defying description. **—**
in′de·scrib·a·bil′i·ty, *n.* **—in′de-
scrib′a·bly,** *adv.*

in·de·struct·i·ble (in′di struk′tə bəl),
adj. that cannot be destroyed. **—in′-
de·struct′i·bil′i·ty, in′de·struct′i·ble-
ness,** *n.* **—in′de·struct′i·bly,** *adv.*

in·de·ter·mi·nate (in′di tûr′mə nit),
adj. **1.** not fixed in extent. **2.** not
clear or precise. **3.** not settled or decided. **—in′de·ter′mi·na·cy** (-nə sē),
**in′de·ter′mi·nate·ness, in′de·ter′mi-
na′tion** (-nā′shən), *n.* **—in′de·ter′mi-
nate·ly,** *adv.*

in·dex (in′deks), *n.,* *pl.* **-dex·es, -di·ces**
(-di sēz′), *v.* **—***n.* **1.** an alphabetical
listing of names, places, etc., along
with the numbers of the pages on
which they are mentioned, as in a
book. **2.** a sign or indication: *a true
index of his character.* **3.** a pointer
in a scientific instrument. **4.** *Print.*
a sign (☞) used to point out a particular note, etc. **5.** Also called **in′-
dex. fin′ger.** the forefinger. **6. a.** a
number or formula expressing some
property, ratio, etc., of something
indicated: *index of growth.* **b.** See
index number. **—***v.t.* **7.** to provide
with an index, as a book. **8.** to enter in an index, as a word. [< L:
informer, pointer] **—in′dex·er,** *n.*

in′dex num′ber, a quantity whose
variation over a period of time measures the change in some phenomenon.

in′dex of refrac′tion, the ratio of the
speed of light in a vacuum, or in
air, to that in the given medium.

In·di·a (in′dē ə), *n.* **1.** a large peninsula in S Asia. **2.** a country covering most of this peninsula.

In′dia ink′, 1. a dense black pigment
used for drawings. **2.** an ink made
from this. Also, **in′dia ink′.**

In·di·an (in′dē ən), *n.* **1.** a member
of the aboriginal peoples of North
and South America. **2.** any of the
indigenous languages of the American Indians. **3.** a member of any of
the peoples native to India or the
East Indies. **—***adj.* **4.** of the Ameri-

can Indians or their languages. **5.**
of India or the East Indies.

In·di·an·a (in′dē an′ə), *n.* a state in
the central United States. *Cap.:* In-
dianapolis. **—In′di·an′i·an,** *adj., n.*

In·di·an·ap·o·lis (in′dē ə nap′ə lis), *n.*
the capital of Indiana.

In′dian corn′, corn¹ (def. 1).

In′dian file′. See **single file.**

In′dian O′cean, an ocean S of Asia,
between Africa and Australia.

In′dian pipe′, a leafless plant having
a solitary flower and resembling a
tobacco pipe.

In′dian sum′mer, a period of mild,
dry weather in late autumn or early
winter.

In′dia pa′per, 1. a fine, thin, but
opaque paper used chiefly for impressions of engravings. **2.** a very
thin, strong paper used for Bibles.

indic., indicative.

in·di·cate (in′də kāt′), *v.t.,* **-cat·ed,
-cat·ing. 1.** to be a sign or index of.
2. to point out or point to. **3.** to
make known. **4.** to express, briefly
or in a general way. **—in′di·ca′tion,**
n.

in·dic·a·tive (in dik′ə tiv), *adj.* **1.**
serving to point out: *behavior indicative of mental disorder.* **2.** *Gram.*
noting the mood of the verb used for
ordinary objective statements, questions, etc. **—***n.* *Gram.* **3.** the indicative mood. **—in·dic′a·tive·ly,** *adv.*

in·di·ca·tor (in′də kā′tər), *n.* **1.** a person or thing that indicates. **2.** a
pointing or directing device, as a
pointer on an instrument.

in·di·ci·a (in dish′ē ə), *n.pl.* envelope
markings substituted for postage
stamps.

in·dict (in dīt′), *v.t.* **1.** to charge with
an offense or crime. **2.** (of a grand
jury) to bring a formal accusation
against. **—in·dict′a·ble,** *adj.* **—in·
dict′ment,** *n.*

in·dif·fer·ent (in dif′ər ənt, -dif′rənt),
adj. **1.** without interest or concern.
2. having no bias or preference. **3.**
not particularly good. **4.** immaterial
or unimportant. **—in·dif′fer·ence,** *n.*
—in·dif′fer·ent·ly, *adv.* **—Syn. 1.**
apathetic, careless.

in·dig·e·nous (in dij′ə nəs), *adj.* originating in and characterizing a particular region or country.

in·di·gent (in′di jənt), *adj.* **1.** lacking
the necessities of life because of
poverty. **—***n.* **2.** an indigent person.
—in′di·gence, *n.* **—in′di·gent·ly,** *adv.*

in·di·gest·i·ble (in′di jes′tə bəl, -dī-),
adj. not easily digested.

in·di·ges·tion (in′di jes′chən, -dī-,
-jesh′-), *n.* incapability of or difficulty in digesting food.

in·dig·nant (in dig′nənt), *adj.* feeling
or characterized by indignation. **—
in·dig′nant·ly,** *adv.*

in·dig·na·tion (in′dig nā′shən), n. strong displeasure at something unworthy, unjust, or base.

in·dig·ni·ty (in dig′ni tē), n., pl. -ties. an injury to one's dignity.

in·di·go (in′də gō′), n., pl. -gos, -goes. 1. a blue dye obtained from plants or manufactured synthetically. 2. a deep violet blue.

in·di·rect (in′də rekt′, -dī-), adj. 1. deviating from a straight line, as a path. 2. not resulting immediately, as consequences. 3. not direct in action or procedure. 4. not straightforward. —**in′di·rec′tion**, n. —**in′di·rect′ly**, adv. —**in′di·rect′ness**, n.

in′direct ob′ject, a word or words representing the person or thing with reference to which the action of verbs is performed.

in′direct tax′, a tax levied indirectly, though ultimately, on one group of persons by taxing another which passes on the expense to the first.

in·dis·creet (in′di skrēt′), adj. lacking prudence or good judgment. —**in′dis·creet′ly**, adv.

in·dis·cre·tion (in′di skresh′ən), n. 1. lack of discretion. 2. an indiscreet act or step.

in·dis·crim·i·nate (in′di skrim′ə nit), adj. 1. choosing at random. 2. making no nice distinctions. 3. confused or jumbled. —**in′dis·crim′i·nate·ly**, adv. —**in′dis·crim′i·nate·ness**, n.

in·dis·pen·sa·ble (in′di spen′sə bəl), adj. absolutely necessary or essential. —**in′dis·pen′sa·bil′i·ty**, n. —**in′dis·pen′sa·bly**, adv.

in·dis·posed (in′di spōzd′), adj. 1. sick or ill, esp. slightly. 2. disinclined or unwilling. —**in′dis·po·si′tion** (-pə zish′ən), n.

in·dis·put·a·ble (in′di spyoo′tə bəl, in dis′pyə-), adj. that cannot be disputed or denied. —**in′dis·put′a·ble·ness**, n. —**in′dis·put′a·bly**, adv.

in·dis·sol·u·ble (in′di sol′yə bəl), adj. incapable of being dissolved, decomposed, undone, or destroyed. —**in′dis·sol′u·bly**, adv.

in·dis·tinct (in′di stingkt′), adj. 1. not clearly marked or defined. 2. not clearly distinguishable or perceptible. —**in′dis·tinct′ly**, adv. —**in′dis·tinct′ness**, n.

in·dite (in dīt′), v.t., -dit·ed, -dit·ing. Archaic. to compose or write, as a speech or poem.

in·di·um (in′dē əm), n. Chem. a rare, silver-white metallic element. Symbol: In; at. wt.: 114.82; at. no.: 49.

in·di·vid·u·al (in′də vij′ōō əl), adj. 1. separate, esp. from similar things. 2. existing as a distinct, indivisible en-

tity. 3. of or pertaining to a particular person or thing: individual tastes. 4. intended for one person only: individual portions. 5. characterized by unique qualities: a highly individual style. —n. 6. a single human being, as distinguished from a group. 7. a person. 8. a distinct, indivisible entity. —**in′di·vid′u·al·ly**, adv.

in·di·vid·u·al·ism (in′də vij′ōō ə liz′əm), n. 1. a social theory advocating the liberty, rights, or independent action of the individual. 2. the principle of independent thought or action. 3. the pursuit of individual rather than common or collective interests. —**in′di·vid′u·al·ly**, adv.

in·di·vid·u·al·ist (in′də vij′ōō ə list), n. 1. a person who is independent in thought or action. 2. an advocate of individualism. —**in′di·vid′u·a·lis′tic**, adj.

in·di·vid·u·al·i·ty (in′də vij′ōō al′i tē), n., pl. -ties. 1. the aggregate of qualities that distinguishes one person or thing from others. 2. existence as a distinct individual.

in·di·vid·u·al·ize (in′də vij′ōō ə līz′), v.t., -ized, -iz·ing. 1. to make individual. 2. to consider individually. 3. to fit for individual tastes. —**in′di·vid′u·al·i·za′tion**, n.

in·di·vid·u·ate (in′də vij′ōō āt′), v.t., -at·ed, -at·ing. 1. to form into an individual entity. 2. to give an individual character to. —**in′di·vid·u·a′tion** (-ā′shən), n.

in·di·vis·i·ble (in′də viz′ə bəl), adj. not separable into parts. —**in′di·vis′·i·bil′i·ty**, n. —**in′di·vis′i·bly**, adv.

In·do·chi·na (in′dō chī′nə), n. a peninsula in SE Asia. —**In′do·chi·nese′**, adj., n.

in·doc·tri·nate (in dok′trə nāt′), v.t., -nat·ed, -nat·ing. to instruct in a doctrine, principle, or ideology, esp. a partisan or sectarian dogma. —**in·doc′tri·na′tion**, n.

In·do-Eu·ro·pe·an (in′dō yoor′ə pē′ən), n. 1. a family of languages including most of the languages of Europe and of countries colonized by Europeans, and extending as far as SW Asia and India. 2. the prehistoric parent language of this family. 3. a member of any of the peoples speaking an Indo-European language. —adj. 4. of or belonging to Indo-European.

in·do·lent (in′dᵊlənt), adj. having a disposition to avoid exertion. —**in′do·lence**, n. —**in′do·lent·ly**, adv.

in·dom·i·ta·ble (in dom′i tə bəl), adj. unable to be subdued or overcome, as courage. —**in·dom′i·ta·bly**, adv.

in′dis·cern′i·ble, adj.
in′dis·cov′er·a·ble, adj.

in′dis·tin′guish·a·ble,
adj.

In·do·ne·sia (in′dɔ nē′zhɔ, -shɔ, -zē ɔ, -dō-), *n.* a country in the Malay Archipelago, consisting of Sumatra, Java, most of Borneo, and many small islands. —**In′do·ne′sian,** *n.*, *adj.*

in·door (in′dōr′, -dôr′), *adj.* done, situated, or used within a house or building.

in·doors (in dōrz′, -dôrz′), *adv.* in or into a house or building.

in·dorse (in dôrs′), *v.t.*, **-dorsed, -dors·ing.** endorse.

in·du·bi·ta·ble (in dōō′bi tɔ bɔl, -dyōō′-), *adj.* not to be doubted. — **in·du′bi·ta·bly,** *adv.*

in·duce (in dōōs′, -dyōōs′), *v.t.*, **-duced, -duc·ing.** 1. to lead by persuasion. 2. to bring about: *sleep induced by drugs.* 3. to produce (magnetism or electric current) by induction. 4. to infer by logical induction. —**in·duc′er,** *n.*

in·duce·ment (in dōōs′mɔnt, -dyōōs′-), *n.* 1. the act of inducing or state of being induced. 2. something that induces, as an incentive.

in·duct (in dukt′), *v.t.* 1. to install in an office, esp. formally. 2. to enlist (a draftee) into military service. 3. to bring in as a member.

in·duct·ance (in duk′tɔns), *n. Elect.* the property of a circuit or a pair of circuits by which a change in current induces an electromotive force.

in·duc·tee (in′duk tē′), *n.* a person inducted into military service.

in·duc·tion (in duk′shɔn), *n.* 1. the process by which a body having electric or magnetic properties produces magnetism, an electric charge, or an electromotive force in a neighboring body without contact. 2. a. the process of reasoning from the specific to the general. b. a conclusion reached by this process. 3. formal installation in an office. 4. the act of enlisting a draftee into military service.

in·duc·tive (in duk′tiv), *adj.* 1. of or pertaining to electrical induction. 2. of, pertaining to, or employing logical induction. —**in·duc′tive·ly,** *adv.* —**in·duc′tive·ness,** *n.*

in·due (in dōō′, -dyōō′), *v.t.*, **-dued, -du·ing.** endue.

in·dulge (in dulj′), *v.*, **-dulged, -dulg·ing.** —*v.i.* 1. to yield to an inclination or desire. —*v.t.* 2. to yield to or gratify (desires, etc.). 3. to yield to the wishes of (oneself or another). —**in·dulg′er,** *n.*

in·dul·gence (in dul′jɔns), *n.* 1. the act of indulging or state of being indulgent. 2. something indulged in. 3. an extension, through favor, of time for payment. 4. *Rom. Cath. Ch.*

a partial remission of the temporal punishment that is still due for sin after absolution.

in·dul·gent (in dul′jɔnt), *adj.* characterized by or showing indulgence.

in·du·rate (*v.* in′dōō rāt′, -dyōō-; *adj.* in′dōō rit, -dyōō-), *v.*, **-rat·ed, -rat·ing,** *adj.* —*v.t.* 1. to make hard, as rock, tissue, etc. 2. to make callous or stubborn. 3. to inure or accustom. —*v.i.* 4. to become hard. —*adj.* 5. hardened or callous. —**in′du·ra′tion** (-rā′shɔn), *n.* —**in′du·ra′tive,** *adj.*

in·dus·tri·al (in dus′trē ɔl), *adj.* 1. of or pertaining to industries or the workers in industries. 2. having many and highly developed industries. —**in·dus′tri·al·ly,** *adv.*

indus′trial arts′, the methods of using tools, machinery, and other industrial materials.

in·dus·tri·al·ism (in dus′trē ɔ liz′ɔm), *n.* an economic organization of society built largely on mechanized industry.

in·dus·tri·al·ist (in dus′trē ɔ list), *n.* a person who owns or manages an industrial enterprise.

in·dus·tri·al·ize (in dus′trē ɔ līz′), *v.*, **-ized, -iz·ing.** —*v.t.* 1. to introduce industry into. —*v.i.* 2. to become industrial. —**in·dus′tri·al·i·za′tion,** *n.*

indus′trial park′, an area of land developed in an orderly, planned way for industry and business.

in·dus·tri·ous (in dus′trē ɔs), *adj.* constantly devoted to one's work. —**in·dus′tri·ous·ly,** *adv.* —**in·dus′tri·ous·ness,** *n.* —**Syn.** assiduous, busy, diligent.

in·dus·try (in′dɔ strē), *n.*, *pl.* **-tries** for 1, 2, 3. 1. the aggregate of manufacturing or technically productive enterprises. 2. any general business field. 3. owners and managers of industry collectively. 4. constant devotion to any work or task.

in·dwell (in dwel′), *v.t.*, *v.i.*, **-dwelt, -dwell·ing.** to be or reside (within), as a guiding force.

-ine[1], a suffix meaning "of or pertaining to," "of the nature of," or "like": *asinine; crystalline.*

-ine[2], a suffix used to form: a. abstract nouns: *doctrine; famine.* b. chemical terms: *bromine; chlorine.* c. names of basic substances: *aniline; caffeine.*

in·e·bri·ate (*v.* in ē′brē āt′, i nē′-; *n.* in ē′brē it, i nē′-), *v.*, **-at·ed, -at·ing,** *n.* —*v.t.* 1. to make drunk or intoxicated. —*n.* 2. a habitual drunkard. —**in·e′bri·a′tion,** *n.*

in·ed·i·ble (in ed′ɔ bɔl), *adj.* unfit to be eaten.

---

in·dul′gent·ly, *adv.*   **in·ed′it·ed,** *adj.*   **in·ed′u·ca·ble,** *adj.*

in·ef·fa·ble (in ef′ə bəl), *adj.* **1.** incapable of being expressed or described. **2.** not to be spoken. —in·ef′fa·bly, *adv.*

in·ef·face·a·ble (in′i fā′sə bəl), *adj.* incapable of being effaced or erased.

in·ef·fec·tive (in′i fek′tiv), *adj.* **1.** not producing results. **2.** inefficient or incompetent. —in·ef·fec′tive·ly, *adv.* —in′ef·fec′tive·ness, *n.*

in·ef·fec·tu·al (in′i fek′chōō əl), *adj.* **1.** without satisfactory or decisive effect. **2.** unavailing or futile. —in′ef·fec′tu·al·ly, *adv.*

in·ef·fi·cient (in′i fish′ənt), *adj.* unable to achieve the desired result with reasonable economy of means. —in′ef·fi′cien·cy, *n.* —in′ef·fi′cient·ly, *adv.*

in·el·e·gant (in el′ə gənt), *adj.* lacking in refinement, gracefulness, or good taste. —in·el′e·gance, *n.* —in·el′e·gant·ly, *adv.*

in·el·i·gi·ble (in el′i jə bəl), *adj.* **1.** not eligible or qualified. **2.** legally disqualified to hold an office. —*n.* **3.** an ineligible person. —in·el′i·gi·bil′i·ty, *n.* —in·el′i·gi·bly, *adv.*

in·e·luc·ta·ble (in′i luk′tə bəl), *adj.* incapable of being evaded or escaped. —in′e·luc′ta·bly, *adv.*

in·ept (in ept′, i nept′), *adj.* **1.** without skill or aptitude, esp. for a particular task. **2.** inappropriate or out of place. **3.** absurd or foolish. —in·ept′i·tude (in ep′ti tōōd′, -tyōōd′, i nep′-), *n.* —in·ept′ly, *adv.* —in·ept′ness, *n.*

in·e·qual·i·ty (in′i kwol′i tē), *n., pl.* **-ties. 1.** the condition or an instance of being unequal, as in size, status, etc. **2.** injustice or partiality. **3.** unevenness, as of surface.

in·er·rant (in er′ənt, -ûr′-), *adj.* free from error.

in·ert (in ûrt′, i nûrt′), *adj.* **1.** having no inherent power of motion or resistance. **2.** *Chem.* having little or no ability to react. **3.** sluggish by habit or nature. —in·ert′ly, *adv.* —in·ert′ness, *n.*

in·er·tia (in ûr′shə, i nûr′-), *n.* **1.** indisposition to action or motion. **2.** the property of matter by which it retains its state of rest or its velocity along a straight line so long as it is not acted upon by an external force. [< L: slothfulness] —in·er′tial, *adj.*

in·es·cap·a·ble (in′e skā′pə bəl), *adj.* incapable of being escaped or avoided. —in′es·cap′a·bly, *adv.*

in·es·ti·ma·ble (in es′tə mə bəl), *adj.* **1.** incapable of being estimated or assessed. **2.** too great to be estimated or appreciated. —in·es′ti·ma·bly, *adv.*

in·ev·i·ta·ble (in ev′i tə bəl), *adj.* unable to be avoided or evaded. —in·ev′i·ta·bil′i·ty, *n.* —in·ev′i·ta·bly, *adv.*

in·ex·act (in′ig zakt′), *adj.* not exact. —in′ex·act′ly, *adv.*

in·ex·cus·a·ble (in′ik skyōō′zə bəl), *adj.* incapable of being justified. —in′ex·cus′a·ble·ness, *n.* —in′ex·cus′a·bly, *adv.*

in·ex·haust·i·ble (in′ig zôs′tə bəl), *adj.* **1.** incapable of being used up. **2.** untiring or tireless. —in′ex·haust′i·bly, *adv.*

in·ex·o·ra·ble (in ek′sər ə bəl), *adj.* **1.** not to be persuaded or moved by entreaties. **2.** unyielding or unalterable. —in·ex′o·ra·bly, *adv.*

in·ex·pe·ri·ence (in′ik spēr′ē əns), *n.* lack of experience or of knowledge or skill gained from experience. —in′ex·pe′ri·enced, *adj.*

in·ex·pert (in eks′pûrt, in′ik spûrt′), *adj.* not expert or skilled. —in·ex′pert·ly, *adv.*

in·ex·pi·a·ble (in eks′pē ə bəl), *adj.* not to be expiated or atoned for.

in·ex·pli·ca·ble (in eks′plə kə bəl, in′ik splik′ə bəl), *adj.* incapable of being explained —in·ex′pli·ca·bly, *adv.*

in·ex·press·i·ble (in′ik spres′ə bəl), *adj.* incapable of being uttered or represented in words. —in′ex·press′i·bly, *adv.*

in·ex·tin·guish·a·ble (in′ik sting′gwi·shə bəl), *adj.* not to be extinguished or quenched.

in ex·tre·mis (in ik strē′mis), *Latin.* **1.** in extremity. **2.** near death.

in·ex·tri·ca·ble (in eks′trə kə bəl), *adj.* **1.** from which one cannot extricate oneself. **2.** incapable of being disentangled or loosed. **3.** hopelessly intricate or perplexing. —in·ex′tri·ca·bly, *adv.*

inf., **1.** infantry. **2.** inferior. **3.** infinitive.

in·fal·li·ble (in fal′ə bəl), *adj.* **1.** exempt from liability to error. **2.** absolutely trustworthy or sure. —in·fal′li·bil′i·ty, in·fal′li·ble·ness, *n.* —in·fal′li·bly, *adv.*

in·fa·mous (in′fə məs), *adj.* **1.** having an extremely bad reputation. **2.** causing a bad reputation. —in′fa·mous·ly, *adv.* —**Syn. 1.** disreputable, notorious. **2.** disgraceful, scandalous.

in·fa·my (in′fə mē), *n., pl.* **-mies** for 3. **1.** extremely bad reputation as the result of a shameful or criminal act. **2.** infamous character or conduct. **3.** an infamous act.

---

in′ef·fi·ca′cious, *adj.*
in·ef′fi·ca·cy, *n.*
in′e·las′tic, *adj.*
in·eq′ui·ta·ble, *adj.*

in·eq′ui·ty, *n.*
in′e·rad′i·ca·ble, *adj.*
in′ex·pe′di·ent, *adj.*

in′ex·pen′sive, *adj.*
in′ex·pen′sive·ly, *adv.*
in′ex·pres′sive, *adj.*

infancy □ infinity

462

in·fan·cy (in′fən sē), *n.*, *pl.* **-cies.** **1.** early childhood. **2.** the corresponding period in the existence of anything.

in·fant (in′fənt), *n.* **1.** a child during the earliest period of its life, esp. before able to walk. —*adj.* **2.** of or for infants. **3.** of or being in infancy. [< L: lit., not speaking]

in·fan·ti·cide (in fan′ti sīd′), *n.* **1.** the act of killing an infant. **2.** a person who kills an infant.

in·fan·tile (in′fən tīl′, -til), *adj.* **1.** like an infant. **2.** of infants or infancy.

in′fantile paral′ysis, poliomyelitis.

in·fan·try (in′fən trē), *n.*, *pl.* **-tries.** a branch of an army composed of soldiers trained and equipped to fight on foot. —**in′fan·try·man,** *n.*

in·farct (in färkt′), *n.* a localized area of tissue that is dying or dead because of an obstruction by embolism. —**in·farct′ed,** *adj.* —**in·farc′tion,** *n.*

in·fat·u·ate (in fach′ōō āt′), *v.t.*, **-at·ed, -at·ing.** to inspire with a foolish or unreasoning passion, as of love. —**in·fat′u·a′tion,** *n.*

in·fect (in fekt′), *v.t.* **1.** to contaminate with disease-producing germs. **2.** to affect with disease. **3.** to affect so as to influence feeling or action. —**in·fec′tor,** **in·fect′er,** *n.*

in·fec·tion (in fek′shən), *n.* **1.** the act of infecting or state of being infected. **2.** an infecting agency or influence. **3.** an infectious disease.

in·fec·tious (in fek′shəs), *adj.* **1.** communicable by infection. **2.** causing or communicating infection. **3.** tending to affect others. Also, **in·fec′tive.** —**in·fec′tious·ly,** *adv.* —**in·fec′tious·ness,** *n.*

in·fe·lic·i·tous (in′fə lis′i təs), *adj.* not well-suited for the occasion: *an infelicitous remark.* —**in′fe·lic′i·ty,** *n.*

in·fer (in fûr′), *v.t.*, **-ferred, -fer·ring.** **1.** to conclude by reasoning from premises or evidence. **2.** to guess or surmise. —**in′fer·ence,** *n.* —**in′fer·en′tial,** *adj.* —**in′fer·en′tial·ly,** *adv.*

—**Usage.** INFER and IMPLY have quite distinct meanings: *One infers from what another has implied.* The use of one of these words for the other is regarded as a solecism by educated persons.

in·fe·ri·or (in fēr′ē ər), *adj.* **1.** low or lower in quality or grade. **2.** low or lower in rank or position. **3.** of little or less value or excellence. —*n.* **4.** an inferior person or thing. —**in·fe′ri·or′i·ty** (-ôr′i tē, -or′-), *n.*

in·fer·nal (in fûr′n°l), *adj.* **1.** of or pertaining to hell. **2.** fiendish. —**in·fer′nal·ly,** *adv.*

in·fer·no (in fûr′nō), *n.*, *pl.* **-nos.** **1.** the infernal regions. **2.** a place or region that resembles hell.

in·fer·tile (in fûr′t°l *or, esp. Brit.,* -tīl), *adj.* not fertile or productive. —**in·fer′tile·ly,** *adv.* —**in·fer·til·i·ty** (in′fər til′i tē), *n.*

in·fest (in fest′), *v.t.* **1.** to overrun in a troublesome manner, as vermin do. **2.** to be numerous in, as anything troublesome. —**in′fes·ta′tion,** *n.* —**in·fest′er,** *n.*

in·fi·del (in′fi d°l), *n.* **1.** a person who has no religious faith. **2.** a person who does not accept a particular faith, esp. Christianity or Islam. [< L *infidēl(is)* unfaithful]

in·fi·del·i·ty (in′fi del′i tē), *n.*, *pl.* **-ties.** **1.** unfaithfulness, esp. in marital relationship. **2.** lack of religious faith.

in·field (in′fēld′), *n. Baseball.* **1.** the diamond. **2.** the positions played by the first base, second base, third base, and shortstop, taken collectively. —**in′field′er,** *n.*

in·fight·ing (in′fī′ting), *n.* **1.** fighting at close range. **2.** fighting, as between members of a group, that is kept secret from outsiders. —**in′fight′er,** *n.*

in·fil·trate (in fil′trāt, in′fil trāt′), *v.t.*, *v.i.*, **-trat·ed, -trat·ing.** **1.** to move into (an organization) surreptitiously, usually as its employee, for covert espionage. **2.** to move into (an enemy area) furtively on special military assignment. **3.** to filter into or through (a substance). —**in′fil·tra′tion,** *n.* —**in′fil·tra′tor,** *n.*

infin., infinitive.

in·fi·nite (in′fə nit), *adj.* **1.** immeasurably great. **2.** unbounded or unlimited. **3.** endless or innumerable. **4.** *Math.* not finite. —*n.* **5.** something infinite. —**in′fi·nite·ly,** *adv.* —**in′fi·nite·ness,** *n.*

in·fin·i·tes·i·mal (in′fin i tes′ə məl), *adj.* **1.** immeasurably minute. **2.** *Math.* of or involving a variable having zero as a limit. —**in′fin·i·tes′i·mal·ly,** *adv.*

in·fin·i·tive (in fin′i tiv), *n.* the simple or basic form of the verb, without inflection, as *to eat* in *I want to eat.*

in·fin·i·tude (in fin′i tōōd′, -tyōōd′), *n.* **1.** infinity (def. 1). **2.** an infinite extent or quantity.

in·fin·i·ty (in fin′i tē), *n.*, *pl.* **-ties.** **1.** the quality or state of being infinite. **2.** infinite space, time, or quantity. **3.** an indefinitely great amount or number.

---

in·fea′si·ble, *adj.*

in·fe′cund, *adj.*

in·firm (in fûrm′), *adj.* **1.** feeble or weak in body or health. **2.** not firm, solid, or strong. —**in·firm′ly,** *adv.*

in·fir·ma·ry (in fûr′mə rē), *n., pl.* **-ries.** a place for the care of the infirm, sick, or injured.

in·fir·mi·ty (in fûr′mi tē), *n., pl.* **-ties.** **1.** a physical weakness or ailment. **2.** a moral weakness or failing.

infl., **1.** influence. **2.** influenced.

in·flame (in flām′), *v.t., v.i.,* **-flamed, -flam·ing. 1.** to set aflame or afire. **2.** to kindle or excite (passions, desires, etc.). **3.** to affect or become affected with inflammation.

in·flam·ma·ble (in flam′ə bəl), *adj.* **1.** capable of being set on fire. **2.** easily aroused to passion or anger. —**in·flam′ma·bil′i·ty,** *n.*

in·flam·ma·tion (in′flə mā′shən), *n.* redness, swelling, pain, heat, and disturbed function of an area of the body, esp. as a reaction of tissues to injurious agents.

in·flam·ma·to·ry (in flam′ə tôr′ē, -tōr′ē), *adj.* **1.** tending to arouse anger, passion, etc. **2.** of or caused by inflammation.

in·flate (in flāt′), *v.,* **-flat·ed, -flat·ing.** —*v.t.* **1.** to swell with gas or air. **2.** to puff up with pride, satisfaction, etc. **3.** to affect with economic inflation. —*v.i.* **4.** to become inflated. —**in·flat′a·ble,** *adj.*

in·fla·tion (in flā′shən), *n.* **1.** a persistent, substantial rise in the general price level, resulting in a fall of purchasing power, caused by any of various factors, as money supply, wages, industrial output, etc. **2.** the act of inflating or state of being inflated. —**in·fla′tion·ar′y,** *adj.*

in·fla·tion·ist (in flā′shə nist), *n.* an advocate of economic inflation. —**in·fla′tion·ism,** *n.*

in·flect (in flekt′), *v.t.* **1.** to modulate (the voice). **2.** to change the form of (a word) by inflection.

in·flec·tion (in flek′shən), *n.* **1.** modulation of the voice. **2.** the change in the form of a word to express grammatical or syntactic functions. Also, *Brit.,* **in·flex·ion.** —**in·flec′tion·al,** *adj.*

in·flex·i·ble (in flek′sə bəl), *adj.* **1.** incapable of being bent or curved. **2.** unyielding or immovable. **3.** not permitting change or variation. —**in·flex′i·bil′i·ty,** *n.* —**in·flex′i·bly,** *adv.* —**Syn. 2.** obstinate, rigid, stern.

in·flict (in flikt′), *v.t.* **1.** to deal or deliver, as a blow. **2.** to afflict, as with punishment. **3.** to impose (anything unwelcome). —**in·flic′tion,** *n.* —**in·flic′tive,** *adj.*

in·flight (in′flīt′), *adj.* done, served, or shown during an air voyage: *an in-flight movie.*

in·flo·res·cence (in′flō res′əns, -flō-, flə-), *n.* **1.** the unfolding of blossoms. **2. a.** the arrangement of flowers on the stem. **b.** a flower cluster. **c.** flowers collectively.

in·flow (in′flō′), *n.* something that flows in.

in·flu·ence (in′flōō əns), *n., v.,* **-enced, -enc·ing.** —*n.* **1.** the power to produce effects on others by intangible or indirect means. **2.** the action or effect of such power. **3.** the power to produce effects on account of one's financial or social standing. **4.** a person or thing that exerts such power. —*v.t.* **5.** to exercise influence on. **6.** to move or impel (a person), as to some action. —**in′flu·en′tial** (-en′shəl), *adj.*

in·flu·en·za (in′flōō en′zə), *n.* an acute, extremely contagious, virus disease, characterized by fever, chills, headache, bronchial inflammation, muscular pains, etc.

in·flux (in′fluks′), *n.* an act of flowing in.

in·fo (in′fō′), *n. Informal.* information.

in·fold (in fōld′), *v.t.* enfold. —**in·fold′er,** *n.*

in·form (in fôrm′), *v.t.* **1.** to impart knowledge or information to. —*v.i.* **2.** to give information, esp. incriminating information. —**in·form′er,** *n.* —**Syn.** advise, notify, tell.

in·for·mal (in fôr′məl), *adj.* **1.** without formality or ceremony. **2.** not according to prescribed, official, or customary forms. **3.** suitable to or characteristic of casual or familiar speech or writing. —**in′for·mal′i·ty** (-mal′i tē), *n.* —**in·for′mal·ly,** *adv.*

in·form·ant (in fôr′mənt), *n.* a person who gives information.

in·for·ma·tion (in′fər mā′shən), *n.* **1.** knowledge communicated or received concerning a particular fact. **2.** any knowledge gained through communication, research, etc. **3.** any data that can be coded for processing by a computer. —**in′for·ma′tion·al,** *adj.*

in·form·a·tive (in fôr′mə tiv), *adj.* giving or providing information. —**in·form′a·tive·ly,** *adv.* —**in·form′a·tive·ness,** *n.*

infra-, a prefix meaning "below": *infrasonic.*

in·frac·tion (in frak′shən), *n.* a breach or violation, as of a law.

in·fra dig (in′frə dig′), beneath one's dignity. [short for L *infrā dignitātem*]

in·fra·red (in′frə red′), *adj.* noting or using the part of the invisible spectrum contiguous to the red end of the visible spectrum.

in·fra·son·ic (in′frə son′ik), *adj.* noting a frequency below the range of human hearing.

in·fra·struc·ture (in′frə struk′chər), n. the basic military installations, communication and transport facilities, etc., of a country.

in·fre·quent (in frē′kwənt), adj. 1. happening or occurring at long intervals or rarely. 2. not habitual or regular. —in·fre′quen·cy, in·fre′quence, n. —in·fre′quent·ly, adv.

in·fringe (in frinj′), v., -fringed, -fringing. —v.t. 1. to commit a breach or infraction of. —v.i. 2. to encroach or trespass: to infringe on someone's privacy. —in·fringe′ment, n.

in·fu·ri·ate (in fyŏŏr′ē āt′), v.t., -at·ed, -at·ing. to make furious. —in·fu′ri·at′ing·ly, adv.

in·fuse (in fyōōz′), v., -fused, -fus·ing. —v.t. 1. to introduce, as by pouring. 2. to imbue or inspire. 3. to steep or soak (leaves, bark, etc.) to extract the soluble properties. —in·fus′er, n. —in·fu′sion, n.

in·fu·si·ble (in fyōō′zə bəl), adj. incapable of being fused or melted.

-ing¹, a suffix meaning: a. act, action, art, or process: eating: printing. b. an instance of such an action: listing. c. product or result of such an action: savings. d. material used in such an action: padding. e. something that performs or receives such an action: covering.

-ing², a suffix used to form: a. the present participle of verbs: I am eating. b. such participles being often used as participial adjectives: warring factions.

-ing³, a suffix meaning "of the kind of": farthing.

in·gen·ious (in jēn′yəs), adj. 1. characterized by cleverness or originality of invention or construction. 2. cleverly inventive or resourceful. —in·gen′ious·ly, adv. —in·gen′ious·ness, n.

in·gé·nue (an′zhə nōō′, -nyōō′), n., pl. -nues (-nōōz′, -nyōōz′). 1. the role of an ingenuous girl, esp. as represented on the stage. 2. an actress who plays such a role. Also, in′ge·nue′.

in·ge·nu·i·ty (in′jə nōō′i tē, -nyōō′-), n. 1. the quality of being ingenious. 2. cleverness or skillfulness of conception or design.

in·gen·u·ous (in jen′yōō əs), adj. 1. free from deceit or disguise. 2. unwarily simple and innocent. —in·gen′u·ous·ly, adv. —in·gen′u·ous·ness, n. —Syn. 1. candid, frank. 2. artless, naive.

in·gest (in jest′), v.t. to take into the body, as food. —in·ges′tion, n.

in·glo·ri·ous (in glôr′ē əs, -glōr′-), adj. 1. not glorious or honorable. 2.

shameful or disgraceful. —in·glo′ri·ous·ly, adv.

in·got (ing′gət), n. a mass of metal cast in a convenient form for shaping, remelting, or refining.

in·graft (in graft′, -gräft′), v.t. engraft.

in·grained (in grānd′, in′grānd′), adj. 1. deep-rooted: ingrained superstition. 2. inveterate or habitual: an ingrained egoist.

in·grate (in′grāt), n. an ungrateful person.

in·gra·ti·ate (in grā′shē āt′), v.t., -at·ed, -at·ing. to establish (oneself) in the favor of others. —in·gra′ti·a′tion, n.

in·grat·i·tude (in grat′i tōōd′, -tyōōd′), n. the state of being ungrateful.

in·gre·di·ent (in grē′dē ənt), n. 1. something that enters as an element into a mixture. 2. a constituent element of anything.

in·gress (in′gres), n. Chiefly Literary. the act of entering.

in·grown (in′grōn′), adj. having grown into the flesh: an ingrown toenail.

in·gui·nal (ing′gwə nəl), adj. of or situated in the groin.

in·hab·it (in hab′it), v.t. to live or dwell in. —in·hab′it·a·ble, adj.

in·hab·it·ant (in hab′i tənt), n. a person or an animal that inhabits a place.

in·hal·ant (in hā′lənt), n. a medicinal substance used for inhaling.

in·ha·la·tor (in′hə lā′tər), n. an apparatus to help one inhale medicinal vapors, oxygen, etc.

in·hale (in hāl′), v.t., v.i., -haled, -hal·ing. to draw in (air) by breathing. —in·ha·la·tion (in′hə lā′shən), n.

in·hal·er (in hā′lər), n. 1. inhalator. 2. respirator (def. 1).

in·here (in hēr′), v.i., -hered, -her·ing. to belong intrinsically.

in·her·ent (in hēr′ənt, -her′-), adj. existing in something as a permanent and inseparable quality. —in·her′ent·ly, adv.

in·her·it (in her′it), v.t., v.i. 1. to receive (property, etc.) by succession or will, as an heir. 2. to receive (a genetic character) by heredity. —in·her′it·a·ble, adj. —in·her′i·tor, n.

in·her·it·ance (in her′i təns), n. 1. something that is or may be inherited. 2. the genetic characters transmitted from parent to offspring. 3. the act or fact of inheriting.

in·hib·it (in hib′it), v.t. 1. to block or hold back (an action, impulse, etc.). 2. Eccles. to prohibit or forbid.

---

in′har·mon′ic, adj.

in′har·mo′ni·ous, adj.

in·hi·bi·tion (in′i bish′ən, in′hi-), *n.* **1.** the act of inhibiting or state of being inhibited. **2.** the blocking or holding back of one psychological process by another.

in·hib·i·tor (in hib′i tər), *n.* a substance that retards or stops a chemical reaction.

in-house (in′hous′), *adj., adv.* within or utilizing an organization's own staff: *in-house research.*

in·hu·man (in hyōō′mən), *adj.* **1.** lacking sympathy, pity, warmth, or compassion. **2.** not human. —in·hu′man·ly, *adv.*

in·hu·mane (in′hyōō mān′), *adj.* lacking humanity or kindness. —in′hu·mane′ly, *adv.*

in·hu·man·i·ty (in′hyōō man′i tē), *n., pl.* -ties. **1.** the state or quality of being inhuman or inhumane. **2.** an inhuman or inhumane act.

in·im·i·cal (i nim′i kəl), *adj.* **1.** tending to be harmful or unfavorable. **2.** unfriendly or hostile. —in·im′i·cal·ly, *adv.*

in·im·i·ta·ble (i nim′i tə bəl), *adj.* incapable of being imitated. —in·im′i·ta·bly, *adv.*

in·iq·ui·ty (i nik′wi tē), *n., pl.* -ties. **1.** gross injustice. **2.** a wicked act. —in·iq′ui·tous, *adj.* —in·iq′ui·tous·ly, *adv.*

init., initial.

in·i·tial (i nish′əl), *adj., n., v.,* -tialed, -tial·ing *or* -tialled, -tial·ing. —*adj.* **1.** of or pertaining to the very beginning. —*n.* **2.** an initial letter, as of a word. **3.** the first letter of a proper name. —*v.t.* **4.** to mark or sign with initials. —in·i′tial·ly, *adv.*

in·i·ti·ate (*v.* i nish′ē āt′; *n.* i nish′ē it, -āt′), *v.,* -at·ed, -at·ing; *n.* —*v.t.* **1.** to begin or set going. **2.** to introduce into the knowledge of some art or subject. **3.** to admit with formal rites into secret knowledge, a society, etc. —*n.* **4.** a person who has been initiated. —in·i′ti·a′tion, *n.* —in·i′ti·a·tor, *n.* —in·i′ti·a·to′ry (-ə tôr′ē), *adj.*

in·i·ti·a·tive (i nish′ē ə tiv, i nish′ə-), *n.* **1.** an introductory act or step. **2.** readiness and ability in initiating action. **3.** one's personal, responsible decision. **4.** a procedure by which a specified number of voters may propose legislation.

in·ject (in jekt′), *v.t.* **1.** to force (a fluid) into a passage, cavity, or tissue. **2.** to interject (a remark, etc.), as into conversation. —in·jec′tion, *n.* —in·jec′tor, *n.*

in·junc·tion (in jungk′shən), *n.* **1.** a court order requiring a person or

corporation to do or refrain from doing a particular act. **2.** the act or an instance of enjoining. **3.** a command or order.

in·jure (in′jər), *v.t.,* -jured, -jur·ing. **1.** to inflict damage or loss on, esp. to a bodily part. **2.** to do wrong or injustice to. —in′jur·er, *n.*

in·ju·ry (in′jə rē), *n., pl.* -ju·ries. **1.** damage or loss sustained, esp. of a bodily part. **2.** wrong or injustice done or suffered. —in·ju′ri·ous (-jōōr′ē əs), *adj.* —in·ju′ri·ous·ly, *adv.*

in·jus·tice (in jus′tis), *n.* **1.** violation of the rights of others. **2.** an unjust act.

ink (ingk), *n.* **1.** a fluid used for writing or printing. —*v.t.* **2.** to mark, stain, or smear with ink.

ink′blot test′ (ingk′blot′), any of various personality tests using blotted patterns of ink, esp. the Rorschach test.

ink·ling (ingk′ling), *n.* **1.** a slight suggestion. **2.** a vague idea.

ink·well (ingk′wel′), *n.* a small pot for ink, esp. one formerly set into a desk-top hole.

ink·y (ingk′kē), *adj.,* ink·i·er, ink·i·est. **1.** black as ink. **2.** stained with ink. **3.** consisting of or containing ink. —ink′i·ness, *n.*

in·laid (in′lād′, in lād′), *adj.* decorated or made with a design set in the surface.

in·land (*adj.* in′lənd; *adv., n.* in′land′, -lənd), *adj.* **1.** of or situated in the interior part of a country. **2.** *Brit.* domestic or internal: *inland revenue.* —*adv.* **3.** in or toward the interior of a country. —*n.* **4.** the inland region.

in-law (in′lô′), *n.* a relative by marriage.

in·lay (*v.* in′lā′, in′lā′; *n.* in′lā′), *v.,* -laid, -lay·ing, *n.* —*v.t.* **1.** to decorate (an object) with layers of fine materials set in its surface. **2.** to insert (layers of fine materials) in the surface of an object. —*n.* **3.** inlaid work or decoration. **4.** a filling, as of gold, that is first shaped to fit a tooth cavity and then cemented into it.

in·let (in′let, -lit), *n.* **1.** an indentation of a shoreline, usually long and narrow. **2.** a narrow passage between islands.

in·mate (in′māt′), *n.* a person who is confined in a hospital, prison, etc.

in me·mo·ri·am (in mə môr′ē əm, -môr′-), in memory (of).

in·most (in′mōst′), *adj.* **1.** situated farthest within. **2.** most intimate.

---

in·hos′pi·ta·ble, *adj.*
in·hos′pi·ta·bly, *adv.*

in′hos·pi·tal′i·ty, *n.*
in′ju·di′cious, *adj.*

in′ju·di′cious·ly, *adv.*
in′ju·di′cious·ness, *n.*

inn (in), *n.* **1.** a usually small, countryside or roadside hotel. **2.** *Obsolesc.* a tavern or pub.

in·nards (in′ərdz), *n.pl. Informal.* **1.** entrails or viscera. **2.** the internal parts of a mechanism or structure.

in·nate (i nāt′, in′āt), *adj.* **1.** existing in one from birth. **2.** inherent in the character of something. —**in·nate′ly,** *adv.* —**in·nate′ness,** *n.* —**Syn. 1.** congenital, inborn, native.

in·ner (in′ər), *adj.* **1.** situated farther within. **2.** more intimate or private: *his inner circle of friends.* **3.** mental or spiritual: *the inner life.*

in′ner cit′y, an older part of a city, densely populated and usually deteriorating.

in·ner-di·rect·ed (in′ər di rek′tid, -dī-), *adj.* guided by internal values rather than external pressures.

in′ner ear′, the internal portion of the ear composed of a vestibule, semicircular canals, and a cochlea.

in·ner·most (in′ər mōst′), *adj.* inmost.

in·ner·sole (in′ər sōl′), *n.* insole.

in·ner·spring (in′ər sprinG′), *adj.* having a number of enclosed helical springs supporting padding: *an innerspring mattress.*

in·ner·vate (i nûr′vāt, in′ər vāt′), *v.t.,* **-vat·ed, -vat·ing. 1.** to communicate nervous energy to. **2.** to furnish with nerves. —**in′ner·va′tion,** *n.*

in·ning (in′inG), *n. Baseball.* a division of a game during which each team has a turn at bat. **2.** *innings, Cricket.* a unit of play in which each team has a turn at bat.

inn·keep·er (in′kē′pər), *n.* a person who owns or operates an inn.

in·no·cent (in′ə sənt), *adj.* **1.** free from moral wrong. **2.** free from legal or specific wrong. **3.** not involving evil intent. **4.** not causing physical or moral injury. **5.** devoid: *innocent of merit.* **6.** naive or simplistic. —*n.* **7.** an innocent person, as a young child. —**in′no·cence,** *n.* —**in′no·cent·ly,** *adv.* —**Syn. 1.** pure, virtuous. **3.** blameless, guiltless.

in·noc·u·ous (i nok′yoo əs), *adj.* **1.** not likely to cause damage or injury. **2.** dull and insipid. —**in·noc′u·ous·ly,** *adv.* —**in·noc′u·ous·ness,** *n.*

in·nom·i·nate (i nom′ə nit), *adj.* having no name.

innom′inate bone′, either of the two bones forming the sides of the pelvis.

in·no·vate (in′ə vāt′), *v.i., v.t.,* **-vat·ed, -vat·ing.** to introduce (something new). —**in′no·va′tive,** *adj.* —**in′no·va′tor,** *n.*

in·no·va·tion (in′ə vā′shən), *n.* **1.** something new introduced. **2.** the introduction of new things or methods.

in·nu·en·do (in′yoo en′dō), *n., pl.* **-dos, -does.** an indirect intimation about a person or thing, esp. of a derogatory nature.

in·nu·mer·a·ble (i noo′mər ə bəl, -nyoo′-), *adj.* too numerous to be numbered or counted.

in·oc·u·late (i nok′yə lāt′), *v.t.* **-lat·ed, -lat·ing.** to inject a serum into, chiefly in order to secure immunity. —**in·oc′u·la′tion,** *n.*

in·of·fen·sive (in′ə fen′siv), *adj.* doing no harm or injury. —**in′of·fen′sive·ly,** *adv.*

in·op·er·a·ble (in op′ər ə bəl), *adj.* **1.** not operable or practicable. **2.** not admitting of a surgical operation without undue risk.

in·op·er·a·tive (in op′ər ə tiv, -ə rā′tiv), *adj.* **1.** not in operation. **2.** without effect.

in·op·por·tune (in op′ər tōōn′, -tyōōn′), *adj.* not opportune or timely. —**in·op′por·tune′ly,** *adv.*

in·or·di·nate (in ôr′d°nit), *adj.* **1.** exceeding proper limits. **2.** not regulated or regular. —**in·or′di·nate·ly,** *adv.* —**Syn. 1.** immoderate, excessive.

in·or·gan·ic (in′ôr gan′ik), *adj.* **1.** not having the structure or organization characteristic of living bodies. **2.** noting or pertaining to compounds that are not hydrocarbons or their derivatives. —**in′or·gan′i·cal·ly,** *adv.*

in·pa·tient (in′pā′shənt), *n.* a patient who stays in a hospital while receiving medical care or treatment.

in·put (in′pŏot′), *n.* **1.** something that is put in. **2.** the power or energy supplied to a machine. **3.** information properly coded for feeding into a computer.

in·quest (in′kwest), *n.* a judicial inquiry, esp. before a jury, as a coroner's inquiry.

in·qui·e·tude (in kwī′i tŏōd′, -tyŏōd′), *n.* restlessness or uneasiness.

in·quire (in kwī°r′), *v.,* **-quired, -quir·ing.** —*v.t.* **1.** to seek to learn by asking. —*v.i.* **2.** to seek information by questioning. **3.** to make investigation: *to inquire into the incident.* —**in·quir′er,** *n.* —**in·quir′ing·ly,** *adv.*

in·quir·y (in kwī°r′ē, in′kwə rē), *n., pl.* **-quir·ies. 1.** a seeking for truth, information, or knowledge. **2.** an investigation, as into an incident. **3.** a question or query.

in·qui·si·tion (in′kwi zish′ən), *n.* **1.** an official investigaton, esp. one of a political or religious nature. **2.** any harsh or prolonged questioning. **3.** (*cap.*) *Rom. Cath. Ch.* a former special tribunal, engaged chiefly in combating and punishing heresy. —**in′qui·si′tion·al,** *adj.* —**in·quis′i·tor,** *n.* —**in·quis′i·to′ri·al** (-kwiz′i tôr′ē-əl), *adj.*

in·quis·i·tive (in kwiz′i tiv), *adj.* **1.** given to inquiry or research. **2.** unduly curious. —in·quis′i·tive·ly, *adv.* —in·quis′i·tive·ness, *n.*

in re (in rē′, rā′), in the matter of.

I.N.R.I., Jesus of Nazareth, King of the Jews. [< L *Iēsus Nazarēnus, Rēx Iūdaeōrum*]

in·road (in′rōd′), *n.* **1.** Usually, *inroads.* a forcible encroachment: *inroads on our savings.* **2.** a hostile raid.

in·rush (in′rush′), *n.* a rushing or pouring in. —in′rush′ing, *n., adj.*

ins., **1.** inches. **2.** insurance.

ins′ and outs′, the intricacies or particulars involved.

in·sane (in sān′), *adj.* **1.** mentally deranged. **2.** of or for insane persons. **3.** utterly senseless. —in·sane′ly, *adv.* —in·san′i·ty (-san′i tē), *n.*

in·sa·tia·ble (in sā′shə bəl, -shē ə-), *adj.* incapable of being satisfied. Also, in·sa′ti·ate (-shē it). —in·sa′-tia·bly, *adv.*

in·scribe (in skrīb′), *v.t.,* -scribed, -scrib·ing. **1.** to write or engrave (words, etc.) on a surface. **2.** to mark (a surface) with words, etc., esp. in a durable way. **3.** to address, autograph, or dedicate (a book, etc.) to someone. **4.** to enroll, as on an official list. **5.** *Geom.* to draw (one figure) within another figure so as to touch at as many points as possible. —in·scrib′er, *n.* —in·scrip′-tion (-skrip′shən), *n.*

in·scru·ta·ble (in skrōō′tə bəl), *adj.* **1.** incapable of being searched into or scrutinized. **2.** not easily understood or known. —in·scru′ta·bil′i·ty, *n.* —in·scru′ta·ble·ness, *n.* —in·scru′ta·bly, *adv.*

in·seam (in′sēm′), *n.* an inner seam, esp. of a trouser leg.

in·sect (in′sekt), *n.* any of a large class of small, air-breathing arthropods having the body divided into three parts, and having three pairs of legs and usually two pairs of wings.

in·sec·ti·cide (in sek′ti sīd′), *n.* a substance or preparation used for killing insects. —in·sec′ti·cid′al, *adj.*

in·sec·tiv·o·rous (in′sek tiv′ər əs), *adj.* adapted to feeding on insects.

in·se·cure (in′si kyŏŏr′), *adj.* **1.** exposed to danger. **2.** not firm or stable. **3.** subject to fear or doubt. —in′se·cure′ly, *adv.* —in′se·cu′ri·ty, *n.* —in′se·cure′ness, *n.*

in·sem·i·nate (in sem′ə nāt′), *v.t.,* -nat-ed, -nat·ing. to inject semen into (the female reproductive tract). —in·sem′i·na′tion, *n.* —in·sem′i·na′tor, *n.*

in·sen·sate (in sen′sāt, -sit), *adj.* **1.** not endowed with sensation. **2.** without feeling or sensitivity. **3.** without sense or judgment. —in·sen′sate·ly, *adv.* —in·sen′sate·ness, *n.*

in·sen·si·ble (in sen′sə bəl), *adj.* **1.** incapable of feeling or perceiving. **2.** not subject to a particular feeling: *insensible to shame.* **3.** unaware or inappreciative. **4.** not perceptible by the senses. **5.** unresponsive in feeling. —in·sen′si·bil′i·ty, *n.* —in·sen′-si·bly, *adv.*

in·sen·si·tive (in sen′si tiv), *adj.* **1.** not physically sensitive. **2.** deficient in acuteness of feeling. —in·sen′si·tive·ly, *adv.* —in·sen′si·tiv′i·ty, *n.*

in·sen·ti·ent (in sen′shē ənt, -shənt), *adj.* without sensation or feeling. —in·sen′ti·ence, *n.*

in·sep·a·ra·ble (in sep′ər ə bəl, -sep′rə-), *adj.* incapable of being separated or disjoined. —in·sep′a·ra·bil′-i·ty, *n.* —in·sep′a·ra·ble·ness, *n.* —in·sep′a·ra·bly, *adv.*

in·sert (v. in sûrt′; n. in′sûrt), *v.t.* **1.** to put or set in. **2.** to introduce into the body of something. —*n.* **3.** something inserted or to be inserted. —in·ser′tion, *n.*

in·set (v. in set′; n. in′set′), *v.t.,* -set, -set·ting. *n.* insert.

in·shore (in′shôr′, -shōr′), *adj.* **1.** carried on or lying close to the shore. —*adv.* **2.** toward the shore.

in·side (*prep.* in′sīd′, in′sīd′; *adv.* in′-sīd′; *n.* in′sīd′; *adj.* in′sīd′, in′-), *prep.* **1.** on the inner part of. **2.** prior to the elapse of. —*adv.* **3.** in or into the inner part. **4.** indoors. **5.** inside of, within the space or period of. —*n.* **6.** the inner part. **7.** the inner side or surface. **8.** insides. *Informal.* the stomach and intestines. **9.** a select circle of power, prestige, etc. **10.** inward nature, mind, feelings, etc. **11.** inside out, a. with the inner side turned out. b. perfectly or completely. —*adj.* **12.** interior or internal. **13.** private or confidential.

in·sid·er (in′sī′dər), *n.* **1.** a member of a certain society, circle of friends, etc. **2.** a person who has some influence or special, usually confidential, information.

in·sid·i·ous (in sid′ē əs), *adj.* **1.** stealthily treacherous or deceitful. **2.** proceeding inconspicuously but with grave effect. **3.** *Rare.* intended to entrap or beguile —in·sid′i·ous·ly, *adv.* —in·sid′i·ous·ness, *n.*

in·sight (in′sīt′), *n.* **1.** an instance of perceiving the true nature of a thing, esp. through intuitive understanding. **2.** penetrating mental vision or discernment. —in′sight′ful, *adj.*

---

in′sa·lu′bri·ous, *adj.*　　　　　　in·san′i·tar′y, *adj.*

in·sig·ni·a (in sig′nē ə), *n., pl.* **-ni·a,** **-ni·as.** 1. a badge or mark of office or honor. 2. a distinguishing mark or sign of anything. Also, **in·sig′ne** (-sig′nē).

in·sin·cere (in′sin sēr′), *adj.* not sincere or honest. —**in′sin·cere′ly,** *adv.* —**in′sin·cer′i·ty** (-ser′i tē), *n.*

in·sin·u·ate (in sin′yōō āt′), *v.,* **-at·ed,** **-at·ing.** —*v.t.* 1. to suggest or hint slyly, esp. something malicious. 2. to instill or infuse subtly or artfully, as into the mind. 3. to introduce into a position by indirect or artful methods. —**in·sin′u·at′ing,** *adj.* — **in·sin′u·a′tion,** *n.* —**in·sin′u·a′tor,** *n.*

in·sip·id (in sip′id), *adj.* 1. without interesting or attractive qualities. 2. without sufficient taste to be pleasing, as food or drink. —**in′si·pid′i·ty,** *n.* —**in·sip′id·ly,** *adv.*

in·sist (in sist′), *v.i.* 1. to be emphatic, firm, or resolute on some matter. —*v.t.* 2. to assert firmly. 3. to persist in demanding. —**in·sist′ing·ly,** *adv.*

in·sist·ent (in sis′tənt), *adj.* emphatic in demanding something. —**in·sist′-ence, in·sist′en·cy,** *n.* —**in·sist′ent·ly,** *adv.*

in si·tu (in sī′tōō, -tyōō), *Latin.* in its original place.

in·so·far as (in′sə fär′, -sō-), to such an extent.

insol.. insoluble.

in·so·la·tion (in′sō lā′shən), *n.* solar radiation received over a given area.

in·sole (in′sōl′), *n.* 1. the inner sole of a shoe or boot. 2. a thickness of material laid as an inner sole within a shoe, esp. for comfort.

in·so·lent (in′sə lənt), *adj.* boldly rude or disrespectful. —**in′so·lence,** *n.* — **in′so·lent·ly,** *adv.*

in·sol·u·ble (in sol′yə bəl), *adj.* 1. incapable of being dissolved. 2. incapable of being solved. —**in·sol′u·bil′i·ty,** *n.* —**in·sol′u·bly,** *adv.*

in·solv·a·ble (in sol′və bəl), *adj.* incapable of being solved or explained.

in·sol·vent (in sol′vənt), *adj.* unable to satisfy creditors or discharge liabilities. —**in·sol′ven·cy,** *n.*

in·som·ni·a (in som′nē ə), *n.* inability to sleep, esp. when chronic. —**in·som′ni·ac′** (-ak′), *n., adj.*

in·so·much (in′sō much′), *adv.* 1. to such an extent. 2. insomuch as, seeing that.

in·sou·ci·ant (in sōō′sē ənt), *adj.* free from concern or care. —**in·sou′ci·ance,** *n.*

insp., 1. inspected. 2. inspector.

in·spect (in spekt′), *v.t.* 1. to look carefully at. 2. to view or examine officially. —**in·spec′tion,** *n.* —**in·spec′tor,** *n.*

in·spi·ra·tion (in′spə rā′shən), *n.* 1. an inspiring or animating action or influence. 2. something inspired, as a thought. 3. the act of inspiring or state of being inspired. 4. the drawing of air into the lungs. —**in′spi·ra′tion·al,** *adj.* —**in′spi·ra′tion·al·ly,** *adv.*

in·spire (in spī°r′), *v.,* **-spired, -spir·ing.** —*v.t.* 1. to infuse an animating, quickening, or exalting influence into. 2. to produce or arouse (a feeling, etc.). 3. to influence or impel. 4. to guide or control by divine influence. 5. to give rise to or cause to take (air, etc.) into the lungs. — *v.i.* 7. to give inspiration. 8. to inhale. —**in·spir′er,** *n.*

in·spir·it (in spir′it), *v.t.* to infuse spirit or life into.

inst., 1. instant (def. 6). 2. institute. 3. institution.

in·sta·bil·i·ty (in′stə bil′i tē), *n.* lack of stability or firmness.

in·stall (in stôl′), *v.t.* 1. to place in position for service or use, as an air conditioner. 2. to establish in an office, position, or place. 3. to induct into an office with formalities. Also, **in·stal′.** —**in·stal·la·tion** (in′-stə lā′shən), *n.* —**in·stall′er,** *n.*

in·stall·ment[1] (in stôl′mənt), *n.* 1. any of several parts into which a debt is divided for payment at successive fixed times. 2. a single portion of something furnished or issued in parts at successive times. Also, **in·stal′ment.**

in·stall·ment[2] (in stôl′mənt), *n. Obs.* the act of installing or fact of being installed. Also, **in·stal′ment.**

install′ment plan′, a system for paying a debt by installments.

in·stance (in′stəns), *n., v.,* **-stanced, -stanc·ing.** —*n.* 1. a thing or person cited to explain a general idea. 2. *Law.* prosecution of a case: *a court of first instance.* 3. at the instance of, at the suggestion of. —*v.t.* 4. to cite as an instance or example. — **Syn.** 1. case, example.

in·stant (in′stənt), *n.* 1. a very short space of time. 2. a particular moment. —*adj.* 3. immediate or direct. 4. pressing or urgent: *instant need.* 5. (of a food) requiring only water, milk, etc., to prepare. 6. *Obsolesc.* of this month.

in·stan·ta·ne·ous (in′stən tā′nē əs), *adj.* occurring or completed in an instant. —**in′stan·ta′ne·ous·ly,** *adv.*

in·stan·ter (in stan′tər), *adv. Facetious.* instantly.

in·stant·ly (in′stənt lē), *adv.* immediately or at once.

---

in·sig·nif′i·cance, *n.*   **in′sig·nif′i·cant,** *adj.*   **in·so·bri′e·ty,** *n.*

in′stant re′play, *Television.* an immediately repeated broadcast of a small segment of a recorded event, esp. of a sports event.

in·state (in stāt′), *v.t.*, **-stat·ed, -stat·ing.** to place in a certain state or position, as in an office.

in·stead (in sted′), *adv.* **1.** as a preferred alternative. **2.** as a replacement. **3. instead of,** in place of.

in·step (in′step′), *n.* the arched upper surface of the human foot between the toes and the ankle.

in·sti·gate (in′stə gāt′), *v.t.*, **-gat·ed, -gat·ing. 1.** to provoke to some action. **2.** to bring about by incitement. —**in′sti·ga′tion,** *n.* —**in′sti·ga′tor,** *n.*

in·still (in stil′), *v.t.* **1.** to infuse slowly into the mind. **2.** to put in drop by drop. Also, **in·stil′.** —**in·still′er,** *n.* —**in·still′ment,** *n.*

in·stinct (in′stingkt), *n.* **1.** an inborn tendency to action common to a given biological species. **2.** a natural inclination or aptitude. **3.** natural intuitive power. —**in·stinc′tive,** *adj.* —**in·stinc′tive·ly,** *adv.* —**in·stinc′tu·al,** *adj.*

in·sti·tute (in′sti tōōt′, -tyōōt′), *v.*, **-tut·ed, -tut·ing,** *n.* —*v.t.* **1.** to set up or establish. **2.** to get under way. —*n.* **3.** an organization for carrying on a particular work, as of scientific character. **4. a.** a college devoted to instruction in technical subjects. **b.** a short instructional program in some specialized activity. **5.** something instituted or established, as an authoritative legal principle. —**in′sti·tu′tor, in′sti·tut′er,** *n.* —**Syn. 2.** inaugurate, initiate.

in·sti·tu·tion (in′sti tōō′shən, -tyōō′-), *n.* **1.** an establishment devoted to the promotion of a particular object, esp. one of a public character. **2.** the building devoted to such work. **3.** a place of confinement, as a mental hospital. **4.** any established law, custom, etc. **5.** any familiar practice or object. —**in′sti·tu′tion·al,** *adj.* —**in′sti·tu′tion·al·ly,** *adv.*

in·sti·tu·tion·al·ize (in′sti tōō′shə·nªliz′, -tyōō′-), *v.t.*, **-ized, -iz·ing. 1.** to make into or treat as an institution. **2.** to confine in an institution, as for rehabilitation. —**in′sti·tu′tion·al·i·za′tion,** *n.*

instr., 1. instructor. **2.** instrument.

in·struct (in strukt′), *v.t.* **1.** to furnish with knowledge, esp. by a systematic method. **2.** to direct or command. —**Syn. 1.** educate, teach, train.

in·struc·tion (in struk′shən), *n.* **1.** the act or practice of instructing. **2.** the knowledge imparted. **3.** Usually, **instructions.** orders or directions. —**in·struc′tion·al,** *adj.*

in·struc·tive (in struk′tiv), *adj.* serving to instruct or inform.

in·struc·tor (in struk′tər), *n.* **1.** a person who instructs. **2.** a college teacher who ranks below an assistant professor. —**in·struc′tor·ship′,** *n.*

in·stru·ment (in′strə mənt), *n.* **1.** a mechanical tool, esp. one used for delicate or precision work: *surgical instruments.* **2.** a contrivance for producing musical sounds. **3.** a formal legal document, as a draft, bond, etc.: *negotiable instruments.* **4.** a mechanical or electronic measuring device, esp. one used in navigation. —*adj.* **5.** relying only on the observation of instruments for navigation: *instrument flying.* —*v.t.* **6.** to equip with instruments.

in·stru·men·tal (in′strə men′tªl), *adj.* **1.** serving as an instrument or means. **2.** of or pertaining to an instrument. **3.** performed on or written for a musical instrument or instruments. —**in′stru·men′tal·ly,** *adv.*

in·stru·men·tal·ist (in′strə men′tªlist), *n.* a person who performs on a musical instrument.

in·stru·men·tal·i·ty (in′strə men tal′i tē), *n., pl.* **-ties.** a means or agency.

in·stru·men·ta·tion (in′strə men tā′shən), *n.* **1.** the arranging of music for instruments, esp. for an orchestra. **2.** the use of, or work done by, instruments.

in·sub·or·di·nate (in′sə bôr′dºnit), *adj.* not submitting to authority. —**in′·sub·or′di·nate·ly,** *adv.* —**in′sub·or′di·na′tion,** *n.*

in·sub·stan·tial (in′səb stan′shəl), *adj.* unsubstantial.

in·suf·fer·a·ble (in suf′ər ə bəl), *adj.* not to be endured or borne. —**in·suf′fer·a·bly,** *adv.*

in·suf·fi·cient (in′sə fish′ənt), *adj.* deficient in force, quality, or amount. —**in′suf·fi′cien·cy,** *n.* **in′suf·fi′cient·ly,** *adv.*

in·su·lar (in′sə lər, ins′yə-), *adj.* **1.** of or pertaining to an island or islands. **2.** detached or isolated. **3.** narrow-minded or illiberal. —**in′su·lar′i·ty** (-lar′i tē), *n.*

in·su·late (in′sə lāt′, ins′yə-), *v.t.*, **-lat·ed, -lat·ing 1.** to cover with nonconducting material to prevent or reduce the transfer of electricity, heat, or sound. **2.** to place in an isolated situation. [< LL *insulāt(us)* made into an island] —**in′su·la′tion,** *n.* —**in′su·la′tor,** *n.*

in·su·lin (in′sə lin, ins′yə-), *n.* **1.** a hormone, produced by the islets of cells of the pancreas, that regulates the metabolism of glucose and other carbohydrates. **2.** any of several commercial preparations of this substance, used in the treatment of diabetes.

in·sult (*v.* in sult′; *n.* in′sult), *v.t.* **1.** to treat insolently or with contemptuous rudeness. —*n.* **2.** an insolent or contemptuously rude action or speech. —**in·sult′ing·ly,** *adv.* —**Syn. 2.** affront, indignity, offense, slight.

in·su·per·a·ble (in soo̅′pər ə bəl), *adj.* incapable of being overcome or surmounted. —**in·su′per·a·bly,** *adv.*

in·sup·port·a·ble (in′sə pôr′tə bəl, -pôr′-), *adj.* **1.** not endurable or bearable. **2.** incapable of being sustained or maintained.

in·sur·ance (in shoor′əns), *n.* **1.** the act, system, or business of insuring property, life, one's person, etc., against loss or harm, in consideration of a payment proportionate to the risk involved. **2.** coverage by contract in which one party agrees to indemnify another for any loss that occurs under the terms of the contract. **3.** the contract itself. **4.** the amount for which anything is insured.

in·sure (in shoor′), *v.t.,* **-sured, -sur-ing. 1.** to issue or obtain insurance on or for. **2.** to ensure. —**in·sur′a·ble,** *adj.*

in·sured (in shoord′), *n.* a person covered by an insurance policy.

in·sur·er (in shoor′ər), *n.* a person or company that insures or issues insurance.

in·sur·gent (in sûr′jənt), *n.* **1.** a person who engages in unorganized outbreak against an established government or authority. **2.** a member of a group, as a political party, who revolts against the policies of the group. —*adj.* **3.** of or characteristic of an insurgent or insurgents. — **in·sur′gence, in·sur′gen·cy,** *n.*

in·sur·mount·a·ble (in′sər moun′tə bəl), *adj.* incapable of being surmounted or overcome. —**in′sur·mount′a·bly,** *adv.*

in·sur·rec·tion (in′sə rek′shən), *n.* the act or an instance of engaging in unorganized outbreak against an established government or authority. —**in′sur·rec′tion·ist,** *n.* —**Syn.** rebellion, revolt.

int., 1. interest. **2.** interior. **3.** interjection. **4.** internal. **5.** international. **6.** intransitive.

in·tact (in takt′), *adj.* remaining uninjured, sound, or whole. —**in·tact′ness,** *n.*

in·tagl·io (in tal′yō, -täl′-), *n., pl.* **-ios.** incised carving, as opposed to carving in relief.

in·take (in′tāk′), *n.* **1.** the place at which a fluid is taken into a channel, pipe, etc. **2.** the act of taking in. **3.** a quantity taken in.

in·tan·gi·ble (in tan′jə bəl), *adj.* **1.** incapable of being perceived by the sense of touch. **2.** not definite or clear to the mind. —*n.* **3.** something intangible, esp. an intangible asset, as good will. —**in·tan′gi·bil′i·ty,** *n.* —**in·tan′gi·bly,** *adv.*

in·te·ger (in′ti jər), *n.* one of the positive or negative numbers 1, 2, 3, 4, etc., or 0, as distinguished from a fraction or a mixed number.

in·te·gral (in′tə grəl), *adj.* **1.** belonging as an essential part of the whole. **2.** necessary to the completeness of the whole. **3.** made up of parts that together constitute a whole. **4.** complete or whole. —**in′te·gral·ly,** *adv.*

in·te·grate (in′tə grāt′), *v.,* **-grat·ed, -grat·ing.** —*v.t.* **1.** to incorporate (parts) into a whole. **2.** to combine to produce a whole or a larger unit. **3.** to make the occupancy or use of (a school, restaurant, etc.) available to persons of all races. —*v.i.* **4.** to become integrated. —**in′te·gra′tion,** *n.* —**in′te·gra′tive,** *adj.*

in′tegrated cir′cuit (in′tə grā′tid), a connected group of circuit elements, as of resistors and transistors, on a single tiny chip of semiconductor material.

in·teg·ri·ty (in teg′ri tē), *n.* **1.** soundness of moral character. **2.** a sound, unimpaired condition. **3.** wholeness or completeness.

in·teg·u·ment (in teg′yə mənt), *n.* a natural covering, as a skin, shell, or rind.

in·tel·lect (in′t[e]lekt′), *n.* **1.** the power of the mind by which one knows or understands. **2.** a particular mind or intelligence, esp. of a high order. **3.** a person possessing a great intellectual capacity.

in·tel·lec·tu·al (in′t[e]lek′choo əl), *adj.* **1.** appealing to or engaging the intellect. **2.** showing a notable mental capacity. **3.** guided or developed by or relying on the intellect. —*n.* **4.** a person of superior intellect. **5.** a person who pursues things of interest to the intellect. —**in′tel·lec′tu·al·ly,** *adv.*

in·tel·lec·tu·al·ism (in′t[e]lek′choo ə-liz′əm), *n.* **1.** the exercise of the intellect. **2.** devotion to intellectual pursuits.

in·tel·lec·tu·al·ize (in′t[e]lek′choo ə-liz′), *v.t.,* **-ized, -iz·ing.** to consider the rational content of, often by ignoring the emotional significance. —**in′tel·lec′tu·al·i·za′tion,** *n.*

in·tel·li·gence (in tel′i jəns), *n.* **1.** capacity for reasoning, understanding, and for similar forms of mental activity. **2.** manifestation of such capacity. **3.** knowledge of an event,

in′sup·press′i·ble, *adj.*

in′sus·cep′ti·ble, *adj.*

circumstance, etc., received or imparted. **4.** the gathering or distribution of secret information, esp. about an enemy. **5.** an agency engaged in gathering such information.

intel'ligence quo'tient, mental age divided by chronological age, usually expressed as a multiple of 100.

in·tel·li·gent (in tel'i jənt), *adj.* having, displaying, or characterized by intelligence or a high mental capacity. —**in·tel'li·gent·ly,** *adv.* —**Syn.** astute, bright, clever, smart.

in·tel·li·gent·si·a (in tel'i jent'sē ə, -gent'sē ə), *n.pl.* intellectuals considered as a group.

in·tel·li·gi·ble (in tel'i jə bəl), *adj.* capable of being understood. —**in·tel'li·gi·bil'i·ty,** *n.* —**in·tel'li·gi·bly,** *adv.*

in·tem·per·ate (in tem'pər it, -prit), *adj.* **1.** given to immoderate indulgence in intoxicating drink. **2.** not temperate or moderate, esp. as regards indulgence of appetite or passion. —**in·tem'per·ance, in·tem'per·ate·ness,** *n.*

in·tend (in tend'), *v.t.* **1.** to have in mind as something to be done or brought about. **2.** to design for a particular purpose or use. **3.** to indicate or mean.

in·tend·ed (in ten'did), *n. Informal.* one's fiancé or fiancée.

in·tense (in tens'), *adj.* **1.** existing in a high or extreme degree: *intense heat.* **2.** acute or vehement, as emotions. **3.** strenuous or earnest: *an intense life.* **4.** having or showing great strength, strong feeling, etc. —**in·tense'ly,** *adv.* —**in·tense'ness,** *n.*

in·ten·si·fy (in ten'sə fī'), *v.t., v.i., -fied, -fy·ing.* to make or become intense or more intense. —**in·ten'si·fi·ca'tion,** *n.* —**in·ten'si·fi'er,** *n.*

in·ten·si·ty (in ten'si tē), *n., pl. -ties.* **1.** the quality or condition of being intense. **2.** energy, strength, etc., as of activity. **3.** a high or extreme degree, as of cold or heat. **4.** magnitude, as of energy or a force per unit of area or time.

in·ten·sive (in ten'siv), *adj.* **1.** of or characterized by intensity. **2.** *Gram.* indicating increased emphasis or force. —*n.* **3.** *Gram.* an intensive element or formation, as *-self* in *himself.* —**in·ten'sive·ly,** *adv.* —**in·ten'sive·ness,** *n.*

inten'sive care', constant medical surveillance provided by nurse-monitored equipment to critically ill patients in a hospital.

in·tent¹ (in tent'), *n.* **1.** the act of intending. **2.** something intended. **3.** meaning or significance. **4.** to all

intents and purposes, practically speaking.

in·tent² (in tent'), *adj.* **1.** firmly fixed or directed. **2.** having the attention sharply fixed: *intent on one's job.* **3.** determined: *intent on revenge.* —**in·tent'ly,** *adv.* —**in·tent'ness,** *n.*

in·ten·tion (in ten'shən), *n.* **1.** the act of determining upon some action. **2.** the end or object intended. —**Syn.** **2.** aim, goal, intent, purpose.

in·ten·tion·al (in ten'shə nºl), *adj.* done deliberately. —**in·ten'tion·al·ly,** *adv.*

in·ter (in tûr'), *v.t., -terred, -ter·ring.* to put (a dead body) in a grave or tomb.

inter-, a prefix meaning: **a.** between or among: *intercollegiate.* **b.** mutually or together: *intercept.*

inter-, **1.** intermediate. **2.** interrogation. **3.** interrogative.

in·ter·act (in'tər akt'), *v.i.* to act one upon another. —**in'ter·ac'tion,** *n.* —**in'ter·ac'tive,** *adj.*

in·ter a·li·a (in'tər ā'lē ə), *Latin.* among other things.

in·ter·breed (in'tər brēd'), *v.t., v.i. -bred, -breed·ing.* to hybridize.

in·ter·ca·lar·y (in tûr'kə ler'ē, in'tər kal'ə rē), *adj.* **1.** inserted in the calendar, as an extra day. **2.** interpolated or interposed.

in·ter·ca·late (in tûr'kə lāt'), *v.t., -lat·ed, -lat·ing.* **1.** to insert (an extra day, etc.) in the calendar. **2.** to interpolate or interpose. —**in·ter'ca·la'tion,** *n.*

in·ter·cede (in'tər sēd'), *v.i., -ced·ed, -ced·ing.* **1.** to plead in behalf of one in trouble. **2.** to offer mediation.

in·ter·cel·lu·lar (in'tər sel'yə lər), *adj.* situated between or among cells.

in·ter·cept (*v.* in'tər sept'; *n.* in'tər sept'), *v.t.* **1.** to take, seize, or halt on the way. **2.** *Math.* to mark off or include, as between two points or lines. —*n.* **3.** the act of intercepting. **4.** *Math.* the distance from the origin to the point at which a curve or line intersects an axis. —**in'ter·cep'tion,** *n.* —**in'ter·cep'tive,** *adj.*

in·ter·cep·tor (in'tər sep'tər), *n.* a high-speed fighter airplane used for the interception of enemy aircraft.

in·ter·ces·sion (in'tər sesh'ən), *n.* **1.** the act of interceding. **2.** a prayer to God on behalf of another. —**in'ter·ces'sion·al,** *adj.* —**in'ter·ces'sor,** *n.* —**in'ter·ces'so·ry,** *adj.*

in·ter·change (*v.* in'tər chānj'; *n.* in'tər chānj'), *v., -changed, -chang·ing, n.* —*v.t.* **1.** to put each (of two things) in the place of the other. **2.**

---

in'ter·ac'a·dem'ic, *adj.*
in'ter·A·mer'i·can, *adj.*
in'ter·a·tom'ic, *adj.*
in'ter·bank', *adj.*
in'ter·branch', *adj.*
in'ter·cap'il·lary, *adj.*

to cause (one thing) to change places with another. **3.** to give and receive reciprocally. —*n.* **4.** reciprocal exchange. **5.** a highway junction consisting of a system of road levels such that vehicles may move without crossing the stream of traffic. —**in′-ter-change′a-ble,** *adj.*

in-ter-col-le-giate (in′tər kə lē′jit, -jē-it), *adj.* taking place between different colleges.

in-ter-com (in′tər kom′), *n. Informal.* an intercommunication system.

in-ter-com-mu-ni-cate (in′tər kə myōō′-nə kāt′), *v.i., v.t.,* -**cat-ed,** -**cat-ing.** to communicate mutually, as people.

in′tercommunica′tion sys′tem (in′tər-kə myōō nə kā′shən), a communication system with a loudspeaker for listening and a microphone for speaking at each of two or more points.

in-ter-con-ti-nen-tal (in′tər kon′t°nen′-t°l), *adj.* **1.** of or between continents. **2.** traveling or capable of traveling between continents.

in-ter-cos-tal (in′tər kos′t°l, -kô′st°l), *adj.* situated between the ribs.

in-ter-course (in′tər kôrs′, -kōrs′), *n.* **1.** dealings or communication between persons or countries. **2.** See sexual intercourse.

in-ter-cul-tur-al (in′tər kul′chər əl), *adj.* between or among different cultures.

in-ter-de-nom-i-na-tion-al (in′tər di-nom′ə nā′shə n°l), *adj.* involving or occurring between different religious denominations.

in-ter-de-part-men-tal (in′tər dē′pärt-men′t°l, di pärt-), *adj.* between or among departments, as of an educational institution.

in-ter-de-pend-ent (in′tər di pen′dənt), *adj.* mutually dependent. —**in′ter-de-pend′ence,** *n.*

in-ter-dict (*n.* in′tər dikt′; *v.* in′tər-dikt′), *n.* **1.** any prohibitory act. —*v.t.* **2.** *Chiefly Eccles.* to forbid or prohibit. **3.** to impede by steady bombardment. —**in′ter-dic′tion,** *n.*

in-ter-dis-ci-pli-nar-y (in′tər dis′ə plə-ner′ē), *adj.* combining or involving two or more academic disciplines.

in-ter-est (in′tər ist, -trist), *n.* **1.** one's feelings of concern or curiosity, as aroused by something or someone. **2.** a person or thing that arouses such feelings. **3.** the power to excite such feelings. **4.** a legal share or right, as in ownership of property or a business. **5.** the enterprise, property, etc., in which one has such a share or right. **6.** Often, **interests.** a group

financially involved in a given enterprise, industry, etc. **7.** benefit or advantage. **8. a.** a sum charged for borrowed money. **b.** the rate for such charge. **9. in the interest or interests of,** to the advantage of. —*v.t.* **10.** to excite the attention or curiosity of. **11.** to be of concern to. **12.** to induce to participate. [< L: it concerns] —**Syn. 10.** absorb, engross, fascinate, intrigue.

in′terest group′, a group of people drawn or acting together because of a common interest, concern, or purpose.

in-ter-est-ing (in′tər i sting, -tri sting, -tə res′ting), *adj.* engaging the attention or curiosity. —**in′ter-est-ing-ly,** *adv.*

in-ter-face (in′tər fās′), *n.* **1.** a surface regarded as the common boundary of two bodies or spaces. **2.** a common boundary between systems or human beings. **3.** computer equipment or programs designed to communicate information from one system to another. —**in′ter-fa′cial,** *adj.*

in-ter-faith (in′tər fāth′), *adj.* between persons belonging to different religions.

in-ter-fere (in′tər fēr′), *v.i.,* -**fered,** -**fer-ing.** **1.** to come into opposition, esp. with the effect of hampering action: *Constant distractions interfere with work.* **2.** to meddle: *to interfere in another's life.* **3.** *Sports.* to obstruct the action of an opposing player in an illegal way. **4.** to create a jumbling of radio signals. —**in′ter-fer′ence,** *n.* —**in′ter-fer′er,** *n.*

in-ter-fer-om-e-ter (in′tər fə rom′i tər), *n.* a device used to measure wavelength and astronomical distances. —**in′ter-fer-om′e-try,** *n.*

in-ter-fer-on (in′tər fēr′on), *n.* a protein substance produced by virus-invaded cells that prevents reproduction of the virus.

in-ter-ga-lac-tic (in′tər gə lak′tik), *adj.* of or existing in the space between galaxies.

in-ter-im (in′tər im), *n.* **1.** an intervening period of time. —*adj.* **2.** belonging to or connected with an interim.

in-te-ri-or (in tēr′ē ər), *adj.* **1.** located within. **2.** situated well inland from the coast. —*n.* **3.** the internal part. **4.** a pictorial representation of the inside of a room. **5.** the inland parts of a country. **6.** the domestic affairs of a country. —**in-te′ri-or-ly,** *adv.*

in′ter-cit′y, *adj.*
in′ter-class′, *adj.*
in′ter-com′pa-ny, *adj.*

in′ter-con-nect′, *v.*
in′ter-con-nec′tion, *n.*
in′ter-coun′ty, *adj.*

in′ter-dis′trict, *adj.*
in′ter-fac′tion-al, *adj.*

inte'rior decora'tion, the designing and furnishing of the interior of a house, office, etc., esp. as an art, business, or profession. Also called **inte'rior design'.** —**inte'rior dec'- orator.**

interj., interjection.

in·ter·ject (in'tər jekt'), *v.t.* to introduce abruptly between statements. —**in'ter·jec'tor,** *n.* —**in'ter·jec'to·ry,** *adj.*

in·ter·jec·tion (in'tər jek'shən), *n.* 1. the act of interjecting. 2. something interjected. 3. a grammatically autonomous word or expression, esp. one conveying emotion, as *alas!* — **in'ter·jec'tion·al,** *adj.* —**in'ter·jec'- tion·al·ly,** *adv.*

in·ter·lace (in'tər lās'), *v.i., v.t.,* -laced, -lac·ing. 1. to unite by or as by lacing together. 2. to mingle or blend.

in·ter·lard (in'tər lärd'), *v.t.* to diversify (a speech, etc.) by interjecting something unique.

in·ter·leaf (in'tər lēf'), *n.* a blank leaf inserted between the regular printed leaves of a book.

in·ter·leave (in'tər lēv'), *v.t.,* -leaved, -leav·ing. to provide blank leaves in (a book).

in·ter·line[1] (in'tər līn'), *v.t.,* -lined, -lin·ing. to write or insert (words, etc.) between the lines of writing or print.

in·ter·line[2] (in'tər līn'), *v.t.,* -lined, -lin·ing. to provide with an interlining.

in·ter·lin·e·ar (in'tər lin'ē ər), *adj.* inserted between lines, as of the lines of print in a book.

in·ter·lin·ing (in'tər li'ning), *n.* an inner lining placed between the ordinary lining and the outer fabric of a garment.

in·ter·lock (in'tər lok'), *v.i., v.t.* 1. to lock or engage together closely. 2. to fit or connect (parts or functions) together so that their action is coordinated.

in·ter·loc·u·tor (in'tər lok'yə tər), *n.* a person who takes part in a conversation or dialogue.

in·ter·loc·u·to·ry (in'tər lok'yə tōr'ē, -tôr'ē), *adj. Law.* not finally decisive: *an interlocutory decree.*

in·ter·lope (in'tər lōp'), *v.i.,* -loped, -lop·ing. 1. to intrude into some region of trade without a proper license. 2. to thrust oneself into the affairs of others. —**in'ter·lop'er,** *n.*

in·ter·lude (in'tər lōōd'), *n.* 1. an intervening episode, period, space, etc. 2. any intermediate performance, as between the acts of a play. 3. an instrumental passage or composition played between the parts of a song, church service, drama, etc.

in·ter·lu·nar (in'tər lōō'nər), *adj.* pertaining to the moon's monthly period of invisibility between the old moon and the new.

in·ter·mar·ry (in'tər mar'ē), *v.i.,* -ried, -ry·ing. 1. to become connected by marriage, as two families, tribes, etc. 2. to marry within one's family. 3. to marry outside one's religion, ethnic group, etc. —**in'ter·mar'riage,** *n.*

in·ter·me·di·ar·y (in'tər mē'dē er'ē), *adj., n., pl.* -ar·ies. —*adj.* 1. being between. 2. serving as an intermediate agent or agency. —*n.* 3. an intermediate agent or agency. —**Syn.** 3. go-between mediator.

in·ter·me·di·ate (in'tər mē'dē it), *adj.* 1. being or acting between two points, stages, etc. —*n.* 2. something intermediate, as a form or class. 3. an intermediary —**in'ter·me'di·a·cy,** *n.* —**in'ter·me'di·ate·ly,** *adv.* —**in'- ter·me'di·ate·ness,** *n.*

in'terme'diate school', 1. a school that enrolls pupils in grades 4 through 6. 2. (formerly) a junior high school.

in·ter·ment (in tûr'mənt), *n.* the act or a ceremony of interring.

in·ter·mez·zo (in'tər met'sō, -med'zō), *n., pl.* -zos, -zi (-sē, -zē). 1. a short musical composition between main divisions of an extended musical work. 2. a short, independent musical composition.

in·ter·mi·na·ble (in tûr'mə nə bəl), *adj.* having no apparent limit or end. — **in·ter'mi·na·bly,** *adv.*

in·ter·min·gle (in'tər ming'gəl), *v.t., v.i.,* -gled -gling. to mingle together.

in·ter·mis·sion (in'tər mish'ən), *n.* an interval between periods of action or activity, as between the acts of a play.

in·ter·mit (in'tər mit'), *v.t., v.i.,* -mit·ted, -mit·ting. to discontinue temporarily.

in·ter·mit·tent (in'tər mit'ənt), *adj.* alternately ceasing and beginning again. —**in'ter·mit'tent·ly,** *adv.*

in·ter·mix (in'tər miks'), *v.t., v.i.* to intermingle. —**in'ter·mix'ture,** *n.*

in·tern[1] (in tûrn'), *v.t.* to restrict to or confine within prescribed limits, as enemy aliens.

in·tern[2] (in'tûrn), *n.* 1. Also, **in'terne.** a recent medical-school graduate serving an apprenticeship under supervision in a hospital. 2. any short-term trainee. —*v.i.* 3. to be or serve as an intern. —**in'tern·ship',** *n.*

---

in·ter·nal (in tûr′n°l), *adj.* 1. of or pertaining to the inside or inner part. 2. *Pharm.* oral (def. 3). 3. inherent or intrinsic. 4. of or pertaining to the domestic affairs of a country: *internal politics.* —in′ter·nal′i·ty, *n.* —in·ter′nal·ly, *adv.*

in·ter′nal-com·bus′tion en′gine (in-tûr′n°l kəm bus′chən), an engine in which the process of combustion takes place within the cylinder or cylinders.

inter′nal med′icine, the branch of medicine dealing with the diagnosis and nonsurgical treatment of diseases.

inter′nal rev′enue, the revenue of a government from any domestic source, excluding the income from customs.

internat., international.

in·ter·na·tion·al (in′tər nash′ə n°l), *adj.* 1. between or among nations. 2. of two or more nations or their citizens. 3. pertaining to the relations between nations. 4. having members or dealings in several nations. —*n.* 5. (*cap.*) any of several international socialist or communist organizations formed in the 19th and 20th centuries. 6. (*sometimes cap.*) a labor union having locals in two or more countries. —in′ter·na′tion·al·ly, *adv.*

in·ter·na·tion·al·ism (in′tər nash′ə-n°liz′əm), *n.* 1. the principle of cooperation among nations, for the promotion of their common good. 2. international character, relations, or control. —in′ter·na′tion·al·ist, *n., adj.*

in·ter·na·tion·al·ize (in′tər nash′ə-n°liz′), *v.t.,* -ized, -iz·ing. to bring under international control. —in′-ter·na′tion·al·i·za′tion, *n.*

in·ter·ne·cine (in′tər nē′sēn, -sīn, -nes′ēn, -īn), *adj.* 1. mutually destructive. 2. pertaining to conflict within a group.

in·tern·ee (in′tûr nē′), *n.* a person who is interned, as a prisoner of war.

in·tern·ist (in′tûr nist, in tûr′nist), a physician who specializes in internal medicine, esp. as distinguished from a surgeon.

in·tern·ment (in tûrn′mənt), *n.* the act of interning or state of being interned.

intern′ment camp′, a prison camp for the confinement of enemy aliens, prisoners of war, political prisoners, etc.

in·ter·node (in′tər nōd′), *n.* a part or space between two nodes, as of a plant stem. —in′ter·nod′al, *adj.*

in·ter·nun·ci·o (in′tər nun′shē ō′, -sē-ō′), *n., pl.* -ci·os. a papal ambassador ranking next below a nuncio.

in·ter-of·fice (in′tər ô′fis, -of′is), *adj.* functioning between the offices of an organization.

in·ter·per·son·al (in′tər pûr′sə n°l), *adj.* of or pertaining to the relations between persons. —in′ter·per′son·al·ly, *adv.*

in·ter·plan·e·tar·y (in′tər plan′i ter′ē), *adj.* being or occurring between planets.

in·ter·play (in′tər plā′), *n.* reciprocal play, action, or influence.

in·ter·po·late (in tûr′pə lāt′), *v.t.,* -lat·ed, -lat·ing. 1. to alter (a text) by the insertion of new matter, esp. without authorization. 2. to introduce (something extraneous) between other things or parts. —in·ter′po·la′tion, *n.* —in·ter′po·la′tor, *n.*

in·ter·pose (in′tər pōz′), *v.t., v.i.,* -posed, -pos·ing. 1. to place or come between (other things). 2. to bring (influence, action, etc.) to bear between parties. 3. to put in (a remark, question, etc.) in the midst of a conversation or discourse. —in·ter·pos′er, *n.* —in′ter·po·si′tion (-pə-zish′ən), *n.*

in·ter·pret (in tûr′prit), *v.t.* 1. to set forth the meaning of. 2. to understand in a particular way. 3. to perform or render (a role in a play, etc.) according to one's understanding or sensitivity. 4. to translate orally. —*v.i.* 5. to translate orally. —in·ter′pret·a·ble, *adj.* —in·ter′pret·er, *n.* —Syn. 1. explain, elucidate.

in·ter·pre·ta·tion (in tûr′pri tā′shən), *n.* 1. the act of interpreting. 2. an elucidation or explanation, as of a creative work, political event, etc. 3. a conception of another's behavior. —in·ter′pre·ta′tion·al, *adj.*

in·ter·pre·ta·tive (in tûr′pri tā′tiv), *adj.* 1. serving to interpret. 2. deduced by interpretation. Also, in·ter′pre·tive (-tiv). —in·ter′pre·ta′tive·ly, *adv.*

in·ter·ra·cial (in′tər rā′shəl), *adj.* for, between, or among persons of different races.

in·ter·reg·num (in′tər reg′nəm), *n., pl.* -nums, -na (-nə). 1. an interval of time between the death of a monarch and the accession of the successor. 2. any interruption in continuity. —in′ter·reg′nal, *adj.*

in·ter·re·late (in′tər ri lāt′), *v.t., vi.,* -lat·ed, -lat·ing. to bring or enter into reciprocal relation. —in′ter·re·lat′ed, *adj.* —in′ter·re·lat′ed·ness,

in′ter·nu′cle·ar, *adj.*
in′ter·o·ce·an′ic, *adj.*
in′ter·or′bi·tal, *adj.;* -ly, *adv.*
in′ter·phone′, *n.*
in′ter·po′lar, *adj.*
in′ter·pro·fes′sion·al, *adj.*
in′ter·re′gion·al, *adj.*
in′ter·re·li′gious, *adj.*

in·ter·re·la·tion,   **in·ter·re·la·tion·ship′,** *n.*

in·ter·rog., interrogative.

in·ter·ro·gate (in ter′ə gāt′), *v.t., v.i.,* **-gat·ed, -gat·ing.** to examine (a person) by questioning, esp. formally. —**in·ter′ro·ga′tion,** *n.* —**in·ter′ro·ga′tor,** *n.*

in·ter·rog·a·tive (in′tə rog′ə tiv), *adj.* **1.** of or conveying a question. **2.** *Gram.* used in or to form a question. —**in′ter·rog′a·tive·ly,** *adv.*

in·ter·rog·a·to·ry (in′tə rog′ə tôr′ē, -tōr′ē), *adj.* interrogative (def. 1). —**in′ter·rog′a·to′ri·ly,** *adv.*

in·ter·rupt (in′tə rupt′), *v.t.* **1.** to break off or cause to cease, as in the middle of something. **2.** to stop (a person) in the midst of doing or saying something, esp. by an interjected remark. —*v.i.* **3.** to interfere with action or speech, esp. by interjecting a remark. —**in′ter·rupt′er, -or.** —**in′ter·rup′tion,** *n.* —**in′ter·rup′tive,** *adj.*

in·ter·scho·las·tic (in′tər skə las′tik), *adj.* between or among schools.

in·ter·sect (in′tər sekt′), *v.t.* **1.** to cut or divide by passing through or across. —*v.i.* **2.** to cross, as lines, wires, etc.

in·ter·sec·tion (in′tər sek′shən, in′tər sek′-), *n.* **1.** a place where two or more roads meet. **2.** the act or fact of intersecting. **3.** *Math.* the set of elements which two or more sets have in common.

in·ter·sperse (in′tər spûrs′), *v.t.,* **-spersed, -spers·ing. 1.** to scatter here and there. **2.** to diversify with something scattered. —**in′ter·sper′sion** (-spûr′zhən, -shən), *n.*

in·ter·state (in′tər stāt′), *adj.* connecting or jointly involving states, esp. of the U.S.

in·ter·stel·lar (in′tər stel′ər), *adj.* between or among the stars.

in·ter·stice (in tûr′stis), *n., pl.* **-stic·es** (-sti siz, -sēz′). a small or narrow space between things or parts. —**in·ter·sti·tial** (in′tər stish′əl), *adj.* —**in′ter·sti′tial·ly,** *adv.*

in·ter·tid·al (in′tər tīd′⁰l), *adj.* of or pertaining to the shore region between the marks of low and high tide.

in·ter·twine (in′tər twīn′), *v.t., v.i.,* **-twined, -twin·ing.** to twine together. —**in′ter·twine′ment,** *n.*

in·ter·ur·ban (in′tər ûr′bən), *adj.* of or connecting two or more cities.

in·ter·val (in′tər vəl), *n.* **1.** an intervening period of time. **2.** a space between things. **3.** *Music.* the difference in pitch between two tones. **4. at intervals, a.** now and then. **b.** at particular places with gaps in between.

in·ter·vene (in′tər vēn′), *v.i.,* **-vened, -ven·ing. 1.** to come between, as in action. **2.** to occur between other events or periods. **3.** to occur incidentally so as to modify. **4.** to interfere, esp. with force or a threat of force. —**in′ter·ven′er, -or.** —**in′ter·ven′tion** (-ven′shən), *n.*

in·ter·ven·tion·ist (in′tər ven′shə nist), *n.* a person who favors intervention, as in the affairs of another state. —**in′ter·ven′tion·ism,** *n.*

in·ter·view (in′tər vyōō′), *n.* **1.** a meeting for obtaining information by questioning a person, as for a magazine article. **2.** the report of such a meeting. **3.** a formal meeting in which a person questions or evaluates another: *a job interview.* —*v.t.* **4.** to have an interview with. —**in′ter·view·ee′,** *n.* —**in′ter·view′er,** *n.*

in·ter·vo·cal·ic (in′tər vō kal′ik), *adj.* immediately following a vowel and preceding a vowel, as the *d* in *widow.*

in·ter·weave (in′tər wēv′), *v.t., v.i.,* **-wove** (-wōv′), or **-weaved; -wo·ven** (-wō′vən) or **-weaved; -weav·ing. 1.** to weave together. **2.** to intermingle as if by weaving. —**in′ter·wo′ven,** *adj.*

in·tes·tate (in tes′tāt, -tit), *adj.* **1.** not having made a will: *He died intestate.* **2.** not disposed of by will: *property intestate.*

in·tes·tine (in tes′tin), *n.* Usually, **intestines.** the lower part of the alimentary canal, extending from the pylorus to the anus and consisting of a narrow, longer part (small′ in·tes′tine) and a broad, shorter part (large′ intes′tine). —**in·tes′tin·al,** *adj.* —**in·tes′ti·nal·ly,** *adv.*

intes′tinal flu′, influenza with abdominal symptoms, as diarrhea, vomiting, etc.

in·ti·mate¹ (in′tə mit), *adj.* **1.** associated in close personal relations. **2.** characterized by warm friendship. **3.** private or closely personal. **4.** suggesting privacy or intimacy. **5.** inmost or deep within. —*n.* **6.** an intimate friend or associate, esp. a confidant. —**in′ti·ma·cy** (-mə sē), *n.* **in′ti·mate·ness,** *n.* —**in′ti·mate·ly,** *adv.* —**Syn. 1. 2.** familiar, friendly.

in·ti·mate² (in′tə māt′), *v.t.,* **-mat·ed, -mat·ing.** to make known indirectly. —**in′ti·mat′er,** *n.* —**in′ti·ma′tion,** *n.*

---

in′ter·school′, *n.*
in′ter·ses′sion, *n.*
in′ter·so·ci′e·tal, *adj.*
in′ter·tan′gle, *v.t.,* -gled, -gling.
in′ter·ri·to′ri·al, *adj.*
in′ter·trib′al, *adj.*
in′ter·trop′i·cal, *adj.*
in′ter·u′ni·ver′si·ty, *adj.*
in′ter·var′si·ty, *adj.*
in′ter·ver′te·bral, *adj.*
in′ter·wrought′, *adj.*

in·tim·i·date (in tim′i dāt′), v.t., -dat-ed, -dat·ing. 1. to make timid. 2. to force into or deter from some action by inducing fear. —in·tim′i·da′·tion, n.

intl., international.

in·to (in′tŏŏ, in′tŏŏ, -tə), prep. 1. to the inside of: He walked into the room. 2. to a point of contact with: backed into a parked car. 3. to the state or form assumed or brought about: went into shock. 4. to the occupation or acceptance of: went into banking. 5. (used to indicate a continuing extent in time or space): lasted into the night.

in·tol·er·a·ble (in tol′ər ə bəl), adj. 1. not tolerable or endurable. 2. excessive or extreme. —in·tol′er·a·bly, adv.

in·tol·er·ant (in tol′ər ənt), adj. 1. not tolerating beliefs, manners, etc., different from one's own, as in political or religious matters. 2. indisposed to tolerate or endure: intolerant of excesses. —in·tol′er·ance, n. —Syn. 1. bigoted, illiberal, prejudiced.

in·to·na·tion (in′tō nā′shən, -tə-), n. 1. the pattern of pitch changes in connected speech. 2. the act of intoning. 3. the manner of producing musical tones. 4. something intoned or chanted.

in·tone (in tōn′), v.t., v.i. -toned, -ton·ing. 1. to speak in a singing voice. 2. to recite in monotone. —in·ton′·er, n.

in to·to (in tō′tō), Latin. in the whole.

in·tox·i·cant (in tok′sə kənt), n. a substance that intoxicates, as an alcoholic liquor.

in·tox·i·cate (in tok′sə kāt′), v.t., -cat-ed, -cat·ing. 1. to stupefy with liquor. 2. to make enthusiastic. —in·tox′i·ca′tion, n.

intr., intransitive.

intra-, a combining form meaning "within" or "inside of": intramural.

in·trac·ta·ble (in trak′tə bəl), adj. not easily managed or controlled.

in·tra·mu·ral (in′trə myŏŏr′əl), adj. 1. involving representatives of a single school: intramural athletics. 2. within the walls or boundaries, as of an institution. —in′tra·mu′ral·ly, adv.

Intrans., intransitive.

in·tran·si·gent (in tran′si jənt), adj. uncompromising, as in politics. Also, **in·tran′si·geant.** —in·tran′si·gence, in·tran′si·geance, n. —in·tran′si·gent·ly, in·tran′si·geant·ly, adv.

in·tran·si·tive (in tran′si tiv), adj. Gram. noting an action without being accompanied by a direct object. —in·tran′si·tive·ly, adv. —in·tran′si·tive·ness, n.

in·tra·state (in′trə stāt′), adj. existing or occurring within a state, esp. one of the states of the U.S.

in·tra·u·ter·ine (in′trə yŏŏ′tər in, -tə-rīn′), adj. located or occurring within the uterus.

intrau′terine device′, any small variously shaped piece of plastic for insertion in the uterus as a continuous contraceptive.

in·tra·ve·nous (in′trə vē′nəs), adj. within or into a vein or the veins. —in·tra·ve′nous·ly, adv.

in·trench (in trench′), v.t. entrench.

in·trep·id (in trep′id), adj. absolutely fearless or dauntless. —in′tre·pid′i·ty, n. —in·trep′id·ly, adv.

in·tri·cate (in′trə kit), adj. 1. having many interrelated parts or facets. 2. hard to understand or solve. —in′tri·ca·cy (-kə sē), n. —in′tri·cate·ly, adv.

in·trigue (v. in trēg′; n. in trēg′, in′trēg), v., -trigued, -tri·guing, n. —v.t. 1. to arouse the curiosity or interest of. 2. to accomplish or force by crafty plotting or underhand machinations. —v.i. 3. to plot craftily or underhandedly. —n. 4. crafty plotting or underhand machinations. 5. the use of such machinations. 6. Obsolesc. a clandestine love affair. —in·tri′guer, n. —in·tri′guing·ly, adv.

in·trin·sic (in trin′sik, -zik), adj. belonging to a thing by its very nature. —in·trin′si·cal·ly, adv.

intro., 1. introduction. 2. introductory.

in·tro·duce (in′trə dŏŏs′, -dyŏŏs′), v.t., -duced, -duc·ing. 1. to present (a person) to another so as to make acquainted. 2. to present (a person, product, etc.) to a group for the first time. 3. to bring (a person) to first experience of or: to introduce someone to skiing. 4. to advance or bring into notice or use. 5. to begin or lead into: to introduce a speech with an anecdote. 6. to put into something for the first time. —in′tro·duc′er, n. —in′tro·duc′tion (-duk′shən), n. —in′tro·duc′to·ry, adv.

in·tro·it (in′trō it, -troit), n. 1. Rom. Cath. Ch. a part of a psalm with antiphon recited at the beginning of the Mass. 2. a choral response sung at the beginning of a religious service.

in·tro·spec·tion (in′trə spek′shən), n. the examination of one's own mental and emotional state. —in′tro·spec′tive, adj. —in′tro·spec′tive·ly, adv. —in′tro·spec′tive·ness, n.

in·tro·vert (in′trə vûrt′), n. a person characterized by concern primarily with his or her own thoughts and feelings. —in′tro·ver′sion (-vûr′zhən), n. —in′tro·vert′ed, adj.

in·trude (in trŏŏd′), v.t., v.i., -trud·ed, -trud·ing. to thrust (oneself) without invitation or welcome. —in-

trud′er, *n.* —**in·tru′sion** (-zhən), *n.* —**in·tru′sive** (-siv), *adj.* —**in·tru′sive·ly,** *adv.* —**in·tru′sive·ness,** *n.*

in·trust (in trust′), *v.t.* entrust.

in·tu·it (in tōō′it, -tyōō-; in′tōō it, -tyōō-), *v.t., v.i. Rare.* to know or understand by intuition.

in·tu·i·tion (in′tōō ish′ən, -tyōō-), *n.* 1. direct perception of truth or fact, independent of any reasoning process. 2. a keen and quick insight. —**in·tu′i·tive,** *adj.* —**in·tu′i·tive·ly,** *adv.*

in·un·date (in′ən dāt′, -un-, in un′dāt), *v.t.,* -**dat·ed, -dat·ing.** to cover with or as with a flood, esp. flood water. —**in′un·da′tion,** *n.*

in·ure (in yŏŏr′, i nŏŏr′), *v.t.,* -**ured, -ur·ing.** to toughen or accustom by extended subjection or experience. —**in·ure′ment,** *n.*

inv., invoice.

in va·cu·o (in vak′yōō ō′), *Latin.* 1. in a vacuum. 2. in isolation.

in·vade (in vād′), *v.t.,* -**vad·ed, -vad·ing.** 1. to enter (another country) by an attacking armed force, esp. for making war. 2. to enter and affect injuriously, as disease. 3. to intrude upon. —**in·vad′er,** *n.*

in·va·lid¹ (in′və lid), *n.* 1. an infirm or sickly person. —*adj.* 2. unable to care for oneself due to sickness or a disability. 3. of or for invalids. —*v.t.* 4. to make an invalid.

in·val·id² (in val′id), *adj.* 1. without force or foundation. 2. deficient in substance or cogency. 3. without legal force, as a contract. —**in′va·lid′i·ty** (-və lid′i tē), *n.* —**in·val′id·ly,** *adv.*

in·val·i·date (in val′i dāt′), *v.t.,* -**dat·ed, -dat·ing.** 1. to render invalid. 2. to deprive of legal force. —**in·val′i·da′tion,** *n.*

in·val·u·a·ble (in val′yōō ə bəl), *adj.* beyond calculable or appraisable value. —**in·val′u·a·bly,** *adv.*

in·var·i·a·ble (in vâr′ē ə bəl), *adj.* not variable or capable of being varied. —**in·var′i·a·bil′i·ty,** *n.* —**in·var′i·a·bly,** *adv.*

in·va·sion (in vā′zhən), *n.* 1. the act or an instance of invading. 2. an entrance into another country by an attacking armed force, esp. for making war. 3. the onset of anything harmful, as disease. 4. infringement by intrusion: *invasion of privacy.* —**in·va′sive** (-siv), *adj.*

in·vec·tive (in vek′tiv), *n.* 1. vehement denunciation, censure, or abuse. 2. insulting or abusive language.

in·veigh (in vā′), *v.i.* to protest strongly or attack vehemently with words: *to inveigh against isolationism.*

in·vei·gle (in vē′gəl, -vā′gəl), *v.t.,* -**gled, -gling.** 1. to entice or lure by

artful talk. 2. to acquire or obtain by such talk. —**in·vei′gler,** *n.*

in·vent (in vent′), *v.t.* 1. to originate as a product of one's own device. 2. to make up or fabricate: *to invent excuses.* —**in·ven′tor,** *n.*

in·ven·tion (in ven′shən), *n.* 1. the act or process of inventing. 2. anything invented. 3. the power or faculty of inventing. 4. something fabricated, as a false statement.

in·ven·tive (in ven′tiv), *adj.* 1. apt at inventing, devising, or contriving. 2. involving or showing invention. —**in·ven′tive·ly,** *adv.* —**in·ven′tive·ness,** *n.* —**Syn.** 1. ingenious, resourceful.

in·ven·to·ry (in′vən tôr′ē, -tōr′ē), *n., pl.* -**to·ries,** *v.,* -**to·ried, -to·ry·ing.** —*n.* 1. a detailed list of current goods, materials, or property, as of a business. 2. the items represented on such a list. 3. the act of making such a list. —*v.t.* 4. to make an inventory of.

in·ver·ness (in′vər nes′), *n.* an overcoat with a long, removable cape. [after a county in NW Scotland]

in·verse (in vûrs′, in′vûrs), *adj.* 1. reversed in position, direction, or tendency. —*n.* 2. that which is inverse. —**in·verse′ly,** *adv.*

in·ver·sion (in vûr′zhən, -shən), *n.* 1. the act of inverting or state of being inverted. 2. anything that is inverted. 3. a reversal in the normal temperature of rising air. —**in·ver′sive,** *adj.*

in·vert (in vûrt′), *v.t.* 1. to turn upside down. 2. to reverse in position, direction, or relationship. 3. to turn inside out. —**in·vert′i·ble,** *adj.*

in·ver·te·brate (in vûr′tə brit, -brāt′), *adj.* 1. without a backbone or spinal column. —*n.* 2. an invertebrate animal.

in·vest (in vest′), *v.t.* 1. to put (money) to use in something offering profitable returns. 2. to use or devote (time, talent, etc.), as to achieve something. 3. to furnish with power, authority, etc. 4. to install in an office or position. 5. to cover, surround, or envelop. 6. *Archaic.* to clothe or attire. —*v.i.* 7. to invest money. —**in·ves′tor,** *n.*

in·ves·ti·gate (in ves′tə gāt′), *v.t., v.i.,* -**gat·ed, -gat·ing.** to search or inquire (into) systematically. —**in·ves′ti·ga·tive,** *adj.* —**in·ves′ti·ga′tion,** *n.* —**in·ves′ti·ga′tor,** *n.*

in·ves·ti·ture (in ves′ti chər), *n.* the act or ceremony of installing in an office or position.

in·vest·ment (in vest′mənt), *n.* 1. the investing of money for profitable returns. 2. money invested. 3. a property or right in which a person invests. 4. investiture.

in·vet·er·ate (in vet′ər it), *adj.* **1.** confirmed in a habit or practice. **2.** firmly established by long continuance, as a disease. —**in·vet′er·a·cy** -ə sē), *n.* —**in·vet′er·ate·ly,** *adv.*

in·vid·i·ous (in vid′ē əs), *adj.* **1.** causing or tending to cause animosity or resentment. **2.** offensively or unfairly discriminating. —**in·vid′i·ous·ly,** *adv.* —**in·vid′i·ous·ness,** *n.*

in·vig·or·ate (in vig′ə rāt′), *v.t.,* -at·ed, -at·ing. to fill with life and energy. —**in·vig′or·a′tion,** *n.*

in·vin·ci·ble (in vin′sə bəl), *adj.* incapable of being conquered, defeated, or subdued. —**in·vin′ci·bil′i·ty,** *n.* —**in·vin′ci·bly,** *adv.* —**Syn.** insuperable, unconquerable.

in·vi·o·la·ble (in vī′ə lə bəl), *adj.* **1.** incapable of being violated or profaned. **2.** secure from breach or infringement. —**in·vi′o·la·bil′i·ty,** *n.* —**in·vi′o·la·bly,** *adv.*

in·vi·o·late (in vī′ə lit, -lāt′), *adj.* free from violation or desecration. —**in·vi′o·late·ly,** *adv.*

in·vis·i·ble (in viz′ə bəl), *adj.* **1.** imperceptible to the eye. **2.** not in sight. **3.** not perceptible or discernible by the mind. —**in·vis′i·bil′i·ty, in·vis′i·ble·ness,** *n.* —**in·vis′i·bly,** *adv.*

in·vi·ta·tion·al (in′vi tā′shə nəl), *adj.* restricted to those invited by the sponsor.

in·vite (in vīt′), *v.t.,* -vit·ed, -vit·ing. **1.** to ask or request the presence or participation of. **2.** to request politely or formally. **3.** to act so as to bring on or render probable. **4.** to attract or entice. —**in′vi·ta′tion,** *n.*

in·vit·ing (in vī′ting), *adj.* temptingly attractive.

in·vo·ca·tion (in′və kā′shən), *n.* **1.** the act of invoking a deity, spirit, etc., for aid, protection, etc. **2.** a prayer at the beginning of a public ceremony.

in·voice (in′vois), *n., v.,* -voiced, -voic·ing. —*n.* **1.** a detailed list of goods sold or services provided, together with the charges and terms. —*v.t.* **2.** to present an invoice to or for.

in·voke (in vōk′), *v.t.,* -voked, -vok·ing. **1.** to call for with earnest desire. **2.** to call on (a deity, Muse, etc.), as in prayer. **3.** to declare to be binding or in effect: *to invoke a veto.* **4.** to petition for help or aid. **5.** to call forth or upon (a spirit) by incantation. **6.** to cause or bring about.

in·vo·lu·cre (in′və lōō′kər), *n.* a collection of bracts surrounding a flower cluster.

in·vol·un·tar·y (in vol′ən ter′ē), *adj.* **1.** done or occurring without choice. **2.** unintentional or unconscious. **3.** acting without volition: *involuntary*

muscles. —**in·vol′un·tar′i·ly,** *adv.* —**in·vol′un·tar′i·ness,** *n.*

in·vo·lute (in′və lōōt′), *adj.* **1.** curled inward or spirally. **2.** involved or complicated.

in·vo·lu·tion (in′və lōō′shən), *n.* **1.** the act of involving or state of being involved. **2.** something involved or complicated.

in·volve (in volv′), *v.t.,* -volved, -volv·ing. **1.** to include as a necessary circumstance, condition, or consequence. **2.** to have a particular effect on. **3.** to include within itself or its scope. **4.** to bring into an intricate form or condition. **5.** to combine inextricably. **6.** to preoccupy or absorb fully. **7.** to bring into a troublesome matter. —**in·volved′** (-volvd′), *adj.* —**in·volve′ment,** *n.*

in·vul·ner·a·ble (in vul′nər ə bəl), *adj.* **1.** incapable of being wounded or hurt. **2.** proof against or immune to attack. —**in·vul′ner·a·bil′i·ty,** *n.* —**in·vul′ner·a·bly,** *adv.*

in·ward (in′wərd), *adv.* Also, **in′wards. 1.** toward the inside, as of a place. **2.** toward the mind or soul. —*adj.* **3.** directed toward the inside. **4.** situated within. **5.** mental or spiritual.

in·ward·ly (in′wärd lē), *adv.* **1.** in, on, or with reference to the inside. **2.** mentally or spiritually. **3.** toward the inside or interior. **4.** privately or secretly.

in·wrought (in rôt′), *adj.* worked with something by way of decoration.

i·o·dide (ī′ə dīd′, -did), *n.* a salt or compound consisting of two elements, one of which is iodine.

i·o·dine (ī′ə dīn′, -din, -dēn′), *n. Chem.* a nonmetallic chemical element consisting of grayish-black crystals, used in medicine and dyes. *Symbol:* I; *at. wt.:* 126.904; *at. no.:* 53. Also, **i·o·din** (ī′ə din).

i·o·dize (ī′ə dīz′), *v.t.,* -dized, -diz·ing. to treat with iodine or an iodide.

i·on (ī′ən, ī′on), *n.* an electrically charged atom or group of atoms. —**i·on′ic** (ī on′ik), *adj.*

I·on·ic (ī on′ik), *adj.* noting a style of ancient Greek architecture characterized by slender, scroll-shaped capitals.

i·on·ize (ī′ə nīz′), *v.,* -ized, -iz·ing. —*v.t.* **1.** to separate or change into ions. **2.** to produce ions in. —*v.i.* **3.** to become ionized. —**i′on·iz′a·ble,** *adj.* —**i′on·i·za′tion,** *n.* —**i′on·iz′er,** *n.*

i·on·o·sphere (ī on′ə sfēr′), *n.* the region of the earth's atmosphere consisting of several ionized layers and extending from about 50 to 250 miles above the surface of the earth. —**i·on′o·spher′ic** (-sfer′ik), *adj.*

I.O.O.F., Independent Order of Odd Fellows.

i·o·ta (ī ō′tə), *n.* **1.** a very small quantity. **2.** the ninth letter of the Greek alphabet (I, ι).

IOU, a written acknowledgment of a debt. Also, **I.O.U.** [from *I owe you*]

I·o·wa (ī′ə wə, ī′ə wä′), *n.* a state in the central United States. *Cap.:* Des Moines. **—I′o·wan,** *adj., n.*

IP, *Baseball.* innings pitched.

IPA, International Phonetic Alphabet.

ip·e·cac (ip′ə kak′), *n.* **1.** a small, creeping plant of tropical South America. **2.** the dried roots of this plant, a drug used as an emetic, purgative, etc.

ips, inches per second. Also, **i.p.s.**

ip·so fac·to (ip′sō fak′tō), by the fact itself.

IQ, See **intelligence quotient.** Also, **I.Q.**

i.q., the same as. [< L *idem quod*]

Ir, Irish.

Ir, iridium.

Ir., **1.** Ireland. **2.** Irish.

I.R., **1.** information retrieval **2.** internal revenue.

IRA, individual retirement account.

I.R.A., Irish Republican Army.

I·ran (i ran′, ī ran′), *n.* a country in SW Asia. **—I·ra·ni·an** (i rā′nē ən, ī rā′-), *adj., n.*

I·raq (i rak′), *n.* a country in SW Asia, W of Iran. Also, **I·rak. —I·ra·qi** (i rak′ē), *n., adj.*

i·ras·ci·ble (i ras′ə bəl, ī ras′-), *adj.* **1.** easily provoked to anger. **2.** produced by anger. **—i·ras′ci·bil′i·ty,** *n.*

i·rate (ī′rāt, ī rāt′), *adj.* **1.** showing bitter anger. **2.** arising from anger. **—i·rate′ly,** *adv.* **—i·rate′ness,** *n.*

IRBM, intermediate range ballistic missile.

ire (ī′r), *n.* bitter anger. **—ire′ful,** *adj.* **—ire′ful·ly,** *adv.*

Ire., Ireland.

Ire·land (ī′ər lənd), *n.* **1.** a large western island of the British Isles, comprising Northern Ireland and the Republic of Ireland. **2.** a republic occupying most of the island of Ireland.

i·ren·ic (ī ren′ik, ī rē′nik), *adj. Chiefly Theol.* tending to promote peace.

ir·i·des·cent (ir′i des′ənt), *adj.* displaying a play of lustrous colors like those of the rainbow. **—ir′i·des′cence,** *n.*

i·rid·i·um (i rid′ē əm, ī rid′-), *n. Chem.* a precious metallic element resembling platinum, used in alloys. *Symbol:* Ir; *at. wt.:* 192.2; *at. no.:* 77.

i·ris (ī′ris), *n., pl.* **i·ris·es, ir·i·des** (ir′i dēz′, ī′ri-), **1.** the circular diaphragm forming the colored portion of the eye. **2.** a plant having showy flowers and sword-shaped leaves.

I·rish (ī′rish), *adj.* **1.** of Ireland, its inhabitants, or their language. **—n.**

2. the inhabitants of Ireland. **3.** the Celtic language of Ireland. **—I′rish·man,** *n.* **—I′rish·wom′an,** *n.fem.*

I′rish bull′, a paradoxical statement that appears to make sense.

I′rish cof′fee, hot coffee and whiskey, sweetened and topped with whipped cream.

I′rish set′ter, one of an Irish breed of setters having a golden-chestnut or mahogany-red coat.

irk (ûrk), *v.t.* to annoy, esp. in a provoking or tedious way.

irk·some (ûrk′səm), *adj.* tending to irk. **—irk′some·ly,** *adv.*

IRO, International Refugee Organization.

i·ron (ī′ərn), *n.* **1.** *Chem.* a ductile, malleable, silver-white metallic element, used in making tools, machinery, etc. *Symbol:* Fe; *at. wt.:* 55.847; *at. no.:* 26. **2.** something hard, strong, rigid, or unyielding: *hearts of iron.* **3.** something made of iron. **4.** an electric appliance with a flat metal underside for pressing or smoothing clothes, linens, etc. **5.** one of a series of metal-headed golf clubs. **6.** **irons,** shackles or fetters. **—adj.** **7.** of, like, or made of iron. **—v.t.,** *v.i.* **8.** to smooth or press (clothes) with an electric iron. **9.** **iron out,** *Informal.* to smooth out or clear up (difficulties, etc.). **—i′ron·er,** *n.*

I′ron Age′, a period of human history following the Stone Age and the Bronze Age, marked by the use of implements and weapons made of iron.

i·ron·bound (ī′ərn bound′), *adj.* **1.** rocky or rugged. **2.** rigid or unyielding.

i·ron·clad (ī′ərn klad′), *adj.* **1.** covered or cased with iron plates, as a vessel. **2.** very rigid or exacting: *an ironclad contract.*

i′ron cur′tain, a barrier of self-imposed isolation around Soviet Russia and its eastern European satellites.

i·ron·ic (ī ron′ik), *adj.* **1.** exhibiting or characterized by irony. **2.** using or prone to irony. Also, **i·ron′i·cal. —i·ron′i·cal·ly,** *adv.*

i·ron·ing (ī′ər ning), *n.* articles of clothing that have been or are to be ironed.

i′ron lung′, a chamber, used esp. in the treatment of polio, which encloses the chest area and in which alternate pulsations of high and low pressure are used to effect normal lung movements.

i′ron ox′ide. See **ferric oxide.**

i′ron py′rites, pyrite.

i·ron·stone (ī′ərn stōn′), *n.* **1.** any iron-bearing mineral or rock. **2.** a hard white stoneware.

i·ron·ware (ī'ərn wâr'), *n.* articles of iron, as pots, kettles, etc.

i·ron·wood (ī'ərn wŏŏd'), *n.* a tree yielding a hard, heavy wood.

i·ron·work (ī'ərn wûrk'), *n.* objects or parts of objects made of iron. —**i'ron·work'er,** *n.*

i·ron·works (ī'ərn wûrks'), *n.* an establishment where iron is smelted or where it is cast or wrought.

i·ro·ny (ī'rə nē, ī'ər-), *n., pl.* **-nies. 1.** a figure of speech in which the words express a meaning that is the direct opposite of the intended meaning. **2.** an outcome of events contrary to what was, or might have been, expected. **3.** the incongruity of this.

Ir·o·quois (ir'ə kwoi', -kwoiz'), *n., pl.* **Ir·o·quois. 1.** a member of the Indian confederacy of New York comprising the Mohawks, Oneidas, Onondagas, Cayugas, and Senecas, and, later, the Tuscaroras. —**Ir'o·quoi'an,** *adj., n.*

ir·ra·di·ate (i rā'dē āt'), *v.,* **-at·ed, -at·ing.** —*v.t.* **1.** to shed rays of light upon. **2.** to illumine intellectually. **3.** to brighten as with light. **4.** to treat by exposure to radiation or other radiant energy. —*v.i.* **5.** *Archaic.* to emit rays. —**ir·ra'di·a'tion,** *n.*

ir·ra·tion·al (i rash'ə nºl), *adj.* **1.** without the faculty of reason. **2.** lacking sound judgment. **3.** utterly illogical. **4.** *Math.* not capable of being expressed exactly as a ratio of two integers. —*n.* **5.** *Math.* an irrational number. —**ir·ra'tion·al'i·ty** (-nal'i tē), **ir·ra'tion·al·ness,** *n.* —**ir·ra'tion·al·ly,** *adv.* —**Syn. 1.** senseless, unreasonable.

ir·re·claim·a·ble (ir'i klā'mə bəl), *adj.* incapable of being reclaimed or reformed. —**ir're·claim'a·bly,** *adv.*

ir·rec·on·cil·a·ble (i rek'ən sī'lə bəl, i rek'ən sī'-), *adj.* **1.** incapable of being brought into harmony or adjustment. **2.** incapable of being made to acquiesce or compromise. —**ir·rec'on·cil'a·bil'i·ty,** *n.* —**ir·rec'on·cil'a·bly,** *adv.*

ir·re·cov·er·a·ble (ir'i kuv'ər ə bəl), *adj.* **1.** incapable of being recovered or regained. **2.** unable to be remedied or rectified. —**ir're·cov'er·a·bly,** *adv.*

ir·re·deem·a·ble (ir i dē'mə bəl), *adj.* **1.** incapable of being bought back or paid off. **2.** beyond redemption or reform. **3.** not convertible into gold or silver.

ir·re·den·tist (ir'i den'tist), *n.* a nationalist who advocates the regaining of a culturally or historically related region now under foreign rule. —**ir're·den'tism,** *n.*

ir·re·duc·i·ble (ir'i dŏŏ'sə bəl, -dyŏŏ'-), *adj.* incapable of being reduced, di-

minished, or simplified. —**ir're·duc'i·bly,** *adv.*

ir·ref·ra·ga·ble (i ref'rə gə bəl), *adj.* not to be disputed or contested.

ir·ref·u·ta·ble (i ref'yə tə bəl, ir'i·fyŏŏ'tə bəl), *adj.* that cannot be refuted or disproved.

irreg., 1. irregular. **2.** irregularly.

ir·re·gard·less (ir'i gärd'lis), *adj. Nonstandard.* regardless.

—**Usage.** IRREGARDLESS is considered nonstandard because it is redundant: once the negative idea is expressed by the *-less* ending, it is excessive to add the negative *ir-* prefix to express the same.

ir·reg·u·lar (i reg'yə lər), *adj.* **1.** without symmetry, even shape, formal arrangement, etc. **2.** not according to rule or to the accepted principle, method, etc. **3.** *Gram.* not conforming to the prevalent pattern of inflection. —*n.* **4.** a soldier not of a regular force, as a guerrilla or partisan. —**ir·reg'u·lar'i·ty,** *n.* —**ir·reg'u·lar·ly,** *adv.*

ir·rel·e·vant (i rel'ə vənt), *adj.* not relevant. —**ir·rel'e·vance,** *n.* —**ir·rel'e·vant·ly,** *adv.*

ir·re·li·gious (ir'i lij'əs), *adj.* **1.** feeling no religious emotions. **2.** showing a lack of religion. **3.** showing hostility to religion. —**ir're·li'gious·ness,** *n.*

ir·re·me·di·a·ble (ir'i me'dē ə bəl), *adj.* not admitting of remedy, cure, or repair. —**ir're·me'di·a·bly,** *adv.*

ir·re·mov·a·ble (ir'i mŏŏ'və bəl), *adj.* incapable of being removed or displaced. —**ir're·mov'a·bly,** *adv.*

ir·rep·a·ra·ble (i rep'ər ə bəl), *adj.* incapable of being repaired, rectified, or made good. —**ir·rep'a·ra·bly,** *adv.*

ir·re·place·a·ble (ir'i plā'sə bəl), *adj.* not admitting of replacement or substitute. —**ir're·place'a·bly,** *adv.*

ir·re·press·i·ble (ir'i pres'ə bəl), *adj.* incapable of being repressed or restrained.

ir·re·proach·a·ble (ir'i prō'chə bəl), *adj.* free from reproach or blame. —**ir're·proach'a·bly,** *adv.*

ir·re·sist·i·ble (ir'i zis'tə bəl), *adj.* **1.** incapable of being resisted or withstood. **2.** extremely tempting or enticing. —**ir're·sist'i·bly,** *adv.*

ir·res·o·lute (i rez'ə lŏŏt'), *adj.* not firmly resolved or determined. —**ir·res'o·lute'ly,** *adv.* —**ir·res'o·lu'tion,** *n.* —**Syn.** indecisive, wavering, vacillating.

ir·re·spec·tive of (ir'i spek'tiv), without regard to.

ir·re·spon·si·ble (ir'i spon'sə bəl), *adj.* **1.** characterized by a lack of a sense of responsibility. **2.** not capable of responsibility. —**ir're·spon'si·bil'i·ty,** **ir're·spon'si·ble·ness,** *n.* —**ir're·spon'si·bly,** *adv.*

ir·re·triev·a·ble (ir'i trē'və bəl), *adj.* that cannot be retrieved or recovered. —**ir're·triev'a·bly,** *adv.*

ir·rev·er·ent (i rev'ər ənt), *adj.* **1.** lacking reverence or respect. **2.** showing disrespect. —**ir·rev'er·ence,** *n.* —**ir·rev'er·ent·ly,** *adv.*

ir·re·vers·i·ble (ir'i vûr'sə bəl), *adj.* incapable of being reversed or changed. —**ir're·vers'i·bly,** *adv.*

ir·rev·o·ca·ble (i rev'ə kə bəl), *adj.* not to be revoked or recalled. —**ir·rev'o·ca·bly,** *adv.*

ir·ri·gate (ir'ə gāt'), *v.t.,* **-gat·ed, -gat·ing. 1.** to supply (land) with water by artificial means, as by diverting streams. **2.** *Med.* to wash (an orifice, wound, etc.) with liquid. —**ir'ri·ga·ble,** *adj.* —**ir'ri·ga'tion,** *n.* —**ir'ri·ga'tor,** *n.*

ir·ri·ta·ble (ir'i tə bəl), *adj.* **1.** easily irritated or exasperated. **2.** *Med.* abnormally sensitive —**ir'ri·ta·bil'i·ty,** *n.* —**ir'ri·ta·bly,** *adv.* —**Syn. 1.** choleric, irascible, touchy.

ir·ri·tate (ir'i tāt'), *v.t.,* **-tat·ed, -tat·ing. 1.** to excite to impatience or anger. **2.** *Med.* to make red or swollen. —**ir'ri·tant** (-t°nt), *adj., n.* —**ir'ri·tat'ing·ly,** *adv.* —**ir'ri·ta'tion,** *n.* —**Syn. 1.** annoy, bother, irk, vex.

ir·rupt (i rupt'), *v.i.* **1.** to break or burst in. **2.** (of animals) to increase suddenly in numbers. —**ir·rup'tion,** *n.* —**ir·rup'tive,** *adj.*

IRS, Internal Revenue Service.

is (iz), *v.* 3rd pers. sing. pres. indic. of **be.**

Is., 1. Isaiah. **2.** Island. **3.** Isle.

is., 1. island. **2.** isle.

Isa., Isaiah.

I·saac (ī'zək), *n.* a Hebrew patriarch, son of Abraham and father of Jacob.

I·sa·iah (ī zā'ə, ī zī'ə), *n.* **1.** a Hebrew prophet of the 8th century B.C. **2.** a book of the Bible bearing his name.

ISBN, International Standard Book Number.

-ise, *Brit.* var. of **-ize:** *organise.*

-ish, a suffix meaning: **a.** belonging to: *Danish.* **b.** like or having the characteristics of: *girlish.* **c.** inclined to: *bookish.* **d.** rather: *reddish.* **e.** approximately as rather: *fiftyish.*

i·sin·glass (ī'zin glas', -gläs', ī'zing-), *n.* **1.** a gelatin obtained from the bladders of certain fish. **2.** thin, translucent sheets of mica.

I·sis (ī'sis), *n.* an Egyptian goddess of fertility.

isl., 1. island. **2.** isle. Also, **Isl.**

Is·lam (is'ləm, iz'-, is läm'), *n.* **1.** the religious faith of Muslims as set forth in the Koran. **2.** the whole body of Muslim believers and countries. [< Ar. submission (to God)] —**Is·lam·ic** (is lam'ik, -lä'mik, iz-), *adj.*

is·land (ī'lənd), *n.* **1.** a land area completely surrounded by water, and not large enough to be called a continent. **2.** something resembling an island, esp. in being isolated.

is·land·er (ī'lən dər), *n.* a native or inhabitant of an island.

isle (īl), *n.* **1.** a small island. **2.** any island.

is·let (ī'lit), *n.* a very small island.

ism (iz'əm), *n.* a distinctive doctrine, theory, system, or dogma.

-ism, a suffix meaning: **a.** action or process: *baptism.* **b.** state or condition: *barbarism.* **c.** doctrine or principle: *Darwinism.* **d.** usage or characteristic: *witticism.* **e.** devotion or adherence: *intellectualism.*

isn't (iz'ənt), contraction of **is not.**

iso-, a combining form meaning: **a.** equal: *isobar.* **b.** isomeric: *isoprene.*

i·so·bar (ī'sə bär'), *n.* a line on a map that connects points at which the barometric pressure is the same. —**i'so·bar'ic** (-bar'ik), *adj.*

i·so·late (ī'sə lāt', is'ə-), *v.,* **-lat·ed, -lat·ing.** to detach or separate so as to be alone. —**i'so·la'tion,** *n.* —**i'so·la'tor,** *n.*

i·so·la·tion·ism (ī'sə lā'shə niz'əm, is'ə-), *n.* a policy of withdrawing one's country from alliances and commitments with other nations. —**i'so·la'tion·ist,** *n., adj.*

i·so·mer (ī'sə mər), *n.* any of two or more chemical compounds that are composed of the same kinds and numbers of atoms but differ from each other in structural arrangement. —**i'so·mer'ic** (-mer'ik), *adj.* —**i·som·er·ism** (ī som'ə riz'əm), *n.*

i·so·met·ric (ī'sə me'trik), *adj.* Also, **i'so·met'ri·cal. 1.** having equality of measure. **2.** of or pertaining to isometrics. —**n. 3. isometrics,** isometric exercises collectively. —**i'so·met'ri·cal·ly,** *adv.*

i'so·met'ric ex'ercise, any of various exercises that pit one muscle against another or against an immovable object in a strong but motionless flexing or contracting.

i·so·prene (ī'sə prēn'), *n.* a volatile liquid used chiefly in the manufacture of synthetic rubber.

i·sos·ce·les (ī sos'ə lēz'), *adj.* having two sides equal: *an isosceles triangle.*

i·sos·ta·sy (ī sos'tə sē), *n.* the equilibrium of the earth's crust in which the forces tending to elevate balance those tending to depress. —**i·so·stat·ic** (ī'sə stat'ik), *adj.* —**i'so·stat'i·cal·ly,** *adv.*

i·so·therm (ī'sə thûrm'), *n.* a line on a weather map connecting points having equal temperature.

i·so·ther·mal (ī'sə thûr'məl), *adj.* occurring at constant temperature.

i·so·ton·ic (ī′sə ton′ik), *adj.* noting solutions characterized by equal osmotic pressure.

i·so·tope (ī′sə tōp′), *n.* any of two or more forms of a chemical element having the same number of protons in the nucleus but having different numbers of neutrons. —i′so·top′ic (-top′ik), *adj.* —i′so·top′i·cal·ly, *adv.*

Isr., 1. Israel. 2. Israeli.

Is·ra·el (iz′rē əl, -rā-), *n.* 1. a country in SW Asia, on the Mediterranean. 2. the Hebrew or Jewish people. 3. a name given to Jacob after he had wrestled with the angel. 4. (formerly) the northern kingdom of the Hebrews. 5. a group considered as God's chosen people.

Is·rae·li (iz rā′lē), *n., pl.* -lis, -li, *adj.* —n. 1. a native or inhabitant of modern Israel. —adj. 2. of modern Israel or its inhabitants.

Is·ra·el·ite (iz′rē ə līt′, -rā-), *n.* a member of the Hebrew people who inhabited ancient Israel.

is·su·ance (ish′ōō ons), *n.* the act of issuing.

is·sue (ish′ōō), *n., v.,* -sued, -su·ing. —n. 1. the act of sending out or putting forth. 2. something that is printed or published and distributed, esp. a given number of a periodical. 3. a quantity sent out or put forth at one time: *a new issue of commemorative stamps.* 4. a point in question or a matter in dispute. 5. a matter the decision of which is of special or public importance. 6. something proceeding from any source, as an effect or consequence. 7. offspring or progeny: *to die without issue.* 8. an outlet or exit. 9. a discharge of blood. 10. **issues,** *English Law.* the profits from land. 11. **at issue,** being disputed. 12. **take issue,** to disagree or dispute. —v.t. 13. to mint, print, or publish for sale or distribution. 14. to distribute (food, etc.) officially. 15. to send out or discharge. —v.i. 16. to go, pass, or flow out. 17. to be published, as a book. 18. to arise as a result. —is′su·er, *n.*

-ist, a suffix meaning: a. a person who makes or produces: *novelist.* b. a person who operates or practices: *machinist.* c. a person skilled in: *cellist.* d. an advocate or supporter: *socialist.*

Is·tan·bul (is′tan bōōl′, -tän-), *n.* a seaport in NW Turkey.

isth·mi·an (is′mē ən), *adj.* of or pertaining to an isthmus.

isth·mus (is′məs), *n., pl.* -mus·es, -mi (-mī). 1. a narrow strip of land, bordered on both sides by water, connecting two larger bodies of land. 2. *Anat.* a connecting part or organ, esp. one that joins structures or cavi-

ties larger than itself. [< L < Gk *isthmós* neck (of land)]

it (it), *pron.* 1. (to represent an inanimate thing previously mentioned.) 2. (to represent a person or animal whose gender is unknown): *Who was it? It was John.* 3. (used as the impersonal subject of the verb *to be*): *It is foggy.* 4. (used as an anticipatory subject or object): *It is necessary that every man do his duty.* —n. 5. (in children's games) the player, as in tag, who must catch the others.

Ital., 1. Italian. 2. Italy. Also, **It.**

ital., 1 italic; italics. 2. italicized.

I·tal·ian (i tal′yən), *adj.* 1. of Italy, its people, or their language. —n. 2. a native or inhabitant of Italy. 3. a Romance language, the language of Italy.

i·tal·ic (i tal′ik, ī tal′-), *adj.* 1. designating a printing type in which the letters slope to the right, used esp. for emphasis. —n. 2. Often, **italics.** italic type.

i·tal·i·cize (i tal′i sīz′, ī tal′-), *v.t.,* -cized, -ciz·ing. to print in italic type.

It·a·ly (it′əl ē), *n.* a country in S Europe.

itch (ich), *v.i.* 1. to feel a tingling irritation of the skin which causes a desire to scratch the part affected. 2. to have a desire to do or to get something. —n. 3. the sensation of itching. 7. a restless longing. 4. a contagious disease caused by a mite that burrows into the skin. —itch′y, *adj.* —itch′i·ness, *n.*

-ite, a suffix meaning: a. an inhabitant: *Tokyoite.* b. a follower: *Darwinite.* c. a mineral or fossil: *anthracite.* d. a commercial product: *vulcanite.*

i·tem (ī′təm), *n.* 1. a separate article or particular. 2. a separate piece of information or news, as a short paragraph in a newspaper. [< L: likewise]

i·tem·ize (ī′tə mīz′), *v.t.,* -ized, -iz·ing. to state by items. —i′tem·i·za′tion, *n.*

it·er·ate (it′ə rāt′), *v.t.,* -at·ed, -at·ing. to say or do again. —it′er·a′tion, *n.*

i·tin·er·ant (ī tin′ər ənt, i tin′-), *adj.* 1. traveling from place to place, esp. for duty or business. —n. 2. a person in itinerant status.

i·tin·er·ar·y (ī tin′ə rer′ē, i tin′-), *n., pl.* -ar·ies. 1. a line or route of travel. 2. a detailed plan for a journey. 3. a record of travel.

-itis, a suffix meaning "inflammation of an organ": *gastritis.*

it′ll (it′°l), contraction of: a. *it will.* b. *it shall.*

its (its), *pron.* the possessive form of **it** (used as an attributive adjective).

it's (its), contraction of: a. *it is.* b. *it has.*

it·self (it self′), *pron.* **1.** a reflexive form of *it*: *The battery recharges itself.* **2.** an emphatic appositive of *it* or a noun: *The bowl itself is beautiful.* **3.** its normal self.

it·ty-bit·ty (it′ē bit′ē), *adj. Baby Talk.* tiny or very small. Also, **it·sy-bit·sy** (it′sē bit′sē).

ITV, instructional television.

-ity, a suffix meaning "state or condition": *civility.*

IUD, See **intrauterine device.**

i.v., intravenous.

I've (īv), contraction of *I have.*

-ive, a suffix meaning: **a.** tending to: *destructive.* **b.** of the nature of: *sportive.*

i·vo·ry (ī′və rē, ī′vrē), *n., pl.* **-ries,** *adj.* —*n.* **1.** the hard white substance composing the main part of the tusks of the elephant, walrus, etc. **2.** any substance resembling ivory. **3.** **ivories,** *Slang.* **a.** the keys of a piano. **b.** dice. **4.** a creamy or yellowish white. —*adj.* **5.** made of ivory. **6.** of the color ivory.

I'vory Coast′, a country in W Africa.

i'vory tow'er, **1.** a place remote from worldly affairs. **2.** an attitude of aloofness from practical affairs.

i·vy (ī′vē), *n., pl.* **i·vies. 1.** a climbing vine having smooth, shiny, evergreen leaves and black berries. **2.** any of various other climbing plants. —**i·vied** (ī′vēd), *adj.*

IWW, Industrial Workers of the World.

-ize, a suffix meaning: **a.** to form or engage in: *theorize.* **b.** to become or form into: *crystallize.* **c.** to treat or affect: *patronize.* **d.** to make or render: *legalize.*

J

J, j (jā), *n., pl.* **J's** or **Js, j's** or **js.** the 10th letter of the English alphabet, a consonant.

J, joule. Also, **j**

J, the 10th in order or in a series.

J., 1. *Cards.* Jack. **2.** Journal. **3.** Judge. **4.** Justice.

Ja., January.

J.A., Judge Advocate.

jab (jab), *v.,* **jabbed, jab·bing,** *n.* —*v.t., v.i.* **1.** to poke sharply, as with the point of something. **2.** to punch, esp. with a short, quick blow. —*n.* **3.** a sharp thrust. **4.** a short, quick blow. —**jab′bing·ly,** *adv.*

jab·ber (jab′ər), *v.i., v.t.* **1.** to speak rapidly, indistinctly, or nonsensically. —*n.* **2.** rapid, indistinct, or nonsensical talk. —**jab′ber·er,** *n.*

ja·bot (zha bō′, zhab′ō), *n.* a ruffle worn at the neck by women.

jac·a·ran·da (jak′ə ran′də), *n.* a tropical American tree having clusters of bluish-violet flowers.

jack (jak), *n.* **1.** any of various portable devices for lifting heavy objects short heights. **2.** a playing card bearing the picture of a servant or soldier. **3.** one of a set of small metal objects having six points, used in a game (**jacks**). **4.** a small national flag flown at the bow of a vessel. **5.** a connecting device in an electrical circuit designed for the insertion of a plug. **6.** *Slang.* money. —*v.t.* **7.** to lift by means of a jack. **8.** *Informal.* to increase or raise: *to jack up prices.*

jack·al (jak′əl, -ôl), *n.* a foxlike carnivore of Asia and Africa. [< Turk *çhakāl* < Pers *shag(h)āl*]

jack·a·napes (jak′ə nāps′), *n.* **1.** an impertinent, presumptuous young man. **2.** *Archaic.* an ape or monkey.

jack·ass (jak′as′), *n.* **1.** a male donkey. **2.** a foolish or stupid person.

jack·boot (jak′bōōt′), *n.* a large leather boot reaching up over the knee.

jack·daw (jak′dô′), *n.* a glossy, black, European bird of the crow family.

jack·et (jak′it), *n.* **1.** a short coat, in any of various forms, usually opening down the front. **2.** a protective outer covering: *a book jacket.* —**jack′et·ed,** *adj.* —**jack′et·less,** *adj.*

Jack′ Frost′, frost or freezing cold personified.

jack·ham·mer (jak′ham′ər), *n.* a portable hammerlike machine for drilling rock, brick, etc., operated by compressed air.

jack-in-the-box (jak′in th̸ə boks′), *n., pl.* **-box·es.** a toy consisting of a box from which, upon release of its lid, a figure springs up. Also, **jack-in-a-box′.**

jack-in-the-pul·pit (jak′in th̸ə pŏŏl′pit, -pul′-), *n., pl.* **-pul·pits.** a North American herb having an upright spadix arched over by a spathe.

jack·knife (jak′nīf′), n., v., **-knifed, -knif·ing.** —n. **1.** a large pocketknife. **2.** a dive during which the diver bends to touch the toes and straightens out immediately before entering the water. —v.i. **3.** to double over like a jackknife. **4.** (esp. of a trailer) to form an inverted V with the cab. —v.t. **5.** to cause to jackknife.

jack·leg (jak′leg′), adj. Slang. **1.** unskilled or untrained. **2.** makeshift or expedient.

jack-of-all-trades (jak′əv ôl′trādz′), n., pl. **jacks-of-all-trades.** a man who is adept at different kinds of work.

jack-o′-lan·tern (jak′ə lan′tərn), n. a lantern made of a hollowed pumpkin with openings cut to represent a human face.

jack·pot (jak′pot′), n. the cumulative stakes or the chief prize in any game.

jack′ rab′bit, a large hare of western North America having very long hind legs and long ears.

jack·screw (jak′skroo′), n. a jack consisting of a screw steadied by a threaded support.

Jack·son (jak′sən), n. **1.** Andrew, 1767–1845, 7th president of the U.S. 1829–37. **2.** the capital of Mississippi.

Jack·son·ville (jak′sən vil′), n. a seaport in NE Florida.

jack·straw (jak′strô′), n. **1.** one of a group of strips of wood, as sticks, used in the game of jackstraws. **2.** **jackstraws,** a game in which players compete in picking up, one by one, as many jackstraws as possible without disturbing the heap.

jack′ tar′, Informal. a sailor or seaman. Also, **Jack′ Tar′.**

Ja·cob (jā′kəb), n. Bible. a son of Isaac.

Ja·cob′s-lad·der (jā′kəbz lad′ər), n. a garden plant whose leaves have a ladderlike arrangement.

jac·quard (jak′ärd, jə kärd′), n. (often cap.) a fabric of elaborate designs.

jade¹ (jād), n. either of two minerals, jadeite or nephrite, sometimes green, widely used for carvings, jewelry, etc.

jade² (jād), n., v., **jad·ed, jad·ing.** —n. **1.** a broken-down, worthless horse. **2.** a vicious or disreputable woman. —v.t., v.i. **3.** to make or become dull or weary, as from overwork. —**jad′ish,** adj.

jad·ed (jā′did), adj. **1.** worn-out or wearied, as by overwork. **2.** dulled or satiated by overindulgence. —**jad′ed·ly,** adv. —**jad′ed·ness,** n.

jade·ite (jā′dīt), n. a mineral occurring in tough masses, whitish to dark green: a form of jade.

jag¹ (jag), n. a sharp projection on an edge or surface.

jag² (jag), n. Informal. a spree or binge: an eating jag.

jag·ged (jag′id), adj. having ragged notches or points. —**jag′ged·ly,** adv. —**jag′ged·ness,** n.

jag·uar (jag′wär), n. a large, ferocious, leopardlike cat of tropical America.

jai a·lai (hī′ lī′, hī′ ə lī′, hī′ ə lī′), a game resembling handball, played on a three-walled court with wicker, basketlike rackets.

jail (jāl), n. **1.** a prison, esp. one for the detention of persons awaiting trial or convicted of minor offenses. —v.t. **2.** to confine in a jail.

jail·bird (jāl′bûrd′), n. a person who is or has been confined in jail.

jail·break (jāl′brāk′), n. an escape from jail by forcible means.

jail·er (jā′lər), n. a person in charge of a jail. Also, **jail′or.**

Ja·kar·ta (jə kär′tə), n. Djakarta.

jal·ap (jal′əp), n. the dried root of a turnip-shaped plant of the morning-glory family, or the yellowish powder derived from it, used chiefly as a purgative.

ja·lop·y (jə lop′ē), n., pl. **-lop·ies.** Informal. an old, decrepit automobile.

jal·ou·sie (jal′ə sē′), n. a blind or shutter made with horizontal slats fixable at an angle.

jam¹ (jam), v., **jammed, jam·ming,** n. —v.t. **1.** to squeeze tightly between bodies or surfaces. **2.** to crush by squeezing. **3.** to press or push violently, as into a confined space. **4.** to block up by crowding. **5.** to make (something) unworkable by causing parts to become stuck or blocked. **6.** to interfere with (radio signals) by sending out others of approximately the same frequency. —v.i. **7.** to become stuck or blocked. **8.** to press or push violently, as into a confined space. **9.** to become unworkable, as through the jamming of a part. **10.** to participate in a jam session. —n. **11.** the act of jamming or state of being jammed. **12.** a mass of objects or vehicles jammed together. **13.** Informal. a difficult or embarrassing situation.

jam² (jam), n. a preserve of whole fruit, slightly crushed, boiled with sugar.

Jam., Jamaica.

Ja·mai·ca (jə mā′kə), n. a country on an island in the West Indies, S of Cuba. —**Ja·mai′can,** adj., n.

jamb (jam), n. either of the upright sides of an opening, as of a doorway.

jam·bo·ree (jam′bə rē′), n. **1.** Informal. any noisy merrymaking. **2.** a large gathering of members of the Boy Scouts.

James·town (jāmz′toun′), *n.* a village in E Virginia: first permanent English settlement in America 1607.

jam-packed (jam′pakt′), *adj.* filled to the greatest possible extent.

jam′ ses′sion, an informal meeting of jazz musicians to perform improvisations.

Jan., January.

jan·gle (jaṅg′gəl), *v.,* **-gled, -gling,** *n.* —*v.i.* 1. to make a harsh, discordant, usually metallic sound. —*v.t.* 2. to cause to jangle. 3. to cause to become irritated or upset. —*n.* 4. a discordant, metallic sound. —**jan′gler,** *n.* —**jan′gly,** *adj.*

jan·i·tor (jan′i tər), *n.* a person who cleans and maintains a building, as an apartment house. [< L: doorkeeper] —**jan′i·to′ri·al** (-tôr′ē əl, -tōr′-), *adj.* —**jan′i·tress,** *n.fem.*

Jan·u·ar·y (jan′yōō er′ē), *n., pl.* **-ar·ies.** the first month of the year, containing 31 days.

Jap., 1. Japan. 2. Japanese.

ja·pan (jə pan′), *n., v.,* **-panned, -panning.** —*n.* 1. a hard, durable, black varnish, used for coating wood, etc. 2. work varnished and figured in the Japanese manner. —*v.t.* 3. to varnish with japan. —**ja·pan′ner,** *n.*

Ja·pan (jə pan′), *n.* a country off the E coast of Asia.

Jap·a·nese (jap′ə nēz′, -nēs′), *adj., n., pl.* **-nese.** —*adj.* 1. of Japan, its people, or their language. —*n.* 2. a native of Japan. 3. the language of Japan.

Jap′anese bee′tle, an oval-shaped beetle, introduced into the eastern U.S. from Japan, the adult of which feeds on the foliage of trees, and the larva of which feeds on plant roots.

jape (jāp), *n., v.i.,* **japed, jap·ing.** *Archaic.* jest. —**jap′er·y,** *n.*

jar¹ (jär), *n.* a broad-mouthed container, usually cylindrical and of glass or earthenware.

jar² (jär), *v.,* **jarred, jar·ring,** *n.* —*v.i.* 1. to produce a harsh, grating sound. 2. to have a harshly unpleasant effect, as on the nerves. 3. to vibrate from concussion. 4. to conflict or clash. —*v.t.* 5. to cause to rattle or shake. —*n.* 6. a harsh, grating sound. 7. a vibrating movement, as from concussion. 8. a sudden, unpleasant effect. 9. a minor disagreement.

jar·di·niere (jär′d⁾nēr′), *n.* an ornamental receptacle for holding plants, flowers, etc.

jar·gon (jär′gən, -gon), *n.* 1. the vocabulary peculiar to a particular trade, profession, or group. 2. unintelligible or meaningless language.

jas·mine (jaz′min, jas′-), *n.* any of several shrubs or vines having fragrant flowers.

jas·per (jas′pər), *n.* a compact, opaque, often highly colored quartz.

ja·to (jā′tō), *n., pl.* **-tos.** an aircraft takeoff using auxiliary rocket motors [*j(et)-a(ssisted) t(ake)o(ff)*]

jaun·dice (jôn′dis, jän′-), *n.* an abnormal body condition due to an increase of bile pigments in the blood, characterized by yellowness of the skin, of the whites of the eyes, etc.

jaun·diced (jôn′dist, jon′-), *adj.* 1. affected with jaundice. 2. exhibiting envy, resentment, etc.

jaunt (jônt, jänt), *v.i.* 1. to make a short journey, esp. for pleasure. —*n.* 2. such a journey.

jaun·ty (jôn′tē, jän′-), *adj.,* **-ti·er, -ti·est.** 1. easy and sprightly in manner or bearing. 2. smartly trim or effective, as clothing. —**jaun′ti·ly,** *adv.* —**jaun′ti·ness,** *n.*

Jav., Javanese.

Ja·va (jä′və), *n.* the main island of Indonesia. —**Jav′a·nese** (-nēz′), *adj., n.*

jave·lin (jav′lin, jav′ə lin), *n.* a light spear, usually thrown by hand, esp. one used in an athletic event.

jaw (jô), *n.* 1. either of two bones forming the framework of the mouth. 2. one of two or more parts, as of a machine, that grasp or hold something: *the jaws of a vise.* —*v.i.* 3. *Slang.* to talk, esp. in a rapid or abusive manner. —**jawed** (jôd), *adj.* —**jaw′less,** *adj.*

jaw·bone (jô′bōn′), *n., v.,* **-boned, -bon·ing,** *adj.* —*n.* a bone of either jaw, esp of the lower jaw. —*v.t. Informal.* to attempt to convince by moral persuasion. —*adj.* 3. *Informal.* resorting to such a practice: *jawbone controls.*

jaw·break·er (jô′brā′kər), *n.* 1. *Informal.* any word that is hard to pronounce. 2. a very hard, opaque candy.

jay (jā), *n.* any of several noisy birds having brownish plumage.

jay·bird (jā′bûrd′), *n.* jay.

Jay·cee (jā′sē′), *n.* a member of a civic group for young men **(Unit′ed States′ Jay′cees′).**

jay·vee (jā′vē′), *n. Informal.* 1. a player on the junior varsity. 2. See **junior varsity.**

jay·walk (jā′wôk′), *v.i.* to cross a street in a heedless manner, as against traffic lights. —**jay′walk′er,** *n.*

jazz (jaz), *n.* 1. a form of native American music marked by improvisation, propulsive rhythms, and polyphonic ensemble playing. 2. *Slang.* insincere or pretentious talk. —*v.t.* 3. to play (music) as jazz. 4. *Slang.* to put liveliness into: *to jazz up a conversation.*

jazz·y (jaz′ē), *adj.*, **jazz·i·er, jazz·i·est.** *Slang.* 1. of or suggestive of jazz music. 2. wildly active or lively. —**jazz′i·ly,** *adv.* —**jazz′i·ness,** *n.*

J.C.S., Joint Chiefs of Staff. Also, **JCS**

jct., junction.

JD, juvenile delinquent.

J.D., 1. Doctor of Jurisprudence. [< L *Juris Doctor*] 2. Doctor of Laws. [< L *Jurum Doctor*] 3. Justice Department. 4. juvenile delinquent.

JDL, Jewish Defense League.

Je., June.

jeal·ous (jel′əs), *adj.* 1. resentful and envious, as of someone's attainments. 2. fearful of losing another's affection. 3. troubled by suspicions of rivalry, unfaithfulness, etc. 4. vigilant in guarding something. —**jeal′ous·ly,** *adv.* —**jeal′ous·y, jeal′ous·ness,** *n.*

jean (jēn), *n.* 1. a stout twilled cotton fabric. 2. **jeans,** trousers made of this fabric.

jeep (jēp), *n.* a small, all-purpose motor vehicle having four-wheel drive, widely used esp. by the armed forces in World War II.

jeer (jēr), *v.i., v.t.* 1. to speak or shout derisively (at). —*n.* 2. a jeering utterance. —**jeer′ing·ly,** *adv.* —Syn. 1. mock, scoff, sneer.

Jef·fer·son (jef′ər sən), *n.* **Thomas,** 1743–1826, 3rd president of the U.S. 1801–09. —**Jef′fer·so′ni·an** (-sō′nē-ən), *adj., n.*

Jef′ferson Cit′y, the capital of Missouri.

Je·ho·vah (ji hō′və), *n.* God, esp. in the Old Testament.

Jeho′vah's Wit′nesses, a Christian sect, founded in the U.S. in the late 19th century, that believes in the imminent end of the world and the establishment of a theocracy under God's rule.

je·june (ji jōōn′), *adj.* 1. *Literary.* lacking in nutritive value. 2. dull or insipid 3. juvenile or immature.

je·ju·num (ji jōō′nəm), *n.* the middle portion of the small intestine, between the duodenum and the ileum. —**je·ju′nal,** *adj.*

jell (jel), *v.i., v.t.* 1. to become or cause to become jellylike in consistency. 2. to become or cause to become clear or definite.

jel·ly (jel′ē), *n., pl.* **-lies,** *v.,* **-lied, -ly·ing.** —*n.* 1. a food preparation of a soft, elastic consistency due to the presence of gelatin, pectin, etc., as fruit juice boiled down with sugar. 2. anything of the consistency of jelly. —*v.t., v.i.* 3. to jell (def. 1). —**jel′ly·like′,** *adj.*

jel·ly·bean (jel′ē bēn′), *n.* a bean-shaped candy with a firm gelatinous filling.

jel·ly·fish (jel′ē fish′), *n., pl.* **-fish, -fish·es.** 1. a marine animal of a soft, gelatinous structure, esp. one with an umbrellalike body and long, trailing tentacles. 2. *Informal.* an indecisive or weak person.

jel′ly roll′, a thin, rectangular layer of sponge cake spread with fruit jelly and rolled up.

jen·net (jen′it), *n.* 1. a small Spanish horse. 2. a female ass or donkey.

jen·ny (jen′ē), *n., pl.* **-nies.** a female donkey or bird.

jeop·ard·ize (jep′ər dīz′), *v.t.,* **-ized, -iz·ing.** to put in jeopardy. —**Syn.** endanger, imperil, risk.

jeop·ard·y (jep′ər dē), *n.* 1. exposure to loss, harm, death, or injury. 2. *Law.* the hazard of being found guilty. —**jeop′ard·ous** (-dəs), *adj.*

Jer., Jeremiah.

jer·e·mi·ad (jer′ə mī′ad), *n.* a mournful complaint.

Jer·e·mi·ah (jer′ə mī′ə), *n.* a prophet of the 6th and 7th centuries B.C.

jerk (jûrk), *n.* 1. a quick, sharp pull, thrust, or twist. 2. a spasmodic, usually involuntary, muscular movement. 3. *Slang.* a fatuous or foolish person. —*v.t.* 4. to move with a jerk. —*v.i.* 5. to give a jerk. —**jerk′y,** *adv.* —**jerk′i·ly,** *adv.* —**jerk′i·ness,** *n.*

jer·kin (jûr′kin), *n.* a closefitting, sleeveless jacket of the 16th and 17th centuries.

jerk·wa·ter (jûrk′wô′tər, -wot′ər), *adj. Informal.* ridiculously insignificant and out-of-the-way: *a jerkwater town.*

jer·ry-build (jer′ē bild′), *v.t.,* **-built, -build·ing.** to build cheaply and flimsily. —**jer′ry-built′,** *adj.*

jer·sey (jûr′zē), *n., pl.* **-seys.** 1. a closefitting knitted pullover sweater or shirt. 2. (*cap.*) a breed of dairy cattle producing milk having a high content of butterfat. 3. a machine-knitted or machine-woven fabric.

Jer′sey Cit′y, a seaport in NE New Jersey.

Je·ru·sa·lem (ji rōō′sə ləm), *n.* the capital of modern Israel.

jess (jes), *n. Falconry.* a short strap fastened around the leg of a hawk and attached to the leash.

jes·sa·mine (jes′ə min), *n.* jasmine.

jest (jest), *n.* 1. a witty remark. 2. a bantering remark. 3. sport or fun. 4. the object of laughter or mockery. —*v.i.* 5. to joke or banter. 6. to gibe or scoff.

jest·er (jes′tər), *n.* 1. a person given to jesting 2. a comic entertainer retained by a medieval prince or noble.

Jes·u·it (jezh′ōō it. jez′yōō-, jez′ōō-), *n.* a member of a Roman Catholic religious order (**Soci′ety of Je′sus**) founded in 1534.

Je·sus (jē′zəs), n. born 4? B.C., crucified A.D. 29?, the source of the Christian religion. Also called **Je′sus Christ′**.

jet¹ (jet), n., v., **jet·ted, jet·ting,** adj. —n. 1. a stream of a liquid or gas forcefully shooting forth from a nozzle or orifice. 2. a spout or nozzle for emitting such a stream. 3. Also called **jet′ plane′**. a jet-propelled aircraft. —v.i., v.i. 4. to shoot (something) forth in a stream. 5. to travel or ship by jet plane. —adj. 6. of or powered by jet propulsion.

jet² (jet), n. 1. a compact black coal, susceptible of a high polish, used for making beads, jewelry, etc. 2. a deep, glossy black. —adj. 3. black as jet.

jet′ lag′, a temporary disruption of one's normal biological rhythms after long-distance travel by airplane through several time zones without sufficient rest en route.

jet·lin·er (jet′lī′nər), n. a commercial jet plane for passengers.

jet·port (jet′pōrt′, -pôrt′), n. an airport for jet planes.

jet′ propul′sion, the propulsion of a body by its reaction to a force ejecting a gas or a liquid from it. —jet′-pro·pelled′ (-prə peld′), adj.

jet·sam (jet′səm), n. goods cast overboard deliberately, as to lighten a vessel in an emergency.

jet′ set′, an international social set composed of affluent people who jet from resort to resort. —jet′ set′ter.

jet′ stream′, 1. strong, generally westerly winds concentrated in a narrow, shallow stream in the upper troposphere. 2. the exhaust of a rocket engine.

jet·ti·son (jet′i san, -zən), v.t. 1. to cast (goods) overboard in order to lighten a vessel in an emergency. 2. to throw off (an obstacle or burden).

jet·ty (jet′ē), n., pl. **-ties.** 1. a structure projecting into a body of water to protect a harbor or coast. 2. Brit. a narrow landing pier.

jeu d'es·prit (zhœ des prē′), pl. **jeux d'es·prit** (zhœ des prē′). French. a witty comment or piece of writing.

Jew (jōō), n. 1. a person whose religion is Judaism. 2. a descendant of the Biblical Hebrews.

jew·el (jōō′əl), n., v., **-eled, -el·ing** or **-elled, -el·ling.** —n. 1. a cut and polished precious stone. 2. a fashioned ornament of a precious metal set with gems. 3. a person or thing of great worth. 4. a durable bearing made of natural or synthetic precious stone, used in fine timepieces. —v.t. 5. to set or adorn with jewels.

jew·el·er (jōō′ə lər), n. a person who makes, sells, or repairs jewelry, watches, etc. Also, Brit., **jew′el·ler.**

jew·el·ry (jōō′əl rē), n. 1. articles of gold, silver, precious stones, etc., for personal adornment. 2. jewels collectively.

jew·el·weed (jōō′əl wēd′), n. a plant having yellow flowers sometimes spotted with brownish red.

Jew·ish (jōō′ish), adj. 1. of or noting the Jews or Judaism. —n. 2. Informal. Yiddish. —**Jew′ish·ness,** n.

Jew·ry (jōō′rē), n. the Jewish people collectively.

Jez·e·bel (jez′ə bel′, -bəl), n. (often l.c.) a wicked, shameless woman.

jg, junior grade. Also, **j.g.**

jib¹ (jib), n. a triangular sail set forward of a foremast

jib² (jib), v.i., **jibbed, jib·bing,** n. Chiefly Brit. (of an animal) to move restively sideways or backward instead of forward.

jibe¹ (jīb), v.i., **jibed, jib·ing.** 1. to shift from one side to the other, as a fore-and-aft sail. 2. to alter course so that a fore-and-aft sail shifts in this manner.

jibe² (jīb), n., v.i., v.t., **jibed, jib·ing.** gibe.

jibe³ (jīb), v.i., **jibed, jib·ing** to be in accord with.

jif·fy (jif′ē), n., pl. **-fies.** Informal. a short time. Also, **jiff.**

jig¹ (jig), n. an open frame for holding work and for guiding tools to the work.

jig² (jig), n., v., **jigged, jig·ging.** —n. 1. a lively dance, usually in triple meter. 2. in jig time, rapidly. 3. **the jig is up,** Slang. it is hopeless. —v.t., v.i. 4. to dance (a jig). 5. to move with a jerky motion.

jig·ger (jig′ər), n. 1. a 1½-ounce measure used in cocktail recipes. 2. a small whiskey glass holding 1½ ounces.

jig·gle (jig′əl), v., **-gled, -gling,** n. — v.t., v.i. 1. to move up and down or to and fro with short, quick jerks. —n. 2. a jiggling movement. —**jig′-gly,** adj.

jig′ saw′, a narrow saw, mounted vertically in a frame, for cutting curves or other difficult lines.

jig′saw puz′zle, a set of irregularly cut pieces of pasteboard that form a picture or design when fitted together.

ji·had (ji häd′), n. 1. a holy war undertaken by Muslims. 2. any bitter crusade for an idea.

jilt (jilt), v.t. 1. to reject or cast aside (a lover or sweetheart). —n. 2. a woman who jilts a lover. —**jilt′er,** n.

Jim Crow (jim′ krō′), a practice or policy of segregating or discriminating against blacks. Also, **Jim′ Crow′ism.** —**jim′-crow′, Jim′-Crow′,** adj.

jim-dan·dy (jim′dan′dē), adj. Informal. of superior quality.

jim·my (jim′ē), *n.*, *pl.* **-mies**, *v.*, **-mied,** **-my·ing.** —*n.* **1.** a short crowbar, esp. used by burglars. —*v.t.* **2.** to force open with a jimmy.

jim′son weed′ (jim′sən), a coarse weed, having white or lavender flowers and poisonous leaves.

jin·gle (jing′gəl), *v.*, **-gled, -gling,** *n.* —*v.i.* **1.** to make clinking or tinkling sounds, as metal objects. —*v.t.* **2.** to cause to jingle. —*n.* **3.** a jingling sound. **4.** a short verse having a succession of repetitious sounds. —**jin′gler,** *n.* —**jin′gly,** *adj.*

jin·go (jing′gō), *n.*, *pl.* **-goes.** a person who professes patriotism excessively, favoring preparedness for war and an aggressive foreign policy. —**jin′go·ism′,** *n.* —**jin′go·ist,** *n.*, *adj.* —**jin′go·is′tic, jin′go·ish,** *adj.*

jinn (jin), *n.*, *pl.* **jinns, jinn.** *Islamic Myth.* a supernatural spirit capable of influencing mankind for good and evil. Also, **jin·ni** (ji nē′, jin′ē).

jin·ri·ki·sha (jin rik′shô, -shä), *n.* a two-wheeled passenger vehicle pulled by one man, formerly used widely in Japan and China. Also, **jin·rick′sha, jin·rik′sha.** [< Jap: man-powered carriage]

jinx (jingks), *n.* **1.** a person, thing, or influence supposed to bring bad luck. —*v.t.* **2.** to place a jinx on.

jit·ney (jit′nē), *n.*, *pl.* **-neys. 1.** a small passenger bus, originally charging each passenger five cents. **2.** *Archaic.* a nickel.

jit·ter (jit′ər), *n.* **1. jitters,** a feeling of fright or uneasiness. —*v.i.* **2.** to behave nervously . —**jit′ter·y,** *adj.*

jit·ter·bug (jit′ər bug′), *n.*, *v.*, **-bugged, -bug·ging.** —*n.* **1.** a strenuous dance performed to swing music, popular esp. in the early 1940's. **2.** a person who dances the jitterbug. —*v.i.* **3.** to dance the jitterbug.

jiu·ji·tsu (jōō ji′tsōō), *n.* jujitsu. Also, **jiu·ju′tsu.**

jive (jīv), *n.*, *v.*, **jived, jiv·ing.** —*n.* **1.** *Slang.* the jargon of jazz and swing musicians. **2.** *Slang.* unintelligible or deceptive talk. **3.** *Obsolesc.* jazz or swing. —*v.i.*, *v.t.* **4.** *Slang.* to fool or kid (someone).

jnt., joint.

Joan of Arc (jōn′ əv ärk′), **Saint,** 1412?–31, French heroine and martyr.

job[1] (job), *n.*, *v.*, **jobbed, job·bing.** —*n.* **1.** a piece of work done as part of the routine of one's occupation. **2.** anything one has to do, as a task. **3.** a post of employment. —*v.i.* **4.** to work at jobs or odd pieces of work. —*v.t.* **5.** to assign or give (work) in separate portions: *to job out a contract.* —**job′less,** *adj.* —**job′lessness,** *n.*

Job (jōb), *n.* the central figure in an Old Testament parable of the righteous sufferer.

job′ ac′tion, any means of organized protest short of a general strike, as a work slowdown, used by employees legally forbidden to strike.

job′ bank′, a governmental computerized data-file for matching unemployed workers with appropriate job openings in a labor market.

job·ber (job′ər), *n.* **1.** a wholesale merchant, esp. one selling to retailers. **2.** a person who does piecework.

job·hold·er (job′hōl′dər), *n.* a person who has a regular job.

job′ lot′, **1.** an assortment of goods sold as a single unit. **2.** a quantity of odds and ends.

job′ shop′, an employment agency that supplies technical personnel on short-term temporary contracts.

jock (jok), *n.* **1.** *Informal.* See **disc jockey. 2.** *Slang.* an athlete.

jock·ey (jok′ē), *n.*, *pl.* **-eys,** *v.*, **-eyed, -ey·ing.** —*n.* **1.** a person who professionally rides hores in races. —*v.t.* **2.** to ride (a horse) as a jockey. **3.** to manipulate cleverly or trickily. **4.** to trick or cheat. —*v.i.* **5.** to aim at an advantage by skillful maneuvering.

jock·strap (jok′strap′), *n.* an elastic supporter for the genitals, worn by men esp. while participating in athletics.

jo·cose (jō kōs′), *adj.* given to or characterized by joking or jesting. —**jo·cose′ly,** *adv.* —**jo·cos′i·ty** (-kos′i tē), **jo·cose′ness,** *n.*

joc·u·lar (jok′yə lər), *adj.* intended for or suited to joking or jesting. —**joc′u·lar′i·ty** (-lar′i tē), *n.*

joc·und (jok′ənd, jō′kənd), *adj. Literary.* tending to inspire cheerfulness or mirth. —**jo·cun·di·ty** (jōkun′di tē), *n.* —**joc′und·ly,** *adv.*

jodh·pur (jod′pər, jōd′-), *n.* **1. jodhpurs,** riding breeches cut very full over the hips and tapering at the knees. **2.** Also called **jodh′pur boot′.** an ankle-high shoe having a strap that buckles on the side.

jog[1] (jog), *v.*, **jogged, jog·ging,** *n.* —*v.t.* **1.** to push slightly, as to arouse the attention. **2.** to stir or jolt into activity: *to jog a person's memory.* **3.** to cause (a horse) to go at a steady trot. —*v.i.* **4.** to run at a leisurely, slow pace, esp. as an outdoor exercise. —*n.* **5.** a slight push or nudge. **6.** a jogging pace or motion. —**jog′ger,** *n.*

jog[2] (jog), *n.* **1.** an irregularity of line or surface. **2.** a bend or turn. —*v.i.* **3.** to bend or turn.

jog·gle (jog′əl), *v.*, **-gled, -gling,** *n.* —*v.t.*, *v.i.* **1.** to shake slightly. —*n.* **2.** a slight shake or jolt.

Jo·han·nes·burg (jō han′is bûrg′), *n.* a city in the N Republic of South Africa.

john (jon), *n. Slang.* a toilet or lavatory.

John (jon), *n.* **1.** the apostle John, believed to be the author of the fourth Gospel. **2.** *Slang.* a prostitute's customer.

John′ Bull′ (bool), **1.** the English people. **2.** the typical Englishman.

John′ Doe′ (dō), (in legal proceedings) a fictitious personage or one whose real name is not known.

john·ny (jon′ē), *n., pl. -nies. Slang.* a short collarless gown fastened in back, worn by hospital patients.

John·ny-jump-up (jon′ē jump′up′), *n.* a small form of the pansy cultivated in flower gardens.

John·son (jon′sən), *n.* **1.** **Andrew,** 1808–75, 17th president of the U.S. 1865–69. **2.** **Lyn·don Baines** (lin′dən bānz), 1908–73, 36th president of the U.S. 1963–69. **3.** **Samuel,** 1709–84, English lexicographer and critic.

John′ the Bap′tist, the forerunner and baptizer of Jesus.

joie de vi·vre (zhwäd° vē′vrᵉ°), *French.* a delight in being alive.

join (join), *v.t., v.i.* **1.** to put together or in contact. **2.** to come into contact or union (with). **3.** to become a member of (a society, party, etc.): *to join a club.* **4.** to participate with (someone) in some act or activity.

join·er (joi′nər), *n.* **1.** a person or thing that joins. **2.** a carpenter, esp. one who constructs doors, window sashes, etc. **3.** a person who belongs to many clubs, etc.

joint (joint), *n.* **1.** the place at which two things are joined or united. **2.** the movable or fixed place or part where two bones or elements of a skeleton join. **3.** a section of meat divided by a butcher, esp. for roasting. **4.** *Slang.* a disreputable place of public accommodation, esp. a cheap restaurant or nightclub. **5.** *Slang.* a marijuana cigarette. **6. out of joint, a.** dislocated, as a bone. **b.** in a disordered state. —*adj.* **7.** shared by or common to two or more. **8.** sharing or acting in common. —*v.t.* **9.** to unite by a joint or joints. **10.** to form or provide with a joint or joints. **11.** to cut (meat) at the joint. —**joint′ly,** *adv.*

joist (joist), *n.* any of the small, parallel beams of timber or steel for supporting floors, ceilings, etc.

joke (jōk), *n., v., joked, jok·ing.* —*n.* **1.** something said or done to provoke laughter. **2.** something that is amusing or ridiculous. **3.** a trifling matter. **4.** something very easy. **5.** See **practical joke.** —*v.i.* **6.** to make or tell jokes. **7.** to say something in fun. [< L *joc(us)* jest] —**jok′ing·ly,** *adv.*

jok·er (jō′kər), *n.* **1.** a person who jokes. **2.** one of two extra playing cards in a pack, used in some games. **3.** a seemingly minor, unsuspected clause or wording that is put into an agreement to change its effect.

jol·li·fi·ca·tion (jol′ə fə kā′shən), *n.* jolly merrymaking.

jol·li·ty (jol′i tē), *n., pl. -ties.* jolly mood, condition, or activity.

jol·ly (jol′ē) *adj* **-li·er, -li·est,** *v.,* **-lied, -ly·ing,** *adv* —*adj.* **1.** in good spirits. **2.** cheerfully festive. **3.** joyous or happy —*v.t* **4.** *Informal.* to keep (a person) in good humor, esp. in the hope of gaining something. —*adv.* **5.** *Brit Informal* extremely: *jolly well.* —**jol′li·ly,** *adv.* —**jol′li·ness,** *n.* —*Syn* 1–3. jovial joyful, jubilant.

jolt (jōlt), *v.t.* **1.** to shake up roughly. **2.** to stun with a blow, esp. in boxing. **3.** to shock psychologically. —*v.i.* **4.** to move with a sharp jerk. —*n.* **5.** a jolting movement or blow. **6.** a psychological shock. —**jolt′er,** *n.* —**jolt′y** (jōl′tē) *adj.*

Jo·nah (jō′nə), *n.* **1.** a Hebrew prophet who was thrown overboard from his ship and swallowed by a large fish that later cast him up onto the shore unhurt. **2.** any person or thing regarded as bringing bad luck.

Jones (jōnz), *n* **John Paul,** 1747–92, American naval commander in the Revolutionary War, born in Scotland.

jon·gleur (jong′glər), *n.* an itinerant medieval minstrel.

jon·quil (jong′kwil, jon′-), *n.* a narcissus having fragrant yellow or white flowers.

Jon·son (jon′sən), *n.* **Ben,** 1573?–1637, English dramatist and poet. —**Jon·so·ni·an** (jon sō′nē ən), *adj.*

Jor·dan (jôr′dᵉn), *n.* **1.** a country in SW Asia. **2.** a river flowing through W Jordan into the Dead Sea.

Jo·seph (jō′zəf, -səf), *n.* **1.** the first son of Jacob: sold into slavery by his brothers, he became governor in Egypt. **2.** the husband of Mary who was the mother of Jesus.

josh (josh), *v.t., v.i. Informal.* to tease by bantering —**josh′er,** *n.*

Josh., Joshua.

Josh·u·a (josh′ōō ə), *n.* the successor of Moses as leader of the Israelites.

Josh′ua tree′, a tree growing in arid regions of the southwestern U.S.

joss (jos), *n.* a Chinese house idol or cult image.

jos·tle (jos′əl), *v.,* **-tled, -tling,** *n.* —*v.t., v.i.* **1.** to bump or shove roughly or rudely, as in a crowd. —*n.* **2.** a bump or shove against someone or something.

jot (jot), v., **jot·ted, jot·ting,** n. —v.t. 1. to write down quickly or briefly. —n. 2. a little bit. —**jot′ter,** n.

jot·ting (jot′ing), n. a quickly written note.

joule (jōōl, joul), n. the meter-kilogram-second unit of work or energy.

jounce (jouns), v., **jounced, jounc·ing,** n. —v.t., v.i. 1. to move joltingly. —n. 2. a jouncing movement. —**jounc′y,** adj.

jour., journal.

jour·nal (jûr′n°l), n. 1. a daily record, as of occurrences or observations. 2. a record, usually daily, of proceedings, as of a legislative body. 3. a newspaper, esp. a daily one. 4. an academic or learned periodical. 5. Bookkeeping. a book of specialized record for particular transactions. 6. the portion of a shaft or axle contained by a bearing [< OF: daily < L diurnāl(is) daily]

jour·nal·ese (jûr′n°lēz′, -n°lēs′), n. a style of writing or expression supposed to characterize newspapers.

jour·nal·ism (jûr′n°liz′əm), n. the profession of gathering, writing, editing, or publishing news, as for a newspaper. —**jour′nal·ist,** n. —**jour′nal·is′tic,** adj. —**jour′nal·is′ti·cal·ly,** adv.

jour·ney (jûr′nē), n., pl. **-neys,** v., **-neyed, -ney·ing.** —n. 1. travel from one place to another, usually taking a rather long time. —v.i. 2. to make a journey. —**jour′ney·er,** n.

jour·ney·man (jûr′nē mən), n. 1. a person who has served an apprenticeship. 2. any experienced, competent worker or performer.

joust (joust, just, jōōst), n. 1. a medieval combat with lances between two armored knights on horseback. —v.i. 2. to contend in a joust. —**joust′er,** n.

jo·vi·al (jō′vē əl), adj. marked by a hearty, joyous humor. —**jo′vi·al′i·ty** (-al′i tē), n. —**jo′vi·al·ly,** adv.

jowl[1] (joul, jōl), n. 1. a jaw, esp. the lower jaw. 2. the cheek.

jowl[2] (joul, jōl), n. a fold of flesh hanging from the jaw, as of a fat person. —**jowl′y,** adj.

joy (joi), n. 1. the emotion of great delight or happiness caused by something good or satisfying. 2. a source of keen pleasure or delight. —**joy′less,** adj.

joy·ance (joi′əns), n. Archaic. joyous feeling.

Joyce (jois), n. **James,** 1882–1941, Irish novelist.

joy·ful (joi′fəl), adj. 1. full of joy. 2. showing or expressing joy. 3. causing or bringing joy. —**joy′ful·ly,** adj. —**joy′ful·ness,** n.

joy·ous (joi′əs), adj. suggesting or promoting joy. —**joy′ous·ly,** adv. —**joy′ous·ness,** n.

joy′ ride′, Informal. a short ride in an automobile driven recklessly. —**joy′ rid′er.** —**joy′ rid′ing.**

JP, jet propulsion.

J.P., Justice of the Peace.

Jpn., 1. Japan. 2. Japanese.

Jr., 1. Journal. 2. Junior.

Ju., June.

ju·bi·lant (jōō′bə lənt), adj. feeling joy and triumph. —**ju′bi·lant·ly,** adv.

ju·bi·la·tion (jōō′bə lā′shən), n. 1. a feeling of joy and triumph. 2. a joyful celebration, as of victory. —Syn. 1. exultation, rejoicing.

ju·bi·lee (jōō′bə lē′, jōō′bə lē′), n. 1. the celebration of an anniversary of a special event, esp. a 25th or 50th anniversary. 2. any season or occasion of rejoicing or festivity. 3. rejoicing or jubilation.

Ju·da·ic (jōō dā′ik), adj. of or pertaining to Judaism or the Jews. Also, **Ju·da′i·cal.**

Ju·da·i·ca (jōō dā′i kə), n.pl. things Jewish, esp. when of a historical or literary nature, as books about Jewish life and customs.

Ju·da·ism (jōō′dē iz′əm, -dā-), n. the monotheistic religion of the Jews.

Ju·das (jōō′dəs), n. 1. Also called **Ju′das Is·car′i·ot** (i skar′ē ət). the disciple who betrayed Jesus. 2. a person treacherous enough to betray a friend.

Ju′das tree′, a Eurasian, purple-flowered, leguminous tree supposed to be the kind upon which Judas hanged himself.

judge (juj), n., v., **judged, judg·ing.** —n. 1. a public officer authorized to hear and determine causes in a court of law. 2. a person appointed to decide in any competition or contest. 3. a person qualified to pass a critical judgment. —v.t. 4. to pass legal judgment on. 5. to form a judgment or opinion of or upon. 6. to decide or settle authoritatively. 7. to think or hold as an opinion. 8. Archaic. to criticize or condemn. —v.i. 9. to act as a judge. 10. to form an opinion or estimate. —**judge′ship,** n.

judg·ment (juj′mənt), n. 1. the act or an instance of judging. 2. the judicial decision of a cause in court. 3. the ability to form an opinion objectively and wisely. 4. the forming of an opinion, estimate, or notion. 5. (usually cap.) the final trial of all mankind. Also, esp. Brit., **judge′ment.** —**judg·men′tal** (-men′t°l), adj.

ju·di·ca·to·ry (jōō′də kə tōr′ē), adj., n., pl. **-to·ries.** —adj. 1. of or pertaining to the administration of justice. —n. 2. a court of law and justice.

ju·di·ca·ture (jōō′də kā′chər), n. 1. the administration of justice. 2. the power of administering justice by legal trial and determination. **3.** judiciary (defs. 2, 3).

ju·di·cial (jōō dish′əl), *adj.* **1.** pertaining to courts of law or to judges. **2.** proper to the character of a judge. **3.** critical or discriminating: *a judicial mind.* **4.** sanctioned or enforced by a court. —**ju·di′cial·ly,** *adv.*

ju·di·ci·ar·y (jōō dish′ē er′ē, -dish′ə-rē), *n., pl.* **-ar·ies,** *adj.* —*n.* **1.** the judicial branch of government. **2.** the system of courts of justice in a country. **3.** judges collectively. —*adj.* **4.** pertaining to the judicial branch, system, or judges.

ju·di·cious (jōō dish′əs), *adj.* having, exercising, or characterized by good judgment. —**ju·di′cious·ly,** *adv.* —**ju·di′cious·ness,** *n.* —**Syn.** reasonable, sensible, wise.

ju·do (jōō′dō), *n.* a method of defending oneself or fighting without weapons, based on jujitsu but banning harmful throws and blows. [< Jap: soft way] —**ju′do·ist,** *n.*

jug (jug), *n.* **1.** a container for liquid, usually made of pottery or glass, commonly having a handle and often a spout. **2.** *Slang.* a jail or prison.

jug·ger·naut (jug′ər nôt′), *n.* any large, overpowering, destructive force or object.

jug·gle (jug′əl), *v.,* **-gled, -gling.** —*v.t.* **1.** to keep (several objects, as balls) in motion in the air simultaneously by tossing and catching. **2.** to manipulate in order to deceive, as by trickery. —*v.i.* **3.** to perform feats of manual dexterity, as tossing up and keeping in motion a number of balls. —**jug′gler,** *n.* —**jug′gler·y,** *n.* —**jug′gling·ly,** *adv.*

jug·u·lar (jug′yə lər, jōō′gyə-), *adj.* **1.** of or situated in the throat or neck. —*n.* **2.** a jugular vein.

juice (jōōs), *n., v.,* **juiced, juic·ing.** —*n.* **1.** the liquid part or contents of plant or animal substance. **2.** the natural fluids of an animal body. **3.** essence, strength, or vitality. **4.** *Slang.* **a.** electricity or electric power. **b.** gasoline, fuel oil, etc. **5.** *Slang.* alcoholic liquor. —*v.t.* **6.** to extract juice from. —**juice′less,** *adj.*

juic·er (jōō′sər), *n.* an appliance for extracting juice from fruits and vegetables.

juic·y (jōō′sē), *adj.,* **juic·i·er, juic·i·est. 1.** full of juice. **2.** very interesting or colorful. —**juic′i·ly,** *adv.* —**juic′i·ness,** *n.*

ju·jit·su (jōō jit′sōō), *n.* a method of defending oneself without weapons by using the strength and weight of an opponent to disable him or her. Also, **ju·jut′su.** [< Jap: soft art]

ju·jube (jōō′jōōb), *n.* **1.** the edible, plumlike fruit of a small, spiny tree. **2.** a fruit-flavored lozenge.

juke·box (jōōk′boks′), *n.* a coin-operated record player.

Jul., July.

ju·lep (jōō′lip), *n.* See **mint julep.**

ju·li·enne (jōō′lē en′), *adj.* (of vegetables) cut into thin strips.

Ju·ly (jōō lī′, jə lī′), *n.* the seventh month of the year, containing 31 days.

jum·ble (jum′bəl), *v.,* **-bled, -bling,** *n.* —*v.t., v.i.* **1.** to mix or be mixed in a confused mass. —*n.* **2.** a mixed or disordered mass.

jum·bo (jum′bō), *n., pl.* **-bos,** *adj.* —*n.* **1.** a very large person, animal, or thing. —*adj.* **2.** very large. [after *Jumbo,* name of large elephant in Barnum circus < Swahili *jumbe* chief]

jump (jump), *v.i.* **1.** to spring clear of the ground or other support by a sudden muscular effort. **2.** to rise suddenly or quickly. **3.** to move or jerk suddenly. **4.** to proceed hastily, as to a conclusion. **5.** to act quickly, as to take advantage of an opportunity. **6.** to rise abruptly, as a price. **7.** *Slang.* to be full of activity. —*v.t.* **8.** to leap or spring over. **9.** to cause to leap. **10.** to bypass or skip. **11.** *Informal.* to flee from: *to jump town.* **12.** to increase abruptly, as a price. **13.** *Informal.* to attack without warning, as from ambush. **14. jump bail,** to abscond while free on bail. —*n.* **15.** the act or an instance of jumping. **16.** an abrupt rise, as of a price. **17.** an abrupt transition. **18.** a sudden start, as from nervous excitement. **19. get** or **have the jump on,** *Informal.* to get or have an initial advantage over. —**jump′a·ble,** *adj.* —**jump′ing·ly,** *adv.*

jump·er¹ (jum′pər), *n.* **1.** a person or thing that jumps. **2.** a person who makes a parachute jump. **3.** a short length of conductor, as to bypass a circuit.

jump·er² (jum′pər), *n.* **1.** a one-piece sleeveless dress worn over a blouse by women and children. **2. jumpers,** rompers.

jump′ing-off′ place′ (jum′ping ôf′, -of′), **1.** the farthest limit of anything settled or civilized. **2.** a place for use as a starting point.

jump′ suit′, 1. a one-piece paratrooper's uniform worn for jumping. **2.** an article of men's or women's lounging attire styled after this.

jump·y (jum′pē), *adj.,* **jump·i·er, jump·i·est. 1.** subject to sudden starts or jumps. **2.** nervous or apprehensive. —**jump′i·ly,** *adv.* —**jump′i·ness,** *n.*

Jun., 1. June. **2.** Junior.

Junc., Junction.

jun·co (jung′kō), *n., pl.* **-cos.** a small North American finch having slate-gray and white plumage.

junc·tion (juŋk′shən), *n.* **1.** the act of joining or state of being joined. **2.** a place or point where things meet or converge. **3.** a meeting place of roads, railroad lines, etc. —**junc′-tion·al,** *adj.*

junc·ture (juŋk′chər), *n.* **1.** a point of time, esp. one made critical by circumstances. **2.** a serious state of affairs. **3.** junction (def. 1).

June (jōōn), *n.* the sixth month of the year, containing 30 days.

Ju·neau (jōō′nō), *n.* the capital of Alaska.

jun·gle (juŋg′gəl), *n.* **1.** wild land over-grown with dense vegetation, esp. in the tropics. **2.** a scene of violence or ruthless competition.

jun·ior (jōōn′yər), *adj.* **1.** younger (often written as *Jr.* following the name of a son bearing the same full name as his father). **2.** lower in rank or standing. **3.** of or for a junior or juniors in schools. —*n.* **4.** a person who is younger than another. **5.** a person who is of lower rank than another. **6.** a student who is in the class or year next below the senior.

jun′ior col′lege, a school offering courses only through the first two years of college.

jun′ior high′ school′, a high school that usually includes grades 7, 8, and 9.

jun′ior var′sity, a team that consists of players who failed to make the varsity.

ju·ni·per (jōō′nə pər), *n.* an evergreen shrub or tree having cones that form purple berries.

junk¹ (juŋk), *n.* **1.** old or discarded material or objects. **2.** anything re-garded as worthless. —*v.t.* **3.** *Informal.* to discard as junk.

junk² (juŋk), *n.* a seagoing ship used in Chinese waters, having a flat bot-tom.

junk³ (juŋk), *n.* *Informal.* narcotics, esp. heroin.

junk·er (juŋg′kər), *n.* *Slang.* a worn-out automobile ready for conversion into scrap.

Jun·ker (yōōng′kər), *n.* a member of the Prussian aristocracy, noted for its militaristic attitudes.

jun·ket (juŋg′kit), *n.* **1.** a sweet, cus-tardlike food of flavored milk cur-dled with rennet. **2.** a pleasure ex-cursion. **3.** a trip, as by an official, made at public expense. —*v.i.* **4.** to go on a junket. —**jun′ke·teer′** (-ki-tēr′), **jun′ket·er,** *n.*

junk′ food′, food that is low in nu-tritious value and usually high in calories, as potato chips.

junk·ie (juŋg′kē), *n.* *Informal.* a drug addict, esp. one addicted to heroin. Also, **junk′y.**

junk′ mail′, *Informal.* unsolicited commercial mail.

Ju·no (jōō′nō), *n.* the ancient Roman queen of heaven, and the wife and sister of Jupiter.

jun·ta (hōōn′tə, hōōn′-, jun′-, hun′-), *n.* a small group ruling a country, esp. immediately after a coup d'état.

jun·to (jun′tō), *n., pl.* **-tos.** a self-appointed committee, esp. with po-litical aims.

Ju·pi·ter (jōō′pi tər), *n.* **1.** the su-preme deity of the ancient Romans. **2.** the planet fifth in order from the sun: the largest in the solar system.

Ju·ras·sic (jōō ras′ik), *adj.* **1.** noting a period of the Mesozoic era char-acterized by the presence of dino-saurs and conifers. —*n.* **2.** the Ju-rassic period.

ju·rid·i·cal (jōō rid′i kəl), *adj.* of or pertaining to legal proceedings. Also, **ju·rid′ic.** —**ju·rid′i·cal·ly,** *adv.*

ju·ris·dic·tion (jōōr′is dik′shən), *n.* **1.** the right, power, or authority to administer justice. **2.** the extent or range of judicial or other authority. —**ju·ris·dic′tion·al,** *adj.*

ju·ris·pru·dence (jōōr′is prōōd′°ns), *n.* **1.** the science or philosophy of law. **2.** a body or system of laws.

ju·rist (jōōr′ist), *n.* **1.** a person versed in the law, as a distinguished judge. **2.** *Brit.* a legal student, writer, or scholar.

ju·ris·tic (jōō ris′tik), *adj.* of or per-taining to a jurist or to jurispru-dence.

ju·ror (jōōr′ər), *n.* a member of a jury. Also called **ju′ry·man.**

ju·ry¹ (jōōr′ē), *n., pl.* **-ries.** **1.** a body of persons sworn to render a verdict or true answer on a law case offi-cially submitted to them. **2.** a com-mittee for deciding winners, as in a competition. —**ju′ry·less,** *adj.*

ju·ry² (jōōr′ē), *adj.* *Naut.* makeshift or temporary, as for an emergency.

just (just), *adj.* **1.** adhering to what is fair, honest, and moral. **2.** rational and informed: *a just appraisal.* **3.** in accordance with correct princi-ples: *just proportions.* **4.** agreeable to truth or fact. **5.** given or awarded rightly. **6.** proper or right. —*adv.* **7.** within a brief preceding time: *The sun had just come out.* **8.** exactly or precisely. **9.** barely: *You've just missed seeing him.* **10.** merely: *just a tramp.* **11.** really or positively: *That's just splendid!* —**just′ly,** *adv.* —**just′ness,** *n.* —Syn. 1. honorable, righteous, upright.

jus·tice (jus′tis), *n.* **1.** rightfulness or lawfulness, as of a claim. **2.** the ad-ministering of deserved punishment or reward. **3.** the administration of what is just according to law. **4.** a judge or magistrate. **5.** do justice, a.

to treat justly or fairly. **b.** to appreciate properly.

jus′tice of the peace′, a local public officer having jurisdiction to try minor cases, administer oaths, or solemnize marriages.

jus·ti·fy (jus′tə fī′), v., **-fied, -fy·ing.** —v.t. **1.** to show to be just or right. **2.** to uphold as warranted or well-grounded. **3.** Theol. to absolve of guilt. —**jus′ti·fi′a·ble,** adj. —**jus′ti·fi′a·bly,** adv. —**jus′ti·fi·ca′tion,** n.

jut (jut), v., **jut·ted, jut·ting,** n. —v.i. **1.** to extend beyond the main body or line: land jutting out into the bay. —n. **2.** something that juts out. —**jut′ting·ly,** adv.

jute (jōōt), n. **1.** a strong, coarse fiber used for making burlap, gunny, etc., obtained from an East Indian plant. **2.** its plant.

juv., juvenile.

ju·ve·nile (jōō′və nəl, -nīl′), adj. **1.** characteristic of or suitable for young persons. **2.** immature or childish. —n. **3.** a young person. **4.** an actor who plays a youthful male role. **5.** a book for children.

ju′venile delin′quency, illegal or antisocial behavior on the part of a minor. —**ju′venile delin′quent.**

jux·ta·pose (juk′stə pōz′), v.t., **-posed, -pos·ing.** to place close together or side by side, as for contrast. —**jux′·ta·po·si′tion,** n.

JV, See junior varsity. Also, **J.V.**

K

K, k (kā), n., pl. **K's** or **Ks, k's** or **ks.** the 11th letter of the English alphabet, a consonant.

K, 1. Kelvin. **2.** kindergarten. **3.** Chess. King. **4.** potassium. [< NL kalium]

k., 1. karat. **2.** kilogram; kilograms. **3.** Chess. king. **4.** kitchen.

ka·bob (kə bob′), n. kebab.

ka·bu·ki (kä bōō′kē, kə-, kä′bōō kē), n. popular drama of Japan characterized by elaborate costuming, highly stylized acting, music, and dancing. [< Jap: singing-and-dancing art]

Kad·dish (kä′dish), n. Judaism. **1.** a liturgical prayer recited during each of the three daily services. **2.** the five-verse form of this prayer that is recited by mourners.

kaf·fee klatsch (kä′fä kläch′, klach′, -fē). See coffee klatsch.

kal·ser (kī′zər), n. a German emperor: the title used from 1871–1918.

kale (kāl), n. a cabbagelike plant having curled or wrinkled leaves. Also, **kail.**

ka·lei·do·scope (kə lī′də skōp′), n. **1.** an optical tube in which bits of glass and beads are shown in changing symmetrical forms by reflection in two or more mirrors as the tube is turned. **2.** anything that shifts continually. —**ka·lei′do·scop′ic** (-skop′ik), adj. —**ka·lei′do·scop′i·cal·ly,** adv.

ka·ma·ai·na (kä′mə ī′nə), n. a long-time resident of Hawaii.

kame (kām), n. a ridge or mound of stratified sand and gravel left by a retreating ice sheet.

ka·mi·ka·ze (kä′mə kä′zē), n. **1.** (in World War II) a member of a corps in the Japanese air force charged with the suicidal mission of crashing his aircraft into an enemy warship. **2.** the airplane used in such a mission.

kan·ga·roo (kang′gə rōō′), n., pl. **-roos, -roo.** a herbivorous marsupial of Australia and adjacent islands, having powerful hind legs used for leaping, and a long, thick tail.

kan′garoo court′, a self-appointed or irregular tribunal, usually disregarding existing principles of law, human rights, etc.

Kans., Kansas.

Kan·sas (kan′zəs), n. a state in the central United States. Cap.: Topeka.

Kan′sas Cit′y, 1. a city in W Missouri. **2.** a city in NE Kansas.

Kant (kant, känt), n. **Im·man·u·el** (i man′yōō əl), 1724–1804, German philosopher. —**Kant′i·an,** adj., n.

ka·o·lin (kā′ə lin), n. a fine white clay used in the manufacture of porcelain. Also, **ka′o·line.**

ka·pok (kā′pok, kap′ək), n. the silky down that covers the seeds of a tropical tree, used as stuffing for pillows, etc.

kap·pa (kap′ə), n. the 10th letter of the Greek alphabet (K, κ).

ka·put (kä pōōt′, -pōōt′, kə-), adj. Slang. ruined or done for.

Ka·ra·chi (kə rä′chē), n. a seaport in S Pakistan.

kar·a·kul (kar′ə kəl), n. **1.** an Asian sheep the young of which have black, glossy fleece. **2.** the fur from this fleece.

kar·at (kar′ət), *n.* a unit for measuring the fineness of gold, pure gold being 24 karats fine.

ka·ra·te (kə rä′tē), *n.* 1. a Japanese method of self-defense in which a person strikes sensitive areas on an attacker's body with the hands, elbows, knees, or feet. 2. a sport based on this. [< Jap: empty hands]

kar·ma (kär′mə), *n.* 1. *Hinduism, Buddhism.* action seen as bringing upon oneself inevitable results, good or bad, either in this life or in a reincarnation. 2. (loosely) fate or destiny. —**kar′mic,** *adj.*

karst (kärst), *n.* an area of limestone formations characterized by sinks, ravines, and underground streams.

kart (kärt), *n.* a small, low-slung motor vehicle, used for racing or recreation.

ka·sha (kä′shə), *n.* a cooked food prepared from hulled and crushed grain, esp. buckwheat. [< Russ]

ka·ty·did (kā′tē did), *n.* a large green American grasshopper, the male of which produces a characteristic song.

kay·ak (kī′ak), *n.* a narrow Eskimo boat with a skin cover on a light framework.

kay·o (kā′ō′), *n., pl.* **kay·os**, **kay·oed, kay·o·ing.** *Boxing Slang.* —*n.* 1. a knockout. —*v.t.* 2. to knock out.

ka·zoo (kə zōō′), *n.* a musical toy consisting of an open tube having a hole in the side covered with membrane, against which the performer sings or hums.

kc, kilocycle; kilocycles.

K.C., 1. Kansas City. 2. King's Counsel. 3. Knights of Columbus.

kc/s, kilocycles per second.

KD, 1. kiln-dried. 2. *Com.* knockdown.

Keats (kēts), *n.* **John,** 1795–1821, English poet.

ke·bab (kā′bob, kə bob′), *n.* Usually, **kebabs.** small pieces of meat, seasoned and broiled on a skewer. Also, **ke·bob′.**

kedge (kej), *v.,* **kedged, kedg·ing,** *n.* —*v.t., v.i.* 1. to pull (a vessel) along by hauling on its anchor cable. —*n.* 2. a small anchor used in kedging.

keel (kēl), *n.* 1. a central structural member in the bottom of a hull, extending from the stem to the stern. 2. *Bot., Zool.* a longitudinal ridge, as on a leaf or bone. 3. **on an even keel,** in a state of balance or stability. —*v.t., v.i.* 4. **keel over,** a. to capsize or overturn. b. to fall or faint, esp. without warning. —**keeled** (kēld), *adj.* **keel′less,** *adj.*

keen[1] (kēn), *adj.* 1. finely sharpened: *a keen edge.* 2. sharp, piercing, or biting: *a keen wind; keen satire.* 3. highly sensitive or perceptive: *a keen mind.* 4. intense: *keen competition.* 5. enthusiastic or ardent. 6. *Slang.* great or wonderful. —**keen′ly,** *adv.* —**keen′ness,** *n.* —**Syn.** 3. acute, discerning, penetrating.

keen[2] (kēn), *n.* (in Ireland) a wailing lament for the dead.

keep (kēp), *v.,* kept, **keep·ing,** *n.* —*v.t.* 1. to continue to hold as one's own: *If you like it, keep it.* 2. to have under one's care or in one's charge. 3. to have or maintain for continued enjoyment, use, or profit: *to keep cows; to keep a store.* 4. to cause to remain in a good condition, or in a specified condition: *to keep meat.* 5. to provide the livelihood of. 6. to cause to stay, as in a certain place: *Keep that dog in the yard.* 7. to maintain or cause to be or remain in a specified condition: *Keep that child quiet.* 8. to prevent or restrain: *Keep that child from yelling.* 9. to withhold from the knowledge of others: *to keep a secret.* 10. to record regularly: *to keep books.* 11. to protect, as from harm or injury. 12. to pay obedient regard to: *to keep a promise.* 13. to fulfill or follow: *to keep one's word.* 14. to observe with formalities or rites: *to keep Christmas.* —*v.i.* 15. to remain or continue as specified: *to keep cool.* 16. to continue as heretofore: *Keep trying.* 17. to remain free of deterioration. 18. to restrain oneself: *Try to keep from smiling.* 19. **keep to oneself,** to remain aloof from others. 20. **keep up,** a. to persist in doing or performing. b. to maintain in good condition. c. to compete successfully. d. to keep oneself informed. —*n.* 21. sustenance or support: *to work for one's keep.* 22. the most heavily fortified building of a medieval castle. 23. **for keeps,** *Informal.* a. with the intention of keeping one's winnings. b. permanently or forever. —**keep′er,** *n.*

keep·ing (kē′ping), *n.* 1. due conformity: *actions in keeping with promises.* 2. care or charge.

keep·sake (kēp′sāk′), *n.* anything kept, or given to be kept, as a token of friendship.

keg (keg), *n.* 1. a small cask. 2. a unit of weight, equal to 100 pounds, used for nails.

keg·ler (keg′lər), *n.* *Slang.* a participant in a bowling game.

kelp (kelp), *n.* 1. any of various large, brown seaweeds. 2. the ash of such seaweeds.

Kelt (kelt), *n.* Celt. —**Kelt′ic,** *n., adj.*

Kel·vin (kel′vin), *adj.* noting a scale of temperature in which 0° equals —273.16° Celsius.

ken (ken), *n.*, *v.*, **kenned** or **kent**, **kenning.** —*n.* 1. range of knowledge or understanding. —*v.t.* 2. *Chiefly Scot.* to know of or about.

Ken·ne·dy (ken'i dē), *n.* **John Fitzger·ald** (fits jer'əld), 1917–63, 35th president of the U.S. 1961–63.

ken·nel (ken'°l), *n.* 1. a house for a dog or dogs. 2. Often, **kennels.** an establishment where dogs are bred, trained, or boarded.

ke·no (kē'nō), *n.* a game of chance, adapted from lotto for gambling purposes.

Ken·tuck·y (kən tuk'ē), *n.* a state in the E central United States. *Cap.:* Frankfort. —**Ken·tuck'i·an**, *adj.*, *n.*

Kentuck'y blue'grass, a grass of the Mississippi valley, used for pasturage and hay.

Ken·ya (ken'yə, kēn'-), *n.* a country in E Africa. —**Ken'yan**, *adj.*, *n.*

kep·i (kā'pē, kep'ē), *n.* a French military cap with a flat, circular top and a visor.

Ke·pone (kē'pōn, -pən), *n.* *Trademark.* a highly toxic chemical pesticide said to contaminate waterways and cause severe nerve damage in humans.

kept (kept), *v.* 1. pt. and pp. of **keep.** —*adj.* 2. provided with financial support in return for sexual favors: *a kept woman.*

ker·a·tin (ker'ə tin), *n.* a fibrous and insoluble protein that is the principal component of horn, hair, nails, etc.

kerb (kûrb), *n.* *Brit.* curb (def. 1).

ker·chief (kûr'chif), *n.* 1. a woman's square scarf worn as a head or neck covering. 2. *Literary.* a handkerchief.

kerf (kûrf), *n.* a cut or incision made by a saw in a piece of wood.

ker·nel (kûr'n°l), *n.* 1. the softer edible part of a nut or the stone of a fruit. 2. a whole seed grain, as of corn. 3. the central part of anything.

ker·o·sene (ker'ə sēn', kar'-, ker'ə-sēn', kar'-), *n.* a white oily liquid obtained by distilling petroleum, used chiefly as a fuel, solvent, etc. Also, **ker'o·sine'.**

kes·trel (kes'trəl), *n.* a common small falcon notable for hovering in the air with its head to the wind.

ketch (kech), *n.* a sailing vessel rigged fore and aft on two masts.

ketch·up (kech'əp, kach'-), *n.* a seasoned sauce whose chief ingredient is usually tomatoes. [< Chin *ke-tsiap* pickled fish brine]

ket·tle (ket'°l), *n.* a metal container in which to boil liquids.

ket·tle·drum (ket'°l drum'), *n.* a drum consisting of a hollow hemisphere of brass or copper over which is stretched a skin.

key¹ (kē), *n.*, *pl.* **keys**, *adj.*, *v.*, **keyed**, **key·ing.** —*n.* 1. a metal instrument

inserted into a lock to move its bolt. 2. something that affords a means of access: *the key to happiness.* 3. something that affords a means of clarifying a problem. 4. a list of explanations, as of symbols or code words. 5. one of a set of levers or parts pressed in operating a typewriter or in playing a piano. 6. the principal tonality of a musical composition: *a symphony in the key of C minor.* 7. tone or pitch, as of voice. 8. mood or characteristic style, as of expression. 9. a device for opening and closing electrical contacts. —*adj.* 10. of cardinal importance. —*v.t.* 11. to adjust (speech, etc.) to a particular state. 12. *Music.* to regulate the pitch of. 13. to fasten or secure with a key. 14. to provide with a key or keys. 15. **key up,** to bring to a great intensity of feeling or energy. —**key'less,** *adj.*

key² (kē), *n.* a reef or low island.

key·board (kē'bōrd', -bôrd'), *n.* a row or set of keys, as on a piano, typewriter, etc.

key' club', a private nightclub to which each member has a door key.

key·hole (kē'hōl'), *n.* a hole in a lock for admitting its key.

key·note (kē'nōt'), *n.*, *v.*, **-not·ed, -not·ing.** —*n.* 1. *Music.* the note or tone on which a key or system of tones is founded. 2. the main idea or theme. —*v.t.* 3. to make a keynote address at. 4. *Music.* to give the keynote of. —**key'not·er**, *n.*

key'note address', a speech, as at a political convention, that presents important issues, principles, policies, etc. Also called **key'note speech'.**

key·punch (kē'punch'), *n.* 1. a machine, operated by a keyboard, for coding information by punching holes in cards for data processing. —*v.t.* 2. to punch holes in with a keypunch. —**key'punch'er**, *n.*

key·stone (kē'stōn'), *n.* 1. the wedge-shaped brick or stone at the summit of an arch. 2. something on which associated things depend.

key' word', a word that serves as a key, as to the meaning of another word, the composition of a cryptogram, etc.

kg, kilogram; kilograms.

KGB, the intelligence and internal-security agency of the Soviet government. [< Russ *K(omitat) G(osudarstvennoy) B(ezopasnosti)*, lit., Committee of State Security]

khak·i (kak'ē, kä'kē), *n.* 1. a dull yellowish brown. 2. a stout twilled cotton uniform cloth of this color. 3. **khakis,** a uniform made of khaki. —*adj.* 4. made of khaki. [< Urdu < Pers: dusty]

khan (kän, kan), *n.* **1.** a medieval ruler of the Tartar and Mongol tribes. **2.** a title of respect used in Iran, Afghanistan, Pakistan, India, etc.

Khar·kov (kär′kof, -kov), *n.* a city in the E Ukraine, in the S Soviet Union in Europe.

Khar·toum (kär tōōm′), *n.* the capital of Sudan.

khe·dive (kə dēv′), *n.* the title of the Turkish viceroys in Egypt from 1867 to 1914.

kHz, kilohertz.

KIA, *Mil.* killed in action.

kib·ble (kib′əl), *v.t.,* **-bled, -bling.** to grind into coarse particles.

kib·butz (ki bōōts′, -bōōts′), *n., pl.* **-but·zim** (-bōōt sēm′). a collective, chiefly agricultural settlement in Israel. [<Heb *quibbūs* gathering]

kib·itz·er (kib′it sər), *n. Informal.* a spectator, esp. at a card game, who gives unsolicited advice to the players. **—kib·itz** (kib′its), *v.i.*

ki·bosh (kī′bosh, ki bosh′), *n. Informal.* **put the kibosh on,** to render inactive or ineffective.

kick (kik), *v.t.* **1.** to strike with a motion of the foot. **2.** to propel or force by striking in such manner. **3.** *Football.* to score (a field goal) by dropkicking the ball. **—v.i. 4.** to make a striking motion with the foot. **5.** *Informal.* to object or complain. **6.** to recoil, as a gun when fired. **7.** *Football.* to make a kick. **8. kick in,** *Slang.* **a.** to contribute (one's share), esp. in money. **b.** to die. **9. kick off, a.** *Football.* to begin play or begin play again by a kickoff. **b.** *Informal.* to initiate. **10. kick over,** *Informal.* (of an internal-combustion engine) to begin ignition. **11. kick the habit,** to get over an addiction, habit, etc. **—n. 12.** the act or an instance of kicking. **13.** a recoil, as of a gun. **14.** *Informal.* an objection or complaint. **15.** *Slang.* **a.** pleasurable excitement. **b.** a strong but temporary interest. **16.** *Football.* **a.** an instance of kicking the ball. **b.** any method of kicking the ball: place kick. **c.** a kicked ball. **—kick·er,** *n.*

kick·back (kik′bak′), *n. Informal.* **1.** a rebate on profits given to the person who influenced a buyer. **2.** a vigorous response.

kick·off (kik′ôf′, -of′), *n.* **1.** *Football.* a kick with which play is begun. **2.** *Informal.* the start of something.

kick·shaw (kik′shô′), *n.* **1.** something showy but without value. **2.** *Archaic.* a tidbit or delicacy.

kick·stand (kik′stand′), *n.* a device for supporting upright a bicycle or motorcycle when not in use.

kick·y (kik′ē), *adj.,* **kick·i·er, kick·i·est.** *Slang.* sprightly, exciting, or charming.

kid[1] (kid), *n.* **1.** a young goat. **2.** Also called **kid′skin′** (-skin′). leather made from the skin of a kid or goat, used in making shoes and gloves. **3.** *Informal.* a child or young person. **—adj. 4.** made of kidskin. **5.** *Informal.* younger: his kid sister. **—kid′dish,** *adj.*

kid[2] (kid), *v.t., v.i.,* **kid·ded, kid·ding.** *Informal.* **1.** to tease or banter. **2.** to deceive as a joke. **—kid′der,** *n.* **—kid′ding·ly,** *adv.*

kid·dy (kid′ē), *n., pl.* **-dies.** *Informal.* a child. Also, **kid·die.**

kid·nap (kid′nap), *v.t.,* **-napped** or **-naped, -nap·ping** or **-nap·ing.** to abduct (a person) by force or fraud, esp. for ransom. **—kid′nap·per, kid′nap·er,** *n.*

kid·ney (kid′nē), *n., pl.* **-neys. 1.** either of a pair of small oval glandular organs in the back part of the abdominal cavity that excrete urine. **2.** *Informal.* kind or sort, esp. as regards disposition or temperament.

kid′ney bean′, the oval-shaped edible seed of a widely cultivated bean.

kid′ney stone′, a concretion abnormally formed in the kidney.

kid·vid (kid′vid′), *n. Slang.* television programs for children.

kiel·ba·sa (kil bä′sə, kēl-), *n., pl.* **-sas, -sy** (-sē). a smoked Polish sausage flavored with garlic.

kie·sel·guhr (kē′zəl gŏōr′), *n.* diatomite.

Ki·ev (kē′ef), *n.* the capital of the Ukraine in the SW Soviet Union in Europe. **—Ki·ev·an** (kē′ef ən, -even), *adj.*

kill (kil), *v.t.* **1.** to cause to die. **2.** to cause to be destroyed. **3.** to defeat or veto (a legislative bill, etc.). **4.** to cause to cease operating: to kill an engine. **5.** to while away (time) so as to avoid boredom or idleness. **6.** to cancel publication of. **—n. 7.** the act of killing, esp. game. **8.** an animal or animals killed. **9.** an aircraft, submarine, etc., destroyed in warfare. **—kill′er,** *n.* **—Syn. 1.** murder, slaughter, slay.

kill·deer (kil′dēr′), *n.* an American plover having two black bands around the upper breast.

kill·ing (kil′ing), *n.* **1.** the act of a person or thing that kills. **2.** *Informal.* a stroke of sizable profit or gain. **—adj. 3.** causing death. **4.** exhausting or tiring. **5.** *Informal.* irresistibly funny.

kill·joy (kil′joi′), *n.* a person or thing that spoils the joy or pleasure of others.

kiln (kil, kiln), *n.* a furnace for burning, baking, or drying something, esp. ceramic objects.

kil·o (kil′ō, kē′lō), *n., pl.* **kil·os. 1.** kilogram. **2.** kilometer.

kilo-, a combining form meaning "thousand": *kilowatt.*

kil·o·cy·cle (kil′ə sī′kəl), *n.* (formerly) kilohertz.

kil·o·gram (kil′ə gram′), *n.* a unit of mass and weight equal to 1000 grams, or 2.2046 pounds. Also, *Brit.*, **kil′o·gramme′.**

kil·o·hertz (kil′ə hûrts′), *n., pl.* **-hertz.** a unit of frequency equal to 1000 cycles per second.

ki·lom·e·ter (ki lom′i tər, kil′ə mē′-), *n.* a unit of length equal to 1000 meters, or 3280.8 feet. Also, *Brit.*, **kil′o·me′tre.**

kil·o·ton (kil′ə tun′), *n.* **1.** one thousand tons. **2.** an explosive force equal to that of 1000 tons of TNT.

kil·o·watt (kil′ə wot′), *n. Elect.* a unit of power equal to 1000 watts.

kil·o·watt-hour (kil′ə wot′our′, -ou′-ər), *n. Elect.* a unit of energy, equivalent to that expanded in one hour by one kilowatt of power.

kilt (kilt), *n.* a short, pleated skirt, esp. of tartan, worn by men in the Scottish Highlands.

kil·ter (kil′tər), *n. Informal.* good condition: *out of kilter.*

ki·mo·no (kə mō′nə, -nō), *n., pl.* **-nos. 1.** a loose, wide-sleeved Japanese robe, fastened at the waist with a wide sash. **2.** a woman's loose dressing gown.

kin (kin), *n.* **1.** a person's relatives collectively. **—adj. 2.** of the same family.

-kin, a suffix meaning "diminutive": *lambkin.*

kind¹ (kīnd), *adj.* **1.** gentle, tender, and good. **2.** showing or based on gentleness and consideration. **— Syn.** benevolent, considerate, humane.

kind² (kīnd), *n.* **1.** a class or group of individual objects, people, etc., of the same nature classified together because they have traits in common. **2.** distinctive nature or character. **3. in kind. a.** in something of the same category. **b.** in goods or services instead of money. **4. kind of,** *Informal.* somewhat. **5. of a kind,** of the same class, nature, etc. **—Usage 4.** KIND OF and SORT OF in this sense are often frowned upon because both phrases characterize vagueness in thinking and inadequacy in expression. If a person wishes to convey vagueness, he is better advised to use RATHER, QUITE, or SOMEWHAT.

kin·der·gar·ten (kin′dər gär′t°n, -d°n), *n.* a school or class for young children, usually four- to six-year-olds.

kin·der·gart·ner (kin′dər gärt′nər, -gärd′-), *n.* **1.** a kindergarten pupil. **2.** *Chiefly Brit.* a kindergarten teacher. Also, **kin′der·gar′ten·er.**

kind·heart·ed (kīnd′här′tid), *adj.* having or showing kindness. **—kind′-heart′ed·ly**, *adv.* **—kind′heart′ed·ness,** *n.*

kin·dle (kin′d°l), *v.,* **-dled, -dling. — *v.t.* 1.** to start (a fire). **2.** to excite or animate, as emotions or actions. **—*v.i.* 3.** to begin to burn. **4.** to become aroused or animated.

kin·dling (kind′ling), *n.* material that can be readily ignited, used in starting a fire.

kind·ly (kīnd′lē), *adj.,* **-li·er, -li·est,** *adv.* **—*adj.* 1.** having a kind disposition. **2.** pleasant or agreeable. — *adv.* **3.** in a kind manner. **4.** cordially or heartily. **5.** obligingly or accommodating: *Would you kindly close the door?* **—kind′li·ness,** *n.*

kind·ness (kīnd′nis), *n.* **1.** the state or quality of being kind. **2.** a kind act.

kin·dred (kin′drid), *n.* **1.** a body of persons related to another. **2.** kin. **—adj. 3.** of a related or similar nature or character. **—kin′dred·ness,** *n.*

kine (kīn), *n.pl. Archaic.* cows or cattle.

kin·e·mat·ics (kin′ə mat′iks, kī′nə-), *n.* the branch of mechanics that deals with pure motion, without reference to the masses or forces involved in it. **—kin′e·mat′ic, kin′e·mat′i·cal,** *adj.* **—kin′e·mat′i·cal·ly,** *adv.*

kin·e·scope (kin′i skōp′), *n.* **1.** See **picture tube. 2.** the motion-picture record of a television program.

ki·ne·sics (ki nē′siks, kī-), *n.* the study of body motion as related to speech. **—ki·ne′sic,** *adj.*

kin·es·the·sia (kin′is thē′zhə), *n.* the sensation of movement or strain in muscles, tendons, and joints. Also, **kin′es·the′sis. —kin′es·thet′ic** (-thet′-ik), *adj.*

ki·net·ic (ki net′ik, kī-), *adj.* of or caused by motion.

kinet′ic en′ergy, the energy of a body with respect to the motion of the body.

ki·net·ics (ki net′iks, kī-), *n.* the branch of mechanics that deals with the actions of forces in producing or changing the motion of masses.

kin·folk (kin′fōk′), *n.pl.* relatives or kindred. Also, **kin′folks′.**

king (king), *n.* **1.** a male sovereign or monarch. **2.** a person or thing preeminent in its class: *an oil king.* **3.** a playing card bearing a picture of a king. **4.** *Chess.* the chief piece capable of moving one square at a time in any direction. **—king′less,** *adj.* **—king′ly,** *adj.* **—king′li·ness,** *n.* **—king′ship,** *n.*

King (king), *n.* **Martin Luther, Jr.,** 1929–68, U.S. minister and civil-rights leader.

king·dom (king'dəm), *n.* **1.** a country having a king or queen as its head. **2.** anything conceived as constituting an independent entity: *the kingdom of thought.* **3.** one of the three great divisions of natural objects, the animal, vegetable, and mineral.

king·fish·er (king'fish'ər), *n.* a fish- or insect-eating bird having a large head and a long, stout bill.

King' James' Ver'sion. See Author- ized Version. Also called **King' James'' Bi'ble.**

king·let (king'lit), *n.* **1.** a king ruling over a small country. **2.** a small, greenish, crested bird.

king·pin (king'pin'), *n.* **1.** *Bowling.* the pin at the center. **2.** *Informal.* the person of chief importance in an undertaking. **3.** one of two pivots on which the front wheels of a motor vehicle turn in steering.

king-size (king'siz'), *adj.* **1.** larger than the usual size. **2.** (of a bed) extra large, usually at least 78 × 80 inches. **3.** of or for a king-size bed. Also, **king'-sized'.**

kink (kingk), *n.* **1.** a twist or curl, as in a rope or hair. **2.** a muscular stiffness or soreness, as in the neck or back. **3.** a flaw or imperfection likely to hinder the successful oper- ation of something, as a plan. **4.** a mental twist. —*v.t., v.i.* **5.** to form or cause to form a kink or kinks. —**kink'y,** *adj.* —**kink'i·ness,** *n.*

kin·ka·jou (king'kə jōō'), *n.* a brown- ish mammal of Central and South America related to the raccoon.

kins·folk (kinz'fōk'), *n.pl.* kinfolk.

kin·ship (kin'ship), *n.* **1.** family rela- tionship. **2.** relationship by nature, qualities, etc.

kins·man (kinz'mən), *n.* a blood rel- ative, esp. a male. —**kins'wom'an,** *n.fem.*

ki·osk (kē osk', ki'osk), *n.* an open circular pavilion used as a band- stand, newsstand, etc. [< F *kiosque* stand in a public park < Turk *köşk* villa < Pers *kūshk* garden pavilion]

Ki·o·wa (ki'ə wə), *n., pl.* -was, -wa. a member of an Indian people of the southwestern U.S.

kip¹ (kip), *n.* the hide of a young or small beast.

kip² (kip), *n.* the monetary unit of Laos.

kip·per (kip'ər), *v.t.* **1.** to cure (her- ring, etc.) by salting and drying in the air or in smoke. —*n.* **2.** a kip- pered fish, esp. a herring.

kirk (kûrk; *Scot.* kirk), *n. Scot. and North Eng.* a church.

kir·tle (kûr'tl), *n.* a woman's loose gown worn in the Middle Ages.

kis·met (kiz'mit, kis'-), *n.* (in Islam) fate or destiny.

kiss (kis), *v.t., v.i.* **1.** to touch or press with the lips in token of greeting, affection, etc. **2.** to touch gently or lightly. —*n.* **3.** the act or an instance of kissing. **4.** a slight touch or con- tact. **5.** any of various small candies. —**kiss'a·ble,** *adj.*

kiss·er (kis'ər), *n.* **1.** a person or thing that kisses. **2.** *Slang.* **a.** the face. **b.** the mouth.

kiss'ing disease', *Slang.* an acute, in- fectious form of mononucleosis characterized esp. by swollen lymph nodes of the neck.

kit (kit), *n.* **1.** a set of tools or sup- plies for performing certain kinds of jobs. **2.** a container for these. **3.** a set of materials or parts from which something can be assembled: *a model kit.* **4.** the whole kit and ca- boodle, *Informal.* the whole lot of certain persons or things.

kitch·en (kich'ən), *n.* **1.** a room or place equipped for cooking. **2.** the staff or equipment of this place.

kitch·en·ette (kich'ə net'), *n.* a very small, compact kitchen. Also, **kitch'- en·et'.**

kitch'en police', *Mil.* **1.** duty as as- sistant to the cooks. **2.** soldiers de- tailed to assist in kitchen duties.

kitch·en·ware (kich'ən wâr'), *n.* cook- ing equipment or utensils.

kite (kit), *n.* **1.** a light frame covered with some thin material, to be flown in the wind at the end of a long string. **2.** a small bird of the hawk family having long, pointed wings. —**kit'er,** *n.*

kith' and kin' (kith), acquaintances and relatives.

kitsch (kich), *n.* art or literature of little or no value. —**kitsch'y,** *adj.*

kit·ten (kit'ən), *n.* a young cat. — **kit'ten·ish,** *adj.* —**kit'ten·ish·ly,** *adv.*

kit·ty¹ (kit'ē), *n., pl.* -ties. **1.** a kitten. **2.** a pet name for a cat.

kit·ty² (kit'ē), *n., pl.* -ties. a pool or reserve of money for some particular purpose.

kit·ty-cor·nered (kit'ē kôr'nərd), *adj., adv. Informal.* cater-cornered. Also, **kit'ty-cor'ner.**

ki·wi (kē'wē), *n.* a grayish-brown flightless bird of New Zealand.

K.J.V., King James Version.

KKK, See **Ku Klux Klan.** Also, **K.K.K.**

Klan (klan), *n.* **1.** See **Ku Klux Klan.** **2.** a chapter of the Ku Klux Klan. — **Klan'ism,** *n.*

klep·to·ma·ni·a (klep'tə mā'nē ə, -mān'yə), *n.* an irresistible impulse to steal, stemming from emotional disturbance. —**klep'to·ma'ni·ac',** *n., adj.*

klieg' light' (klēg), a powerful flood- light with an arc-light source, used esp. in motion-picture studios. Also, **kleig' light'.**

km., kilometer; kilometers. Also, **km kn,** knots; knots.

knack (nak), *n.* **1.** an ability to do a thing easily and well, usually in social situations. **2.** expedient cleverness. —*Syn.* **1.** aptitude, talent.

knack·wurst (nok′wûrst, -wŏŏrst), *n.* a short, thick, highly seasoned sausage.

knap·sack (nap′sak′), *n.* a leather or canvas case for carrying clothes and other supplies on the back.

knave (nāv), *n.* **1.** *Cards.* jack (def. 2). **2.** *Obsolesc.* an unprincipled or dishonest person. —**knav′er·y,** *n.* —**knav′ish,** *adj.* —**knav′ish·ly,** *adv.*

knead (nēd), *v.t.* **1.** to work (dough, clay, etc.) into a uniform mixture by pressing and stretching. **2.** to manipulate by similar movements, as the body in a massage. —**knead′er,** *n.*

knee (nē), *n., v.,* **kneed, knee·ing.** —*n.* **1.** the joint between the thighbone and the lower part of the human leg. **2.** something resembling a bent knee. —*v.t.* **3.** to strike with the knee.

knee·cap (nē′kap′), *n.* the patella.

knee·cap·ping (nē′kap′ing), *n. Slang.* a shooting in the legs in order to maim a person, esp. as a tactic of some terrorist groups.

knee-deep (nē′dēp′), *adj.* **1.** so deep as to reach the knees. **2.** embroiled or involved.

knee·hole (nē′hōl′), *n.* a space for the knees, as under a desk.

kneel (nēl), *v.i.* **knelt** (nelt) or **kneeled, kneel·ing.** to fall or rest on the knees or a knee.

knell (nel), *n.* **1.** the sound made by a bell rung slowly for a death or a funeral. **2.** a sound or sign indicating the end or failure of something. —*v.i.* **3.** to sound, as a funeral bell. **4.** to give forth an ominous sound. —*v.t.* **5.** to proclaim or summon as by a bell.

knew (nŏŏ, nyŏŏ), *v.* pt. of **know.**

knick·ers (nik′erz), *n.* loose-fitting short trousers gathered in at the knee. Also, **knick′er·bock′ers** (-bok′erz).

knick·knack (nik′nak′), *n.* a bit of bric-a-brac.

knife (nīf), *n., pl.* **knives** (nīvz), *v.,* **knifed, knif·ing.** —*n.* **1.** a cutting instrument having a thin, sharp-edged blade fitted with a handle. **2.** any blade for cutting, as in a machine. **3. under the knife,** undergoing surgery. —*v.t.* **4.** to cut or stab with a knife. **5.** *Informal.* to attempt to defeat in an underhanded way.

knight (nīt), *n.* **1.** *Medieval Hist.* **a.** a man, usually of noble birth, raised to honorable military rank and bound to chivalrous conduct. **b.** a mounted soldier serving under a feudal superior. **2.** a man honored by a sovereign because of personal merit or for services rendered to the country and in Great Britain holding the rank next below that of a baronet. **3.** *Chess.* a piece shaped like a horse's head. **4.** a member of any of various orders or associations. —*v.t.* **5.** to dub or make (a man) a knight. —**knight′ly,** *adj.*

knight-er·rant (nīt′er′ənt), *n., pl.* **knights-er·rant.** a medieval knight who traveled in search of adventures.

knight·hood (nīt′hŏŏd), *n.* **1.** the rank, dignity, or vocation of a knight. **2.** knightly character or qualities. **3.** the body of knights.

knish (knish), *n.* a thick patty, as of mashed potato or chopped beef, enclosed in a thin wrapper of dough and fried or baked.

knit (nit), *v.,* **knit·ted** or **knit, knit·ting,** *n.* —*v.t., v.i.* **1.** to make (a garment, fabric, etc.) by joining loops of yarn with needles. **2.** to join closely and firmly together, as members or parts. **3.** to contract into folds or wrinkles: *to knit the brow.* —*n.* **4.** a knitted fabric or garment. **5.** a basic stitch in knitting. —**knit′ter,** *n.*

knit·wear (nit′wâr′), *n.* clothing made of knitted fabric.

knob (nob), *n.* **1.** a rounded handle of a door, drawer, etc. **2.** a rounded lump or protuberance on a surface. **3.** a rounded hill or mountain. —**knobbed,** *adj.* —**knob′by,** *adj.* —**knob′bi·ness,** *n.*

knock (nok), *v.i.* **1.** to strike a sounding blow. **2.** to make a pounding noise: *The engine of our car is knocking badly.* **3.** to strike in collision: *He knocked right into a table.* —*v.t.* **4.** to give a sounding blow to. **5.** to drive or force by striking. **6.** to make by striking: *to knock a hole in the door.* **7.** to strike (a thing) against something else. **8.** *Informal.* to criticize, esp. in a carping manner. **9. knock around** or **about,** *Slang.* **a.** to wander aimlessly. **b.** to mistreat (someone), esp. physically. **10. knock down, a.** to signify the sale of (an article) at auction. **b.** *Com.* to take apart for facility in handling. **c.** *Slang.* to receive, as a salary. **d.** *Informal.* to lower the price of. **11. knock off,** *Slang.* **a.** to cease activity, esp. work. **b.** to dispose of or finish. **c.** to murder or kill. **d.** to get rid of. **e.** to disable or defeat. **12. knock out, a.** to defeat (an opponent) by a knockout. **b.** to render unconscious. **c.** to render exhausted or tired. **13. knock together,** to make or construct in a hurry. —*n.* **14.** the act or sound of knocking. **15.** a rap, as at a door. **16.** a blow or thump. **17.** *Informal.* an adverse criticism. **18.** a pounding noise in an engine.

knock·down (nok′doun′), *adj.* **1.** capable of knocking down or overwhelming. **2.** that can readily be taken apart for easy storage, shipping, etc.

knock·er (nok′ər), *n.* **1.** a person or thing that knocks. **2.** a hinged knob or bar on a door, for use in knocking.

knock-knee (nok′nē′), *n.* inward curvature of the legs at the knees. —**knock′-kneed′**, *adj.*

knock·out (nok′out′), *n.* **1.** the act of knocking out or state of being knocked out. **2.** *Boxing.* a blow that knocks an opponent to the canvas and makes him unable to rise within 10 seconds. **3.** *Informal.* a person or thing overwhelmingly successful or attractive.

knock·wurst (nok′wûrst, -wŏŏrst), *n.* knackwurst.

knoll (nōl), *n.* a small, rounded hill.

knot (not), *n.*, *v.*, **knot·ted, knot·ting.** —*n.* **1.** an interlacing of a cord, rope, etc., drawn tight into a knob or lump. **2.** a bow of ribbon used or worn as an ornament. **3.** a group or cluster of persons or things. **4.** a protuberance on or in a part or process, as in a muscle. **5.** the hard, cross-grained mass of wood at the place where a branch joins the trunk of a tree. **6.** the part of this mass showing in a piece of lumber. **7.** *Naut.* a unit of speed equal to one nautical mile or about 1.15 statute miles per hour. **8.** a complicated problem. **9.** a bond or tie: *the knot of matrimony.* **10.** tie the knot, *Informal.* to marry. —*v.t.*, *v.i.* **11.** to form a knot (in). **12.** to make or become entangled.

knot·hole (not′hōl′), *n.* a hole in a board or plank formed by the falling out of a knot.

knot·ty (not′ē), *adj.*, **-ti·er, -ti·est. 1.** having knots. **2.** intricate or difficult: *a knotty problem.* —**knot′ti·ly,** *adv.* —**knot′ti·ness,** *n.*

knout (nout), *n.* a whip formerly used in Russia for flogging criminals.

know (nō), *v.*, **knew, known** (nōn), **know·ing,** *n.* —*v.t.* **1.** to perceive or understand clearly and with certainty. **2.** to have fixed in the mind or memory. **3.** to be aware of. **4.** to be acquainted with, as by sight. **5.** to understand from experience or attainment: *to know how to make something.* **6.** to be able to distinguish, as one from another. —*v.i.* **7.** to have knowledge, as of fact. **8.** to have information, as about something. —*n.* **9. in the know,** *Informal.* having inside information. —**know′a·ble,** *adj.* —**know′er,** *n.*

know-how (nō′hou′), *n.* knowledge of how to do something.

know·ing (nō′ing), *adj.* **1.** having knowledge or information. **2.** suggesting secret or special knowledge: *a knowing glance.* **3.** deliberate or intentional. —**know′ing·ly,** *adv.* —**know′ing·ness,** *n.* —**Syn. 1.** astute, intelligent, shrewd, wise.

know-it-all (nō′it ôl′), *n. Informal.* a person who acts as though he or she alone knows everything. Also called **know′-all′** (-ôl′).

knowl·edge (nol′ij), *n.* **1.** acquaintance or familiarity gained by experience. **2.** the fact or state of knowing. **3.** what is or may be known. **4.** the sum of what is known. **5.** the body of truths or facts accumulated by mankind.

knowl·edge·a·ble (nol′i jə bəl), *adj.* possessing knowledge or understanding. —**knowl′edge·a·bly,** *adv.*

Knox·ville (noks′vil), *n.* a city in E Tennessee.

Knt., Knight.

knuck·le (nuk′əl), *n.*, *v.*, **-led, -ling.** —*n.* **1.** a joint of a finger, esp. one of the joints at the roots of the fingers. —*v.t.* **2.** to rub or press with the knuckles. **3. knuckle down,** to apply oneself vigorously. **4. knuckle under,** to submit or yield.

knuck·le·bone (nuk′əl bōn′), *n.* a bone forming a knuckle of a finger.

knuck·le·head (nuk′əl hed′), *n. Informal.* a stupid, inept person.

knurl (nûrl), *n.* a small ridge or bead, esp. one of a series, as on the edge of a thumbscrew to assist in obtaining a firm grip. —**knurled** (nûrld), *adj.*

KO (kā′ō′), *n.*, *pl.* **KO's** *v.*, **KO'd, KO′ing.** *Boxing Slang.* —*n.* **1.** a knockout. —*v.t.* **2.** to knock out. Also, **K.O., k.o.**

ko·a·la (kō ä′lə), *n.* a sluggish, tailless, gray, furry marsupial of Australia. Also called **koa′la bear′.**

ko·bold (kō′bold, -bōld), *n.* (in German folklore) a mischievous spirit or goblin that haunts houses.

K. of C., Knights of Columbus.

kohl·ra·bi (kōl rä′bē, kōl′rä′-), *n.*, *pl.* **-bies.** a plant whose stem above ground swells into an edible bulblike formation.

ko·la (kō′lə), *n.* cola[1].

ko′la nut′, the caffeine-containing seed of a tall tree native to western tropical Africa, used in soft drinks.

ko·lin·sky (kə lin′skē), *n.*, *pl.* **-skies.** the fur of an Asian mink.

kook (kŏŏk), *n. Slang.* an unusual, peculiar, or foolish person. —**kook′y, kook′ie,** *adj.* —**kook′i·ness,** *n.*

ko·peck (kō′pek), *n.* a money of account of the Soviet Union, the 100th part of a ruble. Also, **ko′pek.**

Ko·ran (kō rän′, -ran′, kō-), *n.* the sacred book of Islam, regarded by Muslims as the foundation of religion, law, and culture. [< Ar *qur′ān* book, reading]

Ko·re·a (kō rē′ə, kō-), *n.* a peninsula SE of Manchuria divided at 38° N into two countries (**North′ Kore′a** and **South′ Kore′a**). —**Ko·re′an,** *adj., n.*

ko·ru·na (kôr′ə nä′), *n., pl.* **ko·ru·ny** (kôr′ə nē), **ko·ru·nas.** the monetary unit of Czechoslovakia.

ko·sher (kō′shər), *adj.* **1.** fit or allowed to be eaten according to Jewish dietary laws. **2.** adhering to these laws.

kow·tow (kou′tou′, -tou′, kō′-), *v.i.* **1.** to touch the forehead to the ground while kneeling, as an act of worship, reverence, etc., esp. in former Chinese custom. **2.** to act in an obsequious manner. —*n.* **3.** the act of kowtowing. [< Chin: lit., knock (one's head] —**kow′tow′er,** *n.*

K.P., See kitchen police. Also, **KP**

K.P.H., kilometers per hour. Also, **KPH, k.p.h., kph**

Kr, krypton.

kraal (kräl), *n.* **1.** a village of South African natives. **2.** an enclosure for livestock in southern Africa.

kraut (krout), *n.* sauerkraut.

Krem·lin (krem′lin), *n.* **1.** the executive branch of the government of the Soviet Union. **2.** the citadel of Moscow, including within its walls the chief offices of the Soviet government.

Krem·lin·ol·o·gy (krem′li nol′ə jē), *n.* the study of the government and policies of the Soviet Union. —**Krem′lin·ol′o·gist,** *n.*

Krish·na (krish′nə), *n.* an avatar of Vishnu and one of the most popular of Hindu deities.

kro·na (krō′nə), *n., pl.* **-nor** (-nôr), the monetary unit of Sweden.

kró·na (krō′nə), *n., pl.* **kró·nur** (krō′-nər). the monetary unit of Iceland.

kro·ne (krō′nə), *n., pl.* **-ner** (-nər). the monetary unit of Denmark and Norway.

kryp·ton (krip′ton), *n. Chem.* an inert gaseous element, present in very small amounts in the atmosphere: used in high-power light bulbs. *Symbol:* Kr; *at. wt.:* 83.80; *at. no.:* 36.

KS, Kansas.

Kt, *Chess.* knight.

kt., karat.

ku·chen (kōō′ĸнən), *n.* a yeast-raised coffee cake, usually including fruit. [< G: cake]

ku·dos (kōō′dōz, -dōs, -dos, kyōō′-), *n.* praise and glory for an accomplishment.

kud·zu (kōōd′zōō), *n.* a fast-growing climbing vine of China and Japan, now widespread in the southern U.S.: used for fiber, as food and forage, and to prevent soil erosion.

Ku Klux Klan (kōō′ kluks′ klan′, kyōō′), **1.** a secret, chiefly antiblack, terrorist organization in the southern U.S., active for several years after the Civil War. **2.** a secret organization inspired by the former, founded in 1915 and professing Americanism as its object.

ku·lak (kōō läk′, kōō′läk), *n.* a comparatively wealthy Russian peasant whose class stood in the way of collectivized agriculture in the 1920-30's.

kum·quat (kum′kwot), *n.* a small, round or oblong citrus fruit having a sweet rind and acid pulp.

kung fu (kung′ fōō′, gung′-), an ancient Chinese method of self-defense involving soft, fluid movements of hands and legs. [< Chin: accomplished technique]

Ku·wait (kōō wāt′, -wīt′), *n.* a country in NE Arabia.

kW, kilowatt; kilowatts. Also, **kw**

kwa·cha (kwä′chä′), *n.* the monetary unit of Zambia.

Kwang·chow (gwäng′jō′), *n.* a seaport in SE China.

kwash·i·or·kor (kwash′ē ôr′kôr, -kər, kwä′shē-), *n.* a nutritional disease of infants and children, occurring chiefly in Africa, associated with lack of protein.

kWh, kilowatt-hour. Also, **kwhr, K.W.H.**

KY, Kentucky. Also, **Ky.**

kyat (kyät, kē ät′), *n.* the monetary unit of Burma.

Kyo·to (kē ō′tō; *Jap.* kyô′tô), *n.* a city in central Japan.

Kyu·shu (kyōō′shōō), *n.* an island in SW Japan.

L

L, l (el), *n., pl.* **L's** or **Ls, l's** or **ls. 1.** the 12th letter of the English alphabet, a consonant. **2.** something having the shape of an l.

L, 1. large. **2.** *Brit.* pound; pounds. **3.** the Roman numeral for 50.

L., 1. Lake. **2.** Latin. **3.** latitude.

l., 1. left. **2.** length. **3.** *pl.* **ll.,** line. **4.** liter; liters.

la (lä), *n. Music.* the sixth tone of a diatonic scale.

La, lanthanum.

LA, Louisiana. Also, **La.**

L.A., 1. Law Agent. **2.** Los Angeles.

lab (lab), *n. Informal.* a laboratory.

Lab., Labrador.

lab., laboratory.

la·bel (lā′bəl), *n., v.,* **-beled, -bel·ing** or **-belled, -bel·ling. —n. 1.** a slip bearing information or identification concerning something to which it is attached. **2.** a descriptive word or phrase. **—v.t. 3.** to affix a label to. **4.** to designate or describe by or as by a label. **—la′bel·er, la′bel·ler,** *n.*

la·bi·al (lā′bē əl), *adj.* **1.** of the lips or labia. **2.** *Phonet.* involving lip articulation, as *p, v, m, w.* **—la′bi·al·ly,** *adv.*

la·bi·a ma·jo·ra (lā′bē ə mə jôr′ə, -jōr′ə), the outer folds of skin bordering the vulva.

la·bi·a mi·no·ra (lā′bē ə mi nôr′ə, -ōr′ə), the inner folds of skin bordering the vulva.

la·bile (lā′bil, -bīl), *adj.* apt to change, esp. chemically.

la·bi·um (lā′bē əm), *n., pl.* **-bi·a** (-bē ə). **1.** a lip or liplike part. **2.** any of the folds of skin bordering the vulva.

la·bor (lā′bər), *n.* **1.** productive activity, esp. for the sake of economic gain. **2.** the body or organizations of persons engaged in such activity, esp. as distinguished from management and capital. **3.** a job or task done or to be done. **4.** the pains and efforts of childbirth. **—v.i. 5.** to perform labor. **6.** to strive, as toward a goal. **7.** to act at a disadvantage: *to labor under a misapprehension.* **8.** to be in childbirth. **—v.t. 9.** to develop in excessive detail. Also, *Brit.,* **la′bour. —la′bor·er,** *n.* **—la′bor·ing·ly,** *adv.*

lab·o·ra·to·ry (lab′rə tôr′ē, -tōr′ē, lab′-ər ə-), *n., pl.* **-ries.** a place for scientific experiments, tests, or investigations.

La′bor Day′, a legal holiday, the first Monday in September, in honor of labor.

la·bored (lā′bərd), *adj.* **1.** done or made with difficulty: *labored breathing.* **2.** lacking spontaneity. **—la′bored·ly,** *adv.*

la·bo·ri·ous (lə bôr′ē əs, -bōr′-), *adj.* **1.** requiring much labor or exertion. **2.** diligent in labor. **—la·bo′ri·ous·ly,** *adv.* **—Syn. 1.** arduous, difficult. **2.** hardworking, industrious.

la′bor-sav·ing (lā′bər sā′viŋ), *adj.* made to reduce the work required.

la′bor un′ion, an organization of workers for mutual aid and protection, esp. by collective bargaining.

Lab·ra·dor (lab′rə dôr′), *n.* **1.** a peninsula in NE Canada, between the Hudson Bay and the Atlantic. **2.** the portion of Newfoundand in its E part.

lab·ra·dor·ite (lab′rə dô rīt′, lab′rə-dôr′īt), *n.* a feldspar characterized by a brilliant change of colors.

la·bur·num (lə bûr′nəm), *n.* a small leguminous tree having pendulous clusters of yellow flowers.

lab·y·rinth (lab′ə rinth), *n.* a system of many twisting passages or paths out of which it is hard to find one's way. **—lab′y·rin′thine** (-rin′thin, -thēn), *adj.*

lac (lak), *n.* a resinous substance deposited on various trees in southern Asia by a scale insect: used chiefly in producing shellac.

lac·co·lith (lak′ə lith), *n.* a mass of igneous rock formed from lava that has forced overlying strata upward.

lace (lās), *n., v.,* **laced, lac·ing. —n. 1.** a netlike ornamental fabric of threads. **2.** a cord or string for holding or drawing together two flaps, being passed through holes in their edges. **—v.t. 3.** to fasten by means of a lace. **4.** to pass (a cord, etc.), as through holes. **5.** to adorn with lace. **6.** to interlace or intertwine. **7.** *Informal.* to lash or thrash. **8.** to add a small amount of liquor to (food or drink). **—v.i. 9.** to be fastened with a lace. **10. lace into,** to attack physically or verbally. **—lac′er,** *n.* **—lac′y,** *adj.* **—lac′i·ness,** *n.*

lac·er·ate (las′ə rāt′), *v.t.,* **-at·ed, -at·ing,** to tear roughly. **—lac′er·a′tion,** *n.* **—lac′er·a′tive,** *adj.*

lace·wing (lās′wiŋ′), *n.* any of several insects having delicate, lacelike wings.

lach·ry·mal (lak′rə məl), *adj.* **1.** of or producing tears. **2.** lacrimal (def. 1).

lach·ry·mose (lak′rə mōs′), *adj. Literary.* **1.** given to shedding tears. **2.** tending to cause tears.

lack (lak), *n.* **1.** deficiency or absence of something wanted. **2.** something wanted that is insufficient or absent. —*v.i., v.t.* **3.** to be wanting or deficient (in).

lack·a·dai·si·cal (lak′ə dā′zi kəl), *adj.* without vigor, interest, or enthusiasm. —**lack′a·dai′si·cal·ly,** *adv.*

lack·ey (lak′ē), *n., pl.* **-eys. 1.** a servile follower. **2.** a liveried manservant.

lack·lus·ter (lak′lus′tər), *adj.* lacking brilliance or vitality. Also, *Brit.,* **lack′lus′tre.**

la·con·ic (lə kon′ik), *adj.* brief to the point of curtness. —**la·con′i·cal·ly,** *adv.* —**Syn.** concise, succinct, terse.

lac·quer (lak′ər), *n.* **1.** any of various fast-drying resinous or synthetic coatings, used to produce a highly polished, lustrous surface on woods, metals, and porcelain. —*v.t.* **2.** to coat with lacquer. —**lac′quer·er,** *n.*

lac·ri·mal (lak′rə məl), *adj.* **1.** of or situated near the organs that secrete tears. **2.** lachrymal (def. 1).

la·crosse (lə krôs′, -kros′), *n.* a game played by two teams with a ball and long-handled, netted rackets. [< Can F: lit., the crook]

lac·tate (lak′tāt), *v.i., v.t.,* **-tat·ed, -tat·ing.** to produce or secrete milk. —**lac·ta′tion,** *n.*

lac·te·al (lak′tē əl), *adj.* consisting of or resembling milk. —**lac′te·al·ly,** *adv.*

lac·tic (lak′tik), *adj.* of or obtained from milk.

lac′tic ac′id, a colorless or yellowish liquid found in sour milk, used chiefly in food and medicine.

lac·tose (lak′tōs), *n.* a sweet, white, crystalline substance present in milk, used in infant feedings, etc.

la·cu·na (lə kyōō′nə), *n., pl.* **-nae** (-nē) **-nas.** an empty or missing part, esp. in an ancient manuscript.

lad (lad), *n.* a boy or youth.

lad·der (lad′ər), *n.* **1.** a device for climbing, formed of a number of rungs or steps between uprights. **2.** a series of levels, stages, ranks, etc.

lad·die (lad′ē), *n. Chiefly Scot.* a young lad.

lade (lād), *v.t., v.i.,* **lad·ed, lad·en** or **lad·ed, lad·ing.** *Archaic.* **1.** to load (a ship or cargo). **2.** to ladle (water or liquid).

lad·en (lād′ᵊn), *adj.* **1.** loaded, as with cargo. **2.** *Literary.* heavily or painfully burdened: *laden with sin.* —*v.* **3.** a pp. of **lade.**

la·di·da (lä′dē dä′), *adj. Informal.* affected or pretentious: *a la-di-da manner.* Also, **la′-de-da′.**

lad·ing (lā′diñg), *n.* a load or cargo (*rare,* except in combination): *bill of lading.*

la·dle (lād′ᵊl), *n., v.,* **-dled, -dling.** —*n.* **1.** a long-handled utensil with a cup-shaped bowl for dipping or conveying liquids. —*v.t.* **2.** to dip or convey with a ladle. —**la′dler,** *n.*

la·dy (lā′dē), *n., pl.* **-dies. 1.** a woman of good family, social position, breeding, etc. **2.** a polite term for any woman. **3.** any woman or girl: *a cleaning lady.* **4.** (*cap.*) a British title of rank for the wives or daughters of certain nobles. **4.** *Archaic.* a wife.

la·dy·bug (lā′dē bug′), *n.* any of numerous, often brightly colored beetles feeding chiefly on aphids and other small insects. Also called **la′dy bee′tle, la′dy·bird′** (lā′dē bûrd′).

la·dy·fin·ger (lā′dē fiñ′gər), *n.* a small, finger-shaped sponge cake.

la·dy-in-wait·ing (lā′dē in wā′tiñg), *n., pl.* **la·dies-in-wait·ing.** a lady who is in attendance upon a queen or princess.

la·dy·like (lā′dē līk′), *adj.* appropriate to a lady.

la·dy·love (lā′dē luv′), *n. Literary.* a sweetheart.

la·dy·ship (lā′dē ship′), *n.* **1.** (*often cap.*) the form used in speaking of or to a woman having the title of *Lady* (usually prec. by *her* or *your*). **2.** the rank of a lady.

la·dy's-slip·per (lā′dēz slip′ər), *n.* an orchid having flowers somewhat resembling a slipper. Also, **la′dy-slip′per.**

la·e·trile (lā′ə tril′), *n.* a controversial drug prepared from the pits of apricots or peaches, claimed to cure cancer.

La·fa·yette (laf′ē et′, lä′fē-), *n.* **Marquis de,** 1757–1834, French soldier and statesman who served in the American Revolutionary Army.

lag (lag), *v.,* **lagged, lag·ging,** *n.* —*v.i.* **1.** to fail to maintain a speed or pace. **2.** to lose strength or intensity. —*n.* **3.** an instance of lagging. **4.** an amount of lagging. **5.** an interval or lapse of time.

la·ger (lä′gər, lô′-), *n.* a dry, light beer aged up to six months before use. Also called **la′ger beer′.**

lag·gard (lag′ərd), *n.* **1.** a person or thing that lags. **2.** any economic or financial sector whose recovery has not kept pace with the general improving market. —*adj.* **3.** moving or responding slowly. —**lag′gard·ly,** *adv., adj.* —**lag′gard·ness,** *n.*

la·gniappe (lan yap′, lan′yap), *n.* **1.** *Chiefly Southern U.S.* a small gift given with a purchase to a customer. **2.** something given as an extra. Also, **la·gnappe′.**

lagoon (lə gōōn′), *n.* **1.** an area of shallow water separated from the sea by low banks, as in an atoll. **2.** any small, pondlike body of water, esp. one connected with a larger body of water. —**la·goon′al,** *adj.*

La·hore (lə hōr′, -hôr′), *n.* a city in NE Pakistan.

laid (lād), *v.* pt. and pp. of lay¹.

laid-back (lād′bak′), *adj. Slang.* 1. relaxed and unhurried. 2. feeling no psychological pressure.

lain (lān), *v.* pp. of lie².

lair (lär), *n.* a den or resting place of a wild animal.

laird (lârd), *n. Scot.* a landed proprietor.

lais·sez faire (les′ā fâr′), the theory that government should intervene as little as possible in the direction of economic affairs. Also, **lais′ser faire′.** [< F: lit., allow to act] —**lais′sez-faire′, ** *adj.* —**lais′sez-faire′-ism, ** *n.*

la·i·ty (lā′i tē), *n.* 1. the body of religious worshipers, as distinguished from the clergy. 2. the people outside a particular profession, as distinguished from those belonging to it.

lake (lāk), *n.* 1. an inland body of water of considerable size. 2. a pool of liquid suggesting this.

lal·ly·gag (lol′ē gag′), *v.i.,* **-gagged, -gag·ging.** *Informal.* to idle or loaf.

lam¹ (lam), *v.t., v.i.,* **lammed, lamming.** *Slang.* to beat or thrash.

lam² (lam), *v.,* **lammed, lam·ming,** *n. Slang.* —*v.i.* 1. to run away quickly. —*n.* 2. **on the lam,** fleeing or hiding, esp. from the police.

lam., laminated.

la·ma (lä′mə), *n.* a priest or monk in Lamaism.

La·ma·ism (lä′mə iz′əm), *n.* the Buddhism of Tibet and Mongolia.

la·ma·ser·y (lä′mə ser′ē), *n., pl.* **-ser·ies.** a monastery of lamas.

La·maze′ technique′ (lə mäz′), a method by which an expectant mother is prepared for childbirth by psychological and physical conditioning.

lamb (lam), *n.* 1. a young sheep. 2. the meat of a young sheep. 3. an amiable, gentle, or gullible person. 4. **the Lamb,** Christ. —*v.i.* 5. to give birth to a lamb.

lam·baste (lam bāst′, -bast′), *v.t.,* **-bast·ed, -bast·ing.** *Informal.* 1. to beat severely. 2. to reprimand harshly. Also, **lam·bast′.**

lamb·da (lam′də), *n.* the 11th letter of the Greek alphabet (Λ, λ).

lam·bent (lam′bənt), *adj.* 1. moving lightly over a surface: *lambent tongues of flame.* 2. brilliantly playful: *lambent wit.* 3. softly bright: *a lambent light.* —**lam′ben·cy, ** *n.* —**lam′bent·ly, ** *adv.*

lamb·kin (lam′kin), *n.* 1. a little lamb. 2. a young and innocent person, esp. a small child.

lamb·skin (lam′skin′), *n.* 1. the skin of a lamb, esp. when dressed with its wool and used for clothing. 2. leather made from such skin.

lame (lām), *adj.,* **lam·er, lam·est, ** *v.,* **lamed, lam·ing.** —*adj.* 1. crippled or physically disabled, esp. in the foot or leg. 2. impaired through defect or injury. 3. weak or inadequate: *a lame excuse.* —*v.t.* 4. to make lame or defective. —**lame′ly, ** *adv.* —**lame′ness, ** *n.*

la·mé (la mā′), *n.* an ornamental fabric in which metallic threads are woven with silk or rayon.

lame·brain (lām′brān′), *n. Slang.* a fool or half-wit.

**lame′ duck′, ** *Informal.* an elected official who is completing his or her term in office after having failed to be reelected or who is ineligible for an additional term.

la·mel·la (lə mel′ə), *n., pl.* **-mel·lae** (-mel′ē), **-mel·las.** a thin plate or scale.

la·ment (lə ment′), *v.t., v.i.* 1. to express sorrow or deep regret (for or over). —*n.* 2. an expression of sorrow or deep regret. 3. a formal expression of mourning, esp. in verse or song. —**lam′en·ta·ble, ** *adj.* —**lam′en·ta·bly, ** *adv.* —**lam′en·ta′tion, ** *n.* —**la·ment′er, ** *n.* —**Syn.** 1. bewail, grieve, mourn, weep.

la·mi·a (lā′mē ə), *n.* a female monster.

lam·i·na (lam′ə nə), *n., pl.* **-nae** (-nē′), **-nas.** a thin layer of a composite structure. —**lam′i·nar, lam′i·nal, ** *adj.*

lam·i·nate (*v.* lam′ə nāt′; *adj.* lam′ə nāt′, -nit), *v.,* **-nat·ed, -nat·ing, ** *adj.* —*v.t.* 1. to split into thin layers. 2. to form (metal) into a thin plate. 3. to construct by placing layer upon layer. 4. to cover with laminae. —*adj.* 5. Also, **lam′i·nat′ed.** composed of laminae. —**lam′i·na′tion, ** *n.*

lamp (lamp), *n.* 1. a device providing an isolated source of artificial light, as by burning oil or by means of gas or electric energy. 2. a device for providing radiant heat or rays of certain kinds: *infrared lamp.*

lamp·black (lamp′blak′), *n.* a fine black pigment consisting of almost pure carbon.

lam·poon (lam pōōn′), *n.* 1. a sharp, often virulent satire, esp. one directed against an individual. —*v.t.* 2. to mock in a lampoon. —**lam·poon′er, lam·poon′ist, ** *n.* —**lam·poon′er·y, ** *n.*

lamp·post (lamp′pōst′), *n.* a post supporting a street lamp.

lam·prey (lam′prē), *n., pl.* **-preys.** an eellike fish having undeveloped eyes and a circular, sucking mouth.

la·nai (lə nī′), *n.* a veranda, esp. a fully furnished one used as a living room. [< Haw]

lance (lans, läns), *n., v.,* **lanced, lanc-ing.** —*n.* **1.** a long spear with a metal head, used by mounted sol-diers in charging. **2.** an instrument resembling this, esp. a lancet. **3.** a lancer. —*v.t.* **4.** to pierce with a lance. **5.** to open with a lancet.

lance′ cor′poral, *U.S. Marine Corps.* an enlisted person ranking between private first class and corporal.

Lan·ce·lot (lan′sə lət, -lot′, län′-), *n.* the greatest of King Arthur's knights.

lanc·er (lan′sər, län′-), *n.* a mounted soldier armed with a lance.

lan·cet (lan′sit, län′-), *n.* a small sur-gical instrument, usually sharp-pointed and two-edged.

land (land), *n.* **1.** the part of the earth's surface above water. **2.** an area or portion of this. **3.** a nation or country. **4.** a realm or domain. **5.** soil or earth. **6.** any part of the earth's surface which can be owned as property. —*v.t.* **7.** to bring to or set on land. **8.** to bring into a par-ticular place or condition: *His be-havior will land him in jail.* **9.** *In-formal.* to secure or gain: *to land a job.* **10.** to bring (a fish) to land or into a boat. **11.** *Informal.* to de-liver, as a blow. —*v.i.* **12.** to come to land or shore. **13.** to go or come ashore from a ship. **14.** to alight upon a surface from above. **15.** to come to rest or arrive in a particular place or condition.

lan·dau (lan′dô, -dou), *n.* **1.** a four-wheeled, two-seated carriage with a two-part folding top. **2.** a sedanlike automobile with a collapsible top over the rear section.

land·ed (lan′did), *adj.* **1.** owning land: *a landed proprietor.* **2.** consisting of land: *landed property.*

land·er (lan′dər), *n.* a space vehicle capable of landing on a celestial body, as the moon.

land·fall (land′fôl′), *n.* **1.** an approach to or sighting of land. **2.** the land sighted or reached.

land·fill (land′fil′), *n.* **1.** a low area of land that is built up by deposits of solid refuse in layers covered by soil. **2.** the solid refuse itself.

land′ grant′, a tract of land given by the government, as for colleges or railroads. —**land′-grant′,** *adj.*

land·hold·er (land′hōl′dər), *n.* a hold-er or owner of land. —**land′hold′-ing,** *adj., n.*

land·ing (lan′ding), *n.* **1.** the act of a person or thing that lands. **2.** a place where persons or goods are landed, as from a ship. **3.** a platform be-tween flights of stairs.

land′ing gear′, the complete structure on an aircraft or spacecraft for sup-porting it when landing or moving about on the surface.

land·locked (land′lokt′), *adj.* **1.** shut in completely, or almost completely, by land. **2.** living in waters shut off from the sea, as some fish.

land·lord (land′lôrd′), *n.* **1.** a person who owns land, buildings, etc., and leases them to others. **2.** the man-ager of a boardinghouse or rooming house. —**land′la′dy,** *n.fem.*

land·lub·ber (land′lub′ər), *n.* a per-son not accustomed to the sea or seamanship.

land·mark (land′märk′), *n.* **1.** a con-spicuous object on land that serves as a guide. **2.** a distinguishing fea-ture, part, event, etc. **3.** a histori-cally or aesthetically significant building or site. **4.** something used to mark the boundary of land.

land·mass (land′mas′), *n.* a large re-gion of the earth, esp. a continent.

land′ of′fice, a government office for the transaction of business relating to public lands.

land′-of·fice busi′ness (land′ô′fis, -of′-is), *Informal.* a lively, booming business.

land·own·er (land′ō′nər), *n.* an owner or proprietor of land.

land-poor (land′pŏŏr′), *adj.* in need of ready money while owning much unremunerative land.

land·scape (land′skāp′), *n., v.,* **-scaped, -scap·ing.** —*n.* **1.** a section of scenery that may be seen from a single view-point. **2.** a picture representing such scenery. —*v.t.* **3.** to improve the ap-pearance of (an area of land, etc.), as by altering the contours of the ground. —**land′scap′er,** *n.*

land·slide (land′slīd′), *n.* **1.** a fall of a mass of soil or rock on or from a steep slope. **2.** the material that falls. **3.** a sweeping victory, esp. in an election.

lands·man (landz′mən), *n.* a person who lives or works on land.

land·ward (land′wərd), *adv.* **1.** Also, **land′wards.** toward the land. —*adj.* **2.** lying toward the land.

lane (lān), *n.* **1.** a narrow way or passage, as between hedges. **2.** any narrow or well-defined track, route, or course.

lang., language.

lan·guage (lang′gwij), *n.* **1.** a body of words and systems for their use common to a people of the same community or nation. **2.** any sys-tem of formalized symbols, signs, etc., used or conceived as a means of communication. **3.** the means of communication used by animals. **4.** the speech or phraseology peculiar to a class, profession, etc. **5.** a par-ticular manner of verbal expression. [< AF < L *lingua* language, tongue]

lan·guid (lang′gwid), *adj.* **1.** drooping from weakness or fatigue. **2.** lacking in vigor or vitality. **3.** lacking in spirit or interest. —**lan′guid·ly**, *adv.* —**lan′guid·ness**, *n.*

lan·guish (lang′gwish), *v.i.* **1.** to be or become languid. **2.** to pine with desire or longing. **3.** to assume an expression of sentimental melancholy. —**lan′guish·er**, *n.*

lan·guor (lang′gər), *n.* **1.** physical weakness or faintness. **2.** lack of energy or vitality. —**lan′guor·ous**, *adj.* —**lan′guor·ous·ly**, *adv.* —**lan′guor·ous·ness**, *n.*

lank (langk), *adj.* **1.** thin and gaunt. **2.** (of hair) without spring or curl.

lank·y (lang′kē), *adj.*, **lank·i·er**, **lank·i·est.** ungracefully tall, thin, and bony. —**lank′i·ly**, *adv.* —**lank′i·ness**, *n.*

lan·o·lin (lan′ə lin), *n.* a fatty substance extracted from wool, used in ointments.

Lan·sing (lan′sing), *n.* the capital of Michigan.

lan·ta·na (lan tä′na, -tä′-), *n.* a chiefly tropical plant cultivated for aromatic flowers.

lan·tern (lan′tərn), *n.* **1.** a transparent or translucent case for enclosing a light and protecting it from the wind or rain. **2.** the chamber at the top of a lighthouse, surrounding the light.

lan′tern jaw′, a long, thin jaw. —**lan′tern-jawed′,** *adj.*

lan·tha·num (lan′thə nəm), *n. Chem.* a rare-earth, metallic element allied to aluminum. *Symbol:* La; *at. wt.:* 138.91; *at. no.:* 57.

lan·yard (lan′yərd), *n.* **1.** a short rope used on a ship to hold or tighten rigging. **2.** a small cord suspending small objects, as a whistle about the neck.

La·os (lä′ōs, lä′os), *n.* a country in SE Asia. —**La·o·tian** (lä ō′shən), *adj., n.*

lap[1] (lap), *n.* **1.** the front part of the human body from the waist to the knees when in a sitting position. **2.** the part of the clothing that covers this. **3.** a flap or loosely hanging part, as of a garment. **4.** an area of care, charge, or control: *The outcome is in the lap of the gods.*

lap[2] (lap), *v.*, **lapped, lap·ping,** *n.* —*v.t.* **1.** to fold over or about something. **2.** to wrap or enfold in something. **3.** to lay (something) over another. **4.** to get a lap ahead of (a competitor) in racing. —*v.i.* **5.** to fold or wind around something. **6.** to extend beyond a limit. —*n.* **7.** the act of lapping. **8.** a complete circuit of a course in racing. **9.** an overlapping part.

lap[3] (lap), *v.*, **lapped, lap·ping,** *n.* —*v.t., v.i.* **1.** to wash against (something) with a light, splashing sound, as water. **2.** to take in (liquid) with the tongue. **3. lap up,** *Informal.* to receive enthusiastically. —*n.* **4.** the act or sound of lapping. —**lap′per,** *n.*

La Paz (lə päz′), a city and seat of the government of Bolivia.

lap′ belt′, a safety strap for fastening across the lap of the driver or passenger.

lap·board (lap′bōrd′, -bôrd′), *n.* a thin, flat board to be held on the lap for use as a table or desk.

lap′ dog′, a small pet dog.

la·pel (lə pel′), *n.* a part of a garment folded back on the breast, esp. a continuation of a coat collar.

lap·i·dar·y (lap′i der′ē), *n., pl.* **-dar·ies,** *adj.* —*n.* **1.** a person who cuts, polishes, and engraves precious stones. —*adj.* **2.** of or pertaining to the cutting or engraving of precious stones. **3.** of or pertaining to inscriptions on stone monuments.

lap·in (lap′in), *n.* rabbit fur, esp. when trimmed and dyed.

lap·is laz·u·li (lap′is laz′ōō lē, -lī′, laz′yōō-, lazh′ōō-), a deep-blue crystalline rock used as a semiprecious stone.

Lap·land (lap′land′), *n.* a region in N Norway, N Sweden, and N Finland.

Lapp (lap), *n.* **1.** Also called **Lap·land·er** (lap′lan′dər, -lən-). a member of a small, sturdy people inhabiting Lapland. **2.** Also called **Lap·pish.** any of the languages of the Lapps.

lap·pet (lap′it), *n.* a small lap or loosely hanging flap, esp. of a garment or headdress.

lap′ robe′, a fur robe, blanket, etc., to cover the lap, esp. when riding in an automobile, carriage, etc.

lapse (laps), *n., v.,* **lapsed, laps·ing.** —*n.* **1.** a slip or error, often of a trivial sort. **2.** an interval or passage of time. **3.** a moral fall, as from rectitude. **4.** a fall or decline to a lower condition. **5.** *Law.* the termination of a right or privilege through neglect to exercise it. —*v.i.* **6.** to fall, slip, or sink: *to lapse into silence.* **7.** to fall from a previous standard. **8.** to pass away, as time. **9.** to stop or end, as a magazine subscription. **10.** to become void by legal lapse. —**laps′er,** *n.*

lap·wing (lap′wing′), *n.* a large, Old World plover having a long, slender crest.

lar·board (lär′bōrd′, -bôrd′), *n. Naut. Obs.* port[2] (def. 1).

lar·ce·ny (lär′sə nē), *n., pl.* **-nies.** the nonviolent crime of stealing another's money or other personal property. —**lar′ce·nist,** *n.* —**lar′ce·nous,** *adj.*

larch (lärch), *n.* **1.** a tree of the pine family yielding a tough durable wood. **2.** its wood.

lard (lärd), *n.* **1.** the rendered fat of hogs, esp. the internal fat of the abdomen. —*v.t.* **2.** to prepare (lean meat, etc.) for cooking by covering or stuffing with strips of fat. **3.** to intersperse with something for ornamentation. —**lard′y,** *adj.*

lar·der (lär′dər), *n. Chiefly Brit.* a room, usually cool, for storing meat and other foods.

lar′es and pena′tes (lâr′ez ənd pə nā′-tēz), **1.** ancient Roman gods of the household. **2.** the cherished possessions of a household.

large (lärj), *adj.,* **larg·er, larg·est,** *n.* —*adj.* **1.** measuring or amounting to more than average size or quantity. **2.** on a scale beyond the average. **3.** of considerable scope, range, or power. —*n.* **4. at large, a.** free from confinement. **b.** to a considerable extent. **c.** as a whole. **d.** representing the whole of a state or district rather than one division of it. —**large′ness,** *n.* —**larg′ish,** *adj.* —**Syn. 1.** great, huge, immense, massive, vast.

large-heart·ed (lärj′här′tid), *adj.* generous or liberal.

large·ly (lärj′lē), *adv.* **1.** in great part. **2.** in great quantity.

large-scale (lärj′skāl′), *adj.* **1.** of great scope. **2.** made to a large dimensional scale.

lar·gess (lär jes′, lär′jis), *n.* **1.** generous giving of gifts. **2.** a gift so given. Also, **lar·gesse′.**

lar·go (lär′gō), *adj., adv. n., pl.* **-gos.** *Music.* —*adj., adv.* **1.** in a slow, dignified style. —*n.* **2.** a largo movement.

lar·i·at (lar′ē ət), *n.* a long rope used to catch or picket grazing animals.

lark¹ (lärk), *n.* any of numerous, chiefly Old World songbirds, esp. the skylark.

lark² (lärk), *n.* **1.** a merry, carefree adventure. —*v.i.* **2.** to frolic or romp.

lark·spur (lärk′spûr′), *n.* delphinium.

lar·rup (lar′əp), *v.t.,* **-ruped, -rup·ing.** *Dial.* to beat or thrash.

lar·va (lär′və), *n., pl.* **-vae** (-vē). **1.** the immature, wingless, feeding stage of an insect that undergoes complete metamorphosis. **2.** any animal in an analogous immature form. —**lar′val,** *adj.*

lar·yn·gi·tis (lar′ən jī′tis), *n.* inflammation of the larynx.

lar·ynx (lar′ingks), *n., pl.* **la·ryn·ges** (lə rin′jēz), **lar·ynx·es.** the muscular structure at the upper part of the trachea in which the vocal cords are located. —**la·ryn·ge·al** (lə rin′jē əl), *adj.*

la·sa·gna (lə zän′yə, lä-), *n.* a baked dish of large strips of pasta, usually made with meat, cheese, and tomatoes. Also, **la·sa′gne.**

las·car (las′kər), *n.* an East Indian sailor.

las·civ·i·ous (lə siv′ē əs), *adj.* **1.** expressing lust or lewdness. **2.** arousing sexual desire. —**las·civ′i·ous·ly,** *adv.* —**las·civ′i·ous·ness,** *n.*

la·ser (lā′zər), *n.* a device that produces a very narrow beam of extremely intense light, used in communications, industrial processes, etc. [*l*(*ight*) *a*(*mplification by*) *s*(*timulated*) *e*(*mission of*) *r*(*adiation*)]

lash¹ (lash), *n.* **1.** the flexible striking part of a whip. **2.** a swift stroke, as with a whip. **3.** an eyelash. —*v.t.* **4.** to strike or beat, as with a whip. **5.** to attack severely with words. **6.** to dash suddenly and swiftly. —*v.i.* **7.** to make swift strokes, as with a whip. **8.** to attack someone or something with harsh words: *The article lashed out at social injustice.* —**lash′er,** *n.*

lash² (lash), *v.t.* to bind or fasten, as with a rope. —**lash′er,** *n.*

lass (las), *n.* a girl or young woman, esp. one who is unmarried.

las·sie (las′ē), *n. Chiefly Scot.* a young girl.

las·si·tude (las′i tōōd′, -tyōōd′), *n.* weariness of body or mind, as from strain.

las·so (las′ō, la sōō′), *n., pl.* **-sos, -soes,** *v.,* **-soed, -so·ing.** —*n.* **1.** a long rope with a running noose at one end, used for roping horses, cattle, etc. —*v.t.* **2.** to catch with a lasso. —**las′so·er,** *n.*

last¹ (last, läst), *adj., a superl. of* **late** *with* **later** *as compar.* **1.** occurring or coming after all others, as in time or place. **2.** the most recent. **3.** being the only remaining. **4.** conclusive or definitive. **5.** least likely or probable: *the last employee we would fire.* —*adv.* **6.** after all others. **7.** most recently. **8.** in the end. —*n.* **9.** a person or thing that is last. **10.** the end or conclusion. **11. at last,** after a lengthy delay. —**last′ly,** *adv.* —**Syn. 1.** concluding, final, ultimate.

last² (last, läst), *v.i.* **1.** to continue in time or existence. —*v.t.* **2.** to continue to survive for the duration of. —**Syn. 1.** abide, endure.

last³ (last, läst), *n.* **1.** a foot-shaped block or model on which shoes are shaped or repaired. —*v.t.* **2.** to shape on a last. —**last′er,** *n.*

Las·tex (las'teks), *n. Trademark.* a yarn made from a core of rubber thread covered with fabric strands.

last' hurrah', the final, unsuccessful political campaign.

last·ing (las'ting, lä'sting), *adj.* continuing or existing a long time. **—last'ing·ness**, *n.* **—Syn.** durable, enduring, permanent.

Last' Judg'ment, judgment (def. 5).

last' straw', the last of a succession of irritations that strains one's patience to the limit.

Last' Sup'per, the supper of Jesus and His disciples on the eve of His Crucifixion.

last' word', 1. the closing remark, as in an argument. 2. a final or definitive work, statement, etc. 3. *Informal.* the latest, most modern thing.

Lat., Latin.

lat., latitude.

Lat·a·ki·a (lat'ə kē'ə), a variety of Turkish tobacco.

latch (lach), *n.* 1. a device for holding a door or gate closed. **—v.t., v.i.** 2. to close or fasten with a latch. 3. **latch onto,** *Informal.* **a.** to obtain or get. **b.** to attach oneself to.

latch·key (lach'kē'), *n.* a key for releasing a latch, esp. on an outer door.

latch·string (lach'string'), *n.* a string passed through a hole in a door, for raising the latch from the outside.

late (lāt), *adj.,* **lat·er** or **lat·ter, lat·est** or **last,** *adv.,* **lat·er, lat·est.** *—adj.* 1. occurring after the usual or proper time. 2. coming toward the end of day. 3. very recent. 4. recently deceased: *the late Mr. Phipps.* 5. of late, recently. *—adv.* 6. after the usual or proper time. 7. at or to an advanced time or stage. 8. recently but no longer. **—late'ness,** *n.* **—lat'ish,** *adj.*

late·com·er (lāt'kum'ər), *n.* a person who arrives late.

late·ly (lāt'lē), *adv.* recently or not long since.

la·tent (lāt'ənt), *adj.* present or potential but not visible or apparent. **—la'ten·cy,** *n.* **—la'tent·ly,** *adv.*

lat·er·al (lat'ər əl), *adj.* of, situated at, proceeding from, or directed to the side. *—n.* 2. a lateral part or extension. 3. Also called **lat'eral pass'.** *Football.* a pass thrown parallel to the goal line or backward from the position of the passer. **—lat'er·al·ly,** *adv.*

la·tex (lā'teks), *n., pl.* **la·tex·es, lat·i·ces** (lat'i sēz'). 1. a milky liquid in certain plants, as milkweeds, that coagulates on exposure to air. 2. any emulsion in water of finely divided particles of synthetic rubber or plastic.

lath (lath), *n., pl.* **laths** (lathz, laths).

1. a thin, narrow strip of wood, used as a support for plastering, etc. 2. any building material used for similar purpose.

lathe (lāth), *n., v.,* **lathed, lath·ing.** *—n.* 1. a machine for use in working pieces of wood, metal, etc., by rotating them against a tool that shapes them. *—v.t.* 2. to cut or shape on a lathe.

lath·er (lath'ər), *n.* 1. foam made by soap stirred or rubbed in water. 2. froth formed in profuse sweating, as on a horse. 3. *Informal.* a state of excitement. *—v.i., v.t.* 4. to form or cover with lather. **—lath'er·y,** *adj.*

Lat·in (lat'°n, -in), *n.* 1. the language of ancient Rome. 2. a native or inhabitant of ancient Rome. 3. a member of any of the Latin peoples. *— adj.* 4. denoting those peoples using languages derived from Latin, as Spanish, Portuguese, French, Italian, or Rumanian. 5. of ancient Rome, its inhabitants, or their language.

Lat'in Amer'ica, the part of the American continents south of the U.S. in which Romance languages are spoken. **—Lat'in Amer'ican.**

La·ti·no (la tē'nō), *n.* an American citizen or resident of Latin American descent.

lat·i·tude (lat'i tōōd', -tyōōd'), *n.* 1. a. the angular distance north or south from the equator measured in degrees on the meridian of a point. b. a region as marked by this distance. 2. permitted freedom of action, opinion, etc. **—lat'i·tu'di·nal,** *adj.*

lat·i·tu·di·nar·i·an (lat'i tōōd'°när'ē-ən, -tyōōd'-), *n.* a person who is liberal in opinion or conduct, esp. in religious views. **—lat'i·tu'di·nar'i·an·ism,** *n.*

la·trine (lə trēn'), *n.* a communal privy-type toilet, as in a camp.

lat·ter (lat'ər), *adj.* 1. being the second mentioned of two. 2. more advanced in time. 3. near to the end. **—lat'ter·ly,** *adv.*

lat·ter-day (lat'ər dā'), *adj.* 1. of a later or following period. 2. of the present period or time.

Lat'ter-day Saint', a Mormon.

lat·tice (lat'is), *n.* 1. a structure of crossed wooden or metal strips usually arranged to form a diagonal pattern of open spaces. 2. a window or gate consisting of such a structure. 3. an arrangement in space of isolated points in a regular pattern. **—lat'ticed,** *adj.*

lat·tice·work (lat'is wûrk'), *n.* 1. work or structure consisting of lattices. 2. a lattice.

Lat·vi·a (lat'vē ə), *n.* a constituent republic of the Soviet Union in Europe, in the NW part. **—Lat'vi·an,** *adj., n.*

laud (lôd), *v.t.* **1.** to praise highly. —*n.* **2.** a hymn of praise. —**laud′er**, *n.*

laud·a·ble (lô′də bəl), *adj.* highly praiseworthy. —**laud′a·bly**, *adv.*

lau·da·num (lôd′ⁿnəm, lôd′nəm), *n.* **1.** a tincture of opium. **2.** any formerly used preparation in which opium was the chief ingredient.

laud·a·to·ry (lô′də tōr′ē, -tôr′ē), *adj.* containing or expressing high praise. —**laud′a·to′ri·ly**, *adv.*

laugh (laf, läf), *v.i.* **1.** to express mirth, pleasure, or derision with a series of inarticulate sounds and facial or body movements. **2.** to drive, bring, etc., by or with laughter. **3. laugh at, a.** to make fun of. **b.** to find amusement in. **4. laugh off**, to ridicule or dismiss as absurd. —*n.* **5.** the act or sound of laughing. **6.** something that provokes laughter. —**laugh′a·ble**, *adj.* —**laugh′a·bly**, *adv.* —**laugh′ing·ly**, *adv.* —**Syn. 1.** chortle, chuckle, guffaw, roar.

laugh′ing gas′, *Informal*. See **nitrous oxide**.

laugh·ing·stock (laf′ing stok′, läf′ing-), *n.* an object of ridicule.

laugh·ter (laf′tər, läf′-), *n.* the action or sound of laughing.

launch[1] (lônch, länch), *n.* a heavy, open or half-decked motorboat.

launch[2] (lônch, länch), *v.t.* **1.** to float (a newly constructed vessel). **2.** to cause or assist to start. **3.** to put into action or effect. **4.** to send forth forcefully: *to launch a rocket*. **5.** to throw or hurl. —*v.i.* **6.** to plunge boldly or directly into action, speech, etc. **7.** to start out or forth, as a vessel. —*n.* **8.** the act of launching.

launch·er (lônch′ər, länch′ər), *n.* **1.** a person or thing that launches. **2.** a structural device designed to hold a missile in position for launching.

launch′ pad′, a platform from which a rocket is launched. Also called **launch′ing pad′**.

launch′ win′dow, the time period during which a spacecraft must be launched to achieve a desired mission.

laun·der (lôn′dər, län′-), *v.t., v.i.* **1.** to wash or wash and iron (clothes). **2.** *Slang*. to disguise the source of (illegal money) by routing it abroad through a foreign bank. —**laun′der·er**, *n.* —**laun′dress** (-dris), *n.fem.*

Laun·dro·mat (lôn′drə mat′, län′-), *n. Trademark*. a commercial laundry having self-service machines.

laun·dry (lôn′drē, län′-), *n., pl.* **-dries. 1.** articles of clothes, linens, etc., laundered or to be laundered. **2.** a place where such articles are laundered. —**laun′dry·man′**, *n.* —**laun′dry·wom′an**, *n.fem.*

laun′dry list′, *Informal*. a lengthy, usually indiscriminate list of items.

lau·re·ate (lôr′ē it), *adj.* **1.** crowned with laurel as a mark of honor. —*n.* **2.** a person who has been honored in a particular field. —**lau′re·ate·ship′**, *n.*

lau·rel (lôr′əl, lor′-), *n.* **1.** a small, evergreen tree of Europe. **2.** any of various similar trees. **3.** the foliage of the laurel as an emblem of victory or distinction. **4.** a wreath of laurel foliage. **5.** Usually, **laurels.** honor won, as for achievement in a field.

la·va (lä′və, lav′ə), *n.* **1.** the molten rock that issues from a volcano. **2.** the substance formed when this solidifies. [< It: *avalanche* < L *lābēs* a sliding down]

la·va·bo (lə vā′bō, -vä′-), *n., pl.* **-boes.** a large stone washbasin in a medieval monastery.

lav·age (lə väzh′, lav′ij), *n.* a washing, esp. of an organ, as the stomach.

lav·a·liere (lav′ə lēr′, lä′və-), *n.* an ornamental pendant worn on a chain around the neck. Also, **lav′a·lier′**.

lav·a·to·ry (lav′ə tōr′ē, -tôr′ē), *n., pl.* **-ries. 1.** a room equipped with washbowls and usually toilets, esp. one for public accommodation. **2.** a washbowl with its fixtures.

lave (lāv), *v.t., v.i.,* **laved, lav·ing.** *Literary*. to wash or bathe.

lav·en·der (lav′ən dər), *n.* **1.** a pale, bluish purple. **2.** an Old World herb or shrub having spikes of fragrant, pale purple flowers. **3.** its dried flowers or leaves used to scent chests, etc.

lav·ish (lav′ish), *adj.* **1.** using or giving in great amounts. **2.** expended or occurring in profusion. —*v.t.* **3.** to expend or give in great amounts. —**lav′ish·er**, *n.* —**lav′ish·ly**, *adv.* —**lav′ish·ness**, *n.* —**Syn. 1, 2.** bountiful, extravagant, profuse.

law (lô), *n.* **1.** all the rules of conduct established by a government and applicable to a people, whether in the form of legislation or of custom. **2.** any written or positive instance of such rules. **3.** the controlling influence of such rules. **4.** a system or collection of such rules. **5.** the department of knowledge concerned with these rules. **6.** the body of such rules concerned with a particular subject. **7.** the principles applied in the courts of common law. **8.** the profession that deals with legal procedure. **9.** any rule or injunction that must be obeyed. **10.** a principle based on the predictable consequences of an act, condition, etc.

law·a·bid·ing (lô′ə bī′diŋ), *adj.* keeping or obedient to the law.

law·break·er (lô′brā′kər), *n.* a person who breaks or violates the law. —**law′break′ing,** *n., adj.*

law·ful (lô′fəl), *adj.* **1.** allowed or permitted by law. **2.** recognized or sanctioned by law. —**law′ful·ly,** *adv.* —Syn. legal, legitimate.

law·giv·er (lô′giv′ər), *n.* a person who promulgates a law or a code of laws. —**law′giv′ing,** *n., adj.*

law·less (lô′lis), *adj.* **1.** without regard for the law. **2.** uncontrolled by a law. **3.** illegal (def. 1). —**law′-less·ly,** *adv.* —**law′less·ness,** *n.*

law·mak·er (lô′mā′kər), *n.* a person who makes or enacts law, esp. a legislator.

law·man (lô′man′, -mən), *n.* (esp. in the old West) an officer of the law, as a sheriff or marshal.

lawn[1] (lôn, län), *n.* a stretch of grass-covered land, esp. one closely mowed, as in a park. —**lawn′y,** *adj.*

lawn[2] (lôn, län), *n.* a thin or sheer linen or cotton fabric, either plain or printed. —**lawn′y,** *adj.*

lawn′ mow′er, a hand-operated or power-propelled machine for cutting grass.

law·ren·ci·um (lô ren′sē əm, lo-), *n. Chem.* a synthetic, radioactive, metallic element. *Symbol:* Lr; *at. no.:* 103.

law·suit (lô′sōōt′), *n.* a prosecution of a claim in a court of law.

law·yer (lô′yər, loi′ər), *n.* a person whose profession is to conduct lawsuits for clients or to advise or act for them in other legal matters.

lax (laks), *adj.* **1.** lacking in strictness or firmness: *lax morals.* **2.** careless or negligent. **3.** loose or slack: *a lax cord.* —**lax′i·ty, lax′ness,** *n.* —**lax′ly,** *adv.*

lax·a·tive (lak′sə tiv), *n.* **1.** a medicine or agent for relieving constipation. —*adj.* **2.** of or constituting a laxative.

lay[1] (lā), *v.,* **laid, lay·ing,** *n.* —*v.t.* **1.** to put or place in a horizontal position. **2.** to strike or throw to the ground. **3.** to put forth for consideration: *He laid his case before the commission.* **4.** to bring forward, as a claim. **5.** to attribute or ascribe: *to lay blame on someone.* **6.** to bring forth and deposit (an egg). **7.** to bet or wager. **8.** to impose, as a burden or penalty. **9.** to set or apply. **10.** to dispose or place in proper position: *to lay bricks.* **11.** to place along or under a surface: *to lay a pipeline.* **12.** to devise or arrange, as a plan. **13.** to allay or suppress: *to lay a person's doubts at rest.* **14. lay aside,** to save for use at a later time. Also, **lay away, lay by. 15. lay in,** to store away for future use. **16. lay off, a.** to dismiss (a

worker), esp. temporarily. **b.** *Slang.* to stop or cease. **17. lay open, a.** to cut open. **b.** to expose or reveal. **18. lay out, a.** to spread out in order. **b.** *Informal.* to spend or contribute (money). **c.** *Slang.* to knock (someone) unconscious. **d.** to plan or design. **19. lay over,** to make a stop, as during a trip. **20. lay up, a.** to put away for future use. **b.** to cause to be confined to bed. —*n.* **21.** the way or position in which a thing is laid or lies.
—Usage. See **lie**[2].

lay[2] (lā), *v.* pt. of **lie**[1].

lay[3] (lā), *adj.* **1.** of or pertaining to the laity. **2.** not belonging to a specified profession, esp. law or medicine.

lay[4] (lā), *n.* **1.** a short narrative poem, esp. one to be sung. **2.** *Literary.* a song.

lay′ an′alyst, a psychoanalyst who does not have a medical degree.

lay′a·way plan′ (lā′ə wā′), a method of selling merchandise reserved by a down payment and delivered only after full payment of the balance.

lay·er (lā′ər), *n.* **1.** a thickness of some material laid on or spread over a surface. **2.** a person or thing that lays. **3. a.** a shoot or twig that is induced to root while still attached to the living stock, as by bending and covering with soil. **b.** a plant so propagated.

lay·ette (lā et′), *n.* an outfit of clothing, bedding, etc., for a newborn child.

lay′ fig′ure, a jointed model of the human body from which artists work in the absence of a living model.

lay·man (lā′mən), *n.* a member of the laity. —**lay′wom′an,** *n.fem.*

lay·off (lā′ôf′, -of′), *n.* **1.** the act of laying off, as workers. **2.** an interval of enforced unemployment.

lay·out (lā′out′), *n.* **1.** a laying or spreading out. **2.** an arrangement or plan. **3.** a plan or sketch, as of an advertisement.

lay·o·ver (lā′ō′vər), *n.* stopover.

laz·ar (laz′ər, lā′zər), *n. Archaic.* a leper.

Laz·a·rus (laz′ər əs), *n.* a man whom Jesus raised from the dead.

laze (lāz), *v.i., v.t.,* **lazed, laz·ing.** to pass (time) lazily.

la·zy (lā′zē), *adj.,* **la·zi·er, la·zi·est.** **1.** disliking work or effort. **2.** slow-moving or sluggish: *a lazy stream.* —**la′zi·ly,** *adv.* —**la′zi·ness,** *n.* —Syn. **1.** idle, indolent, slothful.

la·zy·bones (lā′zē bōnz′), *n. Informal.* a lazy person.

la′zy Su′san (sōō′zən), a large revolving tray placed at the center of a dining table.

lb., *pl.* **lbs.**, **lb.** pound² (def. 1). Also, **lb** [< L *libra*]

L/C, letter of credit. Also, **l/c**

L.C., Library of Congress.

l.c., **1.** See *loc. cit.* **2.** *Print.* See lower case.

L.C.D., lowest common denominator.

LCD, liquid-crystal diode (used to display the time continuously on digital watches).

LCDR, Lieutenant Commander.

L.C.L., *Com.* less than carload lot.

L.C.M., least common multiple.

LCpl, Lance Corporal.

LD, lethal dose.

Ld., Lord.

ld., load.

LDC, less developed country.

ldg., **1.** landing. **2.** loading.

L-dopa (el′ dō′pə, el′ dō′pä), *n.* a drug for reversing the crippling effects of Parkinson's disease.

lea (lē, lā), *n. Literary.* a grassland.

leach (lēch), *v.t.* **1.** to cause (water) to percolate through something. **2.** to remove soluble substances from (soil) by percolation. —*v.i.* **3.** to undergo the action of percolating water. —**leach′er**, *n.*

lead¹ (lēd), *v.*, **led**, **lead·ing**, *n.* —*v.t.* **1.** to go before or with to show the way. **2.** to influence or induce. **3.** to go at the head of or in advance of: *The school band led the parade.* **4.** to have the advantage over. **5.** to act as leader of (an orchestra, etc.). **6.** to go through or pass (time, life, etc.): *to lead a full life.* —*v.i.* **7.** to act as a guide. **8.** to afford passage to a place. **9.** to go first. **10.** to result in: *The incident led to my resignation.* **11.** *Cards.* to make the first play. **12. lead off**, to take the initiative. **13. lead on**, to lure or tempt. **14. lead up to, a.** to prepare the way for. **b.** to approach (a subject, etc.) gradually or evasively. —*n.* **15.** the position in advance of others. **16.** the extent of such advance. **17.** a person or thing that leads. **18.** a guide to a course, method, etc., to follow. **19.** example or leadership. **20.** the principal part in a play. **21.** *Cards.* **a.** the right of playing first. **b.** the card so played. —**lead′er**, *n.* —**lead′er·less**, *adj.* —**lead′er·ship′**, *n.*

lead² (led), *n.* **1.** *Chem.* a heavy, soft, malleable, bluish-gray metal, used for water pipes, etc. *Symbol:* Pb; *at. wt.:* 207.19; *at. no.:* 82. **2.** something made of this metal. **3.** a plummet or lead for taking soundings. **4.** bullets collectively. **5.** a small stick of graphite, as used in pencils. **6.** a thin strip of metal used for increasing the space between lines of type. —*v.t.* **7.** to cover, weight, or treat with lead. **8.** to fix (window glass) in position with leads.

lead·ed (led′id), *adj.* (of gasoline) containing tetraethyl lead: on combustion it produces a toxic pollutant.

lead·en (led′ən), *adj.* **1.** inertly heavy, like lead. **2.** dull or gloomy. **3.** of a dull gray color. **4.** oppressive or heavy: *a leaden silence.* **5.** sluggish or listless. **6.** made of lead. —**lead′en·ly**, *adv.*

lead·ing (lē′ding), *adj.* **1.** chief or most important. **2.** directing or guiding.

lead′ing ques′tion (lē′ding), a question so worded as to suggest the proper or desired answer.

lead′ poi′soning (led), an acute toxic condition produced by absorption of lead into the body.

lead′ time′ (lēd), the period of time between planning and completing the manufacture of a product.

leaf (lēf), *n., pl.* **leaves** (lēvz), *v.* —*n.* **1.** one of the expanded, usually green organs borne by the stem of a plant. **2.** a petal. **3.** foliage. **4.** a unit generally comprising two printed pages of a book, one on each side. **5.** a thin sheet of metal. **6.** a hinged or detachable flat part, as of a door or table top. —*v.i.* **7.** to put forth leaves. **8.** to turn pages quickly: *to leaf through a book.* —**leaf′less**, *adj.* —**leaf′y**, *adj.*

leaf·age (lē′fij), *n.* foliage.

leafed (lēft), *adj.* leaved.

leaf·hop·per (lēf′hop′ər), *n.* any of numerous leaping insects that suck plant juices, many being serious crop pests.

leaf·let (lēf′lit), *n.* **1.** a small flat or folded sheet of printed matter. **2.** a small or young leaf.

leaf·stalk (lēf′stôk′), *n.* petiole.

league¹ (lēg), *n., v.,* **leagued**, **lea·guing.** —*n.* **1.** an association of persons or states for promotion of common interests. **2.** a group of sports teams organized to compete chiefly among themselves. —*v.t., v.i.* **3.** to unite in a league.

league² (lēg), *n.* a unit of distance, roughly three miles.

League′ of Na′tions, an international organization (1920–46) to promote world peace: replaced by the United Nations.

lea·guer (lē′gər), *n.* a member of a league.

leak (lēk), *n.* **1.** an unintended hole or crack through which fluid or light enters or escapes. **2.** any means of unintended entrance or escape. **3.** a disclosure of secret official information, esp to the news media, by an unnamed source: often deliberately authorized. **4.** the act or an instance of leaking. —*v.i.* **5.** to let fluid or light enter or escape through a leak. **6.** to pass in or out in this manner, as fluid or light. **7.** to become known by information leak: *The news leaked out.* —*v.t.* **8.** to let (fluid or (light) enter or escape. **9.** to allow to become known by information leak. —**leak′er,** *n.* —**leak′y,** *adj.* —**leak′i·ness,** *n.*

leak·age (lē′kij), *n.* **1.** the act or an instance of leaking. **2.** the thing or amount that leaks in or out.

leal (lēl), *adj. Scot.* loyal or true.

lean¹ (lēn), *v.,* **leaned** or **leant** (lent), **lean·ing.** —*v.i.* **1.** to incline or bend from a vertical position. **2.** to incline in feeling, opinion, or action. **3.** to rest against or on something for support. **4.** to depend or rely. —*v.t.* **5.** to cause to lean.

lean² (lēn), *adj.* **1.** without much flesh or fat. **2.** containing little or no fat. **3.** lacking in fullness or productivity. —*n.* **4.** meat containing little or no fat. —**lean′ly,** *adv.* —**lean′ness,** *n.* —**Syn. 1.** lanky, skinny, spare, thin.

lean·ing (lē′ning), *n.* inclination or tendency, as of mind.

lean-to (lēn′tōō′), *n., pl.* **-tos. 1.** a roof of a single pitch with the higher end abutting a wall. **2.** a structure with such a roof.

leap (lēp), *v.,* **leaped** or **leapt** (lept, lēpt), **leap·ing,** *n.* —*v.i.* **1.** to spring from one point to another. **2.** to act hastily or eagerly. —*v.t.* **3.** to jump over. **4.** to cause to leap. —*n.* **5.** a light, springing movement. **6.** the distance jumped. **7.** an abrupt transition. —**leap′er,** *n.*

leap·frog (lēp′frog′, -frôg′), *n., v.,* **-frogged, -frog·ging.** —*n.* **1.** a game in which players take turns leaping over another player who is bent over from the waist. —*v.t., v.i.* **2.** to jump over (a person or thing) in or as if in leapfrog.

leap′ year′, a year that contains 366 days, with February 29 as an additional day.

learn (lûrn), *v.t., v.i.,* **learned** (lûrnd) or **learnt** (lûrnt), **learn·ing. 1.** to acquire knowledge (of) or skill (in) by study, instruction, or experience. **2.** to become informed (of). **3.** to memorize (something). —**learn′er,** *n.*

learn·ed (lûr′nid), *adj.* **1.** having much knowledge or skill. **2.** of or showing much learning. —**Syn. 1, 2.** erudite, scholarly.

learn·ing (lûr′ning), *n.* **1.** knowledge or skill acquired. **2.** the act or process of acquiring knowledge or skill.

lease (lēs), *n., v.,* **leased, leas·ing.** —*n.* **1.** a contract conveying property to another for a specified period in consideration of rent. **2. a new lease on life,** a chance to improve one's circumstances. —*v.t.* **3.** to grant or hold by lease. —**leas′a·ble,** *adj.* —**leas·er,** *n.*

lease·hold (lēs′hōld′), *n.* **1.** property acquired under a lease. **2.** a tenure under a lease. —**lease′hold′er,** *n.*

leash (lēsh), *n.* **1.** a thong or line for holding a dog or other animal in check. —*v.t.* **2.** to secure or hold in or as in a leash.

least (lēst), *adj., a superl. of little with less or lesser as compar.* **1.** smallest in size, amount, or degree. **2.** lowest in consideration or importance. —*n.* **3.** something that is least. **4. at least, a.** at the lowest estimate. **b.** at any rate. Also, **at the least.** —*adv.* **5. superl. of little with less as compar.** to the smallest size, amount, or degree.

least′ com′mon denom′inator, the smallest number that is a common denominator of a given set of fractions.

least′ com′mon mul′tiple. See **lowest common multiple.**

least·wise (lēst′wīz′), *adv. Informal.* at least. Also, *Dial.,* **least′ways′** (-wāz′).

leath·er (leth′ər), *n.* **1.** the skin of an animal prepared for use by tanning or a similar process. —*adj.* **2.** of or made of leather. —**leath′ern,** *adj.*

leath·er·neck (leth′ər nek′), *n. Slang.* a U.S. marine.

leath·er·y (leth′ə rē), *adj.* **1.** like leather. **2.** tough and flexible. —**leath′er·i·ness,** *n.*

leave¹ (lēv), *v.,* **left, leav·ing.** —*v.t.* **1.** to go away from, as a place. **2.** to depart from or quit: *to leave a job.* **3.** to let stay or be as specified: *to leave a door unlocked.* **4.** to let remain in a position to do something without interference: *We left him to his work.* **5.** to stop or abandon. **6.** to have remaining behind: *The wound left a scar.* **7.** to give for use after one's death. —*v.i.* **8.** to go away or depart. **9. leave off,** to stop or cease. **10. leave out,** to omit or exclude. —**leav′er,** *n.*

leave² (lēv), *n.* **1.** permission to be absent, as from duty. **2.** the time this permission lasts. **3.** departure or farewell: *He took his leave abruptly. He took leave of her after dinner.* **4.** *Literary and Often Ironic.* permission or consent: *by your leave.* Also called **leave′ of ab′sence** (for defs. 1, 2).

leave³ (lēv), *v.i.,* **leaved, leav·ing.** to put forth leaves.

leaved (lēvd), *adj.* having leaves.

leav·en (lev′ən), *n.* **1.** a substance, as baking powder, that causes fermentation and expansion of doughs. **2.** fermented dough reserved for use as this substance. **3.** an element that produces an altering or transforming influence. —*v.t.* **4.** to make (dough) rise with a leaven. **5.** to permeate with an altering or transforming element.

leav·en·ing (lev'ə nifg), *n.* **1.** the act or process of causing to ferment by leaven. **2.** leaven (defs. 1–3).

leaves (lēvz), *n.* pl. of **leaf.**

leave-tak·ing (lēv'tā'kifg), *n.* the act of saying goodby.

leav·ings (lē'vifgz), *n.pl.* things left unwanted, as refuse.

Leb·a·non (leb'ə nən), *n.* a country at the E end of the Mediterranean. — **Leb'a·nese'** (-nēz', -nēs'), *adj., n.*

lech·er (lech'ər), *n.* a man given to excessive sexual indulgence. —**lech'·er·ous,** *adj.* —**lech'er·ous·ly,** *adv.* —**lech'er·ous·ness,** *n.* —**lech'er·y,** *n.*

lec·i·thin (les'ə thin), *n.* any of a group of yellow-brown fatty substances, occurring in animal and plant tissues and egg yolk, used in foods, cosmetics, etc.

lect., **1.** lecture. **2.** lecturer.

lec·tern (lek'tərn), *n.* a desk with a slanted top, for a standing reader, lecturer, etc.

lec·ture (lek'chər), *n., v., -tured, -tur·ing.* —*n.* **1.** a discourse read or delivered before an audience or class, esp. for instruction. **2.** a long, tedious reprimand. —*v.t., v.i.* **3.** to deliver a lecture (to or before). **4.** to scold at length. —**lec'tur·er,** *n.* — **lec'ture·ship',** *n.*

led (led), *v.* pt. and pp. of **lead¹.**

LED, light-emitting diode (used to display the time by push button on digital watches).

ledge (lej), *n.* **1.** a horizontal, shelf-like projection on a building or a cliff. **2.** a reef or ridge of rocks in the sea. —**ledge'less,** *adj.*

ledg·er (lej'ər), *n.* an account book of final entry, containing all the transactions of a business.

lee (lē), *n.* **1.** a sheltered place away from the wind. **2.** *Chiefly Naut.* the quarter or region toward which the wind blows. —*adj.* **3.** *Chiefly Naut.* of or pertaining to the lee.

Lee (lē), *n.* **Rob·ert E(dward)** (rob'ərt ed'wərd), 1807–70, Confederate general in the American Civil War.

leech (lēch), *n.* **1.** any bloodsucking aquatic or terrestrial worm, formerly much used in medicine for bloodletting. **2.** a person who clings to another for personal gain. —*v.i.* **3.** to hang on to a person in the manner of a leech.

leek (lēk), *n.* a plant allied to the onion, having a cylindrical bulb and leaves used in cookery.

leer (lēr), *v.i.* **1.** to look with an oblique glance suggestive of lascivious interest or sly and malicious intention. —*n.* **2.** a lascivious or sly look. —**leer'ing·ly,** *adv.*

leer·y (lēr'ē), *adj.,* **leer·i·er, leer·i·est.** cautiously wary. —**leer'i·ness,** *n.* — **Syn.** distrustful, suspicious.

lees (lēz), *n.pl.* sediment or dregs, esp. of wine.

lee·ward (lē'wərd; *Naut.* lōō'ərd), *adj.* **1.** situated or moving away from the wind. —*n.* **2.** the lee side. —*adv.* **3.** toward the lee. —**lee'ward·ly,** *adv.*

lee·way (lē'wā'), *n.* **1.** the drift of a vessel to leeward from its heading. **2.** extra time, space, etc., within which to operate. **3.** a degree of freedom of action or thought.

left¹ (left), *adj.* **1.** of or belonging to the side of a person or thing that is turned toward the west when the subject is facing north. **2.** (*sometimes cap.*) of or belonging to the political left. —*n.* **3.** the left side. **4.** a left-hand turn. **5.** (*sometimes cap.*) a liberal or radical political party or position. —*adv.* **6.** toward the left.

left² (left), *v.* pt. and pp. of **leave¹.**

left-hand (left'hand'), *adj.* **1.** on or to the left. **2.** of, for, or with the left hand.

left-hand·ed (left'han'did), *adj.* **1.** having the left hand more serviceable than the right. **2.** adapted to or performed by the left hand. **3.** ambiguous or doubtful: *a left-handed compliment.* **4.** clumsy or awkward. — *adv.* **5.** with the left hand. —**left'·hand'ed·ly,** *adv.* —**left'-hand'ed·ness,** *n.*

left·ist (lef'tist), (*sometimes cap.*) — *n.* **1.** a member of the Left or a person sympathizing with its views. — *adj.* **2.** of or pertaining to the Left. —**left'ism,** *n.*

left·o·ver (left'ō'vər), *n.* something remaining unused, esp. from a meal.

left' wing', the leftist faction of a political party. —**left'-wing',** *adj.* —**left'-wing'er,** *n.*

left·y (lef'tē), *n., pl.* **left·ies.** *Informal.* a left-handed person.

leg (leg), *n., v.,* **legged, leg·ging.** —*n.* **1.** one of the limbs of animals and human beings that support and move the body. **2.** the lower limb of a human being from the knee to the ankle. **3.** something resembling a leg in use, position, or appearance. **4.** the part of a garment that covers the leg. **5.** one of the sections of any course or travel. **6. pull one's leg,** *Informal.* to make fun of. —*v.t.* **7. leg it,** *Informal.* to walk rapidly or run. —**leg'less,** *adj.*

leg., **1.** legal. **2.** legend. **3.** legislation. **4.** legislative. **5.** legislature.

leg·a·cy (leg'ə sē), *n., pl.* **-cies. 1.** a gift of property, as money, by will. **2.** anything handed down from the past, as from an ancestor or predecessor.

le·gal (lē′gəl), *adj.* **1.** permitted by law. **2.** of or pertaining to law or lawyers. **3.** established or authorized by law. **4.** recognized or enforced by law. —**le·gal·i·ty** (lē gal′i tē), *n.* —**le′gal·ize′**, *v.t.* —**le′gal·i·za′tion**, *n.* —**le′gal·ly**, *adv.*

le′gal age′, the age at which a person acquires full adult legal rights, usually 18 or 21.

le·gal·ese (lē′gə lēz′), *n.* the special, often jargon-filled language of the legal profession.

le′gal hol′iday, a public holiday established by law.

le·gal·ism (lē′gə liz′əm), *n.* strict adherence to law, esp. to the letter rather than the spirit. —**le′gal·is′tic**, *adj.*

le′gal ten′der, currency that may be lawfully tendered or offered in payment of money debts.

leg·ate (leg′it), *n.* a cleric delegated as a representative of the pope. —**leg′ate·ship′**, *n.*

leg·a·tee (leg′ə tē′), *n.* a person to whom a legacy is bequeathed.

le·ga·tion (li gā′shən), *n.* **1.** a diplomatic minister and his or her staff in a foreign mission. **2.** their official headquarters. —**le·ga·tion·ar·y** (li-gā′shə ner′ē), *adj.*

le·ga·to (lə gä′tō), *adj., adv. Music.* without breaks between the successive tones.

leg·end (lej′ənd), *n.* **1.** an unverifiable story handed down by tradition from earlier times and popularly accepted as historical. **2.** an inscription, esp. on a coin or medal. **3.** a table on a map or chart, listing and explaining the symbols used. **4.** a collection of stories about an admirable person. **5.** a person who is the center of such stories.

leg·end·ar·y (lej′ən der′ē), *adj.* of or characteristic of folk legends. —**leg′end·ar′i·ly**, *adv.*

leg·er·de·main (lej′ər də mān′), *n.* **1.** See sleight of hand. **2.** trickery or deception.

leg·ged (leg′id, legd), *adj.* having a specified number or kind of legs: *two-legged; long-legged.*

leg·ging (leg′ing), *n.* a covering for the leg, as of leather. Also, **leg·gin** (leg′in). —**leg′ginged**, *adj.*

leg·gy (leg′ē), *adj.*, **-gi·er**, **-gi·est**. **1.** having awkwardly long legs. **2.** having long, attractive legs.

leg·horn (leg′hôrn′, leg′ərn), *n.* **1.** a fine, smooth, plaited straw. **2.** a hat made of such straw. **3.** (*often cap.*) one of a Mediterranean breed of chickens that are prolific layers of white-shelled eggs.

leg·i·ble (lej′ə bəl), *adj.* capable of being read with ease, as writing. —

leg′i·bil′i·ty, leg′i·ble·ness, *n.* —**leg′i·bly**, *adv.*

le·gion (lē′jən), *n.* **1.** a division of the ancient Roman army usually comprising 4000 to 6000 soldiers. **2.** a multitude of persons or things. —**le′gion·ar′y**, *adj.*

le·gion·naire (lē′jə nâr′), *n.* **1.** (*often cap.*) a member of the American Legion. **2.** a member of any legion.

le′gionnaires′′ disease′, an acute, often fatal disease of unknown cause, characterized by sudden nausea and high fever. [from its first breakout at an American Legion convention in Philadelphia in 1976]

legis., **1.** legislation. **2.** legislative. **3.** legislature.

leg·is·late (lej′is lāt′), *v.*, **-lat·ed**, **-lat·ing**. —*v.i.* **1.** to make or enact laws. —*v.t.* **2.** to create or control by or as by legislation: *attempts to legislate morality.* —**leg′is·la′tor**, *n.*

leg·is·la·tion (lej′is lā′shən), *n.* **1.** the act of legislating. **2.** a law or a body of laws enacted.

leg·is·la·tive (lej′is lā′tiv), *adj.* **1.** having the power to legislate. **2.** of or pertaining to legislation or a legislature. —**leg′is·la′tive·ly**, *adv.*

leg·is·la·ture (lej′is lā′chər), *n.* a body of persons empowered to make, change, or repeal laws.

le·git (lə jit′), *adj. Slang.* legitimate.

le·git·i·mate (li jit′ə mit), *adj.* **1.** according to law: *the legitimate owner of the property.* **2.** in accordance with established principles or standards. **3.** born in wedlock. **4.** reasonable or logical: *a legitimate conclusion.* **5.** justified or genuine: *a legitimate complaint.* **6.** of or pertaining to stage plays, as distinguished from burlesque, vaudeville, etc. —**le·git′i·ma·cy** (-mə sē), *n.* —**le·git′i·mate·ly**, *adv.* —**Syn. 1.** lawful, legal.

le·git·i·mize (li jit′ə mīz′), *v.t.*, **-mized**, **-miz·ing**. **1.** to make lawful or legal. **2.** to sanction or authorize. Also, **le·git′i·ma·tize′**. —**le·git′i·mi·za′tion**, *n.*

leg·man (leg′man′, -mən), *n.* **1.** a person employed to transact business outside an office. **2.** a reporter who gathers information by visiting news sources.

leg·room (leg′rōōm′, -rōōm′), *n.* space sufficient for a person to keep the legs in a comfortable position.

leg·ume (leg′yōōm, li gyōōm′), *n.* **1.** any of a large family of flowering plants having pods that split open when dry, comprising beans, peas, clover, etc. **2.** the pod or seed of such a plant. —**le·gu·mi·nous** (li-gyōō′mə nəs), *adj.*

leg·work (leg′wûrk′), *n. Informal.* work involving extensive walking, as gathering data.

le·ha·yim (lə K͟Hä′yim), *interj. Hebrew.* (a toast used by Jews in drinking to a person's health or well-being.) Also, **le·chay′im.** [lit., to life]

le·i¹ (lā′ē, lā), *n., pl.* **le·is.** (in the Hawaiian Islands) a wreath of flowers.

lei² (lā), *n.* pl. of **leu.**

Leip·zig (līp′sig, -sik), *n.* a city in S East Germany.

lei·sure (lē′zhər, lezh′ər), *n.* **1.** freedom from the demands of work or duty. **2.** free or unoccupied time. —*adj.* **3.** free or unoccupied. **4.** having leisure. —**lei′sure·less,** *adj.*

lei·sure·ly (lē′zhər lē, lezh′ər-), *adj.* **1.** acting or done without haste. —*adv.* **2.** in a leisurely manner.

leit·mo·tif (līt′mō tēf′), *n.* a leading, recurring theme, as in a literary work. Also, **leit′mo·tiv′.**

lek (lek), *n.* the monetary unit of Albania.

LEM, lunar excursion module.

lem·ming (lem′ing), *n.* a small northern rodent, noted for periodic mass migrations.

lem·on (lem′ən), *n.* **1.** the yellowish, acid fruit of a subtropical citrus tree. **2.** the tree itself. **3.** clear, light yellow color. **4.** *Informal.* an inferior, unsatisfactory person or thing. —**lem′on·y,** *adj.*

lem·on·ade (lem′ə nād′), *n.* a beverage of lemon juice, sweetener, and water.

lem·pi·ra (lem pēr′ə), *n.* the monetary unit of Honduras.

le·mur (lē′mər), *n.* a small, chiefly nocturnal mammal, allied to the monkey, having a foxlike face and woolly fur.

lend (lend), *v.,* **lent, lend·ing.** —*v.t.* **1.** to give the temporary use of (money), usually at interest. **2.** to grant the use of (something) with the understanding that it or its equivalent will be returned. **3.** to furnish or impart. **4.** to give or contribute freely. **5.** to adapt (oneself or itself). —*v.i.* **6.** to make loans. —**lend′er,** *n.*

lend-lease (lend′lēs′), *n.* the war materials and other supplies furnished by the U.S. to its allies during World War II.

length (lengkth, length), *n.* **1.** the linear extent of anything as measured from end to end. **2.** extent in time or space. **3.** a piece or portion of a certain extent. **4.** a large extent or expanse of something. **5. at length, a.** completely. **b.** finally. —**length′y,** *adj.* —**length′i·ly,** *adv.*

length·en (lengk′thən, leng′-), *v.t., v.i.* to make or become greater in length. —**length′en·er,** *n.*

length·wise (lengkth′wīz′, length′-), *adv., adj.* in the direction of the length. Also, **length′ways′** (-wāz′).

le·ni·ent (lē′nē ənt, lēn′yənt), *adj.* not harsh or strict, as in disciplining. —**le′ni·en·cy, le′ni·ence,** *n.* —**le′ni·ent·ly,** *adv.* —**Syn.** indulgent, mild, tolerant.

Len·in (len′in), *n.* **Vla·di·mir Il·yich** (vlad′ə mir′ il′yich), 1870–1924, Russian revolutionary leader. —**Len′in·ist,** *adj., n.*

Len·in·grad (len′in grad′), *n.* a seaport in the NW Soviet Union.

len·i·tive (len′i tiv), *adj.* soothing or mitigating, as medicines.

len·i·ty (len′i tē), *n., pl.* **-ties.** the quality or state of being lenient.

lens (lenz), *n., pl.* **lens·es.** **1.** a curved piece of glass or other transparent substance, used in changing the convergence of light rays, as for magnification or correcting defects of vision. **2.** some analogous device, as for affecting sound waves, electromagnetic radiation, etc. **3.** the crystalline body that focuses light rays in the eye.

lent (lent), *v.* pt. and pp. of **lend.**

Lent (lent), *n.* an annual season of fasting and penitence beginning on Ash Wednesday and lasting 40 weekdays to Easter. —**Lent′en, lent′en,** *adj.*

len·til (len′til, -t°l), *n.* **1.** a small annual legume of the bean family having flattened seeds used as food. **2.** the seed itself.

Le·o (lē′ō), *n.* the fifth sign of the zodiac. [< L: lion]

le·one (lē ōn′), *n.* the monetary unit of Sierra Leone.

le·o·nine (lē′ə nīn′), *adj.* of or resembling a lion.

leop·ard (lep′ərd), *n.* **1.** a large, ferocious, spotted Asian or African carnivore of the cat family, usually tawny with black markings. **2.** its fur or pelt.

le·o·tard (lē′ə tärd′), *n.* a skintight, one-piece garment, worn by acrobats, dancers, etc.

lep·er (lep′ər), *n.* a person affected with leprosy.

lep·re·chaun (lep′rə kôn′, -kon′), *n. Irish Folklore.* an elf who looks like a wrinkled old man.

lep·ro·sy (lep′rə sē), *n.* a mildly infectious disease characterized by ulcerations, loss of fingers and toes, anesthesia in certain nerve regions, etc. —**lep′rous,** *adj.*

les·bi·an (lez′bē ən), *n.* a female homosexual. —**les′bi·an·ism′,** *n.*

lese′ maj′esty (lēz), **1.** a crime against the dignity of a ruler. **2.** an attack on any traditional custom, belief, etc. Also, **lèse′ maj·esté.**

le·sion (lē′zhən), *n.* any localized, abnormal structural change in the body caused by injury or disease.

Le·so·tho (le sō'thō, le sōō'tōō), *n.* a country in S Africa.

less (les), *adv., a compar. of* little *with* least *as superl.* **1.** to a smaller extent, amount, or degree. —*adj., a compar. of* little *with* least *as superl.* **2.** smaller in size, amount, or degree. **3.** lower in consideration, dignity, or importance. —*n.* **4.** a smaller amount or quantity. —*prep.* **5.** minus.
—Usage. **3.** See fewer.

-less, a suffix meaning: **a.** without: *childless.* **b.** failure or inability to perform or be performed: *resistless; countless.*

les·see (le sē'), *n.* a person to whom a lease is granted.

less·en (les'ən), *v.t., v.i.* to make or become less. —Syn. abate, diminish.

less·er (les'ər), *adj., a compar. of* little *with* least *as superl.* smaller, as in size, amount, or importance.

les·son (les'ən), *n.* **1.** an exercise, a text, etc., assigned a pupil for study. **2.** a session of formal instruction. **3.** something to be learned or studied. **4.** an instructive example. **5.** a reproof or punishment. **6.** a portion of the Scripture to be read at a divine service.

les·sor (les'ôr, le sôr'), *n.* a person who grants a lease.

lest (lest), *conj.* for fear that.

let[1] (let), *v.,* **let, let·ting.** —*v.t.* **1.** to give opportunity to, esp. by not preventing or stopping. **2.** to allow to pass, go, or come. **3.** to grant the rental or hire of, as for occupancy. **4.** to contract (work) for performance. **5.** to cause or make: *to let one know the truth.* **6.** (used as an auxiliary expressive of a command, suggestion, etc.): *Let me see.* —*v.i.* **7.** to be rented or leased. **8.** let be, to leave alone. **9.** let down, **a.** to disappoint. **b.** to slacken or abate. **c.** to lower, as hair. **10.** let off, **a.** to release by exploding. **b.** to free or excuse. **11.** let on, *Informal.* **a.** to reveal one's true feelings. **b.** to pretend. **12.** let out, **a.** to divulge. **b.** to release, as from confinement. **c.** to enlarge (a garment). **13.** let up, *Informal.* **a.** to slacken or relax. **b.** to stop. —Syn. **1.** allow, permit.

let[2] (let), *n.* **1.** (in tennis, etc.) any play that is voided and must be replayed. **2.** without let or hindrance, *Chiefly Legal.* with no obstacle or impediment.

-let, a suffix meaning: **a.** small: *ringlet.* **b.** an article worn on: *bracelet.*

let·down (let'doun'), *n.* **1.** a minor disappointment. **2.** the descent of an aircraft from a higher to a lower altitude. **3.** letup (def. 1).

le·thal (lē'thəl), *adj.* causing death, as a dose. —**le·thal'i·ty,** *n.* —**le'thal·ly,** *adv.* —Syn. deadly, fatal.

leth·ar·gy (leth'ər jē), *n., pl.* **-gies. 1.** apathetic or sluggish inactivity. **2.** an abnormal state of overpowering drowsiness. —**le·thar·gic** (lə thär'jik), *adj.* —**le·thar'gi·cal·ly,** *adv.*

let's (lets), contraction of *let us.*

let·ter (let'ər), *n.* **1.** a handwritten or typewritten communication, usually transmitted by mail. **2.** an alphabetic character. **3.** a piece of printing type bearing such a character. **4.** actual terms or wording: *the letter of the law.* **5.** letters, **a.** literature in general. **b.** the profession of literature: *a man of letters.* **c.** knowledge, esp. of literature. —*v.t.* **6.** to mark or write with letters. —**let'ter·er** *n.*

let'ter bomb', an explosive device concealed in a postal envelope, intended to injure or kill the addressee.

let'ter box', *Brit.* mailbox.

let'ter car'rier, mailman.

let·tered (let'ərd), *adj.* **1.** marked with letters. **2.** of or characterized by learning or literary culture. **3.** *Literary.* educated or learned.

let·ter·head (let'ər hed'), *n.* **1.** a printed heading on stationery, esp. one giving a name and address. **2.** a sheet of this.

let·ter·ing (let'ər ing), *n.* **1.** the act or process of marking with letters. **2.** the letters themselves.

let·ter·per·fect (let'ər pûr'fikt), *adj.* correct in complete detail.

let·ter·press (let'ər pres'), *n.* **1.** matter printed directly from an inked raised surface. **2.** *Chiefly Brit.* printed text, as distinguished from illustrations.

let'ters pat'ent, a certificate issued by a government giving a person an exclusive right, as to a franchise.

let·tuce (let'is), *n.* an annual herb having crisp leaves used in salads.

let·up (let'up'), *n. Informal.* **1.** a slackening or lessening, as of pace or intensity. **2.** a pause or stop.

le·u (le'ōō), *n., pl.* **lei** (lā). the monetary unit of Rumania.

leu·ke·mi·a (lōō kē'mē ə), *n.* a usually fatal cancerous disease characterized by excessive production of white blood cells. Also, **leu·kae'mi·a.** —**leu·ke'mic, leu·kae'mic,** *adj., n.*

leu·ko·cyte (lōō'kə sīt'), *n.* one of the white or colorless nucleate cells of the blood that help maintain immunity to infection. Also, **leu'co·cyte'.**

lev (lef), *n., pl.* **lev·a** (lev'ə), the monetary unit of Bulgaria.

lev·ee (lev′ē), *n.* **1.** an embankment designed to prevent the flooding of a river. **2.** a landing place for river boats.

lev·el (lev′əl), *adj., n., v.,* -eled, -el·ing or -elled, -el·ling. —*adj.* **1.** having an even and flat surface. **2.** being in a plane parallel to the horizon. **3.** equal in quality or importance. **4.** uniform or steady, as in tone. **5.** balanced or calm, as in judgment. —*n.* **6.** the horizontal line or plane in which anything is situated, with regard to its elevation. **7.** a horizontal position or condition. **8.** a position with respect to a given height. **9.** a position in a graded scale of values. **10.** an instrument for determining or establishing a horizontal surface. —*v.t., v.i.* **11.** to make or become level or even. **12.** to bring (something) to the level of the ground: *to level trees.* **13.** *Informal.* to knock down (a person). **14.** to reduce to equality, as in status. **15.** to aim (a weapon, criticism, etc.) at a mark or objective. **16. level with,** *Slang.* to be frank with. —**lev′el·er, lev′el·ler,** *n.* —**lev′el·ly,** *adv.* —**lev′el·ness,** *n.*

lev·el·head·ed (lev′əl hed′id), *adj.* having common sense and sound judgment. —**lev′el·head′ed·ness,** *n.*

lev·er (lev′ər, lē′vər), *n.* **1.** a bar or rigid body used to lift weight and operating on a fixed axis or fulcrum. **2.** any device that works in this manner, as a crowbar. **3.** a means for wielding power. —*v.t.* **4.** to move with a lever.

lev·er·age (lev′ər ij, lē′vər ij), *n.* **1.** the mechanical advantage gained by using a lever. **2.** power to act or influence.

le·vi·a·than (li vī′ə thən), *n.* **1.** *Bible.* a sea monster. **2.** anything of immense size and power. [< LL *leviathan* < Heb *liwyāthān*]

Le·vi's (lē′vīz), *n. Trademark.* close-fitting trousers made of heavy denim.

lev·i·tate (lev′i tāt′), *v.i., v.t.,* -tat·ed, -tat·ing. to rise or cause to rise in the air, esp. in apparent defiance of gravity. —**lev′i·ta′tion,** *n.*

lev·i·ty (lev′i tē), *n., pl.* -ties. lightness or gaiety of mind, character, or behavior.

lev·y (lev′ē), *n., pl.* **lev·ies,** *v.,* **lev·ied, lev·y·ing.** —*n.* **1. a.** an imposing or collecting, as of a tax, by authority or force. **b.** the amount collected. **2. a.** the conscription of troops. **b.** the troops conscripted. —*v.t.* **3.** to impose (a tax). **4.** to conscript (troops). —*v.i.* **5.** to make a levy. **6.** to seize or attach property by judicial order. **7. levy war,** to start or make war. —**lev′i·er,** *n.*

lewd (lood), *adj.* **1.** inclined to or inciting to lust or lechery. **2.** obscene or indecent. —**lewd′ly,** *adv.* —**lewd′ness,** *n.*

lex., lexicon.

lex·i·cal (lek′si kəl), *adj.* **1.** of the words of a language, as contrasted with its grammar. **2.** of a lexicon. —**lex′i·cal·ly,** *adv.*

lex·i·cog·ra·phy (lek′sə kog′rə fē), *n.* **1.** the editing or making of dictionaries. **2.** the principles and procedures followed in making dictionaries. —**lex′i·cog′ra·pher,** *n.* —**lex′i·co·graph′ic** (-kō graf′ik), **lex′i·co·graph′i·cal,** *adj.* —**lex′i·co·graph′i·cal·ly,** *adv.*

lex·i·con (lek′sə kon′, -kən), *n.* **1.** a dictionary, esp. of Greek, Latin, or Hebrew. **2.** the vocabulary of a particular language or field.

LF, See **low frequency.**

l.f., *Print.* lightface. Also, **lf**

LG, Low German.

lg., **1.** large. **2.** long.

lge., large.

l.h., **1.** left hand. **2.** lower half.

L.H.D., Doctor of Humane Letters. [< L *Litterārum Humāniōrum Doctor*]

Li, lithium.

L.I., Long Island.

li·a·bil·i·ty (lī′ə bil′i tē), *n., pl.* -ties. **1. liabilities,** debts or monetary obligations. **2.** something disadvantageous. **3.** the state or quality of being liable.

li·a·ble (lī′ə bəl), *adj.* **1.** legally responsible. **2.** subject or susceptible. **3.** likely or apt.

li·ai·son (lē′ā zôn′, lē′ə zon′), *n.* **1.** the contact maintained between military units. **2.** any similar connection or relation. **3.** an illicit sexual relationship.

li·ar (lī′ər), *n.* a person who tells lies.

lib (lib), *n. Informal.* liberation, esp. as a social reform: *women's lib; gay lib.* —**lib′ber,** *n.*

li·ba·tion (lī bā′shən), *n.* **1.** a pouring out of wine or other liquid in honor of a deity. **2.** the liquid poured out. **3.** *Often Facetious.* an alcoholic beverage. —**li·ba′tion·ar′y,** *adj.*

li·bel (lī′bəl), *n., v.,* -beled, -bel·ing or -belled, -bel·ling. —*n.* **1. a.** defamation by written or printed words, pictures, or in any form other than by spoken words or gestures. **b.** the crime of publishing it. **2.** anything that is defamatory or that maliciously or damagingly misrepresents. —*v.t.* **3.** to publish a libel against. —**li′bel·er, li′bel·ler, li′bel·ist,** *n.* —**li′bel·ous, li′bel·lous,** *adj.*

lib·er·al (lib′ər əl, lib′rəl), *adj.* **1.** favoring progress and reform, as in politics, religion, etc. **2.** open-minded or tolerant. **3.** characterized by generosity and willingness to give in large amounts. **4.** given freely or abundantly. **5.** not strict or literal. —*n.* **6.** a person of liberal principles or views. —**lib′er·al·ism′,** *n.* —**lib′er·al·i·ty** (lib′ə ral′i tē), *n.* —**lib′er·al·ize′,** *v.t., v.i.* —**lib′er·al·i·za′tion,** *n.* —**lib′er·al·ly,** *adv.* —**lib′er·al·ness,** *n.* —**Syn. 3.** bountiful, munificent.

lib′eral arts′, the course of instruction at a college, comprising the humanities, natural sciences, mathematics, sociology, economics, etc.

lib·er·ate (lib′ə rāt′), *v.t.,* **-at·ed, -at·ing. 1.** to set free, as from bondage, foreign occupation, etc. **2.** to gain full or equal rights for (women). **3.** to free from combination, as a gas. —**lib·er·a′tion,** *n.* —**lib·er·a′tion·ist,** *n., adj.* —**lib′er·a′tor,** *n.*

Li·be·ri·a (lī bēr′ē ə), *n.* a country in W Africa: founded by freed American slaves 1822. —**Li·be′ri·an,** *adj., n.*

lib·er·tar·i·an (lib′ər târ′ē ən), *n.* **1.** a person who advocates liberty, esp. with regard to thought or conduct. **2.** a person who maintains the doctrine of free will.

lib·er·tine (lib′ər tēn′, -tin), *n.* **1.** a person who is morally or sexually unrestrained. —*adj.* **2.** dissolute or licentious.

lib·er·ty (lib′ər tē), *n., pl.* **-ties. 1.** freedom from bondage, captivity, etc. **2.** freedom from external control or interference. **3.** Often, **liberties,** an act of impertinence or excessive familiarity. **4.** permission granted to a sailor or seaman to spend time ashore. **5. at liberty, a.** free from captivity. **b.** out of work. **c.** free to do as specified.

li·bid·i·nous (li bid′ə nəs), *adj.* **1.** of the libido. **2.** full of lust.

li·bi·do (li bē′dō, -bī′dō), *n.* **1.** all of the instinctual energies and desires derived from the id. **2.** the sexual instinct. —**li·bid·i·nal** (li bid′°n°l), *adj.*

Li·bra (lī′brə, lē′-), *n.* the seventh sign of the zodiac. [< L: lit., pair of scales]

li·brar·i·an (lī brâr′ē ən), *n.* a person trained for and engaged in library service.

li·brar·y (lī′brer′ē, -brə rē, -brē), *n., pl.* **-brar·ies. 1.** a place containing books and other material for reading, study, or reference. **2.** a collection of books for similar purposes.

li·bret·to (li bret′ō), *n., pl.* **-bret·tos, -bret·ti** (-bret′ē). **1.** the text of an opera or similar extended musical composition. **2.** a book containing such a text. —**li·bret′tist,** *n.*

Lib·y·a (lib′ē ə), *n.* **1.** a country in N Africa. —**Lib′y·an,** *adj., n.*

lice (līs), *n.* a pl. of **louse.**

li·cense (lī′səns), *n., v.,* **-censed, -censing.** —*n.* Also, *Brit.,* **li′cence. 1.** formal permission from a constituted authority to do a specified thing, as to drive a car. **2.** a certificate of such permission. **3.** intentional deviation from rule, convention, or fact, as for the sake of literary effect. **4.** excessive freedom, esp. licentiousness. —*v.t.* **5.** to issue or grant a license to or for. —**li′cens·a·ble,** *adj.*

li·cen·see (lī′sən sē′), *n.* a person to whom a license is issued or granted.

li·cen·ti·ate (lī sen′shē it, -āt′), *n.* a person who has received a license, as from a university, to practice a profession.

li·cen·tious (lī sen′shəs), *adj.* **1.** sexually unrestrained. **2.** unrestrained by law or morality. —**li·cen′tious·ly,** *adv.* —**li·cen′tious·ness,** *n.*

li·chee (lē′chē), *n.* litchi.

li·chen (lī′kən), *n.* a plant composed of a fungus in union with an alga, growing on rocks, trees, etc. —**li′chen·ous,** *adj.*

lic·it (lis′it), *adj.* permitted by law. —**lic′it·ly,** *adv.*

lick (lik), *v.t.* **1.** to pass the tongue over the surface of. **2.** to pass or play lightly over. **3.** *Informal.* **a.** to hit, esp. as a punishment. **b.** to overcome, as in a fight. —*n.* **4.** a stroke of the tongue over something. **5.** the amount taken up by one stroke of the tongue. **6.** See **salt lick. 7.** *Informal.* **a.** a resounding blow. **b.** a brief, brisk burst of activity. **8. lick and a promise,** *Informal.* a perfunctory doing of something. —**lick′er,** *n.*

lick·e·ty-split (lik′i tē split′), *adv. Informal.* at great speed.

lick·ing (lik′ing), *n.* **1.** *Informal.* **a.** a beating or thrashing. **b.** a reversal or setback. **c.** a severe defeat. **2.** the act of a person or thing that licks.

lic·o·rice (lik′ə ris, -ər ish, lik′rish), *n.* **1.** a leguminous plant of Europe and Asia. **2.** the sweet-tasting, dried root of this plant or an extract made from it, used in medicine, confectionery, etc. **3.** a confection having a licorice flavor.

lid (lid), *n.* **1.** a movable cover, as for a jar. **2.** an eyelid. **3.** *Informal.* a restraint or curb, as on news. —**lid′ded,** *adj.*

li·dar (lī′där), *n.* a device similar to radar in function but utilizing infrared pulses in a laser beam. [*li(ght)* (*ra*)*dar*]

li·do (lē′dō), *n. Brit.* a public swimming pool, usually in the open air.

lie¹ (lī), *n., v.,* **lied, ly·ing.** —*n.* **1.** a false statement made with deliberate intent to deceive. —*v.i.* **2.** to tell a lie. —*v.t.* **3.** to bring or gain by lying. —**Syn. 1.** falsehood, fib, un-truth.

lie² (lī), v., **lay, lain, ly·ing,** n. —v.i. **1.** to be in or get into a reclining or prostrate position. **2.** to rest on a surface, esp. in a horizontal position. **3.** to be found in a particular place or situation. **4.** to be placed or situated. **5.** to be stretched out or extended.
—**Usage.** The two verbs LIE and LAY are not synonymous and should not be confused. LIE means "recline" and is not followed by an object: *He is lying on the couch.* LAY means "place or put" and requires an object: *Lay the book on the table.*

Liech·ten·stein (lik'tən stīn'), n. a country between Austria and Switzerland.

lied (lēd), n., pl. **lied·er** (lē'dər) a German song, lyric, or ballad.

lie' detec'tor, a polygraph used to determine the truth or falsity of a person's answers under questioning.

lief (lēf), adv. *Literary.* gladly: *I would as lief stay as go.*

liege (lēj), n. (in feudal law) **1.** a lord or ruler. **2.** a vassal or subject. —adj. **3.** *Rare.* loyal or faithful.

lien (lēn, lē'ən), n. the legal claim of one person upon the property of another person for the payment of a debt or the satisfaction of an obligation.

lieu (lōō), n. **1.** *Archaic.* place or stead. **2. in lieu of,** instead of.

Lieut., lieutenant.

lieu·ten·ant (lōō ten'ənt), n. **1. a.** See **first lieutenant. b.** See **second lieutenant. 2.** *U.S. Navy.* a commissioned officer ranking next below lieutenant commander. **3.** a person who acts in the place of his or her superior. —**lieu·ten'an·cy,** n.

lieuten'ant colo'nel, *U.S. Mil.* a commissioned officer ranking next above a major.

lieuten'ant comman'der, *U.S. Navy.* a commissioned officer ranking next below a commander.

lieuten'ant gen'eral, *U.S. Mil.* a commissioned officer ranking next above a major general.

lieuten'ant gov'ernor, *U.S.* a state officer next in rank to the governor.

lieuten'ant jun'ior grade', *U.S. Navy.* a commissioned officer ranking next above an ensign.

life (līf), n., pl. **lives,** adj. —n. **1.** the condition that distinguishes animals and plants from inorganic objects and dead organisms, being manifested by metabolism, growth, reproduction, and adaptation to environment. **2.** the animate existence of an individual. **3.** any specified period of animate existence. **4.** the term of existence or activity of something

inanimate, as a machine. **5.** a living being. **6.** living things collectively. **7.** a particular aspect of existence. **8.** the sum of experiences and actions that constitute a person's existence. **9.** a biography. **10.** animation or liveliness. **11.** a mode or manner of living. —**life'less,** adj. —**life'like',** adj.

life' belt', a beltlike life preserver.

life·blood (līf'blud'), n. **1.** the blood, considered as essential to maintain life. **2.** an indispensable element.

life·boat (līf'bōt'), n. a ship's boat designed for use in rescuing lives at sea.

life' buoy', buoy (def. 2).

life·guard (līf'gärd'), n. a trained swimmer employed, as at a beach, to protect bathers from drowning.

life' jack'et, a life preserver in the form of a sleeveless jacket. Also called **life' vest'.**

life·line (līf'līn'), n. **1.** a line or rope for saving life, as one attached to a lifeboat. **2.** the line by which a diver is lowered and raised. **3.** a route over which supplies must be sent to sustain an area or group of persons otherwise isolated.

life·long (līf'lông', -long'), adj. lasting or continuing through life.

life' net', a strong net held by fire fighters to catch persons jumping from a burning building.

life' preserv'er, any of various buoyant or inflatable devices for keeping a person afloat.

lif·er (lī'fər), n. *Slang.* **1.** a person sentenced to or serving life imprisonment. **2.** a career military officer or service person.

life' raft', a raft for use in emergencies at sea.

life·sav·er (līf'sā'vər), n. **1.** a person who rescues another from danger of death, esp. from drowning. **2.** *Informal.* a person or thing that saves a person, as from a difficulty. —**life'sav'ing,** adj., n.

life-size (līf'sīz'), adj. of the size of a living original: *a life-size statue.* Also, **life'-sized'.**

life-style (līf'stīl'), n. a person's general pattern of living.

life·time (līf'tīm'), n. the time that the life of someone or something continues.

life·work (līf'wûrk'), n. the complete or principal work of a lifetime.

LIFO (lī'fō), n. last-in, first-out (a method of inventory evaluation).

lift (lift), v.t. **1.** to bring (something) upward, as from the ground. **2.** to raise in rank, estimation, etc. **3.** to remove or end, as a ban or blockade. **4.** *Slang.* to steal, esp. from a store. **5.** to pay off (a mortgage, etc.) —v.i. **6.** to go up. **7.** to strain upward in lifting something. —*n.* **8.** the act of lifting. **9.** the distance that anything is lifted. **10.** the load or quantity lifted. **11.** a ride in a vehicle, esp. one given to a pedestrian. **12.** assistance of any kind. **13.** a feeling of exaltation. **14.** lifting force or effect. **15.** a device for lifting. **16.** *Brit.* elevator (def. 1). **17.** a rise or elevation of ground. **18.** elevated position, as of the chin. **19.** the component of the aerodynamic force exerted by the air on an airfoil, causing an aircraft to stay aloft.

lift·off (lift′ôf′, -of′), *n.* **1.** a vertical ascent by a spacecraft or aircraft. **2.** the instant of this.

lig·a·ment (lig′ə mənt), *n.* a band of fibrous tissue that connects bones or holds organs in place.

li·gate (lī′gāt), *v.t.,* **-gat·ed, -gat·ing.** to bind with a ligature. —**li·ga′tion,** *n.*

lig·a·ture (lig′ə chər, -choŏr′), *n.* **1.** anything that serves for binding or tying up, as a band, bandage, or cord. **2.** a character or type combining two or more letters, as fi, ffl. **3.** *Music.* a slur. **4.** *Surg.* a thread or wire for constriction of blood vessels.

li·ger (lī′gər), *n.* the offspring of a male lion and a female tiger. [*li*(*on*) + (*ti*)*ger*]

light¹ (līt), *n., adj., v.,* **light·ed** or **lit, light·ing.** —*n.* **1.** something that makes things visible or affords illumination. **2. a.** electromagnetic radiation to which the organs of sight react. **b.** ultraviolet or infrared rays. **3.** an illuminating source, as the sun, a lamp, or a beacon. **4.** radiance or illumination. **5.** daybreak or dawn. **6.** the aspect in which a thing appears or is regarded. **7.** a means of igniting, as a spark or flame. **8.** public notice or knowledge. **9.** one compartment of a window or window sash. **10.** mental or spiritual enlightenment. **11.** a person who is an illuminating example. **12. in the light of,** taking into account. **13. see the light, a.** to come into being. **b.** to be made public. **c.** to begin to understand. **14. shed** or **throw light on,** to clarify. —*adj.* **15.** having light or illumination. **16.** pale and whitish. —*v.t.* **17.** to set burning, as a fire. **18.** to give light to. **19.** to make (an area) bright with light. **20.** to cause to brighten, esp. with joy or animation. —*v.i.* **21.** to take fire or become kindled. **22.** to ignite a cigar, cigarette, or pipe for purposes of smoking: *He lighted up before speaking.* **23.** to become lighted. —**light′ness,** *n.*

light² (līt), *adj.* **1.** of little weight. **2.** not heavy, esp. in proportion to bulk. **3.** of less than the usual weight, amount, intensity, etc. **4.** not difficult or burdensome: *a light task.* **5.** not very profound or serious: *light reading.* **6.** of little importance or consequence. **7.** (of food) easily digested. **8.** airy or buoyant in movement. **9.** characterized by good spirits and gaiety: *a light laugh.* **10.** characterized by lack of proper seriousness: *light conduct.* **11.** slightly delirious. **12.** using small-scale machinery primarily for the production of consumer goods: *light industry.* **13. make light of,** to treat as trivial. —*adv.* **14.** with little load or baggage: *to travel light.* —**light′ly,** *adv.* —**light′ness,** *n.*

light³ (līt), *v.i.,* **light·ed** or **lit, light·ing.** **1.** to come by chance: *to light on a clue.* **2.** to land or settle upon, as a bird. **3.** *Archaic.* to get down, as from a horse. **4. light into,** *Slang.* to attack suddenly. **5. light out,** *Slang.* to leave quickly.

light′ adapta′tion, the reflex adaptation of the eye to bright light. —**light′-a·dapt′ed,** *adj.*

light·en¹ (līt′ən), *v.t., v.i.* to make or become lighter or less dark. —**light′-en·er,** *n.*

light·en² (līt′ən), *v.t., v.i.* **1.** to make or become lighter in weight. **2.** to make or become less gloomy.

light·er¹ (lī′tər), *n.* **1.** a person or thing that lights or ignites. **2.** a device used in lighting cigars, cigarettes, or pipes.

light·er² (lī′tər), *n.* a barge used in loading or unloading ships, or in transporting goods for short distances.

light·face (līt′fās′), *n. Print.* a type characterized by thin lines. —**light′-faced′,** *adj.*

light·fin·gered (līt′fing′gərd), *adj.* having nimble fingers, esp. in picking pockets.

light·foot·ed (līt′foot′id), *adj.* stepping lightly or nimbly.

light·head·ed (līt′hed′id), *adj.* **1.** having a frivolous disposition. **2.** dizzy or delirious.

light·heart·ed (līt′här′tid), *adj.* cheerful or gay. —**light′heart′ed·ly,** *adv.* —**light′heart′ed·ness,** *n.*

light′ heav′yweight, a boxer weighing between 161 and 175 pounds.

light·house (līt′hous′), *n.* a tower displaying a powerful light for the guidance of ships at night.

light·ing (lī′ting), *n.* **1.** the act of igniting or illuminating. **2.** the arrangement of lights to achieve particular effects.

light′ me′ter, a small device that measures the intensity of light in a given place and indicates proper photographic exposure.

light-mind·ed (līt′mīn′did), *adj.* having or showing a lack of serious purpose or attitude.

light·ning (līt′ning), *n.* **1.** a flash of light in the atmosphere caused by an electric charge within a cloud, between clouds, or between a cloud and the ground. —*adj.* **2.** of or like lightning, esp. in regard to speed of movement.

light′ning bug′, firefly.

light′ning rod′, a rodlike conductor installed to divert lightning away from a structure.

light′ op′era, operetta.

lights (līts), *n.pl.* the lungs, esp. of sheep, pigs, etc.

light·ship (līt′ship′), *n.* a ship anchored in a specific location and displaying a light or lights for the guidance of mariners.

light′ show′, a form of entertainment consisting of constantly changing patterns of light and color, usually accompanied by electronically amplified sounds.

light·some (līt′səm), *adj. Literary.* **1.** nimbly buoyant. **2.** gay or light-hearted.

light·weight (līt′wāt′), *adj.* **1.** light in weight. **2.** without seriousness of purpose. —*n.* **3.** a person of less than average weight. **4.** a boxer weighing between 126 and 135 pounds.

light-year (līt′yēr′, -yēr′), *n.* the distance traveled by light in one year, about 5,880,000,000,000 miles.

lig·ne·ous (lig′nē əs), *adj.* of or like wood.

lig·ni·fy (lig′nə fī′), *v.i., v.t., -fied, -fy-ing.* to become or cause to become wood or woody. —**lig′ni·fi·ca′tion**, *n.*

lig·nite (lig′nīt), *n.* a dark-brown coal having a woody texture.

lik·a·ble (lī′kə bəl), *adj.* of a nature that is easily liked. Also, **like′a-ble.** —**lik′a·ble·ness, lik′a·bil′i·ty,** *n.*

like¹ (līk), *adj.* **1.** of the same form, kind, character, etc. —*prep.* **2.** similarly to: *He works like a beaver.* **3.** resembling (someone or something). **4.** characteristic of: *It would be like him to forget our appointment.* **5.** indicative of: *It looks like snow.* **6.** disposed or inclined to: *to feel like going to bed.* **7.** *Nonstandard.* such as: *a hobby like photography.* —*adv.* **8.** *Informal.* likely or probably: *like as not.* —*conj. Nonstandard.* **9.** just as: *It happened like it would.* **10.** as if: *He acted like he was afraid to go home.* —*n.* **11.** a counterpart, match, or equal. **12.** the like, something of a similar nature. **13.** the like or likes of, someone or something like.

—**Usage. 9, 10.** The use of LIKE in place of AS is avoided by educated speakers and writers. *Do as I say, not as I do* does not admit of LIKE instead of AS. In an occasional idiomatic phrase, LIKE is less offensive when substituted for AS IF (*He raced down the street like mad*), but note that this is clearly colloquial.

like² (līk), *v.,* **liked, lik·ing,** *n.* —*v.t.* **1.** to find agreeable or congenial to one's taste. **2.** to wish or prefer: *I'd like to stay.* —*v.i.* **3.** to feel inclined: *Come whenever you like.* —*n.* **4.** Usually, **likes.** the things a person likes or fancies: *likes and dislikes.*

-like, a suffix meaning "like," "similar," or "characteristic of": *childlike; lifelike.*

like·li·hood (līk′lē hŏŏd′), *n.* **1.** the state of being likely or probable. **2.** something likely or probable.

like·ly (līk′lē), *adj.,* **-li·er, -li·est,** *adv.* —*adj.* **1.** reasonably to be expected or believed: *a thing not likely to happen.* **2.** seeming like truth or fact: *a likely story.* **3.** apparently suitable: *a likely spot to build on.* **4.** showing promise of achievement or excellence: *a fine, likely young man.* —*adv.* **5.** probably.

like-mind·ed (līk′mīn′did), *adj.* having a similar opinion, disposition, etc. —**like′-mind′ed·ness,** *n.*

lik·en (lī′kən), *v.t.* to represent as like or similar.

like·ness (līk′nis), *n.* **1.** a representation or image, esp. a portrait. **2.** the semblance or appearance of something. **3.** the state or fact of being like. —*Syn.* **3.** similarity, resemblance.

like·wise (līk′wīz′), *adv.* **1.** in addition. **2.** in like manner.

lik·ing (lī′king), *n.* **1.** a feeling of attraction or fondness. **2.** pleasure or taste. —*Syn.* **1.** inclination, partiality, preference.

li·lac (lī′lək, -lok, -lak), *n.* **1.** a shrub having large clusters of fragrant purple or white flowers. **2.** a pale reddish purple.

Lil·li·pu·tian (lil′l pyŏŏ′shən), *adj.* **1.** extremely small. **2.** petty or trivial.

lilt (lilt), *n.* **1.** rhythmic swing or cadence. **2.** a light, gay song or tune.

lil·y (lil′ē), *n., pl.* **lil·ies,** *adj.* —*n.* **1.** any scaly-bulbed herb having showy, funnel-shaped or bell-shaped flowers. **2.** its flower. **3.** any similar plant, as the calla lily. —*adj.* **4.** white as a lily. **5.** delicately fair.

lil·y-liv·ered (lil′ē liv′ərd), *adj.* weak in courage.

lil′y of the val′ley, *pl.* **lilies of the valley.** a stemless herb having a raceme of drooping, bell-shaped, fragrant, white flowers.

lil′y pad′, the large, floating leaf of a water lily.

lim., limit.

Li·ma (lē′mə), *n.* the capital of Peru.

li′ma bean′ (lī′mə), **1.** a bean having a broad, flat, edible seed. **2.** the seed, used for food.

limb (lim), *n.* **1.** a part or member of an animal body distinct from the head and trunk, as a leg, arm, or wing. **2.** a main branch of a tree. **3. out on a limb,** *Informal.* in a dangerous situation. **—limbed** (limd), *adj.* **—limb′less,** *adj.*

lim·ber (lim′bər), *adj.* **1.** bending readily. **2.** characterized by ease in bending the body. **—**v.t.,* *v.i.* **3.** to make or become limber: *to limber up before the game.* **—lim′ber·ly,** *adv.* **—lim′ber·ness,** *n.*

lim·bo¹ (lim′bō), *n., pl.* **-bos. 1.** (*often cap.*) *Theol.* a region on the border of hell or heaven for some souls, as those of unbaptized infants. **2.** a place or state of oblivion. **3.** a place midway between two extremes. [< ML *in limbo* on hell's border (L: on the edge)]

lim·bo² (lim′bō), *n., pl.* **-bos.** a dance of West Indian origin.

Lim·burg·er (lim′bûr′gər), *n.* a variety of soft cheese of strong odor and flavor. Also called **Lim′burger cheese′.**

lime¹ (līm), *n., v.,* **limed, lim·ing.** **—**n.* **1.** a white or grayish-white solid, obtained from calcium carbonate, limestone, or oyster shells: used chiefly in mortars, plasters, and cements, and in the manufacture of steel, paper, etc. **—**v.t.* **2.** to treat with lime.

lime² (līm), *n.* **1.** the small, greenish-yellow, acid fruit of a tropical tree allied to the lemon. **2.** its tree.

lime³ (līm), *n.* a European linden tree.

lime·ade (līm′ād′), *n.* a beverage consisting of lime juice, a sweetener, and water.

lime-kiln (līm′kil′, -kiln′), *n.* a furnace for making lime by calcining limestone or shells.

lime·light (līm′līt′), *n.* **1.** (formerly) a spotlight used for the stage, using a flame of mixed gases directed at a cylinder of lime. **2.** the center of public notice or interest.

lim·er·ick (lim′ər ik), *n.* a short, humorous and often nonsensical verse of five lines. [after *Limerick,* county in Ireland where it originated]

lime·stone (līm′stōn′), *n.* any stone consisting mainly of calcium carbonate.

lim·it (lim′it), *n.* **1.** the final or furthest bound or point as to extent or continuance. **2. limits,** the premises enclosed within boundaries. **3.** the maximum sum or quantity allowed. **—**v.t.* **4.** to restrict by establishing limits. **5.** to confine within limits. **—lim′it·a·ble,** *adj.* **—lim′i·ta′tion,** *n.* **—lim′i·ta′tive,** *adj.* **—lim′it·er,** *n.* **—lim′it·less,** *adj.* **—lim′it·less·ly,** *adv.*

lim·it·ed (lim′i tid), *adj.* **1.** confined within limits. **2.** *Chiefly Brit.* (of a business firm) owned by stockholders, each having a restricted liability for the company's debts. **3.** (of trains, buses, etc.) making only a restricted number of stops en route. **—lim′it·ed·ly,** *adv.* **—lim′it·ed·ness,** *n.*

lim′ited war′, a war waged with less than total capability or with less than total victory as the purpose.

limn (lim), *v.t. Archaic.* **1.** to draw or paint. **2.** to describe or depict. **—limn·er** (lim′nər), *n.*

lim·o (li′mō), *n., pl.* **lim·os.** *Informal.* a limousine.

li·mo·nite (lī′mə nīt′), *n.* an important iron ore, a hydrated ferric oxide. **—li′mo·nit′ic** (-nit′ik), *adj.*

lim·ou·sine (lim′ə zēn′, lim′ə zēn′), *n.* **1.** any large, luxurious, often chauffeur-driven automobile. **2.** a large sedan or small bus for transporting passengers to and from an airport.

limp¹ (limp), *v.i.* **1.** to walk with a jerky movement, as when lame. **2.** to progress with difficulty. **—**n.* **3.** a lame gait or movement.

limp² (limp), *adj.* **1.** lacking stiffness or firmness, as of substance. **2.** lacking vitality. **3.** without proper strength or force, as of character. **—limp′ly,** *adv.* **—limp′ness,** *n.* **—Syn. 1.** flabby, flaccid, soft.

lim·pet (lim′pit), *n.* a marine mollusk with a low conical shell, found adhering to rocks.

lim·pid (lim′pid), *adj.* clear or transparent, as water. **—lim·pid′i·ty, lim′pid·ness,** *n.* **—lim′pid·ly,** *adv.*

lim·y (lī′mē), *adj.,* **lim·i·er, lim·i·est.** consisting of, containing, or like lime. **—lim′i·ness,** *n.*

lin., **1.** lineal. **2.** linear.

lin·age (lī′nij), *n.* the number of written or printed lines, as in an advertisement. Also, **lin′e·age.**

linch·pin (linch′pin′), *n.* a pin inserted through the end of an axle to secure a wheel.

Lin·coln (ling′kən), *n.* **1.** Abraham, 1809–65, 16th president of the U.S. 1861–65. **2.** the capital of Nebraska.

lin·den (lin′dən), *n.* a large shade tree having fragrant yellowish-white flowers and heart-shaped leaves.

line¹ (līn), *n., v.,* **lined, lin·ing.** **—**n.* **1.** a thin mark made with a pencil, pen, etc., to divide an area, depict an object, etc. **2.** a number of persons or things arranged along an imaginary mark: *to wait in line.* **3.** an indication of demarcation. **4.** outline or contour. **5.** *Math.* the path traced by a moving point. **6.** a furrow or wrinkle, esp. on the face. **7.** a single row of letters or other characters on a page, inscription, etc. **8.** a verse of poetry. **9.** Usually, **lines.** the spoken words of a dramatic performance. **10.** a brief written message. **11.** a course of movement or progress. **12.** a course of action, belief, etc., as one formally adopted by a political group. **13.** a piece of discovered information. **14.** a series of ancestors or of animals or plants of preceding generations. **15.** *Slang.* a form of conversation intended to persuade or impress. **16.** a transportation company or system, or one of its routes. **17.** a person's occupation or business. **18.** a variety of related items for sale. **19.** a cord or rope, esp. a strong one used for fishing, etc. **20.** the wire or wires connecting points or stations in a telegraph or telephone system, or the system itself. **21.** *Mil.* a defensive position or front. **22.** *Football.* the players stationed on the line of scrimmage. **23. down the line,** thoroughly or fully. **24. draw the line,** to impose a limit. **25. hold the line,** to remain firm. **26. in line for,** to be entitled to. **27. in line with,** in conformity with. **28. into line,** a. into alignment. **b.** into agreement or conformity. **29. on the line,** *Slang.* a. at high risk or in a vulnerable position. **b.** in cash rather than on credit. **30. out of line,** *Slang.* a. in disagreement with what is accepted or practiced. **b.** impertinent or presumptuous. —*v.i.* **31.** to take a position in a line: *to line up for play.* —*v.t.* **32.** to bring into a line. **33.** to mark with lines. **34.** to form a line along. **35. line up,** to assemble or rally. —**line′less,** *adj.* —**lin′y, line′y,** *adj.*

line² (līn), *v.t.,* **lined, lin·ing.** to cover the inner side of.

lin·e·age (lin′ē ij), *n.* **1.** lineal descent from an ancestor. **2.** family or race.

lin·e·al (lin′ē əl), *adj.* **1.** being in the direct line, as a descendant, or in a direct line, as succession. **2.** of lineal descent. **3.** linear (def. 1).

lin·e·a·ment (lin′ē ə mənt), *n.* Often, **lineaments.** a distinguishing feature or detail, esp. of the face.

lin·e·ar (lin′ē ər), *adj.* **1.** of, consisting of, or using lines. **2.** pertaining to length. **3.** narrow and elongated: *a linear leaf.* —**lin′e·ar·ly,** *adv.*

line·back·er (līn′bak′ər), *n. Football.* a player on defense who takes a position close behind the linemen.

line′ drive′, *Baseball.* a batted ball that travels low, fast, and straight.

line′ graph′, a graph using lines drawn at right angles to each other.

line·man (līn′mən), *n.* **1.** a person who installs or repairs telephone or telegraph wires. **2.** *Football.* one of the players in the line.

lin·en (lin′ən), *n.* **1.** fabric woven from flax yarns. **2.** Often, **linens.** sheets, towels, etc., made of linen cloth or similar fabric. **3.** yarn or thread made of flax fiber. —**lin′en·y,** *adj.*

line′ of scrim′mage, *Football.* an imaginary line on each side of which the teams line up to start a play.

lin·er¹ (lī′nər), *n.* **1.** one of a commercial line of steamships or airplanes. **2.** a cosmetic used to outline or highlight the eyes.

lin·er² (lī′nər), *n.* **1.** a person who fits or provides linings. **2.** something serving as a lining.

lines·man (līnz′mən), *n.* **1.** lineman (def. 1). **2.** a. an official, as in tennis and soccer, who assists the referee. **b.** *Football.* an official who marks the distances gained and lost.

line·up (līn′up′), *n.* **1.** an orderly arrangement of persons or things in a line. **2.** the persons or things themselves. **3.** *Sports.* the list of the participating players in a game.

ling (liñg), *n.* an elongated, marine food fish.

-ling, a suffix meaning: **a.** a person connected with: *underling.* **b.** little: *duckling.*

ling., linguistics.

lin·ger (liñg′gər), *v.i.* **1.** to remain in a place, as if from reluctance to leave. **2.** to dwell in thought or enjoyment. **3.** to be tardy in action. —**lin′ger·er,** *n.* —**lin′ger·ing,** *adj.*

lin·ge·rie (län′zhə rā′, lan′zhə rē′, -jə-), *n.* women's undergarments.

lin·go (liñg′gō), *n., pl.* **-goes. 1.** language, esp. one that is foreign or strange. **2.** jargon (def. 1).

lin′gua fran′ca (liñg′gwə frañg′kə), any language widely used as a means of communication among speakers of different languages.

lin·gual (liñg′gwəl), *adj.* of or produced by the tongue.

lin·guist (liñg′gwist), *n.* **1.** a specialist in linguistics. **2.** polyglot (def. 3).

lin·guis·tics (liñg gwis′tiks), *n.* **1.** the science of language. **2.** the systematic study of a particular language or dialect. —**lin·guis′tic,** *adj.* —**lin·guis′ti·cal·ly,** *adv.*

lin·i·ment (lin′ə mənt), *n.* a liquid preparation for rubbing on or applying to the skin, as for bruises.

lin·ing (lī′niñg), *n.* material used to line the linner side of something, as a garment.

link (liñgk), *n.* **1.** any of the separate pieces that form a chain. **2.** anything serving to connect one part or thing with another. 3. any of a number of connected sausages. 4. a length unit of 7.92 inches. —*v.t.*, *v.i.* 5. to join by or as by links. —**link′er,** *n.*

link·age (liŋg′kij), *n.* 1. the act of linking or state or manner of being linked. 2. a system of links.

links (liŋks), *n.pl.* a golf course.

link·up (liŋgk′up′), *n.* 1. a contact established, as of troops or spacecraft. 2. something serving as a linking element or system.

lin·net (lin′it), *n.* a small, Old World songbird.

li·no·le·um (li nō′lē əm), *n.* a floor covering formed of canvas coated with linseed oil, powdered cork, and rosin. [< L *līn(um)* flax, linen + *oleum* oil]

Lin·o·type (lī′nə tīp′), *n.* **Trademark.** a typesetting machine that casts solid lines of type from brass dies which are selected automatically by actuating a keyboard.

lin·seed (lin′sēd′), *n.* the seed of flax.

lin′seed oil′, a drying oil obtained by pressing linseed, used in making paints, etc.

lin·sey-wool·sey (lin′zē wŏŏl′zē), *n.* a coarse fabric woven from linen warp and wool filling.

lint (lint), *n.* 1. bits of thread or fluff. 2. staple cotton fiber used to make yarn. 3. *Brit.* a soft surgical dressing. —**lint′y,** *adj.*

lin·tel (lin′t°l), *n.* a horizontal architectural member supporting the weight above an opening, as of a door.

li·on (lī′ən), *n.* 1. a large and powerful carnivorous cat of Africa and southern Asia, the male of which usually has a mane. 2. a man of great strength or courage. 3. a celebrity who is much sought after. 4. **the Lion,** Leo. —**li′on·ess,** *n.fem.*

li·on·heart·ed (lī′ən här′tid), *adj.* very courageous.

li·on·ize (lī′ə nīz′), *v.t.,* **-ized, -iz·ing.** to treat (a person) as a celebrity. —**li′on·i·za′tion,** *n.* —**li′on·iz′er,** *n.*

li′on's share′, an unreasonably large portion.

lip (lip), *n.* 1. either of the two fleshy folds forming the margins of the mouth. 2. a liplike part or structure, as the rim of a pitcher or the edge of a canyon. 3. *Slang.* impudent talk. 4. **keep a stiff upper lip,** to face misfortune bravely. —**lip′less,** *adj.* —**lipped** (lipt), *adj.* —**lip′py,** *adj.* —**lip′pi·ness,** *n.*

lip′ read′ing, the technique by which a deaf person understands speech by watching the lip movements of the speaker. —**lip′-read′,** *v.t., v.i.* —**lip′ read′er.**

lip′ serv′ice, insincere profession of devotion or good will.

lip·stick (lip′stik′), *n.* a crayonlike cosmetic used in coloring the lips.

lip′ sync′, the synchronization of lip movements on film or in live performance with sound recorded previously. Also, **lip′ synch′.** —**lip′-sync′,** **lip′-synch′,** *v.i., v.t.*

liq., 1. liquid. 2. liquor.

liq·ue·fy (lik′wə fī′), *v.t., v.i.,* **-fied, -fy·ing.** to make or become liquid. —**liq′ue·fac′tion** (-fak′shən), *n.* —**liq′ue·fi′a·ble,** *adj.* —**liq′ue·fi′er,** *n.*

li·queur (li kûr′, -kyŏŏr′), *n.* a usually strong, sweet, and highly flavored alcoholic liquor.

liq·uid (lik′wid), *adj.* 1. neither gaseous nor solid. 2. flowing like water. 3. clear or bright: *liquid eyes.* 4. (of tones, etc.) having an agreeable, flowing quality. 5. (of movements, etc.) graceful and unconstricted. 6. readily convertible into cash: *liquid assets.* —*n.* 7. a liquid substance. —**liq·uid′i·ty,** *n.*

liq·ui·date (lik′wi dāt′), *v.t.,* **-dat·ed, -dat·ing.** 1. to settle or pay (a debt). 2. to dissolve (a business or an estate) by apportioning the assets to offset the liabilities. 3. to convert into cash. 4. to get rid of, esp. by killing. —**liq′ui·da′tion,** *n.* —**liq′ui·da′tor,** *n.*

liq·uid·ize (lik′wi dīz′), *v.t.,* **-ized, -iz·ing.** to cause to be of liquid quality.

liq′uid meas′ure, the system of units used in measuring liquid capacity.

liq·uor (lik′ər), *n.* 1. a distilled or spirituous beverage, as brandy or whiskey. 2. the fluid in which food has been cooked.

li·ra (lēr′ə), *n., pl.* **li·re** (lēr′ā), **li·ras.** the monetary unit of Italy and Turkey.

Lis·bon (liz′bən), *n.* the capital of Portugal.

lisle (līl), *n.* a fine, high- and hard-twisted cotton thread, used esp. for hosiery.

lisp (lisp), *n.* 1. a speech defect consisting in pronouncing *s* and *z* like or nearly like the *th* sounds of *thin* and *this,* respectively. 2. the act or sound of lisping. —*v.i., v.i.* 3. to pronounce with a lisp. 4. to speak imperfectly, esp. in a childish manner. —**lisp′er,** *n.* —**lisp′ing·ly,** *adv.*

lis·some (lis′əm), *adj.* 1. lithe, esp. of body. 2. agile or active. Also, **lis′som.** —**lis′some·ly,** *adv.* —**lis′some·ness,** *n.*

list¹ (list), *n.* 1. a series of names or other items set down in a meaningful sequence. —*v.t.* 2. to set down or enter in a list.

list² (list), *n.* 1. a careening to one side, as of a ship. —*v.t., v.i.* 2. to incline or cause to incline to one side.

lis·ten (lis′ən), v.i. 1. to give attention for the purpose of hearing. 2. to heed or pay attention. —**lis′ten·er,** n.

list·ing (lis′tiŋ), n. 1. the act of making a list. 2. an entry in a list.

list·less (list′lis), adj. feeling or showing no inclination toward or interest in anything. —**list′less·ly,** adv. —**list′less·ness,** n. —Syn. languid, indifferent.

list′ price′, the price given by a wholesaler from which a trade discount is computed.

lists (lists), n.pl. an enclosed arena in which knights fought tournaments.

Liszt (list), n. Franz (fränts), 1811–86, Hungarian composer and pianist.

lit¹ (lit), v. a pt. and pp. of light¹.

lit² (lit), v. a pt. and pp. of light².

lit., 1. liter; liters. 2. literal. 3. literally. 4. literary. 5. literature.

lit·a·ny (lit′ən ē), n., pl. -nies. a prayer consisting of a series of invocations with responses.

li·tchi (lē′chē), n. a Chinese tree bearing a fruit consisting of a thin shell enclosing a sweet pulp and a single seed.

li′tchi nut′, the brownish, dried litchi fruit.

li·ter (lē′tər), n. a metric unit of capacity equivalent to 1.0567 liquid quarts or 0.908 dry quart.

lit·er·a·cy (lit′ər ə sē), n. the ability to read and write.

lit·er·al (lit′ər əl), adj. 1. following the words of the original as closely as possible: a literal translation. 2. (of a person) tending to construe words in an unimaginative way. 3. in a primary or strict meaning. 4. true to fact: a literal statement. —**lit′er·al·ly,** adv.

lit·er·al·ism (lit′ər ə liz′əm), n. 1. adherence to the literal sense. 2. exact representation or portrayal, as in art.

lit·er·ar·y (lit′ə rer′ē), adj. 1. of, pertaining to, or characteristic of literature. 2. acquainted with literature. 3. stilted or pedantic. 4. used in writing somewhat formal, elevated poetry or prose. —**lit′er·ar′i·ness,** n.

lit·er·ate (lit′ər it), adj. 1. able to read and write. 2. educated or learned. —n. 3. a literate person. —**lit′er·ate·ly,** adv.

lit·e·ra·ti (lit′ə rä′tē, -rä′tī), n.pl. persons of scholarly or literary attainments.

lit·e·ra·tim (lit′ə rä′tim), adv. letter for letter.

lit·er·a·ture (lit′ər ə chər, -choŏr′, li′trə-), n. 1. writing regarded as having permanent worth through its intrinsic excellence. 2. the entire body of writings of a specific language, period, people, etc. 3. the writings dealing with a particular subject. 4. any kind of printed material, as circulars.

lith., 1. lithograph. 2. lithographic. 3. lithography. Also, **litho., lithog.**

lithe (lĩth), adj., **lith·er, lith·est.** 1. bending readily. 2. smoothly graceful. Also, **lithe′some.** —**lithe′ly,** adv. —**lithe′ness,** n. —Syn. limber, lissome, supple.

lith·i·um (lith′ē əm), n. Chem. a soft, silver-white metallic element, the lightest of all metals. Symbol: Li; at. wt.: 6.939; at. no.: 3.

lith·o·graph (lith′ə graf′, -gräf′), n. 1. a print produced by lithography. —v.t. 2. to produce by lithography. —**li·thog·ra·pher** (li thog′rə fər), n.

li·thog·ra·phy (li thog′rə fē), n. the process of producing an image on a flat, specially prepared stone or plate in such a way that it will absorb and print with special inks. —**lith·o·graph·ic** (lith′ə graf′ik), adj. —**lith′o·graph′i·cal·ly,** adv.

li·thol·o·gy (li thol′ə jē), n. the science of rocks. —**lith·o·log·ic** (lith′ə loj′ik), adj.

lith·o·sphere (lith′ə sfēr′), n. the crust of the earth.

Lith·u·a·ni·a (lith′ōō ā′nē ə), n. a constituent republic of the Soviet Union on the Baltic. —**Lith′u·a′ni·an,** adj. n.

lit·i·gant (lit′ə gənt), n. a person engaged in a lawsuit.

lit·i·gate (lit′ə gāt′), v., -gat·ed, -gat·ing. —v.t. 1. to make the subject of a lawsuit. —v.i. 2. to carry on a lawsuit. —**lit′i·ga′tion,** n. —**lit′i·ga′tor,** n.

li·ti·gious (li tij′əs), adj. 1. of litigation. 2. excessively inclined to litigate. 3. inclined to dispute or disagree. —**li·ti′gious·ness,** n.

lit·mus (lit′məs), n. a coloring matter obtained from certain lichens that turns blue in alkaline solution and red in acid solution, widely used as an indicator.

lit′mus pa′per, a strip of paper impregnated with litmus, used as an indicator.

li·tre (lē′tər), n. Brit. liter.

Litt.D., Doctor of Letters; Doctor of Literature. [< L Lit(t)erārum Doctor]

lit·ter (lit′ər), n. 1. a variety of objects scattered about, esp. scattered rubbish. 2. a number of young brought forth by certain animals at one birth. 3. loose straw, hay, etc., used as bedding for animals. 4. a stretcherlike framework for a sick or wounded person. 5. a vehicle carried by people or animals, consisting of a couch, often covered and curtained, suspended between shafts. 6. slightly decomposed organic material on the floor of a forest. —v.t. 7. to strew (a place) with litter. 8. to scatter (objects) in disorder. 9. to give birth to (young), as a pig.

lit·te·ra·teur (lit′ər ə tûr′), n. a writer of literary works.

lit·ter·bug (lit′ər bug′), n. a person who litters a public place.

lit·tle (lit′ʰl), adj., less or less·er, least or lit·tler, lit·tlest; adv., less, least; n. —adj. 1. not large or below the average in size. 2. short in duration: a little while. 3. of small importance or influence. 4. mean or narrow: a little mind. 5. contemptibly petty: filthy little tricks. —adv. 6. not at all. 7. not much. 8. seldom. —n. 9. a small amount, quantity, or degree. 10. a short distance. 11. a short time. 12. little by little, by degrees. 13. make little of, to belittle or disparage. 14. think little of, to regard as trivial. —lit·tlish (lit′ʰlish, lit′lish), adj. —lit·tle·ness, n.

Lit′tle Dip′per, dipper (def. 3b).

lit·tle·neck (lit′ʰl nek′), n. a young, small quahog clam.

Lit′tle Rock′, the capital of Arkansas.

lit′tle slam′, Bridge. See under slam².

lit′tle the′ater, noncommercial and experimental drama.

lit·to·ral (lit′ər əl), adj. of or located on a shore, esp. of the sea.

lit·ur·gy (lit′ər jē), n., pl. -gies. a form of public worship, esp. in the Christian church. —li·tur′gi·cal (li tûr′ji-kəl), adj. —li·tur′gi·cal·ly, adv. —lit′ur·gist, n.

liv·a·ble (liv′ə bəl), adj. 1. suitable for living in. 2. worth living. Also, **live′a·ble.** —liv·a·bil′i·ty, n.

live¹ (liv), v., lived (livd), liv·ing. —v.i. 1. to have life, as an animal. 2. to remain alive. 3. to continue in existence, operation, memory, etc. 4. to feed or subsist: to live on rice. 5. to dwell or reside. 6. to pass life in a specified manner. —v.t. 7. to pass (one's life). 8. to represent or exhibit in one's life: to live a lie. 9. **live down,** to live so as to allow (a scandal, etc.) to be forgotten or forgiven. 10. **live in** or **out,** to reside at or away from the place of one's employment. 11. **live it up,** Informal. to live in an extravagant manner. 12. **live together,** to cohabit. 13. **live up to,** to live or act in accordance with (some ideal or standard). 14. **live with,** to endure or tolerate.

live² (līv), adj. 1. having life. 2. of or during the life of a living being. 3. full of energy or activity. 4. of current interest: a live issue. 5. burning or glowing, as a coal. 6. being in play, as a football. 7. loaded or unexploded, as a shell. 8. connected to an electric source: a live wire. 9. broadcast or televised at the moment of actual occurrence or performance. 10. made up of actual persons: a live audience.

lived (līvd; sometimes, livd), adj. having life, a life, or lives, as specified: a many-lived cat.

live·li·hood (līv′lē hŏŏd′), n. a means of subsistence.

live·long (liv′lông′, -long′), adj. tediously long in passing: the livelong afternoon.

live·ly (līv′lē), adj., -li·er, -li·est. 1. full of life or vital energy. 2. animated or sprightly. 3. stirring or exciting. 4. strong or keen. 5. rebounding quickly: a lively tennis ball. —live′li·ness, n. —Syn. 1. spirited, vigorous. 2. gay, vivacious.

liv·en (lī′vən), v.t., v.i. to make or become lively or livelier. —liv′en·er, n.

live′ oak′ (līv), an evergreen oak of the southern U.S.

liv·er¹ (liv′ər), n. 1. a large, reddish-brown, glandular organ of the human body, functioning in the secretion of bile and various metabolic processes. 2. an organ in other animals similar to the human liver, often used as food. —liv·ered (liv′ərd), adj.

liv·er² (liv′ər), n. a person who lives in a manner specified: a high liver.

liv·er·ied (liv′ə rēd, liv′rēd), adj. clad in livery, as servants.

liv·er·ish (liv′ər ish), adj. 1. resembling liver, esp. in color. 2. Brit. a. peevish or irascible. b. melancholy or depressed. —liv′er·ish·ness, n.

Liv·er·pool (liv′ər pōōl′), n. a seaport in W England. —Liv′er·pud′li·an (-pud′lē ən), n., adj.

liv·er·wort (liv′ər wûrt′), n. a moss-like plant growing chiefly on damp ground or on tree trunks.

liv·er·wurst (liv′ər wûrst′, -wŏŏrst′), n. a sausage made with a large percentage of liver.

liv·er·y (liv′ə rē, liv′rē), n., pl. -er·ies. 1. a uniform worn by servants, esp. male ones. 2. distinctive attire. 3. the care and feeding of horses for pay. 4. Also called **liv′ery sta′ble.** a stable where horses and carriages are kept for hire.

liv·er·y·man (liv′ə rē mən, liv′rē-), n. a keeper of or an employee in a livery stable.

lives (līvz), n. pl. of life.

live·stock (līv′stok′), n. domestic animals, as horses, cattle, or sheep, kept for their services or raised for food and other products.

live′ wire′ (līv), Slang. an energetic, alert person.

liv·id (liv′id), adj. 1. deathly pale. 2. enraged or furious. 3. having a discolored, bluish appearance due to a bruise. —liv′id·ly, adv. —liv′id·ness, n.

liv·ing (liv'ing), *adj.* **1.** being alive. **2.** in actual existence or use: *living languages.* **3.** active or strong. **4.** true to life, as a picture. **5.** of living persons: *within living memory.* **6.** sufficient for living: *a living wage.* —*n.* **7.** the act or condition of a person or thing that lives. **8.** a particular manner of life. **9.** livelihood. **10. the living,** living persons collectively.

liv'ing room', a room used, esp. by a family, for varied individual and shared social activities.

liz·ard (liz'ərd), *n.* a scaly reptile having an elongated body and a tapering tail.

Lk., Luke.

'll, contraction of: **a.** will[1]: *What'll we do?* **b.** *Informal.* till[1]: *Wait'll she comes.*

LL, Late Latin. Also, **L.L.**

ll., lines.

lla·ma (lä'mə), *n.* a woolly-haired, South American ruminant used as a pack animal.

lla·no (lä'nō), *n.,* *pl.* **-nos.** an extensive grassy plain in Spanish America.

LL.B., Bachelor of Laws. [< L *Legum Baccalaureus*]

LL.D., Doctor of Laws. [< L *Legum Doctor*]

LM (lem), lunar module.

LNG, liquefied natural gas.

lo (lō), *interj. Literary.* look! see!

load (lōd), *n.* **1.** a quantity of material or number of objects carried or supported. **2.** the normal maximum amount of something carried by a vehicle, vessel, etc. **3.** something that burdens like a heavy weight. **4.** the demand on a person, business, or machine, in terms of work. **5. loads,** *Informal.* an enormous amount: *loads of fun.* —*v.t.* **6.** to put a load on or in. **7.** to take on as a load. **8.** to put into (a device) something that it acts upon: *to load a gun.* **9.** to supply in lavish abundance. **10.** to burden or oppress. —*v.i.* **11.** to put on or take on a load. —**load'er,** *n.* —**load'ing,** *n.*

load·ed (lō'did), *adj. Slang.* **1.** under the influence of alcohol or drugs. **2.** very wealthy.

load·star (lōd'stär'), *n.* lodestar.

load·stone (lōd'stōn'), *n.* a black iron ore that possesses magnetic properties.

loaf[1] (lōf), *n., pl.* **loaves. 1.** a portion of bread baked in a mass of definite form. **2.** a shaped or molded mass of food, as of chopped meat.

loaf[2] (lōf), *v.i.* **1.** to lounge lazily and idly. **2.** to idle away time.

loaf·er (lō'fər), *n.* **1.** a person who loafs. **2.** a moccasinlike shoe for casual wear.

loam (lōm), *n.* a rich soil consisting of sand, silt, and clay. —**loam'y,** *adj.*

loan (lōn), *n.* **1.** the act of leanding. **2.** something lent, esp. a sum of money lent at interest. —*v.t., v.i.* **3.** to lend. —**loan'er,** *n.*

loan' shark', *Informal.* a person who lends money at excessive rates of interest. —**loan'shark'ing,** *n.*

loan·word (lōn'wûrd'), *n.* a word in one language that has been borrowed or taken over from another language.

loath (lōth, lōth), *adj.* decidedly unwilling or disinclined. —**loath'ness,** *n.* —**Syn.** averse, reluctant.

loathe (lōth), *v.t.,* **loathed, loath·ing.** to feel intense hatred and disgust for. —**loath'er,** *n.* —**Syn.** abhor, abominate, detest.

loath·ing (lō'thing), *n.* intense hatred and disgust. —**Syn.** antipathy, aversion.

loath·some (lōth'səm, lōth'-), *adj.* exciting or causing loathing. —**loath'some·ly,** *adv.*

loaves (lōvz), *n.* pl. of **loaf**[1].

lob (lob), *v.,* **lobbed, lob·bing,** *n.* —*v.t., v.i.* **1.** to hit (a ball) in a high arc. —*n.* **2.** a lobbed ball. —**lob'ber,** *n.*

lob·by (lob'ē), *n., pl.* **-bies,** *v.,* **-bied, -by·ing.** —*n.* **1.** a corridor or entrance hall, as in a public building, serving as a large waiting room. **2.** a group of private persons engaged in lobbying. —*v.i.* **3.** to try to influence the voting of legislators. —*v.t.* **4.** to influence (legislators) by lobbying. **5.** to urge the passage of (a bill) by lobbying. —**lob'by·ism,** *n.* —**lob'by·ist,** *n.*

lobe (lōb), *n.* **1.** a roundish projection or division, as of an organ or a leaf. **2.** the soft, lower part of the external ear. —**lo'bar,** *adj.* —**lobed** (lōbd), *adj.*

lo·bot·o·my (lō bot'ə mē, lə-), *n., pl.* **-mies.** the surgical cutting into or across a lobe of the brain, esp. in the treatment of mental disorders.

lob·ster (lob'stər), *n.* **1.** an edible marine crustacean having five pairs of legs and two pairs of feelers. **2.** See **spiny lobster.**

lob·ule (lob'yōōl), *n.* **1.** a small lobe. **2.** a subdivision of a lobe. —**lob·u·lar** (lob'yə lər), *adj.*

lo·cal (lō'kəl), *adj.* **1.** of, characteristic of, or restricted to a particular place. **2.** of or affecting a particular part of the body. **3.** stopping at all stations: *a local train.* —*n.* **4.** a local train, bus, etc. **5.** a local branch of a union, fraternity, etc. —**lo'cal·ly,** *adv.*

lo·cale (lō kal', -käl'), *n.* a locality, esp. with reference to events or circumstances connected with it.

lo·cal·i·ty (lō kal′i tē), *n.*, *pl.* **-ties. 1.** a particular location or place. **2.** the condition or fact of being at some specific place.

lo·cal·ize (lō′kə līz′), *v.t.*, **-ized, -iz·ing.** to confine or restrict to a particular place. —**lo′cal·i·za′tion,** *n.*

lo·cate (lō′kāt, lō kāt′), *v.*, **-cat·ed, -cat·ing.** —*v.t.* **1.** to discover the place of. **2.** to establish in a position or locality. **3.** to assign a particular location to (something), as by knowledge. —*v.i.* **4.** to be established in a place. —**lo′ca·tor,** *n.*

lo·ca·tion (lō kā′shən), *n.* **1.** the act of locating. **2.** the place where someone or something is located. **3. on location,** *Motion Pictures.* outside the studio.

loc. cit. (lok′ sit′), in the place cited. [< L *locō citātō*]

loch (lok, loкн), *n. Scot.* **1.** a lake. **2.** a narrow arm of the sea.

lock[1] (lok), *n.* **1.** a mechanical device for securing a door, lid, etc., against intruders. **2.** a mechanism in a firearm, esp. a gunlock. **3.** a chamber in a canal, dam, etc., for raising or lowering vessels by admitting or releasing water. **4.** *Wrestling.* any of various holds: *arm lock.* —*v.t.* **5.** to fasten or secure with a lock. **6.** to shut in a place fastened by a lock: *to lock up a prisoner.* **7.** to make fast or immovable. **8.** to join or unite firmly: *to lock arms.* **9.** to hold fast in an embrace. —*v.i.* **10.** to become locked. **11.** to become interlocked. —**lock′less,** *adj.*

lock[2] (lok), *n.* **1.** a curl or strand of hair. **2. locks,** the hair of the head. **3.** a small portion of wool or flax.

lock·er (lok′ər), *n.* **1.** a chest, closet, etc., that may be locked. **2.** a storage compartment in a quick-freezing plant for rent to users. **3.** a person or thing that locks.

lock·et (lok′it), *n.* a small case for a picture, lock of hair, or other keepsake, usually worn on a necklace.

lock·jaw (lok′jô′), *n.* tetanus in which the jaws become firmly locked together.

lock·out (lok′out′), *n.* the closing of a plant by an employer during a labor controversy to force the workers to come to terms.

lock·smith (lok′smith′), *n.* a person who makes or repairs locks.

lock′ step′, a mode of marching in very close file.

lock·up (lok′up′), *n.* a jail, esp. a local one.

lo·co (lō′kō), *adj. Slang.* crazy or insane.

lo·co·mo·tion (lō′kə mō′shən), *n.* the act or power of moving from place to place.

lo·co·mo·tive (lō′kə mō′tiv), *n.* **1.** a self-propelled vehicle for pulling railroad trains. —*adj.* **2.** of or pertaining to locomotion or locomotives.

lo·co·mo·tor (lō′kə mō′tər), *adj.* of or affecting locomotion.

lo·co·weed (lō′kō wēd′), *n.* a plant of the southwestern U.S. that causes a disease in livestock.

lo·cus (lō′kəs), *n.*, *pl.* **-ci** (-sī). **1.** *Chiefly Law.* a place or locality. **2.** *Math.* the set of all points, lines, or surfaces that satisfies a given requirement.

lo·cust (lō′kəst), *n.* **1.** a grasshopper having short antennae and commonly migrating in swarms. **2.** See **seventeen-year locust. 3.** an American tree having thorny branches and white flowers.

lo·cu·tion (lō kyōō′shən), *n.* **1.** a particular form of expression. **2.** a style of its delivery.

lode (lōd), *n.* a veinlike deposit of ore.

lo·den (lōd′[e]n), *n.* a thick waterproof fabric, used esp. for overcoats.

lode·star (lōd′stär′), *n.* a star that shows the way, esp. the North Star.

lode·stone (lōd′stōn′), *n.* loadstone.

lodge (loj), *n.*, *v.*, **lodged, lodg·ing.** —*n.* **1.** a roughly built shelter or hut, as in the woods. **2.** a main building at a resort or camp. **3.** a branch of a secret society, or its meeting place. **4.** the den of beavers. —*v.i.* **5.** to stay in a place, esp. temporarily. **6.** to live in rented quarters. **7.** to be fixed in a particular place or position. —*v.t.* **8.** to furnish with living quarters, esp. temporarily. **9.** to fix into a particular place or position. **10.** to bring (a complaint, etc.) officially to the proper authorities. **11.** to confer (power or authority) upon. —**lodge′a·ble,** *adj.* —**lodg′ment, lodge′ment,** *n.*

lodg·er (loj′ər), *n. Chiefly Brit.* a person who lives in rented quarters in another's house.

lodg·ing (loj′ing), *n.* **1.** a temporary place to stay or live. **2. lodgings,** a room or rooms rented for residence in another's house.

lo·ess (lō′es, les, lus), *n.* a loamy deposit formed by wind, usually yellowish and calcareous. —**lo·ess′i·al,** *adj.*

loft (lôft, loft), *n.* **1.** an upper story of a warehouse or factory, usually not partitioned into rooms. **2.** *Chiefly Brit.* a room or space under a sloping roof. **3.** a gallery or upper level in a church, hall, etc.: *a choir loft.* —*v.t.* **4.** to hit (a ball) into the air. —**loft′less,** *adj.*

loft·y (lôf'tē, lof'-), *adj.*, **loft·i·er,
loft·i·est. 1.** of imposing height. **2.**
elevated in dignity or character. **3.**
consciously superior or dignified. —
loft'i·ly, *adv.* —**loft'i·ness,** *n.*

log¹ (lôg, log), *n.*, *v.*, **logged, log·ging.**
—*n.* **1.** an unhewn length of the
trunk of a felled tree. **2.** a device
for determining the speed of a vessel. **3.** Also called **log'book'.** a record concerning a trip made by a vessel or aircraft. —*v.t.* **4.** to cut (trees)
into logs. **5.** to enter in a logbook.
6. to travel for (a certain distance
or a certain amount of time). —*v.i.*
7. to cut down trees and get the logs.
—**log'ger,** *n.*

log² (lôg, log), *n.* logarithm.

-log, var. of **-logue:** *analog.*

log., logic.

lo·gan·ber·ry (lō'gən ber'ē), *n.*, *pl.*
-ries. 1. the large, dark-red, acid
fruit of a blackberrylike plant. **2.**
its plant.

log·a·rithm (lôg'ə riŧʰ'əm, -riŧʰ'-, log'-
ə-), *n.* the exponent of the power to
which a base number must be raised
to equal a given number. —**log'a-
rith'mic, log'a·rith'mi·cal,** *adj.*

loge (lōzh), *n.* a box or the front section of the lowest balcony in a
theater.

log·ger·head (lô'gər hed', log'ər-), *n.*
at loggerheads, engaged in dispute.

log·gia (loj'ə, lô'jē ə), *n.*, *pl.* **-gias.** a
gallery or arcade open to the air on
at least one side.

log·ic (loj'ik), *n.* **1.** the science of
correct or reliable reasoning. **2.** a
particular method of reasoning. **3.**
reason or sound judgment. —**lo·gi-
cian** (lō jish'ən), *n.*

log·i·cal (loj'i kəl), *adj.* **1.** of or according to logic. **2.** reasonably to be
expected. —**log'i·cal·ly,** *adv.*

lo·gis·tics (lō jis'tiks), *n.* the military
science dealing with the procure-
ment, maintenance, and movement
of materiel and personnel. —**lo·gis'-
tic, lo·gis'ti·cal,** *adj.* —**lo·gis'ti·cal-
ly,** *adv.* —**lo·gis·ti·cian** (lō'ji stish'-
ən), *n.*

log·jam (lôg'jam', log'-), *n.* **1.** an immovable tangle of logs in a river. **2.**
any blockage resembling this.

lo·go (lô'gō, log'ō), *n.*, *pl.* **-gos.** logo-
type.

log·o·type (lô'gə tīp', log'ə-), *n.* a
distinctive symbol identifying a business company, as in an advertisement.

log·roll·ing (lôg'rō'ling, log'-), *n.* the
exchange of support or favors, esp.
by legislators for mutual political
gain.

-logue, a combining form meaning
"a specified kind of discourse, spok-
en or written": *monologue; trave-
logue.*

lo·gy (lō'gē), *adj.*, **-gi·er, -gi·est.** sluggish and lacking vitality. —**lo'gi-
ness,** *n.* —**Syn.** drowsy, lethargic.

-logy, a combining form meaning: **a.**
a science or study of: *theology.* **b.**
speaking or expression: *tautology.*

loid (loid), *v.t. Slang.* to open (a
door) by sliding a thin piece of
celluloid or plastic along the door
edge to open a spring lock.

loin (loin), *n.* **1.** Usually, **loins.** the
part of the body between the ribs
and hipbone. **2.** a cut of meat from
this region of an animal. **3. loins,**
Chiefly Literary. the area of the
genitals regarded as the seat of
strength and generative power.

loin·cloth (loin'klôŧʰ', -kloŧʰ'), *n.* a
cloth worn around the loins, as by
some tropical inhabitants.

loi·ter (loi'tər), *v.i.* **1.** to linger aimlessly in or about a place. **2.** to move
in a slow, idle manner. —**loi'ter·er,**
n. —**loi'ter·ing·ly,** *adv.* —**Syn. 1.**
dally, dawdle, idle.

loll (lol), *v.i.* **1.** to recline in an indolent manner. **2.** to hang loosely or
droopingly. —*v.t.* **3.** to allow to
hang loosely or droopingly.

lol·li·pop (lol'ē pop'), *n.* a piece of
hard candy stuck on the end of a
stick. Also, **lol'ly·pop'.**

lol·ly·gag (lol'ē gag'), *v.i.*, **-gagged,
-gag·ging.** *Informal.* lallygag.

lon., longitude.

Lond., London.

Lon·don (lun'dən), *n.* the capital of
the United Kingdom, in SE England.

Lon'don broil', a broiled flank steak,
crosscut into thin slices for serving.

lone (lōn), *adj. Chiefly Literary.* **1.**
without companions. **2.** standing by
itself. **3.** sole or single. —**lone'ness,**
n. —**Syn. 1.** solitary, unaccompanied.

lone·ly (lōn'lē), *adj.*, **-li·er, -li·est. 1.**
without company. **2.** destitute of
sympathetic companionship. **3.** remote from places of human habitation. —**lone'li·ly,** *adv.* —**lone'li-
ness,** *n.*

lon·er (lō'nər), *n.* a person who remains alone or avoids the company
of others.

lone·some (lōn'səm), *adj.* **1.** sad because of the lack of friends, companionship, etc. **2.** causing such feeling. **3.** lonely (def. 3). —**lone'some-
ly,** *adv.* —**lone'some·ness,** *n.*

long¹ (lông, long), *adj.*, **long·er** (lông'-
gər, long'-), **long·est** (lông'gist,
long'-), *n.*, *adv.* —*adj.* **1.** having
considerable extent in space. **2.** having considerable duration. **3.** extending or totaling a number of specified
units: *eight miles long.* **4.** containing
many items or units. **5.** tedious or
unpleasant. **6.** extensive or broad:
a long look ahead. **7.** well-endowed
or -supplied: *long on brains.* **8.** be-

ing against great odds: *a long chance.*
9. having the sound of the middle vowels in *mate, meet, mite, mote, moot,* and *mute.* —*n.* **10.** a long time. **11.** before long, soon. **12.** the long and the short of, the substance of. —*adv.* **13.** for a great extent of time. **14.** for or throughout a specified time. **15.** at a point of time far distant from the time indicated: *long before.* **16.** as long as, a. Also, so long as. provided that. b. during the time that.

long² (lông, long), *v.i.* to have an earnest wish. —**Syn.** pine, yearn.

long., longitude.

long·boat (lông'bōt', long'-), *n.* the largest boat formerly carried by a sailing vessel.

long' dis'tance, telephone service between distant points. —**long'-dis'tance,** *adj.*

long-drawn (lông'drôn', long'-), *adj.* drawn out or prolonged.

lon·gev·i·ty (lon jev'i tē), *n.* **1.** a long duration of life. **2.** the length of life.

long' face', an unhappy or glum expression. —**long'-faced',** *adj.*

long-hair (lông'hâr', long'-), *Informal.* —*n.* **1.** *Sometimes Disparaging.* an intellectual. **2.** a lover of classical music. **3.** hippie. —*adj.* **4.** Also, **long'haired'.** of or characteristic of a longhair or his or her taste.

long·hand (lông'hand', long'-), *n.* writing in which words are written out in full by hand.

long·ing (lông'ing, long'-), *n.* **1.** a prolonged, unceasing, or earnest wish. **2.** having such a wish. —**long'ing·ly,** *adv.*

Long' Is'land, an island in SE New York.

lon·gi·tude (lon'ji tōōd', -tyōōd'), *n.* angular distance east or west, between the meridian of a particular place and that of Greenwich, England, expressed in degrees or time.

lon·gi·tu·di·nal (lon'ji tōōd'°n°l, -tyōōd'-), *adj.* **1.** of longitude or length. **2.** extending or set lengthwise. —**lon'gi·tu'di·nal·ly,** *adv.*

long' jump', a jump for distance in track events, usually with a running start.

long-lived (lông'livd', -livd', long'-), *adj.* having a long life or duration.

long' play', a long-playing phonograph record.

long-play·ing (lông'plā'ing, long'-), *adj.* of or pertaining to microgroove records devised to be played at 33⅓ revolutions per minute.

long-range (lông'rānj', long'-), *adj.* **1.** designed to fire a long distance. **2.** allowing for the more distant future.

long·shore·man (lông'shôr'mən, -shôr'-, long'-), *n.* a worker on a pier who loads and unloads vessels.

long' shot', a selection, as of a race horse, that has very little chance of winning.

long-stand·ing (lông'stan'ding, long'-), *adj.* existing or occurring for a long time.

long-suf·fer·ing (lông'suf'ər ing, long'-), *adj.* enduring injury or trouble long and patiently. —**long'-suf'fer·ing·ly,** *adv.*

long-term (lông'tûrm', long'-), *adj.* **1.** covering a relatively long period of time. **2.** *Finance.* maturing over a relatively long period of time.

long-time (lông'tīm', long'-), *adj.* having existed for a long period of time.

long' ton', See under ton (def. 1).

long-wind·ed (lông'win'did, long'-), *adj.* **1.** talking or writing at tedious length. **2.** tediously long. —**long'wind'ed·ly,** *adv.* —**long'-wind'ed·ness,** *n.*

look (lŏŏk), *v.i.* **1.** to set one's eyes upon something in order to see. **2.** to use the sight in searching or examining. **3.** to appear or seem: *to look pale.* **4.** to face or front: *The house looks to the east.* —*v.t.* **5.** to give (someone) a look. **6.** to have an appearance appropriate to: *The actor looked his part.* **7.** look after, to take care of. **8.** look down on or upon, to have contempt for. **9.** look for, a. to seek. b. to anticipate. **10.** look forward to, to anticipate with pleasure. **11.** look in, a. Also, look into. to look briefly inside of. b. Also, look in on. to visit briefly. **12.** look into, to examine. **13.** look out, to be on guard. **14.** look over, to examine, esp. superficially. **15.** look to, a. to give attention to. b. to depend on. **16.** look up, a. *Informal.* to become better. b. to search for. c. to seek out, esp. to visit. **17.** look up to, to respect. —*n.* **18.** the act of looking. **19.** physical appearance or aspect. **20.** looks, general aspect or appearance. —**look'er,** *n.*

look·er-on (lŏŏk'ər on'), *n., pl.* **look-ers-on.** *Informal.* spectator.

look'ing glass', a glass mirror.

look·out (lŏŏk'out'), *n.* **1.** the act of keeping watch. **2.** a person stationed to keep watch. **3.** a station from which watch is kept. **4.** *Informal.* an object of concern.

look-see (lŏŏk'sē'), *n. Slang.* a visual survey.

loom¹ (lōōm), *n.* **1.** a machine for weaving thread into fabrics. —*v.t.* **2.** to weave on a loom.

loom² (lōōm), *v.i.* **1.** to come into view in indistinct and enlarged form. **2.** to assume form as an impending event.

loon¹ (lōōn), *n.* a large, short-tailed, webfooted, fish-eating diving bird.

loon² (lo͞on), *n.* a worthless, lazy, stupid, or insane person.

loon·y (lo͞o′nē), *adj.,* **loon·i·er, loon·i·est.** *Slang.* **1.** lunatic or insane. **2.** extremely foolish. Also, **loon′ey.** —**loon′i·ness,** *n.*

loon′y bin′, *Slang.* an insane asylum.

loop (lo͞op), *n.* **1.** a portion of a cord or ribbon folded or doubled upon itself so as to leave an opening between the parts. **2.** anything shaped like a loop. **3.** a flight maneuver in which an airplane describes a closed curve in a vertical plane. **4. the loop.** See **intrauterine device.** —*v.t.* **5.** to form into a loop. **6.** to make a loop in. —*v.i.* **7.** to make or form a loop or loops.

loop·hole (lo͞op′hōl′), *n.* **1.** a small or narrow opening, as in a wall, for looking or shooting through. **2.** a means of escape or evasion.

loose (lo͞os), *adj.,* **loos·er, loos·est, adv., v., loosed, loos·ing.** —*adj.* **1.** free from anything that binds or restrains. **2.** released from fastening. **3.** sexually promiscuous or wanton: *a loose woman.* **4.** not taut or tight: *a loose rein.* **5.** relaxed in nature. **6.** not compact in structure. **7.** not exact or precise: *loose thinking.* **8.** broad or generous: *a loose interpretation of the law.* **9. on the loose,** free or unconfined. —*adv.* **10.** in a loose manner. —*v.t.* **11.** to let loose. **12.** to unfasten or untie. **13.** to shoot or let fly. **14.** to make less tight. —*v.i.* **15.** to let go a hold. —**loose′ly,** *adv.* —**loose′ness,** *n.* —**Syn. 3.** dissolute, libertine. **7.** indefinite, vague.

loose′ end′, *n.* **1.** an unsettled detail. **2. at loose ends, a.** in an unsettled situation. **b.** having no immediate plans.

loose-leaf (lo͞os′lēf′), *adj.* having punched sheets or pages that can be easily inserted or removed.

loos·en (lo͞o′sən), *v.t., v.i.* **1.** to make or become loose or looser. **2.** to make or become less tight.

loot (lo͞ot), *n.* **1.** goods or valuables taken unlawfully in war or by robbery. **2.** *Informal.* a collection of gifts, purchases, etc. —*v.t., v.i.* **3.** to take (as) loot. —**loot′er,** *n.*

lop¹ (lop), *v.t.,* **lopped, lop·ping. 1.** to cut off the branches or twigs of. **2.** to eliminate as unnecessary or excessive. —**lop′per,** *n.*

lop² (lop), *v.i.,* **lopped, lop·ping.** to hang loosely or limply.

lope (lōp), *v.,* **loped, lop·ing,** *n.* —*v.i.* **1.** to move or run with a long, easy stride. —*n.* **2.** a long, easy stride.

lop·sid·ed (lop′sī′did), *adj.* **1.** inclining to one side. **2.** unevenly balanced. —**lop′sid′ed·ly,** *adv.* —**lop′sid′ed·ness,** *n.*

loq., he (or she) speaks (in stage direction). [< L *loquitur*]

lo·qua·cious (lō kwā′shəs), *adj.* exceedingly talkative. —**lo·qua′cious·ness,** **lo·quac′i·ty** (-kwas′i tē), *n.*

lo·ran (lōr′ən, lôr′-), *n.* a device by which a navigator of a ship or aircraft can locate its position by determining the time displacement between radio signals from two known stations. [*lo(ng)-ra(nge) n(avigation)*]

lord (lôrd), *n.* **1.** a person who has dominion over others, as a feudal superior. **2.** a person who is a leader in a profession. **3.** a titled nobleman or peer, as in Great Britain. **4. Lords.** See **House of Lords. 5.** (*cap.*) God or Jehovah. **6.** (*cap.*) the Savior, Jesus Christ. —*v.t.* **7. lord it over,** to domineer over.

Lord′ Chan′cel·lor, *pl.* **Lords Chancellor.** the presiding officer in the House of Lords. Also called **Lord′ High′ Chan′cel·lor.**

lord·ly (lôrd′lē), *adj.,* **-li·er, -li·est, adv.** —*adj.* **1.** like or befitting a lord. **2.** insolently imperious. —*adv.* **3.** in the manner of a lord. —**lord′li·ness,** *n.* —**Syn. 1.** grand, magnificent.

Lord′s′ day′, the, Sunday.

lord·ship (lôrd′ship), *n.* **1.** (*often cap.*) a term of respect for British judges or certain noblemen: *Your Lordship.* **2.** the status or dignity of a lord.

Lord′s′ Prayer′, the, the prayer given by Jesus to His disciples, and beginning with *Our Father.* Matt. 6:9–13; Luke 11:2–4.

Lord′s′ Sup′per, the, the Holy Communion.

lore (lōr, lôr), *n.* knowledge or learning of a traditional or popular nature.

lor·gnette (lôrn yet′), *n.* a pair of eyeglasses or opera glasses mounted on a handle.

lorn (lôrn), *adj. Literary.* forsaken or forlorn.

lor·ry (lôr′ē, lor′ē), *n., pl.* **-ries.** *Brit.* a motor truck.

Los An·ge·les (lôs an′jə ləs, -lēz′, los), a seaport in SW California.

lose (lo͞oz), *v.,* **lost** (lôst, lost), **los·ing.** —*v.t.* **1.** to come to be without through accident, theft, etc. **2.** to put or leave somewhere subsequently forgotten or mislaid. **3.** to suffer the deprivation of. **4.** to fail to keep or maintain. **5.** to forfeit the possession of. **6.** to get rid of: *to lose weight.* **7.** to have slip from sight, hearing, or attention. **8.** to fail to have or get: *to lose a bargain.* **9.** to fail to win (a prize, etc.). **10.** to cause the loss of. **11.** to let (oneself) go astray or miss the way. **12.** to allow (oneself) to become absorbed in something. —*v.i.* **13.** to suffer loss. —**los′er,** *n.*

loss (lôs, los), *n.* **1.** detriment or disadvantage from losing. **2.** an amount or number lost. **3.** the excess of outlay over income. **4.** Often, **losses.** military casualities. **5. at a loss,** bewildered or uncertain.

loss′ lead′er, an article deliberately sold at a loss for the purpose of drawing customers.

lost (lôst, lost), *adj.* **1.** no longer possessed or retained. **2.** no longer to be found. **3.** having gone astray or missed the way. **4.** not used to good purpose. **5.** not won or gained. **6.** destroyed or ruined. **7.** preoccupied or rapt.

lost′ cause′, a cause that has been defeated or for which defeat is inevitable.

lot (lot), *n.* **1.** any object used in deciding or choosing something by chance. **2.** the method so used. **3.** the decision or choice made by such a method. **4.** allotted share or portion. **5.** one's fortune or fate. **6.** a distinct piece of land. **7.** a number of things or persons collectively. **8.** *Informal.* kind of person. **9.** Often, **lots.** *Informal.* a great many or great deal. **10. draw** or **cast lots,** to settle a question by lot.

loth (lōth, lōth), *adj.* loath.

Lo·thar·i·o (lō thâr′ē ō′), *n., pl.* **-thar·i·os.** a charming man who seduces women.

lo·tion (lō′shən), *n.* a liquid preparation containing external medical or cosmetic agents, as for soothing or softening the skin.

lot·ter·y (lot′ə rē), *n., pl.* **-ter·ies 1.** a gambling game in which numbered tickets are sold and a drawing is held for prizes. **2.** any scheme for the distribution of prizes by chance.

lot·to (lot′ō), *n.* a game of chance in which a leader draws from a stock of numbered disks and the players cover the corresponding numbers on their cards, the winner being the first to cover five in a row.

lo·tus (lō′təs), *n., pl.* **-tus·es. 1.** a plant referred to in Greek legend as yielding a fruit that induced dreamy and contented forgetfulness. **2.** any aquatic plant having shieldlike leaves and showy, solitary flowers. **3.** any of several water lilies.

lo′tus posi′tion, (in Yoga) a sitting posture with the legs crossed and the hands resting on the thighs near the knees.

loud (loud), *adj.* **1.** strongly audible: *loud talking.* **2.** making strongly audible sounds. **3.** clamorous or vociferous. **4.** emphatic or insistent: *a loud denial.* **5.** garish or ostentatious, as colors. **6.** obtrusively vulgar, as manners. —*adv.* **7.** in a loud manner. —**loud′ly,** *adv.* —**loud′ness,** *n.*

—**Syn. 1, 2.** noisy, resounding. **5.** flashy, gaudy, showy.

loud-mouthed (loud′mou*th*d′, -mou*th*t′), *adj.* **1.** loud of voice or utterance. **2.** marked by indiscreet or vulgar speech.

loud-speak·er (loud′spē′kər), *n.* a device for converting electric signals into amplified audible sounds.

Lou·is XIV (lōō′ē), 1638–1715, king of France 1643–1715.

Louis XV, 1710–74, king of France 1715–74.

Louis XVI, 1754–93, king of France 1774–92.

Lou·i·si·an·a (lōō ē′zē an′ə, lōō′ə zē-, lōō′ē-), *n.* a state in the S United States. *Cap.:* Baton Rouge.

Lou·is·ville (lōō′ē vil′), *n.* a port in N Kentucky.

lounge (lounj), *v.,* **lounged, loung·ing,** *n.* —*v.i.* **1.** to recline indolently. **2.** to go or move in a leisurely, indolent manner. **3.** to pass time idly. —*n.* **4.** a large public room, as in a hotel or theater, for lounging, waiting, smoking, etc. **5.** a low-backed sofa for reclining.

loupe (lōōp), *n.* a magnifying glass used by jewelers and watchmakers, intended to fit in the eye socket.

lour (lour, lou′ər), *v.i.* lower².

louse (lous), *n., pl.* **lice** (līs) for **1, 2, lous·es** for **3,** *v.* —*n.* **1.** a small, wingless insect, parasitic on human beings and other mammals. **2.** a plant pest, esp. an aphid. **3.** *Slang.* a contemptible person, esp. an unethical one. —*v.t.* **4. louse up,** *Slang.* to make a mess of.

lous·y (lou′zē), *adj.,* **lous·i·er, lous·i·est. 1.** infested with lice. **2.** *Informal.* **a.** mean or contemptible. **b.** wretchedly bad. **3. lousy with,** *Slang.* well supplied with: *He's lousy with money.* —**lous′i·ly,** *adv.* —**lous′i·ness,** *n.*

lout (lout), *n.* an awkward, stupid person. —**lout′ish,** *adj.* —**lout′ish·ly,** *adv.*

lou·ver (lōō′vər), *n.* **1.** any of a series of narrow openings framed with slanting, overlapping slats, adjustable for admitting light and ventilation while shutting out rain or direct sunlight. **2.** a slat framing such an opening. Also, **lou′vre.** —**lou′-vered,** *adj.*

love (luv), *n., v.,* **loved, lov·ing.** —*n.* **1.** a profoundly tender, passionate affection. **2.** a feeling of warm personal attachment. **3.** sexual desire or its gratification. **4.** a beloved person. **5.** a strong predilection or liking for something. **6.** *Tennis.* a score of zero. **7. in love (with),** feeling deep, affection or passion (for). **8 make love, a.** to woo or court. **b.** to embrace and kiss. **c.** to engage in sexual intercourse. —*v.t.*, *v.i.* 9. to have love or affection (for). 10. to have a strong liking (for): *to love music.* —**lov′a·ble, love′a·ble,** *adj.* —**love′·less,** *adj.*

love·bird (luv′bûrd′), *n.* a small parrot noted for its affection for its mate and often kept as a pet.

love·lorn (luv′lôrn′), *adj.* forsaken by one's lover.

love·ly (luv′lē), *adj.* 1. charmingly beautiful. 2. *Informal.* delightful or highly pleasing. —**love′li·ness,** *n.*

love·mak·ing (luv′mā′king), *n.* the act of making love.

lov·er (luv′ər), *n.* 1. a person who is in love with someone. 2. a person involved in a nonmarital sexual relationship. 3. lovers, a couple in love with each other or having a love affair. 4. a person who has a strong liking for something, as specified: *a music lover.*

love′ seat′, an upholstered seat for two persons.

love·sick (luv′sik′), *adj.* 1. languishing with love. 2. expressive of such languishing. —**love′sick′ness,** *n.*

lov·ing (luv′ing), *adj.* feeling or showing love. —**lov′ing·ly,** *adv.*

lov′ing cup′, a large, two-handled cup, often given as a prize, award, etc.

low[1] (lō), *adj.* 1. not far above the ground or floor. 2. of small extent upward. 3. lying below the general level: *low ground.* 4. of small amount, force, etc. 5. below an acceptable standard: *low intelligence.* 6. depressed or dejected: *low spirits.* 7. humble in status: *a person of low origin.* 8. of inferior quality or character. 9. coarse or vulgar. 10. morally base. 11. deep in pitch, as musical sounds. 12. soft or subdued: *a low murmur.* —*adv.* 13. in or to a low point, place, or level. 14. lay **low,** to overpower or kill. 15. lie **low,** to conceal oneself. —*n.* 16. a low point, place, or level. 17. *Auto.* a transmission gear producing the lowest speed and maximum power. 18. *Meteorol.* a region of relative low pressure. —**low′ness,** *n.*

low[2] (lō), *v.i.*, *n.* moo.

low′ beam′, an automobile headlight beam providing short-range illumination.

low·boy (lō′boi′), *n.* a low chest of drawers on short legs.

low·brow (lō′brou′), *n.* *Informal.* a person without intellectual activities or pursuits.

low-cal (lō′kal′), *adj.* containing a small number of calories.

Low′ Coun′tries, Belgium, Luxembourg, and the Netherlands.

low·down (*n.* lō′doun′; *adj.* lō′doun′), *Informal.* —*n.* 1. the unadorned facts. —*adj.* 2. contemptible or mean.

low·er[1] (lō′ər), *v.t.* 1. to cause to descend. 2. to make lower in height or level. 3. to reduce in amount, degree, force, etc. 4. to bring down in rank or estimation. —*v.i.* 5. to become lower. —*adj.* 6. comparative of **low**[1]. 7. noting the larger branch of a bicameral legislature. 8. (*often cap.*) noting an earlier division of a geological period. —**low′er·most′,** *adj.* —**Syn.** 4. degrade, humble.

low·er[2] (lou′ər, lour), *v.i.* 1. to look sullen or angry. 2. to be dark and threatening, as the weather. —**low′er·ing,** *adj.* —**low′er·ing·ly,** *adv.* —**low′er·y,** *adj.*

low′er case′ (lō′ər), *Print.* small letters as distinguished from capital letters. —**low′er-case′,** *adj.*

low′er class′, a social class comprising the laboring and very poor people, occupying a position below that of the middle class. —**low′er-class′,** *adj.*

low′est com′mon denom′inator. See least common denominator.

low′est com′mon mul′tiple, the smallest number that is a common multiple of a given set of numbers.

low′ fre′quency, a radio frequency between 30 and 300 kilohertz.

low′ gear′, low (def. 17).

Low′ Ger′man, 1. the West Germanic languages not included in the High German group, as English, Dutch, Flemish, etc. 2. the informal German spoken in N Germany.

low-key (lō′kē′), *adj.* restrained or understated, as in style or speech. Also, **low′-keyed′.**

low·land (lō′lənd), *n.* 1. land that is low or level, with respect to the adjacent country. 2. the **Lowlands,** a low region in S, central, and E Scotland.

low·ly (lō′lē), *adj.*, **-li·er, -li·est,** *adv.* —*adj.* 1. having a low status. 2. humble in spirit. —*adv.* 3. in a low manner. —**low′li·ness,** *n.*

low-mind·ed (lō′mīn′did), *adj.* having or showing a low, coarse, or vulgar mind. —**low′-mind′ed·ly,** *adv.* —**low′-mind′ed·ness,** *n.*

low′ pro′file, a deliberately inconspicuous, almost unnoticeable form or manner.

low′ relief′, bas-relief.

low-rise (lō′rīz′), *adj.* (of a building) having a comparatively small number of floors and not equipped with elevators.

low-spir·it·ed (lō′spir′i tid), *adj.* depressed or dejected. —**low′-spir′it·ed·ly,** *adv.* —**low′-spir′it·ed·ness,** *n.*

low-ten·sion (lō′ten′shən), *adj.* operating under relatively low voltage.

low′ tide′, the tide at the point of maximum ebb.

lox¹ (loks), *n.* cured, usually slightly smoked salmon.

lox² (loks), *n.* liquid oxygen, used in liquid rocket propellants. Also, **LOX.**

loy·al (loi′əl), *adj.* **1.** faithful to one's allegiance, as to a government or friends. **2.** faithful to one's oath. —**loy′al·ly,** *adv.* —**loy′al·ty, loy′al·ness,** *n.*

loy·al·ist (loi′ə list), *n.* a supporter of the sovereign or of the existing government, esp. in time of revolt.

loz·enge (loz′inj), *n.* **1.** a small flavored candy, often medicated, originally diamond-shaped. **2.** a four-sided equilateral figure having a diamond shape.

LP, *pl.* **LPs, LP's,** *Trademark.* a long-playing record.

L.P., low pressure.

LPG, liquefied petroleum gas.

LPN, Licensed Practical Nurse.

LR, living room.

Lr, lawrencium.

L.S., 1. left side. **2.** letter signed. **3.** the place of the seal. [< L *locus sigilli*]

LSD, a strongly hallucinogenic compound, used in research on mental disorders and as a psychedelic drug.

LSS, *Med.* life-support system.

Lt., Lieutenant.

lt., light.

L.T., 1. long ton. **2.** *Elect.* low-tension.

Lt. Col., Lieutenant Colonel. Also, **LTC**

Lt. Comdr., Lieutenant Commander. Also, **Lt. Com.**

Ltd., *Com.* Limited.

Lt. Gen., Lieutenant General. Also, **LTG**

LTJG, Lieutenant Junior Grade.

LTL, less than truckload.

ltr., letter.

Lu, lutetium.

lu·au (loo ou′, loo′ou), *n.* a lavish Hawaiian feast.

lub·ber (lub′ər), *n.* **1.** a big, clumsy, stupid person. **2.** an awkward or unskilled seaman. —**lub′ber·ly,** *adj., adv.*

Lub·bock (lub′ək), *n.* a city in NW Texas.

lube (loob), *n. Informal.* **1.** lubricant. **2.** an application of a lubricant, as to a vehicle.

lu·bri·cant (loo′brə kənt), *n.* **1.** a substance, as oil, grease, etc., for lessening friction, esp. in the working parts of a mechanism. —*adj.* **2.** capable of lubricating.

lu·bri·cate (loo′brə kāt′), *v.t.,* **-cat·ed, -cat·ing. 1.** to apply a lubricant to (parts of a mechanism, etc.). **2.** to make slippery or smooth. —**lu′bri·ca′tion,** *n.* —**lu′bri·ca′tor,** *n.*

lu·bri·cous (loo′brə kəs), *adj.* **1.** having an oily smoothness. **2.** sexually wanton. Also, **lu·bri·cious** (loo-brish′əs). —**lu·bric·i·ty** (loo bris′i-tē), *n.*

lu·cent (loo′sənt), *adj.* **1.** shining with light. **2.** translucent or clear.

lu·cid (loo′sid), *adj.* **1.** easily understood. **2.** marked by clear perception or understanding. **3.** *Literary.* lucent. —**lu·cid′i·ty, lu′cid·ness,** *n.* —**lu′cid·ly,** *adv.*

Lu·ci·fer (loo′sə fər), *n.* a rebellious archangel, identified with Satan, expelled from heaven.

Lu·cite (loo′sit), *n. Trademark.* a transparent acrylic resin, used chiefly as a substitute for glass.

luck (luk), *n.* **1.** the force that seems to operate for good or bad in a person's life. **2.** good fortune. —*v.i.* **3. luck out,** *Informal.* to come out all right by luck. —**luck′less,** *adj.*

luck·y (luk′ē), *adj.,* **luck·i·er, luck·i·est. 1.** having good luck. **2.** happening fortunately. **3.** bringing good luck. —**luck′i·ly,** *adv.* —**luck′i·ness,** *n.* —**Syn. 1.** fortunate. **2.** fortuitous. **3.** auspicious.

lu·cra·tive (loo′krə tiv), *adj.* bringing in money or profit. —**lu′cra·tive·ly,** *adv.* —**lu′cra·tive·ness,** *n.*

lu·cre (loo′kər), *n. Facetiously Disparaging.* money or monetary profit: *filthy lucre.*

lu·cu·brate (loo′kyoo brāt′), *v.i.,* **-brat·ed, -brat·ing.** *Literary.* to work, write, or study laboriously, esp. at night. —**lu′cu·bra′tion,** *n.*

lu·di·crous (loo′də krəs), *adj.* causing laughter because of its foolish absurdity. —**lu′di·crous·ly,** *adv.* —**lu′di·crous·ness,** *n.* —**Syn.** incongruous, ridiculous.

luff (luf), *v.i.* to bring the head of a sailing vessel closer to the wind.

lug¹ (lug), *v.t.,* **lugged, lug·ging.** to pull along or carry with effort.

lug² (lug), *n.* **1.** a projecting piece by which anything is held or supported. **2.** a large nut for attaching a wheel to an automobile. **3.** *Slang.* an awkward, clumsy fellow.

lug·gage (lug′ij), *n.* **1.** suitcases, trunks, etc., esp. empty ones as merchandise. **2.** *Chiefly Brit.* baggage (def. 1).

lu·gu·bri·ous (loo goo′brē əs, -gyoo′-), *adj.* mournful or gloomy, esp. exaggeratedly so. —**lu·gu′bri·ous·ly,** *adv.* —**lu·gu′bri·ous·ness,** *n.*

Luke (look), *n.* an early Christian disciple: reputed author of the third Gospel.

luke·warm (look′wôrm′), *adj.* **1.** moderately warm. **2.** having little ardor or zeal. —**luke′warm′ly,** *adv.* —**luke′warm′ness,** *n.*

lull (lul), *v.t.* **1.** to put to sleep or rest by soothing means. **2.** to lead to feel a false sense of safety. —*v.i.* **3.** to quiet down or subside. —*n.* **4.** a temporary stillness. —**lull′ing·ly,** *adv.*

lull·a·by (lul′ə bī′), *n., pl.* **-bies.** a song used to lull a child to sleep.

lum·ba·go (lum bā′gō), *n.* pain in the lower back or lumbar region.

lum·bar (lum′bər, -bär), *adj.* of the loin or loins.

lum·ber[1] (lum′bər), *n.* **1.** timber sawed into planks, boards, etc. **2.** *Brit.* useless articles, furniture, etc., that are stored away. —*v.i.* **3.** to cut timber and prepare it for market. —**lum′-ber·ing,** *n.* —**lum′ber·man,** *n.*

lum·ber[2] (lum′bər), *v.i.* to move clumsily or heavily. —**lum′ber·ing,** *adj.*

lum·ber·jack (lum′bər jak′), *n.* a person who works at lumbering.

lum·ber·yard (lum′bər yärd′), *n.* a yard where lumber is stored for sale.

lu·mi·nar·y (lōō′mə ner′ē), *n., pl.* **-nar·ies.** **1.** a celestial body that gives light, esp. the sun or moon. **2.** an eminent person.

lu·mi·nesce (lōō′mə nes′), *v.i.,* **-nesced, -nesc·ing.** to exhibit luminescence.

lu·mi·nes·cence (lōō′mə nes′əns), *n.* the emission of light occurring at a temperature below that of incandescent bodies. —**lu′mi·nes′cent,** *adj.*

lu·mi·nous (lōō′mə nəs), *adj.* **1.** radiating light. **2.** readily intelligible. —**lu′mi·nance** (-nəns), *n.* —**lu′mi·nos′i·ty** (-nos′i tē), *n.* —**lu′mi·nous·ly,** *adv.*

lum·mox (lum′əks), *n.* *Informal.* a clumsy, stupid person.

lump[1] (lump), *n.* **1.** a piece or mass of no particular shape. **2.** a protuberance or swelling. **3.** a heap or mass. **4. lumps,** *Informal.* deserved or undeserved punishment, criticism, etc. —*adj.* **5.** in a lump or lumps. **6.** in a single, complete payment: *a lump sum.* —*v.t.* **7.** to make or unite into a lump or lumps. —*v.i.* **8.** to form a lump or lumps. —**lump′ish,** *adj.* —**lump′y,** *adj.* —**lump′i·ness,** *n.*

lump[2] (lump), *v.t.* *Informal.* to put up with.

lu·na·cy (lōō′nə sē), *n., pl.* **-cies.** **1.** intermittent insanity. **2.** extreme foolishness.

lu·nar (lōō′nər), *adj.* of or pertaining to the moon.

lu·na·tic (lōō′nə tik), *n.* **1.** an insane person. —*adj.* **2.** insane or demented. **3.** for the insane. **4.** extremely foolish. [< OF *lunatique* < LL *lūnatic(us)* moonstruck]

lu′natic fringe′, members of a usually small group who hold extreme or fanatical views.

lunch (lunch), *n.* **1.** a meal between breakfast and dinner. —*v.i.* **2.** to eat lunch.

lunch·eon (lun′chən), *n.* a lunch, esp. a formal one.

lunch·eon·ette (lun′chə net′), *n.* a small restaurant where light meals are served.

lunch′eon meat′, meat molded in a loaf ready to be served.

lunch·room (lunch′rōōm′, -rŏŏm′), *n.* **1.** a cafeteria or other room used as an eating place, as in a school. **2.** luncheonette.

lu·nette (lōō net′), *n.* any object or space of crescentlike or semicircular outline.

lung (lung), *n.* either of the two saclike respiratory organs in the thorax of human beings and the higher vertebrates. —**lunged** (lungd), *adj.*

lunge (lunj), *n., v.,* **lunged, lung·ing.** —*n.* **1.** a sudden forward thrust, as with a sword. **2.** any sudden forward movement. —*v.i., v.t.* **3.** to move or cause to move with a lunge.

lunk·head (lungk′hed′), *n.* *Slang.* a dull or stupid person. Also called **lunk.**

lu·pine[1] (lōō′pin), *n.* a leguminous plant having blue, pink, or white flowers.

lu·pine[2] (lōō′pīn), *adj.* of or resembling the wolf.

lu·pus (lōō′pəs), *n.* tuberculosis of the skin marked by brownish pimples, esp. about the nose and ears.

lurch[1] (lûrch), *n.* **1.** a sudden tip or roll to one side, as a staggering person. **2.** a swaying or staggering motion or gait. —*v.i.* **3.** to make a lurch, or move in lurches.

lurch[2] (lûrch), *n.* an uncomfortable or desperate situation: *to leave someone in the lurch.*

lure (lŏŏr), *n., v.,* **lured, lur·ing.** —*n.* **1.** anything that attracts irresistibly. **2.** an artificial bait used in angling or trapping. —*v.t.* **3.** to attract or entice. —**lur′ing·ly,** *adv.*

lu·rid (lŏŏr′id), *adj.* **1.** gruesome and revolting. **2.** startlingly sensational. **3.** wildly or garishly red. —**lu′rid·ly,** *adv.* —**lu′rid·ness,** *n.*

lurk (lûrk), *v.i.* **1.** to lie hidden, as in ambush. **2.** to go furtively.

lus·cious (lush′əs), *adj.* **1.** highly pleasing to the taste or smell. **2.** attractive to the senses. —**lus′cious·ly,** *adv.* —**lus′cious·ness,** *n.*

lush[1] (lush), *adj.* **1.** marked by luxuriant vegetation. **2.** marked by luxuriousness or opulence. —**lush′ness,** *n.*

lush[2] (lush), *n.* *Slang.* a habitual excessive drinker.

lust (lust), *n.* **1.** strong sexual desire, esp. when uncontrolled. **2.** a passionate or overmastering desire. —*v.i.* **3.** to have a strong desire, as sexual desire. —**lust′ful,** *adj.* —**lust′ful·ly,** *adv.*

lus·ter (lus'tər), *n.* **1.** the quality of shining by reflected light. **2.** radiant or luminous brightness. **3.** radiance of beauty, merit, or renown. Also, *Brit.,* lus'tre. —lus'ter·less, *adj.* —lus'trous (-trəs), *adj.*

lust·y (lus'tē), *adj.,* lust·i·er, lust·i·est. full of healthy vigor. —lust'i·ly, *adv.* —lust'i·ness, *n.* —Syn. hearty, robust.

lute (lōōt), *n.* a stringed musical instrument having a long, fretted neck and a hollow, pear-shaped body. —lu'te·ist, lu'tan·ist, lut'ist, *n.*

lu·te·ti·um (lōō tē'shē əm), *n. Chem.* a rare-earth, metallic element. *Symbol:* Lu; *at. wt.:* 174.97; *at. no.:* 71. Also, **lu·te'ci·um**.

Lu·ther (lōō'thər), *n.* **Mar·tin** (mär'tⁿn), 1483–1546, German theologian and Reformation leader.

Lu·ther·an (lōō'thər ən), *adj.* **1.** of the Protestant denomination following the doctrines set forth by Luther. —*n.* **2.** a member of the Lutheran Church. —Lu'ther·an·ism, *n.*

Lux·em·bourg (luk'səm bûrg'), *n.* a country between Germany, France, and Belgium. Also, **Lux'em·burg'**.

lux·u·ri·ant (lug zhŏŏr'ē ənt, luk-shŏŏr'-), *adj.* **1.** abundant in growth, as vegetation. **2.** producing abundantly, as soil. **3.** rich or florid, as ornamentation. —lux·u'ri·ance, *n.* —lux·u'ri·ant·ly, *adv.*

lux·u·ri·ate (lug zhŏŏr'ē āt', luk-shŏŏr'-), *v.i.,* -at·ed, -at·ing. **1.** to indulge oneself in luxury. **2.** to grow abundantly. —lux·u'ri·a'tion, *n.*

lux·u·ri·ous (lug zhŏŏr'ē əs, luk-shŏŏr'-), *adj.* **1.** characterized by luxury. **2.** given to or fond of luxury. —lux·u'ri·ous·ly, *adv.* —lux·u'ri·ous·ness, *n.* —Syn. **1.** lush, rich, sumptuous.

lux·u·ry (luk'shə rē, lug'zhə-), *n., pl.* -ries, *adj.* —*n.* **1.** something enjoyed as an addition to the ordinary necessities and comforts of life. **2.** indulgence in the pleasures afforded by such things. —*adj.* **3.** of or affording luxury: *a luxury hotel.*

lv., leave; leaves.

-ly, a suffix meaning: **a.** in a (specified) manner: *loudly.* **b.** in or according to: *theoretically.* **c.** to or from a (specified) direction: *inwardly.* **d.** every: *hourly.* **e.** like or characteristic of: *saintly.*

ly·ce·um (lī sē'əm), *n. U.S.* **1.** an early institution for popular education, providing lectures, concerts, etc. **2.** its building.

lye (lī), *n.* any white, powerful alkaline substance used for washing and in making soap.

ly·ing¹ (lī'ing), *n.* **1.** the telling of lies. —*adj.* **2.** deliberately untruthful. —*v.* **3.** ppr. of lie¹.

ly·ing² (lī'ing), *v.* ppr. of **lie²**.

ly·ing-in (lī'ing in'), *n., pl.* **lyings-in**, **lying-ins**, *adj.* —*n.* **1.** the confinement of a woman giving birth. —*adj.* **2.** pertaining to or for childbirth.

lymph (limf), *n.* a yellowish fluid containing white blood cells that surrounds body cells and carries their wastes to the bloodstream.

lym·phat·ic (lim fat'ik), *adj.* **1.** of or containing lymph. **2.** flabby or sluggish. —lym·phat'i·cal·ly, *adv.*

lymph' node', any of the glandlike masses of tissue that filter microorganisms in the lymph.

lym·phoid (lim'foid), *adj.* **1.** of or resembling lymph. **2.** of or pertaining to the tissue that occurs esp. in the lymph nodes.

lynch (linch), *v.t.* to hang or otherwise kill (a person) by mob action and without legal authority. [perh. after Captain William *Lynch* (1742–1820) of Virginia] —lynch'er, *n.*

lynx (lingks), *n., pl.* **lynx·es**, **lynx.** a wildcat having long limbs, a short tail, and usually tufted ears.

lynx-eyed (lingks'īd'), *adj.* having keen sight.

ly·on·naise (lī'ə nāz'), *adj.* cooked with pieces of onion.

Ly·ons (lī'ənz), *n.* a city in E France. Also, **Ly·on** (lyôn).

lyre (līⁱr), *n.* a harplike musical instrument of ancient Greece.

lyr·ic (lir'ik), *adj.* Also, **lyr'i·cal. 1.** (of a poem) having the form of a song expressing the poet's feelings. **2.** employing or suitable for singing. **3.** (of a voice) relatively light of volume and modest in range. **4.** (of style, etc.) expressing intense spontaneous feeling. —*n.* **5.** a lyric poem. **6.** lyrics, the words of a song. —lyr'i·cal·ly, *adv.*

lyr·i·cist (lir'i sist), *n.* a person who writes the words for songs.

ly·ser'gic ac'id (li sûr'jik, lī-), a crystalline solid used in the synthesis of LSD.

lyser'gic ac'id di·eth'yl·a·mide (dī-eth'əl ə mīd', -mid). See **LSD**.

ly·sin (lī'sin), *n.* an antibody causing the disintegration of bacterial cells.

-lysis, a combining form meaning "a breaking down, loosening, or decomposition": *analysis; paralysis.*

-lyte, a combining form meaning "something subjected to decomposition": *electrolyte.*

LZ, landing zone.

M

M, m (em), *n.*, *pl.* **M's** or **Ms, m's** or **ms.** the 13th letter of the English alphabet, a consonant.

M, 1. Mach. **2.** *Physics.* mass.

M, the Roman numeral for 1000.

m, *Metric System.* meter; meters.

M., 1. Medieval. **2.** Monday. **3.** *pl.* **MM.** Monsieur.

m., 1. male. **2.** married. **3.** masculine. **4.** medium. **5.** noon. [< L *meridies*] **6.** meter. **7.** mile. **8.** minim. **9.** minute. **10.** month. **11.** moon.

ma (mä), *n. Informal.* mother (def. 1).

MA, 1. Massachusetts. **2.** *Psychol.* mental age.

M.A., Master of Arts. [< L *Magister Artium*]

ma'am (mam, mäm; *unstressed* məm), *n. Informal.* madam.

ma·ca·bre (mə kä′brə, -käb′, -kä′bər), *adj.* **1.** bizarre in a gruesome way. **2.** of or dealing with death.

mac·ad·am (mə kad′əm), *n.* **1.** a road made by compacting successive layers of broken stone, often with asphalt or hot tar. **2.** the broken stone used in making such a road. —**mac·ad′am·ize′**, *v.t.*

ma·caque (mə käk′), *n.* a monkey found chiefly in Asia and the East Indies.

mac·a·ro·ni (mak′ə rō′nē), *n.* a wheat pasta in the form of dried, hollow tubes.

mac·a·roon (mak′ə rōōn′), *n.* a cooky made of egg whites, sugar, and almond paste or coconut.

ma·caw (mə kô′), *n.* a large, long-tailed parrot of tropical and subtropical America.

mace[1] (mās), *n.* **1.** a clublike weapon of war with a spiked metal head, used in the Middle Ages. **2.** a ceremonial staff carried before or by certain officials.

mace[2] (mās), *n.* a spice ground from the lacy coating of the nutmeg.

Mace (mās), *n. Trademark.* a chemical solvent that temporarily incapacitates a person by causing eye and skin irritations, used esp. as a means of subduing rioters.

Mac·e·do·ni·a (mas′i dō′nē ə, -dōn′yə), *n.* an ancient country, N of ancient Greece. —**Mac′e·do′ni·an,** *n., adj.*

mac·er·ate (mas′ə rāt′), *v.t.,* **-at·ed, -at·ing. 1.** to soften or separate (a substance) into parts by steeping in a liquid. **2.** to cause to grow thin. —**mac′er·at′er, mac′er·a′tor,** *n.* —**mac′er·a′tion,** *n.*

Mach (mäk), *n.* See **Mach number.** Also, **mach.**

mach., 1. machine. **2.** machinery. **3.** machinist.

ma·chet·e (mə shet′ē, -chet′ē), *n.* a large heavy knife used as a tool in cutting sugar cane and clearing underbrush, esp. in Latin America.

Mach·i·a·vel·li·an (mak′ē ə vel′ē ən), *adj.* unscrupulously cunning or deceptive. [after N. *Machiavelli,* 1469–1527, Ital. statesman]

ma·chic·o·la·tion (mə chik′ə lā′shən), *n.* (in a medieval castle or fortress) an opening in the floor of a projecting parapet through which missiles or molten lead could be cast upon an enemy.

mach·i·na·tion (mak′ə nā′shən), *n.* **1.** the act of plotting. **2.** a crafty scheme.

ma·chine (mə shēn′), *n., v.,* **-chined, -chin·ing.** —*n.* **1.** an apparatus consisting of interrelated parts with separate functions, used in the performance of some kind of work. **2.** a mechanical, electric, or electronic contrivance. **3.** a device that transmits or modifies force or motion, as a lever or pulley. **4.** an organized group of persons that conducts or controls the activities of a political party. **5.** an automobile, airplane, or other mechanical vehicle. —*v.t.* **6.** to make or finish with a machine. —**ma·chin′a·ble,** *adj.*

machine′ gun′, an automatic gun able to deliver a rapid and continuous fire of bullets. —**ma·chine′-gun′,** *v.t.* —**ma·chine′ gun′ner.**

machine′ lan′guage, the coding system for letters, numbers, and instructions that requires no translation by the computer for operation.

ma·chin·er·y (mə shē′nə rē), *n., pl.* **-er·ies. 1.** machines collectively. **2.** the parts of a machine. **3.** any system by which action or order is maintained: *the machinery of government.*

ma·chin·ist (mə shē′nist), *n.* **1.** a person who operates machinery. **2.** a person who makes and repairs machines.

ma·chis·mo (mä chiz′mō), *n.* a strong or exaggerated quality or sense of being masculine.

Mach′ num′ber, the ratio of the speed of an object to the speed of sound in the surrounding atmosphere. Also, **mach′ num′ber.**

ma·cho (mä′chō), *n., pl.* **-chos** (-chōs). *Mexican Spanish.* **1.** a strong, virile man. —*adj.* **2.** strong and manly.

537

mack·er·el (mak′ər əl, mak′rəl), *n.*, *pl.* **-el, -els.** a swift food fish found in the North Atlantic.

mack·i·naw (mak′ə nô′), *n.* a short coat of thick wool, usually plaid.

mack·in·tosh (mak′in tosh′), *n.* 1. a raincoat made of rubberized cloth. 2. such cloth. 3. *Brit.* any raincoat. Also, **mac′in·tosh′.**

mac·ra·mé (mak′rə mā′), *n.* a technique of knotting thread or cord into a coarse fabric, usually in a geometrical pattern, used as a fringe, in belts, etc.

macro-, a combining form meaning "large" or "long": macrocosm.

mac·ro·bi·ot·ic (mak′rō bī ot′ik), *adj.* 1. consisting primarily of grains and vegetables whose use is said to give long life. 2. of or serving such food.

mac·ro·bi·ot·ics (mak′rō bī ot′iks), *n.* the art of lengthening life, esp. by a vegetarian diet.

mac·ro·cosm (mak′rə koz′əm), *n.* 1. the universe considered as a whole. 2. any entire complex structure: *the macrocosm of war.* —**mac′ro·cos′mic,** *adj.*

ma·cron (mā′kron, mak′ron), *n.* a mark (‾) placed over a vowel to indicate that it has a long sound, as in *fate* (fāt).

mac·ro·scop·ic (mak′rə skop′ik), *adj.* visible to the naked eye. Also, **mac′ro·scop′i·cal.** —**mac′ro·scop′i·cal·ly,** *adv.*

mac·u·late (*adj.* mak′yə lit; *v.* mak′yə lāt′), *adj., v.,* **-lat·ed, -lat·ing.** —*adj.* 1. *Rare.* stained or spotted. 2. *Archaic.* to stain or pollute. —*v.t.* 2. *Archaic.* to stain or pollute. —**mac′u·la′tion,** *n.*

mad (mad), *adj., v.,* **mad·der, mad·dest,** *n.* —*adj.* 1. mentally disturbed or deranged. 2. enraged or irritated. 3. wildly excited. 4. extremely unwise. 5. excessively fond. 6. enjoyably hilarious. 7. affected with rabies. —*n.* 8. a spell of ill temper. —**mad′ly,** *adv.* —**mad′ness,** *n.* —**Syn.** 1. crazy, demented, insane. 2. angry, furious, irate.

Mad·a·gas·car (mad′ə gas′kər), *n.* an island country in the Indian Ocean, off the SE coast of Africa.

mad·am (mad′əm), *n., pl.* **mes·dames** (mā dam′) for 1; **-ams** for 2. 1. a polite term of address to a woman. 2. the woman in charge of a brothel. [< OF, orig. *ma dame* my lady]

mad·ame (mad′əm; mə dam′, -dăm′, ma-), *n., pl.* **mes·dames** (mā dam′, dăm′). *French.* Mrs. or madam.

mad·cap (mad′kap′), *adj.* 1. wildly impulsive. —*n.* 2. a madcap person, esp. a girl.

mad·den (mad′ᵊn), *v.t., v.i.* to make or become mad. —**mad′den·ing,** *adj.* —**mad′den·ing·ly,** *adv.*

mad·der (mad′ər), *n.* 1. a plant of Europe and Asia having panicles of small, yellowish flowers. 2. the red root of this plant, used in dyeing. 3. the dye itself.

mad·ding (mad′ing), *adj. Archaic.* acting madly or senselessly.

made (mād), *v.* pt. and pp. of **make.**

Ma·dei·ra (mə dēr′ə, -der′ə), *n.* a rich, strong white wine, resembling sherry.

mad·e·moi·selle (mad′ə mə zel′, mad′mwə-), *n., pl.* **mad·e·moi·selles** (mad′ə mə zelz′, mad′mwə-), **mes·de·moi·settes** (mād′ə mə zel′, mād′mwə zel′). *French.* Miss.

made-to-or·der (mād′tōō ôr′dər, -tə-), *adj.* made in accordance with individual specifications.

made-up (mād′up′), *adj.* 1. concocted, as a story. 2. wearing facial cosmetics. 3. put together or finished.

mad·house (mad′hous′), *n.* 1. an insane asylum. 2. any confused and often noisy place.

Mad·i·son (mad′i sən), *n.* 1. **James,** 1751–1836, 4th president of the U.S. 1809–17. 2. the capital of Wisconsin.

mad·man (mad′man′, -mən), *n.* an insane man. —**mad′wom′an,** *n.fem.*

Ma·don·na (mə don′ə), *n.* 1. the Virgin Mary. 2. a picture or statue representing the Virgin Mary. [< It: *my lady*]

mad·ras (mad′rəs, mə dras′, -dräs′), *n.* a light cotton fabric with woven stripes or figures.

Ma·dras (mə dras′, -dräs′), *n.* a seaport in SE India.

Ma·drid (mə drid′), *n.* the capital of Spain.

mad·ri·gal (mad′rə gəl), *n.* 1. an unaccompanied part song usually for five or six voices: flourished in the 16th century. 2. a medieval lyric poem suitable for being set to music.

mael·strom (māl′strəm), *n.* 1. a powerful or violent whirlpool. 2. a disordered or tumultuous state of affairs.

mae·nad (mē′nad), *n.* 1. a female attendant of Bacchus. 2. any frenzied woman. —**mae·nad′ic,** *adj.* —**mae′nad·ism,** *n.*

maes·tro (mī′strō), *n., pl.* **-tros, -tri** (-trē). 1. an eminent composer, teacher, or conductor of music. 2. a master of any art.

Ma·fi·a (mä′fē ə), *n.* an alleged secret organization of criminals. Also, **Maf′fi·a.** [< It *mafia* boldness]

Ma·fi·o·so (mä fē ō′sō), *n., pl.* **-si** (-sē). a reputed member of the Mafia.

mag (mag), *n. Informal.* magazine (def. 1).

mag., 1. magazine. 2. magnetism. 3. magneto. 4. magnitude.

mag·a·zine (mag'ə zēn', mag'ə zēn'), *n.* **1.** a periodical publication containing stories, essays, poems, etc., often with photographs and drawings. **2.** a room for keeping gunpowder, as on a warship. **3.** a building for keeping military supplies. **4.** a receptacle in a gun or firearm for holding cartridges. **5.** cartridge (def. 3).

mag·da·lene (mag'də lēn'), *n. Rare.* a repentant prostitute. Also, **mag'·da·len** (-lən).

Ma·gel·lan (mə jel'ən), *n.* **Fer·di·nand** (fûr'd°nand'), c1480–1521, Portuguese navigator.

ma·gen·ta (mə jen'tə), *n.* a reddish purple.

mag·got (mag'ət), *n.* a soft-bodied, legless larva of certain insects. —**mag'got·y**, *adj.*

Ma·gi (mā'jī), *n.pl., sing.* **-gus** (-gəs), (*sometimes l.c.*) the three wise men who paid homage to the infant Jesus.

mag·ic (maj'ik), *n.* **1.** the use of various techniques, as spells, charms, etc., that presumably assure human control of supernatural powers. **2.** any extraordinary or mystical influence, charm, or power. **3.** the art of causing illusions as entertainment by sleight of hand, etc. —*adj.* Also, **mag'i·cal. 4.** of or employed in magic. **5.** producing the effects of magic. —**mag'i·cal·ly**, *adv.*

ma·gi·cian (mə jish'ən), *n.* a person skilled in magic.

mag·is·te·ri·al (maj'i stēr'ē əl), *adj.* **1.** of or befitting a magistrate or his or her office. **2.** commanding or authoritative. —**mag'is·te'ri·al·ly**, *adv.*

mag·is·trate (maj'i strāt', -strit), *n.* **1.** a minor judicial officer, as a justice of the peace. **2.** a civil officer charged with the administration of the law. —**mag'is·tra·cy** (-strə sē), *n.*

mag·ma (mag'mə), *n.* molten material beneath or within the earth's crust, from which igneous rock is formed. —**mag·mat'ic** (-mat'ik), *adj.*

Mag·na Char·ta (mag'nə kär'tə), the charter of English liberties granted in 1215. Also, **Mag'na Car'ta.**

mag·nan·i·mous (mag nan'ə məs), *adj.* **1.** generous in forgiving an insult or injury. **2.** high-minded or noble. —**mag'na·nim'i·ty** (-nə nim'i tē), *n.* —**mag·nan'i·mous·ly**, *adv.* —**mag·nan'i·mous·ness**, *n.*

mag·nate (mag'nāt, -nit), *n.* a person of great influence in a particular field of business.

mag·ne·sia (mag nē'zhə, -shə), *n.* a white, tasteless substance, an oxide of magnesium, used as an antacid and laxative. —**mag·ne'sian**, *adj.*

mag·ne·si·um (mag nē'zē əm, -zhəm, -shē əm), *n. Chem.* a light, ductile, silver-white metallic element, used in lightweight alloys. *Symbol:* Mg; *at. wt.:* 24.312; *at. no.:* 12.

mag·net (mag'nit), *n.* **1.** a body or substance that possesses the property of attracting iron. **2.** a thing or person that attracts.

mag·net·ic (mag net'ik), *adj.* **1.** of or pertaining to a magnet or magnetism. **2.** having the properties of a magnet. **3.** capable of being magnetized. **4.** pertaining to the magnetic field of the earth. **5.** exerting a strong attractive power or charm. —**mag·net'i·cal·ly**, *adv.*

magnet'ic field', the space in the vicinity of a magnetic substance through which a magnetic force acts.

magnet'ic north', north as indicated by the end of a compass needle, differing in most places from true north.

magnet'ic record'ing, the process of recording sound, video signals, or data on magnetic tape, cassettes, or cartridges. —**magnet'ic record'er.**

magnet'ic tape', a thin ribbon of plastic material, coated with a substance containing iron oxide or another magnetic material for use in magnetic recording.

mag·net·ism (mag'ni tiz'əm), *n.* **1.** the properties of attraction possessed by magnets. **2.** the agency producing magnetic phenomena. **3.** attractive power or charm.

mag·net·ite (mag'ni tīt'), *n.* a very common black iron oxide: an important iron ore.

mag·net·ize (mag'ni tīz'), *v.t.,* **-ized, -iz·ing. 1.** to impart magnetic properties to. **2.** to exert an attracting influence upon. —**mag'net·iz'a·ble**, *adj.* —**mag'net·i·za'tion**, *n.* —**mag'net·iz'er**, *n.*

mag·ne·to (mag nē'tō), *n., pl.* **-tos.** a small electric generator the armature of which rotates in a magnetic field provided by permanent magnets.

mag·ne·tom·e·ter (mag'ni tom'i tər), *n.* an instrument for measuring the intensity of a magnetic field, esp. the earth's magnetic field.

mag·nif·i·cent (mag nif'i sənt), *adj.* **1.** making a splendid appearance or show. **2.** extraordinarily fine. **3.** noble or sublime. —**mag·nif'i·cence**, *n.* —**mag·nif'i·cent·ly**, *adv.* —**Syn. 1.** grand, lavish, superb.

mag·nif·i·co (mag nif'ə kō'), *n., pl.* **-coes. 1.** a Venetian nobleman. **2.** any lordly personage.

mag·ni·fy (mag'nə fī'), *v.,* **-fied, -fy·ing.** —*v.t.* **1.** to increase the apparent size of, as a lens does. **2.** to cause to seem greater in importance or effect. **3.** *Archaic.* to extol or praise. —*v.i.* **4.** to increase the apparent size of an object. —**mag'ni·fi·ca'tion**, *n.* —**mag'ni·fi'er**, *n.* —**Syn. 2.** exaggerate, overstate.

mag·nil·o·quent (mag nil′ə kwənt), *adj.* marked by a lofty or grandiose style. —**mag·nil′o·quence,** *n.*

mag·ni·tude (mag′ni tōōd′, -tyōōd′), *n.* **1.** greatness in size or extent. **2.** great importance or effect. **3.** volume or loudness of sound. **4.** the brightness of a star or other celestial body as viewed by the unaided eye from the earth.

mag·no·lia (mag nōl′yə, -nō′lē ə), *n.* a shrub or tree having large, usually fragrant flowers and an aromatic bark.

mag·num (mag′nəm), *n.* a large bottle for wine, containing about 50 ounces.

mag′num o′pus, the chief work of a writer or artist.

mag·pie (mag′pī′), *n.* **1.** a bird of the crow family, having a long tail, black-and-white plumage, and noisy habits. **2.** a chatterbox.

Mag·yar (mag′yär), *n.* **1.** a member of the predominant people of Hungary. **2.** the language of Hungary.

ma·ha·ra·jah (mä′hə rä′jə), *n.* a former ruling prince in India, esp. of one of the major states. Also, **ma′·ha·ra′ja.**

ma·ha·ra·nee (mä′hə rä′nē), *n.* **1.** the wife of a maharajah. **2.** a princess having a status like that of a maharajah. Also, **ma′ha·ra′ni.**

ma·ha·ri·shi (mä′hə ri′shē), *n.* a Hindu spiritual guide.

ma·hat·ma (mə hät′mə, -hat′-), *n.* (in India) a person held in the highest esteem for his wisdom and saintliness.

Mahat′ma Gan′dhi. See **Gandhi.**

Ma·hi·can (mə hē′kən), *n., pl.* **-cans, -can.** a tribe or confederacy of North American Indians centralized formerly in the upper Hudson valley.

mah·jongg (mä′jông′, -jong′), *n.* a game of Chinese origin played with dominolike tiles. Also, **mah′-jong′.**

ma·hog·a·ny (mə hog′ə nē), *n., pl.* **-nies. 1.** a tropical American tree yielding a hard, reddish-brown wood used for making furniture. **2.** the wood itself. **3.** a reddish-brown color.

Ma·hom·et (mə hom′it), *n.* Muhammad.

ma·hout (mə hout′), *n.* the keeper or driver of an elephant in India.

maid (mād), *n.* **1.** a female servant. **2.** *Literary.* a girl or young unmarried woman.

maid·en (mād′ən), *n.* **1.** *Literary.* maid (def. 2). —*adj.* **2.** of or befitting a maiden. **3.** unmarried or virgin. **4.** made, tried, or appearing for the frst time: *a maiden voyage.* —**maid′en·hood′,** *n.* —**maid′en·ly,** *adj.*

maid·en·hair (mād′ən hâr′), *n.* a fern having glossy stalks and delicate fronds.

maid·en·head (mād′ən hed′), *n.* **1.** the hymen. **2.** *Archaic.* virginity or maidenhood.

maid′en name′, a woman's surname before marriage.

maid·en·wait·ing (mād′in wā′ting), *n., pl.* **maids-in-wait·ing.** an unmarried lady-in-waiting.

maid′ of hon′or, the chief unmarried attendant of a bride.

maid·ser·vant (mād′sûr′vənt), *n.* maid (def. 1).

mail¹ (māl), *n.* **1.** letters, packages, etc., sent or delivered by the post office. **2.** a single collection of such material as sent or delivered at a given time. **3.** Also, **mails.** a postal system. **4.** *CB Radio Slang.* report or information. —*v.t.* **5.** to send by mail. —**mail′er,** *n.*

mail² (māl), *n.* flexible armor of interlinked metal rings or plates. —**mailed,** *adj.*

mail·box (māl′boks′), *n.* **1.** a public box for depositing outgoing mail. **2.** a private box for receiving incoming mail.

mail·lot (mä yō′), *n.* a closefitting, one-piece bathing suit for women.

mail·man (māl′man′), *n.* a man who carries and delivers mail. —**mail′·wom′an,** *n.fem.*

mail′ or′der, an order received and usually shipped by mail. —**mail′-or′der,** *adj.*

maim (mām), *v.t.* to deprive of the use of some part of the body, esp. by wounding seriously. —**maimed′ness,** *n.*

main (mān), *adj.* **1.** chief in size, extent, or importance. **2.** sheer or utmost, as force. **3.** *Gram.* capable of use in isolation. In *I walked out when the bell rang, I walked out* is the main clause. —*n.* **4.** a principal pipe in a system used to distribute water, gas, etc. **5.** physical effort or strength: *to struggle with might and main.* **6.** the chief part or point. **7.** *Literary.* the open ocean. **8.** *Archaic.* the mainland. **9. in the main,** for the most part. —**main′ly,** *adv.* —**Syn. 1.** primary, principal.

Maine (mān), *n.* a state in the NE United States. *Cap.:* Augusta.

main·frame (mān′frām′), *n.* the device within a computer which contains the central control and arithmetic units.

main·land (mān′land′, -lənd), *n.* the principal land of a country or region, as distinguished from adjacent islands. —**main′land′er,** *n.*

main′ line′, 1. the principal line of a railroad or highway. **2.** *Slang.* a prominent and readily accessible vein that may be used for a narcotic's injection.

main·line (mān′līn′, -līn′), *v.t.*, *v.i.*, **-lined, -lin·ing.** *Slang.* to inject (a drug, esp. heroin) into a vein. —**main′lin′er,** *n.*

main·mast (mān′mast ′, -mäst′, mān′məst), *n.* the principal mast of a ship.

main·sail (mān′sāl′, mān′səl), *n.* the principal sail on a mainmast.

main·spring (mān′spring′), *n.* **1.** the principal spring in a mechanism, as in a watch. **2.** the chief motive power of something.

main·stay (mān′stā′), *n.* **1.** a chief support or part. **2.** the stay that secures the mainmast forward.

main·stream (mān′strēm′), *n.* the dominant course, tendency, or trend.

main·tain (mān tān′), *v.t.* **1.** to keep in existence or continuance. **2.** to keep unimpaired. **3.** to keep in a specified state or position. **4.** to affirm or assert. **5.** to support in speech or argument, as a proposition. **6.** to hold against attack. **7.** to provide for the upkeep or support of. —**main·tain′a·ble,** *adj.* — **main·tain′a·bil′i·ty** (-tā′nə bil′i tē), *n.* —**main·te·nance** (mān′tᵊnəns), *n.*

main·top (mān′top′), *n.* a platform at the head of the lower mainmast.

mai·son·ette (mā′zə net′), *n.* *Brit.* part of a private house rented as a duplex apartment.

mai tai (mī′ tī′), a cocktail of rum and lemon and pineapple juice, sweetened and served with ice.

maî·tre d' (mā′tər dē′, mā′trə), *pl.* **maî·tre d's.** *Informal.* See **maître d'hôtel.**

maî·tre d'hô·tel (mā′tər dō tel′, mā′trə), *pl.* **maî·tres d'ho·tel** (mā′tərz · dō tel′, mā′traz); *n.* **1.** a headwaiter. **2.** a chief steward of a hotel restaurant.

maize (māz), *n.* **1.** *Chiefly Brit.* **corn¹** (def. 1). **2.** a pale yellow.

Maj., Major.

maj·es·ty (maj′i stē), *n., pl.* **-ties. 1.** regal or stately dignity. **2.** supreme greatness or authority. **3.** (*cap.*) a title used when speaking of or to a sovereign (prec. by *His, Her,* or *Your*). —**ma·jes′tic** (mə jes′tik), **ma·jes′ti·cal,** *adj.* —**ma·jes′ti·cal·ly,** *adv.*

Maj. Gen., Major General.

ma·jol·i·ca (mə jol′ə kə, mə yol′-), *n.* Italian glazed earthenware.

ma·jor (mā′jər), *n.* **1.** a commissioned officer ranking next below a lieutenant colonel, as in the U.S. Army. **2. a.** a subject or discipline in which a college student specializes. **b.** a student engaged in such a subject. — *adj.* **3.** greater in size, extent, or importance. **4.** serious or risky: *a ma-*

jor surgical operation. **5.** denoting or based on a major scale. —*v.i.* **6.** to follow an academic major.

ma·jor-do·mo (mā′jər dō′mō), *n., pl.* **-mos. 1.** a chief steward of a noble or royal household. **2.** a butler.

ma·jor·ette (mā′jə ret′), *n.* See **drum majorette.**

ma′jor gen′eral, a commissioned officer ranking next below a lieutenant general, as in the U.S. Army.

ma·jor·i·ty (mə jôr′i tē, -jor′-), *n., pl.* **-ties. 1.** any number larger than half the total, as opposed to the minority. **2.** the amount by which the greater number, as of votes, surpasses the remainder. **3.** the state or time of being of full legal age. **4.** the military rank of a major.

ma·jor-med·i·cal (mā′jər med′i kəl), *adj.* providing insurance coverage for any major injury or sickness, often subject to an initial deduction of a fixed amount.

ma′jor scale′, *Music.* a scale having half steps between the third and fourth and the seventh and eighth degrees.

ma·jus·cule (mə jus′kyōōl, maj′ə-skyōōl′), *n.* a large letter, as a capital or uncial letter.

make (māk), *v.,* **made, mak·ing,** *n.* —*v.t.* **1.** to bring into existence by shaping or changing material: *to make a dress.* **2.** to bring about: *to make war.* **3.** to render: *to make someone happy.* **4.** to fix or prepare: *to make a meal.* **5.** to bring into a certain form: *to make bricks out of clay.* **6.** to cause or compel. **7.** to produce or earn: *to make a good salary.* **8.** to draw up: *to make a will.* **9.** to establish or enact: *to make laws.* **10.** to appoint or name. **11.** to prove to be: *He will make a good lawyer.* **12.** to judge or interpret: *What do you make of it?* **13.** to bring to: *to make an even dozen.* **14.** to assure the success of. **15.** to deliver or utter: *to make a stirring speech.* **16.** to arrive at: *The ship made port on Friday.* **17.** to receive mention or appear in or on: *to make the front page.* —*v.i.* **18.** to cause someone or something to be as specified: *to make sure.* **19.** to show oneself to be in action or behavior: *to make merry.* **20.** to move or proceed: *to make for home.* **21.** to act or start to do something. **22. make away with, a.** to steal. **b.** to destroy or kill. **23. make believe,** to pretend or imagine. **24. make for, a.** to approach. **b.** to help to maintain. **25. make it,** *Informal.* to achieve a specific goal. **26. make off with,** to steal. **27. make out, a.** to complete, as a bill or check. **b.** to establish or prove. **c.** to discern or comprehend.

d. to imply or suggest. **e.** *Informal.* to manage or succeed. **f.** *Slang.* to engage in kissing and caressing. **28. make over, a.** to remodel or alter. **b.** to transfer the title of (property). **29. make up, a.** to constitute or form. **b.** to construct or compile. **c.** to concoct or invent. **d.** Also, **make up for.** to compensate for. **e.** to complete. **f.** to put in order. **g.** to conclude or decide. **h.** to become reconciled, as after a quarrel. **i.** to apply cosmetics. **30. make up to,** *Informal.* to try to become friendly with. —*n.* **31.** style or manner of being made. **32.** type of manufactured item as identified by its name or brand. **33.** disposition, character, or nature. **34.** quantity made. **35. on the make,** *Informal.* **a.** aggressively seeking to improve one's social or financial position. **b.** *Slang.* seeking amorous relations. —**mak′er,** *n.*

make-be·lieve (māk′bi lēv′), *n.* **1.** pretense, esp. of an innocent kind. —*adj.* **2.** pretended or imagined.

make-do (māk′dōō′), *n., adj. Informal.* makeshift.

make·shift (māk′shift′), *n.* **1.** a temporary expedient or substitute. —*adj.* **2.** serving as a makeshift.

make-up (māk′up′), *n.* **1.** cosmetics for the face or other parts of the body. **2.** cosmetics, costumes, etc., used by a performer. **3.** the manner of being made up or put together. **4.** physical or mental constitution.

make-work (māk′wûrk′), *n.* unnecessary work invented to keep workers from being idle.

mak·ings (mā′kingz), *n.* material of which something may be made.

mal-, a prefix meaning "bad," "wrongful," or "ill": *malfunction; malcontent.*

Mal. 1. Malay. **2.** Malayan.

mal·a·chite (mal′ə kīt′), *n.* a green mineral that is an ore of copper, used for making ornamental articles.

mal·a·dapt·ed (mal′ə dap′tid), *adj.* poorly suited to a particular condition or purpose.

mal·ad·just·ed (mal′ə jus′tid), *adj.* badly adjusted, esp. to one's environment. —**mal′ad·just′ment,** *n.*

mal·ad·min·is·ter (mal′əd min′i stər), *v.t.* to manage badly or inefficiently.

mal·a·droit (mal′ə droit′), *adj.* **1.** not adroit or skillful. **2.** bungling or tactless. —**mal′a·droit′ly,** *adv.* —**mal′a·droit′ness,** *n.*

mal·a·dy (mal′ə dē), *n., pl.* **-dies. 1.** any disorder or disease of the body. **2.** any undesirable or disordered condition.

Mal·a·gas′y Repub′lic (mal′ə gas′ē), official name of Madagascar.

ma·laise (ma lāz′), *n.* **1.** a feeling of mental uneasiness. **2.** a condition of general bodily weakness.

mal·a·mute (mal′ə myōōt′), *n.* a large Alaskan dog raised originally for drawing sleds.

mal·a·pert (mal′ə pûrt′), *adj. Archaic.* unbecomingly bold or saucy.

mal·a·prop·ism (mal′ə prop iz′əm), *n.* a ridiculous misuse of words that are similar in sound.

mal·ap·ro·pos (mal′ap rə pō′), *adj.* **1.** out of place. —*adv.* **2.** inappropriately.

ma·lar·i·a (mə lâr′ē ə), *n.* a disease characterized by attacks of chills, fever, and sweating: caused by a parasite transferred by a mosquito. [< It *mal(a) aria* bad air] —**ma·lar′i·al, ma·lar′i·an, ma·lar′i·ous,** *adj.*

ma·lar·key (mə lär′kē), *n. Informal.* nonsense speech or writing. Also, **ma·lar′ky.**

Mal·a·thi·on (mal′ə thī′on), *n. Trademark.* a liquid used as an insecticide.

Ma·la·wi (mä lä′wē), *n.* a country in SE Africa. —**Ma·la′wi·an,** *adj., n.*

Ma·lay (mā′lā, mə lā′), *adj.* **1.** of the Malays or their country or language. —*n.* **2.** a member of the dominant people of the Malay Peninsula and adjacent islands. **3.** the language of the Malays. —**Ma·lay′an,** *adj., n.*

Mal·a·ya·lam (mal′ə yä′ləm), *n.* a language spoken in extreme SW India.

Ma′lay Archipel′ago, an extensive island group in the Indian and Pacific oceans, SE of Asia.

Ma′lay Penin′sula, a peninsula in SE Asia.

Ma·lay·sia (mə lā′zhə, -shə), *n.* a country of SE Asia. —**Ma·lay′sian,** *n., adj.*

mal·con·tent (mal′kən tent′), *adj.* **1.** dissatisfied with prevailing conditions or circumstances. —*n.* **2.** a malcontent person.

mal de mer (mAl də meR′), *French.* seasickness.

Mal′dive Is′lands (mal′dīv), a country on a group of islands in the Indian Ocean.

male (māl), *adj.* **1.** of or belonging to the sex that begets young by fertilizing the female. **2.** of or characteristic of this sex. **3.** *Mach.* made to fit into a corresponding open or recessed part. —*n.* **4.** a male person, animal, or plant. —**male′ness,** *n.*

mal·e·dic·tion (mal′i dik′shən), *n.* a curse or the utterance of a curse.

mal·e·fac·tor (mal′ə fak′tər), *n.* **1.** a person who violates the law. **2.** a person who does evil. —**mal′e·fac′-tion,** *n.* —**mal′e·fac′tress** (-tris), *n.fem.*

ma·lef·ic (mə lef′ik), *adj.* producing evil.

ma·lef·i·cent (mə lef′i sənt), *adj.* doing evil or harm. —**ma·lef′i·cence,** *n.*

ma·lev·o·lent (mə lev′ə lənt), *adj.* 1. wishing evil to another or others. 2. exerting an evil influence. —**ma·lev′o·lence,** *n.* —**ma·lev′o·lent·ly,** *adv.* —**Syn.** 1. malicious, spiteful, vindictive.

mal·fea·sance (mal fē′zəns), *n.* unlawful action by a public official. —**mal·fea′sant,** *adj.,* *n.*

mal·for·ma·tion (mal′fôr mā′shən), *n.* faulty or anomalous structure, esp. in a living body. —**mal·formed′,** *adj.*

mal·func·tion (mal fuŋgk′shən), *n.* 1. failure to function properly. —*v.i.* 2. to fail to function properly.

Ma·li (mä′lē), *n.* a country in W Africa. —**Ma′li·an,** *adj.,* *n.*

mal·ice (mal′is), *n.* 1. a desire to inflict injury on another. 2. *Law.* evil intent or motive. —**ma·li·cious** (məlish′əs), *adj.* —**ma·li′cious·ly,** *adv.* —**Syn.** 1. enmity, malevolence, rancor, spite.

ma·lign (mə līn′), *v.t.* 1. to speak harmful untruths about. —*adj.* 2. evil in effect. 3. having or showing an evil disposition.

ma·lig·nant (mə lig′nənt), *adj.* 1. disposed to cause harm deliberately. 2. harmful in influence or effect. 3. tending to produce death, as a tumor. —**ma·lig′nan·cy,** *n.* —**ma·lig′nant·ly,** *adv.* —**ma·lig′ni·ty** (-ni tē), *n.*

ma·lin·ger (mə liŋ′gər), *v.i.* to pretend illness in order to avoid duty or work. —**ma·lin′ger·er,** *n.*

mall (môl, mäl, mal), *n.* 1. a public walk or promenade lined with shade trees. 2. a. an often covered area or street lined with shops and closed off to motor vehicles. b. a complex of shops in such an area. 3. a strip of land separating a highway.

mal·lard (mal′ərd), *n.,* *pl.* **-lards, -lard.** a common wild duck from which the domestic ducks descended.

mal·le·a·ble (mal′ē ə bəl), *adj.* 1. capable of being extended or shaped by hammering or by pressure from rollers. 2. adaptable or tractable. —**mal′le·a·bil′i·ty,** *n.* —**mal′le·a·bly,** *adv.*

mal·let (mal′it), *n.* 1. a hammerlike tool, usually of wood, used for driving a chisel. 2. the long-handled wooden implement used to strike the balls in croquet or polo.

mal·le·us (mal′ē əs), *n.,* *pl.* **mal·le·i** (mal′ē ī′). the outermost of three small bones in the middle ear.

mal·low (mal′ō), *n.* any of various herbs having lobed or dissected leaves and purple, pink, or white flowers.

mal·nour·ished (mal nûr′isht), *adj.* poorly or improperly nourished.

mal·nu·tri·tion (mal′noo trish′ən, -nyoo-), *n.* inadequate or unbalanced nutrition.

mal·oc·clu·sion (mal′ə kloo′zhən), *n.* irregular contact of opposing teeth in the upper and lower jaws.

mal·o·dor·ous (mal ō′dər əs), *adj.* having an unpleasant odor. —**mal·o′dor·ous·ly,** *adv.* —**mal·o′dor·ous·ness,** *n.*

mal·prac·tice (mal prak′tis), *n.* professional misconduct or improper, negligent practice, esp. by a medical doctor.

malt (môlt), *n.* 1. germinated grain, usually barley, used in brewing and distilling. 2. an alcoholic beverage or liquor fermented from malt. —**malt′y,** *adj.*

Mal·ta (môl′tə), *n.* an island country in the Mediterranean between Sicily and Africa. —**Mal·tese′** (-tēz′), *adj.,* *n.*

malt′ed milk′ (môl′tid), 1. a soluble powder made of dehydrated milk and malted cereals. 2. a beverage made by dissolving this powder, usually in milk.

Mal·thu·si·an (mal thoo′zē ən), *adj.* of or pertaining to the theories of T. R. Malthus (1766–1834), English economist, which state that population tends to increase faster than the means of subsistence, unless checked by such factors as war, famine, etc. —**Mal·thu′si·an·ism,** *n.*

malt·ose (môl′tōs), *n.* a sugar formed by the action of an enzyme on starch, used chiefly as a nutrient.

mal·treat (mal trēt′), *v.t.* to treat badly or roughly. —**mal·treat′ment,** *n.*

ma·ma (mä′mə, mə mä′), *n. Informal.* mother (def. 1). Also, **mam′ma.** [< L: breast]

mam·ba (mäm′bä), *n.* a long, slender African snake.

mam·bo (mäm′bō), *n.,* *pl.* **-bos.** a fast ballroom dance of Haitian origin.

mam·mal (mam′əl), *n.* any of a group of vertebrate animals, including human beings, that feeds its young with milk from the female mammary glands. —**mam·ma·li·an** (mə mā′lēən), *n.,* *adj.*

mam·ma·ry (mam′ə rē), *adj.* of or pertaining to the organs (**mam′mary glands′**) that in the female breast secrete milk.

mam·mog·ra·phy (mə mog′rə fē), *n.* X-ray examination of the breast, esp. for early detection of cancer.

mam·mon (mam′ən), *n.* (*often cap.*) a personification of riches as an evil spirit or deity.

mam·moth (mam′əth), *n.* **1.** an extinct elephantlike mammal having a hairy skin. —*adj.* **2.** immensely large.

man (man), *n., pl.* **men,** *v.,* **manned, man·ning.** —*n.* **1.** an adult male person. **2.** a human being. **3.** the human race. **4.** a male having manly qualities or virtues. **5.** an adult male servant, follower, or employee. **6.** a husband: *man and wife.* **7.** one of the pieces used in playing chess or checkers. **8. as one man,** unanimously. **9. the Man,** *Slang (used by blacks).* a white man, esp. one in a position of authority, as a police officer. **10. to a man,** with no exception. —*v.t.* **11.** to furnish with persons for service or defense. **12.** to strengthen or fortify. —**man′like′,** *adj.*
—**Usage.** The use of *man* in the senses of "human being" and "human race" is now often avoided as sexist.

Man (man), *n.* **Isle of,** an island of the British Isles, in the Irish Sea.

Man., Manitoba.

man., manual.

man′ about town′, a socially active, sophisticated man.

man·a·cle (man′ə kəl), *n., v.,* **-cled, -cling.** —*n.* **1.** a shackle for the hands or feet. **2.** Usually, **manacles.** restraints or checks. —*v.t.* **3.** to handcuff or fetter. **4.** to hamper or restrain.

man·age (man′ij), *v.,* **-aged, -ag·ing.** —*v.t.* **1.** to succeed in accomplishing. **2.** to have charge of or responsibility for: *to manage an estate.* **3.** to dominate or influence by tact or artifice. **4.** to handle or control in action or use. —*v.i.* **5.** to conduct business or affairs. **6.** to continue to get along. —**man′age·a·ble,** *adj.* —**man′age·a·bil′i·ty, man′age·a·ble·ness,** *n.* —**man′age·a·bly,** *adv.*

man·age·ment (man′ij mənt), *n.* **1.** the act or manner of managing. **2.** skill in managing. **3.** the person or persons managing a commercial enterprise. —**man′age·men′tal,** *adj.*

man·ag·er (man′i jər), *n.* a person who manages, esp. one charged with the control or direction of a business. —**man′a·ge′ri·al** (-jēr′ē əl), *adj.*

ma·ña·na (mə nyä′nə), *n., adv. Spanish.* tomorrow.

man-at-arms (man′ət ärmz′), *n., pl.* **men-at-arms.** a soldier, esp. a heavily armed medieval soldier on horseback.

man·a·tee (man′ə tē′, man′ə tē′), *n.* a large aquatic mammal resembling a seal.

Man·ches·ter (man′ches′tər, -chi stər), *n.* a city in NW England.

Man·chu (man chōō′), *n., pl.* **-chus, -chu.** **1.** a member of a Mongolian

people of Manchuria who conquered China and established a dynasty there 1644–1912. **2.** their language.

Man·chu·ri·a (man chŏŏr′ē ə), *n.* a region in NE China. —**Man·chu′ri·an,** *adj., n.*

man·da·mus (man dā′məs), *n.* a writ from a superior court commanding that a specified thing be done.

man·da·rin (man′də rin), *n.* **1.** a high public official in the former Chinese Empire. **2.** (*cap.*) the standard Chinese language. **3.** the loose-skinned fruit of a Chinese citrus tree.

man·date (man′dāt, -dit), *n.* **1.** an authorization to carry out a program or policy, given by the electorate to its representative. **2.** any authoritative order or command. **3.** a commission given by the League of Nations to a member nation to administer a conquered territory. **4.** a territory so administered.

man·da·to·ry (man′də tōr′ē, -tôr′ē), *adj.* **1.** authoritatively ordered or commanded. **2.** of or containing a mandate. —**man′da·to′ri·ly,** *adv.*

man·di·ble (man′də bəl), *n.* **1.** the bone of the lower jaw. **2.** the lower part of a bird's bill. —**man·dib′u·lar** (-dib′yə lər), *adj.*

man·do·lin (man′d°lin, man′d°lin′), *n.* a musical instrument with four or five double strings and a fretted neck. —**man′do·lin′ist,** *n.*

man·drag·o·ra (man drag′ər ə), *n.* mandrake (def. 1).

man·drake (man′drāk, -drik), *n.* **1.** a narcotic, European herb having a fleshy, forked root thought to resemble a human form. **2.** the May apple.

man·drel (man′drəl), *n.* a shaft inserted into a piece of work to hold it during machining. Also, **man′dril.**

man·drill (man′dril), *n.* a large, ferocious-looking baboon of W Africa, the male of which has the face marked with blue and scarlet.

mane (mān), *n.* the long hair growing about the neck of the horse and lion. —**maned,** *adj.*

man-eat·er (man′ē′tər), *n.* **1.** a human cannibal. **2.** an animal that eats or is said to eat human flesh. —**man′-eat′ing,** *adj.*

ma·nège (ma nezh′, -nāzh′), *n.* the art of training and riding horses. Also, **ma·nege′.**

ma·nes (mā′nēz, mä′nes), *n.* **1.** *Rom. Religion.* the souls of the dead. **2.** the spirit of a particular dead person. Also, **Ma′nes.**

ma·neu·ver (mə nōō′vər), *n., v.,* **-vered, -ver·ing.** —*n.* **1.** a planned and regulated movement of troops, war vessels, etc. **2. maneuvers,** a series of tactical exercises in imitation of war. **3.** an adroit move or skillful proceeding, esp. as characterized by craftiness: *political maneuvers.* — *v.t., v.i.* **4.** to perform or cause to perform a maneuver or maneuvers. **5.** to drive or make by maneuvers. **6.** to manage with skill or adroitness. [< F *manoeuvre* < L *manū operāre* to do handwork] —**ma·neu′ver·a·ble,** *adj.* —**ma·neu′ver·a·bil′i·ty,** *n.*

man′ Fri′day, a male administrative assistant with diverse duties.

man·ful (man′fəl), *adj.* having or showing manly spirit. —**man′ful·ly,** *adv.* —**man′ful·ness,** *n.*

man·ga·nese (mang′gə nēs′, -nēz′), *n. Chem.* a hard, brittle, grayish-white, metallic element, used chiefly in alloys. Symbol: Mn; *at. wt.*: 54.938; *at. no.*: 25.

mange (mānj), *n.* a skin disease, esp. of animals, characterized by loss of hair and scabby eruptions.

man·gel-wur·zel (mang′gəl wûr′zəl), *n. Chiefly Brit.* a variety of the beet cultivated as food for livestock.

man·ger (mān′jər), *n.* a box or trough from which horses or cattle eat.

man·gle[1] (mang′gəl), *v.t.,* -**gled, -gling. 1.** to cut, slash, or crush so as to disfigure. **2.** to spoil or ruin. —**man′gler,** *n.*

man·gle[2] (mang′gəl), *n.* a machine for smoothing or pressing clothes by means of heated rollers.

man·go (mang′gō), *n., pl.* -**goes, -gos. 1.** the oblong, slightly acid fruit of a tropical tree. **2.** its tree.

man·grove (mang′grōv, man′-), *n.* any tropical tree that sends roots down from its branches, forming dense thickets, esp. in swampy areas.

man·gy (mān′jē), *adj.,* -**gi·er, -gi·est. 1.** having, caused by, or like the mange. **2.** contemptible or mean. **3.** squalid or shabby. —**man′gi·ness,** *n.*

man·han·dle (man′han′dᵊl, man han′-dᵊl), *v.t.,* -**dled, -dling.** to handle roughly.

Man·hat·tan (man hat′ᵊn, mən-), *n.* **1.** a borough of New York City. **2.** (*often l.c.*) a cocktail of whiskey and sweet vermouth.

man·hole (man′hōl′), *n.* a hole, usually with a cover, affording entrance to a sewer, drain, etc.

man·hood (man′hŏŏd), *n.* **1.** the state of being a man or an adult male person. **2.** manly qualities. **3.** men collectively.

man-hour (man′our′, -ou′ər), *n.* an hour of work by one person, used as an industrial time unit.

man·hunt (man′hunt′), *n.* an intensive search for a criminal, escaped convict, etc.

ma·ni·a (mā′nē ə, mān′yə), *n.* **1.** excessive enthusiasm or desire. **2.** a form of insanity characterized by great excitement and often great violence.

-mania, a combining form meaning "a (specified) type of mania": *megalomania.*

ma·ni·ac (mā′nē ak′), *n.* **1.** a raving or violently insane person. —*adj.* **2.** raving with madness. —**ma·ni·a·cal** (mə nī′ə kəl), *adj.*

man·ic (man′ik, mā′nik), *adj.* pertaining to, resembling or affected by mania.

man·ic-de·pres·sive (man′ik di pres′iv), *adj.* **1.** having a mental disorder marked by alternating extremes of excitement and depression. —*n.* **2.** a person suffering from this disorder.

man·i·cure (man′ə kyŏŏr′), *n., v.,* -**cured, -cur·ing.** —*n.* **1.** a treatment of the hands and fingernails. —*v.t., v.i.* **2.** to take care of (the hands and fingernails) by manicure treatment.

man·i·cur·ist (man′ə kyŏŏr′ist), *n.* a person, esp. a woman, who gives manicures.

man·i·fest (man′ə fest′), *adj.* **1.** readily perceived by the eye or the understanding. —*v.t.* **2.** to show plainly. **3.** to put beyond doubt. —*n.* **4.** a list of the cargo or passengers carried by a vessel or airplane. —**man′i·fest′ly,** *adv.*

man·i·fes·ta·tion (man′ə fe stā′shən), *n.* **1.** the act of manifesting or state of being manifested. **2.** something that manifests. **3.** indication or demonstration.

man·i·fes·to (man′ə fes′tō), *n., pl.* -**toes.** a public declaration of intentions, objectives, or motives.

man·i·fold (man′ə fōld′), *adj.* **1.** of many kinds. **2.** having many different parts or features. **3.** doing or operating several things at once. —*n.* **4.** a copy or facsimile, as of something written. **5.** a pipe having several outlets through which a liquid or gas is distributed or gathered. —*v.t.* **6.** to make copies of, as with carbon paper. **7.** to make manifold. —**man′i·fold′ly,** *adv.* —**man′i·fold′ness,** *n.* —Syn. diverse, varied.

man·i·kin (man′ə kin), *n.* **1.** a little, undersized man. **2.** a model of the human body for teaching anatomy, demonstrating surgical operations, etc. **3.** mannequin. Also, **man′ni·kin.**

Ma·nil·a (mə nil′ə), *n.* a principal city in the Philippines, on S Luzon.

Manil′a hemp′, a fibrous material obtained from the leaves of a Philippine plant, used for making ropes, fabrics, etc.

Manil′a pa′per, a strong, light-brown or buff paper, made originally from Manila hemp.

man′ in the street′, the average person.

man·i·oc (man′ē ok′, mā′nē-), *n.* cassava.

man·i·ple (man′ə pəl), *n.* an ornamental band worn on the left arm as a Eucharistic vestment.

ma·nip·u·la·ble (mə nip′yə lə bəl), *adj.* that can be manipulated.

ma·nip·u·late (mə nip′yə lāt′), *v.t.,* **-lat·ed, -lat·ing. 1.** to handle, manage, or use with skill. **2.** to manage or influence by artful or devious skill. **3.** to change (accounting figures, etc.) to suit one's purpose or advantage. **—ma·nip′u·la′tion,** *n.* **—ma·nip′u·la′tive** (-lā′tiv, lə tiv), *adj.* **—ma·nip′u·la′tor,** *n.*

Man·i·to·ba (man′i tō′bə), *n.* a province in central Canada. *Cap.t* Winnipeg.

man·i·tou (man′i tōō′), *n.* (among the Algonquian Indians) a spirit, deity, or object having supernatural power.

man·kind (man′kīnd′ *for 1;* man′kīnd′ *for 2*), *n.* **1.** human beings collectively. **2.** men, as distinguished from women.

man·ly (man′lē), *adj.,* **-li·er, -li·est,** *adv.* **—adj. 1.** having the qualities usually considered desirable in a man. **2.** pertaining to or befitting a man: *manly sports.* **—adv. 2.** *Archaic.* in a manly manner. **—man′li·ness,** *n.*

man·made (man′mād′), *adj.* produced or made by human beings rather than by nature.

Mann (män), *n.* **Thom·as** (tom′əs), 1875–1955, German novelist.

man·na (man′ə), *n.* **1.** *Bible.* the food miraculously supplied to the Israelites in the wilderness. **2.** something of help given unexpectedly.

manned (mand), *adj.* carrying or operated by one or more persons: *a manned spacecraft.*

man·ne·quin (man′ə kin), *n.* **1.** a model of the human figure used for displaying clothing. **2.** a girl or woman employed to model clothes.

man·ner (man′ər), *n.* **1.** way of doing, being done, or happening. **2.** customary way of acting or doing. **3.** **manners, a.** the prevailing customs of a people or period. **b.** ways of behaving with reference to polite standards. **4.** kind or sort: *All manner of things were happening.* **5.** characteristic style in the arts. **—Syn. 2.** fashion, mode, style.

man·nered (man′ərd), *adj.* **1.** having manners as specified: *ill-mannered people.* **2.** having mannerisms: *a mannered walk.*

man·ner·ism (man′ə riz′əm), *n.* **1.** marked adherence to a particular manner, esp. an affectation. **2.** a habitual or characteristic mode of doing something.

man·ner·ly (man′ər lē), *adj.* having or showing good manners. **—man′ner·li·ness,** *n.*

man·nish (man′ish), *adj.* (esp. of a woman) resembling, characteristic of, or appropriate for a man. **—man′nish·ly,** *adv.* **—man′nish·ness,** *n.*

ma·noeu·vre (mə nōō′vər), *n., v.t., v.i.,* **-vred, -vring.** *Brit.* maneuver.

man-of-war (man′əv wôr′), *n., pl.* **men-of-war.** *Archaic.* a warship.

ma·nom·e·ter (mə nom′i tər), *n.* an instrument for measuring the pressure of a fluid. **—man·o·met·ric** (man′ə me′trik), *adj.*

man·or (man′ər), *n.* **1.** a large landed estate of a medieval lord. **2.** the main mansion on an estate. **—ma·no·ri·al** (mə nôr′ē əl, -nōr′-), *adj.* **—ma·no′ri·al·ism,** *n.*

man·pow·er (man′pou′ər), *n.* **1.** the power supplied by the physical exertions of man. **2.** total personnel available for work or service, as of a nation in time of war.

man·qué (mäṅg kā′), *adj.* *French.* aspiring but unfulfilled: *a poet manqué.*

man·sard (man′särd), *n.* a roof having four sides, each with two slopes, the lower one steep, the upper one nearly flat.

manse (mans), *n.* the residence of a Presbyterian minister, esp. in Scotland.

man·serv·ant (man′sûr′vənt), *n., pl.* **men·serv·ants.** a valet.

man·sion (man′shən), *n.* a very large, impressive residence.

man-sized (man′sīzd′), *adj.* *Informal.* of a size suitable for a man. Also, **man′-size′.**

man·slaugh·ter (man′slô′tər), *n.* the killing of a human being unlawfully but without malice.

man·slay·er (man′slā′ər), *n.* a person who slays a human being.

man·sue·tude (man′swi tōōd′, -tyōōd′), *n.* *Archaic.* mildness or gentleness.

man′ta ray′ (man′tə), a huge ray common in tropical waters, having earlike flaps on each side of the head.

man·tel (man′t°l), *n.* **1.** a construction framing the opening of a fireplace. **2.** a shelf above a fireplace opening.

man·tel·et (man′t°let′, mant′lit), *n.* a short mantle or cloak.

man·tel·piece (man′t°l pēs′), *n.* mantel (def. 2).

man·til·la (man til′ə, -tē′ə), *n.* a lace head scarf, usually covering the shoulders, worn esp. in Spain and Latin America.

man·tis (man′tis), *n., pl.* **-tis·es, -tes** (-tēz). an insect typically holding the forelegs in an upraised position as if in prayer.

man·tis·sa (man tis′ə), *n.* the decimal part of a common logarithm.

man·tle (man′t°l), *n., v.,* **-tled, -tling.** **—n. 1.** a loose, sleeveless cloak. **2.** something that covers or conceals: *the mantle of darkness.* **3.** a hood for a gas jet that gives off a brilliant light when incandescent. **4.** Also called **man′tle·piece′** (-pēs′). mantel (def. 2). **5.** the portion of the earth between the crust and the core. **—v.t. 6.** to cover with or as with a mantle. **—v.i. 7.** to flush or blush. **8.** to be or become covered with a coating, as a liquid.

man·tra (man′trə, mun′-), *n. Hinduism.* a word or formula to be recited or sung.

man·u·al (man′yōō əl), *adj.* **1.** of the hand or hands. **2.** operated by hand. **3.** involving or using work with the hands. **—n. 4.** a handy book, esp. one giving information or instructions. **5.** *Mil.* prescribed drill in handling a rifle. **6.** a keyboard of a pipe organ played with the hands. **—man′u·al·ly,** *adv.*

man′ual al′phabet, an alphabet consisting of a series of finger signals to represent the letters for deaf-mutes to communicate with.

man′ual train′ing, training in the various manual arts and crafts, esp. woodworking.

manuf., 1. manufacture. **2.** manufacturer. **3.** manufacturing.

man·u·fac·to·ry (man′yə fak′tə rē), *n., pl.* **-ries.** *Archaic.* a factory.

man·u·fac·ture (man′yə fak′chər), *v.,* **-tured, -tur·ing,** *n.* **—v.t. 1.** to make (objects or materials), esp. by machinery on a large scale. **2.** to invent fictitiously. **—n. 3.** the act or process of manufacturing. **4.** something that is manufactured. **—man′u·fac′tur·er,** *n.*

man·u·mit (man′yə mit′), *v.t.,* **-mit·ted, -mit·ting.** to release from slavery, as esp. in ancient Rome. **—man′u·mis′sion,** *n.*

ma·nure (mə nŏŏr′, -nyŏŏr′), *n., v.,* **-nured, -nur·ing. —n. 1.** excrement, esp. of animals, or other refuse used as fertilizer. **—v.t. 2.** to apply manure to.

man·u·script (man′yə skript′), *n.* **1.** an original text of an author's work, handwritten or typed, that is submitted to a publisher. **2.** writing, as distinguished from print. **3.** a book or document written by hand before the invention of printing. **—adj. 4.** of, in, or on a manuscript. **5.** written by hand, not printed.

Manx (mangks), *adj.* **1.** of the Isle of Man, its inhabitants, or their language. **—n. 2.** the inhabitants of the Isle of Man. **3.** their language.

man·y (men′ē), *adj.,* **more, most,** *n., pron.* **—adj. 1.** constituting or forming a large number. **—n. 2.** a large or considerable number of persons or things. **—pron. 3.** many persons or things.

Ma·o·ri (mou′rē), *n., pl.* **-ris, -ri,** *adj.* **—n. 1.** a member of a brown-skinned Polynesian people of New Zealand. **2.** their language. **—adj. 3.** of the Maoris or their language.

mao tai (mou′ tī′), a very strong, colorless Chinese liquor distilled from sorghum.

Mao Tse-tung (mou′ dzə dŏŏng′), 1893–1976, Chinese communist leader. **—Mao′ism,** *n.* **—Mao′ist,** *n., adj.*

map (map), *n., v.,* **mapped, map·ping. —n. 1.** a representation, usually on a flat surface, of the features of an area of the earth or a portion of the heavens. **—v.t. 2.** to make a map of. **3.** to sketch or plan: *to map out a new career.* **—map′pa·ble,** *adj.* **— map′per,** *n.*

ma·ple (mā′pəl), *n.* **1.** any of numerous trees or shrubs grown as shade or ornamental trees, for timber, or for sap. **2.** the wood of any such tree.

ma′ple sug′ar, a yellowish-brown sugar produced by boiling down maple syrup.

ma′ple syr′up, a syrup produced by boiling down the sap of maple trees, esp. the sugar maple.

mar (mär), *v.t.,* **marred, mar·ring. 1.** to impair the physical perfection of. **2.** to detract from the quality of. **— Syn. 1.** blemish, deface. **2.** ruin, spoil.

Mar., March.

mar., 1. maritime. **2.** married.

mar·a·bou (mar′ə bŏŏ′), *n.* **1.** a large stork having soft, downy feathers that are used in millinery. **2.** its feather.

mar·ac·a (mə rä′kə, -rak′ə), *n.* a gourd or a gourd-shaped rattle filled with seeds or pebbles and used as a rhythm instrument.

mar·a·schi·no (mar′ə skē′nō, -shē′-), *n.* a cordial or liqueur distilled from a wild cherry.

mar′aschi′no cher′ry, a cherry cooked in syrup and flavored with maraschino.

mar·a·thon (mar′ə thon′, -thən), *n.* **1.** a foot race on a course measuring 26 miles 385 yards. **2.** any long contest of endurance.

ma·raud (mə rôd′), *v.i., v.t.* to rove and raid for plunder. **—ma·raud′er,** *n.*

mar·ble (mär′bəl), *n., adj.* **—n. 1.** a limestone capable of taking a high polish, used for buildings and sculpture. **2.** something resembling marble in hardness, coldness, or smoothness. 3. a little ball made of glass or agate for use in games. 4. **marbles,** a children's game played with such balls, usually of many colors. —*adj.* 5. consisting of or like marble.

mar·ble·ize (mär′bə līz′), *v.t.,* **-ized, -iz·ing.** to color or stain in imitation of variegated marble.

mar·bling (mär′bling), *n.* 1. a decoration or pattern resembling variegated marble. 2. a distribution of fat in streaks through meat.

mar·cel (mär sel′), a series of regular, continuous waves put in the hair by means of a curling iron.

march[1] (märch), *v.i.* 1. to walk with regular, measured steps, as soldiers in military formation. 2. to move forward. —*v.t.* 3. to cause to march. —*n.* 4. the act or course of marching. 5. a regular, measured step. 6. the distance covered in a single period of marching. 7. forward movement. 8. a piece of music with a rhythm suited to marching. 9. **on the march,** moving ahead. 10. **steal a march on,** to gain an advantage over, esp. secretly. —**march′er,** *n.*

march[2] (märch), *n. Archaic.* a border district.

March (märch), *n.* the third month of the year, containing 31 days.

mar·chion·ess (mär′shə nis, mär′shə nes′), *n. Brit.* marquise.

march-past (märch′past′, -päst′), *n.* a parade or procession, esp. of troops past a reviewing stand.

Mar·di gras (mär′dē grä′, grä′), the day before Lent, often celebrated as a day of carnival.

mare[1] (mâr), *n.* a fully mature female horse or other equine animal.

ma·re[2] (mär′ā, mâr′ē), *n., pl.* **ma·ri·a** (mär′ē ə, mâr′-). any of the several large, dark plains on the moon.

mare′s′ nest′, 1. an illusory or false discovery. 2. a confused or disordered situation.

mar·ga·rine (mär′jər in, -jə rēn′, märj′-rin), *n.* a butterlike product made of refined vegetable oils emulsified with milk.

mar·gin (mär′jin), *n.* 1. the space around the printed or written matter on a page. 2. an amount beyond what is necessary: *a margin of safety.* 3. a range or degree of difference. 4. a border or edge. 5. the difference between the cost and the selling price. —**mar′gin·al,** *adj.* —**mar′gin·al·ly,** *adv.*

mar·gi·na·li·a (mär′jə nā′lē ə, -näl′yə), *n.pl.* marginal notes, as in a book.

mar·grave (mär′grāv), *n.* a military governor of a medieval German border province.

mar·gue·rite (mär′gə rēt′), *n.* any of several daisylike flowers, esp. a white chrysanthemum having yellow-centered flowers.

mar·i·a·chi (mä′rē ä′chē), *n.* 1. a small band of Mexican strolling musicians dressed in native costumes. 2. a member of such a band. 3. its dance music.

Mar·i·an (mâr′ē ən), *adj.* of the Virgin Mary.

Ma·rie An·toi·nette (mə rē′ an′twə-net′), 1755–93, queen of France (1774–93) & wife of Louis XVI: guillotined.

mar·i·gold (mar′ə gōld′), *n.* a plant having strong-smelling leaves and bearing orange or yellow flowers.

ma·ri·jua·na (mar′ə wä′nə, -hwä′-, mär′-), *n.* 1. a habit-forming drug obtained from the dried leaves and flowers of an Indian hemp, used as a hallucinogen. 2. its hemp tree. Also, **ma′ri·hua′na.**

ma·rim·ba (mə rim′bə), *n.* a variety of xylophone, often with resonators beneath to reinforce the sound. [< WAfr]

ma·ri·na (mə rē′nə), *n.* a boat basin offering dockage and other service for small craft.

mar·i·nade (*n.* mar′ə nād′, mar′ə nād′; *v.* mar′ə nād′), *n., v.,* **-nad·ed, -nad·ing.** —*n.* 1. a seasoned vinegar-oil mixture in which meat, fish, vegetables, etc., are steeped before cooking. 2. meat or fish steeped in it. —*v.t.* 3. to marinate.

mar·i·nate (mar′ə nāt′), *v.t.,* **-nat·ed, -nat·ing.** to steep (food) in a marinade.

ma·rine (mə rēn′), *adj.* 1. of, existing in, or produced by the sea. 2. pertaining to navigation or shipping. 3. of the marines. —*n.* 4. (*sometimes cap.*) a member of the U.S. Marine Corps. 5. a soldier serving both on shipboard and on land. 6. shipping in general. 7. a marine painting or photograph.

Marine′ Corps′, a branch of the U.S. Navy usually employed in amphibious landing operations.

mar·i·ner (mar′ə nər), *n.* a person who directs or assists in the navigation of a ship.

mar·i·on·ette (mar′ē ə net′), *n.* a puppet manipulated by strings attached to its jointed limbs.

mar·i·tal (mar′i t[ə]l), *adj.* of or pertaining to marriage. —**mar′i·tal·ly,** *adv.*

mar·i·time (mar′i tīm′), *adj.* 1. of or pertaining to commerce and navigation on the sea or to the seagoing vessels and personnel involved. 2. bordering on or making a living from the sea.

mar·jo·ram (mär′jər əm), *n.* an aromatic plant of the mint family, used as a seasoning.

mark¹ (märk), *n.* **1.** something appearing distinctly on a surface, as a dot or dent. **2.** a conspicuous sign used in measuring, etc. **3.** a symbol used in writing or printing: *a punctuation mark.* **4.** a label or brand on merchandise identifying its origin. **5.** something indicative of one's condition or character: *to bow as a mark of respect.* **6.** a symbol used in rating conduct, proficiency, etc., as of pupils. **7.** a required standard of quality: *His dissertation was below the mark.* **8.** something serving as an indication of position. **9.** distinction or importance. **10.** an object aimed at a goal or target. **11.** an object of derision, scorn, etc. **12.** the starting line in a track event. **13. make one's mark,** to attain success. —*v.t.* **14.** to be a distinguishing feature of. **15.** to put a mark or marks on. **16.** to indicate by or as by marks. **17.** to grade or rate. **18.** to make manifest: *to mark approval with a nod.* **19.** to give heed to: *Mark my words!* **20. mark down,** to reduce the price of. **21. mark time, a.** to suspend progress temporarily. **b.** *Mil.* to move the feet alternately as in marching but without advancing. **22. mark up,** to increase the price of. —**mark′er,** *n.*

mark² (märk), *n.* the monetary unit of Germany.

Mark (märk), *n.* **1.** a Christian apostle: reputed author of the second Gospel. **2.** the second Gospel.

mark·down (märk′doun′), *n.* **1.** a reduction in price. **2.** the amount by which a price is reduced.

marked (märkt), *adj.* **1.** strikingly noticeable. **2.** having a mark or marks. —**mark·ed·ly** (mär′kid lē), *adv.*

mar·ket (mär′kit), *n.* **1.** a meeting of people for selling and buying. **2.** a place used for selling and buying. **3.** a store for the sale of food. **4.** a region in which goods and services are bought and sold. **5.** demand for a commodity. **6.** a particular group of potential buyers. —*v.i.* **7.** to buy or sell. **8.** to buy food and provisions for the home. —*v.t.* **9.** to carry or send to market for disposal. **10.** to dispose of in a market. —**mar′ket·a·ble,** *adj.* —**mar′ket·er, mar′ket·eer′,** *n.*

mar·ket·place (mär′kit plās′), *n.* **1.** an open area in a town where a market or markets are held. **2.** the world of commerce.

mark·ka (märk′kä), *n., pl.* **-kaa** (-kä). the monetary unit of Finland.

marks·man (märks′mən), *n.* a person skilled in shooting at a mark. —**marks′man·ship,** *n.* —**marks′wom·an,** *n.fem.*

mark·up (märk′up′), *n.* **1.** the amount added to the cost of a commodity to cover expenses and profit in fixing the selling price. **2. a.** an increase in price. **b.** the amount by which a price is increased.

marl (märl), *n.* an earthy deposit used as a fertilizer for soils deficient in lime.

mar·lin (mär′lin), *n., pl.* **-lin, -lins.** a large, saltwater game fish.

mar·line·spike (mär′lin spīk′), *n.* a pointed iron implement used in separating the strands of rope in splicing. Also, **mar′lin·spike′.**

mar·ma·lade (mär′mə lād′, mär′mə lād′), *n.* a jellylike preserve containing small pieces of fruit and fruit rind, as of oranges.

mar·mo·re·al (mär mōr′ē əl, -môr′-), *adj. Literary.* of or like marble. Also, **mar·mo′re·an.**

mar·mo·set (mär′mə zet′), *n.* a small South and Central American monkey resembling a squirrel.

mar·mot (mär′mət), *n.* any bushytailed, stocky rodent, as the woodchuck.

ma·roon¹ (mə rōōn′), *adj.* dark brownish-red.

ma·roon² (mə rōōn′), *v.t.* **1.** to put ashore and leave on a desolate island or coast. **2.** to isolate without resources or hope.

marque (märk), *n.* a product model or type, as of a sports car.

mar·quee (mär kē′), *n.* **1.** a rooflike shelter over a theater entrance, usually containing the names of a currently featured play or film and its stars. **2.** *Chiefly Brit.* a large tent with open sides, used as for a garden party.

mar·quess (mär′kwis), *n. Brit.* marquis.

mar·que·try (mär′ki trē), *n.* inlaid work of variously colored woods or other materials, esp. in furniture.

mar·quis (mär′kwis, mär kē′), *n., pl.* **-quis·es, -quis** (-kēz′). a nobleman ranking next below a duke and above an earl or count.

mar·quise (mär kēz′), *n., pl.* **-quis·es** (-kē′ziz). **1.** the wife or widow of a marquis. **2.** a lady holding the rank equal to that of a marquis.

mar·qui·sette (mär′ki zet′, -kwi-), *n.* a lightweight open fabric.

mar·riage (mar′ij), *n.* **1.** the state or relationship of being married. **2.** a wedding ceremony. **3.** any close association. —**mar′riage·a·ble,** *adj.* —**Syn. 1.** matrimony, wedlock. **2.** nuptials.

mar·row (mar′ō), *n.* a soft, fatty tissue in the interior cavities of bones.

mar·row·bone (mar′ō bōn′), *n.* a bone containing edible marrow.

mar·ry (mar′ē), *v.,* **-ried, -ry·ing.** — *v.t.* **1.** to take as a husband or wife. **2.** to join in wedlock. **3.** to unite intimately. —*v.i.* **4.** to take a husband or wife. —**mar′ried,** *adj., n.*

Mars (märz), *n.* **1.** the ancient Roman god of war. **2.** the planet fourth in order from the sun.

Mar·seilles (mär sā′), *n.* a seaport in SE France. Also, **Mar·seille′.**

marsh (märsh), *n.* a tract of low wet land. —**marsh′y,** *adj.*

mar·shal (mär′shəl), *n., v.,* **-shaled, -shal·ing** or **-shalled, -shal·ling.** —*n.* **1.** *U.S.* **a.** a federal officer of a judicial district who performs duties similar to those of a sheriff. **b.** the chief of a police or fire department. **2.** the highest-ranking officer of the army in some countries. **3.** an official charged with the arrangement of ceremonies, parades, etc. —*v.t.* **4.** to arrange in proper order. **5.** to usher or lead.

Mar·shall (mär′shəl), *n.* **John,** 1775–1835, U.S. jurist: Chief Justice of the U.S. 1801–35.

marsh′ gas′, a gaseous product consisting primarily of methane.

marsh·mal·low (märsh′mel′ō, -mal′ō), *n.* a spongy confection made from gelatin, sugar, corn syrup, and flavoring.

marsh′ mar′igold, a yellow-flowered plant of the buttercup family that grows in marshes and meadows.

mar·su·pi·al (mär soo′pē əl), *n.* **1.** any of a group of mammals, including kangaroos, opossums, etc., the female of which has a pouch for carrying her young. —*adj.* **2.** of a marsupial. [< L *marsupiāl(is)* pertaining to a pouch]

mart (märt), *n.* a marketplace or trading center.

mar·ten (mär′tən, -tin), *n., pl.* **-tens, -ten. 1.** a slender mammal like a weasel, having a long, glossy coat and bushy tail. **2.** its fur, usually dark brown in color.

mar·tial (mär′shəl), *adj.* **1.** inclined or disposed to war. **2.** appropriate for war: *martial music.* **3.** characteristic of or befitting a warrior. **4.** of or adapted for fighting, esp. without weapons: *Chinese martial arts.* —**mar′tial·ism,** *n.* —**mar′tial·ist,** *n.* —**mar′tial·ly,** *adv.* —**Syn. 1.** military, warlike.

mar′tial law′, the law imposed upon an area by military forces when civil authority has broken down.

Mar·tian (mär′shən), *adj* **1.** of the planet Mars. —*n.* **2.** a supposed inhabitant of the planet Mars.

mar·tin (mär′tən, -tin), *n.* any of several small swallows.

mar·ti·net (mär′tənet′, mär′tənet′), *n.* a strict disciplinarian, esp. a military one.

mar·tin·gale (mär′tən gāl′), *n.* a strap that fastens to a horse's girth and passes between the forelegs: used to steady its head.

mar·ti·ni (mär tē′nē), *n., pl.* **-nis.** a cocktail made with gin or vodka and dry vermouth.

mar·tyr (mär′tər), *n.* **1.** a person who chooses to suffer death rather than renounce his or her religion. **2.** a person who endures great suffering on behalf of any principle or cause. **3.** a person who undergoes severe suffering. —*v.t.* **4.** to make a martyr of. **5.** to torment or torture. —**mar′tyr·dom,** *n.*

mar·vel (mär′vəl), *n., v.,* **-veled, -vel·ing** or **-velled, -vel·ling.** —*n.* **1.** a person or thing that arouses wonder or astonishment. **2.** *Archaic.* the feeling of wonder. —*v.t.* **3.** to wonder at. **4.** to be curious about. —*v.i.* **5.** to be affected with wonder.

mar·vel·ous (mär′və ləs), *adj.* **1.** tending to arouse wonder or astonishment. **2.** superb or excellent. **3.** improbable or incredible. Also, *Brit.,* **mar′vel·lous.** —**mar′vel·ous·ly,** *adv.* —**mar′vel·ous·ness,** *n.*

Marx (märks), *n.* **Karl** (kärl), 1818–83, German founder of communist doctrines.

Marx·ism (märk′siz əm), *n.* the system of economic, social, and political doctrines developed by Karl Marx. —**Marx′ist, Marx′i·an,** *n., adj.*

Mar·y (mâr′ē), *n.* the mother of Jesus.

Mar′y Jane′, *Slang.* marijuana. Also, **mar′y·jane′.**

Mar·y·land (mer′ə lənd), *n.* a state in the E United States. *Cap.:* Annapolis.

mar·zi·pan (mär′zə pan′), *n.* a confection made with almond milk and egg whites.

masc., masculine. Also, **mas.**

mas·car·a (ma skar′ə), *n.* a cosmetic for coloring the eyelashes and sometimes the eyebrows.

mas·con (mas′kon′), *n.* a massive concentration of heavy material beneath the surface of the moon.

mas·cot (mas′kət, -kot), *n.* a person, animal, or thing whose presence is considered as bringing good luck.

mas·cu·line (mas′kyə lin), *adj.* **1.** having qualities, as vigor, strength, etc., characteristic of men. **2.** of or for men. **3.** *Gram.* noting the gender that has among its members most nouns referring to males. **4.** (of a woman) mannish. —*n. Gram.* **5.** the masculine gender. **6.** a noun or other element in that gender. —**mas′cu·line·ly,** *adv.* —**mas′cu·lin′i·ty,** *n.* —**Syn. 1.** manly, virile.

ma·ser (mā′zər), *n.* a device, operating on the principle of the laser, that amplifies microwaves.

mash (mash), *n.* 1. a soft, pulpy mass. 2. a mess of boiled grain, bran, etc., fed warm to horses and cattle. 3. crushed malt or meal of grain mixed with hot water to form wort. —*v.t.* 4. to crush into a soft, pulpy mass. 5. to crush or smash. —**mash′er,** *n.*

MASH (mash), *n.* mobile army surgical hospital.

mask (mask, mäsk), *n.* 1. a covering for all or part of the face, usually for protection or disguise. 2. anything that disguises or conceals. 3. a likeness of a face, as one cast in a mold: *a death mask.* 4. a representation of a face, generally grotesque, used as an ornament. 5. the face or head, as of a fox. 6. masque (def. 1). —*v.t.* 7. to cover or disguise with or as with a mask. —**masked,** *adj.* —**mask′er,** *n.*

mas·och·ism (mas′ə kiz′əm, maz′-), *n.* 1. the condition in which sexual gratification depends on physical pain, esp. inflicted on oneself. 2. neurotic gratification from physical pain and humiliation. —**mas′och·ist,** *n.* —**mas′och·is′tic,** *adj.* —**mas′och·is′ti·cal·ly,** *adv.*

ma·son (mā′sən), *n.* 1. a person whose trade is building with stones, bricks, etc. 2. (*cap.*) a Freemason.

Ma·son·ic (mə son′ik), *adj.* of Freemasons or Freemasonry.

ma·son·ry (mā′sən rē), *n., pl.* **-ries.** 1. the trade of a mason. 2. work constructed by a mason, esp. stonework. 3. (*cap.*) the principles of Freemasonry.

masque (mask, mäsk), *n.* 1. an elaborate entertainment in England in the 16th and 17th centuries, performed chiefly by amateur actors. 2. masquerade (def. 1).

mas·quer·ade (mas′kə rād′), *n., v.,* **-ad·ed, -ad·ing.** —*n.* 1. a festive gathering of persons wearing masks and fancy costumes. 2. a costume worn at such a gathering. 3. false outward show. —*v.i.* 4. to go about under false pretenses. 5. to take part in a masquerade. —**mas′quer·ad′er,** *n.*

mass (mas), *n.* 1. a body of coherent matter of indefinite shape and size. 2. a considerable number or quantity. 3. the greater part. 4. bulk or massiveness. 5. *Physics.* a fundamental property of a body as representing its resistance to acceleration or deceleration. 6. **the masses,** the great body of the common people, esp. the working classes. —*adj.* 7. of or affecting the masses: *mass hysteria.* 8. done repeatedly or in great quantity: *mass attacks.* —*v.i.,*

v.t. 9. to form or gather into a mass or masses. —**mass′y,** *adj.* —**mass′i·ness,** *n.*

Mass (mas), *n.* 1. the celebration of the Eucharist. 2. (*sometimes l.c.*) a musical setting of certain parts of this service.

Mass., Massachusetts.

Mas·sa·chu·setts (mas′ə chōō′sits), *n.* a state in the NE United States. *Cap.:* Boston.

mas·sa·cre (mas′ə kər), *n., v.,* **-cred, -cring.** —*n.* 1. the unnecessary, indiscriminate killing of a number of human beings or animals. 2. *Informal.* a crushing defeat, as in sports. —*v.t.* 3. to kill indiscriminately, esp. in large numbers. —**mas′sa·crer** (mas′ə krər), *n.*

mas·sage (mə säzh′, -säj′), *n., v.,* **-saged, -sag·ing.** —*n.* 1. the rubbing or kneading of the body to stimulate circulation or increase suppleness. —*v.t.* 2. to treat by massage. —**mas·sag′er, mas·sag′ist,** *n.*

massage′ par′lor, a commercial establishment for the massage of males by masseuses, who are sometimes allegedly also engaged in prostitution.

mass·cult (mas′kult′), *n.* a popular culture created esp. by the mass media.

mas·seur (mə sûr′), *n.* a man who provides massage as a profession. —**mas·seuse′** (-sōōs′, -sōōz′), *n.fem.*

mas·sif (mas′if), *n.* a compact portion of a mountain range.

mas·sive (mas′iv), *adj.* 1. consisting of or forming a large mass. 2. great or imposing. —**mas′sive·ly,** *adv.* —**mas′sive·ness,** *n.*

mass·less (mas′lis), *adj. Physics.* having no mass. —**mass′less·ness,** *n.*

mass′-mar′ket pa′per·back, a book bound in a flexible paper cover, typically about 7 x 4½ inches and of low-grade paper stock, often constituting a low-priced edition of a hardcover book: usually distributed on newsstands, in supermarkets, etc., as well as in bookstores.

mass′ me′dia, media (def. 2).

mass′ num′ber, the number of nucleons in the nucleus of the atom.

mass·pro·duce (mas′prə dōōs′, -dyōōs′), *v.t.,* **-duced, -duc·ing.** to manufacture in large quantities, esp. by machinery. —**mass′ produc′tion.**

mast¹ (mast, mäst), *n.* 1. a spar or structure rising above the hull and upper portions of a vessel to hold sails, rigging, etc. 2. any upright pole. —**mast′ed** (mast′id), *adj.*

mast² (mast, mäst), *n.* the fruit of forest trees, used as food for animals.

mas·tec·to·my (ma stek′tə mē), *n.* the operation of removing a breast.

mas·ter (mas′tər, mä′stər), *n.* **1.** a person with the ability or power to control or dispose of something. **2.** an employer of workers or servants. **3.** the captain of a merchant vessel. **4.** the male head of a household. **5.** an owner of a slave, animal, etc. **6.** *Chiefly Brit.* a male teacher. **7.** a workman qualified to carry on his trade independently. **8.** a person eminently skilled in an art or science. **9.** **a.** an academic degree awarded to a student who has completed at least one year of graduate study. **b.** a person having this degree. **10.** a boy or young man (used chiefly as a form of address). **11.** something to be mechanically reproduced. —*adj.* **12.** being master. **13.** chief or principal. **14.** directing or controlling. —*v.t.* **15.** to conquer or subdue. **16.** to become an expert in.

mas′ter chief′ pet′ty of′ficer, a petty officer of the highest rank in the U.S. Navy.

mas·ter·ful (mas′tər fəl, mä′stər-), *adj.* **1.** having or showing the qualities of a master. **2.** showing mastery or skill. —**mas′ter·ful·ly,** *adv.* —**Syn. 1.** authoritative, forceful. **2.** adept, expert.

mas′ter gun′nery ser′geant, *U.S. Marine Corps.* a noncommissioned officer ranking above a master sergeant.

mas′ter hand′, 1. a specially skillful person. **2.** the ability or skill of a master.

mas′ter key′, a key that will open a number of different locks.

mas·ter·ly (mas′tər lē, mä′stər-), *adj.* **1.** worthy of a master. —*adv.* **2.** in a masterly manner.

mas·ter·mind (mas′tər mīnd′, mä′stər-), *v.t.* **1.** to plan and direct (activities) skillfully. —*n.* **2.** a person who is primarily responsible for the execution of a particular project.

mas′ter of cer′emonies, a person who directs the entertainment at a party, dinner, etc.

mas·ter·piece (mas′tər pēs′, mä′stər-), *n.* **1.** a person's most excellent production, as in an art. **2.** any production of masterly skill.

mas′ter ser′geant, *U.S.* **1.** *Army.* a noncommissioned officer ranking next below a staff sergeant major. **2.** *Marine Corps.* a noncommissioned officer ranking next below a master gunnery sergeant. **3.** *Air Force.* a noncommissioned officer ranking next below a senior master sergeant.

mas′ter stroke′, a masterly action or achievement.

mas·ter·work (mas′tər wûrk′, mä′stər-), *n.* masterpiece.

mas·ter·y (mas′tə rē, mä′stə-), *n., pl.* **-ter·ies. 1.** power of command or control. **2.** command or grasp, as

of a subject. **3.** victory or superiority. **4.** expert skill or knowledge.

mast·head (mast′hed′, mäst′-), *n.* **1.** the head of a mast. **2.** that part of a newspaper or magazine which gives its publisher, staff, etc.

mas·tic (mas′tik), *n.* an aromatic resin used in making varnish and adhesive cement.

mas·ti·cate (mas′tə kāt′), *v.t., v.i.,* -cat·ed, -cat·ing. to chew. —**mas′ti·ca′tion,** *n.* —**mas′ti·ca·to·ry** (-kə tōr′ē, -tôr′ē), *adj.*

mas·tiff (mas′tif, mä′stif), *n.* a large, powerful, short-haired dog.

mas·to·don (mas′tə don′), *n.* a large, elephantlike extinct mammal. —**mas′to·don′ic,** *adj.*

mas·toid (mas′toid), *adj.* denoting the nipplelike process of the temporal bone behind the ear. —*n.* **2.** the mastoid process.

mas·tur·ba·tion (mas′tər bā′shən), *n.* the stimulation of one's own or another's genitals to achieve orgasm by practices other than coitus. —**mas′tur·bate′,** *v.i., v.t.* —**mas′tur·ba′tor,** *n.* —**mas·tur·ba·to·ry** (mas′tər bə tōr′ē, -tôr′ē), *adj.*

mat[1] (mat), *n., v.,* mat·ted, mat·ting. —*n.* **1.** a piece of fabric, rubber, etc., used as a covering on a floor, as a pad under a dish of food, etc. **2.** a floor covering for the protection of wrestlers or tumblers. **3.** a thick and tangled mass, as of hair or weeds. —*v.t.* **4.** to cover with or as with mats. **5.** to form into a mat, as by interweaving. —*v.i.* **6.** to form tangled masses.

mat[2] (mat), *n., v.,* mat·ted, mat·ting. —*n.* **1.** a piece of cardboard used to form a border around a picture. —*v.t.* **2.** to provide (a picture) with a mat.

mat[3] (mat), *adj., n., v.,* mat·ted, mat·ting. matte.

mat[4] (mat), *n. Informal,* matrix (def. 2).

mat·a·dor (mat′ə dôr′), *n.* the bullfighter who kills the bull in a bullfight.

match[1] (mach), *n.* a short, slender piece of wood or other material tipped with a chemical substance that produces fire through friction.

match[2] (mach), *n.* **1.** a person or thing that equals or resembles another. **2.** a corresponding or suitably associated pair. **3.** *Chiefly Brit.* a contest or game. **4.** a partner in marriage: *a good match.* **5.** a matrimonial agreement. —*v.t.* **6.** to be equal to. **7.** to be the match or counterpart of. **8.** to cause to correspond. **9.** to fit together, as two things. **10.** to place in opposition or conflict. **11.** to unite in marriage. —*v.i.* **12.** to be equal or suitable. —**match′er,** *n.*

match·book (mach′book′), *n.* a small cardboard folder of paper matches.

match·less (mach′lis), *adj.* having no equal. —**match′less·ly,** *adv.*

match·lock (mach′lok′), *n.* an old type of gunlock in which the priming was ignited by a slow-burning match.

match·mak·er (mach′mā′kər), *n.* a person who arranges marriages by introducing possible mates.

mate (māt), *n., v.,* **mat·ed, mat·ing.** —*n.* **1.** one of a pair. **2.** husband or wife. **3.** one of a pair of mated animals. **4.** a habitual associate. **5.** an officer of a merchant vessel ranking below the captain. —*v.t., v.i.* **6.** to join as a mate or as mates. **7.** to couple in marriage or for breeding.

ma·té (mä′tā, mat′ā), *n.* a tealike South American beverage. Also, **ma′te.**

ma·te·ri·al (mə tēr′ē əl), *n.* **1.** the substance or substances of which a thing is made or composed. **2.** a textile fabric. **3.** materials, the articles or apparatus needed to make or do something. —*adj.* **4.** formed or consisting of matter: *the material world.* **5.** relating to or involving matter: *material force.* **6.** pertaining to the physical rather than the spiritual or intellectual aspect of things. **7.** of much consequence. —**ma·te′ri·al·ly,** *adv.*

ma·te·ri·al·ism (mə tēr′ē ə liz′əm), *n.* **1.** the philosophical theory that regards matter and its motions as constituting the universe, and all phenomena, including those of mind, as due to material agencies. **2.** emphasis on material objects and needs, with a disinterest in spiritual values. —**ma·te′ri·al·ist,** *n., adj.* —**ma·te′ri·al·is′tic,** *adj.* —**ma·te′ri·al·is′ti·cal·ly,** *adv.*

ma·te·ri·al·ize (mə tēr′ē ə līz′), *v.,* **-ized, -iz·ing.** —*v.t.* **1.** to give material form to. —*v.i.* **2.** to become actual fact. **3.** to assume material or bodily form: *The ghost materialized before Hamlet.* —**ma·te′ri·al·i·za′tion,** *n.*

ma·te·ri·el (mə tēr′ē el′), *n.* **1.** the aggregate of things needed in any undertaking. **2.** *Mil.* arms, ammunition, and equipment in general. Also, **ma·té′ri·el′.**

ma·ter·nal (mə tûr′n°l), *adj.* **1.** of, from, or befitting a mother. **2.** related through a mother. —**ma·ter′nal·ly,** *adv.*

ma·ter·ni·ty (mə tûr′ni tē), *n.* **1.** the state of being a mother. —*adj.* **2.** for wear by pregnant women.

math (math), *n. Informal.* mathematics.

math., **1.** mathematical. **2.** mathematics.

math·e·mat·ics (math′ə mat′iks), *n.* the systematic treatment of magnitude, relationships between figures and forms, and relations between quantities expressed symbolically. —**math′e·mat′i·cal,** *adj.* —**math′e·mat′i·cal·ly,** *adv.* —**math′e·ma·ti′cian** (-mə tish′ən), *n.*

mat·i·nee (mat′°nā′, mat′°nā′), *n.* a dramatic or musical performance held in the afternoon. Also, **mat′i·née′.**

mat·ins (mat′°nz, mat′inz) *n.* (*often cap.*) **1.** *Rom. Cath. Ch.* prayers read at daybreak. **2.** *Anglican Ch.* the service of public morning prayer.

matri-, a combining form meaning "mother": *matricide.*

ma·tri·arch (mā′trē ärk′), *n.* a woman who rules a family or tribe. —**ma′tri·ar′chal,** *adj.* —**ma′tri·ar′chy,** *n.*

mat·ri·cide (ma′tri sīd′, mā′-), *n.* **1.** the act of killing one's mother. **2.** a person who kills his or her mother. —**mat′ri·cid′al,** *adj.*

ma·tric·u·late (mə trik′yə lāt′), *v.t., v.i.,* **-lat·ed, -lat·ing.** to enroll in a college or university as a candidate for a degree. —**ma·tric′u·la′tion,** *n.*

mat·ri·mo·ny (ma′trə mō′nē), *n.* **1.** the state of being married. **2.** the rite or ceremony of marriage. —**mat′ri·mo′ni·al,** *adj.* —**mat′ri·mo′ni·al·ly,** *adv.*

ma·trix (mā′triks, ma′-), *n., pl.* **ma·tri·ces** (mā′tri sēz′, ma′-), **ma·trix·es.** **1.** something that gives origin or form to another thing. **2.** *Print.* a mold for casting typefaces.

ma·trix·ing (mā′trik sing, ma′-), *n.* an electronic method of processing four-channel sound for recording in a two-channel form, for reconversion to four channels when played back.

ma·tron (mā′trən), *n.* **1.** a married woman, esp. one with children or one who has an established social position. **2.** a woman who has charge of the housekeeping matters of an institution, as a prison. —**ma′tron·ly,** *adj.* —**ma′tron·li·ness,** *n.*

ma′tron of hon′or, a married woman acting as principal attendant of the bride at a wedding.

Matt., Matthew.

matte (mat), *adj., n., v.,* **mat·ted, mat·ting.** —*adj.* **1.** lusterless and dull in surface. —*n.* **2.** a lusterless and dull finish, as on metals. —*v.t.* **3.** to finish with a matte surface. Also, **matt.**

mat·ter (mat′ər), *n.* **1.** the substance or substances of which any physical object consists or is composed, esp. as distinguished from incorporeal substance, as spirit or mind. **2.** something that occupies space. **3.** a particular kind of substance: *coloring matter.* **4.** a substance discharged by a living body, esp. pus. **5.** things put down in words, esp. printed: *reading matter.* **6.** things sent by mail: *postal matter.* **7.** a situation or affair: *a trivial matter.* **8.** an amount or extent reckoned approximately: *a matter of 10 miles.* **9.** importance or significance. **10.** difficulty or trouble: *There is something the matter.* **11.** ground or cause: *a matter for complaint.* **12.** as a matter of fact, in reality. **13. no matter, a.** it makes no difference. **b.** despite. —*v.i.* **14.** to be of importance. **15.** to discharge pus.

mat·ter-of-fact (mat′ər əv fakt′), *adj.* adhering strictly to fact. —**mat′ter-of-fact′ly,** *adv.* —**mat′ter-of-fact′ness,** *n.*

Mat·thew (math′yōō), *n.* **1.** a Christian apostle: reputed author of the first Gospel. **2.** the first Gospel.

mat·ting (mat′ing), *n.* **1.** a fabric of rushes, hemp, etc., used for floor covering, wrapping material, etc. **2.** mats collectively.

mat·tock (mat′ək), *n.* a pickaxlike implement for loosening the soil in digging.

mat·tress (ma′tris), *n.* a large pad used as or on a bed, consisting of a case of heavy cloth that contains straw, foam rubber, etc.

mat·u·rate (mach′ōō rāt′, mat′yōō-), *v.i.,* **-rat·ed, -rat·ing. 1.** to suppurate. **2.** to mature. —**mat′u·ra′tion,** *n.* —**mat′u·ra′tion·al,** *adj.* —**ma·tur·a·tive** (mə chōōr′ə tiv), *adj.*

ma·ture (mə tōōr′, -tyōōr′, -chōōr′), *adj., v.,* **-tured, -tur·ing.** —*adj.* **1.** ripe, as fruit, or fully aged, as cheese, wine, etc. **2.** fully developed in body or mind, as a person. **3.** of or pertaining to full development. **4.** due or payable, as a bond. —*v.t., v.i.* **5.** to make or become mature. —**ma·ture′ly,** *adv.* —**ma·tu′ri·ty,** *n.*

ma·tu·ti·nal (mə tōōt′ʰn°l, -tyōōt′-), *adj. Literary.* of or occurring in the morning.

mat·zo (mät′sə, -sō), *n., pl.* **mat·zos** (mät′soz, -sōs), **ma·tzoth** (mä tsōt′). **1.** unleavened bread in the form of large crackers, eaten by Jews during Passover. **2.** one of these crackers. Also, **mat′zah.**

maud·lin (môd′lin), *adj.* tearfully or weakly emotional. —**maud′lin·ly,** *adv.*

maul (môl), *n.* **1.** a heavy hammer, as for driving piles. —*v.t.* **2.** to handle roughly. **3.** to injure by a rough beating or shoving. —**maul′er,** *n.*

maun·der (môn′dər), *v.i.* **1.** to talk in a rambling or meaningless way. **2.** to move in an aimless, confused manner. —**maun′der·er,** *n.*

Mau·pas·sant (mō′pə sänt′), *n.* Guy de (gē də), 1850–93, French short-story writer and novelist.

Mau·ri·ta·ni·a (môr′i tā′nē ə), *n.* a country in W Africa. —**Mau′ri·ta′ni·an,** *adj., n.*

Mau·ri·tius (mô rish′əs, -rish′ē əs), *n.* an island country in the Indian Ocean, E of Madagascar. —**Mau·ri′tian,** *adj., n.*

mau·so·le·um (mô′sə lē′əm, -zə-), *n., pl.* **-le·ums, -le·a** (-lē′ə). a stately and magnificent tomb built above ground.

mauve (mōv), *n.* a pale-bluish purple.

mav·er·ick (mav′ər ik, mav′rik), *n.* **1.** an unbranded animal, esp. a motherless calf. **2.** a person who takes an independent stand apart from his associates.

ma·vin (mä′vən), *n.* an expert, esp. in everyday matters. Also, **ma′ven.** [< Yiddish < Heb: connoisseur]

maw (mô), *n.* **1.** the mouth, throat, or gullet of a carnivorous mammal. **2.** the stomach, esp. that of an animal. **4.** a cavernous opening.

mawk·ish (mô′kish), *adj.* sentimental in an objectionably excessive way. —**mawk′ish·ly,** *adv.* —**mawk′ish·ness,** *n.*

max., maximum.

max·i (mak′sē), *n. Informal.* a coat or skirt reaching down to the ankle.

maxi-, a combining form meaning: **a.** very long: *maxiskirt; maxicoat; maxidress.* **b.** of the greatest scope: *maxiservice.*

max·il·la (mak sil′ə), *n., pl.* **max·il·lae** (mak sil′ē). a jaw or jawbone, esp. the upper. —**max·il·lar·y** (mak′sə ler′ē), *adj.*

max·im (mak′sim), *n.* an expression of a general truth or principle, esp. a sententious one.

max·i·mal (mak′sə məl), *adj.* of or being a maximum. —**max′i·mal·ly,** *adv.*

max·i·mize (mak′sə mīz′), *v.t.,* **-mized, -miz·ing.** to increase to a maximum.

max·i·mum (mak′sə məm), *n., pl.* **-mums, -ma** (-mə), *adj.* —*n.* **1.** the greatest quantity, amount, or degree possible or attained. **2.** an upper limit allowable by law or regulation. —*adj.* **3.** amounting to a maximum.

may (mā), *auxiliary verb, past* **might. 1.** (to express wish or prayer): *May you live long!* **2.** (to express contingency): *I may be wrong, but I think you would be wise to go.* **3.** (to express possibility, opportunity, or permission): *It may rain. You may enter.*

May (mā), *n.* the fifth month of the year, containing 31 days.

Ma·ya (mä′yə), *n., pl.* **-yas, -ya. 1.** a member of a highly civilized, ancient Amerindian people in C America. **2.** their language. —**Ma′yan,** *adj., n.*

May′ ap′ple, 1. a perennial, American herb bearing an edible, yellowish, egg-shaped fruit. **2.** its fruit.

may·be (mā′bē), *adv.* perhaps.

May′ Day′, May 1, celebrated with various spring festivities, and, in some countries, with labor parades and political demonstrations.

May·flow·er (mā′flou′ər), *n.* **1.** (*italics*) the ship in which the Pilgrim Fathers sailed from England to America in 1620. **2.** (*l.c.*) any of various plants that blossom in May, as the anemone.

may·fly (mā′flī′), *n.* an insect having delicate, membranous wings and a brief, terrestrial adult stage. Also, **May′ fly′.**

may·hem (mā′hem, mā′əm), *n. Law.* the crime of wilfully inflicting a bodily injury on another.

may·n't (mā′ənt, mānt), contraction of *may not.*

may·o (mā′ō), *n. Informal,* mayonnaise.

may·on·naise (mā′ə nāz′, mā′ə nāz′), *n.* a thick dressing of egg yolks, vinegar or lemon juice, seasonings, and oil.

may·or (mā′ər, mâr), *n.* the chief executive official of a city. —**may′or·al,** *adj.* —**may′or·al·ty,** *n.* —**may′or·ess,** *n.fem.* —**may′or·ship′,** *n.*

May·pole (mā′pōl′), *n.* (*often l.c.*) a high pole, decorated with flowers and ribbons, around which revelers dance during May Day celebrations.

maze (māz), *n.* **1.** a confusing network of paths or passages. **2.** a state of confusion or perplexity. —**maz′y,** *adj.*

ma·zel tov (mä′zel tōv′), a Jewish expression of congratulations and best wishes. [< Yiddish < Heb: lit., good luck]

ma·zur·ka (mə zûr′kə, -zōōr′-), *n.* **1.** a Polish dance in moderately quick triple meter. **2.** music for this dance.

M.B.A., Master of Business Administration.

MC, 1. Marine Corps. **2.** Medical Corps. **3.** Member of Congress.

mc, megacycle; megacycles.

M.C., 1. See **master of ceremonies. 2.** Member of Congress.

Mc·Coy (mə koi′), *n. Slang.* the genuine thing or person as implied (usually prec. by *the* or *the real*).

Mc·Kin·ley (mə kin′lē), *n.* **William,** 1843–1901, 25th president of the U.S. 1897–1901.

MCPO, Master Chief Petty Officer.

MD, Maryland.

Md, mendelevium.

Md., Maryland.

M/D, months after date. Also, **m/d**

M.D., Doctor of Medicine. [< L *Medicīnae Doctor*]

mdnt., midnight.

mdse., merchandise.

me (mē), *pron.* the objective case of **I.**

ME, 1. Maine. **2.** Middle English. **3.** Middle East.

Me., Maine.

M.E., 1. Mechanical Engineer. **2.** Middle English. **3.** Mining Engineer.

mead[1] (mēd), *n.* an alcoholic liquor made by fermenting honey and water.

mead[2] (mēd), *n. Archaic.* meadow.

mead·ow (med′ō), *n.* **1.** a tract of grassland used for pasture or for growing hay. **2.** a low, level tract of grassland along a river. —**mead′ow·land′** (-land′), *n.* —**mead′ow·y,** *adj.*

mead·ow·lark (med′ō lärk′), *n.* any of several American songbirds having a yellow breast, noted for their clear, tuneful song.

mead·ow·sweet (med′ō swēt′), *n.* any plant having white or pink flowers.

mea·ger (mē′gər), *adj.* **1.** lacking fullness or richness: *a meager harvest.* **2.** having little flesh. Also, *Brit.,* **mea′gre.** —**mea′ger·ly,** *adv.* —**mea′ger·ness,** *n.* —Syn. **1.** scanty, sparse.

meal[1] (mēl), *n.* **1.** one of the regular occasions during the day when food is taken. **2.** the food served at such occasions.

meal[2] (mēl), *n.* **1.** a coarse, unsifted powder ground from the edible seeds of any grain. **2.** any powdery substance, as of nuts, resembling this. —**meal′y,** *adj.*

meal·time (mēl′tīm′), *n.* the usual time for a meal.

meal·y·bug (mē′lē bug′), *n.* any of several scalelike insects that are covered with a powdery, waxy secretion.

meal·y·mouthed (mē′lē mouthd′, -moutht′), *adj.* avoiding the use of direct and plain language, as from timidity.

mean[1] (mēn), *v.,* **meant, mean·ing.** —*v.t.* **1.** to have in mind as an intention or purpose. **2.** to intend for a particular purpose or person. **3.** to intend to express or indicate: *What do you mean by "liberal"?* **4.** to have as the sense or significance. **5.** to assume the importance of: *Money means everything to him.* —*v.i.* **6.** to have intentions.

mean[2] (mēn), *adj.* **1.** inferior in quality or character. **2.** unimposing or shabby. **3.** small-minded or ignoble. **4.** *Chiefly Brit.* stingy or miserly. **5.** offensive or selfish. **6.** *Slang.* skillful or impressive. **7.** *Slang.* hard to handle or manage. —**mean′ly,** *adv.* —**mean′ness,** *n.*

mean[3] (mēn), *n.* **1. means,** (*used as sing. or pl.*) a method used to attain an end. **2. means,** great financial resources: *a man of means.* **3.** something midway between two extremes. **4.** *Math.* a quantity having a value intermediate between the values of other quantities, esp. the arithmetic mean. **5. by all means, a.** at any cost. **b.** certainly. **6. by means of,** through the use of. **7. by no means,** in no way. —*adj.* **8.** occupying a middle position or an intermediate place, as in kind or quality.

me·an·der (mē an′dər), *v.i.* **1.** to proceed by a winding or indirect course. **2.** to wander aimlessly. —*n.* **3.** a circuitous movement or journey. — **me·an′der·er,** *n.*

mean·ing (mē′ning), *n.* **1.** what is intended to be expressed or indicated. **2.** the end or purpose of something. —**mean′ing·ful** *adj.* —**mean′ing·ful·ly,** *adv.* —**mean′ing·less,** *adj.*

meant (ment), *v.* pt. and pp. of **mean¹.**

mean·time (mēn′tīm′), *n.* **1.** the intervening time. —*adv.* Also, **mean′while′** (-hwīl′, -wīl′). **2.** in the intervening time. **3.** at the same time.

mean·y (mē′nē), *n., pl.* **mean·ies.** *Informal.* a small-minded, mean, or malicious person. Also, **mean′ie.**

meas., **1.** measurable. **2.** measure.

mea·sles (mē′zəlz), *n.* **1.** an acute infectious disease occurring mostly in children, characterized by fever and an eruption of small red spots. **2.** See **German measles.**

mea·sly (mē′zlē), *adj.,* **-sli·er, -sli·est. 1.** infected with measles. **2.** *Informal.* wretchedly scanty or unsatisfactory.

meas·ure (mezh′ər), *n., v.,* **-ured, -ur·ing.** —*n.* **1.** the extent, dimensions, or quantity of anything ascertained by measuring. **2.** an instrument for measuring. **3.** a unit or standard of measurement. **4.** a definite or known quantity measured out. **5.** a system of measurement. **6.** the act of measuring. **7.** any standard of comparison or judgment. **8.** a quantity or proportion. **9.** a moderate amount. **10.** a legislative bill or enactment. **11.** an action or procedure intended as a means to an end. **12.** a short rhythmical movement or arrangement. **13.** the music contained between two bar lines. **14. beyond measure,** extremely. **15. for good measure,** as an extra. **16. in a measure,** to some degree. —*v.t.* **17.** to ascertain the extent, dimensions, or quantity of, esp. by a standard. **18.** to mark off or deal out by way of measurement. **19.** to estimate the relative amount or value of, by comparison with some standard. **20.** to judge or appraise by comparison with something or someone else. **21.** to serve as the measure of. —*v.i.* **22.** to take measurements. **23.** to be of a specified measure. **24. measure up, a.** to reach a specified standard. **b.** to be qualified. —**meas′ur·a·ble,** *adj.* —**meas′ur·a·bly,** *adv.* —**meas′ure·less,** *adj.* —**meas′ur·er,** *n.*

meas·ure·ment (mezh′ər mənt), *n.* **1.** the process of measuring or being measured. **2.** a measured dimension. **3.** measure (def. 1). **4.** a system of measures.

meat (mēt), *n.* **1.** the flesh of animals as used for food. **2.** the edible part of anything, as a nut. **3.** the essential point or part. **4.** *Informal.* a favorite occupation, activity, etc. **5.** *Literary.* solid food: *meat and drink.* —**meat′y,** *adj.* —**meat′i·ness,** *n.* —**meat′less,** *adj.*

meat·ball (mēt′bôl′), *n.* chopped meat shaped into a ball before cooking.

meat·head (mēt′hed′), *n.* *Slang.* a dunce or fool.

meat′ pack′ing, the industry of slaughtering cattle and preparing their meat for marketing.

Mec·ca (mek′ə), *n.* **1.** the religious capital of Saudi Arabia: birthplace of Muhammad and spiritual center of Islam. **2.** (*often l.c.*) any place that many people visit or hope to visit. —**Mec′can,** *adj., n.*

mech., **1.** mechanical. **2.** mechanics. **3.** mechanism.

me·chan·ic (mə kan′ik), *n.* **1.** a skilled worker with tools, machines, etc. **2.** a person who repairs and maintains machines.

me·chan·i·cal (mə kan′i kəl), *adj.* **1.** having to do with machinery or tools. **2.** caused, operated, or produced by machinery: *mechanical propulsion.* **3.** acting or performed without spirit, individuality, etc. **4.** of or pertaining to mechanics. —**me·chan′i·cal·ly,** *adv.*

mechan′ical advan′tage, the ratio of output force to the input force applied to a mechanism.

mechan′ical draw′ing, drawing, as of machinery, done with the aid of instruments.

mechan′ical engineer′ing, the branch of engineering dealing with the design and production of machinery. —**mechan′ical engineer′.**

me·chan·ics (mə kan′iks), *n.* **1.** the science that deals with the action of forces on bodies and with motion. **2.** the theoretical and practical application of this science to machinery. **3.** the technical aspect of working part.

mech·an·ism (mek′ə niz′əm), *n.* **1.** the structure or arrangement of parts of a machine. **2.** any system of parts working together. **3.** the means by which an effect is produced or a purpose is accomplished. **4.** the theory that everything in the universe is due to mechanical actions or material forces.

mech·a·nis·tic (mek′ə nis′tik), *adj.* **1.** of the theory of mechanism. **2.** of mechanics. —mech'a·nis'ti·cal·ly, adv.

mech·a·nize (mek'ə nīz'), v.t., -nized, -niz·ing. 1. to make mechanical. 2. to introduce machinery into (an industry, enterprise, etc.). 3. *Mil.* to equip with tanks and other armored vehicles. —mech'a·ni·za'tion, n. —mech'a·niz/er, n.

med., 1. medical. 2. medicine. 3. medieval. 4. medium.

M.Ed., Master of Education.

med·al (med'əl), n. 1. a flat piece of metal issued to commemorate a person or event, or given as a reward for bravery or merit. 2. a similar piece of metal bearing a religious image, as of a saint.

med·al·ist (med'list), n. 1. a designer, engraver, or maker of medals. 2. a person awarded a medal. Also, *Brit.,* med'al·list.

me·dal·lion (mə dal'yən), n. 1. a large medal. 2. a decorative design resembling a medal.

med·dle (med'əl), v.i., -dled, -dling. to involve oneself in a matter without right or invitation. —med'dler, n. —med'dle·some (-səm), adj. —Syn. interfere, tamper.

med·e·vac (med'ə vak'), n. a helicopter for evacuating the wounded from a battlefield. [*med(ical-)evac(uation helicopter)*]

me·di·a (mē'dē ə), n. 1. a pl. of medium. 2. the media, the means of communication, as radio and television, newspapers, magazines, etc., that reach or influence very large numbers of people.

me·di·al (mē'dē əl), adj. 1. situated in the middle. 2. ordinary or average.

me·di·an (mē'dē ən), n. 1. the middle number in a given sequence, or the average of the two middle numbers when the sequence has an even number of numbers. 2. Also called me'dian strip'. a dividing strip between opposing lanes of highway traffic. —adj. 3. noting an arithmetic median. 4. medial (def. 1).

me·di·ate (v. mē'dē āt'; adj. mē'dē it), v., -at·ed, -at·ing, adj. —v.t. 1. to settle (disputes, etc.) as an intermediary between parties. —v.i. 2. to act between parties as an intermediary. 3. *Obs.* to occupy an intermediate position. —adj. 4. acting through or involving an intermediate agency. —me'di·ate·ly, adv. —me'di·a'tion, n. —me'di·a'tor, n.

med·ic (med'ik), n. *Slang.* 1. a medical student. 2. a doctor or intern. 3. a corpsman.

med·i·ca·ble (med'ə kə bəl), adj. susceptible of medical treatment. —med'i·ca·bly, adv.

Med·i·caid (med'ə kād'), n. a state and federal program of hospitaliza-

tion and medical insurance for persons of all ages within certain income limits.

med·i·cal (med'i kəl), adj. 1. of or pertaining to the science or practice of medicine. 2. requiring treatment other than surgical. —med'i·cal·ly, adv.

me·dic·a·ment (mə dik'ə mənt, med'ə kə-), n. a healing substance.

Med·i·care (med'ə kār'), n. a federal program of hospitalization and medical insurance for persons aged 65 and over.

med·i·cate (med'ə kāt'), v.t., -cat·ed, -cat·ing. to treat with medicine. —med'i·ca'tion, n. —med'i·ca'tive, adj.

me·dic·i·nal (mə dis'ə nəl), adj. of or having the properties of a medicine. —me·dic'i·nal·ly, adv.

med·i·cine (med'i sin), n. 1. any substance or substances used in treating disease or illness. 2. the art or science of diagnosing, treating, or preventing disease.

med'icine ball', a large, heavy, leather-covered ball thrown and caught for exercise.

med'icine man', (esp. among American Indians) a man supposed to possess supernatural powers.

med·i·co (med'ə kō'), n., pl. -cos. *Slang.* medic.

me·di·e·val (mē'dē ē'vəl, med'ē-), adj. of, pertaining to, or characteristic of the Middle Ages. Also, me'di·ae'val. —me'di·e'val·ism, n. —me'di·e'val·ist, n. —me'di·e'val·ly, adv.

me·di·o·cre (mē'dē ō'kər, mē'dē ō'kər), adj. of only ordinary quality. —me'di·oc'ri·ty (-ok'ri tē), n. —Syn. average, commonplace.

med·i·tate (med'i tāt'), v., -tat·ed, -tat·ing. —v.i. 1. to think contemplatively. —v.t. 2. to intend or plan. —med'i·ta'tion, n. —med'i·ta'tive, adj. —med'i·ta'tive·ly, adv.

Med·i·ter·ra·ne·an (med'i tə rā'nē ən), n. a sea surrounded by Africa, Europe, and Asia. Also called Med'i·terra'nean Sea'.

me·di·um (mē'dē əm), n., pl. -di·a for 1–6, -di·ums for 1–7, adj. —n. 1. a middle state or condition. 2. something intermediate in nature or degree. 3. an intervening substance, as air, through which a force acts. 4. a surrounding condition or environment. 5. an agency, means, or instrument of something specified. 6. the material or technique with which an artist works. 7. a person through whom the spirits of the dead are supposedly able to contact the living. —adj. 8. about halfway between extremes, as of degree, quality, or size.

me·di·um·is·tic (mē'dē ə mis'tik), adj. pertaining to a spiritualistic medium.

med·ley (med′lē), n., pl. **-leys. 1.** a piece of music combining tunes or passages from various sources. **2.** a mixture, esp. of heterogeneous elements.

me·dul·la (mi dul′ə), n., pl. **-dul·las, -dul·lae** (-dul′ē), Anat. **1.** the soft, marrowlike center of an organ. **2.** See medulla oblongata.

medul′la oblonga′ta (ob′lông gä′tə, -lông-), pl. **medulla oblongatas, medullae oblongatae** (-tē). the lowest or hindmost part of the brain.

meed (mēd), n. Archaic. a reward or recompense.

meek (mēk), adj. **1.** overly submissive or spiritless. **2.** humbly patient and mild. —**meek′ly,** adv. —**meek′ness,** n.

meer·schaum (mēr′shəm, -shôm, -shoum), n. **1.** a mineral occurring in white, claylike masses, used for carvings, for pipe bowls, etc. **2.** a tobacco pipe with the bowl made of this substance. [< G: lit., sea foam]

meet¹ (mēt), v., **met, meet·ing,** n. —v.t. **1.** to come upon. **2.** to make oneself acquainted with. **3.** to be present at the arrival of. **4.** to come to or before (one's notice): A peculiar sight met my eyes. **5.** to come into physical contact. **6.** to cope or deal effectively with (a difficulty, etc.). **7.** to satisfy (obligations, demands, etc.). **8.** to encounter in experience. —v.i. **9.** to come together. **10.** to assemble for action or conference. **11.** to become personally acquainted. **12.** to come into contact or form a junction. **13. meet with, a.** to receive or get. **b.** to experience or undergo. **c.** to see, esp. for a lengthy talk. —n. **14.** an assembly, as for a hunt or for an athletic contest. —**meet′er,** n.

meet² (mēt), adj. Archaic. fitting or proper. —**meet′ly,** adv.

meet·ing (mē′tiñg), n. **1.** the act of coming together. **2.** an assembly of persons. **3.** a place or point of contact. **4.** a hostile encounter.

meet′ing house′, a house or building for religious worship, esp. for Quakers.

meg, megohm; megohms.

mega-, a combining form meaning: **a.** large or great: megalith. **b.** 1,000,000 times a given unit: megahertz.

meg·a·cy·cle (meg′ə sī′kəl), n. (formerly) megahertz.

meg·a·death (meg′ə deth′), n. one million deaths: a unit of hypothetical casualties in a nuclear war.

meg·a·hertz (meg′ə hûrts′), n., pl. **-hertz.** one million cycles per second.

meg·a·lith (meg′ə lith), n. a stone of great size, esp. in ancient construction work. —**meg′a·lith′ic,** adj.

meg·a·lo·ma·ni·a (meg′ə lō mā′nē ə), n. a mental illness marked by delusions of greatness, wealth, etc. —**meg′a·lo·ma′ni·ac′,** n., adj.

meg·a·lop·o·lis (meg′ə lop′ə lis), n. an urban region consisting of several large, adjoining cities.

meg·a·phone (meg′ə fōn′), n. a funnel-shaped device for magnifying or directing the voice.

meg·a·ton (meg′ə tun′), n. an explosive force equal to that of one million tons of TNT.

me·gil·lah (mə gil′ə), n. Slang. a lengthy explanation or account. [< Heb: a scroll]

meg·ohm (meg′ōm′), n. one million ohms.

mei·o·sis (mī ō′sis), n. a cell division in which the diploid chromosome number becomes reduced to the haploid. —**mei·ot′ic** (-ot′ik), adj.

Me·kong (mā′kong′), n. a river whose source is in SW China, flowing into the South China Sea.

mel·a·mine (mel′ə mēn′), n. a colorless, crystalline solid used chiefly in the manufacture of synthetic resins.

mel·an·chol·i·a (mel′ən kō′lē ə, -kōl′yə), n. a mental condition characterized by great depression of spirits and gloomy forebodings. —**mel′an·cho′li·ac** (-kō′lē ak′), adj., n. —**mel′an·chol′ic** (-kol′ik), adj. —**mel′an·chol′i·cal·ly,** adv.

mel·an·chol·y (mel′ən kol′ē), n., pl. **-chol·ies,** adj. —n. **1.** a gloomy state of mind. **2.** sober thoughtfulness. —adj. **3.** gloomy and depressed. **4.** soberly thoughtful. —**mel′an·chol′i·ness,** n. —Syn. **3.** downcast, glum.

Mel·a·ne·sia (mel′ə nē′zhə, -shə), n. an island group in the S Pacific NE of Australia. —**Mel′a·ne′sian,** adj., n.

mé·lange (mā länzh′), n. a confused mixture or medley.

me·lan·ic (mə lan′ik), adj. **1.** having dark pigment in the tissues. **2.** of or pertaining to melanism.

mel·a·nin (mel′ə nin), n. a dark pigment in the body of humans and certain animals, as that occurring in the hair.

mel·a·nism (mel′ə niz′əm), n. the condition of having a high amount of dark pigment in the skin, hair, etc.

mel·a·no·ma (mel′ə nō′mə), n., pl. **-mas, -ma·ta** (-mə tə). a darkly pigmented tumor, esp. of the skin or eye.

Mel′ba toast′ (mel′bə), bread sliced thin and toasted until crisp.

Mel·bourne (mel′bərn), n. a seaport in SE Australia.

meld¹ (meld), Cards. —v.t., v.i. **1.** to announce and display (certain cards) for a score. —n. **2.** any combination of cards to be melded.

meld² (meld), *v.t., v.i.* to merge or blend.

me·lee (mā′lā, mā lā′), *n.* **1.** a confused, general, hand-to-hand fight. **2.** confusion or turmoil. Also, **mê′lée.**

mel·io·rate (mēl′yə rāt′, mē′lē ə-), *v.t., v.i.,* **-rat·ed, -rat·ing.** *Literary.* to ameliorate. **—mel′io·ra′tion,** *n.*

mel·lif·lu·ous (mə lif′lŏŏ əs), *adj.* sweetly or smoothly flowing: *a mellifluous voice.* Also, **mel·lif′lu·ent** (-ənt). **—mel·lif′lu·ous·ly,** *adv.*

mel·low (mel′ō), *adj.* **1.** soft and full-flavored from ripeness, as fruit. **2.** well-matured, as wines. **3.** softened or toned down, as by aging or ripening. **4.** soft and rich, as sound, light, etc. **5.** friable or loamy, as soil. **6.** *Informal.* mildly intoxicated. **—v.t., v.i** **7.** to make or become mellow. **—mel′low·ly,** *adv.* **—mel′low·ness,** *n.*

me·lo·di·ous (mə lō′dē əs), *adj.* **1.** pleasing to the ear. **2.** producing or full of melody. **—me·lo′di·ous·ly,** *adv.* **—me·lo′di·ous·ness,** *n.* **—Syn.** musical, tuneful.

mel·o·dra·ma (mel′ə drä′mə, -dram′ə), *n.* a drama in which exaggeration of effect and emotion is produced and plot or action is emphasized at the expense of characterization. **—mel′o·dra·mat′ic** (-drə mat′ik), *adj.* **mel′o·dra·mat′i·cal·ly,** *adv.* **—mel′o·dram′a·tist** (-dram′ə tist, -drä′mə-), *n.*

mel·o·dra·mat·ics (mel′ə drə mat′iks), *n.pl.* melodramatic writing or behavior.

mel·o·dy (mel′ə dē), *n., pl.* **-dies.** **1.** musical sounds in agreeable succession. **2.** *Music.* **a.** the succession of single tones. **b.** the principal part in a harmonic composition. **—mel·lod·ic** (mə lod′ik), *adj.* **—me·lod′i·cal·ly,** *adv.*

mel·on (mel′ən), *n.* the large, fleshy, round or oval fruit of various plants, as the watermelon or cantaloupe.

melt (melt), *v.i., v.t.* **1.** to change to a liquid state by heat. **2.** to make or become liquid. **3.** to pass away or cause to pass away gradually. **4.** to blend or cause to blend gradually. **5.** to soften in feeling, as by pity.

melt·down (melt′doun′), *n.* the faulty melting of uranium-fuel pellets in a nuclear reactor, potentially causing radiation escape.

melt′ing pot′, a country or locality in which a blending of races and cultures is taking place.

melt·wa·ter (melt′wô′tər, -wot′ər), *n.* water from melted snow or ice.

Mel·ville (mel′vil), *n.* **Her·man,** 1819–91, U.S. novelist.

mem., **1.** member. **2.** memorandum.

mem·ber (mem′bər), *n.* **1.** any of the persons composing a group or organization. **2.** a part or organ of a person, animal, or plant. **3.** a constituent part of any composite whole.

mem·ber·ship (mem′bər ship′), *n.* **1.** the state of being a member. **2.** the status of a member. **3.** the total number of members.

mem·brane (mem′brān), *n.* a thin, pliable layer of animal or vegetable tissue, serving to line an organ or connect parts. **—mem′bra·nous** (-brə-nəs), *adj.*

me·men·to (mə men′tō), *n., pl.* **-tos, -toes.** an object or item, often of a personal nature, given or serving as a reminder of a person, event, etc.

mem·o (mem′ō), *n., pl.* **mem·os.** *Informal.* memorandum.

mem·oir (mem′wär, -wôr), *n.* **1.** a record of events written by a person having an intimate knowledge of them, based on his or her personal observation. **2.** an account of one's personal life and experiences. **3.** *Brit.* a report on an academic subject made to a learned society. **4.** *Obs.* a memorandum or note.

mem·o·ra·bil·i·a (mem′ər ə bil′ē ə, -bil′yə), *n.pl.* matters or events worthy to be remembered.

mem·o·ra·ble (mem′ər ə bəl), *adj.* worthy of being remembered. **—mem′o·ra·bil′i·ty, mem′o·ra·ble·ness,** *n.* **—mem′o·ra·bly,** *adv.*

mem·o·ran·dum (mem′ə ran′dəm), *n., pl.* **-dums, -da** (-də). **1.** a note designating something to be remembered, esp. something to be done. **2.** an informal message, esp. one sent between offices.

me·mo·ri·al (mə môr′ē əl, -mōr′-), *n.* **1.** something designed to preserve the memory of a person or event, as a monument. **2.** a statement of facts presented to a legislative body as the ground of a petition. **—adj.** **3.** preserving the memory of a person or event. **—me·mo′ri·al·ize′** (-ə līz′), *v.t.*

Memo′rial Day′, May 30, a day set aside in memory of dead servicemen of all wars: now officially observed on the last Monday in May.

mem·o·rize (mem′ə rīz′), *v.t., v.i.,* **-rized, -riz·ing.** to commit to memory. **—mem′o·ri·za′tion,** *n.* **—mem′o·riz′er,** *n.*

mem·o·ry (mem′ə rē), *n., pl.* **-ries.** **1.** the faculty of recalling or recognizing previous experiences. **2.** the act or fact of remembering. **3.** the length of time over which remembrance reaches. **4.** a mental impression retained. **5.** commemorative remembrance. **6.** the capacity of a computer to store data subject to recall.

Mem·phis (mem'fis), *n.* a port in SW Tennessee, on the Mississippi.

men (men), *n.* pl. of **man.**

men·ace (men'is), *n., v.,* **-aced, -ac·ing.** —*n.* 1. something that threatens to cause evil or harm. 2. a very annoying person. —*v.t., v.i.* 3. to pose a menace (to). —**men'ac·ing·ly,** *adv.*

mé·nage (mā näzh'), *n. Literary.* a household. Also, **me·nage'.**

me·nag·er·ie (mə naj'ə rē, -nazh'-), *n.* a collection of wild or strange animals, esp. for exhibition.

mend (mend), *v.t.* 1. to make sound or usable by repairing. 2. to reform or improve: *to mend one's ways.* —*v.i.* 3. to progress toward recovery, as a sick person. —*n.* 4. the act of mending. 5. a mended place. 6. **on the mend,** recovering from an illness. —**mend'er,** *n.*

men·da·cious (men dā'shəs), *adj.* 1. addicted to telling lies. 2. false or untrue: *a mendacious report.* —**men·da'cious·ly,** *adv.* —**men·dac'i·ty** (-das'i tē), *n.*

Men·del (men'd°l), *n.* **Gre·gor** (greg'ər), 1822–84, Austrian monk and geneticist.

men·de·le·vi·um (men'd°lē'vē əm), *n. Chem.* a synthetic, radioactive element. *Symbol:* Md; *at. no.:* 101.

Men·dels·sohn (men'd°l sən), *n.* **Fe·lix** (fē'liks), 1809–47, German composer.

men·di·cant (men'də kənt), *adj.* 1. living on alms. —*n.* 2. a mendicant friar. 3. *Literary.* a beggar. —**men'di·can·cy** (-kən sē), *n.*

men·folk (men'fōk'), *n.pl.* men, esp. those of a family or community. Also, **men'folks'.**

men·ha·den (men hād'°n), *n., pl.* **-den, -dens.** a marine fish resembling a shad, used for making oil and fertilizer.

me·ni·al (mē'nē əl, mēn'yəl), *adj.* 1. servile and degrading. 2. of or suitable for domestic servants. —*n.* **De·rogatory.** 3. a domestic servant. —**me'ni·al·ly,** *adv.*

me·nin·ges (mi nin'jēz), *n.pl., sing.* **me·ninx** (mē'ningks). the three membranes covering the brain and spinal cord. —**me·nin'ge·al,** *adj.*

men·in·gi·tis (men'in jī'tis), *n.* inflammation of the meninges.

me·nis·cus (mi nis'kəs), *n., pl.* **-nis·ci** (-nis'ī), **-nis·cus·es.** 1. a crescent or a crescent-shaped body. 2. a lens with a crescent-shaped section. 3. *Physics.* the convex or concave upper surface of a column of liquid. —**me·nis'coid** (-koid), *adj.*

Men·non·ite (men'ə nīt'), *n.* a member of an evangelical Protestant sect that rejects military service, the taking of oaths, etc., and is noted for simplicity of living and plain dress.

[after *Menno* Simons (1492–1559), Dutch religious leader]

men·o·pause (men'ə pôz'), *n.* the period of permanent cessation of menstruation. —**men'o·pau'sal,** *adj.*

me·nor·ah (mə nōr'ə, -nôr'ə), *n. Judaism.* a candelabrum, esp. one used during Hanukkah.

mensch (mensh, mench), *n., pl.* **mensch·en** (mensh'ən, mench'ən), *Slang.* a respectable person. [< Yiddish < G: human being]

men·ses (men'sēz), *n.* the menstrual flow or period.

men·stru·a·tion (men'strōo ā'shən), *n.* the periodic discharge of blood and bloody fluid from the uterus, occurring approximately monthly from puberty to menopause in women while not pregnant. —**men'stru·al,** *adj.* —**men'stru·ate,** *v.i.*

men·sur·a·ble (men'shər ə bəl), *adj. Rare.* measurable. —**men'sur·a·bil'i·ty,** *n.*

men·su·ra·tion (men'shə rā'shən), *n. Rare.* the act or process of measuring. —**men'su·ral,** *adj.* —**men'su·ra'tive,** *adj.*

mens·wear (menz'wâr'), *n.* clothing or suits for men.

-ment, a suffix meaning: a. an action or resulting state: *abridgment; refreshment.* b. a product: *fragment.* c. means: *ornament.*

men·tal (men't°l), *adj.* 1. of the mind. 2. affected with a disorder of the mind. 3. for persons so affected: *a mental hospital.* 4. performed by the mind: *mental arithmetic.* —**men'tal·ly,** *adv.*

men'tal age', the level of native mental ability of an individual in relation to the chronological age of the average individual at this level.

men·tal·ist (men't°list), *n.* See **mind reader.**

men·tal·i·ty (men tal'i tē), *n., pl.* **-ties.** 1. mental capacity or endowment. 2. intellectual character.

men'tal reserva'tion, an unspoken or unexpressed qualification of a statement.

men'tal retarda'tion, lack of powers associated with normal intellectual development. Also called **men'tal defi'ciency.**

men·thol (men'thôl, -thol, thol), *n.* 1. a colorless alcohol obtained from peppermint oil or synthesized, used chiefly in perfumes, liqueurs, etc. 2. *Informal.* a mentholated cigarette. —**men'tho·lat'ed** (-thə lā'tid), *adj.*

men·tion (men'shən), *v.t.* 1. to refer briefly to. 2. to cite for a meritorious act. 3. **not to mention,** in addition to. —*n.* 4. a brief or incidental reference. 5. a citation for a meritorious act. —**men'tion·a·ble,** *adj.* **men'tion·er,** *n.*

men·tor (men'tər, -tôr), *n.* a wise and trusted counselor.

men·u (men'yŏŏ, mā'nyŏŏ), *n.* **1.** a list of the dishes or foods available, as in a restaurant. **2.** the dishes served, as at a banquet.

me·ow (mē ou', myou), *n.* **1.** the sound a cat makes. —*v.i.* **2.** to make such a sound.

m.e.p., mean effective pressure.

me·phit·ic (mə fit'ik), *adj.* offensive to the smell.

mer., meridian.

mer·can·tile (mûr'kən tēl', -tīl', -til), *adj.* of or pertaining to merchants or trade.

mer·ce·nar·y (mûr'sə ner'ē), *adj., n., pl.* **-nar·ies.** —*adj.* **1.** working or acting merely for money or other reward. —*n.* **2.** a professional soldier serving in a foreign army solely for pay. —**mer·ce·nar·i·ly** (mûr'sə när'ə lē, mûr'sə ner'-), *adv.* —**mer'ce·nar'i·ness,** *n.* —Syn. 1. avaricious, grasping.

mer·cer (mûr'sər), *n. Brit.* a dealer in textile fabrics.

mer·cer·ize (mûr'sə rīz'), *v.t.,* **-ized, -iz·ing.** to treat (cotton yarns or fabric) with caustic alkali under tension in order to increase strength, luster, and affinity for dye.

mer·chan·dise (*n.* mûr'chən dīz', -dīs'; *v.* mûr'chən dīz'), *n., v.,* **-dised, -dis·ing.** —*n.* **1.** goods, esp. manufactured goods, that are bought and sold. —*v.i.* **2.** to carry on trade. —*v.t.* **3.** to buy and sell. **4.** to plan for and promote the sales of (goods or services). —**mer'chan·dis'er,** *n.*

mer·chant (mûr'chənt), *n.* **1.** a person who buys and sells commodities for profit. **2.** a storekeeper or retailer. —*adj.* **3.** used for trade or commerce: *a merchant ship.* **4.** of the merchant marine: *a merchant seaman.*

mer·chant·a·ble (mûr'chən tə bəl), *adj. Chiefly Law.* suitable for sale.

mer·chant·man (mûr'chənt mən), *n.* a privately owned trading vessel.

mer'chant marine', **1.** the vessels of a nation that are engaged in commerce. **2.** the officers and crews of such vessels.

mer·ci (meʀ sē'), *interj. French.* thank you.

mer·cu·ri·al (mər kyŏŏr'ē əl), *adj.* **1.** changeable and erratic in mood. **2.** lively and sprightly. **3.** pertaining to or caused by the metal mercury. —**mer·cu'ri·al·ly,** *adv.* —**mer·cu'ri·al·ness,** *n.*

mer·cu·ric (mər kyŏŏr'ik), *adj.* of or containing mercury, esp. in the bivalent state.

mercu'ric chlo'ride, a strongly acid, highly poisonous solid, used chiefly as an antiseptic.

Mer·cu·ro·chrome (mər kyŏŏr'ə krōm'), *n. Trademark.* a deep-red liquid of a mercury compound used as an antiseptic.

mer·cu·rous (mər kyŏŏr'əs, mûr'kyər-əs), *adj.* containing univalent mercury.

mer·cu·ry (mûr'kyə rē), *n., pl.* **-ries.** **1.** *Chem.* a heavy, silver-white, metallic element, liquid at ordinary temperatures, used in barometers, thermometers, etc. *Symbol:* Hg; *at. wt.:* 200.59; *at. no.:* 80. **2.** *(cap.)* the ancient Roman god who served as messenger of the gods and was also the god of commerce and science. **3.** *(cap.)* the planet nearest the sun, the smallest in the solar system.

mer·cy (mûr'sē), *n., pl.* **-cies.** **1.** compassion shown toward an offender or enemy. **2.** a disposition to forgive or forbear. **3.** imprisonment instead of the death sentence for a capital offender. **4.** an act of kindness or compassion. **5.** a blessing or fortunate event. **6. at the mercy of,** entirely in the power of. —**mer'ci·ful,** *adj.* —**mer'ci·ful·ly,** *adv.* —**mer'ci·less,** *adj.* —**mer'ci·less·ly,** *adv.* —Syn. 1, 2. clemency, forgiveness, leniency.

mer'cy kill'ing, euthanasia.

mere¹ (mēr), *adj., superl.* **mer·est.** being nothing more nor better than what is specified: *He is still a mere child.* —**mere'ly,** *adv.*

mere² (mēr), *n. Chiefly Brit. Dial.* a lake or pond.

mer·e·tri·cious (mer'i trish'əs), *adj.* **1.** vulgarly attractive. **2.** based on pretense or insincerity. —**mer'e·tri'cious·ly,** *adv.* —**mer'e·tri'cious·ness,** *n.*

mer·gan·ser (mər gan'sər), *n.* a fish-eating diving duck having a narrow bill.

merge (mûrj), *v.t., v.i.,* **merged, merg·ing.** **1.** to lose or cause to lose identity by uniting or blending. **2.** to combine or unite into a single unit.

merg·er (mûr'jər), *n.* **1.** a combination of two or more business enterprises into a single enterprise. **2.** the act or an instance of merging.

me·rid·i·an (mə rid'ē ən), *n.* **1. a.** a great circle of the earth passing through the poles and any given point on the earth's surface. **b.** the half of such a circle included between the poles. **2.** the great circle of the celestial sphere that passes through its poles and the observer's zenith. **3.** *Literary.* the highest point of development or prosperity.

me·ringue (mə rang'), *n.* a frothy topping of beaten egg whites and sugar used for pies or cakes.

me·ri·no (mə rē′nō), n., pl. -nos. 1. (often cap.) one of a breed of sheep, raised originally in Spain, valued for its fine wool. 2. its wool. 3. a yarn or fabric made from this.

mer·it (mer′it), n. 1. claim to respect and praise. 2. something that entitles a person to a reward or commendation. 3. merits, the intrinsic right and wrong of a matter, as a law case. 4. Often, merits. the state or fact of deserving. —v.t. 5. to be worthy of. —mer′it·ed·ly, adv.

mer·i·toc·ra·cy (mer′i tok′rə sē), n. Chiefly Brit. a class of persons making their way on their own ability and talent rather than because of class privileges.

mer·i·to·ri·ous (mer′i tōr′ē əs, -tôr′-), adj. entitled to reward or commendation. —mer′i·to′ri·ous·ly, adv. —mer′i·to′ri·ous·ness, n.

Mer·lin (mûr′lin), n. Arthurian Romance. a venerable magician and seer.

mer·maid (mûr′mād′), n. an imaginary female marine creature, having the head, torso, and arms of a woman and the tail of a fish. —mer′man′, n.masc.

mer·ri·ment (mer′i mənt), n. merry gaiety.

mer·ry (mer′ē), adj., mer·ri·er, mer·ri·est. 1. joyous in disposition or spirit. 2. laughingly gay. 3. make merry, to be gay or festive. —mer′ri·ly, adv. —mer′ri·ness, n. —Syn. blithe, cherry, joyful, mirthful.

mer·ry-go-round (mer′ē gō round′), n. 1. a revolving, circular platform fitted with wooden horses or other animals on which persons, esp. children, may sit for an amusement ride. 2. a busy round, as of social life.

mer·ry·mak·ing (mer′ē mā′king), n. 1. participation in a festive or merry celebration. 2. a merry festivity. —mer′ry·mak′er, n.

me·sa (mā′sə), n. a land formation having a flat top and steep rock walls.

mé·sal·li·ance (mā′zə lī′əns, mā zal′ē-əns), n., pl. mé·sal·li·anc·es (mā′zə-lī′ən sis, mā zal′ē ən sis). a marriage with a social inferior.

mes·cal (me skal′), n. 1. a cactus of Texas and northern Mexico. 2. an intoxicating beverage distilled from the fermented juice of certain species of agave. 3. any agave yielding this.

mes·ca·line (mes′kə lēn′, -lin), n. a hallucinogenic drug obtained from the mescal plant.

mes·dames (mā däm′, -dam′), n. pl. of madame.

mes·de·moi·selles (mā′də mə zel′), n. a pl. of mademoiselle.

mesh (mesh), n. 1. one of the open spaces in a net or other network, as a screen. 2. meshes, the means of catching or holding fast: caught in the meshes of the law. 3. an intertwined structure. 4. any fabric of open texture. 5. the engagement of gear teeth. —v.t., v.i. 6. to entangle or become entangled in or as in a net. 7. to engage or become engaged, as gear teeth. 8. to match or interlock. —meshed (mesht), adj. —mesh′y, adj.

mesh·work (mesh′wûrk′), n. meshed work.

mes·mer·ize (mez′mə rīz′, mes′-), v.t., v.i., -ized, -iz·ing. 1. to fascinate or charm unfailingly. 2. Obs. to hypnotize. —mes′mer·ist, n. —mes·mer·ism′, n. —mes′mer·iz′er, n.

Mes·o·po·ta·mi·a (mes′ə pə tā′mē ə), n. an ancient country in W Asia between the Tigris and Euphrates rivers: now part of Iraq. —Mes′o·po·ta′mi·an, adj., n.

mes·o·sphere (mez′ə sfēr′), n. the region of the earth's atmosphere between the stratosphere and the thermosphere. —mes′o·spher′ic (-sfer′ik), adj.

Mes·o·zo·ic (mez′ə zō′ik, mes′-, mē′-zə-, -sə-), adj. 1. noting an era occurring between 70,000,000 and 220,-000,000 years ago, characterized by the appearance and extinction of dinosaurs. —n. 2. the Mesozoic era.

mes·quite (me skēt′, mes′kēt), n. a spiny shrub of the southwestern U.S. and Mexico, bearing beanlike pods. Also, mes·quit′.

mess (mes), n. 1. a dirty or untidy condition or accumulation of matter or objects. 2. a confusing or difficult state. 3. a group regularly taking meals together. 4. the meal so taken. 5. a quantity of food sufficient for a dish. 6. a dish or quantity of soft or liquid food. —v.t. 7. to make dirty or untidy. 8. to make a mess or muddle of (affairs, etc.). —v.i. 9. to eat in company, esp. as a member of a mess. 10. to make a dirty or untidy mess. 11. mess around or about, Informal. a. to busy oneself without purpose or plan. b. to meddle or interfere. —mess′y, adj. —mess′i·ly, adv. —mess′i·ness, n.

mes·sage (mes′ij), n. 1. a communication, usually of advice or direction, transmitted esp. through an intermediary. 2. the point or idea intended to be conveyed.

Mes·sei·gneurs (Fr. mā se nyœR′), n. pl. of Monseigneur.

mes·sen·ger (mes′ən jər), n. a person who carries a message or runs an errand.

Mes·si·ah (mi sī′ə), n. 1. the promised and expected deliverer of the Jewish people. 2. Jesus Christ. 3. (usually l.c.) any expected deliverer. —**Mes·si·an·ic** (mes′ē an′ik), adj.

mes·sieurs (mes′ərz), n. pl. of **monsieur.**

mess·mate (mes′māt′), n. a member of a group regularly taking meals together.

Messrs. (mes′ərz), pl. of **Mr.**

mes·ti·zo (me stē′zō, mi-), n., pl. **-zos, -zoes.** a person of mixed Spanish and Amerindian blood. —**mes·ti·za** (me stē′zə, mi-), n.fem.

met (met), v. pt. and pp. of **meet**[1].

met., 1. meteorology. 2. metropolitan.

meta-, a prefix meaning: a. after, along with, or beyond: metacarpus. b. change: metamorphosis.

me·tab·o·lism (mə tab′ə liz′əm), n. the sum of the processes in an organism by which protoplasm is produced, maintained, and destroyed, and by means of which energy is made available. —**met·a·bol·ic** (met′ə bol′ik), adj. —**me·tab′o·lize′** (-līz′), v.t., v.i.

me·tab·o·lite (mə tab′ə līt′), n. a product of metabolic action.

met·a·car·pus (met′ə kär′pəs), n., pl. **-pi** (-pī). the part of a hand, esp. of its bony structure, included between the wrist and the fingers. —**met·a·car′pal,** adj., n.

met·a·gal·ax·y (met′ə gal′ək sē), n. the complete system of galaxies.

met·al (met′əl), n. 1. any of a class of elementary substances, as gold, silver, or copper, that are good conductors of electricity and heat, are shiny when polished, and generally can be shaped by hammering. 2. an alloy composed of such substances, as brass. 3. any object made of such substances. 4. Obs. mettle. —**me·tal·lic** (mə tal′ik), adj. —**me·tal′li·cal·ly,** adv.

metall., 1. metallurgical. 2. metallurgy.

met·al·lur·gy (met′əl ûr′jē), n. 1. the science of separating metals from their ores. 2. the science of making alloys. —**met′al·lur′gic, met′al·lur′gi·cal,** adj. —**met′al·lur′gi·cal·ly,** adv. —**met·al·lur·gist** (met′əl ûr′jist, mə tal′ər jist), n.

met·al·ware (met′əl wâr′), n. work of metal, esp. utensils, flatware, etc.

met·al·work (met′əl wûrk′), n. 1. objects made of metal. 2. Also called **met′al·work′ing** (-wûr′kiṅg). the technique of making such objects. —**met′al·work′er,** n.

met·a·mor·phism (met′ə môr′fiz əm), n. 1. a change in the structure of a rock due to natural agencies, as pressure and heat. 2. metamorphosis. —**met′a·mor′phic** (-fik), **met′a·mor′phous** (-fəs), adj.

met·a·mor·phose (met′ə môr′fōz, -fōs), v.t., v.i., **-phosed, -phos·ing.** to subject to or undergo metamorphosis.

met·a·mor·pho·sis (met′ə môr′fə sis), n., pl. **-ses** (-sēz′). 1. a change or successive changes of form from birth or hatching to adulthood in some animals, as of the pupa to the butterfly. 2. a transformation, as by magic or witchcraft. 3. any complete change in appearance or character. [< L < Gk: transformation]

met·a·phor (met′ə fôr′, -fər), n. a figure of speech in which a term or phrase is applied to something to which it is not literally applicable in order to suggest a resemblance, as "A mighty fortress is our God." —**met′a·phor′i·cal** (-fôr′i kəl, -for′-), **met′a·phor′ic,** adj. —**met′a·phor′i·cal·ly,** adv.

met·a·phys·i·cal (met′ə fiz′i kəl), adj. 1. of or pertaining to metaphysics. 2. highly abstract or abstruse. 3. Archaic. supernatural or incorporeal. 4. Archaic. imaginary or fanciful. —**met′a·phys′i·cal·ly,** adv.

met·a·phys·ics (met′ə fiz′iks), n. the branch of philosophy that treats of the ultimate nature of existence, reality, and experience. 2. philosophy, esp. in its more abstruse branches. —**met′a·phy·si′cian** (-fi zish′ən), n.

me·tas·ta·sis (mə tas′tə sis), n., pl. **-ses** (-sēz′). the transfer of disease-producing organisms or of malignant cells to other parts of the body by way of the blood vessels. —**met·a·stat·ic** (met′ə stat′ik), adj. —**me·tas′ta·size′** (-sīz′), v.i.

met·a·tar·sus (met′ə tär′səs), n., pl. **-si** (-sī). the part of a foot, esp. its bony structure, included between the ankle and the toes. —**met′a·tar′sal,** adj., n.

me·tath·e·sis (mə tath′i sis), n., pl. **-ses** (-sēz′). the transposition of letters, syllables, or sounds in a word.

mete (mēt), v.t., **met·ed, met·ing. 1. mete out,** to deal out or administer, as punishment. 2. Archaic. to measure.

me·tem·psy·cho·sis (mə tem′sə kō′sis, -temp′-, met′əm sī-), n., pl. **-ses** (-sēz). the passage of the soul after death to some other human or animal body.

me·te·or (mē′tē ər), n. 1. a transient fiery streak in the sky produced by a meteoroid passing through the earth's atmosphere. 2. a meteoroid or meteorite.

me·te·or·ic (mē′tē ôr′ik, -or′-), adj. 1. of or like a meteor. 2. suggesting a meteor, as in transient brilliance: a meteoric literary career. —**me′te·or′i·cal·ly,** adv.

me·te·or·ite (mē′tē ə rīt′), *n.* a meteor that has reached the earth. —**me′te·or·it′ic** (-rit′ik), *adj.*

me·te·or·oid (mē′tē ə roid′), *n.* any of the small bodies, often remnants of comets, traveling through space.

meteorol., **1.** meteorological. **2.** meteorology.

me·te·or·ol·o·gy (mē′tē ə rol′ə jē), *n.* the science dealing with the atmosphere and its phenomena, including weather and climate. —**me′te·or·o·log′i·cal** (-ər ə loj′i kəl), *adj.* —**me′te·or·ol′o·gist**, *n.*

me·ter¹ (mē′tər), *n.* the fundamental unit of length in the metric system, equivalent to 39.37 inches.

me·ter² (mē′tər), *n.* **1.** an arrangement of words in rhythmic lines or verses. **2.** the rhythmic element in music.

me·ter³ (mē′tər), *n.* **1.** an instrument that automatically measures and registers a quantity consumed, distance traveled, etc. **2.** See **parking meter.** —*v.t.* **3.** to measure by means of a meter. **4.** to process (mail) by means of a postage meter.

-meter, a suffix meaning: **a.** an instrument for measuring: *altimeter.* **b.** a linear meter: *millimeter.*

me·ter-kil·o·gram-sec·ond (mē′tər kil′ə gram′ sek′ənd), *adj.* of the system of units in which the meter, kilogram, and second are the principal units of length, mass, and time.

me′ter maid′, a female employee in a municipal traffic department whose chief duty is the issuance of tickets for parking violations.

meth·a·done (meth′ə dōn′), *n.* a synthetic narcotic drug that blocks the effects of heroin and may be used as a heroin substitute in the treatment of heroin addiction. Also, **meth·a·don** (meth′ə don′).

meth·am·phet·a·mine (meth′am fet′ə mēn, -min), *n.* a stimulating drug of the amphetamine series that suppresses appetite, used in treating obesity.

meth·ane (meth′ān), *n. Chem.* a colorless, odorless, flammable gas, the main constituent of marsh gas and the firedamp of coal mines, obtained commercially from natural gas.

meth·a·nol (meth′ə nōl′, -nôl′), *n.* See **methyl alcohol.**

meth·a·qua·lone (meth′ə kwo′lōn), *n.* a nonbarbiturate sedative-hypnotic drug used to induce sleep.

me·thinks (mi thingks′), *v. impers.; pt.* **me·thought.** *Archaic.* it seems to me.

meth·od (meth′əd), *n.* **1.** an orderly procedure for doing something. **2.** order or system in doing anything. —**me·thod·i·cal** (mə thod′i kəl), *adj.* —**me·thod′i·cal·ly**, *adv.* —**me·thod′i·cal·ness**, *n.*

Meth·od·ist (meth′ə dist), *n.* a member of a Protestant denomination that grew out of the revival of religion led by John Wesley. —**Meth′od·ism′**, *n.*

meth·od·ize (meth′ə dīz′), *v.t.*, **-ized, -iz·ing.** to arrange according to a method.

meth·od·ol·o·gy (meth′ə dol′ə jē), *n., pl.* **-gies. 1.** a system of methods, as those of a science. **2.** the underlying principles and rules of a system or procedure. —**meth′od·o·log′i·cal** (-də loj′i kəl), *adj.* —**meth′od·o·log′i·cal·ly**, *adv.*

Me·thu·se·lah (mə thōō′zə lə, -thōōz′-lə), *n. Bible.* a patriarch said to have lived 969 years.

meth·yl (meth′əl), *n.* a univalent hydrocarbon radical.

meth′yl al′cohol, a colorless poisonous liquid used chiefly as a solvent, fuel, etc.

me·tic·u·lous (mə tik′yə ləs), *adj.* extremely careful about minute details. —**me·tic′u·lous·ly**, *adv.* —**me·tic′u·lous·ness**, *n.* —**Syn.** exact, precise, scrupulous.

mé·tier (mā′tyā, mā tyā′), *n.* a field of activity in which a person has special ability.

me·tre¹ (mē′tər), *n. Brit.* **meter¹.**

me·tre² (mē′tər), *n. Brit.* **meter².**

met·ric¹ (me′trik), *adj.* pertaining to the meter or to the metric system.

met·ric² (me′trik), *adj.* metrical.

met·ri·cal (me′tri kəl), *adj.* **1.** of or composed in poetic meter. **2.** pertaining to measurement. —**met′ri·cal·ly**, *adv.*

met·ri·ca·tion (met′rə kā′shən), *n.* the act of converting into the metric system. —**met′ri·cate′**, *v.t.*

met·ri·cize (met′rə sīz′), *v.t.*, **-cized, -ciz·ing.** to convert into or express in the metric system.

met·rics (me′triks), *n.* **1.** the art of metrical composition. **2.** (not in technical use) the metric system.

met′ric sys′tem, a decimal system of weights and measures based on the meter (39.37 inches) for length, kilogram (2.2 pounds) for mass or weight, and the liter (1.0567 liquid quarts) for volume or capacity.

met′ric ton′, a unit of 1000 kilograms or 2204.6 pounds.

met·ro (me′trō), *n., pl.* **-ros.** a subway, esp. in Paris, France.

Met·ro·lin·er (me′trō lī′nər), *n.* a high-speed, reserved-seat train run by Amtrak.

me·trol·o·gy (mi trol′ə jē), *n., pl.* **-gies.** the science of measures and weights.

met·ro·nome (me′trə nōm′), *n.* an instrument for beating desired time, used esp. as an aid in practicing music. —**met′ro·nom′ic** (-nom′ik), *adj.*

me·trop·o·lis (mə trop'ə lis), *n., pl.* **-lis·es.** 1. the chief, or often capital, city of a country, state, or region. 2. any large, busy city. [< LL < Gk: mother state or city] —**met·ro·pol·i·tan** (me'trə pol'i tⁿn), *adj.*

met·tle (met'ᵊl), *n.* 1. courage and fortitude. 2. characteristic disposition or temperament.

met·tle·some (met'ᵊl səm), *adj.* having or full of mettle.

MEV, million electron volts.

mew¹ (myōō), *n., v.i.* meow.

mew² (myōō), *n.* 1. **mews,** *Brit.* **a.** (formerly) an area of stables built around a small street. **b.** a street having small apartments converted from such stables. —*v.t.* 2. *Archaic.* to shut up or conceal.

mewl (myōōl), *v.i.* to cry feebly, as a baby.

Mex., 1. Mexican. 2. Mexico.

Mex·i·co (mek'sə kō'), *n.* 1. a country in S North America. 2. **Gulf of,** an arm of the Atlantic between the U.S., Cuba, and Mexico. — **Mex'i·can** (-kən), *adj., n.*

Mex'ico Cit'y, the capital of Mexico.

mez·za·nine (mez'ə nēn', mez'ə nēn'), *n.* 1. a low story between two main stories in a building. 2. the lowest balcony or forward part of such a balcony in a theater. [< F < It *.mezzanino,* dim. of *mezzano* middle < L *mediānus* median]

mez·zo·so·pran·o (met'sō sə pran'ō, -prä'nō, mez'ō-), *n., pl.* **-pran·os, -pran·i** (-pran'ē, -prä'nē). 1. a voice or voice part intermediate between soprano and contralto. 2. a person having such a voice. Also, **mez'zo.**

MF, 1. *Radio.* medium frequency. 2. Middle French.

M.F.A., Master of Fine Arts.

mfd., manufactured.

mfg., manufacturing.

mfr., 1. manufacture. 2. manufacturer.

mg, milligram; milligrams.

Mg, magnesium.

Mgr., 1. Manager. 2. Monseigneur. 3. Monsignor.

mgt., management.

M.H., Medal of Honor.

MHz, megahertz; megahertz.

MI, 1. Michigan. 2. Military Intelligence.

mi (mē), *n. Music.* the third tone of a diatonic scale.

mi., 1. mile; miles. 2. mill; mills.

MIA, *Mil.* missing in action.

Mi·am·i (mī am'ē, -am'ə), *n.* a city in SE Florida.

mi·aow (mē ou', myou), *n., v.i.* meow. Also, **mi·aou'.**

mi·as·ma (mī az'mə, mē-), *n., pl.* **-mas, -ma·ta** (-mə tə). 1. noxious exhalations from decaying organic matter that were formerly believed to infect

the atmosphere. 2. a foreboding influence or atmosphere. —**mi·as'mic, mi·as'mal, mi·as·mat'ic** (-mat'ik), *adj.*

mi·ca (mī'kə), *n.* a shiny mineral that can be split into thin, partly transparent sheets, used as an electric insulator.

mice (mīs), *n.* pl of **mouse.**

Mich., Michigan.

Mi·chel·an·ge·lo (mī'kəl an'jə lō', mik'əl-), *n.* 1475–1564, Italian sculptor, painter, architect, and poet.

Mich·i·gan (mish'ə gən), *n.* 1. a state in the N central United States. *Cap.:* Lansing. 2. **Lake,** a lake in the N central U.S., between Wisconsin and Michigan.

micro-, a combining form meaning: **a.** small: *microcosm.* **b.** enlarging (something small): *microphone.* **c.** microscopic: *microorganism.* **d.** a millionth part of a unit: *microgram.*

mi·crobe (mī'krōb), *n.* a microorganism, esp. a disease-producing bacterium. —**mi·cro'bi·al, mi·cro'bic,** *adj.*

mi·cro·bi·ol·o·gy (mī'krō bī ol'ə jē), *n.* the science dealing with microscopic organisms. —**mi'cro·bi'o·log'i·cal** (-bī'ə loj'i kəl), *adj.* —**mi'cro·bi·ol'o·gist,** *n.*

mi·cro·cli·mate (mī'krə klī'mit), *n.* the climate of a small area, as of confined spaces or plant communities. —**mi'cro·cli'ma·tol'o·gy** (-mə tol'ə-jē), *n.*

mi·cro·cop·y (mī'krə kop'ē), *n., pl.* **-cop·ies.** a microphotographic reproduction.

mi·cro·cosm (mī'krə koz'əm), *n.* 1. a world in miniature: *The atom is a microcosm.* 2. humans regarded as epitomizing the universe. —**mi·cro·cos'mic, mi'cro·cos'mi·cal,** *adj.*

mi·cro·e·lec·tron·ics (mī'krō i lek-tron'iks, -ē'lek-), *n.* a branch of electronics dealing with microminiaturization. —**mi'cro·e·lec·tron'ic,** *adj.*

mi·cro·fiche (mī'krə fēsh'), *n.* a flat sheet of microfilm, typically 4 x 6 inches.

mi·cro·film (mī'krə film'), *n.* 1. a film bearing a microphotographic copy of printed or other graphic matter, used esp. for preservation and storage of bulky volumes in a minimum of space. —*v.t., v.i.* 2. to make a microfilm (of).

mi·cro·form (mī'krə fôrm'), *n.* any form or type of film or paper containing microphotographic images.

mi·cro·gram (mī'krə gram'), *n.* one millionth of a gram.

mi·cro·graph (mī'krə graf', -gräf'), *n.* a photograph taken, or a drawing of an object as seen, through a microscope.

mi·cro·groove (mī′krə grōōv′), *n.* the narrow needle groove on a long-playing record.

mi·crom·e·ter (mī krom′i tər), *n.* a device for measuring minute distances, angles, etc., as in connection with a telescope or microscope.

mi·cro·min·i·a·ture (mī′krō min′ē ə chər, -min′ə chər), *adj.* built on an extremely small scale, smaller than subminiature, esp. of electronic equipment. Also, **mi′cro·min′i·a·tur·ized′** (-chə rīzd′).

mi·cro·min·i·a·tur·i·za·tion (mī′krō min′ē ə chər i zā′shən, -chə rī-), *n.* the process of developing and producing microminiaturized equipment, esp. in electronics.

mi·cron (mī′kron), *n., pl.* **-crons, -cra** (-krə). the millionth part of a meter.

Mi·cro·ne·sia (mī′krə nē′zhə, -shə), *n.* the small Pacific islands N of the equator and E of the Philippines. — **Mi′cro·ne′sian,** *adj., n.*

mi·cro·or·gan·ism (mī′krō ôr′gə niz′-əm), *n.* a microscopic plant or animal, as a bacterium or protozoan.

mi·cro·phone (mī′krə fōn′), *n.* an instrument for transforming sound waves into changes in electric currents, used in recording or transmitting sound.

mi·cro·pho·to·graph (mī′krə fō′tə graf′, -gräf′), *n.* 1. a small photograph requiring optical enlargement for viewing. —*v.t.* 2. to make a microphotograph of. — **mi′cro·pho′to·graph′ic** (-graf′ik), *adj.* — **mi′cro·pho·tog′ra·phy** (-fə tog′rə fē), *n.*

mi·cro·scope (mī′krə skōp′), *n.* an optical instrument for magnifying objects too small to be seen by the naked eye. — **mi·cros′co·py** (-kros′kə pē), *n.*

mi·cro·scop·ic (mī′krə skop′ik), *adj.* 1. so small as to be invisible or indistinct without the use of the microscope. 2. very tiny. 3. attentive to minute details. 4. of or involving a microscope. Also, **mi′cro·scop′i·cal.** — **mi′cro·scop′i·cal·ly,** *adv.*

mi·cro·sec·ond (mī′krə sek′ənd), *n.* one millionth of a second.

mi·cro·state (mī′krə stāt′), *n.* a very small country, esp. one newly independent.

mi·cro·sur·ger·y (mī′krō sûr′jə rē), *n.* the dissection of tissue or of individual cells under a microscope. — **mi′cro·sur′gi·cal,** *adj.*

mi·cro·wave (mī′krō wāv′), *n.* an electromagnetic wave of extremely high frequency, usually from 1,000 to 30,000 megahertz.

mi′crowave ov′en, an electric oven using microwaves that penetrate food, generating heat within the food to cook it in a very short time.

mid[1] (mid), *adj.* middle (often used in combination): *midseason; midlife.*

mid[2] (mid), *prep. Literary.* amid. Also, **'mid.**

mid., middle.

mid·air (mid âr′), *n.* any point in the air not close to the earth.

Mi·das (mī′dəs), *n. Class. Myth.* a king who had the power of turning whatever he touched into gold.

mid·day (mid′dā′), *n., adj.* noon.

mid·den (mid′ən), *n. Brit. Dial.* a dunghill or refuse heap.

mid·dle (mid′əl), *adj.* 1. halfway between extremes or limits. 2. intermediate, as in size, quantity, or status. 3. avoiding extremes. 4. (*cap.*) intermediate between linguistic periods classified as Old and Modern or New: *Middle Irish.* —*n.* 5. a middle point, part, or position. 6. the middle part of the human body, esp. the waist. 7. something intermediate.

mid′dle age′, the period of human life between about 40 and about 60. — **mid′dle-aged′,** *adj.*

Mid′dle Ag′es, the time in European history between the 5th century A.D. and 1450 or 1500.

Mid′dle Amer′ica, 1. continental North America S of the U.S., comprising Mexico and Central America. **2.** the average, middle-class Americans as a group. — **Mid′dle Amer′ican.**

mid·dle·brow (mid′əl brou′), *n. Informal.* a person of conventional or widely accepted tastes and cultural interests. — **mid′dle-brow′ism,** *n.*

mid′dle class′, a class of people intermediate in social, economic, and cultural standing. — **mid′dle-class′,** *adj.*

mid′dle ear′, the middle portion of the ear, consisting of the tympanic membrane and an air-filled chamber lined with mucous membrane.

Mid′dle East′, (loosely) the area from Libya to Afghanistan, including the Arabian countries. — **Mid′dle East′ern.**

Mid′dle Eng′lish, the English language of the period c1150–c1475.

mid′dle fin′ger, the finger between the forefinger and the third finger.

mid·dle·man (mid′əl man′), *n.* a person who acts as an intermediary, esp. in the movement of goods from the producer to the consumer.

mid·dle·most (mid′əl mōst′), *adj.* midmost.

mid·dle-of-the-road (mid′əl əv thə-rōd′), *adj.* not favoring any extreme position, esp. in politics. — **mid′dle-of-the-road′er,** *n.*

mid′dle school′, a school, as a private one, usually having grades 5 through 8.

mid·dle·weight (mid′ᵊl wāt′), *n.* **1.** a person of average weight. **2.** a boxer weighing from 147 to 160 pounds. —*adj.* **3.** *Boxing.* of or pertaining to a middleweight or middleweights.

Mid·dle West′, the region of the United States bounded on the W by the Rocky Mountains and on the S by the Ohio River. —**Mid′dle West′ern.** —**Mid′dle West′erner.**

mid·dling (mid′liṅg), *adj.* **1.** medium in size, quality, or grade. **2.** mediocre or ordinary. —*adv.* **3.** moderately or fairly. —**mid′dling·ly,** *adv.*

mid·dy (mid′ē), *n., pl.* **-dies. 1.** *Informal.* a midshipman. **2.** Also called **mid′dy blouse′.** a loose blouse with a sailor collar, worn by children or young girls.

Mid·east (mid′ēst′), *n.* See **Middle East.**

midge (mij), *n.* a minute insect resembling a mosquito.

midg·et (mij′it), *n.* **1.** an extremely small person. **2.** any animal or thing very small of its kind. —*adj.* **3.** extremely small.

mid·i (mid′ē), *n. Informal.* a skirt, coat, or dress of mid-calf length.

mid·land (mid′lənd), *n.* the interior part of a country.

mid·most (mid′mōst′), *adj.* being in or near the middle.

mid·night (mid′nīt′), *n.* **1.** twelve o'clock at night. —*adj.* **2.** of midnight. **3.** like midnight, as in darkness.

mid′night sun′, the sun visible at midnight in midsummer in arctic and antarctic regions.

mid·point (mid′point′), *n.* a point at or near the middle of something, as a line.

mid·rib (mid′rib′), *n. Bot.* the central or middle rib of a leaf.

mid·riff (mid′rif), *n.* **1.** the middle part of the body, between the chest and the waist. **2.** diaphragm (def. 1).

mid·ship·man (mid′ship′mən, mid-ship′-), *n.* a student in training for commission as an officer in the U.S. Navy or Marine Corps.

mid·ships (mid′ships′), *adv.* amidships.

midst[1] (midst), *n.* **1.** the central part or portion. **2.** the figurative area within which a group of persons are gathered: *a traitor in our midst.* **3.** the figurative domain of any kind of environmental condition.

midst[2] (midst), *prep. Literary.* amidst. Also, ′**midst.**

mid·stream (mid′strēm′), *n.* the middle of a stream.

mid·sum·mer (mid′sum′ər, -sum′-), *n.* **1.** the middle of summer. **2.** the summer solstice, around June 21.

mid·term (mid′tûrm′), *adj.* **1.** in or occurring at the halfway point of a term, as a school term. —*n.* **2.** *Informal.* a midterm school examination.

mid·town (mid′toun′, -toun′), *n.* **1.** the part of a city or town between uptown and downtown. —*adv., adj.* **2.** to or situated in midtown.

mid·way (*adv., adj.* mid′wā′; *n.* mid′wā′), *adv., adj.* **1.** in the middle of the way or distance. —*n.* **2.** the area of a fair where sideshows and similar amusements are located.

mid·week (mid′wēk′), *n.* the middle of the week. —**mid′week′ly,** *adj., adv.*

Mid·west (mid′west′), *n.* See **Middle West.** —**Mid′west′ern,** *adj.* —**Mid′west′ern·er,** *n.*

mid·wife (mid′wīf′), *n.* a woman who assists women in childbirth. —**mid′wife′ry** (-wī′fə rē, -wīf′rē), *n.*

mid·win·ter (mid′win′tər), *n.* **1.** the middle of winter. **2.** the winter solstice, around December 22.

mid·year (mid′yēr′), *n.* **1.** in or occurring at the halfway point of a year, as an academic year. —*n.* **2.** *Informal.* a midyear school examination.

mien (mēn), *n.* air, bearing, or aspect, as showing character, feeling, etc.

miff (mif), *v.t. Informal.* to give offense to.

Mig (mig), *n.* a Russian-built fighter aircraft. Also, **MIG.**

might[1] (mīt), *v.* pt. of **may.**

might[2] (mīt), *n.* **1.** superior power or strength. **2.** physical strength.

might·y (mī′tē), *adj.,* **might·i·er, might·i·est,** *adv.* —*adj.* **1.** having or showing superior power or strength. **2.** of great size. **3.** great in degree or importance. —*adv.* **4.** *Informal.* very. —**might′i·ly,** *adv.* —**might′i·ness,** *n.*

mi·gnon·ette (min′yə net′), *n.* a plant having tall spikes of small, fragrant, greenish-white flowers.

mi·graine (mī′grān), *n.* a severe, usually periodic headache, usually confined to one side of the head.

mi·grant (mī′grənt), *adj.* **1.** migrating, esp. of people. —*n.* **2.** a person or animal that migrates. **3.** Also called **mi′grant work′er.** a laborer who moves from one country or region to another to engage temporarily in seasonal farm work.

mi·grate (mī′grāt), *v.i.,* **-grat·ed, -grat·ing. 1.** to go from one country or region to another, esp. repeatedly and in a large group. **2.** to pass periodically from one region or climate to another, as certain birds. —**mi·gra′tion,** *n.* —**mi·gra′tion·al,** *adj.* —**mi′gra·to·ry** (-grə tōr′ē, -tôr′ē), *adj.*

mi·ka·do (mi kä′dō), *n.*, *pl.* **-dos.** *Literary.* an emperor of Japan.

mike (mīk), *n. Informal.* a microphone.

mil (mil), *n.* **1.** a unit of length equal to .001 of an inch. **2.** a thousand: *per mil.*

mil., military.

mi·la·dy (mi lā′dē), *n.* **1.** an English noblewoman. **2.** a woman regarded as having fashionable tastes. Also, **mi·la·di.**

Mi·lan (mi lan′, -län′), *n.* a city in N Italy. —**Mi·lan·ese** (mil′ə nēz′, -nēs′), *n., adj.*

milch (milch), *adj.* yielding milk: *a milch cow.*

mild (mīld), *adj.* **1.** not severe or extreme: *a mild winter.* **2.** not sharp, pungent, or strong: *a mild flavor.* **3.** gentle or kind in feeling or behavior. —**mild′ly,** *adv.* —**mild′ness,** *n.* —Syn. **1.** moderate, temperate. **2.** bland.

mil·dew (mil′dōō′, -dyōō′), *n.* **1.** a cottony, usually whitish coating caused by fungi, growing on plants, fabrics, paper, etc. —*v.t., v.i.* **2.** to affect or become affected with mildew. —**mil′dew′y,** *adj.*

mile (mīl), *n.* **1.** a unit of distance equal to 5280 feet, or 1760 yards (1.609 kilometers). **2.** a unit of distance in sea and air navigation equal to 1.852 kilometers, or 6076 feet.

mile·age (mī′lij), *n.* **1.** the aggregate number of miles traveled over in a given time. **2.** an allowance for traveling expenses at a fixed rate per mile. **3.** the number of miles or relative distance that a vehicle can travel on a quantity of fuel.

mile·post (mīl′pōst′), *n.* a signpost showing the distance in miles to or from a place.

mil·er (mī′lər), *n.* a participant in a one-mile race.

mile·stone (mīl′stōn′), *n.* **1.** a stone functioning as a milepost. **2.** a significant event, as in history.

mi·lieu (mil yōō′, mēl-), *n., pl.* **-lieus, -lieux** (-lyœ′). environment or surroundings, esp. of a social or cultural nature.

mil·i·tant (mil′i tənt), *adj.* **1.** vigorously active and aggressive, esp. in support of a cause. **2.** engaged in warfare or fighting. —*n.* **3.** a militant person. —**mil′i·tan·cy,** *n.* —**mil′i·tant·ly,** *adv.*

mil·i·ta·rism (mil′i tə riz′əm), *n.* **1.** the principle of maintaining a large military establishment. **2.** the tendency to regard military efficiency as the supreme ideal of the state. —**mil′i·ta·rist,** *n.* —**mil′i·ta·ris′tic,** *adj.*

mil·i·ta·rize (mil′i tə rīz′), *v.t.,* **-rized, -riz·ing. 1.** to equip with armed forces and defenses. **2.** to imbue with militarism.

mil·i·tar·y (mil′i ter′ē), *adj., n., pl.* **-tar·ies, -tar·y.** —*adj.* **1.** of, for, or pertaining to armed forces, soldiers, or war. **2.** performed by soldiers. **3.** of the army. —*n.* **4.** the military establishment of a nation. —**mil·i·tar·i·ly** (mil′i târ′ə lē, mil′i ter′ə lē), *adv.*

mil′itary-indus′trial com′plex (mil′i ter′ē in dus′trē əl), a cooperative combination of companies supplying military equipment, etc., and of senior officers of the armed forces.

mil′itary police′, soldiers who perform police duties within the army.

mil·i·tate (mil′i tāt′), *v.i.,* **-tat·ed, -tat·ing.** to operate or work, usually against something.

mi·li·tia (mi lish′ə), *n.* a body of citizens enrolled in military service but serving full-time only in emergencies. —**mi·li′tia·man,** *n.*

milk (milk), *n.* **1.** a white liquid secreted by the mammary glands of female mammals, serving for the nourishment of their young. **2.** this liquid, esp. from cows, used for food by human beings. **3.** any liquid resembling this, as the liquid within a coconut. —*v.t.* **4.** to draw milk from (a cow). **5.** to drain strength, information, or wealth from. —*v.i.* **6.** to yield milk, as a cow. —**milk′er,** *n.* —**milk′y,** *adj.* —**milk′i·ness,** *n.*

milk′ and hon′ey, 1. extraordinary fertility and abundance. **2.** *Informal.* abundantly easy, carefree conditions.

milk′ fe′ver, a disorder often affecting dairy cows immediately after calving, causing drowsiness and paralysis.

milk′ glass′, an opaque white glass.

milk·maid (milk′mād′), *n.* a woman who milks cows or who is employed in a dairy.

milk·man (milk′man′), *n., pl.* **-men.** a man who sells or delivers milk.

milk′ of magne′sia, a milky white suspension in water of hydroxide of magnesium, used as an antacid or laxative.

milk′ shake′, a frothy drink made of milk, flavoring, and ice cream, blended in a mixer.

milk·sop (milk′sop′), *n.* an unmanly or effeminate man or youth.

milk′ tooth′, one of the temporary teeth of a mammal that are replaced by the permanent teeth.

milk·weed (milk′wēd′), *n.* a plant that secretes a milky juice or latex.

Milk′y Way′, the faintly luminous band stretching across the heavens, composed of innumerable stars too distant to be seen clearly with the naked eye.

mill¹ (mil), *n.* **1.** a factory for certain kinds of manufacture, as paper, steel, or textiles. **2.** a building equipped with machinery for grinding grain into flour and other cereal products. **3.** a machine for grinding, crushing, or pulverizing any solid substance. **4.** an establishment that handles important matters in a perfunctory or routine manner: *a divorce mill; a diploma mill.* **5.** **through the mill,** *Informal.* undergoing severe difficulties and trouble. —*v.t.* **6.** to grind, work, or treat in or with a mill. —*v.i.* **7.** to move around aimlessly or confusedly, as a crowd.

mill² (mil), *n.* one tenth of a cent: used as a money of account, esp. in certain tax rates.

mil·lage (mil′ij), *n.* the tax rate, as for property, assessed in mills per dollar.

mill·dam (mil′dam′), *n.* a dam built in a stream to make a millpond.

mil·len·ni·um (mi len′ē əm), *n., pl.* **-ni·ums, -ni·a** (-nē ə). **1.** a period of one thousand years. **2.** a thousandth anniversary. **3. the millennium,** the period of a thousand years during which Christ will reign on earth. **4.** a period of general righteousness and happiness, esp. in the indefinite future. —**mil·len′ni·al,** *adj.*

mill·er (mil′ər), *n.* **1.** a person who owns or operates a mill, esp. a grain mill. **2.** any moth having wings that appear powdery.

mil·let (mil′it), *n.* **1.** a cereal grass cultivated in Asia and Europe and used as food. **2.** its grain.

milli-, a combining form meaning: **a.** thousand: *millipede.* **b.** one thousandth of the specified unit: *millimeter.*

mil·li·am·pere (mil′ē am′pēr), *n.* one thousandth of an ampere.

mil·liard (mil′yərd, -yärd), *n. Brit.* a billion.

mil·li·gram (mil′ə gram′), *n.* one thousandth of a gram. Also, *Brit.,* **mil′li·gramme′.**

mil·li·li·ter (mil′ə lē′tər), *n.* one thousandth of a liter or 0.034 fluid ounce. Also, *Brit.,* **mil′li·li′tre.**

mil·li·me·ter (mil′ə mē′tər), *n.* one thousandth of a meter or 0.04 inch. Also, *Brit.,* **mil′li·me′tre.** —**mil·li·met′ric** (mil′ə me′trik), *adj.*

mil·li·ner (mil′ə nər), *n.* a person who designs, makes, or sells women's hats.

mil·li·ner·y (mil′ə ner′ē, -nə rē), *n.* **1.** women's hats and other articles made or sold by milliners. **2.** the business or trade of a milliner.

mill·ing (mil′iŋg), *n.* the grooved edge on a coin.

mil·lion (mil′yən), *n., pl.* **-lions, -lion. 1.** a cardinal number, a thousand times one thousand. **2.** a symbol for this number, as 1,000,000 or M. **3.** the amount of a thousand thousand in the currency units of a specified country. —**mil′lionth,** *adj., n.*

mil·lion·aire (mil′yə nâr′), *n.* a person whose wealth amounts to a million or more in the currency units of a specified country. Also, **mil′lion·naire′.**

mil·li·pede (mil′ə pēd′), *n.* an arthropod having a cylindrical body composed of from 20 to over 100 segments, each with two pairs of legs.

mil·li·sec·ond (mil′i sek′ənd), *n.* one thousandth of a second.

mil·li·volt (mil′ə vōlt′), *n.* one thousandth of a volt.

mill·pond (mil′pond′), *n.* a pond for supplying water to drive a mill wheel.

mill·race (mil′rās′), *n.* the channel in which the water driving a mill wheel flows to the mill.

mill·stone (mil′stōn′), *n.* **1.** either of a pair of circular stones between which grain is ground, as in a mill. **2.** any heavy burden.

mill·stream (mil′strēm′), *n.* the stream in a millrace.

mill′ wheel′, a water wheel for driving a mill.

mill·wright (mil′rīt′), *n.* a person who erects the machinery of a mill.

milque·toast (milk′tōst′), *n.* a person who is easily dominated or intimidated.

milt (milt), *n.* **1.** the secretion of the male generative organs of fishes. **2.** the organs themselves.

Mil·ton (mil′t°n), *n.* John, 1608–74, English poet.

Mil·wau·kee (mil wô′kē), *n.* a port in SE Wisconsin.

mime (mīm, mēm), *n., v.,* **mimed, mim·ing.** —*n.* **1.** the art of dramatic representation by gestures only, without words. **2.** a performer specializing in this art. **3.** *Archaic.* a mimic, jester, or clown. —*v.t.* **4.** to portray in mime. —*v.i.* **5.** to play a part as a mime. —**mim′er,** *n.*

mim·e·o (mim′ē ō′), *n., v.t. Informal.* mimeograph.

mim·e·o·graph (mim′ē ə graf′, -gräf′), *n.* **1.** a machine for making copies of material typed, written, or drawn on a stencil placed over an ink-filled drum. —*v.t.* **2.** to make copies of (something) on a mimeograph.

mi·me·sis (mi mē′sis, mī-), *n. Rhet.* imitation of the supposed words of another.

mi·met·ic (mi met′ik, mī-), *adj.* **1.** characterized by or exhibiting mimicry. **2.** mimic (defs. 5, 6). —**mi·met′i·cal·ly,** *adv.*

mim·ic (mim′ik), v., **-icked, -ick·ing,** n., adj. —v.t. 1. to imitate in action, speech, etc., often playfully or derisively. 2. to resemble closely. —n. 3. a person who mimics, esp. a performer skilled in mimicking others. 4. a copy or imitation of something. —adj. 5. being merely an imitation of the true thing, often on a smaller scale. 6. given to imitating. —**mim′ick·er,** n. —Syn. 1. ape, copy, mock.

mim·ic·ry (mim′ik rē), n. the act, practice, or art of mimicking.

mi·mo·sa (mi mō′sə, -zə), n. a herb, shrub, or tree of warm regions having small flowers in globular heads or cylindrical spikes.

min., 1. minimum. 2. mining. 3. minister. 4. minor. 5. minute; minutes.

min·a·ret (min′ə ret′, min′ə ret′), n. a slender tower attached to a mosque.

min·a·to·ry (min′ə tôr′ē, -tōr′ē), adj. Literary. menacing or threatening.

mince (mins), v., **minced, minc·ing.** —v.t. 1. to cut into very small pieces. 2. to soften (one's words), esp. for the sake of decorum. 3. to perform or utter with affected elegance. —v.i. 4. to walk or move with short, affectedly dainty steps. —**minc′er,** n. —**minc′ing,** adj.

mince·meat (mins′mēt′), n. a mixture of minced apples, suet, and sometimes meat, together with raisins, currants, etc., used as a filling for a pie (**mince′ pie′**).

mind (mīnd), n. 1. the part in a human being that reasons, understands, perceives, etc. 2. the faculty of reasoning or understanding. 3. a person considered with relation to his or her intellectual powers. 4. reason or sanity: to lose one's mind. 5. opinion or intentions: to change one's mind. 6. psychic or spiritual being. 7. remembrance or recollection. 8. attention or thoughts. 9. **bear** or **keep in mind,** to remember. 10. **blow one's mind,** Slang. to change one's perceptions, etc., esp. through the use of psychedelic drugs. 11. **in mind,** as a plan or intention. 12. **make up one's mind,** to decide or resolve. 13. **on one's mind,** constantly in one's thoughts. 14. **out of one's mind,** a. insane or mad. b. totally distracted. —v.t. 15. to pay attention to. 16. to heed or obey. 17. to look after. 18. to be careful about. 19. to care about. 20. to regard as concerning oneself. —v.i. 21. to pay attention. 22. to obey. 23. to be careful. 24. to care or object.

mind-blow·ing (mīnd′blō′ing), adj. Slang. 1. astounding or overwhelming. 2. producing an effect similar to that of hallucinogenic drugs.

mind·ed (mīn′did), adj. 1. having a certain kind of mind: strong-minded. 2. inclined or disposed.

mind-ex·pand·ing (mīnd′ik span′ding), adj. heightening perceptions disproportionately, esp. as by the use of hallucinogenic drugs.

mind·ful (mīnd′fəl), adj. carefully attentive. —**mind′ful·ly,** adv. —**mind′ful·ness,** n.

mind·less (mīnd′lis), adj. 1. without intelligence. 2. careless or heedless. —**mind′less·ly,** adv. —**mind′less·ness,** n.

mind′ read′er, a person who professes ability to discern the unexpressed thoughts of others. —**mind′ read′ing.**

mind′s′ eye′, mental vision or imagination.

mine¹ (mīn), pron. 1. a form of the possessive case of I: The yellow sweater is mine. 2. that or those belonging to me: Mine is the car with the flat tire.

mine² (mīn), n., v., **mined, min·ing.** —n. 1. an excavation made in the earth for the purpose of extracting ores, coal, etc. 2. a natural deposit of such minerals. 3. an abundant source: a mine of information. 4. Mil.: a. a subterranean passage beneath the enemy's fortifications. b. an encased explosive charge for destroying ships, land vehicles, or personnel. —v.t., v.i. 5. to dig in (the earth) to obtain ores, etc. 6. to extract (ores, etc.) from a mine. 7. to dig or lay military mines (under). 8. to ruin by secret or slow methods. —**min′er,** n.

mine·lay·er (mīn′lā′ər), n. a naval vessel specially equipped for laying underwater mines.

min·er·al (min′ər əl, min′rəl), n. 1. an inorganic substance occurring in nature, as quartz or feldspar, having a definite chemical composition and usually of definite crystal structure. 2. a substance obtained by mining. 3. any substance that is neither animal nor vegetable. 4. **minerals,** Brit. soft drinks. —adj. 5. of or containing minerals.

min·er·al·ize (min′ər ə līz′, min′rə-), v.t., **-ized, -iz·ing.** 1. to transform (a metal) into an ore. 2. to impregnate or supply with mineral substances.

min′eral jel′ly, a kind of petrolatum used to stabilize certain explosives.

min·er·al·o·gy (min′ə rol′ə jē, -ral′ə-), n. the science or study of minerals. —**min·er·al·og·i·cal** (min′ər ə loj′i kəl), adj. —**min·er·al′o·gist,** n.

min′eral oil′, a colorless, oily, tasteless, water-insoluble liquid obtained from petroleum, used as a laxative.

min′eral spring′, a spring of water that contains a significant amount of dissolved minerals.

min′eral wa′ter, water containing dissolved mineral salts or gases, esp. such water for medicinal use.

Mi·ner·va (mi nûr′və), *n.* the ancient Roman goddess of wisdom and arts.

min·e·stro·ne (min′i strō′nē), *n.* a thick Italian soup of vegetables and chicken or meat and bits of pasta.

mine-sweep·er (mīn′swē′pər), *n.* a naval vessel equipped for removing or defusing enemy mines.

min·gle (miṅg′gəl), *v.,* -gled, -gling. —*v.i.* 1. to become mixed or blended. 2. to associate or mix in company. —*v.t.* 3. to put together in a mixture. —min′gler, *n.*

ming′ tree′ (miṅg), an artificially dwarfed tree resembling a bonsai.

min·i (min′ē), *n. Informal.* 1. miniskirt. 2. anything smaller than is normal. 3. subcompact.

mini-, a combining form meaning: a. very short: *miniskirt.* b. lightweight: *minicar.* c. in reduced size: *minicomputer.* d. of limited scope: *minirecession.*

min·i·a·ture (min′ē ə chər, min′ə chər), *n.* 1. a representation or image of something on a reduced scale. 2. a very small painting, esp. a portrait, as on ivory. —*adj.* 3. on or represented on a very small scale. —min′i·a·tur·ist (-chər ist), *n.*

min·i·a·tur·ize (min′ē ə chə rīz′, min′ə-), *v.t.,* -ized, -iz·ing. to make in a miniature size. —min′i·a·tur·i·za′tion, *n.*

min·i·bike (min′ē bīk′), *n.* a small, low-frame motorcycle.

min·i·bus (min′ē bus′), *n. Chiefly Brit.* a very small bus.

min·im (min′əm), *n.* 1. the smallest unit of liquid measure, roughly equivalent to one drop. 2. *Music.* a half note.

min·i·mal (min′ə məl), *adj.* of or being a minimum. —min′i·mal·ly, *adv.*

min·i·mize (min′ə mīz′), *v.t.,* -mized, -miz·ing. 1. to reduce to the smallest possible amount or degree. 2. to belittle. —min′i·miz′er, *n.*

min·i·mum (min′ə məm), *n.,* pl. -mums, -ma (-mə), *adj.* —*n.* 1. the least quantity, amount, or degree possible or attained. 2. a lower limit allowable by law or regulation. —*adj.* 3. amounting to a minimum.

min·ion (min′yən), *n.* 1. a servile follower. 2. *Often Contemptuous.* any favored person. 3. a minor official.

min·is·cule (min′ə skyōōl′), *adj.* minuscule.

min·i·se·ries (min′ē sēr′ēz), *n.* a series of TV dramas, usually based on a novel and presented in several parts.

min·i·skirt (min′ē skûrt′), *n.* a very short skirt ending three or more inches above the knee. —min′i·skirt′ed, *adj.*

min·i·state (min′ē stāt′), *n.* microstate.

min·is·ter (min′i stər), *n.* 1. a person authorized to conduct religious worship, esp. in a Protestant church. 2. a high official appointed to head an executive department of governmental affairs, as in Europe. 3. a diplomatic representative ranking below an ambassador. 4. *Literary.* an agent or instrument of someone or something. —*v.i.* 5. to give care or aid. 6. to contribute, as to comfort or happiness. —*v.t.* 7. *Obs.* to administer or dispense (a sacrament). —min′is·te′ri·al (-stēr′ē əl), *adj.* —min′is·tra′tion, *n.*

min·is·trant (min′i strənt), *n.* 1. a person who ministers or aids. —*adj.* 2. *Obs.* serving as a religious minister.

min·is·try (min′i strē), *n.,* pl. -tries. 1. the service, functions, or profession of a minister of religion. 2. the body or class of ministers of religion. 3. the service, functions, or office of a minister of state. 4. the body of ministers of state. 5. an executive department headed by a minister of state. 6. the building that houses such a department. 7. the term of office of a minister. 8. *Obs.* ministration or service.

mink (miṅgk), *n.,* pl. minks, mink. 1. a weasellike animal of North America, Europe, and Asia. 2. the valuable fur of this animal, brownish with lustrous outside hairs. 3. a garment made of this fur.

Minn., Minnesota.

Min·ne·ap·o·lis (min′ē ap′ə lis), *n.* a city in SE Minnesota.

min·ne·sing·er (min′i siṅg′ər), *n.* one of a class of German lyric poets and singers of the 12th to 14th centuries. [< G = *Minne* love + *Singer* singer]

Min·ne·so·ta (min′i sō′tə), *n.* a state in the N central United States. *Cap.:* St. Paul. —Min′ne·so′tan, *adj., n.*

min·now (min′ō), *n.,* pl. -nows, -now, a small, freshwater fish, often used as live bait.

mi·nor (mī′nər), *adj.* 1. lesser, as in size, amount, extent, or importance. 2. relatively not serious or risky: *a minor wound.* 3. *Music.* smaller by a half step than the corresponding major. —*n.* 4. a person under legal age. 5. *Educ.* a subject course pursued subordinately to a major. —*v.i.* 6. to follow an academic minor.

mi·nor·i·ty (mi nôr′i tē, -nor′-, mī-), *n.,* pl. -ties. 1. any number less than half the total. 2. a group differing, esp. in race, religion, or ethnic background, from the majority of a population. 3. the state or time of being under legal age.

min·ster (min′stər), *n. Brit.* **1.** a church connected with a monastery. **2.** any large or important church, as a cathedral.

min·strel (min′strəl), *n.* **1.** a medieval poet or musician, either belonging to a noble household or traveling about. **2.** a performer in a minstrel show. —**min′strel·sy** (-sē), *n.*

min′strel show′, a stage show, formerly popular in the U.S., in which white performers with blackened faces sang, danced, and joked.

mint¹ (mint), *n.* **1.** an aromatic herb having opposite leaves and small flowers. **2.** a peppermint-flavored candy. —**mint′y,** *adj.*

mint² (mint), *n.* **1.** a place where money is produced under government authority. **2.** *Informal.* a vast amount, esp. of money. —*adj.* **3.** as issued to the public, without having been used: *a mint stamp.* —*v.t.* **4.** to make (coins) by stamping metal. —**mint′age,** *n.* —**mint′er,** *n.*

mint′ ju′lep, a drink made with bourbon, sugar, and ice, and garnished with sprigs of mint.

min·u·end (min′yŏŏ end′), *n.* a number from which another is subtracted.

min·u·et (min′yŏŏ et′), *n.* **1.** a slow, stately dance, popular in the 17th and 18th centuries. **2.** the music for such a dance.

mi·nus (mi′nəs), *prep.* **1.** decreased by: *ten minus six.* **2.** lacking or without: *a book minus its title page.* —*adj.* **3.** noting subtraction. **4.** algebraically negative: *a minus quantity.* **5.** having negative characteristics. —*n.* **6.** See minus sign. **7.** a minus quantity. **8.** a deficiency or loss.

mi·nus·cule (min′ə skyŏŏl′, mi nus′kyŏŏl), *adj.* **1.** very small. —*n.* **2.** a lower-case letter.

mi′nus sign′, *Arith.* the symbol (—) denoting subtraction or a negative quantity.

min·ute¹ (min′it), *n.* **1.** the sixtieth part of an hour. **2.** a short period of time. **3.** an exact point in time. **4. minutes,** an official record of the meeting of an organization. **5.** the sixtieth part of a degree of angle or arc.

mi·nute² (mī nŏŏt′, -nyŏŏt′, mi-), *adj.* -nut·er, -nut·est. **1.** extremely small, as in size. **2.** of minor importance. **3.** attentive to small details: *a minute examination.* —**mi·nute′ly,** *adv.* —**mi·nute′ness,** *n.*

Min·ute·man (min′it man′), *n., pl.* -men. (*sometimes l.c.*) one of a group of American militiamen during the Revolutionary War who held themselves in readiness for immediate military service.

min′ute steak′ (min′it), a thin piece of beefsteak that can be cooked quickly.

mi·nu·ti·ae (mi nŏŏ′shē ē′, -nyŏŏ′-), *n.pl., sing.* -ti·a (-shē ə, -shə). small or trivial details.

minx (mingks), *n.* a pert, flirtatious girl. —**minx′ish,** *adj.*

Mi·o·cene (mī′ə sēn′), *adj.* **1.** of or noting the fourth epoch of the Tertiary period, characterized by the presence of grazing mammals. —*n.* **2.** the Miocene epoch.

mir·a·cle (mir′ə kəl), *n.* **1.** an event that surpasses all known human or natural powers and is ascribed to a divine or supernatural cause. **2.** an unusually marvelous thing or fact. —**mi·rac·u·lous** (mi rak′yə ləs), *adj.* —**mi·rac′u·lous·ly,** *adv.* —**mi·rac′u·lous·ness,** *n.*

mi·rage (mi räzh′), *n.* **1.** an optical phenomenon by which reflected images of distant objects are seen, often inverted. **2.** something illusory, though seemingly real.

mire (mī°r), *n., v.,* **mired, mir·ing.** —*n.* **1.** a stretch of wet, swampy ground. **2.** slimy soil or deep mud. —*v.t.* **3.** to cause to stick fast in mire. **4.** to soil with mire. —*v.i.* **5.** to sink in mire. —**mir′y,** *adj.*

mir·ror (mir′ər), *n.* **1.** a reflecting surface, usually of glass coated with silver on the back. **2.** a faithful representation. **3.** a pattern for imitation. —*v.t.* **4.** to reflect in or as in a mirror.

mirth (mûrth), *n.* gaiety and merriment, esp. as manifested by laughter. —**mirth′ful,** *adj.* —**mirth′ful·ly,** *adv.* —**mirth′ful·ness,** *n.* —**mirth′less,** *adj.* —**Syn.** glee, hilarity, jollity.

MIRV (mûrv), *n.* a guided missile that carries several warheads, each of which can be aimed at a different target. [*m*(ultiple) *i*(ndependently targeted) *r*(eentry) *v*(ehicle)]

mis-, a prefix meaning: a. wrong, wrongly, or incorrectly: *misprint.* b. lack of: *mistrust.*

mis·ad·ven·ture (mis′əd ven′chər), *n.* a mishap or bad fortune.

mis·al·li·ance (mis′ə lī′əns), *n.* an improper alliance or association, esp. in marriage.

mis·an·thrope (mis′ən thrōp′, miz′-), *n.* a hater of mankind. Also, **mis·an·thro·pist** (mis an′thrə pist, miz-). —**mis·an·throp·ic** (mis′ən throp′ik, miz′-), *adj.* —**mis′an·throp′i·cal·ly,** *adv.* —**mis·an′thro·py,** *n.*

---

mis′ad·dress′, *v.t.*
mis′ad·just′, *v.*
mis′ad·min·is·tra′tion, *n.*

mis′ad·vise′, *v.t.,* -vised, -vising.
mis′a·lign′ment, *n.*

mis·al′pha·bet·ize′, *v.t.,* -ized, -iz·ing.

mis·ap·ply (mis′ə plī′), *v.t.*, **-plied,
-ply·ing.** to apply wrongly or improperly. —**mis′ap·pli·ca′tion** (-ap-
lə kā′shən), *n.*

mis·ap·pre·hend (mis′ap ri hend′), *v.t.*
to misunderstand. —**mis′ap·pre·hen′-
sion,** *n.*

mis·ap·pro·pri·ate (mis′ə prō′pre āt′),
v.t., **-at·ed, -at·ing. 1.** to appropriate wrongly. **2.** to appropriate dishonestly. —**mis′ap·pro′pri·a′tion,** *n.*

mis·be·got·ten (mis′bi got′°n), *adj.* unlawfully or irregularly begotten, esp.
illegitimate.

mis·be·have (mis′bi hāv′), *v.i., v.t.,*
-haved, -hav·ing. to behave (oneself) badly or improperly. —**mis′be-
hav′er,** *n.* —**mis′be·hav′ior** (-yər), *n.*
misc., **1.** miscellaneous. **2.** miscellany.

mis·cal·cu·late (mis kal′kyə lāt′), *v.t.,
v.i.,* **-lat·ed, -lat·ing.** to calculate or
judge incorrectly. —**mis′cal·cu·la′-
tion,** *n.*

mis·call (mis kôl′), *v.t.* to call by a
wrong name.

mis·car·ry (mis kar′ē), *v.i.,* **-ried, -ry-
ing. 1.** to fail to attain the right or
desired end. **2.** to go astray or be
lost in transmission. **3.** to give birth
to a fetus before it can survive, esp.
prematurely. —**mis·car′riage** (-ij), *n.*

mis·cast (mis kast′, -käst′), *v.t.,* **-cast,
-cast·ing.** to cast unsuitably, as a
play or an actor or actress.

mis·ce·ge·na·tion (mis′i jə nā′shən, mi-
sej′ə-), *n.* marriage or cohabitation
between a man and woman of different races.

mis·cel·la·ne·ous (mis′ə lā′nē əs), *adj.*
1. consisting of members or elements
of different kinds. **2.** dealing with
various subjects. —**mis′cel·la′ne·ous-
ly,** *adv.* —**mis′cel·la′ne·ous·ness,** *n.*

mis·cel·la·ny (mis′ə lā′nē), *n., pl.*
-nies. 1. a miscellaneous collection
of various items. **2.** a volume of
literary pieces by several authors,
dealing with various topics.

mis·chance (mis chans′, -chäns′), *n.*
a mishap or misfortune.

mis·chief (mis′chif), *n.* **1.** conduct or
action that is annoying but playful,
esp. by children. **2.** a disposition to
annoy or play pranks. **3.** harm or
trouble done or made by a specific
person or thing, often on purpose. **4.**
a source of such harm or trouble.

mis·chie·vous (mis′chə vəs), *adj.* **1.**
causing or tending to cause prankish
mischief. **2.** harmful or injurious.
—**mis′chie·vous·ly,** *adv.* —**mis′chie-
vous·ness,** *n.*

mis·ci·ble (mis′ə bəl), *adj. Chem.* capable of being mixed. —**mis′ci·bil′-
i·ty,** *n.*

mis·con·ceive (mis′kən sēv′), *v.t., v.i.,*
-ceived, -ceiv·ing. to have an erroneous conception of. —**mis′con-
cep′tion** (-sep′shən), *n.*

mis·con·duct (mis kon′dukt), *n.* **1.**
improper conduct. **2.** unlawful conduct by a public official. **3.** bad or
improper management.

mis·con·strue (mis′kən strōō′), *v.t.,*
-strued, -stru·ing. to misunderstand
the meaning of. —**mis′con·struc′-
tion,** *n.*

mis·count (mis kount′), *v.t., v.i.* **1.** to
count or calculate erroneously. —*n.*
2. an erroneous counting or miscal-
culation.

mis·cre·ant (mis′krē ənt), *adj.* **1.** behaving villainously. —*n.* **2.** a scoundrel or villain.

mis·cue (mis kyōō′), *n., v.,* **-cued, -cu-
ing.** *Informal.* —*n.* **1.** a mistake or
error. —*v.i.* **2.** to make a mistake.

mis·deed (mis dēd′), *n.* an immoral
or wicked deed.

mis·de·mean·or (mis′di mē′nər), *n.* **1.**
a criminal offense defined as less
serious than a felony. **2.** misdeed.

mis·di·rect (mis′di rekt′, -dī-), *v.t.* to
direct or instruct incorrectly. —**mis′-
di·rec′tion,** *n.*

mis·do (mis dōō′), *v.t.,* **-did, -done,
-do·ing.** to do wrongly. —**mis·do′-
er,** *n.* —**mis·do′ing,** *n.*

mise en scène (mē zän sen′), *French.*
1. the stage setting of a play. **2.**
physical environment.

mi·ser (mī′zər), *n.* a person who lives
in wretched circumstances in order
to save and hoard money. —**mi′ser-
ly,** *adj.* —**mi′ser·li·ness,** *n.*

mis·er·a·ble (miz′ər ə bəl, miz′rə-),
adj. **1.** wretchedly unhappy or impoverished. **2.** causing misery. **3.** revealing misery. **4.** worthy of pity.
—**mis′er·a·ble·ness,** *n.* —**mis′er·a-
bly,** *adv.* —**Syn. 1.** disconsolate, forlorn. **4.** deplorable, lamentable.

mis·er·y (miz′ə rē), *n., pl.* **-er·ies. 1.**
distress caused by poverty or pain.
2. great distress of mind. **3.** a cause
or source of such distress. —**Syn.**
anguish, grief, suffering, woe.

mis·fea·sance (mis fē′zəns), *n.* the
wrongful performance of a normally
lawful act. —**mis·feas′or,** *n.*

mis·file (mis fīl′), *v.t.,* **-filed, -fil·ing.**
to file (papers, etc.) incorrectly.

---

mis·ar·range′, *v.t.,*
-ranged, -rang·ing.

mis·ar·range′ment, *n.*

mis·charge′, *v.,*
-charged, -charg·ing.

mis′clas·si·fi·ca′tion, *n.*

mis·clas′si·fy′, *v.t.,*
-fied, -fy·ing.

mis·cop′y, *v.,*
-cop·ied, -cop·y·ing.

mis·deal′, *v.t., v.i,*
-dealt, -deal·ing.

mis·de·fine′, *v.t.,*
-fined, -fin·ing.

mis·ed′u·cate′, *v.t.,*
-cat·ed, -cat·ing.

mis′ed·u·ca′tion, *n.*

mis′em·ploy′, *v.t.*

mis·fire (mis fī°r′), v., -fired, -fir·ing, n. —v.i. 1. to fail to fire, as a gun. 2. to fail to produce the intended effect. —n. 3. an act or instance of misfiring.

mis·fit (mis′fit, mis fit′), n. 1. a bad fit. 2. a person who is badly adjusted to his or her environment.

mis·for·tune (mis fôr′chən), n. 1. bad luck. 2. an unlucky event. —Syn. adversity, calamity, hardship.

mis·giv·ing (mis giv′ing), n. a feeling of doubt, distrust, or apprehension.

mis·gov·ern (mis guv′ərn), v.t. to govern or rule badly. —mis·gov′ern·ment, n.

mis·guide (mis gīd′), v.t., -guid·ed, -guid·ing. to guide wrongly. —mis·guid′ance, n. —mis·guid′ed·ly, adv. —mis·guid′er, n.

mis·han·dle (mis han′dəl), v.t., -dled, -dling. 1. to handle badly. 2. to manage badly.

mis·hap (mis′hap, mis hap′), n. an unfortunate accident of a minor nature.

mish·mash (mish′mosh′, -mash′), n. a confused mess.

mis·in·form (mis′in fôrm′), v.t. to give false or misleading information to. —mis′in·form′ant, n. —mis′in·for·ma′tion, n.

mis·in·ter·pret (mis′in tûr′prit), v.t., v.i. to interpret, explain, or understand incorrectly. —mis′in·ter′pre·ta′tion, n.

mis·judge (mis juj′), v.t., v.i., -judged, -judg·ing. to judge or estimate wrongly or unjustly. —mis·judg′ment, n.

mis·la·bel (mis lā′bəl), v.t., -beled, -bel·ing or -belled, -bel·ling. to label wrongly or falsely.

mis·lay (mis lā′), v.t., -laid, -lay·ing. 1. to put in a place afterward forgotten. 2. to lay or place wrongly. —mis·lay′er, n.

mis·lead (mis lēd′), v.t., -led, -lead·ing. 1. to lead wrongly. 2. to lead into error of conduct or judgment. —mis·lead′ing, adj. —mis·lead′ing·ly, adv. —Syn. deceive, delude.

mis·man·age (mis man′ij), v.t., -aged, -ag·ing. to manage badly or incompetently. —mis·man′age·ment, n.

mis·mar·riage (mis mar′ij), n. an unsuitable or unhappy marriage.

mis·match (mis mach′), v.t. 1. to match badly or unsuitably. —n. 2. a bad or unsatisfactory match.

mis·mate (mis māt′), v.t., v.i., -mat·ed, -mat·ing. to mate unsuitably or wrongly.

mis·name (mis nām′), v.t., -named, -nam·ing. to call by a wrong name.

mis·no·mer (mis nō′mər), n. a misapplied name or designation.

mi·sog·a·my (mi sog′ə mē, mī-), n. hatred of marriage. —mi·sog′a·mist, n.

mi·sog·y·ny (mi soj′ə nē, nī-), n. hatred of women. —mi·sog′y·nous, adj. —mi·sog′y·nist, n.

mis·place (mis plās′), v.t., -placed, -plac·ing. 1. to put in a wrong place. 2. mislay (def. 1). 3. to place or bestow improperly or unwisely.

mis·play (mis plā′), Sports, Games. —n. 1. a wrong play. —v.t., v.i. 2. to play wrongly.

mis·print (n. mis′print′, mis print′; v. mis print′), n. 1. a mistake in printing. —v.t. 2. to print incorrectly.

mis·pri·sion (mis prizh′ən), n. a violation of official duty by one in office.

mis·pro·nounce (mis′prə nouns′), v.t., v.i., -nounced, -nounc·ing. to pronounce incorrectly. —mis′pro·nun′ci·a′tion (-nun′sē ā′shən), n.

mis·quote (mis kwōt′), v., -quot·ed, -quot·ing, n. —v.t. 1. to quote incorrectly. —n. 2. an incorrect quotation. —mis′quo·ta′tion (-kwō tā′shən), n.

mis·read (mis rēd′), v.t., v.i., -read (red), -read·ing. 1. to read incorrectly. 2. to misinterpret, esp. in reading.

mis·rep·re·sent (mis′rep ri zent′), v.t. to represent incorrectly or falsely. —mis′rep·re·sen·ta′tion, n.

mis·rule (mis rool′), n., v., -ruled, -rul·ing. —n. 1. bad rule or government. —v.t. 2. to misgovern.

miss[1] (mis), v.t. 1. to fail to hit or strike. 2. to fail to encounter, meet, or catch. 3. to fail to take advantage of. 4. to fail to be present at or for. 5. to notice the absence or loss of. 6. to regret the absence or loss of. 7. to escape or avoid: *He just missed being caught.* 8. to fail to perceive or understand. —v.i. 9. to fail to hit something. 10. to fail of effect or success. 11. to misfire, as a gun. —n. 12. a failure to hit something. 13. a failure of any kind. 14. a misfire.

miss[2] (mis), n., pl. **miss·es.** 1. (cap.) a title prefixed to the name of an unmarried woman or girl. 2. a young unmarried woman or girl. [short for *mistress*]

Miss., Mississippi.

---

mis·hear′, v.t., -heard, -hear·ing.

mis·i·den·ti·fi·ca′tion, n.

mis′i·den′ti·fy′, v., -fied, -fy·ing.

mis′in·struct′, v.t.

mis·in·struc′tion, n.

mis·num′ber, v.

mis′pro·por′tion, n.

mis′re·port′, v.t., n.

mis·sal (mis′əl), *n. Rom. Cath. Ch.* the book containing the prayers and rites of the Mass for the entire year.

mis·shape (mis shāp′, mish-), *v.t.,* **-shaped, -shaped** or **-shap·en, -shap·ing.** to shape badly or wrongly. — **mis·shap′en,** *adj.*

mis·sile (mis′əl), *n.* **1.** an object or weapon thrown, shot, or otherwise propelled to a target. **2.** See **guided missile. 3.** See **ballistic missile.**

mis·sile·ry (mis′əl rē), *n.* the science of the construction and use of guided missiles. Also, **mis′sil·ry.**

miss·ing (mis′ing), *adj.* lacking, absent, or lost.

mis·sion (mish′ən), *n.* **1.** a group of persons acting on behalf of a government in a foreign country. **2.** a permanent diplomatic establishment abroad. **3.** a military operation or task. **4.** a body of persons sent by a church to carry on religious work, esp. in foreign lands. **5.** the place of operation of such persons. **6.** an assigned or self-imposed duty or task.

mis·sion·ar·y (mish′ə ner′ē), *n., pl.* **-ar·ies,** *adj.* —*n.* **1.** a person sent into a newly settled or foreign region to carry on religious work. —*adj.* **2.** of religious missions or missionaries.

Mis·sis·sip·pi (mis′i sip′ē), *n.* **1.** a state in the S United States. *Cap.:* Jackson. **2.** a river flowing S from N Minnesota to the Gulf of Mexico.

Mis·sis·sip·pi·an (mis′i sip′ē ən), *adj.* **1.** of Mississippi or the Mississippi River. **2.** noting a period of the Paleozoic era, occurring from about 300 million to 350 million years ago and characterized by the increase of land areas and the development of winged insects. —*n.* **3.** a native or inhabitant of Mississippi. **4.** *Geol.* the Mississippian period.

mis·sive (mis′iv). *n. Literary.* a letter, esp. a long, serious one.

Mis·sour·i (mi zŏŏr′ē. -zŏŏr′ə), *n.* **1.** a state in the central United States. *Cap.:* Jefferson City. **2.** a river flowing from SW Montana into the Mississippi. **3.** from **Missouri,** *Informal.* skeptical or requiring proof. —**Mis·sour′i·an,** *adj.*

mis·spell (mis spel′), *v.t., v.i.,* **-spelled** or **-spelt, -spell·ing.** to spell incorrectly.

mis·spend (mis spend′), *v.t.,* **-spent, -spend·ing.** to spend wrongly or wastefully.

mis·state (mis stāt′), *v.t.,* **-stat·ed, -stat·ing.** to state wrongly or falsely. —**mis·state′ment,** *n.*

mis·step (mis step′), *n.* **1.** a wrong step. **2.** an error in conduct.

mist (mist), *n.* **1.** a cloudlike mass of minute globules of water suspended in the atmosphere. **2.** a very thin fog. **3.** something that dims or blurs. —*v.i., v.t.* **4.** to make or become misty.

mis·take (mi stāk′), *n., v.,* **-took** (-stŏŏk′), **-tak·en, -tak·ing.** —*n.* **1.** an error caused by a lack of skill, attention, knowledge, etc. **2.** a wrong judgment or idea. —*v.t.* **3.** to regard or identify wrongly. **4.** to understand or interpret wrongly. —*v.i.* **5.** to make a mistake. —**mis·tak′a·ble,** *adj.* —**Syn. 1.** blunder, fault, inaccuracy, oversight.

mis·tak·en (mi stā′kən), *adj.* **1.** being a mistake. **2.** making a mistake. — **mis·tak′en·ly,** *adv.*

mis·ter (mis′tər), *n.* **1.** (*cap.*) (less commonly used, spelled-out form of *Mr.*). **2.** *Informal.* sir (used in direct address, omitting the name of the man addressed).

mis·tle·toe (mis′əl tō′), *n.* an evergreen plant having white berries that grows as a parasite on various trees, used in Christmas decorations.

mis·tral (mis′trəl, mi sträl′), *n.* a cold, dry, northerly wind common in southern Europe.

mis·treat (mis trēt′), *v.t.* to treat badly or abusively. —**mis·treat′ment,** *n.*

mis·tress (mis′tris), *n.* **1.** a woman in authority, as over a household, an institution, or a servant. **2.** a woman who has the power of controlling something. **3.** something regarded as feminine which has supremacy. **4.** a woman who has a continuing, illicit sexual relationship with a man. **5.** *Brit.* a female schoolteacher. **6.** (*cap.*) a former title corresponding to *Mrs.* or *Miss.*

mis·tri·al (mis trī′əl, -trīl′), *n. Law.* **1.** a trial terminated without conclusion because of some error in the proceedings. **2.** an inconclusive trial, as where the jury cannot agree.

mis·trust (mis trust′), *n.* **1.** lack of trust or confidence. —*v.t.* **2.** to regard with mistrust. —*v.i.* **3.** to be suspicious. —**mis·trust′ful,** *adj.* — **mis·trust′ful·ly,** *adv.* —**mis·trust′ful·ness,** *n.* —**mis·trust′ing·ly,** *adv.*

mist·y (mis′tē), *adj.,* **mist·i·er, mist·i·est. 1.** consisting of or like mist. **2.** dimmed or blurred by or as by mist. —**mist′i·ly,** *adv.* —**mist′i·ness,** *n.*

---

mis·sort′, *v.*
mis·term′, *v.t.*
mis·time′, *v.t.,* **-timed, -tim·ing.**

mis·ti′tle, *v.t.,* **-tled, -tling.**
mis′trans·late′, *v.t., v.i.,* **-lat·ed, -lat·ing.**

mis·tune′, *v.,* **-tuned, -tun·ing.**
mis·type′, *n., v.,* **-typed, -typ·ing.**

mis·un·der·stand (mis'un dər stand'), v.t., v.i., -stood (-stŏŏd'), -stand·ing. 1. to understand wrongly. 2. to fail to understand. —Syn. 1. misinterpret.

mis·un·der·stand·ing (mis'un dər stan'ding), n. 1. a failure to understand. 2. disagreement or dissension. —mis'un·der·stand'ing·ly, adv.

mis·use (n. mis yōōs'; v. mis yōōz'), n., v., -used, -us·ing. —n. 1. wrong or improper use. —v.t. 2. to use wrongly or improperly. 3. to treat abusively.

mite[1] (mīt), n. a small animal related to the spider that is parasitic on animals and plants.

mite[2] (mīt), n. 1. a very small sum of money. 2. a very small object or creature.

mi·ter (mī'tər), n. 1. a tall, richly adorned cap worn by bishops and abbots. 2. an oblique surface formed on a piece of wood so as to butt against an oblique surface on another piece to be joined with it. Also, Brit., mi'tre.

mit·i·gate (mit'ə gāt'), v.t., v.i., -gat·ed, -gat·ing. to make or become less severe, intense, or painful. —mit'i·ga'tion, n. —mit'i·ga'tive, mit'i·ga·to'ry (-gə tôr'ē, -tōr'ē), adj. —mit'i·ga'tor, n.

mi·to·sis (mī tō'sis, mi-), n. the process by which a cell divides to produce two identical cells that differ from the parent cell only in size. —mi·tot'ic (-tot'ik), adj.

mitt (mit), n. 1. a mittenlike hand protector worn esp. by a baseball catcher. 2. Slang. a hand. 3. a long glove that leaves the fingers bare, worn by women.

mit·ten (mit'ən), n. a hand covering enclosing the four fingers together and the thumb separately.

mix (miks), v.t. 1. to put (various materials) together in a single uniform mass. 2. to form or make by blending ingredients: to mix mortar. 3. to combine or join: to mix business and pleasure. 4. to hybridize. —v.i. 5. to become mixed. 6. to associate, as in company. 7. mix up. a. to confuse completely. b. to involve or entangle. —n. 8. the result of mixing. 9. a commercially packaged blend of dry ingredients for easy preparation of a food: a cake mix. —mix'a·ble, adj. —mix'er, n. —Syn. 1. blend merge mingle.

mixed' num'ber, a number consisting of a whole number and a fraction, as 4½ or 4.5.

mixed-up (mikst'up'), adj. suffering from mental confusion.

mixt., mixture.

mix·ture (miks'chər), n. 1. a product of mixing. 2. the act of mixing or state of being mixed.

mix·up (miks'up'), n. a confused state of things.

miz·zen (miz'ən), n. a fore-and-aft sail set on a mizzenmast. Also, miz'en.

miz·zen·mast (miz'ən mast', -mäst'; miz'ən məst), n. the third mast from forward in a vessel having three or more masts. Also, miz'en·mast'.

mk., mark.

Mk., mark (German monetary unit).

MKS, meter-kilogram-second.

mkt., market.

ML, Medieval Latin.

ml, milliliter; milliliters.

Mlle., pl. Miles. Mademoiselle.

mm, millimeter; millimeters.

MM., Messieurs.

Mme., pl. Mmes. Madame.

MN, Minnesota.

Mn, manganese.

mne·mon·ic (nē mon'ik, ni-), adj. helping or intended to aid the memory. —mne·mon'i·cal·ly, adv.

MO, Missouri.

Mo, molybdenum.

Mo., 1. Missouri. 2. Monday.

mo., pl. mos., mo. month.

M.O., 1. mail order. 2. Medical Officer. 3. See modus operandi. 4. money order.

moan (mōn), n. 1. a prolonged, low sound uttered from physical or mental suffering. —v.t., v.i. 2. to utter (with) a moan. 3. to lament or bemoan.

moat (mōt), n. a deep, wide trench, usually filled with water, surrounding a castle or fortress.

mob (mob), n., v., mobbed, mob·bing. —n. 1. a disorderly, riotous, or lawless crowd. 2. Sometimes Disparaging. a. any group of persons, animals, or things. b. the mass of common people. 3. a criminal gang. —v.t. 4. to crowd around noisily. 5. to attack violently in or as in a mob.

mo·bile (mō'bəl or, esp. for 5, mō'bēl'), adj. 1. capable of moving or being moved readily. 2. utilizing motor vehicles for ready movement: a mobile library. 3. changeable or changing easily in expression, mood, etc. 4. permitting individual progress from one social group to another. —n. 5. a piece of sculpture having delicately balanced units that move independently, as when stirred by a breeze. —mo·bil'i·ty (-bil'i tē), n.

Mo·bile (mō'bēl, mō bēl'), n. a seaport in SW Alabama.

mo'bile home', a factory-built dwelling unit capable of being hauled to a semipermanent site.

mo·bi·lize (mō'bə līz'), v.t., v.i., -lized, -liz·ing. to make or become assembled, organized, etc., as for war. —mo'bi·li·za'tion, n. —mo'bi·liz'er, n.

mob·ster (mob'stər), *n.* a member of a criminal gang.

moc·ca·sin (mok'ə sin, -zən), *n.* **1.** a heelless shoe made entirely of soft leather. **2.** a slipper resembling this. **3.** cottonmouth.

mo·cha (mō'kə), *n.* **1.** a choice variety of coffee originally grown in Arabia. **2.** a flavoring obtained from a coffee infusion or a combined infusion of chocolate and coffee.

mock (mok), *v.t.* **1.** to treat with scorn and contempt. **2.** to mimic sportively or derisively. **3.** to defy and render futile. —*v.i.* **4.** to use scorn and contempt. —*adj.* **5.** being an imitation or semblance: *a mock battle.* —**mock·er,** *n.* —**mock'er·y,** *n.* —**mock'ing·ly,** *adv.* —**Syn. 1.** deride, ridicule, taunt.

mock·he·ro·ic (mok'hi rō'ik), *adj.* imitating or burlesquing heroic manner, character, or action: *mock-heroic dignity.*

mock·ing·bird (mok'ing bûrd'), *n.* a songbird of the southern U.S. noted for its ability to mimic the songs of other birds.

mock-up (mok'up'), *n.* a model, often full-scale, for study, testing, or teaching.

mod (mod), *adj.* **1.** bold and unconventional in style of dress. —*n.* **2.** a youth who affects mod fashions.

mod., **1.** moderate. **2.** modern.

mode¹ (mōd), *n.* **1.** a manner of acting or doing. **2.** a particular type or form of something. —**mod'al,** *adj.* —**mo·dal'i·ty,** *n.*

mode² (mōd), *n.* **1.** customary or conventional usage in manners, dress, etc. **2.** a style or fashion.

mod·el (mod'ʾl), *n., adj., v.,* **-eled, -el·ing** or **-elled, -el·ling.** —*n.* **1.** a standard or example for imitation or comparison. **2.** a representation, generally in miniature, to show the structure or serve as a copy of something. **3.** an image, as in clay or wax, to be reproduced in more durable material. **4.** a person or thing that serves as a subject for an artist or photographer. **5.** a person employed to pose with, wear, or use a product for purposes of display or advertising. **6.** a typical form or style. —*adj.* **7.** serving as a model. **8.** worthy of serving as a model: *a model student.* —*v.t.* **9.** to form or plan according to a model. **10.** to make a miniature model of. **11.** to display, esp. by wearing: *to model dresses.* —*v.i.* **12.** to serve or be employed as a model. —**mod'el·er,** *n.* —**Syn. 1.** ideal, prototype.

mod·er·ate (*adj., n.* mod'ər it, mod'rit; *v.* mod'ə rāt'), *adj., n., v.,* **-at·ed, -at·ing.** —*adj.* **1.** not extreme, excessive, or intense. **2.** of medium quality, extent, or amount. **3.** mediocre or fair. **4.** calm or mild, as of the weather. **5.** of or pertaining to moderates, as in politics or religion. —*n.* **6.** a person who is moderate in opinion or opposed to extreme views and actions, esp. in politics or religion. —*v.t., v.i.* **7.** to make or become moderate. **8.** to preside (over or at a public forum, debate, etc.). —**mod'er·ate·ly,** *adv.* —**mod'er·ate·ness,** *n.* —**mod·er·a'tion,** *n.* —**Syn. 1.** reasonable, temperate.

mod·er·a·tor (mod'ə rā'tər), *n.* **1.** a person or thing that moderates. **2.** a presiding officer, as over a public forum, debate, etc.

mod·ern (mod'ərn), *adj.* **1.** of or characteristic of present and recent time. **2.** (*cap.*) of or pertaining to the modern period of development of a language, esp. since the Middle Ages. **3.** contemporary in style or form, as in art or music. **4.** a person of modern times. **5.** a person whose views and tastes are modern. —**mod·er·ni·ty** (mo dûr'ni tē, mō-), *n.* —**mod'ern·ly,** *adv.* —**mod'ern·ness,** *n.*

Mod'ern Eng'lish, the English language since c1475.

mod·ern·ism (mod'ər niz'əm), *n.* a method, idea, or usage characteristic of modern times. —**mod'ern·ist,** *n., adj.* —**mod'ern·is'tic,** *adj.*

mod·ern·ize (mod'ər nīz'), *v.t., v.i.,* **-ized, -iz·ing.** to make or become modern. —**mod'ern·i·za'tion,** *n.* —**mod'ern·iz'er,** *n.*

mod·est (mod'ist), *adj.* **1.** having a moderate or humble estimate of oneself. **2.** reserved or reticent. **3.** showing regard for the decencies of behavior or dress. **4.** not showy or ostentatious. **5.** not too large in amount. —**mod'est·ly,** *adv.* —**mod'es·ty,** *n.* —**Syn. 1, 4.** unassuming, unpretentious. **3.** decorous, demure.

mod·i·cum (mod'ə kəm), *n.* a moderate or small quantity.

mod·i·fy (mod'ə fī'), *v.,* **-fied, -fy·ing.** —*v.t.* **1.** to change somewhat the form or qualities of. **2.** to soften, as one's position or demand. **3.** *Gram.* to limit or specify the meaning of. —**mod'i·fi·ca'tion,** *n.* —**mod'i·fi'er,** *n.* —**Syn. 2.** qualify, temper.

mod·ish (mō'dish), *adj.* in the current fashion or style. —**mod'ish·ly,** *adv.* —**mod'ish·ness,** *n.*

mo·diste (mō dēst'), *n. Obsolesc.* a female maker of or dealer in women's dresses and millinery.

mod·u·lar (moj'ə lər, mod'yə-), *adj.* **1.** of modules. **2.** composed of standardized units for easy construction or flexible arrangement: *a modular home.*

mod·u·late (moj'ə lāt', mod'yə-), v., **-lat·ed, -lat·ing.** —v.t. 1. to adjust to a certain measure or proportion. 2. to vary (the voice) in tone, pitch, or volume. 3. *Radio.* to change the amplitude, frequency, or phase of (a carrier wave). —**mod'u·la'tion,** n. —**mod'u·la·tive, mod'u·la·to'ry,** adj. —**mod'u·la'tor,** n.

mod·ule (moj'ōōl, mod'yōōl), n. 1. a standard or unit for measuring. 2. a separable component for assembly into units of differing size or function. 3. any of the self-contained segments of a spacecraft, designed to perform a particular task: *a lunar module.*

mo·dus o·pe·ran·di (mō'dəs op'ə ran'-dī, -dē), pl. **mo·di o·pe·ran·di** (mō'dī op'ə ran'dī, -dē). *Latin.* mode of operating or working.

mo·gul[1] (mō'gul, -gəl), n. an important, powerful, or influential person.

mo·gul[2] (mō'gəl), n. a bump on a ski slope.

mo·hair (mō'hâr'), n. 1. the fleece of an Angora goat. 2. a fabric or yarn made from this.

Mo·ham·med (mō ham'id), n. Muhammad.

Mo·ham·med·an (mō ham'i dən), n., adj. Muslim. —**Mo·ham'med·an'ism,** n.

Mo·hawk (mō'hôk), n., pl. **-hawks, -hawk.** 1. a member of an Indian tribe formerly living in central New York. 2. the language of the Mohawk Indians.

Mo·he·gan (mō hē'gən), n., pl. **-gans, -gan.** a member of a tribe of Algonquian-speaking Indians formerly dwelling chiefly in Connecticut.

Mo·hi·can (mō hē'kən), n., pl. **-cans, -can.** Mahican.

Mohs' scale' (mōz), a scale of hardness used in mineralogy, expressed in 1 for the softest through 10 for the hardest.

moi·e·ty (moi'i tē), n., pl. **-ties.** 1. *Chiefly Law.* a half. 2. an indefinite portion.

moil (moil), v.i. to work hard.

moi·ré (mwä rā', môr'ā), n. a fabric, as silk, having a watery or wavelike appearance. Also, **moire** (mwär).

moist (moist), adj. slightly wet. —**moist'ly,** adv. —**moist'ness,** n.

mois·ten (moi'sən), v.t., v.i. to make or become moist. —**moist'en·er,** n.

mois·ture (mois'chər, moish'-), n. condensed or diffused liquid, esp. water.

mois·tur·ize (mois'chə rīz', moish'-), v.t., v.i., **-ized, -iz·ing.** to add or restore moisture to (something). —**mois'tur·iz'er,** n.

mol., 1. molecular. 2. molecule.

mo·lar (mō'lər), n. 1. a tooth having a broad biting surface adapted for grinding. —adj. 2. of the molar.

mo·las·ses (mə las'iz), n. a thick, dark-colored syrup produced during the refining of sugar.

mold[1] (mōld), n. 1. a hollow form for giving a particular shape to something molten or plastic. 2. something formed in or on this. 3. the shape given by this. 4. a frame on which something is formed or made. 5. shape or form. 6. a distinctive character or type. —v.t. 7. to work into a required shape or form. 8. to shape or form in or on a mold. —**mold'a·ble,** adj. —**mold'er,** n.

mold[2] (mōld), n. 1. a furry growth of minute fungi forming on vegetable or animal matter exposed to damp. 2. a fungus that produces such a growth. —v.i. 3. to become moldy.

mold[3] (mōld), n. loose, crumbly earth rich in organic matter.

mold·board (mōld'bôrd', -bōrd'), n. the curved metal plate in a plow that turns over the earth from the furrow.

mold·er (mōl'dər), v.i. to turn to dust by natural decay.

mold·ing (mōl'ding), n. 1. the act or process of shaping in a mold. 2. something molded. 3. a strip of contoured wood or other material placed on a wall.

mold·y (mōl'dē), adj., **mold·i·er, mold·i·est.** 1. overgrown or covered with mold. 2. musty, as from decay or age. —**mold'i·ness,** n.

mole[1] (mōl), n. a small, congenital spot on the human skin, usually of a dark color and slightly elevated.

mole[2] (mōl), n. a small, burrowing mammal having velvety fur and very small eyes.

mole[3] (mōl), n. a massive structure of stone used as a breakwater.

mole[4] (mōl), n. the molecular weight of a substance expressed in grams.

mol·e·cule (mol'ə kyōōl'), n. 1. the smallest physical unit of an element or compound that can exist separately and still keep the properties of the original substance. 2. any very small particle. —**mo·lec·u·lar** (mō lek'yə lər, mə-), adj.

mole·hill (mōl'hil'), n. a small ridge of earth raised up by burrowing moles.

mole·skin (mōl'skin'), n. 1. the fur of the mole. 2. a sturdy, napped cotton fabric.

mo·lest (mə lest'), v.t. 1. to disturb so as to cause injury. 2. to make indecent sexual advances to. —**mo·les·ta·tion** (mō'le stā'shən, mol'e-), n. —**mo·lest'er,** n. —**Syn.** 1. annoy, bother.

Mo·lière (mōl yâr'), n. 1622–73, French playwright.

moll (mol), *n. Slang.* a girlfriend of a gangster.

mol·li·fy (mol′ə fī′), *v.t.,* **-fied, -fy·ing.** 1. to soften in feeling or temper. 2. to mitigate or reduce. —**mol′li·fi·ca′tion,** *n.* —**mol′li·fi′er,** *n.* —Syn. 1. appease, pacify.

mol·lusk (mol′əsk), *n.* any of a large group of invertebrates comprising the snails, squids, octopuses, etc., having a soft body often protected by a shell. Also, **mol′lusc.** —**mol·lus·can** (mə lus′kən), **mol·lus·kan,** *adj., n.*

mol·ly·cod·dle (mol′ē kod′ºl), *n., v.,* **-dled, -dling.** —*n.* 1. a man or boy who is used to being coddled. —*v.t.* 2. to coddle or pamper. —**mol′ly·cod′dler,** *n.*

molt (mōlt), *v.i.* 1. to cast or shed the feathers, skin, etc., that will be succeeded by a new growth, as birds, insects, etc. —*n.* 2. the act, process, or instance of molting. —**molt′er,** *n.*

mol·ten (mōl′t′n), *adj.* 1. liquefied by heat. 2. produced by melting and casting. —**mol′ten·ly,** *adv.*

mo·lyb·de·num (mə lib′də nəm, mol′ib dē′nəm), *n. Chem.* a silver-white, metal element, used in alloys. *Symbol:* Mo; *at. wt.:* 95.94; *at. no.:* 42.

mom (mom), *n. Informal.* mother (def. 1).

m.o.m., middle of month.

mom-and-pop (mom′ən pop′), *adj. Informal.* of a small retail business owned and operated by a family: *a mom-and-pop grocery.*

mo·ment (mō′mənt), *n.* 1. an indefinitely short period of time. 2. the present or any other particular instant: *busy at the moment.* 3. a definite period or stage. 4. importance or consequence.

mo·men·tar·i·ly (mō′mən târ′ə lē, mo′mən ter′-), *adv.* 1. for a moment. 2. at any moment. 3. *Rare.* from moment to moment.

mo·men·tar·y (mō′mən ter′ē), *adj.* 1. lasting but a moment. 2. occurring at any moment. 3. *Rare.* recurring at every moment. —Syn. 1. ephemeral, transitory. 2. imminent.

mo·men·tous (mō men′təs), *adj.* of great importance or consequence. —**mo·men′tous·ly,** *adv.* —**mo·men′tous·ness,** *n.*

mo·men·tum (mō men′təm), *n., pl.* **-ta** (-tə), **-tums.** 1. the motion of a body or system, equal to the product of the mass of a body and its velocity. 2. **a.** the force of movement. **b.** impetus, as in social event.

mom·my (mom′ē), *n., pl.* **-mies.** *Informal.* mother (def. 1).

Mon., 1. Monday. 2. Monsignor.

Mon·a·co (mon′ə kō′, mə nä′kō), *n.* a principality on the Mediterranean coast, bordering SE France.

mon·arch (mon′ərk), *n.* 1. a hereditary sovereign, as a king, queen, or emperor. 2. a person or thing that holds a dominant position. 3. a large, reddish-brown butterfly having black and white markings. [< LL *monarcha* < Gk *monárchēs* ruling alone] —**mo·nar·chi·cal** (mə när′ki·kəl), **mo·nar′chic,** *adj.*

mon·ar·chism (mon′ər kiz′əm), *n.* 1. the principles of monarchy. 2. the advocacy of monarchical rule. —**mon′ar·chist,** *n., adj.* —**mon′ar·chist′ic,** *adj.*

mon·ar·chy (mon′ər kē), *n., pl.* **-chies.** 1. government by a monarch. 2. a country or nation ruled by a monarch.

mon·as·ter·y (mon′ə ster′ē), *n., pl.* **-ter·ies.** a place of residence occupied by a community of monks. —**mon′as·te′ri·al** (-stēr′ē əl), *adj.*

mo·nas·tic (mə nas′tik), *adj.* of or characteristic of monks or monasteries. Also, **mo·nas′ti·cal.** —**mo·nas′ti·cal·ly,** *adv.*

mo·nas·ti·cism (mə nas′ti siz′əm), *n.* the monastic system, condition, or mode of life.

mon·au·ral (mon ôr′əl), *adj. Obsolesc.* monophonic. —**mon·au′ral·ly,** *adv.*

Mon·dale (mon′dāl′), *n.* **Wal·ter F(rederick)** (wôl′tər) ("Fritz"), born 1928, 42nd vice president of the U.S. since 1977.

Mon·day (mun′dē, -dā), *n.* the second day of the week.

mon·e·tar·ism (mon′i ter′iz əm), *n. Econ.* a theory that changes in the money supply determine the direction of a nation's economy. —**mon′e·tar·ist,** *n., adj.*

mon·e·tar·y (mon′i ter′ē, mun′-), *adj.* 1. of the coinage or currency of a country. 2. of or pertaining to money. —**mon·e·tar·i·ly** (mon′i târ′ə lē, mun′-), *adv.*

mon·ey (mun′ē), *n., pl.* **mon·eys, mon·ies.** 1. any of various objects, esp. coins and banknotes, issued by a government and accepted as a medium of exchange and measure of value. 2. property considered with reference to its pecuniary value. 3. wealth considered in terms of money. 4. pecuniary profit. 5. **in the money,** *Slang.* **a.** having a great deal of money. **b.** first, second, or third place in a contest, esp. a horse or dog race. 6. **make money,** to make a profit.

mon·ey·bag (mun′ē bag′), *n.* 1. a bag for money. 2. **moneybags,** *Informal.* a wealthy person.

mon·eyed (mun'ēd), *adj.* **1.** having money. **2.** consisting of or representing money.

mon·ey·lend·er (mun'ē len'dər), *n.* a person whose business it is to lend money at interest.

mon·ey·mak·er (mun'ē mā'kər), *n.* **1.** a person engaged in or successful at acquiring money. **2.** something that yields pecuniary profit. **—mon'ey·mak'ing,** *adj., n.*

mon'ey of account', a monetary denomination used in reckoning value in transactions or accounts.

mon'ey or'der, an order for the payment of a specified, usually limited amount of money, as one issued by one bank and payable at another.

mon'ey supply', *Econ.* the sum of demand or checking-account deposits and currency in the hands of the public.

mon'ey tree', **1.** a legendary or imaginary tree that, when shaken, sheds coins or paper money. **2.** *Informal.* a good source of money or revenues.

mon·ger (mung'gər, mong'-), *n.* **1.** a person promoting something considered contemptible (used in combination): *a rumormonger.* **2.** *Brit.* a dealer or trader (used in combination): *cheesemonger.*

Mon·gol (mong'gəl, -gol, -gōl, mon'-), *n.* **1.** a member of a pastoral people now living chiefly in Mongolia. **2.** a person having Mongoloid characteristics. **3.** any Mongolian language. **—adj. 4.** Mongolian.

Mon·go·li·a (mong gō'lē ə, mon-), *n.* a region in E central Asia including a country (**Mongo'lian Peo'ple's Repub'lic**) and a region in N China (**In'ner Mongo'lia**).

Mon·go·li·an (mong gō'lē ən, mon-), *adj.* **1.** of Mongolia, its inhabitants, or their languages. **2.** Mongoloid (def. 3). **3.** of the Mongolian languages. **—n. 4.** a native of Mongolia. **5.** a group of languages spoken in Mongolia.

Mon·gol·ic (mong gol'ik, mon-), *adj.* **1.** Mongolian (def. 3). **—n. 2.** Mongolian (def. 5).

Mon·gol·ism (mong'gə liz'əm, mon'-), *n.* the abnormal condition of a child born with a wide, flattened skull and generally a mental deficiency.

Mon·gol·oid (mong'gə loid', mon'-), *n.* **1.** a member of one of the major traditional racial groups of human beings marked by straight black hair, a small nose, and a broad face, usually including the Mongols, Chinese, Koreans, Japanese, etc. **—adj. 2.** of or belonging to this group. **3.** of or affected with Mongolism.

mon·goose (mong'gōōs', mon'-), *n., pl.* **-goos·es.** a slender, ferretlike mammal of India, noted esp. for its ability to kill cobras and other venomous snakes.

mon·grel (mung'grəl, mong'-), *n.* **1.** any animal or plant, esp. a dog, resulting from the crossing of different breeds or varieties. **—adj. 2.** of mixed breed, nature, or origin.

mon·ied (mun'ēd), *adj.* moneyed.

mon·i·ker (mon'ə kər), *n. Slang Obsolesc.* a person's name, esp. a nickname. Also, **mon'ick·er.**

mon·ism (mon'iz əm, mō'niz əm), *n.* a metaphysical view that reality consists of a single element. **—mon'ist,** *n.* **—mo·nis'tic** (mə nis'tik, mō-), *adj.*

mo·ni·tion (mō nish'ən, mə-), *n. Literary.* admonition or warning.

mon·i·tor (mon'i tər), *n.* **1.** a pupil appointed to assist the teacher. **2.** a device for observing, detecting, or recording the operation of a machine or system. **3.** *Radio and Television.* a receiving apparatus used to check the quality of audio or video transmission. **—v.t. 4.** *Radio and Television.* to view or listen to (television or radio transmissions) in order to check video or audio quality. **5.** to observe, detect, or record (an operation or condition) with instruments. **6.** to check and keep track of for purposes of control, surveillance, etc.

mon·i·to·ry (mon'i tōr'ē, -tôr'ē), *adj. Literary.* serving to admonish or warn.

monk¹ (mungk), *n.* a man who is a member of a monastic order within any religion. **—monk'ish,** *adj.* **—monk'ish·ly,** *adv.* **—monk'ish·ness,** *n.*

monk² (mungk), *n. Slang.* a monkey.

mon·key (mung'kē), *n., pl.* **-keys,** *v.,* **-keyed, -key·ing. —n. 1.** any mammal of the primates excluding humans, the anthropoid apes, and the lemurs, esp. one of the group having narrow faces and long tails. **—v.i. 2.** *Informal.* to play or trifle idly.

mon'key busi'ness, *Slang.* **1.** underhanded conduct. **2.** mischievous behavior.

mon·key·shine (mung'kē shīn'), *n.* Usually, **monkeyshines.** *Slang.* a mischievous trick.

mon'key wrench', **1.** a wrench having an adjustable jaw. **2. throw a monkey wrench into,** *Slang.* to interfere with the functioning of.

monk's' cloth', a heavy cotton fabric in a basket weave, used for curtains, etc.

monks·hood (mungks'hŏŏd'), *n.* a poisonous plant with flowers having a large, hood-shaped sepal.

mon·o¹ (mon′ō), *n. Informal* mononucleosis.

mon·o² (mon′ō), *adj.* monophonic.

mono-, a prefix meaning: **a.** alone, single, or one: *monogamy*. **b.** containing one atom of a particular element: *monoxide*.

mon·o·chro·mat·ic (mon′ə krō mat′ik, -ō krə-), *adj.* **1.** of or having one color. **2.** of or producing one-color light of a single wavelength. —**mon′o·chro·mat′i·cal·ly,** *adv.* —**mon′o·chro′ma·tic′i·ty** (-mə tis′i tē), *n.*

mon·o·chrome (mon′ə krōm′), *adj.* of or having tones of one color in addition to the ground hue.

mon·o·cle (mon′ə kəl), *n.* an eyeglass for one eye. —**mon′o·cled,** *adj.*

mon·o·cot·y·le·don (mon′ə kot′°lēd′-°n), *n.* a flowering plant characterized by the presence of only one seed leaf. —**mon′o·cot′y·le′don·ous,** *adj.*

mo·noc·u·lar (mə nok′yə lər), *adj.* **1.** having only one eye. **2.** of or intended for the use of only one eye.

mon·o·dy (mon′ə dē), *n., pl.* -**dies.** a poem in which a single mourner laments. —**mo·nod·ic** (mə nod′ik), *adj.* —**mon′o·dist** (mon′ə dist), *n.*

mo·nog·a·my (mə nog′ə mē), *n.* marriage with only one person at a time. —**mo·nog′a·mist,** *n.* —**mo·nog′a·mous, mon·o·gam·ic** (mon′ə gam′ik), *adj.* —**mo·nog′a·mous·ly,** *adv.*

mon·o·gram (mon′ə gram′), *n., v.,* -**grammed, -gram·ming.** —*n.* **1.** a design consisting of the interlaced initials of a name, often printed on stationery. —*v.t.* **2.** to decorate with a monogram.

mon·o·graph (mon′ə graf′, -gräf′), *n.* a learned treatise on a particular subject. —**mo·nog·ra·pher** (mə nog′rə fər), *n.* —**mon·o·graph·ic** (mon′ə graf′ik), *adj.*

mon·o·lin·gual (mon′ə ling′gwəl), *adj.* **1.** knowing only one language. **2.** expressed in only one language.

mon·o·lith (mon′ə lith), *n.* **1.** a single block of stone, esp. one fashioned as an obelisk or monument. **2.** something having a uniform, massive, or rigid quality or character. —**mon·o·lith′ic,** *adj.*

mon·o·logue (mon′ə lôg′, -log′), *n.* **1.** a prolonged talk by a single speaker. **2.** a dramatic soliloquy. Also, **mon′o·log′.** —**mon·o·log·ist** (mon′ə lôg′-ist, -log′-, mə nol′ə jist), **mon·o·logu·ist** (mon′ə lôg′ist, -log′-), *n.*

mon·o·ma·ni·a (mon′ə mā′nē ə, -mān′yə), *n.* **1.** an exaggerated zeal for or interest in a single subject. **2.** a mental disorder in which the person's mind is confined to one idea. —**mon′o·ma′ni·ac** (-ak′), *n., adj.* —**mon′o·ma·ni′a·cal** (-mə nī′ə kəl), *adj.*

mon·o·mer (mon′ə mər), *n.* a molecule capable of reacting with other molecules to form a polymer.

mo·no·mi·al (mō nō′mē əl, mə-), *Algebra.* —*adj.* **1.** consisting of one term only. —*n.* **2.** a monomial expression or quantity.

mon·o·nu·cle·o·sis (mon′ə nōō′klē ō′sis, -nyōō′-), *n.* an acute infectious disease characterized by sudden fever, a benign swelling of lymph nodes, etc.

mon·o·phon·ic (mon′ə fon′ik), *adj.* of or noting a system of sound recording or reproduction using only a single channel. —**mon′o·phon′i·cal·ly,** *adv.*

mon·o·plane (mon′ə plān′), *n.* an airplane with only one set of wings.

mo·nop·o·ly (mə nop′ə lē), *n., pl.* -**lies.** **1.** exclusive control of a commodity or service in a particular market, or a control that makes possible the manipulation of prices. **2.** an exclusive privilege to carry on a traffic or service, granted by a government. **3.** the exclusive control of something. **4.** something that is the subject of such control. **5.** a company or group that has such control. —**mo·nop′o·list,** *n., adj.* —**mo·nop′o·lis′tic,** *adj.* —**mo·nop′o·lize′** (-līz′), *v.t.* —**mo·nop′o·li·za′tion,** *n.*

mon·o·rail (mon′ə rāl′), *n.* **1.** a railroad whose trains run on a single rail, either on the ground or overhead. **2.** the rail of such a railroad.

mon·o·so·di·um glu·ta·mate (mon′ə sō′dē əm glōō′tə māt′), a white, crystalline, water-soluble powder, used for flavoring foods.

mon·o·syl·la·ble (mon′ə sil′ə bəl), *n.* a word of one syllable, as *yes* or *no.* —**mon′o·syl·lab′ic** (-si lab′ik), *adj.* —**mon′o·syl·lab′i·cal·ly,** *adv.*

mon·o·the·ism (mon′ə thē iz′əm, mon′-ə thē′iz əm), *n.* the doctrine or belief that there is only one God. —**mon′o·the′ist,** *n., adj.* —**mon′o·the·is′tic,** *adj.*

mon·o·tone (mon′ə tōn′), *n.* **1.** a vocal utterance in one unvaried tone. **2.** a single tone without variation in pitch. **3.** sameness of style, as in writing.

mo·not·o·nous (mə not′°nəs), *adj.* **1.** tiresomely uniform. **2.** sounded or uttered in one unvaried tone. —**mo·not′o·nous·ly,** *adv.* —**mo·not′o·nous·ness,** *n.* —**mo·not′o·ny,** *n.* —**Syn. 1.** boring, dull, humdrum, tedious.

mon·ox·ide (mon ok′sīd, mə nok′-), *n.* an oxide containing one oxygen atom in each molecule.

Mon·roe (mən rō′), *n.* **James,** 1758–1831, 5th president of the U.S. 1817–25.

Mon·sei·gneur (môN se nyœR′), *n., pl.* **Mes·sei·gneurs** (mā se nyœR′). a French title of princes and bishops.

mon·sieur (mə syœr′), *n.*, *pl.* **mes·sieurs** (mes′ərz; *Fr.* mā syœr′). *French.* Mr. or sir.

Mon·si·gnor (mon sē′nyər), *n.*, *pl.* **Mon·si·gnors, Mon·si·gno·ri** (mōn′sē nyō′rē). *Rom. Cath. Ch.* a title of certain prelates.

mon·soon (mon sōōn′), *n.* **1.** the seasonal wind of the Indian Ocean and southern Asia. **2.** the season during which this wind blows from the southwest, commonly marked by heavy rains. —**mon·soon′al,** *adj.*

mon·ster (mon′stər), *n.* **1.** an animal or plant of abnormal form or structure. **2.** a fabled animal combining human and animal features, as a centaur. **3.** a person who excites horror, as by wickedness. **4.** any animal or thing of huge size. —*adj.* **5.** huge or enormous. —**mon·stros′i·ty** (-stros′i tē), *n.* —**mon′strous,** *adj.* —**mon′strous·ly,** *adv.* —**mon′strous·ness,** *n.*

mon·strance (mon′strəns), *n. Rom. Cath. Ch.* a receptacle in which the consecrated Host is exposed for adoration.

Mont., Montana.

mon·tage (mon täzh′), *n.* **1.** a photographic image produced by combining parts of different photographs by superimposition, etc. **2.** *Motion Pictures.* juxtaposition or partial superimposition of several shots to form a single image.

Mon·tan·a (mon tan′ə), *n.* a state in the NW United States. *Cap.:* Helena. —**Mon·tan′an,** *adj., n.*

Mon·te Car·lo (mon′tē kär′lō), a town in Monaco: gambling resort.

Mon·tes·so·ri meth·od (mon′ti sōr′ē), a system for instructing young children with special emphasis on the training of the senses. [after Maria Montessori (1870–1952), Ital. educator]

Mon·te·vi·de·o (mon′tə vi dā′ō), *n.* the capital of Uruguay.

Mont·gom·er·y (mont gum′ə rē, -gum′rē), *n.* the capital of Alabama.

month (munth), *n.* **1.** any of the twelve parts into which the calendar year is divided. **2.** a period of about four weeks or 30 days. **3.** one twelfth of the solar year.

month·ly (munth′lē), *adj., n., pl.* **-lies,** *adv.* —*adj.* **1.** happening or done once a month. **2.** continuing or lasting for a month. —*n.* **3.** a periodical published once a month. —*adv.* **4.** once a month.

Mont·pel·ier (mont pēl′yər), *n.* the capital of Vermont.

Mont·re·al (mon′trē ôl′, mun′-), *n.* a seaport in S Quebec, in SE Canada.

mon·u·ment (mon′yə mənt), *n.* **1.** something built or placed to commemorate a person, event, etc. **2.** a building or a natural site preserved for its beauty or historical interest. **3.** any enduring evidence or notable example of something.

mon·u·men·tal (mon′yə men′t°l), *adj.* **1.** of enduring significance. **2.** massive or imposing. **3.** conspicuously great: *monumental stupidity.* **4.** of or serving as a monument. —**mon′u·men′tal·ly,** *adv.*

moo (mōō), *v.,* **mooed, moo·ing,** *n., pl.* **moos.** —*v.i.* **1.** to utter the characteristic sound of a cow. —*n.* **2.** a mooing sound.

mooch (mōōch), *v.t., v.i. Slang.* to obtain (money, food, etc.) by cadging shamelessly. —**mooch′er,** *n.*

mood¹ (mōōd), *n.* **1.** a person's emotional state or outlook. **2.** a prevailing response or feeling.

mood² (mōōd), *n. Gram.* a set of categories for a verb used to indicate whether the verb expresses a statement, a command, or a supposition.

mood·y (mōō′dē), *adj.,* **mood·i·er, mood·i·est.** **1.** given to gloomy moods. **2.** revealing such a mood. **3.** exhibiting varying moods. —**mood′i·ly,** *adv.* —**mood′i·ness,** *n.* —**Syn. 1.** glum, morose. **3.** temperamental.

moon (mōōn), *n.* **1.** the earth's natural satellite, orbiting the earth about every 29½ days and shining by reflecting the sunlight. **2.** any planetary satellite. **3.** something shaped like an orb or a crescent. —*v.i. Informal.* **4.** to indulge in sentimental reveries.

moon·beam (mōōn′bēm′), *n.* a ray of moonlight.

moon·light (mōōn′līt′), *n.* **1.** the light of the moon. —*v.i.* **2.** *Informal.* to work at an additional job after a regular one. —**moon′light′er,** *n.* —**moon′light′ing,** *n.* —**moon′lit′** (-lit), *adj.*

moon·scape (mōōn′skāp′), *n.* **1.** the surface of the moon. **2.** an artistic representation of it.

moon·shine (mōōn′shīn′), *n.* **1.** *Informal.* whiskey illegally distilled in rural areas. **2.** moonlight. **3.** empty or foolish talk. —**moon′shin′er,** *n.*

moon·shot (mōōn′shot′), *n.* the launching of a rocket or spacecraft to the moon.

moon·stone (mōōn′stōn′), *n.* a pearly-blue variety of feldspar used as a gem.

moon·struck (mōōn′struk′), *adj.* **1.** mentally deranged. **2.** dreamily romantic. Also, **moon·strick·en** (mōōn′strik′ən).

moon·walk (mōōn′wôk′), *n.* an exploratory walk by an astronaut on the moon's surface.

moor¹ (mōōr), *n. Brit.* a tract of open, peaty, wasteland, often overgrown with heather.

moor² (mŏŏr), *v.t.* **1.** to secure (a ship, dirigible, etc.) in a particular place. **2.** to fix firmly. —*v.i.* **3.** to moor one's ship, dirigible, etc. —**moor'age,** *n.*

Moor (mŏŏr), *n.* a Muslim of the mixed Berber and Arab people inhabiting NW Africa. —**Moor'ish,** *adj.*

moor·ings (mŏŏr'ĭngz), *n.pl.* **1.** the means by which a vessel is moored. **2.** a place where a vessel may be moored. **3.** sources of one's stability or security.

moor·land (mŏŏr'land'), *n. Brit.* moor¹.

moose (mōōs), *n., pl.* **moose.** a large animal of the deer family, inhabiting Canada and the northern U.S. **2.** the European elk.

moot (mōōt), *adj.* **1.** subject to argument or debate: *a moot point.* **2.** *Law.* for debating or trying hypothetical cases: *a moot court.* —*v.t.* **3.** to present or introduce for debate. —**Syn. 1.** doubtful, unsettled.

mop (mŏp), *n., v.,* **mopped, mop·ping.** —*n.* **1.** a device consisting of a bundle of absorbent yarn or cloth or of a sponge attached to the end of a long handle, used for cleaning floors. **2.** *Slang.* a thick mass of hair. —*v.t.* **3.** to clean with or as with a mop. **4.** **mop up,** *a. Mil.* to clear of surviving enemy combatants. **b.** *Informal.* to complete or finish.

mope (mōp), *v.i.,* **moped, mop·ing.** to be sunk in listless apathy. —**mop'er,** *n.* —**mop'ey, mop'y, mop'ish,** *adj.*

mo·ped (mō'ped), *n.* a low-powered, heavily built motorized bicycle, operable usually without a driver's license. [*mo(tor)* + *ped(al)*] —**mo'ped'er,** *n.*

mop·pet (mŏp'ĭt), *n. Informal.* a young child.

mop-up (mŏp'up'), *n.* the act or an instance of mopping up.

mo·raine (mə rān'), *n.* a mass of boulders, gravel, etc., carried in or on a glacier.

mor·al (môr'əl, mŏr'-), *adj.* **1.** of or concerned with principles of right or wrong conduct. **2.** being in accordance with such principles. **3.** capable of recognizing and conforming to such principles. **4.** behaving according to such principles. **5.** virtuous in sexual matters. **6.** of, pertaining to, or acting on the mind: *moral support.* **7.** depending upon what is observed, as of human nature, rather than upon factual evidence: *moral evidence.* —*n.* **8.** a moral teaching or lesson contained in a story or experience. **9.** **morals,** principles or habits with respect to right or wrong conduct. —**mor'al·ly,** *adv.* —**Syn. 4.** ethical,

honorable, upright. **9.** ethics, standards.

mo·rale (mə ral'), *n.* the moral or mental condition of a person or group with respect to cheerfulness, confidence, etc.

mor·al·ist (môr'ə list, mor'-), *n.* **1.** a person who teaches or studies morals. **2.** a person who believes in regulating the morals of others. —**mor'al·is'tic,** *adj.* —**mor'al·is'ti·cal·ly,** *adv.*

mo·ral·i·ty (mə ral'ĭ tē, mô-), *n., pl.* **-ties. 1.** conformity to the rules of right or wrong conduct. **2.** moral quality or conduct. **3.** a doctrine of morals.

mor·al·ize (môr'ə līz', mor'-), *v.i.,* **-ized, -iz·ing.** to make moral reflections, often on self-righteous grounds. —**mor'al·i·za'tion,** *n.* —**mor'al·iz'er,** *n.*

mo·rass (mə ras'), *n.* **1.** a tract of low, soft, wet ground. **2.** any entangling or troublesome situation.

mor·a·to·ri·um (môr'ə tōr'ē əm, -tôr'-, mor'-), *n., pl.* **-to·ri·ums, -to·ri·a** (-tōr'ē ə, -tôr'-). **1.** a legal authorization to delay the payment of debts. **2.** a temporary cessation of activity.

mo·ray (môr'ā, mor'ā), *n.* a dangerous, vividly colored eel found in tropical seas.

mor·bid (môr'bĭd), *adj.* **1.** suggesting an unhealthy mental state. **2.** affected by or characteristic of disease. **3.** gruesome or grisly. —**mor·bid'i·ty,** *n.* —**mor'bid·ly,** *adv.* —**mor'bid·ness,** *n.*

mor·dant (môr'dⁿnt), *adj.* **1.** caustic or sarcastic, as in expression. —*n.* **2.** a substance used in dyeing to fix the coloring matter. —**mor'dan·cy,** *n.* —**mor'dant·ly,** *adv.*

more (môr, mōr), *adj., compar. of* **much** *or* **many** *with* **most** *as superl.* **1.** in greater amount or degree. **2.** in greater quantity or number. **3.** additional or further: *more pencils; more time.* **4.** a greater amount or degree. **5.** an additional quantity or number. **6.** an additional number of persons or things. —*adv., compar. of* **much** *with* **most** *as superl.* **7.** in or to a greater extent or degree. **8.** in addition. **9.** **more or less,** *a.* to some extent. *b.* approximately.

mo·rel (mə rel'), *n.* any of several edible mushrooms having spongy caps.

more·o·ver (môr ō'vər, mōr-, môr'ō'vər, mōr'-), *adv.* beyond what has been said.

mo·res (môr'āz, -ēz), *n.pl.* folkways of central importance embodying the fundamental moral views of a group.

morgue (môrg), *n.* **1.** a place in which the bodies of unidentifed dead persons are kept pending identification or burial. **2.** a reference file of old clippings, photographs, etc., in a newspaper office.

mor·i·bund (môr′ə bund′, mor′-), *adj.* in a dying state. —**mor′i·bun′di·ty,** *n.* —**mor′i·bund/ly,** *adv.*

Mor·mon (môr′mən), *n.* a member of the Church of Jesus Christ of Latter-day Saints founded in the U.S. in 1830. —**Mor′mon·ism,** *n.*

morn (môrn), *n. Literary.* morning.

morn·ing (môr′ning), *n.* **1.** the first part of the day, from midnight, or esp. dawn, to noon. **2.** the early period of anything.

morn′ing glo′ry, a twining plant having funnel-shaped flowers of various colors.

morn′ing sick′ness, nausea occurring in the early part of the day, as a characteristic symptom in the first months of pregnancy.

morn′ing star′, any bright planet seen in the east immediately before sunrise.

Mo·roc·co (mə rok′ō), *n.* **1.** a country in NW Africa. **2.** (*l.c.*) a fine, pebble-grained leather made from goatskin tanned with sumac. —**Mo·roc′can** (mə rok′ən), *adj., n.*

mo·ron (môr′on, mōr′-), *n.* **1.** *Obsolesc.* a person incapable of developing beyond a mental age of 8–12. **2.** any stupid person. —**mo·ron·ic** (mə ron′ik), *adj.* —**mo·ron′i·cal·ly,** *adv.*

mo·rose (mə rōs′), *adj.* gloomily or sullenly ill-humored. —**mo·rose′ly,** *adv.* —**mo·rose′ness,** *n.*

mor·pheme (môr′fēm), *n.* a minimal grammatical unit that cannot be divided into smaller meaningful parts, as *the, write,* or the *-ed* of *waited.* —**morphem′ic,** *adj.*

mor·phine (môr′fēn), *n.* a bitter alkaloid obtained from opium and used in medicine to relieve acute pain or induce sleep. Also, **mor′phi·a** (-fē ə).

mor·phol·o·gy (môr fol′ə jē), *n.* **1.** the branch of biology dealing with the form and structure of plants and animals. **2.** the study of patterns of word formation in a language. — **mor′pho·log′i·cal** (-fə loj′i kəl), *adj.* —**mor′pho·log′i·cal·ly,** *adv.* —**mor·phol′o·gist,** *n.*

mor·row (môr′ō, mor′ō), *n.* **1.** *Literary.* **a.** tomorrow. **b.** the next day. **2.** *Archaic.* the morning.

Morse′ code′ (môrs), a system of combining dots, dashes, and spaces to represent letters, numbers, etc., used in telegraphy. [after S. F. B. *Morse* (1791–1872), U.S. inventor]

mor·sel (môr′səl), *n.* **1.** a bite or small portion of food. **2.** a delicious tidbit. **3.** a small piece or quantity of anything.

mor·tal (môr′t³l), *adj.* **1.** subject to death. **2.** of humans as subject to death. **3.** of or pertaining to death. **4.** involving spiritual death: *mortal sin.* **5.** causing or liable to cause death. **6.** deadly or implacable: *a mortal enemy.* **7.** severe or dire: *in mortal fear.* —*n.* **8.** a human being. —**mor′tal·ly,** *adv.* —**Syn. 5.** fatal.

mor·tal·i·ty (môr tal′i tē), *n., pl.* **-ties.** **1.** the state or condition of being subject to death. **2.** the relative frequency of death in a population. **3.** death or destruction on a large scale.

mor·tar¹ (môr′tər), *n.* **1.** a thick bowl in which substances are powdered with a pestle. **2.** a cannon very short in proportion to its bore, for throwing shells at high angles.

mor·tar² (môr′tər), *n.* a mixture of lime or cement with sand and water, used to bond bricks or stones into a structure. —**mor′tar·less,** *adj.* —**mor′tar·y,** *adj.*

mor·tar·board (môr′tər bôrd′, -bōrd′), *n.* **1.** a square board used by masons to hold mortar. **2.** an academic cap with a square, flat top and a tassel.

mort·gage (môr′gij), *n., v.,* **-gaged, -gag·ing.** —*n.* **1.** a transfer of real property to a creditor as security for a loan. **2.** the deed by which such a transaction is effected. —*v.t.* **3.** to transfer or place (real property) under a mortgage. **4.** to place under advance obligation. —**mort′ga·gor, mort′gag·er,** *n.*

mort·ga·gee (môr′gə jē′), *n.* a person to whom property is mortgaged.

mor·ti·cian (môr tish′ən), *n.* See **funeral director.**

mor·ti·fy (môr′tə fī′), *v.,* **-fied, -fy·ing.** —*v.t.* **1.** to humiliate, as by a blow to the pride. **2.** to discipline (the body, passions, etc.) by austerities or self-inflicted suffering. —*v.i.* **3.** to become gangrenous. —**mor′ti·fi·ca′tion,** *n.* —**mor′ti·fy′ing·ly,** *adv.*

mor·tise (môr′tis), *n.* a hole made in a piece of wood to receive a tenon, or a projecting part of another piece, for joining the two pieces. Also, **mor′tice.**

mor·tu·ar·y (môr′chōō er′ē), *n., pl.* **-ar·ies.** See **funeral home.**

mos., months.

mo·sa·ic (mō zā′ik), *n.* **1.** a picture or decoration made of small, usually colored pieces of inlaid stones, glass, etc. **2.** the technique of producing this.

Mos·cow (mos′kou, -kō), *n.* the capital of the Soviet Union.

Mo·ses (mō′ziz, -zis), *n,* a Hebrew leader, prophet, and lawgiver. — **Mo·sa′ic** (-zā′ik), *adj.*

mo·sey (mō′zē), *v.i.* **-seyed, -sey·ing.** *Informal.* to shuffle about leisurely.

Mos·lem (mŏz′ləm, mos′-), *n., adj.* Muslim.

mosque (mosk, môsk), *n.* a Muslim place of public worship.

mos·qui·to (mə skē′tō), *n., pl.* **-toes.** a winged insect the female of which sucks the blood of animals and people.

moss (môs, mos), *n.* a small, green, leafy-stemmed plant that grows in mats on moist ground, tree trunks, rocks, etc. —**moss′y,** *adj.* —**moss′i·ness,** *n.*

moss·back (môs′bak′, mos′-), *n.* 1. *Informal.* an extreme conservative. 2. an old turtle. 3. a large and old fish, as a bass.

most (mōst), *adj., superl.* of **much** or **many** with **more** as *compar.* 1. in the greatest amount or degree. 2. in the greatest quantity or number. 3. in the majority of instances. —*n.* 4. the greatest amount or degree. 5. the greatest quantity or number. 6. the majority of persons. 7. **at the most,** at the maximum. Also, **at most. 8. make the most of,** to utilize fully. —*adv., superl.* of **much** with **more** as *compar.* 9. in or to the greatest extent or degree. 10. very: *a most curious event.* 11. *Informal.* almost or nearly.

-most, a suffix occurring in superlatives: *foremost; utmost; lowermost.*

most·ly (mōst′lē), *adv.* 1. for the most part. 2. chiefly or mainly. 3. generally or customarily.

mot (mō), *n.* See **bon mot.**

mote (mōt), *n.* a particle or speck, esp. of dust.

mo·tel (mō tel′), *n.* a roadside hotel for motorists, having rooms adjacent to an outside parking space.

mo·tet (mō tet′), *n.* a vocal composition in polyphonic style, on a Biblical or similar prose text.

moth (môth, moth), *n., pl.* **moths** (môthz, mothz, môths, moths). 1. a soft, winged insect that resembles the butterfly but flies mostly at night. 2. Also called **clothes′ moth′.** a small, yellowish moth whose larvae eat wool, furs, etc.

moth·ball (môth′bôl′, moth′-), *n.* 1. a small ball of naphthalene for placing in closets to repel clothes moths. 2. **in mothballs,** in a condition of being in disuse or in storage.

moth·er (muth′ər), *n.* 1. a female parent. 2. a woman in control or authority. 3. something that gives origin or rise to something else. —*adj.* 4. being a mother: *a mother bird.* 5. of or characteristic of a mother: *mother love.* 6. native: *mother dialect.* —*v.t.* 7. to give origin or rise to. 8. to care for or protect like a mother. —**moth′er·hood′,** *n.* —**moth′er·less,** *adj.*

Moth′er Goose′, a fictitious old woman, reputedly the author of a collection of old English nursery rhymes.

moth·er-in-law (muth′ər in lô′), *n., pl.* **moth·ers-in-law.** the mother of one's husband or wife.

moth·er·land (muth′ər land′), *n.* 1. a person's native land. 2. the land of one's ancestors.

moth·er·ly (muth′ər lē), *adj.* of, like, or befitting a mother. —**moth′er·li·ness,** *n.*

moth·er-of-pearl (muth′ər əv pûrl′), *n.* a hard, rainbow-colored substance forming the inner layer of certain mollusk shells, used for making buttons, beads, etc.

mo·tif (mō tēf′), *n.* a recurring subject, theme, or idea, esp. in an artistic work.

mo·tile (mōt′əl, mō′til), *adj.* capable of moving spontaneously. —**mo·til·i·ty** (mō til′i tē), *n.*

mo·tion (mō′shən), *n.* 1. the action or process of moving or changing place or position. 2. a bodily movement or change of posture, esp. a gesture. 3. a formal proposal, esp. one made to a deliberative assembly. 4. **go through the motions,** to do something half-heartedly. 5. **in motion,** in active operation. —*v.t.* 6. to direct by a motion or gesture. —*v.i.* 7. to make a motion or gesture. —**mo′tion·less,** *adj.* —**mo′tion·less·ly,** *adv.* —**mo′tion·less·ness,** *n.*

mo′tion pic′ture, 1. a sequence of consecutive still pictures on film thrown on a screen in such rapid succession as to give the illusion of natural movement. 2. a play, event, etc., presented in this form. —**mo′tion-pic′ture,** *adj.*

mo′tion sick′ness, a feeling of nausea and dizziness induced by the irregular movement of a passenger vehicle.

mo·ti·vate (mō′tə vāt′), *v.t.,* **-vat·ed, -vat·ing.** to provide with a motive. —**mo′ti·va′tion,** *n.* —**mo′ti·va′tion·al,** *adj.* —*Syn.* impel, incite.

mo·tive (mō′tiv), *n.* 1. an inner urge that prompts a person to action with a sense of purpose. 2. a motif, esp. in music. —*adj.* 3. of or tending to cause motion. 4. prompting to action. 5. constituting a motive. —**mo′tive·less,** *adj.* —*Syn.* 1. incentive, stimulus.

mot·ley (mot′lē), *adj.* 1. exhibiting great diversity of elements. 2. of different colors combined.

mo·tor (mō′tər), *n.* 1. a comparatively small and powerful engine, esp. an internal-combustion engine. 2. any self-powered vehicle. 3. something that imparts motion. 4. a machine that converts electrical energy into mechanical energy. —*adj.* 5.

causing or producing motion. **6.** of or operated by a motor. **7.** of, for, or by motor vehicles: *motor freight.* **8.** of or involving muscular movement. —*v.i.* **9.** to ride or travel in an automobile.

mo·tor·bike (mō′tər bīk′), *n.* **1.** a bicycle propelled by an attached motor. **2.** a small, lightweight motorcycle.

mo·tor·boat (mō′tər bōt′), *n.* a boat propelled by an inboard or outboard motor.

mo·tor·cade (mō′tər kād′), *n.* a procession of automobiles.

mo·tor·car (mō′tər kär′), *n.* Chiefly Brit. an automobile.

mo·tor·cy·cle (mō′tər sī′kəl), *n.* a bicyclelike vehicle propelled by an internal-combustion engine. —**mo′tor·cy′clist** (-sī′klist), *n.*

mo′tor home′, a large motor vehicle designed to serve as a complete traveling and recreational home.

mo·tor·ist (mō′tər ist), *n.* a person who drives or travels in an automobile.

mo·tor·ize (mō′tə rīz′), *v.t.,* **-ized, -iz·ing. 1.** to furnish with a motor. **2.** to supply with motor-driven vehicles. —**mo′tor·i·za′tion,** *n.*

mo′tor lodge′, motel. Also called **mo′tor court′, mo′tor inn′, mo′tor hotel′.**

mo·tor·man (mō′tər mən), *n.* a person who operates an electric vehicle, as a streetcar or subway train.

mo′tor scoot′er, scooter (def. 2).

mo·tor·ship (mō′tər ship′), *n.* a ship driven by an internal-combustion engine.

mo·tor·truck (mō′tər truk′), *n.* truck¹ (def. 1).

mo′tor ve′hicle, any transportation vehicle designed for use on highways, as an automobile, bus, or truck.

mot·tle (mot′ᵊl), *v.t.,* **-tled, -tling.** to mark with blotches of a different color or shade.

mot·to (mot′ō), *n., pl.* **-toes, -tos. 1.** a maxim adopted as an expression of one's guiding principle. **2.** a sentence, phrase, or word inscribed on anything as appropriate to it. [< It < L *muttum* utterance]

moue (mōō), *n. French.* a pouting grimace.

mould (mōld), *n., v.t., v.i. Brit.* mold.

mould·er (mōl′dər), *v.i. Brit.* molder.

mould·ing (mōl′ding), *n. Brit.* molding.

mould·y (mōl′dē), *adj.,* **mould·i·er, mould·i·est.** Brit. moldy.

moult (mōlt), *v.i., n. Brit.* molt.

mound (mound), *n.* **1.** an elevation formed of earth, sand, stones, etc., esp. over a grave or ruins. **2.** a natural elevation of earth. **3.** Baseball. the slightly elevated ground from which the pitcher delivers the ball.

mount¹ (mount), *v.t.* **1.** to go up, esp. in order to reach a level: *He mounted the stairs slowly.* **2.** to get up on (a platform, a horse, etc.). **3.** to furnish with a horse or other animal for riding. **4.** to raise or put into position for use, as a gun. **5.** to prepare and launch, as a campaign or attack. **6.** to fix on or in a support, backing, setting, etc.: *to mount a photograph.* **7.** to prepare (an animal body or skeleton) as a specimen. —*v.i.* **8.** to increase in amount or intensity. **9.** to get up on the back of a horse or other animal for riding. **10.** to ascend or climb. —*n.* **11.** the act or a manner of mounting. **12.** a horse or other animal for riding. **13.** a support, backing, setting, etc., on or in which something is mounted. —**mount′a·ble,** *adj.* —**mount′er,** *n.*

mount² (mount), *n. Chiefly Literary.* a mountain.

moun·tain (moun′tᵊn), *n.* **1.** a natural elevation of the earth's surface, higher than a hill. **2.** a huge amount. —*adj.* **3.** of, on, or in mountains.

moun′tain ash′, a small tree of the rose family, having white flowers and bright-red to orange berries.

moun·tain·eer (moun′tᵊnēr′), *n.* **1.** an inhabitant of a mountainous district. **2.** a climber of mountains, esp. for sport. —*v.i.* **3.** to climb mountains, esp. for sport.

moun′tain goat′, a goatlike antelope of the mountainous regions of North America.

moun′tain lau′rel, a North American laurel having clusters of rose to white flowers.

moun′tain li′on, cougar.

moun·tain·ous (moun′tᵊnəs), *adj.* **1.** abounding in mountains. **2.** resembling a mountain, as being large and high.

moun·tain·top (moun′tᵊn top′), *n.* the top or summit of a mountain.

moun·te·bank (moun′tə bangk′), *n.* **1.** a huckster of quack medicines. **2.** any charlatan or quack.

Moun·tie (moun′tē), *n. Informal.* a member of the Royal Canadian Mounted Police.

mount·ing (moun′ting), *n.* something that serves as a mount, support, setting, etc.

mourn (mōrn, môrn), *v.t., v.i.* **1.** to feel or express sorrow or grief (over). **2.** to grieve or lament over (the dead). —**mourn′er,** *n.*

mourn·ful (mōrn′fəl, môrn′-), *adj.* **1.** feeling or expressing sorrow or grief. **2.** causing grief or lament. —**mourn′ful·ly,** *adv.* —**mourn′ful·ness,** *n.*

mourn·ing (môr′nĭng, mōr′-), n. 1. the conventional manifestation of sorrow for a person's death. 2. the outward tokens of such sorrow, as black garments. 3. a period of time during which a death is mourned.

mouse (n. mous; v. mouz), n., pl. **mice** (mīs), v., **moused, mous·ing.** —n. 1. any of numerous small, furry, thin-tailed rodents, esp. a brownish-gray one (**house′ mouse′**) that infests buildings. 2. *Informal.* a timid, shy person. 3. *Slang.* See **black eye.** —v.i. 4. to hunt for or catch mice.

mous·er (mou′zər), n. an animal that catches mice.

mouse-trap (mous′trap′), n. a trap for catching mice.

mousse (mōos), n. a dessert made with whipped cream and gelatin, and chilled in a mold.

mous·tache (mə stash′, mus′tash), n. *Chiefly Brit.* mustache.

mous·y (mou′sē, -zē), adj., **mous·i·er, mous·i·est.** 1. resembling a mouse, as in color, odor, etc. 2. timid and shy. Also, **mous′ey.** —**mous′i·ness,** n.

mouth (n. mouth; v. mouth), n., pl. **mouths** (mouthz), v. —n. 1. the opening through which an animal or human takes in food and utters sounds. 2. any opening resembling a mouth: *the mouth of a bottle.* 3. **down** in or at the **mouth,** *Informal.* depressed or disheartened. —v.t. 4. to utter softly and indistinctly. 5. to utter in a sonorous or pompous manner. 6. to put or take into the mouth, as food. —**mouthed** (mouthd), adj.

mouth·ful (mouth′fŏol′), n., pl. **-fuls.** 1. as much as a mouth can hold. 2. as much as is taken into the mouth at one time. 3. a small quantity. 4. *Slang.* a spoken remark of special significance: *You said a mouthful!*

mouth′ or′gan, harmonica.

mouth·part (mouth′pärt′), n. the appendage surrounding the mouth in arthropods.

mouth·piece (mouth′pēs′), n. 1. a part, as of a musical instrument, to which the mouth is applied. 2. a person, newspaper, etc., that conveys the opinions of others.

mouth·wash (mouth′wŏsh′, -wôsh′), n. a solution containing antiseptic and breath-sweetening agents used for cleansing the mouth.

mouth-wa·ter·ing (mouth′wô′tər ĭng, -wot′ər-), adj. so appetizing as to cause the saliva to flow.

mouth·y (mou′thē, -thē), adj., **mouth·i·er, mouth·i·est.** garrulous, often in a bombastic manner. —**mouth′i·ly,** adv.

mou·ton (mōo′ton), n. sheepskin processed to resemble seal or beaver.

mov·a·ble (mōo′və bəl), adj. 1. capable of being moved. 2. *Law.* (of property) personal, as distinguished from real. —n. 3. an article of furniture that is not fixed in place. 4. **movables,** *Law.* movable property. Also, **move′a·ble.**

move (mōov), v., **moved, mov·ing,** n. —v.i. 1. to pass from one place or position to another. 2. to go from one place of residence to another. 3. to advance or progress. 4. to have a regular motion, as a machine. 5. to be disposed of by sale, as goods in stock. 6. (of the bowels) to evacuate. 7. to be active in a particular sphere. 8. to take action. 9. to make a formal request, application, or proposal. —v.t. 10. to change from one place or position to another. 11. to set in motion. 12. to prompt or impel to some action. 13. to excite the feelings or passions of: *to move someone to anger.* 14. to propose formally, as for consideration by a deliberative assembly. —n. 15. the act or an instance of moving. 16. a change of residence. 17. an action toward an end. 18. (in chess, checkers, etc.) a player's right or turn to make a play. 19. **on the move,** *Informal.* **a.** busy or active. **b.** advancing or progressing.

move·ment (mōov′mənt), n. 1. the act or process of moving. 2. a manner of moving. 3. a change of position of troops, ships, etc. 4. the course or trend of affairs in a particular field. 5. an organized group of people working toward or favoring a common goal. 6. **a.** an act of defecating. **b.** excrement or stool. 7. the working parts of a mechanism, as of a watch. 8. a principal division or section of a sonata, symphony, etc.

mov·er (mōo′vər), n. 1. a person or thing that moves. 2. a person or company that moves household effects or office equipment from one place to another.

mov·ie (mōo′vē), n. *Informal.* 1. See **motion picture.** 2. a motion-picture theater. 3. **movies, a.** motion pictures as an industry. **b.** the exhibition of a motion picture.

mow[1] (mō), v., **mowed, mowed** or **mown, mow·ing.** —v.t. 1. to cut down (grass, etc.) with a scythe or a machine. 2. to cut grass, etc., from. —v.i. 3. to cut down grass, etc. 4. **mow down,** to kill in great numbers, as soldiers in battle. —**mow′er,** n.

mow[2] (mou), n. 1. the place in a barn where hay or grain is stored. 2. a pile of hay or grain in a barn.

Mo·zart (mōt′särt), n. **Wolf·gang A·ma·de·us** (wōolf′gang am′ə dā′əs), 1756–91, Austrian composer.

moz·za·rel·la (mot'sə rel'la, môt'-), *n.* a mild, white, semisoft Italian cheese.

MP, 1. Military Police. **2.** Military Policeman.

mp., melting point.

M.P., 1. Member of Parliament. **2.** Metropolitan Police. **3.** Military Police. **4.** Military Policeman. **5.** Mounted Police.

mpg, miles per gallon. Also, **m.p.g., MPG**

mph, miles per hour. Also, **m.p.h., MPH**

Mr. (mis'tər), *n., pl.* **Messrs.** (mes'-ərz). a title prefixed to a man's surname or position. Also, *Brit.*, **Mr** [abbr. of *mister*]

Mrs. (mis'iz, miz'-), *n., pl.* **Mmes.** (mā däm', -dam'). a title prefixed to the surname of a married woman. Also, *Brit.*, **Mrs** [abbr. of *mistress*]

MS, 1. Mississippi. **2.** motor ship. **3.** See **multiple sclerosis.**

Ms. (miz, em'es'), *n., pl.* **Mses., Mss.** (miz'es). a title prefixed to a woman's name or position regardless of her marital status or when such status is unknown. Also, **Ms** [*M* (*iss* + *Mr*) *s*.]

MS., *pl.* **MSS.** manuscript.

ms., *pl.* **mss.** manuscript.

M.S., 1. Master of Science. **2.** motor ship. **3.** See **multiple sclerosis.**

msec, millisecond; milliseconds.

MSG, See **monosodium glutamate.**

msg., message.

Msgr., 1. Monseigneur. **2.** Monsignor.

MSgt, Master Sergeant. Also, **M/Sgt**

m.s.l., mean sea level. Also, **M.S.L.**

MST, Mountain Standard Time.

MT, Montana.

Mt., 1. mount. **2.** mountain. Also, **mt.**

M.T., 1. metric ton. **2.** Mountain Time.

mtg., 1. meeting. **2.** mortgage.

mtge., mortgage.

mtn., mountain. Also, **Mtn.**

Mt. Rev., Most Reverend.

Mts., mountains. Also, **mts.**

mu (myōō, mōō), *n.* the 12th letter of the Greek alphabet (M, μ).

much (much), *adj., more, most, n., adv., more, most. —adj. 1.* in great quantity, measure, or degree. —*n. 2.* a great quantity, measure, or degree. **3.** a great, important, or notable thing or matter. —*adv.* **4.** to a great extent or degree. **5.** nearly or about.

mu·ci·lage (myōō'sə lij), *n.* any of various watery preparations of gum, glue, etc., used as an adhesive. —**mu'ci·lag'i·nous** (-laj'ə nəs), *adj.*

muck (muk), *n.* **1.** farmyard dung in a moist state. **2.** a highly organic black soil, often used as a manure. **3.** filth or dirt. —**muck'y,** *adj.*

muck·rake (muk'rāk'), *v.i.,* **-raked, -rak·ing.** to search for and expose real or alleged corruption, scandal, etc., esp. in politics. —**muck'rak'er,** *n.* —**muck'rak'ing,** *n., adj.*

mu·cous (myōō'kəs), *adj.* **1.** consisting of or resembling mucus. **2.** containing or secreting mucus.

mu'cous mem'brane, a lubricating membrane lining an organ, as the alimentary canal.

mu·cus (myōō'kəs), *n.* a viscid secretion of the mucous membranes.

mud (mud), *n.* wet, soft earth.

mud·dle (mud'əl), *v.,* **-dled, -dling,** *n.* —*v.t.* **1.** to mix up in a confused manner. **2.** to confuse mentally. **3.** to confuse with intoxicating drink. **4.** to make muddy or turbid. —*v.i.* **5.** to think or act in a confused manner. —*n.* **6.** a confused mental state. **7.** a confused state of affairs.

mud·dle-head·ed (mud'əl hed'id), *adj.* confused in one's thinking.

mud·dy (mud'ē), *adj.,* **-di·er, -di·est,** *v.,* **-died, -dy·ing.** —*adj.* **1.** abounding in or covered with mud. **2.** not clear or pure, as color. **3.** not clear mentally. —*v.t., v.i.* **4.** to make or become muddy. —**mud'di·ness,** *n.*

mud·guard (mud'gärd'), *n.* a flap behind a rear tire, as on a truck, to prevent mud from being splashed behind.

mud·sling·ing (mud'sling'ing), *n.* an attempt to discredit one's opponent, by malicious personal attacks, as in political campaigning. —**mud'sling'er,** *n.*

muen·ster (mōōn'stər, mun'-, min'-), *n.* a white, semisoft, mild cheese.

mu·ez·zin (myōō ez'in, mōō-), *n.* a Muslim crier who summons the faithful to prayer, usually from a minaret.

muff (muf), *n.* **1.** a thick, tubular covering for the hands, often covered with fur. **2.** *Sports.* a failure to catch a ball that may reasonably be expected to be caught. **3.** any failure. —*v.t., v.i.* **4.** *Informal.* to handle clumsily. **5.** *Sports.* to fail to catch (a ball that may reasonably be expected to be caught).

muf·fin (muf'in), *n.* a small, cup-shaped bread, usually eaten hot with butter.

muf·fle (muf'əl), *v.t.,* **-fled, -fling. 1.** to wrap in a shawl, etc., esp. to keep warm or protect the face and neck. **2.** to wrap with something to deaden sound. **3.** to deaden (sound) by wrappings.

muf·fler (muf'lər), *n.* **1.** a heavy neck scarf. **2.** any device for deadening sound, as that of an internal-combustion engine.

muf·ti (muf'tē), *n.* civilian dress, as opposed to military or other uniform.

mug (mug), *n.*, *v.*, **mugged, mug·ging.**
—*n.* **1.** a drinking cup of earthenware
or metal, usually cylindrical in shape
and having a handle. **2.** the quantity
it holds. **3.** *Slang.* the face. **4.** *Slang.*
a thug or ruffian. —*v.t.* **5.** to assault
(a victim), usually with intent to
rob. **6.** *Slang.* to photograph (a criminal) for police identification. —*v.i.*
7. *Slang.* to grimace voluntarily. —
mug′ger, *n.*

mug·gy (mug′ē), *adj.*, **-gi·er, -gi·est.**
humid and oppressive. —**mug′gi·ly,**
adv. —**mug′gi·ness,** *n.*

mug·wump (mug′wump′), *n.* a person
who is neutral on a controversial
political issue.

Mu·ham·mad (mōō ham′əd), *n.* A.D.
570–632, founder of Islam.

Mu·ham·mad·an (mōō ham′ə dən),
n., *adj.* Muslim. —**Mu·ham′mad-
an′ism,** *n.*

muk·luk (muk′luk), *n.* **1.** a boot worn
by Eskimos, usually of sealskin or
reindeer skin. **2.** a similar boot with
a soft sole.

mu·lat·to (mə lat′ō, myōō-), *n.*, *pl.*
-toes. 1. the offspring of one white
parent and one black parent. **2.** a
person whose racial ancestry is
mixed black and Caucasian.

mul·ber·ry (mul′ber′ē, -bə rē), *n.* **1.**
a tree having dark-purple, edible,
berrylike fruit. **2.** its fruit.

mulch (mulch), *n.* **1.** a covering, as of
straw, leaves, etc., spread or left on
the ground around plants to prevent
evaporation or erosion or enrich the
soil. —*v.t.* **2.** to cover with mulch.

mulct (mulkt), *n.* **1.** a fine, esp. for a
misdemeanor. —*v.t.* **2.** to fine, esp.
for a misdemeanor. **3.** to obtain
(money) from by fraud.

mule¹ (myōōl), *n.* **1.** the offspring of
a male donkey and a mare. **2.** a machine for spinning cotton or other
fibers into yarn. **3.** *Informal.* a stubborn person.

mule² (myōōl), *n.* a backless slipper
for a woman.

mule′ deer′, a deer of western North
America, having large ears.

mu·le·teer (myōō′lə tēr′), *n.* a driver
of mules.

mul·ish (myōō′lish), *adj.* stubborn or
obstinate. —**mul′ish·ly,** *adv.* —**mul′-
ish·ness,** *n.*

mull¹ (mul), *v.i.* to ponder, esp. in an
ineffective way: *to mull over a decision.*

mull² (mul), *v.t.* to heat, sweeten, and
spice, as ale, wine, etc.

mul·lah (mul′ə, mōōl′ə, mōō′lə), *n.* **1.**
a Muslim teacher of the sacred law.
2. his title. Also, **mul′la.**

mul·lein (mul′ən), *n.* a large herb
having coarse, woolly leaves and
spikes of flowers. Also, **mul′len.**

mul·let (mul′it), *n.*, *pl.* **-let, -lets.** any
of several marine or freshwater,
usually gray fishes.

mul·li·gan (mul′ə gən), *n.* *Slang.* a
kind of stew containing meat, vegetables, etc.

mul·li·ga·taw·ny (mul′ə gə tô′nē), *n.* a
curry-flavored soup of East Indian
origin.

mul·lion (mul′yən), *n.* a thin, vertical
bar, as between windowpanes.

multi-, a combining form meaning:
a. many: *multiform.* **b.** many times:
multimillionaire. **c.** more than two:
multilateral.

mul·ti·col·ored (mul′ti kul′ərd, mul′-
ti kul′ərd), *adj.* of many colors.

mul·ti·far·i·ous (mul′tə fâr′ē əs), *adj.*
having wide variety or great diversity. —**mul′ti·far′i·ous·ly,** *adv.* —
mul′ti·far′i·ous·ness, *n.*

mul·ti·form (mul′tə fôrm′), *adj.* having many forms or shapes.

mul·ti·lat·er·al (mul′ti lat′ər əl), *adj.*
1. having many sides. **2.** participated
in by more than two nations.

mul·ti·me·di·a (mul′ti mē′dē ə), *n.pl.*
the simultaneous, combined use of
several media, both audio and visual.

mul·ti·mil·lion·aire (mul′tē mil′yə-
nâr′, mul′tē-), *n.* a person who has
several million dollars, pounds, etc.

mul·ti·na·tion·al (mul′ti nash′ə nəl), *n.*
1. a giant corporation with operations in many foreign countries. —
adj. **2.** of many nations or nationalities. **3.** noting multinationals.

mul·ti·ple (mul′tə pəl), *adj.* **1.** having
many individuals, parts, elements,
etc. —*n.* **2.** a number which contains
another number an integral number
of times without a remainder: *12 is
a multiple of 3.*

mul·ti·ple-choice (mul′tə pəl chois′),
adj. consisting of several possible
answers from which the correct one
must be selected.

mul′tiple sclero′sis, a disease of the
brain and spinal cord characterized
by speech disturbances, muscular in-
coordination, etc.

mul·ti·plex (mul′tə pleks′), *adj.* capable of transmitting two or more signals or messages simultaneously on
the same circuit or channel.

---

mul′ti·cel′lu·lar, *adj.*
mul′ti·di·men′sion·al,
  adj.
mul′ti·di·rec′tion·al, *adj.*
mul′ti·en′gined, *adj.*

mul′ti·eth′nic, *adj.*
mul′ti·faced′, *adj.*
mul′ti·fac′et·ed, *adj.*
mul′ti·fam′i·ly, *adj.*
mul′ti·lin′e·al, *adj.*

mul′ti·lin′gual, *adj.*
mul′ti·mo·lec′u·lar, *adj.*
mul′ti·mo′tored, *adj.*

mul·ti·pli·cand (mul′tə pli kand′), *n.* a number to be multiplied by another.

mul·ti·pli·ca·tion (mul′tə plə kā′shən), *n.* **1.** the act or process of multiplying. **2.** the method of finding the product by repeating a given number a given number of times. **—mul′ti·pli·ca′tion·al,** *adj.*

multiplica′tion sign′, the symbol (×) or (·) used to denote multiplication.

mul·ti·plic·i·ty (mul′tə plis′i tē), *n., pl.* **-ties.** a large number or variety.

mul·ti·pli·er (mul′tə plī′ər), *n.* **1.** a person or thing that multiplies. **2.** a number by which another is multiplied.

mul·ti·ply (mul′tə plī′), *v.t., v.i.,* **-plied, -ply·ing. 1.** to increase in number, quantity, or extent. **2.** to perform the process of multiplication (on).

mul·ti·stage (mul′ti stāj′), *adj.* having more than two sections, esp. of a rocket, each used for different stages of its flight.

mul·ti·tude (mul′ti tōōd′, -tyōōd′), *n.* a great number of persons or things.

mul·ti·tu·di·nous (mul′ti tōōd′nəs, -tyōōd′-), *adj.* occurring or present in great numbers.

mul·ti·ver·si·ty (mul′ti vûr′si tē), *n.* a very large university with a number of campuses located in various places.

mul·ti·vi·ta·min (mul′tə vī′tə min), *adj.* consisting of a combination of several vitamins.

mum[1] (mum), *adj.* not saying a word.

mum[2] (mum), *n. Informal.* chrysanthemum.

mum·ble (mum′bəl), *v.,* **-bled, -bling,** *n.* **—***v.t., v.i.* **1.** to speak indistinctly, as with partly closed lips. **—***n.* **2.** a mumbled utterance or sound. **—mum′bler,** *n.*

mum·ble·ty·peg (mum′bəl tē peg′), *n.* a children's game played with a pocketknife, the object being to cause the blade to stick in the ground. Also, **mum′ble-the-peg′** (-тнə-peg′).

mum·bo jum·bo (mum′bō jum′bō), **1.** a meaningless incantation or ritual. **2.** an object of superstitious awe. **3.** pretentious language designed to confuse.

mum·mer (mum′ər), *n.* a person who wears a mask or disguise, esp. for certain festivals. **—mum′mer·y,** *n.*

mum·mi·fy (mum′ə fī′), *v.t., v.i.,* **-fied, -fy·ing.** to make into or become like a mummy. **—mum′mi·fi·ca′tion,** *n.*

mum·my (mum′ē), *n., pl.* **-mies.** a dead body embalmed and preserved, as by the ancient Egyptians.

mumps (mumps), *n.* an infectious disease characterized by inflammatory swelling of the salivary glands.

mun., municipal. Also, **munic.**

munch (munch), *v.t., v.i.* to chew steadily or vigorously, and often audibly.

mun·dane (mun dān′, mun′dān), *adj.* **1.** of this earthly world. **2.** noting everyday concerns rather than spiritual matters. **3.** ordinary or commonplace. **—mun·dane′ly,** *adv.*

Mu·nich (myōō′nik), *n.* a city in SW West Germany.

mu·nic·i·pal (myōō nis′ə pəl), *adj.* **1.** of a city or its local government. **2.** possessing local self-government. **—mu·nic′i·pal·ly,** *adv.*

mu·nic·i·pal·i·ty (myōō nis′ə pal′i tē), *n., pl.* **-ties.** a city, town, or other district possessing corporate status and usually some form of self-government.

mu·nif·i·cent (myōō nif′i sənt), *adj.* characterized by or displaying great generosity. **—mu·nif′i·cence,** *n.* **—mu·nif′i·cent·ly,** *adv.* **—Syn.** bountiful, lavish.

mu·ni·tions (myōō nish′ənz), *n.pl.* materials used in war, esp. weapons and ammunition.

mu·ral (myōōr′əl), *n.* **1.** a large painting executed on or permanently affixed to a wall. **—***adj.* **2.** of, on, for, or like a wall. **—mu′ral·ist,** *n.*

mur·der (mûr′dər), *n.* **1.** the unlawful killing of a human being with malice aforethought. **2.** *Slang.* something extremely difficult or perilous. **—***v.t.* **3.** to kill by an act constituting murder. **4.** to spoil or mar through incompetence: *to murder a tune.* **—mur′der·er,** *n.* **—mur′der·ess,** *n.fem.*

mur·der·ous (mûr′dər əs), *adj.* **1.** of the nature of or involving murder. **2.** guilty of, bent on, or capable of murder. **3.** extremely difficult or trying. **—mur′der·ous·ly,** *adv.*

mu′ri·at′ic ac′id (myōōr′ē at′ik). See **hydrochloric acid.**

murk (mûrk), *n. Literary.* gloomy darkness.

murk·y (mûr′kē), *adj.,* **murk·i·er, murk·i·est. 1.** gloomily dark. **2.** obscure with mist or haze. **3.** vague, unclear, or confused: *a murky statement.* **—murk′i·ly,** *adv.* **—murk′i·ness,** *n.*

mur·mur (mûr′mər), *n.* **1.** any low, continuous, and often indistinct sound. **2.** a guarded expression of discontent. **3.** an unusual sound produced by abnormal heart action. **—***v.i.* **4.** to make a murmur. **—***v.t.* **5.** to express in murmurs. **—mur′mur·er,** *n.* **—mur′mur·ous,** *adj.*

---

mul′ti·po′lar, *adj.*   **mul′ti·ra′cial,** *adj.*   **mul′ti·sto′ry,** *adj.*
mul′ti·pur′pose, *adj.*   **mul′ti·ra′di·al,** *adj.*

mur·rain (mûr′in), *n.* a contagious disease of cattle.

mus., 1. museum. 2. music.

mus·cat (mus′kət, -kat), *n.* a grape having a sweet aroma and flavor, used for making wine.

mus·ca·tel (mus′kə tel′, mus′kə tel′), *n.* a sweet wine made from muscat grapes.

mus·cle (mus′əl), *n., v.,* -**cled, -cling.** —*n.* 1. a tissue composed of cells or fibers, the contraction of which produces movement in the body. 2. an organ composed of this tissue. 3. muscular strength. —*v.i.* 4. *Informal.* to make one's way by force. — **mus′cled** (-əld), *adj.*

mus·cle-bound (mus′əl bound′), *adj.* having enlarged and somewhat inelastic muscles, as from excessive exercise.

mus·cu·lar (mus′kyə lər), *adj.* 1. of or affected by muscles. 2. having well-developed muscles. —**mus′cu·lar′i·ty** (-lar′i tē), *n.*

mus′cular dys′trophy, a disease characterized by a progressive muscular deterioration and wasting.

mus·cu·la·ture (mus′kyə lə chər), *n.* the muscular system of the body or of its parts.

muse (myōoz), *v.,* **mused, mus·ing.** —*v.i.* 1. to reflect in silence and usually dreamily. —*v.t.* 2. to consider or say reflectively. —**mus′er,** *n.* — **mus′ing·ly,** *adv.* —**Syn.** meditate, ponder, ruminate.

Muse (myōoz), *n.* 1. *Class. Myth.* any of the nine goddesses who presided over various arts and sciences. 2. the power regarded as inspiring a poet.

mu·sette′ bag′ (myōo zet′), a small bag for personal belongings of army officers, carried by a shoulder strap. Also called **mu·sette′.**

mu·se·um (myōo zē′əm), *n.* a building or place where works of art or other objects of permanent value are kept and displayed.

mush[1] (mush), *n.* 1. a thick, soft porridge of boiled cornmeal. 2. any thick, soft mass. 3. mawkish sentimentality.

mush[2] (mush), *v.i.* 1. to travel over snow with a dog sled. —*interj.* 2. (an order to speed up a dog team.)

mush·room (mush′rōom, -rŏom), *n.* 1. any of various fleshy fungi having a dome-shaped cap, esp. an edible species. —*adj.* 2. of or resembling a mushroom. —*v.i.* 3. to spread or grow quickly.

mush·y (mush′ē), *adj.,* **mush·i·er, mush·i·est.** 1. soft and pulpy like mush. 2. *Informal.* overly sentimental. —**mush′i·ness,** *n.*

mu·sic (myōo′zik), *n.* 1. the art of combining sounds of varying pitch to produce compositions expressive of various ideas and emotions. 2. a sequence of sounds produced according to this art. 3. a number of such compositions. 4. any pleasing or harmonious sounds. 5. **face the music,** *Informal.* to accept the consequences bravely.

mu·si·cal (myōo′zi kəl), *adj.* 1. of or producing music. 2. melodious or harmonious. 3. fond of or skilled in music. 4. set to or accompanied by music. —*n.* 5. Also called **mu′sical com′edy.** a play or film based on a slight plot with music, singing, dancing, and dialogue. —**mu′si·cal·ly,** *adv.*

mu·si·cale (myōo′zə kal′), *n.* a program of music forming a social occasion.

mu·si·cian (myōo zish′ən), *n.* a professional performer or composer of music. —**mu·si′cian·ly,** *adj.* —**mu·si′cian·ship′,** *n.*

mu·si·col·o·gy (myōo′zə kol′ə jē), *n.* the scholarly or scientific study of music. —**mu′si·co·log′i·cal** (-kə loj′i kəl), *adj.* —**mu′si·col′o·gist,** *n.*

musk (musk), *n.* a strong-smelling substance secreted in a gland of a hornless Asiatic deer (**musk′ deer′**), used in perfumery. —**musk′y,** *adj.* —**musk′i·ness,** *n.*

mus·keg (mus′keg), *n.* a bog of northern North America.

mus·kel·lunge (mus′kə lunj′), *n., pl.* -**lunge.** a large game fish of the pike family, found in North America.

mus·ket (mus′kit), *n.* a heavy, large-caliber firearm, formerly used by infantry soldiers. —**mus·ket·eer** (mus′ki tēr′), *n.*

mus·ket·ry (mus′ki trē), *n.* 1. the technique of firing muskets or other small arms. 2. muskets or musketeers collectively.

musk·mel·on (musk′mel′ən), *n.* a round or oblong melon having a sweet, edible flesh.

musk′ ox′, a large, shaggy, oxlike animal of arctic regions of North America.

musk·rat (musk′rat′), *n.* 1. a large, aquatic, North American rodent having a musky odor. 2. its fur.

Mus·lim (muz′lim, mŏoz′-, mŏos′-), 1. an adherent of Islam. —*adj.* 2. of Islam or the Muslims.

mus·lin (muz′lin), *n.* a cotton fabric of plain weave, used for sheets, etc.

muss (mus), *n.* 1. a state of disorder or untidiness. —*v.t.* 2. to make disordered or untidy. —**muss′y,** *adj.* —**muss′i·ly,** *adv.* —**muss′i·ness,** *n.*

mus·sel (mus′əl), *n.* any bivalve mollusk, esp. an edible marine bivalve and a freshwater clam.

Mus·so·li·ni (mŏos′ə lē′nē, mōō′sə-), *n.* **Be·ni·to** (bə nē′tō), 1883–1945, Italian Fascist leader.

Mus·sul·man (mus'əl mən), *n., pl.* **-mans, -men.** *Archaic.* a Muslim.

must (must), *auxiliary verb.* **1.** to be compelled to, as by instinct or natural law: *One must eat.* **2.** to be required to: *You must not smoke here.* **3.** to be reasonably expected to: *It must have stopped raining.* **4.** to be inevitably certain to: *Human beings must die.* —*n.* **5.** anything vital.

mus·tache (mus'tash, mə stash'), *n.* the hair growing on the upper lip of men. —**mus'tached,** *adj.*

mus·tang (mus'tang), *n.* a small, hardy horse of the American plains. [< Sp *mestengo* ownerless beast]

mus·tard (mus'tərd), *n.* **1.** a pungent powder or paste prepared from the seeds of a plant related to the cabbage and used as a condiment or medicinally in plasters, etc. **2.** its plant.

mus'tard gas', a liquid chemical-warfare agent blistering the skin and damaging the lungs.

mus·ter (mus'tər), *v.t.* **1.** to assemble (troops, etc.), as for inspection. **2.** to gather or summon: *to muster up one's courage.* —*v.i.* **3.** to assemble for inspection or service. **4.** muster in or out, to enlist into or discharge from military service. —*n.* **5.** an assembling of troops for inspection or service. **6.** pass muster, to meet a certain standard of appearance or performance.

must·n't (mus'ənt), contraction of *must not.*

mus·ty (mus'tē), *adj.,* **-ti·er, -ti·est. 1.** having an odor or flavor suggestive of mold **2.** made obsolete by time. —**mus'ti·ly,** *adv.* —**mus'ti·ness,** *n.*

mu·ta·ble (myōō'tə bəl), *adj.* **1.** liable or subject to change. **2.** given to changing, or constantly changing. —**mu'ta·bil'i·ty,** *n.* —**mu'ta·bly,** *adv.*

mu·tant (myōōt'ənt), *adj.* **1.** undergoing mutation. —*n.* **2.** a new type of organism produced by mutation.

mu·tate (myōō'tāt), *v.t., v.i.,* **-tat·ed, -tat·ing.** to undergo or cause to undergo mutation. —**mu·ta·tive** (myōō'tə tiv), *adj.*

mu·ta·tion (myōō tā'shən), *n.* **1.** the act or process of changing. **2.** a sudden appearance in the offspring, as of an animal or plant, of a characteristic not present in its parents. —**mu·ta'tion·al,** *adj.*

mute (myōōt), *adj., n., v.,* **mut·ed, mut·ing.** —*adj.* **1.** incapable of speech, esp. of a person as because of congenital deafness **2.** refraining from speech or making no sound. —*n.* **3.** a person who is mute, esp. a deaf-mute. **4.** a device for muffling the tone of a musical instrument. —*v.t.* **5.** to deaden or muffle the sound of. —**mute'ly,** *adv.* —**mute'ness,** *n.*

mu·ti·late (myōōt'əlāt'), *v.t.,* **-lat·ed, -lat·ing. 1.** to deprive (an animal) of a limb or other essential part. **2.** to make imperfect by irreparably damaging parts. —**mu'ti·la'tion,** *n.* —**mu'ti·la'tor,** *n.*

mu·ti·ny (myōōt'ənē), *n., pl.* **-nies,** *v.,* **-nied, -ny·ing.** —*n.* **1.** rebellion against constituted authority, esp. by seamen or soldiers against their officers. —*v.i.* **2.** to commit mutiny. —**mu'ti·neer',** *n.* —**mu'ti·nous,** *adj.* —**mu'ti·nous·ly,** *adv.*

mutt (mut), *n. Slang.* a dog, esp. a mongrel.

mut·ter (mut'ər), *v.i., v.t.* **1.** to utter (words) indistinctly or in a low tone. **2.** to grumble feebly. —*n.* **3.** the act or utterance of a person who mutters.

mut·ton (mut'ən), *n.* the flesh of sheep, esp. full-grown sheep, used as food. —**mut'ton·y,** *adj.*

mut·ton·chops (mut'ən chops'), *n.pl.* side whiskers that are narrow at the top and broad and are trimmed short at the bottom.

mu·tu·al (myōō'chōō əl), *adj.* **1.** experienced or performed by each of two or more with respect to the other or others. **2.** having the same relation each toward the other or others. **3.** having in common: *mutual acquaintances.* —**mu'tu·al'i·ty** (-al'i-tē), *n.* —**mu'tu·al·ly,** *adv.*

mu'tual fund', an investment company that invests its pooled funds in a diversified list of securities.

muu·muu (mōō'mōō'), *n.* a loose dress, worn esp. by Hawaiian women.

muz·zle (muz'əl), *n., v.,* **-zled, -zling.** —*n.* **1.** the jaws, mouth, and nose of certain animals. **2.** a device placed over an animal's mouth to prevent biting, eating, etc. **3.** the open end of the barrel of a firearm. —*v.t.* **4.** to put a muzzle on (an animal). **5.** to restrain, as from speech or the expression of opinion.

MV, motor vessel.

mV, millivolt; millivolts.

MVP, *Baseball.* most valuable player.

my (mī), *pron.* **1.** (a form of the possessive case of **I** used as an attributive adjective.) —*interj.* **2.** *Informal.* (an exclamation of surprise.)

my·as·the·ni·a (mī'əs thē'nē ə), *n. Pathol.* muscle weakness. —**my·as·then·ic** (mī'əs then'ik), *adj.*

my·col·o·gy (mī kol'ə jē), *n.* the branch of botany dealing with fungi. —**my·co·log·i·cal** (mī'kə loj'i kəl), *adj.* —**my·col'o·gist,** *n.*

my·e·li·tis (mī'ə lī'tis), *n.* **1.** inflammation of the spinal cord. **2.** inflammation of the bone marrow.

My·lar (mī′lär), *n. Trademark.* a tough film of polyester used esp. in recording tapes, electric insulation, etc.

my·na (mī′nə), *n.* any of several Asian birds of the starling family, esp. certain species that have the ability to mimic human speech. Also, **my′nah.**

my·o·pi·a (mī ō′pē ə), *n.* **1.** a vision defect in which objects are seen distinctly only when near to the eye. **2.** *Informal.* lack of foresight. —**my·op′ic** (-op′ik), *adj.* —**my·op′i·cal·ly,** *adv.*

myr·i·ad (mir′ē əd), *n.* **1.** an indefinitely great number. —*adj.* **2.** of an indefinitely great number.

myr·mi·don (mûr′mi don′, -dən), *n.* a subordinate who executes orders without scruple.

myrrh (mûr), *n.* an aromatic resin obtained from certain plants of Africa and Arabia used for incense, perfume, etc. —**myrrh′ic,** *adj.*

myr·tle (mûr′təl), *n.* **1.** a shrub of southern Europe having evergreen leaves, fragrant white flowers, and aromatic berries. **2.** any of certain unrelated plants as the periwinkle.

my·self (mī self′), *pron.* **1.** (used as an intensifier of *me* or *I*): *I myself told her.* **2.** (used reflexively): *I cut myself.* **3.** my normal self: *A short nap and I was myself again.*

mys·te·ri·ous (mi stēr′ē əs), *adj.* **1.** full of mystery. **2.** obscure or enigmatic. **3.** suggesting a mystery. —**mys·te′ri·ous·ly,** *adv.* —**mys·te′ri·ous·ness,** *n.* —**Syn. 1.** arcane, cryptic, occult. **2.** inexplicable, inscrutable.

mys·ter·y (mis′tə rē, -trē), *n., pl.* **-ter·ies. 1.** something that is secret or impossible to understand. **2.** something that arouses curiosity through its obscure nature. **3.** the quality of being obscure or enigmatic. **4.** a work of fiction concerned with the identification and capture of a criminal or criminals. **5.** any truth unknowable except by divine revelation.

mys′tery play′, a medieval drama about the life, death, and resurrection of Christ.

mys·tic (mis′tik), *adj.* **1.** of esoteric practices, esp. in religion. **2.** mystical. —*n.* **3.** a person who practices mysticism —**mys′tic·ly,** *adv.*

mys·ti·cal (mis′ti kəl), *adj.* **1.** of occult character or power. **2.** of mysticism or mystics. **3.** spiritually symbolic or significant. —**mys′ti·cal·ly,** *adv.*

mys·ti·cism (mis′ti siz′əm), *n.* the belief in a direct, intimate union of the soul with God through contemplation and love.

mys·ti·fy (mis′tə fī′), *v.t.,* **-fied, -fy·ing. 1.** to cause bewilderment in. **2.** to involve in mystery or obscurity. —**mys′ti·fi·ca′tion,** *n.* —**mys′ti·fi′er,** *n.* —**mys′ti·fy′ing·ly,** *adv.*

mys·tique (mi stēk′), *n.* **1.** a profound framework of ideas or beliefs constructed around a person or object. **2.** an aura of mystical power surrounding a particular occupation or pursuit.

myth (mith), *n.* **1.** a traditional or legendary story, usually concerned with deities or demigods. **2.** a story or belief that attempts to explain a basic truth. **3.** a belief or a subject of belief whose truth is accepted uncritically. —**myth′i·cal,** *adj.*

myth., **1.** mythological. **2.** mythology.

my·thol·o·gy (mi thol′ə jē), *n., pl.* **-gies. 1.** a body of myths having a common source or subject. **2.** the study of myths. —**myth·o·log·i·cal** (mith′ə loj′i kəl), *adj.* —**my·thol′o·gist,** *n.*

N

N, n (en), *n., pl.* **N's** or **Ns, n's** or **ns.** the 14th letter of the English alphabet, a consonant.

N, **1.** north. **2.** northern.

N, nitrogen.

N., **1.** Nationalist. **2.** Navy. **3.** New. **4.** Noon. **5.** *Chem.* Normal (strength solution). **6.** Norse. **7.** north. **8.** northern. **9.** November.

n., **1.** name. **2.** net. **3.** neuter. **4.** new. **5.** nominative. **6.** noon. **7.** *Chem* normal (strength solution). **8.** north **9.** northern. **10.** note. **11.** noun. **12.** number.

Na, sodium [< NL *natrium*]

n/a, no account.

N.A., **1.** North America. **2.** not applicable. **3.** not available.

NAACP, National Association for the Advancement of Colored People.

nab (nab), *v.t.*, **nabbed, nab·bing.** *Informal.* **1.** to capture or arrest. **2.** to seize suddenly.

na·bob (nā′bob), *n. Literary.* a very wealthy or powerful person.

na·celle (nə sel′), *n.* a separate enclosure on an airplane, as for housing an engine.

na·cre (nā′kər), *n.* mother-of-pearl. —**na′cre·ous** (-krē əs), *adj.*

na·dir (nā′dər, -dēr), *n.* **1.** the point directly beneath the observer and diametrically opposite to the zenith. **2.** the lowest point.

nae (nā), *adv., adj. Scot.* no.

nag[1] (nag), *v.*, **nagged, nag·ging,** *n.* —*v.t.* **1.** to annoy with persistent demands or complaints. **2.** to keep in a state of troubled awareness or anxiety. —*v.i.* **3.** to find fault or complain in an irritating manner. **4.** to cause persistent discomfort or distress: *This headache has been nagging at me all day.* —*n.* **5.** Also, **nag′ger.** a person who nags, esp. habitually.

nag[2] (nag), *n.* an old, inferior, or worthless horse.

Na·hua·tl (nä′wät′l), *n., pl.* **-hua·tls, -hua·tl. 1.** a member of a group of American Indian peoples of southeastern Mexico and Central America, including the Aztecs. **2.** their language.

nai·ad (nā′ad, -əd, nī′-), *n., pl.* **-ads, -a·des** (-ə dēz′). *Class. Myth.* any of a class of nymphs presiding over rivers and springs.

na·if (nä ēf′), *adj. Rare.* naïve. Also, **na·if′.**

nail (nāl), *n.* **1.** a small, pointed piece of metal, designed to be hammered into wood or other material as a fastener. **2.** the thin, horny plate on the upper side of the end of a finger or toe. **3.** hit the nail on the head, to say or do exactly the right thing. —*v.t.* **4.** to fasten with or as with a nail. **5.** *Informal.* to catch or seize. **6.** *Slang.* to hit (a person). **7.** nail down, *Informal.* to settle once and for all. —**nail′er,** *n.*

nain·sook (nān′sŏŏk, nan′-), *n.* a fine, soft-finished cotton fabric.

Nai·ro·bi (nī rō′bē), *n.* the capital of Kenya.

na·ive (nä ēv′), *adj.* **1.** having genuine simplicity of nature. **2.** lacking social or economic sophistication. Also, **na·ive′.** —**na·ive′ly, na·ive′ly,** *adv.* —**Syn.** artless, ingenuous, unsophisticated.

na·ive·té (nä ēv tā′), *n.* **1.** Also called **na·ive′ness, na·ive′ness.** the quality or state of being naive. **2.** a naive action or remark. Also, **na·ive·té′, na·ive·te′.**

na·ked (nā′kid), *adj.* **1.** without clothing or covering on the body, usually when not supposed to be seen as such for some reason: *naked bathing.* **2.** without the customary covering or container. **3.** unassisted by an optical instrument: *visible to the naked eye.* **4.** unconcealed or unmodified. —**na′ked·ly,** *adv.* —**na′ked·ness,** *n.* —**Syn. 1.** bare, nude, undressed.

NAM, National Association of Manufacturers. Also, **N.A.M.**

nam·by·pam·by (nam′bē pam′bē), *adj., n., pl.* **-bies.** —*adj.* **1.** weakly affected. **2.** without firm methods or policy. —*n.* **3.** a namby-pamby person.

name (nām), *n., v.,* **named, nam·ing,** *adj.* —*n.* **1.** a word or a combination of words by which a person, place, or idea is known or designated. **2.** mere designation, as distinguished from fact: *He was a ruler in name only.* **3.** something that a person is said to be, esp. by way of insult: *to call a person names.* **4.** reputation of any kind. **5.** a widely known or famous person. **6.** a family or clan. **7.** in the name of, a. with appeal to. b. by the authority of. —*v.t.* **8.** to give a name to. **9.** to call by a specified name. **10.** to identify or specify by name. **11.** to designate for an office. **12.** to specify or set: *Name a price.* —*adj.* **13.** widely known. **14.** carrying a name: *a name tag.* —**name′a·ble,** *adj.*

name′ day′, the day of the saint after whom a person is named.

name·less (nām′lis), *adj.* **1.** unknown to fame. **2.** having no name. **3.** left unnamed. **4.** too shocking to be specified. —**name′less·ly,** *adv.*

name·ly (nām′lē), *adv.* that is to say.

name′ of the game′, *Informal.* the central purpose or method.

name·plate (nām′plāt′), *n.* a plate lettered with a name, as on a door.

name·sake (nām′sāk′), *n.* a person given the same name as another.

nan·keen (nan kēn′), *n.* a firm, durable, yellow or buff fabric, originally made from a Chinese cotton. Also, **nan·kin** (nan′kin).

Nan·king (nan′king′), *n.* a port in E China.

nan·ny (nan′ē), *n., pl.* **-nies.** *Chiefly Brit.* a child's nursemaid. Also, **nan′nie.**

nan′ny goat′, a female goat.

na·no·sec·ond (nā′nə sek′ənd, nan′ə-), *n.* one billionth of a second.

nap[1] (nap), *v.,* **napped, nap·ping,** *n.* —*v.i.* **1.** to sleep for a short time. **2.** to be off one's guard. —*n.* **3.** a brief period of sleep. —**nap′per,** *n.*

nap[2] (nap), *n., v.,* **napped, nap·ping.** —*n.* **1.** the downy or fuzzy surface of a fabric, composed of short fibers whose ends are drawn up after weaving. —*v.t.* **2.** to raise a nap on. —**nap′less**, *adj.* —**napped**, *adj.*

na·palm (nā′päm), *n.* **1.** a powder for jelling gasoline for use as an incendiary in firebombs, flamethrowers, etc. **2.** the jelled mixture of this. —*v.t.* **3.** to destroy or attack with napalm.

nape (nāp, nap), *n.* the back of the neck.

na·per·y (nā′pə rē), *n. Archaic.* table linen, as tablecloths, napkins, etc.

naph·tha (naf′thə, nap′-), *n.* a colorless, volatile liquid distilled from petroleum, used as a solvent, fuel, etc. —**naph′thous**, *adj.*

naph·tha·lene (naf′thə lēn′, nap′-), *n.* a white, crystalline, water-insoluble hydrocarbon obtained from coal tar, used in making dyes, as a moth repellant, etc.

nap·kin (nap′kin), *n.* **1.** a small piece of cloth or paper for use in wiping the lips and fingers and to protect the clothes while eating. **2.** See **sanitary napkin.**

Na·ples (nā′pəlz), *n.* a seaport in SW Italy.

na·po·le·on (nə pō′lē ən, -pōl′yən), *n.* a pastry consisting of thin layers of puff paste interlaid with a cream filling.

Na·po·le·on I (nə pō′lē ən), (*Napoleon Bonaparte*) 1769–1821, French general and emperor 1804–15. —**Na·po·le·on′ic** (-on′ik), *adj.*

narc (närk), *n. Slang.* a government narcotics agent or detective.

nar·cis·sism (när′si siz′əm), *n.* **1.** inordinate absorption in oneself. **2.** erotic gratification derived from admiration of one's own body. —**nar′cis·sist**, *n., adj.* —**nar′cis·sis′tic**, *adj.*

nar·cis·sus (när sis′əs), *n., pl.* **-cis·sus, -cis·sus·es, -cis·si** (-sis′ē, -sis′ī) for 1. **1.** any bulbous plant having showy flowers with a cup-shaped crown. **2.** (*cap.*) *Class. Myth.* a youth who fell in love with his own image reflected in a pool and was transformed into the flower narcissus.

nar·co·sis (när kō′sis), *n.* unconsciousness produced by a narcotic drug.

nar·cot·ic (när kot′ik), *n.* **1.** any addictive drug, as morphine, that blunts or distorts the senses and induces sleep. —*adj.* **2.** of or concerned with narcotics. —**nar·cot′i·cal·ly**, *adv.*

nar·co·tism (när′kə tiz′əm), *n.* habitual use of narcotics.

nar·co·tize (när′kə tīz′), *v.t.,* **-tized, -tiz·ing. 1.** to subject to a narcotic. **2.** to deaden the awareness of. —**nar′co·ti·za′tion**, *n.*

nard (närd), *n.* an aromatic ointment used by the ancients.

nar·es (nâr′ēz), *n.pl., sing.* **nar·is** (nâr′-

is). *Anat.* the nostrils.

nark (närk), *n. Slang.* narc.

nar·rate (nar′rāt, na rāt′), *v.t., v.i.,* **-rat·ed, -rat·ing. 1.** to tell (a story, etc.), esp. in an interesting way. **2.** to add an audio running commentary to (a documentary film or television program), usually without being seen on the screen. —**nar·ra′tion**, *n.* —**nar′ra·tor, nar′rat·er**, *n.* —**Syn. 1.** describe, recount, relate.

nar·ra·tive (nar′ə tiv), *n.* **1.** a story of events, experiences, etc. **2.** the art or process of narrating. —*adj.* **3.** of a narrative or narration.

nar·row (nar′ō), *adj.* **1.** of little breadth or width. **2.** limited in range or scope. **3.** lacking breadth of view or sympathy. **4.** limited in amount. **5.** barely adequate or successful: *a narrow escape.* **6.** careful or minute, as a search. —*v.i., v.t.* **7.** to make or become narrower in width or scope. —*n.* **8. narrows,** a narrow part of a body of water. —**nar′row·ish,** *adj.* —**nar′row·ly,** *adv.* —**nar′row·ness,** *n.*

nar·row-mind·ed (nar′ō mīn′did), *adj.* having a prejudiced or self-righteous mind. —**nar′row-mind′ed·ly,** *adv.* —**nar′row-mind′ed·ness,** *n.*

nar·thex (när′theks), *n.* an enclosed passage leading to the nave of a church.

nar·whal (när′wəl), *n.* a small arctic whale, the male of which has a long, twisted tusk.

nar·y (nâr′ē), *adj. Dial.* not one.

NAS, 1. National Academy of Sciences. **2.** Naval Air Station.

NASA (nas′ə), *n.* National Aeronautics and Space Administration.

na·sal (nā′zəl), *adj.* **1.** of the nose. **2.** pronounced with the voice issuing through the nose. —**na·sal′i·ty** (-zal′i tē), *n.* —**na′sal·ly,** *adv.*

na·sal·ize (nā′zə līz′), *v.,* **-ized, -iz·ing.** —*v.t.* **1.** to pronounce as a nasal sound. —*v.i.* **2.** to utter through the nose. —**na′sal·i·za′tion,** *n.*

nas·cent (nas′ənt, nā′sənt), *adj.* beginning to exist or develop. —**nas′cence,** *n.*

Nash·ville (nash′vil), *n.* the capital of Tennessee.

na·stur·tium (nə stûr′shəm, na-), *n.* a plant cultivated for its showy flowers or for its seeds, which are pickled and used like capers.

nas·ty (nas′tē), *adj.,* **-ti·er, -ti·est. 1.** disgustingly unclean. **2.** morally filthy. **3.** very unpleasant: *nasty weather.* **4.** vicious or spiteful. **5.** bad to deal with or experience: *a nasty accident.* —**nas′ti·ly,** *adv.* —**nas′ti·ness,** *n.*

nat., 1. national. **2.** native. **3.** natural.

na·tal (nāt′əl), *adj.* of or pertaining to one's birth.

na·tal·i·ty (nā tal′i tē), *n.* birthrate.

na·tes (nā′tēz), *n.pl. Anat.* the buttocks.

na·tion (nā′shən), *n.* 1. a large body of people possessing its own territory ruled under a unified government. 2. a member tribe of an American Indian confederation. 3. an aggregation of persons of the same ethnic family, often speaking the same language. —**na′tion·hood′,** *n.*

na·tion·al (nash′ə nəl), *adj.* 1. of or maintained by a nation. 2. of or peculiar to a nationality. —*n.* 3. a citizen or subject of a particular country. —**na′tion·al·ly,** *adv.*

Na′tional Guard′, *U.S.* a military reserve force of each state subject to call by the President into federal service in civil emergencies.

na·tion·al·ism (nash′ə nəl liz′əm), *n.* 1. devotion to the interests of one's own nation. 2. the advocacy of or movement for national advancement or independence. —**na′tion·al·ist,** *n.,* *adj.* —**na′tion·al·is′tic,** *adj.* —**na′tion·al·is′ti·cal·ly,** *adv.*

na·tion·al·i·ty (nash′ə nal′i tē), *n., pl.* **-ties.** 1. the status of belonging to a particular nation or country by birth or naturalization. 2. existence as an independent nation. 3. a nation or people. 4. a national quality or character.

na·tion·al·ize (nash′ə nəlīz′), *v.t.,* **-ized, -iz·ing.** 1. to bring under the control or ownership of a nation, as industries or land. 2. to make national in extent or scope. —**na′tion·al·i·za′tion,** *n.*

na·tion·wide (nā′shən wīd′), *adj.* extending throughout the nation.

na·tive (nā′tiv), *adj.* 1. being the place of origin of a person or thing: *one's native land.* 2. belonging to a person at birth or a thing at its origin: *native intelligence.* 3. belonging to the original inhabitants of a region or country. 4. belonging to a person by reason of birthplace: *one's native language.* 5. originating naturally in a particular country or region, as animals or plants. —*n.* 6. a person born in a particular place or country. 7. one of the original inhabitants of a region or country, esp. as distinguished from strangers or foreigners. 8. an animal or plant indigenous to a particular region. [< L *nātīv(us)* inborn, natural] —**Syn.** 2. inborn, innate. 5. indigenous.

na·tiv·ism (nā′ti viz′əm), *n.* 1. the policy of favoring native inhabitants as against immigrants. 2. the doctrine that innate ideas exist.

na·tiv·i·ty (nə tiv′i tē, nā-), *n., pl.* **-ties.** 1. **the Nativity,** a. the birth of Christ. b. Christmas day. 2. the circumstances of one's birth. 3. a horoscope of a person's birth.

natl., national.

NATO (nā′tō), *n.* North Atlantic Treaty Organization.

nat·ty (nat′ē), *adj.,* **-ti·er, -ti·est.** neatly smart in dress or appearance. —**nat′ti·ly,** *adv.* —**nat′ti·ness,** *n.*

nat·u·ral (nach′ər əl, nach′rəl), *adj.* 1. of or pertaining to nature. 2. as formed by nature without human intervention. 3. to be expected or reckoned with. 4. without affectation or constraint. 5. inborn or innate. 6. being such because of one's inborn nature: *a natural mathematician.* 7. reproducing the original state closely: *a natural likeness.* 8. illegitimate: *a natural son.* 9. *Music.* without sharps or flats. —*n.* 10. *Informal.* any person or thing that is well-qualified in some way. 11. *Music.* the sign, placed before a note, canceling the effect of a previous sharp or flat. —**nat′u·ral·ness,** *n.*

nat′ural gas′, combustible gas formed naturally in the earth, consisting chiefly of methane: used as a fuel and to make carbon black and acetylene.

nat′ural his′tory, the study of all objects in nature, esp. in a nontechnical way. —**nat′ural histo′rian.**

nat·u·ral·ism (nach′ər ə liz′əm, nach′rə-), *n.* 1. a technique of rendering artistic or literary subjects so as to reproduce natural appearances or actual events in detail. 2. action arising from or based on natural instincts and desires alone. —**nat′u·ral·is′tic,** *adj.*

nat·u·ral·ist (nach′ər ə list, nach′rə-), *n.* 1. a person who studies natural history, esp. a zoologist or botanist. 2. an adherent of naturalism in literature or art.

nat·u·ral·ize (nach′ər ə līz′, nach′rə-), *v.t.,* **-ized, -iz·ing.** 1. to confer the rights and privileges of a citizen on. 2. to introduce (animals or plants) into a region and cause them to flourish as if native. —**nat′u·ral·i·za′tion,** *n.*

nat·u·ral·ly (nach′ər əl ē, nach′rə lē), *adv.* 1. as would be expected. 2. by inherent nature. 3. in a natural way.

nat′ural sci′ence, a science of objects or processes observable in nature, as biology, physics, etc. —**nat′ural sci′entist.**

nat′ural selec′tion, a process in nature resulting in the survival of only those forms of plant and animal life having certain favorable characteristics that best enable them to adapt to a specific environment.

na·ture (nā′chər), *n.* 1. the particular combination of qualities belonging to a person, animal, or thing. 2. the instincts or inherent tendencies directing conduct. 3. character, kind, or sort. **4.** the characteristic disposition of a person. **5.** natural scenery. **6.** the universe, with all its phenomena. **7.** the sum total of the forces at work throughout the universe. **8.** a primitive, wild condition. **9.** by nature, as a result of inherent qualities.

Nau·ga·hyde (nô′gə hīd′), *n. Trademark.* a strong vinyl fabric used for upholstery, luggage, etc.

naught (nôt), *n.* **1.** the symbol (0) denoting zero. **2.** *Literary.* nothing.

naugh·ty (nô′tē), *adj.,* **-ti·er, -ti·est. 1.** badly behaved or disobedient, esp. of a child. **2.** improper or indecent. —**naugh′ti·ly,** *adv.* —**naugh′ti·ness,** *n.*

nau·se·a (nô′zē ə, -zhə, -sē ə, -shə), *n.* **1.** sickness at the stomach often accompanied by an involuntary impulse to vomit. **2.** extreme disgust.

nau·se·ate (nô′zē āt′, -zhē-, -sē-, -shē-), *v.t., v.i.,* **-at·ed, -at·ing.** to affect or become affected with nausea. —**nau′se·a′tion,** *n.* —**nau′se·at′ing·ly,** *adv.*

nau·seous (nô′shəs, -zē əs), *adj.* **1.** causing nausea. **2.** ill with nausea. —**nau′seous·ness,** *n.*

naut., nautical.

nau·ti·cal (nô′ti kəl), *adj.* of seamen, ships, and navigation. —**nau′ti·cal·ly,** *adv.*

nau′tical mile′, mile (def. 2).

nau·ti·lus (nôt′ələs), *n., pl.* **nau·ti·lus·es, nau·ti·li** (nôt′ə lī′), a deep-sea mollusk having a spiral shell.

nav., 1. naval. **2.** navigable. **3.** navigation.

Nav·a·ho (nav′ə hō′, nä′və-), *n., pl.* **-hos, -hoes, -ho. 1.** a member of an American Indian people located in New Mexico and Arizona. **2.** their language. Also, **Nav′a·jo** (-hō)·

na·val (nā′vəl), *adj.* of, for, or possessing a navy.

nave (nāv), *n.* the principal area of a church, from the main entrance to the chancel.

na·vel (nā′vəl), *n.* umbilicus.

na′vel or′ange, an orange having at the apex a navellike formation containing a small secondary fruit.

nav·i·ga·ble (nav′ə gə bəl), *adj.* **1.** deep and wide enough to afford passage to ships. **2.** capable of being steered, as a vessel. —**nav′i·ga·bil′i·ty,** *n.* —**nav′i·ga·bly,** *adv.*

nav·i·gate (nav′ə gāt′), *v.t., v.i.,* **-gat·ed, -gat·ing. 1.** to move on or through (the sea or the air) in a vessel or aircraft. **2.** to direct or manage (a vessel or aircraft) on its course. **3.** *Informal.* to walk (in or across) safely and soberly. —**nav′i·ga′tion,** *n.* —**nav′i·ga′tor,** *n.*

na·vy (nā′vē), *n., pl.* **-vies. 1.** all the warships belonging to a nation. **2.** (*often cap.*) the complete body of such warships together with their officers and enlisted persons, equipment, yards, etc. **3.** Also called **na′vy blue′.** a dark blue.

na′vy bean′, a small, white bean, dried and used as food.

na′vy exchange′, a post exchange at a naval base.

nay (nā), *adv.* **1.** no (used esp. in voice voting). **2.** and not only so, but: *many good, nay, noble qualities.* —*n.* **3.** a negative vote or voter. **4.** a denial or refusal.

Naz·a·reth (naz′ər əth, -ə rith), *n.* a town in N Israel: the childhood home of Jesus.

Na·zi (nä′tsē, nat′sē), *n.* a member of the fascist political party under Adolf Hitler, which controlled Germany from 1933 to 1945. —**Na′zism, Na′zi·ism,** *n.*

NB, See **nota bene.**

Nb, niobium.

N.B., 1. New Brunswick. **2.** See **nota bene.**

N-bomb (en′bom′), *n.* See **neutron bomb.**

NBS, National Bureau of Standards.

NC, 1. North Carolina. **2.** no charge. **3.** numerical control (used in machine-tool computerization).

N.C., North Carolina.

NCO, Noncommissioned Officer.

NCV, no commercial value.

ND, North Dakota.

Nd, neodymium.

n.d., no date.

N.Dak., North Dakota. Also, **N.D.**

NDEA, National Defense Education Act.

NE, 1. Nebraska. **2.** northeast. **3.** northeastern.

Ne, neon.

N.E., 1. New England. **2.** northeast. **3.** northeastern.

NEA, National Education Association.

Ne·an·der·thal (nē an′dər thôl′, -tôl′, -täl′; nā än′dər täl′), *adj.* **1.** noting an extinct race of prehistoric people that lived in caves. **2.** rugged or uncouth.

Ne·a·pol·i·tan (nē′ə pol′i t°n), *adj.* **1.** of Naples. —*n.* **2.** a native or inhabitant of Naples.

neap′ tide′ (nēp), a tide at the time when the difference between low and high tide is smallest.

near (nēr), *adv.* **1.** at a relatively short distance. **2.** close in time. **3.** close in relation. **4.** almost or nearly. —*adj.* **5.** close in distance. **6.** close at hand in time. **7.** closely related or connected. **8.** intimate or familiar. **9.** narrow or close: *a near escape.* —*prep.* **10.** close to, by, or upon. —*v.t., v.i.* **11.** to come near (to). —**near′ness,** *n.*

near′ beer′, a malt beverage that has an alcoholic content of less than ½ percent.

near·by (nēr′bī′), adj., adv. close at hand.

Near′ East′, the countries of SW Asia and Egypt, and formerly including the Balkan States.

near·ly (nēr′lē), adv. almost: *nearly dead with cold.*

near·sight·ed (nēr′sī′tĭd), adj. 1. affected with myopia. 2. shortsighted (def. 3). —**near′sight′ed·ly,** adv. —**near′sight′ed·ness,** n.

neat (nēt), adj. 1. in a pleasingly orderly condition. 2. orderly in personal appearance or habits. 3. of a simple, pleasing appearance. 4. cleverly effective: *a neat plan.* 5. *Slang.* great or wonderful. 6. net: *neat profits.* 7. (of liquor) unadulterated or undiluted. —**neat′ly,** adv. —**neat′ness,** n.

neath (nēth, nēth), prep. *Literary.* beneath. Also, **'neath.**

neb (neb), n. *Scot.* 1. a bill or beak, as of a bird. 2. the nose, esp. of an animal. 3. **nib.**

NEB, New English Bible.

neb·bish (neb′ĭsh), n. *Slang.* a drab, awkward, insignificant person who is generally ignored. [< Yiddish]

Nebr., Nebraska.

Ne·bras·ka (nə bras′kə), n. a state in the central United States. *Cap.:* Lincoln. —**Ne·bras′kan,** adj., n.

neb·u·la (neb′yə lə), n., pl. **-lae** (-lī′), **-las.** any of the hazy masses of gases and small amounts of dust seen among the stars. —**neb′u·lar,** adj.

neb·u·lize (neb′yə līz′), v.t., **-lized, -liz·ing.** to reduce to fine spray. —**neb′u·liz′er,** n.

neb·u·los·i·ty (neb′yə los′i tē), n., pl. **-ties.** 1. nebulous matter. 2. the state or condition of being nebulous.

neb·u·lous (neb′yə ləs), adj. 1. confusedly hazy or vague. 2. of or resembling a nebula or nebulae. —**neb′u·lous·ly,** adv.

nec·es·sar·i·ly (nes′i sâr′ə lē, nes′i ser′-), adv. 1. by or of necessity. 2. as a necessary result.

nec·es·sar·y (nes′i ser′ē), adj., n., pl. **-sar·ies.** —adj. 1. absolutely needed. 2. happening or existing by necessity. 3. acting or proceeding from compulsion or obligation. —n. 4. something necessary. —**nec′es·sar′i·ness,** n. —**Syn.** 1. essential, indispensable, requisite.

ne·ces·si·tate (nə ses′i tāt′), v.t., **-tat·ed, -tat·ing.** to make necessary.

ne·ces·si·tous (nə ses′i təs), adj. *Literary.* needy or indigent. —**ne·ces′si·tous·ly,** adv.

ne·ces·si·ty (nə ses′i tē), n., pl. **-ties.** 1. something absolutely needed. 2. an imperative requirement or need.

3. the state or fact of being necessary or inevitable. 4. financial poverty. 5. of necessity, as an inevitable result.

neck (nek), n. 1. the part of an animal or human that connects the head and the trunk. 2. the part of a garment covering the neck. 3. a slender part that resembles a neck, as on a bottle, violin, etc. 4. a narrow strip of land, as an isthmus. 5. **neck and neck,** very close, as in a competition. 6. **stick one's neck out,** *Slang.* to take a risk. 7. **win by a neck,** to win by a small amount. —v.i. 8. *Informal.* to kiss and fondle one another. —**necked** (nekt), adj.

neck·er·chief (nek′ər chĭf), n. a cloth worn around the neck by women or men.

neck·lace (nek′lĭs), n. a string of beads, pearls, etc., for wearing around the neck as an ornament.

neck·line (nek′līn′), n. the contour of the neck of a garment.

neck·tie (nek′tī′), n. a decorative band of fabric worn around the neck, and tied in front with a knot or bow.

neck·wear (nek′wâr′), n. articles of dress, as neckties or scarves, to be worn around or at the neck.

ne·crol·o·gy (nə krol′ə jē, ne-), n., pl. **-gies.** a list of persons who have died within a certain time.

nec·ro·man·cy (nek′rə man′sē), n. 1. the art of divination through alleged communication with the dead. 2. sorcery. —**nec′ro·man′cer,** n.

ne·crop·o·lis (nə krop′ə lis, ne-), n., pl. **-lis·es.** a large cemetery of an ancient city.

ne·cro·sis (nə krō′sis, ne-), n. death of a piece of tissue or of an organ. —**ne·crot·ic** (nə krot′ik, ne-), adj.

nec·tar (nek′tər), n. 1. a sweet liquid secreted by plants and used by bees to make honey. 2. *Class. Myth.* the life-giving drink of the gods. 3. the juice of a fruit, esp. when not diluted.

nec·tar·ine (nek′tə rēn′, nek′tə rēn′), n. a peach having a smooth skin.

nee (nā), adj. born (used to introduce the maiden name of a married woman): *Mrs. Mary Johnson, nee Jackson.* Also, **née.**

need (nēd), n. 1. a lack of something wanted or deemed desirable. 2. urgent want, as of something requisite. 3. necessity arising from the circumstances of a case. 4. a situation or time of difficulty: *to help a friend in need.* 5. extreme poverty. 6. **if need be,** should the necessity arise. —v.t. 7. to have need of. 8. to be under an obligation or requirement: *He needs to be alert.* —v.i. 9. to be in need or want. —**need′er,** n.

need·ful (nēd′fəl), *adj.* serving a need or want.

nee·dle (nēd′⁰l), *n., v.,* **-dled, -dling.** —*n.* **1.** a small, slender piece of steel, with a sharp point at one end and a hole for thread at the other, used in sewing. **2.** any of various similar devices, as one for use in knitting or crocheting. **3.** the pointer on a dial, compass, etc. **4.** the hollow, pointed tip of a hypodermic syringe. **5.** a small, slender, pointed instrument, used to transmit vibrations, as from a phonograph record. **6.** a needle-shaped leaf, as of a conifer. —*v.t. Informal.* **7.** to prod or goad. **8.** to tease or annoy.

nee·dle·point (nēd′⁰l point′), *n.* **1.** embroidery worked on open-mesh canvas. **2.** Also called **nee′dlepoint lace′.** a lace in which a needle works out the design on paper.

need·less (nēd′lis), *adj.* not needed or wanted. —**need′less·ly,** *adv.* —**need′less·ness,** *n.*

nee·dle·work (nēd′⁰l wûrk′), *n.* the art of working with a needle, esp. in embroidery or needlepoint.

need·n't (nēd′⁰nt), contraction of *need not.*

needs (nēdz), *adv. Literary.* of necessity (only prec. or fol. by *must*): *It needs must be.*

need·y (nē′dē), *adj.,* **need·i·er, need·i·est.** in a state of need or poverty. —**need′i·ly,** *adv.*

ne'er (nâr), *adv. Literary.* never.

ne'er-do-well (nâr′dōō wel′), *n.* an idle, worthless person.

ne·far·i·ous (ni fâr′ē əs), *adj.* extremely wicked. —**ne·far′i·ous·ly,** *adv.* —**ne·far′i·ous·ness,** *n.*

neg., negative.

ne·gate (ni gāt′, neg′āt, nē′gāt), *v.t.,* **-gat·ed, -gat·ing.** **1.** to destroy the effect or validity of (something). **2.** to deny the truth or existence of (something). —**Syn. 1.** invalidate, nullify.

ne·ga·tion (ni gā′shən), *n.* **1.** the act of negating. **2.** the absence or opposite of something positive. **3.** a negative concept or doctrine.

neg·a·tive (neg′ə tiv), *adj., n., v.,* **-tived, -tiv·ing.** —*adj.* **1.** expressing negation or denial. **2.** lacking positive or affirmative attributes. **3.** lacking in constructiveness or helpfulness. **4.** *Math.* **a.** expressing a quantity less than zero. **b.** measured or proceeding in the direction opposite to that which is considered as positive. **5.** *Photog.* noting an image in which the light and dark tones are reversed. **6.** *Elect.* **a.** of electricity developed on a resin when rubbed with flannel. **b.** charged with electricity thus developed. **c.** caused by an excess of electrons. —*n.* **7.** a negative statement, answer, word, etc. **8.** a person or number of persons arguing against a resolution, statement, etc., as in a debate. **9.** a negative quality or characteristic. **10.** *Photog.* a negative image, as on a film, used chiefly for making positives. **11.** *Elect.* the negative plate or element in a voltaic battery. **12. in the negative,** in expression of refusal or rejection. —*v.t. Chiefly Brit. and Law.* **13.** to deny or contradict. **14.** to refute or disprove. **15.** to refuse assent or consent to. —**neg′a·tive·ly,** *adv.* —**neg′a·tive·ness, neg′a·tiv′i·ty,** *n.*

neg′ative in′come tax′, a system of public assistance whereby families or individuals are paid a guaranteed annual income of a predetermined amount.

neg·a·tiv·ism (neg′ə ti viz′əm), *n.* any negative philosophy, as extreme skepticism.

ne·glect (ni glekt′), *v.t.* **1.** to pay too little attention to, either intentionally or unintentionally. **2.** to be remiss in care for. **3.** to omit, as through carelessness. —*n.* **4.** the fault or an instance of neglecting. **5.** the state of being neglected. **6.** disregard, neglect. —**ne·glect′ful,** *adj.* —**ne·glect′ful·ly,** *adv.* —**Syn. 1.** disregard, ignore, overlook, slight.

neg·li·gee (neg′li zhā′, neg′li zhā′), *n.* **1.** a woman's dressing gown or robe, usually with soft, flowing lines. **2.** easy, informal attire. Also, **neg′li·gée′.**

neg·li·gent (neg′li jənt), *adj.* **1.** characterized by neglect. **2.** indifferent or careless. —**neg′li·gence,** *n.* —**neg′li·gent·ly,** *adv.*

neg·li·gi·ble (neg′li jə bəl), *adj.* being so trifling that it may safely be disregarded.

ne·go·ti·a·ble (ni gō′shē ə bəl, -shə-bəl), *adj.* **1.** (of drafts, securities, etc.) freely transferable for value by endorsement or delivery from one party to another. **2.** capable of being negotiated. —**ne·go′ti·a·bil′i·ty,** *n.*

ne·go·ti·ant (ni gō′shē ənt), *n. Obs.* a person who negotiates.

ne·go·ti·ate (ni gō′shē āt′), *v.,* **-at·ed, -at·ing.** —*v.i.* **1.** to deal or bargain with another or others. —*v.t.* **2.** to arrange for or bring about by discussion and settlement of terms. **3.** to move through or over in a satisfactory manner. **4.** to transfer (negotiable paper) by endorsement or delivery. —**ne·go′ti·a′tion,** *n.* —**ne·go′ti·a′tor,** *n.*

Neg·ri·tude (neg′ri tōōd′, -tyōōd′), *n.* the cultural heritage considered common to blacks or Negroes collectively.

Ne·gro (nē′grō), *n., pl.* **-groes,** *adj.*
Currently Often Offensive. *—n.* **1.** a
person having Negroid characteristics. *—adj.* **2.** of Negroes. [< Sp
and Pg *negro* black < L *niger* black]
—Usage. Many people today consider *Negro* to be derogatory and
offensive, preferring the use of *black.*

Ne·groid (nē′groid), *n.* **1.** a member
of one of the major traditional racial
groups of human beings marked by
brown skin, curly hair, and certain
other genetic features, including the
people of Africa south of the Sahara
and their descendants. *—adj.* **2.** of
or belonging to this group.

Neh·ru (nā′rōō, ne′rōō), *n.* **Ja·wa·har·lal** (jə wə hər läl′), 1889–1964,
Hindu political leader.

neigh (nā), *v.i.* **1.** to utter the cry of
a horse. *—n.* **2.** the cry of a horse.

neigh·bor (nā′bər), *n.* **1.** a person who
lives near another. **2.** one's fellow
human being. *—adj.* **3.** living or situated nearby. *—v.t.* **4.** to live or be
situated near to. Also, *Brit.,* **neigh′·bour.** **—neigh′bor·ing,** *adj.*

neigh·bor·hood (nā′bər hŏŏd′), *n.* **1.**
the area or region surrounding or
near some place, person, etc. **2.** a
district or locality with reference to
its character or inhabitants. **3.** a
number of persons living near one
another. **4. in the neighborhood of,**
Informal. about or approximately.
—Syn. 1. vicinity.

neigh·bor·ly (nā′bər lē), *adj.* showing
qualities befitting a neighbor. **—neigh′bor·li·ness,** *n.*

nei·ther (nē′t͟hər, nī′-), *conj.* **1.** not
either: *Neither John nor Betty is at
home.* **2.** nor: *Bob can't go, and
neither can I.* *—adj.* **3.** not either:
Neither statement is true. *—pron.* **4.**
not the one or the other: *Neither is
to be trusted.*

nel·son (nel′sən), *n.* a wrestling hold
in which pressure is applied to the
head, neck, and arm of an opponent.

nem·a·tode (nem′ə tōd′), *n.* any unsegmented worm having an elongated, cylindrical body.

nem·e·sis (nem′i sis), *n., pl.* **-ses**
(-sēz′). **1.** an agent or act of retribution. **2.** someone or something that
defeats or destroys one. **3.** an opponent whom a person cannot best.

neo-, a combining form meaning: **a.**
new or recent: *neophyte.* **b.** in a
new, modified manner: *neoclassicism.*

ne·o·clas·si·cism (nē′ō klas′ə siz′əm),
n. the movement for a revival or
adaptation of a classic style, as in
art, literature, etc. **—ne′o·clas′sic,
ne′o·clas′si·cal,** *adj.*

ne·o·co·lo·ni·al·ism (nē′ō kə lō′nē ə-
liz′əm), *n.* the policy of a strong na-

tion in seeking political and economic hegemony over a newly independent nation without necessarily
reducing it to the legal status of a
colony. **—ne′o·co·lo′ni·al,** *adj.* **—ne′o·co·lo′ni·al·ist,** *n.*

ne·o·dym·i·um (nē′ō dim′ē əm), *n.*
Chem. a rare-earth, metallic element,
used to color glassware. *Symbol:*
Nd; *at. wt.:* 144.24; *at. no.:* 60.

ne·ol·o·gism (nē ol′ə jiz′əm), *n.* **1.** a
new word, usage, or phrase. **2.** the
use of new words or new senses of
words. Also, **ne·ol′o·gy** (-jē).

ne·on (nē′on), *n.* **1.** a chemically inert gaseous element occurring in the
earth's atmosphere, used chiefly for
filling electrical lamps. *Symbol:* Ne;
at. wt.: 20.183; *at. no.:* 10. **2.** Also
called **ne′on lamp′.** a lamp in which
an electric tube filled with neon
emits a reddish glow, used for nighttime advertising signs.

ne·o·na·tal (nē′ō nāt′l), *adj.* of newborn children. **—ne′o·na′tal·ly,** *adv.*
—ne·o·nate (nē′ə nāt′), *n.*

ne·o·phyte (nē′ə fīt′), *n.* **1.** a person
newly converted to a belief. **2.** a beginner or tyro.

ne·o·plasm (nē′ə plaz′əm), *n.* a new
growth of different or abnormal body
tissue. **—ne′o·plas′tic** (-plas′tik), *adj.*

ne·o·prene (nē′ə prēn′), *n.* an oil-resistant synthetic rubber, used chiefly
in paints, shoe soles, etc.

Ne·pal (nə pôl′, -päl′, -pal′, nā-), *n.*
a country in the Himalayas. **—Nep·a·lese** (nep′ə lēz′), *adj., n.*

ne·pen·the (ni pen′thē), *n.* **1.** a drug
used by the ancients to bring forgetfulness of sorrow or trouble. **2.** anything inducing a pleasurable sensation of forgetfulness.

neph·ew (nef′yōō), *n.* **1.** a son of
one's brother or sister. **2.** a son of
one's husband's or wife's brother or
sister.

neph·rite (nef′rīt), *n.* a whitish to
dark-green form of jade.

ne·phri·tis (nə frī′tis), *n.* inflammation of the kidneys. **—ne·phrit′ic**
(-frit′ik), *adj.*

ne plus ul·tra (nē plus ul′trə), *Latin.*
the highest point.

nep·o·tism (nep′ə tiz′əm), *n.* favoritism shown on the basis of family relationship, as in business or politics.
—nep′o·tis′tic, nep′o·tis′ti·cal, *adj.*

Nep·tune (nep′tōōn, -tyōōn), *n.* **1.** the
ancient Roman god of the sea. **2.** the
planet eighth in order from the sun.
—Nep·tu′ni·an, *adj.*

nep·tu·ni·um (nep tōō′nē əm, -tyōō′-),
n. *Chem.* a radioactive element produced by bombarding uranium with
neutrons. *Symbol:* Np; *at. wt.:* 237;
at. no.: 93.

nerd (nûrd), *n.* *Slang.* a boring, dull,
or unattractive person.

Ne·ro (nēr'ō), *n.* A.D. 37–68, emperor of Rome 54–68.

nerve (nûrv), *n., v.,* **nerved, nerv·ing.** —*n.* **1.** one or more bundles of fibers forming part of a system that conveys impulses of sensation, motion, etc., between the brain or spinal cord and other parts of the body. **2.** firmness or courage. **3.** nerves, nervousness or hysteria. **4.** *Informal.* impertinence or audacity. **5. get on one's nerves,** to irritate or provoke one. —*v.t.* **6.** to give strength or courage to. —**nerved** (nûrvd), *adj.*

nerve' cell', **1.** any of the cells constituting the cellular element of nerve tissue. **2.** one of the essential cells of a nerve center.

nerve' cen'ter, **1.** a group of nerve cells closely working together in the performance of some function. **2.** a source of authority or information.

nerve' gas', a poison gas that paralyzes the nervous system, esp. that part of the system controlling respiration.

nerve·less (nûrv'lis), *adj.* **1.** lacking strength or vigor. **2.** without nervousness, as in emergencies. —**nerve'less·ly,** *adv.* —**nerve'less·ness,** *n.*

nerve-rack·ing (nûrv'rak'ing), *adj.* extremely irritating or trying. Also, **nerve'-wrack'ing.**

nerv·ous (nûr'vəs), *adj.* **1.** easily made fearful or upset. **2.** showing fear or uneasiness. **3.** of or pertaining to the nerves or nervous system. **4.** *Archaic.* sinewy or strong. —**nerv'ous·ly,** *adv.* —**nerv'ous·ness,** *n.* — **Syn.** 1, 2. anxious, apprehensive, high-strung, tense.

nerv'ous break'down, a case of neurasthenia.

nerv'ous sys'tem, the system of nerves and nerve centers in an animal or human, including the brain, spinal cord, nerves, and ganglia.

nerv·y (nûr'vē), *adj.,* **nerv·i·er, nerv·i·est.** **1.** *Informal.* brashly presumptuous. **2.** showing firmness or courage. **3.** *Brit. Informal.* nervous (def. 1). —**nerv'i·ly,** *adv.* —**nerv'i·ness,** *n.*

n.e.s., not elsewhere specified.

-ness, a suffix meaning: a. quality or state: *darkness.* b. something exemplifying a quality or state: *kindness.*

nest (nest), *n.* **1.** the structure of twigs, grass, mud, etc., formed by a bird as a place to lay eggs and rear its young. **2.** a structure built by insects, fishes, etc., for similar purposes. **3.** a snug retreat or refuge. **4.** an assemblage of things lying or set close together or within one another: *a nest of tables.* **5.** a place where something bad is fostered or flourishes: *a robbers' nest.* **6.** the oc-cupants of such a place. —*v.t.* **7.** to settle or place in or as if in a nest. **8.** to fit or place one within another. —*v.i.* **9.** to build or have a nest. — **nest'er,** *n.* —**nest'like',** *adj.*

n'est-ce pas (nes pä'), *French.* isn't that so?

nest' egg', **1.** money saved and held in reserve for emergencies or retirement. **2.** a natural or artificial egg left in a nest to induce a hen to continue laying eggs there.

nes·tle (nes'əl), *v.,* **-tled, -tling.** —*v.i.* **1.** to lie close and snug, like a bird in a nest. **2.** to settle down comfortably. **3.** to lie or be located in a sheltered spot. —*v.t.* **4.** to provide with or settle in a nest, as a bird. **5.** to put or press affectionately. —**nes'tler,** *n.*

nest·ling (nest'ling, nes'ling), *n.* a young bird not yet old enough to leave the nest.

net¹ (net), *n., v.,* **net·ted, net·ting.** —*n.* **1.** a lacelike fabric with a uniform mesh of cotton, silk, etc. **2.** any open, meshed fabric, as a device for catching animals or the barrier across the center of a tennis court. **3.** anything serving to catch or ensnare. —*v.t.* **4.** to cover or enclose with or as with a net. **5.** to catch in or as in a net. —**net'ta·ble,** *adj.*

net² (net), *adj., n., v.,* **net·ted, net·ting.** —*adj.* **1.** remaining after deductions: *net income.* **2.** after deduction of tare: *net weight.* **3.** totally conclusive. —*n.* **4.** a net amount, weight, profit, etc. —*v.t.* **5.** to gain or produce as clear profit. —**net'ta·ble,** *adj.*

NET, National Educational Television.

Neth., Netherlands.

neth·er (nethʹər), *adj.* lying or believed to lie beneath the earth's surface.

Neth·er·lands, the (nethʹər ləndz), a country in W Europe.

neth·er·most (nethʹər mōst', -məst), *adj. Literary.* lowest.

neth'er world', the infernal regions.

net·ting (net'ing), *n.* netted or meshed material, as of fabric or wire.

net·tle (net'əl), *n., v.,* **-tled, -tling.** — *n.* **1.** an herb covered with stinging hairs. —*v.t.* **2.** to arouse to temporary pique. —**net'tler,** *n.* —**Syn.** 2. irritate, provoke, vex.

net·tle·some (net'əl səm), *adj.* causing temporary pique.

net' ton', *Com. Obs.* a short ton.

net·work (net'wûrk'), *n.* **1.** any netlike, crisscross combination of lines, passages, etc. **2.** a netting or net. **3.** *Radio and Television.* a group of stations linked together so that the same programs can be carried.

neu·ral (nŏŏr'əl, nyŏŏr'-), *adj.* of a nerve or the nervous system. —neu'ral·ly, *adv.*

neu·ral·gia (nŏŏ ral'jə, nyŏŏ-), *n.* sharp and paroxysmal pain along a nerve. —neu·ral'gic, *adj.*

neu·ras·the·ni·a (nŏŏr'əs thē'nē ə, nyŏŏr'-), *n.* nervous debility and exhaustion, as from overwork or prolonged mental strain. —neu'ras·then'ic (-then'ik), *adj., n.*

neu·ri·tis (nŏŏ rī'tis, nyŏŏ-), *n.* inflammation of a nerve. —neu·rit'ic (-rit'ik), *adj., n.*

neuro-, a combining form meaning "nerve," "nerves," or "nervous system": *neurology.* Also, neur-.

neurol., neurology.

neu·rol·o·gy (nŏŏ rol'ə jē, nyŏŏ-), *n.* the medical science of the nerves and the nervous system, esp. of the diseases affecting them. —neu·ro·log·i·cal (nŏŏr'ə loj'i kəl, nyŏŏr'-), *adj.* —neu'ro·log'i·cal·ly, *adv.* —neu·rol'o·gist, *n.*

neu·ron (nŏŏr'on, nyŏŏr'-), *n.* a nerve cell with its processes. Also, neu·rone (nŏŏr'ōn, nyŏŏr'-).

neu·ro·sis (nŏŏ rō'sis, nyŏŏ-), *n., pl.* -ses (-sēz). an emotional disorder in which anxieties, phobias, obsessions, etc., dominate the personality.

neu·rot·ic (nŏŏ rot'ik, nyŏŏ-), *adj.* 1. of, having, or characteristic of neurosis. —*n.* 2. a neurotic person. —neu·rot'i·cal·ly, *adv.*

neut., neuter.

neu·ter (nŏŏ'tər, nyŏŏ'-), *adj.* 1. *Gram.* noting the gender containing words not classed as masculine or feminine. 2. *Biol.* having no organs of reproduction. 3. *Zool.* having imperfectly developed sexual organs. 4. *Bot.* having neither stamens nor pistils. —*n.* 5. *Gram.* the neuter gender. 6. a neuter animal or plant. —*v.t.* 7. to spay or castrate (a dog or cat).

neu·tral (nŏŏ'trəl, nyŏŏ'-), *adj.* 1. not taking the part of either side in a dispute or war. 2. of no particular kind or characteristics. 3. (of a color or shade) a. without hue. b. matching well with most other colors or shades. 4. *Chem.* exhibiting neither acid nor alkaline qualities. 5. *Elect.* neither positively nor negatively charged. —*n.* 6. a neutral person or nation. 7. a neutral color. 8. *Mach.* the position of gears when not engaged. —neu'tral·ly, *adv.*

neu·tral·ism (nŏŏ'trə liz'əm, nyŏŏ'-), *n.* the policy or advocacy of maintaining strict neutrality in foreign affairs. —neu'tral·ist, *n., adj.*

neu·tral·i·ty (nŏŏ tral'i tē, nyŏŏ-), *n.* 1. the state of being neutral. 2. the policy or status of a neutral nation.

neu·tral·ize (nŏŏ'trə līz', nyŏŏ'-), *v.t.,* -ized, -iz·ing. 1. to make neutral. 2. to make ineffective. —neu'tral·i·za'tion, *n.* —neu'tral·iz'er, *n.*

neu'tral spir'its, nonflavored alcohol of 190 proof, used for blending with straight whiskeys.

neu·tri·no (nŏŏ trē'nō, nyŏŏ-), *n., pl.* -nos. *Physics.* an elementary particle having neutral charge and no mass.

neu·tron (nŏŏ'tron, nyŏŏ'-), *n. Physics.* an elementary particle having a mass slightly greater than that of a proton, and no charge.

neu'tron bomb', a nuclear bomb with lethal radiation but little blast so that it can kill people without destroying buildings at the target area.

Nev., Nevada.

Ne·va·da (nə vad'ə, -vä'də), *n.* a state in the W United States. *Cap.:* Carson City. —Ne·va'dan, *adj., n.*

nev·er (nev'ər), *adv.* 1. not ever or at no time. 2. not at all or absolutely not.

nev·er·more (nev'ər môr', -mōr'), *adv.* never again.

nev'er-nev'er land' (nev'ər nev'ər), an unreal, imaginary condition or place.

nev·er·the·less (nev'ər thə les'), *adv.* in spite of that.

ne·vus (nē'vəs), *n., pl.* -vi (-vī). any congenital anomaly of the skin, as a birthmark. —ne·void (nē'void), *adj.*

new (nŏŏ, nyŏŏ), *adj.* 1. of recent origin, production, purchase, etc. 2. of a kind now appearing for the first time. 3. having but lately become known. 4. unfamiliar or strange. 5. having but lately come to a place, position, status, etc. 6. unaccustomed: *men new to such work.* 7. coming or occurring afresh: *new gains.* 8. different and better. 9. other than the former or the old. 10. (*cap.*) modern (def. 2). —*adv.* 11. recently or lately. 12. anew or afresh. —new'ness, *n.* —Syn. 1. fresh, novel, original.

New·ark (nŏŏ'ərk, nyŏŏ'-), *n.* a city in NE New Jersey.

New' Bed'ford, a seaport in SE Massachusetts.

new' blood', people recently brought into an organization and expected to revitalize it.

new·born (nŏŏ'bôrn', nyŏŏ'-), *adj., n., pl.* -born, -borns. —*adj.* 1. only just born. 2. born anew. —*n.* 3. a newborn infant.

New' Bruns'wick (brunz'wik), a province in SE Canada. *Cap.:* Fredericton.

new·com·er (nŏŏ'kum'ər, nyŏŏ'-), *n.* a person who has recently come to a place or position.

New′ Deal′, the domestic policies and administration of President Franklin D. Roosevelt for economic recovery and social reforms. —**New′ Deal′er.**

New′ Del′hi, the capital of India, in the N part, adjacent to Delhi.

new·el (nōō′əl, nyōō′-), *n.* **1.** a central pillar from which the steps of a winding stair radiate. **2.** Also called **new′el post′.** a post supporting one end of the handrail of a flight of stairs.

New′ Eng′land, an area in the NE United States, including Connecticut, Maine, Massachusetts, New Hampshire, Rhode Island, and Vermont. —**New′ Eng′lander.**

Newf., Newfoundland.

new·fan·gled (nōō′fang′gəld, nyōō′-), *adj.* **1.** *Often Derogatory.* of a new kind or fashion. **2.** *Rare.* fond of novelty.

new-fash·ioned (nōō′fash′ənd, nyōō′-), *adj.* **1.** lately come into fashion. **2.** modern or up-to-date.

New·found·land (nōō′fənd land′, -lənd), *n.* a province in E Canada, composed of an island off the SE coast and Labrador. *Cap.:* St. John's.

New′ Guin′ea, a large island N of Australia.

New′ Hamp′shire, a state in the NE United States. *Cap.:* Concord.

New′ Ha′ven (hā′vən), a seaport in S Connecticut.

New′ Jer′sey, a state in the E United States. *Cap.:* Trenton. —**New′ Jer′sey·ite** (jûr′zē ĩt′).

New′ Left′, a movement since the mid-1960's in the U.S. by young intellectuals advocating social reform, racial equality, pacifism, and other liberal goals.

new·ly (nōō′lē, nyōō′-), *adv.* **1.** recently or lately. **2.** anew or afresh. **3.** in a new manner or form.

new·ly·wed (nōō′lē wed′, nyōō′-), *n.* a person who has recently married.

new′ math′, mathematics in accord with the theory of sets. Also called **new′ mathemat′ics.**

New′ Mex′ico, a state in the SW United States. *Cap.:* Santa Fe.

new′ moon′, **1.** the moon either when in conjunction with the sun or soon after, being either invisible or visible only as a slender crescent. **2.** the phase of the moon at this time.

New′ Or′le·ans (ôr′lē ənz, ôr lēnz′, ôr′lənz), a seaport in SE Louisiana.

New′port News′ (nōō′pôrt′, -pôrt′, nyōō′-), a seaport in SE Virginia.

news (nōōz, nyōōz), *n.* **1.** a report of a recent event. **2.** a report on current events in a newspaper or on radio or television. **3.** such reports taken collectively: *There's good news tonight.*

news·boy (nōōz′boi′, nyōōz′-), *n.* a boy who sells or delivers newspapers. —**news′girl,** *n.fem.*

news·cast (nōōz′kast′, -käst′, nyōōz′-), *n.* a broadcast of news on radio or television. —**news′cast′er,** *n.*

news·deal·er (nōōz′dē′lər, nyōōz′-), *n.* a person who sells newspapers and periodicals.

news·let·ter (nōōz′let′ər, nyōōz′-), *n.* an analytical news report for periodic distribution to a special audience.

news·man (nōōz′man′, nyōōz′-), *n., pl.* **-men.** **1.** a person employed to gather or report news, as for a newspaper. **2.** newsdealer. —**news′wom′an,** *n. fem.*

news·pa·per (nōōz′pā′pər, nyōōz′-), *n.* a publication, usually issued daily or weekly, containing news, comment, features, photographs, and advertising.

news·pa·per·man (nōōz′pā′pər man′, nyōōz′-), *n.* **1.** a man employed by a newspaper, as a reporter, writer, etc. **2.** the owner of a newspaper. —**news′pa′per·wom′an,** *n.fem.*

new·speak (nōō′spēk′, nyōō′-), *n.* an official style of saying something in the guise of its opposite.

news·print (nōōz′print′, nyōōz′-), *n.* a low-grade paper used chiefly for newspapers.

news·reel (nōōz′rēl′, nyōōz′-), *n.* a short motion picture presenting current events (popular before TV).

news·stand (nōōz′stand′, nyōōz′-), *n.* a stall at which newspapers and periodicals are sold.

news·wor·thy (nōōz′wûr′t͟hē, nyōōz′-), *adj.* of sufficient potential interest to warrant press coverage.

news·y (nōō′zē, nyōō′-), *adj.,* **news·i·er, news·i·est.** *Informal.* **1.** full of news. **2.** chatty or gossipy. —**news′i·ness,** *n.*

newt (nōōt, nyōōt), *n.* any of several brilliantly colored salamanders living in the water.

New Test., New Testament.

New′ Tes′tament, the portion of the Bible recording the experience and teachings of Christ and His disciples.

New·ton (nōōt′ən, nyōōt′-), *n.* **Sir Isaac,** 1642–1727, English philosopher and mathematician. —**New·to′ni·an,** *adj., n.*

new′ town′, a town built according to a preplanned design to contain housing, stores, factories, parks, playgrounds, etc.

new′ wave′, a movement, esp. of French film directors of the late 1950's, that breaks with traditional concepts and techniques. Also, **New′ Wave′.**

New′ World′. See **Western Hemisphere.**

new′ year′, 1. the year approaching or newly begun. **2.** See **New Year's Day.**

New′ Year's′ Day′, January 1.

New′ Year's′ Eve′, the night of December 31.

New′ York′, 1. a state in the NE United States. *Cap.:* Albany. **2.** Also called **New′ York′ Cit′y,** a city and seaport in SE New York. —**New′ York′er.**

New′ Zea′land (zē′lənd), a country in the S Pacific. —**New′ Zea′land·er.**

next (nekst), *adj.* **1.** immediately following. **2.** nearest in space. —*adv.* **3.** in the nearest place, time, importance, etc. **4.** on the first occasion to follow. —*prep.* **5.** adjacent to.

next-door (neks′dôr′, -dōr′, nekst′-), *adj.* situated or living in the next building, house, etc.

nex·us (nek′səs), *n., pl.* **-us·es, -us. 1.** a means of connection. **2.** a connected series or group.

NF, 1. no funds. **2.** Norman French.

Nfld., Newfoundland. Also, **Nfd.**

N.G., 1. National Guard. **2.** no good.

n.g., no good

NGk., New Greek. Also, **N.Gk.**

NH, New Hampshire. Also, **N.H.**

NHI, *Brit.* National Health Insurance.

NHS, *Brit.* National Health Service.

Ni, nickel.

ni·a·cin (nī′ə sin), *n.* See **nicotinic acid.**

Niag′ara Falls′ (nī ag′rə, -ag′ər ə), the falls on a river (**Niag′ara Riv′er**) flowing from Lake Erie into Lake Ontario.

nib (nib), *n.* the writing end of a pen.

nib·ble (nib′əl), *v.,* **-bled, -bling,** *n.* —*v.t., v.i.* **1.** to eat small bits of (something). **2.** to bite slightly or gently. —*n.* **3.** a small or gentle bite. —**nib′bler,** *n.*

nibs (nibz), *n.* **his nibs,** *Slang.* a haughty or tyrannical person.

Nic·a·ra·gua (nik′ə rä′gwə), *n.* a country in Central America. —**Nic′a·ra′guan,** *n., adj.*

nice (nīs), *adj.,* **nic·er, nic·est. 1.** pleasing and agreeable. **2.** amiably pleasant. **3.** respectable and well-mannered. **4.** showing or requiring great accuracy, precision, or skill: *nice workmanship.* **5.** very fine or subtle: *a nice distinction.* **6.** requiring tact or care. **7.** suitable or proper. **8.** *Archaic.* fastidious or particular. [< OF < L *nescius* ignorant, incapable] —**nice′ly,** *adv.* —**nice′ness,** *n.*

nice-nel·ly·ism (nīs′nel′ē iz′əm), *n.* **1.** excessive modesty. **2.** a euphemism. Also, **nice′-Nel′ly·ism.** —**nice′-nel′ly,** *adj.*

ni·ce·ty (nī′si tē), *n., pl.* **-ties. 1.** a delicate or fine point. **2.** Usually,

niceties. a refinement or elegance, as of manners or living. **3.** delicacy of character, as of something requiring care or tact. **4.** exactness or precision. —**Syn. 1.** distinction, subtlety.

niche (nich), *n.* **1.** an ornamental recess in a wall, for a statue or other decorative object. **2.** a place or position suitable for a person or thing.

nick (nik), *n.* **1.** a notch, groove, or chip cut into a surface. **2. in the nick of time,** at the vital moment. —*v.t.* **3.** to make a nick or nicks in. **4.** to injure slightly.

nick·el (nik′əl), *n.* **1.** *Chem.* a hard, silvery-white, ductile and malleable metallic element, used chiefly in alloys. *Symbol:* Ni; *at. wt.:* 58.71; *at. no.:* 28. **2.** a U.S. or Canadian coin equal to five cents.

nick·el·o·de·on (nik′ə lō′dē ən), *n.* **1.** an early motion-picture theater, admission to which cost 5 cents. **2.** an early type of jukebox.

nick′el sil′ver, a silver-white alloy of copper, zinc, and nickel, used in tableware, heating coils, etc.

nick·er (nik′ər), *v., n. Scot.* neigh.

nick·name (nik′nām′), *n., v.,* **-named, -nam·ing.** —*n.* **1.** a name substituted for the name of a person, place, etc., as in ridicule. **2.** a familiar form of a proper name, as *Jim* for *James.* —*v.t.* **3.** to call by a nickname.

nic·o·tine (nik′ə tēn′, -tin, nik′ə tēn′), *n.* a highly toxic liquid alkaloid found in tobacco and valued as an insecticide. —**nic·o·tin·ic** (nik′ə tin′-ik), *adj.*

nic′otin′ic ac′id, an acid that is a component of the vitamin-B complex, used in the treatment of pellagra.

niece (nēs), *n.* **1.** a daughter of one's brother or sister. **2.** a daughter of one's husband's or wife's brother or sister.

Niel′sen rat′ing (nēl′sən), an estimate of the number of viewers of a television program based on monitoring the sets of a selected sample of viewers. [after A. C. *Nielsen* Co., its originator]

Nie·tzsche (nē′chə, -chē), *n.* **Friedrich** (frē′drikɦ), 1844–1900, German philosopher.

nif·ty (nif′tē), *adj.,* **-ti·er, -ti·est.** *Informal.* **1.** smart or stylish. **2.** fine or splendid.

Ni·ger (nī′jər), *n.* a country in NW Africa.

Ni·ger·i·a (nī jēr′ē ə), *n.* a country in W Africa. —**Ni·ge′ri·an,** *adj., n.*

nig·gard (nig′ərd), *n.* **1.** an extremely —**nig′gard·ly,** *adj., adv.* —**nig′gard·li·ness,** *n.*

stingy person. —*adj.* **2.** very stingy.

nig·gling (nig′ling), *adj.* **1.** elaborately petty. **2.** demanding excessive care or attention. **3.** fussy or fastidious. —**nig′gler,** *n.* —**nig′gling·ly,** *adv.*

nigh (nī), *adv., adj.,* **nigh·er, nigh·est,** *prep. Archaic.* near.

night (nīt), *n.* **1.** the period of darkness between sunset and sunrise. **2.** a period of ignorance, misfortune, etc.

night′ blind′ness, poor vision at night or in a dim light. —**night′-blind′,** *adj.*

night·cap (nīt′kap′), *n.* **1.** a cap worn with night clothes. **2.** *Informal.* an alcoholic drink taken at bedtime.

night′ clothes′, garments for wear in bed.

night·club (nīt′klub′), *n.* a restaurant that is open until early in the morning and that also provides drink, music, and other entertainment.

night′ crawl′er, a large earthworm that emerges from its burrow at night.

night·fall (nīt′fôl′), *n.* the coming of night.

night·gown (nīt′goun′), *n.* a loose gown, worn in bed by women or children. Also called **night′dress′** (-dres′).

night·hawk (nīt′hôk′), *n.* **1.** any of several long-winged, night-flying birds related to the whippoorwill. **2.** *Informal.* a night owl.

night·ie (nī′tē), *n. Informal.* a night-gown.

night·in·gale (nīt′ən gāl′, nī′ting-), *n.* a small, Old World migratory thrush noted for the melodious song of the male, esp. at night.

Night·in·gale (nīt′ən gāl′, nī′ting-), *n.* **Florence,** 1820–1910, English nurse and reformer of hospital conditions.

night′ life′, entertainment activities at night, esp. in theaters, nightclubs, etc.

night·ly (nīt′lē), *adj.* **1.** coming or occurring at night or each night. **2.** of or characteristic of the night. —*adv.* **3.** at or by night. **4.** on every night.

night·mare (nīt′mâr′), *n.* **1.** a dream full of great fear or terror. **2.** any terrifying thought or experience. —**night′mar′ish,** *adj.*

night′ owl′, *Informal.* a person who often stays up late at night.

night·rid·er (nīt′rī′dər), *n. U.S.* one of a band of mounted terrorists active at night, esp. during the Reconstruction.

night·shade (nīt′shād′), *n.* any of various plants related to the potato and tomato that bear black or red berries, some species of which are poisonous.

night·shirt (nīt′shûrt′), *n.* a loose shirt for wearing in bed.

night·spot (nīt′spot′), *n. Informal.* a nightclub.

night′ stick′, a heavy stick carried by a policeman or policewoman.

night′ ta′ble, a small table next to a bed. Also called **night·stand** (nīt′-stand′).

night·time (nīt′tīm′), *n.* the time between evening and morning.

night·walk·er (nīt′wôk′ər), *n.* a person who walks or roves about at night, as a thief, prostitute, etc.

night′ watch′man, a watchman who is on duty at night.

night·wear (nīt′wâr′), *n.* See **night clothes.**

nig·ri·tude (nig′ri tōōd′, -tyōōd′, nī′gri-), *n. Literary.* utter darkness.

ni·hil·ism (nī′ə liz′əm, nē′-), *n.* **1.** total rejection of value statements or moral judgments. **2.** absolute destructiveness toward the world at large and oneself. —**ni′hil·ist,** *n., adj.* —**ni′hil·is′tic,** *adj.*

nil (nil), *n.* nothing or zero.

Nile (nīl), *n.* the longest river in Africa, flowing N through Egypt to the Mediterranean Sea.

nim·ble (nim′bəl), *adj.,* **-bler, -blest. 1.** quick and light in movement. **2.** quick to understand and learn. —**nim′ble·ness,** *n.* —**nim′bly,** *adv.*

nim·bus (nim′bəs), *n., pl.* **-bi** (-bī), **-bus·es. 1.** a formless, dark-gray cloud layer. **2.** an aura or atmosphere surrounding a person or thing. **3.** halo (def. 1).

Nim·rod (nim′rod), *n. Bible.* a great hunter.

nin·com·poop (nin′kəm pōōp′, ning′-), *n.* a foolish or stupid person.

nine (nīn), *n.* **1.** a cardinal number, eight plus one. **2.** a symbol for this number, as 9 or IX. —*adj.* **3.** amounting to nine in number. —**ninth** (nīnth), *adj., n.*

nine′ days′′ won′der, an event that arouses short-lived excitement.

nine·pins (nīn′pinz′), *n.* tenpins played without the head pin.

nine·teen (nīn′tēn′), *n.* **1.** a cardinal number, ten plus nine. **2.** a symbol for this number, as 19 or XIX. —*adj.* **3.** amounting to nineteen in number. —**nine′teenth′** (-tēnth′), *adj., n.*

nine·ty (nīn′tē), *n., pl.* **-ties,** *adj.* —*n.* **1.** a cardinal number, ten times nine. **2.** a symbol for this number, as 90 or XC. —*adj.* **3.** amounting to 90 in number. —**nine′ti·eth** (-ith), *adj., n.*

nin·ny (nin′ē), *n., pl.* **-nies.** a fool or simpleton.

ni·non (nē nôn′), *n.* a sturdy chiffon.

ni·o·bi·um (nī ō′bē əm), *n. Chem.* a steel-gray metallic element, used chiefly in alloy steel. *Symbol:* Nb; *at. wt.:* 92.906; *at. no.:* 41.

nip¹ (nip), *v.*, **nipped, nip·ping,** *n.* —
v.t. **1.** to compress tightly between
two surfaces or points. **2.** to sever
by pinching, biting, or snipping. **3.**
to check in growth or development.
4. to affect painfully or injuriously,
as cold does. **5.** *Informal.* **a.** to
snatch away suddenly. **b.** to steal.
—*n.* **6.** a pinch or bite. **7.** a sharp
cold. **8.** a biting taste. **9.** a small
bit or quantity. **10. nip and tuck,**
Informal. very close, as in a contest.

nip² (nip), *n.*, *v.*, **nipped, nip·ping.**
—*n.* **1.** a small drink of liquor. —*v.t.*,
v.i. **2.** to drink (liquor) in nips.

nip·per (nip′ər), *n.* **1.** a person or
thing that nips. **2.** Usually, **nippers.**
a device for nipping, as pincers or
forceps. **3.** one of the large claws of
a crustacean.

nip·ple (nip′əl), *n.* **1.** a protuberance
of the breast or udder where, in
the female, the milk ducts discharge.
2. something resembling it, as the
mouthpiece of a nursing bottle.

Nip·pon (ni pon′, nip′on), *n.* a Japanese name of **Japan.** —**Nip′pon·ese′**
(-ə nēz′), *n., adj.*

nip·py (nip′ē), *adj.*, **-pi·er, -pi·est. 1.**
sharp or biting: *a nippy taste.* **2.**
chilly or chilling.

nir·va·na (nir vä′nə, -van′ə, nər-), *n.*
1. (*often cap.*) *Buddhism.* freedom
from the endless cycle of personal
reincarnations, as a result of the extinction of individual passion, hatred, and delusion. **2.** a state of freedom from worry and the external
world.

Ni·sei (nē′sā′), *n., pl.* **-sei.** a person
of Japanese descent, born and edu-
cated in the U.S. [< Jap: second
generation]

ni·si (nī′sī), *adj., conj. Law.* not yet final or absolute: *to grant a decree nisi.*

nit (nit), *n.* **1.** the egg of a parasitic
insect, esp. of a louse. **2.** the young
of such an insect.

ni·ter (nī′tər), *n.* **1.** See **potassium
nitrate. 2.** See **sodium nitrate.** Also,
esp. Brit., **ni′tre.**

nit·pick (nit′pik′), *v.i. Slang.* to be
excessively concerned with minor details. —**nit′pick′er,** *n.* —**nit′pick/-
ing,** *adj., n.*

ni·trate (nī′trāt), *n., v.,* **-trat·ed, -trat-
ing.** —*n.* **1.** a salt or ester of nitric
acid. **2.** fertilizer consisting of potassium nitrate or sodium nitrate.
—*v.t.* **3.** to treat with nitric acid or a
nitrate. —**ni·tra′tion,** *n.*

ni·tric (nī′trik), *adj.* of or containing
nitrogen.

ni′tric ac′id, a caustic, corrosive liquid, used chiefly in the manufacture
of explosives, fertilizers, etc.

ni·tri·fy (nī′trə fī′), *v.t.,* **-fied, -fy·ing.
1.** to oxidize into nitrites, nitrates,
or their respective acids, esp. by bac-

terial action. **2.** to impregnate with
nitrogen or nitrogen compounds. —
ni′tri·fi·ca′tion, *n.*

ni·trite (nī′trīt), *n.* a salt or ester of
nitrous acid.

nitro-, a combining form indicating
"the univalent radical united through
nitrogen": *nitroglycerin.*

ni·tro·cel·lu·lose (nī′trə sel′yə lōs′), *n.*
See **cellulose nitrate.** —**ni′tro·cel′-
lu·los′ic,** *adj.*

ni·tro·gen (nī′trə jən), *n. Chem.* a
colorless, odorless, gaseous element
that constitutes about four fifths of
the volume of the atmosphere, used
chiefly in the manufacture of ammonia, nitric acid, etc. *Symbol:*
N; *at. wt.:* 14.0067; *at. no.:* 7. —**ni-
trog′e·nous** (-troj′ə nəs), *adj.*

ni·tro·glyc·er·in (nī′trə glis′ər in), *n.* a
highly explosive liquid, used chiefly
as a constituent of dynamite. Also,
ni′tro·glyc′er·ine.

ni′trous ac′id, an unstable
compound of nitrogen known only
in solution.

ni′trous ox′ide, a sweet-smelling,
sweet-tasting gas, used chiefly as an
anesthetic and in aerosol.

nit·ty-grit·ty (nit′ē grit′ē), *n. Slang.*
the crux of a matter or of a problem.

nit·wit (nit′wit′), *n.* a slowwitted or
foolish person.

nix (niks), *Slang.* —*n.* **1.** nothing. —
adv. **2.** no. —*interj.* **3.** (an exclamation of disagreement, warning, etc.)
—*v.t.* **4.** to veto or prohibit.

nix·ie (nik′sē), *n., pl.* **nix·ies.** a letter
or parcel that is undeliverable by the
post office because of a faulty or
illegible address.

Nix·on (nik′sən), *n.* **Richard M(il-
hous)** (mil′hous), born 1913, 37th
president of the U.S. 1969–74 (resigned).

NJ, New Jersey. Also, **N.J.**

NL, New Latin.

n.l., it is not permitted or lawful. [<
L *non licet*]

NLRB, National Labor Relations
Board.

NM, New Mexico.

N/M, *Shipping.* no mark.

nm, nautical mile.

N.M., New Mexico. Also, **N. Mex.**

NNE, north-northeast.

NNW, north-northwest.

no (nō), *adv., adj., n., pl.* **noes, nos.** —
adv. **1.** (a negative used to express
dissent, denial, or refusal.) **2.** (used
to emphasize or introduce a negative statement): *None of the girls
came to the party, no, not a one.* **3.**
not at all (used with a comparative):
He is no better. **4.** not: *whether or
no.* —*adj.* **5.** not any: *no money.*
6. far from being: *He is no genius.*
—*n.* **7.** a denial or refusal. **8.** a negative vote or voter.

No, nobelium.

Nō (nō), *n.* a classic Japanese drama employing verse, prose, choral song, and dance in highly conventionalized forms. Also, **No.**

no., 1. north. 2. northern. 3. number. [< L *numero*] Also, **No.**

No·ah (nō′ə), *n.* the patriarch who built a vessel (**No′ah's Ark′**) in which he, his family, and animals of every species survived the Flood. Gen. 5–9.

No·bel·ist (nō bel′ist), *n.* a person who is awarded a Nobel prize.

no·be·li·um (nō bē′lē əm), *n. Chem.* a synthetic, radioactive element. *Symbol:* No.

No·bel′ prize′ (nō bel′), one of a group of prizes awarded annually from the bequest of Alfred Nobel (1833–96, Swedish scientist) for achievement during the preceding year in physics, chemistry, medicine or physiology, literature, economics, and the promotion of peace.

no·bil·i·ty (nō bil′i tē), *n., pl.* **-ties.** 1. the body of nobles in a country. 2. noble birth or rank. 3. exalted moral excellence.

no·ble (nō′bəl), *adj.,* **-bler, -blest,** *n.* —*adj.* 1. of a hereditary class possessing special social or political status in a country. 2. of an exalted moral excellence. 3. imposing in appearance. 4. of an admirably high quality. —*n.* 5. a person of noble birth or rank. —**no′ble·ness,** *n.* —**no′bly,** *adv.* —**Syn.** 1. aristocratic, highborn. 2. lofty, magnanimous, virtuous. 3. magnificent, stately.

no·ble·man (nō′bəl mən), *n., pl.* **-men.** a man of noble birth or rank. —**no′ble·wom′an,** *n.fem.*

no·blesse o·blige (nō bles′ ō blēzh′), the moral obligation of the highborn to display honorable or charitable conduct.

no·bod·y (nō′bod′ē, -bə dē), *pron., n., pl.* **-bod·ies.** —*pron.* 1. no person. —*n.* 2. *Informal.* a person of no importance, esp. socially.

noc·tur·nal (nok tûr′n°l), *adj.* 1. of or occurring in the night. 2. active by night, as animals. —**noc·tur′nal·ly,** *adv.*

noc·turne (nok′tûrn), *n.* a musical composition appropriate to the night or evening, esp. of a dreamy character.

nod (nod), *v.,* **nod·ded, nod·ding,** *n.* —*v.i.* 1. to make a slight, quick bending of the head, as in assent or greeting. 2. to let the head fall forward with a sudden, involuntary movement when sleepy. 3. (of trees, flowers, etc.) to droop or bend with a swaying motion. —*v.t.* 4. to bend (the head) in a short, quick movement, as of assent or greeting. 5. to express by such a movement. —*n.* 6. a nodding movement. —**nod′der,** *n.*

nod·dle (nod′°l), *n. Informal.* the head.

nod·dy (nod′ē), *n., pl.* **-dies.** 1. a dark-bodied tropical tern. 2. a fool or simpleton.

node (nōd), *n.* 1. a swollen area in the body, as of tissue. 2. a part of a stem that normally bears a leaf. —**nod·al** (nōd′°l), *adj.*

nod·ule (noj′ōōl), *n.* 1. a small node. 2. a small, rounded mass or lump. —**nod·u·lar** (noj′ə lər), *adj.*

No·el (nō el′), *n.* 1. the Christmas season. 2. (*l.c.*) a Christmas carol. Also, **No·ël′.**

no-fault (nō′fôlt′), *n.* 1. a form of automobile insurance designed to enable an injured party to collect compensation promptly from his or her own insurance company without determination of liability. 2. a form of divorce granted without blame attached to either party.

no-frills (nō′frilz′), *adj.* not providing or including certain nonessential features or services: *a no-frills air fare; low-cost, no-frills homes.*

nog·gin (nog′ən), *n.* 1. a small cup or mug. 2. a small amount of liquor, usually a gill. 3. *Informal.* the head.

no-good (nō′gŏod′), *Informal.* —*adj.* 1. worthless or undependable. —*n.* 2. a worthless or undependable person.

Noh (nō), *n.* **Nō.**

no-how (nō′hou′), *adv. Chiefly Dial.* in no manner.

noise (noiz), *n., v.,* **noised, nois·ing.** —*n.* 1. sound, esp. of a loud or harsh kind. 2. loud shouting or clamor. 3. an electric disturbance in a communications system that interferes with a signal. —*v.t.* 4. to spread as a report or rumor. [< OF < L *nausea* seasickness] —**noise′less,** *adj.* —**noise′less·ly,** *adv.*

noise·mak·er (noiz′mā′kər), *n.* a person or thing that makes noise, esp. a rattle, horn, or similar device.

noise′ pollu′tion, environmental contamination generated by excessively loud sound, as of jet engines.

noi·some (noi′səm), *adj.* 1. offensive or disgusting, as an odor. 2. harmful or injurious to health. —**noi′some·ly,** *adv.*

nois·y (noi′zē), *adj.,* **nois·i·er, nois·i·est.** 1. making much noise. 2. full of noise. —**nois′i·ly,** *adv.* —**nois′i·ness,** *n.* —**Syn.** clamorous, vociferous.

no-knock (nō′nok′), *adj. Informal.* noting an authorized police entry by force under search warrant without announcement and identification: *a no-knock narcotics policy.*

no′-load′ fund′ (nō′lōd′), a mutual fund that carries no sales charge. Also called **no′-load′.**

nol·le pros·e·qui (nol'ē pros'ə kwī'), *Law.* an entry made upon the records of a court when the plaintiff or prosecutor will proceed no further in a suit or action.

no·lo con·ten·de·re (nō'lō kən ten'də-rē), *Law.* a defendant's pleading that does not admit guilt but subjects him or her to punishment as though he or she had pleaded guilty.

nol-pros (nol'pros'), *v.t.* **-prossed, -pros·sing.** *Law.* to end by a nolle prosequi.

nom., nominative.

no·mad (nō'mad, nom'ad), *n.* **1.** a member of a tribe that has no fixed abode, but moves about from place to place according to the food supply. **2.** any wanderer. —**no·mad'ic,** *adj.*

no' man's' land', **1.** an uncontrolled area between opposing armies. **2.** an unowned or unclaimed tract of usually barren land.

nom de guerre (nom' də gâr'), *pl.* **noms de guerre** (nomz' də gâr'). *French* a pseudonym.

nom de plume (nom' də plōōm'), *pl.* **noms de plume** (nomz' də plōōm'). See **pen name.**

no·men·cla·ture (nō'mən klā'chər, nō-men'klə-), *n.* a system of names or terms used in a particular science or art.

nom·i·nal (nom'ə nºl), *adj.* **1.** being such in name only. **2.** small in comparison with the actual value. **3.** of or constituting a name or names. —**nom'i·nal·ly,** *adv.*

nom·i·nate (nom'ə nāt'), *v.t.* **-nat·ed, -nat·ing.** **1.** to name as a candidate for appointment or election. **2.** to appoint to a position or office. —**nom'i·na'tion,** *n.* —**nom'i·na'tor,** *n.*

nom·i·na·tive (nom'ə nə tiv, -nā'tiv, nom'nə-), *Gram.* —*adj.* **1.** noting the case of words or phrases used as the subject of a clause or sentence. —*n.* **2.** the nominative case. **3.** a word in the nominative case. —**nom'i·na·tive·ly,** *adv.*

nom·i·nee (nom'ə nē'), *n.* a person nominated, as for an office.

non-, a prefix meaning "not" or "mere negotiation or absence of": *nonpartisan.*

non·age (non'ij, nō'nij), *n.* **1.** legal minority. **2.** any period of immaturity.

non·a·ge·nar·i·an (non'ə jə när'ē ən, nō'nə jə-), *n.* a person between 90 and 100 years old.

non·a·ligned (non'ə līnd'), *adj.* not politically aligned with or favoring the U.S. or the U.S.S.R. —**non'a·lign'ment,** *n.*

nonce (nons), *n.* the present, or immediate, occasion or purpose: *for the nonce.*

non·cha·lant (non'shə länt', non'shə-lənt), *adj.* coolly unconcerned or indifferent. —**non'cha·lance',** *n.* —**non'cha·lant'ly,** *adv.* —**Syn.** casual, carefree, unexcited.

non·com (non'kom'), *n Informal.* a noncommissioned officer.

non·com·bat·ant (non kom'bə t°nt, non'kəm bat'°nt), *n.* **1.** a person connected with a military force in some capacity other than that of a fighter. **2.** a civilian in wartime.

---

non'a·bra'sive, *adj.;*
-ly, *adv.·* -ness, *n.*
non'ab·so·lute', *adj.; n.;*
-ly, *adv.·* -ness, *n.*
non'ab·sorb'a·ble, *adj.*
non'ab·sorb'ent, *adj., n.*
non'ab·stain'er, *n.*
non'ac·a·dem'ic, *adj., n.*
non'ac·cept'ance, *n.*
non·ac'tive, *adj., n.*
non'a·dap'tive, *adj*
non'ad·dict'ing, *adj.*
non'ad·dic'tive, *adj.*
non'ad·dic'tive, *adj.*
non'ad·he'sive, *adj.*
non'ad·ja'cent, *adj.*
non'ad·just'a·ble, *adj.*
non'ad·min'is·tra'tive,
adj.· -ly, *adv.*
non'ad·mis'sion, *n.*
non'a·dult', *adj., n.*
non'ad·van·ta'geous,
adj.· -ly, *adv.*
non'af·fil'i·at·ed, *adj.*
non'ag·gres'sion, *n.*
non'a·gree'ment, *n.*
non'ag·ri·cul'tur·al, *adj.*
non'al·co·hol'ic, *adj.*

non'al·ler·gen'ic, *adj.*
non'an·a·lyt'ic, *adj.*
non'ap·pear'ance, *n.*
non'ap·pli·ca·ble, *adj.*
non·a·quat'ic, *adj.*
non-Ar'y·an, *n., adj.*
non·as·ser'tive, *adj.;*
-ly, *adv.*
non'as·sim'i·la'tion, *n.*
non'ath·let'ic, *adj.*
non'at·tend'ance, *n.*
non'at·trib'u·tive, *adj.;*
-ly, *adv.*
non'au·thor'i·ta'tive,
adj.; -ly, adv
non'au·to·mat'ed, *adj.*
non'au·to·mat'ic, *adj.*
non·ba'sic, *adj.*
non·be'ing, *n.*
non'be·liev'er, *n.*
non'bel·lig'er·ent, *adj., n.*
non·break'a·ble, *adj.*
non'can'cer·ous, *adj.*
non·car'bo·nat'ed, *adj.*
non'car·niv'o·rous, *adj.*
non-Cath'o·lic, *adj., n.*
non'·Cau·ca'sian,
adj., n.

non·caus'al, *adj.;*
-ly, *adv.*
non'ce·les'tial, *adj.*
non·cel'lu·lar, *adj.*
non·cen'tral, *adj.;*
-ly, *adv*
non·charge'a·ble, *adj.*
non-Chris'tian, *adj., n.*
non·civ'i·lized', *adj.*
non·clas'si·cal, *adj.;*
-ly, *adv*
non·cler'i·cal, *adj.;*
-ly, *adv.*
non·clin'i·cal, *adj.;*
-ly, *adv.*
non'co·ag'u·lat'ing, *adj.*
non'co·he'sive, *adj.;*
-ly, *adv.·* -ness, *n.*
non'col·laps'a·ble, *adj.*
non'col·laps'i·ble, *adj.*
non'col·lect'i·ble, *adj.*
non·com'bat. *adj.*
non'com·bin'ing, *adj.*
non'com·bus'ti·ble,
adj., n.
non'com·mer'cial,
adj., n.; -ly, adv

non·com·mis·sioned of·ficer (non′kə-mish′ənd, non′-), an enlisted person holding any of various ranks below commissioned or warrant officers.

non·com·mit·tal (non′kə mit′ºl), adj. not committing oneself to a particular view or course. —**non′com·mit′tal·ly,** adv.

non com·pos men·tis (non kom′pəs ment′is), Latin. mentally incapable.

non·con·duc·tor (non′kən duk′tər), n. a substance that does not readily conduct heat, sound, or electricity. —**non′con·duc′ting,** adj.

non·con·form·ist (non′kən fôr′mist), n. 1. a person who refuses to conform, as to established customs. 2. (often cap.) a Protestant in England who is not a member of the Church of England. —**non′con·form′ism,** n. —**non′con·form′i·ty,** n.

non·co·op·er·a·tion (non′kō op′ə rā′shən), n. 1. failure or refusal to cooperate. 2. a method of showing opposition to policies of the government by refusing to participate in civic life. —**non′co·op′er·a′tive,** adj.

non·dair·y (non′dâr′ē), adj. consisting of no milk or milk ingredients.

non·de·script (non′di skript′, non′di-skript′), adj. of no recognized or definite type or kind. —Syn. amorphous, indistinct.

none (nun), pron. 1. no one. 2. not any. 3. not any persons or things: *None were left when I came.* —adv. 4. to no extent. —adj. 5. Archaic. not any.

—Usage. Since many construe NONE in its sense of "not one," they insist that precision demands its being treated as a singular, followed by a singular verb. However, the word is very often felt to have the sense of def. 3 and there is ample evidence for such use dating back to the earliest English writings.

non·en·ti·ty (non en′ti tē), n., pl. -ties. 1. a person or thing of no importance. 2. something that does not exist, or exists only in imagination.

nones (nōnz), n. the ninth day before the ides in the ancient Roman calendar.

none·such (nun′such′), n. a person or thing without equal.

none·the·less (nun′thə les′), adv. nevertheless.

non′com·mis′sioned, adj.
non′com·mu′ni·ca·ble, adj.
non′com·mu′ni·ca′tive, adj.
non·com′mu·nist, n., adj.
non′com·pet′ing, adj.
non′com·pet′i·tive, adj.
non′com·pli′ance, n.
non′com·ply′ing, adj., n.
non′con·cil′i·a·to′ry, adj.
non′con·clu′sive, adj.; -ly, adv.; -ness, n.
non′con·cur′rence, n.
non′con·cur′rent, adj., n.; -ly, adv.
non′con·duc′tive, adj.
non′con·fi′dence, n.
non′con·fi·den′tial, adj.
non′con·flict′ing, adj.
non′con·form′ing, adj.
non′con·geal′ing, adj.
non′con·nec′tive, adj.
non′con·sec′u·tive, adj.
non′con·sent′ing, adj.
non′con·struc′tive, adj.; -ly, adv.
non′con·sump′tion, n.
non′con·ta′gious, adj.
non′con·tem′po·rar′y, adj.
non′con·tig′u·ous, adj.; -ly, adv.
non′con·tin′u·ance, n.
non′con·tin′u·a′tion, n.
non′con·tin′u·ous, adj.

non′con·tra·band′, n., adj.
non′con·tra·dic′tory, adj.
non′con·trast′a·ble, adj.
non′con·trib′u·ting, adj.
non′con·trib′u·to′ry, adj.
non′con·trol′la·ble, adj.; -ly, adv.
non′con·tro·ver′sial, adj.; -ly, adv.
non′con·ven′tion·al, adj.
non′con·ver′gent, adj.
non′con·ver′sant, adj.
non′con·vert′i·ble, adj.
non′cor·rob′o·ra′tive, adj.
non′cor·rod′ing, adj.
non′cor·ro′sive, adj.
non′cre·a′tive, adj.
non·crim′i·nal, adj.
non·crit′i·cal, adj.
non′crys′tal·line, adj.
non′cu′mu·la′tive, adj.
non·cy′cli·cal, adj.
non′de·duct′i·ble, adj.
non′de·liv′er·y, n.
non′dem·o·crat′ic, adj.
non′de·mon′stra·ble, adj.
non′de·nom′i·na′tion·al, adj.
non′de·part·men′tal, adj.
non′de·pend′ence, n.
non′de·scrip′tive, adj.
non′de·struc′tive, adj.; -ly, adv.; -ness, n.

non′de·tach′a·ble, adj.
non′de·vel′op·ment, n.
non′dif·fer·en′ti·a′tion, n.
non′dip·lo·mat′ic, adj.
non′di·rec′tion·al, adj.
non′dis·ci·pli·nar′y, adj.
non′dis·crim′i·nat′ing, adj.
non′dis·crim′i·na′tion, n.
non′dis·crim′i·na·to′ry, adj.
non′dis·tri·bu′tion, n.
non′di·vis′i·ble, adj.
non′do·mes′ti·cat′ed, adj.
non·dra·mat′ic, adj.
non·drink′er, n.
non·dry′ing, adj.
non′ed·u·ca·ble, adj.
non′ed·u·ca′tion·al, adj.
non′ef·fec′tive, adj.
non′ef·fer·ves′cent, adj.; -ly, adv.
non′e·las′tic, adj.
non′e·lec′tion, n.
non′e·lec′tive, adj.
non′e·lec′tric, adj.
non·el′i·gi·ble, adj.
non′e·mo′tion·al, adj.; -ly, adv.
non′em·pir′i·cal, adj.; -ly, adv.
non′en·force′a·ble, adj.
non′en·force′ment, n.
non·e′qual, adj., n.
non′e·quiv′a·lent, adj.
non′es·sen′tial, adj., n.

non·fic·tion (non fik′shən), *n.* works of prose dealing with facts or theory (contrasted with *fiction* and distinguished from *poetry* and *drama*). —**non·fic′tion·al,** *adj.*

non·he·ro (non′hēr′ō), *n.* antihero.

non·in·ter·ven·tion (non′in tər ven′shən), *n.* **1.** abstention by a nation from interference in the affairs of other nations. **2.** failure or refusal to intervene. —**non′in·ter·ven′tion·al,** *adj.* —**non′in·ter·ven′tion·ist,** *n., adj.*

non·met·al (non′met′ᵊl), *n.* an element not having the character of a metal, as carbon, nitrogen, etc. —**non·me·tal·lic** (non′mə tal′ik), *adj.*

no-no (nō′nō′), *n., pl.* **no-nos, no-no's.** *Slang.* anything that is forbidden, as because it is undesirable. [prob. babytalk based on *No! No!*]

non·ob·jec·tive (non′əb jek′tiv), *adj.* **1.** not objective. **2.** nonrepresentational.

non·pa·reil (non′pə rel′), *adj.* **1.** having no equal. —*n.* **2.** a person or thing having no equal.

non·par·ti·san (non pär′ti zən), *adj.* **1.** without regard to party politics or interests. **2.** not partisan. Also, **non·par′ti·zan.**

non·eth′i·cal, *adj.;*
-ly, *adv.;* -ness, *n.*
non′ex·change′a·ble, *adj.*
non′ex·clu′sive, *adj.*
non′ex·empt′, *adj., n.*
non′ex·ist′ence, *n.*
non′ex·ist′ing, *adj.*
non′ex·pend′a·ble, *adj.*
non′ex·plo′sive, *adj., n.*
non′ex·port′a·ble, *adj.*
non′ex·tant′, *adj.*
non′ex·tra·dit′a·ble, *adj.*
non·fac′tu·al, *adj.;* -ly, *adv.*
non·fas′cist, *n., adj.*
non′fat′, *adj.*
non·fa′tal, *adj.;* -ly, *adv.*
non·fed′er·al, *adj.*
non·fed′er·at′ed, *adj.*
non·fer′rous, *adj.*
non·fil′ter·a·ble, *adj.*
non·flam′ma·ble, *adj.*
non·flex′i·ble, *adj.*
non·flow′er·ing, *adj.*
non·for′feit·a·ble, *adj.*
non·for′fei·ture, *adj., n.*
non·for′ma·tion, *n.*
non·freez′ing, *adj.*
non·ful·fill′ment, *n.*
non·func′tion·al, *adj.*
non·gas′e·ous, *adj.*
non′gov·ern·men′tal, *adj.*
non′gre·gar′i·ous, *adj.*
non·hab′it·a·ble, *adj.*
non·ha·bit′u·al, *adj.*
non·ha·bit′u·at′ing, *adj.*
non·haz′ard·ous, *adj.*
non·he·red′i·tar′y, *adj.*
non·his·tor′ic, *adj.*
non·ho·mo·ge′ne·ous, *adj.*
non·hu′man, *adj.*
non′i·den′ti·cal, *adj.*
non′i·den′ti·ty, *n.*
non·i·de·o·log′i·cal, *adj.*
non′id·i·o·mat′ic, *adj.*
non′im·mu′ni·ty, *n., pl.* -ties.
non′in·clu′sive, *adj.*

non′in·crim′i·nat′ing, *adj.*
non′in·de·pend′ent, *adj.*
non′in·duc′tive, *adj.*
non′in·dus′tri·al, *adj.*
non′in·fec′tious, *adj.*
non′in·flam′ma·ble, *adj.*
non′in·flect′ed, *adj.*
non′in·flec′tion·al, *adj.*
non′in·for′ma·tive, *adj.;* -ly, *adv.*
non′in·hab′it·a·ble, *adj.*
non′in·her′it·a·ble, *adj.*
non′in·ju′ri·ous, *adj.;* -ly, *adv.;* -ness, *n.*
non′in·stinc′tive, *adj.*
non′in·stinc′tu·al, *adj.*
non′in·sti·tu′tion·al, *adj.*
non′in·tel·lec′tu·al, *adj., n.;* -ly, *adv.*
non′in·ter·change′a·ble, *adj.*
non′in·ter·fer′ence, *n.*
non′in·ter·sect′ing, *adj.*
non′in·tox′i·cant, *adj., n.*
non′in·tox′i·cat′ing, *adj.*
non′ir′ri·tant, *adj.*
non′ir·ri·tat′ing, *adj.*
non′ju·di′cial, *adj.*
non·ko′sher, *adj., n.*
non·le′gal, *adj.*
non·le′thal, *adj.*
non·life′, *n.*
non·lin′e·ar, *adj.*
non·lit′er·ar′y, *adj.*
non′li·tur′gi·cal, *adj.;* -ly, *adv.*
non·liv′ing, *adj.*
non·log′i·cal, *adj.*
non·lu′mi·nous, *adj.*
non′mag·net′ic, *adj.*
non′ma·li′cious, *adj.;* -ly, *adv.*
non·ma·lig′nant, *adj.*
non·ma·te′ri·al, *adj.*
non′ma·te′ri·al·is′tic, *adj.*
non′math·e·mat′i·cal, *adj.*

non·meas′ur·a·ble, *adj.*
non′me·chan′i·cal, *adj.;* -ly, *adv.*
non′mech·a·nis′tic, *adj.*
non·mem′ber, *n.*
non·mem′ber·ship′, *n.*
non·mi′gra·to·ry, *adj.*
non·mil′i·tant, *adj., n.;* -ly, *adv.*
non·mil′i·tar·y, *adj.*
non·mor′al, *adj.*
non·mo′tile, *adj.*
non·mys′ti·cal, *adj.;* -ly, *adv.*
non·myth′i·cal, *adj.;* -ly, *adv.*
non·na′tive, *adj.*
non·nat′u·ral, *adj.*
non·nav′i·ga·ble, *adj.*
non′ne·go′ti·a·ble, *adj.*
non′ni·trog′e·nous, *adj.*
non′nu·tri′tious, *adj.*
non′o·be′di·ence, *n.*
non′ob·lig′a·to·ry, *adj.*
non′ob·serv′ance, *n.*
non′oc·cur′rence, *n.*
non·o′dor·ous, *adj.*
non′of·fi′cial, *adj.;* -ly, *adv.*
non·op′er·a·ble, *adj.*
non·op′er·a·tive, *adj.*
non′or·gan′ic, *adj.*
non′or·tho·dox′, *adj.*
non·own′er, *n.*
non′par·al′lel′, *adj.*
non′par·a·sit′ic, *adj.*
non′par·lia·men′ta·ry, *adj.*
non′par·tic′i·pat′ing, *adj.*
non′par·tic′i·pa′tion, *n.*
non·pas′ser·ine, *adj.*
non·pay′ing, *adj.*
non·pay′ment, *n.*
non′per·form′ance, *n.*
non′per·ish·a·ble, *adj., n.*
non·per′ma·nent, *adj.*
non′per·me·a·ble, *adj.*
non·phys′i·cal, *adj.;* -ly, *adv.*
non·phys′i·o·log′i·cal, *adj.;* -ly, *adv.*

non·plus (non plus′, non′plus), *v.t.,* **-plused, -plus·ing** or **-plussed, -plus-sing.** to make utterly perplexed.

non·prof·it (non prof′it), *adj.* not established for the purpose of making money.

non·pro·lif·er·a·tion (non′prō lif′ə rā′-shən), *n.* the action of curbing an excessive, rapid spread: *nonproliferation of nuclear weapons.*

non·rep·re·sen·ta·tion·al (non′rep ri-zen tā′shə n°l), *adj.* not representing or depicting natural objects or forms: *nonrepresentational art.*

non·res·i·dent (non rez′i dənt), *adj.* **1.** not resident in a particular place. **2.** not residing where official duties require a person to reside. —*n.* **3.** a nonresident person. —**non·res′i·dence,** *n.*

non·re·stric·tive (non′ri strik′tiv), *adj. Gram.* noting a clause that supplements but does not limit the antecedent, usually set off by commas.

non·rig·id (non rij′id), *adj.* **1.** not rigid. **2.** designating a type of airship that lacks a supporting structure and is held in shape only by the pressure of the gas within.

non·sched·uled (non skej′ōōld), *adj.* **1.** not scheduled. **2.** supplemental (def. 2).

non·sec·tar·i·an (non′sek tār′ē ən), *adj.* not affiliated with any specific religious denomination.

non·sense (non′sens), *n.* **1.** that which makes no sense or is lacking in sense, esp. meaningless or absurd words or actions. **2.** anything of trifling importance. —**non·sen·si·cal** (non sen′si kəl), *adj.* —**non·sen′si·cal·ly,** *adv.*

non seq., See **non sequitur.**

non se·qui·tur (non sek′wi tər), an inference or a conclusion that does not follow from the premises.

non·sked (non sked′), *n. Informal.* supplemental (def. 3).

non·stand·ard (non′stan′dərd), *adj.* differing in usage from the speech or writing that is generally considered to be correct or preferred.

non·stop (non′stop′), *adj., adv.* without a single stop en route.

non·sup·port (non′sə pōrt′, -pôrt′), *n.* failure to support a dependent as required by law.

---

non′po·et′ic, *adj.*
non′poi′son·ous, *adj.*
non′po·lit′i·cal, *adj.;*
  -ly, *adv.*
non′po′rous, *adj.*
non′pos·ses′sion, *n.*
non′pos·ses′sive, *adj.;*
  -ly, *adv.;* -ness, *n.*
non·pre′cious, *adj.*
non·pred′a·to·ry, *adj.*
non′pre·dict′a·ble, *adj.*
non′prej·u·di′cial, *adj.;*
  -ly, *adv.*
non′pre·scrip′tive, *adj.*
non′pre·serv′a·ble, *adj.*
non′pro·duc′tive, *adj.*
non′pro·fes′sion·al, *adj.*
non·prof′it·a·ble, *adj.*
non′pro·por′tion·al,
  adj.; -ly, *adv.*
non′pro·pri′e·tar′y,
  adj., n., pl. -tar·ies.
non′pro·tec′tive, *adj.;*
  -ly, *adv.*
non·pun′ish·a·ble, *adj.*
non·ra′cial, *adj.*
non·rad′i·cal, *adj.*
non·ra′di·o·ac′tive, *adj.*
non·ra′tion·al, *adj.;*
  -ly, *adv.*
non′re·ac′tive, *adj.*
non·read′er, *n.*
non′re·al·is′tic, *adj.*
non′re·cip′ro·cal,
  adj., n.; -ly, *adv.*
non′rec·og·ni′tion, *n.*
non′re·cov′er·a·ble, *adj.*
non′re·cur′rent, *adj.*
non′re·cur′ring, *adj.*
non′re·deem′a·ble, *adj.*

non′re·fill′a·ble, *adj.*
non′re·flec′tive, *adj.*
non·reg′i·ment′ed, *adj.*
non·reg′is·tered, *adj.*
non′re·li′gious, *adj.*
non′re·mu′ner·a′tive,
  adj.
non′re·new′a·ble, *adj.*
non′rep·re·sent′a-
  tive, *n.*
non′res·i·den′tial, *adj.*
non·re·sid′u·al. *adj.*
non′re·sis′tant, *adj., n.*
non′re·strict′ed. *adj.*
non′re·turn′a·ble, *adj.*
non′re·vers′i·ble, *adj.*
non·rhyth′mic. *adj.*
non·sal′a·ble. *adj.*
non·sal′a·ried. *adj.*
non′scho·las′tic, *adj.*
non′sci·en·tif′ic, *adj.*
non·sea′son·al, *adj.*
non·se′cret, *adj.;*
  -ly, *adv.*
non·sec′u·lar, *adj.*
non′seg·re·gat′ed, *adj.*
non′se·lec′tive, *adj.*
non·sen′si·tive, *adj.;*
  -ly, *adv.*
non·sex′ist, *n., adj.*
non·sex′u·al, *adj.;*
  -ly, *adv.*
non′sig·nif′i·cant, *adj.*
non·sink′a·ble. *adj.*
non′skid′. *adj.*
non·skilled′. *adj.*
non·smok′er. *n.*
non·so′cial. *adj.*
non·speak′ing, *adj.*
non·spe′cial·ist, *n.*

non·spe′cial·ized′, *adj.*
non·spe·cif′ic, *adj.*
non·spir′it·u·al, *adj.*
non·sport′ing, *adj.;*
  -ly, *adv.*
non·sta′ble, *adj.*
non·stain′ing, *adj.*
non·stand′ard·ized′, *adj.*
non·stim′u·lat′ing, *adj.*
non·stra·te′gic, *adj.*
non·strik′er, *n.*
non·strik′ing, *adj.*
non·struc′tur·al, *adj.;*
  -ly, *adv.*
non′sub·mis′sive, *adj.;*
  -ly, *adv.;* -ness, *n.*
non′sub·scrib′er, *n.*
non′suc·cess′, *n.*
non′suc·ces′sive, *adj.;*
  -ly, *adv.;* -ness, *n.*
non′sup·pres′sion, *n.*
non·sur′gi·cal, *adj.*
non′sus·cep′ti·bil′-
  i·ty, *n.*
non′sus·cep′ti·ble, *adj.*
non·sus·tain′ing, *adj.*
non′sym·bol′ic, *adj.*
non·sys·tem·at′ic, *adj.*
non·tax′a·ble, *adj.*
non·tech′ni·cal, *adj.;*
  -ly, *adv.*
non·tem′po·ral, *adj.*
non′the·at′ri·cal, *adj.*
non·think′ing, *adj.*
non·tox′ic, *adj.*
non′tra·di′tion·al, *adj.;*
  -ly, *adv.*
non·trans·fer′a·ble, *adj.*
non′trans·par′ent, *adj.*
non·trop′i·cal, *adj.*

non trop·po (non trop′ō), *Music.* not too much.

non-U (non yōō′), *adj. Informal.* not appropriate to the upper class, esp. of Great Britain.

non·un·ion (non yōōn′yən), *adj.* **1.** not belonging to a labor union. **2.** not recognizing a labor union or union policy. **3.** not manufactured by labor-union workers.

non·vi·o·lence (non vī′ə ləns), *n.* the policy or practice of refraining from the use of violence, as in reaction to oppressive authority. —**non·vi′o·lent,** *adj.* —**non·vi′o·lent·ly,** *adv.*

noo·dle (nōōd′ᵊl), *n.* a narrow strip of dried egg dough, usually boiled and served in soups, etc.

nook (nōōk), *n.* **1.** a corner, as in a room. **2.** any remote, sheltered spot.

noon (nōōn), *n.* **1.** twelve o'clock in the daytime. —*adj.* **2.** of, for, or at noon. Also, **noon′day′** (-dā′), **noon′-time′** (-tīm).

no′ one′, not anyone.

noon·tide (nōōn′tīd′), *n. Archaic.* noon.

noose (nōōs), *n.* a loop with a running knot, as in a snare, that tightens as the rope is pulled.

no-par (nō′pär′), *adj.* without par or face value: *no-par stock.*

nope (nōp), *adv. Informal.* no.

nor (nôr; *unstressed* nər), *conj.* **1.** (used in negative phrases, esp. after *neither,* to introduce the following member or members of a series): *They won't wait for you, nor for me, nor for anybody.* **2.** (used to continue the force of a preceding negative phrase): *I never saw him again, nor did I regret it.*

NORAD (nôr′ad), North American Air Defense Command.

Nor., **1.** Norway. **2.** Norwegian.

Nor·dic (nôr′dik), *adj.* of a Caucasoid people marked by tall stature, blond hair, and blue eyes, exemplified by North Europeans, esp. Scandinavians.

no-re·turn (nō′ri tûrn′), *adj.* (of beverage bottles) that need not be returned, when empty, for refund of a deposit.

Nor·folk (nôr′fək), *n.* a seaport in SE Virginia.

norm (nôrm), *n.* **1.** a typical or standard pattern. **2.** general level or average.

nor·mal (nôr′məl), *adj.* **1.** conforming to the typical or standard pattern. **2.** average in intelligence or personality. **3.** free from mental disorder. —*n.* **4.** anything normal. **5.** the normal form, state, or quantity. —**nor′mal·cy, nor·mal′i·ty** (-mal′i tē), *n.* —**nor′mal·ize′,** *v.t., v.i.* —**nor′-mal·i·za′tion,** *n.* —**nor′mal·ly,** *adv.* —**Syn. 1.** ordinary, regular, usual. **3.** sane.

nor′mal school′, (formerly) a school training teachers, esp. for elementary schools.

Nor·man (nôr′mən), *n.* **1.** a member of the Scandinavians who conquered Normandy in the 10th century. **2.** one of the mixed Scandinavian and French people who inhabited Normandy and conquered England in 1066. **3.** a native or inhabitant of Normandy. —*adj.* **4.** of Normandy, the Normans, or their language.

Nor·man·dy (nôr′mən dē), *n.* a region in N France along the English Channel.

nor·ma·tive (nôr′mə tiv), *adj.* of or pertaining to a norm regarded as correct, as in behavior. —**nor′ma·tive·ly,** *adv.* —**nor′ma·tive·ness,** *n.*

Norse (nôrs), *adj.* **1.** of ancient Scandinavia, its inhabitants, or their language. **2.** Norwegian (def. 1). —*n.* **3.** the Norse, **a.** ancient Scandinavians. **b.** Norwegians. **4.** Norwegian (def. 3).

Norse·man (nôrs′mən), *n.* one of the ancient Scandinavians.

north (nôrth), *n.* **1.** the direction to the left of a person facing the rising sun. **2.** a cardinal point of the compass lying directly opposite south. **3.** (*usually cap.*) a region or territory situated in this direction. **4.** **the North,** the northern area of the United States, lying to the north of the Ohio River and usually including Missouri and Maryland. —*adj.* **5.** lying toward or situated in the north. **6.** coming from the north. —*adv.* **7.** toward or from the north. —**north′-ern** (-ərn), *adj.* —**north′ern·most′** (-mōst′), *adj.*

North′ Amer′ica, the northern continent of the Western Hemisphere. — **North′ Amer′ican.**

North′ Car·o·li′na (kar′ə lī′nə), a state in the SE United States. *Cap.:* Raleigh. —**North′ Car·o·lin′i·an** (-lin′ē ən).

North′ Dako′ta, a state in the N central United States. *Cap.:* Bismarck. —**North′ Dako′tan.**

north·east (nôrth′ēst′), *n.* **1.** a point on the compass midway between north and east. **2.** a region in this direction. **3. the Northeast,** the northeastern part of the U.S., esp. the New England states. —*adj.* **4.** lying toward or situated in the northeast. **5.** coming from the northeast. —*adv.* **6.** toward or from the northeast. —**north′east′er·ly,** *adj., adv.* —**north′east′ern,** *adj.* —**north′east′ward** (-wərd), *adj., adv.* —**north′east′wards,** *adv.*

north·east·er (nôrth′ē′stər; *Naut.* nôr′ē′stər), *n.* a wind or gale from the northeast.

north·er (nôr′thər), *n.* a wind or storm from the north.

north·er·ly (nôr′thər lē), *adj., adv.* **1.** toward the north. **2.** from the north.

North·ern·er (nôr′thər nər), *n.* (*sometimes l.c.*) a native or inhabitant of the North, esp. of the northern U.S.

North′ern Hem′isphere, the half of the earth between the North Pole and the equator.

North′ern Ire′land, a division of the United Kingdom, in NE Ireland.

north′ern lights′. See **aurora borealis.**

North′ Kore′a. See under **Korea.**

North′ Pole′, the northernmost point on the earth.

North′ Sea′, an arm of the Atlantic between Great Britain and the European mainland.

North′ Star′, Polaris.

North′ Vietnam′, a former country in SE Asia, S of China: now part of reunited Vietnam.

north·ward (nôrth′wərd), *adj.* **1.** facing or in the north. —*adv.* **2.** Also, **north′wards.** toward the north. —**north′ward·ly,** *adj., adv.*

north·west (nôrth′west′; *Naut.* nôr′west′), *n.* **1.** a point on the compass midway between north and west. **2.** a region in this direction. **3. the Northwest,** the northwestern part of the United States, esp. Washington, Oregon, and Idaho. —*adj.* **4.** lying toward or situated in the northwest. **5.** coming from the northwest. —*adv.* **6.** toward or from the northwest. —**north′west′er·ly,** *adj., adv.* —**north′west′ern,** *adj.* —**north′west′ward** (-wərd), *adj., adv.* —**north′west′wards,** *adv.*

North′west Ter′ritories, a territory in N Canada. *Cap.:* Yellowknife.

Norw., **1.** Norway. **2.** Norwegian.

Nor·way (nôr′wā), *n.* a country in N Europe.

Nor·we·gian (nôr wē′jən), *adj.* **1.** of Norway, its people, or their language. —*n.* **2.** a native or inhabitant

of Norway. **3.** the language of Norway.

nos., numbers. Also, **Nos.**

nose (nōz), *n., v.,* **nosed, nos·ing.** —*n.* **1.** the part of the face that contains the nostrils and the organs of smell, and functions as the usual passageway for air in respiration. **2.** the sense of smell. **3.** something resembling a nose in location or shape. **4. on the nose,** *Slang.* precisely or correctly. **5. pay through the nose,** to pay an excessive price. **6. turn up one's nose at,** to regard with contempt. **7. under one's nose,** in full view. —*v.t.* **8.** to perceive by or as by smell. **9.** to move or push forward with or as with the nose. **10.** to touch or rub with the nose. —*v.i.* **11.** to smell or sniff. **12.** to move or push forward. **13.** to meddle or pry: *to nose about in someone else's business.* **14. nose out,** to defeat, esp. by a narrow margin. —**nosed** (nōzd), *adj.*

nose′bleed (nōz′blēd′), *n.* bleeding from the nose.

nose′ cone′, the cone-shaped forward section of a rocket or guided missile.

nose′ dive′, **1.** a plunge of an aircraft with the forward part pointing downward. **2.** any sudden drop or decline. —**nose′-dive′,** *v.i.*

nose·gay (nōz′gā′), *n.* a small bunch of esp. fragrant flowers.

nosh (nosh), *v.i.* to eat between meals, esp. to nibble at tidbits. [< Yiddish < G *naschen* to nibble, eat on the sly] —**nosh′er,** *n.*

no-show (nō′shō′), *n. Informal.* a person who makes a reservation, esp. on a plane, and neither uses nor cancels it.

nos·tal·gia (no stal′jə, -jē ə, nə-), *n.* **1.** a longing for pleasures, experiences, or events belonging to the past. **2.** *Obsolesc.* intense homesickness. —**nos·tal′gic,** *adj.* —**nos·tal′gi·cal·ly,** *adv.*

nos·tril (nos′trəl), *n.* one of the external openings of the nose.

nos·trum (nos′trəm), *n.* **1.** *Often Contemptuous.* a patent medicine, esp. of dubious efficacy. **2.** a pet scheme or remedy, as for social ills.

nos·y (nō′zē), *adj.,* **nos·i·er, nos·i·est.** *Informal.* impertinently inquisitive. Also, **nos′ey.** —**nos′i·ly,** *adv.* —**nos′i·ness,** *n.*

not (not), *adv.* (used to express negation, denial, refusal, or prohibition): *It's not far from here.*

no·ta be·ne (nō′tə bē′nē, bä′nā), *Latin.* note well.

no·ta·ble (nō′tə bəl), *adj.* **1.** worthy of note or notice. **2.** successfully accomplished, as persons. —*n.* **3.** a notable person. —**no′ta·bil′i·ty,** *n.* —**no′ta·bly,** *adv.* —**Syn. 2.** distinguished, eminent, prominent.

no·ta·rize (nō′tə rīz′), v.t., **-rized, -riz-ing.** to certify (a document) or cause to become certified through a notary public. —**no′ta·ri·za′tion,** n.

no·ta·ry (nō′tə rē), n., pl. **-ries.** a person legally authorized to authenticate contracts or take affidavits. Also called **no′tary pub′lic.** —**no·tar′i·al,** adj.

no·ta·tion (nō tā′shən), n. **1.** a system of special symbols or signs used to represent or simplify data or ideas: musical notation. **2.** the act or process of utilizing such a system. **3.** a brief note, as in the margin of a book. —**no·ta′tion·al,** adj.

notch (noch), n. **1.** an angular cut in a surface or edge, as one used for keeping a score. **2.** a deep, narrow pass between mountains. **3.** Informal. a step or degree. —v.t. **4.** to cut or make notches in. **5.** to record or score, as in a game. —**notch′y,** adj.

note (nōt), n., v., **not·ed, not·ing.** —n. **1.** a brief written record. **2.** a brief written comment, instruction, reminder, etc. **3.** a short, informal letter. **4.** a formal diplomatic or official communication. **5. notes,** a written summary of something that has been observed or studied. **6.** Brit. a banknote. **7.** any of various types of instruments covering debts, as a promissory note. **8.** notice, observation, or heed: a play worthy of note. **9.** reputation or prominence: a person of note. **10.** importance or consequence: Has anything of note happened? **11.** a hint or underlying expression of a quality, emotion, etc.: a note of triumph. **12.** Music. a sign or character used to represent a tone, its position and form indicating the pitch and duration of the tone. **13.** a sound of musical quality, as one uttered by a bird. **14. compare notes,** to exchange views or impressions. —v.t. **15.** to write or mark down briefly. **16.** to observe or take notice of. **17.** to mention specifically.

note·book (nōt′book′), n. a book with blank pages in which to write notes.

not·ed (nō′tid), adj. widely noticed, esp. for excellence. —**not′ed·ly,** adv. —**Syn.** celebrated, famous, renowned.

note·pa·per (nōt′pā′pər), n. writing paper, esp. that used in personal correspondence.

note·wor·thy (nōt′wûr′t͟hē), adj. worthy of attention or recognition. —**note′wor′thi·ly,** adv.

moth·ing (nuth′ing), n. **1.** no thing or not anything. **2.** no matter of any kind. **3.** a complete absence of something. **4.** something or someone of no importance. **5.** a zero quantity.

6. for nothing, a. free of charge. **b.** for no reason. **c.** to no avail. **7. think nothing of, a.** to treat casually. **b.** to regard as insignificant. —adv. **8.** in no respect or degree.

noth·ing·ness (nuth′ing nis), n. **1.** absence of existence. **2.** absence of significance. **3.** unconsciousness or death.

no·tice (nō′tis), n., v., **-ticed, -tic·ing.** —n. **1.** information or warning of something. **2.** a printed or written statement of this. **3.** notification or warning concerning one's intentions, esp. to terminate an agreement or relation at a specified time. **4.** attention or observation: to take notice of one's surroundings. **5.** a brief review or critique. —v.t. **6.** to be aware of or observe. **7.** to comment on.

no·tice·a·ble (nō′ti sə bəl), adj. **1.** able to attract notice or attention. **2.** deserving of notice or attention. —**no′tice·a·bly,** adv.

no·ti·fy (nō′tə fī′), v.t., **-fied, -fy·ing. 1.** to inform or give formal notice to (someone). **2.** Brit. to make known. —**no′ti·fi·ca′tion** (-fə kā′shən), n. —**no′ti·fi′er,** n.

no·tion (nō′shən), n. **1.** a general or vague idea. **2.** a hastily conceived opinion or view. **3.** a fanciful or foolish idea. **4. notions,** small articles for use in sewing, as buttons, thread, ribbon, etc. —**no′tion·al,** adj.

no·to·ri·ous (nō tōr′ē əs, -tôr′-), adj. **1.** widely but unfavorably known. **2.** generally known. —**no·to·ri·e·ty** (nō′tə rī′i tē), n. —**no·to′ri·ous·ly,** adv.

no-trump (nō′trump′), n. Bridge. a bid to play a hand without a trump suit.

not·with·stand·ing (not′with stan′ding, -with-), prep. **1.** in spite of. —conj. **2.** although. —adv. **3.** nevertheless.

nou·gat (nōo′gət, nōo′gä), n. a paste-like confection containing nuts and sometimes fruit.

nought (nôt), n. Chiefly Brit. naught.

noun (noun), n. Gram. a word that names or designates a person, place, thing, state, or quality.

nour·ish (nûr′ish, nur′-), v.t. **1.** to sustain with food or nutriment. **2.** to strengthen or promote. —**nour′ish·er,** n. —**nour′ish·ing,** adj.

nour·ish·ment (nûr′ish mənt, nur′-), n. **1.** something that nourishes. **2.** the act of nourishing or state of being nourished.

nou·veau riche (nōo′vō rēsh′), pl. **nou·veaux riches** (nōo′vō rēsh′). Usually Disparaging. a person who has newly become rich.

Nov., November.

no·va (nō′və), *n., pl.* **-vas, -vae** (-vē). a star that suddenly becomes thousands of times brighter and then gradually fades.

No·va Sco·tia (nō′və skō′shə), a province in SE Canada. *Cap.:* Halifax. —**No′va Sco′tian.**

nov·el[1] (nov′əl), *n.* a fictitious prose narrative of considerable length. —**nov′el·ist,** *n.* —**nov′el·is′tic,** *adj.* —**nov′el·ize,** *v.t.* —**nov′el·i·za′tion,** *n.*

nov·el[2] (nov′əl), *adj.* of a remarkably new and different kind. —**nov′el·ly,** *adv.*

nov·el·ette (nov′ə let′), *n.* a short novel.

nov·el·la (nō vel′ə), *n., pl.* **-vel·las, -vel·le** (-vel′ā). a form of short novel rich in realism and satire.

nov·el·ty (nov′əl tē), *n., pl.* **-ties.** 1. the state or quality of being novel. 2. a novel occurrence, experience, etc. 3. **novelties,** small, cheap, fancily designed articles, chiefly for adornment or play.

No·vem·ber (nō vem′bər), *n.* the eleventh month of the year, containing 30 days.

no·ve·na (nō vē′nə, nə-), *n., pl.* **-nas, -nae** (-nē). *Rom. Cath. Ch.* a devotion consisting of prayers on nine consecutive days.

nov·ice (nov′is), *n.* 1. a person who is new to a job or position. 2. a person who has been received into a religious order for a period of probation before taking vows. —**Syn.** 1. neophyte, tyro.

no·vi·ti·ate (nō vish′ē it, -āt′), *n.* 1. the state or period of being a novice. 2. the quarters occupied by religious novices.

No·vo·caine (nō′və kān′), *n. Trademark.* procaine.

now (nou), *adv.* 1. at this time or moment. 2. without delay. 3. at the time referred to. 4. in the very recent past. 5. nowadays. 6. as matters stand. 7. (used to introduce a statement or question): *Now, you don't really mean that.* 8. (used to strengthen a command or entreaty): *Now stop that!* 9. **now and again,** occasionally. Also, **now and then.** —*conj.* 10. since. —*n.* 11. the present time or moment. —*adj. Slang.* 12. of the present time. 13. fashionably new. 14. modern and up-to-date.

NOW (nou), **1.** National Organization for Women. **2.** *Banking.* negotiable order of withdrawal (for interest-bearing checking accounts).

now·a·days (nou′ə dāz′), *adv.* in these present times.

no·way (nō′wā′), *adv.* in no way, respect, or degree. Also, **no′ways′.**

no·where (nō′hwâr′, -wâr′), *adv.* 1. not anywhere. 2. **nowhere near,** *Informal.* not nearly. —*n.* 3. the state or place of nonexistence.

no·wise (nō′wīz′), *adv. Literary.* not at all.

nox·ious (nok′shəs), *adj.* 1. injurious to health, as gases. 2. morally harmful. —**nox′ious·ly,** *adv.* —**nox′iousness,** *n.*

noz·zle (noz′əl), *n.* a projecting part forming an outlet for a liquid or gas, as of a hose.

Np, neptunium.

n.p., 1. no pagination. 2. no place (of publication). 3. *Banking.* no protest. 4. notary public. Also, **N.P.**

NPN, nonprotein nitrogen.

NRA, 1. National Recovery Administration. 2. National Rifle Association of America.

NRC, Nuclear Regulatory Commission.

NS, nuclear ship.

N.S., Nova Scotia.

n.s., not specified.

NSA, National Security Agency.

NSC, National Security Council.

NSF, 1. National Science Foundation. 2. not sufficient funds.

NSPCA, National Society for the Prevention of Cruelty to Animals.

NSPCC, National Society for the Prevention of Cruelty to Children.

NT, New Testament.

nth (enth), *adj.* 1. of infinitely decreasing or increasing values, amounts, etc. 2. **the nth degree,** the utmost degree or extent.

N.T.P., normal temperature and pressure.

nt. wt., net weight. Also, **n. wt.**

nu (noō, nyoō), *n.* the 13th letter of the Greek alphabet (N, ν).

n.u., name unknown.

nu·ance (noō′äns, nyoō′-), *n.* a subtle shade of color, meaning, feeling, etc. —**nu′anced,** *adj.*

nub (nub), *n.* 1. a small knob or lump: *a nub of coal.* 2. *Informal.* the gist of something. 3. a small knot of fibers. —**nub′by,** *adj.*

nub·bin (nub′in), *n.* 1. an imperfect ear of corn. 2. a small stunted piece.

nu·bile (noō′bil, nyoō′-), *adj.* (of a girl) suitable for marriage, esp. in regard to age or physical development.

nu·cle·ar (noō′klē ər, nyoō′-), *adj.* 1. of or forming a nucleus. 2. of or involving atomic weapons. 3. operated or powered by atomic energy: *a nuclear submarine.* 4. (of a nation) possessing atomic bombs: *the nuclear powers.*

nu′clear en′ergy. See **atomic energy.**

nu′clear fam′ily, a social unit composed of father, mother, and children.

nu′clear fis′sion, fission (def. 3).

nu′clear fu′sion, fusion (def. 4).

nu'clear phys'ics, the branch of physics that deals with the behavior, structure, and component parts of atomic nuclei.

nu'clear reac'tor, reactor (def. 3).

nu·cle·ate (nōō'klē it, -āt', nyōō'-), *adj., v., -at·ed, -at·ing.* —*adj.* 1. having a nucleus. —*v.t.* 2. to form into a nucleus. —*v.i.* 3. to form a nucleus. —**nu'cle·a'tion,** *n.* —**nu'cle·a'tor,** *n.*

nu·cle'ic ac'id (nōō klē'ik, nyōō-), any of a group of complex acids occurring in all living cells.

nu·cle·o·lus (nōō klē'ə ləs, nyōō-), *n., pl.* **-li** (-lī'). a conspicuous, often rounded body within the nucleus of a cell. —**nu·cle'o·lar** (-lər), *adj.*

nu·cle·on (nōō'klē on', nyōō'-), *n.* a proton or neutron, esp. when considered as a component of a nucleus. —**nu'cle·on'ic,** *adj.*

nu·cle·on·ics (nōō'klē on'iks, nyōō'-), *n.* the branch of science that deals with atomic nuclei, esp. practical applications.

nu·cle·us (nōō'klē əs, nyōō'-), *n., pl.* **-cle·i** (-klē ī'), **-cle·us·es.** 1. a central part or group around which others are grouped. 2. a basis for growth or expansion. 3. a usually spherical mass of protoplasm found in most living cells, forming an essential element in the transmission of genic characters. 4. the positively charged mass within an atom, composed of neutrons and protons, and possessing most of the mass.

nude (nōōd, nyōōd), *adj.* 1. completely unclothed, as a person or the body, usually when supposed to be seen as such for some purpose: *a nude pose.* —*n.* 2. a nude human figure, esp. as represented in art. 3. **the nude,** the condition of being nude. —**nu'di·ty,** *n.*

nudge (nuj), *v.,* **nudged, nudg·ing,** *n.* —*v.t.* 1. to push slightly, esp. with the elbow, as to get attention. —*n.* 2. a slight push. —**nudg'er,** *n.*

nud·ism (nōō'diz əm, nyōō'-), *n.* the practice of going nude, as for health reasons. —**nud'ist,** *n., adj.*

nu·ga·to·ry (nōō'gə tôr'ē, -tōr'ē, nyōō'-), *adj.* 1. of no value or significance. 2. of no force or effect.

nug·get (nug'it), *n.* a lump, esp. of native gold. —**nug'get·y,** *adj.*

nui·sance (nōō'səns, nyōō'-), *n.* an obnoxious or annoying person, thing, practice, etc.

nui'sance tax', a tax paid in small amounts, usually by consumers.

null (nul), *adj.* 1. without value or effect. 2. amounting to nothing. 3. **null and void,** without legal force. —**nul'li·ty,** *n.*

nul·li·fy (nul'ə fī'), *v.t.,* **-fied, -fy·ing.** 1. to render legally null or invalid. 2. to deprive of value or effectiveness. [< LL *nullificāre* to despise] —**nul'li·fi·ca'tion,** *n.* —**nul'li·fi'er,** *n.*

num., numeral; numerals.

numb (num), *adj.* 1. deprived of the physical power of sensation and movement. 2. lacking emotion or feeling. —*v.t.* 3. to make numb. —**numb'ly,** *adv.* —**numb'ness,** *n.*

num·ber (num'bər), *n.* 1. a mathematical unit, having precise relations with other such units. 2. a word or symbol representing such a unit. 3. the sum or total of a group of persons or things. 4. a numeral assigned to an object, person, size, etc., for purposes of identification or classification. 5. a group or quantity amounting to many or several: *a number of persons.* 6. a single item in a series. 7. a single item on the program of a show or concert. 8. a single issue of a periodical or serial. 9. **numbers, a.** many. **b.** numerical strength. **c.** See **numbers game. d.** arithmetic. 10. *Gram.* a form of inflection of a word that indicates whether the word is singular or plural. 11. *Informal.* a person or thing that attracts attention, as a pretty girl. 12. **without** (or **beyond**) **number,** countless or vast. —*v.t.* 13. to amount to in number. 14. to count or enumerate. 15. to mark with numbers. 16. to limit in number. 17. to include in a number. —*v.i.* 18. to be numbered.

num·ber·less (num'bər lis), *adj.* innumerable or countless.

num'bers game', an illegal lottery in which money is wagered on the appearance of certain numbers in some statistical listing or tabulation published in a daily newspaper, racing form, etc.

nu·mer·a·ble (nōō'mər ə bəl, nyōō'-), *adj.* capable of being numbered or counted. —**nu'mer·a·bly,** *adv.*

nu·mer·al (nōō'mər əl, nyōō'-), *n.* 1. one or more words or symbols expressing a number. —*adj.* 2. of or noting a number or numbers.

nu·mer·ate (nōō'mə rāt', nyōō'-), *v.t., -at·ed, -at·ing.* 1. to represent numbers by symbols. 2. to enumerate (def. 2). —**nu'mer·a'tion,** *n.*

nu·mer·a·tor (nōō'mə rā'tər, nyōō'-), *n. Arith.* the number of a fraction above the line.

nu·mer·i·cal (nōō mer'i kəl, nyōō-), *adj.* 1. of or pertaining to numbers. 2. expressed in numbers. Also, **nu·mer'ic.** —**nu·mer'i·cal·ly,** *adv.*

nu·mer·ol·o·gy (nōō'mə rol'ə jē, nyōō'-), *n.* the study of numbers, as in a person's birth date, to interpret his or her character. —**nu'mer·ol'o·gist,** *n.*

nu·mer·ous (nōō′mər əs, nyōō′-), *adj.*
1. in considerable quantity. **2.** consisting of a great number. —**nu′-mer·ous·ly,** *adv.* —**nu′mer·ous·ness,** *n.*

numis., **1.** numismatic. **2.** numismatics.

nu·mis·mat·ics (nōō′miz mat′iks, -mis-, nyōō′-), *n.* the study or collecting of coins, medals, paper money, etc. —**nu′mis·mat′ic,** *adj.* —**nu·mis′ma·tist** (-mə tist), *n.*

num·skull (num′skul′), *n.* *Informal.* a slowwitted person. Also, **numb′-skull′.**

nun (nun), *n.* a woman bound to a religious order, esp. one living in a convent under solemn vows of poverty, chastity, and obedience.

nun·ci·o (nun′shē ō), *n., pl.* **-ci·os.** a papal ambassador in a foreign country.

nun·ner·y (nun′ə rē), *n., pl.* **-ner·ies.** *Obs.* a convent of nuns.

nup·tial (nup′shəl), *adj.* **1.** of or pertaining to marriage or a wedding. —*n.* **2.** Usually, **nuptials.** a wedding or marriage. —**nup′tial·ly,** *adv.*

nurse (nûrs), *n., v.,* **nursed, nurs·ing.** —*n.* **1.** a person, esp. a woman, trained to care for the sick. **2.** nursemaid. **3.** See **wet nurse.** —*v.t.* **4.** to attend to the needs of (the sick). **5.** to seek to cure (an ailment) by taking care of oneself: *to nurse a cold.* **6.** to suckle (an infant). **7.** to promote the growth and development of. **8.** to preserve in an active state: *to nurse a grudge.* **9.** to handle or hold fondly. —*v.i.* **10.** to act as nurse. **11.** to suckle a child. —**nurs′-er,** *n.*

nurse·maid (nûrs′mād′), *n.* a woman or girl employed to take care of children. Also called **nurs′er·y·maid′.**

nurs·er·y (nûr′sə rē), *n., pl.* **-er·ies.** **1.** a room or place set apart for young children. **2.** a nursery school or class. **3.** a place where young trees or other plants are raised for transplanting or for sale.

nurs·er·y·man (nûr′sə rē mən), *n., pl.* **-men.** a person who owns or conducts a plant nursery.

nurs′ery rhyme′, a short, simple poem for children.

nurs′ery school′, a prekindergarten school.

nurs′ing home′, a private establishment that provides nursing care and residential services for the aged or infirm.

nurs·ling (nûrs′ling), *n.* **1.** an infant or young animal being nursed. **2.** any person or thing under fostering care.

nur·ture (nûr′chər), *v.,* **-tured, -tur·ing,** *n.* —*v.t.* **1.** to promote the development of by providing nourishment. **2.** to educate or bring up with care. —*n.* **3.** something that nourishes. **4.** education or upbringing. —**nur′tur·er,** *n.*

nut (nut), *n.* **1.** a dry fruit consisting of an edible kernel enclosed in a woody shell. **2.** the kernel itself. **3.** a small metal block having a threaded hole for screwing onto a bolt. **4.** *Slang.* an insane or highly eccentric person. **5.** *Slang.* an enthusiast or buff.

nut·crack·er (nut′krak′ər), *n.* an instrument for cracking nuts.

nut·hatch (nut′hach′), *n.* a small, short-tailed, sharp-beaked bird that creeps on trees and feeds on small nuts.

nut·meat (nut′mēt′), *n.* the edible kernel of a nut.

nut·meg (nut′meg), *n.* the hard, aromatic seed of the fruit of an East Indian tree, used as a spice.

nut·pick (nut′pik′), *n.* a sharp-pointed table device for removing the meat from nuts.

nu·tri·a (nōō′trē ə, nyōō′-), *n.* the fur of the coypu, used esp. for women's coats.

nu·tri·ent (nōō′trē ənt, nyōō′-), *adj.* **1.** providing nourishment or nutriment. —*n.* **2.** a nutrient substance.

nu·tri·ment (nōō′trə mənt, nyōō′-), *n.* something that nourishes, as food. —**nu·tri·men·tal** (nōō′trə men′t°l, nyōō′-), *adj.*

nu·tri·tion (nōō trish′ən, nyōō-), *n.* **1.** the process by which plants and animals take in and utilize food material. **2.** nutriment. **3.** the science or study of daily diet and health. —**nu·tri′tion·al,** *adj.* —**nu·tri′tion·al·ly,** *adv.* —**nu·tri′tion·ist** (-trish′ə nist), *n.* —**nu′tri·tive** (-tri tiv), *adj.*

nu·tri·tious (nōō trish′əs, nyōō-), *adj.* providing nourishment, esp. to a high degree. —**nu·tri′tious·ly,** *adv.* —**nu·tri′tious·ness,** *n.*

nuts (nuts), *Slang.* —*interj.* **1.** (to express defiance, disgust, etc.) —*adj.* **2.** crazy or insane. **3. be nuts about** or **on,** to be wildly enthusiastic about.

nut·shell (nut′shel′), *n.* **1.** the shell of a nut. **2. in a nutshell,** in brief.

nut·ty (nut′ē), *adj.,* **-ti·er, -ti·est.** **1.** abounding in or producing nuts. **2.** nutlike, esp. in taste. **3.** *Informal.* silly or ridiculous. **4.** *Slang.* insane. —**nut′ti·ly,** *adv.* —**nut′ti·ness,** *n.*

nuz·zle (nuz′əl), *v.t., v.i.,* **-zled, -zling.** **1.** to touch or rub with the nose. **2.** to snuggle or cuddle. —**nuz′zler,** *n.*

NV, Nevada.

NW, **1.** northwest. **2.** northwestern.

NY, New York. Also, **N.Y.**

NYC, New York City. Also, **N.Y.C.**

ny·lon (nī'lon), ²n. **1.** a strong, elastic synthetic material used in hosiery and textiles. **2. nylons,** stockings made of nylon. [formerly a trademark]

nymph (nimf), n. **1.** one of a numerous class of lesser deities of mythology, conceived of as beautiful maidens inhabiting the waters, woods, mountains, etc. **2.** a beautiful young woman. **3.** the young of an insect that undergoes incomplete metamorphosis.

nym·pho·ma·ni·a (nim'fə mā'nē ə), n. abnormal and uncontrollable sexual desire in women. **—nym'pho·ma'ni·ac'** (-ak'), adj., n.

N.Z., New Zealand.

O

O, o (ō), n., pl. **O's** or **Os; o's** or **os** or **oes.** the 15th letter of the English alphabet, a vowel.

O (ō), interj. **1.** (used before a name in direct address, esp. in appeal): *Hear, O Israel!* **2.** (an expression of surprise, pain, etc.)

O, 1. ohm. **2.** Old.

O, 1. the numeral zero. **2.** oxygen.

O., 1. Ocean. **2.** October. **3.** Ohio. **4.** order. **5.** Oregon.

o/a, on or about.

oaf (ōf), n. a clumsy, stupid person. **—oaf'ish,** adj. **—oaf'ish·ly,** adv. **—oaf'ish·ness,** n.

oak (ōk), n. **1.** a tree of the beech family bearing the acorn as fruit. **2.** the hard, durable wood of such a tree. **—oak'en,** adj.

Oak·land (ōk'lənd), n. a seaport in W California.

oa·kum (ō'kəm), n. loose fiber obtained by picking apart old ropes, used for caulking ships.

oar (ōr, ôr), n. **1.** a long shaft with a broad blade at one end, used for rowing or steering a boat. **2. rest on one's oars,** to relax after exertion. **—oared,** adj.

oar·lock (ōr'lok', ôr'-), n. a device, usually U-shaped, used to hold an oar in place.

oars·man (ōrz'mən, ôrz'-), n. a person who rows a boat, esp. in a regatta. **—oars'man·ship',** n.

OAS, Organization of American States.

o·a·sis (ō ā'sis, ō'ə sis), n., pl. **-ses** (-sēz, -sēz'). a fertile or green area in a desert region.

oat (ōt), n. **1.** a cereal grass cultivated for its edible seed. **2.** Usually, **oats.** the seed of this plant. **—oat'en,** adj.

oat·cake (ōt'kāk'), n. a cake, usually thin and brittle, made of oatmeal.

oath (ōth), n., pl. **oaths** (ōthz, ōths). **1.** a solemn appeal to God to witness one's determination to speak the truth or to keep a promise. **2.** a blasphemous use of the name of God or anything sacred.

oat·meal (ōt'mēl', -mēl'), n. **1.** meal made from oats. **2.** a cooked breakfast cereal made from this.

OAU, Organization of African Unity.

ob-, a prefix meaning: **a.** toward or to: *object.* **b.** on or over: *obscure.* **c.** against: *obstruct.*

ob., 1. he (or she) died. [< L *obiit*] **2.** incidentally. [< L *obiter*]

OB, obstetrics.

ob·bli·ga·to (ob'lə gä'tō), n., pl. **-tos, -ti** (-tē). *Music.* an indispensable part or accompaniment.

ob·du·rate (ob'dŏŏ rit, -dyŏŏ-), adj. **1.** stubborn and unyielding. **2.** hardhearted and without remorse. **—ob'du·rate·ly,** adv. **—ob'du·ra·cy,** n.

o·be·di·ent (ō bē'dē ənt), adj. obeying or willing to obey. **—o·be'di·ence,** n. **—o·be'di·ent·ly,** adv. **—** Syn. compliant, docile, tractable.

o·bei·sance (ō bā'səns, ō bē'-), n. **1.** a bodily gesture, as a bow, expressing respect. **2.** deference or homage. **—o·beis'ant,** adj.

ob·e·lisk (ob'ə lisk), n. a four-sided shaft of stone that tapers to a pyramidal apex.

o·bese (ō bēs'), adj. extremely fat. **—o·be'si·ty** (-bē'si tē), n.

o·bey (ō bā'), v.t. **1.** to follow the commands of. **2.** to follow (a command, etc.). **3.** to respond to. **—v.i. 4.** to be obedient. **—o·bey'er,** n.

ob·fus·cate (ob fus'kāt, ob'fə skāt'), v.t., **-cat·ed, -cat·ing. 1.** to confuse or bewilder hopelessly. **2.** to darken or dim. **—ob'fus·ca'tion,** n. **—ob·fus'ca·to'ry** (-kə tōr'ē, -tôr'ē), adj.

o·bi (ō'bē), n. a long, broad sash worn over a Japanese kimono.

o·bit (ō'bit, ob'it), n. *Informal.* obituary.

ob·i·ter dic·tum (ob'i tər dik'təm), pl. **ob·i·ter dic·ta** (ob'i tər dik'tə), an incidental or passing remark or opinion. [< L: (a) saying by the way]

o·bit·u·ar·y (ō bich′ŏō er′ē), *n.*, *pl.* **-ar·ies.** a notice of the death of a person, usually with a brief biographical sketch.

obj., 1. object. 2. objective.

ob·ject (*n.* ob′jikt, -jekt; *v.* əb jekt′), *n.* 1. anything that is visible or tangible. 2. anything that may be perceived intellectually. 3. a thing or person to which thought or action is directed. 4. the end toward which effort is directed. 5. *Gram.* a noun or noun equivalent that receives the action of a verb or follows a preposition. —*v.i.* 6. to offer a reason in opposition. —*v.t.* 7. to put forward in objection. —**ob·jec′tor,** *n.*

ob·jec·tion (əb jek′shən), *n.* 1. a comment or reason offered in opposition, refusal, or disapproval. 2. the act of objecting. 3. a reason or cause for objecting. 4. a feeling of disapproval, dislike, or disagreement.

ob·jec·tion·a·ble (əb jek′shə nə bəl), *adj.* 1. causing objection or disapproval. 2. offensive, as to good taste.

ob·jec·tive (əb jek′tiv), *adj.* 1. being or belonging to the object of perception or thought. 2. not affected by personal feelings or prejudice. 3. being the goal of one's actions. 4. dealing with things external to the mind rather than with thoughts or feelings, as a book. 5. *Gram.* noting the case of words or phrases used as the object of a verb or preposition. —*n.* 6. something that one's efforts are intended to attain. 7. *Gram.* a. the objective case. b. a word in that case. 8. the lens, as in a telescope, that first receives the rays from the object and forms its object. —**ob·jec′tive·ly,** *adv.* —**ob·jec′tive·ness,** *n.* —**ob·jec·tiv·i·ty** (ob′jek tiv′i tē), *n.*

ob′ject les′son, a practical or concrete illustration of a principle.

ob·jet d'art (ôb′zhe dAR′), *pl.* **ob·jets d'art** (ôb′zhe dAR′). *French.* a small object of artistic worth.

ob·jur·gate (ob′jər gāt′, əb jûr′gāt), *v.t.*, **-gat·ed, -gat·ing.** to denounce vehemently. —**ob′jur·ga′tion,** *n.*

obl., 1. oblique. 2. oblong.

ob·late (ob′lāt, o blāt′), *adj.* flattened at the poles, as a spheroid. —**ob′late·ly,** *adv.*

ob·la·tion (o blā′shən), *n.* an offering to God or a deity. —**ob·la′tion·al,** *adj.*

ob·li·gate (ob′lə gāt′), *v.t.*, **-gat·ed, -gat·ing.** to oblige or bind morally or legally.

ob·li·ga·tion (ob′lə gā′shən), *n.* 1. a moral or legal duty. 2. a binding promise, contract, or responsibility. 3. the act of binding oneself by this. 4. an indebtedness or an amount of indebtedness. 5. a debt of gratitude.

ob·lig·a·to·ry (ə blig′ə tôr′ē, -tôr′ē, ob′lə gə-), *adj.* imposing moral or legal obligation. —**ob·lig′a·to′ri·ly,** *adv.* —**Syn.** compulsory, mandatory, required.

o·blige (ə blīj′), *v.t.*, **o·bliged, o·blig·ing.** 1. to bind morally, legally, or physically. 2. to place under a debt of gratitude. 3. to favor or help out. —**o·blig′er,** *n.* —**o·blig′ing,** *adj.* —**o·blig′ing·ly,** *adv.*

ob·lique (ə blēk′), *adj.* 1. neither perpendicular nor parallel to a line. 2. indirectly stated or expressed. —**ob·lique′ly,** *adv.* —**ob·lique′ness,** *n.* —**ob·liq′ui·ty** (-blik′wi tē), *n.*

ob·lit·er·ate (ə blit′ə rāt′), *v.t.*, **-at·ed, -at·ing.** 1. to remove all traces of. 2. to blot out or erase. —**ob·lit′er·a′tion,** *n.* —**ob·lit′er·a′tor,** *n.*

ob·liv·i·on (ə bliv′ē ən), *n.* 1. the state of being forgotten, as by the public. 2. the state of forgetting.

ob·liv·i·ous (ə bliv′ē əs), *adj.* 1. not actively mindful or aware. 2. without memory. —**ob·liv′i·ous·ly,** *adv.* —**ob·liv′i·ous·ness,** *n.* —**Syn.** 1. forgetful, heedless, preoccupied.

ob·long (ob′lông′, -long′), *adj.* 1. in the form of a rectangle one of whose dimensions is greater than the other. —*n.* 2. an oblong figure. —**ob′long·ish,** *adj.* —**ob′long·ly,** *adv.* —**ob′long·ness,** *n.*

ob·lo·quy (ob′lə kwē), *n.*, *pl.* **-quies.** 1. bad repute resulting from public censure. 2. censure or abusive language, esp. as inflicted by the public.

ob·nox·ious (əb nok′shəs), *adj.* extremely objectionable or offensive. —**ob·nox′ious·ly,** *adv.* —**ob·nox′ious·ness,** *n.*

o·boe (ō′bō), *n.* a woodwind instrument having a slender conical body and a double-reed mouthpiece. [< It < F *hautbois* = *haut* high + *bois* wood] —**o′bo·ist,** *n.*

obs., obsolete.

ob·scene (əb sēn′), *adj.* 1. offensive to modesty or decency. 2. intended to cause sexual excitement or lust. 3. abominable or disgusting. —**ob·scene′ly,** *adv.* —**ob·scen′i·ty** (-sen′i tē), *n.*

ob·scu·rant·ism (əb skyŏor′ən tiz′əm, ob′skyŏo ran′tiz əm), *n.* 1. opposition to the increase and spread of knowledge. 2. deliberate evasion of clarity. —**ob·scu′rant·ist,** *n.*, *adj.*

ob·scure (əb skyŏor′), *adj.*, **-scur·er, -scur·est,** *v.*, **-scured, -scur·ing.** —*adj.* 1. not clear to the understanding. 2. not easily noticed or found. 3. not well-known or famous. 4. indistinct to the sight. 5. lacking in light or illumination. —*v.t.* 6. to make obscure. 7. to cover or hide from view. —**ob·scure′ly,** *adv.* —**ob·scu′ri·ty,** *n.* —**Syn.** 1. ambiguous, vague. 2. inconspicuous. 3. undistinguished.

ob·se·qui·ous (əb sē′kwē əs), *adj.* servilely compliant or deferential. —**ob·se′qui·ous·ly,** *adv.* —**ob·se′qui·ous·ness,** *n.*

ob·se·quy (ob′sə kwē), *n., pl.* **-quies.** Usually, **obsequies.** a funeral rite or ceremony.

ob·serv·ance (əb zûr′vəns), *n.* 1. the act of observing or obeying something, as a law. 2. a keeping or celebration of a legal or religious holiday. 3. *Obs.* observation.

ob·serv·ant (əb zûr′vənt), *adj.* 1. observing or regarding attentively. 2. quick to notice or perceive. 3. careful in the observing of a law, religious ritual, etc.

ob·ser·va·tion (ob′zûr vā′shən), *n.* 1. an act or the faculty of observing or noticing. 2. the act of viewing or noting facts or occurrences for scientific research. 3. the record obtained by such an act. 4. a comment on something observed or noticed. 5. the condition of being observed.

ob·serv·a·to·ry (əb zûr′və tôr′ē, -tōr′ē), *n., pl.* **-ries.** a building equipped and used for making observations of astronomical phenomena.

ob·serve (əb zûrv′), *v.t.,* **-served, -serving.** 1. to see and notice. 2. to regard with attention. 3. to make a methodical or scientific observation of. 4. to obey or comply with, as a law. 5. to keep or celebrate by some appropriate procedure, etc.: *to observe a holiday.* 6. to state by way of comment. —**ob·serv′a·ble,** *adj.* —**ob·serv′er,** *n.*

ob·sess (ob ses′), *v.t.* to preoccupy persistently or abnormally. —**ob·ses′sive,** *adj.* —**ob·ses′sive·ly,** *adv.* —**ob·ses′sing·ly,** *adv.* —**ob·ses′sor,** *n.*

ob·ses·sion (əb sesh′ən), *n.* 1. abnormal preoccupation with a persistent idea or desire. 2. the idea or desire itself. —**ob·ses′sion·al,** *adj.*

ob·sid·i·an (əb sid′ē ən), *n.* a volcanic glass similar in composition to granite.

obsolesc., obsolescent.

ob·so·les·cent (ob′sə les′ənt), *adj.* becoming obsolete. —**ob′so·les′cence,** *n.* —**ob′so·les′cent·ly,** *adv.*

ob·so·lete (ob′sə lēt′, ob′sə lēt′), *adj.* 1. having fallen into disuse, esp. by having been replaced. 2. of a discarded or outmoded type. —**ob′so·lete′ly,** *adv.*

ob·sta·cle (ob′stə kəl), *n.* something that stands in the way or obstructs progress.

obstet., 1. obstetric. 2. obstetrics.

ob·stet·rics (əb ste′triks), *n.* the branch of medicine concerned with childbirth and caring for and treating women in or in connection with childbirth. —**ob·stet′ric, ob·stet′ri-**cal, *adj.* —**ob·ste·tri·cian** (ob′sti trish′ən), *n.*

ob·sti·nate (ob′stə nit), *adj.* 1. stubborn and unyielding, esp. without good reason. 2. not easily controlled or overcome. —**ob′sti·na·cy** (-nə sē), **ob′sti·nate·ness,** *n.* —**ob′sti·nate·ly,** *adv.*

ob·strep·er·ous (əb strep′ər əs), *adj.* resisting control in a noisy and difficult manner. —**ob·strep′er·ous·ly,** *adv.* —**ob·strep′er·ous·ness,** *n.* —Syn. boisterous, disorderly, unruly.

ob·struct (əb strukt′), *v.t.* 1. to block with an obstacle, as a road. 2. to hinder the passage, progress, or course of. 3. to block from sight. —**ob·struct′er, ob·struc′tor,** *n.* —**ob·struc′tive,** *adj.* —**ob·struc′tive·ly,** *adv.* —**ob·struc′tive·ness,** *n.*

ob·struc·tion (əb struk′shən), *n.* 1. something that obstructs. 2. the act of obstructing or state of being obstructed.

ob·struc·tion·ist (əb struk′shə nist), *n.* a person who deliberately obstructs progress, esp. of business before a legislative body. —**ob·struc′tion·ism,** *n.*

ob·tain (əb tān′), *v.t.* 1. to get by an effort or by a request. —*v.i.* 2. to be prevalent or in effect. —**ob·tain′a·ble,** *adj.* —**ob·tain′ment,** *n.*

ob·trude (əb trōōd′), *v.,* **-trud·ed, -truding.** —*v.t.* 1. to thrust forward without warrant or invitation. 2. to push out. —*v.i.* 3. to thrust oneself unduly. —**ob·tru′sion** (-trōō′zhən), *n.* —**ob·tru′sive,** *adj.* —**ob·tru′sive·ly,** *adv.* —**ob·tru′sive·ness,** *n.*

ob·tuse (əb tōōs′, -tyōōs′), *adj.* 1. slow in understanding or feeling. 2. not sharp, acute, or pointed. —**ob·tuse′ly,** *adv.* —**ob·tuse′ness,** *n.*

obtuse′ an′gle, an angle greater than 90° but less than 180°.

ob·verse (*n.* ob′vûrs; *adj.* ob vûrs′, ob′vûrs), *n.* 1. the side of a coin or medal that bears the principal design. 2. a counterpart or equivalent. —*adj.* 3. turned toward or facing the observer. 4. serving as a counterpart or equivalent.

ob·vi·ate (ob′vē āt′), *v.t.,* **-at·ed, -ating.** to eliminate (difficulties, etc.) by anticipatory measures. —**ob′vi·a′tion,** *n.*

ob·vi·ous (ob′vē əs), *adj.* 1. easily seen or understood. 2. lacking in subtlety. —**ob′vi·ous·ly,** *adv.* —**ob′vi·ous·ness,** *n.* —Syn. 1. apparent, evident, patent.

oc·a·ri·na (ok′ə rē′nə), *n.* an egg-shaped musical wind instrument having a mouthpiece and finger holes.

OCAS, Organization of Central American States.

occ., occupation.

occas., 1. occasional. 2. occasionally.

oc·ca·sion (ə kā′zhən), *n.* **1.** a particular time, esp. of a certain occurrence. **2.** a special or important time or event. **3.** a convenient or favorable time. **4.** an immediate or incidental cause or reason. **5.** **occasions,** *Obs.* **a.** needs or necessities. **b.** necessary business matters. **6. on occasion,** sometimes or occasionally. —*v.t.* **7.** to cause or bring about.

oc·ca·sion·al (ə kā′zhə nºl), *adj.* **1.** occurring or appearing at infrequent intervals. **2.** of or intended for a special occasion. —**oc·ca′sion·al·ly,** *adv.*

Oc·ci·dent (ok′si dənt), *n.* the Occident, the countries of Europe and America.

Oc·ci·den·tal (ok′si den′tºl), (*sometimes l.c.*) —*adj.* **1.** of the Occident. —*n.* **2.** a native or inhabitant of the Occident.

oc·clude (ə klōōd′), *v.,* **-clud·ed, -clud·ing.** —*v.t.* **1.** to close or stop up (a passage or opening). **2.** to shut in, out, or off. **3.** to incorporate (gases), as by absorption or adsorption. —*v.i.* **4.** *Dentistry.* to meet with the cusps fitting together. —**oc·clu′sion** (-klōō′zhən), *n.* —**oc·clu′sive,** *adj.*

oc·cult (ə kult′, ok′ult), *adj.* **1.** of magic, astrology, and other alleged sciences claiming knowledge of supernatural agencies. **2.** beyond the range of ordinary knowledge. **3.** disclosed only to the initiated. —*n.* **4. the occult,** occult studies or practices. —**oc·cult′ism,** *n.* —**oc·cult′ist,** *n., adj.*

oc·cu·pan·cy (ok′yə pən sē), *n., pl.* **-cies. 1.** the act of taking possession, as of a property. **2.** the period during which a person is an occupant.

oc·cu·pant (ok′yə pənt), *n.* **1.** a person who occupies. **2.** a tenant of premises. **3.** *Law.* an owner through occupancy.

oc·cu·pa·tion (ok′yə pā′shən), *n.* **1.** a person's usual or principal work or business. **2.** any activity in which a person is engaged. **3.** the seizure and control of a territory by a foreign military force. —**oc′cu·pa′tion·al,** *adj.* —**oc′cu·pa′tion·al·ly,** *adv.*

oc′cupa′tional ther′apy, therapy by means of selected creative activity designed to aid recovery. —**oc′cupa′tional ther′apist.**

oc·cu·py (ok′yə pī′), *v.t.,* **-pied, -py·ing. 1.** to take or fill up (space, time, etc.). **2.** to engage or employ (one's attention, etc.). **3.** to take possession and control of (a place), as by military invasion. **4.** to hold a position, office, etc.). **5.** to be a resident or tenant of. —**oc′cu·pi′er,** *n.*

oc·cur (ə kûr′), *v.i.,* **-curred, -cur·ring. 1.** to happen, esp. at a specific time.

2. to appear or present itself. **3.** to suggest itself in thought.

oc·cur·rence (ə kûr′əns, ə kur′-), *n.* **1.** the action or fact of occurring. **2.** something that happens, esp. unexpectedly. —**oc·cur′rent,** *adj.*

OCD, Office of Civil Defense.

o·cean (ō′shən), *n.* **1.** the vast body of salt water that covers almost three fourths of the earth's surface. **2.** any of the five divisions of this body: the Atlantic, Pacific, Indian, Arctic, and Antarctic oceans. **3.** a vast quantity. —**o·ce·an·ic** (ō′shē an′ik), *adj.*

o·cea·naut (ō′shə nôt′, -not′), *n.* aquanaut.

o·cean·go·ing (ō′shən gō′ing), *adj.* of or for sea transportation.

o·ce·a·nog·ra·phy (ō′shē ə nog′rə fē, ō′shə nog′-), *n.* the body of science dealing with the ocean. —**o′ce·a·nog′ra·pher,** *n.* —**o′ce·a·no·graph′ic** (-nə graf′ik), *adj.*

o·cea·nol·o·gy (ō′shə nol′ə jē), *n.* oceanography. —**o′cea·nol′o·gist,** *n.*

o·ce·lot (ō′sə lot′, os′ə-), *n.* a spotted, leopardlike cat, found from Texas through South America.

o·cher (ō′kər), *n.* **1.** a mixture of hydrated oxide of iron with clay, ranging in color from pale yellow to orange and red, and used as a pigment. **2.** its color. Also, **o′chre.**

o′clock (ə klok′), *adv.* of, by, or according to the clock.

OCS, officer candidate school.

Oct., October.

oct., octavo.

oc·ta·gon (ok′tə gon′, -gən), *n.* a polygon having eight angles and eight sides. —**oc·tag′o·nal** (-tag′ə nºl), *adj.*

oc·tane (ok′tān), *n.* **1.** any of several isomeric saturated hydrocarbons. **2.** See **octane number.**

oc′tane num′ber, a designation of antiknock quality of gasoline, numerically equal to the percentage of one specific octane by volume in a given fuel mixture.

oc·tave (ok′tiv, -tāv), *n.* **1.** *Music.* **a.** a tone on the eighth degree from a given tone. **b.** the interval encompassed by such tones. **c.** the harmonic combination of such tones. **2.** a series or group of eight.

oc·ta·vo (ok tā′vō, -tä′-), *n., pl.* **-vos. 1.** a book size of about 6 × 9 inches, determined by printing on sheets folded to form 8 leaves or 16 pages. **2.** a book of this size.

oc·tet (ok tet′), *n.* **1.** a musical composition for eight voices or instruments. **2.** the performers of this. **3.** any group of eight. Also, **oc·tette′.**

Oc·to·ber (ok tō′bər), *n.* the tenth month of the year, containing 31 days.

oc·to·ge·nar·i·an (ok'tə jə när'ē ən), *n.* a person between 80 and 90 years old.

oc·to·pus (ok'tə pəs), *n., pl.* **-pus·es, -pi** (-pī'). a sea mollusk having a soft, oval body and eight sucker-bearing arms. [< NL < Gk *oktṓpous* eight-footed]

oc·to·roon (ok'tə rōōn'), *n.* a person having one-eighth Negroid ancestry.

oc·u·lar (ok'yə lər), *adj.* **1.** of or for the eye. **2.** of or by eyesight. —*n.* **3.** *Optics.* eyepiece. —**oc'u·lar·ly,** *adv.*

oc·u·list (ok'yə list), *n.* **1.** an ophthalmologist. **2.** (loosely) an optometrist.

OD (ō dē'), *n., v.,* **OD'd, OD'ing.** *Slang.* —*n.* **1.** an overdose, esp. of a narcotic drug. —*v.i.* **2.** to take an overdose, esp. of a narcotic drug, to such an extent as to cause death.

O.D., 1. Doctor of Optometry. **2.** *Med.* the right eye. [< L *oculus dexter*] **3.** officer of the day. **4.** olive drab. **5.** overdraft. **6.** overdrawn.

odd (od), *adj.* **1.** differing in nature from what is ordinary. **2.** peculiar in an eccentric way. **3.** leaving a remainder of 1 when divided by 2. **4.** close to or little more than: *300-odd dollars.* **5.** being one of a pair or set: *an odd shoe.* **6.** left over after all others are used. **7.** occasional or various: *odd jobs.* —**odd'ly,** *adv.* —**odd'ness,** *n.* —**Syn. 1.** extraordinary, strange, unusual.

odd·ball (od'bôl'), *Slang.* —*n.* **1.** an eccentric or nonconformist. —*adj.* **2.** eccentric or atypical.

odd·i·ty (od'i tē), *n., pl.* **-ties. 1.** an odd person, thing, or event. **2.** the quality of being odd.

odd·ment (od'mənt), *n.* an extra bit or remnant.

odds (odz), *n.* **1.** the ratio of probability that a contestant will win or lose a contest. **2.** an equalizing allowance given the weaker person or team in a contest. **3.** an advantage favoring one of two contestants. **4. at odds,** in disagreement. **5. by all odds,** by far.

odds' and ends', 1. miscellaneous articles. **2.** miscellaneous matters.

odds-on (odz'on', -ôn'), *adj.* being the one more or most likely to win.

ode (ōd), *n.* a lyric poem expressive of exalted or enthusiastic emotion.

-ode, a suffix meaning "way" or "road": *anode; electrode.*

O·des·sa (ō des'ə), *n.* a seaport in the SW Soviet Union.

O·din (ō'din), *n. Scand. Myth.* the god of war, poetry, and wisdom.

o·di·ous (ō'dē əs), *adj.* **1.** deserving or causing hatred. **2.** highly offensive or disgusting. —**o'di·ous·ly,** *adv.* —**o'di·ous·ness,** *n.* —**Syn. 1.** abominable, hateful, repugnant.

o·di·um (ō'dē əm), *n.* **1.** intense hatred. **2.** the disgrace attaching to something repugnant.

o·dom·e·ter (ō dom'i tər), *n.* an instrument for measuring distance passed over, as by an automobile.

o·dor (ō'dər), *n.* **1.** the property of a substance that affects the sense of smell. **2.** a smell or scent. **3.** repute or esteem: *in bad odor.* Also, *Brit.,* **o'dour.** —**o'dor·less,** *adj.* —**o'dor·ous,** *adj.*

o·dor·if·er·ous (ō'də rif'ər əs), *adj.* yielding or diffusing an odor, esp. a fragrant one.

O·dys·se·us (ō dis'ē əs, ō dis'yōōs), *n.* the hero of Homer's *Odyssey,* and one of the Greek leaders in the Trojan War.

Od·ys·sey (od'i sē), *n.* **1.** (*italics*) an epic poem attributed to Homer, describing Odysseus' adventures after the Trojan War. **2.** (*often l.c.*) any long series of wanderings, esp. when filled with notable experiences. —**Od'ys·se'an,** *adj.*

OE, Old English.

O.E.D., Oxford English Dictionary. Also, **OED**

oed·i·pal (ed'ə pəl, ē'də-), *adj.* (*often cap.*) of or resulting from the Oedipus complex.

Oed'i·pus com'plex (ed'ə pəs, ē'də-), the unresolved desire of a child for sexual gratification through the parent of the opposite sex, esp. the desire of a son for his mother.

oe·no·phile (ē'nə fīl'), *n.* a person who enjoys wines, usually as a connoisseur.

OEO, Office of Economic Opportunity.

o'er (ōr, ôr), *prep., adv. Literary.* over.

O.E.S., Order of the Eastern Star.

oe·soph·a·gus (i sof'ə gəs), *n., pl.* **-gi** (-jī'). esophagus.

oeu·vre (Œ'vR°), *n., pl.* **oeu·vres** (Œ'-vR°). *French.* the works of a writer, painter, or composer taken as a whole.

of (uv, ov, əv), *prep.* **1.** from or away from: *south of Chicago.* **2.** by or coming from: *the plays of Shakespeare.* **3.** from or owing to: *to die of hunger.* **4.** containing or having: *a pitcher of milk.* **5.** made with or consisting of: *a dress of silk.* **6.** so as to be rid of or left without: *to be cured of a bad habit; to be robbed of one's money.* **7.** named: *the city of Berlin.* **8.** belonging to or living in: *the hem of a dress; the wildlife of the desert.* **9.** (used to indicate inclusion within a group or larger whole): *Is he of the royal family?* **10.** ruling or possessing: *the king of Spain.* **11.** possessed or ruled by: *the property of the government.* **12.**

having particular qualities or attributes: *a man of courage.* **13.** about or concerning: *There is talk of peace.* **14.** before or until: *twenty minutes of five.* **15.** set aside for or devoted to: *a minute of prayer.* **16.** on the part of: *It was mean of you to tease him.* **17.** (used to indicate the object of action following a noun or adjective): *the ringing of bells; tired of working.*

OF, Old French.

off (ôf, of), *adv.* **1.** so as to be no longer supported or attached. **2.** so as to be no longer covering or enclosing: *Take your hat off.* **3.** so as to be away or on one's way: *to start off early; to cast off.* **4.** from a charge or price: *10 percent off for cash.* **5.** at a distance in space or future time: *They live two blocks off. Summer is only a week off.* **6.** out of operation or effective existence: *Turn the lights off.* **7.** in absence from work, service, a job, etc. **8. be off,** to depart or leave. **9. off and on,** with intervals between. —*prep.* **10.** so as to be no longer supported by or attached to: *Break off a piece of bread.* **11.** below the usual level or standard: *25 percent off the marked price.* **12.** disengaged or resting from: *off duty.* **13.** *Informal.* refraining or abstaining from: *I'm off liquor.* **14.** apart or distant from: *a village off the main road.* **15.** *Informal.* from: *I bought it off him.* **16.** at the expense of: *She lives off her parents.* **17.** *Naut.* to seaward of: *off Cape of Good Hope.* —*adj.* **18.** in error. **19.** not so good or satisfactory as usual: *Business is off this week.* **20.** no longer in effect: *The agreement is off.* **21.** in a specified state, circumstances, etc.: *to be badly off for money.* **22.** free from work or duty: *a pastime for one's off hours.* **23.** removed or missing: *One of the buttons is off.* **24.** more distant: *the off side of a wall.* **25.** starting to go away: *I'm off to Europe on Monday.* —*v.t.* **26.** *Slang.* to kill or murder. —*interj.* **27.** get away!

off., **1.** office. **2.** officer. **3.** official.

of·fal (ô′fəl, of′əl). *n.* **1.** *Chiefly Brit.* the parts of a butchered animal that are considered inedible by human beings. **2.** refuse in general.

off-beat (*adj.* ôf′bēt′, of′-; *n.* ôf′bēt′, of′-), *adj.* **1.** differing from the usual or expected. —*n.* **2.** *Music.* an unaccented beat of a measure.

off′ Broad′way, (in New York City) experimental and low-budget drama, as produced in theaters other than the traditional commercial theaters in the Broadway area. —**off′-Broad′way,** *adj.*

off′ chance′, a very slight possibility or likelihood.

off-col·or (ôf′kul′ər, of′-), *adj.* **1.** not having the usual color. **2.** of doubtful propriety or taste. **3.** *Brit. Informal.* not in one's usual health.

of·fend (ə fend′), *v.t.* **1.** to cause resentful displeasure in. **2.** to affect (the sense, taste, etc.) disagreeably. —*v.i.* **3.** to cause resentful displeasure. **4.** to err in conduct. —**of·fend′er,** *n.* —**Syn.** **1.** affront, hurt, insult, provoke.

of·fense (ə fens′ *or, esp. for* 6, 7, ô′fens, of′ens), *n.* **1.** a breaking of a law or rule. **2.** a violation of the criminal law that is not a felony. **3.** something that offends or displeases. **4.** the act of offending or displeasing. **5.** a feeling of resentful displeasure: *to give offense.* **6.** the act of attacking. **7.** the side that is attacking or attempting to score in a game. **8. take offense,** to feel displeasure or anger. Also, *Brit.,* **of·fence.**

of·fen·sive (ə fen′siv, ô′fen-, of′en-), *adj.* **1.** unpleasant or disagreeable to the senses. **2.** repugnant, as to the moral sense or good taste. **3.** of offense or attack. —*n.* **4.** the position or attitude of offense or attack. **5.** an aggressive movement or attack. —**of·fen′sive·ly,** *adv.* —**of·fen′sive·ness,** *n.*

of·fer (ô′fər, of′ər), *v.t.* **1.** to present for acceptance or rejection. **2.** to propose for consideration. **3.** to present or volunteer (oneself). **4.** to present solemnly, as a prayer. **5.** to furnish or promise. **6.** to put up or threaten (resistance, etc.). **7.** to introduce or present, as for performance. **8.** to present for sale. **9.** to tender or bid, as a price. —*v.i.* **10.** to make a proposal or suggestion. **11.** to present itself. —*n.* **12.** the act or an instance of offering. **13.** something offered. —**of′fer·er, of′fer·or,** *n.*

of·fer·ing (ô′fər ing, of′ər-), *n.* **1.** something offered as an act of worship or as a gift or contribution. **2.** the act of a person who offers.

of·fer·to·ry (ô′fər tôr′ē, -tōr′ē, of′ər-), *n., pl.* **-ries.** **1.** (*sometimes cap.*) the offering to God of the bread and wine during a Mass. **2.** the part of a church service at which offerings are made. **3.** the prayers or music used during this service.

off-hand (ôf′hand′, of′-), *adv.* **1.** without previous thought or preparation. —*adj.* **2.** Also, **off′hand′ed.** done or made offhand. **3.** informal or casual.

off-hour (ôf′our′, -ou′ər, -our′), *n.* **1.** an hour or other period off duty. **2.** a period outside the hours of greatest activity.

of·fice (ô′fis, of′is), *n.* **1.** a place where business is transacted or professional services are available. **2.** the staff that works there. **3.** a position of duty, trust, or high authority: *the office of President.* **4.** employment or position as an official: *to seek office.* **5.** the duty or function associated with a particular job or position. **6. offices,** something done or said for or to another: *the good offices of a friend.* **7.** a church service or rite.

of·fice·hold·er (ô′fis hōl′dər, of′is-), *n.* a person holding a public office.

of·fic·er (ô′fi sər, of′i-), *n.* **1.** a person holding a commission in the armed services. **2.** a person appointed or elected to a position of responsibility or authority in a government, corporation, or other organization. **3.** a policeman or policewoman.

of·fi·cial (ə fish′əl), *n.* **1.** an officer, esp. in the government. *—adj.* **2.** of or pertaining to an office of duty or authority. **3.** appointed, authorized, or approved by a government or organization. **4.** formal and public, as a ceremony. *—of·fi′cial·dom* (-dəm), *n.* *—of·fi′cial·ly,* *adv.*

of·fi·cial·ism (ə fish′ə liz′əm), *n.* excessive attention to official regulations and routines.

of·fi·ci·ant (ə fish′ē ənt), *n.* a person who officiates at a religious service.

of·fi·ci·ate (ə fish′ē āt′), *v.i.,* **-at·ed, -at·ing. 1.** to perform the duties or functions of an office or position. **2.** to perform the office of a member of the clergy.

of·fi·cious (ə fish′əs), *adj.* objectionably forward in offering unwanted services or advice. *—of·fi′cious·ly,* *adv.* *—of·fi′cious·ness,* *n.* *—Syn.* interfering, meddlesome.

off·ing (ô′fing, of′ing), *n.* **1.** the more distant part of the sea seen from the shore. **2. in the offing, a.** at a distance but within sight. **b.** in the anticipated future.

off·ish (ô′fish, of′ish), *adj.* tending to keep aloof or reserved. *—off′ish·ness,* *n.*

off-key (ôf′kē′, of′-), *adj.* **1.** deviating from the correct tone or pitch. **2.** somewhat irregular or abnormal.

off-lim·its (ôf′lim′its, of′-), *adj.* forbidden to be entered or patronized by certain persons, as soldiers.

off-line (ôf′līn′, of′-), *adj.* operating independently of the main computer.

off·load (ôf′lōd′), *v.t.,* *v.i.* (of a ship or cargo) to unload.

off·print (ôf′print′, of′-), *n.* a reprint in separate form of an article, as from a magazine.

off-sea·son (ôf′sē′zən, of′-), *n.* a time of the year other than the busiest one for a specific activity.

off·set (*n.* ôf′set′, of′-; *v.* ôf′set′, of′-), *n.,* *v.,* **-set, -set·ting.** *—n.* **1.** something that compensates for something else. **2.** Also called **off′set print′ing,** a process in which an inked plate is used to make an impression on the rubber surface of a roller which transfers it to the paper. **3.** a part that branches off from the main part, as a plant, road, pipe, etc. *—v.t.* **4.** to compensate for. **5.** to print by offset. **6.** to form an offset or branch in.

off·shoot (ôf′shoot′, of′-), *n.* **1.** a branch from a main stem, as of a plant. **2.** anything conceived of as springing or proceeding from a main stock.

off·shore (ôf′shôr′, -shōr′, of′-), *adv.* **1.** off or away from the shore. **2.** at a distance from the shore. *—adj.* **3.** moving or tending away from the shore. **4.** located or operating at some distance from the shore. **5.** operated abroad without being regulated at home: *offshore banking.*

off·side (ôf′sīd′, of′-), *adj.,* *adv.* illegally in advance of the ball or puck that is in play.

off·spring (ôf′spring′, of′-), *n.,* *pl.* **-spring, -springs.** an issue or progeny of a person, animal, or plant.

off·stage (ôf′stāj′, of′-), *adj.,* *adv.* in or away from the part of a stage in view of the audience.

off-the-re·cord (ôf′thə rek′ərd, of′-), *adj.* not to be published or quoted.

off-the-shelf (ôf′thə shelf′, of′-), *adj.* **1.** available from merchandise in stock. **2.** easily adaptable for a new or special purpose.

off-the-wall (ôf′thə wôl′, of′-), *adj.* *Slang.* **1.** surprisingly unusual. **2.** bizarre. **3.** impromptu.

off·track (ôf′trak′, of′-), *adj.* of a system of betting on horse races in legalized locations away from the racetrack.

off-white (ôf′hwīt′, -wīt′, of′-), *adj.* white mixed with a small amount of gray or yellow.

off′ year′, 1. a year marked by reduced production or activity. **2.** a year without a major election.

oft (ôft, oft), *adv. Literary.* often.

of·ten (ô′fən, of′ən), *adv.* many times or frequently. Also, *Literary,* **of′ten·times′** (-tīmz′), **oft′times** (ôft′-, oft′-). *—of′ten·ness,* *n.*

o.g., *Philately.* original gum.

o·gle (ō′gəl), *v.,* **o·gled, o·gling,** *n.* *—v.t.,* *v.i.* **1.** to look (at) amorously or flirtatiously. *—n.* **2.** an ogling glance. *—o′gler,* *n.*

o·gre (ō′gər), *n.* **1.** a monster in fairy tales and stories that feeds on human flesh. **2.** a monstrously cruel person. *—o·gress* (ō′gris), *n.fem.*

OH, Ohio.

oh (ō), *interj., n., pl.* **oh's, ohs.** — *interj.* **1.** (an expression of surprise, pain, etc.) —*n.* **2.** the exclamation "oh."

O·hi·o (ō hī′ō), *n.* **1.** a state in the NE central United States. *Cap.:* Columbus. **2.** a river flowing from Pittsburgh, Pennsylvania, to the Mississippi. —**O·hi′o·an,** *adj., n.*

ohm (ōm), *n.* *Elect.* a unit of resistance, equal to the resistance in a conductor in which one volt of potential difference produces a current of one ampere. —**ohm·ic** (ō′mik), *adj.*

ohm·me·ter (ōm′mē′tər), *n.* *Elect.* an instrument for measuring resistance in ohms.

o·ho (ō hō′), *interj.* (an exclamation to express surprise, taunting, exultation, etc.)

-oid, a suffix meaning "resembling" or "like": alkaloid.

oil (oil), *n.* **1.** any of numerous greasy liquids obtained from animals, minerals, or vegetables, insoluble in water, and used for lubricating, illuminating, etc. **2.** petroleum. **3.** See **crude oil. 4.** See oil color. **5.** See **oil painting.** —*v.t.* **6.** to smear, lubricate, or supply with oil —*adj.* **7.** of or like oil. —**oil′er,** *n.*

oil·cloth (oil′klôth′, -kloth′), *n.* a fabric made waterproof by being treated with oil and pigment.

oil′ col′or, a paint made by grinding a pigment in oil. Also called **oil′ paint′.**

oil′ paint′ing, 1. the art of painting with oil colors. **2.** a painting in oil colors. —**oil′ paint′er.**

oil′ shale′, a hard shale from which oil is obtained by distillation.

oil·skin (oil′skin′), *n.* **1.** a cotton made waterproof by treatment with oil. **2.** Often, **oilskins.** a garment made of this.

oil′ well′, a well that yields petroleum.

oil·y (oi′lē), *adj.,* **oil·i·er, oil·i·est. 1.** of, full of, or containing oil. **2.** smeared or covered with oil. **3.** smooth or unctuous, as in manner. —**oil′i·ness,** *n.*

oink (oink), *v.i.* **1.** to grunt as a pig does. —*n.* **2.** an oinking sound.

oint·ment (oint′mənt), *n.* a soft, unctuous preparation, often medicated, for application to the skin.

O·jib·wa (ō jib′wä, -wə), *n., pl.* **-was, -wa. 1.** a member of a North American Indian tribe originally occupying the Lake Superior region. **2.** their language. Also, **O·jib′way.**

OK, Oklahoma.

O.K. (ō′kā′, ō′kā′), *adj., adv., v.,* **O.K.'d, O.K.'ing,** *n., pl.* **O.K.'s** *Informal.* —*adj., adv.* **1.** all right or all correct. —*v.t.* **2.** to approve by saying or writing "O.K." —*n.* **3.** an approval or agreement. Also, **OK, o′kay′.** [prob. after the *O.K. Club,* formed in 1840 by partisans of Martin Van Buren, who named their organization in allusion to "Old Kinderhook," his birthplace being Kinderhook, New York; but cf. also the Bostonian phrase *all correct*]

o·key-doke (ō′kē dōk′), *adj., adv., n. Informal.* O.K. Also, **o′key-do′key** (-ē).

O·ki·na·wa (ō′kə nou′wə, -nä′wə), *n.* the largest of the Ryukyu Islands, in the N Pacific, SW of Japan.

Okla., Oklahoma.

O·kla·ho·ma (ō′klə hō′mə), *n.* a state in the S central United States. *Cap.:* Oklahoma City. —**O′kla·ho′man,** *adj., n.*

O′klaho′ma Cit′y, the capital of Oklahoma.

o·kra (ō′krə), *n.* **1.** a shrub that bears long, green pods. **2.** the pods, used in soups, stews, etc.

O.L., *Med.* the left eye. [< L *oculus laevus*]

old (ōld), *adj.,* **old·er, old·est** or **elder, eld·est,** *n.* —*adj.* **1.** far advanced in years or life: *an old man.* **2.** of the latter part of existence of a person or thing: *old age.* **3.** having lived or existed for a specified time: *a man thirty years old.* **4.** no longer in general use. **5.** belonging to the historical or remote past. **6.** (*cap.*) belonging to the earliest stage of development: *Old English.* **7.** having been such for a long time: *an old trouper.* **8.** deteriorated through age or long use. **9.** wise from mature years. **10.** having been so formerly. —*n.* **11.** old persons collectively: *care for the old.* **12. of old,** in the past. —**old′ish,** *adj.* —**old′ness,** *n.* —**Syn. 1.** aged, elderly. **4.** antiquated, obsolete. **5.** ancient.

old·en (ōl′dən), *adj. Literary.* **1.** old. **2.** of the distant past.

Old′ Eng′lish, the English language of A.D. c450–c1150.

Old′ Fash′ioned, a cocktail made with whiskey, bitters, water, and sugar, garnished with citrus-fruit slices and a cherry.

old-fash·ioned (ōld′fash′ənd), *adj.* reflecting the styles, customs, or methods of the past. —**Syn.** antiquated, outmoded, passé.

old′ fo′gy, fogy. Also, **old′ fo′gey.**

Old′ French′, the French language of the 9th through 13th centuries.

Old′ Glo′ry, See Stars and Stripes.

Old′ Guard′, (*often l.c.*) the conservative members of any group.

old′ hand′, a person who is knowledgeable about something, esp. from long experience.

old′ hat′, *Informal.* trite from having long been used or known.

Old′ High′ Ger′man, High German before c1100.

old·ie (ōl′dē), *n. Informal.* a popular song, joke, or movie of earlier times. Also, **old′y.**

old′ la′dy, *Informal.* **1.** one's mother. **2.** one's wife. **3.** one's steady girlfriend.

old-line (ōld′līn′), *adj.* **1.** following old or traditional ideas, beliefs, or customs. **2.** long or originally established. **—old′-lin′er,** *n.*

Old′ Low′ Ger′man, the language of the German lowlands before c1100.

old′ maid′, *Often Derogatory.* **1.** an elderly or confirmed spinster. **2.** a fussy, timid, or prudish person. **— old-maid·ish** (ōld′mā′dish), *adj.*

old′ man′, *Informal.* **1.** one's father. **2.** one's husband. **3.** (*sometimes caps.*) a person in a position of authority, as an employer.

old′ mas′ter, **1.** an eminent artist of an earlier period, esp. 15th-18th centuries. **2.** a painting by such an artist.

Old′ Norse′, the Germanic language of medieval Scandinavia.

Old′ Sax′on, the Saxon dialect of Low German as spoken before c1100.

old′ school′, adherents of established custom or of conservatism. **—old′-school′,** *adj.*

old·ster (ōld′stər), *n. Informal.* an old or elderly person.

Old′ Tes′tament, the first of the two main divisions of the Christian Bible, regarded as the complete Bible of the Jews.

old-time (ōld′tīm′), *adj.* **1.** of old or former times. **2.** being long established.

old-tim·er (ōld′tī′mər), *n. Informal.* **1.** a person whose residence, membership, or experience dates from long ago. **2.** oldster.

Old′ World′, **1.** Europe, Asia, and Africa. **2.** See **Eastern Hemisphere. —Old′-World′,** *adj.*

old-world (ōld′wûrld′), *adj.* characteristic of a former period of history.

o·lé (ō lā′), *n.* **1.** a shout of approval, acclamation, etc. **—***interj.* **2.** (a shout of approval or encouragement to a bullfighter, performer, etc.)

o·le·ag·i·nous (ō′lē aj′ə nəs), *adj.* **1.** of or containing oil. **2.** oily in manner.

o·le·an·der (ō′lē an′dər, ō′lē an′-), *n.* a poisonous evergreen plant having showy rose-colored or white flowers.

o·le·o (ō′lē ō), *n. Informal.* oleomargarine.

o·le·o·mar·ga·rine (ō′lē ō mär′jə rin, -rēn′, -märj′rin, -rēn), *n.* margarine.

ol·fac·to·ry (ol fak′tə rē, -trē), *adj.* of the sense of smell.

ol·i·gar·chy (ol′ə gär′kē), *n., pl.* **-chies. 1.** a form of government in which the power is controlled by a few persons. **2.** a state so ruled. **3.** the persons or class so ruling. **—ol′i·garch′,** *n.* **—ol′i·gar′chic, ol′i·gar′chi·cal,** *adj.*

Ol·i·go·cene (ol′ə gō sēn′), *adj.* **1.** noting an epoch occurring from 25,-000,000 to 40,000,000 years ago and characterized by the presence of saber-toothed cats. **—***n.* **2.** the Oligocene epoch.

o·li·o (ō′lē ō′), *n., pl.* **o·li·os.** a medley, as of literary selections.

ol·ive (ol′iv), *n.* **1.** an evergreen tree of Mediterranean and other warm regions. **2.** the fruit of this tree, a small oval drupe, used as a relish and as a source of an edible oil (**ol′ive oil′**). **3.** a dull yellow green.

ol′ive branch′, something offered as a token of peace.

ol′ive drab′, *pl.* **olive drabs for 3. 1.** a deep olive color. **2.** woolen cloth of this color used for U.S. Army uniforms. **3.** a uniform made from this.

ol·i·vine (ol′ə vēn′, ol′ə vēn′), *n.* a common mineral that is a silicate of magnesium and iron, occurring in olive-green to gray-green masses.

O·lym·pi·a (ō lim′pē ə), *n.* the capital of Washington.

O·lym′pic Games′, a modern revival of an ancient Greek festival, consisting of international athletic and sports contests, held every four years, each time in a different country. Also called the **O·lym′pics** (-piks).

O·lym·pus (ō lim′pəs), *n.* **Mount,** a mountain in NE Greece: mythical home of the Greek gods and goddesses. **—O·lym′pi·an** (-pē ən), *adj.*

Om (ōm), *n. Hinduism.* a word thought to be an epitome of fulfillment.

O·ma·ha (ō′mə hô′, -hä′), *n., pl.* **-has, -ha for 2. 1.** a city in E Nebraska. **2.** a member of an Indian people formerly living in northeastern Nebraska.

OMB, Office of Management and Budget.

om·buds·man (ôm′bŏŏdz mən′), *n., pl.* **-men.** a public official appointed to hear and investigate complaints by private citizens against government officials or agencies. [< Sw: commissioner]

o·me·ga (ō mē′gə, -mā′-, ō meg′ə), *n.* the 24th and last letter of the Greek alphabet.

om·e·let (om′ə lit, om′lit), *n.* eggs beaten until frothy and cooked, often with other ingredients added, as cheese, ham, etc. Also, **om′e·lette.**

o·men (ō′mən), *n.* any event believed to portend something good or evil.

om·i·cron (om′ə kron′, ō′mə-), *n.* the 15th letter of the Greek alphabet.

om·i·nous (om′ə nəs), *adj.* portending something evil. —**om′i·nous·ly,** *adv.* —**om′i·nous·ness,** *n.* —**Syn.** foreboding, portentous, threatening.

o·mit (ō mit′), *v.t.,* **o·mit·ted, o·mit·ting.** **1.** to leave out or neglect to mention. **2.** to fail to do, make, or use. —**o·mis′sion** (-mish′ən), *n.*

omni-, a combining form meaning "all": *omnipotent.*

om·ni·bus (om′nə bus′, -bəs), *adj., n., pl.* **-bus·es.** —*adj.* **1.** dealing with numerous things at once. —*n.* **2.** *Obsolesc.* a public bus.

om·nip·o·tent (om nip′ə tənt), *adj.* **1.** having unlimited authority or power. —*n.* **2.** **the Omnipotent,** God. —**om·nip′o·tence,** *n.* —**om·nip′o·tent·ly,** *adv.*

om·ni·pres·ent (om′nə prez′ənt), *adj.* present everywhere at the same time. —**om′ni·pres′ence,** *n.*

om·nis·cient (om nish′ənt), *adj.* having infinite knowledge, awareness, or understanding. —**om·nis′cience,** *n.* —**om·nis′cient·ly,** *adv.*

om·ni·um-gath·er·um (om′nē əm gath′-ər əm), *n., pl.* **-ums.** a miscellaneous collection.

om·niv·o·rous (om niv′ər əs), *adj.* **1.** eating all kinds of foods indiscriminately, esp. both animal and plant foods. **2.** taking in everything, as with the mind. —**om·niv′o·rous·ly,** *adv.* —**om·niv′o·rous·ness,** *n.*

on (on, ôn), *prep.* **1.** so as to be supported by: *a hat on a hook.* **2.** attached to or unified with: *a picture on a wall.* **3.** with or among: *to serve on a jury.* **4.** (used to indicate place, location, etc.): *a scar on the face.* **5.** next to or near: *a house on the lake.* **6.** in the direction of: *to go on one's way.* **7.** by means of: *We coasted on our sleds.* **8.** by the agency of: *drunk on wine.* **9.** with respect to: *Write a term paper on Shakespeare.* **10.** in a condition or process of: *The house is on fire!* **11.** (used to indicate a source): *She depends on her father for money.* **12.** (used to indicate a basis or ground): *on my word of honor.* **13.** (used to indicate time or occasion): *on Sunday; We demand cash on delivery.* **14.** occupied with: *She's on the switchboard.* **15.** *Informal.* paid for by, esp. a treat: *The dinner is on me.* **16.** *Slang.* addicted to, esp. narcotics. —*adv.* **17.** in or into a position of being supported. **18.** toward a place, point, activity, etc.: *to look on while others work.* **19.** forward, onward, or along: *Go on now.* **20.** with continuous activity: *to work on.* **21.** in

or into operation: *Turn the gas on.* **22. on and off,** intermittently. **23. on and on,** at great length, so as to become tiresome. —*adj.* **24.** operating or in use: *The television set was on.*

ON, Old Norse.

once (wuns), *adv.* **1.** at one time in the past. **2.** a single time. **3.** even a single time. **4. once and for all,** decisively or finally. Also, **once for all. 5. once in a while,** at intervals. —*conj.* **6.** whenever. —*n.* **7.** one time only: *Once is enough.* **8. at once, a.** immediately or promptly. **b.** at the same time.

once-o·ver (wuns′ō′vər), *n. Informal.* **1.** a quick examination. **2.** a quick, superficial job.

on·com·ing (on′kum′ing, ôn′-), *adj.* approaching or nearing.

one (wun), *adj.* **1.** being a single person or thing. **2.** being unique in kind: *You're the one man I can trust.* **3.** noting some indefinite time: *one evening this week.* **4.** shared by or common to all. **5.** a certain: *One June Smith was chosen.* —*n.* **6.** the first and lowest whole number, being a cardinal number, as 1 or I. **7.** a single person or thing. **8. at one,** in a state of unity. **9. one by one,** singly and successively. —*pron.* **10.** some indefinite person, taken as a typical example: *One could not ask for more.* **11.** a person or thing. **12.** a person or thing of a certain number or kind.

one′ anoth′er, one toward the other or others: *The four women help one another.*

—**Usage.** See **each other.**

O·nei·da (ō nī′də), *n., pl.* **-das, -da.** a member of an Indian people formerly inhabiting central New York.

O′Neill (ō nēl′), *n.* **Eu·gene** (yōō jēn′), 1888–1953. U.S. playwright.

one-lin·er (wun′lī′nər), *n.* a brief, witty or humorous remark.

one·ness (wun′nis), *n.* **1.** the quality of being one. **2.** unity of thought, aim, etc.

on·er·ous (on′ər əs, ō′nər-), *adj.* annoyingly or unfairly burdensome. —**on′er·ous·ness,** *n.*

one·self (wun self′, wunz-), *pron.* **1.** a person's self. **2. be oneself, a.** to be in one's normal state or condition. **b.** to be unaffected and sincere. **3. by oneself, a.** without a companion. **b.** through one's own efforts. Also, **one's′ self′.**

one-sid·ed (wun′sī′did), *adj.* **1.** considering but one side of a matter or question. **2.** with all the advantage on one side: *a one-sided fight.* **3.** having but one side, or but one fully developed side. —**one′-sid′ed·ness,** *n.*

one·time (wun′tīm′), *adj.* having been such at a former time.

one-to-one (wun′tə wun′), *adj.* corresponding element by element.

one-track (wun′trak′), *adj. Informal.* able to concentrate on only one thing at a time.

one′ up′, having gained an advantage, esp. over rivals. —**one-up·man·ship** (wun′up′mən ship′), *n.*

one-way (wun′wā′), *adj.* **1.** moving in one direction only. **2.** providing travel in one direction only: *a one-way ticket.*

on·go·ing (on′gō′ing, ôn′-), *adj.* continuing without interruption.

on·ion (un′yən), *n.* **1.** a plant of the lily family having an edible pungent bulb. **2.** this bulb.

on·ion·skin (un′yən skin′), *n.* a translucent, glazed paper.

on-line (on′līn′, ôn′-), *adj.* directly connected with the main computer.

on·look·er (on′lŏŏk′ər, ôn′-), *n.* spectator.

on·ly (ōn′lē), *adv.* **1.** with nobody or nothing else besides. **2.** no more than. **3.** as recently as. **4.** as a final result. **5.** as the only one. **6.** only too, extremely or very. —*adj.* **7.** being the single one. **8.** alone because of some special quality. —*conj.* **9.** except that.

on·o·mat·o·poe·ia (on′ə mat′ə pē′ə, -mät′-), *n.* **1.** the formation of a word, as *cuckoo,* by imitation of sounds. **2.** the use of suggestive words for rhetorical effect. —**on′o·mat′o·poe′tic, on′o·mat′o·po·et′ic** (-et′ik), *adj.* —**on′o·mat′o·poe′i·cal·ly, on′o·mat′o·po·et′i·cal·ly,** *adv.*

On·on·da·ga (on′ən dô′gə, -dä′-), *n., pl.* **-gas, -ga.** a member of an Indian people formerly inhabiting New York.

on·rush (on′rush′, ôn′-), *n.* a strong forward rush, flow, etc. —**on′rush·ing,** *adj.*

on·set (on′set′, ôn′-), *n.* **1.** the forceful beginning. **2.** an assault or attack. **3.** the initial symptoms, as of a disease.

on·slaught (on′slôt′, ôn′-), *n.* a vigorous or furious attack.

Ont., Ontario.

On·tar·i·o (on târ′ē ō′), *n.* **1.** a province in S Canada. *Cap.:* Toronto. **2. Lake,** a lake between the NE United States and S Canada.

on·to (on′tŏŏ, ôn′-; on′tə, ôn′-), *prep.* **1.** to a position upon. **2.** *Informal.* aware of the true nature, motive, or meaning of. Also **on′ to.**

on·tog·e·ny (on toj′ə nē), *n.* the development of an individual organism.

on·tol·o·gy (on tol′ə jē), *n.* the branch of metaphysics that studies the nature of existence. —**on·to·log·i·cal** (on′t°loj′i kəl), *adj.*

o·nus (ō′nəs), *n.* **1.** an annoying or unfair burden. **2.** a responsibility for wrongdoing.

on·ward (on′wərd, ôn′-), *adv.* **1.** Also, **on′wards.** forward, as in space or time. —*adj.* **2.** directed or moving onward.

on·yx (on′iks, ō′niks), *n.* a variety of chalcedony having parallel bands of alternating colors.

oo·dles (ōōd′°lz), *n. Informal.* a large quantity.

oomph (ōōmf), *n. Slang.* **1.** vigor and vitality. **2.** sex appeal.

ooze[1] (ōōz), *v.,* **oozed, ooz·ing,** *n.* —*v.i.* **1.** to flow or exude slowly, as through holes. —*v.t.* **2.** to exude (moisture, etc.) slowly. —*n.* **3.** something that oozes. —**ooz′y,** *adj.* —**ooz′i·ness,** *n.*

ooze[2] (ōōz), *n.* **1.** mud composed chiefly of the shells of small organisms, covering parts of the ocean bottom. **2.** soft mud or slime. —**ooz′y,** *adj.* —**ooz′i·ness,** *n.*

op (op), *n.* See **op art.**

Op., opus. Also, **op.**

O.P., 1. observation post. **2.** Order of Preachers. **3.** Also, **o.p.** out of print.

o·pal (ō′pəl), *n.* **1.** a mineral, an amorphous form of silica, found in many varieties and colors. **2.** a gem composed of an iridescent variety of this. —**o·pal·ine** (ō′pə lin, -līn′), *adj.*

o·pal·es·cent (ō′pə les′ənt), *adj.* exhibiting a play of colors like that of the opal. —**o′pal·es′cence,** *n.*

o·paque (ō pāk′), *adj.* **1.** not transparent or translucent. **2.** not shining or bright. **3.** hard to understand. **4.** dull or unintelligent. —**o·pac·i·ty** (ō pas′i tē), **o·paque′ness,** *n.* —**o·paque′ly,** *adv.*

op′ art′, a style of abstract art in which forms and space are organized in such a way as to provide optical illusions. —**op′ art′ist.**

op. cit. (op′ sit′), in the work cited. [< L *opere citātō*]

ope (ōp), *adj., v.t., v.i.,* **oped, op·ing.** *Archaic.* open.

OPEC (ō′pek), Organization of Petroleum Exporting Countries.

Op-Ed (op′ed′), *n.* a newspaper page devoted to signed articles by commentators, etc. [*op(posite)*-*ed(itorial page)*]

o·pen (ō′pən), *adj.* **1.** not closed, barred, or shut. **2.** set so as to permit passage through the opening it otherwise closes: *an open door.* **3.** having relatively large or numerous voids or intervals. **4.** relatively unoccupied by buildings, trees, etc.: *open country.* **5.** extended or unfolded. **6.** without restrictions as to who may participate: *an open competition.* **7.** not taken or filled: *Which job is open?* **8.** ready for trade or business: *The store is open on Saturday.* **9.** not restricted as to the hunting of game: *open season.* **10.** undecided or unsettled: *several open questions.* **11.** receptive, as to ideas. **12.** exposed to general view. **13.** frank and unreserved. **14.** generous or liberal. —*v.t., v.i.* **15.** to make or become open. **16.** to make or become accessible or available. **17.** to reveal or become revealed. **18.** to make or become receptive, as to ideas. **19.** to expand or unfold. **20.** to begin or commence. —*n.* **21.** a contest in which both amateurs and professionals may compete. **22.** **the open, a.** the outdoors. **b.** general or public knowledge. —**o′pen·er,** *n.* —**o′pen·ly,** *adv.* —**o′pen·ness,** *n.*

o·pen-air (ō′pən âr′). *adj.* existing or taking place outdoors.

o·pen-and-shut (ō′pən ən shut′), *adj. Informal.* immediately obvious upon consideration.

o·pen-end (ō′pən end′). *adj.* not having fixed limits. Also. **o′pen-end′ed.**

o·pen-eyed (ō′pən īd′). *adj.* having the eyes wide open, as in wonder or alertness.

o·pen-faced (ō′pən fāst′), *adj.* **1.** having a frank and unreserved countenance. **2.** (of a pie, sandwich. etc.) without a layer of crust or bread on top.

o·pen-hand·ed (ō′pən han′did), *adj.* generous in giving. —**o′pen-hand′ed·ly,** *adv.* —**o′pen-hand′ed·ness,** *n.*

o·pen-hearth (ō′pən härth′), *adj.* noting or using a furnace on a shallow hearth over which play flames of burning gas, for making steel.

o′pen-heart′ sur′gery (ō′pən härt′), surgery performed on the exposed heart while a mechanical device pumps the blood.

o′pen house′, 1. a party at a person's home open to all friends and relatives. **2.** a time during which an institution, as a school, is open to the public.

o·pen·ing (ō′pə ning), *n.* **1.** the act or an instance of making or becoming open. **2.** an unobstructed or unoccupied space or place. **3.** the initial stage of anything. **4.** the beginning of a prolonged activity or event. **5.** an unfilled position or job.

o·pen-mind·ed (ō′pən mīn′did), *adj.* having a mind receptive to new ideas or arguments. —**o′pen-mind′ed·ness,** *n.*

o′pen shop′, a company or factory in which union membership is not a condition of employment.

o·pen·work (ō′pən wûrk′), *n.* any kind of work, esp. ornamental, showing openings through its substance.

op·er·a¹ (op′ər ə, op′rə), *n.* a play set to music, with all or most of the words sung to orchestral accompaniment. —**op·er·at·ic** (op′ə rat′ik), *adj.* —**op′er·at′i·cal·ly,** *adv.*

o·per·a² (ō′pər ə, op′ər ə), *n. Rare.* a pl. of **opus.**

op·er·a·ble (op′ər ə bəl), *adj.* **1.** capable of being put into use or practice. **2.** admitting of a surgical operation without undue risk. —**op′er·a·bil′i·ty,** *n.* —**op′er·a·bly,** *adv.*

op′era glass′es, small binoculars for use at plays or concerts.

op·er·ate (op′ə rāt′), *v.,* **-at·ed, -at·ing.** —*v.i.* **1.** to perform work, esp. with effect. **2.** to exert force or influence. **3.** to perform surgery. —*v.t.* **4.** to manage or use (a machine, etc.). **5.** to put or keep in operation.

op·er·a·tion (op′ə rā′shən), *n.* **1.** the act, process, or manner of operating. **2.** the state of something that operates or is in effect. **3.** the exertion of force or influence. **4.** a process of a practical or mechanical nature. **5.** a medical procedure involving surgery. **6.** a mathematical process, as addition. multiplication, etc. **7.** a military campaign or action.

op·er·a·tion·al (op′ə rā′shə nəl), *adj.* **1.** able to function or be used. **2.** of or pertaining to operations or an operation. —**op′er·a′tion·al·ly,** *adv.*

op·er·a·tive (op′ə rā′tiv, -ər ə tiv, op′rə tiv). *n.* **1.** a secret agent. **2.** a worker who operates a machine. esp. in grinding or cutting material. —*adj.* **3.** exerting force or influence. **4.** in effect or operation. **5.** effective or efficient. **6.** pertaining to work or productive activity. **7.** of or involving surgical operations. —**op′·er·a′tive·ly.** *adv.*

op·er·a·tor (op′ə rā′tər), *n.* **1.** a person who operates a mechanical device. as a telephone switchboard. **2.** a symbol for expressing a mathematical operation. **3.** *Slang.* a person who accomplishes his or her purposes by cleverness of method.

op·er·et·ta (op′ə ret′ə), *n.* a short opera. commonly of a light, amusing character.

oph·thal·mic (of thal′mik, op-), *adj.* of or pertaining to the eye.

oph·thal·mol·o·gy (of′thal mol′ə jē, -thəl-. -thə-, op′-), *n.* the branch of medicine dealing with the anatomy, functions. and diseases of the eye. —**oph′thal·mol′o·gist,** *n.*

oph·thal·mo·scope (of thal′mə skōp′, op-). *n.* an instrument for viewing the interior of the eye or examining the retina.

o·pi·ate (ō′pē it, -āt′), *n.* **1.** a medicine containing opium or its derivatives. **2.** anything that soothes or dulls the mind.

o·pine (ō pīn′), *v.t., v.i.,* **o·pined, o·pin·ing.** *Usually Facetious.* to express or hold (an opinion).

o·pin·ion (ə pin′yən), *n.* **1.** a belief that rests on grounds insufficient to produce certainty. **2.** beliefs or judgments shared by many: *social opinion.* **3.** the expression of a formal or professional judgment. —**Syn. 1.** impression, sentiment, view.

o·pin·ion·at·ed (ə pin′yə nā′tid), *adj.* obstinate with regard to one's opinions. —**Syn.** biased, dogmatic.

o·pi·um (ō′pē əm), *n.* a habit-forming narcotic prepared from the bitter thickened juice of a certain poppy.

o·pos·sum (ə pos′əm, pos′əm), *n.* a largely tree-dwelling marsupial, the female of which has an abdominal pouch in which its young are carried.

opp., opposite.

op·po·nent (ə pō′nənt), *n.* a person who opposes, as in a contest or controversy. —**Syn.** adversary.

op·por·tune (op′ər tōōn′, -tyōōn′), *adj.* **1.** favorable for a particular purpose or action. **2.** coming at an appropriate time. —**op′por·tune′ly,** *adv.* —**Syn. 1.** propitious, suitable.

op·por·tun·ism (op′ər tōō′niz əm, -tyōō′-), *n.* the policy or practice of exploiting opportunities without regard to ethical or moral principles. —**op′por·tun′ist,** *n., adj.* —**op′por·tun·is′tic,** *adj.*

op·por·tu·ni·ty (op′ər tōō′ni tē, -tyōō′-), *n., pl.* **-ties. 1.** a favorable time or occasion. **2.** a good chance for self-advancement.

op·pose (ə pōz′), *v.,* **-posed, -pos·ing.** —*v.t.* **1.** to resist forcefully. **2.** to set in opposition. —*v.i.* **3.** to be or act in opposition. —**op·pos′a·ble,** *adj.*

op·po·site (op′ə zit, -sit), *adj.* **1.** situated on the other side of or across from another person or object. **2.** differing greatly or conflicting entirely. —*n.* **3.** a person or thing that is opposite or contrary. **4.** *prep.* across from. —*adv.* **5.** on opposite sides. —**op′po·site·ly,** *adv.* —**op′·po·site·ness,** *n.*

op′posite num′ber, a person's counterpart, esp. in rank or position.

op·po·si·tion (op′ə zish′ən), *n.* **1.** the action of opposing. **2.** antagonism or hostility. **3.** a person or group of persons that opposes, criticizes, or protests. **4.** the major political party that is opposed to the party in power. —**op′po·si′tion·ist,** *n., adj.*

op·press (ə pres′), *v.t.* **1.** to subject to an unjustly harsh exercise of authority or power. **2.** to weigh down, as weariness does. —**op·pres′sor,** *n.*

op·pres·sion (ə presh′ən), *n.* **1.** the unjustly harsh exercise of authority or power. **2.** the act or an instance of oppressing. **3.** the feeling of being oppressed in mind or body.

op·pres·sive (ə pres′iv), *adj.* **1.** unjustly harsh or tyrannical. **2.** causing discomfort. **3.** distressing or upsetting. —**op·pres′sive·ly,** *adv.* —**op·pres′sive·ness,** *n.*

op·pro·bri·ous (ə prō′brē əs), *adj.* **1.** conveying or expressing opprobrium. **2.** outrageously shameful. —**op·pro′bri·ous·ly,** *adv.*

op·pro·bri·um (ə prō′brē əm), *n.* **1.** the disgrace incurred by shameful conduct. **2.** a cause or object of such disgrace.

opt (opt), *v.i.* **1.** to make a choice. **2. opt out,** to decide to leave or withdraw.

opt., 1. optical. **2.** optician. **3.** optics. **4.** optional.

op·ta·tive (op′tə tiv), *adj. Gk. Gram.* designating a verb mood that expresses a wish.

op·tic (op′tik), *adj.* of vision or the eye.

op·ti·cal (op′ti kəl), *adj.* **1.** of or applying optics. **2.** constructed to assist or improve vision. **3.** of or pertaining to eyesight. **4.** of op art. —**op′ti·cal·ly,** *adv.*

op′tical art′. See **op art.**

op′tical scan′ner, a photoelectric device capable of reading characters and converting the information to a computer. —**op′tical scan′ning.**

op·ti·cian (op tish′ən), *n.* a person who makes or sells eyeglasses, contact lenses, and other optical goods.

op·tics (op′tiks), *n.* the branch of physical science that deals with light and vision.

op·ti·mism (op′tə miz′əm), *n.* **1.** the tendency to look on the more favorable side of happenings. **2.** the belief that good ultimately predominates over evil. **3.** the doctrine that the existing world is the best of all possible worlds. —**op′ti·mist,** *n.* —**op′ti·mis′tic,** *adj.* —**op′ti·mis′ti·cal·ly,** *adv.*

op·ti·mum (op′tə məm), *n., pl.* **-ma** (-mə), **-mums,** *adj.* —*n.* **1.** the best or most favorable condition for obtaining a given result. —*adj.* **2.** best or most favorable: *optimum distribution.* —**op′ti·mal,** *adj.* —**op′ti·mal·ly,** *adv.*

op·tion (op′shən), *n.* **1.** the power or right of choosing. **2.** something that may be or is chosen. **3.** the act of choosing. **4.** a privilege of demanding, within a specified time, the carrying out of a transaction upon stipulated terms. —**op′tion·al,** *adj.* —**op′tion·al·ly,** *adv.*

op·tom·e·try (op tom′i trē), *n.* the profession of testing the eyes for defects of vision in order to prescribe corrective glasses. —**op·tom′e·trist,** *n.*

op·u·lent (op′yə lənt), *adj.* **1.** luxuriantly or showily wealthy. **2.** profusely abundant. —**op′u·lence,** *n.* —**op′u·lent·ly,** *adv.*

o·pus (ō′pəs), *n., pl.* **o·pus·es** or, *Rare,* **o·pe·ra** (op′ər ə). a musical composition, esp. one chronologically numbered.

OR, 1. operating room. **2.** Oregon.

or (ôr; *unstressed* ər), *conj.* **1.** (used to represent alternatives): *to be or not to be.* **2.** (used to connect alternative terms for the same thing): *the Sandwich, or Hawaiian, Islands.* **3.** (used in correlation): *whether . . . or.*

-or[1], a suffix meaning "state," "condition," or "quality": *honor.* Also, *Brit.,* **-our.**

-or[2], a suffix meaning "a person or thing that does something": *actor; elevator.*

o.r., *Com.* owner's risk. Also, **O.R.**

or·a·cle (ôr′ə kəl, or′-), *n.* **1.** (in ancient Greece) **a.** a divine utterance made by a god through a priest or priestess in response to an inquiry. **b.** the priest or priestess making such responses. **c.** the shrine at which they were made. **2.** a person who delivers authoritative or wise pronouncements. —**o·rac·u·lar** (ō rak′-yə lər, ə rak′-), *adj.* —**o·rac′u·lar·ly,** *adv.*

o·ral (ôr′əl, ōr′-), *adj.* **1.** uttered in words rather than written. **2.** of or using speech. **3.** of or administered through the mouth. **4.** of the first stage of libidinal development in which sexual desire is undifferentiated from the desire for food. —*n.* **5.** *Informal.* an oral examination. —**o′ral·ly,** *adv.*

o′ral his′tory, tape-recorded interviews made for historic purposes, esp. the reminiscences of notable contemporaries.

or·ange (ôr′inj, or′-), *n.* **1.** a round, reddish-yellow, edible citrus fruit valued esp. for its sweet juice. **2.** the evergreen tree bearing this. **3.** a reddish yellow.

or·ange·ade (ôr′inj ād′, -in jād′, or′-), *n.* a beverage consisting of orange juice, sweetener, and water.

or·ange·ry (ôr′inj rē, or′-), *n., pl.* **-ries.** a place, as a greenhouse, in which orange trees are cultivated in cool climates.

or′ange stick′, a pencillike stick, typically of wood of the orange tree, used in manicuring.

o·rang·u·tan (ō rang′o͞o tan′, ô rang′-), *n.* a large, long-armed anthropoid ape of tree-dwelling habits, found in Borneo and Sumatra. Also, **o·rang′ou·tan′.**

o·rate (ō rāt′, ô rāt′, ōr′āt, ôr′āt), *v.i.,* **-rat·ed, -rat·ing.** to speak pompously or formally.

o·ra·tion (ō rā′shən, ô rā′-), *n.* a formal speech, esp. one delivered on a special occasion.

or·a·tor (ôr′ə tər, or′-), *n.* **1.** a person who delivers an oration. **2.** an eloquent public speaker.

or·a·tor·i·cal (ôr′ə tôr′i kəl, or′ə tor′-), *adj.* of or suggesting an orator or oratory. —**or′a·tor′i·cal·ly,** *adv.*

or·a·to·ri·o (ôr′ə tōr′ē ō′, -tôr′-, or′-), *n., pl.* **-ri·os.** an extended choral and orchestral composition, usually based upon a religious theme.

or·a·to·ry[1] (ôr′ə tōr′ē, -tôr′ē, or′-), *n.* **1.** eloquent speech or language. **2.** the art of public speaking.

or·a·to·ry[2] (ôr′ə tōr′ē, -tôr′ē, or′-), *n., pl.* **-ries.** a small chapel for private devotions.

orb (ôrb), *n. Literary.* **1.** any of the heavenly bodies. **2.** a sphere or globe. —**or·bic·u·lar** (ôr bik′yə lər), *adj.*

or·bit (ôr′bit), *n.* **1.** the curved path that a celestial body takes around another. **2.** the path of a manmade satellite or spacecraft. **3.** a range of activities. —*v.t., v.i.* **4.** to travel in or send into an orbit. —**or′bit·al,** *adj.* —**or′bit·er,** *n.*

orch., orchestra.

or·chard (ôr′chərd), *n.* **1.** an area devoted to the cultivation of fruit trees. **2.** a group of such trees. —**or′chard·ist,** *n.*

or·ches·tra (ôr′ki strə), *n.* **1.** a company of performers who play various musical instruments together. **2.** (in a modern theater) **a.** the space reserved for the musicians, usually the front part of the main floor (**or′chestra pit′**). **b.** the front section of seats on the main floor. —**or·ches′tral** (-kes′trəl), *adj.* —**or·ches′tral·ly,** *adv.*

or·ches·trate (ôr′ki strāt′), *v.t., v.i.,* **-trat·ed, -trat·ing.** to arrange (music) for performance by an orchestra. —**or′ches·tra′tion,** *n.*

or·chid (ôr′kid), *n.* **1.** a terrestrial perennial herb of temperate and tropical regions, having usually showy flowers. **2.** its flower. **3.** a bluish to reddish purple.

ord., 1. order. **2.** ordnance.

or·dain (ôr dān′), *v.t.* **1.** to invest with ministerial or priestly functions. **2.** to decree or order. **3.** to destine or predestine. —*v.i.* **4.** to order or command. —**or·dain′ment,** *n.*

or·deal (ôr dēl′, -dē′əl, ôr′dēl), *n.* any extremely severe or trying test or experience.

or·der (ôr′dər), *n.* **1.** an authoritative communication by which the person addressed is directed to do something. **2.** a system of arrangement or classification of persons or things: *alphabetical order.* **3.** a state of efficiency or neatness. **4.** a state of effective operation. **5.** a state of public peace or conformity to law. **6.** a general classification according to quality or standing. **7.** a social class: *the lower orders.* **8.** a customary mode of procedure. **9.** conformity to this, esp. in parliamentary procedure. **10.** a request or set of instructions by which goods or services are sold, made, or furnished. **11.** something sold, made, or furnished according to this. **12.** a major division of plants and animals consisting of several related families. **13.** a body or society of persons living under the same religious, moral, or social regulations. **14.** any of the grades of the clergy. **15. orders,** the rank or status of an ordained Christian minister. **16.** (*cap.*) *Brit.* **a.** a group of distinguished persons on whom a sovereign has conferred special honor or rank: *the Order of Merit.* **b.** the insignia worn by the members of such a group. **17.** a written direction to pay money or deliver goods. **18.** a style of ancient architecture having a unique design and arrangement of columns. **19. in order, a.** suitable or appropriate. **b.** operating properly. **c.** correct according to the rules. **20. in order that,** to the end that. **21. in order to,** with the purpose of. **22. in short order,** with promptness. **23. on the order of,** resembling to some extent. **24. out of order, a.** unsuitable or inappropriate. **b.** not operating properly. **c.** incorrect according to the rules. **25. to order,** according to one's special instructions. —*v.t., v.i.* **26.** to give an order (to). **27.** to place an order (for). **28.** to put (things) in order.

or·der·ly (ôr′dər lē), *adj., adv., n., pl.* **-lies.** —*adj.* **1.** arranged in a neat, tidy manner. **2.** observant of law, rule, or discipline. —*adv.* **3.** according to established order or rule. —*n.* **4.** an enlisted person assigned to perform various chores for an officer. **5.** a hospital attendant, usually male. —**or′der·li·ness,** *n.* —*Syn.* **1.** methodical, systematic.

or·di·nal (ôr′də nəl), *adj.* of or pertaining to an order, as of animals or plants.

or′dinal num′ber, a number that expresses position in a series, as *first, second, third,* etc.

or·di·nance (ôr′də nəns), *n.* an authoritative rule or law, esp. one enacted by a municipal body.

or·di·nar·i·ly (ôr′də när′ə lē, ôr′də ner′-ə lē), *adv.* in usual cases.

or·di·nar·y (ôr′də ner′ē), *adj., n., pl.* **-nar·ies.** —*adj.* **1.** usually or commonly expected. **2.** average or below average. —*n.* **3. out of the ordinary,** exceptional or unusual. —**or′di·nar′i·ness,** *n.*

or·di·nate (ôr′də nāt′, -dnit), *n.* the distance of a point above or below the horizontal axis of a graph.

or·di·na·tion (ôr′də nā′shən), *n.* the religious ceremony of ordaining.

ord·nance (ôrd′nəns), *n.* **1.** military weapons with their equipment, ammunition, etc. **2.** cannon or artillery.

Or·do·vi·cian (ôr′də vish′ən), *adj.* **1.** noting a period of the Paleozoic era, occurring 440,000,000 to 500,000,000 years ago, and characterized by the presence of algae and seaweeds. —*n.* **2.** the Ordovician period.

or·dure (ôr′jər, -dyŏŏr), *n. Literary.* dung or excrement. —**or′dur·ous,** *adj.*

ore (ōr, ôr), *n.* a metal-bearing mineral or rock, esp. when of value.

Oreg., Oregon. Also, **Ore.**

o·reg·a·no (ə reg′ə nō′, ô reg′-), *n.* a plant related to but spicier than marjoram, used in cookery.

Or·e·gon (ôr′ə gən, -gon′, or′-), *n.* a state in the NW United States. *Cap.:* Salem. —**Or′e·go′ni·an** (-gō′nē ən), *adj., n.*

org., **1.** organic. **2.** organization. **3.** organized.

or·gan (ôr′gən), *n.* **1.** a musical instrument consisting of sets of pipes sounded by compressed air and played from keyboards. **2.** a differentiated part or member having a specific function in a plant or animal. **3.** a means of action or performance. **4.** a periodical publication representing a special group.

or·gan·dy (ôr′gən dē), *n.* a fine, thin, cotton fabric having a crisp finish. Also, **or′gan·die.**

or·gan·ic (ôr gan′ik), *adj.* **1.** of an organ or the organs of an animal or a plant. **2.** of, pertaining to, or derived from living organisms. **3.** noting a class of chemical compounds containing carbon. **4.** characterized by the systematic arrangement of parts. **5.** grown with fertilizers or pesticides of animal or vegetable origin. **6.** inherent or essential. —**or·gan′i·cal·ly,** *adv.*

or·gan·ism (ôr′gə niz′əm), *n.* any form of animal or plant life. —**or′gan·is′-mic, or′gan·is′mal,** *adj.*

or·gan·ist (ôr′gə nist), *n.* a person who plays the organ.

or·gan·i·za·tion (ôr′gə ni zā′shən), *n.*
1. the act or process of organizing,
or state or manner of being organized. **2.** something that is organized.
3. a body of persons organized for
some end or work. —**or′gan·i·za′-**
tion·al, *adj.* —**or′gan·i·za′tion·al·ly,**
adv.

or·gan·ize (ôr′gə nīz′), *v.,* **-ized, -iz**
ing. —*v.t.* **1.** to form as or into a
whole, esp. for united action. **2.** to
arrange in a systematic manner. **3.**
to give organic structure or character to. **4.** to enlist the employees of
(a business) into a labor union. —*v.i.*
5. to become organized. Also, *Brit.,*
or′gan·ise′. —**or′gan·iz′er,** *n.*

or·gan·ized (ôr′gə nīzd′), *adj.* **1.** widespread in operation: *organized crime.*
2. systematically far-reaching: *organized medicine.*

or·gan·za (ôr gan′zə), *n.* a sheer rayon, nylon, or silk fabric for trimmings, etc.

or·gasm (ôr′gaz əm), *n.* the culmination of a sexual act. —**or·gas′mic,**
or·gas′tic, *adj.*

or·gy (ôr′jē), *n., pl.* **-gies. 1.** a party
characterized by unbridled indulgence in drinking, hard drugs, or
promiscuous sexual intercourse. **2.**
uncontrolled indulgence in any activity.

o·ri·el (ôr′ē əl, ôr′-), *n.* a bay window
projecting out from a wall.

o·ri·ent (*n.* ôr′ē ənt, ôr′ē ent′, ôr′-; *v.*
ôr′ē ent′, ôr′-), *n.* **1.** the **Orient, a.**
the countries of Asia, esp. East Asia.
b. (formerly) the countries to the E
of the Mediterranean. —*v.t., v.i.* **2.**
to familiarize (a person or oneself)
with new surroundings or circumstances. **3.** to set in any definite
position with reference to the points
of the compass. —**o′ri·en·ta′tion,** *n.*

O·ri·en·tal (ôr′ē en′t°l, ôr′-), (*sometimes l.c.*) —*adj.* **1.** of the Orient.
—*n.* **2.** a native or inhabitant of the
Orient, esp. a Chinese or Japanese.

o·ri·en·tate (ôr′ē en tāt′, ôr′-, ôr′ē en′
tāt, ôr′-), *v.t., v.i.,* **-tat·ed, -tat·ing.**
to orient.

or·i·fice (ôr′ə fis, or′-), *n.* a mouth or
mouthlike opening. —**or·i·fi·cial** (ôr′
ə fish′əl, or′-), *adj.*

orig., **1.** origin. **2.** original. **3.** originally.

o·ri·ga·mi (ôr′ə gä′mē), *n.* a Japanese
art of folding paper into decorative
or representational forms. [< Jap:
folding paper]

or·i·gin (ôr′i jin, or′-), *n.* **1.** the source
from which anything arises or is derived. **2.** the first stage of existence.
3. birth or parentage. **4.** *Math.* the
point in a coordinate where the axes
intersect.

o·rig·i·nal (ə rij′ə n°l), *adj.* **1.** belonging to the origin or beginning of

something. **2.** inventive or creative.
3. noting the first presentation or performance. **4.** being that from which
a copy or a translation is made. —
n. **5.** a primary form or type from
which varieties are derived. **6.** an
original work or writing, as opposed
to any copy or imitation. —**o·rig′i·**
nal′i·ty (-nal′i tē), *n.* —**o·rig′i·nal·ly,**
adv. —**Syn. 5.** model, prototype.

o·rig·i·nate (ə rij′ə nāt′), *v.,* **-nat·ed,**
-nat·ing. —*v.i.* **1.** to take origin or
rise. **2.** to begin its scheduled run at
a specified place. —*v.t.* **3.** to give
origin or rise to. —**o·rig′i·na′tion,**
n. —**o·rig′i·na′tor,** *n.*

o·ri·ole (ôr′ē ōl′, ôr′-), *n.* a brightly
colored songbird of the Old World.

O·ri·on (ō rī′ən, ô rī′), *n.* a constellation lying on the celestial equator.

or·i·son (ôr′i zən, or′-), *n.* *Archaic.* a
prayer.

Or·lon (ôr′lon), *n.* *Trademark.* a synthetic fiber of light weight and good
wrinkle resistance.

or·mo·lu (ôr′mə loo′), *n.* an alloy of
copper and zinc used to imitate gold.

or·na·ment (*n.* ôr′nə mənt; *v.* ôr′nəment′), *n.* **1.** something added to
improve or enhance the appearance.
2. anything or anyone that adds to
the credit or glory of a group or era.
—*v.t.* **3.** to furnish with ornaments.
—**or′na·men′tal,** *adj.* —**or′na·menta′tion,** *n.*

or·nate (ôr nāt′), *adj.* **1.** elaborately
or sumptuously adorned. **2.** embellished with rhetoric. —**or·nate′ly,**
adv. —**or·nate′ness,** *n.*

or·ner·y (ôr′nə rē), *adj.* *Informal.*
mean in disposition or temper. —
or′ner·i·ness, *n.*

ornith., ornithology.

or·ni·thol·o·gy (ôr′nə thol′ə jē), *n.* the
branch of zoology that deals with
birds. —**or·ni·tho·log·i·cal** (ôr′nəthə loj′i kəl), *adj.* —**or′ni·thol′o·gist,**
n.

o·rog·e·ny (ō roj′ə nē, ô roj′-), *n.*
Geol. the process of mountain formation or upheaval. —**or·o·gen·ic**
(ôr′ə jen′ik, or′ə-), *adj.*

o·ro·tund (ôr′ə tund′, ôr′-), *adj.* **1.**
full, rich, and clear in voice. **2.**
pompous or bombastic in style. —
o·ro·tun·di·ty (ôr′ə tun′di tē, ôr′-), *n.*

or·phan (ôr′fən), *n.* **1.** a child who
has lost both parents through death,
or, less commonly, one parent. —
adj. **2.** bereft of parents. **3.** of or for
orphans. —*v.t.* **4.** to cause to be an
orphan.

or·phan·age (ôr′fə nij), *n.* an institution for the housing and care of orphans.

Or·phe·us (ôr′fē əs, -fyoos), *n.* *Class
Myth.* a poet and musician: reputed
founder of a mystic cult. —**Or′phic**
(-fik), *adj.*

or·ris (ôr′is, or′-), *n.* an iris having a fragrant rootstock (**or′ris·root′**) used in perfumery, etc.

orth., **1.** orthopedic. **2.** orthopedics.

ortho-, a combining form meaning: **a.** straight or upright: *orthodontics.* **b.** right or correct: *orthodox.* Also, **orth-.**

or·tho·don·tics (ôr′thə don′tiks), *n.* the branch of dentistry dealing with the prevention and correction of irregular dentition. Also, **or·tho·don·tia** (ôr′thə don′shə, -shē ə). —**or′-tho·don′tic,** *adj.* —**or′tho·don′tist,** *n.*

or·tho·dox (ôr′thə doks′), *adj.* **1.** conforming to traditional or established doctrine, esp. in religion. **2.** conforming to beliefs, attitudes, or manners that are generally approved. **3.** (*cap.*) of or pertaining to the Eastern Church, esp. the Greek Orthodox Church. [< L *orthodox(us)* < Gk *orthódoxos* < *ortho-* right + *dóx(a)* opinion] —**or′tho·dox′y,** *n.* —**Syn. 2.** conventional, customary.

or·tho·e·py (ôr thō′ə pē, ôr′thō ep′ē), *n.* the study of correct pronunciation. —**or·tho′e·pist,** *n.*

or·thog·ra·phy (ôr thog′rə fē), *n.* **1.** the art of spelling according to accepted usage. **2.** the part of grammar that treats of spelling. —**or·tho·graph·ic** (ôr′thə graf′ik), *adj.* —**or′tho·graph′i·cal·ly,** *adv.*

or·tho·pe·dics (ôr′thə pē′diks), *n.* the correction or cure of deformities and diseases of the skeletal system. —**or′tho·pe′dic,** *adj.* —**or′tho·pe′dist,** *n.*

or·to·lan (ôr′t°lən), *n.* an Old World bunting valued as a food.

Or·well·i·an (ôr wel′ē ən), *adj.* of or suggestive of a dehumanized society manipulated by newspeak. [from theme in *1984,* a novel by Brit. writer George *Orwell* (1903–50)]

-ory¹, a suffix meaning "having the function or effect of": *compulsory.*

-ory², a suffix meaning "a place or an instrument": *dormitory.*

Os, osmium.

o/s, out of stock.

O.S., 1. *Med.* the left eye. [< L *oculus sinister*] **2.** ordinary seaman.

O·sage (ō′sāj, ō sāj′), *n., pl.* **O·sag·es, O·sage.** a member of an Indian people once living in Ohio.

O·sa·ka (ō sä′kə), *n.* a city on S Honshu, in S Japan.

os·cil·late (os′ə lāt′), *v.i.,* **-lat·ed, -lat·ing. 1.** to swing to and fro, as a pendulum does. **2.** to fluctuate between differing opinions, conditions, etc. **3.** *Physics.* to fluctuate repeatedly between two values, as an alternating current. —**os′cil·la′tion,** *n.* —**os′cil·la′tor,** *n.* —**os′cil·la·to′ry** (-lə-tôr′ē, -tōr′ē), *adj.*

os·cil·lo·scope (ə sil′ə skōp′), *n.* a device that depicts on a screen periodic changes in an electric quantity, as voltage, using a cathode-ray tube. —**os·cil′lo·scop′ic** (-skop′ik), *adj.* —**os·cil′lo·scop′i·cal·ly,** *adv.*

os·cu·late (os′kyə lāt′), *v.i., v.t.,* **-lat·ed, -lat·ing.** *Facetious.* to kiss. —**os′cu·la′tion,** *n.*

-ose¹, a suffix meaning "abounding in," "given to," or "like": *jocose; otiose.*

-ose², a suffix forming the names of carbohydrates: *lactose.*

O.S.F., Order of St. Francis.

o·sier (ō′zhər), *n.* **1.** a willow having tough, flexible twigs that are used for wickerwork. **2.** a twig from such a willow.

-osis, a suffix meaning: **a.** action or condition: *metamorphosis.* **b.** a pathological condition: *tuberculosis.*

Os·lo (oz′lō, os′-, ōs′-), *n.* the capital of Norway.

os·mi·um (oz′mē əm), *n. Chem.* a hard, heavy metallic element, used chiefly in alloys. *Symbol:* Os; *at. wt.:* 190.2; *at. no.:* 76.

os·mo·sis (oz mō′sis, os-), *n.* the passage of a fluid through a semipermeable membrane into a solution where its concentration is lower, thus equalizing the conditions on both sides of the membrane. —**os·mot′ic** (-mot′ik, os-), *adj.*

os·prey (os′prē), *n., pl.* **-preys.** a large hawk that feeds on fish.

os·si·fy (os′ə fī′), *v.t., v.i.,* **-fied, -fy·ing. 1.** to convert into bone. **2.** to make or become rigid in habits, attitudes, etc. —**os′si·fi·ca′tion,** *n.*

os·ten·si·ble (o sten′sə bəl), *adj.* given out or outwardly appearing as such. —**os·ten′si·bly,** *adv.* —**Syn.** alleged, professed.

os·ten·ta·tion (os′ten tā′shən), *n.* pretentious display. —**os′ten·ta′tious,** *adj.* —**os′ten·ta′tious·ly,** *adv.*

os·te·op·a·thy (os′tē op′ə thē), *n.* a therapeutic system based upon the premise that health can best be improved or restored by manipulation of the bones and muscles. —**os′te·o·path′** (-ə path′), *n.* —**os′te·o·path′ic** (-ə path′ik), *adj.*

ost·mark (ôst′märk′, ost′-), *n.* the monetary unit of East Germany.

os·tra·cize (os′trə sīz′), *v.t.,* **-cized, -ciz·ing.** to exclude, by general consent, from society or a group. —**os′-tra·cism′,** *n.*

os·trich (ô′strich, os′trich), *n.* a large, two-toed, swift-footed, flightless bird of Africa and Arabia.

Os·we′go tea′ (o swē′gō), a North American herb having showy, bright-red flowers.

OT, 1. Old Testament. **2.** overtime.

OTB, offtrack betting.

OTC, 1. one-stop inclusive tour charter (open to the general public). **2.** over-the-counter.

oth·er (uth′ər), *adj.* **1.** different from the one or ones mentioned or implied: *in some other city.* **2.** being the remaining one or ones of a number: *the other men.* **3.** additional or further: *he and one other person.* **4.** different in nature or kind: *I would not have him other than he is.* **5.** former: *sailing ships of other days.* **6.** every other, every alternate. **7. the other day (night, evening, etc.),** a day (night, evening, etc.) or two ago. *—pron.* **8.** Usually, **others.** other persons or things. **9.** some person or thing else. *—adv.* **10.** otherwise or differently.

oth·er·wise (uth′ər wīz′), *adv.* **1.** under other circumstances. **2.** in another manner. **3.** in other respects: *an otherwise happy life. —adj.* **4.** other or different.

oth′er world′, the world after death.

oth·er·world·ly (uth′ər wûrld′lē), *adj.* of or devoted to another world, as the world of imagination or the world to come. **—oth′er·world′li·ness,** *n.*

o·ti·ose (ō′shē ōs′, ō′tē-), *adj.* **1.** serving no real or useful purpose: *otiose remarks.* **2.** *Rare.* **a.** ineffective or futile. **b.** idle or indolent.

o·to·lar·yn·gol·o·gy (ō′tō lar′ing gol′-ə jē), *n.* the branch of medicine that deals with the ear, nose, and throat. **—o′to·lar′yn·gol′o·gist,** *n.*

OTS, officer training school.

Ot·ta·wa (ot′ə wə), *n., pl.* **-was, -wa** for **2. 1.** the capital of Canada, in SE Ontario. **2.** a member of an Indian people forced into the Lake Superior and Lake Michigan regions by the Iroquois confederacy.

ot·ter (ot′ər), *n., pl.* **-ters, -ter. 1.** an aquatic, fur-bearing mammal having webbed feet and a long, slightly flattened tail. **2.** its fur.

Ot·to·man (ot′ə mən), *n.* **1.** a Turk, esp. of the former Turkish empire. **2.** (*l.c.*) a heavy upholstered sofa or seat, with or without a back. **3.** (*l.c.*) a cushioned footstool. *—adj.* **4.** of Turkey, esp. its former empire.

ou·bli·ette (ōō′blē et′), *n.* a dungeon with an opening only at the top, as in certain old castles.

ouch (ouch), *interj.* (an exclamation expressing sudden pain.)

ought (ôt), *auxiliary verb.* **1.** (used to express duty or moral obligation): *Every citizen ought to help.* **2.** (used to express justice or moral rightness): *He ought to be punished.* **3.** (used to express propriety or appropriateness): *You ought to be home early.* **4.** (used to express probability): *That ought to be the postman.*

oui (wē), *adv., n. French.* yes.

Oui·ja (wē′jə, -jē), *n. Trademark.* a device consisting of a small board moving on a larger board marked with words and letters, used to spell out messages in spiritualistic communication.

ounce (ouns), *n.* **1.** a unit of weight equal to ¹⁄₁₆ pound avoirdupois, or 28.35 grams. **2.** a unit of weight equal to ¹⁄₁₂ pound troy, or 31.103 grams. **3.** See **fluid ounce.**

our (our, ou′ər), *pron.* (a form of the possessive case of **we** used as an attributive adjective.)

ours (ourz, ou′ərz), *pron.* (a form of the possessive case of **we** used as a predicate adjective): *Which house is ours?*

our·selves (är selvz′, our-, ou′ər-), *pron.pl.* **1.** (used as an intensifier of *we* or *us*): *We ourselves would never lie.* **2.** (used reflexively as a substitute for *us*): *We saw television.* **3.** our normal selves: *After a good rest, we're almost ourselves again.*

-ous, a suffix meaning "abounding in," "characterized by," or "having": *glorious; nervous; wonderous.*

oust (oust), *v.t.* to expel from a place or position occupied.

oust·er (ou′stər), *n.* expulsion from a place or position occupied.

out (out), *adv.* **1.** away from the normal place, position, etc. **2.** in or into the outdoors. **3.** to the end or conclusion. **4.** to exhaustion, extinction, or nonexistence: *The lamp went out.* **5.** not in vogue or fashion: *The style has gone out.* **6.** in or into public notice or knowledge. **7.** so as to project or extend: *to stretch out.* **8.** in or into the open: *A rash broke out on her arm.* **9.** from a number, stock, or store: *to pick out.* **10.** aloud or loudly: *to call out.* **11.** thoroughly or completely: *The children tired me out.* **12.** *Baseball.* in a manner resulting in an out: *to strike out.* **13. all out,** with maximum effort. *—adj.* **14.** exposed or made bare: *out at the knees.* **15.** beyond fixed limits: *The ball was declared out.* **16.** beyond the usual range, size, etc.: *an outsize bed.* **17.** incorrect or inaccurate: *His calculations are out.* **18.** having a financial loss: *I'm out 10 dollars.* **19.** *Baseball.* not succeeding in getting on base. **20.** no longer holding (a job, etc.). **21.** not operating or functioning. **22.** not in power or authority. **23.** not stylish or fashionable. **24. out for,** attempting serious efforts to get or do. **25. out of, a.** from within. **b.** beyond the reach of. **c.** without or lacking: *out of fuel.* **d.** from a condition of. **e.** so as to be deprived of. **f.** as a result of: *out of pity.* **g.** from among. **h.** from, as material or a source. **26.**

out to, making serious efforts to. —*prep.* **27.** out from or through: *He ran out the door.* **28.** out along or on: *Let's drive out the old dirt road.* —*n.* **29.** a person or thing that is out. **30.** a means of escape, as from responsibility. **31.** *Baseball.* a put-out. **32. be on the** or **at outs with,** *Informal.* to be on bad terms with. —*v.i.* **33.** to become public or known: *The truth will out.*

out-, a prefix meaning: **a.** outward or external: *outburst.* **b.** outside or at a distance from: *outpost.* **c.** to surpass: *outlast, outlive.*

out·age (ou'tij), *n.* a stoppage in the functioning of a machine or mechanism.

out-and-out (out'°nout', -°nd out'), *adj.* **1.** thoroughgoing or complete. **2.** not concealed or disguised.

out·bal·ance (out'bal'əns), *v.t.,* **-anced, -anc·ing.** outweigh.

out·bid (out'bid'), *v.t.,* **-bid, -bid·den** or **-bid, -bid·ding.** to outdo in bidding.

out·board (out'bōrd', -bôrd'), *adj.* **1.** located on the exterior of a hull or aircraft. **2.** having an outboard motor.

out'board mo'tor, a portable gasoline engine with propeller attached for clamping on the stern of a boat.

out·bound (out'bound'), *adj.* outward bound.

out·break (out'brāk'), *n.* **1.** an outburst, as of war. **2.** a sudden occurrence or incidence as of a disease.

out·build·ing (out'bil'ding), *n.* a detached building subordinate to a main building.

out·burst (out'bûrst'), *n.* a sudden and violent outpouring, as of feeling.

out·cast (out'kast', -käst'), *n.* **1.** a person who is rejected as by society. —*adj.* **2.** rejected or discarded.

out·class (out'klas', -kläs'), *v.t.* to surpass in class or quality.

out·come (out'kum'), *n.* a final or decisive result.

out·crop (out'krop'), *n.* **1.** a coming out, as of a stratum at the surface of the earth. **2.** the emerging part.

out·cry (out'krī'), *n.* **1.** a cry of distress or indignation. **2.** loud clamor.

out·dat·ed (out'dā'tid), *adj.* no longer in use or in fashion.

out·dis·tance (out'dis'təns), *v.t.,* **-tanced, -tanc·ing.** to leave behind, as in running.

out·do (out'dōō'), *v.t.,* **-did, -done, -do·ing.** to surpass in execution or performance.

out·door (out'dōr', -dôr'), *adj.* characteristic of, located, or belonging outdoors.

out·doors (out'dōrz', -dôrz'), *adv.* **1.** in the open air. —*n.* **2.** the world outside of houses.

out·er (ou'tər), *adj.* **1.** farther out. **2.** external or exterior: *an outer garment.*

out·er·most (ou'tər mōst'), *adj.* farthest out.

out'er space', the region beyond the atmosphere of the earth.

out·face (out'fās'), *v.t.,* **-faced, -fac·ing. 1.** to face or stare down. **2.** to face or confront boldly.

out·field (out'fēld'), *n. Baseball.* **1.** the part of the field beyond the diamond. **2.** the players (**out'field'ers**) stationed there.

out·fit (out'fit'), *n., v.,* **-fit·ted, -fit·ting.** —*n.* **1.** the equipment for a special purpose: *an explorer's outfit.* **2.** a complete costume, esp. for a woman. **3.** *Informal.* a group of people associated in an undertaking, as a military unit or a business firm. —*v.t.* **4.** to furnish with an outfit. —**out'fit'ter,** *n.*

out·flank (out'flangk'), *v.t.* to go or extend beyond the flank of (an opposing force).

out·flow (out'flō'), *n.* **1.** the act of flowing out. **2.** something that flows out.

out·fox (out'foks'), *v.t.* to get the better of by cunning or trick.

out·go (out'gō'), *n., pl.* **-goes.** money paid out, esp. as a business expenditure.

out·go·ing (out'gō'ing), *adj.* **1.** leaving or departing. **2.** leaving a position, as for transfer or retirement. **3.** interested in and responsive to others. **4.** take-out.

out·grow (out'grō'), *v.t.,* **-grew, -grown, -grow·ing. 1.** to grow too large for **2.** to leave behind or lose in the changes incident to the passage of time. **3.** to surpass in growing.

out·growth (out'grōth'), *n.* **1.** an additional, supplementary result. **2.** something that grows out, as an offshoot.

out·guess (out'ges'), *v.t.* **1.** to guess correctly the actions of. **2.** to outdo in forethought.

out·house (out'hous'), *n.* an outbuilding with one or more seats and a pit serving as a toilet.

out·ing (ou'ting), *n.* **1.** a short pleasure trip. **2.** an outdoor walk.

---

out'ar'gue, *v.t.*
out'bar'gain, *v.t.*
out'bluff', *v.t.*
out'boast', *v.t.*
out'box', *v.t.*

out'dodge', *v.t.,* **-dodged, -dodg·ing.**
out'fight', *v.t.,* **-fought, -fighting.**

out'gun', *v.t.,* **-gunned, -gun·ning.**
out'hit'. *v.t.,* **-hit, -hit·ting.**

out·land·ish (out lan′dish), *adj.* **1.** grotesquely strange or odd. **2.** having a foreign appearance. —**out′land′ish·ly,** *adv.* —**out·land′ish·ness,** *n.*

out·last (out′last′, -läst′), *v.t.* to last or endure longer than.

out·law (out′lô′), *n.* **1.** a habitual criminal. **2.** (formerly) a person excluded from the benefits and protection of the law. —*v.t.* **3.** to make unlawful. **4.** (formerly) to deprive of the benefits and protection of the law. —**out′law′ry** (-rē), *n.*

out·lay (out′lā′), *n.* **1.** an expenditure of money. **2.** an amount expended.

out·let (out′let, -lit), *n.* **1.** a passage by which anything is let out. **2.** a fixture into which the cord of an electrical appliance may be plugged. **3.** a. a market for goods. b. a retail store selling the goods of a particular manufacturer. **4.** a means of expression or satisfaction.

out·line (out′līn), *n., v.,* -**lined, -lin·ing.** —*n.* **1.** the line by which a figure or object is bounded. **2.** a drawing restricted to line without shading. **3.** a general account or report of only the main features. —*v.t.* **4.** to draw in outline, as a figure. **5.** to give an outline of.

out·live (out′liv′), *v.t.,* -**lived, -liv·ing.** to live or last longer than.

out·look (out′loŏk′), *n.* **1.** the view from a place. **2.** mental view. **3.** prospect of the future.

out·ly·ing (out′lī′ing), *adj.* lying at a distance from a center or main body.

out·ma·neu·ver (out′mə noo′vər), *v.t.* to outdo in maneuvering.

out·mod·ed (out′mō′did), *adj.* **1.** gone out of style. **2.** not acceptable by present standards.

out·num·ber (out′num′bər), *v.t.* to exceed in number.

out-of-date (out′əv dāt′), *adj.* no longer current or used. —**out′-of-date′ness,** *n.*

out′ of doors′, in the open air.

out-of-doors (out′əv dôrz′, -dōrz′), *adj.* **1.** Also, **out′-of-door′.** outdoor. —*n.* **2.** outdoors.

out-of-the-way (out′əv [th]ə wā′), *adj.* **1.** remote from busy or populated regions. **2.** seldom encountered.

out-of-town·er (out′əv tou′nər), *n.* a visitor from another town or city.

out·pa·tient (out′pā′shənt), *n.* a patient receiving treatment at a hospital but not being an inmate.

out·play (out′plā′), *v.t.* to play better than.

out·post (out′pōst′), *n.* **1.** a station established at a distance from the main body of an army to protect it from surprise attack. **2.** the body of troops stationed there. **3.** an outlying settlement.

out·pour·ing (out′pôr′ing, pōr′-), *n.* that which pours out or is poured out.

out·put (out′poŏt′), *n.* **1.** production, esp. the quantity or amount produced in a given time. **2.** the current, voltage, or power produced by an electrical or electronic device. **3.** the information that has been processed by a computer.

out·rage (out′rāj), *n., v.,* -**raged, -rag·ing.** —*n.* **1.** an act of wanton violence. **2.** anything that angers or offends the feelings. **3.** great anger or fury. —*v.t.* **4.** to commit an outrage against. **5.** to arouse outrage in.

out·ra·geous (out rā′jəs), *adj.* **1.** involving gross injury or wrong. **2.** grossly offensive or shocking. **3.** passing reasonable bounds. —**out·ra′geous·ly,** *adv.* —**out·ra′geous·ness,** *n.* —Syn. **2.** insulting, unthinkable.

out·rank (out′rangk′), *v.t.* to rank above.

ou·tré (oo trā′), *adj. French.* passing the bounds of what is usual or proper.

out·reach (*v.* out′rēch′; *n.* out′rēch′), *v.t., v.i.* **1.** to reach beyond. **2.** to reach out. —*n.* **3.** the act or an instance of reaching out. **4.** length of reach.

out·rid·er (out′rī′dər), *n.* **1.** a person on a motorcycle who goes in advance of an automobile, as to clear the way. **2.** a man who rides out or forth, esp. a cowboy. **3.** a mounted attendant riding before or beside a carriage.

out·rig·ger (out′rig′ər), *n.* **1.** a framework supporting a float extended from the side of a boat for adding stability. **2.** a boat equipped with this.

out·right (*adj.* out′rīt′; *adv.* out′rīt′, -rīt′), *adj.* **1.** complete or total. **2.** downright or unqualified. **3.** *Archaic.* directed straight out or on. —*adv.* **4.** completely or entirely. **5.** openly or without restraint. **6.** at once or instantly. —**out′right′ness,** *n.*

out·run (out′run′), *v.t.,* -**ran, -run, -run·ning. 1.** to run faster or farther than. **2.** to exceed or surpass. **3.** to escape by or as by running.

---

out·sell (out'sel'), *v.t.*, **-sold, -sell·ing.** to exceed in volume of sales.

out·set (out'set'), *n.* the beginning or initial stage.

out·shine (out'shīn'), *v.t.*, **-shone, -shin·ing. 1.** to surpass in shining. **2.** to surpass in splendor or excellence.

out·side (*n.* out'sīd', -sīd'; *adj.* out'-sīd', out'-; *adv.* out'sīd'; *prep.* out'-sīd', out'sīd'), *n.* **1.** the outer side, surface, or part. **2.** the external appearance. **3.** the space without or beyond an enclosure or boundary. —*adj.* **4.** of, situated on, or coming from the outside. **5.** not belonging to a specified group or institution: *outside influences.* **6.** slight or remote: *an outside chance for recovery.* **7.** extreme or maximum: *an outside estimate.* **8.** being in addition to one's regular work or duties. — *adv.* **9.** on or to the outside. —*prep.* **10.** on or toward the outside of. **11.** beyond the confines or limits of. **12.** *Informal.* with the exception of. **13.** **outside of,** *Informal.* **a.** other than. **b.** outside (defs. 10–12).

out·sid·er (out'sī'dər), *n.* **1.** a person not belonging to a particular group. **2.** a contestant not classifed among those expected to win.

out·size (out'sīz'), *n.* **1.** an uncommon or irregular size. —*adj.* **2.** Also, **out'sized'.** unusually or abnormally large

out·skirts (out'skûrts'), *n.* the outlying district or region, as of a city.

out·smart (out'smärt'), *v.t.* **1.** to outdo in smartness or cleverness. **2. outsmart oneself.** to defeat oneself unintentionally by intrigue or elaborate scheming

out·spo·ken (out'spō'kən), *adj.* **1.** expressed with boldness or bluntness. **2.** free or unreserved in speech. —**out'spo'ken·ly,** *adv.* —**out'spo'ken·ness.** *n.* —Syn. candid, frank.

out·spread (*v.* out'spred'; *adj.* out'-spred'), *v.* **-spread, -spread·ing,** *adj.* —*v.t., v.i.* **1.** to spread out or extend. —*adj.* **2.** spread out or stretched out.

out·stand·ing (out'stan'ding), *adj.* **1.** prominent as compared with others of its kind. **2.** remaining unsettled or unpaid, as debts. **3.** (of capital stocks) issued and sold or in circulation. **4.** projecting outward or upward. —**out'stand'ing·ly,** *adv.* —Syn. **1.** conspicuous, striking.

out·sta·tion (out'stā'shən), *n.* an auxiliary station, esp. in a remote district.

out·stay (out'stā'), *v.t.* **1.** to stay longer than. **2.** overstay. **3.** outlast.

out·stretch (out'strech'), *v.t.* **1.** to stretch forth or extend. **2.** to stretch beyond. —**out'stretched',** *adj.*

out·strip (out'strip'), *v.t.*, **-stripped, -strip·ping. 1.** to get ahead of in a race. **2.** to outdo or surpass.

out·vote (out'vōt'), *v.t.*, **-vot·ed, -vot·ing.** to outdo or defeat in voting.

out·ward (out'wərd), *adv.* **1.** Also, **out'wards.** toward the outside or exterior. —*adj.* **2.** proceeding or directed toward the outside or exterior. **3.** situated on the outer side. **4.** being what is seen or apparent. —**out'ward·ly,** *adv.*

out·wear (out'wâr'), *v.t.*, **-wore, -worn, -wear·ing. 1.** to wear or last longer than. **2.** to exhaust in strength.

out·weigh (out'wā'), *v.t.* **1.** to exceed in value or importance. **2.** to weigh more than.

out·wit (out'wit'), *v.t.*, **-wit·ted, -wit·ting. 1.** to get the better of by ingenuity or intelligence.

out·work (*v.* out'wûrk'; *n.* out'wûrk'), *v.t.* **1.** to surpass in working. —*n.* **2.** a minor defense lying outside the principal fortification. —**out'work'-er,** *n.*

out·worn (out'wōrn', -wôrn'), *adj.* **1.** no longer used or useful, as ideas. **2.** worn-out, as clothes.

ou·zo (ōō'zō), *n.* an anise-flavored liqueur of Greece.

o·va (ō'və), *n.* pl. of **ovum.**

o·val (ō'vəl), *adj.* **1.** shaped like an egg. **2.** ellipsoidal or elliptical. —*n.* **3.** an object having an oval shape.

O'val Of'fice, 1. the office in which the U.S. President conducts official business, located inside the White House. **2.** the Presidency of the United States.

o·va·ry (ō'və rē), *n., pl.* **-ries. 1.** either of a pair of female reproductive glands in which ova are formed. **2.** *Bot.* the enlarged lower part of the pistil enclosing the ovules. —**o·var'i·an** (ō vâr'ē ən), **o·var'i·al,** *adj.*

o·vate (ō'vāt), *adj.* egg-shaped, esp. a leaf.

o·va·tion (ō vā'shən), *n.* an enthusiastic public reception of a person, esp. loud and prolonged applause.

ov·en (uv'ən), *n.* a compartment, as in a stove, for baking, roasting, or drying.

o·ver (ō'vər), *prep.* **1.** above in place or position. **2.** above and to the other side of: *to leap over a wall.* **3.** above in authority, rank, etc. **4.** so as to rest on or cover: *Throw a sheet over the bed.* **5.** on or upon, so as to cause an effect. **6.** all through. **7.** to the other side of: *to go over a*

---

out'shout', *v.t.*
out'spell', *v.t.*

out'swim', *v.t., v.i.,* **-swam, -swum, -swim·ming.**

out'walk', *v.t.*
out'yell', *v.t.*

bridge. **8.** in excess of. **9.** in preference to. **10.** throughout the duration of: *over a long period of years.* **11.** in reference to or concerning: *to quarrel over a matter.* —*adv.* **12.** beyond the top or upper surface or edge of something: *a roof that hangs over.* **13.** so as to cover the surface or affect the whole surface: *to paint the room over.* **14.** across or beyond the rim: *The soup boiled over.* **15.** from beginning to end: *to read a thing over.* **16.** from one person or party to another: *He made the property over to his brother.* **17.** from one opinion or belief to another: *to win them over to our side.* **18.** on the other side, as of a sea, a river, or any space: *over in Europe.* **19.** from an upright position: *to knock over a glass of milk.* **20.** to a reversed position. **21.** once more: *to do a thing over.* **22.** in repetition or succession: *twenty times over.* **23.** in excess or addition. —*adj.* **24.** upper or higher up. **25.** serving as an outer covering. **26.** remaining or additional. **27.** too great. **28.** ended or past: *when the war was over.* —*interj.* **29.** (to signify in radio communications that the speaker's message is temporarily finished.)

over-, a prefix meaning: **a.** too or too much: *overdo.* **b.** over or above: *overcoat.* **c.** higher in authority or rank: *overlord.*

o·ver·act (ō′vər akt′), *v.t., v.i.* to act in an exaggerated manner.

o·ver·age[1] (ō′vər āj′), *adj.* beyond the required or desired age.

o·ver·age[2] (ō′vər ij), *n.* an excess supply of merchandise.

o·ver·all (*adv.* ō′vər ôl′; *adj., n.* ō′vər ôl′), *adv., adj.* **1.** from one extreme limit of a thing to the other. **2.** covering or including everything. —*n.* **3. overalls,** a man's loose work trous-

ers, usually with a part covering the chest.

o·ver·arm (ō′vər ärm′), *adj.* performed with the arm above the shoulder.

o·ver·awe (ō′vər ô′), *v.t.,* -**awed,** -**aw·ing.** to restrain or subdue by inspiring awe.

o·ver·bal·ance (ō′vər bal′əns), *v.t.,* -**anced,** -**anc·ing.** **1.** to cause to lose balance. **2.** outweigh.

o·ver·bear (ō′vər bâr′), *v.t.,* -**bore,** -**borne,** -**bear·ing.** **1.** to bear over or down by weight or force. **2.** to prevail over or overrule (wishes, etc.).

o·ver·bear·ing (ō′vər bâr′ing), *adj.* haughtily or rudely arrogant. —**o′ver·bear′ing·ly,** *adv.* —**Syn.** domineering, imperious.

o·ver·blown (ō′vər blōn′), *adj.* **1.** inflated with conceit or pretension. **2.** portly or stout.

o·ver·board (ō′vər bōrd′, -bôrd′), *adv.* **1.** over the side of a ship or boat into the water. **2. go overboard,** to go to extremes, esp. because of enthusiasm.

o·ver·cast (ō′vər kast′, -käst′, ō′vər-kast′, -käst′), *adj.* overspread with clouds: *an overcast sky.*

o·ver·charge (*v.* ō′vər chärj′; *n.* ō′vər-chärj′), *v.,* -**charged,** -**charg·ing,** *n.* —*v.t., v.i.* **1.** to charge too high a price. **2.** to fill or load to excess. —*n.* **3.** a charge in excess of a just price. **4.** an excessive load.

o·ver·cloud (ō′vər kloud′), *v.t., v.i.* to overspread or become overspread with or as with clouds.

o·ver·coat (ō′vər kōt′), *n.* a coat worn over the ordinary clothing.

o·ver·come (ō′vər kum′), *v.,* -**came,** -**come,** -**com·ing.** —*v.t.* **1.** to get the better of in a struggle or conflict. **2.** to prevail over (opposition, temptations, etc.). **3.** to overpower or overwhelm in body or mind. —*v.i.* **4.** to gain the victory. —**Syn. 1.** conquer, defeat. **2.** surmount.

o′ver·a·bound′, *n.*
o′ver·a·bund′ance, *n.*
o′ver·a·bun′dant, *adj.*
o′ver·ac′tive, *adj.*
o′ver·a·dorned′, *adj.*
o′ver·ag·gres′sive, *adj.*
o′ver·am·bi′tious, *adj.;* -ly, *adv.*
o′ver·an′a·lyze′, *v.,* -lyzed, -lyz·ing.
o′ver·anx′ious, *adj.*
o′ver·ap′pre·hen′sive, *adj.; -ly, adv.; -ness, n.*
o′ver·ar′gu·men′ta·tive, *adj.*
o′ver·as·ser′tive, *adj.; -ly, adv.; -ness, n.*
o′ver·as·sured′, *adj.*
o′ver·at·tached′, *adj.*
o′ver·at·ten′tive, *adj.; -ly, adv.; -ness, n.*

o′ver·bid′, *v.t., v.i.*
o′ver·bold′, *adj.*
o′ver·bur′den, *v.t.*
o′ver·bur′den·some, *adj.*
o′ver·buy′, *v.t., v.i.*
o′ver·ca·pac′i·ty, *n.*
o′ver·cap′i·tal·ize′, *v.t.*
o′ver·care′ful, *adj.*
o′ver·cas′u·al, *adj.*
o′ver·cau′tious, *adj.*
o′ver·com′mon, *adj.*
o′ver·com′pen·sate′, *v.i.*
o′ver·com·pet′i·tive, *adj.*
o′ver·com·pla′cen·cy, *n.*
o′ver·com·pla′cent, *adj.*
o′ver·con·cern′, *n.*
o′ver·con′fi·dent, *adj.*
o′ver·con·sci·en′tious, *adj.*
o′ver·con·serv′a·tive, *adj.*
o′ver·con·sid′er·ate, *adj.*

o′ver·cook′, *v.t.*
o′ver·cool′, *adj., v.t.*
o′ver·crit′i·cal, *adj.*
o′ver·crowd′, *v.t., v.i.*
o′ver·cu′ri·ous, *adj.*
o′ver·dec′o·rate′, *v.t.* -rat·ed, -rat·ing.
o′ver·de·fen′sive, *adj.*
o′ver·del′i·cate, *adj.*
o′ver·de·pend′ent, *adj.*
o′ver·de·sir′ous, *adj.*
o′ver·de·tailed′, *adj.*
o′ver·de·vel′op, *v.t., v.i.*
o′ver·dil′i·gent, *adj.;* -ly, *adv.*
o′ver·di·ver′si·fi·ca′-tion, *n.*
o′ver·di·ver′si·fy′, *v.,* -fied, -fy·ing.
o′ver·di·ver′si·ty, *n.*

o·ver·do (ō′vər dōō′), v., **-did**, **-done**, **-do·ing.** —v.t. **1.** to do to excess. **2.** to overact (a part). **3.** to cook too much or too long. —v.i. **4.** to do too much or go to an extreme.

o·ver·draft (ō′vər draft′, -dräft′), n. **1.** the act of overdrawing a checking account. **2. a.** a check overdrawn on a checking account. **b.** the amount overdrawn.

o·ver·draw (ō′vər drô′), v.t., **-drew**, **-drawn**, **-draw·ing. 1.** to write checks on (a checking account) in excess of the balance. **2.** to exaggerate in drawing or depicting.

o·ver·drive (ō′ver drīv′), n. a device containing a gear set at such ratio as to provide a drive-shaft speed greater than the engine crankshaft speed.

o·ver·flow (v. ō′vər flō′; n. ō′vər flō′), v.i. **1.** to flow or run over, as rivers, water, etc. **2.** to be filled or supplied with in great measure. —v.t. **3.** to flow over or beyond. **4.** to flow over the edge or brim of. —n. **5.** the act of overflowing. **6.** an excess or superabundance. **7.** an outlet for excess liquid.

o·ver·fly (ō′vər flī′), v.t., v.i., **-flew**, **-flown**, **-fly·ing.** to fly over (a specific area, country, etc.). —**o′ver·flight′** (-flīt′), n.

o·ver·glaze (ō′vər glāz′), n. an outer glaze applied to a ceramic object.

o·ver·grow (ō′vər grō′, ō′vər grō′), v., **-grew**, **-grown**, **-grow·ing.** —v.t. **1.** to cover with growth. **2.** outgrow (def. 1). —v.i. **3.** to grow too fast or too large. —**o′ver·grown′**, adj. — **o′ver·growth′**, n.

o·ver·hand (ō′vər hand′), adv. **1.** with the hand and part or all of the arm raised above the shoulder. —adj. **2.** thrown or performed overhand.

o·ver·hang (v. ō′vər hang′; n. ō′vər-hang′), v., **-hung**, **-hang·ing**, n. —v.t., v.i. **1.** to hang or be suspended over (something). **2.** to threaten, as danger or evil. —n. **3.** something that overhangs, as a roof. **4.** the extent of projection.

o·ver·haul (v. ō′vər hôl′, ō′vər hôl′; n. ō′vər hôl′), v.t. **1.** to investigate or examine thoroughly, as for repair. **2.** to make necessary repairs on. **3.** to gain upon or overtake, as in a race. —n. **4.** a general examination and repair.

o·ver·head (adv. ō′vər hed′; adj., n. ō′vər hed′), adv. **1.** above or over one's head. —adj. **2.** situated or operating above or over the head. **3.** of or pertaining to business overhead. —n. **4.** the general costs of running a business other than the costs of materials and production.

o·ver·hear (ō′vər hēr′), v.t., **-heard**, **-hear·ing.** to hear (speech or a speaker) without the speaker's intention or knowledge.

o·ver·joy (ō′vər joi′), v.t. to cause to feel great joy. —**o′ver·joyed′**, adj.

o·ver·kill (ō′vər kil′), n. **1.** the capacity of a nation to destroy, by nuclear weapons, more of an enemy than would be necessary. **2.** any effect or result that far exceeds what is necessary.

o·ver·land (ō′vər land′, -lənd), adv., adj. by, over, or across the land.

o′ver·dose′, n.	o′ver·ex·ert′, v.t., v.i	o′ver·heat′, v.i., v.t
o′ver·dram′a·tize′, v.t., -tized, -tiz·ing	o′ver·ex·pand′, v.	o′ver·hur′ried, adj
o′ver·dress′, v.t., v.i.	o′ver·ex·pan′sion, n.	o′ver·i·de′al·is′tic, adj.
o′ver·drink′, v.	o′ver·ex·pect′ant, adj.	o′ver·im·ag′i·na′tive, adj.
o′ver·due′, adj.	o′ver·ex·plic′it, adj.	
o′ver·ea′ger, adj.	o′ver·ex·pose′, v.t.	o′ver·im·press′, v.t,
o′ver·eat′, v.i., v.t.	o′ver·ex·tend′, v.t.	o′ver·in·cline′, v., -clined, -clin·ing.
o′ver·ed′u·cate′, v.t., -cat·ed, -cat·ing.	o′ver·fa·mil′iar, adj.	o′ver·in·dulge′, v.t., v.i.
	o′ver·fa·mil′i·ar′i·ty, n.	o′ver·in·dus′tri·al·ize′, v., -ized, -iz·ing.
o′ver·e·lab′o·rate, adj., v.	o′ver·fan′ci·ful. adj.	
o′ver·em·bel′lish, v.t.	o′ver·fas·tid′i·ous, adj.	o′ver·in·flate′, v.t., -flat·ed, -flat·ing.
o′ver·e·mo′tion·al, adj.	o′ver·fa·tigue′, v.t., -tigued, -ti·guing.	o′ver·in·flu·en′tial, adj.
o′ver·em′pha·sis, n.	o′ver·feed′, v., -fed, -feed·ing.	o′ver·in·sist′ence, n.
o′ver·em′pha·size′, v.t., -sized, -siz·ing.	o′ver·fill′, v.	o′ver·in·sist′ent, adj.; -ly, adv.
o′ver·em·phat′ic, adj.	o′ver·fond′, adj.	o′ver·in·sure′, v.t., -sured, -sur·ing.
o′ver·en·thu′si·as′tic, adj.	o′ver·full′, adj.	
	o′ver·fur′nish, v.t.	o′ver·in·tel·lec′tu·al, adj.: -ly, adv.
o′ver·es′ti·mate′, v.t., v.i., n.	o′ver·gen′er·al·ize′, v.t., -ized, -iz·ing.	o′ver·in·tense′, adj.; -ly, adv.
o′ver·ex·cit′a·ble, adj.; -cit′a·bly, adv.	o′ver·gen′er·ous, adj.	o′ver·in′ter·est, n.
o′ver·ex·cite′, v.t., -cit·ed, -cit·ing.	o′ver·graze′, v.t.	o′ver·in·vest′, v.
o′ver·ex′er·cise′, v.t., -cised, -cis·ing; n.	o′ver·hast′i·ly, adv.	o′ver·is′sue, n.
	o′ver·hast′i·ness, n.	
	o′ver·hast′y, adj.	

o·ver·lap (ō'vər lap'), *v.t.*, *v.i.*, **-lapped, -lap·ping. 1.** to extend over and cover a part (of). **2.** to coincide in part (with).

o·ver·lay (ō'vər lā'), *v.t.*, **-laid, -lay·ing. 1.** to lay or place (one thing) over or upon another. **2.** to finish with a layer or applied decoration of something.

o·ver·leap (ō'vər lēp'), *v.t.* **-leaped** or **-leapt, -leap·ing. 1.** to leap over or across. **2.** to overreach (oneself) by leaping too far.

o·ver·lie (ō'vər lī'), *v.t.*, **-lay, -lain, -ly·ing.** to lie over or upon, as a covering, stratum, etc.

o·ver·look (*v.* ō'vər lŏŏk'; *n.* ō'vər-lŏŏk'), *v.t.* **1.** to fail to notice or consider. **2.** to disregard or ignore indulgently, as faults. **3.** to look over, as from a higher position. **4.** to afford a view down over. **5.** *Brit.* to watch or watch over. **6.** *Rare.* to look over in inspection or perusal. —*n.* **7.** terrain, as on a cliff, that affords a view.

o·ver·lord (ō'vər lôrd'), *n.* a person who is lord over another or over other lords.

o·ver·ly (ō'vər lē), *adv.* too or too much.

o·ver·mas·ter (ō'vər mas'tər, -mä'-stər). *v.t.* to gain mastery over.

o·ver·match (ō'vər mach'), *v.t.* **1.** to be more than a match for. **2.** to match against a superior opponent.

o·ver·much (ō'vər much'), *adj.*, *n.*, *adv.* too much.

o·ver·night (ō'vər nīt'; *adj.* ō'vər-nīt'), *adv.* **1.** for or during the night. **2.** very quickly. —*adj.* **3.** done or continuing during the night. **4.** staying for one night **5.** designed to be used on a short trip: *an overnight bag.*

o·ver·pass (ō'vər pas', -päs'), *n.* a highway or railway bridge crossing some barrier. as another highway or railroad tracks.

o·ver·play (ō'vər plā'), *v.t.* **1.** to exaggerate (one's performance in a play, etc.). **2.** to count too heavily on the strength of.

o·ver·pow·er (ō'vər pou'ər), *v.t.* **1.** to subdue by superior force. **2.** to affect or impress excessively.

o·ver·qual·i·fied (ō'vər kwol'ə fīd'), *adj.* with more education or experience than is required in a job or position.

o·ver·reach (ō'vər rēch'), *v.t.* **1.** to reach or extend over or beyond. **2.** to aim at but go beyond. **3.** to defeat (oneself) by overdoing matters. —**o'ver·reach'er,** *n.*

o·ver·ride (ō'vər rīd'), *v.t.*, **-rode, -ridden, -rid·ing. 1.** to set aside or disregard summarily. **2.** to prevail over or supersede. **3. a.** to ride over or across. **b.** to trample or crush.

o·ver·rid·ing (ō'vər rī'ding), *adj.* taking precedence over all other considerations.

o·ver·rule (ō'vər rōōl'), *v.t.*, **-ruled, -rul·ing. 1.** to rule or decide against by superior authority. **2.** override (def. 2).

o·ver·run (ō'vər run'), *v.t.*, **-ran, -run, -run·ning. 1.** to rove over or ravage (a country, etc.), as invaders. **2.** to swarm over in great numbers, as vermin. **3.** to spread or grow rapidly over, as vines. **4.** to run beyond, as a certain limit. **5.** to exceed, as a budget or estimate. **6.** to overflow: *A river overruns its banks.*

o·ver·seas (*adv.* ō'vər sēz'; *adj.* ō'vər-sēz'), *adv.* **1.** across or beyond the sea. —*adj.* **2.** across or over the sea. **3.** of, to, or from countries beyond the sea. Also, *esp. Brit.,* **o·ver·sea** (*adv.* ō'vər sē'; *adj.* ō'vər sē').

o·ver·see (ō'vər sē'), *v.t.*, **-saw, -seen, -see·ing. 1.** to direct (work or workers) as a supervisor. **2.** *Archaic.* to look over or inspect. —**o'ver·se'er,** *n.*

o·ver·sexed (ō'vər sekst'), *adj.* having or showing excessive interest in or need for sexual activity.

o·ver·shad·ow (ō'vər shad'ō), *v.t.* **1.** to render insignificant in comparison. **2.** to cast a shadow over.

o·ver·shoe (ō'vər shōō'), *n.* a shoe worn over another and intended for protection against wet or cold weather.

o'ver·large', *adj.*	**o'ver·pes·si·mis'tic**, *adj.*
o'ver·lav'ish. *adj.*	**o'ver·pop'u·late'**, *v.t.*
o'ver·load', *v.t.*, *n.*	**o'ver·pow'er·ful**, *adj.*
o'ver·long'. *adj.*, *adv.*	**o'ver·praise'**, *v.t.*,
o'ver·mag·ni·fi·ca'tion, *n.*	**-praised. -prais·ing.**
o'ver·mag·ni·fy', *v.t.*,	**o'ver·pre·cise'**, *adj.*
-fied, -fy·ing.	**o'ver·price'**, *v.t.*,
o'ver·mod'est, *adj.*;	**-priced. -pric·ing.**
-ly. *adv.*	**o'ver·print'**, *v.t.*
o'ver·mod'i·fy', *v.*,	**o'ver·pro·duce'**, *v.t.*, *v.i.*
-fied. -fy·ing.	**o'ver·prom'i·nent.** *adj.*
o'ver·nice'. *adj.*	**o'ver·prompt'.** *adj.*,
o'ver·op'ti·mism'. *n.*	**-ly.** *adv.*
o'ver·par·tic'u·lar, *adj.*	**o'ver·pro·por'tion**, *n.*
o'ver·pay', *v.t.*	**o'ver·pro·tect'**, *v.t.*
o'ver·proud', *adj.*	
o'ver·rate', *v.t.*	
o'ver·re·act', *v.i.*	
o'ver·re·fine', *v.t.*	
o'ver·right'eous, *adj.*;	
-ly. *adv.* · **-ness**, *n.*	
o'ver·rig'id. *adj.*	
o'ver·ripe'. *adj.*	
o'ver·roast', *v.t.*	
o'ver·salt'. *v.t.*	
o'ver·scru'pu·lous, *adj.*	
o'ver·sell'. *v.t.*, *v.i.*	
o'ver·sen'si·tive. *adj.*	
o'ver·se·vere'. *adj.*	
o'ver·sharp'. *adj.*	

o·ver·shoot (ō'vər shōot'), *v.t.*, **-shot, -shoot·ing. 1.** to shoot or go over, beyond, or above. **2.** to shoot or project (something) over or above a mark.

o·ver·sight (ō'vər sīt'), *n.* **1.** an error due to carelessness. **2.** watchful care or charge: *oversight of Congressional ethics.* **—Syn. 1.** mistake, slip.

o·ver·size (ō'vər sīz'), *adj.* **1.** of excessive size. **2.** of a size larger than is required. Also, **o'ver·sized'.**

o·ver·sleep (ō'vər slēp'), *v.i.*, **-slept, -sleep·ing.** to sleep beyond the proper time of waking.

o·ver·spread (ō'vər spred'), *v.t.*, **-spread, -spread·ing.** to spread or diffuse over.

o·ver·state (ō'vər stāt'), *v.t.*, **-stat·ed, -stat·ing.** to state too strongly. **—o'ver·state'ment,** *n.* **—Syn.** exaggerate.

o·ver·stay (ō'vər stā'), *v.t.* to stay beyond the time or duration of.

o·ver·step (ō'vər step'), *v.t.*, **-stepped, -step·ping.** to step or pass over or beyond.

o·ver·stuffed (ō'ver stuft'), *adj.* **1.** stuffed or filled to excess. **2.** covered by thick upholstery.

o·ver·sub·scribe (ō'vər səb skrīb'), *v.t.*, **-scribed, -scrib·ing.** to subscribe for in excess of what is available or required. **—o·ver·sub·scrip·tion** (ō'vər·səb skrip'shən), *n.*

o·vert (ō'vûrt, ō vûrt'), *adj.* openly and easily observable. **—o·vert'ly,** *adv.*

o·ver·take (ō'vər tāk'), *v.t.*, **-took, -tak·en, -tak·ing. 1.** to catch up with or pass. **2.** to happen to suddenly or unexpectedly.

o·ver-the-coun·ter (ō'vər thə koun'tər), *adj.* **1.** traded other than on a stock exchange. **2.** sold legally without a prescription.

o·ver·throw (*v.* ō'vər thrō'; *n.* ō'vər·thrō'), *v.*, **-threw, -thrown, -throw·ing,** *n.* **—v.t. 1.** to bring down from power by force. **2.** to throw (something) too far. **3.** overturn (def. 1). **—n. 4.** forcible removal from power. **5.** the act of overthrowing or state or condition of being overthrown. **—o'ver·throw'er,** *n.*

o·ver·time (ō'vər tīm'), *n.* **1.** time worked before or after regularly scheduled working hours. **2.** pay for such time. **—adv. 3.** during overtime. **—adj. 4.** of or for overtime.

o·ver·tone (ō'vər tōn'), *n.* **1.** one of the higher tones in a musical sound that give it fullness and a special quality. **2.** an additional, usually implicit, meaning or quality.

o·ver·top (ō'vər top'), *v.t.*, **-topped, -top·ping. 1.** to rise over or above the top of. **2.** to surpass or excel.

o·ver·ture (ō'vər chər, -chŏŏr'), *n.* **1.** an orchestral prelude to an opera, oratorio, etc. **2.** an opening move toward negotiations, etc.

o·ver·turn (ō'vər tûrn'), *v.t.* **1.** to turn over on its side, face, or back. **2.** overthrow (def. 1). **3.** *Informal.* overrule (def. 1). **—v.i. 4.** to turn on its side, face, or back.

o·ver·view (ō'vər vyōō'), *n.* an overall impression or picture.

o·ver·ween·ing (ō'vər wē'ning), *adj.* **1.** presumptuously conceited or proud. **2.** immoderate or excessive.

o·ver·weigh (ō'vər wā'), *v.t.* **1.** to exceed in weight. **2.** to weigh down excessively.

o·ver·whelm (ō'vər hwelm', -welm'), *v.t.* **1.** to overcome completely in mind or feeling. **2.** to defeat completely with sheer weight of numbers. **3.** to cover or bury beneath a mass of something. **4.** *Archaic.* to overthrow or overturn. **—o'ver·whelm'ing,** *adj.* **—o'ver·whelm'ing·ly,** *adv.*

o·ver·wrought (ō'vər rôt', ō'vər-), *adj.* **1.** excited excessively. **2.** elaborated to excess.

Ov·id (ov'id), *n.* 43 B.C.–A.D. 17?, Roman poet.

o·vi·duct (ō'vi dukt'), *n.* either of a pair of tubes that carry the ova from the ovary to the exterior.

o·vip·a·rous (ō vip'ər əs), *adj.* producing eggs that hatch after being expelled from the body. **—o·vi·par·i·ty** (ō'vi par'i tē), *n.* **—o·vip'a·rous·ly,** *adv.*

o·void (ō'void), *adj.* **1.** having the solid form of an egg. **—n. 2.** an ovoid body.

---

o'ver·sim'ple, *adj.*	**o'ver·stock',** *v.t., n.*	**o'ver·train',** *v.t., v.i.*
o'ver·sim'pli·fy', *v.t.*	**o'ver·stretch',** *v.t.*	**o'ver·use',** *v.t., n.*
o'ver·skep'ti·cal, *adj.*	**o'ver·strict',** *adj.*	**o'ver·val'ue,** *v.t.,*
o'ver·so·lic'i·tous, *adj.*	**o'ver·sub'tle,** *adj.*	**-ued, -u·ing.**
o'ver·so·phis'ti·cat·ed, *adj.*	**o'ver·sub'tle·ty,** *n.,*	**o'ver·vi'o·lent,** *adj.*
o'ver·spar'ing, *adj.*	*pl.* **-ties.**	**o'ver·weal'thy,** *n.*
o'ver·spe'cial·i·za'tion, *n.*	**o'ver·sup·ply',** *n., v.t.*	**o'ver·weight',** *n., adj.*
o'ver·spe'cial·ize', *v.,*	**o'ver·sus·pi'cious,** *adj.*	**o'ver·will'ing,** *adj.;*
-ized, -iz·ing.	**o'ver·sys'tem·at'ic,** *adj.*	**-ly,** *adv.*
o'ver·spend', *v.i.*	**o'ver·tax',** *v.t.*	**o'ver·wise',** *adj.*
o'ver·stim'u·late', *v.,*	**o'ver·tech'ni·cal,** *adj.*	**o'ver·work',** *v.t., n.*
-lat·ed, -lat·ing.	**o'ver·tire',** *v.t.,*	**o'ver·zeal'ous,** *adj.*
	-tired, -tir·ing.	

o·vu·late (ō′vyə lāt′, ov′yə-), *v.i.*, **-lat-ed, -lat·ing.** to shed eggs from an ovary. —**o′vu·la′tion**, *n.*

o·vule (ō′vyōōl), *n.* the body that contains the female germ cell which after fertilization develops into a seed. **2.** *Biol.* a small egg. —**o′vu-lar**, *adj.*

o·vum (ō′vəm), *n., pl.* **o·va** (ō′və). a female reproductive cell.

ow (ou), *interj.* (an expression of pain.)

owe (ō), *v.t.*, **owed, ow·ing. 1.** to be under obligation for the payment or repayment of. **2.** to be in debt to. **3.** to cherish (a certain feeling) toward a person. **4.** to be indebted (to) as the cause or source of.

ow·ing (ō′ing), *adj.* **1.** due for payment. **2. owing to,** because of.

owl (oul), *n.* **1.** a chiefly nocturnal bird of prey having a broad head with large eyes that face forward. **2.** a person of owllike solemnity. **3.** See **night owl.** —**owl′ish,** *adj.* — **owl′ish·ly,** *adv.*

owl·et (ou′lit), *n.* a young owl.

own (ōn), *adj.* **1.** of or belonging to oneself or itself: *He spent only his own money.* —*n.* **2.** something that belongs to one: *This car is my own.* **3. on one's own,** *Informal.* through one's own efforts. —*v.t.* **4.** to have as one's own. **5.** to acknowledge or admit. —*v.i.* **6.** to confess: *I own to being uncertain about that.* —**own′-er,** *n.* —**own′er·ship,** *n.*

ox (oks), *n., pl.* **ox·en. 1.** an adult castrated bull. **2.** any member of the bovine family.

ox·al′ic ac′id (ok sal′ik), a poisonous acid used chiefly for bleaching and as a cleanser.

ox·blood (oks′blud′), *n.* a deep, dull red color.

ox·bow (oks′bō′), *n.* **1.** a U-shaped piece of wood placed under and around the neck of an ox. **2.** a bow-shaped bend in a river.

ox·ford (oks′fərd), *n.* a low shoe laced over the instep.

Ox·ford (oks′fərd), *n.* a city in S England, NW of London: university. —**Ox·o·ni·an** (ok sō′nē ən), *adj., n.*

ox·i·dant (ok′si dənt), *n.* a chemical agent that oxidizes.

ox·i·da·tion (ok′sə dā′shən), *n.* the act or process of oxidizing, or state of being oxidized. —**ox′i·da′tive** (-dā′tiv), *adj.* —**ox′i·da′tive·ly,** *adv.*

ox·ide (ok′sīd, -sid), *n.* a compound containing oxygen and one other element. —**ox·id·ic** (ok sid′ik), *adj.*

ox·i·dize (ok′si dīz′), *v.,* **-dized, -diz-ing.** —*v.t.* **1.** to combine with oxygen. —*v.i.* **2.** to become oxidized. —**ox′i·diz′a·ble,** *adj.* —**ox′i·di·za′-tion,** *n.* —**ox′i·diz′er,** *n.*

ox·y·a·cet·y·lene (ok′sē ə set′ºlēn′, -ºlin), *adj.* noting a mixture of oxygen and acetylene used in cutting steel and welding metals.

ox·y·gen (ok′si jən), *n. Chem.* a colorless, odorless, gaseous element that constitutes about one fifth of the air and is the supporter of life and combustion in air. *Symbol:* O; *at. wt.:* 15.9994; *at. no.:* 8. —**ox′y·gen′ic** (-jen′ik), **ox·yg·e·nous** (ok·sij′ə nəs), *adj.*

ox·y·gen·ate (ok′si jə nāt′), *v.t.,* **-at·ed, -at·ing.** to treat, combine, or enrich with oxygen. —**ox′y·gen·a′tion,** *n.*

ox′ygen tent′, a canopy for placing over a sick person for maintaining a flow of oxygen at critical periods.

oys·ter (oi′stər), *n.* an edible, marine mollusk having an irregularly shaped shell. —**oys′ter·ing,** *n.* —**oys′ter-man,** *n.* —**oys′ter·wom′an,** *n.fem.*

oys′ter crack′er, a small, round, usually salted cracker.

oz., ounce; ounces. Also, **oz**

oz. ap., ounce apothecary's.

oz. av., ounce avoirdupois.

o·zone (ō′zōn, ō zōn′), *n.* **1.** a form of oxygen with a peculiar odor suggesting that of weak chlorine, produced when an electric spark is passed through air or oxygen: used for bleaching, sterilizing water, etc. **2.** *Informal.* clear, fresh air. —**o·zon-ic** (ō zon′ik, ō zō′nik), *adj.*

P

P, p (pē), *n., pl.* **P's** or **Ps, p's** or **ps. 1.** the sixteenth letter of the English alphabet, a consonant. **2. mind one's p's and q's,** to be careful of one's behavior.

P, phosphorus.

p, proton.

P., President.

p., **1.** page. **2.** participle. **3.** past. **4.** *Chess.* pawn. **5.** penny; pence. **6.** per. **7.** pint. **8.** *Baseball.* pitcher. **9.** population. **10.** president. **11.** pressure. **12.** purl.

pa (pä), *n. Informal.* father (def. 1).

PA, 1. Pennsylvania. **2.** public address (system).

Pa, protactinium.

Pa., Pennsylvania.

P.A., 1. power of attorney. **2.** press agent. **3.** purchasing agent.

p.a., See per annum.

pab·u·lum (pab′yə ləm), *n. Literary.* something that gives nourishment.

Pac., Pacific.

pace¹ (pās), *n., v.,* **paced, pac·ing.** —*n.* **1.** a rate of movement, esp. in stepping or walking. **2.** a rate of activity, progress, etc. **3.** a single step. **4.** the distance covered in a step. **5.** a manner of stepping. **6.** a gait of a horse in which the feet on the same side are lifted and put down together. **7. put one through one's paces,** to test one's ability or skill. —*v.t.* **8.** to set or regulate the pace for, as in racing. **9.** to walk up and down or go over with steps. **10.** to measure by paces. **11.** to train to a certain pace. —*v.i.* **12.** to take slow, regular steps. **13.** (of a horse) to travel at a pace. —**pac′er,** *n.*

pa·ce² (pā′sē), *prep. Latin.* with the permission of.

pace·mak·er (pās′mā′kər), *n.* **1.** a person or thing that sets the pace, as in racing. **2.** a person or group that serves as a model to be imitated or followed. **3.** an electronic device implanted beneath the skin to regulate the heartbeat. **4.** a body structure of the heart which functions to maintain the natural beat. —**pace′-mak′ing,** *n.*

pace·set·ter (pās′set′ər), *n.* pacemaker (defs. 1, 2). —**pace′set′ting,** *adj.*

pach·y·derm (pak′i dûrm′), *n.* any of the thick-skinned, nonruminant mammals, esp. the elephant.

pach·y·san·dra (pak′i san′drə), *n.* an evergreen plant often used as a ground cover in the U.S.

pa·cif·ic (pə sif′ik), *adj.* **1.** tending to make peace. **2.** calm or tranquil. —*n.* **3.** (*cap.*) See **Pacific Ocean.** — **pa·cif′i·cal·ly,** *adv.*

Pacif′ic O′cean, an ocean bordered by the American continents, Asia, and Australia.

pac·i·fi·er (pas′ə fī′ər), *n.* **1.** a person or thing that pacifies. **2.** any rubber or plastic device, often shaped into a nipple, for a baby to suck on.

pac·i·fism (pas′ə fiz′əm), *n.* opposition to war or violence as a method of settling disputes. —**pac′i·fist,** *n., adj.*

pac·i·fy (pas′ə fī′), *v.t.,* **-fied, -fy·ing. 1.** to bring or restore to a state of peace. **2.** to calm the anger or agitation of. **3.** to reduce to a submissive state. —**pac′i·fi·ca′tion,** *n.*

pack¹ (pak), *n.* **1.** a group of things wrapped or tied up for easy handling, esp. for carrying on the back. **2.** a definite quantity of merchandise together with its wrapping: *a pack of cigarettes.* **3.** a group of people or things: *a pack of fools.* **4.** a group of certain animals of the same kind: *a pack of wolves.* **5.** deck (def. 3). **6.** an absorbent cloth soaked and put on the skin or body for therapeutic purposes. —*v.t.* **7.** to make into a pack. **8.** to fill compactly with anything: *to pack a trunk.* **9.** to put in a case or box, as for storage. **10.** to press or crowd together within: *The crowd packed the gallery.* **11.** to make airtight or watertight by stuffing. **12.** to load, as with packs or luggage. **13.** to carry or wear, esp. as part of one's usual equipment: *to pack a gun.* **14.** to send off summarily: *We packed them off to my mother.* **15.** *Slang.* to be able to deliver (a blow, etc.). —*v.i.* **16.** to pack goods in compact form, as for shipping. **17.** to move crowded together, as persons. **18.** to become compacted: *Wet snow packs readily.* —*adj.* **19.** used in carrying loads: *pack animals.*

pack² (pak), *v.t.* to manipulate so as to serve one's own purposes: *to pack a jury.*

pack·age (pak′ij), *n., v.,* **-aged, -aging.** —*n.* **1.** a usually small bundle of something packed and wrapped or boxed. **2.** Also called **pack′age deal′.** a series of related parts or elements to be accepted or rejected as a single unit. —*v.t.* **3.** to make or put into a package.

pack′age store′, a store selling sealed bottles of alcoholic beverages for consumption off the premises.

pack·er (pak′ər), *n.* **1.** a person or thing that packs. **2.** a company engaged in food packing.

pack·et (pak′it), *n.* **1.** a small pack or package. **2.** a coastal or river boat that carries cargo and passengers regularly on a fixed route.

pack·horse (pak′hôrs′), *n.* a horse used for carrying goods or supplies.

pack·ing (pak′ing), *n.* **1.** the act or work of an operator of a packing house. **2.** material used to cushion or protect goods packed in a container.

pack′ing house′, an establishment for processing and packing foods, esp. meat, to be sold at wholesale.

pack′ rat′, 1. a large, bushy-tailed rodent of North America which stores away small articles. **2.** *Informal.* a person who collects or saves useless small items.

pack·sad·dle (pak′sad′əl), *n.* a saddle designed for supporting the load on a pack animal.

pack·thread (pak′thred′), *n.* a strong twine for sewing or tying.

pact (pakt), *n.* an agreement of usually limited scope between nations or persons.

pad¹ (pad), *n., v.,* **pad·ded, pad·ding.** —*n.* **1.** a cushionlike mass of soft material used for comfort, protection, or stuffing. **2.** a number of sheets of paper held together at one edge to form a tablet. **3.** the cushionlike protuberance on the underside of the foot of some animals. **4.** the large floating leaf of the water lily. **5.** *Slang.* **a.** one's living quarters. **b.** one's own bed. **6.** See **launch pad.** —*v.t.* **7.** to furnish or stuff with a pad or padding. **8.** to expand with unnecessary or fraudulent material.

pad² (pad), *n., v.,* **pad·ded, pad·ding.** —*n.* **1.** a dull sound, as of footsteps on the ground. —*v.i.* **2.** to walk with a soft, dull sound.

pad·ding (pad′ing), *n.* **1.** material used to pad something. **2.** unnecessary or fraudulent material used to expand something.

pad·dle¹ (pad′əl), *n., v.,* **-dled, -dling.** —*n.* **1.** a short, flat oar for propelling and steering a canoe. **2.** any of various similar implements used for mixing, stirring, or beating. **3.** a blade of a paddle wheel. —*v.i., v.t.* **4.** to propel (a canoe) with a paddle. **5.** to stir or beat with or as with a paddle. —**pad′dler,** *n.*

pad·dle² (pad′əl), *v.i.,* **-dled, -dling.** to move the feet or hands playfully in shallow water. —**pad′dler,** *n.*

pad′dle wheel′, a large steam-driven wheel having projecting paddles, formerly used to propel a ship. —**pad′dle-wheel′,** *adj.*

pad·dock (pad′ək), *n.* **1.** a small, usually enclosed field near a stable for pasturing or exercising animals. **2.** the enclosure in which the horses are saddled and paraded before each race.

pad·dy (pad′ē), *n., pl.* **-dies.** a rice field.

pad′dy wag′on, *Slang.* See **patrol wagon.**

pad·lock (pad′lok′), *n.* **1.** a lock with a sliding shackle that can be passed through a staple or ring. —*v.t.* **2.** to fasten with or as if with a padlock.

pa·dre (pä′drā), *n.* **1.** father (used esp. in addressing or referring to a priest in Spain, Italy, etc.). **2.** *Informal.* a military chaplain. [< Sp, Pg, It: father < L *pater*]

pae·an (pē′ən), *n.* any song of praise, joy, or triumph.

pa·gan (pā′gən), *n.* **1.** a person who is not a Christian, Jew, or Muslim. **2.** an irreligious person. —*adj.* **3.** of pagans or their religion. —**pa′gan·ism,** *n.*

page¹ (pāj), *n., v.,* **paged, pag·ing.** —*n.* **1.** one side of a leaf of something printed or written, as a book. **2.** the entire leaf. **3.** a noteworthy event or period. —*v.t.* **4.** to number or mark the pages of.

page² (pāj), *n., v.,* **paged, pag·ing.** —*n.* **1.** a boy servant in a royal household. **2.** a young person employed to carry messages, run errands, etc. —*v.t.* **3.** to summon (a person) by calling out his or her name repeatedly.

pag·eant (paj′ənt), *n.* **1.** an elaborate public spectacle illustrative of a historical scene. **2.** a costumed procession or parade forming part of public or social festivities. —**pag′eant·ry** (-ən trē), *n.*

page′boy′ (pāj′boi′), *n.* a woman's hairstyle in which the hair is rolled under at shoulder length.

pag·i·na·tion (paj′ə nā′shən), *n.* **1.** the figures by which pages are numbered. **2.** the sequence or number of such figures. —**pag′i·nate′,** *v.t.*

pa·go·da (pə gō′də), *n.* a towerlike, many-storied temple or sacred building in India or China.

paid (pād), *v.* a pt. and pp. of **pay.**

pail (pāl), *n.* a cylindrical container with a handle, used for holding liquids or solids. —**pail′ful′** (-fool′), *n.*

pain (pān), *n.* **1.** bodily suffering or distress, as due to injury or illness. **2.** a distressing sensation in a particular part of the body. **3.** mental or emotional suffering or torment. **4.** pains, laborious or careful efforts. **5.** on or under pain of, liable to the penalty of: *on pain of death.* —*v.t.* **6.** to cause pain to. —**pain′ful,** *adj.* —**pain′ful·ly,** *adv.* —**pain′less,** *adj.* —**pain′less·ly,** *adv.* —**pain′less·ness,** *n.*

Paine (pān), *n.* **Thomas,** 1737–1809, U.S. patriot and writer.

pain·kil·ler (pān′kil′ər), *n. Informal.* something that relieves pain, esp. an analgesic. —**pain′kill′ing,** *adj.*

pains·tak·ing (pān′stā′king, pānz′tā′-), *adj.* making careful and diligent effort. —**pains′tak′ing·ly,** *adv.*

paint (pānt), *n.* **1.** a substance composed of solid coloring matter mixed in a liquid, for application to various surfaces as a protective or decorative coating. **2.** an application of this. **3.** the dried surface pigment. **4.** facial cosmetics designed to heighten natural color. —*v.t.* **5.** to coat, cover, or decorate with or as with paint. **6.** to produce (a picture, etc.) in paint. **7.** to represent in paint. **8.** to describe vividly in words. —*v.i.* **9.** to engage in painting as an art. —**paint′er,** *n.*

paint·brush (pānt′brush′), *n.* any brush for applying paint.

paint·ing (pān'tǐng), *n.* **1.** a picture executed in paints. **2.** the art or work of a person who paints.

pair (pâr), *n., pl.* **pairs, pair,** *v.* —*n.* **1.** two corresponding things that are matched for use together: *a pair of gloves.* **2.** something having two corresponding pieces joined together: *a pair of slacks.* **3.** two people or animals who are in some way associated: *a pair of liars; a pair of horses.* —*v.t., v.i.* **4.** to form (into) a pair. **5.** to mate or cause to mate.

pais·ley (pāz'lē), *adj.* (*often cap.*) having a pattern of colorful and minutely detailed figures.

pa·jam·as (pə jä'məz, -jam'əz), *n.pl.* night clothes consisting of loose-fitting trousers and jacket. —**pa·ja'-maed,** *adj.*

Pa·ki·stan (pak'ī stan', pä'ki stän'), *n.* a country in S Asia, W of India. —**Pa'ki·sta'ni** (pä'ki stä'nē), *n., adj.*

pal (pal), *n. Informal.* an intimate friend.

pal·ace (pal'is), *n.* **1.** the official residence of a sovereign or bishop. **2.** any large and stately building.

pal'ace guard', a group of trusted advisers who seem to control access to a sovereign or president.

pal·a·din (pal'ə din), *n.* **1.** any of the 12 knightly champions in attendance on Charlemagne. **2.** any noble champion.

pal·an·quin (pal'ən kēn'), *n.* a covered or boxlike litter for one person carried by several men, formerly used in India and other Eastern countries.

pal·at·a·ble (pal'ə tə bəl), *adj.* **1.** agreeable to the palate or taste. **2.** acceptable to the mind or feelings. —**pal'-at·a·bil'i·ty,** *n.* —**pal'at·a·bly,** *adv.*

pal·ate (pal'it), *n.* **1.** the roof of the mouth. **2.** the sense of taste. —**pal'-a·tal** (-ə təl), *adj.*

pa·la·tial (pə lā'shəl), *adj.* **1.** of or resembling a palace. **2.** stately and magnificent.

pa·lat·i·nate (pə lat'ᵊnāt', -ᵊnit), *n.* the territory under a palatine.

pal·a·tine (pal'ə tīn', -tin), *adj.* **1.** having royal privileges. **2.** of a palatine or palatinate. —*n.* **3.** a vassal exercising royal privileges in a province. **4.** an important officer of an imperial palace.

pa·lav·er (pə lav'ər, -lä'vər), *n.* **1.** profuse and idle talk. —*v.i.* **2.** to talk profusely and idly. [< Pg *palavra* word, talk]

pale¹ (pāl), *adj.,* **pal·er, pal·est,** *v.,* **paled, pal·ing.** —*adj.* **1.** lacking intensity of color. **2.** approaching white or gray: *pale yellow.* **3.** not bright or brilliant: *the pale moon.* —*v.t., v.i.* **4.** to make or become pale. —**pale'ness,** *n.* —**Syn. 1.** pallid, wan.

pale² (pāl), *n.* **1.** a stake or picket in a fence. **2.** limits or bounds.

pale·face (pāl'fās'), *n.* a white person: a term attributed to American Indians.

Pa·le·o·cene (pā'lē ə sēn', pal'ē-), *adj.* **1.** noting an epoch of the Tertiary period, occurring from 60,000,000 to 70,000,000 years ago, characterized by the advent of birds and the placental mammals. —*n.* **2.** the Paleocene epoch.

Pa·le·o·gene (pā'lē ə jēn', pal'ē-), *adj.* **1.** noting the earlier part of the Cenozoic era, occurring from 25,-000,000 to 70,000,000 years ago. —*n.* **2.** the Paleogene period.

pa·le·og·ra·phy (pā'lē og'rə fē, pal'ē-), *n.* the study of ancient forms of writing. —**pa'le·og'ra·pher,** *n.* —**pa'le·o·graph'ic** (-ə graf'ik), **pa'le·o·graph'i·cal,** *adj.*

paleon., paleontology.

pa·le·on·tol·o·gy (pā'lē ən tol'ə jē, pal'ē-), *n.* the science of the forms of life existing in former geologic periods. —**pa'le·on·tol'o·gist,** *n.*

Pa·le·o·zo·ic (pā'lē ə zō'ik, pal'ē-), *adj.* **1.** noting an era occurring between 220,000,000 and 600,000,000 years ago, characterized by the appearance of fish, insects, and reptiles. —*n.* **2.** the Paleozoic era.

Pal·es·tine (pal'i stīn'), *n.* the territory on the E coast of the Mediterranean occupied by the Hebrews in Biblical times. —**Pal'es·tin'i·an** (-stin'ē ən), *adj., n.*

pal·ette (pal'it), *n.* **1.** a thin board with a thumb hole at one end, used by painters for holding and mixing colors. **2.** the set of colors on such a board.

pal·frey (pôl'frē), *n., pl.* **-freys.** *Archaic.* a saddle horse, esp. a gentle one suitable for a woman.

pal·imp·sest (pal'imp sest'), *n.* a parchment from which writing has been partially or completely erased to make room for another text.

pal·in·drome (pal'in drōm'), *n.* a word, sentence, or verse reading the same backward as forward, as *Madam, I'm Adam.*

pal·ing (pā'ling), *n.* **1.** a fence of pales. **2.** pales collectively. **3.** **pale²** (def. 1).

pal·i·node (pal'ə nōd'), *n.* a poem in which the poet retracts something said in an earlier poem.

pal·i·sade (pal'i sād'), *n.* **1.** a fence of pales or stakes, esp. for defense. **2.** **palisades,** a line of cliffs.

pall¹ (pôl), *n.* **1.** a cloth of velvet for spreading over a coffin. **2.** something that covers, esp. with darkness or gloom.

pall² (pôl), v.i. **1.** to have a wearying effect. **2.** to become satiated or cloyed.

pal·la·di·um (pə lā'dē əm), n. *Chem.* a silver-white, ductile metallic element, used chiefly as a catalyst and in alloys. Symbol: Pd; at. wt.: 106.4; at. no.: 46.

pall·bear·er (pôl'bâr'ər), n. one of several persons who carry or attend the coffin at a funeral.

pal·let¹ (pal'it), n. **1.** a bed or mattress of straw. **2.** a small or makeshift bed.

pal·let² (pal'it), n. a platform on which materials are placed for handling or transportation.

pal·li·ate (pal'ē āt'), v.t., -at·ed, -at·ing. **1.** to conceal the gravity of (an offense) by excuses, apologies, etc. **2.** to relieve without curing, as a disease. —**pal'li·a'tion,** n. —**pal'li·a'tive,** adj., n.

pal·lid (pal'id), adj. faint or deficient in color.

pal·lor (pal'ər), n. unnatural paleness, as from fear.

palm¹ (päm), n. **1.** the inner surface of the hand between the wrist and the fingers. —v.t. **2.** to conceal in the palm, as a playing card used in cheating. **3. palm off,** to dispose of by fraud.

palm² (päm), n. **1.** any of numerous tropical plants, most of which are tall, unbranched trees having a crown of large, feathery leaves at the top. **2.** a leaf of this tree, esp. as formerly borne to signify victory. **3. carry off** or **bear the palm,** to be the victor.

pal·mate (pal'māt, -mit, päl'-, pä'māt), adj. shaped like a hand with the fingers extended, as a leaf. Also, **pal'mat·ed.**

palm·er (pä'mər, päl'mər), n. a pilgrim, esp. of the Middle Ages, who had returned from the Holy Land, in token of which he or she bore a palm branch.

pal·met·to (pal met'ō), n., pl. -tos, -toes. any of various palms having fan-shaped leaves.

palm·is·try (pä'mi strē), n. the practice of reading fortunes and character from the lines and configurations of the palm of the subject's hand. —**palm'ist,** n.

Palm' Sun'day, the Sunday before Easter, celebrating Christ's triumphal entry into Jerusalem.

palm·y (pä'mē), adj., palm·i·er, palm·i·est. **1.** abounding in or shaded with palms. **2.** glorious or prosperous.

pal·o·mi·no (pal'ə mē'nō), n., pl. -nos. a horse having a golden color and a flaxen mane and tail.

pal·pa·ble (pal'pə bəl), adj. **1.** capable of being felt by touch, esp. medi-cally. **2.** readily or plainly perceived. **3.** obvious or evident. —**pal'pa·bil'i·ty,** n. —**pal'pa·bly,** adv.

pal·pate (pal'pāt), v.t., -pat·ed, -pat·ing. *Med* to examine by touch. —**pal·pa'tion,** n.

pal·pi·tate (pal'pi tāt'), v.i., -tat·ed, -tat·ing. **1.** to pulsate with unnatural rapidity, as the heart. **2.** to quiver or throb. —**pal'pi·ta'tion,** n.

pal·sy (pôl'zē), n., pl. -sies. any of various forms of paralysis, as cerebral palsy. —**pal'sied,** adj.

pal·ter (pôl'tər), v.i. **1.** to talk or act insincerely. **2.** to bargain or haggle.

pal·try (pôl'trē), adj., -tri·er, -tri·est. **1.** despicably small: a paltry amount. **2.** utterly worthless. **3.** mean or contemptible. —**pal'tri·ly,** adv. —**pal'tri·ness,** n. —Syn. petty, trifling.

pam., pamphlet.

pam·pas (pam'pəz), n.pl., sing. -pa (-pə). the vast grassy plains of Argentina.

pam·per (pam'pər), v.t. to gratify the wishes of, esp. by catering to physical comforts. —**pam'per·er,** n. —Syn. coddle, indulge, spoil.

pam·phlet (pam'flit), n. **1.** an unbound printed booklet. **2.** (esp. formerly) such a booklet on some subject of current interest. —**pam'phlet·eer'** (-fli tēr'), n.

pan¹ (pan), n., v., panned, pan·ning. —n. **1.** a broad, shallow, metal container used for frying, washing, etc. **2.** any dishlike receptacle or part. **3.** a depression in the ground. **4.** hardpan. —v.t., v.i. **5.** to wash (gravel, etc.) in a pan to separate (gold). **6.** *Informal.* to criticize severely, as in a review of a play. **7. pan out,** *Informal.* to turn out, esp. successfully.

pan² (pan), v., panned, pan·ning, n. *Motion Pictures, Television.* —v.t. **1.** to photograph or televise a scene while rotating the camera through a wide angle. —v.t. **2.** to cause to pan. —n. **3.** the act of panning a camera.

pan-, a combining form meaning: **a.** all: panacea, panorama. **b.** the union of all branches of a group: Pan-American.

Pan., Panama.

pan·a·ce·a (pan'ə sē'ə), n. a remedy for all diseases or troubles.

pa·nache (pə nash', -näsh'), n. **1.** a grand or flamboyant manner. **2.** an ornamental plume, esp. on a helmet.

Pan·a·ma (pan'ə mä'), n. **1.** a country in S Central America. **2.** (sometimes l.c.) See **Panama hat.** —**Pan'a·ma'ni·an** (-mä'nē ən, -mä'-), adj., n.

Pan'ama Canal', a canal extending SE from the Atlantic to the Pacific across Panama.

Pan·ama hat′, a hat made of finely plaited young leaves of a palmlike tropical plant.

Pan·A·mer·i·can (pan′ə mer′i kən), *adj.* of all the countries or peoples of North, Central, and South America.

pan·a·tel·la (pan′ə tel′ə), *n.* a long, slender cigar, usually with straight sides.

pan·cake (pan′kāk′), *n.* a flat cake of batter cooked in a pan or on a griddle.

pan·chro·mat·ic (pan′krō mat′ik, -krə-), *adj.* sensitive to all visible colors, as film.

pan·cre·as (pan′krē əs, pang′-), *n.* a large gland that secretes a digestive fluid into the intestine and also secretes insulin. —**pan′cre·at′ic** (-at′-ik), *adj.*

pan·da (pan′də), *n.* **1.** Also called **less′er pan′da.** a reddish-brown, raccoonlike carnivore of the Himalayas. **2.** Also called **gi′ant pan′da.** a large, black-and-white, bearlike carnivore of Tibet and southwestern China.

pan·dem·ic (pan dem′ik), *adj.* prevalent throughout an entire country or region, as a disease.

pan·de·mo·ni·um (pan′də mō′nē əm), *n.* wild lawlessness or uproar.

pan·der (pan′dər), *n.* Also, **pan′der·er. 1.** a go-between in clandestine love affairs. **2.** a person who caters to or profits from the weaknesses or vices of others. —*v.i.* **3.** to cater basely.

P. and L., profit and loss. Also, **P. & L.**

Pan·do·ra (pan dôr′ə, -dôr′ə), *n.* Class. Myth. the first woman on earth: opened a box holding the troubles that would plague mankind.

pan·dow·dy (pan dou′dē), *n., pl.* **-dies.** a deep pie made with apples, and usually sweetened with molasses.

pane (pān), *n.* a single plate of glass in a frame of a window or door.

pan·e·gyr·ic (pan′i jir′ik, -ji′rik), *n.* **1.** a lofty oration or writing in praise of a person or thing. **2.** an elaborate commendation. —**pan′e·gyr′i·cal,** *adj.* —**pan′e·gyr′ist** (-jir′ist), *n.*

pan·el (pan′ºl), *n., v.,* **-eled, -el·ing** or **-elled, -el·ling.** —*n.* **1.** an area of a wall or door that is distinct from the adjoining areas. **2.** a flat, thin piece of material joined to form a surface. **3.** a flat, broad piece of wood on which a picture is painted. **4.** a vertical strip of fabric set on a skirt, etc. **5.** a list of persons summoned for service as jurors. **6.** a group of persons gathered to participate in a public discussion or quiz game. **7.** a section of a machine containing the controls and dials. —*v.t.* **8.** to furnish with panels.

pan·el·ing (pan′ºling), *n.* **1.** material made into panels, esp. decorative panels. **2.** panels collectively.

pan·el·ist (pan′ºlist), *n.* a member of a public-discussion or quiz-game panel.

pan′el truck′, a small truck having a fully enclosed body.

pang (pang), *n.* **1.** a sudden feeling of emotional distress. **2.** a sudden, brief, sharp pain.

pan·han·dle[1] (pan′han′dºl), *n.* (*sometimes cap.*) a long, narrow, projecting strip of territory that is not a peninsula.

pan·han·dle[2] (pan′han′dºl), *v.i., v.t.,* **-dled, -dling.** Informal. to accost (passersby) on the street and beg (from). —**pan′han′dler,** *n.*

pan·ic (pan′ik), *n., v.,* **-icked, -ick·ing.** —*n.* **1.** a sudden, overwhelming fear that often spreads quickly. —*v.t.* **2.** to affect with panic. **3.** Slang. to keep (an audience) highly amused. —*v.i.* **4.** to be stricken with panic. —**pan′ick·y,** *adj.* —Syn. **1.** alarm, consternation, fright, terror.

pan·i·cle (pan′i kəl), *n.* any loose, diversely branching flower cluster. —**pan′i·cled,** *adj.*

pan·jan·drum (pan jan′drəm), *n.* a self-important or pretentious official.

pan·nier (pan′yər, -ē ər), *n.* one of a pair of baskets to be slung across the back of a pack animal. Also, **pan′ier.**

pan·o·ply (pan′ə plē), *n., pl.* **-plies. 1.** a complete suit of armor. **2.** any complete covering or magnificent array.

pan·o·ram·a (pan′ə ram′ə, -rä′mə), *n.* **1.** a wide, unobstructed view of an extensive area. **2.** a continuously passing scene of events. —**pan′o·ram′ic,** *adj.* —**pan′o·ram′i·cal·ly,** *adv.*

pan·sy (pan′zē), *n., pl.* **-sies. 1.** a plant of the violet family that bears flowers with flat, velvety petals. **2.** its flower.

pant (pant), *v.i.* **1.** to breathe hard and quickly, as after exertion. **2.** to long eagerly: *to pant for fame.* —*v.t.* **3.** to breathe or utter gaspingly. —*n.* **4.** a panting breath. —**pant′ing·ly,** *adv.*

pan·ta·loons (pan′tºloonz′), *n.* a man's closefitting trousers, worn esp. in the 19th century.

pan·the·ism (pan′thē iz′əm), *n.* any philosophical doctrine that identifies God with the universe. —**pan′the·ist,** *n.* —**pan′the·is′tic, pan′the·is′ti·cal,** *adj.*

pan·the·on (pan'thē on', -ən, pan thē'-ən), *n.* **1.** a public building containing tombs or memorials of the illustrious dead of a nation. **2.** a temple dedicated to all the gods. **3.** the gods collectively.

pan·ther (pan'thər), *n.*, *pl.* **-thers, -ther. 1.** a black leopard, esp. one found in southern Asia. **2.** (loosely) **a.** cougar. **b.** jaguar.

pant·ies (pan'tēz), *n.pl.* underpants or undershorts for women and children. Also, **pan'tie, pant'y.**

pan·to·mime (pan'tə mīm'), *n.*, *v.*, **-mimed, -mim·ing.** *—n.* **1.** a play in which the performers express themselves mutely by gestures, often to the accompaniment of music. **2.** significant gesture without speech. — *v.t.*, *v.i.* **3.** to act or express (oneself) in pantomime. **—pan'to·mim'-ic** (-mim'ik), *adj.* **—pan'to·mim'ist** (-mī'mist), *n.*

pan·try (pan'trē), *n.*, *pl.* **-tries.** a room or closet for storing food, dishes, utensils, etc.

pants (pants), *n.pl.* **1.** trousers. **2.** panties.

pant·suit (pant'sōōt'), *n.* a woman's suit for casual wear consisting of slacks and a matching jacket. Also, **pants' suit'.**

pant'y hose', a one-piece garment worn by women, combining panties and stockings.

pant·y·waist (pan'tē wāst'), *n. Informal.* sissy.

pap (pap), *n.* **1.** soft food for infants or invalids. **2.** ideas or writing without substance or real value.

pa·pa (pä'pə, pə pä'), *n. Informal.* father (def. 1).

pa·pa·cy (pā'pə sē), *n.*, *pl.* **-cies.** *Rom. Cath. Ch.* **1.** the office or jurisdiction of the pope. **2.** (*cap.*) the system of Roman Catholic government. **3.** the tenure of a pope's reign. **4.** the succession of the popes.

pa·pa·in (pə pā'in, -pī'in, pā'pə-), *n.* an enzyme found in the fruit of the papaya tree and used as a meat tenderizer.

pa·pal (pā'pəl), *adj.* **1.** of the pope or the papacy. **2.** of the Roman Catholic Church. **—pa'pal·ly,** *adv.*

pa·paw (pô'pô, pə pô'), *n.* **1.** the small fleshy fruit of a North American tree. **2.** its tree. **3.** papaya.

pa·pa·ya (pə pä'yə), *n.* **1.** the large, yellow, melonlike fruit of a tropical American tree. **2.** its tree.

pa·per (pā'pər), *n.* **1.** a substance made from rags, wood, etc., usually in thin sheets, used for writing or printing, for wrapping things, or for covering walls. **2.** a sheet or leaf of this. **3.** a written or printed document. **4.** Often, **papers.** a document or documents of identity. **5.** an essay or dissertation on a particular topic. **6.** newspaper. **7.** wallpaper. *—v.t.* **8.** to cover with paper, esp. wallpaper. *—adj.* **9.** of or made of paper. **—pa'per·er,** *n.* **—pa'per·y,** *adj.*

pa·per·back (pā'pər bak'), *n.* **1.** a softbound book, as distinguished from a hardbound book. **2.** See **mass-market paperback. 3.** See **trade paperback.**

pa·per·board (pā'pər bōrd', -bôrd'), *n.* a thick, stiff cardboard.

pa'per clip', a flat wire clip bent so that it can clasp sheets of paper together.

pa·per·hang·er (pā'pər hang'ər), *n.* a person whose job is to cover walls with wallpaper. **—pa'per·hang'ing,** *n.*

pa'per ti'ger, a person or nation that has the appearance of strength or power but is actually weak or ineffectual.

pa·per·weight (pā'pər wāt'), *n.* a small, heavy object laid on papers to keep them from scattering.

pa·per·work (pā'pər wûrk'), *n.* written or clerical work forming an incidental but necessary part of some work or job.

pa·pier-mâ·ché (pā'pər mə shā'), *n.* a substance made of paper pulp mixed with glue and molded when moist to form various articles, and becoming hard when dry. [< F: lit., chewed paper]

pa·pil·la (pə pil'ə), *n.*, *pl.* **-pil·lae** (-pil'ē). a small, nipplelike process or projection, as on the tongue. **—pap·il·lar·y** (pap'ə ler'ē), *adj.*

pa·pist (pā'pist), *n. Usually Disparaging.* a Roman Catholic.

pa·poose (pa pōōs', pə-), *n.* a North American Indian baby or young child.

pap·ri·ka (pa prē'kə, pə-, pap'rə kə), *n.* a red, powdery condiment derived from dried, ripe sweet peppers.

Pap' test' (pap), a method for the early detection of cancer, esp. uterine. Also called **Pap' smear'.**

pap·ule (pap'yōōl), *n.* a small, pointed, usually inflammatory elevation of the skin. **—pap'u·lar,** *adj.*

pa·py·rus (pə pī'rəs), *n.*, *pl.* **-rus·es, -py·ri** (-pī'rī). **1.** a tall, reedlike plant of Egypt. **2.** an ancient paperlike material made from the pith of this plant.

par (pär), *n.* **1.** an equality in value or standing: *The gains and the losses are on a par.* **2.** an average or normal quality, condition, etc.: *below par.* **3.** the legally established value of the monetary unit of one country. **4.** the nominal or face value of a stock or bond. **5.** *Golf.* the number of strokes set as a standard for a hole or a complete course. *—adj.* **6.** average or normal. **7.** at or pertaining to par.

par., 1. paragraph. 2. parallel. 3. parish.

para-, a prefix meaning: a. beside: *paradigm.* b. beyond: *parapsychology.* c. auxiliary to: *paramedical.*

par·a·ble (par′ə bəl), *n.* a short story designed to convey a truth or moral lesson.

pa·rab·o·la (pə rab′ə lə), *n.* a plane curve formed by the intersection of a cone and a plane parallel to one of its sides. —**par·a·bol·ic** (par′ə-bol′ik), *adj.*

par·a·chute (par′ə shoot), *n., v.,* **-chut-ed, -chut·ing.** —*n.* 1. a large, umbrellalike device of fabric that opens in midair and allows a person or object to descend at a safe rate of speed, as from an airplane. —*v.t., v.i.* 2. to drop by parachute. —**par′-a·chut′ist,** *n.*

pa·rade (pə rād′), *n., v.,* **-rad·ed, -rad-ing.** —*n.* 1. a large public procession, usually of a festive nature. 2. a military ceremony involving the formation and marching of troops. 3. an ostentatious display: *to make a parade of one's beliefs.* 4. *Brit.* promenade (def. 2). —*v.t.* 5. to walk up and down on or in. 6. to display ostentatiously. —*v.i.* 7. to march in a parade. 8. to promenade to show off. —**pa·rad′er,** *n.*

par·a·digm (par′ə dim, -dīm′), *n.* 1. an example serving as a model. 2. *Gram.* a set of all inflected forms based on a single word.

par·a·dise (par′ə dīs′, -dīz′), *n.* 1. heaven, as the final abode of the righteous. 2. *(often cap.)* Eden (def. 1). 3. any place or state of extreme happiness.

par·a·di·si·a·cal (par′ə di sī′ə kəl, -zī′-), *adj.* of, like, or befitting paradise. Also, **par′a·dis′i·ac** (-dis′ē ak′). —**par′a·di·si′a·cal·ly,** *adv.*

par·a·dox (par′ə doks′), *n.* 1. a statement seemingly self-contradictory but in reality expressing a possible truth. 2. any person or situation exhibiting an apparently contradictory nature. —**par′a·dox′i·cal,** *adj.* **par′a·dox′i·cal·ly,** *adv.*

par·af·fin (par′ə fin), *n.* 1. a white, waxy, solid substance obtained from crude petroleum and used for candles or waterproofing paper. 2. *Brit.* kerosene. Also, **par′af·fine** (-fin, -fēn′). —**par′af·fin′ic** (-fin′ik), *adj.*

par·a·gon (par′ə gon′, -gən), *n.* a model of excellence or of a particular excellence.

par·a·graph (par′ə graf′, -gräf′), *n.* 1. a distinct portion of written or printed matter, usually beginning with an indentation on a new line. 2. a mark (¶) indicating the beginning of such a portion. 3. a brief, separate item in a newspaper. —*v.t.* 4. to divide into paragraphs.

Par·a·guay (par′ə gwā′, -gwī′), *n.* a country in central South America. — **Par′a·guay′an,** *adj., n.*

par·a·keet (par′ə kēt′), *n.* a small, slender parrot having a long, graduated tail.

par·al·lax (par′ə laks′), *n.* the apparent displacement of an observed object due to the difference between two points of view.

par·al·lel (par′ə lel′), *adj., n., v.,* **-leled, -lel·ing** or **-lelled, -lel·ling.** — *adj.* 1. extending in the same direction, equidistant at all points, and never converging. 2. having the same direction, nature, or tendency: *parallel interests.* —*n.* 3. a parallel line or plane. 4. anything parallel or similar to something else. 5. a comparison made between two things. 6. an imaginary circle on the earth's surface parallel to the equator and designated in degrees of latitude. — *v.t.* 7. to make parallel. 8. to form a parallel to. 9. to show the similarity of. [< L *parallēl(us)* < Gk *parállēlos* side by side = *para-* + *állēlos* one another] —**par′al·lel′-ism** (-iz′əm), *n.*

par·al·lel·o·gram (par′ə lel′ə gram′), *n.* a four-sided polygon having both pairs of opposite sides parallel to each other.

pa·ral·y·sis (pə ral′i sis), *n., pl.* **-ses** (-sēz′). 1. partial or complete loss of the capacity for motion or feeling in some part of the body. 2. a crippling or stoppage of powers or activity. —**par′a·lyt′ic** (par′ə lit′ik), *n., adj.*

par·a·lyze (par′ə līz′), *v.t.,* **-lyzed, -lyz-ing.** 1. to affect with paralysis. 2. to make powerless, ineffective, or inactive. —**par′a·lyz′er,** *n.* —**par′a-lyz′ing·ly,** *adv.*

par·a·me·ci·um (par′ə mē′shē əm, -sē-əm), *n., pl.* **-ci·a** (-shē ə, -sē ə), **-ci-ums.** or oval freshwater protozoan that swims by cilia.

par·a·med·i·cal (par′ə med′i kəl), *adj.* related to the medical profession in a supplementary capacity. —**par′a-med′ic,** *n.*

pa·ram·e·ter (pə ram′i tər), *n.* 1. *Math.* a constant in a function that determines the specific form of the function. 2. a determining factor or characteristic. —**par·a·met′ric** (par′-ə me′trik) *adj.*

par·a·mil·i·tar·y (par′ə mil′i ter′ē), *adj.* noting an organization operating as a supplement to a regular military force.

par·a·mount (par′ə mount′), *adj.* chief in importance or rank. —**par′a-mount′ly,** *adv.* —**Syn.** foremost, primary.

par·a·mour (par'ə mŏŏr'), n. *Literary.*
an illicit lover, esp. of a married person.

par·a·noi·a (par'ə noi'ə), n. mental
disorder characterized by delusions
that are ascribed to the supposed
hostility of others. —**par'a·noid'**,
par'a·noi'ac (-ak), adj., n.

par·a·pet (par'ə pit, -pet'), n. **1.**
a defensive wall or elevation in a
fortification. **2.** any low protective
wall or barrier at the edge of a balcony or roof.

par·a·pher·nal·ia (par'ə fər nāl'yə, -fə-
nāl'-), n. **1.** articles of equipment
needed for some activity, as a hobby.
2. personal belongings.

par·a·phrase (par'ə frāz'), n., v.,
-phrased, -phras·ing. —n. **1.** a restatement of a passage giving the
meaning in another form, as for
clearness. —v.t., v.i. **2.** to render in
or make a paraphrase. —**par'a·phras'er**, n.

par·a·ple·gi·a (par'ə plē'jē ə, -jə), n.
paralysis of the legs and lower part
of the body. —**par'a·ple'gic** (-plē'-
jik, -plej'ik), adj., n.

par·a·pro·fes·sion·al (par'ə prə fesh'ə-
nəl), n. a person, such as a teacher's
assistant, trained to assist a professional.

par·a·psy·chol·o·gy (par'ə sī kol'ə jē),
n. the branch of psychology that
deals with the investigation of psychic phenomena, as telepathy. —
par'a·psy·chol'o·gist, n.

par·a·site (par'ə sīt'), n. **1.** an animal
or plant that lives on or in another
from whose body it obtains nutriment. **2.** a person who receives support or advantage from another
without giving any useful return. —
par'a·sit'ic (-sit'ik), adj. —**par'a·sit'-
ism** (-sī'tiz əm), n. —**par'a·si·tize'**
(-si tīz', -sī-), v.t.

par·a·sol (par'ə sôl', -sol'), n. a woman's small or light sun umbrella.

par·a·sym·pa·thet·ic (par'ə sim'pə-
thet'ik), adj. pertaining to that part
of the autonomic nervous system
which functions in opposition to
the sympathetic nervous system, as
in inhibiting heartbeat and contracting the pupil of the eye.

par·a·thi·on (par'ə thī'on), n. a poisonous liquid used as an insecticide.

par·a·thy·roid (par'ə thī'roid), adj. **1.**
situated near the thyroid gland. —n.
2. See **parathyroid gland.**

parathy'roid gland', any of several
small glands lying near or embedded
in the thyroid gland, the secretions
of which control the calcium content
of the blood.

par·a·troops (par'ə trōōps'), n.pl.
troops trained to attack or land in
combat areas by parachuting from
airplanes. —**par'a·troop'er**, n.

par·a·ty·phoid (par'ə tī'foid), n. an
infectious disease similar to typhoid
fever but usually milder. Also called
paraty'phoid fe'ver.

par a·vion (pA RA vyôN'), *French.* by
plane (for air mail).

par·boil (pär'boil'), v.t. to boil partially or for a short time.

par·cel (pär'səl), n., v., -celed, -cel·ing or -celled, -cel·ling. —n. **1.** a
quantity of something wrapped or
packed up. **2.** a distinct portion or
tract of land. —v.t. **3.** to divide into
or distribute in parcels or portions:
to parcel out land for campsites.

par'cel post', **1.** a postal service
charged with handling and delivering
parcels. **2.** parcels handled by this.

parch (pärch), v.t. **1.** to make completely dry, as heat, sun, and wind
do. **2.** to make hot or thirsty. —v.i.
3. to suffer from heat or thirst.

parch·ment (pärch'mənt), n. **1.** the
skin of sheep or goats prepared for
writing on. **2.** a manuscript or document on such material.

pard (pärd), n. *Archaic.* a leopard or
panther.

par·don (pär'dən), n. **1.** forgiveness
of an offense or discourtesy. **2.** *Law.*
a. a release from the penalty of an
offense. **b.** the document by which
such release is granted. —v.t. **3.** to
remit the penalty of (an offense). **4.**
to release (a person) from the penalty of an offense. **5.** to make courteous allowance for or to. —**par'-
don·a·ble**, adj. —**par'don·a·bly**, adv.
—**par'don·er**, n.

pare (pâr), v.t., pared, par·ing. **1.** to
cut off the outer coating, layer, or
part of. **2.** to diminish or decrease
gradually. —**par'er**, n.

par·e·gor·ic (par'ə gôr'ik, -gor'-), n.
a camphorated tincture of opium,
used chiefly to check diarrhea.

paren., parenthesis.

par·ent (pâr'ənt, par'-), n. **1.** a father
or a mother. **2.** a source, origin, or
cause. **3.** any organism that produces
or generates another. —**pa·ren'tal**
(pə ren't²l), adj. —**par'ent·hood'**, n.

par·ent·age (pâr'ən tij, par'-), n. derivation or descent from parents or
ancestors.

pa·ren·the·sis (pə ren'thi sis), n., pl.
-ses (-sēz'). **1.** either or both of a
pair of signs ( ) used to enclose a
word, phrase, or clause within a
sentence. **2.** a qualifying or explanatory word, phrase, or clause used
within a sentence. —**par·en·thet'i·-
cal** (par'ən thet'i kəl), **par'en·thet'ic,**
adj.

pa·re·sis (pə rē'sis, par'i sis), n. **1.**
partial paralysis. **2.** a syphilitic disorder characterized by degeneration
of cerebral tissue. —**pa·ret'ic** (-ret'-
ik, -rē'tik), n., adj.

par ex·cel·lence (pär ek′sə läns′), *French.* being an example of excellence.

par·fait (pär fā′), *n.* **1.** a dessert made of layers of ice cream and fruit, syrup, etc., usually topped with whipped cream. **2.** a rich frozen dessert of whipped cream and egg.

pa·ri·ah (pə rī′ə, par′ē ə, pär′-), *n.* **1.** a social outcast. **2.** (*cap.*) a member of a low caste in southern India.

pa·ri·e·tal (pə rī′i t°l), *adj.* **1.** of or situated near the side and top of the skull. **2.** of or pertaining to campus life or its rules, esp. with respect to visiting hours in a dormitory for members of the opposite sex.

par·i·mu·tu·el (par′i myōō′chōō əl), *n.* a form of betting on horse races in which the winners divide the total amount bet less a percentage for the management, taxes, etc.

par·ing (pâr′iŋg), *n.* a piece or part pared off: *apple parings.*

Par·is (par′is; *Fr.* PA Rē′), *n.* the capital of France. —**Pa·ri·sian** (pə rē′zhən, -rizh′ən), *n., adj.*

Par·is (par′is), *n. Class. Myth.* a Trojan prince whose abduction of Helen led to the Trojan War.

Par′is green′, an emerald-green, poisonous powder used as a pigment, insecticide, etc.

par·ish (par′ish), *n.* **1.** an ecclesiastical district having its own church and member of the clergy. **2.** a local church with its field of activity. **3.** (in Louisiana) a county. **4.** the people of a parish.

pa·rish·ion·er (pə rish′ə nər), *n.* a member or inhabitant of a parish.

par·i·ty (par′i tē), *n.* **1.** equality, as in amount, status, or character. **2.** equivalence in value at a fixed ratio between two different currencies. **3.** a system of regulating prices of farm products to provide farmers with the same purchasing power they had in a selected base period.

park (pärk), *n.* **1.** a public area of land having facilities for rest and recreation. **2.** an enclosed area or a stadium used for sports: *a baseball park.* **3.** a considerable extent of land forming the grounds of a country estate. **4.** *Brit.* a space for parking vehicles, esp. automobiles. —*v.t., v.i.* **5.** to halt (a vehicle) with the intention of not using it again immediately. **6.** *Informal.* to put or place (something or someone) somewhere.

par·ka (pär′kə), *n.* **1.** a hooded fur coat for wear in arctic regions. **2.** a similar garment worn for winter sports or by the military.

park′ing me′ter, a coin-operated device for registering and collecting payment for the length of time that a motor vehicle occupies a parking space.

Park′in·son's disease′ (pär′kin sənz), a nerve disease characterized by tremors of fingers and hands and rigidity of muscles.

Park′in·son's law′, any of various facetious "principles" concerning office organization, esp. one which holds that work expands to fill the time allotted to it.

park·way (pärk′wā′), *n.* a broad thoroughfare landscaped with grass, trees, etc.

parl., **1.** parliament. **2.** parliamentary.

par·lance (pär′ləns), *n.* a particular manner of speaking or writing: *legal parlance.*

par·lay (pär′lē, pär lā′), *v.t.* **1.** to bet (an original amount and its winnings) on a subsequent race, contest, etc. —*n.* **2.** a bet parlayed.

par·ley (pär′lē), *n., pl.* **-leys,** *v.,* **-leyed, -ley·ing.** —*n.* **1.** a conference to discuss terms or resolve a dispute, as between opposing forces. —*v.i.* **2.** to hold a parley. —**par′ley·er,** *n.*

par·lia·ment (pär′lə mənt), *n.* **1.** (*cap.*) the legislature of certain countries, esp. Great Britain. **2.** an assembly for conference on public or national affairs. —**par·lia·men′ta·ry** (-men′tə rē, -trē), *adj.*

par·lia·men·tar·i·an (pär′lə men târ′ē ən), *n.* an expert in parliamentary rules and procedures.

par·lor (pär′lər), *n.* **1.** a room or building forming a business place: *billiard parlor.* **2.** *Obsolesc.* a living room. Also, *Brit.,* **par′lour.**

par·lous (pär′ləs), *adj. Archaic.* perilous or dangerous. —**par′lous·ly,** *adv.*

Par·me·san (pär′mi zan′, -zän′, -zən), *n.* a hard, dry Italian cheese made from skim milk, usually grated.

par·mi·gia·na (pär′mə zhä′nə), *adj.* cooked with Parmesan cheese: *veal parmigiana.* Also, **par′mi·gia′no** (-nō).

pa·ro·chi·al (pə rō′kē əl), *adj.* **1.** of a parish church. **2.** of very limited or narrow scope. —**pa·ro′chi·al·ism′** (-ə liz′əm), *n.* —**pa·ro′chi·al·ly,** *adv.*

paro′chial school′, a school maintained and operated by a religious organization.

par·o·dy (par′ə dē), *n., pl.* **-dies,** *v.,* **-died, -dy·ing.** —*n.* **1.** a humorous or satirical imitation of a serious piece of literature or music. —*v.t.* **2.** to make a parody on.

pa·role (pə rōl′), *n., v.,* **-roled, -rol·ing.** —*n.* **1.** the conditional release of a person from prison prior to the end of the maximum sentence imposed. —*v.t.* **2.** to grant or release on parole. [< MF, short for *parole d'honneur* word of honor] —**pa·rol·ee′,** *n.*

par·ox·ysm (par'ək siz'əm), *n.* **1.** any sudden outburst, as of emotion. **2.** a severe attack of a disease, usually recurring periodically. —**par'ox·ys'mal,** *adj.*

par·quet (pär kā', -ket'), *n., v.,* **-queted -quet·ing.** —*n.* **1.** a floor made of parquetry. **2.** the main floor of a theater, esp. the entire floor space for spectators. —*v.t.* **3.** to construct (a floor) of parquetry.

par·quet·ry (pär'ki trē), *n.* mosaic work of wood used for floors.

par·ra·keet (par'ə kēt'), *n.* parakeet.

par·ri·cide (par'i sīd'), *n.* **1.** the act of killing one's father, mother, or other close relative. **2.** a person who commits such an act.

par·rot (par'ət), *n.* **1.** a hook-billed, often brilliantly colored bird having the ability to mimic speech. **2.** a person who merely repeats the words or imitates the actions of another. —*v.t.* **3.** to repeat or imitate without thought or understanding. —**par'rot·er,** *n.*

par·ry (par'ē), *v.,* **-ried, -ry·ing,** *n., pl.* **-ries.** —*v.t.* **1.** to ward off (a thrust, etc.), as in fencing. **2.** to turn aside, esp. by an adroit evasion: *to parry an embarrassing question.* —*n.* **3.** the act or an instance of parrying.

parse (pärs, pärz), *v.t.,* **parsed, pars·ing.** to describe (a word or series of words) grammatically, telling the part of speech, inflectional form, etc.

par·si·mo·ny (pär'sə mō'nē), *n.* extreme or excessive economy or frugality. —**par'si·mo'ni·ous,** *adj.* —**par'si·mo'ni·ous·ly,** *adv.*

pars·ley (pärs'lē), *n.* a garden herb having aromatic leaves used to garnish or season food.

pars·nip (pär'snip), *n.* **1.** a plant having a large, whitish, edible root. **2.** its root.

par·son (pär'sən), *n.* a Protestant clergyman or clergywoman for a parish.

par·son·age (pär'sə nij), *n.* the residence of a parson, as provided by the parish.

part (pärt), *n.* **1.** a portion or division of a whole. **2.** one of the opposing sides in a contest, question, etc. **3.** the dividing line formed in parting the hair. **4.** a constituent piece of a machine or tool. **5.** one's share in some action. **6.** the role given to an actor or actress. **7.** *Music.* **a.** a voice, either vocal or instrumental. **b.** the score for use by a single performer in a group. **8.** Usually, **parts. a.** a region or district. **b.** *Archaic.* abilities or accomplishments: *a man of parts.* **9. for one's part,** as far as concerns one. **10. for the most part,** usually or mostly. **11. in part,** to some extent.. **12 take part,** to partici-

pate. —*v.t.* **13.** to divide (a thing) into parts. **14.** to comb (the hair) away from a dividing line. **15.** to put or keep apart. —*v.i.* **16.** to be or become divided into parts. **17.** to go apart, separate from one another, as persons or things. **18.** to be or become separated from something else. **19.** to depart or leave. **20. part with,** to relinquish. —*adj.* **21.** partial (def. 1). —*adv.* **22.** partly.

part., **1.** participial. **2.** participle. **3.** particular.

par·take (pär tāk'), *v.i.,* **-took** (-tŏŏk'), **-tak·en** (-tā'kən), **-tak·ing.** **1.** to receive, take, or have a share: *to partake of a meal.* **2.** *Literary.* to participate. —**par·tak'er,** *n.*

par·terre (pär târ'), *n.* **1.** the part of a theater floor under the balcony. **2.** an ornamental arrangement of flower beds of different shapes and sizes.

par·the·no·gen·e·sis (pär'thə nō jen'isis), *n.* development of an egg without fertilization. —**par'the·no·ge·net'ic** (-jə net'ik), *adj.*

par·tial (pär'shəl), *adj.* **1.** of or affecting a part only. **2.** favoring one side or party over another. **3. partial to,** particularly fond of. —**par'ti·al'i·ty** (-shē al'i tē, -shal'i-), *n.* —**par'tial·ly,** *adv.*

part·i·ble (pär'tə bəl), *adj.* capable of being divided or separated.

par·tic·i·pate (pär tis'ə pāt'), *v.i.,* **-pated, -pat·ing.** to take or have a part, as with others. —**par·tic'i·pant,** *n.,* *adj.* —**par·tic'i·pa'tion,** *n.* —**par·tic'i·pa'tor,** *n.* —**par·tic'i·pa·to'ry** (-pə tōr'ē, -tôr'ē), *adj.*

par·ti·ci·ple (pär'ti sip'əl, -sə pəl), *n.* an inflected form of a verb that may be used as an adjective or, with an auxiliary, to form certain tenses. —**par'ti·cip'i·al** (-sip'ē əl), *adj.*

par·ti·cle (pär'ti kəl), *n.* **1.** a minute portion, piece, or amount. **2.** See **elementary particle. 3.** a small word of functional or relational use, such as an article, preposition, or conjunction.

par·ti·col·ored (pär'tē kul'ərd), *adj.* having different colors in different parts.

par·tic·u·lar (pər tik'yə lər), *adj.* **1.** of or pertaining to a single or specific person or thing. **2.** distinguished from the ordinary. **3.** being such in an exceptional degree. **4.** exceptionally selective, attentive, or exacting. —*n.* **5.** an individual or distinct part, as an item of a list. **6. in particular,** particularly or especially. —**par·tic'u·lar'i·ty** (-lar'i tē), *n.* —**par·tic'u·lar·ly,** *adv.* —**Syn. 4.** discriminating, fastidious.

par·tic·u·lar·ize (pər tik'yə lə rīz'), *v.t., v.i.,* **-ized, -iz·ing. 1.** to give particulars (of). **2.** to treat in detail.

par·tic·u·late (pər tik′yə lit, -lāt′), *adj.* of or composed of distinct particles.

part·ing (pär′tiŋ), *n.* **1.** the act of a person or thing that parts. **2.** a departure or leave-taking. **3.** a place of division or separation. —*adj.* **4.** given or done at parting. **5.** departing or leaving. **6.** dividing or separating.

par·ti·san (pär′ti zən), *n.* **1.** a firm supporter of a person, party, or cause. **2.** a member of a group of armed civilians engaged in harassing an enemy within an occupied territory during World War II. —*adj.* **3.** of or characteristic of partisans. Also, **par′ti·zan.** —**par′ti·san·ship′,** *n.*

par·ti·tion (pär tish′ən), *n.* **1.** a division into parts or portions. **2.** something that separates or divides, as an interior wall dividing a room. —*v.t.* **3.** to divide into parts or portions. **4.** to divide or separate by a partition.

par·ti·tive (pär′ti tiv), *Gram.* —*adj.* **1.** noting part of a whole. —*n.* **2.** a partitive word or formation.

part·ly (pärt′lē), *adv.* not wholly.

part·ner (pärt′nər), *n.* **1.** a person who shares or partakes. **2.** a person associated with another or others as a principal or a contributor of capital in a business or a joint venture. **3.** a spouse, esp. the wife. **4.** one's companion in a dance. **5.** a player on the same side or team as another. —**part′ner·ship′,** *n.*

part′ of speech′, any of the classes into which words are traditionally divided according to their syntactic function, as noun, pronoun, verb, etc.

par·tridge (pär′trij), *n., pl.* **-tridg·es, -tridge.** any of several game birds including the grouse, bobwhite, etc.

part′ song′, a song with parts for several voices, usually without accompaniment.

part-time (pärt′tīm′), *adj., adv.* working less than the usual or full time. —**part′-tim′er,** *n.*

par·tu·ri·tion (pär′tŏŏ rish′ən, -tyŏŏ-, -chŏŏ-), *n. Med.* the act or process of giving birth to a child.

part·way (pärt′wā′, -wä′), *adv.* in some degree or part.

par·ty (pär′tē), *n., pl.* **-ties,** *adj., v.,* **-tied, -ty·ing.** —*n.* **1.** a social gathering for entertainment or to celebrate an occasion. **2.** a group gathered for some special purpose or task. **3.** a political group organized for gaining governmental control. **4.** *Law.* one of the litigants in a legal proceeding. **5.** *Informal.* a specific individual. —*adj.* **6.** of or for a political party. **7.** of or for a social party. —*v.i.* **8.** to attend or give social parties.

par′ty line′, **1.** a telephone line connecting the telephones of a number of subscribers. **2.** the guiding policy, tenets, or practices of a political party.

par·ve (pär′və), *adj. Judaism.* permissible for use with both meat and dairy meals or dishes: *parve soup.* [< Yiddish *parev*]

par·ve·nu (pär′və nŏŏ′, -nyŏŏ′), *n.* a person who has suddenly acquired wealth or importance, but lacks the proper social qualifications.

pas (pä), *n., pl.* **pas.** a step or series of steps in ballet.

Pas·a·de·na (pas′ə dē′nə), *n.* a city in SW California.

pas·chal (pas′kəl), *adj.* **1.** of the Passover. **2.** of Easter.

pa·sha (pə shä′, pash′ə), *n.* a title formerly held by high officials in countries under Turkish rule.

pass (pas, päs), *v.t.* **1.** to move past. **2.** to leave unconsidered. **3.** to allow to go through or over a barrier or obstacle. **4.** to complete successfully: *to pass an examination.* **5.** to go beyond (a point, degree, etc.). **6.** to cause to go or move onward. **7.** to spend or use (a period of time). **8.** to cause to circulate or spread: *to pass rumors.* **9.** to hand over or deliver: *Pass the salt.* **10.** to discharge from the bowels. **11.** to sanction or approve, esp. by vote: *Congress passed the bill.* **12.** to express or pronounce, as a judgment. **13.** *Baseball.* (of a pitcher) to give a base on balls to (a batter). **14.** *Sports.* to transfer (the ball or puck) to a teammate. —*v.i.* **15.** to go or move onward or forward. **16.** to come to or toward, then go beyond. **17.** to go away or depart. **18.** to slip by, as time. **19.** to come to an end: *The crisis soon passed.* **20.** to take place. **21.** to be transferred, as by inheritance. **22.** to undergo transition or conversion. **23.** to go or get through a barrier or test successfully. **24.** to go unchallenged: *Let the insult pass.* **25.** to express or pronounce an opinion or judgment. **26.** to obtain the approval, as of a legislative body: *The bill finally passed.* **27.** *Cards.* to give up one's chance to bid or play. **28. bring to pass,** to cause to happen. **29. come to pass,** to occur or happen. **30. pass away,** to die. **31. pass for,** to be accepted as. **32. pass off,** to cause to be accepted under a false identity. **33. pass out, a.** to lose consciousness. **b.** to distribute or give out. **34. pass over,** to disregard or ignore. **35. pass up,** *Informal.* to reject, as an opportunity. —*n.* **36.** a permission to enter or leave a place. **37.** a free ticket or permit. **38.** written authorization given a soldier to leave a station or duty for a specified period of time. **39.** a narrow route, esp. between mountains. **40.** *Sports.* the transfer of a ball or puck from one teammate to another. **41.** See **base on balls. 42.** a single movement or effort. **43.** *Informal.* a gesture or action that is intended to be sexually inviting. **44.** a particular state of affairs. **45.** an act of passing. —**pass′er**, *n.*

pass., **1.** passenger. **2.** passive.

pass·a·ble (pas′ə bəl, pä′sə-), *adj.* **1.** capable of being passed, crossed or traveled on. **2.** barely adequate or acceptable. —**pass′a·bly**, *adv.*

pas·sage (pas′ij), *n.* **1.** a short portion of a written work or of a speech. **2.** the act or an instance of passing from one place or condition to another. **3.** the permission, right, or freedom to pass. **4.** the route or course by which a person or thing passes or travels. **5.** *Brit.* a hall or corridor. **6.** a journey by water or air. **7. a.** a passenger accommodation on a ship. **b.** the price charged for this. **8.** a lapse or passing, as of time. **9.** the enactment into law of a legislative measure. **10.** *Archaic.* an exchange of blows: *a passage at arms.*

pas·sage·way (pas′ij wā′), *n.* a way affording passage, as a hall, corridor, etc.

pass·book (pas′bŏŏk′, päs′-), *n.* a book held by a depositor in which the bank enters his or her deposits and withdrawals.

pas·sé (pa sā′, pas′ā), *adj.* **1.** past its interest or usefulness, as an idea. **2.** (esp. of a woman) past one's prime.

pas·sel (pas′əl), *n. Dial.* a fairly large number.

pas·sen·ger (pas′ən jər), *n.* a person who is carried in a public or private conveyance.

passe-par·tout (pas′pär tŏŏ′), *n., pl.* **-touts** (-tŏŏz′). something that passes or provides passage everywhere, as a master key.

pass·er·by (pas′ər bī′, -bī′, pä′sər-), *n., pl.* **pass·ers·by.** a person passing by.

pas·ser·ine (pas′ər in, -ə rīn′, -ə rēn′), *adj.* of or belonging to the large group of birds typically having the feet adapted for perching.

pas·sim (pas′im), *adv. Latin.* here and there: used to indicate the repetition of an idea, phrase, etc., in a book.

pass·ing (pas′iṅg, pä′siṅg), *adj.* **1.** going by or past. **2.** fleeting or transitory. **3.** casual or cursory: *a passing mention.* **4.** indicating that a student has passed: *a passing grade.* —*n.* **5.** the act of a person or thing

that passes. **6.** death or dying. **7. in passing,** incidentally. —**pass′ing·ly**, *adv.*

pas·sion (pash′ən), *n.* **1.** any powerful emotion or feeling, as love or hate. **2.** strong affection. **3.** strong sexual desire. **4.** a strong fondness or enthusiasm. **5.** the object of such a fondness. **6.** an outburst of strong emotion or feeling. **7.** (*often cap.*) the sufferings of Christ on the cross or His sufferings subsequent to the Last Supper. —**pas′sion·less**, *adj.*

pas·sion·ate (pash′ə nit), *adj.* **1.** expressing or revealing strong emotion. **2.** having intense enthusiasm. **3.** easily affected with sexual desire. **4.** filled with anger. —**pas′sion·ate·ly**, *adv.* —**Syn.** 1, 2. ardent, fervent.

pas·sive (pas′iv), *adj.* **1.** acted upon rather than acting or causing action. **2.** submitting without resistance. **3.** *Gram.* noting a voice of verbal inflection indicating that the subject undergoes the action of the verb. —*n.* **4.** *Gram.* the passive voice. —**pas′sive·ly**, *adv.* —**pas·siv·i·ty** (pa siv′ə tē), **pas′sive·ness**, *n.*

pas′sive resist′ance, opposition to a government or to specific laws by the use of noncooperation and other nonviolent methods.

pass·key (pas′kē′, päs′-), *n.* **1.** See **master key. 2.** any private key.

Pass·o·ver (pas′ō′vər, päs′-), *n.* a Jewish festival celebrating the deliverance of the Hebrews from slavery in ancient Egypt.

pass·port (pas′pōrt, -pôrt, päs′-), *n.* a government document issued to a citizen, permitting him or her to leave and reenter the country and authenticating the identification while abroad.

pass·word (pas′wûrd′, päs′-), *n.* a secret word or expression that a person must give in order to pass by a guard.

past (past, päst), *adj.* **1.** gone by in time. **2.** having ended just before the present time. **3.** earlier or former. **4.** *Gram.* designating a verb tense that refers to an action or state in time gone by. —*n.* **5.** the time gone by. **6.** the history of a person, nation, etc. **7.** a person's past life that is characterized by questionable conduct. **8.** *Gram.* **a.** the past tense. **b.** a form in the past tense. —*adv.* **9.** so as to pass by or beyond. —*prep.* **10.** beyond in time, space, amount, or number.

pas·ta (pä′stə), *n.* **1.** an Italian food paste that is shaped and dried as spaghetti, macaroni, etc. **2.** a dish consisting of this paste.

paste (pāst), *n., v., past·ed, past·ing.* —*n.* **1.** a mixture of flour and water, often with starch, used as an adhesive. 2. any soft, smooth mixture of solid and liquid ingredients: *toothpaste*. 3. dough, esp. when prepared with shortening. 4. a brilliant, heavy glass used for making imitation gems. —*v.t.* 5. to fasten or stick with paste. 6. *Slang.* to hit (a person) hard, esp. in the face.

paste·board (pāst′bōrd′, -bôrd′), *n.* a stiff, firm board made of sheets of paper pasted together.

pas·tel (pa stel′, pas′tel), *n.* 1. a color having a soft, subdued shade. 2. a stick of dried colored paste used in drawing or marking. 3. a drawing made with this kind of stick. —**pas·tel′ist, pas′tel·list,** *n.*

pas·tern (pas′tərn), *n.* the part of the foot of a horse between the fetlock and the hoof.

Pas·teur (pa stûr′; *Fr.* pá stœR′), *n.* **Louis** (loo′ē), 1822–95, French chemist and bacteriologist.

pas·teur·ize (pas′chə rīz′, pas′tə-), *v.t.,* **-ized, -iz·ing.** to expose (milk, etc.) to a high temperature to destroy certain microorganisms. —**pas′teur·i·za′tion,** *n.* —**pas′teur·iz·er,** *n.*

pas·tiche (pa stēsh′, pä-), *n.* a literary or musical piece consisting of motifs borrowed from one or more sources.

pas·tille (pa stēl′, -stil′), *n.* 1. a flavored lozenge. 2. a cone of aromatic paste burned as a disinfectant or deodorant. Also, **pas·til** (pas′til).

pas·time (pas′tīm′, päs′-), *n.* any activity that makes time pass agreeably.

past′ mas′ter, a person who is thoroughly expert in a profession, art, etc.

pas·tor (pas′tər), *n.* a member of the clergy in charge of a church or congregation. —**pas′tor·ate** (-it), *n.*

pas·to·ral (pas′tər əl, pä′stor-), *adj.* 1. of or belonging to shepherds. 2. of or pertaining to rural life. 3. having the simplicity or serenity attributed to rural areas. 4. of a pastor or his or her duties. —*n.* 5. a literary work dealing with the life of shepherds or with country life.

pas·to·rale (pas′tə räl′, -ral′, -rä′lē), *n.* a musical composition with a pastoral subject.

past′ par′ticiple, *Gram.* a participle used (a) to express a past action or state or (b) as an adjective.

past′ per′fect, *Gram.* 1. designating a verb tense that refers to an action or state as completed before a past time specified or implied. 2. a verb form or phrase in such a tense.

pas·tra·mi (pə strä′mē), *n.* a highly seasoned cut of smoked beef, esp. from the shoulder. [< Yiddish < Rum *pastramă* < Turk]

pas·try (pā′strē), *n., pl.* **-tries.** 1. a sweet baked food made of paste, esp.

the shortened paste used for pie crust. 2. any item of food of which such paste forms an essential part, as a pie, tart, etc.

pas·tur·age (pas′chər ij, päs′-), *n.* 1. the pasturing of livestock. 2. pasture (defs. 1, 2).

pas·ture (pas′chər, päs′-), *n., v.,* **-tured, -tur·ing.** —*n.* 1. ground used for the grazing of livestock. 2. grass or herbage for feeding livestock. —*v.t.* 3. to put (livestock) to graze on pasture. 4. to graze upon. —**pas′tur·er,** *n.*

past·y (pā′stē), *adj.,* **past·i·er, past·i·est.** 1. of or like paste in consistency. 2. pale and flabby in appearance. —**past′i·ness,** *n.*

pat[1] (pat), *v.,* **pat·ted, pat·ting,** *n.* —*v.t.* 1. to strike lightly with something flat, usually in order to flatten or shape. 2. to stroke or tap gently as an expression of affection or approval. 3. **pat on the back,** to encourage or praise. —*n.* 4. a light stroke or tap with the palm or a flat object. 5. the sound of this. 6. a small piece or mass, usually flat and square: *a pat of butter.* 7. **a pat on the back,** a word of encouragement or praise.

pat[2] (pat), *adj.* 1. exactly to the point. 2. excessively glib. 3. learned perfectly. —*adv.* 4. exactly or perfectly. 5. aptly or opportunely. 6. **stand pat,** to hold firm to one's decision or beliefs.

pat., 1. patent. 2. patented.

patch (pach), *n.* 1. a piece of material used to cover or reinforce a hole or worn place. 2. a piece of material used to cover or protect an injured part. 3. a small piece or area: *a patch of ice.* 4. a small tract of land: *a potato patch.* 5. *Mil.* a cloth emblem worn on the upper uniform sleeve. —*v.t.* 6. to mend or cover with a patch. 7. to repair, esp. in a hasty way. 8. to make by joining patches or pieces together: *to patch a quilt.* 9. to settle or smooth over: *to patch up a quarrel.* —**patch′a·ble,** *adj.* —**patch′er,** *n.*

patch′ test′, a test for allergy in which an impregnated patch is applied to the skin in order to see any reaction.

patch·work (pach′wûrk′), *n.* 1. sewn work made of pieces of cloth of various colors or shapes. 2. something made up of an incongruous variety of pieces.

patch·y (pach′ē), *adj.,* **patch·i·er, patch·i·est.** 1. made up of patches. 2. of inconsistent or irregular quality or texture. —**patch′i·ness,** *n.*

pate (pāt), *n.* the head, esp. the top of the head.

pâ·té (pä tā′), *n.* a paste or spread made of meat or fish, often baked in a pastry.

pa·tel·la (pə tel′ə), *n., pl.* **-las, -tel·lae** (-tel′ē). the flat, movable bone at the front of the knee. —**pa·tel·lar, pa·tel′late** (-tel′it, -āt), *adj.*

pat·en (pat′°n), *n.* a metal plate on which the bread is placed in the celebration of the Eucharist.

pat·ent (pat′°nt *or, esp. Brit. and for def.* 6, pāt′°nt), *n.* **1.** the exclusive right granted by a government to an inventor to manufacture, use, or sell an invention for a certain number of years. **2.** an invention or process protected by this right. **3.** an official document conferring such a right. —*adj.* **4.** protected by a patent. **5.** of or dealing with patents. **6.** unmistakably evident to everyone. **7.** open for inspection by all: *letters patent.* —*v.t.* **8.** to take out a patent on. —**pat′ent·ee,** *n.* —**pat′ent·ly,** *adv.*

pat′ent leath′er, a hard, glossy, smooth leather, used in shoes, bags, etc.

pat′ent med′icine, a medicine sold without a prescription.

pa·ter·fa·mil·i·as (pä′tər fə mil′ē əs, pä′-, pat′ər-), *n. Facetious.* the male head of a household, usually the father.

pa·ter·nal (pə tûr′n°l), *adj.* **1.** of, from, or befitting a father. **2.** related through a father. **3.** inherited from a father. —**pa·ter′nal·ly,** *adv.*

pa·ter·nal·ism (pə tûr′n°liz′əm), *n.* the practice of managing or governing individuals, businesses, or nations in the manner of a father dealing with his children. —**pa·ter′nal·is′tic,** *adj.*

pa·ter·ni·ty (pə tûr′ni tē), *n.* **1.** the state of being a father. **2.** derivation from a father.

pa·ter·nos·ter (pä′tər nos′tər, pat′ər-), *n.* the Lord's Prayer, esp. in the Latin form. Also. **Pa′ter Nos′ter.**

Pat·er·son (pat′ər sən), *n.* a city in NE New Jersey.

path (path, päth), *n., pl.* **paths** (pathz, päthz, paths, päths). **1.** a way beaten or trodden by the feet of people or animals. **2.** a narrow walk or way: *a garden path.* **3.** a route along which something moves. **4.** a course of action, conduct, or procedure. —**path′less,** *adj.*

path., **1.** pathological. **2.** pathology.

pa·thet·ic (pə thet′ik), *adj.* **1.** evoking pity, sorrow, or compassion. **2.** miserably inadequate. —**pa·thet′i·cal·ly,** *adv.* —**Syn. 1.** pitiful, touching.

path·find·er (path′fīn′dər, päth′-), *n.* a person who finds or makes a path, esp. through a wilderness.

path·o·gen (path′ə jən), *n.* any disease-producing organism.

path·o·gen·ic (path′ə jen′ik), *adj.* capable of producing disease. —**path′o·ge·nic′i·ty** (-jə nis′i tē), *n.*

pathol., **1.** pathological. **2.** pathology.

pa·thol·o·gy (pə thol′ə jē), *n., pl.* **-gies. 1.** the science of the origin and nature of diseases. **2.** any deviation from a healthy or normal condition. —**path·o·log·i·cal** (path′ə loj′i kəl), *adj.* —**path/o·log′i·cal·ly,** *adv.* —**pa·thol′o·gist,** *n.*

pa·thos (pā′thos), *n.* the quality in something experienced or understood, as from literature, which evokes pity, sorrow, or compassion.

path·way (path′wā′, päth′-), *n.* path.

-pathy, a combining form meaning: **a.** feeling: *telepathy.* **b.** disease or morbid affection: *psychopathy.*

pa·tience (pā′shəns), *n.* **1.** the quality or capacity of being patient. **2.** *Chiefly Brit.* solitaire (def. 1).

pa·tient (pā′shənt), *n.* **1.** a person under medical or surgical treatment. —*adj.* **2.** bearing misfortune or pain without complaint. **3.** calmly tolerating provocation or delay. **4.** persevering or diligent, esp. over details. —**pa′tient·ly,** *adv.* —**Syn. 2.** enduring, forbearing, long-suffering.

pat·i·na (pat′°nə), *n.* **1.** a green film produced by oxidation on the surface of old bronze. **2.** any ornamental aura.

pa·ti·o (pat′ē ō′, pä′tē ō′), *n., pl.* **-ti·os. 1.** an open courtyard in a traditional Spanish or Spanish-American house. **2.** a paved area adjoining a house used for outdoor living.

pat·ois (pat′wä), *n., pl.* **pat·ois** (pat′wäz). **1.** a provincial dialect of French. **2.** jargon (def. 1).

pat. pend., patent pending.

patri-, a combining form meaning "father": *patriarch.*

pa·tri·arch (pā′trē ärk′), *n.* **1.** the male head of a family or tribe, as in ancient times. **2.** any of the three great progenitors of the Israelites: Abraham, Isaac, or Jacob. **3.** a high-ranking bishop, as in the Eastern Orthodox Church. **4.** a venerable old man. —**pa′tri·ar′chal,** *adj.* —**pa′tri·ar′chate** (-är′kit), *n.* —**pa′tri·ar′chy** (-är′kē), *n.*

pa·tri·cian (pə trish′ən), *n.* any person of noble or high rank.

pat·ri·cide (pa′tri sīd′, pā′-), *n.* **1.** the act of killing one's father. **2.** a person who kills his or her father.

pat·ri·mo·ny (pa′trə mō′nē), *n., pl.* **-nies.** an estate inherited from one's father or ancestors. —**pat′ri·mo′ni·al,** *adj.*

pa·tri·ot (pā′trē ət, -ot′), *n.* a person who loves, supports, and defends his or her country. [< MF *patriote* < L *patriōta* fellow countryman < Gk *patriōtēs* < *pátrio(s)* of one's fathers < *patris* one's fatherland] —**pa′tri·ot′ic** (-ot′ik), *adj.* —**pa′tri·ot′i·cal·ly,** *adv.* —**pa′tri·ot′ism** (-ə tiz′əm), *n.*

pa·tris·tic (pə tris′tik), *adj.* of the fathers of the Christian church or their writings.

pa·trol (pə trōl′), *v.,* **-trolled, -trolling,** *n.* —*v.t.* **1.** to pass regularly through or along (a certain area or route) in order to maintain order and security. —*n.* **2.** a person or group that patrols. **3.** the act of patrolling. —**pa·trol′ler,** *n.*

pa·trol·man (pə trōl′mən), *n.* a police officer assigned to patrol a certain area or route. —**patrol′wom′an,** *n. fem.*

patrol′ wag′on, an enclosed truck used by the police to transport prisoners.

pa·tron (pā′trən), *n.* **1.** a regular customer or client. **2.** a wealthy person who encourages or supports an artist, charity, etc. **3.** See patron saint. —**pa′tron·ess,** *n.fem.*

pa·tron·age (pā′trə nij, pa′-), *n.* **1.** the trade of customers or clients. **2.** the encouragement or support of a patron. **3.** the control of or power to make appointments to government jobs.

pa·tron·ize (pā′trə nīz′, pa′-), *v.t.,* **-ized, -iz·ing. 1.** to give (a commercial establishment) one's patronage. **2.** to behave in an offensively condescending manner toward. **3.** to act as a patron toward. —**pa′tron·iz′er,** *n.*

pa′tron saint′, a saint regarded as the special guardian of a person, group, or place.

pat·ro·nym·ic (pa′trə nim′ik), *n.* a name derived from the name of a father or ancestor, esp. by the addition of a suffix or prefix indicating descent, as *Williamson* (son of William). —**pat′ro·nym′i·cal·ly,** *adv.*

pat·sy (pat′sē), *n., pl.* **-sies.** *Slang.* **1.** a person upon whom the blame for something falls. **2.** a person who is easily deceived or persuaded.

pat·ter¹ (pat′ər), *v.i.* **1.** to make a rapid succession of light taps. —*n.* **2.** a pattering sound. **3.** the act of pattering.

pat·ter² (pat′ər), *n.* **1.** glib and rapid speech used esp. by salesmen or entertainers. **2.** any specialized jargon. —*v.i., v.t.* **3.** to speak glibly and rapidly. —**pat′ter·er,** *n.*

pat·tern (pat′ərn), *n.* **1.** an artistic design, as for decorating a surface. **2.** a mode of behavior regarded as characteristic of persons or things.

3. an original or model considered for or deserving of imitation. **4.** anything designed to serve as a guide in making articles. **5.** a typical example or specimen. —*v.t.* **6.** to make or fashion after a pattern.

pat·ty (pat′ē), *n., pl.* **-ties. 1.** a flat, round piece of ground or chopped food, as of meat. **2.** a little pie.

pau·ci·ty (pô′si tē), *n.* smallness of number or amount.

Paul (pôl), *n.* died A.D. c67, a Christian apostle: author of several of the Epistles. —**Paul·ine** (pô′līn), *adj.*

Paul′ Bun′yan (bun′yən), a legendary giant lumberjack: an American folk hero.

paunch (pônch, pänch), *n.* the belly, esp. when large or protruding. —**paunch′y,** *adj.*

pau·per (pô′pər), *n.* a person without any personal means of support other than from welfare or charity. —**pau′per·ism,** *n.* —**pau′per·ize,** *v.t.* —**pau′per·i·za′tion,** *n.*

pause (pôz), *n., v.,* **paused, paus·ing.** —*n.* **1.** a temporary stop or rest. **2.** a break or rest in speaking or writing, made for emphasis. **3. give pause,** to cause to hesitate, as from surprise or doubt. —*v.i.* **4.** to make a pause.

pave (pāv), *v.t.,* **paved, pav·ing. 1.** to cover (a road, etc.) with concrete, asphalt, or stones so as to make a firm, level surface. **2. pave the way for,** to lead up to. —**pav′er,** *n.*

pave·ment (pāv′mənt), *n.* **1.** a paved surface. **2.** material used for paving.

pa·vil·ion (pə vil′yən), *n.* **1.** a light, usually open building used for shelter, exhibits, etc. **2.** any of a number of separate or attached buildings, as in a hospital. **3.** a large, elaborate tent.

pav·ing (pā′ving), *n.* **1.** the laying of a pavement. **2.** pavement.

Pav·lov (pav′lov), *n.* **I·van Pe·tro·vich** (i vän′ pe trô′vich), 1849–1936, Russian physiologist.

paw (pô), *n.* **1.** the foot of an animal, esp. one having claws. **2.** *Informal.* the human hand. —*v.t., v.i.* **3.** to strike or scrape with the paws. **4.** *Informal.* to handle clumsily, rudely, or with unwelcome familiarity.

pawl (pôl), *n.* a pivoted object adapted to engage with the teeth of a ratchet wheel so as to prevent movement or to impart motion.

pawn¹ (pôn), *v.t.* **1.** to deposit as security, as for money borrowed, esp. with a pawnbroker. **2.** to stake or risk. —*n.* **3.** the state of being pawned: *jewels in pawn.* **4.** something that is pawned.

pawn² (pôn), *n.* **1.** a chessman of the lowest value. **2.** a person who is used or manipulated to further another's purposes.

pawn·bro·ker (pôn′brō′kər), *n.* a person who lends money on goods deposited until redeemed.

Paw·nee (pô nē′), *n., pl.* **-nees, -nee.** a member of an Indian people living in northern Oklahoma.

pawn·shop (pôn′shop′), *n.* the shop of a pawnbroker.

paw·paw (pô′pô′), *n.* papaw.

pay (pā), *v.,* **paid,** *or, for 8,* **payed; pay·ing;** *n.; adj.* —*v.t.* **1.** to settle (a debt or obligation) by giving money. **2.** to give (a certain amount) in exchange for something. **3.** to give money to (a person or organization), as for goods or services. **4.** to give compensation for. **5.** to be profitable to. **6.** to give (attention, compliments, etc.) as if due or fitting. **7.** to make (a call, visit, etc.). **8.** *Naut.* to let out (a rope) by slackening. —*v.i.* **9.** to give money to acquire something or settle an obligation. **10.** to be worthwhile: *It pays to be honest.* **11. pay back, a.** to repay or return. **b.** to retaliate upon or punish. **12. pay down,** to give (partial payment) at the time of purchase as an installment. **13. pay for,** to suffer or be punished for. **14. pay off, a.** to pay a debt in full. **b.** *Slang.* to bribe. **15. pay out,** to expend or disburse. **16. pay up,** to pay fully. —*n.* **17.** wages or salary. **18.** paid employment: *in the pay of the enemy.* **19.** reward or punishment. —*adj.* **20.** requiring payment for service or use: *a pay toilet.* —**pay′a·ble,** *adj.* —**pay·ee′** (-ē′), *n.* —**pay′er,** *n.*

pay·check (pā′chek′), *n.* **1.** a bank check given in lieu of cash as salary or wages. **2.** salary or wages.

pay′ dirt′, **1.** dirt, gravel, or ore that can be mined profitably. **2.** *Informal.* any source of wealth.

pay·load (pā′lōd′), *n.* **1.** the part of a cargo producing revenue or income. **2.** anything carried by an aircraft or spacecraft over what is needed for its operation. **3.** the warhead of a guided missile.

pay·mas·ter (pā′mas′tər, -mä′stər), *n.* a person in charge of paying wages or salaries, as one in the military.

pay·ment (pā′mənt), *n.* **1.** the act of paying. **2.** something paid.

pay·off (pā′ôf′, -of′), *n.* **1.** a settlement or reckoning, as in retribution or reward. **2.** *Informal.* the climax of a story or joke. **3.** *Slang.* a bribe.

pay·roll (pā′rōl′), *n.* **1.** a list of persons to be paid, with the amount due to each. **2.** the total of these amounts.

pay′ sta′tion, a public telephone operated by a coin device. Also called **pay′ phone′.**

payt., payment.

Pb, lead. [< L *plumbum*]

PBB, a toxic industrial chemical contaminating some farm products and causing certain serious health hazards. [*p*(*oly*)*b*(*rominated*) *b*(*iphenyl*)]

PBS, Public Broadcasting Service.

PBX, a telephone system for private use. [*p*(*rivate*) *b*(*ranch e*)*x*(*change*)]

PC, Peace Corps.

p.c., 1. percent. **2.** petty cash. **3.** postal card. **4.** (in prescriptions) after meals. [< L *post cibōs*]

PCB, a poisonous industrial chemical contaminating some river fish and suspected of causing cancer. [*p*(*oly*)-*c*(*hlorinated*) *b*(*iphenyl*)]

PCP, a powerful hallucinogenic drug. [*p*(*hen*)*c*(*ylidine*) + perh. (*peace*) *p*(*ill*), earlier designation]

pct., percent.

Pd, palladium.

pd., paid.

P.D., Police Department.

p.d., 1. per diem. **2.** potential difference.

P.D.Q., *Slang.* immediately or at once. [*p*(*retty*) *d*(*amn*) *q*(*uickly*)]

PDT, Pacific daylight time.

P.E., 1. physical education. **2.** printer's error. **3.** Professional Engineer. **4.** Protestant Episcopal.

pea (pē), *n., pl.* **peas,** (*Archaic*) **pease. 1.** the round, highly nutritious seed of a leguminous plant. **2.** its plant. **3.** any of various related or similar plants or their seed.

peace (pēs), *n.* **1.** the absence of war. **2.** an agreement that ends a war. **3.** a state of harmony among people or groups. **4.** the freedom from disorder normal in a community. **5.** freedom of the mind from fear, anxiety, or annoyance. **6.** silence or stillness. **7. hold** or **keep one's peace,** to keep silent. —**peace′a·ble,** *adj.* —**peace′a·bly,** *adv.* —**peace′ful,** *adj.* —**peace′ful·ly,** *adv.* —**Syn. 1.** amity, concord. **5.** serenity, tranquillity.

Peace′ Corps′, a U.S. government agency that sends volunteers to help developing countries in meeting their needs for skilled manpower.

peace·keep·ing (pēs′kē′ping), *n.* the maintenance of international peace and security, esp. by the United Nations through military force. —**peace′keep′er,** *n.*

peace·mak·er (pēs′mā′kər), *n.* a person who reconciles parties that disagree, quarrel, or fight. —**peace′-mak′ing,** *n., adj.*

peace′ of′ficer, an officer appointed to preserve the public peace, as a sheriff or police officer.

peace′ pipe′, calumet.

peace·time (pēs′tīm′), *n.* **1.** a period of peace. —*adj.* **2.** of or for such a period.

peach (pēch), *n.* **1.** a juicy fruit having a single pit and a fuzzy skin. **2.** the tree bearing this fruit. **3.** a light pinkish yellow. **4.** *Informal.* a person or thing that is especially admired.

pea·cock (pē'kok'), *n.* the male peafowl, noted for its long, spotted, iridescent tail feathers which can be spread in a fan. —**pea'hen'**, *n.fem.*

pea·fowl (pē'foul'), *n.* a large Asiatic forest bird of the pheasant family.

pea' jack'et, a sailor's double-breasted jacket of thick navy-blue wool.

peak (pēk), *n.* **1.** the pointed top of a mountain or ridge. **2.** a mountain with a pointed summit. **3.** the pointed top of anything. **4.** the highest or most important point or level. —*v.t., v.i.* **5.** to bring to or reach a peak.

peak·ed (pē'kid), *adj.* pale and thin, esp. from ill health. —**peak'ed·ness**, *n.*

peal (pēl), *n.* **1.** a loud, prolonged ringing of bells. **2.** a set of bells tuned to one another. **3.** any loud, sustained sound or series of sounds. —*v.t., v.i.* **4.** to sound or give forth in a peal.

pea·nut (pē'nut'), *n.* **1.** a plant related to the pea whose seeds ripen in pods under the ground. **2.** one of its edible seeds. **3.** peanuts, *Slang.* a very small sum.

pea'nut but'ter, a smooth paste made from finely ground roasted peanuts, used as a spread or in cookery.

pear (pâr), *n.* **1.** a sweet, juicy fruit, usually pointed at the stem and rounded at the bottom. **2.** the tree bearing this fruit.

pearl (pûrl), *n.* **1.** a smooth, rounded, lustrous concretion formed within the shells of certain mollusks and valued as a gem. **2.** something similar in form, luster, etc., as a dewdrop. **3.** someone or something precious or choice. **4.** a very pale gray. **5.** mother-of-pearl. —**pearl'y**, *adj.*

Pearl' Har'bor, a harbor near Honolulu in Hawaii: surprise attack by Japan on the U.S. naval base December 7, 1941.

peas·ant (pez'ənt), *n.* **1.** a farm laborer or small farmer, esp. in Europe and Asia. **2.** a rude, uneducated person. —**peas'ant·ry**, *n.*

peat (pēt), *n.* partially decayed vegetable matter found in marshy or damp regions: cut and then dried for use as fuel. —**peat'y**, *adj.*

peat' moss', any moss from which peat may form, used to enrich soil in gardening.

peb·ble (peb'əl), *n., v.,* **-bled, -bling.** —*n.* **1.** a small rounded stone, esp. one worn by the action of water. —*v.t.* **2.** to cover or pave with pebbles.

3. to give a granulated surface to (leather). —**peb'bly**, *adj.*

pe·can (pi kän', pi kan', pē'kan), *n.* **1.** a hickory tree bearing an oval, smooth-shelled nut having a sweet, oily, edible kernel. **2.** its nut.

pec·ca·dil·lo (pek'ə dil'ō), *n., pl.* **-loes, -los.** a petty sin or offense.

pec·ca·ry (pek'ə rē), *n., pl.* **-ries, -ry.** a piglike, hoofed mammal of North and South America, having a dark gray coat with a white collar.

pec·ca·vi (pe kä'vē, -kä'vē), *n.* any confession of guilt or sin.

peck[1] (pek), *v.t.* **1.** to jab with the beak, as a bird does. **2.** to make (a hole) by such strokes. **3.** to pick up bit by bit with the beak. —*v.i.* **4.** to make strokes with the beak or a pointed instrument. **5.** peck at, a. to nibble at food. b. to carp or nag. —*n.* **6.** a quick stroke, as in pecking. **7.** a hole or mark made by pecking. **8.** *Informal.* a hurried kiss.

peck[2] (pek), *n.* a dry measure of 8 quarts or the fourth part of a bushel.

peck'ing or'der, **1.** a social relationship within a flock of poultry in which any one member may assert his or her dominance by pecking weaker members, but is in turn pecked by stronger ones. **2.** a similar relationship within a human social group. Also, **peck' or'der.**

pec·tin (pek'tin), *n.* a white carbohydrate occurring in ripe fruits and used in fruit jellies, cosmetics, etc., because of its ability to solidify to a gel. —**pec'tic, pec'tin·ous,** *adj.*

pec·to·ral (pek'tər əl), *adj.* of, in, or on the chest or breast.

pec·u·late (pek'yə lāt'), *v.t., v.i.,* **-lat·ed, -lat·ing.** to embezzle (public funds). —**pec'u·la'tion,** *n.* —**pec'u·la'tor,** *n.*

pe·cu·liar (pi kyōōl'yər), *adj.* **1.** distinctly strange or unusual. **2.** belonging exclusively to some person, group, or thing. **3.** distinguished in nature or character from others. —**pe·cu·li·ar·i·ty** (pi kyōō'lē ȯr'i tē), *n.* —**pe·cu'liar·ly,** *adv.* —**Syn. 1.** bizarre, eccentric, odd, unique.

pe·cu·ni·ar·y (pi kyōō'nē er'ē), *adj.* of money or monetary payments.

ped·a·gogue (ped'ə gog', -gôg'), *n.* a pedantic, dogmatic teacher. Also, **ped'a·gog'.**

ped·a·go·gy (ped'ə gō'jē, -goj'ē), *n.* the art or science of teaching. —**ped'a·gog'ic** (-goj'ik), **ped'a·gog'i·cal,** *adj.* —**ped'a·gog'i·cal·ly,** *adv.*

ped·al (ped'[ə]l), *n., v.,* **-aled, -al·ing** or **-alled, -al·ling,** *adj.* —*n.* **1.** a foot-operated lever, as on a bicycle or piano. —*v.i.* **2.** to work or use a pedal. **3.** to ride a bicycle. —*v.t.* **4.** to work the pedals of. —*adj.* **5.** *Biol.* of a foot or the feet.

ped·ant (ped′°nt), *n.* **1.** a person who makes an excessive show of learning. **2.** a person who overemphasizes rules or minor details. —**pe·dan·tic** (pə dan′tik), *adj.* —**ped′ant·ry,** *n.* —**pe·dan′ti·cal·ly,** *adv.*

ped·dle (ped′°l), *v.t., v.i.,* **-dled, -dling.** to carry (small articles) from place to place for sale at retail. —**ped′dler, ped′lar,** *n.*

ped·er·as·ty (ped′ə ras′tē, pē′də-), *n.* sexual relations between two males, esp. when one is a minor. —**ped′er·ast′,** *n.*

ped·es·tal (ped′i st°l), *n.* an architectural support for a column, statue, or vase.

pe·des·tri·an (pə des′trē ən), *n.* **1.** a person who goes on foot. —*adj.* **2.** going or on foot. **3.** of or pertaining to walking. **4.** lacking in vitality or imagination, as writing.

pe·des·tri·an·ism (pə des′trē ə niz′əm), *n.* **1.** the exercise or practice of walking. **2.** commonplace or prosaic manner, quality, etc.

pe·di·at·rics (pē′dē a′triks, ped′ē-), *n.* the science dealing with the medical care and diseases of children. —**pe′di·at′ric,** *adj.* —**pe′di·a·tri′cian** (-ə trish′ən), *n.*

ped·i·cab (ped′ə kab′), *n.* a three-wheeled, two-passenger vehicle operated by pedals, formerly used in Southeast Asia.

ped·i·cure (ped′ə kyoor′), *n.* professional care or treatment of the feet and toenails. —**ped′i·cur′ist,** *n.*

ped·i·gree (ped′ə grē′), *n.* **1.** an ancestral line. **2.** a genealogical record, esp. of purebred animals. **3.** distinguished or pure ancestry. —**ped′i·greed′,** *adj.*

ped·i·ment (ped′ə mənt), *n.* a low, triangular gable on the front of an ancient Greek building or a building modeled on its style.

pe·dom·e·ter (pi dom′i tər), *n.* an instrument that measures distance covered in walking.

pe·dun·cle (pi dung′kəl), *n.* **1.** a stalk supporting a flower cluster. **2.** *Zool.* a stalklike part or structure.

peek (pēk), *v.i.* **1.** to look quickly or furtively. **2.** peep¹ (def. 1). —*n.* **3.** a peeking look.

peel (pēl), *v.t.* **1.** to strip (something) of its skin, etc. **2.** to strip (the skin, etc.) from something. —*v.i.* **3.** (of skin, etc.) to come off. **4.** to lose the skin, etc. —*n.* **5.** the skin or rind of a fruit, etc. —**peel′er,** *n.*

peel·ing (pē′ling), *n.* a peeled-off piece of the skin or rind of a fruit.

peen (pēn), *n.* the wedgelike or spherical end of a hammer head opposite the face.

peep¹ (pēp), *v.i.* **1.** to look through a small opening or from a concealed location. **2.** peek (def. 1). **3.** to come partially into view. —*n.* **4.** a quick peek.

peep² (pēp), *n.* **1.** a short, shrill little or furtive look or glance. **5.** *Literary.* the first appearance, as of dawn. —**peep′er,** *n.*

cry or sound, as of a young bird. —*v.i.* **2.** to utter this cry.

peep·hole (pēp′hōl′), *n.* a small hole through which to peep, as in a door.

Peep′ing Tom′, a person who secretly spies on others, esp. for sexual gratification.

peer¹ (pēr), *n.* **1.** a person who is one's equal in rank or ability. **2.** a British nobleman. —**peer′age** (-ij), *n.* —**peer′ess,** *n.fem.*

peer² (pēr), *v.i.* **1.** to look searchingly, as in the effort to discern clearly. **2.** to appear slightly.

peer·less (pēr′lis), *adj.* having no equal. —**Syn.** matchless, nonpareil.

peeve (pēv), *v.,* **peeved, peev·ing,** *n. Informal.* —*v.t.* **1.** to make peevish. —*n.* **2.** a peevish mood. **3.** a source of peevish attitude.

pee·vish (pē′vish), *adj.* querulous from vexation or discontent. —**pee′vish·ly,** *adv.* —**pee′vish·ness,** *n.* —**Syn.** fretful, irritable, petulant.

pee·wee (pē′wē), *n. Informal.* a person or thing that is unusually small.

peg (peg), *n., v.,* **pegged, peg·ging.** —*n.* **1.** a pin driven or fitted into something as a fastening, support, or marker. **2.** *Informal.* a notch or degree. **3.** an occasion or reason. **4.** *Baseball Slang.* a throw. —*v.t.* **5.** to fasten with pegs. **6.** to mark by pegs. **7.** to pierce with a peg. **8.** to keep (a price, etc.) at a set level. **9.** *Baseball Slang.* to throw (a ball). —*v.i.* **10.** to work energetically: *to peg away at homework.*

Peg·a·sus (peg′ə səs), *n. Class. Myth.* a winged horse that stood for poetic inspiration.

peg·board (peg′bôrd′, -bōrd′), *n.* a board having holes into which pegs or hooks are placed.

peg′ leg′, *Informal.* an artificial leg made of wood.

peg·ma·tite (peg′mə tīt′), *n.* a coarsely crystalline granite occurring in veins. —**peg′ma·tit′ic** (-tit′ik), *adj.*

P.E.I. Prince Edward Island.

peign·oir (pān wär′, pen-, pān′wär, pen′-), *n.* a woman's dressing gown.

Pei·ping (bā′ping′), *n.* former name of **Peking.**

pe·jo·ra·tive (pi jôr′ə tiv, -jor′-, pej′ə-rā′-, pē′jə-), *adj.* **1.** having a disparaging effect or force. —*n.* **2.** a pejorative word. —**pe·jo′ra·tive·ly,** *adv.*

Pe·king (pē′king′; *Chin.* bā′ging′), *n.* the capital of the People's Republic of China.

Pe·king·ese (pē′king′ēz′, -ēs′, -kə nēz′, -nēs′), *n.* a small, long-haired dog having a flat face. Also, **Pe′kin·ese′**.

pe·koe (pē′kō, pek′ō), *n.* a superior black tea of Sri Lanka, India, and Java.

pel·age (pel′ij), *n.* the hair or other soft covering of a mammal.

pe·lag·ic (pə laj′ik), *adj.* of open seas or oceans.

pelf (pelf), *n. Disparaging.* money or riches, esp. ill-gotten.

pel·i·can (pel′ə kən), *n.* a large, web-footed, fish-eating bird having a large bill with a distensible pouch.

pel·la·gra (pə lā′grə, -lag′rə, -lā′grə), *n.* a disease caused by a deficiency of niacin in the diet, characterized by skin changes, nervous disorders, and diarrhea. —**pel·la′grous,** *adj.*

pel·let (pel′it), *n.* **1.** a small ball, as of food, medicine, or clay. **2.** a small bullet or shot, as for a shotgun. —**pel′let·ize′** (-īz′), *v.t.*

pell-mell (pel′mel′), *adv.* **1.** in a confused or jumbled manner. **2.** in disorderly, headlong haste. Also, **pell′-mell′.**

pel·lu·cid (pə lōō′sid), *adj.* **1.** allowing the maximum passage of light, as glass. **2.** clear in meaning. —**pel·lu′cid·ly,** *adv.*

pelt[1] (pelt), *v.t., v.i.* to beat or strike in quick succession with or as with blows or missiles. —**pelt′er,** *n.*

pelt[2] (pelt), *n.* the untanned skin of an animal.

pel·vis (pel′vis), *n., pl.* **-vis·es, -ves** (-vēz). **1.** the basinlike cavity in the lower part of the trunk in humans and many other vertebrates. **2.** the bones forming this cavity. [< L: basin] —**pel′vic,** *adj.*

pem·mi·can (pem′ə kən), *n.* a food of shredded dried meat mixed with fat. Also, **pem′i·can.**

pen[1] (pen), *n. v.,* **penned, pen·ning.** —*n.* **1.** any of various instruments for writing or drawing with ink. **2.** such an instrument as a symbol of writing. —*v.t.* **3.** to write with a pen.

pen[2] (pen), *n., v.,* **penned** or **pent, pen·ning.** —*n.* **1.** a small enclosure for animals. **2.** any enclosure used for confinement. —*v.t.* **3.** to confine in or as in a pen.

pen[3] (pen), *n. Slang.* penitentiary.

Pen., peninsula. Also, **pen.**

P.E.N., International Association of Poets, Playwrights, Editors, Essayists, and Novelists.

pe·nal (pēn′°l), *adj.* of or involving legal punishment. —**pe′nal·ly,** *adv.*

pe·nal·ize (pēn′°līz′, pen′-), *v.t.,* **-ized, -iz·ing.** to subject to a penalty. —**pe′nal·i·za′tion,** *n.*

pen·al·ty (pen′°l tē), *n., pl.* **-ties. 1.** punishment for violation of law, rule, or contract. **2.** something forfeited, as a sum of money. **3.** *Sports.* a disadvantage imposed for infraction of the rules.

pen·ance (pen′əns), *n.* **1.** a punishment undergone in token of penitence for sin. **2.** *Rom. Cath. Ch.* a sacrament consisting of confession of a sin followed by forgiveness.

pe·na·tes (pə nā′tēz), *n.pl.* See **lares and penates.**

pence (pens), *n. Brit.* a pl. of **penny.**

pen·chant (pen′chənt), *n.* a strong taste or liking.

pen·cil (pen′səl), *n., v.,* **-ciled, -cil·ing** or **-cilled, -cil·ling.** —*n.* **1.** a slender tube of wood containing a core of graphite or crayon, used for writing or drawing. —*v.t.* **2.** to write, draw, or mark with a pencil.

pen·dant (pen′dənt), *n.* **1.** a hanging ornament, as an earring or locket. —*adj.* **2.** *Rare.* pendent.

pen·dent (pen′dənt), *adj.* **1.** hanging down or suspended. **2.** overhanging or jutting. **3.** *Rare.* pending (def. 3). —*n.* **4.** *Rare.* pendant. —**pen′dent·ly,** *adv.*

pend·ing (pen′ding), *prep.* **1.** while awaiting. **2.** in the period during. —*adj.* **3.** awaiting decision or settlement. **4.** about to take place.

pen·du·lous (pen′jə ləs, pen′də-, -dyə-), *adj.* hanging down loosely.

pen·du·lum (pen′jə ləm, pen′də-, -dyə-), *n.* a long, suspended body whose lower end moves to and fro in an arc when subjected to gravitational force, used esp. in regulating the speed of a clock mechanism. —**pen′du·lar,** *adj.*

pe·ne·plain (pē′nə plān′, pē′nə plān′), *n.* an area reduced almost to a plain by erosion. Also, **pe′ne·plane′.**

pen·e·trate (pen′i trāt′), *v.t., v.i.,* **-trat·ed, -trat·ing. 1.** to pierce or pass into or through. **2.** to enter and be diffused through. **3.** to affect (the mind) deeply. **4.** to understand fully or truly. —**pen′e·tra·ble** (-trə bəl), *adj.* —**pen′e·tra′tion,** *n.* —**pen′e·tra′tive,** *adj.*

pen·e·trat·ing (pen′i trā′ting), *adj.* **1.** of a quality that penetrates, pierces, or pervades: *a penetrating shriek; a penetrating glance.* **2.** acute or discerning: *a penetrating observation.* —**pen′e·trat′ing·ly,** *adv.*

pen·guin (pen′gwin, peng′-), *n.* a flightless, aquatic bird of the Southern Hemisphere, having webbed feet and wings reduced to flippers.

pen·i·cil·lin (pen′i sil′in), *n.* an antibiotic produced by certain molds or manufactured synthetically, used against a variety of diseases and infections.

pen·in·su·la (pə nin′sə lə, -nins′yə lə),
n. an area of land almost completely
surrounded by water. [< L *paenin-
sula,* contr. of *paene insula* almost
island] —**pen·in′su·lar,** *adj.*

pe·nis (pē′nis), *n., pl.* **-nis·es, -nes**
(-nēz). the male organ of urination
and copulation. —**pe·nile** (pēn′ᵊl,
pē′nil), *adj.*

pen·it·ent (pen′i tənt), *adj.* **1.** feeling
sorrow for sin or wrongdoing and
intending atonement. —*n.* **2.** a penitent person. —**pen′i·tence,** *n.* —
pen′i·ten′tial (-ten′shəl), *adj.* —**pen′-
i·tent·ly,** *adv.*

pen·i·ten·tia·ry (pen′i ten′shə rē), *n.,*
pl. **-ries,** *adj.* —*n.* **1.** a state or federal prison for serious offenders. —
adj. **2.** punishable by imprisonment
in a penitentiary.

pen·knife (pen′nif′), *n.* a small pocketknife.

pen·light (pen′lit′), *n.* a flashlight
similar in size and shape to a fountain pen. Also, **pen′lite′.**

pen·man (pen′mən), *n.* **1.** an expert
in penmanship. **2.** a writer or author.
3. *Brit.* a person employed to copy
documents.

pen·man·ship (pen′mən ship′), *n.* the
art of writing with the pen.

Penn (pen), *n.* **William,** 1644–1718,
English Quaker: founder of Pennsylvania 1682.

Penn., Pennsylvania. Also, **Penna.**

pen′ name′, a name used by an author instead of his or her real name.

pen·nant (pen′ənt), *n.* **1.** a long, tapering flag. **2.** such a flag serving
as an emblem of championship.

pen·ni·less (pen′ē lis), *adj.* without
any money whatsoever. —**pen′ni-
less·ness,** *n.* —**Syn.** indigent.

pen·non (pen′ən), *n.* a long, narrow
flag formerly borne on the lance of
a knight. —**pen′noned,** *adj.*

Penn·syl·va·ni·a (pen′səl vā′nē ə,
-vān′yə), *n.* a state in the E United
States. *Cap.:* Harrisburg.

Penn·syl·va·ni·an (pen′səl vā′nē ən,
-vān′yən), *adj.* **1.** of the state of
Pennsylvania. **2.** noting a period of
the Paleozoic era occurring from
270,000,000 to about 300,000,000
years ago and characterized by warm
climates, swampy land areas, and the
development of large reptiles and insects. —*n.* **3.** a native or inhabitant
of Pennsylvania. **4.** *Geol.* the Penn-
sylvanian period.

pen·ny (pen′ē), *n., pl.* **pen·nies,** (*esp.
collectively for 2, 3*) **pence. 1.** a
cent of the U.S. or Canada. **2.**
a coin of the United Kingdom, the
12th part of a shilling: use phased
out in 1971. **3.** Also called **new′
pen′ny.** a bronze coin of the United
Kingdom, the 100th part of a pound.

4. a pretty penny, *Informal.* a considerable sum of money.

pen′ny arcade′, a hall in an amusement park or carnival having coin-
operated games.

pen′ny pinch′er, a miserly or stingy
person —**pen′ny-pinch′ing,** *n., adj.*

pen·ny·roy·al (pen′ē roi′əl), *n.* a plant
yielding a pungent aromatic oil.

pen·ny·weight (pen′ē wāt′), *n.* a unit
of weight equal to 1/20 troy ounce.

pen·ny-wise (pen′ē wiz′), *adj.* **1.** thrifty
with small sums. **2. penny-wise and
pound-foolish,** thrifty and cautious
in small matters, but reckless and
foolish in important matters.

pe·nol·o·gy (pē nol′ə jē), *n.* **1.** the science of the punishment of crime. **2.**
the science of the management of
prisons. —**pe·nol′o·gist,** *n.*

pen·sion (pen′shən), *n.* **1.** a fixed
amount paid regularly by a former
employer to a retired or disabled
person who has met prescribed requirements. —*v.t.* **2.** to grant a pension to. —**pen′sion·er,** *n.*

pen·sive (pen′siv), *adj.* dreamily or
wistfully thoughtful, often in a deep,
sad way. —**pen′sive·ly,** *adv.* —**pen′-
sive·ness,** *n.* —**Syn.** meditative, reflective.

pen·stock (pen′stok′), *n.* a conduit
for conveying water to a water
wheel.

pent (pent), *v.* **1.** a pt. and pp. of
pen². —*adj.* **2.** shut in or confined.

penta-, a combining form meaning
"five": *pentagon.*

pen·ta·cle (pen′tə kəl), *n.* a five-
pointed, star-shaped figure, formerly
used as an occult symbol.

pen·ta·gon (pen′tə gon′), *n.* **1.** a polygon having five angles and five sides.
2. the Pentagon, the U.S. Department of Defense. —**pen·tag′o·nal**
(-tag′ə nᵊl), *adj.*

pen·tam·e·ter (pen tam′i tər), a verse
of five metrical feet.

Pen·ta·teuch (pen′tə tōōk′, -tyōōk′), *n.*
the first five books of the Old Testament. —**Pen′ta·teuch′al,** *adj.*

pen·tath·lon (pen tath′lon), *n.* an athletic contest comprising five different
track-and-field events.

Pen·te·cost (pen′tə kôst′, -kost′), *n.* a
Christian festival celebrated on the
seventh Sunday after Easter, commemorating the descent of the Holy
Spirit upon the apostles. [< L *pen-
tēcostē* < Gk *pentēkostē* fiftieth
(day)] —**Pen′te·cos′tal,** *adj.*

pent·house (pent′hous′), *n.* a separate
apartment on the roof of a high-rise
building.

pent-up (pent′up′), *adj.* not vented or
expressed: *pent-up feelings.*

pe·nu·che (pə nōō′chē), *n.* a candy
made of brown sugar, butter, and
milk.

pe·nul·ti·mate (pi nul′tə mit), *adj.* next to the last.

pe·num·bra (pi num′brə), *n., pl.* **-brae** (-brē), **-bras.** the partial or imperfect shadow surrounding the complete shadow of an opaque body in an eclipse.

pe·nu·ri·ous (pə noõr′ē əs, -nyoõr′-), *adj.* 1. extremely stingy. 2. extremely poor. —**pe·nu′ri·ous·ly,** *adv.* —**pe·nu′ri·ous·ness,** *n.*

pen·u·ry (pen′yə rē), *n.* extreme poverty.

pe·on (pē′ən, pē′on), *n.* 1. a poor farm laborer of Latin America. 2. a person held in servitude to work off debts, esp. in Mexico. —**pe′on·age,** *n.*

pe·o·ny (pē′ə nē), *n., pl.* **-nies.** 1. a shrub having large, many-petaled pink or white flowers. 2. its flower.

peo·ple (pē′pəl), *n., pl.* **-ple, -ples** for 1, *v.,* **-pled, -pling.** —*n.* 1. the whole body of persons constituting a community, tribe, race, or nation. 2. the persons of any particular group or area. 3. the subjects or followers of a ruler or employer. 4. a person's family or relatives. 5. the ordinary persons of a community. 6. persons indefinitely: *Won't people gossip?* 7. human beings, as distinguished from animals. —*v.t.* 8. to fill or supply with people.

pep (pep), *n., v.,* **pepped, pep·ping.** *Informal.* —*n.* 1. vigor or energy. —*v.t.* 2. **pep up,** to inspire or fill with pep. —**pep′py,** *adj.*

pep·per (pep′ər), *n.* 1. a pungent condiment obtained from the dried berries of a tropical, climbing shrub. 2. its shrub. 3. any of several plants bearing hollow green or red fruit having either a sweet or a hot taste. 4. its fruit. —*v.t* 5. to season with pepper. 6. to pelt with shot or missiles.

pep·per·corn (pep′ər kôrn′), *n.* the berry of the pepper plant, dried and used as a spice, often after being ground.

pep·per·mint (pep′ər mint′), *n.* 1. an herb cultivated for its aromatic, pungent oil and used as a flavoring. 2. its oil. 3. a confection flavored with it.

pep·per·y (pep′ə rē), *adj.* 1. of, full of, or resembling pepper. 2. sharp or stinging, as speech. 3. easily angered. —**pep′per·i·ness,** *n.*

pep·sin (pep′sin), *n.* an enzyme, produced in the stomach, that digests proteins.

pep′ talk′, a vigorous talk, as to a person or group, intended to arouse enthusiasm or heighten morale.

pep·tic (pep′tik), *adj.* 1. of or promoting digestion. 2. of or due to the action of pepsin or other digestive secretions.

per (pûr; *unstressed* pər), *prep.* 1. to or for each. 2. *Informal.* according to. 3. (esp. formerly in commercial English) by means of.
—Usage. In commercial use A is preferred to PER by most stylists: *$40 a gross; 5 percent interest a year.*

per-, a prefix meaning: **a.** through: *pervade.* **b.** thoroughly: *peruse.*

Per., 1. Persia. 2. Persian.

per., 1. period. 2. person.

per·ad·ven·ture (pûr′əd ven′chər, per′-), *adv. Archaic.* perhaps.

per·am·bu·late (pər am′byə lāt′), *v.i., v.t.,* **-lat·ed, -lat·ing.** *Literary.* to walk about (or through). —**per·am′bu·la′tion,** *n.*

per·am·bu·la·tor (pər am′byə lā′tər), *n. Brit.* a baby carriage.

per an., See **per annum.** Also, **per ann.**

per an·num (per an′əm), for or in each year.

per·cale (pər kāl′, -kal′), *n.* a closely woven, smooth-finished, cotton cloth, used for sheets, etc.

per cap·i·ta (pər kap′i tə), for each person of population.

per·ceive (pər sēv′), *v.t.,* **-ceived, -ceiv·ing.** 1. to become aware of by means of the senses. 2. to understand or form an idea of. —**per·ceiv′a·ble,** *adj.* —**Syn.** 1. notice, observe.

per·cent (pər sent′), *n.* 1. one part in each hundred . 2. **percentage** (def. 1). —*adv., adj.* 3. Also, **per cent** figured or expressed in hundredths. [short for L *per centum* by the hundred]

per·cent·age (pər sen′tij), *n.* 1. a rate or proportion per hundred. 2. a proportion in general. 3. an allowance, commission, or rate of interest calculated by percent. 4. *Informal.* **a.** a share of earnings or profits. **b.** personal advantage. —**per·cent′aged,** *adj.*

per·cen·tile (pər sen′tīl, -til), *n. Statistics.* a number that divides a series into 100 groups having equal frequencies.

per·cept (pûr′sept), *n.* an impression of something perceived.

per·cep·ti·ble (pər sep′tə bəl), *adj.* capable of being perceived. —**per·cep′ti·bly,** *adv.* —**Syn.** noticeable.

per·cep·tion (pər sep′shən), *n.* 1. the act or result of perceiving. 2. immediate or intuitive recognition. 3. the ability or power to perceive.

per·cep·tive (pər sep′tiv), *adj.* 1. having or showing keenness of perception. 2. of perception. —**per·cep′tive·ly,** *adv.* —**per·cep·tiv′i·ty,** **per·cep′tive·ness,** *n.* —**Syn.** 1. discerning, insightful.

per·cep·tu·al (pər sep′choo əl), *adj.* of or through perception. —**per·cep′tu·al·ly,** *adv.*

perch[1] (pûrch), *n.* **1.** a horizontal pole or rod serving as a roost for birds. **2.** any elevated position or resting place. —*v.i., v.t.* **3.** to rest or set on or as on a perch. —**perch′er,** *n.*

perch[2] (pûrch), *n., pl.* **perch, perch·es. 1.** any spiny-finned, freshwater food fish. **2.** any of various other related fishes.

per·chance (pər chans′, -chäns′), *adv.* **1.** *Literary.* maybe or possibly. **2.** *Archaic.* by chance.

per·cip·i·ent (pər sip′ē ənt), *adj.* perceiving keenly. —**per·cip′i·ence,** *n.*

per·co·late (pûr′kə lāt′), **-lat·ed, -lat·ing.** —*v.t.* **1.** to cause (a liquid) to pass through a porous body. **2.** to brew (coffee) in a percolator. —*v.i.* **3.** to pass through a porous substance. —**per′co·la′tion,** *n.*

per·co·la·tor (pûr′kə lā′tər), *n.* a coffeepot in which boiling water is forced up a hollow stem and filters through ground coffee.

per con·tra (pər kon′trə), on the contrary.

per·cus·sion (pər kush′ən), *n.* **1.** the striking of one body against another with some sharpness. **2.** percussion instruments collectively. **3.** a sharp blow for detonating a small metallic cap (**percus′sion cap′**) containing explosive powder in a firearm. —**per·cus′sion·al,** *adj.*

percus′sion in′strument, a musical instrument in which tones are produced when struck, as a drum or cymbal.

per·cus·sion·ist (pər kush′ə nist), *n.* a musician who plays percussion instruments.

per di·em (pər dē′əm, dī′əm), **1.** by the day. **2.** a daily allowance for living expenses while traveling on business.

per·di·tion (pər dish′ən), *n.* **1.** a state of final spiritual ruin. **2.** hell (def. 1).

per·dur·a·ble (pər dōŏr′ə bəl, -dyōŏr′-), *adj.* extremely durable. —**per·dur′a·bil′i·ty,** *n.*

per·e·gri·na·tion (per′ə grə nā′shən), *n. Literary.* a long journey or wandering.

per·emp·to·ry (pə remp′tə rē, per′emp-tōr′ē, -tôr′ē), *adj.* **1.** leaving no opportunity for denial or refusal. **2.** imperious or dictatorial. **3.** *Law.* absolute or final. —**per·emp′to·ri·ly,** *adv.* —**per·emp′to·ri·ness,** *n.*

per·en·ni·al (pə ren′ē əl), *adj.* **1.** lasting for an indefinitely long time. **2.** regularly continuing or recurrent. **3.** living more than two years, as plants. **4.** continuing throughout the year, as a stream. —*n.* **5.** a perennial plant. —**per·en′ni·al·ly,** *adv.*

perf., 1. perfect. **2.** perforated.

per·fect (*adj., n.* pûr′fikt; *v.* pər fekt′, pûr′fikt), *adj.* **1.** having all the desired qualities. **2.** having no flaws or shortcomings. **3.** correct in every detail. **4.** thorough or utter: *perfect strangers.* **5.** *Gram.* designating a verb tense that refers to a completed action or state. —*n.* **6.** *Gram.* **a.** the perfect tense. **b.** a form in the perfect. —*v.t.* **7.** to bring to perfection. —**per·fect′er,** *n.* —**per′fect·ly,** *adv.* —**per′fect·ness,** *n.*

per·fect·i·ble (pər fek′tə bəl), *adj.* capable of becoming or of being made perfect. —**per·fect′i·bil′i·ty,** *n.*

per·fec·tion (pər fek′shən), *n.* **1.** the state or quality of being perfect. **2.** the highest degree of excellence, as in some art. **3.** the act or fact of perfecting.

per·fec·tion·ism (pər fek′shə niz′əm), *n.* a personal standard or attitude that demands perfection. —**per·fec′tion·ist,** *n.*

per·fec·to (pər fek′tō), *n., pl.* **-tos.** a rather thick, medium-sized cigar tapering toward both ends.

per·fi·dy (pûr′fi dē), *n., pl.* **-dies.** deliberate breach of faith or trust. —**per·fid·i·ous** (pər fid′ē əs), *adj.* —**per·fid′i·ous·ly,** *adv.*

per·fo·rate (pûr′fə rāt′), *v.t., v.i.,* **-rat·ed, -rat·ing. 1.** to make a hole or holes through, as by boring or punching. **2.** to bore or punch (something) with a row of small holes to facilitate separation. —**per′fo·ra′tion,** *n.* —**per′fo·ra′tor,** *n.*

per·force (pər fōrs′, -fôrs′), *adv. Literary.* by or of necessity.

per·form (pər fôrm′), *v.t.* **1.** to do (a job or task) in the proper or established manner. **2.** to fulfill or discharge (a duty, etc.). **3.** to present (a play, musical work, etc.) before an audience. —*v.i.* **4.** to fulfill an undertaking. **5.** to give a performance. —**per·form′er,** *n.*

per·for·mance (pər fôr′məns), *n.* **1.** a musical, dramatic, or other entertainment presented esp. before an audience. **2.** the act of performing. **3.** the execution of work, feats, etc. **4.** a particular action, deed, etc.

perform′ing arts′, arts or skills which require public performance, as acting, dancing, etc.

per·fume (*n.* pûr′fyōōm, pər fyōōm′; *v.* pər fyōōm′), *n., v.,* **-fumed, -fum·ing.** —*n.* **1.** an aromatic substance, usually liquid, esp. one produced from essential oils of plants. **2.** any agreeable odor. —*v.t.* **3.** to fill with perfume or an agreeable odor.

per·fum·er·y (pər fyōō′mə rē), *n., pl.* **-er·ies. 1.** perfumes collectively. **2.** a place where perfumes are made or sold.

per·func·to·ry (pər fuŋk′tə rē), *adj.*
1. performed merely as an uninteresting routine. **2.** without interest or enthusiasm. —**per·func′to·ri·ly,** *adv.* —**per·func′to·ri·ness,** *n.* —**Syn.** indifferent, mechanical.

per·go·la (pûr′gə lə), *n.* an arbor formed of a trellis supported on posts.

perh., perhaps.

per·haps (pər haps′), *adv.* possibly but not sure.

peri-, a prefix meaning: **a.** about or around: *peripheral.* **b.** near: *perigee.*

Per·i·cles (per′ə klēz′), *n.* c495—429 B.C., Athenian statesman.

per·i·cyn·thi·on (per′i sin′(thē ən), *n.* perilune.

per·i·gee (per′i jē′), *n.* the point in the orbit of the moon or an artificial satellite at which it is nearest to the earth.

per·i·he·li·on (per′ə hē′lē ən, -hēl′yən), *n., pl.* **-he·li·a** (-hē′lē ə, -hēl′yə). the point in the orbit of a planet or comet at which it is nearest to the sun. —**per′i·he′li·al,** *adj.*

per·il (per′əl), *n., v.,* **-iled, -il·ing** or **-illed, -il·ling.** —*n.* **1.** a state of grave, imminent danger. **2.** something causing this. —*v.t.* **3.** to expose to peril. —**per′il·ous,** *adj.* —**per′il·ous·ly,** *adv.*

per·i·lune (per′i lōōn′), *n.* the point in a lunar orbit that is nearest to the moon.

pe·rim·e·ter (pə rim′i tər), *n.* **1.** the outer boundary of a closed plane figure. **2.** the length of this.

per·i·ne·um (per′ə nē′əm), *n., pl.* **-ne·a** (-nē′ə). the area in front of the anus extending to the genitals. —**per′i·ne′al,** *adj.*

pe·ri·od (pēr′ē əd), *n.* **1.** a rather large interval of time, as in history, marked by particular qualities or events. **2.** any specified division or portion of time. **3.** any of the parts of equal length into which a game or school day is divided. **4.** the basic unit of geological time comprising several epochs and included with other periods in an era. **5.** the time of menstruation. **6.** the time during which anything runs its course. **7.** a mark of punctuation (.) used to mark the end of a declarative sentence or indicate an abbreviation. —*adj.* **8.** of or noting a historical period: *period costumes.*

pe·ri·od·ic (pēr′ē od′ik), *adj.* **1.** occurring at regular intervals. **2.** repeated at irregular intervals. —**pe′ri·od′i·cal·ly,** *adv.* —**pe′ri·o·dic′i·ty** (-ə dis′i tē), *n.*

pe·ri·od·i·cal (pēr′ē od′i kəl), *n.* **1.** a magazine or other publication that is issued at regular intervals. —*adj.*

2. published at regular intervals. **3.** of such publications. **4.** periodic. —**pe′ri·od′i·cal·ly,** *adv.*

pe·ri·od′ic ta′ble, a chart in which the chemical elements, arranged according to their atomic numbers, are shown in related groups.

per·i·o·don·tal (per′ē ə don′t²l), *adj.* of or concerned with the tissue and gum surrounding and supporting the teeth.

per·i·pa·tet·ic (per′ə pə tet′ik), *adj. Chiefly Literary.* busily walking or traveling about, esp. on assignment: *a peripatetic secretary of state.*

pe·riph·er·al (pə rif′ər əl), *adj.* **1.** of or situated in the periphery. **2.** comparatively superficial or unessential. —*n.* **3.** *Computer Technol.* a device or unit operating outside of a computer but connected to it, as a tape unit. —**pe·riph′er·al·ly,** *adv.*

pe·riph·er·y (pə rif′ə rē), *n., pl.* **-er·ies. 1.** the external boundary of any surface or area. **2.** the external surface of a body. **3.** a surrounding region or area.

pe·riph·ra·sis (pə rif′rə sis), *n., pl.* **-ses** (-sēz′). an unnecessarily long and roundabout style of expression.

pe·rique (pə rēk′), *n.* a rich-flavored tobacco produced in Louisiana.

per·i·scope (per′i skōp′), *n.* an optical instrument for viewing objects that are in an otherwise obstructed field of vision.

per·ish (per′ish), *v.i.* **1.** to die through violence or privation. **2.** to decay or be destroyed.

per·ish·a·ble (per′i shə bəl), *adj.* **1.** subject to decay or destruction. something —*n.* **2.** Usually, **perishables.** something perishable, esp. food. —**per′ish·a·ble·ness,** *n.* —**per′ish·a·bly,** *adv.*

per·i·stal·sis (per′i stôl′sis, -stal′-), *n., pl.* **-ses** (-sēz). the progressive wave of contraction and relaxation of the alimentary canal, by which the contents are forced onward. —**per′i·stal′tic,** *adj.*

per·i·style (per′i stīl′), *n.* a colonnade surrounding a building or an open space. —**per′i·sty′lar,** *adj.*

per·i·to·ne·um (per′i t²nē′əm), *n., pl.* **-to·ne·ums, -to·ne·a** (-t²nē′ə). the serous membrane lining the abdominal cavity. —**per′i·to·ne′al,** *adj.*

per·i·to·ni·tis (per′i t²nī′tis), *n.* inflammation of the peritoneum. —**per·i·to·nit′ic** (per′i t²nit′ik), **per′i·to·nit′al,** *adj.*

per·i·wig (per′i wig′), *n.* peruke.

per·i·win·kle¹ (per′i wiŋ′kəl), *n.* a small sea snail, used for food in Europe.

per·i·win·kle² (per′i wiŋ′kəl), *n.* a trailing, evergreen plant having blue, white, or purple flowers.

per·jure (pûr′jər), v.t., **-jured, -jur·ing.** to make (oneself) guilty of perjury. —**per′jur·er,** n.

per·ju·ry (pûr′jə rē), n., pl. **-ries.** the willful giving of false testimony under oath.

perk[1] (pûrk), v.i. **1.** to become lively or vigorous: She began to perk up during dinner. —v.t. **2.** to raise smartly or briskly: to perk one's head up. **3.** to dress smartly. —**perk′y,** adj. —**perk′i·ness,** n.

perk[2] (pûrk), v.t., v.i. Informal. to percolate.

perks (pûrks), n.pl. Informal. perquisites, esp. those enjoyed by corporate executives.

perm (pûrm), n. Brit. Informal. See **permanent wave.**

perm., permanent.

per·ma·frost (pûr′mə frôst′, -frost′), n. perennially frozen subsoil in arctic regions. [perma(nent) + frost]

per·ma·nent (pûr′mə nənt), adj. **1.** lasting forever or for an indefinitely long time. —n. **2.** See **permanent wave.** —**per′ma·nence, per′ma·nen·cy,** n. —**per′ma·nent·ly,** adv.

per′manent press′, (of a fabric) wrinkle-resistant and requiring little or no ironing after washing.

per′manent wave′, a wave that is set into the hair by the application of a special chemical preparation and that remains for a number of months.

per·me·a·ble (pûr′mē ə bəl), adj. capable of being permeated. —**per′me·a·bil′i·ty,** n. —**per′me·a·bly,** adv.

per·me·ate (pûr′mē āt′), v.t., v.i., **-at·ed, -at·ing. 1.** to pass or penetrate through the pores or spaces (of). **2.** to spread throughout. —**per′me·a′tion,** n.

Per·mi·an (pûr′mē ən), adj. **1.** noting a period of the Paleozoic era occurring from 220,000,000 to 270,000,000 years ago and characterized by the existence of many reptiles. —n. **2.** the Permian period.

per·mis·si·ble (pər mis′ə bəl), adj. that is or can be permitted. —**per·mis′si·bly,** adv.

per·mis·sion (pər mish′ən), n. **1.** formal consent. **2.** authorization to do something.

per·mis·sive (pər mis′iv), adj. **1.** excessively lenient or tolerant. **2.** granting permission. —**per·mis′sive·ly,** adv. —**per·mis′sive·ness,** n.

per·mit (v. pər mit′; n. pûr′mit, pər mit′), v., **-mit·ted, -mit·ting.** —v.t. **1.** to allow formally to do something. **2.** to allow formally to be done or occur. —v.i. **3.** to afford opportunity or possibility. —n. **4.** a written order granting permission.

per·mu·ta·tion (pûr′myə tā′shən), n. **1.** Math. **a.** the act of changing the order of elements arranged in a particular order. **b.** an ordered arrangement of a set with a finite number of elements. **2.** Rare. alteration or transformation. —**per′mu·ta′tion·al,** adj. —**per′mu·ta′tion·ist,** n.

per·ni·cious (pər nish′əs), adj. **1.** causing insidious harm or ruin. **2.** deadly or fatal. —**per·ni′cious·ly,** adv. —**per·ni′cious·ness,** n.

per·o·ra·tion (per′ə rā′shən), n. Rhet. the concluding part of a speech or discourse.

per·ox·ide (pə rok′sīd), n. **1.** a compound in which two oxygen atoms are bonded to each other. **2.** See **hydrogen peroxide.**

perp., perpendicular.

per·pen·dic·u·lar (pûr′pən dik′yə lər), adj. **1.** at exactly a right angle to a flat, level surface. **2.** Geom. meeting a given line or surface at right angles. —n. **3.** a perpendicular line or plane. —**per′pen·dic′u·lar′i·ty,** n. —**per′pen·dic′u·lar·ly,** adv.

per·pe·trate (pûr′pi trāt′), v.t., **-trat·ed, -trat·ing. 1.** to commit (a crime, etc.). **2.** to carry out (a deception, etc.). —**per′pe·tra′tion,** n. —**per′pe·tra′tor,** n.

per·pet·u·al (pər pech′ōō əl), adj. **1.** continuing or enduring forever. **2.** lasting an indefinitely long time. **3.** continuing or continued without interruption. —**per·pet′u·al·ly,** adv. —**per·pet′u·al·ness,** n.

per·pet·u·ate (pər pech′ōō āt′), v.t., **-at·ed, -at·ing. 1.** to make perpetual. **2.** to preserve from extinction or oblivion. —**per·pet′u·a′tion,** n.

per·pe·tu·i·ty (pûr′pi tōō′i tē, -tyōō′-), n., pl. **-ties. 1.** the state or character of being perpetual. **2.** endless duration or existence.

per·plex (pər pleks′), v.t. to trouble with doubt or indecision. —**per·plexed′,** adj. —**per·plex′ed·ly** (-plek′sid lē), adv. —**per·plex′ing,** adj. —**per·plex′i·ty,** n. —Syn. bewilder, confuse, puzzle.

per·qui·site (pûr′kwi zit), n. a payment, benefit, or privilege received in addition to regular income or salary.

Pers., 1. Persia. **2.** Persian.

pers., 1. person. **2.** personal.

per se (pər sā′, sē′), by, of, or in itself.

per·se·cute (pûr′sə kyōōt′), v.t., **-cut·ed, -cut·ing. 1.** to pursue with harassing or oppressive treatment because of religion, race, or beliefs. **2.** to annoy or trouble persistently. —**per′se·cu′tion,** n. —**per′se·cu′tor,** n.

per·se·vere (pûr′sə vēr′), v.i., **-vered, -ver·ing.** to persist in anything undertaken in spite of difficulty or obstacles. —**per′se·ver′ance,** n.

Per·sia (pûr′zhə, -shə), *n.* **1.** former official name of Iran. **2.** an ancient empire located in W and SW Asia.

Per·sian (pûr′zhən, -shən), *adj.* **1.** of Persia, its people, or their language. **—n. 2.** a native or inhabitant of ancient Persia or modern Iran. **3.** the language of the Persians.

Per′sian cat′, a long-haired variety of the domestic cat.

Per′sian Gulf′, an arm of the Indian Ocean, between SW Iran and Arabia.

Per′sian lamb′, 1. the young lamb of the karakul sheep. **2.** the fur of this animal.

per·si·flage (pûr′sə fläzh′), *n.* light, bantering talk or writing.

per·sim·mon (pər sim′ən), *n.* **1.** a tree bearing red or orange, plumlike fruit. **2.** its fruit.

per·sist (pər sist′, -zist′), *v.i.* **1.** to continue steadfastly or often annoyingly, esp. in spite of opposition. **2.** to endure tenaciously. **3.** to be insistent, as in a statement. **—per·sist′ence, per·sist′en·cy,** *n.* **—per·sist′ent, per·sist′ent·ly,** *adv.* **—per·sist′er,** *n.*

per·snick·et·y (pər snik′i tē), *adj. Informal* exceedingly fastidious. **—per·snick′et·i·ness,** *n.*

per·son (pûr′sən), *n.* **1.** a human being. **2.** the individual personality of a human being. **3.** the body of a living human being. **4.** *Gram.* any of the three categories of pronouns or verb inflections that refer to the identity of the speaker, namely, first person, second person, and third person. **5. in person,** in one's own physical presence.

-person, a suffix meaning "a person in a particular function, role, etc.," adopted esp. to eliminate the use of *-man* as traditionally applied to a male: *chairperson.*

per·son·a·ble (pûr′sə nə bəl), *adj.* having a pleasing personal appearance or manner **—per′son·a′ble·ness,** *n.* **—per′son·a·bly,** *adv.*

per·son·age (pûr′sə nij), *n.* a person of distinction or importance.

per·son·al (pûr′sə nəl), *adj.* **1.** of or belonging to a particular person. **2.** referring or directed to a particular person, esp. in a disparaging sense: *personal remarks.* **3.** done or carried out in person: *a personal appearance.* **4.** of the body, clothing, or appearance: *personal cleanliness.* **5.** *Gram.* noting person. **6.** *Law.* of any property consisting of movable articles. **—n. 7.** a short paragraph in a newspaper concerning a particular person or private matters. **—per′son·al·ly,** *adv.*

per′sonal effects′, privately owned articles consisting chiefly of clothing, toilet items, etc.

per·son·al·i·ty (pûr′sə nal′i tē), *n., pl.* **-ties. 1.** the visible aspect of one's character as it impresses others. **2.** the sum total of the physical, mental, emotional, and social characteristics of an individual. **3.** pleasing qualities in a person. **4.** Often, **personalities,** an uncomplimentary remark to a particular person. **5.** a prominent person.

per·son·al·ize (pûr′sə nəlīz′), *v.t.,* **-ized, -iz·ing. 1.** to make personal. **2.** to have marked with one's initials or name.

per·son·al·ty (pûr′sə nəl tē), *n., pl.* **-ties.** *Law.* personal property.

per·so·na non gra·ta (pər sō′nə non grä′tə, grä′-, grat′ə), *pl.* **per·so·nae non gra·tae** (pər sō′nē non grä′tē, grä′-, grat′ē). *Latin.* an unwelcome or unacceptable person.

per·son·i·fy (pər son′ə fī′), *v.t.,* **-fied, -fy·ing. 1.** to represent (an idea or thing) as a person. **2.** to be an embodiment of. **—per·son′i·fi·ca′tion,** *n.*

per·son·nel (pûr′sə nel′), *n.* **1.** the body of persons employed in a service or by an organization. **2.** an organizational department charged with the administration and hiring of employees.

per·spec·tive (pər spek′tiv), *n.* **1.** the art of depicting or drawing objects so as to give the impression of distance and depth. **2.** the manner in which objects appear to the eye in respect to their relative positions and distance. **3.** a broad view of events or ideas in their true nature and relationships.

per·spi·ca·cious (pûr′spə kā′shəs), *adj.* having keen mental perception or understanding. **—per′spi·ca′cious·ly,** *adv.* **—per′spi·cac′i·ty** (-kas′i tē), **per′spi·ca′cious·ness,** *n.*

per·spic·u·ous (pər spik′yōō əs), *adj.* clear in expression or statement. **—per·spic′u·ous·ly,** *adv.* **—per·spi·cu·i·ty** (pûr′spə kyōō′i tē), **per·spic′u·ous·ness,** *n.*

per·spi·ra·tion (pûr′spə rā′shən), *n.* **1.** the act or process of perspiring. **2.** watery fluid excreted in perspiring.

per·spire (pər spīr′), *v.i., v.t.,* **-spired, -spir·ing.** to excrete (watery fluid) through the pores.

per·suade (pər swād′), *v.t.,* **-suad·ed, -suad·ing. 1.** to cause (a person) to do something by appealing to reason or understanding. **2.** to induce to believe. **—per·suad′a·ble,** *adj.* **—per·suad′er,** *n.* **—per·sua′sive** (-swā′siv). *adj.* **—per·sua′sive·ly,** *adv.* **—per·sua′sive·ness,** *n.* **—Syn. 1.** influence. **2.** convince.

per·sua·sion (pər swā′zhən), *n.* **1.** the act of persuading or state of being persuaded. **2.** the power to persuade. **3.** a deep conviction. **4.** a system of religious belief.

pert (pûrt), *adj.* **1.** bold or saucy in speech or behavior. **2.** jaunty and stylish. **3.** *Dial.* lively or sprightly. —**pert′ly,** *adv.* —**pert′ness,** *n.*

pert., pertaining.

per·tain (pər tān′), *v.i.* **1.** to have reference or relation. **2.** to belong or be connected as a part. **3.** to be appropriate or proper.

per·ti·na·cious (pûr′t⁰nā′shəs), *adj.* **1.** holding tenaciously to a purpose. **2.** extremely or stubbornly persistent. —**per′ti·nac′i·ty** (-nas′i tē), *n.*

per·ti·nent (pûr′t⁰nənt), *adj.* directly relating to the matter in hand. —**per′ti·nence, per′ti·nen·cy,** *n.* —**per′ti·nent·ly,** *adv.* —**Syn.** appropriate, relevant.

per·turb (pər tûrb′), *v.t.* to disturb or disquiet greatly in mind. —**per·tur·ba·tion** (pûr′tər bā′shən), *n.*

per·tus·sis (pər tus′is), *n.* See whooping cough.

Pe·ru (pə rōō′), *n.* a country in W South America. —**Pe·ru′vi·an,** *adj., n.*

pe·ruke (pə rōōk′), *n.* a man's wig of the 17th and 18th centuries.

pe·ruse (pə rōōz′), *v.t.,* **-rused, -rus·ing.** to read or examine, esp. with care. —**pe·rus′al,** *n.* —**pe·rus′er,** *n.*

per·vade (pər vād′), *v.t.,* **-vad·ed, -vad·ing.** to spread through every part of. —**per·va′sive** (-vā′siv), *adj.*

per·verse (pər vûrs′), *adj.* **1.** willfully determined not to do what is expected or desired. **2.** persistent or obstinate in what is wrong. **3.** turned away from what is right or good. —**per·verse′ly,** *adv.* —**per·verse′ness, per·ver′si·ty,** *n.*

per·ver·sion (pər vûr′zhən, -shən), *n.* **1.** the act of perverting or state of being perverted. **2.** a perverted form of something. **3.** any means of attaining sexual gratification that is traditionally regarded as abnormal.

per·vert (*v.* pər vûrt′; *n.* pûr′vərt), *v.t.* **1.** to lead astray morally. **2.** to turn to an improper use. **3.** to misinterpret deliberately. **4.** to bring to a less excellent state. —*n.* **5.** a person who practices sexual perversion. —**per·vert′ed,** *adj.*

pe·se·ta (pə sā′tə), *n.* the monetary unit of Spain.

pes·ky (pes′kē), *adj.,* **-ki·er, -ki·est.** *Informal.* annoyingly troublesome. —**pesk′i·ness,** *n.*

pe·so (pā′sō), *n., pl.* **-sos.** the monetary unit of various Spanish-American countries and the Philippines.

pes·si·mism (pes′ə miz′əm), *n.* **1.** the tendency to see only what is gloomy or futile in life. **2.** the belief that the world contains more evil than good. —**pes′si·mist,** *n.* —**pes·si·mis′tic,** *adj.* —**pes′si·mis′ti·cal·ly,** *adv.*

pest (pest), *n.* **1.** a troublesome person, animal, or thing. **2.** a destructive animal or plant. **3.** *Rare.* a pestilence or plague.

pes·ter (pes′tər), *v.t.* to harass with petty annoyances. —**pes′ter·er,** *n.*

pes·ti·cide (pes′ti sīd′), *n.* a chemical for killing pests, as insects or fungi. —**pes′ti·cid′al,** *adj.*

pes·tif·er·ous (pe stif′ər əs), *adj.* **1.** bringing or spreading disease. **2.** pernicious or evil. **3.** *Informal.* troublesome or annoying.

pes·ti·lence (pes′t⁰ləns), *n.* **1.** a deadly epidemic disease, esp. plague. **2.** something considered harmful or evil.

pes·ti·lent (pes′t⁰lənt), *adj.* **1.** producing or tending to produce pestilence. **2.** destructive to life. **3.** injurious to peace or morals. Also, **pest′ti·len′tial** (-len′shəl). —**pes′ti·len′tial·ly,** *adv.* —**pes′ti·lent·ly,** *adv.*

pes·tle (pes′əl, pes′t⁰l), *n.* a tool for pounding or grinding substances in a mortar.

pet[1] (pet), *n., adj., v.,* **pet·ted, pet·ting.** —*n.* **1.** any domesticated or tamed animal that is kept as a companion. **2.** a person or thing especially cherished or indulged: *teacher's pet.* —*adj.* **3.** kept or treated as a pet. **4.** cherished or favorite: *a pet theory.* **5.** showing affection: *a pet name.* —*v.t.* **6.** to treat as a pet. **7.** to fondle, caress, or stroke. —*v.i.* **8.** *Informal.* to make love by fondling and caressing.

pet[2] (pet), *n.* a fit of peevishness.

pet., petroleum.

Pet., Peter.

pet·al (pet′⁰l), *n.* one of the segments of the corolla of a flower. —**pet′aled, pet′alled,** *adj.*

pe·tard (pi tärd′), *n.* **1.** an explosive device formerly used to blow in a door or gate. **2. hoist by or with one's own petard,** caught in one's own trap.

pe·ter (pē′tər), *v.i. Informal.* to diminish gradually and then disappear.

Pe·ter (pē′tər), *n.* Saint, died A.D. 67?, one of the 12 apostles and the reputed author of two of the Epistles.

Peter I, (*"the Great"*) 1672–1725, czar of Russia 1682–1725.

pet·i·ole (pet′ē ōl′), *n.* the slender stalk by which a leaf is attached to a stem.

pe·tite (pə tēt′), *adj.* (of a woman) small in stature or figure.

pet·it four (pet′ē fōr′, fôr′), pl. **pet·its fours** (pet′ē fōrz′, fôrz′). a small tea cake, variously frosted and decorated.

pe·ti·tion (pə tish′ən), n. **1.** a formal request signed by a number of persons and addressed to a government or other authority. **2.** a respectful or humble request. —v.t. **3.** to request (something) by or as by petition. **4.** to address a petition to. —v.i. **5.** to address or present a petition. —**pe·ti′tion·er,** n.

pet′it ju′ry (pet′ē). See **petty jury.**

pet·nap·ping (pet′nap′ing), n. the stealing of pets, as dogs, esp. to sell them for money.

pet·rel (pe′trəl), n. a small seabird having long, pointed wings.

pet·ri·fy (pe′trə fī′), v.t., **-fied, -fy·ing. 1.** to convert into stone or a stony substance. **2.** to make rigid or inert. **3.** to paralyze with astonishment or horror. —**pet′ri·fac′tion** (-fak′shən), n.

petro-, a combining form meaning: **a.** rock or stone: *petrology.* **b.** petroleum: *petrochemical.* **c.** earned through huge export of crude oil: *petrodollars.* **d.** of or pertaining to the petroleum industry: *petroboom; petropolitics.*

pet·ro·chem·i·cal (pe′trō kem′i kəl), n. any chemical obtained from petroleum or natural gas. —**pet′ro·chem′is·try** (-strē), n.

pe·trog·ra·phy (pi trog′rə fē), n. the branch of petrology dealing with the description and classification of rocks. —**pe·trog′ra·pher,** n. —**pet·ro·graph·ic** (pe′trə graf′ik), **pet′ro·graph′i·cal,** adj.

pet·rol (pe′trəl), n. Brit. gasoline.

pet·ro·la·tum (pe′trə lā′təm), n. a semisolid, greaselike substance obtained from petroleum and used for lubrication and in ointments. Also called **pe·tro′leum jel′ly.**

pe·tro·le·um (pə trō′lē əm), n. a dark, oily, flammable, liquid form of bitumen or mixture of hydrocarbons occurring naturally and commonly obtained by drilling: used as fuel or separated by distillation into gasoline, kerosene, etc. —**pe·tro′le·ous,** adj.

pe·trol·o·gy (pi trol′ə jē), n. the science of the origin, structure, and classification of rocks. —**pet·ro·log·ic** (pe′trə loj′ik), **pet′ro·log′i·cal,** adj. —**pet′ro·log′i·cal·ly,** adv. —**pe·trol′o·gist,** n.

pet·ti·coat (pet′ē kōt′), n. **1.** an underskirt, often trimmed and ruffled. **2.** any skirtlike part or covering. —adj. **3.** of or controlled by women: *petticoat government.*

pet·ti·fog·ger (pet′ē fog′ər, -fôg′-), n. a petty, shifty and often dishonest lawyer. —**pet′ti·fog′,** v.i. —**pet′ti·fog′ger·y,** n.

pet·tish (pet′ish), adj. petulant and peevish. —**pet′tish·ly,** adv. —**pet′tish·ness,** n.

pet·ty (pet′ē), adj., **-ti·er, -ti·est. 1.** contemptibly insignificant. **2.** of secondary rank or merit. **3.** narrow in ideas or interests. **4.** mean or spiteful. —**pet′ti·ly,** adv. —**pet′ti·ness,** n. —Syn. **1.** paltry, trivial.

pet′ty cash′, a cash fund for paying for small purchases.

pet′ty ju′ry, a jury, usually of 12 persons, impaneled to hear a civil or criminal proceeding in court.

pet′ty of′ficer, an enlisted person in the navy holding a rank corresponding to that of a noncommissioned officer in the army.

pet′ty of′ficer first′ class′, a petty officer ranking just below a chief petty officer.

pet′ty of′ficer sec′ond class′, a petty officer ranking just below a petty officer first class.

pet′ty of′ficer third′ class′, a petty officer ranking just below a petty officer second class.

pet·u·lant (pech′ə lənt), adj. showing sudden, impatient irritation, esp. over some trifling annoyance. —**pet′u·lance,** n. —**pet′u·lant·ly,** adv.

pe·tu·ni·a (pə tōō′nē ə, -nyə, -tyōō′-), n. a garden plant having funnel-shaped flowers of various colors.

pew (pyōō), n. one of the fixed benches with backs in a church.

pe·wee (pē′wē), n. the phoebe.

pew·ter (pyōō′tər), n. **1.** a metal alloy in which tin is the chief constituent. **2.** articles made of this.

pe·yo·te (pā ō′tē), n. **1.** a hallucinogenic drug obtained from a spineless cactus. **2.** this cactus.

pf., (of stock) preferred. Also, **pfd.**

PFC, Mil. Private First Class. Also, **pfc**

PG, a designation for motion pictures some of whose material may not be suitable for preteenagers, with parental guidance suggested.

P.G., postgraduate.

pg., page.

pH, Chem. a symbol for measuring the acidity or alkalinity of liquid solutions.

pha·e·ton (fā′i t°n), n. **1.** an open four-wheeled carriage used in the 19th century. **2.** a former type of open automobile.

phage (fāj), n. bacteriophage.

pha·lanx (fā′langks, fal′angks), n., pl. **pha·lanx·es** or for 3, **pha·lang·es** (fə-lan′jēz). **1.** (in ancient Greece) a formation of heavily-armed infantry in close ranks and files. **2.** a closely massed body of persons, animals, or things. **3.** any of the bones of the fingers or toes.

phal·a·rope (fal′ə rōp′), *n.* a small, aquatic bird resembling the sandpiper.

phal·lic (fal′ik), *adj.* **1.** of or resembling a phallus. **2.** genital (def. 2b).

phal·lus (fal′əs), *n., pl.* **phal·li** (fal′ī), **phal·lus·es.** **1.** an image of the penis as a symbol of the generative power in nature. **2.** *Anat.* the penis.

phan·tasm (fan′taz əm), *n.* a creation of the imagination or fancy.

phan·tas·ma·go·ri·a (fan taz′mə gôr′ē ə, -gôr′-), *n.* a shifting series of phantasms or deceptive appearances, as in a dream.

phan·ta·sy (fan′tə sē, -zē), *n., pl.* **-sies.** fantasy.

phan·tom (fan′təm), *n.* **1.** an illusory appearance. **2.** any shadowy appearance, as a ghost. —*adj.* **3.** of, like, or of the nature of a phantom. —**phan′tom·like′,** *adj.*

Phar·aoh (fâr′ō, far′ō), *n.* a title of the ancient Egyptian kings.

Phar·i·see (far′ə sē′), *n.* **1.** a member of an ancient Jewish sect that followed religious laws strictly and word for word. **2.** (*l.c.*) a sanctimonious, self-righteous, or hypocritical person. —**phar′i·sa′ic** (-sā′ik), **phar′i·sa′i·cal,** *adj.* —**phar′i·sa′i·cal·ly,** *adv.*

pharm., **1.** pharmaceutical. **2.** pharmacist. **3.** pharmacy.

phar·ma·ceu·ti·cal (fär′mə soo̅′ti kəl), *adj.* **1.** of pharmacy or pharmacists. —*n.* **2.** a pharmaceutical preparation or product. Also, **phar′ma·ceu′tic.**

phar·ma·ceu·tics (fär′mə soo̅′tiks), *n.* pharmacy (def. 1).

phar·ma·cist (fär′mə sist), *n.* a person engaged in pharmacy.

phar·ma·col·o·gy (fär′mə kol′ə jē), *n.* the science dealing with the preparation, uses, and esp. the effects, of drugs. —**phar′ma·co·log′i·cal** (-kə loj′i kəl), **phar′ma·co·log′ic,** *adj.* —**phar′ma·col′o·gist,** *n.*

phar·ma·co·poe·ia (fär′mə kə pē′ə), *n.* **1.** a book containing a list of drugs, their formulas, and other related information. **2.** *Obs.* a stock of drugs. Also, **phar′ma·co·pe′ia.**

phar·ma·cy (fär′mə sē), *n., pl.* **-cies.** **1.** the art and science of preparing and dispensing drugs. **2.** a drugstore.

phar·yn·gi·tis (far′in jī′tis), *n.* inflammation of the mucous membrane of the pharynx.

phar·ynx (far′ingks), *n., pl.* **phar·ynx·es, phar·yn·ges** (fə rin′jēz). the cavity that connects the mouth and nasal passages with the esophagus. —**pha·ryn·ge·al** (fə rin′jē əl), *adj.*

phase (fāz), *n., v.,* **phased, phas·ing.** —*n.* **1.** any of the various views or

aspects of a subject. **2.** a stage in a process of change or development. **3.** one of the recurring appearances or states of the moon in respect to the form, or the absence, of its illuminated disk. —*v.t.* **4. phase in,** to put into use by gradual stages. **5. phase out,** to put out of use by gradual stages. —**pha′sic, pha′se·al,** *adj.*

phase-in (fāz′in′), *n.* the act or an instance of phasing in.

phase-out (fāz′out′), *n.* the act or an instance of phasing out.

Ph.D., Doctor of Philosophy. [< L *Philosophiae Doctor*]

pheas·ant (fez′ənt), *n.* a game bird having a long tail and brilliantly colored feathers.

phe·nac·e·tin (fə nas′i tin), *n.* a crystalline compound used to reduce fever or pain.

phe·no·bar·bi·tal (fē′nō bär′bi tal′, -tôl′, -nə-), *n.* a white soluble powder used as a sedative and a hypnotic.

phe·nol (fē′nōl, -nol), *n.* a white, poisonous mass obtained from coal tar, used chiefly as a disinfectant, as an antiseptic, and in synthetic resins. —**phe·no·lic** (fi nō′lik, -nô′, -nol′ik), *adj.*

phenol′ic res′in, a resin made by condensation of phenol with an aldehyde, used chiefly in the manufacture of paints and plastics, and as adhesives.

phe·nom·e·non (fi nom′ə non′), *n., pl.* **-na** (-nə) for 1, **-nons** for 2, 3. **1.** a fact, occurrence, or circumstance observed or observable. **2.** something that impresses the observer as extraordinary. **3.** a person having some exceptional ability or talent. —**phe·nom′e·nal,** *adj.*

phe·no·type (fē′nə tīp′), *n. Genetics.* **1.** the observable constitution of an organism. **2.** the appearance of an organism resulting from the interaction of the genotype and the environment. —**phe′no·typ′ic** (-tip′ik), *adj.*

pher·o·mone (fer′ə mōn′), *n.* a hormonal substance secreted by an individual and stimulating a behavioral response from an individual of the same species. —**pher′o·mo′nal** (-mō′nəl), *adj.*

phi (fī, fē), *n.* the 21st letter of the Greek alphabet (Φ, φ).

phi·al (fī′əl), *n.* vial.

Phi Be·ta Kap·pa (fī′ bā′tə kap′ə, bē′tə), a national honor society composed of U.S. college students and graduates of high academic distinction.

phil., **1.** philosophical. **2.** philosophy.

Phil·a·del·phi·a (fil′ə del′fē ə), *n.* a city in SE Pennsylvania. —**Phil′a·del′phi·an,** *adj., n.*

Phil·a·del·phia law·yer, *Often Disparaging.* a lawyer skilled in matters involving fine points and technicalities.

phi·lan·der (fi lan′dər), *v.i.* (of a man) to make love without serious intentions. **—phi·lan′der·er,** *n.*

phil·an·throp·ic (fil′ən throp′ik), *adj.* of, for, or engaged in philanthropy.

phi·lan·thro·py (ti lan′thrə pē), *n., pl.* **-pies.** **1.** concern for human beings as expressed by donation of money, property, or work to the needy or to institutions advancing human welfare. **2.** a philanthropic act or gift. **3.** a philanthropic organization. **—phi·lan′thro·pist,** *n.*

phi·lat·e·ly (fi lat′ᵊlē), *n.* the collection and study of postage stamps, postmarks, and related items. **—phil·a·tel·ic** (fil′ə tel′ik), *adj.* **—phil·at′e·list,** *n.*

-phile, a combining form meaning "loving," "friendly," "lover" or "friend": *Anglophile; bibliophile.* Also, **-phil.**

phil·har·mon·ic (fil′här mon′ik, fil′ər-), *adj.* **1.** fond of or devoted to serious music. **2.** of, noting, or presented by a symphony orchestra. **—** *n.* **3.** a philharmonic orchestra, society, or concert.

phi·lip·pic (fi lip′ik), *n. Literary.* a bitter verbal denunciation.

Phil·ip·pines (fil′ə pēnz′, fil′ə pēnz′), *n.* a country comprising 7083 islands (**Phil′ippine Is′lands**) in the Pacific, SE of China. **—Phil′ip·pine,** *adj.*

Phil·is·tine (fil′i stēn′, stīn′, fi lis′tin, -tēn), *n.* **1.** a member of a people inhabiting SW Palestine in Biblical times. **2.** (*l.c.*) a person lacking in or smugly indifferent to culture, aesthetic refinement, etc. **—***adj.* **3.** (*often l.c.*) lacking in or hostile to culture. **4.** of the ancient Philistines.

phil·o·den·dron (fil′ə den′dron), *n.* a tropical American climbing plant.

philol., **1.** philological. **2.** philology.

phi·lol·o·gy (fi lol′ə jē), *n.* **1.** the study of written texts, esp. of literary works, to establish their authenticity. **2.** *Chiefly Brit. Obsolesc.* linguistics. **—phil·o·log·i·cal** (fil′ə loj′i kəl), *adj.* **—phi·lol′o·gist,** *n.*

philos., **1.** philosopher. **2.** philosophy.

phi·los·o·pher (fi los′ə fər), *n.* **1.** a student of or expert in philosophy. **2.** a person who regulates his or her life by a particular system of philosophy. **3.** a person who is rational and calm under trying circumstances.

phi·los·o·phize (fi los′ə fīz′), *v.i.,* **-phized, -phiz·ing.** **1.** to think or reason as a philosopher. **2.** to speculate in a superficial or imprecise manner.

phi·los·o·phy (fi los′ə fē), *n., pl.* **-phies.** **1.** the study of the truths and principles of being, knowledge, or conduct. **2.** a system of doctrine of a particular philosopher. **3.** the study of the basic concepts of a particular branch of knowledge. **4.** a system of principles for guidance in practical affairs. **5.** a calm, patient attitude toward life. **6.** the humanities and sciences, exclusive of law, theology, and medicine: *doctor of philosophy.* **—phil·o·soph·i·cal** (fil′ə sof′i kəl), **phil′o·soph′ic,** *adj.* **—phil′o·soph′i·cal·ly,** *adv.*

phil·ter (fil′tər), *n.* a magic potion, esp. one supposed to induce a person to fall in love. Also, *esp. Brit.,* **phil′tre.**

phle·bi·tis (flə bī′tis), *n.* inflammation of a vein.

phle·bot·o·my (flə bot′ə mē), *n., pl.* **-mies.** the practice of opening a vein for letting blood as a remedial measure.

phlegm (flem), *n.* **1.** thick mucus secreted in the nose and throat, as during a cold. **2.** *Old Physiol.* a humor regarded as causing sluggishness or apathy.

phleg·mat·ic (fleg mat′ik), *adj.* having a sluggish or apathetic disposition. Also, **phleg·mat′i·cal.** **—phleg·mat′i·cal·ly,** *adv.*

phlo·em (flō′em), *n.* the complex vascular tissue through which dissolved food passes to other parts of a plant.

phlox (floks), *n.* a North American garden plant having clusters of small white or pink flowers.

Phnom Penh (nom′ pen′, pə nôm′ pen′), the capital of Cambodia.

-phobe, a suffix meaning "a person who hates or fears": *Anglophobe.*

pho·bi·a (fō′bē ə), *n.* an obsessive or irrational fear or anxiety of some object or situation. **—pho′bic,** *adj.*

-phobia, a combining form meaning "fear" or "dread": *claustrophobia.*

phoe·be (fē′bē), *n.* an American flycatcher having a small crest on its head.

Phoe·ni·cia (fi nish′ə, -nē′shə), *n.* an ancient kingdom on the Ē Mediterranean. **—Phoe·ni′cian,** *n., adj.*

phoe·nix (fē′niks), *n.* a mythical bird fabled to live 500 years, to burn itself to death, and to rise from its ashes.

Phoe·nix (fē′niks), *n.* the capital of Arizona.

phone (fōn), *n., v.t., v.i.,* **phoned, phon·ing.** *Informal.* telephone.

-phone, a combining form meaning "a device producing or transmitting sound": *megaphone; telephone.*

pho·neme (fō′nēm), *n.* any of a small set of basic units of sound, different for each language, by which utterances are represented. **—pho·ne·mic** (fə nē′mik, fō-), *adj.* **—pho·ne′mi·cal·ly,** *adv.*

phonet., phonetics. Also, **phon.**

pho·net·ics (fə net′iks, fō-) *n.* the study of speech sounds and their production, classification, and transcription. —**pho·net′ic,** *adj.* —**pho·ne·ti·cian** (fō′ni tish′ən), *n.*

phon·ics (fon′iks, fō′niks), *n.* a method of teaching reading, pronunciation, and spelling by a system of simple phonetic symbols and rules. —**phon′ic,** *adj.* —**phon′i·cal·ly,** *adv.*

pho·no (fō′nō), *n., pl.* -**nos.** *Informal.* phonograph.

pho·no·graph (fō′nə graf′, -gräf′), *n.* any machine that reproduces sound from records. —**pho′no·graph′ic,** *adj.* —**pho′no·graph′i·cal·ly,** *adv.*

pho·nol·o·gy (fō nol′ə jē, fə-), *n.* the science of speech sounds and their changes. —**pho·no·log·i·cal** (fōn′ə-loj′i kəl), *adj.* —**pho·nol′o·gist,** *n.*

pho·ny (fō′nē), *adj.,* -**ni·er,** -**ni·est,** *n., pl.* -**nies.** *Informal.* —*adj.* **1.** a. not genuine or real. **b.** deliberately misleading or deceptive. —*n.* **2.** something that is phony. **3.** a phony and usually insincere person. Also, **pho′ney.** —**pho′ni·ness,** *n.* —**Syn. 1.** counterfeit, fake, spurious.

phoo·ey (foo′ē), *interj. Informal.* (an exclamation indicating rejection, contempt, or disgust.)

phos·phate (fos′fāt), *n.* **1.** a salt or ester of phosphoric acid, containing phosphorus. **2.** a fertilizing material containing this. **3.** a carbonated drink of water and fruit syrup. —**phos·phat′ic** (-fat′ik), *adj.*

phos·phor (fos′fər), *n.* a substance that exhibits luminescence when struck by radiation.

phos·pho·res·cence (fos′fə res′əns), *n.* **1.** the property of being luminous without perceptible heat, esp. after exposure to light or other radiation. **2.** a luminous appearance resulting from this. —**phos′pho·res′cent,** *adj.* —**phos′pho·res′cent·ly,** *adv.*

phos·phor′ic ac′id (fos fôr′ik, -for′-), a colorless liquid used in soft drinks, fertilizers, etc.

phos·pho·rus (fos′fər əs), *n. Chem.* a solid, nonmetallic element that glows in the dark on exposure to air and whose compounds are used in matches, fertilizers, etc. *Symbol:* P; *at. wt.:* 30.974; *at. no.:* 15. —**phos·pho′rous** (-fôr′əs, -fôr′-), *adj.*

pho·to (fō′tō), *n., pl.* -**tos.** *Informal.* photograph.

photo-, a combining form meaning: **a.** light: *photograph.* **b.** photographic or photograph: *photoengraving.*

pho·to·cell (fō′tō sel′), *n.* See **photoelectric cell.**

pho·to·com·pose (fō′tō kəm pōz′), *v.t.,* -**posed,** -**pos·ing.** to set (type) on a machine that makes photographic negatives of type which are then converted to metal plates for printing. —**pho′to·com′po·si′tion** (-kom′-pi zish′ən), *n.*

pho·to·cop·y (fō′tə kop′ē), *n., pl.* -**cop·ies,** *v.,* -**cop·ied,** -**cop·y·ing.** —*n.* **1.** a photographic reproduction. —*v.t.* **2.** to make a photocopy of.

pho·to·e·lec·tric (fō′tō i lek′trik), *adj.* pertaining to the electronic or other electric effects produced by light. —**pho′to·e·lec′tri·cal·ly,** *adv.*

pho′toelec′tric cell′, an electronic device in which electrons are emitted under illumination, used esp. in an automatic control system where any interruption of a ray of light by a solid object can activate a switch, as for opening a door.

pho·to·en·grave (fō′tō en grāv′), *v.t.,* -**graved,** -**grav·ing.** to make a photoengraving of. —**pho′to·en·grav′er,** *n.*

pho·to·en·grav·ing (fō′tō en grā′ving), *n.* **1.** a process of photographic reproduction by which a relief printing surface is obtained for letterpress printing. **2.** a plate so produced. **3.** a print made from it.

pho′to fin′ish, a finish of a race so close that the winner must be determined by reference to a photograph of the finish.

pho′to·flash lamp′ (fō′tə flash′), flashbulb.

pho·tog (fə tog′), *n. Informal.* a photographer.

photog., **1.** photographer. **2.** photographic. **3.** photography.

pho·to·gen·ic (fō′tə jen′ik), *adj.* being an attractive subject for photography or looking good in a photograph. —**pho′to·gen′i·cal·ly,** *adv.*

pho·to·graph (fō′tə graf′, -gräf′), *n.* **1.** a picture produced by photography. —*v.t.* **2.** to take a photograph of. —*v.i.* **3.** to be photographed in some specified way. —**pho·tog·ra·pher** (fə-tog′rə fər), *n.*

pho·tog·ra·phy (fə tog′rə fē), *n.* **1.** the process or art of producing images of objects by the action of light on sensitized surfaces, esp. a film, in a camera. **2.** cinematography: *director of photography.* —**pho·to·graph·ic** (fō′tə graf′ik), *adj.* —**pho′to·graph′i·cal·ly,** *adv.*

pho·to·jour·nal·ism (fō′tō jûr′n°liz′-əm), *n.* journalism in which photography dominates written copy, as in certain magazines. —**pho′to·jour′nal·ist,** *n.*

pho·to·me·chan·i·cal (fō′tō mə kan′i-kəl), *adj.* noting any of various processes for printing from plates prepared by the aid of photography.

pho·tom·e·ter (fō tom′i tər), *n.* an instrument that measures luminous intensity or brightness. —**pho·to·met·ric** (fō′tə me′trik), *adj.* —**pho·tom′e·try** (-trē), *n.*

pho·to·mi·cro·graph (fō′tə mī′krə graf′, -gräf′), *n.* a photograph taken through a microscope. —**pho′to·mi′cro·graph′ic** (-graf′ik), *adj.* —**pho′to·mi·crog′ra·phy** (-mī krog′rə fē), *n.*

pho·to·mur·al (fō′tə myŏŏr′əl), *n.* a wall decoration consisting of a very large photograph.

pho·ton (fō′ton), *n.* a quantum of electromagnetic radiation.

pho·to·play (fō′tə plā′), *n. Obsolesc.* a motion-picture drama.

pho·to·sen·si·tive (fō′tə sen′si tiv), *adj.* sensitive to light or similar radiation.

pho·to·sen·si·tize (fō′tə sen′si tīz′), *v.t.*, -**tized,** -**tiz·ing.** to make photosensitive. —**pho′to·sen′si·ti·za′tion,** *n.*

pho·to·sphere (fō′tə sfēr′), *n.* **1.** a sphere of light or radiance. **2.** the luminous visible surface of the sun. —**pho′to·spher′ic** (-ik), *adj.*

Pho·to·stat (fō′tə stat′), *n.* **1.** *Trademark.* a type of photocopying machine using sensitized paper. **2.** (*often l.c.*) a copy made by this. —*v.t., v.i.* **3.** (*l.c.*) to copy by this. —**pho′to·stat′ic,** *adj.*

pho·to·syn·the·sis (fō′tə sin′thi sis), *n.* the process by which plants convert water and carbon dioxide into carbohydrates, using sunlight as the source of energy and with the aid of chlorophyll. —**pho′to·syn′the·size′** (-sīz′), *v.t., v.i.* —**pho′to·syn·thet′ic** (-thet′ik), *adj.* —**pho′to·syn·thet′i·cal·ly,** *adv.*

pho·to·vol·ta·ic (fō′tō vol tā′ik), *adj.* providing a source of electric current under the influence of light or similar radiation.

phr., phrase.

phrase (frāz), *n., v.,* **phrased, phrasing.** —*n.* **1.** *Gram.* a sequence of two or more grammatically related words that does not contain a subject and predicate. **2.** a brief expression or remark. **3.** *Music.* a division of a composition, often two to four measures in length. —*v.t.* **4.** to express in words. —**phras′al** (frā′zəl), *adj.*

phra·se·ol·o·gy (frā′zē ol′ə jē), *n.* choice and arrangement of words.

phre·net·ic (fri net′ik), *adj.* frenetic.

phren·ic (fren′ik), *adj.* **1.** of or pertaining to the diaphragm. **2.** relating to the mind or mental activity.

phre·nol·o·gy (fri nol′ə jē, fre-), *n.* a study based on the outmoded idea that a person's mental faculties are indicated by the shape of his or her skull. —**phren′o·log′i·cal,** *adj.* —**phre·nol′o·gist,** *n.*

PHS, Public Health Service.

phy·lac·ter·y (fə lak′tə rē), *n., pl.* -**ter·ies.** either of two small leather cubes containing Biblical verses, worn by orthodox Jewish men during weekday morning prayers, one

strapped to the left arm, the other to the forehead.

phy·log·e·ny (fī loj′ə nē), *n.* the evolution of a kind or type of animal or plant.

phy·lum (fī′ləm), *n., pl.* -**la** (-lə). **1.** a major division of the animal kingdom consisting of one or more related classes. **2.** a category consisting of language stocks considered likely to be related by common origin.

phys., **1.** physical. **2.** physician. **3.** physicist. **4.** physics.

phys·ic (fiz′ik), *n., v.,* -**icked,** -**ick·ing.** *Archaic.* —*n.* **1.** a medicine that purges. —*v.t.* **2.** to treat with a physic or medicine.

phys·i·cal (fiz′i kəl), *adj.* **1.** of or pertaining to the body. **2.** of or pertaining to matter or things existing in nature. **3.** of or pertaining to the properties of matter and energy other than those peculiar to living matter. **4.** of or pertaining to physics. —*n.* **5.** a medical examination of the body. —**phys′i·cal·ly,** *adv.*

phys′ical educa′tion, instruction in sports, exercises, and hygiene, esp. as part of a school or college program.

phys′ical sci′ence, the study of natural laws and processes other than those peculiar to living matter, as in physics, chemistry, or astronomy. —**phys′ical sci′entist.**

phys′ical ther′apy, the treatment of disease by physical remedies, as massage, gymnastics, etc. —**phys′ical ther′apist.**

phy·si·cian (fi zish′ən), *n.* a doctor of medicine. —**phy·si′cian·ly,** *adj.*

phys·i·cist (fiz′i sist), *n.* a scientist who specializes in physics.

phys·ics (fiz′iks), *n.* the science that deals with matter, energy, motion, and force.

phys·i·og·no·my (fiz′ē og′nə mē, -on′ə mē), *n., pl.* -**mies.** the face or countenance, esp. when considered as an index to the character.

phys·i·og·ra·phy (fiz′ē og′rə fē), *n.* geography concerned with natural features of the earth's surface. —**phys′i·o·graph′ic** (-ə graf′ik), *adj.*

physiol., **1.** physiological. **2.** physiologist. **3.** physiology.

phys·i·ol·o·gy (fiz′ē ol′ə jē), *n.* **1.** the science dealing with the functions of living organisms or their parts. **2.** the organic processes of an organism. —**phys′i·o·log′i·cal** (-ə loj′i kəl), **phys′i·o·log′ic,** *adj.* —**phys′i·ol′o·gist,** *n.*

phys·i·o·ther·a·py (fiz′ē ō ther′ə pē), *n.* See **physical therapy.** —**phys′i·o·ther′a·pist,** *n.*

phy·sique (fi zēk′), *n.* the physical structure of a person's body.

pi¹ (pī), *n., pl.* **pis. 1.** the 16th letter of the Greek alphabet (Π, π). **2.** *Math.* **a.** the letter π , used as the symbol for the ratio of the circumference of a circle to its diameter. **b.** the ratio itself: 3.141592 +.

pi² (pī), *n.* printing type mixed together.

pi·a·nis·si·mo (pē′ə nis′ə mō′), *Music.* —*adj.* **1.** very soft. —*adv.* **2.** very softly.

pi·an·ist (pē an′ist, pyan′-, pē′ə nist), *n.* a person who plays the piano, esp. professionally.

pi·an·o¹ (pē an′ō, pyan′ō), *n., pl.* **-an·os.** a musical instrument in which felt-covered hammers, operated from a keyboard, strike metal strings.

pi·a·no² (pē ä′nō), *Music.* —*adj.* **1.** soft. —*adv.* **2.** softly.

pi·an·o·for·te (pē an′ə fôr′tē, -tä, -fôr′-), *n.* (originally) piano¹.

pi·as·ter (pē as′tər), *n.* a money of account of Egypt, Lebanon, the Sudan, and Syria. Also, *Brit.,* **pi·as′tre.**

pi·az·za (pē az′ə, -ä′zə), *n., pl.* **pi·az·zas, piaz·ze** (pyät′tse). **1.** an open square in an Italian town. **2.** *Chiefly New Eng. and Southern U.S.* porch (def. 1).

pi·broch (pē′brоκн), *n.* a piece of martial or sad music performed on the bagpipe.

pic (pik), *n., pl.* **pics, pix,** *Slang.* **1.** a movie. **2.** a photograph.

pi·ca (pī′kə), *n.* **1.** a 12-point type used in typewriters and having 10 characters to the inch. **2.** a similar size of printing type.

pic·a·resque (pik′ə resk′), *adj.* of or describing witty, amusing rogues or their adventures: *a picaresque novel.*

Pi·cas·so (pi kä′sō), *n.* **Pa·blo** (pä′blō), 1881–1973, Spanish painter and sculptor in France.

pic·a·yune (pik′ē yōōn′), *adj* . **1.** of little value or importance **2.** petty or mean.

pic·ca·lil·li (pik′ə lil′ē), *n., pl.* **-lis.** a spiced pickle or relish of chopped vegetables.

pic·co·lo (pik′ə lō′), *n., pl.* **-los.** a small flute, sounding an octave higher than the ordinary flute. [< It: lit., small]

pick¹ (pik), *v.t.* **1.** to choose or select, esp. with care. **2.** to provoke or bring on: *to pick a fight.* **3.** to steal the contents of, as a person's pocket. **4.** to open (a lock) with a device other than the key, as a wire. **5.** to pierce, dig into, or break up (something) with a pointed instrument: *to pick ore.* **6.** to scratch or poke at with the fingers. **7.** to prepare (a fowl) by removing feathers. **8.** to detach piece by piece with the fingers: *She daintily picked the meat from the bones.* **9.** to pluck one by

one: *to pick flowers.* **10.** (of birds) to take up (small bits of food) with the bill or teeth. **11.** to separate or pull to pieces: *to pick fibers.* **12.** *Music.* **a.** to pluck (the strings of an instrument). **b.** to play (a stringed instrument) by plucking with the fingers or a plectrum. —*v.i.* **13.** to use a pointed instrument on something. **14.** to select carefully or fastidiously. **15. pick at, a.** to eat sparingly or without interest. **16. pick off, a.** to remove by pulling or plucking off. **b.** to single out and shoot. **17. pick on,** *Informal.* to torment, tease, or nag. **18. pick out,** to choose or select. **19. pick up, a.** to lift or take up. **b.** to gain or obtain casually: *to pick up a livelihood.* **c.** to take into a car or along with one. **d.** to speed up. **e.** to make progress. **f.** *Informal.* to introduce oneself to and immediately take out socially or date. —*n.* **20.** the act of choosing or selecting. **21.** a person or thing selected. **22.** the choicest or most desirable one. **23.** plectrum. —**pick′er,** *n.*

pick² (pik), *n.* a heavy tool with a curved metal head tapering to a point at one or both ends, mounted on a wooden handle, used for breaking up soil, rock, etc.

pick·a·back (pik′ə bak′), *adv., adj.* piggyback (def. 1).

pick·a·nin·ny (pik′ə nin′ē), *n., pl.* **-nies.** *Usually Offensive.* a black child. Also, **pic′a·nin′ny.**

pick·ax (pik′aks′), *n.* a pick, esp. a mattock. Also, **pick′axe′.**

pick·er·el (pik′ər əl, pik′rəl), *n., pl.* **-el, -els.** a freshwater game fish related to but smaller than the pike.

pick·et (pik′it), *n.* **1.** a pointed stake driven into the ground for use in a fence or to fasten down a tent. **2.** a union member stationed before a struck establishment in order to dissuade workers or shoppers from entering it. **3.** any person engaged in any similar demonstration. **4.** a soldier or group of soldiers serving as a forward lookout against an enemy advance. —*v.t.* **5.** to enclose or confine with pickets. **6.** to fasten or tether to a picket. **7.** to place pickets at (a factory, etc.). **8.** to guard with pickets. —*v.i.* **9.** to act or serve as a picket. —**pick′et·er,** *n.*

pick′et line′, a line of strikers or other demonstrators serving as pickets.

pick·ing (pik′ing), *n.* **1.** the act of a person or thing that picks. **2.** something that is or may be picked or picked up. **3. pickings. a.** remains that are worth saving. **b.** profits obtained by dishonest means.

pick·le (pik′əl), *n., v.,* **-led, -ling.**
—*n.* **1.** a vegetable, esp. a cucumber, preserved in brine or vinegar. **2.** a liquid prepared with salt or vinegar for preserving or flavoring meat, vegetables, etc. **3.** *Informal.* a troublesome or awkward situation. —*v.t.* **4.** to preserve or steep in a pickling liquid.

pick·pock·et (pik′pok′it), *n.* a person who steals from the pockets of people in public places.

pick·up (pik′up′), *n.* **1.** the act or an instance of picking up. **2.** *Auto.* **a.** capacity for rapid acceleration. **b.** a small truck used for deliveries and light hauling. **3.** *Informal.* an improvement, as in business, health, etc. **4.** the device in a phonograph that converts the vibrations of the stylus into electric signals. **5.** *Informal.* a casual, usually unintroduced acquaintance, often one made in hope of a sexual relationship.

pick·y (pik′ē), *adj.,* **pick·i·er, pick·i·est.** extremely fussy or finicky.

pic·nic (pik′nik), *v.,* **-nicked, -nicking.** —*n.* **1.** an outing that includes the eating of food in the open air. **2.** *Informal.* an enjoyable experience or easy task. —*v.i.* **3.** to go on or take part in a picnic. —**pic′nick·er,** *n.*

pi·co·sec·ond (pī′kə sek′ənd), *n.* one trillionth (10^{-12}) of a second.

pi·cot (pē′kō), *n.* one of a number of ornamental loops along the edge of lace, ribbon, etc.

pic·to·graph (pik′tə graf′, -gräf′), *n.* **1.** a pictorial symbol or symbols used to convey an idea. **2.** a graph or chart using symbolic pictures. —**pic′to·graph′ic** (-graf′ik), *adj.*

pic·to·ri·al (pik tōr′ē əl, -tôr′ē əl), *adj.* **1.** of or expressed in pictures. **2.** vivid as a picture. —**pic·to′ri·al·ly,** *adv.*

pic·ture (pik′chər), *n., v.,* **-tured, -turing.** —*n.* **1.** a visual representation of a person, object, or scene made by painting or photography. **2.** a graphic or vivid description. **3.** See **motion picture. 4.** a beautiful or interesting person, thing, group, or scene. **5.** a close resemblance of a person to someone else. **6.** a perfect example of some quality or condition: *the picture of health.* **7.** a situation or set of circumstances. **8.** the image on a television or motion-picture screen. —*v.t.* **9.** to make a picture of. **10.** to form a mental picture of. **11.** to describe vividly in speech or writing. —**pic′tur·er,** *n.*

Pic·ture·phone (pik′chər fōn′), *n. Trademark.* a telephone equipped to receive and transmit a television image of those conversing.

pic·tur·esque (pik′chə resk′), *adj.* **1.** visually charming as if resembling a painting. **2.** (of writing, speech, etc.) strikingly graphic or vivid. **3.** having pleasing or interesting qualities. —**pic′tur·esque′ly,** *adv.* —**pic′tur·esque′ness,** *n.*

pic′ture tube′, a cathode-ray tube forming the screen on which televised images are reproduced.

pic′ture win′dow, a large window in a house designed to frame the exterior view.

pid·dle (pid′ᵊl), *v.i., v.t.,* **-dled, -dling.** to spend (time) idly.

pid·dling (pid′ling), *adj.* negligibly small or trifling.

pidg·in (pij′ən), *n.* a simplified mixture of two languages, usually using words from one language and grammatical features of another.

pidg′in Eng′lish, a pidgin based on English and formerly used in commerce in Chinese ports.

pie¹ (pī), *n.* **1.** a baked food consisting of a pastry crust filled with fruits, preserves, or meat. **2.** *easy as pie, Informal.* very easy or simple.

pie² (pī), *n. Brit.* **pi²**.

pie·bald (pī′bôld′), *adj.* **1.** having patches of black and white or of other colors. —*n.* **2.** a piebald animal, esp. a horse.

piece (pēs), *n., v.,* **pieced, piec·ing.** —*n.* **1.** a portion or quantity of any material, forming a separate entity. **2.** a portion or quantity of a whole. **3.** a particular amount, as of work produced in a factory or cloth to be sold. **4.** an artistic or literary work, as a musical composition or a play. **5.** a soldier's rifle or pistol. **6.** a coin: *a five-cent piece.* **7. go to pieces, a.** to break into fragments. **b.** *Informal.* to lose control of oneself. —*v.t.* **8.** to mend by adding or joining pieces. **9.** to make by joining pieces.

pièce de ré·sis·tance (pyes də RA ZĒ stäns′), *pl.* **pièces de ré·sis·tance** (pyes də RA zē stäns′). *French.* **1.** the principal dish of a meal. **2.** the principal item in a series or group.

piece′ goods′, goods, esp. fabrics, sold at retail by linear measure.

piece·meal (pēs′mēl′), *adv.* **1.** piece by piece. —*adj.* **2.** done piecemeal.

piece·work (pēs′wûrk′), *n.* work done and paid for by the piece. —**piece′work′er,** *n.*

pied (pīd), *adj.* having patches of two or more colors: *a pied horse.*

pied-à-terre (pyä tA teR′), *n., pl.* **pied-à-terre** (pyä tA teR′). *French.* a small dwelling for occasional or temporary use. [lit., foot on ground]

pie-eyed (pī′īd′), *adj. Slang.* drunk or intoxicated.

pie·plant (pī′plant′, -plänt′), *n.* the garden rhubarb.

pier (pēr), *n.* **1.** a structure built to extend from land out into the harbor, used as a landing place for cargo or passengers. **2.** such a structure used as a promenade or an entertainment area. **3.** a support for the ends of a bridge span. **4.** a support of masonry or steel for any structure.

pierce (pērs), *v.,* **pierced, pierc·ing.** —*v.t.* **1.** to penetrate into or run through, as a sharp-pointed instrument does. **2.** to make a hole or opening in. **3.** to force a way into or through. **4.** to penetrate with the eye or mind. **5.** to sound sharply through, as a cry. —*v.i.* **6.** to force a way into or through something. —**pierc′ing·ly,** *adv.*

Pierce (pērs), *n.* **Franklin,** 1804–69, 14th president of the U.S. 1853–57.

Pierre (pēr), *n.* the capital of South Dakota.

pi·e·ty (pī′i tē), *n., pl.* **-ties. 1.** reverence for God. **2.** dutiful respect or regard, as for parents. **3.** a pious act or belief. —**Syn. 1.** devoutness. **2.** veneration.

pi·e·zo·e·lec·tric·i·ty (pī e′zō i lek tris′i tē, -ē′lek-), *n.* electricity produced by mechanical stress on a nonconducting crystal. —**pi·e′zo·e·lec′tric** (-lek′trik), *adj., n.*

pif·fle (pif′əl), *n. Informal.* idle or silly talk. —**pif′fling,** *adj.*

pig (pig), *n.* **1.** a young swine of either sex weighing less than 120 pounds. **2.** pork. **3.** *Informal.* a person of piggish character or habits. **4.** a rough, oblong piece of cast metal. **5.** *Offensive.* a police officer.

pi·geon (pij′ən), *n.* **1.** any of several birds having a compact body and short legs. **2.** *Slang.* a person easily fooled or cheated.

pi·geon·hole (pij′ən hōl′), *n., v.,* **-holed, -hol·ing.** —*n.* **1.** one of a series of small open slots, as in a desk, used for filing or sorting letters, etc. —*v.t.* **2.** to file away, as in a pigeonhole. **3.** to put aside and ignore, often indefinitely. **4.** to put into categories.

pi·geon-toed (pij′ən tōd′), *adj.* having the toes or feet turned inward.

pig·gish (pig′ish), *adj.* like a pig, esp. in being greedy or filthy. —**pig′gish·ness,** *n.*

pig·gy (pig′ē), *n., pl.* **-gies,** *adj.,* **-gi·er, -gi·est.** —*n.* **1.** a small pig. —*adj.* **2.** *Informal.* piggish.

pig·gy·back (pig′ē bak′), *adv., adj.* **1.** on the back or shoulders like a pack. **2.** of or for the carrying of loaded truck trailers on flatcars.

pig·head·ed (pig′hed′id), *adj.* stupidly obstinate. —**pig′head′ed·ness,** *n.*

pig′ i′ron, iron cast into pigs in preparation for conversion into steel.

pig′ Lat′in, a children's jargon in which the first consonant or consonant cluster is moved to the end of each word and followed by "ay," as *eakspay* for "speak."

pig·let (pig′lit), *n.* a little pig.

pig·ment (pig′mənt), *n.* **1.** a coloring matter or substance. **2.** *Biol.* any substance that gives color to the tissues or cells of animals or plants.

pig·men·ta·tion (pig′mən tā′shən), *n. Biol.* coloration with or deposition of pigment.

pig·pen (pig′pen′), *n.* sty¹. Also called **pig′sty′** (-stī′).

pig·skin (pig′skin′), *n.* **1.** the skin of a pig. **2.** leather made from it. **3.** *Informal.* a football.

pig·tail (pig′tāl′), *n.* a braid of hair hanging down the back of the head.

pike¹ (pīk), *n., pl.* **pike, pikes.** a large, slender, freshwater fish having a long, flat snout.

pike² (pīk), *n.* a shafted weapon having a sharp head, formerly used by the infantry.

pike³ (pīk), *n.* turnpike.

pike⁴ (pīk), *n.* a sharply pointed projection or spike.

pik·er (pī′kər), *n. Informal.* a person who does something in a contemptibly small or cheap way.

pike·staff (pīk′staf′, -stäf′), *n., pl.* **-staves** (-stāvz′). the shaft of an infantry pike.

pi·laf (pi läf′, pē′läf), *n.* rice cooked in a meat or poultry broth. Also, **pi·laff, pi·lau** (-lô′).

pi·las·ter (pi las′tər), *n.* a shallow rectangular feature projecting from a wall, usually imitating the form of a column. —**pi·las′tered,** *adj.*

Pi·late (pī′lət), *n.* **Pon·tius** (pon′shəs, -tē əs), Roman procurator of Judea (the S part of ancient Palestine) A.D. 26–36?: condemned Jesus to death.

pil·chard (pil′chərd), *n.* a marine fish related to the herring but smaller and rounder.

pile¹ (pīl), *n., v.,* **piled, pil·ing.** —*n.* **1.** a collection of things laid or lying one upon the other. **2.** pyre. **3.** a large building or mass of buildings. **4.** *Informal.* a large quantity, as of money. **5.** reactor (def. 3). —*v.t.* **6.** to lay or dispose in a pile. **7.** to accumulate or store. **8.** to cover or load with a pile. —*v.i.* **9.** to accumulate, as money, debts, etc.: *The bills keep piling up.* **10.** *Informal.* to move as a group in a confused, disorderly fashion.

pile² (pīl), *n.* a long beam of wood or steel driven into the ground, often under water, as a support for a building, pier, etc.

pile³ (pīl), *n.* a furry surface formed on velvet or other fabrics by short raised loops of yarn. —**piled,** *adj.*

piles (pīlz), *n.* hemorrhoids.

pile·up (pīl′up′), *n.* **1.** an accumulation, as of chores or bills. **2.** a massive collision of several moving vehicles.

pil·fer (pil′fər), *v.i., v.t.* to steal, esp. in small quantities. —**pil′fer·age** (-ij), *n.* —**pil′fer·er,** *n.*

pil·grim (pil′grim, -grəm), *n.* **1.** a person who journeys to some sacred place as an act of devotion. **2.** a wanderer or traveler. **3.** (*cap.*) one of the band of Puritans who founded the colony of Plymouth, Massachusetts in 1620.

pil·grim·age (pil′grə mij), *n.* **1.** a journey of a pilgrim. **2.** any long journey or wandering.

pil·ing (pī′ling), *n.* a number of piles supporting a structure.

pill (pil), *n.* **1.** a small rounded mass of medicine that is to be swallowed whole. **2.** something unpleasant that has to be endured. **3. the pill,** an oral contraceptive for women. **4.** *Slang.* a tiresomely disagreeable person.

pil·lage (pil′ij), *v.,* -**laged, -lag·ing,** *n.* —*v.t., v.i.* **1.** to strip (a conquered land) of money or goods by open violence in war. —*n.* **2.** the act of pillaging. **3.** booty or spoil. —**pil′lag·er,** *n.*

pil·lar (pil′ər), *n.* **1.** an upright, slender structure, as of stone, used as a building support or for a monument. **2.** a person who is a chief supporter of something. —**pil′lared,** *adj.*

pill·box (pil′boks′), *n.* **1.** a small box for holding pills. **2.** a low, concrete structure for enclosing machine guns and used as a minor fortress in warfare.

pil·lion (pil′yən), *n.* a cushion attached behind the saddle of a horse or motorcycle for a second rider.

pil·lo·ry (pil′ə rē), *n., pl.* -**ries,** *v.,* -**ried, -ry·ing.** —*n.* **1.** a wooden framework, with holes for securing the head and hands, formerly used to expose an offender to public derision. —*v.t.* **2.** to set in the pillory. **3.** to expose to public derision.

pil·low (pil′ō), *n.* **1.** a cloth case filled with soft, resilient material, as feathers, used as a rest for the head during sleep. —*v.t.* **2.** to rest on or as on a pillow. **3.** to serve as a pillow for. —**pil′low·y,** *adj.*

pil·low·case (pil′ō kās′), *n.* a removable case for covering a pillow. Also called **pil′low·slip′** (-slip′).

pi·lot (pī′lət), *n.* **1.** a person qualified to operate an aircraft. **2.** a person qualified to steer ships into or out of a harbor. **3.** the steersman of a ship. **4.** a guide or leader. **5.** Also called **pi′lot film′.** a sample film intended

to attract sponsors to a planned television series. —*v.t.* **6.** to act as pilot on, in, or over. **7.** to guide or lead. —*adj.* **8.** serving as a trial undertaking prior to full-scale operation or use. —**pi·lot·age** (pī′lə tij), *n.*

pi·lot·house (pī′lət hous′), *n.* an enclosed structure on the bridge of a vessel from which it may be navigated.

pi′lot light′, a small flame kept burning, as in a gas stove, to relight the burners.

Pil·sner (pilz′nər, pils′-), *n.* (*sometimes l.c.*) **1.** a pale, light lager beer. **2.** a tall glass tapered at the bottom, used esp. for beer. Also, **Pil′sen·er.**

pi·men·to (pi men′tō), *n., pl.* -**tos.** a sweet, red pepper used as a relish and in cooking.

pi·mien·to (pi myen′tō, -men′-), *n., pl.* -**tos.** pimento.

pimp (pimp), *n.* **1.** a man who solicits customers for a prostitute. —*v.i.* **2.** to act as a pimp.

pim·per·nel (pim′pər nel′, -nəl), *n.* an herb having scarlet, purplish, or white flowers that close at the approach of bad weather.

pim·ple (pim′pəl), *n.* a small, usually inflammatory swelling of the skin. —**pim′pled, pim′ply,** *adj.*

pin (pin), *n., v.,* **pinned, pin·ning.** —*n.* **1.** a short, slender piece of metal with a point at one end, used for fastening things together. **2.** a small, slender, often pointed piece of wood, metal, etc., used to fasten, support, or attach things. **3.** an ornament or badge consisting essentially or partly of a pointed or penetrating wire: *a class pin.* **4.** one of the rounded wooden clubs used as the target in bowling. **5.** *Golf.* the flagpole that identifies a hole. **6.** Usually, **pins.** *Informal.* the human legs. —*v.t.* **7.** to fasten with or as with a pin. **8.** to hold fast in a spot or position. **9. pin down,** a. to hold to a course of action, etc. b. to define with precision. **10. pin something on someone,** *Slang.* to blame someone for something on the basis of real or manufactured evidence. —**pin′ner,** *n.*

pin·a·fore (pin′ə fōr′, -fôr′), *n.* a sleeveless dress or full apron closing at the back.

pin′ball machine′, a game device in which a spring-driven ball rolls down a slanted board against pins and through holes that record one's score.

pince-nez (pans′nā′, pins′-), *n., pl.* **pince-nez** (pans′nāz′, pins′-). a pair of eyeglasses held on the face by a spring that pinches the nose.

pin·cers (pin′sərz), *n.* **1.** a gripping tool consisting of a pair of jaws and a pair of handles. **2.** a claw of a lobster or crab. Also, **pinch·ers** (pin′-chərz).

pinch (pinch), *v.t.* **1.** to squeeze between the finger and thumb, the jaws of an instrument, etc. **2.** to press upon so as to cause pain or discomfort. **3.** to affect in such a way as to cause distress, anxiety, etc., as hunger does. **4.** to be stingy or sparing with: *to pinch pennies.* **5.** *Informal.* to arrest. **6.** *Slang.* to steal. —*v.i.* **7.** to exert a painful compressing force: *This shoe pinches.* **8.** to economize unduly. —*n.* **9.** the act of pinching. **10.** an amount taken up between the finger and thumb. **11.** sharp or painful stress, as of hunger. **12.** an emergency. **13.** *Informal.* an arrest. —**pinch′er,** *n.*

pinch-hit (pinch′hit′), *v.i.,* **-hit, -hit·ting. 1.** *Baseball.* to substitute at bat for a teammate. **2.** to substitute for someone, esp. in an emergency. —**pinch′ hit′ter.**

pin′ curl′, a dampened curl secured by a clip or hairpin.

pin·cush·ion (pin′koosh′ən), *n.* a small cushion into which pins are stuck until needed.

pine[1] (pīn), *n.* **1.** any evergreen, cone-bearing tree having long, needle-shaped leaves. **2.** its wood.

pine[2] (pīn), *v.i.,* **pined, pin·ing. 1.** to yearn deeply. **2.** to fail in health or vitality from grief or longing.

pin′e·al bod′y (pin′ē əl), a body of unknown function present in the brain of all vertebrates having a cranium.

pine·ap·ple (pīn′ap′əl), *n.* **1.** the edible juicy fruit of a tropical plant having spiny-edged leaves. **2.** its plant.

pin·feath·er (pin′feth′ər), *n.* an undeveloped feather that has just come through the skin.

ping (ping), *v.i.* **1.** to produce a sharp sound like that of a bullet striking metal. —*n.* **2.** a pinging sound.

Ping-Pong (ping′pong′), *n. Trademark.* See **table tennis.**

pin·head (pin′hed′), *n.* **1.** the head of a pin. **2.** *Slang.* a stupid person.

pin·hole (pin′hōl′), *n.* **1.** a small hole made by or as by a pin. **2.** a hole for a pin to go through.

pin·ion[1] (pin′yən), *n.* a gear with a small number of teeth that engages with a rack or a larger gear.

pin·ion[2] (pin′yən), *n.* **1.** the outer part of a bird's wing. **2.** the wing of a bird. —*v.t.* **3.** to cut off the pinion of (a wing) or bind (the wings), as in order to prevent a bird from flying. **4.** to bind (a person's arms or hands) so as to prevent movement.

pink[1] (pingk), *n.* **1.** a pale red. **2.** any of several garden plants having pink, white, or red flowers resembling carnations. **3.** the highest form or degree: *a runner in the pink of condition.* **4.** Also, **pink′o** (ping′kō). (*often cap.*) *Disparaging.* a person with mildly left-wing political opinions. —*adj.* **5.** of the color pink. **6.** (*often cap.*) *Disparaging.* holding mildly left-wing political views. —**pink′ish,** *adj.*

pink[2] (pingk), *v.t.* **1.** to pierce with a rapier or sword. **2.** to finish at the edge with a toothed or notched pattern.

pink·eye (pingk′ī′), *n.* a contagious, epidemic form of acute conjunctivitis.

pink·ie (ping′kē), *n. Informal.* the little finger. Also, **pink′y.**

pin′ mon′ey, a small sum set aside for minor expenditures.

pin·nace (pin′is), *n.* **1.** a light sailing vessel. **2.** a ship's boat.

pin·na·cle (pin′ə kəl), *n.* **1.** a pointed, towering formation, esp. a mountain peak. **2.** the highest or culminating point, as of success. **3.** a relatively small, upright structure terminating in a gable, a pyramid, or a cone. —**Syn. 2.** acme, summit, zenith.

pin·nate (pin′āt, -it), *adj. Bot.* having leaflets arranged on each side of a common stalk. —**pin′nate·ly,** *adv.*

pi·noch·le (pē′nuk əl, -nok-), *n.* a card game played by two, three, or four persons, with a 48-card deck. Also, **pi′noc·le.**

pi·ñon (pin′yən, pēn′yōn), *n., pl.* **pi·ñons, pi·ño·nes** (pē nyō′nes). any of various pines of the southern Rocky Mountain region, bearing large edible seeds. Also, **pin′yon.**

pin·point (pin′point′), *v.t.* to locate or describe exactly.

pin·prick (pin′prik′), *n.* **1.** any minute puncture made by or as by a pin. **2.** a petty annoyance.

pins′ and nee′dles, 1. a tingly, prickly sensation in a numb limb. **2. on pins and needles,** *Informal.* nervous or anxious.

pin·set·ter (pin′set′ər), *n. Bowling.* a mechanical apparatus that positions the pins and removes struck ones. Also called **pin′spot′ter** (-spot′ər).

pin·stripe (pin′strīp′), *n.* **1.** a very thin stripe in fabrics. **2.** a fabric or garment having such stripes. —**pin′-striped′,** *adj.*

pint (pīnt), *n.* **1.** a liquid measure equal to half a quart or 0.4732 liter. **2.** a dry measure equal to half a quart or 0.550 liter.

pin·to (pin′tō, pēn′-), *adj., n., pl.* **-tos.** —*adj.* **1.** marked with spots or blotches of a different color. —*n.* **2.** a pinto horse.

pin·up (pin′up′), *n. Informal.* **1.** a picture that may be pinned up on a wall, usually of an attractive girl. **2.** a girl in such a picture. —*adj.* **3.** of or suitable for a pinup.

pin·wheel (pin′hwēl′, -wēl′), *n.* **1.** a toy consisting of a wheel with vanes loosely attached to a stick, designed to revolve when blown by the wind. **2.** a kind of firework supported on a pin upon which it revolves when ignited.

pinx., he (or she) painted (it): formerly used on paintings after the artist's name. [< L *pinxit*]

pi·o·neer (pī′ə nēr′), *n.* **1.** one of those who first enter or settle a region. **2.** a person who leads the way in any field of inquiry, enterprise, or progress. —*v.i.* **3.** to be a pioneer. —*v.t.* **4.** to be a pioneer of or in. [< MF *pionier*, OF *peonier* foot soldier]

pi·ous (pī′əs), *adj.* **1.** having or showing reverence for God or a deity. **2.** of or pertaining to religious devotion. **3.** characterized by a hypocritical concern with virtue or religious devotion. —**pi′ous·ly,** *adv.* —**pi′ous·ness,** *n.* —**Syn.** devout.

pip¹ (pip), *n.* one of the spots on dice, playing cards, or dominoes.

pip² (pip), *n.* **1.** a contagious disease of birds, esp. poultry. **2.** *Facetious.* any minor ailment in a person.

pip³ (pip), *n.* a small seed, esp. of an apple or orange.

pip⁴ (pip), *n.* blip (def. 1).

pipe (pīp), *n., v.,* **piped, pip·ing.** —*n.* **1.** a hollow cylinder, as of metal, for conveying water, gas, steam, etc. **2.** a tube of wood or clay, with a small bowl at one end, for smoking tobacco. **3.** a musical wind instrument consisting of a single tube of wood or other material, as a flute. **4. pipes,** *Informal.* the human vocal cords or the voice, esp. as used in singing. **5.** Usually, **pipes. a.** bagpipe. **b.** *Informal.* a tubular organ of a human or animal body. —*v.i.* **6.** to play on a pipe. **7.** to utter a shrill sound like that of a pipe. —*v.t.* **8.** to convey (water, etc.) by means of pipes. **9.** to play (music) on a pipe. **10.** to utter in a shrill sound. **11. pipe down,** *Slang.* to stop talking. **12. pipe up, a.** to begin to sing or to play (a musical instrument). **b.** to speak up. —**pip′er,** *n.*

pipe′ dream′, *Informal.* a baseless fancy or hope.

pipe·line (pīp′līn′), *n.* **1.** a long series of pipes for transporting crude oil, natural gas, water, etc., over great distances. **2.** a direct, often confidential channel for information.

pipe′ or′gan, organ (def. 1).

pi·pette (pī pet′, pi-), *n.* a slender tube for measuring and transferring

quantities of liquids in a laboratory. Also, **pi·pet′.**

pip·ing (pī′ping), *n.* **1.** pipes collectively or a system of pipes. **2.** the act of a person or thing that pipes. **3.** a shrill sound. **4.** the sound or music of pipes. **5.** a tubular band of material used for trimming edges and seams of clothing, upholstery, etc. —*adj.* **6.** emitting a shrill sound. **7. piping hot,** (of food or drink) very hot. —**pip′ing·ly,** *adv.*

pip·it (pip′it), *n.* a small songbird resembling the lark.

pip·pin (pip′in), *n.* any of numerous roundish or oblate varieties of apple.

pip·squeak (pip′skwēk′), *n. Informal.* a small or unimportant person.

pi·quant (pē′kənt, -känt), *adj.* **1.** agreeably pungent in taste or flavor. **2.** interestingly provocative. —**pi′quan·cy,** *n.* —**pi′quant·ly,** *adv.*

pique (pēk), *n., v.,* **piqued, piqu·ing.** —*n.* **1.** irritation or resentment caused by a wound to pride or self-esteem. —*v.t.* **2.** to cause such a feeling in. **3.** to arouse or stimulate.

pi·qué (pi kā′, pē-), *n.* a fabric of cotton, rayon, or silk, woven with raised cords. Also, **pi·que′.**

pi·quet (pi ket′, -kā′), *n.* a card game played by two persons with a 32-card deck.

pi·ra·cy (pī′rə sē), *n., pl.* **-cies. 1.** robbery or illegal violence at sea. **2.** the unauthorized reproduction or use of a copyrighted book, patented invention, etc.

pi·ra·nha (pi rän′yə, -ran′-), *n.* a small, extremely voracious, South American fish, schools of which are known to attack and devour people and large animals.

pi·rate (pī′rət), *n., v.,* **-rat·ed, -rat·ing.** —*n.* **1.** a person who commits piracy. —*v.t.* **2.** to take by piracy. **3.** to reproduce or make use of (a book or invention) without authorization or legal right. —**pi·rat′i·cal** (-rat′i kəl), *adj.*

pir·ou·ette (pir′ōō et′), *n., v.,* **-et·ted, -et·ting.** —*n.* **1.** a whirling about on one foot or on the points of the toes, as in dancing. —*v.i.* **2.** to perform a pirouette.

pis·ca·to·ri·al (pis′kə tōr′ē əl, -tôr′-), *adj.* of fishermen or fishing.

Pis·ces (pī′sēz, pis′ēz), *n.* the twelfth sign of the zodiac. [< L: fishes]

pis·mire (pis′mīr′), *n. Archaic.* an ant.

pis·ta·chi·o (pi stash′ē ō′, -stä′shē ō′), *n., pl.* **-chi·os. 1.** Also called **pista′chio nut′.** the nut of a small tree containing an edible greenish kernel. **2.** its tree.

pis·til (pis′til), *n.* the seed-bearing organ of a flower. —**pis′til·late′**, *adj.*

pis·tol (pis′təl), *n.* a short firearm held and fired with one hand.

pis·tol-whip (pis′təl hwip′, -wip′), *v.t.*, **-whipped, -whip·ping.** to hit repeatedly with a pistol, esp. on the head.

pis·ton (pis′tən), *n.* a disk or cylinder moving within a tube and exerting pressure on, or receiving pressure from, a fluid or gas within the tube.

pit[1] (pit), *n., v.,* **pit·ted, pit·ting.** —*n.* **1.** a deep hole or cavity in the ground. **2.** a covered or concealed excavation, serving as a trap. **3.** a natural hollow or depression in the body. **4.** a small depressed scar left by smallpox. **5.** an enclosure for fights, as of dogs or cocks. **6.** orchestra (def. 2a). **7. a.** hell or limbo. **b.** abyss or bottom. —*v.t.* **8.** to form pits or depressions in. **9.** to make pits or scars in. **10.** to set in opposition, as one against another. —*v.i.* **11.** to become marked with pits.

pit[2] (pit), *n., v.,* **pit·ted, pit·ting.** —*n.* **1.** the stone of a fruit, as a cherry, peach, or plum. —*v.t.* **2.** to remove the pit from (a fruit).

pit·a·pat (pit′ə pat′), *adv.* **1.** with a quick succession of beats or taps. —*n.* **2.** the movement or sound of something going pitapat.

pitch[1] (pich), *v.t.* **1.** to erect or set up firmly, as a tent. **2.** to throw with an aim. **3.** *Baseball.* **a.** to serve (the ball) to the batter. **b.** to fill the position of pitcher in (a game). **4.** to set at a certain point, degree, or level. —*v.i.* **5.** to fall forward or headlong. **6.** *Baseball.* **a.** to serve the ball to the batter. **b.** to fill the position of pitcher. **7.** to slope or dip sharply. **8.** to plunge with alternate fall and rise of bow and stern. **9. pitch in,** *Informal.* **a.** to begin working in earnest. **b.** to contribute to a common purpose. **10. pitch into,** *Informal.* to attack verbally or physically. —*n.* **11.** the act or manner of pitching. **12.** a throw at a target. **13.** relative point or degree. **14.** the angle of slope. **15.** the degree of height or depth of a tone or of sound. **16.** *Baseball.* the serving of the ball to the batter by the pitcher. **17.** a pitching movement, as of a ship. **18.** *Slang.* a high-pressure sales talk.

pitch[2] (pich), *n.* a dark, sticky substance made from wood, coal, or petroleum, used for paving, roofing, etc. —**pitch′y,** *adj.*

pitch-black (pich′blak′), *adj.* extremely black.

pitch·blende (pich′blend′), *n.* a black mineral that is the principal ore of uranium.

pitch-dark (pich′därk′), *adj.* extreme-

ly dark.

pitch·er[1] (pich′ər), *n.* a container, usually with a handle and spout or lip, for holding and pouring liquids.

pitch·er[2] (pich′ər), *n.* a person who pitches, esp. in baseball.

pitch′er plant′, any of various plants having leaves modified into a pitcherlike receptacle.

pitch·fork (pich′fôrk′), *n.* a large, long-handled fork for pitching hay, stalks of grain, etc.

pitch·man (pich′mən), *n.* **1.** an itinerant salesperson of small wares. **2.** *Slang.* any high-pressure salesperson.

pitch′ pipe′, a small flute used for establishing the proper pitch in singing or in tuning a musical instrument.

pit·e·ous (pit′ē əs), *adj.* appealing for pity. —**pit′e·ous·ly,** *adv.* —**pit′e·ous·ness,** *n.*

pit·fall (pit′fôl′), *n.* **1.** a concealed pit for trapping persons or animals. **2.** any danger for the unwary.

pith (pith), *n.* **1.** the soft, spongy tissue at the center of the stem of certain plants. **2.** the important or essential part.

Pith·e·can·thro·pus (pith′ə kan′thrə pəs, -kən thrō′pəs), *n.* an extinct genus of apelike human beings, esp. of the Pleistocene epoch of Java.

pith·y (pith′ē), *adj.,* **pith·i·er, pith·i·est.** **1.** brief and forceful in expression. **2.** of, like, or full of pith. —**pith′i·ly,** *adv.*

pit·i·a·ble (pit′ē ə bəl), *adj.* evoking contemptuous pity. —**pit′i·a·bly,** *adv.*

pit·i·ful (pit′ə fəl), *adj.* **1.** arousing pity. **2.** characterized by contemptible scantiness or smallness. —**pit′i·ful·ly,** *adv.* —**pit′i·ful·ness,** *n.* —Syn. **1.** lamentable, pathetic.

pit·i·less (pit′ē lis, pit′i-), *adj.* feeling or showing no pity. —**pit′i·less·ly,** *adv.* —**pit′i·less·ness,** *n.* —Syn. implacable, merciless.

pi·ton (pē′ton, -tōn), *n. Mountain Climbing.* a metal spike with an eye through which a rope may be passed.

pits (pits), *n.pl. Slang.* an extremely unpleasant or boring thing or person (usually prec. by *the*).

pit·tance (pit′əns), *n.* **1.** a small amount or share. **2.** a small allowance, esp. of money.

pit·ter-pat·ter (pit′ər pat′ər), *n.* the sound of a rapid succession of light beats or taps, as of rain.

Pitts·burgh (pits′bûrg′), *n.* a port in SW Pennsylvania.

pi·tu·i·tar·y (pi tōō′i ter′ē, -tyōō′-), *adj., n., pl.* **-tar·ies.** —*adj.* **1.** of or obtained from the pituitary gland. —*n.* **2.** See **pituitary gland.**

pitu′itary gland′, a small, oval endocrine gland attached to the base of the brain which secretes several hormones controlling body growth.

pit′ vi′per, any of numerous venomous snakes having a heat-sensitive pit on each side of the head between the eye and nostril.

pit·y (pit′ē), *n., pl.* **pit·ies,** *v.,* **pit·ied, pit·y·ing.** —*n.* 1. sympathetic grief or sorrow for the suffering or misfortune of others. 2. a cause or reason for such a feeling. —*v.t., v.i.* 3. to feel pity (for). —**pit′y·ing·ly,** *adv.*

piv·ot (piv′ət), *n.* 1. a pin or short shaft on which something turns or swings. 2. a person or thing on which something depends. 3. the action of pivoting. —*v.i.* 4. to turn on or as on a pivot. —*v.t.* 5. to provide with a pivot or pivots. —**piv′ot·al,** *adj.*

pix¹ (piks), *n.* pyx.

pix² (piks), *n.* a pl. of pic.

pix·y (pik′sē), *n., pl.* **pix·ies.** a mischievous fairy or sprite. Also, **pix′ie.**

pi·zazz (pi zaz′), *n. Slang.* 1. energy or vigor. 2. attractive style. Also, **piz·zazz′.**

piz·za (pēt′sə), *n.* a flat, open-faced pie of Italian origin, consisting of a crust topped with tomato sauce and cheese.

piz·ze·ri·a (pēt′sə rē′ə), *n.* a place where pizzas are made and sold.

piz·zi·ca·to (pit′sə kä′tō), *adj. Music.* played by plucking the strings with the finger, as on a violin.

p.j.'s (pē′jāz′), *n.pl. Informal.* pajamas.

pk., 1. pack. 2. park. 3. peak. 4. peck.

pkg., package.

pkt., 1. packet. 2. pocket.

pkwy., parkway.

pl., 1. place. 2. plate. 3. plural.

plac·ard (plak′ärd, -ərd), *n.* 1. a paperboard sign or notice for display in a public place. —*v.t.* 2. to display placards on or in. —**plac′ard·er,** *n.*

pla·cate (plā′kāt, plak′āt), *v.t.,* **-cat·ed, -cat·ing.** to appease by making some concessions. —**plac·a·ble** (plak′ə bəl, plā′kə-), *adj.* —**pla·ca·tion** (plā kā′shən), *n.*

place (plās), *n., v.,* **placed, plac·ing.** —*n.* 1. a particular portion of space. 2. space in general. 3. the portion of space occupied by a person or thing. 4. any part or spot in a body or surface. 5. a space or seat for a person, as in a theater. 6. position or situation. 7. a job, post, or office. 8. a function or duty. 9. a region or area. 10. a short street. 11. a building set aside for a specific purpose: *a place of worship.* 12. a residence or house. 13. the position occupied by a substitute. 14. a step or point in order of proceeding. 15. the second position at the finish of a horse race. 16. **take place,** to happen or occur. —*v.t.* 17. to put in a particular position, situation, or condition. 18. to put or arrange for: *to place an order.* 19. to appoint (a person) to a post or office. 20. to find employment or living quarters for. 21. to assign a certain position or rank to. 22. to identify by connecting with the proper place, circumstances, etc.: *to place a face.* —*v.i.* 23. to finish second in a horse race. 24. to finish in a specified rank or position.

pla·ce·bo (plə sē′bō), *n., pl.* **-bos, -boes.** a substance having no medicinal value but given to satisfy a patient.

place′ mat′, a mat set on a dining table beneath a place setting.

place·ment (plās′mənt), *n.* 1. the act of placing or state of being placed. 2. location or arrangement. 3. the act of an employment office or employer in filling a position.

pla·cen·ta (plə sen′tə), *n., pl.* **-tas, -tae** (-tē). a vascular organ which connects the fetus to the uterus and through which the embryo obtains nourishment. —**pla·cen′tal,** *adj.*

plac·er (plas′ər), *n.* a superficial gravel or similar deposit containing particles of gold.

place′ set′ting, the dishes and eating utensils set at the place of each person at a meal.

plac·id (plas′id), *adj.* pleasantly calm or peaceful. —**pla·cid·i·ty** (plə sid′i·tē), *n.* —**plac′id·ly,** *adv.*

plack·et (plak′it), *n.* the slit at the top of a garment that facilitates putting it on and taking it off.

pla·gia·rize (plā′jə rīz′, -jē ə rīz′), *v.t., v.i.,* **-rized, -riz·ing.** to steal (the language, ideas, or thoughts) from (another), representing them as one's own original work. —**pla′gia·rism** (-rīz′əm), **pla′gia·ry,** *n.* —**pla′gia·rist,** **pla′gia·riz′er,** *n.*

plague (plāg), *n., v.,* **plagued, pla·guing.** —*n.* 1. an epidemic disease of high mortality, esp. the bubonic plague. 2. any widespread affliction or evil. 3. any cause of unremitting annoyance. —*v.t.* 4. to annoy unremittingly. 5. to infect with a plague. —Syn. 4. bother, trouble.

plaid (plad), *n.* 1. (loosely) a tartan pattern or a pattern suggesting one. 2. a long, rectangular piece of cloth with such a pattern, worn across the shoulder by Scottish Highlanders. —*adj.* 3. (loosely) having a tartan pattern.

plain (plān), *adj.* 1. clear or distinct to the eye or ear: *in plain view.* 2. easily understood. 3. sheer or utter: *plain folly.* 4. free from ambiguity or evasion. 5. without special pretensions, superiority, etc.: *plain people.* 6. not beautiful: *a plain face.* 7. without intricacies or difficulties. 8. with little or no embellishment or elaboration. 9. not rich or highly seasoned, as food. —*adv.* **10.** clearly and simply. —*n.* **11.** an expanse of nearly flat land. —**plain′ly,** *adv.* —**plain′ness,** *n.* —**Syn. 2.** evident, obvious. **4.** candid, outspoken.

plain·clothes·man (plān′klōz′mən, -man′, -klō͝t͟hz′-), *n.* a police detective who wears mufti while on duty.

plains·man (plānz′mən), *n.* an inhabitant of the plains.

plaint (plānt), *n. Literary.* a complaint or lament.

plain·tiff (plān′tif), *n. Law.* a person who brings suit in a court.

plain·tive (plān′tiv), *adj.* expressing sorrow or melancholy. —**plain′tive·ly,** *adv.* —**Syn.** wistful.

plait (plāt, plat), *Chiefly Brit.* —*n.* **1.** a braid, esp. of hair or straw. **2.** pleat. —*v.t.* **3.** to braid, as hair or straw. **4.** to pleat.

plan (plan), *n., v.,* **planned, plan·ning.** —*n.* **1.** a method of doing or proceeding with something formulated beforehand. **2.** a project or definite purpose. **3.** a drawing made to scale to represent the horizontal section of a structure or a machine. —*v.t.* **4.** to arrange a plan or scheme for. **5.** to have in mind as an intention. **6.** to draw a diagrammatic plan of. —*v.i.* **7.** to make plans. —**plan′ner,** *n.* —**Syn. 1.** design, scheme.

pla·nar (plā′nər), *adj.* of or lying in a geometric plane. —**pla·nar·i·ty** (plə-nâr′ə tē), *n.*

plane¹ (plān), *n.* **1.** a flat or level surface. **2.** *Geom.* a surface generated by a straight line on any two points. **3.** a level of existence or development. **4.** an airplane. **5.** *Obsolesc.* a wing of an aircraft. —*adj.* **6.** flat or level. **7.** of or pertaining to planes or plane figures.

plane² (plān), *n., v.,* **planed, plan·ing.** —*n.* **1.** a woodworking tool for smoothing, shaping, or truing. —*v.t.* **2.** to smooth or shape with a plane. —**plan′er,** *n.*

plane³ (plān), *n.* any of several large, spreading shade trees, as the sycamore. Also called **plane′ tree′.**

plan·et (plan′it), *n.* any large heavenly body revolving about the sun and shining by reflected light. —**plan′e·tar′y,** *adj.*

plan·e·tar·i·um (plan′i târ′ē əm), *n., pl.* **-tar·i·ums, -tar·i·a** (-târ′ē ə). **1.** an apparatus or model representing the planetary system. **2.** a device that produces a representation of the heavens by the use of a number of moving projectors. **3.** a building housing such a device.

plan·e·tes·i·mal (plan′i tes′ə məl), *n.* one of the minute bodies that, hypothetically, was an original constituent of the solar system.

plan·et·oid (plan′i toid′), *n.* asteroid (def. 1).

plan·e·tol·o·gy (plan′i tol′ə jē), *n.* a science that deals with the physical features of the planets. —**plan′et·ol′o·gist,** *n.*

plan·gent (plan′jənt), *adj.* resounding loudly, esp. with a plaintive sound, as a bell. —**plan′gen·cy,** *n.*

plank (plangk), *n.* **1.** a long, flat piece of timber, thicker than a board. **2.** one of the expressed principles or objectives comprising the political platform of a party. —*v.t.* **3.** to lay or cover with planks. **4.** to bake or broil and serve on a board. **5. plank down,** to lay or put down with force.

plank·ing (plang′king), *n.* **1.** planks collectively. **2.** the laying or covering of planks.

plank·ton (plangk′tən), *n.* the passively floating or drifting organisms in a body of water. —**plank·ton′ic** (-ton′ik), *adj.*

planned′ par′enthood, the practice by which parents may regulate the number and frequency of their children.

plant (plant, plänt), *n.* **1.** any living organism having rigid cellulose walls, lacking sensory organs and locomotive ability, and mostly living by photosynthesis. **2.** an herb or other soft-stemmed organism, in contrast with a tree or a shrub. **3.** the land, buildings, and machinery necessary for certain kinds of manufacture, as automobiles, chemicals, or electric power. —*v.t.* **4.** to put in the ground for growth. **5.** to furnish or stock (land) with plants. **6.** to establish or implant (ideas, teachings, etc.). **7.** to insert or set firmly. **8.** *Slang.* to station or place covertly or for purposes of deception: *to plant spies.* **9.** to establish or found (a colony).

plan·tain¹ (plan′tin, -tᵊn), *n.* **1.** a tropical plant resembling the banana. **2.** its fruit.

plan·tain² (plan′tin, -tᵊn), *n.* a weed with large, spreading leaves close to the ground and long, slender spikes of small flowers.

plan·tar (plan′tər), *adj.* of the sole of the foot.

plan·ta·tion (plan tā′shən), *n.* **1.** an estate, esp. in a tropical country, on which cotton, tobacco, or coffee is cultivated, formerly by resident laborers. **2.** *Chiefly Brit.* a group of planted trees or plants.

plant·er (plan′tər, plän′-), *n.* **1.** the owner or manager of a plantation. **2.** a machine for planting seeds in the ground. **3.** a person who plants. **4.** a decorative container for growing flowers or ornamental plants.

plant′ louse′, aphid.

plaque (plak), *n.* **1.** a thin, flat plate or tablet, as of metal, intended for ornament, as on a wall. **2.** an inscribed commemorative tablet, as on a monument. **3.** a platelike brooch worn as a badge. **4.** a gelatinous accumulation of bacteria that forms on the teeth.

plash (plash), *n.* **1.** a gentle splash. —*v.t., v.i.* **2.** to splash gently.

plas·ma (plaz′mə), *n.* **1.** the liquid part of blood or lymph. **2.** whey. **3.** a highly ionized gas consisting almost entirely of free electrons and positive ions. Also, **plasm** (plaz′əm) (for defs. 1, 2). —**plas·mat′ic** (-mat′-ik), **plas′mic,** *adj.*

plas·ter (plas′tər, plä′stər), *n.* **1.** a mixture of lime or gypsum, sand, and water, applied in a pasty form to walls, ceilings, etc., and allowed to harden and dry. **2.** See **plaster of Paris. 3.** a preparation for spreading on a cloth and applying to the body for a healing purpose. —*v.t.* **4.** to cover with plaster. **5.** to lay flat like a layer of plaster. **6.** to apply a plaster to (the body). **7.** to overspread with something, esp. excessively: *to plaster posters on a fence.* —**plas′ter·er,** *n.* —**plas′ter·y,** *adj.*

plas·ter·board (plas′tər bôrd′, -bôrd′, plä′stər-), *n.* paper-covered sheets of gypsum and felt for insulating or covering walls.

plas′ter of Par′is, a white powder made from gypsum that hardens quickly after being mixed with water, used for making molds and casts.

plas·tic (plas′tik), *n.* **1.** any of a group of synthetic or natural organic materials that may be shaped when soft and then hardened, used in construction and decoration, and, drawn into filaments, for weaving. —*adj.* **2.** made of a plastic. **3.** capable of being molded or shaped. **4.** having the power of molding or shaping formless material. **5.** *Slang.* **a.** false or insincere: *plastic political speeches.* **b.** superficial or inhuman: *a plastic society.* [< L *plastic(us)* that may be molded < Gk *plastikós*] —**plas·tic·i·ty** (pla stis′i tē), *n.*

plas′tic cred′it, *Informal.* credit granted, esp. by banks, to holders of credit cards: so called because such cards are usually made of plastic.

plas′tic sur′gery, surgery dealing with the repair or replacement of malformed, injured, or lost organs of the body, chiefly by the transplant of living tissues. —**plas′tic sur′geon.**

plat (plat), *n., v.,* **plat·ted, plat·ting.** —*n.* **1.** a plot of ground. **2.** a plan or map of land. —*v.t.* **3.** to make a plat of.

plate[1] (plāt), *n., v.,* **plat·ed, plat·ing.** —*n.* **1.** a shallow, usually circular dish from which food is served or eaten. **2.** the contents of such a dish. **3.** an entire course on one dish. **4.** household dishes, utensils, etc., of or coated with gold or silver. **5.** a thin, flat sheet of metal, esp. of uniform thickness. **6.** a flat, polished piece of metal on which something is engraved. **7.** a flat or curved sheet of material, as metal, on which a picture or text has been engraved, used as a printing surface. **8.** a printed impression from such a piece. **9.** a full-page illustration in a book. **10.** the part of a denture that conforms to the mouth and contains the teeth. **11. the plate,** *Baseball.* See **home plate. 12.** a sheet of glass or metal coated with a sensitized emulsion, used for taking a photograph. —*v.t.* **13.** to coat (metal) with a thin film of gold, silver, etc. **14.** to cover with metal plates for protection. **15.** to make a printing plate from (type). —**plat′ed,** *adj.*

pla·teau (pla tō′), *n., pl.* **-teaus, -teaux** (-tōz′). **1.** a level land area raised above adjoining land on at least one side. **2.** any period of little growth or decline.

plate′ glass′, flat, thick glass ground and polished to a smooth surface, used in large windows, etc.

plat·en (plat′ən), *n.* **1.** a flat plate in a printing press for pressing the paper against the inked type. **2.** the roller of a typewriter.

plat·form (plat′fôrm), *n.* **1.** a raised, flat structure, as in a hall, for use by public speakers, etc. **2.** a set of principles on which a political party takes a public stand.

plat·ing (plā′tiƞg), *n.* **1.** a thin coating of gold, silver, etc. **2.** an external layer of metal plates.

plat·i·num (plat′ən əm, plat′nəm), *n. Chem.* a heavy, grayish-white metallic element, resistant to most chemicals: used esp. in jewelry. *Symbol:* Pt: *at. wt.:* 195.09; *at. no.:* 78.

plat·i·tude (plat′i tōōd′, -tyōōd′), *n.* a flat, dull, or trite remark. —**plat′i·tu′di·nous,** *adj.* —**plat′i·tu′di·nous·ly,** *adv.* —**Syn.** cliché.

Pla·to (plā′tō), *n.* 427—347 B.C., Greek philosopher.

Pla·ton·ic (plə ton′ik, plā-), *adj.* **1.** of Plato or his doctrines. **2.** (*usually l.c.*) free from sensual desire, esp. in a relationship between a man and a woman. **pla·ton′i·cal·ly,** *adv.*

pla·toon (plə tōōn′), *n.* **1.** a military unit consisting of two or more squads. **2.** any similar group or company.

platoon′ ser′geant, *U.S. Army.* a noncommissioned officer ranking below a first sergeant.

plat·ter (plat′ər), *n.* **1.** a large, shallow dish, usually oval in shape, used for serving food, esp. meat. **2.** a meal served on this. **3.** *Slang.* a phonograph record.

plat·y (plat′ē), *n., pl.* **plat·y, plat·ys, plat·ies.** any of several small, freshwater fishes found in Mexico and often kept in aquariums.

plat·y·pus (plat′i pəs), *n., pl.* **-pus·es, -pi** (-pī′). duckbill.

plau·dit (plô′dit), *n.* Usually, **plaudits.** an expression or demonstration of approval, usually by applause.

plau·si·ble (plô′zə bəl), *adj.* **1.** having an appearance of truth or reason but usually open to question: *a plausible excuse.* **2.** apparently worthy of belief or trust but usually not really so: *a plausible adventurer.* —**plau′si·bil′i·ty, plau′si·ble·ness,** *n.* —**plau′si·bly,** *adv.*

play (plā), *n.* **1.** a dramatic composition or piece. **2.** a dramatic performance, as on the stage. **3.** exercise or activity for amusement or recreation. **4.** fun or jest, as opposed to seriousness. **5.** the playing or action of a game. **6.** one's turn to play in a game: *Whose play is it?* **7.** a playing for stakes. **8.** the action or dealing of a specified kind: *fair play.* **9.** action or operation: *the play of fancy.* **10.** light, brisk, or changing movement. **11.** freedom of movement within a space. **12. in** or **out of play,** in or not in the state of being played in a game. **13. make a play for,** *Slang.* to try to attract or gain by impressing favorably. —*v.t.* **14.** to act the part of (a person or character) in a dramatic performance. **15.** to engage in (a game, pastime, etc.). **16.** to contend against in a game. **17.** to employ (a piece of equipment, a player, etc.) in a game. **18.** to bet on. **19.** to imitate in jest or sport: *to play house.* **20.** to perform on (a musical instrument). **21.** to perform (music) on an instrument. **22.** to cause to give forth sound: *to play a radio.* **23.** to do or perform in sport: *to play tricks.* **24.** to cause to move lightly or quickly. —*v.i.* **25.** to exercise oneself in amusement or recreation. **26.** to do something in sport. **27.** to trifle or toy. **28.** to take part in a game. **29.** to conduct oneself in a specified way: *to play fair.* **30.** to act on or as on the stage. **31.** to perform on a musical instrument. **32.** to sound in performance: *Was the radio playing?* **33.** to move about lightly or quickly. **34. play down,** to treat as of little importance. **35. played out,** exhausted or weary. **36. play on** or **upon,** to exploit, as the feelings of another. **37. play up,** to emphasize the importance of. **38. play up to,** *Informal.* to attempt to impress in order to gain someone's favor. —**play′a·ble,** *adj.*

play·act (plā′akt′), *v.i.* **1.** to engage in make-believe. **2.** to perform in a play. —**play′act′ing,** *n.*

play·back (plā′bak′), *n.* the act of reproducing recorded sound, esp. of a tape recorder, right after the recording has been made.

play·bill (plā′bil′), *n.* a program or announcement of a play.

play·boy (plā′boi′), *n.* a wealthy, carefree man who devotes most of his time to the seeking of pleasure. —**play′girl′,** *n.fem.*

play-by-play (plā′bī plā′), *adj.* **1.** pertaining to or being a detailed account of each incident or act of an event. —*n.* **2.** such an account, as a broadcast of a sports event.

play·er (plā′ər), *n.* **1.** a person who takes part or is skilled in a game or sport. **2.** a stage actor. **3.** a performer on a musical instrument. **4.** See **record player.**

play·ful (plā′fəl), *adj.* **1.** full of play or fun. **2.** pleasantly humorous or teasing. —**play′ful·ly,** *adv.* —**play′ful·ness,** *n.*

play·go·er (plā′gō′ər), *n.* a person who attends the theater often or habitually.

play·ground (plā′ground′), *n.* an outdoor area used for recreation, esp. by children.

play·house (plā′hous′), *n.* **1.** a theater. **2.** a small house for children to play in.

play′ing card′, one of a set of cards in four suits, used in playing various games.

play·let (plā′lit), *n.* a short play.

play·mate (plā′māt′), *n.* a child's companion in play. Also called **play′fel′low.**

play-off (plā′ôf′, -of′), *n.* **1.** an extra game or round to settle a tie. **2.** a game or series of games to decide a championship.

play′ on words′, a pun.

play·pen (plā′pen′), *n.* a small enclosure in which an infant or young child can play safely.

play·suit (plā′sōōt′), *n.* a sports costume for women and children.

play·thing (plā′thing′), *n.* toy (def. 1).

play·wright (plā′rīt′), *n.* a writer of plays.

pla·za (plä′zə, plaz′ə), *n.* **1.** a public square or open space in a city or town. **2.** an area along an expressway where public facilities are available. **3.** *Chiefly Canadian.* See **shopping center.**

plea (plē), *n.* **1.** an earnest appeal or request. **2.** an excuse or pretext. **3.** *Law.* a defendant's answer to a charge.

plea′ bar′gaining, a practice in which a criminal defendant is under certain conditions allowed to plead guilty to a lesser charge without a trial, usually resulting in a lenient sentence. —**plea′-bar′gain,** *v.i.*

plead (plēd), *v.*, **plead·ed** or (*Informal or Dial.*) **pled** or **plead** (pled); **plead·ing.** —*v.i.* **1.** to appeal or request earnestly. **2.** *Law.* to put forward a plea in a court. —*v.t.* **3.** to offer as an excuse. **4.** *Law.* **a.** to argue (a case) before a court. **b.** to make a plea of a specific kind: *to plead not guilty.* —**plead′er,** *n.*

pleas·ant (plez′ant), *adj.* **1.** tending to give pleasure. **2.** agreeable or amiable in behavior or manners. —**pleas′ant·ly,** *adv.* —**pleas′ant·ness,** *n.*

pleas·ant·ry (plez′ən trē), *n., pl.* **-ries.** **1.** a courteous social remark, esp. made at the start of a conversation. **2.** a humorous or jesting remark or action.

please (plēz), *v.*, **pleased, pleas·ing.** —*v.t.* **1.** to act to the pleasure or satisfaction of. **2.** to be the pleasure or will of. **3.** be so kind as to: *Please come here.* —*v.i.* **4.** to give pleasure or satisfaction. **5.** to like or wish: *Go where you please.* —**pleas′er,** *n.*

pleas·ing (plē′zing), *adj.* able to produce pleasure. —**pleas′ing·ly,** *adv.*

pleas·ur·a·ble (plezh′ər ə bəl), *adj.* capable of causing pleasure. —**pleas′ur·a·bly,** *adv.*

pleas·ure (plezh′ər), *n.* **1.** enjoyment or satisfaction derived from what is to one's liking. **2.** a cause or source of such a feeling. **3.** a person's will or desire. —**pleas′ure·ful,** *adj.* —Syn. **1.** delight, happiness, joy.

pleat (plēt), *n.* **1.** a fold of even width made by doubling cloth on itself and by pressing or stitching it into place. —*v.t.* **2.** to fold or arrange in pleats.

plebe (plēb), *n.* a freshman at the U.S. Military or Naval Academy.

ple·be·ian (plə bē′ən), *adj.* **1.** of the ancient Roman plebs. **2.** common or vulgar. —*n.* **3.** a member of the ancient Roman plebs. **4.** a member of the common people.

pleb·i·scite (pleb′ī sīt′, -sit), *n.* a direct vote by the people of a country or state on some important public question.

plebs (plebz), *n., pl.* **ple·bes** (plē′bēz). **1.** the common people of ancient Rome. **2.** the common people.

plec·trum (plek′trəm), *n., pl.* **-trums,** **-tra** (-trə). a small piece of metal, plastic, etc., for plucking the strings of a guitar, mandolin, etc.

pled (pled), *v. Informal or Dial.* a pt. and pp. of **plead.**

pledge (plej), *n., v.,* **pledged, pledg·ing.** —*n.* **1.** a solemn promise or agreement. **2.** something given as security, as for the fulfillment of a promise. **3.** the state of being held as security. **4.** a person accepted for membership in a club, fraternity, etc., but not yet formally approved. —*v.t.* **5.** to bind by a pledge. **6.** to promise solemnly. **7.** to give as a pledge. —**pledg′er,** *n.*

Pleis·to·cene (plī′stə sēn′), *adj.* **1.** noting the epoch forming the earlier half of the Quaternary, characterized by widespread glacial ice and by the appearance of humans. —*n.* **2.** the Pleistocene epoch.

ple·na·ry (plē′nə rē, plen′ə-), *adj.* **1.** attended by all qualified members. **2.** complete or absolute, as power or authority. —**ple′na·ri·ly,** *adv.*

plen·i·po·ten·ti·ar·y (plen′ē pə ten′shē er′ē, -shə rē), *n., pl.* **-ar·ies,** *adj.* —*n.* **1.** a diplomatic agent having full authority to represent a government. —*adj.* **2.** having full power or authority.

plen·i·tude (plen′i tōōd′, -tyōōd′), *n.* **1.** fullness in quantity or measure. **2.** the state of being full or complete.

plen·te·ous (plen′tē əs), *adj. Chiefly Literary.* plentiful. —**plen′te·ous·ness,** *n.*

plen·ti·ful (plen′ti fəl), *adj.* **1.** existing in great plenty. **2.** yielding abundantly. —**plen′ti·ful·ly,** *adv.* —Syn. **1.** ample, bountiful, copious.

plen·ty (plen′tē), *n., pl.* **-ties,** *adv.* —*n.* **1.** a fully adequate number or amount. **2.** the state or quality of being plentiful. —*adv.* **3.** *Informal.* fully or quite.

ple·num (plē′nəm, plen′əm), *n. pl.* **ple·nums, ple·na** (plē′nə, plen′ə). **1.** the whole of space filled with matter. **2.** a full assembly, as a joint legislative assembly.

pleth·o·ra (pleth′ər ə), *n.* an over-abundant amount.

pleu·ri·sy (plŏŏr′i sē), *n.* inflammation of the membrane that covers the lungs and lines the chest.

Plex·i·glas (plek′sə glas′, -gläs′), *n. Trademark.* plexiglass.

plex·i·glass (plek′sə glas′, -gläs′), *n.* a lightweight, transparent acrylic plastic material, used chiefly for signs, windows, etc.

plex·us (plek′səs), *n., pl.* **-us·es, -us.** a network of nerves or blood vessels.

pli·a·ble (plī′ə bəl), *adj.* **1.** easily bent. **2.** easily influenced or persuaded. —**pli′a·bil′i·ty,** *n.* —**pli′a·bly,** *adv.*

pli·ant (plī'ənt), *adj.* **1.** bending or yielding readily. **2.** easily yielding to others. **3.** adapting readily to different situations. **—pli'an·cy**, *n.* **—pli'ant·ly**, *adv.*

pli·ers (plī'ərz), *n.* small pincers for bending wire, holding small objects, etc.

plight[1] (plīt), *n.* a distressed or unfortunate condition or state.

plight[2] (plīt), *v.t. Literary.* to give in pledge, as one's word.

plinth (plinth), *n.* a square slab beneath the base of a column.

Pli·o·cene (plī'ə sēn'), *adj.* **1.** noting an epoch occurring from one million to ten million years ago, characterized by an increase in the size and numbers of mammals. **—n.** **2.** the Pliocene epoch.

plod (plod), *v.i.*, **plod·ded**, **plod·ding**. **1.** to walk or move heavily. **2.** to work with constant and monotonous perseverance. **—plod'der**, *n.* **—plod'ding·ly**, *adv.*

PLO, Palestine Liberation Organization.

plop (plop), *v.*, **plopped**, **plop·ping**, *n.* **—v.t.**, *v.i.* **1.** to drop with a sound like that of a flat object striking water without a splash. **—n.** **2.** a plopping sound or fall.

plot[1] (plot), *n.*, *v.*, **plot·ted**, **plot·ting**. **—n.** **1.** a secret plan to do something unlawful or evil. **2.** the plan or main story of a play, novel, etc. **—v.t.** **3.** to plan secretly. **4.** to mark on a map or chart, as a ship's course. **—v.i.** **5.** to make secret plans. **—plot'ter**, *n.* **—Syn.** 5. conspire, scheme.

plot[2] (plot), *n.* a small area of ground.

plov·er (pluv'ər, plō'vər), *n.* a bird having a short tail and a bill like that of a pigeon.

plow (plou), *n.* **1.** a farming implement used for cutting and turning up soil. **2.** any implement resembling this, as a snowplow. **—v.t.** **3.** to cut and turn up (soil) with a plow. **4.** to make (one's way) laboriously through in the manner of a plow. **—v.i.** **5.** to work with a plow. **6.** to move or proceed through something in a slow or forceful manner. Also, *esp. Brit.,* **plough.** **—plow'a·ble,** *adj.* **—plow'er,** *n.* **—plow'man,** *n.*

plow·share (plou'shâr'), *n.* the part of a plow that cuts a furrow in the soil.

ploy (ploi), *n.* a tricky remark or action calculated to gain an advantage by outwitting another.

pluck (pluk), *v.t.* **1.** to pull off or out, as flowers. **2.** to pull by force. **3.** to remove the feathers or hair from by pulling. **4.** to sound (the strings of a musical instrument) by pulling at them with the fingers or a plectrum. **—v.i.** **5.** to pull or tug sharply. **—n.** **6.** the act of plucking. **7.** the heart, liver, and lungs, esp. of an animal used for food. **8.** admirable courage.

pluck·y (pluk'ē), *adj.*, **pluck·i·er**, **pluck·i·est**. admirably courageous. **—pluck'i·ly**, *adv.* **—pluck'i·ness**, *n.*

plug (plug), *n*, *v.*, **plugged**, **plug·ging**. **—n.** **1.** a piece of wood or other material used to stop up a hole. **2.** *Elect.* a device to which the conductors of a cord may be attached and which establishes contact by insertion into an outlet. **3.** a cake of pressed tobacco. **4.** *Slang.* a worn-out horse. **5.** *Informal.* a favorable mention of a product, as on a radio program. **6.** a kind of artificial fishing lure. **—v.t.** **7.** to stop with or as with a plug. **8.** to insert a plug into. **9.** *Informal.* to mention (a product) favorably. **10.** *Slang.* to hit with a bullet. **—v.i.** **11.** *Informal.* to work steadily or doggedly.

plum (plum), *n.* **1.** a round fruit with a smooth skin and a single flat seed. **2.** the tree that bears this fruit. **3.** a raisin when used in a cake or pudding. **4.** a deep purple. **5.** *Slang.* an excellent or desirable thing, as a fine position.

plum·age (plōō'mij), *n.* the feathers of a bird.

plumb (plum), *n.* **1.** a small mass of lead suspended by a line (**plumb' line'**), used to measure the depth of water or to ascertain a vertical line. **—adj.** **2.** exactly straight down, esp. as achieved with the aid of a plumb line. **—adv.** **3.** in a plumb direction. **4.** exactly or precisely. **5.** *Informal.* completely or absolutely. **—v.t.** **6.** to test or measure by a plumb line. **7.** to examine closely in order to understand. [< L *plumbum* lead] **—plumb'a·ble,** *adj.*

plumb·er (plum'ər), *n.* a person who installs or repairs pipes, fixtures, etc., esp. of a water system.

plumb'er's help'er, *Informal.* plunger (def. 2). Also called **plumb'er's friend'.**

plumb·ing (plum'ing), *n.* **1.** the pipes, fixtures, etc., of a water or drainage system. **2.** the work or trade of a plumber.

plume (plōōm), *n.*, *v.*, **plumed**, **plum·ing**. **—n.** **1.** a feather, esp. a large, long, or fluffy one. **—v.t.** **2.** to cover or adorn with plumes. **3.** to preen. **—plumed,** *adj.* **—plum'y,** *adj.*

plum·met (plum'it), *n.* **1.** Also called **plumb' bob'**. a pointed weight attached to a plumb line. **2.** something that weighs down or depresses. **—v.i.** **3.** to plunge straight down.

plump[1] (plump), *adj.* well filled out or rounded in form. —**plump′ly**, *adv.* —**plump′ness**, *n.*

plump[2] (plump), *v.i.*, *v.t.* **1.** to drop heavily or suddenly. **2. plump for**, to support enthusiastically. —*n.* **3.** a heavy or sudden fall. **4.** the sound resulting from this. —*adv.* **5.** heavily or suddenly. **6.** straight down.

plun·der (plun′dər), *v.t.* **1.** to rob of goods by force, as hostile raids. — *v.i.* **2.** to take plunder. —*n.* **3.** the act of plundering. **4.** goods plundered. —**plun′der·a·ble**, *adj.* — **plun′der·er**, *n.* —**Syn. 1.** pillage, ravage, sack.

plunge (plunj), *v.*, **plunged, plung·ing**, *n.* —*v.t.* **1.** to throw or thrust forcibly or suddenly into a liquid, some condition, etc. —*v.i.* **2.** to cast oneself into or as into water, a hole, etc. **3.** *Informal.* to bet or speculate recklessly. **4.** to descend abruptly. —*n.* **5.** the act of plunging.

plung·er (plun′jər), *n.* **1.** a pistonlike part moving within the cylinder of a pump. **2.** a device consisting of a suction cup on a long handle, used for clearing clogged drains. **3.** a person or thing that plunges.

plunk (plungk), *v.t.* **1.** to pluck (a stringed instrument or its strings). **2.** *Informal.* to put down heavily or suddenly. —*v.i.* **3.** to give forth a twanging sound. **4.** *Informal.* to drop heavily or suddenly. **5. plunk down**, *Informal.* to give as payment. —*n.* **6.** a twanging sound.

plu·per·fect (ploo pûr′fikt), *adj.*, *n.* (in older grammars) See **past perfect**.

plu·ral (ploor′əl), *Gram.* —*adj.* **1.** noting the form of a word that refers to more than one. —*n.* **2.** the plural number. **3.** a form in the plural. —**plu′ral·ly**, *adv.*

plu·ral·i·ty (ploo ral′i tē), *n.*, *pl.* **-ties.** **1.** the excess of votes received by the leading candidate, in an election in which there are three or more candidates, over those received by the next candidate. **2.** a number greater than one. **3.** the state of being plural.

plu·ral·ize (ploor′ə līz′), *v.t.*, **-ized, -iz·ing.** to make plural. —**plu′ral·i·za′tion**, *n.*

plus (plus), *prep.* **1.** increased by. **2.** with the addition of. —*adj.* **3.** noting addition. **4.** positive: *a plus quantity.* **5.** more (by a certain amount). **6.** having a certain quality to an unusual degree: *He has personality plus.* —*n.* **7.** a plus quantity. **8.** Also called **plus′ sign′.** the symbol (+) indicating addition or a positive quantity. **9.** something additional. **10.** a surplus or gain.

plush (plush), *n.*, *adj.*, **plush·er, plush·est.** —*n.* **1.** a fabric resembling vel-

vet but having a deeper pile. —*adj.* **2.** Also, **plush′y.** *Informal.* expensively luxurious. —**plush′ly**, *adv.*

Plu·tarch (ploo′tärk), *n.* A.D. c46–c120, Greek biographer.

Plu·to (ploo′tō), *n.* **1.** *Class. Myth.* the god ruling the abode of the dead. **2.** the planet farthest away from the sun.

plu·toc·ra·cy (ploo tok′rə sē), *n.*, *pl.* **-cies.** **1.** government by the wealthy. **2.** a ruling class of wealthy people. —**plu′to·crat′** (-tə krat′), *n.* —**plu′to·crat′ic**, *adj.*

plu·ton (ploo′ton), *n.* any body of igneous rock formed far below the earth's surface. —**plu·ton′ic**, *adj.*

plu·to·ni·um (ploo tō′nē əm), *n.* *Chem.* a radioactive element used as fuel in some nuclear reactors. *Symbol:* Pu; *at. no.:* 94.

plu·vi·al (ploo′vē əl), *adj.* of or having rain, esp. much rain.

ply[1] (plī), *v.*, **plied, ply·ing.** —*v.t.* **1.** to work with or at diligently: *to ply the needle.* **2.** to carry on or practice busily or steadily: *to ply a trade.* **3.** to assail persistently. **4.** to offer something pressingly to: *to ply a person with drink.* **5.** to sail over or along (a river, etc.) steadily. —*v.i.* **6.** to run or travel regularly between certain places, as a boat, bus, etc. **7.** to perform one's work busily or steadily.

ply[2] (plī), *n.*, *pl.* **plies**, *v.*, **plied, ply·ing.** —*n.* **1.** one thickness or layer, as in certain wood products. **2.** any of the strands of which yarn or rope is made. —*v.t.* **3.** to twist together, as strands of yarn.

Plym·outh (plim′əth), *n.* a town in SE Massachusetts: founded by the Pilgrims 1620.

ply·wood (plī′wood′), *n.* a building material made by gluing several thin layers of wood together.

Pm, promethium.

pm., premium.

P.M., 1. Paymaster. **2.** See **p.m. 3.** Police Magistrate **4.** Postmaster. **5.** postmortem. **6.** Prime Minister. **7.** Provost Marshal. Also, **PM**

p.m., the period from 12 noon to 12 midnight. [< L *post meridiem*]

pmk., postmark.

pmt., payment.

P/N, promissory note. Also, **p.n.**

pneu·mat·ic (noo mat′ik, nyoo-), *adj.* **1.** of or containing air, gases, or wind. **2.** operated by compressed air. **3.** filled with compressed air, as a tire. —**pneu·mat′i·cal·ly**, *adv.*

pneu·mo·co·ni·o·sis (noo′mə kō′nē ō′sis, nyoo′-), *n.* a disease of the lungs due to irritation caused by the inhalation of mineral or metallic dust.

pneu·mo·nia (nŏŏ mōn′yə, -mō′nē ə, nyŏŏ-), *n.* acute inflammation of the lungs caused by bacterial or viral infection.

pnxt., See **pinx.**

Po (pō), *n.* a river in N Italy.

Po, polonium.

P.O., 1. petty officer. 2. postal (money) order. 3. post office.

poach[1] (pōch), *v.i., v.t.* 1. to trespass on (another's game preserve) in order to hunt or fish. 2. to take (game or fish) illegally. —**poach′er,** *n.*

poach[2] (pōch), *v.t.* to cook (eggs without shells, fish, etc.) in or over simmering water.

POB, post office box.

POC, port of call.

pock (pok), *n.* 1. a pustule caused by an eruptive disease, as smallpox. 2. pockmark. —**pocked,** *adj.*

pock·et (pok′it), *n.* 1. a small pouch attached in or on a garment, used for carrying small articles. 2. any pouchlike receptacle or cavity. 3. any isolated group, area, or element: *pockets of resistance.* 4. pocketbook (def. 2). 5. a cavity in the earth containing ore. —*adj.* 6. suitable for carrying in the pocket. 7. relatively small. —*v.t.* 8. to put into one's pocket. 9. to take possession of as one's own, often dishonestly. 10. to conceal or suppress: *to pocket one's pride.* 11. to enclose as in a pocket. —**pock′et·ful,** *n.*

pock·et·book (pok′it bŏŏk′), *n.* 1. a woman's purse or handbag. 2. financial resources or means. 3. Also, **pock′et book′,** a book, usually bound in paper, small enough to fit into a pocket. 4. *Brit.* a. a notebook for the pocket. b. *Obsolesc.* a wallet or billfold.

pock·et·knife (pok′it nīf′), *n.* a small knife with one or more blades that fold into the handle.

pock′et park′, a very small park, usually part of a city block containing tall buildings.

pock′et ve′to, a veto of a Congressional bill, automatically effected by the President by not signing the bill before adjournment of the Congress.

pock·mark (pok′märk′), *n.* a scar left by a pock. —**pock′marked′,** *adj.*

po·co (pō′kō), *adv. Music.* somewhat.

po·co a po·co (pō′kō ä pō′kō), *Music.* gradually or little by little.

pod (pod), *n.* 1. a somewhat elongated, two-valved seed vessel, as that of the pea or bean. 2. a compartment under an airplane, for housing a jet engine, cargo, or weapons.

POD, 1. port of debarkation. 2. pay on delivery.

po·di·a·try (pō dī′ə trē, pə-), *n.* the treatment of minor foot ailments, as corns, bunions, etc. —**po·di′a·trist,** *n.*

po·di·um (pō′dē əm), *n., pl.* -**di·ums, -di·a** (-dē ə). 1. a small platform for an orchestra conductor. 2. (loosely) a lectern.

Poe (pō), *n.* **Ed·gar Al·lan** (ed′gər al′ən), 1809–49, U.S. poet, short-story writer, and critic.

POE, 1. port of embarkation. 2. port of entry.

po·em (pō′əm), *n.* a composition in verse, esp. a highly developed, imaginative one.

po·e·sy (pō′i sē, -zē), *n. Archaic.* poetry.

po·et (pō′it), *n.* 1. a person who composes poetry. 2. a person who has the gift of artistic sensitivity. —**po′et·ess,** *n.fem.*

po·et·as·ter (pō′it as′tər), *n.* a writer of low-quality verse.

po·et·ic (pō et′ik), *adj.* 1. of, for, or like poetry or poets. 2. having the qualities of poetry. Also, **po·et′i·cal.** —**po·et′i·cal·ly,** *adv.*

poet′ic jus′tice, an ideal distribution of rewards and punishments such as is common in some poetry and fiction.

poet′ic li′cense, liberty taken by a poet in deviating from rule, form, or logic in order to produce a desired effect.

po·et·ry (pō′i trē), *n.* 1. the art of writing poems. 2. poems collectively. 3. poetic qualities however manifested.

po·grom (pə grum′, -grom′, pō-), *n.* an organized massacre, esp. of Jews. [< Russ: devastation]

poi (poi, pō′ē), *n.* a Hawaiian dish made of taro root.

poign·ant (poin′yənt, poin′ənt), *adj.* 1. keenly distressing to the feelings. 2. affecting or moving the emotions. 3. pungent to the smell. —**poign′an·cy,** *n.* —**poign′ant·ly,** *adv.*

poi·lu (pwä′lŏŏ), *n.* a French soldier in World War I.

poin·ci·an·a (poin′sē an′ə, -ā′nə), *n.* any shrub or small tree having showy orange or scarlet flowers.

poin·set·ti·a (poin set′ē ə, -set′ə), *n.* a plant native to tropical America, having tiny flowers surrounded by large, bright-red, petallike leaves.

point (point), *n.* 1. a sharp or tapering end. 2. a projecting part of anything. 3. a mark made by the sharp end of anything, as a dot. 4. a mark of punctuation, esp. a period. 5. a decimal point. 6. *Geom.* an element having position but not dimensions, as the intersection of two lines. 7. a particular place. 8. any definite position, as in a scale. **9.** any of 32 separate directions, as indicated on a compass. **10.** a degree or stage. **11.** a particular instant of time. **12.** the main idea. **13.** a particular aim or purpose. **14.** a hint or suggestion. **15.** a distinguishing mark or quality. **16.** a single or separate item. **17.** a single unit in counting, measuring, or scoring a game. **18.** a unit of price quotation, as one dollar in stock tradings. **19.** *Print.* a unit of type measurement equal to 1/72 inch. **20.** at the point of, close to. **21.** beside the point, not related to the subject. **22.** in point, pertinent or appropriate. Also, **to the point.** —*v.t.* **23.** to direct (a finger, a weapon, etc.) at or to something. **24.** to indicate the position of: *to point out an object in the sky.* **25.** to furnish with a point, as a pencil. **26.** to mark with one or more points, decimal dots, etc. **27.** to give added force to: *to point up the necessity for caution.* —*v.i.* **28.** to indicate position, as with the finger. **29.** to call attention to. **30.** to face in a particular direction. —**point′y,** *adj.*

point-blank (point′blaṅgk′), *adj.* **1.** aimed or fired straight at the mark, esp. from close range. **2.** straightforward or explicit. —*adv.* **3.** with a direct aim. **4.** bluntly or frankly.

point-ed (poin′tid), *adj.* **1.** having a point. **2.** sharp or piercing: *pointed wit.* **3.** directed particularly, as at a person. **4.** marked or emphasized. —**point′ed-ly,** *adv.* —**point′ed-ness,** *n.*

point-er (poin′tər), *n.* **1.** a long, tapering stick used in pointing things out, as on a map. **2.** a hand on a watch dial, scale, etc. **3.** a short-haired hunting dog. **4.** a piece of advice.

poin-til-lism (pwan′t°liz′əm, -tē iz′əm, poin′-), *n.* a technique in painting of using tiny dots of pure colors instead of brush strokes, the dots being optically mixed into the resulting hue by the viewer. —**poin′til-list,** *n.,* *adj.*

point-less (point′lis), *adj.* **1.** without a point. **2.** without force, meaning, or relevance. —**point′less-ly,** *adv.* —**point′less-ness,** *n.*

point′ of no return′, a crucial point reached in a course of action with no possibility of turning back.

point′ of view′, **1.** a specified manner of consideration or appraisal. **2.** a mental position or attitude.

poise (poiz), *n., v.,* **poised, pois-ing.** —*n.* **1.** a state of balance or equilibrium. **2.** dignified, self-confident manner or bearing. **3.** the way of being poised or carried. —*v.t., v.i.* **4.** to balance or be balanced evenly. —**Syn. 2.** composure, self-possession.

poi·son (poi′zən), *n.* **1.** a substance that can destroy life or impair health by its chemical action inside the body. —*v.t.* **2.** to kill or injure with or as with poison. **3.** to put poison into or upon. **4.** to ruin or corrupt. —*adj.* **5.** causing poisoning. —**poi′son-ous,** *adj.* —**poi′son-ous-ly,** *adv.* —**poi′son-er,** *n.*

poi′son i′vy, a shrub having white berries and pointed leaves in clusters of three, and causing a skin irritation.

poke¹ (pōk), *v.,* **poked, pok-ing,** *n.* —*v.t.* **1.** to prod or push, esp. with something pointed. **2.** to make (a hole, etc.) by or as by prodding or pushing. **3.** *Informal.* to hit with the fist. —*v.i.* **4.** to make a prodding or pushing movement. **5.** to thrust oneself obtrusively. **6.** to search curiously. **7.** to go or proceed in a slow or aimless way. **8.** **poke fun at,** to ridicule, esp. slyly. —*n.* **9.** a prod or push. **10.** *Informal,* a blow with the fist.

poke² (pōk), *n.* *Dial.* a small bag or sack.

pok-er¹ (pō′kər), *n.* a metal rod for stirring a fire.

pok-er² (pō′kər), *n.* a card game in which the players bet on the value of their hands.

pok′er face′, a purposely expressionless face.

pok-y (pō′kē), *adj.,* **pok-i-er, pok-i-est,** *n., pl.* **pok-ies.** —*adj.* **1.** annoyingly slow. **2.** (of a place) small and cramped. —*n.* **3.** *Slang.* a jail. Also, **pok′ey.** —**pok′i-ly,** *adv.* —**pok′i-ness,** *n.*

pol (pol), *n.* *Informal.* a politician.

Pol., **1.** Poland. **2.** Polish.

pol., **1.** political. **2.** politics.

Po-land (pō′lənd), *n.* a country in central Europe.

po-lar (pō′lər), *adj.* **1.** of or pertaining to a pole, as of the earth or a magnet. **2.** of or near the North or South Pole. **3.** opposite in character or action.

po′lar bear′, a large white bear of the arctic regions.

Po-lar-is (pō lâr′is, -lar′-), *n.* the bright star close to the north pole of the heavens.

po-lar-i-ty (pō lar′i tē, -pə-), *n.* **1.** the property or characteristic of having two opposite poles, as in a magnet or storage battery. **2.** the presence of two opposite principles, qualities, or tendencies.

po-lar-i-za-tion (pō′lər i zā′shən), *n.* **1.** a state, or the production of a state, in which rays of light exhibit different properties in different directions. **2.** a wide division of groups or forces into two extreme, opposing positions or views.

po·lar·ize (pō′lə rīz′), v., **-ized, -iz·ing.** —v.t. **1.** to cause polarization in. **2.** to give polarity to. **3.** to divide widely into two extreme, opposing positions or views. —v.i. **4.** to become polarized.

Po·lar·oid (pō′lə roid′), n. Trademark. **1.** Also called **Po′laroid cam′era.** a portable camera that produces a finished picture in seconds after each exposure. **2.** a transparent material for producing polarized light from unpolarized light.

pol·der (pōl′dər), n. a tract of low land, esp. in the Netherlands, reclaimed from the sea or other body of water and protected by dikes.

pole[1] (pōl), n., v., **poled, pol·ing.** —n. **1.** a long, cylindrical, slender piece of wood, metal, etc. —v.t., v.i. **2.** to furnish with poles. **3.** to push or propel (a boat, raft, etc.) with a pole. —**pol′er,** n.

pole[2] (pōl), n. **1.** each of the extremities of an axis, esp. of the earth. **2.** either of the ends of a magnet where the magnetism appears to be concentrated. **3.** either of the connections to an electric cell or battery. **4.** one of two opposite principles, qualities, or tendencies.

Pole (pōl), n. a native or inhabitant of Poland.

pole·cat (pōl′kat′), n., pl. **-cats, -cat. 1.** a European mammal of the weasel family that ejects a fetid fluid when attacked. **2.** skunk (def. 1).

po·lem·ic (pə lem′ik, pō-), n. **1.** a controversial argument, as one against some opinion, doctrine, etc. —adj. **2.** Also, **po·lem′i·cal.** of or pertaining to a polemic. —**po·lem′i·cal·ly,** adv.

po·lem·ics (pə lem′iks, pō-), n. the art or practice of disputation or controversy. —**po·lem′i·cist** (-lem′i sist), n.

pole·star (pōl′stär′), n. **1.** Polaris. **2.** a guiding principle.

pole′ vault′, a field event in which a vault over a crossbar is performed with the aid of a long pole. —**pole′-vault′,** v.i. —**pole′-vault′er,** n.

po·lice (pə lēs′), n., v., **-liced, -lic·ing.** —n. **1.** a force organized, esp. by a city or state government, to maintain order, prevent and detect crime, and enforce the laws. **2.** members of such a force. —v.t. **3.** to regulate or keep in order with or as with police. **4.** Mil. to clean or keep clean (a camp, post, etc.).

po·lice·man (pə lēs′mən), n. a member of a police force. —**po·lice′wom′an,** n.fem.

police′ state′, a nation in which the police, esp. a secret police, suppresses any act that conflicts with governmental policy.

pol·i·cy[1] (pol′i sē), n., pl. **-cies. 1.** a guiding principle or course of action adopted toward an objective or objectives. **2.** prudence or practical wisdom.

pol·i·cy[2] (pol′i sē), n., pl. **-cies.** a document embodying a contract of insurance.

pol·i·cy·hold·er (pol′i sē hōl′dər), n. the individual or firm in whose name an insurance policy is written.

po·li·o (pō′lē ō′), n. poliomyelitis.

po·li·o·my·e·li·tis (pō′lē ō mī′ə lī′tis), n. an acute viral disease, most common in infants, characterized by inflammation of the brain and spinal cord, resulting in paralysis. —**po·li·o·my·e·lit·ic** (pō′lē ō mī′ə lit′ik), adj.

pol·ish (pol′ish), v.t. **1.** to make smooth and glossy, esp. by rubbing. **2.** to make refined or elegant. —v.i. **3.** to become smooth and glossy through polishing. **4. polish off,** Slang. to finish or dispose of quickly. —n. **5.** a substance used to give smoothness or gloss. **6.** the act or an instance of polishing. **7.** smoothness and gloss of a surface. **8.** refinement or elegance. —**pol′ish·er,** n.

Po·lish (pō′lish), adj. **1.** of Poland, its inhabitants, or their language. —n. **2.** the Slavic language of Poland.

polit., **1.** political. **2.** politics.

Po·lit·bu·ro (pol′it byŏor′ō, pə lit′-), n. the chief policy-making and executive division of the Communist Party of the Soviet Union or certain other communist countries.

po·lite (pə līt′), adj. **1.** showing good manners toward others. **2.** refined or cultured. —**po·lite′ly,** adv. —**po·lite′ness,** n. — Syn. **1.** civil, courteous, gracious, mannerly.

pol·i·tesse (pol′i tes′), n. French. politeness.

pol·i·tic (pol′i tik), adj. **1.** sagacious in pursuing a policy. **2.** shrewd in achieving an end.

po·lit·i·cal (pə lit′i kəl), adj. **1.** of or involved in politics or government. **2.** of or characteristic of politicians or political parties. —**po·lit′i·cal·ly,** adv.

pol·i·ti·cian (pol′i tish′ən), n. **1.** a person who is active or skilled in politics, esp. party politics. **2.** a person who engages in politics for his or her own advantage.

po·lit·i·cize (pə lit′i sīz′), v.t., **-cized, -ciz·ing.** to make political.

pol·i·tick (pol′i tik), v.i. to engage in campaign in politics.

po·lit·i·co (pə lit′i kō′), n., pl. **-cos.** a politician.

pol·i·tics (pol′i tiks), *n.* **1.** the science or art of government. **2.** the practice or profession of conducting governmental affairs. **3.** political affairs. **4.** political methods or maneuvers. **5.** political principles or opinions. **6.** use of intrigue in obtaining power or control.

pol·i·ty (pol′i tē), *n., pl.* **-ties.** **1.** a particular form of government. **2.** a state or other organized community.

Polk (pōk), *n.* **James Knox,** 1795–1849, the 11th president of the U.S. 1845–49.

pol·ka (pōl′kə, pō′kə), *n.* **1.** a lively dance of Bohemian origin. **2.** music for such a dance. [< Czech: half (step)]

pol′ka dot′ (pō′kə), a round spot repeated to form a pattern on fabric.

poll (pōl), *n.* **1.** the voting at an election. **2.** the number of votes cast. **3.** Usually, **polls.** the place where votes are taken. **4.** a list of individuals, as for purposes of taxing or voting. **5.** a sampling or collection of opinions on a subject, as in a public survey. **6.** the head, esp. the part on which the hair grows. —*v.t.* **7.** to receive at the polls, as votes. **8.** to take or register the votes of. **9.** to cast at the polls, as a vote. **10.** to canvass in an opinion poll. **11.** to cut short or cut off the hair or wool of (an animal). —**poll′er,** *n.*

pol·lack (pol′ək), *n., pl.* **-lacks, -lack.** a darkly-colored, North Atlantic food fish of the cod family.

pol·len (pol′ən), *n.* the powdery, yellowish grains that are the male reproductive cells of flowering plants.

pol′len count′, a count of the amount of pollen in the air for a given period of time.

pol·li·nate (pol′ə nāt′), *v.t.*, **-nat·ed, -nat·ing.** to convey pollen to the stigma of (a flower). —**pol′li·na′tion,** *n.* —**pol′li·na′tor,** *n.*

pol·li·wog (pol′ē wog′), *n.* tadpole. Also, **pol′ly·wog′.**

poll·ster (pōl′stər), *n.* a person whose occupation is the taking of opinion polls.

poll′ tax′, a tax levied on each adult, sometimes as a prerequisite for voting.

pol·lute (pə lōōt′), *v.t.*, **-lut·ed, -lut·ing.** to make foul or unclean, esp. with waste materials. —**pol·lu′tant,** *n.* —**pol·lut′er,** *n.* —**pol·lu′tion,** *n.*

po·lo (pō′lō), *n.* a game played on horseback between two teams of four players each, using long-handled mallets and a wooden ball.

Po·lo (pō′lō), *n.* **Mar·co** (mär′kō), c1254–1324, Italian traveler to central Asia and China.

pol·o·naise (pol′ə nāz′, pō′lə-), *n.* a slow dance of Polish origin.

po·lo·ni·um (pə lō′nē əm), *n. Chem.* a radioactive chemical element. *Symbol:* Po; *at. wt.:* about 210; *at. no.:* 84.

pol·ter·geist (pōl′tər gīst′), *n.* a ghost or spirit supposed to manifest its presence by poises, knockings, etc.

pol·troon (pol trōōn′), *n. Literary.* a wretched coward.

poly-, a combining form meaning "much" or "many": *polygon.*

pol·y·clin·ic (pol′ē klin′ik), *n.* a clinic or a hospital dealing with various diseases.

pol·y·es·ter (pol′ē es′tər, pol′ē es′tər), *n.* a thermosetting polymeric resin used in making plastics, textile fibers, etc.

pol·y·eth·yl·ene (pol′ē eth′ə lēn′), *n.* a plastic polymer of ethylene used chiefly for containers, electrical insulation, and packaging.

po·lyg·a·my (pə lig′ə mē), *n.* the practice of having more than one spouse, esp. wife, at one time. —**po·lyg′a·mist,** *n.* —**po·lyg′a·mous,** *adj.*

pol·y·glot (pol′ē glot′), *adj.* **1.** able to speak or write several languages. **2.** containing or written in several languages. —*n.* **3.** a polyglot person.

pol·y·gon (pol′ē gon′), *n.* a closed plane figure having three or more usually straight sides. —**po·lyg·o·nal** (pə lig′ə n⁼l), *adj.*

pol·y·graph (pol′ē graf′, -gräf′), *n.* an instrument that records impulses due to changes in certain body activities, as while the person is undergoing emotional stress, often used in detecting lies.

pol·y·he·dron (pol′ē hē′drən), *n., pl.* **-drons, -dra** (-drə). a solid figure having many faces. —**pol·y·he′dral,** *adj.*

pol·y·math (pol′ē math′), *n.* a person learned in many fields.

pol·y·mer (pol′ə mər), *n.* a compound of high molecular weight derived by the addition of many smaller molecules of the same kind. —**pol·y·mer′ic** (-mer′ik), *adj.* —**po·lym·er·ize** (pə lim′ə rīz′, pol′ə mə rīz′), *v.t.* —**po·lym′er·i·za′tion,** *n.*

Pol·y·ne·sia (pol′ə nē′zhə, -shə), *n.* a series of island groups in the Pacific lying E of Micronesia. —**Pol′y·ne′sian,** *adj.*, *n.*

pol·y·no·mi·al (pol′ē nō′mē əl), *adj.* **1.** of or consisting of two or more names or terms. —*n.* **2.** *Algebra.* an expression consisting of two or more terms, as $2x^2 + 7x^2 + 4x + 2$.

pol·yp (pol′ip), *n.* **1.** a tiny water animal having a hollow columnar body and a mouth surrounded by tentacles. **2.** a projecting growth from a mucous surface, as of the rectum.

po·lyph·o·ny (pə lif′ə nē), *n.* music having two or more voices or parts, each with an independent melody. —**pol·y·phon·ic** (pol′ē fon′ik), *adj.* —**pol′y·phon′i·cal·ly**, *adv.*

pol·y·sty·rene (pol′ē stī′rēn), *n.* a clear plastic or stiff foam, used for electric insulation, instrument panels, etc.

pol·y·syl·lab·ic (pol′ē si lab′ik), *adj.* 1. consisting of three or more syllables, as a word. 2. characterized by such words.

pol·y·syl·la·ble (pol′ē sil′ə bəl, pol′ē-sil′-), *n.* a polysyllabic word.

pol·y·tech·nic (pol′ē tek′nik), *adj.* of or offering instruction in many scientific or technical subjects.

pol·y·the·ism (pol′ē thē iz′əm, pol′ə-thē′iz əm), *n.* the doctrine of or belief in more than one god. —**pol′y·the′ist**, *n.* —**pol′y·the·is′tic**, *adj.*

pol·y·un·sat·u·rat·ed (pol′ē un sach′ə-rā′tid), *adj.* of or noting a class of fats of animal or vegetable origin, associated with a low cholesterol content of the blood.

pol·y·vi·nyl (pol′ē vī′nil, -vīn′°l, -vin′il, -°l), *adj.* pertaining to or derived from a vinyl polymer.

pol′yvi′nyl chlo′ride, a white water-insoluble thermoplastic resin, used for making pipes, fabrics, floor coverings, etc.

po·made (pə mād′, -mäd′, pō-), *n. Chiefly Brit.* a scented ointment for dressing the hair.

pome·gran·ate (pom′gran′it, pom′ə-, pum′-; pom′ə gran′it, pəm gran′-), *n.* 1. a fruit having a tough red rind and tart red pulp surrounding many small seeds. 2. the shrub or small tree that bears it.

Pom·er·a·ni·an (pom′ə rā′nē ən, -rān′-yən), *n.* a small dog having long, straight hair, erect ears, and a tail carried over the back.

pom·mel (pum′əl, pom′əl), *n., v.,* -**meled, -mel·ing** or -**melled, -mel·ling.** —*n.* 1. a knob on the hilt of a sword. 2. the protuberant part at the front and top of a saddle. —*v.t.* 3. to pummel.

pomp (pomp), *n.* 1. stately or splendid display. 2. ostentatious or vain display.

pom·pa·dour (pom′pə dôr′, -dōr′, -dōōr′), *n.* an arrangement of a man's or woman's hair in which it is brushed up and back from, or raised high over, the forehead.

pom·pa·no (pom′pə nō′), *n., pl.* -**no, -nos.** a deep-bodied food fish of North and South America.

Pom·peii (pom pā′, -pā′ē), *n.* an ancient city in SW Italy, buried by an eruption of Mount Vesuvius in A.D. 79.

pom·pon (pom′pon), *n.* 1. Also, **pom′pom** (-pom). an ornamental tuft or ball, as of feathers or wool, worn on a hat, etc. 2. a chrysanthemum or dahlia having small, globe-shaped flower heads.

pomp·ous (pom′pəs), *adj.* 1. making an ostentatious display of dignity or importance. 2. ostentatiously lofty or high-flown. 3. full of pomp. —**pom·pos′i·ty** (-pos′i tē), **pomp′ous·ness**, *n.* —**pomp′ous·ly**, *adv.* —Syn. 1. pretentious. 2. bombastic.

pon·cho (pon′chō), *n., pl.* -**chos.** a blanketlike cloak with a hole in the center for the head, often worn as a raincoat.

pond (pond), *n.* a body of water smaller than a lake.

pon·der (pon′dər), *v.i., v.t.* to consider (something) deeply and thoroughly. —**pon′der·er**, *n.* —Syn. meditate, muse, reflect.

pon′der·o′sa pine′ (pon′də rō′sə, pon′-), 1. a large pine of western North America, having yellowish-brown bark. 2. its wood.

pon·der·ous (pon′dər əs), *adj.* 1. of great weight. 2. awkward or unwieldy. 3. dull and labored. —**pon′der·ous·ly**, *adv.*

pone (pōn), *n. Southern U.S.* 1. a baked or fried bread made of cornmeal. 2. an oval-shaped loaf or cake of it.

pon·gee (pon jē′, pon′jē), *n.* a silk cloth of a slightly uneven weave, usually in natural tan color.

pon·iard (pon′yərd), *n.* a small, slender dagger.

pons (ponz), *n., pl.* **pon·tes** (pon′tēz). any tissue connecting two parts of a body organ.

pon·tiff (pon′tif), *n.* 1. the Pope. 2. any high or chief priest. —**pon·tif′i·cal**, *adj.*

pon·tif·i·cate (*n.* pon tif′ə kit, -kāt′; *v.* pon tif′ə kāt′), *n., v.,* -**cat·ed, -cat·ing.** —*n.* 1. the office or term of office of a pontiff. —*v.i.* 2. to speak in a pompous or dogmatic manner. 3. to perform the duties of a pontiff.

pon·toon (pon tōōn′), *n.* 1. *Mil.* a flat-bottomed boat or float used with others to support a temporary bridge. 2. a float fitted to the landing stage of an aircraft.

po·ny (pō′nē), *n.* 1. a small horse. 2. *Slang.* a literal translation, used illicitly in school work.

po·ny·tail (pō′nē tāl′), *n.* a girl's or woman's hairstyle in which the hair is drawn back tightly and fastened at the back of the head.

pooch (pōōch), *n. Slang.* a dog.

poo·dle (pōōd′°l), *n.* an active dog having long, thick, frizzy or curly hair.

pooh (pŏo, pŏo), *interj.* (an exclamation of disdain or contempt.)

pooh-pooh (pŏo′pŏo′), *v.t.* to express disdain or contempt for.

pool[1] (pŏol), *n.* **1.** a small pond. **2.** an outdoor or indoor tank for swimming. **3.** any small collection of liquid on a surface. **4.** a still, deep place in a stream.

pool[2] (pŏol), *n.* **1.** a game resembling billiards but played on a table (**pool′ ta′ble**) having six pockets. **2.** a combination of resources, funds, etc., formed for common advantage. **3.** a group of competing companies joined together for mutual benefit, as to control prices. **4.** the total amount staked by a combination of bettors, as on a race. —*v.t.*, *v.i.* **5.** to contribute to a business pool.

poop[1] (pŏop), *n.* **1.** a superstructure at the stern of a vessel. **2.** See **poop deck.**

poop[2] (pŏop), *v.t. Slang.* to cause to become fatigued.

poop[3] (pŏop), *n. Slang.* information or lowdown.

poop′ deck′, a short deck on top of a poop.

poop′ sheet′, *Slang.* a circular, press release, etc., handed out to give the facts about a particular subject.

poor (pŏor), *adj.* **1.** lacking money or other means of support. **2.** dependent on charity or public support. **3.** indicating or suggesting poverty. **4.** wretchedly lacking. **5.** unfortunate or unlucky. **6.** lacking in resources, capability, etc. **7.** not up to expectations. —**poor′ly,** *adv.* —**Syn. 1.** impoverished, needy, penniless. **4.** meager. **6.** inferior. **7.** unsatisfactory.

poor′ boy′, *Slang.* See **hero sandwich.**

poor·house (pŏor′hous′), *n.* (formerly) an institution in which paupers were maintained at public expense.

poor-mouth (pŏor′mouth′), *v.i. Informal.* to plead or complain about poverty, often as an excuse.

pop[1] (pop), *v.,* **popped, pop·ping,** *n.* —*v.i.* **1.** to make a quick, light, explosive sound. **2.** to burst open with such a sound. **3.** to come or go suddenly. **4.** to swell or stick out, as the eyes. **5.** to shoot with a firearm. **6.** *Baseball.* to hit a pop fly. —*v.t.* **7.** to cause to pop. **8.** to put or thrust suddenly. **9.** *Slang.* to use (a drug in the form of pills), esp. habitually. —*n.* **10.** a light, quick, explosive sound. **11.** an effervescent nonalcoholic beverage. **12.** a shot with a firearm.

pop[2] (pop), *Informal.* —*adj.* **1.** popular (def. 4): *pop culture.* **2.** of or pertaining to popular music: *pop singers.* **3.** of or pertaining to pop

art. —*n.* **4.** popular music. **5.** See **pop art.**

pop[3] (pop), *n. Informal.* father (def. 1).

pop., **1.** popular. **2.** population.

P.O.P., point of purchase.

pop′ art′, a style in the fine arts characterized chiefly by forms and images derived from comic strips and advertising posters. —**pop′ art′ist.**

pop·corn (pop′kôrn′), *n.* **1.** a variety of corn whose kernels burst open and puff out when heated. **2.** such corn when popped.

pope (pōp), *n.* (*often cap.*) the bishop of Rome as head of the Roman Catholic Church.

Pope (pōp), *n.* Alexander, 1688–1744, English poet.

pop-eyed (pop′īd′), *adj.* marked by bulging, staring eyes.

pop′ fly′, *Baseball.* a high fly ball hit to the infield.

pop·gun (pop′gun′), *n.* a toy gun from which a pellet is shot by compressed air.

pop·in·jay (pop′in jā′), *n.* a person given to vain displays and empty chatter.

pop·lar (pop′lər), *n.* **1.** a rapidly growing tree having pointed leaves and light, soft wood. **2.** its wood.

pop·lin (pop′lin), *n.* a finely corded fabric of cotton, rayon, silk, or wool.

pop·o·ver (pop′ō′vər), *n.* a puffed muffin with a hollow center.

pop·per (pop′ər), *n.* a utensil for popping corn.

pop·py (pop′ē), *n., pl.* **-pies.** any of various plants having cup-shaped red, violet, yellow, or white flowers, one kind of which yields opium.

pop·py·cock (pop′ē kok′), *n. Informal.* utter nonsense.

pop·u·lace (pop′yə ləs), *n.* **1.** the common people. **2.** population (def. 2).

pop·u·lar (pop′yə lər), *adj.* **1.** favored or approved by people in general. **2.** favored or approved by acquaintances. **3.** of or representing the people as a whole. **4.** suited to the general masses of people. **5.** suited to the means of ordinary people: *popular prices.* —**pop′u·lar′i·ty** (-lar′i tē), *n.* —**pop′u·lar·ly,** *adv.*

pop·u·lar·ize (pop′yə lə rīz′), *v.t.,* **-ized, -iz·ing.** to make popular. —**pop′u·lar·i·za′tion,** *n.*

pop·u·late (pop′yə lāt′), *v.t.,* **-lat·ed, -lat·ing.** **1.** to live in or on. **2.** to furnish with inhabitants, as by colonization.

pop·u·la·tion (pop′yə lā′shən), *n.* **1.** the total number of persons inhabiting a country, city, etc. **2.** the inhabitants of a place. **3.** the individuals subject to a statistical study. **4.** the act or process of populating.

popula′tion explo′sion, the phenomenon of alarmingly rapid increase in world population since the end of World War II, esp. in developing countries.

pop·u·lism (pop′yə liz′əm), *n.* any political movement aimed chiefly at promoting the rights and interests of the masses. **—pop′u·list,** *n., adj.*

pop·u·lous (pop′yə ləs), *adj.* 1. heavily populated. 2. crowded with people. **—pop′u·lous·ness,** *n.*

pop-up (pop′up′), *n.* See **pop fly.**

p.o.r., pay on return.

por·ce·lain (pôr′sə lin, pôr′-; pôrs′lin, pôrs′-), *n.* a strong, glazed, translucent ceramic ware.

porch (pôrch, pôrch), *n.* 1. an open or glass- or screen-enclosed room attached to the outside of a house. 2. *Chiefly Brit.* a roof-covered structure at an entrance to a building.

por·cine (pôr′sīn, -sin), *adj.* of or resembling swine.

por·cu·pine (pôr′kyə pīn′), *n.* a slow-moving rodent covered with stiff, sharp quills on its back.

pore[1] (pôr, pôr), *v.i.,* **pored, por·ing.** 1. to read or study with steady attention. 2. to ponder intently.

pore[2] (pôr, pôr), *n.* a minute opening, as in the skin or a leaf, for perspiration, absorption, etc.

por·gy (pôr′gē), *n., pl.* **-gy, -gies.** a food fish found in the Mediterranean and off the Atlantic coasts of Europe and America.

pork (pôrk, pôrk), *n.* the flesh of hogs used as food. [< OF < L *porc(us)* hog] **—pork′y,** *adj.*

pork′ bar′rel, *Slang.* a government appropriation designed to ingratiate legislators with their constituents.

pork·er (pôr′kər, pôr′-), *n.* a pig fattened for its meat.

por·no (pôr′nō), *Slang.* **—adj.** 1. pornographic. **—n.** 2. pornography. 3. a pornographic film. Also, **porn** (pôrn).

por·nog·ra·phy (pôr nog′rə fē), *n.* literature, art, or photography of erotic or sexual acts intended to excite prurient feelings. **—por′no·graph′ic** (-nə graf′ik), *adj.* **—por′no·graph′i·cal·ly,** *adv.*

po·rous (pôr′əs, pôr′-), *adj.* 1. full of pores. 2. permeable by water, air, etc. **—po·ros·i·ty** (pō ros′i tē, pô-, pə-), *n.* **—po′rous·ly,** *adv.* **—po′rous·ness,** *n.*

por·phy·ry (pôr′fə rē), *n., pl.* **-ries.** a very hard, purplish-red rock containing small crystals of feldspar. **—por′phy·rit′ic** (-rit′ik), *adj.*

por·poise (pôr′pəs), *n.* 1. a sea mammal resembling a small whale and having a blunt, rounded snout. 2. any of several dolphins.

por·ridge (pôr′ij, por′-), *n. Brit.* oatmeal boiled in water or milk until thick.

por·rin·ger (pôr′in jər, por′-), *n.* a low dish or cup, often with a handle, for soup, porridge, etc.

port[1] (pôrt, pôrt), *n.* 1. a city or town having a harbor with loading and unloading facilities. 2. (loosely) a sea harbor. 3. *Informal.* an airport.

port[2] (pôrt, pôrt), *n.* 1. the left-hand side of a vessel or aircraft, facing forward. **—adj.** 2. of or located to the port. **—v.t., v.i.** 3. to turn or shift to the port side.

port[3] (pôrt, pôrt), *n.* a very sweet, dark-red wine.

port[4] (pôrt, pôrt), *n.* 1. an aperture in a cylinder through which steam or air may pass. 2. porthole.

port[5] (pôrt, pôrt), *v.t.* 1. *Mil.* to carry (a rifle, etc.) in a slanting direction across the body with the barrel near the left shoulder. **—n.** 2. *Archaic.* deportment or carriage.

Port., 1. Portugal. 2. Portuguese.

port·a·ble (pôr′tə bəl, pôr′-), *adj.* 1. capable of being carried or moved. 2. easily carried by hand. 3. (of pension rights) that may be accumulated and transferred from one employer to another. **—n.** 4. something portable, as a small typewriter. **—port′a·bil′i·ty,** *n.*

por·tage (pôr′tij, pôr′-), *n., v.,* **-taged, -tag·ing.** **—n.** 1. the carrying of boats or goods overland from one navigable water to another. 2. the route over which this is done. **—v.i., v.t.** 3. to carry (boats or goods) over a portage.

por·tal (pôr′t[ə]l, pôr′-), *n.* a doorway of imposing appearance. **—por′taled, por′talled,** *adj.*

por·tal-to-por′tal (pôr′t[ə]l tə pôr′t[ə]l, pôr′t[ə]l tə pôr′t[ə]l), *adj.* of a system under which wages are computed for all the time a worker spends on factory premises.

port·cul·lis (pôrt kul′is, pôrt-), *n.* a strong iron grating at the main entrance of a castle that can be let down to prevent passage.

porte-co·chere (pôrt′kō shâr′, -kə-, pôrt′-), *n.* a roofed structure at the door of a building for sheltering persons entering and leaving vehicles. Also, **porte′-co·chère′.**

por·tend (pôr tend′, pôr-), *v.t.* 1. to be a warning of in advance. 2. *Obs.* to signify or mean.

por·tent (pôr′tent, pôr′-), *n.* 1. a warning of what is to happen, esp. of something momentous. 2. foreboding or prophetic significance.

por·ten·tous (pôr ten′təs, pôr-), *adj.* 1. of the nature of a portent. 2. foreboding or prophetic. 3. *Literary.* a. amazing or extraordinary. b. pompous or pretentious. **—por·ten′tous·ly,** *adv.*

por·ter[1] (pōr′tər, pôr′-), *n.* **1.** a person hired to carry baggage, as at a railroad station. **2.** an attendant in a Pullman car.

por·ter[2] (pōr′tər, pôr′-), *n.* Brit. a doorman.

por·ter[3] (pōr′tər, pôr′-), *n.* a heavy, dark-brown ale.

por·ter·house (pōr′tər hous′, pôr′-), *n.* a choice cut of beef from between the prime ribs and the sirloin.

port·fo·li·o (pōrt fō′lē ō′, pôrt-), *n.*, *pl.* **-li·os.** **1.** a flat, portable case for carrying loose papers, drawings, etc. **2.** the securities owned for investment purposes. **3.** the office or post of a minister of state.

port·hole (pōrt′hōl′, pôrt′-), *n.* a small, circular window in a ship's side for light or ventilation.

por·ti·co (pōr′tə kō′, pôr′-), *n.*, *pl.* **-coes, -cos.** a roof-covered structure supported by rows of columns and attached to a building. —**por′ti·coed′**, *adj.*

por·tiere (pōr tyâr′, pôr-, pōr′tē âr′, pôr′-), *n.* a curtain hung in a doorway. Also, **por·tière′.** —**por·tiered′**, *adj.*

por·tion (pōr′shən, pôr′-), *n.* **1.** a part of any whole. **2.** a part of a whole allotted to a person or group. **3.** *Literary.* a person's lot or fate. **4.** *Archaic.* a dowry. —*v.t.* **5.** to divide into portions. **6.** to provide with or as with a portion. —**por′tion·less**, *adj.*

Port·land (pōrt′lənd, pôrt′-), *n.* a seaport in NW Oregon.

Port′land cement′, a hydraulic cement made by burning a mixture of limestone and clay.

port·ly (pōrt′lē, pôrt′-), *adj.*, **-li·er, -li·est. 1.** rather heavy or fat. **2.** *Archaic.* dignified or imposing. —**port′-li·ness**, *n.*

port·man·teau (pōrt man′tō, pōrt′man tō′, pôrt′-), *n.*, *pl.* **-teaus, -teaux** (-tōz, -tō; -tōz′, -tō′). Brit. a leather trunk that opens into two halves.

port′ of call′, a port visited briefly by a ship, usually to take on or discharge passengers and cargo.

port′ of en′try, any place at which customs officials are stationed and through which passengers and cargo are allowed to enter a country.

Por·to Ri·co (pōr′tə rē′kō, pôr′-), former name of **Puerto Rico.** —**Por′to Ri′can.**

por·trait (pōr′trit, -trāt, pôr′-), *n.* a painting or photograph of a person, esp. of the face.

por·trait·ist (pōr′tri tist, -trā-, pôr′-), *n.* a person who makes portraits.

por·trai·ture (pōr′tri chər, pôr′-), *n.* the art of making portraits.

por·tray (pōr trā′, pôr-), *v.t.* **1.** to make a portrait of. **2.** to depict in words. **3.** to act the part of (a character). —**por·tray′al**, *n.*

Por·tu·gal (pōr′chə gəl, pôr′-), *n.* a country in SW Europe.

Por·tu·guese (pōr′chə gēz′, -gēs′, pôr′-; pōr′chə gēz′, -gēs′, pôr′-), *adj.*, *n.*, *pl.* **-guese.** —*adj.* **1.** of Portugal, its inhabitants, or their language. —*n.* **2.** a native or inhabitant of Portugal. **3.** the Romance language of Portugal and Brazil.

Por′tuguese man-of-war′, a large, ocean invertebrate animal having a bladderlike structure by which it is buoyed up and from which are suspended numerous processes capable of severely injuring humans.

por·tu·lac·a (pōr′chə lak′ə, pôr′-), *n.* a fleshy annual plant having showy bright flowers.

pos., 1. position. **2.** positive.

P.O.S., point of sale.

pose (pōz), *v.*, **posed, pos·ing**, *n.* —*v.t.* **1.** to assume or hold a particular physical position, as for an artistic purpose. **2.** to make a pretense of being what one is not: *to pose as a friend.* **3.** to behave in an affected manner. —*v.t.* **4.** to place in a particular physical position, as for a picture. **5.** to state or put forward: *to pose a problem.* —*n.* **6.** a fixed position assumed in posing. **7.** an affected or false appearance or manner. —**pos′ing·ly**, *adv.*

Po·sei·don (pō sīd′ən, pə-), *n.* the ancient Greek god of the sea.

pos·er[1] (pō′zər), *n.* a person who poses.

pos·er[2] (pō′zər), *n.* a confusing question.

po·seur (pō zûr′), *n.* a person who affects a particular manner to impress others.

posh (posh), *adj.* Informal. sumptuously comfortable or elegant. —**posh′ly**, *adv.* —**posh′ness**, *n.*

pos·it (poz′it), *v.t.* Chiefly Logic. to assume as a fact or truth.

po·si·tion (pə zish′ən), *n.* **1.** the location or place of a person or thing at a given moment. **2.** the way in which a person or thing is placed or arranged. **3.** the proper or usual place. **4.** one's stand or opinion. **5.** one's social standing. **6.** a post of employment. —*v.t.* **7.** to put in a particular position. —**po·si′tion·al**, *adj.*

pos·i·tive (poz′i tiv), *adj.* **1.** fully and clearly stated. **2.** admitting of no question: *positive proof.* **3.** confidnt in an opinion or assertion. **4.** overconfident or dogmatic. **5.** practical or helpful: *positive suggestions.* **6.** not speculative or theoretical. **7.** showing approval or agreement. **8.** Elect. **a.** of electricity developed on glass when rubbed with silk. **b.** charged with electricity thus developed. **c.** caused by a deficiency of electrons. **9.** *Photog.* noting an image in which light and dark tones are the same as in the subject. **10.** *Gram.* noting the initial degree of the comparison of adjectives and adverbs, as the positive form *good.* **11.** *Math.* noting a quantity greater than zero. —*n.* **12.** something positive. **13.** *Photog.* a positive image. **14.** *Gram.* **a.** the positive degree. **b.** a form in the positive degree. —**pos'i·tive·ly,** *adv.* —**pos'i·tive·ness,** *n.* —Syn. **1.** definite, explicit, precise. **2.** indisputable. **3.** certain, sure.

pos·i·tron (poz'i tron'), *n. Physics.* the antiparticle of the electron.

poss., 1. possession. **2.** possessive. **3.** possible. **4.** possibly.

pos·se (pos'ē), *n.* the body of persons called by a sheriff to assist in preserving the peace.

pos·sess (pə zes'), *v.t.* **1.** to have as one's property. **2.** to have as a faculty, quality, or attribute. **3.** to have a powerful influence on. **4.** (of an evil spirit) to control (a person) from within. —**pos·ses'sor,** *n.*

pos·sessed (pə zest'), *adj.* **1.** moved or controlled by a strong feeling or a supernatural power. **2.** self-possessed or poised. **3. possessed of,** having or possessing.

pos·ses·sion (pə zesh'ən), *n.* **1.** the act of possessing or state of being possessed. **2.** a thing possessed or owned. **3. possessions,** property or wealth. **4.** a territory belonging to a nation. **5.** *Rare.* self-possession.

pos·ses·sive (pə zes'iv), *adj.* **1.** of or showing possession or ownership. **2.** desiring to dominate or be the only influence on someone. **3.** *Gram.* belonging to the case of a noun, pronoun, or adjective that shows possession. —*n. Gram.* **4.** the possessive case. **5.** a form in the possessive case. —**pos·ses'sive·ly,** *adv.* —**pos·ses'sive·ness,** *n.*

pos·si·ble (pos'ə bəl), *adj.* **1.** that can exist. **2.** that can happen. **3.** that can be done or chosen. **4.** capable of being true. —**pos'si·bil'i·ty** (-bil'i tē), *n.* —**pos'si·bly,** *adv.*

pos·sum (pos'əm), *n. Informal.* **1.** an opossum. **2. play possum,** to feign sleep or death.

post¹ (pōst), *n.* **1.** a strong piece of timber or metal, set upright as a support or marker. **2.** the point

where a horse race begins. —*v.t.* **3.** to fasten (a notice, etc.) to a post, wall, etc. **4.** to bring to public notice, as by a poster. **5.** to publish the name of in a list. **6.** to put up signs forbidding trespassing on or use of.

post² (pōst), *n.* **1.** the place assigned to a person on duty, as a soldier or sentry. **2.** a job, office, or position of trust to which a person is appointed. **3.** a military camp with permanent buildings. **4.** the troops stationed at such a camp. **5.** See **trading post.** —*v.t.* **6.** to station at a post. **7.** to provide, as bail.

post³ (pōst), *n.* **1.** *Brit.* **a.** a single delivery of mail. **b.** the mail itself. **c.** See **post office.** —*v.t.* **2.** *Chiefly Brit.* to mail (a letter). **3.** to supply with up-to-date information: *Keep me posted on him.* **4.** *Bookkeeping.* to enter in due place and form.

post-, a prefix meaning: **a.** after or later than: *postwar.* **b.** behind: *postnasal.*

post·age (pō'stij), *n.* the charge for sending a letter or other matter by mail, usually prepaid by means of a stamp or stamps.

post'age me'ter, an office machine that imprints postage of desired value and a dated postmark on an envelope, the postage having been prepaid at the post office by having the machine set for the lump sum purchased.

post·al (pōs'tᵊl), *adj.* of the post-office or mail service.

post'al card', a card sold by the post office with a stamp printed on it.

post·bel·lum (pōst'bel'əm), *adj.* after the war, esp. the American Civil War.

post·card (pōst'kärd'), *n.* a small, commercially printed card for sending a short message by mail, usually having a picture on one side.

post·date (pōst dāt'), *v.t.,* **-dat·ed, -dat·ing. 1.** to date (a check, etc.) with a date later than the actual one. **2.** to follow in time.

post·er (pō'stər), *n.* a placard or bill for posting in a public place, as for advertising.

pos·te·ri·or (po stēr'ē ər), *adj.* **1.** situated behind or at the rear. **2.** *Rare.* subsequent. **3.** posterior to, after. —*n.* **4.** Often, **posteriors,** the buttocks. —**pos·te·ri·or·i·ty** (po stēr'ē ôr'i tē, -or'-), *n.* —**pos·te'ri·or·ly,** *adv.*

---

post'·Ar·is·to·te'lian, *adj.*

post'·Au·gus'tan, *adj.*

post·Cam'bri·an, *adj.*

post'·Car·bon·if'er·ous, *adj.*

post'·Car·te'sian, *adj.*

post·clas'si·cal, *adj.*

post·con'so·nan'tal, *adj.*

post'con·va·les'cent, *adj.*

post'·Dar·win'i·an, *adj.*

post'·De·vo'ni·an, *adj.*

post'di·ges'tive, *adj.*

post·doc'tor·al, *adj.*

post'e·lec'tion, *adj.*

post·E'o·cene, *adj.*

pos·ter·i·ty (po ster′i tē), *n.* **1.** all future generations collectively. **2.** all descendants of one person.

pos·tern (pō′stərn, pos′tərn), *n.* a back door or gate, esp. in a castle.

post′ exchange′, a store on an army installation that sells goods and services to military personnel and authorized civilians.

post·grad·u·ate (pōst graj′ōō it, -āt′), *adj.* **1.** graduate (def. 4). —*n.* **2.** a postgraduate student.

post·haste (pōst′hāst′), *adv.* with the greatest possible speed.

post·hu·mous (pos′chə məs, -chōō-), *adj.* **1.** published after the death of the author. **2.** born after the death of the father. **3.** occurring after a person's death. —**post′hu·mous·ly,** *adv.*

post·hyp·not·ic (pōst′hip not′ik), *adj.* (of a suggestion) made during hypnosis so as to be effective after awakening.

pos·til·ion (pō stil′yən, po-), *n.* a person who rides the horse on the left of a pair drawing a carriage. Also, **post·il′lion.**

post·lude (pōst′lōōd), *n. Music.* a concluding piece or movement.

post·man (pōst′mən), *n. Chiefly Brit.* a mailman.

post·mark (pōst′märk′), *n.* **1.** an official mark stamped on mail to cancel the postage stamp and indicate the place and date of mailing. —*v.t.* **2.** to stamp with a postmark.

post·mas·ter (pōst′mas′tər, -mä′stər), *n.* the official in charge of a post office. —**post′mis′tress,** *n.fem.*

post′master gen′eral, *pl.* **postmasters general.** the executive head of the postal system of a country.

post me·rid·i·em (pōst′ mə rid′ē əm), See **p.m.**

post-mor·tem (pōst môr′təm), *adj.* **1.** of or occurring in the time following death. **2.** of a postmortem. —*n.* **3.** a postmortem examination, esp. an autopsy. **4.** an evaluation occurring after the end or fact of something.

post′na′sal drip′ (pōst′nā′zəl), a trickling of mucus onto the pharyngeal surface from the posterior portion of the nasal cavity, usually caused by a cold or allergy.

post·na·tal (pōst nāt′əl), *adj.* subsequent to childbirth.

post′ of′fice, 1. any of the local offices of a government postal system at which mail is handled and stamps are sold. **2.** (*often caps.*) the department of a government in charge of the mail.

post·op·er·a·tive (pōst op′ər ə tiv, -ə rā′tiv), *adj.* occurring after a surgical operation. —**post·op′er·a·tive·ly,** *adv.*

post·or·bit·al (pōst ôr′bi t°l), *adj.* located behind the orbit or socket of the eye.

post·paid (pōst′pād′), *adj., adv.* with the postage prepaid.

post·par·tum (pōst′pär′təm), *Obstet. adj.* after childbirth.

post·pone (pōst pōn′), *v.t.,* **-poned, -pon·ing.** to put off to a later time. —**post·pone′ment,** *n.* —**post·pon′er,** *n.*

post·script (pōst′skript′, pōs′skript′), *n.* a note added to a letter after the writer has finished and signed it.

post′ time′, the time set for the start of a horse race.

pos·tu·lant (pos′chə lənt), *n.* a candidate for admission into a religious order.

pos·tu·late (*v.* pos′chə lāt′; *n.* pos′chə lit, -lāt′), *v.,* **-lat·ed, -lat·ing,** *n.* — *v.t.* **1.** to assume the truth of, esp. as a basis for reasoning or arguing. **2.** to assume without proof as self-evident. —*n.* **3.** something postulated. —**pos′tu·la′tion,** *n.*

pos·ture (pos′chər), *n., v.,* **-tured, -tur·ing.** —*n.* **1.** the position or carriage of the body as a whole. **2.** a mental or spiritual attitude. **3.** condition or state, as of affairs. —*v.i.* **4.** to assume a particular posture, esp. for effect. —**pos′tur·al,** *adj.*

post·war (pōst′wôr′), *adj.* following a war.

po·sy (pō′zē), *n., pl.* **-sies.** *Literary.* a flower or nosegay.

pot (pot), *n., v.,* **pot·ted, pot·ting.** —*n.* **1.** a round, deep container of earthenware, metal, etc., used as for cooking. **2.** such a container with its contents. **3.** flowerpot. **4.** all the money bet at a single time. **5.** *Slang.* marijuana. **6. go to pot,** to become ruined. —*v.t.* **7.** to put or transplant into a pot. **8.** to preserve or cook in a pot. —**pot′ful,** *n.*

pot., potential.

po·ta·ble (pō'tə bəl), *adj.* **1.** fit for drinking. —*n.* **2.** something potable. —**po'ta·bil'i·ty,** *n.*

po·tage (pō täzh'), *n.* a thick soup.

pot·ash (pot'ash'), *n.* potassium carbonate, esp. the crude impure form obtained from wood ashes.

po·tas·si·um (pə tas'ē əm), *n. Chem.* a silvery-white metallic element whose compounds are used as fertilizer and in special hard glasses. Symbol: K; *at. wt.:* 39.102; *at. no.:* 19.

potas'sium bro'mide, a white powder used chiefly in making photographic papers and plates, and as a sedative.

potas'sium car'bonate, a white powder used chiefly in making soap, glass, etc.

potas'sium ni'trate, a compound used in gunpowders, fertilizers, and preservatives.

po·ta·tion (pō tā'shən), *n.* **1.** the act of drinking. **2.** a drink of an alcoholic beverage.

po·ta·to (pə tā'tō), *n., pl.* **-toes. 1.** the edible tuber of a perennial, widely grown plant. **2.** its plant.

pota'to chip', a thin slice of potato fried until crisp, usually salted.

pot·bel·ly (pot'bel'ē), *n., pl.* **-lies.** a protruding belly. —**pot'bel'lied,** *adj.*

pot·boil·er (pot'boi'lər), *n. Informal.* a mediocre work of literature or art produced merely for financial gain.

pot' cheese', a cheese similar to cottage cheese but with coarser curds and a drier consistency.

po·teen (pō tēn'), *n.* (in Ireland) illicitly distilled whiskey. Also, **potheen'** (- thēn').

po·tent (pōt'ənt), *adj.* **1.** producing powerful medicinal or chemical effects. **2.** (of a male) capable of sexual intercourse. **3.** convincingly cogent, as an argument. **4.** *Literary.* possessing great controlling or ruling power. —**po'ten·cy,** *n.* —**po'tent·ly,** *adv.*

po·ten·tate (pōt'ən tāt'), *n.* a person who possesses great controlling or ruling power, as a monarch.

po·ten·tial (pə ten'shəl), *adj.* **1.** capable of coming into actuality or realization. —*n.* **2.** something potential. **3.** a latent excellence or ability that may or may not be developed. **4.** *Elect.* the electrification of a point near or within an electrified substance. —**po·ten'ti·al'i·ty** (-shē əl'i-tē), *n.* —**po·ten'tial·ly,** *adv.*

po·ten·ti·ate (pə ten'shē āt'), *v.t.,* **-ated, -at·ing. 1.** to cause to be potent. **2.** to increase the effectiveness of (a drug). —**po·ten'ti·a'tion,** *n.*

pot·head (pot'hed'), *n. Slang.* a person who habitually uses marijuana.

poth·er (poth'ər), *Literary.* —*n.* **1.** an excited disturbance. —*v.t., v.i.* **2.** to bother or disturb.

pot·herb (pot'ûrb', -hûrb'), *n.* any herb prepared as food by cooking in a pot, as spinach, or added as seasoning in cookery, as thyme.

pot·hold·er (pot'hōl'dər), *n.* a quilted or woven pad used in handling hot pots and dishes.

pot·hole (pot'hōl'), *n.* a deep hole, as in a road.

pot·hook (pot'hook'), *n.* **1.** a hook for suspending a pot or kettle over an open fire. **2.** an S-shaped stroke in writing.

po·tion (pō'shən), *n.* a drink, esp. one having or reputed to have medicinal, poisonous, or magical powers.

pot·luck (pot'luk', -luk'), *n.* food that happens to be available without special preparation.

Po·to·mac (pə tō'mək), *n.* a river flowing SE into Chesapeake Bay.

pot·pie (pot'pī'), *n.* **1.** a deep-dish pie containing meat, chicken, etc. **2.** a stew, as of chicken or veal, with dumplings.

pot·pour·ri (pō'poo rē', pot poo'rē), *n.* **1.** a mixture of dried flower petals and spices, kept in a jar for their fragrance. **2.** a medley or any collection of miscellaneous things.

pot' roast', a dish of meat, usually of round or chuck steak, stewed in one piece.

pot·sherd (pot'shûrd'), *n.* a broken pottery fragment, esp. one of archaeological value.

pot·shot (pot'shot'), *n.* **1.** a shot fired at game with little regard to skill. **2.** a shot at an animal or person within easy range. **3.** a casual or aimless criticism.

pot·tage (pot'ij), *n.* a thick soup made of vegetables, with or without meat.

pot·ted (pot'id), *adj.* **1.** transplanted into or grown in a pot. **2.** *Slang.* drunk or intoxicated.

pot·ter¹ (pot'ər), *n.* a person who makes pottery.

pot·ter² (pot'ər), *v.i., v.t. Chiefly Brit.* putter¹.

pot'ter's field', a burial place for strangers and paupers.

pot·ter·y (pot'ə rē), *n., pl.* **-ter·ies. 1.** ceramic ware, esp. earthenware and stoneware. **2.** the art or business of a ceramic potter.

pouch (pouch), *n.* **1.** a small bag, as of leather, esp. one for holding and carrying pipe tobacco. **2.** a bag for carrying mail. **3.** the pocket on the abdomen of certain animals, as kangaroos, in which the young are carried. —*v.t., v.i.* **4.** to put (into) a pouch.

poult (pōlt), *n.* the young of the domestic fowl, as the turkey.

poul·tice (pōl′tis), *n.*, *v.*, **-ticed, -tic·ing.** —*n.* **1.** a soft, moist mass of meal, herbs, etc., spread on a cloth and applied as a medicament to the body. —*v.t.* **2.** to apply a poultice to.

poul·try (pōl′trē), *n.* fowl raised for eggs or meat, including chickens, turkeys, etc.

pounce (pouns), *v.*, **pounced, pounc·ing,** *n.* —*v.i.* **1.** to swoop down suddenly, as a bird does in order to seize its prey. —*n.* **2.** the act of pouncing.

pound¹ (pound), *v.t.* **1.** to strike repeatedly with great force, as with the fist. **2.** to crush into a powder or paste by beating repeatedly. —*v.i.* **3.** to strike heavy blows repeatedly. **4.** to throb violently, as the heart. **5.** to walk or go with heavy steps.

pound² (pound), *n.*, *pl.* **pounds, pound. 1.** a unit of weight 16 ounces avoirdupois (0.4536 kilogram) or 12 ounces troy (0.3732 kilogram). **2.** Also called **pound′ ster′ling.** the monetary unit of the United Kingdom, equal to 20 shillings or 240 pence prior to 1971, and after that date, consisting of 100 new pence. **3.** any of the monetary units of various other countries, as Ireland, Israel, etc.

pound³ (pound), *n.* a public enclosure for confining stray or homeless animals.

pound·age (poun′dij), *n.* **1.** a rate on the pound, as of British currency. **2.** a charge per pound weight. **3.** weight in pounds.

pound′ cake′, a rich, sweet cake made originally with a pound each of butter, sugar, and flour.

pound-fool·ish (pound′fōō′lish), *adj. Chiefly Brit.* foolish in regard to large sums.

pour (pōr, pôr), *v.t.* **1.** to cause to flow in a stream, as from one container to another. **2.** to describe or tell about freely: *to pour out one's troubles.* —*v.i.* **3.** to flow forth or along. **4.** to rain heavily. —*n.* **5.** the act of pouring.

pour·boire (pōōr bwAR′), *n. French.* a tip or gratuity.

pout (pout), *v.i.* **1.** to thrust out the lips, esp. in displeasure. **2.** to appear sullen. —*n.* **3.** the act of pouting. —**pout′er,** *n.*

pov·er·ty (pov′ər tē), *n.* **1.** lack of money, goods, or means of support. **2.** deficiency of desirable or necessary qualities. **3.** scantiness or insufficiency. —**Syn. 1.** destitution, indigence, need, want.

pov·er·ty-strick·en (pov′ər tē strik′ən), *adj.* extremely poor.

POW, prisoner of war. Also, **P.O.W.**

pow·der (pou′dər), *n.* **1.** a mass of fine, loose particles obtained by crushing or grinding any solid substance. **2.** a preparation in this form, as face powder. **3.** gunpowder. —*v.t.* **4.** to reduce to powder. **5.** to sprinkle or cover with powder. —**pow′der·er,** *n.* —**pow′der·y,** *adj.*

pow′der keg′, 1. a small barrel for holding gunpowder. **2.** an explosively dangerous situation.

pow′der room′, a lavatory for women.

pow·er (pou′ər), *n.* **1.** ability to do or act. **2.** physical strength or force. **3.** control, influence, or authority. **4.** a person or thing that possesses or exercises authority or influence. **5.** a state or nation having international authority or influence. **6.** a particular form of mechanical or physical energy: *hydroelectric power.* **7.** *Math.* the product obtained by multiplying a quantity by itself one or more times. **8.** the magnifying capacity of a lens or other optical instrument. —*v.t.* **9.** to supply with power. —*adj.* **10.** operated or driven by mechanical power, as electricity: *a power mower.* **11.** transmitting electricity. **12.** set by pressure from some power source so as to require little energy: *a power brake.*

pow·er·boat (pou′ər bōt′), *n.* a motorboat.

pow′er bro′ker, *Informal.* a person who exerts his or her powerful influence behind the scenes.

pow′er dive′, *Aeron.* a steep dive with the engine delivering thrust at full power. —**pow′er-dive′,** *v.t., v.i.*

pow·er·ful (pou′ər fəl), *adj.* **1.** exerting great power or force. **2.** potent or efficacious, as a drug. **3.** having great authority or influence. —**pow′er·ful·ly,** *adv.* —**Syn. 1.** mighty, strong. **3.** forcible, effective.

pow·er·house (pou′ər hous′), *n.* **1.** a building where electricity is generated. **2.** *Informal.* a person or group having great energy or potential for success.

pow·er·less (pou′ər lis), *adj.* **1.** unable to produce an effect. **2.** lacking power to act. —**pow′er·less·ly,** *adv.*

pow′er of attor′ney, a written document authorizing one person to act for another.

pow·wow (pou′wou′), *n.* **1.** a council or conference of or with American Indians. **2.** *Informal.* any conference or meeting.

pox (poks), *n.* **1.** a disease characterized by multiple skin pustules, as smallpox. **2.** *Informal.* syphilis.

pp, pianissimo.

pp., 1. pages. **2.** past participle.

P.P., 1. parcel post. **2.** postpaid. **3.** prepaid.

ppd., 1. postpaid. **2.** prepaid.

ppr., present participle. Also, **p.pr.**

P.P.S., an additional postscript. Also, **p.p.s.** [< L *post postscriptum*]

ppt., *Chem.* precipitate.

pptn., *Chem.* precipitation.

P.Q., Province of Quebec.

p.q., previous question.

PR, 1. payroll. 2. public relations. 3. Puerto Rico.

Pr, Provençal.

Pr, praseodymium.

pr., 1. pair; pairs. 2. present. 3. price. 4. pronoun.

P.R., 1. proportional representation. 2. public relations. 3. Puerto Rico.

prac·ti·ca·ble (prak′tə kə bəl), *adj.* 1. capable of being put into practice. 2. capable of being used. —**prac′ti·ca·bil′i·ty,** *n.* —**prac′ti·ca·bly,** *adv.*

prac·ti·cal (prak′ti kəl), *adj.* 1. of, involving, or resulting from practice or action rather than theory or thought. 2. suitable for actual use. 3. engaged in actual work. 4. suited for actual work or useful activities: *a practical man.* 5. matter-of-fact or prosaic. 6. being such in practice or effect: *a practical certainty.* —**prac′ti·cal′i·ty** (-tə kal′i tē), *n.*

prac′tical joke′, a trick played mischievously on someone.

prac·ti·cal·ly (prak′tik lē), *adv.* 1. in effect or virtually. 2. in a practical manner. 3. almost or nearly.

prac′tical nurse′, a nurse having shorter training than a registered nurse, usually examined and licensed by the state before practicing.

prac·tice (prak′tis), *n., v.,* **-ticed, -tic·ing.** —*n.* 1. habitual or customary performance. 2. repeated performance or exercise in order to acquire skill. 3. skill so gained. 4. the action of performing or doing something. 5. habit or custom. 6. the pursuit of a profession or occupation, esp. law or medicine. —*v.t.* 7. to perform or do habitually or usually. 8. to perform or exercise repeatedly in order to acquire skill. 9. to pursue as a profession. —*v.i.* 10. to exercise oneself by repeated performance in order to acquire skill. Also, *Brit.,* **prac′tise** (for defs. 7–10).

prac·ticed (prak′tist), *adj.* skilled or proficient through practice.

prac·ti·tion·er (prak tish′ə nər), *n.* a person engaged in the practice of a profession.

prae·tor (prē′tər), *n.* an ancient Roman magistrate subordinate to a consul. —**prae·to′ri·an** (-tōr′ē ən, -tôr′-), *adj.*

prag·mat·ic (prag mat′ik), *adj.* 1. oriented toward practical action or thought. 2. *Philos.* of or pertaining to pragmatism. Also, **prag·mat′i·cal.** —**prag·mat′i·cal·ly,** *adv.*

prag·ma·tism (prag′mə tiz′əm), *n.* 1. orientation toward practical action or thought. 2. a philosophical system stressing practical consequences as constituting the essential criterion in determining truth or value. —**prag′ma·tist,** *n.*

Prague (präg), *n.* the capital of Czechoslovakia.

prai·rie (prâr′ē), *n.* a large, grassy, level or slightly rolling area of land, esp. the broad plain of central North America.

prai′rie dog′, a small burrowing rodent of North American prairies.

prai′rie schoon′er, a covered wagon used by pioneers in crossing the plains of North America.

praise (prāz), *n., v.,* **praised, prais·ing.** —*n.* 1. an expression of approval or admiration. 2. the offering of grateful homage, as to God or a deity, esp. in song. —*v.t.* 3. to express approval or admiration of. 4. to offer grateful homage to (God or a deity), esp. in song. —**Syn.** 3. applaud, commend, extol, laud.

praise·wor·thy (prāz′wûr′thē), *adj.* deserving of praise. —**praise′wor′thi·ly,** *adv.* —**praise′wor′thi·ness,** *n.*

pra·line (prā′lēn, prä′-, prä lēn′), *n.* a candy made of almonds, pecans, or other nuts, cooked in brown sugar.

pram (pram), *n. Brit. Informal.* perambulator.

prance (prans, präns), *v.,* **pranced, pranc·ing,** *n.* —*v.i.* 1. to move by springing from the hind legs, as a horse. 2. to move about in a lively or spirited manner. —*n.* 3. the act of prancing. —**pranc′er,** *n.* —**pranc′ing·ly,** *adv.*

prank (prangk), *n.* a playful or mischievous trick. —**prank′ster,** *n.*

pra·se·o·dym·i·um (prā′zē ō dim′ē əm, prā′sē-), *n. Chem.* a rare-earth, metallic element. *Symbol:* Pr; *at. wt.:* 140.91; *at no.:* 59.

prate (prāt), *v.i., v.t.,* **prat·ed, prat·ing.** to talk excessively and pointlessly. —**prat′er,** *n.*

prat·fall (prat′fôl′), *n. Slang.* a fall on the buttocks, often regarded as comical or humiliating.

pra·tique (pra tēk′, prat′ik), *n.* permission to use a port, given to a ship after quarantine.

prat·tle (prat′əl), *v.,* **-tled, -tling,** *n.* —*v.i., v.t.* 1. to talk in a foolish or simpleminded way. —*n.* 2. the act of prattling. 3. a prattling sound.

prawn (prôn), *n.* a shrimplike crustacean used as food.

pray (prā), *v.t.* 1. to offer devout petition, praise, thanks, etc., to (God or an object of worship). 2. to make an earnest request of (a person). —*v.i.* 3. to say prayers, esp. to God. 4. to make entreaty or supplication, as to a person or for a thing. —**pray′er,** *n.* —**pray′ing·ly,** *adv.*

prayer (prâr), *n.* **1.** the act or practice of praying. **2.** a spiritual communion with God or an object of worship, as in entreaty, thanksgiving, or adoration. **3.** a formula of words used praying. **4.** Often, **prayers.** a religious service consisting wholly or mainly of praying. **5.** the thing prayed for. **6.** an earnest request. **7.** *Slang.* a slim chance.

prayer·ful (prâr′fəl), *adj.* given to or expressive of prayer. —**prayer′ful·ly,** *adv.* —**prayer′ful·ness,** *n.*

pray·ing man·tis, mantis. Also, **pray′ing man′tid** (-tid).

pre-, a prefix meaning: **a.** before or earlier than: *prepay; preschool.* **b.** in front of or ahead of: *prefix.* **c.** above or over: *preeminent.*

preach (prēch), *v.t.* **1.** to deliver (a religious sermon). **2.** to plead strongly in favor of (something). —*v.i.* **3.** to deliver a religious sermon. **4.** to give advice in an obtrusive or tedious way. —**preach′er,** *n.* —**preach′ment,** *n.* —**preach′y,** *adj.*

pre·am·ble (prē′am′bəl), *n.* an introductory statement, as to a formal or legal document, stating the reasons and intent of what follows.

pre·am·pli·fi·er (prē am′plə fī′ər), *n.* an amplifier, esp. in a high-fidelity system, that provides facilities for control and selection of inputs for the main amplifier.

pre·ar·range (prē′ə rānj′), *v.t.,* **-ranged, -rang·ing.** to arrange in advance or beforehand. —**pre′ar·range′ment,** *n.*

pre·ax·i·al (prē ak′sē əl), *adj.* Anat., Zool. situated in front of the body axis. —**pre·ax′i·al·ly,** *adv.*

preb·end (preb′ənd), *n.* a stipend allotted from the revenues of a cathedral to a canon or member of the chapter.

preb·en·dar·y (preb′ən der′ē), *n., pl.* **-dar·ies.** a member of the clergy entitled to a prebend.

prec., **1.** preceded. **2.** preceding.

Pre·cam·bri·an (prē kam′brē ən), *adj.* **1.** noting the earliest era, ending 600,000,000 years ago, during which the earth's crust was formed and the first life appeared. —*n.* **2.** the Precambrian era.

pre·can·cer·ous (prē kan′sə rəs), *adj.* likely to develop into cancer.

pre·car·i·ous (pri kâr′ē əs), *adj.* **1.** dependent on circumstances beyond one's control. **2.** exposed to or involving danger or risk. —**pre·car′i·ous·ly,** *adv.* —**pre·car′i·ous·ness,** *n.* —Syn. **1.** doubtful, insecure, uncertain.

pre·cau·tion (pri kô′shən), *n.* a measure taken in advance to avert danger or failure. —**pre·cau′tion·ar′y,** *adj.*

pre·cede (pri sēd′), *v.t., v.i.,* **-ced·ed, -ced·ing.** to go or come before, as in place, rank, or time. —**pre·ced′a·ble,** *adj.*

prec·e·dence (pres′i dəns, pri sēd′°ns), *n.* the act, fact, or right of preceding.

prec·e·dent¹ (pres′i dənt), *n.* an act, decision, or case that may serve as a guide or justification in subsequent ones.

prec·e·dent² (pri sēd′°nt, pres′i dənt), *adj.* preceding.

pre·ced·ing (prē sē′diñg), *adj.* that precedes.

pre·cen·tor (pri sen′tər), *n.* a person who leads a church choir or congregation in singing.

pre·cept (prē′sept), *n.* a command or direction given as a rule of action or conduct.

pre·cep·tor (pri sep′tər, prē′sep-), *n.* Archaic. a teacher. —**pre·cep′tress,** *n.fem.*

pre·ces·sion (prē sesh′ən), *n.* a slow retrograde motion of the earth's axis of rotation. —**pre·cess′** (-ses′), *v.i.* —**pre·ces′sion·al,** *adj.*

pre·cinct (prē′siñgkt), *n.* **1. a.** a subdivision of a city or town marked off as a district for purposes of police protection. **b.** the police station in such a district. **2.** a small voting district of a city or county. **3.** a space of definite limits. **4.** Often, **precincts.** an enclosing boundary or limit. **5. precincts,** the regions immediately surrounding a place.

pre·ci·os·i·ty (presh′ē os′i tē), *n., pl.* **-ties.** affected refinement, as in language.

---

pre′ac·cept′, *v.*
pre′ac·cept′ance, *n.*
pre′ac·cus′tom, *v.t.*
pre′a·dapt′, *v.t.*
pre′ad·just′, *v.t.*
pre′ad·just′a·ble, *adj.*
pre′ad·just′ment, *n.*
pre′ad·o·les′cence, *n.*
pre′a·dult′, *adj.*
pre′af·firm′, *v.*
pre′af·fir·ma′tion, *n.*
pre′al·lot′, *v.t.,* **-lot·ted, -lot·ting.**

pre′an·nounce′, *v.t.,* **-nounced, -nounc·ing.**
pre′an·nounce′ment, *n.*
pre′ap·pear′ance, *n.*
pre′ap·pli·ca′tion, *n.*
pre′ap·point′, *v.t.*
pre′arm′, *v.t.*
pre′as·cer·tain′, *v.t.*
pre′as·cer·tain′ment, *n.*
pre′as·sem′ble, *v.t.,* **-bled, -bling.**
pre′as·sem′bly, *n.*
pre′as·sign′, *v.t.*

pre′as·signed′, *adj.*
pre·bill′, *v.t.*
pre·bless′, *v.t.*
pre·boil′, *v.t.*
pre·cal′cu·late′, *v.t.,* **-lat·ed, -lat·ing.**
pre′cal·cu·la′tion, *n.*
pre·can′cel, *v.t.*
pre′cap·i·tal·is′tic, *adj.*
pre′cel·e·bra′tion, *n.*
pre·chill′, *v.t.*
pre·Chris′tian, *adj., n.*

pre·cious (presh′əs), *adj.* **1.** of high price or great value. **2.** dear or beloved. **3.** affectedly refined. —**pre′cious·ly,** *adv.* —**pre′cious·ness,** *n.*

prec·i·pice (pres′ə pis), *n.* a cliff with a vertical or nearly vertical face. —**prec′i·piced,** *adj.*

pre·cip·i·tant (pri sip′i tənt), *adj.* precipitate (defs. 6–8). —**pre·cip′i·tan·cy,** *n.*

pre·cip·i·tate (*v.* pri sip′i tāt′; *adj., n.* pri sip′i tit, -tāt′), *v.,* **-tat·ed, -tat·ing,** *adj. n.* —*v.t.* **1.** to hasten the occurrence of. **2.** to cast down headlong. **3.** *Chem.* to separate (a substance) in solid form from a solution. —*v.i.* **4.** *Chem.* to be precipitated. **5.** *Meteorol.* (of moisture) to condense from vapor and fall to the earth as rain, snow, etc. —*adj.* **6.** rushing headlong or rapidly onward. **7.** proceeding rapidly or with great haste: *a precipitate retreat.* **8.** exceedingly sudden or abrupt. —*n.* **9.** *Chem.* a substance precipitated from a solution. —**pre·cip′i·tate·ly,** *adv.* —**pre·cip′i·tate·ness,** *n.* —Syn. **8.** indiscreet, rash, reckless.

pre·cip·i·ta·tion (pri sip′i tā′shən), *n.* **1.** a casting down headlong. **2.** sudden or rash haste. **3.** unwise rapidity. **4.** *Chem.* the precipitating of a substance from a solution. **5.** *Meteorol.* **a.** the products of a precipitate. **b.** the amount precipitated.

pre·cip·i·tous (pri sip′i təs), *adj.* **1.** extremely steep like a precipice. **2.** precipitate (defs. 6–8). —**pre·cip′i·tous·ly,** *adv.* —**pre·cip′i·tous·ness,** *n.*

pré·cis (prā sē′, prā′sē), *n., pl.* **-cis** (-sēz′, -sēz). a concise summary.

pre·cise (pri sīs′), *adj.* **1.** definitely or exactly stated. **2.** minutely accurate. **3.** rigidly particular or strict. —**pre·cise′ly,** *adv.* —**pre·cise′ness,** *n.* —Syn. **3.** meticulous, scrupulous.

pre·ci·sian (pri sizh′ən), *n.* a strict adherent to rules or forms, esp. in matters of religion.

pre·ci·sion (pri sizh′ən), *n.* **1.** the state or quality of being precise. —*adj.* **2.** requiring or characterized by precision: *precision instruments.*

pre·clude (pri klōōd′), *v.t.,* **-clud·ed, -clud·ing.** to make impossible, esp. by previous action. —**pre·clu′sion** (-klōō′zhən), *n.*

pre·co·cious (pri kō′shəs), *adj.* forward in development, esp. mental development. —**pre·co′cious·ly,** *adv.* —

pre·coc·i·ty (-kos′i tē), **pre·co′cious·ness,** *n.*

pre·cog·ni·tion (prē′kog nish′ən), *n.* knowledge of a future event, esp. through extrasensory means. —**pre·cog′ni·tive,** *adj.*

pre·con·ceive (prē′kən sēv′), *v.t.,* **-ceived, -ceiv·ing.** to form an idea of in advance. —**pre′con·cep′tion,** *n.*

pre·con·di·tion (prē′kən dish′ən), *n.* **1.** a condition necessary to a subsequent result. —*v.t.* **2.** to condition or prepare (a person or thing) in advance.

pre·cur·sor (pri kûr′sər, prē′kûr-), *n.* **1.** a person or thing that precedes, as in a job or a method. **2.** a person or thing that goes before and indicates the approach of someone or something else. —**pre·cur′so·ry,** *adj.*

pred., predicate.

pre·da·cious (pri dā′shəs), *adj.* predatory (def. 1). Also, **pre·da′ceous.** —**pre·da′cious·ness, pre·dac·i·ty** (pri das′i tē); *esp. Biol.,* **pre·da′ceous·ness,** *n.*

pre·date (prē dāt′), *v.t.,* **-dat·ed, -dat·ing.** antedate.

pre·da·tion (pri dā′shən), *n.* **1.** a relation between animals in which one organism captures and feeds on others. **2.** *Obs.* the act of plundering or robbing.

pred·a·to·ry (pred′ə tôr′ē, -tōr′ē), *adj.* **1.** habitually preying upon other animals. **2.** of or living by plunder or robbing. —**pred′a·tor** (-tər), *n.* —**pred′a·to′ri·ness,** *n.*

pre·de·cease (prē′di sēs′), *v.t.,* **-ceased, -ceas·ing.** to die before (another person, an event, etc.).

pred·e·ces·sor (pred′i ses′ər, pred′i·ses′or), *n.* a person who precedes another in an office, position, etc.

pre·des·ti·na·tion (pri des′tə nā′shən, prē′des-), *n. Theol.* the foreordination by God of whatever comes to pass, esp. the salvation and damnation of souls. —**pre·des′ti·nate,** *v.t.*

pre·des·tine (pri des′tin), *v.t.,* **-tined, -tin·ing.** to destine in advance.

pre·de·ter·mine (prē′di tûr′min), *v.t.,* **-mined, -min·ing.** to determine in advance. —**pre′de·ter′mi·na′tion,** *n.*

pred·i·ca·ble (pred′ə kə bəl), *adj.* that may be predicated.

pre·dic·a·ment (pri dik′ə mənt), *n.* an unpleasantly difficult or complicated situation. —Syn. dilemma, plight, quandary.

pred·i·cate (v. pred'ə kāt'; adj., n. pred'ə kit), v., -cat·ed, -cat·ing, adj. n. —v.t. **1.** to cause to found or base: *His argument was predicated on sound reasoning.* **2.** to declare or assert as an assumed quality or attribute. —adj. **3.** *Gram.* belonging to the predicate. —n. **4.** *Gram.* the part of a sentence or clause that expresses what is said about the subject. —**pred'i·ca'tion,** n. —**pred'i·ca'tive,** adj.

pre·dict (pri dikt'), v.t. to tell in advance, usually on the basis of facts. —**pre·dict'a·ble,** adj. —**pre·dict'a·bly,** adv. —**pre·dic'tion,** n. —**pre·dic'tor,** n. —Syn. forecast, prophesy.

pre·di·gest (prē'di jest', -dī-), v.t. to treat (food) by an artificial process analogous to digestion to facilitate digestion by the body. —**pre'di·ges'tion,** n.

pre·di·lec·tion (pred'l ek'shən, prēd'-), n. a marked preference.

pre·dis·pose (prē'di spōz'), v.t., -posed, -pos·ing. **1.** to give an inclination to beforehand. **2.** to make susceptible or liable. —**pre'dis·po·si'tion,** n.

pre·dom·i·nant (pri dom'ə nənt), adj. **1.** having power or influence over others. **2.** prevailing or prominent. —**pre·dom'i·nance,** n. —**pre·dom'i·nant·ly,** adv.

pre·dom·i·nate (pri dom'ə nāt'), v.t., -nat·ed, -nat·ing. **1.** to have influence or controlling power. **2.** to surpass others in number, effect, etc. —**pre·dom'i·nate·ly** (-nit lē), adv. —**pre·dom'i·na'tion,** n.

pree·mie (prē'mē), n. *Informal.* a premature infant.

pre·em·i·nent (prē em'ə nənt), adj. eminent above or before others. —**pre·em'i·nence,** n. —**pre·em'i·nent·ly,** adv. —Syn. outstanding.

pre·empt (prē empt'), v.t. **1.** to take possession of for oneself before others can. **2.** to occupy (land) in order to establish a prior right to buy. **3.** *Radio and Television.* to replace or cancel (a scheduled program) with or without notice. —**pre·emp'tion,** n. —**pre·emp'tive,** adj. —**pre·emp'tive·ly,** adv.

preen (prēn), v.t. **1.** (of birds) to smooth or clean (the feathers) with the beak. **2.** to dress (oneself) carefully or smartly. **3.** to pride (oneself) on something. —**preen'er,** n.

pref., **1.** preface. **2.** preference. **3.** preferred. **4.** prefix.

pre·fab (prē'fab'), n. *Informal.* a prefabricated building or house.

pre·fab·ri·cate (prē fab'rə kāt'), v.t., -cat·ed, -cat·ing. to manufacture (a building or house) in standardized parts or sections ready for quick assembly and erection. —**pre'fab'ri·ca'tion,** n.

pref·ace (pref'is), n., v., -aced, -ac·ing. —n. **1.** a short introduction to a book, speech, etc. —v.t. **2.** to provide with or introduce by a preface. —**pref'ac·er,** n. —**pref'a·to'ry** (-fə tôr'e, -tôr'ē), adj.

pre·fect (prē'fekt), n. a chief civil administrator, esp. of a department of France. —**pre'fec·ture** (-fek·chər), n.

pre·fer (pri fûr'), v.t., -ferred, -fer·ring. **1.** to like better: *I prefer summer to winter.* **2.** *Law.* to put forward (a charge, etc.) for consideration or sanction. **3.** *Archaic.* to promote or advance, as in rank or office. —**pre·fer'rer,** n.

pref·er·a·ble (pref'ər ə bəl, pref'rə-), adj. **1.** worthy to be preferred. **2.** more desirable. —**pref'er·a·bly,** adv.

pref·er·ence (pref'ər əns, pref'rəns), n. **1.** the act of preferring or state of being preferred. **2.** something preferred. **3.** a special advantage given to one person or country over others. —**pref'er·en'tial** (-ə ren'shəl), adj.

pre·fer·ment (pri fûr'mənt), n. advancement or promotion, as in rank.

pre·fig·ure (prē fig'yər), v.t., -ured, -ur·ing. **1.** to represent or show beforehand. **2.** to imagine or picture to oneself beforehand.

pre·fix (n. prē'fiks; v. prē fiks', prē'-fiks), n. **1.** *Gram.* an affix placed before a word or stem. —v.t. **2.** to fix or put before or in front. **3.** *Gram.* to add as a prefix. —**pre·fix·al** (prē'fik səl, prē fik'-), adj. —**pre'fix·al·ly,** adv. —**pre·fix·ion** (prē fik'shən), n.

preg·nant (preg'nənt), adj. **1.** having unborn young developing in the uterus. **2.** fraught or abounding. **3.** fertile or rich. **4.** full of meaning. —**preg'nan·cy,** n.

pre·heat (prē hēt'), v.t. to heat before using or before subjecting to some further process.

pre·hen·sile (pri hen'sil, -sīl), adj. adapted for seizing or grasping something: *a prehensile limb.*

---

pre'e·lec'tion, n.
pre'en·gage', v.t.
pre'en·list'ment, adj., n.
pre·es·tab'lish, v.t.
pre·es'ti·mate', v.t., -mat·ed, -mat·ing.

pre'ex·am'i·na'tion, n.
pre'ex·am'ine, v.t., -ined, -in·ing.
pre'ex·ist', v.i.
pre'ex·pose', v.t., -posed, -pos·ing.

pre'ex·po'sure, n.
pre·form', v.t.
pre·game', adj.
pre·gla'cial, adj.
pre·hard'en, v.t.

pre·his·tor·ic (prē′hi stôr′ik, -stor′-), *adj.* of the period prior to recorded history. Also, **pre′his·tor′i·cal.** —**pre′his·tor′i·cal·ly,** *adv.*

pre·judge (prē juj′), *v.t.,* -**judged, -judg·ing.** to judge beforehand or without sufficient investigation. —**pre·judg′ment,** *n.*

prej·u·dice (prej′ə dis), *n., v.,* -**diced, -dic·ing.** —*n.* **1.** an unfavorable opinion formed beforehand or without knowledge. **2.** hatred or dislike directed against a racial, religious, or national group. **3.** *Law.* damage or injury resulting from some judgment or action of another. —*v.t.* **4.** to affect with a prejudice. **5.** *Law.* to damage or injure by some judgment or action. —**prej′u·di′cial** (-dish′əl), *adj.* —**prej′u·diced·ly,** *adv.* —**Syn. 1.** bias, preconception.

prel·ate (prel′it), *n.* a high-ranking member of the clergy, as a bishop. —**prel′a·cy** (-ə sē), *n.*

prelim., preliminary.

pre·lim·i·nar·y (pri lim′ə ner′ē), *adj., n., pl.* -**nar·ies.** —*adj.* **1.** leading up to the main part or business. —*n.* **2.** something preliminary, as an introductory or preparatory step.

pre·lit·er·ate (prē lit′ər it), *adj.* (of a culture) not having written records.

prel·ude (prel′yōōd, prāl′- prē′lōōd, prā′-), *n.* **1.** a preliminary part or work. **2.** a short piece of music, esp. one intended to be played as an introduction to a longer work.

prem., premium.

pre·mar·i·tal (prē mar′i tºl), *adj.* occurring or done before marriage.

pre·ma·ture (prē′mə tōōr′, -tyōōr′, -chōōr′, prē′mə chōōr′), *adj.* occurring, done, or born too soon or before the proper time. —**pre′ma·ture′ly,** *adv.* —**pre′ma·ture′ness,** *n.*

pre·med (prē med′), *Informal.* —*adj.* **1.** premedical. —*n.* **2.** a premedical student.

pre·med·i·cal (prē med′i kəl), *adj.* of or pursuing studies preparatory to the study of medicine.

pre·med·i·tate (pri med′i tāt′), *v.t., v.i.,* -**tat·ed, -tat·ing.** to consider or plan beforehand. —**pre·med′i·tat′ed·ly,** *adv.* —**pre·med′i·ta′tion,** *n.* —**pre·med′i·ta′tor,** *n.*

pre·mier (pri mēr′, prim yēr′), *n.* **1.** See **prime minister.** —*adj.* **2.** first in position or importance. —**pre·mier′ship,** *n.*

pre·miere (pri mēr′, -myâr′), *n., v.,* -**miered, -mier·ing.** —*n.* **1.** a first

public performance of a play, movie, etc. —*v.t., v.i.* **2.** to present or perform publicly for the first time. Also, **pre·mière′.** [< F: first]

prem·ise (prem′is), *n., v.,* -**ised, -is·ing.** —*n.* **1.** *Logic.* a proposition supporting or helping to support a conclusion. **2. premises,** a tract of land including its buildings. —*v.t.* **3.** to set forth beforehand as an introduction.

pre·mi·um (prē′mē əm), *n.* **1.** a bonus or reward given as an inducement, as to purchase products. **2.** an additional amount above the usual price, wages, etc. **3.** *Insurance.* the amount paid for an insurance policy, usually in installments. **4.** an excess value. **5. at a premium, a.** at a very high value because of scarcity.

pre·mo·lar (prē mō′lər), *adj.* situated in front of the molar teeth.

pre·mo·ni·tion (prē′mə nish′ən, prem′ə-), *n.* **1.** an intuitive anticipation of a future event. **2.** a feeling of advance warning. —**pre·mon·i·to·ry** (pri mon′i tôr′ē, -tōr′ē), *adv.* —**Syn.** foreboding, presentiment.

pre·name (prē′nām′), *n. Rare,* forename.

pre·na·tal (prē nāt′ºl), *adj.* previous to birth or to giving birth. —**pre·na′tal·ly,** *adv.*

pre·oc·cu·py (prē ok′yə pī′), *v.t.,* -**pied, -py·ing. 1.** to absorb the full attention of. **2.** to occupy beforehand or before others. —**pre·oc′cu·pa′tion** (-pā′shən), *n.* —**pre·oc′cu·pied,** *adj.* —**Syn. 1.** engross.

pre·op·er·a·tive (prē op′ər ə tiv, -ə rā′tiv), *adj.* occurring before a surgical operation.

pre·or·dain (prē′ôr dān′), *v.t.* to ordain or decree beforehand.

prep (prep), *n., v.,* **prepped, prep·ping.** *Informal.* —*n.* **1.** See **preparatory school.** —*v.t.* **2.** to prepare (a person), as for a surgical operation.

prep., **1.** preparatory. **2.** preposition.

pre·pack·age (prē pak′ij), *v.t.,* -**aged, -ag·ing.** to package (foodstuffs, etc.) before retail distribution or sale.

prep·a·ra·tion (prep′ə rā′shən), *n.* **1.** the act of preparing or state of being prepared. **2.** Usually, **preparations.** a plan or measure by which one prepares for something. **3.** something prepared or manufactured, as a medicine.

pre·par·a·to·ry (pri pâr′ə tôr′ē, -tōr′ē, -par′-, prep′ər ə-), *adj.* serving or designed to prepare or introduce. —**pre·par′a·to′ri·ly,** *adv.*

---

pre·hu′man, *adj.*
pre′in·au′gu·ral, *adj.*
pre′in·dus′tri·al, *adj.*
pre′in·sert′, *v.t.*
pre′in·struct′, *v.t.*

pre′in·struc′tion, *n.*
pre′in·ti·ma′tion, *n.*
pre·kin′der·gar′ten, *adj.*
pre·lim′it, *v.t.*

pre·men′stru·al, *adj.*
pre·mix′, *v.t.*
pre·nup′tial, *adj.*
pre′or·di·na′tion, *n.*
pre′or·gan·i·za′tion, *n.*

prepar'atory school', 1. a private secondary school providing a college-preparatory education. 2. *Brit.* a private elementary school.

pre·pare (pri pâr′), *v.*, **-pared, -par·ing.** —*v.t.* 1. to put in readiness. 2. to provide with what is necessary. 3. to get (a meal) ready for eating. 4. to manufacture or compound, as a medicine. —*v.i.* 5. to put things or oneself in readiness. —**pre·par′er**, *n.*

pre·par·ed·ness (pri pâr′id nis, -pârd′-nis), *n.* the state of being prepared, esp. for war.

pre·pay (prē pā′), *v.t.*, **-paid, -pay·ing.** to pay or pay the charge upon in advance. —**pre·pay′ment**, *n.*

pre·pon·der·ate (pri pon′də rāt′), *v.i.*, **-at·ed, -at·ing.** to be superior in power, force, number, etc. —**pre·pon′der·ance**, *n.* —**pre·pon′der·ant**, *adj.* —**pre·pon′der·ant·ly**, *adv.*

prep·o·si·tion (prep′ə zish′ən), *n.* a word used with a noun or pronoun to form a phrase. —**prep′o·si′tion·al**, *adj.*

pre·pos·sess (prē′pə zes′), *v.t.* 1. to possess or dominate mentally beforehand. 2. to impress favorably at the outset. —**pre′pos·ses′sion**, *n.*

pre·pos·sess·ing (prē′pə zes′ing), *adj.* impressing favorably. —**pre′pos·sess′ing·ly**, *adv.* —**pre′pos·sess′ing·ness**, *n.*

pre·pos·ter·ous (pri pos′tər əs, -trəs), *adj.* amazingly absurd or foolish. —**pre·pos′ter·ous·ly**, *adv.* —**pre·pos′ter·ous·ness**, *n.*

pre·puce (prē′pyoos), *n.* the fold of skin that covers the head of the penis.

pre·re·cord (prē′ri kôrd′), *v.t.* to record (a radio or television program) prior to an actual broadcast or presentation.

pre·req·ui·site (pri rek′wi zit), *adj.* 1. required beforehand. —*n.* 2. something prerequisite.

pre·rog·a·tive (pri rog′ə tiv), *n.* an exclusive right or privilege exercised by virtue of rank or office.

Pres., President.

pres., 1. present. 2. president.

pres·age (*n.* pres′ij; *v.* pres′ij, pri sāj′), *n.*, *v.*, **-aged, -ag·ing.** —*n.* 1. something that portends a future event, as an omen. 2. a feeling of foreboding. —*v.t.* 3. to give an omen of. 4. to portend or foreshadow. 5. to forecast or predict.

pres·by·o·pi·a (prez′bē ō′pē ə, pres′-), *n.* a form of farsightedness. —**pres′by·op′ic** (-op′ik), *adj.*

pres·by·ter (prez′bi tər, pres′-), *n.* 1. a priest in hierarchical churches. 2. an elder in a Presbyterian church.

Pres·by·te·ri·an (prez′bi tēr′ē ən, pres′-), *adj.* 1. designating a Protestant church governed by presbyters and adhering to modified forms of Calvinism. —*n.* 2. a member of a Presbyterian church. —**Pres′by·te′ri·an·ism**, *n.*

pre·school (prē′skōōl′), *adj.* of or intended for a child between infancy and school age. —**pre′school′er**, *n.*

pre·sci·ence (prē′shē əns, -shəns, presh′ē-, presh′əns), *n.* knowledge of things before they exist or happen. —**pre′sci·ent**, *adj.*

pre·scribe (pri skrīb′), *v.t.*, **-scribed, -scrib·ing.** 1. to lay down as a rule or a course of action. 2. *Med.* to order the use of (a medicine or remedy).

pre·script (prē′skript), *n.* something prescribed, as a precept. —**pre·scrip′tive**, *adj.*

pre·scrip·tion (pri skrip′shən), *n.* 1. *Med.* **a.** a written order for the preparation and use of a medicine or remedy. **b.** the medicine prescribed. 2. the act of prescribing.

pres·ence (prez′əns), *n.* 1. the state or fact of being present. 2. immediate nearness of a person or thing. 3. personal appearance or bearing, esp. of a dignified or imposing kind.

pres′ence of mind′, ability to keep calm and act effectively, esp. in an emergency.

pres·ent¹ (prez′ənt), *adj.* 1. existing or occurring now. 2. being at a specified or understood place rather than elsewhere. 3. being actually under consideration: *the present topic.* 4. *Gram.* designating a verb tense that refers to an action or state now going on or to a general truth. —*n.* 5. the present time. 6. *Gram.* **a.** the present tense. **b.** a form in the present tense. 7. **presents**, *Law.* the present document, used as in a deed.

pres·ent² (*v.* pri zent′; *n.* prez′ənt), *v.t.* 1. to give a gift to. 2. to offer or give in a formal way. 3. to introduce (a person) to another, esp in a formal manner. 4. to bring before or introduce to the public. 5. to show or exhibit. 6. to bring before the mind. 7. **present arms**, *Mil.* to bring a rifle to a vertical position in front of the body. —*n.* 8. a thing presented as a gift. —**pre·sent′er**, *n.*

---

pre·plan′, *v.*, **-planned, -plan·ning.**

pre′-Ref·or·ma′tion, *adj.*, *n.*

pre·reg′is·ter, *v.*

pre′reg·is·tra′tion, *n.*

pre-Ren′ais·sance, *adj.*

pre′-Rev·o·lu′tion, *adj.*

pre′-Rev·o·lu′tion·ar′y, *adj.*

pre′sci·en·tif′ic, *adj.*

pre·score′, *v.t.*

pre·sea′son, *adj.*

pre′se·lect′, *v.t.*

pre·sent·a·ble (pri zen′tə bəl), *adj.* **1.** that may be presented or given. **2.** suitable, as in appearance or manners, for being introduced into society or company. —**pre·sent′a·bly,** *adv.*

pres·en·ta·tion (prez′ən tā′shən, prē′zən-), *n.* **1.** the act of presenting or state of being presented. **2.** exhibition or performance, as of a play or film.

pres·ent-day (prez′ənt dā′), *adj.* of the current time.

pre·sen·ti·ment (pri zen′tə mənt), *n.* a feeling of something about to happen, esp. something evil.

pres·ent·ly (prez′ənt lē), *adv.* **1.** in a little while. **2.** *Informal.* at the present time.

pre·sent·ment (pri zent′mənt), *n.* presentation (def. 1).

pres′ent par′ti·ciple, a participle with present meaning, formed by adding the ending -*ing* to the stem of the verb.

pre·serv·a·tive (pri zûr′və tiv), *n.* **1.** a chemical substance used to preserve foods from decomposition or fermentation. —*adj.* **2.** tending to preserve.

pre·serve (pri zûrv′), *v.,* -**served, -serv·ing,** *n.* —*v.t.* **1.** to keep safe from harm or injury. **2.** to keep up or maintain. **3.** to prepare (foods) so as to resist decomposition or fermentation. **4.** to prepare (fruit, vegetables, etc.) by canning or pickling. —*n.* **5.** Usually, **preserves.** preserved fruit, vegetables, etc. **6.** a place set apart for the protection of game or fish. —**pres·er·va·tion** (prez′ər vā′shən), *n.* —**pre·serv′er,** *n.*

pre·set (prē set′), *v.t.,* -**set, -set·ting.** to set beforehand.

pre·shrunk (prē shrungk′), *adj.* (of a fabric) shrunk during manufacture to reduce the potential shrinkage in laundering.

pre·side (pri zīd′), *v.i.,* -**sid·ed, -sid·ing. 1.** to have charge of a meeting, assembly, etc. **2.** to exercise management or control.

pres·i·dent (prez′i dənt), *n.* **1.** (*often cap.*) the highest executive officer of a modern republic, esp. of the United States. **2.** the chief officer of a corporation, university, or other organization. **3.** an officer appointed or elected to preside over an assembly or meeting. —**pres′i·den·cy,** *n.* —**pres′i·den′tial** (-den′shəl), *adj.*

pre·sid·i·um (pri sid′ē əm), *n.* a permanent administrative committee in certain communist countries.

pre·soak (prē sōk′), *v.t., v.i.* **1.** to soak beforehand, esp. chemically. —*n.* **2.** the act or an instance of presoaking. **3.** a chemical substance used to soak laundry before washing, chiefly to remove stains.

pres. part. See present participle.

press¹ (pres), *v.t.* **1.** to act upon with steadily applied weight or force. **2.** to hold closely, as in an embrace. **3.** to make smooth, esp. by ironing. **4.** to extract juice from by pressure. **5.** to squeeze out, as juice. **6.** to trouble or oppress, as by lack of something. **7.** to constrain or compel. **8.** to urge onward or hasten. **9.** to urge repeatedly or insistently. **10.** to emphasize or insist upon. —*v.i.* **11.** to exert weight or force. **12.** to bear heavily, as upon the mind. **13.** to push forward with eagerness or haste. **14.** to crowd or throng. —*n.* **15.** printed publications collectively, esp. newspapers and periodicals. **16.** their editorial employees, taken collectively. **17.** the consensus of critical commentary. **18.** See **printing press. 19.** an establishment for printing books, magazines, etc. **20.** any of various devices or machines for exerting pressure, crushing, or stamping. **21.** a crowding or thronging together. **22.** the desired smooth effect caused by pressing or ironing. **23.** pressure (def. 5). **24.** *Obs.* clothespress. —**press′er,** *n.*

press² (pres), *v.t.* to force into service, esp. naval or military service.

press′ a′gent, a person employed to obtain favorable publicity for his or her client.

press′ con′ference, an interview given to news reporters by a public figure or celebrity.

press·ing (pres′ing), *adj.* demanding immediate attention. —**press′ing·ly,** *adv.* —**press′ing·ness,** *n.*

press·man (pres′mən), *n., pl.* -**men. 1.** a person who operates a printing press. **2.** *Brit.* a newspaper reporter.

pres·sure (presh′ər), *n., v.,* -**sured, -sur·ing.** —*n.* **1.** the exertion of force upon a surface by an object or fluid in contact with it. **2.** *Physics.* force per unit of area. **3.** a state of trouble or strain. **4.** a constraining or compelling force or influence. **5.** the urgency of matters demanding one's energy and time. —*v.t.* **6.** to put pressure on.

pres′sure cook′er, a strong pot for cooking foods quickly under the pressure of steam.

pres′sure group′, a special-interest group that attempts to influence legislation.

pres·su·rize (presh′ə rīz′), *v.t.,* -**rized, -riz·ing.** to maintain normal air pressure inside (an airplane) while flying at high altitudes. —**pres′sur·i·za′tion,** *n.* —**pres′sur·iz′er,** *n.*

---

pre·sift′, *v.t.*   **pre·slav′er·y,** *adj.*

pres·ti·dig·i·ta·tion (pres′ti dij′i tā′-shən), *n. Chiefly Humorous.* See **sleight of hand.** —**pres′ti·dig′i·ta′tor,** *n.*

pres·tige (pre stēzh′, -stēj′, pres′tij), *n.* **1.** high reputation or influence arising from success, achievement, etc. —*adj.* **2.** having or showing prestige or distinction. —**pres·tige′ful,** *adj.* —**pres·tig′ious** (-stij′əs, -stij′ē əs), *adj.* —**pres·tig′i·ous·ly,** *adv.*

pres·to (pres′tō), *adv.* **1.** quickly or immediately. —*adj.* **2.** quick or rapid. [It: quick, quickly < L *praestō* (adv.) at hand]

pre′stressed con′crete (prē strest′), concrete reinforced with wire strands to give an active resistance to loads.

pre·sume (pri zōōm′), *v.,* -**sumed,** -**sum·ing.** —*v.t.* **1.** to assume as true without proof. **2.** to undertake (to do something) without right or permission. —*v.i.* **3.** to reply too much or without reason. —**pre·sum′a·ble,** *adj.* —**pre·sum′a·bly,** *adv.*

pre·sump·tion (pri zump′shən), *n.* **1.** the act of presuming **2.** something presumed. **3.** unbecoming or impertinent boldness. **4.** reason or grounds for presuming or believing something is true. —**pre·sump′tive,** *adj.*

pre·sump·tu·ous (pri zump′chōō əs), *adj.* unbecoming or impertinently bold. —**pre·sump′tu·ous·ly,** *adv.* —**pre·sump′tu·ous·ness,** *n.* —**Syn.** arrogant, forward.

pre·sup·pose (prē′sə pōz′), *v.t.,* -**posed,** -**pos·ing.** **1.** to suppose or assume beforehand. **2.** to require as a necessary condition. —**pre′sup·po·si′tion** (-sup ə zish′ən), *n.*

pre·teen (prē′tēn′), *n.* a child who is not yet a teenager.

pre·tend (pri tend′), *v.t.* **1.** to allege or profess falsely. **2.** to cause (what is not so) to seem so: *to pretend illness.* **3.** to appear falsely so as to deceive: *to pretend to go to sleep.* —*v.i.* **4.** to make believe. **5.** to lay false claim: *He pretended to the throne.* —**pre·tend′er,** *n.* —**pre·tend′ed·ly,** *adv.* —**Syn.** 2. feign, simulate.

pre·tense (pri tens′, prē′tens), *n.* **1.** a false show of something. **2.** a false allegation or justification. **3.** an unwarranted or false claim. **4.** pretension (def. 2). Also, *Brit.,* **pre·tence′.**

pre·ten·sion (pri ten′shən), *n.* **1.** a false claim to something. **2.** an exaggerated outward show, as of wealth.

pre·ten·tious (pri ten′shəs), *adj.* **1.** making claims to importance or dignity. **2.** making an exaggerated outward show. —**pre·ten′tious·ly,** *adv.* —**pre·ten′tious·ness,** *n.* —**Syn.** 1. in-flated, self-important. **2.** ostentatious.

pret·er·it (pret′ər it), (in older grammars) —*adj.* **1.** past (def. 4). —*n.* **2.** past (def. 8). Also, **pret′er·ite.**

pre·ter·nat·u·ral (prē′tər nach′ər əl, -nach′rəl), *adj.* **1.** beyond what is regular in nature. **2.** outside normal experience. —**pre′ter·nat′u·ral·ly,** *adv.*

pre·test (*n.* prē′test; *v.* prē test′), *n.* **1.** an advance testing or trial, as of a new product. —*v.t., v.i.* **2.** to test beforehand.

pre·text (prē′tekst), *n.* a false reason put forward to conceal the true one.

Pre·to·ri·a (pri tōr′ē ə, -tôr′-), *n.* the administrative capital of the Republic of South Africa.

pret·ti·fy (prit′ə fī′), *v.t.,* -**fied,** -**fy·ing.** *Often Disparaging.* to make pretty. —**pret′ti·fi·ca′tion,** *n.* —**pret′ti·fi′er,** *n.*

pret·ty (prit′ē), *adj.,* -**ti·er,** -**ti·est,** *adv.,* *v.,* -**tied,** -**ty·ing.** —*adj.* **1.** pleasing or attractive in a delicate, dainty, or graceful way. **2.** (often used ironically) fine or grand: *a pretty mess!* **3.** *Informal.* fairly great: *a pretty sum.* —*adv.* **4.** fairly or moderately. —*v.t.* **5.** to make pretty. —**pret′ti·ly,** *adv.* —**pret′ti·ness,** *n.*

pret·zel (pret′səl), *n.* a crisp, dry biscuit, usually in the form of a knot or stick, salted on the outside.

prev., **1.** previous. **2.** previously.

pre·vail (pri vāl′), *v.i.* **1.** to exist everywhere or generally. **2.** to be or appear as the more important or conspicuous. **3.** to prove superior in power or influence. **4.** prevail on or upon, to persuade or induce, esp. successfully. —**pre·vail′er,** *n.*

pre·vail·ing (pri vā′ling), *adj.* **1.** having superior power or influence. **2.** prevalent. —**pre·vail′ing·ly,** *adv.*

prev·a·lent (prev′ə lənt), *adj.* **1.** of wide extent or occurrence. **2.** in general use or acceptance. —**prev′a·lence,** *n.* —**prev′a·lent·ly,** *adv.*

pre·var·i·cate (pri var′ə kāt′), *v.i.,* -**cat·ed,** -**cat·ing.** to speak falsely with deliberate intent. —**pre·var′i·ca′tion,** *n.* —**pre·var′i·ca′tor,** *n.*

pre·vent (pri vent′), *v.t.* **1.** to keep from occurring. **2.** to hold back from doing something. —**pre·vent′-a·ble, pre·vent′i·ble,** *adj.* —**pre·ven′tion,** *n.* —**Syn.** 1. avert, forestall. 2. hinder, impede.

pre·ven·tive (pri ven′tiv), *adj.* **1.** noting the prevention of disease. **2.** serving to prevent or hinder. —*n.* **3.** a preventive means or measure. Also, **pre·vent′a·tive** (-ven′tə tiv) (for defs. 2, 3). —**pre·ven′tive·ly,** *adv.* —**pre·ven′tive·ness,** *n.*

---

pre·sur′gi·cal, *adj.*   **pre·un′ion,** *adj.*

pre·view (prē′vyoo͞′), *n.* **1.** an advance showing of a motion picture or play before its public opening. **2.** a showing of brief scenes in a motion picture for purposes of advertisement. —*v.t.* **3.** to view or show beforehand or in advance. Also, **pre′vue′**.

pre·vi·ous (prē′vē əs), *adj.* **1.** coming or occurring before something else. **2. previous to,** before or prior to. —*pre′vi·ous·ly,* *adv.*

pre·war (prē′wôr′), *adj.* existing or done before a war.

prex·y (prek′sē), *n.,* *pl.* **prex·ies.** *Slang.* a president, esp. of a college or university.

prey (prā), *n.* **1.** an animal hunted or seized for food, esp. by another animal. **2.** any victim. **3.** the action or habit of preying: *a beast of prey.* —*v.i.* **4.** to seize and devour prey, as an animal does. **5.** to make attacks for plunder. **6.** to exert a harmful influence, as on one's mind. —**prey′er,** *n.*

pri·ap·ic (prī ap′ik), *adj.* phallic (def. 1).

price (prīs), *n.,* *v.,* **priced, pric·ing.** —*n.* **1.** the amount of money for which anything is bought or sold. **2.** the disadvantage or sacrifice attending something chosen. **3.** *Archaic.* great value or worth. —*v.t.* **4.** to fix the price of. **5.** *Informal.* to ask or find out the price of.

price·less (prīs′lis), *adj.* beyond all price. —**price′less·ness,** *n.*

price′ support′, governmental maintenance of the price of a commodity, product, etc.

price′ war′, a period of intensive competition, esp. among retailers, in which prices are repeatedly cut.

prick (prik), *n.* **1.** a mark or puncture made by something small and sharp. **2.** a sharp pain. **3.** the act of pricking. **4.** the sensation of being pricked. **5.** prickle (def. 1). —*v.t.* **6.** to pierce with something small and sharp. **7.** to affect with sharp pain, as from piercing. **8.** to cause (someone) sharp mental pain. **9.** to mark with a series of pricks or punctures. **10.** to cause to stand erect or point upward. **11. prick up one's ears,** to listen closely.

prick·le (prik′əl), *n.,* *v.,* **-led, -ling.** —*n.* **1.** Also, **prick′er.** something having a sharp point, as a thorn. **2.** a mild pricking sensation. —*v.t.,* *v.i.* **3.** to cause or feel a mild pricking sensation. —**prick′ly,** *adj.* —**prick′li·ness,** *n.*

prick′ly heat′, a skin eruption accompanied by a prickling sensation, caused by an inflammation of the sweat glands.

prick′ly pear′, **1.** the pear-shaped, often prickly fruit of certain kinds of cactus. **2.** a cactus bearing this fruit.

pride (prīd), *n.,* *v.,* **prid·ed, prid·ing.** —*n.* **1.** too high an opinion of one's importance or superiority. **2.** dignified self-respect. **3.** gratification arising from one's accomplishments or possessions. **4.** arrogant behavior. **5.** something that a person is proud of. **6.** a company of lions. —*v.t.* **7.** to indulge (oneself) in pride. —**pride′ful,** *adj.* —**pride′ful·ly,** *adv.*

prie-dieu (prē′dyoo͞′), *n.,* *pl.* **-dieus, -dieux** (-dyoo͞z′). a piece of furniture for kneeling on during prayer, having a shelf above for a book.

pri·er (prī′ər), *n.* a person who pries.

priest (prēst), *n.* **1.** a person who performs the religious rites of a deity. **2.** (in certain Christian, esp. Catholic, churches) a member of the clergy. —**priest′ess,** *n.fem.* —**priest′hood,** *n.* —**priest′ly,** *adj.* —**priest′li·ness,** *n.*

prig (prig), *n.* a person who adheres smugly to rigid standards of propriety or morality. —**prig′gish,** *adj.* —**prig′gish·ly,** *adv.* —**prig′gish·ness,** *n.*

prim (prim), *adj.,* **prim·mer, prim·mest.** formally precise or proper. —**prim′ly,** *adv.* —**prim′ness,** *n.*

prim., **1.** primary. **2.** primitive.

pri·ma·cy (prī′mə sē), *n.,* *pl.* **-cies.** **1.** the state of being first in order, rank, or importance. **2.** the office or rank of an ecclesiastical primate.

pri·ma don·na (prē′mə don′ə, prim′ə), *pl.* **pri·ma don·nas.** **1.** the principal female singer in an opera company. **2.** a vain, temperamental person.

pri·ma fa·ci·e (prī′mə fā′shē ē′, fā′shē, fā′shə), **1.** at first appearance, before investigation. **2.** immediately plain or clear.

pri·mal (prī′məl), *adj.* primary (defs. 1, 2).

pri·mar·i·ly (prī mâr′ə lē, prī′mer ə lē, -mər ə-), *adv.* **1.** mostly or chiefly. **2.** at first.

pri·ma·ry (prī′mer′ē, -mə rē), *adj.,* *n.,* *pl.* **-ries.** —*adj.* **1.** first in order or time. **2.** first or highest in importance. **3.** not dependent on or derived from something else: *a primary cause.* —*n.* **4.** something first in order or importance. **5.** *U.S.* a preliminary election in which voters of each party nominate candidates for office, party officers, etc. —**pri·ma·ri·ness,** *n.* —**Syn.** 1. fundamental, original. 2. chief, main, principal.

pri′mary ac′cent, the principal or strongest stress of a word.

---

pre·warm′, *v.t.*   **pre·wash′,** *n.,* *v.t.*

pri·mary school', 1. a school usually covering the first three or four years of elementary school and sometimes kindergarten. 2. (in certain foreign countries) See **elementary school**.

pri·mate (prī'māt or, *esp.* for 1, prī'mit), *n.* 1. an archbishop or bishop ranking first among the bishops of a province or country. 2. any of an important group of mammals including humans, the apes, monkeys, and lemurs. —**pri·ma'tial** (-mā'shəl), *adj.*

prime (prīm), *adj., n., v.,* **primed, prim·ing.** —*adj.* 1. of first importance or rank. 2. of greatest value or best quality: *prime ribs of beef.* 3. basic or fundamental. 4. *Math.* not divisible without remainder by any number except itself and unity. 5. *Banking.* chargeable as minimum interest on business loans to best-rated clients: *the prime rate.* —*n.* 6. the most flourishing stage or state. 7. the best part of anything. 8. the beginning or earliest stage of something. 9. the spring of the year. 10. *Math.* a prime number. 11. the mark (') often used to distinguish the designations of similar quantities: *a, a'.* 12. *Banking.* the prime interest rate. —*v.t.* 13. to prepare for a particular purpose or operation. 14. to fill (a firearm) with powder. 15. to pour liquid into (a pump) to expel air and make it ready for action. 16. to cover (a surface) with a preparatory coat, as in painting. 17. to supply with information for use.

prime' merid'ian, the meridian running through Greenwich, England, from which longitude east and west is reckoned.

prime' min'ister, the first minister and head of government in certain countries.

prim·er¹ (prim'ər), *n.* 1. a textbook for teaching children to read. 2. any textbook for beginners.

prim·er² (prī'mər), *n.* 1. a person or thing that primes. 2. a small charge of powder used to explode a larger charge. 3. a first coat or layer of paint.

prime' time', *Radio and Television.* the evening broadcasting hours, considered as drawing the largest available audience.

pri·me·val (prī mē'vəl), *adj.* of the first age or ages, esp. of the world. —**pri·me'val·ly,** *adv.*

prim·i·tive (prim'ĭ tiv), *adj.* 1. being the first or earliest of the kind. 2. characteristic of early ages or of an early state of human development. 3. simple or crude. —*n.* 4. a person or thing that is primitive. 5. a naive or unschooled artist. —**prim'·**

i·tive·ly, *adv.* —**prim'i·tive·ness, prim'i·tiv'i·ty,** *n.* —**prim'i·tiv'ism,** *n.*

pri·mo·gen·i·tor (prī'mə jen'i tər), *n.* the earliest ancestor.

pri·mo·gen·i·ture (prī'mə jen'i chər), *n.* 1. the state of being the first-born of the same parents. 2. the system of inheritance by the eldest son.

pri·mor·di·al (prī môr'dē əl), *adj.* of or existing at or from the very beginning. —**pri·mor'di·al·ly,** *adv.*

primp (primp), *v.t., v.i.* to groom (oneself) with extreme or excessive care.

prim·rose (prim'rōz'), *n.* a perennial herb having variously colored flowers.

prim'rose path', 1. a way of life devoted to irresponsible hedonism. 2. a course of action that is easy but treacherous.

prin., 1. principal. 2. principle.

prince (prins), *n.* 1. a nonreigning male member of a royal family. 2. the ruler of a principality. 3. a person that is chief or preeminent in any class or group. —**prince'dom** (-dəm), *n.* —**prince'ly,** *adj.* —**prince'li·ness,** *n.*

prince' con'sort, a prince who is the husband of a reigning female sovereign.

Prince' Ed'ward Is'land (ed'wərd), an island province of SE Canada. *Cap.:* Charlottetown.

prince·ling (prins'ling), *n.* a young prince.

prin·cess (prin'sis, -ses), *n.* 1. a nonreigning female member of a royal family. 2. the consort of a prince.

prin·ci·pal (prin'sə pəl), *adj.* 1. first or highest in importance. —*n.* 2. the head or director of a school. 3. a principal person, as a chief actor or performer. 4. a person who authorizes another, as an agent, to represent him. 5. a capital sum, as distinguished from interest or profit. —**prin'ci·pal·ly,** *adv.*

prin·ci·pal·i·ty (prin'sə pal'i tē), *n., pl.* **-ties.** 1. a state ruled by a prince. 2. the position or authority of a prince.

prin'cipal parts', *Gram.* a set of inflected forms of a verb from which all the other inflected forms can be derived, as *sing, sang, sung; smoke, smoked.*

prin·ci·ple (prin'sə pəl), *n.* 1. a general or fundamental rule or truth on which others are based. 2. a scientific rule or law explaining the action of something in nature. 3. a rule of conduct. 4. devotion or adherence to such a rule or rules. 5. a fundamental doctrine or belief. 6. a chemical constituent of a substance. 7. **in principle,** in theory.

prin·ci·pled (prin′səp pəld), *adj.* imbued with or having moral principles: *high-principled.*

prink (pringk), *v.t., v.i.* primp.

print (print), *v.t., v.i.* **1.** to stamp (words, etc.) on paper with inked type or plates. **2.** to cause (paper, etc.) to receive words, etc., reproduced by such means. **3.** to produce (a book, etc.) in this way, esp. to publish. **4.** to write in letters like those used in print. **5.** *Photog.* to make a positive picture from (a negative). **—n. 6.** the state of being printed. **7.** printed lettering. **8.** printed matter. **9.** a printed publication, as a newspaper. **10.** a mark or impression made by the pressure of one thing on another. **11. a.** a design or pattern on cloth made by printing, as with engraved rollers. **b.** a cloth so treated. **12.** *Photog.* a picture, esp. a positive made from a negative. **13. in** (or **out of**) **print,** (of a book) still (or no longer) available from the publisher. **—adj. 14.** of or by newspapers or magazines (as opposed to *broadcast*): *print media.*

print., printing.

print·a·ble (prin′tə bəl), *adj.* **1.** capable of being printed. **2.** suitable for publication.

print′ed cir′cuit, an electric circuit in which wires have been replaced by conductive strips printed on an insulating sheet.

print·ing (prin′ting), *n.* **1.** the art, process, or business of producing printed texts. **2.** the act of a person or thing that prints. **3.** the total number of copies of a book, etc., printed at one time.

print′ing press′, a machine for printing on paper from type, plates, etc.

print·out (print′out′), *n.* the printed output of a computer.

pri·or[1] (prī′ər), *adj.* **1.** preceding in time or order. **2.** preceding in importance or privilege. **3. prior to,** before. **—pri·or′i·ty** (-ôr′i tē,-ôr′-), *n.*

pri·or[2] (prī′ər), *n.* an officer in a religious house. **—pri′or·ess,** *n.fem.*

pri·or·y (prī′ə rē), *n., pl.* **-ries.** a religious house governed by a prior or prioress.

prism (priz′əm), *n.* **1.** a transparent solid body used for dispersing light into a spectrum or for reflecting rays of light. **2.** *Geom.* a solid having bases or ends that are parallel, congruent polygons and sides that are parallelograms. **—pris·mat·ic** (priz mat′ik), *adj.*

pris·on (priz′ən), *n.* a building for the confinement of persons accused or convicted of crimes.

pris·on·er (priz′ə nər, priz′nər), *n.* a person confined in prison or kept in custody.

pris·sy (pris′ē), *adj.,* **-si·er, -si·est.** excessively or affectedly proper. **—pris′si·ly,** *adv.* **—pris′si·ness,** *n.*

pris·tine (pris′tēn, -tin, -tīn), *adj.* **1.** of the earliest period or state. **2.** having its original purity.

prith·ee (priᵗĦ′ē), *interj. Archaic.* (I) pray thee.

pri·va·cy (prī′və sē), *n.* **1.** the state of being private. **2.** a person's private affairs or life. **3.** secrecy.

pri·vate (prī′vit), *adj.* **1.** belonging to some particular person or persons. **2.** not open to general use. **3.** not established and maintained under public funds: *a private school.* **4.** of or restricted to only one person. **5.** intimate or most personal. **6.** having nothing to do with public life. **7.** undertaken individually or personally: *private research.* **—n. 8.** *U.S.* an enlisted person of one of the two lowest ranks in the Army or of the lowest rank in the Marine Corps. **9. privates.** Also called **pri′vate parts′.** the external genitals. **10. in private,** away from public notice. **—pri′vate·ly,** *adv.* **—pri′vate·ness,** *n.*

pri·va·teer (prī′və tēr′), *n.* (formerly) **1.** a privately owned warship commissioned by a government to fight or harass enemy shipping. **2.** an officer or seaman of a privateer.

pri′vate eye′, *Slang.* a private detective.

pri′vate first′ class′, *U.S.* an enlisted person ranking just below a corporal in the Army or just below a lance corporal in the Marine Corps.

pri·va·tion (prī vā′shən), *n.* **1.** lack of the usual comforts or necessaries of life. **2.** the state of being deprived.

priv·et (priv′it), *n.* a shrub having evergreen leaves, used for hedges.

priv·i·lege (priv′ə lij, priv′lij), *n., v.,* **-leged, -leg·ing. —n. 1.** a special right or benefit enjoyed by a particular person or group. **—v.t. 2.** to grant a privilege to.

priv·i·leged (priv′ə lijd, priv′lijd), *adj.* **1.** enjoying a special privilege or privileges. **2.** *Law.* (of communications) so confidential in nature as not even to be disclosed in court.

priv·y (priv′ē), *adj.,* **priv·i·er, priv·i·est,** *n., pl.* **priv·ies. —adj. 1.** having knowledge of something private or secret: *to be privy to a plot.* **—n. 2.** an outhouse.

priv′y coun′cil, a board or select body of personal advisers, as of a sovereign. **—priv′y coun′cilor.**

prize¹ (prīz), *n.* **1.** a reward for victory or superiority, as in a contest or lottery. **2.** anything striven for or worth striving for. **3.** something, as an enemy's ship, captured at sea in wartime. —*adj.* **4.** having won a prize. **5.** worthy of a prize. **6.** given as a prize.

prize² (prīz), *v.t.,* **prized, priz·ing.** to value or esteem highly.

prize³ (prīz), *v.t.,* **prized, priz·ing.** *Brit.* pry³ (def. 1).

prize·fight (prīz′fīt′), *n.* a contest between boxers for a prize, a sum of money, etc. —**prize′fight′er,** *n.* —**prize′fight′ing,** *n.*

prize·win·ner (prīz′win′ər), *n.* a person or thing that wins a prize. —**prize′win′ning,** *adj.*

p.r.n., (in prescriptions) as occasion arises. [< L *prō rē nātā*]

pro¹ (prō), *adv., n., pl.* **pros.** —*adv.* **1.** in favor. —*n.* **2.** a person who upholds the affirmative in a debate. **3.** an argument or vote in favor of something.

pro² (prō), *adj., n., pl.* **pros.** *Informal.* professional.

pro-, a prefix meaning: **a.** favoring or supporting: *pro-British.* **b.** before or forth: *prolong.* **c.** taking the place of: *pronoun.*

prob., **1.** probable. **2.** probably. **3.** problem.

prob·a·bil·i·ty (prob′ə bil′i tē), *n., pl.* **-ties. 1.** the quality or fact of being probable. **2.** something probable. **3.** in all probability, quite likely.

prob·a·ble (prob′ə bəl), *adj.* **1.** likely to occur or prove true. **2.** supported generally but not conclusively by the evidence. —**prob′a·bly,** *adv.*

pro·bate (prō′bāt), *n., adj. v.,* **-bat·ed, -bat·ing.** —*n.* **1.** the legal proving of a will as authentic or valid. —*adj.* **2.** of or involving probate. —*v.t.* **3.** to establish the authenticity or validity of (a will).

pro·ba·tion (prō bā′shən), *n.* **1.** a testing or trial of the character, ability, or qualifications of a person, as a new employee. **2. a.** a method of dealing with offenders that allows them to go at large under supervision of a person (**proba′tion of′ficer**) appointed for such duty. **b.** the state of having been conditionally released. —**pro·ba′tion·al, pro·ba′tion·ar′y,** *adj.*

pro·ba·tion·er (prō bā′shə nər), *n.* a person undergoing probation or trial.

pro·ba·tive (prō′bə tiv, prob′ə-), *adj.* **1.** designed for testing or trial. **2.**

affording proof or evidence. —**pro′ba·tive·ly,** *adv.*

probe (prōb), *v.,* **probed, prob·ing,** *n.* —*v.t.* **1.** to search into thoroughly. **2.** to examine or explore with a probe. —*v.i.* **3.** to examine or explore with or as with a probe. —*n.* **4.** a slender surgical instrument for exploring a wound, sinus, etc. **5.** a thorough investigation. **6.** a space vehicle for exploring outer space and gathering data. —**probe′a·ble,** *adj.* —**prob′er,** *n.*

pro·bi·ty (prō′bi tē, prob′i-), *n.* integrity and uprightness. [< L *probitās*]

prob·lem (prob′ləm), *n.* **1.** any question or matter involving doubt, uncertainty, or difficulty. **2.** a source of difficulty or trouble. **3.** a question proposed for solution or discussion. —*adj.* **4.** difficult to train or guide.

prob·lem·at·ic (prob′lə mat′ik), *adj.* **1.** causing a problem. **2.** doubtful or questionable. Also, **prob′lem·at′i·cal.**

pro·bos·cis (prō bos′is), *n., pl.* **-bos·cis·es, -bos·ci·des** (-bos′i dēz′). **1.** the trunk of an elephant. **2.** any long flexible snout.

proc., **1.** procedure. **2.** proceedings. **3.** process.

pro·caine (prō kān′, prō′kān), *n.* a compound used chiefly as a local anesthetic.

pro·ca·the·dral (prō′kə thē′drəl), *n.* a church used temporarily as a cathedral.

pro·ce·dure (prə sē′jər), *n.* **1.** a manner of proceeding in any action. **2.** a particular course of action. **3.** any given mode of conducting legal or parliamentary business. —**pro·ce′dur·al,** *adj.*

pro·ceed (prə sēd′), *v.i.* **1.** to go forward, esp. after stopping. **2.** to carry on or continue any action. **3.** to go on to do something. **4.** to begin and carry on a legal action. **5.** to arise or result. —**pro·ceed′er,** *n.*

pro·ceed·ing (prə sē′ding), *n.* **1.** the act of a person or thing that proceeds. **2.** procedure (def. 2). **3.** **proceedings, a.** a series of doings or events. **b.** a record of transactions, as of an academic society. **4.** a legal step or measure.

pro·ceeds (prō′sēdz), *n.* the total amount or the profits derived from a sale or other transaction.

proc·ess (pros′es), *n.* **1.** a systematic series of actions directed to some end. **2.** a specific, continuous action or series of changes. **3.** the act of

pro′a·bor′tion, *adj.*
pro′ad·min′is·tra′tion, *adj.*
pro′a·dop′tion, *adj.*

pro′al·li′ance, *adj.*
pro′a·mend′ment, *adj.*
pro′ap·prov′al, *adj.*

pro′boy′cott, *adj.*
pro′busi′ness, *adj.*
pro·cap′i·tal·ist, *n., adj.*
pro·church′, *adj.*

carrying out or going through a particular series of actions. **4.** the course or lapse, as of time. **5.** *Biol.* a natural outgrowth or projecting part. **6.** *Law.* a court action or summons. —*v.t.* **7.** to treat or prepare by some particular process, as in manufacturing. **8.** to handle in a routine, orderly manner.

pro·ces·sion (prə seşh′ən), *n.* **1.** a line or group of persons or things moving along in an orderly way, as in a parade. **2.** any continuous movement forward.

pro·ces·sion·al (prə seşh′ə n∂l), *n.* a hymn suitable for accompanying a religious procession. —**pro·ces′sion·al·ly,** *adv.*

proc·es·sor (pros′es ər), *n.* **1.** Also, **proc′ess·er.** a person or thing that processes. **2.** the device within a computer that handles data. **3.** See **food processor.**

pro·claim (prō klām′, prə-), *v.t.* to announce formally or publicly. —**pro·claim′er,** *n.* —**proc·la·ma·tion** (prok′lə mā′shən), *n.*

pro·cliv·i·ty (prō kliv′i tē), *n., pl.* -**ties.** a strong habitual inclination or tendency, esp. toward something bad.

pro·con·sul (prō kon′səl), *n.* **1.** a governor or military commander of a province in ancient Rome. **2.** any administrator over a dependency or an occupied area. —**pro·con′su·lar,** *adj.* —**pro·con′su·late,** *n.* —**pro·con′sul·ship′,** *n.*

pro·cras·ti·nate (prō kras′tə nāt′, prə-), *v.i., v.t.,* -**nat·ed, -nat·ing.** to put off (action) habitually till another day or time. —**pro·cras′ti·na′tion,** *n.* —**pro·cras′ti·na′tor,** *n.* —**Syn.** delay.

pro·cre·ate (prō′krē āt′), *v.t., v.i.,* -**at·ed, -at·ing.** to beget or bring forth (offspring). —**pro′cre·a′tion,** *n.* —**pro′cre·a′tive,** *adj.* —**pro′cre·a′tor,** *n.*

Pro·crus·te·an (prō krus′tē ən), *adj.* (*often l.c.*) tending to produce conformity by violent or arbitrary means.

proc·tol·o·gy (prok tol′ə jē), *n.* the branch of medicine dealing with the rectum and anus. —**proc′to·log′ic** (-tº loj′ik), **proc′to·log′i·cal,** *adj.* —**proc·tol′o·gist,** *n.*

proc·tor (prok′tər), *n.* a university official who supervises students during examinations. —**proc·to′ri·al** (-tôr′ē əl, -tōr′-), *adj.*

proc·to·scope (prok′tə skōp′), *n.* an instrument for visual examination of the interior of the rectum. —**proc·to-**

scop·ic (prok′tə skop′ik), *adj.* —**proc·tos·co·py** (prok tos′kə pē), *n.*

proc·u·ra·tor (prok′yə rā′tər), *n.* (in ancient Rome) an imperial official with fiscal or administrative powers.

pro·cure (prō kyŏor′), *v.t.,* -**cured, -cur·ing. 1.** to obtain by effort. **2.** to cause to occur. **3.** to obtain (women) for the purpose of prostitution. —**pro·cur′a·ble,** *adj.* —**pro·cure′ment,** *n.* —**pro·cur′er,** *n.* —**pro·cur′ess,** *n.fem.*

prod (prod), *v.,* **prod·ded, prod·ding,** *n.* —*v.t.* **1.** to poke or jab with something pointed. **2.** to rouse to do something. —*n.* **3.** a poke or jab. **4.** any pointed instrument for prodding, as a goad.

prod., 1. produce. **2.** produced. **3.** producer. **4.** product. **5.** production.

prod·i·gal (prod′ə gəl), *adj.* **1.** wastefully **extravagant. 2.** lavishly abundant. —*n.* **3.** a person who is wastefully **extravagant.** —**prod′i·gal′i·ty** (-gal′i tē), *n.* —**prod′i·gal·ly,** *adv.* —**Syn. 1.** profligate. **2.** bountiful, profuse.

pro·di·gious (prə dij′əs), *adj.* **1.** extraordinary in size or amount. **2.** wonderful or marvelous: *a prodigious feat.* —**pro·di′gious·ly,** *adv.* —**pro·di′gious·ness,** *n.*

prod·i·gy (prod′i jē), *n., pl.* -**gies. 1.** a person, esp. a child, having extraordinary talent or ability. **2.** something wonderful or marvelous.

pro·duce (*v.* prə dōōs′, -dyōōs′; *n.* prod′ōōs, -yōōs, prō′dōōs, -dyōōs), *v.,* -**duced, -duc·ing,** *n.* —*v.t.* **1.** to bring into existence by labor, machine, or thought. **2.** to bring forth or yield. **3.** to present or show for inspection. **4.** to cause or give rise to. **5.** to get (a play, motion picture, etc.) organized for public presentation. —*v.t.* **6.** to bring forth or yield something. —*n.* **7.** something produced, esp. vegetables and fruits. —**pro·duc′er,** *n.* —**pro·duc′i·ble,** *adj.*

prod·uct (prod′əkt, -ukt), *n.* **1.** a thing produced, as by labor. **2.** a result or outcome. **3.** *Math.* the result obtained by multiplying two or more quantities together.

pro·duc·tion (prə duk′shən), *n.* **1.** the act of producing. **2.** product (def. 1). **3.** an amount that is produced. **4.** the organization and presentation of a dramatic entertainment. —**pro·duc′tive,** *adj.* —**pro·duc′tive·ly,** *adv.* —**pro·duc·tiv·i·ty** (prō′duk tiv′i tē, prod′ək-), **pro·duc′tive·ness,** *n.*

pro·em (prō′əm), *n.* an introductory discourse.

---

pro·cler′i·cal, *adj.*
pro·com′mu·nism, *n.*
pro·com′mu·nist, *adj., n.*

pro·com′pro·mise′, *adj.*
pro′con·ser·va′tion, *adj.*

pro′dem·o·crat′ic, *adj.*
pro′dis·ar′ma·ment, *adj.*
pro′en·force′ment, *adj.*

prof (prof), *n. Informal.* professor.

Prof., Professor.

pro·fane (prə fān′, prō-), *adj., v.,* **-faned, -fan·ing.** —*adj.* **1.** irreverent toward God or sacred things. **2.** not for or concerned with religious purposes. **3.** not holy or hallowed. —*v.t.* **4.** to treat (anything sacred) with irreverence. **5.** to misuse (anything revered). —**prof·a·na·tion** (prof′ə nā′shən), *n.* —**pro·fan·a·to·ry** (prə fan′ə tôr′ē, -tōr′ē), *adj.* —**pro·fane′ly,** *adv.* —**pro·fane′ness,** *n.* —Syn. **1.** blasphemous, sacrilegious.

pro·fan·i·ty (prə fan′i tē, prō-), *n., pl.* **-ties. 1.** the quality of being profane. **2.** profane conduct or language.

pro·fess (prə fes′), *v.t.* **1.** to lay claim to, often insincerely. **2.** to admit frankly. **3.** to affirm faith in. **4.** to claim proficiency in (one's profession or business). —**pro·fessed′,** *adj.* —**pro·fess′ed·ly,** *adv.*

pro·fes·sion (prə fesh′ən), *n.* **1.** an occupation requiring advanced education. **2.** the body of persons engaged in such an occupation. **3.** the act of professing something, esp. religious faith.

pro·fes·sion·al (prə fesh′ə nəl), *adj.* **1.** engaged in an activity as a means of livelihood or for gain. **2.** of, connected with, or engaged in a profession. —*n.* **3.** a person who belongs to one of the professions, as law. **4.** a person who earns his or her living in a sport or other occupation frequently engaged in by amateurs. **5.** a person who is expert at his or her work. —**pro·fes′sion·al·ist,** *n.* —**pro·fes′sion·al·ly,** *adv.*

pro·fes·sion·al·ism (prə fesh′ə nºliz′əm), *n.* **1.** professional character, spirit, or methods. **2.** the standing, practice, or methods of a professional, as distinguished from an amateur.

pro·fes·sor (prə fes′ər), *n.* a college or university teacher of the highest rank. —**pro·fes·so·ri·al** (prō′fə sôr′ē əl, -sôr′-, prof′ə-), *adj.* —**pro·fes′sor·ship′, pro·fes′sor·ate,** *n.*

prof·fer (prof′ər), *Literary.* —*v.t.* **1.** to offer, esp. courteously. —*n.* **2.** the act of proffering. —**prof′fer·er,** *n.*

pro·fi·cient (prə fish′ənt), *adj.* well-advanced and competent. —**pro·fi′cien·cy,** *n.* —**pro·fi′cient·ly,** *adv.* —Syn. accomplished, expert, skilled.

pro·file (prō′fīl), *n., v.,* **-filed, -fil·ing.** —*n.* **1.** a human face or head as viewed from one side. **2.** a picture or representation of this. **3.** an outline of an object. **4.** a concise biographical sketch. —*v.t.* **5.** to draw or write a profile of.

prof·it (prof′it), *n.* **1.** Often, **profits.** financial gain resulting from the use of capital in a transaction after all expenses are paid. **2.** an advantage or benefit. —*v.i., v.t.* **3.** to be of benefit (to). **4.** to be of advantage (to). —**prof′it·a·bil′i·ty,** *n.* —**prof′it·a·ble,** *adj.* —**prof′it·a·bly,** *adv.* —**prof′it·less,** *adj.*

prof·it·eer (prof′i tēr′), *n.* **1.** a person who exacts exorbitant profits, as on inferior products. —*v.i.* **2.** to act as a profiteer.

prof·li·gate (prof′li git, -gāt′), *adj.* **1.** utterly and shamelessly immoral. **2.** recklessly prodigal. —*n.* **3.** a profligate person. —**prof′li·ga·cy** (-gə sē), *n.* —**prof′li·gate·ly,** *adv.*

pro for·ma (prō fôr′mə), *Latin.* according to form.

pro·found (prə found′), *adj.* **1.** having deep insight. **2.** penetrating to the depths of one's being: *profound anxiety.* **3.** thorough or pervasive: *profound influence.* **4.** existing far beneath the surface: *the profound depths of the ocean.* —**pro·found′ly,** *adv.* —**pro·fun′di·ty** (-fun′di tē), *n.*

pro·fuse (prə fyoos′), *adj.* **1.** made or done freely and abundantly: *profuse apologies.* **2.** extravagantly generous. —**pro·fuse′ly,** *adv.* —**pro·fu′sion** (-fyoo′zhən), **pro·fuse′ness,** *n.*

pro·gen·i·tor (prō jen′i tər), *n.* **1.** a directly biologically related ancestor. **2.** an original or model for later developments.

prog·e·ny (proj′ə nē), *n., pl.* **-ny, -nies.** descendants or offspring collectively.

prog·na·thous (prog′nə thəs, prog·nā′-), *adj.* having protrusive jaws.

prog·no·sis (prog nō′sis), *n., pl.* **-ses** (-sēz). a forecast of the probable course of a disease.

prog·nos·tic (prog nos′tik), *adj.* **1.** of prognosis. —*n.* **2.** a forecast or prediction. **3.** an omen or portent.

prog·nos·ti·cate (prog nos′tə kāt′), *v.t.,* **-cat·ed, -cat·ing.** to forecast from present indications. —**prog·nos′ti·ca′tion,** *n.* —**prog·nos′ti·ca′tor,** *n.*

pro·gram (prō′gram, -grəm), *n., v.,* **-gramed, -gram·ing or -grammed, -gram·ming.** —*n.* Also, *Brit.,* **pro′gramme. 1.** a plan or schedule to be followed **2.** a list of items, pieces, performers, etc., as in a public entertainment. **3.** a performance or production, esp. on radio or television. **4.** a systematic plan or set of instructions for the solution of a problem by a computer. —*v.t.* **5.** to schedule as part of a program. **6.** to prepare a computer program for. **7.** to supply (a computer) with a program. —**pro′gram·ma·ble,** *adj.* —**pro·gram′ma·bil′i·ty,** *n.* —**pro′gram·mat′ic** (-grə mat′ik), *adj.* —**pro′gram·mer, pro′gram·er,** *n.*

pro′grammed instruc′tion, a set of organized material given in small units allowing a pupil to learn progressively with a minimum of formal instruction. Also called **pro′grammed learn′ing.**

prog·ress (*n.* prog′res; *v.* prə gres′), *n.* **1.** movement toward a specific goal. **2.** cumulative improvement, as of an individual. **3.** onward movement, as in time. —*v.i.* **4.** to advance or proceed. **5.** to improve or better. **6.** to go forward or onward.

pro·gres·sion (prə gresh′ən), *n.* **1.** the act of progressing. **2.** a continuous series. **3.** *Math.* a succession of quantities in which there is a constant relation between each member and the one succeeding it. —**pro·gres′sion·al,** *adj.*

pro·gres·sive (prə gres′iv), *adj.* **1.** of or characterized by progress. **2.** advocating progress, as in technology or politics. **3.** advancing step by step. **4.** *Gram.* noting a verb form that indicates continuing action or state. —*n.* **5.** a person who favors progress or reform, esp. in politics. —**pro·gres′sive·ly,** *adv.* —**pro·gres′sive·ness,** *n.*

pro·hib·it (prō hib′it), *v.t.* **1.** to forbid by authority or law. **2.** to prevent or hinder. —**pro·hib′i·tive, pro·hib′i·to·ry,** *adj.* —**pro·hib′i·tive·ly,** *adv.*

pro·hi·bi·tion (prō′ə bish′ən), *n.* **1.** the act of prohibiting. **2.** the legal prohibiting of the manufacture and sale of alcoholic beverages. —**pro′hi·bi′tion·ist,** *n.*

proj·ect (*n.* proj′ekt; *v.* prə jekt′), *n.* **1.** something planned. **2.** a large or major undertaking. —*v.t.* **3.** to plan or propose. **4.** to throw or cast forward. **5.** to cause to extend or stick out. **6.** to cast (an image, shadow, etc.) onto a surface or into space. —*v.i.* **7.** to extend or stick out. —**pro·jec′tion,** *n.*

pro·jec·tile (prə jek′til, -til), *n.* **1.** a bullet or shell for firing from a gun or similar weapon. **2.** a body projected or impelled forward, as a rocket.

projec′tion booth′, a compartment in a movie theater from which the picture is projected on the screen.

pro·jec·tion·ist (prə jek′shə nist), *n.* a person who operates a motion-picture or slide projector.

pro·jec·tor (prə jek′tər), *n.* an apparatus for throwing an image on a screen, projecting a beam of light, etc.

pro·lapse (prō laps′), *n., v.,* **-lapsed, -laps·ing.** —*n.* **1.** a falling down of

an organ, as the uterus, from its normal position. —*v.i.* **2.** to fall down or out of place.

pro·le·gom·e·non (prō′lə gom′ə non′, -nən), *n., pl.* **-na** (-nə). an introductory essay.

pro·le·tar·i·an (prō′li târ′ē ən), *n.* a member of the proletariat.

pro·le·tar·i·at (prō′li târ′ē ət), *n.* the industrial working class.

pro·lif·er·ate (prō lif′ə rāt′), *v.i., v.t.,* **-at·ed, -at·ing.** to grow or spread excessively and rapidly. —**pro·lif′er·a′tion,** *n.*

pro·lif·ic (prō lif′ik), *adj.* **1.** producing offspring, fruit, etc., abundantly. **2.** producing many literary or creative works. —**pro·lif′i·cal·ly,** *adv.* —Syn. fertile, fruitful, productive.

pro·lix (prō liks′, prō′liks), *adj.* tediously long and wordy. —**pro·lix′i·ty** (-lik′si tē), *n.* —**pro·lix′ly,** *adv.*

pro·logue (prō′lôg, -log), *n.* an introductory part of a play or novel. Also, **pro′log.**

pro·long (prə lông′, -long′), *v.t.* **1.** to lengthen out in time. **2.** to make longer in space. —**pro′lon·ga′tion,** *n.*

prom (prom), *n. Informal.* a formal dance at a school or college. [*prom(enade)*]

prom·e·nade (prom′ə nād′, -näd′), *n., v.,* **-nad·ed, -nad·ing.** —*n.* **1.** a leisurely walk in a public place. **2.** an area used for such walking. **3.** a march of guests opening a formal ball. —*v.i., v.t.* **4.** to take a promenade (through or on). —**prom′e·nad′er,** *n.*

Pro·me·the·us (prə mē′thē əs, -thōos), *n. Class. Myth.* a giant deity who stole fire from heaven and gave it to mankind.

pro·me·thi·um (prə mē′thē əm), *n. Chem.* a rare-earth, metallic element. *Symbol:* Pm; *at. no.:* 61.

prom·i·nence (prom′ə nəns), *n.* **1.** the state of being prominent or conspicuous. **2.** something prominent, as a projection.

prom·i·nent (prom′ə nənt), *adj.* **1.** widely and familiarly known. **2.** easily seen or very noticeable. **3.** standing out beyond a surface or line. —**prom′i·nent·ly,** *adv.* —Syn. **1.** celebrated, distinguished, eminent.

pro·mis·cu·ous (prə mis′kyōō əs), *adj.* **1.** characterized by frequent and indiscriminate changes of one's sexual partners. **2.** composed of a disordered mixture of various kinds of elements. —**prom·is·cu·i·ty** (prom′i·skyōō′i tē, prō′mi-), *n.* —**pro·mis′cu·ous·ly,** *adv.* —**pro·mis′cu·ous·ness,** *n.*

---

pro·in′dus′try, *adj.*   **pro·in′ter·ven′tion,** *adj.*   **pro·mil′i·tar′y,** *adj.*
pro·in′te·gra′tion, *adj.*   **pro·la′bor,** *adj.*

prom·ise (prom′is), *n.*, *v.*, **-ised, -is-ing.** —*n.* **1.** a declaration or assurance that something specified will or will not be done. **2.** indication of future excellence or achievement. **3.** something promised. —*v.t., v.i.* **4.** to make a promise of (something). **5.** to afford ground for expecting.

Prom′ised Land′, Canaan, the land promised by God to Abraham and his descendants.

prom·is·ing (prom′i sing), *adj.* giving favorable promise. —**prom′is·ing·ly,** *adv.*

prom·is·so·ry (prom′i sôr′ē, -sôr′ē), *adj.* containing or implying a promise.

prom′issory note′, a written promise to pay a specified sum of money at a fixed time or on demand.

prom·on·to·ry (prom′ən tōr′ē, -tôr′ē), *n., pl.* **-ries.** a high point of land projecting into the sea.

pro·mote (prə mōt′), *v.t.,* **-mot·ed, -mot·ing. 1.** to encourage the existence or progress of. **2.** to advance in rank or position. **3.** to advertise or aid in developing (a business, product, etc.). —**pro·mo′tion,** *n.* —**pro·mo′tion·al,** *adj.*

pro·mot·er (prə mō′tər), *n.* **1.** a person who aids in developing a company, project, product, etc. **2.** a person or thing that promotes.

prompt (prompt), *adj.* **1.** done or given without delay. **2.** quick to act or respond. —*v.t.* **3.** to induce to action. **4.** to inspire or give rise to. **5.** to supply (an actor or singer) with forgotten words, lines, or actions. —**prompt′er,** *n.* —**prompt′ly,** *adv.* —**prompt′ness, promp′ti·tude′,** *n.*

prompt·book (prompt′book′), *n.* a copy of the script of a play, containing cues and notes.

prom·ul·gate (prom′əl gāt′, prō mul′-gāt), *v.t.,* **-gat·ed, -gat·ing. 1.** to put into operation (a law, etc.) by formal proclamation. **2.** to set forth publicly (a creed, etc.). —**prom′ul·ga′-tion,** *n.* —**prom′ul·ga′tor,** *n.*

pron., 1. pronoun. **2.** pronounced. **3.** pronunciation.

prone (prōn), *adj.* **1.** having a natural tendency: *to be prone to anger.* **2.** lying with the face downward. —**prone′ness,** *n.*

prong (prông, prong), *n.* **1.** one of the pointed tines of a fork. **2.** any pointed, projecting part, as of an antler. —**pronged,** *adj.*

prong·horn (prông′hôrn′, prong′-), *n., pl.* **-horns, -horn.** an antelopelike ruminant of the plains of western North America.

pro·noun (prō′noun′), *n.* a word used in place of a noun or noun phrase. —**pro·nom′i·nal** (-nom′ə nəl), *adj.*

pro·nounce (prə nouns′), *v.t., v.i.,* **-nounced, -nounc·ing. 1.** to utter the sound or sounds of (a word, etc.). **2.** to announce formally or officially. —**pro·nounce′a·ble,** *adj.* —**pro·nun′-ci·a′tion** (-nun′sē ā′shən), *n.*

pro·nounced (prə nounst′), *adj.* clearly apparent. —**pro·nounc·ed·ly** (prə noun′sid lē), *adv.*

pro·nounce·ment (prə nouns′ment), *n.* a formal or official statement.

pron·to (pron′tō), *adv. Slang.* promptly or quickly.

pro·nun·ci·a·men·to (prə nun′sē ə men′tō, -shē ə-), *n., pl.* **-tos.** a political proclamation.

proof (prōōf), *n.* **1.** evidence sufficient to establish a thing as true or factual. **2.** the act of testing for truth or fact. **3.** the establishment of a truth or fact. **4.** the arbitrary standard strength of alcoholic liquor. **5.** *Print.* a trial impression printed to see if corrections are needed. **6.** *Photog.* a trial print from a negative. —*adj.* **7.** impervious or invulnerable: *proof against attack.* **8.** of standard strength, as an alcoholic liquor.

-proof, a suffix meaning: **a.** impervious to: *waterproof.* **b.** protected against: *bulletproof.*

proof·read (prōōf′rēd′), *v.t., v.i.,* **-read (-red′), -read·ing.** to read (printers′ proofs, copy, etc.) to detect and mark errors to be corrected. —**proof′read′er,** *n.*

prop¹ (prop), *n., v.,* **propped, prop-ping.** —*n.* **1.** a rigid object, as a stick or beam, used to hold something up. —*v.t.* **2.** to support with a prop. **3.** to rest (a thing) against a support.

prop² (prop), *n.* property (def. 5).

prop³ (prop), *n. Informal.* a propeller.

prop., 1. property. **2.** proposition. **3.** proprietary. **4.** proprietor.

prop·a·gan·da (prop′ə gan′də), *n.* **1.** information or ideas methodically spread to promote or injure a cause, group, nation, etc. **2.** the deliberate spreading of such information or ideas. —**prop′a·gan′dist,** *n., adj.* —**prop′a·gan′dize** (-dīz), *v.t., v.i.*

prop·a·gate (prop′ə gāt′), *v.,* **-gat·ed, -gat·ing.** —*v.t.* **1.** to cause (a plant or animal) to multiply by natural reproduction. **2.** to reproduce (itself, its kind, etc.), as a plant or an animal does. **3.** to spread (information, customs, etc.) from person to person. —*v.i.* **4.** to multiply by natural reproduction. —**prop′a·ga′tion,** *n.* —**prop′a·ga′tor,** *n.*

pro·pane (prō′pān), *n.* a flammable gas occurring in petroleum and natural gas: used as a fuel.

---

pro·mod′ern, *adj.*   **pro·mon′ar·chist,** *n., adj.*   **pro·na′tion·al·ist,** *adj.*

pro·pel (prə pel'), *v.t.*, **-pelled, -pel·ling.** to drive forward or onward.

pro·pel·lant (prə pel'ənt), *n.* **1.** a propelling agent. **2.** the fuel for propelling a rocket. Also, **pro·pel'lent.**

pro·pel·ler (prə pel'ər), *n.* a device having a revolving hub with radiating blades, for propelling a steamship or airplane.

pro·pen·si·ty (prə pen'si tē), *n., pl.* **-ties.** a strong, often uncontrollable natural inclination or tendency.

prop·er (prop'ər), *adj.* **1.** adapted or appropriate to the purpose. **2.** correct or decorous. **3.** belonging to a particular person, thing, or group. **4.** strict or accurate. **5.** in the strict sense of the word: *Chicago proper.* **6.** *Gram.* noting a particular person or thing. **7.** *Brit. Informal.* complete or thorough. **—prop'er·ly,** *adv.* **—prop'er·ness,** *n.* **—Syn. 1.** fit, suitable. **2.** conventional, polite.

prop·er·tied (prop'ər tēd), *adj.* owning property.

prop·er·ty (prop'ər tē), *n., pl.* **-ties. 1.** something owned. **2.** land or real estate. **3.** right of possession. **4.** an essential or distinctive attribute of something. **5.** any movable item, except scenery and costumes, used on the set in a theatrical production. **—prop'er·ty·less,** *n.*

pro·phase (prō'fāz'), *n.* the first stage in mitosis.

proph·e·cy (prof'i sē), *n., pl.* **-cies. 1.** the foretelling of what is to come. **2.** something declared by a prophet.

proph·e·sy (prof'i sī'), *v.t., v.i.,* **-sied, -sy·ing. 1.** to foretell (future events). **2.** to foretell (something) by divine inspiration. **—proph'e·si'er,** *n.*

proph·et (prof'it), *n.* **1.** a person who speaks with divine inspiration. **2.** a person who foretells future events. **—proph'et·ess,** *n.fem.*

pro·phet·ic (prə fet'ik), *adj.* **1.** of or pertaining to a prophet. **2.** of or containing prophecy. **—pro·phet'i·cal·ly,** *adv.*

pro·phy·lac·tic (prō'fə lak'tik, prof'ə-), *adj.* **1.** protecting from disease or infection. **—n. 2.** *Med.* a prophylactic drug or device, as a condom.

pro·phy·lax·is (prō'fə lak'sis, prof'ə-), *n. Med.* the prevention of disease or a disease, as by treatment.

pro·pin·qui·ty (prō pling'kwi tē), *n.* **1.** nearness in place or time. **2.** nearness of relation.

pro·pi·ti·ate (prə pish'ē āt'), *v.t.,* **-at·ed, -at·ing.** to win or gain the favor of, as an offended deity. **—pro·pi'ti·a'tion,** *n.* **—pro·pi'ti·a·to'ry** (-tōr'ē, -tôr'ē), *adj.*

pro·pi·tious (prə pish'əs), *adj.* **1.** pre-

senting favorable conditions. **2.** favorably disposed.

prop·jet (prop'jet'), *n.* turboprop.

prop·man (prop'man'), *n.* a person responsible for the stage properties, as in a play. **—prop'mis·tress,** *n.fem.*

pro·po·nent (prə pō'nənt), *n.* a person who puts forward a proposition or proposal.

pro·por·tion (prə pôr'shən, -pōr'-), *n.* **1.** the comparative relation between things or magnitudes. **2.** proportions, dimensions or size. **3.** any portion or part in its relation to the whole. **4.** symmetry or balance. **—v.t. 5.** to adjust the proportions of in proper relation. **6.** to balance or harmonize the proportions of. **—pro·por'tion·al,** *adj.* **—pro·por'tion·al'i·ty,** *n.* **—pro·por'tion·al·ly,** *adv.* **—pro·por'tion·ate,** *adj.* **—pro·por'tion·ate·ly,** *adv.*

pro·pose (prə pōz'), *v.,* **-posed, -pos·ing. —v.t. 1.** to offer for consideration or acceptance. **2.** to plan or intend. **3.** to offer (a toast). **—v.i. 4.** to make an offer of marriage. **—pro·pos'al,** *n.* **—pro·pos'er,** *n.*

prop·o·si·tion (prop'ə zish'ən), *n.* **1.** a plan or scheme proposed. **2.** an offer of terms for a business transaction. **3.** *Informal.* a matter considered as something to be dealt with: *a tough proposition.* **4.** anything stated for purposes of discussion. **5.** *Math.* a statement of a truth to be demonstrated. **—prop'o·si'tion·al,** *adj.*

pro·pound (prə pound'), *v.t.* to put forward for consideration or solution. **—pro·pound'er,** *n.*

pro·pri·e·tar·y (prə prī'i ter'ē), *adj.* **1.** of or like a proprietor. **2.** manufactured and sold only by the owner of the patent, as a medicine.

pro·pri·e·tor (prə prī'i tər), *n.* an owner, as of a business or patent. **—pro·pri'e·tor·ship',** *n.* **—pro·pri'e·tress,** *n.fem.*

pro·pri·e·ty (prə prī'i tē), *n., pl.* **-ties. 1.** conformity to established standards of proper behavior or manners. **2.** the proprieties, the conventional standards of behavior in polite society.

pro·pul·sion (prə pul'shən), *n.* **1.** the act of propelling or state of being propelled. **2.** a propelling force. **—pro·pul'sive,** *adj.*

pro ra·ta (prō rā'tə, rä'-), according to a certain rate.

pro·rate (prō rāt', prō'rāt'), *v.i., v.t.,* **-rat·ed, -rat·ing.** to divide, distribute, or calculate proportionately. **—pro·ra'tion,** *n.*

pro·rogue (prō rōg'), *v.t.,* **-rogued, -rogu·ing.** to discontinue a session of (the British Parliament). **—pro'ro·ga'tion,** *n.*

pro're·form', *adj.*   **pro'res·to·ra'tion,** *adj.*   **pro'rev·o·lu'tion·ar'y,** *adj.*

pros., prosody.

pro·sa·ic (prō zā'ik), *adj.* lacking imagination or interest. —**pro·sa'i·cal·ly,** *adv.* —**Syn.** commonplace, humdrum.

pro·sce·ni·um (prō sē'nē əm), *n., pl.* **-ni·a** (-nē ə). the arch that separates a stage from the auditorium.

pro·scribe (prō skrīb'), *v.t.,* **-scribed, -scrib·ing. 1.** to condemn or prohibit as dangerous. **2.** *Obs.* to outlaw or banish. —**pro·scrip'tion** (-skrip'shən), *n.*

prose (prōz), *n.* ordinary language without meter or rhyme.

pros·e·cute (pros'ə kyōōt'), *v.t.,* **-cut·ed, -cut·ing. 1.** to institute legal proceedings against. **2.** to follow up and complete (something undertaken). — **pros'e·cut'a·ble,** *adj.* —**pros'e·cu'tion,** *n.* —**pros'e·cu'tor,** *n.* —**pros'·e·cu·to'ri·al** (-kyōō tôr'ē əl, -tôr'-), **pros'e·cu·to'ry** (-kōō tôr'ē, -tôr'ē), *adj.*

pros·e·lyte (pros'ə līt'), *n., v.,* **-lyt·ed, -lyt·ing.** —*n.* **1.** a person who has changed to a different religion or doctrine. —*v.i., v.t.* **2.** to proselytize. —**pros'e·lyt·ism** (-li tiz'əm, -li-), *n.*

pros·e·lyt·ize (pros'ə li tīz', -li-), *v.t., v.i.,* **-ized, -iz·ing.** to convert or attempt to convert as a proselyte. — **pros'e·lyt·iz'er,** *n.*

pros·o·dy (pros'ə dē), *n.* the study of poetic meters and versification.

pros·pect (pros'pekt), *n.* **1.** Usually, **prospects.** the probability of future success. **2.** expectation or hope. **3.** a potential customer or client. **4.** a potential candidate. **5.** outlook or view over a region. **6.** a mental view or survey. —*v.t., v.i.* **7.** to search or explore (a region), as for gold. — **pros·pec'tor** (pros'pek tər, prə spek'tər), *n.*

pro·spec·tive (prə spek'tiv), *adj.* likely to happen or become. —**pro·spec'tive·ly,** *adv.*

pro·spec·tus (prə spek'təs), *n., pl.* **-tus·es.** a document describing a forthcoming project or enterprise, as one distributed to prospective investors.

pros·per (pros'pər), *v.i.* to be successful, esp. financially.

pros·per·i·ty (pro sper'i tē), *n.* the state or condition of being successful, esp. financially.

pros·per·ous (pros'pər əs), *adj.* **1.** having or characterized by financial success. **2.** *Archaic.* favorable or propitious. —**pros'per·ous·ly,** *adv.*

pros·tate (pros'tāt), *n.* the muscular, glandular organ which surrounds the urethra of males at the base of the bladder. Also called **pros'tate gland'.** —**pro·stat·ic** (prō stat'ik), *adj.*

pros·ta·ti·tis (pros'tə tī'tis), *n.* inflammation of the prostate gland.

pros·the·sis (pros'thi sis, pros thē'sis), *n., pl.* **-ses** (-sēz', -sēz), an artificial part to replace a natural part of the body. —**pros·thet'ic** (-thet'ik), *adj.* **pros·thet'i·cal·ly,** *adv.*

pros·thet·ics (pros thet'iks), *n.* the branch of surgery or of dentistry that deals with the replacement of missing parts with artificial structures.

pros·ti·tute (pros'ti tōōt', -tyōōt'), *n., v.,* **-tut·ed, -tut·ing.** —*n.* **1.** a person, usually a woman, who engages in sexual intercourse for money. —*v.t.* **2.** to sell or offer (oneself) as a prostitute. **3.** to put (one's talent or ability) to unworthy use. —**pros'ti·tu'tion,** *n.*

pros·trate (pros'trāt), *v.,* **-trat·ed, -trat·ing,** *adj.* —*v.t.* **1.** to cast (oneself) face down on the ground, as in humility. **2.** to overcome or reduce to helplessness or exhaustion. —*adj.* **3.** lying flat on the ground. **4.** lying face down. **5.** helpless or exhausted. —**pros·tra'tion,** *n.*

pros·y (prō'zē), *adj.,* **pros·i·er, pros·i·est. 1.** of or resembling prose. **2.** prosaic.

Prot., Protestant.

pro·tac·tin·i·um (prō'tak tin'ē əm), *n. Chem.* a radioactive, metallic element. *Symbol:* Pa; *at. wt:* 231.04; *at. no.:* 91.

pro·tag·o·nist (prō tag'ə nist), *n.* **1.** the leading character of a drama or novel. **2.** a leader of a movement or cause.

pro·te·an (prō'tē ən, prō tē'-), *adj.* readily assuming different forms or characters.

pro·tect (prə tekt'), *v.t.* to cover or shield from injury or danger. —**pro·tec'tor,** *n.* —**pro·tec'tress,** *n.fem.*

pro·tec·tion (prə tek'shən), *n.* **1.** the act of protecting or state of being protected. **2.** a thing, person, or group that protects. **3.** *Informal.* bribe money paid to avoid violence. **4.** *Econ.* **a.** the system of fostering home industries through duties imposed on competitive imports. **b.** the theory or practice of this system. — **pro·tec'tion·al,** *adj.*

pro·tec·tion·ism (prə tek'shə niz'əm), *n.* protection (def. 4b). —**pro·tec'tion·ist,** *n., adj.*

pro·tec·tive (prə tek'tiv), *adj.* **1.** tending to protect. **2.** of or designed for economic protection. —**pro·tec'tive·ly,** *adv.* —**pro·tec'tive·ness,** *n.*

pro·tec·tor·ate (prə tek'tər it), *n.* **1.** the relation of a strong country toward a weaker country that it protects. **2.** a country so protected.

---

pro·slav'er·y, *adj., n.*   **pro·suf'frage,** *adj.*

pro·té·gé (prō′tə zhā′, prō′tə zhā′), *n.* a person who is aided and guided in his career by an influential person. —**pro′té·gée′**, *n.fem.*

pro·tein (prō′tēn, -tē in), *n.* any of a group of nitrogenous organic compounds of high molecular weight that occur in all living cells and that are required for all life processes in animals and plants.

pro tem (prō tem′). See **pro tempore.**

pro tem·po·re (prō tem′pə rē′), *Latin.* for the time being.

Prot·er·o·zo·ic (prot′ər ə zō′ik, prō′tər-), *adj.* **1.** noting a period of the Precambrian era, occurring from 600,000,000 to about 1,500,000,000 years ago, characterized by the appearance of bacteria and marine algae. —*n.* **2.** the Proterozoic period.

pro·test (*n.* prō′test; *v.* prə test′), *n.* **1.** a manifest expression of objection or disapproval. **2.** a solemn or earnest declaration. —*v.i., v.t.* **3.** to make a protest or remonstrance (against). **4.** to make solemn or earnest declaration (of). —**prot·es·ta·tion** (prot′i stā′shən, prō′ti-), *n.* —**pro·test′er, pro·test′or,** *n.*

Prot·es·tant (prot′i stənt), *n.* any Western Christian not an adherent of the Roman Catholic Church or the Eastern Church. —**Prot′es·tant·ism′,** *n.*

pro·tha·la·mi·on (prō′thə lā′mē on′, -ən), *n., pl.* **-mi·a** (-mē ə), a song written to celebrate a marriage. Also, **pro′tha·la′mi·um** (-əm).

proto-, a combining form meaning: **a.** first or original: *prototype.* **b.** chief or essential: *protoplasm.*

pro·to·col (prō′tə kôl′, -kol′, -kōl′), *n.* **1.** the customs and regulations dealing with diplomatic formality, precedence, and etiquette. **2.** an original draft from which a treaty is prepared. **3.** a supplementary international agreement.

pro·ton (prō′ton), *n.* an elementary particle in all atomic nuclei having a positive charge equal to the negative charge on an electron.

pro·to·plasm (prō′tə plaz′əm), *n.* a semifluid, complex substance that is the living matter of all plant and animal cells. —**pro′to·plas′mic, pro′to·plas′mal, pro·to·plas·mat·ic** (prō′tō-plaz mat′ik), *adj.*

pro·to·type (prō′tə tīp′), *n.* the original or model on which something is patterned. —**pro′to·typ′ic,** *adj.*

pro·to·zo·an (prō′tə zō′on), *n.* any of a group of microscopic animals consisting only of a single cell or colony of similar cells. Also, **pro′to·zo′on** (-on, -ən). —**pro′to·zo′ic,** *adj.*

pro·tract (prō trakt′), *v.t.* to draw out or lengthen, esp. in time. —**pro·trac′tion,** *n.*

pro·trac·tor (prō trak′tər), *n.* an instrument having a graduated arc for plotting or measuring angles.

pro·trude (prō trood′), *v.i., v.t.,* **-trud·ed, -trud·ing.** to thrust out or cause to thrust out. —**pro·tru′sion** (-troo′zhən), *n.* —**pro·tru′sive** (-troo′siv), *adj.*

pro·tru·sile (prō troo′sil), *adj.* capable of being thrust out. Also, **pro·trac′tile** (-trak′til).

pro·tu·ber·ance (prō too′bər əns, -tyoo′-), *n.* a thing or part that protrudes. —**pro·tu′ber·ant,** *adj.*

proud (proud), *adj.* **1.** thinking well of oneself because of one's accomplishments, possessions, etc. **2.** feeling honored, as by a distinction conferred on one. **3.** governed in one's words or actions by self-respect. **4.** inclined to excessive self-esteem. **5.** promoting a feeling of pride: *a proud moment.* **6.** stately or majestic. **7.** *Literary.* full of vigor or spirit, as a horse. —**proud′ly,** *adv.* —**proud′ness,** *n.* —**Syn. 1.** self-satisfied. **4.** haughty, overbearing, vain.

proud′ flesh′, a new growth of tissue around the edges of a healing wound.

Prov., **1.** Provençal. **2.** Proverbs.

prov., **1.** province. **2.** provincial. **3.** provisional. **4.** provost.

prove (proov), *v.,* **proved, proved** or **prov·en, prov·ing.** —*v.t.* **1.** to establish the truth or genuineness of. **2.** to establish the quality of, as by a test or demonstration. —*v.i.* **3.** to be found by trial or experience to be: *His story proved false.* —**prov′a·bil′i·ty,** *n.* —**prov′a·ble,** *adj.* —**prov′er,** *n.*

prov·e·nance (prov′ə nəns), *n.* the place of origin, as of a work of art. Also, **pro·ve·ni·ence** (prō vē′nē əns).

Pro·ven·çal (prō′vən säl′, prov′ən-), *n.* **1.** a native or inhabitant of Provence. **2.** a Romance language formerly widely spoken and written in southern France.

Pro·vence (prə väNs′), *n.* a region in SE France.

prov·en·der (prov′ən dər), *n.* **1.** dry food for livestock. **2.** *Facetious.* food for human consumption.

prov·erb (prov′ərb), *n.* a simple, usually concrete saying that expresses practical wisdom. —**pro·ver·bi·al** (prə vûr′bē əl), *adj.*

Prov·erbs (prov′ərbz), *n.* a book of the Bible containing the sayings of sages.

pro·vide (prə vīd′), *v.,* **-vid·ed, -vid·ing.** —*v.t.* **1.** to give what is wanted or needed. **2.** to afford or yield. **3.** to state formally as a condition demanded. —*v.i.* **4.** to take measures with due foresight. **5.** to supply means of sustenance: *to provide for one's family.* —**pro·vid′er,** *n.*

pro·vid·ed (prə vī′did), *conj.* on the condition or understanding. Also, **pro·vid′ing.**

prov·i·dence (prov′i dəns), *n.* **1.** (*often cap.*) the foreseeing care and guidance of God or nature. **2.** (*cap.*) God. **3.** care exercised in providing for the future. **4.** *Archaic.* frugality or thrift.

Prov·i·dence (prov′i dəns), *n.* the capital of Rhode Island.

prov·i·dent (prov′i dənt), *adj.* **1.** careful in providing for the future. **2.** *Archaic.* frugal or thrifty. —**prov′i·dent·ly,** *adv.*

prov·i·den·tial (prov′i den′shəl), *adj.* **1.** of or seeming to come from divine providence. **2.** fortunate or lucky. —**prov′i·den′tial·ly,** *adv.*

prov·ince (prov′ins), *n.* **1.** an administrative division or unit of a country. **2. the provinces,** the parts of a country outside of the capital or the largest cities. **3.** a particular sphere of activity or authority.

pro·vin·cial (prə vin′shəl), *adj.* **1.** belonging to a particular province. **2.** having the manners, viewpoints, etc., considered characteristic of inhabitants of a province. **3.** unsophisticated or narrow. —**pro·vin′cial·ism′,** *n.* —**pro·vin′cial·ly,** *adv.*

prov′ing ground′, any place for testing something, as a new theory.

pro·vi·sion (prə vizh′ən), *n.* **1.** the act of providing or supplying. **2.** provisions, a supply of food. **3.** an arrangement made beforehand. **4.** a formal statement of a condition demanded. —*v.t.* **5.** to supply with provisions.

pro·vi·sion·al (prə vizh′ə nəl), *adj.* **1.** serving only until permanently replaced. **2.** adopted tentatively. —**pro·vi′sion·al·ly,** *adv.*

pro·vi·so (prə vī′zō), *n.*, *pl.* **-sos, -soes.** a clause in a statute or contract by which a condition is introduced.

prov·o·ca·tion (prov′ə kā′shən), *n.* **1.** the act of provoking. **2.** something that serves to provoke.

pro·voc·a·tive (prə vok′ə tiv), *adj.* serving to provoke. —**pro·voc′a·tive·ly,** *adv.*

pro·voke (prə vōk′), *v.t.*, **-voked, -vok·ing. 1.** to stir to anger. **2.** to arouse feelings or activity in. **3.** to incite to action. **4.** to induce or bring about. —**pro·vok′er,** *n.* —**pro·vok′ing·ly,** *adv.* —**Syn. 1.** exasperate, irritate, vex. **2.** excite.

pro·vo·lo·ne (prō′və lō′nē), *n.* a mellow, light-colored, Italian cheese, usually smoked after drying.

prov·ost (prov′əst, prō′vōst), *n.* **1.** a person appointed to superintend or preside. **2.** a high-ranking administrative officer, as of a college. [< L *prōposit(us),* lit., (one) placed before, president]

pro′vost mar′shal (prō′vō), *Army.* an officer on the staff of a commander, charged with police functions.

prow (prou), *n.* the forepart of a ship.

prow·ess (prou′is), *n.* **1.** exceptional bravery in battle. **2.** superior ability or skill.

prowl (proul), *v.i., v.t.* **1.** to move about stealthily, as in search of prey or something to steal. —*n.* **2.** the act of prowling. —**prowl′er,** *n.*

prowl′ car′. See squad car.

prox., proximo.

prox·i·mate (prok′sə mit), *adj.* **1.** immediately before or after. **2.** very near.

prox·im·i·ty (prok sim′i tē), *n.* nearness in space, time, or order.

proxim′ity fuze′, a fuze for detonating a charge, as in a projectile.

prox·i·mo (prok′sə mō′), *adj. Obsolesc.* of next month.

prox·y (prok′sē), *n.*, *pl.* **prox·ies. 1.** the power or function of a person authorized to act for another. **2.** a written authorization granting such power. **3.** the person so authorized.

prs., pairs.

prude (prōōd), *n.* a person who is excessively proper or modest in speech or dress. —**prud′er·y,** *n.* —**prud′ish,** *adj.* —**prud′ish·ness,** *n.*

pru·dent (prōōd′ənt), *adj.* **1.** judicious or wisely cautious in practical affairs. **2.** characterized by or proceeding from such caution and good judgment. **3.** provident (def. 1). —**pru′dence,** *n.* —**pru·den′tial** (-den′shəl), *adj.* —**pru·den′tial·ly,** *adv.* —**pru′dent·ly,** *adv.* —**Syn. 1, 2.** discreet, sensible.

prune¹ (prōōn), *n.* **1.** a plum that dries without spoiling. **2.** such a plum when dried.

prune² (prōōn), *v.t.,* **pruned, prun·ing. 1.** to cut off undesired twigs or branches from. **2.** to remove (something undesirable). —**prun′er,** *n.*

pru·ri·ent (prōōr′ē ənt), *adj.* **1.** tending to have lascivious or lustful thoughts. **2.** causing lasciviousness or lust. —**pru′ri·ence,** *n.* —**pru′ri·ent·ly,** *adv.*

Prus·sia (prush′ə), *n.* a former German kingdom and state in N Europe. —**Prus′sian,** *adj., n.*

pry¹ (prī), *v.i.,* **pried, pry·ing.** to look closely or curiously. —**pry′ing·ly,** *adv.*

---

pro·un′ion, *adj.* **pro·war′,** *adj.*

pry[2] (prī), v., **pried, pry·ing.** n., pl. **pries.** —v.t. **1.** to move, raise, or open by a lever. **2.** to obtain with difficulty, as information. —n. **3.** a tool used for prying. **4.** the leverage exerted.

pry·er (prī′ər), n. prier.

Ps., Psalm; Psalms. Also, Psa.

P.S., 1. postscript. **2.** Public School.

p.s., postscript.

psalm (säm), n. **1.** a sacred song or hymn. **2.** (cap.) any of the songs, hymns, or prayers contained in the Book of Psalms. —**psalm′ist,** n.

psal·mo·dy (sä′mə dē, sal′mə-), n. **1.** psalms collectively. **2.** the art of singing these.

Psalms (sämz), n. a book of the Bible, composed of 150 psalms.

Psal·ter (sôl′tər), n. **1.** the Book of Psalms. **2.** (sometimes l.c.) a book containing the Psalms for devotional use.

pseud., pseudonym.

pseu·do (soo′dō), adj. not true or genuine.

pseudo-, a prefix meaning "false" or "pretended": pseudonym.

pseu·do·nym (sood′°nim), n. a fictitious name used by an author to conceal his or her identity. —**pseudon′y·mous** (-don′ə məs), adj.

psf, pounds per square foot. Also, **p.s.f.**

pshaw (shô), interj. (to express impatience, contempt, etc.)

psi (sī, psē), n. the 23rd letter of the Greek alphabet (ψ, ψ).

psi, pounds per square inch. Also, **p.s.i.**

pso·ri·a·sis (sə rī′ə sis), n. a chronic skin disease characterized by scaly patches.

psst (pst), interj. (to attract someone's attention.)

PST, Pacific Standard Time.

psych (sīk), v.t., **psyched, psych·ing. Slang. 1.** to intimidate or frighten psychologically: to psych out the competition. **2.** to treat or judge by psychoanalysis.

psych., 1. psychologist. **2.** psychology.

psy·che (sī′kē), n. **1.** the human soul or mind. **2.** the mental structure of a person, esp. as a motive force.

psych·e·del·ic (sī′ki del′ik), adj. **1.** of or noting severe perceptual distortion and hallucinations, often accompanied by extreme feelings of either euphoria or despair. **2.** of or noting any of various drugs producing this state, as LSD. **3.** of or reproducing images, sounds, or effects experienced while in such a state. —n. **4.** a psychedelic drug. —**psych′e·del′i·cal·ly,** adv.

psy·chi·a·try (si kī′ə trē, sī-), n. the science of treating mental disorders. —**psy·chi·at′ric** (sī′kē a′trik), adj. —**psy′chi·at′ri·cal·ly,** adv. —**psy·chi′a·trist,** n.

psy·chic (sī′kik), adj. Also, **psy′chi·cal. 1.** of the human soul or mind. **2.** originating outside of normal physiological processes. **3.** specially sensitive to the influence of nonphysical forces. —n. **4.** a person who is specially sensitive to psychic influences. —**psy′chi·cal·ly,** adv.

psy′chic en′ergizer, a drug used in the treatment of mental depression.

psy·cho (sī′kō), n., pl. -**chos.** Slang. a psychopath.

psycho-, a combining form meaning: **a.** the mind: psychology. **b.** mental processes or disorders: psychotherapy. Also, **psych-.**

psychoanal., psychoanalysis.

psy·cho·a·nal·y·sis (sī′kō ə nal′i sis), n. a method for treating neurosis by investigating unconscious mental processes in order to solve mental conflicts. —**psy′cho·an′a·lyst** (-an′°list), n. —**psy′cho·an′a·lyt′ic** (-an′°lit′ik), **psy′cho·an′a·lyt′i·cal,** adj. —**psy′cho·an′a·lyt′i·cal·ly,** adv. —**psy′cho·an′a·lyze′** (-līz′), v.t.

psy·cho·dra·ma (sī′kō drä′mə, -dram′ə), n. a method of group psychotherapy in which patients take roles in improvisational dramatizations of emotionally charged situations.

psy·cho·gen·ic (sī′kō jen′ik), adj. originating in the mind or in a mental process.

psychol., 1. psychologist. **2.** psychology.

psy·chol·o·gy (sī kol′ə jē), n., pl. -**gies. 1.** the science of the human mind and its functions. **2.** the science of human and animal behavior. **3.** the attitudes and behavior typical of a person or group. —**psy′cho·log′i·cal** (-kə log′i kəl), adj. —**psy′cho·log′i·cal·ly,** adv. —**psy·chol′o·gist,** n.

psy·cho·neu·ro·sis (sī′kō noo rō′sis, -nyoo-), n. neurosis.

---

pseu′do·a·ris′to·crat′ic, adj.

pseu′do·ar·tis′tic, adj.

pseu′do·bi′o·graph′i·cal, adj.

pseu′do·clas′sic, adj.

pseu′do·clas′si·cal, adj.

pseu′do·clas′si·cism, n.

pseu′do·his·tor′ic, adj.

pseu′do·his·tor′i·cal, adj.

pseu′do·in′tel·lec′tu·al, n., adj.

pseu′do·leg′end·ar′y, adj.

pseu′do·lib′er·al, adj.

pseu′do·lit′er·ar′y, adj.

pseu′do·mod′ern, adj.

pseu′do·phil′o·soph′i·cal, adj.

pseu′do·pro·fes′sion·al, adj.

pseu′do·schol′ar·ly, adj.

pseu′do·sci′en·tif′ic, adj.

psy·cho·path (sī′kə path′), *n.* a person who is mentally ill or unstable, esp. one who exhibits amoral and antisocial behavior. —**psy′cho·path′ic,** *adj.* —**psy·chop′a·thy** (-kop′ə-thē), *n.*

psy·cho·sex·u·al (sī′kō sek′shōō əl), *adj.* of the relationship of psychological and sexual phenomena.

psy·cho·sis (sī kō′sis), *n., pl.* -**ses** (-sēz). any major severe form of mental disorder or disease affecting the total personality. ·**psy·chot′ic** (-kot′ik), *adj., n.* —**psy·chot′i·cal·ly,** *adv.*

psy·cho·so·mat·ic (sī′kō sō mat′ik, -sə-), *adj.* noting a physical disorder caused or influenced by the emotional state of the patient.

psy·cho·ther·a·py (sī′kō ther′ə pē), *n.* the method of treating mental or emotional disorders by psychological techniques, esp. by psychoanalysis. —**psy′cho·ther′a·pist,** *n.*

psy·cho·trop·ic (sī′kō trop′ik), *adj.* affecting mental activity, as a hallucinogenic drug.

Pt, platinum.

pt., 1. part. 2. past tense. 3. payment. 4. pint; pints. 5. point. 6. port.

P.T., 1. Pacific Time. 2. physical therapy. 3. physical training.

p.t., 1. past tense. 2. pro tempore.

PTA, Parent-Teacher Association.

ptar·mi·gan (tär′mə gən), *n., pl.* -**gans,** -**gan.** a grouse of mountainous and cold northern regions, having feathered feet.

PT boat, a small, fast, lightly armed boat used chiefly for torpedoing enemy shipping. [*p*(*atrol*) *t*(*orpedo*)]

Pte., *Brit. Army.* Private.

pter·o·dac·tyl (ter′ə dak′til), *n.* an extinct flying reptile having the outside digit of the forelimb greatly elongated.

ptg., printing.

P.T.O., *Brit.* please turn over (a page).

Ptol·e·my (tol′ə mē), *n.* lived in 2nd cent. A.D., Greek astronomer. — **Ptol′e·ma′ic** (-mā′ik), *adj.*

pto·maine (tō′mān, tō mān′), *n.* a poisonous substance produced when food decays. ·**pto·main′ic,** *adj.*

pto′maine poi′soning, an acutely painful stomach or intestinal condition caused by eating poisonous or contaminated food.

PTV, public television.

Pty., Proprietary.

Pu, plutonium.

pub (pub), *n. Brit. Informal.* See **public house.**

pub., 1. public. 2. publication. 3. published. 4. publisher. 5. publishing.

pu·ber·ty (pyōō′bər tē), *n.* the period or age at which a person is first capable of sexual reproduction. — **pu′ber·tal,** *adj.*

pu·bes (pyōō′bēz), *n., pl.* **pu·bes.** 1. the lower part of the abdomen covering the genitals. 2. the hair appearing on this part at puberty.

pu·bes·cent (pyōō bes′ənt), *adj.* 1. arriving or arrived at puberty. 2. *Bot., Zool.* covered with down or fine short hair. ·**pu·bes′cence,** *n.*

pu·bic (pyōō′bik), *adj.* of or situated near the pubes or the pubis.

pu·bis (pyōō′bis), *n., pl.* -**bes** (-bēz). the part of the innominate bone that forms the front of the pelvis.

publ., 1. public. 2. publication. 3. published. 4. publisher.

pub·lic (pub′lik), *adj.* 1. of or for the people as a whole. 2. open to all persons. 3. owned by a community. 4. serving a community, as an official. 5. generally known. 6. familiar to the public, as a person. 7. intending good to the community: *public spirit.* —*n.* 8. the people as a whole. 9. a particular group of people having something in common. 10. **in public.** not in private. —**pub′-lic·ly,** *adv.*

pub·li·can (pub′lə kən), *n.* 1. *Brit. Informal.* the keeper of a pub. 2. *Rom. Hist.* a tax collector.

pub·li·ca·tion (pub′lə kā′shən), *n.* 1. the act or process of publishing. 2. something published, esp. a periodical.

pub′lic defend′er, *U.S.* a lawyer employed by a city or county to represent indigents in criminal cases at public expense.

pub′lic domain′, the status of material whose copyright or patent has expired.

pub′lic house′, *Brit.* a tavern or bar.

pub·li·cist (pub′li sist), *n.* a person in the publicity business, esp. a press agent.

pub·lic·i·ty (pu blis′i tē), *n.* 1. information given out to attract public attention to a person, cause, etc. 2. public notice or attention.

pub·li·cize (pub′li sīz′), *v.t.,* -**cized,** -**ciz·ing.** to give publicity to.

pub′lic rela′tions, the efforts of a corporation to promote good will between itself and the public.

pub′lic school′, 1. (in the U.S.) an elementary school or high school that is maintained at public expense. 2. (in England) a privately endowed boarding school for boys that prepares students for university study or public service.

pub′lic serv′ant, a person holding a government office by election or appointment.

pub·lic-spir·it·ed (pub′lik spir′i ted), *adj.* having an unselfish interest in the public welfare.

pub′lic tel′evision, noncommercial television that broadcasts chiefly cultural and educational programs.

pub′lic util′ity, utility (def. 2).

pub·lish (pub′lish), *v.t.* 1. to issue (a book, newspaper, etc.) for sale to the public. 2. to make publicly or generally known. —*v.i.* 3. to engage in the publishing of printed material. —**pub′lish·a·ble,** *adj.* —**pub′lish·er,** *n.*

Puc·ci·ni (pŏŏ chē′nē), **Gia·co·mo** (jä′kô mô), 1858–1924, Italian opera composer.

puce (pyŏŏs), *n.* a dark or brownish purple.

puck (puk), *n.* a black rubber disk used in ice hockey.

Puck (puk), *n.* a mischievous elf in folk tales. —**puck′ish,** *adj.*

puck·er (puk′ər), *v.t., v.i.* 1. to draw or gather into wrinkles or folds. —*n.* 2. a puckered part.

pud·ding (pŏŏd′ing), *n.* a thick, soft dessert, typically containing flour, milk, eggs, and sweetening.

pud·dle (pud′°l), *n.* a small pool of water, esp. muddy or dirty water. —**pud′dly,** *adj.*

pud·dling (pud′ling), *n.* the process of making pig iron into wrought iron by heating in an oxidizing atmosphere to remove the impurities.

pu·den·dum (pyŏŏ den′dəm), *n., pl.* **-da** (-də). Usually, **pudenda.** the external genital organs of the female.

pudg·y (puj′ē), *adj.,* **pudg·i·er, pudg·i·est.** short and fat or thick. —**pudg′i·ness,** *n.*

pueb·lo (pweb′lō), *n., pl.* **pueb·los** (pweb′lōz). 1. the adobe or stone house or group of houses of certain Indians of Arizona and New Mexico. 2. (*cap.*) a member of an Indian people living in such houses.

pu·er·ile (pyŏŏ′ər il, -ə rīl′, pyŏŏr′il, -īl), *adj.* childishly foolish. —**pu′er·ile·ly,** *adv.* —**pu′er·il′i·ty,** *n.*

pu·er·per·al (pyŏŏ ûr′pər əl), *adj.* pertaining to or connected with childbirth.

Puer·to Ri·co (pwer′tə rē′kō, pôr′-, pôr′-), an island in the central West Indies: a commonwealth associated with the U.S. *Cap.:* San Juan. — **Puer′to Ri′can.**

puff (puf), *n.* 1. an abrupt blast or emission of air, breath, vapor, etc. 2. a whiff, as from a cigarette. 3. a light pastry with a filling of whipped cream or jam. 4. a small soft pad: *a powder puff.* 5. a small swelling. 6. an exaggerated commendation made for commercial reasons. —*v.i.* 7. to blow in puffs. 8. to breathe quick and hard. 9. to take puffs in smoking. 10. to become inflated or swollen. —*v.t.* 11. to send forth in puffs. 12. to

smoke (a cigar, pipe, etc.). 13. to inflate or swell. 14. to inflate with pride or vanity. 15. to praise unduly or with exaggeration. —**puff′er,** *n.* —**puff′y,** *adj.* —**puff′i·ness,** *n.*

puff·ball (puf′bôl′), *n.* a fungus having a ball-like fruit body which emits a cloud of spores when broken.

puf·fin (puf′in), *n.* a seabird having a short neck and a large, brightly colored bill.

pug¹ (pug), *n.* a small, short-haired dog having a short, upturned nose. —**pug′gish, pug′gy,** *adj.*

pug² (pug), *n. Slang.* a boxer or pugilist.

pu·gil·ism (pyŏŏ′jə liz′əm), *n.* the art or sport of boxing. —**pu′gil·ist,** *n.* —**pu′gil·is′tic,** *adj.*

pug·na·cious (pug nā′shəs), *adj.* excessively inclined to quarrel or fight. —**pug·na′cious·ly,** *adv.* —**pug·nac′i·ty** (-nas′i tē), *n.* —**Syn.** argumentative, contentious.

pug′ nose′, a short, broad, somewhat turned-up nose. —**pug′-nosed′,** *adj.*

pu·is·sance (pyŏŏ′i səns, pyŏŏ is′əns, pwis′əns), *n. Literary.* power, might, or force. —**pu′is·sant,** *adj.* —**pu′is·sant·ly,** *adv.*

puke (pyŏŏk), *v.i., v.t.,* **puked, puk·ing,** *n. Slang.* vomit.

puk·ka (puk′ə), *adj. Anglo-Indian.* genuine, reliable, or good.

pul·chri·tude (pul′kri tŏŏd′, -tyŏŏd′), *n. Chiefly Literary.* physical beauty. —**pul′chri·tu′di·nous,** *adj.*

pule (pyŏŏl), *v.i.,* **puled, pul·ing.** to cry in a thin voice. —**pul′er,** *n.*

pull (pŏŏl), *v.t.* 1. to use force to cause (something) to move toward or after oneself or itself. 2. to tear or rip. 3. to dislodge or extract, as a nail or tooth. 4. *Informal.* to draw out (a weapon). 5. *Informal.* to attempt or perform: *to pull a robbery.* 6. *Print.* to take (an impression or proof) from type. 7. to strain or stretch (a muscle). —*v.i.* 8. to use force in trying to drag or tug. 9. to move or go. 10. to become or come as specified, by being pulled. 11. **pull for,** *Informal.* to support actively. 12. **pull off,** *Slang.* to perform successfully. 13. **pull oneself together,** to regain command of one's emotions. 14. **pull out, a.** to leave or depart. **b.** to cease action or participation. 15. **pull punches,** *Informal.* to speak with restraint. 16. **pull through,** to come safely through (a crisis, illness, etc.). 17. **pull up, a.** to bring or come to a halt. **b.** to move ahead, esp. in a race. —*n.* 18. the act or an instance of pulling. 19. a force used in pulling. 20. a force that pulls or draws. 21. a device used for pulling, as a handle. **22.** *Slang.* influence, as with persons able to grant favors. **23.** *Informal.* an advantage over others. —**pull′er,** *n.*

pull·back (pool′bak′), *n.* **1.** the act of pulling back. **2.** pullout (def. 2).

pul·let (pool′it), *n.* a young hen.

pul·ley (pool′ē), *n., pl.* **-leys.** a wheel with a grooved edge over which a rope or chain passes, used for transmitting force or performing work, as lifting heavy weights.

Pull·man (pool′mən), *n., pl.* **-mans.** *Trademark.* a railroad passenger car having individual rooms or sleeping berths. [after G. M. *Pullman,* 1831-97, U.S. inventor]

pull·out (pool′out′), *n.* **1.** the act of pulling out. **2.** a planned or arranged withdrawal of military personnel.

pull·o·ver (pool′ō′vər), *adj.* **1.** designed to be put on by drawing over the head. —*n.* **2.** a pullover garment, esp. a sweater.

pull-up (pool′up′), *n.* chin-up.

pul·mo·nar·y (pul′mə ner′ē, pool′-), *adj.* of or affecting the lungs.

Pul·mo·tor (pul′mō′tər, pool′-), *n.* *Trademark.* a mechanical device for artificial respiration.

pulp (pulp), *n.* **1.** the soft, juicy, edible part of a fruit. **2.** the inner substance of the tooth, containing blood vessels and nerves. **3.** a soft, moist mass, as of wood or rags, used in making paper. **4.** a cheap magazine dealing with sensational and lurid material. —**pulp′y,** *adj.*

pul·pit (pool′pit, pul′-), *n.* a platform or raised structure in a church, from which the clergyman or clergywoman delivers the sermon or conducts the service.

pulp·wood (pulp′wood′), *n.* any soft wood suitable for making paper.

pul·sar (pul′sär), *n.* a source of pulsating radio energy located within the Milky Way.

pul·sate (pul′sāt), *v.i.,* **-sat·ed, -sat·ing. 1.** to expand and contract rhythmically, as the heart. **2.** to vibrate or quiver. —**pul·sa′tion,** *n.*

pulse (puls), *n., v.,* **pulsed, puls·ing.** —*n.* **1.** the regular throbbing of the arteries caused by the successive contractions of the heart. **2.** a momentary, sudden fluctuation in an electrical voltage or current. —*v.i.* **3.** to beat or throb.

pul·ver·ize (pul′və rīz′), *v.t., v.i.,* **-ized, -iz·ing.** to reduce or become reduced to dust or powder, as by pounding or grinding. —**pul′ver·i·za′tion,** *n.*

pu·ma (pyoo′mə), *n.* a cougar.

pum·ice (pum′is), *n.* a porous or spongy form of volcanic glass, used as an abrasive.

pum·mel (pum′əl), *v.t.,* **-meled, -mel·ing** or **-melled, -mel·ling.** to beat or pound with the fists.

pump[1] (pump), *n.* **1.** a machine for moving or altering the pressure of fluids or gases, as by suction or pressure. —*v.t.* **2.** to move (a fluid) with a pump. **3.** to empty of a fluid by a pump. **4.** to inflate with a pump. **5.** to drive or force in the way that a pump does. **6.** to question (someone) artfully or persistently to elicit information. —**pump′er,** *n.*

pump[2] (pump), *n.* a lightweight, low-cut shoe without a fastening, worn esp. by women.

pum·per·nick·el (pum′pər nik′əl), *n.* a coarse, slightly sour rye bread.

pump·kin (pump′kin, pung′kin), *n.* **1.** a large, edible, orange-yellow fruit borne by a coarse vine. **2.** its vine.

pun (pun), *n., v.,* **punned, pun·ning.** —*n.* **1.** a humorous use of a word or combination of words so as to emphasize different meanings of the same word or different meanings of words that sound alike. —*v.i.* **2.** to make puns.

punch[1] (punch), *n.* **1.** a thrusting blow with the fist. **2.** *Informal.* a vigorous force. —*v.t.* **3.** to hit with the fist. **4.** *Western U.S.* to drive (cattle). **5.** to poke or prod sharply. —**punch′er,** *n.*

punch[2] (punch), *n.* **1.** a tool for perforating, stamping, or shaping materials. —*v.t.* **2.** to perforate, stamp, or shape with a punch.

punch[3] (punch), *n.* a drink that is a mixture of two or more other drinks, as fruit juice, wine, and soda.

punch′ card′, a card having holes punched in specific positions so as to represent data to be processed by computer.

punch-drunk (punch′drungk′), *adj.* dizzy or groggy from repeated blows to the head in boxing.

pun·cheon (pun′chən), *n.* a large cask or barrel.

punch′ line′, a phrase or sentence that produces the desired effect in a joke.

punch·y (pun′chē), *adj.,* **punch·i·er, punch·i·est.** *Informal.* **1.** vigorously forceful. **2.** punch-drunk.

punc·til·i·o (pungk til′ē ō′), *n., pl.* **-til·i·os** for 1. **1.** a fine point of conduct or ceremony. **2.** strictness or exactness in observing all formalities.

punc·til·i·ous (pungk til′ē əs), *adj.* strict or exact in the observance of all formalities of conduct or actions. —**punc·til′i·ous·ly,** *adv.* —**punc·til′i·ous·ness,** *n.*

punc·tu·al (pungk′choo əl), *adj.* arriving or acting at the time appointed. —**punc′tu·al′i·ty** (-al′i tē), *n.* —**punc′tu·al·ly,** *adv.*

punc·tu·ate (pungk′chōō āt′), *v.t.*, *v.i.*, **-at·ed, -at·ing. 1.** to mark or divide (writing) with punctuation marks. **2.** to interrupt at intervals. **3.** to give emphasis or force (to).

punc·tu·a·tion (pungk′chōō ā′shən), *n.* the use of certain conventional marks (**punctua′tion marks′**), as periods or commas, in writing or printing in order to make the meaning clear.

punc·ture (pungk′chər), *n.*, *v.*, **-tured, -tur·ing. —n. 1.** the act of piercing with a pointed object. **2.** a hole so made. **—v.t., v.i. 3.** to pierce or be pierced with a pointed object.

pun·dit (pun′dit), *n.* a learned person, esp. an expert in a particular field.

pun·gent (pun′jənt), *adj.* **1.** sharp or biting to the sense of taste or smell. **2.** forceful and sharp. **—pun′gen·cy,** *n.* **—pun′gent·ly,** *adv.*

pun·ish (pun′ish), *v.t.* **1.** to subject (a person) to pain, confinement, death, etc., as for a crime. **2.** to inflict a penalty for (an offense). **3.** to handle severely or roughly, as in a fight. **—pun′ish·a·ble,** *adj.* **—Syn. 1.** chastise, discipline, penalize.

pun·ish·ment (pun′ish mənt), *n.* **1.** the act of punishing or fact of being punished. **2.** a penalty inflicted for a crime or offense. **3.** severe treatment.

pu·ni·tive (pyōō′ni tiv), *adj.* inflicting or serving as punishment. **—pu′ni·tive·ly,** *adv.*

punk¹ (pungk), *n.* **1.** any prepared substance that will smolder and can be used to light fireworks, etc. **2.** dry, decayed wood that can be used as tinder.

punk² (pungk), *n. Slang.* **1.** a worthless or unimportant person. **2.** a petty hoodlum. **—adj. 3.** poor in quality.

punk′ rock′, a primitive type of rock-'n'-roll often featuring sociopathic lyrics and sometimes delivered with defiant vulgarity. Also called **punk.** **—punk′ rock′er.**

pun·ster (pun′stər), *n.* a person who makes puns frequently.

punt (punt), *n.* **1.** *Football.* a kick in which the ball is dropped and kicked before it hits the ground. **2.** a small, shallow boat propelled by a pole. **—v.t., v.i. 3.** *Football.* to kick (a ball) in a punt. **4.** to propel (a punt) by a pole. **—punt′er,** *n.*

pu·ny (pyōō′nē), *adj.,* **-ni·er, -ni·est. 1.** small and weak. **2.** feeble or unimportant. **—pu′ni·ly,** *adv.* **—pu′ni·ness,** *n.*

pup (pup), *n.* **1.** a young dog. **2.** a young fox or seal.

pu·pa (pyōō′pə), *n.,* *pl.* **-pae** (-pē), **-pas.** an insect in the transformation stage between the larva and the imago. **—pu′pal,** *adj.*

pu·pil¹ (pyōō′pəl), *n.* a young person in school or under the supervision of a teacher.

pu·pil² (pyōō′pəl), *n.* the expanding and contracting opening in the iris of the eye.

pup·pet (pup′it), *n.* **1.** an artificial figure of a human being or an animal, manipulated by the hand, wires, etc., as on a miniature stage. **2.** a person whose actions are controlled by others. **—pup′pet·ry,** *n.*

pup·pet·eer (pup′i tēr′), *n.* a person who manipulates puppets.

pup·py (pup′ē), *n.,* *pl.* **-pies.** a young dog, esp. one less than a year old.

pup′ tent′ a small, two-person, military tent.

pur·blind (pûr′blīnd′), *adj.* **1.** partially blind. **2.** slow in understanding or imagination. **—pur′blind′ness,** *n.*

pur·chase (pûr′chəs), *v.,* **-chased, -chas·ing,** *n.* **—v.t. 1.** to acquire by payment of money. **—n. 2.** the act or an instance of purchasing. **3.** something purchased. **4.** an effective hold for applying power in moving or raising a heavy object. **—pur′chas·a·ble,** *adj.* **—pur′chas·er,** *n.*

pur·dah (pûr′də), *n.* (in India or Pakistan) the practice of hiding women from the sight of men or strangers.

pure (pyōor), *adj.,* **pur·er, pur·est. 1.** free from anything of a different, inferior, or contaminating kind. **2.** being only that. **3.** absolute or utter: *pure joy.* **4.** clean or spotless. **5.** untainted with evil or guilt. **6.** physically chaste. **7.** abstract or theoretical: *pure science.* **—pure′ly,** *adv.* **—pure′ness,** *n.* **—Syn. 1.** genuine, unadulterated. **5.** blameless, virtuous.

pure·bred (pyōor′bred′), *adj.* of or pertaining to an animal whose ancestors derive over many generations from a recognized breed.

pu·rée (pyōo rā′, -rē′, pyōor′ā), *n.,* *v.,* **-réed, -ré·ing. —n. 1.** a cooked and sieved food, esp. a vegetable or fruit. **2.** a soup made with puréed ingredients. **—v.t. 3.** to make a purée of. Also, **pu·ree′.**

pur·ga·tion (pûr gā′shən), *n.* the act of purging.

pur·ga·tive (pûr′gə tiv), *adj.* **1.** purging or cleansing, esp. by causing evacuation of the bowels. **—n. 2.** a purgative medicine. **—pur′ga·tive·ly,** *adv.*

pur·ga·to·ry (pûr′gə tōr′ē, -tôr′ē), *n.,* *pl.* **-ries. 1.** a condition or place in which, according to Roman Catholics, the souls of those dying penitent are purified from venial sins. **2.** any place of temporary punishment or expiation. **—pur′ga·to′ri·al,** *adj.*

purge (pûrj), *v.*, **purged, purg·ing,** *n.*
—*v.t.* 1. to rid of whatever is impure or undesirable. 2. to free from guilt or sin. 3. to clear or empty (the bowels) by causing evacuation. 4. to put to death or otherwise eliminate by a political purge. —*n.* 5. the act or process of purging. 6. the killing or expulsion of persons considered politically undesirable or disloyal. 7. something that purges, as a purgative medicine. · —**purg′er,** *n.*

pu·ri·fy (pyŏŏr′ə fī′), *v.t., v.i.,* **-fied, -fy·ing.** to make or become pure. —**pu′ri·fi·ca′tion,** *n.* —**pu·rif·i·ca·to·ry** (pyŏŏ rif′ə kə tôr′ē, -tôr′ē), *adj.* —**pu′ri·fi′er,** *n.*

Pu·rim (pŏŏr′im), *n.* a Jewish festival commemorating the deliverance of the Jews in ancient Persia from destruction.

pu·rine (pyŏŏr′ēn, -in), *n.* a compound from which is derived a group of compounds including caffeine.

pur·ism (pyŏŏr′iz əm), *n.* strict observance of or insistence on purity in language, style, etc. —**pur′ist,** *n.*

Pu·ri·tan (pyŏŏr′i t'n), *n.* 1. a member of a sect of Protestants in 16th- and 17th-century England advocating the simplification of the doctrine and worship in the Church of England. 2. (*l.c.*) a person who is strict in moral matters. —**pu′ri·tan′i·cal** (-tan′i kəl), *adj.* —**pu′ri·tan′i·cal·ly,** *adv.* —**Pu′ri·tan·ism′, pu′ri·tan·ism′,** *n.*

pu·ri·ty (pyŏŏr′i tē), *n.* the condition or quality of being pure.

purl¹ (pûrl), *v.t., v.i.* 1. to knit with inversion of the stitch. —*n.* 2. a reverse stitch, used to make ribbing.

purl² (pûrl), *v.i.* 1. to flow with a rippling motion, as a shallow stream does over stones. —*n.* 2. the action or sound of purling.

pur·lieu (pûr′lŏō, pûrl′yŏō), 1. an outlying region, as of a city. 2. purlieus, environs or neighborhood.

pur·loin (pər loin′, pûr′loin), *v.t., v.i. Literary.* to take dishonestly or steal. —**pur·loin′er,** *n.*

pur·ple (pûr′pəl), *n.* 1. any color intermediate between red and blue. 2. cloth or clothing of this hue, esp. as a symbol of royalty. —*adj.* 3. of the color purple. 4. full of exaggerated literary devices and effects. 5. lurid or shocking, as language. —**pur′plish,** *adj.*

pur·port (*v.* pər pôrt′, -pôrt′, pûr′pôrt, -pôrt; *n.* pûr′pôrt, -pôrt), *v.t.* 1. to profess or claim, often falsely. 2. to convey to the mind as the meaning or thing intended. —*n.* 3. the meaning or sense. 4. a purpose or intention. —**pur·port′ed·ly** (-id lē), *adv.*

pur·pose (pûr′pəs), *n., v.,* **-posed, -pos·ing.** —*n.* 1. an intended or desired

result. 2. the reason for which something exists or happens. 3. determination or resoluteness. 4. **on purpose,** by design or intentionally. —*v.t., v.i.* 5. to set as an aim or goal for oneself. · —**pur′pose·ful,** *adj.* —**pur′pose·ful·ly,** *adv.* · —**pur′pose·less,** *adj.* · **pur′pose·ly,** *adv.*

purr (pûr), *v.i.* 1. to utter a low, continuous, murmuring sound, as a cat does when pleased. —*v.t.* 2. to express by or as if by purring. —*n.* 3. the act or sound of purring.

purse (pûrs), *n., v.,* **pursed, purs·ing.** —*n.* 1. a small bag or case for carrying money. 2. a woman's handbag. 3. a sum of money collected as a present or offered as a prize. 4. money available for spending. —*v.t.* 5. to pucker.

purs·er (pûr′sər), *n.* an officer in charge of financial accounts on a ship.

purs·lane (pûrs′lān, -lin), *n.* a low, trailing herb having yellow flowers, used as a salad plant.

pur·su·ance (pər sŏŏ′əns), *n.* the act of carrying out or putting into operation.

pur·su·ant (pər sŏŏ′ənt), *adj.* 1. *Rare.* pursuing. 2. **pursuant to,** in conformity with.

pur·sue (pər sŏŏ′), *v.t.,* **-sued, -su·ing.** —*v.t.* 1. to follow in order to overtake or catch. 2. to strive to gain or accomplish. 3. to carry on or engage in: *to pursue a hobby.* 4. to follow or carry out. —**pur·su′a·ble,** *adj.* —**pur·su′er,** *n.*

pur·suit (pər sŏŏt′), *n.* 1. the act of pursuing. 2. any regular occupation or pastime.

pu·ru·lent (pyŏŏr′ə lənt, pyŏŏr′yə-), *adj.* containing or discharging pus. —**pu′ru·lence,** *n.* —**pu′ru·lent·ly,** *adv.*

pur·vey (pər vā′), *v.t.* to provide (esp. food or provisions) as a business. —**pur·vey′ance** (-əns), *n.* —**pur·vey′or,** *n.*

pur·view (pûr′vyŏō), *n.* 1. the range of operation, authority, or concern. 2. the range of vision, insight, or understanding.

pus (pus), *n.* a thick, yellow-white liquid produced in abscesses, sores, etc. —**pus′like′,** *adj.*

push (pŏŏsh), *v.t., v.i.* 1. to press against in order to move away. 2. to make (one's way, etc.) by thrusting obstacles aside. 3. to press onward or forward. 4. to press the adoption, use, or purchase (of). 5. *Slang.* to sell (narcotics) illicitly. —*n.* 6. the act of pushing. 7. a vigorous onset or effort. 8. a determined advance against opposition. 9. *Informal.* persevering energy. —**push′er,** *n.*

push′ but′ton, a button or knob depressed to open or close an electric circuit.

push-but·ton (pŏosh′but′ᵊn), *adj.* of or involving action subject to easy or instant mechanisms: *the push-button age.*

push·cart (pŏosh′kärt′), *n.* a light cart to be pushed by hand, used esp. by street vendors.

push·o·ver (pŏosh′ō′vər), *n. Slang.* 1. anything done easily. 2. an easily defeated or persuaded person or team.

push·up (pŏosh′up′), *n.* an exercise in which a prone person alternately pushes himself or herself up from the ground by straightening the arms and lets himself or herself down by bending them.

push·y (pŏosh′ē), *adj.,* **push·i·er, push·i·est.** *Informal.* obnoxiously self-assertive. —**push′i·ly,** *adv.* —**push′i·ness,** *n.*

pu·sil·lan·i·mous (pyŏo′sə lan′ə məs), *adj.* lacking courage or resolution. —**pu′sil·la·nim′i·ty** (-lə nim′i tē), *n.* —**pu′sil·lan′i·mous·ly,** *adv.*

puss¹ (pŏos), *n. Informal.* a cat.

puss² (pŏos), *n. Slang.* the face. [< Ir *pus* mouth]

pus·sy (pus′ē), *adj.,* **-si·er, -si·est.** like or containing pus.

puss·y·cat (pŏos′ē kat′), *n.* 1. Also, **puss′y.** a cat, esp. a kitten. 2. *Slang.* an agreeable or well-liked person.

puss·y·foot (pŏos′ē fŏot′), *v.i.* 1. to move in a stealthy or cautious manner. 2. to act cautiously or timidly.

puss′y wil′low (pŏos′ē), a small American willow having silky catkins.

pus·tule (pus′chŏol), *n.* a small elevation of the skin containing pus.

put (pŏot), *v.,* **put, put·ting.** —*v.t.* 1. to move (something) into some place or position. 2. to bring into some condition, state, or relation. 3. to set to a task or action. 4. to render or translate. 5. to assign or attribute. 6. to figure out, as an estimate. 7. to bet or wager. 8. to express or state. 9. to apply for a purpose. 10. to propose or submit, as for consideration. 11. to impose, as a tax. 12. to throw or cast: *to put the shot.* —*v.i.* 13. to go or move: *to put out to sea.* 14. **put across,** *Slang.* to cause to be understood or received favorably. 15. **put aside,** to store up or save. Also, **put by.** 16. **put down, a.** to write down. **b.** to suppress or check. **c.** *Slang.* to belittle or embarrass (a person). 17. **put forth, a.** to propose or present. **b.** to grow buds or leaves. 18. **put in, a.** to interpose or intervene. **b.** to spend (time) as indicated. 19. **put in for,** to apply for or request. 20. **put off, a.** to postpone or defer. **b.** to get rid of by evasion. 21. **put on, a.** to dress oneself with. **b.** to adopt, as an affectation. **c.** to cause to be performed, as a show. **d.** *Slang.* to jest with or tease. 22. **put out, a.** to extinguish, as a fire. **b.** to subject to inconvenience. **c.** *Baseball.* to prevent from reaching base or scoring. **d.** to expel or eject. 23. **put something over on,** *Informal.* to take advantage of. 24. **put through, a.** to accomplish or bring into effect. **b.** to cause to undergo. 25. **put up, a.** to construct or erect. **b.** to preserve or can (food). **c.** to set or arrange (the hair). **d.** to provide (money). **e.** *Informal.* to accommodate or lodge. **f.** to offer, esp. for public sale. **g.** *Slang.* to urge to some action. 26. **put upon,** to take unfair advantage of. 27. **put up with,** *Informal.* to endure or tolerate. 28. **stay put,** *Informal.* to remain in the same place or position.

put-down (pŏot′doun′), *n. Slang.* a remark or act intended to humiliate or snub.

put-on (*n.* pŏot′on′, -ôn′; *adj.* pŏot′on′, -ôn′), *n.* 1. Also, **put′on′.** *Slang.* a teasing lie or prank. —*adj.* 2. assumed or feigned.

put-out (pŏot′out′), *n. Baseball.* an instance of putting out a batter or base runner.

pu·tre·fy (pyŏo′trə fī′), *v.t., v.i.,* **-fied, -fy·ing.** to make or become putrid. —**pu′tre·fac′tion** (-fak′shən), *n.* —**pu′tre·fac′tive,** *adj.*

pu·tres·cent (pyŏo tres′ənt), *adj.* becoming putrid. —**pu·tres′cence,** *n.*

pu·trid (pyŏo′trid), *adj.* 1. in a state of decay or decomposition. 2. very bad or corrupt. —**pu·trid′i·ty, pu′trid·ness,** *n.*

putsch (pŏoch), *n. German.* a revolt or uprising, esp. one that depends upon suddenness and speed.

putt (put), *Golf.* —*v.t., v.i.* 1. to strike (the ball) so as to make it roll into the hole. —*n.* 2. a stroke made in putting.

put·tee (put′ē), *n.* 1. a long strip of cloth wound round the lower leg. 2. a gaiter or legging of leather.

put·ter¹ (put′ər), *v.i.* 1. to busy oneself in a leisurely or ineffective manner. —*v.t.* 2. to waste (time) in puttering. —**put′ter·er,** *n.*

putt·er² (put′ər), *n. Golf.* 1. a person who putts. 2. a relatively short club used in putting.

put·ty (put′ē), *n., pl.* **-ties,** *v.,* **-tied, -ty·ing.** —*n.* 1. a sticky substance made from powdered chalk and linseed oil, used for securing panes of glass in windows. —*v.t.* 2. to secure with putty.

puz·zle (puz′əl), v., **-zled, -zling,** n.
—v.t. **1.** to cause (a person or the
mind) difficulty in solving or understanding a problem or situation.
2. to baffle in an intricate way.
—v.i. **3.** to be baffled in an intricate
way. **4.** to ponder or study, as over
a problem. **5. puzzle out,** to solve
by careful study or effort. —n. **6.** a
problem, game, or device designed
for testing ingenuity or patient effort.
7. a puzzling matter or person. **8.**
a puzzled state or condition. —puz′-
zle·ment, n. —puz′zler, n. —puz′-
zling·ly, adv. —Syn. 1, 2. bewilder,
nonplus, perplex. 6, 7. enigma, riddle.

PVC, See **polyvinyl chloride.**

Pvt., Private.

PW, prisoner of war.

pwt., pennyweight.

PX, See **post exchange.**

Pyg·my (pig′mē), n., pl. **-mies,** adj.
—n. **1. a.** a member of an equatorial
African Negroid race of small stature. **b.** a member of a similar race
of southeastern Asia. **2.** (l.c.) a tiny
person or thing. —adj. **3.** (often l.c.)
of the Pygmies. **4.** (l.c.) of very
small size.

py·jam·as (pə jä′məz, -jam′əz), n.pl.
Brit. pajamas.

py·lon (pī′lon), n. **1.** a marking tower
for guiding aviators. **2.** Chiefly Brit.
a steel tower supporting high-voltage
wires or cable. **3.** a massive structure at the entrance to an ancient
Egyptian temple. [< Gk: gateway]

py·lo·rus (pī lôr′əs, -lōr′-, pī-), n., pl.
-lo·ri (-lôr′ī, -lōr′ī). the opening between the stomach and the duode-
num. —py·lor′ic, adj.

py·or·rhe·a (pī′ə rē′ə), n. **1.** a discharge of pus. **2.** a disease that
causes the formation of pus in the
gums and loosening of the teeth.
Also, **py′or·rhoe′a.**

pyr·a·mid (pir′ə mid), n. **1.** Geom. a
solid having a polygonal base with
triangular sides that meet at an apex.
2. a massive masonry construction of
this shape, built in ancient Egypt as
a royal tomb. —v.i., v.t. **3.** to arrange or build in the form of a pyramid. **4.** to increase on a gradually

expanding basis. —py·ram·i·dal (pi-
ram′i dəl), adj.

pyre (pī′r), n. a pile of wood used to
burn a dead body.

Pyr·e·nees (pir′ə nēz′), n. a mountain
range between Spain and France. —
Pyr′e·ne′an, adj.

py·re·thrin (pī rē′thrin), n. an insecticide made from the dried and powdered flowers of any of several chry-
santhemums.

Py·rex (pī′reks), n. *Trademark.* a
heat- and chemical-resistant glassware used for cooking.

py·rim·i·dine (pī rim′i dēn′, pir′ə mi-
dēn′, -din), n. a compound that is
an important constituent of several
biochemical substances, as thiamine.

py·rite (pī′rīt), n. a brass-yellow mineral that is a compound of sulfur and
iron. —py·rit·ic (pī rit′ik, pə-), adj.

py·ri·tes (pī rī′tēz, pə-, pī′rīts), n., pl.
-tes. any of various metallic sulfides,
as of copper, tin, etc.

pyro-, a combining form meaning
"fire" or "heat": *pyromania.*

py·rol·y·sis (pī rol′i sis), n. the subjection of organic compounds to
very high temperatures.

py·ro·ma·ni·a (pī′rə mā′nē ə), n. a
mania or compulsion to set things on
fire. —py′ro·ma′ni·ac, n., adj.

py·rom·e·ter (pī rom′i tər), n. an apparatus for measuring high temperatures.

py·ro·tech·nics (pī′rə tek′niks), n. **1.**
a display of fireworks. **2.** a brilliant
or sensational display, as of rhetoric.
—py′ro·tech′nic, **py′ro·tech′ni·cal,**
adj.

Pyr′rhic vic′tory (pir′ik), a victory or
goal gained at too great a cost.

Py·thag·o·ras (pi thag′ər əs), n. c582–
c500 B.C., Greek philosopher and
mathematician. —Py·thag′o·re′an
(-ə rē′ən), adj., n.

Pythag′ore′an the′orem, Geom. the
theorem that the square of the hypotenuse of a right triangle is equal
to the sum of the squares of the
other two sides.

py·thon (pī′thon, -thən), n. a large
Old World snake that crushes its
prey to death in its coils.

pyx (piks), n. a container for carrying the Eucharist to the sick.

Q

Q, q (ky$\overline{oo}$), *n.*, *pl.* **Q's** or **Qs, q's** or **qs.** the 17th letter of the English alphabet, a consonant.

Q, *Chess.* queen.

Q., **1.** quarto. **2.** Queen. **3.** question.

q., **1.** quart; quarts. **2.** query. **3.** question. **4.** quire.

Q.C., Queen's Counsel.

Q.E.D., which was to be demonstrated. [< L *quod erat demonstrandum*]

Qi·a·na (kē ä′nə), *n.* *Trademark.* a lightweight silklike manmade fiber chemically classed as nylon.

q.i.d., (in prescriptions) four times a day. [< L *quater in die*]

QM, Quartermaster.

QMC, Quartermaster Corps.

QMG, Quartermaster General.

qq.v., which (words, things, etc.) see. [< L *quae vide*]

qr., **1.** quarter. **2.** quire.

qt., **1.** quantity. **2.** quart.

q.t., *Slang.* **1.** quiet. **2. on the q.t.,** stealthily or secretly.

qto., quarto.

qty., quantity.

qu., question.

qua (kwā, kwä), *adv.* *Latin.* in the character or capacity of.

quack¹ (kwak), *n.* **1.** the harsh, throaty cry of a duck. —*v.i.* **2.** to utter a quack.

quack² (kwak), *n.* **1.** a fraudulent pretender to medical skill. **2.** charlatan. —*adj.* **3.** being a quack. **4.** presented falsely as having curative powers. —**quack′er·y,** *n.* —**quack′ish,** *adj.*

quad¹ (kwod), *n.* *Informal.* a quadrangle, as on a college campus.

quad² (kwod), *n.* *Informal.* a quadruplet.

quad³ (kwod), *adj.* **1.** quadraphonic. —*n.* **2.** quadraphonic sound system.

quad., **1.** quadrangle. **2.** quadrant.

quad·ran·gle (kwod′rang′gəl), *n.* **1.** a plane figure having four angles and four sides. **2.** a square or court surrounded by a building or buildings, as on a college campus. —**quad′ran·gu·lar,** *adj.*

quad·rant (kwod′rənt), *n.* **1.** a quarter of a circle: an arc of 90°. **2.** one of the four parts into which an area is divided by two perpendicular lines. **3.** an instrument, usually containing a graduated arc of 90°, used formerly for measuring altitudes. —**quad·ran′tal** (kwo dran′t°l), *adj.*

quad·ra·phon·ic (kwod′rə fon′ik), *adj.* noting or involving the recording

or reproduction of sound over four separate transmission channels: *quadraphonic records.*

quad·rat·ic (kwo drat′ik), *adj.* *Algebra.* involving the square and no higher power of the unknown quantity.

quad·rat·ics (kwo drat′iks), *n.* the branch of algebra that deals with quadratic equations.

quad·ren·ni·al (kwo dren′ē əl), *adj.* **1.** occurring every four years. **2.** lasting for four years.

quad·ren·ni·um (kwo dren′ē əm), *n.* a period of four years.

quadri-, a combining form meaning "four": *quadrilateral.* Also, **quadru-.**

quad·ri·cen·ten·ni·al (kwod′ri sen ten′ē əl), *n.* a 400th anniversary or its celebration.

quad·ri·lat·er·al (kwod′rə lat′ər əl), *adj.* **1.** having four sides. —*n.* **2.** a polygon with four sides.

qua·drille (kwə dril′, kə-), *n.* a square dance for four couples.

quad·ril·lion (kwo dril′yən), *n.* a cardinal number represented in the U.S. by one followed by 15 zeros, and, in Great Britain, by one followed by 24 zeros. —**quad·ril′lionth,** *n., adj.*

quad·ri·par·tite (kwod′rə pär′tīt), *adj.* **1.** consisting of four parts. **2.** shared by four parties, as a pact.

quad·riv·i·um (kwo driv′ē əm), *n.* (during the Middle Ages) the four liberal arts of arithmetic, geometry, astronomy, and music.

quad·roon (kwo dr$\overline{oo}$n′), *n.* a person who is one-fourth black and three-fourths white.

quad·ru·ped (kwod′r$\overline{oo}$ ped′), *n.* an animal having four feet, esp. a mammal. —**quad·ru·pe·dal** (kwo dr$\overline{oo}$′pi-d°l, kwod′r$\overline{oo}$ ped′°l), *adj.*

quad·ru·ple (kwo dr$\overline{oo}$′pəl, kwod′r$\overline{oo}$-), *adj., n., v.,* **-pled, -pling.** —*adj.* **1.** consisting of four parts. **2.** four times as great. —*n.* **3.** a number or amount four times as great as another. —*v.t., v.i.* **4.** to make or become four times as great.

quad·ru·plet (kwo drup′lit, -dr$\overline{oo}$′plit, kwod′r$\overline{oo}$ plit), *n.* **1.** one of four offspring born of one pregnancy. **2.** any group of four.

quad·ru·pli·cate (*n., adj.* kwo dr$\overline{oo}$′plə kit, -kāt′; *v.* kwo dr$\overline{oo}$′plə kāt′), *n., adj., v.,* **-cat·ed, -cat·ing.** —*n.* **1.** one of four identical items, esp. copies of typewritten matter. **2. in quadruplicate,** in four identical copies. —*adj.* **3.** consisting of four identical parts. **4.** noting the fourth item or copy. —*v.t.* **5.** to make in quadruplicate. **6.** to make four times as great. —**quad·ru'pli·ca'tion,** *n.*

quaff (kwäf, kwaf, kwôf), *Literary.* —*v.t., v.i.* **1.** to drink (a beverage) copiously and heartily. —*n.* **2.** a beverage quaffed. —**quaff'er,** *n.*

quag·mire (kwag'mīr', kwog'-), *n.* an area of miry or boggy ground whose surface yields under the tread.

qua·hog (kwô'hog, -hôg, kwə hog', -hôg'), *n.* a thick-shelled, edible clam of the Atlantic coast. Also, **qua'haug.**

quail¹ (kwāl), *n., pl.* **quails, quail.** a small, migratory game bird of the Old World.

quail² (kwāl), *v.i.* to lose heart or courage, as in danger. —**Syn.** cower, flinch, recoil.

quaint (kwānt), *adj.* **1.** charmingly old-fashioned. **2.** strange or odd in a pleasing way. —**quaint'ly,** *adv.* —**quaint'ness,** *n.*

quake (kwāk), *v.,* **quaked, quak·ing,** *n.* —*v.i.* **1.** to tremble, as from cold or emotional fervor. **2.** to shake, as from shock or internal convulsion. —*n.* **3.** an instance of quaking. **4.** an earthquake. —**quak'ing·ly,** *adv.* —**quak'y,** *adj.*

Quak·er (kwā'kər), *n.* a member of the Society of Friends. —**Quak'er·ism,** *n.*

qual·i·fi·ca·tion (kwol'ə fə kā'shən), *n.* **1.** a skill or quality that fits a person for some job or position. **2.** the act of qualifying or state of being qualified. **3.** a limitation or restriction.

qual·i·fy (kwol'ə fī'), *v.,* **-fied, -fy·ing.** —*v.t.* **1.** to fit by skill or quality for a job or position. **2.** to limit or restrict in some way. **3.** to make less violent or severe. **4.** *Law.* to make legally capable. **5.** to identify (something) according to its qualities. **6.** *Gram.* to modify. **7.** to be or become qualified. **8.** to demonstrate the required ability in a preliminary competition. —**qual'i·fied,** *adj.* —**qual'i·fi'er** (-fī'ər), *n.*

qual·i·ta·tive (kwol'i tā'tiv), *adj.* pertaining to or concerned with quality. —**qual'i·ta'tive·ly,** *adv.*

qual·i·ty (kwol'i tē), *n., pl.* **-ties,** *adj.* —*n.* **1.** a typical and essential feature or characteristic. **2.** character or nature, as belonging to or distinguishing a thing. **3.** fineness or grade of excellence. **4.** great excellence. **5.** *Archaic.* high social position. —*adj.* **6.** of or having superior quality.

qualm (kwäm, kwôm), *n.* **1.** a pang of conscience as to conduct. **2.** a sudden feeling of apprehensive uneasiness. **3.** a sudden onset of illness, esp. of nausea. —**qualm'ish·ly,** *adv.* —**qualm'ish·ness,** *n.*

quan·da·ry (kwon'də rē, -drē), *n., pl.* **-ries.** a state of perplexity and uncertainty. —**Syn.** dilemma.

quan·ti·fy (kwon'tə fī'), *v.t.,* **-fied, -fy·ing.** to determine, indicate, or express the quantity of.

quan·ti·ta·tive (kwon'ti tā'tiv), *adj.* pertaining to or concerned with quantity. —**quan'ti·ta'tive·ly,** *adv.*

quan·ti·ty (kwon'ti tē), *n., pl.* **-ties. 1.** an indefinite amount of anything. **2.** a specified amount or measure. **3.** a considerable amount.

quan·tum (kwon'təm), *n., pl.* **-ta** (-tə). *Physics.* a very small, indivisible quantity of energy.

quar·an·tine (kwôr'ən tēn', kwor'-), *n., v.,* **-tined, -tin·ing.** —*n.* **1.** a strict isolation imposed to prevent the spread of disease. **2.** **a.** the official detention of a ship in port when suspected of carrying a contagious disease. **b.** a place for or period of such detention. **3.** a system of measures maintained by public-health authorities at ports of entry for preventing the spread of disease. —*v.t.* **4.** to put in quarantine.

quark (kwôrk), *n.* any of three types of elementary particles that are believed to form the basis of all matter. [coined word in *Finnegans Wake* by James Joyce]

quar·rel (kwôr'əl, kwor'-), *n., v.,* **-reled, -rel·ing** or **-relled, -rel·ling.** —*n.* **1.** an angry dispute or fight with words. **2.** a cause of dispute. —*v.i.* **3.** to disagree angrily. **4.** to dispute angrily. **5.** to make a complaint. —**quar'rel·er, quar'rel·ler,** *n.* —**quar'rel·some,** *adj.* —**Syn. 1.** argument, altercation, squabble, wrangle.

quar·ry¹ (kwôr'ē, kwor'ē) *n., pl.* **-ries,** *v.,* **-ried, -ry·ing.** —*n.* **1.** a large open pit from which stone is obtained, esp. for use in building. —*v.t.* **2.** to obtain (stone) from a quarry.

quar·ry² (kwôr'ē, kwor'ē), *n., pl.* **-ries. 1.** an animal or bird hunted or pursued. **2.** any object of search or pursuit.

quart (kwôrt), *n.* **1.** a liquid measure equal to ¼ gallon or 0.946 liter. **2.** a dry measure equal to ⅛ peck or 1.101 liters.

quar·ter (kwôr'tər), *n.* **1.** one of four equal parts of something. **2.** one fourth of a dollar, or 25 cents. **3.** a coin of this value. **4.** one fourth of an hour, or fifteen minutes. **5.** one fourth of a year, or three months. **6.** a district of a city or town. **7.** Usually, **quarters.** housing accommodations. **8.** an unspecified source: *information from a high* *quarter.* **9.** one of the four parts of an animal's body, each including a leg. **10.** mercy, esp. as shown to a defeated enemy: *to give quarter.* **11. at close quarters,** close together. —*v.t.* **12.** to divide into four equal parts. **13.** to furnish with housing accommodations. **14.** to cut (a human body) into four parts, esp. formerly in executing for treason. —*adj.* **15.** being one of four equal parts.

quar·ter·back (kwôr′tər bak′), *n.* **1.** a football player who directs the offense of the team. —*v.t.* **2.** to direct the offense of (a football team). **3.** to lead or direct.

quar·ter·deck (kwôr′tər dek′), *n.* the rear part of the uppermost deck of a ship.

quar′ter horse′, one of a breed of strong horses developed in the U.S. for short-distance races, usually a quarter of a mile.

quar·ter·ly (kwôr′tər lē), *adj., n., pl.* **-lies,** *adv.* —*adj.* **1.** occurring, paid, or issued at the end of every quarter of a year. —*n.* **2.** a periodical issued every three months. —*adv.* **3.** once each quarter of a year.

quar·ter·mas·ter (kwôr′tər mas′tər, -mä′stər), *n.* **1.** *Mil.* an officer charged with providing quarters, clothing, transportation, etc. **2.** *Navy.* a petty officer having charge of signals, navigating apparatus, etc.

quar′ter note′, *Music.* a note equivalent to one fourth of a whole note.

quar·ter·staff (kwôr′tər staf′, -stäf′), *n., pl.* **-staves** (-stāvz′, -stavz′, -stävz′). a stout, iron-tipped pole formerly used as a weapon.

quar·tet (kwôr tet′), *n.* **1.** a group of four singers or players. **2.** a musical composition for four voices or instruments. **3.** any group of four persons or things. Also, **quar·tette′.**

quar·to (kwôr′tō), *n., pl.* **-tos.** **1.** a page size of about 9½ × 12 inches, determined by folding printed sheets twice to form four leaves or eight pages. **2.** a book of this size.

quartz (kwôrts), *n.* a very common mineral composed of silicon and oxygen.

quartz′ crys′tal, *Electronics.* a carefully cut slice of quartz which vibrates at a certain rate of speed.

quartz·ite (kwôrt′sīt), *n.* a granular rock consisting essentially of quartz in interlocking grains.

qua·sar (kwā′sär, -sər, -zər), *n.* one of a number of celestial objects, from four to ten billion light-years distant, that are powerful sources of radio energy. Also called **qua′si·stel′lar ob′ject** (kwā′sī stel′ər).

quash[1] (kwosh), *v.t.* to suppress completely, as a rebellion.

quash[2] (kwosh), *v.t.* to annul or set aside, as an indictment.

qua·si (kwā′zī, -sī, kwä′sē, -zē), *adj.* **1.** resembling or seeming to be: *a quasi liberal.* —*adv.* **2.** seemingly but not actually (usually used in combination): *quasi-scientific.*

Qua·ter·nar·y (kwä′tər ner′ē, kwə-tûr′nə rē), *adj.* **1.** noting the present period, forming the latter part of the Cenozoic era, beginning about 1,000-000 years ago and including tthe Recent and Pleistocene epochs. —*n.* **2.** the Quaternary period.

quat·rain (kwo′trān), *n.* a stanza or poem of four lines.

quat·re·foil (kat′ər foil′, ka′trə-), *n.* a leaf composed of four leaflets.

qua·ver (kwā′vər), *v.i.* **1.** to shake tremulously. **2.** to speak or sing tremulously. —*n.* **3.** a quavering shake, esp. in the voice. —**qua′-ver·er,** *n.* —**qua′ver·ing·ly,** *adv.* —**qua′ver·y,** *adj.*

quay (kē), *n.* a landing pier of solid masonry, typically in a small locality.

Que., Quebec.

quean (kwēn), *n. Archaic.* a shrew or hussy.

quea·sy (kwē′zē), *adj.,* **-si·er, -si·est.** **1.** inclined to or feeling nausea. **2.** uneasy or uncomfortable. —**quea′-si·ly,** *adv.* —**quea′si·ness,** *n.*

Que·bec (kwi bek′), *n.* **1.** a province in E Canada. **2.** the capital of this province.

queen (kwēn), *n.* **1.** the wife or widow of a king. **2.** a female sovereign or monarch. **3.** a woman who is foremost or preeminent in any respect. **4.** a playing card bearing a picture of a queen. **5.** *Chess.* the most powerful piece. **6.** a fertile female ant, bee, termite, or wasp. —*v.i.* **7.** to reign as queen. —**queen′ly,** *adj.* —**queen′li·ness,** *n.*

Queens (kwēnz), *n.* a borough of E New York City.

queen-size (kwēn′sīz′), *adj.* **1.** larger than a double bed but smaller than king-size, usually 60 by 72 inches. **2.** made for a queen-size bed.

queer (kwēr), *adj.* **1.** different from what is usual or expected. **2.** *Slang.* homosexual. **3.** *Slang.* worthless or counterfeit. —*v.t.* **4.** to spoil or ruin. —*n.* **5.** *Slang.* a homosexual, esp. a male homosexual. —**queer′ly,** *adv.* —**queer′ness,** *n.* —**Syn. 1.** eccentric, odd, strange, weird.

quell (kwel), *v.t.* **1.** to suppress or crush (a mutiny, etc.). **2.** to quiet or allay (anxieties, etc.). —**quell′er,** *n.*

quench (kwench), v.t. **1.** put an end to (thirst, etc.) by satisfying. **2.** to put out or extinguish (fire, etc.). **3.** to cool suddenly by plunging into a liquid, as in tempering steel by immersion in water. **4.** to subdue or destroy, as an uprising. —**quench′-a·ble,** adj. —**quench′less,** adj.

quer·u·lous (kwer′ə ləs, kwer′yə-), adj. **1.** full of complaints. **2.** peevish or fretful. —**quer′u·lous·ly,** adv. — **quer′u·lous·ness,** n.

que·ry (kwēr′ē), n., pl. **-ries,** v., **-ried, -ry·ing.** —n. **1.** a question, esp. to resolve a doubt. **2.** Print. a question mark (?), esp. as added to a proof sheet. —v.t. **3.** to question as doubtful.

ques., question.

quest (kwest), n. **1.** a search made in order to find something. **2.** an adventurous expedition undertaken by a medieval knight.

ques·tion (kwes′chən, kwesh′-), n. **1.** something asked in order to get information. **2.** a problem for discussion. **3.** a matter of some uncertainty. **4.** a subject of dispute. **5.** a proposal to be debated or voted on. **6. out of the question,** not to be considered. —v.t. **7.** to ask (someone) a question. **8.** to doubt or dispute. —v.i. **9.** to ask a question. —**ques′tion·er,** n. —Syn. **7.** examine, interrogate, quiz.

ques·tion·a·ble (kwes′chə nə bəl, kwesh′-), adj. **1.** of doubtful morality, honesty, etc. **2.** open to question or dispute. —**ques′tion·a·ble·ness, ques′tion·a·bil′i·ty,** n. —**ques′tion·a·bly,** adv.

ques′tion mark′, a punctuation mark (?) placed after a sentence, phrase, or word to show a direct question.

ques·tion·naire (kwes′chə nâr′, kwesh′-), n. a list of questions submitted to gather information.

quet·zal (ket säl′), n., pl. **-zals, -za·les** (-sä′les). **1.** a Central and South American bird having golden-green and scarlet plumage. **2.** the monetary unit of Guatemala.

queue (kyōō), n., v., **queued, queu·ing.** —n. **1.** a braid of hair worn hanging down behind. **2.** Chiefly Brit. a line of people waiting their turn. —v.i., v.t. **3.** to form in a line while waiting.

quib·ble (kwib′əl), n., v., **-bled, -bling.** —n. **1.** a use of ambiguous or irrelevant language to evade a point at issue. **2.** a petty or minor objection. —v.i. **3.** to use a quibble or quibbles. —**quib′bler,** n.

quiche (kēsh), n. French Cookery. a pielike pastry shell filled with a custard and usually flavored with cheese, onion, bacon, etc.

quick (kwik), adj. **1.** done, occur-

ring, or reacting with promptness. **2.** finished or completed in a short time. **3.** prompt to understand, learn, or perceive. **4.** easily excited or aroused. —n. **5.** tender, sensitive flesh, esp. under the nails. **6.** Archaic. living persons: the quick and the dead. **7. cut to the quick,** to injure deeply. —adv. **8.** in a quick manner. —**quick′ly,** adv. —**quick′-ness,** n. —Syn. **1.** expeditious, fleet, rapid, speedy.

quick′ bread′, bread made with a leavening agent that acts quickly, permitting immediate baking.

quick·en (kwik′ən), v.t., v.i. **1.** to make or become more rapid. **2.** to make or become more active or lively. **3.** to bring life (to). **4.** to begin to show signs of life.

quick-freeze (kwik′frēz′), v.t., **-froze, -fro·zen, -freez·ing.** to subject (food) to rapid refrigeration, permitting it to be stored almost indefinitely at freezing temperatures.

quick·ie (kwik′ē), n. Slang. anything done or made hurriedly and sometimes cheaply.

quick·lime (kwik′līm′), n. lime[1] (def. 1).

quick·sand (kwik′sand′), n. a bed of loose sand of considerable depth that is so saturated with water as to yield under weight.

quick·sil·ver (kwik′sil′vər), n. the metallic element mercury.

quick·step (kwik′step′), n. music adapted to a march in quick time.

quick-tem·pered (kwik′tem′pərd), adj. easily angered.

quick′ time′, Mil. a normal rate of marching in which 120 steps, each of 30 inches, are taken in a minute.

quick-wit·ted (kwik′wit′id), adj. having a nimble, alert mind. —**quick′-wit′ted·ness,** n.

quid[1] (kwid), n. a portion of something, esp. tobacco, for chewing.

quid[2] (kwid), n., pl. **quid.** Brit. Slang. one pound sterling.

quid pro quo (kwid′ prō kwō′), Latin. one thing in return for another.

qui·es·cent (kwē es′ənt), adj. at rest or quiet. —**qui·es′cence, qui·es′cen·cy,** n.

qui·et (kwī′it), adj. **1.** making no noise or disturbing sound. **2.** free from disturbance or tumult. **3.** free from trouble or excitement. **4.** motionless or moving very gently. **5.** not busy or active. **6.** gentle or mild. **7.** not showy or obtrusive: quiet colors. —v.t., v.i. **8.** to make or become quiet. —n. **9.** freedom from noise. **10.** freedom from disturbance or tumult. —**qui′et·ly,** adv. —**qui′et·ness,** n.

qui·e·tude (kwī′i tōōd′, -tyōōd′), n. the state of being quiet.

qui·e·tus (kwī ē′təs), *n.*, *pl.* **-tus·es. 1.** *Literary.* the final settlement, as of a debt. **2.** *Archaic.* discharge or release from life.

quill (kwil), *n.* **1.** a large feather of the wing or tail of a bird. **2.** the hard, hollow part of a feather. **3.** Also called **quill′ pen′.** a writing pen formerly made from this. **4.** a hollow spine on a porcupine or hedgehog. —**quill′-like′,** *adj.*

quilt (kwilt), *n.* **1.** a padded covering for a bed, made of two layers of fabric. —*v.t.* **2.** to pad or line like a quilt. —*v.i.* **3.** to make quilts. —**quilt′er,** *n.*

quince (kwins), *n.* **1.** the hard, yellowish, pear-shaped fruit of a small, hardy tree, used in preserves. **2.** its tree.

qui·nine (kwī′nīn), *n.* a bitter alkaloid obtained from cinchona bark, used to treat malaria.

quin·sy (kwin′zē), *n.* a suppurative inflammation of the tonsils.

quint (kwint), *n.* *Informal.* a quintuplet.

quin·tal (kwin′t°l), *n.* a unit of weight equal to 100 kilograms.

quin·tes·sence (kwin tes′əns), *n.* **1.** the pure and concentrated essence of a substance. **2.** the most perfect embodiment of something. —**quin·tes·sen·tial** (kwin′tĭ sen′shəl), *adj.*

quin·tet (kwin tet′), *n.* **1.** a group of five singers or players. **2.** a musical composition for five voices or instruments. **3.** any group of five persons or things. Also, **quin·tette′.**

quin·til·lion (kwin til′yən), *n.* a cardinal number represented in the U.S. by 1 followed by 18 zeros, and, in Great Britain, by 1 followed by 30 zeros. —**quin·til′lionth,** *n.*, *adj.*

quin·tu·ple (kwin tōō′pəl, kwin′tōō pəl, -tyōō′-; v. kwin tōō′pəl kät′, -tyōō′-), *adj.*, *n.*, *v.*, **-pled, -pling.** —*adj.* **1.** consisting of five parts. **2.** five times as great. —*n.* **3.** a number or amount five times as great as another. —*v.t.*, *v.i.* **4.** to make or become five times as great.

quin·tu·plet (kwin tup′lit, -tōō′plit, -tyōō′-, kwin′tōō plit, -tyōō-), *n.* **1.** one of five children born of one pregnancy. **2.** any group of five.

quin·tu·pli·cate (*n.*, *adj.* kwin tōō′plə kit, -tyōō′-; *v.* kwin tōō′plə kāt′, -tyōō′-), *n.*, *adj.*, *v.*, **-cat·ed, -cat·ing.** —*n.* **1.** one of five identical items, esp. copies of typewritten matter. **2. in quintuplicate,** in five identical copies. —*adj.* **3.** consisting of five identical parts. **4.** noting the fifth item or copy. —*v.t.* **5.** to make in quintuplicate. **6.** to make five times as great.

quip (kwip), *n.*, *v.*, **quipped, quipping.** —*n.* **1.** a clever or witty remark, often sarcastic. —*v.i.* **2.** to make quips. —**quip′ster,** *n.*

quire (kwī°r), *n.* a set of 24 or sometimes 25 uniform sheets of paper.

quirk (kwûrk), *n.* **1.** a peculiarity of behavior or personality. **2.** a sudden twist or turn. —**quirk′y,** *adj.* —**quirk′i·ness,** *n.*

quirt (kwûrt), *n.* a riding whip having a short, stout handle and a lash of braided leather.

quis·ling (kwiz′lĭng), *n.* a person who betrays his or her own country by aiding an invading enemy. [after Vidkun *Quisling* (1887–1945), pro-Nazi Norwegian leader]

quit (kwit), *v.*, **quit** or **quit·ted, quit·ting,** *adj.* —*v.t.* **1.** to stop doing or having (something). **2.** to depart from or leave. **3.** to give up or resign. **4.** *Archaic.* to conduct (oneself). —*v.i.* **5.** to stop doing or having something. **6.** to give up or resign one's job. —*adj.* **7.** free or rid, as of an obligation.

quit·claim (kwit′klām′), *Law.* —*n.* **1.** a deed in which one gives up one's claim of title to some property. —*v.t.* **2.** to give up claim to (property).

quite (kwīt), *adv.* **1.** almost completely. **2.** actually or truly. **3.** to a considerable degree. **4. quite a,** unusual or exceptional. **5. quite a few,** a great many.

Qui·to (kē′tô), *n.* the capital of Ecuador.

quits (kwits), *adj.* **1.** on equal terms as a result of repayment or retaliation. **2. call it quits, a.** to end one's activity temporarily. **b.** to abandon an effort.

quit·tance (kwit′°ns), *n.* **1.** discharge from a debt. **2.** recompense or requital.

quit·ter (kwit′ər), *n.* *Informal.* a person who gives up easily or quickly.

quiv·er¹ (kwiv′ər), *v.t.*, *v.i.* **1.** to shake with a slight but rapid motion. —*n.* **2.** the act of quivering. —**quiv′er·er,** *n.* —**quiv′er·ing·ly,** *adv.* —**quiv′er·y,** *adj.*

quiv·er² (kwiv′ər), *n.* a case for holding or carrying arrows.

qui vive (kē vēv′), **1.** *French.* who goes there?: a sentinel's challenge. **2. on the qui vive,** on the alert.

quix·ot·ic (kwik sot′ik), *adj.* extravagantly chivalrous, romantic, and idealistic. [after Don *Quixote*, hero in a novel by Cervantes] —**quix·ot′i·cal·ly,** *adv.* —**Syn.** impractical, visionary.

quiz (kwiz), *v.*, **quizzed, quiz·zing,** *n.*, *pl.* **quiz·zes.** —*v.t.* **1.** to examine (a student or class) informally by questions. —*n.* **2.** an informal test or examination. —**quiz′zer,** *n.*

quiz·zi·cal (kwiz'i kəl), *adj.* 1. mildly puzzled. 2. comically serious. —**quiz'zi·cal'i·ty, quiz'zi·cal·ness,** *n.* —**quiz'zi·cal·ly,** *adv.*

quoin (koin, kwoin), *n.* 1. an external solid angle of a wall. 2. one of the stones forming it. 3. a wedge-shaped piece of wood or stone.

quoit (kwoit), *n.* 1. **quoits,** a game in which rings are thrown at a peg. 2. a ring used in this game.

quon·dam (kwon'dam), *adj. Literary.* that formerly was.

Quon'set hut' (kwon'sit), *Trademark.* a semicylindrical building made of corrugated steel.

quo·rum (kwôr'əm, kwôr'-), *n.* the number of members of an organization required to be present to transact business legally.

quot., quotation.

quo·ta (kwō'tə), *n.* a share or proportional part of a total required or assigned.

quota'tion mark', one of the punctua-

tion marks used to indicate the beginning and end of a quotation, usually shown as (") at the beginning and (") at the end.

quote (kwōt), *v.,* **quot·ed, quot·ing,** *n.* —*v.t.* 1. to repeat (a passage, phrase, etc.), as from a book. 2. to repeat words from (a book, author, etc.). 3. to state (a price), as for merchandise. —*n.* 4. *Informal.* something quoted. 5. See **quotation mark.** —**quot'a·ble,** *adj.* —**quo·ta·tion** (kwō-tā'shen), *n.* —**quo·ta'tion·al,** *adj.* —**quo·ta'tion·al·ly,** *adv.* —**quot'er,** *n.*

quoth (kwōth), *v. Archaic.* said (always placed before the subject): *Quoth the raven, "Nevermore."*

quo·tid·i·an (kwō tid'ē ən), *adj.* 1. *Med.* occurring daily. 2. *Literary.* everyday or ordinary.

quo·tient (kwō'shənt), *n.* the result obtained by dividing one number into another.

q.v., which see. [< L.*quod vide*]

qy., query.

R

R, r (är), *n., pl.* **R's** or **Rs, r's** or **rs.** the 18th letter of the English alphabet, a consonant.

R, 1. *Elect.* resistance. 2. a designation for motion pictures to which those under 17 will be admitted only when accompanied by a parent or adult guardian. 3. *Chess.* rook.

r, *Physics.* roentgen.

R., 1. radius. 2. railroad. 3. railway. 4. Republican. 5. right. 6. river. 7. road.

r., 1. rare. 2. rod. 3. *Baseball.* run; runs.

RA, Regular Army.

Ra, radium.

R.A., Royal Academy.

R.A.A.F., Royal Australian Air Force.

Ra·bat (rä bät'), *n.* the capital of Morocco.

rab·bet (rab'it), *n., v.,* **-bet·ed, -bet·ing.** —*n.* 1. a notch formed in one edge of a board to receive another. —*v.t.* 2. to cut a rabbet in. 3. to join by means of a rabbet. —*v.i.* 4. to become joined by means of a rabbet.

rab·bi (rab'ī), *n., pl.* **-bis.** 1. the spiritual leader of a Jewish congregation. 2. a title of respect for a Jewish scholar or teacher. —**rab·bin·i·cal** (rə bin'i kəl), **rab·bin'ic,** *adj.*

rab·bin·ate (rab'ə nit), *n.* 1. the office of a rabbi. 2. a group of rabbis.

rab·bit (rab'it), *n., pl.* **-bits, -bit.** a small, long-eared, burrowing mammal of the hare family.

rab'bit punch', *Boxing.* a short, sharp blow to the nape of the neck.

rab·ble (rab'əl), *n.* 1. a disorderly crowd. 2. **the rabble,** the lower classes.

rab·ble-rous·er (rab'əl rou'zər), *n.* a person who stirs up the passions or prejudices of the public. —**rab'ble-rous'ing,** *adj., n.*

Rab·e·lais (rab'ə lā'), *n.* Fran·çois (frän swA'), c1490–1553, French satirist and humorist. —**Rab'e·lai'si·an** (-zē ən, -zhən), *adj., n.*

rab·id (rab'id), *adj.* 1. irrationally extreme in opinion or behavior. 2. violently intense. 3. affected with rabies. —**rab·id'i·ty, rab'id·ness,** *n.* —**rab'id·ly,** *adv.*

ra·bies (rā'bēz, -bē ēz'), *n.* an infectious fatal disease transmitted to a human being by the bite of an infected animal.

rac·coon (ra kōōn', rə-), *n., pl.* **-coons, -coon.** 1. a small nocturnal animal of North America having a sharp snout and a bushy ringed tail. 2. its fur.

race[1] (rās), *n.*, *v.*, **raced, rac·ing.** —*n.*
1. a contest of speed, as in running.
2. any contest to achieve something.
3. an onward or regular course. 4. a. a strong or rapid current of water. b. the channel of such a current. —*v.i.* 5. to run a race. 6. to move or go swiftly. —*v.t.* 7. to run a race against. 8. to enter in a race or races. 9. to cause to go at high speed. —**rac′er,** *n.*

race[2] (rās), *n.* 1. a division of the human species characterized by a more or less distinctive combination of physical traits that are transmitted in descent. 2. a group of tribes or peoples forming an ethnic stock. 3. any group or class of persons.

race·horse (rās′hôrs′), *n.* a horse bred or kept for racing.

ra·ceme (rā sēm′, rə-), *n.* a cluster of flowers each of which grows on its own short stalk spaced along the stem. —**rac·e·mose** (ras′ə mōs′), *adj.*

race·track (rās′trak′), *n.* a plot of ground, usually oval, laid out for horse racing. Also, **race′course′** (-kôrs′, -kōrs′).

race·way (rās′wā), *n.* 1. a passage or channel for water, as a millrace. 2. a racetrack for trotting horses harnessed to sulkies.

ra·chi·tis (rə kī′tis), *n.* rickets. —**ra·chit′ic** (-kit′ik), *adj.*

ra·cial (rā′shəl), *adj.* of or characteristic of one race or the races of mankind. —**ra′cial·ly,** *adv.*

ra·cial·ism (rā′shə liz′əm), *n.* the belief in or the practice of racism. —**ra′cial·ist,** *n., adj.* —**ra′cial·is′tic,** *adj.*

rac′ing form′, a sheet providing detailed information about horse races.

rac·ism (rā′siz əm), *n.* 1. the idea that one's own race is superior. 2. a policy or practice based on such an idea. —**rac′ist,** *n., adj.*

rack[1] (rak), *n.* 1. a framework on which articles or materials are arranged or deposited: *a tool rack.* 2. a bar bearing teeth that engages with a gear or pinion. 3. a former instrument of torture on which a victim was slowly stretched. 4. a cause or state of intense suffering. 5. **on the rack,** in a state of distress. —*v.t.* 6. to distress acutely. 7. to strain in mental effort: *to rack one's brains.* 8. to torture by means of a rack. 9. **rack up,** *Slang.* to score or gain.

rack[2] (rak), *n.* 1. *Archaic.* destruction or wreck. 2. **go to rack and ruin,** to become destroyed.

rack·et[1] (rak′it), *n.* 1. a loud, disturbing noise. 2. a dishonest or criminal means of gaining money. 3. any organized illegal activity. —**rack′et·y,** *adj.*

rack·et[2] (rak′it), *n.* any of various light bats having a netting stretched in a more or less oval frame, used in tennis, badminton, etc. Also, **rac′quet.**

rack·et·eer (rak′i tēr′), *n.* a person engaged in an organized illegal activity, as extortion. —**rack′et·eer′ing,** *n.*

rac·on·teur (rak′on tûr′), *n.* a person who is skilled in relating anecdotes.

rac·y (rā′sē), *adj.*, **rac·i·er, rac·i·est.**
1. slightly indecent or improper. 2. having an agreeably peculiar taste or flavor, as wine. 3. full of zest. 4. pungent or piquant. —**rac′i·ly,** *adv.* —**rac′i·ness,** *n.*

rad., 1. *Math.* radical. 2. radio. 3. radius.

ra·dar (rā′där), *n.* a device for determining the presence and location of an object by measuring the time for the echo of a radio wave to return from it and the direction from which it returns. [*ra(dio) d(etecting) a(nd) r(anging)*]

ra·dar·scope (rā′där skōp′), *n.* the viewing screen of radar equipment.

ra·di·al (rā′dē əl), *adj.* 1. extending outward from a central point like rays or radii. 2. of or resembling rays or radii. 3. *Mach.* having pistons moving inward and outward from a central point or shaft: *a radial engine.* —**ra′di·al·ly,** *adv.*

ra′di·al-ply′ tire′ (rā′dē əl plī′), a motor-vehicle tire in which the fabric plies are put straight across at a right angle to the direction of travel.

ra·di·ant (rā′dē ənt), *adj.* 1. emitting rays of light. 2. bright with joy, hope, etc. 3. emitted by radiation. —**ra′di·ance, ra′di·an·cy,** *n.* —**ra′di·ant·ly,** *adv.*

ra′diant en′ergy, energy transmitted in electromagnetic wave motion.

ra·di·ate (rā′dē āt′), *v.*, **-at·ed, -at·ing.** —*v.i.* 1. to spread or move like rays or radii from a center. 2. to emit rays, as of light or heat. —*v.t.* 3. to emit in rays. 4. to show or spread a feeling of (joy, happiness, etc.). —**ra′di·a′tive,** *adj.*

ra·di·a·tion (rā′dē ā′shən), *n.* 1. the act or process of radiating. 2. something radiated, esp. energy emitted as particles or waves.

radia′tion sick′ness, sickness caused by exposure to x-rays or radioactive materials, characterized by nausea, vomiting, loss of hair and teeth, etc.

ra·di·a·tor (rā′dē ā′tər), *n.* 1. a device for warming the air, as in a building. 2. a device for cooling a circulating fluid, as in an automobile engine.

rad·i·cal (rad′i kəl), *adj.* **1.** of or going to the roots or origins of a matter. **2.** thoroughgoing or extreme. **3.** favoring drastic political, economic, or social reforms. —*n.* **4.** a person who advocates radical reforms, esp. in politics. **5.** *Math.* **a.** a quantity expressed as a root of another quantity. **b.** See radical sign. **6.** *Chem.* a group of atoms that act together as a single unit. —**rad′i·cal·ism′,** *n.* —**rad′i·cal·ly,** *adv.* —**rad′i·cal·ness,** *n.* — **Syn. 1.** fundamental. **2.** excessive, immoderate, sweeping.

rad·i·cal·ize (rad′i kə līz′), *v.t., v.i.,* **-ized, -iz·ing.** to make or become radical, esp. in politics. —**rad′i·cal·i·za′tion,** *n.*

rad′ical sign′, *Math.* the symbol √ or ⁿ√, indicating extraction of a root of the quantity that follows it.

ra·di·i (rā′dē ī′), *n.* a pl. of radius.

ra·di·o (rā′dē ō′), *n., pl.* **-di·os,** *adj., v.,* **-di·oed, -di·o·ing.** —*n.* **1.** the transmission of sound and signals through space by means of electromagnetic waves without wires. **2.** a receiver used in such transmission. **3.** the business or industry of producing programs to be transmitted in this manner. —*adj.* **4.** of, used in, or sent by radio. —*v.t., v.i.* **5.** to transmit (messages, etc.) or communicate with (someone) by radio.

radio-, a combining form meaning: **a.** radio: *radiotelegraph.* **b.** radioactive: *radioisotope.* **c.** radiant energy: *radiometer.*

ra·di·o·ac·tiv·i·ty (rā′dē ō ak tiv′i tē), *n.* the property of certain chemical elements causing them to emit radiation as a result of changes in the nuclei of atoms of the element. — **ra′di·o·ac′tive** (-ak′tiv), *adj.* —**ra′di·o·ac′tive·ly,** *adv.*

ra′dio astron′omy, the branch of astronomy that utilizes radio wavelengths rather than visible light to study stars, galaxies, etc.

ra·di·o·car·bon (rā′dē ō kär′bən), *n.* a radioactive isotope of carbon widely used in the dating of archaeological materials.

ra′dio fre′quency, a frequency within the range of radio or television transmission, from about 10 kilohertz to 300,000 megahertz.

ra·di·o·gen·ic (rā′dē ō jen′ik), *adj.* produced by radioactive decay.

ra·di·o·gram (rā′dē ō gram′), *n.* a message transmitted by radiotelegraphy.

ra·di·o·graph (rā′dē ō graf′, -gräf′), *n.* **1.** a photographic image produced by the action of x-rays or rays from radioactive substances. —*v.t.* **2.** to make a radiograph of. —**ra′di·o·graph′ic,** *adj.* —**ra′di·o·graph′i·cal-**

ly, *adv.* —**ra′di·og′ra·phy** (-og′rə-fē), *n.*

ra·di·o·i·so·tope (rā′dē ō ī′sə tōp′), *n.* a radioactive isotope, usually artificially produced.

ra·di·ol·o·gy (rā′dē ol′ə jē), *n.* the science dealing with x-rays or rays from radioactive substances, esp. for medical uses. —**ra′di·o·log′i·cal** (-ō loj′i-kəl), *adj.* —**ra′di·ol′o·gist,** *n.*

ra·di·o·man (rā′dē ō man′), *n.* a person who operates a radio or repairs radio equipment.

ra·di·om·e·ter (rā′dē om′i·tər), *n.* an instrument for detecting and measuring radiant energy. —**ra′di·o·met′ric** (-ō me′trik), *adj.* —**ra′di·o·met′ri·cal·ly,** *adv.* —**ra′di·om′e·try,** *n.*

ra·di·o·phone (rā′dē ō fōn′), *n.* a radiotelephone.

ra·di·os·co·py (rā′dē os′kə pē), *n.* the examination of objects opaque to light by means of other radiation, usually x-rays. —**ra′di·o·scop′ic** (-ō skop′ik), *adj.*

ra·di·o·sonde (rā′dē ō sond′), *n.* an instrument that is carried aloft by a balloon to radio back meteorological information.

ra·di·o·tel·e·graph (rā′dē ō tel′ə graf′, -gräf′), *n.* a telegraph in which messages or signals are sent by radio. —**ra′di·o·tel′e·graph′ic,** *adj.* —**ra′di·o·te·leg′ra·phy,** *n.*

ra·di·o·tel·e·phone (rā′dē ō tel′ə fōn′), *n.* a telephone in which sound or speech is transmitted by radio. —**ra′di·o·tel′e·phon′ic** (-fon′ik), *adj.* — **ra′di·o·te·leph′o·ny,** *n.*

ra′dio tel′escope, a very large instrument for collecting and studying electromagnetic waves from space.

ra·di·o·ther·a·py (rā′dē ō ther′ə pē), *n.* treatment of disease by means of x-rays or of radioactive substances. — **ra′di·o·ther′a·pist,** *n.*

rad·ish (rad′ish), *n.* **1.** the crisp, pungent, edible root of a garden plant, usually eaten raw. **2.** its plant.

ra·di·um (rā′dē əm), *n. Chem.* a highly radioactive metallic element that upon disintegration produces the element radon and alpha particles. *Symbol:* Ra; *at. wt.:* 226; *at. no.:* 88.

ra′dium ther′apy, treatment of disease by means of radium.

ra·di·us (rā′dē əs), *n., pl.* **-di·i** (-dē ī′), **-di·us·es. 1.** a straight line extending from the center of a circle or sphere to the circumference or surface. **2.** a circular area determined by the length of such a line. **3.** field or range of operation or influence. [< L: staff, spoke]

RAdm, Rear Admiral.

ra·dome (rā′dōm′), *n.* a dome-shaped device used to house a radar antenna. [ra(dar) + dome]

ra·don (rā'don), *n. Chem.* a rare, chemically inert, radioactive gaseous element produced by the disintegration of radium. *Symbol:* Rn; *at. wt.:* 222; *at. no.:* 86.

RAF, Royal Air Force.

raf·fi·a (raf'ē ə), *n.* 1. a palm of Madagascar having long, plumelike leaves. 2. the fiber of this palm, used for making matting, baskets, etc.

raff·ish (raf'ish), *adj.* 1. vulgar in a gaudy way. 2. rakish or dissolute. —**raff'ish·ly,** *adv.* —**raff'ish·ness,** *n.*

raf·fle (raf'əl), *n., v., -fled, -fling. —n.* 1. a lottery in which a number of participants buy one or more chances to win a prize. —*v.t.* 2. to give away as a prize in a raffle. —**raf'fler,** *n.*

raft¹ (raft, räft), *n.* a platform for floating on water, esp. one made of logs or planks fastened together. —*v.t.* 2. to transport or travel by raft. 3. to form (logs) into a raft.

raft² (raft, räft), *n. Informal.* a great quantity.

raft·er (raf'tər, räf'-), *n.* one of a series of sloping timbers used to support the covering of a roof.

rag¹ (rag), *n.* a worthless piece of cloth, esp. one torn or worn.

rag² (rag), *v.t.,* **ragged, rag·ging.** *Brit.* to torment with jokes.

rag³ (rag), *n.* a musical composition in ragtime.

ra·ga (rä'gə), *n.* one of the melodic formulas of Hindu music.

rag·a·muf·fin (rag'ə muf'in), *n.* a ragged, dirty person or child.

rage (rāj), *n., v.,* **raged, rag·ing. —n.** 1. angry fury. 2. an intense fad. —*v.i.* 3. to act or speak with fury. 4. to move with violent force. 5. to proceed or spread with violence or intensity.

rag·ged (rag'id), *adj.* 1. wearing tattered or worn-out clothes. 2. torn or worn to rags. 3. shaggy or uneven. 4. having loose or hanging shreds or bits. 5. imperfect or faulty. —**rag'ged·ly,** *adv.* —**rag'ged·ness,** *n.*

rag·lan (rag'lən), *n.* a loose overcoat with raglan sleeves.

rag'lan sleeve', a sleeve that has a long, slanting seam line from the neck to the armhole.

ra·gout (ra gōō'), *n.* a highly seasoned stew of meat or fish.

rag'tag and bob'tail (rag'tag'), *Disparaging.* the rabble.

rag·time (rag'tīm'), *n.* a kind of popular music having a fast, syncopated rhythm.

rag·weed (rag'wēd'), *n.* a common weed with ragged leaves, whose pollen is a major cause of hay fever.

rah (rä), *interj.* hurrah.

raid (rād), *n.* 1. a sudden attack or invasion. —*v.t., v.i.* 2. to make a raid (on). —**raid'er,** *n.*

rail¹ (rāl), *n.* 1. a bar of wood or metal fixed horizontally, as for a support, barrier, or railing. 2. one of a pair of steel bars that provide the running surfaces for the wheels of railroad cars. 3. the railroad. —*v.t.* 4. to furnish with rails.

rail² (rāl), *v.i.* to complain bitterly. —**rail'er,** *n.*

rail³ (rāl), *n.* a short-winged bird found in marshes.

rail·ing (rā'ling), *n.* 1. a fencelike barrier of rails. 2. rails collectively.

rail·ler·y (rā'lə rē), *n., pl.* **-ler·ies.** good-humored ridicule.

rail·road (rāl'rōd'), *n.* 1. a permanent road laid with rails on which locomotives and cars are run. 2. an entire system of such roads together with its rolling stock, buildings, etc. —*v.t.* 3. to transport by railroad. 4. to push (a law or bill) through without enough time to consider objections. 5. *Informal.* to convict (a person) of a crime hastily and unfairly. —*v.i.* 6. to work on a railroad. —**rail'road'er,** *n.* —**rail'road'ing,** *n.*

rail·way (rāl'wā'), *n.* 1. *Chiefly Brit.* a railroad. 2. a line of rails for wheeled equipment.

rai·ment (rā'mənt), *n. Literary.* clothing or apparel.

rain (rān), *n.* 1. water that is condensed from the air and falls in drops from the sky. 2. a fall of such drops. 3. a heavy or thick fall of anything. —*v.i.* 4. (of rain) to fall. 5. to fall like rain. —*v.t.* 6. to send down (rain, etc.). 7. to offer or give in great quantity. 8. **rain out,** to cancel or postpone (an outdoor event) because of rain. —**rain'y,** *adj.* —**rain'i·ness,** *n.*

rain·bow (rān'bō'), *n.* a bow or arc of prismatic colors appearing in the heavens opposite the sun and caused by the sun's rays in drops of rain.

rain' check', 1. a ticket for future use given to spectators at an outdoor event that has been rained out. 2. an offered postponement of an invitation.

rain·coat (rān'kōt'), *n.* a waterproof coat worn as protection against rain.

rain·drop (rān'drop'), *n.* a drop of rain.

rain·fall (rān'fôl'), *n.* 1. a fall or shower of rain. 2. the amount of water falling in rain, expressed as a depth in inches.

rain' for'est, a tropical forest in an area of exceptionally high annual rainfall.

rain·mak·ing (rān'mā'king), *n.* the act or process of making or trying to make rainfall, as by artificial means. —**rain'mak'er,** *n.*

rain·storm (rān'stôrm'), *n.* a storm of a heavy rain.

rain' wa'ter, water fallen as rain.

rain'y day', a time of need or emergency.

raise (rāz), *v.,* **raised, rais·ing,** *n.* — *v.t.* 1. to move to a higher position. 2. to set upright. 3. to build or erect (a structure). 4. to promote the growth of (plants, animals, etc.), as for profit. 5. to rear (a child). 6. to activate or set in motion. 7. to present for consideration, as a question. 8. to assemble or collect, as money. 9. to restore to life, as the dead. 10. to advance in rank or position. 11. to increase in value, amount, or force. 12. to make (one's voice) heard. 13. to utter (a shout, cry, etc.). 14. to cause (dough or bread) to rise. 15. *Mil.* to end (a siege or blockade). —*n.* 16. an increase, esp. in pay or salary. 17. an act of raising. ·—**rais'er,** *n.*

rai·sin (rā'zin), *n.* a sweet dried grape, often used in cakes.

rai·son d' ê·tre (rā'zōn de'tra), reason for being or existence.

ra·jah (rä'jə), *n.* a former prince in India. Also, **ra'ja.**

rake[1] (rāk), *n., v.,* **raked, rak·ing.** —*n.* 1. a long-handled tool having a row of teeth for smoothing out the soil or gathering fallen leaves, etc. —*v.t.* 2. to smooth out or gather with a rake. 3. to search thoroughly through. 4. to sweep (a body of troops, etc.) with gunfire. 5. **rake in,** *Informal.* to get or collect (money, etc.) abundantly and quickly. 6. **rake up,** *Informal.* to discover and bring to light (a scandal, etc.).

rake[2] (rāk), *n.* a dissolute person, esp. formerly in high society.

rake[3] (rāk), *n.* a slope or sloping angle, esp. of a ship's mast.

rake-off (rāk'ôf', -of'), *n. Informal.* a share or amount taken illicitly.

rak·ish[1] (rā'kish), *adj.* like a dissolute rake. —**rak'ish·ly,** *adv.* —**rak'ish·ness,** *n.*

rak·ish[2] (rā'kish), *adj.* 1. smart and dashing. 2. (of a ship) having an appearance suggesting speed. —**rak'ish·ly,** *adv.* —**rak'ish·ness,** *n.*

Ra·leigh (rô'lē, rä'-), *n.* 1. **Sir Walter** (wôl'tər), 1552?–1618, English explorer and writer. 2. the capital of North Carolina.

ral·ly[1] (ral'ē), *v.,* **-lied, -ly·ing,** *n., pl.* **-lies.** —*v.t., v.i.* 1. to bring or gather together again for action, as troops. 2. to bring or come together for a single purpose. 3. to recover or revive, as one's strength. —*n.* 4. a mass meeting for a single purpose.

5. *Finance.* a sharp rise in price after a declining market. 6. Also, **ral'lye.** a long-distance automobile race held on public roads. —**ral'li·er,** *n.*

ral·ly[2] (ral'ē), *v.t.,* **-lied, -ly·ing.** *Brit.* to ridicule in a good-natured way.

ram (ram), *n., v.,* **rammed, ram·ming.** —*n.* 1. a male sheep. 2. **the Ram,** Aries. 3. any of various devices for battering, crushing, or forcing something. —*v.t.* 4. to drive or force by heavy blows. 5. to dash violently against. 6. to cram or stuff.

ram·ble (ram'bəl), *v.,* **-bled, -bling,** *n.* —*v.i.* 1. to roam aimlessly or leisurely. 2. to talk or write in a discursive, aimless way. 3. to grow or spread in a haphazard way, as a vine. —*n.* 4. an aimless walk for pleasure.

ram·bler (ram'blər), *n.* 1. a person or thing that rambles. 2. a climbing rose having clusters of small flowers.

ram·bunc·tious (ram bungk'shəs), *adj.* wild and unruly. ·—**ram·bunc'tious·ness,** *n.* —**Syn.** intractable, obstreperous.

ram·e·kin (ram'ə kin), *n.* a small dish in which food can be baked and served.

ram·ie (ram'ē), *n.* 1. an Asian shrub yielding a fiber used esp. in making textiles. 2. its fiber.

ram·i·fy (ram'ə fī'), *v.t., v.i.* **-fied, -fy·ing.** to divide or spread out into branches or branchlike parts. —**ram'i·fi·ca'tion,** *n.*

ram·jet (ram'jet'), *n.* a jet engine operated by the injection of fuel into a stream of air compressed by the forward speed of the aircraft.

ramp (ramp), *n.* 1. a sloping surface connecting different levels. 2. a movable staircase for entering or leaving an airplane.

ram·page (*n.* ram'pāj; *v.* ram pāj'), *n., v.,* **-paged, -pag·ing.** —*n.* 1. a fit of violent or excited behavior. —*v.i.* 2. to rush furiously or violently. —**ram·pag'er,** *n.* —**ram·pa'geous** (-pā'jəs), *adj.*

ramp·ant (ram'pənt), *adj.* 1. growing luxuriantly, as weeds. 2. prevailing or unbridled, as a rumor.

ram·part (ram'pärt, -pərt), *n.* 1. a broad bank or mound of earth raised as a fortification. 2. anything serving as a bulwark or defense.

ram·rod (ram'rod'), *n.* 1. a rod for ramming down the charge of a muzzle-loading firearm. 2. a cleaning rod for the barrel of a firearm.

ram·shack·le (ram'shak'əl), *adj.* loosely made or held together.

ran (ran), *v.* pt. of **run.**

ranch (ranch), *n.* **1.** an establishment for raising livestock on the range. **2.** *Western U.S.* a large farm used chiefly to raise one crop or kind of animal. **3.** See **ranch house.** —*v.i.* **4.** to work on or manage a ranch. —**ranch′er, ranch′man,** *n.*

ranch′ house′, a long, low house with all the rooms on one level, esp. one built in the suburbs.

ran·cid (ran′sid), *adj.* having a rank, unpleasant, stale smell or taste. —**ran·cid′i·ty** (-sid′i tē), *n.* —**ran′cidness,** *n.*

ran·cor (rang′kər), *n.* bitter, rankling resentment or ill will. Also, *Brit.,* **ran′cour.** —**ran′cor·ous,** *adj.* —**ran′cor·ous·ly,** *adv.* —**Syn.** animosity, malice, venom.

rand (rand), *n., pl.* **rand.** the monetary unit of the Republic of South Africa.

R & B, See **rhythm and blues.**

R&D, research and development.

ran·dom (ran′dəm), *adj.* **1.** without plan or order. **2. at random,** in a random manner. —**ran′dom·ly,** *adv.* —**ran′dom·ness,** *n.*

ran′dom ac′cess, equal access to any desired location in the memory of a computer.

ran·dom·ize (ran′də mīz′), *v.t., v.i.,* **-ized, -iz·ing.** to handle or perform in a random manner. —**ran′dom·i·za′tion** (-mə zā′shən), *n.*

R and R, **1.** rest and recreation. **2.** rest and recuperation. Also, **R & R**

rand·y (ran′dē), *adj.,* **rand·i·er, rand·i·est.** sexually aroused.

ra·nee (rä′nē), *n.* the wife of a rajah.

rang (rang), *v.* pt. of **ring³.**

range (rānj), *n., v.,* **ranged, rang·ing.** —*n.* **1.** the limits within which something varies: *the range of steel prices.* **2.** the extent of the operation or action of something. **3.** the distance of the target from a weapon. **4.** an area for practice in shooting weapons. **5.** an area used for testing missiles in flights. **6.** a row, line, or series, as of persons or things. **7.** an act of ranging or moving around, as over an area. **8.** a large, open region for grazing livestock. **9.** a chain of mountains. **10.** a large stove with burners and an oven. —*v.t.* **11.** to set in rows or lines, esp. in an orderly fashion. **12.** to place in a certain class or group. **13.** to pass over (an area) in all directions, as in exploring. —*v.i.* **14.** to vary within specified limits. **15.** to run or go in a certain direction. **16.** to rove or roam.

rang·er (rān′jər), *n.* **1.** See **forest ranger. 2.** a member of a group of armed persons who patrol a region as guards. **3.** (*cap.*) a soldier special-ly trained for making surprise raids. **4.** a person who ranges or roves.

Ran·goon (rang gōōn′), *n.* the capital of Burma.

rang·y (rān′jē), *adj.,* **rang·i·er, rang·i·est.** slender and long-limbed. —**rang′i·ness,** *n.*

ra·ni (rä′nē), *n.* ranee.

rank¹ (rangk), *n.* **1.** social standing or class. **2.** high social standing. **3.** official position or grade. **4.** a class in any scale of comparison. **5.** relative position or standing: *a writer of the highest rank.* **6.** a line of soldiers standing abreast. **7.** Usually, **ranks.** the members of an armed service apart from its officers. **8.** orderly arrangement. **9.** *Brit.* a line or row of things, esp. taxis: *a cab rank.* —*v.t.* **10.** to arrange in ranks or in regular formation. **11.** to assign to a particular position or class. **12.** to outrank. —*v.i.* **13.** to hold a certain rank or position.

rank² (rangk), *adj.* **1.** growing quickly and coarsely, as grass. **2.** having an offensively strong smell or taste. **3.** offensively strong, as a smell or taste. **4.** utter or absolute: *rank treachery.* —**rank′ly,** *adv.* —**rank′ness,** *n.*

rank′ and file′, **1.** the members of a group or organization, other than its leaders. **2.** rank¹ (def. 7).

rank·ing (rang′king), *adj.* **1.** senior or superior in rank or position. **2.** prominent or highly regarded.

ran·kle (rang′kəl), *v.i., v.t.,* **-kled, -kling.** to cause persistent keen irritation or bitter resentment (in). —**ran′kling·ly,** *adv.*

ran·sack (ran′sak), *v.t.* **1.** to search thoroughly through. **2.** to search through for plunder. —**ran′sack·er,** *n.*

ran·som (ran′səm), *n.* **1.** the payment of a price for the release of a captive, kidnapped person, etc. **2.** the price paid or demanded. —*v.t.* **3.** to free (someone) by the payment of a ransom.

rant (rant), *v.i., v.t.* **1.** to speak wildly and loudly. —*n.* **2.** wild and loud talk. **3.** ranting, extravagant, or violent talk. —**rant′er,** *n.* —**rant′ing·ly,** *adv.*

rap (rap), *v.,* **rapped, rap·ping,** *n.* —*v.t.* **1.** to strike with a quick, light blow. **2.** to utter sharply or vigorously. **3.** to criticize severely. —*v.i.* **4.** to knock quickly or lightly. **5.** *Slang.* **a.** to talk or chat. **b.** to discuss or argue. —*n.* **6.** a quick, light blow. **7.** blame or punishment, esp. for a crime. **8.** *Slang.* **a.** a talk or chat. **b.** a discussion or argument. **9. beat the rap,** *Slang.* to succeed in evading the penalty for a crime. —**rap′per,** *n* ra·pa·cious (rə pā′shəs), *adj.* **1.** given to seizing for plunder. **2.** inordinately greedy. **3.** subsisting on living prey —ra·pa′cious·ly, *adv.* —ra·pac′i·ty (-pas′i tē), ra·pa′cious·ness, *n.*

rape[1] (rāp), *n., v.,* raped, rap·ing. —*n.* **1.** a sexual act committed by force, esp. on a woman. **2.** *Literary.* the act of plundering in war. **3.** *Archaic.* the act of seizing and carrying away by force. —*v.t.* **4.** to commit rape on. **5.** *Literary.* to plunder (a place) in war. **6.** *Archaic.* to seize and carry away by force. —*v.i.* **7.** to commit rape. —rap′er, *n.* —rap′ist, *n.*

rape[2] (rāp), *n.* a plant whose leaves are used for food for hogs, sheep, etc.

Raph·a·el (raf′ē əl, -rā′fē-, rä′fī el′), *n.* 1483–1520, Italian painter.

rap·id (rap′id), *adj.* **1.** moving, happening, or progressing with great speed. —*n.* **2.** Usually, **rapids.** a part of a river where the current runs swiftly. —ra·pid·i·ty (rə pid′i tē), rap′id·ness, *n.* —rap′id·ly, *adv.* —Syn. 1. fast, quick, swift.

rap′id eye′ move′ment. See REM.

rap′id trans′it, a system of rapid mass transportation in a metropolitan area, as the subway.

ra·pi·er (rā′pē ər), *n.* a small sword, esp. of the 18th century, having a narrow blade and used for thrusting. —ra′pi·ered, *adj.*

rap·ine (rap′in), *n. Literary.* the forcible taking of property.

rap·port (ra pōr′, -pôr′), *n.* a harmonious or sympathetic relationship.

rap·proche·ment (Fr. ʀA pROsh mäN′), *n.* an establishment of harmonious relations, as between nations.

rap·scal·lion (rap skal′yən), *n. Archaic.* a rascal or rogue.

rap′ ses′sion, *Slang.* a group discussion, attended esp. by people with specific problems or complaints.

rap′ sheet′, *Slang.* a law-enforcement record of arrest or conviction.

rapt (rapt), *adj.* **1.** deeply engrossed or absorbed. **2.** carried away with emotion. —rapt′ly, *adv.* —rapt′ness, *n.*

rap·ture (rap′chər), *n.* the state of being carried away with deep emotion, esp. joy or love. —rap′tur·ous, *adj.* —Syn. bliss, delight, ecstasy.

ra·ra a·vis (râr′ə ā′vis), *Latin.* a rare person or thing. [< L: rare bird]

rare[1] (râr), *adj.,* rar·er, rar·est. **1.** seldom found. **2.** unusually great or fine. **3.** not dense, as air. —rare′ly, *adv.* —rare′ness, rar·i·ty (râr′i tē), *n.* —Syn. 1. exceptional, infrequent, uncommon.

rare[2] (râr), *adj.,* rar·er, rar·est. (of meat) cooked just slightly. —rare′ness, *n.*

rare·bit (râr′bit), *n.* See **Welsh rabbit.**

rare′-earth′ el′ement (râr′ûrth′), any of a group of closely related metallic elements of atomic numbers 57 to 71 inclusive.

rar·e·fy (râr′ə fī′), *v.t., v.i.,* -fied, -fy·ing. to make or become rare or less dense. —rar′e·fac′tion (-fak′shən), *n.*

rar·ing (râr′ing), *adj. Informal.* very eager or anxious: *raring to go.*

ras·cal (ras′kəl), *n.* **1.** a dishonestly shrewd and tricky person. **2.** a mischievous person or animal. —ras·cal·i·ty (ra skal′i tē), *n.* —ras′cal·ly, *adj., adv.*

rash[1] (rash), *adj.* acting too hastily or without due consideration. —rash′ly, *adv.* —rash′ness, *n.* —Syn. foolhardy, impetuous, reckless.

rash[2] (rash), *n.* **1.** an eruption on the skin. **2.** a flurry of unpleasant occurrences.

rash·er (rash′ər), *n.* **1.** a thin slice of bacon or ham for frying or broiling. **2.** a portion or serving of such slices.

rasp (rasp, räsp), *v.t.* **1.** to scrape with a rough instrument. **2.** to grate upon or irritate. —*v.i.* **3.** to scrape or grate. **4.** to make a grating sound. —*n.* **5.** a coarse file having small, pointed teeth. **6.** a rasping sound. —rasp′er, *n.* —rasp′ing·ly, *adv.* —rasp′y, *adj.*

rasp·ber·ry (raz′ber′ē, -bə rē, räz′-), *n., pl.* -ries. **1.** the small, rounded, red, black, or pale-yellow fruit of a prickly shrub. **2.** its shrub. **3.** *Slang.* a rude sound made with the tongue between the lips to express scorn, dislike, etc.

ras·ter (ras′tər), *n.* an area upon which the image is projected in the picture tube of a television set.

rat (rat), *n., v.,* rat·ted, rat·ting. —*n.* **1.** a long-tailed rodent resembling the mouse but much larger. **2.** *Slang.* a person who betrays or abandons his or her associates, esp. an informer. **3.** smell a rat, to suspect treachery. —*v.i.* **4.** to hunt or catch rats. **5.** *Slang.* to turn informer.

ratch·et (rach′it), *n.* **1.** a bar or wheel with teeth that are engaged by a pawl, usually to prevent reversal of motion. **2.** a mechanism consisting of such a bar or wheel with the pawl.

ratch′et wheel′, a toothed wheel into which a pawl drops or catches.

rate[1] (rāt), *n., v.,* rat·ed, rat·ing. —*n.* **1.** a certain quantity or amount of something considered in relation to a unit of something else. **2.** a fixed price per unit of quantity. **3.** a degree of speed. **4.** rank or rating. **5.** at any rate, a. at all events. b. at least. —*v.t.* **6.** to estimate the value of. **7.** to consider or regard. **8.** *Informal.* to deserve or merit. —*v.i.* **9.** to have value, standing, etc. **10.** to rank very high. —rat′er, *n.*

rate² (rāt), v.t., v.i., **rat·ed, rat·ing.** to scold severely. —**rat′er,** n.

rath·er (rath′ər, räth′ər), adv. **1.** to a certain extent. **2.** more properly or justly. **3.** more readily or willingly. **4.** more correctly. **5.** on the contrary.

raths·kel·ler (rät′skel′ər, rat′-, räth′-), n. a restaurant of the German style, usually located below street level.

rat·i·fy (rat′ə fī′), v.t., **-fied, -fy·ing.** to confirm by expressing approval or formal sanction. —**rat′i·fi·ca′tion,** n. —**rat′i·fi′er,** n.

rat·ing (rā′tĭng), n. **1.** classification according to grade or rank. **2.** a grade in the classification of position. **3.** the credit standing of a person or firm. **4.** Radio and Television. a percentage indicating the number of listeners to or viewers of a specific program.

ra·tio (rā′shō, -shē ō′), n., pl. **-ti·os. 1.** the relation between two similar magnitudes in respect to the number of times the first contains the second. **2.** proportional relation. [< L ratio calculation]

ra·ti·oc·i·nate (rash′ē os′ə nāt′), v.i., **-nat·ed, -nat·ing.** to carry on a process of logical reasoning. —**ra′ti·oc·i·na′tion,** n. —**ra′ti·oc′i·na·tive,** adj. —**ra′ti·oc′i·na·tor,** n.

ra·tion (rash′ən, rā′shən), n. **1.** a fixed allowance of provisions or food, esp. for a soldier or sailor. **2.** an allotted amount of anything. **3. rations,** provisions. —v.t. **4.** to supply as rations. **5.** to provide with rations. **6.** to restrict the consumption of (a commodity, food, etc.).

ra·tion·al (rash′ə nəl), adj. **1.** based on reason. **2.** able to think and reason. **3.** having sound judgment. **4.** Math. of or pertaining to a rational number. —n. **5.** Math. See **rational number.** —**ra′tion·al′i·ty** (-nal′i tē), n. —**ra′tion·al·ly,** adv.

ra·tion·ale (rash′ə nal′), n. **1.** a reasoned exposition of principles. **2.** the fundamental body of reasons serving to account for something.

ra·tion·al·ism (rash′ə nəl iz′əm), n. the principle of accepting reason as the supreme authority in matters of opinion, belief, or conduct. —**ra′tion·al·ist,** n. —**ra′tion·al·is′tic,** adj. —**ra′tion·al·is′ti·cal·ly,** adv.

ra·tion·al·ize (rash′ə nəl īz′, rash′-nəl′īz′), v.t., v.i. **-ized, -iz·ing. 1.** to make or be rational or conformable to reason. **2.** to explain in a rational or rationalistic manner. **3.** to invent plausible explanations for (acts, opinions, etc., that actually have other causes). —**ra′tion·al·i·za′tion,** n. —**ra′tion·al·iz′er,** n.

ra′tional num′ber, Math. a number that can be expressed exactly by a ratio of two integers.

rat·line (rat′lin), n. any of the small ropes that join the shrouds of a ship horizontally and serve as steps for going aloft. Also, **rat′lin.**

rat′ race′, Informal. any exhausting, unremitting activity or regular routine.

rats·bane (rats′bān′), n. rat poison.

rat·tan (ra tan′), n. **1.** a climbing palm having long, tough stems. **2.** these stems, used for wickerwork, canes, etc.

rat·ter (rat′ər), n. an animal used for catching rats, as a terrier or cat.

rat·tle (rat′°l), v., **-tled, -tling,** n. —v.i. **1.** to make a number of short, sharp sounds rapidly. **2.** to move or go rapidly with such sounds. **3.** to talk rapidly. —v.t. **4.** to cause to rattle. **5.** to say or perform in a rapid, lively, or facile manner. **6.** to disconcert or confuse. —n. **7.** a number of rapid short, sharp sounds. **8.** a baby's toy that rattles when shaken. **9.** any of the horny rings at the end of a rattlesnake's tail. —**rat′tly,** adj.

rat·tle·brain (rat′°l brān′), n. an empty-headed, talkative person. —**rat′tle·brained′,** adj.

rat·tler (rat′lər), n. a rattlesnake.

rat·tle·snake (rat′°l snāk′), n. a venomous American snake having a rattle at the end of the tail, with which it produces a rattling sound.

rat·tle·trap (rat′°l trap′), n. a shaky, rattling object, as a rickety vehicle.

rat·tling (rat′lĭng), Informal. —adj. **1.** remarkably lively or fast. —adv. **2.** very: a rattling good time.

rat·trap (rat′trap′), n. **1.** a device for catching rats. **2.** a run-down, filthy place.

rat·ty (rat′ē), adj., **-ti·er, -ti·est. 1.** full of rats. **2.** wretched or shabby.

rau·cous (rô′kəs), adj. **1.** unpleasantly harsh or strident. **2.** rowdy or disorderly. —**rau′cous·ly,** adv. —**rau′cous·ness,** n.

raun·chy (rôn′chē, roun′-, rän′-), adj. Slang. **1.** dirty and slovenly. **2.** obscene or smutty. —**raun′chi·ness,** n.

rau·wol·fi·a (rô wŏŏl′fē ə), n. **1.** an extract from the roots of a tropical tree of India, used to treat hypertension and as a sedative. **2.** its tree.

rav·age (rav′ij), v., **-aged, -ag·ing,** n. —v.t., v.i. **1.** to cause violent destruction (to), as by an invading army. **2.** to affect grievously. —n. **3.** violent destruction. **4.** ravaging action. —**rav′ag·er,** n. —**Syn. 1, 2.** devastate, ruin.

rave (rāv), v., **raved, rav·ing,** n., adj. —v.i. **1.** to talk wildly, as in delirium. **2.** to make a furious disturbance. **3.** to express extravagant praise. —n. **4.** an act of raving. **5.** extravagant praise. —adj. **6.** full of praise.

rav·el (rav′əl), *v.*, **-eled, -el·ing** or **-elled, -el·ling**, *n.* —*v.t.* 1. to unwind or disentangle the threads of (cloth, rope, etc.). 2. to tangle or entangle. 3. to confuse or perplex. —*v.i.* 4. to become raveled. 5. a raveled part. 6. to become tangled. —*n.* 7. a tangle or complication.

ra·ven (rā′vən), *n.* 1. a large black bird of the crow family having a loud, harsh call. —*adj.* 2. of a lustrous black.

rav·en·ing (rav′ə niñg), *adj.* greedy for prey.

rav·en·ous (rav′ə nəs), *adj.* 1. extremely rapacious. 2. extremely hungry. 3. extremely eager, as for satisfaction. —**rav′en·ous·ly,** *adv.* —**rav′en·ous·ness,** *n.*

ra·vine (rə vēn′), *n.* a narrow, steepsided valley, esp. one formed by a river.

rav·ing (rā′viñg), *adj.* 1. talking deliriously. 2. *Informal.* extraordinary or remarkable: *She's a raving beauty.* —*adv.* 3. furiously or wildly. —**rav′ing·ly,** *adv.*

ra·vi·o·li (rav′ē ō′lē, rä′vē-), *n.* small, square envelopes of pasta filled with meat or cheese.

rav·ish (rav′ish), *v.t.* 1. to fill with strong emotion, esp. joy. 2. *Archaic.* to seize and carry off by force. 3. *Literary.* to rape (a woman). —**rav′ish·er,** *n.* —**rav′ish·ment,** *n.*

rav·ish·ing (rav′i shiñg), *adj.* enchantingly pleasing and attractive.

raw (rô), *adj.* 1. uncooked, as food. 2. not finished or manufactured: *raw cotton.* 3. painfully exposed, as a wound. 4. crude in quality or character. 5. inexperienced or untrained: *a raw recruit.* 6. brutally harsh or unfair: *a raw deal.* 7. damp and chilly, as the weather. 8. not diluted, as alcoholic spirits: *raw whiskey.* —*n.* 9. **in the raw, a.** in the natural or unrefined state. **b.** *Slang.* in the nude. —**raw′ly,** *adv.* —**raw′ness,** *n.*

raw-boned (rô′bōnd′), *adj.* lean and bony.

raw·hide (rô′hīd′), *n.* 1. the untanned skin of cattle. 2. a rope or whip made of this.

ray¹ (rā), *n.* 1. a narrow beam of light or other radiation. 2. any form of radiant energy or a stream of radioactive particles. 3. any of the lines or streams in which light appears to radiate from a luminous body. 4. a straight line emanating

from a single point. 5. a slight amount: *a ray of hope.*

ray² (rā), *n.* a fish having a flattened body, very large, flat fins, and a slender whiplike tail.

ray·on (rā′on), *n.* 1. a fiber made by dissolving cellulose and forcing it through tiny holes. 2. fabric made of such fibers.

raze (rāz), *v.t.*, **razed, raz·ing.** to tear down, as an old building.

ra·zor (rā′zər), *n.* a sharp-edged instrument used esp. for shaving.

razz (raz), *Slang.* —*v.t.* 1. to make fun of. —*n.* 2. raspberry (def. 3).

razz·le-dazz·le (raz′əl daz′əl), *n. Informal.* exciting, showy, and often confusing activity. Also called **razz·ma·tazz** (raz′mə taz′).

Rb, rubidium.

r.b.c., red blood cell.

R.B.I., *Baseball.* run batted in; runs batted in.

R.C., 1. Red Cross. 2. Roman Catholic.

RCAF, Royal Canadian Air Force.

R.C.Ch., Roman Catholic Church.

rcd., 1. received. 2 record.

RCMP, Royal Canadian Mounted Police.

rcpt., receipt.

rct, 1. receipt. 2. *Mil.* recruit.

Rd., Road.

rd., 1. road. 2. rod; rods. 3. round.

R.D., rural delivery.

Re, rhenium.

re¹ (rā, rē), *n. Music.* the second tone of a diatonic scale.

re² (rē), *prep. Chiefly Law and Com.* with reference to.

re-, a prefix meaning: **a.** again or anew: *rewrite.* **b.** back or backward: *repay.*

REA, Rural Electrification Administration.

reach (rēch), *v.t.* 1. to get to or as far as. 2. to succeed in touching or getting hold of. 3. to stretch or hold out. 4. to establish communication with. 5. to amount to. 6. to succeed in affecting or influencing. —*v.i.* 7. to make a stretch, as with the hand. 8. to try to touch or seize something. 9. to extend in operation or effect. 10. to penetrate or carry: *as far as the eye could reach.* —*n.* 11. the act or an instance of reaching. 12. the extent or distance of reaching. 13. range of effective action, power, or capacity. 14. a continuous stretch or extent of something.

---

re′a·ban′don, *v.t.*
re′ab·sorb′, *v.t.*
re′ab·sorp′tion, *n.*
re′ac·cede′, *v.t.*, **-ced·ed, -ced·ing.**
re·ac′cent, *v.t.*

re′ac·cept′, *v.t.*
re·ac′cli·mate′, *v.*, **-mat·ed, -mat·ing.**
re′ac·com′mo·date′, *v.*, **-dat·ed, -dat·ing.**
re′ac·com′pa·ny, *v.t.*,

-nied, -ny·ing.
re′ac·cred′it, *v.t.*
re′ac·cuse′, *v.t.*, **-cused, -cus·ing.**
re′ac·cus′tom, *v.t.*

re·act (rē akt′), *v.i.* **1.** to act in response to an agent or influence. **2.** to act reciprocally upon each other. **3.** to act in a reverse manner, esp. so as to return to a prior condition. **4.** to act in opposition. **5.** to respond to a stimulus **6.** to undergo a chemical reaction.

re·ac·tance (rē ak′təns), *n.* *Elect.* the opposition of inductance and capacitance to alternating current.

re·ac·tant (rē ak′tənt), *n.* any substance that undergoes a chemical reaction.

re·ac·tion (rē ak′shən), *n.* **1.** an action in a reverse direction or manner. **2.** movement in the direction of extreme political conservatism. **3.** action in response to some influence, event, etc. **4.** action in response to a stimulus, as of a nerve or muscle. **5.** the action of chemical agents upon each other. **6.** a change in the nucleus of an atom.

re·ac·tion·ar·y (rē ak′shə ner′ē), *adj., n., pl.* -**ar·ies.** —*adj.* **1.** of, marked by, or favoring reaction, esp. in politics. —*n.* **2.** a person who is reactionary, esp. in politics.

re·ac·ti·vate (rē ak′tə vāt′), *v.t., v.i.,* -**vat·ed,** -**vat·ing.** to make or become active or activated again. —**re·ac′ti·va′tion,** *n.*

re·ac·tive (rē ak′tiv), *adj.* **1.** tending to react. **2.** of or characterized by reaction. —**re·ac′tive·ly,** *adv.* —**re′ac·tiv′i·ty,** *n.*

re·ac·tor (rē ak′tər), *n.* **1.** a person or thing that reacts. **2.** a vat in which an industrial chemical reaction takes place. **3.** an apparatus in which a nuclear-fission chain reaction can be initiated and controlled, for generating heat or producing useful radiation.

read¹ (rēd), *v.,* **read** (red), **read·ing** (rē′ding). —*v.t.* **1.** to look at carefully so as to understand the meaning of (something written or printed). **2.** to utter aloud (something written or printed). **3.** to understand the meaning of (signs, symbols, etc.). **4.** to foresee or predict. **5.** to register or indicate, as a thermometer. **6.** (in a computer) to obtain (information), esp. from external units, as punch cards. **7.** *Brit.* to study at a university: *to read law.* **8.** *Informal.* to hear or understand clearly, esp. in radio communication. —*v.i.* **9.** to

read written or printed matter. **10.** to obtain knowledge by reading. **11.** to have a certain wording. **12.** read **into,** to interpret in a particular or different way. **13.** read **out of,** to oust from (a political party or other group). —**read′a·ble,** *adj.* —**read′a·bil′i·ty, read′a·ble·ness,** *n.* —**read′a·bly,** *adv.* —**read′er,** *n.*

read² (red), *adj.* having knowledge gained by reading: *a well-read person.*

read·er·ship (rē′dər ship′), *n.* the people who read a particular book, newspaper, etc.

read·ing (rē′ding), *n.* **1.** the action of a person who reads. **2.** the recital of something written. **3.** the interpretation given in the performance of a dramatic part, musical composition, etc. **4.** matter read or for reading. **5.** the form of a given passage in a particular text. **6.** an interpretation given to anything. **7.** the indication of a graduated instrument.

read·out (rēd′out′), *n.* **1.** the output of information from a computer. **2.** such information represented in printed form. **3.** reading (def. 7).

read·y (red′ē), *adj.,* **read·i·er, read·i·est,** *v.,* **read·ied, read·y·ing,** *n.* —*adj.* **1.** completely prepared for action or use. **2.** willing or not hesitant. **3.** prompt in understanding, replying, etc. **4.** inclined or disposed. **5.** likely at any moment. **6.** immediately available for use: *ready money.* —*v.t.* **7.** to make ready. —*n.* **8.** the ready, the condition or position of being ready. —**read′i·ly,** *adv.* —**read′i·ness,** *n.*

read·y-made (red′ē mād′), *adj.* made in advance for sale rather than to order.

read′y room′, a room in which crew members of an aircraft await their orders for takeoff.

re·a·gent (rē ā′jənt), *n.* a chemical substance that, because of the reactions it causes, is used in analysis and synthesis.

re·al (rē′əl, rēl), *adj.* **1.** existing as a fact rather than imaginary. **2.** not artificial. **3.** *Law.* of or pertaining to immovable or fixed things, as land and buildings. —*adv.* **4.** *Informal.* very or extremely. —*n.* **5.** for real, *Slang.* **a.** in reality. **b.** real or actual. —**re′al·ness,** *n.* —Syn. **1.** actual, true. **2.** authentic, genuine.

---

re′ac·quaint′, *v.t.*
re′ac·quaint′ance, *n.*
re′ac·quire′, *v.t.,* -quired, -quir·ing.
re′ac·qui·si′tion, *n.*
re′a·dapt′, *v.t.*
re′ad·ap·ta′tion, *n.*

re′ad·dress′, *v.t.,* -dressed or -drest, -dres·sing.
re′ad·journ′, *v.*
re′ad·journ′ment, *n.*
re′ad·just′, *v.t.*
re′ad·just′ment, *n.*

re′ad·mis′sion, *n.*
re′ad·mit′, *v.,* -mit·ted, -mit·ting.
re′ad·mit′tance, *n.*
re′a·dopt′, *v.t.*
re′af·firm′, *v.t.*
re′af·fir·ma′tion, *n.*

re′al estate′ (rē′əl, rēl), property, in land and buildings. —**re′al-es-tate′,** *adj.*

re·al·ism (rē′ə liz′əm), *n.* **1.** the tendency to view or represent things as they really are. **2.** the representation in literature or art of things as they really are. —**re′al-ist,** *n., adj.* —**re′al·is·tic,** *adj.* —**re′al·is′ti·cal·ly,** *adv.*

re·al·i·ty (rē al′i tē), *n., pl.* **-ties.** **1.** the state or quality of being real. **2.** a real thing or fact. **3.** *Philos.* the external world that exists independently of perception. **4. in reality,** really or actually.

re·al·ize (rē′ə līz′), *v.,* **-ized, -iz·ing.** —*v.t.* **1.** to grasp or understand clearly. **2.** to make real or fulfill, as a plan. **3.** to obtain as a profit for oneself. **4.** to bring as proceeds, as from a sale. **5.** *Brit.* to convert into cash, as securities. —**re′al·iz′a·ble,** *adj.* —**re′al·i·za′tion,** *n.* —**re′al·iz′er,** *n.*

re·al·ly (rē′ə lē, rē′lē), *adv.* **1.** actually or truly. **2.** indeed.

realm (relm), *n.* **1.** a royal domain. **2.** any field or sphere.

re′al num′ber (rē′əl, rēl), *Math.* a rational number or the limit of a sequence of rational numbers.

re·al·po·li·tik (rē äl′pō′li tēk′), *n.* political realism, esp. policy based on power rather than on ideals. [< G]

re′al time′ (rē′əl, rēl), the actual time elapsed in the performance of a computation by a computer. —**re′al-time′,** *adj.*

Re·al·tor (rē′əl tər, -tôr′), *n. Trademark.* a person in the real-estate business who is a member of the National Association of Realtors.

re·al·ty (rē′əl tē), *n.* See **real estate.**

ream¹ (rēm), *n.* **1.** a quantity of paper consisting of variously 480, 500, or 516 sheets. **2.** Usually, **reams.** a large quantity, as of writing.

ream² (rēm), *v.t.* **1.** to enlarge (a bored hole) with a reamer. **2.** to clean or remove with a reamer.

ream·er (rē′mər), *n.* a sharp-edged rotary tool for finishing or enlarging holes drilled in metal.

reap (rēp), *v.t., v.i.* **1.** to cut (wheat, etc.) with a sickle, scythe, or machine, as in harvest. **2.** to gather or

take (a harvest, etc.). **3.** to get as a return or result.

reap·er (rē′pər), *n.* **1.** a machine for cutting standing grain. **2.** a person who reaps.

rear² (rēr), *n.* **1.** the back part. **2.** the space or position behind. **3.** the hindmost portion of an army, fleet, etc. **4. bring up the rear,** to follow behind. —*adj.* **5.** of or situated at the rear.

rear² (rēr), *v.t.* **1.** to take care of and support up to maturity, esp. a child. **2.** to breed or cultivate (animals or plants). **3.** to raise by building. **4.** to raise upright. —*v.i.* **5.** to rise on the hind legs, as a horse. **6.** to start up in anger. **7.** *Literary.* to rise high, as a building or tower. —**rear′er,** *n.*

rear′ ad′miral, *U.S. Navy, Coast Guard.* a commissioned officer next in rank below a vice admiral.

rear·most (rēr′mōst′), *adj.* farthest in the rear.

rear·ward (rēr′wərd), *adj.* **1.** located at or directed toward the rear. —*adv.* **2.** Also, **rear′wards.** toward or in the rear.

rea·son (rē′zən), *n.* **1.** a basis or circumstance explaining some belief, action, fact, or event. **2.** a statement presented in justification or explanation. **3.** the mental powers concerned with forming conclusions or inferences. **4.** sound judgment. **5.** soundness of mind. **6. stand to reason,** to be clear or logical —*v.i., v.t.* **7.** to think (through) in a logical manner. **8.** to argue or conclude. —**rea′son·er,** *n.* —**rea′son·ing,** *n.*

—**Usage.** Careful writers and speakers avoid the redundant expression "the reason is because." Instead, use "the reason is that": *The reason he isn't coming is that* (not *because*) *he dislikes parties.*

rea·son·a·ble (rē′zə nə bəl, rēz′nə-), *adj.* **1.** in accord with reason. **2.** not exceeding the limit prescribed by reason. **3.** moderate in price. **4.** endowed with reason. —**rea′son·a·ble·ness, rea′son·a·bil′i·ty,** *n.* —**rea′son·a·bly,** *adv.* —**Syn. 1.** judicious, logical, rational, sensible. **2.** equitable, fair.

re′a·lign′, *v.*	**re′an·nex′,** *v.t.*	**re·ar′gue,** *v.,* -gued, -gu·ing.
re′a·lign′ment, *n.*	**re′ap·pear′,** *v.i.*	
re′al·lo·cate′, *v.t.,* -cat·ed, -cat·ing.	**re′ap·pear′ance,** *n.*	**re·arm′,** *v.t.*
re′al·lo·ca′tion, *n.*	**re′ap·pli·ca′tion,** *n.*	**re·ar′ma·ment,** *n.*
re′·al·ly′, *v.t., v.i.,* -lied, -ly·ing.	**re′ap·ply′,** *v.,* -plied, -ply·ing.	**re′a·rous′al,** *n.*
re′a·nal′y·sis, *n., pl.* -ses.	**re′ap·point′,** *v.t.*	**re′a·rouse′,** *v.,* -roused, -rous·ing.
re·an′a·lyze′, *v.t.,* -lyzed, -lyz·ing.	**re′ap·point′ment,** *n.*	**re′ar·range′,** *v.t.,* -ranged, -rang·ing.
re·an′i·mate′, *v.t.,* -mat·ed, -mat·ing.	**re′ap·por′tion,** *v.t.*	**re′ar·range′ment,** *n.*
	re′ap·por′tion·ment, *n.*	**re′ar·rest′,** *v.t., n.*
	re′ap·prais′al, *n.*	**re′as·cend′,** *v.*
	re′ap·praise′, *v.t.,* -praised, -prais·ing.	**re′as·cent′,** *n.*

re·as·sure (rē′ə shŏŏr′), *v.t.*, **-sured,** **-sur·ing.** **1.** to restore the confidence of. **2.** to assure again. **—re′as·sur′ance,** *n.* **—re′as·sur′ing·ly,** *adv.*

re·bate (rē′bāt, ri bāt′), *n.*, *v.*, **-bat·ed,** **-bat·ing.** **—n. 1.** a refund of part of the money paid for some service or charge. **—v.t. 2.** to allow a rebate of or on. **—re′bat·er,** *n.*

reb·el (*n.*, *adj.* reb′əl; *v.* ri bel′), *n.*, *adj.*, *v.*, **-belled,** **-bel·ling.** **—n. 1.** a person who engages in armed resistance against an established government. **2.** a person who resists any authority, control, or tradition. **—** *adj.* **3.** rebellious or defiant. **4.** of or pertaining to rebels. **—v.i. 5.** to act as a rebel. **6.** to show or feel utter repugnance.

re·bel·lion (ri bel′yən), *n.* **1.** armed resistance to one's government or ruler. **2.** resistance to or defiance of any authority. **—Syn. 1.** insurrection, mutiny, revolt.

re·bel·lious (ri bel′yəs), *adj.* **1.** resisting or tefying some authority. **2.** characteristic of rebels or rebellion. **—re·bel′lious·ly,** *adv.* **—re·bel′lious·ness,** *n.* **—Syn. 1.** defiant, insubordinate.

re·birth (rē bûrth′, rē′bûrth′), *n.* **1.** a new or second birth: *the rebirth of the soul.* **2.** a renewed existence, activity, or growth.

re·born (rē bôrn′), *adj.* having undergone rebirth.

re·bound (*v.* ri bound′; *n.* rē′bound′, ri bound′), *v.i.* **1.** to spring back from force of impact. **2.** to recover, as from discouragement. **—n. 3.** the act of rebounding. **4. on the rebound, a.** after a bounce off the ground. **b.** *Informal.* after being rejected by another: *to marry someone on the rebound.*

re·buff (*n.* ri buf′, rē′buf; *v.* ri buf′), *n.* **1.** an abrupt, often blunt refusal, as of a request or offer. **2.** a check to action or progress. **—v.t. 3.** to give a rebuff to.

re·buke (ri byōōk′), *v.*, **-buked, -buk·ing,** *n.* **—v.t. 1.** to express one's stern disapproval to. **—n. 2.** stern disapproval. **—re·buk′ing·ly,** *adv.*

re·bus (rē′bəs), *n.*, *pl.* **-bus·es.** a puzzle in which words or phrases are shown by pictures.

re·but (ri but′), *v.t.*, **-but·ted, -but·ting.** to refute by evidence or argument. **—re·but′tal** (-°l), *n.* **—re·but′ter,** *n.*

rec (rek), *n. Informal.* recreation.

rec., **1.** receipt. **2.** recipe. **3.** record. **4.** recorder. **5** recording.

re·cal·ci·trant (ri kal′si trənt), *adj.* **1.** obstinately defying authority or discipline. **2.** hard to deal with or manage. **—re·cal′ci·trance, re·cal′ci·tran·cy,** *n.* **—Syn.** intractable, unruly.

re·call (*v.* ri kôl′; *n.* ri kôl′, rē′kôl′), *v.t.* **1.** to bring back to conscious memory. **2.** to bring (one's thoughts, etc.) back to matters previously considered. **3.** to summon to return. **4.** to revoke or withdraw. **5.** (of a manufacturer) to call back (esp. an automobile) for inspection or repair of a defective part. **—n. 6.** an act of recalling. **7.** the ability to recall mentally. **8.** the removal or the right of removal of a public official from office by a vote of the people upon petition. **9.** the act of calling back (esp. an automobile) for inspection or repair of a defective part. **—re·call′a·ble,** *adj.*

re·cant (ri kant′), *v.t.* **1.** to withdraw (a belief, opinion, etc.), esp. formally. **—v.i. 2.** to make frank confession of one's mistake. **—re·can·ta·tion** (rē′kan tā′shən), *n.* **—re·cant′er,** *n.* **—re·cant′ing·ly,** *adv.*

re·cap¹ (*v.* rē′kap′, rē kap′; *n.* rē′kap′), *v.*, **-capped, -cap·ping,** *n.* **—v.t. 1.** to recondition (a worn tire) by adding a new strip of rubber and vulcanizing in a mold. **—n. 2.** a recapped tire. **—re·cap′pa·ble,** *adj.*

re·cap² (rē′kap′), *n.*, *v.*, **-capped, -cap·ping.** **—n. 1.** a recapitulation. **—v.t., v.i. 2.** to recapitulate.

---

re·as·sem′ble, *v.*, -bled, -bling.

re·as·sem′bly, *n.*, *pl.* -blies.

re·as·sert′, *v.t.*

re·as·ser′tion, *n.*

re·as·sess′, *v.t.*

re·as·sess′ment, *n.*

re·as·sign′, *v.t.*

re·as·sign′ment, *n.*

re·as·sim′i·late′, *v.*, -lat·ed. -lat·ing.

re·as·sim′i·la′tion, *n.*

re·as·sort′, *v.*

re·as·sort′ment, *n.*

re·as·sume′, *v.t.*, -sumed, -sum·ing.

re·as·sump′tion, *n.*

re·at·tach′, *v.*

re·at·tach′ment, *n.*

re·at·tain′, *v.t.*

re·at·tain′ment, *n.*

re·at·tempt′, *v.t.*

re·a·vow′, *v.t.*

re·a·wake′, *v.*, -woke or -waked, -wak·ing.

re·a·wak′en, *v.*

re·bap′tism, *n.*

re·bap′tize, *v.*, -tized, -tiz·ing.

re·bill′, *v.t.*

re·bind′, *v.*, -bound, -bind·ing.

re·boil′, *v.*

re·broad′en, *v.*

re·broad′cast′, *v.t.*, -cast or -cast·ed, -cast·ing, *n.*

re·build′, *v.t.*, *v.i.*, -built, -build·ing.

re·bur′i·al, *n.*

re·bur′y, *v.t.*, -bur·ied, -bur·y·ing.

re·but′ton, *v.t.*

re·cal′cu·late′, *v.t.*, -lat·ed, -lat·ing.

re·cap′i·tal·ize′, *v.t.*, -ized, -iz·ing.

re·ca·pit·u·late (rē'kə pich'ə lāt'), v.t., v.i., -lat·ed, -lat·ing. to review briefly or sum up (statements). —re'ca·pit'u·la'tion, n. —re'ca·pit'u·la'tive, adj.

re·cap·ture (rē kap'chər), v., -tured, -tur·ing, n. —v.t. 1. to capture again. 2. to recollect vividly. —n. 3. retaking by capture.

recd., received. Also, **rec'd.**

re·cede (ri sēd'), v.i., -ced·ed, -ced·ing. 1. to move back or away. 2. to become more distant. 3. to slope backward.

re·ceipt (ri sēt'), n. 1. a written acknowledgment of having received money or goods. 2. receipts, the amount or quantity received. 3. the act of receiving or state of being received. 4. Dial. a cooking recipe. —v.t. 5. to give a receipt for. 6. to mark as payment received.

re·ceiv·a·ble (ri sē'və bəl), adj. 1. awaiting receipt of payment. 2. capable of being received. —re·ceiv'a·bil'i·ty, n.

re·ceive (ri sēv'), v.t., -ceived, -ceiv·ing. 1. to have (something) given or sent to one. 2. to read or hear (a communication). 3. to experience or undergo: to receive attention. 4. to welcome or accept as a guest, member, etc. 5. to react to (news, etc.) in a specified manner. 6. to hold or bear (something applied, etc.). 7. to accept as true or valid.

re·ceiv·er (ri sē'vər), n. 1. a person or thing that receives. 2. a device that receives electric signals or waves and changes them into sound or pictures, as a television set. 3. Law. a person appointed by a court to take charge of a business or property involved in a lawsuit.

re·ceiv·er·ship (ri sē'vər ship'), n. Law. 1. the condition of being in the hands of a receiver. 2. the position or function of being a receiver.

receiv'ing line', a row formed by the host, hostess, and guests of honor for greeting guests, as at a wedding.

re·cent (rē'sənt), adj. 1. lately happening, done, or made. 2. of a time not long past. 3. (cap.) Geol. noting the present epoch, originating at the end of the glacial period and forming the latter half of the Quaternary. —n. 4. (cap.) Geol. the Recent epoch. —re'cent·ly, adv. —re'cent·ness, re'cen·cy, n.

re·cep·ta·cle (ri sep'tə kəl), n. 1. a container or holder for something. 2. Elect. an outlet.

re·cep·tion (ri sep'shən), n. 1. the act of receiving or state of being received. 2. a manner of being received. 3. a social affair at which persons are formally received. 4. the quality of a radio or television broadcast as received.

re·cep·tion·ist (ri sep'shə nist), n. a person employed to receive callers, as in an office.

re·cep·tive (ri sep'tiv), adj. 1. quick to receive knowledge, ideas, etc. 2. willing to receive suggestions, offers, etc. —re·cep'tive·ly, adv. —re·cep·tiv·i·ty (rē'sep tiv'i tē), re·cep'tive·ness, n.

re·cep·tor (ri sep'tər), n. See sense organ.

re·cess (ri ses', rē'ses), n. 1. a brief period during which work or study is stopped. 2. a space set in a wall. 3. Usually, recesses. a secluded or inner area or part. —v.t. 4. to set in a recess. 5. to make a recess in —v.i. 6. to take a recess.

re·ces·sion (ri sesh'ən), n. 1. the act of receding or withdrawing. 2. a mild but widespread slowdown in business activity. 3. a withdrawing procession, as at the end of a religious service. —re·ces'sion·ar'y, adj.

re·ces·sion·al (ri sesh'ə nəl), n. a hymn or other piece of music played at the end of a service.

re·ces·sive (ri ses'iv), adj. tending to go, move, or slant back.

re·cher·ché (rə shâr'shā), adj. 1. very rare and choice. 2. of studied or excessive refinement.

re·cid·i·vism (ri sid'ə viz'əm), n. repeated or habitual relapse, as into crime. —re·cid'i·vist, n. —re·cid'i·vis'tic, re·cid'i·vous, adj.

recip., 1. reciprocal. 2. reciprocity.

rec·i·pe (res'ə pē'), n. 1. a set of directions for preparing something to eat or drink. 2. a method to attain a desired end.

re·cip·i·ent (ri sip'ē ənt), n. 1. a person or thing that receives.

re·cip·ro·cal (ri sip'rə kəl), adj. 1. given or felt by each toward the other. 2. given or felt in return. 3. Gram. expressing mutual relation. —n. 4. something that is reciprocal to something else. 5. Math. the ratio of unity to a given quantity or expression. —re·cip'ro·cal·ly, adv. —Syn. 1. mutual.

re·cip·ro·cate (ri sip'rə kāt'), v.t., v.i., -cat·ed, -cat·ing. 1. to give or feel in return. 2. to give and take reciprocally. 3. to move alternately

---

re·cast', v., -cast, -cast·ing.
re'cast', n.
re·cel'e·brate', v., -brat·ed, -brat·ing.

re·charge', v.t., -charged, -charg·ing.
re·charge'a·ble, adj.
re·chart', v.t.

re·char'ter, v.t.
re·check', v.,
re'check, n.
re·chris'ten, v.t.

backward and forward. —re·cip'·ro·ca'tion, *n.* —re·cip'ro·ca·tive, *adj.*

rec·i·proc·i·ty (res'ə pros'i tē), *n.* 1. a reciprocal state or relation. 2. the relation or policy in commercial dealings between countries by which corresponding advantages or privileges are granted by each country.

re·cit·al (ri sīt'ºl), *n.* 1. a musical or dance performance, esp. one by individual performers. 2. a formal or public delivery of something memorized. 3. a detailed narration. —re·cit'al·ist, *n.*

rec·i·ta·tion (res'i tā'ghən), *n.* 1. an act of reciting. 2. recital (def. 2). 3. oral response by a pupil or pupils to a teacher on a prepared lesson.

rec·i·ta·tive (res'i tə tēv'), *n.* 1. a style of vocal music intermediate between speaking and singing. 2. a passage or piece in this style.

re·cite (ri sīt'), *v.t., v.i.,* -cit·ed, -cit·ing. 1. to repeat (something) from memory, esp. formally or publicly. 2. to tell in detail, as in class. 3. to repeat or answer a teacher's questions on (a lesson) in class. —re·cit'er, *n.*

reck·less (rek'lis), *adj.* rashly heedless of danger or consequences. —reck'less·ly, *adv.* —reck'less·ness, *n.*

reck·on (rek'ən), *v.t.* 1. *Chiefly Brit.* to count or figure out, often by simple arithmetic. 2. to regard as. 3. *Informal.* to think or suppose. —v.i. 4. *Chiefly Brit.* to count or figure out. 5. *Informal.* to depend or rely, as in expectation. 6. *Informal.* to think or suppose. 7. reckon with, a. to include in consideration. b. to deal with. —reck'on·er, *n.*

reck·on·ing (rek'ə niñg), *n.* 1. *Chiefly Brit.* the act of counting. 2. the settlement of accounts or claims. 3. See dead reckoning.

re·claim (ri klām'), *v.t.* 1. to bring into useful condition, as waste or neglected land. 2. to recover for use from refuse or waste material. 3. to bring back to right conduct. —rec·la·ma·tion (rek'lə mā'ghən), *n.*

ré·clame (*Fr.* Rā klAM'), *n.* French. public attention.

re·cline (ri klīn'), *v.i., v.t.,* -clined, -clin·ing. to lean or cause to lean back. —re·clin'er, *n.*

rec·luse (rek'lōos, ri klōos'), *n.* a person who lives in seclusion or

apart from society. —re·clu'sive, *adj.*

rec·og·ni·tion (rek'əg nish'ən), *n.* 1. the act of recognizing or state of being recognized. 2. approval and acceptance of one's work, efforts, etc., or an expression of this. 3. an official act by which one government acknowledges the existence of another.

re·cog·ni·zance (ri kog'ni zəns, -kon'i-), *n.* an obligation of record entered into before a court binding a person to do a particular act, as to appear in court at a certain date.

rec·og·nize (rek'əg nīz'), *v.t.,* -nized, -niz·ing. 1. to identify as something or someone previously seen or known. 2. to identify from knowledge of appearance or characteristics. 3. to perceive as real or true. 4. to acknowledge as the person entitled to speak, as in a legislature. 5. to acknowledge the existence of (a government) by establishing diplomatic relations. 6. to treat as valid. 7. to acknowledge acquaintance with. 8. to show appreciation of (service, merit, etc.), as by some reward. —rec'og·niz'a·ble, *adj.* —rec'og·niz'a·bly, *adv.*

re·coil (*v.* ri koil'; *n.* rē koil', rē·koil'), *v.i.* 1. to start or shrink back, as in alarm or disgust. 2. to spring back, as a firearm when discharged. —n. 3. an act of recoiling. —re·coil'less, *adj.* —Syn. 1. flinch, quail.

rec·ol·lect (rek'ə lekt'), *v.t., v.i.* to recover knowledge (of) by memory. —rec'ol·lec'tion, *n.*

re·com·bi·nant (rē kom'bi nənt), *adj.* of or resulting from new combinations of genetic material.

rec·om·mend (rek'ə mend'), *v.t.* 1. to present as worthy of acceptance, use, etc. 2. to urge as advisable. 3. to suggest (a choice) as appropriate. 4. to cause to seem desirable or attractive. —rec'om·men·da'tion, *n.* —rec'om·mend'a·to·ry (-də tôr'ē, -tôr'ē), *adj.* —rec'om·mend'er, *n.* —Syn. 1. approve, commend.

rec·om·pense (rek'əm pens'), *v.,* -pensed, -pens·ing, *n.* —v.t. 1. to repay or reward, as for aid. 2. to give compensation for (loss, etc.). —n. 3. a repayment or reward. 4. a compensation or requital.

re·cir'cu·late', *v.,* -lat·ed, -lat·ing.	re·coin'age, *n.*	re'com·mence', *v.,* -menced, -menc·ing.
re·clas'si·fy', *v.t.,* -fied, -fy·ing.	re·col'o·ni·za'tion, *n.*	re'com·mence'ment, *n.*
re·clean', *v.t.*	re·col'o·nize', *v.t.,* -nized, -niz·ing.	re'com·mis'sion, *v.*
re·clothe', *v.t.,* -clothed or -clad, -cloth·ing.	re·col'or, *v.t.*	re'com·mit', *v.t.,* -mit·ted, -mit·ting.
re·coin', *v.t.*	re·comb', *v.*	re'com·par'i·son, *n.*
	re'com·bine', *v.,* -bined, -bin·ing.	

rec·on·cile (rek′ən sīl′), *v.t.*, **-ciled, -cil·ing. 1.** to make friendly again, as after a quarrel. **2.** to cause to accept something not desired. **3.** to harmonize or settle (a quarrel, etc.) **4.** to bring into agreement or consistency. —**rec′on·cil′a·ble,** *adj.* —**rec′on·cile′ment,** *n.* —**rec′on·cil′er,** *n.* —**rec′on·cil·i·a′tion** (-sil′ē ā′shən), *n.* —**Syn. 1.** conciliate, placate.

rec·on·dite (rek′ən dīt′, ri kon′dīt), *adj.* **1.** beyond ordinary knowledge or understanding. **2.** little known or obscure. —**rec′on·dite′ly,** *adv.* —**rec′on·dite′ness,** *n.*

re·con·nais·sance (ri kon′i səns), *n.* a close examination or survey of a region, esp. for obtaining useful information regarding enemy troops.

re·con·noi·ter (rē′kə noi′tər, rek′ə-), *v.t., v.i.* to make a reconnaissance (of). Also, *Brit.*, **rec′on·noi′tre.**

re·con·sid·er (rē′kən sid′ər), *v.t., v.i.* to consider (a matter) again, esp. with a view to change of decision or action. —**re′con·sid′er·a′tion,** *n.*

re·con·sti·tute (rē kon′sti tōōt′, -tyōōt′), *v.t.,* **-tut·ed, -tut·ing.** to constitute again, esp. to add water to dry solids in making a liquid product, as milk.

re·con·struct (rē′kən strukt′), *v.t.* **1.** to construct again. **2.** to re-create in the mind from given or available information.

re·con·struc·tion (rē′kən struk′shən), *n.* **1.** the act of reconstructing or state of being reconstructed. **2.** (*cap.*) **a.** the reintegration of the former Confederate States to the Union after the Civil War. **b.** the period during which this happened, 1865–77.

re·cord (*v.* ri kôrd′; *n., adj.* rek′ərd), *v.t.* **1.** to set down in writing for future use or evidence. **2.** to show or register. **3.** to register (sound or pictures) on a disk or tape for later reproduction. —*n.* **4.** the act of recording or state of being recorded. **5.** a written or printed account of facts or events. **6.** the facts known about a person or thing. **7.** a disk on which sound is recorded for playing on a phonograph. **8.** the greatest achievement or performance of its kind to date. **9. off the record,** not for publication. **10. on record,** ex-

isting in a publication, document, file, etc. —*adj.* **11.** making or constituting a record.

re·cord·er (ri kôr′dər), *n.* **1.** a person who records, esp. as an official duty. **2.** a device for recording sound, esp. on tape or cassette. **3.** a flute having a whistlelike mouthpiece.

re·cord·ing (ri kôr′ding), *n.* **1.** sound recorded on a disk or tape. **2.** such a disk or tape.

re·cord·ist (ri kôr′dist, -kôr′-), *n.* a technician who records sound, esp. on motion-picture film.

rec′ord play′er, an electric machine for playing phonograph records automatically.

re·count (*v.* rē kount′; *n.* rē′kount′, rē kount′), *v.t.* **1.** to count again. —*n.* **2.** a second count, as of votes in an election.

re·count (ri kount′), *v.t.* **1.** to tell in detail. **2.** to tell one by one.

re·coup (ri kōōp′), *v.t.* **1.** to get back an equivalent of (something lost). **2.** to regain or recover. **3.** to reimburse or indemnify.

re·course (rē′kōrs, -kôrs, ri kōrs′, -kôrs′), *n.* **1.** a turning to a person or thing for help or protection. **2.** a person or thing turned to for help or protection. **3. without recourse,** (of an endorser of a check) with no liability to pay in case of default by the original issuer.

re·cov·er (rē kuv′ər), *v.t.* **1.** to get back or regain. **2.** to make up for or make good. **3.** to regain the strength or control of (oneself). **4.** to regain (a useful substance) as from refuse material. —*v.i.* **5.** to regain health, strength, or control. **6.** *Law.* to obtain a favorable judgment in a suit. —**re·cov′er·a·ble,** *adj.* —**re·cov′er·y,** *n.* —**Syn. 5.** mend, recuperate.

recpt, receipt.

rec·re·ant (rek′rē ənt), *Literary.* —*adj.* **1.** unfaithful to duties. **2.** cowardly or craven. —*n.* **3.** a traitor. **4.** a coward. —**rec′re·ance, rec′re·an·cy,** *n.* —**rec′re·ant·ly,** *adv.*

rec·re·ate (rek′rē āt′), *v.t.,* **-at·ed, -at·ing.** to create anew. —**re′·cre·a′·tion,** *n.* —**re′·cre·a′tive,** *adj.*

rec·re·ate (rek′rē āt′), *v.t.,* **-at·ed, -at·ing.** to restore or refresh physically or mentally. —**rec′re·a′tive,** *adj.*

---

re·com·pose′, *v.t.,* -posed, -pos·ing.
re·com·pound′, *v.*
re·con·cen′trate, *v.,* -trat·ed, -trat·ing.
re′con·cen·tra′tion, *n.*
re′con·den·sa′tion, *n.*
re·con·dense′, *v.,* -densed, -dens·ing.
re′con·di′tion, *v.t.*
re′con·firm′, *v.t.*

re′con·fir·ma′tion, *n.*
re′con·nect′, *v.t.*
re·con′quer, *v.t.*
re·con′quest, *n.*
re·con′se·crate′, *v.t.,* -crat·ed, -crat·ing.
re′con·se·cra′tion, *n.*
re·con·sign′, *v.t.*
re′con·sign′ment, *n.*
re′con·sol′i·date′, *v.,* -dat·ed, -dat·ing.

re′con·test′, *v.*
re′con·tract′, *v.*
re′con·vene′, *v.,* -vened, -ven·ing.
re′con·vert′, *v.t.*
re′con·vey′, *v.t.*
re·cook′, *v.t.*
re·cop′y, *v.t.,* -cop·ied, -cop·y·ing.
re·crate′, *v.t.,* -crat·ed, -crat·ing.

rec·re·a·tion (rek′rē ā′shən), *n.* a pastime, sport, or exercise as a means to refresh one's body or mind. —**rec′re·a′tion·al**, *adj.*

re·crim·i·nate (ri krim′ə nāt′), *v.t.*, **-nat·ed, -nat·ing.** to bring a countercharge against an accuser. —**re·crim′i·na′tion**, *n.* —**re·crim′i·na′tive, re·crim′i·na·to·ry** (-nē tōr′ē, -tôr′ē), *adj.*

re·cru·des·cence (rē′krōō des′əns), *n.* a fresh outbreak, esp. of something bad or unwanted. —**re′cru·des′cent**, *adj.*

re·cruit (ri krōōt′), *n.* **1.** a newly enlisted or drafted member of the armed forces. **2.** a new member of any organization. —*v.t., v.i.* **3.** to enlist for military service. **4.** to engage or hire (new employees, members, etc.). **5.** *Rare.* to renew or restore (the health or strength). —**re·cruit′er**, *n.* —**re·cruit′ment**, *n.*

Rec. Sec., Recording Secretary.

rect., 1. receipt. **2.** rectangle. **3.** rectangular. **4.** rectified. **5.** rector. **6.** rectory.

rec·tal (rek′t°l), *adj.* of or for the rectum. —**rec′tal·ly**, *adv.*

rec·tan·gle (rek′tang′gəl), *n.* a parallelogram having four right angles. —**rec·tan′gu·lar** (-gyə lər), *adj.*

rec·ti·fy (rek′tə fī′), *v.t.*, **-fied, -fy·ing. 1.** to put or set right. **2.** *Elect.* to change (an alternating current) into a direct current. —**rec′ti·fi′a·ble**, *adj.* —**rec′ti·fi·ca′tion**, *n.* —**rec′ti·fi′er**, *n.* —**Syn. 1.** correct, redress, remedy.

rec·ti·lin·e·ar (rek′t°lin′ē ər), *adj.* **1.** forming a straight line. **2.** formed by straight lines.

rec·ti·tude (rek′ti tōōd′, -tyōōd′), *n.* **1.** rightness of principle or conduct. **2.** correctness of judgment.

rec·to (rek′tō), *n., pl.* **-tos.** *Print.* a right-hand page.

rec·tor (rek′tər), *n.* **1.** a member of the clergy for a parish. **2.** the head of certain universities, colleges, and schools. —**rec′tor·ate** (-it), *n.* —**rec·to′ri·al** (-tōr′ē əl, -tôr′-), *adj.*

rec·to·ry (rek′tə rē), *n., pl.* **-ries.** a rector's residence.

rec·tum (rek′təm), *n., pl.* **-tums, -ta** (-tə). the lowest section of the intestine, ending in the anus.

re·cum·bent (ri kum′bənt), *adj.* lying down.

re·cu·per·ate (ri kōō′pə rāt′, -kyōō′-), *v.i., v.t.*, **-at·ed, -at·ing. 1.** to regain or restore to health or strength. **2.**

to recover (financial loss). —**re·cu′per·a′tion**, *n.* —**re·cu′per·a′tive,** *adj.*

re·cur (ri kûr′), *v.i.*, **-curred, -cur·ring. 1.** to occur again, as an event or experience. **2.** to return, as in one's thoughts or actions. —**re·cur′rence**, *n.* —**re·cur′rent**, *adj.* —**re·cur′rent·ly,** *adv.*

re·cy·cle (rē sī′kəl), *v.*, **-cled, -cling,** *n.* —*v.t.* **1.** to treat or process (used or waste materials) by making them suitable for reuse. **2.** to cause to pass through a cycle again. —*n.* **3.** the act or process of recycling. —**re·cy′cla·bil′i·ty** (-klə bil′i tē), *n.* —**re·cy′cla·ble,** *adj.*

red (red), *n., adj.,* **red·der, red·dest.** —*n.* **1.** any of various colors resembling the color of blood. **2.** something red, as clothing. **3.** (*often cap.*) a radical leftist in politics, esp. a communist. **4. in the red,** being in debt. **5. see red,** *Informal.* to become enraged. —*adj.* **6.** of the color red. **7.** (*often cap.*) *Informal.* **a.** radically left politically. **b.** of communism or communists. —**red′ly,** *adv.* —**red′ness,** *n.*

red′ blood′ cell′, erythrocyte. Also called **red′ blood′ cor′puscle.**

red-blood·ed (red′blud′id), *adj.* vigorously virile. —**red′-blood′ed·ness,** *n.*

red·breast (red′brest′), *n.* a robin.

red·cap (red′kap′), *n.* a baggage porter in a railroad station.

red′ car′pet, a display of courtesy or welcome, as that shown to very important persons. —**red′-car′pet,** *adj.*

red·coat (red′kōt′), *n.* a British soldier, esp. during the American Revolution.

Red′ Cross′, an international organization to care for the sick and wounded in war and help relieve suffering caused by disasters.

red′ deer′, a deer of Europe and Asia having a reddish-brown summer coat.

red·den (red′°n), *v.t., v.i.* to make or become red, as to blush.

red·dish (red′ish), *adj.* somewhat red. —**red′dish·ness,** *n.*

red dye No. 2, an artificial coloring, most widely used in foods, which is said to contain a cancer-causing agent.

---

re·cross′, *v.*
re·crown′, *v.t.*
re·crys′tal·lize′, *v.*, **-lized, -liz·ing.**

re·dec′o·rate, *v.*, **-rat·ed, -rat·ing.**
re·ded′i·cate′, *v.t.*, **-cat·ed, -cat·ing.**

re·deem (ri dēm′), *v.t.* **1.** to buy back, as something pawned. **2.** to buy or pay off, as a mortgage. **3.** to exchange (bonds, trading stamps, etc.) for money or goods. **4.** to discharge or fulfill (a pledge, etc.). **5.** to make amends for (some fault). **6.** to obtain the release of, as by paying a ransom. **7.** to set free or save, as a sinner. —**re·deem′a·ble,** *adj.* —**re·deem′er,** *n.*

re·demp·tion (ri demp′shən), *n.* **1.** the act of redeeming or state of being redeemed. **2.** deliverance from sin. —**re·demp′tive** (-tiv), *adj.* —**re·demp′to·ry** (-tə rē), *adj.*

red-hand·ed (red′han′did), *adj., adv.* in the very act of a crime or wrongdoing. —**red′-hand′ed·ly,** *adv.*

red·head (red′hed′), *n.* a person having red hair. —**red′head′ed,** *adj.*

red′ her′ring, something intended to divert attention from the real problem.

red-hot (red′hot′), *adj.* **1.** red with heat. **2.** very excited or furious. **3.** fresh or new.

re·dis·trict (rē dis′trikt), *v.t.* to divide anew into districts, as for electoral purposes.

red-let·ter (red′let′ər), *adj.* especially important or happy, as a day.

red′-light′ dis′trict, an area in a city in which many brothels are located.

red·lin·ing (red′lī′ning), *n.* an arbitrary practice by which banks refuse to grant mortgage loans for houses in blighted urban areas. [so called because such areas are said to be encircled by red pencil on the maps] —**red′line′,** *v.t., v.i.*

red′ man′, a North American Indian.

red·neck (red′nek′), *n. Disparaging.* (in the southern U.S.) an uneducated, white farm laborer.

red·o·lent (red′ə lənt), *adj.* **1.** having a pleasant odor. **2.** odorous or smelling. **3.** suggestive or reminiscent. —**red′o·lence, red′o·len·cy,** *n.* —**red′o·lent·ly,** *adv.*

re·doubt (ri dout′), *n.* a small fort used to defend a prominent point.

re·doubt·a·ble (ri dou′tə bəl), *adj.* **1.** that is to be feared. **2.** commanding respect, reverence, or the like. —**re·doubt′a·bly,** *adv.*

re·dound (ri dound′), *v.i.* **1.** to have a good or bad effect or result. **2.** to result or accrue, as to a person.

red′ pep′per, a pepper cultivated in many varieties, the yellow or red pods of which are used for flavoring, sauces, etc.

re·dress (*n.* rē′dres, ri dres′; *v.* ri dres′), *n.* **1.** the setting right of what is wrong. **2.** relief from wrong. **3.** compensation for a wrong. —*v.t.* **4.** to set right. **5.** to correct or reform. **6.** to remedy or relieve.

Red′ Sea′, an arm of the Indian Ocean, extending NW between Africa and Arabia.

red·skin (red′skin′), *n. Often Offensive.* a North American Indian.

red′ snap′per (snap′ər), a large food fish found in the Gulf of Mexico.

red′ tape′, excessive formality and routine required before official action can be taken.

red′ tide′, a brownish-red discoloration of marine waters that is lethal to fish.

re·duce (ri dōōs′, -dyōōs′), *v.,* **-duced, -duc·ing.** —*v.t.* **1.** to lessen in size, number, or amount. **2.** to act destructively upon. **3.** to lower in rank or well-being. **4.** to bring under control. **5.** *Math.* to change the denomination or form of (a fraction or ratio). **6.** *Chem.* **a.** to remove oxygen from a compound, esp. to extract a metal from its oxide. **b.** to lower the positive charge on an ion. —*v.i.* **7.** to become reduced, esp. to lose weight, as by dieting. —**re·duc′er,** *n.* —**re·duc′i·ble,** *adj.* —**re·duc′i·bly,** *adv.* —**re·duc′tive,** *adj.* —**Syn. 1.** decrease, diminish. **3.** degrade, demote.

re·duc·tion (ri duk′shən), *n.* **1.** the act of reducing or state of being reduced. **2.** the amount by which something is reduced. **3.** anything produced by reducing. —**re·duc′tion·al,** *adj.*

---

re′de·fine′, *v.t.,* -fined, -fin·ing.
re′de·lib′er·a′tion, *n.*
re′de·liv′er, *v.t.*
re′de·mand′, *v.t.*
re·dem′on·strate′, *v.,* -strat·ed, -strat·ing.
re′de·ploy′, *v.*
re′de·pos′it, *v., n.*
re′de·scribe′, *v.t.,* -scribed, -scrib·ing.
re′de·sign′, *v.*
re′de·ter′mine, *v.,* -mined, -min·ing.
re′de·vel′op, *v.*

re′de·vel′op·er, *n.*
re′de·vel′op·ment, *n.*
re′di·gest′, *v.t.*
re′di·ges′tion, *n.*
re′di·rect′, *v.t.*
re·dis′count, *v.t.*
re′dis·cov′er, *v.t.*
re′dis·cov′er·y, *n.,* pl. -er·ies.
re′dis·solve′, *v.,* -solved, -solv·ing.
re′dis·till′, *v.t.*
re′dis·trib′ute, *v.t.,* -ut·ed, -ut·ing.
re′dis·tri·bu′tion, *n.*

re′di·vide′, *v.,* -vid·ed, -vid·ing.
re·do′, *v.t.,* -did, -done, -do·ing.
re·don′ble, *v.,* -bled, -bling.
re′draft′, *n., v.t.*
re·draw′, *v.,* -drew, -drawn, -draw·ing; *n.*
re·drill′, *v.*
re·dry′, *v.,* -dried, -dry·ing.

re·dun·dant (ri dun'dənt), *adj.* 1. characterized by unnecessary repetition in expressing ideas. 2. in excess of requirements. —**re·dun'dan·cy,** *n.* —**re·dun'dant·ly,** *adv.*

red·wood (red'wŏŏd'), *n.* 1. a cone-bearing tree of California noted for its height. 2. the brownish-red timber of this tree.

reed (rēd), *n.* 1. the straight stalk of any of various tall grasses growing in marshy places. 2. any of the plants themselves. 3. a musical instrument made from the hollow stalk of such a plant. 4. a thin piece of this stalk or of metal or plastic, whose vibrations produce the sounds of various wind instruments, as the clarinet, harmonica, etc. —**reed'y,** *adj.* —**reed'i·ness,** *n.*

reef¹ (rēf), *n.* a ridge of rock, sand, or coral at or just below the surface of the water. —**reef'y,** *adj.*

reef² (rēf), *Naut.* —*n.* 1. a part of a sail that is rolled and tied down to reduce the area exposed to the wind. —*v.t., v.i.* 2. to shorten (sail) by tying a reef.

reef·er (rē'fər), *n.* 1. *Naut.* a person who reefs. 2. a short coat or jacket of thick cloth. 3. *Slang.* a marijuana cigarette.

reek (rēk), *n.* 1. a strong, unpleasant smell. 2. vapor or steam. —*v.i.* 3. to smell strongly and unpleasantly. 4. to be strongly pervaded with something offensive. 5. to give off steam, smoke, etc. —*v.t.* 6. to emit (smoke, fumes, etc.). —**reek'er,** *n.* —**reek'y,** *adj.*

reel¹ (rēl), *n.* 1. a spool or frame that is used to wind up thread, tape, film, wire, etc. 2. a quantity of something wound on such a device. —*v.t.* 3. to wind on a reel. 4. to pull or draw in by winding a line on a reel. 5. **reel off,** to say quickly and easily. —**reel'a·ble,** *adj.* —**reel'er,** *n.*

reel² (rēl), *v.i.* 1. to sway or rock under a blow, shock, etc. 2. to sway about in standing or walking, as from dizziness or intoxication. 3. to turn round and round. 4. to have a sensation of whirling. —*n.* 5. a reeling movement.

reel³ (rēl), *n.* a lively dance popular in Scotland.

re·en·force (rē'en fôrs', -fōrs'), *v.t.,* -**forced, -forc·ing.** reinforce.

re·en·try (rē en'trē), *n., pl.* -**tries.** 1. a second entry. 2. the return into the earth's atmosphere of an artificial satellite or spacecraft.

reeve (rēv), *v.t.,* **reeved** or **rove, reev·ing.** *Naut.* to pass (a rope) through a hole or ring.

ref (ref), *n., v.t., v.i.,* **reffed, ref·fing.** *Informal.* referee.

ref., 1. referee. 2. reference. 3. referred. 4. refining. 5. reformation. 6. reformed. 7. refund. 8. refunding.

re·fec·tion (ri fek'shən), *n.* *Chiefly Literary.* 1. refreshment, esp. with food or drink. 2. a light meal.

re·fec·to·ry (ri fek'tə rē), *n., pl.* -**ries.** a dining hall, esp. in a cloister.

re·fer (ri fûr'), *v.,* -**ferred, -fer·ring.** —*v.t.* 1. to direct the attention of. 2. to direct to a person or place for information or anything required. 3. to hand over for consideration, decision, etc. 4. to regard as belonging or related. —*v.i.* 5. to allude or call attention. 6. to go for information. —**ref'er·a·ble** (ref'ər ə bəl), *adj.* —**re·fer'rer,** *n.*

ref·er·ee (ref'ə rē'), *n., v.,* -**eed, -ee·ing.** —*n.* 1. a person to whom something is referred, esp. for decision or settlement. 2. a judge in a game or sport. —*v.t., v.i.* 3. to act as referee (for).

ref·er·ence (ref'ər əns, ref'rəns), *n.* 1. an act or instance of referring. 2. a mention or allusion. 3. direction or a direction to some source of information. 4. use or recourse for pur-

---

re·dye', *v.t.,* -dyed, -dye·ing.

re·ech'o, *v.,* -ech·oed, -ech·o·ing; *n.*

re·ed'it, *v.t.*

re·ed·u·cate, *v.t.,* -cat·ed, -cat·ing.

re'e·lect', *v.t.*

re'e·lec'tion, *n.*

re'em·bark', *v.*

re'em·bod'y, *v.t.,* -bod·ied, -bod·y·ing.

re'e·merge', *v.i.,* -merged, -merg·ing.

re'e·mer'gence, *n.*

re·em'pha·size', *v.t.,* -sized, -siz·ing.

re'em·ploy', *v.t.*

re'em·ploy'ment, *n.*

re'en·act', *v.t.*

re'en·close', *v.t.,* -closed, -clos·ing.

re'en·dow', *v.t.*

re'en·gage', *v.,* -gaged, -gag·ing.

re'en·joy', *v.t.*

re'en·large', *v.,* -larged, -larg·ing.

re'en·large'ment, *n.*

re'en·light'en, *v.t.*

re'en·list', *v.*

re'en·list'ment, *n.*

re'en·slave', *v.,* -slaved, -slav·ing.

re·en'ter, *v.*

re·en'trance, *n.*

re'e·nun'ci·a'tion, *n.*

re'e·quip', *v.t.,* -quipped, -quip·ping.

re'e·rect', *v.t.*

re·es·tab'lish, *v.t.*

re·es·tab'lish·ment, *n.*

re·e·val'u·ate, *v.t.,* -at·ed, -at·ing.

re·e·val'u·a'tion, *n.*

re·ex·am'ine, *v.t.,* -ined, -in·ing.

re·ex·change', *v.t.,* -changed, -chang·ing.

re·ex·hib'it, *v.t.*

re·ex·pe'ri·ence, *v.,* -enced, -enc·ing.

re·ex·port', *v.t.*

re·ex·press', *v.t.*

re·fash'ion, *v.t.*

re·fas'ten, *v.t.*

poses of information. **5.** a person to whom one refers for testimony as to one's character, abilities, etc. **6.** a statement, usually written, made by this person. **7.** relation, regard, or respect.

ref′erence book′, a publication consulted for facts or background information, as an encyclopedia, dictionary, atlas, yearbook, etc.

ref·er·en·dum (ref′ə ren′dəm), *n.,* *pl.* **-dums, -da** (-də). **1.** the practice of referring legislative measures to the vote of the electorate for approval or rejection. **2.** a vote on a measure thus referred.

ref·er·ent (ref′ər ənt), *n.* the object or event to which a term or symbol refers.

re·fer·ral (ri fûr′əl), *n.* **1.** an act or instance of referring. **2.** a person recommended to someone or for something.

re·fill (*v.* rē fil′; *n.* rē′fil′), *v.t., v.i.* **1.** to fill again. —*n.* **2.** a material or supply to replace something used up. —**re·fill′a·ble,** *adj.*

re·fine (ri fin′), *v.t., v.i.,* **-fined, -fin·ing. 1.** to bring or cause to change to a fine or a pure state. **2.** to make or become more elegant or polished. —**re·fin′er,** *n.*

re·fined (ri find′), *adj.* **1.** having or showing well-bred feeling, taste, etc. **2.** freed from impurities. **3.** very subtle or precise. —**Syn. 1.** cultivated, elegant, polished.

re·fine·ment (ri fin′mənt), *n.* **1.** elegance of feeling, taste, etc. **2.** the act of refining or state of being refined. **3.** subtle reasoning. **4.** an improved form of something.

re·fin·er·y (ri fī′nə rē), *n., pl.* **-er·ies.** a plant for refining crude or raw materials, as metals, sugar, or petroleum.

refl., 1. reflection. **2.** reflective. **3.** reflex. **4.** reflexive.

re·flect (ri flekt′), *v.t.* **1.** to cast back (light, heat, etc.) from a surface. **2.** to give back or show an image of. **3.** to happen or occur as a result of. —*v.i.* **4.** to be turned or cast back, as light. **5.** to cast back light, heat, etc. **6.** to give back or show an image. **7.** to ponder or meditate. **8.** to bring reproach or discredit by association. —**re·flec′tion,** *n.* —**re·flec′tive,** *adj.* —**re·flec′tive·ly,** *adv.*

re·flec·tor (ri flek′tər), *n.* **1.** a person or thing that reflects. **2.** a polished surface that reflects light, heat, etc. **3.** a telescope using a mirror instead of a lens to form the principal images.

re·flex (rē′fleks), *n.* **1.** an action that takes place automatically in response to the stimulation of a nerve and without conscious effort. —*adj.* **2.** noting or caused by a reflex. **3.** bent or turned back. —**re′flex·ly,** *adv.*

re′flex cam′era, a camera in which the image is reflected by a mirror behind the lens onto a ground glass.

re·flex·ive (ri flek′siv), *Gram.* —*adj.* **1.** (of a verb) taking a subject and object with identical referents, as *shave* in *I shave myself.* **2.** (of a pronoun) used as an object to refer to the subject of a verb, as *myself* in *I shave myself.* —*n.* **3.** a reflexive verb or pronoun. —**re·flex′ive·ly,** *adv.* —**re·flex′ive·ness,** *n.*

re·for·est (rē fôr′ist, -for′-), *v.t., v.i.* to replant trees in (a forest affected by cutting, fire, etc.). —**re′for·est·a′tion,** *n.*

re·form (rē fôrm′, rē′-), *v.t., v.i.* to form again. —**re′for·ma′tion** (-fôr·mā′shən), *n.*

re·form (ri fôrm′), *n.* **1.** the improvement of what is wrong, corrupt, etc. **2.** an improvement in conduct, character, etc. —*v.t.* **3.** to change to a better state, form, etc. **4.** to cause (a person) to abandon evil ways of life or conduct. —*v.i.* **5.** to abandon evil ways of life or conduct. —**re·form′a·ble,** *adj.* —**re·form′a·tive,** *adj.* —**re·formed′,** *adj.*

ref·or·ma·tion (ref′ər mā′shən), *n.* **1.** the act of reforming or state of being reformed. **2.** (*cap.*) the religious movement in the 16th century that led to the establishment of the Protestant churches.

re·form·a·to·ry (ri fôr′mə tôr′ē, -tōr′ē), *adj., n., pl.* **-ries.** —*adj.* **1.** serving or designed to reform. —*n.* **2.** Also called **reform′ school′.** a penal institution for reforming young offenders, esp. minors.

re·form·er (ri fôr′mər), *n.* a person devoted to bringing about reform, as in politics.

re·fract (ri frakt′), *v.t.* to subject to refraction.

---

re·file′, *v.,* **-filed, -fil·ing.**	**re·fire′,** *v.,* **-fired, -fir·ing.**	**re·fold′,** *v.*
re·film′, *v.t.*	**re·fit′,** *v.,* **-fit·ted, -fit·ting.**	**re·forge,** *v.t.,* **-forged, -forg·ing.**
re·fil′ter, *v.t.*		**re·for′mu·late′,** *v.t.,* **-lat·ed, -lat·ing.**
re·fi′nance, *v.t.,* **-nanced, -nanc·ing.**	**re·flow′,** *v.*	**re′for·mu·la′tion,** *n.*
re·fin′ish, *v.t.*	**re·flow′er,** *v.i.*	**re·for′ti·fy′,** *v.t.,* **-fied, -fy·ing.**
	re·fo′cus, *v.,* **-cused, -cus·ing.**	

re·frac·tion (ri frak'shən), *n.* the bending of a ray of light, heat, or sound in passing from one medium into another in which the speed of propagation differs. —**re·frac'tive,** *adj.* —**re·frac'tive·ness, re'frac·tiv'i·ty** (-tiv'i tē), *n.*

re·frac·tor (ri frak'tər), *n.* 1. a person or thing that refracts. 2. a telescope consisting essentially of a lens for forming an image.

re·frac·to·ry (ri frak'tə rē), *adj.* 1. stubbornly disobedient. 2. difficult to melt, reduce, or corrode, as an ore or metal. —**re·frac'to·ri·ly,** *adv.* —**re·frac'to·ri·ness,** *n.*

re·frain¹ (ri frān'), *v.i.* to keep oneself (from doing or indulging in something). —**re·frain'ment,** *n.*

re·frain² (ri frān'), *n.* a phrase or verse recurring at intervals in a song or poem.

re·fresh (ri fresh'), *v.t.* 1. to restore the strength and well-being of, as with food, drink, or rest. 2. to make fresh again, as by cooling or moistening. 3. to quicken or arouse (the memory). —*v.i.* 4. to become fresh or vigorous again. —**re·fresh'er,** *n.,* *adj.* —**re·fresh'ing,** *adj.* —**re·fresh'ing·ly,** *adv.* —**Syn.** 1. reinvigorate, renew.

re·fresh·ment (ri fresh'mənt), *n.* 1. Often, **refreshments.** food and drink, served esp. as snacks. 2. the act of refreshing or state of being refreshed.

refrig., 1. refrigeration. 2. refrigerator.

re·frig·er·ate (ri frij'ə rāt'), *v.t.,* **-at·ed, -at·ing.** to make or keep cold or cool, esp. for preservation. —**re·frig'er·ant,** *adj., n.* —**re·frig'er·a'tion,** *n.*

re·frig·er·a·tor (ri frij'ə rā'tər), *n.* a box or cabinet in which foods and other perishables are kept cool by refrigeration.

ref·uge (ref'yōoj), *n.* 1. shelter from danger, trouble, etc. 2. a place or source of shelter or safety.

ref·u·gee (ref'yōo jē'), *n.* a person who flees for refuge or safety, esp. to a foreign country, as in time of war.

re·ful·gent (ri ful'jənt), *adj.* glowing radiantly. —**re·ful'gence,** *n.* —**re·ful'gent·ly,** *adv.*

re·fund (*v.* ri fund'; *n.* rē'fund), *v.t., v.i.* 1. to give back (esp. money). —*n.* 2. the act of refunding. 3. an amount refunded. —**re·fund'a·ble,** *adj.* —**re·fund'er,** *n.*

re·fur·bish (rē fûr'bish), *v.t.* to restore to a bright and fresh appearance, as furnishings. —**re·fur'bish·ment,** *n.*

re·fuse (ri fyōoz'), *v.t., v.i.,* **-fused, -fus·ing.** 1. to decline to accept (something offered). 2. to express a determination not to (do something). —**re·fus'al,** *n* —**Syn.** 1. reject, spurn.

ref·use² (ref'yōos), *n.* anything discarded as worthless or useless.

re·fute (ri fyōot'), *v.t.,* **-fut·ed, -fut·ing.** 1. to prove to be false, as an opinion. 2. to prove (a person) to be in error. —**re·fut'a·ble,** *adj.* —**ref·u·ta·tion** (ref'yōo tā'shən), *n.* —**re·fut'er,** *n.*

reg., 1. regent. 2. regiment. 3. region. 4. register 5. registered. 6. registrar. 7. registry. 8. regular. 9. regularly. 10. regulation.

re·gain (ri gān'), *v.t.* 1. to gain back. 2. to reach again. —**re·gain'er,** *n.*

re·gal (rē'gəl), *adj.* of or befitting a king, queen, or other monarch, esp. with respect to grandeur. —**re'gal·ly,** *adv.* —**Syn.** majestic, splendid.

re·gale (ri gāl'), *v.t.,* **-galed, -gal·ing.** 1. to entertain or amuse thoroughly. 2. to feed sumptuously. —**re·gale'ment,** *n.*

re·ga·li·a (ri gā'lē ə, -gāl'yə), *n.pl.* 1. the ensigns or emblems of royalty, as the crown, scepter, etc. 2. the insignia of any office or order. 3. rich clothing or finery.

re·gard (ri gärd'), *v.t.* 1. to consider in a particular way. 2. to have or show respect for. 3. to think highly of. 4. to relate to or concern. 5. to look at or observe. —*v.i.* 6. as regards, regarding or concerning. —*n.* 7. thought or concern. 8. respect or esteem. 9. a particular aspect or point. 10. reference or relation. 11. *Archaic.* a look or gaze. 12. **regards,** sentiments of esteem or affection. —**re·gard'ful.** *adj.*

re·gard·ing (ri gär'ding), *prep.* with regard to.

re·gard·less (ri gärd'lis), *adv.* 1. *Informal.* without concern as to advice, warning, etc. 2. **regardless of,** in spite of.

re·gat·ta (ri gat'ə, -gä'tə), *n.* 1. a boat race. 2. an organized series of such races.

regd., registered.

re·gen·cy (rē'jən sē), *n., pl.* **-cies.** —*n.* 1. the office or control of a regent or body of regents. 2. a body of regents. 3. the term of office of a regent.

---

re·frac'ture, *v.,* **-tured, -tur·ing.**

re·frame', *v.t.,* **-framed, -fram·ing.**

re·freeze', *v.,* **-froze, -fro·zen, freez·ing.**

re·fry', *v.,* **-fried, -fry·ing.**

re·fu'el, *v.,* **-eled, -el·ing.**

re·fur'nish, *v.t.*

re·gath'er, *v.*

re·gauge', *v.t.,* **-gauged, -gaug·ing.**

re·gen·er·ate (v. ri jen′ə rāt′; adj. ri-jen′ər it), v., **-at·ed, -at·ing,** adj. —v.t. **1.** to effect a complete moral reform in. **2.** to bring into existence again. **3.** *Biol.* to renew or restore (a lost or injured part). —adj. **4.** made over in a better form. **5.** born again spiritually. —**re·gen′er·a·cy,** n. —**re·gen′er·a′tion,** n. —**re·gen′er·a′tive,** adj. —**re·gen′er·a′tor,** n.

re·gent (rē′jənt), n. **1.** a person who rules a kingdom during the minority, absence, or disability of the sovereign. **2.** a member of a governing board, as of a state university.

reg·i·cide (rej′i sīd′), n. **1.** the killing of a king. **2.** a person who kills a king. —**reg′i·cid′al,** adj.

re·gime (rə zhēm′, rā-), n. **1.** a ruling government. **2.** a system of rule or government. **3.** *Med.* (erroneously) regimen (def. 1). Also, **ré·gime′.**

reg·i·men (rej′ə men′, -mən), n. **1.** a regulated course of diet, exercise, etc., for restoring the health. **2.** *Archaic.* regime (defs. 1, 2). [< L: rule]

reg·i·ment (n. rej′ə mənt; v. rej′ə ment′), n. **1.** a unit of ground forces, consisting of two or more battalions. —v.t. **2.** to manage or treat in a strict, systematic manner with no regard for individual rights and differences. —**reg′i·men′tal,** adj. —**reg′i·men·ta′tion,** n.

Re·gi·na (ri jī′nə), n. the capital of Saskatchewan, Canada.

re·gion (rē′jən), n. **1.** an extensive, continuous part of a surface or space. **2.** a part of the body: *the abdominal region.*

re·gion·al (rē′jə nəl), adj. **1.** of or pertaining to a region, as of a country. **2.** of or localized in a particular bodily region. —**re′gion·al·ly,** adv.

re·gion·al·ism (rē′jē nəliz′əm), n. **1.** a quality or characteristic peculiar to a certain region or area. **2.** an expression or speech pattern peculiar to some region.

reg·is·ter (rej′i stər), n. **1.** a book in which records of acts, events, or names are kept. **2.** a list or record kept in such a book. **3.** a mechanical device by which certain data are automatically recorded. **4.** *Music.* the range of a voice or an instrument. **5.** a device for controlling the flow of warmed air through an opening in a heating system. —v.t. **6.** to enter in a register. **7.** to enroll (a student, voter, etc.). **8.** to re-

cord (mail) at a post office as a protection against loss, theft, etc. **9.** to indicate or show, as on an instrument or scale. **10.** to show (a mood or emotion), as by facial expression or gestures. —v.i. **11.** to enter one's name in a register. **12.** to make some impression. —**reg′is·trant** (-trənt), n.

reg′istered nurse′, a fully trained nurse who has passed a state board examination.

reg·is·trar (rej′i strär′, rej′i strär′), n. a person who keeps official records, esp. at a school or college.

reg·is·tra·tion (rej′i strā′shən), n. **1.** the act of registering. **2.** an entry in a register. **3.** the number registered. **4.** a certificate attesting to the fact that someone or something has been registered.

reg·is·try (rej′i strē), n., pl. **-tries. 1.** the act of registering. **2.** a place where registers are kept. **3.** register (defs. 1, 2).

reg·nal (reg′nəl), adj. of a reigning sovereign or a reign.

reg·nant (reg′nənt), adj. reigning in one's own right and not as a consort.

re·gress (v. ri gres′; n. rē′gres), v.i. **1.** to move in a backward direction, esp. to an earlier or less advanced state or form. —n. **2.** the act of regressing. —**re·gres′sive,** adj. —**re·gres′sor,** n.

re·gres·sion (ri gresh′ən), n. **1.** regress. **2.** the reversion to an earlier pattern of behavior and feeling.

re·gret (ri gret′), v., **-gret·ted, -gret·ting,** n. —v.t., v.i. **1.** to feel sorrow or distress for (a wrong or fault). **2.** to think (of) with a sense of loss. —n. **3.** sorrow or distress for a fault, mistake, etc. **4.** a sense of loss. **5.** **regrets,** a polite, usually formal refusal of an invitation. —**re·gret′ful,** adj. —**re·gret′ful·ly,** adv. —**re·gret′ta·ble,** adj. —**re·gret′ta·bly,** adv. —**re·gret′ter,** n. —Syn. **1.** deplore, lament. **3.** remorse, repentance.

re·group (rē grōōp′), v.t., v.i. **1.** to form into a new group or groups. **2.** to reorganize (troops) after a battle or skirmish.

reg·u·lar (reg′yə lər), adj. **1.** following the normal or customary course of events. **2.** evenly or uniformly arranged. **3.** characterized by fixed principle or procedure. **4.** recurring at fixed intervals. **5.** adhering to a rule or procedure. **6.** being consistently or habitually such: *a regular customer.* **7.** properly qualified for

---

re·gear′, v.
re·ger′mi·nate′, v.,
 -nat·ed, -nat·ing.
re′ger·mi·na′tion, n.
re·ger′mi·na′tive, adj.;
 -ly, adv.

re·gild′, v.t.
re·glaze′, v.t.,
 -glazed, -glaz·ing.
re·gloss′, v.t.
re·glue′, v.t., **-glued,**
 -glu·ing.

re·grade′, v.t., **-grad·ed,**
 -grad·ing.
re·grow′, v., **-grew,**
 -grown, -grow·ing.
re·growth′, n.

an occupation: *a regular physician.*
8. *Informal.* **a.** real or genuine: *a regular fellow.* **b.** absolute or thorough: *a regular rascal.* **9.** *Gram.* following the usual rules of inflection. **10.** *Geom.* having all sides and angles equal. **11.** noting the standing army of a state. **12.** belonging to a religious or monastic order. —*n.* **13.** a customer or client of long standing. **14.** a professional soldier. **15.** a loyal member of a political party. **16.** an athlete who plays in most of the games, usually from the start. —**reg·u·lar·i·ty** (-lar′i tē), *n.* —**reg′u·lar·ize′** (-lə rīz′), *v.t.* —**reg′u·lar·ly,** *adv.*

reg·u·late (reg′yə lāt′), *v.t.,* -**lat·ed,** -**lat·ing.** **1.** to control or direct by a rule, method, etc. **2.** to adjust to some standard or requirement. **3.** to adjust so as to ensure accuracy of operation. **4.** to put in good order. —**reg′u·la′tive, reg′u·la·to′ry** (-lə tôr′ē, -tōr′ē), *adj.* —**reg′u·la·tor,** *n.*

reg·u·la·tion (reg′yə lā′shən), *n.* **1.** a rule or order prescribed by authority, as to regulate conduct. **2.** a governing direction or law. **3.** the act of regulating or state of being regulated. —*adj.* **4.** prescribed by regulation.

re·gur·gi·tate (ri gûr′ji tāt′), *v.i., v.t.,* -**tated,** -**tat·ing.** to surge or cause to surge back, as undigested food from the stomach. —**re·gur′gi·ta′tion,** *n.*

re·ha·bil·i·tate (rē′hə bil′i tāt′), *v.t.,* -**tat·ed,** -**tat·ing.** **1.** to restore to a condition of good health, ability to work, etc. **2.** to restore to good operation or management. **3.** to reestablish the rights, rank, or good reputation of. —**re′ha·bil′i·ta′tion,** *n.* —**re′ha·bil′i·ta′tive,** *adj.*

re·hash (*v.* rē hash′; *n.* rē′hash′), *v.t.* **1.** to work up (old material, as writing) in a new form. —*n.* **2.** the act of rehashing. **3.** something rehashed.

re·hear·ing (rē hēr′ing), *n. Law.* a second presentation of a case.

re·hears·al (ri hûr′səl), *n.* **1.** a practice performance, usually private, in preparation for public presentation, as of a play. **2.** a detailed account or recital.

re·hearse (ri hûrs′), *v.t., v.i.,* -**hearsed,** -**hears·ing.** —*v.t.* **1.** to practice (a performance, etc.) before public presentation. **2.** to drill or train (an actor or actress) by rehearsal. **3.** to relate the facts or details (of). —**re·hears′er,** *n.*

Reich (rīk; *Ger.* RĪKH), *n.* (formerly) the German state. [< G: kingdom]

reign (rān), *n.* **1.** the period during which a sovereign rules. **2.** royal rule. **3.** dominating power or influence. —*v.i.* **4.** to have the power of a sovereign. **5.** to be prevalent or widespread.

re·im·burse (rē′im bûrs′), *v.t.,* -**bursed,** -**burs·ing.** to pay back (someone) an exact equivalent for expense or loss incurred —**re′im·burs′a·ble,** *adj.* —**re′im·burse′ment,** *n.* —**Syn.** indemnify, recompense.

rein (rān), *n.* **1.** a leather strap, fastened to each end of the bit of a bridle, by which the rider controls a horse. **2.** any means of curbing or controlling. **3. give rein to,** to allow freedom to. —*v.t.* **4.** to check or guide by reins. **5.** to curb or restrain.

re·in·car·na·tion (rē′in kär nā′shən), *n.* rebirth of the soul in a new body. —**re′in·car′nate,** *v.t.*

rein·deer (rān′dēr′), *n., pl.* -**deer.** a large deer of northern arctic regions, used as a work animal.

re·in·force (rē′in fōrs′, -fôrs′), *v.t.,* -**forced,** -**forc·ing.** **1.** to strengthen with some added support or material. **2.** to strengthen (a military force) with additional persons, ships, or aircraft. —**re′in·force′ment,** *n.* —**re′in·forc′er,** *n.*

re·in·state (rē′in stāt′), *v.t.,* -**stat·ed,** -**stat·ing.** to put back into a former position or state. —**re′in·state′ment,** *n.*

REIT (rēt, rīt), real-estate investment trust.

---

re·han′dle, *v.t.,* -dled, -dling.	**re′im·pose′,** *v.,* -posed, -pos·ing.	**re′in·fuse′,** *v.t.,* -fused, -fus·ing.
re·hang′, *v.t.,* -hung, -hanged, -hang·ing.	**re′im·pris′on,** *v.t.*	**re′in·fu′sion,** *n.*
re·hard′en, *v.*	**re′in·cor′po·rate′,** *v.,* -rat·ed, -rat·ing.	**re′in·oc′u·late′,** *v.,* -lat·ed, -lat·ing.
re·hear′, *v.t.,* -heard, -hear·ing.	**re′in·cor′po·rate,** *adj.*	**re′in·oc·u·la′tion,** *n.*
re·heat′, *v.t.*	**re′in·cur′,** *v.t.,* -curred, -cur·ring.	**re′in·scribe′,** *v.t.,* -scribed, -scrib·ing.
re·heel′, *v.t.*	**re′in·duce′,** *v.t.,* -duced, -duc·ing.	**re′in·sert′,** *v.t.*
re·hem′, *v.t.,* -hemmed, -hem·ming.	**re′in·duct′,** *v.t.*	**re′in·ser′tion,** *n.*
re·hinge′, *v.t.,* -hinged, -hing·ing.	**re′in·duc′tion,** *n.*	**re′in·spect′,** *v.t.*
re·hire′, *v.t.,* -hired, -hir·ing, *n.*	**re′in·fect′,** *v.t.*	**re′in·stal·la′tion,** *n.*
re·ig·nite′, *v.t.,* -nit·ed, -nit·ing.	**re′in·fec′tion,** *n.*	**re′in·stall′ment,** *n.*
	re′in·flame′, *v.,* -flamed, -flam·ing.	**re′in·struct′,** *v.t.*
	re′in·form′, *v.t.*	**re′in·sure′,** *v.t.,* -sured, -sur·ing.

re·it·er·ate (rē it'ə rāt'), v.t., -at·ed, -at·ing. to say or do repeatedly, esp. with insistence. —re·it'er·a'tion, n. —re·it'er·a'tive, adj.

re·ject (v. ri jekt'; n. rē'jekt), v.t. 1. to refuse to have, take, or act upon. 2. to refuse to grant. 3. to discard as useless or unsatisfactory. —n. 4. a rejected person or thing. —re·jec'tion, n. —re·ject'er, n.

rejec'tion slip', a note from a publisher, rejecting a manuscript submitted.

re·joice (ri jois'), v., -joiced, -joic·ing. —v.i. 1. to feel great joy. —v.t. 2. to fill with great joy. —re·joic'er, n. —re·joic'ing, n.

re·join[1] (ri join'), v.t. 1. to come again into the company of. 2. to join together again. —v.i. 3. to become rejoined.

re·join[2] (ri join'), v.t., v.i. to say as a rejoinder.

re·join·der (ri join'dər), n. an answer to a reply or objection.

re·ju·ve·nate (ri jōō'və nāt'), v.t., -nat·ed, -nat·ing. to restore to youthful vigor, appearance, etc. —re·ju've·na'tion, n.

rel., 1. relating. 2. relative. 3. released. 4. religion. 5. religious.

re·lapse (v. ri laps'; n. ri laps', rē'laps), v., -lapsed, -laps·ing, n. —v.i. 1. to fall or slip back into a former state, esp. into illness after a partial recovery. —n. 2. the act or an instance of relapsing.

re·late (ri lāt'), v., -lat·ed, -lat·ing. —v.i. 1. to tell in an orderly way. 2. to connect in thought or meaning. —v.i. 3. to have reference or relation. 4. to establish a meaningful relationship with a person or thing. —re·lat'a·ble, adj. —re·lat'er, n. — Syn. 1. narrate, recount.

re·lat·ed (ri lā'tid), adj. 1. connected by nature, origin, marriage, etc. 2. connected in thought or meaning. —re·lat'ed·ness, n.

re·la·tion (ri lā'shən), n. 1. a connection between or among things. 2. the mode of connection between one person and another, between people and God, etc. 3. relations, a. connections, dealings, or contacts. b. sexual intercourse. 4. kinship (def. 1). 5. Chiefly Brit. relative (def. 1). 6. Obsolesc. a. the act of narrating. b. a narrative or account. 7. in or with relation to, with reference to. —re·la'tion·al, adj.

re·la·tion·ship (ri lā'shən ship'), n. 1. the state or fact of being related. 2. kinship (def. 1).

rel·a·tive (rel'ə tiv), n. 1. a person connected with another or others by blood or marriage. 2. Gram. a relative pronoun, adjective, or adverb. —adj. 3. considered in relation to something else. 4. having meaning only as related to something else. 5. having relation or connection. 6. having reference or regard. 7. Gram. referring to or modifying an antecedent. —rel'a·tive·ly, adv. —rel'a·tive·ness, n.

rel'ative humid'ity, the amount of water vapor in the air, expressed as a percentage of the maximum amount that the air at the same temperature can hold.

rel·a·tiv·is·tic (rel'ə ti vis'tik), adj. having a value that varies with velocity, equivalent to the value obtained when the velocity is appreciably smaller than the speed of light. —rel'a·tiv·is'ti·cal·ly, adv.

rel·a·tiv·i·ty (rel'ə tiv'i tē), n. 1. the state or fact of being relative. 2. Physics. a theory, formulated essentially by Albert Einstein, that matter and energy are equivalent and form the basis for nuclear energy and that space and time are relative rather than absolute concepts.

re·lax (ri laks'), v.t., v.i. 1. to make or become less tense or rigid. 2. to make or become less strict or severe, as rules or discipline. 3. to release (oneself) from tension, anxiety, etc. —re·lax'er, n.

re·lax·ant (ri lak'sənt), adj. 1. of or causing relaxation. —n. 2. a drug that relaxes, esp. one that lessens strain in muscle.

re·in'te·grate', v., -grat·ed, -grat·ing.	re'in·tro·duc'tion, n.	re·in·volve', v.t., -volved, -volv·ing.
re'in·te·gra'tion, n.	re'in·vent', v.t.	re·in·volve'ment, n.
re'in·ter', v.t., -terred, -ter·ring.	re'in·vest', v.t.	re·is'sue, n., v.t., -sued, -su·ing.
re'in·ter'pret, v.	re'in·ves'ti·gate', v., -gat·ed, -gat·ing.	re·judge', v., -judged, -judg·ing.
re'in·ter'pre·ta'tion, n.	re'in·ves·ti·ga'tion, n.	
re'in·ter'ro·gate', v., -gat·ed, -gat·ing.	re'in·vest'ment, n.	re·kin'dle, v., -dled, -dling.
re'in·ter'ro·ga'tion, n.	re'in·vig'or·ate', v.t., -at·ed, -at·ing.	re·la'bel, v.t., -beled, -bel·ing or -belled, -bel·ling.
re'in·trench', v.	re'in·vig'or·a'tion, n.	
re'in·trench'ment, n.	re'in·vite', v., -vit·ed, -vit·ing.	
re'in·tro·duce', v.t., -duced, -duc·ing	re'in·voke', v.t., -voked, -vok·ing.	re·laun'der, v.t.

re·lax·a·tion (rē′lak sā′shon), n. **1.** relief from work, effort, etc. **2.** an activity or recreation that provides such relief. **3.** the act of relaxing or state of being relaxed.

re·lay (rē lā′), v.t., **-laid, -lay·ing.** to lay again.

re·lay (n. rē′lā; v. rē′lā, ri lā′), n., v., **-layed, -lay·ing.** —n. **1.** a fresh team or shift, as of persons or animals relieving one another or taking turns. **2.** Also called **re′lay race′.** a race between two or more teams of contestants, each contestant running part of the distance. **3.** an electrically operated switch, esp. one that uses a small current to control a much larger one. —v.t. **4.** to pass on by or as by relays. **5.** to provide with or replace by fresh relays.

re·lease (ri lēs′), v., **-leased, -leas·ing.** n. —v.t. **1.** to free from confinement, obligation, pain, etc. **2.** to let loose or go, as an arrow. **3.** to allow to be published, seen, or known. **4.** Law. to relinquish or surrender, as a right. —n. **5.** an act or instance of releasing. **6.** the authorized publication or performance, as of a motion picture. **7.** information released to the public in the form of a bulletin. **8.** Law. a. the surrender of a right to another. b. a document embodying such a surrender. **9.** a device for stopping a machine by releasing a catch, lock, etc. —**re·leas′er,** n.

rel·e·gate (rel′ə gāt′), v.t., **-gat·ed, -gat·ing. 1.** to send or assign to a lower position, place, or rank. **2.** to assign or turn over (a task, etc.) to someone. **3.** to assign or refer (something) to a particular class or kind. **4.** Rare. to send into exile. —**rel′·e·ga′tion,** n.

re·lent (ri lent′), v.i. to become more mild, compassionate, or forgiving.

re·lent·less (ri lent′lis), adj. unyieldingly severe, strict, or harsh. —**re·lent′less·ly,** adv. —**re·lent′less·ness,** n.

rel·e·vant (rel′ə vənt), adj. logically connected with and important to the matter in hand. —**rel′e·vance, rel′e·van·cy,** n. —**rel′e·vant·ly,** adv. —Syn. appropriate, germane, pertinent.

re·li·a·ble (ri lī′ə bəl), adj. that may be relied on. —**re·li′a·bil′i·ty, re·li′a·ble·ness,** n. —**re·li′a·bly,** adv.

re·li·ance (ri lī′əns), n. **1.** confident or trustful dependence. **2.** trust or confidence. **3.** something or someone relied on. —**re·li′ant,** adj.

rel·ic (rel′ik), n. **1.** a thing, idea, or custom that survives from the past. **2.** an object having interest by reason of its age or its association with the past. **3. relics,** remaining parts or fragments. **4.** souvenir or memento. **5.** the body or some personal memorial of a saint, regarded as sacred.

rel·ict (rel′ikt), n. **1.** a plant or animal species surviving from an earlier environment. **2.** Archaic. a widow.

re·lief[1] (ri lēf′), n. **1.** ease or comfort caused by the removal of pain, distress, etc. **2.** a means of such ease or comfort. **3.** help given to those in poverty or need. **4.** something that provides a pleasing change, as from monotony. **5.** release from a duty, as by a replacement. **6.** the person or persons acting as this replacement. **7.** the rescue of a besieged town, fort, etc.

re·lief[2] (ri lēf′), n. **1.** the projection of a figure or part from the ground or plane on which it is formed, as in sculpture or similar work. **2.** a contour variation of the land surface in relation to the surrounding land. **3. in relief, a.** carved or raised. **b.** with sharpness or distinctness.

relief′ pitch′er, Baseball. a pitcher brought into a game to replace another pitcher, often in a critical situation.

re·lieve (ri lēv′), v.t., **-lieved, -liev·ing. 1.** to lighten or alleviate (pain, distress, etc.). **2.** to free from anxiety, fear, etc. **3.** to free from need, poverty, etc. **4.** to break the sameness or monotony of. **5.** to release (a person on duty) by being or providing a replacement. **6.** to set in relief. —**re·liev′er,** n.

relig., religion.

re·li·gion (ri lij′ən), n. **1.** a set of beliefs concerning the cause, nature, and purpose of the universe, esp. belief in or the worship of God or gods. **2.** an organized system of belief in and worship of God or gods. **3.** something one believes in or follows devotedly. —**re·li′gion·ist,** n.

re·li·gi·os·i·ty (ri lij′ē os′i tē), n. affected devotion to religion.

re·li·gious (ri lij′əs), adj., n., pl. **-gious.** —adj. **1.** of or concerned with religion. **2.** devout or pious. **3.** very conscientious or faithful. —n. **4.** a member or members of a religious order. —**re·li′gious·ly,** adv. —**re·li′gious·ness,** n.

---

re·learn′, v., **-learned** or **-learnt, -learn·ing.**
re·let′, v., **-let, -let·ting.**
re·let′ter, v.t.

re·li·cense, v.t., **-censed, -cens·ing.**
re·light′, v., **-light·ed** or **-lit, -light·ing.**

re·line′, v.t., **-lined, -lin·ing.**
re·liq′ui·date′, v., **-dat·ed, -dat·ing.**
re·liq′ui·da′tion, n.

re·lin·quish (ri ling'kwish), v.t. 1. to renounce or surrender (a possession, right, etc.). 2. to give up or put aside. 3. to let go, as a hold or grasp. —**re·lin'quish·er,** n. —**re·lin'quish·ment,** n.

rel·i·quar·y (rel'ə kwer'ē), n., pl. **-quar·ies.** a receptacle for a religious relic or relics.

rel·ique (rel'ik), n. Archaic. relic.

rel·ish (rel'ish), n. 1. liking or enjoyment of the taste of something. 2. pleasurable appreciation or liking of anything. 3. something savory or appetizing, as a sweet pickle of minced vegetables. 4. a pleasing or appetizing flavor. 5. a pleasing or enjoyable quality. —v.t. 6. to take pleasure in. 7. to like the taste or flavor of. —**rel'ish·a·ble,** adj.

re·live (rē liv'), v.t., **-lived, -liv·ing.** 1. to experience again, as an emotion. 2. to live (one's life) again.

re·lo·cate (rē lō'kāt), v.t., v.i., **-cat·ed, -cat·ing.** 1. to locate again. 2. to move (one's business or home) to another place. —**re'lo·ca'tion,** n.

re·luc·tant (ri luk'tənt), adj. 1. not willing or inclined. 2. struggling in opposition. —**re·luc'tance,** or **re·luc'tan·cy,** n. —**re·luc'tant·ly,** adv. —Syn. 1. averse, disinclined, loath.

re·ly (ri lī'), v.i., **-lied, -ly·ing.** to depend confidently.

rem (rem), n. the quantity of ionizing radiation whose biological effect is equal to that produced by one roentgen of x-rays.

REM (rem), n. the quick, darting movement of the eyes during sleep, esp. when dreaming. [r(apid) e(ye) m(ovement)]

re·main (ri mān'), v.i. 1. to continue to be as specified. 2. to stay behind or in the same place. 3. to be left after the removal or loss of all else. 4. to be left to be done or acted upon. —n. 5. Usually, **remains.** something that remains. 6. **remains.** a. writings unpublished at an author's death. b. a dead body.

re·main·der (ri mān'dər), n. 1. a remaining part. 2. Arith. a. the quantity that remains after subtraction. b. the portion of the dividend that is not evenly divisible by the divisor. 3. a copy of a book remaining in the publisher's stock when its sale has practically ceased.

re·mand (ri mand', -mänd'), v.t. to send back (a prisoner) into custody, as to await further proceedings. —**re·mand'ment,** n.

re·mark (ri märk'), v.t. 1. to say casually, as in making a comment. 2. to note or observe. —v.i. 3. to make a remark. —n. 4. the act of remarking. 5. a casual or brief comment.

re·mark·a·ble (ri mär'kə bəl), adj. 1. notably unusual. 2. worthy of notice. —**re·mark'a·ble·ness,** n. —**re·mark'a·bly,** adv. —Syn. extraordinary, singular.

Rem·brandt (rem'brant, -bränt), n. 1606–69, Dutch painter.

re·me·di·a·ble (ri mē'dē ə bəl), adj. capable of being remedied.

re·me·di·al (ri mē'dē əl), adj. 1. affording remedy. 2. intended to correct or improve one's skill in a specified field. —**re·me'di·al·ly,** adv.

rem·e·dy (rem'i dē), n., pl. **-dies,** v., **-died, -dy·ing.** —n. 1. something, as a medicine, that cures or relieves a disease. 2. something that corrects or removes an evil. —v.t. 3. to provide a remedy for.

re·mem·ber (ri mem'bər), v.t. 1. to recall to the mind by using the memory. 2. to keep in mind. 3. to reward, as with a gift or tip. 4. to mention (a person) to another as sending best wishes. —v.t. 5. to possess memory. —**re·mem'ber·a·ble,** adj. —**re·mem'ber·er,** n.

re·mem·brance (ri mem'brəns), n. 1. the act of remembering or state of being remembered. 2. the ability to remember. 3. the length of time over which memory extends. 4. something that serves to bring to or keep in mind. 5. a memory or recollection. 6. **remembrances,** greetings or regards. —Syn. 5. keepsake, memento, souvenir.

re·mind (ri mīnd'), v.t. to cause to remember. —**re·mind'er,** n.

rem·i·nisce (rem'ə nis'), v.i., **-nisced, -nisc·ing.** to recall past experiences, events, etc.

rem·i·nis·cence (rem'ə nis'əns), n. 1. the act or process of reminiscing. 2. a mental impression retained. 3. Often, **reminiscences.** a recollection narrated or told.

---

re·list', v.t.
re·load', v.
re·loan', n., v.t.
re·mail', v.t.
re·make', v.t., -made, -mak·ing.
re'make', n.
re'man·u·fac'ture, v.t., -tured, -tur·ing.

re·mar'riage, n.
re·mar'ry, v., -ried, -ry·ing.
re'match', n.
re·match', v.t.
re·meas'ure, v.t., -ured, -ur·ing.
re·meas'ure·ment, n.
re·melt', v.t.

re·mend', v.
re·mi'grate, v.i., -grat·ed, -grat·ing.
re'mi·li·ta·ri·za'tion, n.
re·mil'i·ta·rize', v.t., -rized, -riz·ing.

rem·i·nis·cent (rem′ə nis′ənt), *adj.* **1.** suggestive of or recalling something because of a certain likeness. **2.** given to reminiscence. **—rem′i·nis′cent·ly,** *adv.*

re·miss (ri mis′), *adj.* negligent, careless, or slow, as in performing one's duty. **—re·miss′ly,** *adv.* **—re·miss′ness,** *n.*

re·mis·sion (ri mish′ən), *n.* **1.** forgiveness, as of sins or offenses. **2.** abatement, as of pain or an illness. **3.** the cancellation of a debt, duty, etc.

re·mit (ri mit′), *v.,* **-mit·ted, -mit·ting.** **—***v.t.* **1.** to send (money) in payment. **2.** to pardon or forgive. **3.** to free someone from, as a debt or punishment. **4.** to make weaker or slacken. **—***v.i.* **5.** to send money, as in payment. **6.** to abate, as a fever.

re·mit·tance (ri mit′ᵊns), *n.* **1.** the sending of money to someone. **2.** the amount of money sent.

rem·nant (rem′nənt), *n.* **1.** a remaining, usually small part or quantity. **2.** a small, unsold or unused piece of fabric. **3.** a trace or vestige.

re·mod·el (rē mod′ᵊl), *v.t.,* **eled, -el·ing** or **-elled, -el·ling.** to make over in a different way. **—re·mod′el·er,** *n.*

re·mon·strance (ri mon′strəns), *n.* the act or an instance of remonstrating. **—re·mon′strant,** *adj.* **—re·mon′strant·ly,** *adv.*

re·mon·strate (ri mon′strāt), *v.,* **-strat·ed, -strat·ing.** **—***v.t.* **1.** to say in protest, objection, or disapproval. **—***v.i.* **2.** to present reasons in complaint or argument **—re·mon·stra·tion** (rē′mon strā′shən, rem′ən-), *n.* **—re·mon′stra·tive** (-strə tiv), *adj.* **—re·mon′stra·tor** (-strā tər), *n.*

rem·o·ra (rem′ər ə), *n.* a fish having a sucking disk on top of the head by which it can attach itself to sharks, ships, etc.

re·morse (ri môrs′), *n.* deep and painful sense of guilt for wrongdoing. **—re·morse′ful,** *adj.* **—re·morse′ful·ly,** *adv.* **—re·morse′less,** *adj.* **—Syn.** contrition, penitence.

re·mote (ri mōt′), *adj.,* **-mot·er, -mot·est.** **1.** far distant in space. **2.** secluded or set apart. **3.** far away in time. **4.** only distantly related: *a remote ancestor.* **5.** slight or faint: *a remote chance.* **—re·mote′ly,** *adv.* **—re·mote′ness,** *n.*

remote′ control′, control of the operation of an apparatus from a distance, as by radio signals.

re·move (ri mōōv′), *v.,* **-moved, -mov·ing,** *n.* **—***v.t.* **1.** to take away or off.

2. to wipe out or get rid of, as a stain. **3.** to dismiss or force from an office or position. **4.** to kill or assassinate. **—***v.i.* **5.** *Brit.* to move from one place, as of residence, to another. **6.** to be capable of being removed or erased. **7.** *Literary.* to go away or depart. **—***n.* **8.** the act of removing. **9.** a degree of distance or separation. **—re·mov′a·ble,** *adj.* **—re·mov′al,** *n.* **—re·mov′er,** *n.*

re·mu·ner·ate (ri myōō′nə rāt′), *v.t.,* **-at·ed, -at·ing.** to pay or reward (a person) for (work or services). **—re·mu′ner·a′tion,** *n.* **—re·mu′ner·a′tive,** *adj.* **—re·mu′ner·a′tive·ly,** *adv.* **—re·mu′ner·a′tive·ness,** *n.* **—re·mu′ner·a′tor,** *n.* **—re·mu′ner·a·to′ry** (-rə·tôr′ē, -tōr′ē), *adj.*

Ren·ais·sance (ren′i säns′, -zäns′, ren′i säns′, -zäns′), *n.* **1.** the vigorous revival of learning and art beginning in 14th-century Florence and extending throughout Europe by the 17th century. **2.** the period of history during which this occurred. **3.** any similar vigorous revival. **4.** (*l.c.*) renascence [< F, MF: rebirth]

re·nal (rēn′ᵊl), *adj.* of the kidneys or the surrounding regions.

re·nas·cence (ri nas′əns, -nās′-), *n.* a renewal of life, vigor, etc. **—re·nas′cent,** *adj.*

ren·coun·ter (ren koun′tər), *n. Rare.* **1.** a casual meeting. **2.** a hostile meeting. Also, **ren·con·tre** (-kon′tər).

rend (rend), *v.t.,* **rent** or **rend·ed, rend·ing.** **1.** to separate into parts with violence. **2.** to tear (one's clothing or hair) in grief. rage, etc. **3.** to distress (the heart) with painful feelings. **—rend′er,** *n.*

ren·der (ren′dər), *v.t.* **1.** to cause to be or become. **2.** to do or perform. **3.** to furnish or provide: *to render aid.* **4.** to present for consideration, payment, etc. **5.** to give in return. **6.** to translate into another language. **7.** to represent or depict, as in painting. **8.** to interpret (a part in a drama, a piece of music, etc.). **9.** to melt down, as fat **—ren′der·er,** *n.*

ren·dez·vous (rän′də vōō′, -dā-), *n., pl.* **-vous** (-vōōz′), *v.,* **-voused** (-vōōd′), **-vous·ing** (-vōō′ing). **—***n.* **1.** an agreement to meet at a certain time and place. **2.** the place of meeting. **3.** the meeting itself. **4.** the meeting of two or more space vehicles in outer space at a prearranged time and point. **—***v.i., v.t.* **5.** to assemble or bring together at a rendezvous.

---

re·mix, *v.,* **-mixed** or **-mixt. -mix·ing.**
re′mod·i·fi·ca′tion, *n.*
re·mod′i·fy, *v.,* **-fied, -fy·ing.**

re·mold′, *v.*
re·mon′e·ti·za′tion, *n.*
re·mon′e·tize′, *v.t.,* **-tized, -tiz·ing.**

re·mort′gage, *v.t.,* **-gaged, -gag·ing.**
re·mount′, *v.*
re·name′, *v.t.,* **-named, -nam·ing.**

ren·di·tion (ren dish′ən), *n.* **1.** the act of rendering. **2.** a translation. **3.** an interpretation, as of a role or a piece of music.

ren·e·gade (ren′ə gād′), *n.* a person who deserts a cause, faith, or party for another.

re·nege (ri nig′, -nĕg′, -nēg′), *v.i.*, **-neged, -neg·ing. 1.** to go back on one's word. **2.** *Cards.* to break a rule of play. **—re·neg′er,** *n.*

re·new (ri nōō′, -nyōō′), *v.t.* **1.** to begin or take up again. **2.** to make effective for an additional period: *to renew a lease.* **3.** to restore or replenish. **4.** to make, say, or do again. **5.** to revive or make fresh again. **6.** to restore to a former state. **—re·new′a·ble,** *adj.* **—re·new′al,** *n.* **—re·new′er,** *n.*

ren·net (ren′it), *n.* an extract from the lining membrane of the stomach of a calf, used to curdle milk, as in making cheese, etc.

ren·nin (ren′in), *n.* an enzyme found in rennet and able to curdle milk.

Re·no (rē′nō), *n.* a city in W Nevada.

Re·noir (ren′wär), *n.* Pierre Au·guste (pyer ō gyst′), 1841–1919, French painter.

re·nounce (ri nouns′), *v.t.*, **-nounced, -nounc·ing. 1.** to give up by formal declaration. **2.** to repudiate or disown. **3.** to give up or put aside voluntarily. **—re·nounce′ment,** *n.* **—re·nounc′er,** *n.*

ren·o·vate (ren′ə vāt′), *v.t.*, **-vat·ed, -vat·ing.** to bring back to a good or earlier condition, esp. by extensive repair. **—ren′o·va′tion,** *n.* **—ren′o·va′tor,** *n.*

re·nown (ri noun′), *n.* widely acclaimed name or honor. **—re·nowned′,** *adj.* **—Syn.** celebrity, eminence, repute.

rent¹ (rent), *n.* **1.** a payment periodically made for the use of another's property, as a house or automobile. **2. for rent,** available in return for rent. **—v.t. 3.** to use or allow the use of in return for rent. **—v.i. 4.** to be leased or let for rent. **—rent′er,** *n.*

rent² (rent), *n.* **1.** an opening made by rending or tearing. **2.** a split or schism, as in a political party. **—v. 3.** a pt. and pp. of **rend.**

rent·al (ren′t°l), *n.* **1.** an amount received or paid as rent. **2.** the act of renting. **3.** a property for rent.

re·nun·ci·a·tion (ri nun′sē ā′shən, -shē-), *n.* an act or instance of renouncing, as a right or claim.

re·or·gan·ize (rē ôr′gə nīz′), *v.t., v.i.,* **-ized, -iz·ing.** to organize again. **—re′or·gan·i·za′tion,** *n.*

rep¹ (rep), *n.* a transversely corded fabric. **—repped,** *adj.*

rep² (rep), *n. Informal.* **1.** repertory. **2.** representative. **3.** reputation.

Rep., 1. Representative. **2.** Republic. **3.** Republican.

rep., 1. repair. **2.** repeat. **3.** report. **4.** reported. **5.** reporter.

re·pair¹ (ri pâr′), *v.t.,* **1.** to put back into good condition after wear, decay, or damage. **2.** to remedy or make up for. **—n. 3.** an act or process of repairing. **4.** Usually, **repairs.** the work done or to be done in repairing. **5.** the good condition resulting from repairing. **—re·pair′a·ble,** *adj.* **—re·pair′er,** *n.*

re·pair² (ri pâr′), *v.i. Chiefly Literary.* to go to a particular place, esp. customarily or as a group.

re·pair·man (ri pâr′man′, -mən), *n.* a person whose occupation is making repairs.

rep·a·ra·tion (rep′ə rā′shən), *n.* **1.** the making of amends for wrong or injury done. **2.** Usually, **reparations.** compensation payable by a defeated country to the victor or victors for damages or loss suffered during war. **—re·par·a·tive** (ri pâr′ə tiv), **re·par′a·to′ry** (-tôr′ē, -tōr′ē), *adj.*

rep·ar·tee (rep′ər tē′, -tā′), *n.* **1.** a quick, witty reply. **2.** conversation full of such replies. **3.** skill in making such replies.

re·past (ri past′, -päst′), *n. Chiefly Literary.* a meal, esp. an enjoyable one.

re·pa·tri·ate (rē pā′trē āt′), *v.t.,* **-at·ed, -at·ing.** to bring or send back (a person) to his or her own country, esp. after a war. **—re·pa′tri·a′tion,** *n.*

re·pay (ri pā′), *v.t.,* **-paid, -pay·ing. 1.** to pay back. **2.** to make a return to or for. **3.** to return: *to repay a visit.* **—re·pay′a·ble,** *adj.* **—re·pay′ment,** *n.* **—Syn. 1.** indemnify, reimburse.

re·ne·go′ti·ate′, *v.,* -at·ed, -at·ing.
re·ne·go′ti·a′tion, *n.*
re·nom′i·nate′, *v.t.,* -nat·ed, -nat·ing.
re·nom·i·na′tion, *n.*
re·no′ti·fy′, *v.t.,* -fied, -fy·ing.
re·num′ber, *v.t.*
re′ob·tain′, *v.t.*

re′ob·tain′a·ble, *adj.*
re′oc·cu·pa′tion, *n.*
re·oc′cu·py′, *v.t.,* -pied, -py·ing.
re′oc·cur′, *v.i.,* -curred, -cur·ring.
re′oc·cur′rence, *n.*
re·o′pen, *v.*
re·or′der, *n., v.t.*
re·or′i·ent, *v.*
re·or′i·en·ta′tion, *n.*

re·pac′i·fy′, *v.t.,* -fied, -fy·ing.
re·pack′, *v.*
re·pack′age, *v.t.,* -aged, -ag·ing.
re·paint′, *v.*
re·pass′, *v.*
re·pave′, *v.t.,* -paved, -pav·ing.

re·peal (ri pēl′), *v.t.* **1.** to revoke or annul by express enactment. —*n.* **2.** the act of repealing. —**re·peal′er**, *n.*

re·peat (ri pēt′), *v.t.* **1.** to say again (something already said). **2.** to say after another. **3.** to tell (something heard). **4.** to do, make, or perform again. —*v.i.* **5.** to do or say something again. —*n.* **6.** the act of repeating. **7.** something repeated, as a rerun on television. **8.** *Music.* **a.** a passage to be repeated. **b.** a sign for this. —**re·peat′a·ble**, *adj.* —**re·peat′er**, *n.* —**Syn.** **1.** recapitulate, reiterate.

re·peat·ed (ri pē′tid), *adj.* done, made, or said again and again. —**re·peat′ed·ly**, *adv.*

repeat′ing dec′imal, a decimal in which a series of digits is repeated indefinitely, as 0.147232323 . . . .

re·pel (ri pel′), *v.t.*, **-pelled**, **-pel·ling**. **1.** to drive or force back. **2.** to keep off or out. **3.** to refuse to accept. **4.** to cause distaste or aversion in.

re·pel·lent (ri pel′ənt), *adj.* **1.** causing distaste or aversion. **2.** impervious or resistant to something. —*n.* **3.** something that repels: *insect repellent.* Also **re·pel′lant.** —**re·pel′lent·ly, re·pel′lant·ly,** *adv.*

re·pent (ri pent′), *v.i., v.t.* **1.** to feel sorry for (a past action, attitude, etc.). **2.** to feel such remorse for (sin or fault) as to change one's ways. —**re·pent′ance,** *n.* —**re·pent′ant,** *adj.* —**re·pent′er,** *n.*

re·per·cus·sion (rē′pər kush′ən), *n.* **1.** an effect or result, often indirect, of some event or action. **2.** an echo or reverberation. **3.** a rebounding or recoil of something after impact. —**re′per·cus′sive,** *adj.*

rep·er·toire (rep′ər twär′, -twôr′), *n.* **1.** the list of dramas, operas, or pieces that a company, actor, or singer is prepared to perform. **2.** the entire stock of skills, techniques, or devices existing in a particular field.

rep·er·to·ry (rep′ər tōr′ē, -tôr′ē), *n., pl.* **-ries. 1.** a theatrical company that presents several performances of its productions regularly or in alternate sequence in one season. **2.** repertoire. —**rep′er·to′ri·al,** *adj.*

rep·e·ti·tion (rep′i tish′ən), *n.* **1.** the act of repeating. **2.** the fact of being repeated.

rep·e·ti·tious (rep′i tish′əs), *adj.* full of repetition, esp. of a tedious kind. —**rep′e·ti′tious·ly,** *adv.* —**rep′e·ti′tious·ness,** *n.*

re·pet·i·tive (ri pet′i tiv), *adj.* characterized by repetition. —**re·pet′i·tive·ly,** *adv.* —**re·pet′i·tive·ness,** *n.*

re·pine (ri pīn′), *v.i.*, **-pined**, **-pin·ing.** to be fretfully discontented. —**re·pin′er,** *n.*

repl., 1. replace. **2.** replacement.

re·place (ri plās′), *v.t.*, **-placed**, **-plac·ing. 1.** to take the place of. **2.** to provide something new in the place of. **3.** to put back in place. —**re·place′a·ble,** *adj.* —**re·place′ment,** *n.* —**re·plac′er,** *n.*

re·play (*v.* ri plā′; *n.* rē′plā′), *v.t.* **1.** to play again, as a record or tape. —*n.* **2.** the act or an instance of replaying. **3.** something replayed, as a portion of a videotape.

re·plen·ish (ri plen′ish), *v.t.* **1.** to make full or complete again. **2.** to supply again or afresh. —**re·plen′ish·er,** *n.* —**re·plen′ish·ment,** *n.*

re·plete (ri plēt′), *adj.* **1.** abundantly filled. **2.** stuffed with food and drink. —**re·ple′tion, re·plete′ness,** *n.*

rep·li·ca (rep′lə kə), *n.* **1.** a copy of a work of art, esp. by the original artist. **2.** any close copy or reproduction.

rep·li·cate (rep′lə kāt′), *v.t.*, **-cat·ed, -cat·ing.** *Biol.* to duplicate or repeat, as an experiment.

rep·li·ca·tion (rep′lə kā′shən), *n.* **1.** *Biol.* duplication of an experiment, esp. to reduce error. **2.** *Law,* a plaintiff's reply to a defendant's answer.

re·ply (ri plī′), *v.*, **-plied, -ply·ing,** *n., pl.* **-plies.** —*v.i., v.t.* **1.** to give (as) an answer, esp. a formal or deliberate one. —*n.* **2.** something replied. —**re·pli′er,** *n.*

re·port (ri pōrt′, -pôrt′), *n.* **1.** a detailed account or statement describing an event, action, etc., usually presented formally. **2.** a rumor or gossip. **3.** reputation or fame. **4.** a loud noise, as from an explosion. —*v.t.* **5.** to write an account of. **6.** to carry and repeat, as a message. **7.** to make a formal report on (a legislative bill). **8.** to make a charge against (a person), as to a superior. **9.** to make known the presence or whereabouts of. —*v.i.* **10.** to make or submit a report. **11.** to work as a reporter, as for a newspaper. **12.** to present oneself duly, as at a place. —**re·port′a·ble,** *adj.*

re·port·age (ri pōr′tij, -pôr′-, rə pōr·täzh′, -pôr-), *n.* **1.** the process of reporting news. **2.** a written account based on direct observation or on documentation.

---

re·peo′ple, *v.t.,* **-pled, -pling.**

re·phrase′, *v.t.,* **-phrased, -phras·ing.**

re·pin′, *v.t.,* **-pinned, -pin·ning.**

re·plan′, *v.t.,* **-planned, -plan·ning.**

re·plant′, *v.t.*

re·pop′u·late′, *v.t.,* **-lat·ed, -lat·ing.**

report′ card′, a periodic written report of a pupil's grades.

re·port·ed·ly (ri pôr′tid lē), *adv.* according to report or rumor.

re·port·er (ri pôr′tər, -pôr′-), *n.* **1.** a person who reports. **2.** a person employed to gather and report news, as for a newspaper. —**rep·or·to·ri·al** (rep′ər tôr′ē əl, -tôr′-), *adj.*

re·pose¹ (ri pōz′), *n., v.,* **-posed, -pos·ing.** —*n.* **1.** the state of being at rest. **2.** peace or tranquillity. **3.** dignified calmness. **4.** absence of movement, animation, etc. —*v.i.* **5.** to lie or be at rest. **6.** to lie dead. **7.** to rest on something. —*v.t.* **8.** to refresh by rest. —**re·pose′ful,** *adj.* —**re·pos′er,** *n.*

re·pose² (ri pōz′), *v.t.,* **-posed, -pos·ing.** to put (confidence or trust) in a person or thing.

re·pos·i·to·ry (ri poz′i tôr′ē, -tôr′ē), *n., pl.* **-tor·ies.** a receptacle or place where things are put or kept.

re·pos·sess (rē′pə zes′), *v.t.* to regain possession of, esp. for nonpayment of money due. —**re′pos·ses′sion,** *n.*

rep·re·hend (rep′ri hend′), *v.t.* to show sharp disapproval of. —**rep′re·hen′sion** (-hen′shən), *n.*

rep·re·hen·si·ble (rep′ri hen′sə bəl), *adj.* deserving to be reprehended. —**rep′re·hen′si·bly,** *adv.* —**Syn.** blameworthy, shameful.

rep·re·sent (rep′ri zent′), *v.t.* **1.** to serve to express or stand for, as a word or symbol does. **2.** to act in place of, as an agent does. **3.** to speak and act for authority. **4.** to act for or in behalf of (a constituency) in exercising a voice in legislation. **5.** to portray or depict. **6.** to picture to the mind. **7.** to describe as having a particular character. **8.** to set forth so as to influence opinion or action. **9.** to act the part of in a play. **10.** to serve as an example or specimen of.

rep·re·sen·ta·tion (rep′ri zen tā′shən), *n.* **1.** the act of representing. **2.** a picture, figure, statue, etc. **3.** the state of being represented by legislative delegates. **4.** the body of representatives of a constituency. **5.** a statement of facts or reasons made in protest. —**rep′re·sen·ta′tion·al,** *adj.*

rep·re·sent·a·tive (rep′ri zen′tə tiv), *n.* **1.** a person who represents another or others. **2.** a person who represents a constituency in a legislative body, esp. a member of the U.S. House of Representatives. **3.** a typical example or specimen. —*adj.* **4.** serving to represent. **5.** representing

a constituency in legislation. **6.** founded on representation in government. **7.** typical of its kind. —**rep′re·sent′a·tive·ly,** *adv.* —**rep′re·sent′a·tive·ness,** *n.*

re·press (ri pres′), *v.t.* **1.** to keep under control. **2.** to put down or quell. **3.** to reject (painful ideas) from the conscious mind. —**re·pres′sion,** *n.* —**re·pres′sive,** *adj.*

re·prieve (ri prēv′), *v., -prieved, -priev·ing, n.* —*v.t.* **1.** to delay temporarily the punishment or execution of. **2.** to relieve temporarily, as from an evil. —*n.* **3.** the act of reprieving or state of being reprieved. —**re·priev′er,** *n.*

rep·ri·mand (rep′rə mand′, -mänd′), *n.* **1.** a severe, usually formal rebuke. —*v.t.* **2.** to rebuke severely, esp. in a formal way.

re·pris·al (ri prī′zəl), *n.* action or an act in retaliation against someone for injuries received.

re·prise (rə prēz′), *n.* **1.** *Music.* a repetition or return to the first theme or subject. **2.** any repeated occurrence.

re·proach (ri prōch′), *v.t.* **1.** to find fault with, usually with a feeling of disappointment. —*n.* **2.** blame conveyed in disapproval. **3.** words expressing blame **4.** a cause of blame. —**re·proach′a·ble,** *adj.* —**re·proach′ful,** *adj.* —**re·proach′ful·ly,** *adv.* —**re·proach′ful·ness,** *n.* —**re·proach′ing·ly,** *adv.* —**Syn.** **1.** admonish, chide, scold.

rep·ro·bate (rep′rə bāt′), *n.* **1.** a wicked, sinful, or unprincipled person. —*adj.* **2.** depraved or unprincipled.

rep·ro·ba·tion (rep′rə bā′shən), *n.* sharp disapproval or condemnation.

re·pro·duce (rē′prə dōōs′, -dyōōs′), *v., -duced, -duc·ing.* —*v.t.* **1.** to make a copy or close imitation of. **2.** to produce again or anew. **3.** to produce by some process of propagation. —*v.i.* **4.** to bear offspring **5.** to undergo reproduction. —**re′pro·duc′er,** *n.* —**re′pro·duc′i·ble,** *adj.* —**re′pro·duc′tion** (-duk′shən), *n.* —**re′pro·duc′tive,** *adj.*

re·prog·ra·phy (ri prog′rə fē), *n.* the art of reproducing documents or books, esp. by electronic means.

re·proof (ri prōōf′), *n.* the act or an expression of reproving.

re·prove (ri prōōv′), *v.t., -proved, -prov·ing.* to censure mildly. —**re·prov′er,** *n.* —**re·prov′ing·ly,** *adv.*

rept., 1. receipt. **2.** report.

---

re′·press′, *v.*
re·price′, *v.t., -priced, -pric·ing.*

re·print′, *v.t.*
re′print′, *n.*

re·probe′, *v., -probed, -prob·ing.*
re·proc′ess, *n.*

rep·tile (rep′til, -tīl), *n.* any cold-blooded, scaly vertebrate, as a turtle, lizard, or snake. —**rep·til·i·an** (rep til′ē ən, -til′yən), *adj., n.*

Repub., **1.** Republic. **2.** Republican.

re·pub·lic (ri pub′lik), *n.* **1.** a country in which the supreme power rests in the body of citizens entitled to vote and is exercised by representatives chosen directly or indirectly by them. **2.** a country in which the head of government is an elected or nominated president, and not a monarch. [< F *république* < L *rēs publica* public matter]

re·pub·li·can (ri pub′li kən), *adj.* **1.** of or favoring a republic. **2.** (*cap.*) of or belonging to the Republican Party. —*n.* **3.** a person who favors a republican form of government. **4.** (*cap.*) a member of the Republican Party. —**re·pub′li·can·ism′,** *n.*

Repub′lican Par′ty, one of the two major political parties in the U.S.: originated 1854–56.

re·pu·di·ate (ri pyōō′dē āt′), *v.t.,* -at·ed, -at·ing. **1.** to reject as having no authority or binding force. **2.** to cast off or disown. **3.** to refuse to acknowledge and pay (a debt). —**re·pu′di·a′tion,** *n.* —**re·pu′di·a′tor,** *n.*

re·pug·nant (ri pug′nənt), *adj.* **1.** highly distasteful or offensive **2.** opposed or contrary, as in nature. —**re·pug′nance,** *n.* —**re·pug′nant·ly,** *adv.*

re·pulse (ri puls′), *v.,* -pulsed, -puls·ing, *n.* —*v.t.* **1.** to drive back, as an invader. **2.** to reject with denial or discourtesy. —*n.* **3.** repulsion (def. 1). **4.** a refusal or rejection.

re·pul·sion (ri pul′shən), *n.* **1.** the act of repulsing or state of being repulsed. **2.** repugnance or aversion. **3.** *Physics.* the force that acts between bodies of like electric charge, tending to separate them.

re·pul·sive (ri pul′siv), *adj.* **1.** causing repugnance or aversion. **2.** tending to reject by denial or discourtesy. —**re·pul′sive·ly,** *adv.* —**re·pul′sive·ness,** *n.*

rep·u·ta·ble (rep′yə tə bəl), *adj.* having a good reputation. —**rep′u·ta·bil′i·ty,** *n.* —**rep′u·ta·bly,** *adv.*

rep·u·ta·tion (rep′yə tā′shən), *n.* **1.** the estimation in which a person or thing is generally held. **2.** a favorable name or standing. **3.** the way in which a person or thing is known or thought of.

re·pute (ri pyōōt′), *n., v.,* -put·ed, -put·ing. —*n.* **1.** reputation (defs. 1,

2). —*v.t.* **2.** to consider or esteem (usually used in the passive).

re·put·ed (ri pyōō′tid), *adj.* considered or supposed to be such. —**re·put′ed·ly,** *adv.*

req., **1.** request. **2.** require. **3.** required. **4.** requisition.

re·quest (ri kwest′), *n.* **1.** the act or an instance of asking for something to be given or done. **2.** something asked for. **3.** the state of being much asked for. —*v.t.* **4.** to ask for, esp. politely or formally. **5.** to ask (someone) to do something. —**re·quest′er,** *n.*

Req·ui·em (rek′wē əm, rē′kwē-), *n.* **1.** *Rom. Cath. Ch.* a Mass for a dead person. **2.** (*often l.c.*) the musical setting for this.

re·quire (ri kwīr′), *v.t.,* -quired, -quir·ing. **1.** to call for as necessary or pressing. **2.** to demand, as by law. —**re·quire′ment,** *n.*

req·ui·site (rek′wi zit), *adj.* **1.** required for a particular purpose. —*n.* **2.** something requisite. —**req′ui·site·ly,** *adv.*

req·ui·si·tion (rek′wi zish′ən), *n.* **1.** an official or formal written order for something needed, as supplies. **2.** the state of being needed or used. —*v.t.* **3.** to demand or take, as for military purposes. —**req′ui·si′tion·er,** *n.*

re·quite (ri kwīt′), *v.t.,* -quit·ed, -quit·ing. **1.** to make return for: to *requite good with good.* **2.** to make return to (a person), as for service or kindness. —**re·quit′al,** *n.* —**re·quit′er,** *n.*

rere·dos (rēr′dos, rēr′i-, râr′i-), *n.* a screen or a decorated part of the wall behind an altar in a church.

re·run (rē′run′), *n.* a showing of a motion picture or television program after its first or previous presentation.

res., **1.** research. **2.** reserve. **3.** residence. **4.** resigned. **5.** resolution.

re·sale (rē′sāl′, rē sāl′), *n.* the act of selling a second time, esp. to a third party. —**re·sal′a·ble,** *adj.*

re·scind (ri sind′), *v.t.* to invalidate (a regulation, etc.) by a later action or a higher authority. —**re·scind′a·ble,** *adj.* —**re·scis′sion** (-sizh′ən), *n.*

re·script (rē′skript′), *n.* an edict or decree issued esp. by a ruler.

res·cue (res′kyōō), *v.,* -cued, -cu·ing, *n.* —*v.t.* **1.** to free or save from danger, captivity, etc. —*n.* **2.** the act of rescuing. —**res′cu·er,** *n.* —**Syn. 1.** deliver, liberate, ransom.

---

re′pub·li·ca′tion, *n.*
re·pub′lish, *v.t.*
re·pur′chase, *v.t.,* -chased, -chasing, *n.*
re·ra′di·ate′, *v.t.,* -at·ed, -at·ing.

re·read′, *v.,* -read, -read·ing.
re′re·cord′, *v.*
re·roll′, *v.*
re·route′, *v.t.,* -rout·ed, -rout·ing.

re·sched′ule, *v.t.,* -uled, -ul·ing.
re·seal′, *v.*
re·seal′a·ble, *adj.*

re·search (ri sûrch´, rē´sûrch), *n.* **1.** systematic inquiry into a subject in order to discover or check facts. — *v.i., v.t.* **2.** to do research (in or on). —re·search´er, *n.*

re·sec·tion (ri sek´shən), *n.* the surgical removal of part of an organ or tissue, esp. bone.

re·sem·blance (ri zem´bləns), *n.* superficial likeness, esp. in appearance. —Syn. similarity.

re·sem·ble (ri zem´bəl), *v.t.,* -bled, -bling. to have a resemblance to.

re·sent (ri zent´), *v.t.* to feel or show bitter indignation at. —re·sent´ful, *adj.* —re·sent´ful·ly, *adv.* —re·sent´·ment, *n.*

res·er·pine (res´ər pin, -pēn´, rə sûr´pin, -pēn), *n.* an alkaloid obtained from the root of the rauwolfia, used to alleviate hypertension and as a tranquilizer.

res·er·va·tion (rez´ər vā´shən), *n.* **1.** Often, **reservations.** an arrangement by which space or accommodations, as a plane seat, are reserved. **2.** the record or assurance of such an arrangement. **3.** an exception or qualification made expressly or tacitly. **4.** a tract of public land set apart, as for an Indian tribe. **5.** the act of reserving.

re·serve (ri zûrv´), *v.,* -served, -serving, *n., adj.* —*v.t.* **1.** to keep back or save for future or special use. **2.** to have kept for oneself in advance, as a hotel room. **3.** to keep as one's own. —*n.* **4.** something reserved for some future use, purpose, or need. **5.** a reservation of land, esp. public land. **6.** an act of reserving. **7.** Mil. **a.** a fraction of a military force held in readiness. **b.** reserves. the enrolled but not regular components of the armed forces. **8.** formality or self-restraint in manner and relationship. **9.** reticence or silence **10.** money held aside, as by a corporation, to meet expected or unexpected demands. **11. in reserve.** put aside for a future need —*adj.* **12.** forming a reserve or reserves.

re·served (ri zûrvd´), *adj.* **1.** kept in reserve or by reservation **2.** withdrawn and self-restrained. —re·serv´ed·ly (ri zûr´vid lē), *adv.* —re·serv´ed·ness, *n.* —Syn. reticent, shy.

re·serv·ist (ri zûr´vist), *n.* a member of a military reserve.

res·er·voir (rez´ər vwär´, -vôr´, rez´ə-), *n.* **1.** a place where water is collected and stored for use, esp. water for supplying a community. **2.** a receptacle for holding a liquid or fluid. **3.** any large or extra supply or stock.

re·side (ri zīd´), *v.i.,* -sid·ed, -sid·ing. **1.** to make one's home for a considerable time. **2.** to lie or be present, as a quality. **3.** to rest or be vested, as a right. —re·sid´er, *n.* —Syn. **1.** abide, dwell, sojourn.

res·i·dence (rez´i dəns), *n.* **1.** the place, esp. the house, in which a person resides. **2.** the act or a period of residing in a place.

res·i·den·cy (rez´i dən sē), *n., pl.* -cies. **1.** residence (def. 2). **2.** the position or tenure of a medical resident.

res·i·dent (rez´i dənt), *n.* **1.** a person who resides in a place. **2.** a physician employed by a hospital while receiving specialized training. —*adj.* **3.** residing in a place. **4.** living or staying at a place in discharge of duty.

res·i·den·tial (rez´i den´shəl), *adj.* **1.** of or pertaining to residence. **2.** suitable or used for residence. —res´i·den´tial·ly, *adv.*

re·sid·u·al (ri zij´ōō əl), *adj.* **1.** of or constituting a residue. —*n.* **2.** a residual quantity. **3.** Usually, **residuals.** additional pay given to a performer for each rerun of a film or TV commercial in which he or she appears. —re·sid´u·al·ly, *adv.*

res·i·due (rez´i dōō´, -dyōō´), *n.* **1.** what remains after a main part is taken away. **2.** a body of matter remaining after evaporation, combustion, distillation, etc.

re·sid·u·um (ri zij´ōō əm), *n., pl.* -sid·u·a (-zij´ōō ə). residue (def. 2).

re·sign (ri zīn´), *v.i., v.t.* **1.** to give up (an office, position, etc.), often formally. **2.** to submit (oneself, one's mind, etc.) without resistance.

res·ig·na·tion (rez´ig nā´shən), *n.* **1.** the act of resigning. **2.** a formal written notification of such an act. **3.** unresisting submission.

re·signed (ri zīnd´), *adj.* unresistingly submissive. —re·sign·ed·ly (ri zī´nid lē), *adv.*

re·sil·i·ent (ri zil´yənt, -zil´ē ənt), *adj.* **1.** capable of returning to the original shape or position after being bent, compressed, or stretched. **2.** recovering readily from illness, depression, etc. —re·sil´ience, re·sil´ien·cy, *n.* —re·sil´ient·ly, *adv.*

---

re·seat´, *v.t.*	re´set´, *n.*	re·sharp´en, *v.*
re·seed´, *v.*	re·set´tle, *v.,* -tled, -tling.	re·ship´, *v.,* -shipped, -ship·ping.
re·sell´, *v.,* -sold, -sell·ing.	re·set´tle·ment, *n.*	re·ship´ment, *n.*
re·set´, *v.t.,* -set, -set·ting.	re·shape´, *v.t.,* -shaped, -shap·ing.	re·shuf´fle, *v.,* -fled, -fling; *n.*

res·in (rez′in), *n.* **1.** a sticky substance obtained esp. from gum trees or pine trees, used in making varnishes, medicines, etc. **2.** any similar synthetic substance used in making plastics, glues, etc. —**res·in·ous** (rez′ə nəs), *adj.*

re·sist (ri zist′), *v.t.* **1.** to fight against. **2.** to withstand the action or effect of. —*v.i.* **3.** to act in opposition. —*n.* **4.** a substance that prevents or inhibits some action, as a coating that inhibits corrosion. —**re·sist′er,** *n.* —**re·sist′i·ble,** *adj.* —**re·sist′less,** *adj.*

re·sist·ance (ri zis′təns), *n.* **1.** the act or power of resisting. **2.** a force that opposes another. **3.** the opposition to the flow of an electric current through a circuit or a piece of conducting material.

re·sist·ant (ri zis′tənt), *adj.* offering or capable of resistance (often used in combination): *flame-resistant pajamas.*

re·sis·tive (ri zis′tiv), *adj.* capable of or inclined to resistance. —**re′sis·tiv′i·ty** (-i tē), *n.*

re·sis·tor (ri zis′tər), *n.* a device used to introduce resistance into an electric circuit.

res·o·lute (rez′ə lōōt′), *adj.* firmly or strongly determined. —**res′o·lute′ly,** *adv.* —**res′o·lute′ness,** *n.* —*Syn.* fixed, persevering, resolved, unwavering.

res·o·lu·tion (rez′ə lōō′shən), *n.* **1.** a formal expression of opinion or intention made, usually after voting, by a formal organization. **2.** the act of resolving or determining, as upon an action or course of action, method, procedure, etc. **3.** firm determination. **4.** the act of resolving into constituent parts. **5.** a solution or explanation, as of a problem.

re·solve (ri zolv′), *v.,* **-solved, -solv·ing,** *n.* —*v.t.* **1.** to come to a definite decision about. **2.** to solve or settle, as a problem. **3.** to separate into constituent parts. **4.** to decide by a formal vote or resolution. —*v.i.* **5.** to make up one's mind. **6.** to become separated into constituent parts. —*n.* **7.** firmness of purpose. **8.** a resolution or decision. —**re·solv′a·ble,** *adj.* —**re·solv′er,** *n.*

re·solved (ri zolvd′), *adj.* firmly fixed in purpose.

res·o·nance (rez′ə nəns), *n.* **1.** an increase or prolongation of a sound or tone caused by secondary vibrations. **2.** the state or quality of being resonant.

res·o·nant (rez′ə nənt), *adj.* **1.** continuing to resound. **2.** deep and full of resonance. **3.** producing resonance. —**res′o·nant·ly,** *adv.*

res·o·nate (rez′ə nāt′), *v.i.,* **-nat·ed, -nat·ing. 1.** to exhibit or produce resonance. **2.** to resound or reecho. —**res′o·na′tion,** *n.*

res·o·na·tor (rez′ə nā′tər), *n.* an appliance for increasing sound by resonance.

re·sort (ri zôrt′), *v.i.* **1.** to have recourse for aid or solution, often as a final choice. **2.** to go, esp. frequently or customarily. —*n.* **3.** a place to which people frequently go, esp. for rest or pleasure. **4.** use of or appeal to a person or thing for aid or solution. **5.** a person or thing resorted to. —**re·sort′er,** *n.*

re·sound (ri zound′), *v.i.* **1.** to ring with sound or an echo. **2.** to sound loudly. —**re·sound′ing,** *adj.* —**re·sound′ing·ly,** *adv.*

re·source (rē′sôrs, -sōrs, ri sôrs′, -sōrs′), *n.* **1.** a source of supply, support, or aid, esp. one held in reserve. **2. resources,** the collective wealth of a country or its means of producing wealth. **3.** the quality of being resourceful.

re·source·ful (ri sôrs′fəl, -sōrs′-), *adj.* able to deal skillfully with new problems, situations, etc. —**re·source′ful·ly,** *adv.* —**re·source′ful·ness,** *n.*

resp., **1.** respective. **2.** respectively.

re·spect (ri spekt′), *n.* **1.** high admiration or esteem for a person or quality. **2.** polite regard or consideration. **3.** relation or reference: *inquiries with respect to a route.* **5. respects,** courtesy and deference as expressed esp. by a visit. —*v.t.* **6.** to hold in admiration or esteem. **7.** to show regard or consideration for. —**re·spect′er,** *n.* —**re·spect′ful,** *adj.* —**re·spect′ful·ly,** *adv.* —**re·spect′ful·ness,** *n.*

re·spect·a·ble (ri spek′tə bəl), *adj.* **1.** worthy of respect or esteem. **2.** proper or decent. **3.** suitable to be seen, as in appearance. **4.** considerable in size, number, or amount. —**re·spect′a·bil′i·ty,** *n.* —**re·spect′a·bly,** *adv.*

re·spect·ing (ri spek′tiṅg), *prep.* regarding or about.

re·spec·tive (ri spek′tiv), *adj.* belonging or proper to each person or thing individually.

re·spec·tive·ly (ri spek′tiv lē), *adv.* in regard to each of a number in the order given.

---

re·sit′u·ate′, *v.t.,*   **-sol·ing.**   **-sow·ing.**
   -at·ed, -at·ing.   **re·sow′,** *v.t.,* **-sowed,**   **re·spell′,** *v.t*
re·sole′, *v.t.,* **-soled,**   **-sown** or **-sowed,**

res·pi·ra·tion (res'pə rā'shən), *n.* **1.** the entire set of physical and chemical processes involved in the taking in of oxygen and the giving off of carbon dioxide by a plant or animal. **2.** the act or process of respiring. —**res·pi·ra·to·ry** (res'pər ə tôr'ē, -tōr'ē, ri spīr'ə-), *adj.*

res·pi·ra·tor (res'pə rā'tər), *n.* **1.** a device, usually of gauze, worn over the mouth, or nose and mouth, to prevent the inhalation of noxious substances. **2.** an apparatus to produce or assist in artificial respiration.

re·spire (ri spīr'), *v.i., v.t.,* -**spired,** -**spir·ing.** to inhale and exhale (air). —**re·spir·a·ble** (res'pər ə bəl, ri spīr'r'ə-), *adj.* —**re·spir'a·bil'i·ty,** *n.*

res·pite (res'pit), *n.* **1.** an interval of relief and rest. **2.** a temporary suspension or reprieve.

re·splend·ent (ri splen'dənt), *adj.* shining brilliantly. —**re·splend'ence,** *n.* —**re·splend'ent·ly,** *adv.* —**Syn.** dazzling, radiant, splendid.

re·spond (ri spond'), *v.i., v.t.* **1.** to return (as) an answer, esp. in an expected way. **2.** to react positively or favorably. —**re·spond'er,** *n.*

re·spond·ent (ri spon'dənt), *adj.* **1.** giving response. —*n.* **2.** a person who responds, esp. a defendant, as in appellate cases.

re·sponse (ri spons'), *n.* **1.** an act or instance of responding by an answer. **2.** any reaction that results from stimulation.

re·spon·si·bil·i·ty (ri spon'sə bil'i tē), *n., pl.* -**ties. 1.** the state or fact of being responsible. **2.** someone or something for which a person is responsible.

re·spon·si·ble (ri spon'sə bəl), *adj.* **1.** answerable or accountable, as for something within one's power or control. **2.** involving duties and obligations. **3.** being the cause or reason of something. **4.** liable for fulfilling a duty. —**re·spon'si·ble·ness,** *n.* —**re·spon'si·bly,** *adv.*

re·spon·sive (ri spon'siv), *adj.* making response, esp. reacting readily to influences, appeals, etc. —**re·spon'sive·ly,** *adv.* —**re·spon'sive·ness,** *n.*

rest¹ (rest), *n.* **1.** the refreshing quiet or repose of sleep. **2.** ease and relaxation after a period of activity. **3.** relief or freedom from troubles or exertion. **4.** one's final repose after death. **5.** cessation or absence of motion. **6.** *Music.* **a.** an interval of silence between tones. **b.** a mark or sign indicating it. **7.** a place that

provides shelter or lodging for travelers. **8.** a supporting device. **9.** **lay to rest,** to inter (a dead body). —*v.i.* **10.** to refresh oneself, as by sleeping or relaxing. **11.** to be quiet or still. **12.** to be quiet or still. **13.** to lie, lean, or be set. **14.** to rely or depend. **15.** to be based or founded. **16.** to be or be found where specified: *The blame rests with them.* —*v.t.* **17.** to refresh with rest. **18.** to lay or place for rest. —**rest'er,** *n.*

rest² (rest), *n.* **1.** a remaining part. **2.** the others: *All the rest are going.* —*v.i.* **3.** to remain as specified: *Rest assured that all is going well.*

res·tau·rant (res'tər ənt, -tə ränt'), *n.* a place where meals are served to customers.

res·tau·ra·teur (res'tər ə tûr'), *n.* the owner or manager of a restaurant.

rest·ful (rest'fəl), *adj.* **1.** full of or giving rest. **2.** quiet or peaceful. —**rest'ful·ly,** *adv.* —**rest'ful·ness,** *n.*

res·ti·tu·tion (res'ti tōō'shən, -tyōō'-), *n.* **1.** the enforced return of property or goods to the rightful owner. **2.** compensation for loss or damage.

res·tive (res'tiv), *adj.* **1.** impatient of control, restraint, or delay. **2.** stubborn or balky. —**res'tive·ly,** *adv.* —**res'tive·ness,** *n.*

rest·less (rest'lis), *adj.* **1.** showing inability to remain at rest. **2.** unquiet or uneasy. **3.** without rest. **4.** unceasingly active. —**rest'less·ly,** *adv.* —**rest'less·ness,** *n.*

res·to·ra·tion (res'tə rā'shən), *n.* **1.** the act of restoring or state or fact of being restored. **2.** something restored, as by renovating.

re·stor·a·tive (ri stôr'ə tiv, -stôr'-), *adj.* **1.** serving to restore something, esp. to health or strength. —*n.* **2.** a restorative medicine or means.

re·store (ri stôr', -stôr'), *v.t.,* -**stored,** -**stor·ing. 1.** to bring back into existence or use. **2.** to bring back to a former or normal state. **3.** to bring back to health or strength. **4.** to put back to a former place or rank. **5.** to give back. —**re·stor'a·ble,** *adj.* —**re·stor'er,** *n.*

re·strain (ri strān'), *v.t.* **1.** to hold back from action. **2.** to limit or hamper. —**re·strain'a·ble,** *adj.* —**re·strained** (-d'), *adj.* —**re·strain'ed·ly** (-strā'nid lē), *adv.* —**re·strain'er,** *n.* —**Syn. 1.** check, curb, repress.

re·straint (ri strānt'), *n.* **1.** a restraining action or influence. **2.** a means

re·stack', *v.t.*
re·staff', *v.t.*
re·stage', *v.t.,* -**staged,** -**stag·ing.**
re·stamp', *v.*

re·start', *v., n.*
re·stock', *v.*
re·state', *v.t.,* -**stat·ed,** -**stat·ing.**
re·state'ment, *n.*

re·straight'en, *v.t.*
re·strength'en, *v.t.*

of restraining. **3.** the act of restraining or state of being restrained. **4.** control or reserve, as of feelings.

re·strict (ri strikt′), *v.t.* to confine or keep within limits, as of action. —**re·strict′ed,** *adj.*

re·stric·tion (ri strik′shən), *n.* **1.** something that restricts, as a law. **2.** the act of restricting or state of being restricted.

re·stric·tive (ri strik′tiv), *adj.* **1.** serving to restrict. **2.** *Gram.* noting a clause that limits or identifies the antecedent and that is usually not set off by commas. —**re·stric′tive·ly,** *adv.* —**re·stric′tive·ness,** *n.*

rest′ room′, a public lavatory.

re·sult (ri zult′), *v.i.* **1.** to come about as an effect. **2.** to end in some particular way. —*n.* **3.** something that results. **4. results,** any effective achievement. **5.** *Math.* a quantity or expression obtained by calculation. —**re·sult′ant,** *adj., n.*

re·sume (ri zōōm′), *v.,* -**sumed,** -**suming.** —*v.t.* **1.** to begin again after interruption. **2.** to take or occupy again. —*v.i.* **3.** to continue after interruption. —**re·sump·tion** (ri-zump′shən), *n.*

ré·su·mé (rez′ŏō mā′, rez′ŏō mā′), *n.* a summary, esp. of one's education, employment, etc., submitted in application for a job. Also, **re′su·me′.**

re·sur·gent (ri sûr′jənt), *adj.* rising or tending to rise again. —**re·sur′gence,** *n.*

res·ur·rect (rez′ə rekt′), *v.t., v.i.* **1.** to bring (something) back into use, practice, etc. **2.** *Theol.* to bring or come back to life again.

res·ur·rec·tion (rez′ə rek′shən), *n.* **1. the Resurrection, a.** the rising again of Christ after His death and burial. **b.** the rising again of people on Judgment Day. **2.** a bringing back into use, practice, etc. **3.** *Theol.* the act of rising again from the dead.

re·sus·ci·tate (ri sus′i tāt′), *v.t., -tated, -tat·ing.* to revive from apparent death or from unconsciousness. —**re·sus′ci·ta′tion,** *n.* —**re·sus′ci·ta′tor,** *n.*

ret., **1.** retain. **2.** retired. **3.** return.

re·tail (rē′tāl), *n.* **1.** the sale of goods directly to consumers, usually in small quantities. —*adj.* **2.** connected with or engaged in such a sale. —*adv.* **3.** at a retail price. —*v.t., v.i.* **4.** to sell or be sold at retail. —**re′tail·er,** *n.*

re·tain (ri tān′), *v.t.* **1.** to keep possession of. **2.** to continue to use or practice. **3.** to keep in mind. **4.** to hold in place or position. **5.** to engage by payment of a retainer. —**re·tain′ment,** *n.*

re·tain·er (ri tā′nər), *n.* **1.** a fee paid to secure services, as of a lawyer. **2.** an attendant or servant, as in a wealthy family. **3.** a person or thing that retains.

retain′ing wall′, a wall for holding in place a mass of earth.

re·take (*v.* rē tāk′; *n.* rē′tāk′), *v.,* -**took, -tak·en, -tak·ing,** *n.* **1.** to take again. **2.** to photograph or film again. —*n.* **3.** a picture or scene photographed or filmed again. —**re·tak′er,** *n.*

re·tal·i·ate (ri tal′ē āt′), *v.i.,* -**at·ed, -at·ing.** to return like for like, esp. evil for evil. —**re·tal′i·a′tion,** *n.* —**re·tal′i·a·to′ry** (-ə tōr′ē, -tôr′ē), *adj.*

re·tard (ri tärd′), *v.t.* to delay the progress of. —**re·tar·da·tion** (rē′-tär dā′shən), *n.* —**re·tard′er,** *n.*

re·tard·ant (ri tär′dənt), *n.* **1.** any substance capable of reducing the speed of a given reaction. —*adj.* **2.** serving to retard.

re·tard·ate (ri tär′dāt), *n.* a mentally retarded person.

re·tard·ed (ri tär′did), *adj.* characterized by mental retardation.

retch (rech), *v.i.* to make efforts to vomit.

retd., **1.** retained. **2.** retired. **3.** returned.

re·ten·tion (ri ten′shən), *n.* **1.** the act of retaining or state of being retained. **2.** the power to retain, esp. in the mind. —**re·ten′tive,** *adj.* —**re·ten′tive·ness,** *n.*

ret·i·cent (ret′i sənt), *adj.* habitually disinclined to speak. —**ret′i·cence,** *n.* —**ret′i·cent·ly,** *adv.* —**Syn.** hesitant, shy, reserved.

ret·i·na (ret′°nə, ret′nə), *n., pl.* **ret·i·nas, ret·i·nae** (ret′°nē′). the innermost coat of the posterior part of the eyeball that receives the image produced by the crystalline lens. —**ret′i·nal,** *adj.*

---

re·string′, *v.,* -strung,
  -string·ing.
re·struc′ture, *v.,* -tured,
  -tur·ing.
re·stud′y, *n., pl.* -stud·ies; *v.,* -stud·ied,
  -stud·y·ing.
re·stuff′, *v.t.*
re·style′, *v.,* styled,
  -styl·ing.
re′sub·mis′sion, *n.*

re′sub·mit′, *v.,* -mit·ted,
  -mit·ting.
re′sub·scribe′, *v.,*
  -scribed, -scrib·ing.
re·sum′mon, *v.t.*
re′sup·ply′, *v.,* -plied,
  -ply·ing; *n., pl.* -plies.
re·sur′face, *v.t.,* -faced,
  -fac·ing.
re′sur·vey′, *v.*
re·sur′vey, *n.*

re·teach′, *v.,* -taught,
  -teach·ing.
re·tell′, *v.,* -told,
  -tell·ing.
re·test′, *v.t.*
re·thread′, *v.t.*
re·think′, *v.,* -thought,
  -think·ing.
re·tie′, *v.t.,* -tied,
  -ty·ing.

ret·i·nue (ret'°nōō', -°nyōō'), *n.* a group of subordinates or attendants of a high-ranking person. —**ret'i·nued'**, *adj.*

re·tire (ri tī°r'), *v.,* **-tired,** **-tir·ing.** —*v.i.* 1. to withdraw or go away to a place of shelter or seclusion. 2. to go to bed. 3. to withdraw from office, business. or active life, usually because of age 4. to fall back or retreat, as from battle. —*v.t.* 5. to withdraw from circulation by paying off, as bonds. 6. to withdraw (troops, etc.), as from battle. 7. to remove from active service, as a military officer. 8. to withdraw (a ship, etc.) permanently from its normal service, usually for scrapping. 9. to put out (a baseball batter, etc.). —**re·tir'ee'**, *n.* —**re·tire'ment,** *n.*

re·tired (ri tī°rd'), *adj.* 1. no longer occupied with one's business or profession 2. withdrawn or secluded.

re·tir·ing (ri tī°r'ing), *adj.* avoiding or withdrawing from contact with others. —**re·tir'ing·ly,** *adv.*

re·tort¹ (ri tôrt'), *v.t.* 1. to reply to, esp. in a sharp way. 2. to return (an accusation, etc.) upon the person uttering it. —*v.i.* 3. to reply, esp. sharply. —*n.* 4. an incisive, witty reply. —**re·tort'er,** *n.*

re·tort² (ri tôrt'), *n.* a glass bulb with a long neck bent downward, used for distilling or decomposing substances by heat

re·touch (rē tuch'), *v.t.* to improve or change details of (a photograph). —**re·touch'a·ble,** *adj.* —**re·touch'er,** *n.*

re·trace (ri trās'), *v.t.,* **-traced, -trac·ing.** to trace backward· *to retrace one's steps.* —**re·trace'a·ble,** *adj.*

re·tract (ri trakt'), *v.t.,* *v.i.* 1. to withdraw (a statement, etc.) as inaccurate or unjustified. 2. to draw back or in. —**re·tract'a·ble,** *adj.* —**re·trac'tion,** *n.*

re·trac·tile (ri trak'til), *adj.* capable of being drawn back or in, as the head of a tortoise

re·tread (*v.* rē tred'. *n.* rē'tred'), *v.,* **-tread·ed, -tread·ing.** *n.* —*v.t.* 1. to put a new tread on (a worn pneumatic tire casing). —*n.* 2. a retreaded tire.

re·treat (ri trēt'), *n.* 1. the forced or strategic withdrawal of a military force before an enemy. 2. the act of withdrawing as into seclusion or privacy. 3. a place of seclusion or privacy. 4. a period of retirement, as for meditation. 5. *Mil.* a. a flag-lowering ceremony held at sunset. b. the bugle call for this. —*v.i.* 6. to make a retreat. 7. to slope backward.

re·trench (ri trench'), *v.t.,* *v.i.* to reduce (expenses). —**re·trench'ment.** *n.*

ret·ri·bu·tion (re'trə byōō'shən), *n.* punishment given in return for some wrong committed. —**re·trib·u·tive** (ri trib'yə tiv), **re·trib'u·to'ry** (-tôr'ē, -tōr'ē), *adj.*

re·trieve (ri trēv'), *v.,* **-trieved, -triev·ing,** *n.* —*v.t.* 1. to get back again. 2. to bring back to a former state. 3. to make amends for. 4. (of hunting dogs) to fetch (killed or wounded game). 5. to obtain (data) stored in the memory of a computer. —*v.i.* 6. *Hunting.* to retrieve game. —*n.* 7. the act of retrieving —**re·triev'a·ble,** *adj* —**re·triev'al,** *n.*

re·triev·er (ri trē'vər), *n.* a large dog trained to retrieve game.

retro-, a prefix meaning· a. backward: *retrogress* b. behind· *retrorocket.*

ret·ro·ac·tive (re'trō ak'tiv), *adj.* effective as of a past date. —**ret'ro·ac'tive·ly,** *adv.*

ret·ro·fire (re'trō fī°r'), *v.t.,* **-fired, -fir·ing.** to ignite (a retrorocket).

ret·ro·grade (re'trə grād'). *adj.,* *v.,* **-grad·ed. -grad·ing** —*adj* 1. having a backward motion or direction. 2. *Chiefly Biol* moving toward a worse condition —*v.i* 3. to move or go backward 4. *Chiefly Biol.* to decline to a worse condition

ret·ro·gress (re'trə gres', re'trə gres'), *v.i.* to go backward into an earlier and usually worse condition. —**ret'ro·gres'sion,** *n.* —**ret'ro·gres'sive,** *adj.*

ret·ro·rock·et (re'trō rok'it), *n.* a small auxiliary rocket used for decelerating a larger rocket or spacecraft.

ret·ro·spect (re'trə spekt'), *n.* 1. a survey of past times, events, etc. 2. **in retrospect,** in looking back on past events. —**ret'ro·spec'tion,** *n.* —**ret'ro·spec'tive,** *adj.,* *n.* —**ret'ro·spec'tive·ly,** *adv.*

re·turn (ri tûrn'), *v.i.* 1. to go or come back, as to a former place or position. 2. to reply or retort. —*v.t.* 3. to put, bring or send back. 4. to give back or repay. 5. to yield (a profit. revenue, etc.). 6. to report or announce officially. 7. to elect, as to a legislative body. —*n.* 8. the act or fact of returning, as by going or coming back or putting, bringing, or sending back 9. a recurrence or

re·ti'tle. *v.t.,* **-tled, -tling.**
re·train', *v.*
re'trans·fer', *v.t.,* **-ferred, -fer·ring.**
re'trans·late', *v.t.,* **-lat·ed. -lat·ing.**
re'trans·mit', *v.t.,* **-mit·ted, -mit·ting.**
re·tri'al, *n.*
re·try', *v.t.,* **-tried, -try·ing.**

reoccurrence. 10. reciprocation or repayment. 11. response or reply. 12. a person or thing that is returned. 13. a yield or profit, as from investment 14. a formal report of taxable income. 15. Usually, **returns**, an official or unofficial report on a count of votes. 16. **in return**, in repayment or reciprocation —*adj.* 17. of or for return or returning: *a return trip* 18. sent, given, or done in return. —**re·turn′a·ble**, *adj.* —**re·turn′er**, *n.*

re·turn·ee (ri tûr nē′, -tûr′nē), *n.* a person who has returned, esp. a serviceman or servicewoman returning from duty overseas.

re·un·ion (rē yōōn′yan), *n.* 1. the act of uniting again or state of being united again 2. a gathering of relatives, friends, or associates after separation.

re-up (rē up′), *v.i., v.t.,* **-upped, -upping**. *Mil. Informal.* to enlist again. [*re* + (*sign*) *up*]

rev (rev), *n., v.,* **revved, rev·ving**. *Informal.* —*n.* 1. a revolution in an engine. —*v.t.* 2. to accelerate sharply the speed of (an engine. [short for *revolution*]

Rev., 1. Revelation; Revelations. 2. Reverend.

rev., 1. revenue. 2. reverse. 3. review. 4. reviewed. 5. revise. 6. revised. 7. revision. 8. revolution. 9. revolving

re·vamp (rē vamp′), *v.t.* 1. to vamp (a shoe) again. 2. to restore by reconstructing, as an ailing business company.

re·veal (ri vēl′), *v.t.* 1. to make known 2. to lay open to view —**re·veal′ing·ly**, *adv.* —**re·veal′ment**, *n.* —Syn. 1. disclose, divulge. 2. display, exhibit.

rev·eil·le (rev′ə lē), *n.* a signal, as of a drum or bugle, for rousing soldiers in the morning.

rev·el (rev′əl), *v.,* **-eled, -el·ing** or **-elled, -el·ling**, *n.* —*v.i.* 1. to take great pleasure 2. to make merry boisterously. —*n.* 3. boisterous merrymaking —**rev′el·er, rev′el·ler,** *n.* —**rev′el·ry,** *n.*

rev·e·la·tion (rev′ə lā′shən), *n.* 1. the act of revealing 2. something revealed, esp something surprising and not known before 3. *Theol.* God's disclosure of Himself to His crea-

tures. 4. (*cap.*) Often, **Revelations**. the last book in the New Testament. —**re·vel·a·to·ry** (ri vel′ə tôr′ē, -tōr′ē, rev′ə lə-), *adj* —**rev′e·la′tion·al**, *adj.*

re·venge (ri venj′), *v.,* **-venged, -veng·ing,** *n.* —*v.t.* 1. to inflict punishment or injury in return for a wrong done. —*n* 2. the act of revenging. 3. something done in vengeance. 4. the desire to revenge. —**re·venge′-ful,** *adj* —Syn. 2. reprisal, retaliation, retribution

rev·e·nue (rev′ən yōō′, -ə nōō′), *n.* the income of a government from taxation and other sources

re·ver·ber·ate (ri vûr′bə rāt′), *v.i., v.t.,* **-at·ed, -at·ing.** 1. to reflect or be reflected many times, as sound waves from the walls of a confined space. —**re·ver′ber·a′tion,** *n.* —**re·ver′ber·a′tor,** *n.*

re·vere (ri vēr′), *v.t.,* **-vered, -ver·ing.** to regard with respect tinged with awe. —**re·ver′er,** *n* —Syn. venerate.

Re·vere (ri vēr′), *n* Paul, 1735-1818, American silversmith and patriot.

rev·er·ence (rev′ər əns, rev′rəns), *n., v.,* **-enced, -enc·ing.** —*n.* 1. a feeling of respect tinged with awe. 2. a gesture showing deep respect, as a bow or curtsy. —*v.t.* 3. to regard or treat with reverence. —**rev′er·enc·er,** *n.*

rev·er·end (rev′ər ənd, rev′rənd), *adj.* 1. (*cap.*) a title of respect prefixed to the name of a clergyman or clergywoman. 2. worthy to be revered. —*n.* 3. *Informal.* a clergyman or clergywoman

rev·er·ent (rev′ər ənt, rev′rənt), *adj.* feeling or exhibiting reverence. —**rev′er·ent·ly,** *adv.*

rev·er·en·tial (rev′ə ren′shəl), *adj.* causing or inspiring reverence.

rev·er·ie (rev′ə rē), *n.* 1. a state of dreamy meditation. 2. a daydream. Also, **rev′er·y.**

re·vers (ri vēr′, -vâr′), *n., pl.* **-vers** (-vērz′, -vârz′) a part of a garment turned back to show the lining, as a lapel. Also, **re·vere** (-vēr′).

re·ver·sal (ri vûr′səl), *n.* the act or an instance of reversing.

re·verse (ri vûrs′) *adj., n., v.,* **-versed, -vers·ing.** —*adj* 1. opposite or contrary in position, direction order, or character. 2. having the back or rear part toward the observer. 3. producing backward movement. —

---

n. **4.** the opposite or contrary of something. **5.** the back or rear of anything, as of a coin. **6.** an adverse change of fortune. **7.** a reversing mechanism, as a gear in an engine. —*v.t.* **8.** to turn in an opposite position. **9.** to turn inside out or upside down. **10.** to turn in the opposite direction. **11.** to revoke or annul, as a verdict. **12.** to cause (a mechanism) to run in a reverse direction. —*v.i.* **13.** to turn or move in the opposite or contrary direction. —**re·verse′ly,** *adv.* —**re·vers′er,** *n.* —**re·vers′i·ble,** *adj.* —**re·vers′i·bil′i·ty, re·vers′i·ble·ness,** *n.* —**re·vers′i·bly,** *adv.*

reverse′ discrimina′tion, the unfair treatment of majority groups (whites, men, etc.) resulting from preference intended to remedy earlier discrimination against minorities (blacks, women, etc.).

re·vert (ri vûrt′), *v.i.* **1.** to return to a former practice, belief, condition, etc. **2.** *Biol.* to return to an earlier or primitive type. **3.** *Law.* to return to the former owner or his or her heirs. —**re·ver′sion** (-vûr′zhən, -shən), *n.* —**re·ver′sion·ar·y,** *adj.* —**re·vert′i·ble,** *adj.*

re·vet·ment (ri vet′mənt), *n.* a facing of masonry, esp. for protecting an embankment.

re·view (ri vyōō′), *n.* **1.** a critical article on a recent book, play, etc. **2.** a magazine containing articles on current events, books, art, etc. **3.** a second or repeated view or study of something. **4.** a formal inspection of any military force or parade. **5.** contemplation of past events or facts. **6.** a general survey of something. **7.** a judicial reexamination, as by a higher court. **8.** *Theat.* revue. —*v.t.* **9.** to look at or look over again. **10.** to go over (studies, etc.) in review. **11.** to inspect formally. **12.** to survey mentally. **13.** to discuss (a book, etc.) in a critical review. —**re·view′er,** *n.*

re·vile (ri vīl′), *v.t., v.i.,* **-viled, -vil·ing.** to speak (of) abusively. —**re·vile′ment,** *n.* —**re·vil′er,** *n.*

re·vise (ri vīz′), *v.,* **-vised, -vis·ing,** *n.* —*v.t.* **1.** to change or otherwise improve on editorially. **2.** to amend or alter. —*n.* **3.** something revised, esp. in printing. —**re·vis′a·ble,** *adj.* —**re·vis′er, re·vi′sor,** *n.* —**re·vi′sion** (-vizh′ən), *n.*

Revised′ Stand′ard Ver′sion, a revision of the Bible prepared by American scholars and completed in 1952.

re·vi·sion·ism (ri vizh′ə niz′əm), *n.* **1.** any deviation from Marxism. **2.** the advocacy of this or other revision. —**re·vi′sion·ist,** *n., adj.*

re·vi·tal·ize (rē vīt′əl īz′), *v.t.,* **-ized, -iz·ing.** to give new life or vitality to. —**re·vi′tal·i·za′tion,** *n.*

re·viv·al (ri vī′vəl), *n.* **1.** the act of reviving or state of being revived. **2.** restoration to life or vigor. **3.** restoration to use or acceptance. **4.** a new performance of an old play or motion picture. **5.** an evangelistic service for the purpose of effecting a religious awakening. —**re·viv′al·ist,** *n.*

re·vive (ri vīv′), *v.t., v.i.,* **-vived, -viv·ing. 1.** to return or restore to life or consciousness. **2.** to return or restore to vigor or strength. **3.** to come back or bring back into use, acceptance, or performance. **3.** to quicken or renew in the mind. —**re·viv′er,** *n.*

re·viv·i·fy (ri viv′ə fī′), *v.t.,* **-fied, -fy·ing.** to restore to life. —**re·viv·i·fi·ca·tion** (ri viv′ə fə kā′shən), *n.*

re·voke (ri vōk′), *v.t.,* **-voked, -vok·ing.** to invalidate by withdrawing or canceling, as a license. —**rev·o·ca·ble** (rev′ə kə bəl), *adj.* —**rev·o·ca·tion** (rev′ə kā′shən), *n.* —**re·vok′er,** *n.*

re·volt (ri vōlt′), *v.i.* **1.** to break away from and refuse to submit to authority. **2.** to turn away in disgust. —*v.t.* **3.** to fill with disgust. —*n.* **4.** the act of revolting. —**re·volt′er,** *n.* —**Syn. 4.** insurrection, rebellion, uprising.

re·volt·ing (ri vōl′ting), *adj.* utterly disgusting or repulsive. —**re·volt′ing·ly,** *adv.*

rev·o·lu·tion (rev′ə lōō′shən), *n.* **1.** a forcible overthrow of an established government by the people governed. **2.** a complete change in something, often one made relatively quickly. **3.** movement in a circular path or orbit. **4.** rotation on an axis. **5.** a single cycle movement or rotation. —**rev′o·lu′tion·ist,** *n., adj.*

rev·o·lu·tion·ar·y (rev′ə lōō′shə ner′ē), *adj., n., pl.* **-ar·ies.** —*adj.* **1.** of, for, or involving a political revolution. **2.** producing or furthering radical change. —*n.* **3.** a person who advocates or takes part in a revolution, esp. a political one.

Revolu′tionary War′. See **American Revolution.**

rev·o·lu·tion·ize (rev′ə lōō′shə nīz′), *v.t.,* **-ized, -iz·ing.** to effect a radical change in.

re·volve (ri volv′), *v.i., v.t.,* **-volved, -volv·ing. 1.** to move or cause to move in a curved orbit. **2.** to rotate or cause to turn around, as on an axis. **3.** to think (about), esp. from all aspects. **4.** to recur periodically. —**re·volv′a·ble,** *adj.*

re·volv·er (ri vol′vər), *n.* a pistol having a revolving cylinder for holding a number of cartridges that may be discharged in succession.

re·vue (ri vyo͞o′), n. a theatrical entertainment consisting of skits, dances, and songs, often parodying recent events, popular fads, etc. —re·vu′ist, n.

re·vul·sion (ri vul′shən), n. 1. a strong feeling of repugnance or distaste. 2. a sudden and violent change of response in sentiment.

re·ward (ri wôrd′), n. 1. something given in return for service, merit, etc. 2. a sum of money offered, as for the recovery of lost property. —v.t. 3. to give a reward to or for.

re·ward·ing (ri wôr′ding), adj. providing a feeling of satisfying return.

re·word (rē wûrd′), v.t. to put into other words.

re·write (rē rīt′), v.t., v.i., -wrote, -writ·ten, -writ·ing. 1. to write in a different form 2. to write again. 3. to write (news submitted by a reporter) for inclusion in a newspaper. —re·writ′er, n.

Rey·kja·vik (rā′kyə vēk′), n. the capital of Iceland

RF, radio frequency.

RFD, rural free delivery.

Rh, rhodium.

r.h., right hand.

rhap·so·dize (rap′sə dīz′), v.i., v.t., -dized, -diz·ing. to speak or write in a rhapsodic form or manner.

rhap·so·dy (rap′sə dē), n., pl. -dies. 1. an exaggerated expression of feeling or enthusiasm 2. an instrument composition irregular in form and suggestive of improvisation. —rhap·sod′ic (-sod′ik), rhap·sod′i·cal, adj. —rhap·sod′i·cal·ly, adv. —rhap′so·dist, n.

rhe·a (rē′ə), n. a flightless South American bird resembling the African ostrich but smaller.

rhe·ni·um (rē′nē əm), n. Chem. a rare, heavy, metallic element. Symbol.: Re: at wt.: 186.2: at no.: 75.

rhe·ol·o·gy (rē ol′ə jē), n. the study of the deformation and flow of matter. —rhe·o·log·ic (rē′ə loj′ik), rhe·o·log′i·cal adj. —rhe·ol′o·gist, n.

rhe·om·e·ter (rē om′i tər), n. an instrument for measuring the flow of fluids, esp blood

rhe·o·stat (rē′ə stat′), n. Elect. an adjustable resistor used for controlling the current in a circuit, as in dimming lights —rhe′o·stat′ic, adj.

rhe′sus mon′key (rē′səs), a small monkey of India, used extensively in medical research.

rhet., 1. rhetoric 2. rhetorical.

rhet·o·ric (ret′ər ik), n. 1. the study of the effective use of language. 2. the use of exaggeration or display in language. —rhe·tor·i·cal (ri tôr′i kəl, -tor′-), adj. —rhe·tor′i·cal·ly, adv. —rhet·o·ri·cian (ret′ə rish′ən), n.

rhetor′ical ques′tion, a question asked solely to produce an effect and not to elicit a reply.

rheum (ro͞om), n. a thin, watery discharge from the eyes or nose. —rheum′y, adj.

rheumat′ic fe′ver, a serious disease, usually affecting children, characterized by fever, swelling and pain in the joints, and cardiac involvement.

rheu·ma·tism (ro͞o′mə tiz′əm), n. any disorder characterized by pain and stiffness of the joints or back. —rheu·mat′ic (-mat′ik), adj., n. —rheu·mat′i·cal·ly, adv. —rheu′ma·toid′ (-mə toid′), adj.

rheu′matoid arthri′tis, a chronic disease characterized by inflammation of the joints frequently accompanied by marked deformities.

Rh factor, a group of antigens in the red blood cells of most persons, that on repeated transfusion into a person lacking such an antigen causes a severe reaction [so called because first found in blood of rh(esus) monkeys]

Rhine (rīn), n. a river flowing from SE Switzerland through West Germany and the Netherlands into the North Sea.

rhine·stone (rīn′stōn′), n. an artificial gem of paste, often cut to resemble a diamond.

rhi·ni·tis (rī nī′tis), n. inflammation of the nose or its mucous membrane.

rhi·no (rī′nō), n., pl. -nos, -no. a rhinoceros.

rhi·noc·er·os (rī nos′ər əs), n., pl. -oses, -os. a large, thick-skinned mammal of Africa and India, having one or two upright horns on the snout.

rhi·zome (rī′zōm), n. a rootlike plant stem that produces roots below and sends up shoots from the upper surface. —rhi·zom·a·tous (rī zom′ə təs, -zō′məs), adj.

Rh-neg·a·tive (är′āch′neg′ə tiv), adj. lacking the Rh factor.

re·warm′, v.

re·wash′, v.

re·weave′, v., -wove or (Rare) -weaved; -wo·ven or -wove; -weav·ing.

re·wed′, v., -wed·ded, -wed·ded or -wed, -wed·ding.

re·weigh′, v.

re·weld′, v.

re·wind′, v.t., -wound, -wind·ing, n.

re·wire′, v.t., -wired, -wir·ing.

re·work′, v., -worked or -wrought, -work·ing.

re·wrap′, v., -wrapped or -wrapt, -wrap·ping.

re·zone′, v.t., -zoned, -zon·ing.

rho (rō), *n., pl.* **rhos.** the 17th letter of the Greek alphabet (P, ρ).

Rhode′ Is′land (rōd), a state in the NE United States. *Cap.*: Providence.

Rho·de·sia (rō dē′zhə), *n.* a country in S Africa. —**Rho·de′sian,** *adj., n.*

rho·di·um (rō′dē əm), *n. Chem.* a metallic element of the platinum family, used to electroplate scientific instruments. Symbol: Rh; *at. wt.:* 102.905; *at. no.:* 45.

rho·do·den·dron (rō′də den′drən), *n.* any evergreen shrub or tree having showy, pink, purple, or white flowers.

rhom·boid (rom′boid), *n.* an oblique-angled parallelogram with only the opposite sides equal.

rhom·bus (rom′bəs), *n., pl.* **-bus·es, -bi** (-bī). an equilateral parallelogram having oblique angles.

Rhone (rōn), *n.* a river flowing from S Switzerland through SE France into the Mediterranean. Also, **Rhône** (rōn).

Rh-pos·i·tive (är′ăch′poz′i tiv), *adj.* possessing the Rh factor.

rhu·barb (rōo′bärb), *n.* **1.** a plant having thick, reddish leafstalks eaten in pies or as stewed fruit. **2.** *Slang.* a quarrel or squabble.

rhyme (rīm), *n., v.,* **rhymed, rhym·ing.** —*n.* **1.** identity in terminal sounds of words or lines of verse. **2.** a word agreeing with another in terminal sound. **3.** verse or poetry having correspondence in the terminal sounds of the lines. —*v.t.* **4.** to turn into rhyme. **5.** to use (a word) as a rhyme to another word. —*v.i.* **6.** to make rhyme or verse. **7.** to form a rhyme, as one word or line with another. —**rhym′er, rhyme′ster,** *n.*

rhy·o·lite (rī′ə līt′), *n.* a fine-grained igneous rock rich in silica.

rhythm (riŧħ′əm), *n.* **1.** movement or activity with uniform or patterned recurrence of a beat, accent, etc. **2.** the pattern of this in speech or music. —**rhyth′mic** (-mik), **rhyth′mi·cal,** *adj.* —**rhyth′mi·cal·ly,** *adv.*

rhythm′ and blues′, an urbanized form of the blues based chiefly on folk songs of popular black American music.

rhythm′ meth′od, a method of birth control by abstaining from sexual intercourse on the days when conception is most likely to occur.

RI, Rhode Island. Also, **R.I.**

ri·al (rē′ôl, -äl), *n.* the monetary unit of Iran.

rib¹ (rib), *n., v.,* **ribbed, rib·bing.** —*n.* **1.** one of a series of curved bones attached to the spine that form the wall of the chest. **2.** something resembling a rib in form, position, or use, as a strengthening part. **3.** a ridge in knitted fabrics. —*v.t.* **4.** to

furnish or strengthen with ribs. **5.** to mark (fabrics) with ridges. —**rib′ber,** *n.*

rib² (rib), *v.t.,* **ribbed, rib·bing.** *Slang.* to make fun of. —**rib′ber,** *n.*

rib·ald (rib′əld), *adj.* vulgar or indecent in speech, language, etc. —**rib′-ald·ry** (-əl drē), *n.* —**rib′ald·ly,** *adv.*

rib·and (rib ənd), *n. Archaic.* ribbon.

rib·bon (rib′ən), *n.* **1.** a woven strip or band of fine material, used for trimming or tying. **2.** ribbons, torn or ragged strips: *clothes torn to ribbons.* **3.** a band of inked material used in a typewriter, etc.

ri·bo·fla·vin (rī′bō flā′vin, rī′bō flā′-), *n.* a factor of the vitamin B complex essential for growth, found in milk, fresh meat, eggs, etc., or made synthetically.

ri·bo·nu·cle′ic ac′id (rī′bō nōō klē′ik, nyōō-, rī′-). See RNA.

ri·bose (rī′bōs), *n.* a sugar obtained by the hydrolysis of RNA.

ri·bo·some (rī′bə sōm′), *n.* any of several minute particles composed of protein and RNA. —**ri·bo·so′mal** (-sō′məl), *adj.*

rice (rīs), *n., v.,* **riced, ric·ing.** —*n.* **1.** the starchy seeds or grain of a grass cultivated in warm climates and used for food. **2.** its grass. —*v.t.* **3.** to reduce to a form resembling rice: *to rice potatoes.* —**ric′er,** *n.*

rich (rich), *adj.* **1.** having wealth or great possessions. **2.** of great value or worth. **3.** expensively elegant or fine, as jewels. **4.** containing much butter, sugar, spices, etc. **5.** deep or strong, as color. **6.** full and mellow in tone. **7.** strongly fragrant. **8.** yielding abundantly, as soil. **9.** abundant or plentiful. **10.** *Informal.* highly amusing. —*n.* **11. the rich,** rich persons collectively. —**rich′ly,** *adv.* —**rich′-ness,** *n.* —Syn. 1. affluent, opulent, wealthy.

Rich·ard I (rich′ərd), ("*Richard the Lion-Hearted*") 1157–99, king of England 1189–99.

rich·es (rich′iz), *n.pl.* abundant and valuable possessions.

Rich·mond (rich′mənd), *n.* **1.** the capital of Virginia. **2.** a borough of SW New York City, comprising Staten Island.

Rich·ter scale (rik′tər), a scale, ranging from 0 to 10, for indicating the intensity of an earthquake. [after C. F. *Richter* (born 1900), U.S. geologist]

rick (rik), *n.* a large pile of hay, straw, etc., esp. when covered by a tarpaulin.

rick·ets (rik′its), *n.* a disease of children, characterized by softening of the bones as a result of lack of vitamin D.

rick·ett·si·a (ri ket′sē ə), *n., pl.* **-si·as** (-sē əz), **-si·ae** (-sē ē′). any of several bacterialike microorganisms parasitic on arthropods. —**rick·ett′si·al,** *adj.*

rick·et·y (rik′i tē), *adj.* **1.** likely to fall or collapse, as a chair. **2.** affected with rickets. —**rick′et·i·ness,** *n.*

rick·rack (rik′rak′), *n.* a narrow, zigzag braid used as a trimming on clothing.

rick·shaw (rik′shô′), *n.* jinrikisha. Also, **rick′sha′.**

ric·o·chet (rik′ə shā′, -shet′), *n., v.,* **-cheted** (-shād′), **-chet·ing** (-shā′ing) or **-chet·ted** (-shet′id), **-chet·ting** (shet′ing). —*n.* **1.** the rebound made by an object after it hits a glancing blow against a surface. —*v.i.* **2.** to move in this way.

ri·cot·ta (ri kot′ə, -kô′tə), *n.* a soft, Italian cottage cheese.

rid (rid), *v.t.,* **rid** or **rid·ded, rid·ding. 1.** to clear or free of something objectionable. **2. get rid of, a.** to get free from. **b.** to eliminate or discard. —**rid′der,** *n.*

rid·dance (rid′ᵊns), *n.* relief or deliverance from something.

rid·den (rid′ᵊn), *v.* pp. of **ride.**

-ridden, a combining form meaning: **a.** obsessed with or overwhelmed by: *guilt-ridden.* **b.** full of or burdened with: *debt-ridden.*

rid·dle¹ (rid′ᵊl), *n.* **1.** a question stated so as to exercise one's ingenuity in answering it. **2.** a puzzling thing or person.

rid·dle² (rid′ᵊl), *v.t.,* **-dled, -dling.** to pierce with many holes suggesting those of a sieve.

ride (rīd), *v.,* **rode, rid·den, rid·ing,** *n.* —*v.i.* **1.** to sit on and manage a horse or other animal in motion. **2.** to be carried in a vehicle. **3.** to move along in any way. **4.** to float on the water. **5.** *Informal.* to continue without interference. —*v.t.* **6.** to sit on and manage (a horse, bicycle, etc.) so as to be carried along. **7.** to ride over, along, or through (a road, region, etc.). **8.** to control or dominate. **9.** *Informal.* to ridicule or harass. —*n.* **10.** a journey on a horse, camel, etc., or on or in a vehicle. **11.** a vehicle or device, as a merry-go-round, on which people ride for amusement.

rid·er (rī′dər), *n.* **1.** a person who rides. **2.** an additional clause attached to a legislative bill in passing it. **3.** an addition or amendment to a document. —**rid′er·less,** *adj.*

rid·er·ship (rī′dər ship′), *n.* the people who ride a particular train, bus, subway, etc.

ridge (rij), *n., v.,* **ridged, ridg·ing.** —*n.* **1.** a long, narrow elevation of land. **2.** the long and narrow crest of something. **3.** any raised, narrow strip, as on cloth. **4.** the horizontal line in which the tops of the rafters of a roof meet. —*v.t., v.i.* **5.** to form into or mark with ridges. —**ridg′y,** *adj.*

ridge·pole (rij′pōl′), *n.* the horizontal timber at the top of a roof, to which the rafters are fastened.

rid·i·cule (rid′ə kyōol′), *n., v.,* **-culed, -cul·ing.** —*n.* **1.** speech or action intended to cause humiliation by making fun of a person or thing. —*v.t.* **2.** to subject to ridicule. —**Syn. 2.** mock, satirize, taunt, tease.

ri·dic·u·lous (ri dik′yə ləs), *adj.* causing or worthy of ridicule. —**ri·dic′u·lous·ly,** *adv.* —**ri·dic′u·lous·ness,** *n.*

riel (rēl), *n.* the monetary unit of Cambodia.

rife (rīf), *adj.* **1.** happening frequently or widely. **2.** abundant or abounding: *a speech rife with clichés.* —**rife′ness,** *n.*

riff (rif), *n.* **1.** an often constantly repeated melodic phrase. —*v.i.* **2.** to perform riffs.

rif·fle (rif′əl), *n., v.,* **-fled, -fling.** —*n.* **1.** a ripple on the shallow surface of a stream. **2.** the method of riffling cards —*v.t., v.i.* **3.** *Cards.* to shuffle by dividing the deck in two, raising the corners slightly, and allowing them to fall alternately together.

riff·raff (rif′raf′), *n.* worthless, low persons.

ri·fle¹ (rī′fəl), *n., v.,* **-fled, -fling.** —*n.* **1.** a shoulder firearm with a rifled barrel to give the bullet a rotatory motion. —*v.t.* **2.** to cut spiral grooves within (a gun barrel, etc.). —**ri′fle·man,** *n.* —**ri′fling,** *n.*

ri·fle² (rī′fəl), *v.t.,* **-fled, -fling.** to ransack and rob. —**ri′fler,** *n.*

rift (rift), *n.* **1.** an opening made by splitting. **2.** a break in friendly relations. —*v.t., v.i.* **3.** to burst open.

rig (rig), *v.,* **rigged, rig·ging,** *n.* —*v.t.* **1.** to fit (a vessel a mast, etc.) with rigging. **2.** to furnish or provide with equipment, clothing, etc. **3.** to assemble or install **4.** to manipulate fraudulently. —*n.* **5.** the arrangement of the masts, spars, sails, etc., on a boat or ship. **6.** apparatus for some purpose. **7.** the equipment used in drilling an oil well. **8.** *Informal.* unusual costume or dress. **9.** *Informal.* a carriage with a horse or horses. —**rig′ger,** *n.*

rig·a·ma·role (rig′ə mə rōl′), *n.* rigmarole.

rig·ging (rig′ing), *n.* the ropes, chains, etc., employed to support and work the masts, sails, etc., on a ship.

right (rīt), *adj.* **1.** in accordance with what is good, proper, or just. **2.** in conformity with truth or fact. **3.** sound or normal, as a person or the mind. **4.** principal, front, or upper: *the right side of cloth.* **5.** most appropriate, desirable, or suitable. **6.** genuine or authentic. **7.** of or belonging to the side of a person or thing that is turned toward the east when the subject is facing north. **8.** (*sometimes cap.*) of or belonging to the political right. **9.** straight or perpendicular. —*n.* **10.** a just claim or title, whether legal or moral. **11.** what is right, just, or correct. **12.** the right side. **13.** a right-hand turn. **14.** (*sometimes cap.*) a conservative or reactionary political party or position. —*adv.* **15.** straight or directly: *right to the bottom.* **16.** quite or completely. **17.** exactly or precisely. **18.** uprightly or righteously. **19.** correctly or accurately: *to guess right.* **20.** properly or fittingly: *to act right.* **21.** toward the right side. **22.** very (used in certain titles): *the right reverend.* **23. right away or off,** without hesitation. **24. right on,** *Slang.* exactly right. —*v.t.* **25.** to put in an upright position. **26.** to put in proper order or condition. **27.** to bring into conformity with truth. **28.** to redress, as a wrong. —**right′er,** *n.* —**right′ness,** *n.*

right′ an′gle, an angle of 90°. — **right′-an′gled,** *adj.*

right·eous (rī′chəs), *adj.* **1.** morally right or justifiable. **2.** acting in an upright, moral way. —**right′eous·ly,** *adv.* —**right′eous·ness,** *n.*

right·ful (rīt′fəl), *adj.* **1.** having a legal or just claim. **2.** equitable or just. —**right′ful·ly,** *adv.* —**right′ful·ness,** *n.*

right-hand (rīt′hand′), *adj.* **1.** on the right. **2.** of, for, or with the right hand. **3.** most efficient or useful, as an assistant.

right-hand·ed (rīt′hand′did), *adj.* **1.** using the right hand or arm more easily than the left. **2.** adapted to or performed by the right hand. —*adv.* **3.** Also, **right′-hand′ed·ly.** with the right hand. —**right′-hand′ed·ness,** *n.*

right·ist (rī′tist), (*sometimes cap.*) — *n.* **1.** a member of the Right or a person sympathizing with its views. —*adj.* **2.** of or pertaining to the Right. —**right′ism,** *n.*

right·ly (rīt′lē), *adv.* **1.** in accordance with truth or fact. **2.** fairly or uprightly. **3.** properly or suitably.

right′ of way′, 1. the right granted to a vehicle to proceed ahead of another. **2.** a path that may lawfully be used. **3.** a right of passage, as over another's land. **4.** the land

acquired by a railroad for tracks. **5.** land covered by a public road. **6.** land over which a power line passes.

right′ wing′, the rightist faction of a political party. —**right′-wing′,** *adj.* —**right′-wing′er,** *n.*

rig·id (rij′id), *adj.* **1.** not pliant or flexible. **2.** firmly fixed or set. **3.** firmly unyielding, as in discipline. —**ri·gid′i·ty, rig′id·ness,** *n.* —**rig′id·ly,** *adv.* —**Syn.** inflexible, strict, unbending.

rig·ma·role (rig′mə rōl′), *n.* **1.** an elaborate or complicated procedure. **2.** meaningless talk.

rig·or (rig′ər), *n.* **1.** strictness or severity, as in dealing with persons. **2.** a severe or harsh circumstance. **3.** inflexible accuracy. Also, *Brit.,* **rig′our.** —**rig′or·ous,** *adj.* —**rig′or·ous·ly,** *adv.* —**Syn. 2.** austerity, hardship.

rig·or mor·tis (rig′ər môr′tis, rī′gôr), the stiffening of the body after death. [< L: stiffness of death]

rile (rīl), *v.t.,* **riled, ril·ing. 1.** to make upset and angry. **2.** roil (def. 1).

rill[1] (ril), *n.* a small stream or brook.

rill[2] (ril), *n.* a long, narrow trench on the moon. Also, **rille.**

rim (rim), *n., v.,* **rimmed, rim·ming.** —*n.* **1.** the outer edge of something, esp. of a circular object. **2.** the outer circle of a wheel. —*v.t.* **3.** to furnish with a rim.

rime[1] (rīm), *n., v.t., v.i.,* **rimed, rim·ing.** rhyme.

rime[2] (rīm), *n.* an opaque coating of ice particles.

rind (rīnd), *n.* a thick outer covering, found on certain fruits or cheeses.

ring[1] (ring), *n., v.,* **ringed, ring·ing.** —*n.* **1.** a circular band, usually of precious metal, for wearing on the finger as an ornament. **2.** anything having a circular form. **3.** a circular or surrounding line or mark. **4.** a number of persons or things situated in a circle. **5.** an enclosed area, often circular, for a sports contest or exhibition: *a circus ring.* **6.** the sport of boxing. **7.** a group of persons cooperating for unethical or illegal purposes. **8. run rings around,** to surpass or outdo. —*v.t.* **9.** to surround with a ring. **10.** to form into a ring. **11.** to provide with a ring. **12.** to toss a ring over (a mark) in certain games. —*v.i.* **13.** to move in a ring or a curving course. —**ring′like,** *adj.*

ring[2] (ring), *v.,* **rang, rung, ring·ing,** *n.* —*v.i.* **1.** to give forth a clear resonant sound, as a doorbell. **2.** to appear to the mind: *His words rang false.* **3.** to cause a bell to sound, esp. as a summons. **4.** to sound loudly. **5.** (of the ears) to have the sensa-

tion of a continued humming sound.
—*v.t.* **6.** to cause (a bell) to ring.
7. to announce or proclaim by or
as by the sound of a bell. **8.** to
telephone. **9. ring a bell,** to remind
one of something. **10. ring up,** to
register (the amount of a sale) on a
cash register. —*n.* **11.** a ringing
sound, as of a bell. **12.** a sound or
tone likened to the ringing of a bell:
rings of laughter. **13.** a telephone
call. **14.** the act or an instance of
ringing a bell. **15.** a specified inherent quality: *the ring of truth.*

ring·er¹ (ring'ər), *n.* **1.** a person or
thing that rings or encircles. **2.** a
quoit or horseshoe so thrown as to
encircle the peg.

ring·er² (ring'ər), *n.* **1.** a person or
thing that rings or makes a ringing
noise. **2.** *Slang.* a horse or athlete
entered in a competition under false
representation. **3.** *Slang.* a person or
thing that closely resembles another.

ring·lead·er (ring'lē'dər), *n.* a person
who leads others, esp. in illegal acts.

ring·let (ring'lit), *n.* a curled lock of
hair.

ring·mas·ter (ring'mas'tər, -mä'stər),
n. a person in charge of the performances in a circus ring.

ring·side (ring'sīd'), *n.* the area occupied by the first row of seats on
all sides of a ring, as at a prizefight.

ring·worm (ring'wûrm'), *n.* a contagious skin disease caused by fungi
and producing ring-shaped patches.

rink (ringk), *n.* **1.** a smooth expanse
of ice for ice skating. **2.** a smooth
floor, usually of wood, for roller
skating. [orig. Scot]

rink·y-dink (ring'kē dingk'), *Slang.*
—*adj.* **1.** outmoded, shabby, or unsophisticated. —*n.* **2.** a rinky-dink
person or thing. Also, **rink'y-tink'**
(-tingk').

rinse (rins), *v.,* **rinsed, rins·ing,** *n.*
—*v.t.* **1.** to drench in clean water
as a final stage in washing or as a
light washing. **2.** to remove (soap,
etc.) by such a process. —*n.* **3.** the
act or an instance of rinsing. **4.** the
water used for rinsing. **5.** any preparation used to rinse or tint the hair.

Ri·o de Ja·nei·ro (rē'ō dā zhə när'ō,
jə-, dē, də), a seaport in SE Brazil.

Ri·o Grande (rē'ō grand', gran'dē),
a river flowing from SW Colorado
into the Gulf of Mexico.

ri·ot (rī'ət), *n.* **1.** a noisy, violent
public disorder caused by a group
or crowd of persons. **2.** a vivid display: *a riot of color.* **3.** *Informal.*
something or someone hilariously
funny. **4. read the riot act to,** to
reprimand or censure. **5. run riot,**
to act or grow without control or
restraint. —*v.i.* **6.** to take part in
a riot. —**ri'ot·er,** *n.* —**ri'ot·ous,**

adj. —**ri'ot·ous·ly,** *adv.* —**ri'ot·ous-
ness,** *n.* —*Syn.* **1.** melee, outbreak.

rip (rip), *v.,* **ripped, rip·ping,** *n.* —*v.t.*
1. to cut or tear apart in a rough
manner. **2.** to saw (wood) in the
direction of the grain. —*v.i.* **3.** to
become ripped. **4.** *Informal.* to move
with speed. **5. rip into,** *Informal.* to
attack physically or verbally. **6. rip
off,** *Slang.* **a.** to steal or pilfer. **b.** to
rob or steal from. **c.** to exploit or
take advantage of. —*n.* **7.** a tear
made by ripping. —**rip'per,** *n.*

R.I.P., may he (or she) rest in peace.
[< L *requiescat in pace*]

ri·par·i·an (ri pâr'ē ən, rī-), *adj.* of,
for, or on the bank of a river.

rip' cord', a cord that opens a parachute or descent when pulled.

ripe (rīp), *adj.,* **rip·er, rip·est. 1.** ready
for reaping, gathering, eating, or
use, as fruit, cheese, etc. **2.** fully
developed or mature, as the mind. **3.**
sufficiently advanced. —**ripe'ly,**
adv. —**ripe'ness,** *n.*

rip·en (rī'pən), *v.t., v.i.* to make or
become ripe.

rip·off (rip'ôf', -of'), *n.* *Slang.* **1.** an
act or instance of ripping off. **2.** exploitation, esp. of unfortunates. **3.** a
person who rips off.

ri·poste (ri pōst'), *n.* **1.** a fencer's
quick thrust given after parry. **2.** a
quick, sharp reply in speech or action. Also, **re·post'.**

rip·ple (rip'əl), *v.,* **-pled, -pling,** *n.*
—*v.i., v.t.* **1.** to form small waves
(on), as a liquid surface. **2.** to un-
dulate in tone or magnitude. —*n.*
3. a small wave. **4.** a sound similar
to water flowing in ripples. —**rip'-
ply,** *adj.*

rip'ple effect', a related series of
consequences set off by a single
event.

rip·roar·ing (rip'rôr'ing, -rōr'-), *adj.*
Informal. boisterously wild and exciting.

rip·saw (rip'sô'), *n.* a saw for cutting
wood with the grain.

rip·tide (rip'tīd'), *n.* a tide that opposes another or other tides, causing
a violent disturbance in the sea.

rise (rīz), *v.,* **rose, ris·en** (riz'ən),
ris·ing, *n.* —*v.i.* **1.** to get up from
a lying or sitting position. **2.** to get
up from bed. **3.** to move or grow
upward. **4.** to appear above the
horizon, as the sun. **5.** to extend
directly upward. **6.** to increase in
amount or price. **7.** to increase in
degree or intensity, as fever. **8.** to
reach a higher status or level of
importance. **9.** to prove oneself
equal to a demand, emergency, or
challenge. **10.** to swell or puff up,
as dough. **11.** to revolt or rebel.
12. to have a source. **13.** *Brit.* to
adjourn, as Parliament. **14.** *Theol.*

to resurrect. —*n.* **15.** the act or an instance of rising. **16.** an increase in amount or price. **17.** an increase in degree or intensity. **18.** elevation in status, fortune, or importance. **19.** origin, source, or beginning. **20.** an upward slope. **21. get a rise out of,** *Informal.* to provoke, as to action or anger. **22. give rise to,** to be the cause of.

ris·er (rī′zər), *n.* **1.** a person who rises, esp. from bed. **2.** the vertical face of a stair step.

ris·i·ble (riz′ə bəl), *adj.* **1.** having the ability or disposition to laugh. **2.** causing laughter. —**ris′i·bil′i·ty** (-bil′i tē), *n.*

risk (risk), *n.* **1.** exposure to the chance of injury or loss. —*v.t.* **2.** to expose to risk. **3.** to take the risk of. —**risk′y,** *adj.* —**risk′i·ness,** *n.* —**Syn. 1.** danger, hazard, jeopardy, peril.

ris·qué (ri skā′), *adj.* daringly close to indecency or impropriety.

rite (rīt), *n.* a ceremonial act or procedure customary in religious or other solemn use.

rit·u·al (rich′ōō əl), *n.* **1.** an established form of conducting a religious or other rite. **2.** any practice or behavior repeated in a prescribed manner. —*adj.* **3.** of, for, or practiced as a ritual. —**rit′u·al·ism′,** *n.* —**rit′u·al·ist,** *n.* —**rit′u·al·is′tic,** *adj.* —**rit′u·al·is′ti·cal·ly,** *adv.* —**rit′u·al·ly,** *adv.*

ritz·y (rit′sē), *adj.,* **ritz·i·er, ritz·i·est.** *Slang.* swanky or elegant. [after *Ritz* hotels, founded by César *Ritz* (1850–1918), Swiss businessman] —**ritz′i·ly,** *adv.* —**ritz′i·ness,** *n.*

riv., river.

ri·val (rī′vəl), *n., adj., v.,* **-valed, -valing** or **-valled, -val·ling.** —*n.* **1.** a person who is competing for the same object or goal as another, or who tries to equal or outdo another. —*adj.* **2.** being a rival. —*v.t.* **3.** to strive to win from, equal, or outdo. **4.** to equal in some quality. —**ri′val·ry,** *n.*

rive (rīv), *v.t., v.i.,* **rived, rived** or **riv·en** (riv′ən), **riv·ing.** *Literary.* **1.** to tear apart. **2.** to distress (the heart, etc.).

riv·er (riv′ər), *n.* a natural stream of water of fairly large size flowing in a definite course.

riv·er·side (riv′ər sīd′), *n.* **1.** a bank of a river. —*adj.* **2.** on or near a bank of a river.

riv·et (riv′it), *n., v.,* **-et·ed, -et·ing** or **-et·ted, -et·ting.** —*n.* **1.** a metal pin having a head at one end, used for passing through holes in two or more plates or pieces to hold them together. —*v.t.* **2.** to fasten with a rivet. **3.** to hold (the attention, etc.) firmly. —**riv′et·er,** *n.*

Riv·i·er·a (riv′ē är′ə), *n.* a resort area along the Mediterranean coast in SE France and NW Italy.

riv·u·let (riv′yə lit), *n.* a small stream.

ri·yal (rē yôl′, -yäl′), *n.* the monetary unit of Saudi Arabia and Yemen Arab Republic.

rm., **1.** ream. **2.** room.

Rn., radon.

R.N., **1.** See **registered nurse. 2.** *Brit.* Royal Navy.

RNA, any of a group of nucleic acids involved in the synthesis of proteins, one type of which bears genetic information.

rnd., round.

ro., rood.

roach[1] (rōch), *n.* **1.** a cockroach. **2.** *Slang.* a very short butt of a marijuana cigarette.

roach[2] (rōch), *n., pl.* **roach·es, roach.** a European freshwater fish of the carp family.

road (rōd), *n.* **1.** a long stretch with a smoothed or paved surface, made for traveling by motor vehicle, carriage, etc. **2.** a way or course: *the road to peace.* **3.** Often, **roads.** a sheltered area of water where vessels may ride at anchor. **4. on the road,** traveling, esp. as a salesman.

road·a·bil·i·ty (rō′də bil′i tē), *n.* the ability of an automobile to ride smoothly under adverse road conditions.

road·bed (rōd′bed′), *n.* the foundation for the track of a railroad or for a road.

road·block (rōd′blok′), *n.* **1.** an obstruction placed across a road for halting or hindering traffic. **2.** anything that obstructs progress.

road′ com/pany, a theatrical group that tours cities and towns, usually performing a single play.

road·run·ner (rōd′run′ər), *n.* a cuckoo of the western U.S. that has a crested head.

road′ show′, a show performed by a touring group of actors.

road·side (rōd′sīd′), *n.* **1.** the side or border of the road. —*adj.* **2.** on or near the roadside.

road·stead (rōd′sted′), *n.* road (def. 3).

road·ster (rōd′stər), *n.* an early type of open automobile having a single seat for two or three passengers.

road·way (rōd′wā′), *n.* **1.** the land over which a road is built. **2.** the part of a road over which vehicles travel.

road·work (rōd′wûrk′), *n.* the exercise of running considerable distances, performed chiefly by boxers in training.

roam (rōm), *v.i., v.t.* to move or travel (about or through) without purpose or direction. —**roam′er,** *n.*

roan (rōn), *adj.* **1.** having a reddish-brown or yellowish-brown coat sprinkled with gray or white, as a horse. —*n.* **2.** a roan horse.

roar (rōr, rôr), *v.i.* **1.** to utter a loud, deep cry or howl. **2.** to laugh loudly. —*v.t.* **3.** to utter or express in a roar. —*n.* **4.** a roaring sound, esp. the characteristic sound of the lion. **5.** a loud outburst of laughter.

roast (rōst), *v.t.* **1.** to cook (meat, etc.) by dry heat, esp. in an oven or on a spit. **2.** to dry or parch by exposure to heat, as coffee beans. **3.** to make extremely or excessively hot. **4.** *Informal.* to criticize mercilessly. —*v.i.* **5.** to roast meat or other food. **6.** to undergo the process of becoming roasted. —*n.* **7.** roasted meat. **8.** a piece of meat for roasting. **9.** a picnic at which food is roasted and eaten: *a corn roast.* —*adj.* **10.** roasted. —**roast′er**, *n.*

rob (rob), *v.*, **robbed, rob·bing.** —*v.t.* **1.** to take from by unlawful force. **2.** to deprive of something unjustly or injuriously. —*v.i.* **3.** to commit or practice robbery. —**rob′ber**, *n.*

rob·ber·y (rob′ə rē), *n.*, *pl.* **-ber·ies.** **1.** the act or an instance of robbing. **2.** the felonious taking of another person's property by violence or intimidation.

robe (rōb), *n.*, *v.*, **robed, rob·ing.** —*n.* **1.** a long, loose or flowing outer garment worn as ceremonial dress. **2.** any long, loose garment, as a bathrobe or dressing gown. **3.** a piece of fur cloth used as a covering or wrap: *a lap robe.* —*v.t.*, *v.i.* **4.** to dress in a robe or robes.

rob·in (rob′in), *n.* **1.** an American thrush having a brownish-gray back and a reddish breast. **2.** any of several small European birds having a reddish breast.

Rob′in Hood′, a legendary English outlaw of the 12th century who robbed the rich to give to the poor.

ro·bot (rō′bət, -bot, rob′ət), *n.* **1.** a machine that resembles a human and does mechanical, routine tasks on command. **2.** a person who works in a mechanical, routine manner. **3.** any machine that operates automatically. [first used in the play *R.U.R.* (by K. Čapek, 1890–1938, Czech playwright), from Czech *robotnik* serf]

ro·bust (rō bust′, rō′bust), *adj.* strong and energetically healthy. —**ro·bust′ly**, *adv.* —**ro·bust′ness**, *n.*

Roch·es·ter (roch′es tər, -i stər), *n.* a city in W New York.

rock¹ (rok), *n.* **1.** a large mass of stone. **2.** the hard, solid mineral matter that makes up much of the earth's crust. **3.** a stone of any size.

4. something resembling or suggesting a rock in firmness or support. **5. on the rocks, a.** *Informal.* in a state of destruction. **b.** served over ice cubes, as a cocktail. —**rock′like′**, *adj.*

rock² (rok), *v.i.*, *v.t.* **1.** to move or swing to and fro or from side to side, esp. gently. **2.** to shake or disturb violently, as an explosion. —*n.* **3.** a rocking movement. **4.** Also called **rock′-'n'-roll** (rok′ən rōl′), **rock′-and-roll′.** popular music marked by a heavily accented rhythm and a simple, repetitious melody structure and esp. played on amplified instruments.

rock′ bot′tom, the very lowest level.

rock-bound (rok′bound′), *adj.* enclosed or covered by rocks.

rock·er (rok′ər), *n.* **1.** one of the curved pieces on which a cradle or a rocking chair rocks. **2.** Also called **rock′ing chair′.** a chair mounted on rockers. **3.** *Informal.* **a.** a rock performer. **b.** a rock song. **4. off one's rocker**, *Slang.* insane or crazy.

rock·et (rok′it), *n.* **1.** any of various simple or complex tubelike devices containing combustibles that on being ignited liberate gases whose action propels the tube through the air. **2.** a space capsule or vehicle put into orbit by such devices. **3.** Also called **rock′et en′gine**. an engine supplied with its own solid or liquid fuel and oxidizer. —*v.i.*, *v.t.* **4.** to move by or like a rocket. —**rock′et·like′**, *adj.*

rock·et·ry (rok′i trē), *n.* the science of rocket design, development, and flight.

rock′ing horse′, a toy horse, as of wood, mounted on rockers or springs, on which children may ride.

rock-ribbed (rok′ribd′), *adj.* **1.** having ribs or ridges of rock. **2.** unyielding and uncompromising.

rock′ salt′, common salt in large crystals.

rock′ wool′, a woollike material made from molten slag or rock, used for heat and sound insulation.

rock·y¹ (rok′ē), *adj.*, **rock·i·er, rock·i·est.** **1.** abounding in or consisting of rocks. **2.** full of difficulties or hazards. **3.** firm or steadfast. —**rock′i·ness**, *n.*

rock·y² (rok′ē), *adj.*, **rock·i·er, rock·i·est.** **1.** inclined to rock or totter. **2.** *Informal.* physically unsteady or weak. —**rock′i·ness**, *n.*

Rock′y Moun′tains, the chief mountain system in North America, extending from central New Mexico to N Alaska. Also called **Rock′ies.**

Rock′y Moun′tain sheep′, bighorn.

ro·co·co (rə kō′kō), *n.* **1.** a style of architecture and decoration marked by very elaborate designs and elegant ornament —*adj.* **2.** of or like rococo. **3.** ornate or florid

rod (rod), *n.* **1.** a straight, slender stick of wood, metal, or other material **2.** a stick or a bundle of sticks used for punishing a person. **3.** punishment or discipline **4.** a scepter carried as a symbol of office or authority **5.** a slender bar or tube, as for suspending curtains. **6.** See **fishing rod. 7.** a unit of length equal to 5½ yards. **8.** *Slang.* a pistol or revolver.

rode (rōd), *v.* pt. of ride.

ro·dent (rōd′°nt), *n.* any of an order of the gnawing or nibbling mammals, including the mice, squirrels, and beavers

ro·de·o (rō′dē ō′, rō dā′ō), *n.*, *pl.* **-de·os. 1.** a public exhibition of cowboy skills, as bronco riding and calf roping. **2.** a roundup of cattle.

Ro·din (rō dan′, -daN′), *n.* (François) Au·guste (Re·né) (frän swA′ ō gYst′ Rə nā′), 1840–1917, French sculptor.

roe[1] (rō), *n.* the eggs of a fish, esp. when used as food.

roe[2] (rō), *n.*, *pl.* **roes, roe.** a small, agile deer of Europe and Asia having three-pointed antlers. Also called **roe′ deer′.**

roe·buck (rō′buk′), *n.*, *pl.* **-bucks, -buck.** a male roe deer.

roent·gen (rent′gən -jən, runt′-), *n.* the international unit for measuring the radiation of x-rays or gamma rays.

roent·gen·ol·o·gy (rent′gə nol′ə jē, -jə-, runt′-), *n.* the branch of medicine dealing with diagnosis and therapy through x-rays. —**roent′gen·o·log′ic** (-n°loj′ik, -jə-, runt′-), **roent′gen·o·log′i·cal,** *adj.* —**roent′gen·ol′o·gist,** *n.*

Roent′gen ray′, x-ray.

ROG, receipt of goods.

rog·er (roj′ər), *interj.* **1.** *Informal.* all right or O.K. **2.** message received and understood (a response to radio communications).

rogue (rōg), *n.* **1.** a criminally dishonest person. **2.** a playfully mischievous person. —**ro·guer·y** (rō′gə rē), *n.* —**ro·guish** (rō′gish) *adj.* —**ro′guish·ly,** *adv.* —**ro′guish·ness,** *n.* —Syn. **1.** knave, scoundrel.

rogues′ gal′lery, a collection of portraits of criminals and suspects maintained by the police for identification.

roil (roil), *v.t.* **1.** to make (water, etc.) unclear or murky by stirring up sediment. **2.** rile (def. 1).

roist·er (roi′stər), *v.i.* to revel noisily or without restraint. —**roist′er·er,** *n.* —**roist′er·ous,** *n.*

role (rōl), *n* **1.** a character acted in a play, film etc **2.** the proper function of a person or thing. Also, **rôle.**

roll (rōl), *v.i* **1.** to move along a surface by turning over and over, as a wheel **2.** to move on wheels. **3.** to flow with an undulating motion, as waves **4.** to extend in undulations, as land **5.** to elapse or pass, as time. **6.** to emit a deep prolonged sound, as thunder or drums **7.** (of a ship) to rock from side to side in open water. —*v.t.* **8.** to cause to move along a surface by turning over and over. **9.** to move along on wheels **10.** to utter with a full flowing, continuous sound. **11.** to pronounce with a trill: *to roll one's r's.* **12.** to turn (the eyes) in different directions. **13.** to cause to rock from side to side, as a ship **14.** to wrap (something) around an axis or around upon itself, or into a rounded shape. **15.** to spread out flat **16.** to wrap or envelop, as in a covering **17.** to spread out or level with a roller. **18. roll back,** to reduce (prices etc.) to a former level, usually by government order **19. roll in.** *Informal* to arrive, esp in large numbers or quantity. **20. roll out.** to spread out or flatten —*n* **21.** a document or paper that is or may be rolled up **22.** a list or register of names **23.** anything rolled up in a cylindrical form **24. a.** a small cake of bread, often rolled or doubled on itself before baking **b.** any food rolled up and cooked **25.** the act or an instance of rolling **26.** undulation, as of a surface **27.** a deep, prolonged sound, as of thunder or drums. **28.** a rolling motion.

roll·back (rōl′bak′), *n.* the act or an instance of rolling back.

roll′ bar′, a sturdy metal bar arching over an automobile to prevent injury to passengers in the event of overturning

roll′ call′, the calling of a list of names for checking attendance.

roll·er (rō′lər), *n* **1.** a person or thing that rolls **2.** a cylinder, wheel, or caster upon which something is rolled along **3.** a cylindrical object on which something is rolled up. **4.** a cylindrical object for crushing, flattening or curling something. **5.** a long, swelling wave

roll′er coast′er, a small railroad, esp. in an amusement park, having open cars that move rapidly along a high, sharply winding track built with steep inclines.

Roll′er Der′by, *Trademark.* a contest between two teams on roller skates, held on a circular, banked board track.

roll′er skate′, a skate with four wheels or rollers for use on a sidewalk or floor. —**roll′er-skate′,** *v.i.* —**roll′er skat′er.**

rol·lick (rol′ik), *v.i.* to move or act in a careless, frolicsome manner. — **rol′lick·ing,** *adj.* —**rol′lick·ing·ly,** *adv.*

roll′ing pin′, a cylinder of wood or other material used for rolling out dough.

roll′ing stock′, the wheeled vehicles of a railroad.

roll-on (rōl′on′, -ôn′), *adj.* packaged in a container equipped with a roller that dispenses the content directly onto the human skin.

roll·o·ver (rōl′ō′vər), *n.* **1.** a rolling or turning over, esp. of an automobile. **2.** an extension or renewal of a monetary obligation, as a loan that has fallen due.

roll′ top′, a flexible, sliding cover for the working area of a desk. — **roll′-top′,** *adj.*

ro·ly-po·ly (rō′lē pō′lē, -pō′lē), *adj.* short and plumply round.

Rom., 1. Roman. **2.** Romance. **3.** Romania. **4.** Romanian.

rom., roman (type).

ro·maine (rō mān′, rə-), *n.* a variety of lettuce havng a cylindrical head of long leaves.

Ro·man (rō′mən), *adj.* **1.** of or characteristic of ancient or modern Rome, its inhabitants, or their customs and culture. **2.** (*usually l.c.*) noting the upright style of printing types most commonly used. **3.** of the Roman Catholic Church. —*n.* **4.** a native, inhabitant, or citizen of ancient or modern Rome. **5.** (*usually l.c.*) roman type or lettering.

ro·man à clef (RÔ mä′ nA klā′), *pl.* **ro·mans à clef** (RÔ mäN′ zA klā′). a novel that represents actual events and real persons under the guise of fiction. [< F: novel with a key]

Ro′man can′dle, a firework consisting of a tube that emits sparks and balls of fire.

Ro′man Cath′olic, 1. of the Roman Catholic Church. **2.** a member of the Roman Catholic Church. —**Ro′man Cathol′icism.**

Ro′man Cath′olic Church′, the Christian church of which the Pope is the supreme head.

ro·mance (*n.* rō mans′, rō′mans; *v.* rō mans′; *adj.* rō′mans), *n.*, *v.*, **-manced, -manc·ing,** *adj.* —*n.* **1.** a story that tells of heroic deeds, adventure, and love. **2.** a medieval story or poem telling of heroic or supernatural events. **3.** a love affair.

4. a made-up, fanciful story. **5.** an appealing or romantic quality. **6.** (*cap.*) Also called **Ro′mance lan′guages.** a group of languages descended from Latin, including French, Spanish, Italian, Portuguese, and a few others. —*v.i.* **7.** to indulge in fanciful stories. **8.** to think or talk romantically. —*v.t.* **9.** *Informal.* to have a love affair with. —*adj.* **10.** (*cap.*) of or pertaining to Romance languages. —**ro·manc′er,** *n.*

Ro′man Em′pire, the empire of the ancient Romans lasting from 27 B.C. to A.D. 395.

Ro·man·esque (rō′mə nesk′), *adj.* noting a style of European architecture prevailing from the 9th through 12th centuries, characterized by heavy masonry construction.

Ro·ma·ni·a (rō mā′nē ə, -mān′yə), *n.* Rumania. —**Ro·ma′ni·an,** *adj.*, *n.*

Ro′man nu′merals, the numerals in the ancient Roman system of notation, still used for certain limited purposes. The common basic symbols are I(=1), V(=5), X(=10), L(= 50), C(=100), D(=500), and M(= 1000).

ro·man·tic (rō man′tik), *adj.* **1.** of or of the nature of romance. **2.** having feelings and thoughts of love and adventure. **3.** fanciful or impractical. **4.** appealing to feelings of romance. **5.** (*often cap.*) of or pertaining to Romanticism. —*n.* **6.** a romantic person. **7.** an adherent of Romanticism. —**ro·man′ti·cal·ly,** *adv.* — **Syn. 2, 4,** ardent, fervent, passionate.

Ro·man·ti·cism (rō man′tï sïz′əm), *n.* (*often l.c.*) a style of literature and art of the 19th century that encouraged freedom of form and emphasized imagination and emotion. —**Ro·man′tï·cist,** *n.*

ro·man·ti·cize (rō man′tï sīz′), *v.*, **-cized, -ciz·ing.** —*v.t.* **1.** to make romantic. —*v.i.* **2.** to hold romantic notions, ideas, etc.

Rom·a·ny (rom′ə nē, rō′mə-), *n.*, *pl.* **-nies, 1.** Gypsy (def. 1). **2.** the language of the Gypsies.

Rome (rōm), *n.* **1.** the capital of Italy. **2.** the ancient Italian kingdom, republic, and empire whose capital was the city of Rome.

Ro·me·o (rō′mē ō′), *n.* any romantic male lover.

romp (romp), *v.i.* **1.** to play in a lively or boisterous manner. **2.** to win without effort, as in racing. —*n.* **3.** a lively or boisterous frolic. **4.** an effortless victory. —**romp′er,** *n.*

romp·ers (rom′pərz), *n.pl.* a loose outer garment combining a waist and short, bloused pants.

rood (rōōd), *n.* **1.** a unit of land area equal to ¼ acre. **2.** a large crucifix.

roof (roof, roof), n., pl. **roofs**, v. —n.
1. the external upper covering of a
house or other building. 2. something resembling this. —v.t. 3. to
cover with a roof. —**roof'er,** n. —
roof'less, adj.

roof' gar'den, 1. a garden on the flat
roof of a building. 2. the top or top
story of a building having a garden
or restaurant.

roof·ing (roo'fing, roof'ing), n. material for roofs.

roof·top (roof'top', roof'-), n. the
roof of a building.

roof·tree (roof'tre', roof'-), n. the
ridgepole of a roof.

rook¹ (rook), n. 1. a black, European
crow noted for its gregarious habits.
—v.t. 2. to cheat or swindle.

rook² (rook), n. a chess piece that
can be moved any unobstructed distance horizontally or vertically.

rook·er·y (rook'ə re), n., pl. **-er·ies.** 1.
a colony of rooks. 2. a breeding
place of rooks.

rook·ie (rook'e), n. 1. any raw recruit, as on a police force. 2. any
novice.

room (room, room), n. 1. a partitioned portion of space within a
building. 2. the persons present in
such a space. 3. space occupied by
or available for something. 4. opportunity or scope for something. 5.
rooms, living quarters. —v.i. 6. to
occupy a room or rooms. —**room'-**
ful, n. —**room'y,** adj. —**room'i·ly,**
adv. —**room'i·ness,** n.

room' and board', lodging and meals.

room·er (roo'mər, room'ər), n. a person who lives in a rented room.

room·ette (room met', room-), n. a small
private compartment in a sleeping
car.

room·ful (room'fool, room'-), n., pl.
-fuls. an amount or number sufficient to fill a room.

room'ing house', a house with furnished rooms to rent.

room·mate (room'mat', room'-), n. a
person who shares a room or apartment with another or others.

Roo·se·velt (ro'zə velt', -volt), n. 1.
Franklin Del·a·no (del'ə no), 1882–
1945, 32nd president of the U.S.
1933–45. 2. **The·o·dore** (the'ə dor,
-dor), 1858–1919, 26th president of
the U.S. 1901–09.

roost (roost), n. 1. a perch upon
which birds or fowls rest at night. 2.
a place with perches for fowls or
birds. 3. **rule the roost,** to be in
charge or control. —v.i. 4. to sit or
rest on a roost. 5. to settle or stay
for the night.

roost·er (roo'stər), n. the adult male
of the domestic fowl.

root¹ (root, root), n. 1. the part of a
plant that develops and spreads under the ground, anchoring the plant
and providing it with water and
nourishment from the soil. 2. any underground part of a plant, as a bulb.
3. the embedded portion of a hair,
tooth, nail, etc. 4. the fundamental
or essential part. 5. the source or
origin of a thing. 6. a quantity that,
when multiplied by itself a specified
number of times, produces a given
quantity. 7. Gram. a basic word or
stem from which other words are
derived. 8. **take root,** a. to begin to
grow. b. to become fixed or established. —v.i. 9. to grow roots. —v.t.
10. to fix by or as by roots. 11. to
pull, tear, or dig up by the roots.
12. to remove completely. —**root'-**
like', adj. —**root'less,** adj.

root² (root, root), v.i. 1. to turn up
the soil with the snout. 2. to search
about. —v.t. 3. to turn over with
the snout.

root³ (root, root), v.i. to encourage
by cheering. —**root'er,** n.

root' beer', a carbonated soft drink
flavored with the extracted juices of
roots, barks, and herbs.

root·stock (root'stok', root'-), n. rhizome.

rope (rop), n., v., **roped, rop·ing.** —n.
1. a strong, thick cord made of
strands of hemp, flax, etc. 2. a
number of things twisted or strung
together in the form of a cord. 3. a
hangman's noose. 4. **know the ropes,**
Informal. to be completely familiar
with the operation or details of
something. —v.t. 5. to tie or fasten
with a rope. 6. to enclose or mark
off with a rope or ropes. 7. to catch
with a lasso. 8. **rope in,** Slang. to
lure or entice, esp. by deceiving.

Roque·fort (rok'fort), n. a strong
cheese made of sheep's milk and
veined with mold.

Ror'schach test' (ror'shäk, ror'-), a
test for revealing the underlying personality structure of an individual
by associations evoked by a series of
inkblot designs

ro·sa·ry (ro'zə re), n., pl. **-ries.** Rom.
Cath. Ch. a string of beads used for
counting a special series of prayers.
[< L rosāri(um), rose garden]

rose¹ (roz), n. 1. any of various prickly garden plants bearing sweet-smelling flowers of various colors. 2. its
flower. 3. something resembling or
suggesting this flower. 4. a purplish
or pinkish red. —adj. 5. of the color
rose.

rose² (roz), v. pt. of **rise.**

ro·sé (ro zā'), n. a pink table wine.

ro·se·ate (ro'ze it, -āt'), adj. 1. tinged
with rose. 2. optimistic or promising.

rose·bud (roz'bud'), n. the bud of a
rose.

rose·bush (rōz′boosh′), *n.* a shrub that bears roses.

rose-col·ored (rōz′kul′ərd), *adj.* **1.** of rose color. **2.** viewing or viewed with optimism.

rose′ fe′ver, hay fever caused by the inhalation of rose pollen.

rose·mar·y (rōz′mâr′ē), *n., pl.* **-mar·ies.** an evergreen shrub, related to mint, whose sweet-smelling leaves are used in cooking.

ro·sette (rō zet′), *n.* **1.** a rose-shaped arrangement of ribbon or other material, used as an ornament or badge. **2.** an ornament resembling a rose.

rose′ wa′ter, water mixed with essential oil of roses.

rose′ win′dow, a circular window decorated with tracery symmetrical about the center.

rose·wood (rōz′wood′), *n.* **1.** the heavy, hard, reddish wood of various tropical trees, used for making furniture, etc. **2.** its tree.

Rosh Ha·sha·nah (rōsh′ hə shä′nə, -shô′-, hä-, rōsh′), the Jewish New Year, celebrated in September or October. Also, **Rosh′ Ha·sha′na.**

ros·in (roz′in), *n.* the brittle resin left after distilling the turpentine from pine pitch, used chiefly in making varnish, inks, etc., and for rubbing on violin bows.

ros·ter (ros′tər), *n.* a list of persons or groups, as of military personnel with their turns of duty.

ros·trum (ros′trəm), *n., pl.* **-trums, -tra** (trə). a platform or stage for public speaking.

ros·y (rō′zē), *adj.,* **ros·i·er, ros·i·est. 1.** pink or pinkish-red. **2.** having a fresh, healthy redness. **3.** cheerful or hopeful. —**ros′i·ly,** *adv.* —**ros′i·ness,** *n.*

rot (rot), *v.,* **rot·ted, rot·ting,** *n.* —*v.i., v.t.* **1** to decompose or decay foully. —*n.* **2.** the process of rotting. **3.** rotting or rotten matter. **4.** any disease characterized by decay. **5.** *Informal.* nonsense or foolish talk.

ro·ta·ry (rō′tə rē), *adj., n., pl.* **-ries.** —*adj.* **1.** turning around on an axis, as a wheel. **2.** having a part or parts that rotate. —*n.* **3.** See **traffic circle. 4.** a rotary device or machine.

ro·tate (rō′tāt, rō tāt′), *v.t., v.i.,* **-tat·ed, -tat·ing. 1.** to turn around an axis or center point. **2.** to alter in a fixed routine of succession. —**ro′tat·a·ble,** *adj.* —**ro·ta′tion,** *n.* —**ro·ta′tion·al,** *adj.* —**ro·ta·tor** (rō′tā tər, rō tā′-), *n.* —**ro′ta·to′ry** (-tə tôr′ē, -tōr′ē), *adj.*

ROTC, Reserve Officers' Training Corps.

rote (rōt), *n.* mere repetition of memorized words or sounds without thought for meaning: *to recite by rote.*

ro·tis·ser·ie (rō tis′ə rē), *n.* a small broiler with a motor-driven spit.

ro·to·gra·vure (rō′tə grə vyoor′, -grā′-vyər), *n.* **1.** a process by which the image to be reproduced is printed from an intaglio copper cylinder. **2.** a newspaper section printed by this process.

ro·tor (rō′tər), *n.* **1.** a rotating part of a machine. **2.** a system of rotating airfoils, as the horizontal ones of a helicopter.

rot·ten (rot′ᵊn), *adj.* **1.** foully decomposing or decaying. **2.** bad-smelling. **3.** morally corrupt. **4.** *Informal.* wretchedly bad or unsatisfactory. —**rot′ten·ly,** *adv.* —**rot′ten·ness,** *n.*

Rot·ter·dam (rot′ər dam′), *n.* a seaport in the SW Netherlands.

ro·tund (rō tund′), *adj.* **1.** round in shape. **2.** plump or fat. —**ro·tund′ly,** *adv.* —**ro·tun′di·ty, ro·tund′ness,** *n.*

ro·tun·da (rō tun′də), *n.* **1.** a round building or hall, esp. one covered by a dome. **2.** a large and high circular room.

rou·ble (roo′bəl), *n.* ruble.

rou·é (roo ā′, roo′ā), *n.* a dissipated and lecherous man.

rouge (roozh), *n., v.,* **rouged, roug·ing.** —*n.* **1.** a red cosmetic for coloring the cheeks or lips. **2.** a reddish powder used for polishing metal, glass, etc. —*v.t., v.i.* **3.** to use rouge (on).

rough (ruf), *adj.* **1.** having a coarse or uneven surface. **2.** shaggy or coarse. **3.** violent or rugged. **4.** stormy or tempestuous, as weather. **5.** unmannerly or rude. **6.** disorderly or riotous. **7.** *Informal.* difficult or unpleasant: *to have a rough time of it.* **8.** without ordinary comforts. **9.** done quickly without attention to detail: *a rough drawing.* **10.** approximate or tentative: *a rough guess.* —*n.* **11.** something rough, esp. rough ground. **12.** *Golf.* any part of the course bordering the fairway on which the grass and weeds are not trimmed **13.** *Chiefly Brit.* a rowdy or ruffian. **14.** **in the rough,** in a rough, crude, or unfinished state. —*adv.* **15.** in a rough manner. —*v.t.* **16.** to make rough. **17.** to treat violently. **18.** to make or do roughly. **19. rough it,** to live without the customary comforts. —**rough′er,** *n.* —**rough′ly,** *adj.* —**rough′ness,** *n.* —**Syn. 1.** bumpy, jagged. **5.** crude, unpolished.

rough·age (ruf′ij), *n.* **1.** rough or coarse material. **2.** food containing a high proportion of indigestible cellulose; as bran.

rough-and-ready (ruf′ən red′ē), *adj.* rough or crude, but good enough for the purpose.

rough-and-tum·ble (ruf′ən tum′bəl), *adj.* **1.** violent, random, and disorderly. —*n.* **2.** rough-and-tumble fighting.

rough·en (ruf′ən), *v.t., v.i.* to make or become rough.

rough-hew (ruf′hyōō′), *v.t.,* **-hewed, -hewed** or **-hewn, -hew·ing. 1.** to hew (timber, etc.) roughly or without smoothing. **2.** to shape roughly.

rough·house (ruf′hous′), *n., v.,* **-housed** (-houst′, -houzd′), **-hous·ing** (-houz′-ing, -hous′-). —*n.* **1.** rough, disorderly playing, esp. indoors. —*v.i.* **2.** to engage in roughhouse. —*v.t.* **3.** to handle roughly but with playful intent.

rough·neck (ruf′nek′), *n. Informal.* **1.** a rough, coarse person. **2.** any laborer working on an oil-drilling rig.

rough·shod (ruf′shod′), *adj.* **1.** shod with horseshoes having projecting nails or points. **2. ride roughshod over,** to treat harshly or domineeringly.

rou·lette (rōō let′), *n.* **1.** a gambling game in which players bet on the space on a rotating wheel at which a spinning ball will rest. **2.** a small wheel with sharp teeth.

Rou·ma·ni·a (rōō mā′nē ə, -mān′yə), *n.* Rumania. —**Rou·ma′ni·an,** *adj., n.*

round (round), *adj.* **1.** shaped like a circle, ring, ball, or cylinder. **2.** consisting of full, curved lines or shapes, as handwriting. **3.** involving circular motion: *a round dance.* **4.** full, complete, or entire: *a round dozen.* **5.** expressed by a whole number with no fraction. **6.** expressed in tens, hundreds, thousands, etc. **7.** roughly correct: *a round guess.* **8.** considerable in amount. **9.** vigorous or brisk: *a round trot.* **10.** outspoken or unqualified: *a round assertion.* —*n.* **11.** any round shape or object. **12.** something circular, as a rung of a ladder. **13.** Sometimes, **rounds.** a completed course of time, series of events or operations, etc. **14.** any complete course, series, or succession. **15.** Often, **rounds.** a going around from place to place, as in a habitual or definite route. **16.** a single outburst, as of applause. **17.** a single discharge of shot by each of a number of guns. **18.** a charge of ammunition for a single shot. **19.** a single serving, as of drinks. **20.** movement in a circle. **21.** the portion of the thigh of beef below the rump and above the leg. **22.** one of a series of periods, as in a boxing match. **23.** a song for several singers, each of whom sings the same melody starting at a different time. **24. in the round, a.** (of a theater) with seats arranged around a central stage, as a theater. **b.** freestanding, as sculpture. —*adv.* **25.** throughout a recurring period of time. **26.** around. —*prep.* **27.** through-

out (a period of time). **28.** around. —*v.t.* **29.** to make round. **30.** to make plump. **31.** to complete or finish. **32.** to encircle or surround. **33.** to go or travel around. **34.** to express as a round number. —*v.i.* **35.** to become round. **36.** to become plump. **37.** to make a circuit. **38.** to turn around, as on an axis. **39. round up, a.** to herd (cattle, etc.) together. **b.** to assemble or gather. —**round′ish,** *adj.* —**round′ness,** *n.*

round·a·bout (round′ə bout′), *adj.* **1.** not straight or direct, as a route. —*n.* **2.** *Brit.* merry-go-round (def. 1).

roun·de·lay (roun′də lā′), *n.* a song in which a phrase or line is continually repeated.

round·house (round′hous′), *n.* **1.** a circular building for the servicing and repair of locomotives. **2.** *Slang.* a punch in which the fist describes a wide arc.

round·ly (round′lē), *adv.* **1.** in a round manner. **2.** vigorously or briskly. **3.** completely or fully.

round-shoul·dered (round′shōl′dərd, -shōl′-), *adj.* having the shoulders bent forward.

round′ ta′ble, 1. a group gathered together for a conference in which each participant has equal status. **2.** (*caps.*) the table around which King Arthur and his knights sat.

round-the-clock (round′the klok′), *adj.* continuing without interruption.

round′ trip′, a trip to a given place and back again. —**round′-trip′,** *adj.*

round·up (round′up′), *n.* **1.** the herding together of cattle, as for inspection or branding. **2.** a gathering together of scattered items or groups of people. **3.** a summary, as of information or news.

round·worm (round′wûrm′), *n.* any nematode that infests the intestines of humans and some mammals.

rouse (rouz), *v.t., v.i.,* **roused, rousing. 1.** to wake up from sleep, inactivity, etc. **2.** to stir up to strong indignation or anger. —**rous′er,** *n.* —*Syn.* animate, stimulate.

Rous·seau (rōō sō′), *n.* **Jean Jacques** (zhän zhäk), 1712–78, French philosopher and author.

roust·a·bout (roust′ə bout′), *n.* any unskilled laborer, as in a circus or oil field.

rout¹ (rout), *n.* **1.** a disastrous defeat. **2.** a confused, disorderly retreat after a defeat. **3.** *Archaic.* a large evening party. —*v.t.* **4.** to defeat badly. **5.** to disperse in disorderly flight.

rout² (rout), *v.t.* **1.** to find or get by searching or rummaging. **2.** to force or drive out. **3.** to hollow out, as with a gouge.

route (rōōt, rout), *n., v.,* **rout·ed, rout·ing.** —*n.* 1. a course or road for travel or shipping. 2. a regular line of travel or shipping. 3. a fixed territory or course covered, as by a milkman. —*v.t.* 4. to fix the route of. 5. to send by a particular route. [< OF < L *rupta* (*via*) broken (road)] —**rout′er,** *n.*

rou·tine (rōō tēn′), *n.* 1. a customary or regular course of procedure. 2. regular, habitual, or unimaginative procedure. —*adj.* 3. like or following routine. 4. dull or uninteresting. —**rou·tine′ly,** *adv.* —**rou·tin′ize** (-tē′nīz), *v.t.*

rove[1] (rōv), *v.i., v.t.,* **roved, rov·ing.** to wander (over or through) without definite destination. —**rov′er,** *n.*

rove[2] (rōv), *v.* a pt. and pp. of **reeve.**

row[1] (rō), *n.* 1. a number of persons or things arranged in a line. 2. a line of adjacent seats facing the same way, as in a theater. 3. a street formed by two continuous lines of buildings. 4. **in a row,** one after another.

row[2] (rō), *v.i., v.t.* 1. to propel (a boat) by using oars. 2. to carry in a rowboat. —*n.* 3. a trip in a rowboat. —**row′er,** *n.*

row[3] (rou), *n.* 1. a noisy dispute or quarrel. —*v.i.* 2. to quarrel noisily.

row·boat (rō′bōt′), *n.* a small boat for rowing.

row·dy (rou′dē), *n., pl.* **-dies,** *adj.,* **-di·er, -di·est.** —*n.* 1. a rough, disorderly person. —*adj.* 2. rough and disorderly. —**row′di·ly,** *adv.* —**row′di·ness,** *n.* —**row′dy·ish,** *adj.* —**row′dy·ism,** *n.*

row·el (rou′əl), *n.* a small wheel with radiating points, forming the end of a spur worn by a horseback rider.

row′ house′ (rō), one of a row of uniform houses, often joined by common walls.

roy·al (roi′əl), *adj.* 1. of a king, queen, or other sovereign. 2. appropriate to or befitting a sovereign. —**roy′al·ly,** *adv.*

roy′al blue′, a deep blue.

roy·al·ist (roi′ə list), *n.* a supporter of a king or royal government.

roy·al·ty (roi′əl tē), *n., pl.* **-ties.** 1. royal persons collectively. 2. royal status, dignity, or power. 3. an agreed portion of the income from a work paid to its author, composer, etc. 4. a portion of the proceeds paid to the owner of a right, as a patent or mineral right, for the use of it.

rpm, revolutions per minute.

rps, revolutions per second.

rpt., 1. repeat. 2. report.

R.R., 1. railroad. 2. rural route.

R.S., 1. Recording Secretary. 2. Revised Statutes. 3. Royal Society.

r.s., right side.

RSFSR, See Russian Soviet Federated Socialist Republic.

RSV, See Revised Standard Version.

R.S.V.P., please reply. Also, **rsvp, r.s.v.p.** [< F r(*épondez*) *s*(*il*) *v*(*ous*) *p*(*lait*) reply, if you please]

rt., right.

RT, radiotelephone.

rte., route.

Ru, ruthenium.

rub (rub), *v.,* **rubbed, rub·bing,** *n.* —*v.t.* 1. to move over the surface of with pressure and friction. 2. to spread or apply with pressure and friction. 3. to move (two things) with pressure and friction over or back and forth over each other. 4. to make sore by friction. 5. to remove by pressure and friction. —*v.i.* 6. to rub something. 7. to move with pressure against something. 8. **rub down, a.** to polish or smooth. **b.** to give a message to. 9. **rub the wrong way,** to annoy or irritate. —*n.* 10. the act or an instance of rubbing. 11. something that annoys or irritates one's feelings. 12. an obstacle or hindrance. 13. a rough area caused by rubbing.

rub·ber[1] (rub′ər), *n.* 1. a highly elastic substance obtained from the milky juice of several tropical trees or made synthetically. 2. a low overshoe made of this material. 3. a person who rubs. 4. *Chiefly Brit.* a pencil eraser. —*adj.* 5. made of rubber. —**rub′ber·y,** *adj.*

rub·ber[2] (rub′ər), *n.* 1. a series or round played until one side wins a specific number of hands, as in bridge. 2. an extra game played to break a tie.

rub′ber band′, a narrow, circular or oblong band of rubber, used for holding things together, as papers.

rub′ber cement′, a liquid adhesive consisting of unvulcanized rubber dispersed in a volatile solvent.

rub·ber·ize (rub′ə rīz′), *v.t.,* **-ized, -iz·ing.** to coat or impregnate with rubber.

rub·ber·neck (rub′ər nek′), *Informal.* —*n.* 1. an extremely curious person. 2. a sightseer or tourist. —*v.i.* 3. to look about or stare with great curiosity.

rub′ber stamp′, 1. a device with a rubber printing surface, used for manually imprinting names, dates, etc. 2. *Informal.* **a.** a person or government agency that gives approval automatically or routinely. **b.** such approval. —**rub′ber-stamp′,** *v.t.*

rub·bish (rub′ish), *n.* 1. worthless, discarded material. 2. nonsense, as in writing, art, etc. —**rub′bish·y,** *adj.*

rub·ble (rub′əl *or, for 1,* rōō′bəl), *n.*
1. rough fragments of broken stone used in masonry. **2.** broken pieces of anything, esp. in a great mass.

rub·down (rub′doun′), *n.* a massage, esp. after a steam bath.

rube (rōōb), *n. Slang.* an unsophisticated country person.

ru·bel·la (rōō bel′ə), *n.* See **German measles.**

Ru·bens (rōō′bənz), *n.* **Peter Paul,** 1577–1640, Flemish painter

ru·bi·cund (rōō′bə kund′), *adj.* unnaturally red or reddish, as the complexion.

ru·bid·i·um (rōō bid′ē əm), *n. Chem.* an active metallic element resembling potassium. *Symbol:* Rb; *at. wt.:* 85.47; *at no.:* 37.

ru·ble (rōō′bəl), *n.* the monetary unit of the Soviet Union.

ru·bric (rōō′brik), *n.* **1.** a title or heading in an early manuscript or book, written or printed in red. **2.** a direction for the conduct of religious services inserted in liturgical books.

ru·by (rōō′bē), *n., pl.* **-bies,** *adj.* —*n.* **1.** a red variety of corundum, used as a gem. **2.** a deep red. —*adj.* **3.** deep-red.

ruck·sack (ruk′sak′, rōōk′-), *n.* a type of knapsack.

ruck·us (ruk′əs), *n. Informal.* a noisy commotion.

rud·der (rud′ər), *n.* a hinged or pivoted vertical blade or flap that is turned to steer a boat or airplane. —**rud′der·less,** *adj.*

rud·dy (rud′ē), *adj.,* **-di·er, -di·est. 1.** having a fresh, healthy red color. **2.** red or reddish. —**rud′di·ly,** *adv.* —**rud′di·ness,** *n.*

rude (rōōd), *adj.,* **rud·er, rud·est. 1.** not courteous or polite. **2.** roughly built or made. **3.** without culture or refinement. **4.** rough or violent. **5.** primitively simple. —**rude′ly,** *adv.* —**rude′ness,** *n.* —**Syn. 1.** fresh, impertinent, unmannerly. **2.** crude. **3.** uncouth, vulgar.

ru·di·ment (rōō′də mənt), *n.* **1.** Usually, **rudiments.** the elemental principles of a subject. **2.** any undeveloped form of something. —**ru′di·men′ta·ry** (-men′tə rē, -trē), *adj.*

rue¹ (rōō), *v.,* **rued, ru·ing,** *n.* —*v.t., v.i.* **1.** to feel remorse or sorrow (for). —*n.* **2.** *Archaic.* remorse or sorrow. —**rue′ful,** *adj.* —**rue′ful·ly,** *adv.* —**rue′ful·ness,** *n.*

rue² (rōō), *n.* a strongly scented plant having yellow flowers and leaves formerly used in medicine.

ruff (ruf), *n.* **1.** a prominent growth of hair or feathers around the neck of an animal. **2.** a wide, pleated collar worn in the 16th and 17th centuries, by both sexes. —**ruffed** (ruft), *adj.* —**ruff′like′,** *adj.*

ruf·fi·an (ruf′ē ən, ruf′yən), *n.* a tough, lawless person. —**ruf′fi·an·ly,** *adj.*

ruf·fle (ruf′əl), *v.,* **-fled, -fling,** *n.* —*v.t.* **1.** to destroy the smoothness of. **2.** to erect (the feathers), as a bird in anger. **3.** to disturb or irritate. **4.** to turn (the pages of a book) rapidly. **5.** to draw up (cloth, lace, etc.) into folds. —*v.i.* **6.** to become ruffled. **7.** to become disturbed or irritated. —*n.* **8.** a strip of fabric drawn up by gathering along one edge and used as a trimming. **9.** disturbance or irritation. **10.** a ripple or undulation. —**ruf′fly,** *adj.* —**ruf′fler,** *n.*

rug (rug), *n.* **1.** a thick fabric for covering part of a floor. **2.** *Chiefly Brit.* See **lap robe.** —**rug′like′,** *adj.*

Rug·by (rug′bē), *n.* (*often l.c.*) a British form of football that developed from soccer.

rug·ged (rug′id), *adj.* **1.** having a roughly broken or jagged surface. **2.** strong and robust. **3.** wrinkled or furrowed, as a face. **4.** roughly irregular or heavy in outline. **5.** rough or harsh. **6.** tempestuous or stormy. —**rug′ged·ly,** *adv.* —**rug′ged·ness,** *n.*

Ruhr (rōōr), *n.* **1.** a river in W West Germany. **2.** a mining and industrial area in this region.

ru·in (rōō′in), *n.* **1.** the downfall or destruction of anything. **2.** something that causes this. **3.** **ruins,** the remains of a destroyed or decaying building or town. **4.** such a building or town. —*v.t.* **5.** to reduce to ruin. **6.** to bring to bankruptcy. **7.** to injure irretrievably. —*v.i.* **8.** to come to ruin. —**ru′in·a′tion,** *n.* —**ru′in·ous,** *adj.* —**ru′in·ous·ly,** *adv.* —**ru′in·ous·ness,** *n.* —**Syn. 5.** demolish, devastate, wreck.

rule (rōōl), *n., v.,* **ruled, rul·ing.** —*n.* **1.** a principle or regulation governing conduct, procedure, etc. **2.** the customary or normal condition, practice, etc. **3.** control or government. **4.** ruler (def. 2). **5.** **as a rule,** generally or usually. —*v.t., v.i.* **6.** to exercise authority or sovereignty (over). **7.** to decide authoritatively or judicially. **8.** to be superior or preeminent (in). **9.** to mark (paper) with lines by using a ruler. **10. rule out,** to eliminate or exclude.

rule′ of thumb′, a rough, practical method of procedure.

rul·er (rōō′lər), *n.* **1.** a person who rules or governs. **2.** a strip of wood or metal having a straight edge used for measuring or drawing lines.

rul·ing (rōō′ling), *n.* **1.** an authoritative or judicial decision. —*adj.* **2.** that rules or governs.

rum (rum), *n.* an alcoholic liquor distilled from molasses or some other fermented sugar-cane product.

Rum., 1. Rumania. 2. Rumanian.

Ru·ma·ni·a (roo mā'nē ə, -mān'yə), *n.* a country in SE Europe. **—Ru·ma'·ni·an,** *adj., n.*

rum·ba (rum'bə, room'-), *n.* a dance, Cuban Negro in origin and complex in rhythm. [< Sp, prob. of Afr origin]

rum·ble (rum'bəl), *v.,* **-bled, -bling,** *n.* **—***v.i., v.t.* 1. to make or cause to make a deep, heavy, somewhat muffled, continuous sound, as thunder. 2. to move with such a sound. **—***n.* 3. a rumbling sound. 4. *Slang.* a street fight between rival teenage gangs. 5. rumbling (def. 1). 6. a rear part of a carriage containing seating accommodations, as for servants, or space for baggage. **—rum'·bler,** *n.* **—rum'bling·ly,** *adv.* **—rum'·bly,** *adj.*

rum·bling (rum'bling), *n.* 1. Often, **rumblings.** a widespread sign of dissatisfaction or grievance. 2. rumble (def. 3).

ru·mi·nant (roo'mə nənt), *n.* 1. any of a group of even-toed, hoofed, cud-chewing mammals, including cattle, deer, camels, etc. **—***adj.* 2. chewing the cud. 3. contemplative or meditative.

ru·mi·nate (roo'mə nāt'), *v.i., v.t.,* **-nat·ed, -nat·ing.** 1. to chew (the cud). 2. to meditate or muse. **—ru'·mi·nat'ing·ly,** *adv.* **—ru'mi·na'tion,** *n.* **—ru'mi·na'tive,** *adj.*

rum·mage (rum'ij), *v.,* **-maged, -maging,** *n.* **—***v.t., v.i.* 1. to search thoroughly through (a place), esp. by turning over or looking through the contents. **—***n.* 2. miscellaneous articles, esp. those for sale at a rummage sale. 3. a rummaging search. **—rum'mag·er,** *n.*

rum'mage sale', a sale of miscellaneous articles, esp. items contributed, to raise money for charity.

rum·my (rum'ē), *n.* any of various card games in which the object is to match cards into sets and sequences.

ru·mor (roo'mər), *n.* 1. a story in general circulation without confirmation or certainty as to facts 2. common hearsay. **—***v.t.* 3. to tell or circulate by rumor. Also, *Brit.,* **ru'mour.**

rump (rump), *n.* 1. the fleshy hind part of an animal's body. 2. a cut of beef from this part. 3. the human buttocks 4. the last, unimportant or inferior part.

rum·ple (rum'pəl), *v.,* **-pled, -pling,** *n.* **—***v.t., v.i.* 1. to crumple or crush into wrinkles. **—***n.* 2. a wrinkle or crease **—rum'ply,** *adj.*

rum·pus (rum'pəs), *n.* a noisy or violent disturbance.

rum'pus room', a room in a house, usually in the basement, for games, parties, etc.

rum·run·ner (rum'run'ər), *n.* a person or ship engaged in smuggling liquor. **—rum'run'ning,** *n., adj.*

run (run), *v.,* **ran, run, run·ning,** *n.* **—***v.i.* 1. to go quickly by moving the legs more rapidly than at a walk. 2. to move or act quickly. 3. to flee or escape. 4. to make a quick trip or informal visit. 5. to go around without restraint. 6. to take part in a race or contest. 7. to be a candidate for election. 8. to migrate, as fish. 9. to ply between places, as a ship. 10. to move or pass freely or smoothly. 11. to creep or climb, as growing vines. 12. to unravel, as stitches or a fabric. 13. to flow, as a liquid. 14. to vary within a certain range. 15. to melt and flow. 16. to undergo a spreading of colors: *materials that run when washed.* 17. to operate or function. 18. to pass into or meet with a certain state or condition. 19. to amount or total. 20. to be stated or worded in a certain manner. 21. to extend in space or time. 22. to return persistently. 23. to be of a certain size, number, etc. **—***v.t.* 24. to move or run along (a route, path, etc.). 25. to perform or compete in by or as by running. 26. to bring into a specified state by running. 27. to drive (an animal) by pursuing. 28. to get past or through: *to run a blockade.* 29. to smuggle (contraband goods). 30. to publish, print, or make copies of. 31. to manage or conduct, as a business. 32. to be exposed to (a chance, risk, etc.). 33. to cause (a liquid) to flow. 34. to draw or trace, as a line. 35. to suffer from, as a fever. **36. run across,** to meet or find accidentally. **37. run down, a.** to collide with and knock down, esp. with a vehicle. **b.** to pursue until captured. **c.** to cease operation. **d.** to exhaust physically. **e.** to criticize severely. **f.** to search for until found. **g.** to give a quick summary of. **38. run in, a.** to visit casually. **b.** *Slang.* to take to jail. **c.** *Print.* to insert (text) without indenting. **39. run into, a.** to collide with. **b.** to meet accidentally. **40. run on, a.** to continue without interruption. **b.** to add something, as at the end of a text. **41. run out, to** terminate or end **42. run out of, to** exhaust a supply of. **43. run over, a.** to hit and knock down, esp. with a vehicle. **b.** to go beyond. **c.** to repeat or review. **44. run through, a.** to pierce or stab. **b.** to use up recklessly. **c.** to rehearse quickly. **45. run up, a.** to sew rapidly. **b.** to amass or incur. **—***n.* 46. the act, an instance, or period of running. 47. a distance covered, as by running. 48. a traveling between two places. 49. a quick trip. **50.** a period during which something, as a machine, operates or continues operating. **51.** the amount of anything produced in such a period. **52.** an unraveled place in knitted work. **53.** onward movement or progress. **54.** the particular course or tendency of something. **55.** freedom to move around in or use something. **56.** a continuous series of performances, as of a play. **57.** an uninterrupted series of things or events. **58.** a sequence of cards in a given suit. **59.** a series of sudden and urgent demands for payment, as on a bank. **60.** a small stream. **61.** a kind or class, as of goods. **62.** an inclined course, as on a slope. **63.** a fairly large enclosure for domestic animals. **64.** large numbers of fish in motion. **65.** *Baseball.* the score unit made by safely running around all the bases. **66. in the long run,** in the end. **67. on the run,** *Informal.* **a.** moving quickly. **b.** escaping or hiding. —**run′less,** *adj.*

run·a·bout (run′ə bout′), *n.* **1.** a small, open automobile. **2.** a small pleasure motorboat.

run·a·round (run′ə round′), *n. Informal.* evasive treatment in response to a request.

run·a·way (run′ə wā′), *n.* **1.** a person or animal that runs away. **2.** the act of running away. —*adj.* **3.** having run away. **4.** accomplished by eloping. **5.** easily won, as a contest. **6.** rising uncontrollably, as inflation.

run·down (run′doun′), *adj.* **1.** entirely fatigued. **2.** in poor health. **3.** fallen into disrepair. **4.** not running because it is unwound, as a clock.

run·down (run′doun′), *n.* a quick summary of information.

rune (rōōn), *n.* **1.** any of the characters of an alphabet used by the ancient Germanic-speaking peoples. **2.** a poem or song written in runes. —**ru′nic,** *adj.*

rung[1] (rung), *v.* pp. of **ring**[2].

rung[2] (rung), *n.* **1.** a rounded crosspiece forming a step of a ladder. **2.** a shaped piece fixed horizontally between the legs of a chair. **3.** any similar piece, as a spoke in a wheel. —**rung′less,** *adj.*

run·in (run′in′), *n.* **1.** *Informal.* a quarrel or argument. **2.** *Print.* matter that is run in.

run·nel (run′°l), *n.* a small stream. Also, **run·let** (run′lit).

run·ner (run′ər), *n.* **1.** a person or thing that runs, as a racer or messenger. **2.** *Baseball.* a player on base or trying to run from one base to another. **3.** either of the long, bladelike strips of metal or wood on which a sled or sleigh slides. **4.** the blade

of an ice skate. **5.** a long, narrow rug suitable for a passageway. **6. a.** a slender stem that runs along the ground, as in the strawberry. **b.** a plant that spreads by such stems.

run·ner-up (run′ər up′), *n., pl.* **runners-up.** a competitor or team finishing in second place.

run·ning (run′ing), *n.* **1.** the act of a person or thing that runs. **2.** competition for a prize, position, etc.: *in the running; out of the running.* —*adj.* **3.** that runs. **4.** extended or measured in a straight line. **5.** going or carried on continuously. —*adv.* **6.** in succession.

run′ning gear′, the working components of a vehicle that are not used to develop or transmit power.

run′ning light′, any of various lights displayed by a vessel or aircraft operating at night.

run·ny (run′ē), *adj.,* -ni·er, -ni·est. **1.** tending to run or drip. **2.** discharging mucus, as a nose.

run·off (run′ôf′, -of′), *n.* a final contest held to break a tie.

run-of-the-mill (run′əv ñə mil′), *adj.* merely average or ordinary.

run-on (run′on′, -ôn′), *adj.* **1.** of or designating something that is added at the end, as of text: *a run-on entry in a dictionary.* —*n.* **2.** run-on matter.

runt (runt), *n.* **1.** a stunted animal. **2.** *Often Contemptuous.* a small person. —**runt′y,** *adj.* —**runt′i·ness,** *n.*

run-through (run′thrōō′), *n.* a quick or informal rehearsal.

run·way (run′wā′), *n.* **1.** a way along which something runs. **2.** a paved strip on which airplanes land and take off. **3.** a narrow ramp extending from a stage into an aisle, as in a theater.

ru·pee (rōō pē′, rōō′pē), *n.* the monetary unit of India, Pakistan, and Sri Lanka.

ru·pi·ah (rōō pē′ə), *n., pl.* -ah, -ahs. the monetary unit of Indonesia.

rup·ture (rup′chər), *n., v.,* -tured, -turing. —*n.* **1.** the act of breaking or bursting. **2.** hernia, esp. abdominal hernia. —*v.t., v.i.* **3.** to cause or suffer a rupture or break.

ru·ral (rōōr′əl), *adj.* of the country, country life, or country people —**ru′ral·ism,** *n.* —**ru′ral·ly,** *adv.* —**Syn.** bucolic, pastoral.

ruse (rōōz), *n.* a cunning stratagem. —**Syn.** artifice, trick.

rush[1] (rush), *v.i., v.t.* **1.** to move, act, or perform with speed, impetuosity, or violence. **2.** to attack suddenly and violently. **3.** to pass or push rapidly or suddenly. **4.** to carry with haste. —*n.* **5.** a rapid, impetuous, or violent onward movement. **6.** an eager rushing of people to one place all at once. **7.** hurried and busy activity. **8.** press of work requiring extraordinary effort or haste. —*adj.* **9.** requiring or done in haste. —**rush′er,** *n.* —**rush′ing·ly,** *adv.*

rush² (rush), *n.* a grasslike marsh herb having pithy or hollow stems used for making mats, baskets, etc. —**rush′y,** *adj.*

rush′ hour′, a time of day in which large numbers of people are going to or returning from work. —**rush′-hour′,** *adj.*

rusk (rusk), *n.* **1.** a slice of sweet raised bread dried and baked again in the oven. **2.** light, soft, sweetened biscuit.

rus·set (rus′it), *n.* **1.** a yellowish brown, light brown, or reddish brown. **2.** a winter apple having a rough brownish skin. **3.** a coarse brownish homespun cloth.

Rus·sia (rush′ə), *n.* **1.** a former empire (**Rus′sian Em′pire**) in E Europe and N Asia: overthrown 1917. **2.** See **Soviet Union.**

Rus·sian (rush′ən), *adj.* **1.** of Russia, its people, or their language. —*n.* **2.** a native or inhabitant of Russia. **3.** the Slavic language of Russia.

Rus′sian roulette′, a game in which each participant in turn, using a revolver into which one bullet has been inserted, spins the cylinder, points the muzzle at his or her head and pulls the trigger.

Rus′sian So′viet Fed′erated So′cialist Repub′lic, the largest of the constituent republics of the Soviet Union.

rust (rust), *n.* **1.** the red or orange coating that forms on iron when exposed to air and moisture. **2.** any coating on metal caused by oxidation. **3.** a plant disease that causes brownish pustules on the leaves, stems, etc. **4.** a reddish brown. —*v.i., v.t.* **5.** to coat or become coated with rust. **6.** to deteriorate or weaken through lack of use. —**rust′y,** *adj.* —**rust′i·ness,** *n.*

rus·tic (rus′tik), *adj.* **1.** artlessly crude and unpolished. **2.** uncouth or boorish. **3.** made of roughly dressed limbs of trees, as furniture. **4.**

Archaic. rural. —*n.* **5.** an unsophisticated country person. —**rus′ti·cal·ly,** *adv.* —**rus·tic′i·ty** (ru stis′i tē), *n.*

rus·ti·cate (rus′tə kāt′), *v.i., v.t.,* **-cated, -cat·ing. 1.** *Chiefly Literary.* to go or send to the country. **2.** to become or make rustic. —**rus′ti·ca′tion,** *n.* —**rus′ti·ca′tor,** *n.*

rus·tle (rus′əl), *v.,* **-tled, -tling,** *n.* —*v.i., v.t.* **1.** to make or cause to make a series of slight, soft sounds, as of parts rubbing gently one on another. **2.** *Informal.* to move or work energetically and speedily. **3.** *Informal.* to steal (livestock, esp. cattle). —*n.* **4.** a rustling sound. —**rus′tler,** *n.* —**rus′tling·ly,** *adv.*

rut¹ (rut), *n., v.,* **rut·ted, rut·ting.** —*n.* **1.** a furrow or track made by the passage of vehicles. **2.** a fixed and dull or unpromising way of life. —*v.t.* **3.** to make ruts in. —**rut′ty,** *adj.* —**rut′ti·ness,** *n.*

rut² (rut), *n.* the periodically recurring sexual excitement of the deer, goat, etc. —**rut′tish,** *adj.*

ru·ta·ba·ga (rōō′tə bā′gə), *n.* a turnip having a large, yellow edible root.

ru·the·ni·um (rōō thē′nē əm), *n. Chem.* a rare metallic element belonging to the platinum group of metals. *Symbol:* Ru; *at. wt.:* 101.07; *at. no.:* 44.

ruth·less (rōōth′lis), *adj.* cruel and unscrupulous, esp. in pursuing a goal. —**ruth′less·ly,** *adv.* —**ruth′less·ness,** *n.* —**Syn.** merciless, pitiless, relentless.

RV, recreational vehicle.

R.W., 1. Right Worshipful. **2.** Right Worthy.

Rwan·da (rōō än′də), *n.* a country in central Africa.

Rx, *Med.* prescription.

-ry, var. of **-ery:** *jewelry.*

Ry., Railway. Also, **Rwy.**

ry·a (rē′ə), *n.* a hand-woven rug with a thick pile.

rye (rī), *n.* **1.** a widely cultivated cereal grass. **2.** the seeds or grain of this plant, used for making flour and whiskey. **3.** a whiskey distilled from a mash containing rye grain.

Ryu′kyu Is′lands (rวōō′kyōō′), a chain of islands in the W Pacific between Kyushu and Taiwan.

S

S, s (es), *n.*, *pl.* **S's** or **Ss, s's** or **ss.** **1.** the 19th letter of the English alphabet, a consonant. **2.** something having the shape of an S.

S, 1. signature. **2.** small. **3.** soft. **4.** South. **5.** Southern.

S, sulfur.

s, 1. signature. **2.** small. **3.** soft. **4.** south. **5.** southern.

's¹, an ending used to form the possessive case of singular nouns and of plural nouns not ending in -*s*: *the men's hats.*

's², contraction of: **a.** is: *She's here.* **b.** has: *She's gone.* **c.** does: *What's she do?* **d.** us: *Let's go.*

-s¹, a suffix used in the formation of adverbs: *unawares.*

-s², an ending marking the third person sing. indicative present of verbs: *asks.*

-s³, an ending marking the regular plural of nouns: *boys.*

S., 1. Saint. **2.** Saturday. **3.** School. **4.** Sea. **5.** Senate. **6.** September. **7.** shilling; shillings. **8.** South. **9.** Southern. **10.** Sunday.

s., 1. saint. **2.** second. **3.** section. **4.** series. **5.** shilling; shillings. **6.** sign. **7.** signed. **8.** singular. **9.** small. **10.** son. **11.** south. **12.** southern. **13.** stere; steres. **14.** substantive.

S.A., 1. Salvation Army. **2.** seaman apprentice. **3.** South Africa.

s.a., 1. sex appeal. **2.** without year or date. [< L *sine annō*] **3.** subject to approval.

Sab·bath (sab'əth), *n.* **1.** the seventh day of the week, Saturday, as the day of rest and religious observance among the Jews and in some Christian churches. **2.** Sunday similarly observed by most Christians.

Sab·bat·i·cal (sə bat'i kəl), *adj.* **1.** of the Sabbath. **2.** (*l.c.*) bringing a period of rest: *a sabbatical leave.* —*n.* **3.** (*l.c.*) See **sabbatical year.**

sabbat'ical year', a year, originally every seventh, of release from normal teaching duties granted to a professor, as for study or travel.

sa·ber (sā'bər), *n.* a heavy, one-edged sword, usually slightly curved, used esp. by cavalry. Also, *Brit.*, **sa'bre.**

sa'ber saw', a portable electric jig saw.

Sa'bin vaccine' (sā'bin), an orally administered polio vaccine. [after A. B. *Sabin*, b. 1906, U.S. virologist]

sa·ble (sā'bəl), *n.* **1.** an Old World weasellike mammal, valued for its dark brown fur. **2.** its fur. **3.** the color black. **4. sables,** *Rare.* mourning garments.

sab·o·tage (sab'ə täzh', sab'ə täzh'), *n.*, *v.*, **-taged, -tag·ing.** —*n.* **1.** any underhand interference with production or work in a plant or factory by enemy agents during wartime or by employees during a labor dispute. **2.** any undermining of a cause. —*v.t.*, *v.i.* **3.** to commit sabotage (against).

sab·o·teur (sab'ə tûr'), *n.* a person who commits sabotage.

sa·bra (sä'brə, -brä), *n.* a native of Israel.

sac (sak), *n.* a baglike structure in an animal or plant. —**sac'like',** *adj.*

Sac (sak, sôk), *n.*, *pl.* **Sacs, Sac. 1.** a tribe of Algonquian-speaking Indians in Iowa and Oklahoma. **2.** a member of this tribe.

SAC, Strategic Air Command.

sac·cha·rin (sak'ə rin), *n.* an extremely sweet, white, soluble powder used as a low-calorie sugar substitute.

sac·cha·rine (sak'ə rin, -rīn'), *adj.* **1.** of or containing sugar. **2.** cloyingly sweet, as in expression. —**sac'cha·rine·ly,** *adv.* —**sac·cha·rin·i·ty** (sak'ə rin'i tē), *n.*

sac·er·do·tal (sas'ər dōt'ºl), *adj.* of or connected with priests. —**sac'er·do'tal·ism,** *n.* —**sac'er·do'tal·ly,** *adv.*

sa·chem (sā'chəm), *n.* the chief of a tribe among some American Indians. —**sa·chem·ic** (sā chem'ik, sā'chə·mik), *adj.*

sa·chet (sa shā'), *n.* a small bag containing scented powder (**sachet' pow'der**), used for scenting clothes.

sack¹ (sak), *n.* **1.** a large bag of strong, coarsely woven material. **2.** any bag, often of paper. **3.** a loose-fitting coat or jacket. **4. the sack,** *Slang.* **a.** dismissal from a job. **b.** bed or sleep. —*v.t.* **5.** to put into sacks. **6.** *Slang.* to dismiss from a job. —**sack'ful,** *n.*

sack² (sak), *v.t.* **1.** to pillage (a place) after capture. —*n.* **2.** the act of sacking or pillaging. —**sack'er,** *n.*

sack³ (sak), *n.* a strong, light-colored wine formerly imported from Spain.

sack·cloth (sak'klôth', -kloth'), *n.* **1.** sacking. **2.** coarse cloth formerly worn as a sign of mourning or penitence.

sack·ing (sak'ing), *n.* coarse woven material, as of hemp, chiefly for sacks.

sac·ra·ment (sak'rə mənt), *n.* **1.** any of various Christian rites, as baptism, believed to have been instituted by Jesus Christ to symbolize or confer grace. **2.** (*often cap.*) the consecrated elements of the Eucharist, esp. the bread. **3.** something regarded as possessing a sacred character. —**sac'ra·men'tal,** adj. —**sac'·ra·men'tal·ly,** adv.

Sac·ra·men·to (sak'rə men'tō), n. the capital of California.

sa·cred (sā'krid), adj. **1.** dedicated to a deity or to some religious purpose. **2.** pertaining to or connected with religion. **3.** reverently dedicated to some person or object. **4.** regarded with reverence. **5.** secured by reverence against violation. —**sa'cred·ly,** adv. —**sa'cred·ness,** n. —**Syn. 1.** consecrated, divine, hallowed, holy.

sa'cred cow', any individual or organization regarded as exempt from criticism.

sac·ri·fice (sak'rə fīs'), n., v., -ficed, -fic·ing. —n. **1.** the offering of something, as an animal, to a deity as an act of worship. **2.** something so offered. **3.** the surrender of something of value for the sake of something else. **4.** something so surrendered. **5.** a loss incurred in selling something below its value. —v.t., v.i. **6.** to make a sacrifice (of). **7.** to surrender for the sake of something else. **8.** to sell at a loss. —**sac'ri·fic'er,** n. —**sac'ri·fi'cial** (-fish'əl), adj. —**sac'ri·fi'cial·ly,** adv.

sac·ri·lege (sak'rə lij), n. the profanation of anything held sacred. —**sac'·ri·le'gious** (-lij'əs, -lē'jəs), adj. —**sac'ri·le'gious·ly,** adv. —**sac'ri·le'·gious·ness,** n.

sac·ris·tan (sak'ri stən), n. an official in charge of the sacristy.

sac·ris·ty (sak'ri stē), n., pl. -ties. a room in a church in which sacred vessels are kept.

sac·ro·il·i·ac (sak'rō il'ē ak', sā'krō-), n. the joint where the sacrum and ilium meet.

sac·ro·sanct (sak'rō sangkt'), adj. extremely sacred and inviolable. —**sac'ro·sanct'ness,** n.

sac·rum (sak'rəm, sā'krəm), n., pl. **sac·ra** (sak'rə, sā'krə), **sac·rums.** the triangular-shaped bone forming the posterior wall of the pelvis.

sad (sad), adj., **sad·der, sad·dest. 1.** feeling unhappiness or grief. **2.** expressing or causing such feeling. —**sad'ly,** adv. —**sad'ness,** n. —**Syn.** dejected, gloomy, melancholy, sorrowful.

sad·den (sad'ən), v.t., v.i. to make or become sad.

sad·dle (sad'əl), n., v., -dled, -dling. —n. **1.** a leather seat for a rider, as on the back of a horse. **2.** a cut of mutton, lamb, etc., including both loins. **3. in the saddle,** in a position of authority. —v.t. **4.** to put a saddle on. **5.** to load or burden.

sad·dle·bow (sad'əl bō'), n. the arched front part of a saddle.

sad'dle horse', a horse suitable for riding.

sad'dle shoe', an oxford with a band of contrasting color across the instep.

Sad·du·cee (saj'ə sē', sad'yə-), n. a member of an ancient Jewish sect that interpreted the Bible literally. —**Sad'du·ce'an,** adj.

sad·i·ron (sad'ī'ərn), n. a solid flatiron having a simple handle.

sad·ism (sad'iz əm, sā'diz om), n. **1.** sexual gratification gained through causing physical pain to others. **2.** any enjoyment in being cruel. [after D. A. F. de *Sade,* 1740–1814, Fr. writer and libertine] —**sad'ist,** n., adj. —**sa·dis·tic** (sə dis'tik, sa-, sā-), adj. —**sa·dis'ti·cal·ly,** adv.

sad·o·mas·o·chism (sad'ō mas'ə kiz'·əm, -maz'-, sā'dō), n sadism and masochism regarded as a fundamental tendency in the same individual. —**sad'o·mas'o·chist,** n. —**sad'o·mas'o·chis'tic,** adj.

sa·fa·ri (sə fär'ē), n. an expedition for hunting, esp. in eastern Africa.

safe (sāf), adj., **saf·er, saf·est,** n. — adj. **1.** free from injury or risk. **2.** secure from liability to injury or risk. **3.** involving little or no risk. **4.** dependable or trustworthy. **5.** denied the chance to do harm. —n. **6.** a secure box of metal for storing valuable articles. —**safe'ly,** adv. — **safe'ness,** n.

safe·con·duct (sāf'kon'dukt), n. a document authorizing safe passage through an enemy region.

safe·guard (sāf'gärd'), n. **1.** something that protects, defends, or ensures safety. —v.t. **2.** to guard or protect.

safe·keep·ing (sāf'kē'ping), n. **1.** the act of keeping in safety. **2.** protection or custody.

safe·ty (sāf'tē), n., pl. -ties. **1.** freedom from injury or risk. **2.** a device to prevent injury. **3.** *Football.* **a.** a play in which the ball is grounded by the offensive on or behind its own goal line. **b.** a defensive back lining up farthest behind the line of scrimmage.

safe'ty glass', shatter-resistant glass made by joining two plates of glass separated by plastic resin.

safe'ty match', a match designed to ignite only when rubbed on a special surface.

safe'ty pin', a pin bent back on itself to form a spring, with a guard to cover the point.

saf·flow·er (saf'lou'ər), n. a thistle-like herb having large, orange-red flower heads that yield a red dye-stuff and seeds from which a cooking oil is extracted.

saf·fron (saf′rən), *n.* **1.** the dried, orange-colored stigmas of a kind of crocus used as a dye and a flavoring. **2.** a yellow orange.

sag (sag), *v.,* **sagged, sag·ging,** *n.* — *v.i.* **1.** to sink downward by weight or pressure, esp. in the middle. **2.** to hang down unevenly. **3.** to lose strength or weaken. —*n.* **4.** a place where something sags. —**sag′gy,** *adj.*

sa·ga (sä′gə), *n.* **1.** a medieval Icelandic or Norse prose narrative of the achievements and events of a person or a family. **2.** any narrative of heroic exploits.

sa·ga·cious (sə gā′shəs), *adj.* having keen mental discernment and sound judgment —**sa·gac′i·ty** (-gas′i tē), *n.* —**sa·ga′cious·ly,** *adv.*

sage¹ (sāj), *n., adj.,* **sag·er, sag·est.** — *n.* **1.** a profoundly wise person. — *adj.* **2.** profoundly wise. —**sage′ly,** *adv.* —**sage′ness,** *n.* —**Syn. 2.** discerning, judicious, prudent.

sage² (sāj), *n.* **1.** an herb of the mint family having grayish-green leaves used in poultry seasoning. **2.** sagebrush.

sage·brush (sāj′brush′), *n.* a sagelike, bushy plant common on the dry plains of the western U.S.

Sag·it·ta·ri·us (saj′i târ′ē əs), *n.* the ninth sign of the zodiac. [< L: archer]

sa·go (sā′gō), *n.* a starchy foodstuff derived from the soft interior of various palms, used in making puddings.

sa·gua·ro (sə gwä′rō, -wä′rō), *n., pl.* **-ros.** a tall cactus of Arizona and neighboring regions, bearing an edible fruit.

Sa·har·a (sə hâr′ə, -har′ə, -här′ə), *n.* a desert in N Africa. —**Sa·har′an,** *adj.*

sa·hib (sä′ib, -ēb, -hib, -hēb), *n.* (formerly in India) sir or master.

said (sed), *v.* **1.** pt. and pp. of **say.** —*adj.* **2.** *Chiefly Law.* aforesaid.

Sai·gon (sī gon′), *n.* the capital of former South Vietnam: renamed **Ho Chi Minh City.**

sail (sāl), *n.* **1.** a piece of fabric extended to the wind in such a way as to cause a ship to move. **2.** some similar piece or apparatus. **3.** a voyage in a sailing vessel. **4.** a sailing vessel or vessels. **5. set sail,** to start a sea voyage. —*v.i.* **6.** to move forward, as a ship. **7.** to travel by water. **8.** to manage a sailboat, esp. for sport. **9.** to begin a journey by water. **10.** to travel through the air, as a kite. —*v.t.* **11.** to sail upon or over. **12.** to navigate (a vessel). **13. sail into,** *Informal.* to begin to act vigorously upon.

sail·boat (sāl′bōt′), *n.* a boat moved by sails.

sail·cloth (sāl′klôth′, -kloth′), *n.* any of various fabrics for boat sails or tents.

sail·fish (sāl′fish′), *n.* a large marine fish related to the swordfishes and having a very large saillike dorsal fin.

sail·or (sā′lər), *n.* **1.** a person whose occupation is sailing or navigation. **2.** Also called **sail′or hat′.** a flat-brimmed straw hat with a low, flat crown.

saint (sānt), *n.* **1.** a person formally recognized by certain Christian churches as being in heaven with God and as being entitled to veneration on earth. **2.** a person of great holiness or benevolence. —**saint′dom,** *n.* —**saint′ed** (-id), *adj.* —**saint′hood,** *n.*

Saint′ Ber·nard′ (bər närd′), one of a breed of very large dogs originally used to rescue lost travelers in the Swiss Alps.

saint·ly (sānt′lē), *adj.,* **-li·er, -li·est.** like or befitting a saint. —**saint′li·ness,** *n.*

Saint′ Val′en·tine′s Day′ (val′ən-tīnz′), February 14, observed in honor of St. Valentine, a 3rd-century martyr, as a day for the exchange of valentines.

saith (seth, sā′əth), *v. Archaic.* third pers. sing. indicative present of **say.**

sake¹ (sāk), *n.* **1.** personal benefit or well-being. **2.** purpose or end: *for the sake of peace.*

sa·ke² (sä′kē), *n.* a Japanese fermented alcoholic beverage made from rice. Also, **sa′ké, sa′ki.**

sa·laam (sə läm′), *n.* **1.** a salutation in Islamic countries. **2.** a very low bow with the palm of the right hand placed on the forehead.

sa·la·cious (sə lā′shəs), *adj.* **1.** grossly indecent or obscene. **2.** lustful or lecherous. —**sa·la′cious·ly,** *adv.* —**sa·la′cious·ness, sa·lac′i·ty** (-las′i tē), *n.*

sal·ad (sal′əd), *n.* a dish, usually served cold, consisting of vegetables, as lettuce, tomatoes, etc., or of fruit, meat, seafood, or eggs, mixed with a dressing.

sal·a·man·der (sal′ə man′dər), *n.* a small amphibian that resembles the lizard but has a smooth, moist skin.

sa·la·mi (sə lä′mē), *n.* a kind of sausage, originally Italian, often flavored with garlic.

sal·a·ry (sal′ə rē), *n., pl.* **-ries.** a fixed compensation periodically paid for regular work. —**sal′a·ried** (-rēd), *adj.*

sale (sāl), *n.* **1.** a transfer of property for money or credit. **2.** an opportunity to sell something. **3.** a selling of goods at reduced prices. **4.** an auction. —**sal′a·ble, sale′a·ble,** *adj.*

Sa·lem (sā′ləm), *n.* the capital of Oregon.

sales·clerk (sālz′klûrk′), *n.* a salesperson in a store.

sales·man (sālz′mən), *n., pl.* **-men.** a man who sells goods or services. —**sales′man·ship′**, *n.* —**sales′girl′**, **sales′wom′an**, **sales′la′dy**, *n.fem.*

sales·per·son (sālz′pûr′sən), *n.* a person who sells goods, esp. in a store.

sal′i·cyl′ic ac′id (sal′i sil′ik), a colorless powder used chiefly in the manufacture of aspirin and other drugs.

sa·li·ent (sā′lē ənt, sāl′yənt), *adj.* **1.** conspicuously noticeable. **2.** projecting or pointing outward. —*n.* **3.** a salient angle or part. —**sa′li·ence**, **sa′li·en·cy**, *n.* —**sa′li·ent·ly**, *adv.*

sa·line (sā′lin, -lēn), *adj.* **1.** of, containing, or resembling salt. —*n.* **2.** a saline medicine. —**sa·lin·i·ty** (sə·lin′i tē), *n.*

Salis′bur·y steak′ (sôlz′ber′ē), ground beef, shaped into a hamburger patty and broiled or fried. [after J. H. *Salisbury,* 19th-century English dietitian]

sa·li·va (sə lī′və), *n.* a watery fluid, secreted into the mouth by glands, that starts the digestion of starches. —**sal·i·var·y** (sal′ə ver′ē), *adj.*

sal·i·vate (sal′ə vāt′), *v.i.,* **-vat·ed, -vat·ing.** to produce saliva. —**sal′i·va′tion**, *n.*

Salk′ vaccine′ (sôlk, sôk), a vaccine for injection against polio. [after J. E. *Salk,* b. 1914, U.S. virologist]

sal·low (sal′ō), *adj.* of a pale, sickly, yellowish color. —**sal′low·ness**, *n.*

sal·ly (sal′ē), *n., pl.* **-lies,** *v.,* **-lied, -ly·ing.** —*n.* **1.** a sortie of troops from a besieged place upon an enemy. **2.** a clever, witty remark **3.** a little excursion. —*v.i.* **4.** to make a sally.

salm·on (sam′ən), *n., pl.* **-ons, -on. 1.** a marine and freshwater food fish having pink flesh. **2.** a light, yellowish pink.

sal·mo·nel·la (sal′mə nel′ə), *n.* any of certain rod-shaped anaerobic bacteria that are pathogenic for humans and warm-blooded animals.

sa·lon (sə lon′), *n.* **1.** a drawing room in a large elegant home **2.** an assembly of leaders in society, art, and politics in such a room, esp. formerly in Paris. **3.** a shop chiefly related to fashion: *a dress salon.*

sa·loon (sə lōōn′), *n.* **1.** a place for the sale and consumption of alcoholic drinks. **2.** a large public room, as on a passenger ship. **3.** *Brit.* sedan (def. 1).

sal·sa (sal′sə), *n.* **1.** a form of Latin American dance music with exciting rhythms. **2.** sauce, esp. chili sauce. [< Sp]

sal′ so′da (sal), the crystalline form of sodium carbonate.

salt (sôlt), *n.* **1.** a crystalline compound of sodium and chlorine, occurring as a mineral, a constituent of seawater, etc., and used for seasoning or preserving food. **2.** a chemical compound usually produced by neutralizing an acid with a base. **3. salts,** any of various salts used as laxatives. **4.** an element that gives liveliness or humor. **5.** *Informal.* a sailor, esp. an experienced one. **6. with a grain of salt,** with skepticism. —*v.t.* **7.** to season, cure, preserve, or treat with salt. **8. salt away,** *Informal.* to keep in reserve. —*adj.* **9.** containing or having the taste of salt. **10.** cured or preserved with salt. —**salt′ed**, *adj.* —**salt′y**, *adj.* —**salt′i·ness**, *n.*

SALT (sôlt), Strategic Arms Limitation Talks.

salt·cel·lar (sôlt′sel′ər), *n.* a shaker or dish for salt.

sal·tine (sôl tēn′), *n.* a crisp, salted cracker.

Salt′ Lake′ Cit′y, the capital of Utah.

salt′ lick′, a place to which wild animals go to lick natural salt deposits.

salt′ of the earth′, an individual or group considered as the best or noblest.

salt·pe·ter (sôlt′pē′tər), *n.* See potassium nitrate.

salt·wa·ter (sôlt′wô′tər, -wot′ər), *adj.* of or inhabiting salt water.

sa·lu·bri·ous (sə lōō′brē əs), *adj.* favorable to health as the air or climate. —**sa·lu′bri·ous·ly**, *adv.* —**sa·lu′bri·ous·ness**, *n*

sal·u·tar·y (sal′yə ter′ē), *adj.* **1.** conducive to some beneficial purpose. **2.** *Rare.* salubrious. —**sal′u·tar′i·ness**, *n.*

sal·u·ta·tion (sal′yə tā′shən), *n.* **1.** something uttered or written by way of saluting. **2.** a word or phrase serving as the prefatory greeting in a letter.

sa·lute (sə lōōt′), *v.,* **-lut·ed, -lut·ing,** *n.* —*v.t., v.i.* **1.** *Mil* to pay respect to (a superior officer) by some formal act, as by raising the right hand to the head **2.** to honor (someone or something) by some ceremonial act, as by firing cannon. **3.** to address (someone) with good will or respect. —*n.* **4.** the act of saluting. —**sa·lut′er**, *n.*

sal·vage (sal′vij), *n., v.,* **-vaged, -vag·ing.** —*n.* **1.** the act of saving a ship or its cargo from perils of the seas. **2.** the act of saving any property from destruction. **3.** the property so saved. **4.** compensation given to those who voluntarily save a ship or its cargo. —*v.t.* **5.** to save from shipwreck, fire, etc. —**sal′vage·a·ble**, *adj.*

sal·va·tion (sal vā′shən), *n.* **1.** the act of saving from harm or loss. **2.** the state of being thus saved. **3.** a means of being thus saved. **4.** *Theol.* deliverance from the power and penalty of sin. —**sal·va′tion·al,** *adj.*

salve (sav, säv), *n., v.,* **salved, salv·ing.** —*n.* **1.** a soothing ointment applied to the skin. **2.** anything that soothes. —*v.t.* **3.** to soothe with or as with salve.

sal·ver (sal′vər), *n.* a serving tray for food, beverages, etc.

sal·vo (sal′vō), *n., pl.* **-vos, -voes.** a discharge of guns in regular succession, often in salute.

SAM (sam), *n.* surface-to-air missile.

sa·mar·i·um (sə mâr′ē əm), *n. Chem.* a lustrous gray rare-earth metallic element. *Symbol:* Sm; *at. wt.:* 150.35; *at. no.:* 62.

same (sām), *adj.* **1.** being the very one mentioned. **2.** agreeing or corresponding in kind, amount, etc. — *pron.* **3.** the same person or thing. **4.** the same, in the same manner. —**same′ness,** *n.*

sam·iz·dat (säm′iz dät′), *n.* a system within the Soviet Union by which dissenting manuscripts whose official publication is forbidden are circulated secretly.

Sa·mo·a (sə mō′ə), *n.* a group of islands in the S Pacific, part of which belong to the U.S. —**Sa·mo′an,** *adj., n.*

sam·o·var (sam′ə vär′, sam′ə vär′), *n.* a Russian metal urn used for heating water for making tea.

sam·pan (sam′pan), *n.* a small boat of the Far East, propelled by a single scull over the stern.

sam·ple (sam′pəl, säm′-), *n., v.,* **-pled, -pling.** —*n.* **1.** a small part of anything or one of a number of things intended to show the quality or nature of the rest. —*v.t.* **2.** to take a sample of, esp. to test by a sample. —**Syn. 1.** example, specimen.

sam·pler (sam′plər, säm′-), *n.* **1.** a person who samples. **2.** an embroidered cloth serving to show a beginner's skill in needlework.

sam·u·rai (sam′oo rī′), *n., pl.* **-rai.** a member of the warrior class in feudal Japan.

San An·to·ni·o (san′ an tō′nē ō′), a city in S Texas. —**San′ Anto′nian.**

san·a·to·ri·um (san′ə tōr′ē əm, -tôr′-), *n., pl.* **-ri·ums, -ri·a** (-rē ə). **1.** a health resort. **2.** *Brit.* sanitarium.

sanc·ti·fy (sangk′tə fī′), *v.t.,* **-fied, -fy·ing. 1.** to make holy. **2.** to purify or free from sin. **3.** to give sanction to. —**sanc′ti·fi·ca′tion,** *n.* —**sanc′ti·fi′er,** *n.*

sanc·ti·mo·ni·ous (sangk′tə mō′nē əs), *adj.* pretending to be devout and righteous. —**sanc′ti·mo′ni·ous·ly,** *adv.* —**sanc′ti·mo′ni·ous·ness,** *n.*

sanc·ti·mo·ny (sangk′tə mō′nē), *n.* affected piety.

sanc·tion (sangk′shən), *n.* **1.** authoritative permission, as for an action. **2.** *Internat. Law.* action by one or more nations toward another nation to force it to comply with legal obligations. —*v.t.* **3.** to authorize or approve. **4.** to ratify or confirm. —**sanc′tion·er,** *n.*

sanc·ti·ty (sangk′ti tē), *n., pl.* **-ties. 1.** holiness or piety of life. **2.** sacred or hallowed character.

sanc·tu·ar·y (sangk′chōō er′ē), *n., pl.* **-ar·ies. 1.** a holy place, as the part of a church around the altar. **2.** a place providing refuge.

sanc·tum (sangk′təm), *n., pl.* **-tums, -ta** (-tə). **1.** a sacred place. **2.** a private place or retreat.

sand (sand), *n.* **1.** tiny, loose grains of worn-down or crushed rock, often found along an ocean shore. —*v.t.* **2.** to smooth or polish, as with sand or sandpaper. **3.** to sprinkle or fill with sand, as a harbor. —**sand′er,** *n.* —**sand′y,** *adj.* —**sand′i·ness,** *n.*

san·dal (san′dəl), *n.* **1.** a shoe consisting of a sole of leather fastened to the foot by straps. **2.** a low shoe or slipper.

san·dal·wood (san′dəl wŏŏd′), *n.* **1.** a fragrant wood of an Asian tree used for carving and burned as incense. **2.** its tree.

sand·bag (sand′bag′), *n., v.,* **-bagged, -bag·ging.** —*n.* **1.** a bag filled with sand, used in fortification, as ballast, or as a blackjack. —*v.t.* **2.** to furnish with sandbags. **3.** to hit with a sandbag. **4.** *Informal.* to coerce into doing something. —**sand′bag′ger,** *n.*

sand·bank (sand′bangk′), *n.* a mass of sand, as on a hillside.

sand′ bar′, a bar of sand formed in a river by tides or currents.

sand·blast (sand′blast′, -bläst′), *n.* **1.** sand blown by compressed air or steam, used to clean or decorate hard surfaces. —*v.t.* **2.** to clean with a sandblast. —**sand′blast′er,** *n.*

sand·box (sand′boks′), *n.* a box for holding sand for children to play in.

sand·hog (sand′hog′, -hôg′), *n.* a laborer who digs underwater tunnels.

San Di·e·go (san′ dē ā′gō), a seaport in SW California.

S&L, savings and loan (association).

sand·lot (sand′lot′), *n.* **1.** a vacant lot, esp. as used by boys for sports. —*adj.* **2.** of or played in such a lot, esp. by amateurs. —**sand′lot′ter,** *n.*

S&M, 1. sadomasochism. **2.** sadomasochist. Also, **s&m**

sand·man· (sand'man'), *n.* the man who, in folklore, puts sand in the eyes of children to make them sleepy.

sand·pa·per (sand'pā'pər), *n.* **1.** strong paper coated with a layer of sand, used for smoothing or polishing. —*v.t.* **2.** to smooth or polish with sandpaper.

sand·pi·per (sand'pī'pər), *n.* a shorebird related to the plover, having a slender bill and a piping call.

sand·stone (sand'stōn'), *n.* a soft, porous rock formed from grains of sand naturally cemented together.

sand·wich (sand'wich, san'-), *n.* **1.** slices of bread with a layer of meat, fish, or cheese between them. **2.** something that resembles a sandwich. —*v.t.* **3.** to insert or squeeze between two other things. [after the fourth Earl of *Sandwich* (1718–92)]

sane (sān), *adj.*, **san·er**, **san·est.** **1.** having a sound, healthy mind. **2.** having sound judgment or good sense. —**sane'ly**, *adv.* —**sane'ness**, *n.* —**Syn.** logical, rational.

San·for·ized (san'fə rīzd'), *adj. Trademark.* (of a fabric) treated to resist shrinking.

San Fran·cis·co (san' fran sis'kō), a seaport in W California.

sang (sang), *v.* a pt. of **sing**.

sang·froid (*Fr.* säN frwA'), *n.* composure under trying conditions. [< F: cold-bloodedness]

san·gri·a (sang grē'ə), *n.* an iced drink, usually of red wine that has been diluted, sweetened, and spiced.

san·gui·nar·y (sang'gwə ner'ē), *adj.* **1.** full of bloodshed. **2.** eager to shed blood. —**san'gui·nar'i·ly**, *adv.*

san·guine (sang'gwin), *adj.* **1.** cheerful and hopeful. **2.** reddish or ruddy. —**san'guine·ly**, *adv.* —**san'guine·ness**, *n.*

sanit., **1.** sanitary. **2.** sanitation.

san·i·tar·i·an (san'i târ'ē ən), *n.* a specialist in public sanitation and health.

san·i·tar·i·um (san'i târ'ē əm), *n.*, *pl.* **-tar·i·ums**, **-tar·i·a** (-târ'ē ə). a hospital for the treatment of chronic diseases, as tuberculosis, or of mental illness.

san·i·tar·y (san'i ter'ē), *adj.* **1.** of or pertaining to health or healthful conditions. **2.** free from dirt, germs, etc.

san'itary nap'kin, an absorbent pad for wear by women during menstruation to absorb the uterine flow.

san·i·ta·tion (san'i tā'shən), *n.* **1.** the development and application of sanitary measures for public health. **2.** disposal of sewage and solid waste.

san·i·tize (san'i tīz'), *v.t.*, **-tized**, **-tiz·ing.** **1.** to make sanitary. **2.** to make less offensive by eliminating anything unwholesome.

san·i·ty (san'i tē), *n.* soundness of mind or judgment.

San Jo·se (san' hō zā'), a city in W California.

San Juan (san' wän', hwän'), the capital of Puerto Rico.

sank (sangk), *v.* a pt. of **sink**.

San Ma·ri·no (san' mə rē'nō), a small country inside E Italy.

sans (sanz; *Fr.* säN), *prep.* without.

San·skrit (san'skrit), *n.* an ancient Indo-European language of India.

San·ta Claus (san'tə klôz'), a jolly man of legend, supposed to bring gifts to children on Christmas Eve.

San·ta Fe (san'tə fā'), the capital of New Mexico.

San·ti·a·go (san'tē ä'gō), *n.* the capital of Chile.

São Pau·lo (souN' pou'lŏŏ), a city in S Brazil.

sap¹ (sap), *n.* **1.** the juice or vital circulating fluid of a woody plant. **2.** vitality and energy. **3.** *Slang.* a fool or dupe. —**sap'less**, *adj.*

sap² (sap), *v.t.*, **sapped**, **sap·ping.** **1.** to weaken or destroy insidiously. **2.** to approach (an enemy position) by digging deep trenches.

sa·pi·ent (sā'pē ənt), *adj. Often Ironic.* wise and discerning. —**sa'pi·ence**, *n.* —**sa'pi·ent·ly**, *adv.*

sap·ling (sap'ling), *n.* a young tree.

sap·phire (saf'ī²r), *n.* a precious gem usually of a deep blue.

sap·py (sap'ē), *adj.*, **-pi·er**, **-pi·est.** **1.** abounding in sap, as a plant. **2.** full of vitality and energy. **3.** *Slang.* silly or foolish. —**sap'pi·ness**, *n.*

sap·ro·phyte (sap'rə fīt'), *n.* any organism that lives on dead organic matter, as certain fungi. —**sap/rophyt'ic** (-fit'ik), *adj.*

sap·suck·er (sap'suk'ər), *n.* an American woodpecker that drills holes in maple, apple, or hemlock to drink the sap.

sap·wood (sap'wŏŏd'), *n.* the soft wood beneath the inner bark through which the sap flows.

Sar·a·cen (sar'ə sən), *n.* **1.** a Muslim, esp. at the time of the Crusades. **2.** (formerly) an Arab. —**Sar·a·cen·ic** (sar'ə sen'ik), *adj.*

sa·ran (sə ran'), *n.* a thermoplastic substance used as a fiber, for packaging, and for making acid-resistant pipe.

sar·casm (sär'kaz əm), *n.* **1.** a sharply sneering or cutting remark. **2.** the use of such remarks intended to hurt or wound another. —**sar·cas'tic** (-kas'tik) , *adj.* —**sar·cas'ti·cal·ly**, *adv.* —**Syn.** derision, irony, mockery, ridicule.

sar·co·ma (sär kō'mə), *n.*, *pl.* **-mas**, **-ma·ta** (-mə tə). a malignant tumor attacking esp. the bones.

sar·coph·a·gus (sär kof′ə gəs), *n., pl.* **-gi** (-jī′), **-gus·es.** a stone coffin, esp. one bearing inscriptions, etc.

sar·dine (sär dēn′), *n.* a small saltwater fish of the herring family, often canned in oil or sauces.

Sar·din·i·a (sär din′e ə, -din′yə), *n.* an Italian island in the Mediterranean, W of Italy.

sar·don·ic (sär don′ik), *adj.* mockingly or tauntingly bitter. —**sar·don′i·cal·ly,** *adv.* —**Syn.** cynical, derisive, sarcastic, scornful.

sarge (särj), *n. Informal.* sergeant.

sa·ri (sär′ē), *n., pl.* **-ris.** an outer garment of Hindu women consisting of a long piece of cotton or silk worn around the body. Also, **sa′ree.**

sa·rong (sə rông′, -rong′), *n.* a loose-fitting, skirtlike garment worn by men and women in the Malay Archipelago and Pacific islands.

sar·sa·pa·ril·la (sär′sə pə ril′ə, sär′-spə-, sas′pə-), *n.* **1.** the root of a trailing tropical American plant used as a flavoring. **2.** a soft drink flavored with an extract of this root.

sar·to·ri·al (sär tôr′ē əl, -tôr′-), *adj.* **1.** of tailors or their trade. **2.** of men's clothing. —**sar·to′ri·al·ly,** *adv.*

sash[1] (sash), *n.* a long band worn over one shoulder or around the waist.

sash[2] (sash), *n.* a fixed or movable frame, as in a window or door, in which panes of glass are set.

sa·shay (sa shā′), *v.i. Informal.* to move or proceed easily or nonchalantly.

Sask., Saskatchewan.

Sas·katch·e·wan (sas kach′ə won′), *n.* a province in W. Canada. *Cap.:* Regina.

sass (sas), *Informal.* —*n.* **1.** impudent back talk. —*v.t.* **2.** to answer back in an impudent manner.

sas·sa·fras (sas′ə fras′), *n.* **1.** an American tree related to the laurel. **2.** the aromatic bark of its root, used esp. for flavoring.

sas·sy[1] (sas′ē), *adj.,* **-si·er, -si·est.** *Informal.* saucy.

sat (sat), *v.* pt. and pp. of **sit.**

SAT, Scholastic Aptitude Test.

Sat., Saturday.

sat., **1.** saturate. **2.** saturated.

Sa·tan (sāt′ən), *n.* the Devil.

sa·tan·ic (sā tan′ik, sə-), *adj.* **1.** of or like Satan. **2.** cruel or diabolic. Also, **sa·tan′i·cal.** —**sa·tan′i·cal·ly,** *adv.*

satch·el (sach′əl), *n.* a small bag, sometimes with a shoulder strap.

sate (sāt), *v.t.,* **sat·ed, sat·ing. 1.** to satisfy (an appetite or desire) fully. **2.** to glut or surfeit.

sa·teen (sa tēn′), *n.* a cotton cloth simulating satin in weave and gloss.

sat·el·lite (sat′əl līt′), *n.* **1.** a celestial body that revolves around a planet.

2. a manmade object launched from the earth into orbit around a celestial body for space travel or for sending worldwide electronic communications, as for television. **3.** a country under the domination of another. **4.** a constant attendant or close subordinate.

sa·ti·ate (sā′shē āt′), *v.t.,* **-at·ed, -at·ing.** to supply with anything to excess, so as to disgust or weary. —**sa′ti·a′tion,** *n.*

sa·ti·e·ty (sə tī′i tē), *n.* the state of being satiated.

sat·in (sat′ən), *n.* a closely woven fabric with a smooth, glossy finish on one side —**sat′in·y,** *adj.*

sat·in·wood (sat′ən wood′), *n.* **1.** the satiny wood of an East Indian tree, used esp. for making furniture. **2.** its tree.

sat·ire (sat′īr), *n.* **1.** the use of sarcasm or irony in exposing human folly, vice, etc. **2.** a literary work in which such use is made. —**sa·tir·i·cal** (sə tir′i kəl), **sa·tir′ic,** *adj.* —**sa·tir′i·cal·ly,** *adv.* —**sat·i·rist** (sat′ər-ist), *n.*

sat·i·rize (sat′ə rīz′), *v.t.,* **-rized, -riz·ing.** to subject to satire. —**sat′i·riz·er,** *n.*

sat·is·fac·tion (sat′is fak′shən), *n.* **1.** the act of satisfying or state of being satisfied. **2.** a person or thing that makes someone satisfied. **3.** compensation, as for a wrong or injury. **4.** payment of a debt, esp. under a court order. **5.** the opportunity to obtain revenge, as by a duel.

sat·is·fac·to·ry (sat′is fak′tə rē), *adj.* giving or causing satisfaction. —**sat′-is·fac′to·ri·ly,** *adv.*

sat·is·fy (sat′is fī′), *v.t.,* **-fied, -fy·ing.** —*v.t.* **1.** to fulfill the desires, needs, or demands of **2.** to solve or dispel, as a doubt. **3.** to discharge fully (a debt, etc.), esp under a court order. **4.** to make reparation to or for. **5.** *Math.* to fulfill the conditions of. —**sat′is·fi′er,** *n.* —**sat′is·fy′ing·ly,** *adv.* —**Syn. 1.** content, gratify.

sa·to·ri (sə tôr′ē, -tôr′ē), *n. Zen.* sudden enlightenment.

sa·trap (sā′trap, sa′-), *n.* a subordinate ruler, often a despotic one.

sat·u·rate (sach′ə rāt′), *v.t.,* **-rat·ed, -rat·ing. 1.** to soak thoroughly or completely. **2.** to fill to excess. **3.** to fill, treat, or charge with the maximum amount of another substance that can be absorbed or combined. —**sat·u·ra·ble** (sach′ər ə bəl), *adj.* —**sat′u·ra′tion,** *n.*

Sat·ur·day (sat′ər dē, -dā′), *n.* the seventh day of the week, following Friday.

Sat′urday-night′ spe′cial, *Slang.* a cheap, small-caliber handgun that is easily obtainable.

Sat·urn (sat'ərn), *n.* **1.** an ancient Roman god of agriculture. **2.** the planet sixth in order from the sun and second largest in the solar system.

sat·ur·nine (sat'ər nīn'), *adj.* having a sluggish, gloomy temperament. —**sat·ur·nin·i·ty** (sat'ər nin'i tē), *n.*

sa·tyr (sā'tər, sat'ər), *n.* **1.** *Class. Myth.* lascivious woodland deity, represented as part human and part goat. **2.** a lascivious man.

sa·ty·ri·a·sis (sā'tə rī'ə sis, sat'ə-), *n.* abnormal, uncontrollable sexual desire in men.

sauce (sôs), *n., v.,* **sauced, sauc·ing.** —*n.* **1.** a liquid or semiliquid relish accompanying food. **2.** stewed fruit. **3.** *Chiefly Brit. Informal.* impertinent insolence. —*v.t.* **4.** to dress or prepare with sauce. **5.** to add special zest to. **6.** *Informal.* to be insolent to.

sauce·pan (sôs'pan'), *n.* a small metal cooking pan with a handle.

sau·cer (sô'sər), *n.* a small, round, shallow dish for holding a cup.

sau·cy (sô'sē), *adj.,* **-ci·er, -ci·est.** **1.** impertinently insolent. **2.** boldly smart. —**sau'ci·ly,** *adv.* —**sau'ci·ness,** *n.*

Sa·u'di Ara'bia (sä ōō'dē, sou'dē, sô'-), a country in N and central Arabia. —**Sa·u'di,** *adj., n.*

sauer·kraut (sour'krout', sou'ər-), *n.* shredded cabbage fermented in brine until sour. [< G = *sauer* sour + *Kraut* greens]

Saul (sôl), *n.* the first king of Israel.

sau·na (sou'nä, -nə, sô'-), *n.* a bath in which the bather is subjected to steam caused by water thrown over heated stones. [< Finn]

saun·ter (sôn'tər, sän'-), *v.i.* **1.** to walk at a leisurely pace. —*n.* **2.** a leisurely walk. —**saun'ter·er,** *n.*

sau·sage (sô'sij), *n.* minced pork or other meats, seasoned and stuffed into a prepared intestine or other casing.

sau·té (sō tā', sô-), *v.t.,* **-téed** (-tād'), **-té·ing** (-tā'ing). to fry lightly with a little oil or fat.

Sau·ternes (sō tûrn', sô-), *n.* a sweet white table wine of France. Also, **sau·terne'.**

sav·age (sav'ij), *adj.* **1.** mercilessly cruel. **2.** uncivilized or barbarous. **3.** fierce or ferocious. **4.** wild or rugged, as country. —*n.* **5.** an uncivilized human being. **6.** a fierce or cruel person. —**sav'age·ly,** *adv.* —**sav'age·ness,** *n.* —**sav'age·ry,** *n.*

sa·van·na (sə van'ə), *n.* a grassy plain with low, scattered trees. Also **sa·van'nah.**

Sa·van·nah (sə van'ə), *n.* a seaport in E Georgia.

sa·vant (sa vänt', sav'ənt), *n.* a person of profound learning.

save¹ (sāv), *v.,* **saved, sav·ing.** —*v.t.* **1.** to rescue from danger or possible injury or loss. **2.** to avoid the spending, consumption, or waste of: *to save energy.* **3.** to set aside or lay up: *to save money.* **4.** to treat carefully in order to reduce wear, fatigue, etc. **5.** *Theol.* to deliver from sin. —*v.i.* **6.** to lay up money for reasons of economy. **7.** to be economical in expenditure. —**sav'a·ble, save'a·ble,** *adj.* —**sav'er,** *n.*

save² (sāv), *prep.* **1.** but or barring. —*conj.* **2.** except or only.

sav·ing (sā'ving), *adj.* **1.** tending or serving to save. **2.** compensating or redeeming. **3.** thrifty or economical. —*n.* **4.** a reduction in expenditure or time. **5.** something saved. **6.** **savings,** sums of money saved. —*prep.* **7.** save¹ (def. 1). —*conj.* **8.** save² (def. 2).

sav'ings certif'icate, a bank receipt similar to a certificate of deposit in offering a high rate of interest in return for a period of nonwithdrawal but available for smaller amounts in deposit.

sav·ior (sāv'yər), *n.* **1.** a person who saves or rescues. **2.** (*cap.*) Christ. Also, *Brit.,* **sav'iour.**

sa·voir-faire (sav'wär fâr'), *n. French.* knowledge of just what to do in any situation.

sa·vor (sā'vər), *n.* **1.** a particular taste or smell. **2.** distinctive quality or property. —*v.i.* **3.** to have a specified savor. —*v.t.* **4.** to taste with enjoyment. Also, *Brit.,* **sa'vour.** —**sa'vor·y,** *adj.* —**sa'vor·i·ness,** *n.*

sav·vy (sav'ē), *v.,* **-vied, -vy·ing,** *n. Slang.* —*v.t.,* **v.i. 1.** to understand, esp. shrewdly. —*n.* **2.** shrewd understanding.

saw¹ (sô), *n., v.,* **sawed, sawed** or **sawn** (sôn), **saw·ing.** —*n.* **1.** a cutting tool consisting of a thin metal blade edged with sharp teeth. —*v.t.* **2.** to cut or shape with a saw. —*v.i.* **3.** to cut with or as with a saw. **4.** to cut as a saw does. —**saw'er,** *n.*

saw² (sô), *v.* pt. of see¹.

saw³ (sô), *n.* a familiar, often hackneyed saying.

saw·bones (sô'bōnz'), *n. Facetious.* a surgeon.

saw·buck (sô'buk'), *n.* **1.** a sawhorse. **2.** *Slang.* a ten-dollar bill.

saw·dust (sô'dust'), *n.* small particles of wood produced in sawing.

saw·horse (sô'hôrs'), *n.* a frame for holding wood while being sawed.

saw·mill (sô'mil'), *n.* a place where logs are sawed into planks, boards, etc.

saw·yer (sô'yər, soi'ər), *n.* a person who saws, esp. as an occupation.

sax (saks), *n. Informal.* saxophone.

Sax·on (sak'sən), *n.* **1.** a member of an ancient Germanic people, some of whom occupied parts of Britain. **2.** their language or dialect

sax·o·phone (sak'sə fōn'), *n.* a musical wind instrument consisting of a conical, usually brass tube with keys or valves and a mouthpiece with one reed. —**sax'o·phon'ist,** *n.*

say (sā), *v.,* **said, say·ing,** *adv., n.* —*v.t.* **1.** to express in words with the voice. **2.** to express in words, esp. in writing. **3.** to state as an opinion. **4.** to recite or repeat. **5.** to report or allege. —*v.i.* **6.** to express oneself **7. that is to say,** in other words. —*adv.* **8.** about or approximately. **9.** for example. —*n.* **10.** the right or chance to say something. **11.** authority to decide. **12.** what a person says or has to say.

say·ing (sā'ing), *n.* something often said, esp. a proverb or maxim.

say-so (sā'sō'), *n. Informal.* **1.** final authority. **2.** an individual's personal assertion.

Sb, antimony. [< L *stibium*]

sb., substantive.

S.B., Bachelor of Science. [< L *Scientiae Baccalaureus*]

SBA, Small Business Administration.

SC, South Carolina. Also, **S.C.**

Sc, scandium.

Sc., Scots.

sc., **1.** scale. **2.** scene. **3.** science.

S.C., South Carolina.

s.c., *Print* small capitals.

scab (skab), *n., v.,* **scabbed, scab·bing.** —*n.* **1.** the crust that forms over a sore or wound during healing. **2.** *Informal.* a worker who refuses to join in a labor strike or who takes a striker's place on the job. —*v.i.* **3.** to become covered with a scab. **4.** *Informal* to work as a scab. —**scab'by,** *adj.* —**scab'bi·ly,** *adv.* —**scab'bi·ness,** *n.*

scab·bard (skab'ərd), *n.* a sheath for a sword, dagger etc.

sca·bies (skā'bēz -bē ēz'), *n.* a contagious skin disease caused by parasitic mites that burrow under the skin.

scab·rous (skab'rəs), *adj.* **1.** having a rough surface because of minute points or projections **2.** indecent or obscene. —**scab'rous·ness,** *n.*

scads (skadz) *n.pl. Slang.* a great number or quantity.

scaf·fold (skaf'əld, -ōld), *n.* **1.** a temporary structure for supporting workers and materials during construction or repair work on a building. **2.** an elevated platform on which a criminal is executed.

scaf·fold·ing (skaf'əl ding, -ōl-), *n.* **1.** a system of scaffolds. **2.** materials for scaffolds.

scal·a·wag (skal'ə wag'), *n. Informal.* a scamp or rascal.

scald (skôld), *v.t.* **1.** to burn with hot liquid or steam. **2.** to use a boiling or hot liquid on. **3.** to heat almost to the boiling point. —*n.* **4.** a burn caused by scalding.

scale¹ (skāl), *n., v.,* **scaled, scal·ing.** —*n.* **1.** one of the thin, flat, horny plates covering certain animals, as fishes, snakes, and lizards. **2.** any thin, platelike piece or flake. **3.** a hard or brittle coating or crust. —*v.t.* **4.** to remove the scales from. —*v.i.* **5.** to come off in scales. —**scaled** (skāld), *adj.* —**scale'less,** *adj.* —**scal'y,** *adj.*

scale² (skāl), *n.* **1.** Often, **scales.** a device or machine for weighing. **2.** either of the pans of a weighing balance. **3. the Scales,** Libra. **4. turn the scales,** to be decisive for or against someone or something.

scale³ (skāl), *n., v.,* **scaled, scal·ing.** —*n.* **1.** a succession or progression of steps or degrees **2.** a ratio between two sets of measurements, as on a map. **3.** a representation of either of these. **4.** an arrangement of things in order of importance, rank, etc. **5.** a series of marks used for measuring. **6.** an instrument that bears such marks. **7.** a relative size or scope **8.** *Music.* a succession of tones ascending or descending according to fixed intervals. —*v.t.* **9.** to climb by or as by a ladder. **10.** to make according to scale. **11.** to reduce or increase according to a fixed scale or proportion.

scale' in'sect, any of numerous small, plant-sucking insects the females of which have scalelike shells.

sca·lene (skā lēn'), *adj.* (of a triangle) having unequal sides.

scal·lion (skal'yən), *n.* any onion that does not form a large bulb.

scal·lop (skol'əp, skal'-), *n.* **1.** a bivalve mollusk that swims by rapidly clapping its shells together. **2.** the edible muscle of such a mollusk. **3.** one of a series of decorative rounded curves along the edge of a fabric. —*v.t.* **4.** to finish (an edge) with scallops. **5.** to escallop. —**scal'lop·er,** *n.*

scalp (skalp), *n.* **1.** the skin and flesh on the top and back of the head, usually covered with hair. —*v.t.* **2.** to cut or tear the scalp from. **3.** *Informal.* to buy and resell (tickets) at higher prices.

scal·pel (skal'pəl), *n.* a small, light, usually straight knife used in surgery.

scam (skam), *n. Slang.* a fraudulent scheme, esp. for making a quck, illegal profit.

scamp (skamp), *n.* a worthless and often mischievous person.

scamp·er (skam′pər), *v.i.* **1.** to run hastily or playfully. —*n.* **2.** the act of scampering.

scam·pi (skam′pē), *n. pl. Italian Cooking.* shrimp fried in oil and garlic. [< It, pl. of *scampo* shrimp]

scan (skan), *v.,* **scanned, scan·ning,** *n.* —*v.t.* **1.** to examine minutely. **2.** to glance at hastily. **3.** to analyze (verse) for its metrical structure. **4.** to sense (characters) for data processing. —*v.i.* **5.** (of verse) to conform to the rules of meter. —*n.* **6.** an act or instance of scanning. — **scan′ner,** *n.*

Scand., 1. Scandinavia. **2.** Scandinavian.

scan·dal (skan′d°l), *n.* **1.** any revealed wrongdoing that causes widespread indignation and disgust. **2.** a disgraceful or discreditable action. **3.** malicious gossip. —**scan′dal·ous,** *adj.* —**scan′dal·ous·ly,** *adv.*

scan·dal·ize (skan′d°līz′), *v.t.,* **-ized, -iz·ing.** to shock or horrify, as by disgraceful conduct. —**scan′dal·iz′er,** *n.*

Scan·di·na·vi·a (skan′də nā′vē ə), *n.* Norway, Sweden, Denmark, and sometimes Iceland and Finland.

Scan·di·na·vi·an (skan′də nā′vē ən), *adj.* **1.** of Scandinavia, its inhabitants, or their languages. —*n.* **2.** a native or inhabitant of Scandinavia. **3.** any of the Germanic languages of Scandinavia.

scan·di·um (skan′dē əm), *n. Chem.* a rare metallic element. *Symbol:* Sc; *at. wt.:* 44.956; *at. no.:* 21.

scan·sion (skan′shən), *n.* the metrical analysis of verse.

scant (skant), *adj.* **1.** barely sufficient in quantity. **2.** having barely enough. —*v.t.* **3.** to limit the supply of.

scant·ling (skant′ling), *n.* a timber of relatively small cross section, used esp. as a rafter.

scant·y (skan′tē), *adj.,* **scant·i·er, scant·i·est. 1.** not adequate in amount or extent. **2.** lacking in something essential. —**scant′i·ly,** *adv.* —**scant′i·ness,** *n.* —**Syn. 1.** meager, sparse.

scape·goat (skāp′gōt′), *n.* a person made to bear the blame for others.

scape·grace (skāp′grās′), *n.* a complete rascal.

scap·u·la (skap′yə lə), *n., pl.* **-lae** (-lē′), **-las.** either of two flat, triangular bones, each forming the back part of the shoulder. —**scap′u·lar,** *adj.*

scar (skär), *n., v.,* **scarred, scar·ring.** —*n.* **1.** the mark left by a healed wound, sore, or burn. **2.** any lasting aftereffect of trouble. —*v.t.* **3.** to

leave a scar on. —*v.i.* **4.** to form a scar, esp. in healing. —**scar′less,** *adj.*

scar·ab (skar′əb), *n.* **1.** a large, dark-shelled beetle, regarded as sacred by the ancient Egyptians. **2.** a representation or image of such a beetle.

scarce (skârs), *adj.,* **scarc·er, scarc·est. 1.** not enough to meet a demand readily. **2.** seldom seen. **3.** **make oneself scarce,** *Informal.* to depart, esp. suddenly. —**scar′ci·ty, scarce′ness,** *n.* —**Syn. 2.** infrequent, rare.

scarce·ly (skârs′lē), *adv.* **1.** by a narrow margin. **2.** definitely not. **3.** probably not. —**Syn. 1.** barely, hardly.

scare (skâr), *v.,* **scared, scar·ing,** *n.* —*v.t.* **1.** to fill suddenly with fear. —*v.i.* **2.** to become scared. **3.** **scare up,** *Informal.* to obtain with effort. —*n.* **4.** a sudden fright or alarm.

scare·crow (skâr′krō′), *n.* a thin figure of a person in old clothes set up to frighten crows or other birds away from crops.

scarf (skärf), *n., pl.* **scarfs, scarves** (skärvz). **1.** a long, broad strip of cloth worn about the neck, shoulders, or head. **2.** a long cover or ornamental cloth for a table, dresser, etc.

scar·i·fy (skar′ə fī′), *v.t.,* **-fied, -fy·ing. 1.** to scratch or cut superficially. **2.** to wound by severe criticism. — **scar′i·fi·ca′tion,** *n.*

scar·let (skär′lit), *n.* a bright red tending toward orange.

scar′let fe′ver, a contagious disease that causes a fever and a scarlet rash. Also called **scar·le·ti·na** (skär′lə tē′nə).

scarp (skärp), *n.* a line of cliffs formed by the fracturing of the earth's crust.

scar·y (skâr′ē), *adj.,* **scar·i·er, scar·i·est.** *Informal.* **1.** causing fright or alarm. **2.** easily frightened. —**scar′i·ness,** *n.*

scat (skat), *v.i.,* **scat·ted, scat·ting,** *Informal.* to go away hastily (usually used in the imperative).

scath·ing (skā′thing), *adj.* bitterly severe, as a remark. —**scath′ing·ly,** *adv.*

sca·tol·o·gy (skə tol′ə jē), *n.* preoccupation with excrement or obscenity, esp. in literature. —**scat′o·log′i·cal,** *adj.*

scat·ter (skat′ər), *v.t.* **1.** to throw or spread loosely over a wide area: *to scatter seeds.* **2.** to send off in different directions. —*v.i.* **3.** to separate and disperse in different directions. —**scat′ter·er,** *n.* —**scat′ter·ing,** *adj., n.*

scat·ter·brain (skat′ər brān′), *n.* a person incapable of serious, connected thought. —**scat′ter·brained′,** *adj.*

scat′ter rug′, a small rug, as one placed in front of a chair.

scat′ter·site′ hous′ing (skat′ər sīt′), a housing program designed to scatter minority or poverty groups throughout an urban area rather than concentrate them in one neighborhood.

scav·enge (skav′inj), v., **-enged, -enging.** —v.t. **1.** to cleanse from filth, as a street. **2.** to collect (something usable) from discarded material. —v.i. **3.** to act as a scavenger. **4.** to search, esp. for food.

scav·en·ger (skav′in jər), n. **1.** an animal that feeds on dead or decaying matter. **2.** a person or animal that searches through refuse for usable articles.

sce·nar·i·o (si när′ē ō′, -när′-), n., pl. **-nar·i·os. 1.** the script of a motion picture, esp. the final version. **2.** an outline of a natural or expected course of events. —**sce·nar′ist,** n.

scene (sēn), n. **1.** the place where some action or event occurs. **2.** any view or picture. **3.** an embarrassing display of emotion or bad manners. **4.** the setting of a story or play. **5.** a division of a play or film that represents a single episode. **6.** a unit of organized action or situation in a play or motion picture. **7.** scenery (def. 2). **8.** Slang. a place or sphere of special activity: *the marijuana scene.*

scen·er·y (sē′nə rē), n., pl. **-er·ies. 1.** the aggregate of features that give character to a landscape. **2.** a representation or illusion of a locale, as for a film or play.

sce·nic (sē′nik, sen′ik), adj. **1.** of natural scenery. **2.** having beautiful natural scenery. **3.** of the stage or stage scenery. —**sce′ni·cal·ly,** adv.

scent (sent), n. **1.** a distinctive odor, esp. when agreeable. **2.** an odor left by an animal or person, by which it may be traced. **3.** Chiefly Brit. perfume. **4.** a sense of smell. —v.t. **5.** to perceive by or as by smell **6.** to fill with an odor. —**scent′less,** adj.

scep·ter (sep′tər), n. a wand carried by a monarch as an emblem of power. Also, Brit., **scep′tre.**

scep·tic (skep′tik), n. skeptic.

sch., school.

sched·ule (skej′ŏŏl, -ŏŏl, -ŏŏ əl; Brit. shed′yŏŏl, shej′ŏŏl), n., v., **-uled, -uling.** —n. **1.** a list of duties, events, etc. **2.** a list or table of details. **3.** a series of things to be done within a given period. **4.** a timetable. —v.t. **5.** to enter in a schedule. **6.** to plan for a certain date. —**sched′u·lar,** adj.

scheel·ite (shā′līt, shē′-), n. a mineral that is an important ore of tungsten.

sche·mat·ic (skē mat′ik), adj. of or pertaining to a scheme or diagram. —**sche·mat′i·cal·ly,** adv.

scheme (skēm), n., v., **schemed, schem·ing.** —n. **1.** an underhand plot. **2.** a plan or program of action to be followed. **3.** any system of correlated things: *a color scheme.* **4.** an outline or diagram. —v.t., v.i. **5.** to make a scheme or plan (for), esp. an underhand one. —**schem′er,** n. —**schem′ing,** adj. —**Syn. 1.** conspiracy, intrigue.

scher·zo (sker′tsō), n., pl. **-zos, -zi** (-tsē). a light or playful movement, as of a symphony.

Schick′ test′ (shik), a skin test to determine immunity to diphtheria. [after Béla *Schick* (1877–1967), U.S. pediatrician]

schil·ling (shil′ing), n. the monetary unit of Austria.

schism (siz′əm), n. a division or split into opposing factions because of disagreement, esp. among religious groups. —**schis·mat′ic** (-mat′ik), adj. —**schis·mat′i·cal·ly,** adv.

schist (shist), n. a crystalline rock that easily splits into thin slabs. —**schis·tose** (shis′tōs), **schis·tous** (shis′təs), adj.

schiz·o·phre·ni·a (skit′sə frē′nē ə, -frēn′yə, skiz′ə-), n. a psychosis marked by withdrawn, bizarre, and sometimes delusional behavior and by intellectual and emotional deterioration —**schiz′oid** (-soid), **schiz′o·phren′ic** (-fren′ik), adj., n.

schle·miel (shlə mēl′), n. Slang. an awkward and unlucky person.

schlepp (shlep), n. Slang. an awkward, spiritless person. Also, **schlep.**

schlock (shlok), Slang. —adj. **1.** grossly inferior in quality and taste. —n. **2.** something of cheap or inferior quality.

schmaltz (shmälts, shmôlts), n. Informal. exaggerated sentimentalism, as in music or soap operas. —**schmaltz′y,** adj.

schmo (shmō), n., pl. **schmoes.** Slang. a foolish, boring, or stupid person. Also, **schmoe.**

schnapps (shnäps, shnaps), n. any strong spirituous liquor. Also, **shnaps.**

schnau·zer (shnou′zər), n. a German dog having a wiry coat.

schnook (shnŏŏk), n. Slang. an unimportant or stupid person.

schol·ar (skol′ər), n. **1.** a learned or erudite person. **2.** Chiefly Brit. a student, esp. one holding a certain scholarship. —**schol′ar·ly,** adj. —**schol′ar·li·ness,** n.

schol·ar·ship (skol′ər ship′), n. **1.** the qualities or attainments of a scholar. **2.** money awarded to a student to help pursue his or her studies.

scho·las·tic (skə las'tik), *adj.* of or pertaining to schools, scholars, or education. —**scho·las'ti·cal·ly,** *adv.*

school[1] (skōōl), *n.* **1.** a place or institution for teaching and learning. **2.** the activities of teaching and learning. **3.** a specialized division of a university. **4.** the body of persons belonging to an educational institution. **5.** any group of persons having common attitudes or beliefs. —*v.t.* **6.** to educate in or as in a school.

school[2] (skōōl), *n.* a large number of fish or other marine animals feeding or migrating together.

school·boy (skōōl'boi'), *n.* a boy attending school. —**school'girl',** *n. fem.*

school·house (skōōl'hous'), *n.* a building in which a school is conducted.

school·marm (skōōl'märm'), *n.* a female schoolteacher, esp. of the old-time country-school type, popularly held to be strict and priggish. Also, **school'ma'am'** (-mam', -mäm').

school·mas·ter (skōōl'mas'tər, -mäs'tər), *n. Obsolesc.* a male schoolteacher. —**school'mis'tress,** *n.fem.*

school·mate (skōōl'māt'), *n.* a companion at school. Also called **school'fel'low.**

school·room (skōōl'rōōm', -rŏŏm'), *n.* a room in which pupils are taught.

school·teach·er (skōōl'tē'chər), *n.* a teacher in a school, esp. in one below the college level.

schoon·er (skōō'nər), *n.* **1.** a sailing vessel having two or more masts and fore-and-aft sails. **2.** a very tall glass for beer.

Schu·bert (shōō'bərt), *n.* Franz (fränts), 1797–1828, Austrian composer.

schuss (shŏŏs, shōōs), *Skiing.* —*n.* **1.** a straight descent with no attempt to decrease speed. —*v.i.* **2.** to execute a schuss.

schuss·boom·er (shŏŏs'bōō'mər, shōōs'-), *n.* a skier who executes a schuss, esp. skillfully.

schwa (shwä, shvä), *n.* **1.** the indeterminate vowel sound or sounds of most unstressed syllables of English, as of *a* in *about.* **2.** the phonetic symbol (ə) for this.

sci., 1. science. **2.** scientific.

sci·at·ic (sī at'ik), *adj.* of or affecting the hip or its nerves.

sci·at·i·ca (sī at'i kə), *n.* a pain in the hip and the back of the thigh.

sci·ence (sī'əns), *n.* **1.** a branch of knowledge or study dealing with a body of facts or truths systematically arranged and showing the operation of general laws. **2.** systematic knowledge of the physical or material world. —**sci·en·tif·ic** (sī'ən tif'ik), *adj.* —**sci'en·tif'i·cal·ly,** *adv.*

sci'ence fic'tion, a form of fiction that draws imaginatively on scientific knowledge and speculation.

sci·en·tist (sī'ən tist), *n.* an expert in science, esp. one of the physical or natural sciences.

sci-fi (sī'fī'), *Slang.* —*adj.* **1.** of or pertaining to science fiction. —*n.* **2.** See **science fiction.**

scil., scilicet.

scil·i·cet (sil'i set'), *adv. Law.* namely [< L]

scim·i·tar (sim'i tər), *n.* a curved, single-edged sword used chiefly by Arabs. Also, **scim'i·ter.**

scin·til·la (sin til'ə), *n.* a minute particle.

scin·til·late (sin't°l·lāt'), *v.i.* **-lat·ed, -lat·ing. 1.** to emit sparks. **2.** to be brilliant or keen, as in talent. —**scin'til·la'tion,** *n.* —**scin'til·lat'ing·ly,** *adv.*

sci·on (sī'ən), *n.* **1.** a descendant, esp. of an illustrious family. **2.** a shoot or twig, esp. one cut for grafting or planting.

scis·sors (siz'ərz), *n.pl.* a cutting instrument for paper, cloth, etc., consisting of two blades so pivoted together that their sharp edges work one against the other.

scis'sors kick', a swimming motion of the legs in which they move somewhat like scissors.

scle·ro·sis (skli rō'sis), *n., pl.* **-ses** (-sēz). an abnormal hardening of a tissue or part, as the walls of the arteries. —**scle·rot'ic** (-rot'ik), *adj.*

scoff (skôf, skof), *v.i.* **1.** to express insolent derision, esp. openly. —*n.* **2.** an expression of insolent derision. —**scoff'er,** *n.* —**scoff'ing·ly,** *adv.* —Syn. **1.** gibe, jeer, mock, scorn.

scoff·law (skôf'lô', skof'-), *n. Informal.* a person who flouts the law, esp. one who fails to pay fines owed.

scold (skōld), *v.t.* **1.** to rebuke angrily. —*v.i.* **2.** to rebuke someone angrily. **3.** to use abusive language. —*n.* **4.** a person, esp. a woman, who is constantly scolding. —**scold'ing,** *adj., n.* —**scold'ing·ly,** *adv.* —Syn. **1.** berate, censure, reprove.

sconce (skons), *n.* a bracket for candles or other lights, placed on a wall.

scone (skōn, skon), *n. Brit.* a flat, round cake or biscuit, as of oatmeal.

scoop (skōōp), *n.* **1.** a small, deep-sided shovel with a short, horizontal handle, for taking up flour, sugar, etc. **2.** the bucket of a dredge, steam shovel, etc. **3.** the quantity that a scoop can hold. **4.** the act of scooping. **5.** *Informal.* a news item first made public in one newspaper, magazine, etc. —*v.t.* **6.** to take up or out with or as with a scoop. **7.** to hollow or dig out. **8.** *Informal.* to make public a news item before (one's competitors).

scoot (sko͞ot), *v.i. Informal.* to go swiftly or hastily.

scoot·er (sko͞o'tər), *n.* **1.** a child's two-wheeled vehicle steered by a handlebar and propelled by pushing one foot against the ground. **2.** a similar but larger and heavier vehicle for adults, propelled by a motor.

scope (skōp), *n.* **1.** the extent or range of one's understanding. **2.** the area or extent covered by something. **3.** opportunity or freedom for movement or activity.

-scope, a combining form meaning "instrument for viewing": *telescope.*

sco·pol·a·mine (skə pol'ə mēn', -min, skō'pə lam'in), *n.* a syrupy alkaloid used chiefly as a sedative.

scor·bu·tic (skôr byo͞o'tik), *adj.* of, like, or affected with scurvy. Also, **scor·bu'ti·cal.**

scorch (skôrch), *v.t.* **1.** to burn slightly or on the surface. **2.** to parch with heat. —*v.i.* **3.** to become scorched. —*n.* **4.** a superficial burn. —**scorch'ing·ly,** *adv.*

score (skōr, skôr), *n., pl.* **scores, score** for 4, *v.,* **scored, scor·ing.** —*n.* **1.** the number of points made in a game or contest **2.** a grade received in an examination or test. **3.** *Music.* **a.** a written or printed piece of music containing all vocal and instrumental parts. **b.** the music for a play, motion picture, etc. **4.** a group or set of 20. **5. scores,** a great many. **6.** a notch or mark, esp. one for noting a single item **7.** any account showing indebtedness. **8.** a reason, ground, or cause. **9.** *Informal.* **a.** the facts of a situation. **b.** a successful move, esp. in obtaining narcotics. **10. pay off** or **settle a score,** to avenge a wrong or injury. —*v.t.* **11.** to add to one's score **12.** to make a score of. **13.** to find or keep the score of. **14.** *Music.* to compose a score for. **15.** to make notches or scratches in, as cardboard to facilitate bending. **16.** to win or achieve: *to score a triumph* **17.** to berate or censure. —*v.i.* **18.** to make points in a game or contest. **19.** to keep score, as of a game. **20.** to achieve an advantage or a success. —**score'less,** *adj.* —**scor'er,** *n.*

sco·ri·a (skōr'ē ə, skôr'-), *n., pl.* **sco·ri·ae** (skōr'ē ē', skôr'-). a cinderlike cellular lava.

scorn (skôrn), *n.* **1.** angry or unqualified contempt. —*v.t.* **2.** to treat or regard with scorn. **3.** to reject with scorn. —**scorn'er,** *n.* —**scorn'ful,** *adj.* —**scorn'ful·ly,** *adv.* —**Syn. 2.** despise, disdain **3.** spurn.

Scor·pi·o (skôr'pē ō'), *n.* the eighth sign of the zodiac. [< L: scorpion]

scor·pi·on (skôr'pē ən), *n.* **1.** an arachnid having a long, narrow tail that terminates in a venomous sting. **2.** **the Scorpion,** Scorpio.

Scot (skot), *n.* a native or inhabitant of Scotland.

Scot., **1.** Scotch. **2.** Scotland. **3.** Scottish.

scotch (skoch), *v.t.* **1.** to put a definite end to: *to scotch a rumor.* **2.** *Archaic.* to injure so as to make harmless.

Scotch (skoch), *adj.* **1.** (used usually outside Scotland and esp. in referring to whiskey, fabrics, etc.) Scottish (def. 1). —*n.* **2.** (*often l.c.*) Also called **Scotch' whis'ky.** whiskey distilled in Scotland, esp. from malted barley. **3.** *Brit.* Scots (def. 1). **4.** Scottish (def. 2).

Scotch·man (skoch'mən), *n.* (used usually outside Scotland) Scot.

Scotch' tape', *Trademark.* a transparent or semitransparent adhesive tape.

scot-free (skot'frē'), *adj.* free from harm or punishment.

Scot·land (skot'lənd), *n.* a division of the United Kingdom in the N part of Great Britain.

Scot'land Yard', the metropolitan police of London, England, esp. the branch engaged in crime detection.

Scots (skots), *n.* **1.** the dialect of English in Scotland. —*adj.* **2.** (used esp. in referring to law, guards, etc.) Scottish (def. 1).

Scots·man (skots'mən), *n.* a Scot.

Scot·tish (skot'ish), *adj.* **1.** of Scotland, its inhabitants, or the dialect of English spoken there. —*n.* **2.** the people of Scotland. **3.** *U.S.* Scots (def. 1).

scoun·drel (skoun'drəl), *n.* an unprincipled, dishonorable person. —**Syn.** knave, rogue, villain.

scour¹ (skour, skou'ər), *v.t., v.i.* **1.** to clean or polish by hard rubbing, esp. with abrasives. **2.** to clean or dig out, esp. by the force of water.

scour² (skour, skou'ər), *v.t.* **1.** to pass quickly over or along. **2.** to range over, as in search.

scourge (skûrj), *n., v.,* **scourged, scourg·ing.** —*n.* **1.** a whip used on human beings. **2.** a person or thing that harasses or destroys. —*v.t.* **3.** to whip with a scourge. **4.** to punish or criticize severely. —**scourg'er,** *n.*

scout¹ (skout), *n.* **1.** a soldier, warship, or airplane sent out to reconnoiter. **2.** a person sent out to obtain information. **3.** a person employed to discover new talent. **4.** a boy scout or girl scout. —*v.i., v.t.* **5.** to reconnoiter. **6.** to find by seeking or searching.

scout² (skout), *v.t.* **1.** to dismiss as absurd or unsound. —*v.i.* **2.** to scoff or flout.

scout·mas·ter (skout′mas′tər, -mä′-stər), *n.* the adult leader of a troop of Boy Scouts.

scow (skou), *n.* a large boat with square ends and a flat bottom.

scowl (skoul), *v.i.* 1. to draw down the brows in a sullen or displeased manner. —*n.* 2. a scowling expression. —**scowl′er**, *n.* —**scowl′ing·ly**, *adv.*

SCPO, Senior Chief Petty Officer.

scrab·ble (skrab′əl), *v.i.,* **-bled, -bling.** 1. to scratch or scrape with claws or hands. 2. to grapple or struggle, esp. with claws or hands. 3. to scramble (def. 2). 4. to scrawl or scribble. —**scrab′bler,** *n.*

scrag·gly (skrag′lē), *adj.,* **-gli·er, -gli·est.** irregular or uneven, as in appearance.

scram (skram), *v.i.,* **scrammed, scramming.** *Informal.* to get out quickly.

scram·ble (skram′bəl), *v.,* **-bled, -bling,** *n.* —*v.i.* 1. to climb or crawl in a hasty, confused way. 2. to compete or struggle with others for possession or gain. —*v.t.* 3. to mix confusedly. 4. to cook (eggs), mixing whites and yolks together. 5. to make (a radio or telephonic message) incomprehensible to interceptors by changing the frequencies. —*n.* 6. a hasty, confused climb or crawl. 7. a confused struggle or competition. —**scram′bler,** *n.*

scrap¹ (skrap), *n., adj., v.,* **scrapped, scrap·ping.** —*n.* 1. a small piece or portion. 2. scraps, bits of leftover food. 3. discarded material that can be reused. —*adj.* 4. consisting of scraps or scrap. 5. discarded or left over. —*v.t.* 6. to make into scrap. 7. to discard as useless. —**scrap′per,** *n.* —**scrap′py,** *adj.*

scrap² (skrap), *n., v.,* **scrapped, scrap·ping.** *Informal.* —*n.* 1. a brief fight or quarrel. —*v.i.* 2. to engage in a scrap. —**scrap′per,** *n.* —**scrap′py,** *adj.* —**scrap′pi·ness,** *n.*

scrap·book (skrap′book′), *n.* a blank book in which to paste pictures, newspaper clippings, etc.

scrape (skrāp), *v.,* **scraped, scrap·ing,** *n.* —*v.t.* 1. to rub (a surface) with something rough or sharp to clean or smooth it. 2. to remove (something) in this manner. 3. to injure by brushing against something rough or sharp. 4. to gather laboriously and with difficulty. 5. to rub roughly on or across (something), often with a grating sound. —*v.i.* 6. to rub against something gratingly. 7. to manage or get by with difficulty or with only the barest margin. —*n.* 8. an act or instance of scraping. 9. a grating or scratching sound. 10. a scraped place. 11. a distressing situation. —**scrap′er,** *n.*

scrap·ple (skrap′əl), *n.* a sausage-like preparation of ground pork, corn meal, and seasonings.

scratch (skrach), *v.t.* 1. to mark or mar the surface of by rubbing or scraping with something sharp or rough. 2. to rub or draw along a rough surface. 3. to rub or scrape slightly, as with the fingernails, to relieve itching. 4. to remove with a scraping action. 5. to cancel (a written item) by drawing a line through it. 6. to withdraw (an entry) from a race. 7. to write or draw by cutting into a surface. —*v.i.* 8. to use the nails or claws, as in digging. 9. to make a slight grating noise. —*n.* 10. a mark left by scratching. 11. an act of scratching. 12. the sound of scratching. 13. **from scratch, a.** from the very beginning. **b.** from nothing. 14. **up to scratch,** up to standard. —*adj.* 15. used for hasty writing, notes, etc.: *a scratch pad.* 16. *Informal.* gathered together hastily: *a scratch crew.* —**scratch′y,** *adj.* —**scratch′i·ly,** *adv.* —**scratch′i·ness,** *n.*

scrawl (skrôl), *v.t., v.i.* 1. to write or draw in a sprawling, awkward manner. —*n.* 2. something scrawled, esp. handwriting. —**scrawl′y,** *adj.*

scrawn·y (skrô′nē), *adj.,* **scrawn·i·er, scrawn·i·est.** excessively thin or lean. —**scrawn′i·ness,** *n.*

scream (skrēm), *v.i.* 1. to utter a loud, sharp, piercing cry. 2. to laugh immoderately. —*v.t.* 3. to utter with or as with a scream. —*n.* 4. a loud, sharp, piercing cry. 5. *Informal.* someone or something that is hilariously funny.

screech (skrēch), *v.i., v.t.* 1. to utter (with) a harsh, shrill sound. —*n.* 2. a screeching sound. —**screech′y,** *adj.*

screen (skrēn), *n.* 1. a movable or fixed device that provides shelter or serves as a partition 2. anything that provides concealment, shelter, etc. 3. a surface on which pictures are projected or formed, as in motion pictures or television. 4. the motion-picture industry. 5. a frame holding a mesh of wire, as to admit air but exclude insects. 6. a sieve or other meshlike device used for sifting or sorting. —*v.t.* 7. to shelter or conceal with or as with a screen. 8. to examine in order to select or reject. 9. to sift or sort through a screen. 10. to project (a motion picture, etc.) on a screen. —**screen′er,** *n.*

screen·play (skrēn′plā′), *n.* the scenario of a motion picture, often adapted from a novel.

screw (skrōō), *n.* **1.** a metal fastener having a spiral ridge winding around it, driven into wood or metal by turning its head. **2.** a rod having a similar spiral ridge that fits into a threaded hole, used as in a clamp or jack. **3.** something having a spiral form. **4.** a rotary propelling device, as for a ship. **5. put the screws on,** to compel by exerting pressure on. —*v.t.* **6.** to attach or fasten with a screw. **7.** to cause to turn as or like a screw. **8.** to twist out of shape. —*v.i.* **9.** to turn as or like a screw. **10.** to be attached or fastened by means of twisting. **11. screw up,** *Slang.* to ruin through stupidity.

screw·ball (skrōō′bôl′), *n.* **1.** *Slang.* an eccentric person. **2.** *Baseball.* a pitched ball that curves toward the side of the plate from which it was thrown.

screw·driv·er (skrōō′drī′vər), *n.* **1.** a hand tool for turning screws. **2.** a mixed drink made with vodka and orange juice.

screw·y (skrōō′ē), *adj.*, **screw·i·er, screw·i·est.** *Slang.* **1.** mentally crazy. **2.** disconcertingly strange.

scrib·ble (skrib′əl), *v.*, **-bled, -bling,** *n.* —*v.t., v.i.* **1.** to write hastily or carelessly. —*n.* **2.** writing made by scribbling. —**scrib′bler,** *n.*

scribe (skrīb), *n.* **1.** a person who copied manuscripts before the invention of printing. **2.** *Facetious.* a writer or author.

scrim (skrim), *n.* a cotton or linen fabric of open weave used for bunting, curtains, etc.

scrim·mage (skrim′ij), *n., v.,* **-maged, -mag·ing.** *Football.* —*n.* **1. a.** the play between the teams from the moment the ball is snapped. **b.** a practice session. —*v.t., v.i.* **3.** to engage in a scrimmage.

scrimp (skrimp), *v.t., v.i.* to be very sparing or frugal (of or with). —**scrimp′y,** *adj.*

scrim·shaw (skrim′shô′), *n.* **1.** a carved or engraved article, esp. of whale ivory made by whalers as a leisure occupation. **2.** such articles collectively.

scrip (skrip), *n.* a certificate of a right to receive payment later in the form of cash or stock.

script (skript), *n.* **1.** the written or typed text of a play, motion picture, etc. **2.** handwriting of the regular cursive type. **3.** *Print.* a type imitating handwriting.

Script., **1.** Scriptural. **2.** Scripture.

Script·ure (skrip′chər), *n.* **1.** Often, **Scriptures.** the sacred writings of the Old or New Testament or both together. **2.** (*often l.c.*) any sacred book or writing. —**scrip′tur·al,** *adj.* —**scrip′tur·al·ly,** *adv.*

scrive·ner (skriv′nər), *n.* *Archaic.* **1.** a scribe or copyist. **2.** a notary.

scrod (skrod), *n.* young Atlantic cod or haddock.

scrof·u·la (skrof′yə lə), *n.* a form of tuberculosis characterized by swelling of the lymphatic glands, esp. of the neck. —**scrof′u·lous,** *adj.*

scroll (skrōl), *n.* **1.** a roll of parchment, paper, etc., esp. one with writing on it. **2.** an ornament having a spiral or coiled form.

scroll′ saw′, a narrow saw used for cutting curved designs.

Scrooge (skrōōj), *n.* (*often l.c.*) a miserly person.

scro·tum (skrō′təm), *n., pl.* **-ta** (-tə), **-tums.** the pouch of skin that contains the testes. —**scro′tal,** *adj.*

scrounge (skrounj), *v.t., v.i.,* **scrounged, scroung·ing.** *Slang.* **1.** to borrow (a small item or amount) without intention of returning it. **2.** to get or take without paying or at another's expense. —**scroung′er,** *n.*

scrub¹ (skrub), *v.,* **scrubbed, scrubbing,** *n.* —*v.t., v.i.* **1.** to rub hard, as with a brush in washing. **2.** to remove (dirt, etc.) by hard rubbing. **3.** *Informal.* to cancel or postpone (a spaceflight). —*n.* **4.** the act of scrubbing. —**scrub′ber,** *n.*

scrub² (skrub), *n.* **1.** a thick growth of low trees or shrubs. **2.** a domestic animal of inferior breeding. **3.** a small or insignificant person. **4.** *Sports.* a player not belonging to the regular team. —*adj.* **5.** small or inferior. —**scrub′by,** *adj.*

scruff (skruf), *n.* the nape or back of the neck.

scruff·y (skruf′ē), *adj.,* **scruff·i·er, scruff·i·est.** shabby and untidy.

scrump·tious (skrump′shəs), *adj.* *Informal.* very pleasing, esp. to the senses. —**scrump′tious·ly,** *adv.* —**scrump′tious·ness,** *n.*

scrunch (skrunch, skrōōnch), *v.t., v.i.* to crunch.

scru·ple (skrōō′pəl), *n., v.,* **-pled, -pling.** —*n.* **1.** a moral or ethical consideration that acts as a restraining force. **2.** a very small quantity. **3.** a unit of apothecaries' weight equal to 20 grains. —*v.i.* **4.** to have scruples.

scru·pu·lous (skrōō′pyə ləs), *adj.* **1.** showing or having scruples. **2.** conscientiously careful. —**scru′pu·los′i·ty** (-los′i tē), **scru′pu·lous·ness,** *n.* —**scru′pu·lous·ly,** *adv.* —**Syn. 2.** exacting, painstaking, punctilious.

scru·ti·nize (skrōōt′°nīz′), *v.t.,* **-nized, -niz·ing.** to examine with critical attention. —**scru′ti·niz′er,** *n.*

scru·ti·ny (skrōōt′°nē), *n., pl.* **-nies.** a critical and minute examination.

scu·ba (skōō′bə), *n.* a portable breathing device used in underwater swimming. [*s*(*elf*)-*c*(*ontained*) *u*(*nderwater*) *b*(*reathing*) *a*(*pparatus*)]

scud (skud), *v.*, **scud·ded, scud·ding,** *n.* —*v.i.* 1. to run or move quickly. —*n.* 2. clouds or spray driven by the wind.

scuff (skuf), *v.i., v.t.* 1. to scrape (one's feet) while walking. 2. to make or become marred or scratched by hard use or wear. —*n.* 3. a flat-heeled slipper open at the back. 4. a marred or scratched spot.

scuf·fle (skuf′əl), *v.*, **-fled, -fling,** *n.* —*v.i.* 1. to struggle or fight in a rough, confused manner. 2. to move or go with a shuffle. —*n.* 3. a rough, confused struggle or fight. 4. a shuffling of the feet. —**scuf′fler,** *n.*

scull (skul), *n.* 1. an oar mounted at the stern of a small boat for moving from side to side to propel the boat. 2. either of a pair of oars rowed by one oarsman. 3. a light, narrow racing boat. —*v.t., v.i.* 4. to propel (a boat) with a scull or sculls. —**scull′er,** *n.*

scul·ler·y (skul′ə rē), *n., pl.* **-ler·ies.** *Chiefly Brit.* a small kitchen in which cooking utensils are cleaned and stored.

scul·lion (skul′yən), *n. Archaic.* a kitchen servant who does menial work.

sculpt (skulpt), *v.t., v.i.* to sculpture.

sculp·tor (skulp′tər), *n.* an artist who works in sculpture. —**sculp′tress,** *n.fem.*

sculp·ture (skulp′chər), *n., v.,* **-tured, tur·ing.** —*n.* 1. the art of carving or modeling statues or figures in stone, wood, clay, etc. 2. a work or works of art produced in this way. —*v.t., v.i.* 3. to carve or model (a piece of sculpture). 4. to make a sculpture (of). —**sculp′tur·al,** *adj.*

scum (skum), *n.* 1. a film of dirt or decayed matter that forms on the surface of a liquid. 2. refuse or waste. 3. a low, worthless person or persons. —**scum′my,** *adj.*

scup·per (skup′ər), *n.* a drain at the edge of a deck, for allowing water to run into the sea.

scurf (skûrf), *n.* 1. small, loose scales of skin, as dandruff. 2. any scaly matter.

scur·ril·ous (skûr′ə ləs), *adj.* grossly or obscenely abusive. —**scur·ril·i·ty** (skə ril′i tē), *n.* —**scur′ril·ous·ly,** *adv.*

scur·ry (skûr′ē, skur′ē), *v.,* **-ried, -ry·ing,** *n., pl.* **-ries.** —*v.i.* 1. to go or move quickly or in haste. —*n.* 2. the act or sound of scurrying.

scur·vy (skûr′vē), *n., adj.* **-vi·er, -vi·est.** —*n.* 1. a disease marked by swollen and bleeding gums, anemia, etc., due to a diet lacking in vitamin C. —*adj.*

2. contemptible or despicable. —**scur′vi·ly,** *adv.*

scutch·eon (skuch′ən), *n.* escutcheon.

scut·tle[1] (skut′əl), *n.* a deep bucket for carrying coal.

scut·tle[2] (skut′əl), *v.,* **-tled, -tling,** *n.* —*v.i.* 1. to run with quick, hasty steps. —*n.* 2. a quick pace.

scut·tle[3] (skut′əl), *v.,* **-tled, -tling,** *n.* —*v.t.* 1. to sink (a ship) by letting water in through holes in the hull. 2. to abandon or destroy (plans, etc.). —*n.* 3. a small opening with a cover in the deck or hull of a ship.

scut·tle·butt (skut′əl but′), *n. Informal.* idle gossip.

scythe (sīth), *n.* a tool having a long, curved blade fastened at an angle to a handle, for cutting grass, grain, etc.

SD, South Dakota.

S.D., 1. South Dakota. 2. special delivery.

s.d., See **sine die.**

S. Dak., South Dakota.

SE, 1. southeast. 2. southeastern.

Se, selenium.

sea (sē), *n.* 1. the salt waters that cover most of the earth's surface. 2. one of the seven seas. 3. a large lake or landlocked body of water. 4. the condition of the surface of the ocean, as caused by the wind. 5. a large wave or waves. 6. an overwhelming quantity: *a sea of faces.* 7. **at sea,** a. on the ocean. b. perplexed or uncertain.

sea′ anem′one, a small marine animal having a tubular body and circles of tentacles.

sea·bed (sē′bed′), *n.* the ocean floor that covers most of the earth's surface.

sea·bird (sē′bûrd′), *n.* a bird frequenting the sea or coast.

sea·board (sē′bôrd′, -bōrd′), *n.* 1. a region bordering a seacoast. —*adj.* 2. bordering on the sea.

sea·coast (sē′kōst′), *n.* the land bordering a sea or ocean.

sea·far·er (sē′fâr′ər), *n. Chiefly Literary.* a traveler on the sea, esp. a sailor.

sea·far·ing (sē′fâr′ing), *adj.* 1. following the sea as a calling. —*n.* 2. the calling of a sailor.

sea·food (sē′fōōd′), *n.* any saltwater fish or shellfish used for food.

sea·go·ing (sē′gō′ing), *adj.* 1. designed for going to sea, as a vessel. 2. seafaring.

sea′ horse′, a small fish having a head slightly resembling that of a horse.

seal[1] (sēl), *n.* 1. an emblem or figure used as evidence of authenticity. 2. a stamp or ring engraved with such a device, used to make an impression on paper, wax, etc. 3. the impression so obtained. 4. a piece of wax so attached to an envelope that it must be broken in order to remove or tamper with the contents. 5. anything that closes or fastens securely. 6. a decorative stamp, esp. as given to contributors to a charitable fund: *a Christmas seal*. 7. anything that serves as a confirmation or guarantee. —*v.t.* 8. to close or fasten securely. 9. to put a seal on, as to authenticate. 10. to confirm or guarantee with or as with a seal. 11. to decide irrevocably. —**seal′er,** *n.*

seal² (sēl), *n., pl.* **seals, seal,** *v.* —*n.* 1. a sea mammal that feeds on fish and has limbs reduced to flippers. 2. the skin or fur of such an animal. —*v.i.* 3. to hunt or capture seals. —**seal′er,** *n.*

Sea·lab (sē′lab′), *n.* any of several U.S. Navy underwater ships for aquanauts in deep-sea research.

seal·ant (sē′lənt), *n.* a substance used for sealing, as a wax, adhesive, etc. —**seal′er,** *n.*

sea′ legs′, the ability to adjust one's sense of balance aboard a rolling ship.

sea′ lev′el, the position of the sea's surface at mean level between high and low tide.

sea′ li′on, a large seal of the Pacific coast of North America.

seal·skin (sēl′skin′), *n.* 1. seal² (def. 2). 2. a garment made of this.

seam (sēm), *n.* 1. a line formed by sewing together pieces of cloth, leather, etc. 2. any line formed by abutting edges. 3. any linear mark, as a wrinkle or scar. 4. *Geol.* a comparatively thin stratum, as of coal. —*v.t.* 5. to join together in a seam. 6. to mark with wrinkles or scars. —**seam′er,** *n.* —**seam′less,** *adj.*

sea·man (sē′mən), *n.* 1. a person skilled in seamanship. 2. *U.S. Navy.* an enlisted man or woman ranking just below a petty officer third class.

sea′man appren′tice, *U.S. Navy.* an enlisted man or woman ranking just below a seaman.

sea′man recruit′, *U.S. Navy.* an enlisted man or woman of the lowest rank.

sea·man·ship (sē′mən ship′), *n.* the knowledge of and skill in the navigation and maintenance of a ship.

seam·stress (sēm′stris), *n.* a woman whose occupation is sewing.

seam·y (sē′mē), *adj.,* **seam·i·er, seam·i·est.** 1. sordid and unpleasant. 2. having or showing seams. —**seam′i·ness,** *n.*

sé·ance (sā′äns), *n.* a meeting in which a spiritualist attempts to communicate with the dead.

sea·plane (sē′plān′), *n.* an airplane equipped with floats for taking off from and landing on water.

sea·port (sē′pōrt′, -pôrt′), *n.* a port or harbor for seagoing vessels.

sear (sēr), *v.t.* 1. to burn the surface of. 2. to mark with a branding iron. 3. to dry up or wither.

search (sûrch), *v.t.* 1. to look through carefully in order to find something missing or lost. 2. to examine carefully in order to find something concealed. 3. to find by examination. —*v.i.* 4. to conduct a search. —*n.* 5. the act or an instance of searching. —**search′er,** *n.* —**search′ing,** *adj.*

search·light (sûrch′līt′), *n.* 1. a powerful lamp that can shine a narrow beam of light in any direction. 2. a beam of light so shined.

sea·scape (sē′skāp′), *n.* 1. a view of the sea. 2. a painting or photograph of the sea.

sea′ shell′, the shell of any marine mollusk.

sea·shore (sē′shōr′, -shôr′), *n.* land along the sea or ocean.

sea·sick·ness (sē′sik′nis), *n.* nausea and dizziness resulting from the rolling of a ship in which one is traveling at sea. —**sea′sick,** *adj.*

sea·side (sē′sīd′), *n.* seashore.

sea·son (sē′zən), *n.* 1. one of the four periods of the year: spring, summer, autumn, or winter. 2. a period of the year marked by certain conditions, activities, etc. 3. a suitable or fitting time. —*v.t.* 4. to add flavor to (food) by the use of seasoning. 5. to add interest or zest to. 6. to harden by experience or by exposure to difficult conditions. 7. to make more resistant to use and wear, as by aging. —*v.i.* 8. to become seasoned. —**sea′son·al,** *adj.* —**sea′son·al·ly,** *adv.* —**sea′son·er,** *n.*

sea·son·a·ble (sē′zə nə bəl), *adj.* 1. suitable for a particular season: *seasonable weather.* 2. timely or opportune. —**sea′son·a·bly,** *adv.*

sea·son·ing (sē′zə niñg), *n.* any substance, as salt, spice, etc., used for adding flavor to food.

sea′son tick′et, a ticket for a specified series of athletic events, concerts, etc.

seat (sēt), *n.* 1. anything used for sitting on, as a chair or bench. 2. the part of a chair or bench on which a person sits. 3. the rump. 4. the part of the garment covering it. 5. a place in which something is established or has its center. 6. a place in which administrative power is centered: *the seat of government.* 7. a right to sit as a member, as in a legislative body. —*v.t.* 8. to place in or on a seat or seats. 9. to accommodate with seats.

seat′ belt′, a strap used to keep a passenger safely secured to his or her seat, as in′ an automobile.

Se·at·tle (sē at′ᵊl), *n.* a seaport in W Washington.

sea′ ur′chin, a small, round sea animal having a shell covered with projecting spines.

sea·ward (sē′wᵊrd), *adv.* 1. Also, **sea′wards.** toward the sea. —*adj.* 2. facing toward the sea. 3. coming from the sea.

sea·wa·ter (sē′wô′tᵊr, -wot′ᵊr), *n.* the salt water of the ocean.

sea·way (sē′wā′), *n* a canal or waterway for oceangoing vessels.

sea·weed (sē′wēd′), *n.* any plant growing in the ocean, esp. a marine alga.

sea·wor·thy (sē′wûr′t͟hē), *adj.* suitable for a voyage at sea, as a ship. —**sea′wor′thi·ness,** *n.*

se·ba·ceous (si bā′shᵊs), *adj.* of, resembling, or secreting a fatty substance.

SEC, Securities and Exchange Commission.

sec., 1. second. 2. secondary. 3. secretary. 4. section. 5. sector.

se·cant (sē′kant, -kᵊnt), *n. Geom.* a line intersecting a curve at two or more points.

se·cede (si sēd′), *v.i.,* **-ced·ed, -ced·ing.** to withdraw from membership in a union or association, esp. a political or religious one —**se·ced′er,** *n.*

se·ces·sion (si sesh′ᵊn), *n.* 1. the act or an instance of seceding. 2. (*often cap.*) *U.S.* the withdrawal of 11 Southern States from the Union in 1860–61. —**se·ces′sion·ist,** *n.*

se·clude (si klōōd′), *v.t.,* **-clud·ed, -clud·ing.** to place or keep apart, esp. from others. —**se·clu′sive,** *adj.*

se·clu·sion (si klōō′zhᵊn), *n.* an act of secluding or state of being secluded. —**se·clu′sive,** *adj.*

sec·ond¹ (sek′ᵊnd), *adj.* 1. being number two in a series. 2. next after the first in grade, rank, quality, or importance 3. other or another: *a second chance.* —*n.* 4. a person or thing that is second. 5. a person who aids another as an assistant, esp. in boxing or dueling. 6. *Auto* the second forward gear in transmission. 7. a flawed article or product —*v.t.* 8. to express formal support of (a motion, etc.), prior to further discussion or voting 9. to further or advance, as aims. 10. to assist or support. —*adv.* 11. Also, **sec′ond·ly.** in the second place. —**sec′ond·er,** *n.*

sec·ond² (sek′ᵊnd), *n.* 1. the sixtieth part of a minute of time. 2. the sixtieth part of a minute of angular measure 3. a moment or instant.

sec·ond·ar·y (sek′ᵊn der′ē), *adj., n., pl.* **-ar·ies.** —*adj.* 1. of minor importance. 2. not primary or original. 3. second in order, place, or time. —*n.* 4. a person or thing that is secondary. —**sec·ond·ar·i·ly** (sek′ᵊn der′ᵊ lē, sek′ᵊn dâr′-), *adv.*

sec′ondary ac′cent, a stress accent weaker than a primary accent.

sec′ondary school′, any school ranking between an elementary school and a college.

sec′ond class′, 1. the class or grade immediately below the first or highest. 2. a class of mail consisting of periodicals. —**sec′ond-class′,** *adj., adv.*

sec·ond-guess (sek′ᵊnd ges′), *v.t., v.i.* 1. to use hindsight in criticizing or correcting (someone or something). 2. to predict (something) or outguess (someone).

sec·ond·hand (sek′ᵊnd hand′), *adj.* 1. not directly known or experienced. 2. previously used or owned. 3. dealing in used goods. —*adv.* 4. after being used or owned by another. 5. not directly.

sec′ond lieuten′ant, a U.S. Army, Air Force, or Marine officer of the lowest commissioned rank.

sec′ond na′ture, an acquired habit that is so deeply ingrained as to appear automatic

sec′ond per′son, *Gram.* the form of a pronoun or verb that refers to the one or ones spoken to.

sec·ond-rate (sek′ᵊnd rāt′), *adj.* 1. of lesser quality or worth. 2. inferior or mediocre.

sec′ond-sto′ry man′, *Informal.* a burglar who enters through upstairs windows.

sec·ond-string (sek′ᵊnd string′), *adj. Informal.* not belonging to the regular team, as in football. —**sec′ond-string′er,** *n.*

sec′ond thought′, Often, **second thoughts.** reservation about a previous action or decision.

sec′ond wind′ (wind), 1. the return of ease in breathing after early exhaustion, as in running. 2. the energy for a renewed effort.

se·cre·cy (sē′kri sē), *n., pl.* **-cies.** 1. the state or condition of being secret. 2. the habit or characteristic of being secretive.

se·cret (sē′krit), *adj.* 1. kept from the knowledge of others. 2. concealed in such a way as to be accessible only to the person or persons concerned. 3. engaged in espionage work: *a secret agent.* 4. unknown or unknowable. —*n.* 5. something that is or is kept secret 6. something unknown or unknowable. 7. a reason or explanation not immediately apparent —**se′cret·ly,** *adv.* —**Syn.** 1. clandestine, hidden, covert. 2. confidential.

sec·re·tar·i·at (sek′ri târ′ē ət), *n.* **1.** a group of officials and employees that performs the administrative and secretarial duties of a large organization. **2.** the building housing this group.

sec·re·tar·y (sek′ri ter′ē), *n., pl.* **-tar·ies. 1.** a person employed to handle correspondence and do clerical work, esp. for an executive, as in a business office. **2.** an official who has charge of a department of government. **3.** a desk with bookshelves on top of it. —**sec′re·tar′i·al** (-târ′ē əl), *adj.* —**sec′re·tar′y·ship′,** *n.*

sec′retary of state′, the Cabinet member of the United States in charge of foreign affairs.

se·crete¹ (si krēt′), *v.t.,* **-cret·ed, -cret·ing.** to generate and discharge as a secretion.

se·crete² (si krēt′), *v.t.,* **-cret·ed, -cret·ing.** to hide in a secret place.

se·cre·tion (si krē′shən), *n.* **1.** the process by which a cell or gland produces a substance that fulfills some function within the organism or is excreted. **2.** the substance itself. —**se·cre′to·ry** (-krē′tə rē), *adj.*

se·cre·tive (sē′kri tiv, si krē′-), *adj.* having the tendency of keeping things secret. —**se′cre·tive·ly,** *adv.* —**se′cre·tive·ness,** *n.*

sect (sekt), *n.* **1.** a religious denomination, esp. one deviating from a generally accepted tradition. **2.** any group united by a specific doctrine or under a leader.

sect., section.

sec·tar·i·an (sek târ′ē ən), *adj.* **1.** of or belonging to a sect. **2.** narrowly limited in interest or scope. —*n.* **3.** a sectarian person. —**sec′tar′i·an·ism,** *n.*

sec·ta·ry (sek′tə rē), *n., pl.* **-ries.** a member of a particular sect.

sec·tile (sek′til), *adj.* capable of being cut smoothly with a knife. —**sec·til′i·ty,** *n.*

sec·tion (sek′shən), *n.* **1.** a part or piece cut off or separated. **2.** a distinct part or subdivision. **3.** a representation of an object as it would appear if cut straight through. —*v.t.* **4.** to cut or divide into sections.

sec·tion·al (sek′shən′l), *adj.* **1.** of or limited to a particular section or district. **2.** composed of several sections. —**sec′tion·al·ism,** *n.* —**sec′tion·al·ly,** *adv.*

sec′tion gang′, a group of workers who take care of a section of railroad track.

sec·tor (sek′tər), *n.* **1.** *Geom.* the part of a circle that is cut off by two radii. **2.** a part of a military area assigned to a particular unit. —**sec′tor·al,** *adj.*

sec·u·lar (sek′yə lər), *adj.* **1.** of or concerned with worldly or nonreligious things. **2.** not bound by monastic vows. —**sec′u·lar·ism,** *n.* —**sec′u·lar·ist,** *n., adj.* —**sec′u·lar·is′·tic,** *adj.* —**sec′u·lar·ly,** *adv.*

sec·u·lar·ize (sek′yə lə rīz′), *v.t.,* **-ized, -iz·ing.** to transfer (property) from ecclesiastical to civil possession or use. —**sec′u·lar·i·za′tion,** *n.* —**sec′u·lar·iz′er,** *n.*

se·cure (si kyŏŏr′), *adj., v.,* **-cured, -cur·ing.** —*adj.* **1.** free from danger or harm. **2.** free from care or anxiety. **3.** firmly fixed or fastened. **4.** sure or certain. —*v.t.* **5.** to get hold or possession of. **6.** to secure or make secure or safe. **7.** to fix or fasten firmly. **8.** to make sure or certain. **9.** to assure payment of by pledging property. —**se·cure′ly,** *adv.* —**se·cure′ness,** *n.* —**se·cur′er,** *n.*

se·cu·ri·ty (si kyŏŏr′i tē), *n., pl.* **-ties,** *adj.* —*n.* **1.** freedom from danger or harm. **2.** freedom from care or anxiety. **3.** something that secures or makes safe. **4.** property deposited as a pledge, as for repayment of a loan. **5.** Usually, **securities.** stocks and bonds.

secu′rity blan′ket, something that gives one a sense of protection.

secy., secretary. Also, **sec′y.**

se·dan (si dan′), *n.* **1.** an enclosed automobile body having two or four doors and two full-length seats. **2.** (formerly) an enclosed vehicle for one person, carried on poles by two persons.

se·date (si dāt′), *adj., v.,* **-dat·ed, -dat·ing.** —*adj.* **1.** undisturbed by passion or excitement. —*v.t.* **2.** to calm or treat with a sedative. —**se·date′ly,** *adv.* —**se·date′ness,** *n.* —**se·da′tion,** *n.* —**Syn. 1.** composed, staid, unperturbed.

sed·a·tive (sed′ə tiv), *adj.* **1.** relieving pain or tension. —*n.* **2.** a sedative drug.

sed·en·tar·y (sed′ᵊn ter′ē), *adj.* characterized by or accustomed to much sitting and little physical activity. —**sed′en·tar′i·ness,** *n.*

Se·der (sā′dər), *n.* a ceremonial dinner celebrated by Jews at Passover, in commemoration of the Exodus.

sedge (sej), *n.* a rushlike or grasslike plant growing in wet places. —**sedg′y,** *adj.*

sed·i·ment (sed′ə mənt), *n.* **1.** loose solid matter that settles to the bottom of a liquid. **2.** *Geol.* organic matter deposited by water, air, or ice. —**sed′i·men·ta′tion,** *n.*

sed·i·men·ta·ry (sed′ə men′tə rē), *adj.* **1.** of, containing, or resembling sediment. **2.** *Geol.* formed by the deposit of sediment, as certain rocks.

se·di·tion (si dish'ən), *n.* incitement of .public disorder .or rebellion against a government. —**se·di'tion·ist,** *n.* —**se·di'tious,** *adj.*

se·duce (si doos', -dyoos'), *v.t.,* **-duced, -duc·ing. 1.** to persuade (someone usually young or inexperienced) to have illicit sexual intercourse, esp. for the first time. **2.** to lead astray, as from duty. **3.** to win over or attract. —**se·duc'er,** *n.* —**se·duc'tion** (-duk'shən), *n.* —**se·duc'tive,** *adj.* —**se·duc'tress,** *n.fem.*

sed·u·lous (sej'ə ləs), *adj.* diligent in attention. **2.** persistently maintained. —**sed'u·lous·ly,** *adv.* —**sed'u·lous·ness,** *n.*

see¹ (sē), *v.,* **saw, seen, see·ing.** —*v.t.* **1.** to perceive with the eyes. **2.** to perceive mentally. **3.** to form a mental image of. **4.** to be cognizant of. **5.** to foresee. **6.** to ascertain or find out. **7.** to undergo or experience. **8.** to make sure: *See that the work is done.* **9.** to visit or meet. **10.** to receive as a visitor. **11.** to attend or escort: *to see someone home.* —*v.i.* **12.** to have the power of sight. **13.** to understand intellectually. **14.** to consider or think *Let me see—how does that song go?* **15. see after,** to take care of. **16. see through, a.** to penetrate to the true nature of. **b.** to stay with until completion. **17. see to,** to take care of. Also, **see about.** —**see'a·ble,** *adj.* —**Syn. 1.** behold, notice. **2.** comprehend, understand.

see² (sē), *n.* the authority, office, or jurisdiction of a bishop.

seed (sēd), *n., pl.* **seeds, seed,** *v.* —*n.* **1.** a fertilized, matured plant ovule containing an embryo that can form a new plant. **2.** such ovules collectively. **3.** the source or cause of anything. **4.** offspring or progeny. **5.** sperm or semen. **6. go or run to seed, a.** to pass to the stage of yielding seed. **b.** to decay or deteriorate. —*v.t.* **7.** to sow with seed **8.** to remove the seeds from (fruit). **9.** to arrange (players in a tournament) so that ranking ones will not meet in early rounds. —*v.i.* **10.** to produce or shed seed. —**seed'er,** *n.* —**seed'less,** *adj.*

seed·ling (sēd'ling), *n.* **1.** a plant grown from a seed. **2.** any young plant.

seed' mon'ey, capital used as initial operating funds for a new enterprise.

seed·y (sē'dē), *adj.,* **seed·i·er, seed·i·est. 1.** abounding in seed. **2.** poorly kept or run-down. **3.** shabbily dressed. —**seed'i·ly,** *adv.* —**seed'i·ness,** *n.*

see·ing (sē'ing), *conj.* in view of the fact that.

seek (sēk), *v.t.,* **sought, seek·ing.** —*v.t.* **1.** to try to find or discover. **2.** to try to obtain. **3.** to try or attempt. —**seek'er,** *n.*

seem (sēm), *v.i.* **1.** to give the outward appearance of being. **2.** to appear to oneself. **3.** to appear to exist. **4.** to appear to be true or evident.

seem·ing (sē'ming), *adj.* appearing to be true or evident —**seem'ing·ly,** *adv.* —**seem'ing·ness,** *n.*

seem·ly (sēm'lē), *adj.,* **-li·er, -li·est. 1.** in propriety or good taste. **2.** *Archaic.* of pleasing appearance. —**seem'li·ness,** *n.* —**Syn. 1.** appropriate, befitting, suitable.

seen (sēn), *v.* pp. of see¹.

seep (sēp), *v.i.* to flow gradually through small openings. —**seep'age** (-ij), *n.*

se·er (sēr), *n.* a person who foretells future events. —**seer'ess,** *n.fem.*

seer·suck·er (sēr'suk'ər), *n.* a light fabric of cotton or rayon with crinkled stripes.

see·saw (sē'sô'), *n.* **1.** a recreation in which two children alternately ride up and down while seated at opposite ends of a plank balanced at the middle. **2.** an up-and-down or a back-and-forth movement or procedure. —*v.i., v.t.* **3.** to move or cause to move in a seesaw manner.

seethe (sēth), *v.i.,* **seethed, seeth·ing. 1.** to surge or foam as if boiling. **2.** to be agitated, as by anger. —**seeth'ing·ly,** *adv.*

see·through (sē'throo'), *adj.* physically transparent: *a see-through blouse.*

seg·ment (*n.* seg'mənt; *v.* seg ment'), *n.* **1.** one of the parts into which something naturally separates or is divided. **2.** *Geom.* a part of a circle cut off by a straight line. —*v.t., v.i.* **3.** to separate or divide into segments. —**seg·men'tal,** *adj.* —**seg'men·ta'tion,** *n.*

seg·re·gate (seg'rə gāt'), *v.t.,* **-gat·ed, -gat·ing. 1.** to set apart from others. **2.** to separate (a specific racial, religious, or other group) from the rest of society. —**seg're·ga'tion,** *n.*

seg·re·ga·tion·ist (seg'rə gā'shə nist), *n.* a person who favors or practices segregation. esp. racial segregation.

seign·ior (sēn'yər), *n.* a feudal lord. —**sei·gnio'ri·al,** *adj.*

seine (sān), *n., v.,* **seined, sein·ing.** —*n.* **1.** a large fishing net having floats at the upper edge and sinkers at the lower. —*v.t., v.i.* **2.** to fish (for) with a seine. —**sein'er,** *n.*

Seine (sān), *n.* a river in N France.

seism (sī'zəm, -səm), *n. Rare,* an earthquake.

seis·mic (sīz'mik, sīs'-), *adj.* of, resembling, or caused by an earthquake. —**seis'mi·cal·ly,** *adv.* —**seis·mic·i·ty** (sīz mis'i tē), *n.*

seis·mo·gram (sīz′mə gram′, sīs′-), *n.* a record made by a seismograph.

seis·mo·graph (sīz′mə graf′, -gräf′, sīs′-), *n.* an instrument for measuring and recording the vibrations of earthquakes. —**seis·mog′ra·pher** (-mog′rə fər), *n.* —**seis′mo·graph′ic,** *adj.* —**seis·mog′ra·phy,** *n.*

seis·mol·o·gy (sīz mol′ə jē, sīs-), *n.* the science or study of earthquakes and their phenomena. —**seis′mo·log′i·cal** (-mə loj′i kəl), *adj.* —**seis·mol′o·gist,** *n.*

seis·mom·e·ter (sīz mom′i tər, sīs-), *n.* a seismograph equipped for measuring the actual movement of the ground. —**seis′mo·met′ric** (-mə me′trik, sīs′-), *adj.*

seize (sēz), *v.t.,* **seized, seiz·ing. 1.** to take hold of suddenly or forcibly. **2.** to take possession of legally. **3.** to arrest or capture. **4.** to take advantage of promptly. **5.** to affect suddenly and deeply.

sei·zure (sē′zhər), *n.* **1.** the act or an instance of seizing. **2.** a sudden attack, as of some disease.

sel., 1. select. **2.** selected. **3.** selection.

sel·dom (sel′dəm), *adv.* on only a few occasions.

se·lect (si lekt′), *v.t., v.i.* **1.** to pick out carefully from among many as most suitable. —*adj.* **2.** chosen in this manner. **3.** of special excellence. **4.** careful in selecting. **5.** carefully chosen. —**se·lec′tive,** *adj.* —**se·lec′tiv′i·ty,** *n.* —**se·lect′ness,** *n.* —**se·lec′tor,** *n.* —**Syn. 2, 3.** choice, preferred. **4.** discriminating. **5.** exclusive.

se·lect·ee (si lek tē′), *n.* a person selected by draft for military service.

se·lec·tion (si lek′shən), *n.* **1.** the act of selecting or state of being selected. **2.** one or a number of persons or things selected. **3.** See **natural selection.**

selec′tive serv′ice, a system for choosing young men for compulsory military service.

se·lect·man (si lekt′mən), *n.* one of a board of town officers in most parts of New England.

sel·e·nite (sel′ə nīt′, si lē′nīt), *n.* a variety of gypsum found in transparent crystals.

se·le·ni·um (si lē′nē əm), *n. Chem.* a nonmetallic element having an electrical resistance that varies under the influence of light, used in photoelectric cells. *Symbol:* Se; *at. wt.:* 78.96; *at. no.:* 34.

sel·e·nog·ra·phy (sel′ə nog′rə fē), *n.* the branch of astronomy that deals with the physical geography of the moon. —**sel′e·nog′ra·pher,** *n.*

sel·e·nol·o·gy (sel′ə nol′ə jē), *n.* the branch of astronomy that deals with the physical characteristics of the moon.

self (self), *n., pl.* **selves,** *adj., pron., pl.* **selves.** —*n.* **1.** a person or thing considered as a complete and separate individual. **2.** a person's nature or character. **3.** self-interest. —*adj.* **4.** of the same material or pattern with the rest: *a self lining.* —*pron.* **5.** *Informal.* myself, yourself, himself, or herself.

self-, a prefix meaning: **a.** of the self: *self-analysis.* **b.** by oneself or itself: *self-appointed.* **c.** to, with, toward, for, on, or in oneself: *self-complacent.* **d.** inherent in oneself or itself: *self-explanatory.* **e.** independent: *self-government.* **f.** automatic: *self-operating.*

self-ad·dressed (self′ə drest′), *adj.* addressed for return to the sender.

self-cen·tered (self′sen′tərd), *adj.* concerned only or primarily with one's self. —**self′-cen′tered·ly,** *adv.* —**self′-cen′tered·ness,** *n.*

self-con·fi·dence (self′kon′fi dəns, self′-), *n.* confidence in one's own abilities, judgment, etc. —**self′-con′fi·dent,** *adj.* —**self′con′fi·dent·ly,** *adv.*

self′-a·ban′don·ment, *n.*	**self′-a·nal′y·sis,** *n.*	**self′-be·tray′al,** *n.*
self′-a·base′ment, *n.*	**self′-ap·plause′,** *n.*	**self′-caused′,** *adj.*
self′-ab·hor′rence, *n.*	**self′-ap·point′ed,** *adj.*	**self′-clean′ing,** *adj.*
self′-ab·sorbed′, *adj.*	**self′-ap·pre′ci·a′tion,** *n.*	**self′-clos′ing,** *adj.*
self′-ac′cu·sa′tion, *n.*	**self′-ap′pro·ba′tion,** *n.*	**self′-com·mand′,** *n.*
self′-ac·cused′, *adj.*	**self′-ap·prov′al,** *n.*	**self′-com·mit′ment,** *n.*
self′-ac·cus′ing, *adj.*	**self′-ap·prov′ing,** *adj.*	**self′-com·pla′cent,** *adj.*
self′-act′ing, *adj.*	**self′-as·sert′ing,** *adj.*	**self′-con·ceit′,** *n.*
self′-ad·just′ing, *adj.*	**self′-as·ser′tion,** *n.*	**self′-con·cern′,** *n.*
self′-ad·min′is·tered, *adj.*	**self′-as·ser′tive,** *adj.*	**self′-con·dem·na′tion,** *n.*
self′-ad′mi·ra′tion, *n.*	**self′-as·sumed′,** *adj.*	**self′-con·demned′,** *adj.*
self′-ad·vance′ment, *n.*	**self′-as·sum′ing,** *adj.*	**self′-con·fessed′,** *adj.*
self′-ad′ver·tise′ment, *n.*	**self′-as·sump′tion,** *n.*	**self′-con·fine′ment,** *n.*
self′-ag·gran′dize·ment, *n.*	**self′-as·sur′ance,** *n.*	**self′-con·fin′ing,** *adj.*
	self′-as·sured′, *adj.*	**self′-con·grat′u·la′tion,** *n.*
self′-ag·gran′diz·ing, *adj.*	**self′-a·ware′,** *adj.;*	
self′-a·lign′ing, *adj.*	**-ness,** *n.*	

self-con·scious (self'kon'shəs, self'-), *adj.* **1.** embarrassed in the presence of others. **2.** made uneasy by the observation of others. —**self'-con'scious·ly**, *adv.* —**self'-con'scious·ness**, *n.*

self-con·tained (self'kən tānd', self'-), *adj.* **1.** having in itself everything necessary. **2.** reserved or restrained. **3.** self-controlled or self-possessed. —**self-con·tain·ed·ly** (self'kən tā'nid-lē, self'-), *adv.* —**self'-con·tain'ed·ness**, *n.*

self-con·trol (self'kən trōl', self'-), *n.* control over one's actions, feelings, etc. —**self'-con·trolled'**, *adj.*

self-de·fense (self'di fens', self'-), *n.* **1.** the use of force in defending oneself against attack. **2.** a claim or plea that one's use of force was necessary for one's own safety. **3.** defense, as by argument, of one's own effort, plan, etc.

self-de·ni·al (self'di nī'əl, self'-), *n.* the denial of one's own desires, pleasures, etc. —**self'-de·ny'ing**, *adj.* —**self'-de·ny'ing·ly**, *adv.*

self-de·struct (self'di strukt'), *v.i.* **1.** to destroy oneself or itself. —*adj.* **2.** causing something to self-destruct. —**self'-de·struc'tion**, *n.* —**self'-de·struc'tive**, *adj.*

self-de·ter·mi·na·tion (self'di tûr'mə-nā'shən, self'-), *n.* **1.** freedom from external control or influence. **2.** the right of a people to determine the way in which they shall be governed. —**self'-de·ter'mined**, *adj.*

self-ef·fac·ing (self'i fā'sing), *adj.*

keeping oneself in the background, as in humility. —**self'-ef·face'ment**, *n.*

self-ev·i·dent (self'ev'i dənt, self'-), *adj.* evident without proof or demonstration.

self-ex·plan·a·to·ry (self'ik splan'ə-tōr'ē, -tôr'ē, self'-), *adj.* needing no explanation.

self-ex·pres·sion (self'ik spresh'ən, self'-), *n.* expression of one's personality, esp. through the arts.

self-gov·ern·ment (self'guv'ərn mənt, -ər mənt, self'-), *n.* government of a nation, state, or other group by its own members. —**self'-gov'erned**, *adj.* —**self'-gov'ern·ing**, *adj.*

self-im·por·tant (self'im pôr't°nt, self'-), *adj.* having or showing too high an opinion of one's own worth. —**self'-im·por'tance**, *n.* —**self'-im·por'tant·ly**, *adv.*

self-in·ter·est (self'in'tər ist, -trist, self'-), *n.* **1.** devotion to one's own interest or advantage, often without regard for others. **2.** personal interest or advantage. —**self'-in'ter·est·ed**, *adj.*

self·ish (sel'fish), *adj.* **1.** concerned only with one's own interests. **2.** revealing care only for oneself. —**self'ish·ly**, *adv.* —**self'ish·ness**, *n.*

self·less (self'lis), *adj.* having little or no concern for oneself. —**self'less·ly**, *adv.* —**self'less·ness**, *n.*

self-made (self'mād'), *adj.* **1.** having succeeded in life unaided, esp. of a person born in poverty: *a self-made millionaire.* **2.** made by oneself or itself.

self'-con·sis'ten·cy, n.
self'-con·sis'tent, adj.
self'-con·sti·tut'ed, adj.
self'-con·sum'ing, adj.
self'-con·tempt', n.
self'-con·tent', adj., n.
self'-con·tent'ed·ly, adv.
self'-con·tent'ment, n.
self'-con·vict'ed, adj.
self'-cor·rect'ing, adj.
self'-cre·at'ed, adj.
self'-crit'i·cal, adj.
self'-de·ceit', n.
self'-de·ceiv'ing, adj.
self'-ded'i·ca'tion, n.
self'-de·feat'ing, adj.
self'-de·fin'ing, adj.
self'-deg'ra·da'tion, n.
self'-de·pend'ence, n.
self'-de·pend'ent, adj.
self'-dep're·cat'ing, adj.
self'-de·pre'ci·a'tion, n.
self'-de·vel'op·ment, n.
self'-di·rect'ed, adj.
self'-di·rect'ing, adj.
self'-di·rec'tion, n.
self'-dis'ci·pline, n.
self'-dis·cov'er·y, n.
self'-dis·sat'is·fac'tion, n.

self'-dis·trust', n.
self'-dis·trust'ful, adj.
self'-dis·trust'ing, adj.
self'-doubt', n.
self'-driv'en, adj.
self'-ed'u·cat'ed, adj.
self'-e·lect'ed, adj.
self'-em·ployed', adj.
self'-em·ploy'ment, n.
self'-en·am'ored, adj.
self'-en·closed', adj.
self'-en·joy'ment, n.
self'-en·rich'ment, n.
self'-es·teem', n.
self'-ex·al·ta'tion, n.
self'-ex·am'i·na'tion, n.
self'-ex·pand'ing, adj.
self'-fer'ti·li·za'tion, n.
self'-fo'cused, adj.
self'-fo'cus·ing, adj.
self'-fo'cused, adj.
self'-fo'cus·sing, adj.
self'-for·get'ful, adj.
self'-ful·fill'ing, adj.
self'-gen'er·at'ing, adj.
self'-giv'ing, adj.
self'-glo'ri·fi·ca'tion, n.
self'-glo'ri·fy'ing, adj.
self'-gov'erned, adj.

self'-grat'i·fi·ca'tion, n.
self'-hate', n.
self'-ha'tred, n.
self'-heal'ing, adj.
self'-help', n.
self'-hu·mil'i·at'ing, adj.
self'-hu·mil'i·a'tion, n.
self'-hyp·no'sis, n.
self'-ig·nite', v.i.,
  -nit·ed, -nit·ing.
self'-im'age, n.
self'-im·posed', adj.
self'-im·prove'ment, n.
self'-in·crim'i·nat'ing,
  adj.
self'-in·duced', adj.
self'-in·dul'gence, n.
self'-in·dul'gent, adj.
self'-in·flict'ed, adj.
self'-in·i'ti·at'ed, adj.
self'-in·i'tia·tive, n.
self'-in·struct'ed, adj.
self'-knowl'edge, n.
self'-lim'i·ted, adj.
self'-loath'ing, n., adj.
self'-love', n.
self'-mas'ter·y, n.
self'-named', adj.
self'-ne·glect', n.

self-pos·ses·sion (self/pə zesh/ən, self/-), n. control of one's feelings, behavior, etc., esp. when under pressure. —self/-pos·sessed/, adj.

self-re·li·ance (self/ri li/əns, self/-), n. reliance on one's own powers, resources, etc. —self/-re·li/ant, adj. —relf/-re·li/ant·ly, adv.

self-re·spect (self/ri spekt/, self/-), n. proper esteem for the dignity of one's own character. —self/-respect/ing, adj.

self-right·eous (self/rī/chəs, self/-), adj. smugly confident of one's own righteousness. —self/-right/eous·ly, adv. —self/-right/eous·ness, n.

self·same (self/sām/), adj. the very same.

self-seek·ing (self/sē/kiṅg), adj. furthering one's own aims and interests. —self/-seek/er, n.

self-serv·ice (self/sûr/vis), n. 1. unaided service of oneself, as in a cafeteria. —adj. 2. operated by means of self-service.

self-start·er (self/stär/tər), n. a device that starts an internal-combustion engine without cranking by hand. —self/-start/ing, adj.

self-styled (self/stīld/), adj. so called or considered by oneself.

self-suf·fi·cient (self/sə fish/ənt, self/-), adj. able to exist and function without outside help. —self/-suf·fi/cien·cy, n.

self-taught (self/tôt/), adj. having taught oneself, with little or no formal instruction.

self-will (self/wil/, self/-), n. stubborn willfulness, as in pursuing one's own aims. —self/-willed/, adj.

self-wind·ing (self/wīn/diṅg), adj. kept wound by an automatic mechanism, as a watch.

sell (sel), v., **sold, sell·ing,** n. —v.t. 1. to transfer (goods) or render (services) in exchange for money. 2. to offer for sale. 3. to persuade or induce to buy. 4. to cause or persuade to accept. —v.i. 5. to engage in selling something. 6. to be sold or offered for sale. 7. to be in demand by buyers. 8. **sell out, a.** to dispose of entirely by selling. **b.** *Informal.* to betray or turn traitor. —n. 9. the act or method of selling. —sell/er, n.

sell/ers' mar/ket, a market in which goods and services are scarce and prices relatively high.

sell·out (sel/out/), n. 1. the act of selling out. 2. an entertainment for which all the seats are sold.

Selt·zer (selt/sər), n. 1. a natural effervescent mineral water containing common salt. 2. *(often l.c.)* a prepared water of similar composition.

sel·vage (sel/vij), n. the edge of woven fabric finished so as to prevent raveling. Also, **sel/vedge.** —sel/vaged, adj.

selves (selvz), n., pron. pl. of **self.**

se·man·tic (si man/tik), adj. 1. of or arising from meanings in language. 2. of or pertaining to semantics. Also, **se·man/ti·cal.** —se·man/ti·cal·ly, adv.

se·man·tics (si man/tiks), n. 1. the study of meanings in language, including its historical changes. 2. the critical study of the functions of words and nonverbal symbols. 3. connotative interpretation. —se·man/ti·cist (-ti sist), n.

sem·a·phore (sem/ə fôr/, -fōr/), n. any device or apparatus for signaling by changing the positions of lights, flags, etc.

sem·blance (sem/bləns), n. 1. outward aspect or appearance. 2. unreal appearance. 3. a likeness or image.

se·men (sē/mən), n. the fluid produced in the male reproductive organs, containing spermatozoa.

---

self/-oc/cu·pied/, adj.	self/-pun/ish·ment, n.	self/-sac/ri·fic/ing, adj.
self/-op/er·at/ing, adj.	self/-re/al·i·za/tion, n.	self/-sat/is·fac/tion, n.
self/-or·dained/, adj.	self/-rec/ol·lec/tion, n.	self/-sat/is·fied/, adj.
self/-o·rig/i·nat/ed, adj.	self/-re·cord/ing, adj.	self/-schooled/, adj.
self/-per·pet/u·at/ing, adj.	self/-re·flec/tion, n.	self/-scru/ti·ny, n.
self/-pit/y, n.	self/-ref/or·ma/tion, n.	self/-seal/ing, adj.
self/-pol/li·na/tion, n.	self/-re·gard/, n.	self/-serv/ing, adj.
self/-por/trait, n.	self/-reg/is·ter·ing, adj.	self/-sup·port/ing, adj.
self/-pow/ered, adj.	self/-reg/u·lat/ing, adj.	self/-sus·tain/ing, adj.
self/-praise/, n.	self/-reg/u·la/tion, n.	self/-tor/ment, n.
self/-pre·oc/cu·pa/tion, n.	self/-re·peat/ing, adj.	self/-tor·ment/ing, adj.
self/-prep/a·ra/tion, n.	self/-re·pres/sion, n.	self/-trained/, adj.
self/-pre·scribed/, adj.	self/-re·proach/, n.	self/-trans/for·ma/tion, n.
self/-pres/er·va/tion, n.	self/-re·proof/, n.	self/-treat/ment, n.
self/-pro·claimed/, adj.	self/-re·sent/ment, n.	self/-trust/, n.
self/-pro·duced/, adj.	self/-re·straint/, n.	self/-un/der·stand/ing, n.
self/-pro·fessed/, adj.	self/-re·strict/ed, adj.	self/-vin/di·ca/tion, n.
self/-pro·pelled/, adj.	self/-re·stric/tion, n.	self/-wor/ship, n.
self/-pro·pul/sion, n.	self/-rule/, n.	
self/-pro·tec/tion, n.	self/-sac/ri·fice, n.	

se·mes·ter (si mes'tər), *n.* either of the two terms into which an academic year is usually divided. —**se·mes'tral, se·mes'tri·al** (-trē əl), *adj.*

semi-, prefix meaning: **a.** half: *semicircle.* **b.** partly: *semiskilled.* **c.** occurring or done twice in a specified period: *semiannual.*

sem·i·an·nu·al (sem'ē an'yōō əl, sem'ī-), *adj.* **1.** occurring or published twice a year. **2.** lasting for half a year. —**sem'i·an'nu·al·ly,** *adv.*

sem·i·au·to·mat·ic (sem'ē ô'tō mat'ik, sem'ī-), *adj.* (of a firearm) automatically ejecting an empty cartridge case but requiring a squeeze of the trigger to fire each individual shot. —**sem'i·au'to·mat'i·cal·ly,** *adv.*

sem·i·cir·cle (sem'i sûr'kəl), *n.* half of a circle. —**sem'i·cir'cu·lar** (-kyə-lər), *adj.*

sem·i·co·lon (sem'i kō'lən), *n.* a punctuation mark (;) used to indicate a more distinct separation than shown by the comma.

sem·i·con·duc·tor (sem'ē kən duk'tər, sem'ī-), *n.* a substance whose electric conductivity is between that of a metal and an insulator, esp. germanium or silicon. —**sem'i·con·duct'ing,** *adj.*

sem·i·fi·nal (sem'ē fīn'ºl, sem'i-), *adj.* **1.** being next to the last in a tournament or competition. —*n.* **2.** a semifinal round or contest.

sem·i·month·ly (sem'ē munth'lē, sem'ī-), *adj.* **1.** occurring or published twice a month. —*adv.* **2.** twice a month.

—**Usage.** See **bimonthly.**

sem·i·nal (sem'ə nºl), *adj.* **1.** of or pertaining to semen or seed. **2.** having possibilities of future develop-

ment. **3.** highly original or creative. —**sem'i·nal·ly,** *adv.*

sem·i·nar (sem'ə när'), *n.* **1.** a small group of advanced students engaged in original research under a professor. **2.** a course for such students.

sem·i·nar·y (sem'ə ner'ē), *n., pl.* -**nar·ies.** a special school that trains students for the priesthood, ministry, or rabbinate. —**sem'i·nar'i·an** (-nâr'-ē ən), *n.*

Sem·i·nole (sem'ə nōl'), *n., pl.* -**noles,** -**nole.** a member of an Indian people in Florida and in Oklahoma.

sem·i·per·me·a·ble (sem'ē pûr'mē ə-bəl, sem'ī-), *adj.* permeable to certain substances only. —**sem'i·per'me·a·bil'i·ty,** *n.*

sem·i·pre·cious (sem'ē presh'əs, sem'ī-), *adj.* having value far lower than precious gems, as a garnet.

sem·i·pri·vate (sem'ē prī'vit, sem'ī-), *adj.* shared with a few other inpatients, as a hospital room.

sem·i·pro (sem'ē prō', sem'ī-), *n., pl.* -**pros.** *Informal,* semiprofessional.

sem·i·pro·fes·sion·al (sem'ē prə fesh'ə-nºl, sem'ī-), *n.* a person who is active in some field or sport for pay on a part-time basis. —**sem'i·pro·fes'sion·al·ly,** *adv.*

sem·i·skilled (sem'ē skild', sem'ī-), *adj.* having or requiring limited training and skill.

Sem·ite (sem'īt), *n.* a member of any of various ancient and modern peoples including the Hebrews and Arabs.

Se·mit·ic (sə mit'ik), *n.* **1.** an important family of Afro-Asiatic languages, including Arabic, Hebrew, etc. —*adj.* **2.** of or pertaining to the Semites or their languages, esp. of the Jews.

---

sem'i·ac'tive, *adj.*	**sem'i·dry',** *adj.*	**sem'i·of·fi'cial,** *adj.*
sem'i·ag'ri·cul'tur·al, *adj.*	**sem'i·e·rect',** *adj.*	**sem'i·per'ma·nent,** *adj.*
sem'i·a·quat'ic, *adj.*	**sem'i·fic'tion·al,** *adj.;*	**sem'i·pet'ri·fied',** *adj.*
sem'i·ar'id, *adj.*	**-ly,** *adv.*	**sem'i·po·lit'i·cal,** *adj.*
sem'i·au·ton'o·mous, *adj.*	**sem'i·fin'ished,** *adj.*	**sem'i·prim'i·tive,** *adj.*
sem'i·bi'o·graph'i·cal,	**sem'i·for'mal,** *adj.*	**sem'i·pub'lic,** *adj.*
adj.; -ly, adv.	**sem'i·formed',** *adj.*	**sem'i·re·fined',** *adj.*
sem'i·civ'i·lized, *adj.*	**sem'i·il·lit'er·ate,** *adj.*	**sem'i·res'o·lute',** *adj.*
sem'i·clas'si·cal, *adj.;*	**sem'i·in·dus'tri·al,** *adj.*	**sem'i·re·spect'a·bil'i·ty,**
-ly, *adv.*	**sem'i·in·dus'tri·al·ized',**	*n.*
sem'i·con'scious, *adj.*	*adj.*	**sem'i·re·spect'a·ble,** *adj.*
sem'i·con'scious·ness, *n.*	**sem'i·in·stinc'tive,** *adj.;*	**sem'i·re·tired',** *adj.*
sem'i·crys'tal·line, *adj.*	**-ly,** *adv.*	**sem'i·re·tire'ment,** *n.*
sem'i·dai'ly, *adj., adv.*	**sem'i·in·tox'i·cat'ed,** *adj.*	**sem'i·rig'id,** *adj.*
sem'i·de·pend'ence, *n.*	**sem'i·leg'end·ar'y,** *adj.*	**sem'i·ru'ral,** *adj.*
semi'i·de·pend'ent, *adj.;*	**sem'i·lit'er·ate,** *adj.*	**sem'i·sa'cred,** *adj.*
-ly, *adv.*	**sem'i·lu'nar,** *adj.*	**sem'i·sa·tir'i·cal,** *adj.;*
sem'i·des'ert, *adj.*	**sem'i·ma·ture',** *adj.*	**-ly,** *adv.*
sem'i·de·tached', *adj.*	**sem'i·mys'ti·cal,** *adj.*	**sem'i·se'ri·ous,** *adj.*
sem'i·di·vine', *adj.*	**sem'i·myth'i·cal,** *adj.*	**sem'i·so'cial·is'tic,** *adj.*
sem'i·do·mes'ti·cat'ed,	**sem'i·nor'mal,** *adj.*	**sem'i·soft',** *adj.*
adj.	**sem'i·nude',** *adj.*	**sem'i·sol'id,** *adj.*
sem'i·do·mes'ti·ca'tion,	**sem'i·nu'di·ty,** *n.*	**sem'i·sweet',** *adj.*
n.	**sem'i·ob·liv'i·ous,** *adj.*	**sem'i·tra·di'tion·al,** *adj.*

sem·i·trail·er (sem′i trā′lər), *n.* a detachable freight trailer resting its forward end on a tractor.

sem·i·vow·el (sem′ē vou′əl), *n.* a speech sound of vowel quality used as a consonant, as (w) in *wet* or (y) in *yet.*

sem·i·week·ly (sem′ē wēk′lē, sem′ī-), *adj.* **1.** occurring or published twice a week. —*adv.* **2.** twice a week. —**Usage.** See biweekly.

sen., **1.** senate. **2.** senator. **3.** senior.

sen·ate (sen′it), *n.* **1.** (*cap.*) the upper house of the U.S. Congress or of many state legislatures. **2.** the supreme council of state in ancient Rome.

sen·a·tor (sen′ə tər), *n.* a member of a senate. —**sen·a·to′ri·al** (-tôr′ē əl, -tōr′-), *adj.*

send (send), *v.t.,* sent, send·ing. **1.** to cause to go. **2.** to cause to be transmitted, as a letter, **3.** to direct or propel, esp. with force. **4.** to emit or discharge. **5.** to cause to happen or befall. **6.** *Slang.* to delight or excite. **7. send for,** to request the coming or delivery of. —**send′·er,** *n.*

send·off (send′ôf′ -of′), *n. Informal.* **1.** a demonstration of good wishes for a person setting out on a trip or career. **2.** a start given to a person or thing.

Sen·e·ca (sen′ə kə), *n., pl.* -cas, -ca. a member of an Indian tribe located in western New York.

Sen·e·gal (sen′ə gôl′), *n.* a country in W Africa. —**Sen′e·ga·lese′,** *adj., n.*

se·nes·cent (se nes′ənt), *adj.* showing signs of growing old. —**se·nes′cence,** *n.*

se·nile (sē′nīl, -nil, sen′īl), *adj.* **1.** suffering from mental or physical decline because of old age. **2.** of or belonging to old age or aged persons. —**se·nil·i·ty** (si nil′i tē), *n.*

sen·ior (sēn′yər), *adj.* **1.** older or elder (often written as *Sr.* following the name of a father bearing the same full name as his son). **2.** having a higher rank or longer service. **3.** of or for a senior or seniors in schools. —*n.* **4.** a senior person. **5.** a student in his or her final year at a high school or college.

sen′ior chief′ pet′ty of′ficer, *U.S. Navy.* a petty officer ranking just below a master chief petty officer.

sen′ior cit′izen, an elderly person, esp. one over 65 years of age.

sen′ior high′ school′, a high school that usually includes grades 10, 11, and 12.

sen·ior·i·ty (sēn yôr′i tē, -yor′-), *n., pl.* -ties. **1.** the state of being senior.

2. rights and privileges resulting from length of service.

sen′ior mas′ter ser′geant, *U.S. Air Force.* a noncommissioned officer ranking just below a chief master sergeant.

sen·na (sen′ə), *n.* **1.** a tropical herb, shrub, or tree of the bean family. **2.** the dried leaflets of such a plant, used as a strong laxative.

se·ñor (sān yôr′, -yôr-, sēn-), *n., pl.* **se·ñors, se·ño·res** (se nyô′Res). *Spanish.* Mr. or sir.

se·ño·ra (sān yôr′ə, -yôr′ə, sēn-), *n. Spanish.* Mrs. or madam.

se·ño·ri·ta (sān yə rē′tə, sen′-), *n. Spanish* Miss.

sen·sa·tion (sen sā′shən), *n.* **1.** the ability or process of perceiving by the senses. **2.** an impression on the body or mind produced by the senses. **3.** a general feeling not directly attributable to any given stimulus, as discomfort, anxiety, or doubt. **4.** a state of excitement produced by some unusual act or event. **5.** the cause of such excitement.

sen·sa·tion·al (sen sā′shə nəl), *adj.* **1.** producing a strong reaction, intense interest, etc. **2.** extraordinary or outstanding. **3.** of physical sensation. —**sen·sa′tion·al·ly,** *adv.*

sen·sa·tion·al·ism (sen sā′shə nə liz′əm), *n.* the use of or interest in sensational subject matter or style. —**sen·sa′tion·al·ist,** *n.*

sense (sens), *n., v.,* sensed, sens·ing. —*n.* **1.** any of the five faculties, as sight, hearing, smell, taste, or touch, by which humans and animals perceive stimuli. **2.** a feeling or perception produced through the sense organs. **3.** any special capacity for reception, understanding, etc.: *a sense of humor.* **4.** Usually, **senses.** clear and sound judgment. **5.** sound, practical intelligence **6.** a more or less vague awareness or impression. **7.** the meaning of a word in a specific context. **8. in a sense,** according to one explanation. **9. make sense,** to be reasonable or sensible. —*v.t.* **10.** to perceive by the senses. **11.** to detect by an automatic means.

sense·less (sens′lis), *adj.* **1.** without sensation or feeling. **2.** stupid or foolish. **3.** meaningless or nonsensical. —**sense′less·ly,** *adv.*

sense′ or′gan, a specialized bodily structure that receives or is sensitive to stimuli.

sen·si·bil·i·ty (sen′sə bil′i tē), *n., pl.* -ties. **1.** capacity for sensation or feeling. **2.** Often, **sensibilities.** capacity for intellectual and aesthetic distinctions, feelings, tastes, etc.

sem′i·trans·lu′cent, *adj.* **sem′i·truth′ful,** *adj.* **sem′i·vol′un·tar′y,** *adj.*

sem′i·trans·par′ent, *adj.* **sem′i·ur′ban,** *adj.* **sem′i·year′ly,** *adj., adv.*

sen·si·ble (sen′sə bəl), *adj.* **1.** having or showing clear and sound judgment. **2.** keenly aware. **3.** capable of being perceived by the senses. **4.** capable of feeling or perceiving. —**sen′si·ble·ness,** *n.* —**sen′si·bly,** *adv.* —Syn. **1.** judicious, rational, wise.

sen·si·tive (sen′si tiv), *adj.* **1.** readily or excessively affected by external stimuli or influences. **2.** having acute sensibility. **3.** hurt or offended easily. **4.** highly responsive to certain agents, as photographic paper. **5.** able to measure or respond to very small amounts or changes, as a thermometer. **6.** sensory. —**sen′si·tive·ly,** *adv.* —**sen′si·tiv′i·ty, sen′si·tive·ness,** *n.* —Syn. **3.** impressionable, susceptible.

sen′sitiv′ity train′ing, a small, educationally oriented group of persons who meet regularly to improve their functioning as group members or leaders through increasing skills and awareness in a social context.

sen·si·tize (sen′si tīz′), *v.t., v.i.,* **-tized, -tiz·ing.** to make or become sensitive. —**sen′si·ti·za′tion,** *n.*

sen·si·tom·e·ter (sen′si tom′i tər), *n. Photog.* an instrument for testing the sensitivity of various types of film. —**sen′si·to·met′ric** (-sə tō me′trik), *adj.*

sen·sor (sen′sər), *n.* a device sensitive to light, temperature, or radiation that transmits a signal to a measuring or control device.

sen·so·ry (sen′sə rē), *adj.* of or pertaining to the senses or sensation.

sen·su·al (sen′shoo əl), *adj.* **1.** preoccupied with the pleasures of the senses, esp. sexual pleasures. **2.** of or pertaining to the body rather than the mind. —**sen′su·al·ist,** *n.* —**sen′su·al′i·ty** (-al′i tē), **sen′su·al·ness,** *n.* —**sen′su·al·ly,** *adv.* —Syn. **1.** voluptuous.

sen·su·ous (sen′shoo əs), *adj.* **1.** perceived by or affecting the senses. **2.** deriving pleasure from things that appeal to the senses. **3.** sensual (def. 1). —**sen′su·ous·ly,** *adv.* —**sen′su·ous·ness,** *n.*

sent (sent), *v.* pt. and pp. of **send.**

sen·tence (sen′təns), *n., v.,* **-tenced, -tenc·ing.** —*n.* **1.** *Gram.* a group of words that contains at least one subject and predicate, and expresses a complete statement. **2.** *Law.* **a.** the judicial determination of punishment. **b.** the punishment itself. —*v.t.* **3.** *Law.* to pronounce sentence upon. [< OF < L *sententia* opinion]

sen·ten·tious (sen ten′shəs), *adj.* **1.** given to excessive moralizing. **2.** abounding in pithy aphorisms or maxims, as style. —**sen·ten′tious·ly,** *adv.* —**sen·ten′tious·ness,** *n.*

sen·tient (sen′shənt), *adj.* **1.** able to perceive by the senses. **2.** experiencing sensation or feeling. —**sen′tient·ly,** *adv.*

sen·ti·ment (sen′tə mənt), *n.* **1.** refined or tender emotion. **2.** attitude toward something. **3.** a feeling or emotion. **4.** a thought influenced by feeling or emotion.

sen·ti·men·tal (sen′tə men′t⁹l), *adj.* **1.** expressing or appealing to tender emotions and feelings. **2.** arising from or serving sentiment. **3.** weakly emotional. —**sen′ti·men′tal·ism,** *n.* —**sen′ti·men′tal·ist,** *n.* —**sen′ti·men·tal′i·ty** (-tal′i tē), *n.* —**sen′ti·men′tal·ly,** *adv.*

sen·ti·men·tal·ize (sen′tə men′t⁹līz′), *v.,* **-ized, -iz·ing.** —*v.i.* **1.** to indulge in sentiment. —*v.t.* **2.** to view with sentiment. —**sen′ti·men′ta·li·za′tion,** *n.*

sen·ti·nel (sen′t⁹n⁹l), *n. Chiefly Literary.* a sentry.

sen·try (sen′trē), *n., pl.* **-tries.** a soldier stationed at a place to stand guard and prevent the passage of unauthorized persons.

Se·oul (sōl), *n.* the capital of South Korea.

Sep., September.

sep., **1.** separate. **2.** separated.

se·pal (sē′pəl), *n.* one of the leaflike parts of a flower calyx.

sep·a·ra·ble (sep′ər ə bəl, sep′rə-), *adj.* capable of being separated. —**sep′a·ra·bly,** *adv.*

sep·a·rate (*v.* sep′ə rāt′; *adj., n.* sep′ər it), *v.,* **-rat·ed, -rat·ing,** *adj., n.* —*v.t.* **1.** to put or keep apart by an intervening barrier or space. **2.** to divide into parts or groups. —*v.i.* **3.** to part or withdraw, as from personal association. **4.** (of a married couple) to stop living together but without getting a divorce. **5.** to become divided or disconnected. **6.** to go in different directions. —*adj.* **7.** not connected or joined. **8.** unconnected or distinct. **9.** existing or maintained independently. **10.** individual or particular; *each separate item.* —*n.* **11.** Usually, **separates.** women's outer garments that may be worn in combination. —**sep′a·rate·ly,** *adv.* —**sep′a·rate·ness,** *n.*

sep·a·ra·tion (sep′ə rā′shən), *n.* **1.** the act of separating or state of being separated. **2.** a place, line, or point of parting. **3.** something that separates or divides.

sep·a·ra·tist (sep′ə rā′tist, -ər ə tist), *n.* a person who practices or advocates separation, esp. from a religious or political body. —**sep′a·ra·tism,** *n.*

sep·a·ra·tive (sep′ə rā′tiv, -ər ə tiv), *adj.* **1.** tending to separate. **2.** causing separation.

sep·a·ra·tor (sep′ə rā′tər), *n.* **1.** a person or thing that separates. **2.** a machine for separating cream from milk.

se·pi·a (sē′pē ə), *n.* **1.** a dark-brown pigment. **2.** a dark brown.

sepn., separation.

sep·sis (sep′sis), *n.* bacterial invasion of the body, esp. by pathogenic organisms.

Sept., September.

Sep·tem·ber (sep tem′bər), *n.* the ninth month of the year, containing 30 days.

sep·tic (sep′tik), *adj.* causing or caused by sepsis.

sep·ti·ce·mi·a (sep′ti sē′mē ə), *n.* See **blood poisoning.**

sep′tic tank′, a tank in which sewage is decomposed and purified by bacteria.

sep·tu·a·ge·nar·i·an (sep′chōō ə jə·nâr′ē ən), *adj.* **1.** of the age of 70 years or between 70 and 80 years old. —*n.* **2.** a septuagenarian person.

Sep·tu·a·gint (sep′tōō ə jint′, -tyōō-, sep′chōō-) *n* the oldest Greek version of the Old Testament. —**Sep′·tu·a·gint′al** *adj.*

sep·tum (sep′təm), *n., pl.* **-ta** (-tə). a dividing wall or membrane in a plant or animal structure

sep·tu·ple (sep′tōō pəl, -tyōō-, sep tōō′pəl, -tyōō′-), *adj., v.,* **-pled, -pling.** —*adj* **1.** consisting of seven parts. **2.** seven times as great. —*v.t.* **3.** to make seven times as great.

sep·ul·cher (sep′əl kər), *n.* **1.** a burial vault built of rock or stone. —*v.t.* **2.** to place in a sepulcher. Also, *Brit.,* **sep′ul·chre.**

se·pul·chral (sə pul′krəl), *adj.* **1.** of or serving as a sepulcher **2.** suggestive of the tomb or burial. **3.** hollow and deep: *a sepulchral voice.* —**se·pul′chral·ly,** *adv.*

sep·ul·ture (sep′əl chər), *n. Archaic.* **1.** the act of entombing. **2.** a sepulcher.

seq., the following (one). [< L *sequens*]

seqq., the following (ones). [< L *sequentia*]

se·quel (sē′kwəl), *n.* **1.** a literary work that continues the narrative of a preceding work **2.** an event following something. **3.** a result or consequence

se·quence (sē′kwəns), *n.* **1.** the following of one thing after another. **2.** order of succession **3.** a connected series. **4.** something that follows. **5.** an uninterrupted portion of a motion-picture story —**se′quent,** *adj., n.* —**se·quen·tial** (si kwen′shəl), *adj.* —**se·quen′ti·al′i·ty,** *n.* —**se·quen′tial·ly,** *adv.*

se·ques·ter (si kwes′tər), *v.t.* **1.** to withdraw into hiding or solitude. **2.** to segregate, as a jury during a trial.

se·ques·trate (si kwes′trāt), *v.t.,* **-trat·ed, -trat·ing** *Law.* to seize and hold (a debtor's property) until legal claims are satisfied. —**se′ques·tra′tion,** *n.*

se·quin (sē′kwin), *n.* a small shining disk used to ornament a dress. —**se′quined,** *adj*

se·quoi·a (si kwoi′ə), *n.* either of two large coniferous trees of California.

ser., 1. serial **2.** series. **3.** sermon.

se·ra (sēr′ə), *n.* a pl. of **serum.**

se·ragl·io (si ral′yō, -räl′-), *n., pl.* **-ragl·ios.** harem (def. 1).

se·ra·pe (sə rä′pē), *n.* a colorful blanketlike shawl worn in Latin America.

ser·aph (ser′əf), *n., pl.* **-aphs, -a·phim** (-ə fim). a member of the highest order of angels —**se·raph′ic** (si raf′ik), *adj.* —**se·raph′i·cal·ly,** *adv.*

Ser·bi·a (sûr′bē ə), *n.* a constituent republic of Yugoslavia, in the SE part.

Ser·bi·an (sûr′bē ən), *adj.* **1.** of Serbia, its inhabitants, or their language. —*n.* **2.** a native or inhabitant of Serbia. **3.** the Slavic language of Serbia. Also **Serb** (sûrb).

sere (sēr), *adj Literary.* dry and withered, as flowers.

ser·e·nade (ser′ə nād′), *n., v.,* **-nad·ed, -nad·ing.** —*n.* **1.** a musical performance in the open air at night by a lover under the window of his lady. —*v.t., v.i.* **2.** to sing or play a serenade (to or for) —**ser′e·nad′er,** *n.*

ser·en·dip·i·ty (ser′ən dip′i tē), *n.* an aptitude for making desirable discoveries by accident. —**ser′en·dip′i·tous,** *adj*

se·rene (sə rēn′), *adj.* **1.** calm and unruffled **2.** clear, as a sky. —**se·rene′ly,** *adv.* —**se·ren′i·ty** (-ren′i tē), **se·rene′ness,** *n* —**Syn. 1.** peaceful, placid tranquil unperturbed.

serf (sûrf), *n.* a person in feudal servitude, attached to a lord's land and transferable with it from one owner to another. [< MF < L *serv(us)* slave] —**serf′dom,** *n.*

Serg., Sergeant. Also, **Sergt.**

serge (sûrj), *n* a strong, twilled fabric used esp for clothing.

ser·geant (sär′jənt), *n.* **1.** a noncommissioned officer ranking just above a corporal, as in the U.S. Army. **2.** a police officer ranking above an ordinary policeman or policewoman. —**ser′gean·cy, ser′geant·ship′,** *n.*

ser′geant at arms′, an officer of a legislative body whose main duty is to preserve order.

ser′geant first′ class′. *U.S. Army.* a noncommissioned officer ranking next above a staff sergeant.

ser′geant ma′jor, 1. *U.S. Army, Air Force, & Marine Corps.* a noncommissioned officer serving as chief administrative assistant in a unit headquarters. 2. *U.S. Marine Corps.* a noncommissioned officer ranking above a first sergeant.

se·ri·al (sēr′ē əl), *n.* 1. anything published or broadcast in short installments at regular intervals. —*adj.* 2. of or pertaining to a serial. 3. of or arranged in a series. —**se′ri·al·ist,** *n.* —**se′ri·al·ize′,** *v.t.* —**se′ri·al·i·za′tion,** *n.* —**se′ri·al·ly,** *adv.*

se′rial num′ber, one of a series of numbers assigned for identification.

se·ries (sēr′ēz), *n., pl.* **-ries.** 1. a number of related or similar things or events following one another in a certain order. 2. a set of related things. 3. *Television.* an ongoing variety, dramatic, or comic program, usually broadcast weekly, involving the same principal performers.

ser·if (ser′if), *n. Print.* a smaller line used to finish off a main stroke of a letter, as at the top and bottom of *M.*

ser·i·graph (ser′ə graf′, -gräf′), *n.* a print made by the silkscreen process. —**se·rig·ra·pher** (si rig′rə fər), *n.* —**se·rig′ra·phy,** *n.*

se·ri·ous (sēr′ē əs), *adj.* 1. of or showing deep and solemn thought. 2. not joking or trifling. 3. requiring careful thought. 4. causing great harm: *a serious illness.* —**se′ri·ous·ly,** *adv.* —**se′ri·ous·ness,** *n.* —**Syn.** 1. earnest, sober. 4. critical, grave.

ser·mon (sûr′mən), *n.* 1. a religious discourse delivered by a clergyman or clergywoman in a church. 2. any serious, often tedious, talk on a moral issue. —**ser′mon·ize′,** *v.i., v.t.*

se·rol·o·gy (si rol′ə jē), *n.* the science dealing with the properties and actions of the serum of the blood. —**se·ro·log·ic** (sēr′ə loj′ik), **se′ro·log′i·cal,** *adj.*

se·rous (sēr′əs), *adj.* of, secreting, or resembling serum.

ser·pent (sûr′pənt), *n.* a snake, esp. a poisonous one.

ser·pen·tine¹ (sûr′pən tēn′, -tīn′), *adj.* 1. of or resembling a serpent. 2. winding and twisting. 3. sly or treacherous.

ser·pen·tine² (sûr′pən tēn′, -tīn′), *n.* an oily, green mineral used for decorative purposes.

ser·rate (ser′it, -āt), *adj.* notched on the edge like a saw: *a serrate leaf.* Also, **ser·rat·ed** (ser′ā tid).

ser·ried (ser′ēd), *adj.* crowded or pressed closely together.

se·rum (sēr′əm), *n., pl.* **se·rums, se·ra** (sēr′ə). 1. the pale-yellow liquid that separates from the clot in the coagulation of blood. 2. a fluid of this kind obtained from an animal rendered immune to some disease by inoculation, used as an antitoxin.

serv., service.

serv·ant (sûr′vənt), *n.* a person employed by another, esp. one employed to perform domestic duties.

serve (sûrv), *v.,* **served, serv·ing,** *n.* —*v.i.* 1. to offer food or drink, as for guests. 2. to work or go through a term of service. 3. to render assistance 4. to answer the purpose. 5. to work as a servant. —*v.t.* 6. to act as a host or hostess in offering a (person) food or drink. 7. to offer (food or drink) to another. 8. to provide regularly or continuously with (goods or services). 9. to render service to. 10. to work or go through (a term, imprisonment, etc.). 11. to render active service to (a king, etc.). 12. to render homage to (God). 13. to answer the requirements of. 14. to work for as a servant. 15. to wait upon at table. 16. to treat in a specified manner. 17. to gratify (wants, needs, etc.). 18. to put (a tennis ball, etc.) in play. 19. *Law.* to make delivery of (a summons). 20. **serve one right,** to treat one as he or she deserves. —*n.* 21. the act, manner, or right of serving, as in tennis. —**serv′er,** *n.*

serv·ice (sûr′vis), *n., adj., v.,* **-iced, -ic·ing.** —*n.* 1. work performed for another or a group. 2. assistance given to someone. 3. goods or utilities that benefit the public. 4. a department of government that serves the public. 5. a. the armed forces. b. any branch of the armed forces. 6. maintenance and repair of machinery, appliances, etc. 7. the act or manner of serving food or drink. 8. Often, **services.** specialized or professional work. 9. a religious ceremony or ritual. 10. a set of dishes, utensils, etc. 11. serve (def. 21). —*adj.* 12. of service or use. 13. of or used by delivery people. 14. of or for the armed forces or one of them: *a service academy.* —*v.t.* 15. to maintain or repair. 16. to supply with services.

serv·ice·a·ble (sûr′vi sə bəl), *adj.* 1. capable of or being of service or use. 2. wearing well or durable. —**serv′ice·a·bil′i·ty, serv′ice·a·ble·ness,** *n.* —**serv′ice·a·bly,** *adv.*

serv·ice·man (sûr′vis man′, -mən), 1. a member of the armed forces. 2. a person whose occupation is to maintain or repair equipment. —**serv′ice·wom′an,** *n.fem.*

serv′ice mark′, a name or symbol, usually registered, that identifies a service provided by a company or other organization.

serv'ice sta'tion, a place equipped for servicing automobiles, esp. by selling gasoline.

ser·vi·ette (sûr'vē et'), n. Brit. a table napkin

ser·vile (sûr'vil, -vīl), adj. 1. slavishly obedient 2. of or for slaves. — **ser'vile·ly,** adv —**ser·vil'i·ty,** n. — Syn. 1. obsequious, subservient.

serv·ing (sûr'ving), n. a single portion of food or drink.

ser·vi·tor (sûr'vi tər), n. Archaic. a manservant

ser·vi·tude (sûr'vi tōōd', -tyōōd'), n. 1. slavery or bondage of any kind. 2. compulsory labor as a punishment for criminals.

ser·vo (sûr'vō) n., pl. -vos. Informal. 1. servomechanism 2. servomotor.

ser·vo·mech·an·ism (sûr'vō mek'ə niz'əm, sûr'vō mek'-) n. an electronic system in which a controlling mechanism is actuated by a low-energy signal

ser·vo·mo·tor (sûr'vō mō'tər), n. a motor forming part of a servomechanism

ses·a·me (ses'ə mē), n. 1. a tropical plant whose edible oval seeds yield an oil 2. its seeds

ses·qui·cen·ten·ni·al (ses'kwi sen ten'ē əl), adj. 1. of a period of 150 years —n 2. a 150th anniversary or its celebration. —**ses'qui·cen·ten'ni·al·ly,** adv

ses·qui·pe·da·li·an (ses'kwi pi dā'lē ən, -dāl'yən) adj. 1. containing many syllables 2. given to using long words

ses·sile (ses'il, -īl), adj. attached by the base, as a leaf issuing from the stem

ses·sion (sesh'ən), n. 1. the meeting of a court or legislature for the transaction of business. 2. a series of such meetings. 3. the period of such a series 4. a period of lessons in the work of a day at school. 5. a period of any particular activity. —**ses'sion·al** adj

set (set) v. **set set·ting.** n., adj. —v.t. 1. to put in a particular place or position 2. to put into a certain condition 3. to put in the proper order or arrangement for use: to set the table for dinner 4. to arrange (the hair) in a particular style 5. to put (a price or value) upon something. 6. to post or station for the purpose of performing some duty 7. to determine or fix definitely 8. to direct or settle resolutely 9. to establish for others to follow 10. to adjust (a clock) according to a certain standard 11. to fix or mount (a gem) in a frame 12. to cause to sit. 13. to put (a broken bone) back in position 14. to fit, as words to music. 15. Print. to arrange (type) in

the order required for printing. 16. to cause (glue) to become fixed or hard. —v.i. 17. to pass below the horizon, as the sun 18. to decline or wane. 19. to become firm or solid, as mortar 20. to sit on eggs to hatch them as a hen 21. to have a certain direction as a wind 22. set about to begin or Also, set in, set to. 23. set aside a. to put to one side, esp for future use b. to discard or annul 24. set back to hinder or impede 25. set down. a. to record in writing or print b. to establish or enact 26. set forth. a. to state or describe b. to begin a journey. 27. set off a. to cause to explode b. to intensify or improve by contrast 28. set on. to attack or cause to attack Also set upon. 29. set out. a. to begin a journey or course b. to undertake or attempt. 30. set up. a. to put upright. b. to inaugurate or establish —n. 31. the act of setting or state of being set. 32. a collection of articles designed for use together 33. a series of volumes as by one author 34. a group of persons associated by occupations status etc 35. the fit, as of an article of clothing 36. fixed direction or inclination 37. receiver (def. 2) 38. Tennis a unit of a match consisting of six or more games 39. scenery for a particular scene of a play or motion picture 40. Math. a collection of objects or elements classed together —adj 41. fixed beforehand 42. deliberately composed. 43. fixed or rigid 44 resolved or determined 45 completely prepared.

set·back (set'bak'). n a sudden, usually temporary reverse, as in progress or recovery

set·tee (se tē'), n a wide seat having a back and usually arms

set·ter (set'ər) n a hunting dog having a silky coat and feathered tail.

set·ting (set'ing) n 1. the act of a person or thing that sets. 2. the surroundings of anything 3. a frame for a jewel etc 4. the place or period in which the action of a story or play takes place 5. stage scenery. 6. a piece of music composed for certain words

set·tle (set'əl), v., **-tled, -tling.** —v.t. 1. to decide or agree upon 2. to put in a definite order or condition. 3. to pay, as a bill or account 4. to move to and populate (a territory, etc.). 5. to establish in a way of life, a business etc 6. to quiet or calm (the nerves, etc.). 7. to make stable —v.i. 8. to decide or agree. 9. to take up residence in a new country or place 10. to become fixed in a particular place. 11. to become clear by the sinking of suspended particles, as a liquid. **12.** to sink to the bottom, as sediment. **13.** to become firm or compact, as the ground - **set′tler,** *n*

set·tle·ment (set′'l mənt), *n.* **1.** the act of settling or state of being settled. **2.** an arrangement or adjustment, as of a disagreement **3.** the establishment of a person in an employer or office or home **4.** a colony, esp. in its early stages. **5.** a small, isolated community **6.** payment of a debt or obligation. **7.** a welfare establishment in an underprivileged area.

set-to (set′tōō′), *n., pl.* **-tos.** *Informal.* a brief sharp fight or argument.

set·up (set′up′), *n.* **1.** a plan or arrangement of something, as an organization **2.** *Informal.* a contest deliberately made easy. **3.** everything required for an alcoholic drink except the liquor

sev·en (sev′ən) *n.* **1.** a cardinal number, 6 plus 1 **2.** a symbol for this number as 7 or VII. —*adj.* **3.** amounting to seven in number. —**sev′enth,** *adj. n.*

sev′en seas′, all the oceans of the world

sev·en·teen (sev′ən tēn′), *n.* **1.** a cardinal number 10 plus 7 **2.** a symbol for this number as 17 or XVII. —*adj.* **3.** amounting to 17 in number. —**sev′en·teenth′** (-tēnth′) *adj. , n.*

sev′en·teen′-year lo′cust (sev′ən tēn′ yēr′), a cicada of the eastern U.S., having nymphs that live in the soil, usually emerging in great numbers after 17 years in the North or 13 years in the South

sev′enth heav′en, a state of intense happiness

sev·en·ty (sev′ən tē), *n., pl.* **-ties,** *adj.* —*n.* **1.** a cardinal number, 10 times 7. **2.** a symbol for this number, as 70 or LXX —*adj.* **3.** amounting to 70 in number. —**sev′en·ti·eth** (-ith), *adj., n.*

78 (sev′ən tē āt′), *n.* an early type of phonograph record that played at 78 revolutions per minute. Also, **sev′-enty-eight′.**

sev·er (sev′ər), *v.t., v.i.* **1.** to separate (a part) from the whole, as by cutting. **2.** to divide into parts, esp. forcibly **3.** to break off (ties, etc.). —**sev′er·ance** *n*

sev·er·al (sev′ər əl, sev′rəl), *adj.* **1.** more than two but fewer than many in number **2.** respective or individual. —*n* **3.** several persons or things. —**sev′er·al·ly,** *adv.*

sev′erance pay′, extra money paid to a dismissed employee in consideration of his or her length of service.

se·vere (si vēr′), *adj., -ver·er, -ver·est.* **1.** very harsh, as in discipline. **2.** serious or grave, as in manner. **3.**

rigidly restrained, as in style. **4.** causing discomfort or distress, as weather. **5.** difficult to endure or fulfill. **6.** rigidly exact or accurate. —**se·vere′ly,** *adv* —**se·ver′i·ty** (-ver′-i tē), *n.* —**se·vere′ness,** *n.*

Se·ville (sə vil′, sev′il), *n.* a port in SW Spain.

sew (sō), *v., sewed, sewn* (sōn) or **sewed, sew·ing.** —*v.t.* **1.** to join or attach by stitches **2.** to make or repair (a garment) in this way. —*v.i.* **3.** to work with a needle and thread or with a sewing machine. **4.** **sew up,** *Informal* **a.** to be certain of. **b.** to have in one's control. —**sew′er,** *n.*

sew·age (sōō′ij), *n* the waste matter that passes through sewers

sew·er (sōō′ər), *n* an artificial conduit, usually underground, for carrying off waste water and refuse.

sew·er·age (sōō′ər ij), *n* **1.** the removal of waste water and refuse by means of sewers **2.** a system of sewers **3.** sewage

sew·ing (sō′ing), *n.* **1.** the act or work of a person or thing that sews. **2.** something sewn or to be sewn.

sew′ing machine′, any of various foot-operated or electric machines for sewing or making stitches.

sex (seks), *n* **1.** either the male or female division of a species, esp. as differentiated with reference to the reproductive functions **2.** the fact or character of being male or female. **3.** the attraction drawing one sex toward another **4.** See **sexual intercourse.** —**sexed** (sekst), *adj.* —**sex′-less,** *adj* —**sex′less·ly,** *adv.* —**sex′-less·ness,** *n.*

sex-, a combining form meaning "six": *sextet.*

sex·a·ge·nar·i·an (sek′sə jə när′ē ən), *adj.* **1.** of the age of 60 years or between 60 and 70 years old. —*n.* **2.** a sexagenarian person

sex′ change′, the transformation from one sex to another, as by surgery.

sex′ chro′mosome a chromosome that affects the determination of sex.

sex·ism (sek′siz əm), *n* discrimination or bias because of sex, esp. that directed against women, as in restricted career choices, etc. —**sex′-ist,** *n., adj.*

sex·pot (seks′pot′), *n. Slang.* a sexually attractive person.

sex′ sym′bol *Slang.* a person having much sex appeal

sex·tant (seks′tənt), *n.* an instrument for measuring angular distances of celestial bodies in determining latitude and longitude, esp. at sea.

sex·tet (seks tet′), *n.* **1.** *Music.* **a.** a group of six singers or players. **b.** a composition for six voices or instruments. **2.** any group of six. Also, **sex·tette′.**

sex·ton (seks′tən), *n.* an official charged with maintaining church property.

sex·tu·ple (seks tōō′pəl, -tyōō′-, -tup′-əl, seks′tōō pəl), *adj., v.,* **-pled, -pling.** —*adj.* 1. consisting of six parts. 2. six times as great or as many. —*v.t., v.i.* 3. to make or become six times as great.

sex·tu·plet (seks tup′lit, -tōō′plit, tyōō′-), *n.* one of six offspring born at one birth.

sex·u·al (sek′shōō əl), *adj.* of or involving sex, the two sexes, or the sexual organs. —**sex′u·al′i·ty** (-al′i-tē), *n.* —**sex′u·al·ly,** *adv.*

sex′ual in′tercourse, an intimate physical relationship, esp. between man and woman, involving use of the sexual organs.

sex·y (sek′sē), *adj.,* **sex·i·er, sex·i·est.** *Informal.* sexually interesting or exciting. —**sex′i·ly,** *adv.* —**sex′i·ness,** *n.*

SF, See **science fiction.** Also, **sf**

Sfc, Sergeant First Class.

SG., 1. senior grade. 2. Secretary General. 3. Solicitor General. 4. Surgeon General.

sgd., signed.

Sgt., Sergeant.

Sgt. Maj., Sergeant Major.

sh (sh), *interj.* hush! be still!

sh., 1. share (of stock). 2. sheet. 3. shilling; shillings.

shab·by (shab′ē), *adj.,* **-bi·er, -bi·est.** 1. reduced in quality by much wear or use. 2. showing neglect or improper care. 3. slovenly or ragged in dress or appearance. 4. meanly ungenerous or unfair. —**shab′bi·ly,** *adv.* —**shab′bi·ness,** *n.*

shack (shak), *n.* 1. a small, crudely built house. —*v.i.* 2. **shack up,** *Slang.* to cohabit.

shack·le (shak′əl), *n., v.,* **-led, -ling.** —*n.* 1. a metal fastening, usually connected by a chain, for securing the wrist or ankle, as of a prisoner. 2. any fastening or coupling device. 3. Often, **shackles.** anything that restricts freedom of thought or action. —*v.t.* 4. to fasten with a shackle or shackles. 5. to restrict in thought or action. —**shack′ler,** *n.*

shad (shad), *n., pl.* **shad, shads.** a deep-bodied food fish that migrates up streams to spawn.

shade (shād), *n., v.,* **shad·ed, shad·ing.** —*n.* 1. a comparative darkness caused by the interception of rays of light. 2. a place or area protected from direct light, esp. sunlight. 3. any device that protects from direct light, as a window shade or lamp shade. 4. **shades,** *Slang.* sunglasses. 5. the degree of darkness of a color. 6. a small amount or degree. 7. a slight difference. 8. *Literary.* a spec-

ter or ghost. —*v.t.* 9. to shield or protect from direct light. 10. to dim or darken. 11. to represent the effects of shade in (a painting). —*v.i.* 12. to change by slight gradations.

shad·ing (shā′ding), *n.* 1. a slight variation of color, character, etc. 2. protection against direct light. 3. the representation of the effects of shade in a painting.

shad·ow (shad′ō), *n.* 1. a dark figure or image cast on a surface by a body intercepting light. 2. partial darkness. 3. a slight trace. 4. a faint indication or suggestion. 5. the dark part of a picture. 6. an oppressive threat or gloomy influence. 7. a phantom or apparition. 8. *Archaic.* shelter or protection. —*v.t.* 9. to overspread with shadow. 10. to follow (a person) about secretly in order to keep watch over his or her movements. 11. to indicate or suggest faintly. —**shad′ow·er,** *n.* —**shad′ow·y,** *adj.* —**shad′ow·i·ness,** *n.*

shad·ow·box (shad′ō boks′), *v.i.* to make the motions of attack and defense, as in boxing, in the absence of an opponent. —**shad′ow·box′ing,** *n.*

shad·y (shā′dē), *adj.,* **shad·i·er, shad·i·est.** 1. abounding in shade. 2. giving shade. 3. *Informal.* of dubious character. 4. **on the shady side of,** beyond (the specified age). —**shad′i·ly,** *adv.* —**shad′i·ness,** *n.*

shaft (shaft, shäft), *n.* 1. a long pole forming the body of various weapons, as the lance or arrow. 2. something directed at someone or something in sharp attack: *shafts of sarcasm.* 3. a round, straight bar forming part of a machine, as for supporting rotating parts. 4. a monument in the form of a column. 5. either of the parallel bars of wood between which the animal drawing a vehicle is hitched. 6. a vertical enclosed space, as in a building. 7. a long, narrow passage dug into the earth. 8. *Slang.* **a.** unfair treatment. **b.** a harsh remark. —*v.t.* 9. to equip with a shaft. 10. *Slang.* **a.** to treat unfairly. **b.** to take advantage of.

shag (shag), *n.* 1. rough, matted hair or wool. 2. a long, rough nap on cloth.

shag·gy (shag′ē), *adj.,* **-gi·er, -gi·est.** 1. having long, rough hair or wool. 2. untidy or unkempt. 3. having a rough nap, as cloth. —**shag′gi·ly,** *adv.* —**shag′gi·ness,** *n.*

shah (shä), *n.* (formerly) the king of Iran. —**shah′dom,** *n.*

shake (shāk), *v.,* **shook, shak·en** (shā′kən), **shak·ing,** *n.* —*v.i., v.t.* 1. to move up and down or back and forth with short, quick movements. 2. to tremble or cause to tremble. 3.

to clasp (a person's hand) in greeting or congratulation. **4.** to come or cause to come off or out by short, quick movements. **5.** to disturb or distress (a person) deeply. **6. shake down, a.** to cause to descend or fall by shaking. **b.** to condition or test, as a ship. **c.** *Slang.* to extort money from. **7. shake off,** to get rid of by shaking. **8. shake up,** to upset or disturb mentally or physically. —*n.* **9.** the act or an instance of shaking. **10. the shakes,** a fit of trembling, esp. from chills or fever. **11.** See **milk shake. 12.** *Informal.* treatment accorded a person: *a fair shake.* **13. no great shakes,** not particularly able or distinguished. —**shak'a·ble, shake'a·ble,** *adj.*

shake·down (shāk'doun'), *n.* **1.** extortion, as by blackmail or threats of violence. **2.** a thorough search. **3.** a makeshift bed. —*adj.* **4.** for conditioning or testing a new vessel or aircraft.

shak·er (shā'kər), *n.* **1.** a person or thing that shakes. **2.** a container with holes in the top, used for holding and sprinkling sugar, salt, etc. **3.** (*cap.*) a member of a Protestant sect in the U.S., practicing celibacy and common ownership of property: now almost extinct.

Shake·speare (shāk'spēr), *n.* **William,** 1564–1616, English poet and dramatist. —**Shake·spear'e·an,** *adj., n.*

shake·up (shāk'up'), *n.* a sudden and thorough change in the personnel of an organization.

shak·o (shak'ō, shā'kō), *n., pl.* **shak·os, shak·oes.** a tall, stiff military cap having a visor and a plume.

shak·y (shā'kē), *adj.,* **shak·i·er, shak·i·est. 1.** tending to shake or tremble. **2.** weak or unsteady. **3.** wavering or unreliable. —**shak'i·ly,** *adv.* —**shak'i·ness,** *n.*

shale (shāl), *n.* a rock, formed from clay, that readily splits into layers.

shale' oil', petroleum distilled from bituminous shale.

shall (shal), *auxiliary v., pt.* **should. 1.** (generally used in the first person to denote simple future time). **2.** (generally used in the second and third persons to denote authority or determination).
—**Usage.** Except in formal or very precise usage, WILL is now generally used in place of *shall.* In questions in which the subject is in the first person (*I* or *we*), however, *shall* is used.

shal·lop (shal'əp), *n.* a small boat formerly used in shallow waters.

shal·lot (shə lot'), *n.* **1.** an onionlike plant whose bulbs are used for flavoring. **2.** its bulb.

shal·low (shal'ō), *adj.* **1.** not deep. **2.** lacking intellectual depth. —*n.* **3.** Usually, **shallows.** the shallow part of a body of water. —**shal'low·ness,** *n.*

sha·lom (shə lōm'), *interj. Hebrew.* peace (used as a Jewish greeting or farewell).

shalt (shalt), *v. Archaic.* 2nd pers. sing. of **shall.**

sham (sham), *n., adj., v.,* **shammed, sham·ming.** —*n.* **1.** a spurious imitation. **2.** a person who assumes a false character. —*adj.* **3.** false or counterfeit. —*v.t., v.i.* **4.** to put on a false appearance (of). —**sham'mer,** *n.*

sha·man (shä'mən, shā'-, sham'ən), *n.* a medicine man among certain peoples, as the Eskimos.

sham·ble (sham'bəl), *v.,* **-bled, -bling,** *n.* —*v.i.* **1.** to walk in an awkward, unsteady way. —*n.* **2.** a shambling gait.

sham·bles (sham'bəlz), *n.pl.* **1.** a scene of utter destruction or disorder. **2.** any place of carnage. **3.** *Rare.* a slaughterhouse.

shame (shām), *n., v.,* **shamed, sham·ing.** —*n.* **1.** the painful feeling arising from the consciousness of something dishonorable or improper. **2.** humiliating dishonor. **3.** something that is cause for regret. **4. put to shame, a.** to cause to suffer shame. **b.** to outdo or surpass. —*v.t.* **5.** to cause to feel shame. **6.** to force through shame. **7.** to bring shame to. —**shame'ful,** *adj.* —**shame'ful·ly,** *adv.* —**shame'ful·ness,** *n.* —**Syn. 1.** chagrin, embarrassment, mortification. **2.** disgrace, ignominy.

shame·faced (shām'fāst'), *adj.* **1.** showing shame or guilt. **2.** very modest or bashful. —**shame'fac'ed·ly** (-fā'sid lē, -fāst'lē), *adv.* —**shame'fac'ed·ness,** *n.*

shame·less (shām'lis), *adj.* lacking any sense of shame. —**shame'less·ly,** *adv.* —**shame'less·ness,** *n.*

sham·poo (sham pōō'), *v.,* **-pooed, -poo·ing,** *n.* —*v.t.* **1.** to wash (the hair), esp. with a shampoo. **2.** to clean (rugs) with a special preparation. —*n.* **3.** the act of shampooing. **4.** a special preparation for washing the hair. —**sham·poo'er,** *n.*

sham·rock (sham'rok), *n.* a three-leafed plant resembling clover: the national emblem of Ireland.

shang·hai (shang'hī, shang hī'), *v.t.,* **-haied, -hai·ing.** to force (a person) to join the crew of a ship, esp. by using drugs or liquor.

Shang·hai (shang hī'), *n.* a seaport in E China.

Shan·gri-la (shang'grə lä', shang'grə-lä'), *n.* an imaginary paradise on earth.

shank (shangk), *n.* **1.** the part of the leg between the knee and the ankle. **2.** a similar part of an animal's leg. **3.** a cut of meat from the upper part of an animal's leg. **4.** a narrow, shaftlike part that connects two portions of a tool. **5.** *Rare.* the early part of a period of time, esp. the evening.

shan't (shant, shänt), contraction of *shall not.*

shan·tung (shan'tung'), *n.* a heavy fabric of raw silk.

shan·ty (shan'tē), *n., pl.* **-ties.** a small, flimsy, often temporary house.

shape (shāp), *n., v.,* **shaped, shap·ing.** —*n.* **1.** appearance with regard to the outline of the surface. **2.** a figure or form seen only in outline. **3.** orderly arrangement. **4.** condition or physical state. **5.** the figure or body of a person. **6. take shape,** to become definite. —*v.t.* **7.** to give definite shape or form to. **8.** to put or express in a particular form. **9.** to adjust or adapt. **10. shape up, a.** to develop to a particular or favorable form. **b.** to improve one's behavior or performance. **c.** to exercise for an attractive or healthy body.

shape·less (shāp'lis), *adj.* **1.** having no definite shape or form. **2.** having an unpleasing shape. —**shape'less·ly,** *adv.* —**shape'less·ness,** *n.*

shape·ly (shāp'lē), *adj.,* **-li·er, -li·est.** having a pleasing shape, esp. with reference to a woman's figure. —**shape'li·ness,** *n.*

shape·up (shāp'up'), *n.* the act of exercising for an attractive or healthy body.

shard (shärd), *n.* a fragment of broken earthenware.

share¹ (shâr), *n., v.,* **shared, shar·ing.** —*n.* **1.** a portion of a whole given or assigned to one person or group. **2.** one of the equal parts into which the capital stock of a corporation is divided. —*v.t.* **3.** to use, own, or receive jointly. **4.** to divide and distribute in shares. —*v.i.* **5.** to take part. —**shar'er,** *n.*

share² (shâr), *n.* a plowshare.

share·crop·per (shâr'krop'ər), *n.* a tenant farmer who pays as rent a share of the crop. —**share'crop',** *v.t., v.i.*

share·hold·er (shâr'hōl'dər), *n.* a holder or owner of shares, esp. in a corporation.

shark¹ (shärk), *n.* a large, often ferocious fish having a rough skin and sharp teeth.

shark² (shärk), *n.* **1.** a person who preys greedily on others, as by cheating. **2.** *Slang.* an expert in a particular field.

shark·skin (shärk'skin'), *n.* **1.** a smooth fabric, or of rayon, with a dull chalklike appearance. **2.** leather made from the hide of a shark.

sharp (shärp), *adj.* **1.** having a thin, keen cutting edge or a fine point. **2.** not blunt or rounded. **3.** involving a sudden change of direction. **4.** clearly defined: *sharp differences of opinion.* **5.** biting in taste. **6.** piercing or shrill in sound. **7.** keenly cold, as weather. **8.** felt acutely, as a pain. **9.** caustic or harsh, as words. **10.** mentally acute or alert. **11.** shrewd or astute. **12.** shrewd to the point of dishonesty. **13.** *Music.* **a.** above the correct pitch. **b.** raised a half step from another note. **14.** *Slang.* very stylish. —*adv.* **15.** keenly or acutely. **16.** abruptly or suddenly. **17.** punctually or promptly. **18.** *Music.* above the correct pitch. —*n.* **19.** *Music.* **a.** a tone a half step above another tone. **b.** the symbol (♯) indicating this. **20.** *Informal.* a shark² (def. 2). **b.** sharper. —*v.t., v.i.* **21.** *Music.* to make or become sharp. —**sharp'ly,** *adv.* —**sharp'ness,** *n.* —**Syn. 8.** intense, severe. **10.** clever, keen, quick, smart.

sharp·en (shär'pən), *v.t., v.i.* to make or become sharp or sharper. —**sharp'en·er,** *n.*

sharp·er (shär'pər), *n.* **1.** a shrewd swindler. **2.** a professional gambler.

sharp·ie (shär'pē), *n.* **1.** a very alert person. **2.** sharper. Also, **sharp'y.**

sharp·shoot·er (shärp'shōō'tər), *n.* an accurate marksman or markswoman. —**sharp'shoot'ing,** *n.*

shat·ter (shat'ər), *v.t., v.i.* **1.** to break into pieces, as by a blow. **2.** to damage or become damaged, as by crushing. —**shat'ter·ing·ly,** *adv.*

shat·ter·proof (shat'ər prōōf'), *adj.* made so as to crack without shattering, as glass.

shave (shāv), *v.,* **shaved, shaved** or **shav·en** (shā'vən), **shav·ing,** *n.* —*v.i.* **1.** to remove hair or a beard with a razor. —*v.t.* **2.** to cut off (hair, esp. the beard) close to the skin with a razor. **3.** to remove hair from (the face, etc.) by cutting it off close to the skin with a razor. **4.** to cut off the beard of (a person). **5.** to cut or scrape thin slices from. **6.** to scrape or come very near to. —*n.* **7.** the act or an instance of shaving or being shaved. —**shav'a·ble, shave'a·ble,** *adj.*

shav·er (shā'vər), *n.* **1.** a person or thing that shaves. **2.** an electric razor. **3.** *Informal.* a small boy.

shav·ing (shā'ving), *n.* **1.** a very thin piece or slice, esp. of wood. **2.** the act of a person or thing that shaves.

Shaw (shô), *n.* George Ber·nard (bər-närd′), 1856–1950, Irish dramatist and critic. —**Sha·vi·an** (shā′vē ən), *adj., n.*

shawl (shôl), *n.* a heavy oblong or square piece of fabric worn for warmth, esp. by women, about the shoulders or the head and shoulders.

Shaw·nee (shô nē′), *n., pl.* **-nees, -nee.** a member of an Indian tribe of the east-central U.S., now in Oklahoma.

shay (shā), *n. Chiefly Dial.* a chaise.

she (shē), *pron.* **1.** the female person or animal previously mentioned. **2.** anything regarded as feminine. —*n.* **3.** a female person or animal.

sheaf (shēf), *n., pl.* **sheaves** (shēvz). **1.** a bundle of cut stalks of grain tied around the middle. **2.** any collection of things bound or tied together.

shear (shēr), *v.,* **sheared, sheared or shorn, shear·ing,** *n.* —*v.t.* **1.** to cut or clip with shears. **2.** to remove (fleece or wool) by cutting or clipping. **3.** to cut or clip the fleece or wool from. **4.** to strip or deprive: *to shear the king of his power.* —*n.* **5.** Usually, **shears. a.** scissors of large size. **b.** any of various other cutting tools or machines having two blades that resemble or suggest those of scissors. **6.** the act or process of shearing or being sheared. —**shear′er,** *n.*

sheath (shēth), *n., pl.* **sheaths** (shēthz). **1.** a case for the blade of a sword or dagger. **2.** any similar case or covering. **3.** a closefitting dress.

sheathe (shēth), *v.t.,* **sheathed, sheath·ing. 1.** to put into a sheath. **2.** to enclose in or as in a case or covering.

sheath·ing (shē′thing), *n.* **1.** a covering or outer layer, as one of metal plates on a ship's bottom. **2.** material for forming any such covering.

sheave (shiv, shēv), *n.* a pulley or wheel having a grooved rim.

she·bang (shə bang′), *n. Informal.* an organization or affair considered in its total structure: *to manage the whole shebang.*

shed¹ (shed), *n.* a slight or rude structure built for shelter or storage.

shed² (shed), *v.,* **shed, shed·ding.** —*v.t.* **1.** to pour forth (water), as a fountain. **2.** to let fall in drops, as tears. **3.** to give or send forth, as light. **4.** to resist being affected by: *cloth that sheds water.* **5.** to cast off or let fall (leaves, etc.) by natural process. —*v.i.* **6.** to fall off, as leaves. **7.** to drop out, as hair, seed, or grain. **8.** to cast off or lose hair, etc. **9. shed blood,** to kill by violence.

she'd (shēd), contraction of: **a.** *she had.* **b.** *she would.*

sheen (shēn), *n.* shining brightness, esp. on a polished surface. —**sheen′y,** *adj.*

sheep (shēp), *n., pl.* **sheep. 1.** a ruminant mammal related to the goat and bred for wool and meat. **2.** a meek and docile person.

sheep·dog (shēp′dôg′, -dog′), *n.* a dog trained to herd and guard sheep.

sheep·fold (shēp′fōld′), *n. Chiefly Brit.* an enclosure for sheep.

sheep·ish (shē′pish), *adj.* **1.** embarrassed, as by having done something wrong. **2.** like sheep, as in meekness. —**sheep′ish·ly,** *adv.* —**sheep′ish·ness,** *n.*

sheep·skin (shēp′skin′), *n.* **1.** the skin of a sheep, esp. when processed with the wool left on. **2.** leather or parchment made from it. **3.** *Informal.* a diploma.

sheer¹ (shēr), *adj.* **1.** transparently thin, as some fabrics. **2.** unqualified or utter: *sheer nonsense.* **3.** very steep. —*adv.* **4.** completely or quite. **5.** very steeply. —**sheer′ly,** *adv.* —**sheer′ness,** *n.*

sheer² (shēr), *v.i., v.t.* to deviate or cause to deviate from a course, as a ship.

sheet¹ (shēt), *n.* **1.** a large rectangular piece of cotton or other material used as an article of bedding. **2.** a rectangular piece of paper. **3.** a broad, thin layer or covering, as of ice. **4.** a relatively thin, usually rectangular piece or slab, as of glass or metal.

sheet² (shēt), *n.* a rope for holding a sail so that it is set at the desired angle.

sheet·ing (shē′ting), *n.* **1.** fabric used to make bed sheets. **2.** material used for covering with or forming into sheets, as of plywood.

sheet′ mu·sic, music, usually for popular songs, printed on unbound sheets of paper.

sheik (shāk, shēk), *n.* **1.** the chief of an Arab family or tribe. **2.** a wealthy or prominent Arab. **3.** (*cap.*) a title of respect prefixed to the name of such a person. Also, **sheikh.** —**sheik′dom** (-dəm), **sheikh′dom,** *n.*

shelf (shelf), *n., pl.* **shelves. 1.** a thin, usually long piece of wood or metal fixed horizontally to a wall or set in a frame, for supporting objects. **2.** something resembling a shelf, as a ledge of rock or a sandbank. **3. on the shelf,** inactive or useless.

shelf′ life′, the period during which a stored commodity remains useful.

shell (shel), *n.* **1.** the hard outer covering of an animal, as an oyster or lobster. **2.** the hard outer covering of an egg or nut. **3.** a hollow projectile for a cannon, mortar, etc. **4.** a metallic cartridge used in small arms. **5.** the lower crust of pastry. **6.** the walls and roof of a building. **7.** a light, long, narrow racing boat, for rowing by oarsmen. —*v.t.* **8.** to remove the shell of. **9.** to fire explosive shells at or on. **10. shell out**, *Informal.* to pay or contribute (money). —**shelled** (sheld), *adj.* —**shell′er**, *n.* —**shell′y**, *adj.*

she'll (shēl), contraction of: **a.** *she will.* **b.** *she shall.*

shel·lac (shə lak′), *n.*, *v.*, **-lacked**, **-lack·ing.** —*n.* **1.** lac that has been purified and formed into thin sheets, used for making varnish. **2.** a varnish made by dissolving this material in alcohol. —*v.t.* **3.** to coat with shellac. **4.** *Slang.* **a.** to defeat decisively. **b.** to thrash soundly. Also, **shel·lack′.** —**shel·lack′er**, *n.*

Shel·ley (shel′ē), *n.* **Per·cy Bysshe** (pûr′sē bish), 1792–1822, English poet.

shell′fire′ (shel′fī⁹r′), *n.* the firing of explosive shells.

shell·fish (shel′fish′), *n.*, *pl.* **-fish**, **-fish·es.** any aquatic animal having a shell, as the oyster or lobster.

shell′ shock′, *Obsolesc.* See **battle fatigue.** —**shell′-shocked′**, *adj.*

shel·ter (shel′tər), *n.* **1.** a limited place or area that provides a temporary cover, as from the elements or an air raid. **2.** the protection or refuge afforded by such a place. —*v.t.* **3.** to provide with a shelter. —*v.i.* **4.** to take shelter.

shelve (shelv), *v.t.*, **shelved**, **shelv·ing. 1.** to place on a shelf. **2.** to put aside from consideration. **3.** to furnish with shelves. —**shelv′er**, *n.*

shelves (shelvz), *n.* pl. of **shelf.**

shelv·ing (shel′ving), *n.* **1.** material for shelves. **2.** shelves collectively.

she·nan·i·gan (shə nan′ə gən), *n.* Usually, **shenanigans.** *Informal.* **1.** wily and dubious conduct. **2.** mischievous nonsense.

Shen·yang (shun′yäng′), *n.* a city in NE China.

shep·herd (shep′ərd), *n.* **1.** a boy or man who herds or tends sheep. —*v.t.* **2.** to herd or tend as a shepherd. —**shep′herd·ess**, *n.fem.*

sher·bet (shûr′bit), *n.* **1.** a frozen fruit-flavored dessert similar to an ice but with milk and egg white or gelatin added. **2.** *Brit.* a drink made of sweetened fruit juice diluted with water and ice.

sher·iff (sher′if), *n.* the chief law-enforcement officer of a county.

Sher·pa (sher′pə, shûr′-), *n.*, *pl.* **-pas**, **-pa.** a member of a Tibetan people living in the Nepalese Himalayas.

sher·ry (sher′ē), *n.*, *pl.* **-ries.** a fortified, amber-colored wine of southern Spain. [< Sp (*vino de*) *Xeres* (wine of) *Jerez*, a city in Spain]

she's (shēz), contraction of: **a.** *she is.* **b.** *she has.*

shew (shō), *v.*, **shewed**, **shewn** (shōn) or **shewed**, **shew·ing**, *n. Archaic.* show.

shib·bo·leth (shib′ə lith, -leth′), *n.* **1.** a peculiarity of usage and speech that distinguishes a particular class or set of persons. **2.** a pet phrase of a group or party.

shied (shīd), *v.* pt. and pp. of **shy.**

shield (shēld), *n.* **1.** a broad piece of armor carried on the arm as a defense against swords, lances, etc. **2.** something shaped like a shield. **3.** a person or thing that protects or guards. **4.** a badge used by a law-enforcement officer. —*v.t.*, *v.i.* **5.** to protect or guard with or as with a shield. —**shield′er**, *n.*

shift (shift), *v.i.* **1.** to move from one place or person to another. **2.** to manage by oneself. —*v.t.* **3.** to transfer from one place or person to another. **4.** to replace (something) by another or others. **5.** *Auto.* to change (gears) from one arrangement to another. —*n.* **6.** a change from one place or person to another. **7.** a person's scheduled period of work. **8.** a group of workers scheduled to work during such a period. **9.** *Auto.* a gearshift. **10.** a loose-fitting dress. **11.** an expedient or evasion, esp. in an emergency. **12.** an artifice or trick. **13. make shift**, to manage with what is at hand.

shift·less (shift′lis), *adj.* lacking in ambition or energy. —**shift′less·ly**, *adv.* —**shift′less·ness**, *n.*

shift·y (shif′tē), *adj.*, **shift·i·er**, **shift·i·est. 1.** given to evasions. **2.** suggesting a deceptive character: *a shifty look.* —**shift′i·ly**, *adv.* —**shift′i·ness**, *n.*

shill (shil), *n. Slang.* a person who poses as a customer in order to decoy others into participating, as for a peddler.

shil·le·lagh (shə lā′lē, -lə), *n.* an Irish cudgel, traditionally of blackthorn or oak. Also, **shil·la′lah.**

shil·ling (shil′ing), *n.* **1.** a money of account of the United Kingdom, the 20th part of a pound, equal to 12 pence: use phased out in 1971. **2.** the monetary unit of Kenya, Tanzania, and Uganda.

shil·ly-shal·ly (shil′ē shal′ē), *v.i.*, **-lied**, **-ly·ing. 1.** to show indecision or hesitation. **2.** to dawdle or trifle. —**shil′ly-shal′li·er**, *n.*

shim (shim), *n.* a thin wedge of metal or wood for driving into crevices or for leveling something.

shim·mer (shim′ər), *v.i.* **1.** to shine with a subdued, tremulous light. —*n.* **2.** a shimmering light. —**shim′mer·ing·ly**, *adv.* —**shim′mer·y**, *adj.*

shim·my (shim′ē), *n., pl.* **-mies,** *v.,* **-mied, -my·ing.** —*n.* 1. a wobbling or shaking in the front wheels of a motor vehicle. —*v.i.* 2. to wobble or shake.

shin (shin), *n., v.,* **shinned, shin·ning.** —*n.* 1. the front part of the leg from the knee to the ankle. —*v.t., v.i.* 2. to climb (a tree, etc.) by holding fast with the arms and legs.

shin·bone (shin′bōn′), *n.* tibia.

shin·dig (shin′dig′), *n. Informal.* an elaborate dance, party, or celebration.

shine (shin), *v.,* **shone** or, esp. for 4, 5, **shined; shin·ing;** *n.* —*v.i.* 1. to give forth or glow with light. 2. to appear with brightness or clearness, as feelings. 3. to excel or be outstanding. —*v.t.* 4. to cause to shine. 5. to direct the light of (a lamp, etc.). 6. to put a gloss or polish on. —*n.* 7. brightness caused by emitted light. 8. luster or polish. 9. sunshine or fair weather. 10. **take a shine to,** *Informal.* to develop a liking for. —**Syn.** 1. gleam, glisten, shimmer, sparkle.

shin·er (shi′nər), *n.* 1. a small glistening fish, esp. a minnow. 2. *Slang.* See **black eye.**

shin·gle[1] (shing′gəl), *n., v.,* **-gled, -gling.** —*n.* 1. a thin piece of wood or asbestos laid in overlapping rows to cover the roof or sides of a house. 2. *Informal.* a small signboard, esp. as hung before a doctor's or lawyer's office. 3. a woman's close-cropped haircut. —*v.t.* 4. to cover with shingles, as a roof. —**shin′gler,** *n.*

shin·gle[2] (shing′gəl), *n. Brit.* 1. water-worn pebbles on the seashore. 2. a beach covered with such pebbles. —**shin′gly,** *adj.*

shin·gles (shing′gəlz), *n.* a painful disease of the skin and nerves, caused by a virus, that produces clusters of blisters.

shin·ny (shin′ē), *v.i.,* **-nied, -ny·ing.** to shin.

Shin·to (shin′tō), *n.* the native religion of Japan, stressing nature and ancestor worship. Also called **Shin′to·ism.** [< Jap: God's Way] —**Shin′to·ist,** *n., adj.* —**Shin′to·is′tic,** *adj.*

shin·y (shi′nē), *adj.,* **shin·i·er, shin·i·est.** 1. bright in appearance. 2. worn to a glossy smoothness, as clothes. —**shin′i·ly,** *adv.* —**shin′i·ness,** *n.*

ship (ship), *n., v.,* **shipped, ship·ping.** —*n.* 1. a vessel, esp. a large oceangoing one propelled by sails or engines. 2. the officers and crew of a vessel. 3. any aircraft or spacecraft. —*v.t.* 4. to transport by ship, rail, truck, or plane. 5. to put or take on board a ship or any other carrier. 6. *Naut.* to take in (water) over the side. 7. to bring (an object) into a ship or boat: *to ship oars.* —*v.i.* 8. to go on board or travel by ship 9. to engage to serve on a ship. —**ship′per,** *n.*

-ship, a suffix meaning: **a.** state or quality: *friendship.* **b.** office or position: *clerkship.* **c.** rank or title: *lordship.* **d.** skill or art: *seamanship.* **e.** all people involved: *ridership.*

ship·board (ship′bōrd′, -bôrd′), *adj.* 1. happening or for use on a ship: *a shipboard romance.* —*n.* 2. *Archaic.* the deck or side of a ship. 3. **on shipboard,** on a ship.

ship·build·er (ship′bil′dər), *n.* a person whose occupation is the designing or constructing of ships. —**ship′build′ing,** *n.*

ship·mate (ship′māt′), *n.* a fellow sailor on the same vessel.

ship·ment (ship′mənt), *n.* 1. a quantity of cargo shipped at one time. 2. the act of shipping cargo.

ship·ping (ship′ing), *n.* 1. the act or business of a person or thing that ships. 2. a number of ships, esp. merchant ships, taken as a whole.

ship·shape (ship′shāp′), *adj.* 1. in good and tidy order. —*adv.* 2. in a shipshape manner.

ship's′ store′, a naval post exchange aboard ship.

shipt., shipment.

ship·wreck (ship′rek′), *n.* 1. the destruction or loss of a ship, as by sinking. 2. the remains of a wrecked ship. 3. ruin, as of one's hopes. —*v.t.* 4. to cause to suffer shipwreck.

ship·wright (ship′rit′), *n.* a skilled carpenter who builds and launches wooden vessels.

ship·yard (ship′yärd′), *n.* a place where ships are built or repaired.

shire (shir′), *n.* one of the counties of Great Britain.

shirk (shûrk), *v.t., v.i.* to evade (work, duty, etc.). —**shirk′er,** *n.*

shirr (shûr), *v.t.* 1. to draw up or gather (fabric) on parallel threads. 2. to bake (eggs) in a shallow dish buttered and lined with crumbs. —*n.* 3. Also, **shirr′ing.** a shirred arrangement of fabric.

shirt (shûrt), *n.* 1. a garment for the upper part of the body, typically having a collar and a front opening, worn chiefly by men. 2. undershirt. 3. **keep one's shirt on,** *Slang.* to remain calm or patient.

shirt·ing (shûr′ting), *n.* fabric for making shirts.

shish ke·bab (shish′ kə bob′), a dish of kebabs of lamb.

shiv (shiv), *n. Slang.* a knife, esp. as a weapon.

Shi·va (shē′və), *n. Hinduism.* the third member of the trinity, along with Brahma and Vishnu.

shiv·er (shiv′ər), *v.i.* **1.** to shake or tremble, esp. with cold or fear. —*n.* **2.** a shivering motion. —**shiv′er·er**, *n.* —**shiv′er·y**, *adj.* —**shiv′er·ing·ly**, *adv.*

shiv·er² (shiv′ər), *v.t., v.i.* **1.** to break or split into fragments. —*n.* **2.** a fragment or splinter.

shlep (shlep), *n. Slang.* schlepp.

shoal¹ (shōl), *n.* **1.** a shallow place in a sea, river, etc. **2.** a sandbank exposed at low tide. —**shoal′y**, *adj.*

shoal² (shōl), *n.* **1.** a school of fish. **2.** any large number or group.

shoat (shōt), *n.* a young, weaned pig.

shock¹ (shok), *n.* **1.** a sudden and violent blow or impact. **2.** a sudden and violent disturbance of the mind or emotions. **3.** the cause of such a disturbance. **4.** the effect produced by the passage of an electric current through the body. **5.** a collapse of circulatory function caused by severe injury, blood loss, or disease. **6.** see **shock absorber.** —*v.t.* **7.** to strike with mental or emotional shock. **8.** to offend or disgust. **9.** to give an electric shock to. —**shock′proof′** (-prōof′), *adj.* —**Syn.** **7.** astound, startle, stun, surprise.

shock² (shok), *n.* a group of sheaves of grain placed on end and supporting one another in the field.

shock³ (shok), *n.* a thick, bushy mass, esp. of hair.

shock′ absorb′er, a device for damping sudden and rapid motion, as the recoil of a spring-mounted object from shock.

shock·er (shok′ər), *n.* **1.** a person or thing that shocks. **2.** a sensational story, motion picture, etc.

shock·ing (shok′ing), *adj.* **1.** causing intense surprise and disgust. **2.** very bad or offensive. —**shock′ing·ly**, *adv.* —**Syn.** indecent, revolting.

shock′ ther′apy, a method of treating certain psychotic disorders, as schizophrenia, by use of drugs or electricity.

shock′ troops′, troops especially trained and equipped for engaging in assault.

shock′ wave′, **1.** an abrupt increase in pressure, density, and velocity caused by an earthquake, etc. **2.** any startling repercussion.

shod·dy (shod′ē), *n., pl.* **-dies,** *adj.,* **-di·er, -di·est.** —*n.* **1.** a fibrous material obtained by shredding rags or waste. **2.** a fabric made from this. **3.** anything inferior made to resemble what is of superior quality. —*adj.* **4.** poorly made or inferior. **5.** mean or nasty. **6.** pretentious or sham. — **shod′di·ly**, *adv.* —**shod′di·ness**, *n.*

shoe (shōo), *n., v.,* **shod** (shod) or **shoed, shoe·ing.** —*n.* **1.** an outer covering, usually of leather, for the human foot. **2.** a horseshoe. **3.** the part of a brake that applies friction to the wheel. **4.** the outer casing of a pneumatic tire. **5.** **fill someone's shoes,** to assume another's position and responsibilities. —*v.t.* **6.** to provide or fit with a shoe or shoes.

shoe·horn (shōo′hôrn′), *n.* a curved device used to help slip one's heel down into a shoe.

shoe·lace (shōo′lās′), *n.* a string or lace for fastening a shoe.

shoe·mak·er (shōo′mā′kər), *n.* a person who makes or mends shoes.

shoe·string (shōo′string′), *n.* **1.** a shoelace. **2.** *Informal.* a very small amount of money.

shoe·tree (shōo′trē′), *n.* a foot-shaped device for placing in a shoe to preserve its shape when not worn.

sho·gun (shō′gun′, -gōon′), *n.* a military dictator in feudal Japan.

shone (shōn), *v.* a pt. and pp. of **shine.**

shoo (shōo), *interj., v.,* **shooed, -shoo·ing.** —*interj.* **1.** (used to drive away a cat, birds, etc.) —*v.t.* **2.** to drive away by shouting "shoo."

shoo-in (shōo′in′), *n. Informal.* a candidate or competitor regarded as certain to win.

shook (shŏok), *v.* **1.** pt. of **shake.** — *adj.* **2.** Also, **shook′ up′.** *Slang.* emotionally unsettled.

shoot (shōot), *v.,* **shot, shoot·ing,** *n.* —*v.t.* **1.** to hit or kill with a bullet or arrow. **2.** to send forth or discharge (a bullet or arrow) from a weapon. **3.** to send forth (words, etc.) rapidly. **4.** to pass rapidly over or down: *to shoot a rapid.* **5.** to emit (a ray of light) suddenly. **6.** to variegate by streaks of another color. **7.** *Sports.* **a.** to throw or kick (a ball, etc.) toward a target or goal. **b.** to score (a goal, points, etc.). **8.** *Photog.* to photograph or film. **9.** to put forth (buds, etc.), as a plant. —*v.i.* **10.** to send forth a bullet or arrow from a weapon. **11.** to hunt with a gun for sport. **12.** to move or pass swiftly. **13.** to put forth buds, etc., as a plant. **14.** *Photog.* to photograph. **15.** *Motion Pictures.* to film or begin to film a scene or movie. **16.** to jut or project. **17.** to permeate the body, as a pain. **18.** **shoot at** or **for,** *Informal.* to strive toward. **19.** **shoot up, a.** to grow rapidly or suddenly. **b.** *Slang.* to inject (a narcotic) intravenously. —*n.* **20.** a new growth of a plant or bud. **21.** a match or contest at shooting. —**shoot′er,** *n.*

shoot′ing i′ron, *Slang.* a firearm, esp. a pistol.

shoot′ing star′, a meteor as seen streaking across the sky at night.

shoot·out (shōot′out′), *n. Slang.* a violent gunfight.

shop (shop), *n.*, *v.*, **shopped, shopping.** —*n.* **1.** a small retail establishment specializing usually in a particular type of goods or services: *a flower shop.* **2.** a place where a certain kind of work is done. **3. talk shop,** to discuss one's trade or business. —*v.i.* **4.** to visit shops or stores to buy or examine goods.

shop·keep·er (shop'kē'pər), *n.* a person who owns or operates a shop.

shop·lift·er (shop'lif'tər), *n.* a person who steals goods from a retail store while posing as a customer. —**shop'-lift',** *v.t.*, *v.i.* —**shop'lift'ing,** *n.*

shoppe (shop), *n.* a small shop (used chiefly on store signs).

shop·per (shop'ər), *n.* **1.** a person who shops. **2.** a retail buyer for another person or a business company.

shop·ping cen'ter, a group of stores within a single architectural plan, esp. in suburban areas.

shop·worn (shop'wôrn', -wōrn'), *adj.* soiled or damaged, as goods handled and exposed in a store.

shore[1] (shōr, shôr), *n.* the land along the edge of a sea, lake, or river. — **shore'less,** *adj.*

shore[2] (shōr, shôr), *n.*, *v.*, **shored, shor·ing.** —*n.* **1.** a supporting post or beam with auxiliary members, as against a ship in drydock. —*v.t.* **2.** to support by shores.

shore·bird (shōr'bûrd'), *n.* a bird that frequents seashores, as the sandpiper.

shore·line (shōr'līn', shôr'-), *n.* the line where shore and water meet.

shore' patrol', members of an organization in the U.S. Navy having police duties.

shorn (shōrn, shôrn), *v.* a pp. of **shear.**

short (shôrt), *adj.* **1.** having little length. **2.** having little height. **3.** brief in duration. **4.** brief or concise, as writing. **5.** rudely brief or abrupt. **6.** below the standard in extent, quantity, etc. **7.** having an insufficient amount of. **8.** crisp and flaky, as pastry. **9.** noting a sale of securities or commodities that the seller does not possess, depending for profit on a decline in prices. **10.** taking a shorter time to pronounce, as certain vowel sounds. **11. short of,** a. less than. b. failing of or excluding. —*adv.* **12.** abruptly or suddenly. **13.** briefly or curtly. **14.** without reaching the intended or particular point. **15. come** or **fall short,** to fail to reach or be sufficient. **16. run short,** to be in insufficient supply. —*n.* **17.** something short. **18. shorts,** a. short trousers. b. short pants worn by men as an undergarment. **19.** See **short circuit. 20.** shortstop. **21. in short,** in brief. —*v.t.*, *v.i.* **22.** to

develop a short circuit (in). —**short'-ness,** *n.* —*Syn.* **4.** succinct, terse. **5.** curt, sharp, testy.

short·age (shôr'tij), *n.* a deficiency in quantity.

short·cake (shôrt'kāk'), *n.* a dessert made of short, baked biscuit dough, topped with fruit and usually whipped cream.

short·change (shôrt'chānj'), *v.t.*, **-changed, -chang·ing. 1.** to give less than the correct change to. **2.** *Informal.* to cheat or defraud.

short' cir'cuit, *Elect.* a condition of relatively low resistance between two points in a circuit, usually resulting in a flow of excess current. —**short'-cir'cuit,** *v.t.*, *v.i.*

short·com·ing (shôrt'kum'ing), *n.* a defect or deficiency in conduct, ability, etc.

short·cut (shôrt'kut'), *n.* **1.** a shorter or quicker way or route. **2.** any method that cuts down on time or energy.

short·en (shôr'tən), *v.t.*, *v.i.* to make or become short or shorter. —**short'-en·er,** *n.*

short·en·ing (shôr'tə·ning, shôrt'ning), *n.* a fat, as butter, used to make pastry crisp or flaky.

short·fall (shôrt'fôl'), *n.* the quantity by which something falls short.

short·hand (shôrt'hand'), *n.* a method of rapid handwriting using simple strokes or symbols that designate letters, words, or phrases.

short·hand·ed (shôrt'han'did), *adj.* not having the necessary number of workers.

short·horn (shôrt'hôrn'), *n.* a breed of beef cattle having short horns.

short-lived (shôrt'līvd', -livd'), *adj.* living or lasting only a little while.

short·ly (shôrt'lē), *adv.* **1.** in a short or brief time. **2.** not at length, as in speech. **3.** *Literary.* curtly, as in reply or behavior.

short' or'der, an order for food that may be quickly prepared.

short-range (shôrt'rānj'), *adj.* having a limited extent, as in distance or time.

short' shrift', little attention or consideration, as in dealing with a matter.

short·sight·ed (shôrt'sī'tid), *adj.* **1.** lacking in foresight. **2.** *Chiefly Brit.* nearsighted (def. 1). —**short'sight'-ed·ly,** *adv.* —**short'sight'ed·ness,** *n.*

short·stop (shôrt'stop'), *n.* *Baseball.* the player covering the area between second and third base.

short' sto'ry, *n.* a piece of prose fiction, usually under 10,000 words.

short-tem·pered (shôrt'tem'pərd), *adj.* having a quick, hasty temper.

short-term (shôrt′tûrm′), *adj.* covering or applying to a relatively short period of time.

short′ ton′. See under **ton** (def. 1).

short·wave (shôrt′wāv′), *n.* a radio wave of 60 meters or less, used for long-distance reception or transmission.

short-wind·ed (shôrt′win′did), *adj.* short of breath.

Sho·sho·ne·an (shō shō′nē ən, shō′shə nē′ən), *adj.* 1. of a family of American Indian languages spoken in the western U.S. —*n.* 2. the Shoshonean languages taken collectively.

Sho·sho·ni (shō shō′nē), *n., pl.* **-nis, -ni.** a member of any of several Indian tribes, ranging from Wyoming to California. Also, **Sho·sho′ne.**

shot¹ (shot), *n., pl.* **shots** or, for 3, 5, **shot.** 1. the act of shooting. 2. the distance traveled by a missile in its flight. 3. a small lead ball or pellet, used esp. as ammunition for a shotgun. 4. a projectile for discharge from a firearm or cannon. 5. such projectiles collectively. 6. a marksman. 7. an iron ball used in shot put. 8. an aimed stroke or throw, as in certain games. 9. an attempt or try. 10. a remark aimed at someone. 11. *Informal.* a hypodermic injection. 12. *Informal.* a small quantity of liquor. 13. a photograph, esp. a snapshot. 14. *Motion Pictures.* a unit of action photographed by one camera. 15. *Archaic.* range or reach. 16. **call the shots,** *Slang.* to exercise control.

shot² (shot), *v.* 1. pt. and pp. of **shoot.** —*adj.* 2. *Slang.* in hopelessly bad condition.

shot·gun (shot′gun′), *n.* a gun used to fire a charge of shot or small pellets.

shot′ put′, a field event in which a heavy metal ball is thrown for distance. —**shot′-put′ter,** *n.* —**shot′-put′ting,** *n.*

should (shŏŏd), *auxiliary v.* 1. pt. of **shall.** 2. ought to: *You should call your mother.* 3. were or were to: *If it should snow, wear your warm boots.* 4. is likely to: *The train should be here any minute now.*

shoul·der (shōl′dər), *n.* 1. the part of each side of the body from the side of the neck to the region where the arm begins. 2. Usually, **shoulders.** these two parts together with the part of the back joining them. 3. a corresponding part in animals. 4. a shoulderlike part or projection. 5. an edge or border on the side of a road. 6. **straight from the shoulder,** without evasion. —*v.t.* 7. to push with or as with the shoulder, esp. roughly. 8. to carry on or as on the shoulder or shoulders. 9. to assume as a responsibility.

shoul′der blade′, scapula.

should·n't (shŏŏd′ənt), contraction of *should not.*

shout (shout), *v.i., v.t.* 1. to call or cry out loudly. —*n.* 2. a loud call or cry. —**shout′er,** *n.*

shove (shuv), *v.,* **shoved, shov·ing,** *n.* —*v.t., v.i.* 1. to move by pushing, esp. from behind. 2. to push roughly or rudely. 3. **shove off, a.** to push a boat from the shore. **b.** *Slang.* to leave or depart. —*n.* 4. the act or an instance of shoving.

shov·el (shuv′əl), *n., v.,* **-eled, -el·ing** or **-elled, -el·ling.** —*n.* 1. a tool having a broad blade or scoop attached to a long handle, used for lifting and moving soil, snow, etc. —*v.t.* 2. to lift and move with a shovel. 3. to dig or clear with a shovel. —**shov′el·ful′,** *n.*

show (shō), *v.,* **showed, shown** or **showed, show·ing,** *n.* —*v.t.* 1. to cause or allow to be seen. 2. to guide or usher. 3. to explain or make clear. 4. to prove or demonstrate. 5. to express by one's behavior, speech, etc. 6. to accord or grant (favor, etc.). —*v.i.* 7. to be or become visible. 8. to be seen in a certain way. 9. to finish third in a horse race. 10. **show off,** to display ostentatiously, esp. to gain attention. 11. **show up, a.** to make known, as faults. **b.** to exhibit in a certain way. **c.** to arrive at a place. —*n.* 12. a display or exhibition. 13. a radio, television, or theatrical presentation. 14. any public exhibition. 15. pretentious display. 16. an unreal appearance. 17. the third position at the finish of a horse race. —**Syn.** 1. display, exhibit. 3. clarify, disclose, reveal.

show′ bill′, a poster advertising a theatrical show.

show·case (shō′kās′), *n.* 1. a glass case for displaying and protecting articles in a shop, museum, etc. 2. anything that exhibits something or someone at its or one's best.

show·down (shō′doun′), *n.* a confrontation for the conclusive settlement of an issue.

show·er (shou′ər), *n.* 1. a brief fall of rain. 2. a fall of many objects, as tears. 3. Also called **show′er bath′.** a bath in which water is sprayed on the body. 4. a party for the giving of gifts, esp. to a prospective bride. —*v.t.* 5. to wet, as with a shower of rain. 6. to pour down, as in a shower. —*v.i.* 7. to rain in a shower. 8. to take a shower bath. —**show′er·y,** *adj.*

show·ing (shō′ing), *n.* 1. the act of putting something on display. 2. show (def. 12). 3. performance, as in a contest.

show·man (shō'mən), *n.* **1.** a person who presents or produces a theatrical show. **2.** a person gifted in presenting things in a dramatic way. — **show'man·ship'**, *n.*

shown (shōn), *v.* a pp. of **show.**

show·off (shō'ôf', -of'), *n.* **1.** a person given to pretentious display. **2.** the act of showing off.

show·piece (shō'pēs'), *n.* something worthy of exhibiting as a fine example of its kind.

show·place (shō'plās'), *n.* a place renowned for its beauty or history and usually open to the public.

show·room (shō'rōom', -rōom'), *n.* a room used for the display of merchandise or samples.

show' win'dow, a display window in a store.

show·y (shō'ē), *adj.,* **show·i·er, show·i·est. 1.** making an imposing display. **2.** ostentatious or gaudy. —**show'i·ly,** *adv.* —**show'i·ness,** *n.* —**Syn. 1.** conspicuous. **2.** flashy, garish.

shpt., shipment.

shr., share.

shrank (shrangk), *v.* a pt. of **shrink.**

shrap·nel (shrap'n³l), *n.* **1.** a. a hollow projectile containing bullets designed to explode before reaching the target. b. such projectiles collectively. **2.** shell fragments. [after H. *Shrapnel* (1761–1842), English inventor]

shred (shred), *n.,* *v.,* **shred·ded** or **shred, shred·ding.** —*n.* **1.** a piece cut or torn off, esp. in a narrow strip. **2.** a bit or scrap. —*v.t.* **3.** to cut or tear into shreds. —**shred'der,** *n.*

Shreve·port (shrēv'pôrt', -pōrt'), *n.* a city in NW Louisiana.

shrew¹ (shrōo), *n.* a woman of violent temper and speech. —**shrew'ish,** *adj.* —**shrew'ish·ness,** *n.*

shrew² (shrōo), *n.* a tiny mouselike animal having a long, sharp snout.

shrewd (shrōod), *adj.* clever or sharp in practical matters. —**shrewd'ly,** *adv.* —**shrewd'ness,** *n.* —**Syn.** acute, astute, keen, quick.

shriek (shrēk), *n.* **1.** a sharp, shrill cry. —*v.i.,* *v.t.* **2.** to cry out in a shriek.

shrift (shrift), *n.* **1.** See **short shrift. 2.** *Archaic.* the act of shriving.

shrike (shrīk), *n.* a predatory bird having a strong, hooked bill.

shrill (shril), *adj.* **1.** high-pitched and piercing in sound quality. —*v.t.,* *v.i.* **2.** to cry shrilly. —**shrill'ness,** *n.* —**shril'ly,** *adv.*

shrimp (shrimp), *n.,* *pl.* **shrimps, shrimp. 1.** a small, long-tailed crustacean, used as food. **2.** *Slang.* a small or insignificant person.

shrine (shrīn), *n.* **1.** a receptacle for sacred relics. **2.** the tomb of a saint.

3. any sacred place for prayer. **4.** any place hallowed by its associations.

shrink (shringk), *v.,* **shrank** or **shrunk; shrunk** or **shrunk·en; shrink·ing;** *n.* —*v.i.* **1.** to contract in size, as with heat or moisture. **2.** to draw back, as in fear. **3.** to become reduced in extent. —*v.t.* **4.** to cause to shrink. —*n.* **5.** shrinkage. **6.** *Slang.* a psychiatrist. —**shrink'a·ble,** *adj.*

shrink·age (shring'kij), *n.* **1.** the act of shrinking. **2.** the amount of shrinking. **3.** reduction or depreciation.

shrink'ing vi'olet, a shy, modest person.

shrink-wrap (shringk'rap'), *v.,* **-wrapped, -wrap·ping,** *n.* —*v.t.* **1.** to wrap and seal in a flexible film that, when exposed to heat, shrinks to the contour of the merchandise. —*n.* **2.** a cover so wrapped. Also, **shrink·pack** (shringk'pak').

shrive (shrīv), *v.t.,* **shrove** (shrōv) or **shrived; shriv·en** (shriv'ən) or **shrived; shriv·ing.** *Archaic.* to hear the confession and absolve (a penitent).

shriv·el (shriv'əl), *v.t.,* *v.i.,* **-eled, -el·ing** or **-elled, -el·ling.** to contract and wrinkle, as through dryness.

shroud (shroud), *n.* **1.** a cloth in which a corpse is wrapped for burial. **2.** something that covers or conceals. **3.** any of the taut ropes running from a masthead to the side of the ship. —*v.t.* **4.** to cover or hide from view.

shrub (shrub), *n.* a woody plant, smaller than a tree, with many separate stems. —**shrub'by,** *adj.*

shrub·ber·y (shrub'ə rē), *n.,* *pl.* **-ber·ies.** shrubs collectively.

shrug (shrug), *v.,* **shrugged, shrug·ging,** *n.* —*v.t.,* *v.i.* **1.** to hunch up (the shoulders), esp. to express doubt or indifference. **2. shrug off, a.** to disregard or minimize. **b.** to rid oneself of. —*n.* **3.** an act of shrugging.

shrunk (shrungk), *v.* a pt. and pp. of **shrink.**

shrunk·en (shrung'kən), *v.* a pp. of **shrink.**

sht., sheet.

shtg., shortage.

shtick (shtik), *n.* *Slang.* a short, comic or attention-getting routine.

shuck (shuk), *n.* **1.** the husk of corn. **2.** Usually, **shucks.** *Informal.* something useless: *not worth shucks.* —*v.t.* **3.** to remove the shucks from. —*interj.* **4. shucks,** (an exclamation of disgust or regret.) —**shuck'er,** *n.*

shud·der (shud'ər), *v.i.* **1.** to tremble convulsively, as from horror. —*n.* **2.** an act of shuddering. —**shud'der·ing·ly,** *adv.*

shuf·fle (shuf'əl), v., **-fled, -fling,** n. —v.i., v.t. **1.** to drag (the feet) clumsily in walking. **2.** to mix (playing cards) in a pack. **3.** to move (an object or objects) around or back and forth. —n. **4.** an act of shuffling. —**shuf'fler,** n.

shuf·fle·board (shuf'əl bōrd', -bôrd'), n. a game in which disks are shoved with a cue toward numbered sections on a floor.

shun (shun), v.t., **shunned, shun·ning.** to avoid habitually, esp. from distaste. —**shun'ner,** n.

shun·pike (shun'pīk'), v.i., **-piked, -pik·ing.** to avoid turnpikes or expressways to travel more leisurely and to avoid tolls. —**shun'pik'er,** n. —**shun'pik'ing,** n.

shunt (shunt), v.t., v.i. **1.** to turn aside or out of the way. **2.** Chiefly Brit. to switch (a railroad car). —n. **3.** the act of shunting. **4.** Chiefly Brit. a railroad switch. —**shunt'er,** n.

shush (shush), interj. **1.** (used as a command to be quiet or silent). —v.t. **2.** to command silence from by saying "shush."

shut (shut), v., **shut, shut·ting,** adj. —v.t. **1.** to put (a door, cover, etc.) in position to close. **2.** to close the doors of. **3.** to close (something) by bringing together or folding its parts. **4.** to confine or enclose. **5.** to cause (a business, etc.) to cease operations. —v.i. **6.** to become shut. **7. shut down,** to close, esp. temporarily, as a factory. **8. shut off,** a. to stop the passage of (water, etc.). b. to isolate or separate. **9. shut out,** a. to keep from entering. b. to prevent (an opposing team) from scoring. **10. shut up,** a. to confine or imprison. b. Informal. to stop or cause to stop talking. —adj. **11.** closed or fastened up.

shut·down (shut'doun'), n. a temporary closing, as of a factory.

shut·eye (shut'ī'), n. Slang. sleep.

shut-in (shut'in'), adj. **1.** confined to one's home, as from illness. —n. **2.** a shut-in invalid.

shut·out (shut'out'), n. any game in which one side does not score.

shut·ter (shut'ər), n. **1.** a solid or louvered cover for a window. **2.** a mechanism for opening and closing the aperture of a camera lens. —v.t. **3.** to close or provide with shutters.

shut·ter·bug (shut'ər bug'), n. Slang. an amateur photographer.

shut·tle (shut'əl), n., v., **-tled, -tling.** —n. **1.** a device in a loom for passing yarn back and forth through the warp. **2.** the sliding container that carries the lower thread in a sewing machine. **3.** a public conveyance, as an airplane, that travels back and forth at regular intervals over a short route. **4.** See **space shuttle.** —v.t., v.i. **5.** to move or cause to move back and forth by or as by a shuttle.

shut·tle·cock (shut'əl kok'), n. a feathered cork head having a plastic crown, used in badminton.

shy[1] (shī), adj., **shy·er** or **shi·er, shy·est** or **shi·est,** v., **shied, shy·ing.** —adj. **1.** not assertive in the presence of others, as persons of the opposite sex. **2.** easily frightened, as an animal. **3.** cautiously distrustful. **4.** Informal. deficient or short. —v.i. **5.** (esp. of a horse) to start back or aside, as in fear. **6.** to draw back, as from caution. —**shi'er, shy'er,** n. —**shy'ly,** adv. —**shy'ness,** n. —Syn. **1.** bashful, retiring, self-conscious. **2.** timid. **4.** wary.

shy[2] (shī), v.t., v.i., **shied, shy·ing.** to throw with a quick, sidelong movement.

shy·lock (shī'lok), n. a hardhearted, extortionate moneylender.

shy·ster (shī'stər), n. Informal. a lawyer who uses questionable methods.

Si, silicon.

S.I., Staten Island.

Si·am (sī am', sī'am), n. former name of Thailand. —**Si·a·mese** (sī'ə mēz', -mēs'), adj., n.

Si'amese twins', any twins who are born joined together in any manner.

Si·be·ri·a (sī bēr'ē ə), n. a wide section of the Soviet Union in N Asia. —**Si·be'ri·an,** adj., n.

sib·i·lant (sib'ə lənt), adj. **1.** characterized by a hissing sound. —n. **2.** a sibilant consonant, as s in this. —**sib'i·lance,** n. —**sib'i·lant·ly,** adv. —**sib'i·late'** (-lāt'), v.i., v.t.

sib·ling (sib'ling), n. a brother or sister.

sib·yl (sib'il), n. a prophetess in ancient Greece or Rome. —**sib·yl·line** (sib'ə lēn', -līn', -lin), adj.

sic[1] (sik), v.t., **sicked, sick·ing.** to urge (a dog) to attack.

sic[2] (sik, sēk), adv. Latin. thus: placed in brackets to indicate that a word or passage which may appear incorrect has been exactly quoted.

Sic·i·ly (sis'ə lē), n. an Italian island in the Mediterranean. —**Si·cil·ian** (si sil'yən, -il'ē ən), adj., n.

sick[1] (sik), adj. **1.** afflicted with disease or bad health. **2.** having nausea. **3.** of or for sick persons. **4.** deeply affected with some unpleasant feeling, as of sorrow. **5.** emotionally or morally disturbed. **6.** disgusted or chagrined. **7.** bored or tired. **8.** Informal. gruesome or sadistic: sick jokes. —n. **9. the sick,** sick persons collectively. —**sick'ish,** adj. —Syn. **1.** ailing, ill, indisposed, infirm.

sick[2] (sik), v.t. Chiefly Brit. sic[1].

sick' bay', a hospital and dispensary aboard ship.

sick·bed (sik′bed′), *n.* the bed used by a sick person.

sick·en (sik′ən), *v.t., v.i.* to make or become sick. —**sick′en·ing,** *adj.* — **sick′en·ing·ly,** *adv.*

sick·le (sik′əl), *n.* a tool having a curved blade mounted in a short handle, for cutting grain, grass, etc.

sick′le-cell′ ane′mia (sik′əl sel′), a hereditary anemia occurring chiefly among blacks, and characterized by acute abdominal pains and ulcerations on the legs.

sick·ly (sik′lē), *adj.,* **-li·er, -li·est. 1.** habitually sick or ailing. **2.** of or arising from ill health. **3.** maudlin and insipid. **4.** faint or feeble, as color. —**sick′li·ness,** *n.*

sick·ness (sik′nis), *n.* **1.** the state of being sick. **2.** a particular disease. **3.** nausea or vomiting.

sick·out (sik′out′), *n.* a form of job action in which some employees refuse to come for work, falsely claiming illness as the reason.

side (sīd), *n., adj., v.,* **sid·ed, sid·ing.** —*n.* **1.** one of the surfaces forming the outside of a thing. **2.** either of the two broad surfaces of a thin, flat object, as a door. **3.** either of the two lateral parts or areas of a thing. **4.** either lateral half of a human or animal body. **5.** an aspect or phase. **6.** any direction or position with reference to a central space or point. **7.** one of two or more contesting teams, parties, etc. **8.** the position or course of a person or group opposing another. **9.** a line of descent through a parent. **10.** a space next to a person or object. **11. on the side,** in addition to one's regular work or interest. **12. side by side,** next to each other. **13. take sides,** to be partial to one side. —*adj.* **14.** at or on one side. **15.** from or toward one side. **16.** subordinate or incidental: *a side issue.* —*v.i.* **17. side with** or **against,** to support or refuse to support (one group, opinion, etc.).

side′ arm′, a weapon, as a pistol, carried at the side or in the belt.

side-arm (sīd′ärm′), *adv., adj.* with the arm extended and moved at or below shoulder level.

side·board (sīd′bōrd′, -bôrd′), *n.* a piece of furniture, as in a dining room, for holding articles of table service.

side·burns (sīd′bûrnz′), *n.pl.* the growth of hair on a man's face that extends downward in front of the ears.

side·car (sīd′kär′), *n.* a small car attached on one side to a motorcycle.

side′ effect′, a secondary and harmful effect, esp. of a medicine.

side·kick (sīd′kik′), *n. Informal.* **1.** a close friend. **2.** a confederate or assistant.

side·light (sīd′līt′), *n.* an item of incidental information.

side·line (sīd′līn′), *n.* **1.** *Sports.* either of the two lines defining the side boundaries of a playing field. **2.** a business or activity pursued in addition to one's primary business.

side·long (sīd′lông′, -long′), *adj.* **1.** directed to one side. —*adv.* **2.** toward the side.

side·man (sīd′man′, -mən), *n.* an instrumentalist in a band or orchestra.

side·piece (sīd′pēs′), *n.* a piece forming a side or a part of a side of something.

si·de·re·al (sī dēr′ē əl), *adj.* of or determined by the stars.

sid·er·ite (sīd′ə rīt′), *n.* a gray-brown mineral that is a minor ore of iron.

side·sad·dle (sīd′sad′əl), *n.* **1.** a woman's saddle on which the rider faces front but with both legs on one side of the horse. —*adv.* **2.** seated on a sidesaddle.

side·show (sīd′shō′), *n.* **1.** a minor show in connection with a principal one, as at a circus. **2.** any subordinate event or matter.

side·split·ting (sīd′split′ing), *adj.* **1.** convulsively uproarious. **2.** producing uproarious laughter.

side·step (sīd′step′), *v.i., v.t.,* **-stepped, -step·ping. 1.** to step to one side. **2.** to evade or avoid (a problem, etc.). —**side′step′per,** *n.*

side·stroke (sīd′strōk′), *n. Swimming.* a stroke in which the body is turned sideways, the hands pull alternately, and the legs perform a scissors kick.

side·swipe (sīd′swīp′), *n., v.,* **-swiped, -swip·ing.** —*n.* **1.** a sweeping blow along the side. —*v.t.* **2.** to strike with such a blow. —**side′swip′er,** *n.*

side·track (sīd′trak′), *v.t., v.i.* **1.** to move from the main track to a siding, as a train. **2.** to move or distract from the main subject or course. —*n.* **3.** siding (def. 1).

side·walk (sīd′wôk′), *n.* a paved path at the side of a street or road.

side·wall (sīd′wôl′), *n.* the part of a tire between the tread and the rim of the wheel.

side·ways (sīd′wāz′), *adv.* **1.** with a side forward. **2.** toward or from one side. —*adj.* **3.** directed toward one side. Also, **side′wise′** (-wīz′).

side·wind·er (sīd′wīn′dər), *n.* a rattlesnake of the southwestern U.S. that moves in loose sand by throwing loops of the body forward.

sid·ing (sī′ding), *n.* **1.** a short railroad track connected with the main track at both ends. **2.** material for covering the outside walls of a frame house.

si·dle (sīd/ᵊl), v.i., -dled, -dling. to move sideways, esp. furtively. —**si′- dling·ly,** adv.

siege (sēj), n. 1. the surrounding and attacking of a fortified place in order to capture it. 2. a prolonged and persistent period, as of illness. 3. **lay siege to,** to surround and attack.

si·er·ra (sē er′ᵊ), n. a chain of mountains whose peaks resemble the teeth of a saw. [< Sp: lit., saw < L serra]

Si·er·ra Le·o·ne (sē er′ᵊ lē ōn′), a country in W Africa.

si·es·ta (sē es′tᵊ), n. a midday nap, esp. as taken in Latin America.

sieve (siv), n. a utensil with a meshed or perforated bottom, used for sifting or straining.

sift (sift), v.t. 1. to pass (flour, etc.) through a sieve to separate larger particles from small ones. 2. to separate by or as by a sieve. 3. to examine closely. —v.i. 4. to pass as through a sieve. —**sift′er,** n.

sig., 1. signal. 2. signature.

sigh (sī), v.i. 1. to let out one's breath audibly, as from sorrow or relief. 2. to yearn or long. —**sigh′er,** n.

sight (sīt), n. 1. the power of seeing. 2. the act or fact of seeing. 3. a person's range of vision. 4. a view or glimpse. 5. something seen or worth seeing. 6. Informal. something shocking or distressing to see. 7. an optical device, as on a firearm, for aiding the eye in aiming. 8. an observation taken with a surveying instrument. 9. **a sight for sore eyes,** Informal. something or someone delightful to see. 10. **at first sight,** at the first glimpse or at once. 11. **at** or **on sight,** immediately upon seeing. 12. **know by sight,** to be able to identify by appearance only. 13. **not by a long sight,** a. probably not. b. definitely not. —v.t. 14. to see or observe. 15. to aim (a firearm) by a sight.

sight·ed (sī′tid), adj. having sight or vision.

sight·less (sīt′lis), adj. 1. lacking sight or vision. 2. Rare. invisible or unseen.

sight·ly (sīt′lē), adj., -li·er, -li·est. pleasing to the sight. —**sight′li·ness,** n.

sight-read (sīt′rēd′), v.t., v.i., -read, -read·ing. to read or perform (written music) without previous practice or study. —**sight′ read′er,** —**sight′ read′ing.**

sight·see·ing (sīt′sē′iṅg), n. 1. the act of visiting places of interest. —adj. 2. of or used for sightseeing. — **sight′se′er,** n.

sig·ma (sig′mᵊ), n. the 18th letter of the Greek alphabet (Σ, σ, ς).

sign (sīn), n. 1. a mark or character used to represent an idea or object, as in arithmetic or music. 2. something that indicates the presence or occurrence of something else. 3. a motion or gesture used to convey an idea, command, etc. 4. a board or metal plate bearing an advertisement, warning, etc. 5. a trace or vestige. 6. an omen or portent. 7. any of the 12 divisions of the zodiac. —v.t. 8. to affix a signature to. 9. to write as a signature. 10. to engage by written agreement. 11. to communicate by means of a sign. —v.i. 12. to write one's signature, as a token of agreement. 13. **sign in** or **out,** to report on arrival or departure. 14. **sign off,** to cease radio or television broadcasting. 15. **sign on,** a. to employ or hire. b. to start radio or television broadcasting. 16. **sign up,** to enlist in the armed forces. —**sign′er,** n.

sig·nal (sig′nᵊl), n., adj., v., -naled, nal·ing or -nalled, -nal·ling. —n. 1. a device or sound that serves as a warning, command, or other message. 2. an act or event that incites some action. 3. an electrical impulse representing sound or picture transmitted or received, as in radio. —adj. 4. serving as a signal. 5. notable or outstanding. —v.t., v.i. 6. to make a signal (to). 7. to communicate by a signal. —**sig′nal·ly,** adv. —**sig′nal·er,** n.

sig·nal·ize (sig′nᵊlīz′), v.t., -ized, -iz·ing. 1. to make conspicuous. 2. to indicate particularly. —**sig′nal·i·za′- tion,** n.

sig·na·to·ry (sig′nᵊ tōr′ē, -tôr′ē), adj., n., pl. -ries. —adj. 1. having joined in signing a document. —n. 2. a signatory person or country.

sig·na·ture (sig′nᵊ chᵊr), n. 1. a person's name signed or written by himself or herself. 2. Music. the sign placed at the beginning of a staff to indicate key or time.

sign·board (sīn′bōrd′, -bôrd′), n. a board bearing a sign, as an advertisement.

sig·net (sig′nit), n. a small seal, as in a finger ring, used to stamp documents.

sig·nif·i·cance (sig nif′ᵊ kᵊns), n. 1. important consequence. 2. meaning or sense. 3. signified expressiveness.

sig·nif·i·cant (sig nif′ᵊ kᵊnt), adj. 1. of important consequence. 2. full of meaning or sense. 3. specially expressive. —**sig·nif′i·cant·ly,** adv. — Syn. 1. critical, momentous, weighty.

sig·ni·fy (sig′nᵊ fī′), v., -fied, -fy·ing. —v.t. 1. to be a sign or indication of. 2. to make known, as by signs or speech. —v.i. 3. to be of impor-

tance. —sig′ni·fi·ca′tion, n. —Syn.
1. betoken, mean, represent. 2. express, indicate.

si·gnor (sēn′yōr, -yôr, sin yōr′, -yôr′), n., pl. -gnors, -gno·ri (-nyô′Rē). *Italian.* Mr. or sir.

si·gno·ra (sin yōr′ə, -yôr′ə), n., pl. -ras, -re (-Rε). *Italian.* Mrs. or madam.

si·gno·ri·na (sēn′yô rē′nə), n., pl. -nas, -ne (-ne). *Italian.* Miss.

sign·post (sīn′pōst′), n. a post bearing a sign that gives information or guidance.

Sikh (sēk), n. a member of a Hindu religious sect refusing to recognize the caste system. —Sikh′ism, n.

si·lage (sī′lij), n. fodder preserved in a silo.

si·lence (sī′ləns), n., v., -lenced, -lenc·ing, *interj.* —n. 1. absence of any sound. 2. the state of being silent. 3. absence of mention. —v.t. 4. to put or bring to silence. 5. to put (fears, etc.) to rest. —*interj.* 6. be silent!

si·lenc·er (sī′lən sər), n. a device for deadening the noise of a firearm.

si·lent (sī′lənt), adj. 1. making no sound. 2. refraining from speech. 3. speechless or mute. 4. habitually talking very little. 5. unspoken or tacit. 6. not sounded or pronounced, as the *b* in doubt. 7. *Motion Pictures.* not having a soundtrack. —si′lent·ly, adv. —si′lent·ness, n. —Syn. 4. reticent, taciturn, uncommunicative.

sil·hou·ette (sil′ōō et′), n., v., -et·ted, -et·ting. —n. 1. an outline drawing uniformly filled in with black. 2. a dark image outlined against a lighter background. —v.t. 3. to show in or as in a silhouette.

sil·i·ca (sil′ə kə), n. a compound of silicon and oxygen occurring esp. as quartz and sand.

sil·i·cate (sil′ə kit, -kāt′), n. a compound containing silicon, oxygen, and a metal.

si·li·ceous (si lish′əs), adj. containing, consisting of, or resembling silica.

sil·i·con (sil′ə kən, -kon′), n. *Chem.* a nonmetallic element occurring in a combined state in minerals and rocks and constituting more than one fourth of the earth's crust. *Symbol:* Si; *at. wt.:* 28.086; *at. no.:* 14.

sil·i·cone (sil′ə kōn′), n. any of a number of polymers containing alternate silicon and oxygen atoms, extremely resistant to heat: used as adhesives, insulators, etc.

sil·i·co·sis (sil′ə kō′sis), n. a lung disease caused by the inhaling of siliceous particles.

silk (silk), n. 1. the soft, lustrous fiber obtained from the cocoon of the silkworm. 2. thread or fabric made from this fiber. 3. any fiber

resembling silk. —silk′en, adj. —silk′y, adj.

silk·screen (silk′skrēn′), n. 1. a process of printing fine colors through a piece of stencil silk stretched over a wooden frame. —v.t. 2. to print by silkscreen.

silk·worm (silk′wûrm′), n. the larva of a Chinese moth that spins a silken cocoon.

sill (sil), n. 1. the horizontal piece beneath a window or door. 2. a horizontal timber or block serving as a foundation of a wall or house.

sil·ly (sil′ē), adj., -li·er, -li·est. pointlessly, often laughably foolish. —sil′li·ness, n. —Syn. absurd, ridiculous, senseless, stupid.

si·lo (sī′lō), n., pl. -los. 1. a structure, typically cylindrical, in which fodder or forage is kept. 2. an underground installation for housing a ballistic missile.

silt (silt), n. 1. fine earth or sand carried by rivers and deposited as sediment. —v.i., v.t. 2. to fill or choke up with silt. —sil·ta′tion, n. —silt′y, adj.

Si·lu·ri·an (si lŏŏr′ē ən, sī-), adj. 1. noting a period of the Paleozoic era, occurring from 400,000,000 to 440,-000,000 years ago and characterized by the appearance of air-breathing animals. —n. 2. the Silurian period.

sil·ver (sil′vər), n. 1. *Chem.* a white, ductile metallic element, used for making coins, jewelry, table utensils, etc. *Symbol:* Ag; *at. wt.:* 107.870; *at. no.:* 47. 2. coins made of this metal. 3. silverware. 4. a shining grayish white. —adj. 5. made of or coated with silver. 6. resembling silver. —v.t. 7. to coat with silver. —sil′ver·er, n.

sil·ver·fish (sil′vər fish′), n. a wingless, silvery-gray insect that feeds on starch and damages books, wallpaper, etc.

sil′ver i′odide, a pale-yellow powder that darkens on exposure to light, used in medicine, photography, and rainmaking.

sil′ver lin′ing, a sign of hope in an unfortunate situation.

sil′ver ni′trate, a corrosive, poisonous powder, used chiefly in making photographic emulsions and as an antiseptic.

sil·ver·smith (sil′vər smith′), n. a person who makes or repairs articles of silver.

sil·ver·ware (sil′vər wâr′), n. 1. articles, esp. tableware, made of or plated with silver. 2. tableware made of stainless steel.

sil·ver·y (sil′və rē), adj. 1. of a shining grayish-white color. 2. having a clear, ringing tone. —sil′ver·i·ness, n.

sim·i·an (sim'ē ən), *adj.* **1.** of or characteristic of apes or monkeys. —*n.* **2.** an ape or monkey.

sim·i·lar (sim'ə lər), *adj.* alike in a general way but not exactly. —**sim'i·lar'i·ty** (-lar'i tē), *n.* —**sim'i·lar·ly**, *adv.* —**Syn.** comparable, resembling.

sim·i·le (sim'ə lē), *n.* a figure of speech in which two unlike things are explicitly compared, as in "she is like a rose [< L. likeness]

si·mil·i·tude (s mil' tōōd', -tyōōd'), *n.* comparative resemblance.

sim·mer (sim'ər), *v.i.* **1.** to cook at or just below the boiling point. **2.** to be in a state of subdued excitement or anger. —*v.t.* **3.** to keep in a state approaching boiling **4.** **simmer down,** to become calm or quiet. —*n.* **5.** the state of simmering.

si·mon·ize (sī'mə nīz'), *v.t.*, *v.i.* to polish (an automobile) with wax. [from *Simoniz* a trademark]

si·mon-pure (sī'mən pyŏor'), *adj.* utterly pure or real

si·mo·ny (sī'mə nē, sim'ə-), *n.* (formerly) the buying or selling of benefices.

sim·pa·ti·co (sim pä'ti kō', -pat'i-), *adj.* compatibly responsive.

sim·per (sim'pər), *n.* **1.** a silly, self-conscious smile —*v.i.* **2.** to put on such a smile —**sim'per·ing·ly**, *adv.* —**sim'per·er**, *n*

sim·ple (sim'pəl), *adj.*, **-pler, -plest,** *n.* —*adj.* **1.** easy to solve, learn, or do. **2.** not complicated or complex. **3.** plain and straightforward. **4.** not pretentious or sophisticated. **5.** without ornament or fancy. **6.** having nothing added *the simple truth.* **7.** lacking in intelligence. **8.** of humble origin —*n* **9.** *Archaic.* a person of humble origin **10.** *Archaic.* a medicinal herb —**sim'ple·ness,** *n.*

sim·ple in'terest. interest payable only on the principal.

sim·ple-mind·ed (sim'pəl mīn'did), *adj.* **1.** free of subtlety or sophistication. **2.** lacking in mental acuteness. **3.** mentally deficient. —**sim'ple·mind'ed·ly**, *adv* —**sim'ple·mind'ed·ness,** *n* —**Syn 1.** artless, guileless.

sim·ple·ton (sim'pəl tən), *n.* a foolish or silly person

sim·plic·i·ty (sim plis'i tē), *n.*, *pl.* **-ties.** **1.** freedom from complexity. **2.** absence of luxury or pretentiousness. **3.** freedom from artificiality or guile. **4.** lack of mental acuteness.

sim·pli·fy (sim'plə fī'), *v.t.*, **-fied, -fy·ing.** to make simple or simpler. —**sim'pli·fi·ca'tion**, *n*

sim·plis·tic (sim plis'tik), *adj.* tending to simplify to the point of error. —**sim·plis'ti·cal·ly**, *adv.*

sim·ply (sim'plē), *adv.* **1.** in a simple manner. **2.** merely or only. **3.** absolutely or utterly.

sim·u·late (sim'yə lāt'), *v.t.*, **-lat·ed, -lat·ing.** **1.** to make a pretense of, esp. something advantageous. **2.** to assume the appearance of. —**sim'u·la'tive,** *adj.* —**sim'u·la'tor,** *n.*

si·mul·cast (sī'məl kast', -käst', sim'-əl-), *n., v.,* **-cast, -cast·ing.** —*n.* **1.** a program broadcast simultaneously on radio and television. —*v.t.* **2.** to broadcast in this way.

si·mul·ta·ne·ous (sī'məl tā'nē əs, sim'-əl-), *adj.* existing or done at the same time. —**si'mul·ta'ne·ous·ly,** *adv.* —**si'mul·ta'ne·ous·ness, si'mul·ta·ne'i·ty** (-tə nē'i tē), *n.*

sin (sin), *n., v.,* **sinned, sin·ning.** —*n.* **1.** a willful violation of some religious or moral principle. **2.** any wrong or evil act. **3. live in sin,** to cohabit —*v.i.* **4.** to commit a sin. —**sin'less,** *adj.* —**sin'ner,** *n.*

Si·nai (sī'nī, sī'nē ī'), *n.* Mount, the mountain on which Moses received the Commandments.

since (sins), *adv.* **1.** from then till now. **2.** between a particular past time and the present. **3.** before now *long since.* —*prep.* **4.** continuously from or counting from **5.** between a past time or event and the present —*conj.* **6.** in the period following the time when **7.** counting from the time when. **8.** because.

sin·cere (sin sēr'), *adj.*, **-cer·er, -cer·est. 1.** free from pretense or falseness. **2.** real or genuine. —**sin·cere'ly,** *adv.* —**sin·cer'i·ty** (-ser'i tē), *n.* —**Syn. 1.** candid, earnest, frank, honest.

si·ne·cure (sī'nə kyŏor', sin'ə-), *n.* a job or position requiring little work, esp. one that pays well.

si·ne di·e (sī'nē dī'ē), *Latin.* without fixing a day for future meeting.

si·ne qua non (sī'nē kwä non'), *Latin.* an indispensable condition.

sin·ew (sin'yōō), *n.* **1.** tendon. **2.** physical strength or power. —**sin'ew·y** (-yōō ē), *adj.*

sin·ful (sin'fəl), *adj.* characterized by or full of sin. —**sin'ful·ly,** *adv.* —**sin'ful·ness,** *n.*

sing (sing), *v.,* **sang** or (*Rare*) **sung, sung, sing·ing.** *n.* —*v.i.* **1.** to use the voice to produce musical sounds. **2.** to produce melodious sounds, as certain birds and insects. **3.** to tell about or praise in verse or song. **4.** to make a ringing or whizzing sound. **5.** *Slang.* to confess or act as an informer. —*v.t.* **6.** to render (a song) by singing. **7.** to bring to a certain state with or by singing: *She sang the baby to sleep.* **8.** to tell or praise in verse or song. —*n.* **9.** a gathering or party for the purpose of singing. —**sing'er,** *n.*

sing., singular.

Sin·ga·pore (sǐng′gə pōr′, -pôr′, sǐng′-ə-), n. an island country in the South China Sea, S of the Malay Peninsula.

singe (sǐnj), v., **singed, singe·ing,** n. —v.t. 1. to burn superficially. 2. to subject (a carcass) to flame in order to remove bristles or feathers. —n. 3. a superficial burn. 4. the act of singeing.

Sin·gha·lese (sǐng′gə lēz′, -lēs′), adj., n., pl. **-lese.** —adj. 1. of a large group of people in Sri Lanka or their language —n 2. a member of the Singhalese people 3. their language.

sin·gle (sǐng′gəl), adj., v., **-gled, -gling,** n. —adj 1. one only 2. of or for one person or family only. 3. solitary or sole 4. not married. 5. of one against one as combat. 6. consisting of only one part, element, or member. 7. sincere and undivided: single devotion 8. separate or individual. —v.t 9. to choose (one) from others. —v.i. 10. Baseball. to hit a single —n. 11. one person or thing. 12. an accommodation for one person 13. Baseball a hit that advances the batter to first base. 14. **singles,** a match with one player on each side, as a tennis match 15. Informal. a one-dollar bill. 16. Usually, **singles** unmarried people collectively. — **sin′gle·ness,** n.

sin·gle-breast·ed (sǐng′gəl bres′tid), adj. having a single button or row of buttons in the front, as a coat.

sin·gle file′, a line of persons or things arranged one behind the other.

sin·gle-hand·ed (sǐng′gəl han′did), adj. 1. done by one person alone. 2. having or using only one hand or one person. —**sin′gle·hand′ed·ly,** adv. —**sin′gle·hand′ed·ness,** n

sin′gle-lens′ re′flex (sǐng′gəl lenz′), a type of reflex camera in which the image passes through the same lens to both the ground glass and the film.

sin·gle-mind·ed (sǐng′gəl mīn′did), adj. having a single aim or purpose. —**sin′gle-mind′ed·ly,** adv. —**sin′gle-mind′ed·ness** n

sin·gle·ton (sǐng′gəl tən), n. Cards. a card that is the only one of a suit in a hand.

sin·gle-track (sǐng′gəl trak′), adj. one-track.

sin·gle·tree (sǐng′gəl trē′), n. whiffletree.

sin·gly (sǐng′glē), adv. 1. one at a time. 2. alone or without aid.

sing·song (sǐng′sông′, song′), n. monotonous, rhythmical cadence or tone.

sin·gu·lar (sǐng′gyə lər), adj. 1. beyond the usual or ordinary. 2. strange or odd. 3. unique or sole. 4. Gram. denoting one person, thing,

or instance. —n. Gram. 5. the singular number 6. a form in the singular. —**sin′gu·lar′i·ty** (-lar′i tē), n. —**sin′gu·lar·ly,** adv.

Sin·ha·lese (sǐn′hə lēz′, -lēs′), adj., n., pl. **-lese.** Singhalese.

sin·is·ter (sǐn′i stər), adj. 1. threatening evil, harm, or trouble. 2. mysteriously wicked. —**sin′is·ter·ly,** adv. —**Syn.** 1. foreboding, ominous. 2. evil, malevolent.

sink (sǐngk), v., **sank** or (Rare) **sunk; sunk** or (chiefly as an adj.) **sunk·en; sink·ing;** n. —v.i. 1. to become submerged or partially submerged in water. 2. to fall or descend gradually to a lower level. 3. to become lower in extent or intensity. 4. to degenerate or decline. 5. to pass or drop gradually into a particular state: to sink into slumber. 6. to fail gradually in strength or health. 7. to enter or permeate the mind. 8. to become hollow, as the cheeks. —v.t. 9. to cause to sink. 10. to bury or lay (a pipe, etc.) in or into the ground. 11. to dig or excavate (a well, etc.). 12. to invest (money) in a business venture. —n. 13. a basin having faucets and a drain, used for washing. 14. a low-lying, poorly drained area. 15. a drain or sewer. —**sink′a·ble,** adj.

sink·er (sǐng′kər), n. 1. a person or thing that sinks. 2. a weight, as of lead, for sinking a fishing line or net.

sink′ing fund′, a fund set aside periodically to pay off a debt, as of a company.

Sino-, a combining form meaning "Chinese": Sino-Japanese.

sin·u·ous (sǐn′yōō əs), adj. having many curves, bends, or turns. —**sin′u·os′i·ty** (-os′i tē), n. —**sin′u·ous·ly,** adv.

si·nus (sī′nəs), n. one of the hollow cavities in the skull that connect with the nasal passages.

si·nus·i·tis (sī′nə sī′tis), n. inflammation of a sinus or the sinuses.

Sioux (sōō), n., pl. **Sioux** (sōō, sōōz). Dakota (def. 1). Also, **Siou·an** (sōō′ən).

sip (sip), v., **sipped, sip·ping,** n. —v.t., v.i. 1. to drink bit by bit. —n. 2. the act of sipping. 3. a small quantity taken by sipping.

SIPC (sip′ik), Securities Investor Protection Corporation.

si·phon (sī′fən), n. 1. a tube bent into legs of unequal length, for use in transferring a liquid from an upper level to a lower one by means of suction created by the weight of the liquid in the longer leg. 2. a bottle from which soda water is forced by a compressed gas. —v.t., v.i. 3. to draw off through a siphon. —**si′phon·al, si·phon′ic** (-fon′ik), adj.

sir (sûr), *n.* **1.** a respectful or formal term of address for a man, used without the name. **2.** (*cap.*) the distinctive title of a knight or baronet, used before the name.

sire (sī′ər), *n., v.,* **sired, sir·ing.** —*n.* **1.** the male parent of a quadruped. **2.** *Archaic.* a respectful term of address for a king. **3.** *Archaic.* a father or forefather. —*v.t.* **4.** (esp. of a quadruped) to be the sire of.

si·ren (sī′rən), *n.* **1.** a device for producing a loud, piercing or wailing sound, used as a warning signal. **2.** (*often cap.*) *Class. Myth.* one of several sea nymphs, part woman and part bird, supposed to lure mariners to destruction by their seductive singing. **3.** a seductively beautiful woman.

sir·loin (sûr′loin), *n.* the portion of the loin of beef in front of the rump.

si·roc·co (sə rok′ō), *n., pl.* **-cos.** a hot, dusty wind blowing from N Africa into S Europe.

sir·up (sir′əp, sûr′-), *n.* syrup.

sis (sis), *n. Informal.* sister.

si·sal (sī′səl, sis′əl), *n.* a strong cordage fiber yielded by an agave.

sis·sy (sis′ē), *n., pl.* **-sies. 1.** an effeminate boy or man. **2.** a timid or cowardly person. —**sis′si·fied,** *adj.*

sis·ter (sis′tər), *n.* **1.** a female having the same parents as another. **2.** a female having only one parent in common with another. **3.** a female fellow member, as of a church. **4.** a female member of a religious community. **5.** *Brit.* a head nurse of a hospital ward. —**sis′ter·ly,** *adj.*

sis·ter·hood (sis′tər hŏŏd′), *n.* **1.** the state of being a sister. **2.** a group of sisters, esp. of nuns.

sis·ter-in-law (sis′tər in lô′), *n., pl.* **sis·ters-in-law. 1.** the sister of one's husband or wife. **2.** the wife of one's brother. **3.** the wife of the brother of one's husband or wife.

Sis·y·phus (sis′ə fəs), *n. Class. Myth.* a ruler of Corinth, an ancient city of Greece, who was punished in Hades by being forced to roll a large stone uphill, which always rolled down again from the top.

sit (sit), *v.,* **sat, sit·ting.** —*v.i.* **1.** to rest with the body supported by the buttocks or thighs. **2.** to be located or situated. **3.** to pose, as for a portrait. **4.** to remain quiet or inactive. **5.** (of a bird) to perch or roost. **6.** (of a hen) to cover eggs to hatch them. **7.** to occupy a seat, as a legislator or judge. **8.** to be in session, as an assembly. **9.** to baby-sit. —*v.t.* **10.** to cause to sit. **11.** to sit astride (a horse). **12. sit in on,** to attend or participate in.

13. sit up, a. to sit upright. **b.** to delay going to bed. **c.** *Informal.* to become interested or aware. —**sit′ter,** *n.*

si·tar (si tär′), *n.* a lute of India.

sit·com (sit′kom′), *n. Informal.* See **situation comedy.**

sit-down (sit′doun′), *n.* **1.** a strike in which workers refuse to leave their place of employment. **2.** a demonstration launched by participants who refuse to move from a public place.

site (sīt), *n.* **1.** the location of a place. **2.** the ground set aside for a building.

sit-in (sit′in′), *n.* a prolonged type of sit-down demonstration, esp. by a civil-rights group.

sit·ting (sit′ing), *n.* **1.** the act or position of a person or thing that sits. **2.** a period of being seated. **3.** a session, as of a legislature.

sit′ting duck′, *Slang.* a helpless or open target or victim.

sit′ting room′, *Chiefly Brit.* See **living room.**

sit·u·ate (sich′ŏŏ āt′), *v.t.,* **-at·ed, -at·ing.** to put in or on a particular site or place.

sit·u·a·tion (sich′ŏŏ ā′shən), *n.* **1.** a state of affairs. **2.** location or position. **3.** a position of employment. —**sit′u·a′tion·al,** *adj.*

sit′ua′tion com′edy, a television comedy series about characters who find themselves in complex, often ludicrous predicaments.

sit·up (sit′up′), *n.* an exercise of lifting the torso from a lying position to a sitting position without bending the legs.

si·tus (sī′təs), *n., pl.* **-tus.** *Law.* a fixed site, as for construction.

sitz′ bath′ (sits, zits), a bath in which the thighs and hips are immersed, esp. as a therapeutic treatment.

six (siks), *n.* **1.** a cardinal number, five plus one. **2.** a symbol for this number, as 6 or VI. —*adj.* **3.** amounting to six in number. — **sixth,** *adj., n.*

six-pack (siks′pak′), *n.* six bottles or cans, as of beer, packaged together for sale as one unit.

six·pence (siks′pəns), *n.* **1.** a sum of six British pennies. **2.** a former British coin worth this sum.

six-shoot·er (siks′shŏŏ′tər, -shŏŏ′-), *n.* a revolver from which six shots can be fired without reloading. Also called **six′-gun′.**

six·teen (siks′tēn′), *n.* **1.** a cardinal number, ten plus six. **2.** a symbol for this number, as 16 or XVI. —*adj.* **3.** amounting to 16 in number. —**six′teenth′,** *adj., n.*

sixth′ sense′, a keen intuitive perception.

six·ty (siks'tē), *n., pl.* **-ties,** *adj.* **—n.**
1. a cardinal number, 10 times 6.
2. a symbol for this number, as
60 or LX. **—adj. 3.** amounting to
60 in number. **—six'ti·eth** (-ith),
adj., n.

siz·a·ble (sī'zə bəl), *adj.* fairly large.
Also, **size'a·ble. —siz'a·bly,** *adv.*

size[1] (sīz), *n., v.,* **sized, siz·ing. —n.**
1. the spatial dimensions, proportions, or extent of anything. **2.** any
of a series of graduated measures
for articles of manufacture or trade.
—v.t. 3. to arrange or sort according
to size. **4. size up,** *Informal.* **a.** to
form an estimate or opinion of.
b. to meet a certain standard.

size[2] (sīz), *n., v.,* **sized, siz·ing. —n. 1.**
a gluelike substance used for filling
the pores of cloth, paper, etc. **—v.t.
2.** to coat or treat with size.

siz·ing (sī'zing), *n.* **1.** size[2]. **2.** the
act or process of treating with size.

siz·zle (siz'əl), *v.,* **-zled, -zling,** *n.*
—v.i. 1. to make a hissing sound,
as in frying. **2.** to be very hot. **—n.
3.** a sizzling sound.

S.J., Society of Jesus.

S.J.D., Doctor of Juridical Science.
[< L *Scientiae Juridicae Doctor*]

skag (skag), *n. Slang.* heroin.

skate[1] (skāt), *n., v.,* **skat·ed, skat·ing.
—n. 1.** a shoe fitted with a metal
blade for gliding on ice. **2.** See
roller skate. —v.i. 3. to glide or
move on skates. **—skat'er,** *n.*

skate[2] (skāt), *n.* an ocean flatfish
having broad fins.

skate·board (skāt'bôrd', -bōrd'), *n.*
1. a short, oblong piece of plastic or
wood mounted on small wheels, used
for gliding on a hard surface. **—v.i.
2.** to glide on a skateboard, esp. as
a sport. **—skate'board'er,** *n.* **—
skate'board'ing,** *n.*

skeet (skēt), *n.* trapshooting in which
targets are hurled at such angles as
to approximate the flight of game
birds.

skein (skān), *n.* a length of yarn
or thread wound on a reel or in a
loose coil.

skel·e·ton (skel'i tºn), *n.* **1.** the bony
framework supporting an animal
body. **2.** any supporting framework,
as of a house. **3.** an outline, as of
a literary work. [< Gk: mummy]
—skel'e·tal, *adj.* **—skel'e·tal·ly,** *adv.*

skel'eton key', a key filed down in
such a way that it can open many
locks.

skep·tic (skep'tik), *n.* **1.** a person who
frequently questions ideas or facts
widely accepted. **2.** a person who
doubts the truth of a religion. **3.**
an adherent of philosophical skepticism.

skep·ti·cal (skep'ti kəl), *adj.* inclined
to doubt or question, often instinc-

tively. **—skep'ti·cal·ly,** *adv.* **—Syn.**
incredulous, unbelieving.

skep·ti·cism (skep'ti siz'əm), *n.* **1.**
skeptical attitude. **2.** doubt with
regard to a religion. **3.** the philosophical doctrine that no knowledge
is trustworthy.

sketch (skech), *n.* **1.** a drawing made
quickly or left unfinished. **2.** a brief,
general outline. **3.** a short play,
esp. a comic one. **—v.t., v.i. 4.** to
make a sketch (of). **—sketch'er,** *n.*
—sketch'y, *adj.* **—sketch'i·ly,** *adv.*
—sketch'i·ness, *n.*

skew (skyoō), *v.i., v.t.* **1.** to take or
give an oblique course (to). **—adj. 2.**
oblique or slanting. **—n. 3.** an
oblique course.

skew·er (skyoō'ər), *n.* **1.** a long pin
for holding meat together while
being cooked. **—v.t. 2.** to fasten
or pierce with a skewer.

ski (skē, shē), *n., pl.* **skis, ski,** *v.,*
skied, ski·ing. —n. 1. one of a
pair of long, slender runners worn
clamped to boots for gliding over
snow. **—v.i. 2.** to glide over snow
on skis. **—ski'er,** *n.*

skid (skid), *n., v.,* **skid·ded, skid·ding.
—n. 1.** a plank or log on which
something heavy may be slid or
rolled. **2.** a low platform on or
by which a load is supported. **3.** a
drag for preventing the wheel of a
vehicle from rotating. **4.** a runner
on the underpart of some airplanes.
5. the act of skidding. **6. the skids,**
Slang. the downward path to ruin
or poverty. **—v.t., v.i. 7.** to slip or
slide, esp. sideways. **8.** to slide
along without rotating, as a wheel.
—skid'dy, *adj.*

skid' row' (rō), a run-down urban
area frequented by vagrants.

skiff (skif), *n.* a boat small enough
for sailing by one person.

ski' lift', an apparatus for carrying skiers up the side of a slope.

skill (skil), *n.* **1.** the ability to do
something well. **2.** a particular craft,
art, or ability. **—skilled,** *adj.*

skil·let (skil'it), *n.* a pan for frying
food.

skill·ful (skil'fəl), *adj.* **1.** having or
using skill. **2.** showing or requiring
skill. Also, **skil'ful. —skill'ful·ly,**
adv. **—skill'ful·ness,** *n.* **—Syn. 1.**
adept, deft, proficient.

skim (skim), *v.t., v.i.,* **skimmed, skim-
ming. 1.** to remove (cream or scum)
from (a liquid). **2.** to move or glide
lightly over or along (a surface). **3.**
to read hurriedly, skipping some
parts.

skim' milk'. milk from which the
cream has been removed.

skim·ming (skim'ing), *n. Slang.* the
practice of hiding part of gambling
earnings for tax evasion.

skimp (skimp), *v.t.*, *v.i.* to scrimp.
skimp·y (skim'pē), *adj.*, **skimp·i·er**, **skimp·i·est.** lacking in size or fullness. —**skimp·i·ly**, *adv.* —**skimp'-i·ness**, *n.* —**Syn.** scanty, stingy.

skin (skin), *n.*, *v.*, **skinned**, **skin·ning.** —*n.* **1.** the external covering of an animal body. **2.** a hide or pelt. **3.** any thin, smooth covering, as the rind of fruit. **4. get under one's skin,** *Slang.* to irritate or bother one. —*v.t.* **5.** to remove or strip the skin from. **6.** to scrape a small piece of skin from. **7.** *Slang.* to fleece, as in gambling. —**skin'less**, *adj.*

skin' div'ing, underwater swimming with a mask, snorkel, and flippers. —**skin'-dive'**, *v.i.* —**skin' div'er.**

skin' flick', *Slang.* a motion picture featuring nudity and sex.

skin·flint (skin'flint'), *n.* a mean, niggardly person.

skin' graft', skin transplanted, as from one to another part of the body. —**skin' graft'ing.**

skin·ny (skin'ē), *adj.*, **-ni·er**, **-ni·est.** very lean or thin. —**skin'ni·ness**, *n.*

skin·ny-dip (skin'ē dip'), *v.i.*, **-dipped**, **-dip·ping**, *n.* *Informal.* —*v.i.* **1.** to swim in the nude. —*n.* **2.** a swim in the nude. —**skin'ny-dip'per**, *n.* —**skin'ny-dip'ping**, *n.*

skin·tight (skin'tīt'), *adj.* fitting closely to the figure.

skip (skip), *v.*, **skipped**, **skip·ping**, *n.* —*v.i.*, *v.t.* **1.** to jump or leap lightly (over). **2.** to pass from one point or thing to another, disregarding or omitting (what intervenes). **3.** to bounce or cause to bounce along a surface. **4.** *Informal.* to leave (a place) hastily and secretly. —*n.* **5.** a light jump or bounce. **6.** a gait marked by alternate steps and hops. —**skip'per**, *n.*

skip·per (skip'ər), *n.* the captain of a vessel.

skir·mish (skûr'mish), *n.* **1.** a brief fight between small bodies of troops. **2.** any brief conflict. —*v.i.* **3.** to engage in a skirmish. —**skir'mish·er**, *n.*

skirt (skûrt), *n.* **1.** the part of a dress or coat that extends downward from the waist. **2.** a woman's garment extending downward from the waist. —*v.t.*, *v.i.* **3.** to pass along the edge or border (of).

skit (skit), *n.* a short, theatrical sketch or act, usually comical.

ski' tour'ing, cross-country skiing as a noncompetitive sport.

ski' tow', a ski lift in which skiers are hauled up while on their skis.

skit·ter (skit'ər), *v.i.* to go, run, or glide lightly or rapidly along a surface.

skit·tish (skit'ish), *adj.* **1.** easily startled. **2.** restlessly lively. **3.** fickle or uncertain. —**skit'tish·ness**, *n.*

skiv·vy (skiv'ē), *n.*, *pl.* **-vies.** *Slang.* **1.** Also called **skiv'vy shirt'.** a cotton T-shirt. **2. skivvies,** underwear consisting of cotton T-shirt and shorts.

skoal (skōl), *interj.* (used as a toast in drinking to someone's health.) [< Scand]

Skt., Sanskrit. Also, **Skr.**

skul·dug·ger·y (skul dug'ə rē), *n.* *Informal.* mean dishonesty or trickery. Also, **skull·dug·gery.**

skulk (skulk), *v.i.* to move stealthily or sneakily. —**skulk'er**, *n.*

skull (skul), *n.* the bony framework of the head, enclosing the brain and supporting the face.

skull·cap (skul'kap'), *n.* a small, brimless, closefitting cap.

skunk (skungk), *n.*, *pl.* **skunks**, **skunk**, *v.* —*n.* **1.** a small, black mammal that can eject a fetid odor when alarmed or attacked. **2.** *Informal.* a thoroughly contemptible person. —*v.t.* **3.** *Slang.* to defeat thoroughly in a game.

sky (skī), *n.*, *pl.* **skies. 1.** the upper atmosphere of the earth. **2.** the celestial heaven. —**sky'ey** (-ē), *adj.*

sky·cap (skī'kap'), *n.* a baggage porter at an air terminal.

sky·div·ing (skī'dī'ving), *n.* the sport of making a parachute jump, delaying the opening of the parachute as long as possible. —**sky'dive'**, *v.i.* —**sky'div'er**, *n.*

sky-high (skī'hī'), *adv.*, *adj.* very high.

sky·jack (skī'jak'), *v.t.* to hijack (an airliner), esp. as a means of making political demands by holding passengers hostage. —**sky'jack'-er**, *n.* —**sky'jack'ing**, *n.*, *adj.*

Sky·lab (skī'lab'), *n.* a space station, launched by the U.S. in 1973, to orbit the earth as a scientific laboratory: fell to earth, prematurely, in 1979.

sky·lark (skī'lärk'), *n.* **1.** a Eurasian lark noted for its song while in flight. —*v.i.* **2.** to frolic playfully. —**sky'lark'er**, *n.*

sky·light (skī'līt'), *n.* an opening in a roof or ceiling.

sky·line (skī'līn'), *n.* **1.** the apparent horizon. **2.** an outline, esp. of buildings, seen against the sky.

sky' mar'shal, an armed federal security guard riding in an airliner to protect it against skyjacking.

sky·rock·et (skī'rok'it), *n.* **1.** a rocket firework that explodes high in the air. —*v.i.*, *v.t.* **2.** to rise or cause to rise suddenly.

sky·scrap·er (skī'skrā'pər), *n.* an extremely tall building of many stories.

sky·ward (skī'wərd), *adv.* **1.** Also, **sky'wards.** toward the sky. —*adj.* **2.** directed toward the sky.

sky·writ·ing (skī'rī'tǐng), *n.* the tracing of words in the sky by releasing smoke from a moving airplane. — **sky'writ'er,** *n.*

S.L., salvage loss.

slab (slab), *n.* a broad, thick, flat piece, as of stone or food.

slack (slak), *adj.* **1.** not tight or taut. **2.** slow or sluggish. **3.** not active or busy. **4.** negligent or careless. —*n.* **5.** a part that is slack or loose. **6.** the condition of being slack or loose. **7.** a lessening in activity, sales, etc. —*v.t.*, *v.i.* **8.** to slacken. **9. slack up,** to become less active or rapid. —**slack'ly,** *adv.* —**slack'ness,** *n.*

slack·en (slak'ən), *v.t.*, *v.i.* **1.** to make or become less active or intense. **2.** to make or become loose or looser. —**Syn. 1.** abate, moderate, reduce.

slack·er (slak'ər), *n.* a person who avoids his or her work or evades military service.

slacks (slaks), *n.* men's or women's trousers for informal wear.

slag (slag), *n.* **1.** fused matter separated during the reduction of a metal from its ore. **2.** lava resembling cinders.

slain (slān), *v.* pp. of **slay.**

slake (slāk), *v.t.*, **slaked, slak·ing. 1.** to satisfy or relieve, as thirst. **2.** to cause disintegration of (lime) by treatment with water.

sla·lom (slä'ləm, -lōm), *n. Skiing.* a downhill race over a winding and zigzag course.

slam¹ (slam), *v.*, **slammed, slam·ming,** *n.* —*v.t.*, *v.i.* **1.** to shut with force and noise. **2.** to throw or thrust with noisy impact. **3.** *Informal.* to criticize harshly. —*n.* **4.** the act or sound of slamming. **5.** *Informal.* a harsh criticism.

slam² (slam), *n. Bridge.* the winning of all the tricks **(grand slam)** or all but one **(little slam** or **small slam).**

slam-bang (slam'bang'), *Informal.* —*adj.* **1.** noisily violent. **2.** quick and careless. —*adv.* **3.** in a slam-bang manner.

slan·der (slan'dər), *n.* **1.** defamation by oral utterance rather than by writing, pictures, etc. —*v.t.* **2.** to utter slander against. —**slan'der·er,** *n.* —**slan'der·ous,** *adj.* —**slan'derous·ly,** *adv.*

slang (slang), *n.* very informal vocabulary that is characteristically more metaphorical and ephemeral than ordinary language. —**slang'y,** *adj.* —**slang'i·ness,** *n.*

slant (slant, slänt), *v.i.*, *v.t.* **1.** to turn at an angle away from a level position. **2.** to present (information) in a way that favors a particular viewpoint. —*n.* **3.** a slanting direction or line. **4.** a particular viewpoint. —*adj.* **5.** sloping or oblique. —**slant'ing·ly,** *adv.* —**slant'wise',** *adv.*, *adj.*

slap (slap), *n.*, *v.*, **slapped, slap·ping.** —*n.* **1.** a sharp blow, esp. with the open hand. **2.** a sharp or sarcastic rebuke. —*v.t.* **3.** to strike with a slap. **4.** to rebuke sharply or sarcastically. **5.** to cast or put forcibly. —**slap'per,** *n.*

slap·dash (slap'dash'), *adj.* **1.** hasty and haphazard. —*adv.* **2.** in a slap-dash manner.

slap·hap·py (slap'hap'ē), *adj.*, **-pi·er, -pi·est.** *Informal.* **1.** severely befuddled. **2.** agreeably foolish.

slap·stick (slap'stik'), *n.* comedy characterized by violently boisterous action.

slash (slash), *v.t.* **1.** to cut with a violent sweeping stroke, as of a knife. **2.** to make slits in. **3.** to reduce or lower sharply. —*v.i.* **4.** to make a violent sweeping stroke, as with a knife. —*n.* **5.** the act of slashing. **6.** a cut or wound made by slashing. **7.** an oblique stroke (/) denoting two alternatives or used as a dividing line in dates, fractions, ratios, etc. —**slash'er,** *n.*

slat (slat), *n.* a thin, narrow strip of wood or metal.

slate (slāt), *n.*, *v.*, **slat·ed, slat·ing.** —*n.* **1.** a dark, blue-gray rock that splits into smooth layers. **2.** a thin piece of this rock used as a roofing material or a small blackboard. **3.** a list of candidates for nomination or appointment. **4. a clean slate,** a record marked by honorable conduct. —*v.t.* **5.** to cover with slate. **6.** to set down for nomination or appointment.

slath·er (slath'ər), *v.t. Informal.* to spread or apply thickly.

slat·tern (slat'ərn), *n.* a slovenly, untidy woman. —**slat'tern·ly,** *adj.*, *adv.*

slaugh·ter (slô'tər), *n.* **1.** the killing of animals, esp. for food. **2.** a brutal, violent killing, esp. of many people. —*v.t.* **3.** to kill (animals), esp. for food. **4.** to kill brutally or massacre. —**slaugh'ter·er,** *n.*

slaugh·ter·house (slô'tər hous'), *n.* a building where animals are butchered.

Slav (släv, slav), *n.* **1.** one of a group of the Slavic-speaking peoples in eastern Europe. —*adj.* **2.** Slavic.

Slav., Slavic.

slave (slāv), *n.*, *v.*, **slaved, slav·ing.** —*n.* **1.** a person who is the property of another and bound to serve him or her without pay. **2.** a person entirely under the domination of some influence or person. —*v.i.* **3.** to work like a slave.

slave′ driv′er, 1. an overseer of slaves. **2.** a hard taskmaster.

slav·er (slav′ər, slā′vər), *v.i., n.* slobber.

slav·er·y (slā′və rē, slāv′rē), *n.* **1.** the owning of slaves as a practice or institution. **2.** the condition of being a slave. **3.** severe toil. —Syn. **1, 2.** bondage, servitude.

Slav·ic (slä′vik, slav′ik), *n.* **1.** a branch of the Indo-European family of languages, including Russian, Polish, Czech, etc. —*adj.* **2.** of the Slavs or their languages.

slav·ish (slā′vish), *adj.* **1.** of or resembling a slave. **2.** deliberately imitative or dependent. —**slav′ish·ly,** *adv.* —**slav′ish·ness,** *n.* —Syn. **1.** abject, base, servile, submissive.

slaw (slô), *n.* coleslaw.

slay (slā), *v.t.,* **slew, slain, slay·ing.** to kill by violence. —**slay′er,** *n.*

sld., 1. sailed. **2.** sealed.

slea·zy (slē′zē, slā′zē), *adj.,* **-zi·er, -zi·est. 1.** thin or poor in texture. **2.** cheap or shoddy. —**slea′zi·ly,** *adv.* —**slea′zi·ness,** *n.*

sled (sled), *n., v.,* **sled·ded, sled·ding.** —*n.* **1.** a small vehicle on runners for sliding over snow or ice. —*v.i., v.t.* **2.** to ride or carry on a sled.

sledge[1] (slej), *n.* a solidly built vehicle mounted on runners, used esp. for carrying loads across snow or ice.

sledge[2] (slej), *n.* a large, heavy hammer wielded with both hands. Also called **sledge′ham′mer.**

sleek (slēk), *adj.* **1.** smooth and glossy. **2.** well-fed or well-groomed. **3.** smooth in manners, speech, etc. —*v.t.* **4.** to make sleek. —**sleek′ly,** *adv.* —**sleek′ness,** *n.*

sleep (slēp), *n., v.,* **slept, sleep·ing.** —*n.* **1.** a periodic state or time of rest in which one loses consciousness at least partly and the body relaxes. **2.** a state of inactivity resembling this. —*v.i.* **3.** to be in the state of sleep. **4.** to be in a state resembling sleep. **5. sleep off,** to get rid of by sleeping. —**sleep′less,** *adj.* —**sleep′less·ness,** *n.*

sleep·er (slē′pər), *n.* **1.** a person or thing that sleeps. **2.** *Informal.* someone or something that suddenly becomes successful or important. **3.** See **sleeping car. 4.** a horizontal timber for supporting something.

sleep′ing bag′, a warmly padded, zippered bag in which a person sleeps outdoors.

sleep′ing car′, a railroad car equipped with sleeping accommodations.

sleep′ing pill′, a pill or tablet containing a drug for inducing sleep. Also called **sleep′ing tab′let.**

sleep′ing sick′ness, a generally fatal African disease characterized by abnormal sleepiness.

sleep·walk·ing (slēp′wô′king), *n.* somnambulism. —**sleep′walk′er,** *n.*

sleep·y (slē′pē), *adj.,* **sleep·i·er, sleep·i·est. 1.** ready or inclined to sleep. **2.** quiet and inactive. —**sleep′i·ly,** *adv.* —**sleep′i·ness,** *n.* —Syn. **1.** drowsy, lethargic, somnolent.

sleep·y·head (slē′pē hed′), *n.* a sleepy person.

sleet (slēt), *n.* **1.** a thin coating of ice formed by freezing rain. **2.** a mixture of hail or snow and rain. —*v.i.* **3.** to fall as sleet. —**sleet′y,** *adj.*

sleeve (slēv), *n.* **1.** the part of a garment that covers the arm. **2.** a tubular piece fitting over a rod. **3. up one's sleeve,** kept secretly ready or close at hand. —**sleeve′less,** *adj.*

sleigh (slā), *n.* a light, usually open vehicle on runners, used for traveling over snow or ice.

sleight′ of hand′ (slīt), **1.** skill in feats requiring quick and clever movements of the hands, esp. for entertainment or deception, as in card tricks. **2.** the performance of such feats.

slen·der (slen′dər), *adj.* **1.** attractively thin and well-formed. **2.** small in proportion to the height or length. **3.** meager or insufficient. **4.** having little value or force. —**slen′der·ly,** *adv.* —**slen′der·ness,** *n.*

slen·der·ize (slen′də rīz′), *v.t., v.i.,* **-ized, -iz·ing.** to make or become slender.

slept (slept), *v.* pt. and pp. of **sleep.**

sleuth (slōōth), *n. Informal.* a detective.

slew[1] (slōō), *v.* pt. of **slay.**

slew[2] (slōō), *n. Informal.* a great number.

slice (slīs), *n., v.,* **sliced, slic·ing.** —*n.* **1.** a thin, broad, flat piece cut from something. **2.** a piece or portion. **3.** a stroke that causes the ball to curve to the right or left. —*v.t.* **4.** to cut into slices. **5.** to separate in a slice or slices. **6.** to hit (a ball) so as to result in a slice. —**slice′a·ble,** *adj.* —**slic′er,** *n.*

slick (slik), *adj.* **1.** smooth and slippery. **2.** smooth in manners, speech, etc., but shallow. **3.** shrewdly adroit. **4.** cleverly devised. —*n.* **5.** a smooth and slippery surface: *an oil slick.* —*v.t.* **6.** to make slick or smooth. **7.** *Informal.* to make smart or fine. —**slick′ly,** *adv.* —**slick′ness,** *n.*

slick·er (slik′ər), *n.* **1.** a loose oilskin raincoat. **2.** *Informal.* a sly cheat. —**slick′ered,** *adj.*

slide (slīd), *v.,* **slid** (slid), **slid·ing.** *n.* —*v.i.* **1.** to move along in continuous contact with a smooth surface: *to slide down a snow-covered hill.* **2.** to slip or skid. —*v.t.* **3.** to cause to slide. **4.** to pass along easily or quietly. **5. let slide,** to allow to deteriorate. —*n.* **6.** the act or an instance of sliding. **7.** a smooth surface for sliding on. **8.** an object intended to slide. **9.** *Geol.* a mass of matter sliding down. **10.** a single transparency, as on a small positive film, for projection on a screen. **11.** a small piece of glass on which objects are placed for microscopic examination. —**slid′a·ble,** *adj.*

slide′ fas′tener, zipper.

slid·er (slī′dər), *n.* **1.** a person or thing that slides. **2.** *Baseball.* a fast pitch that curves slightly.

slide′ rule′, a device for rapid calculation, consisting of a ruler having a sliding center strip with logarithmic scales.

slid′ing scale′, a variable scale, esp. of industrial costs, as wages.

slight (slīt), *adj.* **1.** small in amount or degree. **2.** of little importance or influence. **3.** slender or slim. —*v.t.* **4.** to treat as of little importance. **5.** to ignore contemptuously. **6.** to give only superficial attention. —*n.* **7.** contemptuous discourtesy. —**slight′-ly,** *adv.* —**slight′ness,** *n.*

slim (slim), *adj.,* **slim·mer, slim·mest,** *v.,* **slimmed, slim·ming.** —*adj.* **1.** slender in girth or form. **2.** meager or scanty. —*v.t., v.i.* **3.** to make or become slim. —**slim′ly,** *adv.* —**slim′-ness,** *n.*

slime (slīm), *n.* thin, sticky mud. —**slim′y,** *adj.*

sling (sling), *n., v.,* **slung, sling·ing.** —*n.* **1.** an ancient weapon for hurling stones by hand, usually consisting of a strap with a string at each end. **2.** a bandage suspended from the neck to support an injured arm. **3.** a strap, band, or rope forming a loop by which something is suspended, carried, or hoisted. —*v.t.* **4.** to hurl with or as with a sling. **5.** to support or hang by a sling.

sling′shot (sling′shot′), *n.* a Y-shaped stick with an elastic strip between the prongs for shooting small stones.

slink (slingk), *v.i.,* **slunk, slink·ing.** to move or go in a furtive, abject manner. —**slink′y,** *adj.*

slip¹ (slip), *v.,* **slipped, slip·ping,** *n.* —*v.i.* **1.** to move smoothly or easily. **2.** to slide suddenly and accidentally **3.** to allow something to evade one, as an opportunity. **4.** to elapse or pass quickly or imperceptibly. **5.** to move or go quietly, cautiously, or unobtrusively. **6.** to make a mistake. **7.** to deteriorate, as in health. —*v.t.* **8.** to cause to slip. **9.** to put or pass quickly or stealthily. **10.** to put on or take off (a loose garment). **11.** to pass from or escape (one's memory,

etc.). **12. let slip,** to reveal unintentionally. **13. slip up,** to make an error. —*n.* **14.** the act of slipping. **15.** a mistake or oversight. **16.** a decline or fall in quantity or quality. **17.** a woman's undergarment resembling a light, sleeveless dress or a light skirt. **18.** a pillowcase. **19.** *Rare.* a small berthing dock.

slip² (slip), *n.* **1.** a piece or cutting from a plant, used for growing a new plant. **2.** a small piece of paper, esp. one bearing information. **3.** a young, usually slender person.

slip-cov·er (slip′kuv′ər), *n.* an easily removed fabric cover for a piece of furniture.

slip-knot (slip′not′), *n.* a knot that slips easily along the cord around which it is made.

slip-o·ver (slip′ō′vər), *adj., n.* pullover.

slip·page (slip′ij), *n.* **1.** the act of slipping. **2.** an amount or extent of slipping.

slipped′ disk′, a displacement of a cartilage resulting in severe back pain.

slip·per (slip′ər), *n.* any light, low-cut shoe easily slipped on or off the foot.

slip·per·y (slip′ə rē, slip′rē), *adj.,* **-per·i·er, -per·i·est. 1.** tending to cause slipping, as a wet surface. **2.** likely to slip from one's hold or grasp. **3.** shifty or tricky. —**slip′per·i·ness,** *n.*

slip·shod (slip′shod′), *adj.* carelessly done or made.

slip-up (slip′up′), *n. Informal.* a careless mistake.

slit (slit), *v.,* **slit, slit·ting,** *n.* —*v.t.* **1.** to cut apart or open along a line. **2.** to cut into strips. —*n.* **3.** a straight, narrow cut or opening.

slith·er (slith′ər), *v.i.* to move or slide with a side-to-side motion. —**slith′er·y,** *adj.*

sliv·er (sliv′ər), *n.* **1.** a small, slender piece split or cut off. —*v.t., v.i.* **2.** to split into slivers.

slob (slob), *n. Slang.* a clumsy, slovenly, or boorish person.

slob·ber (slob′ər), *v.i.* **1.** to let saliva run from the mouth. —*n.* **2.** saliva dribbling from the mouth. —**slob′-ber·y,** *adj.*

sloe (slō), *n.* the small, sour, blackish fruit of the blackthorn.

slog (slog), *v.t., v.i.,* **slogged, slog·ging.** to make (one's way) laboriously.

slo·gan (slō′gən), *n.* **1.** a distinctive phrase or motto of any party or group. **2.** a phrase used repeatedly in advertising. [< Gael *sluagh ghairm* army cry]

sloop (sloop), *n.* a single-masted sailing vessel having a jib.

slop (slop), v., **slopped, slop·ping,** n. —v.t., v.i. **1.** to spill (liquid) carelessly. —n. **2.** liquid carelessly spilled. **3.** Often, **slops.** kitchen refuse used as food for swine. **4.** liquid mud. **5.** Slang. badly cooked or unappetizing food or drink.

slope (slōp), v., **sloped, slop·ing,** n. —v.i. **1.** to deviate from the horizontal or vertical. —v.t. **2.** to cause to slope. —n. **3.** a portion of ground having a natural incline, as the side of a hill. **4.** slant, esp. downward or upward. **5.** the amount or degree of slant.

slop·py (slop′ē), adj., **-pi·er, -pi·est. 1.** very wet and splashy, as ground. **2.** careless or loose. **3.** untidy or slovenly. **4.** overly emotional. —**slop′-pi·ly,** adv. —**slop′pi·ness,** n.

slosh (slosh), v.i. **1.** to splash in mud or water. **2.** (of a liquid) to splash about. —**slosh′y,** adj.

slot (slot), n., v., **slot·ted, slot·ting.** —n. **1.** a narrow, straight opening for receiving or admitting something, as a coin. **2.** Informal. a position in a scheduled sequence. —v.t. **3.** to cut a slot in. **4.** Informal. to schedule in sequence.

slot′ car′, a miniature racing automobile electrically operated on a slotted track.

sloth (slôth), n. **1.** extreme or habitual indolence. **2.** a sluggish, tropical animal that hangs from and moves upside down along the branches of trees. —**sloth′ful,** adj. —**sloth′fulness,** n. —Syn. **1.** laziness, sluggishness.

slot′ machine′, a coin-operated machine, esp. one played for gambling purposes.

slouch (slouch), v.i. **1.** to sit, stand, or walk with an awkward, drooping posture. —n. **2.** a slouching posture. **3.** an awkward, clumsy person. **4.** Informal. a lazy or inept person. —**slouch′y,** adj. —**slouch′ing·ly,** adv.

slough[1] (slou), n. **1.** a swamplike region. **2.** a hole full of mire. **3.** a condition of degradation or helplessness.

slough[2] (sluf), n. **1.** the outer layer of the skin of a snake, which is cast off periodically. —v.t. **2.** to shed as or like a slough.

Slo·vak (slō′vak, -väk), n. **1.** one of a Slavic people dwelling in E Czechoslovakia. **2.** their language. —adj. **3.** of the Slovaks or their language.

slov·en (sluv′ən), n. a person who is habitually untidy or careless.

slov·en·ly (sluv′ən lē), adj., **-li·er, -li·est. 1.** habitually untidy or unclean. **2.** careless or slipshod. —**slov′en·li·ness,** n.

slow (slō), adj. **1.** having little speed. **2.** requiring or taking a long time.

3. not quick to learn. **4.** showing less than the proper time, as a clock. **5.** passing heavily, as time. **6.** dull or tedious. —adv. **7.** in a slow manner. —v.t., v.i. **8.** to make or become slow or slower. —**slow′ly,** adv. —**slow′ness,** n. —Syn. **2.** gradual, leisurely, unhurried.

slow·down (slō′doun′), n. a slowing of pace, as by workers.

slow-mo·tion (slō′mō′shən), adj. noting motion pictures in which the images on the screen are made to appear to move more slowly than actually photographed.

slow-wit·ted (slō′wit′id), adj. mentally slow or dull.

SLR, See **single-lens reflex.**

sludge (sluj), n. **1.** a soft, muddy or oozy mass. **2.** a muddy deposit, as in a water tank. —**sludg′y,** adj.

slue (slōō), v.t., v.i., **slued, slu·ing.** to turn or swing (something) around.

slug[1] (slug), n. **1.** a slimy animal that resembles a snail but has no shell. **2.** a piece of metal for firing from a gun. **3.** a small disk used in place of a coin. **4.** Slang. a shot of liquor taken neat.

slug[2] (slug), v., **slugged, slug·ging,** n. Informal. —v.t. **1.** to hit hard, esp. with the fist. —n. **2.** a hard hit, esp. with the fist. —**slug′ger,** n.

slug·gard (slug′ərd), n. a slow, lazy person.

slug·gish (slug′ish), adj. **1.** lacking in energy. **2.** moving slowly. **3.** not acting or working with full vigor. —**slug′gish·ly,** adv. —**slug′gish·ness,** n. —Syn. **1.** indolent, lazy.

sluice (slōōs), n., v., **sluiced, sluic·ing.** —n. **1.** an artificial channel for water, having a gate (**sluice′ gate′**) at the upper end for regulating the flow. **2.** a channel for surplus water. **3.** a long, sloping trough, as for washing ores. —v.t. **4.** to let out (water) through a sluice. **5.** to wash or drench with water as from a sluice. **6.** to send (logs) down a sluice.

slum (slum), n., v., **slummed, slumming.** —n. **1.** a thickly populated, squalid part of a city. —v.i. **2.** to visit slums, esp. out of curiosity.

slum·ber (slum′bər), v.i. **1.** to sleep, esp. peacefully. **2.** to be inactive or calm. —n. **3.** sleep, esp. peaceful sleep. **4.** an inactive or calm state. —**slum′ber·er,** n.

slum·ber·ous (slum′bər əs), adj. **1.** inclined to slumber. **2.** inactive or calm. Also, **slum′brous.**

slum·lord (slum′lôrd′), n. a landlord of slum buildings who charges exorbitant rents.

slump (slump), v.i. **1.** to drop or fall heavily. **2.** to slouch or sag. —n. **3.** the act of slumping.

slung (slung), v. pt. and pp. of **sling.**

slunk (slungk), v. pt. and pp. of **slink.**

slur (slûr), v., **slurred, slur·ring,** n.
—v.t. **1.** to pass over lightly or without
due mention. **2.** to pronounce (a
word, etc.) indistinctly. **3.** to disparage or slight. **4.** *Music.* to sing to
a single syllable or play without a
break (two or more tones of different pitch). —n. **5.** a slurred sound.
6. a disparaging remark. **7.** *Music.*
a curved mark indicating notes to be
slurred. —**Syn. 6.** affront, insult.

slurp (slûrp), *Slang.* —v.t., v.i. **1.** to
eat or drink with loud noises. —n.
2. a slurping sound.

slur·ry (slûr′ē), n., pl. **-ries.** a suspension of a solid in a liquid.

slush (slush), n. **1.** partly melted snow.
2. liquid mud. **3.** silly sentimentality.
—**slush′y,** adj. —**slush′i·ness,** n.

slush′ fund′, a sum of money used
for illicit or corrupt political purposes.

slut (slut), n. **1.** a slovenly woman. **2.**
a dissolute woman. —**slut′tish,** adj.
—**slut′tish·ness,** n.

sly (slī), adj., **sly·er** or **sli·er, sly·est** or
sli·est, n. —adj. **1.** clever in a tricky
way. **2.** secretively underhanded. **3.**
playfully roguish. —n. **4. on the sly,**
secretly or furtively. —**sly′ly,** adv.
—**sly′ness,** n. —**Syn. 1.** crafty, wily.
2. stealthy. **3.** mischievous.

Sm, samarium.

sm., small.

S.M., 1. Master of Science. [< L *Scientiae Magister*] **2.** Sergeant Major.

smack[1] (smak), n. **1.** a slight flavor or
savor. **2.** a small trace. —v.i. **3.** to
have a smack.

smack[2] (smak), v.t. **1.** to close and
open (the lips) smartly so as to produce a sharp sound. **2.** to kiss or
slap with a loud sound. —n. **3.** a
sound made by smacking the lips. **4.**
a loud kiss. **5.** a sharp slap or blow.
—adv. **6.** suddenly and violently. **7.**
directly or squarely.

smack[3] (smak), n. a fishing vessel having a well for keeping the catch alive.

smack[4] (smak). n. *Slang.* heroin.

smack·er (smak′ər), n. *Slang.* a dollar.

SMaj, Sergeant Major.

small (smôl), adj. **1.** of limited size.
2. not great in amount, degree, value,
etc. **3.** of minor importance. **4.** humble or modest. **5.** mean or petty. **6.**
gentle or low, as a voice. **7.** very
young: *a small boy.* **8. feel small,**
to be ashamed. —adv. **9.** in a small
manner. **10.** in low tones. —n. **11.**
a small or narrow part, as of the
back. —**small′ish,** adj. —**small′-
ness,** n.

small′ arms′, firearms that can be
carried in the hand, as rifles.

small′ cap′ital, *Print.* a capital letter whose typeface is as high as a
lower-case *x.*

small′ fry′, 1. young children. **2.** unimportant persons.

small·pox (smôl′poks′), n. a highly
contagious virus disease that causes
fever and skin eruptions.

small-scale (smôl′skāl′), adj. **1.** of
limited extent. **2.** made to a small
dimensional scale.

small′ slam′, *Bridge.* See under **slam**[2].

small′ talk′, light, unimportant conversation.

small-time (smôl′tīm′), adj. of modest importance or influence. —
small′-tim′er, n.

smart (smärt), v.i. **1.** to feel a sharp,
stinging pain. **2.** to cause a sharp,
stinging pain. **3.** to suffer from hurt
feelings. —n. **4.** a smarting sensation. —adj. **5.** bright and clever. **6.**
dashingly neat and trim in appearance. **7.** elegant or fashionable. **8.**
saucy or pert. **9.** brisk or vigorous.
10. sharp and stinging: *a smart pain.*
—**smart′ing·ly,** adv. —**smart′ly,** adv.
—**smart′ness,** n.

smart′ al′eck (al′ik), *Informal.* an
obnoxiously conceited person. Also,
smart′ al′ec.

smart′ bomb′, *Slang.* an air-to-surface
bomb that is guided to its target by
either television or a laser beam.

smart·en (smär′tºn), v.t., v.i. to make
or become smart.

smash (smash), v.t., v.i. **1.** to break
violently into pieces. **2.** to hit or
strike with a shattering force. **3.** to
destroy or be destroyed completely.
—n. **4.** the act or sound of smashing.
5. a smashing blow or hit. **6.** a destructive collision. **7.** a failure or
ruin, esp. financial failure. **8.** a big,
popular success. **9.** a swift overhead
stroke, as in tennis. —**smash′er,** n.

smash·up (smash′up′), n. **1.** a complete crash or collision. **2.** a complete failure or ruin.

smat·ter·ing (smat′ər ing), n. **1.** a
slight or superficial knowledge. **2.** a
small quantity.

smear (smēr), v.t. **1.** to daub (an oily
or sticky substance) on or over. **2.**
to daub an oily or sticky substance
on. **3.** to sully or vilify. —v.i. **4.** to
be or become smeared. —n. **5.** a
stain made by smearing. **6.** vilifica-
tion or defamation. —**smear′er,** n.
—**smear′y,** adj.

smear·case (smēr′kās′), n. *Dial.* See
cottage cheese.

smell (smel), v., **smelled** or **smelt**
(smelt). **smell·ing,** n. —v.t. **1.** to perceive the odor of through the nose.
2. to detect or discover by shrewdness. —v.i. **3.** to give off or have an
odor. **4.** to perceive something by its
odor. —n. **5.** the faculty of smelling.
6. odor or scent. **7.** the act or an
instance of smelling. —**smell′er,** n.
—**Syn. 6.** aroma, bouquet, fragrance.

smell′ing salts′, a strong-smelling ammonium compound used as a stimulant or restorative.

smell·y (smel′ē), *adj.,* **smell·i·er, smell·i·est.** emitting an unpleasant smell. —**smell′i·ness,** *n.*

smelt[1] (smelt), *v.t.* **1.** to fuse or melt (ore) in order to separate the metal contained. **2.** to refine (metal) in this way.

smelt[2] (smelt), *n., pl.* **smelt, smelts.** a small silvery food fish found in Europe.

smelt·er (smel′tər), *n.* **1.** a person who smelts ore. **2.** Also, **smelt′er·y** (-tə rē). a place where ores are smelted.

smid·gen (smij′ən), *n. Informal.* a very small amount. Also, **smid′geon, smid′gin.**

smi·lax (smī′laks), *n.* a twining plant having glossy, bright-green leaves.

smile (smīl), *n., v.,* **smiled, smil·ing.** —*n.* **1.** an expression of the face marked by a turning up of the corners of the mouth, usually indicating pleasure or amusement. —*v.i.* **2.** to have or give a smile. **3.** to show favor. —*v.t.* **4.** to express with a smile. —**smil′er,** *n.* —**smil′ing·ly,** *adv.*

smirch (smûrch), *v.t.* **1.** to soil or smudge, as with soot. **2.** to disgrace or stain. —*n.* **3.** a dirty mark or smear. **4.** a disgrace or stain.

smirk (smûrk), *v.i.* **1.** to smile in an affected or offensively familiar way. —*n.* **2.** such a smile. —**smirk′er,** *n.* —**smirk′ing·ly,** *adv.*

smite (smīt), *v.t.,* **smote, smit·ten** (smit′°n) or **smote, smit·ing. 1.** to strike or hit extremely hard. **2.** to kill by striking hard. **3.** to afflict or affect seriously. —**smit′er,** *n.*

smith (smith), *n.* **1.** a worker in metal. **2.** blacksmith.

smith·er·eens (smith′ə rēnz′), *n.pl. Informal.* small fragments.

smith·y (smith′ē, smith′ē), *n., pl.* **smith·ies.** the workshop of a smith, esp. a blacksmith.

smock (smok), *n.* **1.** a loose, lightweight outer garment worn to protect the clothing while working. —*v.t.* **2.** to draw (a fabric) by needlework into a honeycomb pattern.

smog (smog, smôg), *n.* a mixture of fog and smoke. [*sm(oke)* + *(f)og*] —**smog′gy,** *adj.*

smoke (smōk), *n., v.,* **smoked, smoking.** —*n.* **1.** the visible vapor and gases given off by a burning substance. **2.** something resembling this, as mist. **3.** an act of smoking, esp. tobacco. **4.** a cigar or cigarette. —*v.i.* **5.** to give off smoke. **6.** to inhale and puff tobacco smoke, as from a cigarette. —*v.t.* **7.** to inhale

and puff the smoke of (a cigarette, etc.). **8.** to cure (meat, etc.) by exposure to smoke. **9.** to color or darken by smoke. **10. smoke out, a.** to drive from a hiding place. **b.** to reveal or expose. —**smok′er,** *n.* —**smok′y,** *adj.* —**smok′i·ness,** *n.*

smoke·house (smōk′hous′), *n.* a building in which meat or fish is cured with smoke.

smoke′ screen′, 1. a mass of dense smoke used to hide an area or ship from the enemy. **2.** anything intended to hide or deceive.

smoke·stack (smōk′stak′), *n.* a tall pipe for the escape of smoke or gases, as on a steamboat.

smok·ey (smō′kē), *n. CB Radio Slang.* a policeman or policewoman of any kind.

smok′ing gun′, *Slang.* conclusively incriminating evidence.

smol·der (smōl′dər), *v.i.* **1.** to burn and smoke without flame. **2.** to exist or continue in a suppressed state. —*n.* **3.** dense smoke resulting from slow combustion. Also, *Brit.,* **smoul′der.**

smooch (smōōch), *v.i., v.i., n. Informal.* kiss.

smooth (smōōth), *adj.* **1.** free from roughness or bumps. **2.** free from lumps, as a sauce. **3.** free from jolts or jerks: *smooth driving.* **4.** free from hindrances or difficulties. **5.** polished and agreeable in manner. **6.** bland or mellow. **7.** not harsh to the ear. —*adv.* **8.** in a smooth manner. —*v.t.* **9.** to make smooth of surface. **10.** to free from difficulties. **11.** to refine or polish. **12.** to remove (wrinkles, etc.) from. **13.** to soothe or calm. **14. smooth over,** to make seem less unpleasant or wrong. —**smooth′er,** *n.* —**smooth′ly,** *adv.* —**smooth′ness,** *n.* —Syn. **5.** suave.

smor·gas·bord (smôr′gəs bôrd′, -bôrd′), *n.* a buffet meal of various hot and cold foods. [< Sw]

smote (smōt), *v.* pt. and a pp. of smite.

smoth·er (smuth′ər), *v.t.* **1.** to prevent from breathing freely, as by smoke, or to kill thus. **2.** to cover closely or thickly. **3.** to suppress or repress. —*v.i.* **4.** to become smothered. —*n.* **5.** dense, stifling smoke. —**smoth′er·y,** *adj.*

smudge (smuj), *n., v.,* **smudged, smudg·ing.** —*n.* **1.** a dirty streak or smear. **2.** a smoky fire, esp. one used to protect fruit trees from frost. —*v.t., v.i.* **3.** to make or become dirty with streaks or smears. —**smudg′y,** *adj.*

smug (smug), *adj.,* **smug·ger, smug·gest.** contentedly confident of one's

ability or correctness. —**smug'ly,**
adv. —**smug'ness,** *n.* —**Syn.** complacent, conceited, self-satisfied.

smug·gle (smug'əl), *v.t., v.i.,* **-gled,
-gling. 1.** to import or export (goods)
secretly, esp. without paying customs
duties. **2.** to take or put secretly. —
smug'gler, *n.*

smut (smut), *n.* **1.** indecent language
or an obscene publication. **2.** sooty
matter. **3.** a sooty spot or mark. **4.**
a harmful fungous disease of plants.
—**smut'ty,** *adj.* —**smut'ti·ness,** *n.*

smutch (smuch), *n.* smudge.

Sn, *Chem.* tin. [< L *stannum*]

snack (snak), *n.* a light meal eaten
between regular meals.

snaf·fle (snaf'əl), *n.* a horse's bit
jointed in the middle and without a
curb.

snag (snag), *n., v.,* **snagged, snag·ging.**
—*n.* **1.** any sharp or rough projection. **2.** a tree or part of a tree held
fast under water. **3.** any unexpected
obstacle or difficulty. —*v.t.* **4.** to
catch or tear on a snag. **5.** to obstruct or impede. —**snag'gy,** *adj.*

snail (snāl), *n.* a mollusk having a
spirally coiled shell that moves slowly on a single muscular foot. —**snail'-
like',** *adj.*

snake (snāk), *n., v.,* **snaked, snak·ing.**
—*n.* **1.** a long, limbless, scaly reptile having recurved teeth. **2.** a
treacherous person. —*v.i.* **3.** to
move, twist, or wind like a snake.
—**snake'like',** *adj.* —**snak'y,** *adj.* —
snak'i·ly, *adv.*

snap (snap), *v.,* **snapped, snap·ping,**
n., adj. —*v.i., v.t.* **1.** to make or
cause to make a sudden, sharp
sound. **2.** to move, shut, or catch
with a sharp sound, as a lock. **3.**
to break suddenly, esp. with a
cracking sound. **4.** to flash, as the
eyes. **5.** to move or cause to move
quickly or smartly: *to snap to attention.* **6.** to seize or take with a quick
bite or grab. **7.** to say (something)
quickly and sharply. **8.** to take a
snapshot (of). **9.** *Football.* (of the
center) to put (the ball) into play.
10. snap out of it, to recover or
change quickly. —*n.* **11.** a short,
sharp sound. **12.** a fastening device
that snaps when operating. **13.** a
quick, sharp manner of speaking. **14.**
a quick, sudden bite or grab. **15.** a
short spell, as of cold weather. **16.**
a thin crisp cookie. **17.** *Informal.*
vigor or energy. **18.** *Informal.* an
easy job or task. **19.** *Football.* the
act of snapping the ball. **20.**
made or done suddenly. **21.** *Informal.* easy or simple. **22.** that snaps
when fastened. —**snap'per,** *n.* —
snap'pish, *adj.* —**snap'py,** *adj.*

snap' bean'. See string bean.

snap·drag·on (snap'drag'ən), *n.* a
garden plant cultivated for its spikes
of showy, two-lipped flowers.

snap·shot (snap'shot'), *n.* an informal
photograph taken quickly by a hand-
held camera.

snare[1] (snâr), *n., v.,* **snared, snar·ing.**
—*n.* **1.** a noose for capturing birds
or small animals. **2.** anything that
traps or entangles. **3.** *Surg.* a wire
noose for removing tumors. —*v.t.*
4. to catch with a snare.

snare[2] (snâr), *n.* one of the strings
of gut or wire stretched across the
skin of a drum.

snarl[1] (snärl), *v.i.* **1.** to growl angrily,
showing the teeth, as a dog. **2.** to
speak in a sharp or angry manner.
—*n.* **3.** an angry growl. **4.** a snarling
utterance. —**snarl'er,** *n.* —**snarl'-
ing·ly,** *adv.* —**snarl'y,** *adj.*

snarl[2] (snärl), *n.* **1.** a tangled mass,
as of hair. **2.** a confused condition
or matter. —*v.t., v.i.* **3.** to bring or
get into a snarl. —**snarl'y,** *adj.*

snatch (snach), *v.i.* **1.** to try to seize
something suddenly. —*v.t.* **2.** to
seize by a sudden or hasty grasp.
—*n.* **3.** the act of snatching. **4.** a
bit or fragment. **5.** a brief period.
—**snatch'er,** *n.*

sneak (snēk), *v.,* **sneaked** or (*Dial.*)
snuck, sneak·ing, *n., adj.* —*v.i., v.t.*
to go or move in a stealthy or furtive
manner. —*n.* **2.** a sneaking or underhand person. **3.** a sneaking act or
move. —*adj.* **4.** acting or done in a
sneaking way. —**sneak'ing·ly,** *adv.*
—**sneak'y,** *adj.* —**sneak'i·ness,** *n.*

sneak·er (snē'kər), *n.* a canvas shoe
with a rubber or synthetic sole.

sneer (snēr), *v.i.* **1.** to smile scorn-
fully, as by curling the lip. —*n.* **2.**
a sneering look or expression. **3.** an
act of sneering. —**sneer'er,** *n.* —
sneer'ful, *adj.* —**sneer'ing·ly,** *adv.*

sneeze (snēz), *v.,* **sneezed, sneez·ing,**
n. —*v.i.* **1.** to force out air suddenly
and audibly through the nose and
mouth by involuntary, spasmodic
action. —*n.* **2.** an act of sneezing.
—**sneez'er,** *n.* —**sneez'y,** *adj.*

snick·er (snik'ər), *v.i.* **1.** to laugh in
a half-suppressed manner. —*v.t.* **2.**
to utter with a snicker. —*n.* **3.** a
snickering laugh. Also, **snig·ger**
(snig'ər). —**snick'er·ing·ly,** *adv.*

snide (snīd), *adj.* derogatory in a
nasty manner. —**snide'ness,** *n.* —
Syn. mean, sarcastic, spiteful.

sniff (snif), *v.i., v.t.* **1.** to draw (air)
through the nose in short, audible
inhalations. **2.** to show disdain or
contempt (for). **3.** to perceive by
sniffing or smelling. —*n.* **4.** an act
or sound of sniffing. **5.** anything
sniffed. —**sniff'er,** *n.* —**sniff'ing·ly,**
adv.

snif·fle (snif′əl), v., **-fled, -fling,** n.
—v.i. **1.** to sniff repeatedly, as in
trying not to cry. —n. **2.** an act
or sound of sniffling. **3. the sniffles,**
a cold marked by sniffling. —**snif′-
fler,** n.

snif·ter (snif′tər), n. a pear-shaped
glass for brandy or liqueur.

snip (snip), v., **snipped, snip·ping,** n.
—v.t., v.i. **1.** to cut with a small,
quick stroke or strokes, as with scissors. —n. **2.** the act of snipping. **3.**
a small piece snipped off. **4.** Informal. a small or insignificant person.

snipe (snip), n., pl. **snipes, snipe,** v.,
sniped, snip·ing. —n. **1.** a long-billed
game bird, found in marshy areas.
—v.i. **2.** to shoot or hunt snipe. **3.**
to shoot at individuals from a concealed position. —**snip′er,** n.

snip·pet (snip′it), n. a small bit or
scrap.

snip·py (snip′ē), adj., **-pi·er, -pi·est.**
Informal. haughtily sharp or curt.
—**snip′pi·ly,** adv. —**snip′pi·ness,** n.

snitch¹ (snich), v.t. Slang. to steal,
esp. something of little value.

snitch² (snich), v.i. Slang. to turn
informer.

sniv·el (sniv′əl), v.i., **-eled, -el·ing** or
-elled, -el·ling. 1. to cry with sniffling. **2.** to run at the nose.

snob (snob), n. a person who admires
those with social rank or wealth and
is condescending to others. —**snob′-
ber·y,** n. —**snob′bish,** adj. —**snob′-
bish·ly,** adv. —**snob′bish·ness,** n.

snoop (snōōp), Informal. —v.i. **1.** to
pry in a sly manner. —n. **2.** Also,
snoop′er, a person who snoops.
—**snoop′y,** adj.

snoot (snōōt), n. Slang. **1.** the nose.
2. the face.

snoot·y (snōō′tē), adj., **snoot·i·er,
snoot·i·est.** Informal. snobbishly
conceited. —**snoot′i·ly,** adv. —
snoot′i·ness, n.

snooze (snōōz), v., **snoozed, snooz·ing,**
n. Informal. —v.i. **1.** to nap or doze
briefly. —n. **2.** a brief nap. —**snooz′-
er,** n. —**snooz′y,** adj.

snore (snōr, snôr), v., **snored, snor·ing,**
n. —v.i. **1.** to breathe during sleep
with hoarse sounds. —n. **2.** the act
or sound of snoring. —**snor′er,** n.

snor·kel (snôr′kəl), n. a tube through
which a person may breathe while
swimming face down close to the
surface. [< G *Schnorchel* air intake]

snort (snôrt), v.i. **1.** to force the breath
violently through the nostrils with a
loud, harsh sound, as a horse. **2.** to
express contempt or indignation by a
similar sound. —n. **3.** the act or
sound of snorting. **4.** Slang. a quick
drink of liquor. —**snort′er,** n.

snot (snot), n. Informal. mucus from
the nose. —**snot′ty,** adj.

snout (snout), n. the protruding nose
and jaws of an animal.

snow (snō), n. **1.** white flakes of ice
formed from the freezing of water
vapor in the air. **2.** a fall or layer of
these flakes. —v.i. **3.** to fall as snow.
—v.t. **4.** to let fall as snow. **5.** to
cover or obstruct with or as with
snow. —**snow′y,** adj.

snow·ball (snō′bôl′), n. **1.** a round
mass of snow pressed or rolled together. —v.i. **2.** to become larger
or greater very rapidly.

Snow·belt (snō′belt′), n. Informal.
the northeast region of the U.S.

snow·bound (snō′bound′), adj. shut
in or immobilized by snow.

snow·drift (snō′drift′), n. a mound
of snow driven together by the wind.

snow·drop (snō′drop′), n. a low herb
having drooping, white flowers.

snow·fall (snō′fôl′), n. **1.** a fall of
snow. **2.** the amount of snow at a
particular place or time.

snow′ fence′, a barrier serving as a
protection from drifting snow.

snow·man (snō′man′), n. a figure, resembling a human, made out of
packed snow.

snow·mo·bile (snō′mə bēl′), n. a vehicle adapted for traveling on or
through snow. —**snow′mo·bil′er,** n.
—**snow′mo·bil′ing,** n.

snow·plow (snō′plou′), n. a machine
for clearing away snow from highways, etc.

snow·shoe (snō′shōō′), n. a racket-
shaped frame worn on the foot to
keep the wearer from sinking in
deep snow.

snow·storm (snō′stôrm′), n. a storm
accompanied by a heavy fall of snow.

snub (snub), v., **snubbed, snub·bing,**
n. —v.t. **1.** to treat with disdain and
rudeness, esp. by ignoring. **2.** to
stop (a rope that is running out)
suddenly. —n. **3.** disdainful and
rude treatment. —**snub′ber,** n. —
Syn. **3.** affront, insult, slight.

snub-nosed (snub′nōzd′), adj. having
a nose short and turned up at the
tip.

snuck (snuk), v. Dial. pt. and pp. of
sneak.

snuff¹ (snuf), v.t., v.i. **1.** to sniff
pryingly. **2.** to smell by sniffing.
—n. **3.** an act of snuffing. **4.** powdered tobacco, usually taken by inhaling into the nostrils. **5. up to
snuff,** Informal. up to a certain
standard.

snuff² (snuf), v.t. **1.** to cut off the
burned part of (a candlewick). **2.
snuff out, a.** to put out or extinguish.
b. to suppress or crush.

snuf·fle (snuf′əl), v., **-fled, -fling,** n.
—v.i. **1.** to sniffle noisily. —n. **2.** an
act or sound of snuffling. —**snuf′fly,**
adj.

snug (snug), *adj.*, **snug·ger, snug·gest.**
1. warmly cozy. 2. trim and neat,
as a ship. 3. fitting tightly, as a
garment. 4. *Archaic.* concealed or
hiding. —**snug′ly,** *adv.* —**snug′ness,** *n.*
snug·gle (snug′əl), *v.i., v.t.,* **-gled,**
-gling. to lie or press closely
(against), as for comfort.
so (sō), *adv.* 1. in the manner indicated. 2. in that or this manner.
3. to the degree indicated. 4. very
or extremely. 5. very greatly. 6.
hence or therefore. 7. indeed or
truly. 8. likewise or also. 9. then
or subsequently. 10. **or so,** about or
thereabout: *a day or so.* 11. **so as,**
with the result or purpose. 12. **so
that,** with the effect or result that.
13. **so what?,** why should I care?
—*conj.* 14. in order that. 15. with the
result that. —*pron.* 16. such as has
been stated.
—**Usage.** 4. Although many object
to the use of **so** to mean "very," it
is inoffensive enough to be so used
in all but the most formal context.
So., 1. South. 2. Southern.
s.o., 1. seller's option. 2. strikeout.
soak (sōk), *v.i.* 1. to lie in and become completely wet with liquid. 2.
to pass through something, as a
liquid does. —*v.t.* 3. to wet thoroughly. 4. to absorb or take in. 5.
Slang. to overcharge, as a person.
—*n.* 6. the act of soaking or state
of being soaked. 7. the liquid in
which anything is soaked. 8. *Slang.*
a heavy drinker. —**soak′er,** *n.*
so-and-so (sō′ən sō′), *n., pl.* **so-and-
sos.** someone or something not definitely named.
soap (sōp), *n.* 1. a cleansing substance made by treating fat with an
alkali. 2. **no soap,** *Slang.* absolutely
not. —*v.t.* 3. to rub or lather with
soap. —**soap′y,** *adj.* —**soap′i·ly,**
adv. —**soap′i·ness,** *n.*
soap·box (sōp′boks′), *n.* any platform used by a speaker in the street.
soap·er (sō′pər), *n. Slang.* a soap
opera Also, **soap.**
soap′ op′era, *Informal.* a daytime
serialized melodrama, formerly on
radio but now only on television.
[so called from original sponsorship
by soap companies]
soap·stone (sōp′stōn′), *n.* a variety
of talc with a soapy feel, used for
washtubs, etc.
soar (sōr, sôr), *v.i.* 1. to fly upward
or fly at a great height. 2. to rise
to a higher level. —**soar′er,** *n.*
sob (sob), *v.,* **sobbed, sob·bing,** *n.*
—*v.i.* 1. to weep with short catches
of the breath. —*v.t.* 2. to utter with
sobs. —*n.* 3. the act or sound of
sobbing. —**sob′ber,** *n.* —**sob′bing·ly,**
adv.

so·ber (sō′bər), *adj.* 1. not drunk. 2.
habitually temperate, esp. in the use
of liquor. 3. quiet or sedate. 4. grave
and serious. 5. subdued in tone or
color. 6. free from excess or exaggeration. —*v.t., v.i.* 7. to make or
become sober. —**so′ber·ly,** *adv.* —
so′ber·ness, *n.*
so·bri·e·ty (sə brī′i tē, sō-), *n.* the
state or quality of being sober.
so·bri·quet (sō′brə kā′, -ket′, sō′brə-
kā′, -ket′), *n.* a nickname, esp. one
with a special association, as the
Little Corporal for Napoleon I.
soc., 1. social. 2. socialist. 3. society.
so-called (sō′kôld′), *adj.* called thus
but often falsely or incorrectly.
soc·cer (sok′ər), *n.* a type of football in which the ball is advanced
only by kicking.
so·cia·ble (sō′shə bəl), *adj.* 1. friendly
in company. 2. filled with pleasant
conversation and companionship. —
so′cia·bil′i·ty (-bil′i tē), *n.* —**so′cia-
bly,** *adv.* —**Syn.** 1. companionable,
convivial, gregarious.
so·cial (sō′shəl), *adj.* 1. for or devoted to friendly relations and companionship. 2. of or connected with
fashionable society. 3. living or disposed to live with others or in a
community rather than alone. 4. of
the life, welfare, and relations of
human beings in a community. 5.
sociable (def. 1). 6. living together
in colonies, hives, etc. —*n.* 7. a social gathering. —**so′cial·ly,** *adv.*
so′cial disease′, a disease ordinarily
spread by social contact, esp. a venereal disease.
so·cial·ism (sō′shə liz′əm), *n.* a theory or system of social organization
that advocates the ownership and
control of industry, capital, and land
by the community as a whole. —
so′cial·ist, *n., adj.* —**so′cial·is′tic,**
adj.
so·cial·ite (sō′shə līt′), *n.* a socially
prominent person.
so·cial·ize (sō′shə līz′), *v.,* **-ized, -iz-
ing.** —*v.t.* 1. to establish or regulate
according to the theories of socialism. 2. to adjust to social needs. —
v.i. 3. to associate sociably with
others. —**so′cial·i·za′tion,** *n.* —**so′-
cial·iz′er,** *n.*
so′cialized med′icine, a system for
providing free medical care by the
government.
so′cial secu′rity, a life-insurance and
old-age pension plan maintained by
the federal government.
so′cial work′, work aimed at improving social conditions in a community, as by seeking to relieve poverty. —**so′cial work′er.**

so·ci·e·ty (sə sī′i tē), *n., pl.* **-ties.** 1. a body of individuals living as members of a community. 2. human beings collectively. 3. a system of human organization for large-scale community living. 4. an organized group for a particular purpose or common interest. 5. the fashionable or wealthy class. 6. companionship or company. —**so·ci′e·tal** (-t°l), *adj.*

Soci′ety of Friends′, a Protestant denomination founded in England in the 17th century, opposed to oath-taking and war: commonly called Quakers.

socio-, a combining form meaning "social" or "society": *sociopath.*

sociol., 1. sociological. 2. sociology.

so·ci·ol·o·gy (sō′sē ol′ə jē, sō′shē-), *n.* the study of the origin, development, organization, and functioning of human society. —**so′ci·o·log′i·cal** (-ə loj′i kəl), **so′ci·o·log′ic,** *adj.* —**so′ci·o·log′i·cal·ly,** *adv.* —**so′ci·ol′o·gist,** *n.*

so·ci·o·path (sō′sē ə path′, sō′shē-), *n.* a manifestly antisocial psychopath. —**so′ci·o·path′ic,** *adj.*

sock¹ (sok), *n., pl.* **socks** or, for 1, also **sox.** 1. a short stocking. 2. a lightweight shoe worn in ancient comedy. 3. *Obs.* comic drama.

sock² (sok), *Slang.* —*v.t.* 1. to hit hard. 2. **socked in,** *Informal.* (of an airport) to be closed because of bad weather. —*n.* 3. a hard blow.

sock·et (sok′it), *n.* a hollow into which something fits or is fitted.

Soc·ra·tes (sok′rə tēz′), *n.* 469?-399 B.C., Greek philosopher. —**So·crat·ic** (sə krat′ik, sō-), *adj., n.*

sod (sod), *n., v.,* **sod·ded, sod·ding.** —*n.* 1. the surface of the ground covered with grass. 2. a section of this. —*v.t.* 3. to cover with sod.

so·da (sō′də), *n.* 1. See **sodium hydroxide.** 2. See **sodium carbonate.** 3. sodium. 4. See **sodium bicarbonate.** 5. See **soda water.** 6. a drink made with soda water, flavoring, and often ice cream.

so′da foun′tain, a counter, as in a drugstore, for preparing and serving sodas, light meals, etc.

so′da pop′, a carbonated and artificially flavored soft drink.

so′da wa′ter. 1. water charged with carbon dioxide and often flavored. 2. See **soda pop.**

sod·den (sod′°n), *adj.* 1. soaked with liquid or moisture. 2. soggy (def. 2). 3. dull or listless, as from drunkenness. —**sod′den·ly,** *adv.* —**sod′den·ness,** *n.*

so·di·um (sō′dē əm), *n. Chem.* a metallic element that oxidizes rapidly in moist air, occurring in nature only in the combined state. *Symbol:* Na; *at. wt.:* 22.9898; *at. no.:* 11.

so′dium bicar′bonate, a white, mildly alkaline powder used in cooking and in medicines.

so′dium car′bonate, a grayish-white powder used as a cleanser, for bleaching, etc.

so′dium chlo′ride, salt (def. 1).

so′dium hydrox′ide, a white, solid substance used to make soap and as a caustic.

so′dium ni′trate, a crystalline compound used in fertilizers, explosives, and glass.

so′dium thi·o·sul′fate (thī′ō sul′fāt), a white, crystalline powder used as a fixing agent in photography.

sod·om·y (sod′ə mē), *n.* 1. unnatural, esp. anal or oral, copulation. 2. copulation of a human with an animal. —**sod′om·ite′** (-mīt′), *n.*

so·ev·er (sō ev′ər), *adv.* 1. in any way. 2. of any kind.

so·fa (sō′fə), *n.* a long, upholstered couch with a back and arms.

So·fi·a (sō′fē ə, sō fē′ə), *n.* the capital of Bulgaria.

soft (sôft, soft), *adj.* 1. yielding readily to touch or pressure. 2. relatively deficient in hardness, as metal. 3. smooth and agreeable to the touch. 4. low or subdued in sound. 5. not glaring, as color. 6. gentle or mild, as wind. 7. kind or sympathetic. 8. not strong or robust. 9. not difficult or trying: *a soft job.* 10. (of water) relatively free from mineral salts that interfere with the action of soap. 11. not damaging to the vehicle: *a soft landing on the moon.* 12. not physically addictive, such as marijuana. —*adv.* 13. in a soft manner. —**soft′ly,** *adv.* —**soft′ness,** *n.*

soft·ball (sôft′bôl′, soft′-), *n.* 1. a form of baseball played with a larger and softer ball. 2. the ball itself.

soft-boiled (sôft′boild′, soft′-), *adj.* (of an egg) boiled not long enough to cause the yolk to solidify.

soft·bound (sôft′bound′), *adj.* (of a book) bound with a flexible paper cover. Also, **soft′-cov′er.**

soft′ coal′. See **bituminous coal.**

soft-core (sôft′kôr′, soft′kôr′), *adj.* suggestive rather than explicit: *soft-core pornography.*

soft′ drink′, a beverage that is not alcoholic and is usually carbonated.

sof·ten (sô′fən, sof′ən), *v.t., v.i.* to make or become more soft or softer. —**sof′ten·er,** *n.*

sof·ten·er (sô′fə nər, sof′ə-), *n.* 1. a person or thing that softens. 2. *Chem.* any admixture to a substance for promoting or increasing its softness, smoothness, or plasticity.

soft′ line′, a conciliatory or accommodative stand, esp. in politics. —**soft′-line′,** *adj.* —**soft′-lin′er,** *n.*

soft′ pal′ate, the posterior muscular portion of the palate.

soft′ ped′al, a pedal, as in a piano, for reducing tonal volume.

soft-ped·al (sôft′ped′əl, soft′-), *v.t.*, **-aled, -al·ing** or **-alled, -al·ling.** *Informal.* to obscure the importance of.

soft′ rock′, a type of rock-'n'-roll in which the lyrics are more important than the music.

soft′ sell′, a quietly persuasive and indirect method of advertising or selling.

soft′ soap′, *Informal.* flattery and persuasion. —**soft′-soap′**, *v.t.*

soft-ware (sôft′wâr′, soft′-), *n.* the written programs and other data that may be inserted in computer programs.

soft-wood (sôft′wood′, soft′-), *n.* **1.** any wood that is easily cut. **2.** a coniferous tree or its wood.

soft·y (sôf′tē, sof′-), *n., pl.* **-ties.** *Informal.* a person easily stirred to sentiment. Also, **soft′ie.**

sog·gy (sog′ē), *adj.,* **-gi·er, -gi·est. 1.** thoroughly wet. **2.** damp and heavy, as poorly baked bread. —**sog′gi·ly,** *adv.* —**sog′gi·ness,** *n.*

So·Ho (sō′hō), *n.* a district in lower Manhattan, New York City, noted for art studios, galleries, etc. [so called from its location *so(uth)* of *Ho(uston)* St.]

soi·gné (swän yā′), *adj. French.* **1.** elegantly done or designed. **2.** neat and well-groomed. Also, **soi·gnée′.**

soil[1] (soil), *n.* **1.** the thin layer of the earth's surface in which plants grow. **2.** ground or earth. **3.** a country or region.

soil[2] (soil), *v.t.* **1.** to make unclean or filthy. **2.** to tarnish with disgrace. —*v.i.* **3.** to become soiled. —*n.* **4.** a soiled or dirty spot. **5.** excrement or manure.

soi·ree (swä rā′), *n.* an evening party or gathering. Also, **soi·rée′.**

so·journ (*v.* sō′jûrn, sō jûrn′; *n.* sō′-jûrn), *v.i.* **1.** to stay in a place for a time. —*n.* **2.** a temporary stay. —**so′journ·er,** *n.*

sol[1] (sōl, sol), *n. Music.* the fifth tone of a diatonic scale.

sol[2] (sōl, sol), *n., pl.* **sols, so·les** (sō′-les). the monetary unit of Peru.

sol[3] (sol, sōl), *n.* a colloidal solution in a liquid.

Sol (sol), *n.* **1.** the ancient Roman sun god. **2.** the sun personified.

Sol., 1. Solicitor. **2.** Solomon.

sol., 1. soluble. **2.** solution.

sol·ace (sol′is), *n., v.,* **-aced, -ac·ing.** —*n.* **1.** comfort in sorrow. **2.** something that gives comfort or consolation. —*v.t.* **3.** to comfort or console. —**sol′ac·er,** *n.*

so·lar (sō′lər), *adj.* **1.** of or derived from the sun. **2.** proceeding from or operated by the light or heat of the sun. **3.** of, using, or heated by solar energy: *a solar home.* **4.** determined by the sun.

so′lar bat′tery, a device for converting solar energy into electricity.

so′lar en′ergy, energy obtained from the sun's radiation, as for heating purposes.

so·lar·i·um (sō lâr′ē əm, sə-), *n., pl.* **-ums, -i·a** (-ə). a glass-enclosed room exposed to the sun's rays, as in a hospital.

so′lar plex′us, 1. a network of nerves behind the stomach. **2.** *Informal.* a point between the navel and breastbone.

so′lar sys′tem, the sun with all the celestial bodies that revolve around it.

sold (sōld), *v.* pt. and pp. of **sell.**

sol·der (sod′ər), *n.* **1.** an alloy of tin and lead used when melted to join metal surfaces together. —*v.t., v.i.* **2.** to join with solder. —**sol′der·er,** *n.*

sol′dering i′ron, an instrument for melting and applying solder.

sol·dier (sōl′jər), *n.* **1.** a person who serves in an army. **2.** an enlisted man or woman as distinguished from a commissioned officer. —*v.i.* **3.** to act or serve as a soldier. **4.** to loaf while pretending to work. —**sol′dier·ly,** *adj.*

sol′dier of for′tune, a military adventurer willing to serve any leader or country.

sol·dier·y (sōl′jə rē), *n.* **1.** soldiers collectively. **2.** military skill.

sole[1] (sōl), *adj.* being the only one. —**sole′ly,** *adv.*

sole[2] (sōl), *n., v.,* **soled, sol·ing.** —*n.* **1.** the bottom side of the foot. **2.** the underside of a shoe or boot. —*v.t.* **3.** to furnish with a sole, as a shoe.

sole[3] (sōl), *n., pl.* **sole, soles.** a European flatfish used for food.

sol·e·cism (sol′i siz′əm), *n.* **1.** an ungrammatical usage. **2.** a breach of etiquette.

sol·emn (sol′əm), *adj.* **1.** deeply earnest or serious. **2.** characterized by dignity, awe, or formality. **3.** having a religious or sacred character. **4.** somber or gloomy. —**so·lem·ni·ty** (sə lem′ni tē), *n.* —**sel′emn·ly,** *adv.* —**sol′emn·ness,** *n.*

sol·em·nize (sol′əm nīz′), *v.t.,* **-nized, -niz·ing. 1.** to observe with ceremonies. **2.** to perform the ceremony of (marriage). —**sol′em·ni·za′tion,** *n.*

so·le·noid (sō′lə noid′), *n.* an electric conductor wound on a cylinder that establishes a magnetic field when passing through a current. —**so′le·noi′dal,** *adj.*

so·lic·it (sə lis'it), *v.t.* **1.** to seek for by courteous entreaty. **2.** to lure or tempt. —*v.i* **3.** to solicit something or someone —**so·lic'i·ta'tion,** *n.* —**Syn. 1.** invite petition request.

so·lic·i·tor (sə lis'i tərj, *n.* **1.** a person who solicits business, trade, etc. **2.** See **solicitor general. 3.** *Brit.* a lawyer who advises clients and prepares that case for barristers.

solic·itor gen'eral, *pl.* **solicitors general.** a law officer next in rank to the attorney general

so·lic·i·tous (sə lis'i təs), *adj.* **1.** full of anxiety or concern **2.** anxiously desirous - **so·lic'i·tous·ly,** *adv.* —**so·lic'i·tous·ness,** *n.*

so·lic·i·tude (sə lis'i tōōd' -tyōōd'), *n.* the state of being solicitous.

sol·id (sol'id) *adj.* **1.** having three dimensions (length, width, and thickness). **2.** having the inside completely filled up. **3.** without openings or breaks. **4.** firm, hard, or compact. **5.** having definite shape and size. **6.** consisting entirely of one substance or material **7.** uniform in tone or shades. **8.** real or genuine: *solid comfort.* **9.** sound or good, as an argument **10.** fully reliable or sensible. **11.** written without a hyphen, as a compound word. **12.** united or unanimous, as in opinion. —*n.* **13.** an object having three dimensions. **14.** a solid substance. —**so·lid·i·ty** (sə lid'i tē), *n* —**sol'id·ly,** *adv.* —**sol'id·ness,** *n.*

sol·i·dar·i·ty (sol'i dar'i tē), *n.* union or fellowship, as between members of a group

so·lid·i·fy (sə lid'ə fī'), *v.t.,* *v.i.,* **-fied, -fy·ing.** to make or become solid. —**so·lid'i·fi·ca'tion,** *n.*

sol·id-state (sol'id stāt'), *adj.* utilizing transistors instead of vacuum tubes. **2.** of or dealing with the physical construction of solid materials.

sol·i·dus (sol'i dəs), *n., pl.* **-di** (-dī). **1.** *Brit* slash (def 7) **2.** a gold coin of the Byzantine Empire.

so·lil·o·quize (sə lil'ə kwīz'), *v.i.,* *v.t.,* **-quized, -quiz·ing.** to utter (in) soliloquy.

so·lil·o·quy (sə lil'ə kwē), *n., pl.* **-quies. 1.** the act of talking while or as if alone. **2.** a speech that an actor or actress makes to himself or herself while alone on the stage.

sol·ip·sism (sol'ip siz'əm), *n. Philos.* the theory that only the self exists. —**sol'ip·sist,** *n., adj.* —**sol'ip·sis'tic,** *adj.*

sol·i·taire (sol'i târ'), *n.* **1.** a card game played by one person. **2.** a precious stone, esp. a diamond, set by itself

sol·i·tar·y (sol'i ter'ē), *adj.* **1.** living or being alone. **2.** occurring or done alone. **3.** secluded or lonely. **4.**
sole or only. —**sol'i·tar'i·ness,** *n.* —**Syn. 3.** isolated, remote.

sol·i·tude (sol'i tōōd', -tyōōd'), *n.* **1.** the state of being solitary. **2.** a secluded or lonely place.

soln., solution.

so·lo (sō'lō), *n., pl.* **-los,** *adj., adv., v.* —*n.* **1.** a musical composition for one singer or instrumentalist, with or without accompaniment **2.** any performance by one person —*adj.* **3.** acting or performed by one person. —*adv.* **4.** by oneself. —*v.i.* **5.** to perform a solo. [< It < L *sōlus* alone] —**so'lo·ist,** *n.*

Sol·o·mon (sol'ə mən), *n.* king of Israel in the 10th century B.C., famous for his wisdom.

so' long, *Informal.* goodbye.

sol·stice (sol'stis, sōl'-), *n.* either of the two times a year when the sun is at its greatest distance from the celestial equator about June 21 (**sum'mer sol'stice**) and about December 22 (**win'ter sol'stice**). —**sol·sti'tial** (-stish'əl), *adj*

sol·u·ble (sol'yə bəl), *adj.* **1.** capable of being dissolved or liquefied. **2.** capable of being solved or explained. —*n.* **3.** something soluble. —**sol'u·bil'i·ty,** *n* —**sol'u·bly,** *adv.*

sol·ute (sol'yōōt sō'lōōt), *n.* **1.** the substance dissolved in a given solution. —*adj* **2.** in solution.

so·lu·tion (sə lōō'shən), *n* **1.** the act of solving a problem, question, etc. **2.** an answer or explanation. **3. a.** the act or process by which a gas, liquid, or solid is dispersed homogeneously in a gas, liquid, or solid without chemical change. **b.** the mixture thus formed

solve (solv), *v.t.,* **solved, solv·ing.** to find the answer or explanation for. —**solv'a·ble** *adj* —**solv'er,** *n.*

sol·vent (sol'vənt), *adj.* **1.** able to pay all legal debts. **2.** having the power of dissolving. —*n.* **3.** a substance in a solution that dissolves another substance —**sol'ven·cy,** *n.*

So·ma·li·a (sō mä'lē ə -mäl'yə), *n.* a country on the E coast of Africa.

so·mat·ic (sō mat'ik sə-), *adj.* of the body as distinguished from the mind. —**so·mat'i·cal·ly,** *adv.*

somat'ic cell', any cell other than a germ cell.

som·ber (som'bər), *adj.* **1.** gloomily dark. **2.** depressing or dismal. Also, *Brit.* **som'bre** —**som'ber·ly,** *adv.* —**Syn. 1.** murky, shadowy. **2.** melancholy

som·bre·ro (som brâr'ō), *n., pl.* **-ros.** a man's broad-brimmed hat, worn in Spain and Mexico.

some (sum) *adj.* **1.** being an unknown or unspecified one: *Some person may object.* **2.** of a certain unspecified number or degree: *to some extent.*

3. unspecified but considerable in number or degree: *He was here some .weeks.* **4.** *Informal.* notable of its kind. —*pron* **5.** a certain unspecified number or amount. *Some of the guests came late.* —*adv.* **6.** approximately or about. *Some 300 were present.* **7.** *Informal.* to some extent: *I like baseball some* **8.** *Informal.* to a great extent. *That s going some!*

-some[1], a suffix meaning: **a.** having the quality of *burdensome.* **b.** having a tendency to. *quarrelsome.*

-some[2], a suffix meaning "a group of a certain number" *twosome.*

-some[3], a combining form meaning "body": *chromosome.*

some·bod·y (sum'bod'ē, -bud'ē, -bə-dē), *pron* **1.** some person. —*n.* **2.** a person of importance.

some·day (sum'dā'), *adv.* at an indefinite future time.

some·how (sum'hou'), *adv.* in some way not specified or known.

some·one (sum'wun', -wən), *pron.* somebody

some·place (sum'plās'), *adv. Informal.* somewhere.

som·er·sault (sum'ər sôlt'), *n.* **1.** an acrobatic movement in which a person rolls or jumps completely over, heels over head. —*v.i.* **2.** to perform a somersault. Also, **som'er·set'** (-set').

some·thing (sum'thing), *pron.* **1.** a certain undetermined or unspecified thing. **2. make something of, a.** to benefit or profit from. **b.** to consider useful or valuable. **c.** *Informal.* to question or challenge.

some·time (sum'tīm'), *adv.* **1.** at some indefinite time. **2.** at an indefinite future time. —*adj.* **3.** having been formerly. **4.** *Informal.* sporadic or occasional.

some·times (sum'tīmz'), *adv.* on some occasions

some·way (sum'wā'), *adv. Informal.* somehow Also, **some'ways'.**

some·what (sum'hwut', -hwot', -hwət, -wut', -wot', -wət), *adv.* **1.** in some measure or degree. —*n.* **2.** some part, portion or degree.

some·where (sum'hwâr', -wâr'), *adv.* **1.** in, to, or at a place not specified or known. **2.** at or to some point in amount degree etc.

som·nam·bu·lism (som nam'byə liz'-əm, səm-), *n* the act or habit of walking about while asleep. —**som-nam'bu·list,** *n.*

som·no·lent (som'nə lənt), *adj.* **1.** extremely drowsy. **2.** soporific (def. 1). —**som'no·lence,** *n.* —**som'no·lent·ly,** *adv.*

son (sun), *n.* **1.** a male child or person in relation to his parents. **2.** any male descendant. **3. the Son,** Jesus Christ.

so·nar (sō'när), *n.* a device for detecting and locating objects submerged in water by means of the sound waves they reflect or produce. [*so(und) na(vigation) r(anging)*]

so·na·ta (sə nä'tə), *n. Music.* a composition for one or two instruments, typically in three or four contrasting movements.

song (sông, song), *n.* **1.** a short metrical composition for singing. **2.** poetical composition. **3.** vocal music. **4.** any singing sound. **5. for a song,** at a very low price. —**song'ful,** *adj.* —**song'ful·ly,** *adv.*

song·bird (sông'bûrd', song'-), *n.* a bird that sings a musical song.

song·fest (sông'fest', song'-), *n.* an informal gathering at which people sing folk songs. etc.

song·ster (sông'stər, song'-), *n.* a person skilled in singing. —**song'stress** (-stris), *n.fem*

son·ic (son'ik), *adj.* of or pertaining to sound or the speed of sound.

son'ic boom', an explosive noise generated by an aircraft flying at supersonic speed

son-in-law (sun'in lô'), *n., pl.* **sons-in-law.** the husband of one's daughter.

son·net (son'it), *n.* a poem of 14 lines rhymed according to certain definite schemes.

son·ny (sun'ē), *n., pl.* **-nies.** little son (used in addressing a boy).

so·no·rous (sə nôr'əs, -nōr'-, son'ər-əs), *adj.* **1.** giving out a deep, resonant sound. **2.** rich and full in sound. **3.** high-flown or imposing. —**so·nor'-i·ty** (-i tē), *n* —**so·no'rous·ly,** *adv.*

soon (sōōn), *adv.* **1.** in the near future. **2.** before the usual or expected time. **3.** promptly or quickly. **4.** readily or willingly. **5. sooner or later,** eventually or ultimately.

soot (sŏŏt, sōōt), *n.* a black, powdery substance consisting mostly of carbon, made by the burning of wood, coal, etc. —**soot'y,** *adj.*

sooth (sōōth), *n. Archaic.* truth or fact.

soothe (sōōth), *v.t.,* **soothed, soothing. 1.** to calm or comfort, as with soft words. **2.** to mitigate or allay, as pain. —**sooth'er,** *n.* —**sooth'ing,** *adj.* —**sooth'ing·ly,** *adv.*

sooth·say·er (sōōth'sā'ər), *n.* a person who professes to foretell events. —**sooth'say'ing,** *n.*

sop (sop), *n., v.,* **sopped, sop·ping.** —*n.* **1.** a piece of solid food, as bread, for dipping in liquid food. **2.** something given to pacify or quiet, or as a bribe. —*v.t., v.i.* **3.** to dip or soak in liquid food. **4.** to take up (liquid) by absorption.

SOP, 1. standard operating procedure. **2.** standing operating procedure.

soph (sof), *n. Informal.* a sophomore.

soph·ism (sof′iz əm), *n.* a clever but specious argument.

soph·ist (sof′ist), *n.* a clever but specious reasoner.

so·phis·tic (sə fis′tik), *adj.* of or pertaining to sophists or sophistry. Also, **so·phis′ti·cal.**

so·phis·ti·cate (*v.* sə fis′tə kāt′; *n.* sə fis′tə kit, -kāt′), *v.,* **-cat·ed, -cat·ing,** *n.* —*v.t.* 1. to make worldly-wise. —*n.* 2. a sophisticated person.

so·phis·ti·cat·ed (sə fis′tə kā′tid), *adj.* 1. having or showing worldly knowledge or experience. 2. pleasing to the tastes of sophisticates. 3. complex or intricate, as a system or process. —**so·phis′ti·cat′ed·ly,** *adv.* —**so·phis′ti·ca′tion,** *n.* —**Syn.** 1. cosmopolitan, urbane.

soph·ist·ry (sof′i strē), *n., pl.* **-ries.** the use or practice of sophisms.

Soph·o·cles (sof′ə klēz′), *n.* 495?–406? B.C., Greek dramatist. —**Soph′o·cle′an,** *adj.*

soph·o·more (sof′ə môr′, -môr′; sof′môr, -môr), *n.* a student in his or her second year at a high school or college. [< Gk *soph(ós)* wise + *mōr(ós)* foolish]

soph·o·mor·ic (sof′ə môr′ik, -mor′-), *adj.* 1. of or like sophomores. 2. intellectually pretentious but immature. —**soph′o·mor′i·cal·ly,** *adv.*

sop·o·rif·ic (sop′ə rif′ik, sō′pər-), *adj.* 1. tending to cause sleep. 2. somnolent (def. 1). —*n.* 3. a soporific medicine or drug. —**sop′o·rif′i·cal·ly,** *adv.*

sop·py (sop′ē), *adj.,* **-pi·er, -pi·est.** 1. Also, **sop′ping.** very wet, as ground. 2. *Brit. Slang.* excessively sentimental.

so·pran·o (sə pran′ō, -prä′nō), *n.* 1. the highest singing voice in women and boys. 2. a part for such a voice. 3. a singer with such a voice.

sor·cer·y (sôr′sə rē), *n., pl.* **-cer·ies.** the use of magic through the aid of evil spirits with intent to harm others. —**sor′cer·er,** *n.* —**sor′cer·ess,** *n.fem.*

sor·did (sôr′did), *adj.* 1. wretchedly filthy. 2. morally ignoble or base. 3. meanly selfish. —**sor′did·ly,** *adv.* —**sor′did·ness,** *n.* —**Syn.** 1. foul, squalid. 2. mean, unscrupulous, vile.

sore (sōr, sôr), *adj.,* **sor·er, sor·est,** *n.* —*adj.* 1. physically painful or sensitive. 2. feeling physical pain. 3. distressed or sorrowful. 4. severe or extreme. 5. *Informal.* annoyed or angered. 6. causing irritation: *a sore subject.* —*n.* 7. a sore spot on the body. 8. a source of distress or sorrow. —**sore′ly,** *adv.* —**sore′ness,** *n.*

sore·head (sōr′hed′, sôr′-), *n. Informal.* a disgruntled or vindictive person.

sor·ghum (sôr′gəm), *n.* 1. a cereal grass grown for use as fodder and for its sweet juice. 2. a syrup made from this juice.

so·ror·i·ty (sə rôr′i tē, -ror′-), *n., pl.* **-ties.** a society or club of women or girls, esp. in a college.

sorp·tion (sôrp′shən), *n.* the process of absorption or adsorption. —**sorp′tive,** *adj.*

sor·rel[1] (sôr′əl, sor′-), *n.* 1. a light reddish brown. 2. a horse of this color.

sor·rel[2] (sôr′əl, sor′-), *n.* a plant having sour leaves, used in salads, etc.

sor·row (sor′ō, sôr′ō), *n.* 1. deep, often lengthy anguish caused by loss, disappointment, etc. 2. a cause of such anguish. 3. the expression of such anguish. —*v.i.* 4. to feel or show sorrow. —**sor′row·ful,** *adj.* —**sor′row·ful·ly,** *adv.* —**sor′row·ful·ness,** *n.* —**Syn.** 1. grief, regret, sadness, woe.

sor·ry (sor′ē, sôr′ē), *adj.,* **-ri·er, -ri·est.** 1. feeling regret, sympathy, pity, etc. 2. worthless or pitiful. 3. dismal or miserable. —**sor′ri·ly,** *adv.* —**sor′ri·ness,** *n.*

sort (sôrt), *n.* 1. a kind or type of persons or things distinguished by a common character. 2. quality or nature. 3. *Archaic.* manner or way. 4. **of sorts,** of a mediocre or poor kind. Also, **of a sort.** 5. **out of sorts,** a. in a bad temper. b. in poor health. 6. **sort of,** *Informal.* in a way. —*v.t.* 7. to arrange according to kind or class. —**sort′er,** *n.*

—Usage. 6. See **kind**[2].

sor·tie (sôr′tē), *n.* 1. a rapid movement of troops from a besieged place to attack the besiegers. 2. a combat mission made by one aircraft.

SOS, a radio signal used esp. by ships in distress.

so-so (sō′sō′), *adj.* 1. neither very good nor very bad. —*adv.* 2. in a passable manner.

sot (sot), *n.* a chronic drunkard. —**sot′tish,** *adj.* —**sot′tish·ly,** *adv.*

sou·brette (soo bret′), *n.* a coquettish maidservant in a play or opera.

souf·flé (soo flā′), *n.* a light, baked dish made fluffy with beaten egg whites combined with egg yolks.

sough (sou, suf), *v.i.* 1. to make a sighing or murmuring sound. —*n.* 2. a soughing sound.

sought (sôt), *v.* pt. and pp. of **seek.**

soul (sōl), *n.* 1. the principle of life, feeling, and thought, in humans, regarded as a distinct spiritual entity separate from the body. 2. the emotional part of human nature. 3. a human being. 4. the essential element or part of something. 5. noble warmth of spirit. 6. the inspirer of some action. 7. *Slang.* the general ethnic awareness, pride, and feeling among black Americans. —adj. Slang. **8.** of or characteristic of black Americans or their culture: soul food; soul music. —**soul′less**, adj. —**soul′less·ness**, n.

soul·ful (sōl′fəl), adj. of or expressing deep feeling. —**soul′ful·ly**, adv. — **soul′ful·ness**, n.

sound¹ (sound), n. **1.** the sensation produced by vibrations reaching the organs of hearing through the air or another medium. **2.** that which is heard, as a tone or noise. **3.** the distance within which such a sensation may be heard. **4.** implication or impression. —v.i. **5.** to make a sound. **6.** to convey a certain impression when heard. —v.t. **7.** to cause to sound. **8.** to announce or direct by or as by a sound. **9.** to utter audibly. **10.** to examine by causing to make sound. —**sound′-less**, adj.

sound² (sound), adj. **1.** in good health. **2.** free from defect, decay, etc. **3.** financially secure. **4.** competent or sensible. **5.** having no defect as to truth or reason. **6.** honest or upright. **7.** untroubled or deep: sound sleep. **8.** thorough or severe. —adv. **9.** completely or deeply: sound asleep. —**sound′ly**, adv. —**sound′-ness**, n.

sound³ (sound), v.t., v.i. **1.** to measure the depth of (water), esp. by means of a weighted line. **2.** to seek to elicit the views of (a person) by indirect inquiries, etc. **3.** to plunge downward, as a whale. —**sound′er**, n. —**sound′ing**, n.

sound⁴ (sound), n. **1.** a relatively narrow passage of water between larger bodies of water or between the mainland and an island. **2.** an inlet of the sea.

sound′ing board′, **1.** Also called **sound′board′**. a thin, resonant plate of wood forming part of a musical instrument, as a piano. **2.** a person or group on whom to test ideas or plans.

sound·proof (sound′prōōf′), adj. **1.** impervious to sound. —v.t. **2.** to make soundproof.

sound·track (sound′trak′), n. the narrow strip at one side of a motion-picture film on which sound is recorded.

soup (sōōp), n. **1.** a liquid food made by boiling meat, fish, or vegetables with various added ingredients. **2.** **in the soup**, Slang. in trouble. —v.t. **3.** **soup up**, Slang. to improve the capacity for speed of (an engine).

soup·çon (sōōp sôN′, sōōp′sôN), n. **1.** a slight trace or flavor. **2.** a very small amount.

soup·y (sōō′pē), adj., **soup·i·er**, **soup·i·est**. **1.** resembling soup in consistency. **2.** very thick or dense, as a fog. **3.** overly sentimental.

sour (sour, sou′ər), adj. **1.** having an acid taste resembling that of vinegar, etc. **2.** spoiled or fermented. **3.** disagreeable or unpleasant. **4.** cross or peevish. **5.** Informal. poor or unsuccessful: a sour investment. —v.t., v.i. **6.** to make or become sour. — **sour′ly**, adv. —**sour′ness**, n.

source (sōrs, sôrs), n. **1.** any thing or place from which something comes or is obtained. **2.** the beginning of a stream or river. **3.** a book or person supplying information.

sour·dough (sour′dō′, sou′ər-), n. fermented dough kept from one baking to start the next instead of beginning each time with fresh yeast.

sour′ grapes′, pretended disdain for something one does not or cannot have.

sour·puss (sour′pōōs′, sou′ər-), n. Informal. a person having a grouchy disposition.

souse (sous), v., **soused**, **sous·ing**, n. —v.t., v.i. **1.** to plunge into a liquid. **2.** to make or become wet all over. **3.** to steep in pickling brine. **4.** Slang. to make drunk. —n. **5.** an act of sousing. **6.** something steeped in pickle, esp. a pig's feet. **7.** a liquid used as a pickle. **8.** Slang. a drunkard.

south (south), n. **1.** the direction to the left of a person facing the sunset. **2.** a cardinal point of the compass lying directly opposite north. **3.** (usually cap.) a region or territory situated in this direction. **4. the South**, the general area south of Pennsylvania and the Ohio River and east of the Mississippi. —adj. **5.** lying toward or situated in the south. **6.** coming from the south. —adv. **7.** toward or from the south. —**south·ern** (suth′ərn), adj. —**south′-ern·most′**, adj.

South′ Af′rica, Repub′lic of, a country in S Africa. —**South′ Af′rican**.

South′ Amer′ica, a continent in the S part of the Western Hemisphere. —**South′ Amer′ican**.

South′ Bend′, a city in N Indiana.

South′ Caroli′na, a state in the SE United States. Cap.: Columbia. —**South′ Car·o·lin′i·an** (kar′ə lin′ē-ən).

South′ Chi′na Sea′, a part of the W Pacific, bounded by SE Asia and the Philippines.

South′ Dako′ta, a state in the N central United States. Cap.: Pierre. —**South′ Dako′tan**.

south·east (south'ēst'), *n.* **1.** the direction midway between south and east. **2.** a region in this direction. —*adj.* **3.** lying toward or situated in the southeast. **4.** coming from the southeast. —*adv.* **5.** toward or from the southeast. —**south'east'er·ly,** *adj., adv.* —**south'east'ern,** *adj.* —**south'east'ward,** *adj., adv.* —**south'east'wards,** *adv.*

South'east A'sia, the countries and islands between India and the Philippines.

south·east·er (south'ē'stər), *n.* a gale or storm from the southeast.

south·er (sou'thər), *n.* a wind or storm from the south.

south·er·ly (suth'ər lē), *adj., adv.* **1.** toward the south. **2.** from the south.

south·ern·er (suth'ər nər), *n.* **1.** a native or inhabitant of the south. **2.** (*cap.*) a native or inhabitant of the southern U.S.

South'ern Hem'isphere, the half of the earth between the South Pole and the equator.

south'ern lights'. See aurora australis.

South' Kore'a. See under Korea.

south·paw (south'pô'), *n. Informal.* a person who is left-handed, esp. a left-handed baseball pitcher.

South' Pole', the southernmost point of the earth.

South' Sea' Is'lands, the islands in the S Pacific Ocean.

South' Vietnam', a former country in SE Asia: now part of reunified Vietnam.

south·ward (south'wərd), *adj.* **1.** situated in the south. —*adv.* **2.** Also, **south'wards.** toward the south. —**south'ward·ly,** *adj., adv.*

south·west (south'west'), *n.* **1.** the direction midway between south and west. **2.** a region in this direction. **3. the Southwest,** the southwest region of the United States. —*adj.* **4.** lying toward or situated in the southwest. **5.** coming from the southwest. —*adv.* **6.** toward or from the southwest. —**south'west'er·ly,** *adj., adv.* —**south'west'ern,** *adj.* —**south'west'ward,** *adj., adv.* —**south'west'wards,** *adv.*

south·west·er (south'wes'tər), *n.* **1.** a gale or storm from the southwest. **2.** a sailor's waterproof hat having the brim very broad behind. Also, **sou'·west·er** (sou'wes'tər).

sou·ve·nir (sōō'və nēr', sōō'və nēr'), *n.* something, often a small article of merchandise, given or kept as a reminder, as of a place visited.

sov·er·eign (sov'rin, sov'ər in, suv'-), *n.* **1.** a monarch or other supreme ruler. **2.** a former British gold coin equal to one pound sterling. —*adj.*

3. having supreme rank or power. **4.** having independent power or authority: *a sovereign state.* **5.** superior to all others. —**Syn. 3.** paramount, preeminent.

sov·er·eign·ty (sov'rin tē, suv'-), *n., pl.* **-ties. 1.** the status or rule of a sovereign. **2.** independent power or authority in a state.

so·vi·et (sō'vē et', -it, sō'vē et'), *n.* **1.** any of the elected legislative councils on various levels in the Soviet Union. **2. Soviets,** the governing officials or the people of the Soviet Union. —*adj.* **3.** of or pertaining to a soviet. **4.** (*cap.*) of the Soviet Union. [< Russ *sovyet* council] —**so'vi·et·ism,** *n.* —**so'vi·et·ize',** *v.t.*

So'viet Un'ion, a country of 15 constituent republics in E Europe and W and N Asia.

sow¹ (sō), *v.,* **sowed, sown** (sōn) or **sowed, sow·ing.** —*v.t.* **1.** to scatter (seed) for growth. **2.** to scatter seed over (land). **3.** to spread or disseminate. —*v.i.* **4.** to sow seed. —**.sow'er,** *n.*

sow² (sou), *n.* an adult female swine.

sox (soks), *n.* a pl. of **sock¹.**

soy (soi), *n.* an Oriental salty sauce made from fermented soybeans.

soy·bean (soi'bēn'), *n.* **1.** a bushy plant grown widely for forage and soil improvement. **2.** its seed, processed as oil.

SP, 1. Shore Patrol. **2.** Specialist.

Sp., 1. Spain. **2.** Spaniard. **3.** Spanish.

sp., 1. special. **2.** species. **3.** specimen. **4.** spelling. **5.** spirit.

s.p., (in genealogical tables) without issue or childless. [< L *sine prole*]

spa (spä), *n.* **1.** a mineral spring. **2.** a health resort having such a spring.

space (spās), *n., v.,* **spaced, spac·ing.** —*n.* **1.** the unlimited expanse in which all material objects are contained. **2.** a particular extent of surface. **3.** See **outer space. 4.** a place available for a particular purpose: *a parking space.* **5.** a particular extent of time. **6.** a seat or room on an airplane or ship. —*v.t.* **7.** to divide into spaces. **8.** to set some distance apart.

space·craft (spās'kraft', -kräft'), *n., pl.* **-craft.** any vehicle capable of traveling in outer space.

spaced-out (spāst'out'), *adj. Slang.* dazed by the use of alcohol or drugs.

space·flight (spās'flīt'), *n.* flight into or through outer space.

space' heat'er, a small device for heating a limited space.

space·man (spās'man', -mən), *n.* astronaut. —**space'wom'an,** *n.fem.*

space·ship (spās'ship'), *n.* a spacecraft, esp. a manned one.

space′ shut′tle, a large spacecraft combining a rocket and a glider airplane, planned for eventual routine ferrying of passengers and equipment into orbit and back.

space′ sta′tion, an orbiting artificial satellite from which further space exploration can be undertaken.

space·suit (spās′sōōt′), *n.* a pressurized suit allowing the wearer to survive in outer space.

space·walk (spās′wôk′), *n.* **1.** an extravehicular activity in which an astronaut moves about in outer space. —*v.i.* **2.** to perform a spacewalk. —**space′walk·er,** *n.*

spa·cious (spā′shəs), *adj.* containing much space, as a house. —**spa′cious·ly,** *adv.* —**spa′cious·ness,** *n.*

spade[1] (spād), *n., v.,* **spad·ed, spad·ing.** —*n.* **1.** a digging tool having a long handle and a flat blade. —*v.t., v.i.* **2.** to dig or cut with a spade. —**spade′ful,** *n.*

spade[2] (spād), *n.* **1.** a black figure shaped like an inverted heart with a short stem, used on playing cards. **2.** a playing card so marked.

spa·dix (spā′diks), *n., pl.* **spa·dix·es, spa·di·ces** (spā di′sēz). a floral spike with a fleshy or thickened axis, usually enclosed in a spathe.

spa·ghet·ti (spə get′ē), *n.* a pasta made in the form of long, thin strings for boiling.

Spain (spān), *n.* a country in SW Europe.

spake (spāk), *v. Archaic.* a pt. of **speak.**

span[1] (span), *n., v.,* **spanned, span·ning.** —*n.* **1.** the full extent or stretch of anything. **2.** a space between two supports, as of a bridge. **3.** a short space of time. —*v.t.* **4.** the distance between the tips of the thumb and little finger when fully extended, about 9 inches. **5.** to extend over or across. **6.** to reach or pass over (space or time). **7.** to measure by or as by the span of the hand.

span[2] (span), *n.* a pair of animals harnessed and driven together.

Span., Spanish.

span·gle (spang′gəl), *n., v.,* **-gled, -gling.** —*n.* **1.** a small piece of glittering metal used esp. for decorating garments. —*v.t.* **2.** to decorate with spangles. —**span′gly,** *adj.*

Span·iard (span′yərd), *n.* a native or inhabitant of Spain.

span·iel (span′yəl), *n.* a dog having a long, silky coat and drooping ears.

Span·ish (span′ish), *adj.* **1.** of Spain, its people, or their language. —*n.* **2.** the Spanish people. **3.** the Romance language of Spain and Spanish America.

Span′ish A·mer′ica, the Spanish-speaking countries south of the U.S.

Span·ish-A·mer·i·can (span′ish ə mer′i kən), *n.* **1.** a native or inhabitant of a country of Spanish America. **2.** a person of Spanish descent living in the U.S.

Span′ish fly′, 1. a preparation of powdered beetles formerly used as a diuretic and aphrodisiac. **2.** a green beetle, used in this preparation.

Span′ish moss′, a plant of the southern U.S., growing in long festoons that drape the branches of trees.

spank (spangk), *v.t.* **1.** to strike on the buttocks with the hand, as in punishment. —*n.* **2.** a blow given in spanking.

spank·ing (spang′king), *adj.* **1.** moving rapidly and smartly. **2.** blowing briskly. **3.** *Informal.* unusually fine or large. —*adv.* **4.** *Informal.* extremely or very.

span·ner (span′ər), *n. Brit.* a wrench with fixed jaws.

spar[1] (spär), *n.* a stout pole forming a ship's mast, yard, boom, gaff, etc.

spar[2] (spär), *v.i.,* **sparred, spar·ring. 1.** to engage in boxing, esp. with light blows. **2.** to dispute or argue, esp. cagily.

Spar (spär), *n.* a woman enlisted in the women's reserve of the U.S. Coast Guard: officially disbanded in 1974. Also, **SPAR** [*S(emper)* *par(atus)*, its Latin motto, meaning "always ready"]

spare (spâr), *v.,* **spared, spar·ing,** *adj.,* **spar·er, spar·est,** *n.* —*v.t.* **1.** to refrain from hurting or destroying. **2.** to save from discomfort, annoyance, etc. **3.** to dispense with or do without. **4.** to use economically or frugally. —*adj.* **5.** kept in reserve: *a spare tire.* **6.** free for other use: *spare time.* **7.** lean or thin, as a person. **8.** frugally restricted, as diet. —*n.* **9.** a spare thing, esp. a spare tire. **10.** *Bowling.* the knocking down of all the pins with two bowls. —**spare′ly,** *adv.* —**spare′ness,** *n.*

spare·ribs (spâr′ribz′), *n.pl.* a cut of pork containing ribs having only a small amount of meat.

spar·ing (spâr′ing), *adj.* not giving or spending freely. —**spar′ing·ly,** *adv.* —**Syn.** frugal, thrifty.

spark[1] (spärk), *n.* **1.** a small, glowing particle, esp. one thrown off by burning wood. **2.** a flash of light caused by an electric current passing through air. **3.** any kindling or animating factor. **4.** a small amount or trace. —*v.i.* **5.** to produce sparks. —*v.t.* **6.** *Informal.* to kindle or animate (interest, etc.).

spark² (spärk), n. 1. an elegant or foppish young man. —v.t., v.i. 2. to woo or court.

spar·kle (spär'kəl), v., -kled, -kling, n. —v.i. 1. to shine with little gleams of light. 2. to effervesce, as wine. 3. to be brilliant or lively. —n. 4. a little spark or flash. 5. a sparkling quality or appearance. 6. brilliance or liveliness. —spar'kler, n.

spark' plug', a device for making sparks to ignite the mixture of fuel and air in an engine.

spar·row (spar'ō), n. any small, brownish or grayish bird of the finch family.

sparse (spärs), adj., spars·er, spars·est. thinly scattered or distributed. —sparse·ly, adv. —sparse'ness, spar'si·ty (-si tē), n. —Syn. meager.

Spar·ta (spär'tə), n. an ancient city in S Greece: famous for strict discipline and military power.

Spar·tan (spär't²n), adj. 1. of Sparta or its people. 2. disciplined and austere. —n. 3. a native or inhabitant of Sparta. 4. a person of Spartan characteristics.

spasm (spaz'əm), n. 1. a sudden, abnormal, involuntary muscular contraction. 2. any sudden, brief spell of energy or activity.

spas·mod·ic (spaz mod'ik), adj. 1. of or characterized by spasms. 2. fitful or intermittent. —spas·mod'i·cal·ly, adv.

spas·tic (spas'tik), adj. 1. of or having muscular spasms. —n. 2. a person afflicted with such spasms. —spas'ti·cal·ly, adv.

spat¹ (spat), n., v., spat·ted, spat·ting. —n. 1. a petty quarrel. —v.i. 2. to engage in a spat.

spat² (spat), v. a pt. and pp. of spit¹.

spat³ (spat), n. a short gaiter formerly worn over the instep and around the ankle.

spat⁴ (spat), n. the spawn of an oyster or similar shellfish.

spate (spāt), n. a sudden outpouring, as of words.

spathe (spāth), n. a bract or pair of bracts enclosing a spadix or flower cluster.

spa·tial (spā'shəl), adj. of or existing in space. —spa'tial·ly, adv.

spat·ter (spat'ər), v.t., v.i. 1. to scatter in small particles or drops. 2. to splash, esp. so as to soil. —n. 3. the act or the sound or spattering. 4. a spot of something spattered. —spat'ter·ing·ly, adv.

spat·u·la (spach'ə lə), n. an implement with a broad, flat, flexible blade, used for blending foods, mixing drugs, or spreading plasters, etc. —spat'u·lar, adj.

spav·in (spav'in), n. a disease affecting the hock of a horse, causing lameness. —spav'ined, adj.

spawn (spôn), n. 1. the mass of eggs produced by a fish, amphibian, etc. 2. Usually Disparaging. offspring, esp. when numerous. —v.i., v.t. 3. to produce (spawn). 4. to produce (offspring) in large number. 5. to bring forth, esp. something undesirable. —spawn'er, n.

spay (spā), v.t. to remove the ovaries of (an animal).

S.P.C.A., Society for the Prevention of Cruelty to Animals.

S.P.C.C., Society for the Prevention of Cruelty to Children.

speak (spēk), v., spoke or (Archaic) spake, spo·ken, speak·ing. —v.i. 1. to utter words. 2. to communicate orally. 3. to deliver a public talk or address. —v.t. 4. to utter vocally. 5. to express or make known, esp. with the voice. 6. to use or be able to use in speech, as a foreign language. 7. speak out or up, to speak openly and without fear. —speak'a·ble, adj.

speak·eas·y (spēk'ē'zē), n., pl. -eas·ies. Slang. a saloon illegally selling liquor, esp. during U.S. prohibition.

speak·er (spē'kər), n. 1. a person who speaks. 2. (usually cap.) the presiding officer of a legislative assembly. 3. loudspeaker.

speak'ing in tongues', incomprehensible speech, as in some ecstatic form of prayer.

spear¹ (spēr), n. 1. an early weapon consisting of a sharp metal head on a long wooden shaft, used for thrusting or throwing. 2. a similar instrument used for spearing fish. —v.t. 3. to pierce with or as with a spear. —spear'er, n.

spear² (spēr), n. a sprout or shoot, as of grass.

spear·head (spēr'hed'), n. 1. the sharp-pointed head of a spear. 2. any person or thing that leads an attack, undertaking, etc. —v.t. 3. to act as a spearhead for.

spear·mint (spēr'mint'), n. an aromatic herb used for flavoring.

spec., 1. special. 2. specifically. 3. specification.

spe·cial (spesh'əl), adj. 1. of a distinct or particular kind. 2. different from what is ordinary or usual. 3. peculiar to a particular person, thing, or instance. 4. having a particular function or purpose. 5. great or dear: a special friend. —n. 6. a special person or thing. —spe'cial·ly, adv. —Syn. 2. exceptional, singular.

spe'cial deliv'ery, prompt unscheduled delivery of mail upon payment of an extra fee.

spe·cial·ist (spesh′ə list), *n.* **1.** a person who devotes himself or herself to one particular branch of a subject or pursuit. **2.** *U.S. Army.* any of four enlisted grades having technical or administrative duties, corresponding to the grades of corporal through sergeant first class.

spe·cial·ize (spesh′ə līz′), *v.i.,* **-ized, -iz·ing.** to pursue some special line of study or work. **—spe′cial·i·za′tion,** *n.*

spe·cial·ty (spesh′əl tē), *n., pl.* **-ties. 1.** a special subject of study or line of work. **2.** a product or service specially dealt in or featured. **3.** the state or condition of being special.

spe·cie (spē′shē, -sē), *n.* coined money as distinguished from paper money.

spe·cies (spē′shēz, -sēz), *n., pl.* **-cies. 1.** a group of related plants or animals that can interbreed to produce offspring. **2.** a distinct sort or kind. **specif., 1.** specific. **2.** specifically.

spe·cif·ic (spi sif′ik), *adj.* **1.** distinctly or precisely stated. **2.** peculiar to something or someone. **3.** *Biol.* of or pertaining to a species. **4.** having special curative effect, as a remedy. **—n. 5.** something specific, as a statement or quality. **6.** a specific remedy. **—spe·cif′i·cal·ly,** *adv.* **—spec-i·fic·i·ty** (spes′ə fis′i tē), *n.* **—Syn. 1.** definite, explicit.

spec·i·fi·ca·tion (spes′ə fə kā′shən), *n.* **1.** Usually, **specifications.** a detailed description of measurements, materials, etc., as of a proposed building. **2.** something specified.

specif′ic grav′ity, the ratio of the density of any substance to the density of some other substance taken as standard, water being the standard for liquids and solids.

spec·i·fy (spes′ə fī), *v.t.,* **-fied, -fy·ing. 1.** to state in detail. **2.** to set forth as a specification.

spec·i·men (spes′ə mən), *n.* **1.** a part or individual taken as typifying a whole or group. **2.** a sample, as of urine, for laboratory testing.

spe·cious (spē′shəs), *adj.* apparently good or right but lacking real merit. **—spe′cious·ly,** *adv.* **—spe′cious·ness,** *n.* **—Syn.** false, misleading.

speck (spek), *n.* **1.** a small spot or stain. **2.** a very little bit. **—v.t. 3.** to mark with specks.

speck·le (spek′əl), *n., v.,* **-led, -ling. —n. 1.** a small speck. **—v.t. 2.** to mark with speckles.

specs (speks), *n.pl. Informal.* **1.** specifications. **2.** *Now Chiefly Brit.* spectacles (optical).

spec·ta·cle (spek′tə kəl), *n.* **1.** an impressive sight or view. **2.** a public show or display. **3.** **spectacles,** *Now Chiefly Brit.* eyeglasses.

spec·tac·u·lar (spek tak′yə lər), *adj.* **1.**

impressively showy or striking. **2.** dramatically thrilling or daring. **—n. 3.** a large-scale, elaborate production, as of a film. **—spec·tac′u·lar·ly,** *adv.*

spec·ta·tor (spek′tā tər, spek tā′-), *n.* a person who watches without participating.

spec·ter (spek′tər), *n.* a ghost of a terrifying nature. Also, *Brit.,* **spec′tre.**

spec·tral (spek′trəl), *adj.* **1.** of or resembling a specter. **2.** of or produced by a spectrum.

spec·tro·gram (spek′trə gram′), *n.* a photograph of a spectrum.

spec·tro·graph (spek′trə graf′, -gräf′), *n.* an instrument for photographing a spectrum. **—spec′tro·graph′ic** (-ik), *adj.* **—spec′tro·graph′i·cal·ly,** *adv.*

spec·trom·e·ter (spek trom′i tər), *n.* an optical device for measuring deviation of refracted rays. **—spec′tro·met′ric** (-trə me′trik), *adj.*

spec·tro·scope (spek′trə skōp′), *n.* an optical device for observing the spectrum of light from any source. **—spec′tro·scop′ic** (-skop′ik), **spec′tro·scop′i·cal,** *adj.* **—spec′tro·scop′i·cal·ly,** *adv.* **—spec·tros′co·pist** (-tros′kə pist), *n.* **—spec·tros′co·py** (-pē), *n.*

spec·trum (spek′trəm), *n., pl.* **-tra** (-trə), **-trums. 1.** the band of colors produced when sunlight is passed through a prism, comprising red, orange, yellow, green, blue, indigo, and violet. **2.** a continuous series or sequence.

spec·u·late (spek′yə lāt′), *v.i.,* **-lat·ed, -lat·ing. 1.** to engage in reflective thought, esp. to conjecture. **2.** to engage in any business transaction involving considerable risk for the chance of large gains. **—spec′u·la′tion,** *n.* **—spec′u·la′tive,** *adj.* **—spec′u·la′tive·ly,** *adv.* **—spec′u·la′tor,** *n.* **—Syn. 1.** cogitate, guess, theorize.

speech (spēch), *n.* **1.** the power of speaking. **2.** something spoken. **3.** a public talk or address. **4.** a particular language or dialect. **5.** act or manner of speaking.

speech·less (spēch′lis), *adj.* **1.** temporarily unable to speak, esp. because of strong emotion. **2.** lacking the faculty of speech. **—speech′less·ly,** *adv.*

speed (spēd), *n., v.,* **sped** (sped) or **speed·ed, speed·ing. —n. 1.** rapidity in moving, going, or performing. **2.** rate of motion or progress. **3.** a transmission gear of a motor vehicle. **4.** *Slang.* a stimulating drug, as amphetamine. **—v.i. 5.** to move, go, or perform with speed. **6.** to drive by exceeding the legal speed limit. **—v.t. 7.** to cause to speed. **8.** to increase the rate of speed of: *to speed up one's reading.* **9.** to promote the progress of. **—speed′er,** *n.* **—speed′ing,** *adj.,* *n.* **—speed′y,** *adj.* **—speed′i·ly,** *adv.* **—Syn. 1.** alacrity, celerity, dispatch, haste.

speed·boat (spēd′bōt′), *n.* a motorboat designed for high speeds.

speed·om·e·ter (spē dom′ə tər, spi-), *n.* an instrument on a vehicle for indicating speed and recording the distance traveled.

speed·way (spēd′wā′), *n.* **1.** a road for fast driving. **2.** a track on which automobile or motorcycle races are held.

speed·well (spēd′wel′), *n.* a small tree having spikes of showy blue flowers.

spe·le·ol·o·gy (spē′lē ol′ə jē), *n.* the exploration and study of caves. **—spe′le·ol′o·gist,** *n.*

spell¹ (spel), *v.,* **spelled** or **spelt** (spelt), **spell·ing.** **—v.t. 1.** to name or write the letters of (a word) in order. **2.** (of letters) to form or be (a word, etc.). **3.** to signify or mean. **—v.i. 4.** to spell words. **5. spell out, a.** *Informal.* to explain explicitly. **b.** to write out in full, unabbreviated form.

spell² (spel), *n.* **1.** a word or phrase supposed to have magic power. **2.** any irresistible influence.

spell³ (spel), *n.* **1.** an indefinite space of time. **2.** a period of weather of a specified kind. **3.** a period or bout of an illness. **4.** a period of work. **—v.t. 5.** to take the place of for a time.

spell·bind (spel′bīnd′), *v.t.,* **-bound, -bind·ing.** to make spellbound.

spell·bind·er (spel′bīn′dər), *n.* a speaker who holds his or her audience spellbound.

spell·bound (spel′bound′), *adj.* enchanted or fascinated by or as by a spell.

spell·down (spel′doun′), *n.* a spelling competition in which a contestant who misspells a word is eliminated and sits down.

spell·er (spel′ər), *n.* **1.** a person who spells words. **2.** a textbook to teach spelling.

spell·ing (spel′ing), *n.* **1.** the manner in which words are spelled. **2.** a group of letters representing a word. **3.** the act of a speller.

spe·lun·ker (spi lung′kər), *n.* a person who explores caves. **—spe·lun′king,** *n.*

spend (spend), *v.,* **spent, spend·ing. —v.t. 1.** to pay out (money, etc.). **2.** to employ (labor, time, etc.) on some object. **3.** to pass (time), as in a particular place. **4.** to use up or consume. **—v.i. 5.** to spend money, time, etc. **—spend′er,** *n.* **—Syn. 1.** disburse, expand. **4.** exhaust.

spend·thrift (spend′thrift′), *n.* **1.** a person who spends his or her money extravagantly or wastefully. **—adj. 2.** extravagant or wasteful.

spent (spent), *v.* **1.** pt. and pp. of **spend.** **—adj. 2.** used up or consumed. **3.** tired or worn-out.

sperm (spûrm), *n.* **1.** spermatozoon. **2.** semen. **—sper·mat·ic** (spûr mat′ik), *adj.*

sper·ma·to·zo·on (spûr′mə tə zō′ən, -on, spûr mat′ə-), *n., pl.* **-zo·a** (-zō′ə). a mature male reproductive cell.

sperm′ whale′, a large, square-snouted whale valued for its oil.

spew (spyōō), *v.i.,* *v.t.* **1.** to cast forth or eject. **2.** *Literary.* to vomit. **—n. 3.** something spewed.

sp. gr., See specific gravity.

sphag·num (sfag′nəm), *n.* a soft moss found chiefly on the surface of bogs, used in potting and packing plants.

sphere (sfēr), *n.* **1.** a round object whose surface is at all points equidistant from the center. **2.** any rounded object. **3.** a place or range within which a person or thing exists or operates. **4.** a celestial body, as a planet. [< L *sphaera* globe < Gk *sphaîra* ball] **—spher·i·cal** (sfer′i-kəl), *adj.* **—spher′i·cal·ly,** *adv.* **—sphe·ric·i·ty** (sfi ris′i tē), *n.*

sphe·roid (sfēr′oid), *n.* a solid object like a sphere but not completely round. **—sphe·roi·dal** (sfi roid′ᵊl), *adj.*

sphinc·ter (sfingk′tər), *n.* a circular band of muscle that encircles an orifice of the body.

sphinx (sfingks), *n., pl.* **sphinx·es, sphin·ges** (sfin′jēz). **1.** an ancient Egyptian figure having a human or animal head on the body of a lion. **2.** *(cap.) Class. Myth.* a winged monster, part woman, part lion, that asked difficult riddles and killed those who did not answer correctly. **3.** a mysterious, inscrutable person or thing.

sphyg·mo·ma·nom·e·ter (sfig′mō mə nom′i tər), *n.* a medical instrument for measuring blood pressure.

spice (spīs), *n., v.,* **spiced, spic·ing. —n. 1.** a pungent or aromatic substance of vegetable origin, as pepper or cinnamon, used as seasoning or flavoring **2.** something that gives interest or zest. **—v.t. 3.** to season or flavor with spice. **4.** to give interest or zest. **—spic′y,** *adj.* **—spic′i·ly,** *adv.* **—spic′i·ness,** *n.*

spick-and-span (spik′ən span′), *adj.* **1.** spotlessly clean. **2.** perfectly new.

spic·ule (spik′yōōl), *n.* a small, needlelike part, esp. of a marine sponge. **—spic′u·late′** (-yə lāt′, -lit), **spic′u·lar** (-yə lər), *adj.*

spi·der (spī'dər), *n.* **1.** any of numerous arachnids that spin webs that serve as nests and as traps for prey. **2.** *Obsolesc.* a heavy frying pan. —**spi'der·y,** *adj.*

spiel (spēl, shpēl), *n. Informal.* a colorful talk, esp. one used to persuade.

spiff·y (spif'ē), *adj.,* **spiff·i·er, spiff·i·est.** *Slang.* smart or trim in dress. —**spiff'i·ly,** *adv.*

spig·ot (spig'ət), *n.* **1.** a vent peg or plug of a cask. **2.** *Dial.* a faucet.

spike¹ (spīk), *n., v.,* **spiked, spik·ing.** —*n.* **1.** a very large nail. **2.** a naillike metal projection, as on the sole of a shoe, for improving traction. —*v.t.* **3.** to fasten or provide with spikes. **4.** to pierce with or impale on a spike. **5.** to make ineffective, as a rumor. **6.** *Informal.* to add alcoholic liquor to (a drink). —**spik'y,** *adj.*

spike² (spīk), *n.* **1.** an ear of grain. **2.** a pointed cluster of flowers.

spill (spil), *v.,* **spilled** or **spilt** (spilt), **spill·ing,** *n.* —*v.t.* **1.** to allow to run or fall from a container, esp. unintentionally. **2.** to shed (blood), as in wounding. **3.** *Informal.* to cause to fall, as from a horse. —*v.i.* **4.** to be spilled. —*n.* **5.** a spilling, as of liquid. **6.** a quantity spilled. **7.** *Informal.* a fall, as from a horse. —**spill'a·ble,** *adj.* —**spill'age,** *n.*

spill·way (spil'wā'), *n.* a passageway through which surplus water escapes, as from a reservoir.

spin (spin), *v.,* **spun, spin·ning,** *n.* —*v.t.* **1.** to make (yarn) by drawing out and twisting fibers. **2.** to form (fibers) into yarn. **3.** to produce (a web), as a spider. **4.** to cause to turn around rapidly, as on an axis. **5.** to narrate, esp. lengthily: *to spin a tale.* —*v.i.* **6.** to spin yarn or thread. **7.** to revolve or rotate rapidly. **8.** to produce a web, as a spider. **9.** to move or travel rapidly. **10.** to have a sensation of whirling. —*n.* **11.** a spinning motion. **12.** a short ride for pleasure. **13.** tailspin. —**spin'ner,** *n.* —**spin'ning,** *n., adj.*

spin·ach (spin'ich), *n.* **1.** an herb having large, green edible leaves. **2.** its leaves.

spi·nal (spīn'ᵊl), *adj.* of or pertaining to the spine or spinal cord. —**spi'nal·ly,** *adv.*

spi'nal col'umn, the series of vertebrae in a vertebrate animal forming the axis of the skeleton.

spi'nal cord', the cord of nerve tissue extending through the center of the spinal column.

spin·dle (spin'dᵊl), *n.* **1.** a rounded, slender rod on which thread is

wound in spinning. **2.** a rodlike part of a machine, esp. one that rotates. **3.** a slender, turned piece of wood, used esp. in furniture.

spin·dly (spind'lē), *adj.,* **-dli·er, -dli·est.** long or tall, thin, and usually frail. Also, **spin'dling.**

spine (spīn), *n.* **1.** See **spinal column. 2.** a stiff, pointed process on an animal or plant. **3.** the back edge of a book. —**spin'y,** *adj.*

spine·less (spīn'lis), *adj.* **1.** having no spine or spines. **2.** without strength of character. —**spine'less·ness,** *n.*

spin·et (spin'it), *n.* a small upright piano.

spin·na·ker (spin'ə kər), *n. Naut.* a large, triangular sail set forward of the mast.

spin'ning jen'ny, an early spinning machine having more than one spindle.

spin'ning wheel', a device used for spinning yarn or thread by hand, consisting of a single spindle driven by a large wheel.

spin·off (spin'ôf', -of'), *n.* **1.** a desirable product or effect derived secondarily, as one accruing from technological development. **2.** *Television.* a series developed or extended from characterization in a motion picture or another series that has been popular.

spin·ster (spin'stər), *n.* a woman beyond the usual age for marrying and still unmarried. —**spin'ster·hood',** *n.*

spin'y lob'ster, an edible crustacean differing from the true lobster in having a spiny shell and lacking the large pincers.

spi·ra·cle (spī'rə kəl, spir'ə-), *n.* a minute hole for breathing, as on the abdomen of an insect.

spi·ral (spī'rəl), *n., adj., v.,* **-raled, -ral·ing** or **-ralled, -ral·ling.** —*n.* **1.** the curve generated by a point moving around and away from a central point. **2.** a single circle of a spiral object. **3.** a continuous, accelerating increase or decrease, as in prices. —*adj.* **4.** formed like or running in a spiral. **5.** coiling around a fixed line in a constantly changing series of planes: *a spiral staircase.* —*v.i., v.t.* **6.** to take or cause to take a spiral form. —**spi'ral·ly,** *adv.*

spire (spīᵊr), *n.* **1.** a tall, acutely pointed top of a tower. **2.** any tapering, pointed part of something. **3.** a sprout or shoot of a plant. —**spir'y,** *adj.*

spi·re·a (spī rē'ə), *n.* a shrub of the rose family having small white or pink flowers. Also, **spi·rae'a.**

spir·it (spir′it), *n.* **1.** the incorporeal part of human beings in general or of an individual, as the soul. **2.** a supernatural, incorporeal being, as a ghost. **3.** (*cap.*) the divine influence working in the human heart. **4.** (*cap.*) See **Holy Spirit. 5. spirits,** feelings or mood: *good spirits.* **6.** vigor and courage. **7.** an individual as characterized by disposition: *a few brave spirits.* **8.** a dominant tendency or feeling. **9.** vigorous sense of membership: *college spirit.* **10.** the true meaning or intent: *the spirit of the law.* **11.** Usually, **spirits.** Chiefly *Brit.* hard liquor. —*v.t.* **12.** to carry off mysteriously or secretly. —**spir′it·less,** *adj.* —**spir′it·less·ly,** *adv.*

spir·it·ed (spir′i tid), *adj.* vigorous and courageous. —**spir′it·ed·ly,** *adv.* —**Syn.** animated, vivacious.

spir·it·u·al (spir′i chŏŏ əl), *adj.* **1.** of spirit or the soul. **2.** of sacred things or matters. **3.** of or belonging to the church. —*n.* **4.** a religious song that originated among blacks of the southern U.S. —**spir′it·u·al′i·ty** (-al′i tē), *n.* —**spir′it·u·al·ize′,** *v.t.* —**spir′it·u·al·ly,** *adv.*

spir·it·u·al·ism (spir′i chŏŏ ə liz′əm), *n.* the belief that the spirits of the dead communicate with the living, esp. through mediums. —**spir′it·u·al·ist,** *n.* —**spir′it·u·al·is′tic,** *adj.*

spir·it·u·ous (spir′i chŏŏ əs), *adj.* containing alcohol.

spi·ro·chete (spi′rə kēt′), *n.* any of several spiral-shaped bacteria, a certain species of which causes syphilis. Also, **spi′ro·chaete′.** —**spi′ro·chet′al,** *adj.*

spit[1] (spit), *v.,* **spit** or **spat, spit·ting,** *n.* —*v.i.* **1.** to eject saliva or phlegm from the mouth. —*v.t.* **2.** to eject from the mouth. **3.** to throw out or emit like saliva. —*n.* **4.** saliva, esp. when ejected. **5.** the act of spitting. **6. spit and image,** *Informal.* exact likeness. —**spit′ter,** *n.*

spit[2] (spit), *n., v.,* **spit·ted, spit·ting.** —*n.* **1.** a pointed rod for piercing and holding meat over a fire. **2.** a narrow point of land extending from the shore. —*v.t.* **3.** to pierce with a spit.

spit·ball (spit′bôl′), *n.* **1.** a small ball of chewed paper used as a hand-thrown missile. **2.** *Baseball.* an illegal pitch made to curve by moistening one side of the ball with saliva.

spite (spīt), *n., v.,* **spit·ed, spit·ing.** —*n.* **1.** a malicious desire to harm or humiliate another person. **2. in spite of,** in disregard or defiance of. —*v.t.* **3.** to treat with spite. —**spite′ful,** *adj.* —**spite′ful·ly,** *adv.* —**spite′ful·ness,** *n.* —**Syn. 1.** malevolence, rancor, resentment, spleen.

spit·tle (spit′əl), *n.* spit[1] (def. 4).

spit·toon (spi tŏŏn′), *n.* cuspidor.

splash (splash), *v.t.* **1.** to wet or soil by dashing water or mud upon. **2.** to dash (water, etc.) about in scattered masses. —*v.i.* **3.** to fall, move, or strike with a splash. —*n.* **4.** the act or sound of splashing. **5.** a stain made by splashing. **6.** a striking show or impression. —**splash′er,** *n.* —**splash′y,** *adj.* —**splash′i·ly,** *adv.* —**splash′i·ness,** *n.*

splash·down (splash′doun′), *n.* the landing of a space vehicle in the ocean.

splat[1] (splat), *n.* a broad, flat piece of wood, as in a chair back.

splat[2] (splat), *n.* a sound made by splattering.

splat·ter (splat′ər), *v.t., v.i., n.* spatter.

splay (splā), *v.t., v.i.* **1.** to spread out, esp. awkwardly. —*adj.* **2.** spread or turned outward. **3.** awkward or clumsy.

splay·foot (splā′fŏŏt′), *n.* a broad, flat foot, esp. one turned outward. —**splay′foot′ed,** *adj.*

spleen (splēn), *n.* **1.** an organ near the stomach that produces lymph cells and destroys worn-out red blood cells. **2.** bad temper or spite.

splen·did (splen′did), *adj.* **1.** brilliantly magnificent. **2.** distinguished or glorious. **3.** strikingly admirable or fine. **4.** *Informal.* very good or excellent. —**splen′did·ly,** *adv.* —**Syn. 1.** gorgeous, resplendent, sumptuous.

splen·dor (splen′dər), *n.* **1.** magnificence or grandeur. **2.** great brightness. Also, *Brit.,* **splen′dour.** —**splen′dor·ous,** *adj.*

sple·net·ic (spli net′ik), *adj.* **1.** splenic. **2.** irritable or spiteful.

splen·ic (splen′ik, splē′nik), *adj.* of or affecting the spleen.

splice (splīs), *v.,* **spliced, splic·ing,** *n.* —*v.t.* **1.** to join (two ropes) by weaving the strands together. **2.** to unite (timbers) by overlapping and binding their ends. **3.** to unite (film, tape, etc.) end to end, as by cementing. —*n.* **4.** a joint made by splicing. —**splic′er,** *n.*

splint (splint), *n.* **1.** a thin piece of wood or other rigid material for holding a broken bone in position. **2.** one of a number of thin strips of wood woven together to make a basket, etc.

splin·ter (splin′tər), *n.* **1.** a small, thin, sharp piece, as of wood, split or broken off from the main part. —*v.t., v.i.* **2.** to split or be broken into splinters. —**splin′ter·y,** *adj.*

split (split), v., **split, split·ting,** n., adj.
—v.t., v.i. **1.** to divide from end to
end or into layers. **2.** to tear or
break apart. **3.** to divide into distinct parts or portions. **4.** to divide
into different groups or factions, as
by discord. —n. **5.** the act of splitting. **6.** a crack caused by splitting.
7. a break in unity, as within a
group. —adj. **8.** disunited or divided.

split-lev·el (split′lev′əl), adj. **1.** noting a house having a room or rooms
that are a partial story above or below adjacent rooms. —n. **2.** a split-
level house.

split′ person′ality, a dissociated personality having distinct, autonomous
behavior patterns each of a complexity comparable to that of a normal individual.

split·ting (split′ing), adj. acutely severe, as a headache.

splotch (sploch), n. **1.** a large, irregular spot. —v.t., v.i. **2.** to mark or be
marked with splotches. —**splotch′y,**
adj.

splurge (splûrj), v., **splurged, splurg-
ing,** n. —v.i. **1.** to spend money lavishly. **2.** to show off. —n. **3.** an ostentatious display or expenditure.

splut·ter (splut′ər), v.i., v.t. **1.** to talk
or utter hastily and confusedly. **2.**
sputter (defs. 1, 2). —n. **3.** the act
or sound of spluttering.

spoil (spoil), v., **spoiled** or **spoilt**
(spoilt), **spoil·ing,** n. —v.t. **1.** to
damage or harm the quality, value,
or usefulness of. **2.** to impair the
character of (someone) by excessively indulgent treatment. **3.** Archaic. to plunder or pillage. —v.i.
4. to become spoiled or rotten, as
food. **5. be spoiling for,** Informal.
to be very eager for. —n. **6.** Usually,
spoils. booty or plunder. —**spoil′-
age,** n. —**spoil′er,** n.

spoil·sport (spoil′spôrt′, -spōrt′), n. a
person whose conduct spoils the
pleasure of others.

spoils′ sys′tem, the practice by which
public offices and other political favors are at the disposal of the victorious party.

Spo·kane (spō kan′), n. a city in E
Washington.

spoke[1] (spōk), v. a pt. of **speak.**

spoke[2] (spōk), n. **1.** one of the rods
connecting the rim of a wheel to the
hub. **2.** a rung of a ladder.

spo·ken (spō′kən), v. **1.** pp. of **speak.**
—adj. **2.** expressed by speaking. **3.**
speaking in a specified way: soft-
spoken.

spokes·man (spōks′mən), n. a person
who speaks for another or for a
group. —**spokes′wom′an,** n.fem.

spo·li·a·tion (spō′lē ā′shən), n. the
act of plundering or despoiling. —
spo′li·a′tor, n.

sponge (spunj), n., v., **sponged, sponging.** —n. **1.** a marine animal having
a porous structure. **2.** the light, absorbent, fibrous skeleton of such an
animal, used in cleaning surfaces,
etc. **3.** any of various manmade materials resembling this. —v.t. **4.** to
wipe, rub, absorb, or clean with a
sponge. **5.** Informal. to obtain by
imposing on another's good nature.
—v.i. **6.** Informal. to live at the expense of others. —**spong′er,** n. —
spon′gy, adj.

sponge′ cake′, a light, sweet cake
made with eggs but no shortening.

spon·sor (spon′sər), n. **1.** a person
who vouches for or is responsible for
a person or thing. **2.** a business firm
that buys the time to broadcast a
radio or television program so as
to advertise its product or service.
3. a godfather or godmother. —v.t.
4. to act as sponsor for. —**spon′sor-
ship′,** n.

spon·ta·ne·ous (spon tā′nē əs), adj.
1. acting or resulting from a natural
impulse. **2.** arising from internal
forces or causes. —**spon′ta·ne′i·ty**
(-tə nē′i tē, -nā′-), n. —**spon·ta′ne-
ous·ly,** adv. —**spon·ta′ne·ous·ness,** n.
—**Syn. 1.** impulsive, unpremeditated.

sponta′neous combus′tion, the ignition
of a substance from the rapid oxidation of its own constituents, without
heat from any external source.

spoof (spoof), n. **1.** a light, good-
humored parody. **2.** a hoax or prank.
—v.t., v.i. **3.** to mock lightly and
good-humoredly. **4.** to fool by a
hoax.

spook (spook), n. **1.** Informal. a ghost
or specter. **2.** Slang. a spy. —v.t.,
v.i. **3.** Informal. to frighten or become frightened.

spool (spool), n. any cylindrical device on which thread or wire is
wound.

spoon (spoon), n. **1.** a utensil consisting of a small, shallow bowl with a
handle, used in eating or stirring.
2. a fishing lure consisting of a piece
of metal shaped like this. —v.t. **3.**
to eat with or take up in a spoon.
—**spoon′ful,** n.

spoon·bill (spoon′bil′), n. a wading
bird having a flat bill with a spoon-
like tip.

spoon·er·ism (spoo′nə riz′əm), n. the
accidental transposition of initial
sounds of words, as in a blushing
crow for a crushing blow. [after
W. A. Spooner (1844–1930), Englishman noted for such slips]

spoon-fed (spoon′fed′), adj. **1.** fed
with a spoon. **2.** given no opportunity to act or think for oneself.

spoor (spŏŏr, spōr, spôr), *n.* the track or trail of a wild animal.

spo·rad·ic (spō rad′ik, spô-, spə-), *adj.* 1. appearing or happening at irregular intervals. 2. appearing in scattered or isolated instances. —**spo·rad′i·cal·ly,** *adv.*

spore (spōr, spôr), *n.* a usually single-celled reproductive body of an organism, esp. of a fern or mushroom.

spork (spôrk), *n.* an eating utensil having the features of a spoon and fork. [*sp*(*oon*) + (*f*)*ork*]

sport (spōrt, spôrt), *n.* 1. an athletic activity requiring skill or physical prowess and often of a competitive nature. 2. jest or fun: *to say something in sport.* 3. mockery or ridicule: *to make sport of someone.* 4. an object of mockery. 5. *Informal.* a sportsmanlike or accommodating person. 6. *Informal.* a person interested in sports as an occasion for gambling. 7. an animal or plant that shows an unusual deviation from the normal type. —*adj.* Also, **sports.** 8. of or for a sport or sports. 9. suitable for informal wear: *sport clothes.* —*v.i.* 10. to play or frolic. 11. to trifle or treat lightly. —*v.t.* 12. *Informal.* to wear or display, esp. with ostentation. —**sport′ing,** *adj.*

spor·tive (spōr′tiv, spôr′-), *adj.* 1. fond of sport or play. 2. done in sport or fun. —**spor′tive·ly,** *adv.*

sports·cast (spōrts′kast′, -käst′, spôrts′-), *n.* a newscast concerning sports. —**sports′cast′er,** *n.*

sports·man (spōrts′mən, spôrts′-), *n., pl.* -**men.** 1. a man who engages in sports, esp. in some open-air sport. 2. a person who plays fair and is a good loser. —**sports′man·like′,** *adj.* —**sports′man·ship′,** *n.* —**sports′wom′an,** *n.fem.*

sport·y (spōr′tē, spôr′-), *adj.,* **sport·i·er, sport·i·est.** 1. like or befitting a sportsman or sportswoman. 2. flashy or showy, as in dress.

spot (spot), *n., v.,* **spot·ted, spot·ting,** *adj.* —*n.* 1. a rounded mark made by some foreign matter. 2. a stain or blemish, as on a person's character. 3. a small part of a surface differing from the rest in color or texture. 4. a place or locality. 5. *Informal.* a brief broadcast commercial. 6. **hit the spot,** *Slang.* to satisfy a want or need. 7. **in a (bad) spot,** *Slang.* in an uncomfortable or dangerous situation. 8. **on the spot,** *Slang.* in a difficult or embarrassing position. —*v.t.* 9. to stain with spots. 10. to sully or blemish. 11. *Informal.* to identify by seeing. 12. to position in a particular place. —*v.i.* 13. to make a spot or stain. —*adj.* 14. requiring immediate payment and de-

livery: *a spot sale.* —**spot′less,** *adj.* —**spot′less·ly,** *adv.* —**spot′ted,** *adj.*

spot′ check′, a random or quick sample investigation. —**spot′-check′,** *v.t., v.i.*

spot·light (spot′līt′), *n.* 1. a strong, focused light thrown upon a particular person or object, as on a stage. 2. a lamp for producing such a light. 3. conspicuous public attention.

spot·ter (spot′ər), *n.* a person who observes or watches, as for enemy airplanes.

spot·ty (spot′ē), *adj.,* -**ti·er, -ti·est.** 1. full of or having spots. 2. irregular or uneven in quality. —**spot′ti·ly,** *adv.* —**spot′ti·ness,** *n.*

spous·al (spou′zəl), *n.* Often, **spousals.** *Archaic.* a wedding ceremony.

spouse (spous, spouz), *n.* one's husband or wife.

spout (spout), *v.t., v.i.* 1. to discharge (liquid) forcibly in a jet or stream. 2. to speak or state (something) lengthily in a pompous manner. —*n.* 3. a pipe or tube through which liquid spouts. 4. a jet or stream of liquid.

spp., species (pl. of **specie**).

sprain (sprān), *v.t.* 1. to wrench the muscles or ligaments around (a joint) without dislocation. —*n.* 2. an act of spraining or condition of being sprained.

sprang (sprang), *v.* a pt. of **spring.**

sprat (sprat), *n.* a small, herringlike marine fish of Europe.

sprawl (sprôl), *v.i.* 1. to sit or lie with the limbs spread out carelessly or awkwardly. 2. to spread out in an irregular, straggling manner, as buildings or handwriting. —*n.* 3. a sprawling movement or posture. —**sprawl′er,** *n.*

spray¹ (sprā), *n.* 1. liquid blown or falling through the air in fine particles. 2. a jet of liquid in fine particles, as from an atomizer. 3. a device for discharging such a liquid. —*v.t., v.i.* 4. to discharge a spray (on). 5. to sprinkle with a spray. —**spray′er,** *n.*

spray² (sprā), *n.* a single, slender shoot or twig with its leaves, flowers, or berries.

spray′ gun′, a device for spraying liquid, as insecticide.

spread (spred), *v.,* **spread, spread·ing,** *n.* —*v.t., v.i.* 1. to stretch or open out. 2. to extend or lie stretched out. 3. to distribute or extend over an area of space or time. 4. to make or become known. 5. to apply a thin layer of (something) as a cover or coating. 6. to move or force apart. 7. to prepare (a table) for a meal. —*n.* 8. the act of spreading. 9. an expanse or extent. 10. a cloth covering for a bed or table. 11. *In-*

formal. an abundance of food set out on a table. **12.** any food for spreading on bread, crackers, etc. **13.** printed matter covering several columns, as in a magazine. —**spread′a·ble,** *adj.* —**spread′er,** *n.*

spree (sprē), *n.* **1.** a spell of drinking to intoxication. **2.** an outburst of activity: *a shopping spree.* **3.** a lively frolic.

sprig (sprig), *n.* a small spray.

spright·ly (sprīt′lē), *adj.,* **-li·er, -li·est,** *adv.* —*adj.* **1.** vivacious and gay. —*adv.* **2.** in a sprightly manner. —**spright′li·ness,** *n.* —**Syn. 1.** animated, lively, spirited.

spring (spring), *v.,* **sprang** or **sprung, sprung, spring·ing,** *n.* —*v.i.* **1.** to rise or leap suddenly and swiftly. **2.** to act swiftly upon release, as by elastic force. **3.** to appear suddenly. **4.** to come into being by growth, as a plant. **5.** to originate, as from a source or cause. **6.** to become bent or warped, as boards. —*v.t.* **7.** to cause to spring. **8.** to cause to act swiftly, as a mechanism. **9.** to cause to bend or warp. **10.** to develop: *to spring a leak.* **11.** to bring out or produce suddenly: *to spring a joke.* **12.** *Slang.* to free (someone), as from jail. —*n.* **13.** a leap or bound. **14.** an elastic or bouncing quality or movement. **15.** elasticity or resilience. **16.** an elastic device, as a strip of coiled wire, that recovers its shape after being compressed or bent. **17.** the season between winter and summer. **18.** a flow of water coming from the earth. **19.** a source or cause. —**spring′y,** *adj.* —**spring′i·ness,** *n.* —**Syn. 1.** emanate, issue.

spring·board (spring′bôrd′, -bōrd′), *n.* **1.** a flexible board used in diving or gymnastics. **2.** a starting point.

spring′ fe′ver, a lazy or restless feeling commonly associated with the beginning of spring.

Spring·field (spring′fēld′), *n.* **1.** a city in SW Massachusetts. **2.** the capital of Illinois.

spring·time (spring′tīm′), *n.* the season of spring.

sprin·kle (spring′kəl), *v.,* **-kled, kling,** *n.* —*v.t., v.i.* **1.** to scatter in drops or particles. **2.** to spread (over) with drops or particles of liquid or powder. **3.** to rain slightly. —*n.* **4.** the act of sprinkling. **5.** a light rain. —**sprink′ler,** *n.*

sprin·kling (spring′kling), *n.* a small scattered quantity or amount.

sprint (sprint), *v.i.* **1.** to run at full speed, esp. for a short distance. —*n.* **2.** a short race at full speed. —**sprint′er,** *n.*

sprite (sprīt), *n.* an impish fairy.

sprock·et (sprok′it), *n.* a toothed wheel engaging with a conveyor or power chain. Also called **sprock′et wheel′.**

sprout (sprout), *v.i.* **1.** to put forth buds or shoots, esp. quickly. —*v.t.* **2.** to cause to sprout. —*n.* **3.** a new growth, esp. a bud or shoot.

spruce¹ (sproos), *n.* **1.** an evergreen tree having short, needle-shaped leaves. **2.** its wood.

spruce² (sproos), *adj.,* **spruc·er, spruc·est,** *v.,* **spruced, spruc·ing.** —*adj.* **1.** trim in dress or appearance. —*v.t., v.i.* **2.** to make or become spruce.

sprung (sprung), *v.* a pt. and pp. of **spring.**

spry (sprī), *adj.,* **spry·er, spry·est** or **spri·er, spri·est.** active and brisk, esp. of elderly people. —**spry′ly,** *adv.* —**spry′ness,** *n.* —**Syn.** agile, energetic, nimble.

spud (spud), *n. Informal.* a potato.

spume (spyoom), *n.* foam, esp. tossed up by sea waves.

spu·mo·ne (spə mō′nē), *n.* an Italian ice cream containing layers of various colors and flavors. Also, **spumo′ni.**

spun (spun), *v.* pt. and pp. of **spin.**

spunk (spungk), *n. Informal.* dogged courage. —**spunk′y,** *adj.* —**spunk′i·ness,** *n.*

spur (spûr), *n., v.,* **spurred, spur·ring.** —*n.* **1.** a U-shaped pointed device attached to a rider's boot and used to urge a horse forward. **2.** anything that urges on to action. **3.** a stiff, sharp projection, as on the leg of a rooster. **4.** a ridge projecting from the main mountain range. **5.** a short branch track leading from the main railroad track. **6. on the spur of the moment,** on an impulse. —*v.t.* **7.** to prick with spurs. **8.** to incite or urge on. —*v.i.* **9.** to ride quickly or hurriedly. —**spurred,** *adj.*

spurge (spûrj), *n.* any of numerous plants having milky juice and small, inconspicuous flowers.

spu·ri·ous (spyoor′ē əs), *adj.* of doubtful genuineness. —**spu′ri·ous·ly,** *adv.* —**spu′ri·ous·ness,** *n.* —**Syn.** bogus, false, sham.

spurn (spûrn), *v.t.* to reject with disdain. —**Syn.** rebuff, scorn.

spurt (spûrt), *n.* **1.** a sudden, forceful gush or jet, as of liquid. **2.** a marked increase of effort or activity, esp. for a short period. —*v.i., v.t.* **3.** to make a spurt (in).

sput·nik (spoot′nik, sput′-), *n.* a man-made satellite launched by the Soviet Union. [< Russ: fellow traveler]

sput·ter (sput′ər), *v.i., v.t.* **1.** to make explosive, popping sounds. **2.** to spit out drops of saliva or bits of food, as when speaking excitedly. **3.** splutter (def. 1). —*n.* **4.** the act or sound of sputtering. —**sput′ter·er,** *n.*

spu·tum (spyōō′təm), *n.*, *pl.* **-ta** (-tə). expectorated matter, as saliva mixed with mucus.

spy (spī), *n.*, *pl.* **spies**, *v.*, **spied**, **spy·ing.** —*n.* 1. a person employed by a government to obtain secret information about another country. 2. a person who keeps secret watch on others. —*v.i.* 3. to act as a spy. —*v.t.* 4. to search for or find out by careful observation. 5. to catch sight of suddenly.

spy·glass (spī′glas′, -gläs′), *n.* a small telescope.

sq., 1. the following one. [< L *sequēns*] 2. squadron. 3. square.

sqq., the following ones. [< L *sequentia*]

squab (skwob), *n.*, *pl.* **squabs**, **squab.** a young pigeon.

squab·ble (skwob′əl), *n.*, *v.*, **-bled**, **-bling.** —*n.* 1. a petty quarrel. —*v.i.* 2. to engage in a squabble. —**Syn.** 1. bicker, wrangle.

squab·by (skwob′ē), *adj.*, **-bi·er**, **-bi·est.** short and stout.

squad (skwod), *n.* 1. *Mil.* the smallest unit of persons. 2. any small group organized for a particular purpose.

squad′ car′, a police automobile equipped with a radiotelephone in contact with headquarters.

squad·ron (skwod′rən), *n.* *Mil.* any of various units of persons, aircraft, and vessels.

squal·id (skwol′id, skwôl′-), *adj.* 1. filthy and repulsive. 2. wretched or degraded. —**squal′id·ly**, *adv.* — **squal′id·ness**, *n.* —**Syn.** foul, sordid.

squall¹ (skwôl), *n.* a sudden, violent gust of wind, often with rain or snow. —**squall′y**, *adj.*

squall² (skwôl), *v.i.* 1. to cry or scream loudly and violently. —*n.* 2. the act or sound of squalling.

squal·or (skwol′ər, skwô′lər), *n.* the state or condition of being squalid.

squan·der (skwon′dər), *v.t.* to spend extravagantly or wastefully.

square (skwâr), *n.*, *v.*, **squared**, **squar·ing**, *adj.*, **squar·er**, **squar·est**, *adv.* —*n.* 1. a rectangle having all four sides of equal length. 2. anything having this shape, as a city block. 3. an open area formed by the meeting of two or more streets. 4. an instrument used for drawing or testing right angles. 5. *Math.* the product obtained when a number is multiplied by itself. 6. *Slang.* a person who is behind the times or conventional. —*v.t.* 7. to make square in form. 8. to mark out in one or more squares or rectangles. 9. *Math.* to multiply (a number) by itself. 10. to adjust harmoniously. 11. to pay off or settle: *to square a debt.* —*v.i.* 12. to accord or agree. 13. **square off,** to assume a posture

for fighting, as in boxing. 14. **square oneself,** *Informal.* to make up for something done. —*adj.* 15. formed with or as a right angle. 16. formed as a square. 17. noting any unit of area measurement having the form of a square and designated by a unit of linear measurement forming a side of the square: *one square foot.* 18. having a solid, sturdy form. 19. straight, level, or even, as a surface. 20. having all accounts settled. 21. fair or equal. 22. candid or honest. 23. *Informal.* substantial or satisfying: *a square meal.* 24. *Slang.* conventional or behind the times. —*adv.* 25. in a square manner. —**square′ly**, *adv.* —**square′ness**, *n.* —**squar′ish**, *adj.*

square′ dance′, a dance by a group of four couples arranged in a square or in some set form. —**square′-dance′**, *v.i.*

square′ meas′ure, a system of units for the measurement of areas in squares.

square-rigged (skwâr′rigd′), *adj.* having square sails as the principal sails. —**square′-rig′ger**, *n.*

square′ root′, a number that must be multiplied by itself to yield a particular number.

squash¹ (skwosh), *v.t.* 1. to press into a flat mass or pulp. 2. to quash or suppress. —*v.i.* 3. to be squashed. 4. to make a squashing sound. —*n.* 5. the act or sound of squashing. 6. something squashed. 7. a game played with a ball and rackets on a four-walled court. —**squash′y**, *adj.*

squash² (skwosh), *n.*, *pl.* **squash·es**, **squash.** the fruit of any of various gourdlike plants, used as a vegetable. 2. its plant.

squat (skwot), *v.*, **squat·ted** or **squat**, **squat·ting**, *adj.*, *n.* —*v.i.* 1. to sit on one's haunches or heels. 2. to crouch down, as an animal. 3. to settle without any right or title on another's land. 4. to settle on public land in order to acquire a title to it. —*adj.* 5. Also, **squat′ty.** short and thick or broad. —*n.* 6. the act or position of squatting. —**squat′ness**, *n.* —**squat′ter**, *n.*

squaw (skwô), *n.* *Often Offensive.* an American Indian woman, esp. a wife.

squawk (skwôk), *v.i.* 1. to utter a loud, harsh cry, as a duck. 2. *Slang.* to complain loudly. —*n.* 3. a loud, harsh cry. 4. *Slang.* a loud complaint.

squeak (skwēk), *n.* 1. a short, sharp, shrill cry or sound. —*v.i.*, *v.t.* 2. to utter (with) a squeak. 3. **squeak by** or **through,** to succeed or win by a narrow margin. —**squeak′y**, *adj.*

squeal (skwēl), *n.* **1.** a prolonged, sharp, shrill cry, as of pain. —*v.i.* **2.** to utter a squeal. **3.** *Slang.* to turn informer. —*v.t.* **4.** to utter with a squeal. —**squeal′er,** *n.*

squeam·ish (skwē′mish), *adj.* **1.** easily shocked by anything immodest. **2.** easily nauseated or disgusted. **3.** fastidious or dainty. —**squeam′ish·ly,** *adv.* —**squeam′ish·ness,** *n.*

squee·gee (skwē′jē, skwē jē′), *n.* a T-shaped, rubber-bladed tool for removing water from windows after washing.

squeeze (skwēz), *v.,* **squeezed, squeezing,** *n.* —*v.t.* **1.** to press forcibly together. **2.** to press in order to extract juice. **3.** to force out by pressure. **4.** to embrace or hug firmly. —*v.i.* **5.** to be squeezed. **6.** to exert a compressing force. **7.** to force a way by pressure. —*n.* **8.** the act or an instance of squeezing. **9.** a quantity obtained by squeezing. **10.** a close embrace. **11.** a troubled financial condition. —**squeez′er,** *n.*

squeeze′ bot′tle, a plastic bottle whose contents can be forced out by squeezing.

squelch (skwelch), *v.t.* **1.** to subdue or quell utterly. **2.** *Informal.* to silence (a person), as with a crushing retort. —*n.* **3.** *Informal.* a crushing retort. —**squelch′er,** *n.*

squib (skwib), *n.* **1.** a short and witty or sarcastic saying or writing. **2.** a firework that burns with a hissing noise before exploding.

squid (skwid), *n., pl.* **squid, squids.** a sea animal having a slender body and ten arms.

squig·gle (skwig′əl), *n., v.,* **-gled, -gling.** —*n.* **1.** a short, irregular curve, as in writing. —*v.i., v.t.* **2.** to move or form in squiggles. —**squig′gly,** *adj.*

squint (skwint), *v.i.* **1.** to look with the eyes partly closed. **2.** to look or glance sideways. **3.** to be cross-eyed. —*n.* **4.** the act of squinting. **5.** *Informal.* a quick glance. **6.** cross-eye. —**squint′er,** *n.* —**squint′y,** *adj.*

squire (skwī°r), *n., v.,* **squired, squiring.** —*n.* **1.** the chief landowner in a district in England. **2.** (formerly) an aspirant to knighthood serving a knight. **3.** a man who escorts a woman. **4.** *U.S.* a title formerly applied to a justice of the peace, etc., as in a rural district. —*v.t., v.i.* **5.** to be squire (to).

squirm (skwûrm), *v.i.* **1.** to twist the body like a snake. **2.** to feel or display distress, as from pain. —*n.* **3.** the act of squirming. —**squirm′er,** *n.* —**squirm′y,** *adj.*

squir·rel (skwûr′əl, skwur′-), *n., pl.* **-rels, -rel. 1.** a tree-living, bushy-tailed rodent having thick, soft fur. **2.** its fur.

squirt (skwûrt), *v.i., v.t.* **1.** to eject (liquid) in a jet from a narrow opening. **2.** to wet with a liquid so ejected. —*n.* **3.** a spurt or jet, as of water. **4.** an instrument for squirting. **5.** *Informal.* an insignificant, annoying fellow.

Sr, strontium.

SR., **1.** Seaman Recruit. **2.** shipping receipt.

Sr., **1.** Senior. **2.** *Eccles.* Sister. [< L *Soror*]

Sri Lan·ka (srē lang′kə). an island country in the Indian Ocean, S of India. —**Sri′ Lan′kan.**

S.R.O., standing room only.

SS, Saints.

ss., namely (used on legal documents, as an affidavit, to verify the place of action). [erron. abbr. of *scilicet*]

S.S., 1. steamship. **2.** Sunday School. **3.** sworn statement.

SSA, Social Security Administration.

SSE, south-southeast.

SSgt, Staff Sergeant.

SSR, Soviet Socialist Republic.

SSS, Selective Service System.

SST, supersonic transport.

SSW, south-southwest.

-st, var. of **-est²:** *didst.*

St., 1. Saint. **2.** Strait. **3.** Street.

st., 1. stanza. **2.** state. **3.** statute. **4.** stitch. **5.** stone (weight).

s.t., short ton.

sta., 1. station. **2.** stationary.

stab (stab), *v.,* **stabbed, stab·bing,** *n.* —*v.t., v.i.* **1.** to pierce or wound with or as with a pointed weapon. **2.** to thrust (a pointed weapon) into a person or thing. —*n.* **3.** a thrust with a pointed weapon. **4.** a wound made by stabbing. **5.** *Informal.* a brief attempt.

sta·bile (stā′bēl), *n.* a stationary, abstract sculpture that presents different forms as the viewer walks around it.

sta·bi·lize (stā′bə līz′), *v.t.,* **-lized, -lizing. 1.** to make stable. **2.** to hold at a given level. —**sta′bi·li·za′tion,** *n.* —**sta′bi·liz′er,** *n.*

sta·ble¹ (stā′bəl), *n., v.,* **-bled, -bling.** —*n.* **1.** a building in which horses or cattle are fed and kept. **2.** the group of racehorses belonging to a single owner. —*v.t., v.i.* **3.** to put or live in or as in a stable.

sta·ble² (stā′bəl), *adj.* **1.** able or likely to continue or last. **2.** resistant to sudden change or fluctuation. **3.** reliable and steady, as in emotions. **4.** resisting physical or chemical change. —**sta·bil·i·ty** (stə bil′i tē), *n.* —**sta′bly,** *adv.* —**Syn. 1.** enduring, fixed, permanent. **3.** consistent.

stac·ca·to (stə kä′tō), *adj. Music.* with clear breaks between notes.

stack (stak), *n.* **1.** a large, usually conical pile of hay or straw. **2.** an orderly pile or heap. **3.** stacks, a set of bookshelves, as in a library. **4.** smokestack. **5.** *Informal.* a great number or quantity. —*v.t.* **6.** to pile or arrange in a stack. **7.** to arrange (playing cards) so as to cheat. **8. stack up, a.** to measure up. **b.** to control aircraft waiting to land so that each circles at a certain altitude.

sta·di·um (stā′dē əm), *n., pl.* **-di·ums, -di·a** (-dē ə) a sports arena, usually oval or U-shaped, with tiers of seats. [< L < Gk *stadion* racecourse]

staff (staf, stäf), *n., pl.* **staves** (stāvz) or **staffs** for 1, 2, 5; **staffs** for 3, 4; *v.* —*n.* **1.** a pole, rod, or wand used for supporting as a weapon, or as a symbol of authority. **2.** something that supports or sustains. **3.** a group of assistants to an executive. **4.** *Mil.* a body of officers concerned with planning and administration rather than with participation in combat. **5.** *Music.* a set of five horizontal lines on which music is written. —*v.t.* **6.** to provide with a staff, as of workers.

staff·er (staf′ər, stä′fər), *n.* a member of a staff, esp. of a newspaper.

staff′ ser′geant, *U.S.* **1.** *Air Force.* a noncommissioned officer ranking below a technical sergeant and above a sergeant. **2.** *Army.* a noncommissioned officer ranking above a sergeant and below a sergeant first class. **3.** *Marine Corps.* a noncommissioned officer ranking below a gunnery sergeant and above a sergeant.

stag (stag), *n.* **1.** an adult male deer. —*adj.* **2.** for or of men only: *a stag dinner.* —*adv.* **3.** not accompanied by a female companion.

stage (stāj), *n., v.,* **staged, stag·ing.** —*n.* **1.** a raised platform, as for actors and actresses in a play. **2. the stage,** the theatrical profession. **3.** the scene of any action. **4.** a single period or phase in a process or development **5.** a place of stopping or rest on a journey. **6.** the distance between one such place and the next. **7.** stagecoach **8.** a section of a rocket, usually separable when its propellent is exhausted. —*v.t.* **9.** to represent on or as on a stage. **10.** to organize and carry out. —**stag′y,** *adj.*

stage·coach (stāj′kōch′), *n.* (formerly) a horse-drawn passenger and mail coach traveling over a regular route.

stage·struck (stāj′struk′), *adj.* obsessed with the desire to become an actor or actress

stag·fla·tion (stag′flā shən), *n.* a condition of simultaneously declining business activity, increasing unemployment, and rapid inflation. [*stag(nation)* + (*in*)*flation*]

stag·ger (stag′ər), *v.i.* **1.** to walk or move unsteadily. **2.** to falter or vacillate. —*v.t.* **3.** to cause to stagger. **4.** to astound or shock. **5.** to arrange in a zigzag order. **6.** to arrange in a series of alternating or overlapping intervals. —*n.* **7.** the act or motion of staggering. **8. staggers,** a disease of horses and cattle causing blindness, a staggering gait, etc. —**stag′ger·er,** *n.* —**stag′ger·ing·ly,** *adv.* —**Syn. 1.** reel, totter

stag·ing (stā′jing), *n.* **1.** the process of presenting a play on the stage. **2.** scaffolding (def. 1).

stag·nant (stag′nənt), *adj.* **1.** not flowing or running, as water. **2.** stale or foul from standing. **3.** sluggish or dull.

stag·nate (stag′nāt), *v.i., v.t.,* **-nat·ed, -nat·ing.** to make or become stagnant. —**stag·na′tion,** *n.*

staid (stād), *adj.* **1.** not flighty or capricious. —*v.* **2.** *Archaic.* a pt. and pp. of **stay.** —**staid′ly,** *adv.* —**Syn. 1.** sedate, settled, sober.

stain (stān), *n.* **1.** a color or discoloration caused by a contact with foreign matter. **2.** a moral blemish or stigma. **3.** a dye for coloring woods, etc. —*v.t.* **4.** to discolor with stains. **5.** to dishonor or stigmatize. **6.** to dye (woods, etc.) with a stain. —**stain′er,** *n.* —**stain′less,** *adj.* —**Syn. 4.** soil, spot. **5.** sully, tarnish.

stain′less steel′, alloy steel having a chromium content so as to resist rust and corrosion.

stair (stâr), *n.* **1.** one of a series of steps for going from one level to another. **2. stairs,** a flight of steps. Also called **stair′way′.**

stair·case (stâr′kās′), *n.* a flight of stairs with its framework, banisters, etc.

stair·well (stâr′wel′), *n.* the vertical shaft containing a staircase.

stake¹ (stāk), *n., v.,* **staked, stak·ing.** —*n.* **1.** a post pointed at one end for driving into the ground as part of a fence, support for a plant, etc. **2.** (formerly) a post to which is tied a person for execution by burning. **3. pull up stakes,** *Informal.* to leave or move away. —*v.t.* **4.** to mark with or as with stakes, as boundaries. **5.** to fasten to or support with stakes. **6. stake out,** *Slang.* to keep under police surveillance.

stake² (stāk), *n., v.,* **staked, stak·ing.** —*n.* **1.** something wagered, as the money bet in a gambling game. **2.** Often, **stakes.** a prize or reward, as in a contest. **3. at stake,** in danger or jeopardy. —*v.t.* **4.** to risk or bet. **5.** *Informal.* to furnish with funds or resources.

sta·lac·tite (stə lak′tīt, stal′ək tīt′), *n.* an icicle-shaped deposit, usually of lime, hanging from the roof of a cave.

sta·lag·mite (stə lag′mīt, stal′əg mīt′), *n.* a deposit resembling an inverted stalactite, formed on the floor of a cave.

stale (stāl), *adj.*, **stal·er, stal·est,** *v.* —*adj.* **1.** dry or flat and tasteless, having lost freshness. **2.** trite or not new. **3.** lacking vigor, initiative, etc., as from boredom —*v.t., v.i.* **4.** to make or become stale. —**stale′ness**, *n.*

stale·mate (stāl′māt′), *n., v.,* **-mat·ed, -mat·ing.** —*n.* **1.** *Chess.* a position in which a player cannot move any piece, the result being a draw. **2.** any deadlock. —*v.t.* **3.** to bring to a stalemate.

Sta·lin (stä′lin, -lēn), *n.* **Joseph,** 1879–1953, Russian political leader. — **Sta′lin·ism′,** *n.* —**Sta′lin·ist,** *adj., n.*

stalk¹ (stôk), *n.* **1.** the stem of a plant. **2.** any slender supporting part. —**stalked,** *adj.*

stalk² (stôk), *v.i., v.t.* **1.** to pursue or approach (game) stealthily. **2.** to walk with measured, stiff strides. **3.** to go (through) in a menacing manner. —*n.* **4.** the act of stalking.

stall¹ (stôl), *n.* **1.** a compartment in a stable for one animal **2.** a booth or stand for the display or sale of merchandise. **3.** an enclosed seat in a church choir. **4.** a pew. —*v.t., v.i.* **5.** to stop or cause to stop, esp. unintentionally. **6.** to put or be put in a stall.

stall² (stôl), *Informal.* —*v.i., v.t.* **1.** to delay, esp. by evasion or deception. —*n.* **2.** a ruse or trick used in stalling.

stal·lion (stal′yən), *n.* an uncastrated adult male horse.

stal·wart (stôl′wərt), *adj.* **1.** sturdy and robust **2.** strong and brave. **3.** firm or steadfast —*n.* **4.** a stalwart person —**Syn** **2.** intrepid, valiant.

sta·men (stā′mən) *n., pl.* **sta·mens, stam·i·na** (stam′ə nə). the pollen-bearing organ of a flower. —**stam·i·nate** (stam′ə nit -nāt′), *adj.*

stam·i·na (stam′ə nə), *n.* power to endure disease fatigue, etc.

stam·mer (stam′ər) *v.i., v.t.* **1.** to speak or say with involuntary breaks and pauses. —*n* **2.** the act of stammering. —**stam′mer·er,** *n.* —**stam′mer·ing·ly,** *adv*

stamp (stamp), *v.t.* **1.** to strike forcibly with a downward thrust of the foot. **2.** to bring (the foot) down forcibly. **3.** to imprint or impress with a design, etc **4.** to imprint or impress (a design, etc.) on. **5.** to put an adhesive stamp on. **6.** to characterize or reveal. —*v.i.* **7.** to bring

the foot down forcibly **8.** to walk with heavy, resounding steps. **9. stamp out,** a. to crush or pound. b. to suppress or quell. —*n.* **10.** a small, gummed printed label officially used as evidence of the payment of postage. **11.** the act of stamping. **12.** a die or block for impressing or imprinting. **13.** a design or legend made with such a die or block. **14.** an visible character or quality. **15.** See **trading stamp.** — **stamp′er**, *n.*

stam·pede (stam pēd′), *n., v.,* **-ped·ed, -ped·ing.** —*n.* **1.** a sudden, frenzied rush or flight, as of a herd of frightened animals. —*v.i., v.t.* **2.** to flee or cause to flee in a stampede **3.** to rush or overrun.

stamp′ing ground′, *Informal.* a place that a person frequents.

stance (stans), *n.* **1.** the position of the body and feet while standing. **2.** a mental or emotional attitude.

stanch¹ (stônch, stanch, stänch), *v.t.* **1.** to stop the flow of (a liquid, esp. blood). —*v.i.* **2.** to stop flowing, as blood.

stanch² (stônch, stänch, stanch), *adj.* staunch¹.

stan·chion (stan′shən), *n.* an isolated upright structural support.

stand (stand), *v.,* **stood, stand·ing,** *n.* —*v.i.* **1.** to keep or assume an upright position on the feet **2.** to have a certain height when upright on the feet. **3.** to maintain a steadfast position or attitude, as of support or opposition. **4.** to be placed or situated. **5.** to remain whole or erect. **6.** to remain unchanged or unused. **7.** to be or remain in a certain state or condition. **8.** to be in a certain position or rank. **9.** to cease moving. —*v.t.* **10.** to set upright. **11.** to face or experience, as an ordeal. **12.** to undergo without harm or without giving way. **13.** to endure or tolerate. **14. stand by,** a. to support or help. b. to stand ready. **15. stand for,** a. to represent or symbolize. b. *Informal.* to allow or tolerate. **16. stand off,** to stay at a distance. **17. stand out,** a. to protrude or project. b. to be conspicuous or prominent. **18. stand up.** a. to rise to one's feet. b. to remain convincing. c. to remain durable d. *Slang.* to fail to keep an appointment with. —*n.* **19.** the act of standing **20.** a stop or halt. **21.** a position or attitude taken. **22.** the place in which a person or thing stands **23. the stand.** the place occupied by a person giving testimony in court. **24.** a raised platform, as for a band. **25. stands,** a raised section of seats for spectators. **26.** a piece of furniture on or in which to put articles. **27.** a stall or counter

where articles are displayed for sale.
28. a place occupied by vehicles
available for hire. **29.** the growing
trees in a given area. **30.** a stop of
a theatrical company on tour.

stand·ard (stan′dərd), *n.* **1.** anything
serving as a rule for making judgments or as a basis for comparison.
2. anything authorized as the measure of quantity or quality. **3.** a banner or other object used as an emblem, as of an army or fleet. **4.**
Brit. an upright supporting part. —
adj. **5.** serving as a standard or basis.
6. of recognized excellence. **7.** usual
or customary. —**Syn. 1.** criterion,
guide, model.

stand·ard·bear·er (stan′dərd bâr′ər), *n.*
1. a soldier who carries a standard
or banner. **2.** a conspicuous leader,
as of a political party.

stand·ard·ize (stan′dər dīz′), *v.t.,* **-ized,**
-iz·ing. to bring to an established
standard. —**stand′ard·i·za′tion,** *n.*

stand′ard time′, the time officially
adopted for a region, under a system
that divides the world into 24 zones
for such purpose.

stand·by (stand′bī′), *n., pl.* **-bys. 1.** a
person or thing that can be relied
upon. **2.** a person or thing held
ready to serve as a substitute.

stand·ee (stan dē′), *n. Informal.* a
spectator who stands, as in a theater.

stand-in (stand′in′), *n.* a substitute
for a motion-picture star, as during
the preparation of lighting, cameras,
etc.

stand·ing (stan′ding), *n.* **1.** status
with respect to position, reputation,
or credit. **2.** length of existence or
continuance. —*adj.* **3.** having an
erect or upright position. **4.** performed in or from an erect position:
a standing jump. **5.** still or stagnant,
as water. **6.** lasting or permanent.
7. out of use, as a machine.

stand·off (stand′ôf′, -of′), *n.* a tie in
a game.

stand·off·ish (stand′ô′fish, -of′ish),
adj. cold and unfriendly.

stand·out (stand′out′), *n.* something
or someone remarkably superior.

stand·pipe (stand′pīp′), *n.* a vertical
pipe into which water is pumped to
obtain a required pressure.

stand·point (stand′point′), *n.* See
point of view.

stand·still (stand′stil′), *n.* an absence
of movement or action.

stand-up (stand′up′), *adj.* **1.** standing
upright, as a collar. **2.** delivering a
comic monologue while alone on the
stage, as a comedian.

stank (stangk), *v.* a pt. of **stink.**

stan·za (stan′zə), *n.* a group of lines
forming a division of a poem.

sta·pes (stā′pēz), *n., pl.* **sta·pes, sta-
pe·dez** (stə pē′dēz). the small bone
in the middle ear of mammals.

staph (staf), *n. Informal.* staphylo-
coccus.

staph·y·lo·coc·cus (staf′ə lə kok′əs),
n., pl. **-coc·ci** (-kok′sī). any of several spherical bacteria occurring in
irregular clusters. —**staph′y·lo·coc′-
cal** (-kok′əl), **staph′y·lo·coc′cic**
(-kok′sik), *adj.*

sta·ple[1] (stā′pəl), *n., v.,* **-pled, -pling.**
—*n.* **1.** a short piece of wire bent so
as to bind papers together. **2.** a similar U-shaped piece of wire or metal
with pointed ends for driving into a
surface to hold a hook, bolt, etc. —
v.t. **3.** to attach or fasten with a
staple. —**sta′pler,** *n.*

sta·ple[2] (stā′pəl), *n.* **1.** a principal
raw material or commodity grown
or manufactured in a locality. **2.** a
basic or necessary item of food. **3.**
any basic or chief item or element.
4. the fiber of wool, cotton, or flax.
—*adj.* **5.** chiefly dealt in or consumed. **6.** basic or chief.

star (stär), *n., adj., v.,* **starred, star-
ring.** —*n.* **1.** any of the heavenly
bodies, except the moon and planets,
appearing as luminous points in the
sky at night. **2.** a heavenly body
considered as influencing mankind
and events. **3.** Often, **stars.** a person's destiny or fortune. **4.** a figure
having five or six points radiating
from a center. **5.** asterisk. **6.** an actor or actress who plays a leading
role. **7.** a person who is prominent
in some field. —*adj.* **8.** celebrated
or prominent. **9.** of a star or stars.
—*v.t.* **10.** to decorate with stars. **11.**
to feature as a star. **12.** to mark with
an asterisk. —*v.i.* **13.** to perform
prominently. **14.** to perform as a
star. —**star′dom,** *n.* —**star′less,** *adj.*
—**star′like,** *adj.* —**star′ry,** *adj.*

star·board (stär′bərd), *n.* **1.** the right-
hand side of a vessel or aircraft,
facing forward. —*adj.* **2.** of or located to the starboard.

starch (stärch), *n.* **1.** a white, tasteless, solid carbohydrate found in the
seeds, tubers, and other parts of
plants. **2.** a preparation of this substance used to stiffen fabrics in
laundering. —*v.t.* **3.** to stiffen or
treat with starch. —**starch′y,** *adj.*

stare (stâr), *v.,* **stared, star·ing,** *n.* —
v.i. **1.** to gaze fixedly, esp. with the
eyes wide open. —*v.t.* **2.** to stare at.
—*n.* **3.** a staring gaze. —**star′er,** *n.*

star·fish (stär′fish′), *n., pl.* **-fish, -fish-
es.** a star-shaped sea animal having
five or more rays or arms.

star·gaze (stär′gāz′), *v.i.,* **-gazed, -gaz-
ing. 1.** to observe the stars. **2.** to
daydream. —**star′gaz′er,** *n.*

stark (stärk), *adj.* 1. bluntly plain: *the stark fact.* 2. utter or complete: *stark madness.* 3. harsh or grim. 4. extremely simple or bare. —*adv.* 5. utterly or quite. —**stark′ly,** *adv.* — **stark′ness,** *n.* —Syn. 1. unmistakable. 2. downright, sheer.

stark-nak·ed (stärk′nā′kid), *adj.* absolutely naked.

star·let (stär′lit), *n.* a young actress promoted as a future star.

star·light (stär′līt′), *n.* the light coming from the stars. —**star′lit,** *adj.*

star·ling (stär′ling), *n.* a bird introduced into North America from Europe, having a black body and traveling in large flocks.

Stars′ and Stripes′, the U.S. flag.

Star′-Span·gled Ban′ner, The (stär′-spang′gəld). 1. the national anthem of the U.S. 2. See **Stars and Stripes.**

start (stärt), *v.i.* 1. to begin on a course of action or procedure. 2. to give a sudden jerk or jump, as from surprise. 3. to spring or move suddenly from a position or place. —*v.t.* 4. to set moving or acting. 5. to enter upon or begin. 6. to cause to be an entrant in a game. 7. **start out** or **off,** to begin a trip or career. —*n.* 8. the beginning of an action, journey, etc. 9. the place or time of beginning. 10. a sudden jerking movement of the body. 11. a lead or advance. 12. a chance or aid given to a person starting on a career. 13. *Brit.* startle (def. 3). —**start′er,** *n.*

star·tle (stär′t°l), *v.,* **-tled, -tling,** *n.* —*v.t.* 1. to frighten or disturb suddenly, esp. to cause to start involuntarily. —*v.i.* 2. to become startled. —*n.* 3. something that startles. — **star′tling,** *adj.* —Syn. 1. surprise.

starve (stärv), *v.,* **starved, starv·ing.** —*v.i.* 1. to die from lack of food. 2. to suffer severely from hunger. 3. to feel a strong need. —*v.t.* 4. to cause to starve. 5. to subdue by hunger. —**star·va′tion,** *n.*

starve·ling (stärv′ling), *n.* a person, animal, or plant that is starving.

stash (stash), *Informal.* —*v.t.* 1. to keep or hide away. —*n.* 2. a secret hiding place. 3. something stashed.

-stat, a combining form meaning "stationary" or "set": *thermostat.*

stat., 1. statue. 2. statute.

state (stāt), *n., adj., v.,* **stat·ed, stat·ing.** —*n.* 1. the condition of a person or thing with respect to circumstances, qualities, etc. 2. condition with respect to structure, form, etc. 3. a particular emotional condition. 4. an excited condition: *to leave in a state.* 5. a nation or its government. 6. (*sometimes cap.*) one of the political units that together make up a federal union. 7. governmental activity: *affairs of state.* 8. **the States,** *Informal.* the United States. 9. *Rare.* pomp and grandeur. 10. **lie in state,** to be exhibited publicly before burial. —*adj.* 11. of a state or government. 12. involving ceremony. —*v.t.* 13. to set forth definitely or specifically in speech or writing. —**state′hood,** *n.*

state·craft (stāt′kraft′, -kräft′), *n.* the art of government and diplomacy.

state·house (stāt′hous′), *n.* (*sometimes cap.*) the building in which a state legislature sits.

state·less (stāt′lis), *adj.* lacking nationality.

state·ly (stāt′lē), *adj.* **-li·er, -li·est.** 1. imposing in magnificence or elegance. 2. extremely dignified. — **state′li·ness,** *n.*

state·ment (stāt′mənt), *n.* 1. something stated, as a declaration or assertion. 2. an abstract of an account, as one rendered to show the balance due.

Stat′en Is′land (stat′°n), an island facing New York Bay.

state′ of the art′, the scientific and technical level attained at a given time, as in the computer industry.

state·room (stāt′rōōm′, -rŏŏm′), *n.* a private room or compartment on a ship or train.

state·side (stāt′sīd′), *adj.* 1. being in or toward the U.S. —*adv.* 2. in or toward the U.S.

states·man (stāts′mən), *n.* 1. a person who is experienced in government and government affairs. 2. a person who exhibits great ability in dealing with public issues. —**states′man·like′,** *adj.* —**states′man·ship′,** *n.* —**states′wom′an,** *n.fem.*

stat·ic (stat′ik), *adj.* 1. not moving or changing. 2. of or pertaining to physical force in equilibrium. 3. acting by mere weight without producing motion: *static pressure.* 4. of or pertaining to the electricity contained in or given off by charged bodies. 5. of or pertaining to radio static. —*n.* 6. interference, as a crackling noise, with radio or television signals as a result of electrical disturbances. 7. *Slang.* disturbing remarks. —**stat′i·cal·ly,** *adv.*

sta·tion (stā′shən), *n.* 1. the headquarters of certain public services: *a police station.* 2. a place equipped for a certain kind of service. 3. a starting and stopping place for trains or buses. 4. a place or position in which a person or thing is normally located. 5. *Radio and Television.* a building from which broadcasts originate. 6. social standing. —*v.t.* 7. to assign a station to.

sta·tion·ar·y (stā′shə ner′ē), *adj.* 1. having a fixed position. 2. not moving or changing.

sta'tion break', *Radio and Television.* an interval between or during programs for identifying the station or making announcements.

sta·tion·er (stā'shə nər), *n.* a person who sells stationery.

sta·tion·er·y (stā'shə ner'ē), *n.* **1.** writing materials and office supplies. **2.** letter paper, usually with a letterhead, and envelopes.

sta'tion wag'on, an automobile with one or more rows of folding rear seats and a rear door for access to a cargo area.

sta·tis·tic (stə tis'tik), *n.* a numerical fact or datum.

sta·tis·tics (stə tis'tiks), *n.* **1.** the science that deals with the collection and analysis of numerical facts or data. **2.** the numerical facts or data themselves. —**sta·tis'ti·cal,** *adj.* —**sta·tis'ti·cal·ly,** *adv.* —**stat·is·ti·cian** (stat'i stish'ən), *n.*

stat·u·ar·y (stach'ŌŌ er'ē), *n., pl.* **-ar·ies.** statues collectively.

stat·ue (stach'ŌŌ), *n.* a three-dimensional likeness of a person or animal carved in stone or wood, or cast in metal or plaster.

stat·u·esque (stach'ŌŌ esk'), *adj.* suggesting a statue, as in beauty or dignity of form.

stat·u·ette (stach'ŌŌ et'), *n.* a small statue.

stat·ure (stach'ər), *n.* **1.** the height of a person or animal. **2.** level of achievement.

sta·tus (stā'təs, stat'əs), *n.* **1.** the position or rank of an individual in relation to others. **2.** a state of affairs. **3.** the standing of a person before the law.

sta'tus quo' (kwō), the existing state of affairs.

sta'tus sym'bol, something owned primarily to reflect a person's status.

stat·ute (stach'ŌŌt, -ŌŌt), *n.* **1.** an enactment made by a legislature. **2.** a permanent rule established by an organization or corporation.

stat'ute mile', mile (def. 1).

stat'ute of limita'tions, a statute defining the period within which legal action may be taken.

stat·u·to·ry (stach'ŌŌ tōr'ē, -tôr'ē), *adj.* **1.** prescribed or authorized by statute. **2.** legally punishable, as an offense. —**stat'u·to'ri·ly,** *adv.*

staunch¹ (stônch, stänch), *adj.* **1.** unflinchingly loyal. **2.** strong or well-built. —**staunch'ly,** *adv.* —**staunch'ness,** *n.* —**Syn.** 1. resolute, steadfast.

staunch² (stônch), *v.t., v.i.* stanch¹.

stave (stāv), *n., v.,* **staved** or **stove, stav·ing.** —*n.* **1.** one of the thin, narrow pieces of wood that form the sides of a cask, barrel, etc. **2.** a stick or rod. **3.** stanza. —*v.t.* **4.** to break in the staves of. **5.** to break (a hole)

in, esp. in the hull of a boat. **6. stave off,** to keep off or prevent.

staves (stāvz), *n.* **1.** a pl. of **staff. 2.** pl. of **stave.**

stay¹ (stā), *v.,* **stayed** or (*Archaic*) **staid, stay·ing,** *n.* —*v.i.* **1.** to continue to be at a place or in someone's company. **2.** to spend some time at a place or in a situation. **3.** to halt or pause. **4.** to wait or linger. **5.** *Informal.* to continue or endure, as in a race. —*v.t.* **6.** to stop or halt. **7.** to hold back or restrain. **8.** to suspend or delay. **9.** to appease (one's hunger) temporarily. **10.** to remain through or during. —*n.* **11.** a sojourn or temporary residence. **12.** a stop or halt. **13.** suspension of a judicial proceeding.

stay² (stā), *n., v.,* **stayed, stay·ing.** —*n.* **1.** something used as a support or as a prop. **2.** a flat strip of bone or plastic used esp. for stiffening corsets, collars, etc. **3.** stays, *Brit. Obsolesc.* a corset. —*v.t.* **4.** to support or prop.

stay³ (stā), *n., v.,* **stayed, stay·ing.** —*n.* **1.** a strong rope or wire for steadying masts, funnels, etc. —*v.t.* **2.** to support or steady with stays.

stay'ing pow'er, ability or strength to last or endure.

std., standard.

S.T.D., Doctor of Sacred Theology. [< L *Sacrae Theologiae Doctor*]

Ste., Saint (female). [< F *Sainte*]

stead (sted), *n.* **1.** the place of a person or thing as occupied by a substitute. **2. stand in good stead,** to be useful to, esp. in a time of need.

stead·fast (sted'fast', -fäst', -fəst), *adj.* **1.** firm and unwavering, as in loyalty. **2.** steadily directed. —**stead'fast·ly,** *adv.* —**stead'fast·ness,** *n.*

stead·y (sted'ē), *adj., stead·i·er, stead·i·est, n., pl.* **stead·ies,** *v.,* **stead·ied, stead·y·ing,** *adv.* —*adj.* **1.** firmly placed or fixed. **2.** continuous or free from change. **3.** regular or habitual. **4.** free from excitement. **5.** reliable and careful. **6.** steadfast or unwavering. **7. go steady,** *Informal.* to date exclusively one person of the opposite sex. —*n.* **8.** *Informal.* a person of the opposite sex whom one dates exclusively. —*v.t., v.i.* **9.** to make or become steady. —*adv.* **10.** in a steady manner. —**stead'i·ly,** *adv.* —**stead'i·ness,** *n.*

stead'y-state' the'ory (sted'ē stāt'), the theory that the universe is unlimited and will constantly expand.

steak (stāk), *n.* a slice of meat, esp. beef or fish, cooked by broiling or frying. [< Scand]

steal (stēl), *v.,* **stole, sto·len, steal·ing,** *n.* —*v.t.* **1.** to take (another's property) without permission or right, esp. secretly. **2.** to take or get by sly means. **3.** to gain artfully or surreptitiously. **4.** to move or put secretly or quietly. **5.** *Baseball.* to gain (a base) without the help of a hit or error. —*v.i.* **6.** to commit theft. **7.** to move secretly or quietly. —*n.* **8.** an act of stealing. **9.** *Informal.* something sold at a bargain.

stealth (stelth), *n.* secretly or quietly sly action. —**stealth'y**, *adj.* — **stealth'i·ly**, *adv.* —**stealth'i·ness**, *n.*

steam (stēm), *n.* **1.** the invisible gas or vapor produced when water boils. **2.** the mist formed when this gas condenses in the air. **3.** *Informal.* power or energy. —*v.i.* **4.** to give off steam. **5.** to become covered with condensed steam. **6.** to move or travel by steam power. —*v.t.* **7.** to cook or heat by steam. —*adj.* **8.** operated by or using steam. — **steam'y**, *adj.*

steam·boat (stēm'bōt'), *n.* a small, steam-driven vessel.

steam' en'gine, an engine in which a piston is pushed by the action of the expanding steam generated in a boiler.

steam·er (stē'mər), *n.* **1.** a machine or vehicle driven by steam, as a steamship. **2.** a container in which something is steamed.

steam' fit'ter, a person who installs and repairs steam pipes and their accessories. —**steam' fit'ting.**

steam·roll·er (stēm'rō'lər), *n.* **1.** a heavy, steam-powered vehicle having a roller, used esp. in paving roads. —*v.t.*, *v.i.* **2.** to move or crush with or as with a steamroller.

steam·ship (stēm'ship'), *n.* a large commercial vessel driven by steam.

steam' shov'el, a steam-driven machine for digging or excavating.

ste·a·tite (stē'ə tīt'), *n.* soapstone.

steed (stēd), *n.* a high-spirited horse for riding.

steel (stēl), *n.* **1.** a hard, strong alloy consisting principally of iron and containing carbon and sometimes other metals. **2.** something made of this metal. **3.** great strength or toughness. —*adj.* **4.** of or like steel. —*v.t.* **5.** to make firm or strong. —**steel'y**, *adj.*

steel' wool', a mass of fine, threadlike steel shavings used for scouring or polishing.

steel·yard (stēl'yärd', stil'yərd), *n.* a weighing device consisting of a steel bar suspended from a point near one end.

steep¹ (stēp), *adj.* **1.** having a sharp slant up and down. **2.** *Informal.* unduly high, as a price. —*n.* **3.** a steep place. —**steep'ly**, *adv.* —**steep'- ness**, *n.* —**Syn.** *1.* precipitous.

steep² (stēp), *v.t.*, *v.i.* **1.** to soak in water or other liquid, as to extract

some essence. **2.** to involve or be involved deeply.

steep·en (stē'pən), *v.t.*, *v.i.* to make or become steeper.

stee·ple (stē'pəl), *n.* **1.** a tall construction ending in a spire, esp. on a tower of a church. **2.** such a tower. —**stee'pled**, *adj.*

stee·ple·chase (stē'pəl chās'), *n.* a horse race over a course set with obstacles, as ditches, hedges, etc.

stee·ple·jack (stē'pəl jak'), *n.* a person who builds or repairs steeples, towers, etc.

steer¹ (stēr), *v.t.* **1.** to guide the course of (a vessel or vehicle). **2.** to follow or pursue (a particular course). **3.** *Informal.* to direct the course of, as with advice. —*v.i.* **4.** to steer a vessel or vehicle. **5.** to admit of being steered in a certain manner. **6.** **steer clear of,** to shun or avoid. —*n.* **7.** *Slang.* a piece of advice. —**steer'a·ble**, *adj.* —**steers'- man**, *n.*

steer² (stēr), *n.* a castrated male ox, esp. one raised for beef.

steer·age (stēr'ij), *n.* **1.** (formerly) the lowest class of accommodations on a passenger ship. **2.** the act of steering.

steg·o·saur (steg'ə sôr'), *n.* a dinosaur having a heavy, bony armor. Also, **steg'o·saur'us** (-sôr'əs).

stein (stīn), *n.* an earthenware mug for beer.

stel·lar (stel'ər), *adj.* **1.** of or like stars. **2.** leading or prominent.

stem¹ (stem), *n.*, *v.*, **stemmed, stem- ming.** —*n.* **1.** the main stalk of a plant. **2.** the stalk that supports a leaf, flower, or fruit. **3.** something resembling a stem, as of a tobacco pipe. **4.** the form of a word to which inflectional endings are added. —*v.i.* **5.** to arise or originate. — **stem'less**, *adj.*

stem² (stem), *v.t.*, **stemmed, stem- ming.** to stop or check by or as by damming.

stem³ (stem), *v.t.*, **stemmed, stem- ming.** to make headway against (a tide, etc.).

stem⁴ (stem), *n.* the forward part of a ship.

stemmed (stemd), *adj.* **1.** having a stem. **2.** having the stems taken off.

stem·ware (stem'wâr'), *n.* glassware mounted on footed stems.

stench (stench), *n.* an offensive smell.

sten·cil (sten'səl), *n.*, *v.*, **-ciled, -cil·ing** or **-cilled, -cil·ling.** —*n.* **1.** a thin sheet, as of cardboard, having perforations through which ink or paint applied on one side will pass through to form letters or a design on a surface against which the sheet rests. —*v.t.* **2.** to mark or make by a stencil.

sten·o (sten′ō), *n., pl.* **sten·os** for 1. 1. a stenographer. 2. stenography.

steno., 1. stenographer. 2. stenography. Also, **stenog.**

ste·nog·ra·phy (stə nog′rə fē), *n.* the art of writing in shorthand. —**ste·nog′ra·pher,** *n.* —**sten·o·graph·ic** (sten′ə graf′ik), *adj.* —**sten′o·graph′i·cal·ly,** *adv.*

sten·to·ri·an (sten tôr′ē ən, -tôr′-), *adj.* very loud or strong in sound.

step (step), *n., v.,* **stepped, step·ping.** —*n.* 1. a movement made by lifting one foot and setting it down again in a new position, with the other foot following. 2. the distance covered by such a movement. 3. the sound made by the foot in making such a movement. 4. the manner of walking. 5. a rhythm or pattern in walking, marching, or dancing. 6. one of a number of stages toward reaching a goal. 7. rank, degree, or grade. 8. a support for the foot in ascending or descending. 9. a very short distance. 10. **in step, a.** moving in time to a rhythm. **b.** in harmony or conformity. 11. **out of step, a.** not moving in time to a rhythm. **b.** not in harmony or conformity. 12. **take steps,** to begin to act. —*v.i.* 13. to move in steps. 14. to walk a short distance. 15. to move or go briskly. 16. to get into some situation easily. 17. to put the foot down. —*v.t.* 18. to measure by steps. 19. **step down, a.** to decrease by degrees. **b.** to retire or resign. 20. **step up, a.** to increase by degrees. **b.** to move forward. —**step′per,** *n.*

step-, a prefix meaning "related by remarriage": *stepbrother.*

step·broth·er (step′bruth′ər), *n.* the son of one's stepparent by a former marriage.

step·child (step′chīld′), *n.* a child of one's spouse by a former marriage.

step·daugh·ter (step′dô′tər), *n.* a daughter of one's spouse by a former marriage.

step·down (step′doun′), *n.* a gradual decrease, as in activity.

step·fa·ther (step′fä′thər), *n.* a man who succeeds one's father as the husband of one's mother.

step·lad·der (step′lad′ər), *n.* a ladder with flat treads and a hinged frame opening up to form four supporting legs.

step·moth·er (step′muth′ər), *n.* a woman who succeeds one's mother as the wife of one's father.

step·par·ent (step′pâr′ənt, -par′-), *n.* a stepfather or stepmother.

steppe (step), *n.* a vast plain without trees, as found in the western Soviet Union.

step·ping·stone (step′ing stōn′), *n.* 1. a stone that is stepped on in cross-

ing a stream. 2. any means of advancement or improvement.

step·sis·ter (step′sis′tər), *n.* the daughter of one's stepparent by a former marriage.

step·son (step′sun′), *n.* a son of one's spouse by a former marriage.

step·up (step′up′), *n.* a gradual increase, as in activity.

-ster, a suffix meaning: **a.** a person who is: *oldster.* **b.** a person who does: *trickster.* **c.** a person whose occupation is: *songster.* **d.** a person associated with: *gangster.*

ster., sterling.

stere (stēr), *n.* a unit of capacity equal to one cubic meter.

ster·e·o (ster′ē ō′, stēr′-), *n., pl.* **ster·e·os,** *adj.* —*n.* 1. **a.** stereophonic equipment. **b.** stereophonic sound. **c.** a stereophonic system. 2. a stereoscopic photograph or system. —*adj.* 3. stereophonic.

stereo-, a combining form meaning "solid" or "three-dimensional": *stereoscope.*

ster·e·o·phon·ic (ster′ē ə fon′ik, stēr′-), *adj.* of or noting a system of sound recording or reproduction using two or three channels to produce a more realistic effect. —**ster′e·o·phon′i·cal·ly,** *adv.*

ster·e·o·scope (ster′ē ə skōp′, stēr′-), *n.* a device with two viewing holes that makes photographs appear to be three-dimensional. —**ster′e·o·scop′ic** (-skop′ik), *adj.* —**ster′e·o·scop′i·cal·ly,** *adv.* —**ster′e·os′co·py** (-os′kə pē), *n.*

ster·e·o·tape (ster′ē ə tāp′, stēr′-), *n.* a magnetic tape for recording or reproducing stereophonic sound.

ster·e·o·type (ster′ē ə tīp′, stēr′-), *n., v.,* **-typed, -typ·ing.** —*n.* 1. a printing plate made from a mold cast in type metal. 2. an idea or expression lacking in freshness or originality. 3. a conventional or standardized conception or image. —*v.t.* 4. to make a stereotype of. —**ster′e·o·typ′er,** *n.*

ster·e·o·typed (ster′ē ə tīpt′, stēr′-), *adj.* 1. lacking freshness or originality. 2. reproduced by stereotype plates.

ster·ile (ster′il), *adj.* 1. incapable of producing offspring. 2. free from germs or microorganisms. 3. not producing vegetation. 4. unimaginative and unfruitful. —**ste·ril·i·ty** (stə ril′i tē), *n.*

ster·i·lize (ster′ə līz′), *v.t.,* **-lized, -liz·ing.** to make sterile. —**ster′i·li·za′tion,** *n.* —**ster′i·liz′er,** *n.*

ster·ling (stûr′ling), *adj.* 1. of or noting British money. 2. (of silver) having the standard fineness of .925. 3. made of silver of this fineness. 4. thoroughly excellent. —*n.* 5. British money. 6. sterling silver.

stern[1] (stûrn), *adj.* **1.** severe in conduct or disposition. **2.** expressing severe displeasure. **3.** grim and forbidding. —**stern′ly,** *adv.* —**stern′ness,** *n.* —Syn. **1.** rigid, strict. **2.** harsh, unrelenting.

stern[2] (stûrn), *n.* the rear part of a ship or aircraft.

ster·num (stûr′nəm), *n., pl.* **-nums, -na** (-nə). the flat bone running down the center of the chest and connected to the ribs. —**ster′nal** (-nᵊl), *adj.*

ster·oid (stēr′oid, stĕr′-), *n.* any of a group of fat-soluble compounds, as the bile acids, sex hormones, etc.

ster·to·rous (stûr′tər əs), *adj.* characterized by heavy snoring. **2.** breathing in this manner. —**ster′to·rous·ly,** *adv.*

stet (stet), *v.*, **stet·ted, stet·ting.** —*v.i.* **1.** let it stand (used as a direction, as on a printer's proof, to retain matter previously canceled). —*v.t.* **2.** to mark with "stet."

steth·o·scope (steth′ə skōp′), *n.* an instrument used for hearing sounds produced in the body, esp. those of the lungs and heart. —**steth′o·scop′ic** (-skop′ik), *adj.*

ste·ve·dore (stē′vi dōr′, -dôr′), *n.* a person employed to load or unload ships.

stew (stōō, styōō), *v.t.* **1.** to cook (food) by simmering or slow boiling. —*v.i.* **2.** to undergo cooking in this way. **3.** *Informal.* to fret or worry. —*n.* **4.** a dish cooked by stewing, esp. a mixture of meat and vegetables. **5.** *Informal.* a state of uneasiness or worry.

stew·ard (stōō′ərd, styōō′-), *n.* **1.** a person who manages another's property or financial affairs. **2.** a supervisor of dining and housekeeping services on a passenger ship. **3.** a male employee on a plane or train who serves drinks or food and looks after the comfort of passengers. —**stew′ard·ship′,** *n.*

stew·ard·ess (stōō′ər dis, styōō′-), *n.* a female steward, esp. on an airplane.

stg., sterling.

stick[1] (stik), *n.* **1.** a twig or branch cut or broken off. **2.** any slender, long piece of wood, as a club or drumstick. **3.** *Brit.* cane (def. 1). **4.** anything resembling a stick in shape. **5.** *Informal.* an unenthusiastic person. **6. the sticks,** *Informal.* rural districts.

stick[2] (stick), *v.*, **stuck, stick·ing,** *n.* —*v.t.* **1.** to pierce or puncture with something pointed. **2.** to thrust in (something pointed) so as to pierce or puncture. **3.** to fix in position. **4.** to fasten or attach by glue, moisture, etc. **5.** to render unable to proceed or go back: *The car was stuck in the mud.* **6.** to confuse or puzzle. **7.** *Informal.* to impose something disagreeable upon. —*v.i.* **8.** to have the point or points embedded. **9.** to remain attached by adhesion. **10.** to remain firm, as in resolution. **11.** to keep or remain steadily or unremittingly, as to a task. **12.** to become fastened or stationary by some obstruction. **13.** to be embarrassed or puzzled. **14.** to hesitate or scruple. **15.** to extend or protrude. **16. stick around,** *Slang.* to remain or linger. **17. stick by** or **to,** to remain faithful to. **18. stick up,** *Slang.* to rob, esp. at gunpoint. **19. stick up for,** *Informal.* to support or defend. —*n.* **20.** a thrust with or as with a pointed object.

stick·er (stik′ər), *n.* **1.** an adhesive label. **2.** a person or thing that sticks.

stick′er price′, the manufacturer's suggested retail price, esp. on a new automobile, from which a discount is usually given.

stick-in-the-mud (stik′in t͟he mud′), *n. Informal.* a person who is slow to change.

stick·ler (stik′lər), *n.* **1.** a person who insists on something rigidly: *a stickler for ceremony.* **2.** any puzzling or difficult problem.

stick′ shift′, a manually operated gearshift lever of an automobile, set either in the floor or on the steering column.

stick-to-it·ive (stik′tōō′it iv, -ĭ tĭv), *adj. Informal.* tenaciously resolute. —**stick′-to′-it·ive·ness,** *n.*

stick·up (stik′up′), *n. Slang.* holdup (def. 1).

stick·y (stik′ē), *adj.*, **stick·i·er, stick·i·est. 1.** tending to stick or adhere. **2.** hot and humid. **3.** awkwardly difficult. —**stick′i·ly,** *adv.* —**stick′i·ness,** *n.*

stiff (stif), *adj.* **1.** difficult to bend or flex. **2.** not moving or working easily. **3.** not supple, as from cold. **4.** strong or forceful. **5.** rigidly formal, as manners. **6.** laborious or difficult, as a task. **7.** severe or harsh, as a penalty. **8.** unusually high, as a price. **9.** thick or not liquid. —*adv.* **10.** extremely or completely: *to be scared stiff.* —**stiff′ly,** *adv.* —**stiff′ness,** *n.*

stiff-arm (stif′ärm′), *v.t.* straight-arm.

stiff·en (stif′ən), *v.t., v.i.* to make or become stiff. —**stiff′en·er,** *n.*

stiff-necked (stif′nekt′), *adj.* stubborn and arrogant.

sti·fle (stī'fəl), v., **-fled, -fling.** —v.t.
1. to kill by stopping the breath. 2.
to suppress or withhold. —v.i. 3. to
become stifled. 4. to suffer from
lack of air. —**sti'fler,** n. —**sti'fling·ly,** adv.

stig·ma (stig'mə), n., pl. **stig·mas, stig·ma·ta** (stig'mə tə, stig mä'tə, -mat'ə).
1. a blemish on one's record or reputation. 2. a mark on the skin that
bleeds during certain mental states.
3. the part of a pistil which receives
the pollen. 4. stigmata, marks resembling the wounds on the crucified
body of Christ. —**stig·mat'ic** (-mat'ik), adj.

stig·ma·tize (stig'mə tīz'), v.t., **-tized,
-tiz·ing.** 1. to set a mark of disgrace upon. 2. to mark with a
stigma.

stil·bes·trol (stil bes'trōl, -trôl, -trol),
n. a synthetic estrogen.

stile (stīl), n. a series of steps used
for passing over a wall or fence.

sti·let·to (sti let'ō), n., pl. **-tos, -toes.**
a short dagger with a slender blade.

still¹ (stil), adj. 1. without movement.
2. free from sound or noise. 3.
subdued or hushed. 4. peaceful or
calm. 5. of or noting a single photographic print, esp. of one of the
frames of a motion-picture film. —n.
6. stillness or silence. 7. a still photograph. —adv. 8. up to or at the
time mentioned. 9. in spite of that.
10. even or yet. 11. without sound
or movement: Sit still! —conj. 12.
and yet. —v.t., v.i. 13. to make or
become still. —**still'ness,** n.

still² (stil), n. an apparatus used in
distilling liquids, esp. alcoholic liquors.

still·birth (stil'bûrth'), n. the birth of
a dead child.

still·born (stil'bôrn'), adj. dead at
birth.

still' life', pl. **still lifes.** a representation of inanimate objects.

stilt (stilt), n. 1. one of two poles,
each with a footrest at some distance
above the ground, enabling the
wearer to walk with long steps. 2.
one of several posts supporting a
structure built above the surface of
land or water.

stilt·ed (stil'tid), adj. stiffly dignified
or formal.

Stil·ton (stil'tən), n. a waxy, white
cheese veined with mold.

stim·u·lant (stim'yə lənt), n. 1. something that temporarily quickens the
activity of the mind or body. 2. any
food or beverage that stimulates or
invigorates, as coffee.

stim·u·late (stim'yə lāt'), v.t., **-lat·ed,
-lat·ing.** 1. to rouse to action or
effort, as by encouragement. 2. to
excite (an organism) to its functional
activity. —**stim'u·lat'ing·ly,** adv.

—**stim'u·la'tion,** n. —**stim'u·la'tive**
(-lā'tiv), adj., n. —**Syn.** 1. goad, incite, provoke, stir.

stim·u·lus (stim'yə ləs), n., pl. **-li** (-lī').
something that stimulates psychologically or physiologically.

sting (sting), v., **stung, sting·ing,** n.
—v.t. 1. to prick or wound with a
sharp-pointed, often venom-bearing
organ. 2. to cause sharp pain to. 3.
to cause mental anguish. 4. to goad
or drive, as by sharp irritation. 5.
Slang. to cheat, esp. to overcharge.
—v.i. 6. to use or have a sting. 7.
to cause or feel sharp pain or mental
anguish. —n. 8. the act of stinging.
9. a wound or pain caused by stinging. 10. a sharp-pointed, often venom-bearing organ, as of a bee, capable of inflicting a painful or dangerous wound. —**sting'er,** n. —**sting'ing·ly,** adv.

stin·gy (stin'jē), adj., **-gi·er, -gi·est.**
1. reluctant to give, lend, or spend.
2. scanty or meager. —**stin'gi·ly,**
adv. —**stin'gi·ness,** n. —**Syn.** 1. miserly, niggardly, penurious.

stink (stingk), v., **stank or stunk,
stunk, stink·ing,** n. —v.i. 1. to give
off a strong offensive smell. 2. *Slang.*
to be disgustingly inferior. —n. 3.
a strong offensive smell. —**stink'er,** n.

stint (stint), v.t. 1. to limit to a certain
quantity, often unduly. —v.i. 2. to
be frugal or sparing. —n. 3. an allotted duty or period of work. 4.
limitation or restriction, esp. as to
quantity. —**stint'er,** n. —**stint'ing,**
adj. —**stint'ing·ly,** adv.

sti·pend (stī'pend), n. a periodic payment, usually of a fixed, moderate
amount of money, esp. a scholarship
allowance. —**sti'pend·less,** adj.

stip·ple (stip'əl), v.t., **-pled, -pling.** to
paint, engrave, or draw by means of
dots or small touches rather than
lines.

stip·u·late (stip'yə lāt'), v.t., **-lat·ed,
-lat·ing.** 1. to require as an essential
condition of an agreement. 2. to
specify in the terms of an agreement.
—**stip'u·la'tion,** n. —**stip'u·la'tor,** n.

stir¹ (stûr), v., **stirred, stir·ring,** n.
—v.t., v.i. 1. to agitate (a liquid)
with a continuous or repeated movement of an implement or one's hand.
2. to urge on or incite (someone).
3. to excite the emotion (of). 4. to
rouse from inactivity or sleep. 5.
to move lightly or slightly. —n. 6.
the act of stirring. 7. light or slight
movement. 8. a state of general excitement. —**stir'rer,** n.

stir² (stûr), n. *Slang.* prison.

stir·ring (stûr'ing), adj. 1. intensely
exciting. 2. active or lively. —**stir'ring·ly,** adv. —**Syn.** 1. rousing, thrilling.

stir·rup (stûr′əp, stir′-, stur′-), *n.* either of two rings, as of metal, suspended from a saddle to support the rider's foot.

stitch (stich), *n.* **1.** a complete movement of a threaded needle through a fabric in sewing. **2.** a loop of thread left in place by such a movement. **3.** the slightest bit of clothing. **4.** the least bit of anything. **5.** a sudden, sharp pain, esp. in the side. —*v.t., v.i.* **6.** to make stitches (in). **7.** to mend or fasten with stitches.

stitch·er·y (stich′ə rē), *n.* needlework.

St. John's (sānt′ jonz′), the capital of Newfoundland.

stk., stock.

St. Law·rence (sānt′ lôr′əns, lor′-), a river in SE Canada.

St. Lou·is (sānt′ lōō′is, lōō′ē), a port in E Missouri.

stoat (stōt), *n.* the ermine, esp. when in brown summer coat.

stock (stok), *n.* **1.** a supply of goods kept on hand for sale, as by a shop or company. **2.** a quantity of something accumulated, as for future use. **3.** livestock. **4.** the outstanding capital of a corporation, represented by shares in the form of ownership certificates. **5.** the trunk or main stem of a tree. **6.** a type or breed of plant or animal. **7.** ancestry or descent. **8.** the handle of a whip, fishing rod, etc. **9.** the part to which the barrel and mechanism of a rifle are attached. **10.** the raw material from which something is made. **11.** a broth of meat or fish. **12.** Also called **stock′ com′pany.** a theatrical company that puts on a variety of plays. **13. stocks,** a former instrument of punishment consisting of a frame with holes for securing the ankles and wrists. **14. put** or **take stock in,** *Informal.* to put confidence in. **15. take stock, a.** to make an inventory of stock on hand. **b.** to appraise resources or prospects. —*adj.* **16.** kept regularly in stock. **17.** common or ordinary. —*v.t.* **18.** to furnish with a stock or supply. **19.** to furnish with livestock. **20.** to lay up in store. —*v.i.* **21.** to lay in a stock or supply.

stock·ade (sto kād′), *n.* a defensive barrier consisting of strong posts fixed upright in the ground. **2.** an area enclosed by such posts. **3.** a military prison.

stock·brok·er (stok′brō′kər), *n.* a broker who buys and sells securities for the investing public.

stock′ car′, **1.** a standard automobile converted for racing purposes. **2.** a boxcar for carrying livestock.

stock′ exchange′, **1.** a place where securities are bought and sold. **2.** an association of stockbrokers.

stock·hold·er (stok′hōl′dər), *n.* a person who owns stock in a company.

Stock·holm (stok′hōm, hōlm), *n.* the capital of Sweden.

stock·i·net (stok′ə net′), *n.* an elastic machine-knitted fabric for undergarments.

stock·ing (stok′ing), *n.* a closefitting covering for the foot and leg, usually knitted.

stock′ing cap′, a long, tapering, knitted cap with a tassel at the tip.

stock′ mar′ket, **1.** See stock exchange. **2.** the trading in securities, esp. stocks, throughout a nation.

stock·pile (stok′pīl′), *n., v.,* **-piled, -pil·ing.** —*n.* **1.** a supply of material held in reserve, esp. for use during a shortage. —*v.t., v.i.* **2.** to accumulate a stockpile (of).

stock-still (stok′stil′), *adj.* completely motionless.

stock·y (stok′ē), *adj.,* **stock·i·er, stock·i·est.** solidly built and, usually, short. —**stock′i·ly,** *adv.* —**stock′i·ness,** *n.*

stock·yard (stok′yärd′), *n.* a yard with pens and sheds in which livestock is kept temporarily.

stodg·y (stoj′ē), *adj.,* **stodg·i·er, stodg·i·est.** **1.** commonplace and boring. **2.** unduly old-fashioned. **3.** heavy and thick, as food. —**stodg′i·ly,** *adv.* —**stodg′i·ness,** *n.*

Sto·ic (stō′ik), *n.* **1.** a member of an ancient Greek school of philosophy that held that one should be free from passion in order to attain true happiness. **2.** (*l.c.*) a stoical person. —*adj.* **3.** (*l.c.*) stoical. —**sto′i·cism,** *n.*

sto·i·cal (stō′i kəl), *adj.* showing or marked by great self-control in the face of emotion or pain. —**sto′i·cal·ly,** *adv.* —**Syn.** imperturbable, unflinching.

stoke (stōk), *v.t., v.i.,* **stoked, stoking.** **1.** to poke, stir up, and feed (fire). **2.** to tend the fire of (a furnace). —**stok′er,** *n.*

STOL (es′tôl′), *n.* an aircraft capable of becoming airborne after a short takeoff run. [*s(hort) t(ake)o(ff and) l(anding)*]

stole[1] (stōl), *v.* pt. of steal.

stole[2] (stōl), *n.* **1.** a woman's shoulder scarf of fur or other material. **2.** a narrow strip of cloth worn over the shoulders by some clergymen during services.

sto·len (stō′lən), *v.* pp. of steal.

stol·id (stol′id), *adj.* not easily stirred or excited. —**sto·lid·i·ty** (stə lid′i tē), *n.* —**stol′id·ly,** *adv.* —**Syn.** impassive, phlegmatic.

stom·ach (stum′ək), *n.* **1.** a saclike enlargement of the alimentary canal, as in humans, forming an organ for storing and digesting food. **2.** the belly or abdomen. **3.** appetite for food. **4.** desire or liking. —*v.t.* **5.** to take into or retain in the stomach. —**sto·mach·ic** (stō mak′ik), *adj.*

stom·ach·ache (stum′ok āk′), *n.* pain in the stomach or abdomen.

stom·ach·er (stum′ə kər), *n.* an ornamented garment covering the stomach and chest, formerly worn by women.

stomp (stomp), *v.t., v.i.* to tread heavily and noisily (on). —**stomp′-er,** *n.*

stone (stōn), *n., pl.* **stones** for 1–5; **stone** for 6; *v.,* **stoned, ston·ing.** —*n.* **1.** the hard substance, formed from minerals, of which rocks consist. **2.** a piece of rock. **3.** a jewel or gem. **4.** a mineral concretion in the body, as in the gallbladder. **5.** a hard pit or seed, as of a cherry. **6.** the British unit of weight equal to 14 pounds. —*v.i.* **7.** to throw stones at. **8.** to remove stones from, as fruit. —**stone′ware′,** *n.* —**stone′-work′,** *n.*

stone-, a combining form meaning "completely": *stone-deaf.*

Stone′ Age′, the period in human history marked by the use of stone tools.

stoned (stōnd), *adj. Slang.* under the influence of liquor or a drug.

stone′s′ throw′, a short distance.

stone·wall (stōn′wôl′), *v.t., v.i. Informal.* to block, evade, or stall, esp. intentionally.

ston·y (stō′nē), *adj.,* **ston·i·er, ston·i·est.** **1.** full of or covered with stones. **2.** like stone in hardness. **3.** unfeeling or merciless. —**ston′i·ly,** *adv.* —**ston′i·ness,** *n.*

stood (stŏŏd), *v.* pt. and pp. of **stand.**

stooge (stōōj), *n.* **1.** *Informal.* an entertainer who feeds lines to the main comedian. **2.** *Slang.* any underling or subordinate.

stool (stōōl), *n.* **1.** a single seat without arms or a back. **2.** footstool. **3.** *Med.* feces discharged.

stool′ pi′geon, 1. a pigeon used as a decoy. **2.** *Slang.* a person employed as an informer, esp. for the police.

stoop¹ (stōōp), *v.i.* **1.** to bend the body forward and downward. **2.** to carry the head and shoulders habitually bowed forward. **3.** to lower oneself in dignity. —*n.* **4.** the act of stooping. **5.** a stooping posture. —**stoop′ing·ly,** *adv.*

stoop² (stōōp), *n.* a small raised platform approached by steps at a house entrance.

stop (stop), *v.,* **stopped, stop·ping,** *n.* —*v.t.* **1.** to leave off doing or continuing. **2.** to interrupt or check (a course, process, etc.). **3.** to prevent from proceeding or operating. **4.** to block or obstruct (a passage, hole, etc.) by filling in. **5.** to fill the holes in. —*v.i.* **6.** to come to a standstill, as in a journey. **7.** to cease moving or proceeding. **8.** to come to an end. **9. stop by** or **in,** to make a brief visit. **10. stop off,** to stay at some point, esp. on a journey. **11. stop over,** to stop in the course of a journey, as for the night. —*n.* **12.** the act of stopping. **13.** an end or finish. **14.** a stay or sojourn made at a place. **15.** a place where buses stop to pick up passengers. **16.** stopper. **17.** an obstacle or hindrance. **18.** a part of a musical instrument that regulates, as a hole or key. **19.** *Chiefly Brit.* a punctuation mark, esp. a period. —**Syn. 7.** desist, discontinue.

stop·gap (stop′gap′), *n.* a temporary substitute.

stop·light (stop′līt′), *n.* **1.** a taillight that lights up as the driver of a vehicle steps on the brake pedal to slow down or stop. **2.** a traffic light when red to direct traffic to stop.

stop·o·ver (stop′ō′vər), *n.* a brief stop in the course of a journey, as to eat or sleep.

stop·page (stop′ij), *n.* the act or state of being stopped.

stop·per (stop′ər), *n.* something, as a plug or cork, for closing an opening or hole.

stop·ple (stop′əl), *n., v.,* **-pled, -pling.** —*n.* **1.** a stopper for a bottle. —*v.t.* **2.** to close a stopple.

stop·watch (stop′woch′), *n.* a watch with a hand that can be stopped or started at any instant, used to time races.

stor·age (stôr′ij, stôr′-), *n.* **1** the act of storing or state of being stored. **2.** a building or place for storing goods. **3.** the price charged for storing goods.

stor′age bat′tery, an electric battery capable of being recharged by an electric current.

store (stôr, stōr), *n., v.,* **stored, storing.** —*n.* **1.** a retail establishment engaged usually in selling a wide variety of goods: *a grocery store.* **2.** a supply or stock of something. **3. stores,** supplies of food or other requisites. **4.** *Brit.* warehouse. **5.** *Archaic.* great quantity. **6. in store,** in readiness or reserve. **7. set** or **lay store by,** to have high regard for. —*v.t.* **8.** to gather and put away for future use. **9.** to put in a warehouse. **10.** to supply or stock.

store·front (stôr′frunt′, stōr′-), *n.* the side of a store facing a street, usually containing display windows.

store·house (stôr′hous′, stōr′-), *n.* **1.** an abundant supply or source. **2.** *Brit.* warehouse.

store·keep·er (stôr′kē′pər, stōr′-), *n.* a person who owns or operates a store.

store·room (stôr′rōōm′, -rŏŏm′, stōr′-), *n.* a room in which supplies or goods are stored.

sto·rey (stôr′ē, stōr′ē), *n. Brit.* story².

sto·ried (stôr′ēd, stōr′-), *adj.* celebrated in story or legend.

stork (stôrk), *n.* a large wading bird having long legs and a long neck and bill.

storm (stôrm), *n.* **1.** a violent disturbance of the atmosphere causing high winds, often accompanied by rain, snow, or hail. **2.** any outburst of violent or strong emotion. **3.** a violent military assault. —*v.i.* **4.** to blow, rain, snow, or hail with violence. **5.** to rage or complain violently. **6.** to rush angrily. —*v.t.* **7.** to assault violently. —**storm′y,** *adj.* —**storm′i·ly,** *adv.* —**storm′i·ness,** *n.*

sto·ry¹ (stôr′ē, stōr′ē), *n., pl.* **-ries. 1.** a written or spoken account of something that has happened. **2.** a fictitious tale, shorter than a novel. **3.** the plot of a novel, drama, etc. **4.** an anecdote or joke. **5.** *Journalism.* a news report. **6.** *Informal.* a lie.

sto·ry² (stôr′ē, stōr′ē), *n., pl.* **-ries.** a complete horizontal section of a building, having one continuous floor.

sto·ry·tell·er (stôr′ē tel′ər, stōr′-), *n.* a person who tells or writes stories. —**sto′ry·tell′ing,** *n.*

stoup (stōōp), *n.* a basin for holy water, as at the entrance of a church.

stout (stout), *adj.* **1.** thick or bulky in figure. **2.** brave or dauntless. **3.** strong or sturdy. **4.** solid and heavy. —*n.* **5.** a strong, dark beer. —**stout′ly,** *adv.* —**stout′ness,** *n.* —Syn. **1.** corpulent, plump, portly, thickset.

stove¹ (stōv), *n.* a device for heating or cooking that uses a fuel or electricity.

stove² (stōv), *v.* a pt. and pp. of stave.

stove·pipe (stōv′pīp′), *n.* **1.** a metal pipe used to carry away smoke from a stove. **2.** *Informal.* a tall silk hat.

stow (stō), *v.t.* **1.** to store or pack, as in a ship's hold. **2. stow away, a.** to hide away. **b.** to be a stowaway. —**stow′age,** *n.*

stow·a·way (stō′ə wā′), *n.* a person who hides on a ship or airplane in order to obtain free transportation.

STP, a hallucinogenic drug similar to but more potent than LSD.

S.T.P., standard temperature and pressure.

St. Paul, the capital of Minnesota.

St. Pe·ters·burg (pē′tərz bûrg′), a seaport in W Florida.

stra·bis·mus (strə biz′məs), *n.* a disorder of vision due to the turning of one eye or both eyes from the normal position.

strad·dle (strad′°l), *v.,* **-dled, -dling,** *n.* —*v.i., v.t.* **1.** to stand or sit astride (of). **2.** *Informal.* to favor or appear to favor both sides of (an issue). —*n.* **3.** the act of straddling. —**strad′dler,** *n.*

strafe (strāf, sträf), *v.t.,* **strafed, strafing.** to attack with machine-gun fire from an airplane flying low. —**straf′er,** *n.*

strag·gle (strag′əl), *v.i.,* **-gled, -gling. 1.** to wander about in a scattered manner. **2.** to stray from the main course or line of march. **3.** to grow or spread unevenly. —**strag′gler,** *n.* —**strag′gly,** *adj.*

straight (strāt), *adj.* **1.** without a bend, angle, or curve. **2.** exactly vertical or horizontal. **3.** honest or frank. **4.** right or correct, as thinking. **5.** in the proper order or condition. **6.** continuous or unbroken. **7.** thoroughgoing or unreserved. **8.** undiluted or unmixed, as whiskey. **9.** *Slang.* **a.** normal and conventional. **b.** heterosexual. —*adv.* **10.** in a straight manner. **11. straight away** or **off,** immediately or at once. —*n.* **12.** the condition of being straight. **13.** a straight part, as of a racetrack. **14.** *Poker.* a sequence of five cards. —**straight′ly,** *adv.* —**straight′ness,** *n.*

straight·arm (strāt′ärm′), *v.t.* to push (someone) away by holding the arm out straight.

straight·edge (strāt′ej′), *n.* a strip of wood or metal having a straight edge for use in drawing or testing straight lines.

straight·en (strāt′°n), *v.t., v.i.* **1.** to make or become straight. **2. straighten out, a.** to make or set right. **b.** to correct or reform. —**straight′en·er,** *n.*

straight′ face′, a serious facial expression that conceals one's true feelings. —**straight′-faced′,** *adj.*

straight·for·ward (strāt′fôr′wərd), *adj.* **1.** going or directed straight ahead. **2.** honest and frank. —*adv.* **3.** Also, **straight′for′wards.** in a straightforward manner. —**straight′for′ward·ly,** *adv.* —**straight′for′ward·ness,** *n.*

straight′ man′, an entertainer who plays a foil for a comedian.

straight′ time′, 1. regular working time as distinguished from overtime. **2.** pay for such time.

straight·way (strāt′wā′), *adv.* immediately or right away.

strain[1] (strān), *v.t.* **1.** to draw tight or taut. **2.** to exert to the utmost. **3.** to injure or weaken (a muscle, etc.) by overexertion. **4.** to stretch beyond the proper limit. **5.** to pass (liquid) through a filter or sieve. — *v.i.* **6.** to make violent physical efforts. **7.** to filter, percolate, or ooze. —*n.* **8.** the act of straining or state of being strained. **9.** any strong force or pressure. **10.** great effort or striving. **11.** an injury to a muscle or tendon caused by overexertion. **12.** fatiguing pressure caused by worry, hard work, etc. **13.** Often, **strains.** a melody or tune. **14.** a tone or spirit, as of writing.

strain[2] (strān), *n.* **1.** a line of ancestry or descent. **2.** a particular variety of plants or animals. **3.** an inherited characteristic. **4.** a streak or trace. **5.** *Rare.* a kind or sort.

strained (strānd), *adj.* not natural or spontaneous.

strain·er (strā'nər), *n.* any device for straining liquids, as a filter or sieve.

strait (strāt), *n.* **1.** a narrow passage of water connecting two large bodies of water. **2.** Often, **straits.** a difficulty or bad position. —*adj.* **3.** *Archaic.* narrow or strict.

strait·en (strāt'°n), *v.t.* **1.** to put into difficulties, esp. financial ones. **2.** *Archaic.* to make narrow or strict.

strait′ jack′et, a garment made of strong material and designed to bind the arms, as of a violently delirious person.

strait·laced (strāt'lāst'), *adj.* excessively strict in conduct or morality.

strand[1] (strand), *v.t., v.i.* **1.** to drive or run ashore, as a ship. **2.** to leave or be left in a helpless position. —*n.* **3.** *Literary.* a shore or beach.

strand[2] (strand), *n.* **1.** a number of fibers or threads twisted together to form a rope or cord. **2.** a string of pearls or beads.

strange (strānj), *adj.*, **strang·er**, **strang·est.** **1.** strikingly unusual or peculiar. **2.** previously unknown or unfamiliar. **3.** out of place or uneasy. **4.** unaccustomed to or inexperienced in. **5.** *Obs.* distant or reserved. — **strange′ly,** *adv.* —**strange′ness,** *n.* —**Syn. 1.** bizarre, curious, odd. **2.** alien, foreign.

stran·ger (strān'jər), *n.* **1.** a person with whom one is not acquainted. **2.** a newcomer in a place. **3.** a person who is unused to something.

stran·gle (straṅg'gəl), *v.t., v.i.,* **-gled, -gling.** —*v.t.* **1.** to choke to death with the hands or a tightly drawn cord. **2.** to stifle or restrict. —**stran′gler,** *n.*

stran·gu·late (straṅg'gyə lāt'), *v.t.,* **-lat·ed, -lat·ing.** to constrict so as to prevent circulation, as of blood. — **stran′gu·la′tion,** *n.*

strap (strap), *n., v.,* **strapped, strapping.** —*n.* **1.** a narrow strip of flexible material, esp. leather, for fastening or holding things together. —*v.t.* **2.** to fasten or secure with a strap.

strap·less (strap'lis), *adj.* made without shoulder straps, as a garment.

strapped (strapt), *adj. Informal.* lacking money or funds.

strap·ping (strap'iṅg), *adj.* tall and robust.

stra·ta (strā'tə, strat'ə, strä'tə), *n.* a pl. of **stratum.**

strat·a·gem (strat'ə jəm), *n.* **1.** a plan or trick for deceiving an enemy or opponent. **2.** any tricky scheme.

strat·e·gy (strat'i jē), *n., pl.* **-gies. 1.** the science or art of planning and directing large military movements and operations. **2.** skillful use of a stratagem. **3.** a detailed plan for reaching a goal or advantage. — **stra·te·gic** (strə tē'jik), *adj.* —**strate′gi·cal·ly,** *adv.* —**strat′e·gist,** *n.*

strat·i·fy (strat'ə fī'), *v.t., v.i.,* **-fied, -fy·ing.** to form or become arranged in strata or layers. —**strat′i·fi·ca′tion,** *n.*

stra·tig·ra·phy (strə tig'rə fē), *n.* geology dealing with stratified rocks. — **strat·i·graph·ic** (strat'ə graf'ik), *adj.*

stra·to·cu·mu·lus (strā'tō kyōō'myə-ləs, strat'ō-), *n., pl.* **-li** (-lī). a cloud of a class characterized by large dark, rounded masses.

strat·o·sphere (strat'ə sfēr'), *n.* the region of the upper atmosphere extending upward from about 7 miles to about 15 miles above the earth. —**strat′o·spher′ic** (-sfer′ik), *adj.*

stra·tum (strā'təm, strat'əm, strä'təm), *n., pl.* **stra·ta, stra·tums. 1.** a layer of material, often one of a number of parallel layers one upon another. **2.** a single bed of sedimentary rock. **3.** a social level.

stra·tus (strā'təs, strat'əs), *n., pl.* **-ti** (-tī). a cloud of a class characterized by a gray horizontal layer.

Strauss (strous), *n.* **Johann** (yō'hän'), 1825–1899, Austrian composer.

Stra·vin·sky (strə vin'skē), *n.* **I·gor** (ē'gôr), 1882–1971, U.S. composer, born in Russia.

straw (strô), *n.* **1.** a single stalk of wheat, rye, or other grass. **2.** a mass of such stalks. **3.** a tube for sucking up a beverage. **4.** something almost worthless. —*adj.* **5.** of, like. or made of straw. **6.** yellowish in color. **7.** almost worthless. —**straw′y,** *adj.*

straw·ber·ry (strô'ber'ē, -bə rē), *n., pl.* **-ries.** a juicy, pear-shaped berry that grows on a low plant related to the rose. **2.** its plant.

straw′ boss′, *Informal.* a foreman or forewoman with little or no real authority.

straw′ vote′, an unofficial vote taken to obtain a general trend of opinion.

stray (strā), *v.i.* **1.** to leave the proper course or place. **2.** to go astray from a moral course. **3.** to digress or become distracted. —*n.* **4.** a lost or homeless person or animal. —*adj.* **5.** straying or having strayed, as a domestic animal. **6.** casual or unplanned. —**stray′er,** *n.*

streak (strēk), *n.* **1.** a long, narrow mark or band of color. **2.** a layer or vein: *streaks of fat in meat.* **3.** a strain or trace of anything: *a streak of humor* **4.** *Informal.* **a.** a spell or period, as of luck. **b.** an uninterrupted series. —*v.t.* **5.** to mark with streaks. —*v.i.* **6.** to become streaked. **7.** to go or move rapidly. **8.** to engage in the prank of streaking. —**streak′er,** *n.* —**streak′y,** *adj.* —**streak′i·ness,** *n.*

streak·ing (strē′king), *n.* a prank of dashing briefly in the nude in public view.

stream (strēm), *n.* **1.** a flowing body of water, esp. a small river. **2.** a current or flow of air, gas, liquid, etc. **3.** a continuous flow: *a stream of words.* —*v.i.* **4.** to flow in a stream. **5.** to send forth or throw off a stream. **6.** to move or proceed continuously. —*v.t.* **7.** to send forth in a stream. —**stream′y,** *adj.*

stream·er (strē′mər), *n.* **1.** a long, narrow flag or pennant. **2.** a long, flowing ribbon. **3.** a stream of light, esp. from the aurora borealis. **4.** banner (def. 2).

stream·let (strēm′lit), *n.* a small stream.

stream·line (strēm′līn′), *v.,* **-lined, -lining,** *adj.* —*v.t.* **1.** to make streamlined. **2.** to make simpler and more efficient. —*adj.* **3.** streamlined.

stream·lined (strēm′līnd′), *adj.* **1.** having a surface designed to offer the least possible resistance to a current of air or water. **2.** made simpler and more efficient. **3.** modernized or up-to-date.

stream·lin·er (strēm′lī′nər), *n.* a streamlined passenger train.

street (strēt), *n.* **1.** a public road, usually paved, in a city or town. **2.** such a road together with the sidewalks and buildings. **3.** the people who live or work on a street.

street·car (strēt′kär′), *n.* a public vehicle running on rails along the streets, as a trolley car.

street′ the′ater, the presentation of plays by traveling companies on the streets, in parks, etc.

street·walk·er (strēt′wô′kər), *n.* a prostitute who solicits on the streets.

strength (strengkth, strength), *n.* **1.** bodily or muscular power. **2.** mental or moral power. **3.** force in numbers, as of an army. **4.** effectiveness or potency, as of arguments. **5.** power of resisting force, strain, etc. **6.** intensity or richness, as of light or color. **7.** a source of power. **8.** **on the strength of,** on the basis of.

strength·en (strengk′thən, streng′-), *v.t., v.i.* to make or grow stronger. —**strength′en·er,** *n.*

stren·u·ous (stren′yōō əs), *adj.* **1.** requiring vigorous exertion. **2.** zealously active. —**stren′u·ous·ly,** *adv.* —**stren′u·ous·ness,** *n.* —**Syn. 1.** arduous. **2.** energetic.

strep (strep), *n.* *Informal.* streptococcus.

strep′ throat′, a sore throat caused by a streptococcus and characterized by fever, general weakness, etc.

strep·to·coc·cus (strep′tə kok′əs), *n.,* *pl.* **-coc·ci** (-kok′sī). any of several spherical or oval bacteria occurring in pairs or chains and causing scarlet fever, etc. —**strep′to·coc′cal** (-kok′-əl), *adj.*

strep·to·my·cin (strep′tō mī′sin), *n.* an antibiotic produced by a fungus found in soil and used in the treatment of tuberculosis.

stress (stres), *n.* **1.** physical, mental, or emotional tension. **2.** a situation or factor causing this. **3.** importance or significance attached to a thing. **4.** the relative loudness in the pronunciation of a part of a word or phrase. **5.** the physical pressure exerted on one thing by another. **6.** a balanced force that tends to distort a material body. —*v.t.* **7.** to lay stress or importance on. **8.** to give phonetic stress to. **9.** to subject to material stress. —**stress′or,** *n.* —**Syn. 7.** accent, emphasize.

stretch (strech), *v.t.* **1.** to draw out to full or greater length. **2.** to hold out or extend. **3.** to cause to extend or spread. **4.** to force or make serve beyond the normal or proper limits. —*v.i.* **5.** to lie at full length. **6.** to extend over a distance or area or in a particular direction. **7.** to extend the limbs and contract the muscles. **8.** to become stretched, as any elastic material. —*n.* **9.** the act of stretching or state of being stretched. **10.** an unbroken space or expanse. **11.** an uninterrupted period of time. **12.** the homestretch of a racetrack. **13.** elastic quality. —*adj.* **14.** capable of being stretched elastically. —**stretch′a·ble,** *adj.* —**stretch′y,** *adj.*

stretch·er (strech′ər), *n.* **1.** a canvas-covered, bedlike frame for carrying the sick, wounded, or dead. **2.** a person or thing that stretches.

strew (strōō), *v.t.*, **strewed, strewed** or **strewn** (strōōn), **strew·ing.** 1. to let fall in separate pieces over a surface. 2. to cover with something scattered. 3. to be scattered over (a surface).

stri·a (strī′ə), *n., pl.* **stri·ae** (strī′ē). 1. a slight or narrow furrow or groove. 2. any of a series of parallel lines on the surface of a crystal. —**stri′at·ed** (-ā tid) *adj.* —**stri·a′tion,** *n.*

strick·en (strik′ən), *adj.* 1. a pp. of **strike.** 2. beset or afflicted, as with disease or sorrow. 3. hit or wounded, as by a weapon. —**strick′en·ly,** *adv.*

strict (strikt), *adj.* 1. rigid in following or observing rules. 2. rigidly enforced or maintained. 3. narrowly or carefully limited. 4. absolute or complete: *in strict confidence.* —**strict′ly,** *adv.* —**strict′ness,** *n.* —Syn. 1. rigorous, severe, stringent. 3. exact, precise.

stric·ture (strik′chər), *n.* 1. an adverse criticism. 2. an abnormal contraction of any bodily passage. 3. a restriction or limitation. —**stric′tured,** *adj.*

stride (strīd), *v.,* **strode, strid·den** (strid′ən), **strid·ing,** *n.* —*v.i., v.t.* 1. to walk with long steps, as with vigor or haste. 2. to cross over in one long step. —*n.* 3. a long step. 4. the distance covered by such a step. 5. a striding gait. 6. a step forward, as in progress. 7. **take in (one's) stride,** to deal with calmly. —**strid′er,** *n.*

stri·dent (strīd′ənt), *adj.* making a loud, harsh sound. —**stri′den·cy,** *n.* —**stri′dent·ly,** *adv.*

strife (strīf), *n.* 1. vigorous or bitter conflict or discord. 2. a struggle or clash between rivals.

strike (strīk), *v.,* **struck, struck** or (*esp. for 13, 14*) **strick·en, strik·ing,** *n.* —*v.t.* 1. to deal a blow to, as with the fist. 2. to attack (a target). 3. to produce (fire, etc.) by friction. 4. to cause (a match) to ignite by friction. 5. to hit into or against: *The ship struck a rock.* 6. to enter the mind of: *A happy thought struck him.* 7. to come upon or find (oil, ore, etc.) by digging or drilling. 8. to reach by agreement: *to strike a bargain.* 9. *Naut.* to lower (a sail, mast, or flag). 10. to stamp (a coin, etc.) by punching. 11. to cancel or cross out. 12. to indicate (the hour or day) by a stroke or strokes, as a clock: *to strike 12.* 13. to afflict suddenly, as with disease. 14. to overwhelm emotionally, as with fear. 15. to assume (an attitude or posture). 16. to come upon or reach, as in traveling. 17. to estimate (a mean or average). —*v.i.* 18. to deal a blow. 19. to make an attack. 20. to hit or collide. 21. to come suddenly or unexpectedly. 22. to sound by percussion: *The clock strikes.* 23. to proceed or advance. 24. to leave off work in order to have certain demands met. 25. (of fish) to swallow or take the bait. 26. **strike out, a.** *Baseball.* to put out or be put out by a strikeout.. **b.** to erase or cross out. **c.** to go or set forth.. 27. **strike up, a.** to begin to play or to sing. **b.** to bring into being. —*n.* 28. the act of striking. 29. a deliberate stoppage of work until certain demands are met. 30. *Baseball.* **a.** a pitch that is swung at and missed by the batter. **b.** a pitch that passes through the strike zone and is not swung at by the batter. 31. *Bowling.* the knocking down of all the pins with the first bowl. 32. the discovery of a rich supply of oil or ore. 33. a planned military attack. —**strik′er,** *n.*

strike·break·er (strīk′brā′kər), *n.* a person who takes part in breaking a strike, as by replacing a striking worker.

strike·out (strīk′out′), *n. Baseball.* an out made by a batter to whom three strikes have been charged.

strike′ zone′, *Baseball.* the area above home plate between the batter's knees and shoulders.

strik·ing (strī′king), *adj.* 1. vividly impressive. 2. very conspicuous. —**strik′ing·ly,** *adv.* —Syn. 2. salient.

string (string), *n., v.,* **strung, string·ing.** —*n.* 1. a slender cord or thick thread for binding or tying. 2. a number of objects threaded on a cord: *a string of pearls.* 3. any series of things set close together. 4. (in a musical instrument) a tightly stretched cord or wire that sounds when plucked or struck. 5. **strings,** stringed instruments, esp. those played with a bow. 6. a fiber in a plant. 7. Usually, **strings.** *Informal.* limitations on a proposal: *no strings attached.* 8. **pull strings,** to gain one's objectives by means of influential friends, associates, etc. —*v.t.* 9. to furnish with strings. 10. to stretch (a cord, etc.) from one point to another. 11. to thread on or as on a string: *to string beads.* 12. to arrange in a line or series. 13. to tie or adorn with strings. 14. to strip the strings from: *to string beans.* —**string′y,** *adj.* —**string′i·ness,** *n.*

string′ bean′, a bean whose long, slender pods are used as a vegetable.

stringed (stringd), *adj.* fitted with strings: *a five-stringed banjo.*

strin·gent (strin′jənt), *adj.* 1. rigorously binding or exacting. 2. short in investment funds. —**strin′gent·ly,** *adv.* —**strin′gen·cy,** *n.*

string·er (striṅg′ər), *n.* **1.** a long horizontal timber connecting upright posts. **2.** a part-time newspaper or broadcast correspondent.

strip¹ (strip), *v.,* **stripped, strip·ping.** —*v.t.* **1.** to pull off the covering or clothing from. **2.** to take away or remove. **3.** to clear out or empty, as by removing the contents. **4.** to deprive or divest, as of rank. **5.** to rob or plunder. —*v.i.* **6.** to remove one's clothes. —**strip′per,** *n.*

strip² (strip), *n.* **1.** a long, narrow, flat piece, usually of uniform width. **2.** an airstrip.

stripe (strīp), *n., v.,* **striped, strip·ing.** —*n.* **1.** a band or streak different in color or material from the rest of a surface or thing. **2.** a strip of braid worn on a military or other uniform to indicate rank, service, etc. **3.** sort or kind. —*v.t.* **4.** to mark or furnish with stripes. —**striped** (strīpt, strī′pid), *adj.* —**strip′er,** *n.*

strip·ling (strip′liṅg), *n. Chiefly Literary.* a growing youth.

strip′ mine′, a mine in an open pit formed by removing the earth and rock covering a mineral deposit. —**strip′-mine,** *v.t., adj.* —**strip′ min′er.** —**strip′ min′ing.**

strip·tease (strip′tēz′), *n.* a burlesque act in which a woman dancer removes her garments one at a time to the accompaniment of music. —**strip′teas′er,** *n.*

strive (strīv), *v.i.,* **strove, striv·en** (striv′ən) or **strived, striv·ing. 1.** to make a strong effort. **2.** to struggle vigorously. —**striv′er,** *n.*

strobe (strōb), *n.* **1.** a device used to provide an extremely short flash for high-speed photography. **2.** *Informal.* stroboscope.

stro·bo·scope (strō′bə skōp′, strob′ə-), *n.* an optical device using intermittent illumination to make rapidly moving objects appear to slow down. —**stro′bo·scop′ic** (-skop′ik), *adj., n.*

strode (strōd), *v.* pt. of **stride.**

stroke¹ (strōk), *n., v.,* **stroked, stroking.** —*n.* **1.** the act of striking a blow. **2.** the sound of a striking clock. **3.** an attack of apoplexy or paralysis. **4.** one of a number of complete movements, as in swimming, rowing, etc. **5.** a movement of a pen, pencil, brush, etc. **6.** a mark made by such a movement. **7.** *Brit.* slash (def. 7). **8.** a feat or achievement: *a stroke of genius.* **9.** a sudden or chance action or event, as of luck or fortune. —*v.t.* **10.** to set the stroke for the crew of (a boat).

stroke² (strōk), *v.,* **stroked, strok·ing,** *n.* —*v.t.* **1.** to rub gently, as in soothing or caressing. —*n.* **2.** a stroking movement.

stroll (strōl), *v.i.* **1.** to walk leisurely or idly. —*v.t.* **2.** to walk leisurely along or through. —*n.* **3.** a leisurely walk. —**Syn. 1.** ramble, saunter.

stroll·er (strō′lər), *n.* **1.** a person who strolls. **2.** a chairlike carriage in which a baby rides sitting up.

strong (strôṅg, stroṅg), *adj.,* **stronger** (strôṅg′gər, stroṅg′-), **strong·est** (strôṅg′gist, stroṅg′-). **1.** physically vigorous or powerful. **2.** in good health. **3.** mentally powerful or vigorous. **4.** of great moral power. **5.** powerful in influence, authority, etc. **6.** of great effectiveness or potency: *strong arguments.* **7.** able to resist wear, attack, etc. **8.** strenuous or energetic: *strong efforts.* **9.** intense, as light or color. **10.** having a concentrated flavor or aroma: *strong tea.* **11.** of a designated number: *Marines 20,000 strong.* —**strong′ly,** *adv.* —**Syn. 1, 2.** stalwart, sturdy.

strong-arm (strôṅg′ärm′, stroṅg′-), *Informal.* —*adj.* **1.** using physical force or violence. —*v.t.* **2.** to use force or violence upon.

strong·box (strôṅg′boks′, stroṅg′-), *n.* a small, very sturdy box for storing valuables or money.

strong·hold (strôṅg′hōld′, stroṅg′-), *n.* **1.** a well-fortified place. **2.** a center of influence and support.

strong·man (strôṅg′man′), *n.* a political leader with dictatorial power.

strong·room (strôṅg′rōōm′, -rŏŏm′, stroṅg′-), *n. Brit.* a fireproof, burglarproof room in which valuables are kept.

stron·ti·um (stron′shē əm, -shəm, -tē əm), *n. Chem.* a metallic element whose compounds resemble those of calcium. *Symbol:* Sr; *at. wt.:* 87.62; *at. no.:* 38.

strop (strop), *n., v.,* **stropped, stropping.** —*n.* **1.** a thick leather strap used for sharpening razors. —*v.t.* **2.** to sharpen on a strop.

stro·phe (strō′fē), *n.* a section of a poem, esp. of an ancient Greek ode. —**stroph′ic,** *adj.*

strove (strōv), *v.* pt. of **strive.**

struck (struk), *v.* **1.** pt. and a pp. of **strike.** —*adj.* **2.** shut down or affected by a labor strike.

struc·ture (struk′chər), *n., v.,* **-tured, -tur·ing.** —*n.* **1.** the manner in which something is constructed. **2.** something constructed, as a building. **3.** the manner in which the elements of anything are organized or interrelated. **4.** anything composed of organized or interrelated elements. —*v.t.* **5.** to give a structure to. —**struc′tur·al,** *adj.* —**struc′tur·al·ly,** *adv.*

stru·del (strōōd′əl), *n.* a paper-thin sheet of dough rolled up with fruit or cheese and baked. [< G: whirlpool]

strug·gle (strug'əl), v., **-gled, -gling,** n.
—v.i. **1.** to contend resolutely, as
with an adversary or a problem. **2.**
to advance with violent effort. —n.
3. a resolute fight or competition. **4.**
a violent effort. —**strug'gler,** n. —
Syn. 3, 4. conflict, contest, strife.

strum (strum), v.t., v.i., **strummed,**
strum·ming. to pluck (a stringed
instrument) lightly or casually.

strum·pet (strum'pit), n. Archaic. a
prostitute.

strung (strung), v. pt. and pp. of
string.

strut[1] (strut), v., **strut·ted, strut·ting,**
n. —v.i. **1.** to walk in a vain,
pompous way. —n. **2.** a strutting
walk. —Syn. swagger.

strut[2] (strut), n. a brace set at an
angle into an architectural framework for support.

strych·nine (strik'nin, -nēn, -nīn), n. a
very poisonous substance sometimes
used in medicine as a stimulant.

stub (stub), n., v., **stubbed, stub·bing.**
—n. **1.** a short remaining piece, as
of a pencil, candle, or cigar. **2.** a
short detachable part, as of a check
or ticket, kept as a record. **3.**
a short projecting part. **4.** a tree
stump. —v.t. **5.** to strike (one's toe)
accidentally against a projecting
object. **6.** to put out (a cigarette)
by crushing.

stub·ble (stub'əl), n. **1.** the stumps of
grain left in the ground after harvest.
2. any short rough growth, as of
beard —**stub'bly,** adj.

stub·born (stub'ərn), adj. **1.** unreasonably obstinate in one's ways. **2.**
strong and purposeful. **3.** hard to
handle, manage, or treat. —**stub'-**
born·ly, adv. —**stub'born·ness,** n.
—Syn. **1.** dogged, headstrong, perverse. **2.** resolute. **3.** intractable.

stub·by (stub'ē), adj., **-bi·er, -bi·est.**
short and thick or broad. —**stub'-**
bi·ness, n.

stuc·co (stuk'ō), n., pl. **-coes, -cos,** v.,
-coed, -co·ing. —n. **1.** a plasterlike
material used to coat outside walls.
—v.t **2.** to cover with stucco.

stuck (stuk), v. pt. and pp. of **stick**[2].

stuck-up (stuk'up'), adj. Informal.
snobbishly conceited.

stud[1] (stud), n., v., **stud·ded, stud-**
ding. —n. **1.** a small knob or nail
head projecting from a surface or
part, esp. as an ornament. **2.** a
buttonlike object used to fasten
men's formal shirts. **3.** one of a
number of upright beams in a wall
forming a frame for an outer surface
of wood or plaster. —v.t. **4.** to set
or adorn with studs. **5.** to lie scattered over.

stud[2] (stud), n. a male animal, esp.
a horse (**stud'horse'**), kept for breeding purposes.

stud., student.

stud·book (stud'book'), n. a book
giving the pedigree of horses.

stud·ding (stud'ing), n. **1.** studs, as
in a wall. **2.** material for use as
studs.

stu·dent (stood'ənt, styood'-), n. **1.** a
person who studies, esp. at a secondary school or college. **2.** any person
who studies or carefully examines a
subject.

stud·ied (stud'ēd), adj. **1.** marked by
conscious effort **2.** carefully delib-
erated. —**stud'ied·ly,** adv.

stu·di·o (stoo'dē·ō, styoo'-), n., pl.
-di·os. 1. the workroom of an artist,
as a painter or sculptor. **2.** a place
for instruction in an art, as dancing.
3. a place equipped for broadcasting
radio or television programs, making
phonograph records, etc. **4.** a place
where motion pictures are made.

stu·di·ous (stoo'dē·əs, styoo'-), adj. **1.**
devoted to study. **2.** giving careful
attention —**stu'di·ous·ly,** adv. —
stu'di·ous·ness, n.

stud·y (stud'ē), n., pl. **stud·ies,** v.,
stud·ied, stud·y·ing. —n. **1.** the
acquisition of knowledge, as by reading or reflection **2.** Often, **studies.**
work at school or college. **3.** a detailed examination and analysis of
a subject. **4.** a branch of learning
or knowledge. **5.** zealous endeavor
or deep thought. **6.** a room set apart
for reading or writing. —v.i. **7.** to
set oneself to learn. **8.** to take a
course of study, as at college. **9.** to
think deeply. —v.t. **10.** to set oneself
to learn (a subject). **11.** to examine
or investigate carefully. **12.** to read
carefully or intently. —**stud'i·er,** n.

stuff (stuf), n. **1.** the material of
which anything is made. **2.** material
of some unspecified kind. **3.** things
or belongings. **4.** inward character
or qualities. **5.** Informal. a special
skill: to do one's stuff. **6.** worthless
things or matter. **7.** worthless or
foolish ideas, talk, or writing. **8.**
Brit. woolen fabric. —v.t. **9.** to fill
up. **10.** to fill or cram with food.
11. to fill with stuffing. **12.** to
thrust or cram into an opening or
container. **13.** to pack tightly. **14.**
to stop up or plug. —v.i. **15.** to eat
gluttonously.

stuffed' shirt', Informal. a pompous,
self-satisfied, and inflexible person.

stuff·ing (stuf'ing), n. **1.** seasoned
bread crumbs or other filling used
to stuff poultry or other food. **2.**
material used to fill a mattress, etc.

stuff·y (stuf'ē), adj., **stuff·i·er, stuff-**
i·est. 1. poorly ventilated. **2.** stopped
up or feeling stopped up: a stuffy
nose. **3.** dull or boring. **4.** smug and
pompous. —**stuff'i·ly,** adv. —**stuff'-**
i·ness, n.

stul·ti·fy (stul'tə fī'), *v.t.*, **-fied, -fy·ing.** 1. to make appear foolish or ridiculous. 2. to make futile or ineffectual. —**stul'ti·fi·ca'tion,** *n.*

stum·ble (stum'bəl), *v.,* **-bled, -bling,** *n.* —*v.i.* 1. to trip or stagger while walking or running. 2. to walk or go unsteadily. 3. to make a slip or blunder. 4. to act or speak in a confused, hesitating way. 5. to find or come upon by chance. —*n.* 6. the act of stumbling. —**stum'bler,** *n.* —**stum'bling·ly,** *adv.*

stum'bling block', an obstacle or hindrance, as to progress.

stump (stump), *n.* 1. the lower end of a tree or plant left after the main part falls or is cut off. 2. the part of a limb of the body remaining after the rest has been cut off. 3. a platform for making political campaign speeches. —*v.t.* 4. to make completely at a loss: *This riddle stumps me.* 5. to make political campaign speeches to or in. —*v.i.* 6. to walk heavily or clumsily. 7. to make political campaign speeches. —**stump'er,** *n.* —**stump'y,** *adj.*

stun (stun), *v.t.,* **stunned, stun·ning.** 1. to daze or make unconscious, as by a blow or fall. 2. to amaze or shock.

stung (stung), *v.* pt. and pp. of **sting.**

stunk (stungk), *v.* a pt. and pp. of **stink.**

stun·ning (stun'ing), *adj.* 1. *Informal.* strikingly beautiful or attractive. 2. making unconscious.

stunt¹ (stunt), *v.t.* to stop or slow down the growth or development of. —**stunt'ed·ness,** *n.*

stunt² (stunt), *n.* 1. a display of skill or daring. 2. an act or trick to get attention. —*v.i.* 3. to do a stunt.

stu·pe·fy (stōō'pə fī', styōō'-), *v.t.,* **-fied, -fy·ing.** 1. to dull the sense of. 2. to overwhelm with amazement. —**stu'pe·fa'cient** (-fā'shənt), *adj.* —**stu'pe·fac'tion** (-fak'shən), *n.*

stu·pen·dous (stōō pen'dəs, styōō-), *adj.* 1. immensely astounding. 2. amazingly large or great. —**stu·pen'dous·ly,** *adv.*

stu·pid (stōō'pid, styōō'-), *adj.* 1. mentally slow or dull. 2. senselessly foolish. 3. tediously dull or uninteresting. —**stu·pid'i·ty,** *n.* —**stu'pid·ly,** *adv.* —**Syn.** 2. asinine, inane, witless.

stu·por (stōō'pər, styōō'-), *n.* 1. a dazed or stunned condition. 2. mental torpor or apathy. —**stu'por·ous,** *adj.*

stur·dy (stûr'dē), *adj.,* **-di·er, -di·est.** 1. physically strong and healthy. 2. solid in construction or structure. 3. courageous or indomitable. —**stur'di·ly,** *adv.* —**stur'di·ness,** *n.*

stur·geon (stûr'jən), *n.* a large food fish valued as a source of caviar.

stut·ter (stut'ər), *v.i., v.t.* 1. to speak or say with spasmodic interruptions and repetitions of syllables or sounds. —*n.* 2. the act of stuttering. —**stut'ter·er,** *n.* —**stut'ter·ing·ly,** *adv.*

sty¹ (stī), *n., pl.* **sties.** 1. a pen for pigs. 2. any filthy place.

sty² (stī), *n., pl.* **sties.** an inflamed swelling on the edge of the eyelid.

style (stīl), *n., v.,* **styled, styl·ing.** —*n.* 1. a particular manner of writing, painting, speaking, building, etc., esp. when it is characteristic of a person, group, or period. 2. elegance or luxury. 3. grace or polish in a person's manners or actions. 4. mode or fashion, esp. in dress. 5. the rules according to which printed matter is spelled, punctuated, or arranged. 6. the slender stalk of a pistil. 7. a pointed instrument used in ancient times for writing on waxed tablets. 8. *Rare.* a formal or recognized title. —*v.t.* 9. to design in accordance with a given or new style. 10. to call or name. —**styl'ing,** *n.*

styl·er (stī'lər), *n.* 1. an electric appliance for setting or styling the hair. 2. a person or thing that styles.

styl·ish (stī'lish), *adj.* conforming to the present style, esp. in dress. —**styl'ish·ly,** *adv.* —**styl'ish·ness,** *n.* —**Syn.** chic fashionable, smart.

styl·ist (stī'list), *n.* a master of style, esp. in writing or speaking. —**sty·lis'tic,** *adj.* —**sty·lis'ti·cal·ly,** *adv.*

styl·ize (stī'līz), *v.t.,* **-ized, -iz·ing.** to design or depict according to a particular style, usually sacrificing realism.

sty·lus (stī'ləs), *n., pl.* **-li** (-lī), **-lus·es.** 1. a pointed pen used to make stencils, etc. 2. a needle used for cutting a phonograph record. 3. a phonograph needle. 4. style (def. 7).

sty·mie (stī'mē), *v.,* **-mied, -mie·ing.** —*n.* 1. *Golf.* an instance of a ball's lying on a direct line between the cup and the ball of an opponent about to putt. —*v.t.* 2. to block or thwart. Also, **sty'my.**

styp·tic (stip'tik), *adj.* capable of checking bleeding, as a drug. —**styp'sis,** *n.*

sty·rene (stī'rēn, stēr'ēn), *n.* a liquid that polymerizes to a transparent material.

Sty·ro·foam (stī'rə fōm'), *n. Trademark.* a light, durable polystyrene foam used as packing material.

Styx (stiks), *n. Class. Myth.* a river in Hades over which the souls of the dead must cross. —**Styg·i·an** (stij'ē ən), *adj.*

suave (swäv) adj. smoothly agreeable or polite. —**suave′ly**, adv. —**suav′i·ty**, **suave′ness**, n. —Syn. polished, sophisticated, urbane.

sub (sub), n., v., **subbed**, **sub·bing**. Informal. —n. 1. submarine. 2. substitute. —v.i. 3. to act as a substitute for another.

sub-, a prefix meaning: **a.** below: *substandard*. **b.** beneath: *substratum*. **c.** secondary: *subcommittee*. **d.** subordinate: *subaltern*. **e.** nearly: *subtropical*.

sub., 1. subscription. 2. substitute. 3. suburb. 4. suburban. 5. subway.

sub·al·tern (sub ôl′tərn), n. Brit. Army. a commissioned officer below the rank of captain.

sub·a·tom·ic (sub′ə tom′ik), adj. 1. of a process that occurs within an atom. 2. noting particles contained in an atom.

sub·com·mit·tee (sub′kə mit′ē), n. a secondary committee appointed out of a main committee.

sub·com·pact (sub′kom′pakt), n. an automobile smaller than a compact.

sub·con·scious (sub kon′shəs), adj. 1. existing or operating in the mind beneath or beyond consciousness. —n. 2. subconscious mental processes. —**sub·con′scious·ly**, adv. —**sub·con′scious·ness**, n.

sub·con·ti·nent (sub kon′t′nənt, sub′kon′-), n. a subdivision of a continent. —**sub′con·ti·nen′tal**, adj.

sub·con·tract (n. sub kon′trakt, sub′kon′-; v. sub′kon trakt′), n. 1. a secondary contract made according to the terms of another contract. —v.t., v.i. 2. to make a subcontract (for). —**sub·con′trac·tor**, n.

sub·cul·ture (sub′kul′chər), n. a group having social traits distinctive enough to distinguish it from others within the same society.

sub·cu·ta·ne·ous (sub′kyoo tā′nē əs), adj. 1. lying under the skin, as tissue. 2. situated or introduced under the skin. —**sub′cu·ta′ne·ous·ly**, adv.

sub·deb (sub′deb′), n. Informal. a girl soon to be a debutante.

sub·di·vide (sub′di vīd′, sub′di vīd′), v.t., v.i., **-vid·ed**, **-vid·ing**. 1. to divide into smaller parts. 2. to divide (a plot of land) into building lots. —**sub′di·vi′sion**, n.

sub·due (səb doo′, -dyoo′), v.t., **-dued**, **-du·ing**. 1. to conquer and bring into subjection. 2. to control or calm. 3. to tone down or soften. —Syn. 1. defeat, subjugate, vanquish.

subj., 1. subject. 2. subjunctive.

sub·ject (n., adj. sub′jikt; v. səb jekt′), n. 1. something or someone that forms the basis of a discussion, writing, painting, etc. 2. a branch of knowledge as a course of study. 3. Gram. the part of a sentence or clause that performs or, in the passive voice, receives the action of the verb. 4. a person who owes allegiance to, or is under the domination of, a monarchical state. 5. a person who is treated or experimented upon by others. —adj. 6. being under domination or control. 7. open or exposed: *subject to ridicule*. 8. being dependent upon or influenced by something: *This plan is subject to our approval*. 9. liable or prone: *subject to headaches*. —v.t. 10. to cause to undergo. 11. to make open, liable, or exposed. 12. to subjugate. —**sub·jec′tion**, n.

sub·jec·tive (səb jek′tiv), adj. 1. belonging to the thinking subject rather than to the object of thought. 2. relying upon one's personal feelings or opinions. —**sub·jec′tive·ly**, adv. —**sub·jec·tiv·i·ty** (sub′jek tiv′i tē), **sub·jec′tive·ness**, n.

---

sub′a·cute′, adj.
sub′a·gen·cy, n., pl. -cies.
sub′a′gent, n.
sub′al·li′ance, n.
sub′al′pine, adj.
sub′a′que·ous, adj.
sub′ar′e·a, n.
sub′as·sem′bly, n.
sub′as·so′ci·a′tion, n.
sub′av′er·age, adj.
sub′base′ment, n.
sub′branch′, n.
sub′breed′, n.
sub·cat′e·go′ry, n., pl. -ries.
sub′cell′, n.
sub′cel′lar, n.
sub′chap′ter, n.
sub′chief′, n.

sub′civ·i·li·za′tion, n.
sub′class′, n.
sub′clas·si·fi·ca′tion, n.
sub′clas′si·fy′, v.t., -fied, -fy·ing.
sub′clause′, n.
sub·clin′i·cal, adj.
sub′com·mand′er, n.
sub′com·mis′sion, n.
sub′com·mis′sion·er, n.
sub·coun′cil, n.
sub·cra′ni·al, adj.
sub′cu·ra′tor, n.
sub·dea′con, n.
sub·deb′u·tante′, n.
sub′def·i·ni′tion, n.
sub′de·part′ment, n.
sub′de·part·men′tal, adj.
sub·de′pot, n.

sub′di·a·lect′, n.
sub′di·rec′tor, n.
sub′dis·ci·pline, n.
sub′dis·tinc′tion, n.
sub′dis′trict, n.
sub·ed′i·tor, n.
sub·en′try, n., pl. -tries.
sub·fam′i·ly, n.
sub′floor′, n.
sub·frac′tion, n.
sub·frac′tion·al, adj.
sub′freez′ing, adj.
sub·func′tion, n.
sub·ge′nus, n.
sub·gla′cial, adj.
sub′group′, n.
sub′head′, n.
sub′head′ing, n.
sub·hu′man, adj.
sub·i′tem, n.

sub′ject mat′ter, the substance of a discussion, writing, etc., as distinguished from its form or style.

sub·join (səb join′), *v.t.* to add at the end, as of something written.

sub ju·di·ce (sub jōō′di sē′), *Latin.* awaiting judicial determination.

sub·ju·gate (sub′jə gāt′), *v.t.,* **-gat·ed, -gat·ing.** to bring under subjection or domination. —**sub′ju·ga′tion,** *n.* —**sub′ju·ga′tor,** *n.*

sub·junc·tive (səb jungk′tiv), *Gram.* —*adj.* **1.** noting the mood of a verb used to express a supposition, possibility, wish, etc. —*n.* **2. a.** the subjunctive mood. **b.** a verb form in this mood.

sub·lease (*n.* sub′lēs′; *v.* sub lēs′), *n., v.,* **-leased, -leas·ing.** —*n.* **1.** a lease granted by a person who is himself or herself a lessee. —*v.t.* **2.** to give or take a sublease of.

sub·let (sub let′), *v.t.,* **-let, -let·ting. 1.** to sublease. **2.** to let under a subcontract.

sub·li·mate (sub′lə māt′), *v.t.,* **-mat·ed, -mat·ing. 1.** to redirect (impulses or libido) to more socially constructive ends. **2.** to sublime. —**sub′li·ma′tion,** *n.*

sub·lime (sə blīm′), *adj., v.,* **-limed, -lim·ing.** —*adj.* **1.** elevated or lofty, as in thought. **2.** inspiring awe or veneration. —*v.t.* **3.** to change (a solid substance) by heat to a gas, which on cooling returns to a solid form again. —**sub·lime′ly,** *adv.* —**sub·lim′i·ty** (-blim′i tē), **sub·lime′ness,** *n.* —**Syn. 1.** exalted, noble.

sub·lim·i·nal (sub lim′ə n°l, -lī′mə-), *adj.* existing or operating below the threshold of consciousness. —**sub·lim′i·nal·ly,** *adv.*

sub·lu·nar·y (sub′lōō ner′ē, sub lōō′-nə rē), *adj.* situated beneath the moon. Also, **sub·lu′nar** (-nər).

sub·ma·chine′ gun′ (sub′mə shēn′), a lightweight automatic or semiautomatic gun, fired from the shoulder or hip.

sub·mar·gin·al (sub mär′jə n°l), *adj.* below a required minimum.

sub·ma·rine (*n.* sub′mə rēn′, sub′mə-rēn′; *adj.* sub′mə rēn′), *n.* **1.** a warship designed to operate under the sea. **2.** See **hero sandwich.** —*adj.* **3.** living, growing, or operating under water, esp. the sea.

sub·merge (səb mûrj′), *v.t., v.i.,* **-merged, -merg·ing. 1.** to sink or plunge beneath the surface of water or any liquid. **2.** to cover or overflow with water. —**sub·mer′gence,** *n.* —**sub·mer′gi·ble,** *adj.* —**sub·mer′gi·bil′i·ty,** *n.*

sub·merse (səb mûrs′), *v.t.,* **-mersed, -mers·ing.** to submerge. —**sub·mers′i·bil′i·ty,** *n.* —**sub·mers′i·ble,** *adj.* —**sub·mer′sion,** *n.*

sub·mi·cro·scop·ic (sub′mī krə skop′-ik), *adj.* too small to be seen through a microscope.

sub·min·i·a·ture (sub min′ē ə chər), *adj.* smaller than miniature. —**sub-min′i·a·tur·ize′** (-chə rīz′), *v.t.*

sub·mit (səb mit′), *v.,* **-mit·ted, -mit·ting.** —*v.t.* **1.** to yield (oneself) to the power of another. **2.** to present for consideration. **3.** to present as an opinion. —*v.i.* **4.** to yield oneself to the power of another. —**sub·mis′-sion,** *n.* —**sub·mis′sive,** *adj.* —**Syn. 4.** comply, obey, surrender.

sub·nor·mal (sub nôr′məl), *adj.* below the normal, esp. in intelligence. —**sub′nor·mal′i·ty,** *n.*

sub·or·bit·al (sub ôr′bi t°l), *adj.* falling short of a complete orbit, as a spaceflight.

sub·or·di·nate (*adj., n.* sə bôr′d°nit; *v.* sə bôr′d°nāt′), *adj., n., v.,* **-nat·ed, -nat·ing.** —*adj.* **1.** placed in a lower order or rank. **2.** less important. **3.** under the authority of a superior. **4.** *Gram.* syntactically dependent on other forms: *a subordinate clause.* —*n.* **5.** a subordinate person or thing. —*v.t.* **6.** to put in a subordinate position. —**sub·or′di·nate·ly,** *adv.* —**sub·or′di·na′tion,** *n.*

sub·orn (sə bôrn′), *v.t.* to induce (a witness) unlawfully to commit a misdeed, as perjury. —**sub·or·na·tion** (sub′ôr nā′shən), *n.*

sub·poe·na (sə pē′nə), *n., v.,* **-naed, -na·ing.** —*n.* **1.** a writ for the summoning of witnesses to a court or legislative body. —*v.t.* **2.** to serve with a subpoena. Also, **sub·pe′na.**

sub ro·sa (sub rō′zə), *Latin.* secretly or privately.

sub·scribe (səb skrīb′), *v.t., v.i.,* **-scribed, -scrib·ing. 1.** to obtain a subscription, as to a magazine. **2.** to give or pledge (money), as a contribution or investment. **3.** to sign one's name to (a document), as in approval. **4.** to give one's consent (to). —**sub·scrib′er,** *n.*

sub·script (sub′skript), *n.* a small letter, number, or symbol written or printed low on a line of text.

---

sub·scrip·tion (səb skrip′shən), n. 1. the right to receive a number of issues of a periodical for a sum of money paid. 2. a sum of money subscribed. 3. the act of subscribing.

sub·se·quent (sub′sə kwənt), adj. occurring or coming later or after. —**sub′se·quent·ly,** adv.

sub·ser·vi·ent (səb sûr′vē ənt), adj. 1. servilely submissive. 2. useful or helpful in serving a higher purpose or goal. —**sub·ser′vi·ence, sub·ser′vi·en·cy,** n. —**sub·ser′vi·ent·ly,** adv.

sub·set (sub′set′), n. Math. a set made of elements of a larger set.

sub·side (səb sīd′), v.i. -sid·ed, -sid·ing. 1. to sink to a low or lower level. 2. to become quiet, calm, or less active. —**sub·sid′ence,** n. —Syn. 2. abate, diminish, wane.

sub·sid·i·ar·y (səb sid′ē er′ē), adj., n., pl. -ar·ies. —adj. 1. serving to assist or supplement. 2. subordinate or secondary. —n. 3. a company owned or controlled by another company. 4. a subsidiary thing or person.

sub·si·dize (sub′si dīz′), v.t., -dized, -diz·ing. to furnish or aid with a subsidy. —**sub′si·di·za′tion,** n.

sub·si·dy (sub′si dē), n., pl. -dies. a direct financial aid, esp. by a government, as to farmers or railroads.

sub·sist (səb sist′), v.i. 1. to remain alive, as on food. 2. to continue to exist.

sub·sist·ence (səb sis′təns), n. 1. the state or fact of subsisting. 2. means of supporting life, esp. a minimum livelihood.

sub·soil (sub′soil′), n. a layer of earth below the surface soil.

sub·son·ic (sub son′ik), adj. 1. noting a speed less than that of sound. 2. infrasonic.

sub·spe·cies (sub spē′shēz, sub′spē′shēz), n., pl. -cies. a subdivision of a species, esp. a geographical or ecological subdivision. —**sub·spe·cif′ic** (sub′spi sif′ik), adj. —**sub′spe·cif′i·cal·ly,** adv.

subst., 1. substantive. 2. substantively. 3. substitute.

sub·stance (sub′stəns), n. 1. physical matter or material. 2. a kind of matter of definite chemical composition: a metallic substance. 3. the meaning or gist. 4. substantial or solid character or quality. 5. body or consistency. 6. Philos. the essential part of a thing. 7. wealth or property.

sub·stand·ard (sub stan′dərd), adj. below standard

sub·stan·tial (səb stan′shəl), adj. 1. of ample or considerable amount, size, etc. 2. of a corporeal or material nature. 3. firm, solid, or strong: a substantial fabric. 4. basic or essential. 5. of real worth or effect. 6. financially sound or stable. —**sub·stan′tial·ly,** adv.

sub·stan·ti·ate (səb stan′shē āt′), v.t., -at·ed, -at·ing. to establish by proof or competent evidence. —**sub·stan·ti·a′tion,** n.

sub·stan·tive (sub′stən tiv), n. 1. (in older grammars) a word or phrase used as a noun or noun equivalent. —adj. 2. Brit. having independent existence. 3. meaningful or significant. —**sub′stan·ti′val** (-tī′vəl), adj.

sub·sta·tion (sub′stā′shən), n. a subsidiary station, esp. a branch of a post office.

sub·sti·tute (sub′sti tōōt′, -tyōōt′), n., v., -tut·ed, -tut·ing. —n. 1. a person or thing acting or serving in place of another. —v.t. 2. to put in the place of another. —v.i. 3. to act as a substitute. —**sub′sti·tut′a·bil′i·ty,** n. —**sub′sti·tu′tion,** n.

sub·stra·tum (sub strā′təm, -strat′əm), n., pl. -stra·ta (-strā′tə, -strat′ə), -stra·tums. a stratum or layer lying under another.

sub·struc·ture (sub struk′chər, sub′struk′-), n. a structure forming the foundation of a building.

sub·sume (səb sōōm′), v.t., -sumed, -sum·ing. 1. Logic. to bring under a rule or category. 2. to include in a more comprehensive class or category. —**sub·sum′a·ble,** adj.

sub·teen (sub′tēn′), n. a child about to become a teenager.

sub·tend (səb tend′, sub-), v.t. Geom. to extend under or be opposite to.

sub·ter·fuge (sub′tər fyōōj′), n. a trick or scheme for getting out of something unpleasant.

sub·ter·ra·ne·an (sub′tə rā′nē ən), adj. 1. existing or situated below the surface of the earth. 2. hidden or secret. Also, **sub·ter·ra′ne·ous.** —**sub′ter·ra′ne·ous·ly,** adv.

sub·tile (sut′əl, sub′til), adj. Archaic. subtle.

sub·ti·tle (sub′tīt′əl), n., v., -tled, -tling. —n. 1. a secondary title, as of a book. 2. Motion Pictures, Television. a superimposed caption or translation that appears with the scene at the bottom of the screen. —v.t. 3. to provide a subtitle for.

sub·tle (sut′əl), adj. 1. elusively thin or tenuous, as an odor. 2. fine or delicate in meaning. 3. faint and mysterious. 4. mentally acute. 5. cunning or crafty. —**sub′tle·ty, sub′tle·ness,** n. —**sub′tly,** adv.

---

sub·sec′tion, n.
sub·seg′ment, n.
sub·se′ries, n.

sub·sur′face, adj., n.
sub·sys′tem, n.
sub·ten′ant, n.

sub·top′ic, n.
sub·to′tal, n.

sub·tract (səb trakt′), *v.t., v.i.* **1.** to take (one number) away from another. **2.** to withdraw (a part) from a whole. —**sub·trac′tion,** *n.*

sub·tra·hend (sub′trə hend′), *n.* the number that is subtracted from another.

sub·trop·i·cal (sub trop′i kəl), *adj.* bordering on the tropics.

sub·urb (sub′ûrb), *n.* **1.** a primarily residential community just outside a large city. **2. the suburbs,** the area composed of such communities. —**sub·ur·ban** (sə bûr′bən), *adj.*

sub·ur·ban·ite (sə bûr′bə nīt′), *n.* a person who lives in a suburb.

sub·ur·bi·a (sə bûr′bē ə), *n.* **1.** suburbs or suburbanites collectively. **2.** suburban life.

sub·ven·tion (səb ven′shən), *n.* a public subsidy for science or the arts.

sub·ver·sive (səb vûr′siv), *adj.* **1.** tending or trying to subvert. —*n.* **2.** a subversive person. —**sub·ver′sive·ly,** *adv.*

sub·vert (səb vûrt′), *v.t.* **1.** to overthrow (something established) in an underhanded way. **2.** to undermine or corrupt. —**sub·ver′sion** (-vûr′zhən), *n.* —**sub·vert′er,** *n.*

sub·way (sub′wā′), *n.* an underground electric railroad in a large city.

suc·ceed (sək sēd′), *v.i.* **1.** to turn out successfully. **2.** to accomplish what is attempted or intended. **3.** to take over a position, rank, etc. —*v.t.* **4.** to follow or come after. —**suc·ceed′er,** *n.*

suc·cess (sək ses′), *n.* **1.** a favorable result that one has tried or hoped for. **2.** the attainment of wealth, fame, etc. **3.** a successful person or thing.

suc·cess·ful (sək ses′fəl), *adj.* **1.** finding or having success. **2.** having attained wealth, fame, etc. —**suc·cess′ful·ly,** *adv.*

suc·ces·sion (sək sesh′ən), *n.* **1.** the coming of one person or thing after another. **2.** a number of persons or things following one another. **3.** the act or right by which one person succeeds to the position or rank of another. **4.** the order or line of those entitled to succeed one another. —**suc·ces′sion·al,** *adj.*

suc·ces·sive (sək ses′iv), *adj.* following one after the other. —**suc·ces′sive·ly,** *adv.*

suc·ces·sor (sək ses′ər), *n.* a person who succeeds another in position or rank.

suc·cinct (sək singkt′), *adj.* clearly stated in few words. —**suc·cinct′ly,** *adv.* —**suc·cinct′ness,** *n.* —**Syn.** concise, pithy, terse.

suc·cor (suk′ər), *Literary.* —*n.* **1.** timely aid in distress. —*v.t.* **2.** to render succor to.

suc·co·tash (suk′ə tash′), *n.* a cooked dish of corn kernels and lima beans. [< Am Ind]

Suc·coth (sook′əs, soo kôt′), *n.* Sukkoth.

suc·cu·lent (suk′yə lənt), *adj.* **1.** full of juice. **2.** having fleshy and juicy tissues. —*n.* **3.** a succulent plant. —**suc′cu·lence, suc′cu·len·cy,** *n.* —**suc′cu·lent·ly,** *adv.*

suc·cumb (sə kum′), *v.i.* **1.** to give way to superior force. **2.** to die. —**suc·cumb′er,** *n.*

such (such), *adj.* **1.** of the kind indicated or implied. **2.** like or similar: *tea, coffee,* and *such commodities.* **3.** so very: *such terrible deeds.* **4.** not named but definite. —*adv.* **5.** to so large an extent. —*pron.* **6.** such a person or thing or such persons or things. **7.** someone or something indicated. **8. as such, a.** in that capacity. **b.** in itself. **9. such as,** for example.

such′ and such′, definite or particular but not named or specified.

such·like (such′līk′), *adj.* **1.** of any such kind. —*pron.* **2.** persons or things of such a kind.

suck (suk), *v.t.* **1.** to draw into the mouth by action of the lips and tongue. **2.** to draw (water, etc.) by or as if by suction. **3.** to draw liquid from (fruit, etc.) by action of the lips and tongue. **4.** to put in the mouth and draw upon. —*v.i.* **5.** to suck something. —*n.* **6.** the act of sucking.

suck·er (suk′ər), *n.* **1.** a person or thing that sucks. **2.** *Informal.* a person easily cheated. **3.** a part of an animal adapted for sucking nourishment or for holding fast to something. **4.** a thick-lipped North American freshwater fish. **5.** *Informal.* a lollipop. **6.** *Bot.* a shoot from a subterranean stem or root.

suck·le (suk′əl), *v.t., v.i.,* **-led, -ling.** **1.** to nurse at the breast or udder. **2.** to suck at the breast or udder. **3.** to nourish or bring up.

suck·ling (suk′ling), *n.* an infant or a young animal that suckles.

su·crose (soo′krōs), *n.* a sugar obtained from sugar cane or sugar beet.

suc·tion (suk′shən), *n.* **1.** the act of sucking. **2.** the force created by a vacuum or by reducing the pressure of a gas. —**suc′tion·al,** *adj.*

Su·dan (soo dan′), *n.* **the,** a country in NE Africa. —**Su′da·nese′** (sood′-°nēz′), *n., adj.*

sub·treas′ur·y, *n.*
sub′type′, *n.*
sub·u′nit, *n.*

sub·va·ri·e·ty, *n.,*
  pl. **-ties.**
sub·ze′ro, *adj.*

sud·den (sud′ən), *adj.* **1.** happening or done quickly and unexpectedly. **2.** abrupt or steep. **3.** impetuous or rash. —*n.* **4.** all of a sudden, without warning. —**sud′den·ly,** *adv.* —**sud′den·ness,** *n.* —Syn. **1.** unforeseen. **2.** precipitous. **3.** hasty.

sud′den death′, an overtime period in which a tied contest is won and play is stopped immediately after one team scores.

suds (sudz), *n.pl.* **1.** soapy water. **2.** foam made by soap. —**suds′y,** *adj.*

sue (s o̅o̅), *v.t., v.i.,* **sued, su·ing. 1.** to bring a lawsuit (against). **2.** to petition or appeal. —**su′er,** *n.*

suede (swād), *n.* **1.** leather finished with a soft, napped surface. **2.** a fabric resembling this. Also, **suède.**

su·et (s o̅o̅ ′it), *n.* the hard fat about the loins and kidneys of beef, sheep, etc., used in cooking. —**su′et·y,** *adj.*

Su′ez Canal′, a canal connecting the Mediterranean and the Red Sea.

suf-, var. of sub- before *f: suffix.*

suf., suffix.

suff., **1.** sufficient. **2.** suffix.

suf·fer (suf′ər), *v.i., v.t.* **1.** to undergo or feel (pain or distress). **2.** to undergo or experience (any action or condition). **3.** to tolerate or endure. **4.** to allow or permit. —**suf′fer·a·ble,** *adj.* —**suf′fer·er,** *n.* —**suf′fer·ing·ly,** *adv.*

suf·fer·ance (suf′ər əns, suf′rəns), *n.* **1.** passive permission resulting from lack of interference. **2.** *Archaic.* capacity to endure pain or distress.

suf·fer·ing (suf′ər ing, suf′ring), *n.* **1.** the state of a person who suffers. **2.** something suffered.

suf·fice (sə fis′, -fiz′), *v.i., v.t.,* **-ficed, -fic·ing.** to be enough or adequate, as for needs.

suf·fi·cient (sə fish′ənt), *adj.* adequate for the purpose. —**suf·fi′cien·cy,** *n.* —**suf·fi′cient·ly,** *adv.*

suf·fix (*n.* suf′iks; *v.* suf′iks, sə fiks′), *Gram.* —*n.* **1.** an affix placed at the end of a word or stem. —*v.t.* **2.** to add as a suffix. —**suf·fix·ion** (sə fik′shən), *n.*

suf·fo·cate (suf′ə kāt′), *v.,* **-cat·ed, -cat·ing.** —*v.t.* **1.** to kill by preventing the supply of air to the lungs or gills. **2.** to impede the respiration of. —*v.i.* **3.** to become suffocated. **4.** to be uncomfortable due to a lack of fresh or cool air. —**suf′fo·cat′ing·ly,** *adv.* —**suf′fo·ca′tion,** *n.*

suf·fra·gan (suf′rə gən), *n.* an assistant bishop without ordinary jurisdiction.

suf·frage (suf′rij), *n.* **1.** the right to vote. **2.** a vote. —**suf′fra·gist,** *n.*

suf·fra·gette (suf′rə jet′), *n.* a woman advocate of female suffrage.

suf·fuse (sə fyo̅o̅z′), *v.t.,* **-fused, -fus-**ing. to overspread with or as with a liquid, color, etc. —**suf·fu′sion,** *n.*

sug·ar (sh o̅o̅ g′ər), *n.* **1.** any of a class of sweet, crystalline substances, esp. sucrose. **2.** any of the same class of carbohydrates, as glucose. —*v.t.* **3.** to sprinkle or mix with sugar. **4.** sugarcoat (def. 2). —*v.i.* **5.** to form sugar or sugar crystals. —**sug′ar·less,** *adj.* —**sug′ar·y,** *adj.*

sug′ar beet′, a beet having a white root, cultivated as a source of sugar.

sug′ar cane′, a tall plant of tropical and warm regions, whose sweet juice is the chief source of sugar.

sug·ar·coat (sh o̅o̅ g′ər kōt′), *v.t.* **1.** to cover with sugar. **2.** to make seem more pleasant or acceptable.

sug′ar ma′ple, a maple of eastern North America, whose sweet sap is the chief source of maple sugar.

sug·ar·plum (sh o̅o̅ g′ər plum′), *n. Obsolesc.* a small, rounded piece of candy.

sug·gest (səg jest′, sə-), *v.t.* **1.** to bring up for consideration or possible action. **2.** to bring up through association of ideas. **3.** to propose as possible for some purpose. **4.** to hint at without words. —**sug·gest′i·ble** (-jes′-tə bəl), *adj.* —**sug·gest′i·bil′i·ty,** *n.* —Syn. **1.** propose, recommend. **2.** connote. **4.** imply intimate.

sug·ges·tion (səg jes′chən, -jesh′-, sə-), *n.* **1.** the act of suggesting or state of being suggested. **2.** something suggested. **3.** a slight trace or hint.

sug·ges·tive (səg jes′tiv, sə-), *adj.* **1.** rich in suggestions or ideas. **2.** suggesting or implying something improper or indecent. —**sug·ges′tive·ly,** *adv.* —**sug·ges′tive·ness,** *n.*

su·i·cide (so̅o̅ ′i sid′), *n.* **1.** the act of deliberately killing oneself. **2.** a person who deliberately kills himself or herself. —**su′i·cid′al,** *adj.*

su·i·dol·o·gy (so̅o̅ ′i si dol′ə jē), *n.* the scientific study of suicide and its prevention.

su·i ge·ne·ris (so̅o̅ ′i jen′ər is), *Latin.* unique or singular.

suit (so̅o̅ t), *n.* **1.** a set of clothing, esp. a man's coat and trousers or a woman's short coat and skirt. **2.** lawsuit. **3.** one of the four sets in a pack of playing cards. **4.** *Literary.* the courtship of a woman. **5.** *Archaic.* a plea or appeal, as to ruler. **6.** follow suit, to follow someone else's example. —*v.t.* **7.** to match or make appropriate to. **8.** to be fitting or becoming to. **9.** to satisfy or please. **10.** suit up, to put on the proper or designated suit, as for a spaceflight.

suit·a·ble (so̅o̅ ′tə bəl), *adj.* correct or appropriate for a particular purpose or occasion. —**suit′a·bil′i·ty,** **suit′-a·ble·ness,** *n.* —**suit′a·bly,** *adv.*

suit·case (sōōt′kās′), *n.* a small, flat, rectangular piece of luggage.

suite (swēt *or, often,* sōōt *for* 2), *n.* **1.** a connected series of rooms to be used together, as in a hotel or office building: *an executive suite.* **2.** a set of furniture, esp. for one room. **3.** a musical composition consisting of several short movements, esp. a series of dances. **4.** *Brit.* a group of attendants, as of a queen.

suit·ing (sōō′tĭng), *n.* any fabric for making suits.

suit·or (sōō′tər), *n.* **1.** *Chiefly Literary.* a man who courts a woman. **2.** *Law.* a plaintiff.

su·ki·ya·ki (sōō′kē yä′kē), *n.* a Japanese dish of meat, bean curd, and greens, cooked over direct heat at the table.

Suk·koth (sŏŏk′əs, sŏŏ kôt′), *n.* a Jewish festival celebrating the end of the harvest season. Also, **Suk·kot′.**

sul·fa (sŭl′fə), *adj.* **1.** related chemically to sulfanilamide. **2.** of or involving sulfa drugs.

sul′fa drug′, any of a group of drugs closely related to sulfanilamide, used in treating various bacterial infections.

sul·fa·nil·a·mide (sŭl′fə nĭl′ə mīd′, -mĭd), *n.* a colorless, crystalline compound formerly used in treating gonorrhea, etc.

sul·fate (sŭl′fāt), *n.* a salt or ester of sulfuric acid.

sul·fide (sŭl′fīd), *n.* a compound of sulfur with another element, usually a metal.

sul·fur (sŭl′fər), *n.* *Chem.* a yellow, solid, nonmetallic element, used in making matches, explosives, and medicines. *Symbol:* S; *at. wt.:* 32.064; *at. no.:* 16. —**sul·fu′re·ous** (-fyŏŏr′ē əs), *adj.*

sul′fur diox′ide, a suffocating gas formed when sulfur burns, used chiefly in the manufacture of sulfuric acid.

sul·fu·ric (sŭl fyŏŏr′ĭk), *adj.* of or containing sulfur.

sulfu′ric ac′id, an oily, corrosive liquid usually produced from sulfur dioxide, used chiefly in the manufacture of fertilizers, dyes, etc.

sul·fur·ous (sŭl′fər əs, sŭl fyŏŏr′əs), *adj.* **1.** relating to sulfur. **2.** of the yellow color of sulfur.

sulk (sŭlk), *v.i.* **1.** to be sulky. —*n.* **2.** a state of sulking.

sulk·y (sŭl′kē), *adj.,* **sulk·i·er, sulk·i·est,** *n., pl.* **sulk·ies.** —*adj.* **1.** sullenly ill-humored, resentful, or aloof. —*n.* **2.** a light, two-wheeled, one-horse carriage for one person. —**sulk′i·ly,** *adv.* —**sulk′i·ness,** *n.*

sul·len (sŭl′ən), *adj.* **1.** showing ill humor or resentment in a gloomy and silent way. **2.** gloomy or dismal, as weather. —**sul′len·ly,** *adv.* —

sul′len·ness, *n.* —**Syn. 1.** moody, morose, sulky.

sul·ly (sŭl′ē), *v.t.,* **-lied, -ly·ing.** to stain or defile, esp. by disgracing.

sul·phur (sŭl′fər), *n.* sulfur.

sul·tan (sŭl′tən), *n.* a ruler of a Muslim country. —**sul′tan·ate′** (-āt′), *n.*

sul·tan·a (sul tan′ə, -tä′nə), *n.* a wife, sister, daughter, or mother of a sultan.

sul·try (sŭl′trē), *adj.,* **-tri·er, -tri·est. 1.** oppressively hot and humid. **2.** arousing heated temper or passion. —**sul′tri·ness,** *n.*

sum (sŭm), *n., v.,* **summed, sum·ming.** —*n.* **1.** the result obtained by adding numbers together. **2.** the total amount. **3.** a certain amount of money. **4.** a problem in arithmetic. **5.** summary. —*v.t.* **6.** to add together. **7. sum up,** to summarize.

su·mac (shŏŏ′mak, sōō′-), *n.* any of various shrubs or small trees having feathery leaves and bearing cone-shaped clusters of berries. Also, **su′mach.**

Su·ma·tra (sŏŏ mä′trə), *n.* a large island in the W part of Indonesia. —**Su·ma′tran,** *adj., n.*

sum·ma·rize (sŭm′ə rīz′), *v.t.,* **-rized, -riz·ing.** to make or constitute a summary of. —**sum′ma·ri·za′tion,** *n.*

sum·ma·ry (sŭm′ə rē), *n., pl.* **-ries,** *adj.* —*n.* **1.** a brief, concise restatement of the main facts or points. —*adj.* **2.** brief and concise. **3.** done without due consideration and delay. —**sum·mar·i·ly** (sə mer′ə lē, sŭm′ər ə-), *adv.*

sum·ma·tion (sə mā′shən), *n.* **1.** the act or process of summing or summing up. **2.** *Law.* the final arguments in a case.

sum·mer (sŭm′ər), *n.* **1.** the warmest season of the year, between spring and autumn. —*v.i.* **2.** to spend the summer. —**sum′mer·y,** *adj.*

sum·mer·house (sŭm′ər hous′), *n.* a rustic structure in a garden intended to provide a shady place.

sum·mer·time (sŭm′ər tīm′), *n.* the summer season.

sum·mit (sŭm′ĭt), *n.* **1.** the highest point or part. **2.** the highest state or degree. —*adj.* **3.** between heads of state: *a summit conference.*

sum·mit·ry (sŭm′ĭ trē), *n.* the art or conduct of a summit conference.

sum·mon (sŭm′ən), *v.t.* **1.** to call for the presence of, as by command. **2.** to order to appear before a court. **3.** to call together by authority, as a council. **4.** to arouse or call forth: *to summon up all one's courage.* —**sum′mon·er,** *n.*

sum·mons (sŭm′ənz), *n., pl.* **-mons·es. 1.** an order to appear before a court, as for trial. **2.** any official order to appear at a certain place for some duty.

su·mo (sōō'mō), *n.* a Japanese form of wrestling, usually by men of great height and weight.

sump·tu·ous (sump'chŏŏ əs), *adj.* **1.** costly and lavish. **2.** splendid or superb. —**sump'tu·ous·ly,** *adv.* —**sump'tu·ous·ness,** *n.*

sun (sun), *n., v.,* **sunned, sun·ning.** —*n.* **1.** the star that is the central body of the solar system, around which the earth and other planets revolve and from which they receive light and heat. **2.** sunlight. **3.** any self-luminous heavenly body, esp. one in a planetary system. —*v.t.* **3.** to expose to sunlight. —*v.i.* **4.** to sun oneself.

Sun., Sunday. Also, **Sund.**

sun' bath', exposure of the body to sunlight or a sunlamp, esp. to acquire a suntan. —**sun'bathe',** *v.i.* —**sun'bath'er,** *n.*

sun·beam (sun'bēm'), *n.* a beam or ray of sunlight.

Sun·belt (sun'belt'), *n. Informal.* the southwest region of the U.S.

sun·bon·net (sun'bon'it), *n.* a bonnet with a very wide brim, worn for protection from the sun.

sun·burn (sun'bûrn'), *n., v.,* **-burned** or **-burnt, -burn·ing.** —*n.* **1.** inflammation of the skin caused by overexposure to sunlight or a sunlamp. —*v.t., v.i.* **2.** to affect or be affected with sunburn.

sun·burst (sun'bûrst'), *n.* **1.** a burst of sunlight. **2.** an ornament resembling the sun with rays issuing in all directions.

sun·dae (sun'dē, -dā), *n.* ice cream topped with fruit, syrup, whipped cream, nuts, etc.

Sun·day (sund'ē, -dā), *n.* the first day of the week: the day of rest for most Christians.

sun·der (sun'dər), *v.t., v.i. Literary.* to break apart violently.

sun·di·al (sun'dī'əl, -dīl'), *n.* an instrument that shows time by the shadow cast by a pointer on a dial marked in hours.

sun·down (sun'doun'), *n.* the time of sunset.

sun·dries (sun'drēz), *n.pl.* small, miscellaneous items of small value.

sun·dry (sun'drē), *adj.* various and small in number.

sun·fish (sun'fish'), *n.,* **1.** a large ocean fish having a flattened body. **2.** any of several small, freshwater fishes of North America having a deep, compressed body.

sun·flow·er (sun'flou'ər), *n.* a tall tree having showy, yellow-petaled flowers and edible, oil-producing seeds.

sung (sung), *v.* a pt. and pp. of **sing.**

sun·glass·es (sun'glas'iz, -glä'siz), *n.pl.* eyeglasses with colored lenses to protect the eyes from glare.

sunk (sungk), *v.* a pt. and pp. of **sink.**

sunk·en (sung'kən), *adj.* **1.** having sunk or submerged. **2.** situated on a lower level: *a sunken living room.* **3.** hollow or depressed: *sunken cheeks.*

sun·lamp (sun'lamp'), *n.* a lamp that gives off ultraviolet rays, used for therapeutic purposes.

sun·light (sun'līt'), *n.* the direct light of the sun.

sun·lit (sun'lit'), *adj.* lighted by the sun.

sun·ny (sun'ē), *adj.,* **-ni·er, -ni·est. 1.** abounding in sunshine. **2.** of, like, or from the sun. **3.** cheery or joyous. —**sun'ni·ly,** *adv.* —**sun'ni·ness,** *n.*

sun·rise (sun'rīz'), *n.* **1.** the rising of the sun above the horizon in the morning. **2.** the time when this occurs.

sun·roof (sun'rōof'), *n.* an automobile roof with a section that may be slid open.

sun·set (sun'set'), *n.* **1.** the setting of the sun below the horizon in the evening. **2.** the time when this occurs.

sun'set law', a law requiring a periodic review of justification for the existence of government agencies and programs.

sun·shade (sun'shād'), *n.* something used as a protection from sunlight, as an awning.

sun·shine (sun'shīn'), *n.* sunlight. —**sun'shin'y,** *adj.*

sun'shine law', a law requiring that most government agencies open their official meetings and records to the general public.

sun·spot (sun'spot'), *n.* one of the dark patches that appear periodically on the surface of the sun.

sun·stroke (sun'strōk'), *n.* a sudden and often fatal condition due to prolonged exposure to the sun's rays or to excessive heat. —**sun'struck',** *adj.*

sun·tan (sun'tan'), *n.* a browning of the skin resulting from exposure to sunlight or a sunlamp. —**sun'tanned',** *adj.*

sun·up (sun'up'), *n.* sunrise.

Sun Yat-sen (sōōn' yät'sen'), 1866–1925, Chinese political and revolutionary leader.

sup¹ (sup), *v.i.,* **supped, sup·ping.** *Literary.* to eat supper.

sup² (sup), *v.t., v.i.,* **supped, sup·ping,** *n. Chiefly Dial.* sip.

sup., **1.** superior. **2.** superlative. **3.** supplement. **4.** supplementary. **5.** supply. **6.** supra.

su·per (sōō'pər), *Informal.* —*n.* **1.** superintendent. **2.** supernumerary. —*adj.* **3.** excellent or outstanding. **4.** extremely great.

super., 1. superintendent, 2. superior.

super-, a prefix meaning: **a.** over or above: *superstructure.* **b.** beyond or to excess: *superfine; superpatriotic.* **c.** major or greater: *superhighway; superbomb.* **d.** superior: *supersalesman; superstar.*

su·per·a·bun·dant (soo′pər ə bun′dənt), *adj.* exceedingly abundant. —su′per·a·bun′dance, *n.* —su′per·a·bun′dant·ly, *adv.*

su·per·an·nu·at·ed (soo′pər an′yoo·ā′tid), *adj.* 1. retired because of age or infirmity. 2. too old for use, work, or service. 3. antiquated or obsolete: *superannuated ideas.*

su·perb (soo pûrb′, sə-), *adj.* 1. admirably fine or excellent. 2. sumptuous or grand. 3. imposing or majestic. —su·perb′ly, *adv.*

su·per·car·go (soo′pər kär′gō, soo′pər·kär′-), *n.,* a merchant-ship officer who is in charge of the cargo.

su·per·charge (soo′pər chärj′), *v.t.,* -charged, -charg·ing. to add more power to (an engine) by a supercharger.

su·per·charg·er (soo′pər chär′jər), *n.* a device for forcing air into an internal-combustion engine in order to increase engine power.

su·per·cil·i·ous (soo′pər sil′ē əs), *adj.* haughtily aloof. —su′per·cil′i·ous·ly, *adv.* —su′per·cil′i·ous·ness, *n.* —Syn. arrogant, disdainful, scornful.

su·per·con·duc·tiv·i·ty (soo′pər kon′dok tiv′i tē), *n.* the phenomenon of almost perfect conductivity shown by certain substances at temperatures approaching absolute zero. —su′per·con·duc′tor, *n.*

su·per·e·go (soo′pər ē′gō, -eg′ō), *n., pl.* -gos. the part of the psyche that functions like the conscience in mediating between the drives of the id and moral values.

su·per·e·rog·a·to·ry (soo′pər ə rog′ə·tôr′ē, -tōr′ē), *adj.* doing more than is required or expected. —su′per·er′o·ga′tion (-er′ə gā′shən), *n.*

su·per·fi·cial (soo′pər fish′əl), *adj.* 1. of, on, or near the surface. 2. concerned merely with what is on the surface or obvious. 3. apparent rather than real. —su′per·fi′ci·al′i·ty (-fish′ē al′i tē), su·per·fi′cial·ness, *n.* —su′per·fi′cial·ly, *adv.* —Syn. 2. shallow, trivial.

su·per·flu·ous (soo pûr′floo əs), *adj.* more than sufficient or necessary. —su·per·flu·i·ty (soo′pər floo′i tē), *n.* —su·per′flu·ous·ly, *adv.* —su·per′flu·ous·ness, *n.* —Syn. needless, redundant.

su·per·high·way (soo′pər hī′wā′), *n.* a wide highway designed for traffic at high speeds.

su·per·hu·man (soo′pər hyoo′mən *or, often,* -yoo′-), *adj.* 1. above or

beyond what is human. 2. beyond ordinary human power, ability, etc.

su·per·im·pose (soo′pər im pōz′), *v.t.,* -posed, -pos·ing. to place or put on something else. —su′per·im′po·si′tion, *n.*

su·per·in·tend (soo′pər in tend′, soo′prin-), *v.t.* to act or work as superintendent of. —su′per·in·tend′ence, su′per·in·tend′en·cy, *n.*

su·per·in·tend·ent (soo′pər in ten′dənt, soo′prin-), *n.* 1. a person who has overall charge and control of an organization or district. 2. a person responsible for the maintenance of a building, esp. an apartment house.

su·pe·ri·or (sə pēr′ē ər, soo-), *adj.* 1. above the average in excellence or intelligence. 2. of higher grade or quality. 3. greater in quantity or amount. 4. higher in rank or position. 5. showing a consciousness of superiority to others. 6. not yielding or susceptible: *to be superior to temptation.* —*n.* 7. a superior person or thing. 8. the head of a monastery or convent. —su·pe′ri·or′i·ty (-ôr′i tē, -or′-), *n.* —su·pe′ri·or·ly, *adv.*

Su·pe·ri·or (sə pēr′ē ər, soo-), *n.* **Lake,** a lake in the N central United States and S Canada.

superl., superlative.

su·per·la·tive (sə pûr′lə tiv, soo-), *adj.* 1. of the highest kind or order. 2. *Gram.* noting the highest degree of the comparison of adjectives and adverbs. —*n.* 3. the utmost degree. 4. *Gram.* **a.** the superlative degree. **b.** a form in the superlative. —su·per′la·tive·ly, *adv.* —su·per′la·tive·ness, *n.*

su·per·man (soo′pər man′), *n.* a person of superhuman powers.

su·per·mar·ket (soo′pər mär′kit), *n.* a large, self-service retail market that sells foods and household goods.

su·per·nal (soo pûr′nəl), *adj. Literary.* heavenly or celestial.

su·per·nat·u·ral (soo′pər nach′ər əl), *adj.* 1. above or beyond what is explainable by natural laws or phenomena. 2. of or characteristic of God or a deity. 3. of or relating to ghosts, goblins, etc. —su′per·nat′u·ral·ly, *adv.* —su′per·nat′u·ral·ness, *n.*

su·per·no·va (soo′pər nō′və), *n.* an extremely bright nova.

su·per·nu·mer·ar·y (soo′pər noo′mə·rer′ē, -nyoo′-), *adj., n., pl.* -ar·ies. —*adj.* 1. in excess of the regular or required number. —*n.* 2. a supernumerary person or thing. 3. *Theat.* a performer with no speaking lines.

su·per·pose (soo′pər pōz′), *v.t.,* -posed, -pos·ing. to superimpose so as to coincide. —su′per·pos′a·ble, *adj.* —su′per·po·si′tion, *n.*

su·per·pow·er (soō′pər pou′ər), *n.* any one of the nations, esp. the U.S., the Soviet Union, and Communist China, that dominate world affairs because of their military strength.

su·per·sat·u·rate (soō′pər sach′ə rāt′), *v.t.*, **-rat·ed, -rat·ing.** to increase the concentration of (a solution) beyond saturation. **—su′per·sat′u·ra′tion,** *n.*

su·per·scribe (soō′pər skrīb′, soō′pər-skrīb′), *v.t.*, **-scribed, -scrib·ing.** to write at the top or on the outside (of). **—su′per·scrip′tion** (-skrip′-shən), *n.*

su·per·script (soō′pər skript′), *n.* a small letter, number, or symbol written or printed high on a line of text.

su·per·sede (soō′pər sēd′), *v.t.*, **-sed·ed, -sed·ing.** to set aside as void or obsolete. **—Syn.** displace, supplant.

su·per·son·ic (soō′pər son′ik), *adj.* **1.** greater than the speed of sound. **2.** capable of achieving such speed: *a supersonic plane.* **3.** ultrasonic.

su·per·son·ics (soō′pər son′iks), *n.* the science that deals with supersonic phenomena.

su·per·sti·tion (soō′pər stish′ən), *n.* **1.** an irrational belief in the ominous significance of a particular thing or circumstance. **2.** a custom or act based on such a belief. **—su′per·sti′-tious,** *adj.*

su·per·struc·ture (soō′pər struk′chər), *n.* **1.** the part of a building above its foundation or basement. **2.** any construction built above the main deck of a vessel.

su·per·vene (soō′pər vēn′), *v.i.*, **-vened, -ven·ing.** to occur as something extraneous or unexpected.

su·per·vise (soō′pər vīz′), *v.t.*, **-vised, -vis·ing.** to oversee (work or workers) during execution or performance. **—su′per·vi′sion** (-vizh′ən), *n.* **—su′per·vi′sor,** *n.* **—su′per·vi′so·ry,** *adj.*

su·pine (soō pīn′), *adj.* **1.** lying on the back. **2.** inactive or passive.

supp., 1. supplement. **2.** supplementary. Also, **suppl.**

sup·per (sup′ər), *n.* the evening meal, esp. when dinner is served at midday. **—sup′per·less,** *adj.*

sup′per club′, a small, luxurious nightclub.

sup·plant (sə plant′, -plänt′), *v.t.* **1.** to take the place of, as through force or scheming. **2.** to replace (one thing) by something else. **—supplan·ta·tion** (sup′lan tā′shən), *n.* **—sup·plant′er,** *n.*

sup·ple (sup′əl), *adj.*, **-pler, -plest. 1.** able to bend readily without damage. **2.** limber or lithe: *a supple dancer.* **3.** showing mental adaptability. **4.** compliant or yielding. **—sup′ple-ness,** *n.* **—sup′ply,** *adv.*

sup·ple·ment (*n.* sup′lə mənt; *v.* sup′-lə ment′), *n.* **1.** something added to complete a thing or supply a deficiency. **2.** a part added to a book or an extra part of a newspaper. **—v.t. 3.** to form a supplement to. **—sup′ple·men′ta·ry,** *adj.*

sup·ple·men·tal (sup′lə men′t⁰l), *adj.* **1.** of or forming a supplement. **2.** licensed to provide nonregular flights, esp. charter flights. **—n. 3.** a supplemental airline. **—sup′ple·men′tal·ly,** *adv.*

sup·pli·ant (sup′lē ənt), *n.* **1.** a person who supplicates. **—adj. 2.** supplicating or entreating. Also, **sup′pli·cant** (-kənt).

sup·pli·cate (sup′lə kāt′), *v.i.*, *v.t.*, **-cat·ed, -cat·ing. 1.** to make a humble, earnest entreaty (to), esp. by prayer. **2.** to ask (for) by humble entreaty. **—sup′pli·ca′tion,** *n.*

sup·ply (sə plī′), *v.*, **-plied, -ply·ing,** *n.*, *pl.* **-plies. —v.t., v.i. 1.** to provide (someone) with (something to be used or expended). **2.** to make up for or fill (a need, etc.). **—n. 3.** the act of supplying. **4.** an amount on hand or available as for use. **5.** Usually, **supplies.** a stock of food or other necessary items. **6.** the quantity of a commodity or service that is in the market and available for purchase, esp. at a particular price. **—sup·pli′er,** *n.*

sup·port (sə pōrt′, -pôrt′), *v.t.* **1.** to hold up or bear (a load, etc.). **2.** to sustain or withstand (weight, etc.). **3.** to provide with the means of sustaining life. **4.** to help or comfort. **5.** to uphold and aid. **6.** to corroborate (a statement, etc.). **7.** to endure or tolerate, esp. with patience. **8.** to act with (a star actor or actress), as in a film. **—n. 9.** the act of supporting or state of being supported. **10.** maintenance, as of a family. **11.** a person or thing that supports. **—sup·port′a·ble,** *adj.* **—sup·port′er,** *n.* **—sup·port′ive,** *adj.*

sup·pose (sə pōz′), *v.*, **-posed, -pos·ing. —v.t. 1.** to assume to be true, esp. for the sake of argument. **2.** to think or imagine. **3.** to require logically. **4.** to expect, as facts. **—v.i. 5.** to make a supposition. **—sup·posed′,** *adj.* **—sup·pos′ed·ly,** *adv.*

sup·po·si·tion (sup′ə zish′ən), *n.* **1.** the act of supposing. **2.** something supposed. Also, *Rare,* **sup·pos′al** (-zəl).

sup·pos·i·to·ry (sə poz′i tōr′ē, -tôr′ē), *n.*, *pl.* **-ries.** a solid, conical, easily melted mass of medicinal substance for inserting into the rectum or vagina.

sup·press (sə pres′), *v.t.* **1.** to crush or put down by force. **2.** to hold back or restrain. **3.** to withhold from disclosure or publication. **4.** to inhibit consciously, as an impulse. —**sup·press′i·ble**, *adj.* —**sup·pres′sion** (-presh′ən), *n.* —**sup·pres′sive**, *adj.*

sup·pres·sant (sə pres′ənt), *n.* a drug or chemical that suppresses an undesirable action or condition.

sup·pu·rate (sup′yə rāt′), *v.i.*, **-rat·ed, -rat·ing.** to discharge pus, as a wound. —**sup′pu·ra′tion**, *n.* —**sup′-pu·ra′tive** (-rā′tiv), *adj.*

su·pra (sōō′prə), *adv.* above, esp. when used in referring to parts of a text.

su·pra·na·tion·al (sōō′prə nash′ə nəl), *adj.* beyond the authority of one national government, as a policy.

su·prem·a·cist (sə prem′ə sist, sōō-), *n.* a person who advocates the supremacy of a particular group, esp. a racial group.

su·prem·a·cy (sə prem′ə sē, sōō-), *n.* **1.** the state of being supreme. **2.** supreme authority or power.

su·preme (sə prēm′, sōō-), *adj.* **1.** highest in rank or authority. **2.** of the highest quality or degree. **3.** greatest or extreme. **4.** last or final. —**su·preme′ly**, *adv.* —**su·preme′-ness**, *n.* —**Syn. 1.** paramount, preeminent. **2.** utmost.

Supreme′ Be′ing, God.

Supreme′ Court′, *U.S.* **1.** the highest court of the nation. **2.** the highest court in most states.

Supreme′ So′viet, the legislature of the Soviet Union.

supt., superintendent.

supvr., supervisor.

sur-¹, a prefix meaning: **a.** above or over: *surmount*. **b.** beyond: *surpass.* **c.** additional: *surtax.*

sur-², var. of **sub-** before *r*: *surrogate.*

sur·cease (sûr sēs′), *n.* a temporary halt.

sur·charge (*n.* sûr′chärj′; *v.* sûr chärj′, sûr′chärj′), *n.*, *v.*, **-charged, -charg·ing.** —*n.* **1.** an additional charge or cost. **2.** an inscription that alters the face value of a stamp over which it has been printed. —*v.t.* **3.** to subject to a surcharge. **4.** to print a surcharge on (a stamp). —**sur·charg′er**, *n.*

sur·cin·gle (sûr′sing′gəl), *n.* a girth around the belly of a horse to keep a blanket or saddle in place.

sur·coat (sûr′kōt′), *n.* a garment worn over medieval armor.

sure (shŏŏr), *adj.*, **sur·er, sur·est,** *adv.* —*adj.* **1.** free from doubt as to the truth of something. **2.** certain beyond question. **3.** bound inevitably: *He is sure to come.* **4.** unfailing or unerring. **5.** firm or stable. **6.** re-liable or trustworthy. **7. for sure,** as a certainty. **8. sure enough,** *Informal.* as might have been supposed. —*adv.* **9.** *Informal.* surely. —**sure′-ness**, *n.* —**Syn. 1.** confident, positive.

sure·fire (shŏŏr′fīˀr′), *adj. Informal.* sure to work or perform as expected.

sure·foot·ed (shŏŏr′fŏŏt′id), *adj.* not likely to stumble, slip, or fall. —**sure′foot′ed·ness**, *n.*

sure·ly (shŏŏr′lē), *adv.* **1.** without doubt. **2.** without missing or slipping.

sure·ty (shŏŏr′i tē, shŏŏr′tē), *n.*, *pl.* **-ties. 1.** security against loss or damage. **2.** a person who is legally responsible for the debt or actions of another. **3.** certainty or sureness.

surf (sûrf), *n.* **1.** the waves of the sea that break and foam upon the shore. —*v.i.* **2.** to engage in surfing. —**surf′er**, *n.*

sur·face (sûr′fis), *n.*, *adj.*, *v.*, **-faced, -fac·ing.** —*n.* **1.** the outer face of anything. **2.** any face of a thing. **3.** outward appearance. **4.** land or sea transportation, rather than air transportation. —*adj.* **5.** of or on the surface. **6.** superficial (def. 3). —*v.t.* **7.** to finish the surface of. —*v.i.* **8.** to rise to the surface.

surf·board (sûrf′bôrd′, -bōrd′), *n.* a long, narrow board used in riding the crest of a wave.

sur·feit (sûr′fit), *n.* **1.** an excessive amount. **2.** overindulgence in eating or drinking. **3.** general disgust caused by excess or satiety. —*v.t.* **4.** to bring to a state of surfeit.

surf·ing (sûr′fing), *n.* a sport in which a person stands or lies prone on a surfboard and rides the crest of a wave toward the shore.

surg., **1.** surgeon. **2.** surgery. **3.** surgical.

surge (sûrj), *n.*, *v.*, **surged, surg·ing.** —*n.* **1.** a strong, wavelike forward movement. **2.** any sudden, powerful increase, as of emotion. —*v.i.* **3.** to move in or as in a surge. **4.** to rise suddenly or strongly, as the stock market.

sur·geon (sûr′jən), *n.* a physician who specializes in surgery.

sur·ger·y (sûr′jə rē), *n.*, *pl.* **-ger·ies. 1.** the science of treating diseases, injuries, or deformities by operation on the body, usually with instruments. **2.** treatment performed by a surgeon. **3.** a room for surgical operations.

sur·gi·cal (sûr′ji kəl), *adj.* of or involving surgery or surgeons. —**sur′gi·cal·ly**, *adv.*

Su·ri·nam (sŏŏr′ə näm′), *n.* a country on the NE coast of South America. —**Su·ri′nam′er**, *n.*

sur·ly (sûr′lē), *adj.*, -li·er, -li·est. boorishly rude and bad-tempered. —**sur′li·ly**, *adv.* —**sur′li·ness**, *n.*

sur·mise (*v.* sər mīz′; *n.* sər mīz′, sûr′mīz), *v.*, -mised, -mis·ing, *n.* —*v.t.*, *v.i.* 1. to guess or conjecture intuitively. —*n.* 2. an intuitive conjecture.

sur·mount (sər mount′), *v.t.* 1. to prevail over, as a difficulty. 2. to get over or across (barriers, etc.). 3. to be on top of or above. —**sur·mount′a·ble**, *adj.*

sur·name (sûr′nām′), *n.* the name that a person has in common with the other members of his or her family.

sur·pass (sər pas′, -päs′), *v.t.* 1. to go beyond in excellence or achievement. 2. to be beyond the range or capacity of. —**sur·pass′ing·ly**, *adv.*

sur·plice (sûr′plis), *n.* a loose-fitting, broad-sleeved white vestment, worn over the cassock in some churches.

sur·plus (sûr′plus, -pləs), *n.* 1. an amount or quantity greater than needed. 2. the excess of assets over liabilities accumulated. —*adj.* 3. being a surplus.

sur·prise (sər prīz′), *v.*, -prised, -pris·ing, *n.* —*v.t.* 1. to strike with a sudden feeling of unexpected wonder. 2. to come upon or discover suddenly and unexpectedly. 3. to attack without warning. —*n.* 4. the act of surprising. 5. a feeling of sudden wonder or astonishment. 6. something that surprises. —**sur·pris′er**, *n.* —**sur·pris′ing**, *adj.* —**sur·pris′ing·ly**, *adv.* —**Syn.** 1. amaze, astonish, astound.

sur·re·al·ism (sə rē′ə liz′əm), *n.* a modern style of art and literature stressing the subconscious significance of imagery or the exploitation of unexpected juxtapositions. —**sur·re′al·ist**, *n.*, *adj.* —**sur·re′al·is′tic**, **sur·re′al**, *adj.* —**sur·re′al·is′ti·cal·ly**, *adv.*

sur·ren·der (sə ren′dər), *v.t.* 1. to give up possession of on demand or under duress. 2. to abandon or relinquish (hope, etc.). —*v.i.* 3. to give oneself up, esp. as a prisoner. —*n.* 4. the act of surrendering.

sur·rep·ti·tious (sûr′əp tish′əs), *adj.* obtained, done, or made in an improperly quick, secret manner. —**sur′rep·ti′tious·ly**, *adv.* —**sur′rep·ti′tious·ness**, *n.* —**Syn.** clandestine, stealthy.

sur·rey (sûr′ē, sur′ē), *n.*, *pl.* -reys. a light, four-wheeled, two-seated carriage.

sur·ro·gate (sûr′ə gāt′, -git), *n.* 1. a person appointed to act as a substitute or deputy. 2. (in some states) a judicial officer who presides in a probate court.

sur·round (sə round′), *v.t.* 1. to enclose on all sides. 2. to enclose so as to cut off communication or retreat.

sur·round·ings (sə roun′dingz), *n.pl.* things, circumstances, or conditions that surround a person or thing.

sur·tax (sûr′taks′), *n.* an extra tax on something already taxed.

sur·tout (sər tōō′, -tōōt′), *n.* an earlier type of frock coat.

surv., 1. survey. 2. surveying. 3. surveyor.

sur·veil·lance (sər vā′ləns, -vāl′yəns), *n.* a watch kept over a person, group, etc., esp. over a suspect or prisoner.

sur·vey (*v.* sər vā′; *n.* sûr′vā, sər vā′), *v.*, *n.*, *pl.* -veys. —*v.t.* 1. to take a comprehensive view of. 2. to view in detail. 3. to measure (a tract of land) for size, shape, or the position of boundaries. —*n.* 4. a comprehensive view. 5. a detailed examination of a problem or situation. 6. the act or process of surveying land. 7. the plan or description resulting from this. —**sur·vey′or**, *n.*

sur·vey·ing (sər vā′ing), *n.* the science of surveying land.

sur·vive (sər vīv′), *v.*, -vived, -viv·ing. —*v.i.* 1. to remain or continue alive or in existence or use. —*v.t.* 2. to continue to live or exist after the death or occurrence of. —**sur·viv′al**, *n.* —**sur·vi′vor**, *n.*

sus·cep·ti·ble (sə sep′tə bel), *adj.* 1. especially liable to some influence or agency: *a child susceptible to colds.* 2. capable of being treated in a certain way: *metal susceptible of a high polish.* 3. easily affected or moved. —**sus·cep′ti·bil′i·ty**, *n.* —**sus·cep′ti·bly**, *adv.* —**Syn.** 3. impressionable.

sus·pect (*v.* sə spekt′; *n.* sus′pekt; *adj.* sus′pekt, sə spekt′), *v.t.* 1. to believe to be questionable and unreliable. 2. to believe to be guilty without conclusive proof. 3. to believe to be likely. —*n.* 4. a person who is suspected of a crime. —*adj.* 5. open to or under suspicion. —**Syn.** 1. distrust, doubt. 3. guess, surmise.

sus·pend (sə spend′), *v.t.* 1. to support from above so as to allow free movement. 2. to keep (particles) in suspension. 3. to defer to a later occasion, as a judicial sentence. 4. to halt or interrupt (something in process). 5. to render temporarily void (a rule, etc.). 6. to punish by temporary exclusion from work, school attendance, etc. —*v.i.* 7. to stop payment, as from being unable to meet financial obligations.

sus·pend·er (sə spen′dər), *n.* 1. **suspenders.** adjustable straps worn over the shoulders to support the trousers. 2. *Brit.* garter (def. 1).

sus·pense (sə spens′), *n.* **1.** a state of mental uncertainty or excitement, as from awaiting an outcome. **2.** a state of indecision or anxiety. —**suspense′ful,** *adj.*

sus·pen·sion (sə spen′shən), *n.* **1.** the act of suspending or state of being suspended. **2. a.** the state in which the particles of a substance are mixed with a fluid but are undissolved. **b.** a substance in such a state. **3.** something on or by which something else is suspended. **4.** something suspended.

suspen′sion bridge′, a bridge having a deck suspended from cables that pass over towers and are anchored at each end.

sus·pen·so·ry (sə spen′sə rē), *adj.* **1.** serving to suspend or hold up, as a bandage. **2.** suspending the operation of something.

sus·pi·cion (sə spish′ən), *n.* **1.** the act of suspecting or state of being suspected. **2.** the state of mind of a person who suspects. **3.** a slight trace.

sus·pi·cious (sə spish′əs), *adj.* **1.** causing suspicion. **2.** inclined to suspect. **3.** expressing or indicating suspicion. —**sus·pi′cious·ly,** *adv.* —**sus·pi′cious·ness,** *n.* —**Syn. 1.** questionable. **2.** distrustful.

sus·tain (sə stān′), *v.t.* **1.** to keep going or in effect, as an action or process. **2.** to supply with food and other necessities of life. **3.** to keep (a person, the spirits, etc.) from giving way. **4.** to bear or endure, as a burden. **5.** to undergo (injury, etc.) without yielding. **6.** to support from below. **7.** to uphold as valid, as a claim. **8.** to confirm or corroborate. —**sus·tain′a·ble,** *adj.*

sus·te·nance (sus′tə nəns), *n.* **1.** anything that sustains, esp. food. **2.** means of livelihood. **3.** the process of sustaining or state of being sustained.

sut·ler (sut′lər), *n.* (formerly) a merchant who followed an army and sold provisions to the soldiers.

su·tra (sŏŏ′trə), *n.* any of the sermons of Buddha.

sut·tee (su tē′, sut′ē), *n.* a former Hindu practice in which a widow burned herself on the funeral pyre of her husband.

su·ture (sŏŏ′chər), *n.* **1. a.** a joining of the edges of a wound by stitching. **b.** one of the stitches so used. **2.** the line of junction of two bones, esp. of the skull.

su·ze·rain (sŏŏ′zə rin, -rān′), *n.* **1.** a feudal overlord. **2.** *Obsolesc.* a state exercising political control over a dependent state. —**su′ze·rain·ty,** *n.*

s.v., under the specified word. [< L *sub verbo* or *sub voce*]

svc., service. Also, **svce.**

svelte (svelt, sfelt), *adj.,* **svelt·er, svelt·est. 1.** gracefully slender in figure. **2.** blandly urbane.

svgs., savings.

SW, 1. shipper's weight. **2.** shortwave. **3.** southwest. **4.** southwestern.

Sw., 1. Sweden. **2.** Swedish.

swab (swob), *n., v.,* **swabbed, swabbing.** —*n.* **1.** a bit of cotton fixed to a small stick, for applying medicine to or cleaning the mouth, throat, etc. **2.** a large mop for cleaning decks. —*v.t.* **3.** to clean with a swab.

swad·dle (swod′əl), *v.t.,* **-dled, -dling. 1.** (formerly) to wrap (a newborn infant) with strips of cloth to limit movement. **2.** to wrap (anything) round with bandages.

swag (swag), *n. Slang.* stolen goods or money.

swage (swāj), *n., v.,* **swaged, swag·ing.** —*n.* **1.** a tool for bending metal to a required shape. —*v.t.* **2.** to bend or shape by means of a swage.

swag·ger (swag′ər), *v.i.* **1.** to walk or strut in a bold, haughty way. **2.** to boast or brag noisily. —*n.* **3.** a swaggering walk or manner. —**swag′ger·er,** *n.*

Swa·hi·li (swä hē′lē), *n.* a Bantu language widely used in E Africa. —**Swa·hi′li·an,** *adj.*

swain (swān), *n. Literary.* **1.** a lover or gallant. **2.** a country lad.

swal·low¹ (swol′ō), *v.t.* **1.** to move (food, drink, etc.) from the mouth to the stomach through the throat. **2.** to take in so as to envelop. **3.** *Informal.* to accept without question. **4.** to accept without opposition. **5.** to suppress or hold in, as an emotion. **6.** to take back or retract. —*v.i.* **7.** to perform the act of swallowing. —*n.* **8.** the act of swallowing. **9.** a quantity swallowed.

swal·low² (swol′ō), *n.* a small bird having long wings and a forked tail, noted for its swift, graceful flight.

swal·low·tail (swol′ō tāl′), *n.* **1.** the tail of a swallow or a deeply forked tail like that of a swallow. **2.** any of several butterflies whose long lower wings resemble the tail of a swallow. **3.** cutaway.

swam (swam), *v.* pt. of **swim.**

swa·mi (swä′mē), *n.* a Hindu religious teacher. [< Skt *svāmī* master]

swamp (swomp), *n.* **1.** a tract of wet, spongy land. —*v.t.* **2.** to flood or drench with water. **3.** to overwhelm, esp. with an excess of something. **4.** to sink or fill (a boat) with water. **5.** to plunge in or as if in a swamp. —**swamp′y,** *adj.* —**swamp′i·ness,** *n.*

swamp′ fe′ver, malaria.

swan (swon), *n.* a large, aquatic bird having a long, slender neck and usually pure-white plumage.

swank (swangk), *n. Informal.* **1.** dashing smartness, as in dress or appearance. —*adj.* **2.** Also, **swank′y.** *Informal.* pretentiously stylish.

swans·down (swonz′doun′), *n.* **1.** the under plumage of a swan, used for trimming, powder puffs, etc. **2.** a fine, soft, thick woolen cloth.

swan′ song′, the last work, act, or achievement of a person.

swap (swop), *v.,* **swapped, swap·ping,** *n. Informal.* —*v.t., v.i.* **1.** to exchange by barter. —*n.* **2.** an exchange or barter. —**swap′per,** *n.*

sward (swôrd), *n. Literary.* a stretch of turf.

swarm (swôrm), *n.* **1.** a body of honeybees that leave a hive together to form a new colony. **2.** a body of bees settled together, as in a hive. **3.** a great number of things or persons, esp. in motion. —*v.i.* **4.** (of bees) to emigrate from a hive. **5.** to move about in great numbers. **6.** (of a place) to abound or teem.

swarth (swôrth), *adj. Archaic.* swarthy.

swarth·y (swôr′ẟẖē, -ẟẖē), *adj.,* **swarth·i·er, swarth·i·est.** dark in complexion or color. —**swarth′i·ness,** *n.*

swash (swosh, swôsh), *v.i.* to dash around with a splash, as things in water.

swash·buck·ler (swosh′buk′lər, swôsh′-), *n.* a swaggering swordsman or adventurer. —**swash′buck′ling,** *adj., n.*

swas·ti·ka (swos′ti kə), *n.* **1.** an ancient figure consisting of a cross with arms of equal length, each arm having a continuation at right angles. **2.** this figure with clockwise arms as the official Nazi emblem.

swat (swot), *v.,* **swat·ted, swat·ting,** *n.* —*v.t.* **1.** to hit with a short, crushing blow. —*n.* **2.** a sharp, crushing blow. —**swat′ter,** *n.*

swatch (swoch), *n.* a sample of cloth or other material.

swath (swoth, swôth), *n.* **1.** the space covered by the stroke of a scythe or the cut of a mowing machine. **2.** the piece or strip so cut. **3.** grass or grain cut and thrown together in a line. Also, **swathe.**

swathe (swoẟẖ, swāẟẖ), *v.t.,* **swathed, swath·ing. 1.** to wrap or bind with bandages. **2.** to enfold or envelop.

sway (swā), *v.i.* **1.** to move or swing from side to side or back and forth. **2.** to move or incline to one side. **3.** to fluctuate or vacillate, as in opinion. —*v.t.* **4.** to cause to sway. **5.** to influence or change. —*n.* **6.** a swaying movement. **7.** rule or dominion. **8.** dominating power or influence.

sway·back (swā′bak′), *n.* a deep downward curve in the back, esp. in horses. —**sway′backed′,** *adj.*

Swa·zi·land (swä′zē land′), *n.* a country in SE Africa.

swear (swâr), *v.,* **swore, sworn, swearing.** —*v.i.* **1.** to make a solemn declaration by some sacred being or object. **2.** to bind oneself by an oath. **3.** to use profane language. —*v.t.* **4.** to declare solemnly by swearing by some sacred being. **5.** to bind by an oath. **6. swear in,** to admit to office or service by administering an oath. **7. swear off,** to promise to give up. **8. swear out,** to secure (a warrant for arrest) by making an accusation under oath. —**swear′er,** *n.*

sweat (swet), *v.,* **sweat or sweat·ed, sweat·ing,** *n.* —*v.i.* **1.** to perspire, esp. freely or profusely. **2.** to gather drops of moisture from the air by condensation **3.** *Informal.* to work hard and long. —*v.t.* **4.** to cause to sweat. **5.** to exude in drops or small particles. **6.** *Informal.* to employ (workers) at low wages or for long hours. **7.** *Informal.* to worry or be concerned about. **8. sweat out,** *Slang.* to wait for anxiously or with great interest —*n* **9.** perspiration. **10.** moisture exuded from something or gathered on a surface. **11.** *Informal.* a state of anxiety or impatience. —**sweat′y,** *adj.*

sweat·er (swet′ər), *n.* a knitted jacket or jersey with or without sleeves.

sweat′ gland′, one of the minute, tubular glands of the skin that secrete perspiration.

sweat·shop (swet′shop′), *n.* a shop employing workers at low wages, for long hours, and under poor conditions.

Swed., **1.** Sweden. **2.** Swedish.

Swede (swēd), *n.* a native or inhabitant of Sweden.

Swe·den (swēd′ən), *n.* a country in N Europe.

Swed·ish (swē′dish), *adj.* **1.** of Sweden, its inhabitants, or their language. —*n.* **2.** the people of Sweden collectively. **3.** the Germanic language of the Swedes.

sweep (swēp), *v.,* **swept, sweep·ing,** *n.* —*v.t.* **1.** to move or remove (dust, etc.), as with a broom. **2.** to clear or clean (a room, etc.) of dirt or litter by means of a broom or brush. **3.** to move or take by or as by a steady, driving force. **4.** to pass (something) over a surface with a steady, driving force. **5.** to pass over (a surface, etc.) with a steady, driving force. **6.** to win an overwhelming victory in (a contest). —*v.i.* **7.** to sweep a floor or room with or as with a broom. **8.** to pass in a swift but stately manner. **9.** to extend in a continuous or curving stretch. —*n.*

10. the act of sweeping. **11.** a sweeping movement or stroke. **12.** reach or range. **13.** a continuous extent or stretch. **14.** a widely or gently curving line. **15.** an overwhelming victory in a contest. —**sweep′er,** n.

sweep·ing (swē′pĭng), adj. **1.** of wide range or scope. —n. **2.** the act of a person or thing that sweeps. **3.** sweepings, matter swept out or up. —**sweep′ing·ly,** adv.

sweep·stakes (swēp′stāks′), n. a race or other contest for which the prize consists of the stakes contributed by the various competitors. Also, **sweep′stake′.**

sweet (swēt), adj. **1.** having the taste or flavor of sugar, honey, etc. **2.** not rancid or stale. **3.** not salt or salted: sweet butter. **4.** pleasing to the ear. **5.** pleasing or fresh to the smell. **6.** pleasant in disposition or manners. —n. **7.** Usually, sweets. cake, candy, and other foods containing sugar. —**sweet′ish,** adj. —**sweet′ly,** adv. —**sweet′ness,** n.

sweet·bread (swēt′brĕd′), n. the pancreas or thymus of an animal, esp. a calf or lamb, used for food.

sweet·bri·er (swēt′brī′ər), n. a rose having a tall stem with strong thorns and pink flowers. Also, **sweet′bri′ar.**

sweet′ corn′, any of several kinds of corn having sweet kernels and eaten when young.

sweet·en (swēt′ᵊn), v.t. **1.** to make sweet. **2.** to make mild, soft, or more pleasant. —**sweet′en·er,** n. —**sweet′en·ing,** n.

sweet·heart (swēt′härt′), n. **1.** a person who is loved. **2.** a lover.

sweet′heart con′tract, Slang. a contract made through collusion between dishonest management and labor representatives to pay low wages to union workers.

sweet·meat (swēt′mēt′), n. any highly sweetened delicacy, as candy or preserved fruit.

sweet′ pea′, an annual climbing plant having sweet-scented flowers.

sweet′ pep′per, **1.** a pepper having a mild-flavored, bell-shaped or oblong fruit. **2.** its fruit.

sweet′ pota′to, **1.** a tropical vinelike plant grown for its sweet, edible, tuberous roots. **2.** its root.

sweet-talk (swēt′tôk′), v.t., v.i. Informal. to talk in a flattering manner (to).

sweet′ tooth′, a liking or craving for candy and sweet food.

swell (swĕl), v., **swelled,** swelled or **swol·len,** **swell·ing,** n., adj. —v.i., v.t. **1.** to grow or cause to grow in bulk, as by absorption of moisture. **2.** to bulge out, as a sail. **3.** to increase in amount, degree, or force. **4.** to puff up or become puffed up with pride. —n. **5.** a protuberant part. **6.** a long and unbroken wave. **7.** an increase in amount, degree, or force. **8.** a gradual increase in loudness of sound. **9.** Slang. a fashionably dressed person. —adj. Slang. **10.** fine or excellent. **11.** stylish or elegant.

swelled′ head′, Informal. an inordinately grand opinion of oneself.

swell·head (swĕl′hĕd′), n. Informal. a vain, arrogant person. —**swell′head′ed,** adj.

swell·ing (swĕl′ĭng), n. **1.** the condition of being or becoming swollen. **2.** a swollen part, esp. an abnormal bodily protuberance.

swel·ter (swĕl′tər), v.i. to suffer from oppressive heat.

swel·ter·ing (swĕl′tər ĭng), adj. **1.** suffering from oppressive heat. **2.** characterized by oppressive heat.

swept (swĕpt), v. pt. and pp. of sweep.

swerve (swûrv), v., **swerved,** swerving, n. —v.i., v.t. **1.** to turn aside abruptly in movement or direction. —n. **2.** an act of swerving.

swift (swift), adj. **1.** moving smoothly and speedily. **2.** happening or performed quickly. **3.** quick to act or respond. —n. **4.** a long-winged, swallowlike bird noted for its rapid flight. —**swift′ly,** adv. —**swift′ness,** n.

Swift (swift), n. **Jon·a·than** (jŏn′ᵊthᵊn), 1667–1745, English satirist.

swig (swig), n., v., **swigged,** swig·ging. Informal. —n. **1.** a swallow of liquid, esp. liquor. —v.t., v.i. **2.** to drink heartily.

swill (swil), n. **1.** liquid or partly liquid food for animals. **2.** kitchen garbage. —v.i., v.t. **3.** to drink greedily. **4.** to feed (animals) with swill. —**swill′er,** n.

swim (swim), v., **swam,** swum, swim·ming, n. —v.i. **1.** to move in water by using the limbs, fins, tail, etc. **2.** to float on water. **3.** to move or glide smoothly. **4.** to be surrounded or covered with a liquid. **5.** to be dizzy or giddy. —v.t. **6.** to move along in or cross by swimming. —n. **7.** the act or a period of swimming. **8.** in the swim, interested in or informed about current trends, events, etc. —**swim′mer,** n.

swim·ming (swim′ĭng), n. the sport or a contest based on the ability to swim.

swin·dle (swin′dᵊl), v., **-dled,** -dling, n. —v.t., v.i. **1.** to cheat out of money or property. —n. **2.** the act of swindling. **3.** any fraud. —**swin′dler,** n. —**Syn. 1.** defraud, dupe.

swine (swin), n., pl. **swine. 1.** the domestic hog. **2.** any brutal or vicious contemptible person. —**swin′ish,** adj.

swing[1] (swĭng), v., **swung, swing·ing,**
n. —v.t., v.i **1.** to move or cause to
move back and forth, as something
suspended from above. **2.** to move
or cause to move with a circular or
sweeping movement. **3.** to hang or
cause to move freely. **4.** to cause to
move or turn around a fixed point.
5. to strike with the hand or an object grasped in the hand. **6.** to move
to and fro in a swing. **7.** *Informal.*
to influence or manage as desired:
to swing votes. **8.** *Slang.* **a.** to live
in a lively, stylish way. **b.** to engage
uninhibitedly in sex. **9.** *Informal.* to
suffer death by hanging. —n. **10.**
the act or manner of swinging. **11.**
the amount or extent of such movement. **12.** a swinging blow or stroke.
13. a marked rhythm, as of music.
14. freedom of action or active operation. **15.** a seat suspended from
above by ropes or rods on which a
person may move to and fro for recreation. **16. in full swing,** *Informal.*
in full operation or progress. —
swing'y, *adj.*

swing[2] (swĭng), n. a smooth, flowing
style of jazz, popular esp. in the
1930's.

swing·er (swĭng'ər), n. **1.** a person or
thing that swings. **2.** *Slang.* **a.** a
lively and stylish person. **b.** a person
who is uninhibited sexually.

swing' shift', a work shift in industry from about 4 P.M. until midnight.

swipe (swīp), n., v., **swiped, swip·ing.**
—n. *Informal.* **1.** a strong, sweeping
blow. —v.t. **2.** *Informal.* to strike
with a swipe. **3.** *Slang.* to steal or
filch.

swirl (swûrl), v.i., v.t. **1.** to move or
cause to move with a whirling mo-
tion. —n. **2.** a swirling movement.
3. a twist, as of hair. —**swirl'y,** *adj.*

swish (swĭsh), v.i., v.t. **1.** to move
with a hissing or rustling sound. **2.**
to rustle, as silk. —n. **3.** a swishing
movement or sound.

Swiss (swĭs), adj. **1.** of Switzerland
or its inhabitants. —n. **2.** a native
or inhabitant of Switzerland. **3.** (*l.c.*)
any thin, crisp fabric made in Switzerland. **4.** Also called **Swiss'
cheese'.** a firm pale-yellow cheese
containing many holes.

switch (swĭch), n. **1.** a device for turning an electric appliance on or off or
for changing an electrical connection. **2.** a mechanism for diverting
railroad trains from one track to another. **3.** a shifting or changing. **4.**
a slender, flexible rod, used esp. in
whipping a horse, etc **5.** the act of
whipping with or as with such a rod.
6. a bunch of long hair worn by
women to supplement their own hair.
—v.t. **7.** to shift or change. **8.** to turn
or change by operating an electrical

switch. **9.** to divert (railroad trains)
from one track to another. —v.i.
10. to whip with a switch. **11.** to
swing or whisk, as a fishing line. **12.**
to shift or change. —**switch'er,** n.

switch·back (swĭch'bak'), n. a zigzag
rail or road arrangement for climbing a steep grade.

switch·blade (swĭch'blād'), n. a pocketknife, the blade of which is held
by a spring and released by pressure
on a button.

switch·board (swĭch'bōrd', -bôrd'), n.
a unit containing switches and instruments necessary to complete
telephone circuits manually.

switch' hit'ter, *Baseball.* a player who
can bat either right-handed or left-
handed. —**switch'-hit',** v.i.

switch·man (swĭch'mən), n. a person
who has charge of railroad switches.

Switz., Switzerland.

Swit·zer·land (swĭt'sər lənd), n. a
country in central Europe.

swiv·el (swĭv'əl), n., v., **-eled, -el·ing**
or **-elled, -el·ling.** —n. **1.** a fastening device that allows the thing fastened to turn round freely upon it.
—v.t., v.i. **2.** to turn on or as on a
swivel.

swiz'zle stick' (swĭz'əl), a small rod
for stirring drinks.

swob (swob), n., v.t., **swobbed, swob-
bing.** swab.

swol·len (swō'lən), v. **1.** a pp. of
swell. —adj. **2.** enlarged by or as by
swelling.

swoon (swoon), v.i., n. faint. —
swoon'ing·ly, adv.

swoop (swoop), v.i. **1.** to sweep down
through the air, as a bird upon prey.
—n. **2.** the act of swooping.

swop (swop), v.t., v.i., **swopped, swop-
ping,** n. swap.

sword (sōrd, sôrd), n. **1.** a weapon
with a long, pointed blade fixed in
a hilt. **2.** this weapon as the symbol
of military power or authority. **3. at
swords' points,** mutually ready for
combat.

sword·fish (sōrd'fish', sôrd'-), n. a
large, marine food fish having the
upper jaw elongated into a sword-
like structure.

sword·play (sōrd'plā', sôrd'-), n. the
action or technique of wielding a
sword.

swords·man (sōrdz'mən, sôrdz'-), n.
1. a person who is skilled in the use
of a sword **2.** a fencer or soldier.
—**swords'man·ship',** n.

swore (swōr, swôr), v. pt of **swear.**

sworn (swōrn, swôrn), v. **1.** pp. of
swear. —adj. **2.** bound by an oath
or pledge.

swum (swum), v. pp. of **swim.**

swung (swŭng), v. pt. and pp. of
swing[1].

syb·a·rite (sib′ə rīt′), *n.* a person devoted to luxury and pleasure. —**syb′a·rit′ic** (-rit′ik), *adj.*

syc·a·more (sik′ə môr′, -mōr′), *n.* **1.** a North American shade tree with smooth bark that is easy to flake off. **2.** a European and Asian maple tree.

syc·o·phant (sik′ə fənt), *n.* a self-seeking, servile flatterer. —**syc′o·phan·cy**, *n.* —**syc′o·phan′tic** (fan′-tik), *adj.*

Syd·ney (sid′nē), *n.* a seaport in SE Australia.

syll., **1.** syllable. **2.** syllabus. Also, **syl.**

syl·lab·i·cate (si lab′ə kāt′), *v.t.,* -cated, -cat·ing. to syllabify. —**syl·lab′i·ca′tion,** *n.*

syl·lab·i·fy (si lab′ə fī′), *v.t.,* -fied, -fy·ing. to form or divide into syllables. —**syl·lab′i·fi·ca′tion,** *n.*

syl·la·ble (sil′ə bəl), *n.* **1.** a unit of speech consisting of a single pulse of breath and forming a word or part of a word. **2.** one or more letters used to represent such a unit. —**syl·lab·ic** (si lab′ik), *adj.*

syl·la·bus (sil′ə bəs), *n., pl.* -bus·es, -bi (-bī′). an outline or other brief statement, esp of a course of study.

syl·lo·gism (sil′ə jiz′əm), *n.* a type of deductive argument consisting of two premises by which a conclusion is supported. —**syl′lo·gis′tic** (-jis′tik), *adj.* —**syl′lo·gis′ti·cal·ly,** *adv.*

sylph (silf), *n.* **1.** a slender, graceful girl or woman. **2.** a dainty, imaginary being supposed to inhabit the air.

syl·van (sil′vən), *adj. Chiefly Literary.* **1.** of or inhabiting the woods. **2.** abounding in woods or trees.

sym., **1.** symbol. **2.** symmetrical. **3.** symphony.

sym·bi·o·sis (sim′bī ō′sis, -bē-), *n., pl.* -ses (-sēz). the living together of two dissimilar organisms, esp. when mutually beneficial. —**sym′bi·ot′ic** (-ot′ik, -bē-), *adj.*

sym·bol (sim′bəl), *n.* **1.** a material object representing something, often something immaterial **2.** a letter, figure, or a combination of letters used to represent an object or idea, as in chemistry or astronomy. —**sym·bol′ic** (-bol′ik) **sym·bol′i·cal,** *adj.* —**sym·bol′i·cal·ly,** *adv.*

sym·bol·ism (sim′bə liz′əm), *n.* **1.** the practice of representing things by symbols. **2.** a set of symbols. **3.** symbolic meaning or character.

sym·bol·ize (sim′bə līz′), *v.t.,* -ized, -iz·ing. **1.** to be a symbol of. **2.** to represent by symbols. —**sym′bol·i·za′tion,** *n.*

sym·me·try (sim′i trē), *n., pl.* -tries. **1.** the correspondence in size, form, and arrangement of parts on opposite sides of a plane, line, or point. **2.** beauty based on excellence of proportion. —**sym·met′ri·cal** (si me′-tri kəl), *adj.* —**sym·met′ri·cal·ly,** *adv.*

sym·pa·thet·ic (sim′pə thet′ik), *adj.* **1.** feeling or showing sympathy. **2.** sharing one's ideas, feelings, etc. **3.** pertaining to that part of the autonomic nervous system which functions in opposition to the parasympathetic nervous system, as in stimulating heartbeat and dilating the pupil of the eye. —**sym′pa·thet′i·cal·ly,** *adv.* —**Syn. 1.** commiserating, compassionate. **2.** congenial.

sym·pa·thize (sim′pə thīz′), *v.i.,* -thized, -thiz·ing. **1.** to feel a compassionate sympathy, as for suffering. **2.** to share in a feeling or feelings. —**sym′pa·thiz′er,** *n.*

sym·pa·thy (sim′pə thē), *n., pl.* -thies. **1.** agreement in feeling, as between persons or on the part of one person with respect to another. **2.** the ability to share the feelings of another, esp. in sorrow or trouble. **3.** a relationship between persons or things whereby whatever affects one also affects the other. **4.** favorable or approving accord.

sym·pho·ny (sim′fə nē), *n., pl.* -nies. **1.** an elaborate composition for orchestra, usually in four movements of contrasting tempos. **2.** Also called **sym′phony or′chestra.** a large orchestra organized to perform symphonic compositions. **3.** a concert performed by such an orchestra. **4.** harmony of sounds. —**sym·phon′ic** (-fon′ik), *adj.*

sym·po·si·um (sim pō′zē əm), *n., pl.* -si·ums, -si·a (-zē ə). **1.** a meeting at which several speakers discuss a topic before an audience. **2.** a collection of opinions or articles on a given topic.

symp·tom (simp′təm), *n.* **1.** a phenomenon that arises from and accompanies a particular disease or disorder and serves as an indication of it. **2.** a sign or indication of something. —**symp′to·mat′ic** (-tə-mat′ik), *adj.*

syn-, a prefix meaning: **a.** with or together: *syndrome.* **b.** alike or similar: *synonym.*

syn., **1.** synonym. **2.** synonymous. **3.** synonymy.

syn·a·gogue (sin′ə gog′, -gôg′), *n.* **1.** a Jewish house of worship. **2.** an assembly of Jews for religious worship. Also, **syn′a·gog′.** —**syn′a·gog′al,** *adj.*

syn·apse (sin′aps, si naps′), *n.* the region of contact across which nerve impulses are transmitted in one direction only

sync (singk), *Motion Pictures, Television Informal.* —*n.* **1.** synchronization. —*v.i., v.t.* **2.** to synchronize. Also, **synch** (singk).

syn·chro·nize (sing′krə nīz′), v., -nized, -niz·ing. —v.i. 1. to occur at the same time. 2. to move or operate at the same rate and exactly together. 3. *Motion Pictures, Television.* (of action and sound) to coincide in a scene. —v.t. 4. to cause to synchronize. —syn′chro·ni·za′tion, n. — syn′chro·niz′er, n.

syn·chro·nous (sing′krə nəs), adj. 1. occurring at the same time. 2. moving at the same rate and exactly together. —syn′chro·nous·ly, adv.

syn·co·pate (sing′kə pāt′, sin′-), v.t., -pat·ed, -pat·ing. *Music.* to place (the accents) on beats that are normally unaccented. —syn′co·pa′tion, n.

syn·co·pe (sing′kə pē, -pē′, sin′-), n. the contraction of a word by omitting one or more sounds from the middle, as *ne′er* for *never*.

synd., 1. syndicate. 2. syndicated.

syn·di·cate (n. sin′də kit; v. sin′də-kāt′), n., v., -cat·ed, -cat·ing. —n. 1. a group of individuals or companies combined for carrying out some project requiring large resources of capital. 2. an agency that sells columns or features for simultaneous publication in a number of newspapers. 3. *Informal.* an organized group of gangsters. —v.t. 4. to combine into a syndicate. 5. to distribute or publish through a syndicate. —v.i. 6. to combine to form a syndicate. —syn′di·ca′tion, n.

syn·drome (sin′drōm), n. a group of symptoms that together are characteristic of a specific disease.

syn·er·gism (sin′ər jiz′əm), n. the joint action of agents, as drugs, that when taken together increase each other's effectiveness. —syn′er·gist (-jist), n. —syn′er·gis′tic, adj. — syn′er·gis′ti·cal·ly, adv.

syn·fu·el (sin′fyoo′əl), n. See synthetic fuel. [syn(thetic) + fuel]

syn·od (sin′əd), n. an assembly of church officials or delegates. —syn′od·al, adj. —syn·od·ic (si nod′ik), syn·od′i·cal, adj.

syn·o·nym (sin′ə nim), n. a word having nearly the same meaning as another in the same language. —syn·on·y·mous (si non′ə məs), adj.

syn·on·y·my (si non′ə mē), n. the quality of being synonymous.

syn·op·sis (si nop′sis), n., pl. -ses (-sēz). a brief summary, as of the plot of a novel or motion picture. —syn·op′tic (-nop′tik), syn·op′ti·cal, adj.

syn·tax (sin′taks), n. the pattern or structure of the word order in a phrase, clause, or sentence. —syn·tac′tic (-tak′tik), syn·tac′ti·cal, adj.

syn·the·sis (sin′thi sis), n., pl. -ses (-sēz′). the combining of separate parts or elements to form a whole. —syn′the·size′ (-sīz′), v.t., v.i. —

syn′the·siz′er, n.

syn·thet·ic (sin thet′ik), adj. Also, syn·thet′i·cal. 1. made by artificial, esp. chemical, means. 2. not real or genuine. 3. of or involving synthesis. —n. 4. something synthetic. —syn·thet′i·cal·ly, adv.

synthet′ic fu′el, fuel in the form of liquid or gas made from coal or in the form of oil extracted from shale.

syph·i·lis (sif′ə lis), n. a contagious disease caused by a spirochete, usually venereal, and affecting almost any body organ. —syph′i·lit′ic (-lit′-ik), adj., n.

sy·phon (si′fən), n., v.t., v.i. siphon.

Syr·a·cuse (sir′ə kyoos′, sēr′-), n. a city in central New York.

Syr·i·a (sēr′ē ə), n. a country in SW Asia at the E end of the Mediterranean. —Syr′i·an, adj., n.

sy·ringe (sə rinj′, sir′inj), n., v., -ringed, -ring·ing. —n. 1. a device consisting of a tube and either a plunger or a rubber bulb for taking up fluids from or injecting them into the body. —v.t. 2. to cleanse or inject with a syringe.

syr·up (sir′əp, sûr′-), n. 1. a thick, sweet liquid. 2. liquid made of fruit juices or boiled with sugar. —syr′up·y, adj.

syst., system.

sys·tem (sis′təm), n. 1. a group or combination of things or parts forming a complex or unified whole. 2. an orderly grouping of facts, principles, or methods in a certain field. 3. any formulated method or plan. 4. a manner of arrangement or procedure. 5. a. a set of body organs or related tissues concerned with the same function. b. the body considered as a functioning unit. 6. the structure of society, business, politics, etc. 7. Often, **systems.** an organized set of computer programs. —sys′tem·at′ic, sys′tem·at′i·cal, adj. —sys′tem·at′i·cal·ly, adv.

sys·tem·a·tize (sis′tə mə tīz′), v.t., -tized, -tiz·ing. to arrange according to a system. Also, **sys′tem·ize′.**

sys·tem·ic (si stem′ik), adj. 1. affecting the entire bodily system. 2. absorbed by a plant so as to be lethal to insects that feed on it. —n. 3. a systemic insecticide. —sys·tem′i·cal·ly, adv.

sys′tems anal′ysis, the methodical evaluation of an activity, such as a business, to identify its desired objectives in order to determine procedures by which these objectives can be gained. —sys′tems an′alyst.

sys·to·le (sis′tə lē′, -lē), n. the normal rhythmical contraction of the heart during which the blood in the chamber is forced onward. —sys·tol·ic (si stol′ik), adj.

T

T, t (tē), *n., pl.* **T's** or **Ts, t's** or **ts.**
1. the 20th letter of the English alphabet, a consonant. **2. to a T,** exactly or perfectly.

T., 1. tablespoon; tablespoonful. **2.** Territory **3.** Testament. **4.** true. **5.** Tuesday.

t., 1. teaspoon; teaspoonful. **2.** temperature. **3.** *Gram.* tense. **4.** time. **5.** ton. **6.** transit. **7.** transitive. **8.** troy.

Ta, tantalum.

tab¹ (tab), *n., v.,* **tabbed, tab·bing.**
—n. 1. a small flap or loop, as on a garment, used for pulling or hanging. **2.** a small projection from a card or folder used as an aid in filing. **3. keep tabs on,** *Informal.* to observe closely. **—v.t. 4.** to name or designate

tab² (tab), *n. Informal.* an unpaid bill, as in a restaurant.

tab·by (tab'ē), *n., pl.* **-bies. 1.** a cat with a striped fur. **2.** a female domestic cat.

tab·er·nac·le (tab'ər nak'əl), *n.* **1.** (*often cap.*) the portable sanctuary carried by the Jews during their wanderings after the Exodus **2.** a house of worship for a large congregation **3.** an ornamental receptacle for the Eucharist

ta·ble (tā'bəl), *n., v.,* **-bled, -bling. —n. 1.** a piece of furniture consisting of a flat top supported by one or more legs **2.** such a piece of furniture used for serving food to those seated at it. **3.** the food served at this. **4.** a group of persons sitting at this, as for a meal **5.** an organized arrangement of figures or facts as in columns for quick reference **6.** a concise list or guide *a table of contents.* **7. tables,** tablets on which laws were inscribed by the ancients. **8. turn the tables,** to reverse an existing situation **—v.t. 9.** to lay aside (a resolution, etc.) for future discussion. **10.** *Brit.* to present (a resolution, etc.) for discussion

tab·leau (tab'lō ta blō'), *n., pl.* **tableaux** (tab'lōz, ta blōz'), **tab·leaus. 1.** a vivid or graphic description **2.** a picturesque grouping of persons **3.** a static representation of a scene, by one or more persons suitably costumed and posed esp on a stage.

ta·ble·cloth (tā'bəl klôth', -kloth'), *n.* a cloth for covering a table top.

ta·ble d'hôte (tab'əl dōt'), *pl.* **ta·bles d'hôte** (tab'əlz dōt'). a complete meal served at a fixed time and price at a restaurant.

ta·ble·hop (tā'bəl hop'), *v.i.,* **-hopped, -hop·ping.** to move about in a nightclub, etc., chatting with people at various tables. **—ta·ble·hop'per,** *n.*

ta·ble·land (tā'bəl land'), *n.* an elevated and usually level region.

ta·ble·spoon (tā'bəl spoon', -spoon'), *n.* **1.** a spoon larger than a teaspoon, used in serving food. **2.** a cooking measure equal to ½ fluid ounce. **—ta'ble·spoon'ful,** *n.*

tab·let (tab'lit), *n.* **1.** a number of sheets of writing paper glued together at the edge **2.** a small, flat piece of some solid, as of a drug. **3.** a flat slab, as of stone, bearing an inscription or carving.

ta'ble ten'nis, a variety of tennis played on a table, using small paddles and a hollow plastic ball.

ta·ble·ware (tā'bəl wâr'), *n.* the dishes or utensils, as of china or silver, used at the table

tab·loid (tab'loid), *n.* a newspaper, about half the size of a standard-size newspaper page, concentrating on sensational news, usually heavily illustrated.

ta·boo (tə boo', ta-), *n., pl.* **-boos,** *adj., v.,* **-booed, -boo·ing. —n. 1.** the practice of setting things apart as sacred or forbidden for general use, as among certain primitive peoples. **2.** a ban of any nature based on social convention **—adj. 3.** forbidden by a taboo. **—v.t. 4.** to put under a taboo. **5.** to forbid or prohibit. Also, **ta·bu'.**

ta·bor (tā'bər), *n.* a small drum formerly used to accompany oneself on a pipe or fife Also, **ta'bour.**

tab·u·lar (tab'yə lər), *adj.* **1.** of or arranged in a table or list. **2.** flat like a table or tablet. **—tab'u·lar·ly,** *adv.*

tab·u·late (tab'yə lāt'), *v.t.,* **-lat·ed, -lat·ing.** to put or arrange in a table or list. **—tab'u·la'tion,** *n.* **—tab'u·la'tor,** *n.*

TAC, Tactical Air Command.

tach (tak), *n. Informal,* tachometer.

ta·chom·e·ter (ta kom'i tər, tə-), *n.* an instrument for measuring or indicating the speed of rotation

tach·y·car·di·a (tak'ə kär'dē ə), *n.* excessively rapid heartbeat

tac·it (tas'it), *adj.* **1.** understood without being openly expressed **2.** unvoiced or unspoken. **—tac'it·ly,** *adv.* **—tac'it·ness,** *n.* **—Syn.** implied.

899

tac·i·turn (tas′i tûrn′), *adj.* temperamentally not speaking much. —**tac′·i·tur′ni·ty,** *n.* —**tac′i·turn′ly,** *adv.* — Syn. laconic, reticent, uncommunicative.

tack (tak), *n.* **1.** a short, sharp-pointed nail with a flat, broad head. **2.** a long, temporary stitch used in sewing. **3.** the direction of a sailing vessel sailing close to the wind. **4.** one movement in the zigzag course of a vessel sailing into the wind. **5.** a course of action or conduct. —*v.t.* **6.** to fasten by tacks. **7.** to add something extra. —*v.i.* **8.** to change the course of a sailing vessel. **9.** to change one's course of action or conduct. —**tack′er,** *n.*

tack·le (tak′əl *or, for 2,* tā′kəl), *n.,* *v.,* **-led, -ling.** —*n.* **1.** equipment or gear, esp. for fishing. **2.** a system of ropes and pulleys for hoisting, lowering, or shifting heavy objects. **3.** an act of tackling, as in football. **4.** *Football.* either of the linemen stationed between a guard and an end. —*v.t.* **5.** to undertake to handle or solve. **6.** to seize suddenly, esp. in order to stop. **7.** *Football.* to seize and throw down (a ball carrier). —**tack′ler,** *n.*

tack·y[1] (tak′ē), *adj.,* **tack·i·er, tack·i·est.** a little sticky to the touch. —**tack′i·ness,** *n.*

tack·y[2] (tak′ē), *adj.,* **tack·i·er, tack·i·est.** *Informal.* shabby or dowdy in appearance. —**tack′i·ness,** *n.*

ta·co (tä′kō), *n.,* *pl.* **-cos** (-kōz). a tortilla folded into a turnover or roll with a filling.

Ta·co·ma (tə kō′mə), *n.* a seaport in W Washington.

tac·o·nite (tak′ə nīt′), *n.* a low-grade iron ore.

tact (takt), *n.* a keen sense of the right thing to say or do in dealing with people or situations. —**tact′ful,** *adj.* —**tact′ful·ly,** *adv.* —**tact′less,** *adj.* —**tact′less·ly,** *adv.*

tac·tic (tak′tik), *n.* a method of achieving one's goal.

tac·tics (tak′tiks), *n.* **1.** the science of disposing military forces for battle and maneuvering them in battle. **2.** any maneuvers for gaining advantage or success. —**tac′ti·cal,** *adj.* —**tac′ti·cal·ly,** *adv.* —**tac·ti′cian** (-tish′ən), *n.*

tac·tile (tak′til, -tīl), *adj.* of, pertaining to, or affecting the sense of touch.

tad (tad), *n. Dial.* a small child.

ta·da (tä dä′), *interj.* (used as a jovial fanfare in announcing someone or something.) Also, **ta-dah′.** [imit.]

tad·pole (tad′pōl′), *n.* the aquatic larva of a frog or toad having a tail and gills.

taf·fe·ta (taf′i tə), *n.* a smooth, crisp, lustrous fabric, as of rayon or silk.

taff·rail (taf′rāl′), *n.* a rail around the stern of a ship.

taf·fy (taf′ē), *n.* a candy made of sugar or molasses boiled down.

Taft (taft), *n.* **William How·ard** (hou′ərd), 1857–1930, 27th president of the U.S. 1909–13.

tag[1] (tag), *n.,* *v.,* **tagged, tag·ging.** —*n.* **1.** a piece or strip of strong paper for attaching by one end to something as a mark or label. **2.** any small, hanging part or piece **3.** a hard tip at the end of a shoelace or cord. **4.** a descriptive or representative epithet. **5.** a quotation added for special effect. —*v.t.* **6.** to attach a tag to. **7.** to append as an addition or afterthought. —*v.i.* **8.** *Informal.* to follow closely. —**tag′ger,** *n.*

tag[2] (tag), *n.,* *v.,* **tagged, tag·ging.** —*n.* **1.** a children's game in which one player chases the others till he or she touches one of them. —*v.t.* **2.** to touch in or as in the game of tag. —**tag′ger,** *n.*

TAG, The Adjutant General.

Ta·ga·log (tä gä′log, tag′ə log′), *n.,* *pl.* **-logs, -log** for **1. 1.** a member of a Malayan people native to the Philippines. **2.** the principal Indonesian language of the Philippines.

tag′ sale′, a sale of used household goods, etc., held at one's home.

Ta·hi·ti (tə hē′tē, tä-, tī′tē), *n.* a French island in the S Pacific.

Ta·hi·tian (tə hē′shən, -tē ən, tä-), *adj.* **1.** of Tahiti, its inhabitants, or their language. —*n.* **2.** a native or inhabitant of Tahiti. **3.** the Polynesian language of Tahiti.

tai chi (tī′ jē′), a Chinese form of shadowboxing characterized by extremely slow, stylized movements. Also called **t′ai′ chi′ ch′uan′** (chwän′).

tai·ga (tī′gə), *n.* the coniferous, evergreen forests of subarctic lands.

tail (tāl), *n.* **1.** the hindmost part of an animal, esp. when forming a distinct, flexible appendage. **2.** something resembling this in shape or position. **3.** the bottom or end part of anything. **4.** the reverse of a coin. **5.** *tails,* men's full-dress attire. **6.** *Informal.* a person who keeps a close surveillance of another. **7. turn tail,** to run away from danger. —*adj.* **8.** coming from behind: *a tail breeze.* **9.** being in the rear. —*v.t.,* *v.i.* **10.** *Informal.* to follow close behind. —**tail′less,** *adj.*

tail·coat (tāl′kōt′), *n. Brit.* cutaway.

tail·gate (tāl′gāt′), *n.,* *v.,* **-gat·ed, -gat·ing.** —*n.* **1.** the board or gate at the back of a vehicle which can be removed or let down, as for unloading. —*v.i.,* *v.t.* **2.** to drive hazardously close behind (another vehicle).

tail·light (tāl′līt′), *n.* a warning light, usually red, at the rear of a vehicle.

tai·lor (tā′lər), *n.* **1.** a person whose occupation is the making, mending, or altering of outer garments. —*v.i.* **2.** to do the work of a tailor. —*v.t.* **3.** to make by tailor's work. **4.** to fashion or adapt to a particular taste, purpose, etc.

tail·pipe (tāl′pīp′), *n.* an exhaust pipe located at the rear of a car or jet-engine airplane.

tail·spin (tal′spin′), *n.* a maneuver in which an airplane dives in such a way as to describe a spiral.

taint (tānt), *n.* **1.** a trace of infection or contamination. **2.** a trace of dishonor or discredit. —*v.t.* **3.** to affect with something offensive or harmful. **4.** to contaminate or corrupt.

Tai·pei (tī′pā′), *n.* the capital of the Republic of China.

Tai·wan (tī′wän′), *n.* a Chinese island off the SE coast of China.

take (tāk), *v.,* **took, tak·en** (tā′kən), **tak·ing,** *n.* —*v.t.* **1.** to get into possession, as by voluntary action. **2.** to seize or capture. **3.** to hold, grasp, or grip. **4.** to choose or select. **5.** to receive and accept willingly: *to take advice.* **6.** to receive into some relation: *to take a wife.* **7.** to react or respond to in a specified manner: *She took the news hard.* **8.** to be the recipient of, as a prize. **9.** to gain for use, as by payment or lease. **10.** to subscribe to, as a magazine. **11.** to obtain from a source. **12.** to extract or quote. **13.** to have for one's benefit or use: *to take a nap.* **14.** to be subjected to: *to take punishment.* **15.** to carry off or remove. **16.** to subtract or deduct. **17.** to carry with one. **18.** to use as a means of transportation. **19.** to conduct or escort. **20.** to get or contract, as a disease. **21.** to absorb or become impregnated with: *Waxed paper will not take ink.* **22.** to attract or charm. **23.** to require or demand. **24.** to occupy or fill, as time or space. **25.** to use up or consume. **26.** to do or perform: *to take a walk.* **27.** to make (a photograph). **28.** to write down, as a note. **29.** to study: *to take ballet.* **30.** to deal with: *to take things in their proper order.* **31.** to assume the obligation of: *to take responsibility.* **32.** to experience (a certain feeling). **33.** to apprehend mentally. **34.** to regard or consider. **35.** *Slang.* to cheat or victimize. **36.** *Gram.* to be used with (a certain form, case, etc.). —*v.i.* **37.** to catch or engage, as a lock. **38.** to strike root, as a plant. **39.** to win favor or acceptance, as a person or thing. **40.** to have the intended result or effect, as a medicine. **41.** to make one's way. **42.** to fall or become (sick). **43. take after, a.** to resemble. **b.** to follow or chase. **44. take back, a.** to regain possession of. **b.** to return, as for exchange. **c.** to retract or withdraw. **45. take down, a.** to move from a higher to a lower place. **b.** to pull apart or take apart. **c.** to write down. **46. take for, a.** to assume to be. **b.** to mistake for. **47. take in, a.** to permit to enter. **b.** to make (an article of clothing) smaller. **c.** to include or encompass. **d.** to grasp the meaning of. **e.** to deceive or cheat. **f.** to observe or notice. **48. take it, a.** *Slang.* to endure hardship, abuse, etc. **b.** to understand and consider. **49. take off, a.** to remove. **b.** *Informal.* to depart or leave. **c.** to leave the ground, as an airplane. **d.** to subtract, as a discount. **e.** *Informal.* to burlesque or satirize. **50. take on, a.** to hire or employ. **b.** to undertake or assume. **c.** to acquire or assume. **d.** to contend against. **51. take out, a.** to remove or withdraw. **b.** to obtain by application, as an insurance policy. **c.** *Informal.* to escort or invite. **52. take over,** to assume management of or responsibility for. **53. take to, a.** to devote or apply oneself to. **b.** to begin to like. **c.** to go to. **54. take up, a.** to occupy oneself with the study of. **b.** to lift or pick up. **c.** to occupy (space). **d.** to consume or use up. **e.** to begin to support. **f.** to continue or resume. **g.** to make tighter or smaller. **55. take up with,** *Informal.* to become friendly with. —*n.* **56.** the act of taking. **57.** something that is taken. **58.** *Slang.* money taken in, esp. profits. **59.** *Motion Pictures.* a scene photographed without any interruption or break. **60.** a recording of a musical performance. **61. on the take,** *Slang.* in search of personal profit at the expense of others. — **tak′er,** *n.*

take-off (tāk′ôf′, -of′), *n.* **1.** the leaving of the ground, as in leaping or in beginning a flight in an airplane. **2.** *Informal.* a humorous or satirical imitation.

take-out (tāk′out′), *adj.* made to be carried out of a restaurant or serving food for consumption elsewhere: *take-out coffee.*

take·o·ver (tak′ō′vər), *n.* **1.** the seizure or assumption of authority, control, management, etc. **2.** *Informal.* the acquisition of one company by another, esp. when carried out unexpectedly, often without the general consent of the one acquired.

tak·ing (tā'kĭng), *n.* **1.** the act of a person or thing that takes. **2.** takings, receipts, esp. as a profit. —*adj.* **3.** captivating or pleasing, as a smile.

talc (talk), *n.* **1.** a soft, green-to-gray mineral used in making talcum powder. **2.** See **talcum powder.**

tal'cum pow'der (tal'kəm), a powder made of purified talc, for toilet purposes.

tale (tāl), *n.* **1.** a narrative of some real or imaginary event. **2.** a rumor or piece of gossip, often untrue. **3.** a falsehood or lie.

tale·bear·er (tāl'bâr'ər), *n.* a person who spreads gossip or rumor.

tal·ent (tal'ənt), *n.* **1.** a superior inborn capacity for a special field. **2.** a person or persons with such capacity. **3.** any of various ancient units of weight or money. —**tal'ent·ed,** *adj.* —**Syn. 1.** ability, aptitude, faculty, gift.

ta·ler (tä'lər), *n.* any of various former large coins of various German states.

tal·is·man (tal'is mən, -iz-), *n., pl.* **-mans.** an object engraved with magical symbols that is supposed to bring luck or protection to its bearer.

talk (tôk), *v.i.* **1.** to exchange ideas or information by speaking. **2.** to consult or confer: *Talk with your adviser.* **3.** to chatter or prate. **4.** to deliver a speech, lecture, etc. **5.** to give confidential or incriminating information. **6.** to communicate ideas by means other than speech, as by signs. —*v.t.* **7.** to use in speaking: *to talk French.* **8.** to speak about. **9.** to put or influence by talk: *to talk a person to sleep.* **10.** talk back, to reply rudely. **11.** talk down to, to speak condescendingly to. **12.** talk over, to discuss thoroughly. **13.** talk up, to discuss enthusiastically. —*n.* **14.** the act of talking. **15.** informal conversation. **16.** an informal lecture. **17.** a conference or discussion. **18.** report or rumor. **19.** a subject of talking, esp. of gossip. **20.** dialect or lingo. —**talk'er,** *n.*

talk·a·tive (tô'kə tiv), *adj.* inclined to talk a great deal. Also, **talk'y.** —**talk'a·tive·ly,** *adv.* —**talk'a·tive·ness,** *n.* —**Syn.** garrulous, loquacious, verbose.

talk·ing-to (tô'kĭng tōō'), *n. Informal.* a scolding or reprimand.

talk' show', a radio or TV show in which the host or hostess interviews or chats with guests.

tall (tôl), *adj.* **1.** of more than average height. **2.** having a certain height. **3.** *Informal.* **a.** difficult to believe: *a tall tale.* **b.** large in amount or degree: *a tall price.* —**tall'ness,** *n.*

Tal·la·has·see (tal'ə has'ē), *n.* the capital of Florida.

tal·low (tal'ō), *n.* the harder fat of sheep, cattle, etc., used to make candles, soap, etc. —**tal'low·y,** *adj.*

tal·ly (tal'ē), *n., pl.* **-lies,** *v.,* **-lied, -ly·ing.** —*n.* **1.** (formerly) a stick of wood with notches cut to indicate the amount of a debt or payment. **2.** an account or reckoning, as of the score of a game. **3.** anything corresponding to another thing as a counterpart. —*v.t.* **4.** to count or reckon up. **5.** to mark or enter on a tally. —*v.i.* **6.** to correspond or agree. **7.** to make a point, as in a game. —**tal'li·er,** *n.*

tal·ly·ho (tal'ē hō'), *interj.* (the cry of a rider on first sighting the fox in a fox hunt.)

Tal·mud (täl'mŏŏd, -məd, tal'-), *n.* the collection of writings on Jewish law and tradition. [< Heb: orig., instruction] —**Tal·mud'ic** (-mŏŏ'dĭk, -mŭd'-), *adj.* —**Tal'mud·ist,** *n.*

tal·on (tal'ən), *n.* a claw, esp. of a bird of prey.

tam (tam), *n.* tam-o'-shanter.

ta·ma·le (tə mä'lē), *n.* a Mexican dish made of minced meat that has been packed in cornmeal dough, wrapped in corn husks, and steamed.

tam·a·rack (tam'ə rak'), *n.* **1.** an American larch yielding a useful timber. **2.** its wood.

tam·a·rind (tam'ə rind), *n.* **1.** the pod of a large, tropical tree, containing seeds enclosed in a juicy acid pulp. **2.** its tree.

tam·bou·rine (tam'bə rēn'), *n.* a small drum consisting of a circular frame with a skin stretched over it, played by striking or shaking.

tame (tām), *adj.,* **tam·er, tam·est,** *v.,* **tamed, tam·ing.** —*adj.* **1.** changed from the wild or savage state. **2.** docile or subdued. **3.** spiritless or dull. —*v.t.* **4.** to make tame or domesticated. **5.** to make docile or subdued. —**tam'a·ble, tame'a·ble,** *adj.* —**tame'ly,** *adv.* —**tame'ness,** *n.* —**tam'er,** *n.* —**Syn. 1.** domesticated. **2.** gentle, meek, submissive.

Tam·il (tam'əl, tum'-, tä'məl), *n.* **1.** a member of a people of southern India and Ceylon. **2.** their language.

tam-o'-shan·ter (tam'ə shan'tər), *n.* a woolen cap of Scottish origin, having a round, flat top and often a pompon at its center.

tamp (tamp), *v.t.* to pack in tightly by tapping.

Tam·pa (tam'pə), *n.* a seaport in W Florida.

tam·per (tam'pər), *v.i.* **1.** to meddle improperly or harmfully: *to tamper with another person's camera.* **2.** to make changes, as in order to falsify: *to tamper with a passport.* **3.** to engage in underhand dealings, as in order to influence improperly: *to tamper with a jury.* —**tam′per·er,** *n.*

tam·pon (tam′pon), *n.* a plug of cotton for insertion into a body orifice, wound, etc., chiefly for stopping bleeding.

tan[1] (tan), *v.*, **tanned, tan·ning,** *n., adj.,* **tan·ner, tan·nest.** —*v.t.* **1.** to convert (a hide) into leather, esp. by soaking in a solution containing tannin. **2.** to cause a suntan in. **3.** *Informal.* to thrash or spank. —*v.i.* **4.** to become tanned. —*n.* **5.** suntan. **6.** a yellowish brown. **7.** tanbark. —*adj.* **8.** yellowish-brown.

tan[2] (tan), *n.* tangent (def. 3).

tan·a·ger (tan′ə jər), *n.* any of numerous small American songbirds, the males of which are usually brightly colored.

tan·bark (tan′bärk′), the bark of the oak, hemlock, etc., used in tanning hides.

T&E, travel and entertainment.

tan·dem (tan′dəm), *adv.* **1.** one following the other. **2. in tandem, a.** in single file. **b.** in association or partnership. —*n.* **3.** a two-wheeled carriage drawn by horses in tandem. **4.** a bicycle for two persons with seats arranged in tandem.

tang (tang), *n.* **1.** a strong taste, flavor, or odor. **2.** the part of a chisel or knife attached to the handle or stock. —**tang′y,** *adj.*

tan·ge·lo (tan′jə lō′), *n., pl.* **-los.** a citrus fruit produced by crossing the tangerine and the grapefruit.

tan·gent (tan′jənt), *adj.* **1.** *Geom.* touching a curve at a single point or along one line. **2.** in physical contact. —*n.* **3.** *Geom.* a tangent line, curve, or surface. **4. off on or at a tangent,** changing suddenly from one course of action or thought to another. —**tan·gen′tial** (-jen′shəl), *adj.* —**tan·gen·ti·al′i·ty** (-shē al′i tē), *n.* —**tan·gen′tial·ly,** *adv.*

tan·ge·rine (tan′jə rēn′), *n.* a small, sweet orange with a loose skin that is easily removed.

tan·gi·ble (tan′jə bəl), *adj.* **1.** capable of being touched or grasped. **2.** real or actual, rather than imaginary or visionary. **3.** capable of being assigned a monetary value, as an asset. —*n.* **4.** something tangible, esp. a tangible asset. —**tan′gi·bil′i·ty, tan′gi·ble·ness,** *n.* —**tan′gi·bly,** *adv.*

tan·gle (tang′gəl), *v.,* **-gled, -gling,** *n.* —*v.t.* **1.** to twist into a mass of confusedly interlaced parts. **2.** to involve in something that complicates or obstructs. —*v.i.* **3.** to become tangled. **4.** *Informal.* to argue or quarrel. —*n.* **5.** a tangled or twisted mass. **6.** a complicated condition or situation.

tan·go (tang′gō), *n., pl.* **-gos.** a ballroom dance of Spanish-American origin. [< AmerSp < ?]

tank (tangk), *n.* **1.** a large container or structure for holding a liquid or gas. **2.** an armored, self-propelled combat vehicle, armed with cannon and machine guns. —**tank′ful,** *n.*

tank·ard (tang′kərd), *n.* a large drinking mug, usually with a hinged cover.

tank·er (tang′kər), *n.* a ship, airplane, or truck designed to carry oil or other liquid in bulk.

tan·ner (tan′ər), *n.* a person whose occupation is to tan hides.

tan·ner·y (tan′ə rē), *n., pl.* **-ner·ies.** a place where tanning is done.

tan·nin (tan′in), *n.* any of a group of astringent vegetable compounds used to tan hides and make inks. Also called **tan′nic ac′id** (tan′ik).

tan·sy (tan′zē), *n., pl.* **-sies.** a strong-scented, weedy herb having yellow flowers.

tan·ta·lize (tan′t°līz′), *v.t.,* **-lized, -lizing.** to torment with the sight or prospect of something desired that cannot be had. —**tan′ta·li·za′tion,** *n.* —**tan′ta·liz′er,** *n.* —**tan′ta·liz′ing·ly,** *adv.*

tan·ta·lum (tan′t°ləm), *n. Chem.* a gray, hard, rare, metallic element that resists corrosion: used for chemical and surgical instruments. *Symbol:* Ta; *at. wt.:* 180.948; *at. no.:* 73.

tan·ta·mount (tan′tə mount′), *adj.* equivalent in effect or meaning.

tan·trum (tan′trəm), *n.* a sudden burst of bad temper.

Tan·za·ni·a (tan′zə nē′ə, tan zän′ē ə), *n.* a country in E Africa. —**Tan′za·ni′an,** *adj., n.*

Tao·ism (dou′iz əm, tou′-), *n.* a Chinese religion and philosophical system advocating a life of complete simplicity and naturalness. —**Tao′ist,** *n., adj.*

tap[1] (tap), *v.,* **tapped, tap·ping,** *n.* —*v.t., v.i.* **1.** to strike or touch gently. **2.** to make or put with light blows. —*n.* **3.** a light blow or rap. **4.** a piece of metal attached to the toe or heel of a shoe, as for reinforcement. —**tap′per,** *n.*

tap[2] (tap), *n., v.,* **tapped, tap·ping.** —*n.* **1.** a long plug or stopper for closing an opening, as in a cask. **2.** *Chiefly Brit.* a faucet. **3.** *Elect.* a connection made at some point between the ends of a circuit. **4.** a tool for cutting screw threads inside a hole. —*v.t.* **5.** to draw liquid from (a barrel). **6.** to draw off (liquid) by removing or opening a tap. **7.** to draw upon (resources): *to tap talent.* **8.** to wiretap. **9.** to cut a screw thread inside (a hole). **10.** to open outlets from (power lines, pipes, etc.). —**tap′per,** *n.*

tap′ dance′, a dance in which the rhythm is marked by tapping the heels and toes on the floor. —**tap′-dance′,** v.i. —**tap′ danc′er.**

tape (tāp), n., v., **taped, tap·ing.** —n. **1.** a long, narrow strip of cloth. **2.** a long, narrow strip of paper, metal, or plastic. **3.** See **magnetic tape. 4.** See **tape measure.** —v.t. **5.** to tie up, bind, or attach with tape. **6.** to record on magnetic tape. **7.** to measure with a tape measure.

tape′ deck′, a simplified tape recorder, lacking a power amplifier and speaker of its own.

tape′ meas′ure, a tape marked with subdivisions of the foot or meter and used for measuring.

tape′ play′er, a small machine for playing tape recordings.

ta·per (tā′pər), v.i., v.t. **1.** to make or become smaller or thinner toward one end. **2. taper off,** to decrease gradually. —n. **3.** a very slender candle. **4.** a long wick coated with wax. **5.** a gradual tapering off of width or thickness. —**ta′per·ing·ly,** adv.

tape′ record′er, an electric machine for recording and playing back sound on magnetic tape. —**tape′-re·cord′,** v.t. —**tape′ record′ing.**

tap·es·try (tap′i strē), n., pl. **-tries.** a heavy decorative woven fabric with a pictorial design.

tape·worm (tāp′wûrm′), n. a long, flat worm that lives as a parasite in the intestines.

tap·i·o·ca (tap′ē ō′kə), n. a starchy food substance prepared from cassava and used in puddings, etc.

ta·pir (tā′pər), n., pl. **-pirs, -pir.** a large, hoofed South or Central American swinelike animal having a long, flexible snout.

tap·pet (tap′it), n. a sliding rod, intermittently struck by a cam, for moving another part, as a valve.

tap·room (tap′rōōm′, -rōōm′), n. Chiefly Brit. a barroom.

tap·root (tap′rōōt′, -rōot′), n. a main root descending downward and giving off small lateral roots.

taps (taps), n.pl. a bugle call sounded at night as an order to turn out lights, or performed at a military funeral or a memorial service.

tar¹ (tär), n., v., **tarred, tar·ring.** —n. **1.** a dark, sticky substance obtained by the destructive distillation of coal or wood. **2.** smoke solids or components: *cigarette tar.* —v.t. **3.** to smear or cover with tar.

tar² (tär), n. Informal. a sailor or seaman.

ta·ran·tu·la (tə ran′chə lə), n., pl. **-las, -lae** (-lē). a large, hairy spider that gives a painful but not highly poisonous bite.

tar·dy (tär′dē), adj., **-di·er, -di·est. 1.** not arriving at the designated time. **2.** Chiefly Brit. moving or acting slowly. —**tar′di·ly,** adv. —**tar′di·ness,** n.

tare¹ (târ), n. **1.** vetch. **2.** Bible. a noxious weed, probably the darnel.

tare² (târ), n. the weight of the container or packing materials which must be subtracted to give the net weight of the goods inside.

tar·get (tär′git), n. **1.** an object, as one marked with concentric circles, to be aimed at in shooting practice or competitions. **2.** any thing to be struck with missiles. **3.** a goal or aim. **4.** an object of abuse or scorn. —v.t. **5.** to make a target of.

tar·iff (tar′if), n. **1.** a schedule of duties or taxes imposed by a government, esp. on imported goods. **2.** any duty or tax in such a schedule. **3.** any schedule of charges or rates, as of freight.

Tar·mac (tär′mak), n. **1.** Trademark. a bituminous binder for paving. **2.** (l.c.) Chiefly Brit. apron (def. 3).

tarn (tärn), n. a small mountain lake.

tar·nish (tär′nish), v.t. **1.** to dull the luster of. **2.** to sully or disgrace. —v.i. **3.** to grow dull or discolored. **4.** to become sullied. —n. **5.** a dull coating caused by tarnishing.

ta·ro (tär′ō, târ′ō), n., pl. **-ros.** a stemless, tropical plant cultivated for its tuberous, starchy, edible root. [< Polynesian]

ta·rot (ta rō′), n. any of a set of 22 playing cards used for fortunetelling.

tar·pau·lin (tär pô′lin, tär′pə lin), n. a protective covering of waterproofed canvas or other material.

tar·pon (tär′pon), n., pl. **-pons, -pon.** a large game fish found in the warmer waters of the Atlantic Ocean.

tar·ra·gon (tar′ə gon′, -gən), n. an Old World aromatic plant used for seasoning.

tar·ry¹ (tar′ē), v.i., **-ried, -ry·ing. 1.** to delay in acting or starting. **2.** to remain in a place. —**tar′ri·er,** n.

tar·ry² (tär′ē), adj., **-ri·er, -ri·est.** smeared with tar. —**tar′ri·ness,** n.

tar·sus (tär′səs), n., pl. **-si** (-sī). the collection of bones between the tibia and the metatarsus. —**tar′sal** (-səl), adj., n.

tart¹ (tärt), adj. **1.** slightly or agreeably sharp or sour to the taste. **2.** sharp in tone or expression: *a tart remark.* —**tart′ly,** adv. —**tart′ness,** n. —Syn. **2.** biting, caustic.

tart² (tärt), n. **1.** a small pie filled with fruit, usually having no top crust. **2.** Slang. a prostitute.

tar·tan (tär′t°n), n. a woolen or worsted cloth woven with stripes of different colors and widths crossing at right angles, originally worn chiefly by the Scottish Highlanders.

tar·tar (tär′tər), *n.* **1.** a hard, brownish or yellow substance that collects on the teeth. **2.** a pinkish substance that collects in wine casks, used to make baking powder. —**tar·tar′ic** (-tär′ik, -tär′-), *adj.*

Tar·tar (tär′tər), *n.* **1.** a member of any of the various tribes, chiefly Mongolian and Turkish, that overran Asia and much of eastern Europe in the Middle Ages. **2.** any of several Turkic languages of the Tartars. **3.** (*often l.c.*) a savage, intractable person.

tar′tar sauce′, a mayonnaise dressing with chopped pickles, onions, olives, etc. Also, **tar′tare sauce′.**

task (task, täsk), *n.* **1.** a definite piece of work to be done. **2.** a matter of considerable difficulty. **3.** **take to task,** to blame or censure. —*v.t.* **4.** to put a strain upon.

task′ force, a temporary grouping, esp. of military units, for carrying out a specific operation or mission.

task·mas·ter (task′mas′tər, täsk′mä′stər), *n.* a person who assigns tasks to others, esp. burdensome tasks.

tas·sel (tas′əl), *n., v.,* **-seled, -sel·ing** or **-selled, -sel·ling.** —*n.* **1.** a pendent ornament, consisting of small cords or strands hanging from a roundish knob. **2.** something resembling this, as the inflorescence of certain plants. —*v.t.* **3.** to furnish or adorn with tassels. —*v.i.* **4.** (of corn) to put forth tassels.

taste (tāst), *v.,* **tast·ed, tast·ing,** *n.* —*v.t.* **1.** to recognize the flavor of by the sense of taste. **2.** to try the flavor of by taking some into the mouth. **3.** to eat or drink a little of. **4.** to experience (sorrows, etc.). —*v.i.* **5.** to have a particular flavor. —*n.* **6.** the act of tasting. **7.** the sense by which the flavors of things are perceived when they are brought into contact with the tongue. **8.** the quality perceived by this sense. **9.** a small quantity tasted. **10.** a personal inclination to enjoy or appreciate certain things. **11.** the sense of what is proper, good, or beautiful. **12.** a slight experience, as of sorrow. —**taste′less,** *adj.* —**taste′less·ly,** *adv.* —**tast′er,** *n.* —**Syn. 8.** flavor, savor.

11. discernment, discrimination.

taste′ bud′, one of the cells in the tongue which detect the flavors of dissolved substances.

taste′ful (tāst′fəl), *adj.* having or displaying good taste. —**taste′ful·ly,** *adv.*

tast·y (tā′stē), *adj.,* **tast·i·er, tast·i·est.** having a good flavor. —**tast′i·ness,** *n.* —**Syn.** palatable, savory.

tat (tat), *v.i., v.t.,* **tat·ted, tat·ting.** to do, or make by, tatting.

ta·ta·mi (tə tä′mē), *n., pl.* **-mi, -mis.** any of several large straw mats used as floor ceverings in a Japanese house or restaurant.

Ta·tar (tä′tər), *n.* Tartar.

tat·ter (tat′ər), *n.* **1.** a torn, loosely hanging piece, as of a garment. **2.** **tatters,** torn or ragged clothing. —*v.t., v.i.* **3.** to make or become ragged.

tat·ter·de·mal·ion (tat′ər di māl′yən, -mal′-), *n.* a person in tattered clothing.

tat·ter·sall (tat′ər sôl′), *n.* a fabric with brightly colored crossbars in a tartan pattern.

tat·ting (tat′ing), *n.* **1.** the act or process of making a kind of knotted lace of cotton or linen thread with a shuttle. **2.** such lace.

tat·tle (tat′ᵊl), *v.,* **-tled, -tling.** —*v.i.* **1.** to disclose the secrets of another, esp. out of spite. **2.** to chatter or gossip. —*v.t.* **3.** to disclose by gossiping. —**tat′tler,** *n.*

tat·tle·tale (tat′ᵊl tāl′), *n.* a person who tattles.

tat·too¹ (ta tōō′), *n., pl.* **-toos,** *v.,* **-tooed, -too·ing.** —*n.* **1.** an indelible design or picture made on the skin by puncturing it and inserting pigment. —*v.t.* **2.** to mark (the skin) with tattoos. **3.** to put (tattoos) on the skin. —**tat·too′er, tat·too′ist,** *n.*

tat·too² (ta tōō′), *n., pl.* **-toos.** **1.** a strong beating or drumming. **2.** (formerly) a signal, as of a drum or bugle, sounded at night to call soldiers or sailors to return to their quarters.

tau (tô, tou), *n.* the 19th letter of the Greek alphabet (T,).

taught (tôt), *v.* pt. and pp. of **teach.**

taunt (tônt, tänt), *v.t.* **1.** to challenge or reproach in a sarcastic or insulting manner. —*n.* **2.** an insulting sarcasm. —**taunt′er,** *n.* —**taunt′ing·ly,** *adv.* —**Syn. 1.** gibe, jeer.

taupe (tōp), *n.* a dark brownish gray.

Tau·rus (tôr′əs), *n.* **1.** a constellation of the northern sky. **2.** the second sign of the zodiac. [< L: bull]

taut (tôt), *adj.* **1.** tightly drawn, as a rope. **2.** emotionally tense. **3.** tidy or neat, as a ship. —**taut′ly,** *adv.* —**taut′ness,** *n.*

tau·tol·o·gy (tô tol′ə jē), *n., pl.* **-gies.** **1.** needless repetition of an idea in different words. **2.** an instance of such repetition. —**tau·to·log·i·cal** (tôt′ᵊloj′i kəl), **tau·tol′o·gous** (-gəs), *adj.* —**tau·to·log′i·cal·ly,** *adv.*

tav·ern (tav′ərn), *n.* **1.** a place where liquors are sold and drunk on the premises. **2.** (formerly) an inn. [< OF < L *taberna* inn]

taw (tô), *n.* **1.** a playing marble used as a shooter. **2.** the line from which the players shoot.

taw·dry (tô′drē), *adj.*, **-dri·er, -dri·est.** showy and cheap. —**taw′dri·ness,** *n.*

taw·ny (tô′nē), *adj.*, **-ni·er, -ni·est.** of a dark yellowish color. —**taw′ni·ness,** *n.*

tax (taks), *n.* **1.** a sum of money imposed on incomes, property, or sales by a government for its support. **2.** a burdensome charge or demand. — *v.t.* **3. a.** to impose a tax on (a person, etc.). **b.** to set the amount of a tax on (income, etc.). **4.** to lay a burden on. **5.** to blame or reprove. —**tax′a·ble,** *adj.* —**tax·a′tion,** *n.* —**tax′er,** *n.*

tax·i (tak′sē), *n., pl.* **tax·is** or **tax·ies,** *v.,* **tax·ied, tax·i·ing** or **tax·y·ing.** —*n.* **1.** taxicab. —*v.i.* **2.** to ride or travel in a taxicab. **3.** (of an airplane) to move on the ground or on water under its own power.

tax·i·cab (tak′sē kab′), *n.* a public passenger automobile for hire.

tax·i·der·my (tak′si dûr′mē), *n.* the art of stuffing and mounting the skins of animals in lifelike form. —**tax′i·der′mist,** *n.*

tax′ loss′, a net capital loss established at the year end for the sole purpose of a tax deduction.

tax·on·o·my (tak son′ə mē), *n.* the science dealing with the classification of plants and animals. —**tax′o·nom′-ic** (-sə nom′ik), *adj.* —**tax′o·nom′i·cal·ly,** *adv.* —**tax·on′o·mist,** *n.*

tax·pay·er (taks′pā′ər), *n.* a person who pays a tax. —**tax′pay′ing,** *adj.*

tax′ shel′ter, any financial arrangement, as a certain kind of depreciation allowance, which results in a reduction of taxes due. —**tax′-shel′-tered,** *adj.*

Tay·lor (tā′lər), *n.* **Zach·a·ry** (zak′ə-rē), 1784–1850, 12th president of the U.S. 1849–50.

TB, tuberculosis. Also, **T.B., Tb**

Tb, terbium.

t.b., trial balance.

T′-bar lift′ (tē′bär′), a ski lift having a T-shaped bar against which two skiers may lean.

tbs., tablespoon; tablespoonful. Also, **tbsp.**

TC, Teachers College.

Tc, technetium.

Tchai·kov·sky (chī kôf′skē), *n.* **Peter Il·yich** (il′yich), 1840–93, Russian composer.

TD, **1.** touchdown; touchdowns. **2.** Treasury Department.

TDY, temporary duty.

Te, tellurium.

tea (tē), *n.* **1.** the dried leaves of an evergreen Asian shrub, steeped in boiling water to make a drink. **2.** its shrub. **3.** the drink thus prepared. **4.** any similar drink prepared from the leaves of other plants. **5.** a social gathering at which tea is served. **6.** *Brit.* a light afternoon or evening meal. [< Chin (dial.)]

teach (tēch), *v.*, **taught, teach·ing.** —*v.t.* **1.** to give instruction in. **2.** to give instruction to. **3.** to help to learn, as by example. —*v.i.* **4.** to be employed as a teacher. —**teach′a·ble,** *adj.* —**Syn. 2.** educate, tutor.

teach·er (tē′chər), *n.* a person who teaches or instructs, esp. as a profession.

teach·ing (tē′ching), *n.* **1.** the act or profession of a person who teaches. **2.** Often, **teachings.** something taught, esp. a doctrine.

teach′ing machine′, an automatic device that presents the user with items of information in planned sequence.

tea·cup (tē′kup′), *n.* a cup in which tea is served. —**tea′cup·ful′,** *n.*

teak (tēk), *n.* **1.** a large East Indian tree that yields a hard, resinous, yellowish-brown wood. **2.** its wood.

tea·ket·tle (tē′ket′°l), *n.* a kettle with a cover, spout, and handle, used for boiling water.

teal (tēl), *n., pl.* **-teals, -teal. 1.** a small, wild freshwater duck having a short neck. **2.** a medium to dark greenish blue.

team (tēm), *n.* **1.** a group of persons joined together in some action or contest. **2.** two or more draft animals harnessed together. —*v.i.* **3.** to join or work together in a team. **4.** *Archaic.* to drive a team of animals. —*adj.* **5.** of or performed by a team.

team·mate (tēm′māt′), *n.* a member of the same team.

team·ster (tēm′stər), *n.* **1.** a truck driver: now chiefly used for a member of a large labor union commonly called Teamsters Union. **2.** *Archaic.* the driver of a team of animals.

team·work (tēm′wûrk′), *n.* cooperative effort by a group of persons acting together as a team.

tea·pot (tē′pot′), *n.* a container with a spout and handle, in which tea is made and served.

tear¹ (tēr), *n.* **1.** a drop of salty, watery fluid lubricating the surface of the eye and flowing from it, as when crying. **2. in tears,** weeping or crying. —**tear′ful,** *adj.* —**tear′ful·ly,** *adv.* —**tear′y,** *adj.*

tear² (târ), *v.*, **tore, torn, tear·ing,** *n.* —*v.t.* **1.** to pull apart or in pieces by force. **2.** to produce or make (a hole) by ripping. **3.** to make wounds or scratches in. **4.** to pull or snatch violently. **5.** to divide or disrupt. **6.** to harrow or torment. —*v.i.* **7.** to become torn. **8.** to move with great haste or speed. **9. tear down,** to destroy or demolish. —*n.* **10.** the act of tearing. **11.** a rip or hole. —**tear′·a·ble,** *adj.* —**tear′er,** *n.*

tear-drop (tēr′drop′), *n.* **1.** tear[1] (def. 1). **2.** something shaped like a tear.

tear′ gas′ (tēr), a gas that makes the eyes smart and water, thus producing a temporary blindness. —**tear′-gas′,** *v.t.*

tear-jerk-er (tēr′jûr′kər), *n. Informal.* a pathetic story, play, or movie.

tease (tēz), *v.,* **teased, teas·ing,** *n.* —*v.t.* **1.** to make fun of, esp. playfully or unpleasantly. **2.** to irritate or annoy, as with persistent petty distractions or requests. **3.** to beg or importune repeatedly. **4.** to coax persistently. **5.** to pull apart or separate the fibers of (wool), as in combing. **6.** to ruffle (the hair) by holding it at the ends and combing toward the scalp so as to give body to a hairdo. **7.** to rise a nap on (cloth) with teasels. —*v.i.* **8.** to engage or indulge in teasing. —*n.* **9.** a person who teases. **10.** the act of teasing or state of being teased. —**teas′er,** *n.* —**teas′ing·ly,** *adv.*

tea·sel (tē′zəl), *n.* **1.** a thistlelike herb having prickly leaves and flower heads. **2.** the dried flower head of such an herb used for teasing cloth. **3.** any mechanical device used for this. Also, **tea·zel, tea·zle.**

tea·spoon (tē′spōon′, -spoon′), *n.* **1.** a small spoon for stirring tea, coffee, etc. **2.** a cooking measure equal to 1/6 fluid ounce. —**tea′spoon·ful′,** *n.*

teat (tēt, tit), *n.* a nipple on an udder or breast.

tech., 1. technical. **2.** technically. **3.** technician. **4.** technological. **5.** technology.

tech·ne·ti·um (tek nē′shē əm, -shəm), *n. Chem.* an element of the manganese family, not found in nature but obtained from atomic fission. *Symbol:* Tc; *at. wt.:* 99; *at. no.:* 43.

tech·nic (tek′nik, tek nēk′), *n. Rare.* technique.

tech·ni·cal (tek′ni kəl), *adj.* **1.** of or pertaining to a particular art, science, profession, or trade. **2.** of or concerned with the mechanical or industrial arts and the applied sciences. **3.** of or showing technique. **4.** strictly following the rules of a certain science or art. —**tech′ni·cal·ly,** *adv.* —**tech′ni·cal·ness,** *n.*

tech·ni·cal·i·ty (tek′nə kal′i tē), *n., pl.* **-ties. 1.** the condition of being technical. **2.** the use of technical methods or terms. **3.** a technical point, detail, or expression.

tech′nical ser′geant, *U.S. Air Force.* a noncommissioned officer ranking below a master sergeant and above a staff sergeant.

tech·ni·cian (tek nish′ən), *n.* a person trained or skilled in the technicalities of a certain field, as an applied science.

Tech·ni·col·or (tek′nə kul′ər), *n. Trademark.* a system of making color motion pictures.

tech·nique (tek nēk′), *n.* **1.** the manner with which a person fulfills the technical requirements of his or her particular art or field of endeavor. **2.** technical procedures or methods.

tech·noc·ra·cy (tek nok′rə sē), *n., pl.* **-cies.** government by technologists and engineers. —**tech′no·crat′** (-nə-krat′), *n.* —**tech′no·crat′ic,** *adj.*

tech·nol·o·gy (tek nol′ə jē), *n.* **1.** the branch of knowledge that deals with industrial arts, applied science, engineering, etc. **2.** the practical application of knowledge. —**tech′no·log′i·cal** (-nə loj′i kəl), *adj.* —**tech′no·log′i·cal·ly,** *adv.* —**tech·nol′o·gist,** *n.*

tec·ton·ics (tek ton′iks), *n.* **1.** the constructive arts in general. **2.** the branch of geology dealing with the structure of rocks.

ted′dy bear′ (ted′ē), a stuffed toy bear.

te·di·ous (tē′dē əs, tē′jəs), *adj.* long and tiresome. —**te′di·ous·ly,** *adv.* —**te′di·ous·ness,** *n.* —**Syn.** boring, monotonous, wearisome.

te·di·um (tē′dē əm), *n.* the quality or state of being tedious.

tee (tē), *n., v.,* **teed, tee·ing.** *Golf.* —*n.* **1.** the starting place, usually a hard mound of earth, at the beginning of play for each hole. **2.** a small peg from which the ball is driven, as in teeing off. —*v.t., v.i.* **3.** to place the ball on a tee. **4.** **tee off, a.** to strike the ball from a tee. **b.** *Slang.* to make irritated or disgusted.

teem (tēm), *v.i.* to be overflowingly full.

teen (tēn), *adj.* teenage.

teen·age (tēn′āj′), *adj.* of, being, or like persons in their teens. Also, **teen′aged′.** —**teen′ag′er,** *n.*

teens (tēnz), *n.pl.* **1.** the ages of 13 to 19 inclusive. **2.** the numbers 13 to 19 inclusive.

tee·ny (tē′nē), *adj.,* **-ni·er, -ni·est.** *Informal.* tiny. Also, **teen′sy** (-sē), **teen′sy-ween′sy** (-wēn′sē), **tee·ny-wee·ny** (tē′nē wē′nē).

tee·ny·bop·per (tē′nē bop′ər), *n. Slang.* a rebellious or faddish young teenager of the late 1960's.

tee·pee (tē′pē), *n.* tepee.

tee′ shirt′, T-shirt.

tee·ter (tē′tər), *v.i., v.t.* **1.** to move unsteadily from side to side. **2.** to seesaw. **3.** a wobbling motion.

teeth (tēth), *n.* pl of **tooth.**

teethe (tēth), *v.i.,* **teethed, teeth·ing.** to grow or cut teeth.

tee·to·tal·er (tē tōt′°lər), *n.* a person who abstains totally from alcoholic drinks. Also, *Brit.*, **tee·to′tal·ler.** — **tee·to′tal·ism,** *n.*

Tef·lon (tef′lon), *n. Trademark.* a waxy plastic used as a nonsticking coating, as on frying pans.

Te·he·ran (te′hə ran′, -rän′), *n.* the capital of Iran. Also, **Te·hran′.**

tek·tite (tek′tīt), *n.* a small glassy object, believed to have been dislodged from outer space.

tel., 1. telegram. 2. telegraph. 3. telephone.

Tel A·viv (tel′ ə vēv′), *n.* a city in W Israel.

tele-, a combining form meaning: **a.** at or over a distance: *telegraph.* **b.** of or by television: *telecast.*

tel·e·cast (tel′ə kast′, -käst′), *v.,* **-cast** or **-cast·ed, -cast·ing,** *n.* —*v.t., v.i.* 1. to broadcast by television. —*n.* 2. a television broadcast. —**tel′e·cast′er,** *n.*

tel·e·com·mu·ni·ca·tion (tel′ə kə myōō′nə kā′shən), *n.* Often, **telecommunications.** the science of communication by telephone, telegraph, radio, etc.

teleg., telegraphy.

tel·e·gen·ic (tel′ə jen′ik), *adj.* having physical qualities that look attractive on television.

tel·e·gram (tel′ə gram′), *n.* a message sent by telegraph.

tel·e·graph (tel′ə graf′, -gräf′), *n.* 1. an apparatus or system for transmitting messages over a distance by coded electric signals by wire or cable. —*v.t., v.i.* 2. to transmit or send (a message) to (a person) by telegraph. —**te·leg·ra·pher** (tə leg′rə fər); *Brit.*, **te·leg′ra·phist,** *n.* — **tel′e·graph′ic,** *adj.* —**tel′e·graph′i·cal·ly,** *adv.*

te·leg·ra·phy (tə leg′rə fē), *n.* the construction or operation of telegraphs.

tel·e·ki·ne·sis (tel′ə ki nē′sis, -kī-), *n.* the production of motion in a body, apparently without the application of material force.

te·lem·e·ter (tə lem′i tər, tel′ə mē′tər), *n.* an electronic device for measuring a quantity or value, as of radiation, and transmitting it to a remote station for recording. —**te·lem′et·ric** (tel′ə me′trik), *adj.* —**te·lem·e·try** (tə lem′i trē), *n.*

te·lep·a·thy (tə lep′ə thē), *n.* communication between minds by some means other than sensory perception. —**tel·e·path·ic** (tel′ə path′ik), *adj.* —**tel′e·path′i·cal·ly,** *adv.*

tel·e·phone (tel′ə fōn′), *n., v.,* **-phoned, -phon·ing.** —*n.* 1. an instrument or system for electric transmission of voice over a distance by wire. —*v.t., v.i.* 2. to transmit or convey (a message) to (a

person) by telephone. —**tel′e·phon′er,** *n.* —**tel′e·phon′ic** (-fon′ik), *adj.*

te·leph·o·ny (tə lef′ə nē), *n.* the construction or operation of telephones.

tel·e·pho·to (tel′ə fō′tō), *adj.* noting a lens designed to produce a relatively large image of a distant object. —**tel′e·pho′to·graph′,** *n., v.t., v.i.* —**tel′e·pho′to·graph′ic,** *adj.* —**tel′e·pho·tog′ra·phy,** *n.*

tel·e·play (tel′ə plā′), *n.* a play written or adapted for television.

tel·e·print·er (tel′ə prin′tər), *n. Chiefly Brit.* teletypewriter.

tel·e·scope (tel′i skōp′), *n., v.,* **-scoped, -scop·ing.** —*n.* 1. an instrument that uses lenses or mirrors to make distant objects appear larger and therefore nearer. —*v.t., v.i.* 2. to force or slide together, one into another, like the sliding tubes of a jointed telescope. 3. to shorten or condense. —**tel′e·scop′ic** (-skop′ik), *adj.* —**tel′e·scop′i·cal·ly,** *adv.*

tel·e·thon (tel′ə thon′), *n.* a long television broadcast, esp. one soliciting charity funds. [*tele-* + (*mara*)*thon*]

Tel·e·type (tel′i tīp′), *n. Trademark.* a teletypewriter.

tel·e·type·writ·er (tel′i tīp′rī′tər, tel′i tīp′-), *n.* a typewriterlike machine that sends keyboard characters over a telegraphic wire for printing on a similar machine at a distance. —**tel′e·typ′ist,** *n.*

tel·e·vise (tel′ə vīz′), *v.t., v.i.,* **-vised, -vis·ing.** to send or receive by television.

tel·e·vi·sion (tel′ə vizh′ən), *n.* 1. the broadcasting of images by radio waves to receivers that project them on a picture tube for viewing on a screen at a distance. 2. a set for receiving television broadcasts. 3. the medium or industry of television broadcasting. —**tel·e·vi′sion·al** (tel′ə vizh′ə n°l), *adj.* —**tel′e·vi′sion·al·ly,** *adv.* —**tel·e·vi·sion·ar·y** (tel′ə vizh′ə ner′ē), *adj.*

Tel·ex (tel′eks), *n.* 1. *Trademark.* a two-way teletypewriter service channeled through a public telecommunications system. 2. (*l.c.*) a message transmitted by such a service. [*tele*(*typewriter*) *ex*(*change*)] —**tel′ex,** *v.t.*

tell (tel), *v.,* **told, tell·ing.** —*v.t.* 1. to give an account or narrative of. 2. to express by speech or writing. 3. to inform or notify. 4. to reveal or divulge. 5. to discern or distinguish. 6. to bid or command. —*v.i.* 7. to give an account or narrative. 8. to produce a severe effect: *The strain on him was beginning to tell.* 9. **tell off,** *Informal.* to rebuke severely. 10. **tell on, a.** to tattle on (someone). **b.** to tire or exhaust. —**tell′a·ble,** *adj.* —Syn. 1. describe, relate.

tell·er (tel'ər), *n.* **1.** a person employed in a bank to receive or pay out money over the counter. **2.** a person or thing that tells. —**tell'er·ship'**, *n.*

tell·ing (tel'ing), *adj.* **1.** having force or effect. **2.** revealing much. —**tell'ing·ly**, *adv.*

tell·tale (tel'tāl'), *adj.* **1.** revealing what is not intended to be known, —*n.* **2.** a person who reveals private matters. **3.** a thing serving to reveal something.

tel·lu·ri·um (te lŏŏr'ē əm), *n. Chem.* a brittle, crystalline, silver-white element resembling sulfur in properties, used in making alloys. *Symbol:* Te; *at. wt.:* 127.60; *at. no.:* 52.

tel·ly (tel'ē), *n. Brit. Informal.* television.

te·mer·i·ty (tə mer'i tē), *n.* reckless boldness.

temp., **1.** temperature. **2.** temporary. **3.** in the time of. [< L *tempore*]

tem·per (tem'pər), *n.* **1.** heat of mind or passion, shown in outbursts of anger. **2.** a state of mind or feelings. **3.** calm mood or state of mind: *to lose one's temper.* **4.** the degree of hardness given to a metal. —*v.t.* **5.** to moderate or mitigate. **6.** to bring to a desired consistency, as by blending. **7.** to give strength or toughness to (steel) by heating it and then cooling it. —**Syn.** **1.** rage. **2.** disposition, mood. **3.** composure.

tem·per·a (tem'pər ə), *n.* **1.** a technique of painting in which an emulsion of water and egg or of egg and oil is used as a medium. **2.** a painting executed in this technique.

tem·per·a·ment (tem'pər ə mənt, -prə mənt), *n.* **1.** the unique balance of emotions that affects a person's character. **2.** personal nature that is unusually emotional or unpredictable. —**tem'per·a·men'tal**, *adj.* —**tem'per·a·men'tal·ly**, *adv.* —**Syn.** **1.** disposition, make-up.

tem·per·ance (tem'pər əns, tem'prəns), *n.* **1.** self-restraint in action, statement, etc. **2.** moderation or total abstinence from drinking alcoholic liquors.

tem·per·ate (tem'pər it, tem'prit), *adj.* **1.** showing or characterized by temperance. **2.** moderate in respect to temperature. —**tem'per·ate·ly**, *adv.* —**tem'per·ate·ness**, *n.* —**Syn.** **1.** calm, dispassionate, sober.

Tem'perate Zone', the part of the earth's surface lying between the tropic of Cancer and the Arctic Circle or between the tropic of Capricorn and the Antarctic Circle.

tem·per·a·ture (tem'pər ə chər, -prə-chər), *n.* **1.** a measure of the warmth or coldness of an object or substance. **2. a.** the degree of heat in the human body. **b.** the excess of this above the normal.

tem·pered (tem'pərd), *adj.* **1.** having a certain temper or disposition. **2.** lessened or mitigated.

tem'per tan'trum, a sudden burst of bad temper.

tem·pest (tem'pist), *n.* a severe storm, esp. one accompanied by rain, hail, or snow.

tem·pes·tu·ous (tem pes'chŏŏ əs), *adj.* of or resembling a tempest. —**tem·pes'tu·ous·ly**, *adv.* —**tem·pes'tu·ous·ness**, *n.*

tem·plate (tem'plit), *n.* a pattern, as a thin plate of metal, serving as a gauge or guide in mechanical work. Also, **tem'plet.**

tem·ple¹ (tem'pəl), *n.* **1.** a building dedicated to the worship of a god or gods. **2.** a large building devoted to some public use.

tem·ple² (tem'pəl), *n.* the flattened region on each side of the forehead in human beings.

tem·po (tem'pō), *n., pl.* **-pos**, **-pi** (-pē). **1.** the rate or speed at which a piece of music is played or sung. **2.** rate or rhythm of activity. [< It < L *tempus* time]

tem·po·ral¹ (tem'pər əl, tem'prəl), *adj.* **1.** of or pertaining to time as opposed to space. **2.** concerned with the present life or this world. **3.** temporary or transitory. **4.** not sacred or religious. —**tem'po·ral·ly**, *adv.*

tem·po·ral² (tem'pər əl, tem'prəl), *adj. Anat.* of or near the temples.

tem·po·rar·y (tem'pə rer'ē), *adj., n., pl.* **-rar·ies.** —*adj.* **1.** serving or effective for a time only. —*n.* **2.** a temporary office worker. —**tem'po·rar'i·ly** (-râr'ə lē, -rer'-), *adv.* —**tem'po·rar'i·ness**, *n.* —**Syn.** **1.** ephemeral, provisional, transitory.

tem·po·rize (tem'pə rīz'), *v.i.* **-rized, -riz·ing. 1.** to delay making a decision to gain time. **2.** to comply with the time or occasion. —**tem'po·ri·za'tion**, *n.* —**tem'po·riz'er**, *n.*

tempt (tempt), *v.t.* **1.** to entice or allure to do something unwise or wrong. **2.** to appeal strongly to. **3.** to incline or dispose, esp. strongly. **4.** to risk provoking or defy. —**temp·ta'tion**, *n.* —**tempt'er**, *n.* —**tempt'ing·ly**, *adv.* —**tempt'ress**, *n.fem.*

tem·pu·ra (tem'pŏŏ rä', tem pŏŏr'ə), *n.* a Japanese dish of deep-fried seafood or vegetables. [< Jap: fried food]

ten (ten), *n.* **1.** a cardinal number, nine plus one. **2.** a symbol for this number, as 10 or X. —*adj.* **3.** amounting to ten in number.

ten., tenor.

ten·a·ble (ten′ə bəl), *adj.* capable of being held, maintained, or defended. —**ten′a·bil′i·ty, ten′a·ble·ness,** *n.* —**ten′a·bly,** *adv.*

te·na·cious (tə nā′shəs), *adj.* 1. keeping a firm hold. 2. adhesive or sticky. 3. not easily pulled asunder. 4. persistent or resolute. 5. highly retentive, as memory. —**te·na′cious·ly,** *adv.* —**te·nac′i·ty** (-nas′i tē), *n.*

ten·an·cy (ten′ən sē), *n., pl.* **-cies.** 1. the occupancy of property under a lease. 2. the period of a tenant's occupancy.

ten·ant (ten′ənt), *n.* 1. a person or group that rents and occupies the property of another, as a house. 2. an occupant or inhabitant. —*v.t.* 3. to occupy as a tenant. —**ten′ant·less,** *adj.*

ten′ant farm′er, a person who rents farmland from another and pays in cash or in a portion of the produce.

ten·ant·ry (ten′ən trē), *n.* the body of tenants on an estate.

Ten′ Command′ments, the ten precepts given by God to Moses.

tend[1] (tend), *v.i.* 1. to be disposed or inclined in action or operation. 2. to lead in a particular direction.

tend[2] (tend), *v.t.* 1. to attend to by work or services, care, etc. 2. to watch over and care for.

ten·den·cy (ten′dən sē), *n., pl.* **-cies.** 1. a natural disposition to move, act, or set in some direction or toward some point. 2. an inclination or bent to something.

ten·den·tious (ten den′shəs), *adj.* having a definite tendency, bias, or purpose. Also, **ten·den′cious.** —**ten·den′tious·ly,** *adv.* —**ten·den′tious·ness,** *n.*

ten·der[1] (ten′dər), *adj.* 1. soft or delicate in substance. 2. physically frail. 3. young or immature. 4. light or gentle. 5. easily moved to feeling. 6. affectionate or loving. 7. acutely or painfully sensitive. 8. requiring tactful handling. —**ten′der·ly,** *adv.* —**ten′der·ness,** *n.*

ten·der[2] (ten′dər), *v.t.* 1. to present formally for acceptance. —*n.* 2. an offer or bid made for acceptance. 3. something offered, esp. money, as in payment. —**ten′der·a·ble,** *adj.* —**ten′der·er,** *n.*

ten·der[3] (ten′dər), *n.* 1. a person who tends something. 2. a vessel that attends other vessels, as for supplying provisions. 3. a car attached to a steam locomotive for carrying fuel and water.

ten·der·foot (ten′dər fŏŏt′), *n., pl.* **-foots, -feet** (-fēt′). 1. a newcomer to an unsettled region of the western U.S., unused to hardships. 2. a raw, inexperienced person.

ten·der·heart·ed (ten′dər här′tid), *adj.* easily moved to sympathy. —**ten′der·heart′ed·ness,** *n.*

ten·der·ize (ten′də rīz′), *v.t.,* **-ized, -izing.** to make (meat) tender. —**ten′der·iz′er,** *n.*

ten·der·loin (ten′dər loin′), *n.* the tenderest portion of the loin of beef or pork.

ten·don (ten′dən), *n.* a cord of dense, tough, tissue connecting a muscle with a bone or part.

ten·dril (ten′dril), *n.* a coillike part of a climbing plant which winds around its support.

ten·e·brous (ten′ə brəs), *adj. Archaic.* dark and gloomy. Also, **te·neb·ri·ous** (tə neb′rē əs).

ten·e·ment (ten′ə mənt), *n.* 1. a shabby apartment house in the poorer, crowded part of a city. 2. any apartment house. 3. *Rare.* an apartment or flat.

ten·et (ten′it), *n.* a belief or theory held as true. —**Syn.** doctrine, dogma.

10-4 (ten′fōr′, -fôr′), *CB Radio Slang.* (a commonly used term variously meaning "OK," "message received," "yes, indeed," etc.)

ten′-gal·lon hat′, a man's broadbrimmed hat with a high crown.

Tenn., Tennessee.

Ten·nes·see (ten′i sē′), *n.* a state in the SE United States. *Cap.:* Nashville. —**Ten′nes·se′an,** *adj., n.*

ten·nis (ten′is), *n.* a game played on a court divided by a low net, by opposing players using rackets and a ball.

Ten·ny·son (ten′i sən), *n.* **Alfred, Lord,** 1809–1892, English poet.

ten·on (ten′ən), *n.* a projection formed on the end of a timber for insertion into a hole of another similarly shaped piece to form a joint.

ten·or (ten′ər), *n.* 1. general purport or drift. 2. general course or movement. 3. **a.** the highest adult male voice. **b.** a singer with such a voice. **c.** a musical part for such a part.

ten·pin (ten′pin′), *n.* 1. **tenpins,** a form of bowling played with ten wooden pins. 2. a pin used in this game.

tense[1] (tens), *adj.,* **tens·er, tens·est,** *v.,* **tensed, tens·ing.** —*adj.* 1. showing mental or emotional strain. 2. stretched tight, as a cord. —*v.t., v.i.* 3. to make or become tense. —**tense′ly,** *adv.* —**tense′ness, ten·si·ty** (ten′si tē), *n.* —**Syn.** 1. nervous, suspenseful. 2. rigid, taut.

tense[2] (tens), *n. Gram.* the inflected form of a verb that shows the time of its action or state.

ten·sile (ten′səl, -sil *or, esp. Brit.,* -sīl), *adj.* 1. of or by tension. 2. capable of being stretched or drawn out.

ten·sion (ten'shən), *n.* **1.** the act of
stretching or straining. **2.** the state
of being stretched or strained. **3.**
mental or emotional strain. **2.**
strained relationship between individuals, nations, etc. **5.** a force producing elongation or extension, as
of an elastic material. **6.** voltage.
—**ten'sion·al,** *adj.*

tent (tent), *n.* **1.** a portable shelter
of canvas supported by poles or a
metal frame. —*v.i.* **2.** to live in a
tent. —*v.t.* **3.** to cover with or as
with a tent.

ten·ta·cle (ten'tə kəl), *n.* a slender,
flexible appendage in some invertebrates, used for feeling or grasping.
—**ten'ta·cled,** *adj.* —**ten·tac'u·lar**
(-tak'yə lər), *adj.*

ten·ta·tive (ten'tə tiv), *adj.* **1.** made
or done as a trial, experiment, or
attempt. **2.** unsure or hesitant. —
ten'ta·tive·ly, *adv.* —**ten'ta·tive·ness,**
n. —**Syn. 2.** indefinite, uncertain.

ten·ter·hook (ten'tər hŏŏk'), *n.* **1.** one
of the bent nails that hold cloth
stretched on a drying framework. **2.**
on tenterhooks, in suspense.

tenth (tenth), *adj.* **1.** being number
ten in a series. —*n.* **2.** one of ten
equal parts. **3.** the member of a
series following the ninth.

10-13 (ten'thûr'tēn'), *n. CB Radio
Slang.* a report on road and weather
conditions.

ten·u·ous (ten'yŏŏ əs), *adj.* **1.** thin or
slender in form, as a thread. **2.**
weak or poorly supported, as reasoning. **3.** rare or rarefied, as fog.
—**ten·u·i·ty** (tə nŏŏ'i tē), *n.* —**ten'u-
ous·ly,** *adv.* —**ten'u·ous·ness,** *n.* —
Syn. 2. flimsy, unsubstantial.

ten·ure (ten'yər), *n.* **1.** the act or right
of holding property or an office. **2.**
the period or term of such holding.
3. permanent employment in a position, as a professorship. —**ten'ured,**
adj.

te·pee (tē'pē), *n.* a conical tent of
animal skins used by American Indians.

tep·id (tep'id), *adj.* **1.** moderately
warm, as water. **2.** showing little
enthusiasm. —**te·pid'i·ty, tep'id·ness,**
n. —**tep'id·ly,** *adv.*

te·qui·la (tə kē'lə), *n.* a strong liquor
made from a Mexican agave.

ter., 1. terrace. **2.** territorial. **3.** territory.

ter·bi·um (tûr'bē əm), *n. Chem.* a
rare-earth, metallic element. *Symbol:*
Tb; *at. wt.:* 158.924; *at. no.:* 65.

ter·cen·te·nar·y (tûr sen't'ner'ē, tûr'-
sen ten'ə rē), *n., pl.* -**nar·ies.** tricen-
tennial. Also, **ter'cen·ten'ni·al.**

term (tûrm), *n.* **1.** a word or group of
words designating something, esp.
in a particular field. **2.** the time or
period, usually fixed, through which

something lasts. **3. terms, a.** conditions and stipulations: *the terms of
a contract.* **b.** footing or standing:
We're on friendly terms. **c.** words
expressed in a specified way: *in
harsh terms.* **4.** *Math.* **a.** a group of
numbers or symbols separated from
the rest of an equation by a plus,
minus, or equal sign. **b.** the numerator or denominator of a fraction. **5.**
come to terms, to reach an agreement. **6. in terms of,** with special
reference to. —*v.t.* **7.** to name or
designate.

ter·ma·gant (tûr'mə gənt), *n.* a violent, brawling woman.

ter·mi·nal (tûr'mə nᵊl), *adj.* **1.** situated at or forming the end of something. **2.** final or concluding. **3.** of
or lasting for a term or period. **4.**
causing the end of life, as a cancer.
—*n.* **5.** a terminal part of a structure. **6.** a large installation that
handles one or more transportation
lines: *an airline terminal.* **7.** *Elect.*
a. the point at which a current may
be connected to an electric circuit.
b. a device by means of which such
a connection is made. **8.** a device at
which computer data can be fed in
or out. —**ter'mi·nal·ly,** *adv.*

ter·mi·nate (tûr'mə nāt'), *v.t., v.i.,*
-**nat·ed,** -**nat·ing. 1.** to bring or come
to a definite end. **2.** to form the
boundary (of). —**ter'mi·na·ble** (-nə
bəl), *adj.* —**ter'mi·na'tion,** *n.* —**ter'-
mi·na'tive,** *adj.* —**ter'mi·na'tor,** *n.*

ter·mi·nol·o·gy (tûr'mə nol'ə jē), *n.,
pl.* -**gies.** the special terms used in
a science, art, or technical subject.
—**ter'mi·no·log'i·cal** (-n°loj'i kəl),
adj. —**ter'mi·no·log'i·cal·ly,** *adv.* —
ter'mi·nol'o·gist, *n.*

ter·mi·nus (tûr'mə nəs), *n., pl.* -**ni**
(-nī'), -**nus·es. 1.** the end or extremity of anything. **2.** either end of a
railroad line.

ter·mite (tûr'mīt), *n.* a chiefly tropical, social insect highly destructive
to wooden buildings.

tern (tûrn), *n.* a seabird related to
the gull but having a more slender
body.

ter·na·ry (tûr'nə rē), *adj.* **1.** consisting of or involving three. **2.** third in
order or rank. **3.** based on the number three.

terp·si·cho·re·an (tûrp'sə kə rē'ən,
tûrp'sə kôr'ē ən, -kôr'-), *adj.* pertaining to dancing.

terr., 1. territorial. **2.** territory.

ter·race (ter'əs), *n., v.,* -**raced,** -**racing.** —*n.* **1.** a raised level of earth,
esp. one of a series of levels rising
one above another. **2.** a nearly level
strip of land with a sharp descent
along the edge of a sea, lake, or
river. **3.** an open, often paved area
connected to a house and serving as

an outdoor living area. 4. an outside balcony. 5. the flat roof of an Oriental house. —v.t. 6. to form into a terrace.

ter·ra cot·ta (ter′ə kot′ə), a hard, brownish-red, fired clay, used in pottery, etc.

ter′ra fir′ma (fûr′mə), firm or solid earth.

ter·rain (tə rān′, ter′ān), n. a tract of land considered with reference to its natural features.

ter·ra in·cog·ni·ta (ter′ə in kog′ni tə, in′kog nē′-), Latin. an unexplored land or subject.

ter·ra·pin (ter′ə pin), n. any of several edible North American turtles found in fresh or brackish waters.

ter·rar·i·um (te rârē əm), n., pl. -rar·i·ums, -rar·i·a (-rârē ə). a box or enclosure in which small plants or land animals are kept.

ter·raz·zo (tə raz′ō, -rä′zō), n. a mosaic flooring composed of chips of marble and cement.

ter·res·tri·al (tə res′trē əl), adj. 1. of or representing the earth. 2. of or pertaining to land as distinct from water or air. 3. growing or living on the ground. 4. earthly or worldly. —ter·res′tri·al·ly, adv.

ter·ri·ble (ter′ə bəl), adj. 1. causing prolonged or intense fear. 2. distressingly severe. 3. extremely bad. 4. extreme or excessive. —ter′ri·ble·ness, n. —ter′ri·bly, adv. —Syn. 1. appalling, dreadful, horrible.

ter·ri·er (ter′ē ər), n. any of several usually small dogs, used originally to drive game out of its hole.

ter·rif·ic (tə rif′ik), adj. 1. Informal. a. extraordinarily great or intense. b. extremely fine. 2. arousing great fear or dread. —ter·rif′i·cal·ly, adv.

ter·ri·fy (ter′ə fī′), v.t., -fied, -fy·ing. to fill with terror. —ter·ri·fi′er, n. —ter′ri·fy·ing·ly, adv.

ter·ri·to·ri·al (ter′i tôr′ē əl, -tôr′-), adj. 1. of or pertaining to territory or land. 2. of or restricted to a particular territory or district.

ter·ri·to·ry (ter′i tôr′ē, -tōr′ē), n., pl. -ries. 1. any large tract of land. 2. the land and waters under the jurisdiction of a nation, sovereign, etc. 3. (formerly) a region not admitted to the U.S. as a state but having its own legislature. 4. an assigned district, as of a salesman. 5. a field of action or thought.

ter·ror (ter′ər), n. 1. intense or overpowering fear. 2. a person or thing that causes such fear. 3. terrorism. —Syn. 1. fright, horror, panic.

ter·ror·ism (ter′ə riz′əm), n. the use of violence and threats to intimidate or coerce, esp. for political purposes. —ter′ror·ist, n., adj.

ter·ror·ize (ter′ə rīz′), v.t., -ized, -iz·ing. 1. to overcome with terror. 2. to dominate by intimidation.

ter·ry (ter′ē), n., pl. -ries. a pile fabric with uncut loops on both sides, used for toweling. Also called **ter′ry cloth′.**

terse (tûrs), adj., ters·er, ters·est. neatly or effectively concise. —terse′ly, adv. —terse′ness, n. —Syn. brief, pithy, succinct.

ter·ti·ar·y (tûr′shē er′ē, tûr′shə rē), adj., n., pl. -ar·ies. —adj. 1. of the third order, rank, or formation. 2. being the third stage or degree. 3. (cap.) noting the period forming the earlier part of the Cenozoic era, occurring from 1,000,000 to 70,000,000 years ago. —n. 4. (cap.) Geol. the Tertiary period.

tes·sel·late (tes′ə lāt′), v.t., -lat·ed, -lat·ing. to form or arrange in a mosaic pattern. —tes′sel·la′tion, n.

test (test), n. 1. the means by which the presence, quality, or genuineness of anything is determined. 2. the trial of the quality of something. 3. a form of examination for determining a person's knowledge or achievements. 4. Chem. the process of detecting the presence of an ingredient in a substance or of identifying a substance. —v.t. 5. to subject to a test. —v.i. 6. to undergo or conduct a test. 7. to achieve a specified rating on a test. —test′er, n.

Test., Testament.

test., 1. testator. 2. testimony.

tes·ta·ment (tes′tə mənt), n. 1. Law. a will, esp. one that relates to the disposition of one's personal property. 2. a covenant between God and human beings. 3. (cap.) either the New Testament or the Old Testament. 4. a creed or credo. 5. testimony (def. 2). —tes′ta·men′ta·ry (-men′tə rē), adj.

test·tate (tes′tāt), adj. having made and left a valid will.

tes·ta·tor (tes′tā tər, te stā′tər), n. a person who has died leaving a valid will. —tes·ta′trix (te stā′triks), n.fem.

tes·ter (tes′tər), n. a wooden canopy over a bed.

tes·ti·cle (tes′ti kəl), n. either of two oval glands located in the scrotum.

tes·ti·fy (tes′tə fī′), v., -fied, -fy·ing. —v.i. 1. to give testimony under oath, usually in court. 2. to serve as evidence or proof. —v.t. 3. to declare under oath, usually in court. 4. to demonstrate or show. —tes′ti·fi′er, n.

tes·ti·mo·ni·al (tes′tə mō′nē əl), n. 1. a written declaration recommending a person or thing. 2. something given or done as an expression of esteem or gratitude. —adj. 3. pertaining to or serving as a testimonial.

tes·ti·mo·ny (tes′tə mō′nē), *n.*, *pl.*
-nies. 1. the statement made by a
witness under oath, usually in court.
2. evidence in support of a fact or
statement. **3.** open declaration, as
of faith.

tes·tis (tes′tis), *n.*, *pl.* **-tes** (-tēz). tes-
ticle.

tes·tos·ter·one (te stos′tə rōn′), *n.* the
sex hormone secreted by the testes.

test′ tube′, a glass tube closed at one
end, used in chemical and biological
laboratories.

tes·ty (tes′tē), *adj.,* **-ti·er, -ti·est.** irritably impatient. **—tes′ti·ly,** *adv.* —
tes′ti·ness, *n.*

tet·a·nus (tet′ə nəs), *n.* an infectious,
often fatal disease caused by a bacterium that enters the body through
wounds and characterized by spasms
and rigidity, esp. of the jaw. **—tet′-
a·nal** (-nəl), *adj.*

tetch·y (tech′ē), *adj.,* **tetch·i·er, tetch-
i·est.** *Chiefly Brit.* irritably touchy.

tête-à-tête (tāt′ə tāt′), *adj.* **1.** between
or for two persons only. **—n. 2.** a
private conversation between two
persons. **—adv. 3.** (of two persons)
together in private.

teth·er (teth′ər), *n.* **1.** a cord or chain
by which an animal is fastened to a
fixed object. **2.** the utmost extent of
one's ability or resources. **—v.t. 3.**
to fasten or confine with or as with
a tether.

tetra-, a combining form meaning
"four": *tetrahedron.*

tet′ra·eth·yl lead′ (te′trə eth′əl led′),
a poisonous liquid used as an antiknock agent.

tet·ra·he·dron (te′trə hē′drən), *n.,* *pl.*
-drons, -dra (-drə). a solid contained
by four plane faces. **—tet′ra·he′-
dral,** *adj.*

te·tram·e·ter (te tram′i tər), *n. Pros.*
a verse of four feet.

Teut., **1.** Teuton. **2.** Teutonic.

Teu·ton (tōōt′ⁿn, tyōōt′-), *n.* **1.** a
member of an ancient Germanic
people or tribe. **2.** a native of Germany or a person of German origin.

Teu·ton·ic (tōō ton′ik, tyōō-), *adj.* **1.**
of or characteristic of the Teutons.
—n. 2. Germanic (def. 3).

Tex., Texas.

Tex·as (tek′səs), *n.* a state in the S
United States. *Cap.:* Austin. —
Tex′an, *adj., n.*

text (tekst), *n.* **1.** the main body of
matter on a printed or written page,
as distinguished from notes, illustrations, etc. **2.** the actual words of
an author or speaker. **3.** any form
in which a writing exists. **4.** textbook. **5.** a short passage of the
Scriptures, esp. one chosen as the
subject of a sermon. **6.** *Rare.* a subject or theme. **—tex·tu·al** (teks′chōō-
əl), *adj.*

text·book (tekst′bŏŏk′), *n.* a book
used in the study of a particular subject, esp. one used by students in an
academic course.

tex·tile (teks′til, -tīl), *n.* **1.** any fabric
that is woven or knitted. **2.** any material, as a yarn, suitable for weaving
or knitting. **—adj. 3.** of or pertaining to textiles or their manufacture.

tex·ture (teks′chər), *n.* **1.** the structure of the fibers or yarns that make
up a textile fabric. **2.** the physical
structure given to a material by the
arrangement of its parts. **3.** the visual and tactile quality of a surface.
—tex′tur·al, *adj.*

tex′tured vege′table pro′tein (teks′-
chərd), a nutritious meat substitute
made from soybeans.

T-group (tē′grōōp′), *n.* a group of
persons engaged in sensitivity training. [*T(raining) group*]

Th, thorium.

-th¹, a suffix meaning: **a.** act or action: *growth.* **b.** quality or condition: *warmth.*

-th², a suffix used to form ordinal
numbers: *fourth.*

-th³, var. of **-eth¹:** *doth.*

Th., Thursday.

Thai (tī, tä′ē), *n.* **1.** a native or inhabitant of Thailand. **2.** the official
language of Thailand. **—adj. 3.** of
Thailand, its people, or their language.

Thai·land (tī′land′, -lənd), *n.* a country in SE Asia.

thal·a·mus (thal′ə məs), *n.,* *pl.* **-mi**
(mī′). an oblong mass of gray mat-
ter in the brain through which sensory
impulses pass to the cerebral
cortex. **—tha·lam·ic** (thə lam′ik), *adj.*

tha·lid·o·mide (thə lid′ə mīd′, thə-), *n.*
a drug formerly used as a tranquilizer: when taken during pregnancy
it sometimes causes abnormalities in
the fetus.

thal·li·um (thal′ē əm), *n. Chem.* a
rare metallic element. *Symbol:* Tl;
at. wt.: 204.37; *at. no.:* 81.

Thames (temz), *n.* a river in S England, flowing E through London to
the North Sea.

than (than), *conj.* **1.** (used after comparative adjectives and adverbs to
introduce the second member of a
comparison): *He is taller than I am.*
2. (used after some adverbs and adjectives, as *other,* to denote a difference in kind, style, or identity): *I
had no choice other than that.* —
prep. **3.** by comparison with: *He is a
person than whom I can imagine no
one more courteous.*
—Usage. 2. See **different.**

thane (thān), *n.* **1.** a freeman in early
England holding land in return for
military service. **2.** a clan chief in
early Scotland.

thank (thangk), *v.t.* **1.** to give thanks to. **2. have one** or **oneself to thank,** to hold personally responsible: *We have him to blame for this lawsuit.* —**thank′er,** *n.*

thank·ful (thangk′fəl), *adj.* expressing or feeling thanks. —**thank′ful·ly,** *adv.* —**thank′ful·ness,** *n.* —**Syn.** appreciative, grateful, indebted.

thank·less (thangk′lis), *adj.* **1.** not likely to be appreciated or rewarded. **2.** not expressing or feeling thanks. —**thank′less·ly,** *adv.*

thanks (thangks), *n.pl.* **1.** an acknowledgment of a kindness or favor, expressed by words or otherwise. **2. thanks to, a.** thanks be given to. **b.** because of. —*interj.* **3.** I thank you.

thanks·giv·ing (thangks′giv′ing), *n.* **1.** the act of giving thanks. **2.** an expression of thanks, esp. to God.

Thanksgiv′ing Day′, a U.S. national holiday for giving thanks to God, observed on the fourth Thursday of November.

that (t͟hat), *pron.* and *adj., pl.* **those,** *adv., conj.* —*pron.* **1.** the person or thing pointed out or mentioned: *That is her mother.* **2.** the one more remote in place, time, or thought: *This is Mark and that is John.* **3.** who, whom, or which: *the horse that he bought.* **4.** when: *the year that she left us.* **5. at that, a.** in point of something. **b.** in addition. **6. that is, a.** more accurately. **b.** in other words. Also, **that is to say. 7.** with **that,** at that point. —*adj.* **8.** (indicating the person or thing pointed out or mentioned): *That car is mine.* **9.** (indicating the one more remote in place, time, or thought): *This room is his and that one is mine.* —*adv.* **10.** to that extent: *Don't take that much.* —*conj.* **11.** (used to introduce a subordinate clause expressing cause or reason, purpose or aim, result or consequence, etc.): *That he will come is certain.* **12.** (used elliptically to introduce an exclamation of desire, surprise, etc.): *Oh, that I were young again!*

thatch (thach), *n.* **1.** Also, **thatch′ing.** material, as straw or rushes, used to cover a roof. **2.** a covering of such a material. —*v.t.* **3.** to cover with or as with thatch. —**thatch′er,** *n.*

thaw (thô), *v.i.* **1.** to change from a frozen to a liquid state, esp. slowly. **2.** to be freed from frost or extreme cold. **3.** to become warm enough to melt ice and snow. **4.** to become less unfriendly or cold. —*v.t.* **5.** to cause to thaw. —*n.* **6.** the act of thawing. **7.** weather warm enough to melt ice and snow.

THC, the most active chemical ingredient in marijuana. [*t*(*etra*)-*h*(*ydro*)*c*(*annabinol*)]

Th.D., Doctor of Theology. [< L *Theologiae Doctor*]

the¹ (t͟hə, *before a vowel* t͟hē), *definite article.* **1.** (indicating a particular person or thing): *the book you gave me.* **2.** (marking a noun as being used generically): *The wolf is a wild animal.* **3.** (used before an adjective to make it function as a plural noun): *to visit the sick.*

the² (t͟hə, t͟hē), *adv.* **1.** in or by so much: *He looks the better for his rest.* **2.** by how much . . . by so much: *the more the merrier.*

theat., **1.** theater. **2.** theatrical.

the·a·ter (thē′ə tər, thē′ə-), *n.* **1.** a building or a place for presenting dramatic performances, motion-picture shows, etc. **2.** a room or hall with tiers of seats, used for lectures, etc. **3. the theater,** dramatic performances as a branch of art. **4.** dramatic works collectively. **5.** a field of operations. Also, *esp. Brit.,* **the′a·tre.**

the·a·ter-in-the-round (thē′ə tər in t͟hə round′, thē′ə′-), *n.* See arena theater.

the·at·ri·cal (thē a′tri kəl), *adj.* **1.** of or pertaining to the theater. **2.** produced for showing in the theater rather than on television: *a theatrical film.* **3.** artificial and exaggerated. —*n.* **4. theatricals,** dramatic performances, esp. by amateurs. —**the·at·ri·cal·i·ty** (thē a′tri kal′i tē), *n.* —**the·at′ri·cal·ly,** *adv.* —**Syn.** histrionic, melodramatic.

the·at·rics (thē a′triks), *n.* **1.** the art of staging plays. **2.** artificial and exaggerated mannerisms or actions.

thee (t͟hē), *pron. Archaic.* the objective case of **thou¹.**

theft (theft), *n.* the act or crime of stealing.

thegn (t͟hān), *n.* thane.

their (t͟hâr), *pron.* a form of the possessive of **they** used attributively: *their home.*

theirs (t͟hârz), *pron.* a form of the possessive case of **they** used as a predicate adjective, after or without a noun: *Are you a friend of theirs?*

the·ism (thē′iz əm), *n.* belief in the existence of God or gods. —**the′ist,** *n., adj.* —**the·is′tic,** *adj.* —**the·is′ti·cal·ly,** *adv.*

them (t͟hem), *pron.* the objective case of **they.**

theme (thēm), *n.* **1.** a subject that forms the underlying idea of a discourse or discussion. **2.** the central subject of a work of art. **3.** a short, informal essay. **4.** the main melody of a musical composition. —**the·mat′ic** (thē mat′ik), *adj.* —**the·mat′i·cal·ly,** *adv,*

theme′ park′, a recreational park featuring attractions devoted to one or more particular subjects, esp. animal life.

them·selves (ᵺəm selvz′), *pron. pl.* **1.** an emphatic appositive of *them* or *they: The authors themselves could not agree.* **2.** a reflexive form of *them: They dressed themselves quickly.* **3.** their normal selves.

then (ᵺen), *adv.* **1.** at that time. **2.** soon afterward. **3.** next in order of time. **4.** next in order of place. **5.** in addition. **6.** as a consequence. — *adj.* **7.** existing or being at the time indicated: *the then prince.* —*n.* **8.** that time: *We have been back since then.*

thence (ᵺens), *adv.* **1.** from that place. **2.** from that fact. **3.** *Archaic.* thenceforth.

thence·forth (ᵺens′fôrth′, -fôrth′, ᵺens′fôrth′, -fôrth′), *adv.* from that time onward. Also, **thence′for′ward, thence′for′wards.**

the·oc·ra·cy (ᵺē ok′rə sē), *n., pl.* **-cies. 1.** government in which God or a deity is recognized as the supreme civil ruler or by priests claiming a divine commission. **2.** a state under such a form of government. —**the·o·crat·ic** (ᵺē′ə krat′ik), *adj.* —**the′o·crat′i·cal·ly,** *adv.*

theol., **1.** theological. **2.** theology.

the·ol·o·gy (ᵺē ol′ə jē), *n., pl.* **-gies. 1.** the study of God and His relations to the universe. **2.** a particular form or branch of this study. —**the·o·lo·gian** (ᵺē′ə lō′jən), *n.* —**the′o·log′i·cal** (-ə loj′i kəl), *adj.* —**the′o·log′i·cal·ly,** *adv.*

the·o·rem (ᵺē′ə rəm, ᵺēr′əm), *n.* **1.** *Math.* a proposition or formula containing something to be proved from other propositions or formulas. **2.** a proposition that can be deduced from the premises of a system.

the·o·ret·i·cal (ᵺē′ə ret′i kəl), *adj.* **1.** of or consisting in theory. **2.** existing only in theory. **3.** forming or dealing with theories. Also, **the′o·ret′ic.** —**the′o·ret′i·cal·ly,** *adv.* — **Syn.** hypothetical, speculative.

the·o·rize (ᵺē′ə rīz′), *v.i.,* **-rized, -riz·ing.** to form a theory or theories. —**the′o·re·ti′cian** (-ər i tish′ən), **the′o·rist** (-ə rist), *n.* —**the′o·riz′er,** *n.*

the·o·ry (ᵺē′ə rē, ᵺēr′ē), *n., pl.* **-ries. 1.** a coherent group of general propositions used as principles of explanation for a class of phenomena. **2.** the branch of a science or art that deals with its principles rather than its practice. **3.** an explanation that has not yet been proved true. **4.** a guess or conjecture.

the′ory of games′. See **game theory.**

the·os·o·phy (ᵺē os′ə fē), *n.* a system of religious thought claiming a mys-

tical insight into the divine nature. —**the′o·soph′i·cal** (-ə sof′i kəl), **the′o·soph′ic,** *adj.* —**the′o·soph′i·cal·ly,** *adv.* —**the·os′o·phist,** *n.*

ther·a·peu·tic (ᵺer′ə pyōō′tik), *adj.* of or pertaining to the remedial treatment of disease. —**ther′a·peu′ti·cal·ly,** *adv.*

ther·a·peu·tics (ᵺer′ə pyōō′tiks), *n.* the branch of medicine concerned with the remedial treatment of disease.

ther·a·py (ᵺer′ə pē), *n., pl.* **-pies.** the remedial treatment of a disease or other physical or mental disorder. —**ther′a·pist,** *n.*

there (ᵺâr), *adv.* **1.** in or at that place. **2.** at that point in action. **3.** in that matter. **4.** in or into that place. **5. be not all there,** *Informal.* to be feebleminded. —*pron.* **6.** (used to introduce a sentence or clause in which the verb comes before its subject): *There is no hope.* —*n.* **7.** that place: *He comes from there also.* — *interj.* **8.** (an exclamation of satisfaction, encouragement, etc.): *There! It's done.*

there·a·bouts (ᵺâr′ə bouts′), *adv.* **1.** near that place or time. **2.** about that number, amount, etc. Also, **there′a·bout′.**

there·af·ter (ᵺâr af′tər, -äf′-), *adv.* after that in time.

there·at (ᵺâr at′), *adv.* **1.** at that place. **2.** at that time. **3.** because of that.

there·by (ᵺâr′bī′, ᵺâr′bī′), *adv.* **1.** by means of that. **2.** in that connection or relation.

there·for (ᵺâr′fôr′), *adv.* for or in exchange for that.

there·fore (ᵺâr′fôr′, -fôr′), *adv.* as a result.

there·from (ᵺâr′frum′, -from′), *adv.* from that or it.

there·in (ᵺâr′in′), *adv.* **1.** in or into that place or thing. **2.** in that matter or respect.

there·in·af·ter (ᵺâr′in af′tər, -äf′-), *adv.* afterward in that document or statement.

there·of (ᵺâr′uv′, -ov′), *adv.* **1.** of that or it. **2.** from that origin or cause.

there·on (ᵺâr′on′, -ôn′), *adv.* **1.** on that or it. **2.** *Archaic.* thereupon or at once.

there·to (ᵺâr′tōō′), *adv.* **1.** to that or it. **2.** *Archaic.* in addition to that. Also, **there′un′to.**

there·to·fore (ᵺâr′tə fôr′, -fôr′), *adv.* before or until that time.

there·up·on (ᵺâr′ə pon′, -pôn′), *adv.* **1.** immediately following that. **2.** upon that or it. **3.** in consequence of that.

there·with (t͟hâr'with', -wit͟h'), *adv.* **1.** with that or it. **2.** *Archaic.* thereupon or at once.

there·with·al (t͟hâr'with ôl', -wit͟h-), *adv. Archaic.* **1.** in addition. **2.** with that or it.

therm., thermometer.

ther·mal (thûr'məl), *adj.* **1.** Also, **ther'mic** (-mik). of or caused by heat or temperature. **2.** knitted with air space between layers so as to keep cold air out, as underwear. —**ther'mal·ly,** *adv.*

ther'mal pollu'tion, the discharge into rivers or lakes of heated industrial waste water, destroying plant and animal life.

ther·mis·tor (thər mis'tər), *n.* an electric resistor whose action changes sensitively with temperature.

thermo-, a combining form meaning "heat": *thermoplastic.*

ther·mo·dy·nam·ics (thûr'mō dī nam'-iks, -dī-), *n.* the science concerned with the relations between heat and mechanical energy or work. —**ther'mo·dy·nam'ic,** *adj.* —**ther'mo·dy·nam'i·cal·ly,** *adv.*

ther·mom·e·ter (thər mom'i tər), *n.* an instrument for measuring temperature, typically consisting of a sealed glass tube containing a column of liquid, as mercury, that rises and falls with temperature changes. —**ther·mo·met·ric** (thûr'mə me'trik), **ther'mo·met'ri·cal,** *adj.* —**ther·mo·met'ri·cal·ly,** *adv.* —**ther·mom'e·try,** *n.*

ther·mo·nu·cle·ar (thûr'mō nōō'klē ər, -nyōō'-), *adj.* **1.** of or involving the fusion of atomic nuclei, esp. of a gas, heated to a temperature of several million degrees. **2.** of or involving hydrogen bombs.

ther·mo·plas·tic (thûr'mə plas'tik), *adj.* **1.** noting any plastic that can be repeatedly softened by heat and can harden on cooling. —*n.* **2.** a thermoplastic substance. —**ther'mo·plas·tic'i·ty** (-mō pla stis'i tē), *n.*

ther·mos (thûr'məs), *n.* See **vacuum bottle.**

ther·mo·set·ting (thûr'mō set'ing), *adj.* noting any plastic that sets when heated and cannot be remolded.

ther·mo·sphere (thûr'mə sfēr'), *n.* the region of the upper atmosphere in which temperature increases continuously with altitude.

ther·mo·stat (thûr'mə stat'), *n.* a device that turns a heating or cooling system on and off to maintain a desired temperature automatically. —**ther'mo·stat'ic,** *adj.* —**ther'mo·stat'i·cal·ly,** *adv.*

the·sau·rus (thi sôr'əs), *n., pl.* **-sau·rus·es, -sau·ri** (-sôr'ī). a reference book of synonyms and antonyms.

these (t͟hēz), *pron., adj.* pl. of **this.**

the·sis (thē'sis), *n., pl.* **-ses** (-sēz). **1.** a proposition to be proved or maintained against argument. **2.** a monograph embodying original research, esp. one presented by a candidate for an academic degree.

Thes·pi·an (thes'pē ən), (*often l.c.*) —*adj.* **1.** pertaining to the drama. —*n.* **2.** an actor or actress.

the·ta (thā'tə, thē'-), *n.* the eighth letter of the Greek alphabet (Θ, θ).

thews (thyōōz), *n. Literary.* physical strength.

they (t͟hā), *pron.pl.* **1.** plural of **he, she,** and **it. 2.** people in general.

they'd (t͟hād), contraction of: **a.** *they had.* **b.** *they would.*

they'll (t͟hāl), contraction of: **a.** *they will.* **b.** *they shall.*

they're (t͟hâr), contraction of *they are.*

they've (t͟hāv), contraction of *they have.*

thi·a·mine (thī'ə mēn', -min), *n.* a crystalline compound of the vitamin B complex, essential for normal functioning of the nervous system. Also, **thi'a·min** (-min).

thick (thik), *adj.* **1.** having much extent or space between two surfaces. **2.** measured between opposite surfaces. **3.** dense or packed closely together. **4.** heavy or viscous, as soup. **5.** deep or profound: *thick darkness.* **6.** heavily pronounced: *a thick German accent.* **7.** not properly articulated: *thick speech.* **8.** abounding in things close together. **9.** *Informal.* close and intimate in friendship. **10.** mentally slow. **11.** *Brit. Informal.* disagreeably excessive. —*n.* **12.** the thickest, densest, or most crowded part. —**thick'ly,** *adv.* —**thick'ness,** *n.*

thick·en (thik'ən), *v.t., v.i.* **1.** to make or become thick or thicker. **2.** to make or grow more intense or complex. —**thick'en·er,** *n.* —**thick'en·ing,** *n.*

thick·et (thik'it), *n.* a dense growth of shrubs or small trees.

thick·set (thik'set'), *adj.* **1.** having a heavy, solid body. **2.** set or planted closely together.

thick-skinned (thik'skind'), *adj.* **1.** having a thick skin. **2.** unduly insensitive, as to criticism.

thief (thēf), *n., pl.* **thieves.** a person who steals, esp. secretly.

thieve (thēv), *v.t., v.i.,* **thieved, thiev·ing.** to take by theft. —**thiev'ish,** *adj.*

thiev·er·y (thē'və rē), *n., pl.* **-er·ies.** the practice or an instance of thieving.

thigh (thī), *n.* the part of the lower limb between the hip and the knee.

thigh·bone (thī'bōn'), *n.* femur.

thim·ble (thim′bəl), *n.* a small cap worn to protect the fingertip when pushing a needle in sewing. —**thim′-ble·ful′,** *n.*

thin (thin), *adj.,* **thin·ner, thin·nest,** *adv., v.,* **thinned, thin·ning.** —*adj.* **1.** having little extent or space between two surfaces. **2.** having little flesh. **3.** sparse or widely separated: *thin vegetation.* **4.** of low consistency: *a thin sauce.* **5.** not dense: *thin air.* **6.** without substance: *a thin excuse.* **7.** weak and shrill: *a thin voice.* **8.** lacking richness or strength: *a thin wine.* —*adv.* **9.** in a thin manner. —*v.t., v.i.* **10.** to make or become thin or thinner. —**thin′ly,** *adv.* —**thin′ness,** *n.* —**Syn. 2.** lean, slender, slim. **6.** flimsy.

thine (thīn), *pron.* **1.** the possessive case of **thou** used as an adjective. —*adj.* **2.** (used instead of *thy* before a vowel): *thine eyes.*

thing (thing), *n.* **1.** a material object without life or consciousness. **2.** **things,** matters or affairs. **3.** an action or deed: *to do great things.* **4.** a particular or detail. **5.** a useful object, method, etc. **6. things, a.** clothing or apparel. **b.** personal belongings. **7.** a living being or creature: *She's such a pretty thing.* **8.** a thought or statement. **9.** *Informal.* a peculiar attitude or feeling. **10.** *Slang.* something special that one feels disposed to do: *to do your thing.* **11.** **see** or **hear things,** *Informal.* to have hallucinations.

think (thingk), *v.,* **thought, think·ing.** —*v.i.* **1.** to use the mind rationally, as in dealing with a given situation. **2.** to have in the mind as the subject of one's thoughts. **3.** to call something to one's mind. **4.** to conceive of something. —*v.t.* **5.** to have or form in the mind. **6.** to have as an opinion or belief. **7.** to consider for possible action upon. **8.** to regard as specified: *He thought me unkind.* **9. think up,** to contrive by thinking. —**think′a·ble,** *adj.* — **think′a·bly,** *adv.* —**think′er,** *n.*

think′ tank′, *Informal.* a research institute, esp. one employed by government to solve complex problems. Also called **think′ fac′tory.**

thin·ner (thin′ər), *n.* a liquid used to dilute paint to the proper consistency.

thin-skinned (thin′skind′), *adj.* **1.** having a thin skin. **2.** unduly sensitive, as to criticism.

third (thûrd), *adj.* **1.** being number three in a series. —*n.* **2.** a third part, esp. of one (⅓). **3.** the third member of a series. **4.** *Auto.* the third forward gear in transmission. —*adv.* **5.** Also, **third′ly.** in the third place.

third′ class′, 1. the class or grade immediately below the second. **2.** a class of mail consisting of books, etc. —**third′-class′,** *adj., adv.*

third′ degree′, rough treatment, esp. by the police, in order to get a confession.

third′ dimen′sion, 1. the additional dimension by which a solid object is distinguished from any plane object. **2.** something that heightens reality. —**third′-di·men′sion·al,** *adj.*

third′ per′son, *Gram.* the form of a pronoun or verb that refers to the one or ones spoken about.

third-rate (thûrd′rāt′), *adj.* **1.** of the third rate or quality. **2.** quite inferior.

Third′ World′, (*often l.c.*) nonaligned, developing nations, esp. of Asia and Africa, considered as a political force.

thirst (thûrst), *n.* **1.** a sensation of dryness in the mouth and throat caused by need of liquid. **2.** the physical condition resulting from this need. **3.** a strong or eager desire. —*v.i.* **4.** to feel thirst. **5.** to have a strong desire. —**thirst′y,** *adj.* —**thirst′i·ly,** *adv.* —**thirst′i·ness,** *n.*

thir·teen (thûr′tēn′), *n.* **1.** a cardinal number, 10 plus 3. **2.** a symbol for this number, as 13 or XIII. —*adj.* **3.** amounting to 13 in number. —**thir′teenth′,** *adj., n.*

thir·ty (thûr′tē), *n., pl.* **-ties,** *adj.* —*n.* **1.** a cardinal number, 10 times 3. **2.** a symbol for this number, as 30 or XXX. —*adj.* **3.** amounting to 30 in number. —**thir′ti·eth** (-ith), *adj., n.*

this (this), *pron. and adj., pl.* **these,** *adv.* —*pron.* **1.** the person or thing just indicated or mentioned: *This is my hat.* **2.** the one nearer in place, time, or thought: *This is newer than that.* **3.** what is about to follow: *Now hear this!* —*adj.* **4.** (indicating the person or thing just indicated or mentioned): *This man is my friend.* **5.** (indicating the one nearer in place, time, or thought): *This house is ours and that one is theirs.* —*adv.* **6.** to this extent: *this softly.*

this·tle (this′əl), *n.* any of various prickly plants having purple flower heads. —**this·tly** (this′lē, -ə lē), *adj.*

this·tle·down (this′əl doun′), *n.* the mature down seed ball of a thistle.

thith·er (thith′ər or thith′-), *adv.* **1.** Also, **thith·er·ward.** to or toward that place. —*adj.* **2.** on the farther side.

tho (thō), *conj., adv. Informal.* though. Also, **tho′.**

thole (thōl), *n.* one of a pair of pins inserted into a gunwale to hold an oar in rowing. Also called **thole′-pin′.**

thong (thông, thŏng), *n.* a narrow strip of leather used for fastening or lashing.

Thor (thôr), *n. Scand. Myth.* the god of thunder, rain, and farming.

tho·rax (thôr'aks, thōr'-), *n., pl.* **-rax·es, -ra·ces** (-ə sēz'). **1.** the part of the human trunk between the neck and the abdomen. **2.** (in insects) the portion of the body between the head and the abdomen. **—tho·rac·ic** (thō ras'ik), *adj.*

tho·ri·um (thôr'ē əm, thōr'-), *n. Chem.* a grayish-white metallic element, used as a source of nuclear energy. *Symbol:* Th; *at. wt.:* 232.038; *at no.:* 90.

thorn (thôrn), *n.* **1.** a sharp spine or prickle on a plant. **2.** any of various shrubs or trees bearing such thorns. **3.** a source of continual irritation or suffering. **—thorn'y,** *adj.*

thor·ough (thûr'ō, thur'ō), *adj.* **1.** done without negligence: *a thorough search.* **2.** accustomed to neglecting nothing: *a thorough worker.* **3.** complete or perfect: *thorough enjoyment.* **—thor'ough·ly,** *adv.* **—thor'ough·ness,** *n.*

thor·ough·bred (thûr'ō bred', -ə bred', thur'-), *adj.* **1.** of pure breed, as a horse. **—n. 2.** (*cap.*) any of a breed of racehorses originally developed by crossing Arabian stallions with European mares. **3.** a thoroughbred animal.

thor·ough·fare (thûr'ō fâr', -ə fâr', thur'-), *n.* a road that leads at each end into another road, esp. a major highway.

thor·ough·go·ing (thûr'ō gō'ing, -ə gō'- thur'-), *adj.* extremely thorough.

thorp (thôrp), *n. Archaic.* a hamlet.

those (thōz), *pron., adj.* pl. of **that.**

thou¹ (thou), *pron. Archaic or Literary.* the second person singular in the nominative case.

thou² (thou), *n., pl.* **thous, thou.** *Slang.* thousand.

though (thō), *conj.* **1.** in spite of the fact that. **2.** but or yet: *This is all right, though it's not perfect.* **3.** granting that. *—adv.* **4.** however or nevertheless.

thought¹ (thôt), *n.* **1.** the act or process of thinking. **2.** the capacity of thinking or reasoning. **3.** an idea or notion. **4.** consideration or attention. **5.** an opinion or belief. **6.** *Rare.* a bit or trifle.

thought² (thôt), *v.* pt. and pp. of **think.**

thought·ful (thôt'fəl), *adj.* **1.** showing consideration for others. **2.** occupied with thought. **3.** showing careful thought. **—thought'ful·ly,** *adv.* **—**

thought'ful·ness, *n.* **—Syn. 1.** attentive, solicitous. **2.** pensive, reflective.

thought·less (thôt'lis), *adj.* **1.** lacking in consideration for others. **2.** showing lack of thought. **3.** not thinking enough. **—thought'less·ly,** *adv.* **—thought'less·ness,** *n.*

thou·sand (thou'zənd), *n., pl.* **-sands, -sand,** *adj.* **—n. 1.** a cardinal number, 10 times 100. **2.** a symbol for this number, as 1000 or M. *—adj.* **3.** amounting to 1000 in number. **—thou'sandth** (-th), *adj., n.*

thrall (thrôl), *n.* **1.** a person held in bondage as a slave. **2.** slavery or bondage. **—thrall'dom** (-dəm), **thral'dom,** *n.*

thrash (thrash), *v.t.* **1.** to beat soundly in punishment. **2.** to defeat thoroughly. **3.** thresh (def. 1). *—v.i.* **4.** to toss about wildly. **5. thrash out** or **over,** to resolve by full discussion.

thrash·er (thrash'ər), *n.* **1.** a person or thing that thrashes. **2.** a long-tailed, thrushlike bird.

thread (thred), *n.* **1.** a fine cord of a fibrous material spun out to considerable length, used for sewing. **2.** anything resembling a thread, as in fineness. **3.** something that runs through the whole course of something else. **4.** the helical ridge of a screw. *—v.t.* **5.** to pass the end of a thread through the eye of (a needle). **6.** to make (one's way), as among obstacles. **7.** to cut a thread on or in (a screw). **—thread'er,** *n.*

thread·bare (thred'bâr'), *adj.* **1.** worn out so as to lay bare the threads. **2.** wearing threadbare clothes. **3.** hackneyed or trite.

thread·y (thred'ē), *adj.,* **thread·i·er, thread·i·est.** **1.** consisting of or resembling a thread. **2.** thin and feeble, as a pulse.

threat (thret), *n.* **1.** an expression of an intention to inflict punishment or cause harm. **2.** an indication of probable trouble or danger.

threat·en (thret'ən), *v.t., v.i.* **1.** to utter a threat (against). **2.** to be a threat (to). **3.** to give an ominous indication (of). **—threat'en·er,** *n.* **—threat'en·ing·ly,** *adv.*

three (thrē), *n.* **1.** a cardinal number, 2 plus 1. **2.** a symbol for this number, as 3 or III. *—adj.* **3.** amounting to three in number.

3-D (thrē'dē'), *n. Informal.* a three-dimensional process.

three·di·men·sion·al (thrē'di men'shə-nəl), *adj.* having or seeming to have depth as well as width and height.

three·fold (thrē'fōld'), *adj.* **1.** made up of three parts. **2.** three times as great or as much. *—adv.* **3.** in threefold measure.

three R's, reading, writing, and arithmetic, regarded as the fundamentals of elementary education. [from *r(eading)*, *(w)r(iting)*, and *(a)r(ithmetic)*]

three·score (thrē′skôr′, -skôr′), *n.*, *adj.* *Chiefly Literary.* sixty: *threescore and ten.*

three·some (thrē′səm), *n.* a group of three.

thren·o·dy (thren′ə dē), *n.*, *pl.* **-dies.** a song of lamentation.

thresh (thresh), *v.t.*, *v.i.* **1.** to separate (grain or seeds) from (a cereal plant, etc.) by some mechanical means. **2.** *Rare.* to thrash or beat. —**thresh′er**, *n.*

thresh·old (thresh′ōld, thresh′hōld), *n.* **1.** the sill of a doorway. **2.** any point of beginning. **3.** the point at which a stimulus is strong enough to produce an effect.

threw (thrōō), *v.* pt. of **throw.**

thrice (thrīs), *adv.* **1.** three times. **2.** in threefold quantity or degree.

thrift (thrift), *n.* frugal management, esp. of money. [< Scand] —**thrift′less**, *adj.* —**thrift′y**, *adj.* —**thrift′i·ly**, *adv.* —**thrift′i·ness**, *n.*

thrift′ shop′, a store that sells secondhand goods, esp. for charity.

thrill (thril), *v.t.*, *v.i.* **1.** to feel or cause to feel a sudden, keen excitement. **2.** to move quiveringly. —*n.* **3.** a sudden feeling of keen excitement. **4.** something that causes such a feeling. —**thrill′er**, *n.* —**thrill′ing·ly**, *adv.*

thrive (thrīv), *v.i.*, **throve** or **thrived, thrived** or **thriv·en** (thriv′ən), **thriv·ing.** **1.** to prosper steadily. **2.** to grow vigorously. —**thriv′er**, *n.*

throat (thrōt), *n.* **1.** the passage from the mouth to the stomach or to the lungs. **2.** the front of the neck. **3.** any narrow opening, as of a vase.

throat·y (thrō′tē), *adj.*, **throat·i·er, throat·i·est.** produced deep in the throat, as certain sounds. —**throat′i·ly**, *adv.* —**throat′i·ness**, *n.*

throb (throb), *v.*, **throbbed, throbbing**, *n.* —*v.i.* **1.** to pulsate with increased force or rapidity. **2.** to beat or vibrate. —*n.* **3.** the act of throbbing. **4.** a violent beat or pulsation.

throe (thrō), *n.* **1.** **throes,** any violent convulsion or struggle. **2.** a violent spasm or pang.

throm·bo·sis (throm bō′sis), *n.*, *pl.* **-ses** (-sēz). coagulation of the blood in the heart or veins. —**throm·bot′ic** (-bot′ik), *adj.*

throm·bus (throm′bəs), *n.*, *pl.* **-bi** (-bī). a clot that forms in and obstructs a blood vessel.

throne (thrōn), *n.* **1.** the raised chair occupied by a sovereign or bishop on ceremonial occasions. **2.** the office or dignity of a sovereign. **3.** sovereign power.

throng (thrông, throng), *n.* **1.** a great number of persons or things crowded or considered together. —*v.i.* **2.** to gather or move in a throng. —*v.t.* **3.** to crowd into.

throt·tle (throt′ºl), *n.*, *v.*, **-tled, -tling.** —*n.* **1.** a valve for controlling the flow of fuel to an engine. **2.** the lever or pedal controlling this valve. —*v.t.* **3.** to choke or strangle. **4.** to suppress or censor. **5.** to control the speed of (an engine) with a throttle. —**throt′tler**, *n.*

through (thrōō), *prep.* **1.** in at one end or side and out at the other. **2.** between or among. **3.** by way of. **4.** throughout. **5.** up to and including. **6.** finished with. **7.** by the means of. **8.** in consequence of. —*adv.* **9.** from one end or side to the other. **10.** from the beginning to the end. **11.** to the end. **12.** entirely or completely. —*adj.* **13.** finished or done. **14.** passing or extending from one end, side, or surface to the other. **15.** traveling or moving to a destination without stops or changes: *a through train.* **16.** admitting continuous or direct passage: *a through street.*

through·out (thrōō out′), *prep.* **1.** in, to, or during every part of. —*adv.* **2.** in or during every part.

through·way (thrōō′wā′), *n.* thruway.

throve (thrōv), *v.* a pt. of **thrive.**

throw (thrō), *v.*, **threw, thrown** (thrōn), **throw·ing**, *n.* —*v.t.* **1.** to propel from the hand by a sudden forward motion of the arm and wrist. **2.** to send forth (a glance, etc.). **3.** to put into a certain position or condition as if by hurling: *to throw troops into action.* **4.** to put on, off, or away hastily. **5.** to move (a lever) in order to connect or disconnect. **6.** to cause to fall to the ground. **7.** *Informal.* to lose (a game, etc.) intentionally, as for a bribe. **8.** *Informal.* to astonish or confuse: *Her nastiness really threw me.* **9.** *Informal.* to give or host (a party, etc.). —*v.i.* **10.** to throw or cast something. **11. throw away, a.** to dispose of or discard. **b.** to waste or squander. **12. throw in,** to add as a bonus or extra. **13. throw off, a.** to free oneself of. **b.** to give off or discharge. **c.** to confuse or upset. **14. throw oneself at,** to strive to attract the romantic interest of. **15. throw out, a.** to cast away. **b.** to reject or dismiss. **16. throw over,** to forsake (esp. a lover or spouse). **17. throw together,** to make in a hurried manner. **18. throw up, a.** to vomit. **b.** to build hastily. **c.** to relinquish or abandon. **—n. 19.** the act of throwing. **20.** the distance to which anything is or may be thrown. **21.** a light blanket. **—throw′er,** *n.*

throw·a·way (thrō′ə wā′), *n.* **1.** a handbill distributed free, esp. on the streets. **—adj. 2.** made so as to be discarded after use of the contents, as a container.

throw·back (thrō′bak′), *n.* **1.** the reversion to an ancestral type or character. **2.** an example of this.

throw′ rug′. See scatter rug.

thru (thrōō), *prep., adv., adj. Informal.* through.

thrum (thrum), *v.t., v.i.* **thrummed, thrum·ming.** to strum idly.

thrush (thrush), *n.* any of various songbirds, sometimes having spotted underparts.

thrust (thrust), *v., thrust, thrust·ing. n. —v.t., v.i.* **1.** to push or shove with sudden force. **2.** to put boldly into some position or condition. **3.** to stab or pierce, as with a sword. **—n. 4.** a sudden, forcible shove. **5.** a stab with a sword. **6.** a military attack. **7.** a driving force, as of a remark. **8.** a force exerted by a propeller or propulsive gases to propel a ship, aircraft, or spacecraft. **9.** the downward and outward force exerted by an arch on each side. **— thrust′er, thrust′or,** *n.*

thru·way (thrōō′wā′), *n.* a limited-access high highway.

Thu., Thursday.

thud (thud), *n., v., thud·ded, thud·ding. —n.* **1.** a dull sound of heavy impact. **2.** a blow causing such a sound. **—v.i. 3.** to hit or fall with a thud. **—thud′ding·ly,** *adv.*

thug (thug), *n.* a cruel or vicious ruffian.

thu·li·um (thōō′lē əm), *n. Chem.* a rare-earth metallic element. *Symbol:* Tm; *at. wt.:* 168.934; *at. no.:* 69.

thumb (thum), *n.* **1.** the short, thick, inner digit of the hand. **2.** the part of a glove or mitten for containing the thumb. **3. all thumbs,** clumsy or awkward. **4. thumbs down,** an expression of dissent or disapproval. **5. under one's thumb,** under one's control or influence. **—v.t. 6.** to soil or wear with the fingers in handling. **7.** to glance through (pages) quickly. **8.** to get (a ride) or make (one's way) by hitchhiking.

thumb′ in/dex, a series of labeled notches cut along the fore edge of a book, to indicate the sections.

thumb·nail (thum′nāl′), *n.* **1.** the nail of the thumb. **2.** very small or brief: *a thumbnail description.*

thumb·screw (thum′skrōō′), *n.* **1.** a screw that may be easily turned with

the thumb and a finger. **2.** an old instrument of torture for compressing the thumb.

thumb·tack (thum′tak′), *n.* a tack with a large, flat head, designed to be thrust into a board or wall with the thumb.

thump (thump), *n.* **1.** a blow with something thick and heavy. **2.** the sound made by such a blow. **—v.t. 3.** to beat with a thump. **—v.i. 4.** to beat or fall with a thump.

thump·ing (thum′ping), *adj.* **1.** of or like a thump. **2.** *Informal.* strikingly great.

thun·der (thun′dər), *n.* **1.** the explosive sound following an electrical charge of lightning. **2.** any loud, resounding noise. **—v.i. 3.** to give forth thunder. **4.** to make a loud, resounding noise like thunder. **—v.t. 5.** to utter loudly or threateningly.

thun·der·bolt (thun′dər bōlt′), *n.* a flash of lightning accompanied by thunder.

thun·der·clap (thun′dər klap′), *n.* a crash of thunder.

thun·der·cloud (thun′dər kloud′), *n.* an electrically charged cloud producing lightning and thunder.

thun·der·head (thun′dər hed′), *n.* a thundercloud having a flattened, anvil-shaped top.

thun·der·ous (thun′dər əs), *adj.* producing thunder or a loud noise like thunder. **—thun′der·ous·ly,** *adv.*

thun·der·show·er (thun′dər shou′ər), *n.* a shower accompanied by thunder and lightning.

thun·der·storm (thun′dər stôrm′), *n.* a storm with lightning and thunder.

thun·der·struck (thun′dər struk′), *adj.* overcome with amazement.

Thur., Thursday. Also, **Thurs.**

Thurs·day (thûrz′dē, -dā), *n.* the fifth day of the week, following Wednesday.

thus (thus), *adv.* **1.** in this way. **2.** therefore. **3.** to this extent or degree.

thwack (thwak), *v.t.* **1.** to strike with something flat. **—n. 2.** a sharp blow with something flat. **—thwack′er,** *n.*

thwart (thwôrt), *v.t.* **1.** to oppose successfully. **2.** to frustrate by blocking. **—n. 3.** a seat across a boat, used by an oarsman. **—adj. 4.** passing or lying crosswise. **—adv., prep. 5.** *Archaic.* athwart. **—Syn. 2.** baffle, foil, hinder.

thy (thī), *pron.* the possessive case of **thou** used as an attributive adjective.

thyme (tīm, thīm), *n.* a plant having aromatic leaves used for seasoning.

thy·mine (thī′mēn, -min), *n.* a white crystalline pyrimidine derived from thymus DNA, used chiefly in medical research.

thy·mus (thī′məs), *n.* a gland near the base of the neck in human beings.

thy·roid (thī′roid), *adj.* 1. of or pertaining to the thyroid gland. —*n.* 2. See **thyroid gland.** 3. a preparation made from the thyroid glands of certain animals, used in medicine.

thy′roid gland′, a ductless gland in the neck having a lobe on each side of the windpipe and secreting a hormone that regulates the rates of metabolism and body growth.

thy·self (thī self′), *pron.* the emphatic or reflexive form of *thou* or *thee.*

ti (tē), *n.* the seventh tone of a diatonic scale.

Ti, titanium.

ti·ar·a (tē är′ə, -âr′ə, -âr′ə), *n.* 1. a jeweled, ornamental coronet worn by women. 2. the triple crown of the pope. [< L < Gk: turban]

Ti·ber (tī′bər), *n.* a river in central Italy.

Ti·bet (ti bet′), *n.* an autonomous region of China, in S Asia, N of the Himalayas.

Ti·bet·an (ti bet′ᵊn, tib′i tᵊn), *adj.* 1. of Tibet, its inhabitants, or their language. —*n.* 2. a member of the native Mongolian race of Tibet. 3. the language of Tibet.

tib·i·a (tib′ē ə), *n., pl.* **-ae** (-ē′), **-as.** the inner of the two bones of the leg, extending from the knee to the ankle. —**tib′i·al,** *adj.*

tic (tik), *n.* a spasmodic, involuntary muscular contraction, esp. of the face.

tick[1] (tik), *n.* 1. a slight, sharp, recurring click or beat, as of a clock. 2. a mark used to check off items. —*v.i.* 3. to make a tick, like that of a clock. —*v.t.* 4. *Brit.* to mark with a tick.

tick[2] (tik), *n.* any of numerous bloodsucking insects, some of which transmit diseases.

tick[3] (tik), *n.* a cloth case for a mattress or pillow.

tick[4] (tik), *n. Brit. Informal.* credit or a charge account: *to buy on tick.*

tick·er (tik′ər), *n.* 1. a person or thing that ticks. 2. a telegraphic receiving instrument that automatically prints stock prices on paper tape (**tick′er tape′**). 3. *Slang.* the heart.

tick·et (tik′it), *n.* 1. a printed card or slip giving the holder a right paid for, as admission to a theater. 2. a label or tag. 3. the slate of party candidates running together. 4. *Informal.* a summons issued for a traffic or parking violation. 5. *Brit. Informal.* the license of a ship's officer. —*v.t.* 6. to put a label or tag

on. 7. to attach or serve a traffic ticket to. 8. to issue a ticket to, as on an airline: *ticketed passengers.*

tick·ing (tik′ing), *n.* a strong cotton or linen cloth used for making fabric ticks.

tick·le (tik′əl), *v.,* **-led, -ling,** *n.* —*v.t.* 1. to rub or stroke lightly, as with the fingers, so as to produce a feeling of tingling or twitching. 2. to excite agreeably. —*v.i.* 3. to have or cause a feeling of tingling or twitching. —*n.* 4. the act of tickling or a sensation of being tickled. —**Syn.** 2. amuse, gratify, please.

tick·ler (tik′lər), *n.* a pad or card file used to refresh the memory.

tick·lish (tik′lish), *adj.* 1. sensitive to tickling. 2. requiring careful or delicate handling. 3. easily offended. —**tick′lish·ly,** *adv.* —**tick′lish·ness,** *n.*

tick-tock (tik′tok′), *n.* an alternating ticking sound, as made by a clock.

t.i.d., (in prescriptions) three times a day. [< L *ter in die*]

tid·al (tīd′ᵊl), *adj.* 1. of or caused by tides. 2. dependent on the state of the tide. —**tid′al·ly,** *adv.*

tid′al wave′, 1. a large destructive ocean wave produced by an earthquake, hurricane, or strong wind. 2. any powerful movement or tendency.

tid·bit (tid′bit′), *n.* a choice bit, as of food or gossip.

tide (tīd), *n., v.,* **tid·ed, tid·ing.** —*n.* 1. the periodic rise and fall of the waters of the ocean, produced by the attraction of the moon and sun and occurring about every 12 hours. 2. anything that rises and falls like the tide. 3. a trend or tendency, as of events. 4. a season or period (used only in combination): *Eastertide.* —*v.i.* 5. **tide over,** to assist in getting over a period of difficulty or distress.

tide·land (tīd′land′), *n.* 1. land covered by the tide. 2. **tidelands,** submerged offshore land within the historical boundaries of a U.S. state.

tide·wa·ter (tīd′wô′tər, -wot′ər), *n.* 1. water affected by the tide. 2. low coastal land drained by such water. 3. the water covering tideland at flood tide.

ti·dings (tī′dingz), *n.pl. Chiefly Literary.* news or report.

ti·dy (tī′dē), *adj.,* **-di·er, -di·est,** *v.,* **-died, -dy·ing,** *n., pl.* **-dies.** —*adj.* 1. neat and orderly. 2. *Informal.* fairly large: *a tidy sum.* —*v.t., v.i.* 3. to make tidy or neat. —*n.* 4. an ornamental covering for the backs and arms of an upholstered chair to prevent soiling. —**ti′di·ly,** *adv.* —**ti′di·ness,** *n.*

tie (tī), v., **tied, ty·ing,** n. —v.t. **1.** to bind or fasten with a cord or string drawn together and knotted. **2.** to form by looping and drawing tight. **3.** to form a knot or bow in. **4.** to fasten or join in any way. **5.** to confine or limit. **6.** to make the same score as (an opponent). —v.i. **7.** to make the same score, as in a contest. **8. tie down,** to confine or curtail. **9. tie up, a.** to fasten securely by tying. **b.** to impede or stop. **c.** to engage or occupy completely. **d.** to moor a boat. —n. **10.** anything used to fasten or bind something, as a cord or string. **11.** a necktie or bow tie. **12.** a common interest shared by two or more people or nations. **13.** equality of scores or votes. **14.** a beam or rod used as a brace in a building. **15.** one of the crossbeams used for supporting and fastening the rails of a railroad track.

tie·back (tī′bak′), n. a strip or loop used for holding a curtain back to one side.

tie′ clasp′, an ornamental clasp for securing a necktie to a shirt front. Also called **tie′ bar′, tie′ clip′.**

tie-dye (tī′dī′), n., v., **-dyed, -dye·ing.** —n. **1.** a method of dyeing fabric in pattern by tying off areas of it so that they do not receive the dye. —v.t. **2.** to dye in this method.

tie-in (tī′in′), n. **1.** any direct or indirect link or connection. **2.** a method of advertising or selling two or more often related products together under various inducement arrangements.

Tien·tsin (tin′tsin′), n. a port in NE China.

tier (tēr), n. one of a series of rows rising one behind or above another.

tie′ rod′, Auto. a rod connecting the wheels that turn to steer a vehicle.

tie-up (tī′up′), n. **1.** a temporary stoppage of work, traffic, etc. **2.** an involvement or entanglement.

tiff (tif), n. **1.** a minor quarrel. **2.** a slight fit of annoyance or anger.

ti·ger (tī′gər), n. a large, ferocious animal of the cat family found in Asia and having a tawny coat with narrow black stripes. —**ti′ger·ish** (-ish), adj. —**ti′gress,** n.fem.

tight (tīt), adj. **1.** firmly fixed in place. **2.** stretched so as to be tense. **3.** fitting closely, esp. too closely: *a tight collar.* **4.** difficult to deal with: *to be in a tight situation.* **5.** closely constructed so as to prevent the passage of water, air, etc. **6.** packed closely or full. **7.** set closely together. **8.** hard to obtain, as money. **9.** *Informal.* nearly even: *a tight race.* **10.** *Informal.* miserly or stingy. **11.** *Slang.* drunk or tipsy. —adv. **12.** in a tight manner. **13.**

soundly or deeply: *to sleep tight.* **14.** sit tight, to take no action. —**tight′ly,** adv. —**tight′ness,** n.

tight·en (tīt′ən), v.t., v.i. to make or become tight or tighter. —**tight′en·er,** n.

tight·fist·ed (tīt′fis′tid), adj. very stingy.

tight-lipped (tīt′lipt′), adj. rigidly reluctant to speak.

tight·rope (tīt′rōp′), n. a wire stretched tight, on which acrobats perform.

tights (tīts), n.pl. a skintight garment for the lower part of the body and the legs.

tight·wad (tīt′wod′), n. *Slang.* a stingy person.

ti·glon (tī′glən), n. the offspring of a male tiger and a female lion. [*tig*(er) + *l*(i)*on*]

Ti·gris (tī′gris), n. a river in SW Asia.

til·de (til′də), n. a mark (~) placed over a letter, as in Spanish, to indicate a nasal sound.

tile (tīl), n., v., **tiled, til·ing.** —n. **1.** a thin piece of baked clay, stone, plastic, etc., used for covering roofs, floors, etc. **2.** a small marked piece, used as in dominoes. **3.** an earthenware pipe used for draining land. —v.t. **4.** to cover with tiles. —**til′er,** n. —**til′ing,** n.

till[1] (til), conj., prep. until.

till[2] (til), v.t., v.i. to work (the soil) by plowing and planting, for raising crops. —**till′a·ble,** adj.

till[3] (til), n. (esp. formerly) a money drawer under a counter, as in a store.

till·age (til′ij), n. **1.** the act or work of tilling land. **2.** tilled land.

till·er[1] (til′ər), n. a person who tills land.

till·er[2] (til′ər), n. a bar or lever for turning the rudder in steering.

tilt (tilt), v.t. **1.** to cause to slope, as by lifting one end. —v.i. **2.** to move into a sloping position. **3.** to engage in a tournament tilt. **4.** to attack or charge in or as in a tournament tilt. —n. **5.** a slope or slant. **6.** a form of joust held across lanes separated by railings to prevent collision of the horses. **7.** any contest or dispute.

tilth (tilth), n. *Literary.* tillage.

tilt′-top ta′ble (tilt′top′), a table having a top that can be tilted vertically.

tim·bale (tim′bəl), n. a small pastry shell filled with a meat, fish, or vegetable mixture.

tim·ber (tim′bər), n. **1.** wood suitable for building, making furniture, and other uses. **2.** a piece of such wood. **3.** wooded land. **4.** a single piece of wood forming part of a building, ship, etc. —v.t. **5.** to furnish or support with timber. —**tim′bered,** adj. —**tim′ber·ing,** n.

tim·ber·line (tim′bər līn′), *n.* the altitude above sea level at which timber ceases to grow.

tim·bre (tim′bər, tam′-), *n.* the characteristic quality of a sound, independent of pitch and loudness.

tim·brel (tim′brəl), *n. Archaic.* a tambourine.

time (tīm), *n., adj., v.,* **timed, tim·ing.** —*n.* **1.** the duration of all existence, past, present, and future. **2.** a period or periods. **3.** a system or method of measuring the passage of time. **4.** Often, **times. a.** an age or era. **b.** a period or era in which certain conditions or ideas prevail: *hard times.* **5.** the moment when something is to occur. **6.** a period of work of an employee. **7.** the rate of pay for a particular period of work. **8.** *Informal.* a term of enforced duty or imprisonment: *to do time in prison.* **9.** a period or occasion providing a certain kind of experience: *We had a good time at the party.* **10.** sufficient or spare time. **11.** a particular point in time: *What time is it?* **12.** a particular part of a day, year, etc.: *lunch time.* **13.** each of the occurrences of an act or event that is repeated. **14.** the rate of speed, as in marching. **15.** *Music.* **a.** the relative speed of movement. **b.** the speed and rhythm of a particular kind of music: *waltz time.* **16. ahead of time,** before the time due. **17. at the same time,** nevertheless. **18. at times,** at intervals. **19. for the time being,** for the present. **20. from time to time,** on occasion. **21. in time, a.** early enough. **b.** in the future. **22. make time,** to move quickly, esp. in an attempt to recover lost time. **23. on time, a.** at the specified time. **b.** on the installment plan. **24. time after time,** again and again. Also, **time and again.** —*adj.* **25.** of or showing the passage of time. **26.** set to operate or explode at a certain time. **27.** of or pertaining to installment buying. —*v.t.* **28.** to measure or record the duration or speed of: *to time a race.* **29.** to adjust or regulate according to time, as a clock. **30.** to choose the proper moment for. **31.** to set the rhythm or measure of, as in music. —**tim′er,** *n.*

time′ clock′, a clock that records the exact times of arrival and departure of workers.

time′ frame′, the period of time during which any specific thing occurs.

time-hon·ored (tīm′on′ərd), *adj.* honored because of long continuance or use.

time·keep·er (tīm′kē′pər), *n.* a person who keeps and records the time, as of a sports event.

time·less (tīm′lis), *adj.* **1.** without beginning or end. **2.** restricted to no particular time. —**time′less·ly,** *adv.* —**time′less·ness,** *n.*

time·ly (tīm′lē), *adj.* occurring at a suitable time. —**time′li·ness,** *n.* —Syn. appropriate, opportune.

time-out (tīm′out′), *n.* a brief suspension of activity, as in a sports game.

time-piece (tīm′pēs′), *n.* a device for telling time, usually with hands to indicate the hour and minute.

times (tīmz), *prep.* multiplied by: *Two times four is eight.*

time-serv·er (tīm′sûr′vər), *n.* a person who shapes his or her conduct to conform with the times, esp. for selfish ends. —**time′serv′ing,** *adj., n.*

time′ shar′ing, simultaneous use of a single computer by many subscribers at remote locations.

time-ta·ble (tīm′tā′bəl), *n.* a schedule showing the times of arrival and departure of trains, airplanes, etc.

time-worn (tīm′wôrn′, -wōrn′), *adj.* **1.** showing the effects of age or long use. **2.** commonplace or trite.

tim·id (tim′id), *adj.* lacking in self-confidence or boldness. —**ti·mid′i·ty, tim′id·ness,** *n.* —**tim′id·ly,** *adv.* —Syn. bashful, fearful, shy.

tim·ing (tī′miñg), *n.* the selecting of the best time or speed in order to achieve the desired result.

tim·or·ous (tim′ər əs), *adj.* overly or fearfully timid. —**tim′or·ous·ly,** *adv.* —**tim′or·ous·ness,** *n.*

tim·o·thy (tim′ə thē), *n.* a grass having cylindrical spikes used as fodder.

tim·pa·ni (tim′pə nē), *n.pl.* a set of kettledrums, esp. as used in an orchestra. —**tim′pa·nist,** *n.*

tin (tin), *n., v.,* **tinned, tin·ning.** —*n.* **1.** *Chem.* a soft, silvery metallic element, used for plating and in making solder. *Symbol:* Sn; *at. wt.:* 118.69; *at. no.:* 50. **2.** See **tin plate. 3.** a box or container made from tin plate. **4.** *Brit.* can² (def. 1). —*v.t.* **5.** to cover or coat with tin. **6.** *Chiefly Brit.* to can (food).

tinc·ture (tiñgk′chər), *n., v.,* **-tured, -tur·ing.** —*n.* **1.** a solution of a drug or other substance in alcohol. **2.** a slight trace. **3.** a tint or tinge. —*v.t.* **4.** to give a slight trace or tinge to.

tin·der (tin′dər), *n.* any highly flammable material, esp. as formerly used for kindling.

tin·der·box (tin′dər boks′), *n.* **1.** a box for holding tinder. **2.** a potential source of violence, war, etc.

tine (tīn), *n.* a sharp point or prong, as on a fork.

tin·foil (tin′foil′), *n.* tin, or an alloy of tin and lead, in a thin sheet, for use as a wrapping.

tinge (tinj), n., v., **tinged, tinge·ing** or **ting·ing.** —n. 1. a slight coloration. 2. a slight trace of any quality. —v.t. 3. to add or give a tinge of to.

tin·gle (ting′gəl), v., **-gled, -gling,** n. —v.i. 1. to have a slight prickling or stinging sensation, as from cold, a sharp blow, etc. —n. 2. a tingling sensation. —tin′gler, n. —tin′gly, adj.

tink·er (ting′kər), n. 1. Chiefly Brit. (formerly) an itinerant repairer of pots, pans, etc. 2. a clumsy worker. —v.i. 3. to work clumsily at anything. 4. to putter or fiddle. —tink′er·er, n.

tin·kle (ting′kəl), v., **-kled, -kling,** n. —v.i., v.t. 1. to make or cause to make a series of light, ringing sounds, as of a small bell. —n. 2. a tinkling sound.

tin·ny (tin′ē), adj., **-ni·er, -ni·est.** 1. of or containing tin. 2. like tin in appearance, sound, or taste. —tin′ni·ly, adv. —tin′ni·ness, n.

tin′ plate′, thin sheet steel or iron coated with tin. —tin′-plate′, v.t.

tin·sel (tin′səl), n. 1. thin strips or threads of shiny metal or foil, used for decoration. 2. anything showy or gaudy but of little value.

tin·smith (tin′smith′), n. a person who makes or repairs tinware.

tint (tint), n. 1. a shade or variety of a color. 2. any delicate or pale color. —v.t. 3. to add or give a tint to. —tint′er, n.

tin·tin·nab·u·la·tion (tin′ti nab′yə lā′shən), n. the ringing or sound of bells. [< L tintinnābul(um) bell]

tin·type (tin′tīp′), n. an old type of positive photograph made on a sensitized sheet of enameled tin or iron.

tin·ware (tin′wâr′), n. articles made of tin plate.

ti·ny (tī′nē), adj., **-ni·er, -ni·est.** very small. —ti′ni·ness, n.

-tion, a suffix meaning: a. action or process: reception. b. result of an action: concoction. c. state of condition: dejection.

tip¹ (tip), n., v., **tipped, tip·ping.** —n. 1. a slender or pointed end of anything. 2. a small piece or part forming or covering the end of something. —v.t. 3. to furnish with a tip. 4. to mark or adorn the tip of.

tip² (tip), v., **tipped, tip·ping,** n. —v.t., v.i. 1. to lift one side or end (of). 2. to overturn or topple. —n. 3. the act of tipping or state of being tipped.

tip³ (tip), n., v., **tipped, tip·ping.** —n. 1. a small gift of money given in return for a service. 2. a piece of secret or private information. 3. a useful hint or idea. —v.t. 4. to give a gratuity to. 5. **tip off,** Informal. to give secret information to, esp. as a warning. 6. **tip one's hand,** to reveal one's plans unwittingly. —tip′per, n.

tip⁴ (tip), n., v., **tipped, tip·ping.** —n. 1. a light, smart blow. —v.t. 2. to strike lightly and smartly.

tip-off (tip′ôf′, -of′), n. Informal. secret information given, esp. as a warning.

tip·pet (tip′it), n. a scarf for the neck or the neck and shoulders.

tip·ple (tip′əl), v.t., v.i., **-pled, -pling.** to drink (intoxicating liquor), esp. habitually or to some excess. —tip′pler, n.

tip·ster (tip′stər), n. Informal. a person who furnishes tips, as for betting.

tip·sy (tip′sē), adj., **-si·er, -si·est.** 1. slightly intoxicated or drunk. 2. unsteady or shaky. —tip′si·ly, adv. —tip′si·ness, n.

tip·toe (tip′tō′), n., v., **-toed, -to·ing.** —n. 1. the tip or end of a toe. 2. on tiptoe, a. on the tips of one's toes. b. expectant or eager. c. stealthily or cautiously. —v.i. 3. to move or go on tiptoe, as with caution.

tip-top (tip′top′), n. 1. the highest point. —adj. 2. at the very top. 3. of the highest quality. —adv. 4. very well.

ti·rade (tī′rād, tī rād′), n. a prolonged speech of bitter, outspoken denunciation. —Syn. harangue.

tire¹ (tīr), v.t., v.i. **tired, tir·ing.** 1. to make or become exhausted, as by exertion. 2. to make or become bored or uninterested.

tire² (tīr), n. 1. a rubber covering, either solid or hollow and inflated, for placing over the rim of a wheel to provide traction and absorb shock. 2. a metal band forming the tread of a wagon wheel.

tired (tīrd), adj. 1. exhausted, as by exertion. 2. bored or uninterested. 3. hackneyed or stale. —Syn. 1. enervated, fatigued, weary.

tire·less (tīr′lis), adj. not becoming tired or exhausted. —tire′less·ly, adv. —tire′less·ness, n. —Syn. indefatigable.

tire·some (tīr′səm), adj. causing fatigue or boredom. —tire′some·ly, adv. —tire′some·ness, n.

'tis (tiz), Archaic or Literary. a contraction of it is.

tis·sue (tish′ōo), n. 1. a mass of cells in an animal or plant which form a particular kind of structural material with a definite function. 2. a light, soft, absorbent paper. 3. See tissue paper. 4. a light, woven fabric. 5. an interwoven mass: a tissue of falsehoods.

tis′sue pa′per, a very thin, almost transparent paper used in packing.

tit¹ (tit), n. titmouse.

tit² (tit), *n.* **1.** teat. **2.** *Slang.* a female breast.

ti·tan (tīt′ən), *n.* a person or thing of enormous size or power.

ti·tan·ic (tī tan′ik), *adj.* of enormous size or power.

ti·ta·ni·um (tī tā′nē əm), *n. Chem.* a hard, dark-gray or silvery, corrosion-resistant, metallic element, used to harden steel alloys. *Symbol:* Ti; *at. wt.:* 47.90; *at. no.:* 22.

tit·bit (tit′bit′), *n. Chiefly Brit.* tidbit.

tit′ for tat′, with an equivalent retaliation.

tithe (tīth), *n., v.,* **tithed, tith·ing.** —*n.* **1.** a tenth of one's income offered or levied for the support of a church, as among Mormons. —*v.t., v.i.* **2.** to pay a tithe (of). —**tith′er,** *n.*

ti·tian (tish′ən), *n.* a reddish or golden brown.

tit·il·late (tit′ə lāt′), *v.t.,* **-lat·ed, -lat·ing.** to excite agreeably, esp. superficially. —**tit′il·lat′ing·ly,** *adv.* —**tit′il·la′tion,** *n.*

tit·i·vate (tit′ə vāt′), *v.t., v.i.,* **-vat·ed, -vat·ing.** *Informal.* to make (oneself) smart or spruce. Also, **tit′ti·vate′.**

ti·tle (tīt′ºl), *n., v.,* **-tled, -tling.** —*n.* **1.** the distinguishing name of a book, poem, picture, etc. **2.** a distinctive designation indicating one's rank, position, etc. **3.** *Sports.* the championship. **4.** *Law.* **a.** a legal right to the possession of property, esp. real property. **b.** the instrument constituting evidence of such right. —*v.t.* **5.** to give a title to.

ti′tled (tīt′ºld), *adj.* having a title, esp. of nobility.

tit·mouse (tit′mous′), *n., pl.* **-mice** (-mīs′). a small songbird having soft, thick plumage.

tit·ter (tit′ər), *v.i.* **1.** to laugh in a half-restrained, self-conscious, or affected way. —*n.* **2.** a tittering laugh. —**tit′ter·ing·ly,** *adv.*

tit·tle (tit′ºl), *n.* a very small bit.

tit·tle-tat·tle (tit′ºl tat′ºl), *n.* foolish or idle talk.

tit·u·lar (tich′ə lor, tit′yə-), *adj.* **1.** in title or name only. **2.** of or constituting a title.

tiz·zy (tiz′ē), *n., pl.* **-zies.** *Informal.* a dither.

tk., **1.** tank. **2.** truck.

TKO, *Boxing.* technical knockout.

tkt., ticket.

Tl, thallium.

t.l., total loss.

TLC, tender, loving care.

TM, **1.** trademark. **2.** See **transcendental meditation.**

Tm, thulium.

T-man (tē′man′), *n. Informal.* a special investigator of the U.S. Treasury Department.

T.M.O., telegraph money order.

TN, Tennessee.

tn., **1.** ton. **2.** town. **3.** train.

tng., training.

tnpk., turnpike.

TNT, a high explosive used in warfare and for blasting. [*t*(*ri*)*n*(*itro*)-*t*(*oluene*)]

to (tōō, tŏŏ, tə), *prep.* **1.** so as to reach: *He came to the house.* **2.** in the direction of: *They went to the east.* **3.** to the extent or limit of: *These trees grow to a hundred feet.* **4.** on or upon: *Apply varnish to the surface.* **5.** until: *I studied from three to six.* **6.** (in telling time) before: *It is ten minutes to two.* **7.** (used to express purpose or intention): *Rush to the rescue.* **8.** (used to express destination or end): *He was sentenced to prison.* **9.** so as to result in: *I tore the paper to pieces.* **10.** in honor of: *a toast to your health.* **11.** in recognition of: *a monument to their bravery.* **12.** (used to express addition): *14 added to 16.* **13.** belonging with: *I have the key to the door.* **14.** limited to or reserved for: *We have a table to ourselves.* **15.** for the benefit of: *a gift to the college.* **16.** in accordance with: *an apartment to our liking.* **17.** compared with: *2 is to 10 as 20 is to 100.* **18.** with respect to relation to: *kindness to animals.* **19.** accompanying or accompanied by: *a ballad sung to a guitar.* **20.** contained or included in: *12 eggs to a dozen.* **21.** (used to indicate the indirect object): *Give it to me.* **22.** (used to indicate the infinitive of a verb and sometimes replace the infinitive): *Do you want to go? I don't want to.* —*adv.* **23.** into a closed position: *Pull the door to.* **24.** into action or work: *The crew turned to with a will.* **25.** into a state of consciousness: *When he came to, the room was dark.*

T.O., telegraph office.

t.o., turn over.

toad (tōd), *n.* a froglike amphibian having a dry, warty skin and entering water only during the breeding season.

toad·stool (tōd′stōōl′), *n.* a poisonous mushroom.

toad·y (tō′dē), *n., pl.* **toad·ies,** *v.,* **toad·ied, toad·y·ing.** —*n.* **1.** a fawning flatterer. —*v.i., v.t.* **2.** to be a toady (to).

toast¹ (tōst), *n.* **1.** sliced bread made brown and crisp by heat. —*v.t.* **2.** to make brown and crisp by heat. **3.** to warm thoroughly. —*v.i.* **4.** to become toasted.

toast² (tōst), *n.* **1.** the act of drinking or proposing a drink in honor of a person or event. **2.** a person or event so honored. —*v.t., v.i.* **3.** to propose or drink a toast (to).

toast·er[1] (tō'stər), *n.* an electric appliance for making toast.

toast·er[2] (tō'stər), *n.* a person who proposes drinking a toast.

toast·mas·ter (tōst'mas'tər, -mä'stər), *n.* a person who presides at a dinner, introducing the speakers and proposing toasts. —**toast'mis'tress,** *n.fem.*

to·bac·co (tə bak'ō), *n., pl.* **-cos, -coes.** 1. a plant having large, flat leaves that are prepared for smoking or chewing or as snuff. 2. the prepared leaves, as used in cigarettes. 3. products made from such leaves.

to·bac·co·nist (tə bak'ə nist), *n. Brit.* a retailer in tobacco.

to·bog·gan (tə bog'ən), *n.* 1. a long, narrow sled having a flat bottom, used for coasting. —*v.i.* 2. to coast on a toboggan. 3. to fall rapidly, as prices. —**to·bog'gan·ist,** *n.*

toc·sin (tok'sin), *n.* 1. a signal of alarm. 2. an alarm bell.

to·day (tə dā'), *n.* 1. the present day. 2. the present time or age. —*adv.* 3. on the present day. 4. in these days.

tod·dle (tod'³l), *v.i.,* **-dled, -dling.** to walk with short, unsteady steps, as a child. —**tod'dler,** *n.*

tod·dy (tod'ē), *n., pl.* **-dies.** a drink made of liquor, hot water, sugar, and spices.

to-do (tə dōō'), *n., pl.* **-dos.** *Informal.* noisy disturbance.

toe (tō), *n., v.,* **toed, toe·ing.** —*n.* 1. one of the terminal digits of the foot. 2. a similar part of an animal's foot. 3. any part resembling a toe in shape or position. 4. **on one's toes,** *Informal.* alert or ready. —*v.t.* 5. to touch or reach with the toes. 6. **toe the line,** to conform strictly to a rule or order.

toe·hold (tō'hōld'), *n.* 1. a small space that supports the toes, as in climbing. 2. any slight support or advantage.

toe·nail (tō'nāl'), *n.* a nail of a toe.

tof·fee (tô'fē, tof'ē), *n. Brit.* taffy. Also, **tof'fy.**

to·fu (tō'fōō'), *n.* See **bean curd.** [< Jap]

tog (tog), *n., v.,* **togged, tog·ging.** *Informal.* —*n.* 1. Usually, **togs.** clothes. —*v.t.* 2. to dress or clothe.

to·ga (tō'gə), *n., pl.* **-gas, -gae** (-jē). a loose outer garment worn in public by citizens of ancient Rome. —**to'gaed** (-gəd), *adj.*

to·geth·er (tōō geth'ər, tə-), *adv.* 1. in or into one group, mass, or place: *to gather together.* 2. in or into contact or association with each other: *to bring strangers together.* 3. taken as a whole: *This one cost more than all the others together.* 4. at the same time: *You cannot have both together.* 5. without interruption:

for days together. 6. in or into cooperation or agreement: *to undertake a task together.* —**to·geth'er·ness,** *n.*

tog·ger·y (tog'ə rē), *n. Informal.* togs.

tog'gle switch' (tog'əl), a switch in which a projecting knob causes the contacts to open or close an electric circuit.

To·go (tō'gō), *n.* a country in W Africa.

toil (toil), *n.* 1. hard and continuous work. —*v.i.* 2. to engage in such work. 3. to move with difficulty. —**toil'er,** *n.* —**toil'some,** *adj.* —**Syn.** 1. drudgery, travail.

toi·let (toi'lit), *n.* 1. a room with a fixture consisting of a large bowl and a water-flushing device, used for defecation and urination. 2. the fixture itself. 3. the act or process of grooming or making up. 4. *Archaic.* toilette (def. 2).

toi·let·ry (toi'li trē), *n., pl.* **-ries.** any article or preparation used in cleaning or grooming oneself, as toothpaste or cologne.

toi·lette (twä let'), *n. French.* 1. toilet (def. 3). 2. a woman's particular costume.

toils (toilz), *n.pl. Literary.* entangling hold.

To·kay (tō kā'), *n.* an aromatic, sweet wine. [< Hung]

toke (tōk), *n., v.,* **toked, tok·ing.** *Slang.* —*n.* 1. a puff of a marijuana cigarette. —*v.t.* 2. to light up or puff (a toke).

to·ken (tō'kən), *n.* 1. something meant to represent an act, event, or feeling. 2. a memento or keepsake. 3. a coinlike metal piece used in place of money, as for bus fares. 4. **by the same token,** a. in proof of this. b. similarly or likewise. —*adj.* 5. serving as a token. 6. slight or minimal: *token resistance.* —**Syn.** 1. symbol.

to·ken·ism (tō'kə niz'əm), *n.* the practice or policy of making only token acts, as in racial integration.

To·ky·o (tō'kē ō'), *n.* the capital of Japan. —**To'ky·o·ite',** *n.*

tol·bu·ta·mide (tol byōō'tə mīd'), *n.* an oral drug for mild diabetes.

told (tōld), *v.* 1. pt. and pp. of **tell.** 2. **all told,** in all.

tole (tōl), *n.* enameled or lacquered metalware with gilt decoration, used for trays, lamp shades, etc.

To·le·do (tə lē'dō), *n.* a port in NW Ohio.

tol·er·a·ble (tol'ər ə bəl), *adj.* 1. capable of being tolerated. 2. fairly good. —**tol'er·a·bly,** *adv.* —**Syn.** 1. bearable, endurable. 2. passable.

tol·er·ance (tol'ər əns), *n.* 1. a liberal spirit toward opinions and practices that differ from one's own. 2. the power to endure or resist discomfort, hardship, the action of a drug, poison, etc. **3.** the permissible variation of an object in hardness, weight, or quantity. —**tol′er·ant,** *adj.* —**tol′er·ant·ly,** *adv.*

tol·er·ate (tol′ə rāt′), *v.t.,* **-at·ed, -at·ing. 1.** to allow without hindrance. **2.** to endure without repugnance. **3.** to resist the action of (a drug, etc.). —**tol′er·a′tion,** *n.* —**tol′er·a′tive,** *adj.* —**tol′er·a′tor,** *n.*

toll[1] (tōl), *v.t.* **1.** to ring (a large bell) with slow, repeated strokes. **2.** to announce or summon by this means. —*v.i.* **3.** to sound with slow, repeated strokes, as a bell. —*n.* **4.** the sound of tolling a bell.

toll[2] (tōl), *n.* **1.** a charge paid for some privilege, as for passage over a bridge. **2.** a payment for a long-distance telephone call. **3.** the extent of loss or suffering resulting from some action or calamity.

toll·booth (tōl′boŏth′), *n., pl.* **-booths** (-boŏt͟hz′, -boŏths′). a booth, as at the entrance to a toll road, where a toll is collected.

toll·gate (tōl′gāt′), *n.* a gate where toll is collected.

Tol·stoy (tol′stoi, tōl′-), *n.* Leo, Count, 1828–1910, Russian novelist. Also, **Tol′stoi.**

tol·u·ene (tol′yoŏ ēn′), *n.* a flammable liquid used in the manufacture of TNT.

tom (tom), *n.* **1.** the male of certain animals, as a turkey. **2.** tomcat.

tom·a·hawk (tom′ə hôk′), *n.* **1.** a light ax formerly used by the North American Indians as a weapon and tool. —*v.t.* **2.** to attack or kill with a tomahawk.

to·ma·to (tə mā′tō, -mä′-), *n., pl.* **-toes. 1.** a plant bearing a mildly acid, pulpy fruit, commonly red, used as a vegetable. **2.** its fruit.

tomb (toŏm), *n.* **1.** a vault or chamber for a corpse. **2.** any burial place.

tom·boy (tom′boi′), *n.* a boisterous, boyish young girl.

tomb·stone (toŏm′stōn′), *n.* a stone marker on a tomb or grave.

tom·cat (tom′kat′), *n.* a male cat.

Tom′ Col′lins (tom′ kol′inz), a tall iced drink containing gin.

tome (tōm), *n.* any heavy, large, or learned book.

tom·fool·er·y (tom′foŏl′ə rē), *n.* foolish or silly behavior.

to·mor·row (tə môr′ō, -mor′ō), *n.* **1.** the day following today. —*adv.* **2.** on the day following today.

tom·tit (tom′tit′), *n.* Brit. a titmouse or other small bird.

tom·tom (tom′tom′), *n.* a small primitive drum beaten with the hands.

-tomy, a combining form meaning "a surgical operation": *appendectomy.*

ton (tun), *n.* **1.** a unit of weight, equivalent to 2000 pounds or 907.20 kilograms (**short ton**) in the U.S. and 2240 pounds or 1016.06 kilograms (**long ton**) in Great Britain. **2.** a unit of volume for freight, commonly equal to 40 cubic feet.

to·nal·i·ty (tō nal′i tē), *n., pl.* **-ties.** *Music.* the sum of relations existing between the tones of a scale or musical system.

tone (tōn), *n., v.,* **toned, ton·ing.** —*n.* **1.** a sound of definite pitch, quality, or strength. **2.** quality of sound. **3.** vocal sound. **4.** *Music.* **a.** a musical sound of definite pitch. **b.** an interval equivalent to two half steps. **5.** a particular way of expressing one's feelings or attitudes. **6.** a tint or shade of a color. **7.** the normal state of tension or firmness, as of muscle. **8.** prevailing character or style, as of manners. **9.** distinction or elegance. —*v.t.* **10.** to give a certain tone to. **11. tone down,** to soften or moderate. **12. tone up,** to heighten or intensify. —**ton′al,** *adj.* —**ton′al·ly,** *adv.* —**tone′less,** *adj.*

tone′ arm′, the free-swinging bracket of a phonograph containing the pickup.

tone-deaf (tōn′def′), *adj.* unable to distinguish differences in pitch in musical sounds.

tong (tông, tong), *n.* a Chinese fraternal or secret society in the U.S.

tongs (tôngz, tongz), *n.pl.* a device for holding or lifting objects, consisting of a pair of arms hinged together.

tongue (tung), *n.* **1.** the movable organ in the mouth, functioning in eating, in tasting, and, in human beings, in speaking. **2.** the tongue of an animal, used as food. **3.** the power of speech. **4.** a manner or style of speech. **5.** a language or dialect. **6.** anything resembling a tongue in shape or function. **7. hold one's tongue,** to be or keep silent. **8. tongue in cheek,** mockingly or insincerely. —**tongued,** *adj.* —**tongue′less,** *adj.*

tongue-lash (tung′lash′), *v.t., v.i.* to scold severely. —**tongue′-lash′ing,** *n.*

tongue-tied (tung′tīd′), *adj.* unable to speak, as from shyness or surprise.

tongue′ twist′er, a phrase or sentence difficult to pronounce rapidly, as "Rubber baby buggy bumpers."

ton·ic (ton′ik), *n.* **1.** anything that invigorates or refreshes, as a medicine. **2.** a carbonated quinine water, used esp. as a mixer for highballs. **3.** *Music.* the keynote. —*adj.* **4.** giving or restoring physical or mental vigor or tone. **5.** *Music,* pertaining to or founded on the keynote. —**ton′i·cal·ly,** *adv.*

to·night (tə nīt′), *n.* **1.** this present or coming night. —*adv.* **2.** on or during this present night.

ton·nage (tun′ij), *n.* **1.** the capacity of a merchant vessel, expressed in tons. **2.** the total amount of shipping of a country or a port, measured in tons. **3.** a duty on ships at so much per ton of cargo. **4.** the total weight of anything, expressed in tons.

ton·neau (tu nō′), *n.* a rear compartment for passengers in an early type of automobile.

ton·sil (ton′səl), *n.* either of a pair of soft, oval masses of tissue at the back of the throat. —**ton′sil·lar, ton′sil·ar,** *adj.*

ton·sil·lec·to·my (ton′sə lek′tə mē), *n., pl.* **-mies.** the surgical operation of removing the tonsils.

ton·sil·li·tis (ton′sə lī′tis), *n.* an inflammation of the tonsils.

ton·so·ri·al (ton sôr′ē əl, -sōr′-), *adj.* *Often Facetious.* of or pertaining to a barber or his or her work.

ton·sure (ton′shər), *n.* **1.** the rite of shaving the head of a person becoming a priest or monk. **2.** the part of the head so shaven.

ton·y (tō′nē), *adj.,* **ton·i·er, ton·i·est.** *Slang.* affectedly stylish.

too (tōō), *adv.* **1.** in addition. **2.** to an excessive extent: *too sick to travel.* **3.** extremely or very: *It was too nice of you to come.* **4.** *Informal.* to be sure.

took (tōōk), *v.* pt. of **take.**

tool (tōōl), *n.* **1.** a hand instrument used in performing or facilitating mechanical operations, as a hammer. **2.** the cutting or working part of a machine, as a drill. **3.** anything used to accomplish a definite purpose. **4.** a person manipulated by another for his or her own ends. —*v.t.* **5.** to equip with tools or machinery. **6.** to cut or shape with a tool. —*v.i.* **7.** to work or decorate with a tool. **8.** to drive a vehicle.

toot (tōōt), *v.i., v.t.* **1.** to sound (a horn or whistle) in short, quick blasts. —*n.* **2.** an act or sound of tooting. —**toot′er,** *n.*

tooth (tōōth), *n., pl.* **teeth. 1.** any of the hard, white, bony parts growing from the jaws and used to bite and chew. **2.** any projection resembling a tooth, as on a comb or saw. **3.** effective enforcement power. **4. in the teeth of, a.** so as to confront. **b.** in defiance of. —**toothed** (-t, -d), *adj.* —**tooth′less,** *adj.*

tooth·ache (tōōth′āk′), *n.* a pain in or around a tooth.

tooth′ and nail′, with all one's resources or energy.

tooth·brush (tōōth′brush′), *n.* a small brush for cleaning the teeth.

tooth·paste (tōōth′pāst′), *n.* a dentifrice in paste form.

tooth·pick (tōōth′pik′), *n.* a small pointed piece, as of wood, for removing food particles from between the teeth.

tooth′ pow′der, a dentifrice in powder form.

tooth·some (tōōth′səm), *adj.* **1.** pleasant to the taste. **2.** attractive or pretty. —**tooth′some·ness,** *n.*

tooth·y (tōō′thē, -thē), *adj.,* **-i·er, -i·est.** having or displaying conspicuous teeth: *a toothy smile.* —**tooth′i·ly,** *adv.*

top¹ (top), *n., adj., v.,* **topped, topping.** —*n.* **1.** the highest point, part, or surface of anything. **2.** a lid or cover for a box or other container. **3.** the maximum intensity or amount. **4.** the highest rank, position, or quality. **5.** one's head: *from top to toe.* **6.** the part of a plant that grows above ground. **7. blow one's top,** *Slang.* to lose one's temper. **8. on top of, a.** in addition to. **b.** immediately after. **c.** in complete control, as of a problem. —*adj.* **9.** of, located at, or forming the top. —*v.t.* **10.** to furnish with a top. **11.** to be at the top of. **12.** to reach the top of. **13.** to exceed in height or amount. **14.** to surpass or excel. **15.** to remove the top of (a tree). **16. top off,** to complete, esp. in an exceptional manner. —*Syn.* **1.** apex, pinnacle, summit, zenith.

top² (top), *n.* a child's toy, usually cone-shaped, with a point on which it is made to spin.

to·paz (tō′paz), *n.* a clear yellow or brownish mineral used as a gem.

top′ brass′, *Slang.* high-ranking officers or officials.

top·coat (top′kōt′), *n.* a lightweight overcoat.

top-draw·er (top′drôr′), *adj.* of the highest rank or importance.

top-dress (top′dres′), *v.t.* to manure (land) on the surface.

top′ dress′ing, a covering of manure on the surface of land.

tope (tōp), *v.i., v.t.,* **toped, top·ing.** to drink (liquor) heavily or excessively. —**top′er,** *n.*

To·pe·ka (tə pē′kə), *n.* the capital of Kansas.

top·flight (top′flīt′), *adj.* outstandingly excellent.

top′ hat′, a man's hat with a tall crown, worn esp. on formal occasions.

top-heav·y (top′hev′ē), *adj.* having the top disproportionately heavy. —**top′heav′i·ness,** *n.*

top·ic (top′ik), *n.* a subject of conversation or discussion.

top·i·cal (top′i kəl), *adj.* **1.** dealing with matters of current or local interest. **2.** of or arranged by topics. —**top·i·cal·i·ty** (top′ə kal′i tē), *n.* —**top′i·cal·ly**, *adv.*

top·knot (top′not′), *n.* **1.** a tuft of hair on the top of the head. **2.** a bow of ribbon worn as a headdress.

top·less (top′lis), *adj.* **1.** wearing no clothing above the waist. **2.** featuring dancers or singers who wear no clothing above the waist: *a topless bar.* —**top′less·ness**, *n.*

top-lev·el (top′lev′əl), *adj. Informal.* high-level.

top·mast (top′mast′, -mäst′), *n.* the mast next above a lower mast on a sailing ship.

top·most (top′mōst′), *adj.* at the very top.

top·notch (top′noch′), *adj. Informal.* of the top quality.

topog., topography.

to·pog·ra·phy (tə pog′rə fē), *n., pl.* **-phies. 1.** the art of describing on maps and charts the physical features of an area, as mountains or rivers. **2.** these physical features. —**to·pog′ra·pher,** *n.* —**top·o·graph·ic** (top′ə graf′ik), **top′o·graph′i·cal,** *adj.* —**top′o·graph′i·cal·ly,** *adv.*

top·ping (top′ing), *n.* something that forms a top, esp. a garnish or sauce.

top·ple (top′əl), *v.,* **-pled, -pling.** —*v.i.* **1.** to fall forward, as from weakness. —*v.t.* **2.** to cause to topple. **3.** to overthrow or overturn (a government).

tops (tops), *adj. Informal.* outstanding in performance or quality.

top·sail (top′sāl′), *n.* the sail next above the lowest sail on a mast of a sailing ship.

top-se·cret (top′sē′krit), *adj.* of or designating classified information of the highest level.

top·side (top′sīd′), *adv.* **1.** on the upper side. **2.** up on the deck.

top·sid·er (top′sī′dər), *n. Slang.* a person holding a high public position, as in government.

top·soil (top′soil′), *n.* the upper, fertile layer of soil.

top·sy-tur·vy (top′sē tûr′vē), *adv.* **1.** upside down. **2.** in or into a state of confusion or disorder. —*adj.* **3.** turned upside down. **4.** confused or disorderly.

toque (tōk), *n.* a brimless and close-fitting hat for women.

tor (tôr), *n.* a rocky hill.

To·rah (tōr′ə, tôr′ə), *n.* **1. a.** the Pentateuch. **b.** a large, handwritten scroll containing this, used in a synagogue. **2.** (*often l.c.*) the entire body of Jewish law. [< Heb *tōrāh* instruction, law]

torch (tôrch), *n.* **1.** a portable light consisting of a stick having a flammable substance at the upper end. **2.** such a light as a symbol of enlightenment or learning. **3.** any of various devices that produce a hot flame, as for welding. **4.** *Brit.* flashlight (def. 1).

torch·bear·er (tôrch′bâr′ər), *n.* **1.** a person who carries a torch. **2.** a leader in a movement, cause, etc.

torch·light (tôrch′līt′), *n.* the light of a torch or torches.

torch′ song′, a sentimental popular song of failure in love.

tore (tōr, tôr), *v.* pt. of tear².

tor·e·a·dor (tôr′ē ə dôr′), *n.* a bullfighter. Also, **to·re·ro** (tə râr′ō).

tor·ment (*n.* tôr′ment, *v.* tôr ment′), *n.* **1.** a state of incessant physical or mental suffering. **2.** a source of such suffering. —*v.t.* **3.** to cause torment to. **4.** to worry or annoy excessively. —**tor·ment′ed·ly,** *adv.* —**tor·ment′ing·ly,** *adv.* —**tor·men′tor, tor·ment′er,** *n.* —**Syn.** 1. anguish, misery. 3. distress, harass.

torn (tôrn, tôrn), *v.* pp. of tear².

tor·na·do (tôr nā′dō), *n., pl.* **-does, -dos.** a violent storm in which the winds in a whirling funnel-shaped cloud cause great destruction in their narrow path. [< Sp *tronada* thunderstorm < L *tonāre* to thunder]

To·ron·to (tə ron′tō), *n.* the capital of Ontario, in SE Canada.

tor·pe·do (tôr pē′dō), *n., pl.* **-does,** *v.,* **-doed, -do·ing.** —*n.* **1.** a self-propelled, elongated, underwater missile containing explosives, launched from a submarine, warship, or aircraft, for destroying enemy ships. **2.** any of various detonating devices for other purposes. —*v.t.* **3.** to attack or destroy with a torpedo. —**tor·pe′do·like′,** *adj.*

tor·pid (tôr′pid), *adj.* **1.** extremely sluggish in functioning. **2.** dormant, as a hibernating animal. —**tor·pid′i·ty,** *n.* —**tor′pid·ly,** *adv.* —**Syn.** 1. inactive, lethargic.

tor·por (tôr′pər), *n.* **1.** the state or condition of being torpid. **2.** dullness or apathy.

torque (tôrk), *n.* a force that produces or tends to produce torsion or rotation.

tor·rent (tôr′ənt, tor′-), *n.* **1.** a rapid, violent stream of water. **2.** a rushing or abundant stream of anything. —**tor·ren·tial** (tô ren′shəl), *adj.*

tor·rid (tôr′id, tor′-), *adj.* **1.** subjected to parching heat from the sun. **2.** oppressively hot. **3.** ardent or passionate. —**tor·rid′i·ty, tor′rid·ness,** *n.* —**tor′rid·ly,** *adv.*

Tor′rid Zone′, the part of the earth's surface between the tropics of Cancer and Capricorn.

tor·sion (tôr′shən), n. 1. the act of twisting or state of being twisted. 2. the twisting of an object by two equal and opposite torques. —tor′sion·al, adj. —tor′sion·al·ly, adv.

tor·so (tôr′sō), n., pl. -sos, -si (-sē). the trunk of the human body.

tort (tôrt), n. Law. a civil wrong, not including a breach of contract, for which the injured party is entitled to compensation.

tor·til·la (tôr tē′ə), n. a round, flat Mexican bread made from cornmeal.

tor·toise (tôr′təs), n. a turtle that lives on dry land.

tor′toise shell′, a horny substance of a mottled brown and yellow coloration, composing the upper shell of certain turtles, used for making combs and ornaments. —tor′toise-shell′, adj.

tor·to·ni (tôr tō′nē), n. a rich ice cream containing chopped cherries or topped with crushed almonds.

tor·tu·ous (tôr′chŏo əs), adj. 1. full of twists, turns, or bends. 2. deceitfully indirect. —tor′tu·ous·ly, adv. —tor′tu·ous·ness, n.

tor·ture (tôr′chər), n., v., -tured, -tur-ing. —n. 1. the act of inflicting severe pain, esp. as a means of punishment or coercion. 2. extreme anguish of body or mind. —v.t. 3. to subject to torture. 4. to afflict with extreme anguish of body or mind. 5. to twist, as in shape or meaning. —tor′tured·ly, adv. —tor′-tur·er, n.

To·ry (tôr′ē, tōr′ē), n., pl. -ries. 1. a member of the Conservative Party in Great Britain. 2. (often l.c.) an advocate of conservative principles. 3. a person who supported the British cause in the American Revolution.

toss (tôs, tos), v.t. 1. to throw lightly or carelessly. 2. to move rapidly from place to place. 3. to jerk upward suddenly, as the head. —v.i. 4. to rock or move irregularly. 5. to move about restlessly, esp. on a bed. 6. toss up, to toss a coin to decide something by the side that faces up when it falls. —n. 7. the act of tossing. 8. tossup (def. 1).

toss·up (tŏs′up′, tos′-), n. 1. the act of tossing up. 2. Informal. an even choice or chance.

tot¹ (tot), n. 1. a small child. 2. Chiefly Brit. a small quantity, esp. of liquor.

tot² (tot), v.t., v.i., tot·ted, tot·ting. Chiefly Brit. Informal. to total.

tot., total.

to·tal (tōt′əl), adj., n., v., -taled, -tal-ing or -talled, -tal·ling. —adj. 1. comprising a whole. 2. complete or utter. —n. 3. the total amount. — v.t. 4. to bring to a total. 5. to reach

a total of. 6. Slang. to wreck completely, as a car. —v.i. 7. to amount. —to′tal·ly, adv.

to·tal·i·tar·i·an (tō tal′i târ′ē ən), adj. 1. of or pertaining to a government in which authoritarian political control is concentrated in one party. — n. 2. an adherent of such a government. —to·tal′i·tar′i·an·ism, n.

to·tal·i·ty (tō tal′i tē), n., pl. -ties. 1. the state of being total. 2. the total sum.

to·tal·i·za·tor (tōt′əl ī zā′tər), n. a machine that registers bets and calculates the changing odds and final payoffs, as in a horse race. Also, to′tal·i·sa′tor, to′tal·iz′er (-ī′zər).

tote¹ (tōt), v.t., tot·ed, tot·ing. Informal. to carry, esp. in one's arms. —tot′er, n.

tote² (tōt), v.t., tot·ed, tot·ing. Informal. to total.

tote′ bag′, a large handbag, used by women, esp. when traveling.

to·tem (tō′təm), n. 1. an animal or plant assumed as the emblem of a primitive family or clan. 2. an image of such an object. —to·tem·ic (tō tem′ik), adj.

to′tem pole′, a post carved and painted with totemic figures, erected by Indians of the northwest coast of North America.

tot·ter (tot′ər), v.i. 1. to walk with faltering steps. 2. to show signs of imminent collapse. —tot′ter·er, n.

tou·can (tōō′kan, tōō kän′), n. a brightly colored, fruit-eating, tropical bird having a very large bill.

touch (tuch), v.t. 1. to put the hand or finger on or against (something) so as to feel it. 2. to bring (something) into contact with an object or surface. 3. to strike lightly. 4. to be adjacent to. 5. to consume or use: I rarely touch liquor. 6. to affect, esp. for the worse. 7. to move to gratitude or sympathy. 8. to stop at (a port), as a ship. 9. to succeed in attaining. 10. to be the equal of. 11. to alter slightly the appearance of. 12. Slang. to ask or obtain a loan from. —v.i. 13. to touch someone or something. 14. to come into or be in contact. 15. touch down, (of an airplane) to land. 16. touch off, a. to cause to ignite or explode. b. to give rise to. 17. touch on or upon, a. to treat of in passing. b. to come close to. c. to relate or pertain to. 18. touch up, to modify or improve (a painting, photograph, etc.) by slight changes. —n. 19. the sense by which an object is perceived by physical contact, esp. with the fingers. 20. the act or an instance of touching or of being touched. 21. correspondence or communication. 22. awareness or understanding: out of touch *with reality.* **23.** skill based on acute perception. **24.** a minor stroke that changes or improves something slightly. **25.** the responsiveness of the action of a keyboard instrument. **26.** the characteristic manner of any person practicing an art or skill. **27.** a mild onset of an illness. **28.** a small trace. **29.** *Slang.* the act of asking for or obtaining a loan. —**touch′a·ble,** *adj.*

touch′ and go′, a precarious or delicate state of affairs. —**touch′-and-go′,** *adj.*

touch·down (tuch′doun′), *n.* **1.** *Football.* the act of scoring six points by carrying or passing the ball safely across the opponent's goal line. **2.** the act or moment of an aircraft or spacecraft touching the landing surface.

tou·ché (tōō shā′), *interj.* **1.** *Fencing.* (used to indicate a hit or touch.) **2.** (used for acknowledging a telling remark or rejoinder.)

touch·ing (tuch′ing), *adj.* affecting the emotions deeply. —**touch′ing·ly,** *adv.* —**Syn.** moving, poignant.

touch·stone (tuch′stōn′), *n.* a test or criterion for the qualities of a thing.

touch·y (tuch′ē), *adj.,* **touch·i·er, touch·i·est. 1.** easily hurt or offended. **2.** requiring tactfulness in handling. —**touch′i·ly,** *adv.* —**touch′i·ness,** *n.* —**Syn. 1.** irritable, testy. **2.** delicate, sensitive.

tough (tuf), *adj.* **1.** not easily broken or cut. **2.** hard to chew, as food. **3.** sturdy or hardy. **4.** unyielding or stubborn. **5.** strict and determined, as a policy. **6.** hardened or incorrigible. **7.** difficult to perform or deal with. **8.** vicious or rough. **9.** *Informal.* unlucky or unfortunate. —*n.* **10.** a tough person, esp. a rowdy. —**tough′ly,** *adv.* —**tough′ness,** *n.* —**Syn. 1.** durable, firm, strong.

tough·en (tuf′ən), *v.t., v.i.* to make or become tough or tougher. —**tough′en·er,** *n.*

tou·pee (tōō pā′), *n.* a man's small wig for covering a bald spot.

tour (tōōr), *n.* **1.** a long journey including the visiting of a number of places in sequence. **2.** a journey for fulfilling engagements, as by entertainers. **3.** a brief trip for orientation or inspection, as through an industrial plant. **4.** a period of official duty at one place. —*v.i., v.t.* **5.** to go on a tour (through). **6.** to make a tour (of).

tour de force (tōōr′ də fôrs′, -fôrs′), *pl.* **tours de force** (tōōr′-). a feat requiring unusual strength or skill.

tour·ism (tōōr′iz əm), *n.* **1.** the promotion of tours, esp. by a country as an industry. **2.** the business of providing accommodations for tourists.

tour·ist (tōōr′ist), *n.* a person who makes a tour, esp. for pleasure.

tour′ist class′, the least costly class of accommodations on an ocean liner.

tour·ma·line (tōōr′mə lin, -lēn′), *n.* a mineral having transparent varieties used as gems.

tour·na·ment (tōōr′nə mənt, tûr′-), *n.* **1.** a contest in which a number of competitors take part in a series of matches. **2.** a contest of skill by jousts or tilts. Also, **tour′ney** (-nē).

tour·ni·quet (tûr′nə kit, tōōr′-), *n.* any device for stopping bleeding by compressing a blood vessel, esp. a bandage tightened by twisting with a stick.

tou·sle (tou′zəl), *v.t.,* **-sled, -sling.** to disorder or dishevel, esp. by wind.

tout (tout), *v.t., v.i. Informal.* **1.** to sell or give tips on (racehorses) to bettors. **2.** to praise highly or publicize aggressively.

tow[1] (tō), *v.t.* **1.** to drag or pull by a rope or chain. —*n.* **2.** the act or state of being towed. **3.** something towed. **4. in tow, a.** in the state of being towed. **b.** under one's guidance.

tow[2] (tō), *n.* the fiber of flax, hemp, or jute prepared for spinning.

to·ward (tôrd, tōrd, tə wôrd′), *prep.* **1.** in the direction of. **2.** for: *to save money toward a new house.* **3.** turned to. **4.** shortly before: *toward midnight.* **5.** as a contribution to: *to work toward world peace.* **6.** as regards. Also, **to·wards′.**

tow·el (tou′əl), *n.* **1.** an absorbent cloth or paper for wiping or drying something wet. **2. throw in the towel,** *Slang.* to concede defeat.

tow·el·ing (tou′ə ling), *n.* material used for making towels. Also, *Brit.,* **tow′el·ling.**

tow·er (tou′ər), *n.* **1.** a tall structure either standing alone or forming a top part of a building. **2.** such a structure used as a fort or stronghold. —*v.i.* **3.** to rise high, as a tower does.

tow·er·ing (tou′ər ing), *adj.* **1.** very high or tall. **2.** surpassing others. **3.** extreme or intense: *a towering rage.* —**tow′er·ing·ly,** *adv.*

tow·head (tō′hed′), *n.* a person with very light blond hair. —**tow′head′ed,** *adj.*

tow·hee (tou′hē, tō′hē), *n.* a long-tailed, North American finch.

town (toun), *n.* **1.** a thickly populated area, usually smaller than a city and larger than a village. **2.** any city or center of population. **3.** a township. **4. go to town,** *Slang.* **a.** to do efficiently and speedily. **b.** to be quite successful. **5. on the town,** *Slang.* out to have a good time.

town′ cri′er, (formerly) a person employed by a town to make public proclamations by shouting in the streets.

town′ hall′, a building that houses the officers of a town government.

town·house (toun′hous′), *n.* one of a group of houses that are joined by common side walls.

town′ meet′ing, a meeting of the qualified voters of a town, esp. in New England.

town·ship (toun′ship), *n.* 1. a division of a county having some powers of government. 2. (in U.S. surveys of public land) a district approximately six miles square.

towns·man (tounz′mən), *n.* 1. a native or inhabitant of a town. 2. a fellow citizen.

towns·peo·ple (tounz′pē′pəl), *n.pl.* the inhabitants of a town. Also called **towns′folk′.**

tow·path (tō′path′, -pāth′), *n.* a path along the bank of a canal, for use in towing boats.

tow′ truck′, wrecker (def. 3).

tox·e·mi·a (tok sē′mē ə), *n.* a condition of illness due to the presence of toxins in the bloodstream. Also, **tox·ae′mi·a.** —**tox·e·mic** (tok sē′mik, -sem′ik), *adj.*

tox·ic (tok′sik), *adj.* 1. of or caused by a toxin. 2. having the effect of a poison. —**tox′i·cal·ly,** *adv.* —**tox·ic′i·ty** (-sis′i tē), *n.*

tox·i·col·o·gy (tok′sə kol′ə jē), *n.* the science dealing with the effects, antidotes, and detection of poisons. — **tox′i·co·log′i·cal** (-kə loj′i kəl), **tox′i·co·log′ic,** *adj.* —**tox′i·co·log′i·cal·ly,** *adv.* —**tox′i·col′o·gist,** *n.*

tox·in (tok′sin), *n.* a poisonous substance generated by microorganisms, plants, or animals and causing various diseases.

toy (toi), *n.* 1. an object for a child to play with. 2. something unimportant. 3. a small article of little real value. —*adj.* 4. made or designed for use as a toy. 5. like a toy in smallness of size. —*v.i.* 6. to play or trifle: *Stop toying with your food!*

tp., township.

t.p., title page.

tpk., turnpike.

tr., 1. transitive. 2. translated. 3. translation. 4. translator. 5. transpose. 6. transposition. 7. treasurer. 8. troop.

trace¹ (trās), *n., v.,* **traced, trac·ing.** —*n.* 1. a surviving mark or sign of the former existence or action of a person or thing. 2. a barely discernible quantity or quality. —*v.t.* 3. to follow the track or trail of. 4. to follow the course, development, or history of. 5. to make a plan, diagram, or map of. 6. to copy (a draw-

ing, etc.) by following the lines of the original on a superimposed transparent sheet. —**trace′a·ble,** *adj.* — **trac′er,** *n.* —**Syn.** 1. vestige. 2. hint, suggestion.

trace² (trās), *n.* 1. either of the two straps or chains by which a vehicle is pulled by a harnessed draft animal. 2. **kick over the traces,** to become independent or defiant.

trace′ el′ement, a chemical element found in minute quantities and believed to be a critical factor in physiological processes.

trac·er·y (trā′sə rē), *n., pl.* **-er·ies.** ornamental work of delicate interlacing lines.

tra·che·a (trā′kē ə), *n., pl.* **-ae** (-ē′) **-as.** the tube connecting the throat to the lungs, through which the air passes in breathing. —**tra′che·al,** *adj.*

tra·che·ot·o·my (trā′kē ot′ə mē), *n., pl.* **-mies.** the operation of cutting into the trachea.

tra·cho·ma (trə kō′mə), *n.* a contagious inflammation of the conjunctiva and cornea, characterized by granulations and scarring.

trac·ing (trā′sing), *n.* something made by tracing, esp. a copy of a drawing or plan.

track (trak), *n.* 1. a mark or a series of marks left by a person, animal, or thing in passing. 2. a path or route. 3. a course of action or procedure. 4. a pair of parallel lines of rails providing a road for railroad trains. 5. either of the endless metal treads of a tank or tractor. 6. *Sports.* a. a course laid out for running or racing. b. sports performed on such a course, as running or hurdles. c. track-and-field events. 7. a band of recorded sound laid along the length of a magnetic tape. 8. **in one's tracks,** where one is or is standing at the moment. 9. **keep (or lose) track of,** to keep (or fail to keep) informed about. —*v.t.* 10. to follow or pursue the track of. 11. to follow and record the path of (a satellite or hurricane). 12. to make marks or footprints on or with. 13. **track down,** to pursue until caught or captured. —**track′a·ble,** *adj.* —**track′er,** *n.* — **track′less,** *adj.*

track·age (trak′ij), *n.* the whole quantity of track owned by a railroad.

track′ and field′, a group of sports including running, pole vault, shot put, etc., performed on an oval-shaped track and on its surrounding flat field, whether outdoors or indoors. —**track′-and-field′,** *adj.*

track′ light′ing, a decorative system of electric fixtures consisting of lamps attached anywhere along a rodlike metal track, which is mounted on a ceiling or wall and which permits flexible spotlighting and other effects. —**track′ light′.**

tract¹ (trakt), *n.* **1.** an expanse or stretch of land. **2.** a system of related body organs serving a common function: *the digestive tract.*

tract² (trakt), *n.* a pamphlet, esp. one for propaganda on a religious or political topic.

trac·ta·ble (trak′tə bəl), *adj.* **1.** easily managed or controlled. **2.** easily worked or shaped. —**trac′ta·bly,** *adv.*

trac·tate (trak′tāt), *n. Rare.* a treatise.

trac·tion (trak′shən), *n.* **1.** adhesive friction, as of a tire on a road. **2.** the power to pull a moving vehicle along a surface. **3.** the act of drawing or state of being drawn. —**trac′-tion·al,** *adj.* —**trac′tive,** *adj.*

trac·tor (trak′tər), *n.* **1.** an automotive vehicle with large, heavy treads, used for pulling farm machinery, etc. **2.** a short truck with a driver's cab only, used for pulling a trailer.

trade (trād), *n., v.,* **trad·ed, trad·ing.** —*n.* **1.** the act or process of buying, selling, or exchanging goods or services. **2.** a purchase, sale, or exchange. **3.** an occupation, esp. one of skilled manual or mechanical work. **4.** people engaged in a particular business. **5.** regular or particular customers. —*v.i.* **6.** to carry on trade. **7.** to make an exchange. **8.** *Informal.* to make one's purchases. —*v.t.* **9.** to buy, sell, or exchange. **10. trade in,** to give (a used article) as part payment for a purchase. **11. trade on** or **upon,** to use to one's advantage. —**Syn. 1.** commerce. **3.** craft, livelihood, vocation.

trade′ book′, a book intended for sale in general bookstores, as distinguished from a textbook, etc.

trade-in (trād′in′), *n.* goods given as part payment for a purchase.

trade·mark (trād′märk′), *n.* **1.** a word or symbol distinguishing the product of one company from those of competitors, usually registered with a government to assure its exclusive use by its owner. —*v.t.* **2.** to stamp or put a trademark on. **3.** to register as a trademark.

trade′ name′. 1. a name used by a business or firm to designate its particular line of goods. **2.** such a name that may be or is registered as a trademark. **3.** the name under which a firm does business.

trade-off (trād′ôf′), *n.* the exchange of one thing for another, esp. a concession for a gain: *a tradeoff between inflation and unemployment.*

trade′ pap′erback, a softbound book similar in nature to but usually bigger in size than a mass-market paperback, of better quality paper

stock, in larger type, and at a higher price: usually sold in bookstores as a trade book.

trad·er (trā′dər), *n.* **1.** a person who trades. **2.** (formerly) a ship used in foreign trade.

trades·man (trādz′mən), *n. Brit.* **1.** a shopkeeper. **2.** a craftsman.

trade′ un′ion, *Chiefly Brit.* a labor union of workers in related crafts.

trade′ wind′, a wind that blows regularly toward the equator, coming from the northeast in the Northern Hemisphere and from the southeast in the Southern Hemisphere.

trad′ing post′, a store in a frontier region where goods are obtained by bartering local products.

trad′ing stamp′, a stamp given as a premium by some retailers to a customer, specified quantities of these stamps being exchangeable for various articles.

tra·di·tion (trə dish′ən), *n.* **1.** the handing down of beliefs, legends, and customs from generation to generation, esp. by word of mouth or by practice. **2.** a belief, legend, or custom so handed down. **3.** any long-continued practice or custom. —**tra·di′tion·al,** *adj.* —**tra·di′tion·al·ly,** *adv.* —**tra·di′tion·less,** *adj.*

tra·duce (trə dōōs′, -dyōōs′), *v.t.,* **-duced, -duc·ing.** *Literary.* to attack slanderously. —**tra·duce′ment,** *n.* —**tra·duc′er,** *n.*

traf·fic (traf′ik), *n., v.,* **-ficked, -fick·ing.** —*n.* **1.** the movement of vehicles, airplanes, or pedestrians within a place or between one place and another. **2.** the quantity, intensity, or rate of such movement. **3.** trade or dealing in some commodity or service, often of an illegal nature. **4.** dealings or relations. —*v.i.* **5.** to carry on traffic or trade, esp. illegally. **6.** to have dealings or relations. —**traf′fick·er,** *n.*

traf′fic cir′cle, a circular roadway at a multiple intersection around which traffic moves in a counterclockwise direction.

traf′fic light′, a set of electrically operated signal lights used to direct traffic. Also called **traf′fic sig′nal.**

tra·ge·di·an (trə jē′dē ən), *n.* **1.** an actor of tragedy. **2.** a writer of tragedy.

tra·ge·di·enne (trə jē′dē en′), *n.* an actress of tragedy.

trag·e·dy (traj′i dē), *n., pl.* **-dies. 1.** a serious drama with an unhappy ending. **2.** an unfortunate or dreadful happening.

trag·ic (traj′ik), *adj.* **1.** of or characteristic of tragedy. **2.** unfortunate or dreadful. Also, **trag′i·cal.** —**trag′i·cal·ly,** *adv.* —**Syn. 2.** calamitous, disastrous, fatal.

trag·i·com·e·dy (traj'i kom'i dē), *n.*, *pl.* **-dies.** a drama combining elements of both tragedy and comedy. —**trag'i·com'ic,** *adj.*

trail (trāl), *v.t.* **1.** to draw or drag along behind. **2.** to follow the track or scent of, as in hunting. **3.** to follow along behind, as in a race. —*v.i.* **4.** to draw or drag along the ground or other surface. **5.** to move along slowly. **6.** to become gradually smaller or weaker. **7.** to be losing, in a contest. **8.** (of a plant) to grow along the ground. —*n.* **9.** a path or track across a wild or region. **10.** the track or scent left by an animal, person, or thing, esp. as followed by a hunter, hound, or other pursuer. **11.** something that trails behind, as a stream of dust or smoke. **12.** a series of journeys made or to be made: *the campaign trail.*

trail' bike', a motorcycle adapted for use on rough terrain or trails.

trail·blaz·er (trāl'blā'zor), *n.* **1.** a person who blazes a trail. **2.** a pioneer in any field of endeavor. —**trail'·blaz'ing,** *adj., n.*

trail·er (trā'lər), *n.* **1.** a person or thing that trails. **2.** a large vehicle drawn by another vehicle, used esp. for hauling freight. **3.** a vehicle equipped for use as a movable dwelling or office, drawn by another vehicle. **4.** a trailing plant.

train (trān), *n.* **1.** a group of railroad cars connected together, often drawn by a locomotive. **2.** a line of persons, vehicles, or animals traveling together. **3.** a series of events or ideas. **4.** a succession of connected ideas: *to lose one's train of thought.* **5.** an elongated part of a gown or robe that trails along the ground. **6.** a group of attendants. —*v.t.* **7.** to form the habits, thoughts, or behavior of by discipline and instruction. **8.** to make proficient by instruction and practice. **9.** to make fit by exercise, etc., as for an athletic performance. **10.** to cause to grow in some desired form or direction, as a plant. **11.** to aim or direct, as a firearm. —*v.i.* **12.** to be trained. —**train'a·ble,** *adj.* —**train'er,** *n.* —**train'ing,** *n.*

train·ee (trā nē'), *n.* a person who is being trained, esp. for a job.

train·man (trān'mən), *n.* a member of the crew of a railroad train.

traipse (trāps), *v.i., v.t.,* **traipsed, traips·ing.** *Informal.* to walk (over) idly.

trait (trāt), *n.* a distinguishing quality, esp. of one's personal nature.

trai·tor (trā'tər), *n.* **1.** a person who betrays another, a cause, or any trust. **2.** a person guilty of treason. —**trai'tor·ous,** *adj.* —**trai'tress** (-tris), *n.fem.*

tra·jec·to·ry (trə jek'tə rē), *n., pl.* **-ries.** the curve traced by a projectile object or body in its flight.

tram (tram), *n.* **1.** *Brit.* a streetcar. **2.** a car on rails for carrying loads in a mine.

tram·mel (tram'əl), *n., v.,* **-meled, -mel·ing** or **-melled, -mel·ling.** —*n.* **1.** Usually, **trammels.** anything that hinders freedom of action. —*v.t* **2.** to hinder or restrain.

tramp (tramp), *v.i.* **1.** to walk with heavy, noisy steps. **2.** to travel on foot. —*v.t.* **3.** to step on heavily or steadily. **4.** to travel over on foot. —*n.* **5.** a vagabond living on occasional jobs. **6.** a heavy, noisy footstep. **7.** the sound made by such a step. **8.** a long, steady walk. **9.** a freight ship that takes a cargo wherever shippers desire. **10.** *Slang.* a promiscuous woman. —**tramp'er,** *n.*

tram·ple (tram'pəl), *v.,* **-pled, -pling,** *n.* —*v.i.* **1.** to tread roughly or crushingly. —*v.t.* **2.** to tread heavily and esp. injuriously on or over. —*n.* **3.** the act or sound of trampling. —**tram'pler,** *n.*

tram·po·line (tram'pə lēn', tram'pə len', tram'pə lin), *n.* a sheet of canvas attached by springs to a frame, used as a springboard in tumbling. —**tram'po·lin'er, tram'po·lin'ist,** *n.*

trance (trans, träns), *n.* **1.** a half-conscious and sleeplike state, as that brought on by hypnosis. **2.** a dazed or bewildered condition. **3.** a state of complete mental absorption.

tran·quil (trang'kwil), *adj.* in an enduring state of unagitated quietness. [< L *tranquill(us)*] —**tran·quil'li·ty** (-kwil'i tē), **tran·quil'i·ty,** *n.* —**tran'·quil·ly,** *adv.* —**Syn.** calm, peaceful, placid, serene.

tran·quil·ize (trang'kwə līz'), *v.t., v.i.,* **-ized, -iz·ing.** to make or become tranquil. Also, **tran'quil·lize'.**

tran·quil·iz·er (trang'kwə lī'zər), *n.* a drug that has a calming effect without inducing sleep. Also, **tran'quil·liz'er.**

trans-, a prefix meaning: **a.** across or over: *transport.* **b.** changing thoroughly: *transform.* **c.** beyond: *transequatorial.*

trans., **1.** transaction. **2.** transitive. **3.** translated. **4.** translation. **5.** translator. **6.** transportation. **7.** transverse.

trans·act (tran sakt', -zakt'), *v.t.* to carry on or conduct to a settlement.

trans·ac·tion (tran sak'shən, -zak'-), *n.* **1.** the act of transacting or fact of being transacted. **2.** something transacted, esp. a business agreement. **3.** **transactions,** the published records of the proceedings of a learned society. —**trans·ac'tion·al,** *adj.*

trans·at·lan·tic (trans'ət lan'tik, tranz'-), *adj.* **1.** crossing the Atlantic. **2.** situated beyond the Atlantic.

trans·ceiv·er (tran sē'vər), *n.* a radio transmitter and receiver combined in one unit.

tran·scend (tran send'), *v.t.* **1.** to extend beyond the limits of. **2.** to surpass or excel. —**tran·scend'ent**, *adj.*

tran·scen·den·tal (tran'sen den'tᵊl), *adj.* going beyond ordinary experience, thought, or belief. **2.** abstract or metaphysical. —**tran'scen·den'tal·ly**, *adv.*

tran·scen·den·tal·ism (tran'sen den'tᵊliz'əm), *n.* a philosophy emphasizing the intuitive and spiritual above the empirical. —**tran'scen·den'tal·ist**, *n., adj.*

transcenden'tal medita'tion, a technique of mental discipline for achieving inner serenity and increasing mental power.

trans·con·ti·nen·tal (trans'kon tᵊnen'tᵊl), *adj.* crossing a continent.

tran·scribe (tran skrīb'), *v.t.*, **-scribed, -scrib·ing. 1.** to make a written or typewritten copy of (shorthand notes, a tape recording, etc.). **2.** *Music, Radio and Television.* to make or produce a transcription of. **3.** to represent (sounds) in symbols of another language. —**tran·scrib'er**, *n.*

tran·script (tran'skript), *n.* **1.** something made by transcribing, esp. a typewritten copy of dictated or oral material. **2.** any official reproduction, as of a student's academic record.

tran·scrip·tion (tran skrip'shən), *n.* **1.** the act or process of transcribing. **2.** transcript (def. 1). **3.** *Music.* the arrangement of a composition for a medium other than originally written for. **4.** *Radio and Television.* a recording of a program for later broadcasting.

trans·duc·er (trans dōō'sər, -dyōō'-, tranz-), *n.* a device that receives energy from one system and retransmits it, often in a different form, to another.

tran·sept (tran'sept), *n.* either of the two arms forming right angles to the nave in a church.

trans·fer (*v.* trans fûr', trans'fər; *n.* trans'fər), *v.*, **-ferred, -fer·ring,** *n.* —*v.t.* **1.** to carry or remove from one place, situation, or person to another. **2.** *Law.* to make over the title of: *to transfer land.* **3.** to imprint or impress (a drawing, etc.) from one surface to another. —*v.i.*

4. to transfer oneself or be transferred. **5.** to change from one bus or train to another. —*n.* **6.** Also, **trans·fer'ence** (-əns), the act of transferring or fact of being transferred. **7.** a ticket entitling a passenger to continue the journey on another bus or train. **8.** a person or thing that transfers or is transferred. **9.** *Law.* a conveyance of property to another. —**trans·fer'a·bil'i·ty,** *n.* — **trans·fer'a·ble,** *adj.* —**trans·fer'al** (-əl), **trans·fer'ral,** *n.* —**trans·fer'rer,** *n.*

trans·fig·ure (trans fig'yər), *v.t.*, **-ured, -ur·ing. 1.** to change in outward appearance. **2.** to change so as to glorify or exalt. —**trans·fig'u·ra'tion,** *n.*

trans·fix (trans fiks'), *v.t.*, **-fixed** or **-fixt, -fix·ing. 1.** to make motionless, as with awe. **2.** to pierce through with or as with a pointed weapon.

trans·form (trans fôrm'), *v.t.* **1.** to change in form or structure. **2.** to change in condition, nature, or character. —**trans·for·ma·tion,** *n.* —Syn. **1.** metamorphose, transfigure. **2.** convert.

trans·form·er (trans fôr'mər), *n.* **1.** a person or thing that transforms. **2.** a device for altering the voltage in an electric circuit.

trans·fuse (trans fyōōz'), *v.t.*, **-fused, -fus·ing. 1.** to cause to be instilled, as enthusiasm. **2.** to diffuse into or through. **3.** to give a transfusion to. —**trans·fus'er,** *n.* —**trans·fus'a·ble,** *adj.*

trans·fus·ion (trans fyōō'zhən), *n.* **1.** the act or process of transfusing. **2.** *Med.* **a.** the direct transferring of blood, plasma, or the like, from one person or animal into another. **b.** the injecting of bottled blood or a solution of a salt, sugar, etc., into a blood vessel.

trans·gress (trans gres', tranz-), *v.i., v.t.* **1.** to go beyond the limits imposed by (a law or command). **2.** to pass over (any limit or bound). —**trans·gres'sion** (-gresh'ən), *n.* — **trans·gres'sor,** *n.* —Syn. **1.** infringe, violate.

tran·ship (tran ship'), *v.t., v.i.*, **-shipped, -ship·ping.** transship.

tran·sient (tran'shənt, -zhənt), *adj.* **1.** passing by quickly with time: *transient joys.* **2.** staying only a short time. —*n.* **3.** a person or thing that is transient. **4.** a transient guest, as at a hotel. —**tran'sience, tran'sien·cy,** *n.* —**tran'sient·ly,** *adv.* —Syn. **1.** brief, fleeting, temporary.

tran·sis·tor (tran zis'tər), *n*. **1.** a small electronic semiconductor device performing functions similar to those of a vacuum tube. **2.** a small radio that uses transistors. —**tran·sis'tor·ize'**, *v.t.*

trans·it (tran'sit, -zit), *n*. **1.** a passing across or through, or from one place to another. **2.** conveyance of passengers or goods from one place to another, esp. as a system of local public transportation. **3.** *Survey.* an instrument used by surveyors for measuring angles.

tran·si·tion (tran zish'ən, -sish'-), *n*. passage from one position, state, stage, or subject to another. —**tran·si'tion·al**, *adj*. —**tran·si'tion·al·ly**, *adv*.

tran·si·tive (tran'si tiv, -zi-), *adj*. *Gram.* noting a verb that takes a direct object. —**tran'si·tive·ly**, *adv*. —**tran'si·tive·ness, tran'si·tiv'i·ty**, *n*.

tran·si·to·ry (tran'si tōr'ē, -tôr'ē, -zi-), *adj*. brief or short by its very nature, as human life. —**tran'si·to'ri·ness**, *n*.

transl., **1.** translated. **2.** translation.

trans·late (trans lāt', trans'lāt), *v.t.*, **-lat·ed, -lat·ing. 1.** to turn (something expressed, esp. written) from one language into another. **2.** to change the form, condition, or nature of. **3.** to explain in simpler terms. —**trans·lat'a·ble**, *adj.* — **trans·la'tion**, *n*. —**trans·la'tor**, *n*.

trans·lit·er·ate (trans lit'ə rāt', tranz-), *v.t.*, **-at·ed, -at·ing.** to substitute (letters or words) of one language for those of another. —**trans·lit'er·a'tion**, *n*.

trans·lu·cent (trans lōō'sənt, tranz-), *adj*. permitting light to pass through so diffusedly that objects cannot be clearly seen. —**trans·lu'cence, trans·lu'cen·cy**, *n*. —**trans·lu'cent·ly**, *adv*.

trans·mi·grate (trans mī'grāt, tranz-), *v.i.*, **-grat·ed, -grat·ing.** (of the soul) to be reborn at death in another body. —**trans·mi·gra'tion**, *n*. —**trans·mi'gra·tor**, *n*. —**trans·mi'gra·to'ry** (-grə tōr'ē, -tôr'ē), *adj*.

trans·mis·sion (trans mish'ən, tranz-), *n*. **1.** the act or process of transmitting. **2.** something transmitted. **3.** transference of force between machines or mechanisms. **4.** a compact, enclosed unit of gears for this purpose, as in an automobile. **5.** the broadcasting of radio waves from a transmitter.

trans·mit (trans mit', tranz-), *v.t.*, **-mit·ted, -mit·ting. 1.** to send or convey from one person, place, or thing to another. **2.** to pass on by heredity. **3.** to cause (light, heat, sound, etc.) to pass through a medium. **4.** to send out (radio or television signals). —**trans·mis'si·ble** (-mis'ə bəl), *adj*. —**trans·mit'ta·ble**, *adj*. —**trans·mit'tal, trans·mit'tance**, *n*.

trans·mit·ter (trans mit'ər, tranz-), *n*. **1.** a person or thing that transmits. **2.** a device for transmitting signals, as in radio or telephony.

trans·mog·ri·fy (trans mog'rə fī', tranz-), *v.t.*, **-fied, -fy·ing.** to change in appearance or form, esp. grotesquely. —**trans·mog'ri·fi·ca'tion**, *n*.

trans·mute (trans myōōt', tranz-), *v.t.*, *v.i.*, **-mut·ed, -mut·ing.** to change from one nature, substance, or form into another. —**trans·mut'a·ble**, *adj*. —**trans·mu·ta'tion**, *n*.

trans·na·tion·al (trans nash'ə nəl, tranz-), *adj*. going beyond national boundaries.

trans·o·ce·an·ic (trans'ō shē an'ik, tranz'-), *adj*. **1.** crossing the ocean. **2.** situated beyond the ocean.

tran·som (tran'səm), *n*. **1.** a crosspiece separating a door or window from a window above it. **2.** a small window above a door or other window.

tran·son·ic (tran son'ik), *adj*. close to the speed of propagation of sound. Also, **trans·son'ic**.

transp., transportation.

trans·pa·cif·ic (trans'pə sif'ik), *adj*. **1.** crossing the Pacific. **2.** situated beyond the Pacific.

trans·par·ent (trans pâr'ənt, -par'-), *adj*. **1.** permitting light to pass so that objects situated beyond can be clearly seen. **2.** so sheer in texture as to permit light to pass through. **3.** easily recognized or detected. **4.** candid or frank. —**trans·par'en·cy**, *n*. —**trans·par'ent·ly**, *adv*.

tran·spire (tran spī°r'), *v.i.*, **-spired, -spir·ing. 1.** to become known. **2.** to take place. **3.** to give off moisture, odor, etc., as through pores. —**tran'·spi·ra'tion** (-spə rā'shən), *n*.

trans·plant (*v.* trans plant', *n.* trans'plant'), *v.t.* **1.** to remove (a plant) from one place and plant it in another. **2.** to transfer (an organ, tissue, etc.) from one part of the body to another or from one person to another. **3.** to bring (a family, etc.) from one country or region to another for settlement. —*n.* **4.** the act or process of transplanting. **5.** something transplanted. —**trans'plan·ta'tion**, *n*. —**trans·plant'er**, *n*.

---

trans·isth'mi·an, *adj*.
trans·ma·rine', *adj*.

trans'-Med·i·ter·ra'ne·an, *adj*.
trans·or'bi·tal, *adj*.

tran·spon·der (tran spon'dər), *n.* a transceiver that automatically transmits a certain signal.

trans·port (*v.* trans pōrt', *n.* trans'pōrt'), *v.t.* 1. to carry or convey from one place to another. 2. to carry away by strong emotion. 3. (formerly) to send to a penal colony. —*n.* 4. the act or means of transporting. 5. a ship or airplane employed for transporting troops, etc. 6. strong emotion, as of joy. —**transport'er,** *n.*

trans·por·ta·tion (trans'pər tā'shən), *n.* 1. the act of transporting or state of being transported. 2. the means of conveyance. 3. the business of transporting passengers or goods.

trans·pose (trans pōz'), *v.t., v.i,, -posed, -pos·ing.* 1. to reverse the order or position (of). 2. *Music.* to put (a piece of music) into a different key. —**trans/po·si'tion** (-pə zish'ən), *n.*

trans·sex·u·al (trans sek'shōō əl), *n.* 1. a person who psychologically identifies with the opposite sex. 2. such a person whose sex has been changed by surgery. —**trans·sex'u·al·ism,** *n.*

trans·ship (trans ship'), *v.t., v.i., -shipped, -ship·ping.* to transfer from one ship or vehicle to another for further transportation. —**trans·ship'ment,** *n.*

tran·sub·stan·ti·a·tion (tran'səb stan'shē ā'shən), *n.* (in the Eucharist) the conversion of the whole substance of the bread and wine into the body and blood of Christ, only the external appearance of bread and wine remaining.

trans·verse (trans vûrs', trans'vûrs), *adj.* 1. lying or reaching across. —*n.* 2. something transverse. —**trans-verse'ly,** *adv.*

trans·ves·tism (trans ves'tiz əm, tranz-), *n.* the practice of dressing and behaving like the opposite sex, usually by psychological preference. —**trans·ves'tite** (-ves'tīt), *n., adj.*

trap¹ (trap), *n., v.,* **trapped, trap·ping.** —*n.* 1. a device for catching animals, as one that springs shut suddenly when stepped on. 2. any stratagem for catching a person unawares. 3. a U-shaped section in a drainpipe, for preventing the escape of air or gases. 4. **traps,** the percussion instruments of a jazz band. 5. *Trapshooting.* a device for hurling clay pigeons into the air. 6. *Golf.* a shallow pit serving as a hazard. 7. *Brit.* a light, two-wheeled carriage with springs. —*v.t.* 8. to catch in or as in a trap. —*v.i.* 9. to engage in the business of trapping animals for their furs. —**trap'per,** *n.*

trap² (trap), *v.,* **trapped, trap·ping,** *n.* —*v.t.* 1. to furnish or adorn with trappings. —*n.* 2. **traps,** *Informal.* personal belongings.

trap³ (trap), *n.* fine-grained, dark-colored igneous rock, used for roads. Also called **trap'rock'.**

trap' door', a door set in the surface of a floor or ceiling.

tra·peze (tra pēz'), *n.* a short crossbar attached to the ends of two swinging ropes, used for acrobatics.

trap·e·zoid (trap'i zoid'), *n.* a four-sided plane figure having two sides parallel. —**trap'e·zoi'dal,** *adj.*

trap·pings (trap'ingz), *n.pl.* 1. articles of equipment or dress, esp. of an ornamental character. 2. an ornamental covering for a horse.

trap·shoot·ing (trap'shōō'ting), *n.* the sport of shooting at clay pigeons hurled into the air from a trap.

trash (trash), *n.* 1. anything worthless or useless. 2. a disreputable person. 3. such persons collectively. —**trash'y,** *adj.*

trau·ma (trou'mə, trô'-), *n., pl. -mas, -ma·ta** (-mə tə). 1. a startling experience that has a lasting effect on mental life. 2. a body injury produced by sudden force. —**trau·mat'ic** (-mat'ik), *adj.* —**trau·mat'i·cal·ly,** *adv.* —**trau'ma·tize'** (-tīz'), *v.t.*

tra·vail (trə vāl', trav'āl), *n.* 1. painfully burdensome work. 2. severe mental or physical suffering. 3. *Archaic.* labor in childbirth. —*v.i.* 4. to work painfully. 5. *Archaic.* to suffer labor pains.

trav·el (trav'əl), *v.,* **-eled, -el·ing** or **-elled, -el·ling,** *n.* —*v.i.* 1. to go from one place to another, as by car, esp. to an out-of-town destination. 2. to journey from place to place as a salesman. 3. to pass or be transmitted, as light. 4. *Informal.* to move with speed. 5. *Informal.* to associate or mix. —*v.t.* 6. to travel, journey, or pass through or over. —*n.* 7. the act of traveling, esp. in distant places. 8. **travels,** journeys or wanderings. —**trav'el·er, trav'el·ler,** *n.*

trav·e·logue (trav'ə lôg', -log'), *n.* a motion picture or an illustrated lecture describing travels. Also, **trav'e·log'.**

trav·erse (trav'ərs, trə vûrs'), *v.,* **-ersed, -ers·ing,** *n., adj.* —*v.t.* 1. to pass or move over, along, or through. 2. to extend or reach across or over. 3. to cause to move laterally. —*n.* 4. something that traverses, as a crosspiece or crossbar. —*adj.* 5. extending or reaching across. —**tra·vers'al,** *n.*

trav′erse rod′, a horizontal rod on which drapes slide to open or close when pulled by cords.

trav·er·tine (trav′ər tin, -tēn′), *n.* a form of limestone deposited by hot springs.

trav·es·ty (trav′i stē), *n., pl.* **-ties,** *v.,* **-tied, -ty·ing.** —*n.* **1.** a ridiculous or shameful imitation: *a travesty of justice.* —*v.t.* **2.** to make a travesty on.

trawl (trôl), *n.* **1.** a strong fishing net for dragging along the sea bottom to catch deep-dwelling fish. **2.** a buoyed line used in sea fishing. —*v.i., v.t.* **3.** to fish or catch with a trawl.

trawl·er (trô′lər), *n.* a boat used in trawling.

tray (trā), *n.* a flat, shallow receptacle with raised edges, for carrying, holding, or displaying articles.

treach·er·ous (trech′ər əs), *adj.* **1.** likely to betray trust. **2.** untrustworthy or unreliable. **3.** unstable or insecure, as footing. —**treach′er·ous·ly,** *adv.* —**treach′er·ous·ness,** *n.* — **Syn. 1.** disloyal, faithless, perfidious, traitorous.

treach·er·y (trech′ə rē), *n., pl.* **-er·ies. 1.** betrayal of trust. **2.** violation of allegiance.

trea·cle (trē′kəl), *n. Brit.* molasses.

tread (tred), *v.,* **trod, trod·den** or **trod, tread·ing,** *n.* —*v.t.* **1.** to walk on, over, or along. **2.** to trample or crush underfoot. **3.** to make or form by walking or trampling: *to tread a path.* **4.** to perform by walking or dancing. —*v.i.* **5.** to step or walk. **6.** to trample so as to crush. **7. tread water,** *Swimming.* to maintain the body erect in the water with the head above the surface. —*n.* **8.** the act, sound, or manner of treading. **9.** the part of the undersurface of a shoe that touches the ground. **10.** the upper surface of a step in a stair. **11.** the part of a tire that touches the road.

trea·dle (tred′ᵊl), *n.* a lever operated by the foot to move a machine.

tread·mill (tred′mil′), *n.* **1.** a mill turned by persons or animals walking on moving steps or treading an endless belt. **2.** a monotonous routine of work.

treas., **1.** treasurer. **2.** treasury.

trea·son (trē′zən), *n.* violation of allegiance to one's country, esp. by attempting to overthrow the government. —**trea′son·a·ble,** *adj.* —**trea′son·ous,** *adj.*

treas·ure (trezh′ər), *n., v.,* **-ured, -ur·ing.** —*n.* **1.** accumulated or stored wealth, esp. in the form of jewels, money, etc. **2.** any thing or person highly valued. —*v.t.* **3.** to regard as precious. **4.** to store away, as for future use. [< OF < L *thēsaur(us)*

storehouse] —**treas′ur·a·ble,** *adj.* — **Syn. 3.** cherish, esteem, prize.

treas·ur·er (trezh′ər ər), *n.* an officer charged with the receipt, care, and disbursement of money.

treas′ure trove′, **1.** treasure of unknown ownership, found hidden or buried. **2.** a valuable discovery.

treas·ur·y (trezh′ə rē), *n., pl.* **-ur·ies. 1.** a place where the revenues or funds of a government or corporation are received, kept, and disbursed. **2.** the revenues or funds themselves. **3.** (*cap.*) the department of government in charge of national finances. **4.** a place for keeping or storing treasure.

treat (trēt), *v.t.* **1.** to act or behave toward (a person or thing) in a certain way. **2.** to consider or regard in a certain way. **3.** to give medical or surgical care to. **4.** to deal with in writing or artistically, esp. in a certain style. **5.** to subject to some process or action, as of a chemical. **6.** to provide food, entertainment, gifts, etc., at one's own expense. — *v.i.* **7.** to deal with a subject in speech or writing. **8.** to discuss terms of settlement. —*n.* **9.** food, drink, or entertainment given or paid for by another. **10.** anything that gives pleasure or enjoyment. — **treat′er,** *n.*

trea·tise (trē′tis), *n.* a systematic exposition in writing of a subject.

treat·ment (trēt′mənt), *n.* **1.** the act, manner, or process of treating. **2.** medical or surgical care.

trea·ty (trē′tē), *n., pl.* **-ties.** a formal agreement reached by negotiation between two or more nations.

tre·ble (treb′əl), *adj., n., v.,* **-bled, -bling.** —*adj.* **1.** *Chiefly Brit.* triple. **2.** *Music.* **a.** of the highest part in harmonized music. **b.** of the highest pitch or range, as a voice part, singer, or instrument. **c.** high in pitch. —*n.* **3.** *Music.* **a.** a treble voice, singer, or instrument. **b.** the upper range of an instrument or voice. —*v.t., v.i.* **4.** *Chiefly Brit.* triple (def. 6). [< MF < L *tripl(us)* triple] —**tre′bly,** *adv.*

tre′ble clef′, *Music.* the sign indicating that the second line of the staff is G above middle C.

tree (trē), *n., v.,* **treed, tree·ing.** —*n.* **1.** a perennial plant having a permanent, woody, main stem or trunk and usually branches. **2.** something resembling a tree in shape: *a clothes tree.* **3.** See **family tree.** —*v.t.* **4.** to drive up a tree, as a hunted animal. —**tree′less,** *adj.*

tre·foil (trē′foil), *n.* **1.** a plant having leaves with three leaflets, as the clover. **2.** an ornament or design resembling such a leaf.

trek (trek), v., **trekked, trek·king,** n.
—v.i. **1.** to travel slowly or with difficulty. **2.** (in South Africa) to travel
by ox wagon. —n. **3.** a journey involving hardship. **4.** (in South Africa) a migration by ox wagon. —
trek′ker, n.

trel·lis (trel′is), n. a lattice used as
a support for growing vines.

trem·a·tode (trem′ə tōd′, trē′mə-), n.
any parasitic worm having external
suckers.

trem·ble (trem′bəl), v., **-bled, -bling,**
n. —v.i. **1.** to shake involuntarily,
as from fear or cold. **2.** to be troubled with anxiety or concern. **3.** to
be shaky or wavering, as sound. —n.
4. the act or a state of trembling. —
trem′bler, n. —**trem′bling·ly,** adv.
—**Syn. 1.** quake, shiver, shudder.

tre·men·dous (tri men′dəs), adj. **1.**
extremely large, great, or strong. **2.**
Informal. extraordinary in excellence. **3.** extremely terrifying. —
tre·men′dous·ly, adv. —**tre·men′-
dous·ness,** n.

trem·o·lo (trem′ə lō′), n., pl. **-los.**
Music. a quavering effect produced
by quick repetition of a single tone
or alternating tones.

trem·or (trem′ər, trē′mər), n. **1.** a
shaking or convulsive movement, as
of the earth. **2.** involuntary shaking
of the body, as from disease or excitement.

trem·u·lous (trem′yə ləs), adj. **1.** characterized by trembling or quivering.
2. timid or fearful. —**trem′u·lous·ly,**
adv. —**trem′u·lous·ness,** n.

trench (trench), n. **1.** a long, deep
furrow or ditch. **2.** a long, narrow
excavation in the battle ground, for
protecting soldiers from enemy fire.
—v.t. **3.** to dig trenches in. **4.** to
protect or fortify with trenches. —
v.i. **5.** to dig trenches. **6. trench on**
or **upon, a.** to encroach on. **b.** to
come close to.

trench·ant (tren′chənt), adj. **1.** inci-
sively keen: trenchant wit. **2.** vigorous or effective. **3.** clearly defined.
—**trench′an·cy,** n. —**trench′ant·ly,**
adv. —**Syn. 1.** acute, biting, sharp.

trench′ coat′, a waterproof, belted
overcoat, cut in military style.

trench·er (tren′chər), n. Archaic. a
wooden plate for serving meat.

trench·er·man (tren′chər mən), n. a
heavy eater.

trench′ foot′, a disease of the feet
due to exposure to cold and wet.

trench′ mouth′, a disease characterized by ulceration of the mucous
membranes of the mouth and throat.

trend (trend), n. **1.** a general course
or prevailing tendency. **2.** a current
style or vogue. —v.i. **3.** to have a
general tendency or a certain direction.

trend·y (trend′ē), adj., **-i·er, -i·est.** Informal. of or in the most recent
trend, style, or fashion. —**trend′i-
ness,** n.

Tren·ton (tren′tⁿn), n. the capital of
New Jersey.

tre·pan (tri pan′), n., v., **-panned,
-pan·ning.** —n. **1.** an obsolete form
of the trephine. —v.t. **2.** to trephine.
—**trep·a·na·tion** (trep′ə nā′shən), n.
—**tre·pan′ner,** n.

tre·phine (tri fīn′, -fēn′), n., v.,
-phined, -phin·ing. —n. **1.** a small
circular saw used in surgery to remove disks of bone from the skull.
—v.t. **2.** to operate on with a trephine. —**treph·i·na·tion** (tref′ə nā′-
shən), n.

trep·i·da·tion (trep′l dā′shən), n. **1.**
fearful or nervous anxiety. **2.** Archaic. a trembling movement.

tres·pass (tres′pəs, -pas′), v.i. **1.** to
enter unlawfully or without permission upon the land of another. **2.** to
intrude or encroach. **3.** to commit
an offense or sin. —n. **4.** the act or
an instance of trespassing. —**tres′-
pass·er,** n.

tress (tres), n. Usually, **tresses.** long,
loose locks of hair, esp. of a woman.

tres·tle (tres′əl), n. **1.** a crossbar on
two pairs of spreading legs, used for
forming a barrier or supporting a
table top. **2.** a huge, braced framework of metal or timber, used for
supporting a railroad bridge.

trey (trā), n. a playing card or die
having three pips.

tri-, a combining form meaning: **a.**
having or consisting of: triangle. **b.**
into three parts: trisect. **c.** every
three: triennial.

tri·ad (trī′ad), n. a group of three,
esp. of three closely related persons
or things. —**tri·ad′ic,** adj.

tri·age (trē′äzh, trē äzh′), n. the
sorting out of patients, as in battle,
to determine priority for treatment.

tri·al (trī′əl, trīl), n. **1.** the hearing
and deciding of a criminal or civil
case in a court of law. **2.** the act of
trying, testing, or putting to the
proof. **3.** a distressed or painful
state. **4.** a source of trouble or annoyance. **5.** an attempt or effort. —
adj. **6.** of or used in a trial. **7.** done
or made by way of trial or test.

tri′al and er′ror, a process of solving
problems by trying various methods
and eliminating faulty ones.

tri′al balloon′, a tentative statement
or action designed to test public
reactions.

tri·an·gle (trī′ang′gəl), n. **1.** a plane
figure having three sides and three
angles. **2.** any three-cornered or
three-sided figure or object. —**tri-
an′gu·lar** (-gyə lər), adj. —**tri·an′-
gu·lar·ly,** adv.

tri·an·gu·late (trī ang′gyə lāt′), *v.t.*, **-lat·ed, -lat·ing.** to divide into triangles. —**tri·an′gu·la′tion,** *n.*

Tri·as·sic (trī as′ik), *adj.* **1.** noting a period of the Mesozoic era occurring from 180,000,000 to 220,000,000 years ago, characterized by volcanic activity and the advent of dinosaurs and marine reptiles. —*n.* **2.** the Triassic period.

trib., tributary.

tribe (trīb), *n.* **1.** a group of people descended from a single ancestor, following the same leader and sharing the same customs. **2.** a local division of an aboriginal people. **3.** a group of persons of the same class, profession, or interests. **4.** a class of related animals or plants. —**trib′al,** *adj.*

tribes·man (trībz′mən), *n.* a member of a tribe. —**tribes′wom′an,** *n.fem.*

trib·u·la·tion (trib′yə lā′shən), *n.* **1.** severe trial or suffering. **2.** a cause of this.

tri·bu·nal (trī byōōn′əl, tri-), *n.* **1.** a court of justice. **2.** anything that tries or decides: *the tribunal of public opinion.* **3.** the seat of a judge in ancient Rome.

trib·une (trib′yōōn, tri byōōn′), *n.* **1.** (in ancient Rome) an official elected to protect the rights of the plebeians from the patricians. **2.** a democratic champion: now chiefly used in newspaper names.

trib·u·tar·y (trib′yə ter′ē), *n., pl.* **-tar·ies,** *adj.* —*n.* **1.** a stream flowing into a larger stream or other body of water. **2.** a person or nation that pays tribute. —*adj.* **3.** flowing into a larger stream or other body of water. **4.** paying tribute in money or kind.

trib·ute (trib′yōōt), *n.* **1.** a gift, compliment, or praise given in gratitude, esteem, or regard. **2.** (formerly) a stated payment in money or kind by one sovereign or state to another in acknowledgment of subjugation or as the price of protection. **3.** any enforced payment or contribution.

trice (trīs), *n.* a very short time (used usually in the phrase *in a trice*).

tri·cen·ten·ni·al (trī′sen ten′ē əl), *n.* a 300th anniversary or its celebration.

tri·ceps (trī′seps), *n., pl.* **-ceps·es** (-sep siz), **-ceps.** the muscle on the back of the upper arm whose action straightens the elbow.

tri·cer·a·tops (trī ser′ə tops′), *n.* a dinosaur with a large, bony crest on the neck, a long horn over each eye, and a shorter horn on the nose.

trich·i·no·sis (trik′ə nō′sis), *n.* a disease caused by eating undercooked infected pork and characterized by fever, muscle weakness, etc.

trick (trik), *n.* **1.** an act or device intended to deceive or cheat. **2.** a mischievous act. **3.** a childish act. **4.** a clever act intended to entertain. **5.** the art or knack of doing something. **6.** a feat of magic. **7.** a peculiar habit. **8.** *Cards.* the group or set of cards played in one round. **9.** a turn of duty. **10. do** or **turn the trick,** to achieve the desired result. —*adj.* **11.** inclined to fail suddenly: *a trick knee.* —*v.t.* **12.** to deceive or cheat. **13. trick out** or **up,** to adorn or dress, esp. ostentatiously. —**trick′er,** *n.* —Syn. **1.** artifice, ruse, wile. **2.** prank.

trick·er·y (trik′ə rē), *n., pl.* **-er·ies. 1.** the use of tricks to deceive. **2.** a trick used to deceive.

trick·ish (trik′ish), *adj.* tricky. —**trick′ish·ly,** *adv.* —**trick′ish·ness,** *n.*

trick·le (trik′əl), *v.,* **-led, -ling,** *n.* —*v.i.* **1.** to flow or fall in drops or in a small, slow stream. **2.** to move or pass slowly. —*n.* **3.** a trickling stream. **4.** a small, slow, or irregular quantity of persons or things moving along.

tricks·ter (trik′stər), *n.* a person who tricks or cheats.

trick·y (trik′ē), *adj.,* **trick·i·er, trick·i·est. 1.** given to deceitful or clever tricks. **2.** requiring special handling. **3.** unreliable or unsafe: *a tricky ladder.* —**trick′i·ly,** *adv.* —**trick′i·ness,** *n.* —Syn. **1.** crafty, sly, wily.

tri·col·or (trī′kul′ər), *n.* a flag having three colors, esp. the national flag of France.

tri·cot (trē′kō), *n.* **1.** a warp-knit fabric, usually of nylon, with each side different. **2.** a kind of worsted cloth.

tri·cy·cle (trī′si kəl), *n.* a child's three-wheeled vehicle propelled by foot pedals.

tri·dent (trīd′ənt), *n.* a spear having three prongs.

tried (trīd), *adj.* **1.** tested and proved good or trustworthy. **2.** subjected to hardship. —*v.* **3.** pt. and pp. of **try.**

tri·en·ni·al (trī en′ē əl), *adj.* **1.** occurring every three years. **2.** lasting three years. —**tri·en′ni·al·ly,** *adv.*

tri·fle (trī′fəl), *n., v.,* **-fled, -fling.** —*n.* **1.** something of very little value or importance. **2.** a small quantity or amount. —*v.i.* **3.** to treat lightly or without proper respect. **4.** to play or toy by handling. **5.** to act or talk in a frivolous way. —**tri′fler,** *n.*

tri·fling (trī′fling), *adj.* **1.** negligibly insignificant. **2.** frivolous or shallow. —**tri′fling·ly,** *adv.*

tri·fo·cals (trī fō′kəlz), *n.* eyeglasses having three lenses, one for near, one for intermediate, and one for far vision.

tri·fo·li·ate (trī fō′lē it, -āt′), *adj.* having three leaves, leaflets, or leaflike parts.

trig[1] (trig), *n. Informal.* trigonometry.

trig[2] (trig), *adj. Chiefly Brit.* **1.** smartly neat and trim. **2.** in good physical condition.

trig·ger (trig′ər), *n.* **1.** a small lever in a firearm that, when pressed by the finger, actuates the mechanism for discharging the weapon. —*v.t.* **2.** to initiate or precipitate, as an action. **3.** to explode by pulling a trigger.

tri·glyc·er·ide (trī glis′ə rīd′, -ər id), *n.* an ester obtained from glycerol by linking three molecules of fatty acids.

trig·o·nom·e·try (trig′ə nom′i trē), *n.* the branch of mathematics that deals with the relations between the sides and angles of triangles. —**trig′o·no·met′ric** (-nə me′trik), **trig′o·no·met′ri·cal,** *adj.* —**trig′o·no·met′ri·cal·ly,** *adv.*

tri·lit·er·al (trī lit′ər əl), *adj.* using or consisting of three letters.

trill (tril), *n.* **1.** a succession of high-pitched, rapidly alternating sounds, as made by a bird. **2.** *Music.* the rapid alternation of two adjacent tones. **3.** *Phonet.* a sound, esp. *r*, produced with rapid vibration of the tongue or uvula. —*v.t., v.i.* **4.** to utter, sing, or play with a trill. **5.** *Phonet.* to produce (a trill).

tril·lion (tril′yən), *n.* a cardinal number represented, in the U.S. and France, by one followed by 12 zeros, and, in Great Britain and Germany, by one followed by 18 zeros. —**tril′lionth,** *n., adj.*

tril·li·um (tril′ē əm), *n.* an herb related to the lily, having three leaves from the center of which rises a solitary flower.

tril·o·gy (tril′ə jē), *n., pl.* **-gies.** a series of three plays or novels that are closely related in theme.

trim (trim), *v.,* **trimmed, trim·ming,** *n., adj.,* **trim·mer, trim·mest.** —*v.t.* **1.** to put into a neat or orderly condition by clipping or pruning. **2.** to remove (an excess, etc.) by or as by cutting. **3.** to decorate with ornaments. **4. a.** to balance (a ship) by rearranging the ballast or cargo. **b.** to adjust (the sails or yards) to the direction of the wind. **5.** to level off (an airplane) in flight. **6.** *Informal.* to beat or defeat. —*v.i.* **7.** to change one's views for reasons of expediency. —*n.* **8.** the condition or fitness for action or use. **9.** trimming (def. 1). **10.** the action or result of trimming, as by cutting. **11. a.** the balance of a ship in the water. **b.** the adjustment of a ship to sailing conditions. **12.** woodwork that frames or decorates windows, doors, etc. —*adj.* **13.** pleasingly neat or smart. **14.** in good condition or fitness. —**trim′ly,** *adv.* —**trim′mer,** *n.* —**trim′ness,** *n.*

tri·ma·ran (trī′mə ran′), *n.* a vessel similar to a catamaran but having three hulls.

tri·mes·ter (trī mes′tər, trī′mes-), *n.* **1.** a period of three months. **2.** any of the three terms into which an academic year is divided by some colleges.

trim·ming (trim′ing), *n.* **1.** material used for decoration or ornament. **2.** Usually, **trimmings,** accompaniments to a main dish. **3. trimmings,** pieces cut off in trimming. **4.** *Informal.* a beating or defeat.

tri·month·ly (trī munth′lē), *adj.* occurring or done every three months.

trine (trīn), *adj. Rare.* threefold.

Trin′i·dad and To·ba·go (trin′i dad′ ənd tō bā′gō), an island country in the West Indies.

Trin·i·tar·i·an (trin′i târ′ē ən), *n.* a person who believes in the doctrine of the Trinity. —**Trin′i·tar′i·an·ism,** *n.*

Trin·i·ty (trin′i tē), *n., pl.* **-ties.** **1.** the union of Father, Son, and Holy Spirit in one Godhead. **2.** (*l.c.*) a group of three.

trin·ket (tring′kit), *n.* **1.** a small ornament, usually of little value. **2.** a trivial object.

tri·o (trē′ō), *n., pl.* **-os.** **1.** a musical composition for three voices or instruments. **2.** the three singers or players of such a composition. **3.** any group of three persons or things.

tri·ode (trī′ōd), *n.* a vacuum tube containing three electrodes.

trip (trip), *n., v.,* **tripped, trip·ping.** —*n.* **1.** a course of travel, either for business or pleasure. **2.** a stumble or wrong step. **3.** a quick, light step. **4.** a device for releasing a spring or lever that controls the action of a machine. **5.** *Slang.* the experience of being under the influence of a hallucinogenic drug, esp. LSD. —*v.i., v.t.* **6.** to stumble or cause to stumble. **7.** to make or cause to make a slip or error. **8.** to step or move lightly or quickly. **9.** to release or operate, as a spring or lever. —**trip′per,** *n.* —**Syn. 1.** excursion, expedition, journey, voyage.

tri·par·tite (trī pär′tīt), *adj.* **1.** divided into or consisting of three parts. **2.** shared by three parties, as a treaty.

tripe (trīp), *n.* **1.** a part of the stomach of a ruminant, esp. an ox, used as food. **2.** *Slang.* anything inferior or worthless.

tri·ple (trip′əl), *adj., n., v.,* **-pled, -pling.** —*adj.* 1. consisting of three parts. 2. three times as great or as many. —*n.* 3. an amount three times as great as another. 4. a group of three. 5. *Baseball.* a hit that enables a batter to reach third base safely. —*v.t., v.i.* 6. to make or become three times as great. 7. *Baseball.* to hit a triple. —**tri·ply** (trip′lē), *adv.*

tri·plet (trip′lit), *n.* 1. one of three offspring born at the same birth. 2. any group of three.

tri·plex (trip′leks, trī′pleks), *adj.* 1. triple (def. 1). —*n.* 2. an apartment that has rooms on three floors.

trip·li·cate (*n., adj.* trip′lə kit, -kāt′, *v.* trip′lə kāt′), *n., adj., v.,* **-cat·ed -cat·ing.** —*n.* 1. one of three identical items, esp. copies of typewritten matter. 2. **in triplicate,** in three identical copies. —*adj.* 3. consisting of three identical parts. 4. noting the third item or copy. —*v.t.* 5. to make in triplicate. 6. to make three times as great. —**trip′li·ca′tion,** *n.*

tri·pod (trī′pod), *n.* a three-legged stand or support, as for a camera. —**trip·o·dal** (trip′ə dəl), *adj.*

trip·tych (trip′tik), *n.* a set of three panels side by side, bearing pictures or carvings, often used as an altarpiece.

tri·reme (trī′rēm), *n.* an ancient galley with three tiers of oars on each side.

tri·sect (trī sekt′), *v.t.* to divide into three equal parts. —**tri·sec′tion,** *n.*

tris·kai·dek·a·phobe (tris′kī dek′ə fōb′), *n.* a person who irrationally fears the number 13. —**tris′kai·dek′·a·pho′bi·a,** *n.*

trite (trīt), *adj.,* **trit·er, trit·est.** made stale and uninteresting by repeated use. [< L *trītus* worn] —**trite′ly,** *adv.* —**trite′ness,** *n.* —**Syn.** banal, commonplace, hackneyed.

trit·i·um (trit′ē əm, trish′əm), *n.* an isotope of hydrogen having an atomic weight of three.

trit·u·rate (trich′ə rāt′), *v.t., -rat·ed, -rat·ing.* to reduce to a very fine powder by rubbing or grinding. —**trit′u·ra·ble,** *adj.* —**trit′u·ra′tor,** *n.*

tri·umph (trī′əmf), *n.* 1. a satisfying victory or success. 2. celebration or joy over this. —*v.i.* 3. to gain or win a triumph. 4. to celebrate or rejoice over triumph. —**tri·um′phal** (-um′fəl), *adj.*

tri·um·phant (trī um′fənt), *adj.* 1. having achieved triumph. 2. rejoicing over triumph. —**tri·um′phant·ly,** *adv.*

tri·um·vir (trī um′vər), *n., pl.* **-virs, -vi·ri** (-və rī′). one of the members of a triumvirate.

tri·um·vi·rate (trī um′vər it, -və rāt′), *n.* a government of three persons jointly holding the same authority, as in ancient Rome.

tri·une (trī′yōōn), *adj.* three in one: *a triune God.*

triv·et (triv′it), *n.* 1. a short-legged metal plate put under a hot dish to protect a table. 2. a three-legged metal stand used for supporting cooking vessels over an open fire.

triv·i·a (triv′ē ə), *n.pl.* matters or things of very slight importance.

triv·i·al (triv′ē əl), *adj.* 1. of very slight importance. 2. *Archaic.* commonplace or ordinary. —**triv′i·al′i·ty** (-al′i tē), *n.* —**triv′i·al·ly,** *adv.* —**Syn.** 1. insignificant, negligible, petty, trifling.

triv·i·um (triv′ē əm), *n., pl.* **-i·a** (-ē ə). (in ancient Rome) the three liberal arts of grammar, rhetoric, and logic.

tro·che (trō′kē), *n.* a small medicinal lozenge.

tro·chee (trō′kē), *n. Pros.* a foot of two syllables, the first stressed and the second unstressed. —**tro·cha′ic** (-kā′ik), *adj.*

trod (trod), *v.* pt. and a pp. of **tread.**

trod·den (trod′ⁿn), *v.* a pp. of **tread.**

trog·lo·dyte (trog′lə dīt′), *n.* 1. a primitive cave dweller. 2. a reclusive person.

troi·ka (troi′kə), *n.* 1. a Russian vehicle drawn by three horses abreast. 2. triumvirate. [< Russ]

Tro·jan (trō′jən), *adj.* 1. of Troy or its inhabitants. —*n.* 2. a native or inhabitant of Troy.

Tro′jan War′, the ten-year war waged by the Greeks against the Trojans, ending in the burning of Troy.

troll[1] (trōl), *v.t., v.i.* 1. to sing in a loud, full voice. 2. to sing the parts of (a song) in succession, as in a round. 3. to fish or catch with a moving line. —*n.* 4. a lure used in trolling for fish. —**troll′er,** *n.*

troll[2] (trōl), *n.* (in Scandinavian folklore) a giant or dwarf inhabiting caves.

trol·ley (trol′ē), *n., pl.* **-leys.** 1. a carriage traveling on an overhead track and serving to move a suspended object. 2. a grooved wheel carried on the end of a pole by an electric car and held in contact with a suspended wire from which it collects the current. 3. See **trolley car.** Also, **trol′ly.**

trol′ley bus′, a bus propelled electrically by current taken by means of a trolley.

trol′ley car′, a street car propelled electrically by current taken by means of a trolley.

trol·lop (trol′əp), *n.* 1. a slovenly woman. 2. a promiscuous woman, esp. a prostitute.

trom·bone (trom bōn′, trom′bōn), *n.* a brass wind instrument consisting of a long, U-shaped metal tube, usually with a sliding section to produce different pitches. —**trom·bon·ist** (trom′bō nist, trom bō′-), *n.*

tromp (tromp), *v.i., v.t. Informal.* to tramp.

troop (trōōp), *n.* **1. troops, a.** a group of soldiers, police, etc. **b.** soldiers, esp. enlisted persons. **2.** (formerly) a cavalry unit about the size of an infantry company. **3.** an assemblage of persons or things. **4.** a unit of Boy or Girl Scouts under an adult leader. —*v.i.* **5.** to gather or move in a group.

troop·er (trōō′pər), *n.* **1.** a state police officer. **2.** a mounted police officer. **3.** (formerly) **a.** a horse-cavalry soldier. **b.** a cavalry horse.

troop·ship (trōōp′ship′), *n.* a ship for transporting military troops.

trop., **1.** tropic. **2.** tropical.

trope (trōp), *n.* the use of words in other than their literal sense.

tro·phy (trō′fē), *n., pl.* **-phies.** anything taken or won in war, hunting, competition, etc., esp. when preserved as a memento.

trop·ic (trop′ik), *n.* **1.** either of two corresponding parallels of latitude, one (**trop′ic of Can′cer**) about 23½° N, and the other (**trop′ic of Cap′ri·corn**) about 23½° S of the equator. **2. the tropics,** the regions lying between these parallels of latitude. —*adj.* **3.** of or occurring in the tropics.

trop·i·cal (trop′i kəl), *adj.* **1.** suitable for, characteristic of, or inhabiting the tropics. **2.** very hot and humid. —**trop′i·cal·ly,** *adv.*

tro·pism (trō′piz əm), *n.* an orientation of an organism to an external stimulus, as light.

trop·o·sphere (trop′ə sfēr′), *n.* the inner layer of the atmosphere within which nearly all cloud formations occur. —**trop′o·spher′ic** (-sfer′ik), *adj.*

trot (trot), *n., v.,* **trot·ted, trot·ting.** —*n.* **1.** a gait of a quadruped, as a horse, in which the legs move in diagonal pairs. **2.** the jogging gait of a human being. —*v.i., v.t.* **3.** to move or ride at a trot. **4.** to hurry or bustle. —**trot′ter,** *n.*

troth (trôth, trōth), *n. Archaic.* **1.** fidelity or loyalty. **2.** truth or verity. **3.** one's promise, esp. to marry.

trou·ba·dour (trōō′bə dôr′, -dôr′, -dŏōr′), *n.* one of a class of lyric poets who flourished principally in southern France from the 11th to 13th centuries.

trou·ble (trub′əl), *v.,* **-bled, -bling,** *n.* —*v.t.* **1.** to disturb in mind. **2.** to put to inconvenience or extra effort. **3.** to cause bodily pain or discomfort. **4.** to make murky, as water. —*v.i.* **5.** to put oneself to inconvenience or extra effort. —*n.* **6.** inconvenience or extra effort. **7.** a state of distress or hardship. **8.** a misfortune or affliction. **9.** civil disorder or disturbance. **10.** a physical disorder or ailment. **11.** a mechanical defect or breakdown. —**trou′ble·some,** *adj.* —**trou′ble·some·ly,** *adv.* —**trou′blous** (-ləs), *adj.* —**Syn. 1.** agitate, distress, upset, worry.

trou·ble·mak·er (trub′əl mā′kər), *n.* a person who causes trouble.

trou·ble·shoot·er (trub′əl shōō′tər), *n.* **1.** a person with special skill in resolving disputes or impasses. **2.** an expert in discovering and eliminating the cause of trouble in mechanical equipment. —**trou′ble·shoot′,** *v.i., v.t.*

trough (trôf, trof), *n.* **1.** a long, narrow, open boxlike receptacle, used chiefly to hold water or food for animals. **2.** a gutter from the roof of a building. **3.** any long depression or hollow, as between two ridges or waves.

trounce (trouns), *v.t.,* **trounced, trounc·ing.** **1.** to beat severely. **2.** to defeat decisively. —**trounc′er,** *n.*

troupe (trōōp), *n.* a group of singers, actors, etc. —**troup′er,** *n.*

trou·sers (trou′zərz), *n.pl.* a two-legged outer garment worn chiefly by men and boys, extending from the hips to the ankles.

trous·seau (trōō′sō, trōō sō′), *n., pl.* **-seaux** (-sōz, -sōz′), **-seaus.** a bride's outfit of clothing, linen, etc.

trout (trout), *n., pl.* **trout, trouts.** any of various food or game fishes related to the salmon.

trove (trōv), *n.* See **treasure trove.**

trow (trō), *v.i., v.t. Archaic.* to believe or think.

trow·el (trou′əl), *n.* **1.** a hand tool having a flat blade used for laying or spreading mortar, plaster, etc. **2.** a similar tool with a scooplike blade, used in gardening.

troy (troi), *adj.* measured or expressed in troy weight.

Troy (troi), *n.* an ancient ruined city in NW Asia Minor.

troy′ weight′, a system of weights in use for precious metals and gems, in which 12 ounces equals one pound.

tru·ant (trōō′ənt), *n.* **1.** a student who stays away from school without permission. **2.** a person who shirks his or her duty. —*adj.* **3.** absent from school without permission. **4.** neglectful of one's duties. [< OF: vagrant < Celt] —**tru′an·cy,** *n.*

truce (trōōs), *n.* **1.** a temporary halt in warfare by agreement of both sides. **2.** temporary respite or relief, as from trouble or pain.

truck¹ (truk), *n.* **1.** a large motor vehicle for carrying heavy loads. **2.** a
low platform mounted on wheels,
used for moving heavy objects. **3.** a
frame with two or more pairs of
wheels, for supporting one end of a
railroad car, etc. —*v.t.* **4.** to transport by truck. —*v.i.* **5.** to drive a
truck, esp. as one's work. —**truck′-
er,** *n.*

truck² (truk), *n.* **1.** vegetables grown
for the market. **2.** *Informal.* **a.** dealings or association. **b.** trash or rubbish. —*v.t.* **3.** to exchange (goods).

truck·age (truk′ij), *n.* **1.** transportation by truck. **2.** the charge for this.

truck′ farm′, a farm for the growing
of vegetables for the market. —
truck′ farm′er.

truck·ing (truk′ing), *n.* the act or
business of carrying goods by truck.

truck·le¹ (truk′əl), *v.i.,* **-led, -ling.** to
yield obsequiously. —**truck′ler,** *n.*

truck·le² (truk′əl), *n.* See **trundle bed.**
Also called **truck′le bed′.**

truck·load (truk′lōd′), *n.* a full or
nearly full load on a truck.

truc·u·lent (truk′yə lənt), *adj.* **1.** savagely brutal. **2.** aggressively hostile.
—**truc′u·lence, truc′u·len·cy,** *n.* —
truc′u·lent·ly, *adv.*

Tru·deau (trōō dō′), *n.* **Pi·erre El·li·ot**
(pē âr′ el′ē ət), born 1919, Canadian
political leader: prime minister 1968–
1979 and since 1980.

trudge (truj), *v.,* **trudged, trudg·ing,** *n.*
—*v.i.* **1.** to walk laboriously or
wearily. —*n.* **2.** a laborious or tiring walk. —**trudg′er,** *n.*

true (trōō), *adj.,* **tru·er, tru·est,** *n.,
adv., v.,* **trued, tru·ing** or **true·ing.**
—*adj.* **1.** in accordance with fact or
reality. **2.** not imitation or false. **3.**
loyal or faithful. **4.** agreeing with an
original or standard: *a true copy.* **5.**
having the right form, fit, etc. **6.**
legitimate or rightful. **7.** rightly or
properly so called. —*n.* **8.** accurate
formation or adjustment: *to be out
of true.* **9.** **the true,** truth or reality.
—*adv.* **10.** truly. **11.** in conformity
with the ancestral type: *to breed
true.* —*v.t.* **12.** to form or adjust
accurately. —**true′ness,** *n.* —**Syn. 1.**
actual. **2.** genuine. **4.** accurate, exact.

true′ bill′, a bill of indictment en-
dorsed by a grand jury.

true-blue (trōō′blōō′), *adj.* unwaveringly loyal.

truf·fle (truf′əl, trōō′fəl), *n.* a fungus
that grows underground, eaten as a
delicacy.

tru·ism (trōō′iz əm), *n.* a self-evident,
obvious truth.

tru·ly (trōō′lē), *adv.* **1.** in a true manner. **2.** exactly or accurately. **3.**
really or genuinely.

Tru·man (trōō′mən), *n.* **Har·ry S**
(har′ē), 1884–1972, 33rd president of
the U.S. 1945–53.

trump (trump), *n.* **1.** *Cards.* **a.** any
card of the suit that outranks all
other suits during the playing of a
particular hand or round. **b.** Often,
trumps. the suit itself. —*v.t., v.i.* **2.**
Cards. to take (a trick) with a trump.
3. **trump up,** to devise deceitfully.

trump·er·y (trum′pə rē), *n.* **1.** something showy but without value. **2.**
nonsense or twaddle.

trum·pet (trum′pit), *n.* **1.** a brass
wind instrument consisting of a
curved tube and having a cup-shaped
mouthpiece at one end and a flaring
bell at the other. **2.** something resembling a trumpet, esp. in sound.
—*v.i.* **3.** to blow a trumpet. —*v.t.* **4.**
to proclaim loudly or widely. —
trum′pet·er, *n.*

trun·cate (trung′kāt), *v.t.,* **-cat·ed, -cat-
ing.** to shorten by cutting off a part.
—**trun·ca′tion,** *n.*

trun·cheon (trun′chən), *n.* *Brit.* a
billy or night stick.

trun·dle (trun′dəl), *v.t., v.i.,* **-dled,
-dling.** to roll along on wheels. —
trun′dler, *n.*

trun′dle bed′, a low bed on casters,
usually pushed under another bed
when not in use.

trunk (trungk), *n.* **1.** the main stem
of a tree. **2.** a large, sturdy box for
holding personal effects, used esp.
as luggage. **3.** a large compartment
in an automobile, usually in the rear,
used for luggage, a spare tire, etc. **4.**
the body of a human or an ani-
mal excluding the head and limbs.
5. a telephone line between two central offices. **6.** the main body of an
artery, nerve, etc. **7.** the long snout
of the elephant. **8.** **trunks,** very short
shorts worn by men chiefly for
sports.

trunk′ line′, **1.** a major long-distance
transportation line. **2.** trunk (def. 5).

truss (trus), *n.* **1.** a pad held in place
by a belt, used for supporting a
hernia. **2.** a rigid frame for supporting a bridge, roof, etc. —*v.t.* **3.** to
bind or secure tightly. **4.** to tie (a
fowl) with the limbs held tightly to
the side, as before cooking. **5.** to
furnish or support with a truss. —
truss′er, *n.*

trust (trust), *n.* **1.** unquestioning belief in the integrity, strength, or ability of a person or thing. **2.** confident
expectation. **3.** a person or thing
that can be relied upon. **4.** the responsibility of a person in whom
confidence or authority is placed. **5.**
charge or custody. **6.** something
committed or entrusted to one's
care. **7.** *Law.* **a.** the care and management of property or funds by a

person or a bank for the benefit of another. **b.** the property or funds so held. **8.** an illegal combination of business firms for the purpose of controlling prices or eliminating competition **9.** financial or commercial credit. —*adj.* **10.** *Law.* of or pertaining to a trust. —*v.i.* **11.** to have confidence. —*v.t.* **12.** to have trust or confidence in. **13.** to expect confidently. **14.** to commit or entrust. **15.** to permit to do something without fear of consequences. **16.** to give business credit to. —**trust′er,** *n.* — **Syn.** 1. confidence, faith, reliance.

trus·tee (tru stē′), *n.* one of a body of persons appointed to administer the affairs of an organization, as a college. **2.** a person who holds the title to property for the benefit of another. —**trus·tee′ship,** *n.*

trust·ful (trust′fəl), *adj.* full of trust or confidence. —**trust′ful·ly,** *adv.* — **trust′ful·ness,** *n.*

trust′ fund′, money or securities held in trust.

trust′ ter′ri·tory, a territory under the administrative control of a country designated by the United Nations.

trust·wor·thy (trust′wûr′t͟hē), *adj.* deserving of trust or confidence. — **trust′wor′thi·ness,** *n.*

trust·y (trus′tē), *adj.*, **trust·i·er, trust·i·est,** *n.*, *pl.* **trust·ies.** —*adj.* **1.** that may be trusted or relied on. —*n.* **2.** a convict to whom special privileges are granted

truth (trōōth), *n.*, *pl.* **truths** (trōōt͟hz). **1.** the true or actual state of a matter. **2.** conformity with fact or reality. **3.** a verified or indisputable fact, proposition, or principle. **4.** the state or character of being true. **5. in truth,** truly or actually.

truth·ful (trōōth′fəl), *adj.* **1.** telling the truth, esp habitually. **2.** corresponding with reality. —**truth′ful·ly,** *adv.* —**truth′ful·ness,** *n.*

truth′ se′rum, a drug that induces in the subject a desire to talk, used in interrogation.

try (trī), *v.*, **tried, try·ing,** *n.*, *pl.* **tries.** —*v.t.* **1.** to make a deliberate effort to do. **2.** to test the effect or result of. **3.** to endeavor to evaluate by experiment. **4.** to examine and determine judicially. **5.** to subject to strain, as of patience. **6.** to melt down (fat) to obtain (the oil). —*v.i.* **7.** to make a deliberate effort. **8. try on,** to put on (an article of clothing) to judge the appearance or fit. **9. try out,** to use experimentally. **10. try out for,** to compete for (a place on a team or a role in a play). —*n.* **11.** a deliberate effort. —**Syn.** 1. attempt, essay. 7. endeavor, strive.

try·ing (trī′ing), *adj.* extremely hard to bear or endure. —**try′ing·ly,** *adv.*

try·out (trī′out′), *n.* a trial or test of fitness, strength, or skill.

tryst (trist, trīst), *n.* **1.** a clandestine meeting arranged by lovers. **2.** an appointment or place for such a meeting.

tsar (zär, tsär), *n.* czar. —**tsa·ri·na** (zä rē′nə, tsä-), *n.fem.*

tset′se fly′ (tset′sē, tsē′tsē), a blood-sucking African fly that can transmit sleeping sickness to human beings and animals.

T.Sgt., Technical Sergeant.

T-shirt (tē′s͟hûrt′), *n.* a knit pullover shirt with short sleeves.

tsp., **1.** teaspoon. **2.** teaspoonful.

T square, a T-shaped ruler used in mechanical drawing for making parallel lines.

tsu·na·mi (tsoo nä′mē), *n.* an unusually large sea wave produced by an undersea earthquake or volcanic eruption. [< Jap: harbor wave] — **tsu·na·mic** (tsoo nä′mik, -nam′ik), *adj.*

tub (tub), *n.* **1.** a broad, round, open container, used as for washing clothing. **2.** the amount a tub will hold. **3.** *Informal.* **a.** a bathtub. **b.** *Brit.* a bath in a bathtub.

tu·ba (too′bə, tyoo′-), *n.* a brass wind instrument with valves, having a low range.

tub·by (tub′ē), *adj.*, **-bi·er, -bi·est.** short and fat. —**tub′bi·ness,** *n.*

tube (toob, tyoob), *n.* **1.** a long, hollow pipe, as of glass or rubber, used for conveying liquids. **2.** a small, collapsible cylindrical container from which a paste or liquid may be squeezed. **3.** a tubelike organ or part, as in the human body. **4.** a flexible rubber casing inflated within a pneumatic tire. **5.** See **electron tube. 6.** See **vacuum tube. 7. the tube,** *Informal.* television. **8.** *Brit.* subway. **9. down the tube,** *Informal.* being completely wasted or ruined. —**tube′less,** *adj.*

tu·ber (too′bər, tyoo′-), *n.* a fleshy oblong or rounded outgrowth of an underground stem, as the potato. — **tu′ber·ous,** *adj.*

tu·ber·cle (too′bər kəl, tyoo′-), *n.* **1.** a small, rounded projection, as on a bone or plant. **2.** a small, firm, rounded swelling caused by tuberculosis.

tu′bercle bacil′lus, the bacterium causing tuberculosis.

tu·ber·cu·lar (too bûr′kyə lər, tyoo-), *adj.* **1.** Also, **tu·ber′cu·late** (-lit). of, like, or covered with tubercles. **2.** of or suffering from tuberculosis.

tu·ber·cu·lin (too bûr′kyə lin, tyoo-), *n.* a sterile liquid obtained from the tubercle bacillus, used in the diagnosis and treatment of tuberculosis.

tu·ber·cu·lo·sis (tŏŏ bûr′kyə lō′sis, tyŏŏ-), *n.* **1.** an infectious disease that may affect almost any tissue of the body, esp. the lungs, characterized by tubercles. **2.** this disease when affecting the lungs. —**tu·ber′·cu·lous,** *adj.*

tube·rose (tŏŏb′rōz′, tyŏŏb′-), *n.* a plant that grows from a bulb and has creamy-white, lilylike flowers.

tub·ing (tŏŏ′bing, tyŏŏ′-), *n.* **1.** material in the form of a tube. **2.** a system of tubes. **3.** a piece of tube.

tu·bu·lar (tŏŏ′byə lər, tyŏŏ′-), *adj.* **1.** of or shaped like a tube. **2.** made with tubes. —**tu′bu·lar·ly,** *adv.*

tu·bule (tŏŏ′byŏŏl, tyŏŏ′-), *n.* a small tube.

tuck (tuk), *v.t.* **1.** to thrust in at the edges of (a garment, covering, etc.) to secure in place. **2.** to cram or hide in a close place. **3.** to cover or wrap snugly. **4.** to pull up or gather into folds. **5.** to sew tucks in. —*n.* **6.** a fold sewn into cloth to decorate, shorten, or make a tighter fit.

tuck·er (tuk′ər), *v.t. Informal.* to weary utterly.

Tuc·son (tŏŏ′son, tŏŏ son′), *n.* a city in S Arizona.

-tude, a suffix equivalent to -ness: *platitude.*

Tues., Tuesday. Also, **Tue.**

Tues·day (tŏŏz′dē, -dā, tyŏŏz′-), *n.* the third day of the week, following Monday.

tu·fa (tŏŏ′fə, tyŏŏ′-), *n.* a porous limestone formed from calcium carbonate deposited by springs. —**tu·fa′ceous** (-fā′shəs), *adj.*

tuft (tuft), *n.* **1.** a small bunch of hairs, feathers, or grass growing or fastened closely together. **2.** a cluster of cut threads used as a decorative finish. —*v.t.* **3.** to furnish or decorate with tufts. **4.** to arrange into tufts. —**tuft′ed,** *adj.*

tug (tug), *v.,* **tugged, tug·ging,** *n.* —*v.t., v.i.* **1.** to pull or pull at with strong or persistent effort. **2.** to move by pulling forcibly. **3.** to tow (a ship) with a tugboat. —*n.* **4.** the act of tugging. **5.** tugboat. —**tug′ger,** *n.*

tug·boat (tug′bōt′), *n.* a small, powerful boat for towing or pushing.

tug′ of war′, **1.** an athletic contest between two teams pulling on opposite ends of a rope. **2.** any hard struggle for supremacy.

tu·i·tion (tŏŏ ish′ən, tyŏŏ-), *n.* **1.** the fee for instruction, as at a college. **2.** *Brit.* teaching or instruction.

tu·la·re·mi·a (tŏŏ′lə rē′mē ə), *n.* a disease of rabbits, etc., transmitted to human beings by insects.

tu·lip (tŏŏ′lip, tyŏŏ′-), *n.* **1.** a plant related to the lily, having large, cup-

shaped flowers of various colors. **2.** a flower or bulb of such a plant.

tu′lip tree′, a North American tree having tuliplike flowers and yielding a wood used in making furniture.

tulle (tŏŏl), *n.* a thin, fine net of nylon, rayon, or silk, for millinery, etc.

Tul·sa (tul′sə), *n.* a city in NE Oklahoma.

tum·ble (tum′bəl), *v.,* **-bled, -bling,** *n.* —*v.i.* **1.** to fall or roll end over end. **2.** to fall rapidly. **3.** to perform acrobatic leaps or somersaults. **4.** to stumble or fall. **5.** to move in a hasty, confused way. **6.** *Informal.* to become aware of some fact: *They've tumbled to the secret.* —*v.t.* **7.** to cause to tumble. —*n.* **8.** an act of tumbling. **9.** disorder or confusion.

tum·ble·down (tum′bəl doun′), *adj.* dilapidated as if about to collapse.

tum·bler (tum′blər), *n.* **1.** a performer of acrobatic leaps or somersaults. **2.** a drinking glass without a stem or handle. **3.** a part of a lock that, when lifted by a key, allows the bolt to move.

tum·ble·weed (tum′bəl wēd′), *n.* a plant that becomes detached from its roots in autumn and is driven about by the wind.

tum·brel (tum′brəl), *n.* **1.** a farmer's cart that can be tilted to discharge its load. **2.** a cart used to carry prisoners to the guillotine during the French Revolution. Also, **tum′bril.**

tu·mid (tŏŏ′mid, tyŏŏ′-), *adj.* **1.** affected with swelling. **2.** pompous or bombastic. —**tu·mid′i·ty,** *n.*

tum·my (tum′ē), *n., pl.* **-mies.** *Baby Talk.* stomach or abdomen.

tu·mor (tŏŏ′mər, tyŏŏ′-), *n.* an abnormal or diseased swelling or growth in any part of the body. Also, *Brit.,* **tu′mour.** —**tu′mor·ous,** *adj.*

tu·mult (tŏŏ′məlt, tyŏŏ′-), *n.* **1.** noisy commotion of a crowd. **2.** turbulent mental or emotional disturbance. —**Syn. 1.** clamor, disorder, uproar.

tu·mul·tu·ous (tŏŏ mul′chŏŏ əs, tyŏŏ-), *adj.* **1.** full of tumult. **2.** highly disturbed or agitated.

tun (tun), *n.* a large cask.

tu·na (tŏŏ′nə), *n., pl.* **-na, -nas. 1.** any of several large food and game fishes found in warm seas. **2.** Also called **tu′na fish′.** the flesh of the tuna, used as food.

tun·dra (tun′drə, tŏŏn′-), *n.* a vast, treeless plain of the northern arctic regions.

tune (tŏŏn, tyŏŏn), *n., v.,* **tuned, tuning.** —*n.* **1.** a melody, esp. of short, recognizable nature. **2.** the state of being in the proper pitch. **3.** agreement or harmony. **4.** opinion or mind: *He changed his tune.* **5.** to the tune of, *Informal.* in or about the amount of. —*v.t.* **6.** to adjust (a musical instrument) to the correct pitch. **7.** to bring into harmony. **8.** to adjust (a motor, mechanism, etc.) for proper functioning. **9. tune in,** to adjust a radio or television to receive (a station). —tun·a·bil·i·ty (tōō′nə bil′i tē, tyōō′-), *n.* —tun′a·ble, tune′a·ble, *adj.* —tun′a·bly, *adv.*

tune·ful (tōōn′fəl, tyōōn′-), *adj.* full of musical quality. —tune′ful·ly, *adv.* —tune′ful·ness, *n.* —Syn. harmonious, melodious.

tune·less (tōōn′lis, tyōōn′-), *adj.* without musical quality. —tune′less·ly, *adv.*

tun·er (tōō′nər, tyōō′-), *n.* **1.** a person or thing that tunes. **2.** the portion of a radio receiver that selects a desired signal for amplification.

tune-up (tōōn′up′, tyōōn′-), *n.* an adjustment, as of a motor, to improve working condition.

tung·sten (tung′stən), *n.* *Chem.* a rare, metallic element having a high melting point, used in alloys, electric-lamp filaments, etc. *Symbol:* W; *at. wt.:* 183.85; *at. no.:* 74. —tung·sten·ic (tung sten′ik), *adj.*

tu·nic (tōō′nik, tyōō′-), *n.* **1.** a gownlike outer garment, sometimes belted, worn by men and women in ancient Greece and Rome. **2.** a woman's blouselike garment, usually hip-length. **3.** a military jacket, usually reaching to the hips.

tun′ing fork′, a two-pronged steel instrument producing a tone of constant pitch when struck, and serving as a standard for tuning musical instruments.

Tu·nis (tōō′nis, tyōō′-), *n.* the capital of Tunisia.

Tu·ni·sia (tōō nē′zhə, -shə), *n.* a country in N Africa. —Tu·ni′sian, *adj., n.*

tun·nel (tun′ºl), *n., v.,* -neled, -nel·ing, -nelled, -nel·ling. —*n.* **1.** a passageway, as for trains, etc., through or under a mountain, river, or other obstruction. **2.** a horizontal corridor in a mine. —*v.t., v.i.* **3.** to construct a tunnel (through or under). —tun′nel·er, tun′nel·ler, *n.*

tun′nel vi′sion, an exceedingly narrow viewpoint, as of an issue or problem.

tun·ny (tun′ē), *n., pl.* -ny, -nies. *Chiefly Brit.* tuna.

tuque (tōōk, tyōōk), *n.* a heavy stocking cap worn in Canada.

tur·ban (tûr′bən), *n.* **1.** a man's headdress worn chiefly by Muslims, consisting of a long cloth wound around the head. **2.** any headdress resembling this.

tur·bid (tûr′bid), *adj.* **1.** unclear or murky because of stirred-up sediment. **2.** thick or dense, as clouds.

3. confused or muddled. —tur·bid′i·ty, tur′bid·ness, *n.* —tur′bid·ly, *adv.*

tur·bine (tûr′bin, -bīn), *n.* any of various machines having a rotor with vanes or blades, driven by the pressure of moving steam, water, hot gases, or air.

tur·bo·fan (tûr′bō fan′), *n.* fanjet (def. 1).

tur·bo·jet (tûr′bō jet′), *n.* **1.** Also called tur′bojet en′gine. a jet-propulsion engine in which air from the atmosphere is compressed for combustion by a turbine-drive compressor. **2.** an airplane equipped with such engines.

tur·bo·prop (tûr′bō prop′), *n.* **1.** Also called tur′bo-propel′ler en′gine. a turbojet engine with a turbine-driven propeller. **2.** an airplane equipped with such engines.

tur·bot (tûr′bət), *n., pl.* -bot, -bots. an edible, European flatfish having a diamond-shaped body.

tur·bu·lent (tûr′byə lənt), *adj.* **1.** violently disturbed or agitated. **2.** causing disturbance or disorder. —tur′bu·lence, *n.* —tur′bu·lent·ly, *adv.*

tu·reen (tōō rēn′, tyōō-), *n.* a large, deep dish with a lid, for serving soup, stew, etc.

turf (tûrf), *n.* **1.** a layer of matted earth formed by grass and plant roots. **2.** a piece cut from this. **3.** a block of peat dug for fuel. **4.** the turf, a. a track for horse racing. b. horse racing. —*v.t.* **5.** to cover with turf. —turf′y, *adj.*

tur·gid (tûr′jid), *adj.* **1.** unduly distended or swollen. **2.** inflated or overblown, as writing. —tur·gid′i·ty, *n.* —tur′gid·ly, *adv.*

Tu·rin (tōōr′in, tyōōr′-), *n.* a city in NW Italy.

Turk (tûrk), *n.* a native or inhabitant of Turkey.

Turk., **1.** Turkey. **2.** Turkish.

tur·key (tûr′kē), *n., pl.* -keys, -key. **1.** a large bird of America that typically has green and reddish-brown feathers and that is domesticated in most parts of the world. **2.** its flesh, used as food. **3. talk turkey,** *Informal.* to talk frankly or seriously.

Tur·key (tûr′kē), *n.* a country in W Asia and SE Europe.

tur′key buz′zard, a blackish-brown vulture of tropical and temperate America.

Tur·kic (tûr′kik), *n.* **1.** a subfamily of related languages including Turkish. —*adj.* **2.** of or pertaining to Turkic or Turkic-speaking peoples.

Turk·ish (tûr′kish), *adj.* **1.** of or pertaining to Turkey or the Turks. **2.** of or pertaining to the language of Turkey. —*n.* **3.** the language of Turkey.

tur·mer·ic (tûr′mər ik), *n.* **1.** the aromatic rhizome of an East Indian plant. **2.** a powder prepared from it, used as a condiment or as a yellow dye. **3.** its plant.

tur·moil (tûr′moil), *n.* a condition of great confusion or disturbance. — **Syn.** agitation, ferment, tumult.

turn (tûrn), *v.t.* **1.** to cause to move around on an axis or about a center. **2.** to cause to move partly around. **3.** to reverse the position or placement of. **4.** to change or alter the course of. **5.** to cause to retreat, as an attack. **6.** to change or convert: *to turn water into ice.* **7.** to make by some change. **8.** to cause to become sour or spoiled. **9.** to make nauseated. **10.** to translate or render. **11.** to put to some use or purpose. **12.** to go or pass around or beyond: *to turn a street corner.* **13.** to get beyond or pass: *Her son just turned four.* **14.** to direct or aim. **15.** to send or drive: *He turned the dogs loose.* **16.** to cause to be antagonistic toward. **17.** to wrench, as one's ankle. **18.** to earn or gain: *He turned a huge profit on the sale.* **19.** to shape by grinding, as on a lathe. — *v.i.* **20.** to move around on an axis or about a center. **21.** to move partly around in this manner. **22.** to direct one's interest or effort: *She turned to yoga.* **23.** to change or reverse a course: *to turn to the right.* **24.** to become nauseated. **25.** to become dizzy or giddy. **26.** to attack suddenly: *The dog turned on his master.* **27.** to change or alter, as in appearance. **28.** to become sour or spoiled. **29.** to change color. **30.** to become: *to turn pale.* **31.** to hinge or depend. **32. turn down, a.** to lessen the intensity of. **b.** to refuse or reject. **33. turn in, a.** to hand in. **b.** to inform on. **c.** *Informal.* to go to bed. **34. turn off, a.** to stop the flow of (water, gas, etc.). **b.** to extinguish (a light). **c.** to drive a vehicle onto another road. **d.** *Slang.* to bore or discourage. **35. turn on, a.** to cause (water, gas, etc.) to flow. **b.** to switch on (a light). **c.** *Slang.* to attain euphoria by taking a narcotic drug. **d.** *Slang.* to excite or stimulate. **36. turn out, a.** to extinguish (a light). **b.** to produce as the result of labor. **c.** to result or end. **d.** to appear or be present. **e.** to become ultimately present. **37. turn over, a.** to turn upside down. **b.** to turn from one side to the reverse. **c.** to transfer or hand over. **38. turn to, a.** to appeal to for help. **b.** to begin working in earnest. **39. turn up, a.** to uncover or find. **b.** to intensify or increase. **c.** to appear or arrive. **d.** to be recovered. —*n.* **40.** the act or an instance of turning. **41.** the act of changing course or direction. **42.** the place at which such a change occurs. **43.** one's time or chance to do something. **44.** any change, as in nature or circumstances: *a turn for the better.* **45.** a single revolution, as of a wheel. **46.** a single twist or coil of one thing around another. **47.** a distinctive form or style, as of language. **48.** a short walk or ride. **49.** natural inclination: *the turn of her mind.* **50.** a period of work. **51.** an act of service or disservice: *to do a good turn.* **52.** *Informal.* a shock of surprise or distress. **53. at every turn,** in every instance. **54. in turn,** in proper order. **55. out of turn,** out of proper order. **56. take turns,** to follow one another in order. **57. to a turn,** to perfection. —**turn′er,** *n.*

turn·a·bout (tûrn′ə bout′), *n.* a change of opinion, loyalty, etc.

turn·a·round (tûrn′ə round′), *n.* **1.** a place or area having sufficient room for turning a vehicle around. **2.** a reversal, as in business sales, esp. from loss to profit. **3.** turnabout.

turn·buck·le (tûrn′buk′əl), *n.* a rotating link having one or two internal screw threads, used to unite two threaded parts.

turn·coat (tûrn′kōt′), *n.* a person who disloyally changes to the opposite party or faction.

turn·ing (tûr′ning), *n.* **1.** the act of a person or thing that turns. **2.** a place at which something changes direction.

turn′ing point′, a point at which a decisive change takes place.

tur·nip (tûr′nip), *n.* **1.** the thick, fleshy, edible root of a plant related to the cabbage. **2.** its plant.

turn·key (tûrn′kē′), *n., pl.* -**keys.** a person who has charge of the keys of a prison.

turn·off (tûrn′ôf′, -of′), *n.* a small road that branches off from a larger one.

turn·out (tûrn′out′), *n.* **1.** a gathering of persons, as for a meeting or show. **2.** an output of work. **3.** the act of turning out. **4.** the manner in which a person or thing is dressed or equipped. **5.** a short side passage that enables automobiles to pass one another.

turn·o·ver (tûrn′ō′vər), *n.* **1.** the act of turning over. **2.** the number of workers or employees replaced in a specified period. **3.** the rate of such replacement. **4.** the total amount of business done in a given time. **5.** the rate at which items are sold and restocked. **6.** a change from one position or opinion to another. **7.** a baked pastry with a filling in which half the dough is turned over the filling. —*adj.* **8.** that is or may be turned over.

turn·pike (tûrn′pīk′), *n.* a high-speed highway maintained by tolls.

turn·stile (tûrn′stīl′), *n.* a structure of revolving arms set in an entrance or exit to permit people to go through one at a time.

turn·ta·ble (tûrn′tā′bəl), *n.* a rotating disk on which a phonograph record rests.

tur·pen·tine (tûr′pən tīn′), *n.* a colorless, strong-smelling liquid distilled from cone-bearing trees, used chiefly to thin paints.

tur·pi·tude (tûr′pi tōōd′, -tyōōd′), *n.* shameful wickedness or depravity.

tur·quoise (tûr′koiz, -kwoiz), *n.* **1.** Also, **tur′quois.** a sky-blue or greenish-blue mineral, often used as a gem. **2.** a greenish blue or bluish green.

tur·ret (tûr′it, tur′-), *n.* **1.** a small tower forming part of a larger structure, as of a castle. **2.** a pivoted attachment on a lathe for holding a number of tools. **3.** a low, heavily armored structure, usually revolving horizontally, in which guns are mounted, as on a warship, tank, or aircraft. —**tur′ret·ed,** *adj.*

tur·tle[1] (tur′t°l), *n., pl.* **-tles, -tle. 1.** any of various water and land reptiles having toothless jaws and soft body enclosed in a bony shell. **2. turn turtle,** to overturn or capsize.

tur·tle[2] (tûr′t°l), *n. Archaic.* a turtledove.

tur·tle·dove (tûr′t°l duv′), *n.* a small, wild European dove noted for its sad, cooing call.

tur·tle·neck (tûr′t°l nek′), *n.* **1.** a high, closefitting collar, appearing esp. on pullover sweaters. **2.** a sweater with such a collar.

Tus·ca·ro·ra (tus′kə rôr′ə), *n., pl.* **-ras, -ra.** a member of an Indian people living originally in North Carolina and later in New York.

tusk (tusk), *n.* a tooth developed to great length, as in the elephant, walrus, etc. —**tusked** (tuskt), *adj.*

tusk·er (tus′kər), *n.* an animal with tusks, as an elephant or a wild boar.

tus·sle (tus′əl), *v.,* **-sled, -sling,** *n.* — *v.i.* **1.** to struggle or fight roughly. —*n.* **2.** any vigorous struggle, conflict, etc. —**Syn.** scuffle.

tus·sock (tus′ək), *n.* a tuft or clump of growing grass. —**tus′sock·y,** *adj.*

Tut·ankh·a·men (tōōt′äŋk ä′mən), *n.* 14th century B.C., a king of Egypt of the 18th dynasty.

tu·te·lage (tōōt′°lij, tyōōt′-), *n.* **1.** the act of serving as teacher or guardian. **2.** guidance or protection. **3.** the state of being under a guardian or a tutor. —**tu′te·lar′y** (-ler′ē), **tu′te·lar** (-lər), *adj.*

tu·tor (tōō′tər, tyōō′-), *n.* **1.** a person employed to instruct another, esp. privately. —*v.t., v.i.* **2.** to act as a tutor (to). —**tu·to′ri·al** (-tôr′ē əl, -tōr′-), *adj.*

tut·ti-frut·ti (tōō′tē frōō′tē), *n.* a variety of fruits candied and minced, used in ice cream, confections, etc.

tu·tu (tōō′tōō), *n.* a short, full skirt, worn by ballerinas.

tux (tuks), *n. Informal.* a tuxedo.

tux·e·do (tuk sē′dō), *n., pl.* **-dos.** See **dinner jacket.**

TV, television.

TVA, Tennessee Valley Authority.

TV dinner, a precooked meal packaged in an aluminum tray, quickfrozen, and requiring only heating in oven before serving.

TVP, *Trademark.* See **textured vegetable protein.**

twad·dle (twod′°l), *n., v.,* **-dled, -dling.** —*n.* **1.** silly, idle, or boring talk or writing. —*v.i.* **2.** to talk or write twaddle. —**twad′dler,** *n.*

twain (twān), *n. Archaic.* two.

Twain (twān), *n.* **Mark** (pen name of *Samuel Langhorne Clemens*), 1835–1910, U.S. author and humorist.

twang (twaŋg), *n.* **1.** a sharp, ringing sound made by plucking a string of a musical instrument. **2.** a sharp, nasal tone of voice. —*v.t., v.i.* **3.** to sound or cause to sound with a twang. **4.** to speak or utter with a nasal twang. —**twang′y,** *adj.*

'twas (twuz, twoz; *unstressed* twəz), *Archaic or Literary.* contraction of *it was.*

tweak (twēk), *v.t.* **1.** to pinch and pull with a jerk and twist. —*n.* **2.** an act of tweaking.

tweed (twēd), *n.* **1.** a coarse wool fabric woven in two or more colors. **2. tweeds,** clothing made of this fabric.

tweed·y (twē′dē), *adj.,* **tweed·i·er, tweed·i·est. 1.** made of or resembling tweed. **2.** wearing tweeds, esp. as a mark of a casual or outdoor life.

'tween (twēn), *prep. Literary, Naut.* between.

tweet (twēt), *n.* **1.** a feeble chirping sound, as of a small bird. —*v.i.* **2.** to make such a sound.

tweet·er (twē′tər), *n.* a small loudspeaker that reproduces high-frequency sounds.

tweeze (twēz), *v.t.,* **tweezed, tweezing.** to pluck, as with tweezers.

tweez·ers (twē′zərz), *n.pl.* small pincers for plucking out hairs or picking up small objects.

twelfth (twelfth), *adj.* **1.** being number twelve in a series. —*n.* **2.** one of twelve equal parts. **3.** the twelfth member of a series.

twelve (twelv), *n.* **1.** a cardinal number, 10 plus 2. **2.** a symbol for this number, as 12 or XII. —*adj.* **3.** amounting to 12 in number.

twelve-month (twelv'munth'), *n. Chiefly Brit.* a year.

twen-ty (twen'tē), *n., pl.* **-ties,** *adj.* —*n.* **1.** a cardinal number, 10 times 2. **2.** a symbol for this number, as 20 or XX. —*adj.* **3.** amounting to 20 in number. —**twen'ti-eth** (-ith), *adj., n.*

twen-ty-one (twen'tē wun'), *n.* a card game in which the object is to draw cards adding up to 21.

twen-ty-twen-ty (twen'tē twen'tē), *adj.* having normal visual acuity.

twerp (twûrp), *n. Slang.* an insignificant or despicable fellow.

twice (twīs), *adv.* **1.** two times. **2.** in twofold quantity or degree.

twid-dle (twid'°l), *v.t., v.i.,* **1.** to turn about or play with (something) lightly or idly, esp. with the fingers. **2. twiddle one's thumbs,** to be idle. —**twid'dler,** *n.*

twig (twig), *n.* a slender branch of a tree. —**twig'gy,** *adj.*

twi-light (twī'līt'), *n.* **1.** the dim, scattered light from the sky just after sunset. **2.** the period during which this light prevails. **3.** a period of decline.

twill (twil), *n.* a fabric with a pattern of diagonal, raised lines. —**twilled,** *adj.*

twin (twin), *n., adj., v., twinned, twin-ning.* —*n.* **1.** either of two children or offspring born at the same birth. **2.** either of two persons or things closely related to or resembling each other. **3. the Twins,** Gemini. —*adj.* **4.** being a twin or twins. **5.** being two persons or things closely related to or resembling each other. **6.** being one of a pair: *a twin peak.* —*v.i.* **7.** to give birth to twins.

twine (twīn), *n., v., twined, twin-ing.* —*n.* **1.** a strong thread or string made up of two or more strands twisted together. —*v.t., v.i.* **2.** to twist together. **3.** to coil or wind around (something). —**twin'er,** *n.*

twinge (twinj), *n., v., twinged, twinging.* —*n.* **1.** a sudden, sharp pain or pang. —*v.t., v.i.* **2.** to feel or cause to feel a twinge.

twi-night (twī'nīt'), *adj. Baseball.* noting a doubleheader in which the first game begins in late afternoon and the second in the evening under lights. [*twi(light)* + *night*] —**twi'-night'er,** *n.*

twin-kle (twing'kəl), *v.,* **-kled, -kling,** *n.* —*v.i.* **1.** to shine with a flickering or flashing light. **2.** (of the eyes) to be bright with amusement. **3.** to move flutteringly. —*n.* **4.** a flickering or flashing light. **5.** a sparkling brightness in the eyes. **6.** twinkling. —**twin'kler,** *n.*

twin-kling (twing'kling), *n.* a very short time.

twirl (twûrl), *v.t., v.i.* **1.** to rotate or revolve rapidly. **2.** *Baseball Slang.* to pitch. —*n.* **3.** the act of twirling. **4.** a spiral or coil. —**twirl'er,** *n.*

twist (twist), *v.t.* **1.** to combine (strands or threads) by winding together. **2.** to turn by rotating or revolving. **3.** to wind or coil about something. **4.** to shape into a spiral form. **5.** to wrench or sprain. **6.** to break off by turning forcibly. **7.** to contort, as one's face. **8.** to distort the meaning of. —*v.i.* **9.** to be or become twisted. **10.** to take a spiral form or course. **11.** to rotate or revolve. **12.** to writhe or squirm. —*n.* **13.** a curve or bend. **14.** a rotary motion or spin. **15.** anything formed by or as by twisting. **16.** the act or process of twining things together. **17.** a distortion, as of meaning. **18.** a sudden, unexpected change, as of events. **19.** a novel treatment, method, etc. —**twist'a-ble,** *adj.*

twist' drill', *Mach.* a cylindrical drill bit with one or more deep helical grooves.

twist-er (twis'tər), *n.* **1.** a person or thing that twists. **2.** a ball pitched or moving with a spin. **3.** a whirlwind or tornado.

twit (twit), *v.,* **twit-ted, twit-ting,** *n.* —*v.t.* **1.** to taunt or tease with references to anything embarrassing. —*n.* **2.** the act of twitting.

twitch (twich), *v.t., v.i.* **1.** to pull (at) or move with a sudden, jerking motion. —*n.* **2.** a quick, jerky movement of the body. **3.** a short, sudden pull or tug. —**twitch'ing-ly,** *adv.*

twit-ter (twit'ər), *v.i.* **1.** to make small, tremulous, chirping sounds. **2.** to chatter or jabber. **3.** to titter or giggle. **4.** to tremble with excitement. —*n.* **5.** the act of twittering. **6.** a twittering sound. **7.** a state of tremulous excitement. —**twit'ter-y,** *adj.*

'twixt (twikst), *prep. Archaic.* betwixt.

two (tōō), *n.* **1.** a cardinal number, 1 plus 1. **2.** a symbol for this number, as 2 or II. **3. in two,** into two separate parts. —*adj.* **4.** amounting to two in number.

two-bit (tōō'bit'), *adj. Slang.* trivial or inferior of its kind.

two' bits', *Slang.* twenty-five cents.

two-faced (tōō'fāst'), *adj.* **1.** having two faces. **2.** deceitful or hypocritical. —**two'-fac'ed-ly** (-fā'sid lē), *adv.*

two-fer (tōō'fər), *n.* a card entitling the holder to purchase theater tickets at a reduced price.

two-fist-ed (tōō'fis'tid), *adj. Informal.* strong and vigorous.

two·fold (tōō'fōld'), *adj.* **1.** having two parts. **2.** twice as great or as much. —*adv.* **3.** in twofold measure.

2,4-D, a slightly water-soluble powder used as a weed killer.

2,4,5-T, a water-insoluble solid used chiefly for killing weeds.

two-ply (tōō'plī'), *adj.* consisting of two thicknesses, layers, or strands.

two·some (tōō'səm), *n.* **1.** two people together. **2.** a golf match between two persons.

two-step (tōō'step'), *n.* a ballroom dance marked by sliding steps.

two-time (tōō'tīm'), *v.t.,* -timed, -tim·ing. *Slang.* to be unfaithful to (a lover or spouse). —**two'-tim'er,** *n.*

two-way (tōō'wā'), *adj.* **1.** allowing movement or communication in opposite directions, or both to and from a place. **2.** involving two participants.

twp., township.

TWX, teletypewriter exchange.

TX, Texas.

-ty[1], a suffix meaning "multiples of ten": *twenty.*

-ty[2], a suffix meaning "quality or state": *unity.*

ty·coon (tī kōōn'), *n.* an important person, as in business, having great wealth and power. [< Jap *taikun* great prince]

ty·ing (tī'ing), *v.* ppr. of **tie.**

tyke (tīk), *n.* *Informal.* a small child.

Ty·ler (tī'lər), *n.* **John,** 1790–1862, 10th president of the U.S. 1841–45.

tym·pa·ni (tim'pə nē), *n.pl.* timpani. —**tym'pa·nist,** *n.*

tym·pan'ic mem'brane (tim pan'ik), a membrane separating the tympanum or middle ear from the passage of the external ear.

tym·pa·num (tim'pə nəm), *n.,* pl. -nums, -na (-nə). **1.** See **middle ear. 2.** See **tympanic membrane.**

typ., **1.** typographer. **2.** typographical.

type (tīp), *n., v.,* typed, typ·ing. —*n.* **1.** a number of things or persons sharing certain characteristics that cause them to be regarded as a group. **2.** a thing or person regarded as a member of a class or category. **3.** a thing or person that is typical of a class. **4.** a perfect model or example. **5. a.** a rectangular block of metal having on its upper surface a letter or character in relief, used in printing. **b.** such pieces or blocks collectively. **c.** a printed character or printed characters. —*v.t.* **6.** to typewrite. **7.** to typify or represent. **8.** to classify or identify. —*v.i.* **9.** to typewrite.

-type, a combining form meaning: **a.** type or model: *prototype.* **b.** photographic processes: *daguerreotype.*

type-cast (tīp'kast', -käst'), *v.t.,* -cast, -cast·ing. **1.** to cast (a performer) according to his or her physical type, manner, or personality. **2.** to cast (a performer) repeatedly in the same kind of role.

type·face (tīp'fās'), *n.* the general style or design of printing type.

type' found'er, a person engaged in the making of metal printing type. —**type' found'ing.** —**type' found'ry.**

type·script (tīp'skript'), *n.* a typewritten manuscript.

type·set·ter (tīp'set'ər), *n.* **1.** a person who composes type. **2.** a machine for composing type. —**type'-set',** *v.t., adj.* —**type'set'ting,** *n., adj.*

type·write (tīp'rīt'), *v.t., v.i.,* -wrote, -writ·ten, -writ·ing. to write with a typewriter.

type·writ·er (tīp'rī'tər), *n.* **1.** a machine for writing in letters and characters that resemble printers' type. **2.** *Obs.* a typist.

ty·phoid (tī'foid), *n.* an infectious, often fatal disease characterized by fever and intestinal inflammation. Also called **ty'phoid fe'ver.**

ty·phoon (tī fōōn'), *n.* a tropical hurricane of the western Pacific area and the China seas.

ty·phus (tī'fəs), *n.* an acute, infectious disease caused by a germ transmitted by lice and fleas, and characterized by a peculiar eruption of reddish spots on the body. Also called **ty'phus fe'ver.** —**ty'phous,** *adj.*

typ·i·cal (tip'i kəl), *adj.* **1.** having the characteristics or features of a particular type. **2.** showing distinctive, recognizable features. **3.** conforming to or serving as a type. —**typ'i·cal·ly,** *adv.* —**typ'i·cal·ness,** *n.*

typ·i·fy (tip'ə fī'), *v.t.,* -fied, -fy·ing. **1.** to serve as a typical example of. **2.** to represent by a type or symbol. —**typ'i·fi·ca'tion,** *n.* —**typ'i·fi'er,** *n.*

typ·ist (tī'pist), *n.* a person who types letters, etc., with a typewriter, esp. professionally.

ty·po (tī'pō), *n., pl.* -pos. *Informal.* See **typographical error..**

typo., **1.** typographer. **2.** typographical. **3.** typography. Also, **typog.**

ty·pog·ra·pher (tī pog'rə fər), *n.* a person engaged in typography.

typograph'ical er'ror, an error in typesetting or typing.

ty·pog·ra·phy (tī pog'rə fē), *n.* **1.** the art or process of printing with type. **2.** the work of setting and arranging types and of printing from them. **3.** the general appearance of printed matter. —**ty'po·graph'i·cal** (-pə-graf'i kəl), **ty'po·graph'ic,** *adj.* —**ty'-po·graph'i·cal·ly,** *adv.*

ty·ran·ni·cal (ti ran′i kəl, tī-), *adj.* **1.** of or characteristic of a tyrant. **2.** unjustly cruel or oppressive. Also, **ty·ran′nic.** —**ty·ran′ni·cal·ly,** *adv.* —**ty·ran′ni·cal·ness,** *n.* —**Syn. 2.** arbitrary, despotic, domineering.

tyr·an·nize (tir′ə nīz′), *v.,* **-nized, -niz·ing.** —*v.i.* **1.** to exercise power cruelly or oppressively. **2.** to govern as a tyrant. —*v.t.* **3.** to govern tyrannically. —**tyr′an·niz′er,** *n.*

ty·ran·no·saur (ti ran′ə sôr′, tī-), *n.* a dinosaur that walked upright on its hind feet. Also, **ty·ran′no·saur′us (-sôr′əs).**

tyr·an·nous (tir′ə nəs), *adj. Literary.* tyrannical. —**tyr′an·nous·ly,** *adv.*

tyr·an·ny (tir′ə nē), *n., pl.* **-nies. 1.** arbitrary or unrestrained exercise of power. **2.** the government or rule of a tyrant. **3.** cruel or oppressive government. **4.** a tyrannical act.

ty·rant (tī′rənt), *n.* **1.** a cruel or oppressive ruler. **2.** any despotic person. **3.** an absolute ruler.

tyre (tīər), *n. Brit.* tire².

ty·ro (tī′rō), *n., pl.* **-ros.** a beginner in learning anything. —**Syn.** novice.

tzar (zär, tsär), *n.* czar. —**tza·ri·na (zä rē′nə, tsä-),** *n.fem.*

U

U, u (yōō), *n., pl.* **U's or Us, u's or us. 1.** the 21st letter of the English alphabet, a vowel. **2.** something having the shape of a U.

U (yōō), *adj. Informal,* characteristic of the upper class of Great Britain.

U., **1.** union. **2.** unit. **3.** university. **4.** upper.

UAR, United Arab Republic.

UAW, United Automobile Workers.

u·biq·ui·tous (yōō bik′wi təs), *adj.* being everywhere, esp. at the same time. —**u·biq′ui·tous·ly,** *adv.* —**u·biq′ui·ty,** *n.* —**Syn.** omnipresent.

U-boat (yōō′bōt′), *n.* a German submarine. [< G *U-Boot,* short for *Unterseeboot,* undersea boat]

u.c., *Print.* See upper case.

ud·der (ud′ər), *n.* a baglike mammary gland with more than one teat, as in cows.

UFO (*sometimes* yōō′fō), unidentified flying object.

U·gan·da (yōō gan′də, ōō gän′dä), *n.* a country in E Africa. —**U·gan′dan,** *adj.,n.*

ugh (ōōн, ōō, ug), *interj.* (an exclamation of disgust, aversion, etc.)

ug·li (ug′lē), *n.* a tangelo grown in the West Indies.

ug·ly (ug′lē), *adj.,* **-li·er, -li·est. 1.** very unattractive to look at. **2.** disagreeable or unpleasant. **3.** threatening trouble or danger. **4.** hostile or quarrelsome. —**ug′li·ness,** *n.*

uh (uн, u), *interj.* **1.** (an exclamation of hesitation or pause.) **2.** huh.

u.h., upper half.

UHF, See ultrahigh frequency.

U.K., See United Kingdom.

u·kase (yōō′kas, yōō kāz′), *n.* **1.** an edict of the czar. **2.** any order by an absolute authority.

U·kraine (yōō krān′), *n.* the, a constituent republic of the Soviet Union, in S Europe. Official name, **Ukrain′ian So′viet So′cialist Repub′lic.**

U·krain·i·an (yōō krā′nē ən, -krī′-), *adj.* **1.** of the Ukraine, its people, or their language. —*n.* **2.** a native or inhabitant of the Ukraine. **3.** a Slavic language closely related to Russian.

u·ku·le·le (yōō′kə lā′lē), *n.* a small musical instrument resembling a guitar.

UL, Underwriters' Laboratories.

ul·cer (ul′sər), *n.* **1.** a sore on the surface of the body or in the stomach, intestines, etc., usually containing pus. **2.** any corrupting condition. —**ul′cer·ous,** *adj.*

ul·cer·ate (ul′sə rāt′), *v.i., v.t.,* **-at·ed, -at·ing.** to make or become ulcerous. —**ul′cer·a′tion,** *n.* —**ul·cer·a·tive (ul′sə rā′tiv),** *adj.*

ul·lage (ul′ij), *n.* the amount by which the contents fall short of filling a container.

ul·na (ul′nə), *n., pl.* **-nae (-nē), -nas.** the bone of the forearm on the side opposite to the thumb. —**ul′nar,** *adj.*

ul·ster (ul′stər), *n.* a long, loose, heavy overcoat.

ult., **1.** ultimate. **2.** ultimately. **3.** Also, **ulto.** ultimo.

ul·te·ri·or (ul tēr′ē ər), *adj.* **1.** being beyond what is seen or avowed: *ulterior motives.* **2.** lying on the farther side: *ulterior regions.* —**ul·te′ri·or·ly,** *adv.* —**Syn. 1.** hidden.

ul·ti·mate (ul′tə mit), *adj.* **1.** ending or last in a process or series: *the ultimate cost.* **2.** highest possible: *the ultimate good.* **3.** incapable of being further analyzed or divided: *ultimate* *principles.* **4.** maximum or decisive. —*n.* **5.** something ultimate, as a fundamental fact or principle. —**ul′ti·mate·ly,** *adv.* —**Syn. 1.** final. **2.** absolute, supreme. **3.** fundamental.

ul·ti·ma·tum (ul′tə mā′təm, -mä′-), *n., pl.* **-tums, -ta** (-tə). a final, uncompromising demand or proposal, as in a dispute.

ul·ti·mo (ul′tə mō), *adj. Obsolesc.* of last month.

ul·tra (ul′trə), *adj.* **1.** going beyond what is usual or ordinary. —*n.* **2.** an extremist, as in politics.

ultra-, a prefix meaning: **a.** beyond: *ultraviolet.* **b.** extremely: *ultramodern.*

ul·tra·con·ser·va·tive (ul′trə kən sûr′və tiv), *adj.* extremely conservative, esp. in politics.

ul·tra·fiche (ul′trə fēsh′), *n.* a microfiche of printed matter that is extremely reduced in size.

ul′tra·high fre′quency (ul′trə hī′, -hī′), *Radio.* any frequency between 300 and 3,000 megahertz.

ul·tra·ma·rine (ul′trə mə rēn′), *n.* **1.** a deep-blue pigment. **2.** a deep-blue color. —*adj.* **3.** beyond the sea.

ul·tra·mod·ern (ul′trə mod′ərn), *adj.* extremely modern, as in ideas.

ul·tra·son·ic (ul′trə son′ik), *adj.* noting a frequency above the range of human hearing. —**ul′tra·son′i·cal·ly,** *adv.*

ul·tra·son·ics (ul′trə son′iks), *n.* the branch of science that deals with ultrasonic phenomena.

ul·tra·sound (ul′trə sound′), *n.* ultrasonic waves, used as in industry to test metals for flaws.

Ul·tra·suede (ul′trə swād′), *n. Trademark.* a synthetic suedelike fabric.

ul·tra·vi·o·let (ul′trə vī′ə lit), *adj.* **1.** noting radiation of shorter wavelengths than visible violet light. **2.** utilizing or producing such radiation.

u·lu·late (yōōl′yə lāt′, ul′-), *v.i.,* **-lat·ed, -lat·ing.** to howl or lament loudly. —**ul′u·la′tion,** *n.*

U·lys·ses (yōō lis′ēz), *n.* Latin name for **Odysseus.**

um·bel (um′bəl), *n.* a flower cluster in which a number of flower stalks, nearly equal in length, spread from a common center. —**um′bel·late** (-bə lit), *adj.*

um·ber (um′bər), *n.* **1.** an earthy mineral used as a brown or reddish-brown pigment. **2.** a dark, reddish-brown color.

um·bil·i·cal (um bil′i kəl), *adj.* **1.** of an umbilicus or umbilical cord. **2.** located near the navel.

umbil′ical cord′, a cord connecting the fetus with the placenta of the mother and transmitting nourishment from the mother.

um·bil·i·cus (um bil′ə kəs, um′bə li′-kəs), *n., pl.* **-bil·i·ci** (-bil′i sī′, -bə li′-sī), **-bil·i·cus·es.** the depression in the center of the surface of the abdomen indicating the site of the umbilical cord.

um·bra (um′brə), *n., pl.* **-bras, -brae** (-brē). **1.** a completely shaded area. **2.** the central portion of the shadow of a celestial body where the light from the source of illumination is completely cut off. —**um′bral,** *adj.*

um·brage (um′brij), *n.* **1.** resentful displeasure or personal offense: *to take umbrage at some remark.* **2.** *Archaic.* **a.** shade. **b.** foliage.

um·brel·la (um brel′ə), *n.* **1.** a portable, circular cover consisting of a fabric held on a collapsible frame, used for protection from rain. **2.** any safeguarding arrangement or policy. [< It *ombrella* < L *umbella*]

u·mi·ak (ōō′mē ak′), *n.* an open Eskimo boat covered with skins.

um·laut (ōōm′lout), *n.* **1.** assimilation in which a vowel is influenced by a following vowel or semivowel. **2.** a diacritic (¨) placed over a vowel, esp. as so used in German.

ump (ump), *n., v.t., v.i., Informal.* umpire.

um·pire (um′pīᵊr), *n., v.,* **-pired, -pir·ing.** —*n.* **1.** a person selected to rule on the plays in a sport. **2.** a person selected to settle a dispute. —*v.t., v.i.* **3.** to act as umpire (in or of).

ump·teen (ump′tēn′), *adj. Informal.* of an indefinitely large number. —**ump′teenth′,** *adj.*

UMT, universal military training.

UMW, United Mine Workers.

UN, See **United Nations.**

un-, a prefix meaning: **a.** not: *unfair.* **b.** opposite of: *un-American.* **c.** reversal of an action: *unbend.* **d.** removal or depriving: *unclog.* **e.** completely: *unloose.*

un·a·ble (un ā′bəl), *adj.* lacking ability or power (to do something).

un·a·bridged (un′ə brijd′), *adj.* **1.** not abridged or shortened. **2.** belonging to the most comprehensive kind, as a dictionary.

---

un′a·bashed′, *adj.*
un′a·bash′ed·ly, *adv.*
un′a·bat′ed, *adj.*
un′ab·bre′vi·at′ed, *adj.*
un′ab·solved′, *adj.*
un′ab·sorbed′, *adj.*

un′ab·sorb′ent, *adj.*
un′ac·a·dem′ic, *adj.*
un′ac·cent′ed, *adj.*
un′ac·cen′tu·at′ed, *adj.*
un′ac·cep′ta·ble, *adj.*
un′ac·cept′ed, *adj.*

un′ac·ci·den′tal, *adj.*
un′ac·claimed′, *adj.*
un′ac·cli′mat·ed, *adj.*
un′ac·cli′ma·tized′, *adj.*
un′ac·com′mo·dat′ing, *adj.*

un·ac·com·pa·nied (un'ə kum'pə nēd), *adj.* **1.** not accompanied. **2.** *Music.* without an accompaniment.

un·ac·count·a·ble (un'ə koun'tə bəl), *adj.* **1.** that cannot be accounted for. **2.** not responsible. **—un'ac·count'a·bly,** *adv.*

un·ac·cus·tomed (un'ə kus'təmd), *adj.* **1.** not accustomed or habituated. **2.** unusual or unfamiliar.

un·ad·vised (un'ad vīzd'), *adj.* **1.** without advice or counsel. **2.** imprudent or rash. **—un'ad·vis'ed·ly** (-vī'zid-lē), *adv.*

un·af·fect·ed (un'ə fek'tid), *adj.* **1.** free from affectation. **2.** not affected or influenced. **—un'af·fect'ed·ly,** *adv.* **—Syn. 1.** artless, genuine, natural.

un·al·ien·a·ble (un āl'yə nə bəl), *adj.* *Archaic.* inalienable.

un·A·mer·i·can (un'ə mer'i kən), *adj.* not characteristic of or proper to the U.S., its standards, ideals, etc.

u·nan·i·mous (yōo nan'ə məs), *adj.* **1.** being in complete agreement. **2.** showing complete agreement **—u·na·nim·i·ty** (yōo'nə nim'i tē), *n.* **—u·nan'i·mous·ly,** *adv.*

un·armed (un ärmd'), *adj.* without weapons or armor.

un·as·sail·a·ble (un'ə sā'lə bəl), *adj.* **1.** not open to attack or assault. **2.** not subject to denial or dispute. **—un'as·sail'a·bly,** *adv.*

un·as·sum·ing (un'ə sōō'ming), *adj.* not pretentious or vain. **—un'as·sum'ing·ly,** *adv.* **—Syn.** modest.

un·at·tached (un'ə tacht'), *adj.* **1.** not attached. **2.** not engaged or married.

un·a·vail·ing (un'ə vā'ling), *adj.* being of no use or help. **—un'a·vail'ing·ly,** *adv.*

un·a·void·a·ble (un'ə voi'də bəl), *adj.* incapable of being avoided. **—un'a·void'a·bil'i·ty,** *n.* **—un'a·void'a·bly,** *adv.*

un·a·ware (un'ə wâr'), *adj.* **1.** not aware or conscious. **—adv. 2.** *Archaic.* unawares. **—un'a·ware'ness,** *n.*

un·a·wares (un'ə wârz'), *adv.* **1.** while not aware or knowing. **2.** by surprise or without warning.

un·bal·anced (un bal'ənst), *adj.* **1.** not properly balanced. **2.** mentally disordered. **3.** not brought to an equality of debits and credits.

un·bar (un bär'), *v.t.* to open by or as by removing the bar.

un'ac·com'plished, *adj.*
un'ac·count'ed, *adj.*
un'ac·count'ed-for, *adj.*
un'ac·cred'it·ed, *adj.*
un'ac·knowl'edged, *adj.*
un'ac·quaint'ed, *adj.*
un'ac'tion·a·ble, *adj.*
un'ac'tu·at'ed, *adj.*
un'a·dapt'ed, *adj.*
un'ad·dressed', *adj.*
un'ad·journed', *adj.*
un'ad·ju'di·cat·ed, *adj.*
un'ad·just'a·ble, *adj.*
un'ad·just'ed, *adj.*
un'a·dorned', *adj.*
un'a·dul'ter·at·ed, *adj.*
un'ad·van·ta'geous, *adj.*
un'ad·ven'tur·ous, *adj.*
un'ad·ver'tised', *adj.*
un'ad·vis'a·ble, *adj.*
un'aes·thet'ic, *adj.*
un'af·fil'i·at·ed, *adj.*
un'a·fraid', *adj.*
un'aged', *adj.*
un·ag'ing, *adj.*
un·aid'ed, *adj.*
un·aimed', *adj.*
un·aired', *adj.*
un'a·larm'ing, *adj.*
un'al'ien·at'ed, *adj.*
un'a·ligned', *adj.*
un'a·like', *adj.*
un'al·layed', *adj.*
un'al·le'vi·at·ed, *adj.*
un'al·lied', *adj.*
un'al·low'a·ble, *adj.*
un'al·loyed', *adj.*

un'al·pha·bet·ized', *adj.*
un'al'ter·a·ble, *adj.;*
　-bly, *adv.*
un'am·big'u·ous, *adj.;*
　-ly, *adv.*
un·am·bi'tious, *adj.*
un·am'or·tized', *adj.*
un·am'pli·fied', *adj.*
un'a·mused', *adj.*
un'a·mus'ing, *adj.*
un'a·ni'mat'ed, *adj.*
un'an·nounced', *adj.*
un'an·swer·a·ble, *adj.*
un'an·swered', *adj.*
un'an·tic'i·pat'ed, *adj.*
un'a·pol'o·get'ic, *adj.*
un'a·pol'o·get'i·cal·ly, *adv.*
un'ap·par'ent, *adj.*
un'ap·peal'ing, *adj.*
un'ap·peas·a·ble, *adj.*
un'ap·peased', *adj.*
un'ap·pe·tiz'ing, *adj.;*
　-ly, *adv.*
un'ap'pli·ca·ble, *adj.*
un'ap·plied', *adj.*
un'ap·point'ed, *adj.*
un'ap·por'tioned, *adj.*
un'ap·pre'ci·at'ed, *adj.*
un'ap·pre'ci·a'tive, *adj.*
un'ap·pre·hen'sive, *adj.*
un'ap·proach'a·ble, *adj.*
un'ap·pro·pri·at'ed, *adj.*
un'ap·proved', *adj.*
un'ap·prov'ing, *adj.*
un·ar'mored, *adj.*
un'ar·rest'ed, *adj.*

un·art'ful, *adj.;*
　-ly, *adv.;* -ness, *n.*
un·ar·tic'u·late, *adj.;*
　-ly, *adv.*
un'ar·tic'u·lat'ed, *adj.*
un·ar'tis'tic, *adj.*
un'as·cer·tain'a·ble, *adj.*
un'a·shamed', *adj.*
un·asked', *adj.*
un'as·pi'rat'ed, *adj.*
un'a·spir'ing, *adj.*
un'as·ser'tive, *adj.*
un'as·sessed', *adj.*
un'as·signed', *adj.*
un'as·sim'i·lat'ed, *adj.*
un'as·sist'ed, *adj.*
un'as·sort'ed, *adj.*
un'at·tain'a·ble, *adj.*
un'at·tempt'ed, *adj.*
un'at·tend'ed, *adj.*
un'at·test'ed, *adj.*
un'at·tract'ed, *adj.*
un'at·trac'tive, *adj.*
un'aus·pi'cious, *adj.*
un·au·then'tic, *adj.*
un·au·then'ti·cat'ed, *adj.*
un·au'thor·ized', *adj.*
un'a·vail'a·bil'i·ty, *n.*
un'a·vail'a·ble, *adj.*
un'a·venged', *adj.*
un'a·vowed', *adj.*
un'a·waked', *adj.*
un'a·wak'ened, *adj.*
un·awed', *adj.*
un·backed', *adj.*
un·baked', *adj.*
un·bap'tized', *adj.*

un·bear·a·ble (un bâr′ə bəl), *adj.* not
bearable or tolerable. **—un·bear′a·
bly,** *adv.*

un·beat·en (un bēt′ən), *adj.* 1. not defeated or never defeated. 2. not
trod or traversed. 3. not pounded or
whipped, as eggs.

un·be·com·ing (un′bi kum′ing), *adj.*
1. not becoming or fitting. 2. not attractive or decent. **—un′be·com′ing-
ly,** *adv.* **—Syn.** 1. improper.

un·be·known (un′bi nōn′), *adj.* without one's knowledge. Also, **un′be·
knownst′** (-nōnst′).

un·be·lief (un′bi lēf′), *n.* a habitual
lack of belief, esp. in religion. **—
un′be·liev′er,** *n.* **—un′be·liev′ing,**
adj.

un·be·liev·a·ble (un′bi lē′və bəl), *adj.*
impossible to believe. **—un′be·liev′-
a·bly,** *adv.*

un·bend (un bend′), *v.t.* 1. to straight-
en from a bent form or position. 2.
to relax by being informal or casual. 3. to release from tension, as a
bow. **—v.i.** 4. to become unbent.

un·bend·ing (un ben′ding), *adj.* 1. not
bending or curving. 2. not yielding
or compromising. 3. austere or formal. **—Syn.** 2. inflexible, rigid.

un·bi·ased (un bī′əst), *adj.* not biased
or one-sided. **—un·bi′ased·ly,** *adv.*

un·bid·den (un bid′ən), *adj.* 1. not
bidden or commanded. 2. not asked
or invited. Also, **un·bid′.**

un·bind (un bīnd′), *v.t.* 1. to release
from bonds or restraint. 2. to unfasten or loose.

un·blessed (un blest′), *adj.* 1. not
blessed. 2. wicked or sinful. Also,
un·blest′. **—un·bless′ed·ness** (un-
bles′id nis), *n.*

un·blush·ing (un blush′ing), *adj.* 1.
without remorse or shame. 2. not
blushing. **—un·blush′ing·ly,** *adv.*

un·bolt (un bōlt′), *v.t.* to open by or
as by removing the bolt.

un·born (un bôrn′), *adj.* not yet born.

un·bos·om (un bŏŏz′əm, -bōō′zəm),
v.t. 1. to disclose (a secret, etc.).
—v.i. 2. to disclose one's thoughts
or feelings.

un·bound·ed (un boun′did), *adj.* without limits or bounds. **—un·bound′-
ed·ly,** *adv.* **—Syn.** infinite, vast.

un·bowed (un boud′), *adj.* 1. not
bowed or bent. 2. not subjugated.

un·bri·dled (un brīd′əld), *adj.* 1. not
controlled or restrained. 2. not fitted with a bridle. **—un·bri′dled·ly,**
adv.

un·bro·ken (un brō′kən), *adj.* 1. not
broken or torn. 2. uninterrupted or
continuous. 3. not tamed, as a horse.

un·bur·den (un bûr′dən), *v.t.* 1. to
free from a burden. 2. to relieve
(one's mind, etc.) by revealing or
confessing something.

un·but·ton (un but′ən), *v.t.* to unfasten the buttons of.

un·called-for (un kûld′fôr′), *adj.* 1.
not required or wanted. 2. unwarranted or unjustified.

un·can·ny (un kan′ē), *adj.* 1. having
or seeming to have a supernatural
basis. 2. uncomfortably strange. **—
un·can′ni·ly,** *adv.* **—Syn.** 2. weird.

un·cap (un kap′), *v.t.* to remove a
cap or cover from.

un·ceas·ing (un sē′sing), *adj.* not or
never ceasing. **—un·ceas′ing·ly,** *adv.*

un·cer·e·mo·ni·ous (un′ser ə mō′nē-
əs), *adj.* 1. without ceremony or formalities. 2. abrupt or rude. **—un′-
cer·e·mo′ni·ous·ly,** *adv.* **—un′cer·e·
mo′ni·ous·ness,** *n.*

un·cer·tain (un sûr′tən), *adj.* 1. not
definitely ascertainable or fixed. 2.
not confident or assured. 3. not
precisely determined. 4. not dependable. 5. vague or indistinct. **—un·
cer′tain·ly,** *adv.* **—Syn.** 1. indefinite,
unsure. 2. doubtful.

un·cer·tain·ty (un sûr′tən tē), *n.,* pl.
-ties. 1. the state of being uncertain.
2. something uncertain.

un·char·i·ta·ble (un char′i tə bəl), *adj.*
not charitable or forgiving, as in
judging others. **—un·char′i·ta·ble·
ness,** *n.* **—un·char′i·ta·bly,** *adv.*

un·chart·ed (un chär′tid), *adj.* 1. not
shown or located on a map. 2. unexplored or unknown.

un·beat′a·ble, *adj.*	**un·bridge′a·ble,** *adj.*	**un·car′pet·ed,** *adj.*
un′be·fit′ting, *adj.*	**un·bridged′,** *adj.*	**un·cashed′,** *adj.*
un′be·hold′en, *adj.*	**un·broth′er·ly,** *adj.*	**un·caught′,** *adj.*
un′be·loved′, *adj.*	**un·bruised′,** *adj.*	**un·cel′e·brat′ed,** *adj.*
un·bleached′, *adj.*	**un·brushed′,** *adj.*	**un·cen′sored,** *adj.*
un·blem′ished, *adj.*	**un·buck′le,** *v.t.,*	**un·cen′sured,** *adj.*
un·blink′ing, *adj.*	-led, -ling.	**un·cer′ti·fied′,** *adj.*
un·block′, *v.t.*	**un·budg′et·ed,** *adj.*	**un·chain′,** *v.t.*
un·bod′ied, *adj.*	**un·budg′ing,** *adj.*	**un·chal′lenged,** *adj.*
un·bolt′ed, *adj.*	**un·bur′ied,** *adj.*	**un·change′a·ble,** *adj.*
un·bound′, *adj.*	**un·burned′,** *adj.*	**un·changed′,** *adj.*
un·brand′ed, *adj.*	**un·burnt′,** *adj.*	**un·chang′ing,** *adj.*
un·break′a·ble, *adj.*	**un·can′celed,** *adj.*	**un·chap′er·oned′,** *adj.*
un·bred′, *adj.*	**un·cared′-for′,** *adj.*	**un′char·ac·ter·is′tic,** *adj.*
un·brib′a·ble, *adj.*	**un·car′ing,** *adj.*	**un·charged′,** *adj.*

un·chaste (un chāst′), *adj.* not chaste or virtuous. —**un·chaste′ly,** *adv.* —**un·chaste′ness, un·chas′ti·ty** (-chas′-ti tē), *n.*

un·chris·tian (un kris′chən), *adj.* **1.** not Christian. **2.** not conforming to the Christian spirit.

un·ci·al (un′shē əl, -shəl), *adj.* **1.** of or written in a form of writing having rounded letters used chiefly in Greek and Latin manuscripts from 300 to 900 A.D. —*n.* **2.** uncial writing.

un·cir·cum·cised (un sûr′kəm sīzd′), *adj.* **1.** not circumcised. **2.** not Jewish. **3.** *Archaic.* heathen.

un·civ·il (un siv′əl), *adj.* **1.** without good manners. **2.** uncivilized. —**un·civ′il·ly,** *adv.*

un·civ·i·lized (un siv′ə līzd′), *adj.* not civilized or cultured.

un·clad (un klad′), *adj.* not clad or dressed.

un·clasp (un klasp′, -kläsp′), *v.t.* to open by or as by releasing the clasp.

un·cle (ung′kəl), *n.* **1.** a brother of one's father or mother. **2.** an aunt's husband. **3.** cry or say uncle, *Slang.* to concede defeat.

un·clean (un klēn′), *adj.* **1.** not physically clean. **2.** morally impure. **3.** ceremonially unfit. —**un·clean·ly** (un klēn′lē), *adv.* —**un·clean′ness,** *n.*

un·clean·ly (un klen′lē), *adj.* not cleanly. —**un·clean′li·ness,** *n.*

un·clench (un klench′), *v.t., v.i.* to open from a clenched state or position.

Un′cle Sam′, a personification of the government or people of the U.S.: represented as a tall man with white whiskers.

Un′cle Tom′, *Contemptuous.* a black who is abjectly servile to whites. [so called after the leading character in *Uncle Tom's Cabin* (1852), a novel by Harriet Beecher Stowe]

un·cloak (un klōk′), *v.t.* **1.** to remove the cloak from. **2.** to reveal or expose. —*v.i.* **3.** to take off the cloak.

un·clog (un klog′), *v.t.* to free of an obstruction.

un·close (un klōz′), *v.t., v.i.* to bring or come out of a closed state.

un·clothe (un klōth′), *v.t.* to remove the clothing or a covering from.

un·coil (un koil′), *v.t., v.i.* to unwind from a coiled position.

un·com·fort·a·ble (un kumf′tə bəl, -kum′fər tə bəl), *adj.* **1.** causing discomfort. **2.** in a state of discomfort. —**un·com′fort·a·ble·ness,** *n.* —**un·com′fort·a·bly,** *adv.*

un·com·mit·ed (un′kə mit′id), *adj.* not committed, esp. not pledged to a certain cause, principle, or allegiance.

un·com·mon (un kom′ən), *adj.* **1.** not common or ordinary. **2.** exceptional or remarkable. —**un·com′mon·ly,** *adv.* —**un·com′mon·ness,** *n.*

un·com·mu·ni·ca·tive (un′kə myōo′nə-kā′tiv, -nə kə tiv), *adj.* not disposed to talk or disclose information.

un·com·pro·mis·ing (un kom′prə mī′-zing), *adj.* not making or accepting compromise. —**un·com′pro·mis′ing·ly,** *adv.* —**Syn.** firm, inflexible.

un·con·cern (un′kən sûrn′), *n.* **1.** absence of concern or interest. **2.** freedom from anxiety or care. —**Syn.** indifference, nonchalance.

un·con·cerned (un′kən sûrnd′), *adj.* **1.** not concerned or interested. **2.** free from anxiety or care. —**un′con·cern′ed·ly** (-sûr′nid lē), *adv.*

un·con·di·tion·al (un′kən dish′ə nəl), *adj.* not limited by conditions. —**un′con·di′tion·al·ly,** *adv.* —**Syn.** absolute, categorical.

un·con·di·tioned (un′kən dish′ənd), *adj.* **1.** not subject to conditions. **2.** *Psychol.* natural or innate: *an unconditioned reflex.*

un·con·scion·a·ble (un kon′shə nə-bəl), *adj.* **1.** not guided by conscience. **2.** excessive or unreasonable. —**un·con′scion·a·bly,** *adv.*

un·con·scious (un kon′shəs), *adj.* **1.** without consciousness or awareness.

---

un·chas′tened, *adj.*
un·chas′tised, *adj.*
un·checked′, *adj.*
un·cheer′ful, *adj.;* **-ly,** *adv.*
un·cher′ished, *adj.*
un·chilled′, *adj.*
un·chiv′al·rous, *adj.*
un·cho′sen, *adj.*
un·chris′tened, *adj.*
un·churched′, *adj.*
un·claimed′, *adj.*
un·clar′i·fied′, *adj.*
un·clas′si·fi′a·ble, *adj.*
un·clas′si·fied′, *adj.*
un·cleaned′, *adj.*
un·clear′, *adj.*
un·cleared′, *adj.*
un·cloud′ed, *adj.*

un·clut′tered, *adj.*
un′co·ag′u·lat′ed, *adj.*
un′col·lect′ed, *adj.*
un·col′ored, *adj.*
un·combed′, *adj.*
un·com·bined′, *adj.*
un·com′fort·ed, *adj.*
un·com′fort·ing, *adj.*
un·com·mend′a·ble, *adj.*
un·com·mer′cial, *adj.*
un·com·pen·sat′ed, *adj.*
un·com·pet′i·tive, *adj.*
un·com·plain′ing, *adj.;* **-ly,** *adv.*
un·com·plet′ed, *adj.*
un·com·pli′ant, *adj.*
un·com·pli·cat′ed, *adj.*
un′com·pli·men′ta·ry, *adj.*

un′com·pound′ed, *adj.*
un′com·pre·hend′ed, *adj.*
un′com·pre·hend′ing, *adj.;* **-ly,** *adv.*
un′con·cealed′, *adj.*
un′con·ced′ed, *adj.*
un′con·clud′ed, *adj.*
un′con·densed′, *adj.*
un′con·fined′, *adj.*
un′con·firmed′, *adj.*
un′con·form′a·ble, *adj.*
un′con·fused′, *adj.*
un′con·gen′ial, *adj.*
un′con·nec′ted, *adj.*
un′con′quer·a·ble, *adj.*
un′con′quered, *adj.*
un′con·sci·en′tious, *adj.;* **-ly,** *adv.*

2. temporarily devoid of consciousness. **3.** not consciously realized or done. —*n.* **4. the unconscious,** *Psychoanal.* the part of the mind containing the psychic material of which the ego is unaware. —**un·con′scious·ly,** *adv.* —**un·con′scious·ness,** *n.*

un·con·sti·tu·tion·al (un′kon sti tōō′-shə nᵊl, -tyōō′-), *adj.* unauthorized by or inconsistent with the constitution, as of a country. —**un′con·sti·tu′tion·al′i·ty,** *n.* —**un′con·sti·tu′tion·al·ly,** *adv.*

un·con·ven·tion·al (un′kən ven′shə-nᵊl), *adj.* not conforming to convention or rule. —**un′con·ven′tion·al′i·ty,** *n.* —**un′con·ven′tion·al·ly,** *adv.*

un·cork (un kôrk′), *v.t.* **1.** to draw the cork from. **2.** *Informal.* to set free from a sealed or confined state.

un·count·ed (un koun′tid), *adj.* **1.** not counted. **2.** too many to be counted.

un·cou·ple (un kup′əl), *v.t.* to release the coupling between.

un·couth (un kōōth′), *adj.* **1.** not polished or graceful, as in speech. **2.** awkward or clumsy, as in behavior. —**un·couth′ness,** *n.* —Syn. **1.** coarse, crude. **2.** ungainly.

un·cov·er (un kuv′ər), *v.t.* **1.** to lay bare, as a plot. **2.** to remove the cover or covering from. **3.** to remove a hat from (the head). —*v.i.* **4.** to take off one's hat in respect.

un·cross (un krôs′, -kros′), *v.t.* to change (one's legs) from a crossed position.

UNCTAD, United Nations Conference of Trade and Development.

unc·tion (ungk′shən), *n.* **1.** an act of anointing, esp. as a medical treatment or religious rite. **2.** the oil used in anointing. **3.** something soothing or comforting. **4.** hypocritical or affected earnestness, esp. in language.

unc·tu·ous (ungk′chōō əs), *adj.* **1.** hypocritically smooth or suave. **2.** containing or like oil or ointment. —**unc′tu·ous·ly,** *adv.* —**unc′tu·ous·ness, unc′tu·os′i·ty** (-os′i tē), *n.*

un·cut (un kut′), *adj.* **1.** not cut. **2.** not shortened or condensed. **3.** neither reduced in size nor given shape, as a diamond.

un·daunt·ed (un dôn′tid), *adj.* not dismayed or discouraged. —**un·daunt′ed·ly,** *adv.*

un·de·ceive (un′di sēv′), *v.t.* to free from deception, fallacy, or mistake.

un·de·cid·ed (un′di sī′did), *adj.* **1.** not decided or determined. **2.** not having one's mind firmly made up.

un·de·mon·stra·tive (un′də mon′strə-tiv), *adj.* not given to open exhibition of feeling. —**un′de·mon′stra·tive·ly,** *adv.* —**un′de·mon′stra·tive·ness,** *n.* —Syn. reserved.

un·de·ni·a·ble (un′di nī′ə bəl), *adj.* **1.** not capable of being denied or disputed. **2.** indisputably good. —**un′-de·ni′a·bly,** *adv.* —Syn. **1.** inescapable, obvious.

un·der (un′dər), *prep.* **1.** beneath and covered by: *under a tree.* **2.** below the surface of: *under water.* **3.** protected, controlled, or watched by: *under guard.* **4.** below in amount, rank, importance, etc. **5.** below the specified degree or qualification of: *under age.* **6.** subject to the influence, condition, force, etc.: *under these circumstances.* **7.** subject to the effects of: *under a sedative.* **8.** in the state or process of: *under repair.* **9.** in accordance with: *under the provisions of the law.* **10.** subject to the terms and conditions of: *under contract.* **11.** during the rule

un′con·se·crat′ed, *adj.*
un′con·sent′ing, *adj.*
un′con·sid′ered, *adj.*
un′con·soled′, *adj.*
un′con·sol′i·dat′ed, *adj.*
un′con·strained′, *adj.*
un′con·strict′ed, *adj.*
un′con·sumed′, *adj.*
un′con·sum·mat′ed, *adj.*
un′con·tam′i·nat′ed, *adj.*
un′con·test′ed, *adj.*
un′con·tra·dict′ed, *adj.*
un′con·trite′, *adj.*
un′con·trol′la·ble, *adj.;*
-bly, *adv.*
un′con·trolled′, *adj.*
un′con·ver′sant, *adj.*
un′con·vert′ed, *adj.*
un′con·vert′i·ble, *adj.*
un′con·vinced′, *adj.*
un′con·vinc′ing, *adj.;*
-ly, *adv.*
un·cooked′, *adj.*

un′co·op′er·a′tive, *adj.*
un′co·or′di·nat′ed, *adj.*
un′cor′dial, *adj.*
un′cor·rect′ed, *adj.*
un′cor·rob′o·rat′ed, *adj.*
un′cor·rupt′ed, *adj.*
un′count′a·ble, *adj.*
un·cour′te·ous, *adj.*
un·cov′ered, *adj.*
un·crate′, *v.t.,* -crat·ed,
-crat·ing.
un·crit′i·cal, *adj.*
un·crowd′ed, *adj.*
un′crowned′, *adj.*
un·crys′tal·lized′, *adj.*
un·cul′ti·vat′ed, *adj.*
un·cul′tured, *adj.*
un·curbed′, *adj.*
un·cured′, *adj.*
un·cu′ri·ous, *adj.*
un·curl′, *v.*
un·cur′tained, *adj.*
un·cus′tom·ar′y, *adj.*

un·dam′aged, *adj.*
un·damped′, *adj.*
un·dat′ed, *adj.*
un′de·bat′a·ble, *adj.*
un·de·cayed′, *adj.*
un′de·ci′pher·a·ble, *adj.*
un·de·clared′, *adj.*
un·dec′o·rat′ed, *adj.*
un·de·feat′ed, *adj.*
un·de·fend′ed, *adj.*
un′de·fen′si·ble, *adj.*
un′de·fin′a·ble, *adj.*
un·de·fined′, *adj.*
un′de·liv′er·a·ble, *adj.*
un·de·mand′ing, *adj.*
un′dem·o·crat′ic, *adj.*
un′de·mon′stra·ble, *adj.;*
-bly, *adv.*
un′de·nied′, *adj.*
un′de·nom′i·na′tion·al,
adj.
un′de·pend′a·ble, *adj.*

or administration of: *under King George III.* **12.** within the category of: *entered under anthropology.* **13.** beneath the cover of: *under a pseudonym.* **14.** authorized or attested by: *under seal.* —*adv.* **15.** below or beneath something. **16.** in or to a lower place. **17.** in or to a lower degree, amount, etc.: *selling blouses for $6 and under.* **18.** in or into subjection of submission. —*adj.* **19.** located on the underside: *a bird's under feathers.*

under-, a prefix meaning: **a.** below or beneath: *underbrush.* **b.** lower in grade or dignity: *understudy.* **c.** of lesser degree or amount: *undersized.*

un·der·a·chieve (un′dər ə chēv′), *v.i.* to perform below the potential indicated by tests of mental ability, esp. in school. —**un′der·a·chiev′er,** *n.*

un·der·act (un′dər akt′), *v.t., v.i.* to perform (a role or scene) subtly or with restraint.

un·der·age (un′dər āj′), *adj.* lacking the required age, esp. that of legal maturity.

un·der·arm (un′dər ärm′), *adj.* **1.** situated, used, or appearing in the armpit. **2.** underhand (def. 2). —*adv.* **3.** underhand (def. 4).

un·der·bel·ly (un′dər bel′ē), *n.* **1.** the lower abdomen. **2.** the weaker point.

un·der·bid (un′dər bid′), *v.t., v.i.* **1.** to bid lower than (another bidder). **2.** *Bridge.* to bid less than the value of (one's hand). —**un′der·bid′der,** *n.*

un·der·brush (un′dər brush′), *n.* shrubs and small trees growing under large trees.

un·der·car·riage (un′dər kar′ij), *n.* **1.** the supporting framework underneath a vehicle. **2.** *Chiefly Brit.* See **landing gear.**

un·der·charge (*v.* un′dər chärj′, *n.* un′dər chärj′), *v.t., v.i.* **1.** to charge (a purchaser) too low a price. **2.** to load (a gun) with an insufficient charge. —*n.* **3.** an insufficient charge.

un·der·class·man (un′dər klas′mən, -kläs′-), *n.* a freshman or sophomore in a secondary school or college.

un·der·clothes (un′dər klōz′, -klōt͟hz′), *n.pl.* underwear. Also called **un′der·cloth′ing.**

un·der·coat (un′dər kōt′), *n.* Also, **un′der·coat′ing** (for defs. 1, 2). **1.** a rustproof tarlike seal applied to the underside of a vehicle. **2.** a coat of paint applied under the finishing coat. **3.** a growth of short fur lying

beneath a longer growth in certain animals. **4.** *Rare.* a coat worn under another. —*v.t., v.i.* **5.** to apply an undercoat (to).

un·der·cov·er (un′dər kuv′ər, un′dər-kuv′-), *adj.* **1.** working or done in secret. **2.** engaged in spying or securing confidential information: *an undercover agent.*

un·der·cur·rent (un′dər kûr′ənt, -kur′-), *n.* **1.** a current, as of air or water, that flows beneath another current. **2.** a hidden tendency, attitude, or feeling.

un·der·cut (un′dər kut′), *v.t.* **1.** to cut under or beneath. **2.** to sell at a lower price or work for a lower wage than another. **3.** *Golf.* to hit (the ball) so as to cause a backspin. **4.** *Tennis.* to slice (the ball) using an underhand motion.

un·der·de·vel·oped (un′dər di vel′əpt), *adj.* **1.** improperly or insufficiently developed. **2.** *Often Offensive.* lacking the facilities to develop the economic resources, as a nation.

un·der·dog (un′dər dôg′, -dog′), *n.* **1.** a person who is expected to lose in a contest or conflict. **2.** a victim of social or political injustice.

un·der·done (un′dər dun′), *adj.* not thoroughly cooked.

un·der·draw·ers (un′dər drôrz′), *n.pl.* underpants.

un·der·dress (un′dər dres′), *v.i., -dressed, -dress·ing.* to clothe oneself less completely or formally than is usual or fitting for the circumstances.

un·der·em·ployed (un′dər em ploid′), *adj.* not having the working capacities and time of a population completely utilized by the economy.

un·der·es·ti·mate (un′dər es′tə māt′), *v.t., v.i.* to make too low an estimate (on or for). —**un′der·es′ti·ma′tion,** *n.*

un·der·ex·pose (un′dər ik spōz′), *v.t.* to expose (a film) to insufficient light or for too short a period. —**un′der·ex·po′sure** (-spō′zhər), *n.*

un·der·feed (un′dər fēd′), *v.t., -fed, -feed·ing.* **1.** to feed insufficiently. **2.** to feed with fuel from beneath.

un·der·foot (un′dər fŏŏt′), *adv., adj.* **1.** under the foot or feet. **2.** in the way.

un·der·gar·ment (un′dər gär′mənt), *n.* an article of underwear.

un·der·gird (un′dər gûrd′), *v.t.* to strengthen or secure underneath.

un·der·go (un′dər gō′), *v.t.* **1.** to go through or experience. **2.** to suffer or endure.

un′der·bred′, *adj.*
un′der·clad′, *adj.*
un′der·clerk′, *n.*
un′der·clothed′, *adj.*
un′der·cook′, *v.t.*
un′der·ed′u·cat′ed, *adj.*
un′der·em′pha·size′, *v.t.*
un′der·fi·nance′, *v.t., -nanced, -nanc·ing.*
un′der·fur′, *n.*

un·der·grad·u·ate (un′dər graj′ōo it), *n.* a student in a university or college who has not taken a first degree.

un·der·ground (*adv., adj.* un′dər ground′, *n.* un′dər ground′), *adv.* **1.** beneath the surface of the ground. **2.** in hiding or secret. —*adj.* **3.** existing, placed, or operating underground. **4.** hidden or secret. **5.** *Informal.* **a.** published or produced to reflect nonconformist or radical views: *an underground newspaper.* **b.** avant-garde or experimental: *an underground movie.* **c.** offbeat or inexpensive: *an underground gourmet.* —*n.* **6.** the place or region beneath the surface of the ground. **7.** a secret organization fighting the established government or occupation forces. **8.** *Brit.* subway.

un·der·growth (un′dər grōth′), *n.* shrubs and herbs growing thickly among trees.

un·der·hand (un′dər hand′), *adj.* **1.** not open and aboveboard. **2.** done with the hand below the level of the shoulder. —*adv.* **3.** in an underhand or deceitful manner. **4.** with an underhand motion. —**Syn.** **1.** sly, stealthy, surreptitious.

un·der·hand·ed (un′dər han′did), *adj.* underhand. —**un′der·hand′ed·ly,** *adv.* —**un′der·hand′ed·ness,** *n.*

un·der·lie (un′dər lī′), *v.t.* **1.** to lie under or beneath. **2.** to form the basis of.

un·der·line (un′dər līn′, un′dər līn′), *v.t.* **1.** to mark with a line underneath. **2.** to stress or emphasize.

un·der·ling (un′dər ling), *n.* a subordinate, esp. one of slight importance.

un·der·ly·ing (un′dər lī′ing), *adj.* **1.** lying under or beneath. **2.** fundamental or basic.

un·der·mine (un′dər mīn′), *v.t.* **1.** to injure or destroy underhandedly or gradually. **2.** to wear away at the base. **3.** to dig a tunnel or hole beneath.

un·der·most (un′dər mōst′), *adj., adv.* lowest in position, status, etc.

un·der·neath (un′dər nēth′), *prep., adv.* **1.** below the surface or level of. **2.** under the control of.

un·der·nour·ished (un′dər nûr′isht, -nur′isht), *adj.* not nourished enough for health or normal growth. —**un′der·nour′ish·ment,** *n.*

un·der·pants (un′dər pants′), *n.pl.* drawers or shorts worn under the outer clothing.

un·der·part (un′dər pärt′), *n.* the lower part or side, as of an animal or object.

un·der·pass (un′dər pas′, -päs′), *n.* a passage running underneath, as one crossing under a railroad.

un·der·pay (un′dər pā′), *v.t.* to pay less than is usual or deserved.

un·der·pin·ning (un′dər pin′ing), *n.* **1.** a supporting structure placed beneath a wall or foundation. **2.** Usually, **underpinnings.** the strengthening support, as of a theory. —**un′der·pin′,** *v.t.*

un·der·play (un′dər plā′, un′dər plā′), *v.t., v.i.* **1.** to underact. **2.** to understate or de-emphasize (something).

un·der·priv·i·leged (un′dər priv′ə lijd, -priv′lijd), *adj.* lacking the normal advantages because of low economic and social status.

un·der·pro·duc·tion (un′dər prə duk′shən), *n.* production that is less than normal or than is required by the demand. —**un′der·pro·duce′,** *v.t., v.i.*

un·der·rate (un′dər rāt′), *v.t.* to rate or evaluate too low.

un·der·score (un′dər skōr′, -skôr′), *v.t.* to underline.

un·der·sea (un′dər sē′), *adj.* **1.** located, carried on, or used under the surface of the sea. —*adv.* **2.** Also, **un′der·seas′.** beneath the surface of the sea.

un′der sec′re·tar′y, an official ranking next below a member of the Cabinet.

un·der·sell (un′dər sel′), *v.t.* to sell merchandise cheaper than.

un·der·sexed (un′dər sekst′), *adj.* having or showing less than normal interest in or need for sexual activity.

un·der·shirt (un′dər shûrt′), *n.* a collarless undergarment worn chiefly by men and children.

un·der·shorts (un′dər shôrts′), *n.pl.* short underpants for men and boys.

un·der·shot (un′dər shot′), *adj.* **1.** driven by water passing beneath, as a water wheel. **2.** having the lower jaw projecting from below, as a bulldog.

un·der·side (un′dər sīd′), *n.* a lower or bottom side.

un·der·signed (un′dər sīnd′), *n.* **the undersigned,** the person or persons signing at the end of a document.

un·der·sized (un′dər sīzd′), *adj.* smaller than the usual or normal size. Also, **un′der·size′.**

un·der·skirt (un′dər skûrt′), *n.* a petticoat worn under a skirt or dress.

un·der·slung (un′dər slung′), *adj.* suspended from the axles, as an automobile.

---

un′der·lay′er, *n.*
un′der·lip′, *n.*
un′der·men′tioned, *adj.*
un′der·of·fi′cial, *n.*

un′der·peo′pled, *adj.*
un′der·pop′u·lat′ed, *adj.*
un′der·pow′ered, *adj.*
un′der·price′, *v.t.*

un′der·ri′pened, *adj.*
un′der·run′, *v.t.*
un′der·spend′, *v.,*
　-spent, -spend·ing.

un·der·staffed (un′dər staft′, -stäft′), *adj.* having an insufficient number of personnel.

un·der·stand (un′dər stand′), *v.t.* **1.** to perceive the meaning of. **2.** to have a thorough knowledge of. **3.** to interpret or construe. **4.** to take as agreed or settled **5.** to learn or hear. **6.** to accept as true. **7.** to feel sympathy toward —*v.i.* **8.** to perceive what is meant **9.** to be sympathetic. **10.** to be informed —**un′·der·stand′a·ble**, *adj* - **un′·der·stand′a·bly**, *adv* —**Syn. 1.** comprehend.

un·der·stand·ing (un′dər stan′ding), *n.* **1.** the fact of perceiving what is meant. **2.** the ability to understand. **3.** a particular interpretation. **4.** a mutual agreement, esp of a private or tacit kind —*adj* **5.** having or showing understanding or sympathy. —**un′der·stand′ing·ly,** *adv.*

un·der·state (un′dər stāt′), *v.t.* **1.** to represent less strongly than the facts would bear out. **2.** to set forth in restrained terms. —**un′der·state′·ment,** *n.*

un·der·stood (un′dər stŏŏd′), *adj.* **1.** agreed upon. **2.** implied but not stated.

un·der·stud·y (un′dər stud′ē), *n.* **1.** a person trained to replace an actor or actress if necessary. —*v.t., v.i.* **2.** to study (a part) as an understudy (to).

un·der·sur·face (un′dər sûr′fis), *n.* a lower or bottom surface.

un·der·take (un′dər tāk′), *v.t.* **1.** to take upon oneself, as a project or task. **2.** to promise or obligate oneself to. **3.** to warrant or guarantee.

un·der·tak·er (un′dər tā′kər), *n. Obsolesc.* a funeral director.

un·der·tak·ing (un′dər tā′king *for 1, 2,* un′dər tā′king *for 3*), *n.* **1.** something undertaken, as a task. **2.** a

promises or pledge. **3.** *Obsolesc.* the business of a funeral director.

un·der-the-coun·ter (un′dər thē koun′tər), *adj.* **1.** sold clandestinely. **2.** Also, **un′der-the-ta′ble.** secret or illegal.

un·der·things (un′dər thingz′), *n.pl.* women's underclothes.

un·der·tone (un′dər tōn′), *n.* **1.** a subdued tone of voice. **2.** an underlying quality or element. **3.** a subdued color.

un·der·tow (un′dər tō′), *n.* the seaward flow of water from waves breaking on a beach.

un·der·val·ue (un′dər val′yōō), *v.t.* **1.** to put too low a value on. **2.** to hold too low an opinion of.

un·der·waist (un′dər wāst′), *n.* a blouse worn under another.

un·der·wa·ter (un′dər wô′tər, -wot′ər), *adj.* existing, used, or occurring beneath the water. —*adv.* **2.** beneath the water.

un·der·wear (un′dər wâr′), *n.* clothing worn next to the skin under outer clothes.

un·der·weight (un′dər wāt′), *adj.* weighing less than is normal or required.

un·der·world (un′dər wûrld′), *n.* **1.** the criminal element of human society. **2.** the abode of the dead.

un·der·write (un′dər rīt′), *v.t.* **1.** to guarantee the sale of (a security issue to be offered to the public for subscription). **2.** to bind oneself to support (an undertaking) with money. **3.** to write one's name at the end of (an insurance policy), thereby becoming liable for damage or loss. **4.** to write beneath (used usually in past participle). —**un′der·writ′er,** *n.*

un·de·sir·a·ble (un′di zī°r′ə bəl), *adj.* not desirable or attractive.

un·dies (un′dēz), *n.pl. Informal.* women's or children's underwear.

---

un′der·sup·ply′, *v.t.,* -plied, -ply·ing; *n.*

un′der·trained′, *adj.*

un′der·wind′, *v.t.,* -wound, -wind·ing.

---

un′de·scrib′a·ble, *adj.;* -bly, *adv.*
un′de·served′, *adj.*
un′de·serv′ing, *adj.*
un′de·sired′, *adj.*
un′de·stroyed′, *adj.*
un′de·tach′a·ble, *adj.*
un′de·tached′, *adj.*
un′de·tect′ed, *adj.*
un′de·ter′mi·na·ble, *adj.*
un′de·ter′mined, *adj.*
un′de·terred′, *adj.*
un′de·vel′oped, *adj.*
un′di·ag·nosed′, *adj.*
un′dif·fer·en′ti·at·ed, *adj.*
un′dif·fused′, *adj.*
un′di·gest′ed, *adj.*

un′dig′ni·fied′, *adj.*
un′di·lut′ed, *adj.*
un′di·min′ished, *adj.*
un′dimmed′, *adj.*
un′dip·lo·mat′ic, *adj.*
un′di·rect′ed, *adj.*
un′dis·cerned′, *adj.*
un′dis·cern′i·ble, *adj.;* -bly, *adv.*
un′dis·cern′ing, *adj.*
un′dis·charged′, *adj.*
un·dis′ci·plined, *adj.*
un′dis·closed′, *adj.*
un′dis·cour′aged, *adj.*
un′dis·cov′ered, *adj.*
un′dis·crim′i·nat′ing, *adj.;* -ly, *adv.*
un′dis·guised′, *adj.*

un′dis·mayed′, *adj.*
un′dis·pelled′, *adj.*
un′dis·played′, *adj.*
un′dis·proved′, *adj.*
un′dis·put′a·ble, *adj.*
un′dis·put′ed, *adj.*
un′dis·solved′, *adj.*
un′dis·tilled′, *adj.*
un′dis·tin′guish·a·ble, *adj.*
un′dis·tin′guished, *adj.*
un′dis·tressed′, *adj.*
un′dis·trib′ut·ed, *adj.*
un′dis·turbed′, *adj.*
un′di·ver′si·fied′, *adj.*
un′di·vid′ed, *adj.*
un′di·vulged′, *adj.*

un·do (un dōō′), *v.t.* **1.** to cause to be as if never done. **2.** to unfasten, loosen, or open. **3.** to bring to ruin or disaster.

un·do·ing (un dōō′ing), *n.* **1.** the reversing of what has been done. **2. a.** a bringing to ruin or disaster. **b.** a cause of this. **3.** the act of unfastening, loosing, or opening.

un·doubt·ed (un dou′tid), *adj.* accepted as beyond doubt. —**un·doubt′ed·ly**, *adv.*

un·dress (un dres′), *v.t.* **1.** to remove the clothes of. —*v.i.* **2.** to take one's clothes off. —*n.* **3.** informal or ordinary clothing. **4.** the state of being only partially dressed, as for lounging.

un·due (un dōō′, -dyōō′), *adj.* **1.** more than is necessary or warranted. **2.** inappropriate or improper. **3.** not yet owed, as a bill of exchange.

un·du·lant (un′jə lənt, un′dyə-, -də-), *adj.* wavy in motion or pattern. —**un′du·lance**, *n.*

un·du·late (un′jə lāt′, un′dyə-), *v.i., v.t.*, **-lat·ed, -lat·ing. 1.** to move or cause to move in waves. **2.** to have or cause to have a wavy form or pattern.

un·du·la·tion (un′jə lā′shən, un′dyə-), *n.* **1.** a wavy form or pattern. **2.** a wave of sound or light. —**un′du·la·to′ry**, *adj.*

un·du·ly (un dōō′lē, -dyōō′-), *adv.* **1.** in an undue measure. **2.** inappropriately or improperly.

un·dy·ing (un dī′ing), *adj.* immortal or unceasing, as fame. —**un·dy′ing·ly**, *adv.*

un·earned (un ûrnd′), *adj.* **1.** not earned by work or service. **2.** not merited or deserved.

un·earth (un ûrth′), *v.t.* **1.** to dig out of the earth. **2.** to bring to light, as by search.

un·earth·ly (un ûrth′lē), *adj.* **1.** seeming not to belong to this world. **2.** supernatural or ghostly. **3.** absurdly peculiar.

un·eas·y (un ē′zē), *adj.* **1.** not easy in body or mind. **2.** worried or disturbed. **3.** not easy in manner. —**un·eas′i·ly**, *adv.* —**un·eas′i·ness**, *n.* —**Syn. 1.** restless. **2.** anxious.

un·em·ployed (un′em ploid′), *adj.* **1.** out of work. **2.** not in use. —**un′em·ploy′ment**, *n.*

un·e·qual (un ē′kwəl), *adj.* **1.** not equal, as in size, degree, or amount. **2.** not evenly proportioned or balanced. **3.** not adequate, as in strength or ability. **4.** uneven or variable. —**un·e′qual·ly**, *adv.*

un·e·qualed (un ē′kwəld), *adj.* not surpassed or matched. Also, *Brit.*, **un·e′qualled.** —**Syn.** peerless.

un·e·quiv·o·cal (un′i kwiv′ə kəl), *adj.* impossible to misunderstand or doubt. —**un′e·quiv′o·cal·ly**, *adv.* —**Syn.** explicit, unambiguous.

un·err·ing (un ûr′ing, -er′-), *adj.* **1.** making no error or mistake. **2.** undeviatingly accurate. —**un·err′ing·ly**, *adv.*

UNESCO (yōō nes′kō), United Nations Educational, Scientific, and Cultural Organization.

un·e·ven (un ē′vən), *adj.* **1.** not level or flat. **2.** not uniform in quality. **3.** unequal (def. 1). **4.** (of a number) odd. —**un·e′ven·ly**, *adv.* —**un·e′ven·ness**, *n.*

un·e·vent·ful (un′i vent′fəl), *adj.* without important or special incidents. —**un′e·vent′ful·ly**, *adv.*

un·ex·am·pled (un′ig zam′pəld, -zäm-), *adj.* without precedent or parallel.

un·ex·cep·tion·a·ble (un′ik sep′shə nə bəl), *adj.* beyond reproach or criticism. —**un′ex·cep′tion·a·bly**, *adv.*.

---

un·doc′u·ment·ed, *adj.*
un′dog·mat′ic, *adj.*
un′do·mes′ti·cat′ed, *adj.*
un·done′, *adj.*
un·doubt′ing, *adj.*
un′dra·mat′ic, *adj.*
un·drape′, *v.t.*, -draped, -drap·ing.
un·dreamed′, *adj.*
un·dreamt′, *adj.*
un·dressed′, *adj.*
un·drink′a·ble, *adj.*
un·du′ti·ful, *adj.*
un·dyed′, *adj.*
un·eat′a·ble, *adj.*
un·eat′en, *adj.*
un′e·co·nom′ic, *adj.*
un′e·co·nom′i·cal, *adj.*;
  -ly, *adv.*
un·ed′i·fy′ing, *adj.*
un·ed′u·ca·ble, *adj.*

un·ed′u·cat′ed, *adj.*
un′e·man′ci·pat′ed, *adj.*
un′em·bar′rassed, *adj.*
un′em·bel′lished, *adj.*
un′e·mo′tion·al, *adj.*
un′em·phat′ic, *adj.*
un′en·closed′, *adj.*
un′en·cum′bered, *adj.*
un′en·dan′gered, *adj.*
un·end′ed, *adj.*
un·end′ing, *adj.*; -ly, *adv.*
un′en·dorsed′, *adj.*
un′en·dur′a·ble, *adj.*
un′en·forced′, *adj.*
un′en·gaged′, *adj.*
un′en·joy′a·ble, *adj.*
un′en·light′ened, *adj.*
un′en·riched′, *adj.*
un′en·rolled′, *adj.*
un′en·tan′gled, *adj.*

un′en·tered, *adj.*
un′en·ter·pris′ing, *adj.*
un′en·ter·tain′ing, *adj.*
un′en·thu′si·as′tic, *adj.*
un·en′vi·a·ble, *adj.*
un·en′vi·ous, *adj.*;
  -ly, *adv.*
un′e·quipped′, *adj.*
un′e·rased′, *adj.*
un′es·cap′a·ble, *adj.*;
  -bly, *adv.*
un′es·cort′ed, *adj.*
un′es·sen′tial, *adj.*
un′es·tab′lished, *adj.*
un·es·thet′ic, *adj.*
un·eth′i·cal, *adj.*;
  -ly, *adv.*
un′ex·ag′ger·at′ed, *adj.*
un′ex·ca·vat′ed, *adj.*
un′ex·celled′, *adj.*

un·ex·cep·tion·al (un'ik sep'shə nəl), *adj.* **1.** not exceptional or unusual. **2.** admitting of no exception. **3.** (loosely) unexceptionable.

un·ex·pect·ed (un'ik spek'tĭd), *adj.* occurring or coming without warning. —**un'ex·pect'ed·ly,** *adv.* —**un'ex·pect'ed·ness,** *n.*

un·fail·ing (un fā'lĭng), *adj.* **1.** not failing or diminishing. **2.** completely dependable. **3.** inexhaustible, as resources. —**un·fail'ing·ly,** *adv.* —**un·fail'ing·ness,** *n.*

un·fair (un fâr'), *adj.* **1.** not fair or just. **2.** using unethical business practices. —**un·fair'ly,** *adv.* —**un·fair'ness,** *n.*

un·faith·ful (un fāth'fəl), *adj.* **1.** not faithful or loyal. **2.** guilty of adultery. **3.** not accurate or complete. —**un·faith'ful·ly,** *adv.* —**un·faith'·ful·ness,** *n.*

un·fa·mil·iar (un'fə mil'yər), *adj.* **1.** not familiar or acquainted. **2.** unusual or strange. —**un'fa·mil'i·ar'·i·ty** (-mil'ē ar'i tē), *n.* —**un'fa·mil'iar·ly,** *adv.*

un·fas·ten (un fas'ən, -fä'sən), *v.t.* **1.** to open the fastening of. —*v.i.* **2.** to become unfastened.

un·fa·vor·a·ble (un fā'vər ə bəl), *adj.* **1.** not favorable or advantageous. **2.** adverse or disapproving. —**un·fa'vor·a·bly,** *adv.*

un·feel·ing (un fē'lĭng), *adj.* **1.** without sympathy or compassion. **2.** lacking feeling or sensation. —**un·feel'ing·ly,** *adv.* —**Syn. 1.** callous. **2.** numb.

un·feigned (un fānd'), *adj.* not feigned or hypocritical.

un·fit (un fit'), *adj.*, **1.** not suitable or adapted. **2.** unqualified or incompetent. **3.** not in a physically or mentally good condition. —*v.t.* **4.** to make unfit. —**un·fit'ly,** *adv.* —**unfit'ness,** *n.*

un·fix (un fiks'), *v.t.* **1.** to make no longer fixed. **2.** to unsettle, as the mind.

un·flap·pa·ble (un flap'ə bəl), *adj. Slang.* not easily upset or confused. —**un·flap·pa·bil'i·ty** (un flap'ə bil'i·tē), *n.* —**un·flap'pa·bly,** *adv.*

un·fledged (un flejd'), *adj.* **1.** without feathers sufficiently developed for flight, as a young bird. **2.** immature or inexperienced.

un·flinch·ing (un flin'chĭng), *adj.* not flinching or wavering. —**un·flinch'·ing·ly,** *adv.*

un·fold (un fōld'), *v.t.* **1.** to bring out of a folded state. **2.** to spread out of view. **3.** to reveal gradually or by degrees. —*v.i.* **4.** to become unfolded.

un·for·get·ta·ble (un'fər get'ə bəl), *adj.* impossible to forget. —**un'for·get'·ta·bly,** *adv.*

un·formed (un fôrmd'), *adj.* **1.** not definitely shaped or formed. **2.** not yet developed in character.

un·for·tu·nate (un fôr'chə nit), *adj.* **1.** suffering from bad luck. **2.** causing bad luck. **3.** to be deplored, esp. as being unsuitable. —*n.* **4.** an unfortunate person. —**un·for'tu·nate·ly,** *adv.* —**un·for'tu·nate·ness,** *n.*

un·found·ed (un foun'dĭd), *adj.* without any basis in fact.

un·fre·quent·ed (un frē'kwən tid), *adj.* rarely or never frequented or visited.

un·friend·ly (un frend'lē), *adj.* **1.** not friendly or kind. **2.** not favorable, as a climate. —**un·friend'li·ness,** *n.* —**Syn. 1.** aloof, inimical. **2.** hostile.

un·frock (un frok'), *v.t.* to deprive of ecclesiastical rank and function.

---

un'ex·change'a·ble, *adj.*
un'ex·cit'ed, *adj.*
un'ex·cit'ing, *adj.*
un'ex·cus'a·ble, *adj.;* -bly, *adv.*
un'ex·cused', *adj.*
un·ex'e·cut'ed, *adj.*
un·ex'er·cised', *adj.*
un'ex·pend'ed, *adj.*
un'ex·pe'ri·enced, *adj.*
un'ex·pired', *adj.*
un'ex·plain'a·ble, *adj.;* -bly, *adv.*
un'ex·plained', *adj.*
un'ex·plic'it, *adj.*
un'ex·plod'ed, *adj.*
un'ex·ploit'ed, *adj.*
un'ex·plored', *adj.*
un'ex·posed', *adj.*
un'ex·pressed', *adj.*
un'ex·pres'sive, *adj.*
un·ex'pur·gat'ed, *adj.*
un'ex·tend'ed, *adj.*
un'ex·tin'guished, *adj.*

un·fad'ing, *adj.*
un·fal'ter·ing, *adj.;* -ly, *adv.*
un·fash'ion·a·ble, *adj.;* -bly, *adv.*
un·fath'omed, *adj.*
un·fa'vored, *adj.*
un·feared', *adj.*
un·fear'ing, *adj.*
un·fea'si·ble, *adj.*
un·fed', *adj.*
un·fed'er·at'ed, *adj.*
un·felt', *adj.*
un·fem'i·nine, *adj.*
un·fer·ment'ed, *adj.*
un·fer'ti·lized', *adj.*
un·fes'tive, *adj.*
un·fet'tered, *adj.*
un·filled', *adj.*
un·fil'tered, *adj.*
un·fin'ished, *adj.*
un·fit'ting, *adj.;* -ly, *adv.*
un·flag'ging, *adj.;* -ly, *adv.*

un·flat'ter·ing, *adj.*
un·fla'vored, *adj.*
un'for·bid'den, *adj.*
un'for·bid'ding, *adj.*
un·forced', *adj.*
un'fore·see'a·ble, *adj.*
un'fore·seen', *adj.*
un'for·est'ed, *adj.*
un'fore·told', *adj.*
un'for·giv'a·ble, *adj.;* -bly, *adv.*
un'for·giv'en, *adj.*
un'for·giv'ing, *adj.*
un'for·got'ten, *adj.*
un'for·mu·lat'ed, *adj.*
un'for·sak'en, *adj.*
un·for'ti·fied', *adj.*
un·framed', *adj.*
un·freeze', *v.,* -froze, -fro·zen, -freez·ing.
un·fruit'ful, *adj.*
un·ful·filled', *adj.*
un·fun'ny, *adj.*

un·furl (un fûrl′), *v.t., v.i.* to spread out from a furled state, as a flag.

un·gain·ly (un gān′lē), *adj.* not graceful in form or movement. —**un·gain′li·ness,** *n.* —**Syn.** awkward, clumsy.

un·god·ly (un god′lē), *adj.* **1.** not godly or pious. **2.** sinful or wicked. **3.** *Informal.* dreadful or outrageous. —**un·god′li·ness,** *n.*

un·gov·ern·a·ble (un guv′ər nə bəl), *adj.* impossible to govern, rule, or restrain.

un·gra·cious (un grā′shəs), *adj.* **1.** not gracious or courteous. **2.** unpleasant or disagreeable. —**un·gra′cious·ly,** *adj.* —**un·gra′cious·ness,** *n.*

un·grate·ful (un grāt′fəl), *adj.* **1.** not showing gratitude or appreciation. **2.** distasteful or repellent, as a task. —**un·grate′ful·ly,** *adv.* —**un·grate′ful·ness,** *n.*

un·guard·ed (un gär′did), *adj.* **1.** not guarded or protected. **2.** not cautious or discreet.

un·guent (ung′gwənt), *n.* any ointment used as a salve. —**un·guen·tar·y** (ung′gwən ter′ē), *adj.*

un·gu·late (ung′gyə lit, -lāt′), *adj.* **1.** having hoofs. —*n.* **2.** a hoofed mammal.

un·hand (un hand′), *v.t.* to release from the hand or hands.

un·hap·py (un hap′ē), *adj.* **1.** not happy or cheerful. **2.** unfortunate or unlucky. **3.** unsuitable or inappropriate. —**un·hap′pi·ly,** *adv.* —**un·hap′pi·ness,** *n.* —**Syn. 1.** miserable, sad, wretched.

un·har·ness (un här′nis), *v.t.* to free from or as from harness.

un·health·y (un hel′thē), *adj.* **1.** not in good health. **2.** indicating poor physical or mental health. **3.** harmful to good health. **4.** morally bad or harmful. —**un·health′i·ness,** *n.*

un·heard (un hûrd′), *adj.* **1.** not perceived by the ear. **2.** not given a hearing or audience.

un·heard-of (un hûrd′uv′, -ov′), *adj.* **1.** never heard of. **2.** never known or done before. **3.** shocking or outrageous.

un·hinge (un hinj′), *v.t.* **1.** to remove from hinges. **2.** to upset, as one's mind.

un·hitch (un hich′), *v.t.* to free from a hitch.

un·ho·ly (un hō′lē), *adj.* **1.** not holy or sacred. **2.** ungodly (def. 2). **3.** *Informal.* ungodly (def. 3). —**un·ho′li·ness,** *n.*

un·hook (un hŏŏk′), *v.t.* **1.** to detach from or as from a hook. **2.** to unfasten the hook of.

un·horse (un hôrs′), *v.t.* to dislodge from or as from a horse.

uni-, a prefix meaning "one or only one": *unilateral.*

u·ni·cam·er·al (yōō′nə kam′ər əl), *adj.* of or consisting of a single legislative chamber.

UNICEF (yōō′ni sef′), United Nations Children's Fund. [from its original name, *U(nited) N(ations) I(nternational) C(hildren's) E(mergency) F(und)*]

u·ni·cel·lu·lar (yōō′ni sel′yə lər), *adj.* having or consisting of a single cell.

u·ni·corn (yōō′nə kôrn′), *n.* a mythical creature resembling a horse and having a single horn in the center of its forehead.

u·ni·cy·cle (yōō′ni sī′kəl), *n.* a one-wheeled vehicle, usually driven by pedals.

u·ni·di·rec·tion·al (yōō′ni di rek′shə-nəl, -dī-), *adj.* operating or moving in one direction only.

u·ni·form (yōō′nə fôrm′), *adj.* **1.** having the same form, appearance, or quality as others of its kind. **2.** the same throughout or at all times. —*n.* **3.** dress of distinctive design worn by members of a particular group, as a military force. —*v.t.* **4.** to clothe in or furnish with a uniform. —**u′ni·form′i·ty** (-fôr′mi tē), **u′ni·form′ness,** *n.* —**u′ni·form′ly,** *adv.*

---

un·fur′nished, *adj.*
un·gal′lant, *adj.; -ly, adv.*
un·gath′ered, *adj.*
un·gen′er·ous, *adj.*
un·gen′ial, *adj.; -ly, adv.*
un′gen·teel′, *adj.*
un·gen′tle·man·ly, *adj.*
un·gen′tle, *adj.; -tly, adv.*
un·glazed′, *adj.*
un·gov′erned, *adj.*
un·grace′ful, *adj.; -ly, adv.*
un·grad′ed, *adj.*
un′gram·mat′i·cal, *adj.; -ly, adv.*
un·grat′i·fy′ing, *adj.*
un·ground′ed, *adj.*
un·grudg′ing, *adj.*

un·guid′ed, *adj.*
un·hack′neyed, *adj.*
un·ham′pered, *adj.*
un·hand′i·capped′, *adj.*
un·hand′y, *adj.*
un·hard′ened, *adj.*
un·harmed′, *adj.*
un·harm′ful, *adj.*
un·har·mo′ni·ous, *adj.*
un·har′vest·ed, *adj.*
un·hatched′, *adj.*
un·healed′, *adj.*
un·health′ful, *adj.*
un·heat′ed, *adj.*
un·heed′ed, *adj.*
un·heed′ful, *adj.; -ly, adv.*
un·help′ful, *adj.*

un·her′ald·ed, *adj.*
un′he·ro′ic, *adj.*
un·hes′i·tat′ing, *adj.; -ly, adv.*
un·hin′dered, *adj.*
un·hon′ored, *adj.*
un·housed′, *adj.*
un·hung′, *adj.*
un·hur′ried, *adj.*
un·hurt′, *adj.*
un·hy·gi·en′ic, *adj.*
un·hy′phen·at′ed, *adj.*
un′i·den′ti·fi′a·ble, *adj.*
un′i·den′ti·fied′, *adj.*
un′id·i·o·mat′ic, *adj.*
un′id·i·o·mat′i·cal·ly, *adv.*

u·ni·fy (yoo′nə fī′), *v.t.*, *v.i.*, **-fied, -fy·ing.** to make into or become a single unit. —**u′ni·fi·ca′tion,** *n.* —**u′ni·fi′er,** *n.*

u·ni·lat·er·al (yoo′nə lat′ər əl), *adj.* **1.** involving or done by only one person, group, or nation. **2.** of or on one side only. —**u′ni·lat′er·al·ly,** *adv.*

un·im·peach·a·ble (un′im pē′chə bəl), *adj.* **1.** not liable to be impeached. **2.** above suspicion or reproach. —**un′im·peach′a·bly,** *adv.*

un·in·hib·it·ed (un′in hib′i tid), *adj.* **1.** not inhibited or restricted. **2.** not restrained, as by social convention. —**un′in·hib′it·ed·ly,** *adv.*

un·in·tel·li·gent (un′in tel′i jent), *adj.* deficient in intelligence or intellect. —**un′in·tel′li·gent·ly,** *adv.*

un·in·ten·tion·al (un′in ten′shə n°l), *adj.* not intentional or deliberate. —**un′in·ten′tion·al·ly,** *adv.*

un·in·ter·est·ed (un in′tər i stid, -tris tid), *adj.* **1.** having no interest, as from indifference. **2.** not having a financial interest. —**un·in′ter·est·ed·ly,** *adv.*

un·ion (yoon′yən), *n.* **1.** the act of uniting or state of being united. **2.** something united. **3.** a number of persons, states, or nations joined together for a common purpose. **4.** See **labor union. 5. the Union,** the United States, esp. during the Civil War. **6.** the state of being united in marriage. **7.** a device symbolic of union, used as in a flag. **8.** a device for connecting parts of machinery.

un·ion·ism (yoo′yə niz′əm), *n.* **1.** the principle of forming or supporting union, esp. labor union. **2.** (*cap.*) loyalty to the United States at the time of the Civil War. —**un′ion·ist,** *n.*

un·ion·ize (yoon′yə nīz′), *v.t.*, *v.i.*, **-ized, -iz·ing.** to form (into) a labor union. —**un′ion·i·za′tion,** *n.*

un′ion jack′, 1. (*caps.*) the British national flag. **2.** a flag consisting of a union only.

Un′ion of So′viet So′cialist Repub′- lics, official name of the **Soviet Union.**

u·nique (yoo nēk′), *adj.* **1.** having no like or equal. **2.** being the only one of its kind. **3.** highly unusual. — **u·nique′ly,** *adv.* —**u·nique′ness,** *n.* —Syn. **1.** incomparable, peerless. **2.** singular, sole.

u·ni·sex (yoo′nə seks′), *adj.* **1.** noting or engaged in a design, type, or style that is for use or wear by both sexes alike: *unisex clothes.* —*n.* **2.** the state or condition of being unisex.

u·ni·sex·u·al (yoo′ni sek′shoo əl), *adj.* of or pertaining to one sex only.

u·ni·son (yoo′ni sən, -zən), *n.* **1.** perfect accord or harmony. **2.** agreement in pitch of two or more musical tones, voices, etc.

u·nit (yoo′nit), *n.* **1.** something that forms a united whole. **2.** a specific quantity, as of space, money, etc., used as a standard of measurement. **3.** the smallest whole number. **4.** a single part or group of parts that serves a particular purpose. —**u·ni·tar·y** (yoo′ni ter′ē), *adj.*

U·ni·tar·i·an (yoo′ni târ′ē ən), *n.* a member of a denomination, officially merged with the Universalists in 1961, that rejects the doctrine of the Trinity and emphasizes tolerance of religious opinion. —**U′ni·tar′i·an·ism,** *n.*

u·nite (yoo nīt′), *v.t.*, *v.i.*, **u·nit·ed, u·nit·ing. 1.** to join or combine so as to form a single unit or whole. **2.** to join together for a common purpose. —**u·nit′ed,** *adj.* —Syn. **1.** amalgamate, consolidate, merge.

Unit′ed Ar′ab Em′irates, a federation of seven independent Arab states on the S coast of the Persian Gulf.

Unit′ed Ar′ab Repub′lic, former name (1958–71) of Egypt.

Unit′ed King′dom, a country in NW Europe, consisting of Great Britain and Northern Ireland.

---

un′il·lu′mi·nat′ed, *adj.*	un′in·cum′bered, *adj.*	un′in·sur′a·ble, *adj.*
un·il′lus·trat′ed, *adj.*	un′in·dem′ni·fied′, *adj.*	un′in·sured′, *adj.*
un′im·ag′i·na·ble, *adj.*; -bly, *adv.*	un′in·dorsed′, *adj.*	un·in·tel·lec′tu·al, *adj.*
un′im·ag′i·na′tive, *adj.*; -ly, *adv.*	un′in·fect′ed, *adj.*	un′in·tel′li·gi·ble, *adj.*; -bly, *adv.*
	un′in·flam′ma·ble, *adj.*	
un′im·paired′, *adj.*	un′in·flu·enced, *adj.*	un·in·tend′ed, *adj.*; -ly, *adv.*
un′im·pas′sioned, *adj.*	un′in·flu·en′tial, *adj.*	
un′im·ped′ed, *adj.*	un′in·form′a·tive, *adj.*	un·in′ter·est·ing, *adj.*; -ly, *adv.*
un′im·por′tant, *adj.*	un′in·formed′, *adj.*	
un′im·pos′ing, *adj.*	un′in·hab′it·a·ble, *adj.*	un′in·ter·rupt′ed, *adj.*; -ly, *adv.*
un′im·pressed′, *adj.*	un′in·hab′it·ed, *adj.*	
un′im·pres′sive, *adj.*; -ly, *adv.*	un′in·i′ti·at′ed, *adj.*	un′in·vest′ed, *adj.*
	un′in·jured, *adj.*	un′in·vit′ed, *adj.*
un′im·proved′, *adj.*	un′in·spired′, *adj.*	in·in·vit′ing, *adj.*; -ly, *adv.*
un′in·closed′, *adj.*	un′in·spir′ing, *adj.*; -ly, *adv.*	
un′in·cor′po·rat′ed, *adj.*	un′in·struct′ed, *adj.*	un′in·volved′, *adj.*
		un·i′roned, *adj.*

Unit'ed Na'tions, an international organization with headquarters in New York City, formed to promote international peace, security, and co-operation.

Unit'ed States', a country of 50 states, located in North America, except for Hawaii in the N Pacific. *Cap.:* Washington, D.C. Also called **Unit'ed States' of Amer'ica.**

u·ni·tize (yōō'ni tīz'), *v.t.,* **u·ni·tized, u·ni·tiz·ing. 1.** to make into a single unit. **2.** to make or separate into units.

u'nit pric'ing, the pricing of consumer goods in terms of a standard unit of measure, as so much per pound. —*u'nit price'.*

u'nit trust', *Brit.* See **mutual fund.**

u·ni·ty (yōō'ni tē), *n., pl.* **-ties. 1.** the state or quality of being one. **2.** the state of being combined with others to form a greater whole. **3.** harmony or agreement. **4.** complete accord among persons regarding attitudes, opinions, intentions, etc. **5.** *Math.* the number one. **6.** a harmonious combination of different parts, esp. in art or literature.

Univ., University.

univ., 1. universal. **2.** university.

u·ni·va·lent (yōō'nə vā'lənt, yōō niv'-ə-), *adj.* having a valence of one.

u·ni·valve (yōō'nə valv'), *n.* a mollusk having a single valve, as a snail.

u·ni·ver·sal (yōō'nə vûr'səl), *adj.* **1.** of or affecting all or the whole. **2.** existing or prevailing everywhere. **3.** in all cases or under all conditions. **4.** embracing many or all skills or fields: *a universal genius.* **5.** *Logic.* (of a proposition) asserted of every member of a class. —**u·ni·ver·sal'i·ty** (-vər sal'i tē), *n.* —**u'ni·ver'sal·ly,** *adv.*

U·ni·ver·sal·ist (yōō'nə vûr'sə list), *n.* a member of a denomination, officially merged with the Unitarians in 1961, that emphasizes the universal fatherhood of God and the final salvation of all people. —**U'ni·ver'sal·ism,** *n.*

u·ni·ver·sal·ize (yōō'nə vûr'sə līz'), *v.t.,* **-ized, -iz·ing.** to make universal. —**u'ni·ver'sal·i·za'tion,** *n.*

u'niver'sal joint', a coupling between rotating shafts that permits them to move in any direction. Also called **univer'sal cou'pling.**

u'niver'sal prod'uct code'. See **UPC.**

u·ni·verse (yōō'nə vûrs'), *n.* the totality of known or supposed objects and phenomena throughout space.

u·ni·ver·si·ty (yōō'nə vûr'si tē), *n., pl.* **-ties.** an institution of learning of the highest level, comprising one or more undergraduate colleges and graduate professional schools.

un·just (un just'), *adj.* not just or fair. —**un·just'ly,** *adv.* —**un·just'ness,** *n.*

un·kempt (un kempt'), *adj.* **1.** not combed, as hair. **2.** not neat or tidy. —**Syn.** disheveled, messy.

un·kind (un kīnd'), *adj.* **1.** not kind or considerate. **2.** without sympathy or mercy. —**un·kind'ness,** *n.*

un·kind·ly (un kīnd'lē), *adj.* **1.** not kindly. —*adv.* **2.** in an unkind manner.

un·know·ing (un nō'ing), *adj.* not knowing or aware. —**un·know'ing·ly,** *adv.*

un·known (un nōn'), *adj.* **1.** not known or recognized. **2.** not identified or ascertained. —*n.* **3.** an unknown person or thing.

un·lace (un lās'), *v.t.,* **-laced, -lac·ing.** to loosen the laces of.

un·latch (un lach'), *v.t., v.i.* to unfasten or open by lifting the latch.

un·law·ful (un lô'fəl), *adj.* **1.** against the law. **2.** born out of wedlock. —**un·law'ful·ly,** *adv.* —**un·law'ful·ness,** *n.*

un·learn (un lûrn'), *v.t., v.i.* to forget or lose knowledge (of).

un·learn·ed (un lûr'nid *for 1,* un-lûrnd' *for 2, 3*), *adj.* **1.** not learned or educated. **2.** not by study or training. **3.** indicating ignorance or lack of education.

un·leash (un lēsh'), *v.t.* to release from or as from a leash.

un·less (un les'), *conj.* except under the circumstances that.

un·let·tered (un let'ərd), *adj.* not well educated, esp. in literary culture.

un·like (un līk'), *adj.* **1.** not similar or identical. —*prep.* **2.** different from. **3.** not typical of. —**un·like'ness,** *n.*

un·like·ly (un līk'lē), *adj.* **1.** not likely to be or occur. **2.** not likely to succeed. —**un·like'li·hood', un·like'li·ness,** *n.* —**Syn. 1.** improbable.

un·lim·ber (un lim'bər), *v.t., v.i.* to make (something) ready for use or action.

un·lim·it·ed (un lim'i tid), *adj.* **1.** without limitations or restrictions. **2.** boundless or vast.

---

un·joint'ed, *adj.*	**un·kissed',** *adj.*	**un·leav'ened,** *adj.*
un·jus'ti·fi'a·ble, *adj.;* -bly, *adv.*	**un·know'a·ble,** *adj.*	**un·li'censed,** *adj.*
	un·la'beled, *adj.*	**un·life'like',** *adj.*
un·jus'ti·fied', *adj.*	**un·la'bored,** *adj.*	**un·light'ed,** *adj.*
un·kept', *adj.*	**un·la·ment'ed,** *adj.*	**un·lik'a·ble,** *adj.*
un·king'ly, *adj., adv.*	**un·lead'ed,** *adj.*	**un·lined',** *adj.*

un·load (un lōd′), v.t. 1. to take the load from. 2. to remove or discharge (a load). 3. to remove the charge from (a firearm). 4. to relieve of anything burdensome, oppressive, etc. 5. to get rid of by sale in volume. —v.i. 6. to unload something.

un·lock (un lok′), v.t. 1. to open or unfasten by releasing a lock. 2. to let loose, as one's emotions. 3. to reveal or disclose.

un·looked-for (un lŏŏkt′fôr′), adj. not expected or anticipated.

un·loose (un lōōs′), v.t., -loosed, -loosing. 1. to let loose or set free. 2. to loosen or relax, as one's grasp. Also, **un·loos′en.**

un·luck·y (un luk′ē), adj. 1. not lucky or fortunate. 2. bringing bad luck. —**un·luck′i·ly,** adv.

un·man (un man′), v.t., -manned, -man·ning. to break down the manly spirit of.

un·man·ly (un man′lē), adj. 1. lacking qualities considered desirable in a man. 2. not suitable for a man. —**un·man′li·ness,** n.

un·manned (un mand′), adj. without a human crew.

un·man·ner·ly (un man′ər lē), adj. not mannerly or polite. —**un·man′ner·li·ness,** n. —Syn. discourteous, rude.

un·mask (un mask′, -mäsk′), v.t., v.i. 1. to strip a mask or disguise (from). 2. to reveal the true character (of).

un·mean·ing (un mē′ning), adj. devoid of meaning or sense.

un·men·tion·a·ble (un men′shə nə bəl), adj. unfit or proper to be mentioned.

un·mer·ci·ful (un mûr′si fəl), adj. without mercy or pity. —**un·mer′ci·ful·ly,** adv.

un·mind·ful (un mīnd′fəl), adj. not mindful or careful.

un·mis·tak·a·ble (un′mi stā′kə bəl), adj. not capable of being mistaken or misunderstood. —**un′mis·tak′a·bly,** adv. —Syn. obvious, patent.

un·mit·i·gat·ed (un mit′ə gā′tid), adj. 1. not eased or lessened. 2. complete or absolute. —**un·mit′i·gat·ed·ly,** adv. —Syn. 2. unqualified.

un·mor·al (un môr′əl, -mor′-), adj. amoral. —**un′mo·ral′i·ty** (-mə ral′i·tē, -mô-), n.

un·nat·u·ral (un nach′ər əl, -nach′rəl), adj. 1. not natural or normal. 2. artificial or affected. 3. cruel or inhuman. —**un·nat′u·ral·ly,** adv. —**un·nat′u·ral·ness,** n.

un·nec·es·sar·y (un nes′i ser′ē), adj. not necessary or essential. —**un·nec′es·sar′i·ly** (-sâr′ə lē), adv. —**un·nec′es·sar′i·ness,** n.

un·nerve (un nûrv′), v.t., -nerved, -nerv·ing. to deprive of courage, strength, or determination.

un·num·bered (un num′bərd), adj. 1. not identified by numbers. 2. incapable of being numbered or counted.

un·ob·tru·sive (un′ob trōō′siv), adj. not obtrusive or conspicuous. —**un′ob·tru′sive·ly,** adv.

un·oc·cu·pied (un ok′yə pīd′), adj. 1. having no occupant or occupants. 2. not busy or at work.

un·or·gan·ized (un ôr′gə nīzd′), adj. 1. not formed into a systematized whole. 2. not organized into a labor union.

---

un·list′ed, adj.
un·lit′, adj.
un·liv′a·ble, adj.
un·lo′cat·ed, adj.
un·lov′a·ble, adj.
un·loved′, adj.
un·lov′ing, adj.
un·lu′bri·cat′ed, adj.
un·made′, adj.
un·mag′ni·fied′, adj.
un·man′age·a·ble, adj.
un′man·u·fac′tured, adj.
un·marked′, adj.
un·marred′, adj.
un·mar′riage·a·ble, adj.
un·mar′ried, adj.
un·mas′tered, adj.
un·matched′, adj.
un·meant′, adj.
un·meas′ured, adj.
un′me·chan′i·cal, adj.
un·med′i·cat′ed, adj.
un·me·lo′di·ous, adj.
un·melt′ed, adj.
un·mem′o·rized′, adj.
un·mend′ed, adj.

un·men′tioned, adj.
un·mer′it·ed, adj.
un′me·thod′i·cal, adj.
un·mil′i·tar′y, adj.
un·min′gled, adj.
un·mis·tak′en, adj.
un·mixed′, adj.
un·mold′ed, adj.
un′mo·lest′ed, adj.
un·mol′li·fied′, adj.
un·mo′ti·vat′ed, adj.
un·mount′ed, adj.
un·mourned′, adj.
un·mov′a·ble, adj.
un·moved′, adj.
un·mown′, adj.
un·muf′fle, v.t., -fled, -fling.
un·mu′si·cal, adj.
un·muz′zle, v.t.
un·name′a·ble, adj.
un·named′, adj.
un·nav′i·ga·ble, adj.
un·need′ed, adj.
un·need′ful, adj.; -ly, adv.
un′ne·go′ti·a·ble, adj.
un·neigh′bor·ly, adj.

un·no′tice·a·ble, adj.; -bly, adv.
un·no′ticed, adj.
un′ob·jec′tion·a·ble, adj.
un·ob·liged′, adj.
un′ob·lig′ing, adj.
un′ob·nox′ious, adj.
un′ob·scured′, adj.
un′ob·serv′ant, adj.
un′ob·served′, adj.
un′ob·serv′ing, adj.
un′ob·struct′ed, adj.
un′ob·tain′a·ble, adj.
un′ob·trud′ing, adj.
un′of·fend′ed, adj.
un′of·fend′ing, adj.
un′of·fen′sive, adj.; -ly, adv.
un·of′fered, adj.
un′of·fi′cial, adj.; -ly, adv.
un·o′pened, adj.
un′op·posed′, adj.
un′op·pressed′, adj.
un′or·dained′, adj.
un·o·rig′i·nal, adj.
un·or′na·ment′ed, adj.

un·pack (un pak'), *v.t.*, *v.i.* **1.** to empty (a container) of its contents. **2.** to remove (something) from a container.

un·par·al·leled (un par'ə leld'), *adj.* not paralleled or equaled.

un·per·son (un'pûr'sən), *n.* a person in great disfavor, esp. for political reasons, who is treated as though nonexistent.

un·pin (un pin'), *v.t.* **1.** to remove a pin from. **2.** to unfasten by removing a pin.

un·pleas·ant (un plez'ənt), *adj.* not pleasant or agreeable. —**un·pleas'ant·ly**, *adv.* —**un·pleas'ant·ness**, *n.* —**Syn.** disagreeable, obnoxious.

un·plug (un plug'), *v.t.* **1.** to pull out the plug of (something) from an electric outlet. **2.** to remove a plug or stopper from.

un·plumbed (un plumd'), *adj.* **1.** not measured with a plumb line. **2.** not deeply understood or explored.

un·pop·u·lar (un pop'yə lər), *adj.* not generally liked, approved, or accepted. —**un·pop·u·lar'i·ty** (-lar'i tē), *n.* —**un·pop'u·lar·ly**, *adv.*

un·prec·e·dent·ed (un pres'i den'tid), *adj.* without precedent or parallel.

un·pre·dict·a·ble (un'pri dik'tə bəl), *adj.* not capable of being predicted or foretold. —**un'pre·dict·a·bil'i·ty**, *n.* —**un'pre·dict'a·bly**, *adv.*

un·pre·ten·tious (un'pri ten'shəs), *adj.* not pretentious or affected. —**un'pre·ten'tious·ly**, *adv.* —**un'pre·ten'tious·ness**, *n.* —**Syn.** modest, simple.

un·prin·ci·pled (un prin'sə pəld), *adj.* lacking moral scruples or principles.

un·print·a·ble (un prin'tə bəl), *adj.* improper or unfit for print, as because of obscenity.

un·pro·fes·sion·al (un'prə fesh'ə nəl), *adj.* not professional, esp. contrary to professional standards or ethics.

un·prof·it·a·ble (un prof'i tə bəl), *adj.* not yielding profit or advantage. —**un·prof'it·a·bly**, *adv.*

un·qual·i·fied (un kwol'ə fīd'), *adj.* **1.** lacking the requisite qualifications. **2.** not modified or restricted in any way. —**un·qual'i·fied'ly**, *adv.*

un·ques·tion·a·ble (un kwes'chə nə bəl), *adj.* beyond doubt or dispute. —**un·ques'tion·a·bly**, *adv.*

un·quote (un kwōt'), *v.i.* to close a quotation (often used with the word *quote* opening the quotation).

---

un·or'tho·dox, *adj.;*
 -ly, *adv.*
un·os·ten·ta'tious, *adj.;*
 -ly, *adv.*
un·owned', *adj.*
un·pac'i·fied, *adj.*
un·paid', *adj.*
un·paint'ed, *adj.*
un·paired', *adj.*
un·pal'at·a·ble, *adj.;*
 -bly, *adv.*
un·par'don·a·ble, *adj.;*
 -bly, *adv.*
un·par'doned, *adj.*
un·pas'teur·ized', *adj.*
un·pat'ent·ed, *adj.*
un·pa·tri·ot'ic, *adj.*
un·paved', *adj.*
un·pay'ing, *adj.*
un·ped'i·greed', *adj.*
un·pen'e·trat'ed, *adj.*
un'per·ceived', *adj.*
un'per·cep'tive, *adj.;*
 -ly, *adv.*
un'per·fect'ed, *adj.*
un'per·formed', *adj.*
un'per·suad'ed, *adj.*
un'per·sua'sive, *adj.;*
 -ly, *adv.*
un'per·turb'a·ble, *adj.*
un'per·turbed', *adj.*
un·picked', *adj.*
un·pile', *v.t.*
un·pit'ied, *adj.*
un·pit'y·ing, *adj.*
un·placed', *adj.*
un·planned', *adj.*
un·plant'ed, *adj.*

un·play'a·ble, *adj.*
un·played', *adj.*
un·pleased', *adj.*
un·pleas'ing, *adj.*
un·pledged', *adj.*
un·plowed', *adj.*
un·po·et'ic, *adj.*
un·po·et'i·cal, *adj.;*
 -ly, *adv.*
un·point'ed, *adj.*
un·poised', *adj.*
un·po·lar·ized', *adj.*
un·pol'ished, *adj.*
un·po·lit'ic, *adj.*
un·po·lit'i·cal, *adj.*
un·polled', *adj.*
un·pol'lut'ed, *adj.*
un·pop'u·lat'ed, *adj.*
un·posed', *adj.*
un·pos·ses'sive, *adj.;*
 -ly, *adv.*
un·prac'ti·ca·ble, *adj.*
un·prac'ti·cal, *adj.*
un·prac'ticed, *adj.*
un·pre·dict'ed, *adj.*
un·prej'u·diced, *adj.*
un·pre·med'i·tat'ed, *adj.*
un·pre·pared', *adj.*
un·pre·par'ed·ness, *n.*
un·pre·pos·sess'ing, *adj.*
un·pre·scribed', *adj.*
un·pre·sent'a·ble, *adj.;*
 -bly, *adv.*
un·pre·served', *adj.*
un·pressed', *adj.*
un·pre·sump'tu·ous, *adj.*
un·pre·vent'a·ble, *adj.*
un·proc'essed, *adj.*

un'pro·claimed', *adj.*
un'pro·cur'a·ble, *adj.*
un'pro·duc'tive, *adj.;*
 -ly, *adv.;* -ness, *n.*
un'pro·fessed', *adj.*
un'pro·gres'sive, *adj.;*
 -ly, *adv.*
un'pro·hib'it·ed, *adj.*
un·prom'is·ing, *adj.*
un·prompt'ed, *adj.*
un'pro·nounce'a·ble,
 adj.
un'pro·nounced', *adj.*
un'pro·pi'tious, *adj.;*
 -ly, *adv.*
un'pro·por'tion·ate, *adj.;*
 -ly, *adv.*
un'pro·posed', *adj.*
un'pro·tect'ed, *adj.*
un'pro·test'ing, *adj.;*
 -ly, *adv.*
un·proved', *adj.*
un·prov'en, *adj.*
un'pro·vid'ed, *adj.*
un'pro·voked', *adj.*
un·pub'lished, *adj.*
un·punc'tu·al, *adj.*
un·pun'ished, *adj.*
un·pu'ri·fied, *adj.*
un·quench'a·ble, *adj.*
un·quenched', *adj.*
un·ques'tioned, *adj.*
un·ques'tion·ing, *adj.;*
 -ly, *adv.*
un·qui'et, *adj.*
un·quot'a·ble, *adj.*
un·raised', *adj.*
un·rat'ed, *adj.*

un·rav·el (un rav′əl), *v.t.* **1.** to separate the threads of. **2.** to make plain or clear, as a mystery. —*v.i.* **3.** to become unraveled.

un·read (un red′), *adj.* **1.** not read or perused. **2.** lacking in knowledge gained by reading.

un·re·al (un rē′əl, -rēl′), *adj.* **1.** not real or actual. **2.** imaginary or fanciful. —**un′re·al′i·ty** (-al′i tē), *n.*

un·rea·son·a·ble (un rē′zə nə bəl, -rēz′-nə-), *adj.* **1.** not reasonable or rational. **2.** excessive or exorbitant. —**un·rea′son·a·ble·ness,** *n.* —**un·rea′son·a·bly,** *adv.*

un·rea·son·ing (un rē′zə niñg), *adj.* not reasoning or exercising reason.

un·re·con·struct·ed (un′rē kən struk′tid), *adj.* stubbornly maintaining earlier positions, beliefs, etc.

un·re·gen·er·ate (un′ri jen′ər it), *adj.* **1.** not repentant or reformed. **2.** stubborn or obstinate.

un·re·lent·ing (un′ri len′tiñg), *adj.* **1.** not relenting or yielding. **2.** not slackening in speed, effort, vigor, etc. —**un′re·lent′ing·ly,** *adv.* —**Syn. 1.** implacable, inflexible.

un·re·mit·ting (un′ri mit′iñg), *adj.* not easing or ceasing. —**un′re·mit′ting·ly,** *adv.* —**Syn.** persistent.

un·re·served (un′ri zûrvd′), *adj.* **1.** without reservation or doubt. **2.** frank or open. **3.** not set aside in advance. —**un′re·serv′ed·ly** (-zûr′vid lē), *adv.*

un·rest (un rest′), *n.* **1.** strong dissatisfaction and disturbance. **2.** an uneasy state of mind: *political unrest.*

un·re·strained (un′rē strānd′), *adj.* **1.** not restrained or controlled. **2.** natural or spontaneous. —**un′re·strain′ed·ly,** *adv.*

un·ripe (un rīp′), *adj.* not ripe or mature.

un·ri·valed (un rī′vəld), *adj.* having no rival or competitor. Also, *Brit.,* **un·ri′valled.**

un·roll (un rōl′), *v.t.* **1.** to spread out (something rolled up). **2.** to display or reveal. —*v.i.* **3.** to become unrolled.

un·ruf·fled (un ruf′əld), *adj.* **1.** not agitated or upset. **2.** not ruffled, as a garment. —**Syn. 1.** calm, unperturbed.

un·ru·ly (un rōō′lē), *adj.,* **-li·er, -li·est.** difficult to discipline or rule. —**un·ru′li·ness,** *n.* —**Syn.** disorderly, turbulent.

UNRWA, United Nations Relief and Works Agency.

un·sad·dle (un sad′əl), *v.t., v.i.* to take the saddle from (a horse).

un·sat·u·rat·ed (un sach′ə rā′tid, *adj.* **1.** having the power to dissolve still more of a substance. **2.** *Chem.* having a double or triple bond and capable of forming compounds by addition. —**un·sat′u·rate** (-ər it, -ə rāt′), *n.*

---

un·read′a·ble, *adj.*
un′read′y, *adj.*
un′re·al·is′tic, *adj.*
un′re·al·is′ti·cal·ly, *adv.*
un′re·al′ized′, *adj.*
un′re·buked′, *adj.*
un′re·cep′tive, *adj.;*
   -ly, *adv.*
un′reck′oned, *adj.*
un′re·claimed′, *adj.*
un′rec′og·niz′a·ble, *adj.;*
   -ly, *adv.*
un′rec·og·nized′, *adj.*
un′rec·om·mend′ed, *adj.*
un′rec′om·pensed′, *adj.*
un′rec·on·cil′a·ble, *adj.;*
   -bly, *adv.*
un′rec·on·ciled′, *adj.*
un′re·cord′ed, *adj.*
un·rec′ti·fied, *adj.*
un′re·fined′, *adj.*
un′re·flect′ing, *adj.*
un′re·flec′tive, *adj.*
un′re·formed′, *adj.*
un′re·freshed′, *adj.*
un·reg′i·ment′ed, *adj.*
un·reg′is·tered, *adj.*
un·reg′u·lat′ed, *adj.*
un′re·hearsed′, *adj.*
un′re·lat′ed, *adj.*
un′re·li′a·ble, *adj.;* -bly, *adv.*
un′re·lieved′, *adj.*

un′re·mem′bered, *adj.*
un′re·morse′ful, *adj.;*
   -ly, *adv.*
un′re·mov′a·ble, *adj.*
un′re·moved′, *adj.*
un′re·mu′ner·at′ed, *adj.*
un′re·mu′ner·a′tive, *adj.*
un′re·newed′, *adj.*
un′rent′ed, *adj.*
un′re·paid′, *adj.*
un′re·pealed′, *adj.*
un′re·pent′ant, *adj.*
un′re·pent′ing, *adj.;*
   -ly, *adv.*
un′re·place′a·ble, *adj.*
un′re·placed′, *adj.*
un′re·port′ed, *adj.*
un′rep·re·sent′a·tive, *adj.*
un′rep·re·sent′ed, *adj.*
un′re·pressed′, *adj.*
un′re·prieved′, *adj.*
un′rep·ri·mand′ed, *adj.*
un′re·proved′, *adj.*
un′re·quit′ed, *adj.*
un′re·sent′ful, *adj.;*
   -ly, *adv.*
un′re·signed′, *adj.*
un′re·sist′ant, *adj.*
un′re·sist′ing, *adj.*
un′re·solved′, *adj.*
un′re·spect′ful, *adj.;*
   -ly, *adv.*

un′re·spon′sive, *adj.;*
   -ly, *adv.;* -ness, *n.*
un′re·strict′ed, *adj.;*
   -ly, *adv.*
un′re·tract′ed, *adj.*
un′re·turned′, *adj.*
un′re·vealed′, *adj.*
un′re·venged′, *adj.*
un′re·vised′, *adj.*
un′re·voked′, *adj.*
un′re·ward′ed, *adj.*
un′re·ward′ing, *adj.*
un·rhymed′, *adj.*
un·rhyth′mic, *adj.*
un·right′eous, *adj.*
un·ri′pened, *adj.*
un·ro·man′tic, *adj.*
un′ro·man′ti·cal·ly, *adv.*
un·roof′, *v.t.*
un·ruled′, *adj.*
un·safe′, *adj.;* -ly, *adv.*
un·said′, *adj.*
un′sal·a·bil′i·ty, *n.*
un·sal′a·ble, *adj.*
un·salt′ed, *adj.*
un·sanc′ti·fied′, *adj.*
un·sanc′tioned, *adj.*
un·san′i·tar′y, *adj.*
un·sa′ti·a·ble, *adj.;*
   -bly, *adv.*
un′sat·is·fac′to·ry, *adj.*
un·sat′is·fied′, *adj.*

un·sa·vor·y (un sā′və rē), *adj.* **1.** unpleasant in taste or smell. **2.** morally objectionable. **3.** *Obs.* without flavor or taste. —**un·sa′vor·i·ness,** *n.*

un·scathed (un skā t̸hd′), *adj.* not harmed or hurt.

un·schooled (un skōōld′), *adj.* not schooled, taught, or trained.

un·sci·en·tif·ic (un′sī ən tif′ik), *adj.* not scientific, esp. not conforming to the principles or methods of science. —**un′sci·en·tif′i·cal·ly,** *adv.*

un·scram·ble (un skram′bəl), *v.t.* **1.** to bring out of a scrambled condition. **2.** to make (a scrambled message) comprehensible.

un·screw (un skrōō′), *v.t.* **1.** to loosen a screw from. **2.** to open or remove by turning something.

un·scru·pu·lous (un skrōō′pyə ləs), *adj.* having no scruples or conscience. —**un·scru′pu·lous·ly,** *adv.* —**un·scru′pu·lous·ness,** *n.* —**Syn.** dishonorable, unprincipled.

un·seal (un sēl′), *v.t.* to break or remove the seal of.

un·sea·son·a·ble (un sē′zə nə bəl), *adj.* **1.** not suitable to or normal for the season. **2.** not at the proper time.

un·seat (un sēt′), *v.t.* **1.** to dislodge from a seat or a saddle. **2.** to remove from political office.

un·seem·ly (un sēm′lē), *adj.* **1.** not in keeping with established standards of taste or form. **2.** not suitable to the occasion. —**Syn.** improper, inappropriate.

un·self·ish (un sel′fish), *adj.* not selfish or egotistic. —**un·self′ish·ly,** *adv.* —**un·self′ish·ness,** *n.* —**Syn.** generous, magnanimous.

un·set·tle (un set′°l), *v.t.* **1.** to change from a settled state. **2.** to cause to become uncertain or disturbed. —*v.i.* **3.** to become unsettled. —**un·set′tle·ment,** *n.*

un·set·tled (un set′°ld), *adj.* **1.** not fixed or stable. **2** wavering or uncertain, as in behavior. **3.** undetermined, as a point at issue. **4.** not adjusted or paid, as an account. **5.** not populated, as a region.

un·shack·le (un shak′əl), *v.t.* to free from shackles.

un·sheathe (un shē t̸h′), *v.t.* to draw from a sheath, as a sword.

un·sight·ly (un sīt′lē), *adj.* unpleasant to look at. —**un·sight′li·ness,** *n.* —Syn. ugly, unattractive.

un·skilled (un skild′), *adj.* **1.** having no technical training or skill. **2.** not demanding special training or skill.

un·skill·ful (un skil′fəl), *adj.* not skillful or proficient. —**un·skill′ful·ly,** *adv.* —Syn. awkward, clumsy, inept.

un·snap (un snap′), *v.t.* to undo by or as by opening snaps.

un·snarl (un snärl′), *v.t.* to bring out of a snarled condition.

un·so·phis·ti·cat·ed (un′sə fis′tə kā′tid), *adj.* **1.** not sophisticated or worldly. **2.** not complex or intricate. —**un′so·phis′ti·cat′ed·ly,** *adv.* —Syn. artless, naive, ingenuous.

un·sound (un sound′), *adj.* **1.** not solid or firm, as foundations. **2.** not well-founded, as an argument. **3.** not physically or mentally healthy. —**un·sound′ly,** *adv.* —**un·sound′ness,** *n.*

un·spar·ing (un spâr′ing), *adj.* **1.** not sparing or frugal. **2.** not merciful or forgiving. —**un·spar′ing·ly,** *adv.* —**un·spar′ing·ness,** *n.*

un·speak·a·ble (un spē′kə bəl), *adj.* **1.** too great to express in words. **2.** extremely bad or objectionable. —**un·speak′a·bly,** *adv.*

un·saved′, *adj.*
un·scaled′, *adj.*
un·scarred′, *adj.*
un·scent′ed, *adj.*
un·sched′uled, *adj.*
un·schol′ar·ly, *adj.*
un·scratched′, *adj.*
un·screened′, *adj.*
un·scrip′tur·al, *adj.*
un·sealed′, *adj.*
un·sea′soned, *adj.*
un·sea′wor′thy, *adj.*
un′se·clud′ed, *adj.*
un′se·duced′, *adj.*
un·see′ing, *adj.;* -ly, *adv.*
un·seen′, *adj.*
un·seg′ment·ed, *adj.*
un·seg′re·gat′ed, *adj.*
un′se·lec′tive, *adj.*
un·self-con′scious, *adj.*
un·sen′si·ble, *adj.*
un·sen′si·tive, *adj.*
un·sent′, *adj.*
un·sen′ti·men′tal, *adj.*

un·served′, *adj.*
un·ser′vice·a·ble, *adj.*
un·shak′a·ble, *adj.*
un·sha′ken, *adj.*
un·shamed′, *adj.*
un·shape′ly, *adj.*
un·shared′, *adj.*
un·shaved′, *adj.*
un·shav′en, *adj.*
un·shed′, *adj.*
un·shelled′, *adj.*
un·shel′tered, *adj.*
un·shield′ed, *adj.*
un·shod′, *adj.*
un·shorn′, *adj.*
un·shrink′a·ble, *adj.*
un·shut′, *adj.*
un·sift′ed, *adj.*
un·sight′ed, *adj.*
un·signed′, *adj.*
un·si′lenced, *adj.*
un·sin′ful, *adj.*
un·sink′a·ble, *adj.*
un·slaked′, *adj.*

un·smil′ing, *adj.;* -ly, *adv.*
un·so′cia·ble, *adj.*
un·so′cial, *adj.;* -ly, *adv.*
un·soiled′, *adj.*
un·sold′, *adj.*
un′so·lic′it·ed, *adj.*
un′so·lic′i·tous, *adj.*
un·solv′a·ble, *adj.*
un·solved′, *adj.*
un·soothed′, *adj.*
un·sort′ed, *adj.*
un·sought′, *adj.*
un·spe′cial·ized′, *adj.*
un′spe·cif′ic, *adj.*
un′spe·cif′i·cal·ly, *adv.*
un·spec′i·fied′, *adj.*
un·spec′tac′u·lar, *adj.*
un·spent′, *adj.*
un·spir′i·tu·al, *adj.*
un·spoiled′, *adj.*
un·spo′ken, *adj.*
un·sports′man·like′, *adj.*
un·spot′ted, *adj.*
un·sprung′, *adj.*

un·sta·ble (un stā′bəl), adj. **1.** not firm or firmly fixed. **2.** liable to fall or change. **3.** not emotionally stable. **4.** Chem. tending to decompose easily. —**un·sta′ble·ness,** n. —**un·sta′bly,** adv.

un·stead·y (un sted′ē), adj. **1.** not steady or securely placed. **2.** fluctuating or wavering. **3.** irregular or uneven. —**un·stead′i·ly,** adv. —**un·stead′i·ness,** n.

un·stop (un stop′), v.t. **1.** to remove the stopper from. **2.** to free (a drain, etc.) from any obstruction.

un·strung (un strung′), adj. **1.** having the strings loosened or removed. **2.** weakened or nervously upset.

un·stud·ied (un stud′ēd), adj. **1.** not forced or contrived. **2.** not having studied or learned.

un·sub·stan·tial (un′səb stan′shəl), adj. **1.** lacking strength, firmness, or solidity. **2.** having no foundation in fact. **3.** without substance or reality. —**un′sub·stan′tial·ly,** adv.

un·suit·a·ble (un sōō′tə bəl), adj. not suitable or becoming. —**un·suit·a·bil′i·ty,** n. —**un·suit′a·bly,** adv.

un·sung (un sung′), adj. **1.** not sung. **2.** not celebrated in song or verse.

un·tan·gle (un tang′gəl), v.t. **1.** to bring out of a tangled state. **2.** to straighten out or clear up, as a problem.

un·taught (un tôt′), adj. **1.** not acquired by teaching. **2.** not educated or instructed.

un·think·a·ble (un thing′kə bəl), adj. **1.** not imaginable or conceivable. **2.** not to be considered.

un·think·ing (un thing′king), adj. not thinking, considerate, or heedful.

un·ti·dy (un tī′dē), adj. not tidy or neat. —**un·ti′di·ly,** adv. —**un·ti′di·ness,** n. —**Syn.** disorderly, sloppy.

un·tie (un tī′), v.t. **1.** to loose or unfasten (anything tied). **2.** to free from restraint. —v.i. **3.** to become untied.

un·til (un til′), conj. **1.** up to the time that or when: Wait until she comes. **2.** to the place or extent that: Go north until you see a lake. **3.** before: Don't leave until I return. —prep. **4.** onward to: He worked until 6 P.M. **5.** before: He did not go until night.

un·time·ly (un tīm′lē), adj. **1.** not occurring at a suitable time. **2.** happening too soon or too early. —adv. **3.** unseasonably or prematurely. —**un·time′li·ness,** n.

un·to (un′tōō, un′tə), prep. Archaic. **1.** to. **2.** until.

un·told (un tōld′), adj. **1.** too many or too much to be counted or measured. **2.** not told or revealed. —**Syn. 1.** incalculable, vast.

un·touch·a·ble (un tuch′ə bəl), adj. **1.** that may not or should not be touched. —n. **2.** (formerly) a member of the lowest caste in India. —**un·touch′a·bly,** adv.

un·to·ward (un tôrd′, -tōrd′), adj. **1.** unfavorable or not fortunate. **2.** Archaic. a. improper or unseemly. b. unruly or perverse.

---

un·stained′, adj.
un·stamped′, adj.
un·stand′ard·ized′, adj.
un·sta′pled, adj.
un·starched′, adj.
un·stemmed′, adj.
un·ster′ile, adj.
un·ster′i·lized′, adj.
un·stint′ed, adj.
un·stop′pa·ble, adj.
un·strained′, adj.
un·stressed′, adj.
un·struc′tured, adj.
un·sub·dued′, adj.
un′sub·mis′sive, adj.
un′sub·stan′ti·at·ed, adj.
un·sub′tle, adj.
un′suc·cess′ful, adj.; -ly, adv.
un·suit′ed, adj.
un·sul′lied, adj.
un′su·per·vised′, adj.
un′sup·port′ed, adj.; -ly, adv.
un′sup·pressed′, adj.
un′sup·press′i·ble, adj.
un·sure′, adj.; -ly, adv.; -ness, n.
un′sur·mount′a·ble, adj.

un′sur·pass′a·ble, adj.
un′sur·passed′, adj.
un′sur·prised′, adj.
un′sus·cep′ti·ble, adj.
un′sus·pect′ed, adj.
un′sus·pect′ing, adj.; -ly, adv.
un′sus·pi′cious, adj.; -ly, adv.
un′sus·tained′, adj.
un·swayed′, adj.
un·sweet′ened, adj.
un·swerv′ing, adj.
un′sym·met′ri·cal, adj.; -ly, adv.
un′sym·pa·thet′ic, adj.
un′sym·pa·thet′i·cal·ly, adv.
un′sys·tem·at′ic, adj.
un′sys·tem·at′i·cal, adj.; -ly, adv.
un·tact′ful, adj.; -ly, adv.
un·taint′ed, adj.
un·tal′ent·ed, adj.
un·tamed′, adj.
un·tanned′, adj.
un·tapped′, adj.
un·tar′nished, adj.
un·tast′ed, adj.

un·taste′ful, adj.
un·taxed′, adj.
un·teach′a·ble, adj.
un·tempt′ed, adj.
un·tempt′ing, adj.
un·ten′a·ble, adj.
un·ten′ant·ed, adj.
un·tend′ed, adj.
un·ter′mi·nat′ed, adj.
un·ter′ri·fied′, adj.
un·test′ed, adj.
un·thank′ful, adj.
un·thought′ful, adj.; -ly, adv.
un·thrift′y, adj.
un·till′a·ble, adj.
un·tilled′, adj.
un·tired′, adj.
un·tir′ing, adj.; -ly, adv.
un·tit′led, adj.
un·touched′, adj.
un·trace′a·ble, adj.
un·traced′, adj.
un·trac′ta·ble, adj.
un·trained′, adj.
un·tram′meled, adj.
un′trans·fer′a·ble, adj.
un′trans·ferred′, adj.
un′trans·formed′, adj.

un·true (un trōō′), *adj.* **1.** not true or factual. **2.** not faithful or loyal. **3.** incorrect or inaccurate.

un·truth (un trōōth′), *n.* **1.** something untrue, as a lie. **2.** the state or character of being untrue. —**un·truth′ful**, *adj.* —**un·truth′ful·ness**, *n.*

un·tu·tored (un tōō′tərd, -tyōō′-), *adj.* lacking formal education.

un·twist (un twist′), *v.t., v.i.* to bring out of a twisted condition.

un·used (un yōōzd′ *for 1, 2,* un yōōst′ *for 3*), *adj.* **1.** not put to use. **2.** never having been used. **3.** not accustomed.

un·u·su·al (un yōō′zhōō əl), *adj.* not usual, common, or ordinary. —**un·u′su·al·ly**, *adv.* —**un·u′su·al·ness**, *n.* —**Syn.** extraordinary, rare, remarkable, strange.

un·ut·ter·a·ble (un ut′ər ə bəl), *adj.* **1.** not communicable by speaking. **2.** not pronounceable. —**un·ut′ter·a·bly**, *adv.*

un·var·nished (un vär′nisht), *adj.* **1.** not coated with varnish. **2.** stated without embellishment or disguise: *the unvarnished truth.*

un·veil (un vāl′), *v.t.* **1.** to remove a veil or other covering from. **2.** to reveal or disclose, esp. for the first time. —*v.i.* **3.** to become unveiled.

un·voiced (un voist′), *adj.* **1.** not spoken or expressed. **2.** *Phonet.* voiceless (def. 2).

un·wary (un wâr′ē), *adj.* not watchful or cautious. —**un·war′i·ly**, *adv.* —**un·war′i·ness**, *n.* —**Syn.** needless, unsuspecting.

un·well (un wel′), *adj.* not well or healthy.

un·whole·some (un hōl′səm), *adj.* **1.** injurious to physical or mental health. **2.** unhealthy in appearance. **3.** morally harmful. —**un·whole′some·ly**, *adv.* —**un·whole′some·ness**, *n.*

un·wield·y (un wēl′dē), *adj.* not easily handled or managed, because of size, shape, or weight. —**un·wield′-i·ness**, *n.* —**Syn.** awkward, clumsy.

un·will·ing (un wil′ing), *adj.* **1.** not willing or inclined. **2.** not done or given willingly. —**un·will′ing·ly**, *adv.* —**un·will′ing·ness**, *n.*

un·wind (un wīnd′), *v.t.* **1.** to loosen from a coiled condition. **2.** to disentangle or disengage. —*v.i.* **3.** to become unwound. **4.** to relax, as from one's work.

un·wise (un wīz′), *adj.* lacking in wisdom or good sense. —**un·wise′ly**, *adv.*

un·wit·ting (un wit′ing), *adj.* **1.** not knowing or aware. **2.** not intentional or intended. —**un·wit′ting·ly**, *adv.*

un·wont·ed (un wōn′tid, -wôn′-, -wun′-), *adj.* not customary or habitual. —**un·wont′ed·ly**, *adv.*

un·wor·thy (un wûr′thē), *adj.* **1.** not worthy or deserving. **2.** not suitable or proper. —**un·wor′thi·ly**, *adv.* —**un·wor′thi·ness**, *n.*

un·wrap (un rap′), *v.t.* to remove the wrapping of.

un·writ·ten (un rit′ᵊn), *adj.* **1.** not put in writing or print. **2.** enforced by custom or tradition, as a certain law.

un·zip (un zip′), *v.t.* **1.** to open the zipper of. —*v.i.* **2.** to become unzipped.

up (up), *adv., prep., adj., n., v.,* **upped, up·ping.** —*adv.* **1.** to, toward, or in a higher position. **2.** to or in an erect position. **3.** out of bed. **4.** above the horizon. **5.** to or at any point that is considered higher. **6.** to or at a higher point or degree, as of rank, pitch, etc. **7.** to or at a point of equal advance, extent, etc.: *to catch up.* **8.** into or in activity, operation, etc.: *to stir up a fire.* **9.** into view or consideration: *The*

un·trans·lat′a·ble, *adj.*
un·trans·lat′ed, *adj.*
un·trav′eled, *adj.*
un·trav′ersed, *adj.*
un·treat′ed, *adj.*
un·tried′, *adj.*
un·trimmed′, *adj.*
un·trod′, *adj.*
un·trod′den, *adj.*
un·trou′bled, *adj.*
un·trust′ful, *adj.*
un·trust′wor′thy, *adj.*
un·typ′i·cal, *adj.;*
  -ly, *adv.*
un·us′a·ble, *adj.*
un·u′ti·lized′, *adj.*
un·ut′tered, *adj.*
un·vac′ci·nat′ed, *adj.*
un·van′quished, *adj.*
un·var′ied, *adj.*
un·var′y·ing, *adj.;*
  -ly, *adv.*

un·ven′ti·lat′ed, *adj.*
un·ven′ture·some, *adj.*
un·ver′i·fi′able, *adj.*
un·ver′i·fied′, *adj.*
un·versed′, *adj.*
un·vexed′, *adj.*
un·vis′it·ed, *adj.*
un·want′ed, *adj.*
un·warmed′, *adj.*
un·warned′, *adj.*
un·war′rant·ed, *adj.*
un·washed′, *adj.*
un·watched′, *adj.*
un·wa′ver·ing, *adj.;*
  -ly, *adv.*
un·waxed′, *adj.*
un·weak′ened, *adj.*
un·weaned′, *adj.*
un·wear′a·ble, *adj.*
un·wea′ry, *adj.*
un·wea′ry·ing, *adj.*
un·weave′, *v.i.*

un·wed′, *adj.*
un·wel′come, *adj.*
un·wept′, *adj.*
un·wife′ly, *adj.*
un·wished′, *adj.*
un·wished′-for, *adj.*
un·wit′nessed, *adj.*
un·wom′an·ly, *adj.*
un·won′, *adj.*
un·work′a·ble, *adj.*
un·worked′, *adj.*
un·world′ly, *adj.*
un·worn′, *adj.*
un·wor′ried, *adj.*
un·wov′en, *adj.*
un·wrin′kle, *v.t.,* -kled,
  -kling.
un·yield′ing, *adj.;*
  -ly, *adv.*
un·yoke′, *v.t.*
un·zeal′ous, *adj.;* -ly, *adv.*

lost papers have turned up. **10.** into or in a place of safekeeping, storage, etc.: *to lay up riches.* **11.** into or in a state of union, contraction, etc.: *to fold up.* **11.** to the final point: *to be used up.* **13.** to an end: *He finished it up.* **14.** to a halt. **15.** *Baseball.* at bat. **16.** ahead in points or games. **17.** each: *The score was seven up.* **18. up against,** *Informal.* faced with. **19. up to, a.** as far as. **b.** to the limit of. **c.** capable of. **d.** dependent upon. **e.** engaged in or doing. **20. up with!** reinstate! *Up with the true king!* —*prep.* **21.** to, toward, or at a higher place on or in. **22.** at or to a farther point on. **23.** toward the source or origin of: *up the stream.* **24.** in the interior of (a region). **25.** in a direction contrary to that of. —*adj.* **26.** moving in a direction that is up or is regarded as up. **27.** concluded or ended: *Your time is up.* **28.** going on or happening: *What's up over there?* **29.** in a high condition or position. **30.** in an erect or raised position. **31.** risen above the horizon. **32.** out of bed. **33.** built or constructed. **34.** in a state of agitation or excitement. **35.** higher than: *The price of meat was up.* **36.** in a legal proceeding as defendant: *He is up for murder.* **37.** *Informal.* informed or familiar: *up on current events.* **38.** ahead or in advance, as in a game. **39.** under consideration: *a candidate up for reelection.* **40.** wagered or bet. —*n.* **41.** an upward movement. **42.** an upward slope. **43. on the up and up,** *Informal.* frank or honest. —*v.t.* *Informal.* **44.** to increase or step up. **45.** to raise, as prices. —*v.i.* **46.** *Informal.* to begin something abruptly: *They upped and eloped.*

up-, a combining form meaning "up": *upland.*

up-and-com·ing (up′ən kum′iŋ), *adj.* industrious and likely to succeed.

up·beat (up′bēt′), *n.* **1.** *Music.* an unaccented beat, esp. immediately preceding a downbeat. —*adj.* **2.** optimistic or happy.

up·braid (up brād′), *v.t.* to reproach severely. —**up·braid′er,** *n.*

up·bring·ing (up′briŋ′iŋ), *n.* the care and training of the young.

UPC, the postage-stamp-size series of short black lines imprinted on each package to expedite checkout by an electronic cash register, as in a supermarket. [*u*(*niversal*) *p*(*roduct*) *c*(*ode*)]

up·chuck (up′chuk′), *v.i., v.t. Slang.* to vomit.

up·com·ing (up′kum′iŋ), *adj.* about to take place or appear.

up·coun·try (up′kun′trē), *adj., adv.* **1.** of, toward, or pertaining to the interior of a country. —*n.* **2.** the interior of a country.

up·date (up dāt′, up′dāt′), *v.,* **-dat·ed, -dat·ing,** *n.* —*v.t.* **1.** to bring up to date. —*n.* **2.** information or data updated. —**up′dat′a·ble,** *adj.*

up·draft (up′draft′, -dräft′), *n.* the movement upward of air.

up·end (up end′), *v.t.* **1.** to set on end, as a barrel. —*v.i.* **2.** to become upended.

up·front (up′frunt′), *adj. Informal.* **1.** invested in advance of actual earnings. **2.** conspicuous or prominent. **3.** open or straightforward.

up·grade (*n.* up′grād′, *v.* up′grād′), *n., v.,* **-grad·ed, -grad·ing.** —*n.* **1.** an upward incline or slope. **2.** an increase or improvement. —*v.t.* **3.** to raise to a higher grade, position, or quality.

up·heav·al (up hē′vəl), *n.* **1.** a thrusting upward, esp. of a part of the earth's crust. **2.** violent change or disturbance.

up·hill (up′hil′), *adv.* **1.** up the slope of a hill. **2.** against adversity or difficulties. —*adj.* **3.** going upward on a hill. **4.** laboriously difficult.

up·hold (up hōld′), *v.t.,* **-held, -holding. 1.** to support or defend, as against opposition or criticism. **2.** to keep from sinking. **3.** to lift upward. —**up·hold′er,** *n.*

up·hol·ster (up hōl′stər, ə pōl′-), *v.t.* to provide (sofas, etc.) with fabric, springs, padding, etc. —**up·hol′ster·er,** *n.*

up·hol·ster·y (up hōl′stə rē, ə pōl′-), *n., pl.* **-ster·ies. 1.** the material used in upholstering. **2.** the business of an upholsterer.

UPI, United Press International.

up·keep (up′kēp′), *n.* **1.** the act or state of maintaining in good condition or state of repair. **2.** the cost for this.

up·land (up′lənd, -land′), *n.* land elevated above other land.

up·lift (*v.* up lift′, *n.* up′lift′), *v.t.* **1.** to improve socially, culturally, or morally. **2.** to lift up. —*n.* **3.** an act of lifting up. **4.** a movement to improve social, cultural, or moral conditions. —**up·lift′ment,** *n.*

up·most (up′mōst′), *adj.* uppermost.

up·on (ə pon′, ə pôn′), *prep.* on (usually used more formally or in certain idiomatic phrases).

up·per (up′ər), *adj.* **1.** higher in place or in rank. **2.** noting the smaller branch of a bicameral legislature. **3.** (*often cap.*) noting a later division of a geological period. —*n.* **4.** the part of a shoe above the sole. **5.** *Slang.* a stimulant drug, esp. an amphetamine.

up′per case′, *Print.* capital letters as distinguished from small letters. —**up′per-case′**, *adj.*

up′per class′, a social class comprising the people of the highest status in society. —**up′per-class′**, *adj.*

up·per·class·man (up′ər klas′mən, -kläs′-), *n.* a junior or senior in a secondary school or college.

up′per crust′, *Informal.* the highest social class.

up·per·cut (up′ər kut′), *n.* a swinging blow directed upward, as to an opponent's chin, esp. in boxing.

up′per hand′, the dominating or controlling position.

up·per·most (up′ər mōst′), *adj.* **1.** highest in place or rank. —*adv.* **2.** in or into the highest place or rank.

Up′per Vol′ta (vōl′tə), a country in W Africa.

up·pish (up′ish), *adj. Chiefly Brit. Informal.* uppity.

up·pi·ty (up′i tē), *adj. Informal.* inclined to be haughty or snobbish.

up·raise (up rāz′), *v.t.* to raise or lift up. Also, **up·rear′.**

up·right (up′rīt′, up rīt′), *adj.* **1.** in a position corresponding to that of a person standing up. **2.** righteous or honest. —*n.* **3.** the state of being upright. **4.** something upright. —*adv.* **5.** in an upright position or direction. —**up′right′ly**, *adv.* —**up′right′ness**, *n.* —**Syn. 1.** erect, perpendicular, vertical.

up′right pian′o, a piano with an upright rectangular case.

up·ris·ing (up′rī′zing, up rī′zing), *n.* an outbreak, usually localized, against a government.

up·roar (up′rōr′, -rôr′), *n.* a state of clamor and tumult.

up·roar·i·ous (up rōr′ē əs, -rôr′-), *adj.* **1.** in a state of uproar. **2.** very funny or loud. —**up·roar′i·ous·ly**, *adv.* —**up·roar′i·ous·ness**, *n.*

up·root (up rōōt′, -rōōt′), *v.t.* **1.** to pull out by or as if by the roots, esp. so as to destroy. **2.** to remove violently from a native place or environment.

UPS, United Parcel Service.

ups′ and downs′, good and bad times.

up·scale (up′skāl′), *Slang.* —*n.* **1.** a segment of the population considered above average in income and education. —*adj.* **2.** of or characteristic of people in such a segment.

up·set (*v.,* *adj.,* up set′, *n.* up′set′), *v.,* -set, -set·ting, *n.,* *adj.* —*v.t.* **1.** to turn or tip over. **2.** to throw into disorder or confusion. **3.** to disturb emotionally. **4.** to disturb physically. **5.** to defeat (an opponent that is favored). —*v.i.* **6.** to become upset. —*n.* **7.** an upsetting or instance of being upset. **8.** the unexpected defeat of a person or group that is

favored. **9.** a disturbance or distress. **10.** a disordered or confused arrangement. —*adj.* **11.** disturbed or distressed. **12.** disordered or confused. **13.** turned or tipped over. —**Syn. 3.** agitate, perturb, worry.

up·shift (up′shift′), *v.i.* **1.** to shift the automobile transmission into a higher gear. —*n.* **2.** the act or instance of upshifting.

up·shot (up′shot′), *n.* the final issue.

up·side (up′sīd′), *n.* the upper side.

up′side down′, **1.** with the upper part down. **2.** in or into complete disorder. —**up′side-down′**, *adj.*

up·si·lon (yōōp′sə lon′), *n.* the 20th letter of the Greek alphabet (Υ, υ).

up·stage (up′stāj′), *adv.,* *adj.,* *v.,* -staged, -stag·ing. —*adv.* **1.** on or toward the back of the stage. —*adj.* **2.** of the back of the stage. —*v.t.* **3.** to force (another actor or actress) to act with back to the audience by moving upstage. **4.** to behave snobbishly toward.

up·stairs (up′stârz′), *adv.* **1.** up the stairs. **2.** to or on an upper floor. —*adj.* **3.** of or situated on an upper floor. —*n.* **4.** an upper floor.

up·stand·ing (up stan′ding), *adj.* **1.** standing erect. **2.** upright or honest.

up·start (up′stärt′), *n.* **1.** a person who has risen suddenly from a humble position to wealth or power. **2.** a presumptuous and objectionable person who has so risen. —*adj.* **3.** being or like an upstart.

up·state (up′stāt′), *n.* **1.** the part of a state that is farther north from a chief city. —*adj.,* *adv.* **2.** of, to, or from such an area.

up·stream (up′strēm′), *adv.,* *adj.* toward or in the higher part of a stream.

up·stroke (up′strōk′), *n.* an upward stroke, esp. of a pen.

up·surge (up′sûrj′), *n.* a rapid or sudden increase.

up·swing (up′swing′), *n.* an upward swing, trend, or movement.

up·take (up′tāk′), *n.* **1.** mental grasp: *quick on the uptake.* **2.** a pipe for drawing up smoke or air, as from a mine.

up·tight (up′tīt′), *adj. Slang.* tense, nervous, or jittery. —**up′tight′ness**, *n.*

up-to-date (up′tə dāt′), *adj.* **1.** extending to the present time. **2.** according to the latest ideas, styles, etc. —**up′-to-date′ness**, *n.*

up·town (*adv.,* *n.* up′toun′, *adj.* up′-toun′), *adv.* **1.** to, toward, or in the upper part of a town or city. —*n.* **2.** the uptown section of a town or city.

up·turn (*v.* up tûrn′, *n.* up′tûrn′), *v.t.,* *v.i.* **1.** to turn up or over. —*n.* **2.** an upward turn, as in prices or business.

up·ward (up'wərd), *adv.* Also, **up'wards. 1.** toward a higher place, position, or level. **2. upward** or **upwards of,** more than. —*adj.* **3.** moving or tending upward. —**up'ward·ly,** *adv.* —**up'ward·ness,** *n.*

up'ward mobil'ity, movement from one social level to a higher one.

u·ra·cil (yŏŏr'ə sil), *n.* a crystalline solid used in biochemical research.

U'ral Moun'tains (yŏŏr'əl), a mountain range in the W Soviet Union, forming a natural boundary between Europe and Asia.

u·ran·ic (yŏŏ ran'ik), *adj.* of or containing uranium.

u·ra·ni·um (yŏŏ rā'nē əm), *n. Chem.* a radioactive, metallic element, used in nuclear weapons and as a nuclear fuel. *Symbol:* U; *at. wt.:* 238.03; *at. no.:* 92.

U·ra·nus (yŏŏr'ə nəs, yŏŏ rā'-), *n.* the planet seventh in order from the sun. —**U·ra·ni·an** (yŏŏ rā'nē ən), *adj.*

urb (urb), *n. Informal.* an urban area, as contrasted with its surrounding suburbs.

ur·ban (ûr'bən), *adj.* **1.** of, in, or comprising cities. **2.** characteristic of cities. [< L *urbān(us)* < *urbs* city]

ur·bane (ûr bān'), *adj.* having the polish of sophisticated social life in cities. —**ur·bane'ly,** *adv.* —**ur·ban'i·ty** (-ban'i tē), *n.* —**Syn.** refined, suave, worldly.

ur'ban guerril'la, a member of any underground political group in cities engaged in sporadic violence, kidnapping, etc.

ur·ban·ite (ûr'bə nīt'), *n.* a resident of a city.

ur·ban·ize (ûr'bə nīz'), *v.t.,* **-ized, -izing.** to make urban, as in character or nature. —**ur'ban·i·za'tion,** *n.*

ur·ban·ol·o·gy (ûr'bən ol'ə jē), *n.* the study of urban problems. —**ur'ban·ol'o·gist,** *n.*

ur'ban renew'al, rehabilitation of city areas by demolishing, remodeling, or repairing existing structures in accordance with comprehensive plans.

ur'ban sprawl', the uncontrolled spread of urban development into neighboring regions.

ur·chin (ûr'chin), *n.* **1.** a small, mischievous boy. **2.** a neglected, waiflike child.

Ur·du (ŏŏr'dŏŏ, ûr'-), *n.* one of the official languages of Pakistan.

-ure, a suffix meaning: a. action or result of an action: *pressure.* b. means or instrument: *legislature.*

u·re·a (yŏŏ rē'ə, yŏŏr'ē ə), *n.* **1.** a compound occurring in urine and other body fluids. **2.** a commercial

form of this compound used as a fertilizer.

u·re·mi·a (yŏŏ rē'mē ə), *n.* a disease resulting from accumulation in the blood of substances normally excreted in the urine. —**u·re'mic,** *adj.*

u·re·ter (yŏŏ rē'tər), *n.* a muscular duct carrying urine from a kidney to the bladder.

u·re·thra (yŏŏ rē'thrə), *n., pl.* **-thras, -thrae** (thrē). the canal that extends from the urinary bladder to the exterior and that in the male carries semen as well as urine. —**u·re'thral,** *adj.*

urge (ûrj), *v.,* **urged, urg·ing,** *n.* —*v.t.* **1.** to try to persuade, as by entreaties. **2.** to impel or move to some action. **3.** to recommend or advocate earnestly. **4.** to drive to speed or effort. —*n.* **5.** an act of urging. **6.** a strong impulse.

ur·gent (ûr'jənt), *adj.* **1.** requiring immediate action or attention. **2.** insistent or earnest. —**ur'gent·ly,** *adv.* —**ur'gen·cy,** *n.* —**Syn. 1.** critical, imperative, pressing.

-urgy, a combining form meaning "work or technique": *metallurgy.*

u·ric (yŏŏr'ik), *n.* found in or derived from urine: *uric acid.*

u·ri·nal (yŏŏr'ə nəl), *n.* **1.** a wall fixture for men's use in urinating. **2.** a place having such a fixture or fixtures. **3.** a receptacle for urine.

u·ri·nal·y·sis (yŏŏr'ə nal'i sis), *n.* microscopic or chemical analysis of urine.

u·ri·nar·y (yŏŏr'ə ner'ē), *adj.* **1.** of or pertaining to urine. **2.** pertaining to the organs secreting and discharging urine.

u'rinary blad'der, a membranous sac in which the urine is retained until it is discharged from the body.

u·ri·nate (yŏŏr'ə nāt'), *v.i.,* **-nat·ed, -nat·ing.** to discharge urine.

u·rine (yŏŏr'in), *n.* the liquid excreted by the kidneys and discharged from the body as waste matter.

urn (ûrn), *n.* **1.** a vase with an ornamental pedestal. **2.** a vase for holding the ashes of the cremated dead. **3.** a container with a spigot, used for making tea or coffee in quantity.

u·ro·gen·i·tal (yŏŏr'ō jen'i təl), *adj.* genitourinary.

u·rol·o·gy (yŏŏ rol'ə jē), *n.* a branch of medicine dealing with the genitourinary and urinary tracts and their disorders. —**u·ro·log·ic** (yŏŏr'ə loj'ik), **u'ro·log'i·cal,** *adj.* —**u·rol'o·gist,** *n.*

Ur'sa Ma'jor (ûr'sə), the most prominent northern constellation containing the seven stars that form the Big Dipper.

Ur'sa Mi'nor, the most northern constellation containing the stars that form the Little Dipper, the outermost of which, at the end of the handle, is Polaris.

ur·sine (ûr'sīn, -sin), *adj.* of or resembling a bear.

ur·ti·car·i·a (ûr'tə kâr'ē ə), *n.* skin condition characterized by pale, irregular patches and severe itching.

U·ru·guay (yŏŏr'ə gwä', -gwī'), *n.* a country in SE South America.

us (us), *pron.* the objective case of we.

U.S., See **United States.** Also, **US**

u.s., *Law.* 1. where mentioned above. [< L *ubi supra*] 2. as above. [< L *ut supra*]

U.S.A., 1. United States Army. 2. United States of America. Also, **USA**

us·a·ble (yŏŏ'zə bəl), *adj.* 1. capable of being used. 2. available for use. Also, **use'a·ble.** —**us/a·bil/i·ty, use/a·bil/i·ty, us/a·ble·ness,** *n.*

USAF, United States Air Force.

us·age (yŏŏ'sij, -zij), *n.* 1. manner of doing or handling something. 2. the customary manner of using words and phrases. 3. a particular instance of this. 4. customary or habitual practice.

USCG, United States Coast Guard.

USDA, United States Department of Agriculture.

use (*v.* yŏŏz, *n.* yŏŏs), *v.,* **used, using,** *n.* —*v.t.* 1. to make (something) serve a particular purpose or end. 2. to expend or consume: *to use up the entire allowance.* 3. *Informal.* to take unfair advantage of. 4. to habitually drink or smoke. 5. **used to, a.** was or were in the habit of. **b.** accustomed to. —*n.* 6. the act of using or state of being used. 7. a way of using something. 8. a purpose for which something is used. 9. the power or right of using something. 10. help or profit. 11. occasion or need. 12. continued or repeated practice. 13. **have no use for, a.** to have no occasion or need for. **b.** to dislike. —**us'er,** *n.* —**Syn.** 1. employ, utilize.

used (yŏŏzd), *adj.* having former ownership: *a used car.*

use·ful (yŏŏs'fəl), *adj.* of practical or beneficial use. —**use'ful·ly,** *adv.* —**use'ful·ness,** *n.* —**Syn.** advantageous, serviceable.

use·less (yŏŏs'lis), *adj.* having no practical or beneficial use. —**Syn.** futile, vain, worthless.

USES, United States Employment Service.

ush·er (ush'ər), *n.* 1. a person who escorts people to seats in a church,

theater, etc. 2. a bridegroom's attendant at a wedding. 3. an official having the care of a door, as in a courtroom. —*v.t.* 4. to act as an usher to. 5. to precede or herald: *They ushered in the new theater season.* —**ush/er·ette/** (-ret'), *n.fem.*

USIA, (formerly) United States Information Agency.

USICA, United States International Communication Agency.

USM, United States Mail.

USMC, United States Marine Corps.

USN, United States Navy.

USO, United Service Organizations.

U.S.P., United States Pharmacopeia.

U.S.S., United States Ship.

U.S.S.R., Union of Soviet Socialist Republics. Also, **USSR**

usu., 1. usual. 2. usually.

u·su·al (yŏŏ'zhŏŏ əl, -zhwəl), *adj.* 1. commonly met with or observed in experience. 2. customary or habitual. —**u/su·al·ly,** *adv.* —**u/su·al·ness,** *n.*

u·surp (yŏŏ sûrp', -zûrp'), *v.t., v.i.* to seize and hold (a position, power, etc.) by force or without legal right. —**u·sur·pa·tion** (yŏŏ'sər pā'shən, -zər-), *n.* —**u·surp'er,** *n.*

u·su·ry (yŏŏ'zhə rē), *n., pl.* **-ries.** 1. the lending of money at an exorbitant interest rate. 2. such an interest rate. —**u/su·rer,** *n.* —**u·su·ri·ous** (yŏŏ zhŏŏr'ē əs), *adj.*

UT, Utah. Also, **Ut.**

U·tah (yŏŏ'tô, yŏŏ'tä), *n.* a state in the W U.S. *Cap.:* Salt Lake City.

u·ten·sil (yŏŏ ten'səl), *n.* an instrument or container commonly used in a kitchen.

u·ter·us (yŏŏ'tər əs), *n., pl.* **-ter·i** (-tə-rī'), **-us·es.** the organ of female mammals in which the young develop before birth. —**u/ter·ine** (-in, -tə rīn'), *adj.*

u·tile (yŏŏ'til), *adj. Obs.* useful.

u·til·i·tar·i·an (yŏŏ til/i târ/ē ən), *adj.* 1. of or pertaining to utility. 2. emphasizing usefulness rather than beauty or ornamentation. —**u·til/i·tar/i·an·ism** (-ə niz/əm), *n.*

u·til·i·ty (yŏŏ til/i tē), *n., pl.* **-ties.** 1. the state or quality of being useful. 2. a business enterprise supplying an essential public service, as electricity or gas.

util'ity room', a room containing appliances needed for the upkeep of an establishment.

u·ti·lize (yŏŏt'°līz'), *v.t.,* **-lized, -lizing.** to put to practical or profitable use.

ut·most (ut'mōst'), *adj.* 1. of the greatest degree or amount. 2. being at the farthest point or limit. —*n.* 3. the greatest degree or amount.

U·to·pi·a (yōō tō′pē ə), n. (sometimes l.c.) 1. a place or state of political or social perfection. 2. any visionary system for such perfection. [from imaginary island in Sir Thomas More's Utopia (1516); < NL < Gk ou not + tóp(os) place + -ia] —U·to′pi·an, u·to′pi·an, adj., n.

ut·ter¹ (ut′ər), v.t. 1. to give audible expression to, usually in spoken words. 2. to give forth a sound. —ut′ter·er, n.

ut·ter² (ut′ər), adj. 1. complete in the greatest degree. 2. unconditional or unqualified. —ut′ter·ly, adv.

ut·ter·ance (ut′ər əns), n. 1. a word or words uttered. 2. an act of uttering. 3. a manner of speaking.

ut·ter·most (ut′ər mōst′), adj., n. utmost.

UV, ultraviolet.

u·vu·la (yōō′vyə lə), n., pl. -las, -lae (-lē′). the small mass of tissue hanging downward from the middle of the soft palate. —u′vu·lar, adj.

U/W, underwriter.

ux., Law. wife. [< L uxor]

ux·o·ri·ous (uk sōr′ē əs, -sôr′-, ugzōr′-, -zôr′-), adj. foolishly fond of or extremely submissive to one's wife. —ux·o′ri·ous·ly, adv. —ux·o′ri·ous·ness, n.

V

V, v (vē), n., pl. V's or Vs, v's or vs. 1. the 22nd letter of the English alphabet, a consonant. 2. something having the form of a V.

V, 1. Math. vector. 2. velocity. 3. victory. 4. volt; volts.

V, 1. the Roman numeral for 5. 2. vanadium.

v, 1. velocity. 2. volt; volts.

V., 1. Vice. 2. Village.

v., 1. verb. 2. verse. 3. version. 4. versus. 5. vide. 6. voice. 7. voltage. 8. volume.

VA, 1. Veterans Administration. 2. Vice Admiral. 3. Virginia.

Va., Virginia.

va·can·cy (vā′kən sē), n., pl. -cies. 1. an unoccupied or uninhabited place, esp. one for rent. 2. an unfilled or unheld position or office. 3. the state of being vacant.

va·cant (vā′kənt), adj. 1. not occupied or inhabited, as a house. 2. not filled or held, as a job or position. 3. lacking in thoughtfulness or intelligence: a vacant expression. 4. free from activity or care: vacant hours. —Syn. 1, 2. empty. 3. blank, inane, vacuous.

va·cate (vā′kāt), v.t., -cat·ed, -cat·ing. 1. to cause (a house or position) to be vacant. 2. Law. to make inoperative.

va·ca·tion (vā kā′shən, və-), n. 1. a period of rest or freedom from regular work, study, etc. —v.i. 2. to take or have a vacation. —va·ca′tion·er, va·ca′tion·ist, n.

vac·ci·nate (vak′sə nāt′), v.t., v.i., -nat·ed, -nat·ing. to inject a vaccine into (a person) to protect against a disease, as smallpox or diphtheria. —vac′ci·na′tion, n. —vac′ci·na′tor, n.

vac·cine (vak sēn′, vak′sēn), n. 1. the virus of cowpox used in vaccination against smallpox. 2. the modified virus of any of various other diseases, used in vaccinations.

vac·cin·i·a (vak sin′ē ə), n. cowpox.

vac·il·late (vas′ə lāt′), v.i., -lat·ed, -lat·ing. 1. to sway unsteadily. 2. to shift back and forth between two courses of action. —vac′il·la′tion, n. —vac′il·la′tor, n.

va·cu·i·ty (va kyōō′i tē), n., pl. -ties. 1. absence of ideas or intelligence. 2. a statement revealing such absence. 3. the state of being vacuous. 4. an empty space.

vac·u·ole (vak′yōō ōl′), n. Biol. a cavity within a cell, often containing a watery liquid. —vac·u·o′lar (-ō′lər), adj.

vac·u·ous (vak′yōō əs), adj. 1. lacking in ideas or intelligence. 2. containing a vacuum. —vac′u·ous·ly, adv. —vac′u·ous·ness, n.

vac·u·um (vak′yōō əm, -yōōm), n., pl. -ums, -a (-ə), v. —n. 1. a space entirely devoid of matter. 2. an enclosed space from which air has been partially removed. 3. anything suggesting emptiness. —v.t., v.i. 4. to clean with a vacuum cleaner.

vac′uum bot′tle, a flask having a double wall enclosing a vacuum, used for keeping liquids hot or cold.

vac′uum clean′er, an electrical appliance for cleaning carpets or floors by suction.

vac·u·um-packed (vak′yōō əm pakt′, vak′yōōm-), *adj.* having as much air as possible evacuated before sealing, chiefly to keep freshness.

vac′uum tube′, an electron tube evacuated to a high vacuum.

va·de me·cum (vā′dē mē′kəm, vä′-), *pl.* **va·de me·cums.** *Latin.* something frequently carried about, as a handbook. [< L lit., go with me]

VADM, Vice Admiral.

vag·a·bond (vag′ə bond′), *adj.* **1.** wandering from place to place without any settled home. **2.** leading an unsettled or carefree life. **3.** a person leading a vagabond life. —*n.* **3.** a person leading a vagabond life. —**vag′a·bond′age,** *n.*

va·gar·y (və gãr′ē, vā′gə rē), *n., pl.* **-gar·ies. 1.** an unpredictable or erratic action. **2.** a whimsical or wild idea. —**va·gar′i·ous,** *adj.*

va·gi·na (və jī′nə), *n., pl.* **-nas, -nae** (-nē) the passage leading from the uterus to the vulva. —**vag·i·nal** (vaj′ə nəl), *adj.*

vag·i·ni·tis (vaj′ə nī′tis), *n.* inflammation of the vagina.

va·grant (vā′grənt), *n.* **1.** a person who wanders about with no settled home or job, subsisting usually by begging. —*adj.* **2.** of or characteristic of a vagrant. **3.** not fixed or settled, esp. in course. —**va′gran·cy,** *n.* —**va′grant·ly,** *adv.*

va·grom (vā′grəm), *adj. Archaic.* vagrant.

vague (vāg), *adj.,* **va·guer, va·guest. 1.** not expressed or understood in a clear or precise way. **2.** indefinite in nature, character, or form. —**vague′ly,** *adv.* —**vague′ness,** *n.* —**Syn. 1.** ambiguous, imprecise. **2.** obscure.

vail (vāl), *v.t., v.i. Archaic.* to lower or yield, as in respect or submission.

vain (vān), *adj.* **1.** excessively proud of or concerned about one's own appearance or achievements. **2.** unsuccessful or futile. **3.** without real value or worth. **4. in vain, a.** without result or effect. **b.** in an improper or irreverent manner. —**vain′ly,** *adv.* —**vain′ness,** *n.* —**Syn. 1.** arrogant, conceited, egotistical.

vain·glo·ry (vān′glôr′ē, -glôr′ē), *n.* **1.** excessive vanity. **2.** empty pomp or show. —**vain′glo′ri·ous,** *adj.*

val., **1.** valuation. **2.** value. **3.** valued.

val·ance (val′əns, vā′ləns), *n.* **1.** a short curtain placed across the top of a window. **2.** a short drapery hanging from an edge, as of a canopy or the frame of a bed.

vale (vāl), *n. Chiefly Literary.* a valley.

val·e·dic·tion (val′i dik′shən), *n. Chiefly Literary.* a bidding farewell.

val·e·dic·to·ri·an (val′i dik tôr′ē ən, -tôr′-), *n.* the student of the graduating class who delivers the valedictory.

val·e·dic·to·ry (val′i dik′tə rē), *n., pl.* **-ries.** a farewell address delivered at commencement exercises.

va·lence (vā′ləns), *n.* the relative combining capacity of an atom or group compared with that of the standard hydrogen atom. Also, **va′len·cy.**

Va·len·ci·a (və len′shē ə, -shə), *n.* a seaport in E Spain.

Va·len·ci·ennes (və len′sē enz′), *n.* a flat bobbin lace of linen.

val·en·tine (val′ən tīn′), *n.* **1.** a sentimental card or a gift sent by one person to another on Saint Valentine's Day. **2.** a sweetheart chosen or greeted on this day.

val·et (val′it, va lā′), *n.* **1.** a manservant who cares for his employer's clothes and helps him dress. **2.** an employee, as of a hotel, who provides laundry service, cleaning and pressing, etc.

val′et park′ing, (at a restaurant, etc.) a free service of picking up a customer's car at the entrance, parking it and bringing it back when wanted.

val·e·tu·di·nar·i·an (val′i tōōd′°nâr′ē ən, -tyōōd′-), *n.* an invalid who is excessively concerned about his or her poor health. —**val′e·tu′di·nar′i·an·ism,** *n.*

Val·hal·la (val hal′ə), *n. Teutonic Myth.* the hall of Odin into which the souls of heroes slain in battle were brought to feast.

val·iant (val′yənt), *adj.* heroically courageous. —**val′iance, val′ian·cy,** *n.* —**val′iant·ly,** *adv.*

val·id (val′id), *adj.* **1.** soundly founded on fact or evidence. **2.** legally binding or effective. —**va·lid·i·ty** (və lid′i tē), *n.* —**val′id·ly,** *adv.* —**val′id·ness,** *n.*

val·i·date (val′i dāt′), *v.t.,* **-dat·ed, -dat·ing. 1.** to make legally valid. **2.** to prove to be valid or sound. —**val′i·da′tion,** *n.*

va·lise (və lēs′), *n.* a small or medium piece of hand luggage.

Va·li·um (val′ē əm), *n. Trademark.* a tranquilizer that relieves anxiety and muscular tension.

val·ley (val′ē), *n., pl.* **-leys. 1.** an elongated depression between uplands, hills, or mountains. **2.** a large, flat region drained by a river system.

val·or (val′ər), *n.* heroic courage. Also, *Brit.,* **val′our.** —**val′or·ous,** *adj.* —**val′or·ous·ly,** *adv.* —**Syn.** bravery.

val·or·ize (val′ə rīz′), *v.t.,* **-ized, -iz·ing.** to fix or maintain the price of (a commodity) by government action. —**val′or·i·za′tion,** *n.*

valse (vals), *n. French.* waltz.

val·u·a·ble (val′yōō ə bəl, -yə bəl), *adj.* **1.** having considerable monetary or material value. **2.** of considerable use or service. —*n.* **3.** Usually, **valuables.** valuable personal property, as jewelry or money. — **Syn. 1.** costly, precious. **2.** important.

val·u·ate (val′yōō āt′), *v.t.*, -at·ed, -at·ing. to set a value on. —**val′u·a·tor,** *n.* —**Syn.** appraise.

val·u·a·tion (val′yōō ā′shən), *n.* **1.** the act of valuating something. **2.** an estimated value or worth.

val·ue (val′yōō), *n., v.,* -ued, -u·ing. —*n.* **1.** attributed or relative worth, merit, or usefulness. **2.** monetary or material worth. **3.** equivalent worth or return. **4.** *Math.* the quality or number represented by a figure or symbol. **5.** exact meaning, as of a word. **6. values,** ideals or principles, as of a given society. **7.** degree of lightness or darkness in a color, as in a painting. **8.** *Music.* the relative duration of a tone signified by a note. —*v.t.* **9.** to calculate the monetary value of. **10.** to consider with respect to value, usefulness, or importance. **11.** to regard highly. — **val′u·er,** *n.* —**val′ue·less,** *adj.*

val′ue-add′ed tax′, a sales tax based on the addition to the value of consumer goods or services at each stage of production or distribution.

val·ued (val′yōōd), *adj.* highly regarded.

valve (valv), *n.* **1.** any device for controlling the flow of a fluid. **2.** a movable part that closes or regulates the passage in such a device. **3.** *Anat.* a membranous fold that permits a fluid, as blood, to flow in one direction only. **4.** (in musical wind instruments) a device for changing the length of the air column to alter the pitch of a tone. **5.** one of the separable pieces composing shells, as of a mollusk. **6.** *Brit.* See **vacuum tube.** —**valved** (-d), *adj.* —**valve′less,** *adj.*

val·vu·lar (val′vyə lər), *adj.* having the form or function of a valve, esp. of the heart.

va·moose (va mōōs′), *v.i., v.t.,* -moosed, -moos·ing. *Slang.* to leave hurriedly.

vamp¹ (vamp), *n.* **1.** the portion of a shoe or boot upper that covers the instep and toes. **2.** *Jazz.* an improvised accompaniment consisting of simple chords. —*v.t.* **3.** to furnish or repair with a vamp. **4.** to concoct or invent. **5.** *Jazz.* to improvise (a vamp). —*v.i.* **6.** to improvise a vamp.

vamp² (vamp), *n.* **1.** a charming, unscrupulous woman who exploits or ruins the men she seduces. —*v.t.,*

v.i. **2.** to allure or seduce (a man) by playing the vamp.

vam·pire (vam′pīʳr), *n.* **1.** a reanimated corpse said to suck the blood of sleeping persons at night. **2.** a person who preys ruthlessly upon others. **3.** *vamp².* **4.** Also called **vam′pire bat′.** any of various bats that feed on or are believed to feed on blood.

vam·pir·ism (vam′pīʳr iz′əm, -pə-riz′-), *n.* **1.** belief in the existence of vampires. **2.** the acts or practices of vampires.

van¹ (van), *n.* **1.** a large, closed truck or wagon for moving furniture, animals, etc. **2.** a small, enclosed truck, usually equipped with sleeping, dining, and other facilities. **3.** *Brit.* **a.** a railway baggage car. **b.** a small truck.

van² (van), *n.* vanguard.

va·na·di·um (və nā′dē əm), *n. Chem.* a silvery, metallic element used as a toughening ingredient of steel. *Symbol:* V; *at. wt.:* 50.942; *at. no.:* 23.

Van Al′len belt′ (van al′ən), either of two regions of high-energy, charged particles surrounding the earth. [after J. A. *Van Allen,* b. 1914, U.S. physicist]

Van Bu·ren (van byōōr′ən), **Martin,** 1782–1862, 8th president of the U.S. 1837–41.

Van·cou·ver (van kōō′vər), *n.* a seaport in SW British Columbia, Canada.

van·dal (van′dᵊl), *n.* **1.** a person who willfully destroys or damages public or private property. **2.** (*cap.*) a member of a Germanic people who sacked Rome in A.D. 455. —**van′dal·ism,** *n.*

van·dal·ize (van′dᵊlīz′), *v.t.,* -ized, -iz·ing. to destroy or damage willfully.

Van·dyke′ beard′ (van dīk′), a short, pointed beard.

vane (vān), *n.* **1.** a device that rotates freely and points in the direction from which the wind is blowing. **2.** any of various bladelike parts, as of windmills or propellers.

Van Gogh (van gō′, gôĸʜ′), **Vin·cent** (vin′sənt), 1853–90, Dutch painter.

van·guard (van′gärd′), *n.* **1.** the foremost division or the front part of an army. **2.** the forefront of any movement or activity.

va·nil·la (və nil′ə, -nel′-), *n.* **1.** a flavoring extracted from the podlike fruit of a tropical, climbing orchid, used in ice cream, etc. **2.** Also called **vanil′la bean′.** the fruit of this orchid. **3.** the orchid itself.

van·ish (van′ish), *v.i.* **1.** to disappear from sight, esp. quickly. **2.** to cease to exist. —**van′ish·er,** *n.*

van·i·ty (van'i tē), *n., pl.* **-ties. 1.** excessive pride in one's own appearance or achievements. **2.** lack of real value or worth. **3.** something worthless or unimportant. **4.** Also called **van'ity case'.** a woman's small traveling case for cosmetics and toiletries. —**van'i·tied,** *adj.*

van' line', a transportation company that uses motor vans for long-distance moving of household effects.

van·quish (vang'kwish, van'-), *v.t.* **1.** to overpower (an enemy) completely, esp. in a single battle. **2.** to suppress or overcome, as a feeling. —**van'quish·er,** *n.*

van·tage (van'tij, vän'-), *n.* **1.** a superior position. **2.** Also called **van'tage point'.** a position affording a wide or clear view.

vap·id (vap'id), *adj.* without liveliness or spirit. —**va·pid'i·ty, vap'id·ness,** *n.* —**vap'id·ly,** *adv.*

va·por (vā'pər), *n.* **1.** a visible matter suspended in the air, as fog or smoke. **2.** the gaseous state of a substance that is a liquid under normal conditions. **3.** something insubstantial or transitory. **4. vapors,** *Archaic.* mental depression. Also, *Brit.,* **va'pour.** —**va'por·ish,** *adj.* —**va'por·ish·ness,** *n.*

va·por·ize (vā'pə rīz'), *v.t., v.i.,* **-ized, -iz·ing.** to change into vapor. —**va'por·i·za'tion,** *n.* —**va'por·iz'er,** *n.*

va·por·ous (vā'pər əs), *adj.* **1.** having the form of vapor. **2.** abounding in or giving off vapor. Also, **va'por·y.** —**va'por·ous·ly,** *adv.* —**va'por·ous·ness,** *n.*

va'por trail', contrail.

va·que·ro (vä kâr'ō), *n., pl.* **-ros.** *Southwestern U.S.* a cowboy or herdsman.

var., 1. variable. **2.** variant. **3.** variation. **4.** variety. **5.** various.

var·i·a·ble (vâr'ē ə bəl), *adj.* **1.** apt or likely to vary or change. **2.** capable of being varied or changed. **3.** inconstant or fickle. —*n.* **4.** something variable. **5.** *Math.* **a.** a quantity that may assume any of a set of values. **b.** a symbol that represents this. —**var'i·a·bil'i·ty, var'i·a·ble·ness,** *n.* —**var'i·a·bly,** *adv.*

var·i·ance (vâr'ē əns), *n.* **1.** the state or fact of varying or being variant. **2.** degree of difference. **3.** a dispute or quarrel. **4.** an official permit to do something normally forbidden by regulations, esp. in city zoning. **5. at variance,** in disagreement.

var·i·ant (vâr'ē ənt), *adj.* **1.** differing from others of the same general kind. **2.** showing variation or variety. —*n.* **3.** something variant. **4. a.** a different spelling or pronunciation of the same word. **b.** a different form of the same term or meaning.

var·i·a·tion (vâr'ē ā'shən), *n.* **1.** the act or process of varying. **2.** change in condition or degree. **3.** the extent or rate of change. **4.** a thing different from a standard or norm. **5.** *Music.* the transformation of a melody or theme with changes in harmony or rhythm.

var·i·col·ored (vâr'i kul'ərd), *adj.* having various colors.

var·i·cose (var'ə kōs', vâr'-), *adj.* abnormally swollen: *a varicose vein.* —**var'i·cos'i·ty** (-kos'i tē), *n.*

var·ied (vâr'ēd), *adj.* **1.** consisting of various kinds or items. **2.** changed or altered. —**var'ied·ly,** *adv.*

var·i·e·gate (vâr'ē ə gāt', vâr'ə gāt'), *v.t.,* **-gat·ed, -gat·ing. 1.** to make varied in appearance, esp. by adding different colors. **2.** to give variety to. —**var'i·e·gat'ed,** *adj.* —**var'i·e·ga'tion,** *n.*

va·ri·e·ty (və rī'i tē), *n., pl.* **-ties. 1.** the state or quality of being varied or various. **2.** a number of different types of things, esp. ones in the same category. **3.** a kind or sort. **4.** a category of organisms within a species. **5.** Also called **vari'ety show'.** entertainment consisting of a number of brief, unrelated performances or acts. —**va·ri'e·tal** (-t°l), *adj.* —**va·ri'e·tal·ly,** *adv.*

vari'ety store', a retail store carrying a large variety of low-priced goods.

var·i·o·rum (vâr'ē ōr'əm, -ôr'-), *n.* an edition showing textual differences or notes by a number of scholars.

var·i·ous (vâr'ē əs), *adj.* **1.** of different kinds of the same general thing. **2.** numerous or many. **3.** having many different qualities. **4.** individual or separate. —**var'i·ous·ly,** *adv.* —**var'i·ous·ness,** *n.* —**Syn. 1, 3.** diverse, manifold.

var·let (vär'lit), *n. Archaic.* **1.** an attendant or servant. **2.** a knave or rascal.

var·mint (vär'mənt), *n. Dial.* an objectionable or undesirable animal or person. Also, **var'ment.**

var·nish (vär'nish), *n.* **1.** a preparation made of resins dissolved in an oil or in alcohol, used for finishing or coating wood, metal, etc. **2.** the shiny coating resulting from such preparation. **3.** superficial polish or show. —*v.t.* **4.** to apply varnish to. **5.** to give a superficially pleasing appearance to, esp. in order to deceive.

var·si·ty (vär'si tē), *n., pl.* **-ties. 1.** any principal team that represents a school or college, esp. in sports. **2.** *Brit. Informal.* a university. [var. of *(uni)versity*]

var·y (vâr′ē), v., **var·ied, var·y·ing.** —v.t. **1.** to change in form, appearance, or substance. **2.** to give variety to. —v.i. **3.** to be different from one instance to the next. **4.** to change according to some other changing thing. **5.** to deviate or depart. —**var′y·ing·ly,** adv.

vas·cu·lar (vas′kyə lər), adj. of or provided with vessels or ducts that convey fluids, as blood, lymph, or sap. —**vas′cu·lar·ly,** adv.

vase (vās, vāz, väz), n. a hollow container, as of porcelain, used to hold cut flowers or for decoration.

vas·ec·to·my (va sek′tə mē), n., pl. **-mies.** Surg. excision of all or a portion of the duct that carries sperm from the testis, used for permanent sterilization.

Vas·e·line (vas′ə lēn′, vas′ə lēn′), n. Trademark. petrolatum.

vas·o·mo·tor (vas′ō mō′tər), adj. regulating the diameter of blood vessels, as certain nerves.

vas·sal (vas′əl), n. **1.** (in the feudal system) a person granted the use of land, in return for allegiance to a lord. **2.** a person owing homage to a superior.

vas·sal·age (vas′ə lij), n. **1.** the state or condition of a vassal. **2.** homage or service required of a vassal.

vast (vast, väst), adj. **1.** of very great area or extent. **2.** very great in size, quantity, or degree. —**vast′ly,** adv. —**vast′ness,** n. —Syn. immense.

vast·y (vas′tē, vä′stē), adj. Archaic. vast.

vat (vat), n. a large tub or tank for storing or holding liquids.

VAT, See **value-added tax.**

vat·ic (vat′ik), adj. Rare. of a prophet or prophecy. Also, **vat′i·cal.**

Vat·i·can (vat′i kən), n. **1.** the chief residence of the popes in Vatican City. **2.** the papal government.

Vat′ican Cit′y, an independent papal state within the city of Rome.

vaude·ville (vôd′vil, vōd′-, vô′də-), n. theatrical entertainment consisting of a series of separate performances by comedians, singers, dancers, acrobats, etc. —**vaude·vil·lian** (vôd-vil′yən, vōd-, vô′də-), n.

vault[1] (vôlt), n. **1.** a structure shaped like an arch so as to form a ceiling or roof. **2.** a chamber or passage with an arched ceiling or roof. **3.** an underground storage room. **4.** a strongly built chamber for keeping money or valuable articles. **5.** a burial chamber. —v.t. **6.** to construct or cover with a vault. —v.i. **7.** to curve or bend like a vault. —**vault′ed,** adj. —**vault′y,** adj.

vault[2] (vôlt), v.i., v.t. **1.** to leap or spring (over), esp. with the hands supported on a pole. —n. **2.** the act of vaulting. —**vault′er,** n.

vault·ing (vôl′tiṅg), adj. **1.** leaping up or over. **2.** excessive or exaggerated: vaulting ambition.

vaunt (vônt, vänt), Literary. —v.t., v.i. **1.** to boast (of). —n. **2.** a vaunting assertion. —**vaunt′ed,** adj.

vb., verb.

V.C., Vietcong.

VD, See **venereal disease.**

V-Day (vē′dā′), n. a day of final victory.

veal (vēl), n. the meat of a young calf.

vec·tor (vek′tər), n. **1.** Math. a quantity possessing both magnitude and direction. **2.** an organism that transmits a disease-producing microorganism. —**vec·to′ri·al** (-tōr′ē əl, -tôr′-), adj.

Ve·da (vā′də, vē′-), n. any of the entire collection of Hindu sacred writings. —**Ve′dic,** adj.

Ve·dan·ta (vi dän′tə, -dan′-), n. the chief Indian philosophy that forms the basis for orthodox Hinduism. —**Ve·dan′tic,** adj.

veep (vēp), n. Informal. a vice president.

veer (vēr), v.i., v.t. **1.** to change in direction or course. —n. **2.** a change of direction or course. —**veer′ing·ly,** adv.

veer·y (vēr′ē), n., pl. **veer·ies.** a thrush of the eastern U.S., noted for its song.

veg·e·ta·ble (vej′tə bəl, vej′i tə-), n. **1.** any herbaceous plant whose fruit, roots, bulbs, leaves, or flower parts are used as food. **2.** the edible part of such a plant. **3.** any organism classified as a plant. **4.** an inactive, passive person. —adj. **5.** of or made from edible vegetables. **6.** of or derived from plants. **7.** vegetative (def. 3).

veg·e·tal (vej′i təl), adj. **1.** vegetable (defs. 5, 6). **2.** vegetative (def. 3).

veg·e·tar·i·an (vej′i târ′ē ən), n. **1.** a person who lives on a meatless diet. —adj. **2.** of or pertaining to vegetarians. **3.** consisting solely of vegetables. —**veg′e·tar′i·an·ism,** n.

veg·e·tate (vej′i tāt′), v.i., **-tat·ed, -tat·ing.** **1.** to grow as or like plants. **2.** to live in an inactive, passive way.

veg·e·ta·tion (vej′i tā′shən), n. **1.** all the plants or plant life of a place. **2.** the act or process of vegetating. —**veg′e·ta′tion·al,** adj.

veg·e·ta·tive (vej′i tā′tiv), adj. **1.** growing as or like plants. **2.** of or concerned with plant life. **3.** of or engaged in nutritive and growth processes rather than reproductive processes. **4.** inactive or passive: a vegetative existence.

ve·he·ment (vē′ə mənt), *adj.* **1.** showing intensity of feeling or expression. **2.** forceful or violent. —**ve′he·mence,** **ve′he·men·cy,** *n.* —**ve′he·ment·ly,** *adv.* —**Syn. 1.** ardent, fervent.

ve·hi·cle (vē′i kəl), *n.* **1.** any means in or by which someone or something is carried or transported. **2.** a medium of communication or expression. **3.** a liquid, as oil, in which a pigment is mixed before being applied to a surface. —**ve·hic′u·lar** (-hik′yə lər), *adj.*

veil (vāl), *n.* **1.** a piece of opaque or transparent material worn over the face, esp. by women. **2.** a part of the headdress of a nun. **3.** something that covers or conceals. **4. take the veil,** to become a nun. —*v.t.* **5.** to cover or conceal with or as with a veil. —*v.i.* **6.** to wear a veil. —**veiled** (-d), *adj.*

veil·ing (vā′ling), *n.* **1.** thin material for veils. **2.** veil (def. 3).

vein (vān), *n.* **1.** one of the branching vessels carrying blood from various parts of the body to the heart. **2.** one of the riblike thickenings that form the framework of the wing of an insect. **3.** one of the strands of vascular tissue forming the framework of a leaf. **4.** a mass of igneous rock containing a mineral deposit. **5.** a streak or marking, as in marble. **6.** a distinctive strain or quality. **7.** mood or manner. **8.** a particular mode of expression. —*v.t.* **9.** to mark with or as with veins. —**veined** (-d), *adj.* —**vein′ing,** *n.*

vel., **1.** vellum. **2.** velocity.

Vel·cro (vel′krō), *n. Trademark.* an adhesive nylon tape having tiny, hooked fibers that fasten easily to other surfaces, used in clothing, carpeting, etc.

veld (velt, felt), *n.* the open country bearing few bushes or shrubs, esp. in S Africa. Also, **veldt.**

vel·le·i·ty (və lē′i tē), *n., pl.* **-ties. 1.** volition in its weakest form. **2.** a mere wish.

vel·lum (vel′əm), *n.* **1.** calfskin, lambskin, etc., treated for use as a fine writing surface or as material for bookbinding. **2.** a paper or cloth suggesting vellum.

ve·loc·i·pede (və los′ə pēd′), *n.* an early type of bicycle or tricycle.

ve·loc·i·ty (və los′i tē), *n., pl.* **-ties. 1.** rapidity of motion or operation. **2.** *Mech.* the rate of motion of a body in a certain direction.

ve·lour (və loōr′), *n.* a velvetlike fabric of rayon or wool. Also, **ve·lours** (və loōr′).

ve·lum (vē′ləm), *n., pl.* **-la** (-lə). any of various veillike membranous partitions, as the soft palate. —**ve′lar** (-lər), *adj.*

vel·vet (vel′vit), *n.* **1.** a fabric of silk or nylon with a thick, soft pile. **2.** something like velvet, as in smoothness. **3.** the soft covering of a growing antler. —*adj.* **4.** made of velvet. **5.** resembling velvet. —**vel′vet·y,** *adj.*

vel·vet·een (vel′vi tēn′), *n.* a cotton fabric with short pile, resembling velvet.

Ven., Venerable.

ve·nal (vēn′əl), *adj.* **1.** open to bribery. **2.** influenced by bribery. —**ve·nal′i·ty** (-nal′i tē), *n.* —**ve′nal·ly,** *adv.* —**Syn.** corrupt, mercenary.

ve·na·tion (vē nā′shən, və-), *n.* the arrangement of veins, as in a leaf.

vend (vend), *v.t., v.i. Chiefly Law.* to sell, esp. by peddling. —**vend′i·ble,** *adj.*

vend·ee (ven dē′), *n.* the person to whom a thing is sold.

ven·det·ta (ven det′ə), *n.* any prolonged, bitter feud.

vend′ing machine′, a coin-operated machine for selling small articles.

ven·dor (ven′dər, ven dôr′), *n.* **1.** a person or firm that sells. **2.** See **vending machine.** Also, **vend′er.**

ve·neer (və nēr′), *n.* **1.** a thin layer of fine wood used in covering the surface of cheaper wood or in making plywood. **2.** a deceptive outward appearance. —*v.t.* **3.** to cover or overlay with a veneer.

ven·er·a·ble (ven′ər ə bəl), *adj.* **1.** commanding respect because of great age or associated dignity. **2.** (*cap.*) a title of respect in the Anglican or the Catholic Church. **3.** hallowed by historical or religious association. —**ven′er·a·bil′i·ty,** *n.* —**ven′er·a·bly,** *adv.*

ven·er·ate (ven′ə rāt′), *v.t.,* **-at·ed, at·ing.** to regard with deferential or religious respect. —**ven′er·a′tion,** *n.*

ve·ne·re·al (və nēr′ē əl), *adj.* **1.** arising from sexual intercourse with an infected person. **2.** *Archaic.* of sexual intercourse.

vene′real disease′, any disease transmitted by sexual intercourse, as syphilis or gonorrhea.

Vene′tian blind′, a shade for a window having overlapping horizontal slats that may be opened or closed.

Ven·e·zue·la (ven′i zwā′lə, -zwē′-), *n.* a country in N South America. —**Ven′e·zue′lan,** *adj., n.*

venge·ance (ven′jəns), *n.* **1.** punishment inflicted in retaliation for an injury or bad treatment. **2. with a vengeance, a.** with force or violence. **b.** to an excessive degree. —**Syn. 1.** retribution, revenge.

venge·ful (venj′fəl), *adj.* desiring or seeking vengeance. —**venge′ful·ly,** *adv.* —**venge′ful·ness,** *n.*

V-en·gine (vē′en′jən), *n.* an internal-combustion engine in which the cylinders are arranged in two banks forming a V shape.

ve·ni·al (vē′nē əl, vēn′yəl), *adj.* able to be forgiven, as a sin. —**ve′ni·al·ly,** *adv.*

Ven·ice (ven′is), *n.* a seaport in NE Italy. —**Ve·ne·tian** (və nē′shən), *adj., n.*

ven·i·punc·ture (ven′ə pungk′chər, vē′nə-), *n.* the puncture of a vein for surgical or therapeutic purposes.

ve·ni·re (vi nī′rē), *n.* **1.** a writ directed to the sheriff, requiring him or her to summon persons to act as jurors. **2.** a panel from which a jury is selected.

ve·ni·re·man (vi nī′rē mən), *n.* a person summoned under a venire.

ven·i·son (ven′i sən, -zən), *n.* the flesh of a deer used for food.

ven·om (ven′əm), *n.* **1.** the poisonous fluid secreted by certain snakes or spiders, usually transmitted by biting or stinging. **2.** something suggesting this, as malice.

ven·om·ous (ven′ə məs), *adj.* **1.** secreting and transmitting venom. **2.** full of or containing venom. **3.** spiteful or malignant. —**ven′om·ous·ly,** *adv.*

ve·nous (vē′nəs), *adj.* **1.** of or pertaining to veins. **2.** having, characterized by, or composed of veins. **3.** noting the blood during its passage through the veins.

vent[1] (vent), *n.* **1.** an opening serving as an outlet for air, smoke, or fumes. **2.** a means of exit or escape. **3.** **give vent to,** to give expression to. —*v.t.* **4.** to give free play to (an emotion, etc.). **5.** to release or discharge (smoke, etc.). **6.** to furnish with a vent.

vent[2] (vent), *n.* a slit in the back of a coat or jacket.

ven·ti·late (ven′tᵊlāt′), *v.t.,* **-lat·ed, -lat·ing. 1.** to provide (a room) with fresh air. **2.** to provide with a vent for such air. **3.** to discuss and examine (a problem, etc.) openly and freely. —**ven′ti·la′tion,** *n.* —**ven′ti·la′tor,** *n.* —**ven′ti·la·to·ry** (-lə tôr′ē, -tōr′ē), *adj.*

ven·tral (ven′trəl), *adj.* **1.** of or pertaining to the abdomen or belly. **2.** situated on the abdominal side of the body.

ven·tri·cle (ven′tri kəl), *n.* **1.** either of the two lower chambers on each side of the heart. **2.** one of a series of connecting cavities of the brain. —**ven·tric′u·lar** (-trik′yə lər), *adj.*

ven·tril·o·quism (ven tril′ə kwiz′əm), *n.* the art of speaking so that the voice appears to come from a source other than the speaker. Also called **ven·tril′o·quy** (-kwē). —**ven·tril′o·quist,** *n.*

ven·ture (ven′chər), *n., v.,* **-tured, -tur·ing.** —*n.* **1.** an undertaking, esp. a business enterprise, involving risk or uncertainty. **2.** something risked in such an undertaking. —*v.t.* **3.** to expose to risk or uncertainty. **4.** to take the risk of. **5.** to undertake to express, in spite of possible contradiction or opposition: *to venture a guess.* —*v.i.* **6.** to do or go despite the risk or uncertainty involved. —**ven′tur·er,** *n.*

ven·ture·some (ven′chər səm), *adj.* **1.** inclined to undertake ventures. **2.** involving risk or uncertainty. —**ven′ture·some·ly,** *adv.* —**ven′ture·some·ness,** *n.*

ven·tur·ous (ven′chər əs), *adj.* venturesome. —**ven′tur·ous·ly,** *adv.* —**ven′tur·ous·ness,** *n.*

ven·ue (ven′ōō, ven′yōō), *n.* **1.** *Law.* the place of a crime or cause of action. **2.** the country or place where the jury is gathered and the trial held.

Ve·nus (vē′nəs), *n.* **1.** the Roman goddess of love and beauty. **2.** the planet second in order from the sun and the most brilliant in the solar system.

Ve·nu·si·an (və nōō′sē ən, -shən, -nyōō′-), *adj.* **1.** of or pertaining to the planet Venus. —*n.* **2.** a supposed being inhabiting Venus.

ver., version.

ve·ra·cious (və rā′shəs), *adj.* **1.** habitually speaking the truth. **2.** true or factual —**ve·ra′cious·ly,** *adv.* —**ve·ra′cious·ness,** *n.*

ve·rac·i·ty (və ras′i tē), *n., pl.* **-ties. 1.** habitual truthfulness. **2.** conformity to truth or fact.

ve·ran·da (və ran′də), *n. Chiefly Regional and Brit.* porch (def. 1). Also, **ve·ran′dah.**

verb (vûrb), *n.* a word or phrase that expresses action or state of being. —**verb′less,** *adj.*

ver·bal (vûr′bəl), *adj.* **1.** of or consisting of words. **2.** expressed in spoken words. **3.** concerned with words rather than the ideas expressed. **4.** word for word, as a translation. **5.** derived from a verb, esp. a noun or adjective. —**ver′bal·ly,** *adv.*

ver·bal·ize (vûr′bə līz′), *v.,* **-ized, -iz·ing.** —*v.t.* **1.** to express in words. —*v.i.* **2.** to express something verbally. —**ver′bal·i·za′tion,** *n.*

ver′bal noun′, *Gram.* a noun derived from a verb, as the gerund *smoking,* in *Smoking is forbidden.*

ver·ba·tim (vər bā′tim), *adv., adj.* word for word.

ver·be·na (vər bē′nə), *n.* any of various plants having brightly colored flowers.

ver·bi·age (vûr′bē ij), n. 1. abundance of useless words. 2. manner of useless expression.

ver·bose (vər bōs′), adj. using too many unneeded words to be clear or lively. —ver·bose′ly, adj. —ver·bos′i·ty (-bos′i tē), ver·bose′ness, n. —Syn. talkative, wordy.

ver·bo·ten (vər bōt′°n), adj. German. forbidden, as by law.

ver·dant (vûr′d°nt), adj. 1. green with vegetation. 2. of the color green. 3. immature or inexperienced. —ver′dant·ly, adv.

Ver·di (vâr′dē), n. Giu·sep·pe (jōō-zep′pe), 1813–1901, Italian operatic composer.

ver·dict (vûr′dikt), n. 1. Law. the decision of a jury concerning a matter submitted to their judgment. 2. any judgment or decision.

ver·di·gris (vûr′də grēs′, -gris), n. a green or bluish coating formed on copper, brass, or bronze surfaces.

ver·dure (vûr′jər), n. 1. green vegetation. 2. greenness of fresh vegetation.

verge[1] (vûrj), n., v., verged, verg·ing. —n. 1. the edge or border of something: the verge of a desert. 2. the point beyond which something begins or occurs. 3. a staff carried as an emblem of office, as of a bishop. —v.i. 4. to be on the verge or border.

verge[2] (vûrj), v.i., verged, verg·ing. 1. to tend toward a certain condition. 2. to change gradually into something else.

ver·ger (vûr′jər), n. Chiefly Brit. 1. a general attendant in a church. 2. an official who carries the verge before a bishop.

ver·i·fy (ver′ə fī′), v.t., -fied, -fy·ing. 1. to prove the truth of. 2. to ascertain the truth or correctness of. —ver′i·fi′a·ble, adj. —ver′i·fi·ca′tion (-fə kā′shən), n. —ver′i·fi′er, n. —Syn. 1. confirm.

ver·i·si·mil·i·tude (ver′i si mil′i tōōd′, -tyōōd′), n. 1. the appearance of truth. 2. something having the appearance of truth.

ver·i·ta·ble (ver′i tə bəl), adj. being truly so. —ver′i·ta·bly, adv. —Syn. actual, real.

ver·i·ty (ver′i tē), n., pl. -ties. 1. the state or quality of being true. 2. a true principle, belief, or statement.

ver·meil (vûr′mil), n. 1. vermilion red. 2. gilded silver or bronze.

ver·mi·cel·li (vûr′mi sel′ē, -chel′ē), n. pasta resembling spaghetti but thinner.

ver·mic·u·lite (vər mik′yə līt′), n. any of various minerals that expand markedly on being heated, used for heat insulation.

ver·mi·form (vûr′mə fôrm′), adj. resembling a worm in shape.

ver′miform appen′dix, a narrow, blind tube protruding from the cecum in the lower right-hand part of the abdomen.

ver·mi·fuge (vûr′mə fyōōj′), n. a medicine for expelling worms from the intestines.

ver·mil·ion (vər mil′yən), n. 1. a brilliant scarlet red. 2. a bright-red pigment.

ver·min (vûr′min), n., pl. -min. small, troublesome, and often harmful animals or insects, as lice or fleas. —ver′min·ous, adj.

Ver·mont (vər mont′), n. a state of the NE United States. Cap.: Montpelier. —Ver·mont′er, n.

ver·mouth (vər mōōth′), n. a white or red wine in which aromatic herbs have been steeped.

ver·nac·u·lar (vər nak′yə lər), n. 1. the common native language of a country or region. 2. the language of ordinary, everyday speech. 3. the language or speech peculiar to a profession or class. —adj. 4. of, pertaining to, or expressed in vernacular. —ver·nac′u·lar·ly, adv.

ver·nal (vûr′n°l), adj. 1. of or in spring. 2. like or suggesting spring. 3. youthful or fresh. —ver′nal·ly, adv.

ver′nal e′quinox. See under equinox.

ver·nal·ize (vûr′n°līz′), v.t., -ized, -iz·ing. to shorten the growth period before the blossoming and fruiting of (a plant) by chilling its seed or bulb. —ver′nal·i·za′tion, n.

ver·ni·er (vûr′nē ər), n. a short graduated scale running parallel to a longer scale, used for measuring a fraction part of one of the divisions of the longer scale. [named after P. Vernier (1580–1637), French mathematician]

ve·ron·i·ca (və ron′ə kə), n. speedwell.

Ver·sailles (vər sī′), n. a city in N France, SW of Paris.

ver·sa·tile (vûr′sə til, -tīl′), adj. 1. capable of doing many things well. 2. having many uses or applications. —ver′sa·tile·ly, adv. —ver′sa·til′i·ty, n. —Syn. 1. adaptable, talented.

verse (vûrs), n. 1. one of the lines of a poem. 2. a particular type of metrical line. 3. a poem or a piece of poetry. 4. a section of metrical composition, esp. a stanza. 5. a particular type of poetry. 6. a short division of a chapter in the Bible.

versed (vûrst), adj. acquainted by learning or practice.

ver·si·cle (vûr′si kəl), n. a short sentence said or sung by an officiant and followed by a response from the congregation.

ver·si·fy (vûr'sə fī'), *v.*, **-fied, -fy·ing.** —*v.t.* **1.** to put into verse. —*v.i.* **2.** to compose verses. —**ver'si·fi·ca'·tion** (-fə kā'shən), *n.* —**ver'si·fi'er,** *n.*

ver·sion (vûr'zhən, -shən), *n.* **1.** an account or description from one's point of view. **2.** a particular form or variety of something. **3.** a translation, esp. of the Bible or a part of it. —**ver'sion·al,** *adj.*

vers li·bre (veʀ lē'bʀ°), *French.* See **free verse.**

ver·so (vûr'sō), *n., pl.* **-sos.** *Print.* a left-hand page.

ver·sus (vûr'səs), *prep.* **1.** *Law, Sports.* against. **2.** as compared to: *capitalism versus communism.*

vert., vertical.

ver·te·bra (vûr'tə brə), *n., pl.* **-brae** (-brē'), **-bras.** any of the bones or segments composing the spinal column. —**ver'te·bral,** *adj.*

ver·te·brate (vûr'tə brāt', -brit), *adj.* **1.** having a spinal column. **2.** of or belonging to a group of animals having a spinal column, including mammals, birds, reptiles, amphibians, and fishes. —*n.* **3.** a vertebrate animal.

ver·tex (vûr'teks), *n., pl.* **-tex·es, -ti·ces** (-ti səz'). **1.** the highest point of something. **2.** *Math.* **a.** the point farthest from the base. **b.** a point in a geometrical solid common to three or more sides. **c.** the intersection of two sides of a plane figure.

ver·ti·cal (vûr'ti kəl), *adj.* **1.** at approximately right angles to the plane of the horizon. **2.** of or at a vertex. —*n.* **3.** something vertical, as a line or plane. **4.** a vertical position. —**ver'ti·cal'i·ty, ver'ti·cal·ness,** *n.* —**ver'ti·cal·ly,** *adv.*

ver·tic·il·late (vər tis'ə lit, -lāt'), *adj.* arranged in or forming whorls, as flowers.

ver·tig·i·nous (vər tij'ə nəs), *adj.* **1.** affected with or liable to cause vertigo. **2.** whirling or spinning. —**ver·tig'i·nous·ly,** *adv.*

ver·ti·go (vûr'tə gō'), *n., pl.* **-goes, ver·tig·i·nes** (vər tij'ə nēz'). a disordered feeling a person has that he or she, or his or her surroundings, are whirling about.

ver·vain (vûr'vān), *n.* a plant having elongated or flattened spikes of flowers.

verve (vûrv), *n.* vivacious spirit, esp. in artistic work.

ver·y (ver'ē), *adv.* **1.** in a high degree. **2.** absolutely or exactly. —*adj.* **3.** same or identical: *the very item we have been looking for.* **4.** mere: *The very thought of it is distressing.* **5.** sheer or utter. **6.** actual: *caught in the very act of stealing.* **7.** being such in the extreme: *the very heart of the matter.*

ver·y high' fre'quency, *Radio.* any frequency between 30 and 300 megahertz.

ver·y low' fre'quency, *Radio.* any frequency between 3 and 30 kilohertz.

ves·i·cant (ves'ə kənt), *adj.* **1.** producing blisters. —*n.* **2.** a vesicant substance, as mustard gas.

ves·i·cle (ves'i kəl), *n.* **1.** a small sac or bladderlike cavity filled with fluid. **2.** a blister on the skin. —**ve·sic·u·lar** (və sik'yə lər), **ve·sic'u·late** (-lit, -lāt'), *adj.*

ves·per (ves'pər), *n.* **1.** vespers, (*often cap.*) a religious service in the late afternoon or the evening. **2.** the bell that summons persons to vespers. **3.** (*cap.*) See **evening star. 4.** *Archaic.* evening. —*adj.* **5.** of or pertaining to vespers.

ves·per·tine (ves'pər tin, -tīn'), *adj.* **1.** of or occurring in the evening. **2.** opening or expanding in the evening, as certain flowers.

Ves·puc·ci (ve spōō'chē), *n.* **A·me·ri·go** (ä mer'ə gō), 1451–1512, Italian explorer after whom America was named.

ves·sel (ves'əl), *n.* **1.** a craft larger than a rowboat for traveling on water. **2.** a hollow utensil used esp. for holding liquids. **3.** a tube or duct containing or conveying blood or other body fluid, as a vein.

vest (vest), *n.* **1.** a sleeveless, collarless garment for men, worn under a suit coat. **2.** a similar garment worn by women over a blouse or dress. **3.** *Brit.* an undershirt. —*v.t.* **4.** to clothe, esp. with ecclesiastical vestments. **5.** to place (authority or power) in the control of. **6.** to give authority or power to. —*v.i.* **7.** to become vested in a person, as a right.

Ves·ta (ves'tə), *n.* the ancient Roman goddess of the hearth.

ves·tal (ves'təl), *adj.* **1.** of or pertaining to Vesta or a vestal virgin. **2.** chaste or pure. —*n.* **3.** Also called **ves'tal vir'gin.** one of the virgins consecrated to the tending of the sacred fire in the temple of Vesta.

vest'ed in'terest, a special interest in an existing system, arrangement, or institution for particular personal reasons.

vest·ee (ves tē'), *n.* a decorative front piece worn under a woman's jacket or blouse.

ves·ti·bule (ves'tə byōōl'), *n.* **1.** a passage or hall between the outer and the interior doors of a house. **2.** an enclosed entrance to a railroad passenger car. **3.** a bodily cavity serving as an entrance to another, as that of the internal ear. —**ves·tib·u·lar** (ve stib'yə lər), *adj.*

ves·tige (ves′tij), *n.* **1.** a trace or visible evidence of something that is no longer present or in existence. **2.** *Biol.* an imperfectly developed organ or part having little or no use. —**ves·tig·i·al** (ve stij′ē əl), *adj.* —**ves·tig′i·al·ly,** *adv.*

vest·ing (vest′ing), *n.* the granting to an eligible employee of the right to specified pension benefits, regardless of discontinued employment status.

vest·ment (vest′mənt), *n.* **1.** one of the garments worn by certain members of the clergy during religious service. **2.** a ceremonial robe.

vest-pock·et (vest′pok′it), *adj.* **1.** small enough to be carried in the pocket of the vest. **2.** occupying a small space, as a park.

ves·try (ves′trē), *n., pl.* **-tries. 1.** a room in a church in which the vestments are kept. **2.** (in some churches) a similar room used as a chapel. **3.** *Prot. Episc. Ch.* a committee that manages the temporal affairs of the church.

ves·try·man (ves′trē mən), *n.* a member of a church vestry.

ves·ture (ves′chər), *n. Archaic.* **1.** clothing or garments. **2.** something that covers like a garment.

Ve·su·vi·us (və sōō′vē əs), *n.* an active volcano in SW Italy, near Naples.

vet[1] (vet), *n. Informal.* veterinarian.

vet[2] (vet), *n., adj. Informal.* veteran.

vetch (vech), *n.* a climbing plant grown as food for livestock.

vet·er·an (vet′ər ən, ve′trən), *n.* **1.** a person who has had long service or experience in an occupation or office. **2.** a person who has served in the armed forces, esp. in a war. —*adj.* **3.** experienced through long service. **4.** of or pertaining to veterans.

Vet′erans Day′, November 11, a holiday in the U.S. to honor all armed-service veterans.

vet·er·i·nar·i·an (vet′ər ə nâr′ē ən, ve′trə-), *n.* a person who practices veterinary medicine or surgery.

vet·er·i·nar·y (vet′ər ə ner′ē, ve′trə-), *adj., n., pl.* **-nar·ies.** —*adj.* **1.** noting the medical and surgical treatment of animals, esp. domesticated animals. —*n.* **2.** Also called **vet′erinar′y sur′geon.** *Brit.* a veterinarian.

ve·to (vē′tō), *n., pl.* **-toes,** *v.,* **-toed, -to·ing.** —*n.* **1.** the power vested in one branch of a government to cancel or postpone the decisions or enactments of another branch, esp. the right of a chief executive to reject bills passed by the legislature. **2.** the exercise of this right. **3.** a document exercising such right and setting forth the reasons for it. **4.** a prohibition of any kind. —*v.t.* **5.** to reject (a proposed bill or enactment) by a veto. **6.** to prohibit emphatically. —**ve′to·er,** *n.*

vex (veks), *v.t.* **1.** to irritate and disturb provokingly. **2.** to worry greatly. **3.** *Literary.* to discuss at length: *a vexed question.* **4.** *Archaic.* to stir up, as waves. —Syn. **1.** annoy, irk, fret.

vex·a·tion (vek sā′shən), *n.* **1.** the act of vexing or state of being vexed. **2.** something that vexes. —**vex·a′tious** (-shəs), *adj.* —**vex·a′tious·ly,** *adv.* —**vex·a′tious·ness,** *n.*

VF., **1.** voice frequency. **2.** visual field.

VFD, volunteer fire department.

VFW, Veterans of Foreign Wars.

V.G., 1. very good. **2.** Vicar-General.

VHF, See **very high frequency.**

VI, Virgin Islands. Also, **V.I.**

v.i., 1. verb intransitive. **2.** *Law.* see below. [< L *vide infra*]

vi·a (vī′ə, vē′ə), *prep.* by way of.

vi·a·ble (vī′ə bəl), *adj.* **1.** capable of living or growing, as an infant or seed. **2.** practicable or workable, as a plan. —**vi′a·bil′i·ty,** *n.* —**vi′a·bly,** *adv.*

vi·a·duct (vī′ə dukt′), *n.* a bridge made up of several short spans for carrying a road or railroad, as over a valley.

vi·al (vī′əl, vīl), *n.* a small container, as of glass, for holding liquids.

vi·ands (vī′əndz), *n.pl.* articles of food, esp. choice foods.

vi·at·i·cum (vī at′ə kəm), *n., pl.* **-ca** (-kə), **-cums.** the Eucharist as given to a person dying or in danger of death.

vibes[1] (vībz), *n.pl. Informal.* vibraphone.

vibes[2] (vībz), *n.pl. Slang.* general emotional feelings one has from another person or a place. Also called **vi·bra′tions.**

vi·bra·harp (vī′brə härp′), *n.* vibraphone.

vi·brant (vī′brənt), *adj.* **1.** (of sounds) characterized by perceptible vibration. **2.** pulsating with vigor and energy. **3.** exciting or stimulating. —**vi′bran·cy,** *n.* —**vi′brant·ly,** *adv.*

vi·bra·phone (vī′brə fōn′), *n.* a musical percussion instrument resembling the marimba but having electrically powered resonators.

vi·brate (vī′brāt), *v.,* **-brat·ed, -brat·ing.** —*v.i.* **1.** to move to and fro or up and down quickly and repeatedly. **2.** (of sounds) to produce a quivering effect. **3.** to thrill in emotional response. —*v.t.* **4.** to cause to vibrate. —**vi·bra′tion,** *n.* —**vi·bra′tion·al,** *adj.* —**vi′bra·tor,** *n.* —**vi′bra·to′ry,** *adj.*

vi·bra·to (vi brä′tō, vī-), *n., pl.* **-tos.** *Music.* a pulsating effect produced by a rapid change of pitch.

vi·bur·num (vī bûr′nəm), *n.* any of various shrubs related to the honeysuckle having clusters of small, white flowers.

Vic., 1. Vicar. 2. Victoria.

vic., vicinity.

vic·ar (vik′ər), *n.* 1. *Ch. of Eng.* a parish priest. 2. *Prot. Episc. Ch.* a member of the clergy whose charge is a chapel in a parish. 3. *Rom. Cath. Ch.* an official representing the pope or a bishop. —**vi·car·i·al** (vī kâr′ē əl), *adj.* —**vi·car′i·ate** (-it, -āt′), *n.*

vic·ar·age (vik′ər ij), *n.* the residence or benefice of a vicar.

vic·ar-gen·er·al (vik′ər jen′ər əl), *n., pl.* **vic·ars-gen·er·al.** *Rom. Cath. Ch.* an administrative deputy of a bishop.

vi·car·i·ous (vī kâr′ē əs, vi-), *adj.* 1. performed or suffered in place of another. 2. taking the place of another. 3. felt or enjoyed by imagining oneself to participate in the experience of others. —**vi·car′i·ous·ly,** *adv.* —**vi·car′i·ous·ness,** *n.*

vice¹ (vīs), *n.* 1. an immoral habit or practice. 2. immoral conduct. 3. sexual immorality, esp. prostitution. 4. a fault or flaw.

vice² (vīs), *n. Brit.* vise.

vi·ce³ (vī′sē), *prep.* in the place of, esp. when succeeding to.

vice-, a prefix meaning "deputy or substitute" (now usually written separately without a hyphen): *vice mayor.*

vice′ ad′miral, *U.S. Navy and Coast Guard.* a commissioned officer next in rank below an admiral.

vice·ge·rent (vīs jēr′ənt), *n.* an administrative deputy of a sovereign. —**vice·ge′ren·cy,** *n.*

vi·cen·ni·al (vī sen′ē əl), *adj.* occurring every 20 years.

vice′ pres′ident, 1. an officer next in rank to a president. 2. (*caps.*) the elected officer who is next in authority to the President of the U.S. —**vice′ pres′i·den·cy.** —**vice′ pres′i·den′tial.**

vice·re·gal (vīs rē′gəl), *adj.* of or pertaining to a viceroy. —**vice·re′gal·ly,** *adv.*

vice·roy (vīs′roi), *n.* a person appointed to rule a country or province as the deputy of the sovereign. —**vice′roy′al·ty,** *n.*

vi·ce ver·sa (vī′sə vûr′sə, vīs′ē, vīs′), in reverse order from that of a preceding statement.

vi·chy·ssoise (vish′ē swäz′), *n.* a cream soup of potatoes and leeks, usually served chilled.

vic·i·nage (vis′ə nij), *n. Literary.* vicinity. —**vic′i·nal** (-n°l), *adj.*

vi·cin·i·ty (vi sin′i tē), *n., pl.* **-ties.** 1. the area near or about a place. 2. the state or fact of being near.

vi·cious (vish′əs), *adj.* 1. addicted to or characterized by vice. 2. given to evil. 3. spiteful or malicious. 4. savage or ferocious. 5. unpleasantly severe. —**vi′cious·ly,** *adv.* —**vi′cious·ness,** *n.*

vi′cious cir′cle, a situation in which effort to solve a given problem results in the creation of another problem that in turn leads back to the original problem.

vi·cis·si·tude (vi sis′i tōōd′, -tyōōd′), *n.* 1. vicissitudes, unexpectedly changing circumstances, as of fortune. 2. interchange or alternation.

vic·tim (vik′tim), *n.* 1. a person who suffers from a destructive or injurious action or agency: *war victims.* 2. a person who is deceived or cheated. 3. a living being sacrificed in religious rites.

vic·tim·ize (vik′tə mīz′), *v.t.,* **-ized, -iz·ing.** to make a victim of. —**vic′tim·i·za′tion,** *n.* —**vic′tim·iz′er,** *n.*

vic′timless crime′, a legal offense, such as prostitution or gambling, that generally involves consent and no direct physical violence.

vic·tor (vik′tər), *n.* a winner in any struggle or contest.

Vic·to·ri·a (vik tôr′ē ə, -tōr′-), *n.* 1. 1819–1901, queen of Great Britain 1837–1901. 2. the capital of British Columbia. 3. (*l.c.*) a low, light, four-wheeled carriage with a seat for two passengers and a perch in front for the driver.

Vic·to·ri·an (vik tôr′ē ən, -tōr′-), *adj.* 1. of or pertaining to Queen Victoria or the period of her reign. 2. having the characteristics usually attributed to the Victorians, esp. prudery or stuffiness. —*n.* 3. a person, esp. an author, of that period. —**Vic·to′ri·an·ism,** *n.*

vic·to·ri·ous (vik tôr′ē əs, -tōr′-), *adj.* 1. having achieved a victory. 2. of or characterized by victory. —**vic·to′ri·ous·ly,** *adv.* —**vic·to′ri·ous·ness,** *n.*

vic·to·ry (vik′tə rē), *n., pl.* **-ries.** 1. decisive defeat of an enemy in battle or war. 2. success or superiority in any struggle or contest. —**Syn.** 1. conquest, triumph.

vict·ual (vit′ºl), *n., v.,* **-ualed, -ual·ing, -ualled, -ual·ling.** —*n.* 1. victuals, *Dial. or Informal.* food supplies. —*v.t.* 2. to supply with victuals. —*v.i. Chiefly Naut.* 3. to obtain victuals.

vict·ual·er (vit′ºlər), *n.* 1. *Brit.* an innkeeper licensed to sell liquor. 2. *Obs.* a. a trader in victuals. b. a supply ship. Also, *Brit.,* **vict′ual·ler.**

vi·cu·ña (vĭ kōō′nə, -kyōō′-, və-, və-kōō′nyə), *n.* **1.** a South American animal, related to the llama, yielding a soft, delicate wool. **2.** its wool. **3.** a fabric made from it. Also, **vicu′-na.**

vi·de (vī′dē), *v. Latin.* see (used esp. to refer a reader to a specified part of a text).

vi·de·li·cet (vĭ del′i sit), *adv. Law.* namely. [< L]

vid·e·o (vĭd′ē ō′), *n.* **1.** the visual elements of television. **2.** television. —*adj.* **3.** of or pertaining to television, esp. its visual elements.

vid·e·o·disc (vĭd′ē ō disk′), *n.* a disk on which motion pictures and sound are recorded for later reproduction on a player, esp. on an ordinary television screen. Also, **vid′e·o·disk′.**

vid′eo game′, any of various electronic games that involve moving or movable images controlled by the player on a TV screen.

vid·e·o·tape (vĭd′ē ō tāp′), *n., v.,* **-taped, ·tap·ing.** —*n.* **1.** a type of magnetic tape for picture recording or reproduction, esp. for television. —*v.t.* **2.** to record on videotape.

vid·kid (vĭd′kid′), *n. Slang.* a child who watches television habitually or excessively.

vie (vī), *v.i.*, **vied, vy·ing.** to contend for superiority.

Vi·en·na (vē en′ə), *n.* the capital of Austria. —**Vi·en·nese** (vē′ə nēz′, -nēs′), *adj., n.*

Vi·et·cong (vē′et kong′, vyet′-), *n., pl.* **-cong. 1.** a Communist-led guerrilla force in South Vietnam, supported by North Vietnam, in c1959 through 1973. **3.** a member of this force.

Vi·et·nam (vē′et näm′, vyet′-), *n.* a country in SE Asia, bordering on the South China Sea: formerly divided into North Vietnam and South Vietnam but reunified in 1976. —**Vi′et·nam·ese′** (-nä mēz′, -mēs′), *n., adj.*

view (vyōō), *n.* **1.** the act or an instance of looking at something. **2.** the range of one's vision. **3.** an unobstructed sight of something. **4.** a picture of such a sight. **5.** a personal attitude or opinion. **6.** an aim or purpose. **7.** a prospect or expectation. **8. in view, a.** within range of vision. **b.** under consideration. **c.** as an end sought. **9. in view of,** in consideration of. **10. on view,** on exhibition. **11. with a view to, a.** with the aim of. **b.** with the hope of. —*v.t.* **12.** to see or watch. **13.** to survey or inspect. **14.** to consider or regard.

view·er (vyōō′ər), *n.* **1.** a person or thing that views. **2.** a person who watches television. **3.** any optical apparatus to facilitate viewing, as

of a photographic transparency.

view·find·er (vyōō′fīn′dər), *n.* finder (def. 2).

view·point (vyōō′point′), *n.* See **point of view.**

vi·ges·i·mal (vĭ jes′ə məl), *adj.* based on twenty, as in a system of counting.

vig·il (vij′əl), *n.* **1.** a period of watchfulness or wakefulness that is kept through the night. **2.** the eve before a church festival.

vig′ilance commit′tee, an unauthorized group of citizens organized for the summary punishment of crime, as during pioneer days in the U.S.

vig·i·lant (vij′ə lənt), *adj.* keenly watchful to detect danger or trouble. —**vig′i·lance,** *n.* —**vig′i·lant·ly,** *adv.* —**vig′i·lant·ness,** *n.* —**Syn.** alert.

vig·i·lan·te (vij′ə lan′tē), *n.* a member of a vigilance committee.

vi·gnette (vin yet′), *n., v.,* **-gnet·ted, -gnet·ting.** —*n.* **1.** a short, graceful literary sketch. **2.** a decorative design used on the title page of a book or at the beginning or end of a chapter. **3.** an engraving or photograph that is shaded off gradually at the edges. —*v.t.* **4.** to finish (a photograph) in the manner of a vignette. —**vig·nett′ist,** *n.*

vig·or (vig′ər), *n.* **1.** healthy physical or mental strength. **2.** effective force. Also, *Brit.,* **vig′our.**

vig·or·ous (vig′ər əs), *adj.* **1.** full of vigor. **2.** powerful in action or effect. —**vig′or·ous·ly,** *adv.* —**vig′or·ous·ness,** *n.* —**Syn.** energetic.

Vi·king (vī′king), *n.* any of the Scandinavian pirates who plundered the coasts of Europe from the 8th to 10th centuries.

vil., village.

vile (vīl), *adj.,* **vil·er, vil·est. 1.** morally debased. **2.** foul or repulsive. **3.** degrading or humiliating. **4.** wretchedly bad: *vile weather.* —**vile′-ness,** *n.* —**Syn. 1.** base, corrupt, dissolute. **3.** ignominious.

vil·i·fy (vil′ə fī′), *v.t.,* **-fied, -fy·ing.** to use openly abusive language of or about. —**vil′i·fi·ca′tion,** *n.*

vil·la (vil′ə), *n.* a large, luxurious country residence or estate.

vil·lage (vil′ij), *n.* **1.** a small community in a rural area, usually smaller than a town. **2.** its inhabitants.

vil·lag·er (vil′i jər), *n.* an inhabitant of a village.

vil·lain (vil′ən), *n.* **1.** a cruel, malicious person. **2.** a character in a play or novel who opposes the hero. —**vil′lain·ess,** *n.fem.*

vil·lain·ous (vil′ə nəs), *adj.* **1.** having a cruel, malicious nature. **2.** of or befitting a villain. **3.** very unpleasant. —**vil′lain·ous·ly,** *adv.* —**vil′-lain·ous·ness,** *n.*

vil·lain·y (vil′ə nē), *n.*, *pl.* **-ies. 1.** outrageous wickedness. **2.** a villainous act.

vil·lein (vil′ən), *n.* a feudal serf in England who had certain rights of of a freeman. —**vil·lein·age** (vil′ə nij), *n.*

vil·lus (vil′əs), *n.*, *pl.* **vil·li** (vil′ī). one of the minute processes on the mucous membrane of the small intestine, where they serve in absorbing nutriment. —**vil·lous** (vil′əs), *adj.*

vim (vim), *n.* lively or energetic spirit.

vin (vaN), *n.* French. wine.

vin·ai·grette (vin′ə gret′), *n.* a small ornamental bottle or box for holding aromatic vinegar or smelling salts.

Vin·ci (vin′chē), *n.* Le·o·nar·do da (lē′ə när′dō də), 1452–1519, Italian painter, sculptor, and scientist.

vin·ci·ble (vin′sə bəl), *adj.* capable of being conquered or overcome.

vin·di·ca·ble (vin′də kə bəl), *adj.* capable of being vindicated.

vin·di·cate (vin′də kāt′), *v.t.*, **-cat·ed, -cat·ing. 1.** to clear from an accusation or suspicion. **2.** to maintain or defend against opposition. **3.** to afford justification for. —**vin′di·ca′tion**, *n.* —**vin′di·ca′tor**, *n.* —**Syn. 1.** exonerate.

vin·dic·tive (vin dik′tiv), *adj.* **1.** strongly inclined to revenge. **2.** proceeding from or showing a revengeful spirit. —**vin·dic′tive·ly**, *adv.* —**vin·dic′tive·ness**, *n.* —**Syn.** spiteful, vengeful, unforgiving.

vine (vīn), *n.* **1.** any plant having a long, slender stem that creeps on the ground or climbs a support. **2.** the stem of any such plant. **3.** a grape plant.

vin·e·gar (vin′ə gər), *n.* a sour liquid produced by the fermentation of wine, cider, etc., used to flavor or preserve food. [< OF *vin* wine + *egre* sour]

vin·e·gar·y (vin′ə gə rē), *adj.* **1.** resembling vinegar, esp. in taste. **2.** having a disagreeable character or manner.

vine·yard (vin′yərd), *n.* **1.** a plantation of grapevines. **2.** a sphere of activity, esp. of a spiritual nature.

vi·nous (vī′nəs), *adj.* **1.** of or made with wine. **2.** caused by or given to drinking wine.

vin·tage (vin′tij), *n.* **1.** the wine from a particular harvest or crop. **2.** the annual produce of a grape harvest, esp. with reference to the wine obtained. **3.** an exceptionally fine wine from the crop of a good year. **4.** the act or season of harvesting grapes or of making wine. **5.** the class of dated or old-fashioned objects: *a car of 1917 vintage* —*adj.* **6.** of or pertaining to a vintage. **7.** being or having the best of its kind. **8.** dated or old-fashioned but often of continuing interest.

vint·ner (vint′nər), *n.* **1.** a wine maker. **2.** *Brit.* a wine dealer.

vi·nyl (vīn′əl), *n.* any of various flexible and durable plastics used in coatings, phonograph records, etc.

vi′nyl chlo′ride, a colorless, toxic gas produced by combining vinyl with chlorine, used in making plastics, adhesives, etc.

vi·ol (vī′əl), *n.* a bowed musical instrument differing from the violin in having a greater number of strings, usually six, and frets: common in the 16th and 17th centuries.

vi·o·la (vē ō′lə, vī-), *n.* a four-stringed musical instrument similar to a violin but slightly larger and deeper in tone.

vi·o·la·ble (vī′ə lə bəl), *adj.* capable of being violated: *a violable precept.* —**vi′o·la·bly**, *adv.*

vi·o·late (vī′ə lāt′), *v.t.*, **-lat·ed, -lat·ing. 1.** to break or disregard wrongfully, as a law or rule. **2.** to disturb or interrupt, as one's privacy. **3.** to desecrate or profane. **4.** to rape (a woman). —**vi′o·la′tor**, *n.*

vi·o·la·tion (vī′ə lā′shən), *n.* **1.** the act of violating or state of being violated. **2.** a breach or infringement, as of a law or rule. **3.** a disturbance or interruption. **4.** desecration or profanation. **5.** rape or sexual molestation. —**vi·o·la·tive** (vī′ə lā′tiv, vī′ə lə tiv), *adj.*

vi·o·lence (vī′ə ləns), *n.* **1.** swift and great force that causes damage or injury. **2.** great force, as of feeling. **3.** damage or injury. **4.** rough, brutal force.

vi·o·lent (vī′ə lənt), *adj.* **1.** acting with or characterized by great force. **2.** having or showing great force of feeling. **3.** arising from injurious or destructive force: *a violent death.* **4.** intense in force or effect. —**vi′o·lent·ly**, *adv.*

vi·o·let (vī′ə lit), *n.* **1.** a small, low plant having purple, blue, yellow, or white flowers. **2.** a bluish purple. —*adj.* **3.** bluish-purple.

vi·o·lin (vī′ə lin′), *n.* a four-stringed bowed instrument related to the viola, cello, and double bass but smaller and of highest pitch. —**vi′o·lin′ist**, *n.*

vi·o·list (vē ō′list, vī-), *n.* a viola player.

vi·o·lon·cel·lo (vē′ə lən chel′ō), *n.*, *pl.* **-los.** cello. —**vi′o·lon·cel′list** (-ist), *n.*

VIP, *Informal.* very important person.

vi·per (vī′pər), *n.* **1.** any of various poisonous snakes. **2.** a nasty, spiteful person. **—vi′per·ous, vi′per·ine** (-in, -pə rīn′), *adj.*

vi·ra·go (vi rā′gō, -rä′-), *n., pl.* **-goes, gos.** a loud, ill-tempered, scolding woman.

vi·ral (vī′rəl), *adj.* of or caused by a virus.

vir·e·o (vir′ē ō′), *n., pl.* **-os.** a small American bird having olive-green or gray feathers.

Vir·gil (vûr′jəl), *n.* 70–19 B.C., Roman poet.

vir·gin (vûr′jin), *n.* **1.** a person, esp. a woman, who has never had sexual intercourse. **2.** an unmarried woman. **3. the Virgin,** Mary, the mother of Christ. **4. the Virgin,** Virgo. —*adj.* **5.** of, being, or befitting a virgin. **6.** pure or spotless: *virgin snow.* **7.** untouched or unused: *a virgin forest.*

vir·gin·al[1] (vûr′jə nəl), *adj.* of or proper to a virgin. **—vir′gin·al·ly,** *adv.* **—Syn.** fresh, pure, youthful.

vir·gin·al[2] (vûr′jə nəl), *n.* a rectangular harpsichord popular in the 16th and 17th centuries.

Vir·gin·ia (vir jin′yə), *n.* a state in the E United States. *Cap.:* Richmond. **—Vir·gin′ian,** *adj., n.*

Virgin′ia creep′er, a North American climbing plant having five-pointed leaves and bluish-black berries.

Virgin′ia reel′, an American country dance in which partners start by facing each other in two lines and perform various steps together.

Vir′gin Is′lands, two groups of islands in the West Indies, one belonging to the U.S. and the other, Great Britain.

vir·gin·i·ty (vər jin′i tē), *n.* the state or condition of being virgin or a virgin.

Vir′gin Mar′y, the mother of Jesus.

Vir·go (vûr′gō), *n.* the sixth sign of the zodiac. [< L: *virgin*]

vir·gule (vûr′gyool), *n. Print. Obsolesc.* slash (def. 7).

vir·i·des·cent (vir′i des′ənt), *adj.* slightly green.

vir·ile (vir′əl), *adj.* **1.** of, characteristic of, or befitting a man. **2.** having masculine strength or spirit. **3.** capable of procreation. **—vi·ril·i·ty** (və-ril′i tē), *n.*

vi·rol·o·gy (vī rol′ə jē, vi-), *n.* the science dealing with viruses and viral diseases. **—vi·ro·log·i·cal** (vī′rə loj′i kəl), *adj.* **—vi·rol′o·gist,** *n.*

vir·tu (vər too′, vûr′too), *n.* **1.** excellence in objects of art. **2.** such objects or articles collectively. **3.** a taste for or knowledge of such objects.

vir·tu·al (vûr′choo əl), *adj.* being such in force or effect, though not openly so. **—vir′tu·al·ly,** *adv.*

vir·tue (vûr′choo), *n.* **1.** moral excellence. **2.** a particular good moral quality. **3.** chastity, esp. in a woman. **4.** a good or admirable quality. **5.** *Obsolesc.* potency, as of a medicine. **6. by or in virtue of,** by reason of. **—Syn. 1.** integrity, righteousness.

vir·tu·os·i·ty (vûr′choo os′i tē), *n., pl.* **-ties.** the character, ability, or skill of a virtuoso.

vir·tu·o·so (vûr′choo ō′sō), *n., pl.* **-sos, -si** (-sē). **1.** a person who has great skill in a field, esp. in musical technique. **2.** a person who has a cultivated appreciation of artistic excellence.

vir·tu·ous (vûr′choo əs), *adj.* **1.** having or exhibiting moral virtue. **2.** chaste, as a woman. **—vir′tu·ous·ly,** *adv.* **—vir′tu·ous·ness,** *n.*

vir·u·lent (vir′yə lənt, vir′ə-), *adj.* **1.** actively poisonous or harmful. **2.** intensely bitter or spiteful. **3.** *Med.* **a.** exceedingly infectious. **b.** rapid and severe in its advance, as a disease. **—vir′u·lence, vir′u·len·cy,** *n.* **—vir′u·lent·ly,** *adv.*

vi·rus (vī′rəs), *n.* **1.** any of a group of microscopic infectious agents that reproduce only in living cells and cause diseases, as mumps. **2.** a corrupting influence.

vis., 1. visibility. **2.** visual.

vi·sa (vē′zə), *n.* a permit entered on a passport by a consular officer of a foreign country, allowing the bearer entry into or transit through that country.

vis·age (viz′ij), *n. Literary.* **1.** the face or countenance. **2.** aspect or appearance.

vis-à-vis (vē′zə vē′), *adv., adj., prep., n., pl.* **-vis.** **—***adv., adj.* **1.** face to face. **—***prep.* **2.** in relation to. **3.** facing opposite. **—***n.* **4.** a person situated opposite to another.

vis·cer·a (vis′ər ə), *n.pl., sing.* **vis·cus** (-kəs). **1.** the organs in the cavities of the body, as the stomach, liver, etc. **2.** (loosely) the intestines.

vis·cer·al (vis′ər əl), *adj.* **1.** of or affecting the viscera. **2.** proceeding from instinctive rather than intellectual motivation. **—vis′cer·al·ly,** *adv.*

vis·cid (vis′id), *adj.* viscous. **—vis·cid′i·ty,** *n.* **—vis′cid·ly,** *adv.*

vis·cose (vis′kōs), *n.* a viscous solution obtained from treating cellulose, used in making rayon or cellophane.

vis·cos·i·ty (vi skos′i tē), *n., pl.* **-ties. 1.** the state or quality of being viscous. **2.** *Physics.* the property of a fluid that resists the force tending to cause the fluid to flow.

vis·count (vī′kount′), *n.* a nobleman next below an earl or count and next above a baron. —**vis′count′ess**, *n. fem.*

vis·cous (vis′kəs), *adj.* **1.** having a thick, sticky consistency. **2.** *Physics.* possessing viscosity. —**vis′cous·ly**, *adv.* —**vis′cous·ness**, *n.*

vise (vīs), *n.* a device with two jaws that close together by means of a screw, used to hold in place an object being worked on.

vi·sé (vē′zā), *n. Archaic.* visa.

Vish·nu (vish′nōō), *n. Hinduism.* the second member of the trinity, along with Brahma and Shiva.

vis·i·bil·i·ty (viz′ə bil′i tē), *n.* **1.** the state or fact of being visible. **2.** the degree or distance to which things can be seen under certain conditions of weather.

vis·i·ble (viz′ə bəl), *adj.* **1.** able to be seen. **2.** manifest or obvious. —**vis′i·bly**, *adv.* —**Syn. 1.** discernible, perceptible.

vi·sion (vizh′ən), *n.* **1.** the act or power of seeing. **2.** unusual foresight. **3.** an image or idea of a spiritual nature seen or obtained under the influence of a divine or other agency. **4.** an imaginative conception or anticipation. **5.** a person or thing of extraordinary beauty.

vi·sion·ar·y (vizh′ə ner′ē), *adj., n., pl.* **-ar·ies.** —*adj.* **1.** given to or characterized by unreal or impractical ideas. **2.** seen in a vision. —*n.* **3.** a person who sees visions. **4.** a person with unusual foresight. **5.** a person given to unreal or impractical ideas. —**Syn. 1.** fanciful, imaginary.

vis·it (viz′it), *v.t.* **1.** to go or come to see for social pleasure, business, or sightseeing. **2.** to stay with as a guest. **3.** to go to as a courtesy or for the purpose of official inspection. **4.** to assail or afflict: *a country visited by the plague.* —*v.i.* **5.** to make a visit. **6.** *Informal.* to chat casually. —*n.* **7.** an act or instance of visiting. **8.** a stay as a guest. —**vis′it·a·ble**, *adj.*

vis·i·tant (viz′i tənt), *n. Literary.* a visitor.

vis·it·a·tion (viz′i tā′shən), *n.* **1.** an official visit, as for purposes of church inspection. **2.** a punishment or reward from God. —**vis′it·a′tion·al**, *adj.*

vis′ita′tion rights′, the right of a parent to visit a child in the custody of the other parent, as decreed in a divorce or separation.

vi·sor (vī′zər), *n.* **1.** the projecting front brim of a cap. **2.** an adjustable flap over an automobile windshield for shielding against glare. **3.** the movable front piece of a medieval helmet covering the face. —**vi′sored**, *adj.* —**vi′sor·less′**, *adj.*

vis·ta (vis′tə), *n.* **1.** a view seen through a long, narrow passage. **2.** a mental view or prospect. —**vis′taed** (vis′təd), *adj.*

VISTA (vis′tə), Volunteers in Service to America.

vis·u·al (vizh′ōō əl), *adj.* **1.** of or pertaining to seeing or sight. **2.** used in seeing or sight. **3.** perceptible by the mind. **4.** done by sight and without using instruments: *visual flying.* **5.** noting nonbook materials involving the use of sight, as for educational purposes: *visual aids.* **6.** *Rare.* visible (def. 1). —**vis′u·al·ly**, *adv.*

vis′ual arts′, the arts, such as painting, sculpture, etc., that are appreciated for their aesthetic excellence through the sense of sight.

vis·u·al·ize (vizh′ōō ə līz′), *v.i., v.t.,* **-ized, -iz·ing.** to form a mental image (of). —**vis′u·al·i·za′tion**, *n.* —**vis′u·al·iz′er**, *n.*

vi·tal (vīt′əl), *adj.* **1.** of or pertaining to life. **2.** necessary to life. **3.** energetic or lively. **4.** indispensable or essential. **5.** of critical importance. **6.** *Archaic.* fatal or deadly. —**vi′tal·ly**, *adv.*

vi·tal·i·ty (vī tal′i tē), *n., pl.* **-ties.** **1.** exuberant physical and mental strength. **2.** capacity for survival or endurance. **3.** power to live or grow. —**Syn. 1.** energy, vigor.

vi·tal·ize (vīt′°līz′), *v.t.,* **-ized, -iz·ing.** to give life or vigor to. —**vi′tal·i·za′tion**, *n.* —**vi′tal·iz′er**, *n.*

vi·tals (vīt′°lz), *n.pl.* **1.** the bodily organs that are essential to life, as the brain, heart, etc. **2.** the essential parts of something.

vi′tal signs′, the measurable essential bodily functions, as the pulse, temperature, etc.

vi′tal statis′tics, statistics concerning deaths, births, and marriages.

vi·ta·min (vī′tə min), *n.* any of a group of organic substances essential in small quantities to normal metabolism and health, found in foods and also produced synthetically. [< L *vīt(a)* life + *amin(e)*]

vitamin A, a vitamin found in green and yellow vegetables, egg yolk, etc.: essential to growth and the prevention of night blindness.

vitamin B, 1. a member of the vitamin B complex. **2.** See **vitamin B complex.**

vitamin B₁, thiamine.

vitamin B₂, riboflavin.

vitamin B₁₂, a vitamin obtained from liver, oysters, etc., used chiefly in treating anemia.

vitamin B complex, an important group of vitamins containing vitamin B₁, vitamin B₂, etc.

vitamin C, See ascorbic acid.

vitamin D, a vitamin found esp. in fish-liver oils: essential for the formation of normal bones and teeth.

vitamin E, a vitamin found in wheat-germ oil that promotes fertility and is active in maintaining the nervous and vascular system.

vitamin K, a vitamin occurring esp. in leafy vegetables that promotes blood clotting.

vi·ti·ate (vish′ē āt′), v.t., **-at·ed, -at·ing. 1.** to impair the quality of. **2.** to debase or corrupt. **3.** to make legally invalid. —**vi′ti·a′tion,** n. —**vi′ti·a′tor,** n.

vit·i·cul·ture (vit′ə kul′chər, vī′tə-), n. the cultivation of grapes. —**vit′i·cul′tur·al,** adj. —**vit′i·cul′tur·ist,** n.

vit·re·ous (vi′trē əs), adj. **1.** of or resembling glass, as in glossiness. **2.** obtained from or containing glass.

vit′reous hu′mor, the transparent, jellylike substance filling the eyeball behind the lens.

vit·ri·fy (vi′trə fī′), v.t., v.i., **-fied, -fy·ing.** to change into glass or a glassy substance. —**vit′ri·fi′a·ble,** adj. —**vit′ri·fi·ca′tion** (-fə kā′shən), n.

vi·trine (vi trēn′), n. a glass cabinet esp. for displaying objects of art.

vit·ri·ol (vi′trē əl), n. **1.** See sulfuric acid. **2.** a sulfate made by the action of sulfuric acid on certain metals, as copper. **3.** something severely caustic, as criticism.

vit·tles (vit′əlz), n. Nonstandard. victuals.

vi·tu·per·ate (vī tōō′pə rāt′, -tyōō′-, vi-), v.t., **-at·ed, -at·ing.** to censure severely or abusively. —**vi·tu′per·a′tion,** n. —**vi·tu′per·a′tive,** adj. —**vi·tu′per·a′tive·ly,** adv.

vi·va (vē′və, -vä), interj. Italian, Spanish. long live (the person named)!

vi·va·ce (vi vä′chä), adv., adj. in a lively manner (used as a musical direction).

vi·va·cious (vi vā′shəs, vī-), adj. buoyantly spirited, as in manner. —**vi·va′cious·ly,** adv. —**vi·vac′i·ty** (-vas′i tē), **vi·va′cious·ness,** n. —Syn. animated, lively, sprightly.

vi·var·i·um (vi vâr′ē əm), n., pl. **-i·ums, -i·a** (-ē ə). a place where live animals or plants are kept under natural conditions, as for research.

vi·va vo·ce (vī′və vō′sē), by word of mouth. —**vi′va-vo′ce,** adj.

vive (vēv), interj. French. long live (the person named)!

viv·id (viv′id), adj. **1.** strikingly bright or intense, as color. **2.** clearly perceptible, as an impression. **3.** presenting lifelike freshness or spirit. **4.** full of life or vigor, as a personality. —**viv′id·ly,** adv. —**viv′id·ness,** n.

viv·i·fy (viv′ə fī′), v.t., **-fied, -fy·ing. 1.** to give life or spirit to. **2.** to make vivid or bright. —**viv′i·fi·ca′tion,** n. —**viv′i·fi′er,** n.

vi·vip·ar·ous (vī vip′ər əs), adj. bringing forth living young rather than eggs, as most mammals. —**viv·i·par·i·ty** (viv′ə par′i tē), n. —**vi·vip′a·rous·ly,** adv.

viv·i·sect (viv′i sekt′, viv′i sekt′), v.t. **1.** to dissect the living body of (an animal). —v.i. **2.** to practice vivisection.

viv·i·sec·tion (viv′i sek′shən), n. the practice of dissecting or cutting into living animals, esp. for medical research. —**viv′i·sec′tion·ist,** n.

vix·en (vik′sən), n. **1.** a female fox. **2.** an ill-tempered or quarrelsome woman. —**vix′en·ish,** adj. —**vix′en·ish·ly,** adv.

viz. (viz), Law. videlicet. [by alteration]

viz·ard (viz′ərd), n. Archaic. a protective and disguising mask.

vi·zier (vi zēr′, viz′yər), n. (formerly) a high official in certain Muslim countries. Also, **vi·zir′.**

vi·zor (vī′zər, viz′ər), n. visor.

VL, See Vulgar Latin.

VLF, See very low frequency.

V.M.D., Doctor of Veterinary Medicine. [< L Veterinariae Medicinae Doctor]

V neck, a neckline V-shaped in front.

VOA, Voice of America.

voc., vocative.

vocab., vocabulary.

vo·ca·ble (vō′kə bəl), n. a word considered only as a combination of certain sounds or letters, without regard to meaning.

vo·cab·u·lar·y (vō kab′yə ler′ē), n., pl. **-ies. 1.** the stock of words used by or known to a particular person or group of persons. **2.** an alphabetical list of defined words or phrases. **3.** the words of a language.

vo·cal (vō′kəl), adj. **1.** of or uttered with the voice. **2.** rendered by or intended for singing. **3.** capable of or giving forth sound or speech. **4.** full of voice or voices. **5.** speaking loudly or openly. —n. **6.** a vocal sound. **7.** Music. the part of a composition intended to be sung rather than played on the instruments. —**vo′cal·ly,** adv.

vo′cal cords′, folds of mucous membrane in the larynx that vibrate to produce vocal sound.

vo·cal·ic (vō kal′ik), adj. of, like, or containing a vowel.

vo·cal·ist (vō′kə list), n. a singer, as opposed to an instrumentalist.

vo·cal·ize (vō′kə līz′), v.t., v.i., **-ized, -iz·ing. 1.** to make vocal or articulate. **2.** to speak or sing. —**vo′cal·i·za′tion,** n. —**vo′cal·iz′er,** n.

vocat., vocative.

vo·ca·tion (vō kā′shən), *n.* **1.** any occupation regularly followed for a living. **2.** a strong impulse to follow a particular career. **3.** a religious calling. – **vo·ca′tion·al,** *adj.*

voc·a·tive (vok′ə tiv), *adj. Gram.* (in Latin) noting a case used to indicate the one being addressed. —**voc′a·tive·ly,** *adv.*

vo·cif·er·ate (vō sif′ə rāt′), *v.i., v.t., -at·ed, -at·ing.* to cry out loudly or noisily. —**vo·cif′er·a′tion,** *n.*

vo·cif·er·ous (vō sif′ər əs), *adj.* making a loud or noisy outcry. —**vo·cif′er·ous·ly,** *adv* —**vo·cif′er·ous·ness,** *n.* —**Syn.** clamorous.

vod·ka (vod′kə), *n* a colorless alcoholic liquor, originally made in Russia, distilled from potatoes, etc.

vogue (vōg), *n* **1.** the fashion at a particular time **2.** temporary popularity or favor —**vogu·ish** (vō′gish), *adj.* —**Syn.** fad, mode, style.

voice (vois), *n., v.,* **voiced, voic·ing.** —*n.* **1.** the sound made through the mouth, esp of human beings, in speaking or singing. **2.** the ability to produce such sound. **3.** a sound resembling vocal utterance **4.** expression in words or uttered sounds. **5.** the right or power to be heeded or obeyed. **6.** an expressed will or desire. **7.** any of the vocal parts in a musical score. **8.** *Gram.* a form of verb showing whether the subject performs or receives the action of the verb. **9. with one voice,** in accord or unanimously. —*v.t.* **10.** to give utterance or expression to.

voice′ box′, *Chiefly Phonet.* the larynx.

voiced (voist), *adj.* **1.** having a voice of a specified kind: *gruff-voiced.* **2.** expressed with the voice. **3.** *Phonet.* pronounced with vibration of the vocal cords as the consonant *b.* — **voic·ed·ness** (voi′sid nis, voist′nis), *n.*

voice·less (vois′lis), *adj.* **1.** having no voice. **2.** *Phonet* pronounced without vibration of the vocal cords, as the consonant *k.* —**voice′less·ly,** *adv.* —**voice′less·ness,** *n.*

voice-o·ver (vois′ō′vər), *n.* a voice heard without a narrator being seen, as on television.

voice·print (vois′print′), *n.* a graphic representation of an individually different pattern of a person's speech sound.

void (void), *adj.* **1.** having no legal force. **2.** completely devoid. **3.** containing or holding nothing. **4.** without an incumbent, as a bishopric. **5.** *Literary.* useless or vain. —*n.* **6.** an empty space. **7.** a feeling of loss or emptiness. —*v.t.* **8.** to invalidate or nullify. **9.** to empty or discharge, as

body wastes. —**void′a·ble,** *adj.* —**void′er,** *n.*

voi·là (vwa la′), *interj. French.* there it is!

voile (voil), *n.* a dress fabric, as of wool or cotton, having an open weave.

vol., **1.** volume. **2.** volunteer.

vol·a·tile (vol′ə təl), *adj.* **1.** evaporating rapidly or easily at ordinary temperatures. **2.** tending to break out into open violence. **3.** changeable or flighty, as a disposition. —**vol′a·til′i·ty** (-til′i tē), *n.* —**vol′a·til·ize′** (-īz′), *v.i., v.t.* —**Syn.** **2.** explosive, unstable.

vol·can·ic (vol kan′ik), *adj.* **1.** of or like a volcano. **2.** caused by a volcano. **3.** potentially explosive. —**vol·can′i·cal·ly,** *adv.*

vol·can·ism (vol′kə niz′əm), *n.* volcanic activity.

vol·ca·no (vol kā′nō), *n., pl.* **-noes, -nos.** **1.** a vent in the earth's crust through which lava, steam, and ashes are thrown up. **2.** a mountain formed around such a vent from the materials so expelled.

vol·can·ol·o·gy (vol′kə nol′ə jē), *n.* the scientific study of volcanic phenomena. —**vol′can·o·log′i·cal** (-nˈoj′i kəl), *adj.* —**vol′can·ol′o·gist,** *n.*

vole (vōl), *n.* any of several small mouselike rodents.

Vol·ga (vol′gə), *n.* a river in the W Soviet Union.

vo·li·tion (vō lish′ən), *n.* **1.** the act of willing or choosing. **2.** the power of willing. —**vo·li′tion·al,** *adj.* —**vo·li′tion·al·ly,** *adv.*

vol·ley (vol′ē), *n., pl.* **-leys,** *v.,* **-leyed, -ley·ing.** —*n.* **1.** the simultaneous discharge of a number of missiles or firearms. **2.** the missiles so discharged. **3.** an outburst of many things at once: *a volley of protests.* **4.** *Tennis.* the act of volleying. —*v.t., v.i.* **5.** to discharge or be discharged in or as in a volley. **6.** *Tennis.* to return (the ball) before it hits the ground. —**vol′ley·er,** *n.*

vol·ley·ball (vol′ē bôl′), *n.* **1.** a team game played by striking a large ball over a high net with the hands before it touches the ground. **2.** the ball used.

vol·plane (vol′plān′), *v.i.,* **-planed, -plan·ing.** to glide in an airplane.

volt (vōlt), *n.* the unit of electromotive force equal to the electromotive force that will cause a current of one ampere to flow through a conductor with a resistance of one ohm.

volt·age (vōl′tij), *n.* electromotive force expressed in volts.

vol·ta·ic (vol tā′ik), *adj.* noting electricity produced by chemical action, as in a cell.

Vol·taire (vŏl târ′, vōl-), *n.* 1694–1778, French philosopher and historian.

volt·me·ter (vōlt′mē′tər), *n.* an instrument for measuring the voltage between two points of a circuit.

vol·u·ble (vŏl′yə bəl), *adj.* speaking a ready and easy flow of words. —**vol′u·bil′i·ty,** *n.* —**vol′u·bly,** *adv.* —**Syn.** fluent, glib, talkative.

vol·ume (vŏl′yŏōm -yəm), *n.* **1.** a collection of written or printed sheets bound together and constituting a book **2.** one book of a related set. **3.** all of the issues of a periodical in any one-year period. **4.** the amount of space occupied by an object or substance, as measured in cubic units. **5.** a mass or bulk. **6.** amount or quantity. **7.** the degree of sound intensity.

vol·u·met·ric (vŏl′yə me′trik), *adj.* of or pertaining to measurement by volume. —**vol′u·met′ri·cal·ly,** *adv.*

vo·lu·mi·nous (və lōō′mə nəs), *adj.* **1.** having great volume or bulk. **2.** sufficient to fill many volumes. **3.** *Archaic.* having many coils or windings. —**vo·lu′mi·nos′i·ty** (-nos′i tē), **vo·lu′mi·nous·ness,** *n.* —**vo·lu′mi·nous·ly,** *adv.*

vol·un·tar·y (vŏl′ən ter′ē), *adj.* **1.** done or brought about by one's own free will. **2.** exercising free choice. **3.** done by intention and not by accident. **4.** controlled by the will: *voluntary muscles.* —**vol·un·tar·i·ly** (vŏl′ən ter′ə lē, vŏl′ən târ′-), *adv.*

vol·un·teer (vŏl′ən tēr′), *n.* **1.** a person who offers himself or herself for a service without obligation to do so. —*adj* **2.** of, being, or done by a volunteer. —*v.i.* **3.** to offer oneself for some service of one's own free will. —*v.t.* **4.** to say, give, or offer voluntarily.

vo·lup·tu·ar·y (və lup′chŏō er′ē), *n.,* *pl.* -ies. a person devoted to sensual pleasures.

vo·lup·tu·ous (və lup′chŏō əs), *adj.* **1.** full of, giving, or seeking sensual pleasures. **2.** sensuously attractive, as a woman. —**vo·lup′tu·ous·ly,** *adv.* —**vo·lup′tu·ous·ness,** *n.*

vo·lute (və lōōt′), *n.* a spiral or twisted formation or ornament.

vom·it (vŏm′it), *v.i.,* *v.t.* **1.** to eject (the contents of the stomach) through the mouth. **2.** to throw out or be thrown out with force or violence. —*n.* **3.** the act of vomiting. **4.** the matter ejected in vomiting. —**vom′it·er,** *n.*

voo·doo (vŏō′dŏō), *n.,* *pl.* -doos. **1.** a class of religious rites, as sorcery, prevalent in the West Indies. **2.** a person who practices such rites. **3.** a fetish or charm used in such rites. —**voo′doo·ism,** *n.*

vo·ra·cious (vō rā′shəs, vô-, və-), *adj.* **1.** craving or eating large quantities of food. **2.** eager to absorb or possess: *voracious readers.* —**vo·ra′cious·ly,** *adv.* —**vo·rac′i·ty** (-ras′i tē), **vo·ra′cious·ness,** *n.* —**Syn.** greedy, insatiable, ravenous.

vor·tex (vôr′teks), *n.,* *pl.* **-tex·es, -ti·ces** (-ti sēz′). **1.** a whirling mass of water, as a whirlpool. **2.** a whirling mass of air or fire. **3.** a state of affairs resembling a whirlpool in violence or power to involve. —**vor′ti·cal** (-ti kəl), *adj.*

vo·ta·ry (vō′tə rē), *n.,* *pl.* **-ries. 1.** *Literary.* a person devoted to some pursuit or study **2.** *Archaic.* a person bound by religious vows.

vote (vōt), *n.,* *v.,* **vot·ed, vot·ing.** —*n.* **1.** a formal expression of opinion or choice made by an individual or body of individuals. **2.** the means by which such expression is made, as a ballot. **3.** the right to such expression. **4.** the decision reached by voting. **5.** the expressed choice of a particular group. —*v.i.* **6.** to express an opinion or choice by casting a ballot. —*v.t.* **7.** to enact, elect, or decide by vote. **8.** to declare by general consent. [< L *vōtum* a vow] —**vote′less,** *adj.* —**vot′er,** *n.*

vo·tive (vō′tiv), *adj.* done or given with or as a result of a vow.

vou., voucher.

vouch (vouch), *v.i.* **1.** to give personal guarantee or assurance. **2.** to support as being true or valid.

vouch·er (vou′chər), *n.* **1.** a record of an expense paid. **2.** a person or thing that vouches.

vouch·safe (vouch sāf′), *v.t.,* **-safed, -saf·ing.** to grant or give with graciousness or condescension.

vow (vou), *n.* **1.** a solemn promise or pledge. **2.** a solemn promise made to God. **3.** take vows, to enter a religious order. —*v.t.* **4.** to promise or pledge solemnly. —*v.i.* **5.** to make a vow. —**vow′er,** *n.*

vow·el (vou′əl), *n.* **1.** a speech sound produced without obstructing the flow of air from the lungs. **2.** a letter representing such a sound, as *a, e, i, o, u.* —*adj.* **3.** of or pertaining to a vowel or vowels.

vox po·pu·li (voks′ pop′yə lī′), *Latin.* popular opinion. Also called **vox pop** (pop).

voy·age (voi′ij), *n.,* *v.,* **-aged, -ag·ing.** —*n.* **1.** a journey by ship, esp. for a long distance. **2.** a long journey through air or space. —*v.i., v.t.* **3.** to make or take a voyage (on or over). —**voy′ag·er,** *n.*

vo·ya·geur (vwä′yä zhừr′, voi ə-), *n.* (formerly in Canada) a woodsman or boatman hired by a fur company.

vo·yeur (vwä yûr', voi-), *n.* a person who habitually obtains sexual gratification by looking at sexual objects or acts, esp. in secret. —**vo·yeur'ism,** *n.* —**voy·eur·is'tic** (-yə ris'tik), *adj.*

V.P., Vice President.

vs., **1.** verse. **2.** versus.

v.s., *Law.* see above. [< L *vide supra*]

V/STOL, vertical/short takeoff and landing.

VT, Vermont. Also, **Vt.**

v.t., verb transitive.

VTOL, vertical takeoff and landing.

Vul·can (vul'kən), *n.* the ancient Roman god of fire and metal working.

vul·can·ism (vul'kə niz'əm), *n.* volcanism.

vul·can·ite (vul'kə nīt'), *n.* a hard, polished rubber.

vul·can·ize (vul'kə nīz'), *v.t.,* **-ized, -iz·ing.** to treat (rubber) under heat with sulfur to make it tougher and more durable. —**vul'can·i·za'tion,** *n.* —**vul'can·iz'er,** *n.*

Vulg., Vulgate. Also, **Vul.**

vul·gar (vul'gər), *adj.* **1.** lacking good taste or manners. **2.** indecent or obscene, as in language. **3.** a. vernacular, esp. as distinguished from classical: *the vulgar tongue.* b. of or belonging to the common people, esp. as opposed to the intellectual people. —**vul'gar·ly,** *adv.* —**vul'gar·ness,** *n.* —Syn. **1.** boorish, crude, unrefined. **2.** lewd, profane.

vul·gar·i·an (vul gâr'ē ən), *n.* a person having vulgar taste or manners.

vul·gar·ism (vul'gə riz'əm), *n.* **1.** a vulgar word or phrase used only in common colloquial, and esp. in coarse, speech. **2.** vulgarity (def. 2).

vul·gar·i·ty (vul gar'l tē), *n., pl.* **-ties. 1.** the state or quality of being vulgar. **2.** something vulgar, as an act or expression.

vul·gar·ize (vul'gə rīz'), *v.t.,* **-ized, -iz·ing. 1.** to make vulgar or coarse. **2.** to make (an abstruse theory, etc.) easier to understand, esp. in a popular way. —**vul'gar·i·za'tion,** *n.* —**vul'gar·iz'er,** *n.*

Vul'gar Lat'in, popular Latin, as distinguished from literary or standard Latin.

Vul·gate (vul'gāt, -git), *n.* the Latin version of the Bible used in the Roman Catholic Church.

vul·ner·a·ble (vul'nər ə bəl), *adj.* **1.** capable of being wounded or hurt. **2.** open to criticism or attack. **3.** *Bridge.* having won one of the games of a rubber. —**vul'ner·a·bil'l·ty,** *n.* —**vul'ner·a·bly,** *adv.*

vul·pine (vul'pīn, -pin), *adj.* of or like a fox, esp. in cunning.

vul·ture (vul'chər), *n.* **1.** any of several large birds of prey that feed on dead animals. **2.** a greedy, unscrupulous person. —**vul'tur·ous** (-əs), *adj.*

vul·va (vul'və), *n., pl.* **-vae** (-vē), **-vas.** the external female genitalia. —**vul'val, vul'var,** *adj.*

vv., verses.

v.v., See *vice versa.*

vy·ing (vī'ing), *v.* ppr. of **vie.**

W

W, w (dub'əl yōō'), *n., pl.* **W's** or **Ws, w's** or **ws.** the 23rd letter of the English alphabet, a semivowel.

W, 1. watt; watts. **2.** west. **3.** western. Also, **w**

W, tungsten. [< G wolfram]

W., 1. watt; watts. **2.** Wednesday. **3.** weight. **4.** Welsh. **5.** west. **6.** western. **7.** width.

w., 1. water. **2.** watt; watts. **3.** week; weeks. **4.** wide. **5.** wife. **6.** with.

w/, with.

WA, Washington.

W.A., Western Australia.

wab·ble (wob'əl), *v.i., v.t.,* **-bled, -bling,** *n.* wobble.

Wac (wak), *n.* a member of the Women's Army Corps (**WAC**).

wack·y (wak'ē), *adj.,* **-i·er, -i·est.** *Slang.* absurd or irrational. —**wack'i·ness,** *n.*

wad (wod), *n., v.,* **wad·ded, wad·ding.** —*n.* **1.** a small, soft or pliant mass, as of cotton or paper. **2.** *Informal.* a. a roll of banknotes. b. a large amount of money. **3.** a plug of cotton or felt to hold powder or shot in place in a gun or cartridge. —*v.t.* **4.** to form into a wad. **5.** to roll tightly. **6.** to hold in place by a wad. **7.** to put a wad into.

wad·ding (wod'ing), *n.* **1.** any soft material for stuffing or padding. **2.** material used as wads for guns, etc.

wad·dle (wod'əl), *v.,* **-dled, -dling,** *n.* —*v.i.* **1.** to walk with short steps, swaying from side to side, as a duck does. —*n.* **2.** a waddling gait. —**wad'dler,** *n.*

wade (wād), v., **wad·ed, wad·ing,** n.
—v.i. **1.** to walk partly immersed or sunken, as in water. **2.** to make progress slowly or laboriously. —v.t. **3.** to cross by wading. **4. wade in** or **into,** *Informal.* **a.** to begin energetically. **b.** to attack vigorously. —n. **5.** the act of wading. —**wad′a·ble, wade′a·ble,** adj.

wad·er (wā′dər), n. **1.** a person or thing that wades. **2.** Also called **wad′ing bird′.** a long-legged bird that wades in water in search of food. **3. waders,** high waterproof boots used for wading, as by duck hunters.

wa·di (wä′dē), n. (in Middle East and northern Africa) a stream that is dry except during the rainy season.

Waf (waf), n. a member of the Women in the Air Force (**WAF**).

wa·fer (wā′fər), n. **1.** a thin, crisp cake, biscuit, or candy. **2.** a thin disk of unleavened bread, used in the Eucharist. **3.** any small, thin disk.

waf·fle[1] (wof′əl), n. a thin batter cake baked in a heated hinged appliance (**waf′fle i′ron**), which makes a pattern of square hollows on it.

waf·fle[2] (wof′əl), v.i., **-fled, -fling,** n. *Informal.* —v.i. **1.** to talk or write evasively or indecisively. —n. **2.** waffling language.

waft (waft, wäft), v.t., v.i. **1.** to carry or move lightly and smoothly through the air or over water. —n. **2.** a sound or odor faintly perceived. **3.** a light current or gust. **4.** the act of wafting.

wag (wag), v., **wagged, wag·ging,** n. —v.t., v.i. **1.** to move from side to side, up and down, etc., esp. rapidly and repeatedly. **2.** (of the tongue) to move constantly, as in gossip. —n. **3.** an act of wagging. **4.** a person given to roguish or droll humor.

wage (wāj), n., v., **waged, wag·ing.** —n. **1.** Often, **wages.** money that is paid for labor or services. **2.** Usually, **wages.** recompense or return. —v.t. **3.** to carry on (a war, contest, etc.).

wa·ger (wā′jər), n. **1.** something staked on an uncertain event of any kind. **2.** the act of laying a wager. —v.t., v.i. **3.** to lay a wager (on). —**wa′ger·er,** n. —Syn. bet.

wag·ger·y (wag′ə rē), n., pl. **-ger·ies. 1.** roguish or droll humor. **2.** a jest or joke.

wag·gish (wag′ish), adj. roguishly or drolly humorous.

wag·gle (wag′əl), v., **-gled, -gling,** n. —v.i., v.t. **1.** to move with a short wagging motion. —n. **2.** a waggling motion. —**wag′gly,** adj.

Wag·ner (väg′nər), n. Richard, 1813-83, German composer. —**Wag·ne′ri·an** (-nēr′ē ən), adj., n.

wag·on (wag′ən), n. **1.** a four-wheeled vehicle, esp. a horse-drawn one for hauling heavy loads. **2.** See **station wagon. 3.** See **patrol wagon. 4. on the wagon,** *Slang.* abstaining from alcoholic beverages.

wag·on·er (wag′ə nər), n. a person who drives a wagon.

wag·on·ette (wag′ə net′), n. a light carriage having two lengthwise seats facing each other at the back.

wa·gon-lit (vA gôn lē′), n., pl. **wa·gons-lits** (vA gôn lē′). *French.* a railroad sleeping car. [< F: lit., bed car]

wag′on train′, a group of wagons and horses traveling together.

wag·tail (wag′tāl′), n. a small bird having a long, narrow tail that is habitually wagged up and down.

wa·hi·ne (wä hē′ne, nē), n. (in Hawaii and Polynesia) a girl or young woman.

wa·hoo (wä hōō′, wä′hōō), n., pl. **-hoos.** any of various American shrubs or small trees.

waif (wāf), n. **1.** a homeless and helpless person, esp. a lost child. **2.** something found whose owner is not known, esp. a stray animal.

wail (wāl), v.i. **1.** to make a long, loud mourning cry, as in grief. **2.** to make a similar sound, as the wind. —n. **3.** a wailing cry or any similar sound. —**wail′er,** n.

wail·ful (wāl′fəl), adj. plaintively mournful. —**wail′ful·ly,** adv.

wain (wān), n. *Archaic.* a farm wagon.

wain·scot (wān′skət, -skot), n., v., **-scot·ed, -scot·ing** or **-scot·ted, -scot·ting.** —n. **1.** a paneling of solid wood for an interior wall, esp. the lower part. —v.t. **2.** to panel with wainscot.

wain·scot·ing (wān′skō ting), n. **1.** material for a wainscot. **2.** wainscots collectively. Also, **wain′scot·ting** (-skət ing, -skot-).

wain·wright (wān′rīt′), n. a maker and repairer of wagons.

waist (wāst), n. **1.** the narrowed part of the body between the ribs and the hips. **2.** a garment or part of a garment covering the body from the shoulders to the waistline. **3.** (formerly) a child's undergarment to which other garments may be attached. **4.** the central or middle part of an object which resembles the human waist: *the waist of a violin.*

waist·band (wāst′band′, -bənd), n. a band encircling the waist, esp. as on trousers or a skirt.

waist·coat (wes'kət, wāst'kōt'), *n.*
Brit. vest (def. 1).

waist·line (wāst'līn'), *n.* **1.** an arbitrary line encircling the waist. **2.** the part of a woman's dress which is at this line or may be above or below it according to fashion.

wait (wāt), *v.i.* **1.** to hold oneself ready for an arrival or occurrence. **2.** to be in expectation of something. **3.** to be left undone. **4.** to serve as a waiter or waitress. —*v.t.* **5.** to await patiently. **6.** *Informal.* to cause to be postponed, as a meal. **7. wait on** or **upon, a.** to be an attendant or servant for. **b.** to serve (a customer) as a salesperson or a waiter or waitress. **8. wait table,** to serve food at a table. **9. wait up,** to postpone going to bed to await someone or something. —*n.* **10.** the act or period of waiting. **11. lie in wait,** to wait in ambush.

wait·er (wā'tər), *n.* **1.** a man who waits on table, as in a restaurant. **2.** a salver used in the 18th and 19th centuries.

wait·ing (wā'tiñg), *n.* **1.** the act of a person who waits. **2.** a period of waiting. **3. in waiting,** in attendance, as upon a royal person. —*adj.* **4.** serving or being in attendance.

wait'ing game', a strategy in which action on a matter is postponed to a more advantageous time.

wait'ing list', a list of persons waiting, as for something in limited supply.

wait'ing room', a room to accommodate persons waiting, as in a doctor's office.

wait·ress (wā'tris), *n.* a woman who waits on table, as in a restaurant.

waive (wāv), *v.t.,* **waived, waiv·ing.** **1.** to relinquish intentionally, as a claim or right. **2.** *Archaic.* to defer or postpone. —**Syn.** **1.** forgo, renounce.

waiv·er (wā'vər), *n.* **1.** an intentional relinquishment of a claim or right. **2.** a document stating such relinquishment.

Wa·kash·an (wä kash'ən, wô'kə-shan'), *n.* a family of American-Indian languages spoken in British Columbia and Washington.

wake¹ (wāk), *v.,* **woke** or **waked; waked** or **wok·en; wak·ing;** *n.* —*v.t.* **1.** to become roused from sleep. **2.** to be or continue to be awake. **3.** to become aware or alert. —*v.t.* **4.** to cause to wake. **5.** to rouse from inactivity. **6.** *Dial.* to hold a wake over, as a dead body. —*n.* **7.** a watch kept over a dead body before burial. **8.** *Rare.* awakened state.

wake² (wāk), *n.* **1.** the track of waves left by a moving ship. **2.** the course of anything that has passed. **3. in the wake of,** immediately after.

wake·ful (wāk'fəl), *adj.* **1.** unable to sleep. **2.** characterized by absence of sleep. **3.** watchful or alert. —**wake'ful·ness,** *n.*

wak·en (wā'kən), *v.t., v.i.* to wake or become awake.

wake-rob·in (wāk'rob'in), *n.* trillium.

Wal'dorf sal'ad (wôl'dôrf), a salad of celery, diced apples, nuts, and mayonnaise. [after *Waldorf-Astoria* Hotel in N.Y.C.]

wale (wāl), *n., v.,* **waled, wal·ing.** —*n.* **1.** a mark made on the skin by a rod or whip. **2.** the vertical ridge or rib in knit goods. **3.** the texture of a fabric. —*v.t.* **4.** to mark with wales.

Wales (wālz), *n.* a division of the United Kingdom, in SW Great Britain.

walk (wôk), *v.i.* **1.** to move on foot at a moderate pace. **2.** *Baseball.* to receive a base on balls. **3.** to follow a particular way of life: *He walked in sorrow.* —*v.t.* **4.** to move through, over, or upon by walking. **5.** to cause or help to walk. **6.** to go along with on foot: *I'll walk you to the station.* **7.** *Baseball.* to give a base on balls. **8. walk off** or **away with, a.** to steal. **b.** to win, as in a competition. **9. walk out,** *Informal.* **a.** to go on strike. **b.** to leave in protest. **10. walk out on,** *Informal.* to desert or forsake. —*n.* **11.** the act or an instance of walking. **12.** a distance walked or to be walked: *ten minutes' walk from town.* **13.** a characteristic manner of walking. **14.** a particular form of activity, occupation, or status: *in every walk of life.* **15.** a place or path for walking. **16.** *Baseball.* See **base on balls.** —**walk'er,** *n.*

walk·a·way (wôk'ə wā'), *n.* an easy victory, as in a contest.

walk·ie-talk·ie (wô'kē tô'kē), *n.* a combined radio transmitter and receiver light enough to be carried by hand.

walk-in (wôk'in'), *adj.* **1.** large enough to be walked into. —*n.* **2.** something large enough to be walked into, as a closet. **3.** an assured victory, esp. in an election.

walk'ing pa'pers, *Informal.* a notification of dismissal, esp. from a job.

walk'ing stick', **1.** *Brit.* cane (def. 1). **2.** an insect having a long, slender, twiglike body.

walk-on (wôk'on', -ôn'), *n.* a small part in a play, esp. one without speaking lines.

walk·out (wôk'out'), *n.* **1.** a strike by workers. **2.** the act of leaving a meeting, esp. as an expression of protest.

walk·o·ver (wôk′ō′vər), *n.* walkaway.

walk·up (wôk′up′), *n.* **1.** an apartment building with no elevator. **2.** the apartment itself.

walk·way (wôk′wā′), *n.* a passage for walking.

wall (wôl), *n.* **1.** a solid, upright structure, as of brick or wood, used for support or to enclose an area, esp. in a building. **2.** a rampart raised for defensive purposes. **3.** something that suggests a wall in appearance or function. **4. drive or push to the wall,** to force into a desperate situation. —*v.t.* **5.** to protect, confine, or divide with or as with a wall. **6.** to fill (an opening) with solid construction. —**walled,** *adj.*

wal·la·by (wol′ə bē), *n., pl.* **-bies, -by.** any of various small and medium-sized kangaroos. [< native Austral *wolabā*]

wall·board (wôl′bôrd′, -bōrd′), *n.* a material manufactured in large sheets for use in making or covering walls.

wal·let (wol′it, wô′lit), *n.* a small, folding leather case for paper money, credit cards, etc. **2.** *Archaic.* a pilgrim's knapsack.

wall·eye (wôl′ī), *n.* **1.** an eye having little or no color in the iris. **2.** an eye showing too much white because of divergent squint. **3.** Also called **wall′eyed′ pike′.** a large game fish found in the lakes and rivers of northeastern North America. —**wall′eyed′** (-īd′), *adj.*

wall·flow·er (wôl′flou′ər), *n.* **1.** a European plant having sweet-scented, usually yellow or orange flowers. **2.** a person who sits apart at a party or dance because he or she is shy or unpopular.

Wal·loon (wo lōōn′), *n.* **1.** one of a people living chiefly in S Belgium. **2.** their French dialect.

wal·lop (wol′əp), *Informal.* —*v.t.* **1.** to beat soundly. **2.** to strike vigorously. —*n.* **3.** a vigorous blow. **4.** the ability to create a powerful effect.

wal·lop·ing (wol′ə piñg), *adj. Informal.* impressively big or good.

wal·low (wol′ō), *v.i.* **1.** to roll about or lie in water or mud. **2.** to indulge oneself in a state of mind or way of life: *to wallow in sentimentality.* —*n.* **3.** the act of wallowing. **4.** a place in which animals wallow.

wall·pa·per (wôl′pā′pər), *n.* **1.** a decorative paper for covering the walls of a room. —*v.t.* **2.** to cover or decorate with wallpaper.

Wall′ Street′, a street in New York City: the financial center of the U.S.

wal·nut (wôl′nut′, -nət), *n.* **1.** a round nut with a hard, wrinkled shell and a meaty edible seed. **2.** the tree bearing this nut. **3.** its reddish-brown wood, used for veneer, etc.

wal·rus (wôl′rəs, wol′-), *n., pl.* **-rus·es, -rus.** a large mammal related to the seal, having flippers and large tusks. [< D: lit., whale horse]

waltz (wôlts), *n.* **1.** a ballroom dance in moderately fast triple meter. **2.** music for this dance —*v.i., v.t.* **3.** to dance a waltz (with). **4.** *Informal.* to move breezily or confidently. —**waltz′er,** *n.*

wam·pum (wom′pəm, wôm′-), *n.* small beads made from shells, formerly used by North American Indians for money and ornaments.

wan (won), *adj.,* **wan·ner, wan·nest. 1.** sickly pale or ashen. **2.** showing ill health, fatigue, or sadness: *a .wan smile.* —**wan′ly,** *adv.* —**wan′ness,** *n.*

wand (wond), *n.* **1.** a slender rod, esp. one having magical powers. **2.** a staff carried as an emblem of authority.

wan·der (won′dər), *v.i.* **1.** to move about aimlessly here and there. **2.** to go astray. **3.** to deviate in conduct or thought. —*v.t.* **4.** to move in a meandering course. **5.** to travel aimlessly about, on, or through. —**wan′der·er,** *n.* —**Syn.** 1. meander, roam, stroll.

wan′dering Jew′, any of various trailing or creeping plants, esp. common as indoor plants.

wan·der·lust (wän′dər lust′), *n.* a strong impulse to travel about.

wane (wān), *v.,* **waned, wan·ing,** *n.* —*v.i.* **1.** (of the moon) to lessen in brightness and roundness. **2.** to decline in power or prosperity. **3.** to decrease in strength or intensity. **4.** to approach an end. —*n.* **5.** the act or a period of waning.

wan·gle (wañg′gəl), *v.t.,* **-gled, -gling.** *Informal.* **1.** to accomplish or obtain by scheming or underhand methods. **2.** to manipulate for dishonest ends. —**wan′gler,** *n.*

Wan′kel en′gine (vän′kəl, wän′-), an internal-combustion rotary engine that utilizes a triangular rotor which revolves in a chamber. [after Felix *Wankel* (b. 1902), German inventor]

want (wont, wônt), *v.t.* **1.** to feel a need for. **2.** to crave or desire: *I want to see you.* **3.** to be lacking in. **4.** to seek or hunt: *They want the man for murder.* **5.** *Chiefly Brit.* to require or need: *The house wants painting.* —*v.i.* **6.** to be in a state of need. **7.** to be destitute. —*n.* **8.** something wanted. **9.** absence or lack. **10.** the state of being without something wanted. **11.** destitution or poverty.

want′ ad′, *Informal.* See **classified ad.**

want·ing (wŏn'tĭng, wôn'-), *adj.* **1.** not present when needed. **2.** not up to what is expected. —*prep.* **3.** lacking or without. **4.** less or minus.

wan·ton (wŏn'tᵊn), *adj.* **1.** malicious and unjustifiable: *a wanton attack.* **2.** without regard for what is right or humane. **3.** sexually unrestrained. **4.** *Archaic.* frolicsome or playful. —*n.* **5.** a wanton or lascivious person. —*v.i.* **6.** to become wanton. —**wan'ton·ly,** *adv.* —**wan'ton·ness,** *n.* —**Syn. 1.** reckless. **2.** cruel. **3.** dissolute, lewd.

wap·i·ti (wŏp'ĭ tē), *n., pl.* **-tis, -ti.** elk (def. 2.)

war (wôr), *n., v.,* **warred, war·ring,** *adj.* —*n.* **1.** a major armed conflict, as between nations. **2.** any struggle or fight. **3.** the science of military operations. —*v.i.* **4.** to make or carry on war. **5.** to be in a state of strong opposition. —**war'less,** *adj.*

war., warrant.

War' Between' the States', the U.S. Civil War.

war·ble (wôr'bᵊl), *v.,* **-bled, -bling,** *n.* —*v.i., v.t.* **1.** to sing or whistle with trills, quavers, or melodic embellishments. —*n.* **2.** the act of warbling.

war·bler (wôr'blᵊr), *n.* **1.** a person or thing that warbles. **2.** any of several small, chiefly Old World songbirds.

war' bon'net, an American-Indian headdress consisting of a headband with a tail of ornamental feathers.

war' crime', Usually, **war crimes.** crimes committed against an enemy or captives in wartime that violate international agreements. —**war' crim'inal.**

war' cry', **1.** a sound or expression shouted during an attack in battle. **2.** a slogan used to rally support for a cause.

ward (wôrd), *n.* **1.** an administrative district of a city or town. **2.** a division of a hospital for a particular group of patients. **3.** a section of a prison. **4.** a person under the legal guardianship of another. **5.** the act of keeping guard: *watch and ward.* **6.** the state of being under guard. —*v.t.* **7.** to turn away or aside: *to ward off an attack.*

-ward, a suffix meaning: **a.** at or toward the side of: *backward.* **b.** in the direction of: *skyward.* **c.** at or in the time of: *afterward.* Also, **-wards.**

war' dance', (among primitive peoples) a dance prior to waging war or in celebration of a victory.

war·den (wôr'dᵊn), *n.* **1.** the chief officer in charge of a prison. **2.** an official charged with enforcing certain laws, esp. those regulating game and hunting. **3.** Also called **air'-raid war'den.** a civilian having police duties during an air raid.

ward·er (wôr'dᵊr), *n.* **1.** *Brit.* a prison warden. **2.** *Archaic.* a guard or sentinel.

ward' heel'er, a minor politician who canvasses voters for a party boss.

ward·robe (wôr'drōb), *n.* **1.** a collection or stock of clothes or costumes. **2.** a cabinet or closet for keeping clothes.

ward·room (wôrd'rōōm', -rŏŏm'), *n.* (on a warship) **1.** the living quarters for commissioned officers except the commanding officer. **2.** the dining room and lounge for these officers.

ward·ship (wôrd'shĭp), *n.* **1.** the condition of being under legal guardianship. **2.** the care of a guardian.

ware (wâr), *n.* **1.** Usually, **wares.** articles for sale. **2.** a specific kind of manufactured article: *silverware.* **3.** pottery: *delft ware.*

ware·house (wâr'hous'), *n.* a building for the storage of goods or merchandise. —**ware'house'man, ware'hous'er,** *n.*

ware·room (wâr'rōōm', -rŏŏm'), *n. Obs.* a storeroom or showroom.

war·fare (wôr'fâr'), *n.* **1.** the act or process of engaging in war. **2.** any conflict or struggle.

war·fa·rin (wôr'fᵊ rĭn), *n.* a colorless poisonous powder used chiefly for killing rodents.

war' game', a simulated military operation carried out to test the validity of a war plan.

war·head (wôr'hĕd'), *n.* the forward section of a missile, as a bomb, containing the explosive charge.

war·horse (wôr'hôrs'), *n.* **1.** a horse used in battle. **2.** *Informal.* a veteran, as a soldier or politician, of many struggles.

war·like (wôr'līk'), *adj.* **1.** ready for or fond of war. **2.** threatening war. **3.** of or pertaining to war. —**Syn. 1, 2.** belligerent, hostile.

war·lock (wôr'lŏk'), *n. Archaic.* a male witch.

war·lord (wôr'lôrd'), *n.* **1.** a warlike military leader. **2.** a military commander who has seized power, esp. in one section of a country.

warm (wôrm), *adj.* **1.** having or giving out moderate heat. **2.** having a sensation of bodily heat. **3.** keeping in the body's warmth: *warm clothing.* **4.** (of colors) suggesting warmth, as red or yellow tones. **5.** friendly or loving. **6.** showing strong, lively feelings: *warm interest.* **7.** irritated or angry. **8.** lively or vigorous: *a warm debate.* **9.** strong or fresh: *a warm scent.* **10.** *Informal.* close to something sought, as in a children's game. —*v.t., v.i.* **11.** to make or become warm. **12. warm up, a.** to prepare for a game or other activity by practicing or exercising beforehand.

b. to make or become adequately heated for operation, as an engine. —**warm′er,** *n.* —**warm′ish,** *adj.* —**warm′ly,** *adv.*

warm-blood·ed (wôrm′blud′id), *adj.* having a normal blood temperature that remains relatively constant, irrespective of the temperature of the surroundings, as mammals and birds.

warmed-o·ver (wôrmd′ō′vər), *adj.* **1.** (of cooked foods) heated again. **2.** unimaginatively repeated, as ideas.

warm-heart·ed (wôrm′här′tid), *adj.* having or showing warmth of feeling. —**warm′heart′ed·ly,** *adv.* —**warm′heart′ed·ness,** *n.*

war·mong·er (wôr′mung′gər, -mông′-), *n.* a person who advocates or tries to provoke war. —**war′mon′ger·ing,** *n., adj.*

warmth (wôrmth), *n.* **1.** the quality or state of being warm. **2.** liveliness of feelings. **3.** affection or kindliness.

warm·up (wôrm′up′), *n.* **1.** the act or an instance of warming up. **2. warm-ups,** any outer apparel worn for warmth, esp. in sports or during preliminary exercise.

warn (wôrn), *v.t., v.i.* **1.** to inform (someone) of possible trouble or danger. **2.** to advise (a person) to be cautious about a certain act. **3.** to inform in advance. **4.** to notify (someone) to go or keep at a distance. —**Syn. 1, 2.** admonish, alert. **3.** forewarn.

warn·ing (wôr′ning), *n.* **1.** the act of a person or thing that warns. **2.** something that serves to warn. —*adj.* **3.** serving to warn. —**warn′ing·ly,** *adv.*

warp (wôrp), *v.t., v.i.* **1.** to bend or become bent out of shape. **2.** to turn away from what is right or good. **3.** to move (a ship) by hauling on a rope that has been fastened to a buoy or anchor. —*n.* **4.** a bend or twist from a straight or flat form. **5.** a mental twist or quirk. **6.** the set of yarns placed lengthwise in the loom. —**warp′er,** *n.*

war′ paint′, paint applied by American Indians to their faces and bodies before going to war.

war·path (wôr′path′, -päth′), *n.* **1.** the course taken by American Indians on a warlike expedition. **2. on the warpath, a.** preparing for war. **b.** angry or hostile.

war·plane (wôr′plān′), *n.* an airplane designed for or used in warfare.

war·rant (wôr′ənt, wor′-), *n.* **1.** adequate reason or justification, as for a statement. **2.** a writ authorizing an officer, as of the police, to search, arrest, or seize. **3.** a right to purchase capital stock under certain conditions. —*v.t.* **4.** to give

justification for. **5.** to declare with conviction. **6.** to give a formal assurance or guarantee of: *to warrant safe delivery.* **7.** to guarantee (something sold) to be as represented. **8.** to give authority to.

war′rant of′ficer, an officer in the armed forces ranking below a commissioned officer.

war·ran·ty (wôr′ən tē, wor′-), *n., pl.* **-ties. 1.** a written guarantee given to a purchaser specifying that the manufacturer will repair or replace defective parts free of charge for a stated period of time. **2.** warrant (def. 1).

war·ren (wôr′ən, wor′-), *n.* **1.** a place where rabbits breed or abound. **2.** a crowded building or district.

war·ri·or (wôr′ē ər, wôr′yər, wor′ē ər, wor′yər), *n.* a person engaged or experienced in warfare.

War·saw (wôr′sô), *n.* the capital of Poland.

war·ship (wôr′ship′), *n.* a ship built or armed for combat.

wart (wôrt), *n.* **1.** a small, usually hard, abnormal growth on the skin, caused by a virus. **2.** any small protuberance, as on certain plants. —**wart′y,** *adj.*

wart′ hog′, an African wild hog having large tusks and warts on the face.

war·time (wôr′tīm′), *n.* a time or period of war.

war·y (wâr′ē), *adj.,* **-i·er, -i·est. 1.** habitually watchful. **2.** arising from or showing caution. —**war′i·ly,** *adv.* —**war′i·ness,** *n.* —**Syn. 1.** alert, vigilant. **2.** guarded.

was (wuz, woz), *v.* 1st and 3rd pers. sing. pt. indic. of **be.**

wash (wosh, wôsh), *v.t.* **1.** to clean off dirt or other matter with a liquid, esp. water containing soap. **2.** to remove (dirt or other matter) in this way. **3.** to move by means of water. **4.** to wet or moisten. **5.** to wear or erode by flowing: *The heavy rain washed gullies in the sand.* **6.** to cleanse from guilt. **7.** to cover with a thin layer, as of paint or metal. —*v.i.* **8.** to wash oneself. **9.** to wash clothes. **10.** to undergo washing without damage, esp. shrinking or fading. **11.** to be carried or driven by water. **12.** to move in waves, or with a rushing movement, as water. **13.** to be removed by the action of water: *This topsoil tends to wash away.* **14.** *Informal.* to stand being put to the proof: *That story won't wash.* **15. wash down,** to facilitate the swallowing of (food) by drinking water. **16. wash up,** to wash one's face and hands. —*n.* **17.** the act or process of washing. **18.** a quantity of things washed together, as clothes.

19. the dash or breaking of water. **20.** water moving along in waves or with a rushing movement. **21.** the rough water or air left behind a moving ship or propeller. **22.** a liquid for toilet, cosmetic, or medicinal purposes: *a hair wash.* **23.** a thin coating, as of paint or metal. **24.** *Western U.S.* the dry bed of an intermittent stream. **25.** waste liquid matter, esp. for hogs. —*adj.* **26.** washable.

Wash., Washington.

wash·a·ble (wosh′ə bəl, wô′shə-), *adj.* capable of being washed without damage. —**wash′a·bil′i·ty,** *n.*

wash-and-wear (wosh′ən wâr′, wôsh′-), *adj.* noting a garment that requires little or no ironing after washing.

wash·board (wosh′bôrd′, -bōrd′, wôsh′-), *n.* a corrugated metallic board on which, esp. formerly, clothes were rubbed during washing.

wash·bowl (wosh′bōl′, wôsh′-), *n.* a large bowl or basin used for washing one's hands or face. Also called **wash′ba′sin.**

wash·cloth (wosh′klôth′, -kloth′, wôsh′-), *n.* a small cloth for washing one's face or body. Also called **wash′rag′.**

washed-out (wosht′out′, wôsht′-), *adj.* **1.** faded, esp. from washing. **2.** *Informal.* exhausted or tired-looking.

washed-up (wosht′up′, wôsht′-), *adj. Informal.* having failed completely.

wash·er (wosh′ər, wô′shər), *n.* **1.** a person or thing that washes. **2.** a machine or apparatus for washing. **3.** a flat ring or perforated piece of rubber or metal used to hold a nut or bolt more tightly in place or to prevent leakage.

wash·er·wom·an (wosh′ər wŏŏm′ən, wô′shər-), *n.* a woman who washes clothes for a living.

wash′ goods′, textiles that will not fade by washing.

wash·ing (wosh′ing, wô′shing), *n.* **1.** the act of a person or thing that washes. **2.** wash (def. 18). **3.** material obtained by washing. **4.** a thin coating or covering applied in liquid form: *a washing of gold.*

wash′ing machine′, a household appliance for washing clothes.

wash′ing so′da, a form of sodium carbonate used in cleansers.

Wash·ing·ton (wosh′ing tən, wô′shing-), *n.* **1.** **George,** 1732–99, 1st president of the U.S. 1789–97. **2.** the capital of the United States: coextensive with the District of Columbia. **3.** a state in the NW United States. *Cap.:* Olympia. —**Wash′-ing·to′ni·an** (-tō′nē ən), *adj., n.*

Wash′ington's Birth′day, February 22, the birthday of George Washing-ton: now officially observed as a legal holiday in most states on the third Monday in February.

wash·out (wosh′out′, wôsh′-), *n.* **1.** a washing out or away of earth or gravel by water. **2.** *Informal.* an utter failure.

wash·room (wosh′rōōm′, -rŏŏm′, wôsh′-), *n.* **1.** See **rest room. 2.** *Obs.* a laundry room.

wash·stand (wosh′stand′, wôsh′-), *n.* (formerly) a piece of furniture designed to hold a basin and pitcher of water for washing one's hands or face.

wash·tub (wosh′tub′, wôsh′-), *n.* a tub for use in washing clothes.

wash·wom·an (wosh′wŏŏm′ən, wôsh′-), *n.* washerwoman.

wash·y (wosh′ē, wô′shē), *adj.,* **-i·er, -i·est. 1.** diluted too much, as coffee. **2.** without strength or vigor. —**wash′i·ness,** *n.*

was·n't (wuz′ənt, woz′-), contraction of *was not.*

wasp (wosp), *n.* any of numerous social or solitary winged insects generally having a long, slender body, narrow waist, and often a sharp sting. —**wasp′y,** *adj.*

WASP (wosp), *n.* an American of British or northern European ancestry who belongs to the Protestant church. Also, **Wasp.** [*w(hite) A(nglo-)S(axon) P(rotestant)*] —**WASP′ish, Wasp′ish,** *adj.*

wasp·ish (wos′pish), *adj.* **1.** like a wasp, esp. in behavior. **2.** quick to be angry or resentful. —**wasp′ish·ly,** *adv.* —**wasp′ish·ness,** *n.*

wasp′ waist′, a slender waistline. —**wasp′-waist′ed,** *adj.*

was·sail (wos′əl, -āl, was′-, wo sāl′), *n.* **1.** a former English toast in drinking to a person's health. **2.** the liquor used in such a toast. **3.** a festivity or revel with drinking of healths. —*v.i., v.t.* **4.** to drink a wassail (to). —**was′sail·er,** *n.*

Was′ser·man test′ (wä′sər mən), a diagnostic blood test for syphilis.

wast (wost), *v. Archaic.* a 2nd pers. sing. pt. indic. of *be.*

wast·age (wā′stij), *n.* **1.** loss by use, decay, wastefulness, etc. **2.** anything wasted.

waste (wāst), *v.,* **wast·ed, wast·ing,** *n., adj.* —*v.t.* **1.** to consume, spend, or employ uselessly or carelessly. **2.** to fail to use: *to waste an opportunity.* **3.** to wear away. **4.** to reduce in health or strength. **5.** to destroy or ruin. —*v.i.* **6.** to be consumed, spent, or employed uselessly or carelessly. **7.** to become emaciated or enfeebled. —*n.* **8.** useless consumption or expenditure. **9.** a devastated region. **10.** an uncultivated tract of land. **11.** anything left over from a manufacturing process. **12. wastes,** excrement. **13. lay waste,** to ravage or ruin. —*adj.* **14.** barren or uninhabited. **15.** left over or superfluous. **16.** rejected as useless or worthless. **17.** designed to hold or carry away waste: *a waste pipe.* **18.** unused by or unusable to the organism. — **wast'er,** *n.*

waste·bas·ket (wāst'bas'kit, -bä'skit), *n.* a receptacle for small pieces of trash.

waste·ful (wāst'fəl), *adj.* given to or characterized by waste. —**waste'ful·ly,** *adv.* —**waste'ful·ness,** *n.*

waste·land (wāst'land'), *n.* uncultivated or barren land.

waste·pa·per (wāst'pā'pər), *n.* paper thrown away as useless.

wast·rel (wā'strəl), *n.* a wasteful person.

watch (woch), *v.i.* **1.** to look closely to see what is done or happens. **2.** to look and wait expectantly: *to watch for a signal.* **3.** to maintain a guard or vigil. **4.** to be careful or cautious. —*v.t.* **5.** to look at attentively. **6.** to keep under surveillance. **7.** to look and wait expectantly for. **8. watch oneself,** to be careful. **9. watch out,** to be alert or cautious. —*n.* **10.** the act of watching. **11.** close observation, as to guard or protect. **12.** a period of time for watching or keeping guard. **13.** a person or persons appointed to keep watch. **14.** a small, portable timepiece. **15.** a period of time, usually four hours, during which one part of a ship's crew is on duty. **b.** the crew on duty during this time.

watch·band (woch'band'), *n.* a small strap, as of leather, for fastening a watch to the wrist.

watch·dog (woch'dôg', -dog'), *n.* **1.** a dog kept as a guard. **2.** any watchful guardian.

watch·er (woch'ər), *n.* **1.** a person who watches or keeps watch. **2.** an analytic observer: *a China watcher.*

watch·ful (woch'fəl), *adj.* closely observant. —**watch'ful·ly,** *adv.* —**watch'ful·ness,** *n.* —**Syn.** alert, wary.

watch·mak·er (woch'mā'kər), *n.* a person who makes or repairs watches. —**watch'mak'ing,** *n.*

watch·man (woch'mən), *n.* a person who keeps guard over a building or property. —**watch'wom'an,** *n.fem.*

watch' night', a religious meeting held by some churches on New Year's Eve and terminating after midnight.

watch·tow·er (woch'tou'ər), *n.* a tower on which a guard keeps watch.

watch·word (woch'wûrd'), *n.* **1.** a word or phrase expressing a principle or aim. **2.** *Obs.* a password.

wa·ter (wô'tər, wot'ər), *n.* **1.** a transparent, odorless, tasteless liquid which constitutes rain, oceans, lakes, etc. **2.** a lake, river, or ocean of this liquid. **3.** a special form or variety of this liquid: *mineral water.* **4.** a stage or level of water. **5.** any liquid secretion or exudation, as urine. **6.** a wavy, lustrous pattern on silk and other fabrics. **7. hold water,** to be logical or true. —*v.t.* **8.** to moisten or drench with water. **9.** to supply (animals) with water for drinking. **10.** to furnish with water. **11.** to dilute with, or as with, water. **12.** to produce a wavy, lustrous pattern on (silk, etc.) —*v.i.* **13.** to fill with or secrete water or liquid, as the eyes. **14.** to drink or take in water.

wa'ter ballet', an entertainment consisting of synchronized movements by swimmers, usually to musical accompaniment.

Wa'ter Bear'er, Aquarius.

wat·er·bed (wô'tər bed', wot'ər-), *n.* a vinyl mattress-shaped bag filled with water and used as a bed.

wa'ter bis'cuit, a crackerlike biscuit prepared from flour and water.

wa·ter·borne (wô'tər bôrn', -bōrn', wot'ər-), *adj.* **1.** floating on water. **2.** transported by ship.

wa'ter buf'falo, an oxlike Asiatic buffalo, often domesticated.

Wa·ter·bur·y (wô'tər ber'ē, wot'ər-), *n.* a city in W Connecticut.

wa'ter chest'nut, 1. an aquatic plant bearing an edible, nutlike fruit. **2.** its fruit.

wa'ter clos'et, *Brit.* **1.** a toilet flushed by water. **2.** a room or compartment for this.

wa·ter·col·or (wô'tər kul'ər, wot'ər-), *n.* **1.** a pigment for which water is used as a vehicle. **2.** the art of painting with such pigments. **3.** a painting by this technique.

wa·ter·cool (wô'tər kōōl', wot'ər-), *v.t.* to cool by means of water, as in an engine, etc. —**wa'ter-cooled',** *adj.*

wa'ter cool'er, a device for cooling and dispensing drinking water.

wa·ter·course (wô'tər kôrs', -kōrs', wot'ər-), *n.* **1.** a stream of water. **2.** the bed of a stream.

wa·ter·craft (wô'tər kraft', -kräft', wot'ər-), *n.* boats and ships collectively.

wa·ter·cress (wô'tər kres', wot'ər-), *n.* **1.** a perennial plant growing in clear running water, whose pungent leaves are used esp. in salads. **2.** its leaves.

wa·ter·fall (wô'tər fôl', wot'ər-), *n.* a steep fall of water from a height, as over a precipice.

wa·ter·fowl (wô'tər foul', wot'ər-), *n.* an aquatic bird, esp. a swan, goose, or duck.

wa·ter·front (wô′tər frunt′, wot′ər-), *n.* **1.** land on the edge of a body of water. **2.** the part of a city on such land.

wa′ter gap′, a break in a mountain ridge, cut by and giving passage to a stream.

wa′ter gas′, a fuel gas made by forcing steam over hot coke.

Wa·ter·gate (wô′tər gāt′, wot′ər-), *n.* a political scandal involving illegal activities during and after the re-election campaign in 1972 of President Nixon and which resulted in his resignation in 1974. [from the name of the building in Washington, D.C., that housed Democratic National Committee headquarters and that was broken into by men connected with the Republican campaign]

wa′ter glass′, 1. a drinking glass. **2.** a dense liquid of silicate of sodium, used as an adhesive or in preserving eggs.

wa′ter hole′, a pond used by animals for drinking.

wa′tering hole′, *Slang.* a bar or nightclub.

wa′tering place′, *Chiefly Brit.* a resort featuring mineral springs.

wa′ter lil′y, 1. a water plant having large, floating leaves and showy, fragrant flowers. **2.** its flower.

wa′ter line′, any of a series of lines on the hull of a ship indicating the depth to which it is immersed.

wa·ter·logged (wô′tər lôgd′, -logd′, wot′ər-), *adj.* so filled or saturated with water as to be heavy or unmanageable, as a ship.

Wa·ter·loo (wô′tər loō′, wot′ər-), *n.* **1.** a village in central Belgium: Napoleon decisively defeated, 1815. **2.** a decisive or crushing defeat.

wa′ter main′, a main pipe or conduit in a system for carrying water.

wa·ter·mark (wô′tər märk′, wot′ər-), *n.* **1.** a mark indicating the height to which water has risen. **2.** a faint design pressed on paper during manufacture which can be seen when held up to the light. —*v.t.* **3.** to mark with a watermark.

wa·ter·mel·on (wô′tər mel′ən, wot′ər-), *n.* a large, roundish or elongated melon having a hard, green rind and a sweet, juicy, red pulp.

wa′ter moc′casin, cottonmouth.

wa′ter ou′zel (oō′zəl), any of several stocky, aquatic birds related to the thrushes, having dense, oily plumage.

wa′ter pipe′, 1. a conduit for carrying water. **2.** any tobacco pipe in which the smoke passes through a container of water.

wa′ter po′lo, a water sport played with an inflated ball by two teams of swimmers.

wa·ter·pow·er (wô′tər pou′ər, wot′ər-), *n.* the power of falling or flowing water used to drive machinery.

wa·ter·proof (wô′tər proōf′, wot′ər-), *adj.* **1.** made impervious to water, as by treating with rubber. —*n.* **2.** *Brit.* a raincoat. **3.** any waterproof fabric. —*v.t.* **4.** to make waterproof. —**wa′ter·proof′ing,** *n.*

wa·ter·re·pel·lent (wô′tər ri pel′ənt, wot′ər-), *adj.* repelling water but not entirely waterproof.

wa·ter·re·sist·ant (wô′tər ri zis′tənt, wot′ər-), *adj.* resisting though not entirely preventing the penetration of water.

wa·ter·shed (wô′tər shed′, wot′ər-), *n.* **1.** the ridge dividing two drainage areas. **2.** the area drained by a river. **3.** a major turning point.

wa·ter·side (wô′tər sīd′, wot′ər-), *n.* the land bordering a body of water.

wa′ter ski′, a ski designed to glide over water while being pulled by a speedboat. —**wa′ter-ski′,** *v.i.* —**wa′ter ski′er.**

wa·ter·spout (wô′tər spout′, wot′ər-), *n.* **1.** a pipe for discharging water, esp. rain water. **2.** a funnel-shaped portion of a cloud that touches and draws upon the surface of the water, mixing spray and mist.

wa′ter strid′er, any of several winged insects that dart about on the surface of water.

wa′ter sys′tem, 1. a river and all its branches. **2.** a system of supplying water, as throughout a metropolitan area.

wa′ter ta′ble, the depth below which the ground is saturated with water.

wa·ter·tight (wô′tər tīt′, wot′ər-), *adj.* **1.** so tight that water cannot pass through. **2.** so soundly planned or made that no fault can be found: *a watertight alibi.*

wa′ter tow′er, a tank raised high above the ground, used for storing a water supply.

wa·ter·way (wô′tər wā′, wot′ər-), *n.* any body of water used as a route for vessels.

wa′ter wheel′, a wheel turned by the action of moving water and used to provide power.

wa′ter wings′, an inflated device worn for keeping afloat while swimming.

wa·ter·works (wô′tər wûrks′, wot′ər-), *n.pl.* a complete system for supplying water to an area, including reservoirs, pipes, etc.

wa·ter·y (wô′tə rē, wot′ə-), *adj.* **1.** of or pertaining to water. **2.** containing much or too much water. **3.** tearful, as the eyes. **4.** resembling water, as in appearance. **5.** poor or weak, as writing.

WATS (wots), Wide Area Telecommunications Service (for unlimited long-distance telephone calls for a flat monthly charge).

watt (wot), *n.* a unit of electric power, equal to the power in a circuit in which a current of one ampere flows across a potential difference of one volt. [after James *Watt*, 1736–1819, Scottish engineer and inventor]

watt·age (wot'ij), *n.* electric power measured in watts.

wat·tle (wot'ᵊl), *n.* **1.** a number of rods interwoven with twigs for making fences or walls. **2.** a fleshy lobe hanging down from the beak or chin of certain birds.

wave (wāv), *n., v.,* **waved, wav·ing.** —*n.* **1.** a moving ridge or swell on the surface of the sea, a lake, etc. **2.** a strong rise or increase of something: *a wave of anger.* **3.** a persistent condition in weather temperature: *a heat wave.* **4.** a curve or series of curves, as in the hair. **5.** an act or instance of waving, as with the hand. **6.** *Physics.* a progressive disturbance propagated from point to point in a medium or space, as of sound or light. —*v.i.* **7.** to move to and fro, as a flag stirred by the wind. **8.** to move the hand to and fro as a gesture. **9.** to curve alternately in opposite directions. —*v.t.* **10.** to cause to wave. **11.** to signal by waving. **12.** to brandish (a weapon). **13.** to give a wave to (the hair). —**wave/like/,** *adj.* —**wav/er,** *n.*

Wave (wāv), *n.* a member of the WAVES.

wave/ band/, *Radio.* a range of wave frequencies.

wave/ front/, *Physics.* the locus of all adjacent points at the same phase of oscillation.

wave·length (wāv'length'), *n. Physics.* the distance, measured in the direction of propagation of a wave, between two successive points in the wave.

wave·let (wāv'lit), *n.* a small wave.

wa·ver (wā'vər), *v.i.* **1.** to sway to and fro. **2.** to flicker or quiver, as light. **3.** to falter or begin to fail. **4.** to tremble, as the voice. **5.** to feel or show doubt or indecision, as between choices. —*n.* **6.** an act of wavering. —**wa/ver·er,** *n.* —**wa/ver·ing·ly,** *adv.* —**Syn. 5.** hesitate, vacillate.

WAVES (wāvz), *n.pl.* the commissioned and enlisted women serving in the U.S. Navy: officially in existence 1942–48. [*W*(omen) *A*(ccepted for) *V*(oluntary) *E*(mergency) *S*(ervice)]

wav·y (wā'vē), *adj.,* **-i·er, -i·est. 1.** having or abounding in waves. **2.** moving in waves. —**wav/i·ness,** *n.*

wax¹ (waks), *n.* **1.** a solid, yellowish substance secreted by bees for making their honeycomb. **2.** any of various similar substances, esp. ones composed of hydrocarbons, as paraffin. **3.** earwax. —*v.t.* **4.** to cover or polish with wax. —**wax/er,** *n.*

wax² (waks), *v.i.* **1.** (of the moon) to grow in brightness and roundness. **2.** to increase in strength or intensity. **3.** to become: *to wax eloquent.*

wax/ bean/, a variety of string bean bearing yellowish, waxy pods.

wax·en (wak'sən), *adj. Obsolesc.* waxy.

wax/ myr/tle, a shrub or tree bearing small, wax-coated berries.

wax/ pa/per, a translucent paper made moistureproof by a paraffin coating.

wax·wing (waks'wing'), *n,* a bird having a showy crest and wings with red, waxy tips.

wax·work (waks'wûrk'), *n.* **1.** a life-size figure of a human being, made of wax. **2. waxworks,** an exhibition of wax figures.

wax·y (wak'sē), *adj.,* **wax·i·er, wax·i·est. 1.** resembling wax. **2.** full of, covered with, or made of wax.

way (wā), *n.* **1.** a method or means for attaining a goal **2.** a path or course to a place. **3.** a direction, as of movement: *Look this way.* **4.** passage or progress to a definite goal: *to find one's way.* **5.** distance: *a long way.* **6.** characteristic or habitual manner. **7.** a respect or particular. **8.** the mode of procedure that one chooses or wills: *She always has her own way.* **9.** the course of action that one advocates. **10.** a person's intended path or course of life. **11.** Often, **ways.** habits or customs. **12.** state of health or prosperity. **13.** neighborhood or vicinity. **14.** a structure on which a ship is built. **15. by the way,** incidentally. **16. by way of,** **a.** by the route of. **b.** as a means of. **17. give way, a.** to yield or withdraw. **b.** to collapse or break down. **18. in the way,** making an obstacle or hindrance. **19. make way, a.** to clear the way. **b.** to make progress or headway. **20. out of the way, a.** so as not to obstruct or annoy. **b.** at a distance from the usual route. **c.** improper or amiss. **21. under way, a.** in motion. **b.** in progress. —*adv.* **22.** Also, **'way.** *Informal.* away or far: *way too heavy.*

way·bill (wā'bil'), *n.* a document describing goods shipped by rail or truck.

way·far·er (wā'fâr'ər), *n. Literary.* a traveler on foot. —**way/far/ing,** *adj., n.*

way·lay (wā lā′), *v.t.*, **-laid**, **-lay·ing.**
1. to lie in wait for and attack.
2. to accost unexpectedly. —**way-lay′er,** *n.*

way′ out′, 1. the means by which a predicament may be solved. **2.** *Brit.* exit (def. 1). **3. on the way out,** becoming unfashionable or obsolete.

way-out (wā′out′), *adj. Informal.* far-out.

-ways, a suffix meaning: **a.** in or toward the direction of: *sideways.* **b.** in the position of: *edgeways.*

ways′ and means′, legislation and methods for raising revenue for public expense.

way·side (wā′sīd′), *n.* land adjacent to a road.

way′ sta′tion, a station between principal stations, as on a railroad.

way·ward (wā′wərd), *adj.* **1.** turned or turning away from what is right or proper. **2.** unpredictable or irregular. —**way′ward·ly,** *adv.* —**way′-ward·ness,** *n.* —**Syn. 1.** disobedient, willful.

way·worn (wā′wôrn′, -wôrn′), *adj.* wearied by travel.

W/B, waybill. Also **W.B.**

w.b., water ballast.

W.B.C., white blood cell.

W.C., 1. *Brit.* See **water closet. 2.** without charge.

W.C.T.U., Woman's Christian Temperance Union.

we (wē), *pron.* **1.** nominative pl. of **I. 2.** (used to denote oneself and another or others): *the world we live in.* **3.** I (as in royal proclamations or press editorials).

weak (wēk), *adj.* **1.** easily broken or damaged under pressure or strain. **2.** lacking in strength or vigor. **3.** lacking in courage, resolution, or authority. **4.** unable to satisfy a critical mind, as an argument. **5.** deficient, as in attainment or resources: *weak in spelling.* **6.** of little force, intensity, flavor, etc.: *weak tea.* **7.** showing weakness of body or mind. —**Syn. 1.** delicate, frail. **2.** feeble. **3.** irresolute.

weak·en (wē′kən), *v.t.*, *v.i.* to make or become weak or weaker. —**weak′-en·er,** *n.* —**Syn.** enervate.

weak·fish (wēk′fish′), *n.*, pl. **-fish,** **-fishes.** a food fish found along the Atlantic and Gulf coasts of the U.S.

weak-kneed (wēk′nēd′), *adj.* yielding readily to pressure or intimidation.

weak·ling (wēk′ling), *n.* a person who is physically or morally weak.

weak·ly (wēk′lē), *adj.*, **-li·er, -li·est,** *adv.* —*adj.* **1.** not robust or healthy. —*adv.* **2.** in a weak manner.

weak·ness (wēk′nis), *n.* **1.** the state or quality of being weak. **2.** an inadequate or defective quality, as of character. **3.** a special fondness. **4.** an object of such fondness. —**Syn. 2.** fault, flaw, shortcoming.

weal¹ (wēl), *n. Archaic.* well-being.

weal² (wēl), *n.* wale (def. 1).

weald (wēld), *n. Brit.* wooded or uncultivated country.

wealth (welth), *n.* **1.** a great quantity of money or property of value. **2.** a plentiful amount: *a wealth of detail.* **3.** all goods that have a monetary or exchange value. **4.** valuable contents or produce.

wealth·y (wel′thē), *adj.*, **-i·er, -i·est.** having great wealth. —**wealth′i·ness,** *n.* —**Syn.** affluent, prosperous, rich.

wean (wēn), *v.t.* **1.** to accustom (a child or young animal) to food other than its mother's milk. **2.** to free from a habit or attitude.

weap·on (wep′ən), *n.* **1.** any instrument or device used in fighting. **2.** anything used against an opponent, as in a dispute. —**weap′on·less,** *adj.*

weap·on·ry (wep′ən rē), *n.* **1.** weapons collectively. **2.** the invention and production of weapons.

wear (wâr), *v.*, **wore, worn, wear·ing,** *n.* —*v.t.* **1.** to carry or have on one's person as a covering, support, or ornament. **2.** to show or display, as a smile. **3.** to reduce or damage by strain or rubbing. **4.** to make (a hole, etc.) in something through such action. **5.** to tire or fatigue. —*v.i.* **6.** to deteriorate, as from strain or rubbing. **7.** to endure use or strain. **8.** to reach (a certain state) under the effects of strain or use: *My patience wore thin after I'd waited an hour.* **9.** (of time) to pass slowly or tediously. **10. wear down,** to overcome by persistence. **11. wear off,** to diminish generally. **12. wear out, a.** to make or become unfit or useless through wear. **b.** to exhaust or weary. —*n.* **13.** the act of wearing or state of being worn. **14.** clothing, esp. of a specified kind. **15.** gradual deterioration, as from strain or rubbing. —**wear′a·ble,** *adj.* —**wear′er,** *n.*

wear′ and tear′ (târ), damage or deterioration resulting from ordinary use.

wea·ri·some (wēr′ē səm), *adj.* **1.** causing weariness. **2.** tiresome or tedious. —**wea′ri·some·ly,** *adv.* —**wea′-ri·some·ness,** *n.*

wea·ry (wēr′ē), *adj.*, **-ri·er, -ri·est,** *v.*, **-ried, -ry·ing.** —*adj.* **1.** physically or mentally exhausted, as by hard work. **2.** causing fatigue: *a weary journey.* **3.** having one's patience or tolerance exhausted. —*v.t.*, *v.i.* **4.** to make or become weary. —**wea′-ri·ly,** *adv.* —**wea′ri·ness,** *n.*

wea·sel (wē′zəl), *n.* **1.** a small carnivorous mammal having a long, slender body. —*v.i.* **2.** to be evasive or intentionally misleading. —**wea′sel·ly,** *adj.*

wea′sel words′, an evasive or intentionally misleading statement.

weath·er (we*th*′ər), *n.* **1.** the state of the atmosphere with respect to wind, temperature, moisture, etc. **2.** a strong wind or storm. **3. under the weather,** *Informal.* somewhat ill. —*v.t.* **4.** to expose to the weather. **5.** to discolor or damage by exposure to the weather. **6.** to come safely through (a storm, trouble, etc.). **7.** *Naut.* to pass or sail to the windward. —*v.i.* **8.** to become discolored or damaged by exposure to the weather. —**weath′er·a·bil′i·ty,** *n.*

weath·er-beat·en (we*th*′ər bēt′ən), *adj.* **1.** worn or damaged by exposure to the weather. **2.** tanned and toughened by bad weather: *a weatherbeaten face.*

weath·er·board (we*th*′ər bôrd′, -bōrd′), *n. Brit.* clapboard (def. 1).

weath·er·bound (we*th*′ər bound′), *adj.* delayed or shut in by bad weather, as a ship.

weath·er·cock (we*th*′ər kok′), *n.* **1.** a weather vane in the shape of a rooster. **2.** a fickle person.

weath′er eye′, **1.** alertness to signs of change in the weather. **2.** a careful watch for change, as in circumstance.

weath·er·glass (we*th*′ər glas′, -gläs′), *n.* an early type of barometer.

weath·er·ing (we*th*′ər ing), *n.* the action of frost or other weather conditions upon rocks.

weath·er·man (we*th*′ər man′), *n.* a person who forecasts or reports weather conditions.

weath·er·proof (we*th*′ər prōōf′), *adj.* **1.** able to withstand exposure to all kinds of weather. —*v.t.* **2.** to make weatherproof.

weath·er-strip (we*th*′ər strip′), *n., v.,* **-stripped, -strip·ping.** —*n.* **1.** Also, **weath′er·strip′ping.** a narrow strip of metal or wood placed between a door or window sash and its frame to exclude rain, air, etc. —*v.t.* **2.** to apply weatherstrip to.

weath′er vane′, vane (def. 1).

weath·er-wise (we*th*′ər wīz′), *adj.* skillful in predicting weather.

weath·er·worn (we*th*′ər wôrn′, -wōrn′), *adj. Literary.* weatherbeaten.

weave (wēv), *v.,* **wove** or (*Rare*) **weaved; wo·ven** or **wove; weav·ing;** *n.* —*v.t.* **1.** to interlace (yarns, strips, etc.) so as to form a fabric or material. **2.** to form by such interlacing: *to weave cloth.* **3.** (of a spider or larva) to form (a web). **4.** to form (a plan, etc.) by combining various elements or details. **5.** to combine into a connected whole. **6.** to move along in a winding or zigzag course. —*v.i.* **7.** to make or form by weaving. —*n.* **8.** a pattern or method of weaving. —**weav′er,** *n.*

web (web), *n., v.,* **webbed, web·bing.** —*n.* **1.** a fabric formed by weaving. **2.** a thin, silken material spun by spiders and some other insects. **3.** a membrane that connects the fingers or toes of an animal, as on a frog. **4.** the series of barbs on each side of the shaft of a feather. **5.** any complicated pattern or network. —*v.t.* **6.** to cover or connect with or as with a web. **7.** to ensnare or entrap. —**webbed** (-d), *adj.*

web·bing (web′ing), *n.* a strong, woven material used for belts, straps, harnesses, etc.

web·foot (web′fŏŏt′), *n.* a foot with the toes joined by a web. —**web′foot′ed,** *adj.*

Web·ster (web′stər), *n.* Noah, 1758–1843, U.S. lexicographer.

wed (wed), *v.t., v.i.,* **wed·ded, wed·ded** or **wed, wed·ding.** **1.** to marry (another person) in a formal ceremony. **2.** to unite formally in marriage. **3.** to blend or associate harmoniously.

we'd (wēd), contraction of: **a.** *we had.* **b.** *we should.* **c.** *we would.*

Wed., Wednesday.

wed·ding (wed′ing), *n.* **1.** the act or ceremony of marrying, with its attendant festivities. **2.** the anniversary of a marriage or its celebration. **3.** harmonious blending or association.

wedge (wej), *n., v.,* **wedged, wedging.** —*n.* **1.** a triangular piece of hard material tapering to a thin edge, used to split wood or to adjust the positions of heavy objects. **2.** anything in the shape of a wedge. **3.** something that leads to disunity, change, entrance, etc. —*v.t.* **4.** to separate or split with or as with a wedge. **5.** to fasten tightly by driving in a wedge. **6.** to thrust into or through a narrow space. —*v.i.* **7.** to force a way into or through a narrow space.

wed·lock (wed′lok), *n.* the state of being legally married.

Wednes·day (wenz′dē, -dā), *n.* the fourth day of the week.

wee (wē), *adj.,* **we·er, we·est. 1.** very small. **2.** very early: *in the wee hours.*

weed (wēd), *n.* **1.** a valueless, troublesome plant growing wild, esp. one that crowds or damages the desired crop. —*v.t.* **2.** to free from weeds: *to weed a garden.* **3.** to remove as being undesirable or unwanted: *to weed out inexperienced players.* —**weed′er,** *n.*

weeds (wēdz), *n.pl.* mourning clothes formerly worn esp. by a widow.

weed·y (wē′dē), *adj.*, **weed·i·er, weed·i·est. 1.** full of weeds. **2.** of or like a weed. **3.** thin and scrawny. —**weed′i·ly,** *adv.* —**weed′i·ness,** *n.*

week (wēk), *n.* **1.** a period of seven successive days, usually beginning with Sunday. **2.** the working or school days of such a period: *a 35-hour week.*

week·day (wēk′dā′), *n.* any day of the week except Sunday or, often, Saturday and Sunday.

week·end (wēk′end′), *n.* **1.** the period between Friday evening and Monday morning. —*v.i.* **2.** to spend a weekend.

week·ly (wēk′lē), *adj., adv., n., pl.* -**lies.** —*adj.* **1.** happening or appearing once every week. **2.** computed by the week. **3.** of, for, or lasting a week. —*adv.* **4.** once a week. —*n.* **5.** a periodical appearing once a week.

ween (wēn), *v.t., v.i.* Archaic. to think or suppose.

wee·nie (wē′nē), *n.* Informal. a wiener.

wee·ny (wē′nē), *adj.* Informal. extremely small.

weep (wēp), *v.i., v.t.,* **wept, weep·ing. 1.** to shed (tears) from any overwhelming emotion, as deep sorrow. **2.** to mourn or grieve. **3.** to drip or exude (water or liquid). —**weep′er,** *n.* —**Syn. 1.** cry, sob. **2.** lament.

weep·ing (wē′p'ing), *adj.* **1.** shedding tears from any overwhelming emotion. **2.** dripping or oozing liquid. **3.** (of trees, etc.) having slender, drooping branches.

weep·y (wē′pē), *adj.,* -**i·er,** -**i·est.** easily moved to tears.

wee·vil (wē′vəl), *n.* a beetle with a long snout that attacks farm crops. —**wee′vil·y, wee′vil·ly,** *adj.*

weft (weft), *n.* **1.** filling (def. 3). **2.** a woven fabric.

weigh[1] (wā), *v.t.* **1.** to ascertain the heaviness of, as by use of a scale. **2.** to measure or apportion according to weight. **3.** to consider carefully. **4.** to raise up (an anchor). —*v.i.* **5.** to have a certain weight. **6.** to have importance or influence. **7.** to bear down as a burden. **8. weigh down, a.** to be or cause to become heavy. **b.** to burden or depress. **9. weigh in,** to be weighed officially before a bout, race, etc. —**weigh′er,** *n.*

weigh[2] (wā), *n.* **under weigh,** *Naut.* in motion.

weight (wāt), *n.* **1.** the amount or quantity of heaviness. **2.** *Physics.* the force which gravitation exerts upon a body. **3.** a system of units for expressing heaviness. **4.** a unit of heaviness or mass. **5.** a body of standard heaviness, used on a balance in weighing objects. **6.** a specific quantity determined by weighing. **7.** any heavy load, mass, or object. **8.** a heavy object used to hold something down or open. **9.** a mental burden, as of sorrow. **10.** importance or influence: *an opinion of great weight.* **11.** a metal disk of standard heaviness for lifting in athletic competition or for exercise. —*v.t.* **12.** to add weight to. **13.** to burden or oppress.

weight·less (wāt′lis), *adj.* **1.** having little or no weight. **2.** not affected by gravitational force. —**weight′less·ly,** *adv.* —**weight′less·ness,** *n.*

weight′ lift′ing, the lifting of heavy weights in athletic competition or as an exercise. —**weight′ lift′er.**

weight·y (wā′tē), *adj.,* -**i·er,** -**i·est. 1.** having considerable weight. **2.** burdensome or troublesome. **3.** important or momentous. **4.** having or exerting influence or validity. **5.** solemn or serious. —**weight′i·ly,** *adv.* —**weight′i·ness,** *n.*

weir (wēr), *n.* **1.** a small dam in a river or stream. **2.** a fence, as of brush, set in a stream or channel for catching fish.

weird (wērd), *adj.* **1.** mysterious in an unnatural way. **2.** fantastic or bizarre. —**weird′ly,** *adv.* —**weird′ness,** *n.* —**Syn. 1.** eerie, uncanny.

weird·o (wērd′ō), *n., pl.* -**os.** Slang. an odd or eccentric person or thing. Also, **weird′ie** (-dē).

Welch (welch, welsh), *adj., n.* Rare. Welsh.

wel·come (wel′kəm), *n., v.,* -**comed,** -**com·ing,** *adj.* —*n.* **1.** a kindly greeting or reception. —*v.t.* **2.** to greet with pleasure or courtesy. **3.** to meet, receive, or accept with pleasure: *to welcome a change.* —*adj.* **4.** gladly received: *a welcome visitor.* **5.** given permission (to use or enjoy): *He is welcome to try it.* **6.** without obligation (used as a response to thanks): *You're quite welcome.*

weld (weld), *v.t.* **1.** to join (pieces of metal) by hammering together, esp. after rendering soft by heat. **2.** to unite closely or firmly. —*v.i.* **3.** to be welded. —*n.* **4.** a welded joint. **5.** union or fusion by welding. —**weld′er,** *n.*

wel·fare (wel′fâr′), *n.* **1.** the state of being healthy, properly fed, and comfortable. **2.** organized efforts to improve living conditions for needy persons. **3. on welfare,** receiving public financial aid because of hardship and need.

wel′fare state′, a country in which the government assumes principal responsibility for the general welfare of its people.

wel·kin (wel′kin), *n. Archaic.* the sky.

well[1] (wel), *adv., adj., compar.* **better,** *superl.* **best,** *interj., n.* —*adv.* **1.** in a good or satisfactory manner: *Things are going well.* **2.** in a careful or thorough manner: *Shake well before using.* **3.** comfortably or prosperously: *to live well.* **4.** commendably or excellently: *a difficult task well done.* **5.** with justice or reason: *I could not well refuse.* **6.** with favor or approval: *to think well of someone.* **7.** to a considerable degree: *a sum well over the amount fixed.* **8.** intimately or closely: *I knew him well.* **9.** without doubt. **10.** fortunately or advantageously. **11.** as well, also or too. **12. as well as, a.** as much or as truly as. **b.** in addition to. —*adj.* **13.** in good health: *a well man.* **14.** satisfactory or good: *All is well with us.* **15.** fitting or gratifying: *It is well that you didn't go.* **16.** in a satisfactory position: *I am very well as I am.* —*interj.* **17.** (used to express surprise, reproof, etc.) **18.** (used to introduce a sentence or resume a conversation): *Well, I'd better be going.* —*n.* **19.** good fortune or success: *They wish me well.*
—*Usage.* See **good.**

well[2] (wel), *n.* **1.** a hole drilled or bored into the earth, as to obtain water, oil, gas, etc. **2.** *Literary.* a spring or natural source of water. **3.** an abundant source: *a well of compassion.* **4.** any enclosed space, as for light, stairs, elevator, etc., extending vertically through the floors of a building. **5.** a container for a fluid, as ink. —*v.i., v.t.* **6.** to rise, spring, or gush, as from a well: *Tears welled up in his eyes.*

we′ll (wēl), contraction of: **a.** *we will.* **b.** *we shall.*

well-ad·vised (wel′ad vīzd′), *adj.* **1.** acting with caution or care. **2.** based on or showing wise consideration.

well-ap·point·ed (wel′ə poin′tid), *adj.*
attractively equipped or furnished.

well-bal·anced (wel′bal′ənst), *adj.* **1.** rightly balanced or adjusted. **2.** sensible or sane.

well-be·ing (wel′bē′ing), *n.* good or satisfactory condition of existence.

well-born (wel′bôrn′), *adj.* born of a good or noble family.

well-bred (wel′bred′), *adj.* showing good breeding, as in behavior or manners.

well-con·di·tioned (wel′kən dish′ənd), *adj.* **1.** being in good physical condition. **2.** characterized by proper behavior or disposition.

well-de·fined (wel′di fīnd′), *adj.* clearly stated or distinguished: *a well-defined boundary.*

well-dis·posed (wel′di spōzd′), *adj.* sympathetically or kindly disposed.

well-done (wel′dun′), *adj.* **1.** performed with skill. **2.** (of meat) thoroughly cooked.

well-fa·vored (wel′fā′vərd), *adj. Archaic.* having an attractive appearance.

well-fed (wel′fed′), *adj.* properly nourished.

well-fixed (wel′fikst′), *adj. Informal.* financially secure or stable.

well-found·ed (wel′foun′did), *adj.* based on good reasons, solid evidence, or correct judgment.

well-groomed (wel′grōomd′), *adj.* **1.** clean, neat, and dressed well. **2.** carefully cared for.

well-ground·ed (wel′groun′did), *adj.* **1.** thoroughly instructed in the basic principles of a subject. **2.** well-founded.

well-head (wel′hed′), *n.* **1.** the source of a fountain or spring. **2.** major source. **3.** a shelter for a well.

well-heeled (wel′hēld′), *adj. Informal.* having much money.

well-in·formed (wel′in fôrmd′), *adj.* having extensive knowledge or information, as in one subject.

Wel·ling·ton (wel′ing tən), *n.* the capital of New Zealand.

well-in·ten·tioned (wel′in ten′shənd), *adj.* well-meaning (def. 1).

well-knit (wel′nit′), *adj.* closely or carefully joined together or related: *a well-knit plot.*

well′-ac·cept′ed, *adj.*	**well′-cho′sen,** *adj.*	**well′-earned′,** *adj.*
well′-ac·cus′tomed, *adj.*	**well′-clothed′,** *adj.*	**well′-ed′u·cat′ed,** *adj.*
well′-ac·quaint′ed, *adj.*	**well′-con·cealed′,** *adj.*	**well′-e·quipped′,** *adj.*
well′-ad·just′ed, *adj.*	**well′-con·sid′ered,** *adj.*	**well′-fi·nanced′,** *adj.*
well′-ad′ver·tised′, *adj.*	**well′-con·struct′ed,** *adj.*	**well′-fit′ted,** *adj.*
well′-aimed′, *adj.*	**well′-con·trolled′,** *adj.*	**well′-formed′,** *adj.*
well′-armed′, *adj.*	**well′-cooked′,** *adj.*	**well′-fur′nished,** *adj.*
well′-ar·ranged′, *adj.*	**well′-de·fend′ed,** *adj.*	**well′-guard′ed,** *adj.*
well′-at·tend′ed, *adj.*	**well′-de·scribed′,** *adj.*	**well′-hid′den,** *adj.*
well′-at·tired′, *adj.*	**well′-de·served′,** *adj.*	**well′-housed′,** *adj.*
well′-a·ware′, *adj.*	**well′-de·vel′oped,** *adj.*	**well′-jus′ti·fied′,** *adj.*
well′-be·haved′, *adj.*	**well′-dressed′,** *adj.*	**well′-kept′,** *adj.*
well′-built′, *adj.*		

well-known (wel′nōn′), *adj.* **1.** widely known **2.** fully known.

well-man·nered (wel′man′ərd), *adj.* having polite manners.

well-mean·ing (wel′mē′niñg), *adj.* **1.** having or showing good intentions. **2.** Also, **well′-meant′.** proceeding from good intentions.

well-nigh (wel′nī′), *adv.* very nearly.

well-off (wel′ôf′, -of′), *adj.* **1.** in a fortunate position or condition. **2.** well-to-do.

well-or·dered (wel′ôr′dərd), *adj.* arranged or planned in a desirable way.

well-pre·served (wel′pri zûrvd′), *adj.* having been maintained in good condition.

well-read (wel′red′), *adj.* extensively informed through reading.

well-round·ed (wel′roun′did), *adj.* **1.** having desirably varied abilities or attainments **2.** desirably varied. **3.** fully developed or formed, as a woman's figure

well-spo·ken (wel′spō′kən), *adj.* **1.** aptly or fittingly spoken. **2.** speaking gently or pleasantly. **3.** *Archaic.* polite in speech.

well-spring (wel′spriñg′), *n.* **1.** a source of unfailing supply. **2.** wellhead (def 1).

well-thought-of (wel′thôt′uv′, -ov′), *adj.* of good reputation.

well-timed (wel′tīmd′), *adj.* fittingly or appropriately timed.

well-to-do (wel′tə dōō′), *adj.* having considerable wealth.

well-turned (wel′tûrnd′), *adj.* **1.** gracefully shaped· *a well-turned ankle.* **2.** gracefully and concisely expressed· *a well-turned phrase.*

well-wish·er (wel′wish′ər), *n.* a person who wishes well to another person, a cause, etc. **—well′-wish′ing,** *adj.*, *n.*

well-worn (wel′wôrn′, -wôrn′), *adj.* **1.** showing extensive use or wear. **2.** trite or hackneyed, as a joke. **3.** *Literary.* becomingly worn, as fame.

welsh (welsh, welch), *v.i. Slang.* **1.** to cheat by failing to pay a gambling debt. **2.** to fail deliberately to meet one's obligations. **—welsh′er,** *n.*

Welsh (welsh, welch), *adj.* **1.** of Wales, its people, or their language. **—n. 2.** the people of Wales. **3.** the Celtic language of Wales. **—Welsh′·man,** *n.* **—Welsh′wom′an,** *n.fem.*

Welsh′ cor′gi (kôr′gē), a Welsh breed of dog having short legs, erect ears, and a foxlike head.

Welsh′ rab′bit, a dish consisting of melted cheese, usually mixed with spices, served over toast or crackers. Also, **Welsh′ rare′bit.**

welt (welt), *n.* **1.** a strip, as of leather, set in between the sole of a shoe and its upper. **2.** a strengthening or ornamental finish along a seam of a garment. **3.** wale (def. 1). **—v.t. 4.** to furnish with a welt. **5.** to beat soundly, as with a whip.

wel·ter (wel′tər), *v.i.* **1.** to tumble tumultuously, as the sea. **2.** to roll or writhe. **3.** to lie bathed in something, esp. blood. **—n. 4.** a tossing or tumbling motion. **5.** a confused mass. **6.** a commotion or turmoil.

wel·ter·weight (wel′tər wāt′), *n.* a boxer or wrestler weighing between 136 and 147 pounds.

wen (wen), *n.* a benign sebaceous cyst of the skin, esp. on the scalp.

wench (wench), *n. Archaic.* **1.** a young woman. **2.** a female servant.

wend (wend), *v.t.* to proceed on (one's way).

went (went), *v.* pt. of **go.**

wept (wept), *v.* pt. and pp. of **weep.**

were (wûr), *v.* a 2nd pers. sing. past indic., pl. past indic., and past subj. of **be.**

we're (wēr), contraction of *we are.*

were·n't (wûrnt, wûr′ənt), contraction of *were not.*

were·wolf (wēr′wŏŏlf′, wûr′-, wâr′-), *n., pl.* **-wolves** (-wŏŏlvz′). (in folklore) a human being that has or can be changed into a wolf. Also, **wer′-wolf′.**

wert (wûrt), *v. Archaic.* a 2nd pers. sing. past indic. and subj. of **be.**

wes·kit (wes′kit), *n. Dial.* vest (def. 1).

Wes·ley (wes′lē, wez′-), *n.* **John,** 1703–91, English theologian: founder of Methodism. **—Wes′ley·an,** *adj.*, *n.*

west (west), *n.* **1.** the direction to the left of a person facing north. **2.** a cardinal point of the compass, lying directly opposite east. **3.** (*usually cap.*) a region or territory situated in this direction. **4.** the West, **a.** the western part of the U.S. **b.** the western part of the world, including Europe and the Western Hemisphere. **c.** Western Europe and the Ameri-

well′-liked′, *adj.*	**well′-pro·tect′ed,** *adj.*	**well′-sea′soned,** *adj.*
well′-loved′, *adj.*	**well′-qual′i·fied′,** *adj.*	**well′-spent′,** *adj.*
well′-made′, *adj.*	**well′-rea′soned,** *adj.*	**well′-stat′ed,** *adj.*
well′-man·aged′, *adj.*	**well′-rec′og·nized′,** *adj.*	**well′-sup·plied′,** *adj.*
well′-marked′, *adj.*	**well′-reg′u·lat′ed,** *adj.*	**well′-trav′eled,** *adj.*
well′-paid′, *adj.*	**well′-rep′re·sent′ed,** *adj.*	**well′-treat′ed,** *adj.*
well′-planned′, *adj.*	**well′-sat′is·fied′,** *adj.*	**well′-used′,** *adj.*
well′-pre·pared′, *adj.*		

cas. —*adj.* **5.** lying toward or situated in the west. **6.** coming from the west. —*adv.* **7.** toward or from the west.

West' Berlin', the western zone of Berlin, tied with West Germany.

west·er·ly (wes'tər lē), *adj., adv.* **1.** toward the west. **2.** from the west.

west·ern (wes'tərn), *adj.* **1.** lying toward or situated in the west. **2.** coming from or situated in the west. **3.** (*usually cap.*) of or pertaining to the West. —*n.* **4.** (*often cap.*) a story or motion picture about the U.S. West of the 19th century, esp. about cowboys, Indian wars, etc.

West·ern·er (wes'tər nər), *n.* (*often l.c.*) a native or inhabitant of the West, esp. of the western U.S.

West'ern Hem'isphere, the half of the terrestrial globe that includes North, Central, and South America.

west·ern·ize (wes'tər nīz'), *v.t.,* **-ized, -iz·ing.** to influence with Western ideas or customs.

West'ern Samo'a, a country in the S Pacific.

West' Ger'many, a country in central Europe.

West' In'dies, an archipelago in the N Atlantic between North and South America. —**West' In'dian.**

West' Point', a military reservation in SE New York: U.S. Military Academy.

West' Virgin'ia, a state in the E United States. *Cap.*: Charleston. — **West' Virgin'ian.**

west·ward (west'wərd), *adj.* **1.** moving toward or facing the west. —*adv.* **2.** Also, **west'wards, west'ward·ly.** toward the west.

wet (wet), *adj.,* **wet·ter, wet·test,** *n., v.,* **wet** or **wet·ted, wet·ting.** —*adj.* **1.** covered or soaked with water or other liquid. **2.** not yet dry: *wet paint.* **3.** rainy or misty. **4.** allowing the sale of alcoholic beverages: *a wet town.* **5.** all wet, *Slang.* completely mistaken. —*n.* **6.** wetness or moisture. **7.** rainy or damp weather. **8.** a person in favor of allowing the sale of alcoholic beverages. —*v.t., v.i.* **9.** to make or become wet. — **wet'ly,** *adv.* —**wet'ness,** *n.* —**wet'-ter,** *n.* —**Syn. 9.** drench, saturate, soak.

wet·back (wet'bak'), *n.* a Mexican laborer who enters the U.S. illegally.

wet' blan'ket, a person or thing that dampens enthusiasm, enjoyment, etc.

weth·er (weth'ər), *n.* a castrated male sheep.

wet' nurse', a woman hired to suckle another's infant. —**wet-nurse,** *v.t.*

wet' suit', a closefitting rubber garment worn in cold water by a skin diver for warmth.

wet'ting a'gent, any admixture to a liquid for increasing its ability to penetrate or cover cloth, paper, leather, etc.

we've (wēv), contraction of *we have.*

whack (hwak), *Informal.* —*v.t., v.i.* **1.** to strike with a smart, resounding blow. —*n.* **2.** a smart, resounding blow. **3.** the sound of such a blow. **4.** a trial or attempt: *to take a whack at a job.* **5.** a portion or share. **6.** out of whack, out of order. — **whack'er,** *n.*

whack·ing (hwak'ing), *adj. Chiefly Brit. Informal.* very big.

whack·y (hwak'ē), *adj.,* **-i·er, -i·est.** wacky.

whale[1] (hwāl), *n., pl.* **whales, whale,** *v.,* **whaled, whal·ing.** —*n.* **1.** a very large, air-breathing marine mammal having a fishlike body. **2.** *Informal.* something extraordinarily big or impressive: *a whale of a lot of money.* —*v.i.* **3.** to hunt whales.

whale[2] (hwāl), *v.t.,* **whaled, whal·ing.** *Informal.* to whip or thrash soundly.

whale·boat (hwāl'bōt'), *n.* a long, narrow boat designed for quick turning and use in rough seas.

whale·bone (hwāl'bōn'), *n.* **1.** an elastic, horny substance growing in place of teeth in the upper jaw of certain whales (**whale'bone whale'**). **2.** a thin strip of this substance, formerly used for stiffening a corset.

whal·er (hwā'lər), *n.* **1.** a person engaged in whaling. **2.** a ship used in whaling.

whal·ing (hwā'ling), *n.* the hunting, capturing, and processing of whales.

wham (hwam), *n., v.,* **whammed, wham·ming.** —*n.* **1.** a loud sound produced by an explosion or sharp impact. **2.** a forcible impact —*v.t., v.i.* **3.** to hit with or make a forcible impact, esp. one producing a loud sound.

wham·my (hwam'ē), *n., pl.* **-mies.** *Slang.* a jinx.

wharf (hwôrf), *n., pl.* **wharves** (hwôrvz), **wharfs.** *Chiefly Brit.* pier (def. 1).

wharf·age (hwôr'fij), *n.* **1.** the use of a wharf. **2.** a charge or payment for this.

wharf·in·ger (hwôr'fin jər), *n.* a person who owns or has charge of a wharf.

what (hwut, hwot), *pron.* **1.** which thing or things, action, event, condition, kind, etc.: *What happened?* **2.** that or those which: *Tell me what you want for lunch.* **3.** whatever: *come what may.* **4.** *Nonstandard.* that, which, or who: *She's the one what told me.* **5.** what about, what do you think regarding? **6.** what for, for what reason? —*adj.* **7.** which or which of: *What clothes shall I pack?*

8. whatever or whichever: *Take what supplies you need.* 9. so much or so great: *What trouble I'm having with mathematics!* —*adv.* 10. how much?: *What does it matter?* 11. **what with,** with the addition or complication of: *What with the flu and two colds, I'm a month behind in my work.* —*interj.* 12. (an exclamation of surprise, doubt, or annoyance): *What, aren't you ready yet?*

what·ev·er (hwut ev′ər, hwot-), *pron.* 1. anything that: *Do whatever you like.* 2. no matter what: *He'll do it, whatever happens.* 3. what (for greater emphasis): *Whatever do you mean?* —*adj.* 4. in any amount: *whatever merit the work has.* 5. no matter what: *whatever rebuffs he might receive.* 6. being what or who it may be: *Whatever the reason, he refuses to go.* 7. of any kind: *He eats no sweets whatever.*

what·not (hwut′not′, hwot′-), *n.* a stand with shelves for bric-a-brac, etc.: popular esp. in the 19th century.

what·so·ev·er (hwut′sō ev′ər, hwot′-), *pron., adj.* an emphatic form of **whatever.**

wheal (hwēl), *n.* 1. a small burning or itching swelling on the skin, as from a mosquito bite. 2. wale (def. 1).

wheat (hwēt), *n.* 1. the grain of a cereal grass, ground into flour for making bread, cake, etc. 2. the plant that bears this grain. —**wheat′en,** *adj.*

wheat′ germ′, the embryo of the wheat kernel, used as a concentrated source of vitamins.

whee·dle (hwēd′³l), *v.t., v.i.,* -**dled,** -**dling.** 1. to try to influence (a person) by subtle flattery or slyness. 2. to get (something) by artful persuasions. —**whee′dler,** *n.* —**Syn.** cajole, coax.

wheel (hwēl), *n.* 1. a circular frame or disk arranged to revolve on an axis, as on vehicles, machinery, etc. 2. anything like this in shape or function. 3. a device for steering the gear of a vehicle or vessel. 4. **wheels, a.** the forces that move or control an elaborate system: *the wheels of industry.* **b.** Slang. an automobile, bicycle, or other vehicle. 5. a wheeling or circular movement. 6. Slang. an active and influential person. 7. a former instrument of torture on which the victim was stretched until disjointed. 8. **at the wheel,** steering a vehicle or vessel. —*v.t., v.i.* 9. to turn, rotate, or revolve. 10. to move or carry on wheels. 11. to turn so as to face in a different direction. —**wheeled** (-d), *adj.* —**wheel′er,** *n.* —**wheel′less,** *adj.*

wheel·bar·row (hwēl′bar′ō), *n.* a frame having two handles and mounted on a wheel or wheels, used for carrying small loads.

wheel·base (hwēl′bās′), *n.* the distance measured in inches from the front-wheel spindle to the rear-wheel axle in a motor vehicle.

wheel·chair (hwēl′châr′), *n.* a chair mounted on large wheels used by invalids for moving about.

wheel·er-deal·er (hwē′lər dē′lər), *n.* Slang. a person who operates shrewdly and often unscrupulously, as in big business negotiations.

wheel·wright (hwēl′rīt′), *n.* a person who makes or repairs wheels and wheeled carriages.

wheeze (hwēz), *v.,* **wheezed, wheez·ing,** *n.* —*v.i.* 1. to breathe with difficulty and with a whistling sound. —*n.* 2. a wheezing sound. 3. an old, trite joke or saying.

wheez·y (hwē′zē), *adj.,* -**i·er, -i·est.** afflicted with or characterized by wheezing. —**wheez′i·ness,** *n.*

whelk (hwelk), *n.* a large, edible marine mollusk having a spiral-shaped shell.

whelm (hwelm), *v.t. Literary.* 1. to submerge. 2. to overwhelm.

whelp (hwelp), *n.* 1. the young of a dog, wolf, etc. 2. an ill-bred boy or young man. —*v.t., v.i.* 3. to give birth to (whelps).

when (hwen), *adv.* 1. at or during what time or period?: *When will they leave?* 2. upon what occasion?: *When did you ever see such a crowd?* —*conj.* 3. at what or which time: *I'll tell you when to begin.* 4. at or during the time that: *Call me when dinner is ready.* 5. upon or after which: *I had just come in when the telephone rang.* 6. while on the contrary: *Why are you here when you should be in school?* 7. in view of the fact that: *How can I study when you're making so much noise?* 8. whenever: *He always gets home late when he goes to the movies.* —*pron.* 9. what or which time: *Till when is the store open?* —*n.* 10. the time of anything.
—**Usage. See where.**

whence (hwens), *adv. Literary.* 1. from what place?: *Whence comest thou?* 2. from what source, origin, or cause?: *Whence has he wisdom?*

when·ev·er (hwen ev′ər), *conj.* 1. at whatever time. —*adv.* 2. an emphatic form of **when.** Also, **when′so·ev′er.**

where (hwâr), *adv.* 1. in or at what place or position?: *Where is he?* 2. in what respect or way?: *Where does this affect us?* 3. to or toward what place, point, or end?: *Where are you going?* 4. from what

source?: *Where did you get that idea?* —*conj.* 5. in or at what place: *Find where he is.* 6. in or at the same place that: *The book is where you left it.* 7. in or at whatever place: *I will go where you go.* 8. in or at which place: *They came to the town, where they had lunch.* —*pron.* 9. what place? *Where did you come from?* 10. the place in or at which: *This is where the boat docks.* —*n.* 11. the place or location.
—**Usage.** In careful English, WHERE is not used in place of WHEN: *A holiday is an occasion when we have time off.* WHERE should not be used to replace THAT: *I see by the papers that she is now a full professor.*

where·a·bouts (hwâr′ə bouts′), *n.* 1. the place where a person or thing is. —*adv.* 2. *Literary.* about where?

where·as (hwâr az′), *conj.* 1. while on the contrary. 2. considering that.

where·at (hwâr at′), *conj.* at or upon which.

where·by (hwâr bī′), *conj.* by which.

where·fore (hwâr′fôr, -fōr), *Archaic.* —*conj.* 1. for which cause or reason. —*adv.* 2. for what? —*n.* 3. the cause or reason.

where·from (hwâr frum′, -from′), *conj.* from which.

where·in (hwâr in′), *conj.* 1. in which. —*adv.* 2. in what way or respect?

where·of (hwâr uv′, -ov′), *conj.* 1. of what, which, or whom. —*adv.* 2. *Archaic.* of what?

where·on (hwâr on′, -ôn′), *conj.* 1. on what or which. —*adv.* 2. *Archaic.* on what?

where·so·ev·er (hwâr′sō ev′ər), *conj.* an emphatic form of **wherever.**

where·to (hwâr tōō′), *conj.* 1. to which. —*adv.* 2. *Archaic.* to what end or purpose?

where·up·on (hwâr′ə pon′, -pôn′), *conj.* 1. upon which. 2. at or after which. —*adv.* 3. *Archaic.* upon what?

wher·ev·er (hwâr ev′ər), *conj.* 1. in, at, or to whatever place. 2. in any case or condition in which. —*adv.* 3. an emphatic form of **where.**

where·with (hwâr with′, -with′), *conj.* 1. with which. —*adv.* 2. *Archaic.* with what? —*pron.* 3. the thing or things by or with which.

where·with·al (hwâr′with ôl′), *n.* means for the purpose or need, esp. money.

wher·ry (hwer′ē), *n., pl.* **-ries.** a light rowboat for one person.

whet (hwet), *v.t.*, **whet·ted, whet·ting.** 1. to sharpen (a knife, etc.) by rubbing or grinding. 2. to make keen or eager, as the appetite. —**whet′-ter,** *n.*

weth·er (hweth′ər), *conj.* 1. (used to introduce the first of two or more alternatives): *It doesn't matter whether we go or stay.* 2. (used to introduce a single alternative, the other being implied): *Ask your mother whether you can go.*
—**Usage.** See **if.**

whet·stone (hwet′stōn′), *n.* a stone for whetting cutlery or tools.

whew (hwyōō), *interj.* (a whistling exclamation expressing astonishment, relief, etc.)

whey (hwā), *n.* a watery liquid that separates from milk after it curdles, as in the making of cheese. —**whey′-ey,** *adj.*

whf., wharf.

which (hwich), *pron.* 1. what one or ones?: *Which of these do you want?* 2. whichever (def. 1): *Choose which you like.* 3. the one or ones that: *Tell me which you think will be most useful.* 4. (used in relative clauses to refer to that or those mentioned earlier in the sentence): *The goods which we ordered have been delivered.* —*adj.* 5. what one or ones of (a certain group implied)?: *Which book do you want?* 6. whichever (def. 3): *Use which method you prefer.* 7. being previously mentioned: *It rained all day, during which time we played cards.*

which·ev·er (hwich ev′ər), *pron.* 1. (of a certain group implied) any one or ones that: *Take whichever you like.* 2. no matter which: *Whichever you choose, the others will be offended.* —*adj.* 3. (of an indicated group) no matter which: *whichever day.*

which·so·ev·er (hwich′sō ev′ər), *pron., adj.* an emphatic form of **whichever.**

whiff (hwif), *n.* 1. a slight gust or puff of wind, air, smoke, etc. 2. a slight odor or smell: *a whiff of garlic.* 3. a single inhalation or exhalation. —*v.i.*, *v.t.* 4. to blow or move in whiffs.

whif·fle·tree (hwif′əl trē′), *n.* a crossbar, pivoted at the middle, to which the traces of a harness are fastened for pulling a cart, etc.

Whig (hwig), *n.* 1. *Amer. Hist.* **a.** a supporter of the Revolution. **b.** a member of a political party (c1834–1855) that was formed in opposition to the Democratic Party. 2. a member of a former British political party that held liberal principles and favored reforms.

while (hwīl), *n., conj., v.*, **whiled, whil·ing.** —*n.* 1. a period or interval of time: *to wait a long while.* 2. **worth one's while,** worth one's time, trouble, or effort. —*conj.* 3. during or in the time that. 4. as long as. **5.** even though: *While flattered, I must decline the award.* —*v.t.* **6.** to spend or pass (time) in some easy or pleasant manner: *We whiled away the time singing.*

whi·lom (hwī′ləm), *Archaic.* —*adj.* **1.** former. —*adv.* **2.** formerly.

whilst (hwīlst), *conj. Brit.* while.

whim (hwim), *n.* a sudden, idle, and often willful notion or wish.

whim·per (hwim′pər), *v.i., v.t.* **1.** to cry or utter with low, plaintive, broken sounds. —*n.* **2.** a whimpering cry or sound. —**whim′per·ing·ly,** *adv.*

whim·si·cal (hwim′zi kəl), *adj.* **1.** given to whimsy or fanciful notions. **2.** full of or proceeding from whimsy, as actions. —**whim·si·cal′i·ty** (-kal′i tē), *n.* —**whim′si·cal·ly,** *adv.* —Syn. capricious, erratic.

whim·sy (hwim′zē), *n., pl.* **-sies.** **1.** excessively fanciful or playful humor, esp. in literature. **2.** any odd or fanciful notion. Also, **whim′sey.**

whine (hwīn), *v.,* **whined, whin·ing,** *n.* —*v.i.* **1.** to utter a low, unusually nasal, complaining cry or sound. **2.** to complain in a feeble, peevish way. —*n.* **3.** a whining cry or sound. **4.** a feeble, peevish complaint. —**whin′y,** *adj.* —**whin′er,** *n.* —**whin′ing·ly,** *adv.*

whin·ny (hwin′ē), *v.,* **-nied, -ny·ing,** *n.* —*v.i.* **1.** to neigh gently. —*v.t.* **2.** to express by whinnying. —*n.* **3.** a whinnying sound.

whip (hwip), *n., v.,* **whipped, whip·ping.** —*n.* **1.** a flexible lash with a rigid handle, used for beating a person or animal. **2.** a blow made with or as with this. **3.** a party manager in a legislative body who directs other members. **4.** a dessert made with whipped cream or whipped egg whites. **5.** a whipping stroke or motion. —*v.t.* **6.** to beat with a whip. **7.** to drive (animals) with a whip. **8.** to subject to hard training. **9.** *Informal.* to defeat decisively. **10.** to pull or remove with a quick jerking motion. **11.** to beat (eggs, etc.) to a froth. —*v.i.* **12.** to move or go quickly and suddenly. **13.** to toss or flap about, as with the wind. **14. whip up,** *Informal.* **a.** to put together hurriedly. **b.** to arouse or agitate. —**whip′per,** *n.*

whip·cord (hwip′kôrd′), *n.* **1.** strong, hard-twisted cord. **2.** a worsted fabric with a diagonally ribbed surface.

whip′ hand′, a position of dominance.

whip·lash (hwip′lash′), *n.* **1.** the lash of a whip. **2.** Also called **whip′lash in′jury.** a neck injury caused by a sudden jerking of the head forward or backward.

whip·per·snap·per (hwip′ər snap′ər), *n.* an unimportant but presumptuous person.

whip·pet (hwip′it), *n.* a small, swift dog resembling a greyhound, used for racing.

whip′ping boy′, scapegoat.

whip·ple·tree (hwip′əl trē′), *n.* whiffletree.

whip·poor·will (hwip′ər wil′, hwip′ər-wil′), *n.* a nocturnal, North American bird having a call that sounds like its name.

whip·saw (hwip′sô′), *n.* **1.** a saw for cutting small curves. **2.** a saw for two persons, used to divide timber lengthwise.

whir (hwûr), *v.,* **whirred, whir·ring,** *n.* —*v.i., v.t.* **1.** to move or turn quickly with a humming or buzzing sound. —*n.* **2.** the act or sound of whirring.

whirl (hwûrl), *v.i.* **1.** to turn around, spin, or rotate rapidly. **2.** to face about quickly. **3.** to move or be carried along rapidly. **4.** to reel as from dizziness. —*v.t.* **5.** to cause to whirl. —*n.* **6.** the act of whirling. **7.** a whirling movement. **8.** a rapid series of events or activities. **9.** a state of dizziness. **10.** an attempt or trial: *to give a plan a whirl.* —**whirl′er,** *n.*

whirl·i·gig (hwûr′lə gig), *n.* **1.** a toy for whirling or spinning, as a top. **2.** merry-go-round (def. 1). **3.** something that whirls.

whirl·pool (hwûrl′pōol′), *n.* a rapidly spinning mass of water, exerting a downward sucking force at its center.

whirl·wind (hwûrl′wind′), *n.* **1.** a rapidly spinning mass of air, bringing storms in its path. **2.** anything resembling a whirlwind, as in violent action. —*adj.* **3.** hastily speedy: *a whirlwind trip.*

whirl·y·bird (hwûr′lē bûrd′), *n. Informal.* helicopter.

whish (hwish), *v.i.* **1.** to move with a whiz or swish. —*n.* **2.** a whishing sound.

whisk (hwisk), *v.t., v.i.* **1.** to sweep or brush with light strokes. **2.** to move or carry swiftly. **3.** to whip or beat (eggs, etc.). —*n.* **4.** the act or motion of whisking. **5.** See **whisk broom.** **6.** a small bunch of straw or feathers. **7.** a wire utensil for whipping eggs, etc., by hand.

whisk′ broom′, a small short-handled broom used chiefly to brush clothes, etc.

whisk·er (hwis′kər), *n.* **1.** Usually, **whiskers.** the long hairs growing on the sides of a man's face. **2.** a single hair of the beard. **3.** one of the long, stiff, bristly hairs growing about the mouth of certain animals, as the cat. —**whisk′ered** (-d), *adj.*

whis·key (hwis′kē), *n., pl.* **-keys.** a distilled alcoholic liquor made from a fermented mash of grain, as barley. Also, *esp. Brit. and Canadian,* **whis′ky.**

whis·per (hwis′pər), *v.i., v.t.* **1.** to speak or say with soft, hushed sounds, esp. without vibration of the vocal cords. **2.** to talk or say privately or secretly. **3.** to make a soft, rustling sound. —*n.* **4.** the tone or manner of speaking by whispering. **5.** something whispered. **6.** a hint or rumor. **7.** a soft, rustling sound.

whist (hwist), *n.* a card game resembling bridge, played usually by two players.

whis·tle (hwis′əl), *v.,* **-tled, -tling,** *n.* —*v.i.* **1.** to make a clear musical sound by forcing breath through the pursed lips. **2.** to make such a sound, as by blowing on some device. **3.** to produce a similar sound, as when actuated by steam. **4.** to move or pass with a whistling sound, as a bullet. —*v.t.* **5.** to produce by whistling, as a tune. **6.** to call or signal by whistling. —*n.* **7.** an instrument for producing whistling sounds by means of the breath, steam, etc. **8.** a sound produced by whistling. **9. blow the whistle,** *Slang.* **a.** to turn informer. **b.** to expose or make public: *to blow the whistle on a conspiracy.* —**whis′tler,** *n.*

whis′tle stop′, *n.* **1.** a small town along a railroad line. **2.** a brief appearance in a small town, as during a political campaign.

whit (hwit), *n.* the least amount: *not a whit better.*

white (hwīt), *adj.,* **whit·er, whit·est,** *n.* —*adj.* **1.** of the color of pure snow. **2.** of or belonging to a people having light skin. **3.** of a light or pale color. **4.** pallid or pale. **5.** silvery, as hair. **6.** lacking color. **7.** morally pure. **8.** without malice: *a white lie.* **9.** politically ultraconservative. **10.** blank, as an unoccupied space in printed matter. —*n.* **11.** the color of fresh snow. **12.** a white pigment. **13.** a white material or area, as the albumen of an egg or the white part of the eyeball. **14.** a member of a light-skinned people. **15. whites,** white clothing. —**white′ness,** *n.*

white′ ant′, termite.

white′ blood′ cell′, leukocyte. Also called **white′ blood′ cor′puscle.**

white·cap (hwīt′kap′), *n.* a wave with a broken and foaming white crest.

white-col·lar (hwīt′kol′ər), *adj.* of or belonging to the salaried or professional workers whose jobs do not usually require manual labor.

white′-col′lar crime′, a crime, esp. embezzlement, committed in connection with one's business or professional activities.

white′ el′ephant, **1.** a possession entailing great expense out of proportion to its usefulness to the owner. **2.** a possession unwanted by the owner but difficult to dispose of. [so called because certain rare, light-colored, Asian elephants were regarded as sacred and therefore not used in work]

white′ feath′er, *Chiefly Brit.* a symbol of cowardice.

white-fish (hwīt′fish′), *n.* any of various silvery fishes found in lakes and used as food.

white′ flag′, a white banner used as a symbol of surrender or truce.

white′ gold′, a gold alloy colored white by the presence of nickel or platinum.

white′ goods′, **1.** household linens, as bed sheets, tablecloths, etc. **2.** large household appliances, as refrigerators, washers, etc.

White·hall (hwīt′hôl′), *n.* the British government.

white·head (hwīt′hed′), *n.* a small pimple having a white or yellowish head.

white′ heat′, **1.** an intense heat at which a substance glows white. **2.** a stage of intense activity or feeling. —**white′-hot′,** *adj.*

White·horse (hwīt′hôrs′), *n.* the capital of the Yukon Territory.

White′ House′, the, **1.** the official residence of the President of the U.S. in Washington, D.C. **2.** the executive branch of the U.S. government.

white′ lead′ (led), a white powder used as a pigment and in putty and ceramics.

white′ mat′ter, nerve tissue, esp. of the brain and spinal cord, which is nearly white in color.

whit·en (hwīt′°n), *v.t., v.i.* to make or become white. —**whit′en·er,** *n.* —**whit′en·ing,** *n.*

white′ race′, (loosely) Caucasoid people.

white′ room′. See **clean room.**

white′ sale′, a sale on household linens.

white′ slave′, a girl or woman sold or forced into prostitution. —**white′-slave′,** *adj.* —**white′ slav′ery.**

white·wall (hwīt′wôl′), *n.* a rubber tire having a sidewall with a white band on it.

white·wash (hwīt′wosh′, -wôsh′), *n.* **1.** a composition, as of lime and water, used for whitening walls, fences, etc. **2.** a coverup of wrongdoing by deception in an attempt to exonerate it. **3.** *Informal.* (in sports) a defeat in which the loser fails to score. —*v.t.* **4.** to whiten with whitewash. **5.** to protect from blame by means of a whitewash. **6.** *Informal.* (in sports) to defeat in a whitewash.

white·y (hwī'tē), *n. Slang (used derogatively by blacks).* a white person or white people collectively. Also, **whit'y.**

whith·er (hwiṯẖ'ər), *Archaic.* —*adv.* **1.** to what place? **2.** to what end, point, or action? —*conj.* **3.** to which place. **4.** to whatever place.

whith·er·so·ev·er (hwiṯẖ'ər sō ev'ər), *conj. Archaic.* to whatsoever place.

whit·ing¹ (hwī'tiṇg), *n.* a slender food fish found along the Atlantic coast of North America.

whit·ing² (hwī'tiṇg), *n.* a white powdered chalk used in making putty, whitewash, etc.

whit·ish (hwī'tish), *adj.* somewhat white. —**whit'ish·ness,** *n.*

whit·low (hwit'lō), *n.* felon².

Whit·man (hwit'mən), *n.* **Walt** (wôlt), 1819–92, U.S. poet.

Whit·ney (hwit'nē), *n.* **Mount,** a mountain in E California.

Whit·sun·day (hwit'sun'dē, -dā), *n.* Pentecost.

whit·tle (hwit'°l), *v.,* **-tled, -tling.** —*v.t.* **1.** to cut or shape (a piece of wood) by carving off bits with a knife. **2.** to make (something) in this way. **3.** to reduce the amount of bit by bit: *to whittle down expenses.* —*v.i.* **4.** to whittle a piece of wood. —**whit'tler,** *n.*

whiz (hwiz), *v.,* **whizzed, whiz·zing,** *n.* —*v.i.* **1.** to make a humming or buzzing sound, as of an object passing swiftly through the air. **2.** to move or rush with such a sound. —*n.* **3.** a whizzing sound or movement. **4.** *Informal.* wizard (def. 3).

who (hōō), *pron., possessive* **whose,** *objective* **whom. 1.** what person or persons? **2.** which person or persons? *I know who took it.* **3.** (used in relative clauses to represent someone mentioned previously): *The man who called this morning is here.* **4.** any person or persons that.

WHO, World Health Organization.

whoa (hwō), *interj.* stop! (used esp. to horses).

who·dun·it (hōō dun'it), *n. Informal.* mystery (def. 4).

who·ev·er (hōō ev'ər), *pron.* **1.** any person that. **2.** no matter who: *I won't do it, whoever asks.* **3.** an emphatic form of **who.**

whole (hōl), *adj.* **1.** comprising the full quantity, amount, or extent. **2.** containing all the elements properly belonging. **3.** not cut up or divided. **4.** uninjured, undamaged, or unbroken. **5.** healthy or sound. **6.** *Math.* not fractional. —*n.* **7.** all the

amount or every part of something. **8.** a thing complete in itself. **9. on the whole, a.** considering all the facts. **b.** in general. —**whole'ness,** *n.* —**Syn. 1.** complete, entire, total.

whole·heart·ed (hōl'här'tid), *adj.* completely sincere, enthusiastic, or energetic. —**whole'heart'ed·ly,** *adv.* —**whole'heart'ed·ness,** *n.*

whole' milk', milk containing all its constituents as received from the cow.

whole' note', *Music.* a note equivalent in duration to four quarter notes.

whole' num'ber, integer.

whole·sale (hōl'sāl'), *n., adj., adv., v.,* **-saled, -sal·ing.** —*n.* **1.** the sale of goods in large quantities, as to retailers rather than to consumers directly. —*adj.* **2.** of or engaged in such sale. **3.** broadly indiscriminate: *wholesale discharge of workers.* —*adv.* **4.** on wholesale terms. **5.** broadly and indiscriminately. —*v.t., v.i.* **6.** to sell by wholesale. —**whole'sal'er,** *n.*

whole·some (hōl'səm), *adj.* **1.** conducive to moral or general well-being. **2.** conducive to bodily health. **3.** having or showing physical or mental health. —**whole'some·ly,** *adv.* —**whole'some·ness,** *n.* —**Syn. 1.** beneficial, salutary.

whole·wheat (hōl'hwēt'), *adj.* made from the complete wheat kernel.

who'll (hōōl), contraction of: **a.** *who will.* **b.** *who shall.*

whol·ly (hō'lē, hōl'lē), *adv.* **1.** to the whole amount or extent. **2.** entirely or totally.

whom (hōōm), *pron.* the objective case of **who.**

whom·ev·er (hōōm ev'ər), *pron.* the objective case of **whoever.**

whom·so·ev·er (hōōm'sō ev'ər), *pron.* the objective case of **whosoever.**

whoop (hōōp, hwōōp), *n.* **1.** a loud cry or shout, as of excitement or joy. **2.** the sound made by a person suffering from whooping cough. —*v.i., v.t.* **3.** to utter (with) a whoop. —**whoop'er,** *n.*

whoop'ing cough', an infectious disease, esp. of children, marked by a series of short, gasping coughs followed by a whooping sound.

whoosh (hwōōsh, hwōōsh), *n.* **1.** a loud, rushing noise, as of air or water. —*v.i., v.t.* **2.** to make or cause to make such a noise.

whop·per (hwop'ər), *n. Informal.* **1.** something uncommonly large of its kind. **2.** a big lie.

whop·ping (hwop'iṇg), *adj. Informal.* uncommonly large.

whore (hōr, hôr), *n. Usually Contemptuous.* a prostitute. —**whor'ish,** *adj.*

whorl (hwûrl, hwôrl), *n.* **1.** a circular or spiral arrangement of similar things, as leaves or petals. **2.** one of the central ridges of a fingerprint. —**whorled** (-d), *adj.*

who's (hōōz), contraction of: **a.** *who is.* **b.** *who has.*

whose (hōōz), *pron.* the possessive case of **who** or **which** used as an adjective. **2.** the one or ones belonging to what person or persons.

who·so (hōō'sō), *pron. Archaic.* whoever.

who·so·ev·er (hōō'sō ev'ər), *pron.* an emphatic form of **whoever.**

whse., warehouse. Also, **whs.**

whsle., wholesale.

why (hwī), *adv., conj., n., pl.* **whys,** *interj.* —*adv.* **1.** for what reason, cause, or purpose?: *Why did you leave so early?* —*conj.* **2.** on account of which: *the reason why we refused to go.* **3.** the reason for which: *That is why he returned.* —*n.* **4.** the cause or reason: *the whys of a troublesome situation.* —*interj.* **5.** (used to express surprise, embarrassment, etc.): *Why, it's all gone!*

WI, Wisconsin.

W.I., West Indies.

Wich·i·ta (wich'i tô'), *n.* a city in S Kansas.

wick (wik), *n.* a loosely twisted braid or cord, as in a candle or lamp, for drawing up liquid fuel which is burned at its tip or edge.

wick·ed (wik'id), *adj.* **1.** morally bad or depraved. **2.** mischievous or malicious. **3.** causing or threatening great harm or trouble. **4.** *Slang.* skillful or masterly. —**wick'ed·ly,** *adv.* —**wick'ed·ness,** *n.* —**Syn. 1.** corrupt, iniquitous, nefarious, sinful, vile.

wick·er (wik'ər), *n.* **1.** a slender, pliant twig. **2.** wickerwork. —*adj.* **3.** made of wicker.

wick·er·work (wik'ər wûrk'), *n.* anything made of wicker.

wick·et (wik'it), *n.* **1.** a small door or gate, esp. one in or alongside a larger one. **2.** a small window, as in a ticket office. **3.** *Cricket.* either of the two frameworks at which the bowler aims the ball. **4.** *Croquet.* any of the hoops through which the ball must be hit.

wick·i·up (wik'ē up'), *n.* an American Indian hut made of brushwood or covered with mats.

wid., **1.** widow. **2.** widower.

wide (wīd), *adj.,* **wid·er, wid·est,** *adv.* —*adj.* **1.** having great extent from side to side. **2.** having a certain extent from side to side. **3.** of great range or scope: *wide reading.* **4.** fully opened or extended: *eyes wide with excitement.* **5.** far from an intended point or goal: *a shot wide of the mark.* —*adv.* **6.** over a large area or space. **7.** to the full extent: *Open your mouth wide.* **8.** so as to pass or strike far from an intended point or goal: *The shot went wide.* —**wide'ly,** *adv.* —**wide'ness,** *n.*

wide-a·wake (wīd'ə wāk'), *adj.* **1.** fully awake. **2.** alert or keen.

wide-eyed (wīd'īd'), *adj.* with the eyes open wide, as in amazement.

wide-mouthed (wīd'mouthd', -moutht'), *adj.* **1.** having a wide mouth. **2.** having the mouth opened wide, as in astonishment.

wid·en (wīd'ən), *v.t., v.i.* to make or become wide or wider. —**wid'en·er,** *n.*

wide·spread (wīd'spred'), *adj.* covering or affecting a large area.

widg·eon (wij'ən), *n.* a freshwater duck having a reddish-brown head. Also, **wig'eon.**

wid·ow (wid'ō), *n.* **1.** a woman who has lost her husband by death and has not married again. —*v.t.* **2.** to make a widow of. —**wid'ow·hood',** *n.*

wid·ow·er (wid'ō ər), *n.* a man who has lost his wife by death and has not married again. —**wid'ow·er·hood',** *n.*

width (width, witth), *n.* **1.** extent or measurement from side to side. **2.** a piece of something, esp. cloth, cut across its full wideness.

wield (wēld), *v.t.* **1.** to handle or use (a weapon, etc.), esp. with ease. **2.** to exercise (power, influence, etc.), as in ruling. —**wield'er,** *n.*

wie·ner (wē'nər), *n.* frankfurter. Also, *Informal,* **wie'nie** (-nē).

wife (wīf), *n., pl.* **wives** (wīvz). a woman married to a certain man. —**wife'hood,** *n.* —**wife'less,** *adj.* —**wife'ly,** *adj.*

wig (wig), *n., v.,* **wigged, wig·ging.** —*n.* **1.** a false covering of artificial or natural hair for the head. —*v.t.* **2.** to furnish with a wig. **3.** *Brit. Informal.* to reprimand severely.

wig·gle (wig'əl), *v.,* **-gled, -gling,** *n.* —*v.i., v.t.* **1.** to move with short, quick movements from side to side. —*n.* **2.** a wiggling motion. —**wig'gler,** *n.* —**wig'gly,** *adj.*

wight (wīt), *n. Archaic.* a human being.

wig·let (wig'lit), *n.* a small wig, esp. one used to supplement the existing hair.

wig·wag (wig'wag'), *v.,* **-wagged, -wagging,** *n.* —*v.t., v.i.* **1.** to move to and fro. **2.** to signal by waving flags or lights according to a code. —*n.* **3.** the act or process of wigwagging. **4.** a message wigwagged.

wig·wam (wig'wom), *n.* an American Indian hut formed of an arched framework overlaid with bark, mats, etc.

wild (wīld), *adj.* **1.** living in a state of nature and not tamed. **2.** growing or produced without cultivation, as fruit. **3.** uncivilized or savage. **4.** violent or furious, as a storm. **5.** undisciplined or unruly: *a gang of wild boys.* **6.** unrestrained or unbridled: *wild enthusiasm.* **7.** disregardful of moral restraints as to pleasurable indulgence: *He repented his wild youth.* **8.** reckless or fantastic. **9.** wide of the mark: *a wild throw.* **10.** *Informal.* intensely enthusiastic: *wild about the new styles.* **11.** *Cards.* (of a card) having its value decided by the wishes of the players. —*adv.* **12.** in a wild manner. —*n.* **13.** Often, **wilds.** wilderness or wasteland. —**wild'ly,** *adv.* —**wild'ness,** *n.*

wild·cat (wīld'kat'), *n., adj., v.,* **-cat·ted, -cat·ting.** —*n.* **1.** any of various wild animals closely related to the domestic cat, esp. the lynx. **2.** a fierce, quick-tempered person. **3.** *Informal.* an oil well drilled in a field where no oil has yet been found. —*adj. Informal.* **4.** (of a labor strike) done without the sanction of the union. **5.** fancifully promising quick profits: *a wildcat scheme.* —*v.i., v.t.* **6.** *Informal.* to search (an area of unknown productivity) for oil.

wild'cat bank', *Informal.* a financially unreliable bank in the period before the U.S. Civil War.

wil·de·beest (wil'də bēst'), *n., pl.* **-beests, -beest.** gnu.

wil·der·ness (wil'dər nis), *n.* an uninhabited and uncultivated region.

wild-eyed (wīld'īd'), *adj.* **1.** having an angry or insane expression in the eyes. **2.** extremely irrational or senseless.

wild·fire (wīld'fī°r'), *n.* a fire that burns rapidly and is hard to extinguish.

wild·fowl (wīld'foul'), *n.* a game bird, esp. a wild duck or goose.

wild'-goose' chase' (wīld'gōos'), a search for something unobtainable.

wild·life (wīld'līf'), *n.* animals living in nature.

wild' oat', **1.** any uncultivated weedy grass resembling the cultivated oat. **2. sow one's wild oats,** to lead a dissolute life in one's youth.

wild' rice', **1.** a tall, aquatic grass of North America. **2.** its grain, used for food.

Wild' West', the western frontier of the U.S. during its early rough, lawless period.

wile (wīl), *n., v.,* **wiled, wil·ing.** —*n.* **1.** a beguiling trick intended to ensnare. **2. wiles,** beguiling behavior. —*v.t.* **3.** to lure by wiles. **4. wile away,** to pass (time) leisurely. —Syn. **1.** artifice, deception, stratagem.

wil·ful (wil'fəl), *adj. Chiefly Brit.* willful.

will[1] (wil), *v., pt.* **would.** —*auxiliary.* **1.** (used with subjects of the second and third persons, and often also of the first person, to express simple futurity): *It will rain tomorrow.* **2.** (used esp. with subjects of the first person to express determination): *We will win, no matter what the odds are against us.* **3.** used with any subject to express: **a.** (willingness or inclination): *I will help anyone who is in need.* **b.** (a command): *You will release the prisoners at once.* **c.** (probability): *They will be asleep by this time.* **d.** (customary action): *He will sit by the fire and read for hours.* **e.** (capability or capacity): *A camel will go for days without water.* —*v.t., v.i.* **4.** to wish or desire: *Go where you will.* —Usage. See **shall.**

will[2] (wil), *n., v.,* **willed, will·ing.** —*n.* **1.** the power of the mind to choose and control its own actions: *a strong will.* **2.** an intention or desire: *to submit against one's will.* **3.** a strong purpose or determination. **4.** the wish or purpose as carried out, or to be carried out: *to work one's will.* **5.** disposition, whether good or ill, toward another. **6.** a legal declaration of a person's wishes as to the disposition of his or her property or estate after death. **7. at will,** as one desires. —*v.t.* **8.** to decide upon or bring about by an act of the will. **9.** to compel (a person) to do or be something. **10.** to give or dispose of (property) by a will. **11.** to choose or decide. —**willed** (-d), *adj.*

will·ful (wil'fəl), *adj.* **1.** perversely obstinate. **2.** done deliberately or intentionally. —**will'ful·ly,** *adv.* —**will'ful·ness,** *n.* —Syn. **1.** headstrong, stubborn.

Wil·liam I (wil'yəm), *("the Conqueror")* 1027–87, king of England 1066–87.

wil·lies (wil'ēz), *n.pl. Slang.* feelings of nervousness.

will·ing (wil'ing), *adj.* **1.** favorably inclined or disposed. **2.** doing one's job or one's part cheerfully. **3.** done or offered cheerfully. —**will'ing·ly,** *adv.* —**will'ing·ness,** *n.*

wil·li·waw (wil'ə wô'), *n.* a violent squall that moves seaward down a mountainous coast.

will-o'-the-wisp (wil'ə t͟hə wisp'), *n.* **1.** a light seen flitting about at night over marshy ground, believed to be caused by the burning of marsh gases. **2.** any deceptive aim or hope.

wil·low (wil′ō), *n.* **1.** a tree having tough, pliable twigs or branches used for wickerwork. **2.** its wood.

wil·low·y (wil′ō ē), *adj.* **1.** slender and graceful. **2.** full of willows.

will·pow·er (wil′pou′ər), *n.* strength of one's will, esp. in the exercise of self-control.

wil·ly-nil·ly (wil′ē nil′ē), *adv.* whether one agrees or not.

Wil·son (wil′sən), *n.* **(Thom·as) Wood·row** (tom′əs wōōd′rō), 1856–1924, 28th president of the U.S. 1913–21.

wilt¹ (wilt), *v.i.* **1.** to become limp and drooping, as a fading flower. **2.** to lose strength or confidence. —*v.t.* **3.** to cause to wilt.

wilt² (wilt), *v. Archaic.* second pers. sing. pres. ind. of **will¹**.

Wil·ton (wil′t°n), *n.* a carpet having the loops cut to form a velvet pile. Also called **Wil′ton car′pet, Wil′ton rug′**.

wil·y (wī′lē), *adj.* **-i·er, -i·est.** full of or marked by wiles. —**wil′i·ness,** *n.* —**Syn.** artful, cunning, deceitful, sly.

wim·ble (wim′bəl), *n.* a tool for boring holes.

wim·ple (wim′pəl), *n.* a cloth for covering the head and neck, leaving only the face exposed, worn chiefly by nuns.

win (win), *v.*, **won, win·ning,** *n.* —*v.i.* **1.** to gain the victory. **2.** to finish first in a race. **3.** to succeed by effort. —*v.t.* **4.** to gain a victory in. **5.** to get by effort, as by competition. **6.** to gain the consent or support of. **7.** to gain (favor, etc.) by qualities or influence. **8.** to persuade to marry. **9.** to succeed in reaching (a place, etc.), esp. by great effort. —*n.* **10.** a victory, as in a game. **11.** the first position at the finish of a horse race.

wince (wins), *v.*, **winced, winc·ing,** *n.* —*v.i.* **1.** to draw back involuntarily or tense the body, as from pain. —*n.* **2.** the act or an instance of wincing. —**winc′er,** *n.* —**Syn.** flinch.

winch (winch), *n.* **1.** a machine consisting of a horizontal drum on which to wind a rope or chain, used for hoisting or hauling. **2.** the crank or handle of a revolving machine, as a grindstone.

wind¹ (wind), *n.* **1.** air in natural motion, as along the earth's surface. **2.** a swift current of air. **3.** breath or the power of breathing freely. **4.** any influential force or trend. **5.** air carrying an animal's odor or scent. **6.** empty talk. **7. winds, a.** wind instruments. **b.** players of such instruments. **8.** gas generated in the

intestines. **9. get** or **have wind of,** to receive or have a hint or hints about. **10. in the wind,** occurring or about to occur. —*v.t.* **11.** to make short of breath. **12.** to follow by the scent.

wind² (wīnd), *v.*, **wound, wind·ing,** *n.* —*v.i.* **1.** to move in a bending or curving course. **2.** to coil or twine about something. —*v.t.* **3.** to encircle or wrap about, as with thread or wire. **4.** to roll or coil into a ball or on a spool. **5.** to give power to (a mechanism) by turning a key or crank: *to wind a clock.* **6.** to make (one's way) in a bending or curving course. **7.** to cause to move in a bending or curving course. **8. wind up, a.** to bring or come to a conclusion: *to wind up the campaign.* **b.** *Baseball.* to execute a windup. **c.** to make tense or excited. **d.** to attain to a specified final position or situation. —*n.* **9.** a single turn, twist, or bend. —**wind′er,** *n.*

wind³ (wīnd, wind), *v.t.*, **wind·ed** or **wound, wind·ing.** to sound (a horn, etc.) by blowing.

wind·age (win′dij), *n.* **1.** the influence of the wind in deflecting a missile. **2.** the amount of such deflection.

wind·bag (wind′bag′), *n. Slang.* an empty, pretentious talker.

wind·break (wind′brāk′), *n.* a growth of trees or a structure of boards serving as a shelter from the wind.

wind·bro·ken (wind′brō′kən), *adj.* (of horses) having the breathing impaired.

wind·burn (wind′bûrn′), *n.* skin inflammation caused by overexposure to the wind.

wind′ chill′, the coldness felt on the exposed human flesh by a combination of temperature and wind velocity.

wind·ed (win′did), *adj.* out of breath.

wind·fall (wind′fôl′), *n.* **1.** an unexpected gain or profit. **2.** something blown down by the wind, as fruit.

wind·flow·er (wind′flou′ər), *n.* anemone (def. 1).

wind·ing (wīn′ding), *n.* **1.** something that winds or coils, as a wire. —*adj.* **2.** bending or turning. **3.** helical or spiral, as stairs.

wind′ing sheet′ (wīn′ding), shroud (def. 1).

wind′ in′strument (wind), a musical instrument sounded by the breath or the force of air, as the clarinet.

wind·jam·mer (wind′jam′ər, win′-), *n. Informal.* **1.** any large sailing ship. **2.** a member of its crew.

wind·lass (wind′ləs), *n.* a type of winch operated by a crank, used esp. for hoisting the anchor.

wind·mill (wind′mil′), *n.* a machine driven by the wind blowing against a wheel of blades attached to a shaft, used chiefly for pumping water.

win·dow (win′dō), *n.* **1.** an opening as in a wall or the side of a vehicle, for letting in light or air, or for looking through. **2.** windowpane. **3.** anything likened to a window in appearance or function. —**win′dow·less,** *adj.*

win′dow dress′ing, 1. decoration of the display window of a store, esp. with merchandise. **2.** misrepresentation of facts so as to give a favorable impression. —**win′dow-dress′,** *v.t.* —**win′dow dress′er.**

win·dow·pane (win′dō pān′), *n.* a plate of glass set in the frame of a window.

win·dow-shop (win′dō shop′), *v.i.,* **-shopped, -shop·ping.** to look at articles displayed in shop windows without intending to buy anything. —**win′dow shop′per.**

win′dow sill′, the sill under a window.

wind·pipe (wind′pīp′), *n.* trachea.

wind·row (wind′rō′, win′-), *n.* **1.** a row of hay left to dry before being raked into heaps. **2.** a row of dry leaves swept together by the wind.

wind·shield (wind′shēld′, win′-), *n.* a sheet of glass or plastic set in the front of a vehicle to protect against the wind.

wind·sock (wind′sok′), *n.* a tapered cloth vane installed at airports or elsewhere to indicate wind direction and approximate intensity. Also called **wind′ sleeve′.**

Wind·sor (win′zər), *n.* a city in S Ontario, in SE Canada.

wind·storm (wind′stôrm′), *n.* a storm with heavy wind, but little or no rain.

wind·swept (wind′swept′), *adj.* open or exposed to the wind.

wind·up (wīnd′up′), *n.* **1.** the conclusion of any activity. **2.** *Baseball.* the movements performed by a pitcher before pitching a ball.

wind·ward (wind′wərd), *adv.* **1.** toward the wind. —*adj.* **2.** moving toward the point from which the wind blows. —*n.* **3.** the point or direction from which the wind blows.

wind·y (win′dē), *adj.,* **-i·er, -i·est. 1.** having or marked by wind. **2.** exposed to the wind. **3.** consisting of or resembling wind. **4.** given to prolonged, empty talk. —**wind′i·ly,** *adv.* —**wind′i·ness,** *n.*

wine (wīn), *n., v.,* **wined, win·ing.** —*n.* **1.** the fermented juice of grapes, for use as an alcoholic beverage. **2.** the juice, fermented or unfer-

mented, of various other fruits or plants. —*v.t., v.i.* **3.** to treat with or drink wine. **4. wine and dine,** to entertain lavishly. [< L *vīnum*]

wine′ cel′lar, 1. a cellar for the storage of wines. **2.** a stock of wines.

win·er·y (wī′nə rē), *n., pl.* **-er·ies.** an establishment for making wine.

wing (wing), *n.* **1.** either of the two appendages or parts of most birds and insects and of bats which are used for flying. **2.** anything resembling a wing in shape or use. **3.** the act or manner of flying. **4.** one of the main supporting surfaces of an airplane. **5.** a part of a building projecting on one side of a central or main part. **6.** either of the two side portions of an army or fleet in battle formation. **7.** a tactical unit in an air force. **8.** any one of the team positions on the far side of the center, as in hockey. **9.** the unseen space on the right or left of a theater stage. **10.** a political group considered with respect to their radicalism or conservatism. **11. on the wing,** in flight. **12. take wing,** to begin to fly. **13. under one's wing,** under one's protection or care. —*v.t.* **14.** to equip with wings. **15.** to enable to fly or move rapidly. **16.** to transport on or as on wings. **17.** to wound or disable slightly, esp. in the wing or arm. —*v.i.* **18.** to travel on or as on wings. —**winged** (-d), *adj.* —**wing′less,** *adj.*

wing·ding (wing′ding′), *n. Slang.* a noisy, exciting celebration or party.

wing·span (wing′span′), *n.* the distance between the wing tips of an airplane.

wing·spread (wing′spred′), *n.* **1.** the distance between the tips of the outspread wings of a bird. **2.** wingspan.

wink (wingk), *v.i.* **1.** to close and open one or both eyes quickly. **2.** to close and open one eye quickly as a hint or signal. **3.** to flash or twinkle. —*v.t.* **4.** to make (the eyes or an eye) wink. **5. wink at,** to ignore deliberately. —*n.* **6.** the act of winking. **7.** a hint or signal given by winking. **8.** an instant or twinkling. **9.** a little flash of light. —**wink′er,** *n.*

win·kle (wing′kəl), *n. Brit.* periwinkle[1].

win·ner (win′ər), *n.* a person or thing that wins.

win·ning (win′ing), *n.* **1.** the act of a person or thing that wins. **2.** Usually, **winnings.** something won, esp. money. —*adj.* **3.** successful or victorious. **4.** charming or pleasing. —**win′ning·ly,** *adv.*

Win·ni·peg (win′ə peg′), *n.* the capital of Manitoba, in S Canada.

win·now (win′ō), *v.t.*, *v.i.* **1.** to separate (grain) from chaff, esp. by throwing it into the air. **2.** to drive (chaff) away from grain in this way. **3.** to sort or sift out carefully.

win·o (wī′nō), *n.*, *pl.* **win·os.** *Slang.* a person who is chronically drunk on wine, esp. cheap wine.

win·some (win′səm), *adj.* engagingly charming. **—win′some·ly,** *adv.* **—win′some·ness,** *n.*

win·ter (win′tər), *n.* **1.** the cold season between autumn and spring, usually between December 21st and March 21st. **2.** a period of decline or decay. **—adj. 3.** of, characteristic of, or suitable for winter. **—v.i. 4.** to spend the winter. **—v.t. 5.** to keep or manage during the winter.

win·ter·green (win′tər grēn′), *n.* **1.** an evergreen shrub having white, bell-shaped flowers, a bright-red, berry-like fruit, and aromatic leaves that yield an oil used as a flavoring. **2.** its oil. **3.** the flavor.

win·ter·ize (win′tə rīz′), *v.t.*, **-ized,** **-iz·ing.** to prepare for cold weather, as by adding insulation in a building. **—win′ter·i·za′tion,** *n.*

win·ter·kill (win′tər kil′), *v.t.*, *v.i.* to kill or die from exposure to the cold of winter, as wheat.

win·ter·tide (win′tər tīd′), *n.* *Literary.* wintertime.

win·ter·time (win′tər tīm′), *n.* the season of winter.

win·try (win′trē), *adj.*, **-tri·er,** **-tri·est.** **1.** of or resembling winter or winter weather. **2.** dreary or cheerless. Also, **win′ter·y** (-tə rē).

win·y (wī′nē), *adj.*, **-i·er,** **-i·est.** of or like wine, as in taste.

wipe (wīp), *v.*, **wiped,** **wip·ing,** *n.* **—v.t. 1.** to rub lightly with a cloth, paper, or the hand in order to clean or dry. **2.** to remove by rubbing with or on something. **3.** to put on or apply by rubbing, as with a cloth. **4.** **wipe out, a.** to destroy completely. **b.** *Informal.* to murder or kill. **—n. 5.** the act of wiping. **—wip′er,** *n.*

wire (wī°r), *n.*, *adj.*, *v.*, **wired, wir·ing.** **—n. 1.** a long, slender thread of metal. **2.** a length of such material, consisting either of a single filament or of several filaments woven or twisted together and usually insulated with a dielectric material, used as a conductor of electricity. **3.** a long cable used in telegraph or telephone systems. **4.** **the wire,** the telephone. **5.** *Informal.* the telegraphic system. **6.** a telegram or cablegram. **7.** *Horse Racing.* the finish line. **8.** **pull wires,** *Informal.* to use one's influence to obtain a desired result. **9.** **under the wire,** just within the limit or deadline. **—adj. 10.** made

of wire. **—v.t. 11.** to furnish with wires. **12.** to fasten or bind with wire: *He wired the halves together.* **13.** to send by telegraph. **14.** to send a telegram or cablegram to. **—v.i. 15.** to telegraph or cable.

wire·hair (wī°r′hâr′), *n.* a fox terrier having a wiry coat. Also called **wire′-haired ter′rier.**

wire·less (wī°r′lis), *adj.* **1.** having no wire. **2.** noting a means of communication by radio waves, without the use of wires. **3.** *Brit. Obsolesc.* radio. **—n. 4.** a wireless telegraph or telephone system. **5.** *Brit. Obsolesc.* **a.** a radio receiver. **b.** a radio broadcast.

Wire·pho·to (wī°r′fō′tō), *n.* *Trademark.* a device for transmitting photographs over distances by wire.

wire·pull·er (wī°r′pŏŏl′ər), *n.* a person who uses influence to direct and control the actions of others. **—wire′pull′ing,** *n.*, *adj.*

wire′ record′er, an obsolete type of magnetic recorder using steel wire.

wire′ serv′ice, a business organization that gathers news and news photos for distribution by various means to its subscribers, esp. newspapers: so called from the original transmission of news by telegraph wire.

wire·tap (wī°r′tap′), *v.*, **-tapped, -tapping,** *n.* **—v.t., v.i. 1.** to connect secretly into (a telephone or telegraph wire) so as to obtain information or evidence. **—n. 2.** an act of wiretapping. **3.** a device used in wiretapping. **—wire′tap′per,** *n.*

wir·ing (wī°r′ing), *n.* a system of wires for carrying electric current, as in a building.

wir·y (wī°r′ē), *adj.*, **-i·er,** **-i·est. 1.** made of or resembling wire. **2.** lean and strong. **—wir′i·ness,** *n.*

Wis., Wisconsin. Also, **Wisc.**

Wis·con·sin (wis kon′sən), *n.* a state in the N central United States. *Cap.:* Madison.

wis·dom (wiz′dəm), *n.* **1.** knowledge of what is true or right coupled with good judgment. **2.** scholarly knowledge or learning.

wis′dom tooth′, the third molar on each side of the upper and lower jaws.

wise[1] (wīz), *adj.*, **wis·er, wis·est. 1.** able to judge properly what is true or right. **2.** showing or based on good judgment. **3.** learned or erudite. **4.** *Informal.* crafty or cunning. **5.** *Slang.* **a.** informed or aware. **b.** insolent or impertinent. **—wise′ly,** *adv.* **—Syn. 1, 2,** discerning, judicious, prudent, sage, sensible.

wise[2] (wīz), *n.* *Archaic.* way or manner of doing: *in any wise.*

-wise, a suffix meaning: **a.** in the direction of: *sidewise.* **b.** in the position of: *edgewise.* **c.** in the manner of: *clockwise.* **d.** with regard to: *moneywise.*

wise·a·cre (wīz′ā′kər), *n.* a person who affects to possess great wisdom.

wise·crack (wīz′krak′), *Informal.* —*n.* **1.** a smart or facetious remark. —*v.i.* **2.** to make wisecracks. —**wise′crack′er,** *n.*

wish (wish), *v.t.* **1.** to feel an impulse toward attainment or possession of something: *I wish it were morning.* **2.** to desire (a person or thing) to be (as specified): *I wish you good luck.* **3.** to request or command: *I wish him to come.* —*v.i.* **4.** to desire or yearn. **5.** to make a wish. —*n.* **6.** the act or an instance of wishing. **7.** something wished or desired. **8.** a request or command. **9.** expressed hope for another's success or health: *to send one's best wishes.* —**wish′er,** *n.*

wish·bone (wish′bōn′), *n.* a forked bone in front of the breastbone in most birds.

wish·ful (wish′fəl), *adj.* having or showing a wish. —**wish′ful·ly,** *adv.* —**wish′ful·ness,** *n.*

wish′ful think′ing, interpretation of facts or actions as one would like them to be rather than as they really are.

wish·y-wash·y (wish′ē wosh′ē, -wô′shē), *adj.* **1.** lacking in strength or decisiveness. **2.** thin and weak, as a liquid. —**wish′y-wash′i·ness,** *n.*

wisp (wisp), *n.* **1.** a small bundle, as of straw. **2.** a small tuft, as of hair. **3.** a thin puff, as of smoke. **4.** a person or thing that is small or delicate: *a mere wisp of a girl.* —**wisp′y,** *adj.*

wis·te·ri·a (wi stēr′ē ə), *n.* a climbing shrub having showy clusters of flowers. Also, **wis·tar′i·a** (-stär′-).

wist·ful (wist′fəl), *adj.* feeling or showing a vague, unsatisfied longing. —**wist′ful·ly,** *adv.* —**wist′ful·ness,** *n.* —**Syn.** melancholy, yearning.

wit¹ (wit), *n.* **1.** the ability to perceive unexpected connections between ideas, things, or situations and express them in a brief, clever, and often sharp way. **2.** a person having such ability. **3.** Usually, **wits.** mental balance or sanity. **4.** mental judgment or alertness. **5. at one's wit's end,** utterly at a loss or perplexed. —**Syn. 4.** ingenuity, shrewdness.

wit² (wit), *v.t., v.i.,* **wist** (wist), **wit·ting. 1.** *Archaic.* to know. **2. to wit,** that is to say.

witch (wich), *n.* **1.** a person, esp. a woman, who professes or is supposed to practice sorcery. **2.** an ugly old woman. **3.** *Informal.* an enchanting or charming woman. —*v.t.* **4.** bewitch (def. 1). —**witch′ing,** *n., adj.*

witch·craft (wich′kraft′, -kräft′), *n.* the art or practices of a witch.

witch′ doc′tor, a medicine man in some primitive societies.

witch·er·y (wich′ə rē), *n., pl.* **-er·ies. 1.** witchcraft. **2.** enchanting charm.

witch′ ha′zel, 1. a shrub having small, yellow flowers. **2.** a soothing skin lotion made from its leaves or bark.

witch′ hunt′, an intensive effort to discover and expose disloyalty, subversion, etc., usually based on slight evidence.

with (with, with), *prep.* **1.** accompanied by: *I will go with you.* **2.** in relation to: *to deal with a problem.* **3.** having or showing: *a woman with ambition.* **4.** by means of: *to cut with a knife.* **5.** containing or having: *tea with lemon.* **6.** using or displaying: *to work with diligence.* **7.** in comparison or proportion to: *Their power increased with their numbers.* **8.** in regard to: *to be pleased with a gift.* **9.** because of: *to turn white with fear.* **10.** in the region or sphere of: *It's day with us while it's night with the Chinese.* **11.** from: *to part with something.* **12.** against: *He fought with his brother over the money.* **13.** in the keeping or service of: *to leave something with a friend.* **14.** in the opinion or judgment of: *Her argument carried weight with the judges.* **15.** at the same time as: *He went home with the coming of dark.* **16.** immediately after: *And with that last remark, she turned and left.* **17.** of the same opinion as: *Are you with me or against me?* **18.** as well as: *He can play football with the best of them.* **19.** having been given: *With his parents' consent, he took a long trip.* **20.** in spite of: *With all her wealth, she leads a simple life.* **21.** in the same direction as: *We were driving with the traffic.*

with·al (with ôl′, with-), *adv. Archaic.* **1.** with it all. **2.** in spite of all. **3.** with that.

with·draw (with drô′, with-), *v.,* **-drew, -drawn, -draw·ing.** —*v.t.* **1.** to draw back or away. **2.** to retract or recall, as a remark. —*v.i.* **3.** to go or move back or away. **4.** to remove oneself (from some activity or group).

with·draw·al (with drô′əl, with-), *n.* **1.** the act or an instance of withdrawing. **2.** the act or process of stopping using an addictive substance, as a drug.

with·drawn (wiŧħ drôn′, with-), *adj.* shy and retiring. **—with·drawn′ness**, *n.* **—Syn.** reserved, reticent, unresponsive.

withe (with, wiŧħ, wīŧħ), *n.* a tough, flexible twig suitable for binding things together.

with·er (wiŧħ′ər), *v.i.* **1.** to dry up and shrink, as flowers. **2.** to lose freshness or vitality, as with age. **—v.t. 3.** to cause to wither. **4.** to abash, as by a scathing glance. **—with′er·ing·ly**, *adv.*

with·ers (wiŧħ′ərz), *n.pl.* the highest part of the back at the base of the neck of a horse.

with·hold (wiŧħ hōld′, with-), *v.t.*, **-held, -hold·ing. 1.** to refrain from giving or granting. **2.** to collect (taxes) at the source of income. **3.** to hold back. **—with·hold′er**, *n.*

withhold′ing tax′, a tax collected by withholding at the source.

with·in (wiŧħ in′, with-), *prep.* **1.** in or into the interior of: *within a city.* **2.** in the limits of, as in time. **3.** in the sphere or scope of. **—adv. 4.** as regards the inside. **5.** in the mind, heart, or soul. **6. a.** inside. **b.** indoors. **—n. 7.** the inside of a place.

with-it (wiŧħ′it′, with′-), *adj. Slang.* up-to-date and smart, esp. socially.

with·out (wiŧħ out′, with-), *prep.* **1.** with the absence, omission, or avoidance of. **2.** free from. **3.** not accompanied by. **4.** *Archaic.* outside of. **—adv. 5.** lacking something implied: *We must take this or go without.* **6.** as regards the outside. **7. a.** outside. **b.** outdoors.

with·stand (with stand′, wiŧħ-), *v.t., v.i.,* **-stood, -stand·ing.** to resist or oppose, esp. successfully.

with·y (wiŧħ′ē, with′ē), *n., pl.* **with·ies.** withe.

wit·less (wit′lis), *adj.* lacking wit or intelligence. **—wit′less·ly**, *adv.* **—wit′less·ness**, *n.*

wit·ness (wit′nis), *n.* **1.** a person who is present at an occurrence, esp. one who is able to attest as to what took place. **2.** a person who gives testimony in court. **3.** a person who signs a document in attestation of the genuineness of its execution. **4.** testimony or evidence: *to bear witness to the truth.* **—v.t. 5.** to see or know by personal presence. **6.** to be present at as a formal witness. **7.** to attest by one's signature. **8.** to testify to or give evidence of. **—wit′ness·er**, *n.*

wit·ted (wit′id), *adj.* having intelligence or wits: *dull-witted.*

wit·ti·cism (wit′i siz′əm), *n.* a witty remark or sentence.

wit·ting (wit′iŋ), *adj. Rare.* done or acting knowingly. **—wit′ting·ly**, *adv.*

wit·ty (wit′ē), *adj.*, **-ti·er, -ti·est. 1.** possessing or characterized by wit. **2.** amusingly clever. **—wit′ti·ly**, *adv.* **—wit′ti·ness**, *n.* **—Syn.** droll, humorous, original.

wive (wīv), *v.i., v.t.,* **wived, wiv·ing.** *Obs.* to take (as) a wife.

wives (wīvz), *n. pl.* of **wife.**

wiz·ard (wiz′ərd), *n.* **1.** a male practitioner of black magic. **2.** a conjurer or juggler. **3.** *Informal.* a person of amazing skill or accomplishment.

wiz·ard·ry (wiz′ər drē), *n.* the art or practices of a wizard.

wiz·ened (wiz′ənd), *adj.* shriveled and dried up, as from age.

wk., **1.** week. **2.** work.

wkly., weekly.

WL, wavelength.

wmk., watermark.

WNW, west-northwest.

w/o, without.

WO, Warrant Officer.

woad (wōd), *n.* **1.** a European plant formerly cultivated for a blue dye extracted from its leaves. **2.** its dye.

wob·ble (wob′əl), *v.,* **-bled, -bling,** *n.* **—v.i. 1.** to move unsteadily with a side-to-side motion. **2.** to vacillate or waver. **—v.t. 3.** to cause to wobble. **—n. 4.** a wobbling motion. **—wob′bly**, *adj.* **—wob′bli·ness**, *n.*

woe (wō), *n.* **1.** intense grievous distress. **2.** great misfortune or trouble. **—interj. 3.** (an exclamation of grievous distress.) **—Syn. 1.** anguish, misery, suffering. **2.** affliction, calamity.

woe·be·gone (wō′bi gôn′, -gon′), *adj.* **1.** beset with woe. **2.** showing or expressing woe. **—Syn.** mournful, wretched.

woe·ful (wō′fəl), *adj.* **1.** full of woe. **2.** affected with or causing woe. **3.** of wretched quality. **—woe′ful·ly**, *adv.* **—woe′ful·ness**, *n.*

wok (wäk), *n.* a large bowl-shaped pan used most widely in cooking Chinese food.

woke (wōk), *v.* a pt. of **wake**[1].

wok·en (wō′kən), *v.* a pp. of **wake**[1].

wold (wōld), *n.* an elevated tract of open country, esp. in England.

wolf (wŏŏlf), *n., pl.* **wolves** (wŏŏlvz), *v.* **—n. 1.** a large, carnivorous mammal related to the dog, usually hunting in packs. **2.** a cruelly rapacious person. **3.** *Informal.* a man who makes amorous advances to many women. **4. cry wolf**, to raise a false alarm. **—v.t. 5.** *Informal.* to devour voraciously. **—wolf′ish**, *adj.*

wolf·hound (wŏŏlf′hound′), *n.* a large dog originally used in hunting wolves.

wolf·ram (wŏŏl′frəm), *n.* tungsten.

wolfs·bane (wŏŏlfs′bān′), *n.* a tall plant having yellow flowers.

wol·ver·ine (wŏŏl'və rēn'), n. a stocky, carnivorous, North American mammal of the weasel family, having blackish, shaggy hair with white markings.

wom·an (wŏŏm'ən), n., pl. **wom·en** (wim'in). 1. an adult female person. 2. womankind. 3. feminine nature or feelings. 4. a mistress or sweetheart. 5. a female worker or servant.

wom·an·hood (wŏŏm'ən hŏŏd'), n. 1. the state of being a woman. 2. womanly qualities. 3. women collectively.

wom·an·ish (wŏŏm'ə nish), adj. 1. of or characteristic of a woman. 2. having such qualities as weakness or emotionalism, formerly considered characteristic of women only.

wom·an·ize (wŏŏm'ə nīz'), v., **-ized, -iz·ing.** —v.i. 1. to pursue women habitually. —v.t. 2. to make effeminate. —**wom'an·iz'er,** n.

wom·an·kind (wŏŏm'ən kīnd'), n. women as distinguished from men.

wom·an·like (wŏŏm'ən līk'), adj. womanly (def. 1).

wom·an·ly (wŏŏm'ən lē), adj. 1. like or befitting a woman. 2. having qualities considered appropriate to a woman. —**wom'an·li·ness,** n.

wom'an suf'frage, the right of women to vote.

womb (wŏŏm), n. 1. uterus. 2. the place in which anything is formed or produced. —**wombed,** adj.

wom·bat (wom'bat), n. a burrowing marsupial of Australia, about the size of a badger.

wom·en·folk (wim'in fōk'), n.pl. 1. all women. 2. a particular group of women. Also, **wom'en·folks'.**

wom'en's lib', Sometimes Derogatory. See women's liberation. —**wom'en's lib'ber.**

wom'en's libera'tion, a modern movement to gain full educational, social, and economic opportunities and rights for women equal to those which men are traditionally understood to have.

won¹ (wun), v. pt. and pp. of **win.**

won² (won), n., pl. **won.** the monetary unit of South Korea and North Korea.

won·der (wun'dər), v.i. 1. to speculate curiously. 2. to be filled with curiosity, amazement, and admiration. —v.t. 3. to speculate curiously or be doubtful about. —n. 4. something that causes curiosity, amazement, and admiration. 5. a feeling aroused by this. —**won'der·er,** n. —**Syn.** 1. ponder, question. 2. marvel.

won'der drug', any drug noted for its startling effectiveness.

won·der·ful (wun'dər fəl), adj. 1. causing or arousing wonder. 2. Informal. excellent or fine. —**wonder-**

ful·ly, adv. —**won'der·ful·ness,** n. —Syn. 1. awesome, marvelous, miraculous, remarkable.

won·der·land (wun'dər land'), n. 1. a land of wonders or marvels. 2. a wonderful country or region.

won·der·ment (wun'dər mənt), n. 1. an expression or state of wonder. 2. a cause or occasion of wonder.

won·drous (wun'drəs), adj. Literary. wonderful or marvelous. —**won'drous·ly,** adv. —**won'drous·ness,** n.

wont (wŏnt, wônt, wunt), adj. 1. in the habit: He was wont to rise at dawn. —n. 2. customary practice.

won't (wōnt, wunt), contraction of will not.

wont·ed (wŏn'tid, wôn'-, wun'-), adj. Literary. usual by force of habit.

won ton (won' ton'), a Chinese dumpling filled with minced pork, usually served with soup. [< Chin (dial.)]

woo (wŏŏ), v.t. 1. to seek the love of, esp. with a view to marriage. 2. to seek to win: to woo fame. 3. to importune solicitously. —v.i. 4. to woo a person. —**woo'er,** n.

wood (wŏŏd), n. 1. the hard, fibrous substance composing most of the stem and branches of a tree or shrub. 2. this substance when made suitable for building or burning. 3. Usually, **woods.** a large, thick growth of trees smaller than a forest and larger than a grove. 4. Golf. a club with a wooden head. 5. **out of the woods,** out of a dangerous or difficult situation. —adj. 6. wooden (def. 1). 7. used to work or carry wood. 8. dwelling or growing in woods. —v.t., v.i. 9. to cover or plant with trees. 10. to get supplies of wood (for).

wood' al'cohol. See methyl alcohol.

wood·bine (wŏŏd'bīn'), n. any of various climbing plants, as the European honeysuckle or the Virginia creeper.

wood·block (wŏŏd'blok'), n. 1. a block of wood. 2. woodcut, esp. one engraved in relief.

wood·carv·ing (wŏŏd'kär'ving), n. 1. the art of carving objects by hand from wood. 2. an object so carved. —**wood'carv'er,** n.

wood·chuck (wŏŏd'chuk'), n. a stocky, burrowing, North American marmot that hibernates in the winter.

wood' coal', 1. lignite. 2. Archaic. charcoal (def. 1).

wood·cock (wŏŏd'kok'), n. a game bird having a long bill and short legs.

wood·craft (wŏŏd'kraft', -kräft'), n. 1. skill in anything concerning the woods or forest, as hunting, trapping, etc. 2. woodworking.

wood·cut (wo͝od′kut′), *n.* **1.** a carved block of wood for making prints. **2.** a print made from this. —**wood′cut′ting,** *n.*

wood·cut·ter (wo͝od′kut′ər), *n.* a person who cuts down trees or chops wood. —**wood′cut′ting,** *n.*

wood·ed (wo͝od′id), *adj.* covered with or abounding in trees.

wood·en (wo͝od′ən), *adj.* **1.** made of wood. **2.** stiff or awkward. **3.** dull or spiritless. —**wood′en·ly,** *adv.* — **wood′en·ness,** *n.*

wood·en·ware (wo͝od′ən wâr′), *n.* household articles made of wood.

wood·land (wo͝od′land′, -lənd), *n.* land covered with woods or trees.

wood·man (wo͝od′mən), *n.* woodsman.

wood·note (wo͝od′nōt′), *n.* a natural sound or call, as of a forest bird.

wood·peck·er (wo͝od′pek′ər), *n.* a climbing bird having a hard, chisel-like bill that it hammers into wood in search of insects.

wood·pile (wo͝od′pīl′), *n.* a pile or stack of firewood.

wood·ruff (wo͝od′rəf, -ruf′), *n.* a low aromatic herb having small white flowers.

wood·shed (wo͝od′shed′), *n.* a shed for keeping firewood.

woods·man (wo͝odz′mən), *n.* a person accustomed to life in the woods and skilled in woodcraft.

woods·y (wo͝od′zē), *adj.,* **-i·er, -i·est** of or suggestive of the woods.

wood·wind (wo͝od′wind′), *n.* any of the group of wind instruments comprising the flutes, clarinets, oboes, bassoons, and sometimes the saxophones.

wood·work (wo͝od′wûrk′), *n.* **1.** objects or parts made of wood. **2.** the interior wooden fittings, esp. of a house, as doors.

wood·work·ing (wo͝od′wûr′king), *n.* the act or art of making things of wood.

wood·y (wo͝od′ē), *adj.,* **-i·er, -i·est. 1.** consisting of or containing wood. **2.** resembling wood, as in texture. **3.** wooded. —**wood′i·ness,** *n.*

woof (wo͝of, wo͞of), *n.* **1.** filling (def. 3). **2.** texture, as of fabric.

woof·er (wo͞of′ər), *n.* a loudspeaker designed for the reproduction of low-frequency sounds.

wool (wo͝ol), *n.* **1.** the fine, soft, curly hair that forms the fleece of sheep and certain other animals. **2.** yarn, fabric, or garments made from this hair. **3.** something having fine fibers resembling wool. —**wooled** (-d), *adj.*

wool·en (wo͝ol′ən), *adj.* **1.** made of wool. **2.** of wool or fabrics made from wool. —*n.* **3.** woolens, woolen fabric or clothing. Also, *Brit.,* **wool′len.**

wool·gath·er·ing (wo͝ol′gath′ər ing), *n.* indulgence in fanciful daydreaming.

wool·ly (wo͝ol′ē), *adj.,* **-li·er, -li·est,** *n.,* *pl.* **-lies.** —*adj.* **1.** of or resembling wool. **2.** clothed or covered with wool. **3.** fuzzy or unclear. **4.** *Informal.* rough or vigorous: *a wild and woolly frontier town.* —*n.* **5.** Usually, **woollies,** a knitted undergarment of wool. Also, **wool′y.** —**wool′li·ness,** *n.*

wool′ly bear′, any caterpillar having woolly hairs.

wooz·y (wo͞o′zē, wo͝oz′ē), *adj.,* **-i·er, -i·est.** *Informal.* **1.** stupidly confused. **2.** dazed or dizzy, as from drink. —**wooz′i·ly,** *adv.* —**wooz′i·ness,** *n.*

Worces·ter (wo͝os′tər), *n.* a city in central Massachusetts.

word (wûrd), *n.* **1.** one or a sequence of speech sounds having meaning and making up an independent linguistic unit. **2.** the written or printed letters or characters representing such a unit. **3.** a brief remark or statement. **4.** a short talk or conversation. **5.** news or information. **6.** assurance or promise. **7.** a signal or command. **8. words, a.** speech or talk. **b.** the text or lyrics of a song. **c.** an argument or dispute. **9. the Word, a.** the Bible. **b.** the message of the gospel of Christ. **10. by word of mouth,** through spoken language rather than written language. **11. in a word,** in short. **12. in so many words,** precisely or explicitly. **13. word for word,** in exactly the same words. —*v.t.* **14.** to express in words.

word·age (wûr′dij), *n.* **1.** the number of words used. **2.** verbiage (def. 1). **3.** *Rare.* words collectively.

word·book (wûrd′bo͝ok′), *n.* a book containing a list or lists of words, as for exercise in meanings.

word·ing (wûr′ding), *n.* choice or arrangement of words to express something.

word·play (wûrd′plā′), *n.* use of words in a clever manner, as in a pun.

word′ proc′essing, an automated system for rapid, efficient production of letters, reports, etc., using a special typewriter in conjunction with electronic equipment. —**word′ proc′essor.**

Words·worth (wûrdz′wûrth′), *n.* **William,** 1770–1850, English poet

word·y (wûr′dē), *adj.,* **-i·er, -i·est.** using more words than are needed for communication. —**word′i·ly,** *adv.* —**word′i·ness,** *n.* —**Syn.** redundant, verbose.

wore (wōr, wôr), *v.* pt. of **wear.**

work (wûrk), *n.*, *adj.*, *v.*, **worked** or **wrought, work·ing.** —*n.* **1.** exertion or effort directed to produce or accomplish something. **2.** something that requires exertion or effort. **3.** employment as a means of earning one's living. **4.** the result of exertion or effort. **5.** a product of exertion or effort: *a work of art.* **6.** manner in which something is done. **7. works, a.** a place for manufacturing: *ironworks.* **b.** the working parts of a machine. **c.** engineering structures, as bridges. **8.** *Physics.* the transference of energy equal to the product of the component of a force. **9. the works,** *Slang.* **a.** the entirety of something. **b.** harsh treatment. **10. at work,** working, as at one's job. **11. in the works,** in preparation. **12. out of work,** without a job. —*adj.* **13.** of or for work. —*v.i.* **14.** to do work. **15.** to be employed. **16.** to act or operate effectively. **17.** to attain a specified condition, as if by repeated movement: *The nails worked loose.* **18.** to make way with effort or under stress. **19.** to ferment, as a liquid. —*v.t.* **20.** to use or operate, as a machine. **21.** to bring about by or as by work. **22.** to mold or prepare by work. **23.** to carry on operations in (a district). **24.** to achieve by effort. **25.** to keep at work: *She works her employees hard.* **26.** to make or decorate by needlework or embroidery. **27.** to fashion or shape. **28.** to solve, as an arithmetic problem. **29.** to cause to attain a specified condition, as if by repeated movement. **30.** to cause a strong emotion in: *to work a crowd into a frenzy.* **31. work off,** to lose or dispose of, as by labor. **32. work on** or **upon,** to exercise influence or persuasion on. **33. work out, a.** to bring about. **b.** to solve, as a problem. **c.** to have a result or outcome. **d.** to elaborate or develop. **e.** to prove feasible. **f.** to exercise or train, as for an athletic sport. **34. work up, a.** to stir up or excite. **b.** to prepare or plan. **c.** to rise to a higher position. —**Syn. 1.** labor, toil. **2.** task, undertaking. **3.** calling, occupation, vocation.

work·a·ble (wûr′kə bəl), *adj.* **1.** capable of being put into practice. **2.** capable of being worked. —**work′·a·ble·ness,** *n.*

work·a·day (wûr′kə dā′), *adj.* **1.** of or suitable for working days. **2.** ordinary or commonplace.

work·a·hol·ic (wûrk′ə hô′lik, -hol′ik), *n. Informal.* a person obsessively occupied with work at the expense of normal leisure, human relationships, etc. [*work* + *a*(*lco*)*holic*] —**work′a·hol′ism,** *n.*

work·bench (wûrk′bench′), *n.* a sturdy table at which a craftsman works.

work·book (wûrk′book′), *n.* **1.** a book containing questions, exercises, etc., intended to guide the work of a student. **2.** a book for keeping a record of work completed or planned. **3.** a workman's handbook.

work·day (wûrk′dā′), *n.* **1.** the part of a day during which one works. **2.** a day on which one works.

work·er (wûr′kər), *n.* **1.** a person or thing that works. **2.** a laborer or employee. **3.** a person engaged in a particular field or cause. **4.** a sterile female ant, bee, or termite that does most of the work in a colony.

work′ eth′ic, a moral belief in the sociological importance of work.

work′ farm′, a farm to which juvenile offenders are sent for a period to work.

work·horse (wûrk′hôrs′), *n.* **1.** a horse used for heavy labor. **2.** a person who works arduously.

work·house (wûrk′hous′), *n.* **1.** a prison for petty criminals, who are made to work. **2.** *Brit.* (formerly) a poorhouse for paupers able to work.

work·ing (wûr′king), *n.* **1.** act of a person or thing that works. **2.** operation or action. **3.** Usually, **workings.** a part of a mine or quarry in which work is carried on. —*adj.* **4.** doing some form of work or labor, as for a living. **5.** of or for work. **6.** good or sufficient enough to be useful or effective: *a working model.*

work·ing·man (wûr′king man′), *n.* a man who earns his living usually at manual work. —**work′ing·wom′an,** *n.fem.*

work·load (wûrk′lōd′), *n.* the amount of work that a machine or employee can be or is expected to perform.

work·man (wûrk′mən), *n.* **1.** a man employed in some craft. **2.** workingman. —**work′wom′an,** *n.fem.*

work·man·like (wûrk′mən līk′), *adj.* **1.** like or befitting a workman. **2.** skillful or well-executed.

work·man·ship (wûrk′mən ship′), *n.* **1.** the art or skill of a workman. **2.** the quality or manner of work done.

work·out (wûrk′out′), *n.* **1.** an athletic practice or trial session. **2.** physical exercise.

work·room (wûrk′room′, -room′), *n.* a room in which work is carried on.

work′ sheet′, 1. a sheet of paper on which work schedules or special instructions are recorded. **2.** a piece of paper on which problems or ideas are set down in tentative form.

work·shop (wûrk′shop′), *n.* **1.** a room or building in which mechanical work is carried on. **2.** a seminar which emphasizes exchange of ideas and the demonstration of techniques, skills, etc.

work·ta·ble (wûrk′tā′bəl), *n.* a table at which a person works, often with drawers for materials, tools, etc.

work·up (wûrk′up′), *n.* a thorough medical examination, esp. including various laboratory tests.

work·week (wûrk′wēk′), *n.* the total number of working hours or days in a week.

world (wûrld), *n.* **1.** the earth considered as a planet. **2.** (*often cap.*) a particular division of the earth: *the New World.* **3.** the human race. **4.** the public generally. **5.** the whole system of created things. **6.** a particular class of people, with common interests, aims, etc.: *the literary world.* **7.** secular or social life. **8.** a general grouping of natural things: *the animal world.* **9.** any heavenly body. **10.** a very great quantity or extent: *a world of good.* **11. for all the world,** in every respect.

world·beat·er (wûrld′bē′tər), *n.* a person or thing that surpasses all others of like kind.

world·ling (wûrld′ling), *n.* a person devoted to worldly interests or pleasures.

world·ly (wûrld′lē), *adj.,* **-li·er, -li·est. 1.** devoted to the interests or pleasures of this world. **2.** earthly or mundane. **3.** worldly-wise. **—world′-li·ness,** *n.* **—Syn. 1.** secular, temporal. **3.** cosmopolitan, urban.

world·ly-wise (wûrld′lē wīz′), *adj.* knowledgeable in the ways of the world.

World War I, the war (1914–18) in which France, Great Britain, Russia, the U.S., and their allies defeated Germany, Austria-Hungary, Turkey, and their allies.

World War II, the war (1939–45) in which Great Britain, France, the U.S., and Russia defeated Germany, Italy, and Japan.

world·wide (wûrld′wīd′), *adj.* extending or spread throughout the world.

worm (wûrm), *n.* **1.** any of numerous long, slender, soft-bodied, legless creeping animals, as earthworms, roundworms, tapeworms, etc. **2.** something resembling a worm, as the thread of a screw. **3.** an abject, contemptible person. **4. worms,** any disease caused by parasitic worms in the intestines or other tissues. *—v.i.* **5.** to move or advance like a worm, in a devious or stealthy manner. *—v.t.* **6.** to cause to move or advance in a devious or stealthy man-

ner. **7.** to get by persistent, insidious efforts: *to worm a secret out of a person.* **8.** to free from intestinal worms. **—worm′y,** *adj.*

worm′ gear′, a mechanism consisting of a rotating shaft engaging with and driving a gearwheel.

worm·wood (wûrm′wood′), *n.* **1.** a bitter, aromatic herb used as an ingredient of absinthe. **2.** something bitter or unpleasant.

worn (wôrn, wōrn), *v.* **1.** pp. of **wear.** *—adj.* **2.** damaged through wear or use. **3.** wearied or exhausted.

worn-out (wôrn′out′, wōrn′-), *adj.* **1.** worn or used until no longer fit for use. **2.** completely exhausted or fatigued.

wor·ri·ment (wûr′ē mənt, wur′-), *n.* **1.** harassing annoyance. **2.** a cause of worry.

wor·ri·some (wûr′ē səm, wur′-), *adj.* **1.** causing worry. **2.** inclined to worry. **—wor′ri·some·ly,** *adv.*

wor·ry (wûr′ē, wur′ē), *v.,* **-ried, -ry·ing,** *n., pl.* **-ries.** *—v.i.* **1.** to torment oneself with disturbing thoughts. **2.** to bite or snap repeatedly at something. *—v.t.* **3.** to torment with disturbing thoughts. **4.** to bite or snap repeatedly at. **5.** to seize with the teeth and shake or mangle, as an animal does. *—n.* **6.** a worried condition or feeling. **7.** a cause of this. **—wor′ri·er,** *n.* **—Syn. 1.** fret. **3.** distress, trouble. **6.** anxiety, concern, uneasiness.

wor·ry·wart (wûr′ē wôrt′, wur′-), *n.* a person who tends to worry needlessly.

worse (wûrs), *adj., comparative of* **bad** *and* **ill. 1.** bad or ill in a greater degree. **2.** more unfavorable or injurious. **3.** in poorer health or condition. *—n.* **4.** something worse. *—adv.* **5.** in a worse manner or degree.

wors·en (wûr′sən), *v.t., v.i.* to make or become worse.

wor·ship (wûr′ship), *n., v.,* **-shiped, -ship·ing** *or* **-shipped, -ship·ping.** *—n.* **1.** reverent honor given to a deity. **2.** the expression of such honor, as by prayers. **3.** great admiration or regard. **4.** (*cap.*) *Brit.* a title of honor in addressing a magistrate or mayor (usually prec. by *Your* or *His* or *Her*). *—v.t.* **5.** to show religious worship to. **6.** to feel admiration or regard for. *—v.i.* **7.** to take part in worship. **—wor′ship·er,** *Brit.,* **wor′-ship·per,** *n.* **—Syn. 5.** revere. **6.** adore, idolize.

wor·ship·ful (wûr′ship fəl), *adj.* **1.** feeling or showing worship. **2.** (*cap.*) *Brit.* a title of respect for a justice of the peace, etc. **—wor′ship·ful·ly,** *adv.*

worst (wûrst), *adj.*, *superlative of* **bad** *and* **ill. 1.** bad or ill in the greatest degree. **2.** most unfavorable or injurious. **3.** in poorest health or condition. **4. in the worst way,** *Informal.* very much. Also, **the worst way.** —*n.* **5.** something worst. **6. at worst,** under the worst conditions. **7. if worst comes to worst,** if the very worst happens. **8. make the worst of,** to view only the worst aspects of. —*adv.* **9.** in the worst manner or degree. —*v.t.* **10.** to defeat or beat.

wor·sted (wŏŏs'tid, wûr'stid), *n.* **1.** a firmly twisted yarn or thread spun from wool fibers. **2.** fabric woven from such yarns.

wort (wûrt), *n.* an admixture of malt that becomes beer or ale after fermentation.

-wort, a suffix meaning "a plant or herb": *liverwort.*

worth (wûrth), *prep.* **1.** good or important enough to justify (what is specified). **2.** having a value of. **3.** having property to the amount of. —*n.* **4.** intrinsic excellence of quality as commanding esteem. **5.** value, as in money. **6.** a quantity of something of a specified value: *a dollar's worth of gasoline.*

worth·less (wûrth'lis), *adj.* of no worth or merit. —**worth'less·ness,** *n.*

worth·while (wûrth'hwīl', -wīl'), *adj.* such as to repay one's time or effort.

wor·thy (wûr'thē), *adj.* **-thi·er, -thi·est,** *n., pl.* **-thies.** —*adj.* **1.** having worth or merit. **2.** of commendable excellence: *a book worthy of praise.* —*n.* **3.** a worthy or eminent person. —**wor'thi·ly,** *adv.* —**wor'thi·ness,** *n.*

would (wŏŏd, wəd), *v.* **1.** pt. and pp. of **will¹. 2.** (used to express a wish): *I would it were true.* **3.** (used in place of *will,* to soften a statement or question): *Would you be so kind as to help me?*

would-be (wŏŏd'bē'), *adj.* **1.** wishing to be. **2.** intended to be.

would·n't (wŏŏd'ⁿnt), contraction of *would not.*

wouldst (wŏŏdst), *v. Archaic.* second pers. sing. pt. of **will¹.**

wound¹ (wŏŏnd), *n.* **1.** an injury involving the cutting or tearing of the flesh. **2.** an injury or hurt to the feelings. —*v.t., v.i.* **3.** to inflict a wound (upon). —**wound'ing·ly,** *adv.*

wound² (wound), *v.* **1.** pt. and pp. of **wind². 2.** a pt. and pp. of **wind³.**

wove (wōv), *v.* a pt. and pp. of **weave.**

wo·ven (wō'vən), *v.* a pp. of **weave.**

wow¹ (wou), *v.t.* **1.** *Slang.* to gain an enthusiastic response from. —*n.* **2.** *Slang.* an extraordinary success. —*interj.* **3.** (an exclamation of surprise, pleasure, etc.)

wow² (wou, wō), *n.* a distortion in the pitch fidelity of reproduced sound.

WP, See **word processing.**

wpm, words per minute.

wpn., weapon.

wrack¹ (rak), *n.* **1.** seaweed cast on the shore. **2.** *Obs.* wreck of the sea.

wrack² (rak), *n.* rack².

wraith (rāth), *n.* **1.** an apparition of a living person supposed to portend his or her death. **2.** a ghost or visible spirit.

wran·gle (rang'gəl), *v.,* **-gled, -gling,** *n.* —*v.i.* **1.** to argue or dispute, esp. in a noisy or angry manner. —*v.t.* **2.** to get or bring about by argument. **3.** *Western U.S.* to tend or round up (horses). —*n.* **4.** a noisy or angry dispute. —**wran'gler,** *n.*

wrap (rap), *v.,* **wrapped** *or* **wrapt** (rapt), **wrap·ping,** *n.* —*v.t.* **1.** to enclose or cover in something folded about. **2.** to wind or fold (something) around as a covering. **3.** to enclose and make fast (an article, etc.) with a covering. **4.** to surround, shroud, or hide. —*v.i.* **5.** to become wrapped. **6. wrapped up in,** intensely absorbed in. **7. wrap up,** *Informal.* **a.** to conclude or settle. **b.** to tell in a summary. —*n.* **8.** any outer covering, as a shawl or scarf. **9. under wraps,** in secrecy.

wrap·a·round (rap'ə round'), *n.* a garment that wraps around the body and overlaps at a full-length opening.

wrap·per (rap'ər), *n.* **1.** a person or thing that wraps. **2.** something in which a thing is wrapped. **3.** a long, loose garment, esp. formerly, a woman's bathrobe.

wrap·ping (rap'ing), *n.* Often, **wrappings.** material for wrapping or packing something.

wrap-up (rap'up'), *n. Informal.* a report that summarizes something.

wrasse (ras), *n.* a marine fish having powerful teeth and usually a brilliant color.

wrath (rath, räth *or, Brit.,* rôth), *n.* **1.** fiercely resentful anger. **2.** vengeance motivated by anger. —**wrath'ful,** *adj.* —**wrath'ful·ly,** *adv.* —**wrath'ful·ness,** *n.* —**Syn. 1.** fury, ire, rage.

wreak (rēk), *v.t.* **1.** to carry out or inflict, as vengeance. **2.** to give full expression to, as one's rage.

wreath (rēth), *n., pl.* **wreaths** (rēthz). **1.** a circular band of flowers or leaves twisted together for decoration. **2.** anything resembling a wreath, as in shape: *a wreath of clouds.*

wreathe (rēth), *v.t.,* **wreathed, wreath·ing. 1.** to encircle or adorn with or as with wreaths. **2.** to shape into a wreath. **3.** to curl or twist. **4.** to envelop or cover.

wreck (rek), *n.* **1.** any structure or object reduced to a state of ruin. **2.** shipwreck (defs. 1, 2). **3.** the serious damage or destruction of anything. **4.** a person in poor condition physically or mentally. —*v.t.* **5.** to cause the ruin or destruction of. **6.** to damage or end, as one's career. **7.** to dismantle or demolish.

wreck·age (rek′ij), *n.* **1.** the act of wrecking or state of being wrecked. **2.** the remains of something wrecked.

wreck·er (rek′ər), *n.* **1.** a person or thing that wrecks. **2.** a person who demolishes and removes buildings. **3.** a vehicle equipped to tow wrecked or disabled automobiles.

wren (ren), *n.* a small songbird having brown plumage and a short tail.

wrench (rench), *v.t.* **1.** to pull or force by a violent twist. **2.** to injure by a sudden, violent twist. **3.** to wrest (def. 2). —*n.* **4.** a tool for gripping and turning a bolt or a nut. **5.** a sudden, violent twist. **6.** a painful twist, as of the ankle. **7.** sudden and sharp emotional strain.

wrest (rest), *v.t.* **1.** to take away by force. **2.** to get by great effort. **3.** to twist or turn from the proper meaning or use. —*n.* **4.** the act of wresting. —**wrest′er,** *n.*

wres·tle (res′əl), *v.*, **-tled, -tling,** *n.* —*v.i., v.t.* **1.** to engage in wrestling (with). **2.** to contend, as in a struggle for mastery: *to wrestle with a problem.* —*n.* **3.** the act or a bout of wrestling. —**wres′tler,** *n.*

wres·tling (res′ling), *n.* a sport in which each of two opponents struggles hand to hand in an attempt to force the other down.

wretch (rech), *n.* **1.** a deplorably unfortunate person. **2.** a despicable or mean person.

wretch·ed (rech′id), *adj.* **1.** deplorably unfortunate. **2.** causing misery and sorrow. **3.** despicable or mean. **4.** inferior or worthless. —**wretch′ed·ly,** *adv.* —**wretch′ed·ness,** *n.* —**Syn.** **1.** forlorn, miserable, pitiable.

wrig·gle (rig′əl), *v.*, **-gled, -gling,** *n.* —*v.i.* **1.** to twist from side to side. **2.** to move along by twisting and turning the body, as a snake. **3.** to make one's way by tricks and dodges. —*n.* **4.** the act of wriggling. —**wrig′gly,** *adj.*

wrig·gler (rig′lər), *n.* **1.** a person or thing that wriggles. **2.** the larva of a mosquito.

wright (rīt), *n.* a person who makes or creates something (used in combination): *a playwright.*

wring (ring), *v.*, **wrung, wring·ing,** *n.* —*v.t.* **1.** to twist and press in order to force out liquid. **2.** to force out (liquid) by twisting and pressing. **3.** to twist forcibly. **4.** to extract or get by forceful effort. **5.** to clasp tightly with or without twisting: *to wring one's hands in grief.* **6.** to affect painfully. —*n.* **7.** the act of wringing.

wring·er (ring′ər), *n.* a machine that forces water from anything wet.

wrin·kle¹ (ring′kəl), *n., v.,* **-kled, -kling.** —*n.* **1.** a small furrow in the skin, esp. of the face, as due to aging. **2.** a temporary slight fold in fabric, as due to crushing. —*v.t., v.i.* **3.** to form wrinkles (in). —**wrin′kly,** *adj.*

wrin·kle² (ring′kəl), *n. Informal.* a clever innovation.

wrist (rist), *n.* **1.** the joint between the arm and the hand. **2.** **a slap on the wrist,** a light reprimand.

wrist·band (rist′band′), *n.* the band of a sleeve that covers the wrist.

wrist·watch (rist′woch′), *n.* a watch attached to a strap or band worn around the wrist.

writ (rit), *n.* an order issued by a court requiring the person to whom it is issued to do or refrain from doing something specified.

write (rīt), *v.*, **wrote, writ·ten, writ·ing.** —*v.t.* **1.** to form (letters, words, etc.) on a surface, as with a pen or pencil. **2.** to express or communicate in writing. **3.** to produce as author or composer. **4.** *Computer Technol.* to record (information) in a memory unit. —*v.i.* **5.** to write something, as a letter or book. **6. write down,** to set down in writing. **7. write in,** to insert (a name not printed on a ballot) instead of voting for one on it. **8. write off, a.** to cancel an entry in an account, as an uncollectible debt. **b.** to regard as worthless or lost. **c.** to amortize. **9. write out, a.** to put into writing. **b.** to state completely. **10. write up,** to put into writing, esp. in full detail.

write-in (rīt′in′), *n.* a candidate or vote for a candidate not printed on a ballot but inserted by a voter.

write-off (rīt′ôf′, -of′), *n.* something written off, as an uncollectible debt.

writ·er (rī′tər), *n.* a person engaged in writing, esp. as an occupation.

writer's cramp′, a cramp in the hand and fingers caused by prolonged writing.

write-up (rīt′up′), *n.* a written account, often one favorable to the subject.

writhe (rīth), *v.*, **writhed, writh·ing.** —*v.i.* **1.** to twist the body about, as in pain. **2.** to suffer mentally, as from shame. —*v.t.* **3.** to cause to writhe. —*n.* **4.** a writhing movement. —**writh′ing·ly,** *adv.*

writ·ing (rī'tiṅg), *n.* **1.** the act of a person or thing that writes. **2.** written form. **3.** handwriting (def. 2). **4.** something written. **5.** the profession of a writer.

writ·ten (rit'ⁿn), *v.* pp. of **write.**

wrnt., warrant.

wrong (rôṅg, roṅg), *adj.* **1.** not in accordance with what is morally right. **2.** deviating from truth or fact. **3.** not proper or appropriate. **4.** out of order. **5.** not desired or wanted. **6.** intended to be worn or kept inward or under: *the wrong side of a sweater.* —*n.* **7.** an act that is wrong. **8.** the state or condition of being wrong. **9. in the wrong,** in error. —*adv.* **10.** in a wrong manner. —*v.t.* **11.** to do wrong to. **12.** to impute evil to (someone) unjustly. [perh. < Scand] —**wrong'er,** *n.* —**wrong'-ly,** *adv.* —**wrong'ness,** *n.* —Syn. **1.** sinful, wicked. **2.** erroneous, incorrect, mistaken. **4.** awry, amiss. **11.** maltreat. **12.** malign.

wrong·do·er (rôṅg'dōō'ər, roṅg'-), *n.* a person who does wrong, esp. a sinner. —**wrong'do'ing,** *n.*

wrong·ful (rôṅg'fəl, roṅg'-), *adj.* **1.** full of wrong or unjustness. **2.** unlawful or illegal. —**wrong'ful·ly,** *adv.* —**wrong'ful·ness,** *n.*

wrong·head·ed (rôṅg'hed'id, roṅg'-), *adj.* misguided and stubborn. —**wrong'head'ed·ly,** *adv.* —**wrong'head'ed·ness,** *n.*

wrong·o (rôṅg'ō, roṅg'-), *n., pl.* **-os, -oes.** *Slang.* a serious error.

wrote (rōt), *v.* pt. of **write.**

wroth (rôth, roth), *adj. Archaic.* very angry.

wrought (rôt), *v.* **1.** a pt. and pp. of **work.** —*adj.* **2.** shaped by beating with a hammer, as iron articles. **3.** *Literary.* worked or made.

wrought' i'ron, a form of iron that contains little carbon and is easily forged or welded. —**wrought'-i'ron,** *adj.*

wrought-up (rôt'up'), *adj.* greatly perturbed.

wrung (ruṅg), *v.* pt. and pp. of **wring.**

wry (rī), *adj.,* **wri·er, wri·est. 1.** made by twisting the facial features: *a .wry grin.* **2.** bitterly ironic: *wry humor.* **3.** unusually bent or twisted. —**wry'ly,** *adv.* —**wry'ness,** *n.*

wry·neck (rī'nek'), *n.* **1.** a condition in which the neck is twisted and the head inclined to one side. **2.** a small bird having a peculiar habit of twisting the head and neck.

WSW, west-southwest.

wt., weight.

Wu·han (wōō'hän'), *n.* a city in E China.

WV, West Virginia. Also, **W.Va.**

WW, World War.

WW I. See **World War I.**

WW II. See **World War II.**

WY, Wyoming. Also, **Wyo.**

Wy·o·ming (wī ō'miṅg), *n.* a state in the NW United States. *Cap.:* Cheyenne.

X

X, x (eks) *n., pl.* **X's** or **Xs, x's** or **xs.** the 24th letter of the English alphabet, a consonant.

x (eks), *v.t.,* **x-ed** or **x'd** (ekst), **x-ing** or **x'ing** (ek'siṅg). to cross out or mark with an *x: to x out an error.*

X, 1. the Roman numeral for 10. **2.** Christ. **3.** Christian. **4.** a designation for motion pictures no one under 17 years of age may attend.

x, 1. an unknown quantity, variable, or person. **2.** experimental. **3.** times: $8 \times 8 = 64.$ **4.** by: $3'' \times 4''$ (read: "three by four inches"). **5.** (used to show a particular place or point on a map or diagram.) **6.** x-axis.

Xan·thip·pe (zan tip'ē), *n.* **1.** 5th century B.C., wife of Socrates. **2.** a shrewish, ill-tempered woman. Also, **Xan·tip'pe.**

x-ax·is (eks'ak'sis), *n., pl.* **x'-ax'es** (-sēz). *Math.* (in a plane coordinate system) the horizontal axis along which the abscissa is measured.

X-C, cross-country: *X-C skiing.*

X chromosome, a sex chromosome that carries genes producing female characteristics and that usually occurs in pairs in a female and singly in males.

xd, *Stock Exchange.* without dividend. Also, **x.div.**

Xe, xenon.

xe·bec (zē'bek), *n.* a small three-masted vessel of the Mediterranean.

xen·o·lith (zen'ᵊlith), *n.* a rock fragment foreign to the igneous rock in which it is embedded. —**xen'o·lith'ic,** *adj.*

xe·non (zē′non, zen′on), *n. Chem.* a colorless, chemically inactive gaseous element present in the atmosphere in minute proportions. *Symbol:* Xe; *at. wt.:* 131.30; *at. no.:* 54.

xen·o·pho·bi·a (zen′ə fō′bē ə), *n.* an unreasonable fear or hatred of foreigners or strangers or of what is foreign or strange. **—xen′o·phobe′** (-fōb′), *n.* **—xen′o·pho′bic,** *adj.*

xe·ric (zēr′ik), *adj.* of or adapted to a dry environment.

xe·rog·ra·phy (zi rog′rə fē), *n.* a copying process that uses static electricity to transfer positive images to the paper. **—xe·ro·graph·ic** (zēr′ə graf′ik), *adj.*

Xer·ox (zēr′oks), *n.* **1.** *Trademark.* a process for making instant copies of written or printed matter by xerography. **—***v.t., v.i.* **2.** (*l.c.*) to reproduce by Xerox.

Xerx·es I (zûrk′sēz), 519?–465 B.C., king of Persia 486?–465.

xi (zī, sī; *Gk* ksē), *n.* the 14th letter of the Greek alphabet (Ξ, ξ).

x in, *Stock Exchange.* without interest. Also, **x.i., x.int.**

XL, extra large.

Xmas, Christmas.

Xn., Christian.

Xnty., Christianity.

x-ra·di·a·tion (eks′rā′dē ā′shən), *n.* **1.** exposure to x-rays. **2.** radiation composed of x-rays.

x-ray (eks′rā′), *n.* Also, **x ray. 1.** Often, **x-rays.** a form of electromagnetic radiation similar to light but of shorter wavelength and capable of penetrating solids, to show the interior parts of an object or human body. **2.** a photograph made by x-rays. **—***v.t.* **3.** to examine or treat with x-rays. **—***adj.* **4.** of or by x-rays. Also, **X′-ray′.**

x′ray tube′, an electronic tube for producing x-rays, essentially a cathode-ray tube in which a metal target is bombarded with high-energy electrons.

xy·lem (zī′ləm, -lem), *n.* the part of a vascular bundle forming the woody tissue of a plant.

xy·li·tol (zī′lə tōl′), *n.* a naturally occurring sugar substitute, claimed to reduce tooth decay.

xy·lo·phone (zī′lə fōn′), *n.* a musical instrument consisting of a graduated series of wooden bars, sounded by striking with small wooden hammers. **—xy′lo·phon′ist** (-fō′nist, zī lof′ə-nist, zi-), *n.*

Y

Y, y (wī), *n., pl.* **Y's** or **Ys, y's** or **ys.** the 25th letter of the English alphabet, a semivowel.

Y, yttrium.

y, y-axis.

-y¹, a suffix meaning: **a.** of or like: *woody.* **b.** inclined to: *grouchy.* **c.** full of or containing: *juicy.*

-y², a suffix meaning: **a.** dear: *daddy.* **b.** little: *kitty.*

-y³, a suffix meaning: **a.** action of: *inquiry.* **b.** quality or state: *honesty.* **c.** goods or business establishment specified: *bakery.*

y., **1.** yard; yards. **2.** year; years.

yacht (yot), *n.* **1.** a ship used for private cruising or racing. **—***v.i.* **2.** to cruise or race in a yacht.

yacht·ing (yot′ing), *n.* the sport of cruising or racing in a yacht.

yachts·man (yots′mən), *n.* a person who owns or sails a yacht. **—yachts′man·ship′,** *n.* **—yachts′wom′an,** *n. fem.*

ya·hoo (yä′hōō, yā′-), *n.* a coarse, uncouth person. [< *Yahoos* race of brutes in Swift's *Gulliver's Travels* (1726)]

Yah·weh (yä′we), *n.* a name of God, commonly rendered Jehovah. Also, **Yah′we, Yah′veh** (-ve).

yak¹ (yak), *n.* a shaggy-haired wild ox of the Tibetan highlands.

yak² (yak), *n.,* **yakked, yak·king.** *Slang.* **—***v.i.* **1.** talk steadily and senselessly. **—***n.* **2.** such talk. Also, **yack.**

yam (yam), *n.* **1.** the edible, starchy, tuberous root of a tropical climbing vine. **2.** the sweet potato.

yam·mer (yam′ər), *Informal.* **—***v.i.* **1.** to complain whiningly. **2.** to talk loudly and persistently. **—***v.t.* **3.** to utter complainingly. **—yam′mer·er,** *n.*

yang (yäng, yang), *n.* See under **yin** and **yang.**

Yang·tze (yang′sē), *n.* a river flowing through central China.

yank (yangk), *v.t., v.i.* **1.** to pull abruptly and vigorously. **—***n.* **2.** an abrupt, vigorous pull.

Yank (yangk), *n., adj. Slang.* Yankee.

Yan·kee (yang'kē), *n.* **1.** a native or inhabitant of New England. **2.** a native or inhabitant of the northern U.S. **3.** a native or inhabitant of the United States. —*adj.* **4.** of or characteristic of Yankees. [? < D *Jan Kees* John Cheese, nickname applied by Dutch of colonial New York to English settlers]

yan·qui (yäng'kē), *n.* (*often cap.*) *Spanish.* (in Latin America) Yankee (def. 3).

yap (yap), *v.,* **yapped, yap·ping,** *n.* —*v.i.* **1.** to bark shrilly. **2.** *Slang.* to talk noisily and foolishly. —*n.* **3.** a shrill bark. **4.** *Slang.* **a.** noisy and foolish talk. **b.** the mouth. —**yap'·per,** *n.*

yard¹ (yärd), *n.* **1.** a unit of linear measure equal to 3 feet or 0.9144 meter. **2.** a long spar, supported at its center, by which the head of a sail is supported.

yard² (yärd), *n.* **1.** the ground partially or completely surrounding a house or other building. **2.** an enclosed area for a specific purpose: *a shipyard.* **3.** a system of railroad tracks for switching cars and making them up into trains.

yard·age (yär'dij), *n.* the length or amount of something measured in yards.

yard·arm (yärd'ärm'), *n.* either end of a yard supporting a square sail.

yard' goods'. See **piece goods.**

yard·man (yärd'mən), *n.* a man who works in a railroad yard.

yard·mas·ter (yärd'mas'tər, -mä'stər), *n.* a person who supervises a railroad yard.

yard·stick (yärd'stik'), *n.* **1.** a measuring stick a yard long. **2.** any standard of judgment.

yar·mul·ke (yär'məl kə, yä'məl-), *n.* a Jewish man's skullcap, worn esp. during prayer and religious study. Also, **yar'mel·ke.**

yarn (yärn), *n.* **1.** thread made of fibers and used for knitting or weaving. **2.** *Informal.* a long story of adventure.

yar·row (yar'ō), *n.* a daisylike plant having finely divided leaves and whitish flowers.

yaw (yô), *v.i.* **1.** to deviate temporarily from a straight course, as a ship. **2.** (of an aircraft) to have a motion about its vertical axis. —*n.* **3.** the movement of yawing.

yawl (yôl), *n.* a two-masted, fore-and-aft-rigged sailing vessel having a large mainmast.

yawn (yôn), *v.i.* **1.** to open the mouth wide, esp. involuntarily with deep inhalation, as from sleepiness or boredom. **2.** to extend or stretch wide. —*n.* **3.** the act of yawning. —**yawn'·er,** *n.*

yawp (yôp, yäp), *v.i.* **1.** *Informal.* to utter a loud, harsh cry. **2.** *Slang.* to talk noisily and foolishly. Also, **yaup.** —**yawp'er,** *n.*

yaws (yôz), *n.pl.* a tropical disease characterized by raspberrylike sores on the skin.

y-ax·is (wī'ak'sis), *n., pl.* **y'-ax'es** (-sēz). *Math.* (in a plane coordinate system) the vertical axis along which the ordinate is measured.

Yb, ytterbium.

Y.B., yearbook.

Y chromosome, a sex chromosome that carries genes producing male characteristics and that occurs singly and only in males.

y·clept (ē klept'), *adj. Archaic.* known as. Also, **y·cleped'.**

yd., yard; yards. Also, **yd**

ye¹ (yē), *pron. Archaic or Literary.* you (def. 1).

ye² (th͟e, yē), *definite article. Archaic.* the¹.

yea (yā). *Archaic.* —*adv.* **1. a.** yes. **b.** indeed. —*n.* **2.** aye¹ (def. 2).

yeah (yâ), *adv. Informal.* yes.

year (yēr), *n.* **1.** the period of 365 days, or in leap year 366 days, divided into 12 months, beginning Jan. 1 and ending Dec. 31. **2.** the period of time, 365¼ days, in which the earth makes one complete revolution around the sun. **3.** a period out of every 12 months devoted to a certain pursuit or activity: *the academic year.* **4. years, a.** age, esp. old age. **b.** time, esp. a long time.

year·book (yēr'bŏŏk'), *n.* **1.** a book published annually, containing information about the past year. **2.** a book published by a graduating class, containing photographs, accounts of school activities, etc.

year·ling (yēr'ling), *n.* an animal in its second year.

year·long (yēr'lông', -long'), *adj.* lasting for a year.

year·ly (yēr'lē), *adj.* **1.** annual (defs. 1–3). —*adv.* **2.** once a year.

yearn (yûrn), *v.i.* **1.** to have an anxious longing. **2.** to feel tenderness or affection. —**Syn. 1.** crave, desire, pine.

yearn·ing (yûr'ning), *n.* a persistent or tender longing.

year-round (yēr'round'), *adj.* continuing or active throughout the year.

yeast (yēst), *n.* **1.** a yellowish, semifluid froth consisting of certain minute fungi, used in making beer, as leavening, and in medicine. **2.** a small compressed cake in which this substance is mixed with flour or meal. **3.** mental ferment or agitation. **4.** froth or foam, as of waves.

yeast·y (yē'stē), *adj.,* **-i·er, -i·est. 1.** of, containing, or resembling yeast. **2.** frothy or foamy. **3.** exuberant or ebullient.

yegg (yeg), *n. Slang.* a burglar, esp. one who cracks safes.

yell (yel), *v.i., v.t.* **1.** to cry out with a loud, clear sound, as from pain. —*n.* **2.** a cry uttered by yelling. **3.** a set of words yelled as a cheer to encourage a team, as in a college. —**yell′er,** *n.*

yel·low (yel′ō), *adj.* **1.** of a bright color like that of ripe lemons. **2.** of a complexion or skin somewhat resembling this color. **3.** offensively sensational, as a newspaper. **4.** *Informal.* abjectly cowardly. —*n.* **5.** a yellow color. **6.** the yolk of an egg. —*v.t., v.i.* **7.** to make or become yellow. —**yel′low·ish,** *adj.*

yel·low·bel·ly (yel′ō bel′ē), *n. Slang.* an abject coward. —**yel′low·bel′lied,** *adj.*

yel′low fe′ver, an acute virus disease of warm climates, transmitted by a mosquito and characterized by jaundice, etc. Also called **yel′low jack′.**

yel′low jack′et, a wasp having a black body with bright yellow markings.

Yel·low·knife (yel′ō nīf′), *n.* the capital of the Northwest Territories.

yel′low pag′es, the classified section of a telephone directory, listing subscribers by the type of business or service they offer.

Yel′low Riv′er, a river in W China.

Yel′low Sea′, an arm of the Pacific between China and Korea.

yelp (yelp), *v.i., v.t.* **1.** to give or express in a sharp, shrill cry, as a dog. —*n.* **2.** a sharp, shrill cry.

Yem·en (yem′ən), *n.* **1.** Official name, **Peo′ple's Democrat′ic Repub′lic of Yem′en,** a country in S Arabia. **2.** Official name, **Yem′en Ar′ab Repub′lic,** a country in SW Arabia.

yen¹ (yen), *n., pl.* **yen.** the monetary unit of Japan.

yen² (yen), *n. Informal.* a sharp desire or craving. [? < Chin (Cantonese dial.) *yan* craving]

yeo·man (yō′mən), *n.* **1.** *U.S. Navy.* a petty officer having chiefly clerical duties. **2.** *Brit.* a farmer who cultivates his own land. **3.** (formerly) an attendant or official in a royal or noble household. **4.** *Archaic.* one of a class of freeholders, below the gentry.

yeo·man·ry (yō′mən rē), *n.* yeomen collectively.

yes (yes), *adv., n., pl.* **yes·es.** —*adv.* **1.** (used to express agreement, consent, or approval.) **2.** (used to express emphasis or to introduce a more definite statement): *The play was good, yes, very good indeed.* —*n.* **3.** an affirmative reply.

ye·shi·va (yə shē′və), *n., pl.* **-vahs, -voth** (-vôt′). **1.** an Orthodox Jewish

school for religious and secular education. **2.** an Orthodox Jewish school of higher instruction in Jewish learning. Also, **ye·shi′vah.**

yes′ man′, *Informal.* a person who always agrees with a person of superior rank.

yes·ter (yes′tər), *adj. Archaic.* of or pertaining to yesterday.

yes·ter·day (yes′tər dē, -dā′), *adv.* **1.** on the day preceding this day. **2.** in the recent past. —*n.* **3.** the day preceding this day. **4.** the recent past.

yes·ter·year (yes′tər yēr′), *n.* **1.** last year. **2.** the recent years.

yet (yet), *adv.* **1.** up until the present time. **2.** just now. **3.** in the time remaining. **4.** as previously. **5.** in addition. **6.** even or still. **7.** nevertheless. —*conj.* **8.** though or nevertheless: *It is good, yet it could be improved.*

yet·i (yet′ē), *n.* See **Abominable Snowman.**

yew (yōō), *n.* **1.** an evergreen tree having flat, needlelike leaves. **2.** its fine-grained wood.

Yid·dish (yid′ish), *n.* a language developed from German, written in Hebrew letters and spoken by many Jews, esp. in E Europe.

yield (yēld), *v.t.* **1.** to give forth by natural process, as a crop. **2.** to bring in or earn, as for an investment. **3.** to concede or grant. **4.** to surrender, as to a superior force. —*v.i.* **5.** to be productive, as a farm. **6.** to give oneself up, as to temptation. **7.** to give way to influence or argument. **8.** to collapse, as under pressure. **9.** to surrender voluntarily one's right, privilege, etc. —*n.* **10.** the quantity or amount yielded. —**Syn. 1.** bear, produce. **3, 4.** cede, relinquish.

yield·ing (yēl′ding), *adj.* **1.** inclined to surrender or submit. **2.** flexible or compliant.

yin and yang (yin′ and yäng′, yang′), (in Chinese philosophy) two principles, one negative and feminine (**yin**), and one positive and masculine (**yang**), whose interaction influences the destinies of creatures and things.

yip (yip), *v.,* **yipped, yip·ping,** *n.* —*v.i.* **1.** to bark sharply. —*n.* **2.** a sharp bark.

yip·pie (yip′ē), *n.* a member of a group of politically rebellious students in the late 1960's. [*Y(outh) I(nternational) P(arty)* + *(hip)pie*]

YMCA, Young Men's Christian Association.

YMHA, Young Men's Hebrew Association.

y.o.b., year of birth.

yod (yōd), *n.* the 10th letter of the Hebrew alphabet.

yo·del (yōd′ᵊl), v., **-deled, -del·ing,** or **-delled, -del·ling,** n. —v.t., v.i. **1.** to sing with frequent changes from the ordinary voice to falsetto and back again. —n. **2.** a song or cry yodeled. —**yo′del·er, yo′del·ler,** n.

yo·ga (yō′gə), n. Hinduism. **1.** freedom of the self from its impermanent elements or states. **2.** any of the methods by which such freedom is attained, as certain exercises. [< Hind < Skt]

yo·gi (yō′gē), n., pl. **-gis** (-gēz). a person who practices yoga. Also, **yo′gin** (-gin).

yo·gurt (yō′gərt), n. a custardlike food made from milk curdled by the action of cultures, often sweetened or flavored. Also, **yo′ghurt.**

yoke (yōk), n., pl. **yokes** for 1, 3–6, **yoke** for 2; v., **yoked, yok·ing.** —n. **1.** a bar with bow-shaped pieces for joining a pair of draft animals, esp. oxen, at the neck. **2.** a pair of draft animals joined by this. **3.** something resembling a yoke in form or use. **4.** a shaped piece in a garment, fitted at the shoulders or hips, from which the rest of the garment hangs. **5.** a symbol of subjugation or servitude. **6.** oppressive domination or bondage. —v.t. **7.** to put a yoke on. **8.** to attach (a draft animal) to (a plow or vehicle). **9.** to join or link.

yo·kel (yō′kəl), n. Contemptuous. a country fellow.

Yo·ko·ha·ma (yō′kə hä′mə), n. a seaport on SE Honshu, Japan.

yolk (yōk, yōlk), n. the yellow and principal substance of an egg. —**yolked** (-t), adj.

Yom Kip·pur (yom kip′ər), a major Jewish holy day observed by fasting and recitation of prayers expressing repentance. [< Heb = yōm day + kippur atonement]

yon (yon), adj., adv. Archaic or Dial. yonder.

yon·der (yon′dər), Literary. —adj. **1.** being over there. —adv. **2.** over there.

Yon·kers (yong′kərz), n. a city in SE New York.

yore (yōr, yôr), n. Literary. time past: knights of yore.

you (yōō), pron. **1.** the person or persons being addressed. **2.** one or anyone: a tiny animal you can't even see.

you'd (yōōd), contraction of: **a.** you had. **b.** you would.

you'll (yōōl), contraction of: **a.** you will. **b.** you shall.

young (yung), adj. **young′er** (-gər), **young′est** (-gist). —adj. **1.** being in the first or early stage of life or growth. **2.** of or pertaining to youth. **3.** having the freshness or vigor of youth. **4.** not far advanced in years or experience. —n. **5.** young persons collectively. **6.** young offspring. **7.** with young, pregnant, esp. of an animal. —**young′ish,** adj.

young′ adult′, 1. a teenager (used esp. by publishers and librarians). **2.** a person still in the early years of adulthood.

young′ blood′, 1. youthful people. **2.** fresh, new ideas or vigor.

young·ling (yung′ling), n. a young person or animal.

young·ster (yung′stər), n. a young person.

Youngs·town (yungz′toun′), n. a city in NE Ohio.

youn·ker (yung′kər), n. Archaic. a youngster.

your (yoor, yōr, yôr), pron. **1.** (a form of the possessive case of **you** used as an attributive adjective.) **2.** (cap.) (used as part of a title in addressing certain persons): Your Honor.

you're (yoor), contraction of you are.

yours (yoorz, yōrz, yôrz), pron. **1.** (a form of the possessive case of **you** used as a predicate adjective.) **2.** the one or ones belonging to you.

your·self (yoor self′, yōr-, yər-), n., pl. **-selves** (-selvz′). **1.** an emphatic appositive of you: a letter you yourself wrote. **2.** a reflexive form of you: Did you hurt yourself? **3.** your normal self: You'll soon be yourself again.

yours′ tru′ly, 1. a complimentary close of a letter used before the signature. **2.** Informal. I or me.

youth (yōōth), n., pl. **youths** (yōōths, yōōthz). **1.** the condition of being young. **2.** early life. **3.** the first or early period of anything. **4.** young persons collectively. **5.** a young person, esp. a young man.

youth·ful (yōōth′fəl), adj. **1.** having youth. **2.** of or appropriate to youth. **3.** vigorous or fresh. **4.** in an early period of existence. —**youth′ful·ly,** adv. —**youth′ful·ness,** n.

youth′ hos′tel, hostel.

you've (yōōv), contraction of you have.

yowl (youl), n. **1.** a distressed howl, as of an animal. —v.i. **2.** to utter a yowl.

yo-yo (yō′yō′), n. a spoollike toy which is spun out and reeled in by string wound around it, one end of which is looped around the player's finger.

yr., 1. year; years. **2.** your.

yrs., 1. years. **2.** yours.

Y.T., Yukon Territory.

YTD, year to date.

yt·ter·bi·um (i tûr′bē əm), n. Chem. a rare metallic element. Symbol: Yb; at. wt.: 173.04; at. no.: 70. —**yt·ter′bic,** adj.

yt·tri·um (i′trē əm), *n. Chem.* a rare metallic element. *Symbol:* Y; *at. wt.:* 88.905; *at. no.:* 39.

yu·an (yōō än′), *n., pl.* **-an. 1.** the monetary unit of the Republic of China. **2.** the monetary unit of the People's Republic of China.

yuc·ca (yuk′ə), *n.* a plant having pointed, stiff leaves and white, waxy flowers. [< AmerSp *yuca* < native Indian name]

Yu·go·sla·vi·a (yōō′gō slä′vē ə), *n.* a country in S Europe. —**Yu′go·slav′, Yu′go·sla′vi·an,** *adj., n.*

Yu′kon Ter′ritory (yōō′kon), a territory in NW Canada. *Cap.:* White-horse.

Yule (yōōl), *n. Chiefly Literary.* **1.** Christmas. **2.** the Christmas feast.

Yule′ log′, a large log of wood traditionally burned on Christmas Eve.

Yule·tide (yōōl′tīd′), *n.* Christmas-tide.

yum·my (yum′ē), *adj.,* **-mi·er, -mi·est.** *Informal.* very pleasing, esp. to the taste.

yurt (yōŏrt), *n.* a circular, portable dwelling used by nomads of Mongolia.

YWCA, Young Women's Christian Association.

YWHA, Young Women's Hebrew Association.

Z

Z, z (zē *or, esp. Brit.,* zed), *n., pl.* **Z's** or **Zs, z's** or **zs.** the 26th letter of the English alphabet, a consonant.

Z, See **atomic number.**

z., 1. zero. **2.** zone.

za·ire (zä ēr′), *n., pl.* **zaire.** the monetary unit of Zaire.

Za·ire (zä ēr′), *n.* **1.** a country in central Africa. **2.** a river in central Africa. Also, **Za·ïre′.** —**Za·ir′i·an,** *adj., n.*

Zam·be·zi (zam bē′zē), *n.* a river in S Africa.

Zam·bi·a (zam′bē ə, zäm′-), *n.* a country in S Africa. —**Zam′bi·an,** *adj., n.*

za·ny (zā′nē), *adj.,* **-ni·er, -ni·est,** *n., pl.* **-nies.** —*adj.* **1.** clownishly crazy or silly. —*n.* **2.** an absurdly silly person. **3.** a buffoon, esp. one who formerly mimicked the clown. [< It *zan(n)i,* var. of *Gianni* for *Giovanni* John] —**za′ni·ly,** *adv.* —**za′ni·ness,** *n.*

Zan·zi·bar (zan′zə bär′), *n.* an island off the E coast of Africa: part of Tanzania.

zap (zap), *v.,* **zapped, zap·ping,** *n. Slang.* —*v.t., v.i.* **1.** to kill, shoot, attack, or destroy, esp. with sudden speed. —*n.* **2.** force, energy, or drive.

ZBB, See **zero-base budgeting.**

zeal (zēl), *n.* earnest and diligent enthusiasm, as for a cause. —**Syn.** ardor, fervor, intensity, passion.

zeal·ot (zel′ət), *n.* a person who shows zeal, esp. to an undue or fanatic extent. —**zeal′ot·ry,** *n.*

zeal·ous (zel′əs), *adj.* full of, characterized by, or resulting from zeal. —**zeal′ous·ly,** *adv.* —**zeal′ous·ness,** *n.*

ze·bra (zē′brə), *n., pl.* **-bras, -bra.** a horselike African mammal having a white body covered by dark stripes.

ze·bu (zē′byōō), *n.* a domesticated, Asiatic bovine animal having a large hump over the shoulders.

zed (zed), *n. Brit.* the letter Z or z.

Zeit·geist (tsīt′gīst′), *n. German.* the general trend of thought and feeling of an era.

Zen (zen), *n.* a Buddhist movement whose emphasis is upon enlightenment by means of direct, intuitive insights. [< Jap < Chin < Skt: religious meditation]

ze·na·na (ze nä′nə), *n.* (in India) the part of the house in which the women of a high-caste family were formerly secluded.

ze·nith (zē′nith), *n.* **1.** the point in the sky which is directly overhead. **2.** the highest point or state. —**ze′nith·al** (-nə thəl), *adj.* —**Syn. 2.** acme, culmination, summit.

zeph·yr (zef′ər), *n.* **1.** *Literary.* **a.** a gentle, mild breeze. **b.** (*cap.*) the west wind. **2.** any fine, light fabric or yarn.

Zep·pe·lin (zep′ə lin), *n.* (*often l.c.*) an obsolete type of huge, cigar-shaped, rigid airship. [after Count Ferdinand von *Zeppelin,* 1838–1917, German designer]

ze·ro (zēr′ō), *n., pl.* **-ros, -roes,** *v.,* **-roed, -ro·ing,** *adj.* —*n.* **1.** the figure or numerical symbol 0. **2.** the origin of any kind of measurement on a scale. **3.** nothing or naught. **4.** the lowest point or degree. —*v.t.* **5. zero in,** to aim (a rifle, etc.) at the precise center of a target. **6. zero in on,** a.

to direct fire at the precise center of (a target). **b.** to concentrate upon (a problem, etc.). —*adj.* **7.** having a value of zero. **8.** without change or inflection: *a zero plural.*

ze′ro-base′ budg′eting (zēr′ō bās′), a process of justifying the entire budget every fiscal year or two rather than dealing only with proposed increases, as in government and corporate finance.

ze′ro hour′, 1. *Mil.* the time for the beginning of an attack. **2.** *Informal.* a decisive time.

ze′ro popula′tion growth′, a condition in which the population of a nation remains constant, attainable by having no more than two children in every family.

ze·ro-ze·ro (zēr′ō zēr′ō), *adj.* (of atmospheric conditions) having almost no visibility in both horizontal and vertical directions.

zest (zest), *n.* **1.** hearty enjoyment. **2.** anything added to give flavor or relish. **3.** piquancy or charm. —**zest′ful,** *adj.* —**zest′ful·ly,** *adv.* —**zest′ful·ness,** *n.* —**Syn. 1.** gusto.

ze·ta (zā′tə, zē′-), *n.* the sixth letter of the Greek alphabet (Z, ζ).

Zeus (zōōs), *n.* the supreme deity of the ancient Greeks.

zig·zag (zig′zag′), *n., adj., adv., v.,* **-zagged, -zag·ging.** —*n.* **1.** a line or course consisting of a series of sharp turns or angles in alternating directions. **2.** one of such turns, as in a path. —*adj.* **3.** formed in a zigzag. —*adv.* **4.** in a zigzag manner. —*v.t., v.i.* **5.** to proceed in or form into a zigzag.

zilch (zilch), *n.* *Slang.* zero or nothing.

zil·lion (zil′yən), *n.* *Informal.* an extremely large, indeterminate number.

zinc (zingk), *n., v.,* **zincked** or **zinced** (zingkt), **zinck·ing** or **zinc·ing** (zing′king). —*n.* **1.** *Chem.* a bluish-white metallic element used in making galvanized iron and alloys. *Symbol:* Zn; *at. wt.:* 65.37; *at. no.:* 30. —*v.t.* **2.** to coat with zinc.

zinc′ oint′ment, an ointment containing 20 percent of zinc oxide, used for skin conditions.

zinc′ ox′ide, a white powder used in paints, cosmetics, ointments, etc.

zing (zing), *n.* **1.** a sharp, singing noise. **2.** *Informal.* zestful vitality. —*v.i.* **3.** to move with zing.

zin·ni·a (zin′ē ə), *n.* a common plant grown for its colorful composite flowers.

Zi·on (zī′ən), *n.* **1.** a hill in Jerusalem, on which Solomon's Temple was built. **2.** the Jewish people. **3.** Palestine as the Jewish homeland and symbol of Judaism. **4.** heaven as the final gathering place of true believers.

Zi·on·ism (zī′ə niz′əm), *n.* a worldwide Jewish movement that resulted in the reestablishment and development of the state of Israel. —**Zi′onist,** *n., adj.*

zip[1] (zip), *n., v.,* **zipped, zip·ping.** *Informal.* —*n.* **1.** a sudden, brief hissing sound, as of a bullet. **2.** energy and speed. —*v.i.* **3.** to act or move with zip.

zip[2] (zip), *v.t.,* **zipped, zip·ping.** to fasten or unfasten with a zipper.

zip[3] (zip), *n., v.,* **zipped, zip·ping.** *Slang.* —*n.* **1.** zero or nothing, esp. as a sports score. —*v.t.* **2.** to defeat by keeping an opponent from scoring.

zip′ code′, a five-digit code assigned to each postal area and place with a view to expediting the sorting and delivery of mail. Also, **ZIP′ code′.** [z(*one*) *i*(*mprovement*) *p*(*rogram*)]

zip′ gun′, a makeshift homemade pistol.

zip·per (zip′ər), *n.* a device for joining two pieces of cloth, plastic, etc., consisting of two parallel rows of parts interlocked or parted by the motion of a slide. —**zip′pered,** *adj.*

zip·py (zip′ē), *adj.,* **-pi·er, -pi·est.** *Informal.* full of energy and speed.

zir·con (zûr′kon), *n.* a common mineral sometimes used as a gem.

zir·co·ni·um (zər kō′nē əm), *n.* *Chem.* a ductile metallic element resembling titanium, used in alloys, ceramics, etc. *Symbol:* Zr; *at. wt.:* 91.22; *at. no.:* 40.

zith·er (zith′ər), *n.* a musical instrument with 30 to 40 strings plucked with a plectrum and the fingertips. —**zith′er·ist,** *n.*

zlo·ty (zlô′tē), *n., pl.* **-tys, -ty.** the monetary unit of Poland.

Zn, zinc.

zo·di·ac (zō′dē ak′), *n.* **1.** an imaginary belt of the heavens, within which is the apparent annual path of the sun and which is divided into 12 divisions called *signs,* each named after a constellation. **2.** a diagram representing this belt. —**zo·di′a·cal** (-dī′ə kəl), *adj.*

zom·bie (zom′bē), *n.* **1.** the snake god worshiped in voodoo ceremonies. **2.** a supernatural force that brings a corpse to life. **3.** such a corpse. Also, **zom′bi.**

zon·al (zōn′əl), *adj.* **1.** of, pertaining to, or having the shape of a zone. **2.** Also, **zon·a·ry** (zō′nə rē). resembling a zone. —**zon′al·ly,** *adv.*

zone (zōn), *n., v.,* **zoned, zon·ing.** —*n.* **1.** any of five divisions of the earth's surface, bounded by lines parallel to the equator and named according to the prevailing temperature, comprising two Frigid Zones, two Temperate Zones, and the Torrid Zone. **2.** an area divided off or somehow differentiated from adjoining areas. **3.** any specific district or area, as one in a city under certain restrictions, esp. with regard to building. **4.** *Archaic.* a girdle or belt. —*v.t.* **5.** to divide into zones. **6.** to divide (an urban area) into zones in order to enforce building restrictions. **7.** to surround with a zone. [< L *zōna* < Gk *zōnē* belt] —**zo·na·tion** (zō nā′shən), *n.* —**zoned** (-d), *adj.*

zonked (zoṅgkt, zôṅgkt), *adj. Slang.* intoxicated or stupefied from alcohol or a drug.

zoo (zōō), *n.*, *pl.* **zoos.** See **zoological garden.**

zoo-, a combining form meaning "animal or pertaining to animals": *zoology.*

zool., **1.** zoological. **2.** zoology.

zo′olog′ical gar′den, a park or other enclosure in which live animals are kept for exhibition.

zo·ol·o·gy (zō ol′ə jē), *n.*, *pl.* **-gies.** the science dealing with animals. —**zo·o·log·i·cal** (zō′ə loj′i kəl), **zo·o·log′ic,** *adj.* —**zo·o·log′i·cal·ly,** *adv.* —**zo·ol′o·gist,** *n.*

zoom (zōōm), *v.i.* **1.** to move rapidly with a loud hum or buzz. **2.** to fly an airplane suddenly and sharply upward. **3.** to rise suddenly and sharply, as prices. **4.** to focus a camera with a zoom lens. —*v.t.* **5.** to cause to zoom. —*n.* **6.** the act of zooming.

zoom′ lens′, a lens assembly, as in a television camera, whose focal length can be adjusted continuously to provide various magnifications with no loss of focus.

zo·o·phyte (zō′ə fīt′), *n.* any of various invertebrate animals resembling a plant, as a coral or sea anemone.

zo·o·plank·ton (zō′ə plaṅgk′tən), *n.* the animal organisms in plankton.

zoot′ suit′ (zōōt), a suit with baggy, tapering pants and an oversized coat. —**zoot′-suit′er,** *n.*

Zo·ro·as·ter (zōr′ō as′tər, zôr′-), *n.* 6th century B.C., Persian religious teacher. —**Zo′ro·as′tri·an,** *n.*, *adj.*

Zo·ro·as·tri·an·ism (zōr′ō as′trē ə niz′əm, zôr′-), *n.* an Iranian religion founded by Zoroaster, postulating a supreme deity.

Zou·ave (zōō äv′, zwäv), *n.* one of a former body of French infantry, distinguished by their picturesque uniforms.

zounds (zoundz), *interj. Archaic.* (used as a mild oath.) [(*God*)′s (*w*)*ounds*]

zoy·si·a (zoi′sē ə), *n.* a hardy perennial grass often used for lawns.

ZPG, See **zero population growth.**

Zr, zirconium.

zuc·chet·to (zōō ket′ō), *n.* a small, round skullcap worn by Roman Catholic ecclesiastics.

zuc·chi·ni (zōō kē′nē), *n.*, *pl.* **-ni, -nis.** a cucumberlike summer squash having a smooth, dark-green skin.

Zu·lu (zōō′lōō), *n.*, *pl.* **-lus, -lu,** *adj.* —*n.* **1.** a people of SE Africa. **2.** their language. —*adj.* **3.** of the Zulus or their language.

Zu·ñi (zōō′nyē, -nē, sōō′-), *n.*, *pl.* **-ñis, -ñi. 1.** a member of a pueblo-dwelling tribe of Indians inhabiting western New Mexico. **2.** their language. —**Zu′ñi·an,** *adj.*, *n.*

Zu·rich (zōōr′ik), *n.* a city in N Switzerland.

zwie·back (zwī′bak′, -bäk′, zwē′-, swī′-), *n.* an egg bread that is baked and then sliced and toasted.

zy·gote (zī′gōt, zig′ōt), *n.* **1.** the cell produced by the union of two gametes. **2.** the individual developing from such a cell. —**zy·got·ic** (zī got′ik, zi-), *adj.*

zy·mur·gy (zī′mûr jē), *n.* the branch of chemistry dealing with fermentation, as in brewing.

Common Signs and Symbols

ASTRONOMY

Astronomical Bodies

☉   1. the sun. 2. Sunday.

☽   } 1. the moon. 2. Monday.

} new moon.

} the moon, first quarter.

○ } full moon.

} the moon, last quarter.

☿   1. Mercury. 2. Wednesday.

♀   1. Venus. 2. Friday.

⊕
☉ } Earth.
⊖

♂   1. Mars. 2. Tuesday.

♃   1. Jupiter. 2. Thursday.

♄   1. Saturn. 2. Saturday.

} Uranus.

Ψ   Neptune.

P   Pluto.

✳
✴ } star.

☄   comet.

Signs of the Zodiac

Spring Signs

♈   Aries, the Ram.

♉   Taurus, the Bull.

♊ } Gemini, the Twins.

Summer Signs

♋ } Cancer, the Crab.

♌   Leo, the Lion.

♍   Virgo, the Virgin.

Autumn Signs

♎   Libra, the Scales.

♏   Scorpio, the Scorpion.

♐   Sagittarius, the Archer.

Winter Signs

♑ } Capricorn, the Goat.

♒   Aquarius, the Water Bearer.

♓   Pisces, the Fishes.

BIOLOGY

♂   male; a male organism, organ, or cell; a staminate flower or plant.

♀   female; a female organism, organ, or cell; a pistillate flower or plant.

□   a male.

○   a female.

✕   crossed with; denoting a sexual hybrid.

1036

BUSINESS

@	at; as in: eggs @ 60¢ per dozen.
a/c	account.
B/E	bill of exchange.
B/L	bill of lading.
B/S	bill of sale.
c.&f.	cost and freight.
c/o	care of.
L/C	letter of credit.
O/S	out of stock.
P&L	profit and loss.
w/	with.
w/o	without.
#	**1.** (before a figure or figures) number; numbered; as in: #40 thread. **2.** (after a figure or figures) pound(s); as in: 20#.
%	percent; per hundred.

MATHEMATICS

Arithmetic and Algebra

+   **1.** plus; add. **2.** positive; positive value; as: +64. **3.** denoting underestimated approximate accuracy, with some figures omitted at the end; as in: $\pi = 3.14159+$.

−   **1.** minus; subtract. **2.** negative; negative value; as −64. **3.** denoting overestimated approximate accuracy, with some figures omitted at the end; as in: $\pi = 3.1416-$.

±   **1.** plus or minus; add or subtract; as in: $4 \pm 2 = 6$ or 2. **2.** positive or negative; as in: $\sqrt{a^2} = \pm a$. **3.** denoting the probable error associated with a figure derived by experiment and observation, approximate calculation, etc.

$\left. \begin{array}{c} \times \\ \cdot \end{array} \right\}$ times; multiplied by; as in: $2 \times 4 = 2 \cdot 4$.

$\left. \begin{array}{c} \div \\ / \\ — \end{array} \right\}$ divided by; as in: $8 \div 2 = 8/2 = \frac{8}{2} = 4$.

$\left. \begin{array}{c} : \\ / \\ — \end{array} \right\}$ denoting the ratio of (in proportion).

=   equals; is equal to.

∷   equals; is equal to (in proportion); as in: $6 : 3 :: 8 : 4$.

$\left.\begin{array}{c}\neq \\ \neq\end{array}\right\}$	is not equal to.
≡	is identical with.
$\left.\begin{array}{c}\not\equiv \\ \not\equiv\end{array}\right\}$	is not identical with.
≈	is approximately equal to.
∼.	**1.** is equivalent to. **2.** is similar to.
>	is greater than.
≫	is much greater than.
<	is less than.
≪	is much less than.
≯	is not greater than.
≮	is not less than.
$\left.\begin{array}{c}\geqq \\ \geq\end{array}\right\}$	is equal to or greater than.
$\left.\begin{array}{c}\leqq \\ \leq\end{array}\right\}$	is equal to or less than.
∝	varies directly as; is directly proportional to; as in: $x \propto y$.
$\left.\begin{array}{c}\sqrt{} \\ \sqrt{}\end{array}\right\}$	the radical sign, indicating the square root of; as in: $\sqrt{81} = 9$.
( )	parentheses; as in: $2(a + b)$.'
[ ]	brackets; as in: $4 + 3[a(a + b)]$.
{ }	braces; as in: $5 + b\{(a + b)\ [2 - a(a + b)] - 3\}$.
', ", ''', etc.	prime, double prime, triple prime, etc., used to indicate: *a.* constants, as distinguished from the variable denoted by a letter alone. *b.* a variable under different conditions, at different times, etc.
∪	union
∩	intersection
⊂, ⊆	is a subset of
⊃, ⊇	contains as a subset
⊄	is not a subset of
⊅	does not contain as a subset
∅, ∧, O	set containing no numbers; empty set
∈	is a member of
∉	is not a member of

Geometry

∠   angle; as in: ∠ABC, (*pl.* ∡s).

⊥   **1.** a perpendicular (*pl.* ⊥s). **2.** is perpendicular to; as in: AB ⊥ CD.

‖	**1.** a parallel (*pl.* ‖ s). **2.** is parallel to; as in: AB‖CD.
△	triangle; as in: △ABC, (*pl.* △).
▱	rectangle; as in: ▱ABCD.
□	square; as in: □ABCD.
▱	parallelogram; as in: ▱ABCD.
○	circle (*pl.* ○)
≅	is congruent to; as in:
	△ABD ≅ △CEF.
∼	is similar to; as in:
	△ACE ∼ △BDF.
∴	therefore; hence.
∵	since; because.
π	the Greek letter pi, representing the ratio (3.14159 +) of the circumference of a circle to its diameter.
⌒	(over a group of letters) indicating an arc of a circle; as: ⌒GH, the arc between points G and H.
°	degree(s) of arc; as in: 90°.
′	minute(s) of arc; as in: 90°30′.
″	second(s) of arc; as in: 90°30′15″.

MEDICINE

℞	take (L. *recipe*).
°	degree(s).
A, AA, a, aa	of each.
Э	scruple.
Эss	half a scruple.
Эi	one scruple.
Эiss	a scruple and a half.
Эij	two scruples.
ʒ	dram.
ʒss	half a dram.
ʒi	one dram.
ʒiss	a dram and a half.
ʒij	two drams.
℥	ounce.
℥ss	half an ounce.
℥i	one ounce.
℥iss	an ounce and a half.
℥ij	two ounces.
ℳ	minim.
fʒ	fluid dram.
f℥	fluid ounce.

MISCELLANEOUS

&	the ampersand, meaning *and*.
&c.	et cetera; and others; and so forth; and so on.
′	foot; feet; as in: 6′ = six feet.
″	inch; inches; as in: 6′2″ = six feet, two inches.
×	**1.** by: used in stating dimensions; as in: 2′×4′×1′; a 2″×4″ board. **2.** a sign (the cross) made in place of a signature by a person who cannot write; as in:

his

George × Walsh

mark.

†	died.
©	copyright; copyrighted.
®	registered; registered trademark.
°	degree
*	asterisk
†	dagger
‡	double dagger
/	slash; diagonal
¶	paragraph mark.
§	section mark.
″	ditto; indicating the same as the aforesaid: used in lists, etc.
~	tilde
^	circumflex
¸	(with *c*) cedilla
´	acute accent
`	grave accent
¨	dieresis
¯	macron
˘	breve

MONETARY

$ $	**1.** dollar(s), in the United States, Canada, Liberia, etc. **2.** peso(s), in Colombia, Mexico, etc. **3.** cruzeiro(s), in Brazil. **4.** escudo(s), in Portugal.
¢	cent(s), in the United States, Canada, etc.
£	pound(s), in United Kingdom, Ireland, etc.

p   new penny (new pence), in United Kingdom, Ireland, etc.

/ } (formerly) shilling(s), in United
s. } Kingdom, Ireland, etc.

d.   (formerly) penny (pence), in United Kingdom, Ireland, etc.

¥   yen (yen), in Japan.

RELIGION

†   the cross: a symbol of Christianity.

☩   Celtic cross: used esp. as a symbol of the Presbyterian Church.

☦   three-barred cross; Russian cross: used esp. as a symbol of the Russian Orthodox Church.

✛   Greek cross: used esp. as a symbol of the Greek Orthodox Church.

✠ } **1.** a cross used by the pope and by
+ } Roman Catholic archbishops and bishops before their names. **2.** an indication inserted at those points in the service at which the sign of the cross is made.

✡   star of David: a symbol of Judaism.

☾   crescent: a symbol of Islam.

℟   response: used in prayer books.

✱   an indication used in Roman Catholic service books to separate a verse of a psalm into two parts, showing where the response begins.

℣   an indication used in service books to show the point at which a versicle begins.

☯   ancient Chinese symbol representing the principles of yin and yang.

Foreign Alphabets

GREEK

Letter		Name	Transliter-ation
A	α	alpha	a
B	β	beta	b
Γ	γ	gamma	g
Δ	δ	delta	d
E	ε	epsilon	e
Z	ζ	zeta	z
H	η	eta	e (or ē)
Θ	θ	theta	th
I	ι	iota	i
K	κ	kappa	k
Λ	λ	lambda	l
M	μ	mu	m
N	ν	nu	n
Ξ	ξ	xi	x
O	ο	omicron	o
Π	π	pi	p
P	ρ	rho	r
Σ	σ,ς[1]	sigma	s
T	τ	tau	t
Υ	υ	upsilon	y
Φ	φ	phi	ph
X	χ	chi	ch, kh
Ψ	ψ	psi	ps
Ω	ω	omega	o (or ō)

[1] At end of word.

HEBREW

Letter	Name	Transliter-ation
א	aleph	- or '
ב	beth	b, v
ג	gimel	g
ד	daleth	d
ה	he	h
ו	vav	v, w
ז	zayin	z
ח	cheth	ḥ
ט	teth	ṭ
י	yod	y, j, i
כ ך '	kaph	k, kh
ל	lamed	l
מ ם '	mem	m
נ ן '	nun	n
ס	samekh	s
ע	ayin	'
פ ף '	pe	p, f
צ ץ '	sadi	ṣ
ק	koph	ḳ
ר	resh	r
ש	shin	sh, š
ש	śin	ś
ת	tav	t

[1] At end of word.

RUSSIAN

Letter		Transliteration
А	а	a
Б	б	b
В	в	v
Г	г	g
Д	д	d
E	e	e, ye
Ж	ж	zh
З	з	z
И	и	i
Й	й	ĭ, i
К	к	k
Л	л	l
М	м	m
Н	н	n
О	о	o
П	п	p
Р	р	r
С	с	s
Т	т	t
У	у	u
Ф	ф	f
Х	х	kh, x
Ц	ц	ts, c
Ч	ч	ch, č
Ш	ш	sh, š
Щ	щ	shch, šč
Ы	ы	i
Ь	ь	'
Э	э	e
Ю	ю	yu, ju
Я	я	ya, ja

Basic Manual of Style

The style practices described in this concise guide are those generally prevalent in current English. This manual presents the more commonly accepted alternatives, noting the situations in which a particular usage is preferred. Having made a choice, the writer should maintain the same usage throughout any single document. As in all writing, consistency of style is essential.

PUNCTUATION

PERIOD (.)

Use a period:

1. To end a declarative or imperative sentence (but not an exclamatory sentence).

   The meeting was amicable and constructive.

   Please pass the salt.

   Read the next two chapters before Friday.

2. To end an indirect question.

   He asked when the plane was leaving.

3. To end a polite request even when stated as a question.

   Will you please reply promptly.

4. To end a sentence fragment.

   Not in the least.

   A novel of suspense.

5. To follow most abbreviations.

   Mr., Mrs., Ms., Jr., Dr., N.J., etc., e.g., B.C., A.D.

   (See ABBREVIATIONS below.)

6. To separate dollars from cents in writing figures.

   $25.00 $2.98

7. To use as a decimal point in writing figures.

   98.6 degrees $3.7 million

ELLIPSIS (...or....)

Use an ellipsis mark (three or four consecutive periods) to indicate that part of a quoted sentence has been omitted.

1. If the omission occurs at the beginning or in the middle of the sentence, use three periods in the ellipsis.

   "...the book is lively...and well written."

2. If the last part of the sentence is omitted or if entire sentences are omitted, add a fourth period to the ellipsis to mark the end of the sentence.

   "He left his home....Years later he returned to find everything had changed...."

QUESTION MARK (?)

Use a question mark:

1. To end a sentence, clause, or phrase (or after a single word) that asks a question.

   Who invited him to the party?

   "Is something wrong?" she asked.

   Whom shall we elect? Smith? Jones?

2. To indicate doubt or uncertainty.

   The manuscript dates back to 560 (?) B.C.

EXCLAMATION POINT (!)

Use an exclamation point to end a sentence, clause, phrase, or even a single word that indicates strong emotion or feeling, especially surprise, command, admiration, etc.

> Go away!   Wow!
> What a day this has been!
> "Hey, there!" he shouted.

COMMA (,)

Use a comma only when you have a definite reason for doing so in accordance with the guidelines below. A safe rule to follow is, "When in doubt, leave it out."

Use a comma:

1. To separate words, phrases, and clauses that are part of a series of three or more items.

> The Dutch are an industrious, friendly, generous, and hospitable people.
>
> The chief agricultural products of Denmark are butter, eggs, potatoes, beets, wheat, barley, and oats.

It is permissible to omit the final comma before the *and* in a series of words as long as the absence of a comma does not interfere with clarity of meaning. The final commas in the examples above, while desirable, are not essential.

In many cases, however, the inclusion or omission of a comma before the conjunction can materially affect the meaning. In the following sentence, omission of the final comma might indicate incorrectly that the tanks as well as the vehicles, were amphibious.

> Their equipment included airplanes, helicopters, artillery, amphibious vehicles, and tanks.

Do not use commas to separate two items treated as a single unit within a series.

> For breakfast he ordered orange juice, bread and butter, coffee, and bacon and eggs.

But

> At the supermarket he bought orange juice, bread, butter, bacon, and eggs.

Do not use commas to separate adjectives which are so closely related that they appear to form a single element with the noun they modify. Adjectives which refer to the number, age (old, young, new), size, color, or location of the

noun often fall within this category. A simple test can usually determine the appropriateness of a comma in such instances: If *and* cannot replace the comma without creating a clumsy, almost meaningless effect, it is safe to conclude that a comma is also out of place.

> twenty happy little youngsters
> a dozen large blue dresses
> several dingy old Western mining towns
> beautiful tall white birches

But commas must be used in the following cases where clarity demands separation of the items in a series:

> a dozen large blue, red, yellow, and green crayons
> twenty old, young, and middle-aged spectators

In a series of phrases or dependent clauses, place a comma before the conjunction.

> He sold his business, rented his house, gave up his car, paid his creditors, and set off for Tahiti.
>
> They strolled along the city streets, browsed in the bookshops, and dined at their favorite cafe.

2. To separate independent clauses joined by the coordinating conjunctions *and, but, yet, for, or, nor, so.*

> Almost anyone knows how to earn money, but not one in a million knows how to spend it.

The comma may be omitted in sentences consisting of two short independent clauses.

> We missed the train but we caught the bus in time.

3. To separate a long introductory phrase or subordinate clause from the rest of the sentence.

> Having rid themselves of their former rulers, the people now disagreed on the new leadership.
>
> Although the equipment has not yet been fully developed, scientists are confident of landing astronauts on other planets.

4. To set off words of direct address, interjections, or transitional words used to introduce a sentence (*oh, yes, no, however, nevertheless, still, anyway, well, why, frankly, really, moreover, incidentally,* etc.).

Jim, where have you been?
Oh, here's our new neighbor.
Why, you can't mean that!
Still, you must agree that she knows her business.
Fine, we'll get together.
Well, can you imagine that!

5. To set off an introductory modifier (adjective, adverb, participle, participial phrase) even if it consists of only one word or a short phrase.

Politically, our candidate has proved to be very astute.

Angrily, the delegates stalked out of the conference.

Pleased with the result, he beamed at his painting.

6. To set off a nonrestrictive clause or phrase (an element which is not essential to the basic meaning of the sentence). Place commas both before and after the nonrestrictive portion.

Our professor did not agree that corporations should be protected as "persons" under the Fourteenth Amendment, although the Supreme Court had held that they were.

The old hotel, which had housed visiting celebrities for almost a century, remained outwardly unchanged.

7. To set off appositives or appositive phrases. Place commas both before and after the appositive.

March, the month of crocuses, can still bring snow and ice.

One of our major problems, narcotics, remains unsolved.

Ms. Case, chairperson of the committee, refused to comment.

8. To set off parenthetical words and phrases as well as words of direct address.

You may, if you insist, demand a retraction.

St. Peter's Place, they agreed, is one of the best schools in San Francisco.

The use of pesticides, however, has its disadvantages.

They knew, nevertheless, that all was lost.

Mr. Brown, far younger in spirit than his seventy years, delighted in his grandchildren.

You realize, Nettie, that we may never return to Paris.

9. To set off quoted matter from the rest of the sentence.
(See QUOTATION MARKS below.)

10. To set off items in dates.

Both John Adams and Thomas Jefferson died on July 4, 1826.

A comma is optional when only the month and year are given in a date.

Washington was born in February, 1732, in Virginia.

or

Washington was born in February 1732, in Virginia.

11. To set off elements in addresses and geographical locations when the items are written on the same line. Do not, however, use a comma before the zip code.

35 Fifth Avenue, New York, N.Y. 10002

1515 South Halsted Street, Chicago, Illinois 60607

He lived in Lima, Peru, for fifteen years.

12. To set off titles of individuals.

Dr. Martin Price, Dean of Admissions

Mrs. Rose Winthrop, President

13. To set off the salutation in a personal letter.

Dear Steve,

14. To set off the closing in a letter.

Sincerely yours,
Very truly yours,

15. To denote an omitted word or words in one or more parallel constructions within a sentence.

Ethel is studying Greek; George, Latin.

16. To mark off thousands in numbers of one thousand or more. (The comma is optional in numbers under 10,000.)

7,500 or 7500
11,900   250,631   3,963,426

SEMICOLON (;)

Use a semicolon:

1. To separate independent clauses not joined by a conjunction.

The house burned down; it was the last shattering blow.

The war against poverty must continue; it must be our highest priority.

2. To separate independent clauses that are joined by such conjunctive adverbs as *hence, however, therefore,* etc.

The funds are inadequate; therefore, the project will close down.

Orders exceed all expectations; however, there is a shortage of supplies.

3. To separate long or possibly ambiguous items in a series, especially when the items already include commas.

The elected officers are Jonathan Crane, president; Sarah Huntley, vice president; Edward Stone, secretary; and Susan Morrell, treasurer.

4. To separate elements that are closely related but cannot be joined without creating confusion.

Poverty is unbearable; luxury, insufferable.

5. To precede an abbreviation, word, or phrase (*e.g., i.e., namely, for example*) that introduces an explanatory or summarizing statement.

On the advice of his broker, he chose to invest in major industries; i.e., steel, automobiles, and oil.

COLON (:)

Use a colon:

1. To introduce a series or list of items, examples, or the like.

The three committees are as follows: membership, finance, and legislation. He named his favorite poets: Langston Hughes, W. H. Auden, and Emily Dickinson.

2. To introduce a long formal statement, quotation, or question.

This I believe: All people are created equal and must enjoy equally the rights that are inalienably theirs.

Busch replied: "You are right. There can be no unilateral peace just as there can be no unilateral war. No one will contest that view."

This is the issue: Can an employer dismiss a man simply because he is a member of a union?

3. To follow a formal salutation, as in a business letter or speech.

Dear Mr. Chadwin: Dear Madam:
Dear Ms. Sanchez: Gentlemen:
To Whom It May Concern:
My Fellow Americans:

4. To follow introductory words in a memorandum.

To: Mary Falcon
From: Andrew Casillo

Subject: Book Sales in Quebec

5. To follow the word *Attention* below both the inside and outside address when the writer wishes to bring a letter to the attention of a particular individual within an organization.

Attention: Ms. Jennie Huntley

6. To follow the name of the speaker in a play.

Ghost: Pity me not, but lend thy serious hearing to what I shall unfold.
Hamlet: Speak; I am bound to hear.

7. To separate parts of a citation.

a. Place a colon between chapter and verse numbers in biblical references.
Genesis 3:2.

b. Place a colon between volume and page numbers of periodicals.
Journal of Astronomy 15:237-261.

8. To separate hours from minutes in indicating time.

1:30 p.m. (or P.M.)
2:00 A.M. (or a.m.)

9. To indicate that an initial clause in a sentence will be further explained or illustrated by the material which follows the colon. In effect, the colon is a substitute for such phrases as "for example" or "namely."

It was a city notorious for its inadequacies: its schools were antiquated, its administration was corrupt, and everyone felt the burden of its taxes.

APOSTROPHE (')

Use an apostrophe:

1. To denote the omission of letters, figures, or numerals.

a. The contraction of a word or phrase:

nat'l	o'er	ne'er
ma'am	couldn't	he'll
I'm	you're	it's
she's	we're	they're

Do not confuse *it's* (contraction of *it is*) with the possessive *its*, which does not contain an apostrophe.

b. The contraction of a number, usually a date:

the Spirit of '76   the Class of '48

c. The omission of letters in quoting dialect:

"I ain't goin' back 'cause I'm doin' mighty fine now."

2. To denote the possessive case of nouns.

a. To form the possessive of most singular and plural nouns or of indefinite pronouns not ending in *s*, add an apostrophe and an *s*.

　　the city's industries　　anyone's guess
　　the women's clubs
　　a bachelor's degree

b. To form the possessive of singular nouns of one syllable ending in *s* or the sound of *s*, add an apostrophe and an *s* in most instances.

　　the horse's mane　　Bess's house
　　the class's average　　Lance's car

But if the addition of an *s* would produce an awkward sound or visual effect, add only an apostrophe. This rule applies more frequently, but not exclusively, to words of more than one syllable.

　　Socrates' concepts　　Jesus' teachings
　　Moses' influence
　　for old times' sake

In some cases either form is acceptable.

　　Mr. Jones's (or Jones') employees
　　Keats's (or Keats') poetry

c. To form the possessive of plural nouns (both common and proper) ending in *s*, add only an apostrophe.

　　farmers' problems
　　the Smiths' travels
　　students' views
　　the Joneses' relatives
　　critics' reviews
　　three months' delay

Note, however, that plurals not ending in *s* form their possessive by adding the apostrophe and *s*.

　　men's clothing　　women's hats

d. To denote possession in most compound constructions, add the apostrophe and *s* to the last word of the compound.

　　anyone else's property
　　one another's books
　　brother-in-law's job
　　the attorney general's office

e. To denote possession by two or more proper names, add the apostrophe and *s* to the last name only.

　　Brown, Ross and King's law firm
　　Japan and West Germany's
　　　agreement
　　Lewis and Clark's expedition

f. To denote individual ownership by two or more proper names, add the apostrophe and an *s* to both names.

　　Bruce's and Gina's records.

3. To form the plurals of letters or figures add an apostrophe and an *s*.

　　Dot the i's and cross the t's.
　　33 r.p.m's　　+'s and −'s　　C.O.D.'s
　　figure 8's　　the 1890's (or 1890s)　　V.I.P.'s
　　m's　　PX's　　GI's

QUOTATION MARKS
(" " – Double) (' ' – Single)

NOTE: Unless otherwise noted, double quotation marks are used. For use of single quotation marks, see 1 b.

Use quotation marks:

1. To enclose a direct quotation.

a. To mark words, phrases, sentences, paragraphs, or poetic stanzas which are quoted verbatim from the original.

　　Portia's speech on "The quality of mercy" is one of the most quoted passages from Shakespeare.

　　It was Shaw who wrote: "All great truths begin as blasphemies."

b. To enclose a quotation within a quotation, in which case *single* quotation marks are used.

　　Reading Jill's letter, Pat said, "Listen to this! 'I've just received notice that I made Dean's list.' Isn't she great?"

2. To enclose certain titles:

a. To enclose titles of newspaper and magazine articles, essays, stories, poems, and chapters of books. The quotation marks serve to distinguish such literary pieces from the books or periodicals (these are italicized) in which they appear.

　　Our anthology contains such widely assorted pieces as Bacon's essay "Of Studies," Poe's "The Gold Bug," Keats's "Ode to a Nightingale," and an article on travel from *Mclean's*.

b. To enclose titles of short musical compositions and songs as distinct from symphonies and operas, which are italicized.

　　The national anthem is "The Star-Spangled Banner."

　　Even the youngsters laughed at the "Figaro" aria from *The Barber of Seville*.

c. To enclose titles of works of art such as paintings, drawings, photographs, and sculpture. These may also be italicized.

Most people recognize Da Vinci's "Mona Lisa" and Rodin's "The Thinker."

d. To enclose titles of radio and television programs or of episodes within a series (in which case, the name of the series is italicized).

a recent *Nova* special, "Children of the Forest"

e. To enclose titles of plays only if they are referred to as part of a larger collection. Referred to as single volumes, they are italicized.

"The Wild Duck" is the Ibsen play included in this edition of *Modern European Plays*.

3. To emphasize a word or phrase which is itself the subject of discussion. Italics may be used for the same purpose.

The words "imply" and "infer" are not synonymous.

Such Freudian terms as the "ego," the "superego," the "id," and the "libido" are now considered part of the English language.

4. To draw attention to an uncommon word or phrase, a technical term, or a usage very different in style (e.g., dialect or unusual slang) from the context. Italics are often used for the same purpose.

Teachers are no longer dismayed when students smirk at "square" traditions.

In glass blowing, the molten glass is called "metal."

5. To suggest ironic use of a word or phrase.

The radio blasting forth John's favorite "music" is to his grandfather an instrument of torture.

Bernstein's skiing "vacation" consisted of three weeks with his leg in a cast.

NOTE: If a quotation consists of two or more consecutive paragraphs, use quotation marks at the beginning of each paragraph, but place them at the end of the last paragraph only.

Quotation marks in combination with other punctuation

1. Period. Always place a period *before* the end quotation mark.

One angry commuter complained of "the incredible delays and breakdowns."

2. Comma.

a. Always place a final comma *before* the end quotation mark.

"The delays and breakdowns are incredible," complained one commuter.

b. Use a comma between the quoted matter and such phrases as "according to the report," "she wrote," "he replied," "they asked," etc.

According to the Declaration of Independence, "all men are created equal."

"There never was a good war or a bad peace," wrote Benjamin Franklin.

(CAUTION: Do not use the comma following interrogative or exclamatory quotations. See 3 below.)

3. Question mark or exclamation point.

When a question mark or exclamation point is part of the quoted passage, place these marks *before* the end quotation mark.

"Hurry, please, before it's too late!" she cried.

"Is there any hope of recovering the property?" he asked.

In all other cases, place the exclamation point or question mark *after* the end quotation mark.

Did Pangloss really mean it when he said, "This is the best of all possible worlds"?

How absurd of him to say that "This is the best of all possible worlds"!

4. Colon or semicolon.

Always place a colon or semicolon *after* the end quotation mark.

The boys had always called Tom "the champ"; he began to wonder if the reputation would endure.

There were several reasons why Tom was acknowledged as "the champ": physical strength, intellectual superiority, and qualities of leadership.

5. Dash.

Use a dash to set off the name of the author following a quotation on the same line.

"Pleasure's a sin, and sometimes sin's a pleasure." —Byron.

PARENTHESES ( )

Use parentheses:

1. To enclose material that is not part of the main sentence but is too relevant to omit.

    Faulkner's novels (published by Random House) were selected as prizes.

    The data (see Table 13) was very impressive.

2. To enclose part of a sentence that, if enclosed by commas, would be confusing.

    The authors he published (none other than Schulte, MacGregor and Johnson) were among his best friends.

3. To enclose an explanatory item that is not part of the statement or sentence.

    She wrote to *The Paris* (Illinois) *News.*

4. To enclose numbers or letters that designate each item in a series.

    The project is (1) too time-consuming, (2) too expensive, and (3) poorly staffed.

    He was required to take courses in (a) mathematics, (b) English, (c) history, and (d) geology.

5. To enclose a numerical figure used to confirm a spelled-out number which precedes it.

    Enclosed is a check for ten dollars ($10.00) to cover the cost of the order.

BRACKETS [ ]

Brackets are used in pairs to enclose figures, phrases, or sentences that are meant to be set apart from the context—usually a direct quotation.

Use brackets:

1. To set off a notation, explanation or editorial comment that is inserted in quoted material and is not part of the original text.

    According to the Globe critic, "This [*Man and Superman*] is one of Shaw's greatest plays."

    Or substitute the bracketed proper name for the pronoun: "[*Man and Superman*] is one of Shaw's...."

    "Now that the astronauts have set new records for survival in Space [84 days in *Skylab 4* and 96 days in *Soyuz 26*], space travel for the general public may be realized in our lifetime."

    "Young as they are," he writes, "these students are afflicted with cynicism, world-weariness, and *a total dis-*

regard for tradition and authority." [Emphasis is mine.]

2. To correct an error in a quotation.

    "It was on April 25, 1944 [1945—Ed.] that delegates representing forty-six countries met in San Francisco."

3. To indicate that an error in fact, spelling, punctuation, or language usage is quoted deliberately in an effort to reproduce the original statement with complete accuracy. The questionable fact or expression is followed by the Latin word *sic*, meaning "thus," which is enclosed in brackets.

    "George Washington lived during the seventeenth [*sic*] century."

    "The Missisipi [*sic*] is the longest river in the U.S.," he wrote.

4. To enclose stage directions in plays. Parentheses may also be used for this purpose.

    JULIET: [*Snatching Romeo's dagger*]...O happy dagger! This is thy sheath; [*Stabs herself*] there rest and let me die.

5. To enclose comments made on a verbatim transcription of a speech, debate, or testimony.

    MR. KRINSLEY: The steady rise in taxes must be halted. [*Applause*]

6. To substitute for parentheses within material already enclosed by parentheses. Although it is not seen frequently, this device is sometimes used in footnotes.

    ¹See "René Descartes" (M. C. Beardsley, *The European Philosophers from Descartes to Nietzsche* [New York: Random House, 1960]).

7. To enclose the publication date, inserted by the editor, of an item appearing in an earlier issue of a periodical. This device is used in letters to the editor or in articles written on subjects previously reported. Parentheses may also be used for this purpose.

    Dear Sir: Your excellent article on China [April 15] brings to mind my recent experience...

    When removing old wallpaper [*Handyman's Monthly,* June 1977] make sure that you...

DASH (—)

Use a dash:

1. To mark an abrupt change in thought or

grammatical construction in the middle of a sentence.

> We won the game—but I'm getting ahead of the story.

2. To suggest halting or hesitant speech.

> "Well—er—ah—it's hard to explain," he faltered.

3. To indicate a sudden break or interruption before a sentence is completed.

> "Eric, don't climb up that—" It was too late.

4. To add emphasis to parenthetical material or to mark an emphatic separation between parenthetical material and the rest of a sentence.

> Her influence—she was a powerful figure in the community—was a deterrent to effective opposition.
>
> The excursions for school groups—to museums, zoos, and theaters—are less expensive.
>
> The car he was driving—a gleaming black limousine—was the most impressive thing about him.

5. To set off an appositive or an appositive phrase when a comma would provide less than the desired emphasis on the appositive or when the use of commas might result in confusion with commas within the appositive phrase.

> The premier's promise of changes—land reform, higher wages, reorganization of industry—was not easily fulfilled.

6. To replace an offensive word or part of one.

> Where's that son of a b—?

SLASH (/)

Use a slash:

1. To indicate the end of a line in quoting verse.

> ...the play's the thing/Wherein I'll catch the conscience of the King.

2. To indicate alternative expressions such as *he/she, and/or,* etc. Use this device sparingly.

> The driver must show his/her license to the police.
>
> The tour includes Sweden and/or Norway.
>
> The owner/renter is required to clear the sidewalk.

HYPHEN (-)

The hyphenation of compound nouns and modifiers is often arbitrary, inconsistent, and subject to change. Practices vary. When in doubt, it is best to consult the dictionary.

Use a hyphen:

1. To spell out a word or name.

> r-e-a-s-o-n   C-a-r-l-u-c-c-i

2. To divide a word into syllables.

> hal-lu-ci-na-tion

3. To mark the division of a word of more than one syllable at the end of a line; indicating that the word is to be completed on the following line.

> It is difficult to estimate the damaging psychological effects of racism and sexism.

4. To separate the parts (when spelling out numerals) of a compound number from twenty-one to ninety-nine.

> thirty-six inches to the yard
> Fifty-second Street
> nineteen hundred and forty-three

5. To express decades in words.

> the nineteen-twenties
> the eighteen-sixties

6. To indicate a range of numbers, as in dates or pages.

> the Civil War, 1861-1865
> pages 98-130

7. To separate (when spelling out numerals) the numerator from the denominator of a fraction, especially a fraction which is used as an adjective.

> one-half cup of milk
> a two-thirds majority

When fractions are used as nouns, the hyphen is optional.

> three fourths (or three-fourths) of his constituents
> one fifth (or one-fifth) of the class

Do not use a hyphen to indicate a fraction if either the numerator or denominator is already hyphenated.

> one thirty-second
> forty-five hundredths
> twenty-one thirty-sixths

8. To form certain compound nouns.

> **a.** Nouns consisting of two or more words which show the combination of two or more constituents, qualities, or functions in one person or thing.
>
> secretary-treasurer   city-state

teacher-counselor   AFL-CIO

b. Nouns made up of two or more words, including other parts of speech.

cease-fire	fourth-grader
coat-of-arms	hand-me-down
court-martial	has-been
cure-all	post-mortem

Do not hyphenate compound nouns denoting chemical terms, military rank, or certain governmental positions.

hydrogen sulfide
sodium chloride
carbon tetrachloride
vice admiral
lieutenant governor
justice of the peace
sergeant at arms
brigadier general
lieutenant junior grade
attorney general
private first class

9. To connect the elements of a compound modifier when used *before* the noun it modifies. In most cases, the same modifier is not hyphenated if it *follows* the noun it modifies.

> They engaged in hand-to-hand combat.
>
> They fought hand to hand.
>
> They endured a hand-to-mouth existence.
>
> They lived hand to mouth.
>
> a well-known expert
>
> an expert who is well known
>
> an 8,000-foot peak
>
> The peak was 8000 feet high.

Do not hyphenate a compound modifier which includes an adverb ending in *ly* even when it is used before the noun.

> his loosely fitted jacket
>
> a carefully guarded secret

But a hyphen is used when the compound modifier contains an adverb that does not end in *ly*.

> a well-guarded secret
>
> a fast-growing business

10. To distinguish a less common pronunciation or meaning of a word from its more customary usage.

CUSTOMARY USAGE:
a recreation hall
to recover from an illness
to reform a sinner

HYPHENATED FORM:
re-creation of a scene
re-cover the couch
re-form their lines

11. To prevent possible confusion in pronunciation if a prefix results in the doubling of a letter, especially a vowel.

anti-inflationary	co-op
co-ordinate	pre-empt
pre-eminent	re-enact
re-election	re-entry

The dieresis is sometimes, but less frequently, used over *e* and *o* to accomplish the same result:

coöp   reëntry

12. To join the following prefixes with *proper* nouns or adjectives.

anti	anti-American, anti-British
mid	mid-Victorian, mid-Atlantic, mid-August
neo	neo-Nazi, neo-Darwinism
non	non-European, non-Asian, non-Christian
pan	Pan-American, Pan-Slavic, Pan-African
pro	pro-French, pro-American
un	un-American, un-British

With few exceptions, these prefixes are joined to common nouns without hyphenation:

anticlimax	midsummer
nonintervention	proslavery

13. To join the following prefixes and suffixes with the main word of a compound.

all-	all-powerful, all-embracing, all-star
co-	co-chairman, co-worker, co-author
ex-	ex-sergeant, ex-mayor, ex-wife, ex-premier
self-	self-preservation, self-defeating, self-explanatory, self-educated
-elect	president-elect, governor-elect

14. To form most, but not all, compound nouns and adjectives which begin with the word elements listed below. For words not listed, it is best to consult the dictionary.

cross-

cross-examine	cross-fertilize
cross-purposes	cross-stitch

double-		*ill-*	
double-breasted	double-edged	ill-disposed	ill-organized
double-jointed	double-park	ill-timed	ill-advised
great-		*light-*	
(always used in family relationships)		light-fingered	light-footed
great-grandfather	great-grandson	light-hearted	light-year
great-hearted	great-aunt	*single-*	
heavy-		single-breasted	single-handed
heavy-handed	heavy-hearted	single-minded	
heavy-duty (but heavyweight)		*well-*	
		well-behaved	well-balanced
		well-preserved	well-wisher

DIVISION OF WORDS

The division of a word at the end of a line should be avoided when possible. If it is necessary to divide a word, follow the syllabification shown in the dictionary.

Do not syllabify a word so that only one letter stands alone at the end or beginning of a line. Do not divide a one-syllable word, including words ending in *-ed* (such as *walked, saved, hurled*). Avoid the division of a word that carries only two letters over to

the next line. The following terminal parts of words should never be divided: *-able, -ible; -cial, -sial, -tial; -cion, -sion, -tion; -gion; -ceous, -cious, -tious; -geous.*

If a word that already has a hyphen must be broken, divide the word where only the hyphen already stands.

mother- *or* mother-in- *but not* moth-
in-law   law   er-in-law

ABBREVIATION

In standard academic, scientific, business or other organizational reports and correspondence, abbreviations are generally avoided unless they are the commonly required ones and are specifically known and accepted terms within a particular discipline or trade.

Some abbreviations that are acceptable in journalistic or business writing may not be appropriate in extremely formal announcements or invitations in which even dates are spelled out.

Abbreviations are often used in ordering and billing, catalogs, tabulations, telephone books, classified advertising, and similar cases where brevity is essential.

In some cases, the decision to use an abbreviation is a matter of individual preference. When in doubt, it is usually prudent to use the spelled-out form. Do not, however, spell out a word in one sentence or paragraph only to use the abbreviated form elsewhere.

Use abbreviations in writing:
1. The following titles and forms of address whenever they precede a proper name: *Mr., Mrs., Ms., Dr., Mme., Mlle., M.* Do not spell out these titles even in the most formal situations.

    Mlle. Modiste   Dr. Gerner
    Mr. Carl Sandburg   Mme. Curie
2. Titles of the clergy, government officials, officers of organizations, military and naval personnel (except in an extremely formal context) provided that the title is followed by a first name or initial as well as a surname. If the title is followed only by a surname, it must be spelled out.

    Gen. Arthur Evans   General Evans
    Sgt. Ed Block   Sergeant Block
    Prof. Samuel Page   Professor Page
    Gov. Ella Grasso   Governor Grasso
    Rev. George Ryan

       The Reverend George Ryan *or*
       The Reverend Dr. (*or* Mr.) Ryan
    Hon. Frank Church

The Honorable Frank Church
or The Honorable Mr. Church

Note above that in very formal writing, the titles *Honorable* and *Reverend* are spelled out and are preceded by *The*. When the first name or initial is omitted, the title Mr. or Dr. is substituted.

3. *Jr.* or *Sr.* following a name. These abbreviations should be added only when the names preceding them include a first name or initial.

Paul Thompson, Jr.

4. *Esq.* following a name. This abbreviation should not be used with any other title.

Gerald Hollingsworth, Esq.

5. Academic degrees: *B.A.* (Bachelor of Arts); *M.A.* (Master of Arts); *M.S.* (Master of Science); *Ph.D.* (Doctor of Philosophy); *M.D.* (Doctor of Medicine), etc. When a name is followed by a scholastic degree or by the abbreviations of religious or fraternal orders (BPOE), it should not be preceded by *Mr., Miss., Dr.*, or any other title.

Robert J. Kassan, M.D.

6. The terms used to describe business firms (*Co., Corp., Inc., Bro.* or *Bros., Ltd., R.R.* or *Ry.*) only when these abbreviations are part of the legally authorized name. In all other cases (except for brevity in tables, etc.), *Company, Corporation, Incorporated, Brothers,* and *Limited* should be spelled out.

John Wiley & Sons, Inc.

7. Except in formal writing, the names of states, territories, or possessions that immediately follow the name of a city, mountain, airport, or other identifiable geographic location. Check the dictionary for all such abbreviations.

Detroit, Mich.   San Juan, P.R.

8. Certain expressions:
i.e. (*id est*), that is
e.g. (*exempli gratia*), for example
et al. (*et alii*), and others
etc. (*et cetera*), and so forth

Do not abbreviate:

1. Names of countries, except:
a. The U.S.S.R. (Union of Soviet Socialist Republics) because of its exceptional length.
b. U.S. (United States) when preceding the name of an American ship. The abbreviation U.S. may also be used in tables, footnotes, etc., when modifying a government agency: *U.S. Congress, U.S. Post Office,* etc.

2. The words *street, avenue, boulevard, drive, square, road,* and *court,* except in lists requiring brevity, or when space is limited.

3. The days of the week and the months of the year except in the most informal situations or in tables.

4. Weights and measures except in lists of items, technical writing, etc.

I had hoped to lose ten pounds.
We used ten yards of cloth.

Do not use a period after the following abbreviations or shortened forms:

1. After a contraction, which is not to be confused with an abbreviation. Contractions contain apostrophes which indicate omitted letters; they never end with a period.

sec't'y or sec'y   nat'l

2. After chemical symbols.

H_2O NaCl

3. After *percent*.

4. After initials of military services and specific military terms.

USA	United States Army
USN	United States Navy
RCAF	Royal Canadian Air Force
RCMP	Royal Canadian Mounted Police
MP	military police
SP	shore patrol
POW	prisoner of war
PX	post exchange
GI	government issue
APO	Army post office

5. After the initials of certain governmental agencies or call letters of television and radio stations.

NATO, UNICEF, CIA, CARE, NBC, KQED, WMAQ, CBC, CBET, CFCF

6. After letters that are used as symbols rather than initials.

Let us assume that A and B are playing opposite C and D.

7. After listed items (as in catalogs, outlines, or syllabuses), if none of the items is a complete sentence. If the list includes

only one complete sentence, use a period after this and all other items on the list, including those which are not complete sentences. Consistency is essential: a pe-

riod after each item or no end punctuation whatever.

8. Points of the compass.

   NE ESE SW E by NE

CAPITALIZATION

Many writers have a tendency to use capitals unnecessarily. When in doubt, one can usually learn whether a particular word is generally capitalized by consulting the dictionary. A safe guideline is to capitalize only when there is specific reason to do so.

1. Capitalize the first word of a sentence. Capitalize also, any word (or the first word of a phrase) that stands independently as though it were a sentence.

   H is the new president of the club.
   Where is the chess set?
   Hurrah! No school!

2. Capitalize the first word of each line of verse (unless the poet specifically avoided capitals in such instances).

   Ring forth, ye bells,
   With clarion sound—
   Forget your knells,
   For joys abound.

3. Capitalize the first word of a direct quotation within a sentence (unless the quotation is a fragment).

   He replied, "Vivian prefers to enter in the fall."

   "George," she asked, "don't you want to join us for dinner?"

   He denied that he was "a neurotic editor."

4. Always capitalize the interjection *O* or the pronoun *I*. None of the other pronouns are capitalized unless they occur at the beginning of a sentence or refer to the Deity.

   Here I am.   Exult, O Shores!

5. Capitalize all proper nouns and adjectives.

   Italians   Scottish   Edwardian
   Emily Dickinson   the Cabot family
   Australia   European   Germanic
   Chicago   Chaucerian

6. The German *von* and the Dutch *van* in proper names are commonly not

printed with a capital when part of a name, but usage varies.

   Paul von Hindenburg
   Vincent van Gogh

The French particles *de* and *du* and the Italian *di* and *da* are commonly written in lower case when they are preceded by a first name or title. Without title or first name the particle is sometimes dropped, sometimes capitalized.

   Marquis de Lafayette
      (De) Lafayette
   Count de Mirabeau
      (De) Mirabeau

In English or American names these particles are commonly capitalized in all positions.

   William De Morgan   De Morgan
   Lee De Forest   De Forest

7. Do not capitalize words derived from proper nouns but now having a special meaning distinct from the proper name:

   antimacassar   china
   pasteurize   macadam

8. Capitalize recognized geographical names:

   Ohio River   Sun Valley
   Rocky Mountains   Gulf of Mexico

9. Capitalize the following when they follow a single proper name and are written in the singular:

Butte	County	Delta
Canyon	Creek	Gap
Glacier	Ocean	Range
Harbor	Peninsula	River
Head	Plateau	Valley

   For example, the *Sacramento River*, but the *Tennessee and Cumberland rivers*.

10. Capitalize the following in the singular and plural when they follow a proper name:

    Hill Mountain Island Narrows

11. Capitalize the following in the singular

whether placed before or after the name:

Bay	Sea	Gulf	Mount
Point	Cape	Isle	Peak
Strait	Desert	Lake	Plain

Capitalize in the plural when they come before the name (and sometimes following a single name). For example, *Lakes George and Champlain*, but *Malheur and Goose lakes*.

12. Capitalize geographic directions only when they designate specific regions. Capitalize also special names for regions or districts:

Northwest Passage
Middle Atlantic States
the New World
the South
the Middle East
Western Hemisphere

EXCEPTION: Do not capitalize merely directional parts of states.

eastern Ohio   southern Indiana

13. Do not capitalize compass points when indicating direction.

They went south last year but plan to go west this year.

14. Capitalize the names of streets, parks, buildings, etc.:

Michigan Boulevard
Royal Ontario Museum
Metropolitan Opera House
Golden Gate Bridge
Empire State Building
Yellowstone National Park
Grand Central Parkway

EXCEPTIONS: Do not capitalize such categories of buildings as *library, post office*, or *museum*, written without a proper name, unless local custom makes the classification equivalent to a proper name.

15. Capitalize the various names of God or the Christian Trinity, both nouns and adjectives, and all pronouns clearly referring to the Deity. Capitalize also words that refer to the Bible or other sacred writings.

the Word	Holy Bible
the Savior	the Koran
the Messiah	Ten Commandments
Allah	to do His will
the Almighty	the Virgin Mary

16. Capitalize all personifications.

Come, gentle Death!

17. Capitalize the names of organizations, institutions, political parties, alliances, movements, classes, religious groups, nationalities, races, etc.:

Democratic party (or Party)	Royalist Spain
	Axis powers
Labor party	Soviet Russia
Republicans	Protestants
Dutch Treat Club	Lutherans
United Nations	University of
American Legion	Waterloo
Africans	Caucasians

18. Capitalize divisions, departments, and offices of government, when the official name is used. Do not capitalize incomplete or roundabout designations:

Department of Commerce
Circuit Court of Marion County
Bureau of Labor Statistics
Congress
Senate
House of Commons
United States Army
Board of Aldermen
the council
the lower house (of Congress)
the bureau
the legislature

19. Capitalize the names of wars, battles, treaties, documents, prizes, and important periods or events:

Battle of the Bulge
Declaration of Independence
Nobel Prize
Revolutionary War
Congress of Vienna
Black Death
War of 1812
Golden Age of Pericles
Middle Ages
Treaty of Versailles

Do not capitalize *war* or *treaty* when used without the distinguishing name.

20. Capitalize the numerals used with kings, dynasties, or organizations. Numerals preceding the name are ordinarily spelled out; those following the name are commonly put in Roman numerals:

Second World War	World War II
Nineteenth Amendment	Henry IV
Third Army	Forty-eighth Congress

21. Capitalize titles, military or civil ranks of honor, academic degrees, decorations, etc., when written with the name,

and all titles of honor or rank when used for specific persons in place of the name:

    General Bradstreet
    the Senator from Ohio
    the Earl of Rochester
    Queen Elizabeth
    the Archbishop of Canterbury
    Your Highness

22. Capitalize the main words (nouns, verbs, adjectives, adverbs) of the titles of books, articles, poems, plays, musical compositions, etc., as well as the first word:

    The House of the Seven Gables
    All's Well That Ends Well

    The Kreutzer Sonata

23. Titles of chapters in a book are usually capitalized. Capitalize also any sections of a specific book, such as *Bibliography, Index, Table of Contents*, etc.,

24. In expressions of time, *A.M., P.M., A.D.*, and *B.C.* are usually written or typed in capitals without space between them. It is equally acceptable to show *a.m.* and *p.m.* in lower-case letters.

    9:40 A.M.   6:10 P.M.
    42 B.C.   A.D. 491 (or 491 A.D.)

When A.M., P.M., A.D., and B.C. are to be typeset, one may mark them with double-underlining to indicate that small capitals are to be used.

ITALICS

Indicate italics by underlining in manuscript or typescript.

Use italics:

1. To emphasize a particular word, phrase or statement.

    We *must* appeal for contributions.

2. To refer to the titles of books, magazines, newspapers, motion pictures, plays, longer musical compositions, book-length poems, ships, aircraft, or any other vehicle designated by a proper name. Titles of works of art may be shown in italics or enclosed with quotation marks.

    The Catcher in the Rye   *Mona Lisa*
    Harper's Magazine Rodin's *The Thinker*
    'the *Philadelphia Inquirer*   the *Titanic*
    High Noon   the *Spirit of St. Louis*

    Hamlet   Beethoven's *Ninth Symphony*
    The Raven   *The Faerie Queen*

3. To indicate words or phrases that, although used by English speakers or writers, are still regarded as foreign.

    In his younger days, he was a *bon vivant.*
    Formal dress was *de rigueur* at their annual dance.

4. To refer to a letter, number, word, or expression as such. Quotation marks may be used for the same purpose.

    Her favorite adjective is *fantastic.*
    The present participle ends in *ing.*

5. To indicate stage directions in a play.

    GEORGIA [*turning to* VAN]: Did you hear the bell?
    VAN: Yes, I'll answer it. [*He dashes to the door.*]

NUMERALS

In general, numbers that can be stated in only one or two words are spelled out.

    There were twelve girls and twenty-six boys from Montreal.
    The sweater cost twenty-five dollars.
    He gave one-tenth of his income to charity.

Other numbers are usually shown in figures.

    There are 392 members in the association.
    The radio cost him $136.50.
    The population of Chicago in 1950 was 3,620,962.

The numeral at the beginning of a sentence is usually spelled out. If this is awkward or difficult to read, rewrite the sentence to avoid beginning with a numeral.

> Three hundred and sixty students attended the dance.
>
> Twenty-six million votes were cast for him.
>
> Six thousand dollars was stolen from the safe.

It is important to be consistent in the treatment of numbers when they appear in the same series or in the same sentence or paragraph. Do not spell some out and use figures for others.

> The three chairs are 36, 72, and 122 years old.
>
> He spent $100 on rent, $30 on food, and $265 on clothes.

Use figures (generally) for dates, pages, dimensions, decimals, percentages, measures, statistical data, exact amounts of money, designations of time when followed by A.M. or P.M., and addresses.

June 29, 1945	0.9631	96.8°
124 B.C.	23 percent	86%
p. 263	75 pounds	8:30 A.M.
p. xxvi	93 miles	3:20 P.M.
2' x 4'	$369.27	4262 Brush
10 ft. 3 in.	£ 5.9s.6d	Street

Spell out ordinal numbers whenever possible.

> sixteenth century
> Fifth Avenue
> Eighty-second Congress
> Third Republic
> Twenty-third Psalm
> Third Assembly District

MANUSCRIPT PREPARATION

The manuscript should be typewritten, double-spaced, on white medium-weight paper. The sheets should be of the standard 8½" x 11" size and of good enough quality to permit clear markings in ink. Margins should be about one inch on each side and at the top and bottom. All pages should be numbered consecutively, preferably in the upper right-hand corner, throughout the entire work. Use only one side of the sheet.

A quotation that will run four lines or more is usually set off as a single-spaced, double-indented paragraph.

It is not advantageous to submit the manuscript in any special ornamental

binder. If assembled neatly in a folder, envelope, or cardboard box, the manuscript will be more in keeping with the practice of most professional writers and with the preference of most editors.

IMPORTANT: The author should always retain a complete carbon copy or photocopy of the manuscript, not only to facilitate correspondence between the editor and author, but to serve as insurance against loss of the original copy. Publishers are usually very careful not to lose or damage a manuscript, but their legal responsibility does not extend beyond "reasonable care."

FOOTNOTES AND END NOTES

Footnotes—called "endnotes" when all are placed in a group at the end of the entire text—serve a variety of purposes: to indicate the source of a fact, opinion, or quotation; to provide additional or explanatory material which, although relevant, would interrupt the smooth flow of the main text; and to refer the reader to another part of the text. Excessive use of foot-

notes, however, is distracting; it is the sign, generally, of spurious scholarship.

Material in the text to which footnotes are to be keyed should be numbered with superscript Arabic numerals ([1], [2], [3], [4], etc.). These numerals are usually placed without intervening space at the close of the sentence, quotation, or paragraph, unless doing so would cause confusion or ambiguity (in which case the numeral is placed after the specific word, phrase, or name to which it refers). The superscripts should follow all punctuation marks, except dashes; they should be free of periods, slashes, parentheses or other unnecessary marks.

Footnote numbers should continue consecutively throughout an article or chapter, usually numbering anew in each chapter.

Occasionally a writer will prefer to number the footnotes anew on each page. Because this causes many problems in typesetting, it is preferably avoided. Similarly, some writers prefer to use special symbols (*, †, ‡, §, ¶, , etc.) instead of superscript numerals. Because this system of symbols is limited and confusing, it too is preferably avoided.

Footnotes are placed at the bottom of the page after a quadruple space under the last line of text. (Some style manuals suggest a double space followed by a straight line that extends from the left to the right margins or that extends only two or three inches from the left margin; one line of space is left blank above this separation line and two lines of space are left blank below it.) The footnote, which begins with the appropriate superscript number without a space after it, is usually typed single-space. The first line of the footnote is the same indention used throughout the text itself; subsequent lines are typed to the same margins as the text itself. Use a double space between footnotes. Avoid carrying footnotes onto a following page, if at all possible.

BOOKS:
FIRST FOOTNOTE REFERENCES

When a book is first mentioned in a footnote, the bibliographical information should be as complete as possible. The information should appear in the following order:

1. AUTHOR'S NAME OR AUTHORS' NAMES. The given name or initials are given first, using the form in which the name is generally encountered, the surname being followed by a comma.
2. TITLE OF THE CHAPTER OR PART. When reference is made to an article in a collection, symposium, or the like, the title of the article appears within quotation

marks, the final quotation mark being preceded by a comma.
3. TITLE OF THE BOOK. The title is underlined (to indicate italics) and followed by a comma unless the next information is in parentheses (in which case the comma follows the closing parenthesis). If the title is exceptionally long, it may be shortened by omissions (indicated by three periods in each case). The title should be taken as it is shown on the title page.
4. EDITOR'S OR TRANSLATOR'S NAME. The name of the editor or translator, given in its full and normal form, is preceded by "ed." or "trans." It is followed by a comma unless the next material is in parentheses (in which case the comma follows the closing parenthesis).
5. EDITION USED. If the edition is other than the first one, the edition is identified in Arabic numerals, followed by a comma unless the next material is in parentheses (in which case the comma follows the closing parenthesis).
6. SERIES TITLE. The name of the series is shown without underlining or quotation marks. It is followed by the specific number of the work in the series, preceded and followed by commas. If the next material is in parentheses, the second comma is placed after the closing parenthesis.
7. NUMBER OF VOLUMES. If there is more than one volume in the work and it appears relevant to indicate this fact, the number is shown in Arabic numerals.
8. PUBLICATION DATA. This information is shown within one set of parentheses. The place of publication is usually found on the title page; if more than one city is shown, it is necessary only to show the publisher's main place of activity. If the city is not well known or if it might be confused with another of the same name, add the state or nation. It is followed by a colon. The name of the company, institution, etc., that published the work is shown next, followed by a comma. The date of publication is usually found on the copyright page. If no date is shown on the title page or copyright page, write "n.d." (without quotation marks) to indicate "no date." The parentheses containing the place

of publication, publisher's name, and date of publication are followed by a comma.

9. VOLUME NUMBER. If there are two or more volumes in the work, give the volume number in capital Roman numerals, enclosed by commas. If this information is followed by the page number, omit "Vol." and give the volume number only, followed by a comma.

10. PAGE NUMBER OR NUMBERS. The page number (preceded by "p.") or numbers (preceded by "pp.") are shown in Arabic numerals (unless the original uses Roman numerals), followed by a period. However, if the volume number has been given, the "p." may be omitted.

ARTICLES IN PERIODICALS: FIRST FOOTNOTE REFERENCES

When a magazine or newspaper article is referred to in a footnote for the first time, the bibliographical information is given in the following order:

1. AUTHOR'S OR AUTHORS' NAMES. The name is given in normal order and usual form, followed by a comma.

2. TITLE OF THE ARTICLE. The title is given in full, enclosed by quotation marks, a comma preceding the closing quotation mark.

3. NAME OF THE PERIODICAL. The name of the periodical, underlined to indicate italics, is followed by a comma. If there is a familiar abbreviation of the name of the periodical, it may be used.

4. VOLUME NUMBER. The volume number in capital Roman numerals is followed by a comma unless the next material is within parentheses (in which case the comma follows the closing parenthesis).

5. ISSUE NUMBER OR NAME. If the pagination of each issue is separate and the issue is not designated by month, give the issue number or name.

6. YEAR AND MONTH. The month (if necessary) and year of the volume are enclosed by parentheses followed by a comma.

7. PAGE NUMBER OR NUMBERS. The page number (preceded by "p.") or numbers (preceded by "pp.") are given in Arabic numerals (unless the original text uses Roman numerals) and terminated with

a period. However, if the volume number has been given, the "p." may be omitted.

SUBSEQUENT FOOTNOTE REFERENCES

After the first footnote reference to a book, article, or the like, it is unnecessary to repeat all the bibliographical information in each reference to the same work. Simply give the author's surname (followed by a comma), "p." or "pp.," and the page number(s). If there are several works by the same author that have been referred to, the author's surname is followed by a comma and the title of the work, which may be abridged for easy reference.

COMMON ABBREVIATIONS IN FOOTNOTES

The following abbreviations are commonly encountered in footnotes:

anon.	anonymous
ch. (chs.)	chapter (chapters)
chap. (chaps.)	chapter (chapters)
comp. (s)	compiler(s); compiled by
diss.	dissertation
ed. (s)	editor(s); edition; edited by
f. (ff.)	and the following page (pages)
introd.	introduction; introduced by
n.d.	no date
no. (nos.)	number (numbers)
p. (pp.)	page (pages)
rev.	revised; revised by; revision
ser.	series
tr., trans.	translator; translation; translated by
vol. (vols.)	volume (volumes)

SAMPLE FOOTNOTES: FIRST REFERENCE

A book by one author, first edition:

⁴Loren C. Eiseley, *The Immense Journey* (New York: Random House, 1957), p. 36.

A book by one author, revised or later edition:

⁵Harry Schwartz, *Russia's Soviet Economy*, 2d ed. (Englewood Cliffs, N.J.: Prentice-Hall, 1954), p. 37.

A book by two or more authors:

3Francis P. Shepard and Harold R. Wanless, *Our Changing Coastlines* (New York: McGraw-Hill, 1971), pp. 47-53.

3P. F. Lazarfeld, B. Berelson, and H. Gaudet, *The People's Choice* (New York: Duell, Sloan, and Pearce, 1944), pp. 61-3.

A book having one or more editors:

4Peter Russell, ed., *An Examination of Ezra Pound* (Norfolk, Conn.: New Directions, 1950), pp. 14-23.

5William Van O'Connor and Edward Stone, eds., *A Casebook on Ezra Pound* (New York: Thomas Y. Crowell, 1959), p. 137.

A book having an author and an editor:

3Thomas Robert Malthus, *On Population,* ed. Gertrude Himmelfarb (New York: The Modern Library, 1960), p. xxvii.

A book having a translator:

12Simone Weil, *Oppression and Liberty,* trans. Arthur Wills and John Petrie (Amherst: University of Massachusetts Press, 1973), pp. 106-8.

A book in several volumes:

6Daniel J. Boorstin, *The Americans* (New York: Random House, 1958-73), II, 137.

A book in a series:

3Arthur S. Link, *Woodrow Wilson and the Progressive Era 1910-1917,* New American Nation Series (New York: Harper, 1954), pp. 16-31.

An article in an edited collection of contributions:

2Herbert H. Rowen, "Kingship and Republicanism in the Seventeenth Century: Some Reconsiderations," in *From the Renaissance to the Counter-Reformation,* ed. Charles H. Carter (New York: Random House, 1965), p. 430.

An unsigned article in an encyclopedia:

12"Comets," *Random House Encyclopedia,* 1977 ed., p. 90.

A signed article in an encyclopedia:

2Edgar Frederick Carritt, "Aesthetics," *Encyclopedia Britannica,* 1956 ed., I, 265-267.

An unsigned article in a magazine or newspaper:

5"Controversies in Education: The American High School," *Phi Delta Kappan,* 40 (November, 1958), 26.

A signed article in a magazine or newspaper:

12Zellig Harris, "Grammar on Mathematical Principles," *Journal of Linguistics,* 14, No. 1 (1978), 15-20.

A bulletin report or pamphlet:

13United Nations, *Measures for the Economic Development of Under-Developed Countries* (New York: United Nations, 1951), pp. 8-9.

14The Office of Education and the Office of Economic Opportunity, *Education: An Answer to Poverty* (Washington, D.C.: Government Printing Office, 1965), pp. 68-70.

An unpublished thesis or dissertation:

3Bruce H. Wilson, "The New Democratic Party of Canada: An Example of a Third Party Movement," Diss. New School for Social Research 1976. p. 67.

A private communication:

10Information in a letter to the author from Professor Raven McDavid of the University of Chicago, June 23, 1963.

SAMPLE FOOTNOTES: SUBSEQUENT REFERENCE

8Eiseley, p. 14.

18Schwartz, pp. 43-62.

9Shepard and Wanless, pp. 103-14.

3Link, *Woodrow Wilson,* p. 16.

BIBLIOGRAPHIES

Bibliographies may be organized by subject, types of publications cited, chronological sequence, or alphabetical order. The alphabetical arrangement is, by far, the most common one.

The bibliography should be typed so

that the first line of each item begins flush with the left margin and succeeding lines begin several spaces in. The material is usually double-spaced (and double-spaced between items).

The content of bibliographical entries is the same as that of footnotes with only these major differences:

1. AUTHOR'S NAME. The surname comes first, followed by a comma; then the given name, followed by a period.
2. TITLE. The title is closed by a period.
3. PUBLICATION DATA. The place of publication, name of the publisher, and date of publication are not enclosed by parentheses; a period is placed after the date.

SAMPLE ENTRIES

"Controversies in Education: The American High School." *Phi Delta Kappan,* 40 (November, 1958), pp. 3-126.

Crane, Stephen. *The Red Badge of Courage.* Introd. Robert Wooster Stallman. New York: The Modern Library, 1951.

Shepard, Francis P., and Harold R. Wanless. *Our Changing Coastlines.* New York: McGraw-Hill, 1971.

Johnson, E. L. "Cooperation in Higher Education. *Liberal Education,* 48 (December 1962).

Russell, Peter, ed. *An Examination of Ezra Pound.* Norfolk, Conn.: New Directions, 1950.

Schwartz, Harry. *Russia's Soviet Economy.* 2d ed. Englewood Cliffs, N.J.: Prentice Hall, 1954.

Laurence, Margaret. *The Stone Angel.* Toronto: McClelland & Stewart, 1964.

Boorstin, Daniel J. *The Americans.* 3 vols. New York: Random House, 1958-73.

When writing for a specific publication or publisher, the author should inquire whether there is a preferred style or style manual to be followed. Among the widely used general-purpose style manuals are *A Manual of Style* (published by the University of Chicago) and *The MLA Handbook* (published by the Modern Language Association). Among the style manuals for specific fields and publications are those issued by the American Institute of Biological Sciences, the American Chemical Society, the American Mathematical Society, the American Medical Association, the American Institute of Physics, and the American Psychological Association.

Proofreaders' Marks

The conventional marks shown below are used in preparing a manuscript to be typeset or in proofreading typeset material. The mark should be written in the margin directly in line with the specific part of the text to which it refers; the text should also be marked to indicate the place of the change. If the same line has several changes, vertical or diagonal lines are placed between each of the marginal marks.

EDITORIAL MARKS

Mark in margin:	Instruction:	Mark in text:
[Show change or addition]	Insert at caret	Peter left town in a hurry.
ϑ or ૪	Delete; take out	Stephanie sent me me the book.
⌒	Delete and close up	I haven't seen them for years.
stet	Make no change; keep original	They phoned both Jody and Erik.
tr	Transpose	Put the book on the table.
sp	Spell out	Lunch cost me 6 dollars.
¶	Start new paragraph	up the river. Two years later
No ¶	Do not paragraph; run in	many unnecessary additives. The most dangerous one had been in use for about ten
#	Insert space	It was a small village.
eq #	Equalize spacing	Ronnie got rid of the dog.

PUNCTUATION MARKS

Mark in margin:	Instruction:	Mark in text:
⊙	Period (.)	Claire teaches fifth grade
⎃	Comma (,)	We expect Linda, Nino, and Daniel.
⎧	Semicolon (;)	I came; I saw, I conquered.
⊙	Colon (:)	Alice worked until 6,30 P.M.
⁼	Hyphen (-)	Wu Pan got a two thirds majority.
⌣	Apostrophe (')	Don't mark the authors copy.
!	Exclamation mark (!)	Watch out
?	Question mark (?)	Did Mollie write to you
⌣/⌣	Quotation marks (double) (" ")	I like Rodin's The Thinker.
⌣/⌣	Quotation marks (single) (' ')	He said, "Read The Raven tonight."

1060

PUNCTUATION MARKS

Mark in margin:	Instruction:	Mark in text:
(/)	Parentheses (( ))	Lillian paid 100 pesos₍13¢₎for it.
[/]	Brackets ([ ])	"The play₍Hamlet₎was performed..."
⅟ₘ	One-em dash (—)	TJ finally left₍very reluctantly.
⅟ₙ	One-en dash (–)	See pages 96₍124.

TYPOGRAPHIC MARKS

Mark in margin:	Instruction:	Mark in text:
ital	Set in *italic* type	I've read Paradise Lost twice.
bf	Set in **boldface** type	See the definition of peace.
lf	Set in lightface type	She repaired the motor easily.
rom	Set in roman type	Daphne drove to Winnipeg.
caps	Set in CAPITALS	Prabhuling deserves the nobel prize.
sc	Set in SMALL CAPITALS	He lived about 350 B.C.
c+sc	Set in CAPITALS and SMALL CAPITALS	drive slowly
lc	Set in lower case	Jeanne enjoys Reading.
u+lc	Set in UPPER and lower case	STOP!
⌄	Set as subscript	NaNO₃
^	Set as superscript	A² + B²
‖	Align vertically	‖from one hand to the other without spilling it.
=	Align horizontally	three days later
↓	Push down	She assigned him to Minneapolis.
×	Broken letter	They drove to Miami.
wf	Wrong font	TURN RIGHT
↺	Turn inverted letter	ⓐlert proofread the book.
□	Indent one em	□Rose asked the price.
□□	Indent two ems	□□ The Use of the Comma
⊏	Move to left	⌐What's Maya's last name?
⊐	Move to right	She⌐was born in Jersey City.
⌐	Move up	Please go now.
⌐	Move down	Well, that's that!

1061

Forms of Address

The forms of address shown below cover most of the commonly encountered problems in correspondence. Although there are many alternative forms, the ones given here are generally preferred in conventional usage.

As a complimentary close, use "Sincerely yours," but, when particular formality is preferred, use "Very truly yours."

GOVERNMENT (UNITED STATES)

Addressee	Address on Letter and Envelope	Salutation
The President	The President The White House Washington, D.C. 20500	Dear Mr. *or* Madam President:
The Vice President	The Vice President United States Senate Washington, D.C. 20510	Dear Mr. *or* Madam Vice President:
Members of the Cabinet	The Honorable (*full name*) Secretary of (*name of Department*) Washington, D.C. (*zip code*)	Dear Mr. *or* Madam Secretary:
Attorney General	The Honorable (*full name*) Attorney General Washington, D.C. 20530	Dear Mr. *or* Madam Attorney General:
Senator	The Honorable (*full name*) United States Senate Washington, D.C. 20510	Dear Senator (*surname*):
Speaker of the House of Representatives	The Honorable (*full name*) Speaker of the House of Representatives Washington, D.C. 20515	Dear Mr. *or* Madam Speaker:
Representative	The Honorable (*full name*) House of Representatives Washington, D.C. 20515	Dear Mr. *or* Madam (*surname*):
Chief Justice	The Chief Justice of the United States The Supreme Court of the United States Washington, D.C. 20543	Dear Mr. *or* Madam Chief Justice:
Associate Justice	Mr. *or* Madam Justice (*surname*) The Supreme Court of the United States Washington, D.C. 20543	Dear Mr. *or* Madam Justice:

Addressee	Address on Letter and Envelope	Salutation
Judge of a Federal Court	The Honorable (*full name*) Judge of the (*name of court;* *if a district court, give district*) (*Local address*)	Dear Judge (*surname*):

American Ambassador	The Honorable (*full name*)
	American Ambassador
	(*City*) (*Country*)
		Formal: Sir: *or* Madam:
		Informal:
		   Dear Mr. *or* Madam
		   Ambassador:

American Minister	The Honorable (*full name*)
	American Minister
	(*City*), (*Country*)
		Formal: Sir: *or* Madam:
		Informal:
		   Dear Mr. *or* Madam
		   Minister:

Governor	The Honorable (*full name*) Governor of (*name*) (*City*), (*State*)	Dear Governor (*surname*):
Lieutenant Governor	The Honorable (*full name*) Lieutenant Governor of (*name*) (*City*), (*State*)	Dear (Mr., Ms., Miss *or* Mrs.) (*surname*):
State Senator	The Honorable (*full name*) (*Name of State*) Senate (*City*), (*State*)	Dear (Mr., Ms., Miss *or* Mrs.) (*surname*):

State Representative;
Assemblyman;
Delegate
	The Honorable (*full name*)
	(*Name of State*) House of
	   Representatives (*or* Assembly
	   or House of Delegates)
	(*City*), (*State*)
		Dear (Mr., Ms., Miss *or*
		   Mrs.) (*surname*):

Mayor	The Honorable (*full name*) Mayor of (*name of city*) (*City*), (*State*)	Dear Mayor (*surname*):

GOVERNMENT (CANADA)

Addressee	Address on Letter and Envelope	Salutation

The Governor General	(His *or* Her) Excellency (*full name*)
	Government House
	Ottawa, Ontario K1A 0A1
		Formal: Sir: *or* Madam:
		Informal:
		   Dear Governor
		   General:

The Prime Minister	The Right Honourable (*full name*),
	   P.C., M.P.
	Prime Minister of Canada
	Prime Minister's Office
	Ottawa, Ontario K1A 0A2
		Formal: Dear Sir: *or*
		   Madam:
		Informal:
		   Dear (Mr. *or* Madam)
		   Prime Minister:

Members of the Cabinet	The Honourable (*full name*)
	Minister of (*function*)
	House of Commons
	Parliament Buildings
	Ottawa, Ontario K1A 0A2
		Formal: Dear Sir: *or*
		   Madam:
		Informal:
		   Dear (Mr., Ms., Miss *or*
		   Mrs.) (*surname*):

Senator	The Honourable (*full name*)
	The Senate
	Parliament Buildings
	Ottawa, Ontario K1A 0A4
		Formal: Dear Sir: *or*
		   Madam:
		Informal:
		   Dear Senator:

Addressee	Address on Letter and Envelope	Salutation
Member of House of Commons	(Mr., Ms., Miss *or* Mrs.) *(full name)*, M.P. House of Commons Parliament Buildings Ottawa, Ontario K1A 0A6	*Formal:* Dear Sir: *or* Madam: *Informal:* Dear (Mr., Ms., Miss *or* Mrs.) *(surname)*:
Chief Justice of Canada	The Right Honourable *(full name)* Chief Justice of Canada Supreme Court Building Ottawa, Ontario K1A 0J1	*Formal:* Sir: *or* Madam: *Informal:* Dear Sir: *or* Madam:
Canadian Ambassador	(Mr., Ms., Miss *or* Mrs.) *(full name)* Canadian Ambassador to *(Country)* *(City)*, *(Country)*	*Formal:* Dear Sir: *or* Madam: *Informal:* Dear (Mr., Ms., Miss *or* Mrs.) *(surname)*:
Canadian Minister	(Mrs., Ms., Miss *or* Mrs.) *(full name)* Canadian Minister to *(Country)* *(City)*, *(Country)*	*Formal:* Sir: *or* Madam: *Informal:* Dear (Mr., Ms., Miss *or* Mrs.) *(surname)*:
The Premier of a Province	The Honourable *(full name)*, M.L.A.* Premier of the Province of *(name)*** *(City)*, *(Province)*	*Formal:* Dear Sir: *or* Madam: *Informal:* Dear (Mr., Ms., Miss *or* Mrs.) *(surname):*
Members of provincial governments	(Mr., Ms., Miss *or* Mrs.) *(full name)*, M.L.A.* Member of the Legislative Assembly *(Name)* Building *(City)*, *(Province)*	*Formal:* Dear Sir: *or* Madam: *Informal:* Dear (Mr., Ms., Miss *or* Mrs.) *(surname)*:
Mayor	His *or* Her Worship Mayor *(full name)* City Hall *(City)*, *(Province)*	Dear Sir: *or* Madam:

RELIGIOUS LEADERS

Addressee	Address on Letter and Envelope	Salutation
Minister, Pastor, or Rector	The Reverend *(full name)* *(Title)*, *(name of church)* *(Local address)*	Dear (Mr., Ms., Miss *or* Mrs.) *(surname)*:
Rabbi	Rabbi *(full name)* *(Local address)*	Dear Rabbi *(surname)*:
Catholic Cardinal	His Eminence *(Christian name)* Cardinal *(surname)* Archbishop of *(province)* *(Local address)*	*Formal:* Your Eminence: *Informal:* Dear Cardinal *(surname)*:
Catholic Archbishop	The Most Reverend *(full name)* Archbishop of *(province)* *(Local address)*	*Formal:* Your Excellency: *Informal:* Dear Archbishop *(surname)*:

*For Ontario, use M.P.P.; for Quebec, use M.N.A.
**For Quebec, use "Prime Minister."

Addressee	Address on Letter and Envelope	Salutation
Catholic Bishop	The Most Reverend (*full name*) Bishop of (*province*) (*Local address*)	*Formal:* Your Excellency: *Informal:* Dear Bishop (*surname*):
Catholic Monsignor	The Right Reverend Monsignor (*full name*) (*Local address*)	*Formal:* Right Reverend Monsignor: *Informal:* Dear Monsignor (*surname*):
Catholic Priest	The Reverend (*full name*), (*initials of order, if any*) (*Local address*)	*Formal:* Reverend Sir: *Informal:* Dear Father (*surname*):
Catholic Sister	Sister (*full name*) (*Name of organization*) (*Local address*)	Dear Sister (*full name*):
Catholic Brother	Brother (*full name*) (*Name of organization*) (*Local address*)	Dear Brother (*given name*):
Protestant Episcopal Bishop	The Right Reverend (*full name*) Bishop of (*name*) (*Local address*)	*Formal:* Right Reverend Sir *or* Madam: *Informal:* Dear Bishop (*surname*):
Protestant Episcopal Dean	The Very Reverend (*full name*) Dean of (*church*) (*Local address*)	*Formal:* Very Reverend Sir *or* Madam: *Informal:* Dear Dean (*surname*):
Anglican Archbishop	The Most Reverend (*full name*) Archbishop of (*province*) (*Local address*)	*Formal:* Most Reverend Sir: *Informal:* Dear Archbishop:
Anglican Bishop	The Right Reverend (*full name*) Bishop of (*name*) (*Local address*)	*Formal:* Right Reverend Sir: *Informal:* Dear Bishop:
Anglican Archdeacon	The Venerable Archdeacon (*full name*) (*Local address*)	*Formal:* Venerable Sir: *Informal:* Dear Mr. Archdeacon:
Anglican Dean	The Very Reverend (*full name*) Dean of (*name*) (*Local address*)	*Formal:* Very Reverend Sir: *Informal:* Dear Mr. Dean:
Anglican Canon	The Reverend Canon (*full name*) (*Local address*)	*Formal:* Reverend Sir: *Informal:* Dear Canon:
Methodist Bishop	The Reverend (*full name*) Methodist Bishop (*Local address*)	*Formal:* Reverend Sir: *Informal:* Dear Bishop (*surname*):

Addressee	Address on Letter and Envelope	Salutation
Mormon Bishop	Bishop (*full name*) Church of Jesus Christ of Latter-day Saints (*Local address*)	*Formal:* Sir: *Informal:* Dear Bishop (*surname*):

MISCELLANEOUS

Addressee	Address on Letter and Envelope	Salutation
President of a university or college	Mr. (*full name*) President, (*name of institution*) (*Local address*)	Dear Mr. (*surname*):
Dean of a college or school	Dean (*full name*) School of (*name*) (*name of institution*) (*Local address*)	Dear Dean (*surname*):
Professor	Professor (*full name*) Department of (*name*) (*Name of institution*) (*Local address*)	Dear Professor (*surname*):

Weights and Measures

CUSTOMARY SYSTEM

LINEAR MEASURE

12 inches	= 1 foot
3 feet	= 1 yard
5½ yards	= 1 rod
40 rods	= 1 furlong
8 furlongs (5280 feet)	= 1 statute mile

MARINERS' MEASURE

6 feet	= 1 fathom
1000 fathoms (approx.)	= 1 nautical mile
3 nautical miles	= 1 league

SQUARE MEASURE

144 square inches	= 1 square foot
9 square feet	= 1 square yard
30¼ square yards	= 1 square rod
160 square rods	= 1 acre
640 acres	= 1 square mile

CUBIC MEASURE

1728 cubic inches	= 1 cubic foot
27 cubic feet	= 1 cubic yard

SURVEYORS' MEASURE

7.92 inches	= 1 link
100 links	= 1 chain

LIQUID MEASURE

4 gills	= 1 pint
2 pints	= 1 quart
4 quarts	= 1 gallon
31½ gallons	= 1 barrel
2 barrels	= 1 hogshead

APOTHECARIES' FLUID MEASURE

60 minims	= 1 fluid dram
8 fluid drams	= 1 fluid ounce
16 fluid ounces	= 1 pint
2 pints	= 1 quart
4 quarts	= 1 gallon

DRY MEASURE

2 pints	= 1 quart
8 quarts	= 1 peck
4 pecks	= 1 bushel

WOOD MEASURE

16 cubic feet	= 1 cord foot
8 cord feet	= 1 cord

TIME MEASURE

60 seconds	= 1 minute
60 minutes	= 1 hour
24 hours	= 1 day
7 days	= 1 week
4 weeks (28 to 31 days)	= 1 month
12 months (365-366 days)	= 1 year
100 years	= 1 century

ANGULAR AND CIRCULAR MEASURE

60 seconds	= 1 minute
60 minutes	= 1 degree
90 degrees	= 1 right angle
180 degrees	= 1 straight angle
360 degrees	= 1 circle

TROY MEASURE

24 grains	= 1 pennyweight
20 pennyweights	= 1 ounce
12 ounces	= 1 pound

APOTHECARIES' WEIGHT

20 grains	= 1 scruple
3 scruples	= 1 dram
8 drams	= 1 ounce
12 ounces	= 1 pound

AVOIRDUPOIS WEIGHT

$27\frac{11}{32}$ grains	= 1 dram
16 drams	= 1 ounce
16 ounces	= 1 pound
100 pounds	= 1 short hundred-weight
20 short hundred-weight	= 1 short ton

METRIC SYSTEM

LINEAR MEASURE

10 millimeters	= 1 centimeter
10 centimeters	= 1 decimeter
10 decimeters	= 1 meter
10 meters	= 1 decameter
10 decameters	= 1 hectometer
10 hectometers	= 1 kilometer

LIQUID MEASURE

10 milliliters	= 1 centiliter
10 centiliters	= 1 deciliter
10 deciliters	= 1 liter
10 liters	= 1 decaliter
10 decaliters	= 1 hectoliter
10 hectoliters	= 1 kiloliter

SQUARE MEASURE

100 sq. millimeters	= 1 sq. centimeter
100 sq. centimeters	= 1 sq. decimeter
100 sq. decimeters	= 1 sq. meter
100 sq. meters	= 1 sq. decameter
100 sq. decameters	= 1 sq. hectometer
100 sq. hectomers	= 1 sq. kilometer

WEIGHTS

10 milligrams	= 1 centigram
10 centigrams	= 1 decigram
10 decigrams	= 1 gram
10 grams	= 1 decagram
10 decagrams	= 1 hectogram
10 hectograms	= 1 kilogram
100 kilograms	= 1 quintal
10 quintals	= 1 ton

CUBIC MEASURE

1000 cu. millimeters	= 1 cu. centimeter
1000 cu. centimeters	= 1 cu. decimeter
1000 cu. decimeters	= 1 cu. meter

METRIC AND CUSTOMARY EQUIVALENTS

LINEAR MEASURE

Customary Unit	Metric Unit	Customary Unit	Metric Unit
1 inch =	25.4 millimeters	1 yard =	0.9144 meter
	2.54 centimeters	1 mile =	1609.3 meters
1 foot =	30.48 centimeters		1.6093 kilometers
	3.048 decimeters	0.03937 inch =	1 millimeter
	0.3048 meter	0.3937 inch =	1 centimeter
		3.937 inches =	1 decimeter

Customary Unit	Metric Unit
39.37 inches	
3.2808 feet	= 1 meter
1.0936 yards	
3280.8 feet	
1093.6 yards	= 1 kilometer
0.62137 mile	

SQUARE MEASURE

Customary Unit	Metric Unit
1 square inch =	645.16 square millimeters
	6.4516 square centimeters
1 square foot =	929.03 square centimeters
	9.2903 square decimeters
	0.092903 square meter
1 square yard =	0.83613 square meter
1 square mile =	2.5900 square kilometers
0.0015500 square inch =	1 square millimeter
0.15500 square inch =	1 square centimeter
15.500 square inches	= 1 square decimeter
0.10764 square foot	
1.1960 square yards =	1 square meter
0.38608 square mile =	1 square kilometer

CUBIC MEASURE

Customary Unit	Metric Unit
1 cubic inch =	16.387 cubic centimeters
	0.016387 liter
1 cubic foot =	0.028317 cubic meter
1 cubic yard =	0.76455 cubic meter
1 cubic mile =	4.16818 cubic kilometers
0.061023 cubic inch =	1 cubic centimeter
61.023 cubic inches =	1 cubic decimeter
35.315 cubic feet	= 1 cubic meter
1.3079 cubic yards	
0.23990 cubic mile =	1 cubic kilometer

WEIGHTS

Customary Unit		Metric Unit
1 grain	=	0.064799 gram
1 avoirdupois ounce	=	28.350 grams
1 troy ounce	=	31.103 grams
1 avoirdupois pound	=	0.45359 kilogram
1 troy pound	=	0.37324 kilogram
1 short ton (0.8929 long ton)	=	907.18 kilograms / 0.90718 metric ton
1 long ton (1.1200 short tons)	=	1016.0 kilograms / 1.0160 metric tons
15.432 grains		
0.035274 avoirdupois ounce	=	1 gram
0.032151 troy ounce		
2.2046 avoirdupois pounds = 1 kilogram		
0.98421 long ton	=	1 metric ton
1.1023 short tons		

DRY MEASURE

Customary Unit	Metric Unit
1 quart =	1.1012 liters
1 peck =	8.8098 liters
1 bushel =	35.239 liters
0.90808 quart	
0.11351 peck	= 1 liter
0.028378 bushel	

LIQUID MEASURE

Customary Unit	Metric Unit
1 fluid ounce =	29.573 milliliters
1 quart =	9.4635 deciliters / 0.94635 liter
1 gallon =	3.7854 liters
0.033814 fluid ounce =	1 milliliter
3.3814 fluid ounces =	1 deciliter
33.814 fluid ounces	
1.0567 quarts	= 1 liter
0.26417 gallon	

METRIC CONVERSION FACTORS

APPROXIMATE CONVERSIONS TO METRIC MEASURES

When You Know	Multiply by	To Find
Length		
inches	2.5	centimeters
feet	30	centimeters
yards	0.9	meters
miles	1.6	kilometers
Area		
square inches	6.5	square centimeters
square feet	0.09	square meters
square yards	0.8	square meters
square miles	2.6	square kilometers
acres	0.4	hectares
Mass (weight)		
ounces	28	grams
pounds	0.45	kilograms
short tons	0.9	metric ton
Volume		
teaspoons	5	milliliters
tablespoons	15	milliliters
cubic inches	16	milliliters
fluid ounces	30	milliliters
cups	0.24	liters
pints	0.47	liters
quarts	0.95	liters
gallons	3.8	liters
cubic feet	0.03	cubic meters
cubic yards	0.76	cubic meters
Temperature (exact)		
degrees Fahrenheit	5/9 (after subtracting 32)	degrees Celsius

APPROXIMATE CONVERSIONS FROM METRIC MEASURES

When You Know	Multiply by	To Find
Length		
millimeters	0.04	inches
centimeters	0.4	inches
meters	3.3	feet
meters	1.1	yards
kilometers	0.6	miles
Area		
square centimeters	0.16	square inches
square meters	1.2	square yards
square kilometers	0.4	square miles
hectares	2.5	acres
Mass (weight)		
grams	0.035	ounces
kilograms	2.2	pounds
metric ton	1.1	short tons
Volume		
milliliters	0.03	fluid ounces
milliliters	0.06	cubic inches
liters	2.1	pints
liters	1.06	quarts
liters	0.26	gallons
cubic meters	35	cubic feet
cubic meters	1.3	cubic yards
Temperature (exact)		
degrees Celsius	9/5 (then add 32)	degrees Fahrenheit

THE RANDOM HOUSE 🏠 ENCYCLOPEDIA

THE FIRST one-volume encyclopedia designed for everyday use in today's visually oriented society—a complete, unique reference book of the world's basic knowledge, illuminated with more than 13,800 illustrations, more than 11,300 of them in full color.

THE RANDOM HOUSE ENCYCLOPEDIA provides quick alphabetical access to factual information in its 822-page *Alphapedia* (containing more than 25,000 text entries) and it provides a broader and deeper perspective of human knowledge in its extraordinary 1792-page *Colorpedia* (containing brilliantly integrated text, pictures, and captions).

- Prepared by more than 800 contributors, consultants, editors, designers, artists, etc.
- 2856 pages • 3,000,000 words • 8¼" x 11" in size
- 80-page Atlas in full color • 48-page Time Chart

"Fabulous—the most beautiful and entertaining book of information I have ever seen." —David Elliott, *Chicago Daily News*

"No book on the market can do what *The Random House Encyclopedia* does best: to provide a tremendously informative and rewarding browse." —Curt Suplee, *Washington Post*

"Undeniably unique, merging brilliant illustrations with short texts to survey all areas of knowledge." —*Library Journal*

"If I could only buy one single-volume reference book, would I buy this one? The answer is yes!" —Robert Kirsch, *Los Angeles Times*